The Complete
BIBLICAL LIBRARY

The Complete
BIBLICAL
LIBRARY

THE NEW TESTAMENT GREEK-ENGLISH DICTIONARY

Delta–Epsilon
Word Numbers
1132–2175

The Complete BIBLICAL LIBRARY

The Complete Biblical Library, part 1, a 16-volume study series on the New Testament. Volume 12: GREEK-ENGLISH DICTIONARY, DELTA—EPSILON, Word Numbers 1132–2175. World copyright ©1986 by Thoralf Gilbrant and Tor Inge Gilbrant. © Published 1990 by THE COMPLETE BIBLICAL LIBRARY, Springfield, Missouri 65802, U.S.A. All rights reserved. No part of this publication may be reproduced or transmitted in any form or by any means, electronic or mechanical, including photocopy, recording, or any information storage and retrieval system, without permission in writing from the publisher. Printed in the United States of America 1990 by R.R. Donnelley and Sons Company, Chicago, Illinois 60606. Library of Congress Catalog Card Number 90-85349 International Standard Book Number 0-88243-372-5.

INTERNATIONAL EDITOR
Thoralf Gilbrant

Executive Editor: Ralph W. Harris, M.A.
Computer Systems: Tor Inge Gilbrant

National Editor: Stanley M. Horton, Th.D
Managing Editor: Gayle Garrity Seaver, J.D.

Greek-English Dictionary
Editor: Denis W. Vinyard, M.Div.
Associate Editor: Donald F. Williams, M.Div.

NATIONAL EDITORS

NORWAY
Erling Utnem, Bishop
Arthur Berg, B.D.

DENMARK
Jorgen Glenthoj, Th.M.

HOLLAND
Herman ter Welle, Pastor
Henk Courtz, Drs.

FINLAND
Aapelii Saarisalo, Ph.D.
Valter Luoto, Pastor
Matti Liljequist, B.D.
Toivo Koilo, cand.mag.

SWEDEN
Hugo Odeberg, Ph.D., D.D.
Bertil E. Gartner, D.D.
Thorsten Kjall, M.A.
Stig Wikstrom, D.Th.M.

Project Coordinator: William G. Eastlake

THE COMPLETE BIBLICAL LIBRARY
International and Interdenominational Bible Study System

THE NEW TESTAMENT
Study Bible, Greek-English Dictionary, Harmony of the Gospels

THE OLD TESTAMENT
Study Bible, Hebrew-English Dictionary

THE BIBLE ENCYCLOPEDIA

THE NEW TESTAMENT GREEK-ENGLISH DICTIONARY

Delta–Epsilon
Word Numbers
1132–2175

THE COMPLETE BIBLICAL LIBRARY
Springfield, Missouri, U.S.A.

Table of Contents

	Page
Personnel	5
Greek and Hebrew Alphabets	9
Introduction	10
Greek-English Dictionary	19
Manuscripts	678
Egyptian Papyri	678
Major Codices	680
Majuscules and Minuscules	681
Early Versions	681
Early Church Fathers	682
Books of the Old and New Testament	684
Books of the Apocrypha and Pseudepigrapha	685
Orders and Tractates of the Mishnah and the Talmud	686
Bibliography	687
Resource Tools	687
Modern Greek Texts	687
General Bibliography	687
General References Sources by Title	699
Literature of Antiquity	701

Personnel

INTERNATIONAL EDITOR
Thoralf Gilbrant

Executive Editor: Ralph W. Harris, M.A.

National Editor: Stanley M. Horton, Th.D.

Managing Editor: Gayle A. Seaver, J.D.

Greek-English Dictionary Editor: Denis W. Vinyard, M.Div.

Greek-English Dictionary Associate Editor: Donald F. Williams, M.Div.

BOARD OF REVIEW

John D. Bechtle, D.Min.
Daniel L. Black, Th.D.
David Alan Black, D.Theol.
David R. Bundrick, Th.M.
Vernon D. Doerksen, Th.D.
Thomas E. Friskney, B.D.
Timothy P. Jenney, M.A.

Fred R. Johnson, Ph.D.
Erich H. Kiehl, Th.D.
Oliver McMahan, D.Min.
Siegfried S. Schatzmann, Ph.D.
Virgil Warren, Ph.D.
William C. Williams, Ph.D.
Barney D. Wimer, Ph.D.

STAFF

Senior Editors: Gary L. Leggett, M.A.; Dorothy B. Morris

Editorial Team: Paul S. Ash, B.A., GED Technical Editor; David A. Baca, B.A.; Patti J. Christensen; Charlotte L. Gribben; Melvin M.S. Ho, M.Div.; Carlos E. Johnson, Jr., M.A., GED Background Research; Debra K. King, B.A.; Robert F. Land, B.A., GED Background Research; Gregory A. Lint, M.Div., Septuagint Research; Charles F. Lynch, M.Div., GED Technical Editor; Paul J. Martin, M.A.; Michael Ritchie, M.Div.; Marietta L. Vinyard; Karen D. Wuertz, M.Div.

Production Coordinator, Study Bible, and GED Layout Artist: Cynthia D. Riemenschneider

Art Director: Terry Van Someren, B.F.A.

Word Processing and Secretarial: Sonja Jensen; Rochelle L. Holman; Therese Ritchie; Rachel Wisehart Harvey, B.A.

Personnel Continued

Volume 12 Contributors

The following writers contributed research and original manuscripts for the word studies in Volume 12.

Caroline L. Abshier, M.A.	Bill Brown, Ph.D.
Ben C. Aker, Ph.D.	Mike Cargal, B.A.
French L. Arrington, Ph.D.	John E. Carlson, B.A.
Arden C. Autry, Ph.D.	Joseph L. Castleberry, M.Div.
Gary D. Bailey, M.A.	Gary G. Cohen, Th.D.
Carolyn D. Baker, M.Div.	Lonnie L. Darnell, II, D.Min.
Donald E. Baldwin, Ph.D.	Vernon D. Doerksen, Th.D.
John R. Barlow, M.Div.	Dennis E. DuPont, M.Div.
Freeman Barton, Ph.D.	William E. Elliott, Th.D.
James M. Beaty, Ph.D.	Charles A. Estridge, D.Min.
John D. Bechtle, D.Min.	Steve D. Eutsler, M.A.
David Alan Black, D.Theol.	David A. Fiensey, Ph.D.
Raymond T. Brock, Ed.D.	John C. Fransisco, M.Div.
W. R. Brookman, Ph.D.	Ernest R. Freeman, M.T.S.

Gregory A. Hackett, B.A.	Daniel L. McNaughton, M.A.T.S.
M. Fred Haltom, D.Min.	A. D. Millard, D.Min.
Wesley L. Hansen, B.A.	Kevin B. Miller, B.A.
Ralph W. Harris, M.A.	G. Edward Nelson, M.Div.
David R. Hayward, M.A.T.S.	Matthew L. Neumann, M.Div.
Jerry R. Heady, M.A.	Lori S. O'Dea, B.S.
Kenneth E. Henes, M.Div.	Brian W. O'Grady, M.Div.
David P. Hillis, M.Div.	Robert E. Picirilli, Ph.D.
Michael J. Indest, M.A.	Benno Przybylski, Ph.D.
Richard D. Israel, Ph.D.	Daniel G. Pugerude, Ph.D.
William C. Jackson, M.Div.	David L. Reinhard, M.Div.
Byron D. Klaus, D.Min.	Bernard Rossier, Ph.D.
Richard A. Koffarnus, M.Div.	David D. Rymer
Robert F. Land, M.Div.	Daniel J. Saglimbeni, M.Div.
Philip K. Lohr, M.S.	James B. Shelton, Ph.D.
A. Wayne Lowen, Ph.D.	Norman Shuert, M.Div.

Personnel Continued

Wesley W. Smith, II, M.Div.

Streeter S. Stuart, Jr., Ph.D.

Mary Swanson, B.A.

Stan J. Tharp, M.A.

Francis C. R. Thee, Ph.D.

John Christopher Thomas, Th.M.

Robert E. Tourville, M.A.

Denis W. Vinyard, M.Div.

Paul Walker, Ph.D.

Virgil Warren, Ph.D.

William C. Williams, Ph.D.

Gary D. York, M.Div.

Richard A. Young, Ph.D.

Greek and Hebrew Alphabets

Greek

A	α	alpha	a	(f<u>a</u>ther)
B	β	beta	b	
Γ	γ	gamma	g	(<u>g</u>ot)
Δ	δ	delta	d	
E	ε	epsilon	e	(g<u>e</u>t)
Z	ζ	zeta	z	dz (lea<u>ds</u>)
H	η	eta	ē	(<u>a</u>te)
Θ	θ	theta	th	(<u>th</u>in)
I	ι	iota	i	(s<u>i</u>n or mach<u>i</u>ne)
K	κ	kappa	k	
Λ	λ	lambda	l	
M	μ	mu	m	
N	ν	nu	n	
Ξ	ξ	xi	x	
O	ο	omicron	o	(l<u>o</u>t)
Π	π	pi	p	
P	ϱ	rho	r	
Σ	σ,ς¹	sigma	s	
T	τ	tau	t	
Y	υ	upsilon	u	German ü
Φ	φ	phi	ph	(<u>ph</u>ilosophy)
X	χ	chi	ch	(<u>ch</u>aos)
Ψ	ψ	psi	ps	(li<u>ps</u>)
Ω	ω	omega	ō	(<u>o</u>cean)

Hebrew

א	aleph	ʼ ²	
בּ, ב	beth	b, v	
גּ, ג	gimel	g, gh	
דּ, ד	daleth	d, dh	(<u>th</u>ey)³
ה	he	h	
ו	waw	w	
ז	zayin	z	
ח	heth	ch	(kh)
ט	teth	ṭ	
י	yodh	y	
כּ, כ ך	kaph	k, kh	
ל	lamedh	l	
מ ם	mem	m	
נ ן	nun	n	
ס	samekh	s̱	
ע	ayin	ʻ	
פּ, פ ף	pe	p, ph	
צ ץ	sadhe	ts	
ק	qoph	q	
ר	resh	r	
שׂ	sin	s	
שׁ	shin	sh	
תּ, ת	taw	t, th	(<u>th</u>ing)³

Hebrew Vowels

	ā	father		u	rule		ê	they
	a	dam		ō	role		âh	ah
	e	men		û	tune		ă	hat
	ē	they		ô	hole		ĕ	met
	i	pin		î	machine		e	average
	o	roll		ê	they		ŏ	not

Greek Pronunciation Rules

Before another *g*, or before a *k* or a *ch*, *g* is pronounced and spelled with an *n*, in the transliteration of the Greek word.

In the Greek, *s* is written at the end of a word, elsewhere it appears as σ. The rough breathing mark (ʽ) indicates that an *h*-sound is to be pronounced before the initial vowel or diphthong. The smooth breathing mark (ʼ) indicates that no such *h*-sound is to be pronounced.

There are three accents, the acute (´), the circumflex (^) and the grave (`). These stand over a vowel and indicate that stress in pronunciation is to be placed on the syllable having any one of the accents.

Pronouncing Diphthongs

ai is pronounced like *ai* in aisle
ei is pronounced like *ei* in eight
oi is pronounced like *oi* in oil
au is pronounced like *ow* in cow
eu is pronounced like *eu* in feud
ou is pronounced like *oo* in food
ui is pronounced like *ui* in suite (sweet)

1. Where two forms of a letter are given, the one at the right is used at the end of a word.
2. Not represented in transliteration when the initial letter.
3. Letters underscored represent pronunciation of the second form only.

Introduction

The 6 volumes of the *Greek-English Dictionary* form 1 division of the 16-volume *Complete Biblical Library*. The first division, called the *Study Bible*, is composed of nine volumes. Each one contains an *Interlinear*. It uses a *comparative* Greek text which includes both the *Textus Receptus* and variants from the modern critical texts. All the major variants are found here, plus a multitude of the less significant ones. For our purposes *variant* means a reading which differs from the *Textus Receptus*. A *Textual Apparatus* shows the manuscript background of the variants.

On the page which faces the *Interlinear* is the *Verse-by-Verse Commentary* and the *Various Versions* column. From nearly 100 versions, in addition to the King James Version, the column shows different ways phrases have been translated.

The six-volume *Greek-English Dictionary* is a fitting companion for the *Study Bible*. They are closely linked by a numerical system which identifies each Greek word. The number is placed above the word in the *Interlinear* and is repeated in the *Dictionary* which lists the words in alphabetical order. By this system a person may easily go from the *Study Bible* to an in-depth study in the *Dictionary*. Such an arrangement makes this Greek dictionary as usable for the layman as for the scholar.

Such a combination of Biblical and theological material has not been produced in any previous work. *The Complete Biblical Library* is special because it employs a system which is usable by those who have little or no knowledge of Greek, yet will appeal to theologians at the highest level of scholarship. For all who use this work, it will open wider the door to the richness of the original text of the New Testament.

The *Greek-English Dictionary* is by itself a unique tool. It provides information the user could not obtain without consulting many lexical and theological books. Here all the information is available, saving a great deal of research time for students, ministers, and scholars.

FEATURES OF THE GREEK-ENGLISH DICTIONARY

1. Greek Words of the New Testament
2. Cognate/Synonym Research
3. Septuagint Section
4. Grammatical Forms
5. Greek-English Concordance
6. Word Studies
7. Resource Tools

GREEK WORDS OF THE NEW TESTAMENT

Every Greek word which appears in our *Interlinear* of the New Testament is listed in its alphabetical and numerical order. It is referred to as the "entry word." Including proper nouns, there are more than 5,500 of these. The assigned number also appears above the word each time it occurs in the *Interlinear* of the *Study Bible*. Those who wish more information about a word found in the *Interlinear* can easily locate the word in the *Dictionary* by using this "lexical number," as it is called. The word first appears in its Greek form. As a help to pronunciation, the English transliteration is given. Next appears the grammatical form of the word, such as verb, noun, etc. Finally, the basic meaning or meanings of the word are given.

COGNATE/SYNONYM RESEARCH

Here a majority of the entire vocabulary of the New Testament is subdivided into two main groupings. The first consists of words which have numerous cognates and synonyms, listed by their Greek spelling, English pronunciation, and lexical number. Under them are shown the terms which are related to them, either by descent (cognates) or by meaning (synonyms).

The second group is referred to as cross-reference words. This category was introduced so the long list of cognates which appears with some words would not have to be repeated over and over. The notation *Cross-reference* simply indicates that the reader is being directed to an entry word where there is an extensive listing of related cognates.

Cognates

In analyzing a language the term *cognate* refers to words which share a common derivation or descent. In most languages a verb serves as the root word from which a variety of cognates or related terms (nouns, adjectives, adverbs, etc.) descend. For example, the English words *save, savior, savings, safe,* and *safety* all are cognates; that is, they share a common ancestry.

Considering the cognates of a word is very useful, since words of a common family often share similar characteristics. This is especially helpful in studying the Greek language, where a cognate of a particular word may be used more frequently than the word itself. Knowing the meanings of other members of a cognate "family" helps to define a word from that family which occurs infrequently.

For example, the noun *hagiotēs* occurs only once in the New Testament, at Hebrews 12:10, and is quite rare in both the classical Greek and Septuagint literature. However, the related cognates *hagiazō* ("to sanctify, be holy") and *hagios* ("holy") occur often. One may infer, therefore, that the rare term *hagiotēs* shares with its cognates some overlap in its range of meaning. (The KJV translates it "holiness.")

Synonyms

In this work synonyms are words which have meanings similar to that of the entry word. Thus they are helpful in ascertaining the full meaning of a particular term. In addition, the synonym list indicates the various terms a New Testament writer had available to him. If the Holy Spirit guided the writer to choose one term over another in a given context, it may be important to understand why He did so. It is possible that in some contexts word choice might be simply a matter of style, but on other occasions the choice of one word over another might be very significant.

For example, John 1:12 states that as many as received Jesus as Saviour, "to them gave he power (*exousia*) to become the sons of God." Although several other Greek words have meanings similar to *exousia*, such as *dunamis* ("power, ability") and *ischus* ("strength, power, might"), only *exousia* carries the idea of "authority" or "right" which the context of this verse requires. Use of the English word *power* by the King James' translators tends to cloud the truth conveyed by this text; namely, there is no innate strength or might resident in man which can make him a child of God. Only faith in Christ grants one the "right" or "authority" to become a member of the family of God.

Remember, however, that no two words have exactly the same meaning. The term *semantic range* may be the most accurate description of the actual concept. This expression refers to the range of meanings each word has, depending on how it is used in a specific context. This being true, in order to do an accurate and adequate word study it is important to compare words whose semantic ranges overlap to a significant degree. The synonym lists make such a study possible.

To avoid serious errors in using the cognate/ synonym lists a word of warning may be proper at this point. For example, consider *kērux* ("envoy, herald, messenger") and a synonym, *angelos* ("angel, envoy, messenger"). Although some of their meanings are the same, it is absolutely incorrect to infer that *kērux* means "angel." The full significance of "semantic ranges" must be considered. One should not attach all the meanings of a cognate or a synonym to an entry word. The context helps to determine the specific meaning.

The editors of this massive work feel compelled to present a word of caution to those who use *The Complete Biblical Library's Greek-English Dictionary* and *Study Bible*. These volumes contain a vast amount of facts and information, but all this needs to be analyzed and synthesized before valid conclusions and applications can be derived. Note the following:

(1) While it is true that study of how a word was used over an extended period of time can help define its semantic range (i.e., the parameter of possible meanings a word may have), it will not necessarily disclose its specific meaning in a certain passage. In addition, a word which has a "literal" or "technical" meaning in one place may not have the same meaning every time it is used. For example, the Greek term *sarx*, which is one word used to refer to the human body (1 Peter 4:1), at different times refers to the "flesh" which covers the bones (Luke 24:39), to the human or physical nature (Romans 9:3), or to that aspect of man's fallen nature, i.e., the "flesh," which is subject to sin (Romans 8:3-8).

(2) A study of the historical etymology, including the root components and the cognates and synonyms of a word, does not necessarily determine its exact meaning.

(3) Tracing a word from one language to another (e.g., Hebrew to Greek, Latin to Greek, Greek to English, even Koine Greek to modern Greek) is no guarantee that the specific meaning of the term in its New Testament usage has been discovered.

(4) A Greek word may often have a wide range of meaning. This range is not only present within a particular type of literature (e.g., classical or New Testament) but also throughout the historical use and development of the word. Considering a word's use from one period to another is helpful, and studying all the uses of a word in a given body of literature such as the New Testament is illuminating. However, one must be careful not to impart

Introduction Continued

the entire breadth of meaning to a word everywhere it occurs.

All of these elements of research are of value and can shed light on how the word was used and what it meant in a variety of contexts. Therefore, in doing word studies consideration of the context must work together with the other elements mentioned above to yield a proper understanding of a specific term in a given passage.

This warning must not be allowed to discourage or confuse anyone who is seeking to understand the Bible better through a study of the languages in which it was originally written. Rather, it should be recognized that haphazard treatment of the Scriptures is a mistake that can have eternal consequences. Let this encourage all teachers and students of the Word of God to approach their studies with cautious humility in the effort to "rightly divide the word of truth."

THE SEPTUAGINT SECTION

The Septuagint version is the translation of the Hebrew Old Testament into the Greek Language. The title "Septuagint" (known also by the abbreviation LXX) is derived from the Latin term *septuaginta*, "seventy." This version came into being because of the spread of the Greek language throughout the then-known world. In the Fourth Century B.C. the armies of Alexander the Great swept across the earth, conquering all his enemies and bringing the Greek Empire to its zenith of power. Greek became the universal language.

The earliest written tradition that provides information concerning the origin and history of the Septuagint is the *Letter of Aristeas* (First or Second Century B.C.). This letter claims to be contemporary with the translation of the Torah by 72 Jewish elders who were gathered in Alexandria, Egypt, under the direction of Ptolemy II Philadelphus, ruler of Egypt (285-246 B.C.), hence the title LXX. Many historical inaccuracies and inconsistencies in the letter of Aristeas have caused some modern scholars to reject the reliability of much of the letter's contents. Another explanation is that this title was given to symbolize the 70 elders that accompanied Moses up Mount Sinai (Exodus 24:1,9).

Because of the Assyrian and Babylonian conquests several centuries before, thousands of Jews had been scattered to the far reaches of the empire, and by this time, in the Third Century B.C., Greek had become their everyday language.

Two factors helped to bring the Septuagint version into existence: (1) Some have given credit to Ptolemy II. It is thought that his interest in books led him to encourage the production of the Septuagint (he has also been credited with initiating the development of the great library at Alexandria, Egypt). (2) A more likely explanation, however, was the compelling need of the large number of Greek-speaking Jews at Alexandria and elsewhere who wished to have a text of the Old Testament they could read.

The Septuagint is important because it provides the Hebrew background for so many important Greek words of the New Testament. The Septuagint was of great significance to Greek culture, for through it the riches of the Old Testament were opened to the Greek mind for the first time.

The prominence of the Septuagint in the Early Church also greatly influenced the spread of Christianity and the development of Christian theology—for three reasons: (1) The extensive use of the Septuagint had spread ideas and themes to which the early Christian message could easily be attached. (2) The Septuagint provided a readily accessible pool of theological terminology which could be adopted by the Christian community in communicating the gospel to the Greek mind. (3) A majority of the citations and allusions to the Old Testament found in the New Testament are from the Septuagint.

It is well known that the language of the New Testament is not the classical Greek but the simpler, common, and international Koine Greek from the Hellenistic period of the time of Alexander the Great. But this is not the only characteristic of the New Testament Greek language. Words of deep theological significance in the New Testament text derive much of their content and meaning, not from the secular Greek use of the word, but from the Old Testament use in the history of revelation. In fact, many of these Greek words adopted a Hebrew meaning and spiritual dimension. Words which had little religious significance in secular Greek were used in the Septuagint to express the deep spiritual meaning of their Hebrew equivalents in the Hebrew Old Testament. (For an illustration of this see later information under the heading "Example of Use.")

Features of the Septuagint Section

In the opinion of the editors it is important to provide the information necessary to gain an adequate understanding of the way Old Testament themes, ideas, motifs, and vocabulary were transmitted through the Septuagint version into the Greek mind and the New Testament. Furthermore, this section will provide a bridge between the New Testament *Study Bible* and *Greek-English Dictionary* and the Old Testament *Study Bible* and *Hebrew-English Dictionary*, projected companion projects which will be forthcoming.

The research in this section is based upon the work *A Concordance to the Septuagint*, 3 volumes, edited by Edwin Hatch and Henry A. Redpath, Oxford: The Clarendon Press, 1897, 1906. Reprint, Grand Rapids: Baker Book House, 1983.

Hebrew Words

The first element of the Septuagint section is the Hebrew word(s) and the appropriate transliteration (pronunciation). Provided under each entry word, they represent the terms of the Hebrew Scriptures translated by that Greek word in the Septuagint version.

Note that the relatively small number of Hebrew phrases of two or more words translated by one Greek word are not included. Primarily this is due to the need to maintain a tightly controlled numerical reference system for the *Hebrew-English Dictionary*. In addition, not all words appearing in the Greek New Testament are present in the Septuagint version. Also omitted are any references to Greek particles, conjunctions, prepositions, numerals, or articles.

Hebrew Word Numbers

The second element of the Septuagint section is the number assigned to the Hebrew words. As mentioned earlier, the study system enables the student to move easily between the Old and New Testaments. This number will appear with the word in the *Hebrew-English Dictionary*. Numbers preceded by an *A* identify Aramaic words.

Short Hebrew Word Definitions

The third element of this section provides a brief definition of the Hebrew word and representative references where the Septuagint translates that Hebrew word by the Greek word shown above. This presentation seeks to provide definitions for the Hebrew words which are sensitive to the particular context of the passage cited.

For a more complete treatment of these words see the standard but somewhat dated work by Francis Brown, S.R. Driver, and Charles A. Briggs (*The New Brown-Driver-Briggs—Gesenius Hebrew and English Lexicon*. 1906. Reprint. Peabody, MA: Hendrickson Publishers. 1979). This edition is recommended over the Oxford edition because of its index which allows the student to find the Hebrew word under consideration and directs him to the page and column where the word is found in the lexicon. Furthermore, the Hendrickson edition is also indexed to *Strong's Exhaustive Concordance of the Bible*. The other recommended standard English work is the more recent, though less exhaustive, work by William Holladay (*A Concise Hebrew and Aramaic Lexicon of the Old Testament*. Leiden: E.J. Brill. 1988).

Verb Stems

Occasionally the primary meaning of a Hebrew verb differs from the meaning of that verb in the specific context of the Old Testament verse(s) cited in our research. In these cases the general definition is given first and is followed by the meaning of the specific form or stem being cited (e.g., qal, niphal, piel, etc.). For example: *shālam* (8396), Be complete, sound; piel: repay, return (Dt 7:10, 2 Sm 3:39).

Those who are not familiar with the Hebrew or Aramaic verb stems may want to refer to one of the following grammars: Lambdin, Thomas O. *Introduction to Biblical Hebrew* (New York: Charles Scribner and Sons. 1971); Seow, C.L. *A Grammar for Biblical Hebrew* (Nashville: Abingdon Press. 1987); Gesenius, Wilhelm. *Gesenius' Hebrew Grammar*. 2d English ed., ed. and rev. by E. Kautzsch and A. E. Cowley. (Oxford: Clarendon Press. 1910); Johns, Alger F. *A Short Grammar of Biblical Aramaic*. Rev. ed. (Berrien Springs, MI: Andrews University Printers. 1972).

Biblical and Apocryphal References

These references are simply a representative list of the places in the Septuagint where the given Hebrew word is translated by the Greek word cited. It is not an exhaustive list. For such a list see Hatch and Redpath's *A Concordance to the Septuagint* cited above.

The chapter and verse arrangements of the

Introduction Continued

Septuagint are sometimes different from the English Bible. When this occurs the Septuagint references are placed in brackets or parentheses immediately following the English Bible reference (e.g., Jeremiah 40:5 [47:5]). The Septuagint references are primarily shown according to *The Septuagint with Apocrypha: Greek and English* by Sir Lancelot Brenton, 1851. This work has been reprinted by both Zondervan Publishing House and Hendrickson Publishers and is the only complete English translation of the Septuagint available.

The names of Bible books are shown as they appear in the English Bible. The books affected by this include: 1 and 2 Samuel, which appear as 1 and 2 Kings in the Septuagint; 1 and 2 Kings, which appear as 3 and 4 Kings in the Septuagint; and Ezra, which appears as 2 Esdras in the Septuagint. References to the Theodotion text of Daniel have not been included.

At times a particular Greek rendering may have appeared in only one text. In these cases notations have been provided about the Greek text in which that particular rendering may be found.

As a result of the editing that the Septuagint received in both Jewish and Christian circles after the beginning of the Christian Era, the Septuagint text found in most modern editions does not reflect a single textual tradition. The recovery of a pure text is impossible. Rather, the text of modern printed editions represents the text of one or more of the following three uncials (ancient manuscripts of the Bible from the Third—Tenth Century A.D., written in all capital letters, on parchment or vellum, and bound in book form): Codex Alexandrinus (A) of the Fifth Century A.D.; Codex Sinaiticus (S or Aleph), of the Fourth Century A.D.; and Codex Vaticanus (B), of the Fourth Century A.D. Of the three the Vaticanus text enjoys the place of greatest stature.

In addition to the three texts mentioned above, there are references to the Sixtine Edition in the research part of the Septuagint section. Of the earlier editions the Sixtine is one of the most important. Published under the orders of Pope Sixtus V in 1568 (hence the title "Sixtine"), it was based primarily on the Codex Vaticanus, and any gaps were filled with readings from the Codex Alexandrinus. This edition became the basis for almost all other printed editions in the 300 years which followed its publishing.

For those Greek words which were used to translate five or less Hebrew words in the Septuagint, references are included to Sirach (also known as the Wisdom of Jesus the Son of Sirach, or also Ecclesiasticus), an apochryphal book of the Old Testament. These will provide additional examples of the way the Hebrew language and thought patterns were transmitted into Greek during the Intertestamental Period. Three primary copies of Sirach exist: the Greek of the Septuagint, the Syriac of the Peshitta, and the Hebrew fragments. The content of the book indicates that it was written prior to the Maccabean Revolt in 168 B.C., probably between 195 and 171 B.C.

Why Use the Septuagint?

How can study of the Septuagint increase one's understanding of the New Testament? (1) Most of the Old Testament quotes found in the New Testament come from the Septuagint. (2) More often than actual quotes, allusions to the Septuagint version appear in the New Testament. One such instance is John's use of the phrase *egō eimi* (John 8:58). This term comes directly from the Septuagint's translation of Exodus 3:14 where God reveals himself to Moses as the "I AM." (3) When interpreting specific New Testament passages, the Septuagint can provide the necessary link with the Old Testament which is essential for understanding certain New Testament terms, themes, and concepts.

Example of Use

The most common New Testament word for "law" is *nomos*. In secular Greek *nomos* primarily meant "common usage, custom, or universal principle." This gradually was modified to become what we refer to as "law." *Nomos* also came to mean a law as established by the governing body of a community or country. Through the Septuagint, however, an entirely new dimension for this word was added in the New Testament.

This new dimension came as the result of translating the Old Testament term *tôrāh* by the Greek word *nomos*. To the Jews *tôrāh* was the embodiment of their religion. It was used of the guidance and revelation of God himself, as communicated by the priests and prophets. The priestly instruction concerning the ceremonies and rituals was roughly equivalent to the Greek concept of *nomos*. In the Prophets, however, *tôrāh* was used as parallel in concept with "the word of the Lord" (Isaiah 1:10), and in this use embodied the principles of religion, God's purposes for His people, and the broad guidelines for ethics and morality.

When one comes to the word *nomos* in the Gospel of John, for instance, it is important to know that the word is used exclusively with the Old Testament concept of *tôrāh* in mind. On the other hand, Paul often uses *nomos* in both the common Greek manner, and less frequently in the manner of the Septuagint as equivalent to *tôrāh*. Without understanding the Jewish background of *nomos* as transmitted through the Septuagint, the student of the New Testament would be unaware of this important distinction.

GRAMMATICAL FORMS

In this section of the *Greek-English Dictionary* are listed the various and specific forms which an entry word takes in the text of the New Testament. For example, in the Greek language a noun will have different spellings, depending on how it functions in the sentence (as the subject, direct object, indirect object, etc.). A verb will be spelled differently, depending on whether it is present tense, future tense, singular, plural, etc. The list of grammatical forms simply represents the specific spelling and function in the context of particular verses. Notice the grammatical forms for the word *apostolē* (645):

1. *apostolēs* gen sing fem
2. *apostolēn* acc sing fem

The numbers on the left are a simple listing of the various forms the entry word will have throughout the New Testament. (Note that the word for "apostleship" never appears in the New Testament with its lexical spelling *apostolē*; it appears in the two forms shown above). Next the Greek spelling is shown, along with its English transliteration.

The third element, *gen sing fem*, shows the parsing for each form; that is, the specific information concerning the word's grammatical function in a given context. For example, the first grammatical form shows the word is used in the *gen*itive case, that it is *sing*ular in number, and that it is a *fem*inine noun.

Below is a complete listing of all the abbreviations used in this section (they also appear with the word in the *Interlinear* of the *Study Bible* volumes).

Parts of Speech
prs-pron = personal pronoun
rel-pron = relative pronoun
indef-pron = indefinite pronoun
intr-pron = interrogative pronoun
dem-pron = demonstrative pronoun
noun
verb
inf = infinitive
part = participle
adj = adjective
num = number
art = definite article
prep = preposition
conj = conjunction
partic = particle
intrj = interjection
card = cardinal (number)
ord = ordinal (number)
comp = comparative (adjective)
sup = superlative (adjective)
name
name-adj = name-adjective
name-adv = name-adverb

Mood
indic = indicative
subj = subjunctive
opt = optative
impr = imperative

Tense
pres = present
imperf = imperfect
fut = future
aor = aorist
perf = perfect
plperf = pluperfect

Voice
act = active
mid = middle
pass = passive

Case
nom = nominative
gen = genitive
dat = dative
acc = accusative
voc = vocative

Gender
masc = masculine
fem = feminine
neu = neuter

Person
1 = first person

Introduction Continued

2 = second person
3 = third person

Number
sing = singular
pl = plural

Following is a partial list of the more popular Greek grammars. They are identified as advanced, intermediate, and beginner works.

Blass, F. and A. Debrunner. *A Greek Grammar of the New Testament and Other Early Christian Literature.* Trans. by R.W. Funk. Chicago: Chicago University Press. 1961. (Advanced)

Dana, H.E. and J.R. Mantey. *A Manual Grammar of the Greek New Testament.* New York: Macmillan. 1927. (Intermediate-beginner)

Moulton, J.H., W.F. Howard and N. Turner. *A Grammar of New Testament Greek.* 4 vols. Edinburgh: T. and T. Clark. (Advanced)

Robertson, A.T. *A Grammar of the Greek New Testament in the Light of Historical Research.* Nashville: Broadman Press. 1934. (Advanced)

Story, J. Lyle and Cullen I.K. Story. *Greek to Me: Learning New Testament Through Memory Visualization.* San Francisco: Harper and Row. 1979. (Beginner)

Summers, R. *Essentials of New Testament Greek.* Nashville: Broadman Press. 1950. (Beginner)

Zerwick, M. *Biblical Greek Illustrated by Examples.* Rome: Scripta Pontificii Instituti Biblici. 1963. (Intermediate-advanced)

THE GREEK-ENGLISH CONCORDANCE

This lists all the places the entry word occurs in the KJV New Testament and how it is translated. Furthermore, variants to the KJV are included and identified by bold grammatical form numbers. Important variants are translated by a modern version (NIV, NASB). Less significant variants may retain KJV wording. There is a line for each entry, which includes part of the verse, the word being considered, and the Scripture reference.

Each entry is preceded by a number which identifies the grammatical form (see under "Grammatical Forms" above). Each occurrence of the word itself appears in boldface type so the student may see how it is translated in each context. (Some Greek words of the New Testament are translated by several English words because the context may change the meaning to some degree.) A parenthetical *NT* appears when the entry word can not be precisely translated in English.

Along with the other features, this part of the Dictionary is of great value. A person is able to study a Greek word in every context where it appears in the New Testament. This is the major source of information concerning the basic meaning of a word, and the varied significance it has in different contexts.

WORD STUDIES

The word studies are a focal point and the most prominent feature of the *Greek-English Dictionary*. Here the meaning and use of each Greek word of the New Testament are traced back to secular Greek sources and to the Septuagint. Most important of all, each Greek word is discussed with reference to its meaning within New Testament contexts.

Word Study Procedures

All Greek words found in the New Testament, including the variants to the *Textus Receptus*, have been listed in a dual order, both alphabetical and numerical. The more significant words are discussed in detail. Writers of the word studies have been asked to follow a uniform style so there will be a logical sequence.

First, the usage of the word in nonbiblical Greek literature is described under the heading "Classical Greek." For the purposes of the *Dictionary* this information reports how the entry word was used in secular Greek from as early as the Eighth Century B.C. (e.g., Homer) through the period of the New Testament's authorship. The discussion includes Greek poetry, historical accounts, inscriptions, ostraca, papyri, etc. This usage provides a good basis for understanding the word's significance in the New Testament.

The Septuagint version (*LXX*, see discussion regarding this version) is the next focus of research and study. This Greek translation of the Old Testament was the one used in the First Century A.D. and was a major resource for the New Testament writers. Just as a study of classical Greek literature yields information about the meaning of the Greek words used in the New Testament, study of a term's use within the context of the Septuagint provides additional insights. Moreover (as described earlier in the "Septuagint Section"), comparing a Greek term with the Hebrew word or words it translated may supply further understanding of what certain Greek terms meant to the New Testament writers.

Note: sometimes the Septuagint references are different from those in our English Bible. When this occurs, they follow in brackets or parentheses.

Finally, the study deals with how the word was used in the New Testament itself. This is the most significant factor, since the context is of major importance in determining the meaning of a word.

Sometimes in a word study the writer lists the number of times the word appears in the New Testament. This number may not coincide with the number of occurrences in the *Concordance*. The reason is that variants from the *Textus Receptus* are included in the *Concordance*.

Citations in Text and Bibliography

Our writers, researchers, and editors have cited a wide variety of sources in the word studies. In order to provide consistency in the usage of such a broad range of sources, both in text and in the Bibliography, some adaptations of basic principles have been made.

The fundamental rule concerning citations in text throughout this work is that when there is a reference to another source, the first element of information leads the reader directly to the correct place in the applicable subsection of the Bibliography, with one exception noted below for signed articles.

In-text references to individual books, commentaries, and periodicals are by last name of author, shortened title, volume, and/or page number. Therefore these will be found in the General Bibliography under the author.

Lexicons, dictionaries, and encyclopedias are cited in text by the title of the set, the entry word, and for long articles a volume and page number. In references to signed articles the author's name is listed first, followed by the entry word and title of the set. However, the reader will find this resource along with the others listed above in the Bibliography under "General Reference Sources by Title."

Where a word study refers to the word under discussion in another source, the Greek word is not repeated; only the cited source is given, plus the page number if applicable. For example, the reader may see simply (*Bauer*) in the word study on "agathos." This directs the reader to the article on "agathos" in *Bauer*.

Writings of antiquity are cited differently from modern works, first stating author and title, then usually book, section, and line. In the Bibliography, works of antiquity, early church fathers, the Apocrypha, pseudepigrapha, and Jewish literature are categorized in a section entitled "Literature of Antiquity." This covers secular and noncanonical literature from about the Fifth Century B.C. to the end of the Medieval Period, approximately A.D. 1500.

RESOURCE TOOLS

There are available many other fine works prepared by outstanding scholars. Of these we have selected six standard works which students may consult if they wish to do further research:

STRONG'S = Strong, James. *The Exhaustive Concordance of the Bible.* 1890. Reprint. Nashville: Abingdon Press. 1977.

BAUER = Bauer, Walter, William F. Arndt, and F. Wilbur Gingrich. *A Greek-English Lexicon of the New Testament and other Early Christian Literature.* Rev. ed. by F. Wilbur Gingrich and Frederick W. Danker. Chicago: The University of Chicago Press. 1979.

COLIN BROWN = Brown, Colin, ed. *The New International Dictionary of New Testament Theology.* 4 vols. Grand Rapids: Zondervan Publishing House. 1975.

KITTEL = Kittel, G., and G. Friedrich. *Theological Dictionary of the New Testament.* Trans. by G. W. Bromiley. 10 vols. Grand Rapids: William B. Eerdmans Publishing Co. 1972.

LIDDELL-SCOTT = Liddell, H. G., and R. Scott. *A Greek-English Lexicon.* 9th. ed. Ed. by H. Stuart Jones and R. McKenzie. Oxford: Clarendon. 1940.

MOULTON-MILLIGAN = Moulton, J. H., and G. Milligan. *The Vocabulary of the Greek Testament Illustrated from the Papyri and Other Non-Literary Sources.* London: Hodder and Stoughton. 1914-1930. Reprint. Grand Rapids: William B. Eerdmans Publishing Co. 1985.

They will be listed as follows, by number for Strong's and volume and page for all others: Strong; Bauer; Moulton-Milligan; Kittel; Liddell-Scott; and Colin Brown.

Each has its own special approach and will add to a student's understanding of the New Testament. When any of these six cross-references do not appear, it means that work does not discuss that particular word to any significant degree.

δ

1132. Δαβίδ Dabid name
David.

1. Δαβίδ Dabid masc
2. Δαυίδ Dauid masc

1 the son **of David**, the son of Abraham.	Matt	1:1
1 And Jesse begat **David** the king;		1:6
1 and **David** the king begat Solomon		1:6
1 So all the generations from Abraham to **David**		1:17
1 from **David** until the carrying away into Babylon		1:17
1 saying, Joseph, thou son **of David**,		1:20
1 and saying, Thou son **of David**, have mercy on us.		9:27
1 Have ye not read what **David** did,		12:3
1 Is not this the son **of David**?		12:23
1 Have mercy on me, O Lord, thou son **of David**.		15:22
1 Have mercy on us, O Lord, thou son **of David**.		20:30
1 Have mercy on us, O Lord, thou son **of David**.		20:31
1 cried, saying, Hosanna to the son **of David**:		21:9
1 and saying, Hosanna to the son **of David**;		21:15
1 They say unto him, The son **of David**.		22:42
1 How then doth **David** in spirit call him Lord,		22:43
1 If **David** then call him Lord, how is he his son?		22:45
1 Have ye never read what **David** did,	Mark	2:25
1 Jesus, thou son **of David**, have mercy on me.		10:47
1 Thou son **of David**, have mercy on me.		10:48
1 Blessed be the kingdom of our father **David**,		11:10
1 How say the scribes that Christ is the son **of David**?		12:35
2 How say the scribes that Christ is the son **of David**?		12:35
1 For **David** himself said by the Holy Ghost,		12:36
1 **David** therefore himself calleth him Lord;		12:37
1 whose name was Joseph, of the house **of David**;	Luke	1:27
1 shall give unto him the throne of his father **David**:		1:32
1 salvation for us in the house of his servant **David**;		1:69
1 unto the city **of David**, which is called Bethlehem;		2:4
1 because he was of the house and lineage **of David**:		2:4
1 is born this day in the city **of David** a Saviour,		2:11
1 which was the son **of David**,		3:31
1 Have ye not read so much as this, what **David** did,		6:3
1 Jesus, thou son **of David**, have mercy on me.		18:38
1 but he cried so much the more, Thou son **of David**,		18:39
1 How say they that Christ is **David's** son?		20:41
2 How say they that Christ is **David's** son?		20:41
1 And **David** himself saith in the book of Psalms,		20:42
1 **David** therefore called him Lord, how is he then		20:44
1 That Christ cometh of the seed **of David**,	John	7:42
1 out of the town of Bethlehem, where **David** was?		7:42
1 which the Holy Ghost by the mouth **of David**	Acts	1:16
1 For **David** speaketh concerning him,		2:25
1 freely speak unto you of the patriarch **David**,		2:29
1 For **David** is not ascended into the heavens:		2:34
1 Who by the mouth of thy servant **David** hast said,		4:25
1 unto the days **of David**;		7:45
1 he raised up unto them **David** to be their king;		13:22
2 he raised up unto them **David** to be their king;		13:22
1 I have found **David** the son of Jesse,		13:22
1 I will give you the sure mercies **of David**.		13:34
1 For **David**, after he had served his own generation		13:36
1 and will build again the tabernacle **of David**,	Acts	15:16
1 our Lord, which was made of the seed **of David**	Rom	1:3
1 **David** also describeth the blessedness of the man,		4:6
1 And **David** saith, Let their table be made a snare,		11:9
1 Remember that Jesus Christ of the seed **of David**	2 Tm	2:8
1 Again, he limiteth a certain day, saying in **David**,	Heb	4:7
1 **of David** also, and Samuel, and of the prophets:		11:32
1 he that is true, he that hath the key **of David**,	Rev	3:7
1 the Lion of the tribe of Juda, the Root **of David**,		5:5
1 I am the root and the offspring **of David**,		22:16

The greatest king of Israel, the son of Jesse in the genealogy of Jesus (Matthew 1:6).

1133. δαιμονίζομαι
daimonizomai verb

Be demon-possessed.

CROSS-REFERENCE:
δαίμων daimōn (1136)

1. δαιμονίζεται daimonizetai 3sing indic pres mid
2. δαιμονιζόμενος daimonizomenos
    nom sing masc part pres mid
3. δαιμονιζομένου daimonizomenou
    gen sing masc part pres mid
4. δαιμονιζομένῳ daimonizomenō
    dat sing masc part pres mid
5. δαιμονιζόμενον daimonizomenon
    acc sing masc part pres mid
6. δαιμονιζόμενοι daimonizomenoi
    nom pl masc part pres mid
7. δαιμονιζομένων daimonizomenōn
    gen pl masc part pres mid
8. δαιμονιζομένους daimonizomenous
    acc pl masc part pres mid
9. δαιμονισθείς daimonistheis
    nom sing masc part aor pass

8 and those which **were possessed with devils**,	Matt	4:24
8 they brought unto him many that **were possessed**		8:16
6 there met him two **possessed with devils**,		8:28
7 what was befallen to the **possessed of the devils**.		8:33
5 brought to him a dumb man **possessed with a devil**.		9:32
2 was brought unto him one **possessed with a devil**,		12:22
5 was brought unto him one **possessed with a devil**,		12:22
1 my daughter is grievously **vexed with a devil**.		15:22
8 and them that **were possessed with devils**.	Mark	1:32
5 and see him that **was possessed with the devil**,		5:15
4 to him that **was possessed with the devil**,		5:16

9 he that had been possessed with the devil	Mark	5:18
9 he that was possessed of the devils was healed	Luke	8:36
3 These are not the words of him that hath a devil	John	10:21

Classical Greek

In its earliest uses *daimonizomai* meant "to be possessed by a *daimōn*" (see *daimōn* [1136]). What that means depends upon understanding *daimōn*. Foerster terms it a "solid fact" that *daimōn* could denote a deity and in a philosophical sense it was influenced by popular animistic views; i.e., *daimōn* could be the spirit of any dead person (Foerster, "daimon," *Kittel*, 2:1-20).

The Jewish historian Josephus made an association between *daimonizomai* and supernatural events like oracles or utterances (*Wars of the Jews* 1.8.1, 2.13.4). Some idea of "possession" seems to be behind the usage in *Wars of the Jews* 7.9.1, "as though served by hands other than their own"; (cf. *Antiquities* 8.2.5). Foerster points out the absence of a rabbinic parallel to the verb (Foerster, "daimon," *Kittel*, 2:19). Except for a reading by Aquila in Psalm 91:6 (LXX 90:6), *daimonizomai* does not appear in the Septuagint.

New Testament Usage

In the New Testament *daimonizomai* occurs only in the Gospels (13 times). Those who were "demonized" (i.e., possessed by demons) were often overwhelmed by the evil spirit which took control of their entire personality. At times the demons within the individual controlled both the speech and the actions of the person (e.g., Mark 1:23-26; 5:1-10).

Matthew used the term more than any other writer (seven times); sometimes he replaced Mark's "unclean spirit" with "demon-possessed" (e.g., Matthew 8:28; 12:22, NIV; cf. "possessed with devils" in KJV). Luke and John used *daimonizomai* only once each (Luke 8:36; John 10:21). Except for one text (Matthew 15:22) *daimonizomai* always occurs in a participial form where it means "tormented by a demon." Matthew was also especially fond of the image of the demon-possessed being brought to Jesus (*prosēnenkan autō . . . daimonizomen* [*ous/on*], 4:24; 8:16; 9:32; 12:22).

Matthew linked demon-possession with physical infirmities (9:32; 12:22) and the demon-possessed were ruled by spirits (*pneumata* [see 4011], 8:16) until Jesus cast out the demons (*daimonia*, 9:34).

A common accusation against Jesus was that He himself was demon-possessed (John 7:20; 8:48,52; 10:20f.; cf. Matthew 9:34; 11:18). But His power over the demons demonstrated His authority from the Father (Matthew 12:28), which He gave to His disciples (Luke 10:16,17). The delivering of those who are demon-possessed, i.e., exorcisms, signals that the authority of evil which had enslaved the world (Satan) is broken. Jesus did battle with the enemy and won. These struggles were more than "skirmishes"; they heralded the dawn of the age of salvation. The period of God's rule has begun!

Strong 1139, Bauer 169, Moulton-Milligan 135, Kittel 2:19-20, Liddell-Scott 365, Colin Brown 1:450,453.

1134. δαιμόνιον daimonion noun

Demon.

Cognate:
δαίμων daimōn (1136)

Synonyms:
δαίμων daimōn (1136)
πνεῦμα pneuma (4011)

אֱלִיל 'elîl (462), Idols (Ps 96:5 [95:5]).

גַּד gadh (1440II) Destiny (Is 65:11).

צִי tsî (6984), Desert dweller, crier, demon (Is 34:14).

שָׂעִיר sā'îr (7988), Satyr, demon (Is 13:21).

שֵׁד shēdh (8158), Demon (Dt 32:17, Ps 106:37 [105:37]).

שֹׁד shōdh (8160), Destruction (Ps 91:6 [90:6]).

1. δαιμόνιον daimonion nom/acc sing neu
2. δαιμονίου daimoniou gen sing neu
3. δαιμόνια daimonia nom/acc pl neu
4. δαιμονίων daimoniōn gen pl neu
5. δαιμονίοις daimoniois dat pl neu

3 and in thy name have cast out devils?	Matt	7:22
2 And when the devil was cast out, the dumb spake:		9:33
4 casteth out devils through the prince of the devils.		9:34
3 casteth out devils through the prince of the devils.		9:34
3 cleanse the lepers, raise the dead, cast out devils:		10:8
1 John came ... and they say, He hath a devil.		11:18
3 This fellow doth not cast out devils,		12:24
4 but by Beelzebub the prince of the devils.		12:24
3 And if I by Beelzebub cast out devils,		12:27
3 But if I cast out devils by the Spirit of God,		12:28
1 And Jesus rebuked the devil;		17:18
3 he healed many ... and cast out many devils;	Mark	1:34
3 and suffered not the devils to speak;		1:34
3 preached in their synagogues ... and cast out devils.		1:39
3 power to heal sicknesses, and to cast out devils:		3:15
4 by the prince of the devils casteth he out devils.		3:22
3 by the prince of the devils casteth he out devils.		3:22
3 And they cast out many devils,		6:13
1 he would cast forth the devil out of her daughter.		7:26
1 the devil is gone out of thy daughter.		7:29
1 she found the devil gone out,		7:30
3 Master, we saw one casting out devils in thy name,		9:38
3 Magdalene, out of whom he had cast seven devils.		16:9
3 In my name shall they cast out devils;		16:17
2 which had a spirit of an unclean devil,	Luke	4:33

δαιμόνιον 1134

1 And when the **devil** had thrown him in the midst, ... Luke	4:35
3 And **devils** also came out of many, crying out, ...	4:41
1 For John ... came ... and ye say, He hath a **devil**.	7:33
3 called Magdalene, out of whom went seven **devils**, ...	8:2
3 which had **devils** long time, and ware no clothes, ...	8:27
2 driven by the **demon** into the desert (NASB)	8:29
3 because many **devils** were entered into him.	8:30
3 Then went the **devils** out of the man, ...	8:33
3 out of whom the **devils** were departed, ...	8:35
3 the man out of whom the **devils** were departed	8:38
3 and gave them power and authority over all **devils**, ...	9:1
1 as he was yet a coming, the **devil** threw him down, ...	9:42
3 Master, we saw one casting out **devils** in thy name;	9:49
3 the **devils** are subject unto us through thy name.	10:17
1 And he was casting out a **devil**, and it was dumb.	11:14
2 when the **devil** was gone out, the dumb spake;	11:14
4 **devils** through Beelzebub the chief of the **devils**.	11:15
3 He casteth out **devils** through Beelzebub	11:15
3 ye say that I cast out **devils** through Beelzebub.	11:18
3 And if I by Beelzebub cast out **devils**, ...	11:19
3 But if I with the finger of God cast out **devils**, ...	11:20
3 and tell that fox, Behold, I cast out **devils**, ...	13:32
1 The people answered and said, Thou hast a **devil**: ... John	7:20
1 that thou art a Samaritan, and hast a **devil**?	8:48
1 Jesus answered, I have not a **devil**;	8:49
1 Now we know that thou hast a **devil**.	8:52
1 And many of them said, He hath a **devil**, ...	10:20
1 Can a **devil** open the eyes of the blind?	10:21
4 He seemeth to be a setter forth of strange gods: .... Acts	17:18
5 they sacrifice to **devils**, and not to God: .... 1 Co	10:20
4 not that ye should have fellowship with **devils**.	10:20
4 drink the cup of the Lord, and the cup of **devils**:	10:21
4 of the Lord's table, and of the table of **devils**.	10:21
4 heed to seducing spirits, and doctrines of **devils**; ..... 1 Tm	4:1
3 the **devils** also believe, and tremble. .... Jas	2:19
3 they should not worship **devils**, and idols of gold, ... Rev	9:20
4 For they are the spirits of **devils**, working miracles, ...	16:14
4 is fallen, and is become the habitation of **devils**, ...	18:2

The etymology of this word is uncertain; possibly *daiomai*, "rip, split, tear apart" underlies it. In Greek philosophy *daimon* would then be "one who devours," that is, the spirit of death that separates the body from the soul. Whatever the case, the term conveys the same animistic views characteristic of heathen religion everywhere: the spirits of the dead are able to "possess" or "take over" human or animal bodies.

Classical Greek

In classical and Hellenistic Greek *daimōn* can denote a deity, although it was never entirely divorced from animistic understanding. In mythology *theos* (2292B) was reserved for the central deity of the cult, while *daimōn* was reserved for the minor, lesser deities who were viewed as influencing one's person, life, and fate. In addition, *daimonion* (1134) could carry the sense of "the divine, supernatural, superhuman." It is uncertain whether it is only the neuter of the adjective *daimonios* or the diminutive of the noun *daimōn*, "little deity."

The animistic understanding of *daimōn* continued to influence popular Greek religious and philosophical thought, particularly in magic and exorcism. In an animistic based philosophy all of existence was thought to be filled with—and guided by—*daimonia*. Thus the stars were called *daimonia*.

The authors of the great tragedies used *daimonion* for the "fate" of man (*hē tuchē*, cf. Isaiah 65:11, Septuagint). Thus man does not determine his own destiny, but he is directed by supernatural, divine powers, good and evil, beneficial and detrimental. The individual with "positive" *daimonion* has sort of a "guardian angel" who accompanies him from birth to death. If one has an unfortunate destiny, one's *daimonion* is understood to be evil. There is no way to change one's *daimonion*. In the dualism of the Orphic religion it is proper to speak of *eudaimōn* and *kakodaimōn*, i.e., "good demon" and "evil demon."

Based upon these concepts the Greek "hero" was considered a *daimones*. These powerful men were believed to have a supernatural power which originated in their *daimonion*. And drawing from the animistic beliefs of the populus, Greek tragedians imagined that *daimonia* could possess men, act through them, and occupy their bodies. For example, a demon might awaken evil desires, like an urge for revenge, or a tendency to lie. Therefore *daimonia* could indicate evil passions of a supernatural power and order.

In philosophical discussions *daimonion* denoted the "divine" in each man, like *nous* (3426), "reason," and *suneidēsis* (4743), "conscience," but it was different from *psuchē* (5425), "soul." When Socrates spoke of his *daimonion*, he was not concerned with his "fate" or the "destiny" of his life; rather, he saw it as the positive guiding force, the *internal voice* which whispered warnings and advice.

Daimonia proved useful to philosophers in their defense of "good" gods who allowed evil. Demons thus aided in explaining the problem of evil. The ancient myths about the supernatural feats of the Olympic gods were frequent targets of attack. Apologists found they could attribute such powers to demons or "minor deities" whose character and actions did not have to be explained.

In the face of sickness and suffering *daimonia* also provided a "scapegoat" for the problem of these evils. Sickness and other misfortunes were caused by the activity of evil demons. Many writings tell of demonic possession of men,

δαιμόνιον 1134

women, and animals, and relate accounts of exorcisms and sorcery by invoking the name of a stronger demon.

Philosophy was influenced by beliefs of the Orient and adopted *daimonia* as a word for the link between the world of the immortal gods and mortal men. Neo-Platonism determined that the space between the heaven of the gods and the earth of men was filled with intermediaries which were in charge of the material world and the natural elements. These *daimonia* were diverse in nature. The closer to physical matter they came, the less perfect they were.

Philo, a Hellenistic Jew who was somewhat of an apologist for Judaism at the time of Christ, sought to integrate Judaism with Hellenistic culture and religion. He often used *daimonion* in reference to those intermediary beings mentioned above. His logic, of course, was colored by dualism: God exemplifies that which is perfect—Man at the other end of the spectrum is imperfect and evil. As such, any direct contact between God and Man is impossible. Intermediaries are necessary. In order to express this gap between the two, Philo adopted the vocabulary of Hellenism and joined it with the Old Testament's concept of angels.

Septuagint Usage

Any highly developed "demonology" is remote in the Old Testament. On the other hand, the existence of demons is not denied. For the most part, in Hebrew, "demons" are called by many different names, and understandably so. They are, for instance, called *shēdîm*, perhaps demons of fertility; *seʿîrîm*, demons in the form of hairy goats who reek havoc in the ruins of Babel (Isaiah 13:21, Septuagint), or who reside in the deserts of Edom (Isaiah 34:14, Septuagint) *ʾĕlîlîm*, perhaps originally "worthless gods" (Psalm 96:5); *lîlîth*, probably a demon of the night, perhaps a sex demon or a nightmare (Isaiah 34:14). Other demon names are probably implied in the terms for certain manifestations of evil and in the names of wild animals. The prophet Isaiah warned against leaving the Lord and preparing a table for "Fortune" (RSV) and furnishing drink for "Destiny" (Isaiah 65:11); again, some believe that these were two names for gods. However, the Septuagint reads *tō daimoni* for "Fortune" and *tē tuchē* ("fortune") for "Destiny." The Septuagint most often translates demonic names with *daimonion*, but it also uses *pneuma* (4011), *mataioi* (see 3124), *theoi* (see 2292B), and so on.

Most importantly God forbids any involvement with demons under any circumstances. Demons belong to the powers of wickedness. The sun, the moon, and the stars (which the pagans call demons, divine beings, and which they fear and worship because they imagine the fate of men to be in their hands) are only "lamps" which the Creator himself "lit" for the joy and benefit of His children (Genesis 1:14f.). Israel must never offer sacrifices to evil spirits or practice idolatrous worship with *seʿîrîm* (Leviticus 17:7, Septuagint, *mataioi*). In Moses' Song it is said that when Jeshurun (Israel) waxed fat he forsook the Lord his Creator and sacrificed unto devils (Deuteronomy 32:15,17, Septuagint, *daimonia*). Israel's unfaithfulness toward its Lord is also reflected in Psalm 106:37 (LXX 105:37) which tells of its sacrificing of its sons and daughters unto devils (Septuagint, *daimonia*). To become involved with them was really to adopt the ways of the pagans and break the covenant of the Lord. "For all the gods (Septuagint, *theoi*) of the nations are idols" (Septuagint, *daimonia*) (Psalm 96:5 [LXX 95:5]).

In the Old Testament there is a repeated and explicit prohibition against consulting the spirits of the dead (demons) for advice or guidance. Evidently Israel was strongly tempted by the animistic ideas of the peoples living around them. The prohibition did not deny the existence of demons (cf. 1 Samuel 28:13 [LXX 1 Kings 28:13]: "I saw gods [*theous*] ascending out of the earth"), but it advised that the people of God belong only to Him (Leviticus 19:31; Numbers 23:23; Deuteronomy 18:11f.; Isaiah 8:17; and so on).

The Old Testament also rejects the idea that demons are intermediaries between God and man. Heaven as well as the earth are the property of God, and if He needs special messengers for His word He has His angels at His disposal (Hebrew, *malāʾkhîm*; Septuagint, *angelos* [32]; Genesis 28:12; 48:16; Exodus 14:19; 23:20).

The Lord's sovereignty over all the spirit world is seen in 1 Samuel 16:14 (LXX 1 Kings 16:14). It is said that the Spirit of the Lord (Hebrew *rûach YHWH*, Septuagint, *pneuma Kuriou*) departed from Saul and an evil spirit from the Lord troubled him (Hebrew *rûach-rā'âh*, Septuagint *pneuma ponēron para kuriou*). In the same manner in 1 Kings 22:19-23 (LXX 3 Kings 22:19-23) the Lord deceived the evil Ahab so that judgment was fulfilled on him. The Lord approved the mission of a spirit who offered to be a lying spirit (Hebrew *rûach sheger*, Septuagint *pneuma pseudēs*) in the "mouth of all his prophets" in order to entice Ahab to Ramoth-gilead where he would be defeated. And in Psalm 78:49 (LXX 77:49) it is said that the Lord punished His stubborn people by "sending evil angels among them" (Hebrew, *mal'ăkhê rā'îm* [messengers of judgment]; Septuagint, *angeloi ponēroi*). The Old Testament does not refer to any independent "demons" who exist outside of the omnipotent hand of God.

Intertestamental Period

In spite of the distinct prophetic warning against consorting with *daimonia* rather than the revealed word of the Lord, the thoughts of later Judaism, in part, revolved around demons, their nature and behavior. They developed a sophisticated demonology which is recorded in much of the Apocrypha and Pseudepigrapha of the Old Testament. The influence of Hellenism breached the prohibition of the Old Testament. People investigated demons; they not only believed in their existence, they also gave them place in everyday life. More "names" of demons were contrived.

Their origin was contemplated; some were thought to be created by God, others were perceived to be the offspring of the unnatural union between fallen angels and the "daughters of men" (based upon an interpretation of Genesis 6:1-4). The air was full of demons, and they initiated wars in the realm of men. They had the power to destroy life with sickness, but they were not the cause of every illness. They tempt, they lead men into the unclean practice of paganism, they seduce men with sorcery.

These angels of Satan (The Life of Adam and Eve 16) were led by Asmodius (Tobit 3:8,17), by Mastema (Jubilees 19:28), or by Beliar (The Testament of Levi 3:3). These are subleaders in an army. Most are chained in the abyss or the gulf, until the final judgment (I Enoch 15:1-7; cf. 2 Peter 2:4; Luke 8:31; Jude 6; Revelation 11:7; 17:8). But at the appointed time they will be released and will ravage men on earth (cf. Jubilees). Their abode, as in the Old Testament (cf. Mark 5), is ruins and tombs. The demon of delusion is one of the most dangerous because it is accompanied by seven other demons (cf. Luke 11:26), namely the demons of lewdness, insatiableness, lying, sorcery, impudence, iniquity, and stealing.

The writings of the Qumran community have systematized its members' demonology. Their highly developed theories are even more closely associated with the kingdom of evil spirits, the spiritual army of darkness led by Belial.

The theologians of later Judaism are in agreement about how to avoid the influence of demons: by studying and keeping the Law. But paradoxically, some famous rabbis also practiced both magic and exorcisms.

But there is an additional positive factor within later Jewish demonology: it distinguishes between evil and good spirits. The uncertainty of to whom the evil spirits are obedient disappears. The messengers of Satan are ruled by the ultimate opponent of God, but their activity belongs to this age. When the new age of the Messiah arrives, their time is past.

New Testament Usage

The vocabulary of the New Testament in its comments on demons has largely been adopted from later Judaism. But one cannot infer that it adopts later Judaism's beliefs in a wholesale fashion, nor should one conclude that the New Testament is describing its own unique demonology. In fact, there is no support that the New Testament is even interested in speculating about the nature or origin of demons. On the contrary, it is reserved and reluctant to speculate on demons in comparison with later Judaism.

The form *daimōn* is found at Matthew 8:31, Mark 5:12, Luke 8:29, and Revelation 16:14; 18:2. Otherwise, *daimonion* appears 46 times in the Synoptic Gospels; 6 times in the Gospel of John; 5 times in the letters of Paul; and 3 times in Revelation. But *daimonion* may sometimes seem to be synonymous with *pneuma*, just as it was in the Septuagint; but in those cases there is usually a modifier underlining the nature of the spirit (e.g., *akatharton* [see 167], "unclean," Matthew 10:1; *puthona* [see 4294], "divination," Acts 16:16; cf. Mark 9:25; Acts 19:15; 2 Corinthians 12:7; Revelation 9:11; 12:7,9).

Essentially the Greek usage of *daimonion* lies behind its occurrences in Acts 17:18 where *xenon daimonon* is supposed to refer to a stock expression used since the time of Socrates. The phrase suggests that Paul was perceived as denouncing the accepted gods of the state and was trying to import "foreign" gods.

The same general meaning of the words *deisidaimōn* (1170) and *deisidaimonesteros* (comparative form of the adjective, used positively to mean "pious, religious" and negatively "superstitious") is found in Acts (17:22; 25:19) just as it was in other Greek writings. The adjective *daimoniōdēs* (1135), "demoniac," is found only in James 3:15 in the New Testament where it is linked to false pagan wisdom.

"Being possessed" by demons is often expressed as being "entered" by them (*eiserchetai* [see 1511], e.g., Luke 8:30). The condition is described as having demons "living" within a person (*katoikein* [see 2700], e.g., Matthew 12:45), or one may "have" (*echein* [see 2174]) a demon (e.g., Luke 8:27). John the Baptist was accused of "being possessed" (Matthew 11:18, with parallels), and this same accusation was repeatedly leveled at Jesus (John 7:20; 8:48,52; 10:20). These charges implied not only "He must be crazy," but worse: "He is a Gentile." In other words, it was not the God of Israel who spoke through Him, but it was a demon. To the Jews this was seen as the ultimate rejection of God, His people, and the covenant; that person was a traitor worthy of death. To be possessed by a demon is usually expressed with the verb *daimonizomai* (1133).

Deliverance from being possessed is expressed either by having the demon "cast out" (*ekballein* [see 1531]), as in Matthew 7:22, or the demon might be said to "go out, depart," as in Matthew 17:18. The relationship between sickness and demon possession is not entirely clear in the Gospels. Many illnesses which are not connected with demons are recorded (Matthew 8:5f., 14f.; 9:27; 12:10; 20:30; Mark 7:31, and so on).

Some suffering is clearly attributed to demons: a deaf man was possessed (Matthew 9:32); a blind and mute man was possessed (Matthew 12:22); an epileptic boy was also possessed (Matthew 17:14). In effect, there are sicknesses induced by possession, possession not linked to sickness, and sickness not associated with possession.

Finally, some were possessed without any mention of sickness. The two demoniacs of Gadara (Matthew 8:28f., with parallels), the daughter of the Canaanite woman (Matthew 15:22f.), Mary Magdalene of whom seven evil spirits had "gone out" (Luke 8:2), and the demoniac in the synagogue of Capernaum (Mark 1:23f., with parallels) showed no signs of physical sickness.

In some texts Jesus specifically distinguished between the sick and the possessed. Matthew 4:24 states, "And they brought unto him all sick people that were taken with divers diseases and torments, and those which were possessed with devils, and those which were lunatic, and those that had the palsy; and he healed them." And in Mark 1:32 "they brought unto him all that were diseased, and them that were possessed with devils" (cf. 1:34). The women who ministered to Jesus and His disciples had, in part, been healed of "evil spirits and infirmities" (Luke 8:2).

Thus the picture is not one-dimensional; the accounts of demons and demon possession are different and impossible to systematize. Where the Gospels do not distinguish them we would be wise not to do so either.

Nevertheless, it must be pointed out that all suffering is related to the activity of Satan in the world, inasmuch as all suffering is a result of the fall of man. Suffering, however, whether physical in nature (which may or may not be the result of direct demonic activity) or spiritual (as in the case of demon possession) belongs strictly to this present age. Every miracle of "deliverance" Jesus performs—whether it is the saving of a soul or the healing of a body—serves as a sign (*sēmeion* [4447]) that in Christ, a new age of God's rule and royal dominion has arrived. It is, therefore, not by "magic" but by the power of God ("finger of God" [Luke 11:20]) that Jesus casts out evil spirits. Undoubtedly, the Spirit of God is stronger than all the evil spirits of Satan (Matthew 12:28). Through the power of God, Jesus—the deliverer of fallen mankind, the victorious One, the creator of a new world—restores to men the image of God that was marred by the Fall and by sin. He alone is able to loose all who are chained by the Evil One (Luke 13:16) and thus usher in a new age.

Is it any wonder, then, that demons "know" and fear Jesus (Matthew 8:29; Mark 1:24; James 2:19). The "sentence of death" has been passed on them because God has become man.

They realize their time is short, and therefore they rage (cf. 1 Peter 5:8; Revelation 12:12).

As mentioned above, the demonology of later Judaism systematized a ranking of demons. Organized in the fashion of an army, evil spirits were ostensibly led by Beelzebub, the "prince of the devils" (Matthew 12:24). The Pharisees accused Jesus of being in league with Beelzebub in order to explain by what power He was casting out demons. His response (verse 27) indicates that the disciples of the Pharisees were also engaged in the practice of exorcism. It appears, therefore, that the casting out of a demon does not necessarily result in the salvation of the individual who has been possessed.

This truth is vividly portrayed in Luke 11:24-26 where Jesus used the analogy of an empty house. There Jesus described how a person from whom a demon had been cast out was "reoccupied" by seven spirits more wicked than the first one which originally possessed him. Deliverance is not enough. Christ must become Lord of the "empty house." Real deliverance comes only through the preaching of the gospel concerning Jesus Christ as deliverer. This is why Jesus told the seventy whom He sent out, "Rejoice not, that the spirits are subject unto you; but rather rejoice, because your names are written in heaven" (Luke 10:20). At the same time, however, Jesus saw a foreshadowing of the final defeat of Satan and his demon force—because evil spirits were subject to the seventy through His name (Luke 10:17f.).

The word *daimonion* occurs only five times in the writings of Paul, four of these in the same context (1 Corinthians 10:20f.). The church in Corinth was strongly warned against participating in the pagan idol worship of their relatives or neighbors. They could not in one moment share in the Lord's Supper and in the next participate in the idolatrous meal—an act of worship—of pagan religion. The Lord's Table involves fellowship with Christ and with one another, just as the "table of demons" suggests fellowship with demons/devils. These are mutually exclusive. *Daimonion* here functions just as it did in the Old Testament, to express the worship of idols.

The fifth use of the term in Paul's writings occurs in 1 Timothy 4:1 where it is said that in the latter times some would depart from the faith. False teachers will appear who will follow doctrines which originate with deceiving *pneumata*, "spirits," and from demons. Demonic teaching will oppose the truth in the last days.

The Book of Revelation also speaks of a final assault of demons upon God's Church in the end time. They will purvey false doctrines, and dangerously mislead and entice people with seductive signs (*sēmeia* [4447]). In other words they will perform miracles (Revelation 16:13f.). The worship of demons and idols spoken of in Revelation 9:20 is similar to practices within the emperor cult that arose in the last days of the First Century; nevertheless, it also points to a future "neo-paganism" in which political strength, economic power, and other such demonic forces are worshiped. These have inherent demonic features including the worship of stars and allegiance to Satan.

Every line of the Bible converges upon the final victory of God's kingdom over all the demonic powers in existence. "The time" which the demons fear will come (Matthew 8:29). The "fire, prepared for the devil and his angels" (i.e., demons) will destroy their dominion (Matthew 25:41), and God will condemn them to a punishment of eternal fire (Jude 6).

STRONG 1140, BAUER 169, MOULTON-MILLIGAN 135, KITTEL 2:1-19, LIDDELL-SCOTT 365, COLIN BROWN 1:450-52.

1135. δαιμονιώδης daimoniōdēs adj
Demonic.
CROSS-REFERENCE:
δαίμων daimōn (1136)

1. δαιμονιώδης daimoniōdēs nom sing fem

1 not from above, but is earthly, sensual, devilish....... Jas 3:15

This is an adjective describing that which was associated with an evil spirit (see *daimonion* [1134]). Its usage in James 3:15 describes a knowledge or wisdom which is not of God but from a worldly source or particularly from an evil or unclean spirit.

STRONG 1141, BAUER 169, KITTEL 2:20, LIDDELL-SCOTT 365.

1136. δαίμων daimōn noun
Demon, evil spirit.
COGNATES:
δαιμονίζομαι daimonizomai (1133)
δαιμόνιον daimonion (1134)

δάκνω 1137

δαιμονιώδης daimoniōdēs (1135)
δεισιδαιμονία deisidaimonia (1169)
δεισιδαίμων deisidaimōn (1170)

SYNONYMS:
δαιμόνιον daimonion (1134)
πνεῦμα pneuma (4011)

גַּד gadh (1440II) Destiny (Is 65:11—Codex Sinaiticus only).

1. **δαίμονος** daimonos gen sing masc
2. **δαίμονες** daimones nom pl masc
3. **δαιμόνων** daimonōn gen pl masc

2 So the **devils** besought him, saying,	Matt 8:31
2 And all the **devils** besought him, saying,	Mark 5:12
1 and was driven of the **devil** into the wilderness.	Luke 8:29
3 For they are the spirits of **devils**, working miracles,	Rev 16:14
3 is fallen, and is become the habitation of **devils**,	18:2

In early Greek thought *daimon* was an imprecise term denoting "gods," "lesser deities," or any supernatural being. They could be good or evil depending on the circumstances with which they were associated. By contrast, *daimonion* (1134) narrowly defined those evil spirits that were feared by man. This distinction accounts for the limited use of *daimon* in the Septuagint and the New Testament: "*Daimon* is avoided because it is too closely associated with positive religious elements, whereas *daimonion* indicated from the very first the hostile spirits of popular belief" (Foerster, "daimon," *Kittel*, 2:12). This is confirmed by its lone occurrence in the Septuagint, Isaiah 65:11. Israel is rebuked for attempting to gain the advantage by preparing a table for *gadh*, the "god of fortune." The five uses of *daimon* in the New Testament are an anomaly, for no difference of meaning from the 63 occurrences of *daimonion* is evident. For a more exhaustive study of demonology, see *daimonion* (1134) and *diabolos* (1222).

STRONG 1142, BAUER 169, MOULTON-MILLIGAN 135, KITTEL 2:1-20, LIDDELL-SCOTT 365-66, COLIN BROWN 1:449-54.

1137. δάκνω daknō verb
To bite.

נָשַׁךְ nāshakh (5574), Qal: bite (Gn 49:17, Eccl 10:8, Am 5:19); piel: bite (Nm 21:6, Jer 8:17).

שָׂרָף sārāph (8042), Fiery serpent (Dt 8:15).

1. **δάκνετε** daknete 2pl indic pres act

| 1 But if ye **bite** and devour one another, | Gal 5:15 |

This word is used in the Septuagint primarily to translate the Hebrew word *nāshakh*, which describes the "bite of serpents" (Genesis 49:17; Numbers 21:6,8,9; Deuteronomy 8:15). Its only usage in the New Testament is a figurative reference to fighting within the Galatian church (Galatians 5:15). Paul's understanding of the Mosaic law and the events of Jewish antiquity is evident; he chose this word as part of his strong warning to the Galatians. Today, this word survives in Modern Greek, which puts it among words which have changed very little in 3000 years (*Moulton-Milligan*).

STRONG 1143, BAUER 169-70, MOULTON-MILLIGAN 135, LIDDELL-SCOTT 367.

1138. δάκρυ dakru noun
A tear, teardrop.
CROSS-REFERENCE:
δακρύω dakruō (1140)

1. **δάκρυσιν** dakrusin dat pl neu

| 1 and began to wash his feet with **tears**, | Luke 7:38 |
| 1 but she hath washed my feet with **tears**, | 7:44 |

Since the classical period *dakru* is the poetic form for *dakruon*. It shares plural forms with *dakruon*. The term occurs often in the Septuagint and New Testament but only in plural form: "tears" or "weeping." See word study at *dakruon* (1139).

LIDDELL-SCOTT 367.

1139. δάκρυον dakruon noun
A tear, teardrop.
CROSS-REFERENCE:
δακρύω dakruō (1140)

דִּמְעָה dim'āh (1893), Tears (2 Kgs 20:5, Ps 56:8 [55:8], Jer 9:1).

נָטַף nāṭaph (5382), Hiphil: prophesy (Mi 2:6).

1. **δάκρυον** dakruon nom/acc sing neu
2. **δακρύων** dakruōn gen pl neu

2 and said with **tears**, Lord, I believe;	Mark 9:24
2 and with many **tears**, and temptations,	Acts 20:19
2 to warn every one night and day with **tears**.	20:31
2 I wrote unto you with many **tears**;	2 Co 2:4
2 desiring to see thee, being mindful of thy **tears**,	2 Tm 1:4
2 and supplications with strong crying and **tears**	Heb 5:7
2 though he sought it carefully with **tears**.	12:17
1 God shall wipe away all **tears** from their eyes.	Rev 7:17
1 And God shall wipe away all **tears** from their eyes;	21:4

This term has many references in classical and Koine Greek and is found 35 times in the Septuagint to translate the Hebrew word *dim'āh*. In the New Testament Paul used this word to describe how he ministered to those he discipled (i.e., "with many tears"; cf. Acts

20:19,31; 2 Corinthians 2:4). This was in a manner similar to Jesus' description of the woman who ministered to Him with her "tears" (Luke 7:38,44). Revelation 7:17 and 21:4 both use words from Isaiah 25:8 to say that God will wipe away "every tear" from His people's faces. *Dakruon* appears 11 times in the New Testament. See also *dakru* (1138).
STRONG 1144, BAUER 170, MOULTON-MILLIGAN 135, LIDDELL-SCOTT 367.

1140. δακρύω dakruō verb
Weep, shed tears.

COGNATES:
δάκρυ dakru (1138)
δάκρυον dakruon (1139)

SYNONYM:
κλαίω klaiō (2772)

בָּכָה bākhâh (1098), Weep (Lam 1:2—Codex Alexandrinus only).

דָּמַע dāmaʻ (1891), Qal: weep (Sir 34:13); hiphil: cause to weep (Sir 12:16).

נָטַף nāṭaph (5382), Hiphil: prophesy (Mi 2:6).

נָתַךְ nāthakh (5597), Be poured out (Jb 3:24).

רָעַם rāʻam (7769), Be troubled (Ez 27:35).

1. ἐδάκρυσεν edakrusen 3sing indic aor act
1 Jesus wept. . . . . John 11:35

In classical usage, in the Septuagint, and in Josephus, *dakruō* is used alone to mean "cry," "weep," or "shed tears." It is also used with a direct object to mean "to weep for" something or someone. Its only use in the New Testament is John 11:35, "Jesus wept." The more common word for "weep" in the New Testament is *klaiō* (2772).
STRONG 1145, BAUER 170, MOULTON-MILLIGAN 135, LIDDELL-SCOTT 367.

1141. δακτύλιος daktulios noun
Ring, signet ring.

חוֹתָם chôthām (2460), Signet ring (Gn 38:18).

חוֹתֶמֶת chôthemeth (2966), Signet ring (Gn 38:25).

טַבַּעַת ṭabbaʻath (2995), Ring (Ex 25:12,14 [25:11,13]); signet ring (Est 8:2,8,10).

עִזְקָה ʻizqāh (A6037), Signet ring (Dn 6:17—Aramaic).

1. δακτύλιον daktulion acc sing masc
1 and put a ring on his hand, and shoes on his feet: Luke 15:22

This term means any ring worn on the finger (*daktulos* [1142]) or anything ring shaped, such as a circular handle. It appears most often in the Septuagint to translate the Hebrew word *ṭabbaʻath* which describes a "signet ring" worn to show identity or authority (see Genesis 41:42). The ring was used to place an authorized seal on something (see Esther 8:8,10). In the Parable of the Prodigal Son, the ring indicated full restoration to privilege, position, and authority as a son (Luke 15:22).
STRONG 1146, BAUER 170, MOULTON-MILLIGAN 136, LIDDELL-SCOTT 367.

1142. δάκτυλος daktulos noun
Finger.

אֶצְבַּע ʼetsbaʻ (697), Finger (Lv 4:30, 1 Chr 20:6, Jer 52:21).

יָד yādh (3135), Hand (Is 31:7—only some Sinaiticus texts).

כַּף kaph (3834), Hand (Jb 29:9).

1. δακτύλου daktulou gen sing masc
2. δακτύλῳ daktulō dat sing masc
3. δάκτυλόν daktulon acc sing masc
4. δακτύλων daktulōn gen pl masc
5. δακτύλους daktulous acc pl masc

2 will not move them with one of their fingers. . . . . . . Matt 23:4
5 and put his fingers into his ears, ... Mark 7:33
2 But if I with the finger of God cast out devils, ... Luke 11:20
4 touch not the burdens with one of your fingers. 11:46
1 that he may dip the tip of his finger in water, ... 16:24
2 and with his finger wrote on the ground, ... John 8:6
3 and put my finger into the print of the nails, ... 20:25
3 Then saith he to Thomas, Reach hither thy finger, ... 20:27

Classical Greek
Daktulos is the normal word in Greek of all periods for "finger." Other usages in classical Greek include "toe" (a "finger" of the foot). In another sense *daktulos* is a term of measurement used both of physical length (a "finger's breadth") and of metrical (poetic) pace. It also denotes a "date" (a fruit) and a kind of grape (*Liddell-Scott*).

Septuagint Usage
The Septuagint regularly uses *daktulos* in the literal sense (e.g., Leviticus 4:6,17,25, of the priest who dips his finger [ʼetsbaʻ] in sacrificial blood). "Toes," too, is an attested literal use (2 Samuel 21:20 [LXX 2 Kings 21:20]; Daniel 2:42; cf. 1 Chronicles 20:6, of a huge man with six fingers and toes).

Peculiar to the Septuagint, and undoubtedly influential on the New Testament writers, is the anthropomorphic expression "finger of God" (describing God in "human form" so as to be intelligible). The Egyptian magicians, unable to duplicate the plague of gnats, explained to Pharoah that it was done by "the finger of God" (Exodus 8:19). Elsewhere, the tablets containing the Law are said to be inscribed "by the finger of God" (Exodus 31:18; cf. Deuteronomy 9:10; Daniel 5:5, of the finger that wrote on the wall). The Psalmist used the phrase "the work of thy fingers" referring to God's creative works (8:3). Later, Jewish tradition used this expression frequently in reference to God's miraculous deeds (see Schlier, "daktulos," *Kittel*, 2:20f.).

The works of God's "fingers"—His creative acts—caused the Psalmist to be overwhelmed (Psalm 8:3), but in contrast, Isaiah 2:8, 17:8, and 31:7 speak of human "works of fingers" as the manufacturer of idolatrous altars (cf. Wisdom of Solomon 15:15 which denounces the heathen idols as not having eyes to see, ears to hear, "nor fingers to feel with").

New Testament Usage
Most often the literal sense of "finger" occurs in the New Testament. Jesus placed His fingers in the ears of the deaf man and healed him (Mark 7:33; cf. John 20:25,27 which describes putting a finger in the scars). In a more figurative sense, Jesus condemned the legal experts for not even being willing to lift a "finger" to help God's people live righteous lives (Luke 11:46; cf. Matthew 23:4).

The expression "finger of God" occurs in an important text in Luke 11:20. Jesus declared: "If I with the finger of God cast out devils, no doubt the kingdom of God is come upon you." Here Jesus was using Old Testament language in reference to His own ministry. Theologically it says that Jesus' miracles witness not only to the inbreaking of the Kingdom, but to His source of power as well—"by the finger of God."

STRONG 1147, BAUER 170, MOULTON-MILLIGAN 136, KITTEL 2:20-21, LIDDELL-SCOTT 367-68, COLIN BROWN 2:148,150.

1143. Δαλμανουθά

Dalmanoutha name

Dalmanutha.

1. Δαλμανουθά Dalmanoutha

1 and came into the parts of **Dalmanutha**............ Mark 8:10

Uncertain area near the Sea of Galilee; it may be another name for Magadan (also uncertain) or Magdala (Mark 8:10; cf. Matthew 15:39).

1144. Δαλματία Dalmatia name

Dalmatia.

1. Δαλματίαν Dalmatian acc fem

1 Crescens to Galatia, Titus unto **Dalmatia**.......... 2 Tm 4:10

Mountainous area in southern Illyricum, east of the Adriatic Sea across from Italy (2 Timothy 4:10).

1145. δαμάζω damazō verb

Tame, subdue, control.

חָשַׁל chāshal (A2936), Shatter (Dn 2:40—Aramaic).

1. δαμάσαι damasai inf aor act
2. δαμάζεται damazetai 3sing indic pres mid
3. δεδάμασται dedamastai 3sing indic perf mid

1 neither could any man tame him................... Mark 5:4
2 and of serpents, and of things in the sea, is tamed,... Jas 3:7
3 is tamed, and **hath been tamed** of mankind:............. 3:7
1 the tongue can no man **tame**; it is an unruly evil,...... 3:8

This verb is widely used in classical Greek and later for gaining control of animals, people, nature, or anything requiring effort to master. The *-azō* ending in the verb indicates action and causation, hence to "make tame, get control over, subdue." Its only use in the Septuagint is Daniel 2:40. In the New Testament it refers to man's ability to gain mastery over all kinds of animals, though he cannot "tame" or "gain control over" his own tongue (James 3:7,8). In Mark 5:4 no one but Jesus was able to "tame" or "subdue" the demoniac.

STRONG 1150, BAUER 170, MOULTON-MILLIGAN 136, LIDDELL-SCOTT 368.

1146. δάμαλις damalis noun

Heifer, young cow.

בָּקָר bāqār (1267), Cattle, herd, ox (Nm 7:17,23,29).
עֵגֶל 'ēghel (5903), Calf (1 Sm 28:24, 2 Kgs 10:29, 17:16).
עֶגְלָה 'eghlāh (5904), Heifer (Gn 15:9, 1 Sm 16:2, Hos 10:11).
פַּר par (6749), Young bull (Nm 7:88).
פָּרָה pārāh (6760), Heifer (Nm 19:2,6, Hos 4:16).

1. δαμάλεως damaleōs gen sing fem

1 and the ashes **of an heifer** sprinkling the unclean,.... Heb 9:13

This word is related to *damazō* (1145) and *damalizō*, "to tame" or "subdue." It frequently appears in the Septuagint. An important cleansing ritual required the ashes of a burned red heifer (Numbers 19:2,6,9 and Josephus *Antiquities* 4.4.6). Hebrews 9:13 refers to this Old Testament ritual which cleansed the flesh, but the text adds that only Christ's blood can cleanse the conscience.

STRONG 1151, BAUER 170, MOULTON-MILLIGAN 136, LIDDELL-SCOTT 368.

1147. Δάμαρις Damaris name

Damaris.

1. Δάμαρις Damaris nom fem

1 a woman named **Damaris**, and others with them. ... Acts 17:34

Name of a woman converted by Paul in Athens (Acts 17:34).

1148. Δαμασκηνός

Damaskēnos name-adj

Damascene.

1. Δαμασκηνῶν Damaskēnōn gen pl masc

1 kept the city **of the Damascenes** with a garrison, ... 2 Co 11:32

Belonging to Damascus (2 Corinthians 11:32).

1149. Δαμασκός Damaskos name

Damascus.

1. Δαμασκῷ Damaskō dat fem
2. Δαμασκόν Damaskon acc fem

2 And desired of him letters to **Damascus** .... Acts 9:2
1 And as he journeyed, he came near **Damascus**: 9:3
2 they led him ... and brought him into **Damascus** 9:8
1 And there was a certain disciple at **Damascus**, ... 9:10
1 with the disciples which were at **Damascus**, ... 9:19
1 and confounded the Jews which dwelt at **Damascus**, ... 9:22
1 and how he had preached boldly at **Damascus** 9:27
2 letters unto the brethren, and went to **Damascus**, ... 22:5
1 and was come nigh unto **Damascus** about noon, ... 22:6
2 Arise, and go into **Damascus**; 22:10
2 being led by the hand ... I came into **Damascus** 22:11
1 a good report of all the Jews which dwelt there, ... 22:12
2 Whereupon as I went to **Damascus** with authority 26:12
1 But showed first unto them of **Damascus**, ... 26:20
1 In **Damascus** the governor under Aretas the king ... 2 Co 11:32
2 into Arabia, and returned again unto **Damascus**. ...... Gal 1:17

Ancient city where Paul was baptized (Acts 9:18); ruled in New Testament times by King Aretas (see 696).

1150. δανείζω daneizō verb

Lend money, to borrow.

COGNATES:
δάνειον daneion (1151)
δανειστής daneistēs (1152)

לָוָה lāwâh (4004), Qal: borrow (Neh 5:4, Ps 37:21 [36:21], Is 24:2); hiphil: lend (Dt 28:44, Prv 19:17).

עָבַט 'āvaṭ (5879), Qal: borrow (Dt 15:6); hiphil: lend (Dt 15:8).

שָׁאַל shā'al (8068), Beg (Prv 20:4).

1. δανείζετε daneizete 2pl indic/impr pres act
2. δανείζουσιν daneizousin 3pl indic pres act
3. δανείζητε daneizēte 2pl subj pres act
4. δανείσασθαι daneisasthai inf aor mid
5. δανίσητε danisēte 2pl subj aor act
6. δανίσασθαι danisasthai inf aor mid

4 and from him that would **borrow** of thee .... Matt 5:42
3 if ye **lend** to them of whom ye hope to receive, ... Luke 6:34
5 if ye **lend** to them of whom ye hope to receive, ... 6:34
2 for sinners also **lend** to sinners, ... 6:34
1 But love ye your enemies, and do good, and **lend**, ... 6:35

The active form of this verb means "to lend money" (often for excessive interest). The middle form means "to borrow." It is a very common word from the classical through Koine periods, and it also occurs in the Septuagint. *Daneizō* is often found in contracts, public deeds, and business records. Jesus said to "lend" even to enemies, expecting nothing in return except God's reward (Luke 6:34,35). In a similar context (Matthew 5:42), He said not to turn away from one who wished to "borrow" (middle form).

STRONG 1155, BAUER 170, MOULTON-MILLIGAN 136, LIDDELL-SCOTT 369.

1151. δάνειον daneion noun

Debt, loan.

CROSS-REFERENCE:
δανείζω daneizō (1150)

נָשָׁה nāshâh (5567), Lend (Dt 24:11).

עָבַט 'āvaṭ (5879), Take or give a pledge; hiphil: lend (Dt 15:8).

1. δάνειον daneion nom/acc sing neu

1 and loosed him, and forgave him the **debt**. .... Matt 18:27

From the classical through the Koine period, this noun referred to loans of money. It is so used in the Septuagint. Its root is *daneizō* (1150), "to lend" (Deuteronomy 15:8,10; 28:12; 4 Maccabees 2:8). In Matthew 18:27, the Parable of the Unforgiving Servant, the master canceled the large "debt" of money owed to him by his servant.

δανειστής 1152

STRONG 1156, BAUER 170, MOULTON-MILLIGAN 136, LIDDELL-SCOTT 369.

1152. δανειστής daneistēs noun
Creditor, moneylender.
CROSS-REFERENCE:
 δανείζω daneizō (1150)
 נָשָׁה nāshâh (5567), Creditor (2 Kgs 4:1, Ps 109:11 [108:11]).
 רָשׁ rāsh (7851), Poor (Prv 29:13).

1. δανειστῇ daneistē dat sing masc

1 was a certain **creditor** which had two debtors:....... Luke 7:41

This term refers to a person who lends money or extends credit. It is used this way in classical and Koine Greek, and in the Septuagint. *Daneistēs* is related to *daneizō* (1150), "to lend" (perhaps for interest). In Luke 7:41, a "creditor" who canceled debts owed to him is compared to Jesus who forgives sins.

STRONG 1157, BAUER 170, MOULTON-MILLIGAN 137, LIDDELL-SCOTT 369.

1153. Δανιήλ Daniēl name
Daniel.

1. Δανιήλ Daniēl masc

1 desolation, spoken of by **Daniel** the prophet,....... Matt 24:15
1 of desolation, spoken of by **Daniel** the prophet,.... Mark 13:14

The Old Testament exilic prophet who spoke of the variously interpreted "Abomination of Desolation" (Matthew 24:15).

1154. δαπανάω dapanaō verb
Spend, bear expense, waste, consume.

1. δαπανήσητε dapanēsēte 2pl subj aor act
2. δαπάνησον dapanēson 2sing impr aor act
3. δαπανήσαντος dapanēsantos gen sing masc part aor act
4. δαπανήσασα dapanēsasa nom sing fem part aor act
5. δαπανήσω dapanēsō 1sing indic fut act

4 had **spent** all that she had, ... rather grew worse,.... Mark 5:26
3 And when he **had spent** all,...................... Luke 15:14
2 and **be at charges** with them,...................... Acts 21:24
5 And I will very gladly **spend** and be spent for you; 2 Co 12:15
1 ask amiss, that ye **may consume** it upon your lusts.... Jas 4:3

Classical Greek and Septuagint Usage
The most common meaning of this verb is "to spend money." It is used more broadly, however, to mean spending other things, such as time, energy, or one's strength. It sometimes has the connotation of wastefulness, of using up everything in excessive indulgence. In classical Greek and in the Septuagint it also has the figurative meaning "to wear out, exhaust, or destroy" as in hearts worn out to death, a water supply becoming spent (Judith 11:12), or a burnt offering being spent by the fire (2 Maccabees 1:23).

New Testament Usage
In the New Testament the literal meaning of "spending money" occurs in Acts 21:24 where Paul is asked to pay the temple expenses of four men. It is also used with the bad connotation of wastefulness in the Parable of the Prodigal Son (Luke 15:14). The time came when all his wealth had been spent, obviously wasted indulgently. (See also James 4:3.) Both the broad literal ("spending anything") and the figurative ("being worn out, exhausted, or destroyed") were combined in one sentence by Paul in 2 Corinthians 12:15 when he said, "I will very gladly spend and be spent (*ekdapanaō* [1537], an emphatic form of *dapanaō*) for you."

STRONG 1159, BAUER 171, MOULTON-MILLIGAN 137, LIDDELL-SCOTT 369.

1155. δαπάνη dapanē noun
Cost, expense.

 נִפְקָה niphqāh (A5495), Cost (Ezr 6:4,8—Aramaic).

1. δαπάνην dapanēn acc sing fem

1 sitteth not down first, and counteth the **cost**,....... Luke 14:28

This is the classical word for "cost" or "expenditure," whether reasonable or extravagant. It is commonly used in Koine for "expense" or "price." *Dapanē* is found also in the Septuagint. It is derived from *dapanaō* (1154), "to spend freely" or "consume." In Luke 14:28 Jesus taught that a builder counts the cost before he begins the tower; likewise a person should count the cost of following Jesus (14:26-33).

STRONG 1160, BAUER 171, MOULTON-MILLIGAN 137, LIDDELL-SCOTT 369.

1156. δέ de conj
But, now, more over, yet in fact, indeed.

1. δ' d'
2. δέ de

```
1 and whosoever will lose his life for my sake ....... Matt 16:25
2 The spirit truly is ready, but the flesh is weak..... Mark 14:38
```

Classical Greek and New Testament Usage

This is one of the most common words used in both classical and Koine Greek to connect clauses. Though usually positioned as the second word in the clause, it really begins the clause. Often there is some contrast between the clauses, but often the contrast is barely discernible. If there is a contrast, *de* is translated "but," "however," or "yet." If there is no contrast it is translated "and," "now," or "then." When *de* shows contrast and means "but," it is usually not an emphatic "but." The word *alla* (233), "but," is used to express a strong contrast. Another way of expressing a strong contrast is using *de* along with *mēn* (3173); *mēn* starting the first clause, and *de* starting the second one. (See Matthew 3:11; 9:37.) The Greeks did not use punctuation to mark the end of a sentence. They would simply connect their sentences together with conjunctions, the two most frequent being *de* and *kai* (2504), "and." Often these seem to have no more function than to mark the end of one sentence and the beginning of the next, and sometimes they are left out of the English translation since our period serves that function. *De* is used with *kai* to make the "and" more emphatic. It is then translated "and also" or "but also."

STRONG 1161, BAUER 171, LIDDELL-SCOTT 371-72.

1157. δέησις deēsis noun

Request, petition, prayer, supplication.

COGNATE:
δέομαι deomai (1183)

SYNONYMS:
αἴτημα aitēma (154)
ἔντευξις enteuxis (1767)
εὐχή euchē (2152)
ἱκετηρία hiketēria (2404)
προσευχή proseuchē (4194)

אֲרֶשֶׁת 'āresheth (807), Request (Ps 21:2 [20:2]).

עֱנוּת 'ěnûth (6269), Affliction (Ps 22:24 [21:24]).

צְעָקָה tseʿāqāh (7095), Cry (Ps 9:12).

רְוָחָה rewāchāh (7595), Relief (Lam 3:56—Codex Vaticanus only).

רִנָּה rinnāh (7726), Cry (2 Chr 6:19, Ps 17:1 [16:1], Jer 11:14).

שִׂיחַ sîach (7945), Muse, complain (Ps 142:2 [141:2]).

שֶׁוַע shewaʿ (8210), Cry for help (Ps 5:2).

שׁוּעַ shûaʿ (8213), Cry (Jb 36:19).

שַׁוְעָה shawʿāh (8216), Cry (Pss 34:15 [33:15], 39:12 [38:12], 40:1 [39:1]).

תְּחִנָּה techinnāh (8798), Supplication (1 Kgs 8:38, Pss 6:9, 55:1 [54:1]).

תַּחֲנוּן tachănûn (8800), Supplication (Ps 28:2 [27:2], Jer 3:21, Dn 9:17).

תְּפִלָּה tephillāh (8940), Prayer (2 Chr 6:35, Ps 66:19 [65:19], Is 1:15).

1. **δέησις** deēsis nom sing fem
2. **δεήσεως** deēseōs gen sing fem
3. **δεήσει** deēsei dat sing fem
4. **δέησιν** deēsin acc sing fem
5. **δεήσεσιν** deēsesin dat pl fem
6. **δεήσεις** deēseis acc pl fem

```
1 Fear not, Zacharias: for thy prayer is heard;........ Luke 1:13
5 served God with fastings and prayers night ... day....... 2:37
6 disciples of John fast often, and make prayers,.......... 5:33
3 with one accord in prayer and supplication,......... Acts 1:14
1 my heart's desire and prayer to God for Israel is,.. Rom 10:1
3 Ye also helping together by prayer for us,.......... 2 Co 1:11
3 And by their prayer for you,........................ 9:14
2 Praying always with all prayer and supplication ...... Eph 6:18
3 all perseverance and supplication for all saints;....... 6:18
3 Always in every prayer of mine for you all........ Phlp 1:4
4 Always in every prayer ... making request with joy,..... 1:4
2 shall turn to my salvation through your prayer,......... 1:19
3 by prayer and supplication with thanksgiving.......... 4:6
6 supplications, prayers, intercessions,.............. 1 Tm 2:1
5 in supplications and prayers night and day........... 5:5
5 remembrance of thee in my prayers night and day;..2 Tm 1:3
6 prayers and supplications with strong crying.......... Heb 5:7
1 The effectual fervent prayer of a righteous man...... Jas 5:16
4 and his ears are open unto their prayers:............1 Pt 3:12
```

Classical Greek

Related to the verb *deomai* (1183), "ask, beg, beseech," *deēsis* is basically a "request" or an "entreaty" in a religious context. When addressed to God it can mean a "prayer." Papyri indicate the word was a strong term meaning more than a simple request. It was used of a prisoner's request (probably for freedom or some favor) as well as in requests to deities (*Moulton-Milligan*).

Septuagint Usage

Deēsis occurs quite frequently in the Septuagint where it translates nine Hebrew words including *techinnāh* and *tachănûn*, which are both terms for supplication (favor) (e.g., 1 Kings [LXX 3 Kings] 8:29,30,38; 9:3; 2 Chronicles 6:19,39; Psalms 28:2 [LXX 27:2]; 86:6 [85:6]). "Hear the voice of my supplications, O Lord," the Psalmist cried (Psalm 140:6 [LXX 139:6]). The concepts of prayer and "supplication" are often joined (e.g., 2 Chronicles 6:19; Psalm 6:9; Daniel 9:17; 1 Maccabees 7:37), and *deēsis* is almost exclusively directed to God (but cf. 1 Maccabees 11:49, *Bauer*).

New Testament Usage

The New Testament writers know only of a "supplication" directed to God (but cf. *deomai*). Luke interpreted *deēsis* as an act of piety. He joined it with other such acts like "fasting" (e.g., Luke 2:37; 5:33; cf. 1:13). Paul explicitly linked *deēsis* to prayer four times (Ephesians 6:18; Philippians 4:6; 1 Timothy 2:1; 5:5). At times his "entreaty" was on behalf (*huper* [5065]) of others (Romans 10:1; 2 Corinthians 1:11; 9:14; Philippians 1:4; 1 Timothy 2:1; cf. 2 Timothy 1:2,3 [*peri* (3875)]). Hebrews 5:7 portrays Jesus as offering "prayers and supplications" to God in His role as High Priest.

STRONG 1162, BAUER 171-72, MOULTON-MILLIGAN 137, KITTEL 2:40-41, LIDDELL-SCOTT 372, COLIN BROWN 2:860-61.

1158. δεῖ dei verb

It is necessary, must, has to, should.

CROSS-REFERENCE:
δέω deō (1204)

1. **δεῖ** dei 3sing indic pres act
2. **δέῃ** deē 3sing subj pres act
3. **δέον** deon nom/acc sing neu part pres act
4. **δέοντα** deonta nom/acc pl neu part pres act
5. **δεῖν** dein inf pres act
6. **ἔδει** edei 3sing indic imperf act

1	how that he **must** go unto Jerusalem, and suffer	Matt 16:21
1	Why then say the scribes that Elias **must** first come?	17:10
6	**Shouldest** not thou also have had compassion	18:33
6	these **ought** ye to have done,	23:23
1	for all these things **must** come to pass,	24:6
6	Thou **oughtest** therefore to have put my money to	25:27
2	Though I **should** die with thee,	26:35
1	the scriptures be fulfilled, that thus it **must** be?	26:54
1	that the Son of man **must** suffer many things,	Mark 8:31
1	Why say the scribes that Elias **must** first come?	9:11
1	be ye not troubled: for such things **must** needs be;	13:7
1	gospel **must** first be published among all nations.	13:10
1	see the abomination ... standing where it **ought** not,	13:14
2	If I **should** die with thee, I will not deny thee	14:31
1	that I **must** be about my Father's business?	Luke 2:49
1	I **must** preach the kingdom of God to other cities	4:43
1	Saying, The Son of man **must** suffer many things,	9:22
6	these **ought** ye to have done,	11:42
1	teach you in the same hour what ye **ought** to say.	12:12
1	There are six days in which men **ought** to work:	13:14
6	**ought** not this woman, ... a daughter of Abraham,	13:16
1	Nevertheless I **must** walk to day, and to morrow,	13:33
6	It **was meet** that we should make merry,	15:32
1	But first **must** he suffer many things,	17:25
5	that men **ought** always to pray, and not to faint;	18:1
1	come down; for to day I **must** abide at thy house.	19:5
1	for these things **must** first come to pass;	21:9
6	when the passover **must** be killed.	22:7
1	that this that is written **must** yet be accomplished	22:37
1	**must** be delivered into the hands of sinful men,	24:7
6	**Ought** not Christ to have suffered these things,	24:26
1	that all things **must** be fulfilled,	24:44
6	and thus it **behoved** Christ to suffer,	24:46
1	Marvel not that I said ... Ye **must** be born again.	John 3:7
1	even so **must** the Son of man be lifted up:	John 3:14
1	He **must** increase, but I must decrease.	3:30
6	And he **must** needs go through Samaria.	4:4
1	Jerusalem is the place ... men **ought** to worship.	4:20
1	they that worship him **must** worship him in spirit	4:24
1	I **must** work the works of him that sent me,	9:4
1	which are not of this fold: them also I **must** bring,	10:16
1	The Son of man **must** be lifted up? who is this Son	12:34
1	that he **must** rise again from the dead.	20:9
6	this scripture **must** needs have been fulfilled,	Acts 1:16
1	"It is therefore **necessary** that of the men (NASB)	1:21
1	Whom the heaven **must** receive until the times	3:21
1	is none other name ... whereby we **must** be saved.	4:12
1	We **ought** to obey God rather than men.	5:29
1	and it shall be told thee what thou **must** do.	9:6
1	I will show him how great things he **must** suffer	9:16
1	he shall tell thee what thou **oughtest** to do.	10:6
1	and that we **must** through much tribulation	14:22
1	That it was **needful** to circumcise them,	15:5
1	and said, Sirs, what **must** I do to be saved?	16:30
6	that Christ **must** needs have suffered,	17:3
1	I **must** by all means keep this feast	18:21
1	After I have been there, I **must** also see Rome.	19:21
3	ye **ought** to be quiet, and to do nothing rashly.	19:36
1	that so labouring ye **ought** to support the weak,	20:35
1	the multitude **must** needs come together:	21:22
1	so **must** thou bear witness also at Rome.	23:11
1	Who **ought** to have been here before thee,	24:19
6	Who **ought** to have been present (NASB)	24:19
1	at Caesar's ... where I **ought** to be judged:	25:10
5	crying that he **ought** not to live any longer.	25:24
5	that I **ought** to do many things contrary to ... Jesus.	26:9
1	Sirs, ye **should** have hearkened unto me,	27:21
1	thou **must** be brought before Caesar:	27:24
1	Howbeit we **must** be cast upon a certain island.	27:26
6	that recompense of their error which was meet	Rom 1:27
1	we know not what we should pray for as we **ought**:	8:26
1	not to think of himself more highly than he **ought**	12:3
1	he knoweth nothing yet as he **ought** to know.	1 Co 8:2
1	For there **must** be also heresies among you,	11:19
1	For he **must** reign, till he hath put all enemies	15:25
1	For this corruptible **must** put on incorruption,	15:53
6	sorrow from them of whom I **ought** to rejoice;	2 Co 2:3
1	**must** all appear before the judgment seat of Christ;	5:10
1	If I **must** needs glory, I will glory of the things	11:30
1	Boasting is **necessary**, though it is (NASB)	12:1
1	I may speak boldly, as I **ought** to speak.	Eph 6:20
1	That I may make it manifest, as I **ought** to speak.	Col 4:4
1	ye may know how ye **ought** to answer every man.	4:6
1	that as ye have received of us how ye **ought** to walk	1 Th 4:1
1	For yourselves know how ye **ought** to follow us:	2 Th 3:7
1	A bishop then **must** be blameless,	1 Tm 3:2
1	Moreover he **must** have a good report	3:7
1	**oughtest** to behave thyself in the house of God,	3:15
4	speaking things which they **ought** not.	5:13
1	that laboureth **must** be first partaker of the fruits.	2 Tm 2:6
1	And the servant of the Lord **must** not strive;	2:24
1	a bishop **must** be blameless, as the steward of God;	Tit 1:7
1	Whose mouths **must** be stopped,	1:11
1	teaching things which they **ought** not,	1:11
1	Therefore we **ought** to give the more earnest heed	Heb 2:1
6	For then **must** he often have suffered	9:26
1	for he that cometh to God **must** believe that he is,	11:6
3	though now for a season, if **need** be,	1 Pt 1:6
1	what manner of persons **ought** ye to be in all holy	2 Pt 3:11
1	things which **must** shortly come to pass;	Rev 1:1
1	I will show thee things which **must** be hereafter.	4:1
1	Thou **must** prophesy again before many peoples,	10:11
1	will hurt them, he **must** in this manner be killed.	11:5
1	he that killeth with the sword **must** be killed.	13:10
1	when he cometh, he **must** continue a short space.	17:10
1	and after that he **must** be loosed a little season.	20:3
1	to show ... the things which **must** shortly be done.	22:6

This verb means "it is necessary," and includes the idea that one "must," "ought," or "should" do something. It expresses every sort of compulsion without any indication of the source of that compulsion. The force of the compulsion can range from an absolute must to the much weaker "demands" of etiquette and custom.

Classical Greek
In classical Greek *dei* is used to express what one ought to do because of the demands of grammar, law, or custom. Very frequently it is used to express the necessity of fate. The Greeks had a strong sense that every man had a destiny. Certain things must happen to him, and he must do certain things simply because it was his fate or destiny (see Tiedtke and Link, "Necessity," *Colin Brown*, 2:664).

Septuagint Usage
Dei in itself does not indicate the source of the requirement. However, in the Septuagint it is used to express ethical and religious demands that flowed from the law of God (see Leviticus 4:2).

New Testament Usage
In the New Testament the intensity of the demand and the source of the requirement vary greatly. Usually the source of the demand is the will of God. The will of God expressed in the Law must be obeyed (Luke 11:42). Jesus must die because it was the Father's will (Luke 9:22). Christians must follow God's plan (John 3:7). It is prophesied that things must happen (Revelation 1:1), and that things must happen to fulfill prophecy (Matthew 17:10).

The source of the necessity, however, is not always the will of God. *Dei* sometimes expresses the compulsion of duty (Matthew 18:33) or the requirements of law or custom (Luke 22:7). Occasionally it expresses only the demands of the situation (Matthew 26:35) or what is required in order to obtain a result (Luke 12:12). It may only indicate what is proper or fitting (Romans 8:26). Again, *dei* says that something "must" be done without indicating the source or intensity of the demand.

STRONG 1163, BAUER 172, MOULTON-MILLIGAN 137, KITTEL 2:21-25, LIDDELL-SCOTT 372, COLIN BROWN 2:664-69.

1159. δεῖγμα deigma noun
Example, specimen.
COGNATE:
  δείκνυμι deiknumi (1161)

SYNONYMS:
  ὑπογραμμός hupogrammos (5099)
  ὑπόδειγμα hupodeigma (5100)

1. δεῖγμα deigma nom/acc sing neu

1 Sodom ... are set forth for an example, ... Jude 1:7

In classical Greek this term means "sample," "pattern," or "proof" when an "example" serves as evidence. It is related to *deiknumi* (1161) or *deiknuō*, "to show, point out, make known" or "to prove." It has a similar use in Koine. *Deigma* is not found in the Septuagint. Modern Greek retains the ancient meaning of "proof." The only New Testament use is Jude 7, where Sodom and Gomorrah serve as an "example" of fiery punishment for wickedness. This "example" serves as proof or evidence of sin's consequences.

STRONG 1164, BAUER 172, MOULTON-MILLIGAN 137, LIDDELL-SCOTT 372, COLIN BROWN 3:570.

1160. δειγματίζω deigmatizō verb
Make an example or spectacle of.
CROSS-REFERENCE:
  δείκνυμι deiknumi (1161)

1. ἐδειγμάτισεν edeigmatisen 3sing indic aor act
2. δειγματίσαι deigmatisai inf aor act

2 and not wanting to disgrace her (NASB) .... Matt 1:19
1 he made a show of them openly, triumphing .... Col 2:15

Classical Greek
This verb means "to expose," "to make public," or "to exhibit." It usually has the negative connotation of disgracing someone, of making public what someone would like to keep secret, or of making an example of someone. The noun form of this word, *deigma* (1159), means "example." In classical Greek *deigmatizō* means "to make an example of."

In Koine Greek, however, the negative idea of disgrace is not always strong. *Deigmatizō* was used on the Rosetta stone, for example, with the meaning of verifying records (*Moulton-Milligan*). The sense here is "to make public," with the idea of exposing any possible fraud. It is not used in the Septuagint.

New Testament Usage
In Matthew 1:19 it is used to describe Joseph's feelings when he learned Mary was pregnant and seemingly immoral. It is variously translated as, he did not want to "expose her to public disgrace" (NIV), "make her a public example" (KJV), "disgrace her" (NASB). In Colossians 2:15 the meaning is the same: the powers of

darkness are "made a spectacle of," i.e., they are exposed and mocked as powerless because Jesus triumphed over them on the cross.
STRONG 1165, BAUER 172, MOULTON-MILLIGAN 137-38, KITTEL 2:31-32, LIDDELL-SCOTT 372, COLIN BROWN 3:570.

1161. δείκνυμι deiknumi verb
Show, teach, prove, make known.

COGNATES:
ἀναδείκνυμι anadeiknumi (320)
ἀνάδειξις anadeixis (321)
ἀποδείκνυμι apodeiknumi (579)
ἀπόδειξις apodeixis (580)
δεῖγμα deigma (1159)
δειγματίζω deigmatizō (1160)
ἔνδειγμα endeigma (1714)
ἐνδείκνυμι endeiknumi (1715)
ἔνδειξις endeixis (1716)
ἐπιδείκνυμι epideiknumi (1910)
παραδειγματίζω paradeigmatizō (3718)
ὑπόδειγμα hupodeigma (5100)
ὑποδείκνυμι hupodeiknumi (5101)

SYNONYMS:
ἀναδείκνυμι anadeiknumi (320)
ἀποδείκνυμι apodeiknumi (579)
ἀποκαλύπτω apokaluptō (596)
γνωρίζω gnōrizō (1101)
δηλόω dēloō (1207)
διερμηνεύω diermēneuō (1323)
ἐλέγχω elenchō (1638)
ἐμφανίζω emphanizō (1702)
ἐνδείκνυμι endeiknumi (1715)
ἐξηγέομαι exēgeomai (1817)
ἐπιδείκνυμι epideiknumi (1910)
ἐπιφαίνω epiphainō (1998)
ἑρμηνεύω hermēneuō (2043)
κηρύσσω kērussō (2756)
μηνύω mēnuō (3245)
ὑποδείκνυμι hupodeiknumi (5101)
φανερόω phaneroō (5157)

אָרַךְ 'ārēkh (773), Be long; hiphil: delay (Is 48:9).

בָּרָא bārā' (1282), Create (Nm 16:30).

גָּלָה gālâh (1580), Uncover; niphal: be revealed (Dn 10:1).

יָדַע yādha' (3156), Qal: know (Ex 33:5); hiphil: inform, declare (Gn 41:39, Hos 5:9); teach (Is 40:14).

יָצָא yātsâ' (3428), Go or come out; hiphil: bring out (Jb 28:11).

יָרָה yārâh (3498), Throw, shoot; hiphil: show (Ex 15:25); teach (Mi 4:2).

לָכַד lākhadh (4058), Take (Jos 7:14).

לָמַד lāmadh (4064), Learn; piel: teach (Dt 4:5, Is 40:14).

נָגַד nāghadh (5222), Hiphil: tell (Gn 41:25); describe (Ez 43:10).

נָחָה nāchâh (5328), Hiphil: lead (Ex 13:21).

נָתַן nāthan (5598), Put (2 Kgs 16:14).

רָאָה rā'âh (7495), Qal: see (Nm 24:17, 1 Kgs 13:12, Jer 18:17); hiphil: show (Est 1:4, Ez 11:25); hophal: be shown (Ex 26:30, Lv 13:49).

1. **δείκνυμι** deiknumi 1sing indic pres act
2. **δεικνύεις** deiknueis 2sing indic pres act
3. **δείκνυσιν** deiknusin 3sing indic pres act
4. **δεικνύοντος** deiknuontos
   gen sing masc/neu part pres act
5. **δεικνύειν** deiknuein inf pres act
6. **δείξω** deixō 1sing indic/subj fut/aor act
7. **ἔδειξα** edeixa 1sing indic aor act
8. **ἔδειξεν** edeixen 3sing indic aor act
9. **δεῖξον** deixon 2sing impr aor act
10. **δειξάτω** deixatō 3sing impr aor act
11. **δεῖξαι** deixai inf aor act
12. **δείξει** deixei 3sing indic fut act
13. **δειχθέντα** deichthenta acc sing masc part aor pass
14. **δεικνύντος** deiknuntos
    gen sing masc/neu part pres act
15. **δείξατε** deixate 2pl impr aor act

3	and **showeth** him all the kingdoms of the world,	Matt 4:8
9	**show** thyself to the priest, and offer the gift	8:4
5	began Jesus to **show** unto his disciples,	16:21
9	but go thy way, **show** thyself to the priest,	Mark 1:44
12	And he will **show** you a large upper room	14:15
8	**showed** unto him all the kingdoms of the world	Luke 4:5
9	but go, and **show** thyself to the priest,	5:14
15	**Show** Me a denarius NASB	20:24
12	he shall **show** you a large upper room furnished:	22:12
8	He **showed** them His hands and His feet (NASB)	24:40
2	What sign **showest** thou unto us,	John 2:18
3	and **showeth** him all things that himself doeth:	5:20
12	and he will **show** him greater works than these,	5:20
7	good works have I **showed** you from my Father;	10:32
9	Lord, **show** us the Father, and it sufficeth us.	14:8
9	and how sayest thou then, **Show** us the Father?	14:9
8	he **showed** unto them his hands and his side.	20:20
6	and come into the land which I shall **show** thee.	Acts 7:3
8	but God hath **showed** me that I should not call any	10:28
1	and yet **show** I unto you a more excellent way.	I Co 12:31
12	Which in his times he shall **show**,	I Tm 6:15
13	all things according to the pattern **showed** to thee	Heb 8:5
9	**show** me thy faith without thy works,	Jas 2:18
6	and I will **show** thee my faith by my works.	2:18
10	let him **show** out of a good conversation his works	3:13
11	God gave unto him, to **show** unto his servants	Rev 1:1
6	I will **show** thee things which must be hereafter.	4:1
6	I will **show** unto thee the judgment:	17:1
6	I will **show** thee the bride, the Lamb's wife.	21:9
8	and **showed** me that great city, the holy Jerusalem,	21:10
8	And he **showed** me a pure river of water of life,	22:1
11	sent his angel to **show** unto his servants the things	22:6
4	the feet of the angel which **showed** me these things.	22:8

Classical Greek and Septuagint Usage
Though appearing very early in Greek literature, *deiknumi* maintains the consistent meaning of "reveal," "indicate," or "show" throughout its usage. In the Septuagint *deiknumi* adheres to this and frequently translates the Hebrew *rā'âh*, "see," in the hiphal (causative-active tense). It is mostly used of God (82 of 119 occurrences) who reveals what He desires to whomsoever He wishes. This particular usage dominates in the Pentateuch, Wisdom Literature, Poetical

Books, and the Prophets. However, it either significantly fades or disappears in the historical "conquest" narratives such as Judges, 1 and 2 Samuel, 1 and 2 Kings, and 1 and 2 Maccabees in the Apocrypha.

New Testament Usage

In the New Testament *deiknumi* is used in reference to the devil showing Jesus the kingdoms of the world during His temptation (Matthew 4:8; Luke 4:5) and to the healed leper showing himself to the priest in order to be pronounced clean (Mark 1:44). It also refers to "teaching" (Matthew 16:21; Acts 10:28; 1 Corinthians 12:31). However, it is in John's Gospel and the Apocalypse that the particular divine prerogative noticed in the Septuagint is again expressed. The Apocalypse reports God's "revealing" His purposes and intentions (either through Christ or an angel) to His prophet John (Revelation 1:1). John simply accepted the self-disclosure of God and His ways and transmitted it. The gospel, however, plunges *deiknumi* to new depths by giving to the divine Jesus alone the authority to reveal and show the Father to whomsoever He wished. This was done through a demonstration of God's presence in Him and God's power in His works (see John 14:8-11).

The Shepherd of Hermas also used *deiknumi* extensively in reference to "revealing" divine secrets through the prophet to the people (*Bauer*).

STRONG 1166, BAUER 172, MOULTON-MILLIGAN 138, KITTEL 2:25-30, LIDDELL-SCOTT 373, COLIN BROWN 3:569.

1162. δειλία deilia noun

Cowardice, timidity, fear.
CROSS-REFERENCE:
  δειλιάω deiliaō (1163)

אֵימָה 'êmāh (372), Terror (Ps 55:4 [54:4]).

מְחִתָּה mᵉchittāh (4425), Ruin (Ps 89:40 [88:40]).

מֹרֶךְ mōrekh (4979), Weakness (Lv 26:36—Codex Alexandrinus only).

עַצְלָה 'atslāh (6340), Laziness (Prv 19:15).

1. δειλίας deilias gen sing fem
1 For God hath not given us the spirit of fear;........ 2 Tm 1:7

Deilia is the classical Greek word for "timidity" or "cowardice." It is so used in the Septuagint, as well as in Philo and Josephus. Second Timothy 1:7 states that a spirit of "cowardice," "cowardly fear," or "timidity" is not from God. (Compare *deiliaō* [1163], "to be cowardly, timid," and *deilos* [1164], "cowardly, timid.")

STRONG 1167, BAUER 173, MOULTON-MILLIGAN 138, LIDDELL-SCOTT 374.

1163. δειλιάω deiliaō verb

Be cowardly, timid, or fearful.
COGNATES:
  δειλία deilia (1162)
  δειλός deilos (1164)

חָפַז chāphaz (2753), Niphal: hurry away (Ps 104:7 [103:7]).

חָתַת chāthath (2973), Niphal: be dismayed (Dt 1:21, Jos 8:1, 10:25).

מָסַס māsas (4701), Niphal: melt (Is 13:7).

נוּד nûdh (5290), Have pity (Jer 15:5).

עָרַץ 'ārats (6442), Tremble (Dt 31:6, Jos 1:9).

פָּחַד pāchadh (6585), Be in fear, tremble (Pss 14:5 [13:5], 78:53 [77:53]).

1. δειλιάτω deiliatō 3sing impr pres act
1 not your heart be troubled, neither let it be afraid. John 14:27

This term is found only in the Koine period and later. It is related to *deilia* (1162), "cowardice" or "timidity." The Septuagint contains uses including several exhortations (such as Joshua 1:9) not to fear (*phobeō* [5236]) or "be cowardly" (*deiliaō*). John 14:27 combines "be afraid" (*deiliaō*) with "be troubled" (*tarassō* [4866]), as does Isaiah 13:7,8.

STRONG 1168, BAUER 173, MOULTON-MILLIGAN 138, LIDDELL-SCOTT 374.

1164. δειλός deilos adj

Cowardly, timid.
CROSS-REFERENCE:
  δειλιάω deiliaō (1163)

חָרֵד chārēdh (2830), Trembling (Jgs 7:3).

יָרֵא yārē' (3486), Be afraid (Jgs 7:3—Codex Alexandrinus only).

רַךְ rakh (7679), Weak (2 Chr 13:7); afraid (Dt 20:8).

1. δειλοί deiloi nom pl masc
2. δειλοῖς deilois dat pl masc

1 Why are ye fearful, O ye of little faith?........... Matt 8:26
1 And he said unto them, Why are ye so fearful?..... Mark 4:40
2 But the fearful, and unbelieving,................... Rev 21:8

In the classical Greek this word means "cowardly" or "fearful." There is often implied a note of contempt for the "timid" one. It is also used in a compassionate sense for those made miserable by their fear. *Deilos* is related to *deos* (1183B), "fear" or "alarm." The Septuagint and Koine Greek follow the classical usage. Jesus described the disciples as "fearful" (*deilos*) of the storm (Matthew 8:26; Mark 4:40). Perhaps He rebuked them by this word, but not without compassion. In Revelation 21:8, however, the "fearful" are placed with the unbelieving and the wicked in the lake of fire. Given the contrast between faith and *deilos* in Matthew and Mark (cf. Luke 8:25 where faith is also at risk, but *deilos* is not mentioned) and its association with liars (i.e., those who deny Jesus) in Revelation 21:8, it is perhaps correct to see *deilos* as symptomatic of unbelief.

STRONG 1169, BAUER 173, MOULTON-MILLIGAN 138, LIDDELL-SCOTT 374.

1165. δεῖνα deina noun

A certain person, such a one, someone.

1. δεῖνα deina acc sing masc

1 Go into the city to **such a man**, and say unto him, Matt 26:18

This is a word used in place of someone's name, either to avoid saying the name or to allow anyone's name to be inserted in the sentence. It is found in classical, Koine, and modern Greek. In Matthew 26:18 Jesus referred to "such a man" (*deina*) who was to host Jesus' last Passover meal. More details are given in Mark and Luke, but the man's name is never stated.

STRONG 1170, BAUER 173, MOULTON-MILLIGAN 138, LIDDELL-SCOTT 374.

1166. δεινῶς deinōs adv

Terribly, excessively, vehemently.

1. δεινῶς deinōs

1 servant ... sick of the palsy, **grievously tormented**.... Matt 8:6
1 and the Pharisees began to urge him **vehemently**,...Luke 11:53

An adverb found only twice in the New Testament (Matthew 8:6; Luke 11:53), *deinōs* emphasizes the evil, frightful, or painful force of the action of the verb it modifies. This word is found in Greek literature from Herodotus (Fifth Century B.C.) through the Septuagint, and into the post-New Testament imperial times. In Matthew 8:6 the centurion told Jesus that his, the centurion's, servant was sick of the palsy, "*grievously* (*deinōs*) tormented." Here this adverb has more than the mere force of "much" or "very," or even of "exceedingly." It adds to the quantifier "very" the additional idea of pain and malignity. Thus it might well be translated that his servant was "*viciously* tormented." Likewise, Luke 11:53 states that "the scribes and the Pharisees began to urge him (Jesus) *vehemently*, and to provoke him . . . ." Here too, the idea of *deinōs* is not simply that they urged our Lord a great deal or continuously, but this word conveys the idea that their actions were vicious, mean, and hostile in intent and method.

STRONG 1171, BAUER 173, MOULTON-MILLIGAN 138, LIDDELL-SCOTT 374.

1167. δειπνέω deipneō verb

Eat dinner, dine.

CROSS-REFERENCE:
δεῖπνον deipnon (1168)

לָחַם lācham (4033), Dine (Prv 23:1).

1. δειπνήσω deipnēsō 1sing indic/subj fut/aor act
2. δειπνῆσαι deipnēsai inf aor act

1 Make ready wherewith I **may sup**, and gird thyself, Luke 17:8
2 Likewise also the cup after **supper**, saying,............. 22:20
2 also he took the cup, when he **had supped**, saying, 1 Co 11:25
1 I will come in to him, and **will sup** with him,........ Rev 3:20

This is the classical Greek word for "eating a meal," generally the largest meal of the day. The Koine use includes common meals, feasts, or meals of special religious significance, such as Passover (Josephus *Antiquities* 2.14.6). Luke 17:8, 22:20, and 1 Corinthians 11:25 refer to Christ's Passover meal before His crucifixion. Jesus offers to share a meal ("sup") with those who respond to His "knock" (Revelation 3:20). The meaning here is figurative for the fellowship between Christ and the receptive person (or church, in the context of 3:14ff.).

STRONG 1172, BAUER 173, MOULTON-MILLIGAN 138, KITTEL 2:34-35, LIDDELL-SCOTT 375, COLIN BROWN 2:520-21,536.

1168. δεῖπνον deipnon noun

Dinner, supper, meal.

COGNATE:
δειπνέω deipneō (1167)
SYNONYM:
δοχή dochē (1397)

לֶחֶם lechem (4035), Food (Dn 1:8,13,15f.).

1. **δεῖπνον** deipnon nom/acc sing neu
2. **δείπνου** deipnou gen sing neu
3. **δείπνῳ** deipnō dat sing neu
4. **δείπνοις** deipnois dat pl neu

4	And love the uppermost rooms at **feasts**,	Matt 23:6
1	Herod on his birthday made **a supper** to his lords,	Mark 6:21
4	and the uppermost rooms at **feasts**:	12:39
4	uppermost seats ... and greetings in the markets.	Luke 11:43
1	When thou makest a dinner or **a supper**,	14:12
1	certain man made a great **supper**, and bade many:	14:16
2	And sent his servant at **supper** time to say to them	14:17
2	none of those ... bidden shall taste of my **supper**.	14:24
4	and the chief rooms at **feasts**;	20:46
1	they made him a **supper**; and Martha served:	John 12:2
2	And **supper** being ended,	13:2
2	riseth from **supper**, and laid aside his garments;	13:4
3	which also leaned on his breast at **supper**,	21:20
1	this is not to eat the Lord's **supper**.	I Co 11:20
1	every one taketh before other his own **supper**:	11:21
1	are called unto the marriage **supper** of the Lamb.	Rev 19:9
1	together unto the **supper** of the great God;	19:17

Classical Greek and Septuagint Usage
During classical times a *deipnon* was important in the worship of Greek deities. Participating in a religious "meal" meant one actually participated in the god's nature (Behm, "deipnon," *Kittel*, 2:34f.). In ancient times Jews placed great importance on social interaction through meals. To offer or accept a dinner invitation signaled intents of goodwill, trust, and prosperity. To decline or forbid such an opportunity indicated ill will and also the highest insult (e.g., Luke 14:16-24). The Septuagint makes limited usage of *deipnon* (Daniel 1:8,13,15,16).

New Testament Usage
In the New Testament *deipnon* often refers to the "main meal" of the evening (John 13:2,4; 21:20). In addition, it is a "feast" or "banquet" with the added touch of formality (Matthew 23:6; Mark 12:39; Luke 11:43; 14:17,24; 20:46). *Deipnon* appears in contexts of judgment (Revelation 19:17), celebration (Revelation 19:9), memorial (1 Corinthians 11:20), and farewell (John 12:2; 13:2,4; 21:20).

STRONG 1173, BAUER 173, MOULTON-MILLIGAN 139, KITTEL 2:34-35, LIDDELL-SCOTT 375, COLIN BROWN 2:520,522,536.

1169. δεισιδαιμονία
deisidaimonia adj
Religion.
CROSS-REFERENCE:
δαίμων daimōn (1136)

1. **δεισιδαιμονεστέρους** deisidaimonesterous comp acc pl masc

1 I perceive that in all things ye are too **superstitious**. Acts 17:22

Classical Greek
Deisidaimonia appears in both the classical and intertestamental Greek writings. It appears in three frames of reference: (a) as a neutral word meaning "religion"; (b) in a favorable context, signifying proper and correct fear and worship of God; or (c) in a pejorative, critical sense connected with the idea of improper or false worship.

New Testament Usage
In general, this noun refers to "religion" and occurs in only one place in the New Testament, Acts 25:19. The related adjective *deisidaimōn* (1170), "religious," likewise occurs only once in the New Testament, also in Luke's writings (Acts 17:22).

In Acts 25:19 *deisidaimonia* is translated "superstition." As in Acts 17:22 with the adjective, the word apparently takes an unfavorable sense. However, the majority of commentators understand it here to signify "religion" in its neutral sense, that is, without commendation or criticism. Lenski (*Acts* pp.270-273) argues that Festus would not ridicule the Jewish faith to King Agrippa when Agrippa was by title the Herodian custodian and guardian of that faith, especially at a time when the two were on cordial relations. The word in itself does not convey either approval or disapproval of the religion or worship system addressed. The reader must examine the context to determine any commendation or criticism of the religious system under discussion.

STRONG 1175, BAUER 173, MOULTON-MILLIGAN 139, KITTEL 2:20, LIDDELL-SCOTT 375, COLIN BROWN 1:450,453.

1170. δεισιδαίμων deisidaimōn noun
Religious, superstitious.
COGNATE:
  δαίμων daimōn (1136)
SYNONYM:
  θρῆσκος thrēskos (2334)

1. **δεισιδαιμονίας** deisidaimonias gen sing fem

1 questions against him of their own **superstition**, Acts 25:19

Classical Greek and New Testament Usage
Used by Aristotle the philosopher and Menander the playwright in the Fourth Century B.C., this adjective appears only once in the New

Testament, Acts 17:22. The exact meaning of this usage has occasioned great debate. The word refers either to being "religious," or "god fearing."

The question as to whether it denotes "religion" in a good or bad sense is raised in an examination of Paul's words of introduction to the Areopagus (see 691) assembly in Athens. As he stood in the shadow of the resplendent white-marbled Parthenon he began, "Ye men of Athens, I perceive that in all things ye are *too superstitious*" (Acts 17:22). The "too" is added because here the adjective is used in the Greek comparative form.

R.C.H. Lenski in his commentary on *Acts* translates the term "unusually devoted to divinities," arguing that the Athenians were not superstitious, but rather that their city had more statues and temples devoted to the gods than found anywhere else. The question is this: Was Paul saying to the Athenians (a) "You are *too superstitious*," starting with a rebuke? or (b) "You are *very religious*," starting with a seeming commendation only to explain to them that their religious zeal was not aimed at the correct God? The word is probably best understood as a neutral term, akin to our word *religious*, which can be used with either commendation or condemnation depending on the context and situation (Lenski, *Acts*, pp.720-723).

The adverb *deisidaimōs*, closely related to this adjective, is used in the *Letter of Aristeas* in one place referring to the necessity of obeying the Old Testament dietary laws "scrupulously" (see *Moulton-Milligan*). If this is any clue, then *deisidaimōn* in Acts 17:22 could have the force of saying, "Ye are *very scrupulous in honoring the god* but you have not yet seen the truth nor heard the message of the one true and living God whom I have come to proclaim to you." (See *deisidaimonia* [1169], the related noun, "religion," which also appears only one time in the New Testament, Acts 25:19.)

STRONG 1174, BAUER 173, MOULTON-MILLIGAN 139, KITTEL 2:20, LIDDELL-SCOTT 375, COLIN BROWN 1:450,453.

1171. δέκα deka num

Ten.

CROSS-REFERENCE:
δεκατόω dekatoō (1177)

1. δέκα deka card

1 the ten heard it, they were moved with indignation	Matt 20:24
1 the kingdom of heaven be likened unto ten virgins,	25:1
1 and give it unto him which hath ten talents.	25:28
1 And when the ten heard it, ... much displeased	Mark 10:41
1 eighteen, upon whom the tower	Luke 13:4
1 which had a spirit of infirmity eighteen years,	13:11
1 lo, these eighteen years, be loosed from this bond	13:16
1 with ten thousand to meet him that cometh against	14:31
1 Either what woman having ten pieces of silver,	15:8
1 there met him ten men that were lepers,	17:12
1 Jesus answering said, Were there not ten cleansed?	17:17
1 And he called his ten servants,	19:13
1 his ten servants, and delivered them ten pounds,	19:13
1 saying, Lord, thy pound hath gained ten pounds.	19:16
1 been faithful ... have thou authority over ten cities.	19:17
1 and give it to him that hath ten pounds.	19:24
1 And they said unto him, Lord, he hath ten pounds.	19:25
1 he had tarried among them more than ten days,	Acts 25:6
1 and ye shall have tribulation ten days:	Rev 2:10
1 red dragon, having seven heads and ten horns,	12:3
1 out of the sea, having seven heads and ten horns,	13:1
1 seven heads ... and upon his horns ten crowns,	13:1
1 beast, ... having seven heads and ten horns.	17:3
1 beast ... which hath the seven heads and ten horns.	17:7
1 And the ten horns which thou sawest are ten kings,	17:12
1 And the ten horns which thou sawest are ten kings,	17:12
1 the ten horns which thou sawest upon the beast,	17:16

Classical Greek

Deka, the rounded numeral 10, served as the ancient Hebrews' basic unit of measure. Near Eastern numbering methods also made use of the 10. The number 5 (*pente* [3864]) was used separately or in combination with 10 to indicate other designated amounts (compare 5 foolish and 5 wise virgins, Matthew 25:1-13). The papyri use *deka* to indicate the "one-tenth" Levitical priests should be paid.

Septuagint Usage

Care should be exercised in assigning meaning to Biblical numbers. One should avoid the mystical excesses of ancient and present-day gematria (i.e., the practice of assigning a secret or hidden meaning to the Scriptures by assigning words with a numerical value). Nevertheless, it is generally agreed that *deka* represents completeness. The Mosaic law presented "*ten*" commandments—God's total requirement for righteous living (Exodus 20:1-17; Deuteronomy 5:1-21). The land of Egypt received 10 plagues—a completely thorough and devastating judgment (Exodus 7:8 to 12:31).

New Testament Usage

This sense of entirety can be occasionally and cautiously applied to *deka*'s invested literal or figurative New Testament usages. *Deka*'s separate use in the New Testament indicates 10 things (Luke 15:8; 19:13,24,25), places (Luke 19:17), people (Matthew 25:1; Mark 10:41; Luke 17:12,17), and horns (Revelation 12:3; 13:1; 17:3,7,12,16). It also describes tribulation which lasts a short time (Revelation 2:10).

STRONG 1176, BAUER 173-74, MOULTON-MILLIGAN 139, KITTEL 2:36-37, LIDDELL-SCOTT 375, COLIN BROWN 2:692.

1172. δεκαδύο dekaduo num
Twelve.

1. δεκαδύο dekaduo card

1	And all the men were about **twelve**..............	Acts 19:7
1	that there are yet but **twelve** days since I went up.....	24:11

Classical Greek and Septuagint Usage
In classical Greek the numeral 12 is related to the stars which dictate the 12 months of the lunar calendar. Some believe that the Hebrews associated 12 (literally "10 and 2"; see *deka* [1171] and *duo* [1411]) with the fulfillment of divine purposes. For instance, there are 12 tribes of Israel which would become the nation through which God would fulfill His redemptive plan (Genesis 49; 1 Chronicles 6:63-80).

New Testament Usage
In the New Testament occurrences of the term, Acts 19:7 and 24:11, only the most literal sense is employed, e.g., 12 men and 12 days. The related word *dōdeka* (1420) numbers Christ's 12 apostles (Matthew 10:1ff.), the foundation upon which Christ would build His church.

STRONG 1177, BAUER 174, MOULTON-MILLIGAN 139, LIDDELL-SCOTT 375.

1172B. δεκαοκτώ dekaoktō num
Eighteen.

1. δεκαοκτώ dekaoktō card

1	**eighteen**, upon whom the tower in Siloam fell,.....	Luke 13:4
1	which had a spirit of infirmity **eighteen** years,.........	13:11

A variant to the traditional text (*Textus Receptus*), *dekaoktō* describes the number of fatalities which occurred when a tower at the Pool of Siloam collapsed (see Luke 13:4). It also appears as a variant at Luke 13:11 where the Gospel states that a woman who had a spirit of infirmity for 18 years was supernaturally delivered by a word and a touch from Jesus.

BAUER 174, MOULTON-MILLIGAN 139-40, LIDDELL-SCOTT 375.

1173. δεκαπέντε dekapente num
Fifteen, ten and five.

1. δεκαπέντε dekapente card

1	nigh unto Jerusalem, about **fifteen** furlongs off:....	John 11:18
1	they sounded again, and found it **fifteen** fathoms....	Acts 27:28
1	to see Peter, and abode with him **fifteen** days........	Gal 1:18

Dekapente, occurring in the Septuagint, is related to the earlier classical Greek form *pentekaideka* (*pente* [3864], "five," *kai* [2504], "and," and *deka* [1171], "ten"). This classical form appears later in Luke 3:1 referring to the "fifteenth" year of Tiberius Caesar's reign. *Dekapente*, making use of the then Near Eastern method of counting (see *deka*), occurs three times in the New Testament as a measurement of time (Galatians 1:18) or land distance (John 11:18; Acts 27:28; see *stadios* [4563]).

STRONG 1178, BAUER 174, MOULTON-MILLIGAN 140, LIDDELL-SCOTT 375.

1174. Δεκάπολις Dekapolis name
Decapolis.

1. Δεκαπόλεως Dekapoleōs gen fem

2. Δεκαπόλει Dekapolei dat fem

1	and from **Decapolis**, and from Jerusalem,...........	Matt 4:25
2	and began to publish in **Decapolis**.................	Mark 5:20
1	through the midst of the coasts **of Decapolis**...........	7:31

League of 10 cities formed by Pompey to reduce the threat of isolation. Except for the city of Scythopolic, the league was located east of the Jordon River.

1175. δεκατέσσαρες
dekatessares num
Fourteen, ten and four.

1. δεκατέσσαρες dekatessares card nom masc/fem

2. δεκατεσσάρων dekatessarōn card gen masc/fem

1	from Abraham to David are **fourteen** generations;...	Matt 1:17
1	into Babylon are **fourteen** generations;................	1:17
1	unto Christ are **fourteen** generations...................	1:17
2	I knew a man in Christ above **fourteen** years ago,..	2 Co 12:2
2	Then **fourteen** years after I went up again..........	Gal 2:1

In the Septuagint, *dekatessares* describes the "fourteen" years Jacob served Laban for his two daughters (Genesis 31:41). *Dekatessares* appears five times in the New Testament. Three times Matthew uses this word to speak of "fourteen" generations in Christ's family tree (Matthew 1:17). It can be literally rendered "ten and four" using the "ten" as that day's basic unit of measure. Paul also used *dekatessares* with respect to time (2 Corinthians 12:2; Galatians 2:1) in recounting his personal experience of paradise and his visit to Jerusalem. (See *deka* [1171].)

δεκάτη 1175B

Strong 1180, Bauer 174, Moulton-Milligan 140, Liddell-Scott 376.

1175B. δεκάτη dekatē num
Tenth, tithe.

1. δεκάτη dekatē ord nom sing fem
2. δεκάτην dekatēn ord acc sing fem
3. δεκάτας dekatas ord acc pl fem

1 for it was about the **tenth hour**.	John 1:39
2 To whom also Abraham gave **a tenth part** of all;	Heb 7:2
2 the patriarch Abraham gave the **tenth** of the spoils.	7:4
3 And here men that die receive **tithes**;	7:8
3 who receiveth **tithes**, payed tithes in Abraham.	7:9

Septuagint Usage
This word is an adjective which signifies "a tenth" part of anything. When it is used as a substantive, that is, as a noun, it specifically refers to "the tenth, the tithe." The tithe in the Old Testament economy was to be given to the Lord (Genesis 28:22; Leviticus 27:30; Malachi 3:8), and the Septuagint uses this word in the references noted—except that in Malachi 3:8, *epi-dekatē*, an emphatic form of "tithe," is used in the plural.

New Testament Usage
In the New Testament the word is used four times in Hebrews 7:2,4,8,9 recounting that Abraham paid "tithes" to Melchizedek. Here the writer said there was created by God a priestly order higher than even the Abrahamic/Levitical priesthood, and that Christ's order was like this order. Therefore, His was superior to the Levitical priesthood.

Strong 1181, Bauer 174, Moulton-Milligan 140, Liddell-Scott 376, Colin Brown 2:692-94; 3:851.

1176. δέκατος dekatos num
Tenth.

Cross-Reference:
δεκατόω dekatoō (1177)

1. δέκατος dekatos ord nom sing masc
2. δέκατον dekaton ord acc sing masc

2 earthquake, and the **tenth part** of the city fell,	Rev 11:13
1 the ninth, a topaz; the **tenth**, a chrysoprasus;	21:20

Septuagint Usage
Dekatos, an adjectival form of *deka* (1171), "ten," refers to a "one-tenth portion" in the Septuagint (Exodus 16:36; Leviticus 5:11). It is also used to speak of the tenth (tithe) paid by Abraham to Melchizedek (Genesis 14:20; see Hebrews 7:4).

New Testament Usage
In the New Testament *dekatos* is used as a numeral. For example, in Revelation 21:20 it is used to refer to the "tenth" foundation stone of the New Jerusalem. This was chrysoprasus, a brilliant kind of quartz (the prefix *chryso* means "gold"). In Revelation 11:13 it is used to show that the earthquake destroyed the "tenth" part of Jerusalem.

John 1:39 identifies the time of day that the two disciples came to lodge with Jesus as the "tenth hour" (though the word "hour" is implied, not being in the Greek text). Since the day was considered to start at sunrise, or about 6 a.m., the 10th hour would be about 4 o'clock in the afternoon. It was late in the day and it would soon be dark, so it would not have been wise for the disciples to try to reach their own place of abode.

Strong 1182, Bauer 174, Moulton-Milligan 140, Liddell-Scott 377, Colin Brown 2:692; 3:851.

1177. δεκατόω dekatoō verb
Give (or) receive tithes, pay tithes.

Cognates:
ἀποδεκατεύω apodekateuō (580B)
ἀποδεκατόω apodekatoō (581)
δέκα deka (1171)
δέκατος dekatos (1176)

עָשַׂר 'āsar (6458), Piel: collect the tithe (Neh 10:37).

1. δεδεκάτωκεν dedekatōken 3sing indic perf act
2. δεδεκάτωται dedekatōtai 3sing indic perf mid

1 **received tithes** of Abraham, and blessed him	Heb 7:6
2 Levi also, … **payed tithes** in Abraham.	7:9

In classical Greek *dekatoō* denotes the personal and honorary payment of tithes to the god which made a battle victory possible. *Dekatoō*, occurring in the Septuagint, speaks of the tithe collection procedures by the Levites (Nehemiah 10:37,38). The New Testament employs *dekatoō* only in the Epistle to the Hebrews. It is used once in the active form referring to Melchizedek's receiving of tithes from Abraham (Hebrews 7:6). It occurs again in the passive voice indicating Levi's "paying tithes" (Hebrews 7:9).

Strong 1183, Bauer 174, Moulton-Milligan 140, Liddell-Scott 377, Colin Brown 2:692-94; 3:851.

1178. δεκτός dektos adj
Acceptable, accept, favorable.

δένδρον 1180

COGNATE:
δέχομαι dechomai (1203)
SYNONYMS:
ἀπόδεκτος apodektos (582)
εὐάρεστος euarestos (2080)
εὐπρόσδεκτος euprosdektos (2124)

נָתַן nāthan (5598), Granted (Prv 10:24).

רָצָה rātsâh (7813), Qal: be pleased with, be the favorite (Dt 33:24, Prv 16:7 [15:28]); niphal: be accepted (Lv 1:4).

רָצוֹן rātsôn (7814), What is acceptable (Ex 28:38 [28:34]); favor (Is 49:8).

1. δεκτός dektos nom sing masc
2. δεκτῷ dektō dat sing masc
3. δεκτόν dekton acc sing masc
4. δεκτήν dektēn acc sing fem

3 To preach the **acceptable** year of the Lord	Luke 4:19
1 No prophet is **accepted** in his own country	4:24
1 and worketh righteousness, is **accepted** with him	Acts 10:35
2 For he saith, I have heard thee in a time **accepted**	2 Co 6:2
4 an odour of a sweet smell, a sacrifice **acceptable**	Phlp 4:18

Dektos is actually a verbal adjective derived from the verb *dechomai* (1203), hence it means "acceptable." Although there are no parallel uses of *dektos* prior to the Septuagint (*Moulton-Milligan*), it is doubtful that *dektos* was coined by the Septuagint translators.

Septuagint Usage

Dektos occurs 32 times in the Septuagint, not always with a Hebrew equivalent. Many times it describes a sacrifice or the person offering a sacrifice as "acceptable" to God (e.g., Leviticus 1:3,4; 19:5; 22:19,20; Sirach 35:7 [LXX 32:7]; Isaiah 56:7; Malachi 2:13). God is the judge of what is acceptable which stands in contrast to what God abhors (Proverbs 10:24; 11:1; 12:22; 14:9). Some have associated Isaiah's prophecy that Christ was to "proclaim the acceptable year of the Lord" with the practice of releasing slaves at the year of Jubilee (Isaiah 61:2; cf. Leviticus 25:39-41). The basis for such judgment is not clear; Jubilee is not referred to as an "acceptable," *dektos*, time of any kind. The idea in Isaiah seems more to be a time of "favor" and "grace" (cf. Isaiah 49:8; Luke 4:19-22; 2 Corinthians 6:2).

New Testament Usage

New Testament usage of *dektos* resonates with the concepts expressed in the Septuagint. Except for one instance in the proverb of Luke 4:24, *dektos* is a recognition by God (*Bauer*). Luke 4:19 is a citation of Isaiah 61:2 speaking of "the acceptable (*dekton*) year of the Lord." The same idea is echoed in 2 Corinthians 6:2, a citation of Isaiah 49:8: "In an acceptable (*dektō*) time have I (God) heard thee, and in a day of salvation have I helped thee." This falls in a context in which Paul had just enjoined the Corinthians not to receive "the grace (*charis* [5320B]) of God in vain" (2 Corinthians 6:1). Furthermore, Paul encouraged his readers that "now is the *accepted* (or *acceptable*, NIV; *euprosdektos* [2124]) time; behold, now is the day of salvation" (verse 2).

Anyone fearing God and doing righteousness (*ergazomenos dikaiosunēn*) is acceptable, *dektos*, to God (Acts 10:35; cf. Matthew 6:1). Drawing from the sacrificial imagery of the Old Testament, Paul declared that the gifts sent to him by the Philippians via Epaphroditus were a fragrant offering, "a sacrifice *acceptable*, well-pleasing to God" (Philippians 4:18).

STRONG 1184, BAUER 174, MOULTON-MILLIGAN 140, KITTEL 2:58-59, LIDDELL-SCOTT 377, COLIN BROWN 3:744-46.

1179. δελεάζω deleazō verb

Entrap, lure, entice.

1. δελεάζουσιν deleazousin 3pl indic pres act
2. δελεάζοντες deleazontes nom pl masc part pres act
3. δελεαζόμενος deleazomenos nom sing masc part pres mid

3 he is drawn away of his own lust, and **enticed**	Jas 1:14
2 **beguiling** unstable souls	2 Pt 2:14
1 they **allure** through the lusts of the flesh	2:18

This term appears in classical Greek in both a literal and figurative sense (e.g., "to trap someone because of greed"; see *Liddell-Scott*). Neither the word nor any of its cognates appear in the Septuagint. The three instances in the New Testament are all figurative. The ability of "the sinful nature" *epithumia* to "snare" someone is implicitly warned against (James 1:14; 2 Peter 2:18), and others outside of the community of faith, recognizing the power of temptation, maliciously attempt to "entice" (cf. NIV, "seduce") the weak (2 Peter 2:14,18).

STRONG 1185, BAUER 174, LIDDELL-SCOTT 377.

1180. δένδρον dendron noun

Tree.

SYNONYM:
ξύλον xulon (3448)

אִילָן 'îlān (A367), Tree (Dn 4:10,20,22 [4:7,17,19]—Aramaic).

אֲשֵׁרָה 'ăshērāh (867), Asherim (Is 17:8, 27:9).

δεξιολάβος 1181

עֵץ 'ēts (6320), Tree, wood (Nm 13:20 [13:21], Jb 14:7, Ez 6:13).

1. **δένδρον** dendron nom/acc sing neu
2. **δένδρα** dendra nom/acc pl neu
3. **δένδρων** dendrōn gen pl neu

3	the ax is laid unto the root of the trees:	Matt 3:10
1	every tree which bringeth not forth good fruit	3:10
1	Even so every good tree bringeth forth good fruit;	7:17
1	but a corrupt tree bringeth forth evil fruit.	7:17
1	A good tree cannot bring forth evil fruit,	7:18
1	neither can a corrupt tree bring forth good fruit.	7:18
1	Every tree that bringeth not forth good fruit	7:19
1	Either make the tree good, and his fruit good;	12:33
1	else make the tree corrupt, and his fruit corrupt:	12:33
1	for the tree is known by his fruit.	12:33
1	the greatest among herbs, and becometh a tree,	13:32
3	others cut down branches from the trees,	21:8
2	he looked up, and said, I see men as trees, walking.	Mark 8:24
3	and others cut down branches off the trees,	11:8
3	now also the ax is laid unto the root of the trees:	Luke 3:9
1	every tree therefore which bringeth not forth good fruit	3:9
1	For a good tree bringeth not forth corrupt fruit;	6:43
1	neither doth a corrupt tree bring forth good fruit.	6:43
1	For every tree is known by his own fruit.	6:44
1	and it grew, and waxed a great tree;	13:19
2	a parable; Behold the fig tree, and all the trees;	21:29
2	trees whose fruit withereth, without fruit,	Jude 1:12
1	blow on the earth, nor on the sea, nor on any tree...	Rev 7:1
2	Hurt not the earth, neither the sea, nor the trees,	7:3
3	and the third part of trees was burnt up,	8:7
1	neither any green thing, neither any tree;	9:4

Dendron's figurative usage occasionally occurs in classical Greek, the Septuagint, and some New Testament passages to speak of "good and bad people" (see *Bauer*). Vine says the English rose tree is somewhat like the *dendron* and that the word *rhododendron* is derived from this word (*Expository Dictionary*, "Tree"). The New Testament uses "tree" comparatively, "I see men as trees, walking" (Mark 8:24); literally, "others cut down branches off the trees" (Mark 11:8; see also Revelation 7:1,3; 8:7; 9:4); and parabolically, "the axe is laid unto the root of the trees" (Matthew 3:10; see also Matthew 7:17-19; 12:33; 13:32; Luke 3:9; 6:43,44; 13:19; 21:29).

STRONG 1186, BAUER 174, MOULTON-MILLIGAN 140, LIDDELL-SCOTT 378, COLIN BROWN 3:865-66,868.

1181. δεξιολάβος dexiolabos noun
Spearman, small weapon soldier.
CROSS-REFERENCE:
δεξιός dexios (1182)

1. **δεξιολάβους** dexiolabous acc pl masc

1	and horsemen ... and spearmen two hundred,	Acts 23:23

This military term occurs only once in the New Testament. It is composed of *dexios* (1182) meaning "the right (hand)" and *lambanō* (2956), "to take." Hence, the combination means "to take up by the right hand (for the purpose of throwing, shooting)." Thus, "spearmen," "soldiers equipped with small hand-held ballistic weaponry" (spears or bows), can translate the Acts 23:23 appearance. Some suggest the translation "one posted on the right hand" (*Bauer*). This view would seemingly emphasize the governmental authority possessed by the guards (the right hand is used in the New Testament to indicate authority and privilege), not just their method of guarding.

STRONG 1187, BAUER 174, MOULTON-MILLIGAN 140-41, LIDDELL-SCOTT 379.

1182. δεξιός dexios adj
Right, the right (side), (hand), etc.
COGNATE:
δεξιολάβος dexiolabos (1181)

אָן 'ān (586), Anywhere (1 Kgs 2:42 [3:1]).

יָמִין yāmîn (3332), Right side, right hand (Gn 48:13, 2 Sm 16:6, Ps 110:1 [109:1]).

יָמַן yāman (3340), Hiphil: go or turn to the right (Gn 13:9, Is 30:21, Ez 21:16).

יְמָנִי yᵉmānî (3342), Right hand, right (Ex 29:20, Lv 14:17); south (1 Kgs 6:8).

1. **δεξιόν** dexion nom/acc sing masc/neu
2. **δεξιός** dexios nom sing masc
3. **δεξιά** dexia nom/acc sing/pl fem/neu
4. **δεξιᾶς** dexias gen/acc sing/pl fem
5. **δεξιᾷ** dexia dat sing fem
6. **δεξιάν** dexian acc sing fem
7. **δεξιῶν** dexiōn gen pl neu
8. **δεξιοῖς** dexiois dat pl neu

2	And if thy right eye offend thee, pluck it out,	Matt 5:29
3	And if thy right hand offend thee, cut it off,	5:30
6	but whosoever shall smite thee on thy right cheek,	5:39
3	not thy left hand know what thy right hand doeth:	6:3
7	one on thy right hand, and the other on the left,	20:21
7	but to sit on my right hand, and on my left,	20:23
7	said unto my Lord, Sit thou on my right hand,	22:44
7	And he shall set the sheep on his right hand,	25:33
7	shall the King say unto them on his right hand,	25:34
7	the Son of man sitting on the right hand of power,	26:64
6	and a reed in his right hand:	27:29
5	and a reed in his right hand:	27:29
7	one on the right hand, and another on the left.	27:38
7	one on thy right hand, and the other on thy left...	Mark 10:37
7	But to sit on my right hand and on my left hand	10:40
7	Sit thou on my right hand,	12:36
7	the Son of man sitting on the right hand of power,	14:62
7	the one on his right hand, and the other on his left...	15:27
8	they saw a young man sitting on the right side,	16:5
7	and sat on the right hand of God.	16:19
7	standing on the right side of the altar of incense.	Luke 1:11
3	there was a man whose right hand was withered.	6:6
7	said unto my Lord, Sit thou on my right hand,	20:42
1	smote the servant ... and cut off his right ear.	22:50
7	sit on the right hand of the power of God.	22:69
7	one on the right hand, and the other on the left.	23:33

1	smote the ... servant, and cut off his **right** ear.	John 18:10
3	Cast the net on the **right** side of the ship,	21:6
7	for he is on my **right** hand,	Acts 2:25
5	Therefore being by the **right hand** of God exalted,	2:33
7	said unto my Lord, Sit thou on my **right** hand,	2:34
4	he took him by the **right** hand, and lifted him up:	3:7
5	Him hath God exalted with his **right** hand	5:31
7	and Jesus standing on the **right** hand of God,	7:55
7	the Son of man standing on **the right** hand of God.	7:56
5	who is even at the **right hand** of God,	Rom 8:34
7	by the armour of righteousness on the **right hand**	2 Co 6:7
4	to me and Barnabas the **right hands** of fellowship;	Gal 2:9
5	and set him at his own **right hand** in the heavenly	Eph 1:20
5	where Christ sitteth on the **right hand** of God.	Col 3:1
5	sat down on the **right hand** of the Majesty on high;	Heb 1:3
7	Sit on my **right hand**,	1:13
5	who is set on the **right hand** of the throne	8:1
5	sat down on the **right hand** of God;	10:12
5	is set down at the **right hand** of the throne of God.	12:2
5	gone into heaven, and is on the **right hand** of God;	1 Pt 3:22
5	And he had in his **right** hand seven stars:	Rev 1:16
6	he laid his **right** hand upon me, saying unto me,	1:17
4	seven stars which thou sawest in my **right hand**,	1:20
5	he that holdeth the seven stars in his **right hand**,	2:1
6	saw in the **right hand** of him that sat on the throne	5:1
4	he came and took the book out of the **right hand**	5:7
1	and he set his **right** foot upon the sea,	10:2
6	LIFTED UP HIS RIGHT HAND (NASB)	10:5
4	a mark in their **right** hand, or in their foreheads:	13:16

Classical Greek
Dexios is from the stem *dek*, "take." Its basic meaning is "right" (the opposite of left). Thus it can depict a "right hand, a right eye, a right turn," etc. Classical writers also used *dexios* to refer to "good," i.e., "fortunate" omens. Astrologically speaking, *dexios* indicated a northerly direction. Metaphorically it could refer to something "dexterous," that is, skillful. It was also used of "courteous, kindly" actions (*Liddell-Scott*).

Septuagint Usage
In the Septuagint *dexios* normally translates the Hebrew term *yamîn* (or variations of that word). It is used to contrast "left" (*aristera* [see 704]) (Genesis 13:9; 1 Samuel 6:12 [LXX 1 Kings 6:12]). The right hand suggests power and strength since most people, being right-handed, find their left hand weaker (cf. Judges 5:26). But more importantly, *dexios* symbolizes the divine power of God. The "right" hand or "right" arm of the Lord delivers (Exodus 15:6,12). The Psalmist particularly used the imagery of God's right hand to denote His saving power (Psalms 17:7 [LXX 16:7]; 20:6 [19:6]; 118:15ff. [117:15ff.]), His protection (18:35 [17:35]), and His power to destroy the Psalmist's enemies (Psalms 21:8 [20:8]; cf. 44:3 [43:3]; 45:4 [44:4]).

The expression "to sit at the right hand" of someone suggests a sharing of royal authority. Thus the Psalmist said that the Messiah was invited to sit at God's right hand (Psalm 110:1 [LXX 109:1]; cf. verse 5; 1 Esdras 4:29; cf. Sirach 12:12; 47:5). Therefore, the right side is also the side of honor (1 Kings 2:19 [LXX 3 Kings 2:19]).

Intertestamental Period
The right side continued to be religiously important for Judaism. Torah was said to be at the right hand of God (cf. Deuteronomy 33:2; Grundmann, "dexios," *Kittel*, 2:37ff.). "A wise man's heart is at his right hand; but a fool's heart at his left" (Ecclesiastes 10:2). Similarly the heart of the rich/ungodly is on the left, where riches are found (Proverbs 3:16). Grundmann goes even further and shows that the rabbis continued to exploit this distinction (ibid.).

New Testament Usage
The majority of the New Testament usages of *dexios* occur in the Gospels, Acts, and Revelation (27, 7, and 8 times respectively). Five occurrences are in Hebrews, five in Paul's writings, and one in 1 Peter. The literal use is quite common (e.g., Matthew 5:29 with parallels; Matthew 6:3; John 18:10), but by far the most usual understanding concerns the "right" as the side of honor and power. Many times this is in reference to Christ, who sits at the right hand of God (e.g., Luke 20:42; Acts 2:34; Colossians 3:1). A third feature of "right" involves judgment (ibid.). The latter two usages will be explored below.

By virtue of His resurrection Christ has been exalted to the right hand of God. This exaltation brings with it all privileges, rights, and authority of the Godhead. Thus Psalms like 16:8,9 and 110 became Christologically and messianically interpreted in early Christianity. The exalted Christ is now at the right hand of God (e.g., Acts 2:34; 5:31; Romans 8:34; Ephesians 1:20; Colossians 3:1; Hebrews 1:3,13; 10:12; 12:2; 1 Peter 3:22).

By virtue of His position Christ is not only exalted, He has also been given authority, power, and dominion (Ephesians 1:20ff.; Hebrews 1:13; 1 Peter 3:22). Thus when early Christians confessed Jesus as "exalted to the right hand of God" it was a powerful Christological declaration of who Christ is in relation to God. As Peter said (Acts 2:36), immediately after he cited Psalm 110:1, "Therefore let all the house of Israel know assuredly, that God hath made that same Jesus, whom ye have crucified, both Lord and Christ."

δέομαι 1183

STRONG 1188, BAUER 174-75, MOULTON-MILLIGAN 141, KITTEL 2:37-40, LIDDELL-SCOTT 379, COLIN BROWN 2:146-47.

1183. δέομαι deomai verb
Beg, pray, beseech, request.

COGNATES:
- δέησις deēsis (1157)
- προσδέομαι prosdeomai (4184)

SYNONYMS:
- αἰτέω aiteō (153)
- ἐντυγχάνω entunchanō (1777)
- ἐξαιτέω exaiteō (1793)
- ἐπερωτάω eperōtaō (1890)
- ἐρωτάω erōtaō (2049)
- εὔχομαι euchomai (2153)
- λέγω legō (2978)
- παραιτέομαι paraiteomai (3729)
- παρακαλέω parakaleō (3731)
- προσεύχομαι proseuchomai (4195)
- πυνθάνομαι punthanomai (4299)

אֶבְיוֹן ʾevyôn (33), Poor (Dt 15:11—Codex Alexandrinus only).

אֲהָהּ ʾăhāhh (159), Ah! Intercede (Jos 7:7, 1 Kgs 13:6).

אָנָּה ʾonnāh (588), Oh! (Ex 32:31).

בִּי bî (1031), A petition of entreaty, "Please!" (Gn 44:18).

בָּעוּ bāʿû (A1188), Petition (Dn 6:13—Aramaic).

דָּרַשׁ dārash (1938), Seek (Jb 5:8).

חָלָה chālâh (2571), Piel: seek favor (Ex 32:11, Ps 119:58 [118:58]).

חָנַן chānan (2706), Qal: be gracious (Mal 1:9); piel: make gracious (Prv 26:25); hithpael: plead, cry to (Dt 3:23, 1 Kgs 9:3, Ps 30:8 [29:8]).

נָפַל nāphal (5489), Fall; hiphil: present (Dn 9:18,20); hithpael: lie prostrate (Dt 9:18,25).

עָתַר ʿāthar (6518), Pray (Gn 25:21—Codex Alexandrinus only).

צְלָה tseʿlâh (A7011), Pael: pray (Dn 6:10—Aramaic).

שִׂיחַ sîach (7943), Complaint (Ps 64:1 [63:1]).

שָׁוַע shāwaʿ (8209), Piel: cry for help (Ps 28:2 [27:2]).

1. **δέομαι** deomai 1sing indic pres mid
2. **δεόμεθα** deometha 1pl indic pres mid
3. **δεόμενος** deomenos nom sing masc part pres mid
4. **δεόμενοι** deomenoi nom pl masc part pres mid
5. **ἐδεήθην** edeēthēn 1sing indic aor pass
6. **ἐδεήθη** edeēthē 3sing indic aor pass
7. **δεήθητι** deētheti 2sing impr aor pass
8. **δεήθητε** deēthēte 2pl impr aor pass
9. **δεηθέντων** deēthentōn gen pl masc part aor pass
10. **ἐδέετο** edeeto 3sing indic imperf mid
11. **ἐδεῖτο** edeito 3sing indic imperf mid

8	Pray ye therefore the Lord of the harvest,	Matt 9:38
6	and besought him, saying, Lord, if thou wilt,	Luke 5:12
1	thou Son of God ... I beseech thee, torment me not....	8:28
10	man ... besought him that he might be with him:	Luke 8:38
11	man ... besought him that he might be with him:	8:38
1	saying, Master, I beseech thee, look upon my son:	9:38
5	And I besought thy disciples to cast him out;	9:40
8	pray ye therefore the Lord of the harvest,	10:2
4	Watch ye therefore, and pray always,	21:36
5	But I have prayed for thee, that thy faith fail not:....	22:32
9	And when they had prayed, the place was shaken	Acts 4:31
7	pray God, if perhaps the thought of thine heart	8:22
8	and said, Pray ye to the Lord for me,	8:24
1	I pray thee, of whom speaketh the prophet this?	8:34
3	to the people, and prayed to God alway.	10:2
1	I beseech thee, suffer me to speak unto the people....	21:39
1	wherefore I beseech thee to hear me patiently.	26:3
3	Making request, if by any means now at length....	Rom 1:10
2	we pray you in Christ's stead,	2 Co 5:20
4	Praying us with much entreaty that we would	8:4
1	But I beseech you, that I may not be bold	10:2
1	Brethren, I beseech you, be as I am;	Gal 4:12
4	praying exceedingly that we might see your face,	1 Th 3:10

Classical Greek
Formally *deomai* is the deponent verb from *deō* (1204), "to bind, to want, to need." In classical Greek the form was often *deuomai* (e.g., Homer). It is related to the impersonal verb *dei* (1158), "it is necessary"; thus *denomai* can mean "to lack, to be in need of," or as a participle, "the necessary things" (*ta deomena*). "I pray, ask, beg" are also found along the spectrum of *deomai*'s definition (*Liddell-Scott*).

Septuagint Usage
The lack of any precisely equivalent Hebrew word becomes obvious from a glance at a concordance to the Septuagint. Fifteen different Hebrew terms stand behind *deomai*. Perhaps one of the forms of *chānan* (usually hithpael, "plead for mercy, grace") has a slight edge in terms of number (20 times).

Implicit in *deomai* is the notion of "to request" (cf. Genesis 25:21). Some subordinate relationship between the one making the request and the one with the power to grant it is also implied. The Lord God is normally the one asked (e.g., Exodus 4:10,13; Numbers 12:11,13), but the expression can also be used of human requests to other human beings (e.g., Genesis 43:20; 44:18). Generally, however, *deomai* is the language of prayer and petition to God (Deuteronomy 3:23; Daniel 9:18,20). It suggests humility and dependence upon the Lord (Deuteronomy 9:18,25) (cf. Greeven, "deomai," *Kittel*, 2:41).

New Testament Usage
Twenty-two occurrences of *deomai* are present in the Greek New Testament. Fifteen of these occur in Luke-Acts; there is only one Gospel instance outside of Luke (Matthew 9:38). Paul's writings contain the remaining six instances of *deomai*.

Luke followed the pattern established by the Septuagint, i.e., that *deomai* concerns either a request for divine intervention or a simple human request (cf. Luke 10:2; Acts 8:34; 21:39 of a human's request of another human). When referring to religious requests, it falls in the category of "prayer, petition, request, entreaty." It was used of "requests" made to Jesus for healing mercy (Luke 5:12), and again it implied submission to a higher authority or power (see Luke 8:28; 9:38). The Lord God is the one who hears such petitions, for it is only He who can grant them (Acts 8:22,24).

In the five times Paul used *deomai* he too associated it with "requests" made both to God and man. He used *deomai* in reference to his own personal "prayers" to God (Romans 1:10; 1 Thessalonians 3:10). But he spoke of "pleading" with the Corinthians to be reconciled to Christ (2 Corinthians 5:20; cf. 8:4; 10:2). He also urged the Galatians to imitate him (Galatians 4:12).

STRONG 1189, BAUER 175, MOULTON-MILLIGAN 141, KITTEL 2:40-41, COLIN BROWN 2:860-61,874,885.

1183B. δέος deos noun
Fear, awe.

1. δέους deous gen sing neu

1 serve God acceptably with ... awe (NASB)......... Heb 12:28

Deos appears one time in the New Testament, at Hebrews 12:28 where it is a variant for *aidōs* (127), translated "reverence" in the King James Version. The verse instructs believers to serve the Lord in *awe* and with "godly fear" (*eulabeia* [2105]), remembering that He is a consuming fire (verse 29).

BAUER 175, MOULTON-MILLIGAN 141, KITTEL 9:189-219, LIDDELL-SCOTT 379.

1184. Δερβαῖος Derbaios name-adj
From Derbe.

1. Δερβαῖος Derbaios nom sing masc

1 Secundus; and Gaius of Derbe, and Timotheus;..... Acts 20:4

A term used to describe a person named Gaius in Acts 20:4.

1185. Δέρβη Derbē name
Derbe.

1. Δέρβην Derbēn acc fem

1 and fled unto Lystra and Derbe, cities of Lycaonia, Acts 14:6
1 the next day he departed with Barnabas to Derbe...... 14:20
1 Then came he to Derbe and Lystra:.................. 16:1

City in the province of Galatia evangelized by Paul on his first missionary journey (Acts 14:20).

1186. δέρμα derma noun
Skin (of an animal), hide.

עוֹר 'ôr (5997), Skin (Ex 26:14, Lv 13:2ff., Jer 13:23).

1. δέρμασιν dermasin dat pl neu

1 they wandered about in sheepskins and goatskins;.. Heb 11:37

Derma first occurs in classical Greek. Derived from the verb *derō* (1188), "to peel" or "beat," this noun came to mean the resultant product of butchering efforts, i.e., "skin." *Derma*, occurring only once in the New Testament, is further qualified by its accompanying adjective *aigeios* (122), "that which a goat possesses," in Hebrews 11:37. Since the "skin of a goat" was the apparel of Old Testament prophets (compare Elijah in 2 Kings 1:8), this is probably the reference of Hebrews 11:37. Compare *dermatinos* (1187).

STRONG 1192, BAUER 175, MOULTON-MILLIGAN 141, LIDDELL-SCOTT 379-80.

1187. δερμάτινος dermatinos adj
Made of hides, leather (animal skin).

עוֹר 'ôr (5997), Leather (Lv 13:57ff., 2 Kgs 1:8); skin (Nm 4:10ff.).

1. δερματίνην dermatinēn acc sing fem

1 and a **leathern** girdle about his loins;.............. Matt 3:4
1 and with a girdle **of a skin** about his loins;........ Mark 1:6

Dermatinos is derived from *derma* (1186), meaning "skin, peeling." The suffix *-inos* refers to material. Hence, *dermatinos* is that which belongs to and is peeled off of an animal, i.e., its "skin." *Dermatinos* has a variety of Septuagint usages (e.g., Genesis 3:21; 2 Kings 1:8 [LXX 4 Kings 1:8]). It occurs two times in the New Testament with reference to John the Baptist's waist-fastened belt or strap composed "of a skin" (Mark 1:6). This "leathern girdle" (Matthew 3:4) would provide unhindered movement in the flowing garments of that day. The leather belt often served as a part of the normal clothing of desert dwellers. This would identify John as one like Elijah who wore similar apparel.

STRONG 1193, BAUER 175, MOULTON-MILLIGAN 142, LIDDELL-SCOTT 380.

1188. δέρω derō verb

Beat, strike, scourge.

SYNONYMS:
  κολαφίζω kolaphizō (2826)
  μαστιγόω mastigoō (3118)
  πατάσσω patassō (3822)
  ῥαπίζω rhapizō (4331)
  φραγελλόω phragelloō (5253)

פָּשַׁט pāshaṭ (6838), Hiphil: skin (2 Chr 29:34—Codex Alexandrinus only).

1. **δέρεις** dereis 2sing indic pres act
2. **δέρει** derei 3sing indic pres act
3. **δέρων** derōn nom sing masc part pres act
4. **δέροντες** derontes nom pl masc part pres act
5. **ἔδειραν** edeiran 3pl indic aor act
6. **δείραντες** deirantes nom pl masc part aor act
7. **δαρήσεται** darēsetai 3sing indic fut pass
8. **δαρήσεσθε** darēsesthe 2pl indic fut pass

5 beat one, and killed another, and stoned another...	Matt 21:35
5 and beat him, and sent him away empty............	Mark 12:3
4 and many others; beating some, and killing some......	12:5
8 and in the synagogues ye shall be beaten:.............	13:9
7 shall be beaten with many stripes..................	Luke 12:47
7 shall be beaten with few stripes.....................	12:48
6 husbandmen beat him, and sent him away empty.......	20:10
6 they beat him also, and entreated him shamefully,.....	20:11
4 men that held Jesus mocked him, and smote him.......	22:63
1 but if well, why smitest thou me?.................	John 18:23
6 they had called the apostles, and beaten them,.......	Acts 5:40
6 They have beaten us openly uncondemned,...........	16:37
3 they know that I imprisoned and beat.................	22:19
3 so fight I, not as one that beateth the air:............1	Co 9:26
2 if a man exalt himself, ... smite you on the face....2	Co 11:20

Classical Greek
Most classical writers prior to the time of Aristophanes (ca. Fifth or Fourth Century B.C.) understood *derō* to mean literally "to skin" (as an animal), "to flay." Gradually the term's figurative sense, "to beat," dominated.

Septuagint Usage
Each of the three Septuagint occurrences of *derō* corresponds to the Hebrew verb *pāshaṭ* (hiphil) (manuscripts do vary at each of these texts). Furthermore each text is a literal reference to the priestly practice of skinning the sacrificial offerings (Leviticus 1:6; 2 Chronicles 29:34; 35:11).

New Testament Usage
In the Synoptic Gospels *derō* is used of physical beatings (Mark 12:3,5 with parallels). To "be beaten" may become the disciples' fate (Mark 13:9; cf. Acts 5:40; 16:37; 2 Corinthians 11:20); it was certainly their Master's (Luke 22:63; John 18:23).

Paul recalled that he did not box as one "*beating* the air," i.e., he was no novice boxer in the struggle to win men to Christ (1 Corinthians 9:26). He subdued his own will (literally *sōma* [4835], "body," here) in order to be effective in converting men and women to Christ. For though Paul was free through the Spirit's work, he made himself a slave to all (1 Corinthians 9:19ff.).

STRONG 1194, BAUER 175, MOULTON-MILLIGAN 142, LIDDELL-SCOTT 380, COLIN BROWN 1:161-63.

1189. δεσμεύω desmeuō verb

Bind, tie.

COGNATES:
  δεσμέω desmeō (1190)
  δέσμη desmē (1191)
  δέσμιος desmios (1192)
  δεσμός desmos (1193)
  δεσμοφύλαξ desmophulax (1194)
  δεσμωτήριον desmōtērion (1195)
  δεσμώτης desmōtēs (1196)
  σύνδεσμος sundesmos (4736)

SYNONYMS:
  δεσμέω desmeō (1190)
  δέω deō (1204)

אָלַם 'ālam (487), Piel: bind (Gn 37:7).
אָסַר 'āsar (646), Tie, bind (Gn 49:11, Jgs 16:11).
חָבַל chāval (2341), Pledge (Am 2:8).
חָבַשׁ chāvash (2372), Piel: bind up (Ps 147:3 [146:3]).
צָדָה tsādhāh (6922), Lie in wait (1 Sm 24:11 [24:12]).
צָרַר tsārar (7173), Wrap up (Jb 26:8).

1. **δεσμεύουσιν** desmeuousin 3pl indic pres act
2. **δεσμεύων** desmeuōn nom sing masc part pres act
3. **ἐδεσμεύετο** edesmeueto 3sing indic imperf mid

1 they bind heavy burdens and grievous to be borne,	Matt 23:4
3 and he was bound with chains (NASB).............	Luke 8:29
2 binding and delivering into prisons................	Acts 22:4

Classical Greek and Septuagint Usage
In classical times *desmeuō* spoke of a ship loaded down with heavy contents. In the Septuagint the word refers to Samson's being bound with new ropes (Judges 16:11) and to the sheaves tied up in bundles (Joseph's vision, Genesis 37:7).

New Testament Usage
The New Testament uses this word only twice, for "tying up" or "binding up." In Acts 22:4 *desmeuō* refers to Saul's "binding up" and removing Christians to prison confinement. Figuratively, in Matthew 23:4, *desmeuō* refers

to the burdens of legalism the Pharisees imposed on their followers. Drawing from the customs of Palestine work animals, *desmeuō* likens Pharasaic demands to the heavy loads which were "tied up" and mercilessly tossed upon the beast of burden. See *desmeō* (1190).

STRONG 1195, BAUER 175, MOULTON-MILLIGAN 142, LIDDELL-SCOTT 380, COLIN BROWN 3:591.

1190. δεσμέω desmeō verb
Tie, bind up.
COGNATE:
δεσμεύω desmeuō (1189)
SYNONYMS:
δεσμεύω desmeuō (1189)
δέω deō (1204)

1. ἐδεσμεῖτο edesmeito 3sing indic imperf pass

1 and he **was** kept **bound** with chains and in fetters;...Luke 8:29

Desmeō, used once in the New Testament, refers to the demon possessed man who was "bound" by chains (Luke 8:29). This verb's passive voice indicates the "tying up" was done to him by someone else. Its imperfect tense may indicate this "binding" was done more than simply once. It may have been a repeated and customary occurrence; in other words, the man "was being (and continued to be) bound." See *desmeuō* (1189).

STRONG 1196, BAUER 175, LIDDELL-SCOTT 380.

1191. δέσμη desmē noun
Bundle, bunch.
CROSS-REFERENCE:
δεσμεύω desmeuō (1189)

אֲגֻדָּה 'ăghuddāh (89), Bunch (Ex 12:22).

1. δέσμας desmas acc pl fem

1 the tares, and bind them in **bundles** to burn them: Matt 13:30

The Greek Diodorus used *desmē* to speak of a "bundle of straw." The Septuagint use of *desmē* refers to the "bunch" of hyssop which applied the blood to the doorposts (Exodus 12:22). It later appears in the New Testament within a parabolic context describing the final judgment (Matthew 13:30). *Desmē* is used here in reference to the custom of a Palestine farmer who would gather together both good and bad grain into "bunches." The very similar, but poisonous, imitation grain (darnell) was permitted to grow with the wheat until harvest time. This prevented the wheat from being uprooted and its growth stunted. Later, the darnell would be gathered in "bunches" and burned.

STRONG 1197, BAUER 176, MOULTON-MILLIGAN 142, LIDDELL-SCOTT 380, COLIN BROWN 3:591.

1192. δέσμιος desmios noun
Prisoner.
CROSS-REFERENCE:
δεσμεύω desmeuō (1189)

אָסִיר 'assîr (630), Prisoner (Zec 9:11,12, Lam 3:34).

אָסַר 'āsar (646), Prison (Eccl 4:14—Codex Vaticanus only).

1. δέσμιος desmios nom sing masc
2. δέσμιον desmion acc sing masc
3. δέσμιοι desmioi nom pl masc
4. δεσμίων desmiōn gen pl masc
5. δεσμίους desmious acc pl masc
6. δεσμίοις desmiois dat pl masc

2 was wont to release unto the people a **prisoner**,....Matt 27:15
2 they had then a notable **prisoner**, called Barabbas...... 27:16
2 at that feast he released unto them one **prisoner**,.. Mark 15:6
3 and the **prisoners** heard them......................Acts 16:25
5 supposing that the **prisoners** had been fled............ 16:27
1 Paul the **prisoner** called me unto him,................ 23:18
1 There is a certain man left **in bonds** by Felix:......... 25:14
2 it seemeth to me unreasonable to send **a prisoner**,..... 25:27
5 delivered the **prisoners** to the captain of the guard:.... 28:16
1 yet was I delivered **prisoner** from Jerusalem........... 28:17
1 the **prisoner** of Jesus Christ for you Gentiles,........ Eph 3:1
1 I therefore, the **prisoner** of the Lord,................. 4:1
2 the testimony of our Lord, nor of me his **prisoner**:..2 Tm 1:8
1 Paul, a **prisoner** of Jesus Christ, and Timothy.......Phlm 1:1
1 and now also a **prisoner** of Jesus Christ................ 1:9
6 For you showed sympathy to the **prisoners** (NASB) Heb 10:34
4 Remember them **that are in bonds**,.................... 13:3

Classical Greek
The noun *desmios*, "binding, one who is bound" comes from *deō* (1204), "bind" (cf. *desmos* [1193]). In classical Greek it is used both literally, as in "bound with fetters," or metaphorically, as in "bound with a spell" (*Liddell-Scott*).

Septuagint Usage
The Septuagint shows *desmios* literally referring to "prisoners" (so Lamentations 3:34; Zechariah 9:11; 2 Maccabees 14:27); or, as in Ecclesiastes, a "house of prisoners," i.e., a prison (4:14). "Prisoners of hope" may have been intended to have a double meaning in Zechariah 9:12. Forms of the Hebrew *'āsar*, "to bind," are translated *desmios* in the canonical portions. A figurative usage is intended in the Wisdom of Solomon: "A prisoner of darkness" (17:2, RSV). Another figurative sense can be seen at Hosea 11:4 where God said, "I drew them

... with *bands* of love." Israel, however, rejected His love and rebelled because (in part) they viewed these "bands" as a force which kept them under bondage (cf. Jeremiah 2:20; 5:5).

New Testament Usage
Desmios occurs 16 times in the New Testament. It refers to a "prisoner" in the literal sense in the first and second Gospels (Matthew 27:15,16; Mark 15:6), and this is its purpose in Acts as well (e.g., 16:25,27; 25:14). Often it was the apostle who found himself in prison (e.g., Acts 23:18). The author of Hebrews reminded his readers that those in prison (for the gospel?) were to be remembered (13:3; cf. 10:34).

Paul referred to himself in his letters as a "prisoner of Christ" (*ho desmios tou christou*, Ephesians 3:1; Philemon 1,9; cf. Ephesians 4:1, "prisoner of the Lord"; 2 Timothy 1:8, "his prisoner"). Two ideas are converging: Paul was literally a prisoner, but he was also a *captive* to Christ and imprisoned for His cause.

STRONG 1198, BAUER 176, MOULTON-MILLIGAN 142, KITTEL 2:43, LIDDELL-SCOTT 380, COLIN BROWN 3:591-92.

1193. δεσμός desmos noun
Bond, imprisonment, shackle, ligament.
CROSS-REFERENCE:
δεσμεύω desmeuō (1189)

אָסוּר 'ēsûr (626), Bond, fetter (Jgs 15:14, Eccl 7:26 [7:27]).
אָסוּר 'ēsûr (A627), Imprisonment (Ezr 7:26—Aramaic; Codex Alexandrinus only).
אָסַר 'āsar (646), Bind (Jgs 15:13); prisoner (Is 49:9).
אִסָּר 'issār (647), Vow (Nm 30:14).
חוֹחַ chôach (2430), Hook (2 Chr 33:11).
מוֹטָה môṭāh (4269), Bar of a yoke (Lv 26:13).
מוֹסֵר môsēr (4283), Bond, fetter (Ps 2:3, Is 28:22, Na 1:13).
מַסְגֵּר masgēr (4674), Dungeon (Is 42:7).
מַעֲדַנּוֹת ma'ădhannôth (4730), Fetters, chains (Jb 38:31).
עֲבֹת 'ăvōth (5895), Cord, rope (Ez 3:25, 4:8, Hos 11:4).
צָמִיד tsāmîdh (7051), Covering (Nm 19:15).
צְרוֹר tseˁrôr (7154), Bundle, bag (Gn 42:35, 1 Sm 25:29, Hg 1:6).
קֶשֶׁר qesher (7490), Conspiracy (2 Kgs 12:20—only some Vaticanus texts).

1. δεσμός desmos nom/acc sing masc/neu
2. δεσμοῦ desmou gen sing masc/neu
3. δεσμά desma nom/acc pl masc/neu
4. δεσμῶν desmōn gen pl masc/neu
5. δεσμοῖς desmois dat pl masc/neu
6. δεσμούς desmous nom/acc pl masc/neu

1 and the **string** of his tongue was loosed,	Mark	7:35
3 **chains** and in fetters; and he brake the **bands**,	Luke	8:29
2 be loosed from this **bond** on the sabbath day?		13:16
3 and every one's **bands** were loosed.	Acts	16:26
3 saying that **bonds** and afflictions abide me.		20:23
4 he loosed him from his **bands**,		22:30
4 laid to his charge worthy of death or **of bonds**.		23:29
4 and altogether such as I am, except these **bonds**.		26:29
4 doeth nothing worthy of death or **of bonds**.		26:31
5 in my heart; inasmuch as both in my **bonds**,	Phlp	1:7
6 my **bonds** in Christ are manifest in all the palace,		1:13
5 waxing confident by my **bonds**,		1:14
5 supposing to add affliction to my **bonds**:		1:16
4 Remember my **bonds**. Grace be with you. Amen.	Col	4:18
4 suffer trouble, as an evil doer, even unto **bonds**;	2 Tm	2:9
5 son Onesimus, whom I have begotten in my **bonds**:	Phlm	1:10
5 ministered unto me in the **bonds** of the gospel:		1:13
5 For ye had compassion of me in my **bonds**,	Heb	10:34
4 yea, moreover **of bonds** and imprisonment:		11:36
5 hath reserved in everlasting **chains** under darkness	Jude	1:6

Classical Greek
Classical Greek from Homer (ca. 800-700 B.C.) to Roman times treats *desmos* as "bond" or "fetter." In the singular form it generally describes an impediment or infirmity which afflicts a person. The more common plural form *desma* usually applies to a person's captivity or bondage, as in a prison or to a binding power.

Septuagint Usage
In the Septuagint *desmos*, used over 45 times, replaces several Hebrew terms. But the word most often replaced a form of *'āsar*, "to bind" (cf. the Greek word *pedaō*). It ranges in meaning from "bond," "fetter," "restraint" (e.g., Leviticus 26:13), to a "pouch" used for carrying silver (Genesis 42:35). The more specific idea of "chains" or "bonds" is also present (Psalm 2:3; cf. Isaiah 28:22).

New Testament Usage
Of the 20 times *desmos* appears in the New Testament, only twice is it assigned the singular form—once to describe a speech impediment (Mark 7:35) and once to depict a crippled woman (Luke 13:16).

The primary usage in the New Testament is the plural form *desma*, and in each instance it suggests incarceration or confinement as a prisoner. The frequency of *desma* in the Pauline letters (eight times) shows the apostle's "imprisonment for the gospel" (Philippians 1:13; Philemon 13) which affected his self-understanding in relation to Christ. Paul reckoned himself a prisoner of the Lord (2 Timothy 1:8) as well as "a preacher, and an apostle, and a teacher" (2 Timothy 1:11). His entire future was offered up to the Lord in sacrifice like a prisoner of love.

Strong 1199, Bauer 176, Moulton-Milligan 142, Kittel 2:43, Liddell-Scott 380, Colin Brown 3:591-92.

1194. δεσμοφύλαξ desmophulax noun

Keeper of the prison, jailer, warden.

Cross-References:
δεσμεύω desmeuō (1189)
φυλάσσω phulassō (5278)

1. δεσμοφύλαξ desmophulax nom sing masc
2. δεσμοφύλακι desmophulaki dat sing masc

2 charging the **jailor** to keep them safely:	Acts 16:23
1 the **keeper of the prison** awaking out of his sleep,	16:27
1 the **keeper of the prison** told this saying to Paul,	16:36

Desmophulax is composed of two words: *desmos* (1193), "prison," plus *phulasso* (5278), "guard, watch." Thus, the "one who guards a prison" is deemed a *desmophulax*. A related word, *archidesmophulax*, occurs in the Septuagint. The added *archi* gives the idea of "chief" or "head" indicating the highest ranked prison keeper such as the one who favored Joseph (Genesis 39:21-23). *Desmophulax* appears three times in Acts. On each occasion it denotes the government hired "jailer" responsible for Paul and Silas' safekeeping (Acts 16:23,27,36). His terror, demonstrated by a suicide attempt (Acts 16:27), is understandable. Prison escapes could have meant his disgrace or death at the hands of the Roman government.

Strong 1200, Bauer 176, Moulton-Milligan 142, Liddell-Scott 380, Colin Brown 3:591.

1195. δεσμωτήριον

desmōtērion noun

Place of bondage, prison, jail.

Cross-Reference:
δεσμεύω desmeuō (1189)

אָסִיר 'āṣîr (629), Prisoner (Is 24:22).
אָסַר 'āsar (646), Bind (Jgs 16:21); prison (Jgs 16:25).

1. δεσμωτηρίου desmōtēriou gen sing neu
2. δεσμωτηρίῳ desmōtēriō dat sing neu
3. δεσμωτήριον desmōtērion nom/acc sing neu

2 John had heard in the **prison** the works of Christ,	Matt 11:2
3 and sent to the **prison** to have them brought.	Acts 5:21
3 The **prison** truly found we shut with all safety,	5:23
1 so that the foundations of the **prison** were shaken:	16:26

Classical Greek and Septuagint Usage

Desmōtērion is composed of two Greek words: *desmos* (1193), "bond," plus *tēreō* (4931), "to observe, to keep watch upon." Thus, the place where bound persons are watched and observed for security's sake is a *desmōtērion*. The Septuagint uses *desmōtērion* to indicate the "prison" where Pharaoh confined his chief officers with Joseph (Genesis 40:3).

New Testament Usage

Regarding its New Testament usage, *desmōtērion* occurs only in Matthew and Acts. The first occasion refers to John's confinement at Herod's fortress (Matthew 11:2), which Josephus said was located on the east side of the Dead Sea in Peraea (Josephus *Wars of the Jews* 7.6.1f.). Recent excavations indicate this dungeon was equipped with stocks. These beams were constructed with two widely separated holes for the victim's legs for the purpose of inflicting great weariness and pain. *Desmōtērion*'s other occurrences in Acts 5:21,23 and 16:26, refer to the same kind of confinement. See for contrast *phulakē* (5274).

Strong 1201, Bauer 176, Moulton-Milligan 143, Liddell-Scott 380, Colin Brown 3:591.

1196. δεσμώτης desmōtēs noun

Prisoner, captive.

Cross-Reference:
δεσμεύω desmeuō (1189)

אָסִיר 'aṣṣîr (630), Prisoner (Gn 39:20).
מַסְגֵּר masgēr (4674), Smith (Jer 24:1, 29:2 [36:2]).

1. δεσμώτας desmōtas acc pl masc

1 they delivered Paul and certain other **prisoners**	Acts 27:1
1 And the soldiers' counsel was to kill the **prisoners**,	27:42

Genesis 39:20 records how Joseph was thrown into the place where the "king's prisoners" were kept. In that verse the Septuagint uses a form of *desmōtēs* to translate the Hebrew word *'āsîr*, which means "imprisoned." The word is found in two places in the New Testament: Acts 27:1 and 42. It means a "prisoner"—one who is involuntarily bound, under custody or confinement. It is a derivative of the word *desmos* (1193) which refers to a band or shackle that impedes.

Strong 1202, Bauer 176, Moulton-Milligan 143, Liddell-Scott 380, Colin Brown 3:591.

1197. δεσπότης despotēs noun

Lord, master, owner, ruler.

Cognates:
οἰκοδεσποτέω oikodespoteō (3479)
οἰκοδεσπότης oikodespotēs (3480)

Synonyms:
ἐπιστάτης epistatēs (1972)
κύριος kurios (2935)

אָדוֹן 'ādhôn (112), Lord, master (Jos 5:14, Prv 30:10 [24:33], Is 10:33).

אֱלוֹהַּ 'ĕlôahh (438), God (Dn 9:17,19).

יְהוָה yᵉhwāh (3176), The Lord (Prv 29:25, Is 1:24).

מָשַׁל māshal (5090), Ruler (Prv 6:7).

1. δεσπότης despotēs nom sing masc
2. δεσπότῃ despotē dat sing masc
3. δεσπότην despotēn acc sing masc
4. δέσποτα despota voc sing masc
5. δεσπόταις despotais dat pl masc
6. δεσπότας despotas acc pl masc

```
4 Lord, now lettest thou thy servant depart in peace,.. Luke 2:29
4 Lord, thou art God, which hast made heaven,........ Acts 4:24
6 count their own masters worthy of all honour,...... 1 Tm 6:1
6 And they that have believing masters,................. 6:2
2 sanctified, and meet for the master's use,............ 2 Tm 2:21
5 servants to be obedient unto their own masters,..... Tit 2:9
5 Servants, be subject to your masters with all fear;... 1 Pt 2:18
3 even denying the Lord that bought them,........... 2 Pt 2:1
3 denying the only Lord God, and our Lord Jesus..... Jude 1:4
1 saying, How long, O Lord, holy and true,........... Rev 6:10
```

Classical Greek
In its simplest definition *despotēs* means "master, lord of the house." As a form of address in classical Greek, *despotēs* could denote the positional difference between a master and a slave, between a ruler and subject, or between a god and a man. The emphasis is upon the authority invested in the *despotēs* by virtue of his position (*Liddell-Scott*). Rengstorf notes a certain nuance lies behind *despotēs* in classical usage: "It is in keeping that *despotēs* is always marked by a total lack of enthusiasm in relation to rulers. Originally the only feeling in respect of him is that of the subject toward the one whom he must serve" ("despotes," *Kittel*, 2:44). The distinctive feature of *despotēs* is the absolute authority it represents; thus the term is not relational, but positional.

Septuagint Usage
The term became adapted into the vocabulary of the Septuagint because in itself it carried no pejorative sense, only a sense of power. Nevertheless, it played a subordinate role to *kurios* (2935), "Lord," probably because of its impersonal flavor, which was unsuited to a Biblical view of God (ibid.).

Most frequently (12 of 18 times with Hebrew counterparts) *despotēs* translates *'ādôn*, "Lord, lord, master, owner," and occasionally it equals Yahweh (Genesis 15:2,8; Joshua 5:14; Isaiah 10:33; cf. Proverbs 29:25). Repeatedly it occurs in conjunction with *kurios* (Genesis 15:2,8; Isaiah 1:24; 3:1; 10:33; Jeremiah 1:6). In the material without a Hebrew counterpart the same association of *despotēs* with God continues (Daniel [Septuagint only] 9:8,15,16,17,19). However, *despotēs* is also used in its secular sense (Judith 5:20,24; Sirach 3:7).

New Testament Usage
In the New Testament *despotēs* exhibits the general Biblical pattern of understanding. In the Pastoral Epistles (1 Timothy 6:1,2; Titus 2:9; cf. 2 Timothy 2:21) it is used of human "masters" who are over households containing slaves (*douloi* [see 1395]). But it is also applied to God. Second Peter 2:1 and Jude 4 expressly see a denial (*arneomai* [714]) of God's authority as *despotēs* in the false doctrines that circulated. Thus the unique dimension of *despotēs* is drawn upon. The souls of those "slain for the word of God" cry out to the *despotēs*, the Holy and True One, for vengeance (Revelation 6:10); God alone has the authority to render judgment.

The pious Simeon, a *doulos* (1395), "slave," of God, is ready to die according to the word of his *despotēs* (Luke 2:29). Again, the authority of God is being especially highlighted with this terminology. And in Acts 4:24, the "Lord" who made the heavens is the One who has exerted eternal control over the events surrounding the Cross (4:28).

STRONG 1203, BAUER 176, MOULTON-MILLIGAN 143, KITTEL 2:44-49, LIDDELL-SCOTT 381, COLIN BROWN 2:508-10.

1198. δεῦρο deuro adv
Come, come here, until now, so far.

בּוֹא bô' (971), Come in, come (Gn 24:31, 2 Sm 13:11).

הָלַךְ hālakh (2050), Go, come (Nm 23:7, 1 Kgs 18:5, Neh 6:2).

עָלָה 'ālâh (6148), Go up (2 Kgs 1:3).

1. δεῦρο deuro

```
1 sell that thou hast, ... and come and follow me..... Matt 19:21
1 and come, take up the cross, and follow me....... Mark 10:21
1 have treasure in heaven: and come, follow me...... Luke 18:22
1 he cried with a loud voice, Lazarus, come forth..... John 11:43
1 and come into the land which I shall show thee..... Acts 7:3
1 And now come, I will send thee into Egypt............ 7:34
1 I purposed to come unto you, but was let hitherto,.. Rom 1:13
1 and talked with me, saying unto me, Come hither;.. Rev 17:1
1 and talked with me, saying, Come hither,.............. 21:9
```

Classical Greek and Septuagint Usage
This adverb (cf. *deute* [1199]) appears throughout classical Greek from the time of Homer

onward with two basic senses: (1) as an adverb of place—"come, come here," and (2) as an adverb of time—"now, until now." The usage remains consistent in the Septuagint where it is most often part of the translation of *hālak*, "to go, come" (e.g., Genesis 31:44, "Come now," [NIV]; Exodus 3:10, "Now go"; Numbers 10:29; Judges 4:22).

New Testament Usage

There are nine instances of *deuro* in the New Testament. Three occur in the identical gospel command from Jesus to His disciples: "Come, follow me" (Matthew 19:21; Mark 10:21; Luke 18:22). John's Gospel uses it in a similar manner of Jesus' command to Lazarus to "come forth!" (11:43). On three occasions *deuro* appears as an invitation from God: "Come . . . I shall show thee . . . " (Acts 7:3 [Genesis 12:1]; cf. Revelation 17:1; 21:9).

STRONG 1204, BAUER 176, MOULTON-MILLIGAN 143, LIDDELL-SCOTT 381.

1199. δεῦτε deute adv

Come here, come on.

אָתָה 'āthâh (885), Come (Is 56:9).

בּוֹא bô' (971), Come (Jgs 9:15, Jb 17:10, Ps 95:1 [94:1]).

הַב hav (1957), Come! (Gn 11:3f.,7, Ex 1:10).

הָלַךְ hālakh (2050), Come (Gn 37:20,27, 2 Kgs 7:4, Is 1:18).

1. δεῦτε deute

1 And he saith unto them, Follow me,	Matt 4:19
1 Come unto me, all ye that ... are heavy laden,	11:28
1 This is the heir; come, let us kill him,	21:38
1 and all things are ready: come unto the marriage.	22:4
1 Come, ye blessed of my Father,	25:34
1 Come, see the place where the Lord lay.	28:6
1 And Jesus said unto them, Come ye after me,	Mark 1:17
1 Come ye yourselves apart into a desert place,	6:31
1 This is the heir; come, let us kill him,	12:7
1 saying, This is the heir: come, let us kill him,	Luke 20:14
1 Come, see a man, which told me all things	John 4:29
1 Jesus saith unto them, Come and dine.	21:12
1 Come and gather yourselves together	Rev 19:17

This adverb functions primarily as a hortatory particle used with the plural (see *Bauer*). Its meaning is essentially no different from *deuro* (1198), "come, come now," and in the Septuagint they often replace the same Hebrew term *hālakh* (Genesis 37:20). In the New Testament also it functions in the same kind of passages as *deuro*. Thus Jesus invited Peter and Andrew to "follow me" (Matthew 4:19), and to "come ye after (*opisō* [3557]) me" (Mark 1:17). Jesus invited those who were heavy laden to "come" (Matthew 11:28; cf. 25:34).

Other uses function in essentially the same way to introduce some invitation or command (Matthew 28:6; Revelation 19:17).

STRONG 1205, BAUER 176, LIDDELL-SCOTT 381.

1200. δευτεραῖος deuteraios adj

On the second day.

1. δευτεραῖοι deuteraioi nom pl masc

1 and we came the next day to Puteoli:	Acts 28:13

Found only in Acts 28:13, *deuteraios* is used as an adjective with an adverbial sense meaning "on the second day" or "the next day." In the strict adjective form it refers to something or someone that is from or belongs to the second, or who does something on the second day. It comes from the word *deuteros* (1202) which means "second in order."

STRONG 1206, BAUER 177, LIDDELL-SCOTT 381.

1201. δευτερόπρωτος deuteroprōtos adj

"Second after the first (sabbath)" (KJV); second-first (sabbath).

CROSS-REFERENCE:
πρῶτος prōtos (4270B)

1. δευτεροπρώτῳ deuteroprōtō dat sing masc/neu

1 came to pass on the second sabbath after the first,	Luke 6:1

New Testament Usage

This strange term appears nowhere else in antiquity apart from Luke 6:1, and it is doubtful whether it is an actual word at all. Most modern versions omit it (e.g., RSV, NIV). Because of its rarity, its precise meaning is also disputed. Of the available manuscripts of the New Testament, Western and Byzantine (A C D O f13, TR) manuscripts contain the term while the external witnesses for the term's omission also has support (e.g., p4 p75vid Sinaiticus B W f1 italia Sahidic and Bohairic versions).

Several explanations have been offered as to the meaning of the term. (1) It is the Sabbath following the first day of the Feast of Unleavened Bread. (2) The *Pulpit Commentary* states: "The first sabbath of each of the seven years which made a sabbatical cycle was called first, second, third, etc. Thus the 'second-first' sabbath would signify the first sabbath of the second year" (Spence, *Pulpit Commentary, Luke*, p.139). (3) The *Pulpit Commentary* (ibid.) points out that the civil year of the Jews began in the autumn, and the ecclesiastical year in the spring. So there were two "first sabbaths" every year. The one at the beginning of the civil year would be referred to as the "first first," and the other the "second first." (See Metzger, *Textual Commentary* p.139.)

STRONG 1207, BAUER 177; MOULTON-MILLIGAN 143, LIDDELL-SCOTT 381.

1202. δεύτερος deuteros num
Second.

1. δευτέρου deuterou ord gen sing masc/neu
2. δεύτερος deuteros ord nom sing masc
3. δευτέρῳ deuterō ord dat sing masc
4. δευτέρα deutera ord nom sing fem
5. δευτέρας deuteras ord gen sing fem
6. δευτέρᾳ deutera ord dat sing fem
7. δευτέραν deuteran ord acc sing fem
8. δεύτερον deuteron ord nom/acc sing neu

3	And he came to the **second**, and said likewise.	Matt 21:30
2	Likewise the **second** also, and the third,	22:26
4	And the **second** is like unto it,	22:39
1	He went away again the **second** time, and prayed,	26:42
2	And the **second** took her, and died,	Mark 12:21
4	And the **second** is like, namely this,	12:31
1	And the **second** time the cock crew.	14:72
6	And if he shall come in the **second** watch,	Luke 12:38
2	the **second** came, saying, Lord, thy pound hath	19:18
2	the **second** took her to wife, and he died childless.	20:30
8	enter the **second** time into his mother's womb,	John 3:4
8	This is again the **second** miracle that Jesus did;	4:54
1	Then **again** called they the man that was blind,	9:24
8	He saith to him again the **second** time,	21:16
3	And at the **second** time Joseph was made known	Acts 7:13
1	the voice spake unto him again the **second** time,	10:15
1	But the voice answered me **again** from heaven,	11:9
7	When they were past the first and ... **second** ward,	12:10
3	as it is also written in the **second** psalm,	13:33
8	**secondarily** prophets, thirdly teachers,	1 Co 12:28
2	the **second** man is the Lord from heaven.	15:47
7	that ye might have **a second** benefit;	2 Co 1:15
8	as if I were present, the **second** time;	13:2
4	of the Holy Ghost, be with you all. Amen.	13:14
4	The grace of our Lord ... be with you all. Amen.	2 Th 3:18
4	Grace be with you. Amen.	2 Tm 4:22
1	Grace be with you. Amen.	4:22
7	after the first and **second** admonition reject;	Tit 3:10
5	should no place have been sought **for the second**.	Heb 8:7
8	And after the **second** veil, ... the Holiest of all;	9:3
7	But into the **second** went the high priest alone	9:7
1	appear the **second** time without sin unto salvation.	9:28
8	away the first, that he may establish the **second**.	10:9
7	This **second** epistle, beloved, I now write unto you;	2 Pt 3:1
4	The children of thy elect sister greet thee. Amen.	2 Jn 1:13
8	**afterward** destroyed them that believed not.	Jude 1:5
1	shall not be hurt of the **second** death.	Rev 2:11
8	and the **second** beast like a calf,	4:7
7	And when he had opened the **second** seal,	6:3
1	I heard the **second** beast say, Come and see.	6:3
2	And the **second** angel sounded,	8:8
4	The **second** woe is past; and, behold,	11:14
2	And another angel, a **second** one, followed (NASB)	14:8
2	the **second** angel poured out his vial upon the sea;	16:3
8	**again** they said, Alleluia. And her smoke rose up	19:3
2	on such the **second** death hath no power,	Rev 20:6
2	cast into the lake of fire. This is the **second** death.	20:14
2	lake which burneth ... which is the **second** death.	21:8
2	first foundation was jasper; the **second**, sapphire;	21:19

As a noun *deuteros* can be purely ordinal (numerical) and mean "second in order" or "next to the first" in place or rank (Matthew 22:26,39). *Deuteros* also denotes "second in order" of that which follows in time (Hebrews 8:7). Used in the neuter adverb form of *deuteron*, it refers to "the second time" (John 3:4; 21:16; Acts 7:13; Revelation 19:3). When linked with the word *ek* (1523), "of," *deuteron* is used prepositionally meaning "for the second time" (Mark 14:72; John 9:24; Acts 11:9). In the KJV and RV it is sometimes translated "secondarily, secondly," and "again."

STRONG 1208, BAUER 177, MOULTON-MILLIGAN 143, LIDDELL-SCOTT 381-82.

1203. δέχομαι dechomai verb
Take, receive, accept, approve.

COGNATES:
ἀναδέχομαι anadechomai (322)
ἀπόδεκτος apodektos (582)
ἀποδέχομαι apodechomai (583)
ἀποδοχή apodochē (589)
δεκτός dektos (1178)
διαδέχομαι diadechomai (1231)
διάδοχος diadochos (1234)
δοχή dochē (1397)
εἰσδέχομαι eisdechomai (1509)
ἐκδέχομαι ekdechomai (1538)
ἐνδέχομαι endechomai (1719)
ἐπιδέχομαι epidechomai (1911)
εὐπρόσδεκτος euprosdektos (2124)
παραδέχομαι paradechomai (3720)
προσδέχομαι prosdechomai (4185)
ὑποδέχομαι hupodechomai (5103)

SYNONYMS:
αἱρέω haireō (141)
ἀναδέχομαι anadechomai (322)
ἀπέχω apechō (563)
ἀποδέχομαι apodechomai (583)
ἀπολαμβάνω apolambanō (612)
εἰσδέχομαι eisdechomai (1509)
ἐπιδέχομαι epidechomai (1911)
κομίζω komizō (2837)
λαμβάνω lambanō (2956)
μεταλαμβάνω metalambanō (3205)
παραδέχομαι paradechomai (3720)
παραλαμβάνω paralambanō (3741)
προσδέχομαι prosdechomai (4185)
προσλαμβάνω proslambanō (4213)
ὑποδέχομαι hupodechomai (5103)
ὑπολαμβάνω hupolambanō (5112)

זָרַק zāraq (2323), Sprinkle (2 Chr 30:16).

חָזַק chāzaq (2480), Be strong; hiphil: support (Jb 8:20).

כּוּל kûl (3677), Hiphil: hold (2 Chr 7:7).

δέχομαι 1203

לָקַח lāqach (4089), Accept (Gn 33:10, Ps 50:9 [49:9]).

נָשָׂא nāsā' (5558), Lift, carry; receive (Dt 33:3); forgive (Gn 50:17).

קָבַל qāval (7186), Piel: take (2 Chr 29:16); accept (Jb 2:10).

רָצָה rātsāh (7813), Qal: accept (Dt 33:11); niphal: be accepted (Lv 7:18 [7:8], 22:23,25,27).

שׁוּב shûv (8178), Turn, return; hiphil: recall (Dt 30:1).

1. δέχεται dechetai 3sing indic pres mid
2. δέχονται dechontai 3pl indic pres mid
3. δέχωνται dechōntai 3pl subj pres mid
4. δεχόμενος dechomenos
     nom sing masc part pres mid
5. ἐδέξατο edexato 3sing indic aor mid
6. ἐδεξάμεθα edexametha 1pl indic aor mid
7. ἐδέξασθε edexasthe 2pl indic aor mid
8. ἐδέξαντο edexanto 3pl indic aor mid
9. δέξηται dexētai 3sing subj aor mid
10. δέξωνται dexōntai 3pl subj aor mid
11. δέξαι dexai 2sing impr aor mid
12. δέξασθε dexasthe 2pl impr aor mid
13. δεξάμενος dexamenos
     nom sing masc part aor mid
14. δεξάμενοι dexamenoi nom pl masc part aor mid
15. δεξαμένη dexamenē nom sing fem part aor mid
16. δέξασθαι dexasthai inf aor mid
17. δέδεκται dedektai 3sing indic perf mid
18. δέχηται dechētai 3sing subj pres mid

9	shall not receive you, nor hear your words,	Matt 10:14
4	He that receiveth you receiveth me,	10:40
1	He that receiveth you receiveth me,	10:40
4	he that receiveth me receiveth him that sent me.	10:40
1	he that receiveth me receiveth him that sent me.	10:40
4	receiveth a prophet in the name of a prophet	10:41
4	and he that receiveth a righteous man	10:41
16	And if ye will receive it, this is Elias,	11:14
9	And whoso shall receive one such little child	18:5
1	receive ... little child in my name receiveth me.	18:5
10	whosoever shall not receive you, nor hear you,	Mark 6:11
9	whosoever shall not receive you, nor hear you,	6:11
9	Whosoever shall receive one of such children	9:37
1	receiveth me: and whosoever shall receive me,	9:37
9	receiveth me: and whosoever shall receive me,	9:37
18	receiveth me: and whosoever shall receive me,	9:37
1	receiveth not me, but him that sent me.	9:37
9	Whosoever shall not receive the kingdom of God as ..	10:15
5	Then took he him up in his arms, and blessed God,	Luke 2:28
2	which, when they hear, receive the word with joy;	8:13
10	And whosoever will not receive you,	9:5
3	And whosoever will not receive you,	9:5
13	the people, ... followed him: and he received them,	9:11
9	Whosoever shall receive this child in my name	9:48
1	shall receive this child in my name receiveth me:	9:48
9	whosoever shall receive me receiveth him that sent	9:48
1	whosoever shall receive me receiveth him that sent	9:48
8	And they did not receive him,	9:53
3	city ye enter, and they receive you,	10:8
3	city ye enter, and they receive you not,	10:10
10	they may receive me into their houses.	16:4
11	Take thy bill, and sit down quickly, and write fifty.	16:6
11	said unto him, Take thy bill, and write fourscore.	16:7
10	they may receive you into everlasting habitations.	16:9
9	Whosoever shall not receive the kingdom of God	18:17
13	And he took the cup, and gave thanks, and said,	22:17
8	the Galilaeans received him,	John 4:45
16	Whom the heaven must receive until the times	Acts 3:21
5	who received the lively oracles to give unto us:	7:38
11	and saying, Lord Jesus, receive my spirit.	7:59
17	heard that Samaria had received the word of God,	8:14
8	the Gentiles had also received the word of God.	11:1
8	they received the word with all readiness of mind,	17:11
8	the brethren received us gladly.	21:17
13	from whom also I received letters	22:5
6	We neither received letters out of Judaea	28:21
1	man receiveth not the things of the Spirit of God:	1 Co 2:14
16	that ye receive not the grace of God in vain.	2 Co 6:1
7	how with fear and trembling ye received him.	7:15
16	with much entreaty that we would receive the gift,	8:4
5	For indeed he accepted the exhortation;	8:17
7	or another gospel, which ye have not accepted,	11:4
12	if otherwise, yet as a fool receive me,	11:16
7	nor rejected; but received me as an angel of God,	Gal 4:14
12	And take the helmet of salvation,	Eph 6:17
13	having received of Epaphroditus the things	Phlp 4:18
12	if he come unto you, receive him;	Col 4:10
14	having received the word in much affliction,	1 Th 1:6
7	ye received it not as the word of men,	2:13
8	because they received not the love of the truth,	2 Th 2:10
15	when she had received the spies with peace.	Heb 11:31
12	and receive with meekness the engrafted word,	Jas 1:21

Classical Greek

A widely used term in antiquity, found in both literary and nonliterary sources, *dechomai* essentially means "to receive, to accept"; from that there are many shades of meaning. Material objects can be "received" as well as intangible matters such as instruction or advice. "To receive" a person is "to welcome" him, but the unwelcomed assault of an enemy could also be "received" (*dechomai*) (see *Liddell-Scott*). *Dechomai* also is the primary word in many compounds (e.g., *apodechomai* [583], *katadechomai*, and *prosdechomai* [4185]).

Septuagint Usage

The most common Hebrew counterpart to *dechomai* is *lāqach*, itself a multipurpose term ("to take, seize, remove, acquire"; e.g., Genesis 4:11; Exodus 32:4; Job 4:12). Jacob urged Esau to "accept" his gift (Genesis 33:10). It carries the sense of "accept" as in "forgive" (so RSV; Hebrew *nāsā'*) in Genesis 50:17. Particularly significant is "to receive" discipline or correction (*paideia* [3672]). Israel refused to receive God's correction (Jeremiah 2:30; 5:3; 7:28; 17:23). Proverbs teaches that the wise heart "receives" (RSV, "heeds") commandments, and in a phrase unparalleled by the Hebrew, "the one receiving (*dechomai*) discipline (*paideia*) will be among good things" (Proverbs 16:17).

New Testament Usage

New Testament usage accords with a threefold pattern: (1) "to receive" someone, i.e., "to welcome"; (2) "to take hold of, seize" something; and (3) "to approve or accept" something (intangible).

Most instances of *dechomai* occur in the Synoptic Gospels (33 times), but it occurs only once in all of the Johannine material (John 4:45). Paul used it rather sporadically 14 times; the balance occurs in Acts (9 times), Hebrews (1 time) and James (1 time).

First, the sense of "to receive" someone is evident in Luke 9:5; 10:8; 16:4, and verse 9 especially clearly. A play is being made on *dechomai* in Luke 16:4,9 on the "reception" into a temporal house and the eternal "reception" into an eternal habitation.

Second, "to take hold" is a definition understood by Luke in 2:28. Simeon "takes up" the infant Jesus into his arms and blesses God (cf. Luke 16:6; 22:17; Ephcsians 6:17 for other examples of this understanding).

Finally, of particular interest in New Testament theology is *dechomai*'s function as a description of "receiving" the Word of God (especially Acts 8:14; 11:1; cf. 17:11; 1 Thessalonians 1:6; 2:13; James 1:21) or the kingdom of God (Mark 10:15; parallel Luke 18:17). Note also that the believer is asked to "receive" Jesus (Matthew 10:40; Mark 9:37). In so doing he or she also "receives" or "accepts" or "welcomes" the "one who sent" (*ton aposteilanta*) Jesus. Wrapped up in this transference of authority (cf. Luke 10:16f.) is the technical role of the apostle (*apostolos* [646]).

STRONG 1209, BAUER 177, MOULTON-MILLIGAN 143-44, KITTEL 2:50-54, LIDDELL-SCOTT 382-83, COLIN BROWN 3:744-46.

1204. δέω deō verb
Bind, tie, forbid.

COGNATES:
δεῖ dei (1158)
διάδημα diadēma (1232)
καταδέω katadeō (2582)
περιδέω perideō (3882)
συνδέω sundeō (4737)
ὑποδέομαι hupodeomai (5102)
ὑπόδημα hupodēma (5104)

SYNONYMS:
δεσμεύω desmeuō (1189)
δεσμέω desmeō (1190)

אָסִיר 'assîr (630), Prisoner (Is 42:7).

אָסַר 'āsar (646), Qal: bind (Gn 42:24, Jgs 15:10, Ps 149:8); niphal: be bound (Jgs 16:6,10,13); pual: be taken prisoner (Is 22:3).

חָבַשׁ chāvash (2372), Bind (Ez 27:24).

עָצַר 'ātsar (6352), Shut up (Jer 33:1 [40:1]).

צוּר tsûr (6961), Bind (2 Kgs 5:23—Codex Alexandrinus only).

קָשַׁר qāshar (7489), Bind (Gn 38:28, Jb 39:10); conspire (2 Kgs 12:20).

רָתַק rāthaq (7870), Bind; pual: be bound (Na 3:10).

שִׂים sîm (7947), Lie (Jb 40:21).

1. ἔδησεν edēsen 3sing indic aor act
2. ἔδησαν edēsan 3pl indic aor act
3. δήσῃς dēsēs 2sing subj aor act
4. δήσῃ dēsē 3sing subj aor act
5. δήσητε dēsēte 2pl subj aor act
6. δήσατε dēsate 2pl impr aor act
7. δήσας dēsas nom sing masc part aor act
8. δήσαντες dēsantes nom pl masc part aor act
9. δῆσαι dēsai inf aor act
10. δεδεκώς dedekōs nom sing masc part perf act
11. δήσουσιν dēsousin 3pl indic fut act
12. δεθῆναι dethēnai inf aor pass
13. δέδεμαι dedemai 1sing indic perf mid
14. δέδεσαι dedesai 2sing indic perf mid
15. δέδεται dedetai 3sing indic perf mid
16. δεδεμένον dedemenon nom/acc sing masc/neu part perf mid
17. δεδεμένος dedemenos nom sing masc part perf mid
18. δεδεμένους dedemenous acc pl masc part perf mid
19. δεδεμένην dedemenēn acc sing fem part perf mid
20. δεδεμένα dedemena nom/acc pl neu part perf mid
21. δεδέσθαι dedesthai inf perf mid

4	except he first **bind** the strong man?	Matt 12:29
6	the tares, and **bind** them in bundles to burn them;	13:30
1	For Herod had laid hold on John, and **bound** him,	14:3
3	thou shalt **bind** on earth shall be **bound** in heaven:	16:19
16	thou shalt **bind** on earth shall be **bound** in heaven:	16:19
5	Whatsoever ye shall **bind** on earth	18:18
20	ye shall **bind** on earth shall be **bound** in heaven:	18:18
19	and straightway ye shall find an ass **tied**,	21:2
8	**Bind** him hand and foot, and take him away,	22:13
8	when they had **bound** him, they led him away,	27:2
4	except he will first **bind** the strong man;	Mark 3:27
9	and no man could **bind** him, no, not with chains:	5:3
21	he had been often **bound** with fetters and chains,	5:4
1	and **bound** him in prison for Herodias' sake,	6:17
16	ye shall find a colt **tied**, whereon never man sat;	11:2
16	and found the colt **tied** by the door	11:4
8	and **bound** Jesus, and carried him away,	15:1
17	one named Barabbas, which lay **bound** with,	15:7
1	a daughter of Abraham, whom Satan hath **bound**,	Luke 13:16
16	the which at your entering ye shall find a colt **tied**,	19:30
17	**bound** hand and foot with graveclothes:	John 11:44
2	and officers of the Jews took Jesus, and **bound** him,	18:12
16	Now Annas had sent him **bound** unto Caiaphas	18:24
2	and **wound** it in linen clothes with the spices,	19:40
18	he might bring them **bound** unto Jerusalem.	Acts 9:2
9	to **bind** all that call on thy name.	9:14
18	he might bring them **bound** unto the chief priests?	9:21
16	a great sheet **knit** at the four corners,	10:11
17	between two soldiers, **bound** with two chains:	12:6
17	behold, I go **bound** in the spirit unto Jerusalem,	20:22
7	and **bound** his own hands and feet, and said,	21:11
11	So shall the Jews at Jerusalem **bind** the man	21:11

12	for I am ready not **to be bound** only,	Acts 21:13
12	and commanded him **to be bound** with two chains;	21:33
18	to bring them which were there **bound**	22:5
10	was afraid, ... because he **had bound** him.	22:29
16	and Felix, ... left Paul **bound**.	24:27
15	For the woman which hath an husband is **bound**	Rom 7:2
14	Art thou **bound** unto a wife? seek not to be loosed.	1 Co 7:27
15	is **bound** by the law as long as her husband liveth;	7:39
13	mystery of Christ, for which I am also in **bonds**:	Col 4:3
15	but the word of God is not **bound**.	2 Tm 2:9
18	Loose the four angels which are **bound**	Rev 9:14
1	and Satan, and **bound** him a thousand years,	20:2

Classical Greek and Septuagint Usage

The basic meaning of *deō* is "to bind," either in the sense of "to bind together" or "to bind to (something)." These usages were commonly found in both classical Greek and the Septuagint and led naturally to binding as a synonym for "to chain" or "to take prisoner" (e.g., Psalm 149:8 [LXX 148:8]). Since there were other Hebrew words for the fastening idea, the Septuagint often uses *deō* to convey imprisonment. Important also is the figurative meaning of being bound to law and duty, e.g., to one's spouse.

New Testament Usage

These uses are attested in the New Testament as well. Jesus' body was bound in linen cloths with spices (John 19:40); Peter and Paul were both bound as prisoners (Acts 12:6; 21:33).

In the magical systems of pagan peoples the term "bind" was used to describe the power exercised over someone by a sorcerer, god, or spirit. Release from that power was called "loosing" (*luein* [see 3061]). Luke used this language declaring that Satan has been "bound" with the coming of Jesus (13:16; cf. Revelation 20:2). Paul went to Jerusalem "bound in the Spirit" (*dedemenos egō tō pneumati*, Acts 20:22).

A final matter concerns the "binding" and "loosing" of Matthew 16:19 and 18:18. The scribes and Pharisees of Jesus' day believed they had the prerogative to speak for God on matters of the Law, thus having the power to "bind" and "loose" any Israelite. Jesus announced first to Peter (as a representative disciple, 16:19) and then to all the disciples (18:18) that in contrast to the scribes and Pharisees, who "lock up" the kingdom of heaven, Christians have the keys (i.e., authority based on Jesus' words) to bind and loose (i.e., prohibit and allow certain conduct and exercise Church discipline).

STRONG 1210, BAUER 177-78, MOULTON-MILLIGAN 144, KITTEL 2:60-61, LIDDELL-SCOTT 383, COLIN BROWN 1:171-72; 2:732-34.

1205. δή dē partic

Therefore, now, really, indeed.

1. δή dē

1	which **also** beareth fruit, and bringeth forth,	Matt 13:23
1	Let us **now** go even unto Bethlehem,	Luke 2:15
1	Separate me Barnabas and Saul for the work (NT)	Acts 13:2
1	Let us go again and visit our brethren (NT)	15:36
1	**therefore** glorify God	1 Co 6:20
1	It is not expedient for me doubtless to glory. (NT)	2 Co 12:1

Classical Greek and Septuagint Usage

Dē is vastly more numerous in the Septuagint and the intertestamental literature than in the New Testament. Its total absence in patristic writings shows that this popular classical particle was on the wane during the Koine period.

When added to a word or phrase, *dē* lends exactness or urgency and can be translated by a number of English words such as "therefore, now, indeed, surely," or "really." Sometimes, however, it is better left untranslated (see below). Its most common use is to add urgency to a command. Abraham was commanded to "look now (*dē*) toward heaven" (Genesis 15:5).

New Testament Usage

In the New Testament Paul exhorted the Corinthians, "therefore (*dē*) glorify God in your body" (1 Corinthians 6:20). The deep concern of the risen Lord is highlighted by *dē* in Acts 13:2 (*aphorisate dē moi ton Barnaban kai Saulon*), but it is left out by most translators (e.g., NIV: "Set apart for me Barnabas and Saul"). In Matthew 13:23 it denotes "one who *indeed* bears fruit" (literal translation).

STRONG 1211, BAUER 178, MOULTON-MILLIGAN 144, LIDDELL-SCOTT 383-84.

1205B. δηλαυγῶς dēlaugōs adv

Shining clearly.

1. δηλαυγῶς dēlaugōs

1	and he was restored, and saw every man **clearly**.	Mark 8:25

A variant to the traditional text (*Textus Receptus*), *dēlaug-ōs* substitutes for the more common word *tēlaugōs* (4929) at Mark 8:25. Only Mark's Gospel records this unique healing of a blind man who after being touched *twice* by Jesus was able to see all things "clearly."

BAUER 178, MOULTON-MILLIGAN 144, LIDDELL-SCOTT 384.

1206. δῆλος dēlos adj

Clear, evident.

δηλόω 1207

COGNATE:
δηλόω dēloō (1207)
SYNONYMS:
κατάδηλος katadēlos (2583)
πρόδηλος prodēlos (4130)

אוּר 'ûr (216), Urim (Nm 27:21, 1 Sm 28:6).
תָּמִים tāmîm (8879), Perfect (1 Sm 14:41).
תֻּמִּים tummîm (8880), Thummin (Dt 33:8).
תְּרָפִים tᵉrāphîm (8994), Household god (Hos 3:4).

1. δῆλον dēlon nom/acc sing masc/neu

1 thou also art one ... for thy speech **bewrayeth** thee.	Matt 26:73
1 it is **manifest** that he is excepted,	1 Co 15:27
1 it is **evident**: for, The just shall live by faith.	Gal 3:11
1 and it is **certain** we can carry nothing out.	1 Tm 6:7

Classical Greek and Septuagint Usage
Although this term is not commonly used, it does appear in classical Greek from the time of Homer (800-600 B.C.) to mean "clear, plain, evident." In the Septuagint, when Saul petitioned God for "*clear* manifestations" (1 Samuel 14:41 [LXX 1 Kings 14:41]), a form of *dēlos* is used to translate the Hebrew term *tāmîm*, meaning "complete, sound." When used as an adjective in reference to God, it describes the completeness and integrity of His acts.

New Testament Usage
The word is found four times in the New Testament. A literal translation of Matthew 26:73 reveals that Peter was identified as a follower of Christ by his manner of speech, "For thy speech betrayeth thee" (literally, "maketh thee *manifest*"). Paul's use of *dēlos* in 1 Corinthians 15:27 concurs with Matthew's meaning ("manifest"); however, in Galatians 3:11 and 1 Timothy 6:7, its meaning can be taken as "evident, certain."

STRONG 1212, BAUER 178, MOULTON-MILLIGAN 144, LIDDELL-SCOTT 385, COLIN BROWN 3:316.

1207. δηλόω dēloō verb
Reveal, manifest, bring to light, signify.
COGNATES:
ἄδηλος adēlos (81)
ἀδηλότης adēlotēs (82)
ἀδήλως adēlōs (83)
δῆλος dēlos (1206)
ἔκδηλος ekdēlos (1539)
κατάδηλος katadēlos (2583)
πρόδηλος prodēlos (4130)
SYNONYMS:
ἀναδείκνυμι anadeiknumi (320)
ἀποδείκνυμι apodeiknumi (579)
ἀποκαλύπτω apokaluptō (596)
γνωρίζω gnōrizō (1101)
δείκνυμι deiknumi (1161)
ἐμφανίζω emphanizō (1702)
ἐπιδείκνυμι epideiknumi (1910)
ἐπιφαίνω epiphainō (1998)
μηνύω mēnuō (3245)
φανερόω phaneroō (5157)

גְּלָה gᵉlāh (A1581), Reveal (Dn 2:47—Aramaic).
חֲוָה chăwâh (A2426), Pael: show, make known (Dn 2:11,24—Aramaic); haphel: make known, show (Dn 2:6,9,16—Aramaic).
יָדַע yādhaʿ (3156), Qal: know (Ps 147:20 [147:9]); niphal: be known (Est 2:22); make oneself known (Ex 6:3); hiphil: let know, make know, declare (Ex 33:12, Jer 16:21); teach (Ps 51:6 [50:6]).
יְדַע yᵉdhaʿ (A3157), Know; haphel: make know (Dn 2:25,26, 7:16—Aramaic).
יָרָה yārāh (3498), Throw, shoot; hiphil: teach (Dt 33:10, 1 Kgs 8:36, 2 Chr 6:27).
רָאָה rāʾâh (7495), See; niphal: appear (1 Sm 3:21).
שָׁמַע shāmaʿ (8471), Hear; hiphil: declare (Is 42:9).

1. δηλοῖ dēloi 3sing indic pres act
2. δηλοῦντος dēlountos gen sing neu part pres act
3. ἐδήλωσεν edēlōsen 3sing indic aor act
4. δηλώσας dēlōsas nom sing masc part aor act
5. δηλώσει dēlōsei 3sing indic fut act
6. ἐδήλου edēlou 3sing indic imperf act
7. ἐδηλώθη edēlōthē 3sing indic aor pass

7 For it hath been **declared** unto me of you,	1 Co 1:11
5 be made manifest: for the day **shall declare** it,	3:13
4 Who also **declared** unto us your love in the Spirit.	Col 1:8
2 The Holy Ghost this **signifying**,	Heb 9:8
1 **signifieth** the removing of those things	12:27
6 the Spirit of Christ which was in them did **signify**,	1 Pt 1:11
3 even as our Lord Jesus Christ hath **showed** me.	2 Pt 1:14

Classical Greek and Septuagint Usage
The common verb *dēloō* retains its classical sense in the Septuagint and New Testament. It means to "reveal," "manifest," or "show." In the Septuagint it is used especially in relation to God's self-revelation to His people and is interchangeable with *gnōrizō* (1101), "to make known." God reveals His name (Exodus 6:3), His plans (Exodus 33:12), and His demands (2 Chronicles 6:27). In Jeremiah 16:21 His manifestation is both judgment and mercy (*egō dēlōsō ... tēn cheira mou*: "I will reveal ... my hand"). There is also a special sense of "to interpret" (of mysteries; e.g., Daniel 5:15). Worth noting is that the outcome of the Urim and Thummim is referred to as *tēn dēlōsin kai tēn alētheian* ("revelation and truth"; cf. Leviticus 8:8).

New Testament Usage
In the New Testament the writers often used the synonyms *apokaluptō* (596) and *phaneroō* (5157) when speaking of God's self-revelation.

Dēloō is used in this way only in 1 Corinthians 3:13: *hē gar hēmera dēlōsei* ("for the day will be revealed"). It was used, however, to denote messages given by the Spirit (through the prophets, 1 Peter 1:11; in the Scriptures, Hebrew 9:8) and by the exalted Lord (2 Peter 1:14).

STRONG 1213, BAUER 178, MOULTON-MILLIGAN 144, KITTEL 2:61-62, LIDDELL-SCOTT 385, COLIN BROWN 3:316-17.

1208. Δημᾶς Dēmas name
Demas.

1. Δημᾶς Dēmas nom masc

1 Luke, the beloved physician, and Demas,	Col 4:14
1 For Demas hath forsaken me,	2 Tm 4:10
1 Aristarchus, Demas, Lucas, my fellowlabourers.	Phlm 1:24

A companion of Paul who later abandoned him (Colossians 4:14; 2 Timothy 4:10).

1209. δημηγορέω dēmēgoreō verb
Deliver a public oration, speak publicly.
CROSS-REFERENCE:
δῆμος dēmos (1211B)

1. ἐδημηγόρει edēmēgorei 3sing indic imperf act

1 upon his throne, and made an oration unto them.	Acts 12:21

This term is used only once in the New Testament, at Acts 12:21. It means "make a speech, deliver a public address" and comes from the word *dēmos* (1213), "people, crowd, public," and the word *agora* (57), "market place."

STRONG 1215, BAUER 178, LIDDELL-SCOTT 385.

1210. Δημήτριος Dēmētrios name
Demetrius.

1. Δημήτριος Dēmētrios nom masc
2. Δημητρίῳ Dēmētriō dat masc

1 For a certain man named Demetrius, a silversmith,	Acts 19:24
1 Demetrius, and the craftsmen which are with him,	19:38
2 Demetrius hath good report of all men,	3 Jn 1:12

The name *Dēmētrios* refers to two individuals in the New Testamant. The first was an Ephesian silversmith who incited a riot against Paul (Acts 19:24-38). The second was a highly esteemed Christian mentioned in John's third epistle (3 John 12).

1211. δημιουργός dēmiourgos noun
Maker, craftsman, creator.
COGNATES:
δῆμος dēmos (1211B)
ἐργάζομαι ergazomai (2021)

1. δημιουργός dēmiourgos nom sing masc

1 whose builder and maker is God.	Heb 11:10

Classical Greek
Two questions demand attention when examining *dēmiourgos*: (1) why this common classical term is found infrequently in the Septuagint and, in light of this, (2) why it appears at all in the New Testament (only in Hebrews 11:10).

Dēmiourgos in Homer, et al., is used to mean "one who builds, fashions, or forms," i.e., the "craftsman" (e.g., potter, sculptor, builder, etc.). Of significance here is the adaptation of this word in Greek religion and philosophy to a technical status denoting the power which created the world. This power (e.g., Zeus), however, forms the world out of already existing materials (*ataxia*, "chaos").

Septuagint Usage
The Septuagint translators, therefore, rejected equating *theos* (2292B) "God," with *dēmiourgos* for theological reasons. They taught that God created the world "out of nothing" (Latin, *ex nihilo*; see Genesis 1:1 and the Hebrew verb *bārā'*). Thus God is protected from images of a worker limited to the physical world; His absolute sovereignty is maintained. The Greek words chosen to convey God's creative work are *poieō* (4020), *plassō* (3972), and *ktizō* (2908). While not the most prominent in the Septuagint, *ktizō* attains preeminence in the New Testament.

New Testament Usage
In light of the foregoing, why is *dēmiourgos* found at all in Hebrew 11:10? Given the Hellenistic flavor to this epistle and its literary Alexandrian Greek style, it is not surprising to find in it the adaptation of secular concepts. Indeed, here the writer has retained a common phrase (*technitēs kai dēmiourgos*: "architect and builder," NASB) carrying none of the feared connotations. Besides, the writer is speaking about building a city which would not have to be created out of nothing.

STRONG 1217, BAUER 178-79, MOULTON-MILLIGAN 144, KITTEL 2:62, LIDDELL-SCOTT 386, COLIN BROWN 1:387.

1211B. δῆμος dēmos noun
People, assembly.

COGNATES:
ἀποδημέω apodēmeō (584)
ἀπόδημος apodēmos (585)
δημηγορέω dēmēgoreō (1209)
δημιουργός dēmiourgos (1211)
δημόσιος dēmosios (1212)
ἐκδημέω ekdēmeō (1540)
ἐνδημέω endēmeō (1720)
ἐπιδημέω epidēmeō (1912)
παρεπίδημος parepidēmos (3789)
συνέκδημος sunekdēmos (4748)

SYNONYMS:
γλῶσσα glōssa (1094)
ἔθνος ethnos (1477)
λαός laos (2967)
ὅμιλος homilos (3521)
ὄχλος ochlos (3657)
πλῆθος plēthos (3988)
φυλή phulē (5279)

מִשְׁפָּחָה mishpāchāh (5121), Clan, tribe (Nm 4:18, Jos 7:14, Jgs 17:7).

עַם 'am (6194I), People (Dn 8:24, 9:16, 11:32).

רֹבַע rōva' (7545), Dust (Nm 23:10).

שֵׁבֶט shēveṭ (8101), Tribe (Nm 18:2).

1. δῆμος dēmos nom sing masc
2. δήμῳ dēmō dat sing masc
3. δῆμον dēmon acc sing masc

1	And the **people** gave a shout,	Acts 12:22
3	and sought to bring them out to the **people**.	17:5
3	when Paul would have entered in unto the **people**,	19:30
2	and would have made his defence unto the **people**.	19:33

Classical Greek and Septuagint Usage
Dēmos is used extensively in classical Greek and the Septuagint to denote the general population of a country, i.e., the commoners. The plural (*dēmoi*) refers to a township or parish. The Septuagint translators, especially in Numbers, used *dēmos* to translate the Hebrew *mishpāchāh*, "extended family, clan, subtribe." Later occurrences of the word show a more general meaning of "people" or "crowd".

New Testament Usage
In Acts 12:22 it is used of the people of Tyre and Sidon gathered to hear Herod Agrippa I. It refers to the assembled crowd who were citizens of those cities. In Acts 17:5 it is used of the rioting mob in Thessalonica and parallels *ochlos* (3657), "crowd." In Acts 19:30 and 33, with reference to the rioting mob which rushed into the theater, it is also called the *ekklēsia* (1564) the "assembly of citizens" (Acts 19:32).

Both Ephesus and Thessalonica were free Greek cities, a special privilege granted by the Roman government. All citizens of each of these two cities were part of the *dēmos* or *ekklēsia* that handled the government of the city and elected the officials. Both terms are used of an assembly or crowd of citizens, whether called together officially or whether coming together as an unorganized, confused mob. *Demos* seems to draw attention to them as a crowd. *Ekklesia* seems to emphasize that they were citizens. (See also Bruce, *New International Commentary on the New Testament, Acts.*)

STRONG 1218, BAUER 179, MOULTON-MILLIGAN 144-45, KITTEL 2:63, LIDDELL-SCOTT 386-87, COLIN BROWN 2:788-89.

1212. δημόσιος dēmosios adj
Public.

CROSS-REFERENCE:
δῆμος dēmos (1211B)

1. δημοσίᾳ dēmosia dat sing fem

1	and put them in the **common** prison.	Acts 5:18
1	They have beaten us **openly** uncondemned,	16:37
1	he mightily convinced the Jews, and that **publicly**,	18:28
1	have showed you, and have taught you **publicly**,	20:20

This term is used four times in the New Testament, all occurring in the Book of Acts (5:18; 16:37; 18:28; 20:20). It means "public" or "common" when referring to something "belonging to the state" (Acts 5:18). When used alone as an adverb (*dēmosia*), it means "publicly" (Acts 16:37). Its root is the word *dēmos* (1211B) meaning "public, people, crowd."

STRONG 1219, BAUER 179, MOULTON-MILLIGAN 145, LIDDELL-SCOTT 387, COLIN BROWN 2:788,790.

1213. δῆμος dēmos
See word study at number 1211B.

1214. δηνάριον dēnarion noun
Denarius.

1. δηναρίου dēnariou gen sing neu
2. δηνάριον dēnarion nom/acc sing neu
3. δηναρίων dēnariōn gen pl neu
4. δηνάρια dēnaria nom/acc pl neu

4	which owed him an hundred **pence**:	Matt 18:28
1	agreed with the labourers for **a penny a day**,	20:2

2	they received every man **a penny**	Matt 20:9
2	and they likewise received every man **a penny**	20:10
1	didst not thou agree with me **for a penny**?	20:13
2	And they brought unto him **a penny**	22:19
3	go and buy two hundred **pennyworth** of bread,	Mark 6:37
2	bring me **a penny**, that I may see it.	12:15
3	might ... sold for more than three hundred **pence**,	14:5
4	one owed five hundred **pence**, and the other fifty.	Luke 7:41
4	morrow when he departed, he took out two **pence**,	10:35
2	Show me a **penny**. Whose image and	20:24
3	Two hundred **pennyworth** of bread	John 6:7
3	sold for three hundred **pence**,	12:5
1	A measure of wheat **for a penny**,	Rev 6:6
1	and three measures of barley **for a penny**;	6:6

Classical Greek
Dēnarion is actually a Greek transliteration of the Latin *denarius*, a silver coin minted by the Romans from 268 B.C. until around A.D. 200. The term is not found in the Septuagint. Gradually, by the time of Diocletian, the Roman denarius replaced the Greek drachma. Diocletian actually reintroduced the denarius as an equivalent to the drachma (*Moulton-Milligan*). Its value is relative; it equaled approximately 1 day's wage during the New Testament period (Matthew 20:2,9,10,13) and weighed about 3.8 grams ("Denarius," *Interpreters' Dictionary of the Bible* 1:824).

New Testament Usage
The term itself occurs only in the Gospels and in Revelation (e.g., Mark 6:37; Luke 7:41; 10:35; John 6:7; 12:5; Revelation 6:6), and it always denotes the piece of money. The phrases "a quart of wheat for a denarius, three quarts of barley for a denarius" (RSV, Revelation 6:6) depict the hardship of obtaining the necessities of life. The real value of luxuries like oil and wine will be exposed then—their price will be unaffected.

STRONG 1220, BAUER 179, MOULTON-MILLIGAN 145, LIDDELL-SCOTT 388.

1215. δήποτε dēpote adv
Whatever.

1. δήποτε dēpote

1	was made whole of **whatsoever** disease he had.	John 5:4

In classical Greek (since Homer) and the Septuagint, *dēpote* was used to mean "at any time." This adverb is found only once in the New Testament, occurring at John 5:4. It means "whatever, some kind." *Dēpote* comes from *dē* (1205), an emphatic particle, and from *pote* (4077) meaning "sometime."

STRONG 1221, BAUER 179, MOULTON-MILLIGAN 145, LIDDELL-SCOTT 388.

1216. δήπου dēpou partic
Of course, surely.

1. δήπου dēpou

1	For verily he took not on him the nature of angels;	Heb 2:16

This adverb is used only once in the New Testament, occurring at Hebrews 2:16 where it means "it is clear, surely of course." *Dēpou* comes from *dē* (1205), a particle of emphasis, and from *pou* (4084), an indefinite pronoun.

STRONG 1222, BAUER 179, LIDDELL-SCOTT 388.

1217. διά dia prep
Through, by, with, because of, for the sake of.

1. δι' di'
2. διά dia

2	fulfilled ... spoken of the Lord **by** the prophet,	Matt 1:22
2	for thus it is written **by** the prophet,	2:5
2	their own country by another way. (NASB)	2:12
2	fulfilled ... was spoken of the Lord **by** the prophet,	2:15
2	which was spoken **through** Jeremiah (NASB)	2:17
2	be fulfilled which was spoken **by** the prophets,	2:23
2	who was spoken of **through** the prophet (NIV)	3:3
2	word that proceedeth **out of** the mouth of God.	4:4
2	was spoken **by** Esaias the prophet, saying,	4:14
2	**Therefore** I say unto you,	6:25
2	Enter ye in **at** the strait gate: for wide is the gate,	7:13
1	and many there be which go **in thereat**:	7:13
2	fulfilled which was spoken by Esaias the prophet,	8:17
2	so that no man might pass **by** that way.	8:28
2	Why does your Teacher eat **with** (NASB) (NT)	9:11
2	Why do we and the Pharisees fast (NASB) (NT)	9:14
2	ye shall be hated of all men **for** my name's **sake**:	10:22
2	he sent [word] **by** his disciples (NASB)	11:2
2	Jesus went on the sabbath day **through** the corn;	12:1
2	spoken **by** Esaias the prophet, saying,	12:17
2	**therefore** they shall be your judges.	12:27
2	**Wherefore** I say unto you,	12:31
1	he walketh **through** dry places, seeking rest,	12:43
2	**because** they had no deepness of earth:	13:5
2	and **because** they had no root, they withered away.	13:6
2	speak to them in parables? (NASB) (NT)	13:10
2	**Therefore** speak I to them in parables:	13:13
2	persecution ariseth **because** of the word,	13:21
2	fulfilled which was spoken **by** the prophet,	13:35
2	**Therefore** every scribe which is instructed	13:52
2	not ... mighty works ... **because** of their unbelief.	13:58
2	and **therefore** mighty works do show forth	14:2
2	and put him in prison **for** Herodias' **sake**,	14:3
2	nevertheless **for** the oath's **sake**,	14:9
2	Why do Your disciples transgress (NASB) (NT)	15:2
2	why do you yourselves transgress (NASB) (NT)	15:3
2	transgress the commandment ... **by** your tradition?	15:3
2	commandment ... of none effect **by** your tradition.	15:6
2	Why could we not cast it out? (NASB) (NT)	17:19
2	**Because** of your unbelief:	17:20
1	but woe to that man **by** whom the offence cometh!	18:7
2	angels do **always** behold the face of my Father	18:10
2	**Therefore** is the kingdom of heaven likened	18:23
2	eunuchs for the kingdom of heaven's sake.	19:12
2	easier for a camel to go **through** the eye of a needle,	19:24
2	be fulfilled which was spoken **by** the prophet,	21:4
2	Then why did you not believe him? (NASB) (NT)	21:25
2	**Therefore** say I unto you,	21:43
2	**therefore** ye shall receive the greater damnation.	23:14
2	**Wherefore**, behold, I send unto you prophets,	23:34
2	ye shall be hated of all nations **for** my name's **sake**.	24:9

διά

2 And **because** iniquity shall abound,	Matt 24:12
2 desolation, spoken of **by** Daniel the prophet,	24:15
2 **for** the elect's sake those days shall be shortened.	24:22
2 **Therefore** be ye also ready:	24:44
1 woe ... **by** whom the Son of man is betrayed!	26:24
2 destroy the temple ... and to build it **in** three days.	26:61
2 fulfilled that which was spoken **by** Jeremy	27:9
2 For he knew that **for** envy they had delivered him.	27:18
1 suffered many things this day ... **because of** him.	27:19
1 again he entered into Capernaum **after** some days;	Mark 2:1
2 they could not come nigh unto him **for** the press,	2:4
2 Why do John's disciples (NASB) (NT)	2:18
2 went **through** the corn fields on the sabbath day;	2:23
2 The sabbath was made **for** man, and not man for	2:27
2 was made for man, and not man **for** the sabbath:	2:27
2 a small ship ... **because of** the multitude,	3:9
2 **because** it had no depth of earth:	4:5
2 and **because** it had no root, it withered away.	4:6
2 or persecution ariseth **for** the word's **sake**,	4:17
2 **Because** that he had been often bound with fetters	5:4
2 And constantly night and day (NASB) (NT)	5:5
2 even such mighty works are wrought **by** his hands?	6:2
2 And he marvelled **because of** their unbelief.	6:6
2 and **therefore** mighty works do show forth	6:14
2 and bound him in prison for Herodias' **sake**,	6:17
2 yet **for** his oath's **sake**, and for their sakes	6:26
2 Why do Your disciples not walk (NASB) (NT)	7:5
2 And he said unto her, For this saying go thy way;	7:29
2 region of Tyre and came **through** Sidon (NASB)	7:31
2 they departed thence, and passed **through** Galilee;	9:30
2 the coasts of Judaea by the farther side of Jordan:	10:1
2 It is easier for a camel to go **through**	10:25
2 man should carry any vessel **through** the temple.	11:16
2 **Therefore** I say unto you,	11:24
2 Then why did you not believe him? (NASB) (NT)	11:31
2 answering said unto them, Do ye not **therefore** err,	12:24
2 ye shall be hated of all men **for** my name's **sake**:	13:13
2 no flesh should be saved: but **for** the elect's **sake**,	13:20
1 but woe to that man by whom the Son of man	14:21
2 and **within** three days I will build another	14:58
2 that the chief priests had delivered him **for** envy.	15:10
2 confirming the word **with** signs following. Amen.	16:20
2 As he spake **by** the mouth of his holy prophets,	Luke 1:70
2 **Through** the tender mercy of our God;	1:78
2 **because** he was of the house and lineage of David:	2:4
2 he passing **through** the midst of them went his way,	4:30
1 have toiled all the night, (NT)	5:5
2 And when they could not find **by** what way	5:19
2 they might bring him in **because of** the multitude,	5:19
2 and let him down **through** the tiling with his couch	5:19
2 Why do you eat and drink with (NASB) (NT)	5:30
2 that he went **through** the corn fields;	6:1
2 **because** it had been well built. (NASB)	6:48
2 to him out of every city, he spake **by** a parable:	8:4
2 it withered away, **because** it lacked moisture.	8:6
2 and could not come at him **for** the press.	8:19
1 before all ... **for** what cause she had touched him,	8:47
2 he was perplexed, **because** that it was said of some,	9:7
2 **because** he is his friend, yet because ... importunity	11:8
2 yet **because of** his importunity he will rise and give	11:8
2 **therefore** shall they be your judges.	11:19
2 he walketh **through** dry places, seeking rest;	11:24
2 **Therefore** also said the wisdom of God,	11:49
2 said unto his disciples, **Therefore** I say unto you,	12:22
2 Strive to enter in **at** the strait gate:	13:24
2 I have married a wife, ... **therefore** I cannot come.	14:20
1 but woe unto him, **through** whom they come!	17:1
2 passed **through** the midst of Samaria and Galilee.	17:11
2 Yet **because** this widow troubleth me,	18:5
2 is easier for a camel to go **through** a needle's eye,	18:25
2 and all things that are written **by** the prophets	18:31
1 tree to see him: for he was to pass (NT)	19:4
2 **because** he was nigh to Jerusalem,	19:11
2 why do you not put the money (NASB) (NT)	19:23
2 Why are you untying it? (NASB) (NT)	19:31
2 Why did you not believe him? (NASB) (NT)	20:5
2 ye shall be hated of all men **for** my name's **sake**.	21:17
2 but woe unto that man **by** whom he is betrayed!	Luke 22:22
2 **because** he had heard many things of him;	23:8
2 Who **for** a certain sedition made in the city,	23:19
2 that **for** sedition and murder was cast into prison,	23:25
2 and why do doubts arise in your (NASB) (NT)	24:38
2 and were continually in the temple (NASB) (NT)	24:53
1 All things were made **by** him;	John 1:3
1 that all men **through** him might believe.	1:7
1 and the world was made **by** him,	1:10
2 For the law was given **by** Moses,	1:17
2 but grace and truth came **by** Jesus Christ.	1:17
2 **therefore** am I come baptizing with water.	1:31
2 **because** he knew all men,	2:24
1 but that the world **through** him might be saved.	3:17
2 **because of** the bridegroom's voice:	3:29
2 And he must needs go **through** Samaria.	4:4
2 believed on him **for** the saying of the woman,	4:39
2 And many more believed **because of** his own word;	4:41
2 Now we believe, not **because of** thy saying:	4:42
2 And **therefore** did the Jews persecute Jesus,	5:16
2 **Therefore** the Jews sought the more to kill him,	5:18
2 and I live **by** the Father:	6:57
1 so he that eateth me, even he shall live **by** me.	6:57
2 And he said, **Therefore** said I unto you,	6:65
2 no man spake openly of him **for** fear of the Jews,	7:13
2 Moses **therefore** gave unto you circumcision;	7:22
1 was a division among the people **because of** him.	7:43
2 Why did you not bring Him? (NASB) (NT)	7:45
2 Why do you not understand (NASB) (NT)	8:43
2 why do you not believe Me? (NASB) (NT)	8:46
2 ye ... hear them not, **because** ye are not of God.	8:47
2 going **through** the midst of them, and so passed by.	8:59
2 **Therefore** said his parents, He is of age; ask him.	9:23
2 entereth not **by** the door into the sheepfold,	10:1
2 But he that entereth in **by** the door	10:2
1 **by** me if any man enter in, he shall be saved,	10:9
2 **Therefore** doth my Father love me,	10:17
2 was a division ... among the Jews for these sayings.	10:19
2 **for** which of those works do ye stone me?	10:32
1 that the Son of God might be glorified **thereby**.	11:4
1 And I am glad **for** your **sakes** that I was not there,	11:15
2 but **because of** the people which stand by I said it,	11:42
2 Why was this ointment not sold (NASB) (NT)	12:5
2 and they came not **for** Jesus' **sake** only,	12:9
1 **by reason of** him many of the Jews went away,	12:11
2 For this **cause** the people also met him,	12:18
2 but **for** this **cause** came I unto this hour.	12:27
1 voice came not **because of** me, but for your sakes.	12:30
1 voice came not because of me, but **for** your **sakes**.	12:30
2 **Therefore** they could not believe,	12:39
2 **because of** the Pharisees they did not confess him,	12:42
2 **therefore** said he, Ye are not all clean.	13:11
2 Lord, why can I not follow You (NASB) (NT)	13:37
1 no man cometh unto the Father, but **by** me.	14:6
2 or else believe me **for** the very works' **sake**.	14:11
2 ye are clean **through** the word which I have spoken	15:3
2 **therefore** the world hateth you.	15:19
2 things will they do unto you for my name's **sake**,	15:21
2 **therefore** said I, that he shall take of mine,	16:15
2 **for** joy that a man is born into the world.	16:21
2 which shall believe on me **through** their word;	17:20
2 **therefore** he that delivered me unto thee	19:11
1 without seam, woven from the top **throughout**.	19:23
2 but secretly **for** fear of the Jews,	19:38
2 **because of** the Jews' preparation day;	19:42
2 the disciples were assembled for fear of the Jews,	20:19
2 **through** the Holy Ghost had given commandments	Acts 1:2
1 **over a period of** forty days, (NASB)	1:3
2 which the Holy Ghost **by** the mouth of David	1:16
2 this is that which was spoken **by** the prophet Joel;	2:16
1 which God did **by** him in the midst of you,	2:22
2 and **by** wicked hands have crucified and slain:	2:23
2 I foresaw the Lord **always** before my face,	2:25
2 **Therefore** did my heart rejoice,	2:26
2 wonders and signs were done **by** the apostles,	2:43
1 yea, the faith which is **by** him hath given him	3:16
2 had showed **by** the mouth of all his prophets,	3:18

διά 1217

2	which God hath spoken by the mouth ... prophets ... Acts	3:21
2	Being grieved that they taught the people,	4:2
1	miracle hath been done by them is manifest to all	4:16
2	because of the people: for all men glorified God	4:21
2	Who by the mouth of thy servant David hast said,	4:25
2	may be done by the name of thy holy child Jesus.	4:30
2	Ananias, why hath Satan filled (NASB) (NT)	5:3
2	And by the hands of the apostles were many signs	5:12
2	But the angel ... by night opened the prison doors,	5:19
2	how that God by his hand would deliver them:	7:25
2	because that of long time he had bewitched them	8:11
2	through laying on of the apostles' hands	8:18
2	that the gift of God may be purchased with money	8:20
2	and let him down by the wall in a basket.	9:25
2	as Peter passed throughout all quarters,	9:32
2	and prayed to God continually (NASB) (NT)	10:2
1	what is the cause wherefore ye are come?	10:21
2	preaching peace by Jesus Christ: he is Lord of all:	10:36
2	that through his name whosoever believeth in him	10:43
2	and signified by the Spirit that there should be	11:28
2	and sent it to the elders by the hands of Barnabas	11:30
2	that it was true which was done by the angel;	12:9
2	desired peace; because their country was	12:20
2	that through this man is preached unto you	13:38
1	was published throughout all the region.	13:49
2	signs and wonders to be done by their hands.	14:3
2	and that we must through much tribulation	14:22
2	by my mouth should hear the word of the gospel,	15:7
2	But we believe that through the grace of the Lord	15:11
1	God had wrought among the Gentiles by them.	15:12
2	And they wrote letters by them after this manner;	15:23
2	who shall also tell you the same things by mouth.	15:27
2	exhorted the brethren with many words,	15:32
2	and took and circumcised him because of the Jews	16:3
2	And a vision appeared to Paul in the night;	16:9
2	sent away Paul and Silas by night unto Berea:	17:10
2	because that Claudius had commanded all Jews	18:2
2	And because he was of the same craft,	18:3
1	spake the Lord to Paul in the night by a vision,	18:9
2	helped them ... which had believed through grace:	18:27
2	showing by the scriptures that Jesus was Christ.	18:28
2	And God wrought special miracles by ... Paul:	19:11
2	that they be no gods, which are made with hands:	19:26
2	he purposed to return through Macedonia.	20:3
2	which he hath purchased with his own blood.	20:28
2	who said to Paul through the Spirit,	21:4
2	had wrought among the Gentiles by his ministry.	21:19
2	he could not know the certainty for the tumult,	21:34
2	that he was borne of the soldiers for the violence	21:35
1	might know wherefore they cried	22:24
1	known the cause wherefore they accused him,	23:28
2	took Paul, and brought him by night to Antipatris.	23:31
2	Seeing that by thee we enjoy great quietness,	24:2
2	deeds are done unto this nation by thy providence,	24:2
2	maintain always a blameless (NASB) (NT)	24:16
1	Now after many years I came to bring alms	24:17
2	under Cyprus, because the winds were contrary,	27:4
2	dangerous, because the fast was now already past,	27:9
2	because of the present rain, and ... the cold.	28:2
2	the present rain, and because of the cold.	28:2
2	because there was no cause of death in me.	28:18
2	For this cause therefore have I called for you,	28:20
2	Well spake the Holy Ghost by Esaias the prophet	28:25
2	Which he had promised afore by his prophets ... Rom	1:2
1	By whom we have received grace and apostleship,	1:5
2	I thank my God through Jesus Christ for you all,	1:8
2	That is, that I may be comforted together with you	1:12
2	For this cause God gave them up	1:26
2	have sinned in the law shall be judged by the law;	2:12
2	judge ... by Jesus Christ according to my gospel.	2:16
2	through breaking the law dishonourest thou God?	2:23
1	blasphemed among the Gentiles through you,	2:24
2	if it fulfil the law, judge thee, who by the letter	2:27
2	for by the law is the knowledge of sin.	3:20
2	the righteousness of God which is by faith of Jesus	3:22
2	through the redemption that is in Christ Jesus:	3:24
2	to be a propitiation through faith in his blood,	3:25
2	for the remission of sins that are past, ... Rom	3:25
2	By what law? of works? Nay: ... by the law of faith.	3:27
2	By what law? of works? Nay: ... by the law of faith.	3:27
2	which shall justify ... uncircumcision through faith.	3:30
2	Do we then make void the law through faith?	3:31
1	that believe, though they be not circumcised;	4:11
2	not to Abraham, or to his seed, through the law,	4:13
2	but through the righteousness of faith.	4:13
2	Therefore it is of faith, that it might be by grace;	4:16
1	Now it was not written for his sake alone,	4:23
1	But for us also, to whom it shall be imputed,	4:24
2	Who was delivered for our offences,	4:25
2	and was raised again for our justification.	4:25
2	we have peace with God through our Lord Jesus	5:1
1	By whom also we have access by faith	5:2
2	by the Holy Ghost which is given unto us.	5:5
1	we shall be saved from wrath through him.	5:9
2	we were reconciled to God by the death of his Son,	5:10
2	we also joy in God through our Lord Jesus Christ,	5:11
1	by whom we have now received the atonement.	5:11
2	Wherefore, as by one man sin entered	5:12
1	as by one man sin entered into the world,	5:12
2	sin entered into the world, and death by sin;	5:12
1	And not as it was by one that sinned, so is the gift:	5:16
2	For if by one man's offence death reigned by one;	5:17
2	the gift of righteousness shall reign in life by one,	5:17
1	Therefore as by the offence of one judgment	5:18
1	even so by the righteousness of one the free gift	5:18
2	For as by one man's disobedience many were	5:19
2	so by the obedience of one shall many be	5:19
2	even so might grace reign through righteousness	5:21
2	unto eternal life by Jesus Christ our Lord.	5:21
2	we are buried with him by baptism into death:	6:4
2	raised up from the dead by the glory of the Father,	6:4
2	I speak after the manner of men	6:19
2	are become dead to the law by the body of Christ;	7:4
2	the motions of sins, which were by the law,	7:5
2	I had not known sin, but by the law:	7:7
2	But sin, taking occasion by the commandment,	7:8
2	For sin, taking occasion by the commandment,	7:11
1	deceived me, and by it slew me.	7:11
2	working death in me by that which is good;	7:13
2	that sin by the commandment might become	7:13
2	I thank God through Jesus Christ our Lord.	7:25
2	in that it was weak through the flesh,	8:3
1	if Christ be in you, the body is dead because of sin;	8:10
2	if Christ be in you, the body is dead because of sin;	8:10
2	but the Spirit is life because of righteousness.	8:10
2	shall also quicken your mortal bodies by his Spirit	8:11
2	but by reason of him who hath subjected the same	8:20
1	then do we with patience wait for it.	8:25
2	more than conquerors through him that loved us.	8:37
2	Why? Because they did not pursue (NASB) (NT)	9:32
2	and hearing by the word of God.	10:17
2	And bend their backs forever (NASB) (NT)	11:10
1	they are enemies for your sakes:	11:28
2	they are beloved for the fathers' sakes.	11:28
1	For of him, and through him, and to him,	11:36
2	I beseech you ... brethren, by the mercies of God,	12:1
2	For I say, through the grace given unto me,	12:3
2	not only for wrath,	13:5
2	but also for conscience sake.	13:5
2	For for this cause pay ye tribute also:	13:6
1	that there is nothing unclean of itself:	14:14
2	But if thy brother be grieved with thy meat,	14:15
2	but it is evil for that man who eateth with offence.	14:20
2	we through patience and comfort of the scriptures	15:4
2	and the encouragement of the (NASB) (NT)	15:4
2	For this cause I will confess to him,	15:9
2	because of the grace that is given to me of God,	15:15
1	those things which Christ hath not wrought by me,	15:18
1	I will come by you into Spain.	15:28
2	beseech you, ... for the Lord Jesus Christ's sake,	15:30
2	Jesus Christ's sake, and for the love of the Spirit,	15:30
2	I may come unto you with joy by the will of God,	15:32
2	and by good words and fair speeches deceive	16:18
2	and by the scriptures of the prophets,	16:26

61

διά 1217

2 be glory **through** Jesus Christ for ever. Amen.	Rom 16:27
2 be glory **through** Jesus Christ for ever. Amen.	16:27
2 an apostle of Jesus Christ **through** the will of God,	1 Co 1:1
1 **by** whom ye were called unto the fellowship	1:9
2 **by** the name of our Lord Jesus Christ,	1:10
2 the world **by** wisdom knew not God,	1:21
2 it pleased God **by** the foolishness of preaching	1:21
2 But God hath revealed them unto us **by** his Spirit:	2:10
1 is Apollos, but ministers **by** whom ye believed,	3:5
2 but he himself shall be saved; yet so as **by** fire.	3:15
2 in a figure ... myself and to Apollos **for** your **sakes**;	4:6
2 We are fools **for** Christ's **sake**, but ye are wise	4:10
2 I have begotten you **through** the gospel.	4:15
2 For this **cause** have I sent unto you Timotheus,	4:17
2 Why not rather be wronged? (NASB) (NT)	6:7
2 Why not rather be defrauded? (NASB) (NT)	6:7
2 and will also raise up us **by** his own power.	6:14
2 Nevertheless, **to avoid** fornication,	7:2
2 that Satan tempt you not **for** your incontinency.	7:5
2 that this is good **for** the present distress,	7:26
1 and one Lord Jesus Christ, **by** whom are all things,	8:6
1 Christ, **by** whom are all things, and we **by** him,	8:6
1 the weak brother perish, **for** whom Christ died?	8:11
1 Or saith he it altogether **for** our **sakes**?	9:10
1 **For** our **sakes**, no doubt, this is written:	9:10
2 And this I do **for** the gospel's **sake**,	9:23
2 and all passed **through** the sea;	10:1
2 that eat, asking no question **for** conscience **sake**:	10:25
2 eat, asking no question **for** conscience **sake**.	10:27
1 eat not **for** his **sake** that showed it,	10:28
2 Neither was the man created **for** the woman;	11:9
2 but the woman **for** the man.	11:9
2 **For** this **cause** ought the woman to have power	11:10
2 to have power on her head **because** of the angels.	11:10
2 even so is the man also **by** the woman;	11:12
2 **For** this **cause** many are weak and sickly	11:30
2 to one is given **by** the Spirit the word of wisdom;	12:8
1 For now we see **through** a glass, darkly;	13:12
2 utter by the tongue words easy to be understood,	14:9
2 rather speak five words **with** my understanding,	14:19
1 **By** which also ye are saved,	15:2
1 For since **by** man came death,	15:21
1 **by** man came also the resurrection of the dead.	15:21
2 which giveth us the victory **through** our Lord Jesus	15:57
1 whomsoever ye shall approve **by** your letters,	16:3
2 My love be with you all in Christ Jesus. Amen.	16:24
2 Paul, an apostle of Jesus Christ **by** the will of God,	2 Co 1:1
2 **by** the comfort wherewith we ourselves are	1:4
2 so our consolation also aboundeth **by** Christ.	1:5
2 thanks may be given **by** many on our behalf.	1:11
1 And to pass **by** you into Macedonia,	1:16
1 Jesus Christ, who was preached among you **by** us,	1:19
1 even **by** me and Silvanus and Timotheus,	1:19
1 Wherefore also **by** Him is our Amen (NASB)	1:20
1 and in him Amen, unto the glory of God **by** us.	1:20
2 I wrote unto you **with** many tears;	2:4
2 **for** your **sakes** forgave I it in the person of Christ;	2:10
1 the savour of his knowledge **by** us in every place.	2:14
2 such trust have we **through** Christ to God-ward:	3:4
2 the face of Moses **for** the glory of his countenance;	3:7
2 that which fades away was **with** glory, (NASB)	3:11
2 **Therefore** seeing we have this ministry,	4:1
2 and ourselves your servants **for** Jesus' **sake**.	4:5
2 are alway delivered unto death **for** Jesus' **sake**,	4:11
2 shall raise up us also **by** Jesus,	4:14
1 For all things are **for** your **sakes**,	4:15
2 might **through** the thanksgiving of many redound	4:15
2 For we walk **by** faith, not by sight:	5:7
2 For we walk by faith, not **by** sight:	5:7
2 every one may receive the things done **in** his body,	5:10
2 who hath reconciled us to himself **by** Jesus Christ,	5:18
1 as though God did beseech you **by** us:	5:20
2 **by** the armour of righteousness on the right hand	6:7
2 **By** honour and dishonour,	6:8
2 **by** evil report and good report:	6:8
2 **Therefore** we were comforted in your comfort:	7:13
2 and unto us **by** the will of God.	8:5
2 but **by** occasion of the forwardness of others,	2 Co 8:8
1 he was rich, yet **for** your **sakes** he became poor,	8:9
2 praise is in the gospel **throughout** all the churches;	8:18
1 which causeth **through** us thanksgiving to God.	9:11
2 is abundant also by many thanksgivings unto God;	9:12
2 Whiles **by** the experiment of this ministration	9:13
2 **for** the exceeding grace of God in you.	9:14
2 **by** the meekness and gentleness of Christ,	10:1
2 I may not seem as if I would terrify you **by** letters.	10:9
1 as we are in word **by** letters when we are absent,	10:11
2 Why? Because I do not love you? (NASB) (NT)	11:11
2 And **through** a window in a basket I let down	11:33
2 in a basket was I let down **by** the wall,	11:33
1 gain of you **by** any of them whom I sent unto you?	12:17
2 **Therefore** I write these things being absent,	13:10
2 of the Holy Ghost, be with you all. Amen.	13:14
1 Paul, an apostle, not of men, neither **by** man,	Gal 1:1
2 neither by man, but **by** Jesus Christ, and God	1:1
1 but **by** the revelation of Jesus Christ.	1:12
2 it pleased God, who ... called me **by** his grace,	1:15
2 Then fourteen years **after** I went up again	2:1
2 **because** of false brethren unawares brought in,	2:4
2 but **by** the faith of Jesus Christ,	2:16
2 For I **through** the law am dead to the law,	2:19
2 for if righteousness come **by** the law,	2:21
2 receive the promise of the Spirit **through** faith.	3:14
1 but God gave it to Abraham **by** promise.	3:18
1 was ordained by angels in the hand of a mediator.	3:19
2 are all the children of God **by** faith in Christ Jesus.	3:26
2 and if a son, then an heir of God **through** Christ.	4:7
1 how **through** infirmity of the flesh I preached	4:13
1 but he of the freewoman was **by** promise.	4:23
2 but he of the freewoman was **by** promise.	4:23
1 but faith which worketh **by** love.	5:6
2 but **by** love serve one another.	5:13
1 cross ... **by** whom the world is crucified unto me,	6:14
2 an apostle of Jesus Christ **by** the will of God,	Eph 1:1
2 the adoption of children **by** Jesus Christ to himself,	1:5
2 In whom we have redemption **through** his blood,	1:7
2 **Wherefore** I also, after I heard of your faith	1:15
2 God, ... **for** his great love wherewith he loved us,	2:4
2 For by grace are ye saved **through** faith;	2:8
2 reconcile both unto God in one body **by** the cross,	2:16
1 For **through** him we both have access by one Spirit	2:18
2 partakers of his promise in Christ **by** the gospel:	3:6
2 hid in God, who created all things **by** Jesus Christ:	3:9
2 known **by** the church the manifold wisdom of God,	3:10
2 and access with confidence **by** the faith of him.	3:12
2 to be strengthened with might **by** his Spirit	3:16
2 That Christ may dwell in your hearts **by** faith;	3:17
2 who is above all, and **through** all, and in you all.	4:6
2 compacted **by** that which every joint supplieth,	4:16
2 **through** the ignorance that is in them,	4:18
2 **because** of the blindness of their heart:	4:18
2 **for because** of these things cometh the wrath	5:6
2 **Wherefore** be ye not unwise,	5:17
2 **Wherefore** take unto you the whole armour	6:13
2 Praying always **with** all prayer and supplication	6:18
2 that love our Lord Jesus Christ in sincerity. Amen.	6:24
2 to think this ... **because** I have you in my heart;	Phlp 1:7
2 fruits of righteousness, which are **by** Jesus Christ,	1:11
2 Some ... preach Christ even **of** envy and strife;	1:15
1 preach Christ ... and some also **of** good will:	1:15
2 shall turn to my salvation **through** your prayer,	1:19
2 whether it be **by** life, or by death,	1:20
2 whether it be by life, or **by** death.	1:20
1 to abide in the flesh is more needful **for** you.	1:24
2 in Jesus Christ for me **by** my coming to you again.	1:26
2 **for** the work of Christ he was nigh unto death,	2:30
2 were gain to me, those I counted loss **for** Christ.	3:7
2 loss **for** the excellency of the knowledge of Christ	3:8
1 **for** whom I have suffered the loss of all things,	3:8
2 but that which is **through** the faith of Christ,	3:9
1 grace of our Lord Jesus ... be with you all. Amen.	4:23
2 Paul, an apostle of Jesus Christ **by** the will of God,	Col 1:1
2 **For** the hope which is laid up for you in heaven,	1:5
2 **For** this **cause** we also, since the day we heard it,	1:9

62

διά 1217

2	In whom we have redemption **through** his blood,	Col 1:14
1	all things were created **by** him, and for him:	1:16
1	**by** him to reconcile all things unto himself;	1:20
2	having made peace **through** the blood of his cross,	1:20
1	**by** him, I say, whether they be things in earth,	1:20
2	In the body of his flesh **through** death,	1:22
2	Beware lest any man spoil you **through** philosophy	2:8
2	**through** the faith of the operation of God,	2:12
2	from which all the body **by** joints and bands	2:19
1	For which things' sake the wrath of God cometh	3:6
1	giving thanks to God and the Father **by** him.	3:17
1	mystery of Christ, **for** which I am also in bonds:	4:3
2	Remember my bonds. Grace be with you. Amen.	4:18
1	manner of men we were among you **for** your **sake**.	1 Th 1:5
2	For this cause also thank we God without ceasing,	2:13
2	For this cause, when I could no longer forbear,	3:5
2	**Therefore**, brethren, we were comforted over you	3:7
2	we were comforted over you ... **by** your faith:	3:7
1	for all the joy wherewith we joy **for** your **sakes**	3:9
2	commandments we gave you **by** the Lord Jesus.	4:2
2	even so them also which sleep **in** Jesus	4:14
2	but to obtain salvation **by** our Lord Jesus Christ,	5:9
2	very highly in love **for** their work's sake	5:13
2	or be troubled, neither **by** spirit, nor **by** word,	2 Th 2:2
2	or be troubled, neither **by** spirit, nor **by** word,	2:2
1	nor **by** word, nor **by** letter as from us,	2:2
1	nor **by** word, nor **by** letter as **from** us,	2:2
2	**for** this cause God shall send them strong delusion,	2:11
2	Whereunto he called you **by** our gospel,	2:14
2	whether **by** word, or our epistle.	2:15
1	whether **by** word, or our epistle.	2:15
2	we command and exhort **by** our Lord Jesus Christ,	3:12
2	And if any man obey not our word **by** this epistle,	3:14
2	the Lord ... give you peace always **by** all means.	3:16
2	Howbeit **for** this **cause** I obtained mercy,	1 Tm 1:16
1	professing godliness **with** good works.	2:10
2	Notwithstanding she shall be saved in childbearing,	2:15
2	For it is sanctified **by** the word of God and prayer.	4:5
2	the gift ... which was given thee **by** prophecy,	4:14
2	but use a little wine **for** thy stomach's **sake**	5:23
2	Paul, an apostle of Jesus Christ **by** the will of God,	2 Tm 1:1
1	**Wherefore** I put thee in remembrance that thou	1:6
2	which is in thee **by** the putting on of my hands.	1:6
2	**by** the appearing of our Saviour Jesus Christ,	1:10
2	life and immortality to light **through** the gospel:	1:10
1	For the which cause I also suffer these things:	1:12
2	keep **by** the Holy Ghost which dwelleth in us.	1:14
2	that thou hast heard of me **among** many witnesses,	2:2
2	**Therefore** I endure all things **for** the elect's sakes,	2:10
2	**Therefore** I endure all things **for** the elect's **sakes**,	2:10
2	**through** faith which is in Christ Jesus.	3:15
1	that **by** me the preaching might be fully known,	4:17
1	witness is true. **Wherefore** rebuke them sharply,	Tit 1:13
2	**by** the washing of regeneration,	3:5
2	Which he shed on us abundantly **through** Jesus	3:6
2	the bowels of the saints are refreshed **by** thee,	Phlm 1:7
2	Yet **for** love's **sake** I rather beseech thee,	1:9
2	For perhaps he **therefore** departed for a season,	1:15
2	**through** your prayers I shall be given unto you.	1:22
2	grace of our Lord ... be with your spirit. Amen.	1:25
1	**by** his Son, ... **by** whom also he made the worlds;	Heb 1:2
1	when he had **by** himself purged our sins,	1:3
2	**therefore** God, even thy God, hath anointed thee	1:9
2	minister **for** them who shall be heirs of salvation?	1:14
2	**Therefore** we ought to give the more earnest heed	2:1
1	For if the word spoken by angels was stedfast,	2:2
2	which at the first began to be spoken **by** the Lord,	2:3
2	lower than the angels **for** the suffering of death,	2:9
1	For it became him, **for** whom are all things,	2:10
2	whom are all things, and **by** whom are all things,	2:10
2	of their salvation perfect **through** sufferings.	2:10
1	**for** which cause ... not ashamed to call ... brethren,	2:11
2	that **through** death he might destroy him	2:14
2	**through** fear of death were ... subject to bondage.	2:15
2	howbeit not all that came out of Egypt **by** Moses.	3:16
1	they could not enter in **because** of unbelief.	3:19
1	entered not in **because** of unbelief:	4:6
2	And **by reason** hereof he ought, as for the people,	Heb 5:3
1	And **by reason** hereof he ought, as for the people,	5:3
2	For when **for** the time ye ought to be teachers,	5:12
2	**by reason** of use have their senses exercised	5:14
1	herbs meet for them **by** whom it is dressed,	6:7
2	**through** faith and patience inherit the promises.	6:12
2	That **by** two immutable things,	6:18
2	Levi also, ... payed tithes **in** Abraham.	7:9
1	Levi also, ... payed tithes **in** Abraham.	7:9
2	If ... perfection were **by** the Levitical priesthood,	7:11
2	for the weakness and unprofitableness thereof.	7:18
1	**by** the which we draw nigh unto God.	7:19
2	but this with an oath **by** him that said unto him,	7:21
2	were not suffered to continue **by reason** of death:	7:23
2	But this man, **because** he continueth ever,	7:24
1	to save them ... that come unto God **by** him,	7:25
2	are continually entering the outer (NASB) (NT)	9:6
2	**by** a greater and more perfect tabernacle,	9:11
1	Neither **by** the blood of goats and calves,	9:12
2	but **by** his own blood he entered	9:12
2	who **through** the eternal Spirit offered himself	9:14
2	And **for this cause** he is the mediator	9:15
2	to put away sin **by** the sacrifice of himself.	9:26
2	**because** that the worshippers once purged,	10:2
2	sanctified **through** the offering of the body of Jesus	10:10
2	which he hath consecrated for us, **through** the veil,	10:20
1	**by** which he obtained witness ... he was righteous,	11:4
1	and **by** it he being dead yet speaketh.	11:4
1	**by** the which he condemned the world,	11:7
2	they passed through the Red sea as **by** dry land:	11:29
2	Who **through** faith subdued kingdoms,	11:33
2	having obtained a good report **through** faith,	11:39
1	compassed about with so great a cloud of witnesses,	12:1
1	unto them which are exercised thereby.	12:11
2	trouble you, and **thereby** many be defiled;	12:15
1	and **by** it many be defiled (NASB)	12:15
2	**whereby** we may serve God acceptably	12:28
2	**thereby** some have entertained angels unawares.	13:2
2	into the sanctuary **by** the high priest for sin,	13:11
2	he might sanctify the people **with** his own blood,	13:12
1	By him therefore let us offer the sacrifice of praise	13:15
2	continually offer up a sacrifice (NASB) (NT)	13:15
2	**through** Jesus Christ; to whom be glory for ever	13:21
2	for I have written a letter unto you **in** few words.	13:22
2	Grace be with you all. Amen.	13:25
2	as they that shall be judged **by** the law of liberty.	Jas 2:12
2	yet ye have not, **because** ye ask not.	4:2
1	unto a lively hope **by** the resurrection of Jesus	1 Pt 1:3
2	Who are kept **by** the power of God **through** faith	1:5
2	of gold that perisheth, **though** it be tried with fire,	1:7
2	which are now reported unto you **by** them that	1:12
1	but was manifest in these last times **for** you,	1:20
2	Who **by** him do believe in God,	1:21
2	in obeying the truth **through** the Spirit	1:22
2	Being born again, ... **by** the word of God,	1:23
2	acceptable to God **by** Jesus Christ.	2:5
2	to every ordinance of man **for** the Lord's sake:	2:13
1	are sent **by** him for the punishment of evildoers,	2:14
2	if a man **for** conscience toward God endure grief,	2:19
2	be won **by** the conversation of the wives;	3:1
2	if ye suffer **for** righteousness' sake, happy are ye:	3:14
1	few, that is, eight souls were saved **by** water.	3:20
1	**by** the resurrection of Jesus Christ:	3:21
2	in all things may be glorified **through** Jesus Christ,	4:11
2	By Silvanus, a faithful brother unto you,	5:12
1	I have written briefly, exhorting, (NT)	5:12
2	**through** the knowledge of him that hath called us	2 Pt 1:3
2	him that hath called us **to** glory and virtue:	1:3
1	**Whereby** are given unto us ... precious promises:	1:4
2	that **by** these ye might be partakers of the divine	1:4
1	**by reason** of whom the way ... be evil spoken of.	2:2
1	earth standing out of the water and in the water:	3:5
1	**Whereby** the world that then was, ... perished:	3:6
1	wherein the heavens being on fire,	3:12
2	your sins are forgiven you **for** his name's sake.	1 Jn 2:12
2	**therefore** the world knoweth us not,	3:1
2	**therefore** speak they of the world,	4:5

διαβαίνω 1218

1 into the world, that we might live **through** him.	1 Jn 4:9
1 This is he that came **by** water and blood,	5:6
2 For the truth's **sake**, which dwelleth in us,	2 Jn 1:2
2 I would not write **with** paper and ink:	1:12
2 Wherefore, if I come, I will remember his deeds	3 Jn 1:10
2 but I will not **with** ink and pen write unto thee:	1:13
2 God our Saviour, **through** Jesus (NASB)	Jude 1:25
2 signified it **by** his angel unto his servant John:	Rev 1:1
2 **for** the word of God, and **for** the testimony of Jesus	1:9
2 **for** the word of God, and **for** the testimony of Jesus	1:9
2 and **for** my name's sake hast laboured,	2:3
2 **for** thou hast created all things,	4:11
2 souls of them that were slain **for** the word of God,	6:9
2 and **for** the testimony which they held:	6:9
2 Therefore are they before the throne of God,	7:15
2 And they overcame him **by** the blood of the Lamb,	12:11
2 and **by** the word of their testimony;	12:11
2 Therefore rejoice, ye heavens,	12:12
2 deceiveth them ... **by the means of** those miracles	13:14
2 angel said to me, why do you marvel (NASB) (NT)	17:7
2 Therefore shall her plagues come in one day,	18:8
2 Standing afar off **for** the fear of her torment,	18:10
2 shall stand afar off **for** the fear of her torment,	18:15
2 them that were beheaded **for** the witness of Jesus,	20:4
2 **for** the witness of Jesus, and **for** the word of God,	20:4
2 and the nations shall walk **by** its light (NASB)	21:24

Dia is a preposition which shows relationship between words or groups of words. It is used with two Greek noun cases. (1) With the genitive its primary meaning is "through," and (2) with the accusative the basic meaning is "on account of."

Dia is also added as a prefix to other words to intensify or modify their meanings. For example, *diakrinō* (1246) means "to separate," "to discern," and "to discriminate." *Krinō* (2892) alone means "to judge," yet by the added *dia* the word is intensified (Acts 11:12). Another example is *diablepō* (1221) which means "to see through or across." *Blepō* (984) means "to see," but by adding the prefix *dia* the word is modified to mean "to see clearly" (Luke 6:42).

Classical Greek

In classical Greek usage *dia* occurs in the genitive case showing several nuances: of *place* or *space* in the sense of "through, in the midst of," and "intervals"; of *time* in the sense of duration, "between" and "throughout"; of the *causal* sense, "through" or "by"; to express *conditions*, by "through" (see *Liddell-Scott*).

Dia occurs with the accusative case in the sense of place meaning "through, among," and "in"; of time with persons in the sense of "thanks to, on account of," and "by reason of"; of things, to indicate the reason, occasion, or purpose in the sense of "for the sake of, because of," and "on account of." Without a case, *dia* is used as an adverb to mean "throughout." Its meaning in compound words are: "through, in different directions, asunder, thoroughly, out and out, between, partly," and "interval" (ibid.).

New Testament Usage

According to the Greek papyri, the Koine use of *dia* is basically the same as the classical. The Biblical use of *dia* in the Septuagint and the Greek New Testament are also fundamentally alike. It appears little change occurred in meaning and usage of *dia* during the three centuries between the Septuagint's translation and the New Testament's origin.

In the New Testament *dia* occurs about 670 times as a preposition with the genitive and accusative cases. The usual translation of *dia* with the genitive is "through" or "by" when it is used of place or medium (Matthew 7:13; Luke 6:1; 2 Corinthians 11:33). When *dia* is used of time, the meaning is "during" or "in the course of" (Luke 5:5; Acts 5:19). *Dia* with the genitive often expresses secondary agency, causation, and instrumentality and is rendered "by means of" and "by" (John 1:3,10,17; Acts 3:18; 1 Corinthians 3:5; Ephesians 2:8).

The usual translation of *dia* with the accusative case is "on account of" and "on this account," thus "because of" or "for the sake of" (Matthew 10:22; 24:12; John 1:31; 6:57; Ephesians 2:4). *Dia* with the accusative gives the basis of an action and *dia* with the genitive states the instrument of an action. Compare *dia* with the accusative in Romans 15:15 and *dia* with the genitive in Romans 12:3. In the Romans 15:15 sense, grace is the basis for the apostle's being made an instrument of grace in the Romans 12:3 reference.

STRONG 1223, BAUER 179-81, MOULTON-MILLIGAN 145-46, KITTEL 2:65-70, LIDDELL-SCOTT 388-89, COLIN BROWN 3:1171-74,1176-78,1181-84, 1186,1189-91,1193,1197-98,1201,1210-11.

1218. διαβαίνω diabainō verb

Go through, cross, go over.
CROSS-REFERENCE:
ὑπερβαίνω huperbainō (5070)

בּוֹא bô' (971), Go in (Dt 11:29).

הָלַךְ hālakh (2050), Walk (Prv 30:29 [24:64]).

יָרַד yāradh (3495), Flow (Ps 119:136 [118:136]—Codex Alexandrinus only).

מָלַט mālaṭ (4561), Niphal: get away (1 Sm 20:29—Sixtine Edition only).

עָבַר 'āvar (5882), Qal: pass over (Nm 32:29, Jos 4:1); pass through (Is 43:2); niphal: be crossed (Ez 47:5);

hiphil: bring over (2 Sm 19:41 [19:40]); cross (Gn 32:10).

עָלָה ʿālâh (6148), Arise (Jer 6:5—Codex Alexandrinus only).

עָמַד ʿāmadh (6198), Get up (Ex 21:21—Codex Alexandrinus only).

צָעַד tsāʿadh (7081), March (Ps 68:7 [67:7]).

1. διέβησαν diebēsan 3pl indic aor act
2. διαβάς diabas nom sing masc part aor act
3. διαβῆναι diabēnai inf aor act

3 they which would **pass** from hence to you cannot;..Luke 16:26
2 saying, **Come over** into Macedonia, and help us..... Acts 16:9
1 By faith they **passed through** the Red sea..........Heb 11:29

Classical Greek and Septuagint Usage
This word is used extensively in classical Greek and appears over 120 times in the Septuagint to translate different forms of the Hebrew term ʿāvar, meaning "pass over, through, by."

New Testament Usage
Diabainō occurs three times in the New Testament and means "cross over, go through." Its roots are *dia* (1217), "through," and *bainō*, meaning "walk." Although the KJV translates the word three different ways, in each case the idea involves movement from one place to another.

STRONG 1224, BAUER 181, MOULTON-MILLIGAN 146, LIDDELL-SCOTT 389.

1219. διαβάλλω diaballō verb
Throw across, slander, accuse.
COGNATES:
βάλλω ballō (900)
διάβολος diabolos (1222)

שָׂטָן sāṭān (7931), Adversary (Nm 22:22—Sixtine Edition only).

1. διεβλήθη **dieblēthē** 3sing indic aor pass

1 had a steward; and the same **was accused** unto him Luke 16:1

Classical Greek
In classical Greek *diaballō* (from *dia* [1217], "through," and *ballō* [900], "I throw") means "to throw over or across." But an understanding different from its root words' meanings takes precedence: *diaballō* also means "to quarrel, to slander," and "to deceive through hostile slanderous information" (*Liddell-Scott*). The term occurs regularly in these senses. According to *Bauer* it means to "bring charges against (with) hostile intent." However, *Moulton-Milligan* challenges the notion that *diaballō* always implied a malicious intent.

Septuagint Usage
The idea of "malicious intent" is attested in the Septuagint: "Certain Chaldeans came forward and maliciously accused the Jews" (Daniel 3:8, RSV). Further, there is also the more classical sense of "giving slanderous information" (2 Maccabees 3:11; 4 Maccabees 4:1); these, too, suggest a malevolent spirit.

New Testament Usage
The single use of *diaballo* in the New Testament occurs in Luke 16:1 in the Parable of the Unjust Steward. In light of the parable itself, it is apparent that the charges leveled against the steward were neither malicious nor based upon false information. *Diaballō* in this case means only that "charges were brought against him," and the veracity of those charges is indicated by the reactions of the master and the steward.

STRONG 1225, BAUER 181, MOULTON-MILLIGAN 146-47, KITTEL 2:71, LIDDELL-SCOTT 389-90, COLIN BROWN 3:468.

1220. διαβεβαιόομαι
diabebaioomai verb
Speak confidently, affirm, assert strongly.
COGNATE:
βεβαιόω bebaioō (943)
SYNONYM:
διϊσχυρίζομαι diischurizomai (1334)

1. διαβεβαιοῦνται diabebaiountai 3pl indic pres mid
2. διαβεβαιοῦσθαι diabebaiousthai inf pres mid

1 neither what they say, nor whereof they **affirm**...... 1 Tm 1:7
2 and these things I will that thou **affirm constantly**,.... Tit 3:8

Diabebaioomai is used only twice by Paul in the New Testament to mean "speak confidently, affirm, insist on, special emphasis." It comes from the word *dia* (1217), "through," denoting the channel of an act, and from the word *bebaioō* (943) meaning "to confirm." Paul used it only in the Pastorals at 1 Timothy 1:7 and Titus 3:8.

STRONG 1226, BAUER 181, MOULTON-MILLIGAN 147, LIDDELL-SCOTT 390.

1221. διαβλέπω diablepō verb
Look intently, see through, see clearly.
CROSS-REFERENCE:
βλέπω blepō (984)

1. διαβλέψεις diablepseis 2sing indic fut act
2. διέβλεψεν dieblepsen 3sing indic aor act

1 and then **shalt thou see clearly** to cast out the mote .. Matt 7:5
2 and he **looked intently** and was restored (NASB)... Mark 8:25
1 and then **shalt thou see clearly** to pull out the mote Luke 6:42

In classical Greek this word is often used literally to mean "look intently" or "open one's eyes (wide)" (see *Bauer*).

Diablepō is used two times in the New Testament. Both Matthew 7:5 and Luke 6:42 used *diablepō* to mean "see clearly" in describing the same teaching. *Diablepō* comes from *dia* (1217), "through," and *blepō* (984), "to look at."

STRONG 1227, BAUER 181, MOULTON-MILLIGAN 147, LIDDELL-SCOTT 390.

1222. διάβολος diabolos adj

Slanderous, false accuser, the adversary, the devil.

CROSS-REFERENCE:
διαβάλλω diaballō (1219)

צַר tsar (7141), Enemy (Est 7:4).

צָרַר tsārar (7173), Enemy (Est 8:1).

שָׂטָן sāṭān (7931), Satan (1 Chr 21:1, Jb 1:6,7, Zec 3:1,2).

1. διάβολος **diabolos** nom sing masc
2. διαβόλου **diabolou** gen sing masc
3. διαβόλῳ **diabolō** dat sing masc
4. διάβολον **diabolon** acc sing masc
5. διάβολοι **diaboloi** nom pl masc
6. διαβόλους **diabolous** acc pl fem

2 into the wilderness to be tempted of the **devil**....... Matt 4:1
1 Then the **devil** taketh him up into the holy city,........ 4:5
1 the **devil** taketh him up into an ... mountain,.......... 4:8
1 Then the **devil** leaveth him, and, behold,.............. 4:11
1 The enemy that sowed them is the **devil**;.............. 13:39
3 fire, prepared for the **devil** and his angels:............ 25:41
2 Being forty days tempted of the **devil**.......... Luke 4:2
1 And the **devil** said unto him,........................... 4:3
1 the **devil**, taking him up into an high mountain,....... 4:5
1 And the **devil** said unto him,........................... 4:6
1 And when the **devil** had ended all the temptation,...... 4:13
1 then cometh the **devil**, and taketh away the word...... 8:12
1 chosen you twelve, and one of you is a **devil**?..... John 6:70
2 Ye are of your father the **devil**,..................... 8:44
2 the **devil** having now put into the heart of Judas....... 13:2
2 and healing all that were oppressed of the **devil**;.... Acts 10:38
2 thou child of the **devil**,............................... 13:10
3 Neither give place to the **devil**..................... Eph 4:27
2 be able to stand against the wiles of the **devil**.......... 6:11
2 he fall into the condemnation of the **devil**........ 1 Tm 3:6
2 lest he fall into reproach and the snare of the **devil**..... 3:7
6 Even so must their wives be grave, not **slanderers**,..... 3:11
2 recover themselves out of the snare of the **devil**,.... 2 Tm 2:26
5 trucebreakers, false **accusers**, incontinent, fierce,........ 3:3
6 not **false accusers**, not given to much wine,......... Tit 2:3
4 him that had the power of death, that is, the **devil**;.. Heb 2:14
3 Resist the **devil**, and he will flee from you........... Jas 4:7
1 the **devil**, as a roaring lion, walketh about,.......... 1 Pt 5:8
2 He that committeth sin is of the **devil**;.............. 1 Jn 3:8
1 for the **devil** sinneth from the beginning................. 3:8
2 that he might destroy the works of the **devil**............ 3:8
2 of God are manifest, and the children of the **devil**:..... 3:10
3 Yet Michael ... when contending with the **devil**..... Jude 1:9

1 the **devil** shall cast some of you into prison,......... Rev 2:10
1 the **devil** shall cast some of you into prison,............ 2:10
1 that old serpent, called the **Devil**, and Satan,.......... 12:9
1 for the **devil** is come down unto you,................. 12:12
1 that old serpent, which is the **Devil**, and Satan,........ 20:2
1 the **devil** that deceived them was cast into the lake.... 20:10

Classical Greek
Related to the noun *diabolē* (from *diaballō* [1219], "to set against"), "false accusation, slander," this adjective occurs rather infrequently in classical Greek. Its use as a substantive ("slanderer") is attested, but it lacks the precision common to the New Testament.

Septuagint Usage
For the Septuagint translators, *diabolos* served as an equivalent to two Hebrew words, most often *sāṭān*, from which comes the name "Satan." *Satan* was also transliterated by the Septuagint translators. The Lord raised up a (literally) "satan" (Hadad the Edomite) against Solomon (1 Kings 11:14,23 [LXX 3 Kings 11:14,23]).

Where *diabolos* translates *satan* it usually refers to the adversary of God, Satan (most often in Job 1:6,7,9,12 etc.; used with article; cf. Zechariah 3:1,2,3). On other occasions *diabolos* is less precise (e.g., Psalm 109:6 [LXX 108:6], "an evil man," NIV). The presence of the article does not guarantee the more technical sense of "the devil" (e.g., Esther 7:4). The Angel of Yahweh is described as a *satan* when opposing Balaam (Numbers 22:22,23).

Intertestamental Period
Later Jewish traditions viewed this figure as present in the Garden and responsible for the entrance of death into the world (Wisdom of Solomon 2:24; some also point to Ezekiel 28:12-16 and Isaiah 14:12-15). Satan was not yet seen as having been cast out of heaven (cf. 1 Enoch 86:1-6; Luke 10:18), otherwise he could not have been the "accuser" (cf. Zechariah 3:1ff.). The devil is a principal character in the sophisticated angelology created by later Judaism. Such figures as Belial in Qumran (who resembles Satan but who is distinct), Mastema, Azazel, and Beelzeboul (a chief demon in the hierarchy [cf., Mark 3:22]) developed during the intertestamental period (Bietenhard, "Satan," *Colin Brown*, 3:468).

New Testament Usage
All of this comes together in the New Testament where Satan and his demons are seen as supernatural powers that control not only the world but the "present evil age" (Galatians 1:4, NIV; cf. Ephesians 6:10ff.). With the coming

of Jesus, however, Satan's reign was shattered and the new age of God's Spirit began. Jesus demonstrated His absolute authority over Satan in the Temptation and in His ensuing ministry. He cast out demons and healed the sick, thus signifying the overthrow of Satan's stronghold (cf. Mark 3:23ff.; Luke 10:17).

The Gospels also picture a present tension between these two ages—(1) when Satan's forces rule, and (2) the age ushered in by Jesus. Thus the Church experiences both victory and momentary defeats during this present struggle (cf. Ladd, *The Presence of the Future*, pp.171-94). In Jesus, Satan has been tethered. In the Crucifixion, Resurrection, and Ascension he is defeated. Satan and his demons only await being put away forever (Revelation 20:1ff.). See the word study at *satanas* (4423).

STRONG 1228, BAUER 182, KITTEL 2:72-81, LIDDELL-SCOTT 390, COLIN BROWN 3:468-73.

1223. διαγγέλλω diangellō verb

Proclaim, declare, announce everywhere.

CROSS-REFERENCE:
ἀγγέλλω angellō (31B)

אָמַר 'āmar (569), Command (Jos 6:10 [6:9]).

סָפַר sāphar (5807), Count; piel: proclaim, tell (Ex 9:16, Ps 2:7 [2:6]).

עָבַר 'āvar (5882), Pass over; hiphil: sound, blow (Lv 25:9).

1. διάγγελλε diangelle 2sing impr pres act
2. διαγγέλλων diangellōn nom sing masc part pres act
3. διαγγελῇ diangelē 3sing subj aor pass

1 but go thou and **preach** the kingdom of God........ Luke 9:60
2 to signify the accomplishment of the days.......... Acts 21:26
3 name might be **declared** throughout all the earth..... Rom 9:17

Classical Greek
In classical Greek *diangellō* means "to give notice by a messenger," and thus "to noise abroad" and "to proclaim." (The noun *diangelia* means a "notification.") The word is a compound of *dia* (1217), "through," and *angellō* (31B), "proclaim." By its addition the preposition *dia* intensifies *angellō*.

Septuagint Usage
In the Septuagint *diangellō* occurs in Exodus 9:16, Leviticus 25:9, Joshua 6:10, Psalms 2:6, and 59:13 (LXX 58:13). In each of these references one detects that *diangellō* means "to publish the message far and near" (cf. 2 Maccabees 1:33; 3:34).

New Testament Usage
The New Testament is rich in words for preaching, proclaiming, and announcing. Some of these words have the root word of *angellō*: *Anangellō* (310), "to bring back words" (Acts 14:27); *apangello* (514) meaning to "report," "announce," and "proclaim" (Acts 5:22); *diangellō* meaning "to make known" and "to proclaim far and wide" (Romans 9:17); *exangellō* (1788), "to tell out" and "to proclaim" (1 Peter 2:9); *katangellō* (2576) meaning "to declare" (Acts 17:13); and *prokatangellō* (4152) meaning "to foretell" or "to announce beforehand" (Acts 3:24).

The New Testament uses *diangellō* only three times (Luke 9:60; Acts 21:26; Romans 9:17). The context of Acts 21:26 indicates it was of utmost importance that the Jews knew the apostle Paul had cooperated with Jewish customs by fulfilling his vow. The Luke 9:60 and Romans 9:17 references emphasize a thorough preaching of the kingdom and reality of God.

STRONG 1229, BAUER 182, KITTEL 1:67-69, LIDDELL-SCOTT 391, COLIN BROWN 3:44-47.

1224. διαγίνομαι diaginomai verb

Go through, pass time, elapse.

CROSS-REFERENCE:
γίνομαι ginomai (1090)

1. διαγενομένου diagenomenou
gen sing masc/neu part aor mid
2. διαγενομένων diagenomenōn
gen pl fem part aor mid

1 And when the sabbath **was past**, Mary Magdalene, Mark 16:1
2 after certain days king Agrippa and Bernice came.. Acts 25:13
1 Now when much time **was spent**,..................... 27:9

Diaginomai is a compound composed of *dia* (1217), "through," and *ginomai* (1090), "to happen, to take place," and "to come to pass." However, *diaginomai* means "to pass through." The definition of this compound word shows how inappropriate it is to assume that root components of a word supply its "basic" or "literal" meaning.

Classical Greek
In classical Greek the word occurs with an alternative spelling, *diagignomai*. The basic meaning is "to go through," "to pass," "to go through life," and "to continue through." Sometimes the verb means "intervene" or "elapse."

διαγινώσκω 1225

Septuagint Usage
In the Septuagint the verb *diaginomai* is not listed except in a disputed text in 2 Maccabees (11:26), yet its root verb *ginomai* occurs numerous times. Thus the word *diaginomai* seems to have had little circulation among the Jews until the Christian Era.

New Testament Usage
The New Testament use of *diaginomai* is limited to three references (Mark 16:1; Acts 25:13; 27:9). Mark's use is in regard to the passing of the Sabbath. The genitive absolute construction makes the Sabbath the subject of *diaginomai* ("was past"). The idea is that the Sabbath had come and was now over. The Sabbath had to pass before the women could resume their intention to complete the preparation of the Lord's body with spices.

The use of *diaginomai* in both Acts references (Acts 25:13; 27:9) also has to do with time elapse. In the former reference, days intervened between Paul's trial before the governor Festus and the arrival of King Agrippa. In the latter reference, too much time had passed between the ship's arrival at Fair Havens and the passengers' embarking on the voyage to Rome. Due to the excessive time spent at the fair city of Lasea, there was great danger of winter storms at sea. *Diaginomai* emphasizes the interval of time.

STRONG 1230, BAUER 182, MOULTON-MILLIGAN 147, LIDDELL-SCOTT 391.

1225. διαγινώσκω diaginōskō verb
Decide, determine by examination.
CROSS-REFERENCE:
γινώσκω ginōskō (1091)

דָּמָה dāmâh (1880), Be like; piel: plan (Nm 33:56).
יָדַע yādha' (3156), Qal: know (Dt 2:7, 8:2); niphal: make known (Prv 14:33).

1. διαγινώσκειν **diaginōskein** inf pres act
2. διαγνώσομαι **diagnōsomai** 1sing indic fut mid

1 inquire something more perfectly concerning him:.. Acts 23:15
2 I will know the uttermost of your matter............... 24:22

Classical Greek and Septuagint Usage
In classical Greek *diaginōskō* was used since the time of Homer to mean "decide, determine." The Septuagint used a form of *diaginōskō* in the place of two Hebrew words, *dāmâh* and *yādha'*. God told Moses that what He had "determined" (Hebrew *dāmâh*) to do to the Canaanites would be done to the Israelites if they did not obey (Numbers 33:56). Proverbs states that the wisdom of obedience is found in the good heart, but in the heart of fools it is not *discerned* (Hebrew *yādha'*, Proverbs 14:33).

New Testament Usage
Diaginōskē is used only twice in the New Testament, both times in the Book of Acts (23:15; 24:22). It means to "investigate, examine, decide, determine." Its component parts are the words *dia* (1217) and *ginōskō* (1091), "to know."

STRONG 1231, BAUER 182, MOULTON-MILLIGAN 147, LIDDELL-SCOTT 391.

1226. διαγνωρίζω diagnōrizō verb
Give an exact report, publish abroad.
CROSS-REFERENCE:
γινώσκω ginōskō (1091)

1. διεγνώρισαν **diegnōrisan** 3pl indic aor act

1 they made known abroad the saying which was...... Luke 2:17

This term is used only once in the New Testament, occurring at Luke 2:17. It means "to give an exact report, to make known" and comes from the word *dia* (1217), "through," and *gnōrizō* (1101), "to make known, reveal." The term is very rare in classical Greek literature.

STRONG 1232, BAUER 182, LIDDELL-SCOTT 391.

1227. διάγνωσις diagnōsis noun
Decision.
CROSS-REFERENCE:
γινώσκω ginōskō (1091)

1. διάγνωσιν **diagnōsin** acc sing fem

1 to be reserved unto the hearing of Augustus,....... Acts 25:21

In both classical Greek and intertestamental literature, *diagnōsis* is used as a legal term meaning "decision." It occurs only once in the New Testament (Acts 25:21) and has the meanings "examination, decision, hearing." It comes from the word *diaginōskō* (1225) meaning to "investigate, decide, examine." (Compare the English word *diagnosis*.)

STRONG 1233, BAUER 182, MOULTON-MILLIGAN 147, LIDDELL-SCOTT 391.

1228. διαγογγύζω diagonguzō verb
Grumble, complain aloud.

CROSS-REFERENCE:
γογγύζω gonguzō (1105)

לוּן lûn (4021), Niphal: murmur, grumble (Ex 15:24, Nm 14:2, Jos 9:18); hiphil: murmur, grumble (Ex 16:8).

רָגַז rāghaz (7553), Be upset emotionally (Sir 34:24).

רָגַן rāghan (7566), Niphal: murmer (Dt 1:27).

1. διεγόγγυζον diegonguzon 3pl indic imperf act

1 And the Pharisees and scribes **murmured**, saying,.. Luke 15:2
1 And when they saw it, they all **murmured**, saying,..... 19:7

There is no record of the use of *diagonguzō* prior to the Septuagint where it appears nine times in reference to Israel's grumbling toward God (cf. Exodus 15:24; Numbers 14:2,36; 16:11). It occurs twice in the New Testament, both times in the Gospel of Luke (15:2; 19:7). It means to "murmur, complain, grumble (out loud)." Its roots are *dia* (1217) (used here to intensify the meaning) and *gonguzō* (1105), "grumble, murmur, mutter, complain."

STRONG 1234, BAUER 182, KITTEL 1:735, LIDDELL-SCOTT 391.

1229. διαγρηγορέω diagrēgoreō verb
Fully awake, stay awake.

1. διαγρηγορήσαντες diagrēgorēsantes
nom pl masc part aor act

1 and when they were **awake**, they saw his glory,...... Luke 9:32

Diagrēgoreō is a compound word consisting of *dia* (1217), "through" or "thorough," and *grēgoreō* (1121) meaning "to be awake."

Classical Greek
In the classical writings *diagrēgoreō* means the state of "full wakefulness" or "to keep awake." The more common use of the concept is expressed by omitting *dia* (which strengthens the verb) and using the root word *grēgoreō*. *Grēgoreō* occurs quite often in classical literature meaning "watch," "to be fully awake," or "become fully awake."

Septuagint Usage
The Septuagint does not have the strengthened form *diagrēgoreō*, but the weaker form *grēgoreō* occurs 7 times (and once in Theodotion's version of Daniel 9:14). Nehemiah 7:3, for example, shows the alert condition expressed by the weaker word translated "watch." Nehemiah and the guards on the wall were expecting an attack, therefore they were "watchful."

New Testament Usage
In the New Testament *diagrēgoreō* occurs once, in Luke 9:32. The disciples were weighed down with sleep, but when Christ's transfiguration began to occur, they became thoroughly awake. It was while they were "totally awake" that they saw Christ's glory. The testimony of their experience is emphasized by the strong verb for "completely awake."

STRONG 1235, BAUER 182, LIDDELL-SCOTT 392.

1230. διάγω diagō verb
Live, pass time.

CROSS-REFERENCE:
ἄγω agō (70)

בּוֹא bô' (971), Come, go; hiphil: bring (Zec 13:9).

הָלַךְ hālakh (2050), Go, walk; hiphil: lead (Jb 12:17, Ps 136:16 [135:16]).

עָבַר 'āvar (5882), Go over; hiphil: cause to pass (2 Kgs 17:17, Ps 78:13 [77:13], Ez 20:37).

פָּשַׂק pāsaq (6834), Open; piel: spread one's legs (Ez 16:25).

1. διάγωμεν diagōmen 1pl subj pres act
2. διάγοντες diagontes nom pl masc part pres act

1 that we may **lead** a quiet and peaceable life........ 1 Tm 2:2
2 **living** in malice and envy, hateful, and hating........Tit 3:3

The term *diagō* is very common in Greek writings in the sense of "spend one's life" (see *Bauer*). It occurs twice in the New Testament. Paul used it in the Pastorals (1 Timothy 2:2; Titus 3:3) to mean "lead a life, living." *Diagō* comes from *dia* (1217), often denoting the channel of an act, and *agō* (70), "lead."

STRONG 1236, BAUER 182, MOULTON-MILLIGAN 147, LIDDELL-SCOTT 392.

1231. διαδέχομαι diadechomai verb
Receive in turn.

CROSS-REFERENCE:
δέχομαι dechomai (1203)

מִשְׁנֶה mishneh (5112), Second (2 Chr 31:12, Est 10:3).

פַּרְבָּר parbār (6753), Court (1 Chr 26:18).

1. διαδεξάμενοι diadexamenoi
nom pl masc part aor mid

1 Which also our fathers that **came after**............. Acts 7:45

Diadechomai is used only once in the New Testament, occurring at Acts 7:45. It means to "succeed after, come after, receive in turn (from a previous owner)." The term comes from *dia* (1217) and *dechomai* (1203), "take, receive, accept, approve."

διάδημα 1232

STRONG 1237, BAUER 182, MOULTON-MILLIGAN 147-48, LIDDELL-SCOTT 392.

1232. διάδημα diadēma noun
Diadem, crown.
COGNATE:
δέω deō (1204)
SYNONYM:
στέφανος stephanos (4586)

כֶּתֶר kether (3933), Crown (Est 1:11, 2:17).

צָנִיף ts*niwph (7068), Turban, diadem (Is 62:3).

תַּכְרִיךְ takhrîkh (8838), Mantle (Est 8:15).

1. διαδήματα diadēmata nom/acc pl neu

1 seven heads ... and seven **crowns** upon his heads....	Rev 12:3
1 seven heads ... and upon his horns ten **crowns**,........	13:1
1 and on his head were many **crowns**;..................	19:12

Classical Greek
The Greek word *diadēma* means royal "crown." The term is related to the word *diadeō*, "to bind around." Xenophon referred to the "band" of the tiara around the head of the Persian king (see *Bauer*). Such a crown was worn by Alexander the Great and by later Grecian monarchs.

Septuagint Usage
The Septuagint often reads *diadēma* for the Hebrew *kether*, "crown"; in the Book of Esther it was used in reference to the crown of the Persian queen Vashti (1:11, cf. 2:17) and to the king (6:8). Redeemed Israel will be a "crown" (*diadēma*) in the hand of God (Isaiah 62:3).

New Testament Usage
The New Testament records *diadēma* 3 times, all in the Book of Revelation: of the 7 diadems of the dragon (12:3); of the 10 "crowns" upon the horns of the beast (13:1); and of the many crowns of Christ—the One called Faithful and True (19:12).

STRONG 1238, BAUER 182, LIDDELL-SCOTT 393, COLIN BROWN 1:405.

1233. διαδίδωμι diadidōmi verb
Distribute, give out, hand over.
COGNATE:
δίδωμι didōmi (1319)
SYNONYMS:
ἀναδίδωμι anadidōmi (323)
ἀποδίδωμι apodidōmi (586)
διαιρέω diaireō (1238)
διαμερίζω diamerizō (1260)
δίδωμι didōmi (1319)
δωρέομαι dōreomai (1426)
ἐπιδίδωμι epididōmi (1914)
κοινωνέω koinōneō (2814)
μερίζω merizō (3177)
μεταδίδωμι metadidōmi (3200)
παραδίδωμι paradidōmi (3722)
παρέχω parechō (3792)
χαρίζομαι charizomai (5319)

חָלַק chālaq (2606), Piel: divide (Gn 49:27—Codex Alexandrinus only).

נָפַל nāphal (5489), Fall; hiphil: allot (Jos 13:6).

נָתַן nāthan (5598), Give; yield (Gn 49:20—Codex Alexandrinus only).

1. διαδίδωσιν diadidōsin 3sing indic pres act
2. διέδωκεν diedōken 3sing indic aor act
3. διάδος diados 2sing impr aor act
4. διαδιδώσουσιν diadidōsousin 3pl indic fut act
5. διεδίδοτο diedidoto 3sing indic imperf mid
6. διεδίδετο diedideto 3sing indic imperf pass

1 armour wherein he trusted, and **divideth** his spoils.	Luke 11:22
3 sell all that thou hast, and **distribute** unto the poor,....	18:22
2 he **distributed** to the disciples,.....................	John 6:11
5 and **distribution was made** unto every man...........	Acts 4:35
6 and **distribution was made** unto every man.............	4:35
4 shall **give** their power and strength unto the beast...	Rev 17:13

Diadidōmi comes from *dia* (1217), denoting the channel of an act, and *didōmi* (1319), "give, bestow, grant." In three of its five New Testament uses *diadidōmi* refers to a literal distribution of material goods, e.g., financial wealth (Luke 18:22; Acts 4:35), food (John 6:11). In Luke 11:22 the word occurs in an allegory Jesus used to present one of His rare teachings involving the devil. Referring to Satan as a "strong man" (verse 21), Jesus said, "when someone (i.e., Christ) stronger attacks and overpowers him, he takes away the armor in which he trusted and *divides up* the spoils" (NIV). Finally, *diadidōmi* is used in an eschatological context describing 10 future kings who will *give* their power (*dunamis* [1405]) and authority (*exousia* [1833]) to the "beast."

STRONG 1239, BAUER 182, MOULTON-MILLIGAN 148, LIDDELL-SCOTT 393.

1234. διάδοχος diadochos noun
Successor.
CROSS-REFERENCE:
δέχομαι dechomai (1203)

חָלַף chālaph (2599), Hiphil: replace, substitute, change (Sir 48:8).

מִשְׁנֶה mishneh (5112), Second (2 Chr 28:7).

שַׂר sar (8015), Captain (2 Chr 26:11).

שָׁרַת shārath (8664), Piel: be an attendant, serve (Sir 46:1).

1. διάδοχον diadochon acc sing masc

1 Felix was **succeeded** by Porcius Festus (NASB) ..... Acts 24:27

Used only once in the New Testament, this term occurs at Acts 24:27. It means "successor" and has a companion form, the word *diadechomai* (1231) meaning "succeed after, come after, receive in turn."
Strong 1240, Bauer 182, Moulton-Milligan 148, Liddell-Scott 393.

1235. διαζώννυμι diazōnnumi verb
Tie around oneself, gird tightly.
Cognate:
ζώννυμι zōnnumi (2207)
Synonyms:
ἀναζώννυμι anazōnnumi (326)
ζώννυμι zōnnumi (2207)
περιζώννυμι perizōnnumi (3887)

חָגוֹר chāghôr (2381), Belt (Ez 23:15—Codex Alexandrinus only).

1. διέζωσεν diezōsen 3sing indic aor act
2. διεζώσατο diezōsato 3sing indic aor mid
3. διεζωσμένος diezōsmenos
nom sing masc part perf mid

1 and took a towel, and **girded** himself............ John 13:4
3 wipe ... with the towel wherewith he was **girded**....... 13:5
2 **girt** his fisher's coat unto him, for he was naked,..... 21:7

This term is used three times in the New Testament, all in the Gospel of John (13:4,5; 21:7). It means "to gird tightly, wrap or tie around, put on." *Diazōnnumi* comes from *dia* (1217), often denoting the channel of an act, and *zōnnumi* (2207), "to bind around, gird."
Strong 1241, Bauer 182, Moulton-Milligan 148 (see "diazōnnuō"), Kittel 5:302-8, Liddell-Scott 394, Colin Brown 3:120.

1236. διαθήκη diathēkē noun
Last will and testament, covenant, will, contract, dispostion.
Cross-Reference:
τίθημι tithēmi (4935)

אַחֲוָה 'achāwāh (263), Brotherhood (Zec 11:14—Codex Alexandrinus only).
בְּרִית berîth (1311), Covenant (Gn 17:2, Jos 3:6, Ez 16:59ff.).
דָּבָר dāvār (1745), Word; oath (Dt 9:5).

כָּתַב kāthav (3918), Write (2 Chr 25:4).
עֵדוּת 'ēdhûth (5925), Testimony (Ex 27:21, 31:7, 39:35 [39:15]).
תּוֹרָה tôrāh (8784), Law (Dn 9:13).

1. διαθήκη diathēkē nom sing fem
2. διαθήκης diathēkēs gen sing fem
3. διαθήκῃ diathēkē dat sing fem
4. διαθήκην diathēkēn acc sing fem
5. διαθῆκαι diathēkai nom pl fem
6. διαθηκῶν diathēkōn gen pl fem

2 For this is my blood of the new **testament**,........ Matt 26:28
2 This is my blood of the new **testament**,........... Mark 14:24
2 the mercy ... and to remember his holy **covenant**;.... Luke 1:72
1 This cup is the new **testament** in my blood,........... 22:20
2 of the **covenant** which God made with our fathers,... Acts 3:25
4 And he gave him the **covenant** of circumcision:......... 7:8
5 and the glory, and the **covenants**,.................... Rom 9:4
1 and the glory, and the **covenants**,.................... 9:4
2 For this is my **covenant** unto them,................. 11:27
1 This cup is the new **testament** in my blood:........ 1 Co 11:25
2 hath made us able ministers of the new **testament**;.. 2 Co 3:6
2 untaken away in the reading of the old **testament**;...... 3:14
2 Though it be but a man's **covenant**,................. Gal 3:15
4 this I say, that the **covenant**, that was confirmed 3:17
5 are an allegory: for these are the two **covenants**;....... 4:24
6 and strangers from the **covenants** of promise,........ Eph 2:12
2 was Jesus made a surety of a better **testament**......Heb 7:22
2 much also he is the mediator of a better **covenant**,..... 8:6
4 make a new **covenant** with the house of Israel.......... 8:8
4 Not according to the **covenant** that I made............. 8:9
3 because they continued not in my **covenant**,............ 8:9
1 For this is the **covenant** that I will make............. 8:10
2 and the ark of the **covenant** overlaid ... with gold,..... 9:4
2 and the tables of the **covenant**;...................... 9:4
2 he is the mediator of the new **testament**,............. 9:15
3 transgressions that were under the first **testament**,... 9:15
1 For where a **testament** is, there must also............ 9:16
1 For a **testament** is of force after men are dead:........ 9:17
2 Saying, This is the blood of the **testament**........... 9:20
1 This is the **covenant** that I will make with them..... 10:16
2 and hath counted the blood of the **covenant**,......... 10:29
2 And to Jesus the mediator of the new **covenant**,...... 12:24
2 through the blood of the everlasting **covenant**,....... 13:20
2 was seen in his temple the ark of his **testament**:.....Rev 11:19

Classical Greek

In classical Greek *diathēkē* exclusively denotes a "last will or testament." It is considered a legal, technical term for that agreement. However, there are indications that previously *diathēkē* included an even wider range of definition, and it may have been used as a religious term as well (*Moulton-Milligan*; Behm, "diathēkē," *Kittel*, 2:124ff.). The papyri confirm that the meaning "testament" dominates completely in Hellenism. However, such a restricted sense of the word does not take into account the reality that equivalent Hebrew and Aramaic terms from which *diathēkē* draws much of its meaning, meant not only "testament" but also a "decree" or "disposition." Since nothing indicates the term had acquired a new meaning, one must consequently assume that the Greek word also covered these areas. This forms an interesting background for understanding the use of the word in the Septuagint.

Only rarely does *diathēkē* seem to have been used as a synonym for *suntēkē*, "agreement." One single case is known (Aristophanes), but this case, too, concerns an agreement between two parties which was dictated by one and could be accepted or rejected by the other. This meaning lies close to the idea of "covenant" so prominent in Israel's religion.

Septuagint Usage

Diathēkē is the principal equivalent for the Hebrew *b^{e}rîth*, "covenant," in the Septuagint. Evidently the Greek term did not entirely capture the meaning of *b^{e}rîth*, but as so often happens in the Septuagint, the full sense of the Hebrew is transferred to the Greek. Thus, in the Greek of the New Testament *diathēkē* connotes something much more than its meaning in common Greek. The Old Testament concept of covenant affected the language itself.

The covenant idea is one of the foremost ideas of the Old Testament. Understanding it is essential for comprehending both the law of Israel and its religious position. *B^{e}rîth*, the conveyer of this idea, is perhaps derived from *bārā'*, "to eat, eat together with," and from this, "to have fellowship with." It describes "covenant" in the normal sense of the word, "a solemn agreement" in which two parties mutually assume certain obligations as foundations for fellowship. The word also denotes the conditions or stipulations of the covenant. In addition, *berith* can describe a decree that is imposed on only one party, or where one party assumes the obligations. Sometimes *diathēkē* carries the limited meaning of "oath" (Genesis 26:3).

Old Testament Background

The Old Testament provides many examples of covenants. Some are covenants between men (either persons or groups); some are covenants between God and men. Covenants between men represent either a new purely legal relationship between the parties, or else they can define the ethical, sacral, or legal obligations involved in a previous relationship. The most simple transaction can be a friendly agreement between two persons, like David and Jonathan, for instance (1 Samuel [LXX 1 Kings] 18:1-3; 20:8; 23:18). The marriage "covenant" may also fall into this category (Malachi 2:14).

Even though covenants involve only a human relationship, such an agreement also has a sacred character; in other words, it is conducted "before the Lord" (1 Samuel 23:18 [LXX 1 Kings 23:18]). This means the Lord witnesses the covenant and enforces it. The Lord is the guardian of the covenant, and upon a violation of the agreement He punishes the violator. In Israel a covenant was not imaginable apart from this background which assumed the sacredness of such events.

A covenant enacted solely to outline the legal responsibilities between two parties is much more difficult than a covenant having friendship as its original basis. The covenant between Jacob and Laban is illustrative here (Genesis 31:44f.). Any covenant between men must be understood as a positive shift in their relationship—a step toward brotherhood. In an alliance one enters into a strange "blood covenant"; the other party is to be treated as one's own kin. That means that a legally binding kinship comes into existence between those of the same covenantal blood. This explains why Israel was categorically forbidden to make a covenant with the idolatrous and morally corrupt Canaanites (Exodus 23:32; 34:12-16; Deuteronomy 7:2-4). When Israel transgressed this interdict they incurred the wrath and judgment of God (Judges 2:1f.).

To break a covenant was a monumental sin. Essentially it was an overt act of sin against God which carries serious consequences (Amos 1:9; cf. 2 Samuel 21:1f. [LXX 2 Kings 21:1f]; Ezekiel 17). But it was also a sin against the covenant party. The guilty one was held in utter contempt (cf. Genesis 34:30). Even under circumstances in which the establishing of a covenant has taken place by deceit the covenant carried its binding force (Joshua 9:3ff.; 9:14-21). A broken agreement must be atoned for, as David illustrated (2 Samuel 21 [LXX 2 Kings 21]).

Covenants were also established between men, such as between a prince and his people. David made a covenant with the elders in Israel (2 Samuel 5:3 [LXX 2 Kings 5:3]); King Zedekiah made a covenant with his entire people which proclaimed liberty for the slaves (Jeremiah 34:8f. [LXX 41:8]; cf. Exodus 21:2; Deuteronomy 15:12).

Alliances could also be made between races, tribes, and peoples. That the concept of covenant can also be applied to idols is evident from the names like *Ba'al B^{e}rîth* ("Baal of the covenant," Judges 8:33; 9:4) and *'El B^erith* ("the god of the covenant," Judges 9:46).

However, it is the covenant between the Lord and Israel which completely dominates the Old Testament concept of covenant. When God enters into a covenant with men the initiative is always His. An agreement with someone equal with God is impossible. Through the making of a covenant with God the human party can never demand anything as a right. When God makes himself a participant in such a covenant, thus obliging himself to fulfill the obligations of the covenant, man can depend upon His faithfulness to bless him according to the covenant. This always happens according to God's own free will; His covenants are agreements based upon grace. When He enters into such a covenant He is sovereign. He alone chooses the instruments of His plans (cf. Genesis 15:17f.; 2 Samuel 7 [LXX 2 Kings 7]). Five such "grace covenants" described in the Old Testament hold special importance.

The first was God's covenant with Noah (Genesis 9:8-17) which guaranteed the continued existence of mankind and the creation. In it the Lord promised that He would never again send a flood to destroy the earth (verse 11). The rainbow was to be a sign of this covenant between God and the earth (verse 13).

In a second covenant God promised Abraham that he and his wife Sarah would be progenitors of a great people (Genesis 17:2-16). Abraham would be a "father of many nations" (verses 4-6) and Sarah "a mother of nations" (verse 16). In a clearly messianic prophecy, Abram was told that "in thee shall all families of the earth be blessed" (Genesis 12:3). Later, the Lord unilaterally extended this promise (which included title to a portion of land in Palestine [Genesis 15:18-21]) to Abraham's descendants. Again, this was a covenant by grace; the condition of the covenant was faith alone. Obedience to the Law, which was added "because of transgressions," was not a condition of inheriting the promise (cf. Galatians 3:15-19). The sign of this covenant was to be circumcision (Genesis 17:10-14).

God's covenant with Israel at Sinai comprised a third "grace covenant," one which served as the foundation of the theocracy existing in the Old Testament. By this covenant God selected Israel to be "a peculiar (special) treasure ... above all people ... a kingdom of priests, and a holy nation" (Exodus 19:5f.). The relationship which already existed between the Lord and Israel, and which was the basis of their wonderful deliverance from Egypt, here received a more binding, legal force—the establishment of a covenant through a historical action, namely, the Exodus event.

The goal of this covenant was not only the deliverance of Israel from Egypt but an ongoing, enduring gift from God to His people. The Lord bound himself to His people through this legally obliging promise. However, the sign of the covenant would be Israel's obedience to the Law, especially to the belief that there is only one real and true God. The so-called "great *shemah*," recorded at Deuteronomy 6:4, became the great symbol of Israel's faith and their principal dogma: "Hear, O Israel: The Lord our God is one Lord." The great declaration of Deuteronomy 6:4 provided Israel with the foundation of authority from which God gave the Law. Only God could "cut" such a covenant, and only God could see that it was successfully fulfilled. In order to communicate the Law to the Israelites in the intended spirit and specificity, God chose to use a Near Eastern covenant form known as a suzerainty treaty. This type of covenant treaty was well known to the culture of their time and was typically used between a suzerain (king) and a vassal (loyal servant). The Israelites would have been familiar with this covenant form and thus would have understood that: (1) it was unilateral in nature, and (2) it was given by the rightful king in order to establish a firm relationship between both parties, so the king's concerns for his people might be carried out.

Research in Biblical archaeology, notably by G.E. Mendenhall and M.G. Kline, has identified six primary elements in a typical suzerainty treaty, all of which can be found in the texts pertaining to the giving of the Law as follows:

(1) Preamble—identifies the author of the treaty along with his title and/or attributes. See Exodus 19:3; 20:2; 24:1.

(2) Historical Prologue—recounts the benevolent deeds of the suzerain on the vassal's behalf. See Exodus 19:4; 20:26; 24:16 (instructions concerning respect for God's power and holiness implied knowledge of His deeds which revealed those attributes).

(3) Stipulations—establishes principles, general and specific, upon which future relations were

to be based. See Exodus 19:5; Exodus 20:3-17 (the Decalogue); Exodus 24:3 (refers to all the Lord's words and laws previously spoken in Exodus 20—23).

(4) Blessings and/or Curses—delineates the results of the responses to the treaty. See Exodus 19:5,6; 20:5,6,7,12.

(5) List of divine witnesses and/or Oath—acknowledges the treaty's authority. See Exodus 19:8; 24:7 (Deuteronomy 32:1 and Isaiah 1:2 also summon heaven and earth as witnesses to Israel's relationship with their God).

(6) Provisions for deposit of treaty and for public reading. See Exodus 25:21 and Deuteronomy 10:1-5; 28; 31:10-13.

These parallels were not intended for a rigid division of treaty parts but were familiar enough to the Israelites so they would understand the implications, as well as the imperatives, of the Law. In God's covenant, His love for His people is revealed—declared by His deeds and guaranteed to continue for the sake of those loyal to Him. Their obedience to the Law would strengthen that love bond and foreshadowed the day when the Covenant Maker would write His law on tablets of human hearts (Jeremiah 31:33 [LXX 38:33]).

In essence, the covenant God made with Israel at Sinai was as thoroughly "by grace" as was His covenant with Abraham. By giving the Law God did not change the condition of the covenant, that is, from faith to works. Righteousness before God was established by faith alone. Israel was God's chosen people before the Law was given, and no one could become "the people of God" solely by obeying the Law. Notice that in Exodus 19:4, before giving Israel the Law, God reminded them of the grace He had shown them.

The Law could not bring life (cf. Galatians 3:21), but through the Law, Israel might live lives pleasing to God (Ezekiel 20:13). Nevertheless, when Israel rejected the Law, God's wrath came upon them, for they were actually rejecting God himself. Therefore, the great error and delusion of the Jews was that they interpreted the Law itself as the way to salvation, and in doing so went "about to establish their own righteousness" (Romans 10:3).

A fourth covenant of grace was established by God with Phinehas (Numbers 25:11-13). It was described by the Lord as a "covenant of peace" (verse 12), and it placed the Levites in an "everlasting priesthood." Jeremiah 33:21,22 states that this covenant was as firm as the covenant God had made with David (see below).

A fifth covenant, then, was the one God made with David. It gave to David the promise that he would always have a "son" established as king over God's people. This promise culminated (and will culminate) in the coming of Jesus, the Messiah (cf. Revelation 22:5).

It was by covenant, then, that God created and maintained a relationship with Israel. And although Israel broke the covenant with God, He did not abolish the conditions of the covenant. Instead, the Lord promised to establish a "new covenant," one in which His Spirit would write His laws in the hearts of His people (Jeremiah 31:31-34 [LXX 38:31-34]). This eschatological covenant is realized in the person of Jesus Christ.

New Testament Usage

The New Testament writers appropriated their understanding of the covenant and the promises of a new covenant directly from the Old Testament. Nevertheless, it is somewhat puzzling that the term *diathēkē* appears only about 30 times in the New Testament, whereas *berith* occurs no less than 300 times in the Old Testament. One must, however, take into consideration that the thought of the covenant in the New, more than in the Old Testament, is bound to its key theme—the kingdom of God. Through the covenant God appointed Israel as the people of God; likewise, the new covenant, in a spiritual sense established the Messianic Kingdom and the community of the new age. This comes across linguistically in Luke 22:29 where the expression *diatithēmai . . . baseleian*, "to promise or transfer the kingdom," is equivalent to *kārath bᵉrîth* of the Old Testament, "to make a covenant." In the Septuagint this expression is translated as *diathēkēn diatithēmai*.

Diathēkē thus conveys the Hebraic, Biblical understanding of covenant rather than the secular Greek. In Hebrews 9:16 the word is used in its common definition of "last will," a meaning also echoed in Galatians 3:15. Otherwise, the term always means "covenant." The covenant between God and His people is the point of contact between the New Testament and the prophecies of the Old

Testament concerning a new covenant (e.g., Jeremiah 31:31-34). This thought has a central place, especially in the Servant Songs of Isaiah (42:6; 49:8). A mark of this new covenant was to be its individuality and spirituality. Laws and covenant terms would be "written in the hearts" of individuals—in conscience, will, feelings, and thought. As a result a general knowledge of God would be based upon revelation and personal experience. Total and complete forgiveness of sins would be the cornerstone of the new life with God. The gift of the Spirit was also included in the covenant (e.g., Isaiah 59:21). Inspired with a sense of awe of God in the heart (Jeremiah 32:40), humanity was to experience this covenant as a covenant of liberty, joy, and peace (Ezekiel 34:25).

These thoughts are developed throughout the New Testament. From the writer of the Book of Hebrews we learn that the old covenant, with its "types," its earthly priesthood, and its sacrificial system, was incomplete and imperfect; everything was only a shadow of the true and heavenly (Hebrews 8:5). Therefore the old *diathēkē* was obsolete, destined to disappear (Hebrews 8:13; cf. 2 Corinthians 3:14). It had to be replaced by a new covenant (Hebrews 8:7) because it could not take sin away (Hebrews 10:4). The old covenant was being interpreted based upon letter, not Spirit; as a result, it was a "ministry that brought death," not Spirit and life (2 Corinthians 3:7f., NIV). Judaism allowed the covenant to become a rule of law; consequently it could only place its children in bondage (Galatians 4:24).

Drawing upon this heritage of the old, the new covenant appeared in all its perfection and glory, the fulfillment of the covenant God made with the fathers (Luke 1:72; Acts 3:25), with Israel (Romans 9:4). The new covenant (Hebrews 8:8ff.; 10:16f.) was promised by the prophets (Jeremiah 31:31ff.; cf. Ephesians 2:12). It was new in both time (*nea* [see 3363C]; Hebrews 12:24) and nature (*kainos* [2508]; Hebrews 9:15). Compared with the first covenant the new covenant is superior (Hebrews 7:22), because it is founded upon better promises (8:6). Contrary to the first covenant, this one is eternal (Hebrews 13:20). The guarantor of this new agreement is the eternal Son of God (7:22), its Mediator (9:15).

Just as the first covenant was consecrated with blood, the death of Christ was the inevitable requirement for putting the new covenant into force. His death brought redemption from the transgressions under the first covenant, and His blood ratified the new (Hebrews 9:15ff.). The blood of Christ which was shed for many for the forgiveness of sins (Matthew 26:28 with parallels), is the blood of the eternal covenant (Hebrews 10:29; 13:20). The covenant meal, the Lord's Supper, is reminiscent of the institution of the covenant through the sacrifice of Christ. It permits the believer to share in the benefits and obligations of the covenant (1 Corinthians 11:23ff., cf. 10:16f.). There may be a parallel between the death of Christ and the sacrifice offered at the institution of the first covenant at Sinai (Exodus 24:6).

According to Paul, the new, heavenly covenant—symbolized by Sarah, the free wife of Abraham—gives the believer rights as a child and provides liberty (Galatians 4:22f.). According to its nature it is spirit and life, and it offers its members a share in the Spirit of God. Only the living God and His Spirit can enable a person to participate in a covenant of this nature (2 Corinthians 3:5f.).

The prophets foretold this time of refreshing (Acts 3:25). But not only Israel will share in this new agreement. The Gentiles were previously excluded from joining the people of God and were strangers to the covenants and their promises, without hope and without God. But no longer are they strangers and aliens; rather, they have become fellow citizens with the "elect." They are members of the household of faith (Ephesians 2:11-19). They have been included in the covenant and enjoy its blessings.

STRONG 1242, BAUER 183, MOULTON-MILLIGAN 148-49, KITTEL 2:106-34, LIDDELL-SCOTT 394-95, COLIN BROWN 1:365-66,368-69,371-72,374,376

1237. διαίρεσις diairesis noun
Differences, distinction.

CROSS-REFERENCE:
αἱρέω haireō (141)

גֶּזֶר gezer (1536), Parts (Ps 136:13 [135:13]).

מַחֲלֹקֶת machălōqeth (4393), Portion, division (1 Chr 27:1,2,4ff., 2 Chr 35:10).

מִפְלַגָּה miphlaggāh (4815), Division (2 Chr 35:12).

נַחֲלָה nachălāh (5338), Territories, inheritance (Jos 19:51).

פְּלַגָּה pᵉlaggāh (6634), Division (Jgs 5:15—Codex Alexandrinus only).

פְּלֻגָּה pᵉluggāh (6635), Division (2 Chr 35:5).

1. διαιρέσεις diaireseis nom pl fem

1 there are **diversities** of gifts, but the same Spirit....	1 Co 12:4
1 **differences** of administrations, but the same Lord......	12:5
1 And there are **diversities** of operations,..............	12:6

Classical Greek
In classical Greek *diairesis* means "divisibility." It is used as a medical term to refer to "dissection," "surgical operation," and "wounds." In the economic sense *diairesis* means a "dividing" or "distributing" of money. In technical usage of speech, rhetoric, and grammar, *diairesis* refers to the "division" of a composition into outline form, "separation" of the sentences into parts of speech, and the resolution of diphthongs into syllables.

The papyri sources follow the basic meanings of *diairesis* indicated by the classical writings. Referring to agriculture *diairesis* is used to mean the "surveying" of land, the "division" of wheat land to farmers, and the proper "period" of time to plant crops.

Septuagint Usage
In the Septuagint *diairesis* occurs 32 times. The basic meaning is "division" or "distribution." Joshua 19:51, for example, states that the land of Canaan was "distributed" by lot at the tent of meeting. In Judges 5:16 *diairesis* means "division" in referring to the clans of Reuben. Most Septuagint references of *diairesis* bear the meaning of "divisions" of gatekeepers, and "households" of Levites or priests. In Psalm 136:13 (LXX 135:13) *diairesis* is rendered "divided."

New Testament Usage
The New Testament uses *diairesis* three times in one passage in which the apostle Paul explained spiritual matters (1 Corinthians 12:4-6). The primary meaning of *diairesis* in the Septuagint ("divisions") is apparent, but the semantic range includes "diversities, distributions," and "varieties." The same Spirit infuses believers with "diversities" of gifts. The same Lord "distributes" different functions to members of His body. The same God works within believers to effect "varieties" of results.

Strong 1243, Bauer 183, Moulton-Milligan 149, Kittel 1:184-85, Liddell-Scott 395.

1238. διαιρέω diaireō verb
Divide, distribute.

Cognate:
αἱρέω haireō (141)

Synonyms:
ἀποδίδωμι apodidōmi (586)
διαδίδωμι diadidōmi (1233)
διαμερίζω diamerizō (1260)
δίδωμι didōmi (1319)
δωρέομαι dōreomai (1426)
κοινωνέω koinōneō (2814)
μερίζω merizō (3177)
μεταδίδωμι metadidōmi (3200)
μετέχω metechō (3218)

בָּדַל bādhal (950), Hiphil: sever (Lv 1:17, 5:8).

בָּתַר bāthar (1363), Qal: cut in two (Gn 15:10); piel: cut in two (Gn 15:10).

גָּזַר gāzar (1535), Divide (1 Kgs 3:25,26).

חָלַק chālaq (2606), Qal: divide, share (Jos 22:8, 2 Sm 19:29, Prv 17:2); niphal: be divided (1 Chr 23:6); piel: divide (Prv 16:19, Is 9:3); hithpael: divide (Jos 18:5).

חָצָה chātsâh (2779), Qal: divide (Gn 32:7, Jgs 7:16); niphal: be divided (Ez 37:22).

חָצַץ chātsāts (2788), Divide; pual: curtailed (Jb 21:21).

נָחַל nāchal (5336), Take possession of; hiphil: inherit (Jos 1:6—only in some Vaticanus texts).

נָתַח nāthach (5591), Piel: cut in pieces (Lv 1:12).

1. διαιροῦν diairoun nom/acc sing neu part pres act
2. διεῖλεν dieilen 3sing indic aor act

2 And he **divided** unto them his living...............	Luke 15:12
1 **dividing** to every man severally as he will..........	1 Co 12:11

A common term in classical Greek, *diaireō* has several meanings including "divide, distinguish, distribute, decide, disperse," and "determine" (*Liddell-Scott*). It is comprised of *dia* (1217), denoting the channel of an act, and *haireō* (141), "choose, prefer, decide." It is used only twice in the New Testament (Luke 15:12; 1 Corinthians 12:11). Its use in Corinthians indicates it is by the will of the Holy Spirit that the *charismata* (see 5321) are "dispensed" or "distributed" among members of the body of Christ.

Strong 1244, Bauer 183, Moulton-Milligan 149, Kittel 1:184-85, Liddell-Scott 395.

1238B. διακαθαίρω diakathairō verb
Clean out.
Cross-Reference:
καθαίρω kathairō (2480)

1. διακαθᾶραι diakatharai inf aor act

1 to **clean out** His threshing floor (NASB)............	Luke 3:17

The prefix *dia* (1217), which often intensifies the verb, adds the expression "thoroughly" to the root verb *kathairō* (2480), meaning "to cleanse." It is found in Aristotle, Plato, and other early writers, although it does not appear in the Septuagint. This verb appears twice in the New Testament as variants to the *Textus Receptus*. Both instances describe how John the Baptist spoke of the coming Messiah as One who would *thoroughly clean out* His threshing floor, removing all the chaff (Matthew 3:12; Luke 3:17).

BAUER 183, MOULTON-MILLIGAN 149, LIDDELL-SCOTT 396.

1239. διακαθαρίζω diakatharizō verb
Cleanse thoroughly, to winnow.
CROSS-REFERENCE:
 καθαίρω kathairō (2480)

1. **διακαθαριεῖ** diakathariei 3sing indic fut act

1 and he will **thoroughly purge** his floor,	Matt 3:12
1 and he will **thoroughly purge** his floor,	Luke 3:17

This term, found nowhere in either classical Greek or the Septuagint, is used twice in the New Testament. Matthew 3:12 and Luke 3:17 record the same saying of John the Baptist. The word means "to cleanse perfectly, clean out, thresh out." It comes from *dia* (1217), denoting the channel of an act (used here to intensify the word), and *katharizō* (2483), "to clean, purify." Modern editions of the Greek text read *diakathairō* (1238B) in these verses.

STRONG 1245, BAUER 183, LIDDELL-SCOTT 396.

1240. διακατελέγχομαι
diakatelenchomai verb
Refute (completely, thoroughly).
CROSS-REFERENCE:
 ἐλέγχω elenchō (1638)

1. **διακατηλέγχετο** diakatelencheto
   3sing indic imperf mid

1 he mightily **convinced** the Jews, and that publicly,	Acts 18:28

This long word comes from *dia* (1217), denoting the channel of an act; *kata*, expressing opposition and intensity; and *elenchō* (1638), meaning "convict, convince, reprove." It is used once in the New Testament, occurring at Acts 18:28, where it means "convince, refute, prove." The NIV translates the verb "vigorously refuting" ("mightily convince," KJV).

STRONG 1246, BAUER 184, LIDDELL-SCOTT 397.

1241. διακονέω diakoneō verb
Serve, wait upon tables, minister, help, serve as deacon.
COGNATES:
 διακονία diakonia (1242)
 διάκονος diakonos (1243)
SYNONYMS:
 ἀντιλαμβάνομαι antilambanomai (479)
 βοηθέω boētheō (990)
 ἐλεέω eleeō (1640)
 λατρεύω latreuō (2973)
 λειτουργέω leitourgeō (2982)
 συμβάλλω sumballō (4671)
 συναντιλαμβάνομαι sunantilambanomai (4729)
 ὑπηρετέω hupēreteō (5094)

1. **διακονεῖ** diakonei 3sing indic pres act
2. **διακονῇ** diakonē 3sing subj pres act
3. **διακονείτωσαν** diakoneitōsan 3pl impr pres act
4. **διακονῶν** diakonōn nom sing masc part pres act
5. **διακονοῦντες** diakonountes
    nom pl masc part pres act
6. **διακονούντων** diakonountōn
    gen pl masc part pres act
7. **διακονοῦσαι** diakonousai
    nom pl fem part pres act
8. **διακονεῖν** diakonein inf pres act
9. **διακόνει** diakonei 2sing impr pres act
10. **διηκόνησεν** diēkonēsen 3sing indic aor act
11. **διηκονήσαμεν** diēkonēsamen 1pl indic aor act
12. **διακονήσαντες** diakonēsantes
    nom pl masc part aor act
13. **διακονῆσαι** diakonēsai inf aor act
14. **διακονήσει** diakonēsei 3sing indic fut act
15. **διηκόνει** diēkonei 3sing indic imperf act
16. **διηκόνουν** diēkonoun 3pl indic imperf act
17. **διακονουμένῃ** diakonoumenē
    dat sing fem part pres mid
18. **διακονηθεῖσα** diakonētheisa
    nom sing fem part aor pass
19. **διακονηθῆναι** diakonēthēnai inf aor pass

16 angels came and **ministered** unto him.		Matt 4:11
15 and she arose, and **ministered** unto them.		8:15
19 the Son of man came not to be **ministered** unto,		20:28
13 came not to be **ministered** unto, but to **minister**,		20:28
11 or in prison, and did not **minister** unto thee?		25:44
7 followed Jesus from Galilee, **ministering** unto him:		27:55
16 and the angels **ministered** unto him.		Mark 1:13
15 the fever left her, and she **ministered** unto them.		1:31
19 the Son of man came not to be **ministered** unto,		10:45
13 not to be **ministered** unto, but to **minister**,		10:45
16 followed him, and **ministered** unto him;		15:41
16 immediately she arose and **ministered** unto them.		Luke 4:39
16 which **ministered** unto him of their substance.		8:3
8 not care that my sister hath left me **to serve** alone?		10:40
14 and will come forth and **serve** them.		12:37

διακονία 1242

9	and serve me, till I have eaten and drunken;	Luke 17:8
4	and he that is chief, as he that doth serve.	22:26
4	he that sitteth at meat, or he that serveth?	22:27
4	but I am among you as he that serveth.	22:27
15	they made him a supper; and Martha served:	John 12:2
2	If any man serve me, let him follow me;	12:26
2	if any man serve me, him will my Father honour.	12:26
8	leave the word of God, and serve tables.	Acts 6:2
6	Macedonia two of them that ministered unto him,	19:22
4	I go unto Jerusalem to minister unto the saints.	Rom 15:25
18	to be the epistle of Christ ministered by us,	2 Co 3:3
17	which is administered by us to the glory	8:19
17	in this abundance which is administered by us:	8:20
3	then let them use the office of a deacon.	1 Tm 3:10
12	For they that have used the office of a deacon well	3:13
10	and in how many things he ministered unto me	2 Tm 1:18
2	that in thy stead he might have ministered unto me	Phlm 1:13
12	in that ye have ministered to the saints,	Heb 6:10
5	ye have ministered to the saints, and do minister.	6:10
16	not unto themselves, but unto us they did minister	1 Pt 1:12
5	even so minister the same one to another,	4:10
1	if any man minister,	4:11

Classical Greek
This verb member of the *diakon-* word group means chiefly "serve" or (passively) "be served." Not especially common in classical Greek, in its earliest uses *diakoneō* probably did not have any religious connotations and simply meant "to render a service" of any kind. Herodotus has the first-known instance; there it simply means "to wait table" (Beyer, "diakoneō," *Kittel*, 2:82ff.). More general senses include "to care for, provide for," or "to do the work of a servant." *Beyer* notes that in the eyes of the Greek serving was viewed with disdain, and "ruling and not serving is proper to a man . . . " (ibid.). (See word studies on *doulos* [1395], *douleuō* [1392].)

Septuagint Usage
Somewhat surprisingly the Septuagint does not use the verb *diakoneō* at all. Its translators, instead, elected to render Hebrew verbs of service (e.g., '*āvadh*) with *douleō*, *latreuō* (2973), and *leitourgeō* (2982). The nouns *diakonos* (1243) and *diakonia* (1242), however, do appear, although in limited numbers (e.g., Esther 1:10; 2:2; cf. 1 Maccabees 11:58).

New Testament Usage
Slightly over one-half of the instances of *diakoneō* occur in the Gospels. At times the term denotes the kind of "waiting on tables" or "serving" described in its classical usage (e.g., Matthew 8:15; Mark 1:31; Luke 10:40; 17:8). In more general terms, it refers to the kind of "care" that women followers of Jesus provided (e.g., Matthew 27:55; Mark 15:41).

Of more theological significance is the place of "service" in the life of the disciple, which of course is predicated upon Jesus' own model as servant. Jesus himself "did not come to be served (*ouk diakonethēnai*), but to serve (*diakonesai*)" (Matthew 20:28, NIV; Mark 10:45). He was in their midst as a servant (*ho dianonōn*) (Luke 22:26). Jesus invited His followers to serve if they wished to lead (Luke 22:27; cf. John 12:26; cf. Matthew 20:26; Mark 9:35).

Outside of the Gospels the idea of "to wait tables" is seen, most clearly in Acts 6:2 (in this case, money tables as in Matthew 21:12). Gradually "to serve" (*diakoneō*) took on more religious significance. "Service" was directed to the church (Romans 15:25; 2 Corinthians 3:3; Hebrews 6:10; cf. 1 Peter 4:10,11) and individuals (2 Timothy 1:18; Philemon 13). This included tangible support (2 Corinthians 8:19,20). The drift toward associating *diakoneō* with the "office" of deacon is also reflected in some letters (1 Timothy 3:8,10; cf. Philippians 1:1) although the transition would not be complete until later. Paul did not hesitate to describe his ministry as *diakonos*; however, his description was obviously without the later technical and ecclesiastical overtones (Romans 16:1; 1 Corinthians 3:5; 2 Corinthians 3:6; Colossians 1:23; cf. Acts 19:22).

STRONG 1247, BAUER 184, MOULTON-MILLIGAN 149, KITTEL 2:81-87, LIDDELL-SCOTT 398, COLIN BROWN 3:544-48.

1242. διακονία diakonia noun
Service, ministry.

COGNATE:
διακονέω diakoneō (1241)
SYNONYM:
λειτουργία leitourgia (2983)
נַעַר na'ar (5470), Boy, youth; servant (Est 6:5—Codex Alexandrinus only).

1. διακονία diakonia nom sing fem
2. διακονίας diakonias gen sing fem
3. διακονίᾳ diakonia dat sing fem
4. διακονίαν diakonian acc sing fem
5. διακονιῶν diakoniōn gen pl fem

4	But Martha was cumbered about much serving,	Luke 10:40
2	and had obtained part of this ministry.	Acts 1:17
2	he may take part of this ministry and apostleship,	1:25
3	widows were neglected in the daily ministration.	6:1
3	to prayer, and to the ministry of the word.	6:4
4	determined to send relief unto the brethren	11:29
4	when they had fulfilled their ministry,	12:25
4	ministry, which I have received of the Lord Jesus,	20:24
2	had wrought among the Gentiles by his ministry.	21:19
4	the apostle of the Gentiles, I magnify mine office:	Rom 11:13
4	Or ministry, let us wait on our ministering:	12:7
3	Or ministry, let us wait on our ministering:	12:7
1	and that my service which I have for Jerusalem	15:31

5	differences **of administrations**, but the same Lord...	1 Co 12:5
4	addicted themselves to the **ministry** of the saints,......	16:15
1	But if the **ministration** of death,.....................	2 Co 3:7
1	the **ministration** of the spirit be rather glorious?........	3:8
1	For if the **ministration** of condemnation be glory,.......	3:9
1	much more doth the **ministration** of righteousness.......	3:9
4	Therefore seeing we have this **ministry**,................	4:1
4	and hath given to us the **ministry** of reconciliation;.....	5:18
1	that the **ministry** be not blamed:......................	6:3
2	the fellowship of the **ministering** to the saints...........	8:4
2	For as touching the **ministering** to the saints,...........	9:1
1	For the **administration** of this service....................	9:12
2	Whiles by the experiment of this **ministration**...........	9:13
4	taking wages of them, to do you **service**...............	11:8
2	for the work of the **ministry**,.......................	Eph 4:12
4	the **ministry** which thou hast received in the Lord,....	Col 4:17
4	counted me faithful, putting me into the **ministry**;...	1 Tm 1:12
4	make full proof of thy **ministry**.....................	2 Tm 4:5
4	Mark, ... for he is profitable to me for the **ministry**.....	4:11
4	**minister** for them who shall be heirs of salvation?....	Heb 1:14
4	I know thy works, and charity, and **service**,..........	Rev 2:19

Classical Greek

A member of the *diakoneō* (1241)/*diakonos* (1243) word group, *diakonia* is the noun for the activity of "service" which is rendered by a *diakonos* ("servant"). It also denotes the position of a servant. In many Greek circles the idea of service was almost unbearable since service almost always involved submission to another person's will. This opinion is most clearly reflected by the Sophists who believed that a free man should only serve his own interests and wishes. Many felt that service to another contradicted the very intent and goal of life: i.e., the full development and expansion of the individual personality.

Beyer notes that the *diakoneō* word group is distinct from other terms of service (e.g., *douleuō* [1392], *therapeuō* [2300], *latreuō* [2973], *leitourgeō* [2982], *hupereteō*) in that *diakoneō* is a very personal service, often suggesting a "service" of love (Beyer, "diakoneō," *Kittel*, 2:81ff.). Its relative absence in the papyri before the Fourth Century A.D. suggests it was more of a literary term than a popular expression. It may have been understood in a technical sense, which only later was absorbed into common speech (*Moulton-Milligan*).

Septuagint Usage

The Septuagint records *diakonia* only three times, twice in the Book of Esther (6:3,5) and once in the apocryphal 1 Maccabees (11:58). *Diakonos*, the only other member of the word group appearing in the Septuagint, also makes five of its seven appearances in Esther. There, too, both words are always in reference to the *diakonoi*, "servants," of the king who attended him. In the Old Testament the ideas of service and servanthood were not as negative as they were in Greek culture. The commandments which exhorted the Israelites to love the Lord above all else and to love one's neighbor as oneself laid the foundation for a God-directed life-style characterized by service. While the title "servant" did reflect a position of inferiority, at the same time it can be seen as a title of honor. For example, the greatest men in the history of Israel—Abraham, Jacob, Moses, David, Elijah, etc.—are called "servants" of the Lord. Even more notably, the Messiah is referred to as the *Servant* of the Lord (cf. Isaiah 42–53, the Servant Songs).

The Maccabean usage links *diakonia* to "table vessels of gold" (Beyer, "diakonia," *Kittel*, 2:87) which the Revised Standard Version translates as a "table service." This reflects the relationship to *diakoneō* which in secular Greek primarily meant "to wait, to serve at table" (e.g., Josephus, *Antiquities* 2.12.1; 11.5.6, both times of service to a king). However, it could also mean "to provide or care for" in a general sense (Beyer, *Kittel*, 2:82).

New Testament Usage

New Testament usage evolves out of the Greek understanding of the term, but it adopts a positive attitude toward *diakonia* in contrast to the Greek notion that "service" was not dignified (ibid.). In Christianity *diakonia* becomes the central attitude toward life. No longer is service something to be despised.

The teaching of Jesus concerning service parallels the positive elements of the term as it was understood in the Old Testament, particularly in His exhortations to serve God and neighbor. By His own example Jesus modeled a life-style of service for others. The Greek culture of the day thought it unimaginable to live in such a way. They were more concerned with the endless pursuit for wisdom and self-realization. The very characteristics of the life of Christ represent a total contrast to this still popular ideology. Matthew 20:28 states, "The Son of man came not to be ministered unto, but to minister, and to give his life a ransom for many." This type of *self*-abandonment is a required element of every Christian's life. The challenge to Christ's followers is, "We ought to lay down our lives for the brethren" (1 John 3:16).

Of its 35 appearances in the New Testament, *diakonia* occurs only once in the third Gospel (Luke 10:40). Martha, to her detriment, was more anxious about *diakonia*—preparing the meal—than listening to her Master. This follows the normal secular usage which linked *diakonia* to table service. This understanding is repeated in Acts 6:2: "It is not right that we (the apostles) should give up preaching the word of God to serve tables (*diakonein trapezais*)" (RSV). The apostles recognized that the "service" (*diakonia*) of the Word and prayer must take precedence (6:4, the play on the word is obvious in the Greek) over the distribution of food.

The notion of "providing for" or "supporting" (tangibly) was also common in secular Greek. That meaning was also employed by the New Testament writers. This is probably more the intent of its use in Acts 6:1 (see above), and in Acts 11:29 the sense of "relief" (RSV) captures the idea of "provision" (cf. Acts 12:25, "mission" [RSV]; Romans 12:7; 1 Corinthians 16:15; 2 Corinthians 8:4; 9:1,12,13; Revelation 2:19). *Diakonia* in this sense was especially directed to fellow Christians in need.

The former covenant of the written code kills (2 Corinthians 3:6); it was a "ministration (*diakonia*) of death" (2 Corinthians 3:7). But the "ministry" (*diakonia*) of the Spirit, through which Paul had been enabled to become a "servant" (*diakonos*, 3:6), is life (*to de pneuma zōopoiei*).

Diakonia also acquired the somewhat technical sense in early Christianity of "the ministry of the gospel"—the role of the apostle (see Romans 11:13; 15:31; cf. Acts 20:24; 21:19). *Diakonia* may describe the "service" of the apostle or the prophet and others but not the "office" (despite Philippians 1:1). Its resistance to becoming a technical term is evidenced by its use in connection with many figures in the Church in early Christianity.

Diakonia is *not* the job description of the deacon (*diakonos*) (cf. 1 Timothy 1:12 where Paul applied it to himself as apostle) until later when deacon became an office in the church (Ignatius *To the Magnesians* 6:1; *To the Philadelphians* 10:2; Shepherd of Hermas *Similitude* 9.26.2). However, it would be erroneous to conclude *diakonia* exclusively referred to the activity of the deacon since it is also applied to other church officials (Ignatius *To the Philadelphians* 1:1; 10:2; *To the Smyrnaeans* 12:1).

At its heart the gospel summons every disciple to *diakonia*. Service must first and foremost be service to God. As His servants we are to offer ministry to His body (Ephesians 4:12). Thus, we note the charismatic gifts are *diakoniai* (1 Corinthians 12:5), performed on behalf of the Body as a whole. *Diakonia* expresses itself also in tangible acts of love—the sharing of food and sustenance, money, and possessions—not only within the Body but without, to other churches (Acts 11:29). The subjects of the kingdom of God are servants, just as their King is a servant (Luke 22:26ff.) to the purposes of His Father. "He that is greatest among you, let him be as the younger; and he that is chief, as he that doth serve. For whether is greater, he that sitteth at meat, or he that serveth? is not he that sitteth at meat? but I am among you as he that serveth" (Luke 22:26,27).

Strong 1248, Bauer 184, Moulton-Milligan 149, Kittel 2:87-88, Liddell-Scott 398, Colin Brown 3:544-48.

1243. διάκονος diakonos noun
Servant, waiter, deacon.

Cognate:
διακονέω diakoneō (1241)
Synonyms:
βοηθός boēthos (991)
θεράπων therapōn (2301)
λειτουργός leitourgos (2985)
συνεργός sunergos (4754)
ὑπηρέτης hupēretēs (5095)

נַעַר na'ar (5470), Boy, youth; attendant (Est 6:5).
שָׁרַת shārath (8664), Piel: serve (Est 1:10).

1. **διάκονος** diakonos nom sing masc
2. **διάκονον** diakonon acc sing masc
3. **διάκονοι** diakonoi nom pl masc
4. **διακόνοις** diakonois dat pl masc
5. **διακόνους** diakonous acc pl masc
6. **διακόνου** diakonou gen sing fem

1 will be great among you, let him be your **minister**;	Matt 20:26
4 Then said the king to the **servants**,	22:13
1 he that is greatest among you shall be your **servant**.	23:11
1 the same shall be last of all, and **servant** of all.	Mark 9:35
1 will be great among you, shall be your **minister**:	10:43
4 His mother saith unto the **servants**,	John 2:5
3 but the **servants** which drew the water knew;	2:9
1 and where I am, there shall also my **servant** be:	12:26
1 For he is the **minister** of God to thee for good.	Rom 13:4
1 for he is the **minister** of God,	13:4
2 a **minister** of the circumcision for the truth of God,	15:8
2 is a **servant** of the church which is at Cenchrea:	16:1
6 be glory through Jesus Christ for ever. Amen.	16:27
3 is Apollos, but **ministers** by whom ye believed,	1 Co 3:5
5 hath made us able **ministers** of the new testament;	2 Co 3:6
3 approving ourselves as the **ministers** of God,	6:4
3 no great thing if his **ministers** also be transformed	11:15
3 be transformed as the **ministers** of righteousness;	11:15
3 Are they **ministers** of Christ?	11:23
1 is therefore Christ the **minister** of sin? God forbid.	Gal 2:17
1 Whereof I was made a **minister**,	Eph 3:7

1 beloved brother and faithful **minister** in the Lord,	Eph 6:21
4 to all the saints ... with the bishops and **deacons**:	Phlp 1:1
1 who is for you a faithful **minister** of Christ;	Col 1:7
1 whereof I Paul am made a **minister**;	1:23
1 Whereof I am made a **minister**,	1:25
1 a faithful **minister** and fellowservant in the Lord:	4:7
2 sent Timotheus, our brother, and **minister** of God,	1 Th 3:2
5 Likewise must the **deacons** be grave,	1 Tm 3:8
3 Let the **deacons** be the husbands of one wife,	3:12
1 thou shalt be a good **minister** of Jesus Christ,	4:6

Classical Greek

The secular use of *diakonos* in Greek literature follows the pattern established by the verb *diakoneō* (1241) (cf. *diakonia* [1242]). The *diakonos* was essentially one who "waited at table," but the *diakonos* performed a wide range of duties including those of a "baker, messenger, (of a woman) maid, cook, etc." (see Beyer, "diakonos," *Kittel*, 2:91, for the primary references).

In all likelihood the term was used in association with religious duties. Moulton-Milligan points to a "college" of *diakonoi* who were overseen by a priest (*hiereus* [2385]) in the cult of Serapis and Isis. Josephus used *diakonos* in reference to a servant of God, but not in any technical sense (*Wars of the Jews* 3.8.3). It seems unlikely, though, that the New Testament developed its understanding of *diakonos* in compliance with any of these religious uses; rather, the New Testament concept of servanthood evolved directly from Jesus' own model as the servant of God (e.g., Luke 22:26ff.).

Septuagint Usage

The uses of *diakonos* in the Septuagint are restricted to Esther, Proverbs, and 4 Maccabees. In Esther *diakonoi* is a versional variant at 6:3,5, which otherwise read *diakonia*. In Esther 1:10 and 2:2 (as in 6:3,5) *diakonos* is the king's "attendant." The Hebrew behind *diakonos* is *na'ar* and *sharath* in Esther. *Diakonos* is a term of derogation in 4 Maccabees 9:17 ("you abominable *lackeys*," RSV). This recalls the Greek notion that "to serve" was degrading.

New Testament Usage

New Testament usage patterns itself to some degree after common Greek use. A *diakonos* was an "attendant, servant" (of a king, Matthew 22:13). *Diakonoi* were "servants" at the marriage at Cana (John 2:5,9). But far more crucial to the New Testament is the idea that the "servant" is the disciple who models servanthood of his or her Lord (e.g., Matthew 20:26; 23:11; John 12:26).

From the basis of Jesus' own model, "serving" became the means of proclaiming the gospel. "Servants" proclaimed the word to elicit faith and to encourage the saints (1 Corinthians 3:5; 2 Corinthians 3:6; Ephesians 3:7; Colossians 1:7,23,25; 1 Thessalonians 3:2). "Service" is also expressed in enduring hardship, just as God's Servant did on behalf of His people (2 Corinthians 6:4ff.).

Evidently Paul referred to an established group of *diakonoi* in Philippi (Philippians 1:1). It is probably a general term for workers in the "ministry" (as in Ephesians 6:21; Colossians 4:7; 1 Timothy 4:6). Paul's application of *diakonos* to Timothy (1 Timothy 4:6)—who was also a preacher and teacher (1 Timothy 4:13,14) and evangelist (2 Timothy 4:5)—suggests the term was flexible and not nearly so technical as some would imagine.

By the time of Ignatius (ca. A.D. 110) and Clement of Rome (ca. A.D. 90–100) *diakonos* did carry a more restricted, technical sense (see 1 Clement 42:4,5; Ignatius *To the Ephesians* 2:1; *To the Magnesians* 6:1).

As to the question in Romans 16:1 of whether or not Phoebe was a "deaconess," the answer is most certainly, "yes." The forms (masculine and feminine) of *diakonos* would be identical here, but the grammar and common sense suggest that *diakonos* was referring to Phoebe. The *real* question, however, is does "deaconess" here carry any kind of technical sense? The answer to that, as we have seen, is probably "no." It was only in the later church that *diakonos* became a technical term for a church office, at least later than Romans.

STRONG 1249, BAUER 184-85, MOULTON-MILLIGAN 149, KITTEL 2:88-93, LIDDELL-SCOTT 398, COLIN BROWN 3:544-46,548-49.

1244. διακόσιοι diakosioi num

Two hundred.

1. **διακοσίων** diakosiōn card gen masc
2. **διακοσίους** diakosious card acc masc
3. **διακόσιαι** diakosiai card nom fem
4. **διακοσίας** diakosias card acc fem

1 go and buy **two hundred** pennyworth of bread,	Mark 6:37
1 **Two hundred** pennyworth of bread	John 6:7
1 but as it were **two hundred** cubits,	21:8
2 Make ready **two hundred** soldiers	Acts 23:23
2 and horsemen ... and spearmen **two hundred**,	23:23
3 **two hundred** threescore and sixteen souls.	27:37
4 a thousand **two hundred** and threescore days,	Rev 11:3
4 a thousand **two hundred** and threescore days.	12:6

This is a term used eight times in the New Testament, occurring in four different books. It comes from *dis* (1357A) meaning "twice" and *hekaton* (1526) meaning "hundred." See Mark 6:37; John 6:7; 21:8 for examples of its use.
STRONG 1250, BAUER 185, LIDDELL-SCOTT 398.

1245. διακούω diakouō verb
Give (someone) a hearing.
COGNATE:
  ἀκούω akouō (189)
SYNONYMS:
  ἀκούω akouō (189)
  εἰσακούω eisakouō (1508)
  ἐνωτίζομαι enōtizomai (1785)
  ἐπακούω epakouō (1858)
  ἐπακροάομαι epakroaomai (1859)
  ὑπακούω hupakouō (5057)

שָׁמַע shāmaʿ (8471), Hear (Dt 1:16).

1. διακούσομαι diakousomai 1sing indic fut mid

1 I will hear thee, said he,....................Acts 23:35

This term is used only once in the New Testament, occurring at Acts 23:35. It can be translated "hear throughout, give (someone) a hearing, listen patiently." *Diakouō* comes from *dia* (1217), denoting the channel of an act, and *akouō* (189), meaning "hear, understand." In Acts 23:35 Felix told Paul that when his accusers arrived in Caesarea from Jerusalem, "I (Felix) will *hear* thee," i.e., give a formal hearing of the charges against Paul as well as his defense.
STRONG 1251, BAUER 185, MOULTON-MILLIGAN 150, LIDDELL-SCOTT 399.

1246. διακρίνω diakrinō verb
Make a distinction, decide, judge, dispute, doubt.
COGNATES:
  ἀδιάκριτος adiakritos (86)
  διάκρισις diakrisis (1247)
  κρίνω krinō (2892)
SYNONYMS:
  ἀνακρίνω anakrinō (348)
  ἀποδιορίζω apodiorizō (587)
  ἀποχωρίζω apochōrizō (667)
  διαχωρίζω diachōrizō (1310)
  κρίνω krinō (2892)
  μερίζω merizō (3177)
  συζητέω suzēteō (4653)
  σχίζω schizō (4829)
  χωρίζω chōrizō (5398)

בָּחַן bāchan (1010), Test, try (Jb 12:11, 23:10).

בָּחַר bāchar (1013), Choose (Jb 9:14—Codex Alexandrinus only).
בָּרַר bārar (1331), Test (Eccl 3:18).
דִּין dîn (1833), Defend (Prv 31:9, Zec 3:7 [3:8]).
מָדוֹן mādhôn (4209II) Contend (Jer 15:10).
מִשְׁפָּט mishpāṭ (5122), Dispute (Ez 44:24).
פָּרַשׁ pārash (6817), Inform precisely (Lv 24:12).
רִיב rîv (7662), Defend, conduct a lawsuit (Dt 33:7).
שָׁפַט shāphaṭ (8570), Qal: decide, judge (Ex 18:16, 1 Kgs 3:9, Jl 3:12); niphal: enter into controversy or judgment (Ez 20:35,36, Jl 3:2).

1. διακρίνει diakrinei 3sing indic pres act
2. διακρινέτωσαν diakrinetōsan 3pl impr pres act
3. διακρίνων diakrinōn nom sing masc part pres act
4. διακρίνειν diakrinein inf pres act
5. διέκρινεν diekrinen 3sing indic aor act
6. διακρῖναι diakrinai inf aor act
7. διεκρίνομεν diekrinomen 1pl indic imperf act
8. διακρινόμενος diakrinomenos
  nom sing masc part pres mid
9. διακρινόμενον diakrinomenon
  acc sing masc part pres mid
10. διακρινόμενοι diakrinomenoi
  nom pl masc part pres mid
11. διεκρίθη diekrithē 3sing indic aor pass
12. διεκρίθητε diekrithēte 2pl indic aor pass
13. διακριθῆτε diakrithēte 2pl subj aor pass
14. διακριθῇ diakrithē 3sing subj aor pass
15. διεκρίνοντο diekrinonto 3pl indic imperf mid
16. διακρίναντα diakrinanta
  nom/acc sing/pl masc/neu part pres mid
17. διακρινομένους diakrinomenous
  acc pl masc part pres mid

4 O ye hypocrites, ye can **discern** the face of the ....Matt 16:3
13 If ye have faith, and **doubt** not, ... 21:21
14 and **shall** not **doubt** in his heart, but shall believe Mark 11:23
8 **doubting** nothing: for I have sent them............Acts 10:20
15 they ... of the circumcision **contended** with him,...... 11:2
9 Spirit bade me go with them, nothing **doubting**...... 11:12
16 Spirit bade me go with them, nothing **doubting**..... 11:12
5 And put no **difference** between us and them,........ 15:9
11 He **staggered** not at the promise of God...........Rom 4:20
8 And he that **doubteth** is damned if he eat,.......... 14:23
1 For who **maketh** thee to **differ** from another?...... 1 Co 4:7
6 that shall be able **to judge** between his brethren?...... 6:5
3 not **discerning** the Lord's body...................... 11:29
7 For if we **would judge** ourselves, ... not be judged..... 11:31
2 speak two or three, and let the other **judge**.......... 14:29
8 But let him ask in faith, nothing **wavering**.........Jas 1:6
8 For he that **wavereth** is like a wave of the sea......... 1:6
12 Are ye not then **partial** in yourselves, ... 2:4
8 Michael ... he **disputed** about the body of Moses,...Jude 1:9
10 of some have compassion, **making a difference**:........ 1:22
17 have mercy on some, who are doubting (NASB)........ 1:22

Classical Greek
Diakrinō is one of the many *krinō*- compounds found in Greek (e.g., *anakrinō* [348], *katakrinō* [2602]). It is formed from *dia* (1217) and *krinō* (2892) and literally means "I judge through." Originally the *dia* intensified the *krinō* stem,

and the term meant "to (spatially) separate one item from another" (Buchsel, "diakrinō," *Kittel,* 3:946). Passively it could mean "to be dissolved." The meaning found in the New Testament, "to doubt," is unknown in ancient Greek. Gradually the original sense of "to separate" (spatially) disappeared. *Diakrinō* also acquired the figurative sense of "to distinguish"; finally, it means "to judge" or "to decide" (see *Liddell-Scott*).

The papyri suggest that the figurative sense came to dominate in popular use. *Diakrinō* occurs in judicial decisions and in documents which refer to the process of making a decision either through examination or testing (see *Moulton-Milligan*).

Septuagint Usage
The Septuagint translators found *diakrinō* useful for translating eight Hebrew terms, but two—*dîn* ("to judge") and *shāphaṭ* ("to judge or govern")—dominate. Many passages reflect *diakrinō's* legal overtones (Exodus 18:16; 1 Chronicles 26:29; Job 9:33f.; Psalm 50:4 [LXX 49:4]) as well as its simple meaning of "choice" and "discernment" (Job 9:14; 12:11).

New Testament Usage
The New Testament shares the heritage of secular Greek in its understanding of *diakrinō*. In many cases it means "to discern, to judge," or "to make distinction." Jesus argued that His opponents could "discern" the signs of the heavens, but they could not judge correctly or interpret the signs of the times (Matthew 16:3).

The idea of "to make a distinction" (cf. the English word *discriminate*) is also prevalent. No "distinction" was made between the Gentile and the Jewish believers (Acts 11:12; cf. 1 Corinthians 4:7; 4 Maccabees 1:14).

A peculiar use of *diakrinō* (in a middle form) meaning "to doubt" appears in the New Testament several times. James exemplified this use when he reminded his audience that prayers are to be asked "in faith", nothing wavering (*en pistei mēden diakrinomenos*). For the one doubting (*ho diakrinomenos*) "is like a wave of the sea driven with the wind and tossed" (James 1:6). This same understanding of *diakrinō* recurs in Matthew 21:21 (of faith, prayer; parallel Mark 11:23); Romans 4:20 (of Abraham's faith); Romans 14:23; and Jude 22.

STRONG 1252, BAUER 185, MOULTON-MILLIGAN 150, KITTEL 3:946-49, LIDDELL-SCOTT 399, COLIN BROWN 1:503-5.

1247. διάκρισις diakrisis noun
Judicial differentiation, distinction.

COGNATE:
διακρίνω diakrinō (1246)

SYNONYMS:
διαλογισμός dialogismos (1255)
συζήτησις suzētēsis (4654)

מִפְלָשׂ miphlās (4819), Hanging clouds, cloud layers (Jb 37:16).

1. **διάκρισιν** diakrisin acc sing fem
2. **διακρίσεις** diakriseis nom/acc pl fem

2 but not to **doubtful** disputations.		Rom 14:1
2 to another **discerning** of spirits;		1 Co 12:10
1 senses exercised to **discern** both good and evil.		Heb 5:14

Classical Greek
The word *diakrisis* is a noun form of the verb *diakrinō* (1246) which means "to differentiate, discern, and assess" in the sense of judgment or judging through with the goal of rendering an impartial decision. It also carries with it the understanding of "separation" and "division." Within this context the classical usage of *diakrisis* (the noun form) picks up the idea of "separation" and "division" together with such additional meanings as "quarrel" and "struggle." It is also used in a special way to describe an interval.

Septuagint Usage
In the Septuagint the verb form *diakrinō* essentially means "to make a distinction, examine, choose, and render judgment" in the sense of dispensing justice. In this regard, the noun form *diakrisis* is found only once in the Septuagint in Job 37:16 where it is used in a rather unique translation of the statement, "Do you know about the layers of the thick clouds?" It is thought by some scholars that a parallel usage is found in Matthew 16:13 with regard to understanding Christ's divine identity, but this is open to question.

New Testament Usage
In the New Testament *diakrisis* essentially means the "differentiation" between good and bad (Hebrews 5:14) and the "discerning" of spirits (1 Corinthians 12:10). In the Corinthian passage the word is used to describe one of the gifts or enablements of the Spirit and implies the supernatural power of spiritual insight to detect and expose satanic strategies and demonic activities. It also carries the meaning of "quarrel" in Romans 14:1.

STRONG 1253, BAUER 185, MOULTON-MILLIGAN 150, KITTEL 3:949-50, LIDDELL-SCOTT 399, COLIN BROWN 1:503-4.

1248. διακωλύω diakōluō verb
Prevent, hinder.
COGNATE:
κωλύω kōluō (2940)
SYNONYMS:
ἀνακόπτω anakoptō (346)
ἐγκόπτω enkoptō (1458)
κατέχω katechō (2692)
κωλύω kōluō (2940)

1. διεκώλυεν diekōluen 3sing indic imperf act

1 But John forbad him, saying,......................Matt 3:14

This is a term occurring only once in the New Testament. It can be translated "prevent, prohibit, forbid." The word comes from *dia* (1217), denoting the channel of an act, and *kōluō* (2940), "hinder, prevent, keep from." The *dia* gives it an intensive meaning. In Matthew 3:14 John the Baptist, having recognized Jesus as the promised Messiah, tried to prevent the Lord from being baptized by him. John felt a need to be baptized by Jesus.

STRONG 1254, BAUER 185, MOULTON-MILLIGAN 150, LIDDELL-SCOTT 400.

1249. διαλαλέω dialaleō verb
Discuss, converse together.
CROSS-REFERENCE:
λαλέω laleō (2953)

1. διελάλουν dielaloun 3pl indic imperf act
2. διελαλεῖτο dielaleito 3sing indic imperf pass

2 and all these sayings **were noised abroad** .... Luke 1:65
1 **communed** one with another what they might do 6:11

This term has a variety of meanings. In its active voice it can be translated "discuss, talk with, commune." In the passive voice, "to noise abroad, talk about, be talked of everywhere." *Dialaleō* is a compound verb from *laleō* (2953), "to speak," and *dia* (1217), which means here "by turns." Robertson (*Word Pictures in the New Testament*, 2:18) defines its active form as "continuous talk back and forth between people."

STRONG 1255, BAUER 185, MOULTON-MILLIGAN 150, LIDDELL-SCOTT 400.

1250. διαλέγομαι dialegomai verb
Discuss, reason, dispute, say thoroughly.
COGNATE:
λέγω legō (2978)
SYNONYMS:
ἀναγγέλλω anangellō (310)
ἀνατίθημι anatithēmi (392)
ἀπαγγέλλω apangellō (514)
ἀποδείκνυμι apodeiknumi (579)
ἀποκρίνω apokrinō (605B)
διαλογίζομαι dialogizomai (1254)
ἐρεύγομαι ereugomai (2027)
καταγγέλλω katangellō (2576)
κηρύσσω kērussō (2756)
λαλέω laleō (2953)
λέγω legō (2978)
ὁμιλέω homileō (3519)
συζητέω suzēteō (4653)
φθέγγομαι phthengomai (5187)
φωνέω phōneō (5291)

דָּבַר dāvar (1744), Piel: speak (Ex 6:27, Is 63:1).
רִיב rîv (7662), Contend (Jgs 8:1).
שָׁעָה shāʿâh (8541), Look at favorably (Sir 14:20).

1. διαλέγεται dialegetai 3sing indic pres mid
2. διαλεγόμενος dialegomenos nom sing masc part pres mid
3. διαλεγομένου dialegomenou gen sing masc part pres mid
4. διαλεγόμενον dialegomenon acc sing masc part pres mid
5. διελέχθη dielechthē 3sing indic aor pass
6. διελέχθησαν dielechthēsan 3pl indic aor pass
7. διελέγετο dielegeto 3sing indic imperf mid
8. διελέξατο dielexato 3sing indic aor mid

6 held their peace: for by the way they **had disputed** .. Mark 9:34
7 and three sabbath days **reasoned** with them .... Acts 17:2
8 and three sabbath days **reasoned** with them 17:2
7 **disputed** he in the synagogue with the Jews, ... 17:17
7 And he **reasoned** in the synagogue every sabbath, ... 18:4
5 into the synagogue, and **reasoned** with the Jews....... 18:19
8 into the synagogue, and **reasoned** with the Jews....... 18:19
2 **disputing** and persuading the things concerning 19:8
2 **disputing** daily in the school of one Tyrannus.......... 19:9
7 Paul **preached** unto them, ... 20:7
3 Paul was long **preaching**, he sunk down with sleep, ... 20:9
4 they neither found me ... **disputing** with any man, ... 24:12
3 And as he **reasoned** of righteousness, ... 24:25
1 ye have forgotten the exhortation which **speaketh** ... Heb 12:5
7 Michael ... he **disputed** about the body of Moses, ... Jude 1:9

In general the Greek word *dialegomai* means "to think about certain things from a number of different perspectives." It is to ponder, intellectually weigh, or revolve the different aspects of an idea in the mind.

Classical Greek
Developmentally the word has its roots in the classical Greek concept of conversing together or discussing ideas in general verbal interaction. However, in Socrates, Plato, and Aristotle the process became more refined in striving to persuade someone or to establish an idea by pure thought or dialectic interaction. Finally in Polybius (a Greek historian of third- and second-century Rome) it came to be predominantly used for the art of conferring, negotiating, or presenting an idea as in an address or speech.

Septuagint Usage

In the Septuagint the word's essential meaning is much like its classical derivation: "to speak or communicate verbally." On occasion the word is used in the sense of teaching or contending with someone. In general, however, the Septuagint usage denotes regular conversation along with some references to the idea of God speaking with others (Isaiah 63:1). In only one instance is the sense of disputation or controversial discussion portrayed (Schrenk, "dialogeomai," *Kittel*, 2:94; Josephus *Antiquities* 7.11.6).

New Testament Usage

From the New Testament standpoint *dialegomai* finds its meaning in the sphere of the revelation of God. In this sense there is no philosophical dialogue to reach an idea. There is no process of thesis and antithesis with subsequent interaction to arrive at synthesis. Rather, God speaks and reveals His Word which calls for obedience and full acceptance of His will spoken in His Word.

Thus, in Hebrews 12:5 God speaks words of encouragement in the intimacy of a familial relationship, and in the Book of Acts (17:2,17; 18:4,19; 19:9; 20:7,9; 24:12) Paul delivered spiritual sermons expounding the revelation of God rather than posing the propositions of Greek philosophy. In these passages it was not a question of information for disputation, contention, or debate but revelation for consideration, perception, assimilation, and action. The listeners were to weigh the evidence intellectually regarding the appropriate response.

Only in Mark 9:34 is there the issue of argument and dispute as the disciples contended with one another over the question, "Who is the greatest?"

STRONG 1256, BAUER 185, MOULTON-MILLIGAN 150, KITTEL 2:93-95, LIDDELL-SCOTT 400 (see "dialegō"), COLIN BROWN 3:820-21.

1251. διαλείπω dialeipō verb

Pause, stop in the middle.

COGNATE:
λείπω leipō (2981)

SYNONYMS:
ἀνίημι aniēmi (445)
ἡσυχάζω hēsuchazō (2248)
καταλύω kataluō (2617)
καταπαύω katapauō (2634)
κοπάζω kopazō (2841)
παύω pauō (3835)

דָּמָה dāmâh (1880), Come to the end, cease (Jer 14:17).

חָדַל chādhal (2403), Stop (1 Kgs 15:21).
יָחַל yāchal (3282), Hiphil: wait (1 Sm 10:8).
מוּשׁ mûsh (4318), Fail (Jer 17:8).
מָנַע mānaʿ (4661), Restrain (Jer 31:16 [38:16]).
שׁוּב shûv (8178), Repent (Jer 8:6).
שָׁלָה shālâh (8347), Have quiet, be quiet; niphal: be negligent (2 Chr 29:11).

1. **διέλιπεν** dielipen 3sing indic aor act
2. **διέλειπεν** dieleipen 3sing indic imperf act

1 since ... I came in hath not **ceased** to kiss my feet... Luke 7:45
2 since ... I came in hath not **ceased** to kiss my feet....... 7:45

This compound verb, comprised of *dia* (1217), "between," and *leipō* (2981), "leave," means "to stop" or "to cease." When used as a medical term it means "to be intermittent" and "to discontinue giving remedies for a time." The interval left can refer to space or time. In the New Testament *dialeipō* is used only in Luke 7:45 where the woman who washed the feet of Jesus with her tears did not "cease" to kiss her Master's feet (an act of worship and repentance).

STRONG 1257, BAUER 185, MOULTON-MILLIGAN 150, LIDDELL-SCOTT 401, COLIN BROWN 3:247-48,251.

1252. διάλεκτος dialektos noun

Language, dialect.

CROSS-REFERENCE:
λέγω legō (2978)

לָשׁוֹן lāshôn (4098), Language (Dn 1:4).

1. **διαλέκτῳ** dialektō dat sing fem

1 in their proper **tongue**, Aceldama, ... field of blood. Acts 1:19
1 every man heard them speak in his own **language**....... 2:6
1 And how hear we every man in our own **tongue**,....... 2:8
1 he spake unto them in the Hebrew **tongue**, saying,..... 21:40
1 heard that he spake in the Hebrew **tongue** to them,.... 22:2
1 and saying in the Hebrew **tongue**, Saul, Saul,.......... 26:14

This term can refer to the language of a country or nation (*glōssa* [1094] is used more often) but usually refers to the specific dialect of a region or special district within a nation. It is used in the New Testament only by Luke primarily in connection with the various visitors on the Day of Pentecost (Acts 2:6,8) and with Paul's preaching to the people of Jerusalem (Acts 21:40; 22:2).

STRONG 1258, BAUER 185, MOULTON-MILLIGAN 150-51, LIDDELL-SCOTT 401.

1253. διαλλάσσομαι diallassomai verb

Reconcile, change the mind of.

CROSS-REFERENCE:
ἀλλάσσω allassō (234)

διαλογίζομαι 1254

סוּר sûr (5681), Turn aside; hiphil: take away, send away (Jb 12:20,24).

פָּרַר pārar (6815), Hiphil: thwart (Jb 5:12).

רָצָה rātsâh (7813), Be pleased with; hithpael: make oneself acceptable (1 Sm 29:4).

שׁוּב shûv (8178), Return, turn; hiphil: bring back (Jgs 19:3—Codex Alexandrinus only).

1. διαλλάγηθι diallagēthi 2sing impr aor pass

1 and go thy way; first **be reconciled** to thy brother, ... Matt 5:24

Diallassomai has a wide variety of meaning including "to alter or exchange, to distinguish oneself," and "to reconcile." Found in the New Testament only in Matthew 5:24, it is in the aorist tense, passive voice, second person. It means "become reconciled" and denotes mutual concession after mutual hostility, i.e., to see to it that the offended brother renounces his anger, chooses to alter his attitude, and exchanges his hostility for peace. *Katallassō* (2614), which also means "to change, exchange, reconcile," refers to the kind of reconciliation in which the hostility and enmity is all man's; he needs to be reconciled to God, not God to him (see 2 Corinthians 5:18-20).

STRONG 1259, BAUER 186, MOULTON-MILLIGAN 151 (see "diallassō"), KITTEL 1:253-54 (see "diallassō"), LIDDELL-SCOTT 401-2 (see "diallassō"), COLIN BROWN 3:166-67,173.

1254. διαλογίζομαι dialogizomai verb

Consider, ponder thoroughly, reason, deliberate.

COGNATES:
 διαλογισμός dialogismos (1255)
 λέγω legō (2978)

SYNONYMS:
 ἀναλογίζω analogizō (355)
 βλέπω blepō (984)
 βουλεύομαι bouleuomai (1003)
 διαλέγομαι dialegomai (1250)
 δοκέω dokeō (1374)
 εἶδον eidon (1481)
 ἐνθυμέομαι enthumeomai (1744)
 ἐπιβλέπω epiblepō (1899)
 ἔχω echō (2174)
 ἡγέομαι hēgeomai (2216)
 κατανοέω katanoeō (2627)
 κρίνω krinō (2892)
 λογίζομαι logizomai (3023)
 νοέω noeō (3401)
 νομίζω nomizō (3406)
 οἴομαι oiomai (3496)
 συζητέω suzēteō (4653)
 συμβάλλω sumballō (4671)
 συμβουλεύω sumbouleuō (4674)
 ὑπολαμβάνω hupolambanō (5112)
 φρονέω phroneō (5262)

זָמַם zemām (2247), Plan (Ps 140:8 [139:8]).

חָשַׁב chāshav (2913), Qal: devise (Ps 10:2 [9:23]); piel: consider (Ps 77:5 [76:5]).

1. διαλογίζεσθε dialogizesthe 2pl indic pres mid
2. διαλογίζονται dialogizontai 3pl indic pres mid
3. διαλογιζόμενοι dialogizomenoi
  nom pl masc part pres mid
4. διαλογιζομένων dialogizomenōn
  gen pl masc part pres mid
5. διαλογίζεσθαι dialogizesthai inf pres mid
6. διελογίζετο dielogizeto 3sing indic imperf mid
7. διελογίζεσθε dielogizesthe 2pl indic imperf mid
8. διελογίζοντο dielogizonto 3pl indic imperf mid

8 And they **reasoned** among themselves, saying, ... Matt 16:7
1 ye of little faith, why **reason** ye among yourselves, ... 16:8
8 And they **reasoned** with themselves, saying, ... 21:25
3 of the scribes ... and **reasoning** in their hearts, ... Mark 2:6
2 that they so **reasoned** within themselves, ... 2:8
1 Why **reason** ye these things in your hearts? 2:8
8 And they **reasoned** among themselves, saying, ... 8:16
1 Why **reason** ye, because ye have no bread? 8:17
7 What was it that ye **disputed** among yourselves 9:33
8 they began **reasoning** with one another (NASB) 11:31
6 and **cast** in her **mind** what manner of salutation ..... Luke 1:29
4 and all men **mused** in their hearts of John, ... 3:15
5 And the scribes and the Pharisees began **to reason**, ... 5:21
1 What **reason** ye in your hearts? 5:22
6 he **thought** within himself, saying, What shall I do, ... 12:17
8 **reasoned** among themselves, ... This is the heir: 20:14
1 Nor **consider** that it is expedient for us, ... John 11:50

Classical Greek

This deponent verb (a verb with a middle form but an active sense) is a compound from *dia* (1217), "through," and *logizomai* (3023), "reckon, count, compute," and essentially means "consider, reason, discuss" in classical Greek. In addition, it still reflects the heritage of its parent verb *logizomai* and under many circumstances has the technical meaning "balance accounts." In later papyri *dialogizomai* could function as a legal term meaning "hold an inquiry." The purpose of such an investigation was to review financial or administrative services (Schrenk, "dialogizomai," *Kittel*, 2:95; *Liddell-Scott*).

Septuagint Usage

Since few of the manuscripts of the Septuagint agree on when and where *dialogizomai* should be read, it is difficult to be specific about its usage. If one assumes every appearance as genuine then there are 16 occurrences. In every case but one (Psalm 140:8 [LXX 139:8]) the Hebrew behind it is *chāshav*, "be reckoned" (niphal) or "consider, plan" (piel).

Shimei requested that David "not reckon" him guilty of his past wrongdoings (2 Samuel 19:19 [LXX 2 Kings 19:19]). Similarly, Judas Maccabaeus' act of providing for a sin offering was praiseworthy, for it "took into account" the resurrection (2 Maccabees 12:43). A dominant idea of mental "reasoning" or "devising," especially in the sense of evil scheming, is recurrent in the Psalms (Psalms 10:2 [LXX 9:22]; 21:11 [20:11]; 35:20 [34:20]; 36:4 [35:4]; 140:8 [139:8]). More positively the Psalmist "considers" his ways and turns to God (119:59 [LXX 118:59]). God also "plans" the defeat and destruction of Babylon (Jeremiah 50:45).

New Testament Usage
The Gospels use the verb *dialogizomai* (cf. the noun *dialogismos* [1255]) most often to convey the idea of "consider, discuss, ponder." Thus it is used of the disciples' discussion of Jesus' comment about the yeast of the Pharisees and Sadducees (Matthew 16:7,8; Mark 8:16,17). Luke used it when he wrote of Mary's consideration of the greeting of the angel (Luke 1:29), but he also used it of the scribes and Pharisees as they were "thinking to themselves" about Jesus' claims and identity (Luke 5:21,22; cf. 20:14). Thus in the New Testament *dialogizomai* moves from mere cognitive "thinking" to verbal "discussion" in many instances (e.g., Mark 8:16; Luke 20:14, all used with *pros* [4172B], "to, with," rather than *en* [1706], "in").

STRONG 1260, BAUER 186, MOULTON-MILLIGAN 151, KITTEL 2:95-96, LIDDELL-SCOTT 402, COLIN BROWN 3:820.

1255. διαλογισμός dialogismos noun
Thought, inward reasoning, doubt, questioning.
COGNATE:
διαλογίζομαι dialogizomai (1254)
SYNONYMS:
γνώμη gnōmē (1100)
διάκρισις diakrisis (1247)
διανόημα dianoēma (1264)
διάνοια dianoia (1265)
ἐνθύμησις enthumēsis (1745)
ἔννοια ennoia (1755)
ἐπίνοια epinoia (1948)
λογισμός logismos (3027)
νόημα noēma (3402)
νοῦς nous (3426)
συζήτησις suzētēsis (4654)

חִשָּׁבוֹן chishshāvôn (2920), Plan, invention (Sir 27:5).

מְזִמָּה mᵉzimmāh (4343), Intention (Ps 139:20 [138:20]).

מַחֲשֶׁבֶת machsheveth (4422III Thought, plot (Pss 56:5 [55:5], 94:11 [93:11], Lam 3:60).

עֶשְׁתֹּנֶת ʿeshtōneth (6491), Plan, thought (Ps 146:4 [145:4]).

רֵעַ rēaʿ (7740), Thought (Ps 139:2 [138:2]).

1. **διαλογισμός** dialogismos nom sing masc
2. **διαλογισμοῦ** dialogismou gen sing masc
3. **διαλογισμόν** dialogismon acc sing masc
4. **διαλογισμοί** dialogismoi nom pl masc
5. **διαλογισμῶν** dialogismōn gen pl masc
6. **διαλογισμοῖς** dialogismois dat pl masc
7. **διαλογισμούς** dialogismous acc pl masc

4	For out of the heart proceed evil **thoughts**,........	Matt 15:19
4	out of the heart of men, proceed evil **thoughts**,.....	Mark 7:21
4	that the **thoughts** of many hearts may be revealed...	Luke 2:35
7	But when Jesus perceived their **thoughts**,...............	5:22
7	But he knew their **thoughts**, and said to the man.......	6:8
1	Then there arose **a reasoning** among them,............	9:46
3	And Jesus, perceiving the **thought** of their heart,........	9:47
4	and why **do thoughts** arise in your hearts?.............	24:38
6	but became vain in their **imaginations**,..............	Rom 1:21
5	but not to doubtful **disputations**.......................	14:1
7	again, The Lord knoweth the **thoughts** of the wise,..	1 Co 3:20
5	Do all things without murmurings and **disputings**:...	Phlp 2:14
2	lifting up holy hands, without wrath and **doubting**...	1 Tm 2:8
5	and are become judges of evil **thoughts**?.............	Jas 2:4

The noun *dialogismos* comprises a combination of *dia* (1217), "through" in the sense of separation, and *logismos* (3027), "reasoning." The result of this merger gives *dialogismos* the general meaning of "thinking through by personal thought, deliberation, and inward reasoning."

Classical Greek
In classical Greek the root word embodies what may be referred to as "modern dialogue." In its everyday usage it means "general conversation," but in the language of the philosophers it denotes "verbal interaction and debate" with the objective in mind of a teaching/learning experience. Related to this meaning the noun form *dialogismos* emerges as "a process of deliberating, considering, reckoning, weighing, and discussing."

Septuagint Usage
In the Septuagint *dialogismos* stands primarily for the Hebrew counterpart *machăshāvāh* which means "a plan or purpose devised in thought or reflection." Furst states: "The noun *dialogismos* also often means the perverse, vain thinking which contemplates destruction (Psalm 94:11 [LXX 93:11]), and is turned against God (Isaiah 59:7; Jeremiah 4:14) and against the pious (Psalm 56:5 [LXX 55:5]) .... But the word is also used for God's profound (Psalm 92:5 [91:5]) and wonderful (Psalm 40:5 [39:5]) thoughts" (Furst, "Think," *Colin Brown*, 3:820).

New Testament Usage
In the New Testament *dialogismos* seems to be used primarily with a depreciatory connotation

διαλύω 1256

whereby the inner thought life causes both sinful and carnal motives. This idea is in contrast to the Greek understanding of thought leading to truth (cf. 1 Corinthians 1:21-25) and clearly shows the unredeemed thought life to be evil (Matthew 15:19; Mark 7:21), suspicious (Luke 2:35; 6:8), cynical (Luke 5:22; 24:38), and worthless (Romans 1:21; 1 Corinthians 3:20).

Also, in the same regard, there is the constant danger of the redeemed person reverting to spiritually immature motives which breed selfish ambition (Matthew 9:33ff.; Luke 9:46ff.), argumentative attitudes (Romans 14:1; Philippians 2:14; 1 Timothy 2:8), and bigoted relationships (James 2:4).

Christ, however, put the thought life in proper perspective with the illustration of a child who represents the principle that "he that is least among you all, the same shall be great" (Luke 9:46-48).

STRONG 1261, BAUER 186, MOULTON-MILLIGAN 151, KITTEL 2:96-98, LIDDELL-SCOTT 402, COLIN BROWN 3:820-21.

1256. διαλύω dialuō verb

Disperse, utterly dissolve.

COGNATE:
 λύω luō (3061)

אָבָה 'āvâh (13), Consent (Prv 6:35).

חָבַל chăval (2341), Act corruptly (Neh 1:7).

מָסַס māsas (4701), Niphal: be burned (Jgs 15:14—Codex Alexandrinus only).

נָתַר nāthar (5609), Fall, start up; hiphil: untie (Is 58:6).

פָּרַק pāraq (6811), Piel: shatter (1 Kgs 19:11).

שָׁבַר shāvar (8132), Break; niphal: be broken up (Jon 1:4).

1. διελύθησαν dieluthēsan 3pl indic aor pass

1 and all, as many as obeyed him, were scattered, ... Acts 5:36

Dialuō is a derivative of the Greek verb *luō* (3061) meaning "to loose." In the broadest classical sense *dialuō* takes on the understanding of "to break up" or "dissolve." The word also appears in the Septuagint often with the meaning of "loosen" (Isaiah 58:6). It is used in the New Testament as an aorist passive verb (*dialuthēsan*) meaning "were scattered" (Acts 5:36).

As one of many rich combinations of the root word *luō*, *dialuō* denotes God's breaking up of sin and destroying its grip (Isaiah 40:2).

The same idea is found in Acts 5:36. Gamaliel warned the Sanhedrin (about A.D. 32) to be careful of their treatment of the apostles. He believed that if God had the power to destroy the movement of Theudas (a self-appointed false prophet) by scattering his followers, He could certainly do something similar with the followers of Jesus.

STRONG 1262, BAUER 186, MOULTON-MILLIGAN 151-52, LIDDELL-SCOTT 402, COLIN BROWN 2:33-34.

1257. διαμαρτύρομαι diamarturomai verb

Charge, warn, testify, confirm.

COGNATE:
 μαρτυρέω martureō (3113)
SYNONYMS:
 διαστέλλω diastellō (1285)
 διατάσσω diatassō (1293)
 ἐντέλλομαι entellomai (1765)
 ἐξορκίζω exorkizō (1828)
 ἐπιμαρτυρέω epimartureō (1942)
 ἐπιτάσσω epitassō (1988)
 ἐπιτρέπω epitrepō (1994)
 κελεύω keleuō (2724)
 λέγω legō (2978)
 μαρτυρέω martureō (3113)
 ὁρκίζω horkizō (3589)
 παραγγέλλω parangellō (3715)
 προστάσσω prostassō (4225)
 συντάσσω suntassō (4781)
 τάσσω tassō (4872)

זָהַר zāhar (2178), Hiphil: warn (Ex 18:20).

יָדַע yādha' (3156), Know; hiphil: cause to know, announce, inform (Ez 16:2, 20:4).

עוּד 'ûdh (5967), Hiphil: warn (Ex 19:21); hophal: be warned (Ex 21:29).

1. διαμαρτύρομαι diamarturomai
 1sing indic pres mid
2. διαμαρτύρεται diamarturetai
 3sing indic pres mid
3. διαμαρτύρηται diamarturētai 3sing subj pres mid
4. διαμαρτυρόμενος diamarturomenos
 nom sing masc part pres mid
5. διεμαρτύρω diemarturō 2sing indic aor mid
6. διεμαρτύρατο diemarturato 3sing indic aor mid
7. διεμαρτυράμεθα diemarturametha
 1pl indic aor mid
8. διεμαρτυράμενοι diemarturamenoi
 nom pl masc part aor mid
9. διαμαρτύρασθαι diamarturasthai inf aor mid
10. διεμαρτύρετο diemartureto
 3sing indic imperf mid

3 have five brethren; that he **may testify** unto them, Luke 16:28
10 with many other words **did he testify** and exhort, ... Acts 2:40
6 with many other words **did he testify** and exhort, ... 2:40
8 **had testified** and preached the word of the Lord, ... 8:25

9 and to testify that it is he which was ordained	Acts 10:42
4 and testified to the Jews that Jesus was Christ	18:5
4 Testifying both to the Jews, and also to the Greeks,	20:21
2 Save that the Holy Ghost witnesseth in every city,	20:23
9 to testify the gospel of the grace of God	20:24
5 for as thou hast testified of me in Jerusalem,	23:11
4 he expounded and testified the kingdom of God,	28:23
7 as we also have forewarned you and testified	1 Th 4:6
1 I charge thee before God, and the Lord Jesus	1 Tm 5:21
4 charging them before the Lord that they strive not	2 Tm 2:14
1 I charge thee therefore before God,	4:1
6 But one in a certain place testified, saying,	Heb 2:6

Classical Greek

Formally, the deponent verb *diamarturomai* comes from the preposition *dia* (1217) plus the verb *marturomai*, "witness, affirm" (cf. *martureō* [3113], "bear witness"). The *dia* functions in an intensifying capacity, thus *diamarturomai* means first of all "charge to witness, invoke as a witness." This was used both in reference to gods and men in classical Greek; in this sense it was synonymous with *marturomai*. Other meanings stemming from this include "'to declare emphatically,' whether with ref.(erence) to facts or truths ... or in the sense of a summons, admonition, or warning" (Strathmann, "marturomai," *Kittel*, 4:511; cf. *Liddell-Scott*). In a general sense it means "protest solemnly" (against someone or something [especially false]; *Liddell-Scott*).

Septuagint Usage

Except for three instances *diamarturomai* translates a form of the Hebrew word *'ûdh* meaning either "warn" or "call as a witness." The Lord instructed Moses to go down from Mount Sinai and "warn" the people to consecrate themselves (Exodus 19:10 [Septuagint only]). The recurrent idea of "call a witness" and "admonish or warn" converge typically in Deuteronomy 4:26. Here God called heaven and earth as His witnesses against Israel. If Israel became idolatrous or corrupt God declared surely He would not let their sin go unpunished (cf. Deuteronomy 8:19; 30:19; 31:28; 32:46). Thus *diamarturomai* carries the idea of a "solemn warning," i.e., a certainty verified by witnesses. The prophets and seers and covenant decrees "warned" or "testified to" Israel of the consequences of sin (2 Kings 17:13,15 [LXX 4 Kings 17:13,15]; cf. 2 Chronicles 24:19; Nehemiah 9:26). God himself testified against Israel; still she refused to listen (Psalms 50:7 [LXX 49:7]; 81:8 [80:8]; cf. Jeremiah 6:10; Malachi 2:14).

New Testament Usage

The majority of instances of *diamarturomai* occur in the writings of Luke (one in his Gospel; nine in Acts) and Paul (four times). The writer of Hebrews also used it once. The familiar convergence of warning and testimony are reflected in Luke's use. The rich man pleaded that Abraham would send Lazarus to "warn" (NIV) his brothers. Abraham's response is reminiscent of the Septuagint's use: "They have Moses and the Prophets, let them listen to them" (Luke 16:28f.). The Law and the Prophets "testify to" (i.e., "warn") those who heed their advice (cf. Hebrews 2:6, a similar idea of "testimony").

Acts Account

In the Book of Acts *diamarturomai* occurs during the preaching of the Word on the Day of Pentecost and elsewhere (Acts 2:40; cf. 8:25; 10:42; 18:5). Here the testimony to the truth of the gospel, witnessed by the apostles who experienced Jesus' ministry and who saw the risen Lord, admonished the listeners to repent and to serve God (Acts 20:21; cf. 20:24; 23:11; 28:23).

In another use, "being warned" by the Holy Spirit Paul was certain of the fate awaiting him in Jerusalem (Acts 20:23); nevertheless, he was compelled to preach the gospel entrusted to him.

Pauline Epistles

Implicit in *diamarturomai*, then, is the notion that dire consequences await the one ignoring the divine warning of the gospel. To neglect such testimony is to risk punishment or worse (cf. 1 Thessalonians 4:6). Paul's admonition to Timothy "before God" (*enōpion tou theou*) is charged with legal overtones. Paul was "testifying" to Timothy of the certainty of consequences if he (Timothy) or others ignored Paul's instructions. Although the idea of a formal entrusting with duties is implied in some translations of *diamarturomai* (cf. NIV's "charge," 1 Timothy 5:21; 2 Timothy 4:1; "warn," 2 Timothy 2:14), this does not fully convey the seriousness of the warning and the urgency of the moment. Timothy must act or face the consequences (cf. 1 Timothy 5:1; 2 Timothy 2:14; 4:1).

STRONG 1263, BAUER 186, MOULTON-MILLIGAN 152, KITTEL 4:510-12, LIDDELL-SCOTT 403, COLIN BROWN 3:1038-39,1041,1044.

1258. διαμάχομαι diamachomai verb

Contend sharply, fight fiercely.

διαμένω 1259

CROSS-REFERENCE:
μάχομαι machomai (3136)

לָחַם lācham (4032), Niphal: fight (Dn 10:20).

נָצָה nātsāh (5510), Strive (Sir 8:3).

רִיב rîv (7662), Dispute, quarrel (Sir 8:1).

1. διεμάχοντο diemachonto 3pl indic imperf mid
1 and strove, saying, We find no evil in this man:.... Acts 23:9

This term comes from the verb *machomai* (3136) meaning "to fight, quarrel, dispute, strive with." The prefix *dia* (1217) intensifies the meaning yielding the idea of "to struggle against, contend sharply." It is used only in Acts 23:9 of the portion of the Sanhedrin, i.e., "the scribes that were of the Pharisees' part," which defended Paul against the Sadducees who "say that there is no resurrection, neither angel, nor spirit" (verse 8). Robertson says, "It was a lively scrap!" (*Word Pictures in the New Testament*, 3:402).

STRONG 1264, BAUER 186, LIDDELL-SCOTT 403.

1259. διαμένω diameno verb
Remain, be constant, continue.

COGNATE:
μένω meno (3176)

SYNONYMS:
ἀπολείπω apoleipō (614)
αὐλίζομαι aulizomai (829)
διατελέω diateleō (1294)
διατρίβω diatribō (1298)
ἐμμένω emmenō (1682)
ἐπιμένω epimenō (1946)
καθίζω kathizō (2495)
καταμένω katamenō (2620)
μένω menō (3176)
παραμένω paramenō (3748)
περιλείπομαι perileipomai (3898)
ὑπομένω hupomenō (5116)

יָצַב yātsav (3429), Hithpael: take one's stand (Ps 5:5).

יָשַׁב yāshav (3553), Sit enthroned (Ps 61:7 [60:7]).

נָטַר nātar (5387), Keep on being angry (Jer 3:5).

נִין nîn (5396), Hiphil: continue (Ps 72:17 [71:17]).

נָצַב nātsav (5507), Niphal: stand firm (Ps 119:89 [118:89]).

עָמַד 'āmadh (6198), Stand, endure (Pss 19:9 [18:9], 102:26 [101:26], 119:90,91 [118:90,91]).

1. διαμένεις diameneis 2sing indic pres act
2. διαμένει diamenei 3sing indic pres act
3. διαμείνῃ diameinē 3sing subj aor act
4. διαμεμενηκότες diamemenēkotes
   nom pl masc part perf act
5. διέμενεν diemenen 3sing indic imperf act

5 he beckoned unto them, and remained speechless.... Luke 1:22
4 which have continued with me in my temptations....... 22:28
3 the truth of the gospel might continue with you....... Gal 2:5
1 They shall perish; but thou remainest;............... Heb 1:11
2 for since the fathers fell asleep, all things continue... 2 Pt 3:4

This word is a compound verb from *dia* (1217), "through," and *menō* (3176), "to stay, abide, remain." It means "to remain throughout without intermission or interruption." Jesus complimented His disciples as "they which have continued with me in my temptations" (Luke 22:28). It is contrasted with *apollumi* (616), "perish, pass away," in Hebrews 1:11, "They (heaven and earth) shall perish, but thou (God) remaineth."

STRONG 1265, BAUER 186, MOULTON-MILLIGAN 152, LIDDELL-SCOTT 403.

1260. διαμερίζω diamerizō verb
Divide, separate into parts, distribute.

COGNATE:
μερίζω merizō (3177)

SYNONYMS:
ἀποδίδωμι apodidōmi (586)
διαδίδωμι diadidōmi (1233)
διαιρέω diaireō (1238)
δίδωμι didōmi (1319)
μερίζω merizō (3177)
μεταδίδωμι metadidōmi (3200)

חָלַק chālaq (2606), Qal: be smooth (Ps 55:21 [54:21]); piel: disperse, scatter (Gn 49:7, 2 Sm 6:19, Ps 108:7 [107:7]); pual: be divided (Zec 14:1).

חֵלֶק chēleq (2610), Reward (Ps 17:14 [16:14]).

נָחַל nāchal (5336), Take posession of; hiphil: give hereditary possession of (Dt 32:8).

פָּלַג pālagh (6629), Niphal: be divided (Gn 10:25, 1 Chr 1:19).

1. διαμερίσατε diamerisate 2pl impr aor act
2. διεμέριζον diemerizon 3pl indic imperf act
3. διαμεριζόμενοι diamerizomenoi
   nom pl masc part pres mid
4. διαμεριζόμεναι diamerizomenai
   nom pl fem part pres mid
5. διεμερίσθη diemeristhē 3sing indic aor pass
6. διεμερίσαντο diemerisanto 3pl indic aor mid
7. διαμερισθεῖσα diameristheisa
   nom sing fem part aor pass
8. διαμεμερισμένοι diamemerismenoi
   nom pl masc part perf mid
9. διαμερισθήσεται diameristhēsetai
   3sing indic fut pass
10. διαμερίζονται diamerizontai 3pl indic pres mid
11. διαμερισθήσονται diameristhēsontai
   3pl indic fut pass

6 and parted his garments, casting lots:............. Matt 27:35
6 They parted my garments among them,............... 27:35

2 they **parted** his garments, casting lots upon them, **Mark 15:24**	
10 they **parted** his garments, casting lots upon them, ... 15:24	
7 Every kingdom **divided** against itself ... desolation; **Luke 11:17**	
5 If Satan also **be divided** against himself, ... 11:18	
8 there shall be five in one house **divided**, ... 12:52	
9 The father **shall be divided** against the son, ... 12:53	
11 The father **shall be divided** against the son, ... 12:53	
1 Take this, and **divide** it among yourselves: 22:17	
3 And they **parted** his raiment, and cast lots. 23:34	
6 They **parted** my raiment among them, ... **John 19:24**	
4 appeared unto them **cloven** tongues like as of fire, .. **Acts 2:3**	
2 **parted** them to all men, as every man had need. 2:45	

Classical Greek
Diamerizō comes from the verb *merizō* (3177), "divide," plus the preposition *dia* (1217), "through." The preposition intensifies the meaning; thus *diamerizō* means "divide thoroughly." Among classical writers it was used by Plato of a butcher who cuts animals into pieces (see Thayer, *Greek-English Lexicon*; cf. *Liddell-Scott*). Other meanings include simply "divide, distribute part," or "separate."

Septuagint Usage
The Septuagint uses the term with regard to dividing the earth (Genesis 10:25), the nations (Deuteronomy 32:8), land (Psalms 60:6 [LXX 59:6]; 108:7 [107:7]; Isaiah 34:17; Ezekiel 47:21), plunder (Judges 5:30; Zechariah 14:1), and food (2 Samuel 6:19 [2 Kings 6:19]).

New Testament Usage
In the New Testament *diamerizō* is found in a passage common to the four Gospels (Matthew 27:35; Mark 15:24; Luke 23:34; John 19:24): The soldiers who crucified Jesus divided His clothes among themselves. Jesus said that any kingdom that experiences internal conflict, including Satan's, is doomed to failure (Luke 11:17,18). According to Luke 12:52,53 (also see verse 51), Jesus' coming forces people to make a choice for Him or against Him. The different choices made inevitably lead to disunity within families. At the Last Supper (Luke 22:17) Jesus instructed His disciples to divide (share) among themselves the Passover cup for the purpose of uniting them (Marshall, *New International Greek Testament Commentary, Luke*, pp.798f.). This same idea of "dividing among" ("distributing, sharing"; cf. *Bauer*) can be seen in Acts 2:45. The believers made a regular practice (note the imperfect tenses here) of selling their material possessions and dividing the proceeds among themselves according to individual needs (Bruce, *Acts of the Apostles*, p.101). Of Acts 2:3 Marshall says, "A flame divided itself into several tongues, so that each (tongue) rested upon one of the persons present" (Marshall, *Tyndale New Testament Commentaries*, 5:68).

For the best explanation of the theological significance of this extraordinary experience consult Horton, *What the Bible Says About the Holy Spirit*, pp.141f.

STRONG 1266, BAUER 186, MOULTON-MILLIGAN 152, LIDDELL-SCOTT 403.

1261. διαμερισμός diamerismos noun
Division, dissension.
COGNATE:
μερίζω merizō (3177)
SYNONYM:
διχοστασία dichostasia (1364)

מַחֲלֹקֶת machălōqeth (4393), Portion (Ez 48:29).

1. διαμερισμόν diamerismon acc sing masc

1 I tell you, Nay; but rather **division**: .... **Luke 12:51**

In its only use in the New Testament Jesus contrasted *diamerismos* with *eirēnē* (1503), "peace." "Suppose ye that I am come to give on earth? I tell you, Nay; but rather *division*" (Luke 12:51). "Division" in this context goes beyond the literal meaning found in the Septuagint at Ezekiel 48:29 which discusses the *division* of the land" by lot unto the tribes of Israel for an inheritance." Matthew's Gospel reads *machaira* (3134), "sword," for *diamerismos* and reveals that the word is referring to "dissension."

STRONG 1267, BAUER 186, LIDDELL-SCOTT 403.

1262. διανέμω dianemō verb
Distribute, spread about.
CROSS-REFERENCE:
νόμος nomos (3414)

חָלַק chālaq (2606), Give to (Dt 29:26).

1. διανεμηθῇ dianemēthē 3sing subj aor pass

1 But that it **spread** no further among the people, ... **Acts 4:17**

The primary meaning of *dianemō* is "spread", as in "to spread a report among a group of people." Its only use is in Acts 4:17 as a passive verb. The Sanhedrin attempted to silence Peter and John from "spreading" the good news of Christ among the people.

STRONG 1268, BAUER 186, MOULTON-MILLIGAN 152, LIDDELL-SCOTT 405.

1263. διανεύω dianeuō verb
Beckon, nod, signal.
COGNATE:
νεύω neuō (3368)

διανόημα 1264

SYNONYMS:
κατανεύω kataneuō (2626)
νεύω neuō (3368)

קָרַץ qārats (7460), Wink (Ps 35:19 [34:19]).

1. διανεύων dianeuōn nom sing masc part pres act

1 he **beckoned** unto them, and remained speechless.... Luke 1:22

This is the intensive form of *neuō* (3368), "to nod," meaning "to express one's thoughts by a sign or motion." In the New Testament it is used only in reference to the "signs" made by Zechariah when he could not speak about the birth of his son John (Luke 1:22). As a participle being used with a finite verb it means "repeated beckoning."

STRONG 1269, BAUER 187, LIDDELL-SCOTT 405.

1264. διανόημα dianoēma noun
Though.

COGNATE:
νοέω noeō (3401)

SYNONYMS:
διαλογισμός dialogismos (1255)
διάνοια dianoia (1265)
ἐνθύμησις enthumēsis (1745)
ἔννοια ennoia (1755)
ἐπίνοια epinoia (1948)
λογισμός logismos (3027)
νόημα noēma (3402)
νοῦς nous (3426)

גִּלּוּל gillûl (1585), Idols (Ez 14:3,4).

מַחֲשֶׁבֶת machsheveth (4422III Thought (Is 55:9).

שֵׂכֶל sēkhel (7961I), Shrewdness, deceit (Dn 8:25).

1. διανοήματα dianoēmata nom/acc pl neu

1 But he, knowing their **thoughts**, said unto them, ... Luke 11:17

This term is akin to the verb *noeō* (3401), "to consider," but emphasizes the result of the activity of thought. It overlaps into the realm of purpose, intent, and motive. It was a favorite word of Plato, but in the New Testament it is used only in Luke 11:17 of Jesus knowing the thoughts of the Pharisees in relation to His activity of casting out demons. It emphasizes their real motive toward Him.

STRONG 1270, BAUER 187, KITTEL 4:968, LIDDELL-SCOTT 405, COLIN BROWN 3:122-23,125,128.

1265. διάνοια dianoia noun
Mind, understanding, intellect, feelings, dispostion.

COGNATE:
νοέω noeō (3401)

SYNONYMS:
γνώμη gnōmē (1100)
διαλογισμός dialogismos (1255)
διανόημα dianoēma (1264)
ἐνθύμησις enthumēsis (1745)
ἔννοια ennoia (1755)
ἐπίνοια epinoia (1948)
λογισμός logismos (3027)
νόημα noēma (3402)
νοῦς nous (3426)
πρόθεσις prothesis (4145)
σύνεσις sunesis (4757)

בִּינָה bînāh (1035), Insight (Dn 9:22).

גִּלּוּל gillûl (1585), Idols (Ez 14:4).

לֵב lēv (3949), Heart (Ex 36:1, Is 55:9); self (Gn 27:41).

מַחֲשֶׁבֶת machsheveth (4422III Thought (Is 55:9).

קֶרֶב qerev (7419), Heart (Jer 31:33 [38:33]).

1. διανοίας dianoias gen sing fem
2. διανοίᾳ dianoia dat sing fem
3. διάνοιαν dianoian acc sing fem
4. διανοιῶν dianoiōn gen pl fem

2 and with all thy soul, and with all thy **mind**........ Matt 22:37
1 with all thy soul, and with all thy **mind**,.......... Mark 12:30
2 the proud in the **imagination** of their hearts........ Luke 1:51
1 and with all thy strength, and with all thy **mind**;...... 10:27
2 and with all thy strength, and with all thy **mind**;...... 10:27
1 The eyes of your **understanding** being enlightened;... Eph 1:18
4 fulfilling the desires of the flesh and of the **mind**;...... 2:3
2 Having the **understanding** darkened,.................. 4:18
2 and enemies in your **mind** by wicked works,......... Col 1:21
3 I will put my laws into their **mind**,................. Heb 8:10
4 and in their **minds** will I write them;................ 10:16
3 and in their **minds** will I write them;................ 10:16
1 Wherefore gird up the loins of your **mind**,.......... 1 Pt 1:13
3 I stir up your pure **minds** by way of remembrance:.. 2 Pt 3:1
3 and hath given us an **understanding**,................ 1 Jn 5:20

Classical Greek
This is a very common word in classical Greek; its principal meaning is "a thought, a reflection," but it is open to many interpretations (e.g., "meditations" [either good or evil]).

Septuagint Usage
Dianoia often translated the Hebrew term *leb*, "mind, character, heart," or "disposition" (e.g., Genesis 8:21; Exodus 35:10,22), and it was often linked to the term *kardia* (2559), "heart," as the different Septuagintal texts make clear (e.g., at Exodus 35:10; Numbers 32:7; Deuteronomy 6:5; 28:47 [different versions read *kardia* instead of *dianoia*]). In the New Testament its relationship to *kardia* is to be noted in Luke 1:51.

New Testament Usage
Most of the New Testament writers used the word, but they did not follow the Greek philosophical use. Rather, their view was like that of the Septuagint. Classical Greek employs *dianoia* as an expression of the mind's ability to engage in philosophical and theoretical

speculation or some other creative thought. The New Testament associates it with the internal ability of man to express thoughts, desires, and feelings.

The legal expert replied to Jesus' question regarding the greatest commandment in the Law: "Thou shalt love the Lord thy God with all thy heart, and with all thy soul, and with all thy strength, and with all thy mind (*dianoia*); and thy neighbor as thyself" (Luke 10:27). The true godly life is lived from the heart, and it asserts itself through feelings, compassion, and understanding. The believer has received discernment to know the true One (1 John 5:20). Through this avenue of the mind he is able to seek His help and assistance. A disciple must be renewing his or her mind on a continual basis in order to keep this channel of communication open (Romans 12:2).

Dianoia is used in reference to the mind as the seat of understanding, emotions, and desire in Matthew 22:37, Mark 12:30, Luke 10:27, and Ephesians 1:18. In 1 John 5:20 it refers to discernment in Colossians 1:21 and Luke 1:51 to a way of thinking; and in Ephesians 2:3, the only place *dianoia* occurs in the plural, of evil thoughts.

Sin is, in part, generated by a "darkened understanding"; this, in turn, is futile because it leads only to further alienation from God. Only the power of God can break the vicious cycle and renew the mind of human beings (Ephesians 4:17ff.).

STRONG 1271, BAUER 187, MOULTON-MILLIGAN 152, KITTEL 4:963-67, LIDDELL-SCOTT 405, COLIN BROWN 3:122-25,127-28.

1266. διανοίγω dianoigō verb
Open fully, explain, expound.
CROSS-REFERENCE:
ἀνοίγω anoigō (453)

יָצָא yātsâ' (3428), Come out, go out; hiphil: lead forth (Jb 38:32).
פּוּץ pûts (6571), Hiphil: scatter (Hb 3:14).
פֶּטֶר peṭer (6605), Firstborn (Ex 13:2,12,13, Ez 20:26).
פִּטְרָה piṭrāh (6606), Firstborn (Nm 8:16).
פָּעַר pā'ar (6720), Open wide (Is 5:14).
פָּצָה pātsâh (6722), Open (Lam 2:16, 3:46).
פָּקַח pāqach (6741), Qal: open (2 Kgs 6:17,20, Jb 27:19, Zec 12:4); niphal: be opened (Gn 3:5,7).
פָּרַשׂ pāras (6816), Extend (Prv 31:20).

פָּתַח pāthach (6858), Qal: spread out, open (Jb 29:19, Ez 3:2, Zec 11:1); niphal: be opened (Ez 24:27, Na 2:6, Zec 13:1).
פֶּתַח pethach (6860), Door (Hos 2:15).

1. **διανοίγων** dianoigōn nom sing masc part pres act
2. **διανοῖγον** dianoigon nom/acc sing neu part pres act
3. **διήνοιξεν** diēnoixen 3sing indic aor act
4. **διήνοιγεν** diēnoigen 3sing indic imperf act
5. **διηνοίχθησαν** diēnoichthēsan 3pl indic aor pass
6. **διανοίχθητι** dianoichthēti 2sing impr aor pass
7. **διηνοιγμένους** diēnoigmenous
acc pl masc part perf mid

6 and saith unto him, Ephphatha, that is, **Be opened**...Mark 7:34
5 And straightway his ears **were opened**,................. 7:35
2 Every male that **openeth** the womb shall be called...Luke 2:23
5 And their eyes **were opened**, and they knew him;...... 24:31
4 and while he **opened** to us the scriptures?............. 24:32
3 Then **opened** he their understanding,.................. 24:45
7 Behold, I see the heavens **opened** up (NASB)....... Acts 7:56
3 whose heart the Lord **opened**,....................... 16:14
1 **Opening** and alleging,................................ 17:3

Classical Greek
According to its limited classical sources *dianoigō* means "lay open" (eyes) or "open for connecting." The *dia* (1217) in all likelihood intensifies the verb *anoigō* (453), "open" (cf. *Liddell-Scott*).

Septuagint Usage
In the Septuagint *dianoigō* means "open." In a literal sense it is used of a male child "opening" the womb (i.e., "being born"; Exodus 13:2; cf. Luke 2:23). Specifically it refers to the firstborn child. It is also used of God's opening blinded eyes (2 Kings 6:20 [LXX 4 Kings 6:17,20]). Figuratively *dianoigō* depicts the opening of the mouth of the grave (Isaiah 5:14), the mouths of one's enemies (Lamentations 2:16), the fountain for cleansing (Zechariah 13:1), and the eyes of perception (Genesis 3:5,7).

New Testament Usage
The New Testament shows two distinct understandings. Jesus commanded the hearing and speaking faculties of the deaf man who "could hardly talk" (Mark 7:32, NIV) to "Be opened!" (verse 34). Figuratively the eyes of Cleopas and his companion were opened (Luke 24:31), so they recognized the significance of Jesus' actions (cf. verse 16). The mind (Luke 24:45), the heart (Acts 16:14), and the ears were all opened (cf. Acts 16:14 with John 6:44 and Ephesians 1:18,19). In these the movement to the second meaning is seen (e.g., Luke 24:45, "opened he their understanding").

The second meaning of *dianoigō* in the New Testament is "to explain, interpret." Thus in

Luke 24:32 the Old Testament is "opened" ("explained") in terms of its fulfillment in Jesus. Twice more this sense occurs in Luke's writings (Luke 24:45; Acts 17:3). According to Luke, both the Scriptures (Luke 24:32; Acts 17:3) and the understanding (Luke 24:45) require God's opening.

Strong 1272, Bauer 187, Liddell-Scott 405, Colin Brown 2:726,729.

1267. διανυκτερεύω
dianuktereuō verb
Spend the whole night.

1. διανυκτερεύων dianuktereuōn
nom sing masc part pres act

1 and **continued all night** in prayer to God............Luke 6:12

This term refers to all-night vigils. It means literally to "continue all night" or "spend the whole night," coming from *dia* (1217), "through," and *nux* (3433), "night." In the New Testament it is used in connection with Jesus praying all night before choosing His 12 disciples (Luke 6:12). This is the only occurrence of *dianuktereuō* in the New Testament.

Strong 1273, Bauer 187, Moulton-Milligan 152, Liddell-Scott 405.

1268. διανύω dianuō verb
Complete, finish.
Synonyms:
  ἀναπληρόω anaplēroō (376)
  ἀνταναπληρόω antanaplēroō (463)
  ἀποτελέω apoteleō (652)
  ἐκπληρόω ekplēroō (1590)
  ἐκτελέω ekteleō (1602)
  ἐξαρτίζω exartizō (1806)
  ἐπιτελέω epiteleō (1989)
  καταρτίζω katartizō (2645)
  πληρόω plēroō (3997)
  συντελέω synteleō (4783)
  τελειόω teleioō (4896)
  τελέω teleō (4903)

1. διανύσαντες dianusantes nom pl masc part aor act

1 And when we **had finished** our course from Tyre,...Acts 21:7

Classical Greek authors used *dianuō* with the meaning "to complete" (see *Bauer*). Later Greek writers, for example Xenophon (Second Century A.D.), used the word in the sense "to continue," for instance, a voyage (Bruce, *Acts of the Apostles*, p.386). *Dianuō* occurs in the New Testament only in Acts 21:7 which refers to Paul's voyage from Cyprus to Tyre; once "completed" they continued on to Ptolemais.

Strong 1274, Bauer 187, Moulton-Milligan 152, Liddell-Scott 406.

1269. διαπαντός diapantos adv
Always, continually.
Cognate:
  πᾶς pas (3817B)
Synonyms:
  ἀεί aei (103)
  ἑκάστοτε hekastote (1525)
  πάντοτε pantote (3704)

1. διαπαντός diapantos

1 And **always**, night and day,....................Mark 5:5
1 And were **continually** in the temple,..........Luke 24:53
1 to the people, and prayed to God **alway**......Acts 10:2
1 **always** a conscience void of offence toward God,...... 24:16
1 and bow down their back **alway**................Rom 11:10
1 the priests went **always** into the first tabernacle,.....Heb 9:6
1 offer the sacrifice of praise to God **continually**,........ 13:15

Usually written *dia pantos*, this word nevertheless appears seven times in this compound form. It describes a period of time throughout or during which anything is done. It emphasizes the whole period of time to its very end.

Strong 1275, Bauer 187, Liddell-Scott 406.

1269B. διαπαρατριβή
diaparatribē noun
Constant strife.

1. διαπαρατριβαί diaparatribai nom pl fem

1 **constant friction** between men NASB..............1 Tm 6:5

The preposition *dia* (1217), "through," compounds with the noun *paratribē*, "rubbing against one another," to form a double compound word meaning "incessant or constant wrangling or strife." This double compound is found in the New Testament only at 1 Timothy 6:5 where Paul described those teaching false doctrine as causing constant strife.

Aside from this one use in the New Testament *diaparatribē* also appears in Polybius (Second Century B.C.).

Bauer 187, Liddell-Scott 406.

1270. διαπεράω diaperaō verb
Pass over, cross.

עָבַר 'āvar (5882), Cross over (Dt 30:13, Is 23:2).

1. διαπερῶσιν diaperōsin 3pl subj pres act
2. διαπερῶν diaperōn nom/acc sing neu part pres act
3. διεπέρασεν dieperasen 3sing indic aor act
4. διαπεράσαντος diaperasantos
    gen sing masc part aor act
5. διαπεράσαντες diaperasantes
    nom pl masc part aor act

3 And he entered into a ship, and **passed over**,........Matt 9:1
5 And when they **were gone over**,......................14:34
4 And when Jesus **was passed over** again by ship......Mark 5:21
5 And when they **had passed over**,......................6:53
1 neither **can** they **pass** to us, ... from thence........Luke 16:26
2 And finding a ship **sailing over** unto Phenicia,......Acts 21:2

    The basic meaning of this term is "cross." Often the point of departure, the destination, or both are included. Related to *peran* (3871), "across, on the other side," and *peras* (3872), "boundary," it is the source of the English words *portal* or *port*. Most New Testament references are to Jesus and His disciples' activity of crossing the Sea of Galilee. See Matthew 9:1; 14:34; Mark 5:21; 6:53.
STRONG 1276, BAUER 187, MOULTON-MILLIGAN 152, LIDDELL-SCOTT 406.

1271. διαπλέω diapleō verb
Sail through or across the sea.
CROSS-REFERENCE:
    πλέω pleō (3986)

1. διαπλεύσαντες diapleusantes
    nom pl masc part aor act

1 had **sailed over** the sea of Cilicia and Pamphylia,... Acts 27:5

    This is a compound verb from *dia* (1217), "through" or "across," and *pleō* (3986), "sail" or "travel by sea." It was used only by Luke as he described an aspect of Paul's journey to Rome (Acts 27:5).
STRONG 1277, BAUER 187, MOULTON-MILLIGAN 152-53, LIDDELL-SCOTT 407.

1272. διαπονέω diaponeō verb
Toil through; be worried, troubled.

עָצַב 'ātsav (6321), Hurt; niphal: injure oneself (Eccl 10:9).

1. διαπονούμενοι diaponoumenoi
    nom pl masc part pres mid
2. διαπονηθείς diaponētheis
    nom sing masc part aor pass

1 **Being grieved** that they taught the people,..........Acts 4:2
2 **being grieved**, turned and said to the spirit,..........16:18

    This verb is found only in a passive voice in the New Testament which is why some lexicons spell the word *diaponeomai*. In its two occurrences (Acts 4:2; 16:18), the word is translated "grieved" which does not show the stronger meaning "greatly disturbed or annoyed." For example, at Acts 4:2 the priests, the captain of the temple, and the Sadducees were not simply "grieved" at the preaching of the apostles; they were *greatly annoyed*—to the point of throwing Peter and John into prison (see Acts 4:3).
STRONG 1278, BAUER 187 (see "diaponeomai"), MOULTON-MILLIGAN 153, LIDDELL-SCOTT 408.

1273. διαπορεύω diaporeuō verb
Go through.
SYNONYMS:
    διέρχομαι dierchomai (1324)
    διοδεύω diodeuō (1347)
    ἔρχομαι erchomai (2048)
    παραπορεύομαι paraporeuomai (3760)
    παρέρχομαι parerchomai (3790)
    πορεύομαι poreuomai (4057)

אָחַד 'echādh (258), Hithpael: show oneself sharp (Ez 21:16).

בּוֹא bô' (971), Go, come; withstand (Nm 31:23).

דָּרַךְ dārakh (1931), Tread; hiphil: let walk, cross over (Is 11:15).

הָלַךְ hālakh (2050), Qal: go, walk (1 Kgs 18:35, Ps 91:6 [90:6], Ez 33:15); piel: move about, go (Ps 104:26 [103:26]); hithpael: walk around, move back and forth (Jb 22:14, Pss 77:17 [76:17], 101:2 [100:2]).

יָצָא yātsâ' (3428), Come out, go out, march, go up (Jos 15:3).

עָבַר 'āvar (5882), Qal: pass over, pass through (2 Chr 7:21, Ez 33:28); hiphil: make pass through (Ez 20:26).

פֶּלֶג pelegh (6631), Spring (Prv 5:16).

שׁוּט shût (8198), Go about (Nm 11:8, Jb 2:2).

1. διαπορευόμενος diaporeuomenos
    nom sing masc part pres mid
2. διαπορευομένου diaporeuomenou
    gen sing masc part pres mid
3. διαπορεύεσθαι diaporeuesthai inf pres mid
4. διεπορεύετο dieporeueto 3sing indic imperf mid
5. διεπορεύοντο dieporeuonto 3pl indic imperf mid

3 that he **went through** the corn fields;..............Luke 6:1
4 he **went through** the cities and villages, teaching,......13:22
2 the multitude **pass by**, he asked what it meant........18:36
5 And as they **went through** the cities,..............Acts 16:4
1 for I trust to see you in my **journey**,..............Rom 15:24

    This term is accompanied by the name of a place in the accusative case. It is a compound verb from *dia* (1217), "through," and *poreuomai* (4057), "go" or "proceed." With the exception of Romans 15:24 it is used only in Luke's writings. Occurring as a participial form in Romans 15:24 *diaporeuō* is best translated there as "on the way" or "in passing" (*Bauer*).

STRONG 1279, BAUER 187 (see "diaporeuomai"), MOULTON-MILLIGAN 153 (see "diaporeuomai"), LIDDELL-SCOTT 408.

1274. διαπορέω diaporeō verb
Be greatly perplexed, be at a loss, be in doubt.

1. διηπόρει diēporei 3sing indic imperf act
2. διηπόρουν diēporoun 3pl indic imperf act
3. διαπορεῖσθαι diaporeisthai inf pres mid
4. διηποροῦντο diēporounto 3pl indic imperf mid

1	he **was perplexed**, because that it was said of some,	Luke 9:7
3	as they **were** much **perplexed** thereabout, behold,	24:4
2	And they were all amazed, and **were in doubt**,	Acts 2:12
4	And they were all amazed, and **were in doubt**,	2:12
2	they **doubted** of them whereunto this would grow,	5:24
1	Now while Peter **doubted** in himself	10:17

Vincent (*Word Studies in the New Testament*, 1:338) says *diaporeō* describes "one who goes through the whole list of possible solutions, but finds no way out." *Diaporeō* may emphasize a growing sense of despair. It is a very important Lukan word used as a reaction by people to a manifestation of God's power.

STRONG 1280, BAUER 187, LIDDELL-SCOTT 408.

1275. διαπραγματεύομαι diapragmateuomai verb
Earn, engage in trade.
CROSS-REFERENCE:
πράσσω prassō (4097)

1. διεπραγματεύσατο diepragmateusato 3sing indic aor mid
2. διεπραγματεύσαντο diepragmateusanto 3pl indic aor mid

1	how much every man **had gained by trading**	Luke 19:15
2	how much every man **had gained by trading**	19:15

In classical Greek this word was used by Plato to mean "discern" or "examine thoroughly" (*Phaedrus* 77d; 95e). In a first-century B.C. use it means "gain by trading" or "earn" (Dionysius of Halicarnassus 3.72).

The prefix *dia* (1217) makes this the intensive form of the verb *pragmateuomai* (4090), "conduct business or trade." Luke states that the king in the Parable of the Talents "commanded (his) servants to be called unto him, to whom he had given the money, that he might know how much every man *had gained by trading*" (Luke 19:15).

STRONG 1281, BAUER 187, MOULTON-MILLIGAN 153, KITTEL 6:641-42, LIDDELL-SCOTT 408, COLIN BROWN 3:1158.

1276. διαπρίω diapriō verb
Cut apart, sawn through, furious.

שׂוּר sûr (7917), Cut (1 Chr 20:3).

1. διεπρίοντο dieprionto 3pl indic imperf pass

1	When they heard that, they **were cut to the heart**,	Acts 5:33
1	they **were cut to the heart**,	7:54

Diapriō means "to saw through, to divide by a saw." In this literal sense it is found in the Septuagint translation of 1 Chronicles 20:3. Figuratively it means "to cut to the heart." The term is used twice in the New Testament by Luke. In both Acts 5:33 and 7:54 the Jewish leaders were "infuriated" or "enraged" (cf. NIV's "furious") when they heard Peter and Stephen (respectively) speak. This effect on the Sanhedrin is to be attributed to the convicting work of the Holy Spirit.

STRONG 1282, BAUER 187, MOULTON-MILLIGAN 153, LIDDELL-SCOTT 409.

1277. διαρπάζω diarpazō verb
Plunder thoroughly.
CROSS-REFERENCE:
ἁρπάζω harpazō (720)

בַּז baz (993), Plunder (Ez 7:21).
בָּזַז bāzaz (997), Qal: plunder (Gn 34:27,29, 1 Sm 14:36, Zep 2:9); niphal: be plundered (Am 3:11).
גָּזַל gāzal (1528), Rob (Dt 28:29, Jer 21:12, Ez 22:29).
עָזַב 'āzav (6013), Abandon (Zep 2:4).
עָשַׁק 'āshaq (6479), Defraud (Mi 2:2).
שָׁסָה shāsāh (8536), Plunder (1 Sm 23:1, Ps 44:10 [43:10], Jer 50:11 [27:11]).
שָׁסַס shāsas (8537), Qal: plunder (Ps 89:41); niphal: be plundered (Zec 14:2).

1. διαρπάσαι diarpasai inf aor act
2. διαρπάσει diarpasei 3sing indic fut act
3. διαρπάσῃ diarpasē 3sing subj aor act

1	into a strong man's house, and **spoil** his goods,	Matt 12:29
2	and then he will **spoil** his house	12:29
3	and then he will **spoil** his house	12:29
1	into a strong man's house, and **spoil** his goods,	Mark 3:27
2	and then he will **spoil** his house	3:27

Classical Greek and Septuagint Usage
The classical Greek meanings of the word *diarpazō* include "plunder, seize as plunder,

snatch away from." It is used in the Septuagint of looting which occurred in connection with battle (1 Samuel [LXX 1 Kings] 14:36; 23:1; 2 Kings 17:20 [LXX 4 Kings 17:20]), even if there was not much of a fight (Genesis 34:27,29; 2 Kings 7:16 [LXX 4 Kings 7:16]). The Septuagint also employs this term for the robbery of individuals (Jeremiah 21:12; 22:3; Ezekiel 22:29; Micah 2:2).

New Testament Usage
In the New Testament *diarpazō* occurs only in Mark 3:27 (twice) and in the parallel passage in Matthew 12:29 (only once in some texts) with the meaning "plunder thoroughly." The passage, which stresses the supreme might and authority of Christ, says that only a stronger man can tie up a strong man and plunder his goods. Only Jesus can plunder Satan's goods, i.e., rescue those enslaved by the devil. The compound word *diarpazō* expresses how thoroughly the rule of God in Jesus is displacing Satan's rule among men.

STRONG 1283, BAUER 188, MOULTON-MILLIGAN 153, LIDDELL-SCOTT 410.

1278. διαρρήσσω diarrhēssō verb
Tear (one's clothes), break asunder.
COGNATE:
πήγνυμι pēgnumi (3939)
SYNONYMS:
ῥήγνυμι rhēgnumi (4342)
σπαράσσω sparassō (4535)
συσπαράσσω susparassō (4804)
σχίζω schizō (4829)

בָּצֵק bātseq (1242), Swell (Neh 9:21).

בָּקַע bāqa‘ (1260), Qal: split, break through (2 Sm 23:16, 1 Chr 11:18, Ps 78:13 [77:13]); niphal: break to pieces (2 Chr 25:12); piel: split, break open (Ps 78:15 [77:15]); pual: be ripped open (Hos 13:16 [14:1]).

חָצָה chātsâh (2779), Divide; niphal: be divided (2 Kgs 2:14).

נָתַק nāthaq (5607), Tear away; niphal: be pulled up (Is 33:20); piel: break off (Pss 2:3, 107:14 [106:14], Jer 5:5).

פָּרַם pāram (6785), Tear to pieces (Lv 10:6, 21:10).

פָּתַח pāthach (6858), Qal: open (Ps 105:41 [104:41]); piel: loosen, strip (Ps 30:11 [29:11], Is 45:1).

קָרַע qāra‘ (7458), Qal: tear (Gn 37:29, 2 Sm 1:2,11, Jl 2:13); niphal: be torn (1 Sm 15:27).

קְרָעִים qᵉrā‘îm (7459), Rags (Prv 23:21).

1. διαρρήσσων **diarrhēssōn**
nom sing masc part pres act

2. διέρρηξεν **dierrhēxen** 3sing indic aor act
3. διαρρήξας **diarrhēxas** nom sing masc part aor act
4. διαρρήξαντες **diarrhēxantes**
nom pl masc part aor act
5. διερρήγνυτο **dierrhēgnuto** 3sing indic imperf pass
6. διαρήσσων **diarēssōn** nom sing masc part pres act
7. διερρήσσετο **dierrhēsseto** 3sing indic imperf pass
8. διαρήξας **diarēxas** nom sing masc part aor act

2 Then the high priest rent his clothes, saying,....... Matt 26:65
3 Then the high priest rent his clothes, and saith,.... Mark 14:63
8 Then the high priest rent his clothes, and saith,........ 14:63
5 a great multitude of fishes: and their net brake...... Luke 5:6
7 a great multitude of fishes: and their net brake......... 5:6
1 chains and in fetters; and he brake the bands;.......... 8:29
4 they rent their clothes, and ran in among.......... Acts 14:14

In both the Septuagint (Genesis 37:29,34; 44:13; Leviticus 10:6; Numbers 14:6; Joshua 7:6; Judges 11:35, etc.; compare Joel 2:13) and the New Testament (Matthew 26:65; Mark 14:63; Acts 14:14) *diarrēssō* is used of tearing one's clothes as a sign of grief or other deep emotion. The high priest (cf. Matthew/Mark) tore his clothes because he felt that Jesus blasphemed God. Likewise Paul and Barnabas tore their clothes to express their objection and revulsion at the Lycaonians' attempt to regard them as divine.

Both in the Septuagint (Jeremiah 30:8 [LXX 37:8]; Nahum 1:13) and the New Testament (Luke 8:29) *diarrēssō* also means "break" as, for instance, in the breaking of chains or fetters. Intransitively the word is used of nets that began to tear, i.e., "burst," due to the weight of the large catch (Luke 5:6).

STRONG 1284, BAUER 188, MOULTON-MILLIGAN 153 (see "diarrēgnumi"), LIDDELL-SCOTT 410.

1279. διασαφέω diasapheō verb
Explain, declare, make clear.

בָּאַר bā’ēr (907), Piel: explain (Dt 1:5).

חֲוָה chăwâh (A2426), Haphel: tell (Dn 2:6—Aramaic).

1. διεσάφησαν **diesaphēsan** 3pl indic aor act
2. διασάφησον **diasaphēson** 2sing impr aor act

2 Explain to us the parable of the tares (NASB)..... Matt 13:36
1 came and told unto their lord all that was done........ 18:31

Various meanings for the word *diasapheō* are derived by context: (1) "explain" or "make clear" (as one would a parable, i.e., Matthew 13:36); (2) "tell plainly and in detail" or "report" accurate information (i.e., Matthew 18:31). It is an intensive verb form of *sapheō*, "explain," and is related to the noun *saphas*, "clear."

διασείω 1280

STRONG 1285, BAUER 188, MOULTON-MILLIGAN 153, LIDDELL-SCOTT 411.

1280. διασείω diaseiō verb
Extort by force, terrify, shake thoroughly.
CROSS-REFERENCE:
σείω seiō (4434)

פָּחַד pāchadh (6585), Fear; hiphil: cause to shake (Jb 4:14).

1. διασείσητε diaseisēte 2pl subj aor act

1 Do violence to no man, neither accuse any falsely; ...Luke 3:14

This is a legal term which literally means "shake violently." Vincent (*Word Studies in the New Testament*, 1:283) says it describes the process of taking money from someone "by terrifying them." The English slang expression "shake down" possesses the same connotation. Socrates referred to it as blackmail. It was used by the medical community to describe diseases that caused shaking reactions. *Diaseiō* is found only in Luke 3:14. In this passage is found evidence of how forceful John the Baptist's preaching must have been. Even soldiers (as well as tax collectors [verse 12] and the multitudes in general [verse 10]) were asking what they must do to "brink forth fruits worthy of repentance" (verse 8). To the soldiers John replied, "Don't *extort money* and don't accuse people falsely—be content with your pay" (verse 14, NIV).

STRONG 1286, BAUER 188, MOULTON-MILLIGAN 153, LIDDELL-SCOTT 411, COLIN BROWN 3:556-58.

1281. διασκορπίζω diaskorpizō verb
Scatter, disperse, waste, winnow.
CROSS-REFERENCE:
σκορπίζω skorpizō (4505)

בָּזַז bāzaz (997), Plunder, pual: be plundered (Jer 50:37 [27:37]).

בָּזַר bāzar (1002), Piel: disperse (Ps 68:30 [67:30]).

זָרָה zārâh (2306), Qal: scatter (Ps 106:27 [105:27]); piel: scatter (Ez 5:10, Zec 1:19,21).

זָרַק zāraq (2323), Scatter (Ez 10:2).

מַפֵּץ mappēts (4823), War club (Jer 51:20 [28:20]).

נָדַח nādhach (5258), Hiphil: scatter (Dt 30:1, Dn 9:7).

נוּעַ nûaʻ (5309), Qal: shake, tremble; wander (Ps 59:15 [58:15]); hiphil: scatter (Ps 59:11 [58:11]).

נַעַר naʻar (5470), Young one? wanderer? (Zec 11:16—Codex Alexandrinus only).

נָפַץ nāphats (5492), Piel: smash, break up (Jer 13:14, 51:22 [28:22]).

פּוּץ pûts (6571), Qal: scatter (Nm 10:35, Ps 68:1 [67:1], Ez 46:18); niphal: be scattered (Jer 10:21, Ez 28:25); hiphil: cause to be scattered or dispersed (Dt 30:3, Neh 1:8, Ez 11:16).

פָּזַר pāzar (6582), Niphal: be scattered (Ps 141:7 [140:7]); piel: scatter (Ps 89:10 [88:10]).

פָּרַד pāradh (6754), Spread out; hithpael: be out of joint, be scattered (Pss 22:14 [21:14], 92:9 [91:9]).

1. διασκορπίζων diaskorpizōn
    nom sing masc part pres act
2. διεσκόρπισα dieskorpisa 1sing indic aor act
3. διεσκόρπισας dieskorpisas 2sing indic aor act
4. διεσκόρπισεν dieskorpisen 3sing indic aor act
5. διεσκορπίσθησαν dieskorpisthēsan
    3pl indic aor pass
6. διεσκορπισμένα dieskorpismena
    nom/acc pl neu part perf mid
7. διασκορπισθήσεται diaskorpisthēsetai
    3sing indic fut pass
8. διασκορπισθήσονται diaskorpisthēsontai
    3pl indic fut pass

```
3 and gathering where thou hast not strowed: ....... Matt 25:24
2 and gather where I have not strowed: ................ 25:26
7 and the sheep of the flock shall be scattered abroad.... 26:31
8 and the sheep of the flock shall be scattered abroad.... 26:31
7 smite the shepherd, ... the sheep shall be scattered. Mark 14:27
8 smite the shepherd, ... the sheep shall be scattered..... 14:27
8 smite the shepherd, ... the sheep shall be scattered..... 14:27
4 strength with his arm; he hath scattered the proud .. Luke 1:51
4 and there wasted his substance with riotous living...... 15:13
1 accused unto him that he had wasted his goods........ 16:1
6 the children of God that were scattered abroad..... John 11:52
5 all, even as many as obeyed him, were dispersed..... Acts 5:37
```

Classical Greek
This verb means "to scatter" or "to disperse." Secular Greek writers, such as the historian Polybius (see *Bauer*), as well as nonliterary papyri dated around 117 B.C. attest to its early usage (*Moulton-Milligan*).

Septuagint Usage
In religious literature *diaskorpizō* occurs regularly in the Septuagint where it translates some 12 Hebrew verbs. Nehemiah 1:8 links God's warning that He would "scatter" unfaithful Israel among the nations to a prophecy given to Moses hundreds of years earlier (see Leviticus 26:33). Their current state at the time of the writing was that of a vanquished, exiled people. A noun form, *diaskorpismos*, is also found in the Septuagint.

New Testament Usage
The sense of "scatter" or "disperse" predominates the New Testament understanding. Matthew and Mark recall Zechariah's words that the sheep of the smitten shepherd would be

"dispersed" (Matthew 26:31; Mark 14:27; cf. Zechariah 13:7). The Prodigal Son's poverty and downfall came largely because he "squandered" (NIV; i.e., "wasted") his wealth (Luke 15:13). This reflects a slightly different understanding of the term when used with regard to property.

John reported that the high priest unknowingly prophesied that Jesus would die not only for the Jewish nation but for the "dispersed" children of God in order to unite them together into one (John 11:51,52).

STRONG 1287, BAUER 188, MOULTON-MILLIGAN 153, KITTEL 7:418-22, LIDDELL-SCOTT 412, COLIN BROWN 2:33-34.

commander of the Roman troops in Jerusalem was afraid Paul would be "torn apart" by the furious crowd (NIV, "torn to pieces"). He wisely elected to place Paul under protective custody until he could be safely transported to Felix (Acts 23:10).

The early Christian writer Clement harshly condemned the divisions, splits, schisms, and differences within the church which, in his words, were "tearing apart" the body of Christ (1 Clement 46:7).

STRONG 1288, BAUER 188, MOULTON-MILLIGAN 153-54, LIDDELL-SCOTT 412.

1282. διασπάω diaspaō verb
Tear apart, break asunder.
CROSS-REFERENCE:
σπάω spaō (4538)

בָּקַע bāqaʿ (1260), Piel: tear open (Hos 13:8).

נָתַץ nāthats (5606), Break down (Jb 19:10).

נָתַק nāthaq (5607), Pull away, tear away; niphal: be snapped (Jgs 16:9, Jer 10:20); tear away (Jer 2:20); piel: snap in two, break (Jgs 16:12, Is 58:6).

פּוּץ pûts (6571), Disperse (Zep 3:10—only some Sinaiticus texts).

שָׁסַע shāsaʿ (8538), Piel: tear, tear in pieces (Jgs 14:6—Codex Alexandrinus only).

1. **διασπασθῇ** diaspasthē 3sing subj aor pass
2. **διεσπάσθαι** diespasthai inf perf mid

2 and the chains **had been plucked asunder** by him, ... Mark 5:4
1 fearing lest Paul should have been **pulled in pieces** ... Acts 23:10

Classical Greek and Septuagint Usage
In classical Greek literature *diaspaō* means to "tear apart, tear down." In one military context the word referred to an army that was scattered and in disorder. In the Septuagint *diaspaō* occurs 11 times. The lion that attacked Samson on his way to Timnah (the lion later became the object of his riddle) was "torn apart" by Samson's bare hands (Judges 14:6). It also describes the ease with which Samson broke the thongs with which Delilah had tied him (Judges 16:9).

New Testament Usage
Mark, the only Gospel writer to use *diaspaō*, dramatically depicted the Gadarene demoniac's strength (an aspect which Luke and Matthew neglect). Mark stated that the demoniac had been bound with chains and fetters many times, but he "broke" them (Mark 5:4).

Diaspaō occurs only one other time, in Acts. Because Paul had created such an uproar, the

1283. διασπείρω diaspeirō verb
Sow, scatter, or spread abroad.
CROSS-REFERENCE:
διασπορά diaspora (1284)

זָרָה zārāh (2306), Qal: winnow (Jer 15:7); piel: scatter (Lv 26:33, Ps 44:11 [43:11], Ez 12:14).

נָדַח nādhach (5258), Niphal: outcast (Is 56:8); be driven away (Jer 49:5 [30:5]); hiphil: drive out (Jer 32:37 [39:37]).

נָכָה nākhâh (5409), Hiphil: smite (Ez 32:15).

נָפַץ nāphats (5492), Be dispersed (Gn 9:19, Is 11:12, 33:3).

פָּאָה pāʾāh (6522), Hiphil: scatter (Dt 32:26).

פּוּץ pûts (6571), Qal: Be scattered, disperse (1 Sm 14:34, Ez 34:5); niphal: be scattered (1 Kgs 22:17, Jer 52:8); spread abroad (Gn 10:18); hiphil: scatter (Dt 28:64, Is 24:1, Ez 29:12).

פָּזַר pāzar (6582), Piel: scatter (Jl 3:2); pual: scattered (Est 3:8).

פָּרַד pāradh (6754), Niphal: be separated (Gn 10:32); pual: dispersed (Est 3:8); hiphil: separate from each other (Dt 32:8).

פְּרָזִי pᵉrāzî (6772), Open, rural country (Est 9:19).

פָּרַשׂ pāras (6816), Spread out; niphal: be scattered (Ez 17:21).

רִיק rîq (7671), Hiphil: leave unfed (Is 32:6).

שָׁגָה shāghâh (8146), Wander (Ez 34:6).

1. **διεσπάρησαν** diesparēsan 3pl indic aor pass
2. **διασπαρέντες** diasparentes
   nom pl masc part aor pass

1 and they were all **scattered abroad** .... Acts 8:1
2 Therefore they that were **scattered abroad** went 8:4
2 Now they which were **scattered abroad** 11:19

This is a compound verb from *dia* (1217), "throughout," and *speirō* (4540), "to sow seed." Vine says, "The word in general is suggestive of the effects of the scattering in the sowing of the spiritual seed of the word of life" (*Expository Dictionary*, "Scatter"). It was used by Luke (Acts 8:1,4; 11:19) in the passive form to refer to the dispersion of the Church from its Jerusalem origins. The noun *diaspora* (1284) was used 12 times in the Septuagint for the dispersion of the Jews among the Gentiles (Deuteronomy 28:25; 30:4; Jeremiah 41:17). (See James 1:1; 1 Peter 1:1 for New Testament references.)

STRONG 1289, BAUER 188, MOULTON-MILLIGAN 154, LIDDELL-SCOTT 412, COLIN BROWN 2:33-34.

1284. διασπορά diaspora noun
Dispersion.
COGNATES:
διασπείρω diaspeirō (1283)
σπάω spaō (4538)

זַוֲעָה zawă'āh (2196I), Horror (Jer 34:17 [41:17]).

חֶרְפָּה cherpāh (2887), Shame (Dn 12:2).

מִזְרֶה mizreh (4348), Winnowing fork (Jer 15:7).

נָדַח nādhach (5258), Niphal: outcasts, exiles (Dt 30:4, Neh 1:9, Ps 147:2 [146:2]).

נְצִירֵי nᵉtsyyrê (5521), Preserved ones (Is 49:6).

שָׁחַת shāchath (8271), Hiphil: destroy (Jer 13:14—only in some Sinaiticus texts).

1. **διασπορᾶς** diasporas gen sing fem
2. **διασπορᾷ** diaspora dat sing fem
3. **διασπορᾶν** diasporan acc sing fem

3 will he go unto the **dispersed** among the Gentiles, ... John 7:35
2 to the twelve tribes which are scattered **abroad**, ... Jas 1:1
1 to the strangers **scattered** throughout Pontus, ... 1 Pt 1:1

Classical Greek and Septuagint Usage
The term *diaspora*, "dispersion," occurs infrequently in secular Greek, but it appears regularly in Jewish and Christian documents where it is a technical term of the Jewish settlements outside the borders of Palestine (see Rothenberg, "Foreign," *Colin Brown*, 1:685f.).

The Septuagint used *diaspora* 12 times. The word renders loosely several Hebrew terms. On three occasions it translates *nādhach* which means "dispersed" (Deuteronomy 30:4; Nehemiah 1:9; Psalm 147:2 [LXX 146:2]). The translators of the Septuagint evidently preferred other, stronger language to convey the Hebrew record of the exile and captivity of the Jews. The technical sense was not known here.

Early in Israel's history God had warned Israel that it would be "scattered" or "dispersed" (cf. the verb *diaspeirō* [1283], "scatter") among the people of the earth (Deuteronomy 28:63-68). This dispersion began when Israel was carried off to Assyria (ca. 722 B.C.) and when Judah went into captivity in Babylon (ca. 586 B.C.). Many of the descendants of those who were exiled never returned to the land of Israel even when the opportunity to return arose (cf. Ezra). Later, many Jews also emigrated of their own free will to foreign lands.

New Testament Usage
During the time of the New Testament most of the Jews actually lived outside the borders of Israel. Egypt, Syria, Asia Minor, Greece, and Rome knew of numerous Jewish settlements. These "Diaspora Jews" enjoyed considerable religious freedom; they even built synagogues and won many adherents, or proselytes, to their religion. They maintained a connection with their homeland by sending temple taxes and offerings to the temple in Jerusalem.

Jesus warned of a new and total dispersion (Luke 21:24). This took place in part after the destruction of Jerusalem (A.D. 70), and it was realized further after the Bar Kochba revolt (ca. A.D. 135).

The same Old Testament prophecies which forewarned of the impending "dispersion" of Israel tell also that in the last days God will once more gather His people to their own land (Isaiah 11:12; 49:12; Jeremiah 31:8-10 [LXX 38: 8-10]; Ezekiel 20:32-38; 37:21).

In later Judaism *diaspora* was the usual term for describing those Jews who lived in areas which were formerly places of exile. The New Testament understands it in this sense of Jews who lived among the Greeks (John 7:35). The story of the dispersion of the Hellenists from Jerusalem following the stoning of Stephen uses the verb *diaspeirō* to describe the event (Acts 8:1,4; 11:19).

When James wrote of "the twelve tribes which are *scattered* abroad" (1:1) and when Peter wrote to "the strangers *scattered* throughout" (1 Peter 1:1), *diaspora* should probably be read in its traditional technical sense.

STRONG 1290, BAUER 188, KITTEL 2:98-104, LIDDELL-SCOTT 412, COLIN BROWN 1:685-86; 2:33-35.

1285. διαστέλλω diastellō verb
Command, give orders, admonish.
COGNATE:
στέλλομαι stellomai (4575)

διαστολή 1287

Synonyms:
διαμαρτύρομαι diamarturomai (1257)
διατάσσω diatassō (1293)
ἐντέλλομαι entellomai (1765)
ἐπιτάσσω epitassō (1988)
ἐπιτρέπω epitrepō (1994)
κελεύω keleuō (2724)
λέγω legō (2978)
ὁρκίζω horkizō (3589)
παραγγέλλω parangellō (3715)
προστάσσω prostassō (4225)
συντάσσω suntassō (4781)
τάσσω tassō (4872)

בָּדַל bādhal (950), Niphal: be set apart (1 Chr 23:13); be excluded from (Ezr 10:8); hiphil: distinguish (Lv 10:10); set apart (Dt 10:8, Ezr 8:24).

בָּטָא bāṭā' (1017II) Piel: speak rashly or thoughtlessly (Lv 5:4, Ps 106:33 [105:33]).

גָּזַז gāzaz (1525), Shear; niphal: be cut off (Na 1:12).

גָּעַר gā'ar (1647), Rebuke (Mal 3:11).

זָהַר zāhar (2178), Niphal: be warned (Ez 3:21); hiphil: warn (2 Chr 19:10, Ez 3:19ff.).

חָלַק chālaq (2606), Assign (2 Chr 23:18).

יָדַע yādha' (3156), Know; hiphil: teach (Ez 22:26).

נָקַב nāqav (5529), Pierce; designate (Gn 30:28).

סוּר ṣûr (5681), Turn aside; hiphil: remove (Gn 30:35).

פָּלָא pālā' (6623), Be extraordinary; piel: fulfill something hard or special (Lv 22:21).

פָּצָה pātsâh (6722), Utter (Ps 66:14 [65:14]).

פָּרָא pārā' (6750), Hiphil: flourish (Hos 13:15).

פָּרַד pāradh (6754), Niphal: be separated (Gn 25:23); hiphil: separate, separate from each other (Gn 30:40, Ru 1:17, 2 Kgs 2:11).

פָּרַע pāra' (6797), Let alone, relent (Ez 24:14).

פָּרַץ pārats (6805), Make a breach; niphal: be frequent (1 Sm 3:1).

פָּרַשׂ pāras (6816), Piel: scatter (Ps 68:14 [67:14]).

קָדַשׁ qādhash (7227), Be holy; hiphil: set apart (Jos 20:7).

קָרָה qārâh (7424), Happen; hiphil: select (Nm 35:11).

קָרַע qāra' (7458), Cut out (Jer 22:14).

רָמַס rāmaṣ (7717), Trample (Mi 5:8).

שִׂים śîm (7947), Put, set; give (Neh 8:8).

1. διαστελλόμενον diastellomenon
nom/acc sing neu part pres mid
2. διεστείλατο diesteilato 3sing indic aor mid
3. διεστειλάμεθα diesteilametha 1pl indic aor mid
4. διεστέλλετο diestelleto 3sing indic imperf mid

2 **charged** he his disciples that they should tell no .... Matt 16:20
2 **charged** them straitly that no man should know it; .. Mark 5:43
2 And he **charged** them that they should tell no man: 7:36
4 but the more he **charged** them, ... 7:36
4 And he **charged** them, saying, Take heed, ... 8:15
2 **he charged** them that they should tell no man 9:9
3 to whom we **gave** no such **commandment**: .... Acts 15:24
1 they could not endure that which **was commanded**, .. Heb 12:20

Vine says *diastellō* is a compound verb from *dia* (1217), "asunder," and *stellomai* (4575), "to draw" (*Expository Dictionary*, "Charge"). It is stronger than *entellomai* (1765), "command." *Diastellō* was used by Mark to lay great stress on the messianic secret. (In Mark 5:43; 7:36; and 9:9 Jesus "commands" those present to keep certain of His activities quiet.) It is also found in Hebrews 12:20.

STRONG 1291, BAUER 188, MOULTON-MILLIGAN 154, KITTEL 7:591-92, LIDDELL-SCOTT 412-13, COLIN BROWN 1:335.

1286. διάστημα diastēma noun
Space, interval.

בּוֹא bô' (971), Go in (Ez 41:6).
אֲצִילָה 'atstsîlah (701I), Height (Ez 41:8).
בִּנְיָן binyān (1177), Building (Ez 42:5).
גְּדֶרֶת gᵉdhereth (1481), Wall (Ez 42:12).
גִּזְרָה gizrāh (1539), Courtyard (Ez 42:13).
מִגְרָעוֹת mighrā'ôth (4192), Ledge (1 Kgs 6:6).
מִגְרָשׁ mighrāsh (4194), Open space (Ez 45:2, 48:15,17).
מִדָּה middāh (4201), Measure (1 Kgs 7:9).
מוּסָדָה mûsādhāh (4281), Base (Ez 41:8).
רֶוַח rewach (7592), Space (Gn 32:16).

1. διάστημα diastēma nom/acc sing neu

1 And it was about the space of three hours after, ... Acts 5:7

Classical Greek and Septuagint Usage
This term comes from *dia* (1217), "through," and *histēmi* (2449), "stand, set, place." In classical Greek *diastēma* was frequently used since the time of Plato to mean an "interval" of music, but it could also refer to (geometric) "radius" and "distance" (see *Liddell-Scott*). The primary use of this term in the Septuagint seems related to the idea of "distance" in that it is most often used to translate *mighrāsh*, "open land or space" (Ezekiel 45:2; 48:15,17).

New Testament Usage
In the New Testament it is used only once in Acts 5:17 to refer to the interval or space of time between Ananias' death and Sapphira's similar offense which resulted in her death as well.

STRONG 1292, BAUER 188, MOULTON-MILLIGAN 154, LIDDELL-SCOTT 413.

1287. διαστολή diastolē noun
Difference, distinction, separation.

διαστρέφω 1288

CROSS-REFERENCE:
στέλλομαι stellomai (4575)

חֻקָּה chuqqāh (2807), Statute (Nm 19:2).
מִבְטָא miṭṭā' (4147), Rash vow (Nm 30:6 [30:7]).
פְּדוּת pᵉdhûth (6545), Division (Ex 8:23).

1. **διαστολή** diastolē nom sing fem
2. **διαστολήν** diastolēn acc sing fem

1 for there is no **difference**:	Rom 3:22
1 is no **difference** between the Jew and the Greek:	10:12
2 except they give a **distinction** in the sounds,	1 Co 14:7

Classical Greek and Septuagint Usage
In classical Greek *diastolē* means "dilatation" or "separation." This could be used literally in a medical sense of "dilating" or in the sense of physical "separation" by a boundary or fence. With regard to people, *diastolē* is used to mean "discrimination" or "distinction."

The Septuagint uses *diastolē* to translate three Hebrew terms in a manner consistent with classical usage. In Exodus 8:23 God instructed Moses to tell Pharaoh how He would "put a division (difference)" between the Israelites and the Egyptians so the plague of flies would afflict only the Egyptians (see also Numbers 19:2; 30:7).

New Testament Usage
In the New Testament Paul is the only writer to use this word. In two of its three uses Paul referred to the lack of "difference" between Jew and Gentile because of the "righteousness of God which is by faith of Jesus Christ unto all and upon all them that believe" (Romans 3:22; cf. 10:12).

STRONG 1293, BAUER 188, MOULTON-MILLIGAN 154, KITTEL 7:592-93, LIDDELL-SCOTT 413.

1288. διαστρέφω diastrephō verb
Pervert, turn away, seduce, oppose, corrupt.
COGNATE:
στρέφω strephō (4613)
SYNONYMS:
μεταστρέφω metastrephō (3214)
στρέφω strephō (4613)

הָפַךְ hāphakh (2089), Turn, overturn; hithpael: change direction (Jb 37:12).
הֵפֶךְ hēphekh (2090), Opposite (Ez 16:34).
כָּאַב kā'av (3628), Be in pain; hiphil: cause grief (Ez 13:22).
כָּאָה kā'āh (3630), Be disheartened; hiphil: dishearten (Ez 13:22).
נָטָה nāṭāh (5371), Extend, stretch out; hiphil: pervert (Ex 23:6).

עָוַת 'āwath (6003), Piel: make crooked (Eccl 7:13 [7:14]); pual: crooked (Eccl 1:15); hithpael: stoop (Eccl 12:3).
עָכַר 'ākhar (6138), Trouble (1 Kgs 18:17,18).
עָקַל 'āqal (6365), Pual: perverted (Hb 1:4).
עֲקַלְקַל 'ăqalqāl (6366), Winding (Jgs 5:6).
עָקַשׁ 'āqash (6378), Piel: pervert (Prv 10:9, Mi 3:9).
עִקֵּשׁ 'iqqēsh (6379), Perverted (Prv 11:20).
פָּרַע pāra' (6797), Let go; hiphil: cause to rest (Ex 5:4).
פָּתַל pāthal (6871), Twist; hithpael: prove oneself astute (Ps 18:26 [17:26]).
פְּתַלְתֹּל pᵉthaltōl (6872), Crooked (Dt 32:5).
צוּד tsûdh (6942), Pilpel: hunt (Ez 13:18).
תַּהְפֻּכָה tahpukhāh (8749), Perverse thing (Prv 8:13, 16:30).
תּוּר tûr (8780), Follow (Nm 15:39).
תָּפַשׂ tāphas (8945), Capture (Ez 14:5—Codex Alexandrinus only).

1. **διαστρέφων** diastrephōn
   nom sing masc part pres act
2. **διαστρέφοντα** diastrephonta
   acc sing masc part pres act
3. **διαστρέψαι** diastrepsai inf aor act
4. **διεστραμμένης** diestrammenēs
   gen sing fem part perf mid
5. **διεστραμμένη** diestrammenē
   nom sing fem part perf mid
6. **διεστραμμένα** diestrammena
   nom/acc pl neu part perf mid

5 O faithless and **perverse** generation,	Matt 17:17
5 O faithless and **perverse** generation,	Luke 9:41
2 We found this fellow **perverting** the nation,	23:2
3 seeking **to turn away** the deputy from the faith.	Acts 13:8
1 wilt thou not cease **to pervert** the right ways	13:10
6 speaking **perverse** things, to draw away disciples	20:30
4 in the midst of a crooked and **perverse** nation,	Phlp 2:15

Classical Greek
Diastrephō is actually a compound word formed from *dia* (1217) and *strephō* (4613), "turn." It can in most cases be literally translated "make crooked" or "misshape" as in a craftsman's poor workmanship. As a technical term *diastrephō* acquired moral overtones. According to the ethical system of ancient Stoics, "The nature of man, which is originally good and oriented to the good, is 'twisted' (*diastrephetai*) by bad teaching and example and by environmental influences of all kinds" (Bertram, "diastrephō," *Kittel*, 7:717).

Septuagint Usage
Diastrephō occurs a number of times in the Septuagint, generally with a negative sense, such as the "crooked" generation of Israel (Deuteronomy 32:5). Ironically Ahab called

Elijah the "troubler" of Israel (1 Kings 18:17). The Lord abhors mankind's "crooked ways" (Proverbs 8:13).

New Testament Usage

The New Testament reflects the figurative sense very plainly in Matthew 17:17 (cf. Luke 9:41). Jesus lamented that His "generation" was unbelieving or faithless (*apistos* [566]) and "crooked." The conjoining of *diastrephō* with *apistos* shows the desperate condition of the people.

Four of the remaining instances of *diastrephō* are credited to Luke (23:2; Acts 13:8,10; 20:30). Before Pilate Jesus was accused by the chief priests and elders of "turning away" (NIV, "subverting") the nation. Paul called Elymas' acts of sorcery and magic a "perversion" of the right ways of God (Acts 13:8). Elymas had attempted to "turn" (*diastrephō*) the proconsul, Sergius Paulus, from the faith.

Paul used *diastrephō* in Philippians 2:15 in a way similar to the Gospel writers. The Philippians were urged to be "faultless" (*amōmos* [297]) in the midst of a "crooked" (*skolios* [4501]) and "perverse" (*diastrephō*) generation.

STRONG 1294, BAUER 189, MOULTON-MILLIGAN 154, KITTEL 7:717-19, LIDDELL-SCOTT 413.

1289. διασῴζω diasōzō verb

Save, recover, heal perfectly, convey safely through.

COGNATE:
σῴζω sōzō (4834)

SYNONYMS:
ἐξαιρέω exaireō (1791)
λυτρόω lutroō (3056)
σῴζω sōzō (4834)

חָיָה chāyâh (2513), Be alive; piel: let live (Jos 9:15).

יָשַׁע yāshaʻ (3588), Niphal: be saved, be rescued (Nm 10:9, Jer 8:20); hiphil: save (Dt 20:4, Zec 8:13, Hos 13:10).

מָלַט mālaṯ (4561), Niphal: escape (Gn 19:19, Jgs 3:29, Am 9:1); piel: deliver (Jb 29:12, Eccl 8:8).

עָשַׁת ʻāshath (6486), Hithpael: take notice of (Jn 1:6).

פָּלַט pālaṯ (6647), Escape; piel: give birth (Jb 21:10); save (Mi 6:14); hiphil: save (Mi 6:14).

פָּלִיט pālîṭ (6654), Fugitive (Jgs 12:4,5).

פָּלֵט pālêṭ (6655), Fugitive (Nm 21:29).

פְּלֵיטָה pᵉlêṭāh (6656), What has escaped, survivor (Jgs 21:17, Dn 11:42).

שָׂרַד sāradh (8018), Escape (Jos 10:20).

שָׂרִיד sārîdh (8032), Survivor (Jos 10:28,30,37,39).

1. **διασώσῃ** diasōsē 3sing subj aor act
2. **διασώσωσιν** diasōsōsin 3pl subj aor act
3. **διασῶσαι** diasōsai inf aor act
4. **διεσώθησαν** diesōthēsan 3pl indic aor pass
5. **διασωθέντα** diasōthenta acc sing masc part aor pass
6. **διασωθέντες** diasōthentes nom pl masc part aor pass
7. **διασωθῆναι** diasōthēnai inf aor pass
8. **διασώσωσι** diasōsōsi 3pl subj aor act

```
4 as many as touched were made perfectly whole...... Matt 14:36
1 beseeching him that he would come and heal....... Luke 7:3
2 and bring him safe unto Felix the governor......... Acts 23:24
3 willing to save Paul, kept them from their purpose;.... 27:43
7 that they escaped all safe to land..................... 27:44
6 And when they were escaped,......................... 28:1
5 whom, though he hath escaped the sea,.............. 28:4
4 few, that is, eight souls were saved by water........ 1 Pt 3:20
```

Classical Greek

In classical Greek this verb—from *dia* (1217), "through," and *sōzō* (4834), "to save"—in the active voice means "to preserve through" (a danger). Passively it means "to be rescued, to pass safely through." It is also used of things which were "maintained" and of "recovering" from an illness (*Liddell-Scott*).

Septuagint Usage

Diasōzō occurs over 60 times in the Septuagint where it corresponds to six Hebrew words and six additional forms of those words. Most commonly *mālaṯ*, "to get to safety," and forms of *pālaṯ*, "to escape, to be delivered, to be spared," occur. Lot did not feel he could "escape" the disaster the Lord was about to bring upon Sodom and Gomorrah by fleeing to the mountains (see Genesis 19:19). The Lord went with Israel to "deliver" her from her enemies (cf. Numbers 10:9; Deuteronomy 20:4). Joshua, following the instructions of the Lord, allowed no "survivors" in his sweeping victory over the five kings (Joshua 10:20,28,30,37,39,40; 11:8).

New Testament Usage

The New Testament understanding of *diasōzō* (eight times) varies. It is used in the sense of "to recover" (from an illness) in the Gospels (Matthew 14:36; Luke 7:3). But in Acts, Luke employed *diasōzō* of Paul's "safe passage" from Jerusalem to Felix the governor (23:24). In Acts chapter 27 *diasōzō* describes the "safe arrival" on land of Paul's shipwrecked captors and companions who "escaped" the clutches of the sea (Acts 27:43,44; 28:1,4).

A most significant text is 1 Peter 3:20 which speaks of Noah's being "preserved," "rescued,"

διαταγή 1290

or "delivered" through the water (*diesōthēsan di hudatos*) of the Flood by the ark. Josephus also used *diasōzō* twice in reference to Noah's being "saved" from the waters of the Flood by the ark (*Against Apion* 1.19; *Antiquities* 1.3.2), but he had no other image in his mind of this "deliverance." However, Peter drew a parallel between Noah's rescue "through" (*dia*, not "from") the waters of the Flood to the believers' passage from death to life in the waters of baptism (3:21). That is, just as Noah's coming safely through the waters of the Flood was a testimony to the faith he had before the Flood, so going through baptism testifies to the faith one has for salvation before baptism.

Strong 1295, Bauer 189, Moulton-Milligan 154, Liddell-Scott 414, Colin Brown 3:205,211-12.

1290. διαταγή diatagē noun
Ordinance, direction, arrangement, disposition.
Cross-Reference:
τάσσω tassō (4872)

פַּרְשֶׁגֶן parsheghen (A6823), Copy (Ezr 4:11—Aramaic).

1. **διαταγῇ** diatagē dat sing fem
2. **διαταγάς** diatagas acc pl fem

2 have received the law by the **disposition** of angels,...Acts 7:53
1 resisteth the **ordinance** of God:................. Rom 13:2

This word is related to the verb *tassō* (4872), "place in order, arrange, appoint," and its intensive form *diatassō* (1293), "command" or "prescribe." It is translated "disposition" in Acts 7:53. Vincent (*Word Studies in the New Testament*, 1:484f.) comments that this "disposition" is in the "sense of arrangement as we say a general disposed his troops." The reference here is most likely to the Jewish tradition that the Law was given through the agency of angels (Deuteronomy 33:2; Psalm 68:17 [LXX 67:17]; Galatians 3:19). See Romans 13:2 for the only other New Testament use of this noun.

Strong 1296, Bauer 189, Moulton-Milligan 155, Kittel 8:36, Liddell-Scott 414.

1291. διάταγμα diatagma noun
Mandate, decree, edict, command.
Cognate:
τάσσω tassō (4872)
Synonyms:
δόγμα dogma (1372)
ἔνταλμα entalma (1762)
ἐντολή entolē (1769)
ἐπιταγή epitagē (1987)

נִשְׁתְּוָן nisht^ewān (5588), Letter (Ezr 7:11).

1. **διάταγμα** diatagma nom/acc sing neu

1 they were not afraid of the king's **commandment**.... Heb 11:23

This is a term used to indicate an official "command," "edict," or "decree" by an emperor or a king. It is related to *tagma* (4852) meaning "that which is ordered." *Diatagma* is used once in the New Testament, Hebrews 11:23, in reference to the king of Egypt's "edict" to kill all male babies.

Strong 1297, Bauer 189, Moulton-Milligan 155, Liddell-Scott 414, Colin Brown 1:330.

1292. διαταράσσω diatarassō verb
Agitate, trouble greatly, confuse.
Cross-Reference:
ταράσσω tarassō (4866)

1. **διεταράχθη** dietarachthē 3sing indic aor pass

1 when she saw him, she **was troubled** at his saying,...Luke 1:29

This word comes from *dia* (1217), which means "throughout," and *tarassō* (4866), "to stir up, disturb, throw into confusion." In Luke 1:29 it refers to Mary's intense feeling when she was greeted by the angel who told her she would become pregnant with Jesus. This is the only occurrence of *diatarassō* in the New Testament.

Strong 1298, Bauer 189, Liddell-Scott 414.

1293. διατάσσω diatassō verb
Give orders, command, direct, arrange, prescribe.
Cognate:
τάσσω tassō (4872)
Synonyms:
διαμαρτύρομαι diamarturomai (1257)
διαστέλλω diastellō (1285)
ἐντέλλομαι entellomai (1765)
ἐπιτάσσω epitassō (1988)
ἐπιτρέπω epitrepō (1994)
κελεύω keleuō (2724)
λέγω legō (2978)
ὁρκίζω horkizō (3589)
παραγγέλλω parangellō (3715)
προστάσσω prostassō (4225)
συντάσσω suntassō (4781)
τάσσω tassō (4872)

אָמַר 'āmar (569), Say; appoint (1 Kgs 11:18).
חָקַק chāqaq (2809), Commander (Jgs 5:9).
מָדַד mādhadh (4200), Measure (Ez 42:20).
פְּטִירִים p^etִyyrîm (6601), Free from duty (1 Chr 9:33).

שִׂים sîm (7947), Appoint (Ez 21:19).

שָׁמַר shāmar (8490), Retain, keep (2 Chr 5:11, Ez 44:8).

1. **διατάσσων diatassōn** nom sing masc part pres act
2. **διέταξα dietaxa** 1sing indic aor act
3. **διέταξεν dietaxen** 3sing indic aor act
4. **διατεταχέναι diatetachenai** inf perf act
5. **διατάσσομαι diatassomai** 1sing indic pres mid
6. **διεταξάμην dietaxamēn** 1sing indic aor mid
7. **διετάξατο dietaxato** 3sing indic aor mid
8. **διαταγείς diatageis** nom sing masc part aor pass
9. **διαταξάμενος diataxamenos** nom sing masc part aor mid
10. **διαταχθέντα diatachthenta** nom/acc pl neu part aor pass
11. **διατεταγμένος diatetagmenos** nom sing masc part perf mid
12. **διατεταγμένον diatetagmenon** nom/acc sing neu part perf mid
13. **διατάξομαι diataxomai** 1sing indic fut mid

```
1  made an end of commanding his twelve disciples, Matt 11:1
12 Exact no more than that which is appointed you.... Luke 3:13
3  she arose ... and he commanded to give her meat......  8:55
10 he did the things that were commanded him?.........  17:9
10 done all those things which are commanded you,......  17:10
7  as he had appointed, speaking unto Moses,......... Acts 7:44
4  Claudius had commanded all Jews to depart..........  18:2
11 intending to take in Paul: for so had he appointed,... 20:13
12 Then the soldiers, as it was commanded them,.......  23:31
9  And he commanded a centurion to keep Paul,........  24:23
5  And so ordain I in all churches................... 1 Co 7:17
3  Even so hath the Lord ordained......................  9:14
13 And the rest will I set in order when I come.........  11:34
2  as I have given order to the churches of Galatia,.....  16:1
8  was ordained by angels in the hand of a mediator... Gal 3:19
6  ordain elders ... as I had appointed thee:............ Tit 1:5
```

Classical Greek and Septuagint Usage
The verb *diatassō* occurs in Greek writings from the time of Herodotus. It is used in the Septuagint (e.g., Judges 5:9; 1 Kings 11:18 [LXX 3 Kings]; Ezekiel 21:24 [LXX 21:19]) to translate eight different Hebrew words that all refer to "order, direct or command."

New Testament Usage
There are 16 instances of *diatassō* in the New Testament. Most are attributed to Luke (nine times) or Paul (six times). It can denote God's "directing" Moses (Acts 7:44) or the Emperor Claudius' "commanding" that Jews must leave Rome (Acts 18:2). Paul wrote that in all the churches he "commanded" that people should remain as they had been called (1 Corinthians 7:17; cf. other instructions, 1 Corinthians 11:34; Titus 1:5). The Lord "ordered" that those preaching the gospel should receive their living from it (1 Corinthians 9:14).

Strong 1299, Bauer 189, Moulton-Milligan 155, Kittel 8:34-35, Liddell-Scott 414, Colin Brown 3:854.

1294. διατελέω diateleō verb
Continue, remain.

Cognate:
τελέω teleō (4903)

Synonyms:
ἀπολείπω apoleipō (614)
αὐλίζομαι aulizomai (829)
διαμένω diamenō (1259)
διατρίβω diatribō (1298)
ἐμμένω emmenō (1682)
ἐπιμένω epimenō (1946)
καθίζω kathizō (2495)
καταμένω katamenō (2620)
μένω menō (3176)
παραμένω paramenō (3748)
περιλείπομαι perileipomai (3898)
ὑπομένω hupomenō (5116)

הָיָה hāyâh (2030), Be, is (Dt 9:7).

כָּלָה kālâh (3735), Come to an end (Jer 20:18).

1. **διατελεῖτε diateleite** 2pl indic pres act

```
1 and continued fasting, having taken nothing........Acts 27:33
```

This intransitive verb appears in classical Greek from the time of Herodotus to mean "continue being or doing" and could also be used as "persevere" with regard to something done zealously (see *Liddell-Scott*). The Septuagint uses this term only three times (Deuteronomy 9:7; Jeremiah 20:7,18) in a manner consistent with the classical usage. Its only occurrence in the New Testament is in Acts 27:33 where Paul exhorted the soldiers in the midst of a storm to end their "*continued* fasting."

Strong 1300, Bauer 189, Moulton-Milligan 155, Liddell-Scott 415.

1295. διατηρέω diatēreō verb
Guard, keep, preserve, abstain.

Cross-Reference:
τηρέω tēreō (4931)

הָלַךְ hālakh (2050), Go, walk; hiphil: bring, take (Ex 2:9).

מִשְׁמֶרֶת mishmereth (5111), What is kept (Ex 12:6).

נָצַר nātsar (5526), Keep (Ex 34:7, Dt 33:9, Prv 22:12).

עָמַד 'āmadh (6198), Stand; hiphil: let remain (Ex 9:16).

שָׁמַר shāmar (8490), Keep (Gn 17:9, Prv 21:23).

1. **διατηροῦντες diatērountes** nom pl masc part pres act
2. **διετήρει dietērei** 3sing indic imperf act

```
2 but his mother kept all these sayings in her heart....Luke 2:51
1 from which if ye keep yourselves, ye shall do well. Acts 15:29
```

Classical Greek
A common word in antiquity (e.g., Plato, Josephus, Philo, and the Septuagint) but

relatively rare in the New Testament (only two times), *diatēreō* means "keep" and "keep oneself from" something. It is a compound verb of the preposition *dia* (1217) and the verb *tēreō* (4931), "keep."

Septuagint Usage
The Septuagint uses *diatēreō* 16 times. For example, God commanded that His covenant (*diathēkē* [1236]) be "kept" (Genesis 17:9,10; Deuteronomy 33:9). In Theodotion's version of Daniel, Daniel "keeps" the matter of the interpretation of the dream of the four beasts to himself (Daniel 7:28, *diatēreō*; cf. Daniel 7:28 [Septuagint], *stērizō* [4592]).

New Testament Usage
A usage very similar to Theodotion's use occurs in Luke 2:51 of Mary who "keeps," "treasures" (*diatēreō*), in her heart the words of the boy Jesus that He must be about His Father's business. Luke is responsible for the only other instance of *diatēreō*. In Acts 15:29 the second sense of "keep oneself from" is preferred. The Gentile believers were advised by the Jerusalem Council to "keep themselves from" food that had been sacrificed to idols, from blood, from the meat of any strangled animal, and from sexual immorality.

STRONG 1301, BAUER 189, MOULTON-MILLIGAN 155, KITTEL 8:151, LIDDELL-SCOTT 415.

1296. διατί diati adv
Why? Wherefore.

1. διατί diati

1 Why eateth your Master with publicans and	Matt 9:11
1 Why do we and the Pharisees fast oft,	9:14
1 Why speakest thou unto them in parables?	13:10
1 Why do thy disciples transgress the tradition	15:2
1 Why do ye also transgress the commandment	15:3
1 Why could not we cast him out?	17:19
1 Why did ye not then believe him?	21:25
1 Why do the disciples of John and ... Pharisees fast,	Mark 2:18
1 Why walk not thy disciples according to	7:5
1 he will say, Why then did ye not believe him?	11:31
1 saying, Why do ye eat and drink with publicans	Luke 5:30
1 Why do the disciples of John fast often,	5:33
1 Wherefore then gavest not thou my money into the	19:23
1 And if any man ask you, Why do ye loose him?	19:31
1 he will say, Why then believed ye him not?	20:5
1 and why do thoughts arise in your hearts?	24:38
1 Why have ye not brought him?	John 7:45
1 Why do ye not understand my speech?	8:43
1 And if I say the truth, why do ye not believe me?	8:46
1 Why was not this ointment sold	12:5
1 Lord, why cannot I follow thee now?	13:37
1 Ananias, why hath Satan filled thine heart	Acts 5:3
1 Wherefore? Because they sought it not by faith,	Rom 9:32
1 Why do ye not rather take wrong?	1 Co 6:7
1 why do ye not rather suffer yourselves	6:7
1 Wherefore? because I love you not? God knoweth.	2 Co 11:11
1 angel said unto me, Wherefore didst thou marvel!..	Rev 17:7

This term is used in a direct question to someone meaning "why?" or "for what reason?" It is a compound word from *dia* (1217), which means "because of" or "for the sake of," and from *ti* (see 4949), which means "what?" or "why?" Many critical editions do not read *diati* as one word but as two separate words, *dia ti*. This in no way affects the sense (e.g., Matthew 15:2,3; 17:19; 21:25; Mark 11:31; Acts 5:3; etc.).

STRONG 1302, BAUER 189.

1297. διατίθημι diatithēmi verb
Decree, ordain, assign.
CROSS-REFERENCE:
τίθημι tithēmi (4935)

כָּרַת kārath (3901), Make a covenant (Dt 5:2, 2 Sm 3:13, Is 55:3).

נָתַן nāthan (5598), Give (Hos 11:8).

צָוָה tsāwâh (6943), Piel: command (Jos 7:11).

קוּם qûm (7251), Stand up, arise; hiphil: establish (Gn 9:17).

שָׁלַם shālam (8396), Be complete; hiphil: make peace (1 Chr 19:19).

1. διατίθεμαι diatithemai 1sing indic pres mid
2. διέθετο dietheto 3sing indic aor mid
3. διαθέμενος diathemenos
  nom sing masc part aor mid
4. διαθεμένου diathemenou
  gen sing masc part aor mid
5. διαθήσομαι diathēsomai 1sing indic fut mid

1 And I appoint unto you a kingdom,	Luke 22:29
2 a kingdom, as my Father hath appointed unto me;	22:29
2 of the covenant which God made with our fathers,	Acts 3:25
5 For this is the covenant that I will make	Heb 8:10
4 must also of necessity be the death of the testator.	9:16
3 it is of no strength at all while the testator liveth.	9:17
5 This is the covenant that I will make with them	10:16

Classical Greek and Septuagint Usage
Diatithēmi, which in our literature appears only in the middle voice (*diatithemai*), occurs often in every kind of Greek literature. Its definition means "decree, ordain" (found regularly in the Septuagint), "confer," or "assign" or "make a will" (see *Bauer*). Ordinarily *diatithēmi* replaces the Hebrew *kārath* in the Septuagint. Its association with covenant language (cf. *diathēkē* [1236]) is clear from its first uses in Genesis 9:17, the account of the covenant sign of the rainbow (Genesis 15:18 [manuscript R]; cf. Genesis 26:28; 31:44; Deuteronomy 5:2; etc.)

It thus means "make an agreement, establish a covenant."

New Testament Usage

Only Luke and the writer of Hebrews utilized *diatithēmi* in the New Testament. In a solemn, almost ceremonial setting, Jesus "confers" (NIV) a kingdom to the disciples just as the Father "conferred" to Him (Luke 22:29). Acts 3:25 makes an even closer association of *diatithēmi* with the idea of "make a will" by linking it to *diathēkē*, "covenant, will, testament." Literally, Peter declared to his listeners that they were heirs to the "covenant God covenanted" with their ancestors.

Covenant language—that of making a will—occurs exclusively in the Hebrews' use of *diatithēmi*. Two allusions are to Jeremiah 31:31 (LXX 38:31), speak of the new covenant God promised "to covenant" with His people (*diathēkē hen diathēsomai*; cf. Hebrews 8:10; 10:16). Likewise, in Hebrews 9:16,17 the language of "will making" or "covenant" provides the context for understanding *diatithēmi*. The death of Christ effected the new covenant, for "a will is in force only when somebody has died" (verse 17, NIV). Thus the New Testament, even Luke's Gospel, seems to take *diatithēmi* to be formally associated with the death of Christ as the signal that the new testament of God was now in force.

Strong 1303, Bauer 189-90, Moulton-Milligan 155-56, Kittel 2:104-6, Liddell-Scott 415.

1298. διατρίβω diatribō verb

Spend time, pass time, stay.

Synonyms:
ἀπολείπω apoleipō (614)
αὐλίζομαι aulizomai (829)
διαμένω diamenō (1259)
διατελέω diateleō (1294)
εἰμί eimi (1498)
ἐμμένω emmenō (1682)
ἐπιμένω epimenō (1946)
καθίζω kathizō (2495)
καταμένω katamenō (2620)
μένω menō (3176)
παραμένω paramenō (3748)
περιλείπομαι perileipomai (3898)
ὑπομένω hupomenō (5116)

גּוּר gûr (1513), Stay (Jer 35:7 [42:7]).
יָשַׁב yāshav (3553), Dwell (Lv 14:8).

1. **διατρίβοντες diatribontes** nom pl masc part pres act
2. **διετρίψαμεν dietripsamen** 1pl indic aor act
3. **διέτριψαν dietripsan** 3pl indic aor act
4. **διατρίψας diatripsas** nom sing masc part aor act
5. **διέτριβεν dietriben** 3sing indic imperf act
6. **διέτριβον dietribon** 3pl indic imperf act

5	and there he **tarried** with them, and baptized.	John 3:22
5	and there **continued** with his disciples.	11:54
5	from Judaea to Caesarea, and there **abode**.	Acts 12:19
3	Long time therefore **abode** they speaking boldly	14:3
6	And there they **abode** long time with the disciples.	14:28
6	Paul also and Barnabas **continued** in Antioch,	15:35
1	and we were in that city **abiding** certain days.	16:12
2	to Troas in five days; where we **abode** seven days.	20:6
4	he **had tarried** among them more than ten days,	25:6
6	And when they **had been** there many days,	25:14

Classical Greek

Diatribō (from *dia* [1217], "through," and *tribō*, "rub") occurs as early as Homer (ca. 8–6 B.C.). A very rare meaning of the term is "rub hard." More frequently it means "spend time, reside, stay, remain, waste time" (*Liddell-Scott*). It was utilized by the Septuagint translators as well as Hellenistic writers contemporary with the New Testament (e.g., Josephus *Antiquities* 6.8.6, 8.11.1).

Septuagint Usage

The more common classical meaning is found in the Septuagint at Leviticus 14:8; the unclean individual must "spend" 7 days outside his or her own residence. Tobit, one of the apocryphal writings of the Septuagint, used *diatribō* in its rare sense of "rub" (11:8,12). Sometimes *diatribō* is in reference to a locality rather than time. "Nicanor stayed on in Jerusalem ..." (2 Maccabees 14:23; cf. Judith 10:2; the RSV translates *diatribō* "lived").

New Testament Usage

Of its 10 appearances in the New Testament 8 occur in Acts (12:19; 14:3,28; 15:35; 16:12; 20:6; 25:6,14). In Acts, every use of *diatribō* follows the common classical usages. Herod traveled from Judea to Caesarea and "stayed" (NIV) there for a while (12:19). So, too, Paul and Barnabas *spend* considerable time in the Iconium synagogue boldly proclaiming the gospel (14:3).

John's Gospel is credited with an instance of *diatribō* at 3:22. Jesus went into the Judean countryside and *spends* time with His disciples. In a similar account at John 11:54, some manuscripts read *diatriben* (aorist, *diatribō*), but the others read *emeinen*, from *menō* (3176), "abide, remain." One can easily see that the two words were understood to mean the same thing.

Strong 1304, Bauer 190, Moulton-Milligan 156, Liddell-Scott 416.

1299. διατροφή diatrophē noun
Nourishment, food.
Cross-Reference:
τρέφω trephō (4982)

1. διατροφάς diatrophas acc pl fem

1 food and raiment let us be therewith content........ 1 Tm 6:8

Used only once, in 1 Timothy 6:8, this word denotes food for the physical body. It is from *trophē* (5001), "food." Vine suggests that *dia* (1217) adds strength: "suggesting a sufficient supply" (*Expository Dictionary*, "Food").
Strong 1305, Bauer 190, Moulton-Milligan 156, Liddell-Scott 416.

1300. διαυγάζω diaugazō verb
Shine through, break of dawn.
Cross-Reference:
αὐγάζω augazō (820)

1. διαυγάσῃ diaugasē 3sing subj aor act

1 that shineth in a dark place, until the day dawn,..... 2 Pt 1:19

This is a compound verb from *dia* (1217), "through," and *augazō* (820), "see" or "shine forth." In classical Greek this term is used mostly to mean "shine through." However, it could also mean "transparent" (especially as a perfect participle), "translucent." Metaphorically it means "being enlightened." Despite the varied usage of this term in classical Greek, the Septuagint has no Old Testament reference for it, and it is used only once in the New Testament. Peter exhorted his hearers to "take heed, as unto a light that shineth in a dark place, until the day *dawn*," for the day of Christ's return will surely come (2 Peter 1:19).
Strong 1306, Bauer 190, Moulton-Milligan 156, Liddell-Scott 417, Colin Brown 2:289.

1300B. διαυγής diaugēs adj
Transparent.
Cross-Reference:
αὐγάζω augazō (820)

1. διαυγής diaugēs nom sing masc

1 was pure gold, like transparent glass (NASB)....... Rev 21:21

This hapax legomenon, a composite of the preposition *dia* (1217), "through," and the noun *augē* (821), "light of the sun," literally means "translucent" or "transparent." Aristotle (Fourth Century B.C.) and other early writers used this word to describe the transparency of water. Callimachus (Third Century B.C.) used it of metal, giving it the meaning of "radiant." Its only New Testament occurrence is in Revelation 21:21 where John described the streets of the New Jerusalem: "the street of the city was pure gold, as it were *transparent* glass."
Bauer 190, Liddell-Scott 417.

1301. διαφανής diaphanēs adj
Transparent.
Cross-Reference:
φαίνω phainō (5154)

זַךְ zakh (2217), Pure (Ex 30:34).

1. διαφανής diaphanēs nom sing masc

1 was pure gold, as it were transparent glass......... Rev 21:21

This is a compound from *dia* (1217), "through," and *phainō* (5154), "shine, give light." In Revelation 21:21 it is used to denote transparent glass. Some modern critical editions (e.g., *Nestle-Aland 26th*, *UBS 3rd*), however, read *diaugēs* (1300B) instead of *diaphanēs* here.
Strong 1307, Bauer 190, Moulton-Milligan 156, Liddell-Scott 417.

1302. διαφέρω diapherō verb
Carry, spread, be worth more than, differ, be different.
Cross-Reference:
φέρω pherō (5179)

שְׁנָה sh^{e}nāh (A8522), Peal: be different (Dn 7:3,23,24); hithpaal: change (Dn 7:28—Aramaic).

1. διαφέρει diapherei 3sing indic pres act
2. διαφέρετε diapherete 2pl indic pres act
3. διαφέροντα diapheronta nom/acc pl neu part pres act
4. διενέγκῃ dienenkē 3sing subj aor act
5. διαφερομένων diapheromenōn gen pl masc part pres mid
6. διεφέρετο diephereto 3sing indic imperf pass

2 Are ye not much better than they?................. Matt 6:26
2 ye are of more value than many sparrows............. 10:31
1 How much then is a man better than a sheep?........ 12:12
4 man should carry any vessel through the temple....Mark 11:16
2 ye are of more value than many sparrows........Luke 12:7
2 how much more are ye better than the fowls?......... 12:24
6 And the word of the Lord was published...........Acts 13:49
5 as we were driven up and down in Adria,................ 27:27
3 and approvest the things that are more excellent,.... Rom 2:18
1 for one star differeth from another star in glory.... 1 Co 15:41
1 whatsoever they were, it maketh no matter to me:....Gal 2:6

1 differeth nothing from a servant, though he be lord...Gal 4:1
3 That ye may approve things that are excellent;......Phlp 1:10

Classical Greek
Diapherō occurs frequently in classical Greek and has a variety of meanings: "to differ" or "be different," also "to carry over or across, to go through, to bear, endure, spread, separate," etc. When the meaning is "to differ," it may have both positive ("to excel or surpass") and negative ("to quarrel") connotations (Weiss, "diapherō," *Kittel*, 9:62).

Septuagint Usage
In the Septuagint *diapherō* occurs 17 times as the translation of the Hebrew (or Aramaic) *shᵉnāh*. Noteworthy in the Septuagint are Proverbs 20:2 which depicts the rage of a king as not different from the roar of a lion, 1 Esdras 5:55 which speaks of cedar trees being brought or carried on floats to Joppa, and Wisdom of Solomon 18:10 which is commonly held to refer to enemies who are at variance with or who differ from the Israelites.

New Testament Usage
Diapherō is found in the New Testament just 13 times. In three cases it means basically "to carry": Mark 11:16 which refers to a man carrying a vessel or container, Acts 13:49 which speaks of the word of the Lord being carried or published through the whole area, and Acts 27:27 where Paul's Rome-destined ship was carried or driven by the storm. In five instances (Matthew 6:26; 10:31; 12:12; Luke 12:7,24) it is used to compare the value of a human being with nature (birds, sheep, etc.). In each case it is claimed that the value of human life is much greater in God's eyes, thus placing humanity in a special sphere of His love and care. In 1 Corinthians 15:41, while writing of the resurrected body which he contrasted with the natural body, Paul noted that one star is "different" from another. In Galatians 4:1 it is used to distinguish between a child and a slave.

Romans 2:18 and Philippians 1:10 are quite similar with the participle of *diapherō* used as a noun to give the effect of approving those things which are different. In the case of Romans 2:18 the concern is for the Jew who makes decisions about life and conduct on the basis of the Law, while Philippians 1:10 speaks of the distinction pertaining to life and conduct which should characterize the Christian until the Day of Christ. In both cases there is implied a moral and ethical judgment and perspective which is able to deal with the good and bad of life.

STRONG 1308, BAUER 190, MOULTON-MILLIGAN 156-57, KITTEL 9:62-64, LIDDELL-SCOTT 417-18.

1303. διαφεύγω diapheugō verb
To go free, escape (from being a prisoner).
COGNATE:
    φεύγω pheugō (5180)
SYNONYMS:
    ἀποφεύγω apopheugō (662)
    ἐκφεύγω ekpheugō (1614)
    καταφεύγω katapheugō (2672)
    φεύγω pheugō (5180)

מָלַט mālaṭ (4561), Niphal: escape (Prv 19:5).
נָדַד nādhadh (5252), Flap (Is 10:14).
נוּס nûs (5308), Escape (Am 9:1).
עָלַז ʻālaz (6159), Rejoice (Jer 11:15).
פָּלִיט pālîṭ (6654), Fugitive (Jos 8:22, 2 Kgs 9:15).
שָׂגַב sāghav (7891), Be inaccessibly high (Dt 2:36).
שָׂרִיד sārîdh (8032), Survivor (Jos 10:28,30,33).

1. **διαφύγοι** diaphugoi 3sing opt aor act
2. **διαφύγῃ** diaphugē 3sing subj aor act

1 lest any of them should swim out, and escape.......Acts 27:42
2 lest any of them should swim out, and escape.......... 27:42

From *pheugō* (5180), "to flee," this term is found in classical Greek from the time of Herodotus (Fifth Century B.C.) meaning "get away from," "escape," and by implication "survive." Less commonly it was also used figuratively to mean "escape one's notice or memory" (see *Liddell-Scott*).

It is used 15 times in the Septuagint to translate 7 different Hebrew terms, most frequently *sārîdh* meaning "survivor" (as a noun) and "escape" (as a verb). (See Deuteronomy 2:36; Joshua 8:22; Isaiah 10:14; Jeremiah 11:15.) Acts 27:42 contains the only appearance of *diapheugō* in the New Testament, where some of the Roman soldiers suggested the prisoners (Paul among them) be killed rather than risk an "escape." But the centurion in charge, probably mindful of how Paul's vision had saved all of their lives (Acts 27:22-31), kept the soldiers from carrying out their suggestion.

STRONG 1309, BAUER 190, MOULTON-MILLIGAN 157, LIDDELL-SCOTT 418.

1304. διαφημίζω diaphēmizō verb
Report, publish abroad, disseminate.
CROSS-REFERENCE:
    φημί phēmi (5183)

1. **διαφημίζειν** diaphēmizein inf pres act

διαφθείρω 1305

2. διεφήμισαν diephēmisan 3pl indic aor act
3. διεφημίσθη diephēmisthē 3sing indic aor pass

2 **spread abroad** his fame in all that country.......... Matt 9:31
3 **commonly reported** among the Jews until this day...... 28:15
1 publish it much, and to **blaze abroad** the matter,.... Mark 1:45

This compound verb comes from *phēmizō*, which means "spread a report" or "express with words," and *dia* (1217), "through" or "by." Used in Matthew 9:31; 28:15; and Mark 1:45, it means "spreading the news about" someone or something.

STRONG 1310, BAUER 190, MOULTON-MILLIGAN 157, LIDDELL-SCOTT 418.

1305. διαφθείρω diaphtheirō verb
Destroy, ruin, corrupt.
COGNATE:
  φθείρω phtheirō (5188)
SYNONYMS:
  ἀναιρέω anaireō (335)
  ἀνατρέπω anatrepō (394)
  ἀπόλλυμι apollumi (616)
  ἀφανίζω aphanizō (846)
  καθαιρέω kathaireō (2479)
  καταλύω kataluō (2617)
  καταργέω katargeō (2643)
  καταστρέφω katastrephō (2660)
  καταφθείρω kataphtheirō (2673)
  κενόω kenoō (2729)
  λύω luō (3061)
  ὀλοθρεύω olothreuō (3508)
  πορθέω portheō (4058)
  φθείρω phtheirō (5188)

חָבַל chāval (2341), Act ruinously, corruptly; piel: destroy (Eccl 5:6 [5:5], Mi 2:10).

חָרֵב chārēv (2817), Pual: be dried (Jgs 16:7,8).

מוּת mûth (4322), Die; hiphil: kill (1 Kgs 2:25).

פָּלַל pālal (6663), Piel: judge (Ez 16:52—Codex Alexandrinus only).

רִיק rîq (7671), Hiphil: keep hungry (Is 32:6—Codex Alexandrinus only).

שָׁחַת shāchath (8271), Niphal: be ruined (Jer 13:7); be corrupt (Ez 20:44); piel: destroy (Jgs 6:5, 2 Sm 14:11, Na 2:2); hiphil: destroy (Ru 4:6, Ps 78:38 [77:38], Lam 2:8); hophal: blemished (Mal 1:14).

שָׁמֵם shāmēm (8460), Be desolated (Is 49:19—Codex Alexandrinus and some Sinaiticus manuscripts only).

1. διαφθείρει diaphtheirei 3sing indic pres act
2. διαφθείροντας diaphtheirontas
                acc pl masc part pres act
3. διαφθεῖραι diaphtheirai inf aor act
4. διαφθείρεται diaphtheiretai 3sing indic pres mid
5. διεφθάρη diephtharē 3sing indic aor pass
6. διεφθαρμένων diephtharmenōn
                gen pl masc part perf mid

7. διέφθειρε diephtheire 3sing indic imperf/aor act
8. διεφθάρησαν diephtharēsan 3pl indic aor pass

1 no thief approacheth, neither moth **corrupteth**...... Luke 12:33
4 but though our outward man **perish**,................. 2 Co 4:16
6 Perverse disputings of men of **corrupt** minds,....... 1 Tm 6:5
5 and the third part of the ships were **destroyed**....... Rev 8:9
8 and the third part of the ships were **destroyed**........... 8:9
3 **shouldest destroy** them which destroy the earth......... 11:18
2 shouldest destroy them which **destroy** the earth......... 11:18

Classical Greek
Found frequently in classical Greek, *diaphtheirō* means basically "to destroy," although it is often capable of varied translations such as "to kill," "to ruin or corrupt" (both physically and morally), "to spoil, disable," etc. Throughout Greek literature it tends to emphasize the resultant state of action rather than the act itself. It is applied to both outward or physical destruction as well as to the destruction of that which is not simply physical, such as the mind or soul, etc.

Septuagint Usage
In the Septuagint *diaphtheirō* occurs more than 75 times, primarily as a translation of *shāchath*. Usually it is applied to some kind of personal destruction or corruption. Thus Judges 20:21 indicates that the sons of Benjamin destroyed 22,000 men of Israel, while Psalm 14:1 (LXX 13:1) speaks of a man who corrupted himself by saying, "There is no God."

New Testament Usage
The verb *diaphtherō* occurs just six times in the New Testament. While outward or physical destruction or corruption appears to be the principal concern of *diaphtheirō* in the New Testament, another emphasis is clearly present. First Timothy 6:5 speaks of the corruption of the mind which is associated with erroneous doctrine that does not conform to godliness. Revelation 11:18, which depicts the judgment and destruction of those who destroy the earth, has implications that go beyond just physical judgment and destruction or punishment.

STRONG 1311, BAUER 190, MOULTON-MILLIGAN 157, KITTEL 9:93-106, LIDDELL-SCOTT 418.

1306. διαφθορά diaphthora noun
Destruction, corruption (of the body), decay.
COGNATE:
  φθείρω phtheirō (5188)
SYNONYM:
  φθορά phthora (5193)

חֶבֶל chevel (2346), Cord (Hos 11:4).

מַדְחֵפָה madhchēphāh (4215), A thrust (Ps 140:11 [139:11]).
מַכְאוֹב makh'ôv (4480), Pain (Jer 51:8 [28:8]).
מַשְׁחִית mashchîth (5072), Destruction (Ez 21:31).
שְׁחוּת sh°chûth (8248), Pit (Prv 28:10).
שְׁחִית sh°chîth (8255), Pit (Ps 107:20 [106:20], Lam 4:20).
שָׁחַת shāchath (8271), Piel: destroy (Hos 13:9); hiphil: destroy (Jer 13:14, 15:3).
שַׁחַת shachath (8273), Pit (Jb 33:28, Ps 35:7 [34:7], Ez 19:4).

1. διαφθοράν diaphthoran acc sing fem

1 wilt thou suffer thine Holy One to see **corruption**....	Acts 2:27
1 neither his flesh did see **corruption**..................	2:31
1 now no more to return to **corruption**,................	13:34
1 shalt not suffer thine Holy One to see **corruption**.....	13:35
1 and was laid unto his fathers, and saw **corruption**:....	13:36
1 he, whom God raised again, saw no **corruption**........	13:37

This term refers to the decay or decomposition of the physical body. It is used only in Acts and always in reference to bodily decay after death (2:27,31; 13:34-37). In the Septuagint it is used in Job 33:28; Psalms 16:10 (LXX 15:10); 30:9 (29:9).

STRONG 1312, BAUER 190, KITTEL 9:93-106, LIDDELL-SCOTT 418.

1307. διάφορος diaphoros adj

Different, diverse; outstanding, excellent.
CROSS-REFERENCE:
φέρω pherō (5179)

כִּלְאַיִם kil'ayim (3731), Two kinds (Lv 19:19, Dt 22:9).
שְׁנַיִם sh°nayim (8530), Two (Ezr 8:27).

1. διαφόροις diaphorois dat pl masc
2. διάφορα diaphora nom/acc pl neu
3. διαφορωτέρας diaphorōteras comp gen sing fem
4. διαφορώτερον diaphorōteron comp nom/acc sing neu

2 **differing** according to the grace that is given to us,	Rom 12:6
4 obtained **a more excellent** name than they............	Heb 1:4
3 now hath he obtained **a more excellent** ministry,......	8:6
1 and **divers** washings, and carnal ordinances,..........	9:10

In classical Greek since the time of Herodotus (Fifth Century B.C.) this term means "different" but later (by the time of Josephus) came to include the meaning "outstanding, excellent." It is used 12 times in the Septuagint to translate 3 different Hebrew words. In Leviticus 19:19 it refers to "diverse" seed, and in Theodotion's version of Daniel (7:17,19) the reference of the beast being "different" has a qualitative sense of "greater" (in terms of power) as well as "different" (in terms of its description).

In Romans 12:6 it refers to the diversity of spiritual gifts among believers. In Hebrews 9:10 it refers to the various kinds of ceremonial washings. A comparative form of the adjective, *diaphorōteros*, meaning "much different from, much better than, or superior to something or someone," occurs twice in the New Testament. It is used in Hebrews 1:4 and 8:6 in reference to Christ's name being superior to that of the angels and His ministry being superior to or more excellent than that of the high priests.

STRONG 1313, BAUER 190-91, MOULTON-MILLIGAN 157-58, LIDDELL-SCOTT 418-19.

1308. διαφυλάσσω diaphulassō verb

Guard, protect, watch over (someone).
CROSS-REFERENCE:
φυλάσσω phulassō (5278)

חָרַף chāraph (2884), Niphal: acquire (Lv 19:20).
נָצַר nātsar (5526), Watch, guard (Dt 32:10).
שָׁמַר shāmar (8490), Qal: keep, preserve (Dt 7:12, Jos 24:17, Prv 2:8); niphal: be kept (Hos 12:13).

1. διαφυλάξαι diaphulaxai inf aor act

1 give his angels charge over thee, **to keep** thee:......	Luke 4:10

The meaning "watch closely, guard carefully" occurs in classical Greek where it is used especially of providential care. This usage continues into the New Testament where the term is found only in Luke 4:10 when Satan was tempting Jesus to throw himself from the pinnacle of the temple. In this verse we find the Septuagint's reading of Psalm 91:11,12 (LXX 90:11,12), "He will command his angels *to protect* you."

STRONG 1314, BAUER 191, MOULTON-MILLIGAN 158, LIDDELL-SCOTT 419.

1309. διαχειρίζομαι
diacheirizomai verb

Lay violent hands on, murder, put to death.
COGNATE:
χείρ cheir (5331)
SYNONYMS:
ἀναιρέω anaireō (335)
ἀποκτείνω apokteinō (609)
ἀπόλλυμι apollumi (616)
θανατόω thanatoō (2266)
θύω thuō (2357)
νεκρόω nekroō (3362)

διαχλευάζω 1309B

σφάζω sphazō (4821)
φονεύω phoneuō (5244)

1. διεχειρίσασθε diecheirisasthe 2pl indic aor mid
2. διαχειρίσασθαι diacheirisasthai inf aor mid

1 Jesus, whom ye **slew** and hanged on a tree......... Acts 5:30
2 the Jews caught me ... and went about **to kill** me...... 26:21

Related to *cheir* (5331), "hand," the word literally means "to lay hands on someone in a violent manner with the result being death." It is used only twice in Acts and means "to kill" (Acts 5:30; 26:21).

STRONG 1315, BAUER 191 (see "diacheirizō"), MOULTON-MILLIGAN 158 (see "diacheirizō"), LIDDELL-SCOTT 420 (see "diacheirizō").

1309B. διαχλευάζω diachleuazō verb
Mock, scoff.

1. διαχλευάζοντες diachleuazontes
nom pl masc part pres act

1 But others were **mocking** and saying (NASB)........Acts 2:13

The prefix *dia* (1217) intensifies the meaning of *chleuazō* (5348), "to mock or jest," thus producing a word used for "severe jesting" or "mocking in derision." This word appears in the New Testament only in Acts 2:13 where on the Day of Pentecost some of the crowd mocked the believers as they spoke in tongues and said that they were babbling from drunkenness. The word does not appear in the Septuagint.

BAUER 191, LIDDELL-SCOTT 420.

1310. διαχωρίζω diachōrizō verb
Separate; (passive) be separated, to depart from.

COGNATE:
χωρίζω chōrizō (5398)

SYNONYMS:
ἀναλύω analuō (358)
ἀναχωρέω anachōreō (400)
ἀπαλλάσσω apallassō (521)
ἀπέρχομαι aperchomai (562)
ἀποβαίνω apobainō (571)
ἀποδιορίζω apodiorizō (587)
ἀπολύω apoluō (624)
ἀποχωρέω apochōreō (666)
ἀποχωρίζω apochōrizō (667)
ἀφίημι aphiēmi (856)
ἀφίστημι aphistēmi (861)
διακρίνω diakrinō (1246)
ἐγκαταλείπω enkataleipō (1452)
ἐξέρχομαι exerchomai (1814)
ἐξιέναι exienai (1821)
ἐξίστημι existēmi (1822)
κρίνω krinō (2892)

μερίζω merizō (3177)
μεταίρω metairō (3202)
παράγω paragō (3717)
σχίζω schizō (4829)
ὑπάγω hupagō (5055)
χωρέω chōreō (5397)
χωρίζω chōrizō (5398)

בָּדַל bādhal (950), Niphal: separate oneself (1 Chr 12:8—Codex Alexandrinus only); hiphil: separate (Gn 1:6,7); dismiss (2 Chr 25:10).

סוּר sûr (5681), Turn aside; hiphil: remove (Gn 30:32).

פָּלָא pālā' (6623), Be extraordinary; hiphil: perform a miracle (Jgs 13:19).

פָּרַד pāradh (6754), Niphal: separate, be separated (Gn 13:9,11, 2 Sm 1:23); hiphil: separate (Prv 16:28).

פָּרַשׁ pārash (6817), Make distinct, declare; niphal: scatter (Ez 34:12).

שִׁית shîth (8308), Set apart (Gn 30:40).

1. διαχωρίζεσθαι diachōrizesthai inf pres mid

1 And it came to pass, as they **departed** from him,.... Luke 9:33

Classical Greek and Septuagint Usage
In classical Greek the meaning of the word *diachōrizō* is "separate." In its passive form it can also mean "divorced" in the sense of "separating from someone" (see *Liddell-Scott*). In the Septuagint *diachōrizō* is used to translate six Hebrew words. The two most frequently used are *bādhal*, "be divided, separate," and *pāradh*, "divide." (See Genesis 1:4; Numbers 32:12; Ezekiel 34:12.)

New Testament Usage
While its meaning can include separation "of things," its use for "people" separating is continued into the New Testament. The only occurrence of this term is found in Luke 9:33 to describe how Moses and Elijah "departed" from Jesus while Peter and John watched. Peter, not understanding their "departure," then suggested to Jesus that they make three tabernacles so their fellowship might continue there on the mountain.

STRONG 1316, BAUER 191, MOULTON-MILLIGAN 158, LIDDELL-SCOTT 420.

1311. διδακτικός didaktikos adj
Skillful in teaching, well able to teach (or) instruct.

CROSS-REFERENCE:
διδάσκω didaskō (1315)

1. διδακτικόν didaktikon acc sing masc

1 given to hospitality, **apt to teach**;................... 1 Tm 3:2
1 but be gentle unto all men, **apt to teach**, patient,....2 Tm 2:24

The use of this term meaning "skillful in teaching" can be traced back to the First Century B.C. (Philodemus). Even though it does not appear in the Septuagint (as an adjective) its original meaning has been preserved in the New Testament. In its only two uses, at 1 Timothy 3:2 and 2 Timothy 2:24, *didaktikos* means "able or apt to teach." In those two contexts it also suggests an ability to refute errors.

STRONG 1317, BAUER 191, MOULTON-MILLIGAN 158, KITTEL 2:165, LIDDELL-SCOTT 421, COLIN BROWN 3:759,765.

1312. διδακτός didaktos adj
Taught, instructed.

CROSS-REFERENCE:
διδάσκω didaskō (1315)

לִמֻּד limmudh (4065), Taught (Is 54:13).

1. **διδακτοί** didaktoi nom pl masc
2. **διδακτοῖς** didaktois dat pl masc

1	And they shall be all **taught** of God	John 6:45
2	not in the words which man's wisdom **teacheth**	1 Co 2:13
2	but which the Holy Ghost **teacheth**;	2:13

From classical Greek comes the meaning "that which can be taught by study and experience" (see *Liddell-Scott*). This teaching carries with it the idea of demonstration by the instructor; the student learns by imitating his instructor. In the Septuagint the idea of "instruction" (of persons) is found in 1 Maccabees 4:7 and that people may be taught "by God" (Isaiah 54:13). John used this verse from Isaiah in his Gospel (John 6:45). The only other New Testament usage is in 1 Corinthians 2:13 where Paul contrasted man's teaching with the teaching of the Holy Spirit.

STRONG 1318, BAUER 191, MOULTON-MILLIGAN 158, KITTEL 2:165, LIDDELL-SCOTT 421, COLIN BROWN 3:759,764.

1313. διδασκαλία didaskalia noun
Teaching, instruction.

COGNATE:
διδάσκω didaskō (1315)

SYNONYM:
διδαχή didachē (1316)

אַלּוּף 'allûph (443), Friend (Prv 2:17).

לָמַד lāmadh (4064), Learn; pual: be taught (Is 29:13).

1. **διδασκαλίας** didaskalias gen/acc sing/pl fem
2. **διδασκαλία** didaskalia nom sing fem
3. **διδασκαλίᾳ** didaskalia dat sing fem
4. **διδασκαλίαν** didaskalian acc sing fem
5. **διδασκαλίαις** didaskaliais dat pl fem

1	teaching for **doctrines** the commandments of men	Matt 15:9
1	teaching for **doctrines** the commandments of men	Mark 7:7
3	or he that teacheth, on **teaching**;	Rom 12:7
4	were written for our **learning**,	15:4
1	and carried about with every wind of **doctrine**,	Eph 4:14
1	after the commandments and **doctrines** of men?	Col 2:22
3	any other thing that is contrary to sound **doctrine**;	1 Tm 1:10
5	heed to seducing spirits, and **doctrines** of devils;	4:1
1	in the words of faith and of good **doctrine**,	4:6
3	attendance to reading, to exhortation, to **doctrine**.	4:13
3	Take heed unto thyself, and unto the **doctrine**;	4:16
3	they who labour in the word and **doctrine**.	5:17
2	that the name of God and his **doctrine**	6:1
3	and to the **doctrine** which is according to godliness;	6:3
3	But thou hast fully known my **doctrine**,	2 Tm 3:10
4	and is profitable for **doctrine**, for reproof,	3:16
1	when they will not endure sound **doctrine**;	4:3
3	may be able by sound **doctrine** both to exhort and	Tit 1:9
3	the things which become sound **doctrine**:	2:1
3	in **doctrine** showing uncorruptness, gravity,	2:7
4	that they may adorn the **doctrine** of God	2:10

Classical Greek
In classical Greek *didaskalia* functions much as it does later in Hellenistic Greek where it means "teaching, instruction." One sense not found in the New Testament is that of the "rehearsing" of a drama (see *Liddell-Scott*). "Teaching" could be either the activity of instruction or the passive reception of education (Rengstorf, "didaskalia," *Kittel*, 2:160).

Septuagint Usage
Didaskalia occurs only four times in the Septuagint. Two of those instances are outside the canon (Sirach 24:33; 39:8). The two canonical uses are Proverbs 2:17 and Isaiah 29:13. The text in Proverbs suggests that the "guide" (RSV, "companion," Hebrew *'allûph*) of her youth is the covenant (*b^erîth*) of God. The Septuagint translates *'allûph* here as *didaskalia*. This links *didaskalia* to God's covenant and suggests a relationship between *didaskalia* (as God's alone) and *nomos* (3414), "law." Sirach reflects a similar understanding. Isaiah (alluded to by Matthew and Mark and possibly Colossians) implies God's *didaskalia* (singular) is in stark contrast to the *didaskalias* (accusative plural) of men; i.e., proper theologies are no replacement for a contrite heart before the Lord which is expressed in love and obedience (cf. Leviticus 19:18; Deuteronomy 6:3-6).

New Testament Usage
Apart from the two Gospel texts, which are allusions to Isaiah 29:13 (Matthew 15:9; Mark 7:7), only Paul used *didaskalia* in the New Testament (19 times). In Romans 12:7 and 15:4 it is to be understood in the ordinary sense of

διδάσκαλος 1314

"teaching" or "instruction." More importantly, *didaskalia* (singular) came to describe proper Christian "doctrine" in contrast to the false "teachings" (plural) of men which threatened the Early Church.

Correct *didaskalia* was a crucial plea from Paul in the Pastoral Epistles. The communities—indeed, "sound teaching" itself (1 Timothy 1:10)—were threatened by false teachers who had imported their own "teachings" (plural). They could not stand sound doctrine, preferring instead the "doctrines of devils" (1 Timothy 4:1). The solution to these erroneous teachings was the "good doctrine" (*tēs kalēs didaskalias*, 1 Timothy 4:6; cf. 1 Timothy 4:13; 6:3; 2 Timothy 3:10; 4:3; Titus 1:9; 2:1,10).

STRONG 1319, BAUER 191, MOULTON-MILLIGAN 158, KITTEL 2:160-63, LIDDELL-SCOTT 421, COLIN BROWN 3:768-71.

1314. διδάσκαλος didaskalos noun

Teacher. THE PERSON DOING THE
COGNATE: TEACHING (DIDASKO)
διδάσκω didaskō (1315)

SYNONYMS:
καθηγητής kathēgētēs (2491)
παιδευτής paideutēs (3673)

1. διδάσκαλος didaskalos nom sing masc
2. διδάσκαλον didaskalon acc sing masc
3. διδάσκαλε   didaskale   voc sing masc
4. διδάσκαλοι didaskaloi nom pl masc
5. διδασκάλων didaskalōn gen pl masc
6. διδασκάλους didaskalous acc pl masc

3	a certain scribe came, and said unto him, **Master**,...	Matt 8:19
1	Why eateth your **Master** with publicans and............	9:11
2	The disciple is not above his **master**,.................	10:24
1	enough for the disciple that he be as his **master**,......	10:25
3	saying, **Master**, we would see a sign from thee........	12:38
1	and said, Doth not your **master** pay tribute?..........	17:24
3	behold, one came and said unto him, Good **Master**,...	19:16
3	saying, **Master**, we know that thou art true,..........	22:16
3	Saying, **Master**, Moses said, If a man die,............	22:24
3	**Master**, which is the great commandment............	22:36
1	for One is your **Teacher**, (NASB).....................	23:8
1	The **Master** saith, My time is at hand;...............	26:18
3	**Master**, carest thou not that we perish?........ Mark	4:38
2	why troublest thou the **Master** any further?..........	5:35
3	**Master**, I have brought unto thee my son,............	9:17
3	**Master**, we saw one casting out devils in thy name,...	9:38
3	and asked him, Good **Master**, what shall I do.........	10:17
3	**Master**, all these have I observed from my youth:....	10:20
3	come unto him, saying, **Master**,....................	10:35
3	**Master**, we know that thou art true,................	12:14
3	**Master**, Moses wrote unto us,......................	12:19
3	Well, **Master**, thou hast said the truth:.............	12:32
3	one of his disciples saith unto him, **Master**,.........	13:1
1	The **Master** saith, Where is the guestchamber,.......	14:14
5	in the temple, sitting in the midst of the **doctors**,... Luke	2:46
3	and said unto him, **Master**, what shall we do?.......	3:12
2	The disciple is not above his **master**:...............	6:40
1	but every one that is perfect shall be as his **master**... Luke	6:40
3	to say unto thee. And he saith, **Master**, say on........	7:40
2	Thy daughter is dead; trouble not the **Master**..........	8:49
3	saying, **Master**, I beseech thee, look upon my son:....	9:38
3	lawyer stood up, and tempted him, saying, **Master**,...	10:25
3	one of the lawyers, and said unto him, **Master**,.......	11:45
3	And one of the company said unto him, **Master**,......	12:13
3	Good **Master**, what shall I do to inherit ... life?.....	18:18
3	said unto him, **Master**, rebuke thy disciples..........	19:39
3	And they asked him, saying, **Master**, we know......	20:21
3	Saying, **Master**, Moses wrote unto us,..............	20:28
3	scribes answering said, **Master**, thou hast well said....	20:39
3	saying, **Master**, but when shall these things be?......	21:7
1	**Master** saith unto thee, Where is ... guestchamber,...	22:11
3	Rabbi, which is to say, being interpreted, **Master**,... John	1:38
1	we know that thou art **a teacher** come from God:.....	3:2
1	Art thou a **master** of Israel,.......................	3:10
3	They say unto him, **Master**,.......................	8:4
1	saying, The **Master** is come, and calleth for thee.....	11:28
1	Ye call me **Master** and Lord: and ye say well;.......	13:13
1	I ... your Lord and **Master**, have washed your feet;...	13:14
3	saith unto him, Rabboni; which is to say, **Master**,...	20:16
4	in the church ... certain prophets and **teachers**;.... Acts	13:1
2	An instructor of the foolish, **a teacher** of babes,..... Rom	2:20
6	secondarily prophets, thirdly **teachers**,............ 1 Co	12:28
4	Are all apostles? are all prophets? are all **teachers**?...	12:29
6	some, evangelists; and some, pastors and **teachers**;... Eph	4:11
1	**a teacher** of the Gentiles in faith and verity........ 1 Tm	2:7
1	and an apostle, and a **teacher** of the Gentiles....... 2 Tm	1:11
6	shall they heap to themselves **teachers**,............	4:3
4	For when for the time ye ought to be **teachers**,...... Heb	5:12
4	My brethren, be not many **masters**,................ Jas	3:1

Classical Greek

Didaskalos, "teacher," is derived from the verb *didaskō* (1315), "to teach" (see the cognate noun *didaskalia* [1313], "teaching"). In secular Greek *didaskalos* denotes "the teacher" who instructs his pupils. Most often this concerns cognitive learning (in a didactic manner) rather than practical experience. The teacher may be an educator, or he may be a leader of a philosophical "school" of thought.

Septuagint Usage

The canonical portions of the Septuagint record *didaskalos* only once (Esther 6:1). There the word stands for a "reader." There is not, however, a corresponding Hebrew term in this verse. In 2 Maccabees, Aristobulus is called a "teacher" of Ptolemy (1:10).

New Testament Usage

Although *didaskalos* is relatively infrequent in the Septuagint, it appears 58 times in the New Testament, most frequently in the Gospels. No less than 41 times the term is applied to Jesus. The vocative form *didaskale* is an equivalent to the Hebrew *rabbi*—"master, lord, teacher"—which appears in a transliterated form (e.g., Matthew 23:7,8; 26:25,49; Mark 9:5; 10:51 [or *rhabboni*]; 11:21; 14:45). Despite the fact that *didaskalos* functions as an equivalent for *rabbi* (4318), there is a great difference between the Greek and Hebrew understandings of the role of the "teacher." *Didaskalos* should be interpreted in the New Testament especially in light of the place of *rhabbi* in Judaism (see Wegenast, "Teach," *Colin Brown*, 3:767).

Additionally, in the New Testament, *didaskalos* is clearly indebted to the Old Testament. "Teaching" is particularly defined as knowledge of God. God uses men in history as teachers of His purpose. Parents are to instruct their children in the knowledge of God and are to educate them to His purposes (Genesis 18:19; Deuteronomy 6:6,7). One duty of Moses was to teach the people the commandments, laws, and prescriptions of the Lord (Deuteronomy 6:1f.). God intended that Israel should become a teacher of the rest of mankind. This becomes initially realized in the restoration of the people of God in Christ (Isaiah 2:1-4; 60:1-3; 66:19).

Jesus Christ came from God as "The Teacher"—God's spokesman (John 3:2; Hebrews 1:1). Other than *kurios*, *didaskalos* is the primary form of address to Jesus. However, Jesus was not educated as a teacher (rabbi) in the traditional formal sense. He was not an authorized teacher in the eyes of the religious community (John 7:15; cf. Matthew 13:54). This caused some to be "offended"; but the opposition that Jesus encountered as "teacher" involved more. Jesus did not follow traditional schools of thought, neither did He teach following (exclusively) traditional rabbinic methods. He taught in the power and authority of His messianic consciousness. Frequently, but not exclusively, He based His arguments on an interpretation of the Scriptures, because they testified of Him. At other times, when He answered, "Thus saith the Lord!" He challenged tradition—"You have heard it said"—by His own authority from God—"But I say to you . . . " (e.g., Matthew 5:33,34). Jesus' words, like the Scriptures themselves, will never pass away (Matthew 5:18; Mark 13:31).

Following the ascension of Jesus and the arrival of the Spirit on the Day of Pentecost, the Holy Spirit became the Divine Teacher. He brought to the disciples remembrance and illumination of the teaching of Jesus (John 14:26). From this foundation He then instructed the disciples on matters which they were unable to understand during Jesus' ministry on earth (John 16:12-14). As a teacher, Jesus is unique. In Him the revelation of God reaches its climax, its fulfillment, and therefore its end (cf. John 1:17,18). The plainness in style and expression, the cleanness of thought, the vivid and forceful use of commonplace illustrations, and the dynamic, illuminating presentation of spiritual truths all combine to make Jesus a teacher who is unsurpassed. All who heard Him agreed: "Never man spake like this man" (John 7:46). The teaching activity of the Spirit is inseparably joined with the teaching ministry of Jesus. "He shall not speak of himself; but whatsoever he shall hear, that shall he speak" (John 16:13). The role of teacher was uniquely carried out in the inspiration of the New Testament writers.

The apostles were to be teachers above all else (Matthew 28:20; cf. Acts 6:4). Paul as the apostle to the Gentiles was a "teacher of the Gentiles" (1 Timothy 2:7; 2 Timothy 1:11). The apostles were teachers who were distinct from all later teachers in the church of Jesus Christ. They were bearers of revelation on a level equal to the prophetic disclosure of the Old Testament. The promise that the Spirit would teach (John 14:26; 16:12-14) was fulfilled in part by the apostles. Through the Spirit, Jesus himself teaches through the apostles: "He that heareth you heareth me" (Luke 10:16).

The teacher in the Church after the time of the apostles does not have any authority to introduce any new teaching but only to teach the doctrine of Christ and the apostles. The overseers of the Church ought to have such a teaching ability (1 Timothy 3:2). The duty of the teachers is to express the "unsearchable riches of Christ" (Ephesians 3:8). The teacher is also responsible for protecting the Church against the false teachings that may threaten it (Ephesians 4:14; cf. 1 Timothy 4:13,16). Teachers assume a tremendous personal responsibility and will be accountable before God (James 3:1f.). Therefore, only the one called by God should exercise the gift of teaching. (See also *didachē* [1316]).

STRONG 1320, BAUER 191, MOULTON-MILLIGAN 158-59, KITTEL 2:148-59, LIDDELL-SCOTT 421, COLIN BROWN 3:765-68.

1315. διδάσκω didaskō verb

Teach.

COGNATES:
- διδακτικός didaktikos (1311)
- διδακτός didaktos (1312)
- διδασκαλία didaskalia (1313)
- διδάσκαλος didaskalos (1314)
- διδαχή didachē (1316)

διδάσκω 1315

ἑτεροδιδασκαλέω heterodidaskaleō (2064)
θεοδίδακτος theodidaktos (2289)
καλοδιδάσκαλος kalodidaskalos (2538)
νομοδιδάσκαλος nomodidaskalos (3410)
ψευδοδιδάσκαλος pseudodidaskalos (5407)

SYNONYMS:
ἀναγγέλλω anangellō (310)
κατηχέω katēcheō (2697)
μαθητεύω mathēteuō (3072)
παιδεύω paideuō (3674)
παραδίδωμι paradidōmi (3722)
συμβιβάζω sumbibazō (4673)

אָלַף 'ālaph (509), Learn; piel: teach (Jb 33:33).

בִּין bîn (1032), Discern; hiphil: give understanding (Jb 32:8).

חָוָה chāwâh (2425), Piel: show (Jb 36:2).

חָיָה chāyâh (2513), Live; piel: give life (Jb 33:4).

יָדַע yādha' (3156), Know; hiphil: cause to know (Jb 10:2, 13:23); teach (Jb 37:19).

יָצָא yātsā' (3428), Go out, come out; hiphil: bring forth (Jb 8:10—Codex Alexandrinus only).

יָרָה yārāh (3498), Throw, shoot; hiphil: teach (Jb 6:24, Prv 4:4, 6:13).

לָמַד lāmadh (4064), Qal: learn (Prv 30:3 [24:26]); piel: teach (Dt 6:1, 2 Chr 17:7, Jer 9:14); pual: trained, taught (1 Chr 25:7, S/S 3:8, Is 29:13).

סָכַן sākhan (5725), Be of benefit (Jb 22:2).

פָּרַשׁ pārash (6817), Make distinct, declare; pual: translate (Neh 8:8).

1. διδάσκω didaskō 1sing indic pres act
2. διδάσκεις didaskeis 2sing indic pres act
3. διδάσκει didaskei 3sing indic pres act
4. διδάσκῃ didaskē 3sing subj pres act
5. δίδασκε didaske 2sing impr pres act
6. διδάσκων didaskōn nom sing masc part pres act
7. διδάσκοντος didaskontos gen sing masc part pres act
8. διδάσκοντι didaskonti dat sing masc part pres act
9. διδάσκοντες didaskontes nom pl masc part pres act
10. διδάσκειν didaskein inf pres act
11. ἐδίδαξα edidaxa 1sing indic aor act
12. ἐδίδαξας edidaxas 2sing indic aor act
13. ἐδίδαξεν edidaxen 3sing indic aor act
14. ἐδίδαξαν edidaxan 3pl indic aor act
15. διδάξῃ didaxē 3sing subj aor act
16. διδάξωσιν didaxōsin 3pl subj aor act
17. δίδαξον didaxon 2sing impr aor act
18. διδάξαι didaxai inf aor act
19. διδάξει didaxei 3sing indic fut act
20. ἐδίδασκεν edidasken 3sing indic imperf act
21. ἐδίδασκον edidaskon 3pl indic imperf act
22. ἐδιδάχθην edidachthēn 1sing indic aor pass
23. ἐδιδάχθητε edidachthēte 2pl indic aor pass
24. ἐδιδάχθησαν edidachthēsan 3pl indic aor pass

6	Jesus went about ... **teaching** in their synagogues,..	Matt 4:23
20	And he opened his mouth, and **taught** them,.........	5:2
15	break ... commandments, and **shall teach** men so,.....	5:19
15	but whosoever shall do and **teach** them,...............	5:19
6	For he **taught** them as one having authority,..........	7:29
6	**teaching** in their synagogues, and preaching	9:35
10	he departed thence to **teach** and to preach	11:1
20	he **taught** them in their synagogue,................	13:54
9	**teaching** for doctrines the commandments of men.....	15:9
8	came unto him as he was **teaching**, and said,.........	21:23
2	and **teachest** the way of God in truth,................	22:16
6	I sat daily with you **teaching** in the temple,.........	26:55
6	I sat daily with you **teaching** in the temple,.........	26:55
24	they took the money, and did as they were **taught**:...	28:15
9	**Teaching them** to observe all things whatsoever	28:20
20	he entered into the synagogue, and **taught**........	Mark 1:21
6	for he **taught** them as one that had authority,........	1:22
20	multitude resorted unto him, and he **taught** them.....	2:13
10	And he began again to **teach** by the sea side:........	4:1
20	And he **taught** them many things by parables,......	4:2
10	he began **to teach** in the synagogue:................	6:2
6	And he went round about the villages, **teaching**.......	6:6
14	what they had done, and what they had **taught**.......	6:30
10	and he began **to teach** them many things,............	6:34
9	**teaching** for doctrines the commandments of men.....	7:7
10	And he began **to teach** them,......................	8:31
20	For he **taught** his disciples, and said unto them,......	9:31
20	and, as he was wont, he **taught** them again.........	10:1
20	And he **taught**, saying unto them, Is it not written,...	11:17
2	but **teachest** the way of God in truth:................	12:14
6	answered and said, while he **taught** in the temple,...	12:35
6	I was daily with you in the temple **teaching**,........	14:49
20	**taught** in their synagogues, being glorified of all....	Luke 4:15
6	of Galilee, and **taught** them on the sabbath days......	4:31
20	he sat down, and **taught** the people out of the ship....	5:3
6	as he was **teaching**, that there were Pharisees and.....	5:17
10	that he entered into the synagogue and **taught**:........	6:6
17	**teach** us to pray, as John also **taught** his disciples.....	11:1
13	**teach** us to pray, as John also **taught** his disciples.....	11:1
19	the Holy Ghost **shall teach** you in the same hour	12:12
6	And he was **teaching** in one of the synagogues	13:10
6	he went through the cities and villages, **teaching**,.....	13:22
12	and thou hast **taught** in our streets..................	13:26
6	And he **taught** daily in the temple....................	19:47
7	as he **taught** the people in the temple,................	20:1
2	we know that thou sayest and **teachest** rightly,........	20:21
2	but **teachest** the way of God truly:...................	20:21
6	And in the day time he was **teaching** in the temple;...	21:37
6	**teaching** throughout all Jewry.....................	23:5
6	in the synagogue, as he **taught** in Capernaum.......	John 6:59
20	Jesus went up into the temple, and **taught**...........	7:14
6	Then cried Jesus in the temple as he **taught**.........	7:28
10	among the Gentiles, and **teach** the Gentiles?.........	7:35
20	and he sat down, and **taught** them...................	8:2
6	as he **taught** in the temple:........................	8:20
13	as my Father hath **taught** me, I speak these things,...	8:28
2	and dost thou **teach** us? And they cast him out.......	9:34
19	the Holy Ghost, ... he **shall teach** you all things,......	14:26
11	I ever **taught** in the synagogue, and in the temple,....	18:20
10	of all that Jesus began both to do and **teach**,.......	Acts 1:1
10	Being grieved that they **taught** the people,...........	4:2
10	not to speak at all nor **teach** in the name of Jesus....	4:18
21	into the temple early in the morning, and **taught**......	5:21
9	standing in the temple, and **teaching** the people.......	5:28
10	that ye **should not teach** in this name?..............	5:28
9	they ceased not **to teach** and preach Jesus Christ.....	5:42
18	with the church, and **taught** much people............	11:26
21	from Judaea **taught** the brethren, and said,..........	15:1
9	**teaching** and preaching the word of the Lord,.......	15:35
6	**teaching** the word of God among them...............	18:11
20	spake and **taught** diligently the things of the Lord,....	18:25
18	have showed you, and have **taught** you publicly,.....	20:20
2	that thou **teachest** all the Jews......................	21:21
6	**teacheth** all men every where against the people,......	21:28
6	**teaching** those things which concern the Lord Jesus...	28:31
6	Thou therefore which **teachest** another,............	Rom 2:21
2	which teachest another, **teachest** thou not thyself?......	2:21

διδάσκω 1315

6	or he that **teacheth**, on teaching;	Rom 12:7
1	as **I teach** every where in every church.	1 Co 4:17
3	**Doth** not even nature itself **teach** you, that,	11:14
22	neither received it of man, neither **was I taught** it,	Gal 1:12
23	**have been taught** by him, as the truth is in Jesus:	Eph 4:21
9	and **teaching** every man in all wisdom;	Col 1:28
23	and stablished in the faith, as ye **have been taught**,	2:7
9	**teaching** and admonishing one another in psalms	3:16
23	and hold the traditions which ye **have been taught**,	2 Th 2:15
10	But I suffer not a woman **to teach**,	1 Tm 2:12
5	These things command and **teach**.	4:11
5	These things **teach** and exhort.	6:2
18	men, who shall be able **to teach** others also.	2 Tm 2:2
9	**teaching** things which they ought not,	Tit 1:11
10	ye have need that one **teach** you again	Heb 5:12
16	And they **shall** not **teach** every man his neighbour,	8:11
4	and ye need not that any man **teach** you:	1 Jn 2:27
3	as the same anointing **teacheth** you of all things,	2:27
13	even as it **hath taught** you, ye shall abide in him.	2:27
20	who **taught** Balac to cast a stumblingblock	Rev 2:14
10	Jezebel, ... **to teach** and to seduce my servants	2:20
3	Jezebel, ... **to teach** and to seduce my servants	2:20

Classical Greek

In the most basic terms *didaskō* (cf. *didaskalia* [1313], *didachē* [1316]) means "to teach." In its various voices it can also mean "to learn" (passive) or "to teach oneself" (middle). Classical writers applied *didaskō* to everything from "to educate" (as in imparting information) to "to train" (as in horsemanship or even warfare) (see *Liddell-Scott*).

Rengstorf notes that *didaskō* especially was used "for the impartation of practical or theoretical knowledge" which was basic to the development of skill of any kind. He also points out that the practice of teaching through example was not intended to elicit rote imitation; rather, the aim was to develop the skills and talents of the student without jeopardizing individuality ("didaskō," *Kittel*, 2:135). Rengstorf also notes the rather infrequent use of *didaskō* in religious contexts in secular Greek writings (ibid.).

Septuagint Usage

From the Septuagint we learn that *didaskō* (over 100 times) served many purposes, translating 11 Hebrew terms as well as additional forms. Most commonly *didaskō* translated the intensive form of *lāmadh* ("to teach, to learn"). God taught Israel the Law through Moses (Deuteronomy 4:1; 6:1; cf. Job 21:22; Psalm 25:4,5,9 [LXX 24:4,5,9]). These ordinances and traditions were to be "taught" to Israel's children (Deuteronomy 11:19). Job wished God would teach him what he had done wrong (cf. 6:24; 10:2). However, it would be a mistake to restrict *didaskō* (or *lāmadh*) exclusively to a religious connotation in the Septuagint. The Psalmist was "trained" in warfare (Psalm 18:34 [LXX 17:34]; cf. 2 Samuel 22:35 [2 Kings 22:35]).

Rengstorf comments on the distinctive character of *didaskō* in the Septuagint from secular Greek: "The idea of total claim (i.e., the total effect) is not to be detected in secular Greek .... In the LXX, on the other hand, the concern is with the whole man and his education ... " (ibid.). He further notes that later Judaism did come to associate *didaskō* (*lāmadh*) with the learning of the intent and purpose of Torah. *Lāmadh* became a "specialized term for the translation of the Torah into concrete directions for the life of the individual" (ibid.).

New Testament Usage

The Gospels indicate that "teaching" was a primary characteristic of Jesus' ministry (consult Stein, *Method and Message of Jesus' Teachings*, for a thorough discussion of this topic). After all, as a rabbi or teacher (John 20:16; see also Bornkamm, *Jesus of Nazareth*, pp.96ff.) that would have been an essential task. Whether from the synagogue (e.g., Matthew 4:23; 9:35; 13:54) or the temple (Matthew 26:55; Mark 12:35; 14:49; Luke 20:1) or simply "by the sea side" (Mark 4:1), Jesus' teaching focused upon the "way of God" (Matthew 22:16; Luke 20:21)—the Kingdom. Thus, "to teach" summarizes His ministry (Matthew 11:1; Mark 2:13; Luke 4:15; 19:47; John 7:14,28). Teaching and preaching might as well be synonymous (Matthew 11:1; Acts 1:1; 15:35) (see Wegenast, "Teach," *Colin Brown*, 3:764, in reference to Acts especially.)

Remarkably the disciples "taught" even prior to Pentecost, presumably about Jesus (Mark 6:30). The disciples were promised they would be tutored even more by the Holy Spirit (John 14:26). In Acts (*didaskō*, 16 times) the apostles continued the work which Jesus began (1:1; 4:2; cf. 4:18). The "words of this Life" (RSV) were proclaimed (*didaskō*) in the temple (Acts 5:21,42; cf. 5:25,28). Again the similarity between "preaching" and "teaching" is seen (Acts 15:35; 18:25; cf. 20:20ff.; 28:31). Paul taught and encountered the same kind of opposition experienced by Jesus. Thus "to teach" was to challenge the religious system of Judaism; it was not the simple impartation of information (Acts 21:21,28).

Even the Epistles show the close connection between proclamation and teaching (Romans 2:21; Ephesians 4:21; Colossians 1:28). The

διδαχή 1316

role of teaching in the structure of the assembly began to take shape (Romans 12:7; 1 Corinthians 4:17; cf. Ephesians 4:11f.; Colossians 3:16). Even the traditions which were taught overlaped. Timothy was "to teach" in order to stimulate godly behavior in himself and others (1 Timothy 4:11; 6:2), but at the heart of such instruction must be Christ—the Saviour of all mankind (1 Timothy 4:10). Thus teaching was to be both the locus of the truth of the gospel and the point of attack (1 & 2 Timothy passim; cf. Hebrews 5:12; Revelation 2:14,20) by outsiders and insiders alike.

In short, in the New Testament "to teach" is to proclaim the message of salvation. This may transpire on the basic level of proclaiming the arrival of the Kingdom—the consequence of the Cross, or it can unfold on the secondary level of teaching "godliness," i.e., the proper reaction to the primary message of the Cross.

The writings of the Early Church suggest that "teaching" became the vehicle for passing on the proclamation of the apostles and Jesus, and that it came to have the more technical meaning of passing on "information." Evidently time moved the concept of "teaching" away from its original moorings of teaching the whole man (or woman) to teaching the correct doctrine. The New Testament hints at this movement (perhaps in 1 Corinthians 12:28; Ephesians 4:11; 2 Thessalonians 2:15; and throughout the Pastoral Epistles), but it has not fully materialized. The New Testament still views "teaching" as closely related to the total message of salvation.

STRONG 1321, BAUER 192, MOULTON-MILLIGAN 159, KITTEL 2:135-48, LIDDELL-SCOTT 421-22, COLIN BROWN 3:759-65.

1316. διδαχή didachē noun

Act of teaching, instruction, doctrine, that which is taught.
COGNATE:
    διδάσκω didaskō (1315)
SYNONYM:
    διδασκαλία didaskalia (1313)
לָמַד lāmadh (4064), Learn; piel: teach (Ps 60, title [59, title]).

1. διδαχή didachē nom sing fem
2. διδαχῆς didachēs gen sing fem
3. διδαχῇ didachē dat sing fem
4. διδαχήν didachēn acc sing fem
5. διδαχαῖς didachais dat pl fem

3	the people were astonished at his **doctrine**:	Matt 7:28
2	the **doctrine** of the Pharisees and of the Sadducees.	16:12
3	they were astonished at his **doctrine**.	22:33
3	And they were astonished at his **doctrine**:	Mark 1:22
1	What thing is this? what new **doctrine** is this?	1:27
3	and said unto them in his **doctrine**,	4:2
3	all the people was astonished at his **doctrine**.	11:18
3	And he said unto them in his **doctrine**,	12:38
3	And they were astonished at his **doctrine**:	Luke 4:32
1	My **doctrine** is not mine, but his that sent me.	John 7:16
2	shall know of the **doctrine**, whether it be of God,	7:17
2	asked Jesus of his disciples, and of his **doctrine**.	18:19
3	stedfastly in the apostles' **doctrine** and fellowship,	Acts 2:42
2	ye have filled Jerusalem with your **doctrine**,	5:28
3	being astonished at the **doctrine** of the Lord.	13:12
1	saying, May we know what this new **doctrine**,	17:19
2	that form **of doctrine** which was delivered you.	Rom 6:17
4	contrary to the **doctrine** which ye have learned;	16:17
3	by knowledge, or by prophesying, or by **doctrine**?	1 Co 14:6
4	every one of you hath a psalm, hath a **doctrine**,	14:26
3	rebuke, exhort with all longsuffering and **doctrine**.	2 Tm 4:2
4	Holding fast the ... word as he hath been taught,	Tit 1:9
2	Of the **doctrine** of baptisms,	Heb 6:2
5	carried about with divers and strange **doctrines**.	13:9
3	and abideth not in the **doctrine** of Christ,	2 Jn 1:9
3	He that abideth in the **doctrine** of Christ,	1:9
4	come any unto you, and bring not this **doctrine**,	1:10
4	hast there them that hold the **doctrine** of Balaam,	Rev 2:14
4	them that hold the **doctrine** of the Nicolaitanes,	2:15
4	rest in Thyatira, as many as have not this **doctrine**,	2:24

Classical Greek

Another member of the *didaskō* (1315) word group (cf. *didaskalia* [1313]; *didaskalos* [1314]), *didachē* is, like *didaskalia*, a noun meaning "a teaching." At times *didachē* means "something which is demonstrated or proven." Here, there is a close affinity to the cognate verb *didaskō* which has *dek-* ("to accept, to stretch forth the hand in order to receive something") as its etymological root. The term *didaskō* then means "to make someone accept something." Like its companions, *didachē* could refer to the exchange of information or to the training in some skill or art. Papyri confirm that *didachē* was known in the sense of "training" (military) in common speech. One instance of *didachē* in connection with religious "doctrine" also occurs (see *Moulton-Milligan*).

Septuagint Usage

Didachē appears only one time in the Septuagint in the title (probably not originally part of the Psalm) of Psalm 60 (LXX 59): "To the choirmaster: according to Shushan Eduth. A Miktam of David; for instruction (*didachē*); ..." (RSV). The Hebrew behind this is the piel (intensive) of *lāmadh* ("to teach").

New Testament Usage

New Testament usage reflects two senses. Teaching (*didachē*) can refer to "instruction," either of Jesus (Matthew 7:28; Mark 1:22; 11:18) or of others (Matthew 16:12, of the Pharisees and Sadducees; Acts 2:42, of the apostles; Hebrews 13:9, of the opponents of the gospel).

Didachē also carries the more developed understanding of "doctrine," i.e., a set of truths or practices to be learned and followed (e.g., Titus 1:9; Hebrews 6:2; 2 John 9,10; cf. Revelation 2:14,15) which are entrusted to the Church (e.g., Romans 16:17; Titus 1:9). As such, the only true "doctrine" or "teaching" is that of Christ. In one sense Jesus' general instruction is ultimately this same "doctrine." It comes from God (John 7:16) and has the authority of God (John 7:17f.; cf. Mark 1:27).

The form of Jesus' teachings resembled that which was customary for Jewish teachers of the day. His practice of teaching in the synagogue was quite common (cf. Luke 4:16-32). This rabbinic teaching style played an important role in transmitting the doctrines of Jesus to the Church. This same style was employed by rabbis in an effort to convey oral traditions from generation to generation. Because these traditions were not written down until nearly 200 years after the death of Christ (forming what is called the "Mishnah"), students of the rabbi memorized the words of their teachers.

The rabbis were very careful in the transmission of their sacred teachings. The process was highly regulated, and only authorized teachers were permitted to convey these materials to a select few chosen learners. The goal of the disciple was to be able to state, "I have not spoken one word which I have not heard from the mouth of my teachers." They were to be like cisterns, not losing one drop of what they had received.

To advance His doctrine most effectively, Jesus chose concise, and at times rhythmic sayings that would be easy to memorize and to transmit orally. The limited record of the actual words of Christ and the existence of an established oral tradition of His teachings (cf. 1 Corinthians 7:10,25; 11:23-25, for example) seem to verify this. In addition, the same language used to describe receiving and transmitting the teaching of the rabbis was employed by writers of the New Testament (see Luke 1:1 and 1 Corinthians 15:1f.).

In light of the similarities seen between the teaching methods of Jesus and those of the rabbis, it is unlikely that the words of instruction He gave to His disciples were extremely verbose and unrestrained. Instead, Jesus seems to have put forth doctrines, words of wisdom, etc., as succinct precepts which the disciples memorized by paraphrasing them and by constantly quoting them. These, then, are the sayings of Christ which are recorded in the Gospels. The disciples did not, as some suppose, mix the doctrines of the Early Church with a fraction of all the instruction conveyed to them by Jesus in order to produce a Gospel. We find, rather, a collection of sayings which they had been taught after the style of the rabbis. Therefore, the "sermons" of Jesus recorded in the Synoptic Gospels are not sermons in the usual meaning of the word.

John's Gospel is a somewhat different case. In it the sermons of Jesus appear to be paraphrases which were built around the central sayings of Christ. Jesus, realizing that His disciples would be messengers or carriers of His teachings, conveyed that which He viewed as the essential doctrines for His church. For this reason there is probably no teaching from antiquity which has been transmitted more precisely—and which bears the exact form of its originator—than the teachings of Jesus Christ.

In contrast to Hellenistic teachers, Jesus' instruction was directed toward the entire man. The intention of His teaching was not merely to create intellectual understanding but to create faith which would inspire obedience. In this way Jesus' style of teaching also resembled that of Jewish rabbis.

However, what set Jesus' apart from that of the other Jewish teachers of His day was that He taught as one who had authority (Matthew 7:29). This is not to imply that Jesus sought to annul or replace the Law and the Prophets. On the contrary, His teachings confirmed the validity of the Law. He made it quite clear that not a "jot" of it would perish. Jesus constantly referred to the Scriptures when discussing doctrine with the Jewish teachers, and He emphatically stated that "the Scripture cannot be broken" (John 10:35). Nevertheless, knowing that He was the Messiah, He placed His own words on the same authoritative plane as the Scriptures (cf. Matthew 5:21f. which reads, "Ye have heard that it was said by them of old time . . . but I say unto you . . . ").

Often Jesus used the phrase "Amen, amen" (translated "Verily, verily" or "Truly, truly") to introduce His teachings. This is unparalleled in Judaism. It is an expression which demonstrates

His unequaled authority and His immediate knowledge of the will of God. As a result, His listeners marveled at His teaching because it came with a demonstration of power unlike that of the scribes (Matthew 13:54).

The authority of Christ's teachings rested in His knowledge that what He taught was really the Father's doctrine (John 7:16). Since He was taught by God (John 8:28) He knew that those who sincerely sought to hear and to do God's will would recognize that His doctrine was the Father's (John 7:17). This doctrine stood in contrast to the "dangerous leaven" of the scribes and Pharisees whom He called "blind leaders" (Matthew 15:14). Jesus invited men who were pressed down under the burdens of the Law that Jewish teachers laid upon them to learn from Him and to find rest for their souls (Matthew 11:28-30).

Through the apostles, the teachings of Jesus continued under the anointing of the Holy Spirit. Acts 1:1, for example, states that Luke had written in his Gospel that which Jesus "*began* both to do and teach." Therefore, "the apostles' doctrine" (Acts 2:42) and "the doctrine of Christ" (2 John 9) are one and the same.

Upon His departure Jesus charged His apostles to win disciples, "*teaching* them to observe all things whatsoever I have commanded you" (Matthew 28:20). Teaching, therefore, became a prevailing feature of the Early Christian Church. Not only was this true among Jewish believers in Jerusalem (Acts 2:42; 4:2; 5:28,42) but also among the Gentile converts. In the churches established by Paul and his coworkers, purposeful, systematic instruction was an ongoing process (Acts 15:35; 17:1-3,10-13,16f.; 18:1-11; 19:8-10). Even while in prison Paul persisted in a ministry of teaching (Acts 28:23,30f.). As was the case when Jesus taught, the teaching of the apostles came with a demonstration of the power of God (cf. Romans 15:18f.).

Several features characterize the Church's ongoing ministry of instruction. These include repeating and interpreting the doctrines set forth by Jesus himself and explaining Old Testament Scriptures in the light of their present and future fulfillment (including the "Christ-event" itself). In addition, admonitions for ethical Christian conduct along with the transmission of wisdom for living form a large part of this ministry.

The continuing duty of this office also includes contending "for the faith which was once delivered unto the saints" (Jude 3). Transmitting revealed truth and divine salvation history, now written down with nothing to be added or subtracted, is a privilege entrusted to the Church until the end of time.

A study of the Scriptures reveals that the teaching ministry of the Church has both a positive as well as a negative aspect. While it involves presenting eternal truths, it also combats delusion and false doctrine. To readers of the present time it is at times shocking to read how aggressive, almost violent are the Bible's attacks upon false teachers. Jesus himself exemplified this fact. Consider, for example, His fierce condemnation of the scribes and Pharisees. "Whited sepulchres," "serpents and vipers," and "blind leaders" are but a few samples of the harsh words He used. Others in the New Testament were just as severe as Jesus. Paul pronounced a curse on those who were preaching another gospel (Galatians 1:8,9) and called his opponents "dogs" and "evil workers" (Philippians 3:2). Peter compared false teachers to unreasoning animals, condemning them with the certainty that their destruction was inevitable (2 Peter 2:1; 3:12-14). The same denouncement is expressed in the Epistle of Jude which attacks false teachers who had slipped into the church.

The apostles had an unceasing struggle against a variety of strange teaching which ran counter to "sound doctrine" (1 Timothy 1:10; Titus 2:1). Among the most serious were the following: the denial of the resurrection of the body (1 Corinthians 15:12); the mingling of Christianity with Judaism known as "Judaizing" (cf. the books of Galatians, Colossians, and Hebrews); gnosticism (see study on *gnōsis* [1102]); the denial of Jesus Christ as having come in the flesh (1 John 2:22,23; 4:1; 2 John 7); and attacks against Christian morality (Revelation 2:14,15,20,24; see also Romans 16:17; 1 Timothy 1:3ff.; 4:1ff.; 6:3ff.; Hebrews 13:9). (For further information see *hairesis* [138].)

STRONG 1322, BAUER 192, MOULTON-MILLIGAN 159, KITTEL 2:163-65, LIDDELL-SCOTT 422, COLIN BROWN 3:60-61,63,768-71.

1317. δίδραχμον didrachmon noun

Two silver coins (a double drachma, two-drachma piece).

CROSS-REFERENCE:

δραχμή drachmē (1400)

כֶּסֶף keseph (3826B), Silver (Gn 20:16).

שֶׁקֶל sheqel (8621), Shekel (Gn 23:15,16, Ex 21:32).

1. δίδραχμα didrachma nom/acc pl neu

1 they that received **tribute money** came to Peter, ... Matt 17:24
1 and said, Doth not your master pay **tribute**? 17:24

Drachmon is a silver coin, and *di* means "two." This was the sum required from each person annually as a temple tax (Matthew 17:24). It was nearly equivalent to a half-shekel among the Jews.

STRONG 1323, BAUER 192, MOULTON-MILLIGAN 159, LIDDELL-SCOTT 422, COLIN BROWN 3:752-53.

1318. Δίδυμος Didumos name
Didymus.

1. Δίδυμος Didumos nom masc

1 Then said Thomas, which is called **Didymus**, ... John 11:16
1 But Thomas, one of the twelve, called **Didymus**, ... 20:24
1 Simon Peter, and Thomas called **Didymus**, ... 21:2

The Greek name of the apostle Thomas which means "twin" (John 11:16).

1319. δίδωμι didōmi verb
Give, give out, hand over, entrust, give back, give up.

COGNATES:

ἀναδίδωμι anadidōmi (323)
ἀποδίδωμι apodidōmi (586)
διαδίδωμι diadidōmi (1233)
δόσις dosis (1388)
δότης dotēs (1389)
δῶμα dōma (1423)
δωρεά dōrea (1424)
δῶρον dōron (1428)
ἐκδίδωμι ekdidōmi (1541)
ἔκδοτος ekdotos (1547)
ἐπιδίδωμι epididōmi (1914)
εὐμετάδοτος eumetadotos (2111)
μεταδίδωμι metadidōmi (3200)
παραδίδωμι paradidōmi (3722)
πατροπαράδοτος patroparadotos (3832)
προδίδωμι prodidōmi (4131)
προδότης prodotēs (4132)

SYNONYMS:

ἀναδίδωμι anadidōmi (323)
ἀποδίδωμι apodidōmi (586)
διαδίδωμι diadidōmi (1233)
διαιρέω diaireō (1238)
διαμερίζω diamerizō (1260)
δωρέομαι dōreomai (1426)
ἐπιδίδωμι epididōmi (1914)
ἐπιφέρω epipherō (2002)
ἐπιχορηγέω epichorēgeō (2007)

μερίζω merizō (3177)
μεταδίδωμι metadidōmi (3200)
παραβάλλω paraballō (3708)
παραδίδωμι paradidōmi (3722)
παρέχω parechō (3792)
προστίθημι prostithēmi (4227)
χαρίζομαι charizomai (5319)

אוֹר 'ôr (213), Be or become light; hiphil: give light (Ez 32:7—Codex Alexandrinus only).

בּוֹא bô' (971), Come, go; hiphil: apply (Prv 23:12); bring in (Dn 9:24).

בָּזַר bāzar (1002), Scatter (Dn 11:24).

בָּנָה bānâh (1161), Build (1 Kgs 6:5).

הָיָה hāyâh (2030), Become, be (Ex 5:13, Jos 24:32, Ez 45:16).

הָלַךְ hālakh (2050), Go, walk; hiphil: cause to walk (Ez 36:12—Codex Alexandrinus only).

הָלַל hālal (2054), Shine; hiphil: give light (Is 13:10).

חָזַק chāzaq (2480), Be strong; piel: make firm (Is 22:21).

חָלַק chālaq (2606), Piel: divide (Gn 49:27).

יְהַב y^ehav (A3162), Peal: give (Ezr 5:12, Dn 2:21,23,37—Aramaic); peil: be given (Ezr 5:14, Dn 5:28, 7:4,11,12—Aramaic); hithpeel: be given, be paid (Ezr 6:8,9—Aramaic).

יָהַב yāhav (3163), Give, provide (Gn 30:1, Jos 18:4, Zec 11:12).

יָסַף yāsaph (3362), Add, increase; hiphil: give (Jb 42:10).

יָצַק yātsaq (3441), Pour (Is 44:3).

יָצַת yātsath (3448), Burn; niphal: be burned (Neh 2:17).

יָרַד yāradh (3495), Come or go down; hiphil: cause to come down (Ez 34:26).

יָרַשׁ yārash (3542), Take possession of, inherit; hiphil: give as an inheritance (2 Chr 20:11).

כּוּן kûn (3679), Hiphil: devote (Ezr 7:10).

כָּלָה kālâh (3735), Be complete; piel: spend (Is 49:4).

מָכַר mākhar (4513), Sell (Ru 4:3).

מָלַךְ mālakh (4566), Be or become king; hiphil: make king (1 Kgs 3:7).

מָנָה mānâh (4630), Count; piel: appoint (Jb 7:3, Dn 1:5).

נָגַהּ nāghahh (5226), Shine; hiphil: give light (Is 13:10).

נָגַשׂ nāghas (5241), Exact (2 Kgs 23:35).

נוּחַ nûach (5299), Rest; hiphil: leave (1 Kgs 7:47 [7:48]—Codex Alexandrinus only).

נָשָׂא nāsâ' (5558), Piel: take (2 Sm 19:42).

נָתִין nāthîn (5595), Nethinim, temple servants (1 Chr 9:2).

נָתַן nāthan (5598), Qal: give (Nm 35:6,7,8, 2 Kgs 15:20, Is 43:4); niphal: be given (Gn 38:14, 1 Chr 5:20); hophal: be given (Nm 26:54, 1 Kgs 2:21, Jb 28:15).

נְתַן n^ethan (A5599), Provide (Ezr 7:20—Aramaic).

עָטָה 'āṭâh (6057), Hiphil: cover (Ps 84:6 [83:6]).

עָמַד 'āmadh (6198), Stand; hiphil: appoint (2 Chr 33:8).

δίδωμι 1319

עָרַב 'ārav (6386), Pledge oneself (Jer 30:21 [37:21]).

עָשָׂה 'āsâh (6449), Honor (2 Chr 32:33); make (Ez 37:22).

פּוּק pûq (6572), Hiphil: give, grant (Is 58:10).

צָוָה tsāwâh (6943), Piel: command (Ezr 9:11).

צָפַן tsāphan (7121), Hide; niphal: stored up (Jb 15:20).

קָשַׁב qāshav (7477), Listen (Is 32:3).

רוּם rûm (7597), Be high, exalted; hiphil: contribute (2 Chr 35:8).

שִׂים sîm (7947), Give (Ex 4:11, Jos 7:19); appoint (Is 60:17).

שׁוּב shûv (8178), Hiphil: return (Prv 12:14).

שִׁית shîth (8308), Put, set, station, take one's stand (Jb 38:36, Ps 21:6 [20:6], Jer 51:39 [28:39]).

שָׁלַם shālam (8396), Be complete; piel: restore (Is 57:18).

שָׁפַת shāphath (8609), Ordain (Is 26:12).

תּוּב tûv (A8752), Haphel: return (Ezr 6:5—Aramaic).

תָּנָה tānâh (8896), Piel: recount (Jgs 5:11).

1. **δίδωμι** didōmi 1sing indic pres act
2. **δίδωσιν** didōsin 3sing indic pres act
3. **δίδου** didou 2sing impr pres act
4. **δίδοτε** didote 2pl impr pres act
5. **διδούς** didous nom sing masc part pres act
6. **διδόντος** didontos gen sing masc part pres act
7. **διδόντι** didonti dat sing masc part pres act
8. **διδόντα** didonta acc sing masc part pres act
9. **διδόντες** didontes nom pl masc part pres act
10. **διδόναι** didonai inf pres act
11. **δέδωκας** dedōkas 2sing indic perf act
12. **ἔδωκα** edōka 1sing indic aor act
13. **ἔδωκας** edōkas 2sing indic aor act
14. **ἔδωκεν** edōken 3sing indic aor act
15. **ἐδώκαμεν** edōkamen 1pl indic aor act
16. **ἐδώκατε** edōkate 2pl indic aor act
17. **ἔδωκαν** edōkan 3pl indic aor act
18. **δῷς** dōs 2sing subj aor act
19. **δῷ** dō 3sing subj aor act
20. **δώσῃ** dōsē 3sing subj aor act
21. **δῶμεν** dōmen 1pl subj aor act
22. **δῶτε** dōte 2pl subj aor act
23. **δῶσιν** dōsin 3pl subj aor act
24. **δῴη** dōē 3sing opt aor act
25. **δός** dos 2sing impr aor act
26. **δότω** dotō 3sing impr aor act
27. **δότε** dote 2pl impr aor act
28. **δούς** dous nom sing masc part aor act
29. **δόντος** dontos gen sing masc part aor act
30. **δόντα** donta acc sing masc part aor act
31. **δοῦναι** dounai inf aor act
32. **δέδωκα** dedōka 1sing indic perf act
33. **δέδωκεν** dedōken 3sing indic perf act
34. **δεδώκει** dedōkei 3sing indic plperf act
35. **δεδώκεισαν** dedōkeisan 3pl indic plperf act
36. **δώσω** dōsō 1sing indic fut act
37. **δώσεις** dōseis 2sing indic fut act
38. **δώσει** dōsei 3sing indic fut act
39. **δώσουσιν** dōsousin 3pl indic fut act
40. **ἐδίδου** edidou 3sing indic imperf act
41. **ἐδίδουν** edidoun 3pl indic imperf act
42. **δίδοται** didotai 3sing indic pres mid
43. **διδόμενον** didomenon nom/acc sing neu part pres mid
44. **ἐδόθη** edothē 3sing indic aor pass
45. **ἐδόθησαν** edothēsan 3pl indic aor pass
46. **δοθῇ** dothē 3sing subj aor pass
47. **δοθείη** dotheiē 3sing opt aor pass
48. **δοθεῖσα** dotheisa nom sing fem part aor pass
49. **δοθείσης** dotheisēs gen sing fem part aor pass
50. **δοθείσῃ** dotheisē dat sing fem part aor pass
51. **δοθεῖσαν** dotheisan acc sing fem part aor pass
52. **δοθέντος** dothentos gen sing neu part aor pass
53. **δοθῆναι** dothēnai inf aor pass
54. **δέδοται** dedotai 3sing indic perf mid
55. **δεδομένην** dedomenēn acc sing fem part perf mid
56. **δεδομένον** dedomenon nom/acc sing neu part perf mid
57. **δοθήσεται** dothēsetai 3sing indic fut pass
58. **διδόασιν** didoasin 3pl indic pres act
59. **διδῶ** didō 1sing subj pres act
60. **δεδωκότι** dedōkoti dat sing masc/neu part pres act
61. **δοῖ** doi 3sing subj aor act
62. **δῴη** dōē 3sing subj aor act
63. **δώσωμεν** dōsōmen 1pl subj aor act
64. **δώσωσιν** dōsōsin 3pl subj aor act
65. **δόντι** donti dat sing masc part aor act
66. **δώσομεν** dōsomen 1pl indic fut act
67. **ἐδίδοσαν** edidosan 3pl indic imperf act

36	saith unto him, All these things **will I give** thee,	Matt 4:9
26	let him **give** her a writing of divorcement:	5:31
3	**Give** to him that asketh thee,	5:42
25	**Give** to him that asketh thee,	5:42
25	**Give** us this day our daily bread.	6:11
22	**Give** not that which is holy unto the dogs,	7:6
57	Ask, and it **shall be given** you;	7:7
10	know how to **give** good gifts unto your children,	7:11
38	your Father which is in heaven **give** good things	7:11
30	God, which **had given** such power unto men.	9:8
14	he **gave** them power against unclean spirits,	10:1
27	freely ye have received, freely **give**.	10:8
57	for it shall **be given** you in that same hour	10:19
57	and there **shall** no sign **be given** to it,	12:39
40	and brought forth fruit, some an hundredfold,	13:8
54	Because it **is given** unto you to know the mysteries	13:11
54	it is given unto you ... but to them it **is not given**.	13:11
57	For whosoever hath, to him **shall be given**,	13:12
31	promised ... to **give** her whatsoever she would ask.	14:7
25	**Give** me here John Baptist's head in a charger.	14:8
53	he commanded it **to be given** her.	14:9
44	his head ... **given** to the damsel:	14:11
27	They need not depart; **give** ye them to eat.	14:16
14	and **gave** the loaves to his disciples,	14:19
14	and brake them, and **gave** to his disciples,	15:36
40	and brake them, and **gave** to his disciples,	15:36
57	and there **shall** no sign **be given** unto it,	16:4

δίδωμι 1319

36	And **I will give** unto thee the keys of the kingdom Matt	16:19
38	or what **shall** a man **give** in exchange for his soul?	16:26
25	that take, and **give** unto them for me and thee.	17:27
31	command **to give** a writing of divorcement,	19:7
54	All men cannot ... save they to whom it is **given**.	19:11
25	go and sell that thou hast, and **give** to the poor,	19:21
36	and whatsoever is right **I will give** you.	20:4
31	**I will give** unto this last, even as unto thee.	20:14
31	is not mine **to give**, but it shall be given to them	20:23
31	and **to give** his life a ransom for many.	20:28
14	and who **gave** thee this authority?	21:23
57	**given** to a nation bringing forth the fruits thereof.	21:43
31	Is it lawful **to give** tribute unto Caesar, or not?	22:17
39	and **shall show** great signs and wonders;	24:24
38	and the moon **shall** not **give** her light,	24:29
10	wise servant, ... **to give** them meat in due season?	24:45
31	wise servant, ... **to give** them meat in due season?	24:45
27	**Give** us of your oil; for our lamps are gone out.	25:8
14	And unto one he **gave** five talents, to another two,	25:15
27	and **give** it unto him which hath ten talents.	25:28
57	For unto every one that hath **shall be given**,	25:29
16	For I was an hungered, and **ye gave** me meat:	25:35
16	For I was an hungered, and **ye gave** me no meat:	25:42
53	might ... sold for much, and **given** to the poor,	26:9
31	And said unto them, What will ye **give** me,	26:15
40	blessed it, and brake it, and **gave** it to the disciples,	26:26
28	blessed it, and brake it, and **gave** it to the disciples,	26:26
14	and **gave** thanks, and **gave** it to them, saying,	26:27
14	Now he that betrayed him **gave** them a sign,	26:48
17	And **gave** them for the potter's field,	27:10
17	**They gave** him vinegar to drink mingled with gall:	27:34
17	**they gave** large money unto the soldiers,	28:12
44	All power **is given** unto me in heaven and in earth.	28:18
14	and **gave** also to them which were with him? Mark	2:26
41	immediately began **taking** counsel (NASB)	3:6
14	and choked it, and it **yielded** no fruit.	4:7
40	and **did yield** fruit that sprang up and increased;	4:8
54	Unto you it **is given** to know the mystery	4:11
57	For he that hath, to him **shall be given**:	4:25
53	commanded that something **should be given** her	5:43
48	and what wisdom is this which is **given** unto him,	6:2
40	and **gave** them power over unclean spirits;	6:7
36	Ask of me whatsoever ... and **I will give** it thee.	6:22
36	**I will give** it thee, unto the half of my kingdom.	6:23
18	I will that **thou give** me ... the head of John	6:25
14	and **gave** it to the damsel:	6:28
14	and the damsel **gave** it to her mother.	6:28
27	answered and said unto them, **Give** ye them to eat.	6:37
21	go and buy ... bread, and **give** them to eat?	6:37
66	go and buy ... bread, and **give** them to eat?	6:37
63	go and buy ... bread, and **give** them to eat?	6:37
40	and **gave** them to his disciples to set before them;	6:41
40	and **gave** to his disciples to set before them;	8:6
57	There **shall** no sign **be given** unto this generation.	8:12
38	Or what **shall** a man **give** in exchange for his soul?	8:37
61	Or what **shall** a man **give** in exchange for his soul?	8:37
25	sell whatsoever thou hast, and **give** to the poor,	10:21
25	**Grant** unto us that we may sit, one on thy right	10:37
31	But to sit on my right hand ... is not mine **to give**;	10:40
31	to minister, and **to give** his life a ransom for many.	10:45
14	and who **gave** thee this authority to do these things?	11:28
38	and **will give** the vineyard unto others.	12:9
31	Is it lawful **to give** tribute to Caesar, or not?	12:14
21	**Shall we give**, or shall we not give?	12:15
21	**Shall we give**, or shall we not give?	12:15
46	but whatsoever **shall be given** you in that hour,	13:11
39	For false Christs ... **shall show** signs and wonders,	13:22
38	and the moon **shall** not **give** her light,	13:24
28	left his house, and **gave** authority to his servants,	13:34
53	been sold ... and **have been given** to the poor.	14:5
31	they were glad, and promised **to give** him money.	14:11
14	**gave** to them, and said, Take, eat: this is my body.	14:22
14	he **gave** it to them: and they all drank of it.	14:23
34	And he that betrayed him **had given** them a token,	14:44
41	they **gave** him to drink wine mingled with myrrh:	15:23
38	and the Lord God **shall give** unto him the throne. Luke	1:32
31	That he **would grant** unto us,	1:74
31	**To give** knowledge of salvation unto his people. Luke	1:77
31	**to offer** a sacrifice according to that which is said	2:24
36	devil said unto him, All this power **will I give** thee,	4:6
1	and to whomsoever **I will give** it.	4:6
14	and **gave** also to them that were with him;	6:4
3	**Give** to every man that asketh of thee;	6:30
4	**Give**, and it shall be given unto you;	6:38
57	**Give**, and it **shall be given** unto you;	6:38
39	and running over, **shall** men **give** into your bosom.	6:38
14	And he **delivered** him to his mother.	7:15
13	thou **gavest** me no water for my feet:	7:44
13	Thou **gavest** me no kiss: but this woman since	7:45
54	Unto you it **is given** to know the mysteries	8:10
57	for whosoever hath, to him **shall be given**;	8:18
53	she arose ... and he commanded **to give** her meat.	8:55
14	and **gave** them power and authority over all devils,	9:1
27	But he said unto them, **Give** ye them to eat.	9:13
40	**gave** to the disciples to set before the multitude.	9:16
1	Behold, **I give** unto you power to tread on serpents	10:19
32	Behold, **I give** unto you power to tread on serpents	10:19
14	and **gave** them to the host, and said unto him,	10:35
3	**Give** us day by day our daily bread.	11:3
31	I cannot rise and **give** thee.	11:7
38	Though he **will** not rise and **give** him, because he is	11:8
38	yet because of his importunity he will rise and **give**	11:8
57	And I say unto you, Ask, and it **shall be given** you;	11:9
10	know how **to give** good gifts unto your children:	11:13
38	how much more **shall** your heavenly Father **give**	11:13
57	and there **shall** no sign **be given** it,	11:29
27	But rather **give** alms of such things as ye have;	11:41
31	for it is your Father's good pleasure **to give** you	12:32
27	Sell that ye have, and **give** alms;	12:33
10	**to give** them their portion of meat in due season?	12:42
44	For unto whomsoever much **is given**,	12:48
31	Suppose ye that I am come **to give** peace on earth?	12:51
25	**give** diligence that thou mayest be delivered from	12:58
25	come and say to thee, **Give** this man place;	14:9
25	**give** me the portion of goods that falleth to me.	15:12
40	that the swine did eat: and no man **gave** unto him.	15:16
27	and **put** a ring on his hand, and shoes on his feet;	15:22
13	and yet thou never **gavest** me a kid,	15:29
38	who **shall give** you that which is your own?	16:12
31	are not found that returned **to give** glory to God,	17:18
25	sell all that thou hast, and **distribute** unto the poor,	18:22
14	people, when they saw it, **gave** praise unto God.	18:43
1	Lord, the half of my goods **I give** to the poor,	19:8
1	Lord, the half of my goods **I give** to the poor;	19:8
14	his ten servants, and **delivered** them ten pounds,	19:13
14	called unto him, to whom he **had given** the money,	19:15
34	called unto him, to whom he **had given** the money,	19:15
13	then **gavest** not thou my money into the bank,	19:23
27	and **give** it to him that hath ten pounds.	19:24
57	That unto every one which hath **shall be given**;	19:26
28	or who is he that **gave** thee this authority?	20:2
23	they **should give** him of the fruit of the vineyard:	20:10
39	they **should give** him of the fruit of the vineyard:	20:10
38	and **shall give** the vineyard to others.	20:16
31	Is it lawful for us **to give** tribute unto Caesar,	20:22
36	For **I will give** you a mouth and wisdom,	21:15
31	were glad, and covenanted **to give** him money.	22:5
14	and **gave** unto them, saying, This is my body.	22:19
43	This is my body which is **given** for you:	22:19
10	and forbidding **to give** tribute to Caesar,	23:2
14	to them **gave** he power to become the sons of God, John	1:12
44	For the law was **given** by Moses,	1:17
21	that we **may give** an answer to them that sent us.	1:22
14	that he **gave** his only begotten Son,	3:16
56	nothing, except it be **given** him from heaven.	3:27
2	for God **giveth** not the Spirit by measure unto him.	3:34
33	and hath **given** all things into his hand.	3:35
14	parcel of ground that Jacob **gave** to his son Joseph.	4:5
25	Jesus saith unto her, **Give** me to drink.	4:7
25	and who it is that saith to thee, **Give** me to drink;	4:10
14	he **would have given** thee living water.	4:10
14	which **gave** us the well, and drank thereof himself,	4:12
36	of the water that **I shall give** him shall never thirst;	4:14
36	but the water that **I shall give** him shall be in him	4:14

123

δίδωμι 1319

25	give me this water, that I thirst not,	John 4:15
33	but **hath committed** all judgment unto the Son:	5:22
14	so **hath** he **given** to the Son to have life in himself;	5:26
14	**hath given** him authority to execute judgment also,	5:27
14	for the works which the Father **hath given** me	5:36
33	for the works which the Father **hath given** me	5:36
14	he **distributed** to the disciples,	6:11
38	meat ... which the Son of man **shall give** unto you:	6:27
2	meat ... which the Son of man **shall give** unto you:	6:27
14	written, He **gave** them bread from heaven to eat.	6:31
33	Moses **gave** you not that bread from heaven;	6:32
14	Moses **gave** you not that bread from heaven;	6:32
2	my Father **giveth** you the true bread from heaven.	6:32
5	and **giveth** life unto the world.	6:33
25	Lord, evermore **give** us this bread.	6:34
2	All that the Father **giveth** me shall come to me;	6:37
33	all which he **hath given** me I should lose nothing,	6:39
36	and the bread that I **will give** is my flesh,	6:51
36	my flesh, which I **will give** for the life of the world.	6:51
31	How can this man **give** us his flesh to eat?	6:52
56	except it were **given** unto him of my Father.	6:65
33	Did not Moses **give** you the law,	7:19
14	Did not Moses **give** you the law,	7:19
33	Moses therefore **gave** unto you circumcision;	7:22
25	and said unto him, **Give** God the praise:	9:24
1	And I **give** unto them eternal life;	10:28
33	My Father, which **gave** them me,	10:29
38	whatsoever thou wilt ask ... God **will give** it thee.	11:22
35	and the Pharisees **had given** a commandment,	11:57
44	Why was not this ... sold ... and **given** to the poor?	12:5
14	he **gave** me a commandment, what I should say,	12:49
33	he **gave** me a commandment, what I should say,	12:49
33	that the Father **had given** all things into his hands,	13:3
14	that the Father **had given** all things into his hands,	13:3
12	For I **have given** you an example,	13:15
32	For I **have given** you an example,	13:15
36	I shall dip the morsel and **give** it (NASB)	13:26
2	he **gave** it to Judas Iscariot, the son of Simon.	13:26
19	or, that he **should give** something to the poor.	13:29
1	A new commandment I **give** unto you,	13:34
38	and he **shall give** you another Comforter,	14:16
1	Peace I leave with you, my peace I **give** unto you:	14:27
2	my peace I **give** unto you: not as the world **giveth**,	14:27
1	not as the world **giveth**, **give** I unto you.	14:27
14	as the Father **gave** me commandment, even so I do.	14:31
19	whatsoever ye shall ask of ... he **may give** it you.	15:16
38	ask the Father in my name, he **will give** it you.	16:23
13	As thou **hast given** him power over all flesh,	17:2
11	**give** eternal life to as many as thou **hast given** him.	17:2
20	that he **should give** eternal life	17:2
38	that he **should give** eternal life	17:2
11	I have finished the work which thou **gavest** me	17:4
11	the men which thou **gavest** me out of the world:	17:6
13	the men which thou **gavest** me out of the world:	17:6
11	thine they were, and thou **gavest** them me;	17:6
13	thine they were, and thou **gavest** them me;	17:6
11	that all things whatsoever thou **hast given** me	17:7
13	that all things whatsoever thou **hast given** me	17:7
11	given unto them the words which thou **gavest** me;	17:8
13	given unto them the words which thou **gavest** me;	17:8
32	For I **have given** unto them the words	17:8
11	them which thou **hast given** me; for they are thine.	17:9
11	keep ... those whom thou **hast given** me,	17:11
11	those that thou **gavest** me I have kept,	17:12
32	I **have given** them thy word;	17:14
11	the glory which thou **gavest** me I have given them;	17:22
32	the glory which thou gavest me I **have given** them;	17:22
11	I will that they also, whom thou **hast given** me,	17:24
13	may behold my glory, which thou **hast given** me:	17:24
11	may behold my glory, which thou **hast given** me:	17:24
11	Of them which thou **gavest** me have I lost none.	18:9
33	the cup which my Father **hath given** me,	18:11
14	**gave** Jesus a blow, (NASB)	18:22
41	and to **give** Him blows (NASB)	19:3
67	and to **give** Him blows in the face (NASB)	19:3
14	Whence art thou? But Jesus **gave** him no answer.	19:9
56	except it were **given** thee from above:	19:11
2	taketh bread, and **giveth** them, and fish likewise.	John 21:13
17	And they **gave** forth their lots;	Acts 1:26
40	as the Spirit **gave** them utterance.	2:4
36	And I **will show** wonders in heaven above,	2:19
37	neither **wilt** thou **suffer** thine Holy One	2:27
1	but such as I have **give** I thee:	3:6
14	**hath given** him this perfect soundness	3:16
56	none other name under heaven **given** among men,	4:12
25	and **grant** unto thy servants,	4:29
31	and a Saviour, for **to give** repentance to Israel,	5:31
14	whom God **hath given** to them that obey him.	5:32
14	And he **gave** him none inheritance in it,	7:5
31	yet he promised that he **would give** it to him	7:5
14	And he **gave** him the covenant of circumcision:	7:8
14	and **gave** him favour and wisdom	7:10
2	that God **was granting** them deliverance (NASB)	7:25
31	who received the lively oracles **to give** unto us:	7:38
42	of the apostles' hands the Holy Ghost **was given**,	8:18
27	Saying, **Give** me also this power,	8:19
28	And he **gave** her his hand, and lifted her up,	9:41
14	and **granted** that He should become (NASB)	10:40
14	as God **gave** them the like gift as he did unto us,	11:17
14	the Gentiles **granted** repentance unto life.	11:18
14	smote him, because he **gave** not God the glory:	12:23
14	And after that **he gave** unto them judges	13:20
14	and God **gave** unto them Saul the son of Cis,	13:21
36	I **will give** you the sure mercies of David.	13:34
37	**shalt** not **suffer** thine Holy One to see corruption.	13:35
7	and **granted** signs and wonders to be done	14:3
5	in that he did good, and **gave** us rain from heaven,	14:17
28	**giving** them the Holy Ghost,	15:8
5	seeing he **giveth** to all life, and breath,	17:25
31	desiring him that he **would** not **adventure**	19:31
31	and **to give** you an inheritance among all them	20:32
10	It is more blessed **to give** than to receive.	20:35
57	He hoped also that money **should have been given**	24:26
28	but was strong in faith, **giving** glory to God;	Rom 4:20
52	by the Holy Ghost which **is given** unto us.	5:5
14	God **hath given** them the spirit of slumber,	11:8
49	For I say, through the grace **given** unto me,	12:3
51	differing according to the grace that **is given** to us,	12:6
27	but rather **give** place unto wrath:	12:19
38	every ... of us **shall give** account of himself to God.	14:12
24	Now the God of patience and consolation **grant** you	15:5
51	because of the grace that **is given** to me of God,	15:15
50	grace of God which **is given** you by Jesus Christ;	1 Co 1:4
14	even as the Lord **gave** to every man?	3:5
51	According to the grace of God which **is given**	3:10
1	have no commandment ... yet I **give** my judgment,	7:25
21	that we **may cause** no hindrance (NASB)	9:12
54	for her hair **is given** her for a covering.	11:15
42	But the manifestation of the Spirit **is given**	12:7
42	to one **is given** by the Spirit the word of wisdom;	12:8
28	**having given** more abundant honour to that part	12:24
8	And even things without life **giving** sound,	14:7
19	except they **give** a distinction in the sounds,	14:7
19	For if the trumpet **give** an uncertain sound,	14:8
22	utter by the tongue words easy to be understood,	14:9
2	But God **giveth** it a body as it hath pleased him,	15:38
7	which **giveth** us the victory through our Lord Jesus	15:57
28	and **given** the earnest of the Spirit in our hearts.	2 Co 1:22
28	also **hath given** unto us the earnest of the Spirit.	5:5
9	but **give** you occasion to glory on our behalf,	5:12
29	and **hath given** to us the ministry of reconciliation;	5:18
9	**Giving** no offence in any thing,	6:3
55	grace ... **bestowed** on the churches of Macedonia;	8:1
17	but first **gave** their own selves to the Lord,	8:5
1	And herein I **give** my advice:	8:10
7	which **put** the same earnest care into the heart	8:16
65	which **put** the same earnest care into the heart	8:16
14	hath dispersed abroad; he **hath given** to the poor:	9:9
14	which the Lord **hath given** us for edification,	10:8
44	there **was given** to me a thorn in the flesh,	12:7
14	according to the power which the Lord **hath given**	13:10
29	Who **gave** himself for our sins,	Gal 1:4
51	perceived the grace that **was given** unto me,	2:9
17	**they gave** to me and Barnabas the right hands	2:9

δίδωμι 1319

44	had been a law given which could have given life, ... Gal	3:21
46	the promise by faith of Jesus Christ **might be given**	3:22
16	your own eyes, and **have given** them to me.............	4:15
62	**may give** unto you the spirit of wisdom ....Eph	1:17
14	and **gave** him to be the head over all things	1:22
49	of the grace of God which **is given** me to you-ward: ...	3:2
51	to the gift of the grace of God **given** unto me	3:7
49	to the gift of the grace of God **given** unto me	3:7
44	Unto me, who am less ... is this grace **given**, ...	3:8
24	That he **would grant** you, according to the riches	3:16
19	That he **would grant** you, according to the riches	3:16
44	unto every one of us **is given** grace according to	4:7
14	he led captivity captive, and **gave** gifts unto men.....	4:8
14	And he **gave** some, apostles; and some, prophets;	4:11
4	Neither **give** place to the devil......................	4:27
19	that it **may minister** grace unto the hearers...........	4:29
47	And for me, that utterance **may be given** unto me, ...	6:19
46	And for me, that utterance **may be given** unto me, ...	6:19
51	**is given** to me for you, to fulfil the word of God; ... Col	1:25
15	commandments we **gave** you by the Lord Jesus, ... 1 Th	4:2
30	God, who **hath** also **given** unto us his holy Spirit.	4:8
8	God, who **hath** also **given** unto us his holy Spirit.	4:8
6	taking vengeance on them that know not God, ... 2 Th	1:8
28	and **hath given** us everlasting consolation	2:16
21	but **to make** ourselves an ensample unto you	3:9
24	Now the Lord of peace himself **give** you peace	3:16
28	Who **gave** himself a ransom for all, ... 1 Tm	2:6
44	the gift ... which **was given** thee by prophecy, ...	4:14
10	**give** none occasion to the adversary	5:14
14	For God **hath** not **given** us the spirit of fear; ...... 2 Tm	1:7
51	and grace, which **was given** us in Christ Jesus	1:9
24	Lord **give** mercy unto the house of Onesiphorus;	1:16
24	The Lord **grant** unto him that he may find mercy	1:18
24	and the Lord **give** thee understanding in all things	2:7
38	and the Lord **give** thee understanding in all things	2:7
19	if God peradventure **will give** them repentance	2:25
62	if God peradventure **will give** them repentance	2:25
14	Who **gave** himself for us, ... Tit	2:14
14	I and the children which God **hath given** me........ Heb	2:13
14	the patriarch Abraham **gave** the tenth of the spoils.	7:4
5	I **will put** my laws into their mind, ...	8:10
5	I **will put** my laws into their hearts, ...	10:16
6	let him ask of God, that **giveth** to all men liberally, Jas	1:5
57	let him ask of God, ... and it **shall be given** him........	1:5
22	notwithstanding ye **give** them not those things	2:16
2	But he **giveth** more grace. Wherefore he saith, ...	4:6
2	but **giveth** grace unto the humble.	4:6
14	And he prayed again, and the heaven **gave** rain, ...	5:18
30	raised him up from the dead, and **gave** him glory; .. 1 Pt	1:21
2	and **giveth** grace to the humble.	5:5
51	also according to the wisdom **given** unto him .... 2 Pt	3:15
33	manner of love the Father **hath bestowed** upon us, ... 1 Jn	3:1
14	love one another, as he **gave** us commandment.	3:23
14	by the Spirit which he **hath given** us.	3:24
33	because he **hath given** us of his Spirit.	4:13
14	is the record, that God **hath given** to us eternal life, ...	5:11
38	**shall give** him life for them that sin not unto death.	5:16
33	and **hath given** us an understanding.	5:20
14	The Revelation ... which God **gave** unto him, ... Rev	1:1
36	that overcometh **will I give** to eat of the tree of life, ...	2:7
36	**will I give** thee a crown of life.	2:10
36	**will I give** to eat of the hidden manna, ...	2:17
36	and **will give** him a white stone, ...	2:17
12	And I **gave** her space to repent of her fornication;	2:21
36	I **will give** unto every ... according to your works.	2:23
36	to him **will I give** power over the nations:	2:26
36	And I **will give** him the morning star.	2:28
32	behold, I **have set** before thee an open door, ...	3:8
1	I **will make** them of the synagogue of Satan, ...	3:9
59	I **will make** them of the synagogue of Satan, ...	3:9
36	**will I grant** to sit with me in my throne, ...	3:21
39	And when those beasts **give** glory and honour	4:9
44	and a crown **was given** unto him:	6:2
44	and power **was given** to him ... to take peace	6:4
44	and there **was given** unto him a great sword, ...	6:4
44	power **was given** unto them over the fourth part	6:8
45	white robes **were given** unto every one of them;	6:11
44	white robes **were given** unto every one of them; .... Rev	6:11
44	to whom it **was given** to hurt the earth and the sea, ...	7:2
45	and to them **were given** seven trumpets.	8:2
44	and there **was given** unto him much incense, ...	8:3
20	that he **should offer** it with the prayers of all saints	8:3
38	that he **should offer** it with the prayers of all saints	8:3
44	and to him **was given** the key of the bottomless pit.....	9:1
44	locusts ... and unto them **was given** power, ...	9:3
44	to them it **was given** that they should not kill them, ...	9:5
25	and said unto him, **Give** me the little book............	10:9
31	and said unto him, **Give** me the little book............	10:9
44	And there **was given** me a reed like unto a rod:	11:1
44	measure it not; **for** it is given unto the Gentiles:	11:2
36	And I **will give** power unto my two witnesses, ...	11:3
17	affrighted, and **gave** glory to the God of heaven.	11:13
31	that thou **shouldest give** reward unto thy servants	11:18
45	the woman **were given** two wings of a great eagle, ...	12:14
14	and the dragon **gave** him his power, and his seat, ...	13:2
14	they worshipped the dragon which **gave** power	13:4
44	**was given** unto him a mouth speaking great things	13:5
44	and power **was given** unto him to continue	13:5
44	it **was given** unto him to make war with the saints, ...	13:7
44	and power **was given** him over all kindreds, ...	13:7
44	means of those miracles which he **had power** to do ...	13:14
44	**had power** to give life unto the image of the beast,...	13:15
31	had power **to give** life unto the image of the beast, ...	13:15
20	he causeth all, ... free and bond, **to receive** a mark ...	13:16
23	he causeth all, ... free and bond, **to receive** a mark ...	13:16
27	with a loud voice, Fear God, and **give** glory to him; ...	14:7
14	one of the four beasts **gave** unto the seven angels	15:7
13	and thou **hast given** them blood to drink;	16:6
11	and thou **hast given** them blood to drink;	16:6
44	power **was given** unto him to scorch men with fire....	16:8
31	and they repented not **to give** him glory...............	16:9
31	**to give** unto her the cup of the wine..................	16:19
58	**shall give** their power and strength unto the beast.....	17:13
14	For God **hath** put in their hearts to fulfil his will, ...	17:17
31	to agree, and **give** their kingdom unto the beast, ...	17:17
27	so much torment and sorrow **give** her:	18:7
21	be glad and rejoice, and **give** honour to him:	19:7
63	be glad and rejoice, and **give** honour to him:	19:7
44	And to her **was granted** that she should be arrayed ...	19:8
44	and judgment **was given** unto them:	20:4
14	And the sea **gave** up the dead which were in it;	20:13
17	hell **delivered** up the dead which were in them:	20:13
36	I **will give** unto him that is athirst of the fountain	21:6

Classical Greek

The basic meaning of *didōmi* throughout Greek literature is "to give," although it is also often translated "to offer, grant, assign, render," etc.

Septuagint Usage

In the Septuagint *didōmi* occurs many times. Usually it is a translation of *nāthan*, although it is also used for words such as *yᵉhav* (as in Genesis 47:15; Deuteronomy 32:3) and *soom* (as in Jeremiah 42:15 [LXX 49:15] where the Lord warned the Israelites not to set or fix their minds upon Egypt, etc.).

New Testament Usage

Didōmi is one of the most frequently used verbs of the New Testament, occurring more than 400 times. In the New Testament *do*, the root of *didōmi*, lends itself to many other important words such as *dōrea* (1424) and *dōron* (1428), "gift"; *dōrean* (1425), "freely"; *apodidōmi* (586), "to pay back, deliver, reward," etc.

The frequency of *didōmi* in the New Testament allows for several general categories of usage. First we may note those instances where it refers to the giving of physical items and articles such as the head of John the Baptist (Matthew 14:7), the giving of money (Mark 14:11), meat or food (Luke 8:55), oil (Matthew 25:8), vinegar (Matthew 27:34), etc.

Second, there are many occurrences of what may be considered divine giving or blessing from either God, Jesus, or the Holy Spirit. This is of two kinds: physical or material blessing such as bread or sustenance (Matthew 6:11), gifts (Matthew 7:11), physical healing (Acts 3:16), rain (Acts 14:17), etc. But more frequently it refers to that divine blessing or giving which is spiritual or immaterial. Thus, man is given knowledge of salvation (Luke 1:77), eternal life (John 17:2), the Spirit (John 3:34), gifts of the Spirit (1 Corinthians 12:7), laws (Hebrews 8:10), grace (Romans 12:3), mercy (2 Timothy 1:16,18), power (2 Corinthians 13:10), etc.

A third category of giving in the New Testament has to do with what humanity gives to God, especially in terms that are immaterial or spiritual such as ourselves (2 Corinthians 8:5), praise (John 9:24), glory (Luke 17:18).

Finally it is important to note the use of *didōmi* for God's giving to Jesus. John's Gospel. It states that God gave to Jesus all things (3:35), all authority (5:27), sheep or followers (10:29), and disciples (17:2ff.).

There are several instances in the New Testament where *didōmi* is associated with objects in a type of personification. Thus, the seed gives (yields) fruit (Matthew 13:8), and the moon gives light (Matthew 24:29).

A number of other occurrences of *didōmi*, some of them unusual or significant, may be noted. Matthew 20:28 indicates that Jesus gave His life as a ransom. Jesus promised to give His followers a mouth (words to speak) when apprehended by the authorities (Luke 21:15). According to Acts 2:4 it was the Spirit who gave the early disciples the power to speak with tongues at Pentecost. Acts 11:18 says that God granted (gave) repentance to Gentiles as well as Jews. Both Acts 2:27 and Acts 13:35 refer to Psalm 16 indicating that God would not allow (give) His Holy One to see corruption. Romans 14:12 says that Christians will give an account of themselves at the judgment. In Ephesians 4:27 Paul warned his readers not to "give place (an opportunity) to the devil." And Revelation 20:13 pictures death and hell as delivering (giving up) the dead.

Luke 12:58, which speaks of being diligent (giving an effort) to agree with one's legal opponent, may be based on a Latin idiom which had entered Greek usage by the time of the New Testament (*Bauer*).

STRONG 1325, BAUER 192-93, MOULTON-MILLIGAN 159-60, KITTEL 2:166, LIDDELL-SCOTT 422-23, COLIN BROWN 2:39-41.

1320. διεγείρω diegeirō verb

Wake up thoroughly, excite, stir up, arouse.

COGNATE:
  ἐγείρω egeirō (1446)
SYNONYMS:
  ἐγείρω egeirō (1446)
  ἐξανίστημι exanistēmi (1801)
  ἐξεγείρω exegeirō (1809)
  ἐπεγείρω epegeirō (1877)
  παροτρύνω parotrunō (3813)

1. διεγείρω diegeirō 1sing indic pres act
2. διεγείρουσιν diegeirousin 3pl indic pres act
3. διεγείρειν diegeirein inf pres act
4. διήγειραν diēgeiran 3pl indic aor act
5. διεγερθείς diegertheis nom sing masc part aor pass
6. διηγείρετο diēgeireto 3sing indic imperf pass
7. διεγείρετο diegeireto 3sing indic imperf pass

5 Then Joseph **being raised** from sleep . . . . Matt 1:24
2 and they **awake** him, and say unto him, Master, ... Mark 4:38
5 And he **arose**, and rebuked the wind, ... 4:39
4 and **awoke** him, saying, Master, master, we perish. . . Luke 8:24
5 And **being aroused**, He rebuked the wind (NASB) 8:24
6 the sea **arose** by reason of a great wind that blew. . . John 6:18
7 the sea **arose** by reason of a great wind that blew. 6:18
3 to **stir** you **up** by putting you in remembrance; . . . . . . 2 Pt 1:13
1 I **stir up** your pure minds by way of **remembrance**: 3:1

This word is from *egeirō* (1446) meaning "to raise" and *dia* (1217) meaning "through" or "by." It is used in the New Testament to mean "wake up" physically. It can also mean "to arouse or stir up someone's emotions." John 6:18 says "the sea arose," meaning the water became rough. Also see Matthew 1:24; Mark 4:38,39; Luke 8:24; 2 Peter 1:13 and 3:1.

STRONG 1326, BAUER 193-94, MOULTON-MILLIGAN 160, LIDDELL-SCOTT 423.

1320B. διενθυμέομαι

dienthumeomai verb

Reflect, think about, ponder.

1. διενθυμουμένου dienthumoumenou
gen sing masc part pres mid

1 While Peter **was reflecting** on the vision (NASB) ... Acts 10:19

According to *Bauer* this word occurs nowhere outside of Christian literature. Its single occurrence in the New Testament is at Acts 10:19 which relates that Peter was "pondering" the vision God had given him. In that vision Peter, a devout Jewish Christian, was told by a voice to eat many kinds of food considered unclean by the rules of Judaism. As he was "thinking through" the implications of this vision, the Holy Spirit spoke, directing him to go with the three Gentile men who just then had called out from the gate of the house where he was staying. Peter followed them back to the house of Cornelius, a Roman centurion.

BAUER 194, LIDDELL-SCOTT 424.

1320C. διεξέρχομαι
diexerchomai verb

Pass through, come out.

CROSS-REFERENCE:
ἔρχομαι erchomai (2048)

יָצָא yātsâ' (3428), Qal: come out (Jb 20:25); hiphil: bring out (Ez 12:5).

צָנַח tsānach (7070), Go down into (Jgs 4:21).

1. διεξελθοῦσα diexelthousa
nom sing fem part aor act

Found in classical Greek literature since Sophocles (Fifth Century B.C.), *diexerchomai* is a doubly compounded verb (*dia* [1217] + *ek* [1523] + *erchomai* [2048]) which means "to go through" or "pass through completely." In its only New Testament occurrence, at Acts 28:3, it has the meaning "come out." Although it is a variant, replacing the word *exerchomai* (1814) in some manuscripts, the form *diexerchomai* also exists in the Septuagint and in the writings of Philo and Josephus.

BAUER 194, MOULTON-MILLIGAN 160, LIDDELL-SCOTT 424-25.

1321. διέξοδος diexodos noun

Street crossing.

CROSS-REFERENCE:
ὁδός hodos (3461)

יָצָא yātsâ' (3428), Go out (Ps 144:14 [143:14]).

מוֹצָא môtsâ' (4296), Spring (2 Kgs 2:21, Ps 107:33 [106:33]).

מִפְרָץ miphrāts (4825), Landing place (Jgs 5:17).

פֶּלֶג pelegh (6631), Irrigation canal (Ps 1:3).

תּוֹצָאוֹת tôtsâ'ôth (8777), Boundary (Nm 34:4,5, Jos 15:4,7); escape (Ps 68:20 [67:20]).

1. διεξόδους diexodous *acc pl fem*

1 Go ye therefore into the **highways**, ... Matt 22:9

Classical Greek and Septuagint Usage

In secular Greek *diexodos* is used primarily of an "outlet" or "passage, a road leading out of town, a means of escape, an exposition," etc. The focus is upon the conclusion or the end of the way or road and not so much on the road itself.

In Philo it is used variously, sometimes suggesting an "exposition" or "clarification." In the Greek papyri it is used of the "conclusion of a trial." In the Septuagint *diexodos* occurs more than 25 times, principally for variations of *yātsâ'*, and in most of these cases, especially in Numbers 34 and Joshua 15-19, it is used to designate boundary lines.

New Testament Usage

Diexodos is used only once in the New Testament in the Parable of the Marriage Feast (Matthew 22:9). Luke's parallel of the great feast uses *plateia* (3973B) and *rhume* (4362) in 14:21. The singular use of *diexodos* in Matthew 22:9 surely requires some distinction from the common *hodos* (3461), "road," although Matthew 22:10 indicates that the slaves went out to the "streets" (*hodos*), so one cannot be too rigid. Perhaps it is best to think of *diexodos* as designating "that point of any road leading out of (or into) a city"; a place where the road seemed to end and the open road or country road seemed to begin. Thus Matthew's reference may imply that the slaves went out on the regular city roads and continued their search up to the point where the roads emptied into the open country. Here they might meet many people coming into and going from a city.

STRONG 1327, BAUER 194, MOULTON-MILLIGAN 160, KITTEL 5:103-9, LIDDELL-SCOTT 424-25, COLIN BROWN 3:940.

1322. διερμηνευτής
diermēneutēs noun

Interpreter, one who explains.

CROSS-REFERENCE:
ἑρμηνεύω hermēneuō (2043)

1. διερμηνευτής diermēneutēs *nom sing masc*

διερμηνεύω 1323

1 But if there be no **interpreter**,	1 Co 14:28

Not found prior to its single Biblical use in 1 Corinthians 14:28, *diermēneutēs* specifically denotes the "interpreter" or "translator" of a gift of tongues. The expression is very rare after its first appearance in 1 Corinthians. It did not appear again until the 12th Century A.D.

STRONG 1328, BAUER 194, MOULTON-MILLIGAN 160, KITTEL 2:661-66, LIDDELL-SCOTT 425, COLIN BROWN 1:579,581.

1323. διερμηνεύω diermēneuō verb

Explain, interpret, translate.

COGNATE:
  ἑρμηνεύω hermēneuō (2043)

SYNONYMS:
  δείκνυμι deiknumi (1161)
  ἐμφανίζω emphanizō (1702)
  ἐξηγέομαι exēgeomai (1817)
  ἑρμηνεύω hermēneuō (2043)
  μεθερμηνεύω methermēneuō (3148)
  ὁρίζω horizō (3587)
  φράζω phrazō (5255)

1. **διερμηνεύουσιν** diermēneuousin 3pl indic pres act
2. **διερμηνεύῃ** diermēneuē 3sing subj pres act
3. **διερμηνευέτω** diermēneuetō 3sing impr pres act
4. **διηρμήνευεν** diērmēneuen 3sing indic imperf act
5. **διερμηνευομένη** diermēneuomenē
              nom sing fem part pres mid
6. **διηρμήνευσεν** diērmēneusen 3sing indic aor act
7. **διερμήνευσεν** diermēneusen 3sing indic aor act

4 he **expounded** unto them in all the scriptures	Luke 24:27
7 he **expounded** unto them in all the scriptures	24:27
6 he **expounded** unto them in all the scriptures	24:27
5 which by **interpretation** is called Dorcas:	Acts 9:36
1 do all speak with tongues? do all **interpret**?	1 Co 12:30
2 he that speaketh with tongues, except he **interpret**,	14:5
2 him that speaketh ... pray that he may **interpret**.	14:13
3 and that by course; and let one **interpret**.	14:27

Classical Greek

The basic meaning of *diermēneuō* is "to explain, interpret," or "translate." It is formed from the word *hermēneuō* (2043) from which the English "hermeneutics" is derived. In classical Greek *hermēneuō* is more common, yet the verb *diermēneuō*, "translate" or "explain," does occur.

Septuagint Usage

The term occurs only once in the Septuagint, in the apocryphal Second Book of Maccabees. Here it follows the classical sense of "to interpret, translate" (*nephthar*, which is translated as purification [2 Maccabees 1:36]).

New Testament Usage

The New Testament uses *diermēneuō* in the sense of "explain" or "interpret" (Luke 24:27: "He explained to them what was said in all the Scriptures concerning himself" [NIV]). *Diermēneuomenē* carries the sense of "translate" (Acts 9:36, "In Joppa there was a disciple named Tabitha [which, when translated, is Dorcas]," NIV).

The other four occurrences of *diermēneuō* in the New Testament all pertain to the interpretation of speaking in tongues (1 Corinthians 12:30; 14:5,13,27). In these instances it would seem to mean "taking the unintelligible and making it understandable." Thus "explaining, interpreting" seems more reasonable when concerned with glossolalia.

STRONG 1329, BAUER 194, MOULTON-MILLIGAN 160, KITTEL 2:661-66, LIDDELL-SCOTT 425, COLIN BROWN 1:579-81.

1324. διέρχομαι dierchomai verb

Go through, come, go, go about.

COGNATE:
  ἔρχομαι erchomai (2048)

SYNONYMS:
  διαπορεύω diaporeuō (1273)
  διοδεύω diodeuō (1347)
  ἐπέρχομαι eperchomai (1889)
  ἔρχομαι erchomai (2048)
  ἐφικνέομαι ephikneomai (2167)
  ἥκω hēkō (2223)
  καταντάω katantaō (2628)
  παραγίνομαι paraginomai (3716)
  παραπορεύομαι paraporeuomai (3760)
  παρέρχομαι parerchomai (3790)
  παρίστημι paristēmi (3798)
  πορεύομαι poreuomai (4057)
  προσέρχομαι proserchomai (4193)
  φθάνω phthanō (5185)

אָהַל 'āhal (163), Piel: pitch a tent (Is 13:20).

אוֹר 'ôr (213), Be or become light; hiphil: give light (Ex 14:20).

בּוֹא bô' (971), Qal: come, go (Nm 31:23, 2 Kgs 4:42, Is 52:1); hiphil: put in (Jer 13:1).

הָלַךְ hālakh (2050), Qal: go, walk (Gn 22:5, 1 Kgs 3:6, Ps 73:9 [72:9]); piel: flow (Ps 104:10 [103:10]); walk (Lam 5:18); hithpael: walk, walk about (1 Sm 2:30, 1 Chr 17:6, Ps 105:13 [104:13]).

חָלַף chālaph (2599), Pass through (Is 21:1).

יָצָא yātsâ' (3428), Go or come out (Jos 19:12,13, Jer 37:4 [44:4]).

יָרַד yāradh (3495), Go down (Jos 16:3).

נָחַל nāchal (5336), Inherit (Prv 28:10).

סָבַב sāvav (5621), Qal: go through (2 Chr 17:9); niphal: turn around (Jos 18:14—Codex Alexandrinus only).

עָבַר 'āvar (5882), Qal: pass through (Nm 20:17, Mi 2:13);

pass on (Jos 18:18); hiphil: bring (Nm 31:23, Ez 47:3); send (2 Chr 30:5).

עָמַד ʻāmadh (6198), Stand (1 Sm 6:20).

פָּגַע pāghaʻ (6534), Reach (Jos 16:7—Codex Alexandrinus only).

רָכַב rākhav (7680), Ride; hiphil: lead on horseback (Est 6:11).

רָמַשׂ rāmas (7718), Prowl (Ps 104:20 [103:20]).

שׁוּט shûṭ (8198), Go or rove about (2 Sm 24:2).

שׁוּר shûr (8227), Descend (S/S 4:8).

תָּאַר tāʼar (8716), Turn (Jos 18:14—Codex Alexandrinus only).

תַּהֲלֻכֹת tahălukhōth (8748), Procession (Neh 12:31).

1. διῆλθον diēlthon 1/3sing/pl indic aor act
2. διῆλθεν diēlthen 3sing indic aor act
3. διέλθω dielthō 1sing subj aor act
4. διέλθωμεν dielthōmen 1pl subj aor act
5. διελθών dielthōn nom sing masc part aor act
6. διελθόντα dielthonta acc sing masc part aor act
7. διελθόντες dielthontes nom pl masc part aor act
8. διελθεῖν dielthein inf aor act
9. διεληλυθότα dielēluthota acc sing masc part perf act
10. διέρχομαι dierchomai 1sing indic pres mid
11. διέρχεται dierchetai 3sing indic pres mid
12. διερχόμενος dierchomenos nom sing masc part pres mid
13. διερχόμενον dierchomenon acc sing masc part pres mid
14. διέρχεσθαι dierchesthai inf pres mid
15. διελεύσεται dieleusetai 3sing indic fut mid
16. διήρχετο diērcheto 3sing indic imperf mid
17. διήρχοντο diērchonto 3pl indic imperf mid
18. διέρχωμαι dierchōmai 1sing pres mid

11	he walketh through dry places, seeking rest,	Matt 12:43
8	easier for a camel to go through the eye of a needle,	19:24
4	Let us pass over unto the other side.	Mark 4:35
8	It is easier for a camel to go through (NASB)	10:25
4	Let us now go even unto Bethlehem,	Luke 2:15
15	a sword shall pierce through thy own soul also,	2:35
5	he passing through the midst of them went his way,	4:30
16	But so much the more went there a fame abroad	5:15
4	Let us go over unto the other side of the lake.	8:22
17	And they departed, and went through the towns,	9:6
11	he walketh through dry places, seeking rest;	11:24
16	passed through the midst of Samaria and Galilee.	17:11
8	is easier for a camel to go through a needle's eye,	18:25
16	And Jesus entered and passed through Jericho.	19:1
14	tree to see him: for he was to pass that way.	19:4
14	And he must needs go through Samaria.	John 4:4
18	nor come all the way here to draw (NASB)	4:15
5	going through the midst of them, and so passed by	8:59
1	Therefore they that were scattered abroad went	Acts 8:4
12	and passing through he preached in all the cities,	8:40
13	as Peter passed throughout all quarters,	9:32
8	desiring him that he would not delay to come	9:38
2	Jesus of Nazareth ... who went about doing good,	10:38
1	travelled as far as Phenice and Cyprus,	11:19
8	Barnabas, that he should go as far as Antioch.	11:22
7	When they were past the first and ... second ward,	12:10
7	when they had gone through the isle unto Paphos,	13:6
7	But when they departed from Perga,	Acts 13:14
7	And after they had passed throughout Pisidia,	14:24
17	they passed through Phenice and Samaria,	15:3
16	And he went through Syria and Cilicia,	15:41
7	Now when they had gone throughout Phrygia	16:6
1	Now when they had gone throughout Phrygia	16:6
12	For as I passed by, and beheld your devotions,	17:23
12	and went over all the country of Galatia	18:23
8	And when he was disposed to pass into Achaia,	18:27
6	Paul having passed through the upper coasts	19:1
5	when he had passed through Macedonia	19:21
5	And when he had gone over those parts,	20:2
1	among whom I have gone preaching the kingdom	20:25
2	and so death passed upon all men,	Rom 5:12
1	and all passed through the sea;	1 Co 10:1
3	when I shall pass through Macedonia:	16:5
10	for I do pass through Macedonia.	16:5
8	And to pass by you into Macedonia,	2 Co 1:16
9	high priest, that is passed into the heavens,	Heb 4:14

Classical Greek and Septuagint Usage
In classical and Septuagint Greek this term is used to mean "pass through." It is used over 100 times in the Septuagint to translate 17 Hebrew words with their variations. Most often it is used to translate ʻāvar which generally means "pass over, through, by, pass on." (See Genesis 15:17; Exodus 12:12; 2 Samuel 11:27 [LXX 2 Kings 11:27]; Psalm 18:12 [LXX 17:12].)

New Testament Usage
As in classical and Septuagint Greek, the New Testament uses dierchomai with a somewhat wide range in meaning. The general concept of dierchomai is to "go through." Most often it is used to convey "moving about from one geographic location to another" (see Luke 17:11; John 4:4; Acts 14:24; 15:41). There are many instances of this use of dierchomai in the New Testament.

It may also be used in the sense of "going through without any particular geographic notion." For instance, Matthew 19:24 speaks of the camel "going through" the eye of a needle, and Luke 4:30 uses dierchomai for Jesus "passing through" the crowd. In Hebrews 4:14 it is used in reference to Jesus, the "great high priest, that is passed into the heavens." Dierchomai is also used in Romans 5:12 which speaks of death "passed upon all men." In addition to the above uses, dierchomai may simply mean "come" or "go" (see Mark 4:35; Luke 8:22; Acts 9:38).

STRONG 1330, BAUER 194, MOULTON-MILLIGAN 160, KITTEL 2:676, LIDDELL-SCOTT 425-26, COLIN BROWN 1:320-21.

1325. διερωτάω dierōtaō verb
Find by inquiry, ascertain.

διετής 1326

CROSS-REFERENCE:
ἐρωτάω erōtaō (2049)

1. διερωτήσαντες dierōtēsantes
nom pl masc part aor act

1 had made inquiry for Simon's house, ... Acts 10:17

The amplified definition of *dierōtaō* is "to find out something through inquiry, to ask a question and find out the answer." It occurs only in Acts 10:17 in the New Testament. Cornelius' messengers had inquired in Joppa concerning the location of Simon's house, where Peter was staying.

STRONG 1331, BAUER 194, LIDDELL-SCOTT 426.

1326. διετής dietēs adj
Two years old.

1. διετοῦς dietous gen sing masc

1 all the children ... from two years old and under, ... Matt 2:16

The meaning "2 years old" comes to us from classical and Septuagint Greek. However, in its only New Testament appearance (Matthew 2:16) its context includes "two years old and under," in reference to Herod's murder of Bethlehem's children in an effort to kill the infant Jesus. Vine concurs, stating that it denotes "lasting two years, two years old" (*Expository Dictionary*, "Year").

STRONG 1332, BAUER 194, MOULTON-MILLIGAN 160, LIDDELL-SCOTT 426.

1327. διετία dietia noun
A period of 2 years.

1. διετίας dietias gen sing fem
2. διετίαν dietian acc sing fem

1 But after two years Porcius Festus came .... Acts 24:27
2 Paul dwelt two whole years in his own ... house, ... 28:30

This term was not found prior to the Christian Era. It occurs only twice in the New Testament, in Acts 24:27 and 28:30. Both of these passages refer to the periods of time that Paul waited for his "judgment," once by Festus and the other by Caesar.

STRONG 1333, BAUER 194, MOULTON-MILLIGAN 160-61, LIDDELL-SCOTT 426.

1328. διηγέομαι diēgeomai verb
Describe, show, or tell; relate fully; conduct a narration through to the end.

COGNATE:
ἐξηγέομαι exēgeomai (1817)
SYNONYMS:
ἀγγέλλω angellō (31B)
ἀναγγέλλω anangellō (310)
ἀνατίθημι anatithēmi (392)
ἀπαγγέλλω apangellō (514)
ἐκδιηγέομαι ekdiēgeomai (1542)
ἐξηγέομαι exēgeomai (1817)
ἐρεύγομαι ereugomai (2027)
ἑρμηνεύω hermēneuō (2043)
καταγγέλλω katangellō (2576)
κηρύσσω kērussō (2756)
λέγω legō (2978)
φθέγγομαι phthengomai (5187)
φράζω phrazō (5255)

אָמַר 'āmar (569), Command (Est 1:17).

דָּבַר dāvar (1744), Qal: speak (Est 10:3); piel: speak (Jer 23:28).

חוּד chûdh (2424), Propound a riddle (Ez 17:2).

כָּרָה kārâh (3868), Dig (Ps 119:85 [118:85]).

נָשָׂא nāsâ' (5558), Lift, carry; recite (Sir 44:5).

סָפַר sāphar (5807), Qal: count (Pss 48:12 [47:12], 87:6 [86:6]); piel: tell (Ex 18:8, 2 Kgs 8:4, Jl 1:3); pual: be declared (Ps 88:11 [87:11]).

שִׂיחַ sîach (7943), Qal: consider, complain, talk about, sing about (Jgs 5:10, Pss 105:2 [104:2], 145:5 [144:5]); polel: meditate, consider (Is 53:8).

1. διηγοῦ diēgou 2sing impr pres mid
2. διηγούμενον diēgoumenon
acc sing masc part pres mid
3. διηγήσατο diēgēsato 3sing indic aor mid
4. διηγήσαντο diēgēsanto 3pl indic aor mid
5. διηγήσωνται diēgēsōntai 3pl subj aor mid
6. διηγήσεται diēgēsetai 3sing indic fut mid

4 And they that saw it told them how it befell to him Mark 5:16
5 he charged them that they should tell no man 9:9
1 show how great things God hath done unto thee ..... Luke 8:39
4 told him all that they had done. And he took them, ... 9:10
6 and who shall declare his generation? .... Acts 8:33
3 and declared unto them how he had seen the Lord 9:27
3 declared unto them how the Lord had 12:17
2 for the time would fail me to tell of Gedeon, ... Heb 11:32

Classical Greek and Septuagint Usage
In classical Greek this term primarily means "set out in detail" or "describe." It appears over 50 times in the Septuagint, usually to translate *sāphar* which means "recount, relate" in the variations used (see Genesis 24:66; Exodus 10:2; 2 Kings 8:4 [LXX 4 Kings 8:4]; Psalm 22:22 [LXX 21:22]).

New Testament Usage
Diēgeomai comes from the two words *dia* (1217), "through," and *hēgeomai*, "to lead," and means "to recount, to relate in full." It is found primarily in the Gospels and Acts (e.g., Mark 5:16; Luke 8:39; 9:10; Acts 8:33; 9:27;

12:17). In Mark 9:9 and Hebrews 11:32 the KJV renders the word *diēgeomai* "to tell."
STRONG 1334, BAUER 195, MOULTON-MILLIGAN 161, LIDDELL-SCOTT 427, COLIN BROWN 1:573,575-76.

1329. διήγησις diēgēsis noun
Narrative, account, declaration.
CROSS-REFERENCE:
ἐξηγέομαι exēgeomai (1817)

חִידָה chîdhāh (2512), Saying (Hb 2:6).
מִסְפָּר mispār (4709), Account (Jgs 7:15—Codex Alexandrinus only).
סוֹד sôdh (5660), Council, counsel (Sir 9:15).
שִׂיחָה sîchāh (7946), Complaint, study, meditation (Sir 6:35).

1. διήγησιν diēgēsin acc sing fem
1 to set forth in order **a declaration** of those things .... Luke 1:1

This unique word is found in the New Testament only in Luke 1:1. In classical Greek literature it was used in a speech by Aristotle, for example, where it means "the statement of a case" (*Liddell-Scott*). Similarly, Luke described the many who had undertaken to compile a "narrative" (RSV); "declaration" (KJV); "account" (NIV), of the things concerning Jesus.
STRONG 1335, BAUER 195, MOULTON-MILLIGAN 161, KITTEL 2:909, LIDDELL-SCOTT 427, COLIN BROWN 1:573-76.

1330. διηνεκής diēnekēs adj
Unbroken, continuous, for all time.
SYNONYMS:
ἀΐδιος aidios (126)
αἰώνιος aiōnios (164)

1. διηνεκές diēnekes nom/acc sing neu
1 abideth a priest **continually**........................ Heb 7:3
1 which they offered year by year **continually** 10:1
1 after he had offered one sacrifice for sins **for ever**,..... 10:12
1 he hath perfected **for ever** them that are sanctified..... 10:14

In classical Greek this term appears since the time of Homer and generally means "continuous, uninterrupted (of time)." In the New Testament this adjective is found only in Hebrews (7:3; 10:1,12,14) and is used in a phrase with *eis* (1506B), "unto," and the article, signifying "perpetually, continually," or "forever."
STRONG 1336, BAUER 195, MOULTON-MILLIGAN 161, LIDDELL-SCOTT 427.

1331. διθάλασσος dithalassos adj
Surrounded by two seas, lying between two seas.
CROSS-REFERENCE:
θάλασσα thalassa (2258)

1. διθάλασσον dithalasson acc sing masc
1 And falling into a place **where two seas met**,....... Acts 27:41

This term appears from the First Century B.C. to mean "with the sea on both sides." Its use as an adjective in the New Testament is consistent with this idea. It is found only in Acts 27:41 and refers to a place that is "divided into two seas" or "where two seas meet." It describes something like a sandbar or reef, at some distance from the shore, with deep water on each side (see *Bauer*). The KJV translates *dithalassos* as a place "where two seas met"; RSV, "a shoal"; NIV, "a sandbar."
STRONG 1337, BAUER 195, LIDDELL-SCOTT 427.

1332. διϊκνέομαι diikneomai verb
Pass through, pierce.
SYNONYMS:
ἐκκεντέω ekkenteō (1561)
νύσσω nussō (3434)

בָּרַח bārach (1300), Flee; hiphil: pass through (Ex 26:28).

1. διϊκνούμενος diiknoumenos
nom sing masc part pres mid
1 **piercing even to the dividing asunder** of soul........ Heb 4:12

This compound verb is made up of *dia* (1217), which means "through" (in the spatial sense), and *ikneomai*, "to go." It appears as far back as the Fifth Century B.C. and is used in the Septuagint to translate *bārach*, which means "pass through," as a bar passed through the middle of the tabernacle in order to support its roof (Exodus 26:28). It is used only in Hebrews 4:12 in reference to the Word of God "piercing" or "penetrating" even to the point of dividing soul and spirit.
STRONG 1338, BAUER 195, LIDDELL-SCOTT 428.

1333. διΐστημι diistēmi verb
Put apart, proceed, depart, part.
CROSS-REFERENCE:
ἵστημι histēmi (2449)

חָלַק chālaq (2606), Piel: divide (Ez 5:1).
עָרַם 'āram (6429), Niphal: be heaped up (Ex 15:8).
פָּרַד pāradh (6754), Hiphil: separate (Prv 17:9).

διϊσχυρίζομαι 1334

1. διέστη **dieste** 3sing indic aor act
2. διαστήσαντες **diastesantes** nom pl masc part aor act
3. διαστάσης **diastases** gen sing fem part aor act

3 the space of one hour after another ... affirmed, ... Luke 22:59
1 while he blessed them, he was parted from them, ... 24:51
2 and when they had gone a little further, ... Acts 27:28

Classical Greek and Septuagint Usage

From the time of Homer this term was used in classical Greek to mean "go away, set apart, separate" when used as an intransitive verb and "divide, farther" when used as a transitive verb. It is used in the Septuagint to translate four different Hebrew terms that also indicate "parting, separating" (Exodus 15:8; Proverbs 17:9).

New Testament Usage

Diistēmi appears only three times in the New Testament in a manner consistent with the classical and Septuagint usage. In Luke 22:59 the form *diastasēs* is employed to demonstrate a passing of time, "about an hour later ... " (NIV), "and about the space of one hour after ... " (KJV).

Luke 24:51 uses *diestē* to relate a going away or parting from someone: "While he blessed them, he was parted from them" (KJV). The final occurrence of *diistēmi* is Acts 27:28: "A short time later ... " (NIV); "and when they had gone a little further ... " (KJV).

Thus, the basic idea of "separation" or "going away" may relate to the passing of time (the separation of one hour from the next) or physical separation of individuals or objects.

STRONG 1339, BAUER 195, MOULTON-MILLIGAN 161, LIDDELL-SCOTT 428.

1334. διϊσχυρίζομαι

diischurizomai verb

Insist, maintain firmly, confidently affirm.

COGNATE:
  ἰσχύω ischuō (2453)

SYNONYM:
  διαβεβαιόομαι diabebaioomai (1220)

1. διϊσχυρίζετο **diischurizeto** 3sing indic imperf mid

1 one hour after another confidently affirmed, ... Luke 22:59
1 But she constantly affirmed that it was even so. ..... Acts 12:15

This infrequently used word comes from *dia* (1217), "through," and *ischurizomai*, "to strengthen" or "persist." Found in Luke 22:59 and Acts 12:15, *diischurizomai* carries the sense of "intense corroboration or affirmation." In Luke, "another (maid, young woman) *confidently affirmed*" that Peter was with Jesus at the time of His arrest. In Acts, even though the disciples had been praying for the imprisoned Peter, they thought Rhoda was "mad" when she told them that he was standing at the gate. Nevertheless, Rhoda "constantly affirmed" that Peter was waiting to be let into the house.

STRONG 1340, BAUER 195, LIDDELL-SCOTT 428.

1335. δικαιοκρισία **dikaiokrisia** noun

Righteous judgment.

CROSS-REFERENCES:
  δικαιόω dikaioō (1338)
  κρίνω krinō (2892)

1. δικαιοκρισίας **dikaiokrisias** gen sing fem

1 and revelation of the righteous judgment of God; .... Rom 2:5

This word is formed from two terms: the adjective *dikaios* (1335B), "righteous," and the noun *krisis* (2893), "decision" or "judgment." *Dikaiokrisia* is found only once in the New Testament, at Romans 2:5, where it speaks of a day in which "righteous judgment" shall be visited upon those whose hearts are hard and impenitent. In 2 Thessalonians 1:5 the two words *dikaias* and *kriseōs* are used separately to denote the "righteous judgment" of God.

STRONG 1341, BAUER 195, MOULTON-MILLIGAN 161, KITTEL 2:174-78, 224-25, LIDDELL-SCOTT 428.

1335B. δίκαιος **dikaios** adj

Just, righteous, right, upright, impartial.

CROSS-REFERENCE:
  δικαιόω dikaioō (1338)

אֱמֶת 'ĕmeth (583), Faithfulness, truth (Ex 18:21, Jer 42:5 [49:5], Zec 7:9).

דִּין dîn (1835), Judgment (Prv 20:8).

חֶסֶד cheṣedh (2721), Righteous (Is 57:1).

טָהוֹר ṭāhôr (2999), Pure (Prv 30:12 [24:35]).

יָשָׁר yāshār (3596), Righteous, just (Nm 23:10, Prv 3:32, 11:4).

יֹשֶׁר yōsher (3598), Uprightness (Prv 17:26).

מִשְׁפָּט mishpāṭ (5122), Decision (Prv 16:33); justice, judgment (Prv 21:7, 29:4).

נָדִיב nādhîv (5259), Noble (Prv 17:7).

נָקִיא nāqî' (5538I), Innocent (Jl 3:19, Jon 1:14).

נָקִי nāqî (5538II) Innocent (Jb 9:23, Prv 1:11).

נָקָם nāqām (5542), Vengeance (Is 47:3).

צַדִּיק tsaddîq (6926), Just, righteous (Dt 4:8, 2 Chr 12:6, Ez 18:5).

δίκαιος 1335B

צֶדֶק tsedheq (6928), Righteous, righteousness (Dt 16:18, Jb 36:3, Is 32:1).

צְדָקָה tsᵉdhāqāh (6930), Righteousness, truthfulness (Jb 37:23, Prv 21:3).

שָׁלֵם shālēm (8400), Full, accurate (Prv 11:1).

תָּמִים tāmîm (8879), Blamelessly (Prv 28:18—some Sinaiticus manuscripts only).

1. δίκαιον dikaion nom/acc sing masc/neu
2. δικαίου dikaiou gen sing masc/neu
3. δίκαιος dikaios nom sing masc
4. δικαίῳ dikaiō dat sing masc
5. δίκαιε dikaie voc sing masc
6. δίκαιοι dikaioi nom pl masc
7. δικαίων dikaiōn gen pl masc
8. δικαίοις dikaiois dat pl masc
9. δικαίους dikaious acc pl masc
10. δικαία dikaia nom sing fem
11. δικαίας dikaias gen sing fem
12. δικαίαν dikaian acc sing fem
13. δίκαιαι dikaiai nom pl fem
14. δίκαια dikaia nom/acc pl neu

3	Then Joseph her husband, being a **just** man,	Matt 1:19
9	and sendeth rain on the **just** and on the unjust.	5:45
9	for I am not come to call the **righteous**,	9:13
1	and he that receiveth a **righteous** man	10:41
2	a righteous man in the name of a **righteous** man	10:41
2	shall receive a **righteous** man's reward.	10:41
6	That many prophets and **righteous** men ... desired	13:17
6	Then shall the **righteous** shine forth as the sun	13:43
7	and sever the wicked from among the **just**,	13:49
1	and whatsoever is **right** I will give you.	20:4
1	and whatsoever is **right**, that shall ye receive.	20:7
6	so ye also outwardly appear **righteous** unto men,	23:28
7	and garnish the sepulchres of the **righteous**,	23:29
1	That upon you may come all the **righteous** blood	23:35
2	from the blood of **righteous** Abel unto the blood	23:35
6	Then shall the **righteous** answer him, saying,	25:37
6	punishment: but the **righteous** into life eternal.	25:46
1	sinned in that I have betrayed the innocent blood.	27:4
4	Have thou nothing to do with that **just** man:	27:19
2	I am innocent of the blood of this **just** person:	27:24
9	I came not to call the **righteous**, but sinners	Mark 2:17
1	knowing that he was a **just** man and an holy,	6:20
6	And they were both **righteous** before God,	Luke 1:6
7	the disobedient to the wisdom of the **just**;	1:17
3	and the same man was **just** and devout,	2:25
9	I came not to call the **righteous**, but sinners	5:32
1	why even of yourselves judge ye not what is **right**?	12:57
7	be recompensed at the resurrection of the **just**.	14:14
8	more than over ninety and nine **just** persons,	15:7
6	that they were **righteous**, and despised others:	18:9
9	which should feign themselves **just** men,	20:20
3	saying, Certainly this was a **righteous** man.	23:47
3	a counsellor; and he was a good man, and a **just**:	23:50
10	as I hear, I judge: and my judgment is **just**;	John 5:30
12	but judge **righteous** judgment.	7:24
5	**righteous** Father, the world hath not known thee:	17:25
1	But ye denied the Holy One and the **Just**,	Acts 3:14
1	Whether it be **right** in the sight of God	4:19
2	showed before of the coming of the **Just One**;	7:52
3	And they said, Cornelius the centurion, a **just** man,	10:22
1	shouldest know his will, and see that **Just One**,	22:14
7	be a resurrection ... both of the **just** and unjust.	24:15
3	as it is written, The **just** shall live by faith.	Rom 1:17
6	For not the hearers of the law are **just** before God,	2:13
3	As it is written, There is none **righteous**, no,	3:10
1	that he might be **just**, and the justifier of him	3:26
2	For scarcely for a **righteous** man will one die:	Rom 5:7
6	by the obedience ... shall many be made **righteous**.	5:19
10	and the commandment holy, and **just**, and good.	7:12
3	it is evident: for, The **just** shall live by faith.	Gal 3:11
1	obey your parents in the Lord: for this is **right**.	Eph 6:1
1	Even as it is **meet** for me to think this of you all,	Phlp 1:7
14	whatsoever things are **just**,	4:8
1	Masters, give unto your servants that which is **just**	Col 4:1
11	a manifest token of the **righteous** judgment of God,	2 Th 1:5
1	Seeing it is a **righteous** thing	1:6
4	that the law is not made **for a righteous** man,	1 Tm 1:9
3	which the Lord, the **righteous** judge, shall give me	2 Tm 4:8
1	a lover of good men, sober, **just**, holy, temperate;	Tit 1:8
3	Now the **just** shall live by faith:	Heb 10:38
3	he obtained witness that he was **righteous**,	11:4
7	and to the spirits **of just** men made perfect,	12:23
1	Ye have condemned and killed the **just**;	Jas 5:6
2	The effectual fervent prayer of a **righteous** man	5:16
9	For the eyes of the Lord are over the **righteous**,	1 Pt 3:12
3	hath once suffered for sins, the **just** for the unjust,	3:18
3	And if the **righteous** scarcely be saved,	4:18
1	I think it **meet**, as long as I am in this tabernacle,	2 Pt 1:13
1	And delivered **just** Lot,	2:7
3	For that **righteous** man dwelling among them,	2:8
12	in seeing and hearing, vexed his **righteous** soul	2:8
3	he is faithful and **just** to forgive us our sins,	1 Jn 1:9
1	we have an advocate ... Jesus Christ the **righteous**:	2:1
3	If ye know that he is **righteous**,	2:29
3	he that doeth righteousness is **righteous**,	3:7
3	righteousness is righteous, even as he is **righteous**.	3:7
14	own works were evil, and his brother's **righteous**.	3:12
13	**just** and true are thy ways, thou King of saints.	Rev 15:3
3	Thou art **righteous**, O Lord, which art, and wast,	16:5
13	Almighty, true and **righteous** are thy judgments.	16:7
13	For true and **righteous** are his judgments:	19:2
3	and he that is **righteous**, let him be righteous still:	22:11

Classical Greek

This extremely pivotal term in Biblical literature is multifaceted in classical writings. Even here, however, *dikaios/dikē* (1343) is linked to the fulfillment of religious obligations (Schrenk, "dikaios," *Kittel*, 2:182), but it serves a more crucial role in the language of ethics. *Dikaios*, an adjective, especially describes persons who, according to social standards, are "civilized, upright," or "decent" (*Liddell-Scott*). *Dikaios* also echoes the language of the courts and can mean "lawful, just"; this sense always affects the term. But by far the most important role of this term is its function in the realm of ethics, which naturally is bound to law. The "just" person is the "virtuous" man (see *aretē* [697] for the concept of virtue in the ancient world). To be "righteous" is to be sensible (*phronimos* [5265]), wise (*sophos* [4533]), and manly (*andreios*) (Schrenk, "dikaios," *Kittel*, 2:182; see also Seebass, "Righteousness," *Colin Brown*, 3:352-373).

Hellenistic Judaism, as represented by Josephus and Philo, imported and modified the Greek concept of *dikaios*. Josephus applied *dikaios* to Old Testament figures (*Antiquities* 9.3.1), and he occasionally applied it to God (*Antiquities* 2.6.4; 11.3.6; *Wars of the Jews*

7.8.6). Philo followed this practice more frequently than Josephus (e.g., *On Dreams* 2.29; *Life of Moses* 2.50) (cited by Schrenk, "dikaios," *Kittel*, 2:183). Both also used *dikaios* in reference to "things" as "proper," "right," or "fitting." This usage becomes even more common as papyri confirm; nevertheless, its forensic nature seems always in the background (*Moulton-Milligan*).

Septuagint Usage

Dikaios occurs extensively in the Septuagint. Most often (180 times, cf. Seebass; "Righteousness," *Colin Brown*, 3:354) it translates *tsāddîq*, although it serves as an equivalent (roughly) to 11 other words including *'ĕmeth* ("reliable, true, faithful"; Jeremiah 42:5 [LXX 49:5]) and *yāshār* ("correct, upright"; Numbers 23:10; Proverbs 3:32).

Here, as has already been noted previously, the Old Testament's understanding colors the meaning of the Greek rather than vice versa. Its meaning in the New Testament is also shaped by the Hebrew rather than the Hellenistic understanding. *Dikaios* moves away from its ethical and forensic moorings to a relational position. The *dikaios* one is the one "who fulfills his duties toward God and the theocratic society, meeting God's claim in this relationship" (Schrenk, "dikaios," *Kittel*, 2:185). God is "just" not only in His judgments (the legal sense), but in His "uprightness" He loves the "just deeds" of His people (Psalm 11:7 [LXX 10:8]), and He watches over them to redeem them (Psalm 34:15ff. [LXX 33:15ff.]). The association of God's "just" character with His salvation forms the foundation of New Testament understanding.

New Testament Usage

Understandably, *dikaios* is a common term in the New Testament with a wide range of meaning. It appears over 75 times. Although the New Testament was not totally unaffected by the Hellenistic concept of *dikaios* ("just" [ethically], "correct," or "innocent"; cf. e.g., Matthew 23:35; 27:24 ["innocent"]; perhaps Acts 10:22 [of Cornelius]; see also Mark 6:20; Acts 4:19; Ephesians 6:1), the Septuagint was the primary source of direction for the New Testament writers. *Dikaios* is first and foremost a relational term—specifically describing man's relationship to God.

Dikaios still retains its connection with correct judgment (John 5:30; 7:24; Acts 4:19); God is the *dikaios* Judge (2 Timothy 4:8; cf. Revelation 16:5,7; 19:2; cf. John 17:25; 1 Peter 2:23) who forgives sin. Thus His *dikaios* nature is especially present in the atoning work of Christ—the Just One (Acts 3:14; 7:52; 22:14; 1 John 2:1)—who makes us *dikaios* before God (2 Thessalonians 1:5; 1 John 1:9). God shows His "righteous, just, upright" judgment through the sacrifice of Christ, the propitiation to be received by faith (Romans 3:25f.). As Paul said, "It (Christ's sacrifice) was to prove at the present time that he (God) himself is righteous and that he justifies him who has faith in Jesus" (Romans 3:26, RSV).

God shows His righteousness to men—who cannot possibly be righteous of their own accord (Romans 3:10) or through keeping the Law (Romans 3:20; cf. Romans 2:13)—by allowing them to trust Him who justifies the ungodly (Romans 4:5). Thus, the existence of the *dikaios* one (e.g., Abraham [Romans 4:3; cf. Romans 1:17; Habakkuk 2:4]) is grounded upon trust in God, and it is lived out in obedience (Romans 2:13). Righteousness, therefore, is never as much a *state* as it is a *relationship* with a living God.

Consequently the New Testament can speak of *dikaios* men and women not because of their ability to keep the Law or even to perform good deeds (Luke 18:19; 20:20). They are *dikaios* because of their relation to God (e.g., Luke 1:6; 2:25; Acts 10:22). These *dikaioi* are the people of God throughout all generations, even before Christ (Hebrews 12:23; 1 Peter 3:12). They are especially those who have died or who have been persecuted for that relationship (Matthew 23:29,35; 2 Thessalonians 1:6; cf. Matthew 10:41; 13:17; 2 Timothy 4:8; 2 Peter 2:7ff.).

STRONG 1342, BAUER 195-96, MOULTON-MILLIGAN 162, KITTEL 2:174-78,182-91, LIDDELL-SCOTT 429, COLIN BROWN 3:352-55,358,360-63,365-70.

1336. δικαιοσύνη dikaiosunē noun

Righteousness, equity, justice.

CROSS-REFERENCE:
δικαιόω dikaioō (1338)

אֱמֶת 'ĕmeth (583), Faithfulness (Gn 24:49); truth (Dn 8:12).

זָכוּ zākhû (A2219), Innocence (Dn 6:22—Aramaic).

חֶסֶד cheṣedh (2721), Kindness (Gn 21:23, Is 63:7); love (Prv 20:28).

טוֹב ṭôv (3005), Good (Ps 38:20 [37:20]).

δικαιοσύνη 1336

מָדוֹן mādhôn (4209II) Adversity (Prv 17:14).

מֵישָׁרִים mêshārîm (4478), Uprightness (1 Chr 29:17).

מִשְׁפָּט mishpāṭ (5122), Just (Prv 16:11); justice (Prv 17:23); law (Ez 18:17,19).

נִקָּיוֹן niqqāyôn (5539), Innocence (Gn 20:5).

פֶּתִי pethî (6864), Simple (Prv 1:22).

צַדִּיק tsaddîq (6926), Righteous (Prv 15:6 [15:5]).

צֶדֶק tsedheq (6928), Righteousness (Jb 8:6, Is 11:5); fairness (Lv 19:15).

צְדָקָה tsᵉdhāqāh (6930), Righteousness (Dt 9:5,6, 1 Kgs 8:32, Hos 10:12).

שָׂכַל sākhal (7959), Hiphil: understand (Prv 21:16).

1. δικαιοσύνη dikaiosunē nom sing fem
2. δικαιοσύνης dikaiosunēs gen sing fem
3. δικαιοσύνῃ dikaiosunē dat sing fem
4. δικαιοσύνην dikaiosunēn acc sing fem

4	for thus it becometh us to fulfil all **righteousness**....	Matt 3:15
4	which do hunger and thirst after **righteousness**:.........	5:6
2	they which are persecuted for **righteousness**' sake:......	5:10
1	That except your **righteousness** shall exceed...........	5:20
4	Beware of practicing your **righteousness** (NASB)........	6:1
4	first the kingdom of God, and his **righteousness**;........	6:33
2	John came unto you in the way of **righteousness**,......	21:32
3	In holiness and **righteousness** before him,.............	Luke 1:75
2	of sin, and of **righteousness**, and of judgment:.........	John 16:8
2	Of **righteousness**, because I go to my Father,..........	16:10
4	and worketh **righteousness**, is accepted with him....	Acts 10:35
2	thou enemy of all **righteousness**,.....................	13:10
3	he will judge the world in **righteousness**..............	17:31
2	And as he reasoned of **righteousness**,.................	24:25
1	For therein is the **righteousness** of God revealed....	Rom 1:17
4	commend the **righteousness** of God,....................	3:5
1	**righteousness** of God without the law is manifested,.....	3:21
1	the **righteousness** of God which is by faith of Jesus.....	3:22
2	declare his **righteousness** for the remission of sins.......	3:25
2	To declare, I say, at this time his **righteousness**:......	3:26
4	and it was counted unto him for **righteousness**..........	4:3
4	his faith is counted for **righteousness**...................	4:5
4	whom God imputeth **righteousness** without works,......	4:6
4	faith was reckoned to Abraham for **righteousness**.......	4:9
2	a seal of the **righteousness** of the faith	4:11
4	**righteousness** might be imputed unto them also:........	4:11
2	but through the **righteousness** of faith.................	4:13
4	therefore it was imputed to him for **righteousness**......	4:22
2	the gift of **righteousness** shall reign in life by one,......	5:17
2	even so might grace reign through **righteousness**.......	5:21
2	and your members as instruments of **righteousness**......	6:13
4	or of obedience unto **righteousness**?...................	6:16
3	ye became the servants of **righteousness**...............	6:18
3	servants to **righteousness** unto holiness..................	6:19
3	ye were free from **righteousness**........................	6:20
4	but the Spirit is life because of **righteousness**............	8:10
3	finish the work, and cut it short in **righteousness**:.......	9:28
4	Gentiles, which followed not after **righteousness**,......	9:30
4	have attained to **righteousness**,........................	9:30
4	even the **righteousness** which is of faith................	9:30
2	which followed after the law of **righteousness**,.........	9:31
2	hath not attained to the law of **righteousness**...........	9:31
4	For they being ignorant of God's **righteousness**,........	10:3
4	going about to establish their own **righteousness**,......	10:3
3	not submitted ... unto the **righteousness** of God........	10:3
4	for **righteousness** to every one that believeth............	10:4
4	describeth the **righteousness** which is of the law,......	10:5
1	But the **righteousness** which is of faith	10:6
1	not meat and drink; but **righteousness**, and peace,......	14:17
1	**righteousness**, and sanctification, and redemption:...	1 Co 1:30
2	much more doth the ministration of **righteousness**...	2 Co 3:9
1	might be made the **righteousness** of God in him.....	2 Co 5:21
2	by the armour of **righteousness** on the right hand.......	6:7
3	fellowship ... **righteousness** with unrighteousness?.......	6:14
1	his **righteousness** remaineth for ever.....................	9:9
2	and increase the fruits of your **righteousness**;..........	9:10
2	be transformed as the ministers of **righteousness**;.......	11:15
1	for if **righteousness** come by the law,.................	Gal 2:21
4	and it was accounted to him for **righteousness**...........	3:6
1	verily **righteousness** should have been by the law.......	3:21
2	wait for the hope of **righteousness** by faith.............	5:5
3	which after God is created in **righteousness**...........	Eph 4:24
3	is in all goodness and **righteousness** and truth;........	5:9
2	and having on the breastplate of **righteousness**,........	6:14
2	Being filled with the fruits of **righteousness**,........	Phlp 1:11
4	touching the **righteousness** which is in the law,.........	3:6
4	mine own **righteousness**, which is of the law,..........	3:9
4	the **righteousness** which is of God by faith:..............	3:9
4	flee these things; and follow after **righteousness**,....	1 Tm 6:11
4	Flee also youthful lusts: but follow **righteousness**,...	2 Tm 2:22
3	for correction, for instruction in **righteousness**:........	3:16
2	there is laid up for me a crown of **righteousness**,.......	4:8
3	Not by works of **righteousness** which we have done,..	Tit 3:5
4	Thou hast loved **righteousness**, and hated iniquity;...	Heb 1:9
2	is unskilful in the word of **righteousness**................	5:13
2	first being by interpretation King of **righteousness**,....	7:2
2	became heir of the **righteousness** which is by faith.....	11:7
4	wrought **righteousness**, obtained promises,.............	11:33
2	it yieldeth the peaceable fruit of **righteousness**.........	12:11
4	wrath of man worketh not ... **righteousness** of God....	Jas 1:20
4	and it was imputed unto him for **righteousness**:........	2:23
2	And the fruit of **righteousness** is sown in peace........	3:18
3	being dead to sins, should live unto **righteousness**:...	1 Pt 2:24
2	if ye suffer for **righteousness**' sake, happy are ye:......	3:14
3	faith with us through the **righteousness** of God......	2 Pt 1:1
2	saved Noah ... a preacher of **righteousness**,............	2:5
2	not to have known the way of **righteousness**,...........	2:21
1	and a new earth, wherein dwelleth **righteousness**,......	3:13
4	every one that doeth **righteousness** is born of him....1 Jn 2:29
4	he that doeth **righteousness** is righteous,................	3:7
4	whosoever doeth not **righteousness** is not of God,......	3:10
3	and in **righteousness** he doth judge and make war...	Rev 19:11
4	righteous, still practice **righteousness** (NASB)...........	22:11

Classical Greek

Dikaiosunē ("righteousness, justice, uprightness") one of the many derivations from *dikē* (1343) ("justice") represents an abstract concept in classical Greek, although a concrete act underlies the abstraction.

The concept of *dikaiosunē* involves two basic meanings: First, "righteousness" is seen from a legal/political standpoint. Second, it is viewed from the religious/ethical/moral perspective. All *dikē* language has been colored by these different backgrounds, and quite naturally the two cannot be separated entirely.

The legal overtones of *dikaiosunē* are inescapable, for even as the term invades the language of ethics it continues to carry forensic (legal) baggage. At the outset it denoted a life governed by law and order and a sense of duty. In Plato's Utopia (ideal society) *dikaiosunē* is the foundational governing principle (see Plato *Republic* 433a).

The realms of ethics and religion incorporated *dikaiosunē* into their language and discussions. In the notion of "virtue," which plays such

δικαιοσύνη 1336

an important role in Greek (especially Stoic) philosophy, *dikaiosunē* became a major virtue; often it is among the most important (e.g., Bultmann, *Primitive Christianity*, pp.141f.).

Septuagint Usage

Dikaiosunē functions in the Septuagint as the equivalent of the Hebrew *tsᵉdhāqāh* and *tsedeq* as well as other words. The Greek word absorbs the Hebraic understanding into New Testament usage.

The concept of righteousness in the Old Testament is wholly a religiously determined idea. It does not express any abstract ethical norm or concept. Neither is it any ideal moral system or set of universal laws. Righteousness describes the relationship which Israel had with Yahweh. Essential for the basis of righteousness is the covenant relationship. This alliance presupposes a mutual righteousness between the two parties which is expressed most fully in faithfulness to the covenant relationship. The righteous or just one fulfills to the other party the obligations that are dictated by the covenant.

This is not to say that the covenantal parties of the Old Testament were equal; on the contrary, God was the Master, and Israel was the servant. The covenant relationship was created in the first place because of God's merciful initiative to choose a sinful people.

Such an association is indicative of the righteousness of God. True righteousness is God-oriented. God proves His righteousness by His faithfulness to the covenant, and He fulfills His covenant promises because He is just (Nehemiah 9:8). God himself is the fountain of all righteousness. Righteousness as a human responsibility is also primarily being faithful to the covenant. The righteous one is godly and pious, walking in the ordinances of the Lord (Psalms 32:11 [LXX 31:11]; 33:1 [32:1]; 97:11 [96:11]; 140:13 [139:13]; Ezekiel 18:5f.).

God protects the righteous (Psalms 5:12; 7:9f.; 34:15 [LXX 33:15]), He supports them (Psalm 37:17,39 [LXX 36:17,39]) and He blesses them (Psalm 37:26,29 [LXX 36:26,29]). Righteousness leads to God's favor in this life as well as in death (Deuteronomy 6:25; Proverbs 11:4-6; 12:28; 13:6). Yet to be "righteous" is not identical to being ethically or morally perfect. Righteousness is essentially a religious choice. The just live in faithful obedience to the covenant and seek God's grace. They accept the Lord as judge (Psalms 7:11; cf. 119:137 [LXX 118:137]; Jeremiah 12:1). They are the "poor in spirit," the humble, those with "a broken and a contrite heart" (Psalm 51:17 [LXX 50:17]). God promises that they shall inherit the earth (Psalm 37:29 [LXX 36:29]). The Lord acknowledges and rewards righteousness and punishes the unjust.

The Lord is altogether just by nature and by the proclamation of His Word. The righteous one accepts this as truth. All the Lord does is just and fair. His judgments, at times unsearchable and incomprehensible, cannot be questioned (cf. the Book of Job). Therefore, the righteous and godly submit themselves to His judgments, for God is not arbitrary or whimsical in His decisions (cf. Psalms 9:8; 96:13 [LXX 95:13]). Because by His very nature God is righteous and just, His dealings with men never produce injustice. God, in fact, is the advocate of all who suffer injustice (Psalms 35:23f. [LXX 34:23]; 43:1 [42:1]; 94:2 [93:2]; 143:1-12 [142:1-12]; Isaiah 50:8f.; 54:17).

But God's righteous judgments are also His saving justice; judgment and salvation coalesce. Under the wrath of God the repentant remnant wait for the saving eschatological manifestation of justice: "I will bear the indignation of the LORD ... until he plead my cause, and execute judgment for me: he will bring me forth to the light, and I shall behold his righteousness" (Micah 7:9; cf. Isaiah 1:26). Especially in the closing chapters of Isaiah (from chapter 45 on), righteousness, *tsᵉdhāqāh*, is synonymous with the eschatological salvation (45:8; 46:13; 51:5; 59:17; 61:11). Here *tsᵉdhāqāh* depicts the redemptive work of God who establishes His kingdom in the world—His royal saving power. "By terrible things in righteousness wilt thou answer us, O God of our salvation" (Psalm 65:5 [LXX 64:5]). Through the Just One, the eschatological King of salvation, the Lord will reveal His justice in salvation. Early in Israel's history the idea of righteousness was particularly associated with the king as God's representative who dispenses justice (2 Samuel 8:15 [LXX 2 Kings 8:15]; 1 Kings 10:9 [3 Kings 10:9]; Isaiah 16:5). Messiah, as the saving righteousness of God, comes to deliver God's people. His kingdom will be established "with judgment and with justice ... even for ever" (Isaiah 9:7;

cf. 11:5; 60:16-21; Jeremiah 23:5; 33:13 [LXX 40:13]; Malachi 4:2).

Isaiah 42:4 proclaims that Messiah will establish justice on the earth. Even Gentiles have opportunity to share in that covenant blessing: "He shall bring forth judgment (justice) to the Gentiles" (Isaiah 42:1). This kingdom of the Messiah described in Isaiah is characterized by righteousness. It also shows that the work of righteousness is peace. (Cf. Psalm 85:10f. [LXX 84:10] where it is said that "righteousness and peace have kissed each other.") These concepts, then, serve as a background for the Greek term *dikaiosunē* as it is used in the New Testament.

In later Judaism righteousness became primarily a human activity, a human virtue alongside other virtues. To practice "justice" was defined as "being merciful," "giving alms," or "praying" (cf. Matthew 6:2). *Righteousness* also came to mean "the fulfillment of legal obligations." The concept of righteousness as a relationship was replaced by a legal ideal. The Law was held to be a collection of judicial ordinances; God was believed to be the Supreme Judge who would evaluate "righteousness" in terms of a man's deeds (i.e., "keeping the Law" and "doing righteousness"). On the basis of God's judgment He would either vindicate or condemn the man. Thus "salvation" totally depended upon man's ability to do deeds of righteousness and to keep the Law.

New Testament Usage

The New Testament concept of justice is remote from the Greek doctrine of virtue and also from the Jewish concept of earning righteousness through keeping the Law. The term *dikaiosunē* is applied both to God and to people in the New Testament. In reference to people it is concerned with the imputed righteousness "in Christ" and the practical righteousness of everyday living and conduct. The righteous judgment of God as well as His saving grace are particularly described in *dikaiosunē* language.

Since the New Testament is by nature diverse, a single usage or definition should not be forced upon any word apart from its context; this is doubly so for *dikaiosunē*. Nevertheless, some basics—which have been largely patterned after the Old Testament's understanding—can be outlined. One primary feature of New Testament use is its distinctive character from the Hellenistic view (see above). First and foremost "righteousness" (apart from the Pauline usage which will be examined separately) is a relational term. A second primary feature of New Testament usage is that true "righteousness" ("right conduct") is born out of faith in God, particularly in His ability to judge and to save. Since Paul's writings have such a highly developed understanding of *dikaiosunē*, it is appropriate to analyze *dikaiosunē* in terms of Pauline and non-Pauline usage.

Synoptic Gospels

Matthew used *dikaiosunē* more than any other Gospel writer. His own Jewish-Christian context necessitated a corrective instruction about true righteousness (the term is entirely absent in Mark, who was probably writing to Gentiles). Righteousness from the Jewish perspective was "attained" by doing both works of righteousness—almsgiving, prayer, fasting—and works of the Law (cf. Matthew 6:2). Matthew's Gospel does not try to eliminate these charitable acts themselves; however, they are understood as responses to God's forgiveness rather than a means to His favor. God's followers should not "do righteousness" to be seen by men (i.e., in public) but to be seen by God (in private); this is the response of faith. Simply "doing" is inadequate (5:20). Righteousness is a relationship to be desired (5:6) and sought after (6:33), although it is a free gift of God which cannot be earned. This is what irritated the religious leaders so much. They thought the way to righteousness was through their acts.

Luke's Gospel uses *dikaiosunē* in much the same way as Matthew. For example, Luke 1:74f. states that when God redeemed His people, they would be free to serve Him "without fear, in holiness and righteousness."

Gospel of John

John's Gospel, somewhat more Christological in its orientation, says much the same thing in the single passage containing *dikaiosunē*. Righteousness will be realized in Jesus' return to the Father and in the coming of the Spirit. This world does not have at its disposal the possibility of true righteousness apart from God's providing it himself (John 16:8,10).

Acts Account

Acts records that Cornelius feared God and worked righteousness (10:35). Evidently Cornelius' actions were a response to his fear of God. They were not motivated by any

δίκαιος 1337

desire to manipulate God or to be approved by men. Righteousness also characterizes God's judgment in Acts (17:31). The implication is that repentance (17:30) is the only means of being justified, i.e., of being "saved" (cf. Luke 1:75).

General Epistles

Dikaiosunē occurs six times in Hebrews. No developed understanding seems present here. However, the relationship between righteousness, judgment, salvation, and faith in God to judge does occur (Hebrews 11:7, cf. Genesis 15:6; Hebrews 12:11; cf. Psalm 119:137; Jeremiah 12:1; especially Micah 7:9). James echoed this Old Testament principle that faith is the response of those who are truly righteous (James 2:23). Peter tied judgment, justice, and salvation with the life lived in righteous obedience to the sacrifice of Christ (cf. 2 Peter 1:1; 2:5,21). Righteousness is present in the life of the believer who lives in faith that God's justice/judgment/salvation will usher in a new heaven and a new earth where righteousness dwells (2 Peter 3:13; cf. Revelation 19:11).

Righteousness is not passive though; it is to be pursued (cf. 1 Timothy 6:11; 2 Timothy 2:22). It is the mark of the believer, and without active "doing" there is no real relationship (i.e., righteousness) with God (1 John 2:29; 3:7,10; cf. James 2:17). The one practicing righteousness may even have to suffer for it (1 Peter 3:14).

Pauline Epistles

The magnitude and complexity of the Pauline discernment of *dikaiosunē* is obvious. The debate over works-righteousness/law-faith will continue to rage. But some issues are conceded by almost everyone. Paul's writings share with the rest of the New Testament the recognition that the righteousness initiated by the Christ-event has eliminated any popular ideologies that saw righteousness as attainable through man's efforts. Righteousness is solely experienced because of God's sovereign act, His "gracious and decisive intervention for man in Christ" (Schrenk, "dikaiosunē," *Kittel*, 2:203).

The righteousness of God (*dikaiosunē theou*) is revealed in the gospel (Romans 1:17), which is apart from the Law but confirmed by it (Romans 3:21). Justification—"the establishment of a right relationship with God"—is based upon God's gift (Romans 3:21-24), to be received by faith, not by man's actions (Romans 3:25; 10:6ff; cf. Romans 4:3-22; 9:30; 10:3; Galatians 3:6; Philippians 3:9; Titus 3:5). Belief averts judgment (Romans 10:9-13).

Christ accomplishes what the Law could not do: through His death (God's gift) believers are made righteous (Romans 8:3,4; 2 Corinthians 5:21; Galatians 2:21; cf. Romans 10:4).

Righteousness is expressed by our actions; Christians thus confirm their relationship to God (Romans 6:13,16ff.; 2 Corinthians 6:7; 9:10; Philippians 1:11; 2 Timothy 3:16). Indeed their very lives testify to that relationship (Romans 1:17; 2:13). Having been freed from sin is to become "servants to God" (Romans 6:22) and "servants of righteousness" (Romans 6:18). God's righteousness revealed in the present (Romans 1:17; 3:26) has provided true righteousness for the believer.

Therefore, since righteousness is by faith alone, any supposed "righteousness by works," i.e., obedience to the Law, has been abolished. The righteousness of God comes only through faith (Romans 1:17; 3:22,26; 4:3f.; 9:30; 10:4,6,10). The object of this faith is Jesus Christ and His redemptive act. God's righteousness is revealed in the substitutionary death of the innocent One on behalf of the guilty. Redemption, then, is not outside God's justice. Sin is still abhorrent to God and deserves His wrath. However, "He hath made him to be sin for us, who knew no sin; that we might be made the righteousness of God in him" (2 Corinthians 5:21).

The great central truth in all of this is that the righteousness of God is now on the side of men. A renewed understanding of this truth sparked a reformation of unparalleled proportions. When Martin Luther grasped this concept, that righteousness comes through faith alone, the God and the Scriptures which before were a source of fear and guilt suddenly became a mighty fortress which guaranteed his salvation. His time of personal bondage gave way to liberty. Likewise, this same freedom comes to all who receive Paul's clear message concerning the righteousness which is from God through faith.

STRONG 1343, BAUER 196-97, MOULTON-MILLIGAN 162, KITTEL 2:174-78,192-210, LIDDELL-SCOTT 429, COLIN BROWN 3:352-54,358,360,365,369-72.

1337. δίκαιος dikaios

See word study at number 1335B.

1338. δικαιόω dikaioō verb

Justify, render innocent, pronounce righteous.

COGNATES:
- ἀδικέω adikeō (90)
- ἀντίδικος antidikos (473)
- δικαιοκρισία dikaiokrisia (1335)
- δίκαιος dikaios (1335B)
- δικαιοσύνη dikaiosunē (1336)
- δικαίωμα dikaiōma (1339)
- δικαίως dikaiōs (1339B)
- δικαίωσις dikaiōsis (1340)
- δικαστής dikastēs (1342)
- δίκη dikē (1343)
- ἐκδικέω ekdikeō (1543)
- ἐκδίκησις ekdikēsis (1544)
- ἔκδικος ekdikos (1545)
- ἔνδικος endikos (1722)
- καταδικάζω katadikazō (2584)
- ὑπόδικος hupodikos (5105)

בָּחַן bāchan (1010), Try; pual: testing (Ez 21:13).

זָכָה zākhâh (2218), Qal: be justified (Mi 6:11); piel: keep pure (Ps 73:13 [72:13]).

צָדֵק tsādheq (6927), Qal: be justified, be righteous (Gn 38:26, Ps 19:9 [18:9], Is 43:9); piel: justify, make righteous (Jb 33:32, Jer 3:11, Ez 16:51); hiphil: justify, vindicate (Ex 23:7, Is 50:8); give justice (2 Sm 15:4); hithpael: prove one's innocence (Gn 44:16).

צֶדֶק tsedheq (6928), Righteousness (Is 42:21).

רִיב rîv (7662), Plead one's case (Is 1:17, Mi 7:9).

שָׁפַט shāphaṭ (8570), Judge, decide; niphal: plead (1 Sm 12:7—Codex Alexandrinus only).

1. δικαιοῖ dikaioi 3sing indic pres act
2. δικαιῶν dikaiōn nom sing masc part pres act
3. δικαιοῦντα dikaiounta acc sing masc part pres act
4. δικαιοῦντες dikaiountes nom pl masc part pres act
5. δικαιοῦν dikaioun inf pres act
6. ἐδικαίωσεν edikaiōsen 3sing indic aor act
7. ἐδικαίωσαν edikaiōsan 3pl indic aor act
8. δικαιώσει dikaiōsei 3sing indic fut act
9. δικαιοῦται dikaioutai 3sing indic pres mid
10. δικαιοῦσθε dikaiousthe 2pl indic pres mid
11. δικαιούμενοι dikaioumenoi nom pl masc part pres mid
12. δικαιοῦσθαι dikaiousthai inf pres mid
13. ἐδικαιώθη edikaiōthē 3sing indic aor pass
14. ἐδικαιώθητε edikaiōthēte 2pl indic aor pass
15. δικαιωθῇς dikaiōthēs 2sing subj aor pass
16. δικαιωθῶμεν dikaiōthōmen 1pl subj aor pass
17. δικαιωθέντες dikaiōthentes nom pl masc part aor pass
18. δικαιωθῆναι dikaiōthēnai inf aor pass
19. δικαιωθήτω dikaiōthētō 3sing impr aor pass
20. δεδικαίωμαι dedikaiōmai 1sing indic perf mid
21. δεδικαίωται dedikaiōtai 3sing indic perf mid
22. δεδικαιωμένος dedikaiōmenos nom sing masc part perf mid
23. δικαιωθήσῃ dikaiōthēsē 2sing indic fut pass
24. δικαιωθήσεται dikaiōthēsetai 3sing indic fut pass
25. δικαιωθήσονται dikaiōthēsontai 3pl indic fut pass
26. δικαιῶσαι dikaiōsai inf aor act

13	But wisdom is **justified** of her children............	Matt 11:19
23	For by thy words **thou shalt be justified**,.............	12:37
7	heard him, and the publicans, **justified** God,.......	Luke 7:29
13	But wisdom is **justified** of all her children...........	7:35
5	But he, willing **to justify** himself, said unto Jesus,...	10:29
26	But he, willing **to justify** himself, said unto Jesus,...	10:29
4	Ye are they which **justify** yourselves before men;.....	16:15
22	down to his house **justified** rather than the other:.....	18:14
18	from which ye could not **be justified** by the law...	Acts 13:39
9	by him all that believe **are justified** from all things,...	13:39
25	but the doers of the law **shall be justified**..........	Rom 2:13
15	That thou mightest **be justified** in thy sayings,.........	3:4
24	there shall no flesh **be justified** in his sight:............	3:20
11	**Being justified** freely by his grace.....................	3:24
3	and the **justifier** of him which believeth in Jesus.......	3:26
12	is **justified** by faith without the deeds of the law.......	3:28
8	God, which **shall justify** the circumcision by faith,......	3:30
13	For if Abraham were **justified** by works,..............	4:2
3	but believeth on him that **justifieth** the ungodly,.......	4:5
17	Therefore **being justified** by faith,.....................	5:1
17	Much more then, **being now justified** by his blood,.....	5:9
21	For he that is dead **is freed** from sin.................	6:7
6	and whom he called, them he also **justified**:...........	8:30
6	and whom he **justified**, them he also glorified..........	8:30
2	It is God that **justifieth**................................	8:33
20	yet am I not hereby **justified**:.....................	1 Co 4:4
14	but ye **are justified** in the name of the Lord Jesus,.....	6:11
9	that a man is not **justified** by the works of the law,	Gal 2:16
16	that we might **be justified** by the faith of Christ,......	2:16
24	by the works of the law **shall** no flesh **be justified**,...	2:16
18	But if, while we seek **to be justified** by Christ,......	2:17
1	the scripture, foreseeing that God **would justify**........	3:8
9	no man is **justified** by the law in the sight of God,....	3:11
16	that we might **be justified** by faith..................	3:24
10	whosoever of you **are justified** by the law;...........	5:4
13	manifest in the flesh, **justified** in the Spirit,...........	1 Tm 3:16
17	That **being justified** by his grace,....................	Tit 3:7
13	Was not Abraham our father **justified** by works,.....	Jas 2:21
9	Ye see then how that by works a man is **justified**,......	2:24
13	also was not Rahab the harlot **justified** by works,......	2:25
19	and he that is righteous, **let him be righteous** still:	Rev 22:11

The term *dikaioō*, "justify," is a cognate of the noun *dikaios* (1335B), "just." Both belong to the family of words related to the root form *dikē* (1343), "penalty, punishment." (See also the word studies at *dikaiosunē* [1336] and *dikaiōma* [1339].)

Classical Greek

From classical writers we discover that *dikaioō* is first of all a forensic term meaning "to make or establish as right, to judge" or "to execute justice." This legal heritage is never fully shaken as the word moves into the realm of ethics ("to regard as right or fair"). In Hellenistic literature and nonliterary sources we find that understanding to be the most common (cf. *Moulton-Milligan*). Josephus said that Moses "*did not regard it fair* that the children should be punished for the sins of their fathers" (*Antiquities* 9.9.1). Schrenk notes that Josephus "never deviates from Gk. usage" ("dikaioō," *Kittel*, 2:211). The influence of its legal heritage becomes evident in that *dikaioō* could mean either "to secure justice," i.e., "acquit" someone, or "to judge, punish," i.e., "condemn" someone (ibid.; *Liddell-Scott*).

Septuagint Usage

The *tsedeq* word group was usually translated by the *dikaios* group in the Septuagint. But *zākhâh* (qal, "be [morally] pure"; piel, "keep [something] pure") and *rîv* (a legal dispute) were also conveyed by *dikaioō* (e.g., Psalm 73:13 [LXX 72:13]; Micah 6:11; 7:9). As noted before, the Septuagint actually shaped the meaning of the Greek for the New Testament writers. It often absorbed—in this case almost totally—the Hebraic understanding of *tsedheq*, "to be just, righteous" or "to be justified" (in the sense of being right).

Dikaioō is used in the sense of "to acquit" (*tsedheq*, hiphil) in several texts (Exodus 23:7; Deuteronomy 25:1; Isaiah 5:23). "To render justice" in the process of judging is another meaning (2 Samuel 15:4 [LXX 2 Kings 15:4]; Job 33:32). God is "justified," His sentencing blameless in His judgment (Psalm 51:4 [LXX 50:4]; cf. Sirach 1:21; 10:29; 13:22). To seek justice, correct oppression, defend the fatherless and "plead" for the widow are the responsibilty of God's people (Isaiah 1:17, *rib* Hebrew). God is the one who ultimately declares "righteousness" (Isaiah 45:24; 50:8; 53:11).

From the Septuagint we can glean some important observations: The ability to justify is God's prerogative and His domain, particularly in the covenant relationship. "Relationship" is the key word for understanding what it means to be "just" in God's sight. To ask whether being "justified" is simply a status or a status with ethical qualities is to miss the relational aspect of *dikaioō* which finds its fullest expression in the covenant relationship. Nevertheless, the godly Israelite was fully aware of the fact that his own righteousness, i.e., "ethical behavior," could never form the foundation of his relationship with God. When the righteous God and His law serve as the basis of comparison, he realizes that no man is righteous in himself. "Who can say, I have made my heart clean, I am pure from my sin?" (Proverbs 20:9; cf. Psalm 143:2 [LXX 142:2]). Thus the way Paul used "righteousness"—emerging directly out of the Old Testament—indicates that he perceived righteousness only in terms of God's activity "in Christ," i.e., in the relationship believers have with Him.

New Testament Usage

Clearly the New Testament concept of justification is rooted in the Old Testament. The writers of the New Testament built upon truths established in the Old and often referred to these Scriptures to support and to prove doctrine. For example, Paul quoted the prophet Habakkuk (2:4) in his letter to the Romans (1:17) stating, "The just shall live by faith." (See also Romans 4:3/Genesis 15:6; Romans 4:8/Psalm 32:2.) It is evident that the message of grace and forgiveness so apparent in the New Testament is also a central theme in the Old Testament. Salvation never came through obedience to the Law, and yet the principles of the Law stand firm. "The wages of sin is death" (Romans 6:23), and man is reconciled to God only through the death of a substitute. In the Old Testament animals served as substitutes in the sacrificial system which brought atonement; in the New Testament Jesus made himself a "sin offering" for all men (cf. 2 Corinthians 5:21; also Hebrews 7:27; 9:14,22-28; passim).

A theological question still in debate arises here: If a man *could* obey the Law perfectly would he be "justified" or "righteous" in God's sight? Some believe the New Testament never denies this possibility. If a person fulfilled the Law he would be justified. When Galatians 2:16 states that "a man is not justified by the works of the law," the claim is made that this statement is rooted in the fact that no man ever *did* fulfill the Law. All have sinned; the class of the "righteous ones" has no members.

In contrast to the above viewpoint, others would say that even if a man could obey the Law perfectly, he could not justify himself. The argument involves an understanding of the true nature of sin; i.e., *sin*, and the inevitable guilt it brings in the eyes of a holy God, involves more than sinful actions. It is possible that one's actions could reflect obedience to the Law, while one's attitudes were quite sinful in God's sight. Even more important to this viewpoint is the concept of imputed guilt which involves all mankind. Stated simply, not only has a sentence of death been passed on to all men (Romans 5:12), but guilt before God is also inherited by every offspring of Adam. Only the sacrificial death of Jesus Christ can atone for this imputed guilt and leave in its place an imputed righteousness.

In any case, the question becomes mute in light of Psalm 14:1-3 and Romans 3:10 which proclaims, in part, "There is none righteous, no, not one." Therefore, it is evident that justification is only by grace whether the Old or New Testament is examined. Under the old covenant, true conversion and upright conduct were demanded. The same also holds true for those living under the new covenant.

Likewise, the provision for forgiveness and justification are identical in the two Testaments. God always justifies on the basis of the offering, and as Hebrews 9:22 makes clear, "Without shedding of blood (there) is no remission (of sin)." Faith in the efficacy of the animal sacrifice was prerequisite to forgiveness of sins under the old covenant; likewise, only faith in the atoning self-sacrifice of the Lamb of God brings justification under the new (cf. Isaiah 53:5,6). Isaiah 53:11 says, "By his knowledge shall my righteous servant justify many; for he shall bear their iniquities." It is by the abandonment of faith to the Messiah and by trust in His work that justification takes place. This New Testament truth is prophesied in Jeremiah 23:6 where one of the Old Testament names of God is translated "The Lord our Righteousness." However, in later Judaism a radical shift occurred in the Jewish understanding of righteousness and justification. While a true fear of God and a messianic expectation continued, most of Judaism—including the religious leaders—had a corrupted view of the Law. This led to a salvation-by-works religion which hinged upon self-righteousness.

At the time of Jesus several contrasting opinions on the subject of justification existed. The dominating viewpoint, however, was that of the Pharisees. It maintained that he who kept the Law would be judged as righteous before God. Emphasis was placed on building up one's own righteousness (cf. Romans 10:3). Eventually the domineering feature in the "salvation" doctrine of Judaism was the accumulation of a treasury of good deeds.

At this point the pharisaic term *zakut* is central. Originally the term meant "innocence," "to possess innocence," or "to be declared innocent of a charge." The meaning of the term eventually evolved in the direction of "being ascribed a greater right." To possess *zakut*, therefore, meant "to be declared innocent or worthy, to be accepted" and by extension "to have obtained a special preference." The Pharisees taught that God awards *zukut* and enables men to win *zakut*. Thus we see the Pharisee in the temple praising and thanking God because he is who he is (Luke 18:9-14). The Pharisee is grateful on the basis of his own goodness and fulfillment of the Law and supposes that God will therefore judge him as righteous.

In conjunction with these teachings, the Pharisees held that man's free will was a determining factor in achieving righteousness. They were convinced that if a man's desire was to live in accordance to the Law, God would let him succeed to the extent that even an imperfect life would be seen as fulfilling the Law. In other words, God could accept even a defective fulfillment of the Law if the will to do good was present. The entire New Testament stands in distinct contrast to these ideas of salvation which, in spite of all disguise, are nothing but self-redemption and works-righteousness.

Jesus himself stirred up the strongest opposition; first, by maintaining flawlessly the requirements of the Law and second by preaching that only by grace can salvation be obtained. The message of Christ was much more radical than the teachings of the Pharisees. Jesus called for a conversion quite different from theirs. The conversion Jesus called for was not one which attempted to make a bad tree produce good fruit. It did not hinge on what man's free will could accomplish but, on the contrary, emphasized a total capitulation and surrender to God. In addition, the conversion Jesus spoke of was not only a turning away from sin but also a conversion from dead works (cf. Matthew 11:28,29; Hebrews 6:1). This involved nothing less than a total abandonment of trusting in obedience to the Law as the means of salvation.

In part, therefore, it is understandable why the religious leaders of the day so bitterly opposed the Lord Jesus. His words and His life seemed to contradict everything which their system of salvation and justification was built upon. But perhaps the greatest offense to these leaders was that the justification by faith preached by Christ was not a faith in one's own works but faith in a person: Christ himself! "This is the work of God, that ye believe on him whom he hath sent" (John 6:29). It is not the fulfillment of the Law that God looks upon; He looks upon a person's attitude toward Jesus, the Messiah (Matthew 10:32). The doctrine of justification seen throughout the New Testament, therefore, has its foundation in the words of Jesus. Paul's teaching on the subject rests on truths expressed by Christ in the Gospels, e.g., His power to forgive sin and His atoning death.

Paul's writings (especially Romans) present the clearest, most thorough theological examination of the theme of "justification" in the New Testament. For Paul, the word *dikaioō* expressed the central evangelical truth that God does not ascribe to the sinner the penalty for his sin but by grace ascribes to him righteousness by faith in Jesus Christ (Romans 3:23-26; 4:5-8; 5:19). This same topic is discussed in the Epistle to the Galatians. There Paul reemphasized that just as grace and not works brings salvation, so too continued growth and a righteous life occur only through grace and not through obedience to the Law.

On this point Paul obviously battled the Judaizers. The thought that righteousness was imputed by faith in a Person and not through the Law was revolutionary, even blasphemous to most religious leaders of the day. The propitiation which comes through faith in the redemptive work of Christ supersedes the Law. Paul summarized by saying, "We conclude that a man is justified by faith without the deeds of the law" (Romans 3:28).

Paul did not speak of justification simply from a theoretical standpoint. On the contrary, his heart broke for the Jews who were bound to legalism. His own bitter experience as well proved to him that the Law could not produce righteousness (cf. Romans 8:3f.; Galatians 2:16). Even though Paul testified that he was blameless with respect to the "righteousness which is in the law" (Philippians 3:6), his experience with Christ on the road to Damascus proved that his zeal for the Law could not justify him before God. Just the opposite occurred: his zeal made him an opponent of the Messiah and a persecutor of the Church. His experience with the risen Saviour destroyed forever his optimism that by fulfilling the Law one could obtain righteousness.

After the Damascus experience Paul recognized the delusion his fellow Jews were under. He realized that the system of self-justification was an abomination in the sight of God (cf. Luke 16:15). These insights given to him by the Holy Spirit led him to conclude, "He is not a Jew, which is one outwardly . . . but he is a Jew, which is one inwardly" (Romans 2:28f.). Paul further recognized that even circumcision, the very symbol of the covenant between Israel and God, was merely "outward." Paul wrote, "We are the circumcision, which worship God in the spirit, and rejoice in Christ Jesus, and have no confidence in the flesh" (Philippians 3:3). In reality, therefore, Christianity—with its doctrine of justification by faith—is the true Jewish religion, not the legalistic system of the Pharisees. Christianity is not an appendage to Judaism. Rather, it is the goal and fulfillment of the Old Testament, for justification by faith is in full agreement with its teachings (compare Romans 1:17 with Habakkuk 2:4; Romans 4:3 with Genesis 15:6; Romans 4:8 with Psalm 32:1f.).

Furthermore, Paul's teaching on justification fixes the universal character of Christianity (Romans 3:28-30). He depicted more than a doctrinal conflict between the legalism of Pharisaism and the true nature of holiness presented in the gospel. For if salvation was through the Law, Judaism would have been the way to salvation for Gentiles also. Instead, the work of Christ created the same basis for both Jew and Gentile to come into fellowship with God (Ephesians 2:11f.).

On this point Paul testified concerning his own conversion. If he, a zealous Jew and a son of the Law, could find no help but only condemnation in the Law (cf. Romans 7), it was equally unreasonable to expect Gentiles to conform their lives to the Law in order to find salvation (Galatians 2:15f.). Justification by faith alone is God's plan of salvation, and Paul verified that even the Old Testament confirms this truth. For example, Galatians 3:8 states, "And the Scripture, foreseeing that God would justify the heathen through faith, preached before the gospel unto Abraham, saying, In thee shall all nations be blessed." If salvation was through the Law, only Jews could be saved, but the gospel is for all men. Therefore, "They which be of faith are blessed with faithful Abraham" (Galatians 3:9). (See also the analogy of the "first Adam" and the "second man" or "last Adam" in Romans 5:12f. and 1 Corinthians 15:45f.)

In Paul's writings, then, the doctrine of justification finds its most complete presentation. These teachings—grace and righteousness, atonement and reconciliation, conversion and faith—represent the central and fundamental beliefs of Christianity.

Elsewhere in the New Testament the verb *dikaioō* is used in only a few places. Most important, however, is its use in the Epistle of James which provides a necessary complement to the doctrine of justification presented in the Pauline epistles. While Paul maintained that justification is not through works but through faith, James emphasized that this faith is not a dead faith. Instead, it is a faith which is *proven* by good works. Paul was aware that the doctrine of justification could be misused (Romans 3:8); James' intent, however, was to correct those who had misunderstood this doctrine and to punish those who deliberately distorted it (see also 2 Peter 3:16).

Some try to suggest that the themes contained in James contradict Paul's teachings. This misconception, however, is a result of not understanding each writer's use of key words. For example, when Paul spoke of "faith," he had in mind a faith, such as his own, which revolutionizes one's very existence. In James, the term "faith" is applied to heartless so-called "believers" who claim salvation but refuse to help brothers and sisters who are in need of clothing and who lack daily food (James 2:15f.). James said that this type of "faith," which does not produce works, is no better than the "faith" of demons (2:19). In addition, when Paul spoke of "works," he was referring to a legalistic obedience to the Law which was an attempt to secure salvation. Obviously James used the term "works" much differently. His use of the word conveys the same message found in 1 John 3:7: "Little children, let no man deceive you: he that *doeth righteousness* is righteous, even as he is righteous" (cf. 1 John 3:17f.).

Therefore, when James stated that "by works a man is justified, and not by faith only" (2:24), he did *not* contradict Paul's statement that "a man is justified by faith without the deeds of the law" (Romans 3:28). Again, James was emphasizing that deeds "justify" the genuineness of faith (cf. James 2:22: "By works was faith made perfect"). By his works the believer shows God and man that he is justified by faith. This in no way contradicts what Paul taught. (For examples of where Paul maintains the necessity of deeds see 1 Corinthians 7:19; Galatians 5:6; 6:15; Ephesians 2:10; Philippians 1:10.) Both James and Paul taught that good works are the natural and necessary result of justification.

By way of summary, then, the majority of the appearances of *dikaioō* in the New Testament appear in Paul's writings (27 out of 40). The association of *dikaioō* with judgment/acquittal occurs (Matthew 12:37; 1 Corinthians 4:4), and the sense of "proven right" is also found (Matthew 11:19; Luke 7:35) as is "proven just" (Luke 7:29, of God; cf. Romans 8:33; 1 Timothy 3:16). Justifying oneself in the covenant relationship is impossible (Luke 16:15); neither can the Law justify anyone; only faith can do that (Acts 13:38,39; Romans 2:13; 3:20; 4:2; Galatians 2:16; 3:11; 5:4). Even as the New Testament looks back on the Old, its writers recognize this truth was always in God's design (Romans 4:2; James 2:21,24,25; cf. Romans 8:30).

"Justification" or "righteousness" in the covenantal alliance can only be provided by faith in Christ (Romans 3:21ff.; 4:5; 5:1; Galatians 2:16; 3:24) which by His grace is a gift (Romans 3:30; Titus 3:7). The death of Christ and our own death with Him has imputed this righteousness (Romans 5:9; 6:7; cf. 1 Corinthians 6:11; Galatians 2:17).

STRONG 1344, BAUER 197-98, MOULTON-MILLIGAN 162-63, KITTEL 2:174-78,211-19, LIDDELL-SCOTT 429, COLIN BROWN 3:352,354,358,360-63,365,369-7

1339. δικαίωμα dikaiōma noun

Requirement, commandment, righteous deed, equitable deed.

CROSS-REFERENCE:
δικαιόω dikaioō (1338)

דֶּרֶךְ derekh (1932), Way (Jb 34:27).

חֹק chōq (2805), Statute (Ex 15:25,26, 2 Kgs 17:37, Ez 36:27).

חֻקָּה chuqqāh (2807), Statute (Dt 6:2, 2 Sm 22:23, Mi 6:16).

יָרִיב yārîv (3516), Opponent (Jer 18:19).

מִצְוָה mitswāh (4851), Commandment (1 Kgs 2:3).

מִשְׁפָּט mishpāt (5122), Ordinance (Ex 21:1, Ez 20:18); justice (1 Sm 8:3).

פִּקּוּדִים piqqûdhîm (6740), Precepts (Pss 19:8 [18:8], 119:27,93,94,141 [118:27,93,94,141]).

δικαίως 1339B

צְדָקָה tsᵉdhāqāh (6930), Legal right (2 Sm 19:28).
צוּרָה tsûrāh (6965), Pattern (Ez 43:11).
רִיב rîv (7663), Cause, case (Jer 11:20).

1. δικαίωμα dikaiōma nom/acc sing neu
2. δικαιώματος dikaiōmatos gen sing neu
3. δικαιώματα dikaiōmata nom/acc pl neu
4. δικαιώμασιν dikaiōmasin dat pl neu

```
4 walking in all the commandments and ordinances ... Luke 1:6
1 Who knowing the judgment of God, ............... Rom 1:32
3 uncircumcision keep the righteousness of the law, ...... 2:26
1 the free gift is of many offences unto justification. ...... 5:16
2 even so by the righteousness of one the free gift ....... 5:18
1 That the righteousness of the law might be fulfilled .... 8:4
3 Then verily the first covenant had also ordinances ... Heb 9:1
4 and divers washings, and carnal ordinances, ........... 9:10
3 and divers washings, and carnal ordinances, ........... 9:10
3 worship ... for thy judgments are made manifest ..... Rev 15:4
3 for the fine linen is the righteousness of saints. ........ 19:8
```

Classical Greek
This multipurpose noun is a member of the *dikaiōs* (1335B) family which is derived from *dikē* (1343). In secular Greek *dikaiōma* often meant a "legal claim or right." The papyri attest to this usage in the common vernacular as well. Furthermore, it could imply a "legal document" or "proof" in a legal case. In particular, a *dikaiōma* could refer to a "decree" or an "ordinance."

Sometimes *dikaiōma* means a "judgment" or, negatively, "punishment"; like its companion *dikaioō* (1338), though, it also assumes a more positive meaning. It is of special interest to note that in Aristotle *dikaiōma* is employed in the sense of something "restored," a "compensation" to a victim of a crime, an "amendment of a wrong."

Septuagint Usage
The same positive nuance carries over into the Septuagint. *Dikaiōma* never occurs in reference to the Ten Commandments; however, it does appear in association with the social and cultic ordinances (e.g., Genesis 26:5; Exodus 15:25f.; Deuteronomy 4:1). Approximately 70 times *dikaiōma* is equated with *chōq* or *chuqqāh*; about 40 times, *mishpāṭ*. It corresponds to five other terms as well.

New Testament Usage
In the New Testament *dikaiōma* covers a broad range of definition. It may refer to "regulation, requirement, commandment." In Luke 1:6 Zechariah and Elisabeth are described as "walking in all the commandments and *ordinances* of the Lord blameless." Elsewhere, the wicked who know "the judgment of God" nevertheless disobey, even delighting in the disobedience of others (Romans 1:32). This idea of "decree" or "commandment" can be seen in several additional texts (Romans 2:26; 8:4; Hebrews 9:1,10). Similarly, Revelation 15:4 uses *dikaiōma* in connection with God's just actions, that is, His "judgments."

The one act of righteousness (*dikaiōma*) of Christ secured justification (*dikaiōsis* [1340], "acquittal," RSV) for all men (Romans 5:18). Here the word incorporates the various aspects of the Christ-event: His life, death, and resurrection. In this passage the focus is on the substitutionary death of Jesus, the antithesis of the fall of Adam. *Dikaiōma* is God's justification of sinners—given by grace on the basis of Christ's death and received by faith (Romans 5:16; cf. Romans 3:24; Ephesians 2:8). This, perhaps, is the central meaning of the word as it is used in the New Testament, although it carries a significant portion of its classical use having to do with "restitution" or "compensation" (see above). Paul's usage clearly corresponds with the Septuagintal occurrences.

Finally *dikaiōma* depicts the "righteous deeds" (RSV) of the saints (Revelation 19:8). This probably refers to the endurance of the saints in times of persecution and distress (e.g., Revelation 7:14). Similarly, 1 John 2:29 states, "Every one that doeth righteousness is born of him," although the aspect of persecution is not mentioned in this context.

From the above discussion it is clear that no single definition can express the varied meanings and uses of the term *dikaiōma*. However, one can conclude that the word serves as a concrete expression for righteousness. Vine (*Expository Dictionary*, "Justification") states that this Greek word for justification is the "expression for and effect of *dikaiosis*".

STRONG 1345, BAUER 198, MOULTON-MILLIGAN 163, KITTEL 2:174-78,219-23, LIDDELL-SCOTT 429, COLIN BROWN 3:352,354,361-63,371-72.

1339B. δικαίως dikaiōs adv
Justly, uprightly, rightly, properly.
CROSS-REFERENCE:
δικαιόω dikaioō (1338)

צֶדֶק tsedheq (6928), Righteous, just (Dt 1:16, 16:20).
תָּמִים tāmîm (8879), Blameless (Prv 28:18).

1. δικαίως dikaiōs

```
1 we indeed justly; ... but this ... done nothing amiss. Luke 23:41
1 Awake to righteousness, and sin not; ............. 1 Co 15:34
```

| 1 and justly and unblameably we behaved ourselves ... 1 Th 2:10
| 1 we should live soberly, **righteously**, and godly, ... Tit 2:12
| 1 committed himself to him that judgeth **righteously:** ... 1 Pt 2:23

Classical Greek
This is the adverbial form in the *dikaios* (1335B) word group meaning "truly" or "with reason, justly, uprightly." It occurs both in classical and secular sources from the time of Homer (see *Bauer*).

Septuagint Usage
The Septuagint's usage is sporadic. Eight of its 13 occurrences are found outside the canon (e.g., Wisdom of Solomon, Sirach, and the Maccabean writings). Of its five canonical appearances it means "rightly, correctly" most of the time (of judgment, Deuteronomy 1:16; with justice, Proverbs 31:9, Hebrew *tsedeq*; cf. Wisdom of Solomon 9:12; Sirach 35:18 [LXX 32:18]; Genesis 27:36, Hebrew *hakhiy*, "truly").

New Testament Usage
Five texts read *dikaiōs* in the New Testament. Only Luke used *dikaiōs* in the Gospels (23:41). One of the thieves being crucified with Jesus considered his own punishment "just" (cf. 1 Peter 2:23). First Thessalonians (2:10) and Titus (2:12) use *dikaiōs* in reference to the conduct and life-style that are to mark believers' lives. They are to live "soberly, righteously (*dikaiōs*), and godly (*eusebōs* [2134])" (Titus 2:12). Paul (1 Corinthians 15:34) used *dikaiōs* of "coming to one's correct senses" (i.e., "right mind," RSV).

STRONG 1346, BAUER 198, LIDDELL-SCOTT 429, COLIN BROWN 3:352,361,363,370.

1340. δικαίωσις dikaiōsis noun
Acquittal, justification.
CROSS-REFERENCE:
δικαιόω dikaioō (1338)

מִשְׁפָּט mishpāṭ (5122), Law (Lv 24:22).

1. δικαίωσιν dikaiōsin acc sing fem
| 1 and was raised again for our **justification**. .... Rom 4:25
| 1 gift came upon all men unto **justification** of life. 5:18

Classical Greek
The noun *dikaiōsis*, like its companions *dikaios* (1335B), *dikaiosunē* (1336), etc., is rather imprecise in its meaning in classical Greek. It could refer to the activity of "doing justice" or of demanding a "right" as in a "just claim" (Thucydides; see *Liddell-Scott*).

Septuagint Usage
Dikaiōsis occurs only once in the Septuagint not counting a variant versional reading of Psalm 35:23 (Symmachus, "vindication" is properly understood here, cf. verse 24). The Lord commanded one *dikaios* ("law," RSV; Hebrew, *mishpāṭ*; "legal decision," "ruling") for the sojourner and one for the native (Leviticus 24:22).

New Testament Usage
Dikaiōsis occurs only twice in our New Testament, both times in Romans. Jesus was put to death for (*dia* [1217], causal) our transgressions (*paraptōma* [3761], cf. Isaiah 52:13 to 53:12) and raised for (*dia*, result) our "justification," *dikaiōsis* (Romans 4:25). Our righteousness comes from faith, through Christ who vindicates us. The parallel use of the preposition *dia* indicates that "through" His death on the cross and "through" His resurrection on the third day, Jesus procured all that was necessary for our justification. Paul always considered the death and resurrection of Christ as one interrelated act. The importance of the Resurrection is based on His victorious death on the cross; likewise, the Resurrection is God's vindication, His validation or justification of the life and the death of Jesus.

Romans 5:18 echoes that the *paraptōma* ("transgressions") of one man (Adam) brought a sentence of *death* upon *all* mankind, but one man's death (Christ's) brings justification (Romans 5:17), i.e., "acquittal" (RSV), and *life* for *all* (Romans 5:18).

STRONG 1347, BAUER 198, KITTEL 2:174-78,223-24, LIDDELL-SCOTT 429, COLIN BROWN 3:352,354,361,363,371-72.

1341. δικαίως dikaiōs
See word study at number 1339B.

1342. δικαστής dikastēs noun
Judge.
CROSS-REFERENCE:
δικαιόω dikaioō (1338)

שָׁפַט shāphaṭ (8570), A judge (Ex 2:14, Jos 24:1, Is 3:2).

1. δικαστήν dikastēn acc sing masc
| 1 Man, who made me **a judge** or a divider over you? Luke 12:14
| 1 Who made thee a ruler and **a judge** over us? .... Acts 7:27
| 1 saying, Who made thee a ruler and **a judge?** 7:35

This word denotes "the person who settles differences between two parties involved in a controversy." It is found only in Luke 12:14 and Acts 7:27,35. It is a derivative of *dikē* (1343), "what is right," and is similar to *dikazō*, "to judge." Unlike the other word for "judge," *kritēs* (2896), *dikastēs* can be used only in the forensic sense to describe someone who belongs to or is used in courts or public forums of adjudication, arbitration, or public discussion and debate.

STRONG 1348, BAUER 198, MOULTON-MILLIGAN 163, LIDDELL-SCOTT 429-30.

1343. δίκη dikē noun
Penalty, punishment, judicial condemnation or sentence.
CROSS-REFERENCE:
δικαιόω dikaioō (1338)

דָּבָר dāvār (1745), Word; plague (Hos 13:14).

דִּין dîn (1835), Cause (Ps 9:4).

חָרוּץ chārûts (2844), Decision (Jl 3:14).

מִשְׁפָּט mishpāṭ (5122), Cause (Ps 140:12 [139:12]).

נָקַם nāqam (5541), Punish (Ex 21:20).

נָקָם nāqām (5542), Vengeance (Lv 26:25, Dt 32:41,43).

רִיב rîv (7662), Contend (Am 7:4).

רִיב rîv (7663), Case, cause (Jb 29:16, Pss 35:23 [34:23], 43:1 [42:1], Mi 7:9).

1. δίκη dikē nom sing fem
2. δίκην dikēn acc sing fem

2 desiring to have **judgment** against him............Acts 25:15
1 yet **vengeance** suffereth not to live.................... 28:4
2 Who shall **be punished** with everlasting destruction.. 2 Th 1:9
2 an example, suffering the **vengeance** of eternal fire... Jude 1:7

Classical Greek
Dikē, which forms the background of the entire *dikaios* (1335B) word group, was a term of no small significance in classical Greek, particularly in the philosophical systems (e.g., Plato, Aristotle, Hesiod). *Dikē*, ranging in meaning from "custom, law, judgment," to "trial, penalty, punishment," is of disputed etymological origin (see Schrenk, "dikē," *Kittel*, 2:179f.). However, the association between *dikē* and the goddess of the same name is a basic point of departure for understanding *dikē*. *Dikē* was the Greek goddess of recompense who sat beside the throne of Zeus and watched over the earth to insure that justice was satisfactorily maintained. The term *dikē*, therefore, is the divine principle of law not instituted by man (because it is itself divine); it is a universal law of the world, a universal immanent force (ibid.). From this, *dikē* and its cognates filtered into forensic and ethical language.

As early as Homer, a double meaning could be seen in the term, i.e., "justice" in the legal sense along with the concept of that which was "common practice" or "acceptable behavior." These meanings are reflected in many of *dikē*'s cognate forms. To be "righteous" (*dikaios*) was to do externally the legal ordinances prescribed by government or dictated by society. The New Testament, in contrast, influenced by the Septuagint, transforms this understanding. *Dikaios* becomes an inward property indicative of a relationship with God (see comments on *dikaiosunē* [1336], *dikaios* [1335B], *dikaioō* [1338]).

Septuagint Usage
The breadth of definition of *dikē* carries over into the Septuagint. Six Hebrew terms are translated by *dikē*, but verbal and substantival forms of *rîv* ("legal decision, ruling") are most common (cf. *mishpāṭ*, Psalm 140:12 [LXX 139:12]; *dîn*, "judge," Psalm 9:4). *Rib* often has legal significance (e.g., Psalm 35:23 [LXX 34:23]; 43:1 [LXX 42:1]; 74:22 [73:22]; Proverbs 22:23; Micah 7:9).

Also in the Old Testament we see a second dominant sense: "punishment" = judgment (Leviticus 26:25; Deuteronomy 32:41; Esther 8:13); nevertheless, this too is woven in with "justice" (Deuteronomy 32:43).

New Testament Usage
The New Testament reflects the classical heritage, but it moves closer to the Septuagintal understanding of *dikē* as "divine retribution or punishment"—usually eschatological. Acts 28:4 reveals the popular personification of *dikē*, "justice," executed by that immanent power (cf. comments above). The inhabitants of Malta believed the snake was carrying out *dikē*, because Paul had, in their estimation, been a murderer who had escaped the "justice" of the sea in the shipwreck.

But *dikē* as "punishment," most notably "punishment dispensed by God," the supreme Judge, is also known. At the coming of the Lord the ungodly will suffer "punishment"—the vengeance of the Lord (2 Thessalonians 1:8,9). Jude 7 compares the punishment Sodom and Gomorrah received to the judgment God will soon bring upon the earth.

STRONG 1349, BAUER 198, MOULTON-MILLIGAN 163,

KITTEL 2:174-82, LIDDELL-SCOTT 430, COLIN BROWN 3:92-93,96.

1344. δίκτυον diktuon noun

Fishing net.

חֲרַכִּים chărakkîm (2867), Lattice (S/S 2:9).
רֶשֶׁת resheth (7862), Net (Prv 1:17, Ez 12:13, Hos 5:1).
שְׂבָכָה sᵉvākhāh (7877), Network (1 Kgs 7:17,41, 2 Chr 4:12,13).

1. δίκτυον diktuon nom/acc sing neu
2. δίκτυα diktua nom/acc pl neu

2	straightway left their **nets**, and followed him........	Matt 4:20
2	he saw other two brethren, ... mending their **nets**;.....	4:21
2	And straightway they forsook their **nets**,............	Mark 1:18
2	who also were in the ship mending their **nets**........	1:19
2	and were washing their **nets**.......................	Luke 5:2
2	Launch out into the deep, and let down your **nets**.....	5:4
1	nevertheless at thy word I will let down the **net**.....	5:5
2	nevertheless at thy word I will let down the **net**.....	5:5
1	a great multitude of fishes: and their **net** brake.....	5:6
2	a great multitude of fishes: and their **net** brake.....	5:6
1	Cast the **net** on the right side of the ship,.........	John 21:6
1	dragging the **net** with fishes........................	21:8
1	and drew the **net** to land full of great fishes,......	21:11
1	yet was not the **net** broken..........................	21:11

This is a general term for "net," a device for catching fish, birds, or insects. It is a derivative of the classical verb *dikō* which means "to cast." In the Septuagint the term *diktuon* is used to describe a "net" for catching birds in Proverbs 1:17 and figuratively as a "snare" in Job 18:8 and Proverbs 29:5. In the New Testament *diktuon* refers to the type of net that captures fish (Matthew 4:20,21; Mark 1:18,19; Luke 5:2,4-6; John 21:6,8,11).

STRONG 1350, BAUER 198, MOULTON-MILLIGAN 163, LIDDELL-SCOTT 431.

1345. διλόγος dilogos adj

Double-tongued, insincere, deceitful.

CROSS-REFERENCE:
λόγος logos (3030)

1. διλόγους dilogous acc pl masc

1 must the deacons be grave, not **doubletongued**,..... 1 Tm 3:8

This word comes from *dis* (1357A), meaning "twice," and *logos* (3030), which means "a word" or "speech." In one piece of extant literature (i.e., Pollux, Second Century A.D.) the word means "repetition." Aside from this rare use, there is no other occurrence of the term in classical Greek (*Moulton-Milligan*). In 1 Timothy 3:8, the only New Testament occurrence, *dilogos* is translated "double-tongued," saying one thing to one person and then changing the story to another (giving different versions of a story perhaps with the intent to deceive).

STRONG 1351, BAUER 198, MOULTON-MILLIGAN 163, LIDDELL-SCOTT 431.

1346. διό dio conj

Therefore, wherefore, on this account, because of this, for this reason.

1. διό dio

1	**Wherefore** that field was called, The field of blood,	Matt 27:8
1	**therefore** also that holy thing which shall be born...	Luke 1:35
1	**Wherefore** neither thought I myself worthy............	7:7
1	**Therefore** came I unto you without gainsaying,.....	Acts 10:29
1	**Wherefore** he saith also in another psalm,..........	13:35
1	**Wherefore** my sentence is,...........................	15:19
1	**Wherefore** I take you to record this day,...........	20:26
1	**Therefore** watch, and remember,.....................	20:31
1	**wherefore** he sent for him the oftener,.............	24:26
1	**Wherefore** I have brought him forth before you,.....	25:26
1	**wherefore** I beseech thee to hear me patiently.......	26:3
1	**Wherefore**, sirs, be of good cheer:.................	27:25
1	**Wherefore** I pray you to take some meat:............	27:34
1	**Wherefore** God also gave them up to uncleanness...	Rom 1:24
1	**Therefore** thou art inexcusable, O man,.............	2:1
1	**therefore** it was imputed to him for righteousness......	4:22
1	**Wherefore** ye must needs be subject,................	13:5
1	**Wherefore** receive ye one another,...................	15:7
1	**For which cause** also I have been much hindered.....	15:22
1	**Wherefore** I give you to understand,................	1 Co 12:3
1	**Therefore** let one who speaks in a tongue (NASB).....	14:13
1	**Wherefore** also by Him is our Amen (NASB)........	2 Co 1:20
1	**Wherefore** I beseech you that ye would confirm.......	2:8
1	I believed, and **therefore** have I spoken;............	4:13
1	we also believe, and **therefore** speak;...............	4:13
1	**For which cause** we faint not;.......................	4:16
1	**Wherefore** we labour, that, whether present or.......	5:9
1	**Wherefore** come out from among them,...............	6:17
1	**for this reason**, to keep me from exalting (NASB).....	12:7
1	**Therefore** I take pleasure in infirmities,...........	12:10
1	**So then**, brethren, we are not children of (NASB)....	Gal 4:31
1	**Wherefore** remember, that ye being in time past.....	Eph 2:11
1	**Wherefore** I desire that ye faint not................	3:13
1	**Wherefore** he saith, When he ascended up on high,.....	4:8
1	**Wherefore** putting away lying,......................	4:25
1	**Wherefore** he saith, Awake thou that sleepest,.......	5:14
1	**Wherefore** God also hath highly exalted him,........	Phlp 2:9
1	**Wherefore** we would have come unto you,.............	1 Th 2:18
1	**Wherefore** when we could no longer forbear,..........	3:1
1	**Wherefore** comfort yourselves together,..............	5:11
1	**Wherefore**, though I might be much bold in Christ..	Phlm 1:8
1	**Wherefore** as the Holy Ghost saith,.................	Heb 3:7
1	**Wherefore** I was grieved with that generation,.......	3:10
1	**Therefore** leaving the principles of the doctrine......	6:1
1	**Wherefore** when he cometh into the world,...........	10:5
1	**Therefore** sprang there even of one,................	11:12
1	**wherefore** God is not ashamed.......................	11:16
1	**Wherefore** lift up the hands which hang down,.......	12:12
1	**Wherefore** we receiving a kingdom...................	12:28
1	**Wherefore** Jesus also, that He might sanctify........	13:12
1	**Wherefore** lay apart all filthiness and superfluity......	Jas 1:21
1	But he giveth more grace. **Wherefore** he saith,.........	4:6
1	**Wherefore** gird up the loins of your mind,..........	1 Pt 1:13
1	**Wherefore** also it is contained in the scripture,........	2:6
1	**Wherefore** the rather, brethren, give diligence.....	2 Pt 1:10
1	**Wherefore** I will not be negligent...................	1:12
1	**Wherefore**, ... seeing that ye look for such things,.....	3:14

This is an inferential conjunction meaning "wherefore, therefore, for this reason, for which cause" (e.g., Matthew 27:8; Luke 1:35; and others). It is used to pass from one proposition, statement, or judgment considered as true to another whose truth is believed to follow the former, denoting that the inference is self-evident (see *Bauer*).

STRONG 1352, BAUER 198, MOULTON-MILLIGAN 163-64, LIDDELL-SCOTT 432.

1347. διοδεύω diodeuō verb
To go through, go about, journey, travel.
SYNONYMS:
διαπορεύω diaporeuō (1273)
διέρχομαι dierchomai (1324)
ἔρχομαι erchomai (2048)
παραπορεύομαι paraporeuomai (3760)
παρέρχομαι parerchomai (3790)
πορεύομαι poreuomai (4057)

דָּרַךְ dārakh (1931), Tread (Is 59:8).

הָלַךְ hālakh (2050), Go, walk; hithpael: walk about (Gn 13:17).

עָבַר 'āvar (5882), Pass through, pass by (Ez 5:14, Zep 3:6, Zec 7:14).

1. διοδεύσαντες diodeusantes
    nom pl masc part aor act
2. διώδευεν diōdeuen 3sing indic imperf act

2 that he went throughout every city and village,...... Luke 8:1
1 Now when they had passed through Amphipolis.... Acts 17:1

Diodeuō generally means "to go" or "to pass." It is translated "went throughout" in Luke 8:1 and "passed through" in Acts 17:1. This compound word comes from *dia* (1217), "through," and *hodos* (3461), "way." It is used over 20 times in the Septuagint, most often to translate *'āvar*, "pass over, through, by, pass on" (see Genesis 12:6; Psalm 89:41 [LXX 88:41]; Jeremiah 2:6).

STRONG 1353, BAUER 198, MOULTON-MILLIGAN 164, LIDDELL-SCOTT 432.

1348. Διονύσιος Dionusios name
Dionysius.

1. Διονύσιος Dionusios nom masc

1 among the which was **Dionysius the Areopagite,**.... Acts 17:34

Member of the Areopagite (692) converted by Paul (Acts 17:34).

1349. διόπερ dioper conj
For this very reason, therefore, wherefore.

1. διόπερ dioper
1 **Wherefore,** if meat make my brother to offend,..... 1 Co 8:13
1 **Wherefore,** my dearly beloved, flee from idolatry....... 10:14
1 **Wherefore** let him that speaketh in an unknown....... 14:13

Dioper appears in classical literature, the Septuagint (e.g., Judith 8:17; 2 Maccabees 5:20; 6:16), the papyri, and three times in the New Testament (all in 1 Corinthians: at 8:13; 10:14; and 14:13). It is an inferential conjunction (*di hoper*) which signals a conclusion is about to be drawn on the basis of preceding information.

STRONG 1355, BAUER 199, MOULTON-MILLIGAN 164, LIDDELL-SCOTT 433.

1350. διοπετές diopetes noun
Fallen from heaven, fallen from Jupiter (Zeus).

1. διοπετοῦς diopetous gen fem

1 and of the image which fell down from Jupiter?..... Acts 19:35

Diopetēs is found in classical literature and the papyri but not in the Septuagint. In the New Testament it is used once in Acts 19:35 to refer to the image or sacred stone of Artemis (Diana) which was believed to have fallen from heaven. *Diopetēs* comes from two words: *dios*, which means "heaven," and the verb *piptō* (3959), meaning "to fall."

1350B. διόρθωμα diorthōma noun
Reform, a successful achievement, making straight, setting right.
CROSS-REFERENCE:
ὀρθός orthos (3580)

1. διορθωμάτων diorthōmatōn gen pl neu

1 reforms are being carried out (NASB)............. Acts 24:2

In its classical uses *diorthōma* describes something that was "made straight" or "set right." It has a figurative use which refers to a "revision" of a law. The only New Testament occurrence is at Acts 24:2 where it appears as a variant to the term *katorthōma* (2705). There, Ananias the high priest employed a certain orator, Tertullus, to argue the Jews' case against Paul before Felix the governor. Tertullus introduced his appeal using flattery which included the highly debatable statement that Felix, through his "providence" (*pronoia* [4166], "foresight"), had instituted "very worthy deeds" (*diorthōma*) which brought great peace to the region.

BAUER 199, MOULTON-MILLIGAN 164, LIDDELL-SCOTT 434.

1351. διόρθωσις diorthōsis noun
Reformation, a thorough straightening, rectification.
CROSS-REFERENCE:
ὀρθός orthos (3580)

1. διορθώσεως diorthōseōs gen sing fem

1 imposed on them until the time **of reformation**....... Heb 9:10

Diorthōsis is composed of two Greek words: *dia* (1217), meaning "through," and *orthos* (3580), meaning "straight" or "upright." It therefore means a "setting in order" or a "bringing back to an early order." The term is used in classical literature and the papyri, but not in the Septuagint. In the New Testament *diorthōsis* appears only in Hebrews 9:10 where it refers to the new order established in Christ, in contrast with the provisional nature of the old covenant.

STRONG 1357, BAUER 199, MOULTON-MILLIGAN 164, KITTEL 5:450, LIDDELL-SCOTT 434, COLIN BROWN 3:351.

1352. διορύσσω diorussō verb
Break in, dig through.
SYNONYM:
ἀπορέω aporeō (633)

חָתַר chāthar (2972), Dig through (Jb 24:16, Ez 12:5,12).

1. διορύσσουσιν diorussousin 3pl indic pres act
2. διορυγῆναι diorugēnai inf aor pass
3. διορυχθῆναι dioruchthēnai inf aor pass

1 and where thieves **break through** and steal:......... Matt 6:19
1 and where thieves do not **break through** nor steal:...... 6:20
2 not have suffered his house to be broken up........... 24:43
3 not have suffered his house to be broken up........... 24:43
2 not have suffered his house to be broken through... Luke 12:39
3 not have suffered his house to be broken through...... 12:39

Diorussō is a combination of two Greek words: the preposition *dia* (1217), which means "through," and the verb *orussō* (3599), which means "to dig." It appears in classical literature, the Septuagint, and the papyri. In the New Testament it occurs four times in the teachings of Jesus (Matthew 6:19,20; 24:43; Luke 12:39), always describing the illegal entry of a thief into a home, accomplished by digging through a sun-dried brick wall.

STRONG 1358, BAUER 199, MOULTON-MILLIGAN 164, LIDDELL-SCOTT 434, COLIN BROWN 2:831.

1353. Διόσκουροι Dioskouroi name
Dioskouroi.

1. Διοσκούροις Dioskourois dat pl masc

1 in a ship ... whose sign was **Castor and Pollux**...... Acts 28:11

The twin sons of Zeus, Castor and Pollus, who were the patron deities of sailors (Acts 28:11).

1354. διότι dioti conj
Because, for, on this account, therefore.

1. διότι dioti

1 Fear not, Zacharias: **for** thy prayer is heard;........ Luke 1:13
1 **because** there was no room for them in the inn......... 2:7
1 look up, ... **for** your redemption draweth nigh.......... 21:28
1 doubting nothing: **for** I have sent them............. Acts 10:20
1 **Therefore** he also says in another Psalm (NASB)...... 13:35
1 **Because** he hath appointed a day,................... 17:31
1 **For** I am with thee, and no man shall set on thee..... 18:10
1 **for** I have much people in this city................... 18:10
1 **Therefore** I testify to you this day (NASB)............ 20:26
1 **for** they will not receive thy testimony............... 22:18
1 **Because** that which may be known of God.......... Rom 1:19
1 **Because** that, when they knew God,.................... 1:21
1 **Therefore** by the deeds of the law there shall no........ 3:20
1 **Because** the carnal mind is enmity against God:...... 8:7
1 **Because** the creature itself also shall be delivered....... 8:21
1 **because** I persecuted the church of God............. I Co 15:9
1 **for** by the works ... shall no flesh be justified......Gal 2:16
1 **because** that ye had heard that he had been sick.....Phlp 2:26
1 also our own souls, **because** ye were dear unto us.... 1 Th 2:8
1 **For** we wanted to come to you (NASB)................. 2:18
1 **because** that the Lord is the avenger of all such,........ 4:6
1 was not found, **because** God had translated him:.... Heb 11:5
1 **because** they saw he was a proper child;............. 11:23
1 Ye ask, and receive not, **because** ye ask amiss,........ Jas 4:3
1 **Because** it is written, Be ye holy; **for** I am holy...... 1 Pt 1:16
1 **For** all flesh is as grass,............................... 1:24
1 **For** this is contained in Scripture (NASB)............. 2:6

In classical, Septuagint, and New Testament Greek *dioti* is a conjunction with several nuances. First, it may introduce causal clauses and be translated "because" or "for" (*Bauer*). Examples of this use are Luke 2:7, " ... because there was no room for them in the inn"; 1 Thessalonians 2:8, " ... because ye were dear unto us."

Dioti at times replaces *hoti* (3617) to demonstrate cause and is usually rendered "for" in these instances (see Luke 1:13; Acts 22:18; Galatians 2:16). In two instances *dioti* begins a clause with inference and is translated as "therefore" or "so" (see Acts 13:35; 20:26). Finally, in Romans 8:21 (some manuscripts read *hoti* here) *dioti* is used and requires a translation of "that" (ibid.).

STRONG 1360, BAUER 199, MOULTON-MILLIGAN 164-65, LIDDELL-SCOTT 435.

1355. Διοτρέφης Diotrephēs name
Diotrephes.

δıπλοῦς 1356

1. Διοτρέφης Diotrephēs nom masc

1 Diotrephes, who loveth to have the preeminence..... 3 Jn 1:9

A haughty Christian whose actions and attitudes proved a hindrance to the church (3 John 9).

1356. διπλοῦς diplous adj
Double, twofold.

כָּפַל kāphal (3843), Fold double (Ex 28:16, 39:9 [36:16]).

כֶּפֶל kephel (3844), Double (Jb 11:6, Is 40:2).

מַכְפֵּלָה makhpēlah (4512), Machpelah, the place called Machpelah (Gn 23:9).

מִשְׁנֶה mishneh (5112), Twice, double (Ex 16:22, Zec 9:12).

שְׁנַיִם shᵉnayim (8530), Two (Ex 22:9).

1. διπλῆς diplēs gen sing fem
2. διπλοῦν diploun nom/acc sing neu
3. διπλᾶ dipla nom/acc pl neu
4. διπλότερον diploteron comp acc sing masc

4 twofold more the child of hell than yourselves...... Matt 23:15
1 be counted worthy of double honour,................ 1 Tm 5:17
3 double unto her double according to her works:.... Rev 18:6
2 in the cup which she hath filled fill to her double..... 18:6

Diplous (also spelled *diploos*) means "twice as much, double." It derives from the cognate verbal form *diploō* (1357) meaning "to double." The term appears in classical literature, the Septuagint, and the papyri. In the New Testament it occurs twice: In Revelation 18:6 it is used negatively to describe the judgment against Babylon, and in 1 Timothy 5:17 it is used positively to indicate the proper reward for dedicated "elders that rule well." A comparative form, *diploteros*, occurs once in the New Testament, in Matthew 23:15, where it describes the morally deplorable condition of a proselyte to Pharisaical Judaism. He is said to be "*twofold more* the child of hell" than the Pharisee.

STRONG 1362, BAUER 199, MOULTON-MILLIGAN 165, LIDDELL-SCOTT 436.

1357. διπλόω diploō verb
Double.

1. διπλώσατε diplōsate 2pl impr aor act

1 double unto her double according to her works:..... Rev 18:6

Diploō appears in classical literature and once in the New Testament, but not in the Septuagint or the papyri. Its meanings in classical Greek include "double, multiply by two." In Revelation 18:6 it is used to describe the severity of the punishment that will be meted out to Babylon.

STRONG 1363, BAUER 199, LIDDELL-SCOTT 436.

1357A. δίς dis adv
Twice.

פַּעַם paʿam (6718), Twice (Gn 41:32, 43:10, 1 Kgs 11:9).

שְׁתִיל shāthîl (8691), Twice (Neh 13:20).

1. δίς dis

1 before the cock crow twice, thou shalt deny me....Mark 14:30
1 Before the cock crow twice, thou shalt deny me....... 14:72
1 I fast twice in the week, I give tithes of all........ Luke 18:12
1 For even in Thessalonica ye sent once and again....Phlp 4:16
1 come unto you, even I Paul, once and again;....... 1 Th 2:18
1 without fruit, twice dead, plucked up by the roots;.. Jude 1:12

Dis appears in classical literature, the Septuagint, the papyri, and six times in the New Testament. Four times it expresses the idea of "twice" or "a second time": in Mark 14:30,72 in reference to the cock's crowing; in Luke 18:12 to describe the self-righteous Pharisee's routine of fasting twice each week; and in Jude 12 to describe the double deadness of false teachers. *Dis* is used in Philippians 4:16 and 1 Thessalonians 2:18 in conjunction with *hapax* (526) to mean "again and again," that is, "more than twice" or "repeatedly."

STRONG 1364, BAUER 199, MOULTON-MILLIGAN 165, LIDDELL-SCOTT 436.

1357B. δισμυριάς dismurias noun
A double myriad; 20,000.

1. δισμυριάδες dismuriades nom pl fem

1 horsemen were two hundred million (NASB)......... Rev 9:16

Classical usage from the Fifth Century B.C. attests to the existence of this term which means "two myriads" (cf. *murias* [3323]). At times the term is used as "an indefinite number of incalculable immensity" (*Bauer*). It occurs once in the New Testament at Revelation 9:16 where it specifies the total "number of the army of the horsemen" as *dismuriades muriadōn*, that is, "two myriads of myriads." The KJV translates this phrase "two hundred thousand thousand," i.e., 200 million.

BAUER 199.

1358. διστάζω distazō verb
To doubt, waver.

SYNONYM:
ἀπορέω aporeō (633)

1. ἐδίστασας edistasas 2sing indic aor act
2. ἐδίστασαν edistasan 3pl indic aor act

1 O thou of little faith, wherefore **didst thou doubt?** .. Matt 14:31
2 they worshipped him: but some doubted. 28:17

Distazō comes from two Greek words: *dis* (1357A), meaning "double," and *stasis* (4565), meaning "standing." Thus *distazō* means "to stand in two ways, to be uncertain, to doubt." *Distazō* appears in classical literature where it carries two meanings: "to doubt" and "to hesitate" because of doubt. It also appears in the papyri, but not in the Septuagint. The New Testament uses *distazō* twice in Matthew, both times in reference to doubting Jesus. In Matthew 14:31 Peter is the subject, and in 28:17 some of the 11 disciples doubted Jesus in His post-Resurrection appearance.

STRONG 1365, BAUER 200, MOULTON-MILLIGAN 165, LIDDELL-SCOTT 437, COLIN BROWN 1:504.

1359. δίστομος distomos adj
Two-edged, double-edged.

CROSS-REFERENCE:
στόμα stoma (4601)

פִּיּוֹת pēyôth (6610), Double-edged (Prv 5:4).
פִּיפִיּוֹת pîphîyôth (6617), Double-edged (Ps 149:6).

1. δίστομος distomos nom sing fem
2. δίστομον distomon acc sing fem

2 and sharper than any **twoedged** sword, ... Heb 4:12
1 out of his mouth went a sharp **twoedged** sword: ...... Rev 1:16
2 he which hath the sharp sword with **two edges**; 2:12

Distomos is the combination of two Greek words: *dis* (1357A), meaning "two," and *stoma* (4601), meaning "mouth." *Distomos* thus functions as an adjective to describe things which have two mouths. It is used of rivers, branching roads, and swords which have two mouths or edges. *Distomos* occurs in classical literature and the papyri, as well as three times in the Septuagint (Judges 3:16; Psalm 149:6 [LXX 148:6]; Proverbs 5:4) and three times in the New Testament (Hebrews 4:12; Revelation 1:16; 2:12). In the Bible *distomos* always describes a sword.

STRONG 1366, BAUER 200, MOULTON-MILLIGAN 165, LIDDELL-SCOTT 437.

1360. δισχίλιοι dischilioi num
Two thousand.

CROSS-REFERENCE:
χιλιάς chilias (5342)

1. δισχίλιοι dischilioi card nom masc

1 they were about two thousand; .... Mark 5:13

Dischilioi is the combination of two Greek numbers: *dis* (1357A), meaning "two," and *chilioi* (5343), meaning "thousand." Thus *dischilioi* means "2,000." It is used in classical literature, the Septuagint, the papyri, and once in the New Testament in Mark 5:13 to denote the size of the herd of pigs into which Jesus cast the legion of demons.

STRONG 1367, BAUER 200, LIDDELL-SCOTT 437, COLIN BROWN 2:699.

1361. δίς dis
See word study at number 1357A.

1362. διυλίζω diulizō verb
Strain out, filter through.

מִזְרָק mizrāq (4353), Sprinkling basin (Am 6:6).

1. διϋλίζοντες diulizontes nom pl masc part pres act

1 which **strain** at a gnat, and swallow a camel. .... Matt 23:24

Diulizō means "to strain or filter out" as in removing sediment from new wine. It appears in classical literature and the Septuagint (e.g., Amos 6:6, "Filtered" wine). In the New Testament *diulizō* is used once, in Matthew 23:24, as part of Jesus' hyperbolic description of the Pharisees who "strain (out) a gnat, and swallow a camel."

STRONG 1368, BAUER 200, LIDDELL-SCOTT 438.

1363. διχάζω dichazō verb
Divide, set at variance, cause disunion.

1. διχάσαι dichasai inf aor act

1 to set a man at variance against his father, ... Matt 10:35

The root of this word, *dicha*, generally means "divide in two, apart" (see *Liddell-Scott*). In classical Greek *dichazō* was used by Plato and others to mean "divide in two" when referring to a logical dichotomy. It does not appear in the Septuagint but is used once in the New Testament. In Matthew 10:35 Jesus used this word metaphorically to describe how the effects of His coming will "set a man at variance" against his family. Jesus' intent was not to

δικοστασία 1364

divide or destroy families, but He knew that some division would occur, separating those who accepted Him from those who did not.

Strong 1369, Bauer 200, Moulton-Milligan 165, Liddell-Scott 439.

1364. διχοστασία dichostasia noun
Dissension.
Cognate:
ἵστημι histēmi (2449)
Synonym:
διαμερισμός diamerismos (1261)

1. διχοστασίαι dichostasiai nom pl fem
2. διχοστασίας dichostasias acc pl fem

2 mark them which cause **divisions** and offences ...... Rom 16:17
1 and **divisions**, are ye not carnal, and walk as men? .. 1 Co 3:3
1 emulations, wrath, strife, **seditions**, heresies, ... Gal 5:20

Classical Greek
This noun is related to *dichostateō* (from *dicha*, which is both an adverb and a preposition meaning "in two, apart," and *histēmi* [2449], "I stand"). *Dichostasia*, therefore, is a "standing apart," thus it is a "dissension" or (an act of) "sedition."

Septuagint Usage
Only 1 Maccabees 3:29 in the apocryphal portion of the Septuagint reads *dichostasia*. King Antiochus realized that his abolishment of long-standing laws had caused "*dissension* and disaster" (RSV) in the land.

New Testament Usage
Paul alone used *dichostasia* in the New Testament. In every case "dissension" is an adequate translation (Romans 16:17; 1 Corinthians 3:3; Galatians 5:20). Paul was apparently referring to internal dissension in the church, which he regarded as totally contrary to godly behavior ("dissension" or "variance" is in the "vice-list" of the "works of the flesh," Galatians 5:19-21). Another reading of *dichostasia* occurs in 1 Corinthians 3:3 which has diverse manuscript support for its authenticity (e.g., p46 D F G Majority text).

Strong 1370, Bauer 200, Moulton-Milligan 165, Kittel 1:514, Liddell-Scott 439.

1365. διχοτομέω dichotomeō verb
Cut in two, severely scourge, flog.
Cross-Reference:
περιτέμνω peritemnō (3919)

נָתַח nāthach (5591), Piel: cut in pieces (Ex 29:17).

1. διχοτομήσει dichotomēsei 3sing indic fut act

1 And shall **cut him asunder**, ... Matt 24:51
1 when he is not aware, and **will cut him in sunder**, .. Luke 12:46

In classical Greek *dichotomeō* is used in reference to the ancient method of punishment by "cutting into pieces" or the "dismemberment" of a convicted and condemned person. In the Septuagint it appears in Exodus 29:17, "Cut the ram in pieces." Here *dichotomeō* translates the Hebrew word *nāthach* which simply means "cut up, cut in pieces," although *nāthach* is usually translated into Greek as *melizein*. (See also Leviticus 1:8; Ezekiel 24:4.) In the New Testament *dichotomeō* occurs only in Matthew 24:51, "He will cut him to pieces" (NIV), and the parallel passage of Luke 12:46. Here it seems to mean "cut in two for the purpose of punishment."

Strong 1371, Bauer 200, Moulton-Milligan 165, Kittel 2:225-26, Liddell-Scott 439.

1366. διψάω dipsaō verb
Thirst for, desire earnestly.
Cognate:
δίψος dipsos (1367)

חֹרֶב chōrev (2822), Heat (Is 25:4,5).

עָיֵף 'āyēph (6106), Faint, exhausted (Jb 22:7, Is 29:8, Jer 31:25 [38:25]).

צִיָּה tsîyāh (6993), Desert (Is 35:1, 41:18).

צָמֵא tsāmē' (7039), Be thirsty (Ex 17:3, Jgs 4:19, Ps 42:2 [41:2]).

צָמֵא tsāmē' (7041), Thirsty (2 Sm 17:29, Ps 107:5 [106:5], Is 21:14).

שָׁקַק shāqaq (8630), Rush (Prv 28:15).

1. διψῶ dipsō 1sing indic/subj pres act
2. διψῶμεν dipsōmen 1pl indic pres act
3. διψᾷ dipsa 3sing subj pres act
4. διψῶν dipsōn nom sing masc part pres act
5. διψῶντι dipsonti dat sing masc part pres act
6. διψῶντα dipsonta acc sing masc part pres act
7. διψῶντες dipsontes nom pl masc part pres act
8. ἐδίψησα edipsēsa 1sing indic aor act
9. διψήσῃ dipsēsē 3sing subj aor act
10. διψήσει dipsēsei 3sing indic fut act
11. διψήσουσιν dipsēsousin 3pl indic fut act

7 which do hunger and **thirst** after righteousness: .... Matt 5:6
8 I was **thirsty**, and ye gave me drink: 25:35
6 or **thirsty**, and gave thee drink? 25:37
8 I was **thirsty**, and ye gave me no drink: 25:42
6 Lord, when saw we thee an hungered, or **athirst**, ... 25:44
10 Whosoever drinketh of this water **shall thirst** .... John 4:13
9 of the water that I shall give him **shall** never **thirst**; 4:14
10 of the water that I shall give him **shall** never **thirst**; 4:14
1 give me this water, that I **thirst** not, ... 4:15

9 and he that believeth on me **shall** never **thirst**..... John 6:35	
10 and he that believeth on me **shall** never **thirst**..... 6:35	
3 If any man **thirst**, let him come unto me,..... 7:37	
1 that the scripture might be fulfilled, saith, I **thirst**..... 19:28	
3 if he **thirst**, give him drink:..... Rom 12:20	
2 unto this present hour we both hunger, and **thirst**, 1 Co 4:11	
11 shall hunger no more, neither **thirst** any more;..... Rev 7:16	
5 I will give unto him that is **athirst** of the fountain.... 21:6	
4 And let him that is **athirst** come..... 22:17	

The root of this word, *dipsa*, generally means "thirst". It is found throughout classical Greek and the Septuagint in a variety of forms. In the New Testament *dipsaō* is found 16 times to describe 3 kinds of "thirst." The first kind of "thirst" depicts an actual physical thirst that may even cause physical suffering (see Matthew 25:35,37,42,44; John 4:13,15; 19:28; Romans 12:20). The second and third kinds of "thirst" use *dipsaō* in a figurative sense. John wrote of the "thirst" for the water of life (John 4:14,16; 6:35; 7:37; Revelation 21:6; 22:17), while Matthew used "thirst" to describe a longing or strong desire for righteousness (Matthew 5:6). See word study at *dipsos* (1367).

STRONG 1372, BAUER 200, MOULTON-MILLIGAN 165, KITTEL 2:226-29, LIDDELL-SCOTT 439-40, COLIN BROWN 2:264-68,277.

1367. δίψος dipsos noun
Thirst.
CROSS-REFERENCE:
διψάω dipsaō (1366)

צָמָא tsāmā' (7040), Thirst (Ex 17:3, Jgs 15:18, Lam 4:4).
צָמֵא tsāmē' (7041), Thirsty (Is 44:3).
צִמְאָה tsim'āh (7042), Thirst (Jer 2:25).
תֹּהוּ tōhû (8744), Wilderness (Dt 32:10).

1. δίψει dipsei dat sing neu

1 in hunger and **thirst**, in fastings often,..... 2 Co 11:27	

Classical Greek and Septuagint Usage
Individually as well as collectively the images of hunger and thirst were used metaphorically in classical Greek in reference to human longings of various kinds (e.g., freedom, honor, wealth). The verb *dipsaō* (1366), "to thirst," and the noun *dipsos*, "thirst," are used about 50 times combined in the Septuagint. There they translate many Hebrew words, for example: *tsāmē'*, "thirst"; *tsîyāh*, "dry"; *'āyēph*, "tired, exhausted." The terms describe the land which thirsts for rain, or in a similar metaphor "thirst" involves a deep longing for God (Psalms 42:2 [LXX 41:2]; 63:1 [62:1]; 143:6 [142:6]).

Later Judaism spoke of "thirst" as a description of the torment of hell (2 Esdras 8:59). A parallel thought is present in the New Testament (Luke 16:24) in the Parable of Lazarus and the Rich Man.

New Testament Usage
In the New Testament the verb *dipsaō* is found 16 times, while the noun occurs only once (2 Corinthians 11:27). Both the verb and the noun are used literally and figuratively. In the context of judgment Jesus identified himself with the "little ones" who have been hungry and thirsty. Those who did not show mercy to these are condemned, but the one who offers even a drink of water will not be without reward (Matthew 25:35f.; cf. Matthew 10:42).

Jesus used physical thirst as a point of departure for speaking about spiritual thirst to the Samaritan woman (John 4:13f.). "Hungering and thirsting" after righteousness characterize the disciple. Those who are thirsty for spiritual matters are invited to come and take of the water of life—without cost (Revelation 22:17). Hunger and thirst will be no more in God's eternal kingdom. There thirst will be quenched by the fountain of Life (cf. Revelation 7:16 and 21:6).

STRONG 1373, BAUER 200, MOULTON-MILLIGAN 166, KITTEL 2:226-29, LIDDELL-SCOTT 440, COLIN BROWN 2:265.

1368. δίψυχος dipsuchos adj
Double-minded.
COGNATE:
ψυχή psuchē (5425)

1. δίψυχος dipsuchos nom sing masc
2. δίψυχοι dipsuchoi nom pl masc

1 A **double minded** man is unstable in all his ways...... Jas 1:8	
2 and purify your hearts, ye **double minded**...... 4:8	

Dipsuchos, meaning "two souls," is a figurative expression for indecision or wavering (cf. *diakrinō* [1246], which parallels *dipsuchos* in James 1:8; 4:8, the "double-minded" man). It implies doubt. The form of the word is unknown in Greek of any type prior to its appearance in James. Here the Old Testament's idea of a "divided" or "undivided" heart may be what is meant.

The Old Testament endorses loving God with all our hearts (Deuteronomy 6:5), seeking Him with all our hearts (Jeremiah 29:13 [LXX 36:13]), trusting in the Lord with all our hearts (Proverbs 3:5), praising God with all our hearts (Psalm 138:1 [LXX 137:1]), and keeping the

διωγμός 1369

law of God with all our hearts (Psalm 119:34 [LXX 118:34]). God looks for men with whole hearts (2 Chronicles 16:9), and the Psalmist prays for an undivided heart (Psalm 86:11 [LXX 85:12]). David desired that Solomon would have a whole heart (1 Chronicles 29:19). Solomon desired the same for the people (1 Kings 8:61 [LXX 3 Kings 8:61]). The people gave with a "perfect heart" (1 Chronicles 29:9).

STRONG 1374, BAUER 201, MOULTON-MILLIGAN 166, KITTEL 9:665, LIDDELL-SCOTT 440, COLIN BROWN 3:686-87.

1369. διωγμός diōgmos noun
Persecution.
CROSS-REFERENCE:
διώκω diōkō (1371)

מָרוּד mārûdh (4950), Wandering (Lam 3:19).
רָדַף rādhaph (7579), Piel: pursue (Prv 11:19).

1. **διωγμός** diōgmos nom sing masc
2. **διωγμοῦ** diōgmou gen sing masc
3. **διωγμόν** diōgmon acc sing masc
4. **διωγμῶν** diōgmōn gen pl masc
5. **διωγμοῖς** diōgmois dat pl masc
6. **διωγμούς** diōgmous acc pl masc

2 for when tribulation or **persecution** ariseth .... Matt 13:21
2 afterward, when affliction or **persecution** ariseth ..... Mark 4:17
4 and children, and lands, with **persecutions**; 10:30
1 And at that time there was a great **persecution** ...... Acts 8:1
3 and raised **persecution** against Paul and Barnabas, ... 13:50
1 shall tribulation, or distress, or **persecution**, ... Rom 8:35
5 in reproaches, in necessities, in **persecutions**, ... 2 Co 12:10
5 your **persecutions** and tribulations that ye endure: ... 2 Th 1:4
5 **Persecutions**, afflictions, which came unto me .... 2 Tm 3:11
6 at Lystra; what **persecutions** I endured: 3:11

Classical Greek
Classical writers regarded *diōgmos* as the "chase" or the "pursuit" of someone or something. It could also mean "persecution," although many of the modern nuances associated with that expression would be foreign to ancient Greeks.

Septuagint Usage
We find the familiar sense of religious persecution (see especially *diōkō* [1371]) in the Septuagint, particularly in the Psalms. Oepke notes that the Septuagint has been faithful to the Masoretic text in conveying this theme (e.g., Psalms 7:1; 31:15 [LXX 30:15]; 35:3 [34:3]; 71:11 [70:11]; 109:16 [108:16]; 119:84 [118:84]). It has also imported the concept "independently" of itself (Oepke, "diōkō," Kittel, 2:229). The noun *diōgmos* occurs only in Proverbs 11:19 (Hebrew *rādhaph*) and Lamentations 3:19 (*mārûdh*). The sense of persecution (religious/national) may be intended in Lamentations.

Although the term is rarely used in the Septuagint, the concept of persecution is prevalent throughout the Old Testament. The writer of Hebrews listed many individuals who suffered persecution: Abel, at the hands of Cain; Joseph by his brothers; David by Saul. Elijah was forced to flee for his life (1 Kings 19 [LXX 3 Kings 19]), Jeremiah was dropped into a well (Jeremiah 38 [LXX 45]), Amos was driven out of the sanctuary (Amos 7), and Daniel was thrown to the lions (Daniel 6).

As a nation, Israel experienced persecution all during its existence but especially so during the period of the Maccabees (168 through 163 B.C.). Thousands of Jews emigrated to surrounding countries. Under the reign of Antiochus IV Epiphanes (175 through 163 B.C.) many Jews were murdered because they refused to participate in the idol worship of their captors.

New Testament Usage
In the New Testament *diōgmos* consistently means "religious persecution." Mark notes that *diōgmos* comes *dia ton logon*—"because of the word" (Mark 4:17; parallel Matthew 13:21). Likewise, in Acts *diōgmos* comes upon (*epi* [1894]) the Church (8:1) or individuals of the Church (13:50, Paul and Barnabas). The sense in Romans 8:35 might possibly be ambiguous except it is certain from other instances that Paul was referring to "persecution because of Christ" (2 Corinthians 12:10; 2 Timothy 3:11; cf. 2 Thessalonians 1:4). Thus *diōgmos* is virtually a technical term for "persecution" in the New Testament.

Persecution is a prevalent topic in the New Testament as well as in the Old. John the Baptist was thrown into prison and subsequently beheaded (Matthew 14:3f.). As a young child Jesus himself was threatened with persecution in all its intensity (Matthew 2). Throughout His ministry Jesus showed an awareness of His own demise (Matthew 17:12), and in the final months of His earthly life He discussed the subject frequently with His disciples. From the onset of His public ministry, Jesus suffered tremendous persecution which culminated in His violent death on the cross.

Before His death Jesus warned the disciples that they too would be persecuted if they continued to follow Him (Matthew 5:11f.; 10:16-25; John 15:18-21). He told them they would be hated (Matthew 24:9; John 16:2), mocked, and spoken evil of (Matthew 5:11), ill-treated (Matthew 24:9), brought into court (Matthew 10:17f.; Mark 13:9), excluded from the synagogues (John 16:2), and even murdered (Matthew 10:21; 23:34; 24:9). All of this would take place for Jesus' sake (Matthew 5:11; 24:9) and for the cause of righteousness (Matthew 5:10).

However, the Bible teaches that persecution should not cause the disciple of Jesus to lose courage. In fact, proof of genuine discipleship is patient endurance in times of persecution. The one whose commitment to Christ is shallow will stumble when persecution arises (Matthew 13:20f.). But by enduring persecution, the believer shows his spiritual relationship with past heroes of the faith (Matthew 5:12). He in turn shall receive a rich blessing (Matthew 5:11), and his reward in heaven will be great (Matthew 5:12). Therefore, the believer should not fear but should persevere, even to the point of praying for those who bring persecution (Matthew 5:44).

Shortly after its "birth," the church in Jerusalem met severe persecution. Repeated accusations by the apostles against the leaders of Israel that they had crucified Messiah (Acts 2:36; 3:13-15; 4:10-12; 5:30), along with the preaching of the Resurrection, caused great fury and opposition (Acts 4:2,17,18,21; 5:17f.). After Stephen was martyred (Acts 7:28), a storm of persecution arose which led to the dispersion of the Christian congregation into Judea and Samaria (Acts 8:1).

During the period of Paul's missionary activities Christianity met little or no organized persecution from the Roman officials. It was seen as a sect within Judaism, which was accepted in the Roman Empire. Persecution by government officials was more localized and personalized (i.e., toward individuals rather than toward a "movement").

This situation changed completely, however, during the reign of Nero (ca. 64 A.D.) and Domitian. State-sanctioned persecution increased as emperor worship became more developed. Eventually, emperors called themselves gods and saviors, terms which were blasphemous to Christians. As a result, they refused to obey the demands of the emperor cult. Disobedience by believers then resulted in their massive persecution.

The Scriptures teach that persecution is inevitable for the true follower of Jesus (2 Timothy 3:12). The anti-Christian principles of the world's system are bound to clash with the values and morality of God-fearing Christians. As evil men and wickedness increase, persecution will not lessen but will come to a climax during the reign of the Antichrist. For this reason the Book of Revelation is replete with descriptions involving the persecutions which are yet to come.

STRONG 1375, BAUER 201, LIDDELL-SCOTT 440, COLIN BROWN 2:805-6.

1370. διώκτης diōktēs noun

Persecutor.
CROSS-REFERENCE:
διώκω diōkō (1371)

1. διώκτην diōktēn acc sing masc
1 Who was before a blasphemer, and a **persecutor**,... 1 Tm 1:13

This term is used only in 1 Timothy 1:13 where Paul described himself as a "persecutor" of righteousness. The implied meaning is "to persecute in an active sense" including the idea of pursuit, pressing toward the work of persecuting. In secular use, records of a harsh ruler, Apollonius, refer to him as a "persecutor" who relentlessly abused slaves, subjecting them to ill-treatment and hard labor in stone quarries (*Moulton-Milligan*).

STRONG 1376, BAUER 201, MOULTON-MILLIGAN 166, LIDDELL-SCOTT 440.

1371. διώκω diōkō verb

Pursue, follow after, press forward, persecute.
COGNATES:
διωγμός diōgmos (1369)
διώκτης diōktēs (1370)
ἐκδιώκω ekdiōkō (1546)
καταδιώκω katadiōkō (2584C)

אָיַב 'āyav (342), Enemy (Ps 69:4 [68:4]—Codex Sinaiticus only).

בָּרַח bārach (1300), Flee, run away; hiphil: put to flight (1 Chr 12:15—Codex Sinaiticus only).

דָּהַר dāhar (1777), Gallop (Na 3:2).

דָּחַף dāchaph (1821), Hurry (Est 8:14—only some Sinaiticus texts).

הָלַךְ hālakh (2050), Go (Mi 2:10).

διώκω 1371

חָרַד chāradh (2829), Tremble; hiphil: make afraid (Is 17:2).

חָרֵד chārēdh (2830), Trembling (Ezr 9:4).

נָדַף nādhaph (5264), Drive away; niphal: pursue (Prv 21:6).

נוּס nûs (5308), Flee (Am 2:16).

רָדָה rādhâh (7575), Rule (Lv 26:17).

רָדַף rādhaph (7579), Qal: pursue (Ex 15:9); run (2 Kgs 5:21); persecute (Jer 17:18); niphal: be pursued (Lam 5:5); the past (Eccl 3:15); piel: pursue (Prv 12:11, Na 1:8); pual: be chased (Is 17:13); hiphil: pursue (Jgs 20:43).

רוּץ rûts (7608), Run (Hb 2:2); be busy (Hg 1:9).

שָׁדַד shādhadh (8161), Destroyer (Is 16:4).

שָׁפַט shāphaṭ (8570), Judge (Ps 109:31 [108:31]—only in some Sinaiticus texts).

1. **διώκω** diōkō 1sing indic pres act
2. **διώκεις** diōkeis 2sing indic pres act
3. **διώκωμεν** diōkōmen 1pl subj pres act
4. **διώκωσιν** diōkōsin 3pl subj pres act
5. **δίωκε** diōke 2sing impr pres act
6. **διώκετε** diōkete 2pl impr pres act
7. **διώκων** diōkōn nom sing masc part pres act
8. **διώκοντες** diōkontes nom pl masc part pres act
9. **διωκόντων** diōkontōn gen pl masc part pres act
10. **διώκοντας** diōkontas acc pl masc part pres act
11. **διώκοντα** diōkonta nom/acc pl neu part pres act
12. **ἐδίωξα** ediōxa 1sing indic aor act
13. **ἐδίωξεν** ediōxen 3sing indic aor act
14. **ἐδίωξαν** ediōxan 3pl indic aor act
15. **διώξητε** diōxēte 2pl subj aor act
16. **διώξωσιν** diōxōsin 3pl subj aor act
17. **διωξάτω** diōxatō 3sing impr aor act
18. **διώξετε** diōxete 2pl indic fut act
19. **διώξουσιν** diōxousin 3pl indic fut act
20. **ἐδίωκον** ediōkon 1/3sing/pl indic imperf act
21. **ἐδίωκεν** ediōken 3sing indic imperf act
22. **διώκομαι** diōkomai 1sing indic pres mid
23. **διώκωνται** diōkōntai 3pl subj pres mid
24. **διωκόμενοι** diōkomenoi nom pl masc part pres mid
25. **δεδιωγμένοι** dediōgmenoi nom pl masc part perf mid
26. **διωχθήσονται** diōchthēsontai 3pl indic fut pass
27. **διώκομεν** diōkomen 1pl indic pres act
28. **διώκονται** diōkontai 3pl indic pres mid

25	Blessed are they which **are persecuted**	Matt 5:10
16	when men shall revile you, and **persecute you**,	5:11
14	for so **persecuted** they the prophets ... before you.	5:12
9	which despitefully use you, and **persecute** you;	5:44
4	But when they **persecute** you in this city,	10:23
4	**persecute** you in this city, flee ye into another:	10:23
18	and **persecute** them from city to city:	23:34
19	will kill and some they will **persecute** (NASB)	Luke 11:49
15	or, see there: go not after them, nor **follow** them.	17:23
19	shall lay their hands on you, and **persecute** you,	21:12
20	And therefore did the Jews **persecute** Jesus,	John 5:16
14	If they have **persecuted** me,	15:20
19	they will also **persecute** you;	15:20
14	of the prophets **have not** your fathers **persecuted**?	Acts 7:52
2	Saul, Saul, why **persecutest** thou me?	9:4
2	the Lord said, I am Jesus whom thou **persecutest**:	9:5
12	And I **persecuted** this way unto the death,	22:4
2	Saul, Saul, why **persecutest** thou me?	22:7
2	I am Jesus of Nazareth, whom thou **persecutest**.	22:8
20	I **persecuted** them even unto strange cities.	26:11
2	Saul, Saul, why **persecutest** thou me?	26:14
2	And he said, I am Jesus whom thou **persecutest**.	26:15
11	Gentiles, which **followed** not after righteousness,	Rom 9:30
7	which **followed** after the law of righteousness,	9:31
8	**given** to hospitality.	12:13
10	Bless them which **persecute** you: bless,	12:14
3	**follow** after the things which **make** for peace,	14:19
27	**follow** after the things which **make** for peace,	14:19
24	**being persecuted**, we suffer it:	1 Co 4:12
6	**Follow** after charity, and desire spiritual gifts,	14:1
12	because I **persecuted** the church of God.	15:9
24	**Persecuted**, but not forsaken;	2 Co 4:9
20	beyond measure I **persecuted** the church of God,	Gal 1:23
7	That he which **persecuted** us in times past	1:23
21	**persecuted** him that was born after the Spirit,	4:29
22	why do I yet **suffer persecution**?	5:11
23	only lest they **should suffer persecution**	6:12
28	only lest they **should suffer persecution**	6:12
7	Concerning zeal, **persecuting** the church;	Phlp 3:6
1	Not ... already perfect: but I **follow after**,	3:12
1	I press toward the mark for the prize	3:14
6	but ever **follow** that which is good,	1 Th 5:15
5	flee these things; and **follow** after righteousness,	1 Tm 6:11
5	Flee also youthful lusts: but **follow** righteousness,	2 Tm 2:22
26	all that will live godly ... **shall suffer persecution**.	3:12
6	**Follow** peace with all men, and holiness,	Heb 12:14
17	let him seek peace, and **ensue** it.	1 Pt 3:11
13	was cast unto the earth, **he persecuted** the woman	Rev 12:13

Classical Greek and Septuagint Usage

In classical Greek *diōkō* means "to pursue after something, try to achieve something, run after, persecute." In the Septuagint *diōkō* is often used of pursuit by enemies (see Exodus 15:9; Psalms 7:1; 31:15 [LXX 30:15]; 35:3 [34:3]). *Diōkō* is also used in the Septuagint in the sense of pursuing a goal or something good (see Deuteronomy 16:20; Psalm 34:14 [LXX 33:14]; Proverbs 15:9). In this sense it is used to translate at least 13 different Hebrew verbs.

New Testament Usage

In the New Testament *diōkō* is most often used to mean "persecute." Persecution is a consistent theme in the New Testament. The prophets had been persecuted (Matthew 5:12). Jesus met with persecution (John 5:16; Acts 22:8). But perhaps most prevalent are the references to the followers of Jesus, members of His church (Matthew 5:10; Luke 21:12; John 15:20; Romans 12:14) who met with persecution.

Quite aside from persecution, *diōkō* is also used in the New Testament to express the quest of Christian values. Paul exhorted us to "follow after the things which make for peace, and things wherewith one may edify another" (Romans 14:19); and to "follow after righteousness, godliness, faith, love, patience, meekness" (1 Timothy 6:11). In this sense *diōkō* means "to aspire, to seek after something." Finally, *diōkō* is also used to mean "drive out" or "drive away" as in Matthew 23:34.

STRONG 1377, BAUER 201, MOULTON-MILLIGAN 166, KITTEL 2:229-30, LIDDELL-SCOTT 440, COLIN BROWN 2:805-6.

1372. δόγμα dogma noun
Decree, edict, ordinance.
COGNATE:
δογματίζω dogmatizō (1373)
SYNONYMS:
γνώμη gnōmē (1100)
διάταγμα diatagma (1291)
ἔνταλμα entalma (1762)
ἐντολή entolē (1769)
ἐπιταγή epitagē (1987)

דָּת dāth (1944), Edict (Est 9:1—only some Sinaiticus texts).

1. **δόγμα dogma** nom/acc sing neu
2. **δογμάτων dogmatōn** gen pl neu
3. **δόγμασιν dogmasin** dat pl neu
4. **δόγματα dogmata** nom/acc pl neu

1 that there went out a decree from Caesar Augustus, Luke 2:1
4 they delivered them the decrees for to keep, ... Acts 16:4
2 and these all do contrary to the decrees of Caesar, ... 17:7
3 law of commandments contained in ordinances; ...... Eph 2:15
3 the handwriting of ordinances that was against us, ... Col 2:14

Classical Greek
In classical Greek two meanings dominate the definition of *dogma*: a "decree or an ordinance" and a "doctrine or a dogma" (see *Bauer*). Also, the local assemblies made "resolutions" (*dogmata*) for governing the people. More formally, a *dogma* was a published official "decree" or "edict" (Kittel, "dogma," *Kittel*, 2:230ff.).

Septuagint Usage
Dogma occurs over 20 times in the Septuagint including the Apocrypha. "Decree" (royal) should be read at Esther 4:8; 9:1 (Hebrew, Aramaic *dāth*; cf. Daniel 6:13; 4 Maccabees 4:23,26). Perhaps the idea of "doctrines" (RSV, "traditions") is intended in 3 Maccabees 1:3; this is probably a reference to the Law.

New Testament Usage
Luke wrote of the imperial "decree" of Caesar Augustus that "the world should be taxed" (2:1; cf. Acts 17:7). But in Acts he recorded the *dogmata*, the "decisions" or "resolutions" that had been ratified by the Jerusalem Council (cf. 16:4). In Ephesians 2:15 *dogma* carries an even more heightened sense of an "authoritative decision" or "ordinance"; particularly here the legal ordinances of the Mosaic code are in mind. The use of the word in Colossians 2:14 may be a play upon legal demands of the Law which formerly indicted the believer.

STRONG 1378, BAUER 201, MOULTON-MILLIGAN 166, KITTEL 2:230-32, LIDDELL-SCOTT 441, COLIN BROWN 1:330-31.

1373. δογματίζω dogmatizō verb
Impose an ordinance, submit to a decree.
COGNATES:
δόγμα dogma (1372)
δοκέω dokeō (1374)

דָּת dāth (A1945), Decree (Dn 2:15—Aramaic).
כָּתַב kāthav (3918), Write; niphal: be decreed (Est 3:9).

1. **δογματίζεσθε dogmatizesthe** 2pl indic pres mid

1 living in the world, are ye subject to ordinances, ... Col 2:20

This term, from *dogma* (1372), "law, decree," implies submission to decrees ordained by governing human authority. Kittel asserts such ordinances to be matters of taste, touch, and other behavior-guiding legalities ("dogmatizō," *Kittel*, 2:230ff.). Its only New Testament occurrence is in Colossians 2:20. There it is used in a negative sense. Paul asked, "Wherefore if ye be dead with Christ from the rudiments of the world, why, as though living in the world, are ye *subject to ordinances*?"

STRONG 1379, BAUER 201, MOULTON-MILLIGAN 166, KITTEL 2:230-32, LIDDELL-SCOTT 441, COLIN BROWN 1:330.

1374. δοκέω dokeō verb
Think, seem, suppose, appear.
COGNATES:
δογματίζω dogmatizō (1373)
δοκιμάζω dokimazō (1375)
δοξάζω doxazō (1386)
εὐδοκέω eudokeō (2085)
παράδοξος paradoxos (3723)
SYNONYMS:
ἀναλογίζω analogizō (355)
βλέπω blepō (984)
βουλεύομαι bouleuomai (1003)
διαλογίζομαι dialogizomai (1254)
εἶδον eidon (1481)
ἐνθυμέομαι enthumeomai (1744)
ἐπιβλέπω epiblepō (1899)
ἔχω echō (2174)
ἡγέομαι hēgeomai (2216)
κατανοέω katanoeō (2627)
κρίνω krinō (2892)

δοκέω 1374

λογίζομαι logizomai (3023)
νοέω noeō (3401)
νομίζω nomizō (3406)
οἴομαι oiomai (3496)
συμβάλλω sumballō (4671)
συμβουλεύω sumbouleuō (4674)
ὑπολαμβάνω hupolambanō (5112)
ὑπονοέω huponoeō (5120)
φρονέω phroneō (5262)

אָמַר 'āmar (569), Say (Prv 28:24).

חָשַׁב chāshav (2913), Qal: think (Gn 38:15); niphal: be reckoned (Prv 27:14).

טוֹב tôv (3004), Be pleasing (Est 1:19, 3:9, 5:4, 8:5).

יָשַׁר yāshar (3595), Be pleasing (Jer 27:5 [34:5]).

נָדַב nādhav (5246), Prompt (Ex 25:2, 35:21).

נָדִיב nādhîv (5259), Willing (Ex 35:22).

נָשָׂא nāsâ' (5558), Lift, carry; stir (Ex 35:26).

1. **δοκεῖτε** dokeite 2pl indic/impr pres act
2. **δοκοῦσιν** dokousin dat pl masc indic/part pres act
3. **δοκῶ** dokō 1sing indic pres act
4. **δοκεῖς** dokeis 2sing indic pres act
5. **δοκεῖ** dokei 3sing indic pres act
6. **δοκοῦμεν** dokoumen 1pl indic pres act
7. **δοκῇ** dokē 3sing subj pres act
8. **δοκῶν** dokōn nom sing masc part pres act
9. **δοκοῦντες** dokountes nom pl masc part pres act
10. **δοκούντων** dokountōn gen pl masc part pres act
11. **δοκοῦσα** dokousa nom sing fem part pres act
12. **δοκοῦν** dokoun nom/acc sing neu part pres act
13. **δοκοῦντα** dokounta nom/acc pl neu part pres act
14. **δοκεῖν** dokein inf pres act
15. **ἔδοξα** edoxa 1sing indic aor act
16. **ἔδοξεν** edoxen 3sing indic aor act
17. **ἔδοξαν** edoxan 3pl indic aor act
18. **δόξω** doxō 1sing subj aor act
19. **δόξῃ** doxē 3sing subj aor act
20. **δόξητε** doxēte 2pl subj aor act
21. **δόξαντες** doxantes nom pl masc part aor act
22. **ἐδόκει** edokei 3sing indic imperf act
23. **ἐδόκουν** edokoun 3pl indic imperf act
24. **ἔδοξε** edoxe 3sing indic aor act

20	And **think** not to say within yourselves,......	Matt 3:9
2	for they **think** ... be heard for their much speaking.....	6:7
5	Jesus ... saying, What **thinkest** thou, Simon?..........	17:25
5	How **think** ye? if a man have an hundred sheep,......	18:12
5	But what **think** ye? A certain man had two sons;.....	21:28
5	Tell us therefore, What **thinkest** thou?..............	22:17
5	What **think** ye of Christ? whose son is he?..........	22:42
1	an hour as ye **think** not the Son of man cometh....	24:44
4	**Thinkest** thou that I cannot now pray to my Father,..	26:53
5	What **think** ye? They answered and said,.............	26:66
17	they **supposed** it had been a spirit, and cried out:..	Mark 6:49
9	they which **are accounted** to rule over the Gentiles...	10:42
16	It **seemed good** to me also, having had perfect.....	Luke 1:3
5	shall be taken even that which he **seemeth** to have.....	8:18
5	Which now of these three, **thinkest** thou,.............	10:36
1	Son of man cometh at an hour when ye **think** not....	12:40
1	**Suppose** ye that I am come to give peace on earth?..	12:51
1	**Suppose** ye that these Galilaeans were sinners........	13:2
1	**think** ye that they were sinners above all men........	13:4
3	Doth he thank that servant ... I **trow** not........	Luke 17:9
14	and because they **thought** that the kingdom of God...	19:11
5	which of them **should be accounted** the greatest.......	22:24
23	and **supposed** that they had seen a spirit...........	24:37
1	for in them ye **think** ye have eternal life:..........	John 5:39
1	Do not **think** that I will accuse you to the Father:.....	5:45
17	but they **thought** that he had spoken of ... rest.......	11:13
21	**supposing** that she was going to the tomb (NASB)...	11:31
5	What **think** ye, that he will not come to the feast?....	11:56
23	For some of them **thought**,.........................	13:29
19	killeth you **will think** that he doeth God service.......	16:2
11	She, **supposing** him to be the gardener,..............	20:15
22	but **thought** he saw a vision....................Acts	12:9
16	Then **pleased** it the apostles and elders,..............	15:22
16	It **seemed** good unto us,.............................	15:25
16	For it **seemed** good to the Holy Ghost, and to us,.....	15:28
16	Notwithstanding it **pleased** Silas to abide there still....	15:34
5	He **seemeth** to be a setter forth of strange gods:.....	17:18
5	it **seemeth** to me unreasonable to send a prisoner,....	25:27
15	I verily **thought** with myself,........................	26:9
21	**supposing** that they had obtained their purpose,.....	27:13
5	If any man among you **seemeth** to be wise..........I Co	3:18
3	I **think** that God hath set forth us the apostles last,....	4:9
3	and I **think** also that I have the Spirit of God.........	7:40
5	And if any man **think** that he knoweth any thing,......	8:2
8	that **thinketh** he standeth take heed lest he fall......	10:12
5	But if any man **seem** to be contentious,...............	11:16
13	those members ... which **seem** to be more feeble,....	12:22
6	members ... which we **think** to be less honourable,....	12:23
5	If any man **think** himself to be a prophet,............	14:37
18	I may not **seem** as if I would terrify you by letters.2 Co	10:9
19	I say again, Let no man **think** me a fool;.............	11:16
1	Again, **think** ye that we excuse ourselves unto you? ...	12:19
2	but privately to them **which were of reputation**,......Gal	2:2
10	But of these **who seemed** to be somewhat,..............	2:6
9	for they who **seemed** to be somewhat.................	2:6
9	Cephas, and John, who **seemed** to be pillars,..........	2:9
5	For if a man **think** himself to be something,..........	6:3
5	If any other man **thinketh** that he hath whereof....Phlp	3:4
19	believed on in the world, received up into **glory**....1 Tm	3:16
7	any of you **should seem** to come short of it.........Heb	4:1
1	Of how much sorer punishment, **suppose** ye,...........	10:29
12	a few days chastened us after their own **pleasure**;.....	12:10
5	no chastening for the present **seemeth** to be joyous,...	12:11
5	If any man among you **seem** to be religious,........Jas	1:26
1	Do ye **think** that the scripture saith in vain,...........	4:5

Classical Greek

There are two basic functions of *dokeō* in classical Greek, and these largely continued to dominate throughout the early history of the term. First, *dokeō* is used with an object (transitive use); thus: "I think (that ...)" or "I believe (something)." Second, *dokeō* is used without an object (intransitive use); thus: "It seems (to me)," "to be supposed." Sometimes in this usage *dokeō* was contrasted with reality—the supposed versus the real. Such an antithesis marked its role in the language of ethics (Kittel, "dokeō," *Kittel*, 2:232ff.).

Septuagint Usage

The imprecise character of *dokeō* as well as its subjective nature made it highly difficult to find direct Hebrew equivalents. In the Septuagint *dokeō* translates 8 Hebrew words in only 17 instances with Hebrew originals. Many Hebrew texts have no counterpart to the Greek (e.g., Proverbs 14:12; 16:25; 17:28; 26:12).

Other texts have doubtful correspondence (e.g., Job 15:21; 20:7,22). The intransitive use predominates in the Septuagint (e.g., Genesis 38:15; Exodus 25:2; Esther 1:19; 3:9).

New Testament Usage
The New Testament usage accords with the classical pattern. *Dokeō* is employed transitively: "... for they think (*dokousin*) that they shall be heard for their much speaking" (Matthew 6:7; with *hoti* [3617]; see also Matthew 26:53; Mark 6:49; 2 Corinthians 12:19; James 4:5); or, "Think not to say within yourselves, We have Abraham" (Matthew 3:9; cf. Luke 24:37; John 5:39; 1 Corinthians 3:18; 7:40).

Intransitively *dokeō* can mean "to seem, to appear." Jesus asked Peter, "What thinkest thou, Simon?" (Matthew 17:25). Here Peter was asked to subjectively interpret his own thoughts and feelings (cf. Matthew 18:12; 21:28; 22:17,42; see Luke 10:36). A second intransitive usage meaning "be influential, be recognized as being something" (see *Bauer*) also occurs (cf. Mark 10:42: "those who are *regarded* as rulers ... " [NIV]; see also Galatians 2:2,6).

STRONG 1380, BAUER 201-2, MOULTON-MILLIGAN 166-67, KITTEL 2:232-33, LIDDELL-SCOTT 441-42, COLIN BROWN 3:821-22.

1375. δοκιμάζω dokimazō verb

To try, scrutinize, prove, test, examine.

COGNATES:
ἀδόκιμος adokimos (95)
ἀποδοκιμάζω apodokimazō (588)
δοκέω dokeō (1374)
δοκιμασία dokimasia (1375B)
δοκιμή dokimē (1376)
δοκίμιον dokimion (1377)
δόκιμος dokimos (1378)

SYNONYMS:
ἀνακρίνω anakrinō (348)
πειράζω peirazō (3847)

בָּחַן bāchan (1010), Test (Jb 34:3, Pss 17:3 [16:3], 66:10 [65:10]).

בָּחַר bāchar (1013), Choose; niphal: be tested, be selected (Prv 8:10).

חָקַר chāqar (2811), Spy out, try, taste (Ps 139:1,23 [138:1,23]).

יָקַר yāqar (3478), Be valued (Zec 11:13).

מַצְרֵף matsrēph (4876), Crucible (Prv 17:3).

צָרַף tsāraph (7170), Test (Jgs 7:4—Codex Alexandrinus only).

1. **δοκιμάζετε** dokimazete 2pl indic/impr pres act
2. **δοκιμάζεις** dokimazeis 2sing indic pres act
3. **δοκιμάζει** dokimazei 3sing indic pres act
4. **δοκιμαζέτω** dokimazetō 3sing impr pres act
5. **δοκιμάζων** dokimazōn
    nom sing masc part pres act
6. **δοκιμάζοντι** dokimazonti
    dat sing masc part pres act
7. **δοκιμάζοντες** dokimazontes
    nom pl masc part pres act
8. **δοκιμάζειν** dokimazein inf pres act
9. **ἐδοκιμάσαμεν** edokimasamen 1pl indic aor act
10. **ἐδοκίμασαν** edokimasan 3pl indic aor act
11. **δοκιμάσητε** dokimasēte 2pl subj aor act
12. **δοκιμάσαι** dokimasai inf aor act
13. **δοκιμάσει** dokimasei 3sing indic fut act
14. **δοκιμαζέσθωσαν** dokimazesthōsan
    3pl impr pres mid
15. **δοκιμαζομένου** dokimazomenou
    gen sing neu part pres mid
16. **δεδοκιμάσμεθα** dedokimasmetha
    1pl indic perf mid

```
8  ye can discern the face of the sky and of the earth;Luke 12:56
1  but how is it that ye do not discern this time?........ 12:56
8  but how is it that ye do not discern this time?........ 12:56
12 I go to prove them: I pray thee have me excused..... 14:19
10 they did not like to retain God in their knowledge, Rom 1:28
2  and approvest the things that are more excellent,...... 2:18
8  that ye may prove what is that good,................ 12:2
3  condemneth not himself in that ... he alloweth........ 14:22
13 fire shall try every man's work of what sort it is....1 Co 3:13
4  But let a man examine himself,...................... 11:28
11 whomsoever ye shall approve by your letters,......... 16:3
5  and to prove the sincerity of your love............. 2 Co 8:8
9  we have oftentimes proved diligent in many things,.... 8:22
1  whether ye be in the faith; prove your own selves..... 13:5
4  But let every man prove his own work,................ Gal 6:4
7  Proving what is acceptable unto the Lord........... Eph 5:10
8  That ye may approve things that are excellent;..... Phlp 1:10
16 But as we were allowed of God to be put in trust..1 Th 2:4
6  as pleasing men, but God, which trieth our hearts..... 2:4
1  Prove all things; hold fast that which is good.......... 5:21
14 And let these also first be proved;................. 1 Tm 3:10
10 proved me, and saw my works forty years.......... Heb 3:9
15 of gold that perisheth, though it be tried with fire,..1 Pt 1:7
1  but try the spirits whether they are of God:........1 Jn 4:1
```

Classical Greek

In classical Greek the term was used for "testing" the genuineness of metals and coins. Furthermore, persons could be "put to the test" or "scrutinized." And if this tested person were "approved" *dokimazō* could also describe that state of acceptance.

Septuagint Usage

The Septuagint authors understood *dokimazō* in reference to the testing of precious metals (Proverbs 8:10; 17:3; Zechariah 13:9); of people (Judges 7:4; Psalms 66:10 [LXX 65:10]; 139:1 [138:1]); of other objects (the ear "tests" words; Job 34:3); of the heart by the Lord (Psalms 17:3 [LXX 16:3]; 26:2 [25:2]); and of the Lord by people (Psalms 81:7 [LXX 80:7]; 95:9 [94:9]).

δοκιμασία 1375B

New Testament Usage

Probably influenced by the Septuagint, the New Testament understands *dokimazō* as the testing process which salvages the good and discards the useless. Whereas *peirazō* (3847) often means "to try" in the sense of "to tempt to sin," the intent of *dokimazō* is primarily to eliminate the dross and recover the valuable or genuine remains. That which has endured this process or trial is then "accepted" or "approved." These are *dokimos* (1378), the opposite of *adokimos* (95) ("a castaway," KJV; "disqualified," RSV, Phillips; "rejected" NEB, TEV; in 1 Corinthians 9:27).

The Lord must be behind any valid trial. Paul expressed it thus: "For not he that commendeth himself is approved (*dokimos*), but whom the Lord commendeth" (2 Corinthians 10:18). But this does not exclude our own duty to "examine" ourselves (2 Corinthians 13:5; 1 Corinthians 11:28) and to "examine" God's will and plan and purpose for His church (Romans 12:2; Ephesians 5:10; Philippians 1:10). The final judgment will determine whether the believer's lives and service pass the test (1 Corinthians 3:13).

STRONG 1381, BAUER 202, MOULTON-MILLIGAN 167, KITTEL 2:255-60, LIDDELL-SCOTT 442, COLIN BROWN 3:808-10.

1375B. δοκιμασία dokimasia noun

Act of testing, proving.

CROSS-REFERENCE:
δοκιμάζω dokimazō (1375)

1. δοκιμασίᾳ dokimasia dat sing fem

1 proved me, and saw my works forty years.......... Heb 3:9

As a variant to the traditional text (i.e., *Textus Receptus*) this term is used once in the New Testament at Hebrews 3:9. *Liddell-Scott* reports that *dokimasia* was used "of magistrates after election, to see if they fulfilled the legal requirements of legitimacy." The passage in Hebrews says that Israel's fathers tempted God by "proving" Him in the wilderness. Verse 10 states that their testing "grieved" (angered) God.

BAUER 202, MOULTON-MILLIGAN 167, KITTEL 2:255-60, LIDDELL-SCOTT 442, COLIN BROWN 3:808.

1376. δοκιμή dokimē noun

Test, ordeal, trial, approved character, proof.

CROSS-REFERENCE:
δοκιμάζω dokimazō (1375)

1. δοκιμή dokimē nom sing fem
2. δοκιμῆς dokimēs gen sing fem
3. δοκιμῇ dokimē dat sing fem
4. δοκιμήν dokimēn acc sing fem

4 And patience, experience; and experience, hope:....	Rom 5:4
1 And patience, experience; and experience, hope:........	5:4
4 that I might know the proof of you,.................	2 Co 2:9
3 How that in a great trial of affliction.................	8:2
2 Whiles by the experiment of this ministration...........	9:13
4 Since ye seek a proof of Christ speaking in me,........	13:3
4 But ye know the proof of him,.....................	Phlp 2:22

Classical Greek and Septuagint Usage

The noun *dokimē*—"the quality of being approved," "a test" or "proof"—is not found in classical Greek and is a rare word in Hellenistic Greek. It was actually a new formation of the Hellenistic period, perhaps being derived from the verb *dokimazō* (1375) (*Moulton-Milligan*; see also *Bauer*). It occurs only once in a textual variant in the Septuagint (Psalm 68:31 [LXX 67:31]).

New Testament Usage

Paul alone used *dokimē* in the New Testament (six times). *Dokimē* should be understood in its sense of "character" or an "approved" (state) in Romans 5:4; 2 Corinthians 2:9; 9:13; and Philippians 2:22. Paul proclaimed in a famous crescendo of encouragement: "Suffering produces endurance, (*hupomonē* [5119]) and endurance produces character (*dokimē*), and character produces hope" (Romans 5:3,4; RSV). Likewise, 2 Corinthians 2:9 and 9:13 carry the implication that *dokimē* results from testing. Furthermore, Paul endorsed Timothy to the Philippians because he had "proved himself" (Philippians 2:22, NIV) in the service of the gospel.

The less abstract concept of *dokimē* as "a test," "authentication," or "proof of genuineness" occurs in 2 Corinthians 13:3. Paul advised the agitators in Corinth that he would indeed give them "proof" of his authority as spokesman for Christ. The "proof" they would receive, however, would not be what they wanted, for Paul promised to prove his authority by "not (sparing) those who sinned earlier or any of the others" (2 Corinthians 13:2, NIV).

STRONG 1382, BAUER 202, MOULTON-MILLIGAN 167, KITTEL 2:255-60, LIDDELL-SCOTT 442, COLIN BROWN 3:808-9.

1377. δοκίμιον dokimion noun

Testing, genuineness, sterling quality.

CROSS-REFERENCE:
δοκιμάζω dokimazō (1375)

זָקַק zāqaq (2298), Wash, strain; pual: refined (1 Chr 29:4).

יְקָר yeqār (3480), Preciousness; high (Zec 11:13—only some Sinaiticus texts).

מַצְרֵף matsrēph (4876), Crucible (Prv 27:21).

עֲלִיל ʿălîl (6172), Furnace (Ps 12:6 [11:6]).

1. δοκίμιον dokimion nom/acc sing neu

1 that the **trying** of your faith worketh patience.........Jas 1:3
1 That the **trial** of your faith,......................1 Pt 1:7

Classical Greek
Dokimion (or *dokimeion*) is a term of some small controversy. Two basic definitions are usually presented: (1) a "testing" or a "means of testing"; or (2) "something tested," hence, "genuine" (as a neuter adjective of *dokimos* [1378]). The distinction is subtle but nonetheless important.

Since *dokimion* occurs only twice in the New Testament and is virtually absent from literary Greek, evidence from the papyri and the Septuagint are invaluable for understanding the texts of James 1:3 and 1 Peter 1:7.

Septuagint Usage
Evidence from the Septuagint (1 Chronicles 29:4; Psalm 12:6 [LXX 11:6]; Proverbs 27:21; Zechariah 11:13) reveals the relationship between metal (especially silver and gold) that had been refined and the word *dokimion*. Papyri confirm this association (see *Moulton-Milligan*). Therefore, when used adjectivally it means "pure" or "tested."

New Testament Usage
Most problematic is James 1:3. Many versions understand James 1:3 to mean that the "testing" (*to dokimion*) of one's faith produces "patience" (*hupomonē* [5119]) (see e.g., KJV, RSV, NEB, NIV). These versions have undoubtedly been influenced by Romans 5:4 which clearly indicates that *hupomonē* produces *dokimē*, which, in turn, produces hope. But Turner raises this question of James 1:3, "Is patience produced by the tested faith itself or by the actual testing of faith?" (*Grammatical Insights*, pp.168ff.).

The context of refining metals in 1 Peter 1:7 easily allows for the "something tested" understanding. If the same understanding were applied to James 1:3 one might read: "Your genuine faith brings about endurance" or, "Tested faith produces perseverance." Thus, evidence seems to favor that *to dokimion* is actually a neuter adjective of *dokimos*; as such, it means "that which is tested, pure, genuine." From this perspective one should reevaluate many translations of James 1:3.

STRONG 1383, BAUER 203, KITTEL 2:255-60, LIDDELL-SCOTT 442, COLIN BROWN 3:808-9.

1378. δόκιμος dokimos adj
Approved, acceptable, tried.
CROSS-REFERENCE:
δοκιμάζω dokimazō (1375)

זָקַק zāqaq (2298), Wash, strain; pual: refined (1 Chr 28:18).

טָהוֹר ṭāhôr (2999), Pure (2 Chr 9:17).

יְקָר yeqār (3480), Preciousness; high (Zec 11:13).

עָבַר ʿāvar (5882), Current (Gn 23:16).

פָּזַז pāzaz (6581), Hophal: overlaid with gold (1 Kgs 10:18).

1. δόκιμος dokimos nom sing masc
2. δόκιμον dokimon acc sing masc
3. δόκιμοι dokimoi nom pl masc

1 is acceptable to God, and **approved** of men.........Rom 14:18
2 Salute Apelles **approved** in Christ......................16:10
3 they which are **approved** may be made manifest....1 Co 11:19
1 For not he that commendeth himself is **approved**,..2 Co 10:18
3 not that we should appear **approved**,..................13:7
2 Study to show thyself **approved** unto God,..........2 Tm 2:15
1 when he is tried, he shall receive the crown of life,...Jas 1:12

Classical Greek
Dokimos is a companion term of *dokimē* (1376), *dokimazō* (1375), *dokimion* (1377), *dokimasia* (1375B), and other compounds of the same word group. Properly speaking, in antiquity the entire group recalls a refining process of metal; hence, metal (especially silver or gold) that is *dokimos* is "tested." The implication is that having been "tested" the metal is now "approved, pure, genuine." The term became easily applied to individuals whose characters were "esteemed, approved" or of "quality" (e.g., Philo; Josephus *Against Apion* 1.3).

Septuagint Usage
Consistently in the Septuagint *dokimos* is associated with precious metals (gold and silver), and it translates some five different Hebrew words in its six appearances. It describes the silver Abraham paid Ephron the Hittite. Literally the text says that he weighed out "four hundred 'didrachma' (all together about 10 pounds) of silver *approved* by merchants" (cf. 1 Kings 10:18 [LXX 3 Kings 10:18], "fine gold"; 1 Chronicles 28:18, "refined gold"; 1 Chronicles 29:4, "refined silver"; and so on). The figurative

use of *dokimos* as applied to individuals was foreign to the Septuagint writers.

New Testament Usage
By the New Testament period the trend had shifted to an exclusively figurative, religious function. Notwithstanding, 1 Peter 1:7 reveals that the imagery behind the term was realized.

Paul called upon *dokimos* more than any other writer, and, in fact, six of its seven instances may be ascribed to Paul (Romans 14:18; 16:10; 1 Corinthians 11:19; 2 Corinthians 10:18; 13:7; 2 Timothy 2:15). The only other occurrence is attributed to James (1:12).

At the heart of Paul's understanding of *dokimos*, "approved, tested," lies the Old Testament principle that God tests and judges those He loves. Salvation calls for conduct that attests to it, especially in the face of adversity and trial. The individual who has successfully endured testing is thus *dokimos* (see Romans 5:3f.). This "approval, certification, authentication," or whatever one wishes to call it, can only be established through testing by "God, who tests (*dokimazō*) our hearts" (1 Thessalonians 2:4, NIV). Paul considered his being entrusted with the gospel to be a result of testing (*dedokimasmetha hupo tou theou*, 1 Thessalonians 2:4) that proved him able to bear the weight of responsibility.

On one hand, one cannot declare himself "attested, approved," or "proven". Only God—as Judge—has that prerogative (2 Corinthians 10:18). On the other hand, Paul urged Timothy to "present yourself to God as one *approved* (judgment language), a workman who has no need to be ashamed, rightly handling the word of truth" (2 Timothy 2:15, RSV). Having been approved by God, believers will be rewarded with the "crown of life" (James 1:12).

STRONG 1384, BAUER 203, MOULTON-MILLIGAN 168, KITTEL 2:255-60, LIDDELL-SCOTT 442, COLIN BROWN 3:808.

1379. δοκός dokos noun
Beam of wood, log, or joist.

מְחַבְּרוֹת mᵉchabbᵉrôth (4360), Couplings (2 Chr 34:11).

סִפֻּן sippun (5803), Ceiling (1 Kgs 6:15).

קוֹרָה qôrāh (7264), Beam (2 Kgs 6:2).

קִיר qîr (7306), Ceiling (1 Kgs 6:16).

1. δοκός dokos nom sing fem
2. δοκόν dokon acc sing fem

2	considerest not the **beam** that is in thine own eye?... Matt 7:3
1	and, behold, a **beam** is in thine own eye?............. 7:4
2	first cast out the **beam** out of thine own eye;........... 7:5
2	perceivest not the **beam** that is in thine own eye?... Luke 6:41
2	when thou thyself beholdest not the **beam** that is....... 6:42
2	cast out first the **beam** out of thine own eye,........... 6:42

This word appears in the Synoptic accounts of Christ's analogy of judging and removing objects from one's vision (Matthew 7:3ff.; Luke 6:41ff.). Extra-Biblical references commonly indicate that this word is generally used to indicate very large beams of wood suitable to provide heavy foundational support for large buildings and construction needs.

STRONG 1385, BAUER 203, MOULTON-MILLIGAN 168, LIDDELL-SCOTT 443.

1380. δόλιος dolios adj
Deceitful, treacherous.

CROSS-REFERENCE:
δολόω doloō (1383)

דָּלַק dālaq (1875), Burn (Prv 26:23—Codex Sinaiticus only).

חֶלְקָה chelqāh (2613), Flattering (Ps 12:2,3 [11:2,3]).

מִרְמָה mirmāh (4983), Deceit (Ps 17:1 [16:1], Jer 9:8).

עַוְלָה 'awlāh (5983), Unjust (Ps 43:1 [42:1]).

רְמִיָּה rᵉmîyāh (7711), Deceit (Ps 120:2,3 [119:2,3], Prv 12:24,27).

שֶׁקֶר sheqer (8632), Contempt (Ps 31:18 [30:18]); lie (Ps 109:2 [108:2]).

תַּרְמִית tarmîth (8988), Deceit (Zep 3:13).

1. δόλιοι dolioi nom pl masc

1	For such are false apostles, **deceitful** workers,...... 2 Co 11:13

From a root word implying trickery or a decoy, a false representation, this word communicates deceitful intent with destructive motives. In the New Testament it is used only in 2 Corinthians in a description of "false apostles, *deceitful* workers" who were representing themselves as "apostles of Christ."

STRONG 1386, BAUER 203, MOULTON-MILLIGAN 168, LIDDELL-SCOTT 443.

1381. δολιόω dolioō verb
Deceive, lie.

CROSS-REFERENCE:
δολόω doloō (1383)

חָלַק chālaq (2606), Be false, smooth; hiphil: flatter (Ps 5:9).

נָכַל nākhal (5417), Act deceitfully; piel: be hostile (Nm 25:18); hithpael: deal subtly (Ps 105:25 [104:25]).

1. ἐδολιοῦσαν edoliousan 3pl indic imperf act

1 with their tongues they **have used deceit**;............ Rom 3:13

Dolioō has a cognate noun form *dolos* (1382) which bears a literal meaning of "bait" or "snare" and the related metaphoric meaning "deceit." In the New Testament it is used once, in Romans 3:13. There Paul quoted Psalm 5:9 as part of his description of the sinful condition of mankind: "their tongues *practice deceit*" (NIV).

STRONG 1387, BAUER 203, LIDDELL-SCOTT 443.

1382. δόλος dolos noun

Deceit, fraud, craftiness, treachery.

COGNATE:
δολόω doloō (1383)
SYNONYM:
ἀπάτη apatē (535)

דָּבָר dāvār (1745), Word, matter, thing (2 Sm 14:20—Codex Vaticanus only).

חָנֵף chānēph (2715), Godless (Jb 13:16).

מִלָּה millāh (4543), Word, utterance (Ps 139:4 [138:4]—only in some Sinaiticus texts).

מִרְמָה mirmāh (4983), Fraud, deceit, betrayal, disappointment (Gn 27:35, Ps 24:4 [23:4], Mi 6:11).

מַשָּׁאוֹן mashshā'ôn (5046), Deception (Prv 26:26).

סֵתֶר sēther (5848), Hiding place, secrecy (Dt 27:24).

עָרְמָה 'ormāh (6430), Cunning (Ex 21:14).

רָכִיל rākhîl (7689), Slanderer (Lv 19:16).

רְמִיָּה remîyāh (7711), Slackness, looseness, deceit (Jb 13:7, Ps 52:2 [51:2]).

רַעַשׁ ra'ash (7783), Quaking, roar, clatter, commotion (Is 9:5).

תֹּךְ tōkh (8826), Oppression, oppressor, extortioner (Ps 10:7 [9:28]).

1. δόλος dolos nom sing masc
2. δόλου dolou gen sing masc
3. δόλῳ dolō dat sing masc
4. δόλον dolon acc sing masc

3 consulted that they might take Jesus by **subtlety**,... Matt 26:4
1 Thefts, covetousness, wickedness, **deceit**,......... Mark 7:22
3 scribes sought how they might take him by **craft**,...... 14:1
1 Behold an Israelite indeed, in whom is no **guile**!... John 1:47
2 And said, O full of all **subtlety** and all mischief,.... Acts 13:10
2 full of envy, murder, debate, **deceit**, malignity;...... Rom 1:29
3 nevertheless, being crafty, I caught you with **guile**...2 Co 12:16
3 was not of **deceit**, nor of uncleanness, nor in guile:... 1 Th 2:3
4 Wherefore laying aside all malice, and all **guile**,..... 1 Pt 2:1
1 neither was **guile** found in his mouth:................ 2:22
4 and his lips that they speak no **guile**:............... 1 Pt 3:10
1 And in their mouth was found no **guile**:........... Rev 14:5

Classical Greek

Properly *dolos* is a "bait" for fish; from that it can refer to any "trickery" or "deception." The Trojan horse is a classic example of *dolos* (see *Liddell-Scott*). Early (Second Century B.C.) inscriptions link *dolos* to *ponēros* (4050), "wickedness." Papyri of the Third Century A.D. speak of "tainted" silver and gold (see *Moulton-Milligan*).

Septuagint Usage

The versatility of *dolos* is substantiated most plainly by the Septuagint where *dolos* translates 11 Hebrew expressions, most regularly *mirmāh* ("fraud, deceit"). Jacob's act of "deceit" (one meaning of the name Jacob is "supplanter") resulted in his receiving Isaac's blessing which was intended for Esau (Genesis 27:35ff.). Any "treacherous act" of murder deserved death according to the legal code of Israel (Exodus 21:14, Hebrew *'ormāh*). See also Psalms 10:7 (LXX 9:27); 24:4 (23:4); 32:2 (31:2); 34:13 (33:13); 36:3 (35:3) which refer to verbal "deceit" or "falsehood" (cf. 1 Maccabees 1:30; 7:10,27, of pretended words of peace).

New Testament Usage

Dolos appears 12 times in the New Testament. It marks the plotting of the religious leaders to arrest and kill Jesus in Matthew 26:4 (parallel Mark 14:1). *Dolos* indicates extreme wickedness; often it appears in conjunction with other heinous sins (e.g., Mark 7:22; Romans 1:29; 1 Peter 2:1). Paul was accused of "guile" by the Corinthians (2 Corinthians 12:16), but he insisted otherwise (cf. 2 Corinthians 4:2). Jesus' character is precisely the opposite of deceitfulness. He operated on the basis of honesty (John 1:47; 1 Peter 2:22).

STRONG 1388, BAUER 203, MOULTON-MILLIGAN 168, LIDDELL-SCOTT 443.

1383. δολόω doloō verb

Falsify, adulterate, corrupt.

COGNATES:
ἄδολος adolos (96)
δόλιος dolios (1380)
δολιόω dolioō (1381)
δόλος dolos (1382)

חָלַק chālaq (2606), Be smooth, slippery, false; hiphil: beat smooth, flatter (Ps 36:2 [35:2]).

רָגַל rāghal (7558), Slander, gossip (Ps 15:3 [14:3]).

δόμα 1384

1. δολοῦντες dolountes nom pl masc part pres act
1 nor **handling** the word of God **deceitfully;** .... 2 Co 4:2

Used only in 2 Corinthians 4:2, *doloō* is variously translated "adulterating," "handling deceitfully," or "to distort." In essence the word means "to falsify by presenting a distorted mixture of truth and falsehood." The intent of such deception is progressive—first to ensnare, then to corrupt.

STRONG 1389, BAUER 203, MOULTON-MILLIGAN 168, LIDDELL-SCOTT 443.

1384. δόμα doma noun
Gift.
COGNATE:
δῶρον dōron (1428)
SYNONYMS:
δόσις dosis (1388)
δωρεά dōrea (1424)
δώρημα dōrēma (1427)
δῶρον dōron (1428)
κορβᾶν korban (2850)
χάρις charis (5320B)
χάρισμα charisma (5321)

אֶתְנַן 'ethnan (900), Harlot's wages (Hos 9:1).
גְּמוּל gᵉmûl (1618), Repayment (Prv 19:17).
מִגְדָּנוֹת mighdānôth (4169), Gifts (2 Chr 32:23).
מֹהַר mōhar (4258), Dowry (1 Sm 18:25).
מַשָּׂא massā' (5014), Tribute (2 Chr 17:11).
מַתָּן mattān (5150), Gift (Prv 18:16).
מַתָּנָה mattānāh (5153), Gift (Gn 25:6, Nm 18:6, Ez 20:31).
מַתְּנָה mattᵉnāh (A5154), Gift (Dn 2:6—Aramaic).
מַתַּת mattath (5164), Gift (1 Kgs 13:7).
נְדָבָה nᵉdhāvāh (5249), Something voluntary (Dt 23:23); freewill offering (2 Chr 31:14).
נָשָׂא nāsā' (5558), Lift, take; niphal: be taken (2 Sm 19:42).
נָתַן nāthan (5598), Give (Nm 27:7 [27:6], Eccl 5:1 [4:17]).
תְּנוּפָה tᵉnûphāh (8901), Wave offering (Lv 7:30 [7:20]).

1. δόμα doma nom/acc sing neu
2. δόματα domata nom/acc pl neu

2 know how to give good **gifts** unto your children, ... Matt 7:11
2 know how to give good **gifts** unto your children: ... Luke 11:13
2 he led captivity captive, and gave **gifts** unto men..... Eph 4:8
1 Not because I desire a **gift**: but I desire fruit .... Phlp 4:17

Related to the verb *didōmi* (1319), "to give," the emphasis of this noun is upon the concrete nature of what has been given, i.e., the gift itself. It appears over 30 times in the Septuagint, translating 10 different Hebrew words. Most often it translates a form of *mattān*, generally "gift" with the implication that it is an appropriate gift for a specific reason or occasion (see Genesis 25:6; 47:22; Exodus 28:38 [LXX 28:34]; Numbers 3:9; Psalm 68:18 [67:18]; Ezekiel 46:5,16,17; Hosea 9:1). It is found in only four New Testament passages: Matthew 7:11; Luke 11:13; Ephesians 4:8; Philippians 4:17. The more common words for "gift" are *dōrea* (1424) and *dōron* (1428).

STRONG 1390, BAUER 203, MOULTON-MILLIGAN 168, LIDDELL-SCOTT 444.

1385. δόξα doxa noun
Glory, splendor, radiance, fame, renown, honor.
CROSS-REFERENCE:
δοξάζω doxazō (1386)

אוֹן 'ôn (202), Power (Is 40:26).
בָּשָׂר bāsār (1340), Flesh (Is 17:4).
גָּאוֹן gā'ôn (1377), Majesty (Ex 15:7, Mi 5:4); pomp (Is 14:11).
גֵּאוּת gē'ûth (1378), Majesty (Is 26:10).
הָדָר hādhār (1994), Splendor (Is 2:10, Ez 27:10); honor (Ps 149:9).
הֲדַר hădhar (A1995), Majesty (Dn 4:30,36 [4:27,33]—Aramaic).
הֶדֶר hedher (1996), Adornment (Dn 11:20).
הֲדָרָה hădhārāh (1997), Glory (Prv 14:28).
הוֹד hôdh (2003), Majesty (1 Chr 29:25, Jb 37:22, Ps 21:5 [20:5]).
הוֹן hôn (2019), Wealth (Ps 112:3 [111:3]).
זְבֻל zᵉvul (2166), Dwelling (Ps 49:14 [48:14]).
חֶסֶד cheṣedh (2721), Beauty (Is 40:6).
טוּב ṭûv (3008), Goodness (Ex 33:19).
יֳפִי yŏphî (3418), Beauty (Is 33:17, Lam 2:15).
יְקָר yᵉqār (3480), Honor (Est 1:4, 6:3).
כָּבֵד kāvēdh (3632), Be honored; piel: glorify (Is 24:15).
כָּבֵד kāvēdh (3633), Glorious (Ps 45:13 [44:13]).
כֹּבֶד kōvedh (3635), Denseness (Is 30:27).
כָּבוֹד kāvôdh (3638), Glory (Ex 40:34, Ps 3:3, Ez 3:12).
מַשָּׂא massā' (5014), Load (Is 22:25).
נֵס nēṣ (5438), Banner (Ez 27:7).
עֹז 'ōz (6010), Strength (Ps 68:34 [67:34], Is 12:2).
פָּאַר pā'ar (6526), Hithpael: be glorified (Is 60:21).
פְּאֵר pᵉ'ēr (6527), Garland (Is 61:3).
קֹדֶשׁ qōdhesh (7231), Something holy (Jer 23:9).
שׁוּל shûl (8201), Train of a robe (Is 6:1).
תֹּאַר tō'ar (8717), Appearance (Is 52:14).

δόξα 1385

תְּהִלָּה tehillāh (8747), Glory (Ex 15:11, Is 61:3).

תּוֹעָפוֹת tô'āphôth (8776), Horns, strength (Nm 23:22, 24:8).

תְּמוּנָה temûnāh (8874), Form, likeness (Nm 12:8, Ps 17:15 [16:15]).

תִּפְאֶרֶת tiph'ereth (8930), Glory (Ex 28:2); pride (Is 10:12).

1. **δόξα** doxa nom sing fem
2. **δόξης** doxēs gen sing fem
3. **δόξῃ** doxē dat sing fem
4. **δόξαν** doxan acc sing fem
5. **δόξας** doxas acc pl fem

4	the kingdoms of the world, and the **glory** of them;	Matt 4:8
1	and the power, and the **glory**, for ever. Amen.	6:13
3	That even Solomon in all his **glory**	6:29
3	For the Son of man shall come in the **glory**	16:27
2	in the throne **of** his **glory**,	19:28
2	Son of man coming ... with power and great **glory**.	24:30
3	When the Son of man shall come in his **glory**,	25:31
2	then shall he sit upon the throne of his **glory**:	25:31
3	in the **glory** of his Father with the holy angels.	Mark 8:38
3	and the other on thy left hand, in thy **glory**.	10:37
2	coming in the clouds with great power and **glory**.	13:26
1	and the **glory** of the Lord shone round about them:	Luke 2:9
1	**Glory** to God in the highest, and on earth peace,	2:14
4	and the **glory** of thy people Israel.	2:32
4	this power will I give thee, and the **glory** of them:	4:6
3	when he shall come in his own **glory**,	9:26
3	Who appeared in **glory**, and spake of his decease	9:31
4	and when they were awake, they saw his **glory**,	9:32
3	that Solomon in all his **glory** was not arrayed like	12:27
1	Friend, go up higher: then shalt thou have **worship**	14:10
4	are not found that returned to give **glory** to God,	17:18
1	peace in heaven, and **glory** in the highest.	19:38
2	coming in a cloud with power and great **glory**.	21:27
4	suffered these things, and to enter into his **glory**?	24:26
4	dwelt among us, and we beheld his **glory**,	John 1:14
4	the **glory** as of the only begotten of the Father,	1:14
4	and manifested forth his **glory**;	2:11
4	I receive not **honour** from men.	5:41
4	which receive **honour** one of another,	5:44
4	seek not the **honour** that cometh from God only?	5:44
4	He that speaketh of himself seeketh his own **glory**:	7:18
4	but he that seeketh his **glory** that sent him,	7:18
4	And I seek not mine own **glory**:	8:50
1	If I honour myself, my **honour** is nothing:	8:54
4	and said unto him, Give God the **praise**:	9:24
2	sickness is not unto death, but for the **glory** of God,	11:4
4	thou shouldest see the **glory** of God?	11:40
4	These things said Esaias, when he saw his **glory**,	12:41
4	For they loved the **praise** of men more	12:43
4	the praise of men more than the **praise** of God.	12:43
3	glorify thou me with thine own self with the **glory**	17:5
4	the **glory** which thou gavest me I have given them;	17:22
4	that they may behold my **glory**,	17:24
2	God of **glory** appeared unto our father Abraham,	Acts 7:2
4	stedfastly into heaven, and saw the **glory** of God,	7:55
4	smote him, because he gave not God the **glory**:	12:23
2	when I could not see for the **glory** of that light,	22:11
4	And changed the **glory** of the uncorruptible God	Rom 1:23
4	seek for **glory** and honour and immortality,	2:7
1	But **glory**, honour, and peace,	2:10
4	more abounded through my lie unto his **glory**;	3:7
4	sinned, and come short of the **glory** of God;	3:23
4	but was strong in faith, giving **glory** to God;	4:20
2	and rejoice in hope of the **glory** of God.	5:2
2	raised up from the dead by the **glory** of the Father,	6:4
4	are not worthy to be compared with the **glory**	8:18
2	into the **glorious** liberty of the children of God.	8:21
1	and the **glory**, and the covenants,	9:4
2	the riches of his **glory** on the vessels of mercy,	9:23
4	which he had afore prepared unto **glory**,	Rom 9:23
1	are all things: to whom be **glory** for ever. Amen.	11:36
4	as Christ also received us to the **glory** of God.	15:7
1	be **glory** through Jesus Christ for ever. Amen.	16:27
4	God ordained before the world unto our **glory**:	1 Co 2:7
4	they would not have crucified the Lord of **glory**.	2:8
4	or whatsoever ye do, do all to the **glory** of God.	10:31
1	forasmuch as he is the image and **glory** of God:	11:7
1	but the woman is the **glory** of the man.	11:7
1	But if a woman have long hair, it is a **glory** to her:	11:15
1	but the **glory** of the celestial is one,	15:40
1	There is one **glory** of the sun,	15:41
1	and another **glory** of the moon,	15:41
1	and another **glory** of the stars:	15:41
3	for one star differeth from another star in **glory**.	15:41
3	It is sown in dishonour; it is raised in **glory**:	15:43
4	and in him Amen, unto the **glory** of God by us.	2 Co 1:20
3	written and engraven in stones, was **glorious**,	3:7
4	the face of Moses for the **glory** of his countenance;	3:7
3	the ministration of the spirit be rather **glorious**?	3:8
1	For if the ministration of condemnation be **glory**,	3:9
3	the ministration of righteousness exceed in **glory**.	3:9
2	by reason of the **glory** that excelleth.	3:10
2	For if that which is done away was **glorious**,	3:11
3	much more that which remaineth is **glorious**.	3:11
4	beholding as in a glass the **glory** of the Lord,	3:18
2	are changed into the same image from **glory**	3:18
4	into the same image from **glory** to **glory**,	3:18
2	lest the light of the **glorious** gospel of Christ,	4:4
2	of the **glory** of God in the face of Jesus Christ.	4:6
4	thanksgiving of many redound to the **glory** of God.	4:15
2	a far more exceeding and eternal weight **of glory**;	4:17
2	By **honour** and dishonour,	6:8
4	which is administered by us to the **glory**	8:19
1	and the **glory** of Christ.	8:23
1	To whom be **glory** for ever and ever. Amen.	Gal 1:5
2	To the praise of the **glory** of his grace,	Eph 1:6
2	That we should be to the praise of his **glory**,	1:12
2	unto the praise of his **glory**.	1:14
2	the God of our Lord Jesus ... the Father of **glory**,	1:17
2	and what the riches of the **glory** of his inheritance	1:18
2	at my tribulations for you, which is your **glory**.	3:13
2	grant you, according to the riches of his **glory**,	3:16
1	Unto him be **glory** in the church by Christ Jesus	3:21
4	unto the **glory** and praise of God.	Phlp 1:11
4	Christ is Lord, to the **glory** of God the Father.	2:11
1	**glory** is in their shame, who mind earthly things.	3:19
2	it may be fashioned like unto his **glorious** body,	3:21
3	according to his riches in **glory** by Christ Jesus.	4:19
1	Now unto God and our Father be **glory** for ever	4:20
1	Strengthened ... according to his **glorious** power,	Col 1:11
2	the **glory** of this mystery among the Gentiles;	1:27
2	which is Christ in you, the hope of **glory**:	1:27
3	then shall ye also appear with him in **glory**.	3:4
4	sought we **glory**, neither of you, nor yet of others,	1 Th 2:6
4	who hath called you unto his kingdom and **glory**.	2:12
1	For ye are our **glory** and joy.	2:20
2	of the Lord, and from the **glory** of his power;	2 Th 1:9
2	to the obtaining of the **glory** of our Lord Jesus.	2:14
2	the **glorious** gospel of the blessed God,	1 Tm 1:11
1	God, be honour and **glory** for ever and ever.	1:17
2	salvation which is in Christ ... with eternal **glory**.	2 Tm 2:10
1	to whom be **glory** for ever and ever. Amen.	4:18
2	and the **glorious** appearing of the great God	Tit 2:13
2	Who being the brightness of his **glory**,	Heb 1:3
3	thou crownedst him **with glory** and honour,	2:7
3	we see Jesus, ... crowned **with glory** and honour;	2:9
4	in bringing many sons unto **glory**,	2:10
2	was counted worthy of more **glory** than Moses,	3:3
2	the cherubims of **glory** shadowing the mercyseat;	9:5
1	Jesus Christ; to whom be **glory** for ever and ever.	13:21
2	the Lord of **glory**, with respect of persons.	Jas 2:1
4	might be found unto praise and honour and **glory**	1 Pt 1:7
5	the sufferings ... and the **glory** that should follow.	1:11
2	raised him up from the dead, and gave him **glory**;	1:21
1	and all the **glory** of man as the flower of grass.	1:24
1	to whom be **praise** and dominion for ever	4:11

2 that, when his **glory** shall be revealed,	1 Pt 4:13
2 for the spirit of **glory** and of God resteth upon you:	4:14
2 also a partaker of the **glory** that shall be revealed:	5:1
2 receive a crown of **glory** that fadeth not away.	5:4
4 called us unto his eternal **glory** by Christ Jesus,	5:10
1 To him be **glory** and dominion for ever and ever.	5:11
2 him that hath called us to **glory** and virtue:	2 Pt 1:3
3 him that hath called us to **glory** and virtue:	1:3
4 received from God the Father honour and **glory**,	1:17
2 came such a voice to him from the excellent **glory**,	1:17
5 they are not afraid to speak evil of **dignities**.	2:10
1 To him be **glory** both now and for ever. Amen.	3:18
5 despise dominion, and speak evil of **dignities**.	Jude 1:8
2 before the presence of his **glory** with exceeding joy,	1:24
1 be **glory** and majesty, dominion and power,	1:25
1 to him be **glory** and dominion for ever and ever.	Rev 1:6
4 And when those beasts give **glory** and honour	4:9
4 worthy, ... to receive **glory** and honour and power:	4:11
4 and strength, and honour, and **glory**, and blessing.	5:12
1 heard I saying, Blessing, and honour, and **glory**,	5:13
1 Saying, Amen: Blessing, and **glory**, and wisdom,	7:12
4 affrighted, and gave **glory** to the God of heaven.	11:13
4 with a loud voice, Fear God, and give **glory** to him;	14:7
2 the temple was filled with smoke from the **glory**	15:8
4 and they repented not to give him **glory**.	16:9
2 angel ... the earth was lightened with his **glory**.	18:1
1 and **glory**, and honour, and power, unto the Lord	19:1
4 be glad and rejoice, and give **honour** to him:	19:7
4 Having the **glory** of God: and her light was like	21:11
1 for the **glory** of God did lighten it,	21:23
4 and the kings of the earth do bring their **glory**	21:24
4 bring the **glory** and honour of the nations into it.	21:26

Classical Greek

The Greek noun *doxa* is derived from the verb *dokeō* (1374), "to consider, to believe, to think." The sense of the noun in classical Greek thus becomes: "belief, opinion," and later "reputation." The "opinion" a person has about something may be involved, or it may refer to a belief someone has about another (i.e., "reputation"). However, the secular understanding of *doxa* is rarely, if ever, present in the New Testament. This provides another example of how the Septuagint and later the New Testament take a Greek term and radically alter it by invoking upon it the contents of a Hebrew counterpart. It has absorbed the more objective and absolute character associated in the Hebrew term *kābod* which denotes the majesty and splendor of God.

Septuagint Usage and Old Testament Background

The Septuagint records *doxa* nearly 450 times, translating 25 different Hebrew words, and in the majority of these occurrences *doxa* corresponds to the Hebrew *kāvôdh*. Consequently, these two terms became virtually synonymous from the perspective of the Biblical writers.

The term *kāvôdh* originally meant "that which makes something heavy, heaviness, weight, dignity." But it rapidly acquired the meaning of "honor, splendor, power." This has become the principal definition in the Old Testament (Genesis 45:13; Exodus 16:10; Leviticus 9:6,23).

Kāvôdh also functions in a secular sense for whatever gives an individual "honor, prestige, reputation," or "influence." In these cases the term(s) may refer to the *doxa* of men rather than God. The material riches of Abraham and Jacob (Genesis 13:2, *kāvôdh*; Genesis 31:1) and the properties and estates of others afforded them honor (*doxa*, Psalm 49:17 [LXX 48:17]). Also the "honor" or "reputation" of a country can consist of its resources and power and the subsequent influence which these possessions exert (Isaiah 4:5; 16:14; 17:4; 21:16). The prestige of countries and people can consist of their beautiful landscapes and aesthetic qualities which impress others (Isaiah 10:16-18; 35:2; 60:13).

Nevertheless, the Old Testament predominantly tells of God's glory. First, the invisible God manifested himself in the history of Israel, such as through the manifestation of His *doxa*— His glory, *Kᵉvôdh-'El*. The cosmic character of the splendor and glory of creation reveal the Creator: "The heavens declare the glory of God" (Psalm 19:1 [LXX 18:1]; cf. 8:1). The glory of the Creator is also expressed in frightening natural phenomena such as thunder and lightning (cf. Psalm 29:3f. [LXX 28:3f]).

Second, and more significantly, *Kᵉvôdh Yᵉwāh* expresses God's action in salvation history. In the exodus from Egypt and during the entire wandering in the desert, God revealed His glory in the form of a cloud during the day and a pillar of fire during the night. This symbolized the redemption, help, and guidance available to the people. It expressed the constant saving presence of God in the midst of His people (Exodus 14:17; 16:7,10; 40:34f.; cf. Numbers 14:10f.). The glory of God is presented as a dense cloud which covered Mount Sinai and as thunder and lightning at the giving of the Law (Exodus 19:16f.; 24:15f.).

But God's *kāvôdh* is uniquely connected with the ark of the covenant, with the tabernacle in the desert, and with the temple in Jerusalem (Exodus 29:42f.; 40:34f.). God's glory is His presence (1 Samuel 4:1-21). When the ark was taken by the Philistines, and Israel was defeated, the people cried, "The glory is departed from Israel" (1 Samuel 4:22 [LXX 1 Kings 4:22]). Likewise the glory of the Lord resided in the temple of Solomon when it was consecrated and when the fire fell consuming the offerings (1 Kings 8:11 [LXX 3 Kings 8:11]; cf. 2 Chronicles 5:14; 7:1). Isaiah saw this glory when he entered into the temple and received his call as a prophet (Isaiah 6:3f.; cf. Ezekiel 1:28). Later, when the Maccabeans reconsecrated the temple after the Syrians had defiled it (ca. 164 B.C.), they spoke of the glory of the Lord which once more was present in the midst of the people (1 Maccabees chapter 1).

The vision Ezekiel saw beside the Chebar River in Chaldea was another representation of the glory of God (see Ezekiel 1:28; cf. Isaiah's vision of the angels which surrounded the throne of God [Isaiah 6:1f.]). In later chapters the prophet saw the glory departing from Israel. Toward the end of the book, however, there is recorded Ezekiel's vision of God's glory once again entering the temple (Ezekiel 43:3f.). In the Book of Ezekiel the glory of God is often characterized by dazzling splendor and light.

God's redeeming His people from exile in Babylon (Isaiah chapters 40—66 especially) is seen as a manifestation of the glory of God both for Israel and for the nations. The universal gift of salvation available to all anticipates the future and final revelation of the glory of the Lord—the eschatological hope of the Old Testament (Isaiah 43:7; 44:23; 46:13; 49:3; 60:1f.; Habakkuk 2:14).

New Testament Usage

Echoing the use of and understanding of *kāvôdh* of the Old Testament as a term of salvation history, *doxa* functions in the New Testament as a universal expression for the visible "glory of God" and for His "honor and power." However, the word can also function more generally in reference to the "brightness" of light (Acts 22:11), to human "grandeur and imposing beauty" (Matthew 4:8; 6:29; 1 Peter 1:24), and to "honor and praise" (John 5:44; 7:18; 8:50; 1 Thessalonians 2:6,20). But as a theological expression *doxa* uniquely capsulizes the essence of the divine existence. It describes the revelation of God's glory in Christ Jesus and the essential nature of the kingdom of God in the eschatological consummation (Ephesians 1:6,17,18; 1 Timothy 1:11; see below).

The writings of the New Testament endorse and advance the Old Testament's comments about God's glory: The God who revealed himself in the history of Israel is the "God of glory" (Acts 7:2), and He alone is the God and Lord of the creation. Thus to Him alone belong glory and power (Romans 1:23f.). However, this glory is not a static condition; rather, it is manifested in the history of Israel, in God's redeeming power. To the community of the New Testament it was a present power of salvation (Romans 6:4; 9:23; Ephesians 1:18; Colossians 1:11). This glory and power of God will be ultimately revealed on the Last Day (Matthew 19:28; 1 Peter 5:1; Revelation 15:8). Jesus taught His disciples to pray to the Father that He might receive the "kingdom, the power, and the glory (*doxa*)" (Matthew 6:13, *Textus Receptus*). In that regard the New Testament echoes the liturgical tradition of Judaism to give "glory to God" (Luke 2:14; 19:38; Romans 11:36; Galatians 1:5; Philippians 1:11; 2:11). This does not imply that man can create honor or glory for God, but implicitly mankind exalts God in His true essence because of His power and might (John 9:24; as reflected by angels, Luke 9:26; Jude 8; Revelation 18:1).

But by far the most important understanding for the New Testament writers is that the glory of God has been revealed in and through Jesus Christ whom the writer of Hebrews says is "the brightness of his glory" (Hebrews 1:3). Paul spoke of Christ as "the Lord of glory" (1 Corinthians 2:8; cf. James 2:1; Psalm 24:7,10).

The theme of the glory of the Lord permeates the birth narratives in Luke's Gospel (Luke 2:9,14; cf. John 2:11). Jesus' glory "as of the only begotten of the Father" is revealed to the eye of faith (John 1:9-14), especially in the miracles (John 2:11; 11:40). Jesus also spoke to others of His glory, a glory He has from eternity (John 5:44; 17:5,22,24). On the Mount of Transfiguration the glory of Jesus broke forth and shone through in its fullness to the three disciples (Matthew 17:1f.; 2 Peter 1:16f.).

John's Gospel promotes the thought that the glory of Christ was expressed in His affliction and suffering. The Cross is the central locus of the glorification of Christ, the tangible witness that the saving power and glory of God are operating in and through Him. "The hour is come, that the Son of Man should be glorified" (John 12:23-28; 13:31; cf. Luke 24:26; Philippians 2:5-11).

With Paul and the Epistles it is essentially the risen, living, and soon-to-return Christ who testifies to God's saving glory. The Resurrection was a demonstration of the enormous power of the Father (Romans 6:4; 1 Peter 1:11). Christ has received this glory as the ascended and living Lord (2 Corinthians 4:4f.; Philippians 3:21; 1 Peter 1:21; Revelation 5:9-12); it shall be revealed finally at His return (Titus 2:13; 1 Peter 4:13; 5:1; cf. Mark 8:38; 10:37; 13:26; with parallels).

Therefore, the glory of God which is revealed in and through Jesus Christ is a redeeming and transforming power which is presently at work. Believers may already participate in the glory of Christ (Romans 8:17f.; 1 Peter 5:1f.). The believer realizes his or her sharing in this glory in the context of the Christian community which is being transformed into the image of Christ (2 Corinthians 3:18; cf. Genesis 1:26f.; Romans 8:17f.; 1 Corinthians 15:20-49). Union with Christ and participation in His glory is the work of the Spirit who offers a foretaste of the future glory ("the Spirit of glory," 1 Peter 4:14).

The Gospel of John presents a unique picture of the glory of Christ relating it to His abasement and suffering. Because the Cross is the demonstration of the saving power of God made manifest, it becomes the first stage in the glorification of Jesus. It was immediately preceding His suffering and crucifixion that Jesus said the hour had come for the Son of Man to be glorified. This statement is followed by the parable of a grain of wheat needing to "die" before it is able to bear fruit (cf. John 12:23,24,28; 13:31; cf. Luke 24:26).

A parallel thought is found in Philippians 2:5-11 where the topic relates to Christ's self-humbling, i.e., leaving His exalted position as deity to take on the form (see *homoiōma* [3530] and *schēma* [4828]) of a man. Because Jesus was willing to humble himself and be obedient even to death, God has given Him a name above all names and has "exalted him to the highest place" (verse 9, NIV). As a result (cf. verse 11), the "glory" of the Father is manifested in heaven, on earth, and under the earth.

In Paul's epistles, therefore, it is the resurrected, living Saviour who expresses God's saving glory. It was in the Resurrection God revealed His tremendous glory (Romans 6:4; 1 Peter 1:11), and Jesus now carries out and effects that glory as the living and ascended Lord (2 Corinthians 4:4f.; Philippians 3:21; 1 Peter 1:21; Revelation 5:9). This glory shall be fully revealed at His return (Titus 2:13; 1 Peter 4:13; 5:1; likewise, the Synoptics discuss Christ's *doxa* in connection with the *parousia* [3814] [i.e., His return; cf. Mark 8:38; 10:37; 13:26]). The return of Jesus in His glory, then, has become the hope of the believer.

Although the hope of the believer connotes a looking forward, the glory of God revealed in Christ is active *now* in the redeeming, transforming power of the Holy Spirit. The New Testament emphasizes that believers already participate in His glory (Romans 8:17; 1 Peter 5:1f.) and are being changed into the image of Christ "from glory to glory" (2 Corinthians 3:18). The Holy Spirit, who is called "the Spirit of glory" (1 Peter 4:14), is continually active in the lives of believers, giving them a foretaste of future glory *now*.

The Gospel of John emphasizes to a somewhat stronger degree that the believer presently participates in the glory of Christ (John 17:22). The key to this realization is that believers, by the power of the Spirit, will perform the same works as Christ and will consequently glorify (*doxazō* [1386]) the Father, i.e., make manifest the saving power of God in the name of Christ (John 14:13; cf. 14:12-20; 16:12-15). Paul, from a slightly different perspective, accented the future sharing in the glory of God and Christ; this is the "hope of glory" (Colossians 1:27; 2 Thessalonians 2:14; 1 Peter 5:10). God desires to bring His children in Christ forth "into the glorious liberty of the children of God" (Romans 8:21; cf. Ephesians 1:18; Hebrews 2:10) which is totally realized in the resurrection at the return of Jesus (Colossians 3:4; cf. Romans 8:28-30; 2 Corinthians 4:17; 5:5; Philippians 3:21; 1 John 3:2).

STRONG 1391, BAUER 203-4, MOULTON-MILLIGAN 168-69, KITTEL 2:233-53, LIDDELL-SCOTT 444, COLIN BROWN 2:44-52.

1386. δοξάζω doxazō verb

Ascribe glory to, honor, praise.

COGNATES:
  δοκέω dokeō (1374)
  δόξα doxa (1385)
  ἐνδοξάζω endoxazō (1724)
  ἔνδοξος endoxos (1725)
  κενοδοξία kenodoxia (2725)
  κενόδοξος kenodoxos (2726)
  συνδοξάζω sundoxazō (4738)

SYNONYMS:
  μεγαλύνω megalunō (3141)
  τιμάω timaō (4939)

δοξάζω 1386

אָדַר 'ādhar (139), Niphal: be majestic (Ex 15:6,11).

גָּאָה gā'âh (1371), Be high (Ex 15:1).

גָּבַהּ gāvahh (1391), High (Is 52:13).

גָּדוֹל gādhôl (1448), Great (Est 10:3, Mal 1:11).

גָּדַל gādhal (1461), Become great; piel: promote (Est 3:1).

הָדַר hādhar (1991), Honor; niphal: be respected (Lam 5:12).

יְקָר yeqār (3480), Honor (Es 6:6,7,9,11); glory (Ps 37:20 [36:20]).

יְקָר yeqār (A3481), Honor (Dn 2:6—Aramaic).

כָּבֵד kāvēdh (3632), Qal: be glorified (Is 66:5); niphal: be honored (Lv 10:3, Is 43:4); distinguish oneself (2 Sm 6:20); piel: honor (1 Sm 2:29, Ps 22:23 [21:23], Mal 1:6); pual: be honored (Prv 13:18).

כָּבוֹד kāvôdh (3638), Glory, honor (1 Chr 17:18, Is 24:23).

נָוָה nāwâh (5294), Dwell; hiphil: praise (Ex 15:2).

נָזִיר nāzîr (5319), Separated one (Dt 33:16).

נָשָׂא nāsā' (5558), Lift, take; niphal: be exalted (Is 52:13); piel: support (Ezr 8:36).

פָּאַר pā'ar (6526), Piel: glorify (Is 60:7,13); hithpael: show one's glory (Is 44:23); boast (Is 10:15).

קָדַשׁ qādhash (7227), Be holy; niphal: show oneself holy (Is 5:16).

קָרַן qāran (7450), Shine, be radiant (Ex 34:29,30,35).

רוּם rûm (7597), Be high, exalted; polel: exalt (Is 25:1, 33:10).

תִּפְאֶרֶת tiph'ereth (8930), Glory (Is 4:2).

1. δοξάζω doxazō 1sing indic pres act
2. δοξάζητε doxazēte 2pl subj pres act
3. δοξαζέτω doxazetō 3sing impr pres act
4. δοξάζων doxazōn nom sing masc part pres act
5. δοξάζοντες doxazontes nom pl masc part pres act
6. δοξάζειν doxazein inf pres act
7. δοξάσω doxasō 1sing indic/subj fut/aor act
8. ἐδόξασα edoxasa 1sing indic aor act
9. ἐδόξασεν edoxasen 3sing indic aor act
10. ἐδόξασαν edoxasan 3pl indic aor act
11. δοξάσῃ doxasē 3sing subj aor act
12. δοξάσωσιν doxasōsin 3pl subj aor act
13. δόξασον doxason 2sing impr aor act
14. δοξάσατε doxasate 2pl impr aor act
15. δοξάσαι doxasai inf aor act
16. δοξάσει doxasei 3sing indic fut act
17. ἐδόξαζεν edoxazen 3sing indic imperf act
18. ἐδόξαζον edoxazon 3pl indic imperf act
19. δοξάζεται doxazetai 3sing indic pres mid
20. δοξάζηται doxazētai 3sing subj pres mid
21. δοξαζόμενος doxazomenos nom sing masc part pres mid
22. ἐδοξάσθη edoxasthē 3sing indic aor pass
23. δοξασθῇ doxasthē 3sing subj aor pass
24. δοξασθῶσιν doxasthōsin 3pl subj aor pass
25. δεδόξασμαι dedoxasmai 1sing indic perf mid
26. δεδόξασται dedoxastai 3sing indic perf mid
27. δεδοξασμένη dedoxasmenē dat sing fem part perf mid
28. δεδοξασμένον dedoxasmenon nom/acc sing neu part perf mid

12	and **glorify** your Father which is in heaven.	Matt 5:16
24	hypocrites do ... that **they may have glory** of men.	6:2
10	they marvelled, and **glorified** God,	9:8
10	and **they glorified** the God of Israel.	15:31
18	and **they glorified** the God of Israel.	15:31
6	that they were all amazed, and **glorified** God,	Mark 2:12
5	**glorifying** and praising God for all the things	Luke 2:20
21	taught in their synagogues, **being glorified** of all.	4:15
4	and departed to his own house, **glorifying** God.	5:25
18	And they were all amazed, and **they glorified** God,	5:26
18	there came a fear on all: and they **glorified** God,	7:16
17	she was made straight, and **glorified** God.	13:13
4	turned back, and with a loud voice **glorified** God,	17:15
4	and followed him, **glorifying** God:	18:43
9	the centurion saw what was done, he **glorified** God,	23:47
17	the centurion saw what was done, he **glorified** God,	23:47
22	because that Jesus **was** not yet **glorified**.	John 7:39
1	If I **honour** myself, my honour is nothing:	8:54
7	If I **honour** myself, my honour is nothing:	8:54
4	it is my Father that **honoureth** me;	8:54
23	that the Son of God **might be glorified** thereby.	11:4
22	when Jesus **was glorified**, then remembered they	12:16
23	that the Son of man **should be glorified**.	12:23
13	Father, **glorify** thy name.	12:28
8	I have both **glorified** it, and will glorify it again.	12:28
7	I have both glorified it, and **will glorify** it again.	12:28
22	Now is the Son of man **glorified**,	13:31
22	And **God is glorified** in him.	13:31
22	If God **be glorified** in him,	13:32
16	God shall also **glorify** him in himself,	13:32
16	and **shall** straightway **glorify** him.	13:32
23	that the Father may **be glorified** in the Son.	14:13
22	Herein is my Father **glorified**, that ye bear ... fruit;	15:8
16	He shall **glorify** me: for he shall receive of mine,	16:14
13	Father, the hour is come; **glorify** thy Son,	17:1
11	that thy Son also **may glorify** thee:	17:1
8	I have **glorified** thee on the earth:	17:4
13	**glorify** thou me with thine own self with the glory	17:5
25	and thine are mine; and I **am glorified** in them.	17:10
16	signifying by what death he should **glorify** God.	21:19
9	God of our fathers, hath **glorified** his Son Jesus;	Acts 3:13
18	for all men **glorified** God for that which was done,	4:21
18	they held their peace, and **glorified** God, saying,	11:18
10	they held their peace, and **glorified** God, saying,	11:18
18	they were glad, and **glorified** the word of the Lord:	13:48
18	And when they heard it, they **glorified** the Lord,	21:20
10	they knew God, **they glorified** him not as God,	Rom 1:21
9	and whom he justified, them he also **glorified**.	8:30
1	the apostle of the Gentiles, I **magnify** mine office;	11:13
2	ye may with one mind and one mouth **glorify** God,	15:6
15	that the Gentiles might **glorify** God for his mercy;	15:9
14	therefore **glorify** God in your body,	1 Co 6:20
19	or one member **be honoured**,	12:26
26	**was made glorious** had no glory in this respect,	2 Co 3:10
28	**made glorious** had no glory in this respect,	3:10
5	they **glorify** God for your professed subjection	9:13
18	And they **glorified** God in me.	Gal 1:24
20	the word ... may have free course, and **be glorified**,	2 Th 3:1
9	So also Christ **glorified** not himself	Heb 5:5
27	ye rejoice with joy unspeakable and **full of glory**:	1 Pt 1:8
12	**glorify** God in the day of visitation.	2:12
20	that God in all things **may be glorified**	4:11
19	but on your part he is **glorified**.	4:14
3	but let him **glorify** God on this behalf.	4:16
11	shall not fear thee, O Lord, and **glorify** thy name?	Rev 15:4
16	shall not fear thee, O Lord, and **glorify** thy name?	15:4
9	How much she **hath glorified** herself,	18:7

In the New Testament the word *doxazō* reflects two distinct meanings. First, it means "to praise or pay honor to someone" (either God [e.g., Mark 2:12; Luke 2:20; John 21:19] or men [1 Corinthians 12:26], although the latter is rare). A common phrase incorporating this sense is "glorify God" (nearly 20 times). Second it means "to adorn or clothe with glory, splendor, or luster, celebrating the value or nature of someone or something" (e.g., John 8:54; 13:31f.; 1 Peter 1:8).

STRONG 1392, BAUER 204, MOULTON-MILLIGAN 169, KITTEL 2:253-54, LIDDELL-SCOTT 444, COLIN BROWN 2:44-45,874.

1387. Δορκάς Dorkas name
Dorcas.

1. Δορκάς Dorkas nom fem

1 which by interpretation is called **Dorcas:** .... Acts 9:36
1 the coats and garments which **Dorcas** made, ... 9:39

The Greek name of Tabitha, a Christian from Joppa, whom Peter raised from the dead (Acts 9:36ff.); the name means "gazelle."

1388. δόσις dosis noun
Gift, giving.

COGNATE:
δίδωμι didōmi (1319)

SYNONYMS:
δόμα doma (1384)
δωρεά dōrea (1424)
δώρημα dōrēma (1427)
δῶρον dōron (1428)
κορβᾶν korban (2850)
χάρις charis (5320B)
χάρισμα charisma (5321)

חֹק chōq (2805), Allotment (Gn 47:22).

מַתָּן mattān (5150), Gift (Prv 21:14).

מַתַּת mattath (5164), Gift (Prv 25:14).

1. δόσις dosis nom sing fem
2. δόσεως doseōs gen sing fem

2 as concerning **giving** and receiving, ... Phlp 4:15
1 good **gift** and every perfect gift is from above, ... Jas 1:17

Common in extra-Biblical usage in reference to financial transactions (installments, debit, credit, purchase and rental prices, etc.), this word refers to a "free gift." The emphasis is upon the act of giving as a response to a petition or granting favor.

STRONG 1394, BAUER 204-5, MOULTON-MILLIGAN 169, LIDDELL-SCOTT 446.

1389. δότης dotēs noun
Giver.

CROSS-REFERENCE:
δίδωμι didōmi (1319)

1. δότην dotēn acc sing masc

1 or of necessity: for God loveth a cheerful **giver**...... 2 Co 9:7

This word appears only in 2 Corinthians 9:7 and apparently is nonexistent in pre-Christian writings. It communicates the idea of one who willfully surrenders, gives, or delivers up something. In this passage the *attitude* seems equal in importance to the act of giving.

STRONG 1395, BAUER 205, MOULTON-MILLIGAN 169, LIDDELL-SCOTT 446.

1390. δουλαγωγέω doulagōgeō verb
Bring into subjection, enslave.

CROSS-REFERENCES:
ἄγω agō (70)
δουλόω douloō (1396)

1. δουλαγωγῶ doulagōgō 1sing indic pres act

1 and bring it into **subjection:** .... 1 Co 9:27

In classical Greek *doulagōgeō* refers to the act of making slaves from captives after battle. This word stresses the idea of "bringing into bondage" in either a literal or moral sense, as a slave driver subdues and rules his slaves. It is used once in the New Testament, in 1 Corinthians 9:27, where Paul told the Corinthians how he must control his bodily desires in order to practice what he preached without hypocrisy.

STRONG 1396, BAUER 205, MOULTON-MILLIGAN 169, KITTEL 2:279-80, LIDDELL-SCOTT 446, COLIN BROWN 1:647.

1391. δουλεία douleia noun
Slavery, bondage.

CROSS-REFERENCE:
δουλεύω douleuō (1392)

עָבַד 'āvadh (5856), Labor (1 Kgs 9:21—Codex Alexandrinus only).

עֶבֶד 'evedh (5860), Servant (Ex 13:3, Jer 34:13 [41:13]).

עֲבֹדָה 'āvōdhāh (5865), Work, service (Lv 25:39, 2 Chr 10:4, Ps 104:14 [103:14]).

עֲבְדֻת 'avdhuth (5874), Bondage (Ezr 9:8,9, Neh 9:17).
עֲבִידָה 'ăvîdhāh (A5881), Service (Ezr 6:18—Aramaic).
פְּעֻלָּה pᵉ'ullah (6715), Reward (Ez 29:20—Codex Alexandrinus only).

1. **δουλείας** douleias gen sing fem
2. **δουλείαν** douleian acc sing fem

1	not received the spirit **of bondage** again to fear;	Rom 8:15
1	shall be delivered from the **bondage** of corruption	8:21
2	the mount Sinai, which gendereth to **bondage,**	Gal 4:24
1	be not entangled again with the yoke **of bondage.**	5:1
1	were all their lifetime subject **to bondage.**	Heb 2:15

Classical Greek
From *douleuō*, this noun denotes the condition of "slavery" or "bondage." It can also collectively refer to the "slave class" (see *Liddell-Scott*). The entire word group was widely employed in the ancient world in virtually every kind of literature from around the Fifth Century B.C. onward.

Septuagint Usage
Douleia and another form, *doulia*, occur in the Septuagint over 40 times; in every case but one the Hebrew original is some form of *'evedh*, "slave, servant," or "a subject." Typical is the expression "house of bondage" as an epithet for Egypt (e.g., Exodus 13:3,14; 20:2; Deuteronomy 5:6; 6:12; Judges 6:8; cf. Nehemiah 9:17; Jeremiah 34:13 [LXX 41:13]; Micah 6:4). *Douleia* can be somewhat ambiguous. It can refer to "servitude" in God's house (1 Chronicles 25:6; Nehemiah 10:32), but in another context it means "exile" (Lamentations 1:3; cf. Isaiah 14:3). Nevertheless, whether figurative or literal, the lowly status of the one enslaved and the dependency of the slave upon the master are usually implied.

New Testament Usage
Douleia occurs only five times in the New Testament, though the motif "slave/free" is particularly common. Each of the five usages is figurative. The Spirit signals that believers belong to Christ (Romans 8:9); He makes them alive and is the seal of sonship. As sons and daughters Christians have been set free from the Law, sin, and death (Romans 8:2; cf. Galatians 4:24). Thus, Paul could write about receiving the Spirit of sonship (freedom), not the spirit of slavery (Law) (Romans 8:15; cf. Galatians 5:1). The Book of Hebrews resonates with this thought. "Fear of death" enslaved people to "lifelong bondage" (*douleia*), but Christ destroyed the power of death and "deliver(ed)" (or "freed," *apallassō* [521]) the captives (Hebrews 2:15).

STRONG 1397, BAUER 205, MOULTON-MILLIGAN 169, KITTEL 2:261-79, LIDDELL-SCOTT 446, COLIN BROWN 3:592-93,595-98.

1392. δουλεύω douleuō verb
Be a slave, be subject to obey.

COGNATES:
δουλεία douleia (1391)
δουλόω douloō (1396)

SYNONYMS:
διακονέω diakoneō (1241)
θεραπεύω therapeuō (2300)
λατρεύω latreuō (2973)
λειτουργέω leitourgeō (2982)
ὑπηρετέω hupēreteō (5094)

עָבַד 'āvadh (5856), Qal: serve (Gn 25:23, 1 Sm 7:3, Jer 8:2); pual: be enslaved (Is 14:3); hiphil: honor (Is 43:23).

עֶבֶד 'evedh (5860), Servant (Prv 11:29, Is 65:8).

שָׁרַת shārath (8664), Piel: serve (Is 56:6).

1. **δουλεύετε** douleuete 2pl indic/impr pres act
2. **δουλεύω** douleuō 1sing indic pres act
3. **δουλεύει** douleuei 3sing indic pres act
4. **δουλεύουσιν** douleuousin 3pl indic pres act
5. **δουλευέτωσαν** douleuetōsan 3pl impr pres act
6. **δουλεύων** douleuōn nom sing masc part pres act
7. **δουλεύοντες** douleuontes nom pl masc part pres act
8. **δουλεύειν** douleuein inf pres act
9. **ἐδούλευσεν** edouleusen 3sing indic aor act
10. **ἐδουλεύσατε** edouleusate 2pl indic aor act
11. **δουλεύσωσιν** douleusōsin 3pl subj aor act
12. **δεδουλεύκαμεν** dedouleukamen 1pl indic perf act
13. **δουλεύσει** douleusei 3sing indic fut act
14. **δουλεῦσαι** douleusai inf pres act
15. **δουλεύσουσιν** douleusousin 3pl indic fut act

8	No man can **serve** two masters:	Matt 6:24
8	Ye cannot **serve** God and mammon.	6:24
2	Lo, these many years do I **serve** thee,	Luke 15:29
8	No servant can **serve** two masters:	16:13
8	Ye cannot **serve** God and mammon.	16:13
12	and were never **in bondage** to any man:	John 8:33
11	And the nation to whom they **shall be in bondage**	Acts 7:7
15	And the nation to whom they **shall be in bondage**	7:7
6	**Serving** the Lord with all humility of mind,	20:19
8	that henceforth we should not **serve** sin.	Rom 6:6
8	that we should **serve** in newness of spirit,	7:6
2	with the mind I myself **serve** the law of God;	7:25
13	The elder **shall serve** the younger.	9:12
7	fervent in spirit; **serving** the Lord;	12:11
6	For he that in these things **serveth** Christ	14:18
4	they that are such **serve** not our Lord Jesus Christ,	16:18
10	ye **did service** unto them which ... no gods.	Gal 4:8
8	whereunto ye desire again **to be in bondage?**	4:9
14	whereunto ye desire again **to be in bondage?**	4:9
3	this Agar ... and **is in bondage** with her children.	4:25
1	but by love **serve** one another.	5:13

δούλη 1393

7	With good will **doing service**, as to the Lord,	Eph 6:7
9	he **hath served** with me in the gospel.	Phlp 2:22
1	receive the reward ... for ye **serve** the Lord Christ.	Col 3:24
8	to God from idols **to serve** the living and true God;	1 Th 1:9
5	not despise them, ... but rather **do them service**,	1 Tm 6:2
7	deceived, **serving** divers lusts and pleasures,	Tit 3:3

Classical Greek
The ordinary meaning of *douleuō* in the ancient world is "be a slave" (to someone) or "perform the duties of a slave." *Moulton-Milligan* records no use of *douleuō* in a religious sense. It does, however, point out the reading of "temple slaves" (*heirodouloi*) in some of the cults.

Septuagint Usage
The Septuagint attests to extensive use of *douleuō*, usually as an equivalent of the Hebrew *'āvadh* ("serve") or one of its derivatives. *Douleuō* speaks of Jacob's service to Laban for Rachel (Genesis 29:18,20,25,30). In a religious connection 2 Chronicles describes Israel's idolatrous worship of Asherah poles: *edouleuon tais Astartais* (24:18; cf. Judges 10:6,10,13). Allegiance to Yahweh is also described in terms of servitude (Judges 10:16; Nehemiah 9:35; Ezekiel 20:40).

New Testament Usage
Douleuō occurs in the Synoptic Gospels in the material common to Matthew and Luke (Matthew 6:24; Luke 16:13) and in the Lucan Parable of the Prodigal Son (Luke 15:29). The tradition shared by Matthew and Luke fluctuates between a literal statement of the inability of man to serve two masters and the religious implication that it is equally impossible for man to serve both God and the material mind-set of the world.

John's Gospel uses *douleuō* only once, but the idea permeates his story. The opposing Jewish leaders claimed to have served no one (John 8:33). Jesus declared they were actually slaves (*douloi* [see 1395]) to sin (8:34) and not free at all. Only the truth makes one free (John 8:32).

Paul is famous for his portrayal of the enslaving effect of the Law. He contrasted this with the freedom that the slave of Christ experiences (Romans 7:6,25; cf. 2 Corinthians 3:17; Galatians 5:1). Such freedom calls for service to one another (*douleuete allēlois*, Galatians 5:13) as well as service to God (Romans 12:11; Colossians 3:23,24; 1 Thessalonians 1:9).

Strong 1398, Bauer 205, Moulton-Milligan 170, Kittel 2:261-79, Liddell-Scott 446, Colin Brown 3:592-95,598.

1393. δούλη doulē noun
A female slave, bondmaid, bondwoman.
Cross-Reference:
δουλόω douloō (1396)

אָמָה 'āmāh (526), (Female) servant (Lv 25:44, 1 Sm 25:31, 1 Kgs 1:13).

עֶבֶד 'evedh (5860), Servant (Ex 21:7).

שִׁפְחָה shiphchāh (8569), (Female) servant (Ru 2:13, 1 Sm 25:27, 2 Kgs 4:2).

1. **δούλη** doulē nom sing fem
2. **δούλης** doulēs gen sing fem
3. **δούλας** doulas acc pl fem

1	And Mary said, Behold the **handmaid** of the Lord;	Luke 1:38
2	hath regarded the low estate of his **handmaiden**:	1:48
3	And on my servants and on my **handmaidens**	Acts 2:18

Whether voluntarily or involuntarily assumed, this refers to a woman serving as a slave and indicates at the same time the humble station of the slave. New Testament usage deals with the status or attitude of a slave. It also emphasizes serving another, and being in subjection.

Strong 1399, Bauer 205, Kittel 2:261-79, Liddell-Scott 446.

1394. δοῦλος doulos adj
Servile, slavish, subservient.

עֶבֶד 'evedh (5860), Servant (Ps 119:91 [118:91]).

1. **δοῦλα** doula nom/acc pl neu

| 1 | **servants** to uncleanness and to iniquity | Rom 6:19 |
| 1 | **servants** to righteousness unto holiness. | 6:19 |

Classical Greek
Although identical in form to the noun *doulos* (1395), "slave," this *doulos* is the adjective member of that word group. Its basic meaning is "servile, subservient, slavish." It could be applied to persons or objects such as a "subservient city" (see *Liddell-Scott*).

Septuagint Usage
Only two instances of the adjective are attested in the Septuagint; one is canonical. The Psalmist declared that everything is "subject" to God (Psalm 119:91 [LXX 118:91]). In the apocryphal Wisdom of Solomon the writer spoke of the potter who designs vessels of "service" (15:7).

New Testament Usage
The New Testament's use is restricted to two, both in Romans 6:19. Paul reminded his readers that formerly they offered the members of their bodies "in slavery" (NIV) to uncleanness, but

now they were to offer them "in slavery" (NIV) to righteousness (cf. verses 20-22).

STRONG 1400, BAUER 205, MOULTON-MILLIGAN 170, KITTEL 2:261-79, LIDDELL-SCOTT 447, COLIN BROWN 3:592-97.

1395. δοῦλος doulos noun
Slave, bondman, servant.

COGNATE:
δουλόω douloō (1396)

SYNONYMS:
οἰκέτης oiketēs (3473)
παιδάριον paidarion (3671)
παῖς pais (3679)

נַעֲרָה naʻărāh (5472), Maiden (Prv 9:3).
עָבַד ʻāvadh (5856), Serve, work (2 Kgs 10:21ff., Eccl 5:12 [5:11]).
עֲבַד ʻăvadh (A5857), Make (Ezr 4:15—Aramaic).
עֲבֵד ʻăvēdh (A5859), Servant (Ezr 5:11—Aramaic).
עֶבֶד ʻevedh (5860), Servant (Lv 26:13, Neh 1:6, Hg 2:23 [2:24]).
עַם ʻam (6194I), People (Ps 80:4 [79:4]).

1. δοῦλος doulos nom sing masc
2. δούλου doulou gen sing masc
3. δούλῳ doulō dat sing masc
4. δοῦλον doulon acc sing masc
5. δοῦλε doule voc sing masc
6. δοῦλοι douloi nom pl masc
7. δούλων doulōn gen pl masc
8. δούλοις doulois dat pl masc
9. δούλους doulous acc pl masc

3	and to my **servant**, Do this, and he doeth it.	Matt 8:9
1	nor the **servant** above his lord.	10:24
1	be as his master, and the **servant** as his lord.	10:25
6	So the **servants** of the householder came and said	13:27
6	enemy hath done this. The **servants** said unto him,	13:28
7	king, which would take account of his **servants**.	18:23
1	**servant** therefore fell down, and worshipped him,	18:26
2	lord of that **servant** was moved with compassion,	18:27
1	But the same **servant** went out,	18:28
5	O thou wicked **servant**, I forgave thee all that debt,	18:32
1	will be chief among you, let him be your **servant**:	20:27
9	he sent his **servants** to the husbandmen,	21:34
9	And the husbandmen took his **servants**,	21:35
9	Again, he sent other **servants** more than the first:	21:36
9	And sent forth his **servants** to call them	22:3
9	Again, he sent forth other **servants**, saying,	22:4
9	And the remnant took his **servants**,	22:6
8	saith he to his **servants**, The wedding is ready,	22:8
6	So those **servants** went out into the highways,	22:10
1	Who then is a faithful and wise **servant**,	24:45
1	Blessed is that **servant**, whom his lord ... find so	24:46
1	But and if that evil **servant** shall say in his heart,	24:48
2	The lord of that **servant** shall come in a day	24:50
9	who called his own **servants**,	25:14
7	After a long time the lord of those **servants** cometh,	25:19
5	Well done, thou good and faithful **servant**:	25:21
5	Well done, good and faithful **servant**;	25:23
5	Thou wicked and slothful **servant**,	25:26
4	And cast ye the unprofitable **servant** ... darkness:	25:30
4	and struck a **servant** of the high priest's,	26:51
1	will be the chiefest, shall be **servant** of all.	Mark 10:44
4	at the season he sent to the husbandmen a **servant**,	12:2
4	And again he sent unto them another **servant**;	12:4
8	left his house, and gave authority to his **servants**,	13:34
4	smote a **servant** of the high priest, ... cut off his ear.	14:47
4	Lord, now lettest thou thy **servant** depart in peace,	Luke 2:29
1	And a certain centurion's **servant**, who was dear	7:2
4	that he would come and heal his **servant**.	7:3
3	and to my **servant**, Do this, and he doeth it.	7:8
4	found the **servant** whole that had been sick.	7:10
6	Blessed are those **servants**,	12:37
6	and find them so, blessed are those **servants**.	12:38
1	Blessed is that **servant**, whom his lord when he	12:43
1	But and if that **servant** say in his heart,	12:45
2	The lord of that **servant** will come in a day when	12:46
1	And that **servant**, which knew his lord's will,	12:47
4	And sent his **servant** at supper time to say to them	14:17
1	So that **servant** came, and showed his lord these	14:21
3	master of the house being angry said to his **servant**,	14:21
1	And the **servant** said, Lord, it is done as thou	14:22
4	And the lord said unto the **servant**,	14:23
9	But the father said to his **servants**,	15:22
7	having a **servant** plowing or feeding cattle,	17:7
3	Doth he thank that **servant** because he did	17:9
6	say, We are unprofitable **servants**:	17:10
9	And he called his ten **servants**,	19:13
9	commanded these **servants** to be called unto him,	19:15
5	And he said unto him, Well, thou good **servant**:	19:17
5	own mouth will I judge thee, thou wicked **servant**.	19:22
4	at the season he sent a **servant** to the husbandmen,	20:10
4	And again he sent another **servant**:	20:11
4	one of them smote the **servant** of the high priest,	22:50
6	his **servants** met him, and told him, saying,	John 4:51
1	Whosoever committeth sin is the **servant** of sin.	8:34
1	And the **servant** abideth not in the house for ever:	8:35
1	The **servant** is not greater than his lord;	13:16
9	Henceforth I call you not **servants**;	15:15
1	for the **servant** knoweth not what his lord doeth:	15:15
1	The **servant** is not greater than his lord.	15:20
4	and smote the high priest's **servant**,	18:10
3	The **servant's** name was Malchus.	18:10
6	And the **servants** and officers stood there,	18:18
7	One of the **servants** of the high priest,	18:26
9	And on my **servants** and on my handmaidens	Acts 2:18
8	and grant unto thy **servants**,	4:29
6	These men are the **servants** of the most high God,	16:17
1	Paul, a **servant** of Jesus Christ,	Rom 1:1
9	that to whom ye yield yourselves **servants** to obey,	6:16
6	his **servants** ye are to whom ye obey;	6:16
6	that ye were the **servants** of sin,	6:17
4	For when ye were the **servants** of sin,	6:20
1	Art thou called being a **servant**? care not for it:	1 Co 7:21
1	For he that is called in the Lord, being a **servant**,	7:22
1	he that is called, being free, is Christ's **servant**.	7:22
6	bought with a price; be not ye the **servants** of men.	7:23
6	whether we be **bond** or free;	12:13
9	and ourselves your **servants** for Jesus' sake.	2 Co 4:5
1	pleased men, I should not be the **servant** of Christ.	Gal 1:10
1	there is neither **bond** nor free,	3:28
2	differeth nothing **from a servant**, though he be lord	4:1
1	Wherefore thou art no more a **servant**, but a son;	4:7
6	**Servants**, be obedient to ... your masters	Eph 6:5
6	but as the **servants** of Christ,	6:6
1	receive of the Lord, whether he be **bond** or free.	6:8
6	Paul and Timotheus, the **servants** of Jesus Christ,	Phlp 1:1
2	and took upon him the form of **a servant**,	2:7
1	Barbarian, Scythian, **bond** nor free:	Col 3:11
6	**Servants**, obey in all things your masters	3:22
8	Masters, give unto your **servants** that which is just	4:1
1	Epaphras, who is one of you, a **servant** of Christ,	4:12
6	Let as many **servants** as are under the yoke	1 Tm 6:1
4	And the **servant** of the Lord must not strive;	2 Tm 2:24
1	Paul, a **servant** of God, and an apostle of Jesus	Tit 1:1
9	Exhort **servants** to be obedient unto ... masters,	2:9
4	Not now as a **servant**, but above a **servant**,	Phlm 1:16
4	but above a **servant**, a brother beloved,	1:16
1	a **servant** of God and of the Lord Jesus Christ,	Jas 1:1

δοῦλος 1395

6 cloak of maliciousness, but as the **servants** of God...	1 Pt 2:16
1 Peter, a **servant** and an apostle of Jesus Christ,......	2 Pt 1:1
6 they themselves are the **servants** of corruption:.........	2:19
1 Jude, the **servant** of Jesus Christ,...................	Jude 1:1
8 God gave unto him, to show unto his **servants**.......	Rev 1:1
3 signified it by his angel unto his **servant** John:..........	1:1
9 and to seduce my **servants** to commit fornication,......	2:20
1 and the mighty men, and every **bondman**,..............	6:15
9 sealed the **servants** of our God in their foreheads.......	7:3
9 as he hath declared to his **servants** the prophets........	10:7
8 that thou shouldest give reward unto thy **servants**.....	11:18
9 small and great, rich and poor, free and **bond**,.........	13:16
2 And they sing the song of Moses the **servant** of God,..	15:3
7 hath avenged the blood of his **servants** at her hand.....	19:2
6 saying, Praise our God, all ye his **servants**,.............	19:5
7 and the flesh of all men, both free and **bond**,..........	19:18
6 and his **servants** shall serve him:.....................	22:3
8 sent his angel to show unto his **servants** the things.....	22:6

Classical Greek

Doulos, "slave," is a member of the *douleuō* (1392) word group. Generally a Greek *doulos* was born into that condition rather than being made a slave at some later point in time (see *Liddell-Scott*; cf. Jewish "slaves" in Jeremias, *Jerusalem in the Time of Jesus*, pp.312ff.). It is of no small consequence for understanding the New Testament concept of a slave that to the Greeks to be a slave was to be subject to an utterly debasing social and anthropological position. Autonomy was the highest prize of the Hellenistic world; thus servitude was the absence of any such freedom. Although the position of slaves within households differed, the dependence of the slave upon another and his or her subjection in service made it repulsive to Greeks.

The Greeks did speak of "serving gods"; however, the ultimate goal of worship was to experience "freedom" from both internal and external bonds (i.e., obligations to others). The only positive association of *doulos* was to be a *doulos* to the laws of society (Plato). This was the mark of the ideal citizen (Plato *Leges* 3.698c,700a; cited by Rengstorf, "doulos," *Kittel*, 2:261ff.). "Within the Gr(eek) concept of God there is in fact no place for this word group as an expression of religious relationship and service" (ibid., 2:264).

Septuagint Usage

'Avadh and its derivatives are overwhelmingly the Hebrew counterpart to *doulos* (just as it was so with *douleia*) in the Septuagint, although *pais* is the preferred equivalent when the reference is to slaves who are at the disposal of others. The idea of slavery in Israel was far removed from the Greek notion.

First, people could become slaves as a result of choice. Second, in contrast to the Hellenistic idea, slaves served only for 6 years (Exodus 21:2), and the Old Testament also provided for the protection of slaves from mistreatment (Exodus 21:14,26,27). Third, a religious relationship was regularly conveyed by servanthood (*douleia* [1391]).

David referred to himself as God's slave (often translated "servant" in the RSV; 1 Samuel 23:10,11 [LXX 1 Kings 23:10,11]; Psalm 89:50 [88:50]), but he also considered himself Saul's servant (1 Samuel 19:4 [LXX 1 Kings 19:4]) and Jonathan's servant (1 Samuel 20:7,8 [LXX 1 Kings 20:7,8]). Here one can observe the sharp contrast with the Hellenistic mind-set which would have despised such a relationship. God referred to David as His slave (2 Samuel 3:18 [LXX 2 Kings 3:18]; Psalm 89:3,20 [LXX 88:3,20]) who would effect His salvation. God's people are His chosen servants (Psalms 105:6 [LXX 104:6]; 134:1 [133:1]; Isaiah 49:3; cf. 2 Kings 10:21-23 [LXX 4 Kings 10:21,23]), especially the prophets (2 Kings 17:23 [LXX 4 Kings 17:23]; Amos 3:7; Zechariah 1:6).

The slave of God, therefore, carries out the will and purpose of God. The slave also depends upon his Lord to provide protection and sustenance. One can see the appropriateness of such a metaphor as a description of God's people.

The Psalmist considered himself the slave of God who had been free by God (Psalm 116:16 [LXX 115:16]; cf. Psalms 34:22 [LXX 33:22]; 102:28 [101:28]; 144:10 [143:10]; Isaiah 48:20; 2 Maccabees 7:33; 8:29). Service to God is not, however, expressed in single acts; rather, the servant continually does the bidding of his Lord.

The most unique role of the word *slave* is its function as an image of the Messiah. This is developed in the closing chapters of Isaiah where the term *'evedh* occurs 20 times in the singular (chapters 39–53, Kaiser, "'evedh," *Theological Wordbook of the Old Testament*, pp.639f.; note, *doulos* occurs only six times here in the Septuagint). This is vital for understanding Jesus' mission as God's Servant (Mark 10:43ff.; Philippians 2:7).

New Testament Usage

Doulos in the New Testament plays a major theological role. Apart from the use of *doulos* as a character in a parable (e.g., Matthew 25:14ff.; Mark 12:2; Luke 14:17) and excluding its normal literal use (e.g., Luke

7:2ff.; John 18:10; Ephesians 6:5ff.; Colossians 3:22ff.; 1 Timothy 6:1), it usually functions in a figurative sense. This figurative use covers three basic areas: (1) the Christian as a *doulos* of God; (2) the Christian as a *doulos* to other Christians; (3) Christ as the *doulos* of God.

The Christian as a "doulos" of God. John's Gospel and Paul's epistles agree that people are either "slaves" (*douloi*) of sin, or they are slaves of righteousness (i.e., they are obedient; John 8:34; cf. Acts 7:6; Romans 6:16,17,20). Believing in Christ's atoning work makes it possible for people to be freed from their enslavement to sin and to enjoy a new status as sons and daughters of God (Galatians 4:7; cf. 2 Peter 2:19).

Doulos is a frequent appellation adopted by the writers of the New Testament for their own position (e.g., Romans 1:1; Galatians 1:10; Philippians 1:1; Titus 1:1, *doulos tou theou*; James 1:1; 2 Peter 1:1; Revelation 1:1). It is difficult to determine the precise origin of this concept. It may be linked to the Old Testament image of the prophets as God's servants (Septuagint, *douloi*; Hebrew, ʿ*evedh*; 2 Kings 17:23 [LXX 4 Kings 17:23]; Amos 3:7; Zechariah 1:6; cf. Revelation 10:7; 11:18) (see Rengstorf, "doulos," *Kittel*, 2:273ff.). Like the Old Testament prophet, New Testament servants proclaimed the good news (Acts 16:17; 2 Corinthians 4:5).

The believing community is God's/Christ's *douloi* (1 Corinthians 7:22). That is, the *doulos* of God is under obligation to be totally committed to his (or her) Lord (Matthew 6:24: "No man can serve two masters"; cf. Matthew 8:9). God's servants may have to pay with their lives (Revelation 19:2).

The Christian as a "doulos" to other Christians. Believers are to model the servanthood of Jesus (see below). "Whosoever will be chief among you, let him be your servant" (Matthew 20:27; cf. 1 Corinthians 7:23). Service to one another is an expression of love (*agapē* [26], Galatians 5:13), kindness, and social responsibility (2 Timothy 2:4). Nevertheless, slaves are no longer a social class in the Christian community as far as the eschatological reality is concerned (Galatians 3:28; Colossians 3:11; Philemon 16). Notwithstanding, practical concerns forbid the forcible exercise of this truth (1 Corinthians 7:21ff.; Ephesians 6:5ff.; Colossians 3:22).

Christ as the "doulos" of God. The servanthood of Jesus is capsulized in Philippians 2:6ff.: "Who being in the form of God, thought it not robbery to be equal with God: but made himself of no reputation, and took upon him the form of a servant (*doulos*)." The Lord (*kurios* [2935]) becomes the slave (*doulos*)—the ultimate reversal of roles. Christ's example in the washing of the disciples' feet is an object lesson for the Christian community (John 13:15)—not just of washing feet but of service. Christ's role as *doulos* welds Him solidly with humanity's condition. He identified with mankind's subjection to the Law, sin, and death (Hebrews 2:15). Servanthood to God is uniquely expressed in Christ's obedience even unto death (cf. Philippians 2:8).

STRONG 1401, BAUER 205-6, MOULTON-MILLIGAN 170, KITTEL 2:261-79, LIDDELL-SCOTT 447, COLIN BROWN 592-97.

1396. δουλόω douloō verb

Enslave, subject, be in bondage.

COGNATES:
δουλαγωγέω doulagōgeō (1390)
δουλεύω douleuō (1392)
δούλη doulē (1393)
δοῦλος doulos (1394)
δοῦλος doulos (1395)
καταδουλόω katadouloō (2585)
ὀφθαλμοδουλεία ophthalmodouleia (3651)
σύνδουλος sundoulos (4739)

עָבַד ʿāvadh (5856), Qal: be enslaved (Gn 15:13); hiphil: bring (Is 43:23—Sixtine Edition only).

1. ἐδούλωσα edoulōsa 1sing indic aor act
2. δουλώσουσιν doulōsousin 3pl indic fut act
3. ἐδουλώθητε edoulōthēte 2pl indic aor pass
4. δουλωθέντες doulōthentes
   nom pl masc part aor pass
5. δεδούλωται dedoulōtai 3sing indic perf mid
6. δεδουλωμένοι dedoulōmenoi
   nom pl masc part perf mid
7. δεδουλωμένας dedoulōmenas
   acc pl fem part perf mid

2 and that they should bring them into bondage, ... Acts 7:6
3 ye became the servants of righteousness. .... Rom 6:18
4 free from sin, and become servants to God, ... 6:22
5 A brother or a sister is not under bondage .... 1 Co 7:15
1 yet have I made myself servant unto all, ... 9:19
6 were in bondage under the elements of the world: .... Gal 4:3
7 not false accusers, not given to much wine, ... Tit 2:3
5 of the same is he brought in bondage. .... 2 Pt 2:19

Classical Greek

Unlike *douleuō* (1392), which refers to carrying out the duties of a slave or servant or to the relationship between a slave and master, *douloō* conveys the idea of "enslaving" someone, "to make another or oneself a slave or a subject" (cf. *katadouloō* [2585]). Passively, one can "be enslaved."

Septuagint Usage

Four out of eight times in the Septuagint *douloō* translates the Hebrew *'āvadh*, "serve." The other four instances appear in the Greek writings (Wisdom of Solomon 19:14; 1 Maccabees 8:11; 4 Maccabees 3:2; 13:2). First Maccabees recalls the practice of enslaving the conquered by the victor (cf. Genesis 15:13), while 4 Maccabees picks up the figurative kind of enslavement—enslavement by desire (cf. 4 Maccabees 3:2; 13:2, "enslaved to emotion [*pathos* (3669)]" [RSV]).

New Testament Usage

The New Testament follows the figurative use reflected in the Maccabean writings (but cf. Acts 7:6 and Genesis 15:13). Paul, in a classic paragraph, underscored the radical change instituted by the gospel. Believers were formerly slaves to sin (Romans 6:17; cf. Galatians 4:3; 2 Peter 2:19), but now they have been set free from sin (Romans 6:18). They have been "enslaved" for righteousness and have become "servants to God" (Romans 6:22). In one other use of the word, Paul said he was willing to enslave himself to others if it would win men and women to Christ (1 Corinthians 9:19).

Strong 1402, Bauer 206, Moulton-Milligan 170, Kittel 2:279, Liddell-Scott 447.

1397. δοχή dochē noun

Reception, feast.

Cognate:
  δέχομαι dechomai (1203)
Synonym:
  δεῖπνον deipnon (1168)

לֶחֶם l°chem (A4036), Feast (Dn 5:1—Aramaic).

מִשְׁתֶּה mishteh (5136), Feast, banquet (Gn 26:30, Est 1:3, 5:4).

1. δοχήν dochēn acc sing fem

1 And Levi made him a great **feast** in his own house: Luke 5:29
1 But when thou makest **a feast**, call the poor,........... 14:13

Translated "feast" or "banquet," the word *dochē* refers to a festive occasion. (It is from the root word meaning "reception.") The joyous nature of the event implies a sense of entertainment and celebration. It is found twice in the New Testament. In Luke 5:29 it denotes the banquet that Matthew gave in honor of Jesus. At Luke 14:13 *dochē* occurs in the context of a lesson Jesus taught concerning the subject of giving: Those who "make a feast" should invite the poor rather than those who will be able to pay them back.

Strong 1403, Bauer 206, Moulton-Milligan 170, Kittel 2:54, Liddell-Scott 447, Colin Brown 3:744-45.

1398. δράκων drakōn noun

Dragon, serpent.

Synonym:
  ὄφις ophis (3653)

כְּפִיר k°phîr (3841), Young lion (Jb 4:10, 38:39).

לִוְיָתָן liwyāthān (4018), Leviathan, sea monster, crocodile (Jb 41:1 [40:20], Ps 104:26 [103:26], Is 27:1).

נָחָשׁ nāchāsh (5357), Serpent (Jb 26:13, Am 9:3).

עַתּוּד 'attûdh (6500), Ram (Jer 50:8 [27:8]).

פֶּתֶן pethen (6874), Asp (Jb 20:16).

תַּן tan (8895), Jackal (Mi 1:8, Jer 9:11).

תַּנִּין tannîn (8906I), Sea monster, serpent (Ex 7:9,10, Jb 7:12, Jer 51:34 [28:34]).

1. δράκων drakōn nom sing masc
2. δράκοντος drakontos gen sing masc
3. δράκοντα drakonta acc sing masc
4. δράκοντι drakonti dat sing masc

1 wonder in heaven; and behold a great red **dragon**,.. Rev 12:3
1 and the **dragon** stood before the woman............... 12:4
2 Michael and his angels fought against the **dragon**;...... 12:7
1 and the **dragon** fought and his angels,.................. 12:7
1 the great **dragon** was cast out, that old serpent,........ 12:9
1 the **dragon** saw that he was cast unto the earth,...... 12:13
1 swallowed up the flood which the **dragon** cast out..... 12:16
1 And the **dragon** was wroth with the woman,............ 12:17
1 and the **dragon** gave him his power, and his seat,...... 13:2
3 they worshipped the **dragon** which gave power........ 13:4
4 they worshipped the **dragon** which gave power........ 13:4
1 two horns like a lamb, and he spake as a **dragon**...... 13:11
2 like frogs come out of the mouth of the **dragon**,....... 16:13
3 And he laid hold on the **dragon**, that old serpent,..... 20:2

Drakōn occurs exclusively in the Book of Revelation in the New Testament (13 times). In ancient literature it was commonly relied upon to translate "serpent" or "dragon." Jewish and Christian writers used it figuratively to depict the devil (e.g., Philo; Sybilline Oracles 3.794; the Testament of Asher 7.3). *Bauer* reports that *drakōn* was a synonym of *ophis* (3653), "snake, serpent." The Septuagint translators seem to have been more discreet in using them interchangeably; of the nine Hebrew words which translate the two Greek terms, they coincide only on one, *nāchāsh*. It occurs only four times as an equivalent of either *drakōn* or *ophis* (Job 26:13; Amos 9:3; cf. Numbers

21:9; Isaiah 14:29). By the time of the New Testament, however, *ophis* and *drakōn* were virtually the same. The Book of Revelation especially testifies to this.

The image of *drakōn* has been largely responsible for popular misconceptions of the devil or Satan as being a fiery-faced, pitchfork-carrying, horned creature. The dragon of Revelation 12 is "red" (NIV, KJV, RSV; from *purros* [4308], "red" [as of fire]); he has a powerful tail and 10 horns (12:3,4). The dragon is specifically identified as Satan—"that old serpent (*ophis*), called the Devil, and Satan" (12:9; cf. 12:15; 20:2). The dragon can almost certainly be associated with the serpent in the Garden of Eden. Responsible for deceiving the nations (20:3), he will be chained for a thousand years in the abyss. Then he will be released for a short time.

STRONG 1404, BAUER 206, MOULTON-MILLIGAN 170, KITTEL 2:281-83, LIDDELL-SCOTT 448, COLIN BROWN 1:507-8.

1399. δράσσομαι drassomai verb

Grasp, take, capture, seize.

SYNONYMS:
ἀγρεύω agreuō (63)
ἁρπάζω harpazō (720)
ἐπιλαμβάνομαι epilambanomai (1934)
ἔχω echō (2174)
ζωγρέω zōgreō (2204)
θηρεύω thēreuō (2317)
καταλαμβάνω katalambanō (2608)
κρατέω krateō (2875)
λαμβάνω lambanō (2956)
πιάζω piazō (3945)
συλλαμβάνω sullambanō (4666)
συναρπάζω sunarpazō (4734B)

נָשַׁק nāshaq (5583), Piel: kiss (Ps 2:12).
קָמַץ qāmats (7346), Take a handful (Lv 2:2, 5:12, Nm 5:26).

1. δρασσόμενος drassomenos
nom sing masc part pres mid
1 He taketh the wise in their own craftiness..........1 Co 3:19

This word means "to apprehend or capture something or someone," especially by firmly taking hold with the hands. Its use in the Septuagint takes a literal meaning, to physically "take a handful" (see Leviticus 2:2; 5:12; Numbers 5:26). The New Testament uses *drassomai* only once, in 1 Corinthians 3:19, where it is used figuratively to describe how God will handle those who think they are wise in their own eyes.

STRONG 1405, BAUER 206, MOULTON-MILLIGAN 170, LIDDELL-SCOTT 448.

1400. δραχμή drachmē noun

Drachma. (Possibly worth 18 or 19 cents.)

CROSS-REFERENCE:
δίδραχμον didrachmon (1317)

אֲדַרְכּוֹן ’ādharkôn (147), Daric (Ezr 8:27—Codex Alexandrinus only).
בֶּקַע beqaʽ (1261), Half shekel (Ex 38:26 [39:2]).
דַּרְכְּמוֹנִים darkᵉmônîm (1933), Drachmas (Ezr 2:69—Codex Alexandrinus only).
שֶׁקֶל sheqel (8621), Shekel (Jos 7:21—only some Vaticanus texts).

1. δραχμήν drachmēn acc sing fem
2. δραχμάς drachmas acc pl fem

2 Either what woman having ten pieces of silver,.....Luke 15:8
1 if she lose one piece, doth not light a candle,..........15:8
1 for I have found the piece which I had lost..........15:9

The *drachmē* was a silver coin of the Grecian empire. It is mentioned once in the New Testament (Luke 15:8,9). Coinage of New Testament times was principally the gold and silver currencies of the Roman government and copper issues of local rulers. However, the silver *drachmē* (and *tetradrachmē*, four times the value of a *drachmē*) continued to circulate in Palestine during the time of Christ.

The *drachmē* first appeared after the conquest of Persia (332–323 B.C.) by Alexander the Great. He, for the first time, standardized currency for trade and commerce. The Alexandrian standard of weights valued the *drachmē* at just over 66 grams of silver. At first it bore the inscription and image of Alexander but later this was changed.

Following the division of the Greek Empire into the Seleucid and Ptolemaic dynasties, the Alexandrian standard was kept by the Seleucids who were seated in Antioch. The Ptolemies of Alexandria adopted the Phoenician standard revising the *drachmē* to weigh 56 grams. The Ptolemaic *drachmē* was preferred currency to the Jews who met severe persecution at the hands of the Seleucids.

Despite Jewish preference for the Ptolemaic *drachmē*, the *drachmē* struck in Antioch prevailed in circulation in Palestine because of its equal exchange value for the Roman silver denarius. The denarius was a Roman soldier's daily wage. The Antiochan *drachmē* is the one probably referred to in the New Testament (cf.

δρέπανον 1401

Perkin, "Money," *International Standard Bible Encyclopedia*, 3:402).

STRONG 1406, BAUER 206, MOULTON-MILLIGAN 170-71, LIDDELL-SCOTT 449.

1401. δρέπανον drepanon noun
Sickle, pruning hook.

דָּרְבָן dār°vān (1921II) Goad (1 Sm 13:21).
חֶרְמֵשׁ chermēsh (2876), Sickle (Dt 16:9, 23:25).
מַגָּל maggāl (4177), Sickle (Jer 50:16 [27:16], Jl 3:13).
מַזְמֵרָה mazmērāh (4345), Plowshare (Is 2:4, 18:5, Jl 3:10, Mi 4:3).
מַחֲרֵשָׁה mach°rēshāh (4419I), Plowshare (1 Sm 13:20—Codex Vaticanus only).

1. δρέπανον drepanon nom/acc sing neu

1 immediately he putteth in the **sickle**,	Mark 4:29
1 a golden crown, and in his hand a sharp **sickle**.	Rev 14:14
1 Thrust in thy **sickle**, and reap: for the time is come	14:15
1 And he that sat on the cloud thrust in his **sickle**	14:16
1 another angel ... he also having a sharp **sickle**.	14:17
1 with a loud cry to him that had the sharp **sickle**,	14:18
1 saying, Thrust in thy sharp **sickle**,	14:18
1 And the angel thrust in his **sickle** into the earth,	14:19

Found in Mark 4:29 and Revelation 14:15-19, *drepanon* is commonly translated "sickle." This word refers to a tool that was used both for harvesting grain (Mark 4:29) and clusters of grapes (Revelation 14:15-19). Its use in the New Testament is consistent with classical Greek writings where the word described a pruning knife, scythe, scimitar, curved sword, or even a tool used for cutting down trees and tree branches (see *Bauer; Liddell-Scott*).

STRONG 1407, BAUER 206, MOULTON-MILLIGAN 171, LIDDELL-SCOTT 449, COLIN BROWN 3:527.

1402. δρόμος dromos noun
Course, career.
COGNATES:
πρόδρομος prodromos (4133)
συνδρομή sundromē (4740)

מֵרוֹץ mērôts (4955), Race (Eccl 9:11).
מְרוּצָה m°rûtsāh (4956), Running (2 Sm 18:27); course (Jer 8:6).
שִׁפְעָה shiph°āh (8599), Flood (Jb 38:34—Codex Alexandrinus only).

1. δρόμον dromon acc sing masc

1 And as John fulfilled his **course**, he said,	Acts 13:25
1 so that I might finish my **course** with joy,	20:24
1 I have finished my **course**, I have kept the faith:	2 Tm 4:7

Classical Greek and Septuagint Usage
In classical Greek the proper meaning of *dromos* is applied to the "course" of heavenly bodies. Astral science of the period took for granted the invisible influence of the stars and planets on human events. To chart the "course" of a star gave meaning to one's fate and shaped everyday trivia.

Figurative usage of *dromos* soon developed the meaning to chart the "course" of runners in a race. In this earthly plane, a runner's fate was determined by whether he continued in or completed the "course." In the Septuagint and rabbinic literature *dromos* was stripped of its astrological meanings and became a loanword from the field of racing.

New Testament Usage
In the New Testament and in the writings of second-century Christians *dromos* was used figuratively to depict the "course" of one's life. The word appears only three times in the New Testament; twice in Acts (13:25; 20:24) and once in the Pauline letters (2 Timothy 4:7). Each instance borrows from the imagery of racing to metaphorically describe the completing of one's life. Second-century Christians found it natural to ascribe *dromos* to the death of martyrs who "securely reached the goal in the race of faith" (1 Clement 6:2).

STRONG 1408, BAUER 206-7, MOULTON-MILLIGAN 171, KITTEL 8:233-34, LIDDELL-SCOTT 450, COLIN BROWN 3:945,947.

1403. Δρούσιλλα Drousilla name
Drusilla.

1. Δρουσίλλῃ Drousillē dat fem

1 when Felix came with his wife **Drusilla**,	Acts 24:24

The youngest daughter of Agrippa I who heard Paul speak before her husband, Felix (Acts 24:24).

1404. δύναμαι dunamai verb
Be able, have power to do, have capacity for.
COGNATES:
ἀδυνατέω adunateō (100)
ἀδύνατος adunatos (101)
δύναμις dunamis (1405)
δυναμόω dunamoō (1406)
δυνάστης dunastēs (1407)
δυνατέω dunateō (1408)
δυνατός dunatos (1409)
ἐνδυναμόω endunamoō (1727)

δύναμαι 1404

Synonyms:
ἐξισχύω exischuō (1823)
ἰσχύω ischuō (2453)

גִּבּוֹר gibbôr (1399), Warrior (Jb 16:14 [16:15]).
יָכֹל yākhōl (3310), Be able (Gn 29:8, Neh 6:3); overpower (Ob 7).
יְכִל yᵉkhil (A3311), Be able (Dn 2:10,47, 3:29—Aramaic).
יָסַף yāṣaph (3362), Add, increase; hiphil: do again (Is 24:20).
כְּהַל kᵉhal (A3666), Be able (Dn 5:8—Aramaic).
כּוּל kûl (3677), Lay hold of; hiphil: hold (1 Kgs 8:64, Jer 2:13).
כָּלָה kālâh (3735), End; piel: finish (Neh 4:2—Sixtine Edition only).
מָצָא māṣā' (4834), Find (Jb 32:3).
עָצַר 'āṣar (6352), Refrain (2 Chr 20:37).

1. δύναμαι dunamai 1sing indic pres mid
2. δύνῃ dunē 2sing indic pres mid
3. δύνασαι dunasai 2sing indic pres mid
4. δύναται dunatai 3sing indic pres mid
5. δυνάμεθα dunametha 1pl indic pres mid
6. δύνασθε dunasthe 2pl indic pres mid
7. δύνανται dunantai 3pl indic pres mid
8. δύνηται dunētai 3sing subj pres mid
9. δύνωνται dunōntai 3pl subj pres mid
10. δυναίμην dunaimēn 1sing opt pres mid
11. δύναιντο dunainto 3pl opt pres mid
12. δυναμένου dunamenou
     gen sing masc/neu part pres mid
13. δυνάμενος dunamenos
     nom sing masc part pres mid
14. δυναμένῳ dunamenō dat sing masc part pres mid
15. δυνάμενον dunamenon
     acc sing masc part pres mid
16. δυνάμενοι dunamenoi nom pl masc part pres mid
17. δυναμένων dunamenōn gen pl masc part pres mid
18. δυναμένους dunamenous
     acc pl masc part pres mid
19. δυναμένη dunamenē nom sing fem part pres mid
20. δυνάμεναι dunamenai nom pl fem part pres mid
21. δυνάμενα dunamena
     nom/acc pl neu part pres mid
22. δύνασθαι dunasthai inf pres mid
23. ἠδυνήθην ēdunēthēn 1sing indic aor pass
24. ἠδυνήθη ēdunēthē 3sing indic aor pass
25. ἠδυνήθημεν ēdunēthēmen 1pl indic aor pass
26. ἠδυνήθητε ēdunēthēte 2pl indic aor pass
27. ἠδυνήθησαν ēdunēthēsan 3pl indic aor pass
28. δυνηθῆτε dunēthēte 2pl subj aor pass
29. δυνήσῃ dunēsē 2sing indic fut mid
30. δυνήσεται dunēsetai 3sing indic fut mid
31. δυνησόμεθα dunēsometha 1pl indic fut mid
32. δυνήσεσθε dunēsesthe 2pl indic fut mid
33. δυνήσονται dunēsontai 3pl indic fut mid
34. ἠδύνατο ēdunato 3sing indic imperf mid
35. ἐδύνατο edunato 3sing indic imperf mid
36. ἠδύναντο ēdunanto 3pl indic imperf mid
37. ἠδύνασθε ēdunasthe 2pl indic imperf mid
38. ἠδυνάσθη ēdunasthē 3sing indic aor pass
39. ἐδύνασθε edunasthe 2pl indic imperf mid
40. ἠδύναντο ēdunanto 3pl indic imperf mid
41. ἠδύνασθε ēdunasthe 2pl indic imperf mid

4	God **is able** of these stones to raise up children	Matt 3:9
4	A city that is set on an hill **cannot** be hid	5:14
3	**thou canst** not make one hair white or black	5:36
4	No man **can** serve two masters:	6:24
6	Ye **cannot** serve God and mammon	6:24
4	**can** add one cubit unto his stature?	6:27
4	A good tree **cannot** bring forth evil fruit,	7:18
3	Lord, if thou wilt, **thou canst** make me clean	8:2
7	**Can** the children of the bridechamber mourn,	9:15
1	Believe ye that **I am able** to do this?	9:28
17	kill the body, but are not **able** to kill the soul:	10:28
15	fear him which **is able** to destroy ... soul and body	10:28
4	else how **can** one enter into a strong man's house,	12:29
6	how **can** ye, being evil, speak good things?	12:34
6	but **can** ye not discern the signs of the times?	16:3
27	and they **could** not cure him	17:16
25	Why **could** not we cast him out?	17:19
13	He that **is able** to receive it, let him receive it	19:12
4	amazed, saying, Who then **can** be saved?	19:25
6	Are ye **able** to drink of the cup that I shall drink of,	20:22
5	They say unto him, **We are able**	20:22
35	And no man **was able** to answer him a word,	22:46
34	For this ointment **might** have been sold for much,	26:9
35	For this ointment **might** have been sold for much,	26:9
4	if this cup **may** not pass away from me,	26:42
1	Thinkest thou that I **cannot** now pray	26:53
1	This fellow said, **I am able** to destroy the temple	26:61
4	He saved others; himself he **cannot** save	27:42
3	If thou wilt, **thou canst** make me clean	Mark 1:40
22	Jesus **could** no more openly enter into the city,	1:45
16	they **could** not come nigh unto him for the press,	2:4
4	who **can** forgive sins but God only?	2:7
7	**Can** the children of the bridechamber fast,	2:19
7	have the bridegroom with them, they **cannot** fast	2:19
22	so that they **could** not so much as eat bread	3:20
4	said ... in parables, How **can** Satan cast out Satan?	3:23
4	divided against itself, that kingdom **cannot** stand	3:24
4	be divided against itself, that house **cannot** stand	3:25
30	that house will not **be able** to stand (NASB)	3:25
4	Satan ... he **cannot** stand, but hath an end	3:26
4	No man **can** enter into a strong man's house,	3:27
22	so that the fowls of the air **may** lodge	4:32
36	spake he the word ... as they **were able** to hear it	4:33
40	spake he the word ... as they **were able** to hear it	4:33
34	and no man **could** bind him, no, not with chains:	5:3
35	and no man **could** bind him, no, not with chains:	5:3
34	And he **could** there do no mighty work,	6:5
35	And he **could** there do no mighty work,	6:5
34	and would have killed him; but she **could** not:	6:19
4	that entering into him **can** defile him:	7:15
4	entereth into the man, it **cannot** defile him;	7:18
24	have no man know it: but he **could** not be hid	7:24
38	have no man know it: but he **could** not be hid	7:24
30	From whence **can** a man satisfy these men	8:4
4	as snow; so as no fuller on earth **can** white them	9:3
3	if **thou canst do** any thing, have compassion on us,	9:22
2	if **thou canst do** any thing, have compassion on us,	9:22
3	Jesus said unto him, If **thou canst** believe,	9:23
2	Jesus said unto him, If **thou canst** believe,	9:23
25	asked ... privately, Why **could** not we cast him out?	9:28
4	This kind **can** come forth by nothing, but by	9:29
30	in my name, that **can** lightly speak evil of me	9:39
4	saying among themselves, Who then **can** be saved?	10:26
6	**can** ye drink of the cup that I drink of?	10:38
5	And they said unto him, **We can**	10:39

179

δύναμαι 1404

34	might have been sold for more than three hundred	Mark 14:5
6	and whensoever ye will ye **may** do them good:	14:7
4	He saved others; himself he **cannot** save.	15:31
13	behold, thou shalt be dumb, and not **able** to speak,	Luke 1:20
34	when he came out, he **could** not speak unto them:	1:22
35	when he came out, he **could** not speak unto them:	1:22
4	That God **is able** of these stones to raise up	3:8
3	Lord, if thou wilt, thou **canst** make me clean.	5:12
4	Who **can** forgive sins, but God alone?	5:21
6	**Can** ye make the children of the bridechamber fast,	5:34
4	**Can** the blind lead the blind?	6:39
3	Either how **canst** thou say to thy brother, Brother,	6:42
36	and **could** not come at him for the press.	8:19
27	thy disciples to cast him out; and they **could** not.	9:40
1	I **cannot** rise and give thee.	11:7
4	And which of you with taking thought **can** add	12:25
6	If ye then **be** not **able** to do that ... which is least,	12:26
19	and **could** in no wise lift up herself.	13:11
1	I have married a wife, ... therefore I **cannot** come.	14:20
4	and his own life also, he **cannot** be my disciple.	14:26
4	doth not bear his cross, ... **cannot** be my disciple.	14:27
4	that forsaketh not all ... he **cannot** be my disciple.	14:33
29	for thou **mayest** be no longer steward.	16:2
2	for thou **mayest** be no longer steward.	16:2
4	No servant **can** serve two masters:	16:13
6	Ye **cannot** serve God and mammon.	16:13
9	they which would pass from hence to you **cannot**;	16:26
4	they that heard it said, Who then **can** be saved?	18:26
34	and **could** not for the press, because he was little of	19:3
7	Neither **can** they die any more:	20:36
33	adversaries **shall** not **be able** to gainsay nor resist.	21:15
4	**Can** there any good thing come out of Nazareth?	John 1:46
4	for no man **can** do these miracles that thou doest,	3:2
4	he **cannot** see the kingdom of God.	3:3
4	How **can** a man be born when he is old?	3:4
4	**can** he enter the second time into his mother's	3:4
4	he **cannot** enter into the kingdom of God.	3:5
4	How **can** these things be?	3:9
4	A man **can** receive nothing, except it be given him	3:27
4	The Son **can** do nothing of himself,	5:19
1	I **can** of mine own self do nothing:	5:30
6	How **can** ye believe, which receive honour	5:44
4	No man **can** come to me, except	6:44
4	How **can** this man give us his flesh to eat?	6:52
4	This is an hard saying; who **can** hear it?	6:60
4	no man **can** come unto me, except it were given	6:65
4	The world **cannot** hate you; but me it hateth,	7:7
6	and where I am, thither ye **cannot** come.	7:34
6	and where I am, thither ye **cannot** come?	7:36
6	whither I go, ye **cannot** come.	8:21
6	because he saith, Whither I go, ye **cannot** come.	8:22
6	It is because you **cannot** hear My word. (NASB)	8:43
4	the night cometh, when no man **can** work.	9:4
4	How **can** a man that is a sinner do such miracles?	9:16
34	If this man were not of God, **he could** do nothing.	9:33
4	**Can** a devil open the eyes of the blind?	10:21
4	**is able** to pluck them out of my Father's hand.	10:29
4	and the scripture **cannot** be broken;	10:35
34	**Could** not this man, which opened the eyes	11:37
35	**Could** not this man, which opened the eyes	11:37
36	Therefore they **could** not believe,	12:39
6	Whither I go, ye **cannot** come;	13:33
3	Whither I go, thou **canst** not follow me now;	13:36
1	Lord, why **cannot** I follow thee now?	13:37
5	and how **can** we know the way?	14:5
4	the Spirit of truth; whom the world **cannot** receive,	14:17
4	As the branch **cannot** bear fruit of itself,	15:4
6	for without me ye **can** do nothing.	15:5
6	but ye **cannot** bear them now.	16:12
5	miracle hath been done ... and we **cannot** deny it.	Acts 4:16
5	For we **cannot** but speak ... which we have seen	4:20
6	But if it be of God, ye **cannot** overthrow it;	5:39
32	But if it be of God, ye **cannot** overthrow it;	5:39
10	How **can** I, except some man should guide me?	8:31
4	**Can** any man forbid water,	10:47
26	from which ye **could** not be justified by the law	13:39
6	Except ye be circumcised ... ye **cannot** be saved.	15:1
5	saying, **May** we know what this new doctrine,	Acts 17:19
31	whereby we **may** give an account of this concourse.	19:40
14	word of his grace, which **is able** to build you up,	20:32
13	he **could** not know the certainty for the tumult,	21:34
12	he **could** not know the certainty for the tumult,	21:34
29	examining of whom thyself **mayest** take knowledge	24:8
12	Because that thou **mayest** understand,	24:11
7	Neither **can** they prove the things	24:13
4	no man **may** deliver me unto them.	25:11
35	This man **might** have been set at liberty,	26:32
11	if by any means they **might** attain to Phenice,	27:12
12	**could** not bear up into the wind, we let her drive.	27:15
6	Except these abide in the ship, ye **cannot** be saved.	27:31
11	if it **were possible**, to thrust in the ship.	27:39
18	and commanded that they which **could** swim	27:43
4	is not subject to the law ... neither indeed **can** be.	Rom 8:7
7	then they that are in the flesh **cannot** please God.	8:8
30	**shall be able** to separate us from the love of God,	8:39
16	**able** also to admonish one another.	15:14
14	is **of power** to stablish you according to my gospel,	16:25
4	foolishness unto him: neither **can** he know them,	1 Co 2:14
23	**could** not speak unto you as unto spiritual,	3:1
41	for hitherto ye **were** not **able** to bear it,	3:2
39	for hitherto ye **were** not **able** to bear it,	3:2
6	not able to bear it, neither yet now **are** ye **able**.	3:2
4	other foundation **can** no man lay than that is laid,	3:11
30	that **shall be able** to judge between his brethren?	6:5
3	but if thou **mayest** be made free, use it rather.	7:21
6	suffer you to be tempted above that ye **are able**;	10:13
22	a way to escape, that ye **may be able** to bear it.	10:13
6	Ye **cannot** drink the cup of the Lord,	10:21
6	ye **cannot** be partakers of the Lord's table,	10:21
4	and that no man **can** say that Jesus is the Lord, but	12:3
4	And the eye **cannot** say unto the hand,	12:21
6	**may** all prophesy one by one, that all may learn,	14:31
7	that flesh and blood **cannot** inherit the kingdom	15:50
4	that flesh and blood cannot inherit the kingdom	15:50
22	**be able** to comfort them which are in any trouble,	2 Co 1:4
22	so that the children of Israel **could** not	3:7
5	**can** do nothing against the truth, but for the truth.	13:8
13	had been a law given **which could** have given life,	Gal 3:21
6	Whereby, when ye read, ye **may** understand	Eph 3:4
14	Now unto him that is **able** to do	3:20
22	that ye **may be able** to stand against the wiles	6:11
28	that ye **may be able** to withstand in the evil day,	6:13
32	wherewith ye **shall be able** to quench all ... darts	6:16
22	he is **able** even to subdue all things unto himself.	Phlp 3:21
16	when we **might** have been burdensome,	1 Th 2:6
5	what thanks **can** we render to God again for you,	3:9
4	and they that are otherwise **cannot** be hid.	1 Tm 5:25
7	and they that are otherwise **cannot** be hid.	5:25
5	and it is certain we **can** carry nothing out.	6:7
4	whom no man hath seen, nor **can** see:	6:16
4	yet he abideth faithful: he **cannot** deny himself.	2 Tm 2:13
21	never able to come to the knowledge of the truth.	3:7
21	which **are able** to make thee wise unto salvation,	3:15
4	he is **able** to succour them that are tempted.	Heb 2:18
27	they **could** not enter in because of unbelief.	3:19
15	have not an high priest which **cannot** be touched	4:15
13	Who **can** have compassion on the ignorant,	5:2
15	unto him that **was able** to save him from death,	5:7
4	Wherefore he **is able** also to save them	7:25
20	could not make him that did the service perfect,	9:9
4	**can** never with those sacrifices	10:1
7	**can** never with those sacrifices	10:1
7	same sacrifices, which **can** never take away sins:	10:11
15	engrafted word, which **is able** to save your souls.	Jas 1:21
4	and have not works? **can** faith save him?	2:14
4	the tongue **can** no man tame; it is an unruly evil,	3:8
4	**Can** the fig tree, my brethren, bear olive berries?	3:12
6	ye kill, and desire to have, and **cannot** obtain:	4:2
13	is one lawgiver, who is **able** to save and to destroy:	4:12
4	for his seed remaineth in him: and he **cannot** sin,	1 Jn 3:9
4	how **can** he love God whom he hath not seen?	4:20
14	Now unto him that **is able** to keep you from falling,	Jude 1:24
2	and how thou **canst** not bear them which are evil:	Rev 2:2
4	before thee an open door, and no man **can** shut it:	3:8

34	was able to open the book, neither to look thereon.	Rev 5:3
35	was able to open the book, neither to look thereon....	5:3
4	his wrath is come; and who shall be able to stand?.....	6:17
34	lo, a great multitude, which no man could number,....	7:9
35	lo, a great multitude, which no man could number,....	7:9
4	idols ... which neither can see, nor hear, nor walk:.....	9:20
7	idols ... which neither can see, nor hear, nor walk:.....	9:20
4	the beast? who is able to make war with him?........	13:4
8	might buy or sell, save he that had the mark,........	13:17
4	might buy or sell, save he that had the mark,........	13:17
34	and no man could learn that song but...............	14:3
35	and no man could learn that song but...............	14:3
34	and no man was able to enter into the temple,.......	15:8
35	and no man was able to enter into the temple,.......	15:8

Classical Greek

In classical Greek *dunamai* is used in three ways. First, in its weakest and most common reference *dunamai* means "I can, I am able," or "I am capable of." From the time of Homer such usage is found universally in ancient Greek literature. Second, in a stronger sense it is translated "I am able" and is reinforced with a subjective spiritual or moral attitude to show the force of one's will to do or not to do something. Third, in some instances *dunamai* is used with the meaning "to be equal to, to count as," or "to signify."

Septuagint Usage

The Septuagint uses *dunamai* to translate more than a dozen Hebrew words associated with ability or capacity (or lack of it) to perform a task. It is especially used for *yākhōl*. In numerous occurrences *dunamai* is used in a negative sense to show the contrast between the limits or loss of human power over personal fate (cf. Exodus 8:18; Leviticus 26:37; Isaiah 24:20; Daniel 2:26; 5:8) and the omnipotency of Yahweh.

New Testament Usage

As in the Septuagint, the New Testament uses *dunamai* to express ability and capacity to accomplish something in deed, attitude, or thought. For example, Jesus questioned the charge of the scribes by asking, "How can Satan cast out Satan?" (Mark 3:23). The context indicates Satan cannot rise up against himself and be divided. If he did, his "kingdom" would come to an end (verse 26).

STRONG 1410, BAUER 207, MOULTON-MILLIGAN 171, KITTEL 2:284-317, LIDDELL-SCOTT 451-52, COLIN BROWN 2:601-4,615.

1405. δύναμις dunamis noun

Power, might, ability, force.

COGNATE:
δύναμαι dunamai (1404)

SYNONYMS:
ἐξουσία exousia (1833)
ἰσχύς ischus (2452)
κράτος kratos (2877)
κυριότης kuriotēs (2936)

אוֹן 'ôn (202), Power (Jb 40:16 [40:11]).

אֵל 'ēl (417), Power (Neh 5:5).

אֱנוֹשׁ 'ĕnôsh (596), Men (Jer 40:7 [47:7]—Codex Alexandrinus only).

גֹּבַהּ gōvahh (1394), Majesty (Jb 40:10 [40:5]).

גִּבּוֹר gibbôr (1399), Warrior (Hos 10:13).

גְּבוּרָה geᵛûrāh (1400), Strength (Jgs 8:21, 2 Kgs 18:20, Eccl 10:17).

גְּדוּד geᵈhûdh (1447), Band, troop (1 Chr 12:18, 2 Chr 25:9,10,13).

הוֹן hôn (2019), Wealth (Ez 27:18,27).

הָמוֹן hāmôn (2066), Multitude, crowd (2 Sm 6:19, Jer 3:23, Ez 32:24).

חֹזֶק chōzeq (2484), Strength (Hg 2:22 [2:23]).

חַיִל chayil (2524), Army (Ex 14:28); mighty man (2 Sm 17:10).

חָלָץ chālats (2603), Army (2 Chr 20:21—Codex Vaticanus only).

יָד yādh (3135), Hand (Jos 4:24).

כָּבוֹד kāvôdh (3638), Glory (Is 8:7—Codex Sinaiticus only).

כֹּחַ kōach (3699), Ability (1 Chr 29:2); be able (Ezr 10:13).

מְאֹד meᵒōdh (4108), Might (Dt 6:5).

מַחֲנֶה machăneh (4402), Army (1 Chr 12:22, 2 Chr 14:13).

מִלְחָמָה milchāmāh (4560), Battle (2 Chr 13:3).

מַתָּנָה mattānāh (5152), Gift (Dt 16:17).

עֶבֶד 'evedh (5860), Servant (Est 2:18).

עֹז 'ōz (6010), Strength (Jb 41:22 [41:13]).

עֱזוּז 'ĕzûz (6020), Strength (Ps 145:6 [144:6]).

עַם 'am (6194II) People (1 Chr 21:2).

פֶּה peh (6552), Vow (Nm 6:21).

פָּלָא pālā' (6623), Niphal: be wondrous (Jb 37:14).

צָבָא tsāvā' (6893), Army, host (Gn 21:22, 2 Sm 10:16).

1. δύναμις dunamis nom sing fem
2. δυνάμεως dunameōs gen sing fem
3. δυνάμει dunamei dat sing fem
4. δύναμιν dunamin acc sing fem
5. δυνάμεις dunameis nom/acc pl fem
6. δυνάμεων dunameōn gen pl fem
7. δυνάμεσιν dunamesin dat pl fem
8. δυνάμεσι dunamesi dat pl fem

1	and the **power**, and the glory, for ever. Amen.......	Matt 6:13
5	and in thy name done many **wonderful works**?..........	7:22
5	wherein most of his **mighty works** were done,.........	11:20
5	for if the **mighty works**, which were done in you,......	11:21

δύναμις 1405

5	if the **mighty works**, which have been done in thee,	Matt 11:23
5	Whence ... this wisdom, and these **mighty works**?	13:54
5	And he did not many **mighty works** there	13:58
5	**mighty works** do show forth themselves in him.	14:2
4	not knowing the scriptures, nor the **power** of God.	22:29
5	and the **powers** of the heavens shall be shaken:	24:29
2	Son of man coming ... with **power** and great glory.	24:30
4	to every man according to his several **ability**;	25:15
2	the Son of man sitting on the right hand of **power**,	26:64
4	knowing in himself that **virtue** had gone out	Mark 5:30
5	even such **mighty works** are wrought by his hands?	6:2
4	And he could there do no **mighty work**,	6:5
5	**mighty works** do show forth themselves in him.	6:14
3	have seen the kingdom of God come with **power**.	9:1
4	man which shall do a **miracle** in my name,	9:39
4	know not the scriptures, neither the **power** of God?	12:24
5	and the **powers** that are in heaven shall be shaken.	13:25
2	coming in the clouds with great **power** and glory.	13:26
2	the Son of man sitting on the right hand of **power**,	14:62
3	And he shall go before him in the spirit and **power**	Luke 1:17
1	the **power** of the Highest shall overshadow thee:	1:35
3	And Jesus returned in the **power** of the Spirit	4:14
3	and **power** he commandeth the unclean spirits,	4:36
1	the **power** of the Lord was present to heal them.	5:17
1	there went **virtue** out of him, and healed them all.	6:19
4	for I perceive that **virtue** is gone out of me.	8:46
4	and gave them **power** and authority over all devils,	9:1
5	for if the **mighty works** had been done in Tyre	10:13
4	and over all the **power** of the enemy:	10:19
6	for all the **mighty works** that they had seen;	19:37
5	for the **powers** of heaven shall be shaken.	21:26
2	see the Son of man coming in a cloud with **power**	21:27
2	sit on the right hand of the **power** of God.	22:69
4	until ye be endued with **power** from on high.	24:49
4	until ye be endued with **power** from on high.	24:49
4	But ye shall receive **power**,	Acts 1:8
7	a man approved of God among you by **miracles**	2:22
3	as though by our own **power** or holiness	3:12
3	what **power**, or by what name, have ye done this?	4:7
3	And with great **power** gave the apostles witness	4:33
2	And Stephen, full of faith and **power**,	6:8
1	saying, This man is the great **power** of God.	8:10
3	beholding the **miracles** and signs which were done.	8:13
3	Jesus ... with the Holy Ghost and with **power**:	10:38
5	And God wrought special **miracles** by ... Paul:	19:11
3	And declared to be the Son of God with **power**,	Rom 1:4
1	for it is the **power** of God unto salvation	1:16
1	even his eternal **power** and Godhead;	1:20
5	nor angels, nor principalities, nor **powers**,	8:38
5	nor angels, nor principalities, nor **powers**,	8:38
4	that I might show my **power** in thee,	9:17
3	through the **power** of the Holy Ghost.	15:13
3	Through **mighty** signs and wonders,	15:19
3	by the **power** of the Spirit of God;	15:19
1	but unto us which are saved is the **power** of God.	1 Co 1:18
4	Christ the **power** of God, and the wisdom of God.	1:24
2	but in demonstration of the Spirit and **of power**:	2:4
3	in the wisdom of men, but in the **power** of God.	2:5
4	not the speech of them ... but the **power**.	4:19
3	the kingdom of God is not in word, but in **power**.	4:20
3	with the **power** of our Lord Jesus Christ,	5:4
2	and will also raise up us by his own **power**.	6:14
6	To another the working of **miracles**;	12:10
5	after that **miracles**, then gifts of healings,	12:28
5	Are all apostles? ... are all **workers of miracles**?	12:29
4	Therefore if I know not the **meaning** of the voice,	14:11
4	put down all rule and all authority and **power**.	15:24
3	it is sown in weakness; it is raised in **power**:	15:43
1	and the **strength** of sin is the law.	15:56
4	we were pressed out of measure, above **strength**,	2 Co 1:8
2	that the excellency of the **power** may be of God,	4:7
3	By the word of truth, by the **power** of God,	6:7
4	For to their **power**, I bear record,	8:3
4	yea, and beyond their **power** they were willing	8:3
1	for my **strength** is made perfect in weakness.	12:9
1	that the **power** of Christ may rest upon me.	12:9
7	in signs, and wonders, and **mighty deeds**.	12:12
2	yet he liveth by the **power** of God.	2 Co 13:4
2	but we shall live with him by the **power** of God.	13:4
5	and worketh **miracles** among you,	Gal 3:5
2	And what is the exceeding greatness of his **power**	Eph 1:19
2	Far above all principality, and **power**, and might,	1:21
2	given ... by the effectual working of his **power**.	3:7
3	to be strengthened **with might** by his Spirit	3:16
4	according to the **power** that worketh in us,	3:20
4	may know him, and the **power** of his resurrection,	Phlp 3:10
3	Strengthened with all **might**,	Col 1:11
3	his working, which worketh in me **mightily**.	1:29
3	but also in **power**, and in the Holy Ghost,	1 Th 1:5
2	be revealed from heaven with his **mighty** angels,	2 Th 1:7
3	and the work of faith with **power**:	1:11
3	with all **power** and signs and lying wonders,	2:9
2	hath not given us the spirit of fear; but **of power**,	2 Tm 1:7
4	be thou partaker ... according to the **power** of God;	1:8
4	form of godliness, but denying the **power** thereof:	3:5
2	and upholding all things by the word of his **power**,	Heb 1:3
7	with signs and wonders, and with divers **miracles**,	2:4
5	word of God, and the **powers** of the world to come,	6:5
4	but after the **power** of an endless life.	7:16
4	Through faith also Sara herself received **strength**	11:11
4	Quenched the **violence** of fire,	11:34
3	Who are kept by the **power** of God through faith	1 Pt 1:5
6	and **powers** being made subject unto him.	3:22
2	for the spirit of glory and of God resteth upon you:	4:14
2	According as his divine **power** hath given unto us	2 Pt 1:3
4	the **power** and coming of our Lord Jesus Christ,	1:16
3	angels, which are greater in power and **might**,	2:11
3	countenance was as the sun shineth in his **strength**.	Rev 1:16
4	no man can shut it: for thou hast a little **strength**,	3:8
4	worthy, ... to receive glory and honour and **power**:	4:11
4	the Lamb that was slain to receive **power**,	5:12
1	and thanksgiving, and honour, and **power**,	7:12
4	because thou hast taken to thee thy great **power**,	11:17
1	and **strength**, and the kingdom of our God,	12:10
4	and the dragon gave him his **power**, and his seat,	13:2
2	smoke from the glory of God, and from his **power**;	15:8
4	shall give their **power** and strength unto the beast.	17:13
2	rich through the **abundance** of her delicacies.	18:3
1	and honour, and **power**, unto the Lord our God:	19:1

Among the many words of the root *duna* (e.g., *dunamai* [1404], *dunastēs* [1407], *dunamoō* [1406], *endunamoō* [1727]) *dunamis* is the most important. *Dunamis* denotes "might, power, strength." In order to comprehend the background and content of *dunamis* in classical and Hellenistic Greek, a knowledge of the role of the term in the realm of philosophy is necessary.

Classical Greek

Greek philosophy in its earliest stages assigned *dunamis* an important part. Pythagoras' numerological speculations afforded *dunamis* a place as the creative power of the *kosmos* (2862), the "created world." Plato saw *dunamis* as the essence of existence. Poseidonius developed this speculation to its zenith when he considered *dunamis* to be the true and absolute cosmic principle, the dominant force in the microcosm and macrocosm. He maintained that *dunamis* was the original primeval force in all of nature and existence. Poseidonius built his entire cosmological theory upon the premise of *dunamis*.

These theories were decisive for the development of the Hellenistic concept of God. Stoics spoke of a self-created, self-generating energy which governed the world; this force was identified as God. Whereas God in Platonic philosophy and in Aristotelian theory was transcendent, here God was held to be a neutral impersonal force—*dunamis*. This force disclosed itself in lesser deities—*dunameis* ("powers, demons"). On this basis the gods of the Orient were imported into Greek thought; thus the Greek world became Hellenized under the pressure of the spirit of the Orient (see Reinhardt, *Poseidonius* as cited by Grundmann, "dunamis," *Kittel*, 2:288ff.). From this, Greek philosophy branched into more popular speculations about how these forces could be controlled, which led to the practice of magic. "Controlling fate" ordered the circumstances of a given individual in every aspect of life.

Septuagint Usage

It must be noted that *dunamis* as a New Testament term can be enlightened only to a limited degree from the vantage point of normal Greek usage. It is primarily Septuagintal usage which sheds light on its New Testament meaning. *Dunamis* is equated with 26 Hebrew terms. Nearly 140 times it stands for *chayil* and over 110 times for *tsāvā'*, most often in the meaning of "powers" or "military forces."

The great difference between "power" in Greek and "power" in Hebrew lies in the attitude toward God. In the Hellenistic world, with its impersonal concept of God, only a neutral principle of force which was active in the universe as powers of nature was recognized. This is quite different from the Old Testament concept. There the personal God appears. Instead of inactive natural powers, God is a personal power and might. While natural powers regulate the world, they do not operate exclusively according to fixed laws or principles (forces) of nature. Rather, these powers are determined and controlled by the personal will of God. In Greek literature the gods of heathenism are themselves subject to the powers of nature; in contrast, the God of Israel appears as the God of history who himself controls the world by His might. He is the Creator who governs history, and His *dunamis* is especially present in His redeeming acts in history which are exercised for the sake of His people.

The ongoing work of sustaining creation reflects a series of immeasurable divine manifestations of power (Isaiah 40:26; Jeremiah 27:5; 32:17). Phenomena of nature like those of Psalm 29:7 (cf. Exodus 24:15f.) are not the fury of arbitrary blind powers of nature; these are the glorious manifestations of the will of the Creator. They are revealed for judgment and salvation.

Salvation history as well as its setting—secular history—shows the power of God as He fulfills His eternal purpose (Exodus 9:13-16; cf. Romans 9:17f.). The entire history of Israel—the existence of the chosen people, their development, and their affect upon other nations—is proof of the power of God (cf. Exodus 15:6,13; 32:11; Deuteronomy 9:26,29; 26:8). Even one of the Old Testament names of God, the Lord Sabaoth (translated *kurios tōn dunameōn* in the Septuagint), represents the Almighty One who is master of the heavenly forces.

One of the great differences between the religion of Israel and the pagan nations which surrounded her was the attitude toward the "powers" of nature. In religions where an impersonal natural power is worshiped, there is also a belief that spells, charms, and magical rites can be used to master "the power." Israel was strictly forbidden to engage in any such practices. "Power" was only to be viewed with respect to the personal being of God; in place of magic the Scriptures elevated prayer, offerings, and obedience which was a result of faith.

Even such holy objects as the ark of the covenant were never permitted to be used in magical ways. When Israel attempted to secure a victory over the Philistines by bringing the ark into the battle, God allowed it to be captured by the enemy rather than encouraging heathen practices. The revelation of God's power in connection with the ark was always related to moral and religious truths; that is, Israel's faith in God and obedience to His precepts brought His protection and victory over the enemy. At a later period in Israel's history God even allowed the temple to be destroyed rather than to let Israel continue to believe that its presence in Jerusalem would guarantee the blessing of the Lord.

There were times in the history of Israel when God uniquely revealed His power through His instruments the prophets (e.g., Micah 3:8, of Micah; and Luke 1:17, a reference to Elijah). Moses was in a special way equipped with the power of God (Deuteronomy 34:10-12; cf. Acts 7:22). Later God's power worked through the judges (Judges 6:34; cf. Psalm 18:40; 2 Samuel 22:40f.).

The promise of the coming Messiah is linked to the power of God. He is furnished with the Spirit of power (Isaiah 11:2; cf. Micah 5:4; Isaiah 61:1ff./Luke 4:18ff.). Messiah carries the name "mighty God" (Isaiah 9:6). Judaism regarded this title as reserved for the Sovereign and Almighty God of the Old Testament. One of the major roles that Judaism expected the Messiah to fulfill was to crush the demonic powers of the spiritual realm. Thus the exorcism of demons and the curing of the sick were signs of the arrival of the Messianic Age.

New Testament Usage

The New Testament employs *dunamis* over 120 times, where it has various meanings. It may refer to God's power (Matthew 22:29), to the power of Jesus Christ (1 Corinthians 5:4), to the power of the Holy Spirit (Romans 15:13), to the power of the gospel (Romans 1:16), or to the power of the Cross (1 Corinthians 1:18). Romans 8:38 is one passage in the New Testament which refers to some type of hostile spiritual poweres, perhaps demon spirits, conquered by Christ but still waging battle against Christians (see discussion in Classical Greek section). Other verses may contain this same meaning of the word *dunamis*, for example, Mark 13:25, Luke 21:26, Hebrews 6:5, and 1 Peter 3:22.

Christ's incarnation was a result of the "power of the Highest," which indicated the keynote of the salvation the infant would provide (Luke 1:35ff.). Christ's coming, His life, His deeds, His death, and His resurrection confirm the entrance of redemption into history. Jesus the Prophet, mighty in deeds and words (Luke 24:19), possesses a unique power (Luke 4:14; cf. Acts 10:38). In the Synoptic Gospels the miracles of Jesus are termed "mighty works" (*dunameis*). They are understood as manifestations of the power of God (Matthew 11:20f.; 13:58; Luke 19:37). His deeds testified that God had sent Him as His agent (Acts 2:22) to bare a divine message (John 3:2).

The miracles of Jesus were radically distinct from the wonders and "miracles" which the exorcists and conjurers performed (Acts 8:9-11; 19:13). The revelation of the power of God is conditional upon a personal religious commitment to faith in God. The disciples could not heal the sick boy because they lacked faith (Mark 9:14f.). Even Jesus was hindered in Nazareth because the inhabitants lacked faith (Matthew 13:58). But nothing is impossible for those who have faith (Mark 9:23). Faith invokes the mighty power of God, and the one who has faith experiences His wonder-working power.

Jesus' miracles (*dunameis*) were worked by His powerful words. He overcame demonic forces like those found in sickness, sin, and death (Acts 10:38). The miracles of Jesus signaled the inbreaking of God's rule over the world, and marked the overthrow of demonic and satanic dominion. His wonders were "signs" (*sēmeia* [see 4447]) which indicated the eschatological time of redemption had arrived. They were signs of the divine kingdom and thus were messianic signs. They not only legitimized the divinity of Jesus, they also saved and released men from the power of the enemy.

Whereas the deliverance of Israel from their bondage in Egypt stands as the great demonstration of God's power in the Old Testament, the resurrection of Jesus Christ from the dead is the great demonstration of God's power in the New Testament (Acts 2:24; Ephesians 1:19,20). Through the Resurrection the power of death is broken (1 Corinthians 15:24f.). The resurrection life of Christ is lived through the power of the Resurrection—the power of the age to come (Romans 1:4; 2 Corinthians 13:4). It is the "power of an endless life" (Hebrews 7:16).

The return of Christ, which will consummate salvation, will take place with great power (Matthew 24:30), with His mighty angels (2 Thessalonians 1:7). By His power He will finally subdue all things and grant believers a share in His incorruptible and eternal glory (Philippians 3:21).

The period between the first coming of Christ and His return is the time of gospel proclamation. The resurrected Lord, who commanded His church to proclaim the gospel, also promised her power (Acts 1:8): "But ye shall receive power, after that the Holy Ghost is come upon you; and ye shall be witnesses unto me both in Jerusalem, and in all Judea, and in Samaria, and unto the uttermost part of the earth" (Acts 1:8). The gospel is the power of God unto salvation (Romans 1:16). It will be preached in the demonstration of the power of the Spirit (1

Corinthians 2:4f.), not with words of wisdom which render its power ineffective. The Word of God is alive in those who receive it. It is not simply a story of historical facts, but it has in itself creative power which can deliver man from the power of darkness and can translate him into the kingdom of Christ (Colossians 1:11-13).

The Church is the custodian of the power of God through the ministry of the Holy Spirit. The life and activity of the Church reflects a spontaneous expression of the power of God (Ephesians 1:17f). By the power of the Spirit it is possible to overcome the power of the flesh and to live a life commensurate with God's will. In the struggles of the Church against the power of the spiritual world the mighty power of the Lord stands as the only surety of victory and salvation (Ephesians 6:10).

In their service to and for God Christians are equipped with His supernatural power. On the Day of Pentecost the promise of power for the life and service of the believer was fulfilled (Acts 2:1f.). The variety of gifts of the Spirit enable the believer to both witness and live for the Lord. This power to witness not only concerned the power available to the apostles but the power at the disposal of every believer (Ephesians 4:8f.; 1 Corinthians 12–14). This *dunamis* of the Spirit will remain in the Church until the day of Christ's return.

STRONG 1411, BAUER 207-8, MOULTON-MILLIGAN 171-72, KITTEL 2:284-317, LIDDELL-SCOTT 452, COLIN BROWN 2:601-6,608.

1406. δυναμόω dunamoō verb
Strengthen, confirm.
COGNATE:
δύναμαι dunamai (1404)
SYNONYMS:
βεβαιόω bebaioō (943)
ἐνδυναμόω endunamoō (1727)
ἐνισχύω enischuō (1749)
ἐπιστηρίζω epistērizō (1975)
κυρόω kuroō (2937)
σθενόω sthenoō (4454)
στερεόω stereoō (4583)
στηρίζω stērizō (4592)

גָּבַר gāvar (1428), Be strong; piel: exert strength (Eccl 10:10).
עָזַז ʻāzaz (6022), Be strong (Ps 68:28 [67:28]).

1. δυναμούμενοι dunamoumenoi
nom pl masc part pres mid
2. ἐδυναμώθησαν edunamōthēsan 3pl indic aor pass

1 Strengthened with all might,......................Col 1:11
2 from weakness were made strong (NASB).........Heb 11:34

This comes from the root word *dunamis* (1405), "power, might, strength," and means "empowered" or "endowed with strength." Implied in its New Testament usage is the adding of power, i.e., having passed from weakness to a place of strength.

STRONG 1412, BAUER 208, MOULTON-MILLIGAN 172, KITTEL 2:284-317, LIDDELL-SCOTT 452, COLIN BROWN 2:601,603.

1407. δυνάστης dunastēs noun
Ruler, sovereign, court official, prince, potentate.
CROSS-REFERENCE:
δύναμαι dunamai (1404)

אָבִיר ʼāvîr (47), Strong (Gn 49:24).
אַדִּיר ʼaddîr (116), Noble person (Na 3:18).
אֵיתָן ʼêthān (393), Secure (Jb 12:19).
בַּיִת bayith (1041), Household (Gn 50:4).
גִּבּוֹר gibbôr (1399), Mighty man (1 Chr 28:1, 29:24).
גָּדוֹל gādhôl (1448), Great (Lv 19:15, Prv 18:16, 25:6).
חָזָק chāzāq (2481), Mighty ones (Jb 5:15).
יָרָה yārâh (3498), Hiphil: teach (Jb 36:22).
מִבְחָר mivchār (4144), Best (Dn 11:15).
מָשַׁל māshal (5090), Ruler (Prv 23:1).
נָדַב nādhav (5246), Compel; hithpael: volunteers (Jgs 5:9—Codex Alexandrinus only).
נָדִיב nādhîv (5259), Princes, officials (1 Sm 2:8, Prv 17:26, 25:7).
סָרִיס sārîs (5835), Court official (Jer 34:19 [41:19]).
עָצוּם ʻātsûm (6335), Mighty ones (Prv 18:18—Codex Alexandrinus only).
עָרִיץ ʻārîts (6422), Ruthless ones (Jb 6:23, 15:20).
פָּרָז pārāz (6769I), Warriors, throng (Hb 3:14).
רָזוֹן rāzôn (7615), Prince (Prv 14:28).
רָזַן rāzan (7619), Ruler (Prv 8:15).
רָשָׁע rāshāʻ (7857), Wicked (Jb 9:22).
שַׂר sar (8015), Prince (Dn 9:6,8, 11:5).

1. δυνάστης dunastēs nom sing masc
2. δυνάστας dunastas acc pl masc

2 He hath put down the mighty from their seats,......Luke 1:52
1 a man of Ethiopia, an eunuch of great authority.....Acts 8:27
1 who is the blessed and only Potentate,..............1 Tm 6:15

This word often refers to a potentate or other government official. The greatest authority is that of God, the only sovereign ruler of all creation. Its New Testament uses refer to authority which mightily govern, ranging from earthly authority to divine sovereignty. See Luke 1:52; 1 Timothy 6:15. In Acts 8:27 *dunastēs* could be translated "court official."

STRONG 1413, BAUER 208, MOULTON-MILLIGAN 172, KITTEL 2:284-317, LIDDELL-SCOTT 452-53, COLIN BROWN 2:601.

1408. δυνατέω dunateō verb
Be powerful, able.
CROSS-REFERENCE:
δύναμαι dunamai (1404)

1. δυνατεῖ dunatei 3sing indic pres act

1 for the Lord **is able** to make him stand (NASB)	Rom 14:4
1 God **is able** to make all grace abound (NASB)	2 Co 9:8
1 to you-ward is not weak, but **is mighty** in you	13:3

Although not found prior to the Christian period in either classical or Septuagintal Greek, *dunateō* is roughly equivalent to the verb *dunamai* (1404), "be able, strong enough," etc. (*Liddell-Scott*). It is related to the adjective *dunatos* (1409), "powerful, mighty."

In the New Testament there are three occurrences of *dunateō*, all in the writings of the apostle Paul. Paul informed those who would judge others that God is the only One before whom men appear; moreover, He is able (*dunateō*) to make the weak stand before Him just as He enables all men by His grace (Romans 14:4). In 2 Corinthians 9:8 again it is God who "is able to make all grace abound." Taking a slightly different tack in which he emphasized the "power" (*dunamis* [1405]) of Christ, Paul declared that Christ was not weak in dealing with the Corinthians, but He was among them in power (*dunateō*), for He lives by the power of God (2 Corinthians 13:3).

STRONG 1414, BAUER 208, KITTEL 2:284-317, LIDDELL-SCOTT 453, COLIN BROWN 2:601,603.

1409. δυνατός dunatos adj
Having power, mighty, capable, possible.
COGNATE:
δύναμαι dunamai (1404)
SYNONYMS:
ἐνεργής energēs (1740)
ἰσχυρός ischuros (2451)
κραταιός krataios (2873)

אַבִּיר 'abbîr (48), Mighty (Jgs 5:22—Codex Alexandrinus only).

אַדִּיר 'addîr (116), Nobles (2 Chr 23:20).

בָּחוּר bāchûr (1005), Chosen men (of war) (2 Chr 13:3,17, 25:5).

בִּין bîn (1032), Discern, understand; hiphil: teach (2 Chr 35:3).

אִישׁ הַבֵּנַיִם בֵּנַיִם 'îsh habbēnayim bēnayim (1174), Champion (1 Sm 17:4).

גִּבּוֹר gibbôr (1399), Mighty man, warrior (Jos 8:3, 1 Kgs 1:10, Zep 3:17).

גָּבַר gāvar (1428), Prevail (1 Sm 2:9).

גֶּבֶר gever (1429), Chief man (1 Chr 24:4).

גָּדוֹל gādhôl (1448), Great (Prv 25:6—only some Sinaiticus texts).

חָזָק chāzāq (2481), Strong (Jgs 18:26).

חַיִל chayil (2524), Mighty man (1 Sm 9:1, Na 2:3); capable man (Gn 47:6 [47:4]).

חָלַץ chālats (2603), Equip for war (1 Chr 12:24, 2 Chr 17:18).

חָסִין chāsîn (2731), Strong, mighty (Ps 89:8 [88:8]).

יָכֹל yākhōl (3310), Have the power to, be able to (Nm 13:30 [13:31], 22:38).

יְכִל yᵉkhil (A3311), Be able (Dn 3:17—Aramaic).

כַּבִּיר kabbîr (3642), Mighty (Jb 36:5).

כּוּן kûn (3679), Niphal: be right or proper (Ex 8:26).

עַז 'az (6006), Strong (Ps 18:17 [17:17]).

עֹז 'ōz (6010), Strength (Jgs 5:21).

עָצוּם 'ātsûm (6335), Strong (Mi 4:7).

פְּרָזוֹן pᵉrāzôn (6770), Peasantry (Jgs 5:7).

רַב rav (7521), Great (Jer 32:19 [39:19]).

רוּם rûm (7597), Be tall (Dt 1:28, 2:21).

שָׁלִישׁ shālîsh (8388), (Chariot) commander (2 Chr 8:9).

1. δυνατός dunatos nom sing masc
2. δυνατοί dunatoi nom pl masc
3. δυνατόν dunaton nom/acc sing neu
4. δυνατά dunata nom/acc pl neu

4 but with God all things are **possible**	Matt 19:26
3 if it were **possible**, they shall deceive the very elect	24:24
3 if it be **possible**, let this cup pass from me:	26:39
4 all things **are possible** to him that believeth	Mark 9:23
4 for with God all things **are possible**.	10:27
3 to seduce, if it were **possible**, even the elect	13:22
3 if it were **possible**, the hour might pass from him	14:35
4 Abba, Father, all things are **possible** unto thee;	14:36
1 For he **that is mighty** hath done to me great things;	Luke 1:49
1 sitteth ... first, and consulteth whether he be **able**	14:31
4 are impossible with men are **possible** with God	18:27
1 which was a prophet **mighty** in deed and word	24:19
3 it was not **possible** that he should be holden of it	Acts 2:24
1 and was **mighty** in words and in deeds	7:22
1 what was I, that I **could** withstand God?	11:17
1 an eloquent man, and **mighty** in the scriptures,	18:24
3 if it were **possible** for him, to be at Jerusalem	20:16
2 which among you **are able**, go down with me,	25:5
3 if it **were possible**, to thrust in the ship.	27:39
1 what he ... promised, he was **able** also to perform	Rom 4:21
3 to show his wrath, and to make his **power** known,	9:22
1 for God **is able** to graft them in again.	11:23
3 If it be **possible**, ... live peaceably with all men.	12:18
1 be holden up: for God is **able** to make him stand	14:4
2 **strong** ought to bear the infirmities of the weak,	15:1
2 not many **mighty**, not many noble, are called:	1 Co 1:26
1 God is **able** to make all grace abound toward you;	2 Co 9:8

4 but **mighty** through God to the pulling down	2 Co 10:4
1 for when I am weak, then am I **strong**.	12:10
2 we are glad, when we are weak, and ye are **strong**:	13:9
3 if ... been **possible**, ... plucked out your own eyes,	Gal 4:15
1 and am persuaded that he is **able** to keep that	2 Tm 1:12
1 may be **able** by sound doctrine both to exhort and	Tit 1:9
1 Accounting that God was **able** to raise him up,	Heb 11:19
1 and **able** also to bridle the whole body.	Jas 3:2
2 and the **mighty** men, and every bondman,	Rev 6:15

Classical Greek and Septuagint Usage

In the classical Greek of the Fifth Century B.C. *dunatos* first appears in the writings of Pindar and Herodotus. The etymology is undiscovered, but the intent is clear: It means "strong," "mighty," "powerful," or "able." It is used over 150 times in the Septuagint to translate 25 different Hebrew words. Most often it translates the Hebrew *gibbôr*, an adjective which generally means "strong" or "mighty" (see Joshua 6:2; Judges 6:12; Psalm 24:8 [LXX 23:8]). It is often descriptive of someone who magnifies himself, behaves proudly, acts boldly and audaciously, demonstrates valor, or acts like a tyrant. It may depict a strong hunter like Nimrod (Genesis 10:8,9), or the mighty Yahweh (Deuteronomy 10:17). There are other Hebrew words translated by *dunatos* that further broaden its meaning. For example, the Hebrew *'addîr* means "majestic" (2 Chronicles 23:20) and *bāchûr* means "valiant" (2 Chronicles 13:3).

New Testament Usage

In the New Testament *dunatos* appears 33 times. The Synoptic Gospels use it 12 times, but it is conspicuously absent in John's Gospel. In most other instances it occurs in Acts or the Pauline letters. As in classical Greek, three separate uses of *dunatos* are evident in the New Testament. First, it ascribes power to a person's being or attributes, for example, gods, angelic beings, powerful and prominent people, or persons who demonstrate faith and strong character. Similarly, *dunatos* may assign power to things such as weapons, commandments, and works of creation (including man). (See 2 Corinthians 10:4; 12:10; Revelation 6:15.) The second common usage of *dunatos* shows the ability of someone by virtue of personal effort or position to do something or wield power to effect change. This emphasis is *to do* more than *to be*. For example, a king with 10,000 troops must reckon whether "he is able" to defeat an army of 20,000 foot soldiers (Luke 14:31). (Also see 2 Timothy 1:12 and James 3:2.) The third usage treats the word as a neuter adjective instead of the verbal adjective of *dunamai* (1404). In this sense *dunatos* means "it is possible, practical, or can happen." (See Matthew 16:26; Mark 10:27; Luke 18:27.)

STRONG 1415, BAUER 208-9, MOULTON-MILLIGAN 172, KITTEL 2:284-317, LIDDELL-SCOTT 453, COLIN BROWN 2:601.

1410. δύνω dunō verb

Set, go down.

COGNATES:
    ἀπεκδύομαι apekduomai (550)
    ἀπέκδυσις apekdusis (551)
    ἐκδύω ekduō (1549)
    ἔνδυμα enduma (1726)
    ἔνδυσις endusis (1729)
    ἐνδύω enduō (1730)
    ἐπενδύομαι ependuomai (1887)
    ἐπενδύτης ependutēs (1888)

אָסַף 'āsaph (636), Withdraw (Jl 2:10, 3:15).

בּוֹא bô' (971), Qal: come (Gn 28:11, 2 Sm 2:24, Eccl 1:5); hiphil: make go (Am 8:9).

חָבַשׁ chāvash (2372), Bar (Jon 2:6).

חָלַץ chālats (2603), Equip for war; niphal: be delivered (Prv 11:8—Codex Alexandrinus only).

צָלַל tsālal (7019), Sink (Ex 15:10).

שָׁחַח shāchach (8249), Bow down; niphal: whisper (Is 29:4).

1. δύνοντος dunontos gen sing masc part pres act
2. ἔδυ edu 3sing indic aor act
3. ἔδυσεν edusen 3sing indic aor act

2 And at even, when the sun **did set**,		Mark 1:32
3 And at even, when the sun **did set**,		1:32
1 Now when the sun **was setting**,		Luke 4:40

This word is used to describe the setting of the sun. From the word that means "sink," this astronomer's term commonly refers to the setting of heavenly bodies (suns, stars) as they appear to "go down" and "sink" behind or into the horizon. *Dunō* is used in this literal sense in Mark 1:32 and Luke 4:40.

STRONG 1416, BAUER 209, MOULTON-MILLIGAN 172, COLIN BROWN 1:314.

1411. δύο duo num

Two, both.

1. δυσίν dusin card dat
2. δυσί dusi card dat
3. δύο duo card

3 walking by the sea of Galilee, saw **two** brethren,	Matt 4:18
3 he saw other **two** brethren, James ... and John	4:21
3 compel thee to go a mile, go with him **twain**.	5:41
2 No man can serve **two** masters:	6:24
3 there met him **two** possessed with devils,	8:28
3 **two** blind men followed him, crying, and saying,	9:27

δύο 1411

3	Nor scrip for your journey, neither **two** coats,	Matt 10:10
3	Are not **two** sparrows sold for a farthing?	10:29
3	John had heard ... he sent **two** of his disciples,	11:2
3	We have here but five loaves, and **two** fishes.	14:17
3	and took the five loaves, and the **two** fishes,	14:19
3	rather than having **two** hands or **two** feet to be cast	18:8
3	rather than having **two** hands or **two** feet to be cast	18:8
3	than having **two** eyes to be cast into hell fire.	18:9
3	then take with thee one or **two** more,	18:16
3	that in the mouth **of two** or three witnesses	18:16
3	That if **two** of you shall agree on earth as touching	18:19
3	**two** or three are gathered together in my name,	18:20
3	and they **twain** shall be one flesh?	19:5
3	Wherefore they are no more **twain**, but one flesh.	19:6
3	Grant that these my **two** sons may sit,	20:21
3	moved with indignation against the **two** brethren.	20:24
3	behold, **two** blind men sitting by the way side,	20:30
3	then sent Jesus **two** disciples,	21:1
3	But what think ye? A certain man had **two** sons;	21:28
3	Whether of them **twain** did the will of his father?	21:31
1	On these **two** commandments hang all the law	22:40
3	Then shall **two** be in the field;	24:40
3	**Two** women shall be grinding at the mill;	24:41
3	And unto one he gave five talents, to another **two**,	25:15
3	And likewise he that had received **two**,	25:17
3	he that had received **two**, he also gained other **two**.	25:17
3	also that had received **two** talents came and said,	25:22
3	Lord, thou deliveredst unto me **two** talents:	25:22
3	I have gained **two** other talents beside them.	25:22
3	after **two** days is the feast of the passover,	26:2
3	took with him Peter and the **two** sons of Zebedee,	26:37
3	At the last came **two** false witnesses,	26:60
3	Whether of the **twain** will ye that I release	27:21
3	Then were there **two** thieves crucified with him,	27:38
3	behold, the veil of the temple was rent in **twain**	27:51
3	behold, the veil of the temple was rent in **twain**	27:51
3	and began to send them forth by **two** and **two**;	Mark 6:7
3	and began to send them forth by **two** and **two**;	6:7
3	be shod with sandals; and not put on **two** coats.	6:9
3	when they knew, they say, Five, and **two** fishes.	6:38
3	taken the five loaves, and the **two** fishes,	6:41
3	and the **two** fishes divided he among them all.	6:41
3	than having **two** hands to go into hell,	9:43
3	than having **two** feet to be cast into hell,	9:45
3	than having **two** eyes to be cast into hell fire:	9:47
3	And they **twain** shall be one flesh:	10:8
3	so then they are no more **twain**, but one flesh.	10:8
3	And James and John, the sons of Zebedee,	10:35
3	he sendeth forth **two** of his disciples,	11:1
3	and she threw in **two** mites, which make a farthing.	12:42
3	After **two** days was the feast of the passover,	14:1
3	And he sendeth forth **two** of his disciples,	14:13
3	And with him they crucify **two** thieves;	15:27
3	And the veil of the temple was rent in **twain**	15:38
1	After that he appeared in another form **unto two**	16:12
3	A pair of turtledoves, or **two** young pigeons.	Luke 2:24
3	He that hath **two** coats, let him impart to him that	3:11
3	And saw **two** ships standing by the lake:	5:2
3	And John calling unto him **two** of his disciples	7:19
3	was a certain creditor which had **two** debtors:	7:41
3	neither money; neither have **two** coats apiece.	9:3
3	We have no more but five loaves and **two** fishes;	9:13
3	Then he took the five loaves and the **two** fishes,	9:16
3	And, behold, there talked with him **two** men,	9:30
3	glory, and the **two** men that stood with him.	9:32
3	the Lord appointed seventy-**two** others (NIV)	10:1
3	sent them **two** and **two** ... into every city and place,	10:1
3	and sent them **two** and **two** ahead of Him (NASB)	10:1
3	The seventy-**two** returned with joy (NIV)	10:17
3	morrow when he departed, he took out **two** pence,	10:35
3	Are not five sparrows sold for **two** farthings,	12:6
1	three against **two**, and **two** against three.	12:52
3	three against **two**, and **two** against three.	12:52
3	And he said, A certain man had **two** sons.	15:11
2	No servant can serve **two** masters:	16:13
3	in that night there shall be **two** men in one bed;	17:34
3	**Two** women shall be grinding together;	17:35
3	**Two** men shall be in the field;	Luke 17:36
3	**Two** men went up into the temple to pray;	18:10
3	the mount of Olives, he sent **two** of his disciples,	19:29
3	a certain poor widow casting in thither **two** mites.	21:2
3	And they said, Lord, behold, here are **two** swords.	22:38
3	And there were also **two** other, malefactors,	23:32
3	**two** men stood by them in shining garments:	24:4
3	**two** of them went that same day to a village	24:13
3	next day after John stood, and **two** of his disciples;	John 1:35
3	And the **two** disciples heard him speak,	1:37
3	One of the **two** which heard John speak,	1:40
3	containing **two** or three firkins apiece.	2:6
3	and he abode there **two** days.	4:40
3	Now after **two** days he departed thence,	4:43
3	five barley loaves, and **two** small fishes:	6:9
3	that the testimony of **two** men is true.	8:17
3	he abode **two** days still in the same place	11:6
3	and **two** others with him, on either side one,	19:18
3	So they ran **both** together:	20:4
3	And seeth **two** angels in white sitting,	20:12
3	the sons of Zebedee, and **two** other of his disciples.	21:2
3	behold, **two** men stood by them in white apparel;	Acts 1:10
3	And they appointed **two**, Joseph called Barsabas,	1:23
3	show whether of these **two** thou hast chosen,	1:24
3	in the land of Madian, where he begat **two** sons.	7:29
3	Peter was there, they sent unto him **two** men,	9:38
3	he called **two** of his household servants,	10:7
3	with recurrent fever and **dysentery** (NASB)	10:19
3	Peter was sleeping between **two** soldiers,	12:6
1	between **two** soldiers, bound with **two** chains:	12:6
3	And this continued by the space of **two** years;	19:10
3	Macedonia **two** of them that ministered unto him,	19:22
3	all with one voice about the space of **two** hours,	19:34
1	and commanded him to be bound with **two** chains;	21:33
3	And he called unto him **two** centurions, saying,	23:23
3	for two, saith he, shall be one flesh.	1 Co 6:16
3	let it be by **two**, or at the most by three,	14:27
3	Let the prophets speak **two** or three,	14:29
3	In the mouth **of two** or three witnesses	2 Co 13:1
3	For it is written, that Abraham had **two** sons,	Gal 4:22
3	are an allegory: for these are the **two** covenants;	4:24
3	for to make in himself of **twain** one new man,	Eph 2:15
3	unto his wife, and they **two** shall be one flesh.	5:31
3	For I am in a strait betwixt **two**,	Phlp 1:23
3	an accusation, but before **two** or three witnesses.	1 Tm 5:19
3	That by **two** immutable things,	Heb 6:18
1	died without mercy under **two** or three witnesses:	10:28
3	and, behold, there come **two** woes more hereafter.	Rev 9:12
3	horsemen were **two** hundred thousand thousand:	9:16
3	shall they tread under foot forty and **two** months.	11:2
1	And I will give power unto my **two** witnesses,	11:3
3	the **two** olive trees, and the **two** candlesticks	11:4
3	the **two** olive trees, and the **two** candlesticks	11:4
3	because these **two** prophets tormented them	11:10
3	the woman were given **two** wings of a great eagle,	12:14
3	given unto him to continue forty and **two** months.	13:5
3	**two** horns like a lamb, and he spake as a dragon.	13:11
3	These **both** were cast alive into a lake of fire.	19:20

The use of this word dates back as far as the Fifth Century B.C. It is widely used throughout classical Greek and the Septuagint to mean "two" (especially in the nominative form when used with a substantive; cf. "two demoniacs," Matthew 8:28; also 9:27; 10:10,29). When used with *ek* (1523) following, *duo* can mean "two of them" or "a couple" (Luke 24:13; John 1:35; 21:2). It can also be used as a general approximation for a small number ("where *two* or three are gathered," Matthew 18:20; cf. John 2:6; 1 Corinthians 14:27). Finally, it can be used as part of a distributive phrase when accompanied by a preposition: "in two," "two apiece," "two by two" (see Matthew 27:51; Mark 6:7; 15:38; Luke 9:3; 10:1).

Strong 1417, Bauer 209, Moulton-Milligan 172-73, Liddell-Scott 453.

1412. δυσβάστακτος
dusbastaktos adj

Difficult or burdensome to carry, hard to bear (burdens).

נֵטֶל nêṭel (5377), Burden (Prv 27:3).

1. δυσβάστακτα dusbastakta nom/acc pl neu

1 they bind heavy burdens and **grievous to be borne**, Matt 23:4
1 for ye lade men with burdens **grievous to be borne**, Luke 11:46

This compound, a form of *bastazō* (934), can be found in classical Greek as early as the First Century A.D. to mean "intolerable, grievous to be borne." Its single appearance in the Septuagint is found in Proverbs 27:3 where a fool's wrath is said to be heavier than both a heavy stone and *cumbersome* sand. In the two New Testament occurrences, Jesus used *dusbastaktos* to refer to the "burdens" the Pharisees and scribes put on the people, while they themselves never touched such things (Matthew 23:4; Luke 11:46). The implication goes beyond "heaviness" and suggests something about the burden that makes it a "grievous" experience, "hard to bear." This is contrasted by Jesus' invitation and promise of an easy yoke and a light burden (Matthew 11:29,30).

Strong 1419, Bauer 209, Moulton-Milligan 173, Liddell-Scott 454.

1413. δυσεντερία dusenteria noun
Dysentery.

1. δυσεντερίᾳ dusenteria dat sing fem

1 of Publius lay sick of a fever and of a **bloody flux:** Acts 28:8

This term, used since the time of Herodotus, has been transliterated into today's medical term *dysentery*. Although it did not originate as a technically medical term, Vine says it is formed from *enteron* which denotes an intestine (*Expository Dictionary*, "Dysentery"). Classical Greek clearly associates it with an "affliction," something one "suffers" from and which is usually accompanied by fever (see *Liddell-Scott*). There are no occurrences in the Septuagint to describe this ailment; however, its only New Testament appearance is consistent with the classical meaning. In Acts 28:8 Paul prayed and laid hands on the father of Publius while shipwrecked on the island of Melita. He apparently suffered from some form of dysentery. The KJV renders this term "bloody flux" in that same passage.

Strong 1420, Bauer 209 (see "dusenterion"), Moulton-Milligan 173, Liddell-Scott 456.

1413B. δυσεντέριον
dusenterion noun
Dysentery.

1. δυσεντερίῳ dusenteriō dat sing neu

1 of Publius lay sick of a fever and of a **bloody flux:** Acts 28:8

This term is the late Hellenistic Greek form of *dusenteria*. See the word study at number 1413.

1414. δυσερμήνευτος
dusermēneutos adj
Hard to explain, or interpret.
Cross-Reference:
ἑρμηνεύω hermēneuō (2043)

1. δυσερμήνευτος dusermēneutos nom sing masc

1 **hard to be uttered**, seeing ye are dull of hearing...... Heb 5:11

This is a compound word from *dus*, "hard," and *hermēneuō* (2043), "to interpret." Thus the meaning is "hard to interpret" or "hard to explain." It occurs in the New Testament only in Hebrews 5:11. The writer said his meaning was hard to explain because his audience had failed to grow spiritually, and they were spiritually hard of hearing.

Strong 1421, Bauer 209, Liddell-Scott 456.

1415. δύσκολος duskolos adj
Hard, difficult.

אֵיד 'êdh (344), Disaster (Jer 49:8 [29:8]).

1. δύσκολον duskolon nom/acc sing neu

1 how **hard** is it for them that trust in riches........ Mark 10:24

In classical Greek *duskolos* is used to refer to people who were hard to please or discontented and to things which were troublesome, harassing, or unpleasant. It occurs in the Septuagint in Jeremiah 49:8 (LXX 29:8) in reference to Edom's having "done unpleasant things" (*duskola epoiēsen*). The Hebrew text actually concerns God's promise to punish (cf. NIV's "bring disaster") Esau. In Mark 10:24 the meaning is "unpleasant" or "difficult." Thus, to give up riches is unpleasant and troublesome for rich men.

STRONG 1422, BAUER 209, MOULTON-MILLIGAN 173, LIDDELL-SCOTT 458.

1416. δυσκόλως duskolōs adv
Hardly, with difficulty.
SYNONYMS:
μόγις mogis (3289)
μόλις molis (3296)

1. δυσκόλως duskolōs
1 a rich man shall **hardly** enter into the kingdom .... Matt 19:23
1 How **hardly** shall they that have riches enter ..... Mark 10:23
1 How **hardly** shall they that have riches enter ..... Luke 18:24

This is the adverbial form of *duskolos* (1415). It is used three times in the New Testament, all in reference to rich men entering the kingdom of God (Matthew 19:23; Mark 10:23; Luke 18:24). The KJV translation, "hardly," should not be taken in its modern sense of "by no means" but rather in the sense of "with difficulty."

STRONG 1423, BAUER 209, LIDDELL-SCOTT 458.

1417. δυσμή dusmē noun
West, setting (of sun).

אַחֲרוֹן 'achărôn (315), Western (Dt 11:24).
בּוֹא bô' (971), Go (Gn 15:12, Ex 17:12, Jos 10:13).
יָם yām (3328), West (2 Chr 4:4, Dn 8:4).
מָבוֹא māvô' (4136), Setting of sun (Jos 1:4, Ps 50:1 [49:1]); west (Zec 8:7).
מֵעַל me'al (A4763), Sunset (Dn 6:14—Aramaic).
מַעֲרָב ma'ărāv (4790), West (1 Chr 7:28, Ps 107:3 [106:3], Is 59:19).
עֲרָב 'ărav (6386), Trade (Ez 27:9).
עֲרָבָה 'ărāvāh (6400), Desert, wilderness (Dt 1:1, Ps 68:4 [67:4]); plain (Nm 22:1).

1. δυσμῶν dusmōn gen pl fem
1 That many shall come from the east and **west**, ... Matt 8:11
1 and shineth even unto the **west**; 24:27
1 When ye see a cloud rise out of the **west**, ... Luke 12:54
1 they shall come from the east, and from the **west**, ... 13:29
1 south three gates; and on the **west** three gates ..... Rev 21:13

In classical Greek *dusmē* means "going down" or "setting" and usually refers to the sun but occasionally to "old age." It also means "the place of sunset," i.e., "the west."

In the Septuagint it refers to the time of sunset (Genesis 15:12), to the plains of Moab (Numbers 22:1), and to the west (Joshua 1:4). An interesting example is found in Psalm 50:1 (LXX 49:1) where it is ambiguous whether the reference is to time or location. In the New Testament *dusmē* always refers to the west, but "west" retains its cosmic significance (that is, meaning the "uttermost parts of the earth") in Matthew 8:11; 24:27; and Luke 13:29.

STRONG 1424, BAUER 209, MOULTON-MILLIGAN 173, LIDDELL-SCOTT 458.

1418. δυσνόητος dusnoētos adj
Hard to understand.
CROSS-REFERENCE:
νοέω noeō (3401)

1. δυσνόητα dusnoēta nom/acc pl neu
1 in which are some things **hard to be understood**, ... 2 Pt 3:16

From *dus*, "hard," and *noeō* (3401), "to think," *dusnoētos* occurs in the New Testament only in 2 Peter 3:16 where it refers to some hard-to-understand aspects of Paul's teaching which had been twisted by false teachers.

STRONG 1425, BAUER 209, KITTEL 4:963, LIDDELL-SCOTT 459, COLIN BROWN 3:122,124,129.

1418B. δυσφημέω dusphēmeō verb
Speak evil of, defame, slander.
CROSS-REFERENCE:
φημί phēmi (5183)

1. δυσφημούμενοι dusphēmoumenoi
nom pl masc part pres mid
1 we are **slandered**, we try to conciliate (NASB) ..... 1 Co 4:13

A rare word in classical Greek literature, *dusphēmeō* is found one time in the New Testament as a variant to the traditional text (i.e., the *Textus Receptus*) at 1 Corinthians 4:13. This passage records some of the hardships Paul endured for the sake of the gospel. Verse 13 says, "When we are *slandered*, we answer kindly" (NIV). The more common Greek term for "slander" is the word *blasphēmeō* (980).

BAUER 209, MOULTON-MILLIGAN 173, LIDDELL-SCOTT 461.

1419. δυσφημία dusphēmia noun
Slander, evil report, defamation.

CROSS-REFERENCE:
φημί phēmi (5183)

1. δυσφημίας dusphēmias gen sing fem

1 by **evil report** and good report: .... 2 Co 6:8

In classical Greek *dusphēmia* means "words of ill omen, things unlucky to say." It also means "slander, blasphemy, curses." In 1 and 3 Maccabees it bears the meaning of both "blasphemy" and "evil reports" (1 Maccabees 7:38; 3 Maccabees 2:26). In the New Testament *dusphēmia* occurs only in 2 Corinthians 6:8 where it is paired with its opposite, *euphēmia* (2143), "commendation, good report." It is used in reference to accusations brought against Paul and thus means "slander" or "bad report" rather than "blasphemy."

STRONG 1426, BAUER 209-10, MOULTON-MILLIGAN 173, LIDDELL-SCOTT 461.

1420. δώδεκα dōdeka num
Twelve; the Twelve.

1. δώδεκα dōdeka card

1 was diseased with an issue of blood **twelve** years, ... Matt 9:20
1 when he had called unto him his **twelve** disciples, ... 10:1
1 Now the names of the **twelve** apostles are these; 10:2
1 These **twelve** Jesus sent forth, ... 10:5
1 made an end of commanding his **twelve** disciples, ... 11:1
1 of the fragments that remained **twelve** baskets full. 14:20
1 ye also shall sit upon **twelve** thrones, ... 19:28
1 twelve thrones, judging the **twelve** tribes of Israel. 19:28
1 took the **twelve** disciples apart in the way, ... 20:17
1 Then one of the **twelve**, called Judas Iscariot, ... 26:14
1 the even was come, he sat down with the **twelve**. 26:20
1 lo, Judas, one of the **twelve**, came, ... 26:47
1 give me more than **twelve** legions of angels? 26:53
1 he ordained **twelve**, that they should be with him, ... Mark 3:14
1 And He appointed the **twelve**: Simon (NASB) 3:16
1 they ... with the **twelve** asked of him the parable. 4:10
1 which had an issue of blood **twelve** years, ... 5:25
1 for she was of the age of **twelve** years, ... 5:42
1 And he called unto him the **twelve**, ... 6:7
1 they took up **twelve** baskets full of the fragments, ... 6:43
1 They say unto him, **Twelve**. 8:19
1 and called the **twelve**, and saith unto them, ... 9:35
1 he took again the **twelve**, and began to tell them 10:32
1 he went out unto Bethany with the **twelve**. 11:11
1 And Judas Iscariot, one of the **twelve**, ... 14:10
1 And in the evening he cometh with the **twelve**. 14:17
1 one of the **twelve**, that dippeth with me in the dish. 14:20
1 while he ... spake, cometh Judas, one of the **twelve**, ... 14:43
1 And when he was **twelve** years old, ... Luke 2:42
1 his disciples: and of them he chose **twelve**, ... 6:13
1 preaching ... and the **twelve** were with him, ... 8:1
1 had one only daughter, about **twelve** years of age, ... 8:42
1 a woman having an issue of blood **twelve** years, ... 8:43
1 Then he called his **twelve** disciples together, ... 9:1
1 then came the **twelve**, and said unto him, ... 9:12
1 of fragments that remained to them **twelve** baskets. 9:17
1 he took unto him the **twelve**, and said unto them, ... 18:31
1 Iscariot, being of the number of the **twelve**. 22:3
1 he sat down, and the **twelve** apostles with him. 22:14
1 sit on thrones judging the **twelve** tribes of Israel. 22:30
1 he that was called Judas, one of the **twelve**, ... 22:47

1 and filled **twelve** baskets with the fragments .... John 6:13
1 said Jesus unto the **twelve**, Will ye also go away? 6:67
1 Have not I chosen you **twelve**, ... one ... is a devil? 6:70
1 Judas Iscariot ... being one of the **twelve**. 6:71
1 Are there not **twelve** hours in the day? 11:9
1 But Thomas, one of the **twelve**, called Didymus, ... 20:24
1 the **twelve** called the multitude of the disciples .... Acts 6:2
1 and Jacob begat the **twelve** patriarchs. 7:8
1 And there were in all about **twelve** men (NASB) 19:7
1 no more than **twelve** days ago I went up (NASB) 24:11
1 that he was seen of Cephas, then of the **twelve**: .... I Co 15:5
1 to the **twelve** tribes which are scattered abroad, ... Jas 1:1
1 from the tribe of Judah **twelve** thousand (NASB) ..... Rev 7:5
1 from the tribe of Reuben **twelve** thousand (NASB) 7:5
1 from the tribe of Gad **twelve** thousand (NASB) 7:5
1 from the tribe of Aser **twelve** thousand (NASB) 7:6
1 tribe of Nephthalim **twelve** thousand (NASB) 7:6
1 tribe of Manasses **twelve** thousand (NASB) 7:6
1 from the tribe of Simeon **twelve** thousand (NASB) 7:7
1 from the tribe of Levi **twelve** thousand (NASB) 7:7
1 from the tribe of Issachar **twelve** thousand (NASB) 7:7
1 from the tribe of Zebulun **twelve** thousand (NASB) 7:8
1 from the tribe of Joseph **twelve** thousand (NASB) 7:8
1 the tribe of Benjamin **twelve** thousand (NASB) 7:8
1 and upon her head a crown of **twelve** stars: 12:1
1 had a wall great and high, and had **twelve** gates, ... 21:12
1 had **twelve** gates, and at the gates **twelve** angels, ... 21:12
1 names of the **twelve** tribes of the children of Israel: 21:12
1 And the wall of the city had **twelve** foundations, ... 21:14
1 and in them the names of the **twelve** apostles 21:14
1 and in them the names of the **twelve** apostles 21:14
1 he measured the city ... **twelve** thousand furlongs. 21:16
1 And the **twelve** gates were **twelve** pearls: 21:21
1 And the **twelve** gates were **twelve** pearls: 21:21
1 the tree of life, which bare **twelve** manner of fruits, ... 22:2

Classical Greek
Although *dōdeka* simply means "12," this number has special significance from very ancient times. Rengstorf suggests that this is because of the division of the year in Babylon into 12 months which spread to the west by way of Egypt and Rome ("dedeka," *Kittel*, 2:321ff.). When used symbolically *dōdeka* suggests completeness. Vine says it is the number of "Divine administration"(*Expository Dictionary*, "Twelve").

New Testament Usage
In the New Testament it is most often used to refer to the 12 special disciples (Matthew 10:1; John 6:70) and occasionally to the 12 tribes (Luke 22:30), though some believe the reference in James 1:1 may refer symbolically to all Christians. The number is used as a round number (a dozen) in Matthew 9:20; 26:53; Mark 5:42; Luke 8:42,43.

STRONG 1427, BAUER 210, MOULTON-MILLIGAN 173, KITTEL 2:321-28, LIDDELL-SCOTT 463, COLIN BROWN 2:694,703.

1421. δωδέκατος dōdekatos num
Twelfth.

1. δωδέκατος dōdekatos ord nom sing masc

δωδεκάφυλον 1422

1 the eleventh, a jacinth; the twelfth, an amethyst..... Rev 21:20

This term occurs only in Revelation 21:20. See *dōdeka* (1420) for a discussion of the significance of "12."

STRONG 1428, BAUER 210, MOULTON-MILLIGAN 173, KITTEL 2:321-28, LIDDELL-SCOTT 464.

1422. δωδεκάφυλον
dōdekaphulon noun

The 12 tribes.

1. δωδεκάφυλον dōdekaphulon nom/acc sing neu

1 Unto which promise our twelve tribes,............. Acts 26:7

This is a compound word, from *dōdeka* (1420), "12," and *phulē* (5279), "tribe," meaning "the 12 tribes." It occurs in the New Testament only in Acts 26:7. The singular form of the word points to the perception of the 12 tribes as 1 unit.

STRONG 1429, BAUER 210, MOULTON-MILLIGAN 174, KITTEL 2:321-28, LIDDELL-SCOTT 464, COLIN BROWN 2:695.

1423. δῶμα dōma noun

Roof, housetop.

CROSS-REFERENCE:
δίδωμι didōmi (1319)

גָּג gāgh (1437), Roof (Dt 22:8, Jos 2:6, Ps 102:7 [101:7]).

1. δώματος dōmatos gen sing neu
2. δῶμα dōma nom/acc sing neu
3. δωμάτων dōmatōn gen pl neu

3 hear in the ear, that preach ye upon the **housetops**. Matt 10:27
1 Let him which is on the **housetop** not come down..... 24:17
1 And let him that is on the **housetop** not go down..Mark 13:15
2 they went upon the **housetop**,...................... Luke 5:19
3 shall be proclaimed upon the **housetops**."............ 12:3
1 In that day, he which shall be upon the **housetop**,..... 17:31
2 Peter went up upon the **housetop** to pray.......... Acts 10:9

Classical Greek
In classical Greek *dōma* generally means a "building" or a "house." Since the time of Homer, Eighth Century B.C., the word was used for any "room" of a house such as a hallway or dining room.

Septuagint Usage
The Septuagint uses *dōma* 25 times to translate the Hebrew *gāgh* meaning "roof, top." This narrower interpretation is the meaning that is consistently used throughout Scripture. (See Deuteronomy 22:8; Job 2:6; Judges 9:51; Psalm 102:7 [LXX 101:7]; Jeremiah 19:13.)

New Testament Usage
Throughout Biblical times the roof was an important part of private, family, and public life. Most roofs were flat and accessible by a flight of stairs adjoining an outside wall (cf. Matthew 24:17; Mark 13:15). Because of frequent use, Jewish law required rooftops to have a parapet or guardrail to protect family members and guests from falling (Deuteronomy 22:8).

While the roof was adaptable to drying and storing grains (Joshua 2:6), it served other fundamental purposes. The Jews used the roof as a place to retreat (2 Samuel 11:2), commemorate deliverance from captivity (Nehemiah 8:16), publicly mourn the loss of loved ones (Jeremiah 48:38; Isaiah 22:1), privately worship (2 Kings 23:12; Acts 10:9), conduct meetings (1 Samuel 9:25), and shout public announcements (Luke 12:3).

The proverbial phrase "to shout or proclaim on the housetops" is equivalent to the making of a public announcement or proclamation (Matthew 10:27; Luke 12:3).

STRONG 1430, BAUER 210, MOULTON-MILLIGAN 174, LIDDELL-SCOTT 464.

1424. δωρεά dōrea noun

Gift, bounty.

COGNATES:
δίδωμι didōmi (1319)
δῶρον dōron (1428)

SYNONYMS:
δόμα doma (1384)
δόσις dosis (1388)
δώρημα dōrēma (1427)
δῶρον dōron (1428)
κορβᾶν korban (2850)
χάρις charis (5320B)
χάρισμα charisma (5321)

חִנָּם chinnām (2703), Without cost, free (Nm 11:5, 1 Chr 21:24, Is 52:3).

מְחִיר mᵉchîr (4379), Price (Dn 11:39).

מַתְּנָה mattᵉnāh (A5154), Gift (Dn 2:48—Aramaic).

1. δωρεά dōrea nom sing fem
2. δωρεᾶς dōreas gen sing fem
3. δωρεᾷ dōreā dat sing fem
4. δωρεάν dōrean acc sing fem

4 If thou knewest the **gift** of God,.................... John 4:10
4 and ye shall receive the **gift** of the Holy Ghost...... Acts 2:38
4 that the **gift** of God may be purchased with money...... 8:20
1 was poured out the **gift** of the Holy Ghost............ 10:45
4 as God gave them the like **gift** as he did unto us,..... 11:17
1 and the **gift** by grace, which is by one man,.... Rom 5:15
2 the **gift** of righteousness shall reign in life by one,...... 5:17
3 Thanks be unto God for his unspeakable **gift**........2 Co 9:15
4 according to the **gift** of the grace of God........... Eph 3:7

| 2 grace according to the measure of the gift of Christ. | Eph 4:7 |
| 2 and have tasted of the heavenly gift, | Heb 6:4 |

Classical Greek
Greek writers of the classical period understood *dōrea* to refer to a "gift" or a "present," especially a "free gift." Josephus recalled that Moses received the laws of Sinai as a "gift of God" (*Antiquities* 3.8.10). Papyri show that "gift" or "benefit" was understood in the vernacular as well (see *Moulton-Milligan*). Closely related to this word is the adverb *dōrean* (1425), "freely."

Septuagint Usage
The Septuagint is familiar with both the noun and the adverb, but the adverbial usage dominates. The substantive use is witnessed more regularly in the portions without a Hebrew original (e.g., 1 Esdras 3:5; Wisdom of Solomon 7:14; but cf. Daniel 2:48 [Septuagint], Hebrew *matt‛nāh*). The writer of 2 Maccabees informs us that "cities had been given as a *present*" (*dōrēa*) (4:30, RSV; cf. 3 Maccabees 1:7).

New Testament Usage
The New Testament writers often used *dōrea* to refer to God's gift of the Holy Spirit (*dōrean tou theou*, John 4:10; Acts 8:20; cf. *tēn dōrean tou hagiou pneumatos*, Acts 2:38; 10:45; 11:17 [cf. verse 16]; Hebrews 6:4). God's supreme gift of Jesus Christ as the Saviour of the world is the demonstration of God's grace (*charis* [5320B]) (Romans 5:15,17).

Paul viewed his ministry as a herald of the good news as a "gift" (*dōrea*, not *charisma*; Ephesians 3:7; 4:7). The emphasis here is upon the "freeness" or unearned nature of God's gift bestowed upon Paul. Otherwise it is unwise to press any minor points of differences between the two terms.

STRONG 1431, BAUER 210, MOULTON-MILLIGAN 174, KITTEL 2:166-67, LIDDELL-SCOTT 464, COLIN BROWN 2:40-42.

1425. δωρεάν dōrean adv
Freely, without cause, without reason, undeservedly.
CROSS-REFERENCE:
  δῶρον dōron (1428)

1. δωρεάν dōrean

1 freely ye have received, freely give	Matt 10:8
1 freely ye have received, freely give	10:8
1 They hated me **without a cause**	John 15:25
1 Being justified **freely** by his grace	Rom 3:24
1 have preached to you the gospel of God freely?	2 Co 11:7
1 by the law, then Christ is dead **in vain**	Gal 2:21
1 Neither did we eat any man's bread **for nought;**	2 Th 3:8
1 athirst of the fountain of the water of life freely.	Rev 21:6
1 let him take the water of life freely	22:17

Classical Greek
Formally *dōrean* is the accusative of *dōrea* (1424), but since around the Fifth Century before Christ (Herodotus) it has functioned as an adverb meaning both "freely, without cost" and "without cause, reason."

Septuagint Usage
The adverbial usage dominates the portions of the Septuagint with Hebrew originals. Laban suggested that Jacob should not work "for nought" simply because they were kinsmen (Genesis 29:15). Elsewhere, the slave was permitted freedom "for nothing" after serving for 6 years (Exodus 21:2). A sense of "without cause" (frequently RSV) is also to be understood. This is often found in contexts alluding to killing "without cause" (e.g., 1 Samuel 25:31 [LXX 1 Kings 25:31]; cf. Psalms 35:7 [LXX 34:7]; 109:3 [108:3]; 119:161 [118:161]).

New Testament Usage
The adverb occurs nine times in the New Testament. The sense of "freely ye have received, freely give" (Matthew 10:8) is not so much an expression of liberality or generosity as it is "without cause, without expecting a return." Christians do not need a reason to give.

Psalm 35:19 (LXX 34:19), "(They) hate me *without a cause*" was applied to Jesus specifically (John 15:25). Jesus was not guilty of any crime. In another use, justification is "freely" given by God (Romans 3:24; cf. 2 Corinthians 11:7; 2 Thessalonians 3:8) to those having faith in Jesus (Romans 3:24). However, Christ died "without cause" (*dōrean*) if justification came through the keeping of the Law (Galatians 2:21). The "water of life" is also "freely" given (i.e., "without cost" by God). Again, the idea is not how valuable the water is (some might be tempted to say "priceless," making "without price" function as an adjective); rather, the emphasis is upon the "freeness" of God's gift (Revelation 21:6; 22:17).

STRONG 1432, BAUER 210, KITTEL 2:167, COLIN BROWN 2:40-41.

1426. δωρέομαι dōreomai verb
Give, present, bestow.

δώρημα 1427

COGNATE:
δῶρον dōron (1428)

SYNONYMS:
ἀναδίδωμι anadidōmi (323)
ἀποδίδωμι apodidōmi (586)
διαδίδωμι diadidōmi (1233)
δίδωμι didōmi (1319)
ἐπιδίδωμι epididōmi (1914)
ἐπιφέρω epipherō (2002)
ἐπιχορηγέω epichorēgeō (2007)
κοινωνέω koinōneō (2814)
μεταδίδωμι metadidōmi (3200)
παραδίδωμι paradidōmi (3722)
παρέχω parechō (3792)
παρίστημι paristēmi (3798)
προσάγω prosagō (4175)
προστίθημι prostithēmi (4227)
προσφέρω prospherō (4232)
χαρίζομαι charizomai (5319)

זָבַד zāvadh (2149), Endow (Gn 30:20).
חָבַר chāvar (2357), Piel: join (Sir 7:25).
נָתַן nāthan (5598), Give (Est 8:1, Prv 4:2).
קָרְבָּן qorbān (7421), Offering (Lv 7:15 [7:5]).

1. ἐδωρήσατο edōrēsato 3sing indic aor mid
2. δεδώρηται dedōrētai 3sing indic perf mid
3. δεδωρημένης dedōrēmenēs
   gen sing fem part perf mid

1 when he knew it ... he gave the body to Joseph.... Mark 15:45
3 According as his divine power hath given unto us.... 2 Pt 1:3
2 Whereby are given unto us ... precious promises:........ 1:4

In the Septuagint *dōreomai* is used of God's presenting Leah with children (Genesis 30:20), of offering a sacrifice (Leviticus 7:5), of the king presenting a ring to Mordecai (Esther 8:2), and of a father giving sound advice to his son (Proverbs 4:2). In the New Testament it is used of Pilate's giving Jesus' body to Joseph of Arimathea (Mark 15:45), of God's giving us everything we need for life and godliness (2 Peter 1:3), and of His giving very great and precious promises (2 Peter 1:4).

STRONG 1433, BAUER 210, MOULTON-MILLIGAN 174, KITTEL 2:166-67, LIDDELL-SCOTT 464, COLIN BROWN 2:40-41.

1427. δώρημα dōrēma noun
Present, free and undeserved gift.

COGNATE:
δῶρον dōron (1428)

SYNONYMS:
δόμα doma (1384)
δόσις dosis (1388)
δωρεά dōrea (1424)
δῶρον dōron (1428)
κορβᾶν korban (2850)
χάρις charis (5320B)
χάρισμα charisma (5321)

1. δώρημα dōrēma nom/acc sing neu

1 And not as it was by one that sinned, so is the gift: Rom 5:16
1 good gift and every perfect gift is from above,........ Jas 1:17

This word refers to "a gift or present freely bestowed on someone." It occurs rarely in classical prose, being a poetic form of *dōrea* (1424). It occurs twice in the New Testament (Romans 5:16; James 1:17). In James 1:17 it appears in conjunction with *dosis* (1388), "gift," in the phrase "every good *dosis* and every perfect *dōrēma*." J.B. Mayor notes that Philo (20 B.C. to 45 A.D.) used the words *dosis* and *dōrea* together, giving *dosis* the sense of "giving" and *dōrea* that of "gift" (*James*, pp.57f.). Thus *dosis* may refer to "the gradual giving of sustenance and guidance" and *dōrēma* as "the final gift of eternal life." Since the words of James 1:17 make a hexameter poetic line, this may be a verse from a lost poem. This would explain the poetic form *dōrēma* instead of *dōrea*.

STRONG 1434, BAUER 210, MOULTON-MILLIGAN 174, KITTEL 2:166-67, LIDDELL-SCOTT 464, COLIN BROWN 2:40-42.

1428. δῶρον dōron noun
Gift, offering, present.

COGNATES:
δίδωμι didōmi (1319)
δόμα doma (1384)
δωρεά dōrea (1424)
δωρεάν dōrean (1425)
δωρέομαι dōreomai (1426)
δώρημα dōrēma (1427)
δωροφορία dōrophoria (1428B)

SYNONYMS:
δόμα doma (1384)
δόσις dosis (1388)
δωρεά dōrea (1424)
δώρημα dōrēma (1427)
κορβᾶν korban (2850)
χάρις charis (5320B)
χάρισμα charisma (5321)

אֶשְׁכָּר 'eshkār (841), Tribute (Ps 72:10 [71:10]).
בֶּצַע betsaʻ (1240), Plunder (Jgs 5:19).
זֶבֶד zēvedh (2150), Gift (Gn 30:20).
לֶחֶם lechem (4035), Food (Lv 21:6,8, Nm 28:24).
לֶקַח leqach (4090), Teaching (Prv 4:2).
מְאוּם mu'wm (4113II) Spot (Jb 31:7).
מִגְדָּנוֹת mighdānôth (4169), Precious things (Gn 24:53).
מִנְחָה minchāh (4647), Present (Gn 33:10, Jgs 3:15, Is 39:1).
מַשְׂאֵת mas'ēth (5020), Tribute (Am 5:11).
מַתָּנָה mattānāh (5152), Gift (Prv 15:27, Ez 20:39).
נֶדֶר nēdher (5266II) Vow (Dt 12:11).

δῶρον 1428

קָרְבָּן qorbān (7421), Offering (Lv 1:2,3, 2:1, 3:6ff., Nm 7:3,10ff.).
קֻרְבָּן qurbān (7422), Supply (Neh 13:31).
שֹׁחַד shōchadh (8245), Bribe (Ex 23:8, Mi 3:11); present (2 Kgs 16:8).
שַׁי shay (8282), Gift (Ps 76:11 [75:11]).
תּוֹדָה tôdhāh (8756), Thank offering (Jer 33:11 [40:11]).

1. **δῶρον dōron** nom/acc sing neu
2. **δώρῳ dōrō** dat sing neu
3. **δῶρα dōra** nom/acc pl neu
4. **δώροις dōrois** dat pl neu

```
3 they presented unto him gifts;.....................Matt 2:11
1 Therefore if thou bring thy gift to the altar,...........5:23
1 Leave there thy gift before the altar,..................5:24
1 and then come and offer thy gift.......................5:24
1 and offer the gift that Moses commanded,..............8:4
1 say to his father or his mother, It is a gift,..........15:5
2 but whosoever sweareth by the gift that is upon it,....23:18
1 the gift, or the altar that sanctifieth the gift?.......23:19
1 the gift, or the altar that sanctifieth the gift?.......23:19
1 It is Corban, that is to say, a gift,.................Mark 7:11
3 the rich men casting their gifts into the treasury....Luke 21:1
3 their abundance cast in unto the offerings of God:.....21:4
1 and that not of yourselves: it is the gift of God:.....Eph 2:8
3 that he may offer both gifts and sacrifices for sins:...Heb 5:1
3 For every high priest is ordained to offer gifts..........8:3
3 are priests that offer gifts according to the law;.......8:4
3 in which were offered both gifts and sacrifices,........9:9
4 God testifying of his gifts:...........................11:4
3 make merry, and shall send gifts one to another;...Rev 11:10
```

Classical Greek

Any "gift" or "present," including the votive offerings of religion, could be deemed a *dōron* by classical writers. A second meaning of the word in classical Greek is "the breadth of the hand, the palm" (see *Liddell-Scott*). Its presence in the papyri shows that *dōron* was a term of the common people as well as a literary word. Sometimes "temple offerings" are called *dōra* (see *Moulton-Milligan*).

Septuagint Usage

The Septuagint reveals that *dōron* was frequently selected as an equivalent to *qorbān* (see the Greek term *korban* [2850]), an "offering" or "gift" which was usually offered to God. A *dōron* could include a "sacrificial offering" of any kind (e.g., Leviticus 2:5,7,13; Numbers chapter 7 passim). *Minchāh*, "gift," is also a popular equivalent for *dōron*. Its scope is even broader than *qorbān*, though, as it can refer to "tribute" (usually offered to kings). The Lord regarded the *dōron* of Abel but not of Cain (Genesis 4:4). Jacob sent Esau a "present" (perhaps "tribute" or even "bribe") to insure his safe passage (Genesis 32:13-21).

In the Old Testament, gifts were given on many different occasions: between friends (1 Samuel 18:4), on days of rejoicing (2 Samuel 6:19; Nehemiah 8:10; Esther 9:19f.), when coming before kings (1 Kings 10:24f.), and when visiting people in authority (1 Samuel 9:7). Subjects sent gifts to their rulers (1 Kings 4:21), and victors received gifts from those they had conquered (Judges 3:17; 2 Chronicles 17:11). While judges and witnesses were forbidden to receive gifts (Deuteronomy 16:19), judges were often bribed (1 Samuel 8:3 [LXX 1 Kings 8:3]; Isaiah 5:23; Micah 3:11).

The size of the gift varied with the ability of the giver and could be great (2 Kings 8:9) or small (1 Samuel 9:8). The type of gift varied also: money (2 Samuel 18:11); objects of gold or silver, clothes and weapons (1 Kings 10:25); provisions (1 Samuel 16:20); and cattle (2 Chronicles 17:11). There were also gifts given for religious purposes (Exodus 25:2f.; Ezra 8:25f.).

The Lord himself is the greatest giver of gifts. He is good, and He does good (Psalm 119:68). He satisfies the desire of every living thing (Psalm 145:16) and gives His people good gifts (Psalms 37:4; 104:27f.). The people of God, therefore, are urged not to forget all His benefits (Psalm 103) but to repay His goodness (Psalm 116:12).

The greatest gifts of God are salvation and forgiveness of sin (Psalms 6:5; 25:11; 32:1; 33:18f.; 86:5; 103:3). The free gift of this salvation reaches its fullness at the coming of the Messiah (Isaiah 53:5,11; 61:1-3). The concept of salvation through merit, which gradually became so prominent in Judaism, stands in direct conflict with the teachings and prophecies of the Old Testament.

New Testament Usage

The entire life of Jesus was an extension of the clear teachings of the Old Testament. His very life represented the service of giving, and He himself is the gift of God (John 3:16). Second Corinthians 9:15 calls Christ the "unspeakable gift (*dōrea* [1424]) of God." In addition, the salvation which comes to man through faith is by grace. This grace is God's "gift" (*dōron*) so that no one may boast of good works (see Ephesians 2:8f.). Salvation, which is "according to the riches of his grace" (Ephesians 1:7), is also referred to as the "gift of righteousness" made available through the obedience of one Man, Jesus Christ (Romans 5:15-19, especially verse 17). The God who "spared not his own Son, but delivered him up for us all" gives the believer all things (Romans 8:32); that is, He gives all things which pertain to life and godliness (2 Peter 1:3) both now and in the future (1 Timothy 4:8).

God's love, then, is expressed in His giving gifts to men, His greatest gift being His own Son. The Son of God perfectly expressed this attribute of God by giving His life as a ransom. In turn He commanded His disciples to lay down their lives in sacrificial giving. However, Jesus reminded them, "It is more blessed to give than to receive" (Acts 20:35). The entire Christian life, therefore, should be characterized by giving with a view toward serving God with a grateful heart in the process (cf. Romans 12:1; 1 Peter 2:5). This service of giving is to be effected with joy and with no thought of honor or compensation (Matthew 6:2f.; Luke 14:13f.). God will reward those who give out of love (Luke 6:38); however, the motive must be right in the eyes of God (1 Corinthians 13:3).

For the New Testament Evangelists (only in the Synoptics) *dōron* is specifically understood to be the "religious offering." Matthew used it explicitly in this manner eight out of nine times (e.g., 5:23,24; 15:5; but cf. Matthew 2:11 of the Magi's gift to the child Jesus); Luke used *dōron* twice in this way (21:1,4). "Offerings" were prescribed by Old Testament law (Matthew 8:4). Mark, in his single usage, linked *dōron* to the Hebrew *qorbān* which he transliterated into Greek (*korban*). By the time of the New Testament period *qorbān* was a type of "vow in which one's goods were ideally given to the temple (but in reality retained) and hence could not be given to others (Mark 7:11; Matthew 15:5)." (See also Coppes, "qorbān," *Theological Wordbook of the Old Testament*, 2:813.)

The Book of Hebrews, too, is particularly fond of the religious or ceremonial understanding of the term. One duty of the high priest, according to the Law, was to offer gifts (*dōra*) and sacrifices (*thusia* [2355]) on behalf of the people (Hebrews 5:1; 8:3). Nonetheless, such offerings were inadequate since they were only a "copy" of the real thing. Jesus, in His role as High Priest, offered himself as the true gift, i.e., sacrifice, which secured eternal redemption (9:11ff.). Such may indirectly be the imagery behind Ephesians 2:8: Salvation is the gift of God, i.e., God's offering.

Revelation 11:10 is unique in that there does not appear to be any religious imagery present. Simply "gifts" or "presents" is the best translation (as in Matthew; see also *didōmi* [1319]).

STRONG 1435, BAUER 210-11, MOULTON-MILLIGAN 174-75, KITTEL 2:166-67, LIDDELL-SCOTT 465, COLIN BROWN 2:39-43.

1428B. δωροφορία dōrophoria noun
The bringing of a gift.
CROSS-REFERENCE:
δῶρον dōron (1428)

1. δωροφορία dōrophoria nom sing fem

1 and that my service which I have for Jerusalem .... Rom 15:31

The word *dōrophoria* is a variant which replaces the term *diakonia* (1242), "service," in a few manuscripts at Romans 15:31. It may refer to the "collection" or "gift" Paul brought to Jerusalem. While the term may reflect Paul's original language, the only other extant occurrence did not appear until over 100 years later (see *Moulton-Milligan*). Perhaps the "service" Paul hoped would be acceptable to the Jerusalem saints was the collection he was bringing to them.

BAUER 211, MOULTON-MILLIGAN 175, LIDDELL-SCOTT 465.

ε

1429. ἔα ea intrj
Ah! Ha!

1. ἔα ea
1 Let us alone; what have we to do with thee, (NT)	Mark	1:24
1 Let us alone; what have we to do with thee,	Luke	4:34

This short word is an expression of great surprise. It is used in Attic poetry but only rarely in classical prose. Although *ea* can possibly be a command form of the verb *eaō* (1432), "to leave alone," it is unlikely that it means this in the New Testament passages where it occurs (Mark 1:24; Luke 4:34). Given the context of astonishment of the crowd, it is likely that the demons were crying out in astonishment as well. The word is used in the Septuagint only in Job, where it translates the Hebrew word for "yea!" or "behold!" (Job 15:16; 19:5; 25:6).

STRONG 1436, BAUER 211, LIDDELL-SCOTT 465.

1430. ἐάν ean partic
If, whenever.

1. ἐάν ean
1 if thou wilt fall down and worship me.	Matt 4:9
1 but if the salt have lost his savour,	5:13
1 except he first bind the strong man?	12:29
1 Except ye be converted, and become as ... children,	18:3
1 not pass away ... except I drink it, thy will be done.	26:42
1 And if a kingdom be divided against itself,	Mark 3:24
1 he will first bind the strong man;	3:27
1 except they wash their hands oft, eat not,	7:3
1 except they wash, they eat not.	7:4
1 Salt is good: but if the salt have lost his saltness,	9:50

Classical Greek
Ean is a conditional particle (derived from *ei an*) which indicates that something *may* take place (e.g., "if"). The form *eian* appeared after 400 B.C. along with other contractions such as *kan* (2550) (*kai* plus *ean*).

New Testament Usage
The use of *ean* in the contracted form *an* (300) seems to have led Biblical writers to connect *ean* with relative pronouns ("whosoever"). This use of *ean* for *an*, which occurs over 60 times in the New Testament, was a scarce usage in the papyri *except* for the period from 100 B.C. to A.D. 200. Deissman (*Bible Studies*, p.203) lists nearly 50 uses of *ean* in a great variety of documents while counting only 8 uses of *an*. The papyri evidence supporting the use of *ean* (as opposed to *an* as a relative pronoun) during the limited time period from 100 B.C. to A.D. 200 provides philological evidence for the dating of the New Testament.

In the New Testament *ean* occurs over 350 times. The predominant use of the word parallels its use in the Septuagint where it translates the Hebrew word *im* meaning "if." At times it even expresses the unimaginable future (1 Corinthians 12:15, "If the foot [were to] say ... "). The second use of *ean* is with a relative pronoun, such as *hos ean* (literally "who if"), translated as "whoever." The third use of *ean* is in conjunction with other particles including *ean de kai* ("even if"), *ean kai* ("if also"), *ean me* ("if not" or "unless"), *eanper* (1430B), "if only," and *ean te* ("whether or").

STRONG 1437, BAUER 211, MOULTON-MILLIGAN 177, LIDDELL-SCOTT 465.

1430B. ἐάνπερ eanper conj
If indeed, if only.

1. ἐάνπερ eanper
1 whose house are we, if we hold fast the confidence	Heb 3:6
1 if we hold the beginning of our confidence stedfast	3:14
1 And this will we do, if God permit.	6:3

Although some New Testament manuscripts divide this term into its two component parts—*ean* (1430), a conditional particle meaning "if," and *per*, an enclitic particle which intensifies or extends the force of words compounded with it (cf. *Bauer*)—many write it as a single word.

Moulton-Milligan shows a somewhat limited use of this construction but attests to its form as early as 14 B.C. However, Hatch and Redpath indicate a common usage of the term in the Septuagint (ca. 250 B.C.)(*Concordance to the Septuagint*).

Its three occurrences in Hebrews highlight the conditional element the term brings into a context. For example, Hebrews 3:6 (in the *Textus Receptus*) states that believers are Christ's "house" *if* they hold fast the confidence and the rejoicing of the hope firm to the end (see also Hebrews 3:14). Also, in Hebrews 6:3 a similar construction is used: "And this will we do, *if* God permit." Notice that in each of these occurrences *eanper* is found in clauses which contain a subjunctive mood verb (a mood which expresses potential action). This type of a construction (usually with *ean* but also with *eanper*) is called a "third-class conditional" clause and implies a *probable* future condition. Using Hebrews 6:1-3 as an example then, one can interpret the passages as saying, "*If* God permits, and it is likely that He will, we will move beyond teaching the basic doctrines of Christ and press on toward 'perfection' (*teleiōtēs* [4899], 'completeness' or 'maturity')."

BAUER 211, MOULTON-MILLIGAN 177, LIDDELL-SCOTT 465.

1431. ἑαυτοῦ heautou prs-pron
Himself, herself, of one's self.

1. αὐτῶν hautōn gen pl masc/fem/neu
2. ἑαυτῶν heautōn gen pl masc/fem/neu
3. αὐτοῦ hautou gen sing masc/neu
4. ἑαυτοῦ heautou gen sing masc/neu
5. ἑαυτῷ heautō dat sing masc
6. ἑαυτόν heauton acc sing masc
7. ἑαυτοῖς heautois dat pl masc
8. ἑαυτούς heautous acc pl masc
9. ἑαυτῆς heautēs gen sing fem
10. ἑαυτῇ heautē dat sing fem
11. ἑαυτήν heautēn acc sing fem
12. ἑαυταῖς heautais dat pl fem
13. ἑαυτάς heautas acc pl fem
14. ἑαυτό heauto nom/acc sing neu
15. αὐτόν hauton acc sing masc
16. αὐτούς hautous acc pl masc
17. ἑαυτά heauta nom/acc pl neu
18. αὐτοῖς hautois dat pl masc

9 morrow shall take thought for the things **of itself**.... Matt 6:34
7 They parted my garments **among them**,............... 27:35
6 and to love his neighbour as **himself**,............. Mark 12:33
7 provide **yourselves** bags which wax not old,........ Luke 12:33

Classical Greek and Septuagint Usage
Heautou is a third person reflexive pronoun generally translated "himself." In classical Greek this reflexive pronoun is very common, although a contracted form *autou* (841) was often used rather than *heautou*. From the time of the Tragic writers onward (Sophocles, Herodotus) the pronoun was also used on occasion for the first and second person, e.g., "ourself." Likewise, there are some 70 examples of *heautou* used for the first and second person plural pronouns in the New Testament. This reflexive pronoun is frequently spelled *heatou* in the papyri and inscriptions. *Heautou* is used throughout the Septuagint. Like classical Greek, the plural *heautoun* is often used for the first and second person plural.

New Testament Usage
In the New Testament *heautou* is the common word for "himself," appearing over 320 times. Whereas older Greek often used *autou* rather than *heautou*, this use appears only 20 times in the New Testament. The primary purpose of this reflexive pronoun is to indicate that the agent and the person acted upon are the same. Many of these actions upon oneself are attitudes which reflect internal, spiritual growth. Examples of internal things a person does to himself include: deny, humble, exalt, know, love, justify, condemn, deceive, examine, trust, and rejoice. External actions which one does to "himself" include save, cut loose, kill, gird, drink, give, and purify.

Heautou is also used in the New Testament, to a much lesser extent, to express the idea of possession of very personal things. In these instances it is translated "his own." Such uses include the possession of his own life, body, soul, wife, work, flesh, and things.

STRONG 1438, BAUER 211-12, MOULTON-MILLIGAN 177, LIDDELL-SCOTT 466, COLIN BROWN 1:547; 2:815-16.

1432. ἐάω eaō verb
Allow, permit, leave one alone, let be.
COGNATE:
προσεάω proseaō (4188)
SYNONYM:
ἐπιτρέπω epitrepō (1994)
דָּמַם dāmam (1887), Keep silent (Jb 31:34).
הַב hav (1957), Give (Gn 38:16).

חָדַל chādhal (2403), Cease (Jb 10:20).

נוּחַ nûach (5299), Settle; hiphil: leave alone (Ex 32:10, Est 3:8).

נָתַן nāthan (5598), Permit (Jb 9:18).

רָפָה rāphâh (7791), Relax, withdraw; hiphil: leave alone (Dt 9:14, Jgs 11:37).

שְׁבַק sh^evaq (A8131), Leave; hithpeel: be left (Dn 2:44—Aramaic).

1. ἐᾷς eas 2sing indic pres act
2. ἐᾶτε eate 2pl impr pres act
3. εἴασεν eiasen 3sing indic aor act
4. εἴασαν eiasan 3pl indic aor act
5. ἐάσαντες easantes nom pl masc part aor act
6. ἐάσατε easate 2pl impr aor act
7. ἐάσει easei 3sing indic fut act
8. εἴα eia 3sing indic imperf act
9. εἴων eiōn 3pl indic imperf act

```
3 not have suffered his house to be broken up....... Matt 24:43
8 And he rebuking them suffered them not to speak:.. Luke 4:41
2 And Jesus answered and said, Suffer ye thus far...... 22:51
6 Refrain from these men, and let them alone:........ Acts 5:38
3 suffered all nations to walk in their own ways.......... 14:16
3 but the Spirit suffered them not........................ 16:7
9 the disciples suffered him not.......................... 19:30
5 the morrow they left the horsemen to go with him,.... 23:32
4 cut off the ropes of the boat, and let her fall off...... 27:32
9 they committed themselves unto the sea,............... 27:40
3 yet vengeance suffereth not to live..................... 28:4
7 suffer you to be tempted above that ye are able;... 1 Co 10:13
1 because thou sufferest that woman Jezebel,........... Rev 2:20
```

Classical Greek

Eaō, which generally is translated "suffer," "allow," or "permit," is used in the passive voice in classical literature and means "giving up," as in conceding in an argument. It also carries the sense of "letting alone." It is occasionally joined with the negative (*ouk eaō*) to mean "not permit," i.e., "forbid" or "prevent."

Septuagint Usage

The Septuagint translators used *eaō* as a replacement for nine Hebrew terms, none of which predominate. Very often the sense reflected is "to allow" (e.g., Genesis 38:16) or "to leave alone" (e.g., Exodus 32:10; Deuteronomy 9:14). The negative construction (*ouk + eaō*) occurs as well (Joshua 19:47, Septuagint only; Job 9:18,28).

New Testament Usage

In the New Testament *eaō* appears 13 times and generally follows the classical usage. Ten of the thirteen appearances of *eaō* are from the hand of Luke (Luke and Acts). The primary meaning is "to allow or permit," although the word most often appears in the negative, as in Luke 4:41, Jesus "would not *allow* them (demons) to speak" (NIV).

Other uses include the idea of "letting alone," as in Acts 27:40, "Cutting loose the anchors, they left them (*eaō*) in the sea" (NIV). Perhaps the most unusual use of this word is the strong concept of "letting alone" found in Luke 22:51 where Jesus responded to Peter's having cut off the ear of the high priest's slave by saying, "Suffer ye thus far," i.e., "leave him alone."

STRONG 1439, BAUER 212, MOULTON-MILLIGAN 177-78, LIDDELL-SCOTT 466.

1433. ἑβδομήκοντα
hebdomēkonta num

Seventy.

1. ἑβδομήκοντα hebdomēkonta card

```
1 the Lord appointed other seventy also,............ Luke 10:1
1 And the seventy returned again with joy, saying,....... 10:17
1 all his kindred, threescore and fifteen souls........... Acts 7:14
1 and horsemen threescore and ten, and spearmen ...... 23:23
1 two hundred and seventy-six persons (NASB)......... 27:37
```

This number is used in Luke 10:1,17 as the number of apostles Jesus sent out to minister (there is some question as to whether Jesus sent out 70 or 72 disciples; a discussion of this is found in Metzger, *Textual Commentary* p.150). This number may have been based on the 70 elders appointed by Moses in Numbers 11:16 and perhaps was selected because of its connection with the universal number 7 (see *hepta* [2017]). The fact that there were 70 nations in the rabbinic conception of the world suggests that an apostle was sent out for each nation, pointing to the universal scope of the gospel (Rengstorf, "hepta," *Kittel*, 2:634). This theme of universalism is strongly emphasized in Luke.

STRONG 1440, BAUER 212-13, MOULTON-MILLIGAN 178, KITTEL 2:627-35, LIDDELL-SCOTT 466.

1434. ἑβδομηκονταέξ
hebdomēkontaex num

Seventy-six.

1. ἑβδομηκονταέξ hebdomēkontaex card

```
1 two hundred threescore and sixteen souls.......... Acts 27:37
```

Found nowhere in classical Greek nor in the Septuagint, this term is used once in the New Testament. In Acts 27:37 the number of people on board the ship that eventually ran aground on the shore of Melita was listed as *diakosiai*, "two hundreds," and *hebdomēkontoex*, "76."

ἑβδομηκοντάκις 1435

(Many modern texts divide this term into its two component words *hebdomēkonta* [1433], "70," and *hex* [1787], "6.")

1435. ἑβδομηκοντάκις
hebdomēkontakis adv
Seventy times (seventy times seven?).

שֶׁבַע sheva' (8124), Seventy (Gn 4:24).

1. ἑβδομηκοντάκις hebdomēkontakis
1 Until seven times: but, Until seventy times seven... Matt 18:22

It is unclear whether this word refers to 70 plus 7 or 70 times 7. It occurs only in Matthew 18:22 (in reference to Peter's question concerning how many times one must forgive) and in the Septuagint reading of Genesis 4:24 (in reference to the number of times Lamech wished to be avenged). The number is certainly symbolic and refers to universal, unlimited forgiveness.

STRONG 1441, BAUER 213, MOULTON-MILLIGAN 178, KITTEL 2:627-35, LIDDELL-SCOTT 466.

1436. ἕβδομος hebdomos num
Seventh.

1. ἑβδόμου hebdomou ord gen sing masc/neu
2. ἕβδομος hebdomos ord nom sing masc
3. ἑβδόμης hebdomēs ord gen sing fem
4. ἑβδόμῃ hebdomē ord dat sing fem
5. ἑβδόμην hebdomēn ord acc sing fem

5 Yesterday at the **seventh** hour the fever left him..... John 4:52
3 For he spake in a certain place of the **seventh** day... Heb 4:4
4 God did rest the **seventh** day from all his works......... 4:4
2 Enoch also, the **seventh** from Adam, prophesied..... Jude 1:14
5 And when he had opened the **seventh** seal,.......... Rev 8:1
1 But in the days of the voice of the **seventh** angel,...... 10:7
2 And the **seventh** angel sounded;........................ 11:15
2 the **seventh** angel poured out his vial into the air;..... 16:17
2 the **seventh**, chrysolyte; the eighth, beryl;.............. 21:20

This term occurs in such passages as John 4:52; Hebrews 4:4; Jude 14; and Revelation 8:1 as the ordinal for "seven." See *hepta* (2017). Its meaning from the time of Homer through the Septuagint and into the New Testament remains the same.

STRONG 1442, BAUER 213, MOULTON-MILLIGAN 178, KITTEL 2:627-35, LIDDELL-SCOTT 466.

1437. Ἔβερ Eber name
Eber.

1. Ἔβερ Eber masc

1 which was the son **of Heber**,....................... Luke 3:35

The son of Shelah in the genealogy of Jesus (Luke 3:35). The term *Hebrew* is possibly derived from it.

1438. Ἑβραϊκός Hebraikos name-adj
Hebrew.

1. Ἑβραϊκοῖς Hebraikois dat pl masc/neu
1 in letters of Greek, and Latin, and **Hebrew**,........Luke 23:38

Pertaining to writing, the inscription placed above Jesus was written in Greek, Latin, and *Hebrew* (Luke 23:38).

1439. Ἑβραῖος Hebraios name
A Hebrew person.

1. Ἑβραῖος Hebraios nom sing masc
2. Ἑβραῖοι Hebraioi nom pl masc
3. Ἑβραίων Hebraiōn gen pl masc
4. Ἑβραίους Hebraious acc pl masc

4 a murmuring of the Grecians against the **Hebrews**,... Acts 6:1
2 Are they **Hebrews**? so am I. Are they Israelites?... 2 Co 11:22
1 the tribe of Benjamin, an **Hebrew** of the **Hebrews**;.. Phlp 3:5
3 the tribe of Benjamin, an **Hebrew** of the **Hebrews**;...... 3:5
4 Grace be with you all. Amen..................... Heb 13:25

Hebraios is one of four New Testament words with the base *Hebra-*, all translated "Hebrew": (1) *Hebraikos* (1438), an adjective meaning "Hebrew/Aramaic" (language); (2) *Hebrais* (1439B), a noun with the same meaning; (3) *Hebraisti* (1440), an adverb for "in Hebrew/Aramaic"; and (4) *Hebraios*, a noun referring to a Hebrew *person*. *Hebra-ios* transliterates the Hebrew base and adds different endings to indicate case usage and to form related words.

Old Testament Background
The origin of the Hebrew word is debated. Some consider it a derivative of the name *Eber* (*-ber*), an ancestor in the sixth generation before Abraham (Genesis 1:14,27; cf. Luke 3:34,35). However, Scripture never applies "Hebrew" to anyone before Abraham or anyone except his descendants, nor is it found outside Biblical writings.

A more likely explanation takes the word from the Semitic root meaning "to pass over," whether "passing over" the Euphrates (from the viewpoint of Canaan), "passing over" from Canaan (from the viewpoint of Egypt), or "passing over" the Jordan (from the viewpoint of western Palestine). In a generalized way it could have meant "immigrant," which fits with Abraham and his descendants as sojourners in Canaan, Egypt, and Canaan once more respectively.

Septuagint Usage

In support of this view, the Hebrew word first occurs in Genesis 14:13 as a description of Abraham in Palestine. In this one case the Septuagint translates the term: "Abraham *the emigrant (peratēs)*." Later his descendants emigrated to Egypt, where the term appears again in the Joseph narratives (Genesis 39:14, etc.) and the Exodus account (Exodus 1:15, etc.). Later still it shows up in 1 Kings (LXX 3 Kings), when Israelites have long been settled in Palestine (4:6, etc.). The Israelites regarded themselves and were regarded by others as a people that came out of Egypt (Numbers 22:5; Psalm 114:1; etc.).

Some have wondered about connecting *Hebrew* with *Habiru* (ʿapiru), a recurring term in Near Eastern literature for "nomadic" peoples from varied ethnic backgrounds. In a more disparaging sense *Hebrews* might have meant "trespassers," although usage does not particularly suggest a negative connotation in the term itself.

The Old Testament uses *Hebrews* then as an ethnic term equivalent to "Israelites," that is, descendants of Jacob, in distinction from other such groups. First Samuel 14:21 (LXX 1 Kings 14:21) does use both words together but not in a clearly contrasting way. *Hebrews* does not mean slaves versus masters, as has been proposed, since Abraham was not subject to any master (Genesis 14:13; cf. 40:15; 43:32) and since "Hebrew" slaves stood in contrast to foreign slaves (Exodus 21:2; Deuteronomy 15:12; etc.). Genesis and Exodus contrast *Hebrews* with Egyptians; 1 Kings (LXX 3 Kings) contrasts it with Philistines, and in several places it contrasts Israelite and foreign slaves. In these connections the Septuagint uses *Hebraios* about 30 times for various forms of this Hebrew root.

The Apocrypha contrasts *Hebraios* with Babylonians in Judith 10:12; 12:11; 14:18 and with foreigners under Antiochus Epiphanes in the books of Maccabees (2 Maccabees 7:31; 11:13; etc.).

New Testament Usage

The three New Testament occurrences of *Hebraios* bring in a new distinction among the Jews by setting "Hebrews" in contrast to "Hellenists." The Hebrews retained Hebrew (that is, Aramaic) as their mother tongue and maintained a more distinctive Jewish culture. The distinction showed itself early in the Jerusalem church when Hellenists murmured against Hebrews, because widows among the Hellenists had been overlooked in the Christians' welfare ministry (Acts 6:1).

Later Paul twice called himself a Hebrew while defending his apostleship against Judaizers. Not only was he a descendant of Abraham and an Israelite, he was a Hebrew like his critics (2 Corinthians 11:22). Paul spoke Hebrew when he addressed the temple mob—conceivably classical Hebrew rather than Aramaic in this case (Acts 21:40 and 22:2). In Philippians 3:5 Paul said he was a "Hebrew of Hebrews," possibly meaning that he was a "top-notch" Hebrew in the sense of a Semitic superlative (cf. "Lord of Lords"). More likely, Paul meant that he was a "Hebrew-speaking (Jew born) of Hebrew-speaking (parents)" that retained Jewish customs while residing in Tarsus. Paul himself evidently grew up in Jerusalem, since he studied at the feet of Gamaliel (Acts 22:3; cf. 5:34). In both 2 Corinthians and Philippians the apostle to the Gentiles depreciated such distinctions as "foolishness" and "refuse" in comparison to the high calling of God in the Jewish Messiah (2 Corinthians 11:16-21; Philippians 3:7,8).

STRONG 1445, BAUER 213, MOULTON-MILLIGAN 178 (see "Ebraios"), KITTEL 3:356-91, LIDDELL-SCOTT 467, COLIN BROWN 2:304-5.

1439B. Ἑβραΐς Hebrais name-adj
Hebrew.

1. Ἑβραΐδι Hebraidi dat sing fem

1 he spake unto them in the **Hebrew** tongue, saying, ..Acts 21:40
1 heard that he spake in the **Hebrew** tongue to them, ... 22:2
1 and saying in the **Hebrew** tongue, Saul, Saul, ... 26:14

Hebrew dialect, that is, Aramaic (Acts 21:40).

1440. Ἑβραϊστί Hebraisti name-adv
In Hebrew.

1. Ἑβραϊστί Hebraisti

1 which is called in the **Hebrew** tongue Bethesda, ... John 5:2
1 the Pavement, but in the **Hebrew**, Gabbatha. 19:13
1 which is called in the **Hebrew** Golgotha: 19:17

ἑβραΐς 1441

1 it was written in Hebrew, and Greek, and Latin....	John 19:20
1 said to Him in Hebrew, "Rabboni!" (NASB)..........	20:16
1 whose name in the Hebrew tongue is Abaddon,......	Rev 9:11
1 a place called in the Hebrew tongue Armageddon.....	16:16

Adverb meaning "in Hebrew" or "in Aramaic" (John 5:2; 19:20).

1441. ἑβραΐς hebrais
See word study at number 1439B.

1442. ἐγγεγράφω engegraphō
See word study at number 1443B.

1443. ἐγγίζω engizō verb
Come near, approach, bring near.

COGNATES:
  ἐγγύς engus (1445)
  προσεγγίζω prosengizō (4189)

SYNONYMS:
  ἐντυγχάνω entunchanō (1777)
  ἐφίστημι ephistēmi (2168)
  παραβάλλω paraballō (3708)
  παρίστημι paristēmi (3798)
  προσάγω prosagō (4175)
  προσεγγίζω prosengizō (4189)
  προσέρχομαι proserchomai (4193)
  προσπορεύομαι prosporeuomai (4223)
  φθάνω phthanō (5185)

הָרַס hāraṣ (2117), Force through (Ex 19:21).

חוּשׁ chûsh (2456), Hiphil: hasten (Is 5:19).

יָחַל yāchal (3282), Piel: wait, make one hope (Ps 69:3 [68:3]—only some Vaticanus texts).

יָקֹשׁ yāqosh (3483), Catch; niphal: be snared (Is 8:15).

כָּנַף kānaph (3795), Niphal: hide oneself (Is 30:20).

מְטָא mᵉṭā' (A4428), Extend, reach, arrive, come (Dn 4:11,22—Aramaic).

נָגַע nāghaʻ (5236), Qal: reach (Jon 3:6, Jer 51:9 [28:9]); hiphil: come, draw near (Pss 88:3 [87:3], 107:18 [106:18]).

נֶגַע neghaʻ (5237), Wound, sore (Ps 38:11 [37:11]).

נָגַשׁ nāghash (5242), Qal: come near, approach (Gn 27:21, Jgs 9:52); niphal: come near (Ex 19:22, Is 29:13); hiphil: bring near (Gn 48:13, Is 41:22, Am 6:3).

קָוָה qāwâh (7245), Piel: wait for (Hos 12:6).

קָרֵב qārēv (7414), Qal: draw near, approach (Gn 27:41, 1 Kgs 2:1, Is 41:5); piel: bring near, approach (Is 46:13); hiphil: bring near, offer (Gn 12:11, Hg 2:14 [2:15]).

קָרֵב qārēv (7416), Approaching (2 Sm 18:25, Ez 40:46).

קְרָב qᵉrāv (7417), Battle (Ps 55:18,21 [54:18,21]).

קֶרֶב qerev (7419), In midst of (Hb 3:2).

קִרְבָה qirᵉvāh (7420), Approaching, seek (Is 58:2).

קָרוֹב qārôv (7427), Near, approach (Lv 10:3, Ru 2:20, Is 51:5).

1. ἐγγίζομεν engizomen 1pl indic pres act
2. ἐγγίζουσιν engizousin 3pl indic pres act
3. ἐγγίζοντος engizontos gen sing masc part pres act
4. ἐγγίζοντι engizonti dat sing masc part pres act
5. ἐγγίζοντες engizontes nom pl masc part pres act
6. ἐγγιζόντων engizontōn gen pl masc part pres act
7. ἐγγίζουσαν engizousan acc sing fem part pres act
8. ἐγγίζειν engizein inf pres act
9. ἤγγισεν ēngisen 3sing indic aor act
10. ἤγγισαν ēngisan 3pl indic aor act
11. ἐγγίσατε engisate 2pl impr aor act
12. ἐγγίσας engisas nom sing masc part aor act
13. ἐγγίσαντος engisantos gen sing masc part aor act
14. ἐγγίσαι engisai inf aor act
15. ἤγγικεν ēngiken 3sing indic perf act
16. ἐγγιεῖ engiei 3sing indic fut act
17. ἐγγίζει engizei 3sing indic pres act
18. ἤγγιζεν ēngizen 3sing indic imperf act
19. ἐγγίσει engisei 3sing indic fut act

15 Repent ye: for the kingdom of heaven is at hand...	Matt 3:2
15 Repent: for the kingdom of heaven is at hand..........	4:17
15 preach, saying, The kingdom of heaven is at hand.....	10:7
17 people draweth nigh unto me with their mouth,......	15:8
10 And when they drew nigh unto Jerusalem,............	21:1
9 And when the time of the fruit drew near,...........	21:34
15 hour is at hand, and the Son of man is betrayed......	26:45
15 behold, he is at hand that doth betray me...........	26:46
15 and the kingdom of God is at hand: repent ye,.....	Mark 1:15
2 And when they came nigh to Jerusalem,.............	11:1
15 let us go; lo, he that betrayeth me is at hand........	14:42
9 let us go; lo, he that betrayeth me is at hand.........	14:42
9 Now when he came nigh to the gate of the city,....	Luke 7:12
15 The kingdom of God is come nigh unto you..........	10:9
15 that the kingdom of God is come nigh unto you......	10:11
17 no thief approacheth, neither moth corrupteth.......	12:33
5 Then drew near unto him all the publicans...........	15:1
9 and as he came and drew nigh to the house,........	15:25
8 that as he was come nigh to Jericho,................	18:35
13 and when he was come near, he asked him,.........	18:40
9 when he was come nigh to Bethphage and Bethany,...	19:29
3 when he was come nigh, even now at the descent....	19:37
9 he was come near, he beheld the city, and wept.....	19:41
15 I am Christ; and the time draweth near:\..........	21:8
15 then know that the desolation thereof is nigh........	21:20
17 look up, ... for your redemption draweth nigh........	21:28
18 Now the feast of unleavened bread drew nigh,.......	22:1
9 Judas, ... drew near unto Jesus to kiss him.........	22:47
12 Jesus himself drew near, and went with them........	24:15
10 drew nigh unto the village, whither they went:.......	24:28
18 But when the time of the promise drew nigh,......Acts 7:17
8 And as he journeyed, he came near Damascus:.......	9:3
6 and drew nigh unto the city,......................	10:9
12 Then the chief captain came near, and took him,.....	21:33
4 and was come nigh unto Damascus about noon,......	22:6
14 we, or ever he come near, are ready to kill him......	23:15
15 the day is at hand:.............................	Rom 13:12
9 for the work of Christ he was nigh unto death,.....Phlp 2:30
1 by the which we draw nigh unto God.............Heb 7:19
7 so much the more, as ye see the day approaching....	10:25
11 Draw nigh to God, and he will draw nigh to you.... Jas 4:8
16 Draw nigh to God, and he will draw nigh to you......	4:8
19 Draw nigh to God, and he will draw nigh to you......	4:8

15 for the coming of the Lord draweth nigh.	Jas 5:8
15 But the end of all things is at hand:	1 Pt 4:7

Classical Greek
In classical Greek *engizō* means "to approach" or "bring near," often referring to drawing near to God. One form (*hoi engista*) is used by Antipho (4.4.1) to refer to the "next of kin," e.g., "those closest." The word is rarely found in the papyri.

Septuagint Usage
In the Septuagint *engizō* is a common word referring to both spatial nearness (Genesis 12:11) and time nearness (Isaiah 26:17). It is particularly used to describe both the approaching Day of Judgment and to describe one drawing near to God.

New Testament Usage
In the New Testament *engizō* occurs 42 times. It describes the approaching of events or people (harvest, Passover, the commander, men). *Engizō* is often used to describe the approaching of the kingdom of God (Matthew 3:2, etc.). It likewise refers to the imminence of various aspects of that spiritual kingdom: the hour of betrayal (Matthew 26:45), redemption (Luke 21:28), and the Second Coming (Hebrews 10:25).

Finally *engizō* was used to describe one drawing near to God spiritually: to worship (Matthew 15:8) and to meditate (James 4:8).

STRONG 1448, BAUER 213, MOULTON-MILLIGAN 178, KITTEL 2:330-32, LIDDELL-SCOTT 467, COLIN BROWN 2:53-55.

1443B. ἐγγράφω engraphō verb
Inscribe, engrave, write upon.
CROSS-REFERENCE:
γράφω graphō (1119)

כָּתַב kāthav (3918), Qal: write down, record (Dn 12:1); niphal: be written, recorded (Jer 17:13—only some Sinaiticus texts).

פִּתּוּחַ pittûach (6855), Engraving (Ex 39:14 [36:21]—Codex Vaticanus only).

1. ἐγγεγραμμένη engegrammenē
   nom sing fem part perf mid
2. ἐνγέγραπται engegraptai 3sing indic perf mid
3. ἐγγέγραπται engegraptai 3sing indic perf mid

2 rejoice, because your names are **written** in heaven.	Luke 10:20
3 rejoice that your names are **recorded** (NASB)	10:20
1 Ye are our epistle **written** in our hearts,	2 Co 3:2
1 **written** not with ink, but with the Spirit	3:3

In classical Greek the term *engraphō* is used with the sense of "to be enrolled or registered." This explains what Jesus said in Luke 10:20 to the 70 disciples, "Rejoice, because your names are *written* in heaven." Paul's use of the word in 2 Corinthians 3:2,3 is better explained in reference to Jeremiah 31:33 (LXX 38:33) and Proverbs 3:3 (although the Septuagint uses *graphō* [1119] rather than *engraphō*). Schrenk notes that the expression "to inscribe on the heart" was widespread in the ancient world ("*engraphō*," *Kittel*, 1:769f.). Paul stressed that Christ himself by the Spirit had "inscribed" the Corinthians on Paul's heart with the result that his ministry to them was divinely ordained *and* publicly obvious. See 2 Corinthians 3:7 for the further implications of this "inscription."

STRONG 1449, BAUER 213-14, MOULTON-MILLIGAN 178, KITTEL 1:769-70, LIDDELL-SCOTT 468, COLIN BROWN 3:482-83,486,490.

1444. ἔγγυος enguos adj
Guarantee, pledged.

1. ἔγγυος enguos nom sing masc

1 was Jesus made a **surety** of a better testament.	Heb 7:22

Classical Greek
Enguos is an adjective formed by the compounding of the preposition *en* (1706) and *enguē*, "security" (which according to Moulton and Howard is probably from an old form for *hand* [*Grammar of New Testament Greek*, 2:307]). It is found in both classical and common Greek. *Enguos* can mean "offering a pledge, surety" (as an adjective), or "one who guarantees" (as a substantive). It is attested in ancient writings of all kinds (Preisker, "enguos," *Kittel*, 2:329).

Septuagint Usage
Only the apocryphal portions of the Septuagint witness to *enguos*. In Sirach 29:15 a personal "surety" (RSV) or "guarantor" is pictured as investing his life in an almost saving act (cf. verse 16, *rhuomai*). The idea of "certain" or "guaranteed" (of victory) is plain in 2 Maccabees 10:28.

New Testament Usage
Hebrews 7:22 is the only instance of *enguos* in the New Testament. Jesus is the "Guarantor" (RSV "surety"; NIV "guarantee") of the superiority of the new covenant. Through God's oath (i.e., promise), which had to be carried out (cf. Hebrews 6:14f.), Jesus is a priest forever. Therefore He is able to "save completely" because He always lives to intercede (Hebrews 7:25). Jesus as God's pledge is the certainty of

God's promises and His ultimate salvation. He is the basis for hope—our "anchor of the soul" (Hebrews 6:19; cf. 6:11; 7:19; 10:23).

Strong 1450, Bauer 214, Moulton-Milligan 179, Kittel 2:329, Liddell-Scott 468, Colin Brown 1:372-73.

1445. ἐγγύς engus adv
Near, close to.
Cognate:
  ἐγγίζω engizō (1443)
Synonym:
  πλησίον plēsion (3999)
אָח 'ách (250), Brother, blood relative (Jb 6:15).
אֵצֶל 'ētsel (703), Above, over (Jer 35:4 [42:4]).
מוּל mûl (4272II) Opposite (Dt 4:46).
קָרוֹב qārôv (7427), Near (Ex 13:17, 2 Chr 6:36, Is 13:6).

1. ἐγγύς engus
2. ἐγγύτερον enguteron comp

1 ye know that summer is **nigh**:	Matt 24:32
1 know that it is **near**, even at the doors.	24:33
1 The Master saith, My time is **at hand**;	26:18
1 putteth forth leaves, ye know that summer is **near**:	Mark 13:28
1 know that it is **nigh**, even at the doors.	13:29
1 because he was **nigh** to Jerusalem,	Luke 19:11
1 see and know ... that summer is now **nigh at hand**.	21:30
1 know ye that the kingdom of God is **nigh at hand**.	21:31
1 And the Jews' passover was **at hand**,	John 2:13
1 John also was baptizing in Aenon **near** to Salim,	3:23
1 And the passover, a feast of the Jews, was **nigh**.	6:4
1 and drawing **nigh** unto the ship;	6:19
1 **nigh** unto the place where they did eat bread,	6:23
1 Now the Jews' feast of tabernacles was **at hand**.	7:2
1 Now Bethany was **nigh** unto Jerusalem,	11:18
1 went thence unto a country **near** to the wilderness,	11:54
1 And the Jews' passover was nigh **at hand**:	11:55
1 where Jesus was crucified was **nigh** to the city:	19:20
1 for the sepulchre was **nigh at hand**.	19:42
1 which is **near** Jerusalem, a Sabbath (NASB)	Acts 1:12
1 And forasmuch as Lydda was **nigh** to Joppa,	9:38
1 fair havens; **nigh** whereunto was the city of Lasea.	27:8
1 The word is **nigh** thee, even in thy mouth,	Rom 10:8
2 for now is our salvation **nearer** than when we	13:11
1 are made **nigh** by the blood of Christ.	Eph 2:13
1 which were afar off, and to them that were **nigh**.	2:17
1 The Lord is **at hand**.	Phlp 4:5
1 is rejected, and is **nigh** unto cursing;	Heb 6:8
1 that which decayeth ... is ready to vanish away.	8:13
1 for the time is **at hand**.	Rev 1:3
1 Seal not the sayings ... for the time is **at hand**.	22:10

Classical Greek
Engus is a versatile adverb in classical Greek. "Near" is its simplified meaning, but it can mean "near" in reference to place, in reference to time, in reference to quantity, or in reference to relationships (see *Liddell-Scott*). The comparative "nearer," *enguteron*, is also common in classical Greek.

Septuagint Usage
In the Septuagint *engus*, together with its various forms (*engion, engutatos, engista*), translates seven Hebrew terms. The most common equivalent (43 out of 50 times with a Hebrew original) is *qārôv*, "near." Spatial use is common (Genesis 19:20, the city is "near"), as is temporal (Deuteronomy 32:35, of the day of destruction that is "near"; cf. Isaiah 13:6). A relational use is attested in Psalm 34:18: The Lord is "near" the brokenhearted.

New Testament Usage
Thirty-two instances of *engus* are recorded in the New Testament including the comparative and superlative forms *enguteron* and *engista* (Mark 6:36; Romans 13:11). The Gospels and Acts are more fond of *engus* (23 times)—probably due to their travel narratives—than the epistles (9 times). *Engus* as an adverb of place is common (e.g., Luke 19:11; John 3:23; 6:19,23; Acts 27:8), but its use as an adverb of time is equally apparent (e.g., Matthew 24:32 with parallels; John 2:13; 6:4; 7:2). Many times its temporal function has an eschatological flavor (e.g., Luke 21:31; Philippians 4:5; Hebrews 8:13; cf. Revelation 1:3; 22:10).

Engus functions as a relational term in Ephesians 2:13, although a play on the term as an adverb of place is also to be allowed. Those who were "far off," *makran* (3084), have been brought "near" by the blood of Christ (Ephesians 2:18; cf. 2:17).

Strong 1451, Bauer 214, Moulton-Milligan 179, Kittel 2:330-32, Liddell-Scott 468, Colin Brown 2:52-54.

1446. ἐγείρω egeirō verb
Raise, be raised, rise, appear, wake up, arouse!
Cognates:
  διεγείρω diegeirō (1320)
  ἔγερσις egersis (1447)
  ἐξεγείρω exegeirō (1809)
  ἐπεγείρω epegeirō (1877)
  συνεγείρω sunegeirō (4741)
Synonyms:
  διεγείρω diegeirō (1320)
  ἐξανίστημι exanistēmi (1801)
  ἐξεγείρω exegeirō (1809)
בָּקַשׁ bāqash (1272), Seek, try to get (Prv 17:11).
גָּרָה gārâh (1667), Piel: begin a dispute (Prv 29:22).
הָלַךְ hālakh (2050), Go (Ex 5:8).
יָדַע yādhaʻ (3156), Know, observe (Ez 38:14).
יָקַץ yāqats (3477), Awake, wake up (Gn 41:4,7).
לָקַח lāqach (4089), Take, lay hold of (1 Sm 5:3).
נוּעַ nûaʻ (5309), Hiphil: shake, tremble (Dn 10:10).
עוּר ʻâwar (5996), Qal: be awake (Ps 108:2 [107:2]);

ἐγείρω 1446

niphal: be stirred up, be set in motion (Jer 6:22—Codex Vaticanus only); polel: stir up, disturb (Is 10:26); hiphil: rouse, stir up (S/S 2:7, Jer 51:11 [28:11]).

עָלָה ʿālâh (6148), Hiphil: stirs up (Prv 15:1).

עָמַד ʿāmadh (6198), Stand, take one's stand; hiphil: set, raise up (Dn 8:18).

קוּם qûm (7251), Qal: rise up (1 Chr 10:12, Prv 6:9); hiphil; raise up, establish (Jgs 2:16, Ps 113:7 [112:7], Is 14:9).

קִיץ qîts (7301), Hiphil: awake (2 Kgs 4:31).

רוּם rûm (7597), Be high, arise; hiphil: raise, lift up (1 Sm 2:8).

שָׁכַם shākham (8326), Hiphil: get up, rise early (Is 5:11).

שָׁקַד shāqadh (8613), Be vigilant, watchful (Jer 44:27 [51:27]).

תָּמַךְ tāmakh (8881), Take hold of, grasp (Prv 29:23—only some Sinaiticus texts).

1. ἐγείρει egeirei 3sing indic pres act
2. ἐγείρετε egeirete 2pl impr pres act
3. ἐγείροντι egeironti dat sing masc part pres act
4. ἐγείρειν egeirein inf pres act
5. ἤγειρεν ēgeiren 3sing indic aor act
6. ἤγειραν ēgeiran 3pl indic aor act
7. ἐγείρας egeiras nom sing masc part aor act
8. ἐγείραντος egeirantos gen sing masc part aor act
9. ἐγείραντα egeiranta acc sing masc part aor act
10. ἐγεῖραι egeirai inf aor act
11. ἐγερῶ egerō 1sing indic fut act
12. ἐγερεῖς egereis 2sing indic fut act
13. ἐγερεῖ egerei 3sing indic fut act
14. ἐγείρομαι egeiromai 1sing indic pres mid
15. ἐγείρεται egeiretai 3sing indic pres mid
16. ἐγείρονται egeirontai 3pl indic pres mid
17. ἐγείρηται egeirētai 3sing subj pres mid
18. ἐγείρεσθε egeiresthe 2pl impr pres mid
19. ἐγείρου egeirou 2sing impr pres mid
20. ἠγέρθη ēgerthē 3sing indic aor pass
21. ἠγέρθησαν ēgerthēsan 3pl indic aor pass
22. ἐγερθῇ egerthē 3sing subj aor pass
23. ἐγέρθητι egerthēti 2sing impr aor pass
24. ἐγέρθητε egerthēte 2pl impr aor pass
25. ἐγερθείς egertheis nom sing masc part aor pass
26. ἐγερθέντι egerthenti dat sing masc part aor pass
27. ἐγερθῆναι egerthēnai inf aor pass
28. ἔγειραι egeirai 2sing impr aor mid
29. ἐγήγερται egēgertai 3sing indic perf mid
30. ἐγηγερμένον egēgermenon acc sing masc part perf mid
31. ἐγερθήσεται egerthēsetai 3sing indic fut pass
32. ἐγερθήσονται egerthēsontai 3pl indic fut pass
33. ἐγείρουσιν egeirousin 3pl indic pres act
34. ἔγειρε egeire 2sing impr pres act

25	And Joseph **arose** from his sleep (NASB)	Matt 1:24
25	angel of the Lord ... saying, **Arise**,	2:13
25	When he **arose**, he took ... child and his mother	2:14
25	Saying, **Arise**, and take the young child	2:20
25	And he **arose**, and took the young child	2:21
10	of these stones **to raise up** children unto Abraham	3:9
20	and **she arose**, and ministered unto them	8:15
6	And his disciples came to him, and **awoke him**,	8:25
25	Then he **arose**, and rebuked the winds and the sea;	8:26
28	or to say, **Arise**, and walk?	9:5
34	or to say, **Arise**, and walk?	9:5
25	**Arise**, take up thy bed, and go unto thine house	9:6
34	**Arise**, take up thy bed, and go unto thine house	9:6
25	And he **arose**, and departed to his house	9:7
25	And Jesus **arose**, and followed him,	9:19
20	and took her by the hand, and the maid **arose**	9:25
2	Heal the sick, cleanse the lepers, **raise** the dead,	10:8
16	the deaf hear, the dead **are raised up**,	11:5
29	there hath not **risen** a greater than John the Baptist	11:11
13	will he not lay hold on it, and **lift it out**?	12:11
1	will he not lay hold on it, and **lift it out**?	12:11
31	queen of the south **shall rise up** in the judgment	12:42
20	John the Baptist; he **is risen** from the dead;	14:2
27	and be killed, and **be raised** again the third day	16:21
24	touched them, and said, **Arise**, and be not afraid	17:7
22	until the Son of Man **has risen** (NASB)	17:9
31	and the third day he **shall be raised** again	17:23
31	and on the third day He **will be raised up** (NASB)	20:19
31	For nation **shall rise** against nation,	24:7
32	false prophets **shall rise**, and shall deceive many,	24:11
32	there **shall arise** false Christs, and false prophets,	24:24
21	all those virgins **arose**, and trimmed their lamps	25:7
27	But after **I am risen again**, I will go before you	26:32
18	**Rise**, let us be going: ... is at hand that ... betray	26:46
20	and many bodies of the saints which slept **arose**,	27:52
21	and many bodies of the saints which slept **arose**,	27:52
14	After three days **I will rise** again	27:63
20	say unto the people, He **is risen** from the dead:	27:64
20	He is not here: for **he is risen**, as he said	28:6
20	and tell his disciples that he **is risen** from the dead;	28:7
5	came and took her by the hand, and **lifted her up**;	Mark 1:31
28	Thy sins be forgiven thee; or to say, **Arise**,	2:9
34	Thy sins be forgiven thee; or to say, **Arise**,	2:9
19	Thy sins be forgiven thee; or to say, **Arise**,	2:9
28	**Arise**, and take up thy bed, and go thy way	2:11
34	**Arise**, and take up thy bed, and go thy way	2:11
20	And immediately **he arose**, took up the bed,	2:12
28	saith unto the man ... **Stand forth**	3:3
34	saith unto the man ... **Stand forth**	3:3
17	And should sleep, and **rise** night and day,	4:27
33	and they **awoke Him** and said (NASB)	4:38
28	Talitha cumi; ... I say unto thee, **arise**	5:41
34	Talitha cumi; ... I say unto thee, **arise**	5:41
20	That John the Baptist **was risen** from the dead,	6:14
29	That John the Baptist **was risen** from the dead,	6:14
20	John, whom I beheaded: he **is risen** from the dead	6:16
5	But Jesus took him by the hand, and **lifted him up**;	9:27
28	Be of good comfort, **rise**; he calleth thee	10:49
34	Be of good comfort, **rise**; he calleth thee	10:49
16	And as touching the dead, that **they rise**:	12:26
31	For nation **shall rise** against nation,	13:8
32	For false Christs and false prophets **shall rise**,	13:22
27	But after **I am risen**, I will go before you	14:28
18	**Rise up**, let us go; lo, he that betrayeth me	14:42
20	which was crucified: he **is risen**; he is not here:	16:6
30	them which had seen him after he **was risen**	16:14
5	And hath **raised up** an horn of salvation for us	Luke 1:69
10	That God is able of these stones **to raise up**	3:8
28	to say, Thy sins be forgiven thee; or to say, **Rise up**	5:23
34	to say, Thy sins be forgiven thee; or to say, **Rise up**	5:23
28	I say unto thee, **Arise**, and take up thy couch,	5:24
34	I say unto thee, **Arise**, and take up thy couch,	5:24
28	**Rise up**, and stand forth in the midst	6:8
34	**Rise up**, and stand forth in the midst	6:8
23	And he said, Young man, I say unto thee, **Arise**	7:14
29	saying, That a great prophet **is risen up** among us;	7:16
20	saying, That a great prophet **is risen up** among us;	7:16

ἐγείρω 1446

16	the deaf hear, the dead **are raised**,	Luke 7:22
25	Then he **arose**, and rebuked the wind	8:24
19	by the hand, and called, saying, Maid, **arise**.	8:54
34	by the hand, and called, saying, Maid, **arise**.	8:54
29	it was said ... that John **was risen** from the dead;	9:7
20	it was said ... that John **was risen** from the dead;	9:7
27	and be slain, and **be raised** the third day.	9:22
25	yet because of his importunity he **will rise** and give	11:8
31	queen of the south **shall rise up** in the judgment	11:31
22	When once the master of the house **is risen up**,	13:25
16	Now that the dead **are raised**,	20:37
31	said he unto them, Nation **shall rise** against nation,	21:10
20	He is not here, but **is risen:**	24:6
20	Lord **is risen** indeed, and hath appeared to Simon.	24:34
11	and in three days I **will raise** it **up**.	John 2:19
12	and wilt thou **rear** it **up** in three days?	2:20
20	When therefore he **was risen** from the dead,	2:22
28	Jesus saith ... **Rise**, take up thy bed, and walk.	5:8
34	Jesus saith ... **Rise**, take up thy bed, and walk.	5:8
1	For as the Father **raiseth up** the dead,	5:21
29	for out of Galilee **ariseth** no prophet.	7:52
15	for out of Galilee **ariseth** no prophet.	7:52
15	she **arose** quickly, and came unto him.	11:29
20	she **arose** quickly, and came unto him.	11:29
5	Lazarus was ... whom he **raised** from the dead.	12:1
5	see Lazarus ... whom he **had raised** from the dead.	12:9
5	called Lazarus ... and **raised** him from the dead,	12:17
15	**riseth** from supper, and laid aside his garments;	13:4
18	even so I do. **Arise**, let us go hence.	14:31
25	after that he **was risen** from the dead,	21:14
28	In the name of Jesus Christ of Nazareth **rise up**	Acts 3:6
5	he took him by the right hand, and **lifted** him **up:**	3:7
5	whom God **hath raised** from the dead;	3:15
5	ye crucified, whom God **raised** from the dead,	4:10
5	The God of our fathers **raised up** Jesus,	5:30
20	And Saul **arose** from the earth;	9:8
5	But Peter **took** him **up**, saying, Stand up;	10:26
5	Him God **raised** up the third day,	10:40
5	and he smote Peter on the side, and **raised** him **up**,	12:7
5	he **raised up** unto them David to be their king;	13:22
5	hath God ... **raised** unto Israel a Saviour, Jesus;	13:23
5	But God **raised** him from the dead:	13:30
5	he, whom God **raised again**, saw no corruption.	13:37
1	incredible ... that God **should raise** the dead?	26:8
9	if we believe on him **that raised** up Jesus our Lord	Rom 4:24
20	and **was raised again** for our justification.	4:25
20	that like as Christ **was raised up** from the dead	6:4
25	Knowing that Christ **being raised** from the dead	6:9
26	even to him who **is raised** from the dead,	7:4
8	But if the Spirit of him that **raised up** Jesus	8:11
7	he that **raised up** Christ from the dead shall also	8:11
25	yea rather, that **is risen again**,	8:34
5	that God hath **raised** him from the dead,	10:9
27	that now it is high time **to awake** out of sleep:	13:11
5	And God hath both **raised up** the Lord,	1 Co 6:14
29	and that he **rose again** the third day	15:4
29	if Christ be preached that he **rose** from the dead,	15:12
29	if ... be no resurrection ... then is Christ not **risen:**	15:13
29	if Christ be not **risen**, then is our preaching vain,	15:14
5	we have testified of God that he **raised up** Christ:	15:15
5	whom **he raised** not up, if ... the dead rise not.	15:15
16	if so be that the dead **rise** not.	15:15
16	For if the dead **rise** not, then is not Christ **raised:**	15:16
29	For if the dead **rise** not, then is not Christ **raised:**	15:16
29	And if Christ **be** not **raised**, your faith is vain;	15:17
29	But now is Christ **risen** from the dead,	15:20
16	baptized for the dead, if the dead **rise** not at all?	15:29
16	what advantageth it me, if the dead **rise** not?	15:32
16	some man will say, How **are** the dead **raised up**?	15:35
15	is sown in corruption; it **is raised** in incorruption:	15:42
15	It is sown in dishonour; it **is raised** in glory;	15:43
15	it is sown in weakness; it **is raised** in power;	15:43
15	is sown a natural body; it **is raised** a spiritual body	15:44
32	and the dead **shall be raised** incorruptible,	15:52
3	but in God which **raiseth** the dead:	2 Co 1:9
7	Knowing that he which **raised up** the Lord Jesus	4:14
13	**shall raise up** us also by Jesus,	4:14
26	but unto him which died for them, and **rose again**.	2 Co 5:15
8	God the Father, who **raised** him from the dead;	Gal 1:1
7	in Christ, when he **raised** him from the dead,	Eph 1:20
28	Wherefore he saith, **Awake** thou that sleepest,	5:14
34	Wherefore he saith, **Awake** thou that sleepest,	5:14
4	thinking to **cause** me **distress** (NASB)	Php 1:16
8	of God, who **hath raised** him from the dead.	Col 2:12
5	whom **he raised** from the dead, even Jesus,	1 Th 1:10
30	**was raised** from the dead according to my gospel:	2 Tm 2:8
4	Accounting that God was able to **raise** him up,	Heb 11:19
13	and the Lord **shall raise** him **up;**	Jas 5:15
9	God, that **raised** him **up** from the dead,	1 Pt 1:21
28	angel stood, saying, **Rise**, and measure the temple	Rev 11:1
34	angel stood, saying, **Rise**, and measure the temple	11:1

Classical Greek

In classical Greek the word *egeirō* is used for three basic ideas: (1) "to awaken, stir up, rouse," (2) "to set up, erect," (3) "to raise, raise (the dead)," and intransitively, "to rise (from the dead)." All of these ideas find common usage in one context or another from classical Greek writings down through the Koine Greek period.

Septuagint and New Testament Usage

The Septuagint uses this word and another very common Greek word, *anistēmi* (448), to translate a wide range of Hebrew words. The two Greek words really act with a high degree of semantic overlap. This becomes quite clear when one examines 1 Corinthians 15, where *egeirō* is always used for *resurrection*, and Mark 9:9,10,31, where *anistēmi* is used. Mark 5:41,42 has both verbs with the same sense in close proximity.

The New Testament utilized these two verbs from the Septuagint and from common speech in order to communicate its distinctive message concerning the resurrection of Jesus Christ. Oepke makes the point that *egeirō* is preferred over *anistēmi* in texts on the resurrection "because it brings out better the concrete nature of the divine action" (Oepke, "egeirō," *Kittel*, 2:335). This is difficult to sustain over the numerous references on the Resurrection which employ *anistēmi*. In fact, the noun *anastasis* (384) (formed from *anistēmi*), "resurrection," is used exclusively for the event. (Matthew 27:53, the only exception, has *egersis* [1447], formed from *egeirō*). Whereas the New Testament prefers the verb *egeirō* (73 times) over *anistēmi* (28 times) in speaking of resurrection, the noun usage is more than a reversal of the case! What we see here is a convention of language in which the speakers (Koine Greek, in this case) settle on one form of a word for no particular or observable reason. The perfectly acceptable noun *egersis* never found popular usage.

In conclusion, the verb *egeirō* is seen with all its classical meanings and is generally preferred over the other verb, *anistēmi*, to speak of rising from the dead.

STRONG 1453, BAUER 214-25, MOULTON-MILLIGAN 179, KITTEL 2:333-37, LIDDELL-SCOTT 469, COLIN BROWN 3:279-80.

1447. ἔγερσις egersis noun
Resurrection, awakening.
CROSS-REFERENCE:
ἐγείρω egeirō (1446)

קוּם qûm (7251), Qal: get up, rise up (Ps 139:2 [138:2]); hiphil: set up, establish (Jgs 7:19—Codex Alexandrinus only).

1. ἔγερσιν egersin acc sing fem

1 And came out of the graves after his resurrection,..Matt 27:53

This term is used in classical Greek from the Fifth Century B.C. (especially by Hippocrates) to mean "rousing or stimulation of the spirit." It is used in reference to the erection of walls or buildings, recovery from sickness, rising from sleep or from sitting (see Psalm 139:2 for a Septuagint usage), or for the resurrection of the dead. See *egeirō* (1446) for further discussion. See also *anastasis* (384), "resurrection." *Anastasis* is used more commonly to refer to resurrection. *Egersis* occurs only in Matthew 27:53 where it is used of Jesus' "resurrection."

STRONG 1454, BAUER 215, MOULTON-MILLIGAN 179, KITTEL 2:337-38, LIDDELL-SCOTT 469, COLIN BROWN 3:279-80.

1448. ἐγκάθετος enkathetos adj
Lying in wait, spy.
COGNATE:
συνίημι suniēmi (4770)
SYNONYM:
κατάσκοπος kataskopos (2655)

אָרַב 'ārav (717), Lie in ambush, lie in wait (Jb 31:9).
חָנָה chānâh (2684), Encamp, pitch a camp (Jb 19:12).

1. ἐγκαθέτους enkathetous acc pl masc

1 And they watched him, and sent forth spies,.......Luke 20:20

In classical Greek *enkathetos* means "one put in secretly" or "one paid to spy." In the Septuagint (Job 14:12; 31:9) this word is used to refer to soldiers encamped around a city under siege and a "peeping tom" who lurks at a woman's door. Luke 20:20 follows the classical meaning of "men paid to spy."

STRONG 1455, BAUER 215, LIDDELL-SCOTT 469.

1449. ἐγκαίνια enkainia noun
Feast of Dedication.
CROSS-REFERENCE:
καινός kainos (2508)

חֲנֻכָּה chănukkāh (2700), Dedication (Neh 12:27).
חֲנֻכָּה chănukkāh (A2701), Dedication (Ezr 6:16,17—Aramaic).

1. ἐγκαίνια enkainia nom/acc pl neu
2. ἐνκαίνια enkainia nom/acc pl neu

1 And it was at Jerusalem the feast of the dedication, John 10:22
2 And it was at Jerusalem the feast of the dedication,.... 10:22

The word *enkainia* appears only in the Bible, Apocrypha, and ecclesiastical writings. In the Septuagint *enkainia* is used twice in Nehemiah 12:27 to translate the Hebrew word *chănukkāh*, referring to the dedication, *enkainia*, of the walls of Jerusalem. Several verb forms also appear in the Septuagint conveying the idea of "dedicate" or "consecrate." *Enkainia* appears in the Apocrypha (1 Maccabees 4:54) where it is used for the feast instituted by Judas Maccabaeus (165 B.C.) in memory of the cleansing of the temple following the desecration by Antiochus Epiphanes. In Patristic literature *enkainia* is used for the dedication of the temple (Clement of Alexandria) and of churches (Eusebius).

Enkainia occurs only once in the New Testament (John 10:22) where it also refers to the Feast of Dedication, or Hanukkah. Jesus was in Jerusalem at the time of the Feast of Dedication, an 8-day feast which begins on the 25th of the month Chislev (in the middle of December). A verb form of this word appears in two places in the New Testament (Hebrews 9:18 and 10:20) where the idea of "making new" or "restoring" is continued as the old (9:18) and new (10:20) covenants are inaugurated.

STRONG 1456, BAUER 215, LIDDELL-SCOTT 469.

1450. ἐγκαινίζω enkainizō verb
Inaugurate, dedicate, renew.
CROSS-REFERENCE:
καινός kainos (2508)

חָדַשׁ chādhash (2412), Piel: renew, restore (1 Sm 11:14, Ps 51:10 [50:10]).
חָנַךְ chānakh (2699), Dedicate (Dt 20:5, 1 Kgs 8:63, 2 Chr 7:5).

ἐγκακέω **1450B**

1. ἐνεκαίνισεν enekainisen 3sing indic aor act
2. ἐγκεκαίνισται enkekainistai 3sing indic perf mid

2 neither ... testament was dedicated without blood. .... Heb 9:18
1 which he hath consecrated for us, through the veil, ... 10:20

In extra-Biblical literature *enkainizō* occurs only in two texts with the meaning "innovate." This idea has reference to the establishment of conditions or realities which had no prior existence. In the Septuagint the word translates two different Hebrew words, *chādhash*, "renew," and *chānakh*, "inaugurate, dedicate." The latter of the two uses is dominant. Although texts such as 1 Samuel 11:14 (LXX 1 Kings 11:14) show *enkainizō* (for *chādhash*) in the sense of "renew" ("Let us... renew the kingdom"), most references of *enkainizō* stand for the Hebrew word *chānakh*, as in 1 Kings 8:63 (LXX 3 Kings 8:63) referring to the opening of Solomon's Temple, a development which had no precedent.

The New Testament texts are limited to Hebrews 9:18 and 10:20. Both texts must be understood, not as the renewing of some previously existing condition, but rather as the inauguration of completely new circumstances, a point which agrees with the evidences given above. Hebrews 9:18 speaks in legal terminology about the inauguration of the "first" covenant. Since there could be no prior covenant to this "first," we know the word refers to what had no prior existence. So also in Hebrews 10:20, the "new and living way" had no prior existence until Jesus brought it into being. This is new territory for the believer, a mystery disclosed in this age of New Testament blessing!

STRONG 1457, BAUER 215, KITTEL 3:453-54, LIDDELL-SCOTT 469, COLIN BROWN 2:670,673.

1450B. ἐγκακέω enkakeō verb
Grow weary, faint.
CROSS-REFERENCE:
    κακός kakos (2527)

1. ἐγκακῶμεν enkakōmen 1pl subj pres act
2. ἐνκακεῖν enkakein inf pres act
3. ἐγκακεῖν enkakein inf pres act
4. ἐγκακήσητε enkakēsēte 2pl subj aor act
5. ἐγκακοῦμεν enkakoumen 1pl indic pres act

3 they ought to pray and not to lose heart (NASB) ... Luke 18:1
2 that men ought always to pray, and not to faint; 18:1
5 received mercy, we do not lose heart (NASB) .... 2 Co 4:1
5 Therefore we do not lose heart (NASB) 4:16
1 And let us not lose heart in doing good (NASB) ..... Gal 6:9
3 I ask you not to lose heart (NASB) .... Eph 3:13
4 do not grow weary of doing good (NASB) .... 2 Th 3:13

Although the *Textus Receptus* spells this word *ekkakeō* (1560), many early manuscripts and modern Greek texts replace the first *kappa* with a *gamma*. (In our volumes, a *gamma* which preceeds a *kappa*, a *chi*, a *xi*, or another *gamma*, is transliterated as an *n* to aid in its pronunciation.) Other texts spell the word *enk-*, with the letter *nu* replacing the *gamma*. In any case, the term means "to faint" or "become tired" (2 Thessalonians 3:13; cf. Galatians 6:9). In several places it takes on the understanding of "to lose heart" or "to despair" (2 Corinthians 4:1,16; Ephesians 3:13; see *Bauer*).

BAUER 215, KITTEL 3:486, LIDDELL-SCOTT 469, COLIN BROWN 1:561,563.

1451. ἐγκαλέω enkaleō verb
Accuse, bring charges against.
COGNATES:
    ἔγκλημα enklēma (1455)
    καλέω kaleō (2535)
SYNONYM:
    κατηγορέω katēgoreō (2693)

אָמַר 'āmar (569), Say, call (Ex 22:9).
עָנָה 'ānâh (6257), Answer; accuse (Sir 46:19).
פּוּחַ pûach (6558), Hiphil: utters, pours out (Prv 19:5).

1. ἐγκαλείτωσαν enkaleitōsan 3pl impr pres act
2. ἐγκαλέσει enkalesei 3sing indic fut act
3. ἐνεκάλουν enekaloun 3pl indic imperf act
4. ἐγκαλοῦμαι enkaloumai 1sing indic pres mid
5. ἐγκαλούμενον enkaloumenon
                            acc sing masc part pres mid
6. ἐγκαλεῖσθαι enkaleisthai inf pres mid

1 there are deputies: let them implead one another. ... Acts 19:38
6 to be called in question for this day's uproar, ... 19:40
3 known the cause wherefore they accused him, ... 23:28
5 to be accused of questions of their law, ... 23:29
4 all the things whereof I am accused of the Jews: 26:2
4 For which hope's sake, ... I am accused of the Jews. ... 26:7
2 shall lay any thing to the charge of God's elect? ..... Rom 8:33

Classical Greek
This word developed quite early as a legal technical term meaning "to bring charges against, prosecute." This sense is clearly exemplified in the papyri, along with an extended sense, to "make an appeal." For instance, at the point of satisfying a loan by making the last payment, the creditor would write, " ... (I) make no further claim (*enkaleō*)." In both cases the word has to do with taking legal action.

Septuagint Usage
The Septuagint usage of this word sheds light on how it is used in the New Testament. In Proverbs 19:5, a false witness is "one who

presses (legal) charges deceitfully." (See also Zechariah 1:4, "to whom the prophets made an appeal.")

New Testament Usage

The New Testament sometimes uses *enkaleō* in Acts where it has the full legal sense of "press charges," especially in connection with Paul's defense of the gospel. The Jews, of course, were the "prosecutors" and the Roman tribunal was the court (Acts 23:28,29; 26:2,7). But Paul also suffered the threat of prosecution at the hands of the Ephesian pagans (Acts 19:38,40).

There is, however, one grand exception to all this overt "legal" language, but it is not without the general meaning given above. Romans 8:33 describes the scene of a heavenly court, before which no prosecutor can stand to speak against the believer.

STRONG 1458, BAUER 215, MOULTON-MILLIGAN 179, KITTEL 3:496, LIDDELL-SCOTT 469-70, COLIN BROWN 1:84.

1452. ἐγκαταλείπω enkataleipō verb

Desert, abandon, leave remaining.

COGNATE:
λείπω leipō (2981)

SYNONYMS:
ἀναλύω analuō (358)
ἀναχωρέω anachōreō (400)
ἀνίημι aniēmi (445)
ἀπαλλάσσω apallassō (521)
ἀπέρχομαι aperchomai (562)
ἀποβαίνω apobainō (571)
ἀπολείπω apoleipō (614)
ἀπολύω apoluō (624)
ἀποτάσσω apotassō (651)
ἀποχωρέω apochōreō (666)
ἀφίημι aphiēmi (856)
ἀφίστημι aphistēmi (861)
διαχωρίζω diachōrizō (1310)
ἐξέρχομαι exerchomai (1814)
ἐξιέναι exienai (1821)
καταλείπω kataleipō (2611)
μεταίρω metairō (3202)
παράγω paragō (3717)
ὑπάγω hupagō (5055)
ὑπολιμπάνω hupolimpanō (5115)
χωρέω chōreō (5397)

בָּגַד bāghadh (931), Treat faithlessly (Hos 5:7, Mal 2:10,11,14,15,16).

יָשַׁב yāshav (3553), Dwell, live (Lv 18:25—Codex Alexandrinus only).

יָתַר yāthar (3613), Niphal: be left over (Is 1:8); hiphil: leave over (Is 1:9).

כָּרַת kārath (3901), Cut off, cut down; niphal: be cut off (Prv 24:14).

מָאַס māʾas (4128), Cast away, reject (Is 41:9).

נָטַשׁ nāṭash (5389), Qal: forsake (Ps 27:9 [26:9]); niphal: spread out (Is 16:8); pual: be deserted (Is 32:14).

עָבַר ʿāvar (5882), Go over, go through; transgress, (Dn 9:11).

עָזַב ʿāzav (6013), Qal: left, forsake, set free (1 Kgs 21:21 [20:21], Ps 71:9 [70:9], Jer 4:29); niphal: be set, be left to (Neh 13:11); pual: be abandoned, be forsaken (Jer 49:25 [30:25]).

פּוּק pûq (6572), Hiphil: grant (Ps 140:8 [139:8]).

רָפָה rāphâh (7791), Hiphil: abandon, forsake (Dt 4:31, Jos 1:5).

שְׁאִיָּה sheʾîyāh (8067), Desolation (Is 24:12).

שָׁאַר shāʾar (8080), Niphal: be left over, remain (Ezr 9:15—only some Sinaiticus texts).

שׁוּב shûv (8178), Return, come back (Hos 11:9).

שָׁיָה shāyāh (8286), Forget (Dt 32:18).

שָׁכַח shākhach (8319), Forget (Is 17:10—Codex Alexandrinus only).

1. ἐγκαταλείποντες enkataleipontes nom pl masc part pres act
2. ἐγκατέλιπες enkatelipes 2sing indic aor act
3. ἐγκατέλιπεν enkatelipen 3sing indic aor act
4. ἐγκατέλιπον enkatelipon 3pl indic aor act
5. ἐγκαταλίπω enkatalipō 1sing subj aor act
6. ἐγκαταλείψεις enkataleipseis 2sing indic fut act
7. ἐγκαταλειπόμενοι enkataleipomenoi nom pl masc part pres mid
8. ἐγκατελείφθη enkateleiphthē 3sing indic aor pass
9. ἐγκαταλείπω enkataleipō 1sing indic pres act
10. ἐγκατέλειπεν enkateleipen 3sing pres/imperf act
11. ἐγκατέλειπον enkateleipon 3pl pres/imperf act

2	My God, my God, why hast thou forsaken me?...	Matt 27:46
2	My God, my God, why hast thou forsaken me?..	Mark 15:34
6	Because thou wilt not leave my soul in hell,........	Acts 2:27
8	HE WAS NEITHER ABANDONED (NASB)..........	2:31
3	Except the Lord of Sabaoth had left us a seed,.....	Rom 9:29
7	Persecuted, but not forsaken;.....................	2 Co 4:9
3	For Demas hath forsaken me,....................	2 Tm 4:10
10	For Demas hath forsaken me,...................	4:10
4	no man stood with me, but all men forsook me:......	4:16
11	no man stood with me, but all men forsook me:......	4:16
1	Not forsaking the assembling of ourselves together,	Heb 10:25
5	I will never leave thee, nor forsake thee.............	13:5
9	I will never leave thee, nor forsake thee.............	13:5

Classical Greek and Septuagint Usage

The frequent use of this word in classical Greek can be shown in three meanings: (1) "leave behind," (2) "leave in the lurch, abandon," (3) "omit." The Septuagint also uses the word very frequently, most often for the Hebrew *ʿāzav*, "leave, forsake." A colorful papyrus text illustrates the word: "Your brother went away and left me in the lurch with bandits lying about" (see *Moulton-Milligan*). Psalm 22:1 certainly has that sense, as this is precisely the meaning which gives us understanding when this psalm is quoted by Jesus on the cross (Matthew 27:46; Mark 15:34), "My God, my God, why hast thou forsaken me?" This rejection of Jesus has, of course, been answered by the Resurrection.

New Testament Usage
Peter uses *enkataleipō* in Acts 2:27,31 when he says that God's Holy One was not left to rot in the grave. All in all, of the 10 occurrences of the word in the New Testament, 6 are direct quotes from the Old Testament, and 2 concern those who had "abandoned" Paul (for example, 2 Timothy 4:16). Another passage exhorts not to "abandon" the assembling (in fellowship) of ourselves (Hebrews 10:25).

Of special note is the use of the word *enkataleipō* at 2 Corinthians 4:8,9 (NIV) where Paul draws a line on how far suffering extends: "We are . . . persecuted, but not *abandoned* (of God)." Hebrews 13:5, also an Old Testament quote (Deuteronomy 31:6), contains the unique promise of God's enduring presence in strong terms saying, "He will never leave you nor forsake you" (NIV). This could only be the case because of the abandonment Jesus endured.

STRONG 1459, BAUER 215-16, MOULTON-MILLIGAN 179, LIDDELL-SCOTT 470.

1453. ἐγκατοικέω enkatoikeō verb
Live, dwell among.
CROSS-REFERENCE:
οἰκέω oikeō (3474)

1. ἐγκατοικῶν enkatoikōn nom sing masc part pres act
1 For that righteous man **dwelling among them,** .... 2 Pt 2:8

This word has essentially the same meaning as *katoikeō*, "live, dwell, inhabit," however, the prefix *en* is added to indicate and intensify a transitive use of *katoikeō*. This can be seen in its only New Testament occurrence, where Peter speaks of how God delivered Lot ("that righteous man") from the evil environment in which he lived before the city was reduced to ashes (2 Peter 2:8).

STRONG 1460, BAUER 216, LIDDELL-SCOTT 471.

1453B. ἐγκαυχάομαι
enkauchaomai verb
Boast.

CROSS-REFERENCE:
καυχάομαι kauchaomai (2714)

הָלַל hālal (2054), Praise; hithpael: boast (Pss 52:1 [51:1], 97:7 [96:7]).

שָׁאַג shā'agh (8057), Roar (Ps 74:4 [73:4]).

שָׁבַח shāvach (8099), Praise, glorify; hithpael: glory in (Ps 106:47 [105:47]).

1. ἐγκαυχᾶσθαι enkauchasthai inf pres mid
1 we ourselves **speak proudly of you** (NASB)......... 2 Th 1:4

According to *Moulton-Milligan*, this word is found in the classics (e.g., Aesop's Fables), the Septuagint (e.g., Psalms 51:3; 73:4; 96:7), and once in the New Testament at 1 Thessalonians 1:4 (the *Textus Receptus* reads *kauchaomai* [2714]). In each occurrence the verb means "to boast." Because the Thessalonian believers endured persecution and tribulation with patience and faith, Paul "bragged" about them ("glorified"—KJV) to other churches. (Notice in 2 Corinthians 9:2 that Paul had boasted to the Thessalonians about the zealous generosity of the Christians in Corinth.)

BAUER 216, KITTEL 3:653, LIDDELL-SCOTT 471, COLIN BROWN 1:227-28.

1454. ἐγκεντρίζω enkentrizō verb
Graft (in).

1. ἐγκεντρίσαι enkentrisai inf aor act
2. ἐνεκεντρίσθης enekentristhēs 2sing indic aor pass
3. ἐγκεντρισθῶ enkentristhō 1sing subj aor pass
4. ἐγκεντρισθήσονται enkentristhēsontai 3pl indic fut pass

2 a wild olive tree, wert grafted in among them,...... Rom 11:17
3 broken off, that I might be grafted in.................. 11:19
4 they abide not still in unbelief, shall be grafted in:..... 11:23
1 for God is able to graft them in again................. 11:23
2 and wert grafted contrary to nature into a good........ 11:24
4 branches, be grafted into their own olive tree?......... 11:24

Classical Greek
This relatively rare word means "to graft in," as in trees, plants, or their branches. *Moulton-Milligan* suggests *enkentrizō* "belongs to higher Koinē" Greek. *Bauer* cites Aristotle and Theophrastes as examples of classical usage.

Septuagint Usage
The Septuagint attests to only one puzzling reading of *enkentrizō* in the apocryphal Wisdom of Solomon (6:11). There the RSV translates it as "bitten" (as in "to bite" or "to sting" [of an insect or snake]). But perhaps the better sense is "to goad" or "to prod" (cf. the classical noun *enkentris*, "a sting" or a "goad").

New Testament Usage

New Testament usage is restricted to Paul in Romans chapter 11 (verses 17,19,23,24). Apparently Paul is picking up on a known metaphor in order to authenticate the "engrafting" of Gentiles into the "tree" of Israel. The rabbis spoke of the "engrafting" of Ruth (a Moabite and a foreigner) or Naamah (an Ammonite) into Abraham (the root of the tree of Israel). Jewish proselytes were said to be "grafted" into Abraham by the Jewish Hellenistic historian Philo (*De Exsecrationibus* 6 cited in Embry, "Tree," *Colin Brown*, 3:867).

STRONG 1461, BAUER 216, LIDDELL-SCOTT 471, COLIN BROWN 3:865,867,869.

1455. ἔγκλημα enklēma noun

Charge, accusation.
CROSS-REFERENCE:
ἐγκαλέω enkaleō (1451)

1. ἐγκλήματος enklēmatos gen sing neu
2. ἔγκλημα enklēma nom/acc sing neu

2 to have nothing **laid to his charge** worthy of death..Acts 23:29
1 to answer ... concerning the **crime laid against** him..... 25:16

This word appears in classical Greek from the Fifth Century B.C. but is not used in the Septuagint. Its only two occurrences in the New Testament are in Acts 23:29 and 25:16. Acts 23:29 shows how *enklēma* can be used in a more general sense, "reproach" or "charge," while Acts 25:16 uses *enklēma* as a legal term, the "accusation" of criminal offense.

STRONG 1462, BAUER 216, MOULTON-MILLIGAN 179-80, KITTEL 3:496, LIDDELL-SCOTT 472, COLIN BROWN 1:84.

1456. ἐγκομβόομαι enkomboomai verb

Clothe oneself with; put on, cover oneself with.

1. ἐγκομβώσασθε enkombōsasthe 2pl impr aor mid

1 and **be clothed with** humility:...................... 1 Pt 5:5

This rare verb is not found in classical Greek or the Septuagint and appears only once in the New Testament. Delling suggests that the word means "to invest oneself with," "to make one's essential characteristic" ("enkomboomai," *Kittel*, 2:339). Its figurative use in 1 Peter 5:5 is consistent with this meaning, "*be clothed with* humility," referring to what should be the visible attitude and conduct of Christians.

STRONG 1463, BAUER 216, MOULTON-MILLIGAN 180, KITTEL 2:339, LIDDELL-SCOTT 473.

1457. ἐγκοπή enkopē noun

Hindrance.
CROSS-REFERENCE:
ἐγκόπτω enkoptō (1458)

1. ἐγκοπήν enkopēn acc sing fem

1 lest we **should hinder** the gospel of Christ........... 1 Co 9:12

Peisker suggests that this word comes from the verb *enkoptō* (1458). It is composed of *en* (1706), "in," and *koptō* (2847), "to strike," and originally meant "to knock in or cut into" (Peisker, "Hinder," *Colin Brown*, 2:220f.). The meaning "hinder" came out of its use as a military term where a retreating army would cut up (break up) the road behind it in order to temporarily delay or hinder the pursuing enemy. Neither verb nor noun occur in the Septuagint; however, in the New Testament it appears once, in 1 Corinthians 9:12. Paul did not allow himself to receive money from the churches which began as a result of his preaching because he saw that as a hindrance to the gospel.

STRONG 1464, BAUER 216, MOULTON-MILLIGAN 180, KITTEL 3:855-57, LIDDELL-SCOTT 473, COLIN BROWN 2:220-21.

1458. ἐγκόπτω enkoptō verb

Hinder, prevent, weary.
COGNATES:
ἐγκοπή enkopē (1457)
κόπτω koptō (2847)
SYNONYMS:
ἀνακόπτω anakoptō (346)
κατέχω katechō (2692)
κωλύω kōluō (2940)

1. ἐγκόπτω enkoptō 1sing subj pres act
2. ἐνέκοψεν enekopsen 3sing indic aor act
3. ἐνεκοπτόμην enekoptomēn 1sing indic imperf pass
4. ἐγκόπτεσθαι enkoptesthai inf pres mid

1 that I be not further **tedious** unto thee,............ Acts 24:4
3 I have been much **hindered** from coming to you..... Rom 15:22
2 who **hindered** you from obeying the truth? (NASB).. Gal 5:7
2 come unto you, ... but Satan **hindered** us............ 1 Th 2:18
4 so that your prayers may not be **hindered** (NASB)... 1 Pt 3:7

Classical Greek and Septuagint Usage

This word has the meanings (1) "engrave," (2) "oppose," and (3) "check, hinder" in classical Greek. There is a text which has *enkoptō* as an intransitive verb, "come to a stop." The basic semantic idea of "obstacle" originally derived from the word's use in the military practice of making slits in a road to slow down a pursuing enemy; from this came the meaning "engrave." A noun form, *enkopos*, is present in a few Old Testament texts with the meaning "burden" (Job 19:2, Ecclesiastes 1:8), but the verb *enkoptō* is not found in the Septuagint.

New Testament Usage
Key to the discussion of the New Testament use of the word is the fact that all of the occurrences, except Acts 24:4, have the word in the sense of "check, hinder," and that this is always a hindering of spiritual activity (e.g., ministry, obedience, or prayer). The interesting passage in 1 Thessalonians 2:18, "but Satan hindered us," is illuminated from a papyrus text, "You kept good things from us." For "hinder" in a more general sense, see *kōluō* (2940). The text of Acts 24:4 has *enkoptō* meaning, "to burden, weary." Here Tertullus, one of Paul's enemies, used the word in a very polite address to Felix the Roman official in deferring to launch into a lengthy introduction.

Strong 1465, Bauer 216, Moulton-Milligan 180, Kittel 3:855-57, Liddell-Scott 473, Colin Brown 2:220-21.

1459. ἐγκράτεια enkrateia noun
Temperance, self-control.

Cross-Reference:
ἐγκρατεύομαι enkrateuomai (1460)

1. ἐγκράτεια enkrateia nom sing fem
2. ἐγκρατείας enkrateias gen sing fem
3. ἐγκρατεία enkrateia dat sing fem
4. ἐγκράτειαν enkrateian acc sing fem

2 righteousness, temperance, and judgment to come,.. Acts 24:25
1 Meekness, temperance: against such ... is no law...... Gal 5:23
4 And to knowledge temperance; and ... patience;..... 2 Pt 1:6
3 to temperance patience; and to patience godliness;...... 1:6

Classical Greek
This word is very important in Greek ethical philosophy. The Stoics understood the concept as someone having control over all things and maintaining personal freedom in spite of anything which sought to deprive him of it. For Philo, a Jewish philosopher in Egypt during the time of Christ, the word signifies restraint in relation to bodily desires, especially sex, food, or idle chatter. The concept was also important to the Essenes, a Jewish sect in Palestine during the time of Christ. The Essenes stressed absolute purity of life, abstaining from sex, and following a rigid dietary regimen (Grundmann, "enkrateia," *Kittel*, 2:340f.).

Septuagint Usage
Enkrateia occurs only in the more Hellenized writings of the Septuagint—Sirach 18:15,30 and 4 Maccabees 5:34. The influence of Greek ethical philosophy is obvious; for example, it is the Jewish law which is credited with teaching "self-control" (4 Maccabees 5:34).

New Testament Usage
In the New Testament *enkrateia* means "self-control." That characteristic is seen to be a result of the indwelling of the Spirit, not primarily of the willpower of humans, as is the case with the Greek and Jewish thought. (See Acts 24:25; Galatians 5:23; and 2 Peter 1:6 for the only New Testament occurrences.)

Strong 1466, Bauer 216, Moulton-Milligan 180, Kittel 2:339-42, Liddell-Scott 473, Colin Brown 1:494-96.

1460. ἐγκρατεύομαι enkrateuomai verb
Exercise self-control, abstain from something.

Cognates:
ἐγκράτεια enkrateia (1459)
ἐγκρατής enkratēs (1461)
κρατέω krateō (2875)

אָפַק 'aphaq (681), Encompass; hithpael: restrain oneself (Gn 43:31).

1. ἐγκρατεύεται enkrateuetai 3sing indic pres mid
2. ἐγκρατεύονται enkrateuontai 3pl indic pres mid

2 But if they cannot contain, let them marry:......... 1 Co 7:9
1 striveth for the mastery is temperate in all things........ 9:25

Classical Greek
The verb *enkrateuomai* contains the root *krat-*, which means "power" or "control" (Baltensweiler, "Discipline," *Colin Brown*, 1:494). The word therefore is used of having power or control over oneself. The related noun form, *enkrateia* (1459), is usually rendered "self-control" or "abstinence." This definition is consistent with *enkrateuomai* in classical Greek.

The idea of self-control was emphasized by the ancient Greeks. Socrates considered it to be one of man's principle virtues. The Stoics felt self-control to be a sign of human freedom: one was truly free if he could control his sexual drive or his desire for food. Occasionally this self-control developed into asceticism. Even in the days of Jesus the Essenes were known for their ascetic attitudes toward life (ibid., 1:494f.).

Septuagint Usage

In the Septuagint *enkrateuomai* occurs three times. Rather than being primarily an ascetic term, it denotes one that is in control or has gained control of something (ibid.). In Genesis 43:31 it describes Joseph's struggle to control his tears after seeing his brother Benjamin again. Saul, in 1 Samuel 13:12 (LXX 1 Kings 13:12), recounted how he had to force himself to offer God a burnt offering. Finally, in Esther 5:10, Haman, though filled with anger, is said to have controlled himself upon seeing Mordecai refuse to tremble before him.

New Testament Usage

The New Testament contains only two instances of *enkrateuomai*, both in Paul's first letter to the Corinthians. In 1 Corinthians 7:9 Paul emphasized that marriage was advisable for those who cannot "contain" (KJV), i.e., "control themselves" (NIV). His point is that marriage is a concession to those who cannot constrain the human drive (ibid.). In 1 Corinthians 9:25 Paul commended the Christian who, like an athlete, "is temperate" (KJV), i.e., "experiences self-control" (NIV). In both of these passages the term *enkrateuomai* is the opposite of self-gratification. The proper attitude of the believer is to be one of self-control over all desires, especially his sexual desires. This does not mean that asceticism is to be enjoined upon the Christian. For Paul, marriage was good so long as it did not stand in the way of following Jesus. Marriage is a beautiful picture of the relationship between Christ and the Church (cf. Ephesians 5:21-23). Even though Paul himself preferred celibacy (1 Corinthians 7:7), he never gave it any inherent value.

STRONG 1467, BAUER 216, MOULTON-MILLIGAN 180, KITTEL 2:339-42, LIDDELL-SCOTT 473, COLIN BROWN 1:494-96.

1461. ἐγκρατής enkratēs adj

In full control of oneself, disciplined.

CROSS-REFERENCE:
 ἐγκρατεύομαι enkrateuomai (1460)

1. ἐγκρατῆ enkratē acc sing masc

1 a lover of good men, sober, just, holy, temperate;..... Tit 1:8

Classical Greek

Enkratēs comes from the verb stem *krat-*, meaning "power, lordship," and the prefix *en*, although the latter is only a formal association (Grundmann, "enkratēs," *Kittel*, 2:339f.). This adjective means, "in possession of power, in control." It can describe something as "strong," such as a "firm" grip. It also implies "possession." When used to describe people, it can speak of "self-control." The *enkratēs* person is the "master" of his emotions, "self-disciplined" (cf. the related term *enkrateia* [1459], a significant expression in Greek philosophical discussions, see *Liddell-Scott*).

Septuagint Usage

Because *enkratēs* and its cognates play such a prominent role in Hellenistic philosophical discussions, it is not surprising that *enkratēs* occurs in the Septuagint only in the apocryphal wisdom literature or in the writings influenced by Hellenism. Nevertheless, one should not suppose that philosophical Hellenism has influenced the usage there. No usage prefigures the philosophical understanding except for perhaps one appearance in Sirach 26:15, which speaks of the value of an "*enkratēs* soul" (*psuchē* [5425]).

None of the terms figure prominently in the Septuagint, but *enkratēs* is used the most (11 times). It occurs in Tobit of "controlling, overpowering" an enormous fish (6:8; cf. Susanna 39). It functions similarly in 2 Maccabees of militarily "taking possession" of "exceedingly high strongholds" (8:30; cf. 10:15,17; 13:13). Positively, both the Law and Wisdom are things desired to be "possessed" (Sirach 6:27; 15:1).

New Testament Usage

Enkratēs appears a single time in the Greek New Testament, at Titus 1:8 (cf. *enkrateia*, Acts 24:25; Galatians 5:23; 2 Peter 1:6; and *enkrateuomai* [1460], 1 Corinthians 7:9; 9:25). Obviously Paul used the philosophical understanding of *enkratēs* as an ideal of behavior in this text on behalf of his readers. But Paul's understanding of "self-control" (also expressed as *sōphrosunē* [4849]) was different. Self-control moves beyond public definition. Now it is defined in terms of godliness. Obviously this includes the Hellenistic morality, but it also exceeds it, especially where leaders of the Church are concerned.

STRONG 1468, BAUER 216, MOULTON-MILLIGAN 180, KITTEL 2:339-42, LIDDELL-SCOTT 473, COLIN BROWN 1:494-96.

1462. ἐγκρίνω enkrinō verb

Class (someone in a certain group).

CROSS-REFERENCE:
κρίνω krinō (2892)

1. ἐγκρῖναι enkrinai inf aor act

1 For we dare not **make** ourselves **of the number**, ... 2 Co 10:12

Classical Greek
Enkrinō is actually a compound formed from the preposition *en* (1706) (*eg* before a gutteral in a compound) and the verb *krinō* (2892), "to judge." Its meaning in classical Greek includes "to reckon in, or among." From this it means "to accept, approve" and thus "adopt" (see *Liddell-Scott*).

New Testament Usage
Enkrinō does not appear at all in the Septuagint, and it occurs only once in the New Testament. This single usage of *enkrinō* comes from Paul in his second letter to Corinth (10:12). In that passage he used it in conjunction with another *krin-* compound, *sunkrinō* (4644), "to combine or compare." Paul, guided by the Spirit, adopted the basic classical understanding. He did not want to "reckon himself among" those who were "self-endorsing" (literally "who commend themselves"). Paul did not wish to be considered a part of that group which boasted of its own success. Paul wanted, rather, to confine his boasting "to the field God has assigned" (2 Corinthians 10:13, NIV).

STRONG 1469, BAUER 216, KITTEL 3:951, LIDDELL-SCOTT 473.

1463. ἐγκρύπτω enkruptō verb
Put in, hide.

CROSS-REFERENCE:
κρύπτω kruptō (2900)

חָבָא chāvā' (2331), Niphal: hide, be safe (Am 9:3—Codex Alexandrinus only).

טָמַן ṭāman (3045), Hide, bury (Jos 7:21, Prv 19:24).

עוּג 'ûgh (5964), Bake (Ez 4:12).

צָפַן tsāphan (7121), Hide, store up (Hos 13:12).

1. ἐνέκρυψεν enekrupsen 3sing indic aor act

1 leaven, ... and **hid** in three measures of meal, ... Matt 13:33
1 a woman took and **hid** in three measures of meal, ..Luke 13:21

Classical Greek and Septuagint Usage
Appearing first in the writings of Homer, this verb and its related terms most frequently indicate the act of hiding or concealing something, or denote something hidden. There are seven instances of *enkruptō* in the Septuagint. Of the six with a Hebrew original, three are translations of *ṭāman*, "hide." Achan admitted that he "hid" the plunder "in" the ground inside his tent (Joshua 7:21,22). Its use in Proverbs 19:24 contributes to a larger image of laziness. The sluggard "buries" (NIV) his hand in a dish. Here the idea of concealment gives way to a picture of laziness where the sluggard's hand is "enveloped" as it were by what he needs for his sustenance, but he is too lazy to bring even the smallest portion to his mouth. Figuratively Hosea speaks of "hidden" sin (13:12) and in 1 Maccabees 16:15 addresses men "hidden" in ambush.

New Testament Usage
Enkruptō occurs in the New Testament one or two times. It unquestionably occurs in Matthew 13:33 in the similitude of the woman who took yeast and "put it in" (cf. the NIV's "mixed in") a lot of flour. (There is no suggestion of "hiding" here.) Some manuscripts (P75 Aleph A D W et al.) also read *enkruptō* in Luke's parallel account (13:21), while other manuscripts read *kruptō* (B K L N 892 et al.).

STRONG 1470, BAUER 216, LIDDELL-SCOTT 474.

1464. ἔγκυος enkuos adj
Pregnant.

1. ἐγκύῳ enkuō dat sing fem

1 Mary his espoused wife, **being great with child**. ...... Luke 2:5

This adjective is from the verb *kuō*, "to be or make pregnant." *Enkuos*, therefore, notes the condition of being "pregnant." It is used figuratively of the Trojan horse which surreptitiously carried Greek soldiers into the city of Troy, thus allowing them to "impregnate" the fortress (see *Liddell-Scott*).

Enkuos is rare in the Septuagint occurring only once in Sirach 42:10. There it follows the customary usage when the writer speaks of a father who worries about his virgin daughter becoming "pregnant." Likewise, the single New Testament use holds no surprises. Only Luke has it, and he used it of the virgin Mary who was "great with child" (Luke 2:5).

STRONG 1471, BAUER 216-17, LIDDELL-SCOTT 474.

1465. ἐγχρίω enchriō verb
Rub (or) put on.

COGNATE:
χρίω chriō (5383)
SYNONYM:
ἐπιχρίω epichriō (2009)

קָרַע qāra' (7458), Enlarge, shade (Jer 4:30).

1. ἔγχρισον **enchrison** 2sing impr aor act
2. ἐγχρίσῃ **enchrisē** 3sing subj aor act
3. ἐγχρῖσαι **enchrisai** inf aor act

1 and **anoint** thine eyes with eyesalve,................. Rev 3:18
3 and **anoint** thine eyes with eyesalve,................... 3:18

Classical Greek
Enchriō is a compound derived from the preposition *en* (1706), "in, within," and the verb *chriō* (5383), "to anoint, to rub on, smear." There are two classical definitions for *enchriō*, "to anoint" or "to sting, prick, inject." It is used both literally and figuratively.

Septuagint Usage
The apocryphal Book of Tobit records *enchriō* two times, and once it appears in the Book of Jeremiah. In all three cases *enchriō* is associated with "anointing" someone's eyes. After his father was blinded by sparrow droppings (Tobit 2:9,10; NB: Codex Sinaiticus reads *enchriō* in this account), Tobias is instructed by an angel that the gall of a great fish he has captured is useful for "anointing" the eyes of a "man with white films in his eyes" (6:8). Later, Tobias "anoints" his father's eyes and he regains his sight (Tobit 11:7-15, especially verse 8).

The use in Jeremiah, although pertaining to eyes, is somewhat different. In that text "to anoint" means "to rub on, smear on" cosmetically. Thus it describes a woman "applying" eyeshadow (Jeremiah 4:30).

New Testament Usage
The only occurrence of *enchriō* in the New Testament is at Revelation 3:18, resembling the use in Tobit. The Lord God wants to "anoint" the eyes of the church in Laodicea with salve so it can see. (In two occurrences in papyri [Third and Fourth Centuries A.D.] *enchriō* is again connected with "anointing" eyes [*Moulton-Milligan*].)

STRONG 1472, BAUER 217, MOULTON-MILLIGAN 180, LIDDELL-SCOTT 476.

1466. ἐγώ egō prs-pron
I.

1. ἐγώ **egō** nom 1sing
2. μου **mou** gen 1sing
3. ἐμοῦ **emou** gen 1sing
4. μοι **moi** dat 1sing
5. ἐμοί **emoi** dat 1sing
6. με **me** acc 1sing
7. ἐμέ **eme** acc 1sing

2 a Governor, that shall rule my people Israel......... Matt 2:6
4 when ye have found him, bring **me** word again,......... 2:8
2 saying, Out of Egypt have I called my son............. 2:15
1 I indeed baptize you with water unto repentance:....... 3:11
2 but he that cometh after **me** is mightier than I,......... 3:11
2 but he that cometh after **me** is mightier than I,......... 3:11
1 I have need to be baptized of thee,.................... 3:14
6 need ... baptized of thee, and comest thou to **me**?...... 3:14
2 my beloved Son, in whom I am well pleased........... 3:17
4 if thou wilt fall down and worship **me**................... 4:9
2 Then saith Jesus unto him, Get thee hence, Satan:...... 4:10
2 And he saith unto them, Follow **me**,.................... 4:19
3 shall say ... evil against you falsely, for my sake........ 5:11
1 But I say unto you, That whosoever is angry........... 5:22
1 But I say unto you, ... whosoever looketh on 5:28
1 But I say unto you, ... shall put away his wife,......... 5:32
1 But I say unto you, Swear not at all;................... 5:34
1 But I say unto you, That ye resist not evil:............. 5:39
1 But I say unto you, Love your enemies,................ 5:44
4 Not every one that saith **unto me**, Lord, Lord,.......... 7:21
2 but he that doeth the will of my Father................. 7:21
4 Many will say **to me** in that day, Lord, Lord,........... 7:22
3 depart from **me**, ye that work iniquity................... 7:23
2 Therefore whosoever heareth these sayings **of mine**,..... 7:24
2 And every one that heareth these sayings **of mine**,..... 7:26
6 Lord, if thou wilt, thou canst make **me** clean............. 8:2
2 Lord, my servant lieth at home sick of the palsy,...... 8:6
1 Jesus saith unto him, I will come and heal him.......... 8:7
2 that thou shouldest come under **my** roof:................ 8:8
2 speak the word ... and **my** servant shall be healed....... 8:8
1 For I am a man under authority,...................... 8:9
2 and to **my** servant, Do this, and he doeth it............. 8:9
4 Lord, suffer **me** first to go and bury my father........... 8:21
4 Lord, suffer **me** first to go and bury my father........... 8:21
4 Follow **me**; and let the dead bury their dead............. 8:22
4 and he saith unto him, Follow **me**...................... 9:9
2 **My** daughter is even now dead:......................... 9:18
1 I send you forth as sheep in the midst of wolves:...... 10:16
3 brought before governors and kings for my sake:...... 10:18
2 ye shall be hated of all men for my name's sake:...... 10:22
5 Whosoever therefore shall confess **me** before men,..... 10:32
2 him will I confess also before my Father............... 10:32
6 But whosoever shall deny **me** before men,.............. 10:33
2 him will I also deny before my Father................. 10:33
7 He that loveth father or mother more than **me**......... 10:37
2 loveth father ... more than **me** is not worthy **of me**..... 10:37
7 and he that loveth son or daughter more than **me** 10:37
2 loveth son ... more than **me** is not worthy **of me**...... 10:37
2 he that taketh not his cross, and followeth after **me**,... 10:38
2 he that taketh not his cross, is not worthy **of me**...... 10:38
3 and he that loseth his life for my sake shall find it..... 10:39
7 He that receiveth you receiveth **me**,.................... 10:40
7 he that receiveth **me** receiveth him that sent **me**....... 10:40
6 he that receiveth **me** receiveth him that sent **me**....... 10:40
5 blessed ... whosoever shall not be offended in **me**..... 11:6
1 Behold, I send my messenger before thy face,......... 11:10
2 Behold, I send my messenger before thy face,......... 11:10
4 All things are delivered **unto me** of my Father:......... 11:27
2 All things are delivered unto **me** of **my** Father:......... 11:27
6 Come unto **me**, all ye that ... are heavy laden,......... 11:28
2 Take **my** yoke upon you, and learn of **me**;.............. 11:29
3 and learn **of me**; for I am meek and lowly in heart:... 11:29
2 For **my** yoke is easy, and **my** burden is light............ 11:30
2 For **my** yoke is easy, and **my** burden is light............ 11:30
2 Behold **my** servant, whom I have chosen;............... 12:18
2 **my** beloved, in whom **my** soul is well pleased:.......... 12:18
2 **my** beloved, in whom **my** soul is well pleased:.......... 12:18
2 I will put **my** spirit upon him,......................... 12:18
1 And if I by Beelzebub cast out devils,................. 12:27
1 But if I cast out devils by the Spirit of God,........... 12:28
3 He that is not with **me** is against **me**;................... 12:30

ἐγώ 1466

3	He that is not with me is against **me**;	Matt **12**:30
3	he that gathereth not with **me** scattereth abroad.	12:30
6	he that gathereth not with **me** scattereth abroad.	12:30
2	will return into **my** house from whence I came out;	12:44
2	will return into **my** house from whence I came out;	12:44
2	Who is **my** mother? and who are **my** brethren?	12:48
2	Who is **my** mother? and who are **my** brethren?	12:48
2	Behold **my** mother and **my** brethren!	12:49
2	Behold **my** mother and **my** brethren!	12:49
2	For whosoever shall do the will of **my** Father	12:50
2	the same is **my** brother, and sister, and mother.	12:50
2	but gather the wheat into **my** barn.	13:30
2	saying, I will open **my** mouth in parables;	13:35
4	Give **me** here John Baptist's head in a charger.	14:8
4	He said, Bring them hither to **me**.	14:18
1	Be of good cheer; it is **I**; be not afraid.	14:27
6	if it be thou, bid **me** come unto thee on the water.	14:28
6	he cried, saying, Lord, save **me**.	14:30
3	by whatsoever thou mightest be profited by **me**;	15:5
4	people draweth nigh **unto me** with their mouth,	15:8
6	and honoureth **me** with their lips;	15:8
3	but their heart is far from **me**.	15:8
6	But in vain they do worship **me**,	15:9
2	which **my** heavenly Father hath not planted,	15:13
6	Have mercy on **me**, O Lord, thou son of David;	15:22
2	**my** daughter is grievously vexed with a devil.	15:22
4	and worshipped him, saying, Lord, help **me**.	15:25
4	because they continue with **me** now three days,	15:32
6	Whom do men say that I the Son of man am?	16:13
6	He saith unto them, But whom say ye that I am?	16:15
2	but **my** Father which is in heaven.	16:17
2	and upon this rock I will build **my** church;	16:18
2	said unto Peter, Get thee behind **me**, Satan:	16:23
2	behind me, Satan: thou art an offence **unto me**:	16:23
3	behind me, Satan: thou art an offence **unto me**:	16:23
2	any man will come after **me**, let him deny himself,	16:24
4	deny himself, and take up his cross, and follow **me**.	16:24
3	will lose his life for **my** sake shall find it.	16:25
2	This is **my** beloved Son,	17:5
2	Lord, have mercy on **my** son: for he is a lunatic,	17:15
4	Jesus answered ... bring him hither **to me**.	17:17
3	that take, and give unto them for **me** and thee.	17:27
2	receive ... little child in **my** name receiveth **me**.	18:5
2	receive ... little child in **my** name receiveth **me**.	18:5
7	offend one of these little ones which believe in **me**,	18:6
2	angels do always behold the face of **my** Father	18:10
2	Even so it is not the will of your Father	18:14
2	done for them of **my** Father which is in heaven.	18:19
7	how oft shall my brother sin against **me**,	18:21
2	how oft shall my brother sin against **me**,	18:21
5	have patience with **me**, and I will pay thee all.	18:26
7	have patience with **me**, and I will pay thee all.	18:26
4	took him by the throat, ... Pay **me** that thou owest.	18:28
5	Have patience with **me**, and I will pay thee all.	18:29
7	Have patience with **me**, and I will pay thee all.	18:29
6	I forgave thee all ... because thou desiredst **me**:	18:32
1	Shouldest not thou ... even as **I** had pity on thee?	18:33
2	So likewise shall **my** ... Father do also unto you,	18:35
6	and forbid them not, to come unto **me**:	19:14
7	and forbid them not, to come unto **me**:	19:14
6	And he said unto him, Why callest thou **me** good?	19:17
2	All these things have I kept from **my** youth up:	19:20
4	sell that thou hast, ... and come and follow **me**.	19:21
4	That ye which have followed **me**,	19:28
2	or wife, or children, or lands, for **my** name's sake,	19:29
3	or wife, or children, or lands, for **my** name's sake,	19:29
2	And said unto them; Go ye also into the vineyard,	20:4
2	He saith unto them, Go ye also into the vineyard;	20:7
4	didst not thou agree with **me** for a penny?	20:13
1	I will give unto this last, even as unto thee.	20:14
2	not lawful **for me** to do what I will with mine own?	20:15
1	Is thine eye evil, because **I** am good?	20:15
2	Grant that these **my** two sons may sit,	20:21
1	Are ye able to drink of the cup that **I** shall drink of,	20:22
1	baptized with the baptism that **I** am baptized with?	20:22
2	saith unto them, Ye shall drink indeed of **my** cup,	20:23
1	baptized with the baptism that **I** am baptized with:	20:23
2	but to sit on **my** right hand, and on my left,	Matt **20**:23
2	but to sit on **my** right hand, and on my left,	20:23
2	for whom it is prepared of **my** Father.	20:23
4	loose them, and bring them **unto me**.	21:2
2	**My** house shall be called the house of prayer;	21:13
4	I also will ask you one thing, which if ye tell **me**,	21:24
1	Neither tell **I** you by what authority **I** do these	21:27
2	and said, Son, go work to day in **my** vineyard.	21:28
1	And he answered and said, **I** go, sir: and went not.	21:30
2	saying, They will reverence **my** son.	21:37
2	Behold, **I** have prepared **my** dinner:	22:4
2	**my** oxen and **my** fatlings are killed,	22:4
6	Why tempt ye **me**, ye hypocrites?	22:18
4	Show **me** the tribute money.	22:19
1	**I** am the God of Abraham, and the God of Isaac,	22:32
2	The Lord said unto **my** Lord, Sit thou on my right	22:44
2	said unto my Lord, Sit thou on **my** right hand,	22:44
1	Wherefore, behold, **I** send unto you prophets,	23:34
6	Ye shall not see **me** henceforth, till ye shall say,	23:39
2	many shall come in **my** name, saying, **I** am Christ;	24:5
1	many shall come in my name, saying, **I** am Christ;	24:5
2	ye shall be hated of all nations for **my** name's sake.	24:9
2	but **my** words shall not pass away.	24:35
2	no, not the angels of heaven, but **my** Father only.	24:36
2	shall say in his heart, **My** lord delayeth his coming;	24:48
4	saying, Lord, thou deliveredst **unto me** five talents:	25:20
4	Lord, thou deliveredst **unto me** two talents:	25:22
2	therefore to have put **my** money to the exchangers,	25:27
1	**I** should have received mine own with usury.	25:27
2	Come, ye blessed of **my** Father,	25:34
4	For **I** was an hungered, and ye gave **me** meat:	25:35
6	**I** was thirsty, and ye gave **me** drink:	25:35
6	**I** was a stranger, and ye took **me** in:	25:35
6	Naked, and ye clothed **me**:	25:36
6	**I** was sick, and ye visited **me**:	25:36
6	**I** was in prison, and ye came unto **me**.	25:36
2	done it unto one of the least of these **my** brethren,	25:40
5	of these my brethren, ye have done it **unto me**.	25:40
3	Depart from **me**, ye cursed, into everlasting fire,	25:41
4	For **I** was an hungered, and ye gave **me** no meat:	25:42
6	**I** was thirsty, and ye gave **me** no drink:	25:42
6	**I** was a stranger, and ye took **me** not in:	25:43
6	naked, and ye clothed **me** not:	25:43
6	sick, and in prison, and ye visited **me** not.	25:43
5	not to one of the least of these, ye did it not **to me**.	25:45
7	for she hath wrought a good work upon **me**.	26:10
7	poor always with you; but **me** ye have not always.	26:11
2	in that she hath poured this ointment on **my** body,	26:12
6	ointment on my body, she did it for **my** burial.	26:12
4	And said unto them, What will ye give **me**,	26:15
1	and **I** will deliver him unto you?	26:15
2	The Master saith, **My** time is at hand;	26:18
2	keep the passover at thy house with **my** disciples.	26:18
6	I say unto you, that one of you shall betray **me**.	26:21
1	to say unto him, Lord, is it **I**?	26:22
3	He that dippeth his hand with **me** in the dish,	26:23
6	He that dippeth ... the same shall betray **me**.	26:23
1	Master, is it **I**? He said unto him, Thou hast said.	26:25
2	and said, Take, eat; this is **my** body.	26:26
2	For this is **my** blood of the new testament,	26:28
2	I drink it new with you in **my** Father's kingdom.	26:29
5	All ye shall be offended because of **me** this night:	26:31
6	But after I am risen again, I will go before you	26:32
1	Peter answered ... yet will **I** never be offended.	26:33
6	before the cock crow, thou shalt deny **me** thrice.	26:34
6	Though I should die with thee, yet will I not deny	26:35
2	**My** soul is exceeding sorrowful, even unto death:	26:38
3	tarry ye here, and watch with **me**.	26:38
2	O **my** Father, if it be possible, let this cup pass	26:39
5	if it be possible, let this cup pass from **me**:	26:39
1	nevertheless not as **I** will, but as thou wilt.	26:39
3	What, could ye not watch with **me** one hour?	26:40
2	O **my** Father, if this cup may not pass away	26:42
5	if this cup may not pass away from **me**,	26:42
6	behold, he is at hand that doth betray **me**.	26:46
2	Thinkest thou that I cannot now pray to **my** Father,	26:53
4	and he shall presently give **me** ... twelve legions	26:53

ἐγώ **1466**

6	with swords and staves for to take me?	Matt 26:55
6	daily with you ... and ye laid no hold on me.	26:55
6	Before the cock crow, thou shalt deny me thrice.	26:75
4	for the potter's field, as the Lord appointed me.	27:10
2	They parted my garments among them,	27:35
2	and upon my vesture did they cast lots.	27:35
2	My God, my God, why hast thou forsaken me?	27:46
2	My God, my God, why hast thou forsaken me?	27:46
6	My God, my God, why hast thou forsaken me?	27:46
2	go tell my brethren that they go into Galilee,	28:10
2	go into Galilee, and there shall they see me.	28:10
4	All power is given unto me in heaven and in earth.	28:18
1	I am with you alway,	28:20
1	Behold, I send my messenger before thy face,	Mark 1:2
2	Behold, I send my messenger before thy face,	1:2
2	There cometh one mightier than I after me,	1:7
2	There cometh one mightier than I after me,	1:7
1	I indeed have baptized you with water:	1:8
2	Thou art my beloved Son, ... I am well pleased.	1:11
2	And Jesus said unto them, Come ye after me,	1:17
6	If thou wilt, thou canst make me clean.	1:40
4	Follow me. And he arose and followed him.	2:14
2	saying, Who is my mother, or my brethren?	3:33
2	saying, Who is my mother, or my brethren?	3:33
2	and said, Behold my mother and my brethren!	3:34
2	and said, Behold my mother and my brethren!	3:34
2	shall do the will of God, the same is my brother,	3:35
2	the same is my brother, and my sister, and mother.	3:35
5	What have I to do with thee, Jesus, thou Son	5:7
6	I adjure thee by God, that thou torment me not.	5:7
4	saying, My name is Legion: for we are many.	5:9
2	My little daughter lieth at the point of death:	5:23
2	turned ... and said, Who touched my clothes?	5:30
2	and sayest thou, Who touched me?	5:31
1	he said, It is John, whom I beheaded:	6:16
6	Ask of me whatsoever thou wilt, and I will give	6:22
6	sware unto her, Whatsoever thou shalt ask of me,	6:23
2	I will give it thee, unto the half of my kingdom.	6:23
4	I will that thou give me ... the head of John	6:25
1	Be of good cheer: it is I; be not afraid.	6:50
6	This people honoureth me with their lips,	7:6
3	but their heart is far from me.	7:6
6	Howbeit in vain do they worship me,	7:7
3	by whatsoever thou mightest be profited by me;	7:11
2	Hearken unto me every one ... and understand:	7:14
4	because they have now been with me three days,	8:2
6	saying unto them, Whom do men say that I am?	8:27
2	he saith unto them, But whom say ye that I am?	8:29
2	rebuked Peter, saying, Get thee behind me, Satan:	8:33
2	he said unto them, Whosoever will come after me,	8:34
4	and take up his cross, and follow me.	8:34
3	but whosoever shall lose his life for my sake	8:35
6	Whosoever therefore shall be ashamed of me	8:38
2	saying, This is my beloved Son: hear him.	9:7
2	Master, I have brought unto thee my son,	9:17
2	how long shall I suffer you? bring him unto me.	9:19
2	Lord, I believe; help thou mine unbelief.	9:24
1	Thou dumb and deaf spirit, I charge thee,	9:25
2	such children in my name, receiveth me:	9:37
7	receiveth me: and whosoever shall receive me,	9:37
7	receiveth me: and whosoever shall receive me,	9:37
7	receiveth not me, but him that sent me.	9:37
6	receiveth not me, but him that sent me.	9:37
2	man which shall do a miracle in my name,	9:39
6	in my name, that can lightly speak evil of me.	9:39
2	shall give you a cup of water to drink in my name,	9:41
7	offend one of these little ones that believe in me,	9:42
6	Suffer the little children to come unto me,	10:14
2	Jesus said unto him, Why callest thou me good?	10:18
2	Master, all these have I observed from my youth.	10:20
4	and come, take up the cross, and follow me.	10:21
3	or lands, for my sake, and the gospel's,	10:29
6	What would ye that I should do for you?	10:36
1	can ye drink of the cup that I drink of?	10:38
1	baptized with the baptism that I am baptized with?	10:38
1	Ye shall indeed drink of the cup that I drink of;	10:39
1	and with the baptism that I am baptized withal	10:39
2	But to sit on my right hand and on my left hand	Mark 10:40
2	But to sit on my right hand and on my left hand	10:40
2	Jesus, thou son of David, have mercy on me.	10:47
6	Thou son of David, have mercy on me.	10:48
2	My house shall be called ... the house of prayer?	11:17
4	I will also ask of you one question, and answer me,	11:29
2	was it from heaven, or of men? answer me.	11:30
1	Neither do I tell you by what authority I do these	11:33
2	he sent him also ... They will reverence my son.	12:6
6	Why tempt ye me? bring me a penny,	12:15
4	bring me a penny, that I may see it.	12:15
1	I am the God of Abraham, ... of Isaac, ... of Jacob?	12:26
2	The LORD said to my Lord,	12:36
2	Sit thou on my right hand,	12:36
2	many shall come in my name, saying, I am Christ;	13:6
1	saying, I am Christ; and shall deceive many.	13:6
3	be brought before rulers and kings for my sake,	13:9
2	ye shall be hated of all men for my name's sake:	13:13
3	but my words shall not pass away.	13:31
7	she hath wrought a good work on me.	14:6
5	she hath wrought a good work on me.	14:6
7	ye may do them good: but me ye have not always.	14:7
2	come aforehand to anoint my body to the burying.	14:8
2	come aforehand to anoint my body to the burying.	14:8
2	"Where is My guest room NASB)	14:14
2	where I shall eat the passover with my disciples?	14:14
6	One of you which eateth with me shall betray me.	14:18
3	One of you which eateth with me shall betray me.	14:18
1	one by one, Is it I? and another said, Is it I?	14:19
1	one by one, Is it I? and another said, Is it I?	14:19
3	one of the twelve, that dippeth with me in the dish.	14:20
2	gave to them, and said, Take, eat: this is my body,	14:22
2	This is my blood of the new testament,	14:24
5	All ye shall be offended because of me this night:	14:27
6	But after that I am risen, I will go before you	14:28
1	Although all shall be offended, yet will not I.	14:29
6	before the cock crow ... thou shalt deny me thrice.	14:30
6	If I should die with thee, I will not deny thee	14:31
2	My soul is exceeding sorrowful unto death:	14:34
3	take away this cup from me: nevertheless not what	14:36
1	nevertheless not what I will, but what thou wilt.	14:36
6	let us go; lo, he that betrayeth me is at hand.	14:42
6	with swords and with staves to take me?	14:48
2	in the temple teaching, and ye took me not:	14:49
1	I will destroy this temple that is made with hands,	14:58
1	said, I am: and ye shall see the Son of man sitting	14:62
6	the cock crow twice, thou shalt deny me thrice.	14:72
2	My God, my God, why hast thou forsaken me?	15:34
2	My God, my God, why hast thou forsaken me?	15:34
6	My God, my God, why hast thou forsaken me?	15:34
2	In my name shall they cast out devils;	16:17
1	Whereby shall I know this? for I am an old man,	Luke 1:18
2	am an old man, and my wife well stricken in years.	1:18
1	the angel answering said unto him, I am Gabriel,	1:19
2	be dumb, ... because thou believest not my words,	1:20
4	Thus hath the Lord dealt with me	1:25
2	to take away my reproach among men.	1:25
4	Mary said, ... be it unto me according to thy word.	1:38
4	whence is this to me, that the mother of my Lord	1:43
2	that the mother of my Lord should come to me?	1:43
6	that the mother of my Lord should come to me?	1:43
7	that the mother of my Lord should come to me?	1:43
2	the voice of thy salutation sounded in mine ears,	1:44
2	salutation ... the babe leaped in my womb for joy.	1:44
2	And Mary said, My soul doth magnify the Lord,	1:46
2	And my spirit hath rejoiced in God my Saviour.	1:47
2	And my spirit hath rejoiced in God my Saviour.	1:47
6	henceforth all generations shall call me blessed.	1:48
4	For he that is mighty hath done to me great things;	1:49
2	For mine eyes have seen thy salvation,	2:30
6	he said unto them, How is it that ye sought me?	2:49
2	that I must be about my Father's business?	2:49
2	that I must be about my Father's business?	2:49
1	I indeed baptize you with water;	3:16
2	but one mightier than I cometh,	3:16
2	which said, Thou art my beloved Son;	3:22
5	for that is delivered unto me;	4:6

217

ἐγώ 1466

#	Text	Ref
2	If thou ... wilt worship **me**, all shall be thine.	Luke 4:7
3	If thou ... wilt worship **me**, all shall be thine.	4:7
2	Get thee behind **me**, Satan: for it is written,	4:8
7	The Spirit of the Lord is upon **me**,	4:18
6	because he hath anointed **me** to preach the gospel	4:18
6	he hath sent **me** to heal the brokenhearted,	4:18
4	Ye will surely say unto **me** this proverb, Physician,	4:23
6	I must preach the kingdom of God to other cities	4:43
3	Depart from **me**; for I am a sinful man, O Lord.	5:8
6	Lord, if thou wilt, thou canst make **me** clean.	5:12
4	named Levi, ... and he said unto him, Follow **me**.	5:27
6	And why call ye **me**, Lord, Lord, and do not	6:46
6	Whosoever cometh to **me**, and heareth **my** sayings,	6:47
2	and heareth **my** sayings, and doeth them,	6:47
2	worthy that thou shouldest enter under **my** roof:	7:6
2	but say in a word, and **my** servant shall be healed.	7:7
1	For I also am a man set under authority,	7:8
2	and to **my** servant, Do this, and he doeth it.	7:8
5	blessed ... whosoever shall not be offended in **me**.	7:23
1	Behold, I send **my** messenger before thy face,	7:27
2	Behold, I send **my** messenger before thy face,	7:27
2	thou gavest **me** no water for **my** feet:	7:44
4	thou gavest **me** no water for **my** feet:	7:44
2	but she hath washed **my** feet with tears,	7:44
4	Thou gavest **me** no kiss: but this woman since	7:45
2	since ... I came in hath not ceased to kiss **my** feet.	7:45
2	**My** head with oil thou didst not anoint:	7:46
2	this woman hath anointed **my** feet with ointment.	7:46
2	**My** mother and **my** brethren are these which hear	8:21
2	**My** mother and **my** brethren are these which hear	8:21
5	What have I to do with thee, Jesus, ... Son of God	8:28
6	thou Son of God ... I beseech thee, torment **me** not.	8:28
2	Jesus said, Who touched **me**? When all denied,	8:45
2	and press thee, and sayest thou, Who touched **me**?	8:45
2	And Jesus said, Somebody hath touched **me**:	8:46
1	for I perceive that virtue is gone out of **me**.	8:46
2	for I perceive that virtue is gone out of **me**.	8:46
1	Herod said, John have I beheaded: but who is this,	9:9
1	but who is this, of whom I hear such things?	9:9
6	he asked them, ... Whom say the people that I am?	9:18
6	He said unto them, But whom say ye that I am?	9:20
2	If any man will come after **me**, let ... deny himself,	9:23
4	and take up his cross daily, and follow **me**.	9:23
3	but whosoever will lose his life for **my** sake,	9:24
6	shall be ashamed of **me** and of **my** words,	9:26
2	saying, This is **my** beloved Son: hear him.	9:35
2	look upon **my** son: for he is mine only child.	9:38
4	look upon **my** son: for he is **mine** only child.	9:38
2	Whosoever shall receive this child in **my** name	9:48
7	shall receive this child in **my** name receiveth **me**:	9:48
7	whosoever shall receive **me** receiveth him that sent	9:48
6	receive **me** receiveth him that sent **me**:	9:48
4	And he said unto another, Follow **me**. But he said,	9:59
4	Lord, suffer **me** first to go and bury **my** father.	9:59
2	Lord, suffer **me** first to go and bury **my** father.	9:59
4	but let **me** first go bid them farewell,	9:61
2	bid them farewell, which are at home at **my** house.	9:61
1	behold, I send you forth as lambs among wolves.	10:3
3	He that heareth you heareth **me**;	10:16
7	and he that despiseth you despiseth **me**;	10:16
7	he that despiseth **me** despiseth him that sent **me**.	10:16
6	he that despiseth **me** despiseth him that sent **me**.	10:16
4	All things are delivered to **me** of **my** Father:	10:22
2	All things are delivered to **me** of **my** Father:	10:22
2	said unto Jesus, And who is **my** neighbour?	10:29
1	when I come again, I will repay thee.	10:35
6	when I come again, I will repay thee.	10:35
2	dost thou not care that **my** sister hath left **me**	10:40
2	dost thou not care that **my** sister hath left **me**	10:40
4	to serve alone? bid her therefore that she help **me**.	10:40
4	and say unto him, Friend, lend **me** three loaves;	11:5
2	For a friend of **mine** in his journey is come to **me**,	11:6
6	For a friend of **mine** in his journey is come to **me**,	11:6
4	from within shall answer and say, Trouble **me** not:	11:7
2	and **my** children are with **me** in bed; I cannot rise	11:7
3	and **my** children are with **me** in bed; I cannot rise	11:7
6	ye say that I cast out devils through Beelzebub	11:18
1	And if I by Beelzebub cast out devils,	Luke 11:19
1	But if I cast out demons (NASB)	11:20
3	He that is not with **me** is against **me**:	11:23
3	He that is not with **me** is against **me**:	11:23
3	and he that gathereth not with **me** scattereth.	11:23
2	I will return unto **my** house whence I came out.	11:24
2	And I say unto you **my** friends,	12:4
5	Whosoever shall confess **me** before men,	12:8
6	But he that denieth **me** before men shall be denied	12:9
2	speak to **my** brother, that he divide the inheritance	12:13
3	that he divide the inheritance with **me**.	12:13
6	Man, who made **me** a judge or a divider over you?	12:14
2	because I have no room where to bestow **my** fruits?	12:17
2	I will pull down **my** barns, and build greater;	12:18
2	and there will I bestow all **my** fruits and **my** goods.	12:18
2	and there will I bestow all **my** fruits and **my** goods.	12:18
2	And I will say to **my** soul, Soul, thou hast much	12:19
2	say in his heart, **My** lord delayeth his coming;	12:45
3	depart from **me**, all ye workers of iniquity.	13:27
6	Nevertheless I must walk to day, and to morrow,	13:33
6	and verily I say unto you, Ye shall not see **me**,	13:35
6	needs go and see it: I pray thee have **me** excused.	14:18
6	I go to prove them: I pray thee have **me** excused.	14:19
2	and compel them ... that **my** house may be filled.	14:23
2	none of those ... bidden shall taste **of my** supper.	14:24
6	If any man come to **me**, and hate not his father,	14:26
2	and his own life also, he cannot be **my** disciple.	14:26
2	doth not bear his cross, and come after **me**,	14:27
2	doth not bear his cross, ... cannot be **my** disciple.	14:27
2	that forsaketh not all ... he cannot be **my** disciple.	14:33
4	saying unto them, Rejoice with **me**;	15:6
2	for I have found **my** sheep which was lost.	15:6
4	saying, Rejoice with **me**; for I have found the piece	15:9
4	give **me** the portion of goods that falleth to **me**.	15:12
2	hired servants of **my** father's have bread enough	15:17
1	I have bread enough ... and I perish with hunger!	15:17
2	I will arise and go to **my** father, and will say	15:18
6	make **me** as one of thy hired servants.	15:19
2	For this **my** son was dead, and is alive again;	15:24
2	and yet thou never gavest **me** a kid,	15:29
2	that I might make merry with **my** friends:	15:29
3	thou art ever with **me**, and all that I have is thine.	15:31
2	for **my** lord taketh away from **me** the stewardship:	16:3
2	for **my** lord taketh away from **me** the stewardship:	16:3
6	they may receive **me** into their houses.	16:4
2	How much owest thou unto **my** lord?	16:5
1	And I say to you, make friends (NASB)	16:9
6	Abraham, have mercy on **me**, and send Lazarus,	16:24
6	the tip of his finger in water, and cool **my** tongue;	16:24
2	that thou wouldest send him to **my** father's house:	16:27
4	and serve **me**, till I have eaten and drunken;	17:8
6	was a widow ... Avenge **me** of mine adversary.	18:3
2	was a widow ... Avenge **me** of mine adversary.	18:3
4	Yet because this widow troubleth **me**,	18:5
6	lest by her continual coming she weary **me**.	18:5
4	saying, God be merciful to **me** a sinner.	18:13
6	Suffer little children to come unto **me**,	18:16
6	Jesus said unto him, Why callest thou **me** good?	18:19
2	he said, All these have I kept from **my** youth up.	18:21
4	have treasure in heaven: and come, follow **me**.	18:22
2	Jesus, thou son of David, have mercy on **me**.	18:38
6	the more, Thou son of David, have mercy on **me**.	18:39
6	come down; for to day I must abide at thy house.	19:5
2	Lord, the half of **my** goods I give to the poor;	19:8
2	Lord, the half of **my** goods I give to the poor;	19:8
1	Thou knewest that I was an austere man,	19:22
2	then gavest not thou **my** money into the bank,	19:23
1	I might have required mine own with usury?	19:23
2	But those **mine** enemies, which would not that I	19:27
6	which would not that I should reign over them,	19:27
2	bring hither, and slay them before **me**.	19:27
2	It is written, **My** house is the house of prayer:	19:46
4	I will also ask you one thing; and answer **me**:	20:3
1	Neither tell I you by what authority I do these	20:8
2	What shall I do? I will send **my** beloved son:	20:13
6	and said unto them, Why tempt ye **me**?	20:23
4	Show **me** a penny. Whose image and	20:24

ἐγώ 1466

2	The Lord said unto **my** Lord, Sit thou on my right	Luke 20:42
2	said unto **my** Lord, Sit thou on my right hand,	20:42
2	many shall come in **my** name, saying, I am Christ;	21:8
1	**I** am Christ; and the time draweth near:	21:8
2	before kings and rulers for **my** name's sake	21:12
1	For **I** will give you a mouth and wisdom,	21:15
2	ye shall be hated of all men for **my** name's sake	21:17
2	but **my** words shall not pass away.	21:33
2	where I shall eat the passover with **my** disciples?	22:11
6	to eat this passover with you before **I** suffer:	22:15
2	This is **my** body which is given for you:	22:19
2	This cup is the new testament in **my** blood,	22:20
6	the hand of him that betrayeth **me** is with me	22:21
3	the hand of him that betrayeth me is with **me**	22:21
1	but **I** am among you as he that serveth.	22:27
3	which have continued with **me** in my temptations.	22:28
2	which have continued with me in **my** temptations.	22:28
4	a kingdom, as my Father hath appointed **unto me**;	22:29
2	a kingdom, as **my** Father hath appointed unto me;	22:29
2	ye may eat and drink at **my** table in my kingdom,	22:30
2	ye may eat and drink at my table in **my** kingdom,	22:30
1	But **I** have prayed for thee, that thy faith fail not:	22:32
6	thou shalt thrice deny that thou knowest **me**.	22:34
5	that is written must yet be accomplished in **me**,	22:37
3	for the things concerning **me** have an end.	22:37
3	if thou be willing, remove this cup from **me**:	22:42
2	nevertheless not **my** will, but thine, be done.	22:42
2	When **I** was daily with you in the temple,	22:53
7	ye stretched forth no hands against **me**:	22:53
6	Before the cock crow, thou shalt deny **me** thrice.	22:61
4	And if **I** also ask you, ye will not answer me,	22:68
1	And he said unto them, Ye say that **I** am.	22:70
4	Ye have brought this man **unto me**,	23:14
1	and, behold, **I**, having examined him before you,	23:14
7	Daughters of Jerusalem, weep not for **me**,	23:28
2	remember **me** when thou comest into thy kingdom.	23:42
3	To day shalt thou be with **me** in paradise.	23:43
2	Father, into thy hands **I** commend my spirit:	23:46
1	stood in the midst of them, ... Peace be unto you.	24:36
2	Behold **my** hands and my feet, that it is I myself:	24:39
2	Behold my hands and **my** feet, that it is I myself:	24:39
1	Behold my hands and my feet, that it is **I** myself:	24:39
6	handle **me**, and see; for a spirit hath not flesh	24:39
7	spirit hath not flesh and bones, as ye see **me** have.	24:39
2	These are **My** words which I spoke to you (NASB)	24:44
3	in the prophets, and in the psalms, concerning **me**.	24:44
1	And, behold, **I** send the promise of my Father	24:49
2	behold, I send the promise of **my** Father upon you:	24:49
2	He that cometh after **me** is preferred before me:	John 1:15
2	He that cometh after me is preferred before **me**:	1:15
2	John bare witness of him, ... for he was before **me**.	1:15
1	and denied not; but confessed, **I** am not the Christ.	1:20
1	**I** am the voice of one crying in the wilderness,	1:23
1	John answered them, saying, **I** baptize with water:	1:26
2	who coming after **me** is preferred before me,	1:27
2	who coming after me is preferred before **me**,	1:27
1	whose shoe's latchet **I** am not worthy to unloose.	1:27
1	whose shoe's latchet I am not worthy to unloose.	1:27
1	This is he of whom **I** said,	1:30
2	After **me** cometh a man ... preferred before me:	1:30
2	After me cometh a man ... preferred before **me**:	1:30
2	is preferred before **me**: for he was before me.	1:30
1	therefore am **I** come baptizing with water.	1:31
6	but he that sent **me** to baptize with water,	1:33
4	he that sent me ... the same said **unto me**,	1:33
4	and findeth Philip, and saith unto him, Follow **me**.	1:43
6	Nathanael saith ... Whence knowest thou **me**?	1:48
5	Woman, what have **I** to do with thee?	2:4
2	**mine** hour is not yet come.	2:4
2	not **my** Father's house an house of merchandise.	2:16
6	The zeal of thine house hath eaten **me** up.	2:17
4	Ye yourselves bear **me** witness, that I said,	3:28
1	that I said, **I** am not the Christ,	3:28
3	He must increase, but **I** must decrease.	3:30
4	Jesus saith unto her, Give **me** to drink.	4:7
3	thou, being a Jew, askest drink of **me**,	4:9
4	and who it is that saith to thee, Give **me** to drink;	4:10
1	of the water that **I** shall give him shall never thirst;	John 4:14
1	but the water that I shall give him shall be in him	4:14
4	give **me** this water, that I thirst not,	4:15
4	Jesus saith unto her, Woman, believe **me**	4:21
1	Jesus saith unto her, **I** that speak unto thee am he	4:26
4	see a man, which told **me** all things that ever I did:	4:29
1	**I** have meat to eat that ye know not of.	4:32
6	My meat is to do the will of him that sent **me**,	4:34
1	**I** sent you to reap	4:38
4	which testified, He told **me** all that ever I did.	4:39
2	Sir, come down ere **my** child die.	4:49
6	**I** have no man, ... to put me into the pool:	5:7
1	but while I am coming, another steppeth down	5:7
3	**I** am coming, another steppeth down before me.	5:7
6	He that made **me** whole, the same said unto me,	5:11
4	He that made me whole, the same said **unto me**,	5:11
2	**My** Father worketh hitherto, and I work.	5:17
2	He that heareth **my** word,	5:24
6	and believeth on him that sent **me**,	5:24
1	**I** can of mine own self do nothing:	5:30
6	but the will of the Father which hath sent **me**.	5:30
1	If **I** bear witness of myself, my witness is not true.	5:31
2	If I bear witness of myself, **my** witness is not true.	5:31
3	There is another that beareth witness of **me**;	5:32
3	that the witness which he witnesseth of **me** is true.	5:32
1	But **I** receive not testimony from man:	5:34
1	But **I** have greater witness than that of John:	5:36
4	for the works which the Father hath given **me**	5:36
1	the same works that **I** do, bear witness of me,	5:36
3	the same works that I do, bear witness of **me**,	5:36
6	bear witness of me, that the Father hath sent **me**.	5:36
6	And the Father himself, which hath sent **me**,	5:37
3	the Father himself, ... hath borne witness of **me**.	5:37
3	and they are they which testify of **me**.	5:39
6	ye will not come to **me**, that ye might have life.	5:40
1	**I** am come in my Father's name,	5:43
2	I am come in **my** Father's name,	5:43
6	come in my Father's name, and ye receive **me** not:	5:43
1	Do not think that **I** will accuse you to the Father:	5:45
5	ye would have believed **me**: for he wrote of me.	5:46
3	ye would have believed me: for he wrote of **me**.	5:46
1	But he saith unto them, It is **I**; be not afraid.	6:20
6	Ye seek **me**, not because ye saw the miracles,	6:26
2	**my** Father giveth you the true bread from heaven.	6:32
1	And Jesus said unto them, **I** am the bread of life:	6:35
6	he that cometh to **me** shall never hunger;	6:35
7	he that cometh to me shall never hunger;	6:35
7	and he that believeth on **me** shall never thirst.	6:35
6	That ye also have seen **me**, and believe not.	6:36
4	All that the Father giveth **me** shall come to me;	6:37
7	All that the Father giveth me shall come to **me**;	6:37
6	him that cometh to **me** I will in no wise cast out.	6:37
7	him that cometh to me I will in no wise cast out.	6:37
6	not ... own will, but the will of him that sent **me**.	6:38
6	And this is the Father's will which hath sent **me**,	6:39
4	all which he hath given **me** I should lose nothing,	6:39
6	And this is the will of him that sent **me**,	6:40
2	And this is the will of him that sent me,	6:40
1	and **I** will raise him up at the last day.	6:40
1	**I** am the bread which came down from heaven.	6:41
6	No man can come to **me**, except	6:44
7	No man can come to me, except	6:44
6	except the Father which hath sent **me** draw him:	6:44
1	and **I** will raise him up at the last day.	6:44
6	and hath learned of the Father, cometh unto **me**.	6:45
7	and hath learned of the Father, cometh unto me.	6:45
7	He that believeth on **me** hath everlasting life.	6:47
1	**I** am that bread of life.	6:48
1	**I** am the living bread which came down	6:51
1	and the bread that I will give is **my** flesh,	6:51
2	and the bread that I will give is my flesh,	6:51
1	**my** flesh, which I will give for the life of the world.	6:51
2	Whoso eateth **my** flesh, and drinketh my blood,	6:54
2	Whoso eateth my flesh, and drinketh **my** blood,	6:54
1	and **I** will raise him up at the last day.	6:54
2	For **my** flesh is meat indeed,	6:55
2	and **my** blood is drink indeed.	6:55

219

ἐγώ 1466

2	He that eateth my flesh, and drinkest my blood, ... John	6:56
2	He that eateth my flesh, and drinkest my blood,	6:56
5	drinketh my blood, dwelleth in me, and I in him.	6:56
6	As the living Father hath sent me,	6:57
6	so he that eateth me, even he shall live by me.	6:57
7	so he that eateth me, even he shall live by me.	6:57
1	the words that I speak unto you, they are spirit,	6:63
6	no man can come unto me, except it were given	6:65
7	no man can come unto me, except it were given	6:65
2	except it were given unto him of my Father.	6:65
1	Have not I chosen you twelve, ... one ... is a devil?	6:70
7	The world cannot hate you; but me it hateth,	7:7
1	but me it hateth, because I testify of it,	7:7
1	I go not up yet unto this feast:	7:8
6	My doctrine is not mine, but his that sent me.	7:16
1	whether it be of God, or whether I speak of myself.	7:17
6	Why go ye about to kill me?	7:19
5	Moses should not be broken; are ye angry at me,	7:23
6	Ye both know me, and ye know whence I am:	7:28
1	But I know him: for I am from him,	7:29
6	for I am from him, and he hath sent me.	7:29
6	and then I go unto him that sent me.	7:33
6	Ye shall seek me, and shall not find me:	7:34
6	You shall seek Me, and shall not find Me (NASB)	7:34
1	and where I am, thither ye cannot come.	7:34
6	Ye shall seek me, and shall not find me:	7:36
1	and where I am, thither ye cannot come?	7:36
6	If any man thirst, let him come unto me,	7:37
7	He that believeth on me, as the scripture hath said,	7:38
1	Jesus said unto her, Neither do I condemn thee:	8:11
1	I am the light of the world:	8:12
5	he that followeth me shall not walk in darkness,	8:12
4	he that followeth me shall not walk in darkness,	8:12
1	Though I bear record of myself,	8:14
2	I bear record of myself, yet my record is true:	8:14
1	Ye judge after the flesh; I judge no man.	8:15
1	And yet if I judge, my judgment is true:	8:16
1	I am not alone, but I and the Father that sent me.	8:16
6	I am not alone, but I and the Father that sent me.	8:16
1	I am one that bear witness of myself,	8:18
3	and the Father that sent me beareth witness of me.	8:18
6	and the Father that sent me beareth witness of me.	8:18
7	Ye neither know me, nor my Father:	8:19
2	Ye neither know me, nor my Father:	8:19
7	if ye had known me, ... known my Father also.	8:19
2	ye should have known my Father also.	8:19
1	Then said Jesus again unto them, I go my way,	8:21
6	and ye shall seek me, and shall die in your sins:	8:21
1	whither I go, ye cannot come.	8:21
1	because he saith, Whither I go, ye cannot come.	8:22
1	Ye are from beneath; I am from above:	8:23
1	ye are of this world; I am not of this world.	8:23
1	believe not that I am he, ye shall die in your sins.	8:24
3	but he that sent me is true:	8:26
1	then shall ye know that I am he,	8:28
6	as my Father hath taught me, I speak these things.	8:28
2	as my Father hath taught me, I speak these things.	8:28
6	And he that sent me is with me:	8:29
3	And he that sent me is with me:	8:29
6	the Father hath not left me alone;	8:29
1	for I do always those things that please him.	8:29
2	in my word, then are ye my disciples indeed;	8:31
6	that ye are Abraham's seed; but ye seek to kill me,	8:37
1	I speak that which I have seen with my Father:	8:38
2	I speak that which I have seen with my Father:	8:38
6	But now ye seek to kill me,	8:40
7	If God were your Father, ye would love me:	8:42
1	for I proceeded forth and came from God;	8:42
6	neither came I of myself, but he sent me.	8:42
1	because I tell you the truth, ye believe me not.	8:45
4	because I tell you the truth, ye believe me not.	8:45
6	Which of you convinceth me of sin?	8:46
4	And if I say the truth, why do ye not believe me?	8:46
1	Jesus answered, I have not a devil;	8:49
6	but I honour my Father, and ye do dishonour me.	8:49
6	but I honour my Father, and ye do dishonour me.	8:49
1	And I seek not mine own glory:	8:50

2	And I seek not mine own glory: .... John	8:50
2	thou sayest, If a man keep my saying,	8:52
1	If I honour myself, my honour is nothing:	8:54
2	If I honour myself, my honour is nothing:	8:54
2	it is my Father that honoureth me:	8:54
6	it is my Father that honoureth me;	8:54
1	Yet ye have not known him; but I know him:	8:55
1	I say unto you, Before Abraham was, I am.	8:58
7	I must work the works of him that sent me,	9:4
6	I must work the works of him that sent me,	9:4
1	others said, He is like him: but he said, I am he.	9:9
2	Jesus made clay, and anointed mine eyes,	9:11
4	and said unto me, Go to the pool of Siloam,	9:11
2	clay upon mine eyes, and I washed, and do see.	9:15
2	and yet he hath opened mine eyes.	9:30
1	For judgment I am come into this world,	9:39
1	I am the door of the sheep.	10:7
3	that ever came before me are thieves and robbers:	10:8
1	I am the door: ... shall be saved,	10:9
3	by me if any man enter in, he shall be saved,	10:9
1	I am come that they might have life,	10:10
1	I am the good shepherd.	10:11
1	I am the good shepherd, and know my sheep,	10:14
6	I know My own, and My own know Me (NASB)	10:14
6	As the Father knoweth me,	10:15
2	and I lay down my life for the sheep.	10:15
6	which are not of this fold: them also I must bring,	10:16
2	and they shall hear my voice;	10:16
6	Therefore doth my Father love me,	10:17
1	my Father love me, because I lay down my life,	10:17
2	my Father love me, because I lay down my life,	10:17
3	No man taketh it from me,	10:18
1	but I lay it down of myself.	10:18
2	This commandment have I received of my Father.	10:18
1	the works that I do in my Father's name,	10:25
2	the works that I do in my Father's name,	10:25
3	in my Father's name, they bear witness of me.	10:25
2	My sheep hear my voice, and I know them,	10:27
4	and I know them, and they follow me:	10:27
2	neither shall any man pluck them out of my hand.	10:28
2	My Father, which gave them me,	10:29
4	My Father, which gave them me,	10:29
2	is able to pluck them out of my Father's hand.	10:29
1	I and my Father are one.	10:30
2	good works have I showed you from my Father;	10:32
6	for which of those works do ye stone me	10:32
7	for which of those works do ye stone me?	10:32
1	Is it not written in your law, I said, Ye are gods?	10:34
2	If I do not the works of my Father, believe me not.	10:37
4	If I do not the works of my Father, believe me not.	10:37
5	though ye believe not me, believe the works:	10:38
5	and believe, that the Father is in me, and I in him.	10:38
2	if thou hadst been here, my brother had not died.	11:21
1	I am the resurrection, and the life:	11:25
7	he that believeth in me, though he were dead,	11:25
7	liveth and believeth in me shall never die.	11:26
1	I believe that thou art the Christ, the Son of God,	11:27
2	if thou hadst been here, my brother had not died.	11:32
2	Father, I thank thee that thou hast heard me.	11:41
1	And I knew that thou hearest me always:	11:42
2	And I knew that thou hearest me always:	11:42
6	that they may believe that thou hast sent me.	11:42
2	against the day of my burying hath she kept this.	12:7
7	poor always ye have ... but me ye have not always.	12:8
5	If any man serve me, let him follow me;	12:26
5	If any man serve me, let him follow me;	12:26
1	and where I am, there shall also my servant be:	12:26
5	if any man serve me, him will my Father honour.	12:26
2	Now is my soul troubled; and what shall I say?	12:27
6	what shall I say? Father, save me from this hour:	12:27
7	voice came not because of me, but for your sakes.	12:30
7	Jesus cried and said, He that believeth on me,	12:44
7	believeth not on me, but on him that sent me.	12:44
6	believeth not on me, but on him that sent me.	12:44
7	And he that seeth me seeth him that sent me.	12:45
6	And he that seeth me seeth him that sent me.	12:45
1	I am come a light into the world,	12:46

ἐγώ 1466

7	believeth on **me** should not abide in darkness...... John	12:46
2	And if any man hear **my** words, and believe not,......	12:47
1	I judge him not: for I came not to judge the world,....	12:47
7	He that rejecteth **me**, and receiveth not **my** words,.....	12:48
2	He that rejecteth **me**, and receiveth not **my** words,.....	12:48
1	For I have not spoken of myself;......................	12:49
6	but the Father which sent **me**,.......................	12:49
4	he gave **me** a commandment, what I should say,......	12:49
1	whatsoever I speak therefore, ... the Father said......	12:50
4	even as the Father said **unto me**, so I speak...........	12:50
2	Peter saith ... Lord, dost thou wash **my** feet?..........	13:6
1	What I do thou knowest not now;.....................	13:7
2	Peter saith ... Thou shalt never wash **my** feet,.......	13:8
3	If I wash thee not, thou hast no part with **me**........	13:8
2	not **my** feet only, but also **my** hands and **my** head.....	13:9
6	Ye call **me** Master and Lord: and ye say well;........	13:13
1	If I then, your Lord and Master,.....................	13:14
1	example, that ye should do as I have done to you.....	13:15
1	I know whom I have chosen:.........................	13:18
3	He that eateth bread with **me**	13:18
2	He that eateth bread with **me**	13:18
7	hath lifted up his heel against **me**...................	13:18
1	when ... come to pass, ye may believe that I am he....	13:19
7	He that receiveth whomsoever I send receiveth **me**;....	13:20
7	he that receiveth **me** receiveth him that sent **me**.......	13:20
6	he that receiveth **me** receiveth him that sent **me**.......	13:20
6	I say unto you, that one of you shall betray **me**.......	13:21
1	He it is, to whom I shall give a sop,.................	13:26
6	Ye shall seek **me**: and as I said unto the Jews,........	13:33
1	Whither I go, ye cannot come;.......................	13:33
1	Whither I go, thou canst not follow **me** now;..........	13:36
4	Whither I go, thou canst not follow **me** now;..........	13:36
4	but thou shalt follow **me** afterwards..................	13:36
2	I will lay down **my** life for thy sake.................	13:37
3	Wilt thou lay down thy life for **my** sake?.............	13:38
6	cock shall not crow, till thou hast denied **me** thrice.....	13:38
7	ye believe in God, believe also in **me**................	14:1
2	In **my** Father's house are many mansions:.............	14:2
1	that where I am, there ye may be also...............	14:3
1	And whither I go ye know, and the way ye know.....	14:4
1	I am the way, the truth, and the life:................	14:6
3	no man cometh unto the Father, but by **me**...........	14:6
6	If ye had known **me**, ... known **my** Father also:.......	14:7
7	If ye had known **me**, ... known **my** Father also:.......	14:7
2	ye should have known **my** Father also:...............	14:7
6	and yet hast thou not known **me**, Philip?.............	14:9
7	he that hath seen **me** hath seen the Father;...........	14:9
1	Believest thou not that I am in the Father,...........	14:10
5	that I am in the Father, and the Father in **me**?........	14:10
1	words that I speak unto you I speak not of myself:....	14:10
5	Father that dwelleth in **me**, he doeth the works........	14:10
4	Believe **me** that I am in the Father,...................	14:11
1	Believe **me** that I am in the Father,...................	14:11
5	that I am in the Father, and the Father in **me**:........	14:11
4	or else believe **me** for the very works' sake...........	14:11
7	He that believeth on **me**,............................	14:12
1	the works that I do shall he do also;.................	14:12
1	because I go unto **my** Father.......................	14:12
2	because I go unto **my** Father.......................	14:12
2	whatsoever ye shall ask in **my** name, that will I do,....	14:13
6	If you ask **Me** anything in My name, (NASB)........	14:14
2	If ye shall ask any thing in **my** name, I will do it.....	14:14
1	If ye shall ask any thing in **my** name, I will do it.....	14:14
6	If ye love **me**, keep **my** commandments...............	14:15
1	And I will pray the Father, and he shall give you.....	14:16
6	Yet a little while, and the world seeth **me** no more;...	14:19
6	but ye see **me**: because I live, ye shall live also.......	14:19
1	but ye see **me**: because I live, ye shall live also.......	14:19
1	I am in **my** Father, and ye in **me**, and I in you........	14:20
2	I am in **my** Father, and ye in **me**, and I in you........	14:20
5	I am in **my** Father, and ye in **me**, and I in you........	14:20
2	He that hath **my** commandments,....................	14:21
6	hath **my** commandments, ... he it is that loveth **me**:....	14:21
6	and he that loveth **me** shall be loved of **my** Father,....	14:21
2	and he that loveth **me** shall be loved of **my** Father,....	14:21
1	and I will love him, and will manifest myself.........	14:21
6	If a man love **me**, he will keep **my** words:............	14:23

2	If a man love **me**, he will keep **my** words:.......... John	14:23
2	will keep **my** words: and **my** Father will love him,.....	14:23
6	He that loveth **me** not keepeth not **my** sayings:........	14:24
2	He that loveth **me** not keepeth not **my** sayings:........	14:24
6	word ... not mine, but the Father's which sent **me**.....	14:24
2	Ghost, whom the Father will send in **my** name,........	14:26
1	all that I said to you (NASB) (NT)....................	14:26
1	not as the world giveth, give I unto you.............	14:27
1	Ye have heard how I said unto you, I go away,.......	14:28
6	If ye loved **me**, ye would rejoice,....................	14:28
2	for **my** Father is greater than I.......................	14:28
2	for **my** Father is greater than I.......................	14:28
5	prince of this world ... and hath nothing in **me**.......	14:30
4	as the Father gave **me** commandment, even so I do....	14:31
1	I am the true vine,................................	15:1
2	and **my** Father is the husbandman....................	15:1
5	Every branch in **me** that beareth not fruit.............	15:2
5	Abide in **me**, and I in you..........................	15:4
5	no more can ye, except ye abide in **me**...............	15:4
1	I am the vine, ye are the branches:..................	15:5
5	He that abideth in **me**, and I in him,.................	15:5
3	for without **me** ye can do nothing...................	15:5
5	If a man abide not in **me**, he is cast forth.............	15:6
5	If ye abide in **me**, and **my** words abide in you,........	15:7
2	If ye abide in **me**, and **my** words abide in you,........	15:7
2	Herein is **my** Father glorified, that ye bear ... fruit;....	15:8
6	As the Father hath loved **me**, so have I loved you:....	15:9
2	If ye keep **my** commandments, ye shall abide..........	15:10
2	keep ... commandments, ye shall abide in **my** love;....	15:10
1	even as I have kept **my** Father's commandments.......	15:10
2	even as I have kept **my** Father's commandments,.......	15:10
2	Ye are **my** friends, if ye do whatsoever I command....	15:14
1	Ye are **my** friends, if ye do whatsoever I command....	15:14
2	for all things that I have heard of **my** Father..........	15:15
6	Ye have not chosen **me**, but I have chosen you,........	15:16
1	Ye have not chosen **me**, but I have chosen you,........	15:16
2	whatsoever ye shall ask of the Father in **my** name,.....	15:16
2	ye know that it hated **me** before it hated you..........	15:18
1	but I have chosen you out of the world,..............	15:19
1	Remember the word that I said unto you,.............	15:20
7	If they have persecuted **me**,.........................	15:20
2	if they have kept **my** saying,........................	15:20
2	things will they do unto you for **my** name's sake,......	15:21
6	because they know not him that sent **me**..............	15:21
7	He that hateth **me** hateth **my** Father also.............	15:23
2	He that hateth **me** hateth **my** Father also.............	15:23
7	both seen and hated both **me** and **my** Father..........	15:24
2	both seen and hated both **me** and **my** Father..........	15:24
6	They hated **me** without a cause......................	15:25
1	whom I will send unto you from the Father,..........	15:26
3	the Spirit of truth, ... he shall testify of **me**:.........	15:26
3	because ye have been with **me** from the beginning.....	15:27
7	because they have not known the Father, nor **me**......	16:3
1	ye may remember that I told you of them.............	16:4
6	But now I go **my** way to him that sent **me**;...........	16:5
6	and none of you asketh **me**, Whither goest thou?......	16:5
1	Nevertheless I tell you the truth;....................	16:7
1	It is expedient for you that I go away:...............	16:7
1	for if I go not away, the Comforter will not come.....	16:7
7	Of sin, because they believe not on **me**;..............	16:9
2	Of righteousness, because I go to **my** Father,.........	16:10
6	because I go to **my** Father, and ye see **me** no more;...	16:10
7	He shall glorify **me**: for he shall receive of mine,......	16:14
6	A little while, and ye shall not see **me**:...............	16:16
6	and again, a little while, and ye shall see **me**,........	16:16
1	ye shall see **me**, because I go to the Father...........	16:16
6	A little while, and ye shall not see **me**:...............	16:17
6	and again, a little while, and ye shall see **me**:........	16:17
1	and, Because I go to the Father?.....................	16:17
6	A little while, and ye shall not see **me**:...............	16:19
6	and again, a little while, and ye shall see **me**?........	16:19
7	And in that day ye shall ask **me** nothing..............	16:23
2	Whatsoever ye shall ask the Father in **my** name,.......	16:23
2	Hitherto have ye asked nothing in **my** name:..........	16:24
2	At that day ye shall ask in **my** name:................	16:26
1	that I will pray the Father for you:...................	16:26
7	Father ... loveth you, because ye have loved **me**,......	16:27

221

ἐγώ 1466

1 and have believed that I came out from God......John	16:27	
7 every man to his own, and shall leave me alone:......	16:32	
3 yet I am not alone, because the Father is with me....	16:32	
5 that in me ye might have peace......................	16:33	
1 but be of good cheer; I have overcome the world.....	16:33	
1 I have glorified thee on the earth:...................	17:4	
4 I have finished the work which thou gavest me.......	17:4	
6 glorify thou me with thine own self with the glory....	17:5	
4 the men which thou gavest me out of the world:.....	17:6	
5 thine they were, and thou gavest them me;..........	17:6	
4 that all things whatsoever thou hast given me........	17:7	
4 given unto them the words which thou gavest me.....	17:8	
6 and they have believed that thou didst send me......	17:8	
1 I pray for them: I pray not for the world,...........	17:9	
4 them which thou hast given me; for they are thine....	17:9	
1 but these are in the world, and I come to thee.......	17:11	
4 keep ... those whom thou hast given me,............	17:11	
1 I kept them in thy name:...........................	17:12	
4 those that thou gavest me I have kept,..............	17:12	
1 I have given them thy word;.......................	17:14	
1 even as I am not of the world......................	17:14	
1 are not of the world, even as I am not of the world...	17:16	
7 As thou hast sent me into the world,................	17:18	
1 And for their sakes I sanctify myself,...............	17:19	
7 but for them also which shall believe on me..........	17:20	
5 as thou, Father, art in me, and I in thee,...........	17:21	
6 that the world may believe that thou hast sent me.....	17:21	
1 the glory which thou gavest me I have given them;....	17:22	
4 the glory which thou gavest me I have given them;....	17:22	
1 I in them, and thou in me, ... made perfect in one;...	17:23	
5 I in them, and thou in me, ... made perfect in one;...	17:23	
6 that the world may know that thou hast sent me,.....	17:23	
7 and hast loved them, as thou hast loved me.........	17:23	
4 I will that they also, whom thou hast given me,......	17:24	
1 whom thou hast given me, be with me where I am;....	17:24	
3 whom thou hast given me, be with me where I am;....	17:24	
4 may behold my glory, which thou hast given me:.....	17:24	
6 lovedst me before the foundation of the world.......	17:24	
1 world hath not ... but I have known thee,..........	17:25	
6 and these have known that thou hast sent me.......	17:25	
6 that the love wherewith thou hast loved me.........	17:26	
1 Jesus saith unto them, I am he.....................	18:5	
1 As soon then as he had said unto them, I am he,....	18:6	
1 Jesus answered, I have told you that I am he:.......	18:8	
7 if therefore ye seek me, let these go their way:......	18:8	
4 Of them which thou gavest me have I lost none......	18:9	
4 the cup which my Father hath given me,............	18:11	
1 Jesus answered him, I spake openly to the world;.....	18:20	
1 I ever taught in the synagogue, and in the temple,...	18:20	
6 Why askest thou me? ask them which heard me,.....	18:21	
1 behold, they know what I said.....................	18:21	
6 but if well, why smitest thou me?..................	18:23	
1 saith, Did not I see thee in the garden with him?....	18:26	
3 or did others tell it thee of me?....................	18:34	
1 Pilate answered, Am I a Jew?......................	18:35	
5 and the chief priests have delivered thee unto me:.....	18:35	
1 Jesus answered, Thou sayest that I am a king......	18:37	
1 I am a king. To this end was I born,...............	18:37	
2 Every one that is of the truth heareth my voice......	18:37	
1 unto the Jews, ... I find in him no fault at all........	18:38	
1 and crucify him: for I find no fault in him...........	19:6	
5 Speakest thou not unto me?.......................	19:10	
3 Thou couldest have no power at all against me,.....	19:11	
6 he that delivered me ... hath the greater sin..........	19:11	
2 They parted my raiment among them,...............	19:24	
2 They parted my raiment among them,...............	19:24	
2 Because they have taken away my Lord,...........	20:13	
4 tell me where thou hast laid him,....................	20:15	
2 Jesus saith unto her, Touch me not;................	20:17	
2 for I am not yet ascended to my Father:.............	20:17	
2 but go to my brethren, and say unto them,..........	20:17	
2 I ascend unto my Father, and your Father,..........	20:17	
2 I ascend unto ... to my God, and your God...........	20:17	
6 as my Father hath sent me, even so send I you......	20:21	
2 and put my finger into the print of the nails,.........	20:25	
2 and thrust my hand into his side,...................	20:25	
2 Reach hither thy finger, and behold my hands;.......	20:27	
2 reach hither thy hand, and thrust it into my side: .. John	20:27	
2 Thomas answered ... My Lord and my God...........	20:28	
2 Thomas answered ... My Lord and my God...........	20:28	
6 because thou hast seen me, thou hast believed:.......	20:29	
6 son of Jonas, lovest thou me more than these?........	21:15	
2 He saith unto him, Feed my lambs..................	21:15	
6 Simon, son of Jonas, lovest thou me?...............	21:16	
2 He saith unto him, Feed my sheep..................	21:16	
6 Simon, son of Jonas, lovest thou me?...............	21:17	
6 he said unto him the third time, Lovest thou me?.....	21:17	
2 Jesus saith unto him, Feed my sheep................	21:17	
4 he saith unto him, Follow me......................	21:19	
4 what is that to thee? follow thou me.................	21:22	
2 which, saith he, ye have heard of me..........Acts	1:4	
4 ye shall be witnesses unto me both in Jerusalem,......	1:8	
2 ye shall be witnesses unto me both in Jerusalem,......	1:8	
2 be this known unto you, and hearken to my words:....	2:14	
2 I will pour out of my Spirit upon all flesh:............	2:17	
2 And on my servants and on my handmaidens.........	2:18	
2 And on my servants and on my handmaidens.........	2:18	
2 I will pour out in those days of my Spirit;............	2:18	
2 I foresaw the Lord always before my face,...........	2:25	
2 for he is on my right hand,.........................	2:25	
2 Therefore did my heart rejoice,.....................	2:26	
2 and my tongue was glad;..........................	2:26	
2 moreover also my flesh shall rest in hope:...........	2:26	
2 Because thou wilt not leave my soul in hell,..........	2:27	
4 Thou hast made known to me the ways of life;......	2:28	
6 shalt make me full of joy with thy countenance.......	2:28	
2 The Lord said unto my Lord, Sit thou on my right.....	2:34	
2 said unto my Lord, Sit thou on my right hand,.......	2:34	
4 Then Peter said, Silver and gold have I none;........	3:6	
4 raise up unto you of your brethren, like unto me;......	3:22	
4 Tell me whether ye sold the land for so much?.......	5:8	
1 they shall be in bondage will I judge, said God:.......	7:7	
4 shall they come forth, and serve me in this place.....	7:7	
6 Wilt thou kill me, as thou diddest the Egyptian........	7:28	
1 Saying, I am the God of thy fathers,................	7:32	
2 the affliction of my people which is in Egypt,.........	7:34	
7 like unto me; him shall ye hear....................	7:37	
4 have ye offered to me slain beasts and sacrifices.......	7:42	
4 Heaven is my throne, and earth is my footstool:......	7:49	
2 Heaven is my throne, and earth is my footstool:......	7:49	
4 what house will ye build me? saith the Lord:.........	7:49	
2 or what is the place of my rest?....................	7:49	
2 Hath not my hand made all these things?...........	7:50	
2 and saying, Lord Jesus, receive my spirit.............	7:59	
3 and said, Pray ye to the Lord for me,...............	8:24	
7 these things which ye have spoken come upon me....	8:24	
6 How can I, except some man should guide me?......	8:31	
6 here is water; what doth hinder me to be baptized?.....	8:36	
6 Saul, Saul, why persecutest thou me?...............	9:4	
1 the Lord said, I am Jesus whom thou persecutest:.....	9:5	
6 Lord, what wilt thou have me to do?................	9:6	
1 Ananias. And he said, Behold, I am here, Lord......	9:10	
4 for he is a chosen vessel unto me,..................	9:15	
2 to bear my name before the Gentiles,...............	9:15	
1 I will show him how great things he must suffer......	9:16	
2 great things he must suffer for my name's sake.......	9:16	
6 the Lord, even ... hath sent me,....................	9:17	
1 doubting nothing: for I have sent them..............	10:20	
1 and said, Behold, I am he whom ye seek:...........	10:21	
1 Stand up; I too am just a man (NASB)...............	10:26	
5 but God hath showed me that I should not call any....	10:28	
6 I ask therefore for what intent ye have sent for me?...	10:29	
2 and at the ninth hour I prayed in my house,.........	10:30	
2 behold, a man stood before me in bright clothing,.....	10:30	
1 I was in the city of Joppa praying:..................	11:5	
3 by four corners; and it came even to me:............	11:5	
4 a voice saying unto me, Arise, Peter; slay and eat.....	11:7	
2 unclean hath at any time entered into my mouth.....	11:8	
4 But the voice answered me again from heaven,.......	11:9	
6 were three men ... sent from Caesarea unto me......	11:11	
4 And the Spirit bade me go with them,..............	11:12	
5 Moreover these six brethren accompanied me,.......	11:12	
6 as I began to speak, the Holy Ghost fell on them,.....	11:15	
1 what was I, that I could withstand God?.............	11:17	

ἐγώ 1466

4	Cast thy garment about thee, and follow me.	Acts 12:8
6	and hath delivered me out of the hand of Herod,	12:11
4	Separate me Barnabas and Saul for the work	13:2
2	a man after mine own heart,	13:22
2	which shall fulfil all my will.	13:22
6	Whom think ye that I am? I am not he.	13:25
7	Whom think ye that I am? I am not he.	13:25
1	Whom think ye that I am? I am not he.	13:25
7	But, behold, there cometh one after me,	13:25
2	Thou art my Son, this day have I begotten thee.	13:33
1	Thou art my Son, this day have I begotten thee.	13:33
1	and perish: for I work a work in your days,	13:41
2	by my mouth should hear the word of the gospel,	15:7
2	saying, Men and brethren, hearken unto me:	15:13
2	all the Gentiles, upon whom my name is called,	15:17
1	Wherefore my sentence is,	15:19
6	If ye have judged me to be faithful to the Lord,	16:15
2	come into my house, and abide there.	16:15
6	and said, Sirs, what must I do to be saved?	16:30
1	that this Jesus, whom I preach unto you, is Christ.	17:3
1	ignorantly worship, him declare I unto you.	17:23
1	Your blood be upon your own heads; I am clean:	18:6
1	For I am with thee, and no man shall set on thee	18:10
4	for I have much people in this city.	18:10
1	look ye to it; for I will be no judge of such matters.	18:15
6	I must by all means keep this feast	18:21
6	After I have been there, I must also see Rome.	19:21
6	After I have been there, I must also see Rome.	19:21
4	which befell me by the lying in wait of the Jews:	20:19
1	behold, I go bound in the spirit unto Jerusalem,	20:22
4	not knowing the things that shall befall me there:	20:22
5	not knowing the things that shall befall me there:	20:22
4	Holy Spirit solemnly testifies to me (NASB)	20:23
6	saying that bonds and afflictions abide me,	20:23
2	neither count I my life dear unto myself,	20:24
2	so that I might finish my course with joy,	20:24
1	And now, behold, I know that ye all,	20:25
2	shall see my face no more.	20:25
1	that I am pure from the blood of all men.	20:26
1	For I know this, that after my departing	20:29
2	that after my departing shall grievous wolves enter	20:29
2	these hands have ministered unto my necessities,	20:34
3	my necessities, and to them that were with me.	20:34
2	What mean ye to weep and to break mine heart?	21:13
2	for I am ready not to be bound only,	21:13
4	unto the chief captain, May I speak unto thee?	21:37
1	Paul said, I am a man which am a Jew of Tarsus,	21:39
4	I beseech thee, suffer me to speak unto the people.	21:39
2	hear ye my defence which I make now unto you.	22:1
1	I am verily a man which am a Jew, born in Tarsus,	22:3
4	As also the high priest doth bear me witness,	22:5
4	And it came to pass, that, as I made my journey,	22:6
7	shone from heaven a great light round about me.	22:6
4	and heard a voice saying unto me, Saul, Saul,	22:7
6	Saul, Saul, why persecutest thou me?	22:7
1	And I answered, Who art thou, Lord?	22:8
6	And he said unto me, I am Jesus of Nazareth,	22:8
7	And he said unto me, I am Jesus of Nazareth,	22:8
1	I am Jesus of Nazareth, whom thou persecutest.	22:8
5	And they that were with me saw indeed the light,	22:9
4	they heard not the voice of him that spake to me.	22:9
6	And the Lord said unto me, Arise,	22:10
4	being led by the hand of them that were with me,	22:11
6	Came unto me, and stood, and said unto me,	22:13
7	Came unto me, and stood, and said unto me,	22:13
4	and said unto me, Brother Saul, receive thy sight.	22:13
4	when I was come again to Jerusalem,	22:17
2	while I prayed in the temple, I was in a trance;	22:17
6	while I prayed in the temple, I was in a trance;	22:17
4	And saw him saying unto me, Make haste,	22:18
3	they will not receive thy testimony concerning me.	22:18
1	they know that I imprisoned and beat	22:19
6	And he said unto me, Depart: for I will send thee	22:21
1	for I will send thee far hence unto the Gentiles.	22:21
4	Tell me, art thou a Roman? He said, Yea.	22:27
1	With a great sum obtained I this freedom.	22:28
1	And Paul said, But I was free born.	22:28

1	I have lived in all good conscience before God	Acts 23:1
6	for sittest thou to judge me after the law,	23:3
6	commandest me to be smitten contrary to the law?	23:3
3	Men and brethren, I am a Pharisee,	23:6
1	resurrection of the dead I am called in question.	23:6
3	for as thou hast testified of me in Jerusalem,	23:11
6	Paul the prisoner called me unto him,	23:18
4	What is that thou hast to tell me?	23:19
6	that thou hast showed these things to me.	23:22
7	that thou hast showed these things to me.	23:22
4	when it was told me how that the Jews laid wait	23:30
4	that there are yet but twelve days (NT)	24:11
6	neither found me in the temple disputing	24:12
6	prove the things whereof they now accuse me.	24:13
2	prove the things whereof they now accuse me.	24:13
2	I came to bring alms to my nation, and offerings.	24:17
6	Jews from Asia found me purified in the temple,	24:18
6	and object, if they had ought against me.	24:19
7	and object, if they had ought against me.	24:19
5	if they have found any evil doing in me,	24:20
2	while I stood before the council,	24:20
1	I am called in question by you this day.	24:21
3	and there be judged of these things before me?	25:9
6	at Caesar's ... where I ought to be judged:	25:10
2	if ... none of these things whereof these accuse me,	25:11
6	no man may deliver me unto them.	25:11
2	About whom, when I was at Jerusalem,	25:15
1	none accusation of such things as I supposed:	25:18
1	because I doubted of such manner of questions,	25:20
4	Jews have dealt with me, both at Jerusalem,	25:24
1	But when I found that he had committed nothing	25:25
4	it seemeth to me unreasonable to send a prisoner,	25:27
2	wherefore I beseech thee to hear me patiently.	26:3
2	My manner of life from my youth,	26:4
2	which was at the first among mine own nation	26:4
6	Which knew me from the beginning,	26:5
1	I verily thought with myself,	26:9
1	and many of the saints did I shut up in prison,	26:10
6	shining round about me	26:13
5	about me and them which journeyed with me.	26:13
4	I heard a voice speaking unto me,	26:14
6	Saul, Saul, why persecutest thou me?	26:14
1	And I said, Who art thou, Lord?	26:15
1	And he said, I am Jesus whom thou persecutest.	26:15
6	what thou have seen of me (NIV)	26:16
1	the Gentiles, to whom I am sending (NASB)	26:17
7	them which are sanctified by faith that is in me.	26:18
6	For these causes the Jews caught me in the temple,	26:21
6	Almost thou persuadest me to be a Christian.	26:28
2	but also all that hear me this day,	26:29
1	might become such as I am, except (NASB)	26:29
4	Sirs, ye should have hearkened unto me,	27:21
4	For there stood by me this night the angel of God,	27:23
1	the angel of God, whose I am, and whom I serve,	27:23
4	that it shall be even as it was told me.	27:25
1	I have committed nothing against the people,	28:17
6	they had examined me, would have let me go,	28:18
5	because there was no cause of death in me.	28:18
2	not that I had ought to accuse my nation of.	28:19
2	I thank my God through Jesus Christ for you all,	Rom 1:8
2	God is my witness, whom I serve with my spirit	1:9
2	I serve with my spirit in the gospel of his Son,	1:9
2	in my prayers making request, (NASB)	1:10
3	with you by the mutual faith both of you and me.	1:12
7	So, as much as in me is, I am ready to preach	1:15
2	judge ... by Jesus Christ according to my gospel.	2:16
2	Wherefore, my brethren, ye also are become dead	7:4
5	wrought in me all manner of concupiscence.	7:8
1	For I was alive without the law once:	7:9
1	the commandment came, sin revived, and I died.	7:9
4	the commandment, ... I found to be unto death.	7:10
6	deceived me, and by it slew me.	7:11
5	Was then that which is good made death unto me?	7:13
4	working death in me by that which is good;	7:13
1	but I am carnal, sold under sin.	7:14
1	Now then it is no more I that do it,	7:17
5	is no more I that do it, but sin that dwelleth in me.	7:17

223

ἐγώ 1466

5	For I know that in me that is, in my flesh,	Rom 7:18
2	For I know that in me that is, in my flesh,	7:18
4	for to will is present with me;	7:18
1	Now if I do that I would not,	7:20
1	no more I that do it, but sin that dwelleth in me	7:20
5	no more I that do it, but sin that dwelleth in me	7:20
5	when I would do good, evil is present with me	7:21
5	when I would do good, evil is present with me	7:21
2	But I see another law in my members,	7:23
2	warring against the law of my mind,	7:23
6	and bringing me into captivity to the law of sin	7:23
2	captivity to the law of sin which is in my members	7:23
1	O wretched man that I am!	7:24
6	who shall deliver me from the body of this death?	7:24
1	with the mind I myself serve the law of God;	7:25
6	hath made me free from the law of sin and death	8:2
4	I lie not, my conscience also bearing me witness	9:1
2	I lie not, my conscience also bearing me witness	9:1
4	That I have great heaviness and continual sorrow	9:2
2	great heaviness and continual sorrow in my heart	9:2
1	For I could wish that myself were accursed	9:3
2	myself were accursed from Christ for my brethren,	9:3
2	my brethren, my kinsmen according to the flesh:	9:3
2	that I might show my power in thee,	9:17
2	that my name might be declared throughout all	9:17
4	wilt say then unto me, Why doth he yet find fault?	9:19
6	Why hast thou made me thus?	9:20
2	call them my people, which were not my people;	9:25
2	I will call them my people, which were not	9:25
2	it was said unto them, Ye are not my people;	9:26
1	First Moses saith, I will provoke you to jealousy	10:19
7	I was found of them that sought me not;	10:20
7	made manifest unto them that asked not after me	10:20
2	All day long I have stretched forth my hands	10:21
1	For I also am an Israelite, of the seed of Abraham,	11:1
2	and I am left alone, and they seek my life	11:3
1	inasmuch as I am the apostle of the Gentiles,	11:13
2	the apostle of the Gentiles, I magnify mine office:	11:13
2	provoke to emulation them which are my flesh,	11:14
1	broken off, that I might be grafted in	11:19
3	For this is my covenant unto them,	11:27
4	For I say, through the grace given unto me,	12:3
5	for it is written, Vengeance is mine;	12:19
1	Vengeance is mine; I will repay, saith the Lord	12:19
1	For it is written, As I live, saith the Lord,	14:11
5	saith the Lord, every knee shall bow to me,	14:11
7	of them that reproached thee fell on me	15:3
2	I myself also am persuaded of you, my brethren,	15:14
1	I myself also am persuaded of you, my brethren,	15:14
4	because of the grace that is given to me of God,	15:15
6	That I should be the minister of Jesus Christ	15:16
3	those things which Christ hath not wrought by me,	15:18
6	so that from Jerusalem, (NT)	15:19
4	that ye strive together with me in your prayers	15:30
3	together with me in your prayers to God for me;	15:30
2	and that my service which I have for Jerusalem	15:31
3	hath been a succourer of many, and of myself also	16:2
2	Greet Priscilla and Aquila my helpers in Christ	16:3
2	Who have for my life laid down their own necks:	16:4
1	unto whom not only I give thanks,	16:4
2	Salute my wellbeloved Epaenetus,	16:5
2	Salute Andronicus and Junia, my kinsmen,	16:7
2	and Junia, my kinsmen, and my fellowprisoners,	16:7
3	who also were in Christ before me	16:7
2	Greet Amplias my beloved in the Lord	16:8
2	our helper in Christ, and Stachys my beloved	16:9
2	Salute Herodion my kinsman	16:11
3	Salute Rufus ... and his mother and mine	16:13
2	Timotheus my workfellow, and Lucius, and Jason,	16:21
2	and Jason, and Sosipater, my kinsmen, salute you	16:21
1	I Tertius, who wrote this epistle, salute you	16:22
2	Gaius mine host, and of the whole church,	16:23
2	is of power to stablish you according to my gospel,	16:25
2	I thank my God always on your behalf,	1 Co 1:4
4	For it hath been declared unto me of you,	1:11
2	hath been declared unto me of you, my brethren,	1:11
1	I am of Paul; and I of Apollos; and I of Cephas;	1:12
1	I am of Paul; and I of Apollos; and I of Cephas;	1 Co 1:12
1	I am of Paul; and I of Apollos; and I of Cephas;	1:12
1	and I of Apollos; and I of Cephas; and I of Christ	1:12
6	For Christ sent me not to baptize, but to preach	1:17
1	And I was with you in weakness, and in fear,	2:3
2	And my speech and my preaching was not	2:4
2	my preaching was not with enticing words	2:4
1	And I, brethren, could not speak unto you as	3:1
1	For while one saith, I am of Paul;	3:4
1	and another, I am of Apollos; are ye not carnal?	3:4
1	I have planted, Apollos watered;	3:6
4	to the grace of God which is given unto me,	3:10
5	But with me it is a very small thing,	4:3
6	but he that judgeth me is the Lord	4:4
2	but as my beloved sons I warn you	4:14
1	for in Christ Jesus I have begotten you	4:15
2	Wherefore I beseech you, be ye followers of me	4:16
2	I sent unto you Timotheus, who is my beloved son,	4:17
2	who shall bring you into remembrance of my ways	4:17
2	are puffed up, as though I would not come to you	4:18
1	I verily, as absent in body, but present in spirit,	5:3
3	when ye are gathered together, and my spirit,	5:4
4	have I to do to judge them also that are without?	5:12
4	All things are lawful unto me,	6:12
4	all things are lawful for me,	6:12
1	but I will not be brought under the power of any	6:12
4	concerning the things whereof ye wrote unto me:	7:1
1	And unto the married I command, yet not I,	7:10
1	But to the rest speak I, not the Lord:	7:12
1	shall have trouble in the flesh: but I spare you	7:28
2	Wherefore, if meat make my brother to offend,	8:13
2	lest I make my brother to offend	8:13
2	are not ye my work in the Lord?	9:1
2	you are the seal of my apostleship (NASB)	9:2
7	Mine answer to them that do examine me is this,	9:3
1	Or I only and Barnabas, have not we power	9:6
1	But I have used none of these things:	9:15
5	that it should be so done unto me:	9:15
4	for it were better for me to die,	9:15
2	than that any man should make my glorying void	9:15
1	I have nothing to glory of:	9:16
4	for necessity is laid upon me;	9:16
4	yea, woe is unto me, if I preach not the gospel!	9:16
4	What is my reward then?	9:18
4	What is my reward then?	9:18
2	that I abuse not my power in the gospel	9:18
1	I therefore so run, not as uncertainly;	9:26
2	But I keep under my body,	9:27
2	Wherefore, my dearly beloved, flee from idolatry	10:14
4	All things are lawful for me,	10:23
4	all things are lawful for me,	10:23
2	is my liberty judged of another man's conscience?	10:29
1	For if I by grace be a partaker,	10:30
1	evil spoken of for that for which I give thanks?	10:30
2	Be ye followers of me, even as I also am of Christ	11:1
2	brethren, that ye remember me in all things,	11:2
1	For I have received of the Lord	11:23
2	eat: this is my body, which is broken for you:	11:24
2	my brethren, when ye come together to eat,	11:33
2	And though I bestow all my goods to feed the poor,	13:3
2	and though I give my body to be burned,	13:3
5	and he that speaketh shall be a barbarian unto me	14:11
2	if I pray in an unknown tongue, my spirit prayeth,	14:14
2	spirit prayeth, but my understanding is unfruitful	14:14
2	I thank my God, I speak with tongues more than	14:18
2	rather speak five words with my understanding,	14:19
2	and yet for all that will they not hear me,	14:21
2	my brethren, desire earnestly (NASB)	14:39
1	For I am the least of the apostles,	15:9
7	and his grace which was bestowed upon me	15:10
1	yet not I, but the grace of God which was with me	15:10
5	yet not I, but the grace of God which was with me	15:10
1	Therefore whether it were I or they, so we preach,	15:11
4	what advantageth it me, if the dead rise not?	15:32
2	Therefore, my beloved brethren, be ye stedfast,	15:58
5	if it be meet that I go also, they shall go with me	16:4
6	may bring me on my journey whithersoever I go	16:6

ἐγώ 1466

4	For a great door and effectual is opened unto me,.. 1 Co	16:9
1	for he worketh the work of the Lord, as I also do.....	16:10
6	that he may come unto me:................................	16:11
2	My love be with you all in Christ Jesus. Amen.........	16:24
5	with me there should be yea yea, and nay nay?..... 2 Co	1:17
3	even by me and Silvanus and Timotheus,..............	1:19
1	Moreover I call God for a record upon my soul,.......	1:23
1	For if I make you sorry,...................................	2:2
6	who is he then that maketh me glad,...................	2:2
3	but the same which is made sorry by me?.............	2:2
6	sorrow from them of whom I ought to rejoice;.........	2:3
7	if any have caused grief, he hath not grieved me,.....	2:5
1	To whom ye forgive any thing, I forgive also:.........	2:10
1	for if I forgave any thing, to whom I forgave it,........	2:10
4	and a door was opened unto me of the Lord,...........	2:12
2	I had no rest in my spirit,................................	2:13
6	because I found not Titus my brother:.................	2:13
6	because I found not Titus my brother:.................	2:13
4	I will be their God, and they shall be my people.......	6:16
2	I will be their God, and they shall be my people.......	6:16
4	and ye shall be my sons and daughters,...............	6:18
4	Great is my boldness of speech toward you,............	7:4
4	great is my glorying of you:...............................	7:4
3	your mourning, your fervent mind toward me;.........	7:7
6	so that I rejoiced the more................................	7:7
4	it is superfluous for me to write to you:................	9:1
5	Lest haply if they of Macedonia come with me,........	9:4
1	Now I Paul myself beseech you by the meekness.....	10:1
2	ye could bear with me a little in my folly:..............	11:1
2	a little in my folly: and indeed bear with me...........	11:1
2	for that which was lacking to me.......................	11:9
5	As the truth of Christ is in me,.........................	11:10
7	no man shall stop me of this boasting..................	11:10
6	I say again, Let no man think me a fool;...............	11:16
6	if otherwise, yet as a fool receive me,..................	11:16
1	ministers of Christ? I speak as a fool I am more;......	11:23
2	that which cometh upon me daily,......................	11:28
4	that which cometh upon me daily,......................	11:28
1	who is offended, and I burn not?.......................	11:29
2	glory of the things which concern mine infirmities.....	11:30
6	the king kept the city ... desirous to apprehend me:....	11:32
4	It is not expedient for me doubtless to glory..........	12:1
2	of myself I will not glory, but in mine infirmities.......	12:5
7	think of me above that which he seeth me to be,......	12:6
6	think of me above that which he seeth me to be,......	12:6
3	which he seeth me to be, or that he heareth of me....	12:6
4	there was given to me a thorn in the flesh,............	12:7
6	the messenger of Satan to buffet me,..................	12:7
3	besought ... thrice, that it might depart from me.....	12:8
4	he said unto me, My grace is sufficient for thee:......	12:9
2	he said unto me, My grace is sufficient for thee:......	12:9
5	for my strength is made perfect in weakness.........	12:9
2	therefore will I rather glory in my infirmities,.........	12:9
7	that the power of Christ may rest upon me...........	12:9
6	become a fool in glorying; ye have compelled me:.....	12:11
1	for I ought to have been commended of you:...........	12:11
1	except it be that I myself was not burdensome........	12:13
4	not burdensome to you? forgive me this wrong.........	12:13
1	And I will very gladly spend and be spent for you;....	12:15
1	But be it so, I did not burden you:.....................	12:16
6	And lest, when I come again,............................	12:21
2	And lest, when I come again,............................	12:21
6	my God may humiliate me before you (NASB)........	12:21
2	my God will humble me among you,...................	12:21
5	Since ye seek a proof of Christ speaking in me,........	13:3
4	which the Lord hath given me to edification,..........	13:10
5	And all the brethren which are with me,............ Gal	1:2
3	gospel which was preached of me is not after man......	1:11
1	For I neither received it of man,........................	1:12
2	above many my equals in mine own nation,...........	1:14
2	exceedingly zealous of the traditions of my fathers.....	1:14
6	God, who separated me from my mother's womb,......	1:15
2	God, who separated me from my mother's womb,......	1:15
5	To reveal his Son in me,..................................	1:16
3	to them which were apostles before me;...............	1:17
4	And they glorified God in me.............................	1:24
5	neither Titus, who was with me, being a Greek,........	2:3
4	whatsoever they were, it maketh no matter to me:.... Gal	2:6
5	be somewhat in conference added nothing to me:.......	2:6
5	the same was mighty in me toward the Gentiles:........	2:8
4	perceived the grace that was given unto me,..........	2:9
5	to me and Barnabas the right hands of fellowship;......	2:9
1	For I through the law am dead to the law,.............	2:19
1	yet not I, but Christ liveth in me:......................	2:20
1	yet not I, but Christ liveth in me:......................	2:20
6	live by the faith of the Son of God, who loved me,.....	2:20
3	who loved me, and gave himself for me................	2:20
1	Brethren, I beseech you, be as I am;...................	4:12
6	for I am as ye are: ye have not injured me at all........	4:12
2	And my temptation which was in my flesh.............	4:14
2	temptation which was in my flesh ye despised not,.....	4:14
6	nor rejected; but received me as an angel of God,......	4:14
4	your own eyes, and have given them to me.............	4:15
6	and not only when I am present with you...............	4:18
2	My little children, of whom I travail in birth...........	4:19
2	to change my voice; for I stand in doubt of you........	4:20
4	Tell me, ye that desire to be under the law,............	4:21
1	I Paul say unto you, that if ye be circumcised,.........	5:2
1	I have confidence in you through the Lord,............	5:10
1	And I, brethren, if I yet preach circumcision,...........	5:11
5	But God forbid that I should glory,.....................	6:14
5	cross ... by whom the world is crucified unto me,......	6:14
4	From henceforth let no man trouble me:...............	6:17
1	for I bear in my body the marks of the Lord Jesus.....	6:17
2	for I bear in my body the marks of the Lord Jesus.....	6:17
2	making mention of you in my prayers;............. Eph	1:16
1	For this cause I Paul, the prisoner of Jesus Christ......	3:1
4	of the grace of God which is given me to you-ward:....	3:2
4	How that by revelation he made known unto me.......	3:3
2	understand my knowledge in the mystery of Christ.....	3:4
4	to the gift of the grace of God given unto me.........	3:7
5	Unto me, who am less than the least of all saints,......	3:8
2	I desire that ye faint not at my tribulations for you,.....	3:13
2	For this cause I bow my knees unto the Father........	3:14
1	I therefore, the prisoner of the Lord,...................	4:1
1	but I speak concerning Christ and the church.........	5:32
2	Finally, my brethren, be strong in the Lord,...........	6:10
3	And for me, that utterance may be given unto me,.....	6:19
4	And for me, that utterance may be given unto me,.....	6:19
2	that I may open my mouth boldly,.....................	6:19
6	I may speak boldly, as I ought to speak...............	6:20
7	But that ye also may know my affairs,.................	6:21
2	I thank my God upon every remembrance of you,.... Phlp	1:3
2	Always in every prayer of mine for you all............	1:4
5	Even as it is meet for me to think this of you all,......	1:7
6	to think this ... because I have you in my heart;......	1:7
2	in my heart; inasmuch as both in my bonds,...........	1:7
2	ye all are partakers of my grace.........................	1:7
2	For God is my record, how greatly I long after you.....	1:8
7	that the things which happened unto me.............	1:12
2	my bonds in Christ are manifest in all the palace,......	1:13
2	waxing confident by my bonds,.........................	1:14
2	supposing to add affliction to my bonds:...............	1:16
4	For I know that this shall turn to my salvation.......	1:19
2	According to my earnest expectation and my hope,.....	1:20
2	so now also Christ shall be magnified in my body,.....	1:20
5	For to me to live is Christ, and to die is gain...........	1:21
4	if I live in the flesh, this is the fruit of my labour:.....	1:22
5	in Jesus Christ for me by my coming to you again.....	1:26
5	Having the same conflict which ye saw in me,.........	1:30
5	the same conflict ... and now hear to be in me........	1:30
2	Fulfil ye my joy, that ye be likeminded,...............	2:2
2	Wherefore, my beloved, as ye have always obeyed,.....	2:12
2	ye have always obeyed, not as in my presence only,....	2:12
2	but now much more in my absence,...................	2:12
5	that I may rejoice in the day of Christ,.................	2:16
4	the same cause also do ye joy, and rejoice with me.....	2:18
5	he hath served with me in the gospel..................	2:22
7	so soon as I shall see how it will go with me...........	2:23
2	to send to you Epaphroditus, my brother,.............	2:25
2	and he that ministered to my wants...................	2:25
7	God had mercy on him; ... but on me also,............	2:27
6	to supply your lack of service toward me...............	2:30
2	Finally, my brethren, rejoice in the Lord................	3:1

ἐγώ 1466

#	Text	Ref
5	to me indeed is not grievous, but for you it is safe...	Phlp 3:1
1	Though I might also have confidence in the flesh.......	3:4
1	If any ... might trust in the flesh, I more:.............	3:4
4	But what things were gain to me,....................	3:7
2	the knowledge of Christ Jesus my Lord:...............	3:8
1	Brethren, I count not myself to have apprehended:.....	3:13
2	Brethren, be followers together of me,...............	3:17
2	my brethren, dearly beloved and longed for,..........	4:1
2	dearly beloved and longed for, my joy and crown,.....	4:1
4	help those women which laboured with me............	4:3
2	Clement also, and with other my fellowlabourers,.....	4:3
5	Those things, ... and heard, and seen in me, do:.....	4:9
3	your care of me hath flourished again;................	4:10
1	for I have learned, in whatsoever state I am,........	4:11
6	all things through Christ which strengtheneth me.......	4:13
2	that ye did communicate with my affliction...........	4:14
4	no church communicated with me ... but ye only.......	4:15
4	ye sent once and again unto my necessity............	4:16
2	But my God shall supply all your need................	4:19
5	The brethren which are with me greet you............	4:24
1	whereof I Paul am made a minister;.................. Col	1:23
2	Who now rejoice in my sufferings for you,...........	1:24
2	afflictions of Christ in my flesh for his body's sake,.....	1:24
1	Whereof I am made a minister,......................	1:25
4	is given to me for you, to fulfil the word of God;.......	1:25
5	his working, which worketh in me mightily............	1:29
2	for as many as have not seen my face in the flesh;......	2:1
6	That I may make it manifest, as I ought to speak.....	4:4
7	All my state shall Tychicus declare unto you,.........	4:7
2	Aristarchus my fellowprisoner saluteth you,...........	4:10
4	which have been a comfort unto me..................	4:11
2	Remember my bonds. Grace be with you. Amen.......	4:18
1	come unto you, even I Paul, once and again;..... 1 Th	2:18
1	gospel ... which was committed to my trust........ 1 Tm	1:11
6	hath enabled me, for that he counted me faithful,.....	1:12
6	hath enabled me, for that he counted me faithful,.....	1:12
1	into the world to save sinners; of whom I am chief.....	1:15
5	that in me first Jesus Christ might show forth.........	1:16
1	Whereunto I am ordained a preacher,................	2:7
2	remembrance of thee in my prayers night and day;... 2 Tm	1:3
2	which is in thee by the putting on of my hands........	1:6
7	the testimony of our Lord, nor of me his prisoner:.....	1:8
1	Whereunto I am appointed a preacher,...............	1:11
2	which I have committed unto him against that day.....	1:12
3	sound words, which thou hast heard of me,..........	1:13
6	they which are in Asia be turned away from me;......	1:15
6	Onesiphorus; for he oft refreshed me,...............	1:16
2	refreshed me, and was not ashamed of my chain:.....	1:16
4	he sought me out very diligently, and found me.......	1:17
2	Thou therefore, my son, be strong in the grace.......	2:1
3	And the things that thou hast heard of me...........	2:2
2	was raised from the dead according to my gospel:.....	2:8
2	But thou hast fully known my doctrine,................	3:10
4	afflictions, which came unto me at Antioch...........	3:11
6	but out of them all the Lord delivered me............	3:11
1	I charge thee therefore before God,.................	4:1
1	For I am now ready to be offered,..................	4:6
2	and the time of my departure has come (NASB)......	4:6
4	there is laid up for me a crown of righteousness,.....	4:8
4	the righteous judge, shall give me at that day:.......	4:8
5	shall give me at that day: and not to me only,.......	4:8
6	Do thy diligence to come shortly unto me:...........	4:9
6	For Demas hath forsaken me,......................	4:10
3	Only Luke is with me..............................	4:11
4	Mark, ... for he is profitable to me for the ministry.....	4:11
4	Alexander the coppersmith did me much evil:........	4:14
2	At my first answer no man stood with me,...........	4:16
4	At my first answer no man stood with me,...........	4:16
6	no man stood with me, but all men forsook me:......	4:16
4	the Lord stood with me, and strengthened me;.......	4:17
6	the Lord stood with me, and strengthened me;.......	4:17
3	that by me the preaching might be fully known,.....	4:17
6	the Lord shall deliver me from every evil work,......	4:18
1	through preaching, which is committed unto me ...... Tit	1:3
1	ordain elders ... as I had appointed thee:............	1:5
6	be diligent to come unto me to Nicopolis:...........	3:12
3	All that are with me salute thee.....................	3:15
2	I thank my God, making mention of thee always....	Phlm 1:4
2	making mention of thee always in my prayers,.......	1:4
3	I beseech thee for my son Onesimus,................	1:10
2	son Onesimus, whom I have begotten in my bonds:.....	1:10
5	but now profitable to thee and to me:...............	1:11
1	Whom I would have retained with me,...............	1:13
4	that in thy stead he might have ministered unto me.....	1:13
5	a brother beloved, specially to me,.................	1:16
7	If thou count me therefore a partner,................	1:17
6	If thou count me therefore a partner,................	1:17
7	If thou count me ... partner, receive him as myself.....	1:17
5	or oweth thee ought, put that on mine account;......	1:18
1	I Paul have written it with mine own hand,..........	1:19
1	written it with mine own hand, I will repay it:.......	1:19
4	thou owest unto me even thine own self besides......	1:19
1	Yea, brother, let me have joy of thee in the Lord:.....	1:20
2	Yea, brother, ... refresh my bowels in the Lord........	1:20
4	But withal prepare me also a lodging:................	1:22
2	Epaphras, my fellowprisoner in Christ Jesus;........	1:23
2	Aristarchus, Demas, Lucas, my fellowlabourers,.....	1:24
2	Thou art my Son, this day have I begotten thee?.... Heb	1:5
1	Thou art my Son, this day have I begotten thee?.....	1:5
1	And again, I will be to him a Father,...............	1:5
4	be to him a Father, and he shall be to me a Son?.....	1:5
2	Sit on my right hand,.............................	1:13
2	I will declare thy name unto my brethren,...........	2:12
1	And again, I will put my trust in him................	2:13
1	I and the children which God hath given me.........	2:13
4	I and the children which God hath given me.........	2:13
6	When your fathers tempted me, proved me,.........	3:9
6	proved me, and saw my works forty years..........	3:9
2	proved me, and saw my works forty years..........	3:9
2	and they have not known my ways.................	3:10
2	So I sware in my wrath, They shall not enter.......	3:11
2	They shall not enter into my rest...................	3:11
2	as he said, As I have sworn in my wrath,...........	4:3
2	if they shall enter into my rest:....................	4:3
2	in this place again, If they shall enter into my rest......	4:5
2	Thou art my Son, to day have I begotten thee........	5:5
1	Thou art my Son, to day have I begotten thee.......	5:5
2	by the hand to lead them out of the land of Egypt;.....	8:9
2	because they continued not in my covenant,.........	8:9
2	For this is the covenant that I will make............	8:10
2	I will put my laws into their mind,.................	8:10
4	and they shall be to me a people:..................	8:10
6	saying, Know the Lord: for all shall know me,.....	8:11
4	but a body hast thou prepared me:.................	10:5
3	in the volume of the book it is written of me,.......	10:7
2	I will put my laws into their hearts,................	10:16
5	Vengeance belongeth unto me, I will recompense,.....	10:30
1	Vengeance belongeth unto me, I will recompense,.....	10:30
2	For ye had compassion of me in my bonds,.........	10:34
2	But My righteous one shall live by faith (NASB).....	10:38
2	my soul shall have no pleasure in him..............	10:38
6	for the time would fail me to tell of Gedeon,.......	11:32
2	My son, despise not thou the chastening............	12:5
2	Yet once more I shake not the earth only,..........	12:26
5	So that we may boldly say, The Lord is my helper,.....	13:6
4	and I will not fear what man shall do unto me.......	13:6
2	My brethren, count it all joy when ye..............	Jas 1:2
2	Do not err, my beloved brethren...................	1:16
2	my beloved brethren, let ... man be swift to hear,.....	1:19
2	My brethren, have not the faith of our Lord.........	2:1
2	Stand thou there, or sit here under my footstool:.....	2:3
2	Hearken, my beloved brethren,....................	2:5
2	What doth it profit, my brethren,...................	2:14
4	show me thy faith without thy works,...............	2:18
2	and I will show thee my faith by my works..........	2:18
2	and I will show thee my faith by my works..........	2:18
2	My brethren, be not many masters,................	3:1
2	My brethren, these things ought not so to be........	3:10
2	Can the fig tree, my brethren, bear olive berries?.....	3:12
2	Take, my brethren, the prophets, who have spoken.....	5:10
2	But above all things, my brethren, swear not,......	5:12
2	My brethren, if any among you strays (NASB)......	5:19
1	Because it is written, Be ye holy; for I am holy......	1 Pt 1:16
2	saluteth you; and so doth Marcus my son...........	5:13

ἐγώ 1466

2 that shortly I must put off this **my** tabernacle,	2 Pt	1:14
4 even as our Lord Jesus Christ hath showed **me**.		1:14
2 from the excellent glory, This is **my** beloved Son,		1:17
1 **my** beloved Son, in whom I am well pleased.		1:17
2 **My** little children, these things write I unto you,	1 Jn	2:1
2 Marvel not, **my** brethren, if the world hate you.		3:13
2 **My** little children, let us not love in word,		3:18
1 and her children, whom I love in the truth;	2 Jn	1:1
1 whom I love in the truth; and not I only,		1:1
1 the wellbeloved Gaius, whom I love in the truth.	3 Jn	1:1
1 I am Alpha and Omega,	Rev	1:8
1 I John, who also am your brother,		1:9
2 heard behind **me** a great voice, as of a trumpet,		1:10
1 I am Alpha and Omega, the first and the last:		1:11
3 And I turned to see the voice that spake with **me**.		1:12
7 he laid his right hand upon **me**, saying unto **me**,		1:17
4 he laid his right hand upon **me**, saying **unto me**,		1:17
1 Fear not; I am the first and the last:		1:17
2 seven stars which thou sawest in **my** right hand,		1:20
2 and for **my** name's sake hast laboured,		2:3
2 and thou holdest fast **my** name,		2:13
2 and hast not denied **my** faith,		2:13
2 days wherein Antipas was **my** faithful martyr,		2:13
2 **My** faithful one, who was killed (NASB)		2:13
2 fight against them with the sword of **my** mouth.		2:16
1 Behold, I will cast her into a bed,		2:22
1 that I am he which searcheth the reins and hearts:		2:23
2 overcometh, and keepeth **my** works unto the end,		2:26
2 even as I received of **my** Father.		2:27
2 completed in the sight of **My** God (NASB)		3:2
3 shall walk with **me** in white: for they are worthy.		3:4
2 but I will confess his name before **my** Father,		3:5
2 hast kept **my** word, and hast not denied **my** name.		3:8
2 hast kept **my** word, and hast not denied **my** name.		3:8
1 and to know that I have loved thee.		3:9
2 Because thou hast kept the word of **my** patience,		3:10
2 will I make a pillar in the temple of **my** God,		3:12
2 and I will write upon him the name of **my** God,		3:12
2 and the name of the city of **my** God,		3:12
2 which cometh down out of heaven from **my** God:		3:12
2 and I will write upon him **my** new name.		3:12
2 art lukewarm, ... I will spue thee out of **my** mouth.		3:16
3 I counsel thee to buy of **me** gold tried in the fire,		3:18
1 As many as I love, I rebuke and chasten:		3:19
2 if any man hear **my** voice, and open the door,		3:20
3 and will sup with him, and he with **me**.		3:20
3 will I grant to sit with **me** in **my** throne,		3:21
2 will I grant to sit with **me** in **my** throne,		3:21
2 and am set down with **my** Father in his throne.		3:21
3 was as it were of a trumpet talking with **me**;		4:1
1 I wept much, because no man was found worthy		5:4
4 And one of the elders saith **unto me**, Weep not:		5:5
4 And one of the elders answered, saying **unto me**,		7:13
2 And I said to him, "My lord, you know." (NASB)		7:14
4 And he said **to me**, These are they which came out		7:14
4 and I heard a voice from heaven saying **unto me**,		10:4
3 The voice ... from heaven spake unto **me** again,		10:8
4 and said unto him, Give **me** the little book.		10:9
4 And he said **unto me**, Take it, and eat it up;		10:9
2 and it was in **my** mouth sweet as honey:		10:10
2 and as soon as I had eaten it, **my** belly was bitter.		10:10
4 And he said **unto me**, Thou must prophesy again		10:11
4 And there was given **me** a reed like unto a rod:		11:1
2 And I will give power unto **my** two witnesses,		11:3
4 And I heard a voice from heaven saying **unto me**,		14:13
3 and talked with **me**, saying **unto me**, Come hither;		17:1
4 and talked with **me**, saying **unto me**, Come hither;		17:1
6 carried **me** away in the spirit into the wilderness:		17:3
4 angel said **unto me**, Wherefore didst thou marvel?		17:7
1 I will tell thee the mystery of the woman,		17:7
4 he saith **unto me**, The waters which thou sawest,		17:15
2 voice from heaven, ... Come out of her, **my** people,		18:4
4 And he saith **unto me**, Write,		19:9
4 saith **unto me**, These are the true sayings of God.		19:9
4 And he said **unto me**, See thou do it not:		19:10
1 And I John saw the holy city, new Jerusalem,		21:2
4 And he said **unto me**, Write:		21:5
4 said **unto me**, It is done. I am Alpha and Omega,	Rev	21:6
1 said **unto me**, It is done. I am Alpha and Omega,		21:6
1 I will give unto him that is athirst of the fountain		21:6
4 and I will be his God, and he shall be **my** son.		21:7
6 And there came unto **me** one of the seven angels		21:9
3 and talked with **me**, saying, Come hither,		21:9
6 And he carried **me** away in the spirit		21:10
4 and showed **me** that great city, the holy Jerusalem,		21:10
3 And he that talked with **me** had a golden reed:		21:15
4 And he showed **me** a pure river of water of life,		22:1
4 And he said **unto me**, These sayings are faithful		22:6
1 And I John saw these things, and heard them.		22:8
4 the feet of the angel which showed **me** these things.		22:8
4 Then saith he **unto me**, See thou do it not:		22:9
4 And he saith **unto me**, Seal not the sayings		22:10
2 behold, I come quickly; and **my** reward is with **me**,		22:12
3 behold, I come quickly; and **my** reward is with **me**,		22:12
1 I am Alpha and Omega,		22:13
1 I Jesus have sent mine angel to testify unto you		22:16
2 I Jesus have sent **mine** angel to testify unto you		22:16
1 I am the root and the offspring of David,		22:16
1 I testify to everyone who hears (NASB)		22:18

Egō is actually the first person personal pronoun—"I." Naturally, according to its case it changes meaning: (*e*)*mou*, "of, from me"; (*e*)*moi*, "to, for, with, by, in, at me"; and (*e*)*me*, "me" (and the respective plurals: *hēmeis* [2231], *hēmōn*, *hēmin*, *hēmas*). When used with a verb *egō* emphasizes the personal aspect of the action of the subject. *Egō* is part of the word *kagō* (2476), which is actually a combination of *kai* (2504) and *egō*, "I also." There are many theological questions involving the use of "I" or "we" throughout the New Testament. Is Paul's "I" in Romans chapter 7 an autobiographical "I" or is it merely a convenient literary device to strengthen his argument? What do the "We" sections of Acts reveal about its author? Other such questions merit attention, but here the focus will primarily rest upon the examination of the theological significance of "I," especially in the "I am" sayings of Jesus.

Classical Greek

One of the most unique and significant aspects of Jesus' ministry is His self-identification as the *egō eimi* ("I AM," John 4:26; 6:20; 8:12,18,24,28,58; 13:19). It is, of course, not unusual in ancient literature, whether Greek, Egyptian, or Hebrew, for a divine figure to assert "I am such and such" whether "I am the truth," or "I am the grace of the aeon," etc. (cf. Harner, *Facet Books Biblical Series*, 26:26,27). However, there is no parallel in ancient nonbiblical literature for a divine figure to assert *egō eimi* without any predicate (Harner, ibid., 26:26-30).

Although some scholars, e.g., G.P. Wetter and Adolf Deissman, have argued that Jesus utilized already existing religious ideas for His claim to be the *egō eimi* (implying that there was

227

nothing special in Jesus' claims to be divine), a thorough examination of Hellenistic, Gnostic, and Christian Gnostic writings illustrates that no pagan religious figure ever claimed to be the *egō eimi* (see Stauffer, "egō," *Kittel*, 2:343ff.). The only background for this expression is the Old Testament, particularly Exodus 3:14 and Isaiah chapters 40 to 55 where God (Yahweh) states, "I AM." The only conclusion to be drawn from this is that Jesus' claim to be God, in terms of the expression *egō eimi*, is unique.

Septuagint Usage and Intertestamental Period

Jesus does not draw as much from the deposits of antiquity as He does from His own "roots"—the Old Testament and Judaism. Clearly the formula *egō eimi* is much developed as a special designation for God in the Pentateuch (Exodus 3:14), and in the entire Septuagint for that matter. The exclusivity of God over any other gods is foundational to Old Testament theology. This idea of God as unparalleled lies at the heart of Yahweh (Hebrew, *YHWH*). "I Am That I Am" Yahweh declares to Moses (Exodus 3:14, *egō eimi* in the Septuagint). "I AM" is the very name of God.

In Judaism that was contemporary with Jesus the "I am" style became even more developed, especially in apocalyptic literature. For example, in the Apocalypse of Abraham (ca. A.D. 100) God declares: "... I am before-the-World and Mighty ... I am the protector for you and I am your helper ..." (Apocalypse of Abraham 9:3,4).

In addition, *egō* occurs throughout antiquity in all kinds of literature. It functions both to add emphasis (Daniel [Theodotion] 7:15,28; 8:1,15) and as the subject of the verb (e.g., Judges 5:3; 6:18; Ruth 4:4; Isaiah 28:28).

New Testament Usage

The New Testament's use of the "I style" is generally applied to Christ. But God is also acknowledged with this style in certain instances. Paul cited Isaiah 45:23 in Romans 14:11 and added *egō* to the Old Testament text (he adds *zō egō*). Here the *egō* almost certainly refers to God rather than Christ (so Cranfield, *The International Critical Commentary, Romans*, 2:710). It seems barely possible that Paul may have picked up the Old Testament text from Isaiah 45:22, *egō eimi ho theos kai ouk estin allos*, "I am God and there is not any other." Thus Paul was incorporating a Septuagintal usage of *egō eimi* to point to God. (See also Stauffer, "egō," *Kittel*, 2:345.) For the most part, though, the New Testament reserves the "I am" proclamation for Jesus.

All of the Gospel writers seem to be aware of the "I am" significance. The Synoptic writers did not develop this motif to the extent that John did, but they were certainly aware of it. Matthew especially understood the "I am" statement in the classic Old Testament declaration of God's identity, Exodus 3:6 (cf. Matthew 22:32). Mark and Luke, however, were hesitant to make the point (cf. Mark 12:26: *egō ho theos Abraam* ... ; Luke, *kurion ton theou Abraam* ... ; Matthew, *egō eimi ho theos Abraam*). During the passion of Jesus His true identity is couched in "I am" language (Mark 14:62; Luke 22:70; cf. Luke 24:39). (For other instances see Mark 6:50 [with parallels]; 13:6.)

But John developed the "I am" motif more fully than any of the other Gospel writers. Most obvious are his famous metaphors: "I am the bread of life" (6:35, cf. 6:41,48,51); "I am the light of the world" (8:12, cf. 12:46); "I am the door" (10:9, cf. 10:7); "I am the good shepherd" (10:11,14); "I am the resurrection, and the life" (11:25); "I am the way, the truth, and the life" (14:6); "I am the true vine" (15:1, cf. 15:5).

Not only does the *egō eimi* formula dominate John, it coincides dramatically with the book's theme that the Word became flesh (1:14). The eternal Christ confronts His listeners: "Before Abraham was, I am (*egō eimi*)" (John 8:58).

Outside of the Gospels—which by their very nature are concerned with the ministry of Jesus—the *egō eimi* motif plays only a minor role. But the writer of the Revelation apparently picked up on the motif. The Lord declares: "I am the Alpha and the Omega, ... who is, and who was, and who is to come, the Almighty" (Revelation 1:8, NIV; cf. 21:6; 22:13). Likewise, "I am the first and the last" (Revelation 1:17) speaks of God's eternality. "I am" searches the hearts and minds of humanity (Revelation 2:23). The interchange of speakers between God (e.g., 1:8) and Christ (e.g., 21:6) proclaim the deity of Christ in no uncertain terms.

STRONG 1473, BAUER 217, MOULTON-MILLIGAN 180, KITTEL 2:343-62, LIDDELL-SCOTT 477, COLIN BROWN 2:278-83.

1467. ἐδαφίζω edaphizō verb
Dash to the ground, raze.
COGNATE:
ἔδαφος edaphos (1468)
SYNONYM:
κατασκάπτω kataskaptō (2649)

יָשַׁב yāshav (3553), Sit down (Is 3:26).
נָטַשׁ nāṭash (5389), Leave to oneself, abandon (Ez 31:12).
נָפַץ nāphats (5492), Piel: smash, break up (Ps 137:9 [136:9]).
רָטַשׁ rāṭash (7660), Smash; pual: be smashed (Hos 10:14, Na 3:10).

1. ἐδαφιοῦσιν edaphiousin 3pl indic fut act
1 And shall lay thee even with the ground,..........Luke 19:44

Classical Greek
Occurring from around the Fourth Century B.C. onward, this verb denotes "to beat level and firm" like the floor. It can refer also to the action of "providing a floor," or in a harsh sense "to dash to the ground" (cf. the noun *edaphos* [1468], "bottom, ground") (see also *Liddell-Scott*).

Septuagint Usage
In the Septuagint both of the latter meanings are evident. It occurs in the most peculiar statement of the Psalmist that "happy is he who . . . seizes your infants and 'dashes' them against the rocks" (NIV, Psalm 137:9 [LXX 136:9], Hebrew *nāphats*, "smash"; cf. Hosea 10:14; Nahum 3:10). Obviously this is an image of destruction. Isaiah 3:26 continues the imagery of defeat of the city of Zion (cf. the imagery in Ezekiel 31:12).

New Testament Usage
The imagery of the Old Testament continues in the single New Testament use. Jesus lamented over Jerusalem's failure to recognize the visitation of God in His ministry. Because of this refusal Jesus declared they would be judged harshly. Jerusalem will be "razed" to the ground and the children within her will be "dashed" to pieces (Luke 19:44).

STRONG 1474, BAUER 217, MOULTON-MILLIGAN 180, LIDDELL-SCOTT 477.

1468. ἔδαφος edaphos noun
Ground.
COGNATE:
ἐδαφίζω edaphizō (1467)
SYNONYM:
γῆ gē (1087)

אֶרֶץ 'erets (800), Ground, piece of land (Ez 41:20).
מוֹסָד môṣādh (4279), Foundation (Jer 31:37 [38:37]).
עָפָר 'āphār (6312), Dust, dry dirt (Ps 119:25 [118:25], Is 29:4).
קַרְקַע qarqaʿ (7463), Floor (Nm 5:17, 1 Kgs 6:15,16).

1. ἔδαφος edaphos nom/acc sing neu
1 And I fell unto the ground,......................Acts 22:7

Classical Greek
"Bottom, foundation, base," and thus "ground" are among the classical definitions of *edaphos*. It denotes everything from "pavement" to the "ground, soil." It can even describe the "text" of a manuscript (in contrast to the margin area, see *Liddell-Scott*).

Septuagint Usage
In 15 instances in the Septuagint *edaphos* translates 5 different Hebrew words. It is used of the earthen "floor" in the tabernacle (Numbers 5:17; cf. Sirach 33:10) or the temple floor which was covered with gold (1 Kings [LXX 3 Kings] 6:15,16,30; cf. 7:7) (Hebrew *qarqaʿ*). God alone "walks on the 'bottom' of the ocean" (Job 9:8, Septuagint). The Psalmist used it figuratively of his present inner condition (his "soul is joined with the ground," Psalm 44:25 [LXX 43:25]), but certainly this was brought on by external forces (cf. verses 22,23).

New Testament Usage
The single New Testament use concerns the "ground" upon which Saul fell during his encounter with the risen Lord on the road to Damascus (Acts 22:7).

STRONG 1475, BAUER 217, MOULTON-MILLIGAN 180, LIDDELL-SCOTT 477.

1469. ἑδραῖος hedraios adj
Firm, steadfast.
COGNATE:
ἑδραίωμα hedraiōma (1470)
SYNONYM:
στερεός stereos (4582)

1. ἑδραῖος hedraios nom sing masc
2. ἑδραῖοι hedraioi nom pl masc

1 Nevertheless he that standeth stedfast in his heart,...1 Co 7:37
2 Therefore, my beloved brethren, be ye stedfast,........ 15:58
2 If ye continue in the faith grounded and settled,......Col 1:23

Classical Greek and Septuagint Usage
This adjective denotes something or someone "sitting, stationary." Classical meanings also include "steady, steadfast, firm." *Hedraios*

occurs only in Symmachus' version of the Old Testament (e.g., Psalms 33:14 [LXX 32:14]; 57:7 [56:7]; 89:37 [LXX 88:37]).

New Testament Usage

The three appearances of *hedraios* in the New Testament are attributed to the apostle Paul. Paul used it of a "firm" conviction (1 Corinthians 7:37). He reminded believers to remain "firm, steadfast" in the Faith on two occasions (1 Corinthians 15:58; Colossians 1:23). Papyrus Bodmer (p72) reads *hedraios* instead of *stereos* (4582), "steadfast, firm," at 1 Peter 5:9. The usage here closely resembles Paul's.

Strong 1476, Bauer 217, Moulton-Milligan 180, Kittel 2:362-64, Liddell-Scott 478, Colin Brown 1:660-63.

1470. ἑδραίωμα hedraiōma noun
Foundation.
Cognate:
  ἑδραῖος hedraios (1469)

1. ἑδραίωμα hedraiōma nom/acc sing neu

1 the pillar and **ground** of the truth.................. 1 Tm 3:15

This unusual word occurs nowhere outside of Christian literature. It is almost certainly related to *hedraios* (1469), an adjective meaning "firm, steadfast," which does occur in classical writings as well as our literature.

As to its meaning in the New Testament at 1 Timothy 3:15, *Moulton-Milligan* notes that Hort—probably drawing upon the "almost universal Latin rendering *firmamentum*"—translates *hedraiōma* as "stay or bulwark." That, however, seems to miss the imagery Paul was utilizing in 1 Timothy 3:15.

Paul was addressing the issue of proper lifestyle for those of God's house (*oikos* [3486])—his assembly (church, *ekklēsia* [1564])—itself a "pillar" (*stulos* [4620]), and *hedraiōma*, "foundation," of the truth. The building imagery, found elsewhere in Paul in reference to the Church (e.g., 1 Corinthians 3:16,17; 2 Corinthians 6:16; Ephesians 2:21), was certainly used to influence the interpretation of *hedraiōma* as a building term.

Thus, the Church is the pillar and *foundation* of the truth. As such its members must conduct themselves accordingly. This is especially true for any of those who are assuming posts of leadership (cf. 1 Timothy 3:1-13, a discussion of particular *behavioral* qualities of leaders). Proper life-style and conduct are the marks of the truth. These contrast the behavior of the false teachers who threaten the Church in their assault on the truth (cf. 1 Timothy 1:3-11; 4:1-3; 6:3ff.).

Strong 1477, Bauer 218, Moulton-Milligan 180-81, Kittel 2:362-64, Liddell-Scott 478, Colin Brown 1:660-62.

1471. Ἐζεκίας Hezekias name
Hezekiah.

1. Ἐζεκίας Hezekias nom masc
2. Ἐζεκίαν Hezekian acc masc

2 and Achaz begat **Ezekias**;........................ Matt 1:9
1 And **Ezekias** begat Manasses;........................ 1:10

The son of Ahaz in the genealogy of Jesus (Matthew 1:9).

1472. ἐθελοθρησκεία ethelothrēskeia noun
Self-made religion, would-be religion.
Cross-Reference:
  θρησκεία thrēskeia (2333)

1. ἐθελοθρησκείᾳ ethelothrēskeia dat sing fem
2. ἐθελοθρησκίᾳ ethelothrēskia dat sing fem

1 have indeed a show of wisdom in **will worship**,....... Col 2:23
2 have indeed a show of wisdom in **will worship**,......... 2:23

Ethelo- compounds denote either "to do or be something" on purpose or "to wish to do or be something" outside of the realm of possibility (see *Bauer*). When coupled with *thrēskia* (2333), "worship, religion," the result is "self-made" or "would-be" religion. *Ethelothrēskeia* (also spelled *ethelothrēskia*) is not present in classical Greek or in the Septuagint. *Moulton-Milligan* suggest that it was coined by the apostle Paul himself who used it once in the New Testament at Colossians 2:23. It is thought that *ethelothrēskeia* thus could mean either "self-made religion" or "voluntary worship".

P.T. O'Brien (*Word Biblical Commentary*, 44:153) takes a different tack toward unravelling the meaning of the term. He views its origination in the language of Paul's opponents. He connects it to their apparent "worship of angels" (*thrēskeia ton angelon*) in Colossians 2:18, and argues that Paul was using it sarcastically. "Freely chosen worship" is thus how O'Brien renders it, but with a sarcastic twist: "The apostle regards this worship as freely chosen but wrong!" (ibid.).

STRONG 1479, BAUER 218, MOULTON-MILLIGAN 181, KITTEL 3:155-59, LIDDELL-SCOTT 479.

1473. ἐθίζω ethizō verb
Accustom.

1. εἰθισμένον eithismenon
nom/acc sing neu part perf mid
1 Jesus, to do for him after the **custom** of the law,.... Luke 2:27

Classical Greek
Most often *ethizō* means "to be accustomed" (passively or when used intransitively) or "to accustom." However it can also denote "according to custom or what is customary." Classical Greek evidences many related words from the *eth-* stem, most of which pick up on the idea of "custom, habit, etc." (see *Liddell-Scott*).

Septuagint Usage
Appearing in the Septuagint only three times, *ethizō* occurs only in the apocryphal writings of Sirach and 2 Maccabees. Sirach 23:9 (cf. 23:14) advises not to "get in the habit of" taking oaths. Maccabeus noticed that Nicanor dealt with him more harshly than had been his "custom" (2 Maccabees 14:30).

New Testament Usage
Ethizō occurs only in Luke's Gospel (2:27) and the use there is perhaps shaded in meaning, although the basic sense remains. According to the "custom" of the Law, Mary and Joseph brought the child Jesus to the temple to have Him circumcised and to offer sacrifices according to the prescriptions of the Law (Luke 2:23,24). Luke used another member of this word group in reference to the customs of the Law—*ethos* (1478). Often this word, too, recalls that "customs" of the Law are as binding as the laws themselves (cf. Acts 6:14; 15:1; 16:21).

STRONG 1480, BAUER 218, MOULTON-MILLIGAN 181, LIDDELL-SCOTT 479-80.

1474. ἐθνάρχης ethnarchēs noun
Governor, ethnarch.
CROSS-REFERENCES:
ἀρχή archē (741)
ἔθνος ethnos (1477)

1. ἐθνάρχης ethnarchēs nom sing masc

1 In Damascus the **governor** under Aretas the king...2 Co 11:32

Classical Greek
Ethnarchēs is a compound form of *ethnos* (1477), "nation," and *archō* (751), "to rule." An ethnarch would be the "ruler of a nation." The ethnarch actually "ruled" only in the stead of a higher power. Such a subordinate "governor" was, according to Josephus, in charge of people under foreign rule "just as if he were the head of a sovereign state" (*Antiquities* 14.7.2).

Septuagint Usage
The word is found only in the later writings of the Septuagint, specifically three times in 1 Maccabees. There it refers to the position outlined above (14:47; 15:1,2), particularly as it affected the Jewish people.

New Testament Usage
Ethnarchēs occurs only once in the New Testament at 2 Corinthians 11:32. Paul referred to an order issued by the "governor" under King Aretas IV—because of pressure by the Jews—to have Paul arrested while he was in Damascus.

STRONG 1481, BAUER 218, MOULTON-MILLIGAN 181, LIDDELL-SCOTT 480.

1475. ἐθνικός ethnikos adj
Gentile, heathen.
CROSS-REFERENCE:
ἔθνος ethnos (1477)

1. ἐθνικός ethnikos nom sing masc
2. ἐθνικοί ethnikoi nom pl masc
3. ἐθνικῶν ethnikōn gen pl masc

2 Do not even the **Gentiles** do the same? (NASB).... Matt 5:47
2 use not vain repetitions, as the **heathen** do:............. 6:7
1 let him be unto thee as a **heathen** man 18:17
3 accepting nothing from the **Gentiles** (NASB)........ 3 Jn 1:7

Classical Greek and Septuagint Usage
Related to *ethnos* (1477), "a group of people, a nation," *ethnikos* is an adjective depicting in classical Greek the ideas of "national, foreign, the nationality of someone." In later Greek it can depict a "tax collector" when used substantively. Apart from one variant reading at Leviticus 21:7, *ethnikos* is absent in the Septuagint (cf. the related term *ethnos* which is used extensively).

New Testament Usage
National origin continues to be an important factor for understanding *ethnikos* in the New Testament. In each of its four occurrences (Matthew 5:47; 6:7; 18:17; 3 John 7) it functions as a plural noun. "Pagans" is the idea

in each of these texts, and this especially refers to the Gentiles in contrast to the Jews.
STRONG 1482, BAUER 218, MOULTON-MILLIGAN 181, KITTEL 2:372, LIDDELL-SCOTT 480, COLIN BROWN 2:790,795.

1476. ἐθνικῶς ethnikōs adv
Like the heathen, like a Gentile.
CROSS-REFERENCE:
  ἔθνος ethnos (1477)

1. ἐθνικῶς ethnikōs
1 being a Jew, livest after the manner of Gentiles, ... Gal 2:14

Classical Greek
Ethnikōs is an adverb from the same family as the adjective *ethnikos* (1475). Thus its meaning in Greek would be "like a national." However, apparently *ethnikōs* comes on the scene only in the Christian period and beyond. It does not occur in the Septuagint and occurs only once in the New Testament.

New Testament Usage
Ethnikōs is found in Galatians 2:14 where Paul plainly understood it in a neutral sense of "like a pagan, like a Gentile." He reprimanded Peter for his hypocrisy (2:13) of living like a Gentile on the one hand—he had eaten with them and fellowshiped with them—and yet on the other hand, when Jews arrived from James he separated himself from Gentile fellowship. By doing this Peter imposed upon Gentiles the requirement to live in accordance with Jewish customs. *Ethnikōs* here merely refers to Peter's life-style in contrast to Jewish practice. Paul was not condemning Peter for "living like a Gentile"; on the contrary, Paul was condemning Peter for stopping that activity when confronted with the possibility of Jewish opposition. By restricting himself to Jewish customs and rules Peter thereby sent a silent message to the Gentiles that they must conform to Jewish practices. Such legalism appalled the apostle Paul, and he challenged Peter concerning his actions.
STRONG 1483, BAUER 218, COLIN BROWN 2:790,795.

1477. ἔθνος ethnos noun
Nation, people, heathen, pagans, Gentiles.
COGNATES:
  ἐθνάρχης ethnarchēs (1474)
  ἐθνικός ethnikos (1475)
  ἐθνικῶς ethnikōs (1476)

SYNONYMS:
  δῆμος dēmos (1211B)
  λαός laos (2967)
  ὄχλος ochlos (3657)
  πλῆθος plēthos (3988)
  φυλή phulē (5279)

אִי 'î (339), Coast, island (Is 41:5, 42:4).
אֻמָּה 'ummāh (531), Nation (Nm 25:15).
אֻמָּה 'ummāh (A532), Nation (Ezr 4:10, Dn 7:14—Aramaic).
אֶרֶץ 'erets (800), Ground, territory, earth (Ezr 9:7,11, Ez 31:12).
גּוֹי gôy (1504), People, nation (Ex 9:24, 1 Chr 14:17, Ez 12:15).
הָמוֹן hāmôn (2066), Multitude, army (2 Chr 32:7, Is 13:4).
זֶרַע zera' (2320), Brethren, descendants (Est 10:3).
חַבָּר chabbār (2362), Traders (Jb 41:6 [40:25]).
חַיִל chayil (2524), Forces, riches (Is 60:5).
לְאֹם le'ōm (3947), People, ethnic community (Pss 47:3 [46:3], 67:4 [66:4], Hb 2:13).
מַי may (4448), Water (Nm 24:7).
נָשִׂיא nāsî' (5562), Princes, rulers (Gn 17:20).
עֶבֶד 'evedh (5860), Servant, official (Est 1:3).
עַם 'am (6194I), People, inhabitants (Gn 49:10, Jos 24:18, Is 17:12).
צָבָא tsāvā' (6893), Multitude, army (Is 13:4).

1. ἔθνος ethnos nom/acc sing neu
2. ἔθνους ethnous gen sing neu
3. ἔθνει ethnei dat sing neu
4. ἔθνη ethnē nom/acc pl neu
5. ἐθνῶν ethnōn gen pl neu
6. ἔθνεσιν ethnesin dat pl neu

5 beyond Jordan, Galilee of the **Gentiles**; .... Matt 4:15
4 For after all these things do the **Gentiles** seek: 6:32
5 Go not into the way of the **Gentiles**, ... 10:5
6 for a testimony against them and the **Gentiles**. 10:18
6 and he shall show judgment to the **Gentiles**. 12:18
4 And in his name shall the **Gentiles** trust. 12:21
6 And shall deliver him to the **Gentiles** to mock, ... 20:19
5 Ye know that the princes of the **Gentiles** 20:25
3 given to a **nation** bringing forth the fruits thereof. 21:43
1 For **nation** shall rise against **nation**, ... 24:7
1 For **nation** shall rise against **nation**, ... 24:7
5 ye shall be hated of all **nations** for my name's sake. ... 24:9
6 in all the world for a witness unto all **nations**; 24:14
4 And before him shall be gathered all **nations**: 25:32
4 Go ye therefore, and teach all **nations**, ... 28:19
6 and shall deliver him to the **Gentiles**: .... Mark 10:33
5 they which are accounted to rule over the **Gentiles** 10:42
6 be called of all **nations** the house of prayer? 11:17
1 For **nation** shall rise against **nation**, ... 13:8
1 For **nation** shall rise against **nation**, ... 13:8
4 gospel must first be published among all **nations**. 13:10
5 A light to lighten the **Gentiles**, ... Luke 2:32
1 For he loveth our **nation**, ... built us a synagogue. 7:5
4 these things do the **nations** of the world seek after: 12:30
6 For he shall be delivered unto the **Gentiles**, ... 18:32
1 said he unto them, **Nation** shall rise against **nation**, ... 21:10
1 said he unto them, **Nation** shall rise against **nation**, ... 21:10
4 and shall be led away captive into all **nations**: 21:24

ἔθνος 1477

5	Jerusalem shall be trodden down of the **Gentiles**,...Luke	21:24
5	until the times of the **Gentiles** be fulfilled.............	21:24
5	upon the earth distress **of nations**, with perplexity;.....	21:25
5	kings of the **Gentiles** exercise lordship over them;......	22:25
1	We found this fellow perverting the **nation**,............	23:2
4	among all **nations**, beginning at Jerusalem.............	24:47
1	and take away both our place and **nation**.......... John	11:48
1	and that the whole **nation** perish not.................	11:50
2	prophesied that Jesus should die for that **nation**;.......	11:51
2	And not for that **nation** only,.......................	11:52
1	Thine own **nation** and the chief priests	18:35
2	devout men, out of every **nation** under heaven....... Acts	2:5
4	Why did the **heathen** rage,..........................	4:25
6	both Herod, and Pontius Pilate, with the **Gentiles**,......	4:27
1	And the **nation** to whom they shall be in bondage	7:7
5	with Jesus into the possession of the **Gentiles**,..........	7:45
1	and bewitched the **people** of Samaria,..................	8:9
5	to bear my name before the **Gentiles**,..................	9:15
2	of good report among all the **nation** of the Jews,......	10:22
3	But in every **nation** he that feareth him,..............	10:35
4	because that on the **Gentiles** also was poured out	10:45
4	the **Gentiles** had also received the word of God........	11:1
6	the **Gentiles** granted repentance unto life..............	11:18
4	destroyed seven **nations** in the land of Chanaan,......	13:19
4	the **Gentiles** besought that these words	13:42
4	lo, we turn to the **Gentiles**..........................	13:46
5	I have set thee to be a light of the **Gentiles**,...........	13:47
4	And when the **Gentiles** heard this, they were glad,.....	13:48
5	But the unbelieving Jews stirred up the **Gentiles**,.......	14:2
5	there was an assault made both of the **Gentiles**,.......	14:5
4	suffered all **nations** to walk in their own ways.........	14:16
6	he had opened the door of faith unto the **Gentiles**.....	14:27
5	declaring the conversion of the **Gentiles**:...............	15:3
4	that the **Gentiles** by my mouth should hear	15:7
6	God had wrought among the **Gentiles** by them........	15:12
5	declared how God at the first did visit the **Gentiles**,...	15:14
4	all the **Gentiles**, upon whom my name is called,........	15:17
5	which from among the **Gentiles** are turned to God:....	15:19
5	which are of the **Gentiles** in Antioch and Syria and....	15:23
1	And hath made of one blood all **nations** of men	17:26
4	from henceforth I will go unto the **Gentiles**............	18:6
5	shall deliver him into the hands of the **Gentiles**.......	21:11
6	what things God had wrought among the **Gentiles**	21:19
4	which are among the **Gentiles** to forsake Moses,......	21:21
5	As touching the **Gentiles** which believe,................	21:25
4	for I will send thee far hence unto the **Gentiles**.......	22:21
3	deeds are done unto this **nation** by thy providence,....	24:2
3	hast been of many years a judge unto this **nation**,.....	24:10
1	I came to bring alms to my **nation**, and offerings......	24:17
3	which was at the first among mine own **nation**	26:4
5	from the **Gentiles**, unto whom now I send thee,.......	26:17
6	all the coasts of Judaea, and then to the **Gentiles**,....	26:20
6	show light unto the people, and to the **Gentiles**,......	26:23
2	not that I had ought to accuse my **nation** of..........	28:19
6	that the salvation of God is sent unto the **Gentiles**,....	28:28
6	for obedience to the faith among all **nations**,........ Rom	1:5
6	fruit among you ... even as among other **Gentiles**.......	1:13
4	For when the **Gentiles**, which have not the law,.......	2:14
6	name of God is blasphemed among the **Gentiles**	2:24
5	is he not also of the **Gentiles**?.........................	3:29
5	not also of the **Gentiles**? Yes, of the **Gentiles** also:.....	3:29
5	I have made thee a father of many **nations**,...........	4:17
5	that he might become the father of many **nations**,......	4:18
5	not of the Jews only, but also of the **Gentiles**?.........	9:24
4	What shall we say then? That the **Gentiles**,............	9:30
3	jealousy by them that are no **people**,..................	10:19
3	and by a foolish **nation** I will anger you..............	10:19
6	through ... fall salvation is come unto the **Gentiles**,....	11:11
5	the diminishing of them the riches of the **Gentiles**;.....	11:12
6	For I speak to you **Gentiles**,..........................	11:13
5	inasmuch as I am the apostle of the **Gentiles**,..........	11:13
5	until the fulness of the **Gentiles** be come in...........	11:25
4	that the **Gentiles** might glorify God for his mercy;.....	15:9
5	this cause I will confess to thee among the **Gentiles**,...	15:9
4	And again he saith, Rejoice, ye **Gentiles**,...............	15:10
4	And again, Praise the Lord, all ye **Gentiles**;...........	15:11
4	And again, Praise the Lord, all ye **Gentiles**;...........	15:11
5	and he that shall rise to reign over the **Gentiles**;... Rom	15:12
4	in him shall the **Gentiles** trust........................	15:12
4	be the minister of Jesus Christ to the **Gentiles**,........	15:16
5	the offering up of the **Gentiles** might be acceptable,.....	15:16
5	to make the **Gentiles** obedient, by word and deed,.....	15:18
4	For if the **Gentiles** have been made partakers..........	15:27
5	but also all the churches of the **Gentiles**...............	16:4
4	known to all **nations** for the obedience of faith:.......	16:26
6	and to **Gentiles** foolishness (NASB) .... 1 Co	1:23
6	fornication as is not ... named among the **Gentiles**,......	5:1
4	that the things which the **Gentiles** sacrifice,............	10:20
4	Ye know that ye were **Gentiles**,........................	12:2
5	in perils by the **heathen**, in perils in the city,.......2 Co	11:26
6	that I might preach him among the **heathen**;......... Gal	1:16
6	that gospel which I preach among the **Gentiles**,........	2:2
4	the same was mighty in me toward the **Gentiles**:........	2:8
4	that we should go unto the **heathen**,...................	2:9
5	he did eat with the **Gentiles**:..........................	2:12
4	compellest thou the **Gentiles** to live as do the Jews?....	2:14
5	are Jews by nature, and not sinners of the **Gentiles**,.....	2:15
4	that God would justify the **heathen** through faith,.......	3:8
4	In thee shall all **nations** be blessed....................	3:8
4	come on the **Gentiles** through Jesus Christ;............	3:14
4	that ye being in time past **Gentiles** in the flesh,..... Eph	2:11
5	the prisoner of Jesus Christ for you **Gentiles**,...........	3:1
4	That the **Gentiles** should be fellowheirs,................	3:6
6	that I should preach among the **Gentiles**	3:8
4	that ye henceforth walk not as other **Gentiles** walk,.....	4:17
6	the glory of this mystery among the **Gentiles**;...... Col	1:27
6	to speak to the **Gentiles** that they might be saved,...1 Th	2:16
4	even as the **Gentiles** which know not God:.............	4:5
5	a teacher of the **Gentiles** in faith and verity......... 1 Tm	2:7
6	seen of angels, preached unto the **Gentiles**,.............	3:16
5	and an apostle, and a teacher of the **Gentiles**....... 2 Tm	1:11
4	and that all the **Gentiles** might hear:...................	4:17
1	priesthood, an holy **nation**, a peculiar people;....... 1 Pt	2:9
6	your conversation honest among the **Gentiles**:...........	2:12
5	to have wrought the will of the **Gentiles**,...............	4:3
5	they went forth, taking nothing of the **Gentiles**......3 Jn	1:7
5	to him will I give power over the **nations**:........... Rev	2:26
2	and tongue, and people, and **nation**;...................	5:9
2	all **nations**, and kindreds, and people, and tongues,.....	7:9
6	many peoples, and **nations**, and tongues, and kings.....	10:11
6	measure it not; for it is given unto the **Gentiles**:.......	11:2
5	the people and kindreds and tongues and **nations**	11:9
4	the **nations** were angry, and thy wrath is come,.......	11:18
4	who was to rule all **nations** with a rod of iron:........	12:5
1	over all kindreds, and tongues, and **nations**............	13:7
1	that dwell on the earth, and to every **nation**,..........	14:6
4	because she made all **nations** drink of the wine	14:8
5	Thou King of the **nations**. (NASB)	15:3
4	for all **nations** shall come and worship before thee;....	15:4
5	and the cities of the **nations** fell:......................	16:19
4	peoples, and multitudes, and **nations**, and tongues......	17:15
4	For all **nations** have drunk of the wine of the wrath ...	18:3
4	for by thy sorceries were all **nations** deceived..........	18:23
4	sword, that with it he should smite the **nations**:........	19:15
4	that he should deceive the **nations** no more,...........	20:3
4	And shall go out to deceive the **nations**	20:8
4	the **nations** of them which are saved shall walk	21:24
4	bring the glory and honour of the **nations** into it.......	21:26
5	the leaves ... were for the healing of the **nations**......	22:2

Classical Greek

Ethnos is a rather broad term for any group of people, a nation, a tribe or caste, or a group of animals (as in a swarm of insects) in classical writings (see *Liddell-Scott*). Papyri and inscriptions indicate the term continued to be very diverse in later periods. *Ethnos* could describe a limited association (of priests or gravediggers) as well as a broader group (a province of people). Generally *ethnos* could include any of those people who lived outside of the city (*polis* [4032]) (see *Moulton-Milligan*).

Septuagint Usage

The diversity of *ethnos* carries over to the Septuagint where it translates 15 Hebrew terms. Nevertheless, *ethnos* assumes a particular role as a term for non-Jewish peoples. Two Hebrew terms, *goi*, "people, nation" (Genesis 12:2; 2 Kings 18:33 [LXX 4 Kings 18:33]), and *'am*, "people" (e.g., Genesis 28:3; 1 Chronicles 16:26), dominate as equivalents to *ethnos*. Often these contrast Israel (Exodus 34:24), but *ethnos* can also refer to a swarm of insects (Joel 1:6). Originally, there was no racial or "ethnic" distinction in the Hebrew or Greek. But, over time, the Hebrew and the Greek acquired specific meanings. For example, *gôyim* became a technical term for Gentiles while *'am* was reserved for Israel (Bertram, "ethnos," *Kittel*, 2:365). Later in Hellenistic Judaism *ta ethnē* became a technical term for "Gentiles," and *ho laos*, "the people," denoted the (chosen) people of God (cf. *Bauer*).

New Testament Usage

The flexibility of *ethnos* in the New Testament is also attested. *Ethnos* can denote nations in general (e.g., Matthew 25:32; Luke 12:30; Romans 4:18), or the nation of Israel (Luke 7:5; John 11:48ff.; 18:35; Acts 10:22). God's people are even called a "holy nation" *ethnos hagion* (1 Peter 2:9). Yet, it can also refer to all, *panta* (see 3817B), nations (e.g., Matthew 24:9,14; 28:19; Mark 11:17; Romans 1:5; 15:11; 16:26).

But the technical sense of "Gentiles" is not overlooked by the New Testament writers. Christ was handed over to the Gentiles in fulfillment of prophecy (Mark 10:33, parallel Luke 18:32; cf. Luke 21:24; Acts 4:27; 11:1,18; 14:2,5). Gentiles are contrasted with Israel frequently in Romans (2:14,24; 3:29; 9:24,30), Galatians (2:8,12,14,15), Ephesians (2:11; 3:6,8), and 1 Thessalonians (2:16).

Being a Gentile was often considered a sinful condition that was totally alienated from God and marked by sinful behavior (Ephesians 2:11; 4:17; 1 Peter 2:12; 4:3). Gentiles specifically "do not know God" (1 Thessalonians 4:5, NIV). Here the Septuagint rather than classical Greek has done more to shape the understanding of *ethnos* in the New Testament. This is in contrast to Philo and Josephus—Jewish contemporaries of the New Testament authors—who do not make such distinction (Schmidt, "ethnos," *Kittel*, 2:371).

In a religious sense, the *ethnos* were not only non-Jews, but were also "without hope and without God" (Ephesians 2:12, NIV), separated from God because the Law and the covenant was given only to the Jew. Nevertheless, the New Testament clearly testifies that Jesus is the Saviour of *all* men, Paul himself being called the apostle of the Gentiles (*ethos*). Through His death, Jesus tore down the middle wall of partition between Jews and Gentiles, making the two into one (see Ephesians 2:11-16). While many Jews rejected the Gospel and therefore judged themselves "unworthy of everlasting life" (Acts 13:46), God extended His call to the Gentile. This great grace toward the Gentiles was a secret which had been hidden before, but which Paul said "now is made manifest to his saints" (Colossians 1:26f.).

STRONG 1484, BAUER 218, MOULTON-MILLIGAN 181, KITTEL 2:364-72, LIDDELL-SCOTT 480, COLIN BROWN 2:790-91,793-96,805.

1478. ἔθος ethos noun

Habit, usage, custom, law.

COGNATE:
ἦθος ēthos (2222)

SYNONYMS:
νόμος nomos (3414)
συνήθεια sunētheia (4764)

1. **ἔθος** ethos nom/acc sing neu
2. **ἔθει** ethei dat sing neu
3. **ἐθῶν** ethōn gen pl neu
4. **ἔθεσιν** ethesin dat pl neu
5. **ἔθη** ethē nom/acc pl neu
6. **ἔθεσι** ethesi dat pl neu

1 According to the **custom** of the priest's office,	Luke 1:9
1 went up to Jerusalem after the **custom** of the feast.	2:42
1 and went, as he **was wont**, to the mount of Olives;	22:39
1 as the **manner** of the Jews is to bury.	John 19:40
5 change the **customs** which Moses delivered us.	Acts 6:14
2 Except ye be circumcised after the **manner**	15:1
5 And teach **customs**, which are not lawful	16:21
4 neither to walk after the **customs**.	21:21
1 **manner** of the Romans to deliver any man to die,	25:16
3 to be expert in all **customs** ... among the Jews:	26:3
4 against the people, or **customs** of our fathers,	28:17
1 as the **manner** of some is;	Heb 10:25

Classical Greek

Ethos carries two basic meanings: (1) an informal sense of "custom," i.e., "habit"; and (2) a formal "custom" or "law." For example, Jesus' "habit" (*ethos*) was to go to the Mount of Olives (Luke 22:39; cf. NIV "as usual"). Here the informal sense is plain. The formal idea of "custom" is reflected in 4 Maccabees. Its writer recalls Antiochus' unsuccessful efforts to make the Israelites "abandon their ancestral customs" (4 Maccabees 18:5, RSV). The informal sense dominated classical literature, whereas the formal sense predominates in religious literature. This phenomenon may in large measure be explained by the role of tradition (*paradosis*) in the religion of Israel.

Septuagint Usage

Only the apocryphal writings of the Septuagint use *ethos* (6 times). Wisdom of Solomon conveniently illustrates the relationship between informal and formal "custom": "Then the ungodly *custom* (making idols), grown strong with time, was kept as law" (Wisdom of Solomon 14:16, RSV). The Maccabean writings reflect the versatility of the term (1 Maccabees 10:89; 2 Maccabees 13:4 [informal]; cf. 2 Maccabees 11:25; 4 Maccabees 18:5 [informal]).

New Testament Usage

The New Testament picture mirrors the two senses of *ethos* as well. Luke, who uses *ethos* more than any other writer (of its 12 uses 10 are Luke's), utilizes both meanings, although he favors the formal sense (only 22:39 seems to be informal, cf. Hebrews 10:25). The customs of Moses and the "fathers" (Acts 6:14; 28:17; cf. John 19:40) are the heartbeat of the Jewish religion. If one were a Jew, one's life revolved around the *ethos* of the religion (Acts 16:21; 21:21; 26:3; cf. Josephus *Antiquities* 15.8.4). Even Roman "customs" were understood as binding (Acts 25:16; cf. Sherwin-White, *Roman Society and Roman Law*, pp.48f.).

STRONG 1485, BAUER 218-19, MOULTON-MILLIGAN 181, KITTEL 2:372-73, LIDDELL-SCOTT 480, COLIN BROWN 2:436-38.

1479. εἰ ei conj

If, since.

1. εἰ ei

1	the tempter ... said, If thou be the Son of God,	Matt 4:3
1	And saith unto him, If thou be the Son of God,	4:6
1	thenceforth good for nothing, **but** to be cast out,	5:13
1	And if thy right eye offend thee, pluck it out,	5:29
1	And if thy right hand offend thee, cut it off,	5:30
1	**otherwise** ye have no reward of your Father	6:1
1	If therefore the light that is in thee be darkness,	6:23
1	Wherefore, if God so clothe the grass of the field,	6:30
1	If ye then, being evil, know how to give good gifts	7:11
1	If thou cast us out, suffer ... into the herd of swine.	8:31
1	**else** the bottles break, and the wine runneth out,	9:17
1	If they have called the master of the house	10:25
1	And **if** ye will receive it, this is Elias,	11:14
1	for if the mighty works, which were done in you,	11:21
1	if the mighty works, which have been done in thee,	Matt 11:23
1	and no man knoweth the Son, **but** the Father;	11:27
1	neither knoweth any man the Father, **save** the Son,	11:27
1	not lawful for him ... **but** only for the priests?	12:4
1	But if ye had known what this meaneth,	12:7
1	saying, Is it lawful to heal (NT)	12:10
1	**but** by Beelzebub the prince of the devils.	12:24
1	And if Satan cast out Satan, he is divided	12:26
1	And if I by Beelzebub cast out devils,	12:27
1	But if I cast out devils by the Spirit of God,	12:28
1	no sign be given to it, **but** the sign of ... Jonas:	12:39
1	not without honour, **save** in his own country,	13:57
1	We have here **but** five loaves, and two fishes.	14:17
1	if it be thou, bid me come unto thee on the water.	14:28
1	I am not sent **but** unto the lost sheep ... of Israel.	15:24
1	no sign ... **but** the sign of the prophet Jonas.	16:4
1	If any man will come after me, ... deny himself,	16:24
1	if thou wilt, let us make here three tabernacles;	17:4
1	they saw no man, **save** Jesus only.	17:8
1	this kind goeth not out **but** by prayer and fasting.	17:21
1	Wherefore if thy hand or thy foot offend thee,	18:8
1	And if thine eye offend thee, pluck it out,	18:9
1	Pay back what you owe (NASB)	18:28
1	Is it lawful for a man to put away his wife (NT)	19:3
1	except it be for fornication, ... shall marry another,	19:9
1	If the case of the man be so with his wife,	19:10
1	there is none good **but** one, that is, God:	19:17
1	but if thou wilt enter into life,	19:17
1	If thou wilt be perfect, go and sell that thou hast,	19:21
1	Is thine eye evil, because I am good? (NT)	20:15
1	and found nothing thereon, **but** leaves only,	21:19
1	If David then call him Lord, how is he his son?	22:45
1	If we had been in the days of our fathers,	23:30
1	And except those days should be shortened,	24:22
1	if it were possible, they shall deceive the very elect.	24:24
1	no, not the angels of heaven, **but** my Father only.	24:36
1	that if the goodman of the house had known	24:43
1	been good for that man if he had not been born.	26:24
1	**Though** all men shall be offended because of thee,	26:33
1	if it be possible, let this cup pass from me:	26:39
1	if this cup may not pass away from me,	26:42
1	tell us **whether** thou be the Christ, the Son of God.	26:63
1	If thou be the Son of God, come down	27:40
1	If he be the King of Israel, let him now come down	27:42
1	let him deliver him now, if he will have him:	27:43
1	let us see **whether** Elias will come to save him.	27:49
1	who can forgive sins **but** God only?	Mark 2:7
1	**else** the new piece that filled it up taketh away	2:21
1	**else** the new wine doth burst the bottles,	2:22
1	which is not lawful to eat **but** for the priests,	2:26
1	**whether** he would heal him on the sabbath day;	3:2
1	if Satan rise up against himself, and be divided,	3:26
1	If any man have ears to hear, let him hear.	4:23
1	**save** Peter, and James, and John the brother	5:37
1	is not without honour, **but** in his own country,	6:4
1	**save** that he laid his hands upon a few sick folk,	6:5
1	nothing for their journey, **save** a staff only;	6:8
1	If any man have ears to hear, let him hear.	7:16
1	There shall no sign be given (NT)	8:12
1	except for one loaf they had with them (NIV)	8:14
1	he asked him if he saw ought.	8:23
1	If anyone wishes to come after Me (NASB)	8:34
1	no man any more, except Jesus only (NASB) (NT)	9:8
1	till the Son of man were risen from the dead.	9:9
1	if thou canst do any thing, have compassion on us,	9:22
1	Jesus said unto him, If thou canst believe,	9:23
1	come forth by nothing, **but** by prayer and fasting.	9:29
1	and saith unto them, If any man desire to be first,	9:35
1	that a millstone were hanged about his neck,	9:42
1	Is it lawful for a man to put away his wife? (NT)	10:2
1	there is none good **but** one, that is, God.	10:18
1	he came, if haply he might find any thing thereon:	11:13
1	when he came to it, he found nothing **but** leaves:	11:13
1	answering saith unto them, Have faith in God.	11:22
1	forgive, if ye have ought against any:	11:25
1	But if ye do not forgive, neither will your Father	11:26
1	but teachest the way of God in truth:	12:14

εἰ 1479

1 And **except** that the Lord had shortened those days,Mark 13:20	
1 to seduce, **if** it were possible, even the elect............ 13:22	
1 no man, ... neither the Son, **but** the Father............. 13:32	
1 good were it ... **if** he had never been born.............. 14:21	
1 **Although** all shall be offended, yet will not I.......... 14:29	
1 **if** it were possible, the hour might pass from him..... 14:35	
1 see **whether** Elias will come to take him down.......... 15:36	
1 And Pilate marvelled **if** he were already dead:......... 15:44	
1 he asked him **whether** he had been any while dead..... 15:44	
1 **If** thou be the Son of God, command this stone that Luke 4:3	
1 **If** thou be the Son of God, cast thyself down......... 4:9	
1 unto none ... was Elias sent, **save** unto Sarepta,....... 4:26	
1 none ... cleansed, **saving** Naaman the Syrian........... 4:27	
1 Who can forgive sins, **but** God alone?................. 5:21	
1 **if** otherwise, then both the new maketh a rent,....... 5:36	
1 **else** the new wine will burst the bottles.............. 5:37	
1 which it is not lawful to eat **but** for the priests......... 6:4	
1 **whether** he would heal on the sabbath day;............. 6:7	
1 is it lawful on the Sabbath (NASB) (NT)................. 6:9	
1 For **if** ye love them which love you, what thank........ 6:32	
1 **if** he were a prophet, would have known who and...... 7:39	
1 suffered no ... **save** Peter, and James, and John,........ 8:51	
1 **except** we should go and buy meat for all this........... 9:13	
1 **If** any man will come after me, let ... deny himself,..... 9:23	
1 shall rest upon it: **if** not, it shall turn to you again..... 10:6	
1 for **if** the mighty works had been done in Tyre........ 10:13	
1 no man knoweth who the Son is, **but** the Father;...... 10:22	
1 but the Father; and who the Father is, **but** the Son,... 10:22	
1 **Though** he will not rise and give him, because he is ... 11:8	
1 or **if** he ask a fish, ... give him a serpent?............ 11:11	
1 **If** ye then, being evil, know how to give good gifts.... 11:13	
1 **If** Satan also be divided against himself,................ 11:18	
1 And **if** I by Beelzebub cast out devils,................... 11:19	
1 **But if** I with the finger of God cast out devils,......... 11:20	
1 **but** the sign of Jonas the prophet...................... 11:29	
1 **If** thy whole body therefore be full of light,............ 11:36	
1 **If** ye then be not able to do that ... which is least,..... 12:26	
1 **If** then God so clothe the grass, which is to day...... 12:28	
1 **if** the goodman of the house had known what hour.... 12:39	
1 and what will I, **if** it be already kindled?............. 12:49	
1 and **if** not, then after that thou shalt cut it down...... 13:9	
1 Lord, are there few that be saved? (NT)............... 13:23	
1 Is it lawful to heal on the sabbath day? (NT)........... 14:3	
1 **If** any man come to me, and hate not his father,..... 14:26	
1 the cost, **whether** he have sufficient to finish it?....... 14:28	
1 sitteth ... first, and consulteth **whether** he be able..... 14:31	
1 **Or else**, while the other is yet a great way off,........ 14:32	
1 **If** therefore ye have not been faithful in the........... 16:11	
1 And **if** ye have not been faithful in that which is..... 16:12	
1 **If** they hear not Moses and the prophets,............. 16:31	
1 It were better for him **that** a millstone were hanged.... 17:2	
1 **If** ye had faith as a grain of mustard seed,............. 17:6	
1 returned to give glory to God, **save** this stranger....... 17:18	
1 **Though** I fear not God, nor regard man;............... 18:4	
1 me good? none is good, **save** one, that is, God......... 18:19	
1 and **if** I have taken any thing from any man......... 19:8	
1 **If** thou hadst known, even thou, ... in this thy day,.... 19:42	
1 **if** thou be willing, remove this cup from me:......... 22:42	
1 Lord, shall we smite with the sword? (NT)............ 22:49	
1 "**If** You are the Christ, tell us." (NASB).............. 22:67	
1 he asked **whether** the man were a Galilaean............ 23:6	
1 For **if** they do these things in a green tree,............ 23:31	
1 **if** he be Christ, the chosen of God..................... 23:35	
1 saying, **If** thou be the king of the Jews, save thyself.... 23:37	
1 saying, **If** thou be Christ, save thyself and us........... 23:39	
1 **if** thou be not that Christ, nor Elias,............. John 1:25	
1 **If** I have told you earthly things,..................... 3:12	
1 **but** he that came down from heaven,................... 3:13	
1 **If** thou knewest the gift of God,....................... 4:10	
1 For **if** you believed Moses, (NASB)................... 5:46	
1 **But if** ye believe not his writings,..................... 5:47	
1 **save** that one whereinto his disciples were entered,..... 6:22	
1 **save** he which is of God, he hath seen the Father....... 6:46	
1 **If** thou do these things, show thyself to the world...... 7:4	
1 **If** a man on the sabbath day receive circumcision,..... 7:23	
1 **if** ye had known me, ... known my Father also....... 8:19	
1 **If** ye were Abraham's children,....................... 8:39	
1 **If** God were your Father, ye would love me:........John 8:42	
1 And **if** I say the truth, why do ye not believe me?..... 8:46	
1 **Whether** he be a sinner or no, I know not:............. 9:25	
1 **If** this man were not of God, he could do nothing...... 9:33	
1 **If** ye were blind, ye should have no sin:................ 9:41	
1 The thief cometh not, **but** for to steal, and to kill,..... 10:10	
1 **If** thou be the Christ, tell us plainly................... 10:24	
1 **If** he called them gods,.............................. 10:35	
1 **If** I do not the works of my Father, believe me not.... 10:37	
1 **But if** I do, though ye believe not me,................. 10:38	
1 Lord, **if** he sleep, he shall do well..................... 11:12	
1 **if** thou hadst been here, my brother had not died...... 11:21	
1 **if** thou hadst been here, my brother had not died...... 11:32	
1 He ... needs only to wash his feet (NASB) (NT)....... 13:10	
1 **If** I then, your Lord and Master,...................... 13:14	
1 **If** ye know these things,............................. 13:17	
1 **If** God be glorified in him,........................... 13:32	
1 **if** it were not so, I would have told you................ 14:2	
1 no man cometh unto the Father, **but** by me............ 14:6	
1 **If** ye had known me, ... known my Father also:........ 14:7	
1 or **else** believe me for the very works' sake............ 14:11	
1 **If** ye loved me, ye would rejoice,..................... 14:28	
1 **If** the world hate you, ye know that it hated me..... 15:18	
1 **If** ye were of the world,.............................. 15:19	
1 **If** they have persecuted me,.......................... 15:20	
1 **if** they have kept my saying,......................... 15:20	
1 **If** I had not come and spoken unto them,.............. 15:22	
1 **If** I had not done among them the works............. 15:24	
1 and none of them is lost, **but** the son of perdition;..... 17:12	
1 **if** therefore ye seek me, let these go their way:......... 18:8	
1 **If** I have spoken evil, bear witness of the evil:......... 18:23	
1 but **if** well, why smitest thou me?..................... 18:23	
1 **If** he were not a malefactor,.......................... 18:30	
1 **if** my kingdom were of this world,..................... 18:36	
1 **except** it were given thee from above:................. 19:11	
1 priests answered, We have no king **but** Caesar......... 19:15	
1 saith unto him, Sir, **if** thou have borne him hence,..... 20:15	
1 they asked of him, saying, Lord, (NT)............. Acts 1:6	
1 **If** we this day be examined of the good deed........... 4:9	
1 **Whether** it be right in the sight of God................. 4:19	
1 Tell me **whether** ye sold the land for so much?........ 5:8	
1 **But if** it be of God, ye cannot overthrow it;............ 5:39	
1 said the high priest, Are these things so? (NT)......... 7:1	
1 pray God, **if** perhaps the thought of thine heart....... 8:22	
1 **If** thou believest with all thine heart, thou mayest...... 8:37	
1 asked **whether** Simon, which was surnamed Peter,..... 10:18	
1 **Forasmuch** then as God gave them the like gift........ 11:17	
1 preaching the word to none **but** unto the Jews......... 11:19	
1 Ye men and brethren, **if** ye have any word........... 13:15	
1 **If** ye have judged me to be faithful to the Lord,...... 16:15	
1 **whether** those things were so......................... 17:11	
1 **if** haply they might feel after him, and find him,...... 17:27	
1 **If** it were a matter of wrong or wicked lewdness,...... 18:14	
1 **But if** it be a question of words and names,........... 18:15	
1 Have ye received the Holy Ghost (NT)................ 19:2	
1 not ... heard **whether** there be any Holy Ghost......... 19:2	
1 Wherefore **if** Demetrius, and the craftsmen............ 19:38	
1 **if** ye inquire any thing concerning other matters,...... 19:39	
1 **if** it were possible for him, to be at Jerusalem......... 20:16	
1 **save** only that they keep themselves from............ 21:25	
1 unto the chief captain, May I speak (NT)............. 21:37	
1 Is it lawful for you to scourge a man that is (NT)..... 22:25	
1 Tell me, art thou a Roman? He said, Yea. (NT)....... 22:27	
1 but **if** a spirit or an angel hath spoken to him,......... 23:9	
1 and object, **if** they had ought against me.............. 24:19	
1 **if** they have found any evil doing in me,.............. 24:20	
1 accuse this man, **if** there be any wickedness in him..... 25:5	
1 For **if** I be an offender,.............................. 25:11	
1 but **if** there be none of these things whereof these..... 25:11	
1 I asked him **whether** he would go to Jerusalem......... 25:20	
1 incredible ... **that** God should raise the dead?......... 26:8	
1 **That** Christ should suffer,........................... 26:23	
1 and **that** he should be the first that should rise......... 26:23	
1 set at liberty, **if** he had not appealed unto Caesar...... 26:32	
1 **if** somehow they could reach Phoenix (NASB)........ 27:12	
1 **if** it were possible, to thrust in the ship................ 27:39	
1 making request, **if** perhaps now at last (NASB)..... Rom 1:10	

εἰ

1 But if you bear the name "Jew," (NASB) .... Rom 2:17	1 but if against my will, a dispensation of the gospel.. 1 Co 9:17
1 For what if some did not believe? 3:3	1 no temptation ... but such as is common to man: 10:13
1 But if our unrighteousness commend 3:5	1 If any of them that believe not bid you to a feast, ... 10:27
1 For if the truth of God hath more abounded 3:7	1 For if I by grace be a partaker, ... 10:30
1 For if Abraham were justified by works, ... 4:2	1 if the woman be not covered, let her also be shorn: ... 11:6
1 For if they which are of the law be heirs, ... 4:14	1 but if it be a shame for a woman to be shorn 11:6
1 For while we were still helpless (NASB) 5:6	1 But if any man seem to be contentious, ... 11:16
1 For if, when we were enemies, we were reconciled 5:10	1 For if we would judge ourselves, ... not be judged..... 11:31
1 For if through the offence of one many be dead, ... 5:15	1 And if any man hunger, let him eat at home; 11:34
1 For if by one man's offence death reigned by one; 5:17	1 say that Jesus is the Lord, but by the Holy Ghost..... 12:3
1 For if we have been planted together 6:5	1 If the whole body were an eye, ... 12:17
1 Now if we be dead with Christ, ... 6:8	1 If the whole were hearing, ... 12:17
1 I had not known sin, but by the law: 7:7	1 if they were all one member, where ... the body? 12:19
1 for I had not known lust, except the law had said, ... 7:7	1 he that speaketh with tongues, except he interpret, ... 14:5
1 If then I do that which I would not, ... 7:16	1 it may be, so many kinds of voices (NT) 14:10
1 Now if I do that I would not, ... 7:20	1 And if they will learn any thing, ... 14:35
1 Now if any man have not the Spirit of Christ, ... 8:9	1 If any man think himself to be a prophet, ... 14:37
1 if Christ be in you, the body is dead because of sin; 8:10	1 But if any man be ignorant, let him be ignorant. 14:38
1 But if the Spirit of him that raised up Jesus 8:11	1 if ye keep in memory what I preached unto you, ... 15:2
1 For if ye live after the flesh, ye shall die: 8:13	1 unless ye have believed in vain. 15:2
1 but if ye through the Spirit do mortify the deeds 8:13	1 if Christ be preached that he rose from the dead, ... 15:12
1 And if children, then heirs; heirs of God, ... 8:17	1 But if there be no resurrection of the dead, ... 15:13
1 But if we hope for that we see not, ... 8:25	1 if Christ be not risen, then is our preaching vain, ... 15:14
1 If God be for us, who can be against us? 8:31	1 For if the dead rise not, then is not Christ raised: 15:16
1 What if God, willing to show his wrath, ... 9:22	1 And if Christ be not raised, your faith is vain; 15:17
1 Except the Lord of Sabaoth had left us a seed, ... 9:29	1 If in this life only we have hope in Christ, ... 15:19
1 And if by grace, then is it no more of works: 11:6	1 baptized for the dead, if the dead rise not at all? 15:29
1 But if it be of works, then is it no more grace: 11:6	1 If after the manner of men I have fought, ... 15:32
1 Now if the fall of them be the riches of the world, ... 11:12	1 what advantageth it me, if the dead rise not? 15:32
1 If by any means I may provoke to emulation 11:14	1 it may chance of wheat, (NT) 15:37
1 For if the casting away of them be the reconciling 11:15	1 If there is a natural body, there is also (NASB) 15:44
1 the receiving of them be, but life from the dead? 11:15	1 If any man love not the Lord Jesus Christ, ... 16:22
1 For if the firstfruit be holy, the lump is also holy: 11:16	1 For if I make you sorry, ... 2 Co 2:2
1 and if the root be holy, so are the branches. 11:16	1 but the same which is made sorry by me? 2:2
1 And if some of the branches be broken off, ... 11:17	1 if any have caused grief, he hath not grieved me, ... 2:5
1 But if thou boast, thou bearest not the root, ... 11:18	1 whether ye be obedient in all things. 2:9
1 For if God spared not the natural branches, ... 11:21	1 for if I forgave any thing, to whom I forgave it, ... 2:10
1 For if thou wert cut out of the olive tree 11:24	1 or need we, ... epistles of commendation to you, ... 3:1
1 If it be possible, ... live peaceably with all men. 12:18	1 But if the ministration of death, ... 3:7
1 For there is no power but of God: 13:1	1 For if the ministration of condemnation be glory, ... 3:9
1 but to love one another: 13:8	1 For if that which is done away was glorious, ... 3:11
1 and if there be any other commandment, ... 13:9	1 if our gospel be hid, it is hid to them that are lost: 4:3
1 but to him that esteemeth any thing to be unclean, ... 14:14	1 but though our outward man perish, (NT) 4:16
1 But if thy brother be grieved with thy meat, ... 14:15	1 inasmuch as we, having put it on, (NASB) (NT) 5:3
1 For if the Gentiles have been made partakers 15:27	1 that if one died for all, then were all dead: 5:14
1 I baptized none of you, but Crispus and Gaius; ..... 1 Co 1:14	1 yea, though we have known Christ after the flesh, ... 5:16
1 besides, I know not whether I baptized any other. 1:16	1 if any man be in Christ, he is a new creature: 5:17
1 save Jesus Christ, and him crucified. 2:2	1 For though I made you sorry with a letter, ... 7:8
1 for if they had understood it, (NASB) 2:8	1 I do not repent, though I did repent: 7:8
1 save the spirit of man which is in him? 2:11	1 made you sorry, though it were but for a season. 7:8
1 of God knoweth no man, but the Spirit of God. 2:11	1 Wherefore, though I wrote unto you, ... 7:12
1 Now if any man build upon this foundation gold, ... 3:12	1 For if I have boasted any thing to him of you, ... 7:14
1 If any man's work abide which he hath built 3:14	1 For if there be first a willing mind, ... 8:12
1 If any man's work shall be burned, ... 3:15	1 If any man trust to himself that he is Christ's, ... 10:7
1 If any man defile the temple of God, ... 3:17	1 For if he that cometh preacheth another Jesus, ... 11:4
1 If any man among you seemeth to be wise 3:18	1 But though I be rude in speech, ... 11:6
1 now if thou didst receive it, why dost thou glory, ... 4:7	1 no great thing if his ministers also be transformed 11:15
1 and if the world shall be judged by you, ... 6:2	1 if otherwise, yet as a fool receive me, ... 11:16
1 except it be with consent for a time, ... 7:5	1 For ye suffer, if a man bring you into bondage, ... 11:20
1 But if they cannot contain, let them marry: 7:9	1 if a man devour you, if a man take of you, ... 11:20
1 If any brother hath a wife that believeth not, ... 7:12	1 if a man devour you, if a man take of you, ... 11:20
1 And if a woman has a husband (NIV) 7:13	1 if a man exalt himself, ... smite you on the face. 11:20
1 But if the unbelieving depart, let him depart. 7:15	1 if a man smite you on the face. 11:20
1 whether thou shalt save thy husband? 7:16	1 If I must needs glory, I will glory of the things 11:30
1 whether thou shalt save thy wife? 7:16	1 of myself I will not glory, but in mine infirmities. 12:5
1 But as God hath distributed to every man, ... 7:17	1 in nothing am I behind ... though I be nothing. 12:11
1 but if thou mayest be made free, use it rather. 7:21	1 except it be that I myself was not burdensome 12:13
1 But if any man think that he behaveth himself 7:36	1 though the more abundantly I love you, ... 12:15
1 And if any man think that he knoweth any thing, ... 8:2	1 For though he was crucified through weakness, ... 13:4
1 if any man love God, the same is known of him. 8:3	1 Examine yourselves, whether ye be in the faith; 13:5
1 and that there is none other God but one. 8:4	1 that ... Christ is in you, except ye be reprobates? 13:5
1 Wherefore, if meat make my brother to offend, ... 8:13	1 but there be some that trouble you, ... Gal 1:7
1 If I be not an apostle unto others, ... 9:2	1 If any man preach any other gospel unto you 1:9
1 If we have sown unto you spiritual things, ... 9:11	1 do I seek to please men? for if I yet pleased men, ... 1:10
1 a great thing if we shall reap your carnal things? 9:11	1 of the apostles ... save James the Lord's brother. 1:19
1 If others be partakers of this power over you, ... 9:12	1 unto Peter before them all, If thou, being a Jew, ... 2:14
1 For if I do this thing willingly, I have a reward: 9:17	1 But if, while we seek to be justified by Christ, ... 2:17

1 For **if** I build again the things which I destroyed,	Gal 2:18
1 for **if** righteousness come by the law,	2:21
1 For **if** the inheritance be of the law,	3:18
1 for **if** there had been a law given which could	3:21
1 And **if** ye be Christ's, then are ye Abraham's seed,	3:29
1 and **if** a son, then an heir of God through Christ.	4:7
1 for I bear you record, that, **if** it had been possible,	4:15
1 And I, brethren, **if** I yet preach circumcision,	5:11
1 But **if** ye bite and devour one another,	5:15
1 **if** ye be led of the Spirit, ye are not under the law.	5:18
1 **If** we live in the Spirit, let us also walk	5:25
1 For **if** a man think himself to be something,	6:3
1 glory, **save** in the cross of our Lord Jesus Christ,	6:14
1 **if** indeed you have heard (NASB)	Eph 3:2
1 what is it **but** that he also descended first	4:9
1 **if** indeed you have heard Him (NASB)	4:21
1 but **that** which is good to the use of edifying,	4:29
1 **if** I live in the flesh, this is the fruit of my labour:	Phlp 1:22
1 **If** there be therefore any consolation in Christ,	2:1
1 any consolation in Christ, **if** any comfort of love,	2:1
1 any comfort of love, **if** any fellowship of the Spirit,	2:1
1 fellowship of the Spirit, **if** any bowels and mercies,	2:1
1 Yea, and **if** I be offered upon the sacrifice	2:17
1 **If** any other man thinketh that he hath whereof	3:4
1 **If** by any means I might attain	3:11
1 but I follow after, **if** that I may apprehend that	3:12
1 and **if** in any thing ye be otherwise minded,	3:15
1 **if** there be any virtue, and **if** there be any praise,	4:8
1 **if** there be any virtue, and **if** there be any praise,	4:8
1 no church communicated with me ... **but** ye only.	4:15
1 **if** indeed you continue in the faith firmly (NASB)	Col 1:23
1 For **though** I be absent in the flesh,	2:5
1 Wherefore **if** ye be dead with Christ	2:20
1 **If** ye then be risen with Christ,	3:1
1 For **if** we believe that Jesus died and rose again,	1 Th 4:14
1 that **if** any would not work, neither should he eat.	2 Th 3:10
1 And **if** any man obey not our word by this epistle,	3:14
1 **if** there be any ... contrary to sound doctrine;	1 Tm 1:10
1 **If** a man desire the office of a bishop,	3:1
1 For **if** a man know not how to rule his own house,	3:5
1 But **if** any widow have children or nephews,	5:4
1 But **if** any provide not for his own,	5:8
1 **if** she have brought up children,	5:10
1 **if** she have lodged strangers,	5:10
1 **if** she have washed the saints' feet,	5:10
1 **if** she have relieved the afflicted,	5:10
1 **if** she have diligently followed every good work.	5:10
1 **If** any man or woman that believeth have widows,	5:16
1 an accusation, **but** before two or three witnesses.	5:19
1 **If** any man teach otherwise, and consent not	6:3
1 For **if** we be dead with him, we shall also live	2 Tm 2:11
1 **If** we suffer, we shall also reign with him:	2:12
1 **if** we deny him, he also will deny us:	2:12
1 **If** we believe not, yet he abideth faithful:	2:13
1 **If** any be blameless, the husband of one wife,	Tit 1:6
1 **If** thou count me therefore a partner,	Phlm 1:17
1 **If** he hath wronged thee, or oweth thee ought,	1:18
1 For **if** the word spoken by angels was stedfast,	Heb 2:2
1 They shall **not** enter into my rest.	3:11
1 but to them that believed not?	3:18
1 **if** they shall enter into my rest:	4:3
1 in this place again, **If** they shall enter into my rest.	4:5
1 For **if** Jesus had given them rest,	4:8
1 that accompany salvation, **though** we thus speak.	6:9
1 saying, "I will surely bless you (NASB) (NT)	6:14
1 **If** therefore perfection were by the Levitical	7:11
1 **for** that after the similitude of Melchisedec	7:15
1 For **if** he were on earth, he should not be a priest,	8:4
1 For **if** that first covenant had been faultless,	8:7
1 For **if** the blood of bulls and of goats,	9:13
1 truly, **if** they had been mindful of that country	11:15
1 **If** ye endure chastening,	12:7
1 But **if** ye be without chastisement,	12:8
1 For **if** they escaped not who refused him that spake	12:25
1 **If** any of you lack wisdom, let him ask of God,	Jas 1:5
1 For **if** any be a hearer of the word, and not a doer,	1:23
1 **If** any man among you seem to be religious,	1:26
1 **If** ye fulfil the royal law according to the scripture,	Jas 2:8
1 But **if** ye have respect to persons, ye commit sin,	2:9
1 Now **if** thou commit no adultery, yet **if** thou kill,	2:11
1 **If** any man offend not in word, ... is a perfect man,	3:2
1 Now **if** we put the bits into (NASB)	3:3
1 **if** ye have bitter envying and strife in your hearts,	3:14
1 but **if** thou judge the law, thou art not a doer	4:11
1 though now for a season, **if** need be,	1 Pt 1:6
1 And **if** ye call on the Father,	1:17
1 **if** you have tasted the kindness of (NASB)	2:3
1 **if** a man for conscience toward God endure grief,	2:19
1 **if**, when ye be buffeted for your faults,	2:20
1 but **if**, when ye do well, and suffer for it,	2:20
1 that, **if** any obey not the word,	3:1
1 **if** ye suffer for righteousness' sake, happy are ye:	3:14
1 For it is better, **if** the will of God be so,	3:17
1 **If** any man speak,	4:11
1 **if** any man minister,	4:11
1 **If** ye be reproached for the name of Christ,	4:14
1 Yet **if** any man suffer as a Christian,	4:16
1 at the house of God: and **if** it first begin at us,	4:17
1 And **if** the righteous scarcely be saved,	4:18
1 For **if** God spared not the angels that sinned,	2 Pt 2:4
1 For **if** after they have escaped the pollutions	2:20
1 but they were not of us; for **if** they had been of us,	1 Jn 2:19
1 is a liar **but** he that denieth that Jesus is the Christ?	2:22
1 Marvel not, my brethren, **if** the world hate you.	3:13
1 but try the spirits **whether** they are of God:	4:1
1 **if** God so loved us, we ought also to love	4:11
1 but he that believeth that Jesus is the Son of God?	5:5
1 **If** we receive the witness of men,	5:9
1 **If** there come any unto you,	2 Jn 1:10
1 or **else** I will come unto thee quickly,	Rev 2:5
1 Repent; or **else** I will come unto thee quickly,	2:16
1 which no man knoweth **saving** he that receiveth it.	2:17
1 but only those men which have not the seal of God	9:4
1 And **if** any man will hurt them,	11:5
1 **if** any man will hurt them, he must ... be killed.	11:5
1 **If** any man have an ear, let him hear.	13:9
1 **If** anyone is to go into captivity, (NIV)	13:10
1 **if** anyone kills with the sword,	13:10
1 might buy or sell, **save** he that had the mark,	13:17
1 **but** the hundred and forty and four thousand,	14:3
1 **If** any man worship the beast and his image,	14:9
1 and **whosoever** receiveth the mark of his name.	14:11
1 a name written, that no man knew, **but** he himself.	19:12
1 And **whosoever** was not found written in the book	20:15
1 but they which are written in the Lamb's book	21:27

Classical Greek

This conditional particle occurs in all kinds of ancient literature of every period. It has a variety of functions that are determined especially by the mood and tense of the verb, or by the particle's relationship to other words in the sentence. Within such flexible surroundings the word still retains its basic meaning of "if" or "since." The multiple functions stem from this base.

New Testament Usage

The most ordinary use of *ei* is with the indicative mood. Under that condition *ei* can mean "if" with the assumption that what is being asserted is actually true: "If thou be the Son of God ..." (Matthew 4:3; 5:29f.; 6:23; 8:31). In other words, "since you really are the Son of God ..." is the implication of that sentence.

Another function with the indicative mood is the use of *ei* in a "contrary to fact" conditional sentence, when an assumption is being made about something that has not actually taken place. Jesus knows that the Pharisees feel that "if we (the Pharisees) had been in the days of our fathers, we would not have been partakers with them in the blood of the prophets" (Matthew 23:30). Here it is obvious that they could not have actually done it. Likewise, Mary, the sister of Lazarus, laments: "Lord, if (*ei*) you had been here (and You were not), my brother would not have died" (John 11:32, NIV).

Following verbs of emotion and sometimes verbs of knowing, *ei* can mean "that." The following verses could be translated as: "Pilate marveled that (*ei*) he (Jesus) had already died" (Mark 15:44); "Do not be surprised that (*ei*) the world hates you . . ." (1 John 3:13); "I do not know that (*ei*) he is a sinner" (John 9:25).

Ei can also serve as an interrogative particle as the following possible translations show: "Is it lawful (*ei exestin*) on the sabbath days to do good, or to do evil?" (Luke 6:9); "Lord, are (only) few being saved?" (*ei oligoi hoi sōzomenoi*, Luke 13:23). Sometimes the question is indirectly implied by "whether." "Let us see whether Elijah will come," in other words, "Will he come?" (Matthew 27:49).

Not infrequently *ei* combines with other particles. In those cases it assumes a different meaning, for example, *ei kai*, "even if, although"; *ei men oun*, "if then, but"; *ei mē*, "except, but." In association with the indefinite pronoun *tis* (4948), *ei ti* means "everyone who, whoever" (e.g., Luke 9:23; 1 Timothy 3:1).

For a more thorough analysis of the multi-purpose particle *ei*, and for the source of much of the above material, see *Bauer*.

STRONG 1487, BAUER 219-20, MOULTON-MILLIGAN 181-82, LIDDELL-SCOTT 480-81.

1480. εἴγε eige conj
If indeed, inasmuch as.

1. εἴγε eige

1 If so be that being clothed we shall not	2 Co 5:3
1 suffered so many things in vain? if it be yet in vain	Gal 3:4
1 If ye have heard of the dispensation of the grace	Eph 3:2
1 If so be that ye have heard him,	4:21
1 If ye continue in the faith grounded and se⁺tled,	Col 1:23

Eige is actually a combination of the conditional particle *ei*, "if, since," and the enclitic particle *ge* (1058), "whose exact force is difficult to define" (Moule, *Idiom Book of New Testament Greek*, p.164). Generally, however, the effect of *ge* is to emphasize the word with which it is used. Thus, *eige* means "if indeed, that is, inasmuch as." The form *eige* occurs only twice in the Septuagint; the Hebrew in those texts—both in Job—is uncertain.

New Testament Usage

Since early Greek manuscripts of the books of the New Testament were written in *scriptio continua*, that is, there were no spaces left between words or sentences, it is uncertain whether or not *eige* appears at all (cf. *Bauer*). Those texts in which it is thought to appear all belong to Paul (2 Corinthians 5:3; Galatians 3:4; Ephesians 3:2; 4:21; Colossians 1:23). Its meaning in those texts follows the usage outlined above.

STRONG 1489, BAUER 152 (see "ge"), LIDDELL-SCOTT 482.

1480B. εἰδέα eidea noun
Appearance, face.

דְּמוּת d^emûth (1883), Image (Gn 5:3—Codex Alexandrinus only).

1. εἰδέα eidea nom sing fem

1 And his **appearance** was like lightning (NASB)	Matt 28:3

A later form of the Greek term *idea* (2374), this word appears in Matthew 28:3 and means "appearance" or "face." While modern versions such as the NIV use the word "appearance," the KJV describes the angel which sat upon the stone that had blocked Jesus' sepulcher saying, "His *countenance* was like lightning." ("Countenance" is a word often used with respect to faces.) In the Septuagint, Genesis 5:3 reflects a related understanding of the word *eidea*: "And Adam lived a hundred and thirty years, and begat a son in his own *likeness*."

BAUER 220, MOULTON-MILLIGAN 182, KITTEL 2:373-75, LIDDELL-SCOTT 482.

1481. εἶδον eidon verb
Saw, perceived, look after, visit.

COGNATES:
ἀπεῖδον apeidon (538)
εἶδος eidos (1482)
ἐπεῖδον epeidon (1881)
οἶδα oida (3471)
προεῖδον proeidon (4134)
συνείδησις suneidēsis (4743)

εἶδον 1481

συνεῖδον suneidon (4744)
ὑπερεῖδον hupereidon (5074)

SYNONYMS:
ἀναλογίζω analogizō (355)
ἀντιλαμβάνομαι antilambanomai (479)
ἀτενίζω atenizō (810)
βλέπω blepō (984)
βουλεύομαι bouleuomai (1003)
γινώσκω ginōskō (1091)
διαλογίζομαι dialogizomai (1254)
δοκέω dokeō (1374)
ἐμβλέπω emblepō (1676)
ἐνθυμέομαι enthumeomai (1744)
ἐπιβλέπω epiblepō (1899)
ἐπιγινώσκω epiginōskō (1906)
ἐποπτεύω epopteuō (2013)
ἔχω echō (2174)
ἡγέομαι hēgeomai (2216)
θεάομαι theaomai (2277)
θεωρέω theōreō (2311)
κατανοέω katanoeō (2627)
κρίνω krinō (2892)
λογίζομαι logizomai (3023)
νοέω noeō (3401)
νομίζω nomizō (3406)
οἶδα oida (3471)
ὁράω horaō (3571)
σκοπέω skopeō (4503)
συμβάλλω sumballō (4671)
συμβουλεύω sumbouleuō (4674)

אוֹר 'ôr (213), Become bright (1 Sm 14:29).

בּוּר bûr (987B), Consider, reflect (Eccl 9:1 [8:17]).

הִנֵּה hinnēh (2079), Behold (Gn 27:6).

חָזָה chāzâh (2463), See, look (Nm 24:4,16, Jb 36:25, Ez 13:23).

חֲזָה chāzâh (A2464), See, witness (Ezr 4:14, Dn 2:26,41,43, 7:1—Aramaic).

חָלַם chālam (2593), Dream (Gn 37:9, 40:5,8, 41:1,11).

יָדַע yādha' (3156), Qal: know, understand (Ex 33:13, Jos 24:31, 2 Kgs 10:10); piel: cause to know (Jb 38:12); pual: friend (Jb 19:14—Codex Alexandrinus only).

לָקַח lāqach (4089), Bring (2 Kgs 3:15—Codex Alexandrinus only).

מָצָא mātsâ' (4834), Find, obtain (Lam 2:9).

מַרְאָה mar'eh (4920), Form, image (Jos 22:10, Jb 4:16).

נָבַט nāvaṭ (5202), Hiphil: behold, see (Nm 12:8, Jb 6:19, Is 38:11).

פּוּק pûq (6572), Hiphil: finds (Prv 3:13).

צָפָה tsāphâh (7099), Observe attentively, watch (Is 56:10).

רָאָה rā'âh (7495), Qal: see, perceive (Gn 1:10, 1 Chr 10:5, Is 6:1); niphal: appear (Ez 19:11, Dn 8:1); hiphil: let see, show (Jos 5:6, Is 39:4).

1. **εἶδον** eidon 1/3sing/pl indic aor act
2. **εἶδες** eides 2sing indic aor act
3. **εἶδεν** eiden 3sing indic aor act
4. **εἶδε** eide 3sing indic aor act
5. **εἴδομεν** eidomen 1pl indic aor act
6. **εἴδετε** eidete 2pl indic aor act
7. **εἶδαν** eidan 3pl indic aor act
8. **ἴδω** idō 1sing subj aor act
9. **ἴδῃς** idēs 2sing subj aor act
10. **ἴδῃ** idē 3sing subj aor act
11. **ἴδωμεν** idōmen 1pl subj aor act
12. **ἴδητε** idēte 2pl subj aor act
13. **ἴδωσιν** idōsin 3pl subj aor act
14. **ἴδε** ide 2sing impr aor act
15. **ἴδετε** idete 2pl impr aor act
16. **ἰδών** idōn nom sing masc part aor act
17. **ἰδόντες** idontes nom pl masc part aor act
18. **ἰδοῦσα** idousa nom sing fem part aor act
19. **ἰδεῖν** idein inf aor act
20. **ἰδού** idou 2sing impr aor mid
21. **ἴδον** idon 1/3sing/pl indic aor act
22. **ἴδεν** iden 3sing indic aor act
23. **εἴδαμεν** eidamen 1pl indic aor act
24. **ἴδαν** idan 3pl indic aor act

20	But while he thought on these things, **behold**,	Matt 1:20
20	**Behold**, a virgin shall be with child,	1:23
20	**behold**, there came wise men from the east	2:1
5	for **we have seen** his star in the east,	2:2
20	and, **lo**, the star, which they **saw** in the east,	2:9
1	and, **lo**, the star, which **they saw** in the east,	2:9
17	**saw** the star, ... rejoiced with exceeding great joy.	2:10
1	and **saw** the Child with Mary (NASB)	2:11
20	And when they were departed, **behold**,	2:13
16	when he **saw** that he was mocked of the wise men,	2:16
20	**behold**, an angel of the Lord appeareth in a dream	2:19
16	But when he **saw** many of the Pharisees	3:7
20	and, **lo**, the heavens were opened unto him,	3:16
3	he **saw** the Spirit of God descending like a dove,	3:16
20	And **lo** a voice from heaven, saying,	3:17
20	Then the devil leaveth him, and, **behold**,	4:11
4	The people which sat in darkness **saw** great light;	4:16
3	The people which sat in darkness **saw** great light;	4:16
3	walking by the sea of Galilee, **saw** two brethren,	4:18
3	he **saw** other two brethren, James ... and John	4:21
16	**seeing** the multitudes, he went up into a mountain:	5:1
13	that **they may see** your good works,	5:16
20	and, **behold**, a beam is in thine own eye?	7:4
20	And, **behold**, there came a leper and worshipped	8:2
3	he **saw** his wife's mother laid, and sick of a fever.	8:14
16	Now when Jesus **saw** great multitudes about him,	8:18
20	And, **behold**, there arose a great tempest in the sea,	8:24
20	And, **behold**, they cried out, saying,	8:29
20	and, **behold**, the ... swine ran violently down	8:32
20	**behold**, the whole city came out to meet Jesus:	8:34
17	the whole city came out ... and when they **saw** him,	8:34
20	And, **behold**, they brought to him a man sick	9:2
16	and Jesus **seeing** their faith said unto the sick	9:2
20	And, **behold**, certain of the scribes said	9:3
16	And Jesus **knowing** their thoughts said,	9:4
17	But when the multitude **saw** it, they marvelled,	9:8
3	he **saw** a man, named Matthew,	9:9
20	**behold**, many publicans and sinners came	9:10
17	And when the Pharisees **saw** it,	9:11
20	**behold**, there came a certain ruler,	9:18
20	And, **behold**, a woman, which was diseased	9:20
16	But Jesus turned him about, and when he **saw** her,	9:22
16	**saw** the minstrels and the people making a noise,	9:23
20	**behold**, they brought to him a dumb man	9:32
16	But when he **saw** the multitudes,	9:36
20	**Behold**, I send you forth as sheep	10:16
19	But what went ye out **for to see**?	11:8
20	**behold**, ... wear soft clothing are in kings' houses.	11:8
19	But what went ye out **for to see**? A prophet?	11:9
20	**Behold**, I send my messenger before thy face,	11:10
20	**Behold** a man gluttonous, and a winebibber,	11:19

εἶδον 1481

17	But when the Pharisees **saw** it, they said unto him, Matt	12:2
20	**Behold**, thy disciples do that which is not lawful	12:2
20	And, **behold**, ... man which had his hand withered	12:10
20	**Behold** my servant, whom I have chosen;	12:18
16	Jesus **knew** their thoughts, and said unto them,	12:25
19	saying, Master, we would **see** a sign from thee	12:38
20	and, **behold**, a greater than Jonas is here	12:41
20	and, **behold**, a greater than Solomon is here	12:42
20	**behold**, his mother and his brethren stood without,	12:46
20	**Behold** thy mother and my brethren	12:47
20	**Behold** my mother and my brethren!	12:49
20	saying, **Behold**, a sower went forth to sow;	13:3
12	and seeing ye shall see, and shall not **perceive:**	13:14
13	lest at any time **they should see** with their eyes	13:15
19	have desired to **see** those things which ye see,	13:17
1	many ... desired to see ... and **have not seen** them;	13:17
7	many ... desired to see ... and **have not seen** them;	13:17
24	many ... desired to see ... and **have not seen** them;	13:17
3	And Jesus went forth, and **saw** a great multitude,	14:14
17	And when the disciples **saw** him walking on the sea,	14:26
20	And, **behold**, a woman of Canaan came	15:22
13	till **they see** the Son of man coming in his kingdom	16:28
20	And, **behold**, there appeared unto them Moses and	17:3
20	**behold**, a bright cloud overshadowed them:	17:5
20	and **behold** a voice out of the cloud, which said,	17:5
1	they **saw** no man, save Jesus only	17:8
17	So when his fellowservants **saw** what was done,	18:31
20	**behold**, one came and said unto him, Good Master,	19:16
20	**Behold**, we have forsaken all, and followed thee;	19:27
3	and **saw** others standing idle in the marketplace,	20:3
20	**Behold**, we go up to Jerusalem;	20:18
20	**behold**, two blind men sitting by the way side,	20:30
20	**Behold**, thy King cometh unto thee,	21:5
17	And when the chief priests and scribes **saw**	21:15
16	when he **saw** a fig tree in the way, he came to it,	21:19
17	And when the disciples **saw** it, they marvelled,	21:20
17	and ye, when ye **had seen** it, repented not	21:32
17	But when the husbandmen **saw** the son,	21:38
20	**Behold**, I have prepared my dinner:	22:4
3	he **saw** there a man ... not on a wedding garment:	22:11
20	Wherefore, **behold**, I send unto you prophets,	23:34
20	**Behold**, your house is left unto you desolate	23:38
12	Ye **shall** not **see** me henceforth, till ye shall say,	23:39
12	therefore **shall see** the abomination of desolation,	24:15
20	if any man shall say unto you, **Lo**, here is Christ;	24:23
20	**Behold**, I have told you before	24:25
20	**Behold**, he is in the desert; go not forth:	24:26
20	**behold**, he is in the secret chambers; believe it not	24:26
12	So likewise ye, when ye **shall see** all these things,	24:33
20	**Behold**, the bridegroom cometh;	25:6
14	**behold**, I have gained beside them five talents	25:20
14	**behold**, I have gained two other talents beside	25:22
14	afraid, ... **lo**, there thou hast that is thine	25:25
5	when **saw** we thee an hungered, and fed thee?	25:37
23	when **saw** we thee an hungered, and fed thee?	25:37
5	When **saw** we thee a stranger, and took thee in?	25:38
5	**saw** we thee sick, or in prison, and came unto thee?	25:39
5	Lord, when **saw** we thee an hungered, or athirst,	25:44
17	But when his disciples **saw** it, they had indignation,	26:8
20	**behold**, the hour is at hand,	26:45
20	**behold**, he is at hand that doth betray me	26:46
20	**lo**, Judas, one of the twelve, came,	26:47
20	And, **behold**, one of them which were with Jesus	26:51
19	went in, and sat with the servants, **to see** the end	26:58
14	**behold**, now ye have heard his blasphemy	26:65
3	gone out into the porch, another maid **saw** him,	26:71
16	Judas, ... when he **saw** that he was condemned,	27:3
16	When Pilate **saw** that he could prevail nothing,	27:24
11	**let us see** whether Elias will come to save him,	27:49
20	**behold**, the veil of the temple was rent in twain	27:51
17	**saw** the earthquake, and those things ... were done,	27:54
20	And, **behold**, there was a great earthquake:	28:2
15	Come, **see** the place where the Lord lay	28:6
20	and, **behold**, he goeth before you into Galilee;	28:7
20	there shall ye see him: **lo**, I have told you	28:7
20	**behold**, Jesus met them, saying, All hail	28:9
20	**behold**, some of the watch came into the city,	28:11
17	And when they **saw** him, they worshipped him: Matt	28:17
20	and, **lo**, I am with you alway,	28:20
20	**Behold**, I send my messenger before thy face, Mark	1:2
3	he **saw** the heavens opened, and the Spirit	1:10
3	he **saw** Simon and Andrew his brother	1:16
3	he **saw** James the son of Zebedee, and John	1:19
16	When Jesus **saw** their faith, he said unto the sick	2:5
5	saying, We never **saw** it on this fashion	2:12
23	saying, We never **saw** it on this fashion	2:12
3	he **saw** Levi the son of Alphaeus sitting	2:14
17	And when the scribes and Pharisees **saw** him eat	2:16
14	**Behold**, why do they on the sabbath day	2:24
20	**Behold**, thy mother and thy brethren without	3:32
14	and said, **Behold** my mother and my brethren!	3:34
20	and said, **Behold** my mother and my brethren!	3:34
20	Hearken; **Behold**, there went out a sower to sow:	4:3
13	That seeing they may see, and not **perceive**;	4:12
16	he **saw** Jesus afar off and ran and worshipped him,	5:6
19	And they went out **to see** what it was that was done,	5:14
17	And they **that saw** it told them how it befell to him	5:16
20	And, **behold**, there cometh one of the rulers	5:22
16	Jairus ... and when he **saw** him, he fell at his feet,	5:22
19	And he looked round about **to see** her	5:32
1	people **saw** them departing, and many knew him,	6:33
3	And Jesus, when he came out, **saw** much people,	6:34
15	How many loaves have ye? go and **see**	6:38
3	And he **saw** them toiling in rowing;	6:48
16	And he **saw** them toiling in rowing;	6:48
17	But when they **saw** him walking upon the sea,	6:49
1	For they all **saw** him, and were troubled	6:50
7	For they all **saw** him, and were troubled	6:50
17	And when they **saw** some of his disciples eat bread	7:2
16	he had turned about and **looked on** his disciples,	8:33
13	till they **have seen** the kingdom of God come	9:1
1	they **saw** no man any more, save Jesus only	9:8
1	they should tell no man what things they **had seen**,	9:9
3	he **saw** a great multitude about them,	9:14
1	they **saw** a large crowd around them (NASB)	9:14
16	when they **beheld** him, were greatly amazed,	9:15
17	when they **beheld** him, were greatly amazed,	9:15
16	when he **saw** him, straightway the spirit tare him;	9:20
16	Jesus **saw** that the people came running together,	9:25
5	Master, **we saw** one casting out devils in thy name,	9:38
16	when Jesus **saw** it, he was much displeased,	10:14
20	**Lo**, we have left all, and have followed thee	10:28
20	Saying, **Behold**, we go up to Jerusalem;	10:33
16	And **seeing** a fig tree afar off having leaves,	11:13
1	they **saw** the fig tree dried up from the roots	11:20
14	Master, **behold**, the fig tree which thou cursedst	11:21
16	But he, **knowing** their hypocrisy, said unto them,	12:15
8	bring me a penny, that **I may see** it	12:15
16	**recognizing** that He had answered them (NASB)	12:28
16	And when Jesus **saw** that he answered discreetly,	12:34
14	**see** what manner of stones and what buildings	13:1
12	when ye **shall see** the abomination of desolation,	13:14
20	if any man shall say to you, **Lo**, here is Christ;	13:21
14	if any man shall say to you, **Lo**, here is Christ;	13:21
20	or, **lo**, he is there; believe him not:	13:21
14	or, **lo**, he is there; believe him not:	13:21
20	**behold**, I have foretold you all things	13:23
12	when ye **shall see** these things come to pass,	13:29
20	the hour is come; **behold**, the Son of man is betrayed	14:41
20	let us go; **lo**, he that betrayeth me is at hand	14:42
18	And when she **saw** Peter warming himself,	14:67
18	a maid **saw** him again, and began to say to them	14:69
14	**behold** how many things they witness against thee	15:4
11	from the cross, that we **may see** and believe	15:32
20	when they heard it, said, **Behold**, he calleth Elias	15:35
14	when they heard it, said, **Behold**, he calleth Elias	15:35
11	Let alone; **let us see** whether Elias will come	15:36
16	**saw** that he so cried out, and gave up the ghost,	15:39
1	they **saw** a young man sitting on the right side,	16:5
14	is not here: **behold** the place where they laid him	16:6
16	And when Zacharias **saw** him, he was troubled, Luke	1:12
20	**behold**, thou shalt be dumb, and not able to speak,	1:20
18	when she **saw** him, she was troubled at his saying,	1:29
20	And, **behold**, thou shalt conceive in thy womb,	1:31

241

εἶδον 1481

#	Text	Ref
20	And, **behold,** thy cousin Elisabeth, she hath also...	Luke 1:36
20	And Mary said, **Behold** the handmaid of the Lord;	1:38
20	**lo,** as soon as the voice of thy salutation sounded	1:44
20	for, **behold,** from henceforth all generations	1:48
20	And, **lo,** the angel of the Lord came upon them,	2:9
20	**behold,** I bring you good tidings of great joy,	2:10
11	and **see** this thing which is come to pass,	2:15
17	when they **had seen** it, they made known abroad	2:17
1	for all the things that they had heard and **seen,**	2:20
21	for all the things that they had heard and **seen,**	2:20
20	And, **behold,** there was a man in Jerusalem,	2:25
19	revealed unto him ... that he should not **see** death,	2:26
10	before he **had seen** the Lord's Christ.	2:26
1	For mine eyes **have seen** thy salvation,	2:30
20	**Behold,** this child is set for the fall and rising again	2:34
17	And when they **saw** him, they were amazed:	2:48
20	**behold,** thy father and I have sought thee	2:48
3	And **saw** two ships standing by the lake:	5:2
22	And **saw** two ships standing by the lake:	5:2
16	Simon Peter **saw** it, he fell down at Jesus' knees,	5:8
20	was in a certain city, **behold** a man full of leprosy:	5:12
16	who **seeing** Jesus fell on his face,	5:12
20	And, **behold,** men brought in a bed a man	5:18
16	And when he **saw** their faith, he said unto him,	5:20
5	saying, We **have seen** strange things to day.	5:26
20	for, **behold,** your reward is great in heaven:	6:23
20	**behold,** there was a dead man carried out,	7:12
16	when the Lord **saw** her, he had compassion on her,	7:13
6	and tell John what things ye **have seen** and heard;	7:22
19	But what went ye out for to **see?**	7:25
20	**Behold,** they which were gorgeously apparelled,	7:25
19	But what went ye out for to **see?** A prophet? Yea,	7:26
20	**Behold,** I send my messenger before thy face,	7:27
20	**Behold** a gluttonous man, and a winebibber,	7:34
20	**behold,** a woman in the city, which was a sinner,	7:37
16	Now when the Pharisee which had bidden him **saw**	7:39
19	thy brethren stand without, desiring to **see** thee.	8:20
16	When he **saw** Jesus, he cried out, and fell down	8:28
17	When they that fed them **saw** what was done,	8:34
19	Then they went out to **see** what was done;	8:35
17	They also which **saw** it told them by what means	8:36
20	And, **behold,** there came a man named Jairus,	8:41
18	And when the woman **saw** that she was not hid,	8:47
19	hear such things? And he desired to **see** him.	9:9
13	not taste of death, till they **see** the kingdom of God.	9:27
20	And, **behold,** there talked with him two men,	9:30
1	and when they were awake, they **saw** his glory,	9:32
7	and when they were awake, they **saw** his glory,	9:32
20	And, **behold,** a man of the company cried out,	9:38
20	**lo,** a spirit taketh him, and he suddenly crieth out;	9:39
16	And Jesus, **perceiving** the thought of their heart,	9:47
5	Master, we **saw** one casting out devils in thy name;	9:49
17	And when his disciples James and John **saw** this,	9:54
20	**behold,** I send you forth as lambs among wolves.	10:3
20	**Behold,** I give unto you power to tread on serpents	10:19
19	that many prophets and kings have desired to **see**	10:24
1	have desired to **see** ... and **have not seen** them;	10:24
24	have desired to **see** ... and **have not seen** them;	10:24
7	have desired to **see** ... and **have not seen** them;	10:24
20	And, **behold,** a certain lawyer stood up,	10:25
16	when he **saw** him, he passed by on the other side.	10:31
16	**looked** on him, and passed by on the other side.	10:32
16	and when he **saw** him, he had compassion on him,	10:33
20	and, **behold,** a greater than Solomon is here.	11:31
20	and, **behold,** a greater than Jonas is here.	11:32
16	And when the Pharisee **saw** it, he marvelled	11:38
20	and, **behold,** all things are clean unto you.	11:41
12	When ye **see** a cloud rise out of the west,	12:54
20	**Behold,** these three years I come seeking fruit	13:7
20	**behold,** there was a woman which had a spirit	13:11
16	And when Jesus **saw** her, he called her to him,	13:12
20	**lo,** these eighteen years, be loosed from this bond,	13:16
20	And, **behold,** there are last which shall be first,	13:30
20	and tell that fox, **Behold,** I cast out devils,	13:32
20	**Behold,** your house is left unto you desolate:	13:35
12	and verily I say unto you, Ye **shall** not **see** me,	13:35
20	And, **behold,** there was a certain man before him	14:2
19	bought ... ground, and I must needs go and **see** it:	Luke 14:18
3	his father **saw** him, and had compassion, and ran,	15:20
20	**Lo,** these many years do I serve thee,	15:29
16	And when he **saw** them, he said unto them,	17:14
16	And one of them, when he **saw** that he was healed,	17:15
20	Neither shall they say, **Lo** here! or, **lo** there!	17:21
20	Neither shall they say, **Lo** here! or, **lo** there!	17:21
20	for, **behold,** the kingdom of God is within you.	17:21
19	when ye shall desire **to see** one of the days	17:22
20	**See** here; or, **see** there: go not after them,	17:23
20	or, **see** there: go not after them, nor follow them.	17:23
17	but when his disciples **saw** it, they rebuked them.	18:15
16	And when Jesus **saw** that he was very sorrowful,	18:24
20	Peter said, **Lo,** we have left all, and followed thee.	18:28
20	said unto them, **Behold,** we go up to Jerusalem,	18:31
16	people, when they **saw** it, gave praise unto God.	18:43
20	And, **behold,** there was a man named Zacchaeus,	19:2
19	And he sought **to see** Jesus who he was;	19:3
10	and climbed up into a sycamore tree to **see** him:	19:4
3	he looked up, and **saw** him, and said unto him,	19:5
17	And when they **saw** it, they all murmured, saying,	19:7
20	**Behold,** Lord, the half of my goods I give	19:8
20	Lord, **behold,** here is thy pound, which I have kept	19:20
1	for all the mighty works that they **had seen,**	19:37
16	come near, he **beheld** the city, and wept over it,	19:41
17	they will reverence him when they **see** him.	20:13
17	But when the husbandmen **saw** him,	20:14
3	he looked up, and **saw** the rich men casting their gifts	21:1
3	he **saw** also a certain poor widow casting in thither	21:2
12	ye **shall see** Jerusalem compassed with armies,	21:20
15	he spake to them a parable; **Behold** the fig tree,	21:29
12	likewise ye, when ye **see** these things come to pass,	21:31
20	**Behold,** when ye are entered into the city,	22:10
20	But, **behold,** the hand of him that betrayeth me	22:21
20	Simon, **behold,** Satan hath desired to have you,	22:31
20	And they said, Lord, **behold,** here are two swords;	22:38
20	**behold** a multitude, and he that was called Judas,	22:47
17	they which were about him **saw** what would follow,	22:49
18	But a certain maid **beheld** him as he sat by the fire,	22:56
16	And after a little while another **saw** him, and said,	22:58
16	when Herod **saw** Jesus, he was exceeding glad:	23:8
19	for he was desirous **to see** him of a long season,	23:8
19	he hoped to **have seen** some miracle done by him.	23:8
20	and, **behold,** I, having examined him before you,	23:14
20	and, **lo,** nothing worthy of death is done unto him.	23:15
20	For, **behold,** the days are coming, ... they shall say,	23:29
16	Now when the centurion **saw** what was done,	23:47
20	And, **behold,** there was a man named Joseph,	23:50
20	as they were much perplexed thereabout, **behold,**	24:4
20	And, **behold,** two of them went that same day	24:13
1	went to the sepulchre, ... but him they **saw** not.	24:24
15	**Behold** my hands and my feet, that it is I myself:	24:39
15	and **see;** for a spirit hath not flesh and bones,	24:39
20	And, **behold,** I send the promise of my Father	24:49
14	**Behold** the Lamb of God, ... taketh away the sin	John 1:29
9	Upon whom thou shalt **see** the Spirit descending,	1:33
14	looking upon Jesus ... **Behold** the Lamb of God!	1:36
15	He saith unto them, Come and **see.**	1:39
1	They came and **saw** where he dwelt,	1:39
7	They came and **saw** where he dwelt,	1:39
14	Philip saith unto him, Come and **see.**	1:46
3	Jesus **saw** Nathanael coming to him,	1:47
14	**Behold** an Israelite indeed, in whom is no guile!	1:47
1	when thou wast under the fig tree, I **saw** thee.	1:48
1	I **saw** thee under the fig tree, believest thou?	1:50
19	he cannot **see** the kingdom of God.	3:3
14	to whom thou barest witness, **behold,**	3:26
15	**see** a man, which told me all things that ever I did:	4:29
20	**behold,** I say unto you, Lift up your eyes,	4:35
12	Except ye **see** signs and wonders, ye ... not believe.	4:48
16	When Jesus **saw** him lie,	5:6
14	and said unto him, **Behold,** thou art made whole;	5:14
17	when they **had seen** the miracle that Jesus did,	6:14
16	**saw** that there was none other boat there,	6:22
1	**saw** that there was none other boat there,	6:22
3	the people therefore **saw** that Jesus was not there,	6:24
6	Ye seek me, not because ye **saw** the miracles,	6:26

εἶδον 1481

11	What sign showest thou then, that we **may see**,.... John	6:30
14	But, **lo**, he speaketh boldly,.........................	7:26
14	Art thou also of Galilee? Search, and **look**:..........	7:52
10	Your father Abraham rejoiced **to see** my day:.........	8:56
3	and he **saw** it, and was glad.........................	8:56
3	he **saw** a man which was blind from his birth..........	9:1
14	Lord, **behold**, he whom thou lovest is sick............	11:3
17	when they **saw** Mary, that she rose up hastily.........	11:31
18	Mary was come where Jesus was, and **saw** him,.......	11:32
3	When Jesus therefore **saw** her weeping,...............	11:33
14	They said unto him, Lord, come and **see**.............	11:34
14	Then said the Jews, **Behold** how he loved him!.......	11:36
13	but that they **might see** Lazarus also,.................	12:9
20	**behold**, thy King cometh, sitting on an ass's colt.....	12:15
14	**behold**, the world is gone after him....................	12:19
19	and desired him, saying, Sir, we would **see** Jesus......	12:21
13	that they **should** not **see** with their eyes,.........	12:40
3	These things said Esaias, when he **saw** his glory,.....	12:41
14	**Lo**, now speakest thou plainly,.......................	16:29
20	**Behold**, the hour cometh, yea, is now come,..........	16:32
14	**behold**, they know what I said.......................	18:21
1	saith, Did not I **see** thee in the garden with him?.....	18:26
14	saith unto them, **Behold**, I bring him forth to you,...	19:4
14	And Pilate saith unto them, **Behold** the man!........	19:5
20	And Pilate saith unto them, **Behold** the man!........	19:5
1	the chief priests therefore and officers **saw** him,......	19:6
21	the chief priests therefore and officers **saw** him,.....	19:6
14	and he saith unto the Jews, **Behold** your King!......	19:14
16	When Jesus therefore **saw** his mother,................	19:26
20	he saith unto his mother, Woman, **behold** thy son!...	19:26
14	he saith unto his mother, Woman, **behold** thy son!...	19:26
20	Then saith he to the disciple, **Behold** thy mother!.....	19:27
14	Then saith he to the disciple, **Behold** thy mother!.....	19:27
1	came to Jesus, and **saw** that he was dead already,....	19:33
3	that other disciple, ... and he **saw**, and believed......	20:8
17	were the disciples glad, when they **saw** the Lord.....	20:20
8	Except I **shall see** in his hands the print of ... nails,...	20:25
14	Reach hither thy finger, and **behold** my hands;.......	20:27
17	blessed are they that **have** not **seen**,.................	20:29
16	Peter **seeing** him saith to Jesus,.......................	21:21
20	**behold**, two men stood by them in white apparel;...Acts	1:10
20	**Behold**, are not all these which speak Galilaeans?.....	2:7
19	wilt thou suffer thine Holy One **to see** corruption.....	2:27
3	neither his flesh **did see** corruption....................	2:31
16	**seeing** Peter and John about to go into the temple....	3:3
3	all the people **saw** him walking and praising God:.....	3:9
16	And when Peter **saw** it, he answered..................	3:12
5	speak the things which we **have seen** and heard.......	4:20
23	speak the things which we **have seen** and heard.......	4:20
20	**behold**, the feet of them which have buried...........	5:9
20	Then came one and told them, saying, **Behold**,......	5:25
20	and, **behold**, ye have filled Jerusalem.................	5:28
1	saw his face as it had been the face of an angel........	6:15
7	saw his face as it had been the face of an angel........	6:15
16	**seeing** one of them suffer wrong, he defended him,...	7:24
16	When Moses **saw** it, he wondered at the sight:........	7:31
16	**I have seen**, I have seen the affliction of my people...	7:34
1	I have seen, **I have seen** the affliction of my people....	7:34
3	stedfastly into heaven, and **saw** the glory of God,.....	7:55
20	And said, **Behold**, I see the heavens opened,.........	7:56
16	Now when Simon **saw** that the Spirit (NASB)........	8:18
20	he arose and went: and, **behold**, a man of Ethiopia,...	8:27
20	**See**, here is water; what doth hinder me..............	8:36
3	away Philip, that the eunuch **saw** him no more:......	8:39
20	Ananias. And he said, **Behold**, I am here, Lord.......	9:10
20	one called Saul, of Tarsus: for, **behold**, he prayeth,....	9:11
3	And **hath seen** in a vision a man named Ananias......	9:12
3	and declared unto them how he **had seen** the Lord.....	9:27
1	And all that dwelt at Lydda and Saron **saw** him,......	9:35
7	And all that dwelt at Lydda and Saron **saw** him,......	9:35
18	And she opened her eyes: and when she **saw** Peter,...	9:40
3	He **saw** in a vision evidently about the ninth hour.....	10:3
3	what this vision which he **had seen** should mean,.....	10:17
20	**behold**, the men which were sent from Cornelius......	10:17
20	Spirit said unto him, **Behold**, three men seek thee....	10:19
20	and said, **Behold**, I am he whom ye seek:.............	10:21
20	**behold**, a man stood before me in bright clothing,....	10:30

1	and in a trance I **saw** a vision,.................... Acts	11:5
1	and **saw** fourfooted beasts of the earth,................	11:6
20	And, **behold**, immediately there were three men......	11:11
3	showed us how he **had seen** an angel in his house,....	11:13
16	when he came, and **had seen** the grace of God,.......	11:23
16	And because he **saw** it pleased the Jews,..............	12:3
20	**behold**, the angel of the Lord came upon him,........	12:7
1	and when they had opened the door, and **saw** him,...	12:16
7	and when they had opened the door, and **saw** him,...	12:16
20	now, **behold**, the hand of the Lord is upon thee,......	13:11
16	when he **saw** what was done, believed,................	13:12
20	But, **behold**, there cometh one after me,..............	13:25
19	shalt not suffer thine Holy One **to see** corruption.....	13:35
3	and was laid unto his fathers, and **saw** corruption:....	13:36
3	he, whom God raised again, **saw** no corruption.......	13:37
15	**Behold**, ye despisers, and wonder, and perish:........	13:41
17	But when the Jews **saw** the multitudes,...............	13:45
20	**lo**, we turn to the Gentiles.............................	13:46
16	and **perceiving** that he had faith to be healed,........	14:9
17	And when the people **saw** what Paul had done,......	14:11
19	elders came together for **to consider** of this matter....	15:6
20	and, **behold**, a certain disciple was there,.............	16:1
3	And after he **had seen** the vision,.....................	16:10
17	masters **saw** that the hope of their gains was gone,...	16:19
16	and **seeing** the prison doors open,.....................	16:27
17	and when they **had seen** the brethren,................	16:40
19	After I have been there, I must also see Rome........	19:21
20	**behold**, I go bound in the spirit unto Jerusalem,......	20:22
20	And now, **behold**, I know that ye all,.................	20:25
17	when they **saw** the chief captain and the soldiers,.....	21:32
19	shouldest know his will, and **see** that Just One,.......	22:14
19	And **saw** him saying unto me, Make haste,...........	22:18
1	I **saw** in the way a light from heaven,................	26:13
2	a witness both of these things which thou **hast seen**,..	26:16
20	and, **lo**, God hath given thee all them that sail.......	27:24
1	And when the barbarians **saw** the venomous beast....	28:4
16	whom when Paul **saw**, he thanked God,..............	28:15
19	**to see** you, and to speak with you:....................	28:20
12	and seeing ye shall **see**, and shall not **perceive**:..........	28:26
13	lest they **should see** with their eyes,...................	28:27
19	For I long **to see** you, that I may impart unto you..Rom	1:11
14	**Behold**, thou art called a Jew,........................	2:17
20	it is written, **Behold**, I lay in Sion a stumblingstone,...	9:33
14	**Behold** therefore the goodness and severity...........	11:22
3	as it is written, Eye hath not **seen**, nor ear heard,.. 1 Co	2:9
10	For if any man **see** thee which hast knowledge........	8:10
20	**Behold**, I show you a mystery;.......................	15:51
19	For I will not see you now by the way;...............	16:7
20	**behold**, all things are become new................. 2 Co	5:17
20	**behold**, now is the accepted time;.....................	6:2
20	**behold**, now is the day of salvation...................	6:2
20	as dying, and, **behold**, we live;........................	6:9
20	For **behold** this selfsame thing,........................	7:11
20	**Behold**, the third time I am ready to come to you;...	12:14
1	But other of the apostles **saw** I none, save James... Gal	1:19
20	**behold**, before God, I lie not...........................	1:20
17	But contrariwise, when they **saw** that the gospel.......	2:7
1	But when **I saw** that they walked not uprightly.......	2:14
14	**Behold**, I Paul say unto you,..........................	5:2
15	Ye see how large a letter I have written unto you,.....	6:11
16	that whether I come and **see** you, or else be absent, Phlp	1:27
15	Having the same conflict which ye **saw** in me,........	1:30
6	Having the same conflict which ye **saw** in me,........	1:30
19	he longed after you all, and was full of heaviness,.....	2:26
17	that, when ye **see** him again, ye may rejoice,..........	2:28
6	Those things, ... and heard, and **seen** in me, do:......	4:9
19	endeavoured the more abundantly **to see** your face 1 Th	2:17
19	desiring greatly **to see** us, as we also to see you:......	3:6
19	praying exceedingly that we **might see** your face,.....	3:10
3	whom no man **hath seen**, nor can see:............. 1 Tm	6:16
19	whom no man hath seen, nor can see:.................	6:16
19	Greatly desiring to see thee,....................... 2 Tm	1:4
20	And again, **Behold** I and the children............. Heb	2:13
1	proved me, and **saw** my works forty years............	3:9
20	**Behold**, the days come, saith the Lord,...............	8:8
20	Then said I, **Lo**, I come.............................	10:7
20	Then said he, **Lo**, I come to do thy will, O God......	10:9

243

εἶδον 1481

19	Enoch was translated that he should not **see** death;	Heb 11:5
17	but **having seen** them afar off,	11:13
1	because **they saw** he was a proper child;	11:23
20	**Behold**, we put bits in the horses' mouths,	Jas 3:3
20	**Behold** also the ships, which ... be so great,	3:4
20	**Behold**, how great a matter a little fire	3:5
20	**Behold**, the hire of the labourers who have reaped	5:4
20	**Behold**, the husbandman waiteth	5:7
20	**behold**, the judge standeth before the door.	5:9
20	**Behold**, we count them happy which endure.	5:11
6	and **have seen** the end of the Lord;	5:11
15	and **have seen** the end of the Lord;	5:11
17	and though you have not **seen** Him, (NASB)	1 Pt 1:8
20	**Behold**, I lay in Sion a chief corner stone,	2:6
19	For he that will love life, and **see** good days,	3:10
15	**Behold**, what manner of love the Father hath	1 Jn 3:1
10	**see** his brother sin a sin which is not unto death,	5:16
19	But I trust I shall shortly **see** thee,	3 Jn 1:14
20	**Behold**, the Lord cometh with ten thousands	Jude 1:14
3	testimony of Jesus ... and of all things that he **saw**.	Rev 1:2
20	**Behold**, he cometh with clouds;	1:7
1	And being turned, **I saw** seven golden candlesticks;	1:12
1	And when **I saw** him, I fell at his feet as dead.	1:17
20	and, **behold**, I am alive for evermore, Amen;	1:18
2	Write the things which thou **hast seen**,	1:19
2	The mystery of the seven stars which thou **sawest**	1:20
2	and the seven candlesticks which thou **sawest**	1:20
20	**behold**, the devil shall cast some ... into prison,	2:10
20	**Behold**, I will cast her into a bed,	2:22
20	**behold**, I have set before thee an open door,	3:8
20	**Behold**, I will make them of the synagogue	3:9
20	**behold**, I will make them to come and worship	3:9
20	**Behold**, I come quickly: hold that fast	3:11
20	**Behold**, I stand at the door, and knock:	3:20
1	After this **I looked**, and, **behold**,	4:1
20	and, **behold**, a door was opened in heaven:	4:1
20	and, **behold**, a throne was set in heaven,	4:2
1	upon the seats **I saw** four and twenty elders sitting,	4:4
1	**saw** in the right hand of him that sat on the throne	5:1
1	**I saw** a strong angel proclaiming with a loud voice,	5:2
20	**behold**, the Lion of the tribe of Juda,	5:5
1	And **I beheld**, and, lo, in the midst of the throne	5:6
20	And **I beheld**, and, lo, in the midst of the throne	5:6
1	And **I beheld**, and I heard the voice of many angels	5:11
1	And **I saw** when the Lamb opened one of the seals,	6:1
1	And **I saw**, and behold a white horse:	6:2
20	And I saw, and **behold** a white horse:	6:2
1	And **I beheld**, and lo a black horse;	6:5
20	And I beheld, and **lo** a black horse;	6:5
1	And **I looked**, and behold a pale horse:	6:8
20	And I looked, and **behold** a pale horse:	6:8
1	**I saw** under the altar the souls of them	6:9
1	And **I beheld** when he had opened the sixth seal,	6:12
20	and, **lo**, there was a great earthquake;	6:12
1	And after these things **I saw** four angels	7:1
1	And **I saw** another angel ascending from the east,	7:2
1	After this **I beheld**, and, lo, a great multitude,	7:9
20	After this I beheld, and, **lo**, a great multitude,	7:9
1	**I saw** the seven angels which stood before God;	8:2
1	And **I beheld**, and heard an angel flying	8:13
1	and **I saw** a star fall from heaven unto the earth:	9:1
20	and, **behold**, there come two woes more hereafter.	9:12
1	And thus **I saw** the horses in the vision,	9:17
1	And **I saw** another mighty angel come down	10:1
1	And the angel which **I saw** stand upon the sea	10:5
20	and, **behold**, the third woe cometh quickly.	11:14
1	wonder in heaven; and **behold** a great red dragon,	12:3
3	the dragon **saw** that he was cast unto the earth,	12:13
1	and **saw** a beast rise up out of the sea,	13:1
1	And the beast which **I saw** was like unto a leopard,	13:2
1	**saw** one of his heads as it were wounded to death;	13:3
1	**I beheld** another beast coming up out of the earth;	13:11
1	**I looked**, and, lo, a Lamb stood on the mount	14:1
20	and, **lo**, a Lamb stood on the mount Sion.	14:1
1	And **I saw** another angel fly in the midst of heaven,	14:6
1	And **I looked**, and behold a white cloud,	14:14
20	And I looked, and **behold** a white cloud,	14:14
1	**saw** another sign in heaven, great and marvellous,	Rev 15:1
1	**I saw** as it were a sea of glass mingled with fire:	15:2
1	And after that **I looked**, and, behold, the temple	15:5
20	and, **behold**, the temple of the tabernacle	15:5
1	**I saw** three unclean spirits like frogs come out of	16:13
20	**Behold**, I come as a thief.	16:15
1	**I saw** a woman sit upon a scarlet coloured beast,	17:3
1	And **I saw** the woman drunken with the blood	17:6
16	when **I saw** her, I wondered with great admiration.	17:6
2	The beast that thou **sawest** was, and is not;	17:8
2	And the ten horns which thou **sawest** are ten kings,	17:12
2	waters which thou **sawest**, where the whore sitteth,	17:15
2	the ten horns which thou **sawest** upon the beast,	17:16
2	the woman which thou **sawest** is that great city,	17:18
1	**I saw** another angel come down from heaven,	18:1
8	queen, and am no widow, and **shall see** no sorrow.	18:7
1	**I saw** heaven opened, and behold a white horse;	19:11
20	I saw heaven opened, and **behold** a white horse;	19:11
1	And **I saw** an angel standing in the sun;	19:17
1	And **I saw** the beast, and the kings of the earth,	19:19
1	And **I saw** an angel come down from heaven,	20:1
1	And **I saw** thrones, and they sat upon them,	20:4
1	**I saw** a great white throne, and him that sat on it,	20:11
1	And **I saw** the dead, small and great,	20:12
1	And **I saw** a new heaven and a new earth:	21:1
1	And I John **saw** the holy city, new Jerusalem,	21:2
1	And I John **saw** the holy city, new Jerusalem,	21:2
20	**Behold**, the tabernacle of God is with men,	21:3
20	**Behold**, I make all things new.	21:5
1	And **I saw** no temple therein:	21:22
20	**Behold**, I come quickly: blessed is he that	22:7
20	**behold**, I come quickly; and my reward is with me,	22:12

Classical Greek

Originally *eidon* is the second aorist of the classical verb *eidō* ("I see, know"; cf. *oida* [3471]), which does not appear in the present active even in classical writings and is usually translated in the past tense. However, in the classical period *eidon* came to be used as the second aorist of *horaō* (3571) rather than *eidō*. In the New Testament *eidon* is much more common than the present tense, *horaō* (Michaelis, "horaō," *Kittel*, 5:367). Various shades of meaning were associated with *eidon*, among them "to see, experience, behold, look at, perceive, (passively) to appear, etc." (*Liddell-Scott*). "In Philo *horaō* (including *eidon*) occupies the most important place among the verbs of seeing" (Michaelis, "horaō," *Kittel*, 5:334).

Septuagint Usage

Eidon (including the infinitive form *idein*) appears in the Septuagint as a replacement for approximately 14 Hebrew expressions. "*Horaō* with its aorist form *eidon* occurs some 1450 times in the Septuagint" (Dahn, "See," *Colin Brown*, 3:513). Most often, however, a form of *yādah* ("to know") stands behind it. Its usage in the Septuagint conforms with its common understanding. Thus it can describe someone seeing something (e.g., Genesis 1:21,25,31; etc.). Implied in seeing is a "knowing" or "perceiving" of something (e.g. Genesis 16:4,5).

It can also mean visionary-ecstatic prophetic seeing, being substituted for *rā'âh* and *chāzâh* (Michaelis, "horaō," *Kittel*, 5:329).

At times *eidon* appears as an imperative, *ide*: "Look!" or "Consider . . ." (e.g., Ecclesiastes 1:10; 7:13). The demonstrative particle *idou*, being the aorist middle imperative of *eidon*, is related to this form. It is even more common (e.g., Genesis 1:29; Leviticus 13:5,6; 1 Samuel 1:8 [LXX 1 Kings 1:8]; etc.). *Eidon* is also used figuratively of water, the sea, or the earth seeing (Psalms 76:16 [LXX 75:16]; 96:4 [95:4]; 113:3 [112:3]).

New Testament Usage

Eidon occurs throughout the New Testament with its expected wide range of definition. As in classical and Septuagint usage, seeing has predominance over hearing. It regularly denotes physical sight (e.g., Matthew 2:2,9; John 1:47; Acts 3:3). Often *eidon* means "to perceive" or "to realize" something (Matthew 2:16; cf. Mark 7:2) as a result of seeing. "To see" in the sense of "to experience" is also to be understood in some passages. Thus "to see death" (Luke 2:26) is another way of saying "to die," or "to see good days" (1 Peter 3:10) means "to experience a good life" (cf. Acts 2:27,31). "To see" someone in the sense of "to visit or meet with" occurs in a few texts: thus Jesus' family hopes to "see" Him (Luke 8:20); and Paul, "having seen" the brothers at Lydia's house, encouraged them (Acts 16:40) (see *Bauer*). In John the verb sometimes takes on special significance. It can even refer to the perception of supernatural events and things (e.g., John 1:33).

BAUER 220-21, MOULTON-MILLIGAN 182, KITTEL 5:315-67, COLIN BROWN 3:511,513,515.

1482. εἶδος eidos noun

Appearance, form, sight, kind.

COGNATE:
εἶδον eidon (1481)

SYNONYMS:
εἰκών eikōn (1494)
ἰδέα idea (2374)
μορφή morphē (3307)
μόρφωσις morphōsis (3309)
ὁμοίωμα homoiōma (3530)
σχῆμα schēma (4828)
τύπος tupos (5020)
χάραγμα charagma (5316)

מַרְאֶה mar'eh (4920), Behold, appearance (Gn 41:2, 2 Sm 11:2, Is 52:14).

מִשְׁפָּחָה mishpāchāh (5121), Kind (Jer 15:3).
מִשְׁפָּט mishpāṭ (5122), Conformity (Ex 26:30).
עַיִן 'ayin (6084), Look, appearance (Nm 11:7, Ez 1:16).
עַפְעַפַּיִם 'aph'appayim (6310), Rays, flashes (Jb 41:18).
שִׁית shîth (8308), Dressed (Prv 7:10).
תֹּאַר tō'ar (8717), Form, appearance (Gn 29:17, 1 Sm 25:3, Jer 11:16).

1. εἶδος eidos nom/acc sing neu
2. εἴδους eidous gen sing neu
3. εἴδει eidei dat sing neu

3 And the Holy Ghost descended in a bodily **shape**... Luke 3:22
1 the **fashion** of his countenance was altered,............. 9:29
1 neither heard his voice ... nor seen his **shape**........ John 5:37
2 For we walk by faith, not by **sight**:................... 2 Co 5:7
2 Abstain from all **appearance** of evil.................. 1 Th 5:22

Classical Greek

In classical Greek *eidos* is related to the verb *eidō*, "see." It denotes a person or thing's visible form, but it also stresses the link between appearance and reality. For example, when Homer praised the *eidos* of a woman, he meant not only her outward beauty but her inward character (see Braumann, "Form, Substance," *Colin Brown*, 1:703f.). Other classical uses included *eidos* as meaning "form" or "nature" and "class" or "kind" (*Liddell-Scott*).

Septuagint Usage

In the Septuagint *eidos* translates both *mar'eh*, "sights, appearance," and *tō'ar*, "form." The word emphasizes the outward appearance of the whole being (e.g., Isaiah 53:2,3; the suffering Servant has nothing in His "appearance" that would attract men to Him). God himself is said to have spoken to Moses *en eidei* (Numbers 12:8). The "form" or "appearance" of the Lord looked like fire to the Israelites (Exodus 24:17).

New Testament Usage

Eidos occurs only five times in the New Testament. In 1 Thessalonians 5:22 Paul declared that believers are to "abstain from all appearance of evil." The context may show that the apostle's injunction refers specifically to those prophetic utterances that were "evil" (i.e., opposed to the truth). In 2 Corinthians 5:7 Paul declared, "We walk by faith, not by sight." Paul apparently meant that the Christian life "is a matter of faith, not of sight" (TEV). In other words, the Christian is guided by faith in Christ and not by the things he can see.

According to Luke 3:22, at Jesus' baptism the Holy Spirit descended in "a bodily shape" ("in bodily form," NIV). Luke's account stresses the reality of the event. Similarly, Luke 9:29 uses *eidos* to describe the change in Jesus' appearance at the Transfiguration: "The fashion of his countenance was altered." In John 5:37 Jesus stated that his addressee had never seen the "shape" (*eidos*) of the Father. The implication of the context (5:17-47) may be that Jesus *had* seen God's form and thus had an authority and relationship with the Father which no man has ever had (Braumann, "Form, Substance," *Colin Brown*, 1:704). The Jews refused to hear Jesus—the spokesman of God (5:24). They did not recognize God's Son who makes the invisible Father known (1:18).

STRONG 1491, BAUER 221, MOULTON-MILLIGAN 182, KITTEL 2:373-75, LIDDELL-SCOTT 482, COLIN BROWN 1:703-4.

1483. εἰδωλεῖον eidōleion noun
Idol's temple.
CROSS-REFERENCE:
εἴδωλον eidōlon (1487)

1. εἰδωλείῳ eidōleiō dat sing neu

1 if any ... see thee ... sit at meat in the **idol's temple**, 1 Co 8:10

Classical Greek
Eidōleion or *eidōlion* means an "idol's temple." According to current evidence, the term does not occur in secular, classical Greek, although there are some "analogous forms" (see *Moulton-Milligan*).

Septuagint Usage
Five instances of *eidōleion* appear in the Septuagint, but only one of these is canonical (Daniel 1:2). All, however, have essentially the same meaning, "an idol's temple." The use in Daniel and 1 Esdras 2:10 occur in the identical phrase, "he stored these things in his idol's temple." Both texts are alluding to Nebuchadnezzar's seizing of the holy vessels of the Lord from the temple in Jerusalem and taking them back to Babylon where he put them in his god's temple. In every case *eidōleion* carries an unfavorable sense. It is the site of pagan worship. If Israel participated in any such events it was one of the most serious sins it could commit (cf. 1 Maccabees 1:47).

New Testament Usage
An understanding of the sole New Testament usage certainly depends upon the precedent set by the Septuagint. Again *eidōleion* is an "idol's temple" (1 Corinthians 8:10). Paul cautioned his Corinthian readers against exercising their "freedom" to eat anything—even meat that has been sacrificed to idols—at the detriment to others. Thus being seen "eating in an idol's temple" would imply an endorsement of a practice the "weaker brother" would be unable to adopt. Although in actuality the eating of idol meat was in itself not a crime or sin—one need not think of the meat as sacrificed to idols (8:7f.)—Paul urged discretion on the part of the "strong." The whole discussion beginning in chapter 8 of 1 Corinthians actually extends into chapter 10. To grasp the issue here, a basic understanding of customs in the ancient world is necessary. First, almost all meat eaten in the ancient world was a sacrifice. People did not simply "eat meat" without first having sacrificed it. Thus, even meat bought in the marketplace was formerly a sacrifice. Second, Paul clearly did not encourage participation in idol worship—which would have certainly included eating—but neither did he want his Corinthian readers to allow their freedom to be judged by another (10:28f.). (See also the terms *eidōlothutos* [1484], *eidōlolatreia* [1485], *eidōlolatrēs* [1486], *eidōlon* [1487].)

STRONG 1493, BAUER 221, MOULTON-MILLIGAN 182-83, KITTEL 2:379, LIDDELL-SCOTT 483, COLIN BROWN 2:284.

1484. εἰδωλόθυτος eidōlothutos adj
Sacrificed to idols.
CROSS-REFERENCE:
εἴδωλον eidōlon (1487)

1. εἰδωλόθυτον eidōlothuton nom/acc sing neu
2. εἰδωλοθύτων eidōlothutōn gen pl neu
3. εἰδωλόθυτα eidōlothuta nom/acc pl neu

2 That ye abstain **from meats offered to idols**, ... Acts 15:29
1 keep themselves from **things offered unto idols**, ... 21:25
2 Now as touching **things offered unto idols**, ... 1 Co 8:1
2 those things that are offered in **sacrifice unto idols**, ... 8:4
1 eat it as a **thing offered unto an idol**; 8:7
3 to eat those **things which are offered to idols**; 8:10
1 That a **thing sacrificed to idols** is anything (NASB) 10:19
1 which is offered in **sacrifice to idols** is any thing? 10:19
1 This is **offered in sacrifice unto idols**, ... 10:28
3 to eat **things sacrificed unto idols**, ... Rev 2:14
3 and to eat **things sacrificed unto idols**. 2:20

The word denotes "something sacrificed to an idol" and is the Jewish equivalent of the Gentile word *hierothutos*, "sacred sacrifice." The Jewish term carries a disparaging connotation since the word *eidōlon* (1487) normally means "phantom" or "likeness" and thus, "unreal." Some of the meat in the market only arrived there after part of it was thrown on a pagan altar and part of it eaten in a sacred meal devoted to a deity. Yet not all the meat in the market had such a history.

New Testament Usage
The Apostolic decree of Acts (15:29; 21:25) prohibited the eating of such meat, and this prohibition received later support from the Book of Revelation (2:14,20). Both New Testament books connect eating meat offered to idols with fornication, and Revelation seems to equate eating such meat with idolatry. Later Christianity continued the prohibition, e.g., the Didache, Justin Martyr, and Irenaeus.

In his instructions to Corinthian Christians Paul allowed anyone whose own conscience was not offended and who would not be offending a weaker brother to eat such meat. Paul may have given this permission to prevent cutting off Christians from contact with non-Christians and also because idols were really nothing (1 Corinthians 5:9,10; 8:4). Still, in 1 Corinthians 10:14, Paul forbade "idolatry" (*eidōlolatreia* [1485]).

STRONG 1494, BAUER 221, KITTEL 2:378-79 (see "eidōlothuton"), LIDDELL-SCOTT 483, COLIN BROWN 2:284-85; 3:417,432 (see "eidōlothuton").

1485. εἰδωλολατρεία
eidōlolatreia noun

Idolatry.
CROSS-REFERENCE:
εἴδωλον eidōlon (1487)

1. εἰδωλολατρεία eidōlolatreia nom sing fem
2. εἰδωλολατρείας eidōlolatreias gen sing fem
3. εἰδωλολατρείαις eidōlolatreiais dat pl fem
4. εἰδωλολατρία eidōlolatria nom sing fem
5. εἰδωλολατρίας eidōlolatrias gen sing fem
6. εἰδωλολατρίαις eidōlolatriais dat pl fem

2 Wherefore, my dearly beloved, flee from **idolatry**... 1 Co 10:14
1 **Idolatry**, witchcraft, hatred, variance, emulations, ... Gal 5:20
4 **Idolatry**, witchcraft, hatred, variance, emulations, ... 5:20
1 and covetousness, which is **idolatry**: .... Col 3:5
4 and covetousness, which is **idolatry**: 3:5
3 revellings, banquetings, and abominable **idolatries**: ... 1 Pt 4:3
6 revellings, banquetings, and abominable **idolatries**: 4:3

Eidōlolatreia (or the form *eidōlolatria*) and its companion *eidōlolatrēs* (1486) are generally held to be Christian formations (see *Moulton-Milligan*, "eidōlolatrēs") since they are not found prior to the Christian period. Nonetheless, a similar thought if not identical language does occur (e.g., Testament of Judah 19:1; cf. *Bauer*). Basically it means "idolatry," from *eidōlon* (1487), "image," and *latreia* (2972), "service."

New Testament Usage
Eidōlolatreia is specifically linked to monetary greed in the New Testament as well as other literature (Ephesians 5:5; Colossians 3:5; cf. Testament of Judah 19:1; Polycarp to the Philippians 11:2; cf. also Matthew 6:24; 1 Corinthians 5:10,11). But it can additionally refer to participation in idolatrous practices. This is explicitly described as participating in the cultic meal (i.e., "eating and drinking") of paganism (1 Corinthians chapter 8 passim; 10:14,18; cf. 10:7). *Eidōlolatreia* also falls in general "vice-lists" of more heinous crimes (Galatians 5:20; 1 Peter 4:3; cf. Barnabas 20:1; Didache 3:4; 5:1). It is often mentioned in connection with *pleonexia* (3984), "covetous" (cf. Ephesians 4:19).

Very simply, *eidōlolatreia* is active rejection of God by willful participation in sin. Allegiance is sworn to sin rather than to God. As the writer of the Testament of Judah expresses it: "They (those led to idolatry) designate as gods those who are not gods" (Testament of Judah 19:11).

STRONG 1495, BAUER 221 (see "eidōlolatria"), KITTEL 2:379-80 (see "eidōlolatria"), LIDDELL-SCOTT 483 (see "eidōlolatria"), COLIN BROWN 2:284-86 (see "eidōlolatria").

1486. εἰδωλολάτρης
eidōlolatrēs noun

Idolater.
CROSS-REFERENCE:
εἴδωλον eidōlon (1487)

1. εἰδωλολάτρης eidōlolatrēs nom sing masc
2. εἰδωλολάτραι eidōlolatrai nom pl masc
3. εἰδωλολάτραις eidōlolatrais dat pl masc

3 the covetous, or extortioners, or with **idolaters**; ...... 1 Co 5:10
1 a fornicator, or covetous, or an **idolater**, or a railer, ... 5:11
2 neither fornicators, nor **idolaters**, nor adulterers, ... 6:9
2 Neither be ye **idolaters**, as were some of them; 10:7
1 nor covetous man, who is an **idolater**, ... Eph 5:5
3 and sorcerers, and **idolaters**, and all liars, ... Rev 21:8
2 **idolaters**, and whosoever loveth and maketh a lie. 22:15

This expression does not occur prior to the Christian period in either classical or Septuagintal Greek. It appears seven times in the Greek New Testament, five of which are credited to Paul and two to John the Revelator. "Idolater" is the basic definition of *eidōlolatrēs*, and of course this always has an unfavorable sense in the New Testament.

The idolater is among the people of this world (1 Corinthians 5:10), but he might call himself a "brother." Paul gave differing advice to the church as to how to respond to the "idolater" of the world or the "idolater" in the church. Of the former he advised the church to continue to have dealings with him; but of the latter Paul said, "Do not associate with them, do not even eat with them" (1 Corinthians 5:11, author's translation).

Idolaters will have no part in the inheritance of the Kingdom (1 Corinthians 6:9). Their destiny is the lake of fire in the company of the cowardly, false, unbelieving, sexually immoral, and the like (Revelation 21:8; cf. 22:15). Make no mistake, however, "idolatry" is not only worshiping in pagan temples; it is a sin taking place as much—if not more—today than ever before. Paul equated impure and covetous persons with the idolatrous (Ephesians 5:5).

STRONG 1496, BAUER 221, MOULTON-MILLIGAN 183, KITTEL 2:379-80, LIDDELL-SCOTT 483, COLIN BROWN 2:284-85.

1487. εἴδωλον eidōlon noun

Idol, image.

COGNATES:
εἰδωλεῖον eidōleion (1483)
εἰδωλόθυτος eidōlothutos (1484)
εἰδωλολατρεία eidōlolatreia (1485)
εἰδωλολάτρης eidōlolatrēs (1486)
κατείδωλος kateidōlos (2682)

אֵל 'ēl (416), Oak, mighty tree (Is 57:5).
אֱלָהּ 'ĕlāhh (A434), God, gods (Dn 3:12,18, 5:4,23—Aramaic).
אֱלוֹהַּ 'ĕlôahh (438), God, gods (Nm 25:2, 1 Kgs 11:8, Is 37:19).
אֱלִיל 'ĕlîl (462), Worthless, idols (Lv 19:4, 1 Chr 16:26, Hb 2:18).
בָּמָה bāmāh (1154), Shrine, high place (Ez 16:16).
בַּעַל ba'al (1197), Baal (2 Chr 17:3, Jer 9:14 [9:13]).
גִּלּוּל gillûl (1585), Idols (Lv 26:30, 2 Kgs 17:12, Ez 6:4).
הֶבֶל hevel (1961), False gods, worthless idols (Dt 32:21, Jer 14:22, 16:19).
חַמָּן chammān (2658), Incense altar (2 Chr 14:5 [14:4], Is 27:9).
מִפְלֶצֶת miphletseth (4818), Disgraceful image, idol (2 Chr 15:16).
עָצָב 'ātsāv (6322), Image, idol (1 Sm 31:9, 2 Chr 24:18, Hos 8:4).
עֹצֶב 'ōtsev (6326), Idol (Is 48:5).
פָּסִיל pāsîl (6702), Idol (2 Chr 33:22, Is 30:22).
פֶּסֶל pesel (6705), Idol (Ex 20:4).
צֶלֶם tselem (7021), Statue, image (Nm 33:52).
שָׂעִיר sā'îr (7988), Goat idol (2 Chr 11:15).
שִׁקּוּץ shiqqûts (8617), Abominable idol (1 Kgs 11:7).
תְּרָפִים tᵉrāphîm (8994), Idols (Gn 31:19,34,35).

1. εἴδωλον eidōlon nom/acc sing neu
2. εἰδώλου eidōlou gen sing neu
3. εἰδώλῳ eidōlō dat sing neu
4. εἰδώλων eidōlōn gen pl neu
5. εἴδωλα eidōla nom/acc pl neu

```
3 and offered sacrifice unto the idol, .................. Acts 7:41
4 that they abstain from pollutions of idols, ............ 15:20
5 that abhorrest idols, dost thou commit sacrilege? .... Rom 2:22
1 we know that an idol is nothing in the world, ........ 1 Co 8:4
2 for some with conscience of the idol unto this hour ..... 8:7
1 What say I then? that the idol is any thing, ........... 10:19
1 that an idol is anything? (NASB) ..................... 10:19
5 were Gentiles, carried away unto these dumb idols, .... 12:2
4 what agreement hath the temple of God with idols? 2 Co 6:16
4 to God from idols to serve the living and true God; 1 Th 1:9
4 Little children, keep yourselves from idols. Amen. ... 1 Jn 5:21
5 they should not worship devils, and idols of gold, .... Rev 9:20
```

Classical Greek

In classical Greek *eidōlon* is only rarely used for "false gods" or "idols." But it was often employed for describing "ghosts" or "phantoms" in Hades (see 85) or for any phenomenon without a physical, material existence. The term also served to depict an image of either a mental or physical nature. The expression is derived from *eidos* (1482), "that which is seen."

Septuagint Usage

The Septuagint calls upon *eidōlon* to translate several Hebrew terms, all of which refer to pagan deities. Normally it carries a disparaging nuance. Typically, pagan deities are "vanities" (Jeremiah 14:22; 18:15); in fact, they are "gods" which do not exist, in contrast to the only true God who can say "I am."

New Testament Usage

These thoughts are picked up and developed in the New Testament. Idols are "vain things" (RSV) and false gods (Acts 14:15). In truth they have no existence (1 Corinthians 8:4); rather, behind the idols lurk evil spiritual powers which are indeed real. Participation in any pagan religion will subject the participant to the control and influence of these evil forces of darkness. Ultimately idolatry will invite the wrath and judgment of God (1 Corinthians 10:19-21).

The New Testament cautions against patent idolatry in any of its variegated forms (e.g., 1 Corinthians 5:10f.; 10:7) as well as giving a warning against idolatry in more undetectable forms (e.g., the "worship" of Mammon, Matthew

6:24; cf. Ephesians 5:5). Magic and sorcery are also forms of subtle idolatry (Galatians 5:19f.; Ephesians 5:5; Colossians 3:5; Revelation 9:20f.; 21:8; 22:15).

STRONG 1497, BAUER 221, MOULTON-MILLIGAN 183, KITTEL 2:375-78, LIDDELL-SCOTT 483, COLIN BROWN 2:284,292.

1488. εἰκῇ eikē adv
Without cause, in vain, without purpose.

1. εἰκῇ eikē

1 **without a cause** shall be in danger of the judgment:	Matt 5:22
1 for he beareth not the sword **in vain**:	Rom 13:4
1 unless ye have believed **in vain**.	1 Co 15:2
1 Have ye suffered so many things **in vain**?	Gal 3:4
1 suffered so many things in vain? if it be yet **in vain**.	3:4
1 lest I have bestowed upon you labour **in vain**.	4:11
1 **vainly** puffed up by his fleshly mind,	Col 2:18

Classical Greek and Septuagint Usage
In classical Greek *eikē* usually means "at random." The word refers to an action done without a plan or purpose. The papyri demonstrate a similar usage.

The Septuagint translators used the word once at Proverbs 28:25 to mean "without due consideration." The Hebrew follows a different text here.

New Testament Usage
The New Testament exhibits four meanings for this word. In Matthew 5:22, the meaning appears to be "without cause," "Whosoever is angry with his brother *without a cause* shall be in danger of the judgment." *Eikē*, however, does not appear in some manuscripts in this verse.

In Galatians Paul used the word to mean "without result" or "in vain," "I am afraid of you, lest I have bestowed upon you labor in vain" (4:11). "Without purpose" is the meaning in Romans 13:4, "If you do wrong, be afraid, for he does not bear the sword for nothing" (NIV). The same sense may be intended in 1 Corinthians 15:2, "... unless ye have believed in vain."

STRONG 1500, BAUER 221-22, MOULTON-MILLIGAN 183, KITTEL 2:380-81, LIDDELL-SCOTT 484.

1489. εἴκοσι eikosi num
Twenty, a score.

1. εἴκοσιν eikosin card
2. εἴκοσι eikosi card

2 that cometh against him with twenty thousand?	Luke 14:31
2 rowed about three or four miles (NASB) (NT)	John 6:19
2 together were about an hundred and **twenty**,	Acts 1:15
2 And sounded, and found it **twenty** fathoms:	27:28
2 about the throne were four and **twenty** seats:	Rev 4:4
2 upon the seats I saw four and **twenty** elders sitting,	4:4
2 The four and **twenty** elders fall down before him	4:10
2 living creatures and the twenty-four elders (NASB)	5:8
2 the four and **twenty** elders, which sat before God	11:16
2 And the four and **twenty** elders and the four beasts	19:4

This word appears in classical Greek (since Homer), papyri, and throughout the Septuagint. It simply means "20." It occurs in Luke 14:31; John 6:19; Acts 1:15; 27:28; 1 Corinthians 10:8. It is also used in reference to the "four and twenty elders" in Revelation 4:4 (twice); 4:10; 5:8,14; 11:16; 19:4 (see word study at *eikositessares* [1491]).

STRONG 1501, BAUER 222, MOULTON-MILLIGAN 183, LIDDELL-SCOTT 485.

1490. εἰκοσιπέντε eikosipente num
Twenty-five.

1. εἰκοσιπέντε eikosipente card

1 rowed about **five and twenty** or thirty furlongs,	John 6:19

While most modern Greek texts show this term as two separate words—*eikosi*, (1489) "20," and *pente* (3864), "5"—*Liddell-Scott* indicates that other classical literature may have combined the two into one word. In either case the term is used once in the New Testament at John 6:19. The Gospel records that Jesus walked to meet His disciples *on* the Sea of Galilee after they had rowed 25 or 30 "furlongs" (KJV)—about halfway across the 7- to 8-mile-wide lake.

LIDDELL-SCOTT 485.

1491. εἰκοσιτέσσαρες
eikositessares num

Twenty-four.

1. εἰκοσιτέσσαρες eikositessares card nom masc/fem

1 four beasts and **four and twenty** elders fell down	Rev 5:8
1 And the **four and twenty** elders fell down	5:14

The number 24 is found numerous times in the New Testament, either as one compound word or two separate words (*eikosi* [1489], "20," and *tessares* [4911B], "4"), all occurring in the Book of Revelation (e.g., 4:4,10; 5:8; 11:16; 19:4). The word specifies either the number of elders who worship God and the Lamb in heaven or the thrones that the elders sit upon. Perhaps these 24 are, as some suggest, the 12 patriarchs and the 12 apostles. In any case, they are the representatives of God's people who have finished their course on earth and are now in a state of glory.

LIDDELL-SCOTT 485.

1492. εἰκοσιτρεῖς eikositreis num
Twenty-three.
CROSS-REFERENCE:
ἀπουσία apousia (660)

1. εἰκοσιτρεῖς eikositreis card nom/acc masc/fem
1 and fell in one day **three and twenty** thousand...... 1 Co 10:8

Found once in the New Testament, at 1 Corinthians 10:8 (in either a compound form or as two separate words; *eikosi* [1489], "20," and *treis* [4980], "3"), the word represents the number "23." In this context it is combined with the word for 1,000, *chiliades* (see 5342), and records the number of Israelites who died in a plague under God's judgment having committed fornication during the wilderness wanderings. (For an explanation of the supposed discrepancy between the figure 23,000 given in 1 Corinthians and the figure 24,000 stated in Numbers 25:9, see the *Romans-Corinthians Study Bible*, p.381.)

BAUER 222, LIDDELL-SCOTT 485.

1493. εἴκω eikō verb
Yield.

עָנָה ʻānâh (6257), Answer (1 Kgs 12:7—Codex Alexandrinus only).

1. εἴξαμεν eixamen 1pl indic aor act
1 To whom we **gave place** by subjection, no,.......... Gal 2:5

Classical Greek
Eikō is a versatile, widely used verb in classical Greek. Its range of definition includes: "to yield, withdraw"; "to yield (something)"; and in an impersonal sense, "it is allowable or possible" (see *Liddell-Scott*).

Septuagint Usage
Only two occurrences of *eikō* are certain in the Septuagint. Yielding to someone or something may be because of fear (Wisdom of Solomon 18:25). Reason is able to "rule" emotions and keep them from being "given in to" (4 Maccabees 1:6).

There is possibly one other instance of *eikō* in the Septuagint. At 1 Kings 12:7 (LXX 3 Kings 12:7) Codex Alexandrinus reads *eikō*. The Hebrew behind *eikō* in 1 Kings 12:7 (LXX 3 Kings 12:7) would be ʻānâh, "to bow down, to humble oneself." The imagery in the overall passage recalls a slave's "yielding." The elders advise Rehoboam to "yield" to the request of the assembly of Israel to lighten their load. Rehoboam rejects this counsel and subsequently incites the house of Israel to rebellion against the house of David (cf. 1 Kings 12:19 [LXX 3 Kings 12:19]).

New Testament Usage
The only usage in the New Testament conforms to the classical and Septuagintal definition of *eikō*: "to give in, yield." Paul wrote to the Galatian church advising them that he did not "yield" to pressure from the "false brethren" who were trying to compel Paul and his companions to follow the law of circumcision (Galatians 2:4,5).

STRONG 1502, BAUER 222, LIDDELL-SCOTT 485, COLIN BROWN 2:256.

1494. εἰκών eikōn noun
Image, likeness, form, appearance.
SYNONYMS:
εἶδος eidos (1482)
ἰδέα idea (2374)
μορφή morphe (3307)
μόρφωσις morphōsis (3309)
σχῆμα schēma (4828)
τύπος tupos (5020)
χάραγμα charagma (5316)

דְּמוּת dᵉmûth (1883), Likeness (Gn 5:1).
סֶמֶל semel (5761), Idol, image (2 Chr 33:7).
פֶּסֶל peṣel (6705), Idol (Is 40:19,20).
צֶלֶם tselem (7021), Image, model (Gn 1:26, Ez 16:17).
צְלֵם tsᵉlēm (A7022), Image, statue (Dn 2:31,34,35, 3:1ff.—Aramaic).
תְּבוּנָה tᵉvûnâh (8722), Understanding, skill (Hos 13:2).

1. εἰκών eikōn nom sing fem
2. εἰκόνος eikonos gen sing fem
3. εἰκόνι eikoni dat sing fem
4. εἰκόνα eikona acc sing fem

1 Whose is this **image** and superscription?.......... Matt 22:20
1 Whose is this **image** and superscription?.......... Mark 12:16
4 a penny. Whose **image** and superscription hath it?..Luke 20:24
2 into **an image** made like to corruptible man,........ Rom 1:23
2 to be conformed to the **image** of his Son,.......... 8:29
1 forasmuch as he is the **image** and glory of God:....1 Co 11:7
4 And as we have borne the **image** of the earthy,....... 15:49
4 we shall also bear the **image** of the heavenly.......... 15:49
4 are changed into the same **image** from glory...... 2 Co 3:18
1 who is the **image** of God, should shine unto them....... 4:4
1 Who is the **image** of the invisible God,.............. Col 1:15

4 after the **image** of him that created him:	Col 3:10
4 and not the very **image** of the things,	Heb 10:1
4 that they should make an **image** to the beast,	Rev 13:14
3 had power to give life unto the **image** of the beast,	13:15
1 that the **image** of the beast should both speak,	13:15
4 would not worship the **image** ... should be killed.	13:15
3 would not worship the **image** ... should be killed.	13:15
4 If any man worship the beast and his **image**,	14:9
4 who worship the beast and his **image**,	14:11
2 the victory over the beast, and over his **image**,	15:2
3 and upon them which worshipped his **image**.	16:2
3 and them that worshipped his **image**.	19:20
4 had not worshipped the beast, neither his **image**,	20:4

Classical Greek

The term *eikōn*, "image, picture, reflection," is derived from *eoika* (1842), "to be like." In classical Greek *eikōn* could refer to "pictures" or "statues" or "idols." The Greeks believed that an image—of whatever kind—possessed part of the reality which it represented. If the image, picture, or statue was that of a deity they contended that a deity was present and worked through that representation (cf. *eidōlon* [1487]; Flender, "Image," *Colin Brown*, 2:287).

Septuagint Usage

Eikōn stands for five Hebrew words in the Septuagint. Negatively the term is used for the idols—often graven "images"—of Israel's pagan neighbors. Positively it refers to man as created in the "image" of God. Any images of God were strictly forbidden in Israel (Exodus 20:4; Deuteronomy 27:15); they were not to serve any purpose in Israel's worship of the invisible God.

New Testament Usage

Eikōn functions in the New Testament in an assortment of ways. It can refer to the "image" of the emperor on a Roman coin (Matthew 22:20) to "idols" made by men in exchange for the glory of God (Romans 1:23), or to the "image" of the beast who was wounded but survived (Revelation 13:14).

Picking up on the Genesis account, Paul described man as being in the "image ... of God" (1 Corinthians 11:7). Adam's descendants bear His "image" or "likeness" (1 Corinthians 15:49).

Hebrews 10:1 explains that the Law is not the ultimate image of spiritual matters; it is only a shadow. Like the shadow a statue makes, the Law affords only a vague representation of the reality behind it.

Furthermore, *eikōn* is used concerning the born-again man whose image is renewed in the likeness of Christ; he is reborn in the image of the Creator (Colossians 3:10; cf.; Ephesians 4:24). When the believer is finally glorified, he or she will be conformed to the image of God's Son (Romans 8:29; 1 Corinthians 15:49).

Finally Christ is the image (*eikōn*) of God (2 Corinthians 4:4; Colossians 1:15; cf. John 14:9; Hebrews 1:3). That this wording denotes the deity of Christ is undeniable.

STRONG 1504, BAUER 222, MOULTON-MILLIGAN 183, KITTEL 2:381-97, LIDDELL-SCOTT 485, COLIN BROWN 2:286-88,292-93.

1495. εἰλικρίνεια eilikrineia noun

Sincerity, purity of motive.
CROSS-REFERENCE:
κρίνω krinō (2892)

1. εἰλικρινείας eilikrineias gen sing fem
2. εἰλικρινείᾳ eilikrineia dat sing fem

1 with the unleavened bread **of sincerity** and truth.	1 Co 5:8
2 that in simplicity and godly **sincerity**,	2 Co 1:12
1 but as of **sincerity**, but as of God,	2:17

Classical Greek

Eilikrineia does not appear in classical Greek, but it does occur in later secular documents (see *Moulton-Milligan*). Its origin is not certain, but it possibly is derived from *hēilē* or *hēl* (see 2229), "sun" or "sunlight," and *krinō* (2892), "I judge." Thus, according to Thayer it means something judged "pure" under the light of the sun (*Greek-English Lexicon*). *Eilikrineia*, therefore, is the quality of "purity, sincerity."

Septuagint Usage

Eilikrineia occurs one time in the Septuagint (Codex Alexandrinus), at Wisdom of Solomon 7:25 (the text may also be *eilikrinēs* [1496]). Writing about the virtues of wisdom the author comments that "she" (wisdom) is a "pure emanation" of God's glory.

New Testament Usage

Eilikrineia appears only three times in the New Testament, and each of these belongs to Paul (1 Corinthians 5:8; 2 Corinthians 1:12; 2:17). The meaning "sincerity or pure motive" is behind Paul's usage. Instead of celebrating Passover with bread contaminated with old leaven—symbolizing wickedness and malice—Christians are to use the "bread of sincerity and truth" (1 Corinthians 5:8).

A "godly sincerity" is the mark of the life of the believer. This sincerity is characterized by pure motives (2 Corinthians 2:17; cf. 2 Peter 3:1). This kind of "sincerity" cannot even be attacked by outsiders; in fact, it testifies to them. Such sincerity itself originates in God (2 Corinthians 1:12).

εἰλικρινής 1496

STRONG 1505, BAUER 222, MOULTON-MILLIGAN 183-84, KITTEL 2:397-98, LIDDELL-SCOTT 486.

STRONG 1506, BAUER 222, MOULTON-MILLIGAN 184, KITTEL 2:397-98, LIDDELL-SCOTT 486.

1496. εἰλικρινής eilikrinēs adj
Pure, unsullied, sincere.
COGNATE:
  κρίνω krinō (2892)
SYNONYMS:
  ἀμίαντος amiantos (281)
  καθαρός katharos (2485)

1. εἰλικρινεῖς eilikrineis nom pl masc
2. εἰλικρινῆ eilikrinē acc sing fem

1 that ye may be **sincere** and without offence .... Phlp 1:10
2 I stir up your **pure** minds by way of remembrance: .. 2 Pt 3:1

Classical Greek
Although the origin of *eilikrinēs* is uncertain, it is possible that it is derived from *hilē* (*hēlios* [2229], "sun") and *krinō* (2892), "to judge." From that it perhaps meant something like "to judge in the light of the sun" (as in a garment) to see if it was free of spots (Hawthorne, *Word Biblical Commentary*, 43:28). It appears to be a picture word, showing how a cloth merchant might show a garment to a customer in the full light of the sun, so he may see it as it really is. Thus *eilikrinēs* means "spotless, pure." It could also mean "unalloyed" (of metals) or "unmixed" (see *Liddell-Scott*). From the time of Plato on, the term bore moral overtones (Büchsel, "eilikrines," *Kittel*, 2:397).

Septuagint Usage
Eilikrinēs occurs only in the apocryphal Wisdom of Solomon (7:25) in the Septuagint. Its author refers to Wisdom as a "pure emanation" (*aporroia eilikrinēs*) of the glory of the Almighty.

New Testament Usage
The two New Testament usages of *eilikrinēs* both refer to moral "purity." Paul prayed that the Philippians might be "pure" (*eilikrinēs*) and "blameless" (*aproskopos* [671]) at the return of Christ. Such purity is further defined as being "filled with the fruits of righteousness" (Philippians 1:11, RSV; cf. verse 10).

Second Peter 3:1 is a reminder to the "sincere mind" (RSV) of his reader that the predictions of the prophets are certain. "Pure" may also be an appropriate translation here, as a contrast to the corrupted character of the opponents who were predicted to come by the prophets (e.g., 2 Peter 2:1ff.; cf. 3:11,14). Again, there is an eschatological precedent for such a quality.

1497. εἱλίσσω eilissō verb
Roll up.

1. εἱλισσόμενον heilissomenon
  nom/acc sing neu part pres mid
1 departed as a scroll when it **is rolled together**; .... Rev 6:14

This is a variant spelling of *helissō*. See the word study at number 1654.

1498. εἰμί eimi verb
To be, exist, live, stay, reside, occur; am.
COGNATES:
  ἄπειμι apeimi (545)
  ἀπουσία apousia (660)
  εἴσειμι eiseimi (1510)
  ἑκούσιος hekousios (1582)
  ἑκουσίως hekousiōs (1583)
  ἔνειμι eneimi (1735)
  ἔξεστιν exestin (1815)
  ἐξιέναι exienai (1821)
  ἐξουσιάζω exousiazō (1834)
  ἐπιοῦσα epiousa (1951)
  ἐπιούσιος epiousios (1952)
  οὐσία ousia (3639)
  παρουσία parousia (3814)
  περιούσιος periousios (3904)
  σύνειμι suneimi (4745)
SYNONYMS:
  αὐλίζομαι aulizomai (829)
  γίνομαι ginomai (1090)
  διατρίβω diatribō (1298)
  ἐμμένω emmenō (1682)
  ἐπιμένω epimenō (1946)
  καταμένω katamenō (2620)
  μένω menō (3176)
  παραμένω paramenō (3748)
  ὑπομένω hupomenō (5116)

1. ἦτε ēte 2pl indic/subj pres/imperf act
2. εἰμί eimi 1sing indic pres act
3. εἶ ei 2sing indic pres act
4. ἐστίν estin 3sing indic pres act
5. ἐσμέν esmen 1pl indic pres act
6. ἐστέ este 2pl indic pres act
7. εἰσίν eisin 3pl indic pres act
8. ὦ ō 1sing subj pres act
9. ᾖς ēs 2sing subj pres act
10. ᾖ ē 3sing subj pres act
11. ὦμεν ōmen 1pl subj pres act
12. ὦσιν ōsin 3pl subj pres act
13. εἴης eiēs 2sing opt pres act
14. εἴη eiē 3sing opt pres act

εἰμί 1498

15. ἴσθι isthi 2sing impr pres act
16. ἤτω ētō 3sing impr pres act
17. ἔστω estō 3sing impr pres act
18. ὄντα onta nom/acc sing/pl masc/neu part pres act
19. ὄντος ontos gen sing masc/neu part pres act
20. ὄντων ontōn gen pl masc/neu part pres act
21. ὤν ōn nom sing masc part pres act
22. ὄντι onti dat sing masc part pres act
23. ὄντες ontes nom pl masc part pres act
24. οὖσιν ousin dat pl masc part pres act
25. ὄντας ontas acc pl masc part pres act
26. οὖσα ousa nom sing fem part pres act
27. οὔσης ousēs gen sing fem part pres act
28. οὔσῃ ousē dat sing fem part pres act
29. οὖσαν ousan acc sing fem part pres act
30. οὖσαι ousai nom pl fem part pres act
31. οὐσῶν ousōn gen pl fem part pres act
32. εἶναι einai inf pres act
33. ἔστωσαν estōsan 3pl impr pres act
34. ἦν ēn 1/3sing indic imperf act
35. ἦς ēs 2sing indic imperf act
36. ἦμεν ēmen 1pl indic imperf act
37. ἦσαν ēsan 3pl indic imperf act
38. ἔσομαι esomai 1sing indic fut mid
39. ἔσῃ esē 2sing indic fut mid
40. ἔσται estai 3sing indic fut mid
41. ἐσόμεθα esometha 1pl indic fut mid
42. ἔσεσθε esesthe 2pl indic fut mid
43. ἔσονται esontai 3pl indic fut mid
44. ἐσόμενον esomenon
    nom/acc sing neu part fut mid
45. ἔσεσθαι esesthai inf fut mid
46. ἤμην ēmēn 1sing indic imperf mid
47. ἦσθα ēstha 2sing indic imperf mid
48. ἐστί esti 3sing indic pres act
49. ὄν on nom/acc sing neu part pres act
50. ἤμεθα ēmetha 1pl indic imperf mid

34	Now the birth of Jesus Christ **was** on this wise:	Matt 1:18
21	Then Joseph her husband, **being** a just man,	1:19
4	that which is conceived in her is of the Holy Ghost.	1:20
4	which being interpreted **is**, God with us.	1:23
4	Saying, Where **is** he that is born King of the Jews?	2:2
3	**art** not the least among the princes of Juda:	2:6
34	it came and stood over where the young child **was**.	2:9
15	and **be** thou there until I bring thee word:	2:13
34	And **was** there until the death of Herod:	2:15
7	and would not be comforted, because **they are** not.	2:18
4	For this is he that was spoken of by the prophet	3:3
34	and his meat **was** locusts and wild honey.	3:4
4	but he that cometh after me **is** mightier than I,	3:11
2	whose shoes **I am** not worthy to bear:	3:11
4	for thus it **becometh** us to fulfil all righteousness.	3:15
4	This is my beloved Son, ... well pleased.	3:17
3	the tempter ... said, If **thou be** the Son of God,	4:3
3	And saith unto him, If **thou be** the Son of God,	4:6
37	casting a net into the sea: for **they were** fishers.	4:18
4	for theirs is the kingdom of heaven.	5:3
4	persecuted ... for theirs is the kingdom of heaven.	5:10
6	Blessed **are** ye, when men shall revile you,	5:11
6	Ye **are** the salt of the earth:	5:13
6	Ye **are** the light of the world.	5:14
40	kill **shall be** in danger of the judgment:	Matt 5:21
40	without a cause **shall be** in danger of the judgment:	5:22
40	say ... Raca, **shall be** in danger of the council:	5:22
40	say, Thou fool, **shall be** in danger of hell fire.	5:22
15	Agree with thine adversary quickly, (NT)	5:25
3	whiles **thou art** in the way with him;	5:25
4	neither by heaven; for it is God's throne:	5:34
4	Nor by the earth; for it is his footstool:	5:35
4	by Jerusalem; for it is the city of the great King.	5:35
17	let your communication **be**, Yea, yea; Nay, nay:	5:37
40	let your communication **be**, Yea, yea; Nay, nay:	5:37
4	for whatsoever is more than these **cometh** of evil.	5:37
42	Be ye therefore perfect, even as your Father ... **is**	5:48
4	even as your Father which is in heaven is perfect.	5:48
10	That thine alms **may be** in secret:	6:4
39	thou **shalt** not **be** as the hypocrites are:	6:5
42	thou **shalt** not **be** as the hypocrites are:	6:5
4	For thine is the kingdom, and the power,	6:13
4	For where your treasure **is**, there will your heart	6:21
40	treasure is, there will your heart be also.	6:21
4	The light of the body is the eye:	6:22
10	if therefore thine eye be single,	6:22
40	thy whole body **shall be** full of light.	6:22
10	But if thine eye **be** evil, thy whole body	6:23
40	thy whole body **shall be** full of darkness.	6:23
4	If therefore the light that is in thee be darkness,	6:23
4	Is not the life more than meat,	6:25
18	which to day **is**, ... to morrow is cast into the oven,	6:30
4	Or what man **is there** of you, ... his son ask bread,	7:9
23	If ye then, **being** evil, know how to give good gifts	7:11
4	for this is the law and the prophets.	7:12
7	and many there **be** which go in thereat:	7:13
7	narrow is the way, ... and few there **be** that find it.	7:14
7	but inwardly they **are** ravening wolves.	7:15
34	and it fell: and great **was** the fall of it.	7:27
34	for He **was** teaching them (NASB)	7:29
2	I am not worthy that thou shouldest come	8:8
2	For I **am** a man under authority,	8:9
40	there **shall be** weeping and gnashing of teeth.	8:12
6	Why **are ye** fearful, O ye of little faith?	8:26
4	saying, What manner of man is this,	8:27
34	And there **was** a good way off from them	8:30
4	For whether is easier, to say,	9:5
4	But go ye and learn what that **meaneth**,	9:13
4	as long as the bridegroom **is** with them?	9:15
37	because they **were** distressed and downcast (NASB)	9:36
4	Now the names of the twelve apostles **are** these;	10:2
4	for the workman **is** worthy of his meat.	10:10
4	or town ye shall enter, inquire who in it **is** worthy;	10:11
10	house be worthy, let your peace come upon it:	10:13
10	but if **it be** not worthy,	10:13
40	It **shall be** more tolerable for the land of Sodom	10:15
6	For it is not ye that speak, but the Spirit	10:20
42	ye **shall be** hated of all men for my name's sake:	10:22
4	The disciple is not above his master,	10:24
4	Fear them not ... for there is nothing covered,	10:26
7	But the very hairs of your head **are** all numbered.	10:30
4	loveth father ... more than me is not worthy of me:	10:37
4	loveth son ... more than me is not worthy of me.	10:37
4	he that taketh not his cross, ... is not worthy of me.	10:38
3	And said unto him, **Art** thou he that should come,	11:3
4	And blessed is he, whosoever shall not be offended	11:6
7	they that wear soft clothing **are** in kings' houses.	11:8
4	For this is he, of whom it is written,	11:10
4	least in the kingdom of heaven is greater than he.	11:11
4	And if ye will receive it, this is Elias,	11:14
4	It is like unto children sitting in the markets,	11:16
40	It **shall be** more tolerable for Tyre and Sidon	11:22
40	it **shall be** more tolerable for the land of Sodom	11:24
2	and learn of me; for **I am** meek and lowly in heart:	11:29
4	For my yoke is easy, and my burden is light.	11:30
34	which **was** not lawful for him to eat,	12:4
7	priests ... profane the sabbath, and **are** blameless?	12:5
4	That in this place is one greater than the temple.	12:6
4	But if ye had known what this **meaneth**,	12:7
4	the Son of man is Lord even of the sabbath day.	12:8
40	What man **shall there be** among you,	12:11

253

εἰμί 1498

4	Is not this the son of David?	Matt	12:23
43	therefore they **shall be** your judges.		12:27
21	He that is not with me is against me;		12:30
4	He that is not with me is against me;		12:30
23	how can ye, **being** evil, speak good things?		12:34
34	For as Jonas **was** three days ... in the whale's belly;		12:40
40	so **shall** the Son of man **be** three days		12:40
40	Even so **shall** it **be** also unto this wicked generation.		12:45
4	Who is my mother? and who are my brethren?		12:48
7	Who is my mother? and who **are** my brethren?		12:48
4	the same **is** my brother, and sister, and mother.		12:50
4	This is he which received seed by the way side.		13:19
4	the same is he that heareth the word,		13:20
4	root in himself, but is only temporary, (NASB)		13:21
4	is he that heareth the word;		13:22
4	is he that heareth the word, and understandeth it;		13:23
4	The kingdom ... is like to a grain of mustard seed,		13:31
4	Which indeed is the least of all seeds:		13:32
4	it is the greatest among herbs,		13:32
4	The kingdom of heaven is like unto leaven,		13:33
4	He that soweth the good seed is the Son of man;		13:37
4	The field is the world;		13:38
7	the good seed **are** the children of the kingdom;		13:38
7	but the tares **are** the children of the wicked one;		13:38
4	The enemy that sowed them is the devil;		13:39
4	the harvest is the end of the world;		13:39
7	and the reapers **are** the angels.		13:39
40	so **shall** it **be** in the end of this world.		13:40
40	there **shall be** wailing and gnashing of teeth.		13:42
4	the kingdom ... is like unto treasure hid in a field;		13:44
4	kingdom of heaven is like unto a merchant man,		13:45
4	the kingdom of heaven is like unto a net,		13:47
40	So **shall** it **be** at the end of the world:		13:49
40	there **shall be** wailing and gnashing of teeth.		13:50
4	is like unto a man that is an householder,		13:52
4	Is not this the carpenter's son?		13:55
7	And his sisters, **are** they not all with us?		13:56
4	A prophet is not without honour,		13:57
4	said unto his servants, This is John the Baptist;		14:2
4	This **is** a desert place, and the time is now past;		14:15
37	they that had eaten **were** about five thousand men,		14:21
34	when the evening was come, **he was** there alone.		14:23
34	But the ship **was** now in the midst of the sea,		14:24
34	tossed with waves: for the wind **was** contrary.		14:24
4	saying, It is a spirit; and they cried out for fear.		14:26
2	Be of good cheer; it is I; be not afraid.		14:27
3	if it **be** thou, bid me come unto thee on the water.		14:28
3	Of a truth **thou art** the Son of God.		14:33
7	Let them alone: **they be** blind leaders of the blind.		15:14
6	Are ye also yet without understanding?		15:16
4	These **are** the things which defile a man:		15:20
4	It is not meet to take the children's bread,		15:26
37	they that did eat **were** about four thousand men,		15:38
32	Whom do men say that I the Son of man **am**?		16:13
32	He saith unto them, But whom say ye that I **am**?		16:15
3	Thou **art** the Christ, the Son of the living God.		16:16
3	Blessed **art thou**, Simon Barjona:		16:17
3	And I say also unto thee, That thou **art** Peter,		16:18
40	thou shalt bind on earth **shall be** bound in heaven:		16:19
40	thou shalt loose on earth **shall be** loosed in heaven.		16:19
4	should tell no man that he **was** Jesus the Christ.		16:20
40	Lord: this shall not **be** unto thee.		16:22
3	behind me, Satan: **thou art** an offence unto me:		16:23
7	**There be** some standing here,		16:28
4	Lord, it is good for us to be here:		17:4
32	Lord, it is good for us to **be** here:		17:4
4	This is my beloved Son,		17:5
38	how long **shall I be** with you?		17:17
7	Jesus saith unto him, Then are the children free.		17:26
4	Who is the greatest in the kingdom of heaven?		18:1
4	the same is greatest in the kingdom of heaven.		18:4
4	for it must needs **be** that offences come;		18:7
4	it is better for thee to enter into life halt or		18:8
4	it is better for thee to enter into life with one eye,		18:9
4	Even so it is not the will of your Father,		18:14
17	**let him be** unto thee as a heathen man		18:17
40	ye shall bind on earth **shall be** bound in heaven:		18:18

40	ye shall loose on earth **shall be** loosed in heaven.	Matt	18:18
7	two or three **are** gathered together in my name,		18:20
2	two or three are ... there **am** I in the midst of them.		18:20
43	and they twain **shall be** one flesh?		19:5
7	Wherefore **they are** no more twain, but one flesh.		19:6
4	If the case of the man **be** so with his wife,		19:10
7	For **there are** some eunuchs,		19:12
7	and **there are** some eunuchs,		19:12
7	and **there be** eunuchs, ... made themselves eunuchs		19:12
4	for of such is the kingdom of heaven.		19:14
4	There is only One who **is** good (NASB)		19:17
32	If thou wilt **be** perfect, go and sell that thou hast,		19:21
34	for he **was** one who owned much (NASB)		19:22
4	It is easier for a camel to go through		19:24
4	With men this is impossible; but with God		19:26
4	but with God all things **are** possible.		19:26
40	have forsaken all, ... what **shall** we **have** therefore?		19:27
43	But many that are first **shall be** last;		19:30
4	For the kingdom of heaven **is** like unto a man		20:1
10	and whatsoever is right I will give you.		20:4
10	and whatsoever is right, that shall ye receive.		20:7
4	Is thine eye evil, because I am good?		20:15
2	Is thine eye evil, because I **am** good?		20:15
43	So the last **shall be** first, and the first last:		20:16
7	for many **are** called, but few chosen.		20:16
4	is not mine to give, but it shall be given to them		20:23
40	But it **shall** not **be** so among you:		20:26
4	But it **shall** not **be** so among you:		20:26
17	will be great among you, **let him be** your minister;		20:26
40	will be great among you, **let him be** your minister;		20:26
32	And whosoever will **be** chief among you,		20:27
17	will be chief among you, **let him be** your servant:		20:27
40	will be chief among you, **let him be** your servant:		20:27
4	all the city was moved, saying, Who is this?		21:10
4	This is Jesus the prophet of Nazareth of Galilee.		21:11
34	The baptism of John, whence **was** it?		21:25
34	**There was** a certain householder,		21:33
4	This is the heir; come, let us kill him,		21:38
4	and it is marvellous in our eyes?		21:42
4	saith he to his servants, The wedding is ready,		22:8
37	but they which were bidden were not worthy.		22:8
40	there **shall be** weeping and gnashing of teeth.		22:13
7	For many **are** called, but few are chosen.		22:14
3	saying, Master, we know that **thou art** true,		22:16
32	Sadducees, which say that there is no resurrection,		22:23
37	Now **there were** with us seven brethren,		22:25
40	in the resurrection whose wife **shall she be**		22:28
7	but **are** as the angels of God in heaven.		22:30
2	I **am** the God of Abraham, and the God of Isaac,		22:32
4	God is not the God of the dead, but of the living.		22:32
4	This is the first and great commandment.		22:38
4	What think ye of Christ? whose son **is he**?		22:42
4	If David then call him Lord, how is he his son?		22:45
4	for one is your Master, even Christ;		23:8
6	one is your Master, ... and all ye **are** brethren.		23:8
4	for one is your Father, which is in heaven.		23:9
4	for one is your Master, even Christ.		23:10
40	he that is greatest among you **shall be** your servant:		23:11
4	Whosoever shall swear by the temple, it is nothing;		23:16
4	Ye fools and blind: for whether is greater,		23:17
4	Whosoever shall swear by the altar, it is nothing;		23:18
6	but within ye **are** full of hypocrisy and iniquity.		23:28
36	If we **had been** in the days of our fathers,		23:30
50	If we **had been** in the days of our fathers,		23:30
36	we **would** not **have been** partakers with them		23:30
50	we **would** not **have been** partakers with them		23:30
6	that ye **are** the children of them which killed		23:31
40	Tell us, when **shall** these things **be**?		24:3
2	many shall come in my name, saying, I **am** Christ;		24:5
4	things must come to pass, but the end is not yet.		24:6
43	and **there shall be** famines, and pestilences,		24:7
42	ye **shall be** hated of all nations for my name's sake.		24:9
40	For then **shall be** great tribulation,		24:21
4	Behold, he is in the desert; go not forth:		24:26
40	so **shall** also the coming of the Son of man **be**.		24:27
10	For wheresoever the carcase is,		24:28
4	know that it is near, even at the doors.		24:33

εἰμί 1498

40	so **shall** also the coming of the Son of man **be**....	Matt 24:37
37	**they were** eating and drinking,	24:38
40	so **shall** also the coming of the Son of man **be**.	24:39
43	Then **shall** two **be** in the field;	24:40
4	Who then **is** a faithful and wise servant,	24:45
40	there **shall be** weeping and gnashing of teeth.	24:51
37	And five of them **were** wise, and five **were** foolish....	25:2
35	**thou hast been** faithful over a few things,	25:21
35	**thou hast been** faithful over a few things,	25:23
3	Lord, I knew thee that **thou art** an hard man,	25:24
40	there **shall be** weeping and gnashing of teeth.	25:30
46	**I was** a stranger, and ye took me in:	25:35
46	**I was** in prison, and ye came unto me.	25:36
46	**I was** a stranger, and ye took me not in:	25:43
4	The Master saith, My time **is** at hand;	26:18
2	to say unto him, Lord, **is** it I?	26:22
34	it **had been** good ... if he had not been born.	26:24
2	Master, **is** it I? He said unto him, Thou hast said.	26:25
4	and said, Take, eat; this **is** my body.	26:26
4	For this **is** my blood of the new testament;	26:28
4	My soul **is** exceeding sorrowful, even unto death:	26:38
4	if it **be** possible, let this cup pass from me:	26:39
37	asleep again: for their eyes **were** heavy.	26:43
4	Whomsoever I shall kiss, that same **is** he:	26:48
3	tell us whether thou **be** the Christ, the Son of God....	26:63
4	They answered and said, He **is** guilty of death.	26:66
4	Prophesy unto us, ... Who **is** he that smote thee?	26:68
47	Thou also **wast** with Jesus of Galilee.	26:69
34	This fellow **was** also with Jesus of Nazareth.	26:71
3	said to Peter, Surely thou also **art** one of them;	26:73
4	because it **is** the price of blood.	27:6
3	**Art** thou the King of the Jews?	27:11
2	**I am** innocent of the blood of this just person:	27:24
4	Golgotha, that **is** to say, a place of a skull,	27:33
4	THIS **IS** JESUS THE KING OF THE JEWS.	27:37
3	If **thou be** the Son of God, come down	27:40
4	If he **be** the King of Israel, let him now come down..	27:42
2	for he said, **I am** the Son of God.	27:43
4	that **is** to say, My God, my God, why hast thou	27:46
34	Truly this **was** the Son of God.	27:54
37	And many women **were** there beholding afar off,	27:55
34	Among which **was** Mary Magdalene, and Mary	27:56
34	there **was** Mary Magdalene, and the other Mary,	27:61
4	which **is** the one after the preparation, (NASB)	27:62
40	so the last error **shall be** worse than the first.	27:64
34	His countenance **was** like lightning,	28:3
4	He **is** not here: for he is risen, as he said.	28:6
2	**I am** with you alway,	28:20
34	And John **was** clothed with camel's hair,	Mark 1:6
2	the latchet of whose shoes **I am** not worthy	1:7
3	Thou **art** my beloved Son, ... I am well pleased.	1:11
34	And he **was** there in the wilderness forty days,	1:13
34	tempted of Satan; and **was** with the wild beasts;	1:13
37	casting a net into the sea: for **they were** fishers.	1:16
34	for He **was** teaching them (NASB)	1:22
34	And there **was** in their synagogue a man	1:23
3	I know thee who **thou art**, the Holy One of God.	1:24
4	What thing **is** this? what new doctrine **is** this?	1:27
34	And all the city **was** gathered together at the door.	1:33
34	And he preached in their synagogues (NT)	1:39
34	but **was** without in desert places:	1:45
4	and it was noised that he **was** in the house.	2:1
34	they uncovered the roof where he **was**:	2:4
37	But **there were** certain of the scribes sitting there,	2:6
4	Whether **is** it easier to say to the sick of the palsy,	2:9
37	for **there were** many, and they followed him.	2:15
37	and the Pharisees **were** fasting; (NASB)	2:18
4	fast, while the bridegroom **is** with them?	2:19
24	and gave also to them which **were** with him?	2:26
4	the Son of man **is** Lord also of the sabbath.	2:28
34	**there was** a man there which had a withered hand.	3:1
3	and cried, saying, Thou **art** the Son of God.	3:11
32	charged ... that they should not make him known.	3:12
12	he ordained twelve, that they **should be** with him,	3:14
4	Boanerges, which **is**, The sons of thunder:	3:17
4	but **is** in danger of eternal damnation:	3:29
40	but **is** in danger of eternal damnation:	3:29
4	saying, Who **is** my mother, or my brethren?	Mark 3:33
4	shall do the will of God, the same **is** my brother,	3:35
34	the whole multitude **was** by the sea on the land.	4:1
37	the whole multitude **was** by the sea on the land.	4:1
7	And these **are** they by the way side,	4:15
7	And these **are** they likewise which are sown	4:16
7	root in themselves, but **are** only (NASB)	4:17
7	And these **are** they which are sown among thorns;	4:18
7	**are** sown among thorns; such as hear the word,	4:18
7	And these **are** they which are sown on good ground;	4:20
4	For there **is** nothing hid, which shall not	4:22
4	And he said, So **is** the kingdom of God,	4:26
49	though it **is** smaller than all the seeds (NASB)	4:31
4	**is** less than all the seeds that be in the earth:	4:31
34	they took him even as **he was** in the ship.	4:36
34	And there **were** also with him other little ships.	4:36
37	And there **were** also with him other little ships.	4:36
34	And he **was** in the hinder part of the ship,	4:38
6	And he said unto them, Why **are** ye so fearful?	4:40
4	said one to another, What manner of man **is** this,	4:41
34	night and day, **he was** in the mountains,	5:5
4	saying, My name **is** Legion: for we are many.	5:9
5	saying, My name **is** Legion: for **we are** many.	5:9
34	Now **there was** there nigh unto the mountains	5:11
37	**they were** about two thousand;	5:13
4	And they went out to see what it **was** that was done...	5:14
10	prayed him that **he might be** with him.	5:18
34	and he **was** nigh unto the sea.	5:21
26	which had an issue of blood twelve years, (NT)	5:25
15	go in peace, and **be** whole of thy plague.	5:34
34	and entereth in where the damsel **was** lying.	5:40
4	Talitha cumi; which is, being interpreted, Damsel,	5:41
34	for she **was** of the age of twelve years.	5:42
4	**Is** not this the carpenter, the son of Mary,	6:3
7	and **are** not his sisters here with us?	6:3
4	A prophet **is** not without honour, but in his own	6:4
40	**shall be** more tolerable for Sodom and Gomorrha	6:11
4	Others said, That it **is** Elias,	6:15
4	And others said, That **it is** a prophet,	6:15
4	he said, It **is** John, whom I beheaded:	6:16
37	for there **were** many coming and going,	6:31
37	because **they were** as sheep not having a shepherd:	6:34
4	This **is** a desert place,	6:35
37	that did eat ... **were** about five thousand men.	6:44
34	the ship **was** in the midst of the sea,	6:47
34	for the wind **was** contrary unto them:	6:48
32	they supposed it **had been** a spirit, and cried out:	6:49
4	they supposed it **had been** a spirit, and cried out:	6:49
2	Be of good cheer: it **is** I; be not afraid.	6:50
34	for their heart **was** hardened.	6:52
4	began to carry about ... where they heard **he was**.	6:55
4	that **is** to say, with unwashen, hands,	7:2
4	And many other things **there be**,	7:4
4	It **is** Corban, that **is** to say, a gift,	7:11
4	**There is** nothing from without a man,	7:15
4	those **are** they that defile the man.	7:15
6	**Are** ye so without understanding also?	7:18
34	woman **was** a Greek, a Syrophenician by nation;	7:26
4	for it **is** not meet to take the children's bread,	7:27
4	and saith unto him, Ephphatha, that **is**, Be opened.	7:34
19	In those days the multitude **being** very great,	8:1
7	for divers of them came from far.	8:3
37	And they that had eaten **were** about four thousand:	8:9
32	saying unto them, Whom do men say that **I am**?	8:27
32	he saith unto them, But whom say ye that **I am**?	8:29
3	And Peter answereth ... Thou **art** the Christ.	8:29
7	That **there be** some of them that stand here,	9:1
37	Elias with Moses: and **they were** talking with Jesus.	9:4
4	Master, it **is** good for us to **be** here:	9:5
32	Master, it **is** good for us **to be** here:	9:5
37	he wist not what to say; for **they were** sore afraid.	9:6
4	saying, This **is** my beloved Son: hear him.	9:7
4	what the rising from the dead **should mean**.	9:10
38	faithless generation, how long **shall** I **be** with you?	9:19
4	How long **is** it ago since this came unto him?	9:21
32	and saith unto them, If any man desire **to be** first,	9:35
40	desire to be first, the same **shall be** last of all,	9:35

255

εἰμί 1498

4	for there is no man which shall do a miracle	Mark	9:39
4	For he that is not against us is on our part.		9:40
4	For he that is not against us is on our part.		9:40
6	give you a cup ... because ye belong to Christ,		9:41
4	it is better for him that a millstone were hanged		9:42
4	it is better for thee to enter into life maimed,		9:43
4	it is better for thee to enter halt into life,		9:45
4	it is better for thee to enter into the kingdom		9:47
43	And they twain shall be one flesh:		10:8
7	so then they are no more twain, but one flesh.		10:8
4	for of such is the kingdom of God.		10:14
34	for he was one who owned much (NASB)		10:22
4	how hard is it for them that trust in riches		10:24
4	It is easier for a camel to go through		10:25
4	for with God all things are possible.		10:27
4	There is no man that hath left house,		10:29
43	many that are first shall be last; and the last first.		10:31
37	And they were in the way going up to Jerusalem;		10:32
34	and Jesus was walking on ahead of them; (NASB)		10:32
4	But to sit on my right hand ... is not mine to give;		10:40
40	But so shall it not be among you:		10:43
4	But so shall it not be among you:		10:43
40	will be great among you, shall be your minister:		10:43
32	and whoever wishes to be first among you (NASB)		10:44
40	will be the chiefest, shall be servant of all.		10:44
4	And when he heard that it was Jesus of Nazareth,		10:47
27	and now the eventide was come,		11:11
34	for the time of figs was not yet.		11:13
40	not doubt ... he shall have whatsoever he saith.		11:23
40	believe that ye receive ... and ye shall have them.		11:24
34	The baptism of John, was it from heaven,		11:30
34	counted John, that he was a prophet indeed.		11:32
4	This is the heir; come, let us kill him,		12:7
40	let us kill him, and the inheritance shall be ours.		12:7
4	the Lord's doing, and it is marvellous in our eyes?		12:11
3	we know that thou art true, and carest for no man;		12:14
32	the Sadducees, which say there is no resurrection;		12:18
37	Now there were seven brethren: and the first		12:20
40	whose wife shall she be of them? for the seven had		12:23
7	but are as the angels which are in heaven.		12:25
4	He is not the God of the dead, but ... of the living:		12:27
4	Which is the first commandment of all?		12:28
4	"The foremost is (NASB)		12:29
4	Hear, O Israel; The Lord our God is one Lord:		12:29
4	There is none other commandment greater		12:31
4	there is one God; and there is none other but he:		12:32
4	there is one God; and there is none other but he:		12:32
4	is more than all whole burnt offerings		12:33
3	Thou art not far from the kingdom of God.		12:34
4	How say the scribes that Christ is the son of David?		12:35
4	and whence is he then his son?		12:37
4	and she threw in two mites, which make a farthing.		12:42
40	Tell us, when shall these things be?		13:4
2	saying, I am Christ; and shall deceive many.		13:6
43	and there shall be earthquakes in divers places,		13:8
43	and there shall be famines and troubles:		13:8
6	for it is not ye that speak, but the Holy Ghost.		13:11
42	ye shall be hated of all men for my name's sake:		13:13
21	And let him that is in the field not turn back again		13:16
43	For in those days shall be affliction,		13:19
43	And the stars of heaven shall fall,		13:25
4	putteth forth leaves, ye know that summer is near:		13:28
4	know that it is nigh, even at the doors.		13:29
4	watch and pray: for ye know not when the time is.		13:33
34	After two days was the feast of the passover,		14:1
40	the feast day, lest there be an uproar of the people.		14:2
19	being in Bethany in the house of Simon the leper,		14:3
37	were some that had indignation within themselves,		14:4
4	The Master saith, Where is the guestchamber,		14:14
34	good were it ... if he had never been born.		14:21
4	gave to them, and said, Take, eat: this is my body.		14:22
4	This is my blood of the new testament,		14:24
4	My soul is exceeding sorrowful unto death:		14:34
4	if it were possible, the hour might pass from him.		14:35
37	asleep again, for their eyes were heavy,		14:40
21	cometh Judas, one of the twelve, (NT)		14:43
4	saying, Whomsoever I shall kiss, that same is he;		14:44
46	I was daily with you in the temple teaching,	Mark	14:49
34	he was sitting with the officers, (NASB)		14:54
37	but their witness agreed not together. (NT)		14:56
34	But neither so did their witness (NT)		14:59
3	Art thou the Christ, the Son of the Blessed?		14:61
2	said, I am: and ye shall see the Son of man sitting		14:62
32	And they all condemned him to be guilty of death.		14:64
19	And as Peter was beneath in the palace,		14:66
47	And thou also wast with Jesus of Nazareth.		14:67
4	a maid saw him again, ... This is one of them.		14:69
3	Surely thou art one of them: ... art a Galilaean,		14:70
3	thou art one of them: for thou art a Galilaean,		14:70
3	Pilate asked him, Art thou the King of the Jews?		15:2
34	And there was one named Barabbas,		15:7
4	led him away into the hall, called Praetorium; (NT)		15:16
4	which is, being interpreted, The place of a skull.		15:22
34	And it was the third hour, and they crucified him.		15:25
34	superscription of his accusation was written over,		15:26
4	which is, being interpreted, My God, my God,		15:34
34	he said, Truly this man was the Son of God.		15:39
37	There were also women looking on afar off:		15:40
34	afar off: among whom was Mary Magdalene,		15:40
34	Who also, when he was in Galilee, followed him,		15:41
34	the even was come, because it was the preparation,		15:42
4	preparation, that is, the day before the sabbath,		15:42
34	which also waited for the kingdom (NT)		15:43
34	in a sepulchre which was hewn out of a rock,		15:46
34	the stone has was rolled away: for it was very great.		16:4
4	which was crucified: he is risen; he is not here:		16:6
37	And they were both righteous before God,	Luke	1:6
34	And they had no child, ... Elisabeth was barren,		1:7
34	no child, because that Elisabeth was barren,		1:7
37	and they both were now well stricken in years.		1:7
34	the whole multitude of the people were praying		1:10
40	And thou shalt have joy and gladness;		1:14
40	For he shall be great in the sight of the Lord,		1:15
2	Whereby shall I know this? for I am an old man,		1:18
2	the angel answering said unto him, I am Gabriel,		1:19
39	behold, thou shalt be dumb, and not able to speak,		1:20
34	And the people waited for Zacharias, (NT)		1:21
34	he beckoned unto them, (NT)		1:22
14	what manner of salutation this should be.		1:29
40	He shall be great, and shall be called the Son of		1:32
40	and of his kingdom there shall be no end.		1:33
40	Then said Mary unto the angel, How shall this be,		1:34
4	and this is the sixth month with her,		1:36
40	for there shall be a performance of those things		1:45
4	There is none of thy kindred that is called		1:61
34	saying, His name is John. And they marvelled all.		1:63
40	saying, What manner of child shall this be!		1:66
34	And the hand of the Lord was with him.		1:66
34	and was in the deserts till the day of his showing		1:80
32	because he was of the house and lineage of David:		2:4
28	Mary his espoused wife, being great with child.		2:5
32	while they were there, the days were accomplished		2:6
34	because there was no room for them in the inn.		2:7
37	And there were in the same country shepherds		2:8
40	tidings of great joy, which shall be to all people.		2:10
4	is born ... a Saviour, which is Christ the Lord.		2:11
34	And, behold, there was a man in Jerusalem,		2:25
34	a man in Jerusalem, whose name was Simeon;		2:25
34	And it was revealed unto him by the Holy Ghost,		2:26
34	And Joseph and his mother marvelled (NT)		2:33
34	And there was one Anna, a prophetess,		2:36
34	and the grace of God was upon him.		2:40
32	supposing him to have been in the company,		2:44
32	that I must be about my Father's business?		2:49
34	and came to Nazareth, and was subject unto them:		2:51
40	and the crooked shall be made straight,		3:5
14	whether he were the Christ, or not;		3:15
2	latchet of whose shoes I am not worthy to unloose:		3:16
3	which said, Thou art my beloved Son;		3:22
34	Jesus himself began to be about thirty years of age,		3:23
21	being as was supposed the son of Joseph,		3:23
3	If thou be the Son of God, command this stone that		4:3
40	If thou ... wilt worship me, all shall be thine.		4:7
3	If thou be the Son of God, cast thyself down		4:9

256

εἰμί 1498

34	came to Nazareth, where he **had been** brought up:	Luke 4:16
34	he found the place where it **was** written,	4:17
37	the eyes of all … **were** fastened on him.	4:20
4	And they said, **Is** not this Joseph's son?	4:22
4	No prophet **is** accepted in his own country.	4:24
37	many widows **were** in Israel in the days of Elias,	4:25
37	many lepers **were** in Israel in the time of Eliseus	4:27
34	and taught them on the sabbath days. (NT)	4:31
34	at his doctrine: for his word **was** with power.	4:32
34	And in the synagogue there **was** a man,	4:33
3	I know thee who thou **art**; the Holy One of God.	4:34
34	Simon's wife's mother **was** taken with a … fever;	4:38
3	and saying, Thou **art** Christ the Son of God.	4:41
32	not to speak: for they knew that he **was** Christ.	4:41
34	And he preached in the synagogues (NT)	4:44
34	he stood by the lake of Gennesaret, (NT)	5:1
34	entered into one of the ships, which **was** Simon's,	5:3
2	Depart from me; for I **am** a sinful man, O Lord.	5:8
37	sons of Zebedee, which **were** partners with Simon.	5:10
39	from henceforth thou shalt catch men. (NT)	5:10
32	And it came to pass, when he **was** in a certain city,	5:12
34	And he withdrew himself into the wilderness, (NT)	5:16
34	as he **was** teaching, that there were Pharisees and …	5:17
37	that there **were** Pharisees and doctors of the law	5:17
37	which **were** come out of every town of Galilee,	5:17
34	the power of the Lord **was** present to heal them.	5:17
34	in a bed a man which **was** taken with a palsy:	5:18
4	saying, Who **is** this which speaketh blasphemies?	5:21
4	Whether **is** easier, to say, Thy sins be forgiven	5:23
34	and there **was** a great company of publicans	5:29
37	publicans and of others that sat down (NT)	5:29
4	fast, while the bridegroom **is** with them?	5:34
4	desireth new: for he saith, The old **is** better.	5:39
23	was an hungered, and they which **were** with him;	6:3
4	That the Son of man **is** Lord also of the sabbath.	6:5
34	there **was** a man whose right hand was withered.	6:6
34	there **was** a man whose right hand was withered.	6:6
34	and continued all night in prayer to God. (NT)	6:12
4	ye poor: for yours **is** the kingdom of God.	6:20
6	Blessed **are** ye, when men shall hate you,	6:22
4	ye love them which love you, what thank **have** ye?	6:32
4	them which do good to you, what thank **have** ye?	6:33
4	of whom ye hope to receive, what thank **have** ye?	6:34
40	and your reward shall **be** great,	6:35
42	and ye **shall be** the children of the Highest:	6:35
4	for he **is** kind unto the unthankful and to the evil.	6:35
4	Be ye … merciful, as your Father also **is** merciful.	6:36
4	The disciple **is** not above his master:	6:40
40	but every one that is perfect **shall be** as his master.	6:40
4	a good tree bringeth not forth corrupt (NT)	6:43
4	I will show you to whom he **is** like:	6:47
4	He **is** like a man which built an house,	6:48
4	**is** like a man that without a foundation built	6:49
34	who **was** dear unto him, was sick, and ready to die.	7:2
4	That he **was** worthy for whom he should do this:	7:4
2	for I **am** not worthy that thou shouldest enter	7:6
2	For I also **am** a man set under authority,	7:8
34	the only son of his mother, and she **was** a widow:	7:12
34	crowd from the city **was** with her (NASB)	7:12
3	saying, **Art thou** he that should come?	7:19
3	**Art thou** he that should come?	7:20
4	And blessed **is** he, whosoever shall not be offended	7:23
4	they which … live delicately, **are** in kings' courts.	7:25
4	This **is** he, of whom it is written,	7:27
4	Among those that are born of women there **is** not	7:28
4	**is** least in the kingdom of God is greater than he.	7:28
7	men of this generation? and to what **are** they like?	7:31
7	They **are** like unto children sitting in the	7:32
34	behold, a woman in the city, which **was** a sinner,	7:37
34	if he **were** a prophet, would have known who and	7:39
4	for she **is** a sinner.	7:39
37	There **was** a certain creditor which had two	7:41
4	Who **is** this that forgiveth sins also?	7:49
37	which had **been** healed of evil spirits and	8:2
14	disciples asked him, … What **might** this parable **be**?	8:9
4	the parable **is** this: The seed is the word of God.	8:11
4	the parable **is** this: The seed is the word of God.	8:11
7	Those by the way side **are** they that hear;	Luke 8:12
7	And that which fell among thorns **are** they, which,	8:14
7	But that on the good ground **are** they,	8:15
4	nothing **is** secret, that shall not be made manifest;	8:17
7	My mother and my brethren **are** these which hear	8:21
4	And he said unto them, Where **is** your faith?	8:25
4	What manner of man **is** this! for he commandeth	8:25
4	Gadarenes, which **is** over against Galilee.	8:26
4	And Jesus asked him, saying, What **is** thy name?	8:30
34	And **there was** there an herd of many swine	8:32
32	man … besought him that he **might be** with him:	8:38
37	received him: for they **were** all waiting for him.	8:40
34	**had** one only daughter, about twelve years of age,	8:42
26	a woman **having** an issue of blood twelve years,	8:43
4	Herod said, John have I beheaded: but who **is** this,	9:9
5	and get victuals: for we **are** here in a desert place.	9:12
7	We **have** no more but five loaves and two fishes;	9:13
37	For they **were** about five thousand men.	9:14
32	And it came to pass, as he **was** alone praying,	9:18
32	he asked them, … Whom say the people that I **am**?	9:18
32	He said unto them, But whom say ye that I **am**?	9:20
7	I tell you of a truth, **there be** some standing here,	9:27
37	with him two men, which **were** Moses and Elias:	9:30
37	they that **were** with him were heavy with sleep:	9:32
4	Master, **it is** good for us to be here:	9:33
32	Master, it is good for us **to be** here:	9:33
4	saying, This **is** my beloved Son: hear him.	9:35
4	look upon my son: for he **is** mine only child.	9:38
38	perverse generation, how long **shall** I **be** with you,	9:41
34	it **was** hid from them, that they perceived it not:	9:45
14	which of them **should be** greatest.	9:46
40	**is** least among you all, the same **shall be** great.	9:48
4	**is** least among you all, the same **shall be** great.	9:48
4	for he that **is** not against us is for us.	9:50
4	for he that is not against us **is** for us.	9:50
34	his face **was** as though he would go to Jerusalem.	9:53
6	Ye know not what manner of spirit ye **are** of.	9:55
4	and looking back, **is** fit for the kingdom of God.	9:62
10	if the son of peace be there, your peace shall rest	10:6
4	for the labourer **is** worthy of his hire.	10:7
40	it **shall be** more tolerable in that day for Sodom,	10:12
40	But it **shall be** more tolerable for Tyre and Sidon	10:14
4	no man knoweth who the Son **is**, but the Father;	10:22
4	but the Father; and who the Father **is**, but the Son,	10:22
4	said unto Jesus, And who **is** my neighbour?	10:29
34	And she **had** a sister called Mary,	10:39
4	But one **thing is** needful:	10:42
32	that, as he **was** praying in a certain place,	11:1
7	and my children **are** with me in bed; I cannot rise	11:7
32	because he **is** his friend, yet because … importunity	11:8
34	And he **was** casting out a devil, and it was dumb.	11:14
34	And he was casting out a devil, and it **was** dumb.	11:14
43	therefore **shall** they **be** your judges.	11:19
4	armed keepeth his palace, his goods **are** in peace:	11:21
21	He that is not with me **is** against me:	11:23
4	He that is not with me **is** against me:	11:23
4	This **is** an evil generation: they seek a sign;	11:29
40	so **shall** also the Son of man **be** to this generation.	11:30
4	The light of the body **is** the eye:	11:34
10	therefore when thine eye **is** single,	11:34
4	thy whole body also **is** full of light;	11:34
10	but when thine eye **is** evil,	11:34
4	that the light which **is** in thee be not darkness.	11:35
40	the whole **shall** be full of light,	11:36
4	and, behold, all things **are** clean unto you.	11:41
6	for ye **are** as graves which appear not,	11:44
6	you **are** witnesses and approve the deeds (NASB)	11:48
4	leaven of the Pharisees, which **is** hypocrisy.	12:1
4	**is** nothing covered, that shall not be revealed;	12:2
4	and not one of them **is** forgotten before God?	12:6
4	for a man's life **consisteth** not in the abundance	12:15
40	**shall** those things **be**, which thou hast provided?	12:20
4	The life **is** more than meat,	12:23
4	ravens: … which neither **have** storehouse nor barn;	12:24
18	God so clothe the grass, **which is** to day in the field,	12:28
4	where your treasure **is**, there will your heart be	12:34
40	where your treasure is, there **will** your heart **be**	12:34

257

εἰμί

#	Text	Ref
33	Let your loins be girded about,	Luke 12:35
7	and find them so, blessed are those servants.	12:38
4	Who then is that faithful and wise steward,	12:42
43	there shall be five in one house divided,	12:52
40	There will be heat; and it cometh to pass.	12:55
34	And he was teaching in one of the synagogues	13:10
34	behold, there was a woman which had a spirit	13:11
34	infirmity eighteen years, and was bowed together,	13:11
7	There are six days in which men ought to work:	13:14
29	this woman, being a daughter of Abraham,	13:16
4	Unto what is the kingdom of God like?	13:18
4	It is like a grain of mustard seed,	13:19
4	It is like leaven, which a woman took and hid	13:21
6	say unto you, I know you not whence ye are:	13:25
6	I know you not whence ye are; depart from me,	13:27
40	There shall be weeping and gnashing of teeth,	13:28
7	And, behold, there are last which shall be first,	13:30
43	And, behold, there are last which shall be first,	13:30
7	and there are first which shall be last.	13:30
43	and there are first which shall be last.	13:30
37	the sabbath day, that they watched him. (NT)	14:1
34	And, behold, there was a certain man before him	14:2
10	lest a more honourable man than thou be bidden	14:8
40	Friend, go up higher: then shalt thou have worship	14:10
39	thou shalt be blessed; for they cannot recompense	14:14
4	were bidden, Come; for all things are now ready.	14:17
7	were bidden, Come; for all things are now ready.	14:17
4	as thou hast commanded, and yet there is room.	14:22
32	and his own life also, he cannot be my disciple.	14:26
32	doth not bear his cross, ... cannot be my disciple.	14:27
4	sitteth ... first, and consulteth whether he be able	14:31
19	Or else, while the other is yet a great way off,	14:32
32	that forsaketh not all ... he cannot be my disciple.	14:33
4	It is neither fit for the land, nor ... the dunghill;	14:35
37	Then drew near unto him all the publicans	15:1
40	I say unto you, that likewise joy shall be in heaven	15:7
2	And am no more worthy to be called thy son.	15:19
2	and am no more worthy to be called thy son.	15:21
34	For this my son was dead, and is alive again;	15:24
34	dead, and is alive again; he was lost, and is found.	15:24
34	Now his elder son was in the field:	15:25
14	of the servants, and asked what these things meant.	15:26
3	thou art ever with me, and all that I have is thine.	15:31
4	thou art ever with me, and all that I have is thine.	15:31
34	for this thy brother was dead, and is alive again;	15:32
34	and is alive again; and was lost, and is found.	15:32
34	There was a certain rich man, ... had a steward;	16:1
7	children of this world are in their generation wiser,	16:8
4	He that is faithful in that which is least is faithful	16:10
4	he that is unjust in the least is unjust also in much.	16:10
6	Ye are they which justify yourselves before men;	16:15
4	among men is abomination in the sight of God.	16:15
4	And it is easier for heaven and earth to pass,	16:17
34	There was a certain rich man,	16:19
34	And there was a certain beggar named Lazarus,	16:20
4	It is impossible but that offences will come:	17:1
5	say, We are unprofitable servants:	17:10
34	giving him thanks: and he was a Samaritan.	17:16
4	for, behold, the kingdom of God is within you.	17:21
40	so shall also the Son of man be in his day.	17:24
40	so shall it be also in the days of the Son of man.	17:26
40	Even thus shall it be in the day when the Son	17:30
40	In that day, he which shall be upon the housetop,	17:31
43	in that night there shall be two men in one bed;	17:34
43	Two women shall be grinding together;	17:35
43	Two men shall be in the field;	17:36
34	There was in a city a judge, which feared not God,	18:2
34	And there was a widow in that city;	18:3
7	that they were righteous, and despised others;	18:9
2	God, I thank thee, that I am not as other men are,	18:11
4	children ... for of such is the kingdom of God.	18:16
34	he was very sorrowful: for he was very rich.	18:23
4	For it is easier for a camel to go through a needle's	18:25
4	are impossible with men are possible with God.	18:27
4	There is no man that hath left house, or parents,	18:29
34	and this saying was hid from them,	18:34
14	the multitude pass by, he asked what it meant.	18:36
34	which was the chief among the publicans,	Luke 19:2
34	the chief among the publicans, and he was rich.	19:2
4	And he sought to see Jesus who he was;	19:3
34	not for the press, because he was little of stature.	19:3
4	forsomuch as he also is a son of Abraham.	19:9
32	because he was nigh to Jerusalem,	19:11
15	have thou authority over ten cities. (NT)	19:17
3	I feared thee, because thou art an austere man:	19:21
2	Thou knewest that I was an austere man,	19:22
40	MY HOUSE SHALL BE A HOUSE (NASB)	19:46
4	It is written, My house is the house of prayer:	19:46
34	And he taught daily in the temple. (NT)	19:47
4	or who is he that gave thee this authority?	20:2
34	baptism of John, was it from heaven, or of men?	20:4
4	for they be persuaded that John was a prophet.	20:6
32	for they be persuaded that John was a prophet.	20:6
4	saying, This is the heir: come, let us kill him,	20:14
4	What is this then that is written,	20:17
32	which should feign themselves just men, (NT)	20:20
32	which deny that there is any resurrection;	20:27
10	AND HE IS CHILDLESS (NASB)	20:28
37	There were therefore seven brethren:	20:29
7	for they are equal unto the angels;	20:36
7	and are the children of God,	20:36
23	being the children of the resurrection.	20:36
4	For he is not a God of the dead, but of the living:	20:38
32	How say they that Christ is David's son?	20:41
4	therefore calleth him Lord, how is he then his son?	20:44
40	saying, Master, but when shall these things be?	21:7
2	I am Christ; and the time draweth near:	21:8
43	And great earthquakes shall be in divers places,	21:11
40	and fearful sights and great signs shall there be.	21:11
42	ye shall be hated of all men for my name's sake.	21:17
7	For these be the days of vengeance,	21:22
40	for there shall be great distress in the land,	21:23
40	Jerusalem shall be trodden down of the Gentiles,	21:24
40	there shall be signs in the sun, and in the moon,	21:25
43	there shall be signs in the sun, and in the moon,	21:25
4	see and know ... that summer is now nigh at hand.	21:30
4	know ye that the kingdom of God is nigh at hand.	21:31
34	And in the day time he was teaching in the temple;	21:37
18	Iscariot, being of the number of the twelve.	22:3
4	Where is the guestchamber, where I shall eat	22:11
4	This is my body which is given for you:	22:19
14	which of them it was that should do this thing.	22:23
32	which of them should be accounted the greatest.	22:24
2	but I am among you as he that serveth.	22:27
6	Ye are they which have continued with me	22:28
2	Lord, I am ready to go with thee, both into prison,	22:33
4	two swords. And he said unto them, It is enough.	22:38
44	they which were about him saw what would follow,	22:49
19	When I was daily with you in the temple,	22:53
4	but this is your hour, and the power of darkness.	22:53
34	maid beheld him ... This man was also with him.	22:56
3	Thou art also of them. And Peter said, ... I am not.	22:58
2	Thou art also of them. And Peter said, ... I am not.	22:58
34	Of a truth this fellow also was with him:	22:59
4	this fellow also was with him: for he is a Galilaean.	22:59
4	saying, Prophesy, who is it that smote thee?	22:64
3	Art thou the Christ? tell us. And he said	22:67
40	shall the Son of man sit on the right (NT)	22:69
3	Then said they all, Art thou then the Son of God?	22:70
2	And he said unto them, Ye say that I am.	22:70
32	saying that he himself is Christ a King.	23:2
3	Art thou the King of the Jews?	23:3
4	he asked whether the man were a Galilaean.	23:6
4	knew that he belonged unto Herod's jurisdiction,	23:7
18	who himself also was at Jerusalem at that time.	23:7
34	for he was desirous to see him of a long season,	23:8
23	before they were at enmity between themselves.	23:12
4	and, lo, nothing worthy of death is done unto him.	23:15
34	Who ... for murder, was cast into prison.	23:19
4	if he be Christ, the chosen of God.	23:35
3	saying, If thou be the king of the Jews, save thyself.	23:37
34	And a superscription also was written over him	23:38
4	and Hebrew, THIS IS THE KING OF THE JEWS.	23:38
3	saying, If thou be Christ, save thyself and us.	23:39

εἰμί **1498**

3	seeing thou **art** in the same condemnation?	Luke 23:40
39	To day shalt thou be with me in paradise.	23:43
34	And it **was** about the sixth hour,	23:44
34	saying, Certainly this **was** a righteous man.	23:47
34	The same had not consented to the counsel (NT)	23:51
34	a sepulchre ... wherein never man before **was** laid.	23:53
34	And that day **was** the preparation,	23:54
37	which came with him from Galilee, (NT)	23:55
4	He is not here, but is risen:	24:6
21	how he spake unto you when he **was** yet in Galilee,	24:6
37	It **was** Mary Magdalene, and Joanna, and Mary the	24:10
37	two of them went that same day to a village (NT)	24:13
6	ye have one to another, as ye walk, and **are** sad?	24:17
4	it **had been** he which should have redeemed Israel:	24:21
4	for it is toward evening, and the day is far spent.	24:29
34	Did not our heart burn within us, (NT)	24:32
2	stood in the midst of them, ... Peace be unto you.	24:36
6	And he said unto them, Why **are** ye troubled?	24:38
2	Behold my hands and my feet, that it is I myself:	24:39
21	I spake unto you, while I **was** yet with you,	24:44
6	And ye **are** witnesses of these things.	24:48
37	And **were** continually in the temple,	24:53
34	In the beginning **was** the Word,	John 1:1
34	the Word **was** with God, and the Word was God.	1:1
34	the Word was with God, and the Word **was** God.	1:1
34	The same **was** in the beginning with God.	1:2
34	In him **was** life; and the life was the light of men.	1:4
4	In him was life; and the life was the light of men.	1:4
34	In him was life; and the life **was** the light of men.	1:4
34	He **was** not that Light, but was sent to bear witness	1:8
34	That **was** the true Light, which lighteth every man	1:9
34	He was in the world,	1:10
34	John bare witness ... This **was** he of whom I spake,	1:15
34	John bare witness of him, ... for **he was** before me.	1:15
21	begotten Son, which is in the bosom of the Father,	1:18
4	And this is the record of John,	1:19
3	from Jerusalem to ask him, Who **art** thou?	1:19
2	and denied not; but confessed, I **am** not the Christ.	1:20
3	And they asked him, What then? **Art** thou Elias?	1:21
2	**Art** thou Elias? And he saith, I **am** not.	1:21
3	**Art** thou that prophet? And he answered, No.	1:21
3	Then said they unto him, Who **art** thou?	1:22
37	And they which were sent **were** of the Pharisees.	1:24
3	if thou be not that Christ, nor Elias,	1:25
4	He it is, who coming after me	1:27
2	whose shoe's latchet I **am** not worthy to unloose.	1:27
34	beyond Jordan, where John **was** baptizing.	1:28
4	This is he of whom I said,	1:30
34	is preferred before me: for **he was** before me.	1:30
4	same is he which baptizeth with the Holy Ghost.	1:33
4	I saw, and bare record that this is the Son of God.	1:34
34	for it **was** about the tenth hour.	1:39
34	followed him, **was** Andrew, Simon Peter's brother.	1:40
4	the Messias, which is, being interpreted, the Christ.	1:41
3	Thou **art** Simon the son of Jona:	1:42
34	Now Philip **was** of Bethsaida,	1:44
32	Can there any good thing **come** out of Nazareth?	1:46
4	Behold an Israelite indeed, in whom is no guile!	1:47
18	when thou **wast** under the fig tree, I saw thee.	1:48
3	thou **art** the Son of God; ... the King of Israel.	1:49
3	**art** the Son of God; thou **art** the King of Israel.	1:49
34	and the mother of Jesus **was** there:	2:1
4	They have no wine.	2:3
37	And there **were** set there six waterpots of stone,	2:6
4	and knew not whence it **was**:	2:9
34	And the Jews' passover **was** at hand,	2:13
4	And his disciples remembered that it **was** written,	2:17
34	Now when he **was** in Jerusalem at the passover,	2:23
34	for he knew what **was** in man.	2:25
34	There **was** a man of the Pharisees,	3:1
10	miracles that thou doest, except God **be** with him.	3:2
21	How can a man be born when he is old?	3:4
4	That which is born of the flesh is flesh;	3:6
4	and that which is born of the Spirit is spirit.	3:6
4	so is every one that is born of the Spirit.	3:8
3	**Art** thou a master of Israel,	3:10
21	even the Son of man which **is** in heaven.	3:13
4	And this is the condemnation,	John 3:19
34	because their deeds **were** evil.	3:19
4	that they **are** wrought in God.	3:21
34	John also **was** baptizing in Aenon near to Salim,	3:23
34	baptizing ... because there **was** much water there:	3:23
34	For John **was** not yet cast into prison.	3:24
34	he that **was** with thee beyond Jordan,	3:26
10	nothing, except it **be** given him from heaven.	3:27
2	that I said, I **am** not the Christ,	3:28
2	I am not the Christ, but that I **am** sent before him.	3:28
4	He that hath the bride is the bridegroom:	3:29
4	He that cometh from above is above all:	3:31
21	he that **is** of the earth is earthly,	3:31
4	he that is of the earth is earthly,	3:31
4	he that cometh from heaven is above all.	3:31
4	hath set to his seal that God is true.	3:33
34	Now Jacob's well **was** there.	4:6
34	and it **was** about the sixth hour.	4:6
21	How is it that thou, **being** a Jew,	4:9
27	askest drink of me, which **am** a woman of Samaria?	4:9
4	and who it is that saith to thee, Give me to drink;	4:10
4	nothing to draw with, and the well is deep:	4:11
3	**Art** thou greater than our father Jacob,	4:12
4	and he whom thou now hast is not thy husband:	4:18
3	I perceive that thou **art** a prophet.	4:19
4	Jerusalem is the place ... men ought to worship.	4:20
4	for salvation is of the Jews.	4:22
4	But the hour cometh, and now is,	4:23
2	Jesus saith unto her, I that speak unto thee **am** he.	4:26
4	Come, see a man, ... is not this the Christ?	4:29
4	My meat is to do the will of him that sent me,	4:34
4	Say not ye, There **are** yet four months,	4:35
7	for they **are** white already to harvest.	4:35
4	And herein is that saying true,	4:37
4	One soweth, and another reapeth. (NT)	4:37
4	and know that this is indeed the Christ,	4:42
34	And **there was** a certain nobleman,	4:46
34	After this there **was** a feast of the Jews;	5:1
4	there is at Jerusalem by the sheep market a pool,	5:2
34	And a certain man **was** there,	5:5
34	and on the same day **was** the sabbath.	5:9
4	It is the sabbath day: it is not lawful for thee	5:10
4	What man is that which said unto thee,	5:12
4	And he that was healed wist not who it **was**:	5:13
19	a multitude **being** in that place.	5:13
4	man departed, and told the Jews that it **was** Jesus,	5:15
4	The hour is coming, and now is,	5:25
4	execute judgment ... because he is the Son of man.	5:27
4	as I hear, I judge: and my judgment is just;	5:30
4	If I bear witness of myself, my witness is not true.	5:31
4	There is another that beareth witness of me;	5:32
4	that the witness which he witnesseth of me is true.	5:32
34	He **was** a burning and a shining light:	5:35
7	and they **are** they which testify of me.	5:39
4	there is one that accuseth you, even Moses,	5:45
34	And the passover, a feast of the Jews, was nigh.	6:4
4	There is a lad here, which hath five barley loaves,	6:9
4	but what **are** they among so many?	6:9
34	Now there **was** much grass in the place.	6:10
4	This is of a truth that prophet that should come	6:14
2	But he saith unto them, It is I; be not afraid.	6:20
34	saw that there **was** none other boat there,	6:22
4	the people therefore saw that Jesus **was** not there,	6:24
4	This is the work of God, that ye believe	6:29
4	as it is written, He gave them bread from heaven	6:31
4	For the bread of God is he which cometh down	6:33
2	And Jesus said unto them, I **am** the bread of life:	6:35
4	And this is the Father's will which hath sent me,	6:39
4	And this is the will of him that sent me,	6:40
2	I **am** the bread which came down from heaven.	6:41
4	And they said, Is not this Jesus, the son of Joseph,	6:42
4	It is written in the prophets,	6:45
43	And they **shall** be all taught of God.	6:45
21	save he which is of God, he hath seen the Father.	6:46
2	I **am** that bread of life.	6:48
4	This is the bread which cometh down from heaven,	6:50
2	I **am** the living bread which came down	6:51

259

εἰμί 1498

4	and the bread that I will give is my flesh,	John 6:51
4	For my flesh is meat indeed,	6:55
4	and my blood is drink indeed.	6:55
4	This is that bread which came down from heaven:	6:58
4	This is an hard saying; who can hear it?	6:60
34	the Son of man ascend up where he was before?	6:62
4	It is the spirit that quickeneth;	6:63
4	the words that I speak unto you, they are spirit,	6:63
4	the words ... they are spirit, and they are life.	6:63
7	But there are some of you that believe not.	6:64
7	For Jesus knew from the beginning who they were	6:64
4	who should betray him. (NT)	6:64
10	except it were given unto him of my Father.	6:65
3	we believe and are sure that thou art that Christ,	6:69
4	chosen you twelve, and one of you is a devil?	6:70
21	Judas Iscariot ... being one of the twelve.	6:71
34	Now the Jews' feast of tabernacles was at hand.	7:2
32	and he himself seeketh to be known openly.	7:4
4	but your time is alway ready.	7:6
4	I testify of it, that the works thereof are evil.	7:7
4	sought him at the feast, and said, Where is he?	7:11
34	And there was much murmuring among the people	7:12
4	for some said, He is a good man:	7:12
4	My doctrine is not mine, but his that sent me.	7:16
4	shall know of the doctrine, whether it be of God,	7:17
4	seeketh his glory that sent him, the same is true,	7:18
4	the same is true, and no unrighteousness is in him.	7:18
4	not because it is of Moses, but of the fathers;	7:22
4	Is not this he, whom they seek to kill?	7:25
4	Do the rulers know indeed that this is ... Christ?	7:26
4	Howbeit we know this man whence he is:	7:27
4	Christ cometh, no man knoweth whence he is.	7:27
2	Ye both know me, and ye know whence I am;	7:28
4	but he that sent me is true, whom ye know not.	7:28
2	But I know him: for I am from him,	7:29
4	Yet a little while am I with you,	7:33
2	and where I am, thither ye cannot come.	7:34
4	What manner of saying is this that he said,	7:36
2	and where I am, thither ye cannot come?	7:36
34	for the Holy Ghost was not yet given;	7:39
4	Many ... said, Of a truth this is the Prophet.	7:40
4	Others said, This is the Christ.	7:41
34	out of the town of Bethlehem, where David was?	7:42
7	this people who knoweth not the law are cursed.	7:49
21	he that came to Jesus by night, being one of them,	7:50
3	Art thou also of Galilee? Search, and look:	7:52
26	with the woman still standing there (NIV) (NT)	8:9
7	Woman, where are those thine accusers?	8:10
2	I am the light of the world:	8:12
4	bearest record of thyself; thy record is not true.	8:13
4	I bear record of myself, yet my record is true:	8:14
4	And yet if I judge, my judgment is true:	8:16
2	my judgment is true: for I am not alone,	8:16
4	It is also written in your law,	8:17
4	that the testimony of two men is true.	8:17
2	I am one that bear witness of myself,	8:18
4	Then said they unto him, Where is thy Father?	8:19
6	Ye are from beneath; I am from above:	8:23
2	Ye are from beneath; I am from above:	8:23
6	ye are of this world; I am not of this world.	8:23
2	ye are of this world; I am not of this world.	8:23
4	believe not that I am he, ye shall die in your sins.	8:24
3	Then said they unto him, Who art thou?	8:25
4	but he that sent me is true;	8:26
2	then shall ye know that I am he,	8:28
4	And he that sent me is with me:	8:29
6	in my word, then are ye my disciples indeed;	8:31
5	They answered him, We be Abraham's seed,	8:33
4	Whosoever committeth sin is the servant of sin.	8:34
42	Son ... make you free, ye shall be free indeed.	8:36
6	I know that ye are Abraham's seed;	8:37
4	Abraham is our father. Jesus saith unto them,	8:39
1	If ye were Abraham's children,	8:39
6	If ye were Abraham's children,	8:39
34	If God were your Father, ye would love me:	8:42
6	Ye are of your father the devil,	8:44
34	He was a murderer from the beginning,	8:44
4	because there is no truth in him.	John 8:44
4	for he is a liar, and the father of it.	8:44
21	He that is of God heareth God's words:	8:47
6	ye ... hear them not, because ye are not of God.	8:47
3	Say we not well that thou art a Samaritan,	8:48
4	there is one that seeketh and judgeth.	8:50
3	Art thou greater than our father Abraham,	8:53
4	If I honour myself, my honour is nothing:	8:54
4	it is my Father that honoureth me;	8:54
4	of whom ye say, that he is your God:	8:54
38	if I should say, I know him not, I shall be a liar	8:55
2	I say unto you, Before Abraham was, I am.	8:58
4	the works of him that sent me, while it is day:	9:4
8	As long as I am in the world, I am the light	9:5
2	I am the light of the world.	9:5
34	they which before had seen him that he was blind,	9:8
4	Is not this he that sat and begged?	9:8
4	Some said, This is he: ... but he said, I am he.	9:9
4	others said, He is like him: but he said, I am he.	9:9
2	others said, He is like him: but he said, I am he.	9:9
4	Then said they unto him, Where is he?	9:12
34	it was the sabbath day when Jesus made the clay,	9:14
4	This man is not of God,	9:16
34	And there was a division among them.	9:16
4	He said, He is a prophet.	9:17
34	that he had been blind, and received his sight,	9:18
4	Is this your son, who ye say was born blind?	9:19
4	We know that this is our son, ... was born blind:	9:20
34	Then again called they the man that was blind,	9:24
4	we know that this man is a sinner.	9:24
4	Whether he be a sinner or no, I know not:	9:25
21	I know, that, whereas I was blind, now I see.	9:25
3	Thou art his disciple; but we are Moses' disciples.	9:28
5	Thou art his disciple; but we are Moses' disciples.	9:28
4	as for this fellow, we know not from whence he is.	9:29
4	Why herein is a marvellous thing,	9:30
4	that ye know not from whence he is,	9:30
10	but if any man be a worshipper of God,	9:31
34	If this man were not of God, he could do nothing.	9:33
4	Who is he, Lord, that I might believe on him?	9:36
4	and it is he that talketh with thee.	9:37
23	Pharisees which were with him heard these words,	9:40
5	and said unto him, Are we blind also?	9:40
1	If ye were blind, ye should have no sin:	9:41
4	the same is a thief and a robber.	10:1
4	in by the door is the shepherd of the sheep.	10:2
34	what things they were which he spake unto them.	10:6
10	what things they were which he spake unto them.	10:6
2	I am the door of the sheep.	10:7
7	that ever came before me are thieves and robbers:	10:8
2	I am the door: ... shall be saved,	10:9
2	I am the good shepherd:	10:11
21	But he that is an hireling, and not the shepherd,	10:12
7	not the shepherd, whose own the sheep are not,	10:12
4	not the shepherd, whose own the sheep are not,	10:12
4	The hireling fleeth, because he is an hireling,	10:13
2	I am the good shepherd, and know my sheep,	10:14
4	And other sheep I have, which are not of this fold:	10:16
4	These are not the words of him that hath a devil.	10:21
34	the feast of the dedication, and it was winter.	10:22
3	If thou be the Christ, tell us plainly.	10:24
6	But ye believe not, because ye are not of my sheep,	10:26
4	My Father, ... is greater than all;	10:29
5	I and my Father are one.	10:30
21	that thou, being a man, makest thyself God.	10:33
4	Is it not written in your law, I said, Ye are gods?	10:34
6	Is it not written in your law, I said, Ye are gods?	10:34
2	because I said, I am the Son of God?	10:36
34	into the place where John at first baptized; (NT)	10:40
34	all things that John spake of this man were true.	10:41
34	Now a certain man was sick, named Lazarus,	11:1
34	It was that Mary which anointed the Lord	11:2
4	This sickness is not unto death,	11:4
34	two days still in the same place where he was.	11:6
7	Are there not twelve hours in the day?	11:9
4	because there is no light in him.	11:10
46	And I am glad for your sakes that I was not there,	11:15

εἰμί 1498

34	Now Bethany **was** nigh unto Jerusalem, ... John	11:18
35	if thou **hadst been** here, my brother had not died.....	11:21
2	I **am** the resurrection, and the life:	11:25
3	I believe that thou **art** the Christ, the Son of God, ...	11:27
34	but **was** in that place where Martha met him........	11:30
23	The Jews then which **were** with her in the house, ...	11:31
34	Then when Mary was come where Jesus **was**, ...	11:32
35	if thou **hadst been** here, my brother had not died.....	11:32
34	It **was** a cave, and a stone lay upon it.	11:38
4	he stinketh: for he **hath been** dead four days.	11:39
34	the stone from the place where the dead **was** laid. ...	11:41
21	Caiaphas, **being** the high priest that same year, ...	11:49
21	but **being** high priest that year, he prophesied	11:51
34	And the Jews' passover **was** nigh at hand:	11:55
4	if any man knew where he **were**, he should show it, ...	11:57
34	where Lazarus **was** which had been dead, ...	12:1
34	Lazarus **was** one of them that sat at the table	12:2
34	but because he **was** a thief, and had the bag, ...	12:6
4	people of the Jews ... knew that he **was** there:	12:9
4	found a young ass, sat thereon; as it is written, ...	12:14
34	remembered ... these things **were** written of him, ...	12:16
21	The people therefore that **was** with him	12:17
37	And **there were** certain Greeks among them	12:20
2	and where I **am**, there shall also my servant be:	12:26
40	and where I am, there **shall** also my servant **be**:	12:26
4	Now **is** the judgment of this world:	12:31
4	Son ... must **be** lifted up? who is this Son of man? ...	12:34
4	Yet a little while **is** the light with you.	12:35
4	I know that his commandment **is** life everlasting:	12:50
34	wipe ... with the towel wherewith he **was** girded.	13:5
4	but is clean every whit: and ye **are** clean, ...	13:10
6	but is clean every whit: and ye **are** clean, ...	13:10
6	therefore said he, Ye **are** not all clean.	13:11
2	call me Master ... and ye say well; for so I **am**.	13:13
4	The servant **is** not greater than his lord;	13:16
6	happy **are** ye if ye do them.	13:17
2	when ... come to pass, ye may believe that I **am** he...	13:19
34	Now **there was** leaning on Jesus' bosom one	13:23
14	he should ask who it **should be** of whom he spake....	13:24
4	he should ask who it **should be** of whom he spake....	13:24
4	lying on Jesus' breast saith ... Lord, who is it?	13:25
4	He it **is**, to whom I shall give a sop, ...	13:26
34	went immediately out: and it **was** night.	13:30
2	Little children, yet a little while I **am** with you.	13:33
6	By this shall all men know that ye **are** my disciples, ..	13:35
7	In my Father's house **are** many mansions:	14:2
2	that where I **am**, there ye may be also.	14:3
1	that where I **am**, there ye may be also.	14:3
2	I **am** the way, the truth, and the life:	14:6
2	Have I **been** so long time with you, ...	14:9
4	I **am** in the Father, and the Father is in Me? (NASB)	14:10
10	that He **may be** with you forever;	14:16
10	Comforter, that he may abide with you for ever;	14:16
10	Comforter, that he may abide with you for ever;	14:16
40	for he dwelleth with you, and **shall be** in you.	14:17
4	for he dwelleth with you, and **shall be** in you.	14:17
4	hath my commandments, ... he it is that loveth me: ...	14:21
4	word which ye hear **is** not mine, but the Father's:	14:24
4	for my Father **is** greater than I.	14:28
2	I **am** the true vine, ...	15:1
4	and my Father **is** the husbandman.	15:1
6	ye **are** clean through the word which I have spoken ...	15:3
2	I **am** the vine, ye are the branches:	15:5
10	that My joy **may be** in you (NASB)	15:11
4	This **is** my commandment, ... love one another, ...	15:12
6	Ye **are** my friends, if ye do whatsoever I command ...	15:14
1	If ye **were** of the world, ...	15:19
6	but because ye **are** not of the world, ...	15:19
4	The servant **is** not greater than his lord.	15:20
6	because ye **have been** with me from the beginning. ...	15:27
46	at the beginning, because I **was** with you.	16:4
4	All things that the Father hath **are** mine:	16:15
4	What **is** this that he saith unto us, A little while?, ...	16:17
4	What **is** this that he saith, A little while?	16:18
10	ask, and ye shall receive, that your joy **may be** full....	16:24
2	yet I **am** not alone, because the Father is with me....	16:32
4	yet I am not alone, because the Father is with me....	16:32

4	And this **is** life eternal, that they might know thee John	17:3
32	glory which I had with thee before the world **was**.....	17:5
37	thine they **were**, and thou gavest them me;	17:6
4	that all things whatsoever ... **are** of thee.	17:7
7	that all things whatsoever ... **are** of thee.	17:7
7	them which thou hast given me; for they **are** thine. ...	17:9
4	And all mine **are** thine, and thine are mine;	17:10
2	And now I **am** no more in the world, ...	17:11
7	but these **are** in the world, and I come to thee.	17:11
12	that they **may be** one, as we are.	17:11
46	While I **was** with them in the world, ...	17:12
7	because they **are** not of the world, ...	17:14
2	even as I **am** not of the world.	17:14
7	They **are** not of the world, ...	17:16
2	are not of the world, even as I **am** not of the world....	17:16
4	Sanctify them through thy truth: thy word **is** truth....	17:17
12	they also **might be** sanctified through the truth.	17:19
12	they all **may be** one; as thou, Father, art in me, ...	17:21
12	and I in thee, that they also **may be** one in us:	17:21
12	that they **may be** one, even as we are one:	17:22
5	that they may be one, even as we **are** one:	17:22
12	that they **may be** made perfect in one;	17:23
2	whom thou hast given me, be with me where I **am**; ...	17:24
12	whom thou hast given me, **be** with me where I am; ...	17:24
10	love wherewith thou hast loved ... **may be** in them, ...	17:26
34	over the brook Cedron, where **was** a garden, ...	18:1
2	Jesus saith unto them, I **am** he.	18:5
2	As soon then as he had said unto them, I **am** he, ...	18:6
2	Jesus answered, I have told you that I **am** he:	18:8
34	The servant's name **was** Malchus.	18:10
34	for he **was** father in law to Caiaphas, ...	18:13
34	which **was** the high priest that same year.	18:13
34	Caiaphas **was** he, which gave counsel to the Jews, ...	18:14
34	that disciple **was** known unto the high priest, ...	18:15
34	disciple, which **was** known unto the high priest, ...	18:16
3	Art not thou also one of this man's disciples?	18:17
2	one of this man's disciples? He saith, I **am** not.	18:17
34	who had made a fire of coals; for it **was** cold:	18:18
34	and Peter stood with them, (NT)	18:18
34	And Simon Peter stood and warmed himself. (NT) ...	18:25
3	Art not thou also one of his disciples? He denied it, ..	18:25
2	He denied it, and said, I **am** not.	18:25
21	being his kinsman whose ear Peter cut off, ...	18:26
34	and it **was** early; and they themselves went not	18:28
34	If he **were** not a malefactor, ...	18:30
3	and said unto him, Art thou the King of the Jews? ...	18:33
2	Pilate answered, Am I a Jew?	18:35
4	Jesus answered, My kingdom is not of this world:	18:36
34	if my kingdom **were** of this world, ...	18:36
4	but now **is** my kingdom not from hence.	18:36
3	Pilate therefore said ... **Art** thou a king then?	18:37
3	Jesus answered, Thou sayest that I **am** a king.	18:37
21	Every one that **is** of the truth heareth my voice, ...	18:37
4	Pilate saith unto him, What is truth?	18:38
4	But ye **have** a custom, that I should release ... one ...	18:39
34	but Barabbas. Now Barabbas **was** a robber.	18:40
3	and saith unto Jesus, Whence **art** thou?	19:9
34	except it **were** given thee from above:	19:11
3	If thou let this ... go, thou **art** not Caesar's friend:	19:12
34	And it **was** the preparation of the passover, ...	19:14
34	it **was** about the sixth hour. (NASB)	19:14
34	and put it on the cross. And the writing **was**, ...	19:19
34	where Jesus was crucified **was** nigh to the city:	19:20
34	was written in Hebrew, and Greek, and Latin.	19:20
2	but that he said, I **am** King of the Jews.	19:21
34	now the coat **was** without seam, ...	19:23
40	but cast lots for it, whose it **shall be**:	19:24
34	because it **was** the day of preparation (NASB)	19:31
34	The Jews therefore, because it **was** the preparation, ...	19:31
34	for that sabbath day **was** an high day, ...	19:31
4	he that saw it bare record, and his record **is** true:	19:35
21	Joseph of Arimathaea, **being** a disciple of Jesus, ...	19:38
4	as the manner of the Jews **is** to bury.	19:40
34	place where he was crucified there **was** a garden;	19:41
34	in which no one had yet been laid. (NASB) (NT) ...	19:41
34	for the sepulchre **was** nigh at hand.	19:42
27	early, when it **was** yet dark, unto the sepulchre, ...	20:1

261

#	Text	Ref
34	And the napkin, that **was** about his head,	John 20:7
4	saw Jesus standing, and knew not that it **was** Jesus.	20:14
4	She, supposing him **to be** the gardener,	20:15
27	**being** the first day of the week,	20:19
37	when the doors were shut where the disciples **were**	20:19
34	Thomas, ... **was** not with them when Jesus came.	20:24
37	after eight days again his disciples **were** within,	20:26
4	other signs ... which **are** not written in this book:	20:30
4	that ye might believe that Jesus **is** the Christ,	20:31
37	**There were** together Simon Peter, and Thomas	21:2
4	but the disciples knew not that it **was** Jesus.	21:4
4	whom Jesus loved saith unto Peter, It **is** the Lord.	21:7
4	Now when Simon Peter heard that it **was** the Lord,	21:7
34	girt his fisher's coat unto him, for **he was** naked,	21:7
37	for they **were** not far from land,	21:8
20	and for all there **were** so many,	21:11
3	none of the disciples durst ask him, Who **art** thou?	21:12
4	knowing that it **was** the Lord.	21:12
35	When thou **wast** young, thou girdedst thyself,	21:18
4	and said, Lord, which **is** he that betrayeth thee?	21:20
4	This **is** the disciple which testifieth of these things,	21:24
4	and we know that his testimony **is** true.	21:24
4	there **are** also many other things which Jesus did,	21:25
4	It **is** not for you to know the times or the seasons,	Acts 1:7
42	ye **shall be** witnesses unto me both in Jerusalem,	1:8
37	And while they looked stedfastly (NT)	1:10
4	which **is** from Jerusalem a sabbath day's journey.	1:12
37	where abode both Peter, and James, (NT)	1:13
37	These all continued with one accord in prayer (NT)	1:14
34	together **were** about an hundred and twenty,	1:15
34	For he **was** numbered with us,	1:17
4	Haceldama, that **is**, Field of Blood (NASB)	1:19
17	and let no man dwell therein:	1:20
37	they **were** all with one accord in one place.	2:1
37	and it filled all the house where they **were** sitting.	2:2
37	And there **were** dwelling at Jerusalem Jews,	2:5
7	Behold, **are** not all these which speak Galilaeans?	2:7
32	saying one to another, What **meaneth** this?	2:12
7	These men **are** full of new wine.	2:13
17	**be** this known unto you, and hearken to my words:	2:14
4	seeing it **is** but the third hour of the day.	2:15
4	this is that which was spoken by the prophet Joel;	2:16
40	it **shall come to pass** in the last days, saith God,	2:17
40	And it **shall come to pass,**	2:21
34	it **was** not possible that he should be holden of it.	2:24
4	for he **is** on my right hand,	2:25
4	and his sepulchre **is** with us unto this day.	2:29
5	hath God raised up, whereof we all **are** witnesses.	2:32
4	For the promise **is** unto you, and to your children,	2:39
37	they continued stedfastly (NT)	2:42
34	wonders and signs were done by the apostles.	2:43
37	And all that believed **were** together,	2:44
34	And they knew that it **was** he which sat for alms	3:10
5	raised from the dead; whereof we **are** witnesses.	3:15
40	And it **shall come to pass,** that every soul,	3:23
6	Ye **are** the children of the prophets,	3:25
34	in hold unto the next day: for it **was** now eventide.	4:3
37	as many as **were** of the kindred of the high priest,	4:6
17	**Be** it known unto you all, and to all the people	4:10
4	This **is** the stone which was set at nought of you	4:11
4	Neither **is there** salvation in any other:	4:12
4	for **there is** none other name under heaven given	4:12
7	and perceived that they **were** unlearned	4:13
37	that they **had been** with Jesus.	4:13
4	Whether it **be** right in the sight of God	4:19
34	For the man **was** above forty years old,	4:22
37	was shaken where they **were** assembled together;	4:31
34	that believed **were** of one heart and of one soul:	4:32
32	the things which he possessed **was** his own;	4:32
34	but they **had** all things common.	4:32
34	and great grace **was** upon them all.	4:33
34	there **was** not a needy person among them (NASB)	4:34
4	which **is**, being interpreted, The son of consolation,	4:36
37	they **were** all with one accord in Solomon's porch.	5:12
26	which **is** the sect of the Sadducees,	5:17
7	whom ye put in prison **are** standing in the temple,	5:25
5	And we **are** his witnesses of these things;	5:32
32	Theudas, boasting himself **to be** somebody;	Acts 5:36
10	for if this counsel or this work **be** of men,	5:38
4	But if it **be** of God, ye cannot overthrow it;	5:39
4	It **is** not reason that we should leave	6:2
22	Abraham, when he **was** in Mesopotamia,	7:2
19	to his seed after him, when as yet he **had** no child.	7:5
40	That his seed **should** sojourn in a strange land;	7:6
34	sold Joseph into Egypt: but God **was** with him,	7:9
18	when Jacob heard that there **was** corn in Egypt,	7:12
34	Moses was born, and **was** exceeding fair,	7:20
34	and **was** mighty in words and in deeds.	7:22
6	ye **are** brethren; why do ye wrong one to another?	7:26
4	for the place where thou standest **is** holy ground.	7:33
4	This **is** that Moses,	7:37
4	This **is** he, that was in the church	7:38
34	Our fathers **had** the tabernacle	7:44
34	And Saul **was** consenting unto his death.	8:1
32	giving out that himself **was** some great one:	8:9
4	saying, This man **is** the great power of God.	8:10
34	when he **was** baptized, he continued with Philip,	8:13
34	For as yet he **was** fallen upon none of them:	8:16
14	Thy money perish with thee, (NT)	8:20
4	Thou **hast** neither part nor lot in this matter:	8:21
4	for thy heart **is** not right in the sight of God.	8:21
18	I perceive that thou **art** in the gall of bitterness,	8:23
4	down from Jerusalem unto Gaza, which **is** desert.	8:26
34	who **had** the charge of all her treasure,	8:27
34	**Was** returning, and sitting in his chariot	8:28
34	The place of the scripture which he read **was** this,	8:32
32	I believe that Jesus Christ **is** the Son of God.	8:37
25	whether they **were** men or women,	9:2
3	And he said, Who **art** thou, Lord?	9:5
2	the Lord said, I **am** Jesus whom thou persecutest:	9:5
34	And he **was** three days without sight,	9:9
34	And **there was** a certain disciple at Damascus,	9:10
4	for he **is** a chosen vessel unto me,	9:15
4	preached Christ ... that he **is** the Son of God.	9:20
4	**Is** not this he that destroyed them	9:21
4	proving that this **is** very Christ.	9:22
4	and believed not that he **was** a disciple.	9:26
34	And he **was** with them coming in and going out	9:28
34	kept his bed eight years, and **was** sick of the palsy.	9:33
34	**was** at Joppa a certain disciple named Tabitha,	9:36
34	this woman **was** full of good works.	9:36
27	And forasmuch as Lydda **was** nigh to Joppa,	9:38
4	and the disciples had heard that Peter **was** there,	9:38
26	while she **was** with them.	9:39
34	**was** a certain man in Caesarea called Cornelius,	10:1
4	What **is** it, Lord? And he said unto him,	10:4
4	whose house **is** by the sea side:	10:6
14	what this vision which he had seen **should** mean,	10:17
2	and said, Behold, I **am** he whom ye seek:	10:21
34	And Cornelius waited for them, (NT)	10:24
2	Stand up; I myself also **am** a man.	10:26
4	Ye know how that it **is** an unlawful thing,	10:28
46	Four days ago I **was** fasting until this hour;	10:30
4	I perceive that God **is** no respecter of persons:	10:34
4	and worketh righteousness, **is** accepted with him.	10:35
4	preaching peace by Jesus Christ: he **is** Lord of all:	10:36
34	and healing all ... for God **was** with him.	10:38
5	And we **are** witnesses of all things	10:39
4	and to testify that it **is** he which was ordained	10:42
23	And the apostles and brethren that **were** in Judaea	11:1
46	I **was** in the city of Joppa praying:	11:5
46	men already come unto the house where I **was**,	11:11
36	before the house in which we were staying (NASB)	11:11
46	what **was** I, that I could withstand God?	11:17
37	some of them **were** men of Cyprus and Cyrene,	11:20
34	And the hand of the Lord **was** with them:	11:21
27	of the church at Jerusalem (NASB) (NT)	11:22
34	For he **was** a good man, and full of the Holy Ghost	11:24
45	should **be** great dearth throughout all the world:	11:28
4	And because he saw it pleased the Jews, (NT)	12:3
37	Then **were** the days of unleavened bread.	12:3
34	but prayer **was** made without ceasing of the church	12:5
34	Peter **was** sleeping between two soldiers,	12:6
4	that it **was** true which was done by the angel;	12:9

εἰμί 1498

37 where many **were** gathered together praying....... Acts	12:12
4 Then said they, **It is** his angel......................	12:15
34 **there was** no small stir among the soldiers,...........	12:18
34 Herod **was** highly displeased with them of Tyre.......	12:20
37 Now **there were** in the church that was at Antioch....	13:1
29 Now there were in the church that **was** at Antioch....	13:1
34 Which **was** with the deputy of the country,...........	13:7
39 thou **shalt be** blind, not seeing the sun for a season...	13:11
4 Ye men and brethren, if ye **have** any word...........	13:15
32 Whom think ye that I **am**? I am not he..............	13:25
2 Whom think ye that I **am**? I am not he...............	13:25
2 whose shoes of his feet I **am** not worthy to loose.....	13:25
7 who **are** his witnesses unto the people................	13:31
3 Thou **art** my Son, this day have I begotten thee......	13:33
17 **Be** it known unto you therefore,......................	13:38
34 It **was** necessary that the word of God should first....	13:46
32 that thou shouldest **be** for salvation..................	13:47
37 as many as **were** ordained to eternal life believed.....	13:48
37 part **held** with the Jews, and part with the apostles.....	14:4
37 And there they preached the gospel. (NT)............	14:7
34 Mercurius, because he **was** the chief speaker..........	14:12
19 which **was** before their city,.......................	14:13
5 We also **are** men of like passions with you,...........	14:15
37 had **been** recommended to the grace of God.........	14:26
4 Known unto God **are** all his works...................	15:18
23 Judas and Silas, **being** prophets also themselves,......	15:32
34 and, behold, a certain disciple **was** there,.............	16:1
25 because of the Jews which **were** in those quarters:....	16:3
34 There stood a man of Macedonia (NT)...............	16:9
4 which **is** the chief city of that part of Macedonia,.....	16:12
36 and we **were** in that city abiding certain days.........	16:12
32 where prayer was wont to **be made**;...................	16:13
32 If ye have judged me **to be** faithful to the Lord,......	16:15
7 These men **are** the servants of the most high God,....	16:17
24 not lawful for us ... **being** Romans..................	16:21
5 Do thyself no harm: for we **are** all here.............	16:28
7 feared, when they heard that they **were** Romans......	16:38
34 Thessalonica, where **was** a synagogue of the Jews:.....	17:1
4 that this Jesus, whom I preach unto you, **is** Christ....	17:3
32 saying that there is another king, one Jesus...........	17:7
37 These **were** more noble than those in Thessalonica,...	17:11
29 when he saw the city wholly given to idolatry. (NT)..	17:16
32 He seemeth to **be** a setter forth of strange gods:......	17:18
32 we would know therefore what these things **mean**.....	17:20
5 For in him we live, and move, and **have** our **being**;...	17:28
5 For we **are** also his offspring.........................	17:28
32 not to think that the Godhead is like unto gold,......	17:29
32 he **was** of the same craft, he abode with them,........	18:3
37 for by their occupation they **were** tentmakers..........	18:3
32 testifying ... that Jesus **was** the Christ (NASB)........	18:5
34 whose house joined hard to the synagogue. (NT).....	18:7
2 For I **am** with thee, and no man shall set on thee	18:10
4 for I **have** much people in this city...................	18:10
19 But while Gallio **was** proconsul of Achaia (NASB)...	18:12
34 If it **were** a matter of wrong or wicked lewdness,.....	18:14
4 But if it **be** a question of words and names,...........	18:15
32 look ye to it; for I will **be** no judge of such matters...	18:15
21 and mighty in the scriptures, (NT)..................	18:24
34 This man **was** instructed in the way of the Lord;.....	18:25
32 showing by the scriptures that Jesus **was** Christ......	18:28
32 that, while Apollos **was** at Corinth,...................	19:1
4 not ... heard whether **there be** any Holy Ghost........	19:2
4 coming after him, that **is**, in Jesus (NASB)...........	19:4
37 And all the men were about twelve..................	19:7
37 And **there were** seven sons of one Sceva, a Jew,.......	19:14
6 Jesus I know, and Paul I know; but who **are** ye?.....	19:15
34 man in whom the evil spirit **was** leaped on them,.....	19:16
4 ye know that by this craft we **have** our wealth.........	19:25
7 saying that they **be** no gods,........................	19:26
23 certain of the chief of Asia, which **were** his friends,...	19:31
34 and some another: for the assembly **was** confused;....	19:32
4 But when they knew that he **was** a Jew,.............	19:34
4 he said, Ye men of Ephesus, what man is there	19:35
29 **is** a worshipper of the great goddess Diana,..........	19:35
20 these things cannot be spoken (NT)..................	19:36
4 ye ought to be quiet, (NT).........................	19:36
7 **there are** deputies: let them implead one another......	19:38
37 And there **were** many lights in the upper chamber, Acts	20:8
37 where they **were** gathered together....................	20:8
36 where we **were** gathered together (NASB)............	20:8
4 Trouble not yourselves; for his life **is** in him..........	20:10
34 intending to take in Paul: for so **had** he appointed,...	20:13
34 if it **were** possible for him, to be at Jerusalem........	20:16
14 if it **were** possible for him, to be at Jerusalem........	20:16
2 that I **am** innocent of the blood of all men (NASB)..	20:26
24 my necessities, and to them that **were** with me.......	20:34
4 **It is** more blessed to give than to receive..............	20:35
34 for there the ship **was** to unlade her burden............	21:3
19 Philip the evangelist, which **was** one of the seven;...	21:8
37 And the same man **had** four daughters, virgins,......	21:9
4 at Jerusalem bind the man that **owneth** this girdle,....	21:11
7 many thousands of Jews **there are** which believe;.....	21:20
4 What **is** it therefore?...............................	21:22
7 We **have** four men which have a vow on them;.......	21:23
4 they were informed concerning thee, **are** nothing;.....	21:24
4 Crying out, Men of Israel, help: This is the man,.....	21:28
37 For they had seen before with him in the city (NT)...	21:29
14 and demanded who he **was**, and what he had done...	21:33
4 and demanded who he **was**, and what he had done....	21:33
3 **Art** not thou that Egyptian,..........................	21:38
2 Paul said, I **am** a man which am a Jew of Tarsus,.....	21:39
2 I **am** verily a man which am a Jew, born in Tarsus,...	22:3
6 and was zealous toward God, as ye all **are** this day...	22:3
25 to bring them which **were** bound.................	22:5
3 And I answered, Who **art** thou, Lord?................	22:8
2 I **am** Jesus of Nazareth, whom thou persecutest.......	22:8
23 And they that **were** with me saw indeed the light,....	22:9
39 For thou **shalt** be his witness unto all men............	22:15
46 they know that I imprisoned and beat (NT)..........	22:19
46 I also **was** standing by, and consenting..............	22:20
4 Take heed ... for this man is a Roman................	22:26
3 Tell me, **art** thou a Roman? He said, Yea.............	22:27
4 was afraid, after he knew that he **was** a Roman,......	22:29
34 found out that he **was** a Roman (NASB)..............	22:29
4 I wist not, brethren, that he **was** the high priest:......	23:5
4 one part **were** Sadducees, and the other Pharisees,....	23:6
2 Men and brethren, I **am** a Pharisee,.................	23:6
32 For the Sadducees say that there is no resurrection,..	23:8
37 And **they** were more than forty which had...........	23:13
5 we, or ever he come near, **are** ready to kill him.......	23:15
4 What **is** that thou hast to tell me?....................	23:19
7 and now **are** they ready, looking for a promise.......	23:21
4 having understood that he **was** a Roman..............	23:27
45 there **would be** a plot against, (NASB)...............	23:30
4 he asked of what province he **was**....................	23:34
18 **hast been** of many years a judge unto this nation,...	24:10
7 that there **are** yet but twelve days since I went up....	24:11
45 that there shall **be** a resurrection of the dead,........	24:15
28 came with his wife Drusilla, which was a Jewess,...	24:24
45 temperance, and judgment to come, (NT)...........	24:25
4 accuse this man, if there **be** any wickedness in him....	25:5
2 Then said Paul, I stand at Caesar's judgment seat,....	25:10
4 but if there **be** none of these things whereof these....	25:11
4 **There is** a certain man left in bonds by Felix:.........	25:14
4 **It is** not the manner of the Romans..................	25:16
24 captains, and principal men of the city, (NT).........	25:23
18 Especially because I know thee to **be** expert..........	26:3
3 And I said, Who **art** thou, Lord?.....................	26:15
2 And he said, I **am** Jesus whom thou persecutest......	26:15
18 some Jews seized me in the temple (NASB) (NT)....	26:21
4 for this thing **was** not done in a corner................	26:26
2 and altogether such as I **am**, except these bonds......	26:29
19 a Macedonian of Thessalonica, **being** with us.........	27:2
32 under Cyprus, because the winds **were** contrary.......	27:4
34 fair havens; nigh whereunto **was** the city of Lasea.....	27:8
19 and when sailing was now dangerous,...............	27:9
45 I perceive that this voyage will **be** with hurt..........	27:10
40 for there **shall be** no loss of any man's life............	27:22
2 the angel of God, whose I **am**, and whom I serve,....	27:23
40 that it **shall be** even as it was told me................	27:25
36 we **were** in all in the ship two hundred ... souls......	27:37
50 we **were** in all in the ship two hundred ... souls......	27:37
4 No doubt this man is a murderer,....................	28:4
32 changed their minds, and said that he **was** a god......	28:6

263

εἰμί

25	Paul called the chief of the Jews together: (NT)	Acts 28:17
4	every where it is spoken against. (NT)	28:22
23	And when they agreed not among themselves, (NT)	28:25
17	**Be** it known therefore unto you,	28:28
6	Among whom **are** ye also the called of Jesus	Rom 1:6
24	To all that **be** in Rome, beloved of God,	1:7
4	God **is** my witness, whom I serve with my spirit	1:9
4	That **is**, that I may be comforted together with you	1:12
2	I **am** debtor both to the Greeks, and ... Barbarians;	1:14
4	for it **is** the power of God unto salvation	1:16
4	which may be known of God **is** manifest in them;	1:19
32	so that they **are** without excuse:	1:20
32	Professing themselves **to be** wise, ... became fools,	1:22
4	the Creator, who **is** blessed for ever. Amen.	1:25
7	which commit such things **are** worthy of death,	1:32
3	Therefore thou **art** inexcusable, O man,	2:1
4	the judgment of God **is** according to truth	2:2
4	For **there is** no respect of persons with God.	2:11
7	having not the law, **are** a law unto themselves:	2:14
32	confident that thou thyself **art** a guide of the blind,	2:19
9	but if thou **be** a breaker of the law,	2:25
4	For he **is** not a Jew, which **is** one outwardly;	2:28
4	that good may come? whose damnation **is** just.	3:8
32	both Jews and Gentiles, that they **are** all under sin;	3:9
4	As it is written, **There is** none righteous, no,	3:10
4	**There is** none that understandeth,	3:11
4	**there is** none that seeketh after God.	3:11
4	**there is** none that doeth good, no, not one.	3:12
4	there is none that doeth good, no, not one.	3:12
4	**There is** no fear of God before their eyes.	3:18
4	for **there is** no difference:	3:22
32	that he **might be** just, and the justifier of him:	3:26
22	when he **was** in circumcision, or ... uncircumcision?	4:10
32	that he **might be** the father of all them that believe,	4:11
32	promise, that he **should be** the heir of the world,	4:13
4	for where no law **is**, there is no transgression.	4:15
32	the end the promise **might be** sure to all the seed:	4:16
4	of the faith of Abraham; who **is** the father of us all,	4:16
18	those things which **be** not as though they were.	4:17
18	those things which **be** not as though they **were**.	4:17
40	So shall thy seed **be**.	4:18
4	what he ... promised, he **was** able also to perform.	4:21
20	For when we **were** yet without strength,	5:6
20	love toward us, in that, while we **were** yet sinners,	5:8
23	when we **were** enemies, we were reconciled to God	5:10
34	For until the law sin **was** in the world:	5:13
19	but sin is not imputed when there **is** no law.	5:13
4	who **is** the figure of him that was to come.	5:14
41	we **shall be** also in the likeness of his resurrection:	6:5
32	Likewise reckon ye also yourselves **to be** dead	6:11
32	Likewise reckon ye also yourselves **to be** dead	6:11
4	for ye **are** not under the law, but under grace.	6:14
5	shall we sin, because we **are** not under the law,	6:15
6	his servants ye **are** to whom ye obey;	6:16
1	that ye **were** the servants of sin,	6:17
1	For when ye **were** the servants of sin,	6:20
1	ye **were** free from righteousness.	6:20
4	she **is** free from that law;	7:3
32	so that she **is** no adulteress,	7:3
36	For when we **were** in the flesh, the motions of sins,	7:5
4	For we know that the law **is** spiritual:	7:14
2	but I **am** carnal, sold under sin.	7:14
4	dwells in me, that **is**, in my flesh (NASB)	7:18
22	captivity to the law of sin which **is** in my members.	7:23
23	**are** after the flesh do mind the things of the flesh;	8:5
23	then they that **are** in the flesh cannot please God.	8:8
6	But ye **are** not in the flesh, but in the Spirit,	8:9
4	man have not the Spirit of Christ, he **is** none of his.	8:9
4	brethren, we **are** debtors, not to the flesh,	8:12
7	led by the Spirit of God, they **are** the sons of God.	8:14
5	beareth witness ... that we **are** the children of God:	8:16
4	saved by hope: but hope that is seen **is** not hope:	8:24
24	them who **are** the called according to his purpose.	8:28
32	**to be** conformed to the image of his Son,	8:29
4	who **is** even at the right hand of God,	8:34
4	That I **have** great heaviness and continual sorrow	9:2
32	myself **were** accursed from Christ for my brethren,	9:3
7	Who **are** Israelites; to whom pertaineth	Rom 9:4
21	who **is** over all, God blessed for ever. Amen.	9:5
7	Neither, because they **are** the seed of Abraham,	9:7
4	That **is**, it is not the children of the flesh (NASB)	9:8
40	this time will I come, and Sarah **shall have** a son.	9:9
3	who **art** thou that repliest against God?	9:20
40	And it **shall come to pass**,	9:26
10	children of Israel **be** as the sand of the sea,	9:27
4	my heart's desire and prayer to God for Israel **is**,	10:1
4	that **is**, to bring Christ down from above:	10:6
4	that **is**, to bring Christ again from the dead.	10:7
4	The word is nigh thee, even in thy mouth,	10:8
4	that **is**, the word of faith, which we preach;	10:8
4	For **there is** no difference between the Jew	10:12
2	For I also **am** an Israelite, of the seed of Abraham,	11:1
4	But if it be of works, then is it no more grace:	11:6
4	otherwise work **is** no more work.	11:6
2	inasmuch as I **am** the apostle of the Gentiles,	11:13
21	and thou, **being** a wild olive tree,	11:17
4	for God **is** able to graft them in again.	11:23
1	lest ye **should be** wise in your own conceits;	11:25
22	to every man that **is** among you,	12:3
5	So we, being many, are one body in Christ,	12:5
4	For **there is** no power but of God:	13:1
30	the powers that **be** are ordained of God.	13:1
7	the powers that be **are** ordained of God.	13:1
7	For rulers **are** not a terror to good works,	13:3
4	For he **is** the minister of God to thee for good.	13:4
4	for he **is** the minister of God,	13:4
7	for they **are** God's ministers,	13:6
3	Who **art** thou that judgest another man's servant?	14:4
4	be holden up: for God **is** able to make him stand.	14:4
5	whether we live ... or die, we **are** the Lord's.	14:8
32	but to him that esteemeth any thing **to be** unclean,	14:14
4	For the kingdom of God **is** not meat and drink;	14:17
4	for whatsoever is not of faith **is** sin.	14:23
40	Esaias saith, **There shall be** a root of Jesse,	15:12
6	that ye also **are** full of goodness,	15:14
32	That I **should be** the minister of Jesus Christ	15:16
7	pleased them verily; and their debtors they **are**.	15:27
29	**is** a servant of the church which is at Cenchrea:	16:1
4	who **is** the firstfruits of Achaia unto Christ.	16:5
7	who **are** of note among the apostles,	16:7
25	the household of Narcissus, which **are** in the Lord.	16:11
32	yet I would **have** you wise unto that which is good,	16:19
28	Unto the church of God which **is** at Corinth,	1 Co 1:2
10	and that **there be** no divisions among you;	1:10
1	but that ye **be** perfectly joined together	1:10
7	that **there are** contentions among you.	1:11
2	I **am** of Paul; and I of Apollos; and I of Cephas;	1:12
4	the cross **is** to them that perish foolishness;	1:18
4	but unto us which are saved it **is** the power of God.	1:18
4	Because the foolishness of God **is** wiser than men;	1:25
4	and the weakness of God **is** stronger than men.	1:25
18	which **are** not, to bring to nought things that are:	1:28
18	which are not, to bring to nought things that **are**:	1:28
6	But of him **are** ye in Christ Jesus,	1:30
10	faith should not stand in the wisdom (NT)	2:5
4	for they **are** foolishness unto him:	2:14
6	For ye **are** yet carnal: ... is among you envying,	3:3
6	and divisions, **are** ye not carnal, and walk as men?	3:3
2	For while one saith, I **am** of Paul;	3:4
6	and another, I am of Apollos; **are** ye not carnal?	3:4
4	Who then **is** Paul, and who **is** Apollos,	3:5
4	What then is Apollos? And what **is** Paul? (NASB)	3:5
4	So then neither **is** he that planteth any thing,	3:7
7	he that planteth and he that watereth **are** one:	3:8
5	For we **are** labourers together with God:	3:9
5	ye **are** God's husbandry, ye **are** God's building.	3:9
4	foundation ... that is laid, which **is** Jesus Christ.	3:11
4	fire shall try every man's work of what sort it **is**.	3:13
6	Know ye not that ye **are** the temple of God,	3:16
4	for the temple of God is holy, which temple ye **are**.	3:17
6	for the temple of God is holy, which temple ye **are**.	3:17
32	If any man among you seemeth **to be** wise	3:18
4	the wisdom of this world **is** foolishness with God.	3:19
7	the thoughts of the wise, that they **are** vain.	3:20

εἰμί 1498

4	let no man glory in men. For all things are yours;	1 Co 3:21
4	or things present, or things to come; all are yours;	3:22
4	But with me it is a very small thing	4:3
4	but he that judgeth me is the Lord.	4:4
6	Now ye are full, now ye are rich,	4:8
4	I sent unto you Timotheus, who is my beloved son,	4:17
6	ye are puffed up, and have not rather mourned,	5:2
1	that ye may be a new lump, as ye are unleavened.	5:7
6	that ye may be a new lump, as ye are unleavened.	5:7
10	brother if he should be an immoral person (NASB)	5:11
6	are ye unworthy to judge the smallest matters?	6:2
4	Is it so, that there is not a wise man among you?	6:5
4	Now therefore there is utterly a fault among you,	6:7
1	And such were some of you: but ye are washed,	6:11
4	that your bodies are the members of Christ?	6:15
4	that he which is joined to an harlot is one body?	6:16
43	for two, saith he, shall be one flesh.	6:16
4	But he that is joined unto the Lord is one spirit.	6:17
4	Every sin that a man doeth is without the body;	6:18
4	is the temple of the Holy Ghost which is in you,	6:19
6	which ye have of God, and ye are not your own?	6:19
4	in your body, and in your spirit, which are God's.	6:20
1	and come together again (NASB) (NT)	7:5
32	For I would that all men were even as I myself.	7:7
4	It is good for them if they abide even as I.	7:8
4	for it is better to marry than to burn.	7:9
4	else were your children unclean;	7:14
4	your children unclean; but now are they holy.	7:14
4	Circumcision is nothing,	7:19
4	and uncircumcision is nothing,	7:19
4	being a servant, is the Lord's freeman:	7:22
4	he that is called, being free, is Christ's servant.	7:22
32	hath obtained mercy of the Lord to be faithful.	7:25
32	I say, that it is good for a man so to be.	7:26
4	those who have wives should be as though (NASB)	7:29
12	they that have wives be as though they had none;	7:29
32	But I would have you without carefulness.	7:32
10	that she may be holy both in body and in spirit:	7:34
10	if she should be of full age, (NASB)	7:36
4	she is at liberty to be married to whom she will;	7:39
4	she is happier if she so abide, after my judgment:	7:40
7	For though there be that are called gods,	8:5
7	as there be gods many, and lords many,	8:5
26	and their conscience being weak is defiled.	8:7
19	shall not the conscience of him which is weak	8:10
2	Am I not an apostle? am I not free?	9:1
2	Am I not an apostle? am I not free?	9:1
6	are not ye my work in the Lord?	9:1
2	If I be not an apostle unto others,	9:2
2	yet doubtless I am to you:	9:2
6	for the seal of mine apostleship are ye in the Lord.	9:2
4	Mine answer to them that do examine me is this,	9:3
4	I have nothing to glory of:	9:16
4	yea, woe is unto me, if I preach not the gospel!	9:16
4	What is my reward then?	9:18
21	For though I be free from all men,	9:19
21	not being myself under the Law (NASB)	9:20
21	being not without law to God,	9:21
37	how that all our fathers were under the cloud,	10:1
34	that spiritual Rock ... and that Rock was Christ.	10:4
32	to the intent we should not lust after evil things,	10:6
4	is it not the communion of the blood of Christ?	10:16
4	is it not the communion of the body of Christ?	10:16
5	For we being many are one bread, and one body:	10:17
7	are not they which eat of the sacrifices partakers	10:18
4	What say I then? that the idol is any thing,	10:19
4	which is offered in sacrifice to idols is any thing?	10:19
5	provoke the Lord ... are we stronger than he?	10:22
4	This is offered in sacrifice unto idols,	10:28
4	that the head of every man is Christ;	11:3
4	for that is even all one as if she were shaven.	11:5
4	but the woman is the glory of the man.	11:7
4	For the man is not of the woman;	11:8
4	Judge in yourselves: is it comely that a woman	11:13
4	if a man have long hair, it is a shame unto him?	11:14
4	But if a woman have long hair, it is a glory to her:	11:15
32	But if any man seem to be contentious,	11:16
32	For there must be also heresies among you,	1 Co 11:19
4	this is not to eat the Lord's supper.	11:20
4	eat: this is my body, which is broken for you:	11:24
4	This cup is the new testament in my blood:	11:25
40	shall be guilty of the body and blood of the Lord.	11:27
1	Ye know that ye were Gentiles,	12:2
7	there are diversities of gifts, but the same Spirit.	12:4
7	And there are differences of administrations,	12:5
7	And there are diversities of operations,	12:6
4	but it is the same God which worketh all in all.	12:6
4	For as the body is one, and hath many members,	12:12
18	being many, are one body: so also is Christ.	12:12
4	being many, are one body: so also is Christ.	12:12
4	For the body is not one member, but many.	12:14
2	Because I am not the hand, I am not of the body;	12:15
2	Because I am not the hand, I am not of the body;	12:15
4	is it therefore not of the body?	12:15
2	Because I am not the eye, I am not of the body;	12:16
2	Because I am not the eye, I am not of the body;	12:16
4	is it therefore not of the body?	12:16
34	if they were all one member, where ... the body?	12:19
4	which seem to be more feeble, are necessary:	12:22
32	members ... which we think to be less honourable,	12:23
10	That there should be no schism in the body;	12:25
6	are the body of Christ, and members in particular.	12:27
2	and have not charity, I am nothing.	13:2
46	When I was a child, I spake as a child,	13:11
42	for ye shall speak into the air. (NT)	14:9
4	There are, ... so many kinds of voices in the world,	14:10
7	There are, ... so many kinds of voices in the world,	14:10
38	I shall be unto him that speaketh a barbarian,	14:11
6	forasmuch as ye are zealous of spiritual gifts,	14:12
4	spirit prayeth, but my understanding is unfruitful.	14:14
4	What is it then? I will pray with the spirit,	14:15
7	tongues are for a sign, not to them that believe,	14:22
4	and report that God is in you of a truth.	14:25
4	How is it then, brethren? when ye come together,	14:26
10	But if there be no interpreter,	14:28
4	God is not the author of confusion, but of peace,	14:33
4	for it is a shame for women to speak in the church.	14:35
32	If any man think himself to be a prophet,	14:37
7	are the commandments of the Lord.	14:37
4	are the commandments of the Lord.	14:37
2	For I am the least of the apostles,	15:9
2	that am not meet to be called an apostle,	15:9
2	But by the grace of God I am what I am:	15:10
2	But by the grace of God I am what I am:	15:10
4	that there is no resurrection of the dead?	15:12
4	But if there be no resurrection of the dead,	15:13
4	your faith is worthless (NASB)	15:17
6	if Christ be not raised, ... ye are yet in your sins.	15:17
5	we are of all men most miserable.	15:19
5	If in this life only we have hope in Christ,	15:19
5	we are of all men most miserable.	15:19
10	that God may be all in all.	15:28
4	There is a natural body, and there is a spiritual	15:44
4	is a natural body, and there is a spiritual body.	15:44
4	know that your labour is not in vain in the Lord.	15:58
10	if it be meet that I go also, they shall go with me.	16:4
34	but his will was not at all to come at this time;	16:12
4	that it is the firstfruits of Achaia,	16:15
16	let him be Anathema Maranatha.	16:22
28	unto the church of God which is at Corinth,	2 Co 1:1
24	with all the saints which are in all Achaia:	1:1
6	knowing, that as ye are partakers of the sufferings,	1:7
11	that we should not trust in ourselves,	1:9
4	rejoicing is this, the testimony of our conscience,	1:12
5	that we are your rejoicing,	1:14
10	with me there should be yea yea, and nay nay?	1:17
4	our word to you is not yes and no (NASB)	1:18
5	but are helpers of your joy: for by faith ye stand.	1:24
4	who is he then that maketh me glad,	2:2
4	that my joy is the joy of you all.	2:3
4	whether ye be obedient in all things.	2:9
5	For we are unto God a sweet savour of Christ,	2:15
5	For we are not as many,	2:17
6	Ye are our epistle written in our hearts,	3:2

265

εἰμί 1498

6	**to be** the epistle of Christ ministered by us,	2 Co 3:3
5	Not that we **are** sufficient of ourselves	3:5
40	the ministration of the spirit **be** rather glorious?	3:8
4	Now the Lord **is** that Spirit:	3:17
4	if our gospel **be** hid, it is hid to them that are lost:	4:3
4	if our gospel be hid, it **is** hid to them that are lost:	4:3
4	who **is** the image of God, should shine unto them.	4:4
10	that the excellency of the power **may be** of God,	4:7
23	For we that **are** in this tabernacle do groan,	5:4
32	present or absent, we **may be** accepted of him.	5:9
34	To wit, that God **was** in Christ,	5:19
6	for ye **are** the temple of the living God;	6:16
5	For we **are** the temple of the living God; (NASB)	6:16
38	I **will be** their God, and they shall be my people.	6:16
43	I will be their God, and they **shall be** my people.	6:16
38	And **will be** a Father unto you,	6:18
42	and ye **shall be** my sons and daughters,	6:18
6	that ye **are** in our hearts to die and live with you.	7:3
32	approved yourselves **to be** clear in this matter.	7:11
4	his inward affection **is** more abundant toward you,	7:15
21	he **was** rich, yet for your sakes he became poor,	8:9
18	in many ways that he **is** zealous, (NIV)	8:22
4	it **is** superfluous for me to write to you:	9:1
1	that, as I said, ye **may be** ready:	9:3
32	that the same **might be** ready;	9:5
4	not only supplieth the want of the saints, (NT)	9:12
32	If any man trust to himself that he **is** Christ's,	10:7
5	as **we are** in word by letters when we are absent,	10:11
4	For not he that commendeth himself **is** approved,	10:18
4	As the truth of Christ **is** in me,	11:10
40	whose end **shall be** according to their works.	11:15
32	I say again, Let no man think me a fool; (NT)	11:16
23	suffer fools gladly, seeing ye yourselves **are** wise.	11:19
7	**Are** they Hebrews? so am I. Are they Israelites?	11:22
7	**Are** they Israelites? so am I.	11:22
7	**Are** they the seed of Abraham? so am I.	11:22
7	**Are** they ministers of Christ?	11:23
21	Lord Jesus Christ, which **is** blessed for evermore,	11:31
38	I would desire to glory, I **shall** not **be** a fool;	12:6
2	for when I am weak, then **am** I strong.	12:10
2	in nothing am I behind ... though I **be** nothing,	12:11
4	**is** it wherein ye were inferior to other churches,	12:13
17	But **be** it so, I did not burden you:	12:16
6	Examine yourselves, whether ye **be** in the faith;	13:5
4	how that Jesus Christ **is** in you,	13:5
6	that ... Christ is in you, except ye **be** reprobates?	13:5
5	trust that ye shall know that we **are** not reprobates.	13:6
11	though we **be** as reprobates.	13:7
1	we are glad, when we are weak, and ye **are** strong;	13:9
40	and the God of love and peace **shall be** with you.	13:11
4	Which **is** not another; but there be some	Gal 1:7
7	but **there be** some that trouble you,	1:7
17	preach any other gospel ... let him **be** accursed.	1:8
17	preach any other gospel ... let him **be** accursed.	1:9
46	pleased men, I **should** not **be** the servant of Christ.	1:10
4	gospel which was preached of me **is** not after man.	1:11
46	**was** unknown by face unto the churches of Judaea	1:22
37	they **had** heard only, That he which persecuted us	1:23
21	neither Titus, who was with me, **being** a Greek,	2:3
32	But of these who seemed **to be** somewhat,	2:6
37	whatsoever they **were**, it maketh no matter to me:	2:6
32	Cephas, and John, who seemed **to be** pillars,	2:9
34	I withstood him ... because he **was** to be blamed.	2:11
6	**Are** ye so foolish? having begun in the Spirit,	3:3
7	are of faith, the same **are** the children of Abraham.	3:7
7	are of the works of the law **are** under the curse:	3:10
7	are of the works of the law are under the curse:	3:10
4	And the law **is** not of faith:	3:12
4	but as of one, And to thy seed, which **is** Christ.	3:16
4	mediator is not a mediator of one, but God **is** one.	3:20
4	mediator is not a mediator of one, but God is one.	3:20
34	verily righteousness **should have been** by the law.	3:21
5	we **are** no longer under a schoolmaster.	3:25
6	**are** all the children of God by faith in Christ Jesus.	3:26
6	for ye **are** all one in Christ Jesus.	3:28
6	And if ye be Christ's, then **are** ye Abraham's seed,	3:29
4	Now I say, That the heir, as long as he **is** a child,	4:1
21	differeth nothing ... though he **be** lord of all;	Gal 4:1
4	But **is** under tutors and governors until the time	4:2
36	Even so we, when we **were** children,	4:3
36	**were** in bondage under the elements of the world:	4:3
50	were in bondage under the elements of the world:	4:3
6	because ye **are** sons, God hath sent forth the Spirit	4:6
3	Wherefore thou **art** no more a servant, but a son;	4:7
24	service unto them which by nature **are** no gods.	4:8
34	Where **is** then the blessedness ye spake of?	4:15
32	Tell me, ye that desire **to be** under the law,	4:21
4	Which things **are** an allegory:	4:24
7	are an allegory: for these **are** the two covenants,	4:24
4	Sinai, which gendereth to bondage, which **is** Agar.	4:24
4	For this Agar **is** mount Sinai in Arabia,	4:25
4	But Jerusalem which **is** above is free,	4:26
4	But Jerusalem which is above **is** free,	4:26
5	we, ... as Isaac was, **are** the children of promise.	4:28
6	we, ... as Isaac was, **are** the children of promise.	4:28
5	brethren, we **are** not children of the bondwoman,	4:31
4	that he **is** a debtor to do the whole law.	5:3
10	shall bear his judgment, whosoever he **be**.	5:10
6	if ye be led of the Spirit, ye **are** not under the law.	5:18
4	Now the works of the flesh **are** manifest,	5:19
4	works of the flesh ... which **are** these;	5:19
4	But the fruit of the Spirit **is** love, joy, peace,	5:22
4	against such **there is** no law.	5:23
32	For if a man think himself **to be** something,	6:3
21	think himself to be something, when he **is** nothing,	6:3
4	For neither **is** circumcision anything, (NASB)	6:15
24	an apostle ... to the saints which **are** at Ephesus,	Eph 1:1
32	that we **should be** holy and without blame	1:4
32	That we should **be** to the praise of his glory,	1:12
4	Which **is** the earnest of our inheritance	1:14
4	that ye may know what **is** the hope of his calling,	1:18
4	Which **is** his body, the fulness of him	1:23
25	who **were** dead in trespasses and sins:	2:1
36	and **were** by nature the children of wrath,	2:3
50	and were by nature the children of wrath,	2:3
21	But God, who **is** rich in mercy,	2:4
25	Even when we **were** dead in sins,	2:5
6	by grace ye **are** saved;	2:5
6	For by grace **are** ye saved through faith;	2:8
5	For we **are** his workmanship,	2:10
1	That at that time ye **were** without Christ,	2:12
23	now in Christ Jesus ye who sometimes **were** far off	2:13
4	For he **is** our peace, who hath made both one,	2:14
6	therefore ye **are** no more strangers and foreigners,	2:19
6	but you **are** fellow-citizens with the saints (NASB)	2:19
19	Jesus Christ himself **being** the chief corner stone;	2:20
32	That the Gentiles **should be** fellowheirs,	3:6
4	at my tribulations for you, which **is** your glory.	3:13
4	what **is** it but that he also descended first	4:9
4	He that descended **is** the same also that ascended	4:10
11	That we henceforth **be** no more children,	4:14
4	which **is** the head, even Christ:	4:15
23	**being** alienated from the life of God	4:18
29	through the ignorance that **is** in them,	4:18
4	have been taught by him, as the truth **is** in Jesus:	4:21
5	for we **are** members one of another.	4:25
6	For of this you can **be** sure: No immoral, (NIV)	5:5
4	nor covetous man, who **is** an idolater,	5:5
1	For ye **were** sometimes darkness,	5:8
4	Proving what **is** acceptable unto the Lord.	5:10
4	For **it is** a shame even to speak of those things	5:12
4	for whatsoever doth make manifest **is** light.	5:13
4	Redeeming the time, because the days **are** evil.	5:16
4	And be not drunk with wine, wherein **is** excess;	5:18
4	For the husband **is** the head of the wife,	5:23
4	even as Christ **is** the head of the church:	5:23
10	but that it **should be** holy and without blemish.	5:27
5	For we **are** members of his body, of his flesh,	5:30
43	unto his wife, and they two **shall be** one flesh.	5:31
4	This **is** a great mystery:	5:32
4	obey your parents in the Lord: for this **is** right.	6:1
4	which **is** the first commandment with promise:	6:2
39	and thou **mayest** live long on the earth.	6:3
4	knowing that your Master also **is** in heaven;	6:9

εἰμί

4	neither **is there** respect of persons with him.	Eph 6:9
4	For we wrestle not against flesh and blood, (NT)	6:12
4	the sword of the Spirit, which **is** the word of God:	6:17
24	all the saints in Christ Jesus **which are** at Philippi,	Php 1:1
4	Even as **it is** meet for me to think this of you all,	1:7
25	ye all **are** partakers of my grace.	1:7
4	For God **is** my record, how greatly I long after you	1:8
1	that ye **may be** sincere and without offence	1:10
32	having a desire to depart, and **to be** with Christ;	1:23
4	which **is** to them an evident token of perdition,	1:28
32	thought it not robbery **to be** equal with God:	2:6
4	For it **is** God which worketh in you	2:13
34	he longed after you all, and **was** full of heaviness,	2:26
8	and that I **may be** the less sorrowful.	2:28
5	For we **are** the circumcision,	3:3
34	But what things **were** gain to me,	3:7
32	loss for the excellency of the knowledge (NT)	3:8
32	count them but dung, that I may win Christ, (NT)	3:8
4	Finally, brethren, whatsoever things **are** true,	4:8
40	do: and the God of peace **shall be** with you.	4:9
2	in whatsoever state **I am**, therewith to be content.	4:11
32	in whatsoever state I am, therewith **to be** content.	4:11
4	also it is constantly bearing fruit (NASB)	Col 1:6
4	who **is** for you a faithful minister of Christ;	1:7
4	Who **is** the image of the invisible God,	1:15
4	And he **is** before all things,	1:17
4	And he **is** the head of the body, the church:	1:18
4	who **is** the beginning, the firstborn from the dead;	1:18
25	you, that **were** sometime alienated and enemies	1:21
4	for his body's sake, which **is** the church:	1:24
4	which **is** Christ in you, the hope of glory:	1:27
7	In whom **are** hid all the treasures of wisdom	2:3
2	absent in the flesh, yet **am I** with you in the spirit,	2:5
40	lest any man spoil you through philosophy (NT)	2:8
6	And ye **are** complete in him, which is the head	2:10
4	which **is** the head of all principality and power:	2:10
25	And you, **being** dead in your sins	2:13
34	the handwriting of ordinances that **was** against us,	2:14
4	Which **are** a shadow of things to come;	2:17
4	Which all **are** to perish with the using;	2:22
4	These **are** matters which have (NASB)	2:23
4	where Christ **is**, seated at the right (NASB)	3:1
4	and covetousness, which **is** idolatry:	3:5
4	put on charity, which **is** the bond of perfectness.	3:14
4	obey ... for this is well pleasing unto the Lord.	3:20
4	and **there is** no respect of persons.	3:25
4	a faithful and beloved brother, who **is** one of you.	4:9
23	called Justus, who **are** of the circumcision.	4:11
32	when we might **have been** burdensome,	1 Th 2:6
4	but as it **is** in truth, the word of God,	2:13
31	the churches of God which in Judaea **are** in Christ	2:14
6	For ye **are** our glory and joy.	2:20
36	when we **were** with you, we told you before	3:4
4	For this **is** the will of God, even your sanctification,	4:3
6	for ye yourselves **are** taught of God to love	4:9
41	and so **shall** we ever **be** with the Lord.	4:17
6	But ye, brethren, **are** not in darkness,	5:4
6	Ye **are** all the children of light,	5:5
5	**we are** not of the night, nor of darkness.	5:5
23	But let us, who **are** of the day, be sober,	5:8
4	We are bound to thank God ... as **it is** meet,	2 Th 1:3
4	showing himself that he **is** God.	2:4
21	when **I was** yet with you, I told you these things?	2:5
4	him, whose coming **is** after the working of Satan	2:9
4	But the Lord **is** faithful, who shall stablish you,	3:3
36	when we **were** with you, this we commanded you,	3:10
4	which **is** the token in every epistle: so I write.	3:17
4	Now the end of the commandment **is** charity	1 Tm 1:5
32	Desiring **to be** teachers of the law;	1:7
18	Who **was** before a blasphemer, and a persecutor,	1:13
2	into the world to save sinners; of whom I **am** chief.	1:15
4	Of whom **is** Hymenaeus and Alexander;	1:20
20	For kings, and for all that **are** in authority;	2:2
32	suffer not a woman to teach, ... but **to be** in silence.	2:12
32	A bishop then must **be** blameless,	3:2
23	also first be proved; ... **being** found blameless.	3:10
33	Let the deacons **be** the husbands of one wife,	3:12
4	which **is** the church of the living God,	1 Tm 3:15
4	great **is** the mystery of godliness:	3:16
39	thou **shalt be** a good minister of Jesus Christ,	4:6
4	for bodily discipline is only of little profit, (NASB)	4:8
4	but godliness **is** profitable unto all things,	4:8
4	the living God, who **is** the Saviour of all men,	4:10
15	**be absorbed** in them, (NASB)	4:15
10	that thy profiting may appear to all. (NT)	4:15
4	for that **is** good and acceptable before God.	5:4
12	these ... give in charge, that they **may be** blameless.	5:7
4	hath denied the faith, and **is** worse than an infidel.	5:8
7	Some men's sins **are** open beforehand,	5:24
4	the good works of some **are** manifest beforehand;	5:25
7	Let as many servants as **are** under the yoke	6:1
7	not despise them, because they **are** brethren;	6:2
7	because they **are** faithful and beloved,	6:2
32	supposing that gain **is** godliness:	6:5
4	But godliness with contentment **is** great gain.	6:6
4	For the love of money **is** the root of all evil:	6:10
32	**to be** generous and ready to share, (NASB)	6:18
4	Grace **be** with thee. Amen.	6:21
4	which is in thee by the putting on of my hands.	2 Tm 1:6
4	and am persuaded that he **is** able to keep that	1:12
4	of whom **are** Phygellus and Hermogenes.	1:15
43	men, who **shall be** able to teach others also.	2:2
4	a canker: of whom **is** Hymenaeus and Philetus;	2:17
25	The Lord knoweth them that **are** his.	2:19
4	**there are** not only vessels of gold and of silver,	2:20
40	he **shall be** a vessel unto honour, sanctified,	2:21
32	but **be** gentle unto all men, apt to teach, patient,	2:24
43	For men **shall be** lovers of their own selves,	3:2
7	For of this sort **are** they which creep into houses,	3:6
40	for their folly **shall be** manifest unto all men,	3:9
10	That the man of God **may be** perfect,	3:17
40	the time **will come** ... not endure sound doctrine;	4:3
4	Only Luke **is** with me.	4:11
4	Mark, ... for **he is** profitable for me for the ministry.	4:11
4	If any **be** blameless, the husband of one wife,	Tit 1:6
32	a bishop must **be** blameless, as the steward of God;	1:7
10	**may be** able by sound doctrine both to exhort and	1:9
7	For **there are** many unruly and vain talkers	1:10
4	This witness **is** true. Wherefore rebuke them	1:13
23	deny him, **being** abominable, and disobedient,	1:16
32	That the aged men **be** sober, grave, temperate,	2:2
32	to love their husbands, to love their children, (NT)	2:4
32	in everything, **to be** well-pleasing, (NASB)	2:9
32	obey magistrates, **to be** ready to every good work,	3:1
32	To speak evil of no man, **to be** no brawlers,	3:2
36	For we ourselves also **were** sometimes foolish,	3:3
4	These things **are** good and profitable unto men.	3:8
7	for they **are** unprofitable and vain.	3:9
21	and sinneth, **being** condemned of himself.	3:11
12	maintain good works ... that they **be** not unfruitful.	3:14
21	**being** such an one as Paul the aged,	Phlm 1:9
4	receive him, that **is**, sending my very heart (NASB)	1:12
10	thy benefit should not **be** as it were of necessity,	1:14
21	Who **being** the brightness of his glory,	Heb 1:3
3	Thou **art** my Son, this day have I begotten thee?	1:5
38	And again, I **will be** to him a Father,	1:5
40	be to him a Father, and he **shall be** to me a Son?	1:5
7	and the heavens **are** the works of thine hands:	1:10
3	and they shall be changed: but thou **art** the same,	1:12
7	**Are** they not all ministering spirits,	1:14
4	What **is** man, that thou art mindful of him?	2:6
38	And again, I **will** put my trust in him.	2:13
4	him that had the power of death, that **is**, (NASB)	2:14
37	**were** all their lifetime subject to bondage.	2:15
18	Who **was** faithful to him that appointed him,	3:2
5	whose house **are** we, if we hold fast the confidence	3:6
40	lest there **be** in any of you an evil heart of unbelief,	3:12
5	For unto us **was** the gospel preached,	4:2
4	Neither **is there** any creature that is not manifest	4:13
3	Thou **art** my Son, to day have I begotten thee.	5:5
21	Though he were a Son, yet learned he obedience	5:8
32	For when for the time ye ought **to be** teachers,	5:12
4	unskilful in the word ... for he **is** a babe.	5:13
4	strong meat **belongeth** to them that are of full age,	5:14

4	also King of Salem, which **is**, King of peace;	Heb 7:2
4	tithes ... that **is**, from their brethren (NASB)	7:5
34	For he **was** yet in the loins of his father,	7:10
34	If ... perfection **were** by the Levitical priesthood,	7:11
4	And **it** is yet far more evident:	7:15
7	For those priests **were** made without an oath;	7:21
7	And they truly **were** many priests,	7:23
34	For if he were on earth, he should not **be** a priest,	8:4
34	For if he were on earth, he should not **be** a priest,	8:4
20	**seeing** that there are priests that offer gifts	8:4
4	much also he is the mediator of a better covenant,	8:6
34	For if that first covenant **had been** faultless,	8:7
38	and I **will be** to them a God,	8:10
43	and they **shall be** to me a people:	8:10
38	For I **will be** merciful to their unrighteousness,	8:12
4	of which we cannot now speak particularly. (NT)	9:5
4	**that is** to say, not of this creation; (NASB)	9:11
4	he **is** the mediator of the new testament,	9:15
5	which will we **are** sanctified through the offering	10:10
4	**that is**, His flesh (NASB)	10:20
5	we **are** not of them who draw back unto perdition;	10:39
4	Now faith **is** the substance of things hoped for,	11:1
32	he obtained witness that he **was** righteous,	11:4
4	for he that cometh to God must believe that he **is**,	11:6
7	that they **were** strangers and pilgrims on the earth.	11:13
4	they desire a better country, **that is** (NASB)	11:16
34	Of whom the world **was** not worthy:	11:38
4	for what son **is** he whom the father chasteneth not?	12:7
6	**be** without chastisement, ... then **are** ye bastards,	12:8
6	then **are** ye bastards, and not sons.	12:8
32	no chastening for the present seemeth **to be** joyous,	12:11
34	And so terrible **was** the sight, that Moses said,	12:21
2	I exceedingly fear and quake: (NT)	12:21
23	as **being** yourselves also in the body.	13:3
4	**that is**, the fruit of lips that give thanks (NASB)	13:15
1	ye may **be** perfect and entire, wanting nothing.	Jas 1:4
4	for God cannot **be** tempted with evil,	1:13
4	good gift and every perfect gift **is** from above,	1:17
32	we **should be** a kind of firstfruits of his creatures.	1:18
17	let every man **be** swift to hear, slow to speak,	1:19
4	For if any **be** a hearer of the word, and not a doer,	1:23
34	straightway forgetteth what manner of man he **was**.	1:24
40	this man **shall be** blessed in his deed.	1:25
32	If any man among you seem **to be** religious,	1:26
4	undefiled before God and the Father **is** this,	1:27
12	or sister **be** naked, and destitute of (NT)	2:15
4	faith, if it hath not works, **is** dead, being alone.	2:17
4	believest that there **is** one God; thou doest well:	2:19
4	know, ... that faith without works **is** dead?	2:20
4	For as the body without the spirit **is** dead, so faith	2:26
4	so faith without works **is** dead also.	2:26
18	also the ships, which though they **be** so great,	3:4
4	Even so the tongue **is** a little member,	3:5
4	This wisdom descendeth not from above, (NT)	3:15
4	But the wisdom that **is** from above is first pure,	3:17
4	the friendship of the world **is** enmity with God?	4:4
32	whosoever therefore **will be** a friend of the world	4:4
3	thou **art** not a doer of the law, but a judge.	4:11
4	**is** one lawgiver, who is able to save and to destroy:	4:12
3	who **art** thou that judgest another?	4:12
4	It **is** even a vapour, that appeareth for a little time,	4:14
6	It **is** even a vapour, that appeareth for a little time,	4:14
4	rejoice in your boastings: all such rejoicing **is** evil,	4:16
4	knoweth to do ... and doeth it not, to him **it is** sin.	4:17
40	and the rust of them **shall be** a witness against you,	5:3
4	that the Lord **is** very pitiful, and of tender mercy.	5:11
16	but let your yea **be** yea; and your nay, nay;	5:12
10	he have committed sins, they shall (NT)	5:15
34	Elias **was** a man subject to like passions as we are,	5:17
4	though now for a season, if need **be**,	1 Pt 1:6
42	YOU **SHALL BE** HOLY, FOR I AM (NASB)	1:16
2	Because it is written, Be ye holy; for I **am** holy.	1:16
32	that your faith and hope might **be** in God.	1:21
4	this **is** the word which by the gospel is preached	1:25
4	For so **is** the will of God, that with well doing	2:15
1	For ye **were** as sheep going astray;	2:25
17	Whose adorning let it not **be** that outward	3:3

4	which **is** in the sight of God of great price.	1 Pt 3:4
4	in which a few, that **is**, eight persons (NASB)	3:20
4	Who **is** gone into heaven, and is on the right hand	3:22
4	to whom **be** praise and dominion for ever	4:11
32	and testifying that this **is** the true grace of God	5:12
4	But he that lacketh these things **is** blind,	2 Pt 1:9
2	I think it meet, as long as I **am** in this tabernacle,	1:13
4	that shortly I must put off this **is** my tabernacle, (NT)	1:14
4	from the excellent glory, This **is** my beloved Son,	1:17
23	when we **were** with him in the holy mount.	1:18
43	even as there **shall be** false teachers among you,	2:1
23	angels, which **are** greater in power and might,	2:11
7	These **are** wells without water,	2:17
34	For it **had been** better for them not to have known	2:21
4	And saying, Where **is** the promise of his coming?	3:4
37	that by the word of God the heavens **were** of old,	3:5
7	the earth, ... by the same word **are** kept in store,	3:7
4	in which **are** some things hard to be understood,	3:16
34	That which **was** from the beginning,	1 Jn 1:1
34	that eternal life, which **was** with the Father,	1:2
10	write we unto you, that your joy **may be** full.	1:4
4	This then **is** the message which we have heard	1:5
4	that God **is** light, and in him is no darkness at all.	1:5
4	that God is light, and in him **is** no darkness at all.	1:5
4	But if we walk in the light, as he **is** in the light,	1:7
4	we deceive ourselves, and the truth **is** not in us.	1:8
4	he **is** faithful and just to forgive us our sins,	1:9
4	we make him a liar, and his word **is** not in us.	1:10
4	And he **is** the propitiation for our sins:	2:2
4	and keepeth not his commandments, **is** a liar,	2:4
4	**is** a liar, and the truth is not in him.	2:4
5	hereby know we that we **are** in him.	2:5
4	The old commandment **is** the word	2:7
4	which thing **is** true in him and in you:	2:8
32	that saith he **is** in the light, and hateth his brother,	2:9
4	hateth his brother, **is** in darkness even until now.	2:9
4	and **there is** none occasion of stumbling in him.	2:10
4	But he that hateth his brother **is** in darkness,	2:11
6	young men, because ye **are** strong,	2:14
4	love the world, the love of the Father **is** not in him.	2:15
4	**is** not of the Father, but is of the world.	2:16
4	is not of the Father, but **is** of the world.	2:16
4	Little children, **it is** the last time:	2:18
4	whereby we know that **it is** the last time.	2:18
37	They went out from us, but they **were** not of us;	2:19
37	but they were not of us; for if they **had been** of us,	2:19
37	but they were not of us; for if they **had been** of us,	2:19
7	be made manifest that they **were** not all of us.	2:19
4	because ye know it, and that no lie **is** of the truth.	2:21
4	**is** a liar but he that denieth that Jesus is the Christ?	2:22
4	is a liar but he that denieth that Jesus **is** the Christ?	2:22
4	**is** antichrist, that denieth the Father and the Son.	2:22
4	And this **is** the promise that he hath promised us,	2:25
4	anointing teacheth you of all things, and **is** truth,	2:27
4	and is truth, and **is** no lie,	2:27
4	If ye know that he **is** righteous,	2:29
5	called the sons of God: and such we **are**. (NASB)	3:1
5	Beloved, now **are** we the sons of God,	3:2
41	and it doth not yet appear what we **shall be**:	3:2
41	we **shall be** like him; for we shall see him as he is.	3:2
4	we shall be like him; for we shall see him as he **is**.	3:2
4	hope in him purifieth himself, even as he **is** pure.	3:3
4	for sin **is** the transgression of the law.	3:4
4	to take away our sins; and in him **is** no sin.	3:5
4	he that doeth righteousness **is** righteous,	3:7
4	righteousness is righteous, even as he **is** righteous.	3:7
4	He that committeth sin **is** of the devil,	3:8
4	In this the children of God **are** manifest,	3:10
4	whosoever doeth not righteousness **is** not of God,	3:10
4	For this **is** the message that ye heard	3:11
34	Not as Cain, who **was** of that wicked one,	3:12
34	Because his own works **were** evil,	3:12
4	Whosoever hateth his brother **is** a murderer:	3:15
5	And hereby we know that we **are** of the truth,	3:19
4	heart condemn us, God is greater than our heart,	3:20
4	And this **is** his commandment,	3:23
4	but try the spirits whether they **are** of God:	4:1

εἰμί

4	that Jesus Christ is come in the flesh **is** of God:	1 Jn 4:2
4	that Jesus Christ is come in the flesh **is** not of God:	4:3
4	and this **is** that spirit of antichrist,	4:3
4	and even now already **is** it in the world.	4:3
6	Ye **are** of God, little children,	4:4
4	because greater **is** he that is in you,	4:4
7	They **are** of the world:	4:5
5	We **are** of God: he that knoweth God heareth us;	4:6
4	he that is not of God heareth not us.	4:6
4	let us love one another: for love **is** of God;	4:7
4	that loveth not knoweth not God; for God **is** love.	4:8
4	Herein **is** love, not that we loved God,	4:10
4	God dwelleth in us, and his love **is** perfected in us.	4:12
4	shall confess that Jesus **is** the Son of God,	4:15
4	believed the love that God hath to us. God **is** love;	4:16
4	because as he **is**, so are we in this world.	4:17
5	because as he is, so **are** we in this world.	4:17
4	**There is** no fear in love;	4:18
4	and hateth his brother, he **is** a liar:	4:20
4	believeth that Jesus **is** the Christ is born of God:	5:1
4	For this **is** the love of God,	5:3
7	and his commandments **are** not grievous.	5:3
4	and this **is** the victory that overcometh the world,	5:4
4	Who **is** he that overcometh the world,	5:5
4	but he that believeth that Jesus **is** the Son of God?	5:5
4	This **is** he that came by water and blood,	5:6
4	And it **is** the Spirit that beareth witness,	5:6
4	that beareth witness, because the Spirit **is** truth.	5:6
7	For there **are** three that bear record in heaven,	5:7
7	Father, ... Word, ... Ghost: and these three **are** one.	5:7
7	And there **are** three that bear witness in earth,	5:8
7	and these three **agree** in one.	5:8
4	the witness of God **is** greater:	5:9
4	this **is** the witness of God which he hath testified	5:9
4	And this **is** the record,	5:11
4	given to us eternal life, and this life **is** in his Son.	5:11
4	And this **is** the confidence that we have in him,	5:14
4	**There is** a sin unto death:	5:16
4	All unrighteousness **is** sin:	5:17
4	and **there is** a sin not unto death.	5:17
5	And we know that we **are** of God,	5:19
5	and we **are** in him that is true,	5:20
4	even in his Son Jesus Christ. This **is** the true God,	5:20
40	which dwelleth in us, and **shall be** with us for ever.	2 Jn 1:2
40	Grace **be** with you, mercy, and peace, from God	1:3
4	this **is** love, that we walk after his commandments.	1:6
4	This **is** the commandment,	1:6
4	This **is** a deceiver and an antichrist.	1:7
10	and speak face to face, that our joy **may be** full.	1:12
4	He that doeth good **is** of God:	3 Jn 1:11
4	and ye know that our record **is** true.	1:12
4	These **are** spots in your feasts of charity,	Jude 1:12
7	These **are** murmurers, complainers,	1:16
43	told you **there should be** mockers in the last time,	1:18
7	These **be** they who separate themselves, sensual,	1:19
21	and peace, from him which **is**, and which was,	Rev 1:4
34	and peace, from him which is, and which **was**,	1:4
4	from the seven Spirits which **are** before his throne;	1:4
2	**I am** Alpha and Omega,	1:8
21	which **is**, and which was, and which is to come,	1:8
34	which is, and which **was**, and which is to come,	1:8
2	**I am** Alpha and Omega, the first and the last:	1:11
2	Fear not; **I am** the first and the last:	1:17
2	and, behold, **I am** alive for evermore, Amen;	1:18
4	which thou hast seen, and the things which **are**,	1:19
7	seven stars **are** the angels of the seven churches:	1:20
7	the seven candlesticks ... **are** the seven churches.	1:20
32	thou hast tried them which say they **are** apostles,	2:2
7	them which say they are apostles, and are not,	2:2
4	which **is** in the midst of the paradise of God.	2:7
3	but thou **art** rich and I know the blasphemy	2:9
32	the blasphemy of them which say they **are** Jews,	2:9
7	and are not, but **are** the synagogue of Satan.	2:9
2	that **I am** he which searcheth the reins and hearts:	2:23
3	thou hast a name that thou livest, and **art** dead.	3:1
7	shall walk with me in white: for **they are** worthy.	3:4
32	which say they **are** Jews, and are not, but do lie:	3:9

7	which say they are Jews, and **are** not, but do lie;	Rev 3:9
3	know thy works, that thou **art** neither cold nor hot:	3:15
13	I would thou **wert** cold or hot.	3:15
35	I would thou **wert** cold or hot.	3:15
3	thou **art** lukewarm, and neither cold nor hot,	3:16
2	thou sayest, **I am** rich, and increased with goods,	3:17
3	and knowest not that thou **art** wretched,	3:17
7	which **are** the seven Spirits of God.	4:5
34	God Almighty, which **was**, and is, and is to come.	4:8
21	God Almighty, which was, and **is**, and is to come.	4:8
3	Thou **art** worthy, O Lord, to receive glory	4:11
7	and for thy pleasure they **are** and were created.	4:11
37	and for thy pleasure they are and **were** created.	4:11
4	Who **is** worthy to open the book,	5:2
21	behold, the Lion of the tribe of Juda, (NT)	5:5
7	which **are** the seven Spirits of God sent forth	5:6
7	vials full of odours, which **are** the prayers of saints.	5:8
3	Thou **art** worthy to take the book,	5:9
34	number of them **was** myriads (NASB)	5:11
4	Saying with a loud voice, Worthy **is** the Lamb	5:12
4	And every creature which **is** in heaven,	5:13
4	such as are in the sea, and all that **are** in them,	5:13
7	What **are** these which are arrayed in white robes?	7:13
7	These **are** they which came out of great tribulation,	7:14
7	Therefore **are** they before the throne of God,	7:15
37	and their teeth **were** as the teeth of lions.	9:8
34	and their power **was** to hurt men five months.	9:10
7	their power **is** in their mouth, and in their tails:	9:19
4	their power is in their mouth, and in their tails:	9:19
40	And sware ... that there **should be** time no longer:	10:6
40	but it **shall be** in thy mouth sweet as honey.	10:9
34	and it **was** in my mouth sweet as honey:	10:10
7	These **are** the two olive trees,	11:4
21	Almighty, which **art**, and wast, and art to come;	11:17
34	Almighty, which art, and **wast**, and art to come;	11:17
34	And the beast which I saw **was** like unto a leopard,	13:2
4	Here **is** the patience and the faith of the saints.	13:10
4	Here **is** wisdom. Let him that hath understanding	13:18
4	for it **is** the number of a man; and his number is	13:18
7	These **are** they which were not defiled with women;	14:4
7	were not defiled with women; for they **are** virgins.	14:4
7	are virgins. These **are** they which follow the Lamb	14:4
7	they **are** without fault before the throne of God.	14:5
4	Here **is** the patience of the saints:	14:12
3	Thou **art** righteous, O Lord, which art, and wast,	16:5
21	O Lord, which **art**, and wast, and shalt be,	16:5
34	O Lord, which art, and **wast**, and shalt be,	16:5
7	given them blood to drink; for they **are** worthy.	16:6
7	For they **are** the spirits of devils, working miracles,	16:14
4	hail; for the plague thereof **was** exceeding great.	16:21
34	woman **was** clothed in purple and scarlet (NASB)	17:4
34	The beast that thou sawest **was**, and is not;	17:8
4	The beast that thou sawest was, and **is not**;	17:8
34	behold the beast that **was**, and is not, and yet is.	17:8
4	behold the beast that was, and **is not**, and yet is.	17:8
4	behold the beast that was, and is not, and yet **is**.	17:8
7	The seven heads **are** seven mountains,	17:9
7	And there **are** seven kings: five are fallen,	17:10
4	and one **is**, and the other is not yet come;	17:10
34	And the beast that **was**, and is not,	17:11
4	And the beast that was, and **is not**,	17:11
4	even he **is** the eighth, and is of the seven,	17:11
4	even he is the eighth, and **is** of the seven,	17:11
4	And the ten horns which thou sawest **are** ten kings,	17:12
4	for he **is** Lord of lords, and King of kings:	17:14
7	waters ... where the whore sitteth, **are** peoples,	17:15
4	the woman which thou sawest **is** that great city,	17:18
2	queen, and **am** no widow, and shall see no sorrow.	18:7
37	for thy merchants **were** the great men of the earth;	18:23
4	for the fine linen **is** the righteousness of saints.	19:8
7	saith unto me, These **are** the true sayings of God.	19:9
2	See thou do it not: **I am** thy fellowservant,	19:10
4	for the testimony of Jesus **is** the spirit of prophecy.	19:10
4	that old serpent, which **is** the Devil, and Satan,	20:2
43	but they **shall be** priests of God and of Christ,	20:6
4	which **is** the book of life: and the dead were judged	20:12
4	cast into the lake of fire. This **is** the second death.	20:14

4	were passed away; and there **was** no more sea.....	Rev 21:1
43	will dwell with them, and they **shall be** his people,....	21:3
40	God himself **shall be** with them, and be their God....	21:3
40	and there **shall be** no more death, neither sorrow,....	21:4
40	neither **shall** there be any more pain:................	21:4
7	Write: for these words **are** true and faithful.........	21:5
2	said unto me, It is done. **I am** Alpha and Omega,....	21:6
38	and I **will be** his God, and he shall be my son.......	21:7
40	and I will be his God, and he **shall be** my son.......	21:7
4	lake which burneth ... which **is** the second death.....	21:8
4	which **are** the names of the twelve tribes.............	21:12
4	and the length **is** as large as the breadth:...........	21:16
4	length and the breadth and the height ... **are** equal....	21:16
4	to the measure of a man, that **is**, of the angel.......	21:17
34	And the building of the wall of it **was** of jasper:......	21:18
34	twelve pearls: every several gate **was** of one pearl:....	21:21
4	God Almighty and the Lamb **are** the temple of it.....	21:22
40	not be shut ... for there **shall be** no night there.......	21:25
40	And there **shall be** no more curse:....................	22:3
40	the throne of God and of the Lamb **shall be** in it;....	22:3
40	**shall be** no night there; and they need no candle,.....	22:5
2	See thou do it not: for **I am** thy fellowservant,.......	22:9
4	Seal not the sayings ... for the time **is** at hand........	22:10
40	to give every man according as his work **shall be**.....	22:12
4	to give every man according as his work **shall be**.....	22:12
2	**I am** Alpha and Omega,...........................	22:13
40	that they **may have** right to the tree of life,...........	22:14
2	**I am** the root and the offspring of David,............	22:16

Eimi means "to be," "to exist," "to live," "to reside," or "to occur." For example, *eimi* can express "God *exists*" (literally "is") in Hebrews 11:6 and also, "If we had *been* in the days of our fathers ..." in Matthew 23:30.

Septuagint Usage
Jewish and Christian writers used *eimi*, especially in the participial form *ōn*, as an attribute of God. The background for this practice lies in the Septuagint translation of Exodus 3:14 where God replies to Moses' question about God's name by saying, "I am the *existing one* (*ho ōn*)." Because of this translation, Philo and Josephus used the same expression to refer to God. The New Testament Book of Revelation (1:4,8; 11:17; 16:5) also employed *ōn* to refer to God.

Eimi can also function as a copula to unite a subject together with a predicate. In Greek the reader may have difficulty deciding which is the subject and which is the predicate nominative since word order is relatively unimportant. Context must often decide.

New Testament Usage
In this category—*eimi* as a copula—belong Jesus' numerous "I am" statements of the Gospels and especially of the Gospel of John. Again the background for this expression lies in the Old Testament. The verse mentioned above (Exodus 3:14) is also an "I am" statement. Further, in the Old Testament, frequently at the end of a prophetic oracle God said, "I am the Lord" (*'ani YHWH*, "Yahweh"), e.g., Ezekiel 33:29. Finally, a few times God referred to himself simply by saying, "I, am he" (*'ani hu*), e.g., Deuteronomy 32:39. The "I am" statement as a means of a deity's self-revelation is also strongly established in the ancient orient and Hellenism.

Jesus used this expression frequently. Sometimes the expression appears absolutely or without a stated predicate: "Before Abraham was, I am" (John 8:58, cf. Mark 14:61ff.). At Jesus' arrest He spoke the words "I am," and His arresters fell to the ground (John 18:6). More often Jesus used a predicate: "I am the living bread" (John 6:51). In the Gospel of John, Jesus identified himself in such a way as the light of the world, the door, the good shepherd, the Son of God, the resurrection, the way, the truth, the life, and the vine.

STRONG 1510, BAUER 222-26, MOULTON-MILLIGAN 184-85, KITTEL 2:398-400, LIDDELL-SCOTT 487-89, COLIN BROWN 2:278-83.

1499. εἴπερ eiper conj
If indeed, provided that, since.

1. εἴπερ eiper

1	since indeed God who will justify (NASB)..........	Rom 3:30
1	if so be that the Spirit of God dwell in you.............	8:9
1	if so be that we suffer with him,......................	8:17
1	For **though** there be that are called gods,...........	1 Co 8:5
1	if so be that the dead rise not.......................	15:15
1	Seeing it is a righteous thing........................	2 Th 1:6
1	**If so be** ye have tasted that the Lord is gracious.....	1 Pt 2:3

Eiper is a compound word consisting of the conditional particle *ei* (1479) and the enclitic particle *per*. Some Greek texts show two separate words. However, since *per* is an enclitic, i.e., "an unaccented word which is pronounced as part of the preceding word" (similar to the word *not* in *cannot*), and because Greek manuscripts do not show separation between words, grammarians debate whether it should be read as one or two words. In either case, the resultant meaning is an intensification of the conditional particle *ei*.

New Testament Usage
New Testament examples of this construction can be found at Romans 3:30; 8:9; and 2 Thessalonians 1:16 where the word is best translated "if indeed" or "since." Here its use follows a pattern seen also in the Attic (a Greek dialect which predates the Koine of the New Testament) in which the supposition agrees with the fact. In 1 Corinthians 8:5, however, the translation "for even if" indicates that the

supposed "fact" is in question: "For even if there are so-called gods . . . " (NIV). (See also 1 Corinthians 15:15.)

STRONG 1512, BAUER 226, MOULTON-MILLIGAN 185, LIDDELL-SCOTT 489.

1500. εἶπον eipon verb
Say, speak.

אָמַר 'āmar (569), Qal: say (Gn 6:13, Jos 22:2, Ez 33:10); niphal: be said (Gn 10:9, 2 Kgs 4:26, Zep 3:16).

אֲמַר 'āmar (A570), Say, ask (Ezr 5:3,4, Jer 10:11, Dn 2:5,7—Aramaic).

אֹמֶר 'ōmer (575), Say (Jb 9:27).

בִּין bîn (1032), Perceive, consider; hithpolel: look at, consider closely (Is 14:16).

דָּבַר dāvar (1744), Piel: speak to, command (Ex 6:10, 1 Kgs 2:31, Ez 40:4).

דָּבָר dāvār (1745), Word (Gn 45:27, 2 Sm 3:17, Prv 15:23).

דָּמָה dāmâh (1880), Piel: thought, planned (Est 4:13, Is 14:24).

חֲוָה chăwâh (A2426), Hafel: interpret (Dn 2:10—Aramaic).

יָדַע yādha‘ (3156), Know, understand (Is 19:12, 48:6).

יָרָה yārâh (3498), Hiphil: teach (Jb 12:7).

מְלַל melal (A4590), Pael: speak (Dn 6:21—Aramaic).

מָשָׁל māshal (5090), Say, quote (a proverb) (Ez 16:44, 17:2, 24:3).

נָאַם nā'am (5176), Speak (Ps 110:1 [109:1], Is 56:8, Jer 30:8 [37:8]).

נָגַד nāghadh (5222), Hiphil: report, inform (2 Kgs 22:10, Is 41:22).

נָתַן nāthan (5598), Give, ascribe (Jb 36:3).

סוּת sûth (5684), Hiphil: incite (Jb 2:3).

עוּת ‘ûth (6003B), Sustain (Is 50:4).

עָנָה ‘ānâh (6257), Answer, reply (Jb 38:1).

עֲנָה ‘ănâh (A6258), Answer, begin to speak (Dn 2:8, 3:24, 6:13—Aramaic).

עָרַךְ ‘ārakh (6424), Put (Jb 23:4).

פֶּה peh (6552), Mouth; command (Gn 45:21).

צָוָה tsāwâh (6943), Piel: commanded, charged (Lv 9:6, Ps 148:5).

קָרָא qārā' (7410), Qal: call, cry out (Gn 45:1, 1 Sm 3:16, Zec 7:13); niphal: be called (Is 32:5).

רָאָה rā'âh (7495), See; approve (Lam 3:36).

רָדַף rādhaph (7579), Persecute (Jb 19:28).

שָׁמַע shāma‘ (8471), Hear; hiphil: tell (Is 41:23).

תּוּב tûv (A8752), Return; haphel: answer (Dn 2:14—Aramaic).

1. εἴπατε eipate 2pl indic/impr aor act
2. εἶπας eipas 2sing indic aor act
3. εἶπον eipon 1/3sing/pl indic aor act
4. εἶπα eipa 1sing indic aor act
5. εἶπεν eipen 3sing indic aor act
6. εἴπω eipō 1sing subj aor act
7. εἴπῃς eipēs 2sing subj aor act
8. εἴπῃ eipē 3sing subj aor act
9. εἴπωμεν eipōmen 1pl subj aor act
10. εἴπητε eipēte 2pl subj aor act
11. εἴπωσιν eipōsin 3pl subj aor act
12. εἰπέ eipe 2sing impr aor act
13. εἰπάτω eipatō 3sing impr aor act
14. εἰπάτωσαν eipatōsan 3pl impr aor act
15. εἰπών eipōn nom sing masc part aor act
16. εἰπόντος eipontos gen sing masc part aor act
17. εἰπόντι eiponti dat sing masc part aor act
18. εἰπόντα eiponta acc sing masc part aor act
19. εἰπόντες eipontes nom pl masc part aor act
20. εἰποῦσα eipousa nom sing fem part aor act
21. εἰπεῖν eipein inf aor act
22. ἐρρήθη errhēthē 3sing indic aor pass
23. ἐρρέθη errhethē 3sing indic aor pass
24. ἐρρήθησαν errhēthēsan 3pl indic aor pass
25. ῥηθείς rhētheis nom sing masc part aor pass
26. ῥηθέν rhēthen nom/acc sing neu part aor pass
27. εἶπες eipes 2sing indic aor act
28. εἶπαν eipan 3pl indic aor act
29. εἰπόν eipon 2sing impr aor act
30. εἴπας eipas nom sing masc part aor act
31. ἐρρέθησαν errhethēsan 3pl indic aor pass
32. εἴπασα eipasa nom sing fem part aor act

26	that it might be fulfilled which **was spoken**	Matt 1:22
3	And they **said** unto him, In Bethlehem of Judaea:	2:5
28	And they **said** unto him, In Bethlehem of Judaea:	2:5
5	And he sent them to Bethlehem, and **said**,	2:8
6	and be thou there until I bring thee **word**:	2:13
26	that it might be fulfilled which **was spoken**	2:15
26	Then was fulfilled that which **was spoken**	2:17
26	that it might be fulfilled which **was spoken**	2:23
25	For this is he that **was spoken** of by the prophet	3:3
5	he **said** unto them, O generation of vipers,	3:7
5	And Jesus answering **said** unto him,	3:15
5	And when the tempter came to him, he **said**,	4:3
12	**command** that these stones be made bread.	4:3
5	But he answered and **said**, It is written,	4:4
5	he **said** to Him, "All these things (NASB)	4:9
26	That it might be fulfilled which **was spoken**	4:14
11	and shall **say** all manner of evil against you falsely,	5:11
23	Ye have heard that it **was said** by them of old time,	5:21
22	Ye have heard that it **was said** by them of old time,	5:21
8	and whosoever **shall say** to his brother, Raca,	5:22
8	but whosoever **shall say**, Thou fool,	5:22
23	Ye have heard that it **was said** by them of old time,	5:27
22	Ye have heard that it **was said** by them of old time,	5:27
23	It **hath been said**, Whosoever ... put away his wife,	5:31
22	It **hath been said**, Whosoever ... put away his wife,	5:31
23	that it **hath been said** by them of old time,	5:33
22	that it **hath been said** by them of old time,	5:33
23	Ye have heard that it **hath been said**, An eye for an ...	5:38
22	Ye have heard that it **hath been said**, An eye for an ...	5:38
23	Ye have heard that it **hath been said**,	5:43
22	Ye have heard that it **hath been said**,	5:43

εἶπον 1500

7	See **thou tell** no man; but go thy way,	Matt 8:4
12	but **speak** the word only,	8:8
5	and **said** to them that followed, Verily I say	8:10
5	And Jesus **said** unto the centurion, Go thy way;	8:13
26	That it might be fulfilled which **was spoken**	8:17
5	And a certain scribe came, and **said** unto him,	8:19
5	And another of his disciples **said** unto him,	8:21
5	But Jesus **said** unto him, Follow me;	8:22
5	And **he said** unto them, Go.	8:32
5	and Jesus seeing their faith **said** unto the sick	9:2
3	certain of the scribes **said** within themselves,	9:3
28	certain of the scribes **said** within themselves,	9:3
5	And Jesus knowing their thoughts **said**,	9:4
21	For whether is easier, **to say**,	9:5
21	or **to say**, Arise, and walk?	9:5
3	they **said** unto his disciples,	9:11
5	But when Jesus heard that, he **said** unto them,	9:12
5	And Jesus **said** unto them,	9:15
5	he **said**, Daughter, be of good comfort;	9:22
1	What I tell you in darkness, that **speak** ye in light:	10:27
5	And **said** unto him, Art thou he that should come,	11:3
5	Jesus answered and **said** unto them,	11:4
5	At that time Jesus answered and **said**,	11:25
3	But when the Pharisees saw it, they **said** unto him,	12:2
28	But when the Pharisees saw it, they **said** unto him,	12:2
5	But he **said** unto them, ... not read what David did,	12:3
5	And he **said** unto them, What man shall there be	12:11
26	That it might be fulfilled which **was spoken**	12:17
3	But when the Pharisees heard it, they **said**,	12:24
5	Jesus knew their thoughts, and **said** unto them,	12:25
8	whosoever **speaketh** a word against the Son of man,	12:32
8	but whosoever **speaketh** against the Holy Ghost,	12:32
5	But he answered and **said** unto them,	12:39
5	Then one **said** unto him,	12:47
5	But he answered and **said** unto him that told him,	12:48
17	But he answered and **said** unto him that **told** him,	12:48
5	and **said**, Behold my mother and my brethren!	12:49
3	And the disciples came, and **said** unto him,	13:10
28	And the disciples came, and **said** unto him,	13:10
5	He answered and **said** unto them,	13:11
3	So the servants of the householder came and **said**	13:27
3	enemy hath done this. The servants **said** unto him,	13:28
26	That it might be fulfilled which **was spoken**	13:35
5	He answered and **said** unto them,	13:37
5	Then **said** he unto them,	13:52
5	they were offended ... But Jesus **said** unto them,	13:57
5	**said** unto his servants, This is John the Baptist;	14:2
5	But Jesus **said** unto them, They need not depart;	14:16
5	He **said**, Bring them hither to me.	14:18
5	And Peter answered him and **said**, Lord,	14:28
5	And he **said**, Come.	14:29
5	But he answered and **said** unto them,	15:3
5	For God **said**, (NASB)	15:4
8	Whosoever **shall say** to his father or his mother,	15:5
5	And he called the multitude, and **said** unto them,	15:10
3	Then came his disciples, and **said** unto him,	15:12
5	But he answered and **said**,	15:13
5	Then answered Peter and **said** unto him,	15:15
5	And Jesus **said**, ... yet without understanding?	15:16
5	But he answered and **said**,	15:24
5	But he answered and **said**,	15:26
5	And she **said**, Truth, Lord: yet the dogs eat	15:27
5	Then Jesus answered and **said** unto her,	15:28
5	Then Jesus called his disciples unto him, and **said**,	15:32
3	And they **said**, Seven, and a few little fishes.	15:34
28	And they **said**, Seven, and a few little fishes.	15:34
5	He answered and **said** unto them,	16:2
5	Then Jesus **said** unto them, Take heed and beware	16:6
5	Which when Jesus perceived, he **said** unto them,	16:8
3	that **I spake** it not to you concerning bread,	16:11
5	**he bade** them not beware of the leaven of bread,	16:12
3	And they **said**, Some say that thou art John	16:14
28	And they **said**, Some say that thou art John	16:14
5	And Simon Peter answered and **said**,	16:16
5	And Jesus answered and **said** unto him,	16:17
11	**should tell** no man that he was Jesus the Christ.	16:20
5	But he turned, and **said** unto Peter,	16:23
5	Then **said** Jesus unto his disciples,	Matt 16:24
5	Then answered Peter, and **said** unto Jesus,	17:4
5	And Jesus came and touched them, and **said**,	17:7
10	Jesus ... saying, **Tell** the vision to no man,	17:9
5	And Jesus answered and **said** unto them,	17:11
5	that he **spake** unto them of John the Baptist.	17:13
5	Then Jesus answered and **said**,	17:17
3	Then came the disciples to Jesus apart, and **said**,	17:19
5	And Jesus **said** unto them,	17:20
5	while they abode in Galilee, Jesus **said** unto them,	17:22
3	and **said**, Doth not your master pay tribute?	17:24
28	and **said**, Doth not your master pay tribute?	17:24
16	And upon his **saying**, "From strangers," (NASB)	17:26
5	And **said**, Verily I say unto you,	18:3
12	neglect to hear them, **tell** it unto the church:	18:17
29	neglect to hear them, **tell** it unto the church:	18:17
5	Then came Peter to him, and **said**, Lord,	18:21
5	And he answered and **said** unto them,	19:4
5	And **said**, For this cause shall a man leave father	19:5
5	But he **said** unto them, All men cannot receive this	19:11
5	But Jesus **said**, Suffer little children,	19:14
5	behold, one came and **said** unto him, Good Master,	19:16
5	And he **said** unto him, Why callest thou me good?	19:17
5	He saith unto him, Which? Jesus **said**,	19:18
5	Then **said** Jesus unto his disciples,	19:23
5	But Jesus beheld them, and **said** unto them,	19:26
5	Then answered Peter and **said** unto him,	19:27
5	And Jesus **said** unto them, Verily I say unto you,	19:28
5	And **said** unto them; Go ye also into the vineyard,	20:4
5	But he answered one of them, and **said**, Friend,	20:13
5	disciples apart in the way, and **said** unto them,	20:17
5	And he **said** unto her, What wilt thou?	20:21
12	**Grant** that these my two sons may sit,	20:21
5	Jesus answered and **said**, Ye know not what ye ask	20:22
5	But Jesus called them unto him, and **said**,	20:25
5	And Jesus stood still, and called them, and **said**,	20:32
8	And if any man **say** ought unto you, ye shall say,	21:3
26	be fulfilled which **was spoken** by the prophet,	21:4
1	**Tell** ye the daughter of Sion,	21:5
3	And **said** unto him, Hearest thou what these say?	21:16
28	And **said** unto him, Hearest thou what these say?	21:16
5	Jesus answered and **said** unto them,	21:21
10	but also if **ye shall say** unto this mountain,	21:21
5	And Jesus answered and **said** unto them,	21:24
10	I also will ask you one thing, which if **ye tell** me,	21:24
9	If **we shall say**, From heaven; he will say unto us,	21:25
9	But if **we shall say**, Of men; we fear the people;	21:26
3	And they answered Jesus, and **said**, We cannot tell.	21:27
28	And they answered Jesus, and **said**, We cannot tell.	21:27
5	and he came to the first, and **said**, Son,	21:28
5	He answered and **said**, I will not:	21:29
5	And he came to the second, and **said** likewise.	21:30
5	And he answered and **said**, I go, sir: and went not.	21:30
3	they **said** among themselves, This is the heir;	21:38
5	And Jesus answered and **spake** unto them	22:1
1	**Tell** them which are bidden, ... I have prepared	22:4
5	Then **said** the king to the servants,	22:13
12	**Tell** us therefore, What thinkest thou?	22:17
29	**Tell** us therefore, What thinkest thou?	22:17
5	But Jesus perceived their wickedness, and **said**,	22:18
5	Moses **said**, If a man die, having no children,	22:24
5	Jesus answered and **said** unto them, Ye do err,	22:29
26	not read that which **was spoken** unto you by God,	22:31
5	Jesus **said** unto him, Thou shalt love the Lord	22:37
5	The Lord **said** unto my Lord, Sit thou on my right	22:44
11	All therefore whatsoever **they bid** you observe,	23:3
10	Ye shall not see me henceforth, till **ye shall say**,	23:39
5	Jesus **said** unto them, See ye not all these things?	24:2
12	**Tell** us, when shall these things be?	24:3
5	And Jesus answered and **said** unto them,	24:4
26	desolation, **spoken** of by Daniel the prophet,	24:15
8	if any man shall **say** unto you, Lo, here is Christ,	24:23
11	Wherefore if **they shall say** unto you,	24:26
8	But and if that evil servant **shall say** in his heart,	24:48
3	And the foolish **said** unto the wise,	25:8
28	And the foolish **said** unto the wise,	25:8
5	But he answered and **said**, Verily I say unto you,	25:12

εἶπον 1500

5	also that had received two talents came and **said,** Matt	25:22	
5	which had received the one talent came and **said,**	25:24	
5	His lord answered and **said** unto him, ...	25:26	
5	Jesus had finished ... he **said** unto his disciples, ...	26:1	
5	When Jesus understood it, he **said** unto them, ...	26:10	
5	And **said** unto them, What will ye give me, ...	26:15	
5	And he **said,** Go into the city to such a man, ...	26:18	
1	Go into the city to such a man, and **say** unto him, ...	26:18	
5	And as they did eat, **he said,** Verily I say unto you, ..	26:21	
5	And he answered and **said,** He that dippeth	26:23	
5	Judas, which betrayed him, answered and **said,**	26:25	
2	Master, is it I? He **said** unto him, Thou **hast said.** ..	26:25	
5	brake it, and gave it to the disciples, and **said,**	26:26	
5	Peter answered and **said** unto him, ...	26:33	
3	Likewise also **said** all the disciples.	26:35	
28	Likewise also **said** all the disciples.	26:35	
15	and prayed the third time, **saying** the same words.	26:44	
5	to Jesus, and **said,** Hail, master; and kissed him.	26:49	
5	And Jesus **said** unto him, Friend, ...	26:50	
5	In that same hour **said** Jesus to the multitudes, ...	26:55	
3	And **said,** This fellow said, I am able to destroy	26:61	
28	And **said,** This fellow said, I am able to destroy	26:61	
5	And the high priest arose, and **said** unto him, ...	26:62	
5	And the high priest answered and **said** unto him, ...	26:63	
7	**tell** us whether thou be the Christ, the Son of God...	26:63	
2	Jesus saith unto him, Thou **hast said:**	26:64	
3	They answered and **said,** He is guilty of death.	26:66	
28	They answered and **said,** He is guilty of death.	26:66	
3	after a while came unto him ... and **said** to Peter, ...	26:73	
3	And they **said,** What is that to us? see thou to that...	27:4	
28	And they **said,** What is that to us? see thou to that...	27:4	
3	and **said,** It is not lawful for to put them	27:6	
28	and **said,** It is not lawful for to put them	27:6	
26	fulfilled that which **was spoken** by Jeremy	27:9	
5	when they were gathered ... Pilate **said** unto them, ...	27:17	
5	The governor answered and **said** unto them, ...	27:21	
3	Whether of the twain ... They **said,** Barabbas.	27:21	
28	Whether of the twain ... They **said,** Barabbas.	27:21	
5	Then answered all the people, and **said,**	27:25	
26	be fulfilled which **was spoken** by the prophet, ...	27:35	
5	for **he said,** I am the Son of God.	27:43	
28	The rest **said,** Let be, let us see whether Elias will	27:49	
5	Saying, Sir, we remember that that deceiver **said,**	27:63	
11	steal him away, and **say** unto the people, ...	27:64	
5	And the angel answered and **said** unto the women, ..	28:5	
5	He is not here: for he is risen, as **he said.**	28:6	
1	and **tell** his disciples that he is risen from the dead; ..	28:7	
3	there shall ye see him: lo, **I have told you.**	28:7	
1	Saying, **Say** ye, His disciples came by night, ...	28:13	
5	And Jesus **said** unto them, Come ye after me, ... Mark	1:17	
16	And as soon as he **had spoken,** ... leprosy departed	1:42	
7	saith unto him, See thou **say** nothing to any man:	1:44	
5	he **said** unto them, Why reason ye these things;	2:8	
21	Whether is it easier **to say** to the sick of the palsy, ...	2:9	
21	Thy sins be forgiven thee; or **to say,** Arise, ...	2:9	
5	And Jesus **said** unto them, ...	2:19	
5	And he **spake** to his disciples, ...	3:9	
3	multitude sat about him, and they **said** unto him, ...	3:32	
5	and **said** unto the sea, Peace, be still.	4:39	
5	And **he said** unto them, Why are ye so fearful?	4:40	
5	And cried with a loud voice, and **said,**	5:7	
5	fell down before him, and **told** him all the truth.	5:33	
5	And he **said** unto her, Daughter, ...	5:34	
5	**commanded** that something should be given her	5:43	
5	he **said,** It is John, whom I beheaded:	6:16	
5	the king **said** unto the damsel, ...	6:22	
5	and **said** unto her mother, What shall I ask?	6:24	
5	And she **said,** The head of John the Baptist.	6:24	
5	And he **said** unto them, ...	6:31	
5	answered and **said** unto them, Give ye them to eat.	6:37	
5	He answered and **said** unto them, ...	7:6	
5	Moses **said,** Honour thy father and thy mother;	7:10	
8	If a man **shall say** to his father or mother, ...	7:11	
5	But Jesus **said** unto her, ...	7:27	
5	And he **said** unto her, For this saying go thy way;	7:29	
11	And he charged them that they **should tell** no man:	7:36	
3	How many loaves have ye? And they **said,** Seven.	8:5	

28	How many loaves have ye? And they **said,** Seven. Mark	8:5	
5	and **commanded** to set them also before them.	8:7	
3	And they **said,** Seven.	8:20	
7	nor **tell** it to any in the town.	8:26	
28	And they **told** Him, saying, "John (NASB)	8:28	
11	charged them that they **should tell** no man of him.	8:30	
5	he **said** unto them, Whosoever will come after me, ...	8:34	
5	And he answered and **told** them, ...	9:12	
5	And one of the multitude answered and **said,**	9:17	
3	and I **spake** to thy disciples that ... cast him out;	9:18	
4	and I **spake** to thy disciples that ... cast him out;	9:18	
5	And he **said,** Of a child.	9:21	
5	Jesus **said** unto him, If thou canst believe, ...	9:23	
5	And **he said** unto them, ... by prayer and fasting.	9:29	
5	had taken him in his arms, **he said** unto them, ...	9:36	
5	But Jesus **said,** Forbid him not:	9:39	
5	And he answered and **said** unto them, ...	10:3	
3	And they **said,** ... to write a bill of divorcement, ...	10:4	
28	And they **said,** ... to write a bill of divorcement, ...	10:4	
5	And Jesus answered and **said** unto them, ...	10:5	
5	he was much displeased, and **said** unto them, ...	10:14	
5	Jesus **said** unto him, Why callest thou me good?	10:18	
5	And he answered and **said** unto him, ...	10:20	
5	and **said** unto him, One thing thou lackest:	10:21	
5	Jesus answered and **said,** Verily I say unto you, ...	10:29	
5	And he **said** unto them, ...	10:36	
3	They **said** unto him, Grant unto us	10:37	
28	They **said** unto him, Grant unto us	10:37	
5	Jesus **said** unto them, Ye know not what ye ask:	10:38	
3	And they **said** unto him, We can.	10:39	
28	And they **said** unto him, We can.	10:39	
5	And Jesus **said** unto them, ...	10:39	
5	Jesus stood still, and **commanded** him to be called. ...	10:49	
5	And answering him, Jesus **said,** (NASB)	10:51	
5	The blind man **said** unto him, Lord, ...	10:51	
5	And Jesus **said** unto him, ...	10:52	
8	And if any man **say** unto you, Why do ye this?	11:3	
1	**say** ye that the Lord hath need of him;	11:3	
3	**said** unto them even as Jesus had commanded:	11:6	
28	**said** unto them even as Jesus had commanded:	11:6	
5	**said** unto them just as Jesus had **told** (NASB)	11:6	
5	And Jesus answered and **said** unto it, ...	11:14	
8	That whosoever **shall say** unto this mountain, ...	11:23	
8	not doubt ... he shall have whatsoever he **saith.**	11:23	
5	And Jesus answered and **said** unto them, ...	11:29	
9	If we **shall say,** From heaven;	11:31	
9	But if we **shall say,** Of men;	11:32	
3	But those husbandmen **said** among themselves, ...	12:7	
28	But those husbandmen **said** among themselves, ...	12:7	
5	knew that he **had spoken** the parable against them: ...	12:12	
12	but teachest the way of God in truth:	12:14	
5	But he, knowing their hypocrisy, **said** unto them, ...	12:15	
3	superscription? And they **said** unto him, Caesar's.	12:16	
28	superscription? And they **said** unto him, Caesar's.	12:16	
5	And Jesus answering **said** unto them, ...	12:17	
5	answering **said** unto them, Do ye not therefore err, ...	12:24	
5	how in the bush God **spake** unto him, saying, ...	12:26	
5	And the scribe **said** unto him, Well, Master, ...	12:32	
2	Well, Master, thou **hast said** the truth:	12:32	
27	Well, Master, thou **hast said** the truth:	12:32	
5	he **said** unto him, Thou art not far from	12:34	
5	For David himself **said** by the Holy Ghost, ...	12:36	
5	The LORD **said** to my Lord, ...	12:36	
5	calling His disciples ... He **said** (NASB)	12:43	
5	And Jesus answering **said** unto him, ...	13:2	
12	Tell us, when shall these things be?	13:4	
29	Tell us, when shall these things be?	13:4	
26	of desolation, **spoken** of by Daniel the prophet, ...	13:14	
8	if any man shall **say** to you, Lo, here is Christ;	13:21	
5	And Jesus **said,** Let her alone; why trouble ye her? ...	14:6	
1	**say** ye to the goodman of the house, ...	14:14	
5	into the city, and found as **he had said** unto them, ...	14:16	
5	And as they sat and did eat, Jesus **said,** Verily I say ..	14:18	
5	And he answered and **said** unto them, ...	14:20	
5	gave to them, and **said,** Take, eat: this is my body....	14:22	
5	And **he said** unto them, This is my blood	14:24	
15	went away, and prayed, and **spake** the same words. ...	14:39	

εἶπον 1500

5	And Jesus answered and said unto them,	Mark	14:48
5	And Jesus said, I am: and ye shall see the Son		14:62
5	And Peter called to mind the word that Jesus said		14:72
5	And he answering said unto him, Thou sayest it.		15:2
5	And Pilate answered and said again unto them,		15:12
5	he said, Truly this man was the Son of God.		15:39
1	tell his disciples and Peter that he goeth before you		16:7
5	Galilee: there shall ye see him, as he said unto you.		16:7
3	neither said they any thing to any man;		16:8
5	And he said unto them, Go ye into all the world,		16:15
5	But the angel said unto him, Fear not, Zacharias:	Luke	1:13
5	And Zacharias said unto the angel,		1:18
5	the angel answering said unto him, I am Gabriel,		1:19
5	And the angel came in unto her, and said, Hail,		1:28
5	And the angel said unto her, Fear not, Mary:		1:30
5	Then said Mary unto the angel, How shall this be,		1:34
5	And the angel answered and said unto her,		1:35
5	And Mary said, Behold the handmaid of the Lord;		1:38
5	And she spake out with a loud voice, and said,		1:42
5	And Mary said, My soul doth magnify the Lord,		1:46
5	And his mother answered and said, Not so;		1:60
3	they said unto her, There is none of thy kindred		1:61
28	they said unto her, There is none of thy kindred		1:61
5	And the angel said unto them, Fear not: for,		2:10
3	the shepherds said one to another,		2:15
5	up in his arms, and blessed God, and said,		2:28
5	Simeon blessed ... and said unto Mary his mother,		2:34
5	and his mother said unto him, Son,		2:48
5	he said unto them, How is it that ye sought me?		2:49
3	and said unto him, Master, what shall we do?		3:12
28	and said unto him, Master, what shall we do?		3:12
5	And he said unto them, Exact no more than that		3:13
5	And what shall we do? And he said unto them,		3:14
5	And the devil said unto him,		4:3
12	command this stone that it be made bread.		4:3
5	And the devil said unto him,		4:6
5	And Jesus answered and said unto him,		4:8
5	and said unto him, If thou be the Son of God,		4:9
5	And Jesus answering said unto him, It is said,		4:12
5	And he said unto them, Ye will surely say		4:23
5	And he said, Verily, I say unto you,		4:24
5	And he said unto them, I must preach the kingdom		4:43
5	when he had left speaking, he said unto Simon,		5:4
5	And Simon answering said unto him, Master,		5:5
5	And Jesus said unto Simon, Fear not;		5:10
15	and touched him, saying, I will: be thou clean.		5:13
21	And he charged him to tell no man:		5:14
5	And when he saw their faith, he said unto him,		5:20
5	he answering said unto them,		5:22
21	Whether is easier, to say, Thy sins be forgiven		5:23
21	to say, Thy sins be forgiven thee; or to say, Rise up		5:23
5	he said unto the sick of the palsy, I say unto thee,		5:24
5	named Levi, ... and he said unto him, Follow me.		5:27
5	And Jesus answering said unto them,		5:31
3	And they said unto him, Why do the disciples		5:33
28	And they said unto him, Why do the disciples		5:33
5	he said unto them, Can ye make the children of		5:34
3	And certain of the Pharisees said unto them,		6:2
28	And certain of the Pharisees said unto them,		6:2
5	And Jesus answering them said,		6:3
5	and said to the man which had the withered hand,		6:8
5	Then said Jesus unto them, I will ask you		6:9
5	he said unto the man, Stretch forth thy hand.		6:10
11	Woe ... when all men shall speak well of you!		6:26
5	And he spake a parable unto them,		6:39
12	but say in a word, and my servant shall be healed.		7:7
5	and said unto the people that followed him,		7:9
5	he had compassion on her, and said unto her,		7:13
5	And he said, Young man, I say unto thee, Arise.		7:14
3	When the men were come unto him, they said,		7:20
28	When the men were come unto him, they said,		7:20
5	Jesus answering said unto them, Go your way,		7:22
5	And the Lord said, Whereunto then shall I liken		7:31
5	he spake within himself, saying, This man,		7:39
5	And Jesus answering said unto him, Simon,		7:40
21	I have somewhat to say unto thee. And he saith,		7:40
12	to say unto thee. And he saith, Master, say on.		7:40
12	he frankly forgave them both. Tell me therefore,	Luke	7:42
5	Simon answered and said, I suppose that he,		7:43
5	And he said unto him, Thou hast rightly judged.		7:43
5	And he said unto her, Thy sins are forgiven.		7:48
5	he said to the woman, Thy faith hath saved thee;		7:50
5	to him out of every city, he spake by a parable:		8:4
5	And he said, Unto you it is given to know		8:10
5	And he answered and said unto them,		8:21
5	and he said unto them, Let us go over unto the		8:22
5	And he said unto them, Where is your faith?		8:25
5	fell down before him, and with a loud voice said,		8:28
5	And he said, Legion: because many devils were		8:30
5	Jesus said, Who touched me? When all denied,		8:45
5	all denied, Peter and they that were with him said,		8:45
5	And Jesus said, Somebody hath touched me:		8:46
5	he said unto her, Daughter, be of good comfort:		8:48
5	And all wept, and bewailed her: but he said,		8:52
21	but he charged them that they should tell no man		8:56
5	he said unto them, Take nothing for your journey,		9:3
5	Herod said, John have I beheaded: but who is this,		9:9
3	then came the twelve, and said unto him,		9:12
28	then came the twelve, and said unto him,		9:12
5	But he said unto them, Give ye them to eat.		9:13
3	And they said, We have no more but five loaves		9:13
28	And they said, We have no more but five loaves		9:13
5	And he said to his disciples,		9:14
3	They answering said, John the Baptist;		9:19
28	They answering said, John the Baptist;		9:19
5	He said unto them, But whom say ye that I am?		9:20
5	Peter answering said, The Christ of God.		9:20
21	and commanded them to tell no man that thing;		9:21
15	Saying, The Son of man must suffer many things,		9:22
5	Peter said unto Jesus, Master, it is good for us		9:33
5	And Jesus answering said,		9:41
5	he said unto his disciples,		9:43
5	said unto them, Whosoever shall receive this child		9:48
5	And John answered and said, Master,		9:49
5	And Jesus said unto him, Forbid him not:		9:50
3	they said, Lord, wilt thou that we command fire		9:54
28	they said, Lord, wilt thou that we command fire		9:54
9	wilt thou that we command fire to come down		9:54
5	But he turned, and rebuked them, and said,		9:55
5	a certain man said unto him, Lord,		9:57
5	And Jesus said unto him, Foxes have holes,		9:58
5	And he said unto another, Follow me. But he said,		9:59
5	And he said unto another, Follow me. But he said,		9:59
5	Jesus said unto him, Let the dead bury their dead:		9:60
5	And another also said, Lord, I will follow thee;		9:61
5	And Jesus said unto him, No man,		9:62
1	go ... out into the streets of the same, and say,		10:10
5	said unto them, I beheld Satan as lightning fall		10:18
5	In that hour Jesus rejoiced in spirit, and said,		10:21
5	All things are delivered to me of my Father: (NT)		10:22
5	turned him unto his disciples, and said privately,		10:23
5	He said unto him, What is written in the law?		10:26
5	And he answering said, Thou shalt love the Lord		10:27
5	And he said unto him, Thou hast answered right:		10:28
5	said unto Jesus, And who is my neighbour?		10:29
5	And Jesus answering said, A certain man		10:30
5	and gave them to the host, and said unto him,		10:35
5	And he said, He that showed mercy on him.		10:37
5	said Jesus unto him, Go, and do thou likewise.		10:37
5	and came to him, and said, Lord,		10:40
12	to serve alone? bid her therefore that she help me.		10:40
29	to serve alone? bid her therefore that she help me.		10:40
5	And Jesus answered and said unto her, Martha,		10:41
5	when he ceased, one of his disciples said unto him,		11:1
5	And he said unto them, When ye pray, say,		11:2
5	said unto them, Which of you shall have a friend,		11:5
8	and say unto him, Friend, lend me three loaves;		11:5
8	from within shall answer and say, Trouble me not:		11:7
3	But some of them said, He casteth out devils		11:15
28	But some of them said, He casteth out devils		11:15
5	But he, knowing their thoughts, said unto them,		11:17
5	lifted up her voice, and said unto him,		11:27
5	But he said, Yea rather, blessed are they that hear		11:28
5	And the Lord said unto him,		11:39

εἶπον 1500

5	And he **said**, Woe unto you also, ye lawyers!	Luke 11:46
5	Therefore also **said** the wisdom of God,	11:49
1	Therefore whatsoever ye **have spoken** in darkness	12:3
10	or what thing ye shall answer, or what ye **shall say**:	12:11
21	teach you in the same hour what ye ought **to say**.	12:12
5	And one of the company **said** unto him, Master,	12:13
12	**speak** to my brother, that he divide the inheritance	12:13
5	And he **said** unto him, Man, who made me a judge	12:14
5	And he **said** unto them, Take heed, and beware	12:15
5	And he **spake** a parable unto them, saying,	12:16
5	he **said**, This will I do: I will pull down my barns,	12:18
5	God **said** unto him, Thou fool, this night thy soul	12:20
5	**said** unto his disciples, Therefore I say unto you,	12:22
5	Then Peter **said** unto him, Lord, speakest thou this	12:41
5	And the Lord **said**, Who then is that faithful	12:42
8	But and if that servant **say** in his heart,	12:45
5	And Jesus answering **said** unto them,	13:2
5	Then **said** he unto the dresser of his vineyard,	13:7
5	he called her to him, and **said** unto her,	13:12
5	The Lord then answered him, and **said**,	13:15
5	And again he **said**, Whereunto shall I liken	13:20
5	Then **said** one unto him, Lord, are there few	13:23
5	few that be saved? And he **said** unto them,	13:23
5	And he **said** unto them, Go ye, and tell that fox,	13:32
1	and **tell** that fox, Behold, I cast out devils,	13:32
10	until the time come when ye **shall say**,	13:35
5	And Jesus answering **spake** unto the lawyers	14:3
5	And answered them, **saying**, Which of you	14:5
8	he **may say** unto thee, Friend, go up higher:	14:10
5	he **said** unto him, Blessed is he that shall eat bread	14:15
5	**said** he unto him, A certain man made a ... supper,	14:16
21	And sent his servant at supper time **to say** to them	14:17
5	began to make excuse. The first **said** unto him,	14:18
5	And another **said**, I have bought five yoke of oxen,	14:19
5	And another **said**, I have married a wife,	14:20
5	master of the house being angry **said** to his servant,	14:21
5	And the servant **said**, Lord, it is done as thou	14:22
5	And the lord **said** unto the servant,	14:23
5	multitudes ... and he turned, and **said** unto them,	14:25
5	And he **spake** this parable unto them, saying,	15:3
5	And he **said**, A certain man had two sons:	15:11
5	And the younger of them **said** to his father,	15:12
5	And when he came to himself, he **said**,	15:17
5	And the son **said** unto him, Father, I have sinned	15:21
5	But the father **said** to his servants,	15:22
5	And he **said** unto him, Thy brother is come;	15:27
5	And he answering **said** to his father,	15:29
5	And he **said** unto him, Son, thou art ever with me,	15:31
5	And he called him, and **said** unto him,	16:2
5	Then the steward **said** within himself,	16:3
5	And he **said**, An hundred measures of oil.	16:6
5	And he **said** unto him, Take thy bill, ... write fifty.	16:6
5	Then **said** he to another, ... how much owest thou?	16:7
5	And how much owest thou? And he **said**,	16:7
5	And he **said** unto them, Ye are they which justify	16:15
5	And he cried and **said**, Father Abraham,	16:24
5	But Abraham **said**, Son, remember that thou in thy	16:25
5	Then he **said**, I pray thee therefore, father,	16:27
5	And he **said**, Nay, father Abraham: but if one went	16:30
5	And he **said** unto him, If they hear not Moses and	16:31
5	Then **said** he unto the disciples,	17:1
3	the apostles **said** unto the Lord, Increase our faith.	17:5
28	the apostles **said** unto the Lord, Increase our faith.	17:5
5	the Lord **said**, If ye had faith as a grain of mustard	17:6
5	And when he saw them, he **said** unto them,	17:14
5	Jesus answering **said**, Were there not ten cleansed?	17:17
5	And he **said** unto him, Arise, go thy way: thy faith	17:19
5	he answered them, and **said**, The kingdom of God	17:20
5	And he **said** unto the disciples, The days will come,	17:22
5	And he **said** unto them, Wheresoever the body is,	17:37
5	but afterward he **said** within himself,	18:4
5	the Lord **said**, Hear what the unjust judge saith.	18:6
5	And he **spake** this parable unto certain	18:9
5	But Jesus called them unto him, and **said**,	18:16
5	Jesus **said** unto him, Why callest thou me good?	18:19
5	he **said**, All these have I kept from my youth up.	18:21
5	when Jesus heard these things, he **said** unto him,	18:22

5	Jesus saw that he was very sorrowful, he **said**,	Luke 18:24
3	they that heard it **said**, Who then can be saved?	18:26
28	they that heard it **said**, Who then can be saved?	18:26
5	he **said**, The things which are impossible with men	18:27
5	Peter **said**, Lo, we have left all, and followed thee.	18:28
5	And he **said** unto them, Verily I say unto you,	18:29
5	he took unto him the twelve, and **said** unto them,	18:31
5	And he **said**, Lord, that I may receive my sight.	18:41
5	And Jesus **said** unto him, Receive thy sight:	18:42
5	he looked up, and saw him, and **said** unto him,	19:5
5	And Zacchaeus stood, and **said** unto the Lord;	19:8
5	Jesus **said** unto him, This day is salvation come	19:9
5	he added and **spake** a parable,	19:11
5	He **said** therefore, A certain nobleman went into	19:12
5	delivered them ten pounds, and **said** unto them,	19:13
5	**commanded** these servants to be called unto him,	19:15
5	And he **said** unto him, Well, thou good servant:	19:17
5	**said** likewise to him, Be thou also over five cities.	19:19
5	And he **said** unto them that stood by,	19:24
3	And they **said** unto him, Lord, he hath ten pounds.	19:25
28	And they **said** unto him, Lord, he hath ten pounds.	19:25
15	And when he **had** thus **spoken**, he went before,	19:28
15	**Saying**, Go ye into the village over against you;	19:30
5	and found even as he **had said** unto them.	19:32
3	owners ... **said** unto them, Why loose ye the colt?	19:33
28	owners ... **said** unto them, Why loose ye the colt?	19:33
3	And they **said**, The Lord hath need of him.	19:34
28	And they **said**, The Lord hath need of him.	19:34
3	of the Pharisees from among the multitude **said**	19:39
28	of the Pharisees from among the multitude **said**	19:39
5	he answered and **said** unto them, I tell you that,	19:40
3	And **spake** unto him, saying, ... by what authority	20:2
28	And **spake** unto him, saying, ... by what authority	20:2
12	Tell us, by what authority doest thou these things?	20:2
29	Tell us, by what authority doest thou these things?	20:2
5	he answered and **said** unto them, I will also ask	20:3
1	I will also ask you one thing; and **answer** me:	20:3
9	If we **shall say**, From heaven; he will say,	20:5
9	and if we **say**, Of men; all the people will stone us:	20:6
5	And Jesus **said** unto them, Neither tell I you	20:8
5	**said** the lord of the vineyard, What shall I do?	20:13
3	And when they heard it, they **said**, God forbid.	20:16
28	And when they heard it, they **said**, God forbid.	20:16
5	And he beheld them, and **said**,	20:17
5	that he **had spoken** this parable against them.	20:19
5	he perceived their craftiness, and **said** unto them,	20:23
3	They answered and **said**, Caesar's.	20:24
28	They answered and **said**, Caesar's.	20:24
5	he **said** unto them, Render therefore unto Caesar	20:25
5	And Jesus answering **said** unto them,	20:34
3	Then certain of the scribes answering **said**, Master,	20:39
28	Then certain of the scribes answering **said**, Master,	20:39
2	scribes answering said, Master, thou **hast** well **said**.	20:39
5	And he **said** unto them, How say they that Christ is	20:41
5	The Lord **said** unto my Lord, Sit thou on my right	20:42
5	Then in the audience of all the people he **said**	20:45
5	And he **said**, Of a truth I say unto you,	21:3
5	And as some spake of the temple, ... he **said**,	21:5
5	And he **said**, Take heed that ye be not deceived:	21:8
5	he **spake** to them a parable; Behold the fig tree,	21:29
15	he sent Peter and John, **saying**, Go and prepare	22:8
3	**said** unto him, Where wilt thou that we prepare?	22:9
28	**said** unto him, Where wilt thou that we prepare?	22:9
5	And he **said** unto them,	22:10
5	**said** unto them, With desire I have desired to eat	22:15
5	And he took the cup, and gave thanks, and **said**,	22:17
5	And he **said** unto them, The kings of the Gentiles	22:25
5	And the Lord **said**, Simon, Simon, behold,	22:31
5	he **said** unto him, Lord, I am ready to go with thee,	22:33
5	And he **said**, I tell thee, Peter,	22:34
5	he **said** unto them, When I sent you without purse,	22:35
3	lacked ye any thing? And they **said**, Nothing.	22:35
28	lacked ye any thing? And they **said**, Nothing.	22:35
5	Then **said** he unto them, But now,	22:36
3	And they **said**, Lord, behold, here are two swords.	22:38
28	And they **said**, Lord, behold, here are two swords.	22:38
5	two swords. And he **said** unto them, It is enough.	22:38

275

εἶπον 1500

5	And when he was at the place, he **said** unto them, Luke	22:40
5	And **said** unto them, Why sleep ye? rise and pray,...	22:46
5	But Jesus **said** unto him, Judas, betrayest thou......	22:48
3	saw what would follow, they **said** unto him, Lord,......	22:49
28	saw what would follow, they **said** unto him, Lord,....	22:49
5	And Jesus answered and **said**, Suffer ye thus far.....	22:51
5	Then Jesus **said** unto the chief priests,...............	22:52
5	and earnestly looked upon him, and **said**,............	22:56
5	Thou art also of them. And Peter **said**, ... I am not...	22:58
5	And Peter **said**, Man, I know not what thou sayest...	22:60
5	the word of the Lord, how he **had said** unto him,.....	22:61
12	Art thou the Christ? **tell** us. And he said...........	22:67
29	Art thou the Christ? **tell** us. And he said...........	22:67
5	he **said** unto them, If I tell you, ye will not believe:..	22:67
6	he **said** unto them, If I tell you, ye will not believe:..	22:67
3	Then **said** they all, Art thou then the Son of God?...	22:70
28	Then **said** they all, Art thou then the Son of God?...	22:70
3	And they **said**, What need we any further witness?...	22:71
28	And they **said**, What need we any further witness?...	22:71
5	**said** Pilate to the chief priests and to the people,...	23:4
5	**Said** unto them, ... have brought this man unto me,..	23:14
5	And he **said** unto them the third time, Why,.........	23:22
5	turning unto them **said**, Daughters of Jerusalem,.....	23:28
5	And Jesus **said** unto him, Verily I say unto thee,.....	23:43
5	when Jesus had cried with a loud voice, he **said**,.....	23:46
15	and **having said** thus, he gave up the ghost...........	23:46
3	they **said** unto them, Why seek ye the living among ..	24:5
28	they **said** unto them, Why seek ye the living among ..	24:5
5	**said** unto them, What manner of communications	24:17
5	Cleopas, answering **said** unto him,...................	24:18
5	And he **said** unto them, What things?...............	24:19
3	they **said** unto him, Concerning Jesus of Nazareth,...	24:19
28	they **said** unto him, Concerning Jesus of Nazareth,...	24:19
3	and found it even so as the women **had said**:........	24:24
5	Then he **said** unto them, O fools,...................	24:25
3	And they **said** one to another,......................	24:32
28	And they **said** one to another,......................	24:32
5	And he **said** unto them, Why are ye troubled?.......	24:38
15	And when he **had** thus **spoken**,........................	24:40
5	he **said** unto them, Have ye here any meat?.........	24:41
5	And he **said** unto them,.............................	24:44
5	And **said** unto them, Thus it is written,..............	24:46
5	John bare witness ... This was he of whom I **spake**, John	1:15
3	Then **said** they unto him, Who art thou?.............	1:22
28	Then **said** they unto him, Who art thou?.............	1:22
5	straight the way ... as **said** the prophet Esaias........	1:23
3	And they asked him, and **said** unto him,..............	1:25
28	And they asked him, and **said** unto him,..............	1:25
3	This is he of whom I **said**,...........................	1:30
5	he that sent me ... the same **said** unto me,...........	1:33
3	What seek ye? They **said** unto him, Rabbi,...........	1:38
28	What seek ye? They **said** unto him, Rabbi,...........	1:38
5	And when Jesus beheld him, he **said**,.................	1:42
5	And Nathanael **said** unto him,.......................	1:46
5	Jesus answered and **said** unto him,...................	1:48
5	Jesus answered and **said** unto him,...................	1:50
3	Because I **said** unto thee,............................	1:50
5	And **said** unto them that sold doves,.................	2:16
3	Then answered the Jews and **said** unto him,...........	2:18
28	Then answered the Jews and **said** unto him,...........	2:18
5	Jesus answered and **said** unto them,..................	2:19
3	Then **said** the Jews,.................................	2:20
28	Then **said** the Jews,.................................	2:20
5	and the word which Jesus **had said**....................	2:22
5	came to Jesus by night, and **said** unto him, Rabbi,...	3:2
5	Jesus answered and **said** unto him,...................	3:3
3	Marvel not that I **said** ... Ye must be born again......	3:7
5	Nicodemus answered and **said** unto him,..............	3:9
5	Jesus answered and **said** unto him,...................	3:10
3	If I **have told** you earthly things,.....................	3:12
6	shall ye believe, if I **tell** you of heavenly things?......	3:12
3	And they came unto John, and **said** unto him,.......	3:26
28	And they came unto John, and **said** unto him,.......	3:26
5	John answered and **said**,.............................	3:27
3	that I **said**, I am not the Christ,.....................	3:28
5	Jesus answered and **said** unto her,...................	4:10
5	Jesus answered and **said** unto her,...................	4:13
5	woman answered and **said**, I have no husband......John	4:17
2	Jesus said unto her, Thou hast well **said**,..............	4:17
27	Jesus said unto her, Thou hast well **said**,..............	4:17
5	yet no man **said**, What seekest thou?.................	4:27
5	see a man, which **told** me all things that ever I did:...	4:29
5	But he **said** unto them, I have meat to eat...........	4:32
5	which testified, He **told** me all that ever I did.........	4:39
5	Then **said** Jesus unto him,............................	4:48
5	the man believed the word that Jesus had **spoken**......	4:50
3	they **said** unto him, Yesterday at the seventh hour.....	4:52
28	they **said** unto him, Yesterday at the seventh hour.....	4:52
5	in the which Jesus **said** unto him, Thy son liveth:.....	4:53
5	He that made me whole, the same **said** unto me,.....	5:11
15	What man is that which **said** unto thee,...............	5:12
5	and **said** unto him, Behold, thou art made whole:.....	5:14
5	man departed, and **told** the Jews that it was Jesus,.....	5:15
5	Then answered Jesus and **said** unto them,.............	5:19
5	And Jesus **said**, Make the men sit down...............	6:10
3	**said** unto him, Rabbi, when camest thou hither?......	6:25
5	Jesus answered them and **said**, Verily, verily,..........	6:26
3	Then **said** they unto him, What shall we do,..........	6:28
5	Jesus answered and **said** unto them,..................	6:29
3	They **said** therefore unto him,.......................	6:30
5	Then Jesus **said** unto them, Verily, verily, I say	6:32
3	Then **said** they unto him, ... give us this bread.......	6:34
5	And Jesus **said** unto them, I am the bread of life:.....	6:35
3	But I **said** unto you, That ye also have seen me,......	6:36
5	The Jews then murmured at him, because he **said**,.....	6:41
5	Jesus therefore answered and **said** unto them,.........	6:43
5	Then Jesus **said** unto them, Verily, verily, I say.........	6:53
5	These things **said** he in the synagogue,................	6:59
3	when they had heard this, **said**,......................	6:60
28	when they had heard this, **said**,......................	6:60
5	he **said** unto them, Doth this offend you?............	6:61
5	**said** Jesus unto the twelve, Will ye also go away?......	6:67
3	His brethren therefore **said** unto him,.................	7:3
15	When he **had said** these words unto them,..............	7:9
5	Jesus answered them, and **said**,......................	7:16
5	The people answered and **said**, Thou hast a devil:.....	7:20
5	Jesus answered and **said** unto them,..................	7:21
5	Then **said** Jesus unto them,...........................	7:33
3	Then **said** the Jews among themselves,................	7:35
5	What manner of saying is this that he **said**,............	7:36
5	He that believeth on me, as the scripture hath **said**,...	7:38
5	But this **spake** he of the Spirit,........................	7:39
5	Hath not the scripture **said**,..........................	7:42
3	Then came the officers ... and they **said** unto them,....	7:45
3	They answered and **said** unto him,...................	7:52
28	They answered and **said** unto him,...................	7:52
5	he lifted up himself, and **said** unto them,.............	8:7
5	and saw none but the woman, he **said** unto her,......	8:10
5	She **said**, No man, Lord.............................	8:11
5	Jesus **said** unto her, Neither do I condemn thee:......	8:11
3	The Pharisees therefore **said** unto him,................	8:13
5	Jesus answered and **said** unto them,..................	8:14
5	Then **said** Jesus again unto them, I go my way,......	8:21
5	And he **said** unto them, Ye are from beneath;.......	8:23
3	I **said** therefore unto you,............................	8:24
5	Who art thou? And Jesus **saith** unto them,............	8:25
5	Then **said** Jesus unto them,...........................	8:28
3	They answered and **said** unto him,...................	8:39
28	They answered and **said** unto him,...................	8:39
3	Then **said** they to him,...............................	8:41
28	Then **said** they to him,...............................	8:41
5	Jesus **said** unto them, If God were your Father,.......	8:42
3	Then answered the Jews, and **said** unto him,..........	8:48
28	Then answered the Jews, and **said** unto him,..........	8:48
3	Then **said** the Jews unto him,........................	8:52
28	Then **said** the Jews unto him,........................	8:52
6	and if I **should say**, I know him not,..................	8:55
3	Then **said** the Jews unto him,........................	8:57
28	Then **said** the Jews unto him,........................	8:57
5	Jesus **said** unto them, Verily, verily,..................	8:58
15	When he **had** thus **spoken**, he spat on the ground,.....	9:6
5	And **said** unto him, Go,..............................	9:7
5	He answered and **said**, A man that is called Jesus.....	9:11
5	and **said** unto me, Go to the pool of Siloam,..........	9:11

εἶπον 1500

3	Then **said** they unto him, Where is he?	John	9:12
28	Then **said** they unto him, Where is he?		9:12
5	He **said** unto them, He put clay upon mine eyes,		9:15
5	He **said**, He is a prophet.		9:17
3	His parents answered them and **said,**		9:20
28	His parents answered them and **said,**		9:20
3	These words **spake** his parents,		9:22
28	These words **spake** his parents,		9:22
3	Therefore **said** his parents, He is of age; ask him.		9:23
28	Therefore **said** his parents, He is of age; ask him.		9:23
3	called they the man ... and **said** unto him,		9:24
28	called they the man ... and **said** unto him,		9:24
5	He answered and **said,**		9:25
3	Then **said** they to him again, What did he to thee?		9:26
28	Then **said** they to him again, What did he to thee?		9:26
3	He answered them, I **have told** you already,		9:27
3	Then they reviled him, and **said,**		9:28
28	Then they reviled him, and **said,**		9:28
5	The man answered and **said** unto them,		9:30
3	They answered and **said** unto him,		9:34
28	They answered and **said** unto him,		9:34
5	and when he had found him, he **said** unto him,		9:35
5	He answered and **said,** Who is he, Lord,		9:36
5	And Jesus **said** unto him, Thou hast both seen him,		9:37
5	And Jesus **said,**		9:39
3	and **said** unto him, Are we blind also?		9:40
28	and **said** unto him, Are we blind also?		9:40
5	Jesus **said** unto them,		9:41
5	This parable **spake** Jesus unto them:		10:6
5	Then **said** Jesus unto them again, Verily, verily,		10:7
12	If thou be the Christ, **tell** us plainly.		10:24
29	If thou be the Christ, **tell** us plainly.		10:24
3	I **told** you, and ye believed not:		10:25
3	because ye are not of my sheep, as I **said** unto you.		10:26
4	Is it not written in your law, I **said,** Ye are gods?		10:34
5	If he **called** them gods,		10:35
3	because I **said,** I am the Son of God?		10:36
5	all things that John **spake** of this man were true.		10:41
5	When Jesus heard that, he **said,**		11:4
5	These things **said** he:		11:11
3	Then **said** his disciples,		11:12
28	Then **said** his disciples,		11:12
5	**said** Jesus unto them plainly, Lazarus is dead.		11:14
5	Then **said** Thomas, which is called Didymus,		11:16
5	Then **said** Martha unto Jesus, Lord,		11:21
5	Jesus **said** unto her, I am the resurrection,		11:25
20	And when she **had so said,** she went her way,		11:28
20	**saying,** The Master is come, and calleth for thee.		11:28
32	**saying,** The Master is come, and calleth for thee.		11:28
5	And **said,** Where have ye laid him?		11:34
3	And some of them **said,** Could not this man,		11:37
28	And some of them **said,** Could not this man,		11:37
3	**Said** I not unto thee, that, if thou wouldest believe,		11:40
5	And Jesus lifted up his eyes, and **said,** Father,		11:41
3	but because of the people which stand by I **said** it,		11:42
15	he thus **had spoken,** he cried with a loud voice,		11:43
3	and **told** them what things Jesus had done.		11:46
28	and **told** them what things Jesus had done.		11:46
5	**said** unto them, Ye know nothing at all,		11:49
5	And this **spake** he not of himself:		11:51
5	This he **said,** not that he cared for the poor;		12:6
5	Then **said** Jesus, Let her alone;		12:7
3	The Pharisees therefore **said** among themselves,		12:19
28	The Pharisees therefore **said** among themselves,		12:19
6	Now is my soul troubled; and what **shall I say**?		12:27
5	Jesus answered and **said,**		12:30
5	Then Jesus **said** unto them,		12:35
5	the saying of Esaias ... fulfilled, which he **spake,**		12:38
5	could not believe, because that Esaias **said** again,		12:39
5	These things **said** Esaias, when he saw his glory,		12:41
5	Jesus cried and **said,** He that believeth on me,		12:44
6	he gave me a commandment, what I **should say,**		12:49
5	Jesus answered and **said** unto him,		13:7
3	therefore **said** he, Ye are not all clean.		13:11
5	he **said** unto them,		13:12
15	When Jesus **had thus said,**		13:21
5	he was troubled in spirit, and testified, and **said,**		13:21
12	he should ask who it should be of whom he spake.	John	13:24
5	no ... knew for what intent he **spake** this unto him.		13:28
3	Ye shall seek me: and as I **said** unto the Jews,		13:33
3	if it were not so, I **would have told** you.		14:2
5	Jesus answered and **said** unto him,		14:23
3	whatsoever I **have said** unto you.		14:26
3	Ye have heard how I **said** unto you, I go away,		14:28
3	rejoice, because I **said,** I go unto the Father;		14:28
3	Remember the word that I **said** unto you,		15:20
3	ye may remember that I **told** you of them.		16:4
3	these things I **said** not unto you at the beginning,		16:4
3	therefore **said** I, that he shall take of mine,		16:15
3	Then **said** some of his disciples among themselves,		16:17
28	Then **said** some of his disciples among themselves,		16:17
5	Now Jesus knew ... and **said** unto them,		16:19
3	Do ye inquire among yourselves of that I **said,**		16:19
5	and lifted up his eyes to heaven, and **said,**		17:1
15	When Jesus **had spoken** these words,		18:1
5	went forth, and **said** unto them, Whom seek ye?		18:4
5	As soon then as he **had said** unto them, I am he,		18:6
3	Whom seek ye? And they **said,** Jesus of Nazareth.		18:7
28	Whom seek ye? And they **said,** Jesus of Nazareth.		18:7
3	Jesus answered, I **have told** you that I am he:		18:8
5	That the saying might be fulfilled, which he **spake,**		18:9
5	Then **said** Jesus unto Peter,		18:11
5	and **spake** unto her that kept the door,		18:16
3	behold, they know what I **said.**		18:21
16	And when he **had spoken,**		18:22
15	**saying,** Answerest thou the high priest so?		18:22
3	They **said** therefore unto him,		18:25
5	He denied it, and **said,** I am not.		18:25
5	Pilate then went out unto them, and **said,**		18:29
3	They answered and **said** unto him,		18:30
28	They answered and **said** unto him,		18:30
5	Then **said** Pilate unto them, Take ye him,		18:31
3	The Jews therefore **said** unto him,		18:31
5	saying of Jesus might be fulfilled, which he **spake,**		18:32
5	and **said** unto him, Art thou the King of the Jews?		18:33
3	or **did** others tell it thee of me?		18:34
5	Pilate therefore **said** unto him,		18:37
15	And when he **had said** this, he went out again		18:38
5	but that he **said,** I am King of the Jews:		19:21
3	They **said** therefore among themselves,		19:24
28	They **said** therefore among themselves,		19:24
5	he **said,** It is finished: ... and gave up the ghost.		19:30
20	when she had thus **said,** she turned herself back,		20:14
12	**tell** me where thou hast laid him,		20:15
12	but go to my brethren, and **say** unto them,		20:17
5	and that he **had said** these things unto her.		20:18
15	And when he **had so said,**		20:20
5	Then **said** Jesus to them again, Peace be unto you:		20:21
15	And when he **had said** this, he breathed on them,		20:22
5	But he **said** unto them, Except I shall see		20:25
5	stood in the midst, and **said,** Peace be unto you.		20:26
5	Thomas answered and **said** unto him, My Lord		20:28
5	And he **said** unto them,		21:6
5	Peter was grieved because he **said** unto him		21:17
5	And he **said** unto him, Lord, thou knowest all		21:17
5	This **spake** he, signifying by what death he should		21:19
15	And when he **had spoken** this, he saith unto him,		21:19
5	and **said,** Lord, which is he that betrayeth thee?		21:20
5	yet Jesus **said** not unto him, He shall not die;		21:23
5	And **he said** unto them,	Acts	1:7
15	And when he **had spoken** these things,		1:9
3	Which also **said,** Ye men of Galilee,		1:11
28	Which also **said,** Ye men of Galilee,		1:11
5	stood up in the midst of the disciples, and **said,**		1:15
3	And they prayed, and **said,** Thou, Lord,		1:24
28	And they prayed, and **said,** Thou, Lord,		1:24
21	let me freely **speak** unto you of the patriarch		2:29
5	The Lord **said** unto my Lord, Sit thou on my right		2:34
3	and **said** unto Peter and to the rest of the apostles,		2:37
5	Peter, fastening his eyes upon him with John, **said,**		3:4
5	Then Peter **said,** Silver and gold have I none;		3:6
5	For Moses truly **said** unto the fathers,		3:22
5	Peter, filled with the Holy Ghost, **said** unto them,		4:8
3	But Peter and John answered and **said** unto them,		4:19

277

εἶπον 1500

3	the chief priests and elders had **said** unto them.....	Acts 4:23
28	the chief priests and elders had **said** unto them........	4:23
3	and **said**, Lord, thou art God,..........................	4:24
28	and **said**, Lord, thou art God,..........................	4:24
15	Who by the mouth of thy servant David **hast said**,.....	4:25
5	But Peter **said**, Ananias, why hath Satan filled........	5:3
12	Tell me whether ye sold the land for so much?........	5:8
5	And she **said**, Yea, for so much.........................	5:8
5	Peter **said** unto her, How is it that ye have agreed.....	5:9
5	opened the prison ... brought them forth, and **said**,....	5:19
3	Peter and the other apostles answered and **said**,........	5:29
28	Peter and the other apostles answered and **said**,........	5:29
5	And **said** unto them, Ye men of Israel,.................	5:35
3	multitude of the disciples unto them, and **said**,.........	6:2
28	multitude of the disciples unto them, and **said**,.........	6:2
5	Then **said** the high priest, Are these things so?........	7:1
5	And **said** unto him, Get thee out of thy country,.......	7:3
5	they shall be in bondage will I judge, **said** God:.......	7:7
15	**saying**, Sirs, ye are brethren;...........................	7:26
15	did his neighbour wrong thrust him away, **saying**,.....	7:27
5	Then **said** the Lord to him,.............................	7:33
19	**saying**, Who made thee a ruler and a judge?..........	7:35
15	which **said** unto the children of Israel,.................	7:37
30	which **said** unto the children of Israel,.................	7:37
19	**Saying** unto Aaron, Make us gods to go before us:....	7:40
5	And **said**, Behold, I see the heavens opened,...........	7:56
15	And when he **had said** this, he fell asleep..............	7:60
5	Peter **said** unto him, Thy money perish with thee,.....	8:20
5	and **said**, Pray ye to the Lord for me,..................	8:24
5	Then the Spirit **said** unto Philip, Go near,.............	8:29
5	and heard him read the prophet Esaias, and **said**,......	8:30
5	he **said**, How can I, except some man should guide....	8:31
5	And the eunuch answered Philip, and **said**,............	8:34
5	Philip **said**, If thou believest with all thine heart,......	8:37
5	And he answered and **said**, I believe..................	8:37
5	And he **said**, Who art thou, Lord?.....................	9:5
5	the Lord **said**, I am Jesus whom thou persecutest:.....	9:5
5	And he trembling and astonished **said**, Lord,...........	9:6
5	Ananias; and to him **said** the Lord in a vision,........	9:10
5	Ananias. And he **said**, Behold, I am here, Lord.......	9:10
5	But the Lord **said** unto him, Go thy way:.............	9:15
5	and putting his hands on him **said**, Brother Saul,.....	9:17
5	And Peter **said** unto him, AEneas,.....................	9:34
5	and turning him to the body **said**, Tabitha, arise......	9:40
18	**saying** unto him, Cornelius.............................	10:3
5	when he looked on him, he was afraid, and **said**,.....	10:4
5	What is it, Lord? And he **said** unto him,.............	10:4
5	But Peter **said**, Not so, Lord;..........................	10:14
5	Spirit **said** unto him, Behold, three men seek thee.....	10:19
5	and **said**, Behold, I am he whom ye seek:.............	10:21
3	And they **said**, Cornelius the centurion, a just man,...	10:22
28	And they **said**, Cornelius the centurion, a just man,...	10:22
5	Then Peter opened his mouth, and **said**,..............	10:34
3	But I **said**, Not so, Lord:...............................	11:8
5	And the Spirit **bade** me go with them,.................	11:12
18	angel in his house, which stood and **said** unto him,...	11:13
5	And the angel **said** unto him, Gird thyself,............	12:8
5	And when Peter was come to himself, he **said**,.......	12:11
3	And they **said** unto her, Thou art mad.................	12:15
28	And they **said** unto her, Thou art mad.................	12:15
28	Then **said** they, It is his angel.........................	12:15
5	And he **said**, Go show these things unto James,......	12:17
5	Holy Ghost **said**, Separate me Barnabas and Saul.....	13:2
5	And **said**, O full of all subtlety and all mischief,......	13:10
5	Paul stood up, and beckoning with his hand **said**,.....	13:16
5	to whom also he gave testimony, and **said**,...........	13:22
3	Then Paul and Barnabas waxed bold, and **said**,.......	13:46
28	Then Paul and Barnabas waxed bold, and **said**,.......	13:46
5	**Said** with a loud voice, Stand upright on thy feet.....	14:10
5	Peter rose up, and **said** unto them,.....................	15:7
5	And some days after Paul **said** unto Barnabas,........	15:36
5	being grieved, turned and **said** to the spirit,...........	16:18
3	And brought them to the magistrates, **saying**,.........	16:20
28	And brought them to the magistrates, **saying**,.........	16:20
3	And they **said**, Believe on the Lord Jesus Christ,.....	16:31
28	And they **said**, Believe on the Lord Jesus Christ,.....	16:31
3	and others **said**, We will hear thee again.............	17:32
28	and others **said**, We will hear thee again..........Acts	17:32
5	he shook his raiment, and **said** unto them,............	18:6
5	**spake** the Lord to Paul in the night by a vision,......	18:9
5	Gallio **said** unto the Jews,.............................	18:14
15	But bade them farewell, **saying**,.......................	18:21
5	**said** unto them, Have ye received the Holy Ghost....	19:2
3	And they **said** unto him,...............................	19:2
5	And he **said** unto them,................................	19:3
3	And they **said**, Unto John's baptism..................	19:3
28	And they **said**, Unto John's baptism..................	19:3
5	Then **said** Paul, John verily baptized with............	19:4
5	And the evil spirit answered and **said**,................	19:15
15	**saying**, After I have been there,.......................	19:21
5	and **said**, Sirs, ye know that by this craft.............	19:25
15	And when he had thus **spoken**,.......................	19:41
5	and embracing him **said**, Trouble not yourselves;.....	20:10
5	when they were come to him, he **said** unto them,.....	20:18
5	the words of the Lord Jesus, how he **said**,............	20:35
15	And when he **had thus spoken**, he kneeled down,.....	20:36
5	and bound his own hands and feet, and **said**,........	21:11
19	**saying**, The will of the Lord be done..................	21:14
3	they glorified the Lord, and **said** unto him,...........	21:20
28	they glorified the Lord, and **said** unto him,...........	21:20
21	unto the chief captain, May I speak unto thee?........	21:37
5	Paul **said**, I am a man which am a Jew of Tarsus,....	21:39
5	And he **said** unto me, I am Jesus of Nazareth,.......	22:8
3	And I **said**, What shall I do, Lord?...................	22:10
5	And the Lord **said** unto me, Arise,...................	22:10
5	and **said** unto me, Brother Saul, receive thy sight.....	22:13
5	he **said**, The God of our fathers hath chosen thee,...	22:14
3	And I **said**, Lord, they know that I imprisoned.......	22:19
5	And he **said** unto me, Depart: for I will send thee....	22:21
15	**bade** that he should be examined by scourging;.......	22:24
30	**bade** that he should be examined by scourging;.......	22:24
5	Paul **said** unto the centurion that stood by,...........	22:25
5	Then the chief captain came, and **said** unto him,.....	22:27
5	And Paul, earnestly beholding the council, **said**,......	23:1
5	Then **said** Paul unto him, God shall smite thee,......	23:3
3	And they that stood by **said**,..........................	23:4
28	And they that stood by **said**,..........................	23:4
16	he **said** this, there arose a dissension (NASB)........	23:7
5	the Lord stood by him, and **said**, Be of good cheer,..	23:11
3	came to the chief priests and elders, and **said**,.......	23:14
28	came to the chief priests and elders, and **said**,.......	23:14
5	And he **said**, The Jews have agreed to desire.........	23:20
5	And he called unto him two centurions, **saying**,......	23:23
14	Or else let these same here say,.......................	24:20
15	he deferred them, and **said**,...........................	24:22
30	he deferred them, and **said**,...........................	24:22
5	But Festus, ... answered Paul, and **said**,..............	25:9
5	Then **said** Paul, I stand at Caesar's judgment seat,....	25:10
3	And I **said**, Who art thou, Lord?.....................	26:15
4	And I **said**, Who art thou, Lord?.....................	26:15
5	And he **said**, I am Jesus whom thou persecutest:.....	26:15
5	And Paul **said**, I would to God, that not only thou,..	26:29
16	And when he **had thus spoken**, the king rose up,.....	26:30
5	Paul stood forth in the midst of them, and **said**,.....	27:21
5	Paul **said** to the centurion and to the soldiers,........	27:31
15	And when he **had thus spoken**, he took bread,......	27:35
30	And when he **had thus spoken**, he took bread,......	27:35
3	And they **said** unto him,...............................	28:21
28	And they **said** unto him,...............................	28:21
16	after that Paul **had spoken** one word,................	28:25
5	Saying, Go unto this people, and **say**,................	28:26
29	Saying, Go unto this people, and **say**,................	28:26
16	when he **had said** these words, the Jews departed,...	28:29
22	It **was said** unto her, The elder shall serve..........Rom	9:12
23	It **was said** unto her, The elder shall serve...........	9:12
22	that in the place where it **was said** unto them,.......	9:26
23	that in the place where it **was said** unto them,.......	9:26
7	**Say** not in thine heart, Who shall ascend.............	10:6
8	should **say** that I had baptized in mine own name...1 Co	1:15
8	But if any man **say** unto you,........................	10:28
6	What **shall** I **say** to you? shall I praise you in this?...	11:22
5	and **said**, Take, eat: this is my body,................	11:24
21	and that no man can **say** that Jesus is the Lord, but..	12:3
8	If the foot **shall say**, Because I am not the hand,.....	12:15

8	And if the ear **shall say**, Because I am not the eye,	1 Co 12:16
21	And the eye cannot **say** unto the hand,	12:21
8	But when he **saith** all things are put under him,	15:27
15	who **commanded** the light to shine out of darkness,	2 Co 4:6
5	as God hath **said**, I will dwell in them,	6:16
3	**I said** unto Peter before them all,	Gal 2:14
24	to Abraham and his seed were the promises **made**.	3:16
31	to Abraham and his seed were the promises **made**.	3:16
1	And **say** to Archippus, Take heed to the ministry	Col 4:17
5	even a prophet of their own, **said**,	Tit 1:12
5	For unto which of the angels **said** he at any time,	Heb 1:5
3	I was grieved with that generation, and **said**,	3:10
21	as I may so **say**, Levi also, who receiveth tithes,	7:9
3	Then **said** I, Lo, I come	10:7
18	For we know him that hath **said**,	10:30
5	that Moses **said**, I exceedingly fear and quake:	12:21
10	have respect to him ... and **say** unto him,	Jas 2:3
10	Sit thou here in a good place; and **say** to the poor,	2:3
15	For he that **said**, Do not commit adultery,	2:11
5	Do not commit adultery, **said** also, Do not kill.	2:11
8	And one of you **say** unto them, Depart in peace,	2:16
9	If we **say** that we have fellowship with him,	1 Jn 1:6
9	If we **say** that we have no sin,	1:8
9	If we **say** that we have not sinned,	1:10
8	If a man **say**, I love God, and hateth his brother,	4:20
5	but **said**, The Lord rebuke thee.	Jude 1:9
23	and it **was said** unto them, that they should rest	Rev 6:11
5	And he **said** to me, These are they which came out	7:14
23	**was commanded** them ... should not hurt the grass	9:4
5	angel **said** unto me, Wherefore didst thou marvel?	17:7
5	And he that sat upon the throne **said**,	21:5
5	**said** unto me, It is done. I am Alpha and Omega,	21:6
5	And he **said** unto me, These sayings are faithful	22:6
13	And let him that heareth **say**, Come.	22:17

Classical Greek

Eipon, used from Homer on, is the second aorist of the obsolete verb *epō*. It is regularly used as the second aorist of *legō* (2978), "to utter in words, speak, say, tell," and sometimes of *phēmi* (5183), "to say, assert, affirm," and *agoreuō*, "to speak, address, proclaim." Its classical use is extremely widespread where it is translated by a variety of English words depending upon the context. They include "speak, say, recite, address, call, tell, proclaim, command," and "order," among others (see Liddell-Scott).

Septuagint Usage

The Septuagint translates 27 Hebrew words with the word *eipon* or one of its related grammatical forms. The most common word translated as *eipon* is the word *'āmar*, "say, speak, tell" or "proclaim." The New Testament also conveys a wide semantic range similar to those in classical Greek and Septuagint usage.

New Testament Usage

The variety of ways in which *eipon* is used in the New Testament is completely dependent upon the grammatical and situational context. For example, Bauer shows that the verb is often followed by the phrase *ton logo*, "the word," with the accusative case (Matthew 26:44; Luke 12:3). In other places *eipon* introduces a direct discourse, such as at Matthew 9:22. At other times it is used with *hoti* (3617), "that," in direct discourse (1 John 1:6,8,10, "If we say *that* we ... "). Occasionally *eipon* is used with a double accusative in the sense "to call or name" (John 15:15, "I have *called* you friends") or in the sense of saying a certain thing to someone (Luke 12:16, "He spake a parable unto them"). The verb may have a single object (cf. Mark 5:33; 14:72). It may also be modified by an adverb (Matthew 21:30; Luke 6:26) or by a prepositional phrase (Luke 8:41). Often *eipon* is used with an interrogative pronoun (John 12:27, "What shall I say?") or an indefinite pronoun (Luke 7:40, "I have somewhat to say").

Frequently the perfect form of *eipon* is used to introduce quotations from the Old Testament (Luke 2:24; Acts 2:16; 13:40). This tense emphasizes the continuing authority of what was spoken in the Old Testament. (Consider the similar expression, "It is written" [Luke 4:4,8,10], the perfect tense of *graphō* [1119], "to write.") *Eipon* may also be used with the reflexive pronoun *heautou* (1431), "oneself," carrying the idea of "to say to oneself" (Luke 16:3; 18:41).

The wide range of classical and Septuagint meanings can be seen in the New Testament in many places (Mark 5:43—Jesus "*commanded* that something should be given her to eat"; John 10:35—"If he *called* them gods, unto whom the word of God came ... "). It is used in John 16:4 with the idea of "foretelling" and at Romans 6:1 with the idea of "concluding," i.e., "What shall we *say* (conclude) then?" One more sense can be seen at Luke 1:30, which could read "announce." The flexibility of *eipon* shows the importance of examining a Greek word within its contextual setting before deciding on a precise meaning. Not every aspect of a term's definition can be forced into each of its New Testament occurrences. Proper exegesis places a limit upon the range of possible meanings a word may carry. (See also *legō* [2978].)

BAUER 226, MOULTON-MILLIGAN 185, LIDDELL-SCOTT 489-90, COLIN BROWN 1:341.

1501. εἴπως eipōs conj

If by any means, if perhaps, if somehow.

1. εἴπως eipōs

1	**if by any means** they might attain to Phenice,	Acts 27:12
1	Making request, **if by any means** now at length	Rom 1:10

εἰρηνεύω 1502

Classical Greek and Septuagint Usage
Modern Greek texts of the New Testament often break this term into its component parts—*ei* (1479), a conditional particle translated "if," and *pōs* (4316), an enclitic particle meaning "somehow" or "perhaps." (By definition an "enclitic" is "a word which has no accent of its own and so is pronounced as a part of the preceding word.") Nevertheless, some grammarians support the existence of the compound particle *eipōs* which has the resultant idea of "if perhaps" or "if somehow." (A "particle" is simply "a unit of speech which expresses a general meaning or some type of connective or limiting relationship." Some grammars group articles, prepositions, conjunctions, and even some interjections and adverbs under the category of "particle.") Hatch and Redpath indicate that the term *eipōs* is used eight times in the Septuagint (*Concordance to the Septuagint*, "eipos"). It is found both in the subjunctive and optative moods, reflecting the conditional aspect that *ei* brings into the particle. Second Samuel 16:12 (LXX 2 Kings 16:12), for example, shows a typical conditional (optative in this instance) usage: "It *may be* that the Lord will look on mine affliction."

New Testament Usage
This same conditional quality is evident in the four New Testament occurrences of this construction. In Acts 27:12 the optative mood follows: "... *if by any means* they might attain to Phoenix." (The centurion who was transporting Paul to Rome, along with the ship's captain and owner, *hoped* to reach a port more "commodious to winter in.") The remaining three New Testament usages (Romans 1:10; 11:14; Philippians 3:11) are found in constructions which employ a future tense which once again introduces a conditional element. In each of these, however, one can sense that the final outcome, though conditional, is not uncertain. For example, in Philippians 3:11 Paul wrote, "If by any means I might attain unto the resurrection of the dead." From his other writings we are convinced that Paul was *certain* he would attain this resurrection.

STRONG 1513, BAUER 226.

1502. εἰρηνεύω eirēneuō verb
Be at peace, live in peace.

CROSS-REFERENCE:
εἰρήνη eirēnē (1503)

שָׁלָה shālâh (8347), Be at ease, quiet (Jb 3:26).

שָׁלוֹם shālôm (8361), Quiet, silent (Jb 5:24, 15:21).

שָׁלַם shālam (8396), Be finished, keep peace; hiphil: make peace (1 Kgs 22:44 [22:45]); hophal: be brought into peace (Jb 5:23).

שָׁקַט shāqat (8618), Have peace, be at peace (2 Chr 14:5,6, 20:30).

1. εἰρηνεύετε eirēneuete 2pl impr pres act
2. εἰρηνεύοντες eirēneuontes
   nom pl masc part pres act

1 Have salt ... and **have peace** one with another....... Mark 9:50
2 If it be possible, ... live peaceably with all men..... Rom 12:18
1 be of good comfort, be of one mind, **live in peace**; 2 Co 13:11
1 And **be at peace** among yourselves.................. 1 Th 5:13

Classical Greek and Septuagint Usage
Eirēneuō can signify in nonbiblical Greek "to bring to peace" (transitive use [i.e., needing a direct object]) or "to live peaceably" (intransitive use). The Septuagint version demonstrates both meanings. The word can translate the hiphil of *shalam* to describe the cessation of hostilities between two warring nations ("And Jehoshaphat made peace with the king of Israel" [1 Kings 22:44 (LXX 3 Kings 22:44)]). The Septuagint translators also used the term intransitively of internal peace in translating the Hebrew word *shālâh* "be at ease" (Job 3:26).

The papyri used the term intransitively to mean "to be at peace" as in an inscription found at Halicarnassus describing the peaceful age of Augustus: "Earth and sea are at peace."

New Testament Usage
The noun "peace" (*eirēnē* [1503]) in the New Testament can refer to external security (Luke 14:32; Acts 24:2), harmony among men (Acts 7:26), and especially to salvation (Luke 1:79). God's peace is equal to God's salvation.

Eirēneuō is used four times in the New Testament, all intransitively. Paul used the term three of the four times in sections containing admonitions on Christian living, and evidently he echoed the words of Jesus in Mark 9:50. In Paul's three admonitions (Romans 12:18; 2 Corinthians 13:11; 1 Thessalonians 5:13) Christians must live in peace with themselves and with all men. Because the salvation of God gives peace, Christians must demonstrate their new status by living harmoniously.

STRONG 1514, BAUER 227, MOULTON-MILLIGAN 185, KITTEL 2:417-18, LIDDELL-SCOTT 490, COLIN BROWN 2:776,780.

1503. εἰρήνη eirēnē noun

Peace, harmony, tranquility, health.

Cognates:

εἰρηνεύω eirēneuō (1502)
εἰρηνικός eirēnikos (1504)
εἰρηνοποιέω eirēnopoieō (1505)
εἰρηνοποιός eirēnopoios (1506)

בֶּטַח beṭach (1020), Safety, secure (Jb 11:18, Prv 3:23, Is 14:30).

הָלַךְ hālakh (2050), Go, walk (2 Sm 3:24).

לֶקַח leqach (4090), Teaching (Is 29:24).

צַח tsach (6970), Clear (Is 32:4).

שַׁלְוָה shalwāh (8358), Quiet (Prv 17:1).

שָׁלוֹם shālôm (8361), Peace (Lv 26:6, 2 Sm 15:9, Mi 3:5).

שָׁלֵם shālēm (8401), Salem, Jerusalem (Ps 76:2 [75:2]).

שְׁלָם sh*lām (A8404), Well-being, peace (Ezr 4:17, 5:7, Dn 4:1 [3:31]—Aramaic).

שָׁקַט shāqaṭ (8618), Peaceful (1 Chr 4:40).

1. εἰρήνη eirēnē nom sing fem
2. εἰρήνης eirēnēs gen sing fem
3. εἰρήνῃ eirēnē dat sing fem
4. εἰρήνην eirēnēn acc sing fem

1	And when ye come into an house, salute it.	Matt 10:12
1	house be worthy, let your **peace** come upon it:	10:13
1	if it be not worthy, let your **peace** return to you.	10:13
4	Think not that I am come to send **peace** on earth:	10:34
4	I came not to send **peace**, but a sword.	10:34
4	go in **peace**, and be whole of thy plague.	Mark 5:34
2	to guide our feet into the way of **peace**.	Luke 1:79
1	Glory to God in the highest, and on earth **peace**,	2:14
3	Lord, now lettest thou thy servant depart in **peace**,	2:29
4	Thy faith hath saved thee; go in **peace**.	7:50
4	thy faith hath made thee whole; go in **peace**.	8:48
1	house ye enter, first say, **Peace** be to this house.	10:5
2	if the son of **peace** be there, your peace shall rest	10:6
1	your **peace** shall rest upon it: if not, it shall turn to	10:6
3	armed keepeth his palace, his goods are in **peace**:	11:21
4	Suppose ye that I am come to give **peace** on earth?	12:51
4	an ambassage, and desireth conditions of **peace**.	14:32
1	**peace** in heaven, and glory in the highest.	19:38
4	the things which belong unto thy **peace**!	19:42
1	stood in the midst of them, ... **Peace** be unto you.	24:36
4	**Peace** I leave with you, my peace I give unto you:	John 14:27
4	**Peace** I leave with you, my **peace** I give unto you:	14:27
1	that in me ye might have **peace**.	16:33
1	and saith unto them, **Peace** be unto you.	20:19
1	Then said Jesus to them again, **Peace** be unto you:	20:21
1	stood in the midst, and said, **Peace** be unto you.	20:26
4	and would have set them at one again,	Acts 7:26
4	Then had the churches rest throughout all Judaea:	9:31
4	preaching **peace** by Jesus Christ: he is Lord of all:	10:36
4	desired **peace**; because their country was	12:20
2	go in **peace** from the brethren unto the apostles.	15:33
3	now therefore depart, and go in **peace**.	16:36
2	Seeing that by thee we enjoy great **quietness**,	24:2
1	Grace to you and **peace** from God our Father,	Rom 1:7
1	But glory, honour, and **peace**,	2:10
2	And the way of **peace** have they not known:	3:17
4	we have **peace** with God through our Lord Jesus	5:1
1	but to be spiritually minded is life and **peace**.	8:6
4	the feet of them that preach the gospel of **peace**,	10:15
1	not meat and drink; but righteousness, and **peace**,	14:17
2	follow after the things which make for **peace**,	14:19
2	of hope fill you with all joy and **peace** in believing,	15:13
2	Now the God of **peace** be with you all. Amen.	15:33
2	God of **peace** shall bruise Satan under your feet	16:20
1	Grace be unto you, and **peace**, from God	1 Co 1:3
3	but God hath called us to **peace**.	7:15
2	God is not the author of confusion, but of **peace**,	14:33
3	but conduct him forth in **peace**,	16:11
1	Grace be to you and **peace** from God our Father,	2 Co 1:2
2	and the God of love and **peace** shall be with you.	13:11
1	Grace be to you and **peace** from God the Father,	Gal 1:3
1	But the fruit of the Spirit is love, joy, **peace**,	5:22
1	**peace** be on them, and mercy, and upon the Israel	6:16
1	Grace be to you, and **peace**, from God our Father,	Eph 1:2
1	For he is our **peace**, who hath made both one,	2:14
4	make ... of twain one new man, so making **peace**;	2:15
4	and preached **peace** to you which were afar off,	2:17
4	**PEACE TO THOSE WHO WERE NEAR; (NASB)**	2:17
2	to keep the unity of the Spirit in the bond of **peace**:	4:3
4	shod with the preparation of the gospel of **peace**;	6:15
1	**Peace** be to the brethren, and love with faith,	6:23
1	Grace be unto you, and **peace**, from God	Phlp 1:2
1	the **peace** of God, which passeth all understanding,	4:7
2	do: and the God of **peace** shall be with you.	4:9
1	Grace be unto you, and **peace**, from God	Col 1:2
1	And let the **peace** of God rule in your hearts,	3:15
1	Grace be unto you, and **peace**, from God	1 Th 1:1
1	For when they shall say, **Peace** and safety;	5:3
2	And the very God of **peace** sanctify you wholly;	5:23
1	Grace unto you, and **peace**, from God our Father	2 Th 1:2
2	Now the Lord of **peace** himself give you peace	3:16
2	Now the Lord of peace himself give you **peace**	3:16
1	Grace, mercy, and **peace**, from God our Father	1 Tm 1:2
1	Grace, mercy, and **peace**, from God the Father	2 Tm 1:2
4	but follow righteousness, faith, charity, **peace**,	2:22
1	Grace, mercy, and **peace**, from God the Father,	Tit 1:4
1	Grace to you, and **peace**, from God our Father	Phlm 1:3
2	also King of Salem, which is, King of **peace**;	Heb 7:2
2	when she had received the spies with **peace**.	11:31
4	Follow **peace** with all men, and holiness,	12:14
2	Now the God of **peace**,	13:20
3	And one of you say unto them, Depart in **peace**,	Jas 2:16
3	And the fruit of righteousness is sown in **peace**	3:18
4	sown in peace of them that make **peace**.	3:18
1	Grace unto you, and **peace**, be multiplied.	1 Pt 1:2
4	let him seek **peace**, and ensue it.	3:11
1	**Peace** be with you all that are in Christ Jesus.	5:14
1	Grace and **peace** be multiplied unto you	2 Pt 1:2
3	be diligent that ye may be found of him in **peace**,	3:14
1	mercy, and **peace**, from God the Father,	2 Jn 1:3
1	**Peace** be to thee. Our friends salute thee.	3 Jn 1:14
1	Mercy unto you, and **peace** and love,	Jude 1:2
1	and **peace**, from him which is, and which was,	Rev 1:4
4	him that sat thereon to take **peace** from the earth,	6:4

Classical Greek

The term *eirēnē*, "peace," primarily functions as the antithesis to war in secular Greek (Beck and Brown, "Peace," *Colin Brown*, 2:776). The word does not imply so much "peace" as an ideal behavior or as fellowship between men; rather, it is more related to a condition of peace, a respite during an endless series of wars.

We see this principal understanding of the word reflected in the Latin phrase *pax Romana*, the "Roman peace," which Augustus the emperor instituted by force in the countries along the Mediterranean coast. Among the people of this time the longing for peace was deep; consequently, this new condition of law and order was welcomed as the Golden Age. Furthermore, the Greeks considered peace (the absence of war) as the foundation for national and personal welfare and prosperity. The goddess Eirene was believed to give gifts of wealth and well-being.

Gradually *eirēnē* denoted a peaceful attitude. It came to be understood as a contrast to boisterous behavior, and it tended to mean "peace and quiet." The Stoic philosophers sometimes used the word to indicate "inner peace, tranquility" or "peace of mind." These variations, however, do not alter the fact that to the Greeks *eirēnē* was first and foremost "a state of peace in contrast to war."

Septuagint Usage

When the term was adopted by the Septuagint translators, *eirēnē* was an inadequate equivalent to the Hebrew *shālôm*. *Shālôm* served more purposes and had more diversity of meaning than the limited term *eirēnē*. To have "shalom" in the Old Testament period meant not only to have "peace" as it is understood today; it also meant to feel "healthy" or to be "whole." "Peace" was a state of well-being.

Peace is also viewed in relation to God. God grants peace to His covenant community. Peace was the harmonious condition which reigned in Israel when the communion with God was intact. Peace signals that the blessings of the Lord flow to the people. Justice and salvation from all distress are carried out in the land of promise (cf. Psalm 85:9-14 [LXX 84:9-14]). Peace—for both the individual and for the nation—depended upon whether or not they obeyed the commandments of God (Isaiah 48:18; Leviticus 26:3-6; cf. Deuteronomy 28 concerning the blessings and the curses of the covenant). The prophets considered all the troubles in the land as the by-product of disobedience and the stubbornness of the people (Isaiah 48:22; 59:8; Jeremiah 6:13,14; 16:5; Zechariah 8:9,10). From the time of Micaiah, son of Imlah, to Ezekiel there was in Israel an enormous struggle between the genuine prophets and the false "prosperity" prophets who overlooked the sins of the people and preached "peace" (usually political peace). For true prophecy peace was the condition of justice (*tsᵉdāqāh*) (Isaiah 32:17; 48:18; 54:13; 60:17). There is no peace for a backslidden, disobedient people.

In spite of a sense of hopelessness (Ecclesiastes 3:8) and the ever-present disobedience of Israel, through almost every prophetic utterance one can see dimly a hope for a future in which peace reigned. A new covenant with God will come, the prophets declared, a covenant of peace which will not be moved (Isaiah 54:10f.; Ezekiel 34:25f.; 37:26). The coming Servant of the Lord, through His suffering and death, will bear "the chastisement of our peace" upon himself (Isaiah 53:5).

In the Old Testament *shālôm* was inherently an expression of the period of the eschatological salvation and of the conditions of the Messianic Age. Israel will no longer suffer at the hands of its enemies. It will live safely (Isaiah 57:17f.; Jeremiah 29:11f.; 33:6f.; Haggai 2:9; Zechariah 6:12,13). In the last days the people will not "learn war any more" (Micah 4:1-4). All of this will be fully realized when the Messiah comes; He will be the prince of peace (Isaiah 9:6; Micah 5:1-4; Zechariah 9:9,10). The Messianic Kingdom means that the conditions of paradise (i.e., the Garden of Eden) will be restored (Isaiah 11:1f.; Hosea 2:20f.; Amos 9:13f.).

Where the blessings of the new covenant are poured out upon the people of God, everything will be healed, everything will be whole again. Then the status of "very good" which God proclaimed at creation (Genesis 1:31) will return (cf. Revelation chapters 21 and 22). So *shālôm* is an all-encompassing expression for salvation—the normal condition of the "new creature."

New Testament Usage

It is primarily in the light of this rich heritage from the Old Testament that *eirēnē* is understood in the New Testament. Now the prophetic hope of the future *shālôm*, "peace," is about to be fulfilled in Jesus Christ. At His birth the angels sang of peace on earth (Luke 2:14). When Jesus entered Jerusalem on His journey to suffering and death, the multitude sang, in accordance with Zechariah 9:9,10, of "peace in heaven" (Luke 19:38).

From the day of the Fall man has been at enmity, at war, with God. People are "alienated and enemies" not only because of their deeds but because of their disposition (Colossians 1:21; the carnal mind is at enmity against God [Romans 8:7]). If there was to be peace between God and man, God himself had to take the initiative. He did so when He sent His Son, He who "is our peace" (Ephesians 2:14). At His atoning death for our sins we were reconciled to God in spite of our sins. The message of reconciliation is called "the gospel of peace" (Acts 10:36; Ephesians 2:17; 6:15), and the God who has performed this is called "the God of peace" (cf. Romans 5:2-5).

The Holy Spirit bears the fruit of peace in the life of the believer (Galatians 5:22). The attitude of peace within the Christian is acquired through the new relationship with God. In turn, believers can also affect their surroundings: "Blessed are the peacemakers"—literally "those who make peace" (Matthew 5:9). The Christian is admonished to live peaceably with all men, if it is possible (Romans 12:18; Hebrews 12:14). Believers are to seek peace and to pursue it (1 Peter 3:11). This is especially applicable in relationships with other believers (2 Corinthians 13:11; Ephesians 4:3; 1 Thessalonians 5:13; 2 Timothy 2:22).

Thus *eirēnē* as a fruit of the Spirit concerns the heart of the individual. Peace is not only a condition in relation to God and men; it is also a blessed experience in concrete life situations. It affords a good conscience (Luke 7:50; 8:48), and the believer can experience the peace of God. Still, the peace he feels is something much more than a matter of feelings. The peace of the soul which he experiences is grounded on the real declaration of peace with God that has been made through Christ. This is the background of the words of Jesus when He promised His disciples "my peace" (John 14:27). No external circumstances can rob this peace from a believer, not even the greatest tribulation (John 16:33; Romans 8:35-39).

This peace will be with a believer (1 Corinthians 1:3), it will reign in his or her heart (Colossians 3:15), and it will keep his or her heart and thoughts in Christ Jesus (Philippians 4:7).

The New Testament does not imagine any permanent political peace in the world during this age. On the contrary, war and strife should be expected right into the last days (Matthew 24:6; Revelation 12:17; 13:7; 19:19; passim). When the new heaven and the new earth are created, peace will reign. The prophecies of the Old Testament of eternal peace will have their total fulfillment in the new earth where righteousness lives (2 Peter 3:13). Thus peace corresponds to the language of the Old Testament; peace is the consummation of the eschatological salvation.

STRONG 1515, BAUER 227-28, MOULTON-MILLIGAN 185-86, KITTEL 2:400-417, LIDDELL-SCOTT 490, COLIN BROWN 2:776-83.

1504. εἰρηνικός eirēnikos adj
Peaceable, peaceful.
CROSS-REFERENCE:
  εἰρήνη eirēnē (1503)

כֵּן kēn (3773), True, honest (Gn 42:11,19,31,33,34).

שָׁלוֹם shālôm (8361), Peace (Dt 20:12 [20:11], Ps 37:37 [36:37], Ob 7).

שָׁלַם shālam (8396), Be peaceable (2 Sm 20:19).

שֶׁלֶם shelem (8399), Fellowship offering, peace offering (2 Sm 6:18, 1 Kgs 8:64, Prv 7:14).

שָׁלֵם shālēm (8400), Peaceable, undivided (Gn 34:21, 1 Chr 12:38).

1. **εἰρηνικόν** eirēnikon acc sing masc
2. **εἰρηνική** eirēnikē nom sing fem

1 it yieldeth the **peaceable** fruit of righteousness ...... Heb 12:11
2 from above is first pure, then **peaceable**, gentle, ... Jas 3:17

This word connotes the "peaceful" quality of righteous Christian living. Related to the common word *eirēnē* (1503), in Hebrews 12:11, it is the result of painful discipline. James 3:17 asserts that it is the result of spiritual discernment.

STRONG 1516, BAUER 228, MOULTON-MILLIGAN 186, KITTEL 2:418-19, LIDDELL-SCOTT 490, COLIN BROWN 3:776,780,782.

1505. εἰρηνοποιέω eirēnopoieō verb
Make peace.
CROSS-REFERENCES:
  εἰρήνη eirēnē (1503)
  ποιέω poieō (4020)

לָבַט lāvat (3964), Niphal: be ruined, fall (Prv 10:10).

1. **εἰρηνοποιήσας** eirēnopoiēsas
              nom sing masc part aor act

1 **having made peace** through the blood of his cross, ... Col 1:20

This is a compound word from *eirēnē* (1503), "peace," and *poieō* (4020), "to make." Only Jesus can "make peace" once and for all through His blood on the cross (Colossians 1:20).

STRONG 1517, BAUER 228, KITTEL 2:419-20, LIDDELL-SCOTT 490, COLIN BROWN 2:776,782.

1506. εἰρηνοποιός eirēnopoios adj
Making peace.

εἰς 1506A

CROSS-REFERENCES:
εἰρήνη eirēnē (1503)
ποιέω poieō (4020)

1. εἰρηνοποιοί eirēnopoioi nom pl masc

1 Blessed are the **peacemakers**: ... children of God..... Matt 5:9

Jesus described the "peacemakers" in the Beatitudes. There is probably a connection between Jesus' act of "making peace" on the cross (Colossians 1:20) and those who become sons of God by imitating Jesus and taking up that cross (Matthew 5:9).

STRONG 1518, BAUER 228, KITTEL 2:419, LIDDELL-SCOTT 490, COLIN BROWN 2:776,780,782.

1506A. εἷς heis num

One, alone, one and the same, only one, someone, anyone.

COGNATE:
ἑνότης henotēs (1759)

1. **ἑνός henos** card gen masc/neu
2. **ἑνί heni** card dat masc/neu
3. **εἷς heis** card nom masc
4. **ἕνα hena** card acc masc
5. **μία mia** card nom fem
6. **μιᾶς mias** card gen fem
7. **μιᾷ mia** card dat fem
8. **μίαν mian** card acc fem
9. **ἕν hen** card nom/acc neu

9	**one** jot or **one** tittle shall in no wise pass	Matt	5:18
5	one jot or **one** tittle shall in no wise pass		5:18
8	Whosoever therefore shall break **one** of these least		5:19
9	that **one** of thy members should perish,		5:29
9	that **one** of thy members should perish,		5:30
8	thou canst not make **one** hair white or black.		5:36
9	And whosoever shall compel thee to go **a** mile,		5:41
4	for either he will hate the **one**, and love the other;		6:24
1	else he will hold to the **one**, and despise the other.		6:24
4	can add **one** cubit unto his stature?		6:27
9	Solomon ... was not arrayed like **one** of these.		6:29
3	And **a** certain scribe came, and said unto him,		8:19
3	a ruler came and knelt before him (NIV) (NT)		9:18
9	and **one** of them shall not fall on the ground		10:29
4	shall give to drink unto **one** of these little ones		10:42
9	that shall have **one** sheep,		12:11
4	Who, when he had found **one** pearl of great price,		13:46
4	and others, Jeremias, or **one** of the prophets.		16:14
8	**one** for thee, and one for Moses, and one for Elias.		17:4
8	one for thee, and **one** for Moses, and one for Elias.		17:4
8	one for thee, and one for Moses, and **one** for Elias.		17:4
9	And whoso shall receive **one** such little child		18:5
4	But whoso shall offend **one** of these little ones		18:6
1	that ye despise not **one** of these little ones;		18:10
9	hundred sheep, and **one** of them be gone astray,		18:12
3	that **one** of these little ones should perish.		18:14
9	that **one** of these little ones perish. (NASB)		18:14
4	then take with thee **one** or two more,		18:16
3	**one** was brought unto him,		18:24
4	went out, and found **one** of his fellowservants,		18:28
8	and they twain shall be **one** flesh?		19:5
5	Wherefore they are no more twain, but **one** flesh.		19:6
3	behold, **one** came and said unto him, Good Master,		19:16
3	there is none good but **one**, that is, God:		19:17
8	Saying, These last have wrought but **one** hour,	Matt	20:12
2	But he answered **one** of them, and said, Friend,		20:13
3	**one** on thy right hand, and the other on the left,		20:21
3	one on thy right hand, and the **other** on the left,		20:21
8	henceforth **for** ever		21:19
4	I also will ask you **one** thing, which if ye tell me,		21:24
3	Then **one** of them, which was a lawyer, asked him		22:35
3	for **one** is your Master, even Christ;		23:8
3	for **one** is your Father, which is in heaven.		23:9
3	for **one** is your Master, even Christ.		23:10
4	for ye compass sea and land to make **one** proselyte,		23:15
3	the **one** shall be taken, and the other left.		24:40
3	the one shall be taken, and the **other** left.		24:40
3	the **one** shall be taken, and the other left.		24:41
3	the one shall be taken, and the **other** left.		24:41
9	five talents, to another two, and to another **one**;		25:15
9	had received **one** went and digged in the earth,		25:18
9	which had received the **one** talent came and said,		25:24
2	done it **unto one** of the least of these my brethren,		25:40
2	as ye did it not **to one** of the least of these,		25:45
3	Then **one** of the twelve, called Judas Iscariot,		26:14
3	I say unto you, that **one** of you shall betray me.		26:21
3	they each **one** began to say to Him, (NASB)		26:22
8	What, could ye not watch with me **one** hour?		26:40
3	lo, Judas, **one** of the twelve, came,		26:47
3	And, behold, **one** of them which were with Jesus		26:51
5	and **a** damsel came unto him, saying,		26:69
9	And he answered him to never **a** word;		27:14
4	was wont to release unto the people **a** prisoner,		27:15
3	**one** on the right hand, and another on the left.		27:38
3	one on the right hand, and **another** on the left.		27:38
3	straightway **one** of them ran, and took a sponge,		27:48
8	it began to dawn toward the **first** day of the week,		28:1
3	who can forgive sins but God **only**?	Mark	2:7
9	**some** thirty, and some sixty, and some an hundred.		4:8
9	some **thirty**, and some sixty, and some an hundred.		4:8
9	some thirty, and **some** sixty, and some an hundred.		4:8
9	some thirty, and some **sixty**, and some an hundred.		4:8
9	some thirty, and some sixty, and **some** an hundred.		4:8
9	some thirty, and some sixty, and some an **hundred**.		4:8
9	**some** thirtyfold, some sixty, and some an hundred.		4:20
9	some thirtyfold, **some** sixty, and some an hundred.		4:20
9	some thirtyfold, some sixty, and **some** an hundred.		4:20
3	there cometh **one** of the rulers of the synagogue,		5:22
3	That it is a prophet, or as **one** of the prophets.		6:15
4	they in the ship with them more than **one** loaf.		8:14
4	some say, Elias; and others, One of the prophets.		8:28
3	but others, **one** of the prophets. (NASB)		8:28
8	**one** for thee, and one for Moses, and one for Elias.		9:5
8	one for thee, and **one** for Moses, and one for Elias.		9:5
8	one for thee, and one for Moses, and **one** for Elias.		9:5
3	And **one** of the multitude answered and said,		9:17
9	Whosoever shall receive **one** of such children		9:37
4	And whosoever shall offend **one** of these little ones		9:42
8	And they twain shall be **one** flesh:		10:8
5	so then they are no more twain, but **one** flesh.		10:8
3	there came **one** running, and kneeled to him,		10:17
3	there is none good but **one**, that is, God.		10:18
9	**One thing** thou lackest: ... sell whatsoever		10:21
3	**one** on thy right hand, and the other on thy left		10:37
3	and the **other** on thy left hand, in thy glory.		10:37
4	I will also ask of you **one** question, and answer me,		11:29
4	Having yet therefore **one** son, his wellbeloved,		12:6
3	And **one** of the scribes came,		12:28
3	Hear, O Israel; The Lord our God is **one** Lord:		12:29
3	there is **one** God; and there is none other but he:		12:32
5	And there came a **certain** poor widow,		12:42
3	**one** of his disciples saith unto him, Master,		13:1
3	And Judas Iscariot, **one** of the twelve,		14:10
3	**One** of you which eateth with me shall betray me.		14:18
3	**one** by one, Is it I? and another said, Is it I?		14:19
3	one by **one**, Is it I? and another said, Is it I?		14:19
3	**one** of the twelve, that dippeth with me in the dish.		14:20
9	one of the twelve, **one** who dips with Me (NASB)		14:20
8	sleepest thou? couldest not thou watch **one** hour?		14:37
3	while he ... spake, cometh Judas, **one** of the twelve,		14:43
3	And **one** of them that stood by drew a sword,		14:47

εἷς 1506A

3	And there followed him a certain young man, (NT)	Mark 14:51
5	there cometh **one** of the maids of the high priest:	14:66
4	at that feast he released unto them **one** prisoner,	15:6
4	the **one** on his right hand, and the other on his left.	15:27
4	the **one** on his right hand, and the **other** on his left.	15:27
6	very early in the morning the **first** day of the week,	16:2
7	very early in the morning the **first** day of the week,	16:2
7	very early in the morning the **first** day of the week,	16:2
2	and he laid his hands on every **one** of them,	Luke 4:40
9	And he entered into **one** of the ships,	5:3
7	And it came to pass, when he was in a **certain** city,	5:12
7	And it came to pass on a **certain** day,	5:17
3	**one** owed five hundred pence, and the other fifty.	7:41
7	Now it came to pass on a **certain** day,	8:22
8	**one** for thee, and **one** for Moses, and one for Elias:	9:33
8	one for thee, and **one** for Moses, and one for Elias:	9:33
8	one for thee, and **one** for Moses, and **one** for Elias:	9:33
1	But **one** thing is needful:	10:42
1	But **one** thing is needful:	10:42
2	touch not the burdens with **one** of your fingers.	11:46
9	and not **one** of them is forgotten before God?	12:6
4	taking thought can add to his stature **one** cubit?	12:25
9	Solomon ... was not arrayed like **one** of these.	12:27
2	there shall be five in **one** house divided,	12:52
7	And he was teaching in **one** of the synagogues	13:10
6	they all with **one** consent began to make excuse.	14:18
9	if he lose **one** of them, doth not leave the ninety	15:4
2	joy ... be in heaven over **one** sinner that repenteth,	15:7
8	if she lose **one** piece, doth not light a candle,	15:8
2	there is joy ... over **one** sinner that repenteth.	15:10
2	joined himself **to a** citizen of that country;	15:15
4	make me as **one** of thy hired servants.	15:19
4	And he called **one** of the servants, and asked	15:26
4	So he called every **one** of his lord's debtors	16:5
4	for either he will hate the **one**, and love the other;	16:13
1	else he will hold to the **one**, and despise the other.	16:13
8	and earth to pass, than **one** tittle of the law to fail.	16:17
4	than that he should offend **one** of these little ones.	17:2
3	And **one** of them, when he saw that he was healed,	17:15
8	when ye shall desire to see **one** of the days	17:22
6	in that night there shall be two men in **one** bed;	17:34
3	the **one** shall be taken, and the other shall be left.	17:34
5	the **one** shall be taken, and the other left.	17:35
3	the **one** shall be taken, and the other left.	17:36
3	the **one** a Pharisee, and the other a publican.	18:10
3	me good? none is good, save **one**, that is, God.	18:19
9	Yet lackest thou **one thing**: sell all that thou hast,	18:22
7	And it came to pass, that on **one** of those days,	20:1
4	I will also ask you **one** thing; and answer me:	20:3
3	he that was called Judas, **one** of the twelve,	22:47
3	**one** of them smote the servant of the high priest,	22:50
6	one hour after another confidently affirmed,	22:59
4	he must release **one** unto them at the feast.	23:17
3	And **one** of the malefactors ... railed on him,	23:39
7	Now upon the **first** day of the week,	24:1
3	And the **one** of them, whose name was Cleopas,	24:18
9	and without him was not **any** thing made	John 1:3
9	In him was life; and the life was the light of men.	1:4
3	**One** of the two which heard John speak,	1:40
3	**One** of his disciples, Andrew,	6:8
9	There is a lad here, which hath five barley loaves,	6:9
9	save that **one** whereinto his disciples were entered,	6:22
3	chosen you twelve, and **one** of you is a devil?	6:70
3	Judas Iscariot ... being **one** of the twelve.	6:71
9	I have done one work, and ye all marvel.	7:21
3	he that came to Jesus by night, being **one** of them,	7:50
3	went out **one** by one, beginning at the eldest,	8:9
3	went out one by **one**, beginning at the eldest,	8:9
4	we have one Father, even God.	8:41
9	one thing I know, that, whereas I was blind,	9:25
3	and there shall be **one** fold, and one shepherd.	10:16
3	and there shall be one fold, and **one** shepherd.	10:16
9	I and my Father are **one**.	10:30
3	**one** of them, named Caiaphas, ... the high priest	11:49
3	that **one** man should die for the people,	11:50
3	but that also he should gather together in **one**	11:52
5	Lazarus was **one** of them that sat at the table	12:2
3	Then saith **one** of his disciples, Judas Iscariot,	John 12:4
3	I say unto you, that **one** of you shall betray me.	13:21
3	was leaning on Jesus' bosom **one** of his disciples,	13:23
9	that they may be **one**, as we are.	17:11
9	they all may be **one**; as thou, Father, art in me,	17:21
9	and I in thee, that they also may be **one** in us:	17:21
9	that they may be **one**, even as we are one:	17:22
9	that they may be one, even as we are **one**:	17:22
9	that they may be made perfect in **one**;	17:23
4	expedient that **one** man should die for the people.	18:14
3	one of the officers which stood by struck Jesus	18:22
3	**One** of the servants of the high priest,	18:26
4	that I should release unto you **one** at the passover:	18:39
3	**one** of the soldiers with a spear pierced his side,	19:34
7	The **first** day ... cometh Mary Magdalene early,	20:1
4	but wrapped together in a place by itself.	20:7
4	the **one** at the head,	20:12
4	and the **other** at the feet,	20:12
7	being the **first** day of the week,	20:19
3	But Thomas, **one** of the twelve, called Didymus,	20:24
9	the which, if they should be written every **one**,	21:25
4	must **one** be ordained to be a witness with us	Acts 1:22
4	show whether of these two thou hast chosen, (NT)	1:24
4	cloven tongues ... and it sat upon each (NT)	2:3
3	each **one** heard them speaking (NIV)	2:6
5	that believed were of one heart and of **one** soul:	4:32
3	No one claimed that any of his (NIV)	4:32
3	And there stood up **one** of them named Agabus,	11:28
8	they went out, and passed on through **one** street;	12:10
1	And hath made of **one** blood all nations of men	17:26
1	though he be not far from every **one** of us:	17:27
5	all with **one** voice about the space of two hours	19:34
7	And upon the **first** day of the week,	20:7
4	to warn every **one** night and day with tears.	20:31
8	to Ptolemais, ... and abode with them **one** day.	21:7
9	declared particularly what things God had wrought	21:19
1	offering should be offered for every **one** of them.	21:26
9	**one** part were Sadducees, and the other Pharisees,	23:6
4	Then Paul called **one** of the centurions unto him,	23:17
6	Except it be for this **one** voice,	24:21
8	and after **one** day the south wind blew,	28:13
9	after that Paul had spoken **one** word,	28:25
3	There is none righteous, no, not **one**:	Rom 3:10
1	there is none that doeth good, no, not **one**.	3:12
3	Seeing it is **one** God, which shall justify	3:30
1	as by **one** man sin entered into the world,	5:12
1	For if through the offence of **one** many be dead,	5:15
1	and the gift by grace, which is by **one** man,	5:15
1	And not as it was by **one** that sinned, so is the gift:	5:16
1	for the judgment was by **one** to condemnation,	5:16
1	For if by **one** man's offence death reigned by one;	5:17
1	For if by one man's offence death reigned by **one**;	5:17
1	the gift of righteousness shall reign in life by **one**,	5:17
1	Therefore as by the offence of **one** judgment	5:18
1	even so by the righteousness of **one** the free gift	5:18
1	**one** man's disobedience many were made sinners,	5:19
1	so by the obedience of **one** shall many be	5:19
1	but when Rebecca also had conceived by **one**,	9:10
2	For as we have many members in **one** body,	12:4
9	So we, being many, are **one** body in Christ,	12:5
3	and every **one** members one of another.	12:5
2	ye may with one mind and **one** mouth glorify God,	15:6
9	he that planteth and he that watereth are **one**:	1 Co 3:8
3	that no **one** of you be puffed up for one	4:6
1	of you be puffed up for **one** against another.	4:6
9	that he which is joined to an harlot is **one** body?	6:16
8	for two, saith he, shall be **one** flesh.	6:16
9	But he that is joined unto the Lord is **one** spirit.	6:17
3	and that there is none other God but **one**.	8:4
3	But to us there is but **one** God, the Father,	8:6
3	and **one** Lord Jesus Christ, by whom are all things,	8:6
3	run in a race run all, but **one** receiveth the prize?	9:24
7	and fell in **one** day three and twenty thousand.	10:8
3	For we being many are **one** bread, and one body:	10:17
9	For we being many are one bread, and **one** body:	10:17
1	for we are all partakers of that **one** bread.	10:17
9	for that is even all **one** as if she were shaven.	11:5

2	To another faith by the same Spirit;	1 Co 12:9
9	all these worketh that **one** and the selfsame Spirit,	12:11
9	For as the body is **one**, and hath many members,	12:12
1	and all the members of that **one** body,	12:12
9	being many, are **one** body: so also is Christ.	12:12
2	by **one** Spirit are we all baptized into one body,	12:13
9	by **one** Spirit are we all baptized into one body,	12:13
9	and have been all made to drink into **one** Spirit.	12:13
9	For the body is not **one** member, but many.	12:14
9	the members every **one** of them in the body,	12:18
9	if they were all **one** member, where ... the body?	12:19
9	now are they many members, yet but **one** body.	12:20
9	And whether **one** member suffer,	12:26
9	or **one** member be honoured,	12:26
3	and that by course; and let **one** interpret.	14:27
4	may all prophesy **one** by one, that all may learn,	14:31
8	Upon the **first** day of the week let every one of you	16:2
3	that if **one** died for all, then were all dead:	2 Co 5:14
2	for I have espoused you to **one** husband,	11:2
8	five times received I forty stripes save **one**.	11:24
1	but as of **one**, And to thy seed, which is Christ.	Gal 3:16
1	mediator is not a mediator **of one**, but God is one.	3:20
3	mediator is not a mediator of one, but God is **one**.	3:20
3	for ye are all **one** in Christ Jesus.	3:28
4	the **one** by a bondmaid, the other by a freewoman.	4:22
4	the one by a bondmaid, the **other** by a freewoman.	4:22
5	the **one** from the mount Sinai,	4:24
2	For all the law is fulfilled in **one** word,	5:14
9	For he is our peace, who hath made both **one**,	Eph 2:14
4	for to make in himself of twain **one** new man,	2:15
2	reconcile both unto God in **one** body by the cross,	2:16
2	we both have access by **one** Spirit unto the Father.	2:18
9	There is **one** body, and one Spirit,	4:4
9	There is one body, and **one** Spirit,	4:4
7	even as ye are called in **one** hope of your calling;	4:4
3	**One** Lord, one faith, one baptism,	4:5
5	One Lord, **one** faith, one baptism,	4:5
9	One Lord, one faith, **one** baptism,	4:5
3	**One** God and Father of all, who is above all,	4:6
2	unto every **one** of us is given grace according to	4:7
1	the effectual working in the measure of **every** part,	4:16
8	unto his wife, and they two shall be **one** flesh.	5:31
4	Nevertheless let every **one** of you in particular	5:33
2	hear of your affairs, that ye stand fast in **one** spirit,	Phlp 1:27
7	with **one** mind striving together for the faith	1:27
9	being of one accord, of **one** mind.	2:2
9	but this **one** thing I do,	3:13
2	to the which also ye are called in **one** body;	Col 3:15
2	ye may know how ye ought to answer every **man**.	4:6
4	and comforted and charged every **one** of you,	1 Th 2:11
3	and edify **one** another, even as also ye do.	5:11
4	and edify one **another**, even as also ye do.	5:11
1	charity of every **one** of you all toward each other	2 Th 1:3
3	For there is **one** God, and one mediator	1 Tm 2:5
3	one God, and **one** mediator between God and men,	2:5
6	must be blameless, the husband of **one** wife,	3:2
6	Let the deacons be the husbands **of one** wife,	3:12
1	a widow ... having been the wife **of one** man,	5:9
6	If any be blameless, the husband of **one** wife,	Tit 1:6
8	after the **first** and second admonition reject;	3:10
1	and they who are sanctified are all of **one**:	Heb 2:11
8	after he had offered **one** sacrifice for sins for ever,	10:12
7	For **by one** offering he hath perfected for ever	10:14
1	sprang there even of **one**, and him as good as dead,	11:12
6	who for **one** morsel of meat sold his birthright.	12:16
2	and yet offend in **one** point, he is guilty of all.	Jas 2:10
3	believest that there is **one** God; thou doest well:	2:19
3	is **one** lawgiver, who is able to save and to destroy:	4:12
4	and continue there **a** year, and buy and sell,	4:13
9	But, beloved, be not ignorant of this **one** thing,	2 Pt 3:8
5	that **one** day is with the Lord as a thousand years,	3:8
5	and a thousand years as **one** day.	3:8
9	Father, ... Word, ... Ghost: and these three are **one**.	1 Jn 5:7
9	and these three agree in **one**.	5:8
9	And the four beasts had **each** of them six wings	Rev 4:8
9	And the four beasts had each of them six wings	4:8
3	And **one** of the elders saith unto me, Weep not:	5:5
8	And I saw when the Lamb opened **one** of the seals,	Rev 6:1
1	**one** of the four beasts saying, Come and see.	6:1
3	And **one** of the elders answered, saying unto me,	7:13
1	heard **an** angel flying through the midst of heaven,	8:13
5	**One** woe is past; and, behold, there come two woes	9:12
8	I heard **a** voice from the four horns of the ... altar	9:13
8	saw **one** of his heads as it were wounded to death;	13:3
9	**one** of the four beasts gave unto the seven angels	15:7
3	And there came **one** of the seven angels	17:1
3	and **one** is, and the other is not yet come;	17:10
8	but receive power as kings **one** hour with the beast.	17:13
8	These have **one** mind, and shall give their power	17:13
8	For God hath put **in** their hearts	17:17
7	Therefore shall her plagues come in **one** day,	18:8
7	mighty city! for in **one** hour is thy judgment come.	18:10
7	For **in one** hour so great riches is come to nought.	18:17
7	for **in one** hour is she made desolate.	18:19
3	And **a** mighty angel took up a stone	18:21
4	And I saw **an** angel standing in the sun;	19:17
3	twelve pearls: **every** several gate was of one pearl:	21:21
1	twelve pearls: every several gate was of **one** pearl:	21:21
4	and yielded her fruit every month: (NT)	22:2

Classical Greek

Heis (masculine; *mia*, feminine; *hen*, neuter) is an extraordinarily diverse term throughout antiquity. Basically it denotes "one," the number. From that point it moves to assume various shades of meaning depending upon context and grammatical construction. It can mean "alone"; it can emphasize the "oneness" of something or someone; it can also be joined with a negative for emphasis (Matthew 27:14; Luke 11:26). The term joins with the relative pronoun *tis* (4948) for a more specific effect; hence, "a certain someone." However, it may simply mean "someone, anyone" when *tis* does not appear (Mark 14:51 [some manuscripts]; Luke 22:50). The sense of a numerical "one" is absent in the New Testament. Classical literature, papyri, and other Hellenistic writings all attest to these usages; hence, they are only secondarily important for understanding the New Testament uses which merely follow these already grammatically established principles.

New Testament Usage

Heis commonly means the uniqueness of something; i.e., the single or only one of its kind. In that respect the "oneness" or "uniqueness" of God is a vital tenet of the Biblical faith—both Old and New Testaments. God "alone" is one. The *shema* of Israel reflects the centrality of this distinction in the religion of Israel: "Hear, O Israel: The Lord our God is one Lord" (Deuteronomy 6:4; cf. Mark 12:29ff.). There is no other beside Him (Mark 12:32).

The Biblical religion allows for no other God but Yahweh. God's desire to bring all men to the knowledge of the truth is grounded in His status as the only God. Paul writes in 1 Timothy 2:5, "For there is one God" (*heis gar theos*). He continues that there is "one mediator between God and men" (*heis kai mesitēs theou kai anthrōpōn*), "the man Christ Jesus" (*anthrōpos Christos Iēsous*). No other is God except the one, the one God the Father, the one Lord Jesus Christ through whom all things came into existence (1 Corinthians 8:4,6; Ephesians 4:5,6).

Christ is unique in His role as Second Adam (1 Corinthians 15:22,45ff.). Just as sin and death entered the world through a single man (*henos anthrōpou*), in the same way, but even more effectively, a single Man, Jesus Christ (*tou henos Iēsou Christou*), was the bearer of God's grace (Romans 5:12,14, but see verses 12-20). He is the pivot of all history (Romans 5:14). The *one* died on behalf of many (2 Corinthians 5:14; cf. John 11:50ff.). The death of *one* for many brings unity to the many: "For ye are all one in Christ Jesus" (*pantes gar humeis heis este en Christō Iēsou*; Galatians 3:28). Christ is head over all His church (Ephesians 1:22; Colossians 1:18) which is one.

The unity of the Church through the one Spirit is fundamental to the message of the gospel. "There is one body, and one Spirit" (*Hen sōma kai hen pneuma*, Ephesians 4:4; cf. 2:18; 4:15,16). Unity becomes the basis for behavior as well as the criterion for the exercise of spiritual gifts (1 Corinthians 12-14), even though unity is expressed in diversity.

STRONG 1520, BAUER 230-32, MOULTON-MILLIGAN 187, KITTEL 2:434-42, LIDDELL-SCOTT 492, COLIN BROWN 2:716,719-20,722.

1506B. εἰς eis prep

Into, to, toward, unto, opposed to.

1. εἰς eis

1	there came wise men from the east **to** Jerusalem,	Matt 2:1
1	And he sent them **to** Bethlehem, and said,	2:8
1	And when they were come **into** the house,	2:11
1	they departed **into** their own country another way.	2:12
1	young child and his mother, and flee **into** Egypt,	2:13
1	young child and ... and departed **into** Egypt:	2:14
1	take the ... child ... and go **into** the land of Israel:	2:20
1	and came **into** the land of Israel.	2:21
1	he turned aside **into** the parts of Galilee:	2:22
1	And he came and dwelt in a city called Nazareth:	2:23
1	is hewn down, and cast **into** the fire.	3:10
1	I indeed baptize you with water **unto** repentance:	3:11
1	and gather his wheat **into** the garner;	3:12
1	was Jesus led up of the Spirit **into** the wilderness	4:1
1	Then the devil taketh him up **into** the holy city,	4:5
1	devil taketh ... **into** an exceeding high mountain,	4:8
1	John was cast **into** prison, he departed **into** Galilee;	4:12
1	he came and dwelt in Capernaum,	4:13
1	casting a net **into** the sea: for they were fishers.	4:18
1	And his fame went **throughout** all Syria:	Matt 4:24
1	seeing the multitudes, he went up **into** a mountain:	5:1
1	it is thenceforth good **for** nothing,	5:13
1	in no case enter **into** the kingdom of heaven.	5:20
1	say, Thou fool, shall be in danger **of** hell fire.	5:22
1	and thou be cast **into** prison.	5:25
1	not that thy whole body should be cast **into** hell.	5:29
1	not that thy whole body should be cast **into** hell.	5:30
1	neither **by** Jerusalem; ... the city of the great King.	5:35
1	whoever slaps you **on** your right cheek, (NASB)	5:39
1	when thou prayest, enter **into** thy closet,	6:6
1	And lead us not **into** temptation,	6:13
1	and the power, and the glory, **for** ever. Amen.	6:13
1	Behold the fowls of the air: for they sow not, (NT)	6:26
1	neither do they reap, nor gather **into** barns;	6:26
1	to day is, and to morrow is cast **into** the oven,	6:30
1	Take therefore no thought **for** the morrow:	6:34
1	and broad is the way, that leadeth **to** destruction,	7:13
1	and narrow is the way, which leadeth **unto** life,	7:14
1	is hewn down, and cast **into** the fire.	7:19
1	shall enter **into** the kingdom of heaven;	7:21
1	and offer the gift ... for a testimony **unto** them.	8:4
1	And when Jesus was entered **into** Capernaum,	8:5
1	shall be cast out **into** outer darkness:	8:12
1	And when Jesus was come **into** Peter's house,	8:14
1	gave commandment to depart **unto** the other side.	8:18
1	And when he was entered **into** a ship,	8:23
1	And when he was come **to** the other side	8:28
1	**into** the country of the Gergesenes,	8:28
1	suffer us to go away **into** the herd of swine.	8:31
1	they went **into** the herd of swine:	8:32
1	swine ran violently down a steep place **into** the sea,	8:32
1	and went their ways **into** the city,	8:33
1	behold, the whole city came out **to** meet Jesus:	8:34
1	And he entered **into** a ship, and passed over,	9:1
1	passed over, and came **into** his own city.	9:1
1	Arise, take up thy bed, and go **unto** thine house.	9:6
1	And he arose, and departed **to** his house.	9:7
1	not ... righteous, but sinners **to** repentance.	9:13
1	Neither do men put new wine **into** old bottles:	9:17
1	but they put new wine **into** new bottles,	9:17
1	And when Jesus came **into** the ruler's house,	9:23
1	And the fame hereof went abroad **into** all that land.	9:26
1	And when he was come **into** the house,	9:28
1	that he will send forth labourers **into** his harvest.	9:38
1	Go not **into** the way of the Gentiles,	10:5
1	and **into** any city of the Samaritans enter ye not:	10:5
1	Provide neither gold, ... nor brass in your purses,	10:9
1	Nor scrip **for** your journey, neither two coats,	10:10
1	And **into** whatsoever city or town ye shall enter,	10:11
1	And when ye come **into** an house, salute it.	10:12
1	for they will deliver you up to the councils,	10:17
1	**for** a testimony against them and the Gentiles	10:18
1	the brother shall deliver up the brother **to** death,	10:21
1	but he that endureth to the end shall be saved.	10:22
1	persecute you in this city, flee ye **into** another:	10:23
1	persecute you in this city, flee ye into another:	10:23
1	and what ye hear in the ear, that preach ye	10:27
1	receiveth a prophet in the name of a prophet	10:41
1	a righteous man in the name of a righteous man	10:41
1	a cup of cold water only in the name of a disciple,	10:42
1	What went ye out **into** the wilderness to see?	11:7
1	How he entered **into** the house of God,	12:4
1	he went **into** their synagogue:	12:9
1	and if it fall **into** a pit on the sabbath day,	12:11
1	my beloved, **in** whom my soul is well pleased:	12:18
1	till he send forth judgment **unto** victory.	12:20
1	else how can one enter **into** a strong man's house,	12:29
1	because they repented **at** the preaching of Jonas;	12:41
1	will return **into** my house from whence I came out;	12:44
1	will return **into** my house from whence I came out;	12:44
1	great multitudes ... so that he went **into** a ship,	13:2
1	He also that received seed **among** the thorns	13:22
1	the tares, and bind them in bundles to burn them:	13:30
1	but gather the wheat **into** my barn.	13:30
1	leaven, ... and hid **in** three measures of meal,	13:33
1	sent the multitude away, and went **into** the house:	13:36

εἰς 1506B

1 And shall cast them **into** a furnace of fire:	Matt 13:42
1 is like unto a net, that was cast **into** the sea,	13:47
1 and sat down, and gathered the good **into** vessels,	13:48
1 And shall cast them **into** the furnace of fire:	13:50
1 which is instructed **unto** the kingdom of heaven	13:52
1 And when he was come **into** his own country,	13:54
1 departed thence by ship **into** a desert place apart:	14:13
1 go **into** the villages, and buy themselves victuals.	14:15
1 and looking up **to** heaven, he blessed, and brake,	14:19
1 Jesus constrained his disciples to get **into** a ship,	14:22
1 and to go before him **unto** the other side,	14:22
1 he went up **into** a mountain apart to pray:	14:23
1 O thou of little faith, **wherefore** didst thou doubt?	14:31
1 And when they were come **into** the ship,	14:32
1 they came **into** the land of Gennesaret.	14:34
1 they came to land **at** Gennesaret. (NASB)	14:34
1 they sent out **into** all that country round about,	14:35
1 Not ... which goeth **into** the mouth defileth a man;	15:11
1 blind lead the blind, both shall fall **into** the ditch.	15:14
1 entereth in at the mouth goeth **into** the belly,	15:17
1 entereth in at the mouth goeth **into** the belly,	15:17
1 and is cast out **into** the draught?	15:17
1 and departed **into** the coasts of Tyre and Sidon.	15:21
1 I am not sent but **unto** the lost sheep ... of Israel.	15:24
1 and went up **into** a mountain, and sat down there.	15:29
1 He got **into** the boat, (NASB)	15:39
1 and came **into** the coasts of Magdala.	15:39
1 And when his disciples were come **to** the other side,	16:5
1 Jesus came **into** the coasts of Caesarea Philippi,	16:13
1 how that he must go **unto** Jerusalem, and suffer	16:21
1 and bringeth them up **into** an high mountain apart,	17:1
1 for ofttimes he falleth **into** the fire,	17:15
1 he falleth **into** the fire, and oft **into** the water.	17:15
1 Son ... shall be betrayed **into** the hands of men:	17:22
1 And when they were come **to** Capernaum,	17:24
1 And when he was come **into** the house,	17:25
1 go thou **to** the sea, and cast an hook,	17:27
1 ye shall not enter **into** the kingdom of heaven.	18:3
1 offend one of these little ones which believe **in** me,	18:6
1 that a millstone were hanged **about** his neck,	18:6
1 better for thee to enter **into** life halt or maimed,	18:8
1 hands or two feet to be cast **into** everlasting fire.	18:8
1 it is better for thee to enter **into** life with one eye,	18:9
1 than having two eyes to be cast **into** hell fire.	18:9
1 Moreover if thy brother shall trespass **against** thee,	18:15
1 two or three are gathered together **in** my name,	18:20
1 how oft shall my brother sin **against** me,	18:21
1 And his fellowservant fell down at his feet,	18:29
1 he would not: but went and cast him **into** prison,	18:30
1 and came **into** the coasts of Judaea beyond Jordan;	19:1
1 and they twain shall be one flesh? (NT)	19:5
1 thou wilt enter **into** life, keep the commandments.	19:17
1 a rich man shall hardly enter **into** the kingdom	19:23
1 for a rich man to enter **into** the kingdom of God.	19:24
1 went out ... to hire labourers **into** his vineyard.	20:1
1 he sent them **into** his vineyard.	20:2
1 And said unto them; Go ye also **into** the vineyard,	20:4
1 He saith unto them, Go ye also **into** the vineyard;	20:7
1 And Jesus going up **to** Jerusalem took the twelve	20:17
1 Behold, we go up **to** Jerusalem;	20:18
1 and they will condemn Him **to** death, (NASB)	20:18
1 And shall deliver him **to** the Gentiles to mock,	20:19
1 And when they drew nigh **unto** Jerusalem,	21:1
1 and were come **to** Bethphage,	21:1
1 come to Bethphage, **to** the Mount (NASB)	21:1
1 Go **into** the village over against you,	21:2
1 And when he was come **into** Jerusalem,	21:10
1 And Jesus went **into** the temple of God,	21:12
1 left the, and went out of the city **into** Bethany;	21:17
1 Now in the morning as he returned **into** the city,	21:18
1 Let no fruit grow on thee henceforward **for** ever.	21:19
1 Be thou removed, and be thou cast **into** the sea;	21:21
1 And when he was come **into** the temple,	21:23
1 the harlots go **into** the kingdom of God before you.	21:31
1 the same is become the head of the corner: (NT)	21:42
1 they held Him **to** be a prophet. (NASB)	21:46
1 to call them that were bidden **to** the wedding:	22:3
1 and all things are ready: come **unto** the marriage.	Matt 22:4
1 one **to** his farm, another to his merchandise:	22:5
1 one to his farm, another **to** his merchandise:	22:5
1 and as many as ye shall find, bid **to** the marriage.	22:9
1 So those servants went out **into** the highways,	22:10
1 and cast him **into** outer darkness;	22:13
1 for You are not partial **to** any. (NASB)	22:16
1 and persecute them from city **to** city:	23:34
1 Then shall they deliver you up **to** be afflicted,	24:9
1 But he that shall endure **unto** the end, ... be saved.	24:13
1 in all the world **for** a witness unto all nations;	24:14
1 who are in Judea flee **to** the mountains; (NASB)	24:16
1 until the day that Noe entered **into** the ark,	24:38
1 and went forth **to** meet the bridegroom.	25:1
1 the bridegroom cometh; go ye out **to** meet him.	25:6
1 that were ready went in with him **to** the marriage:	25:10
1 enter thou **into** the joy of thy lord.	25:21
1 enter thou **into** the joy of thy lord.	25:23
1 cast ye ... unprofitable servant **into** outer darkness:	25:30
1 Depart from me, ye cursed, **into** everlasting fire,	25:41
1 these shall go away **into** everlasting punishment:	25:46
1 punishment: but the righteous **into** life eternal.	25:46
1 Son of man is betrayed **to** be crucified. (NT)	26:2
1 **unto** the palace of the high priest;	26:3
1 saying, To what purpose is this waste?	26:8
1 for she hath wrought a good work **upon** me.	26:10
1 also this, ... be told **for** a memorial of her.	26:13
1 Go **into** the city to such a man, and say unto him,	26:18
1 which is shed for many **for** the remission of sins.	26:28
1 they went out **into** the mount of Olives.	26:30
1 risen again, I will go before you **into** Galilee.	26:32
1 Jesus with them **unto** a place called Gethsemane,	26:36
1 Watch and pray, that ye enter not **into** temptation:	26:41
1 Son of man is betrayed **into** the hands of sinners.	26:45
1 Put up again thy sword **into** his place:	26:52
1 Then did they spit **in** his face, and buffeted him;	26:67
1 And when he was gone out **into** the porch,	26:71
1 the pieces of silver **into** the sanctuary (NASB)	27:5
1 It is not lawful for to put them **into** the treasury,	27:6
1 bought ... the potter's field, **to** bury strangers in.	27:7
1 And gave them **for** the potter's field,	27:10
1 the soldiers ... took Jesus **into** the common hall,	27:27
1 And they spit **upon** him,	27:30
1 and took the reed, and smote him **on** the head.	27:30
1 and led him away to crucify him. (NT)	27:31
1 when they were come **unto** a place called Golgotha,	27:33
1 behold, the veil of the temple was rent **in** twain	27:51
1 behold, the veil of the temple was rent **in** twain	27:51
1 went **into** the holy city, and appeared unto many.	27:53
1 it began to dawn **toward** the first day of the week,	28:1
1 and, behold, he goeth before you **into** Galilee;	28:7
1 go tell my brethren that they go **into** Galilee,	28:10
1 behold, some of the watch came **into** the city,	28:11
1 Then the eleven disciples went away **into** Galilee,	28:16
1 **into** a mountain where Jesus had appointed them.	28:16
1 baptizing them in the name of the Father, and	28:19
1 the baptism of repentance **for** the remission of sins.	Mark 1:4
1 and was baptized of John **in** Jordan.	1:9
1 Spirit descending **on** him like a dove. (NIV)	1:10
1 the Spirit driveth him **into** the wilderness.	1:12
1 Jesus came **into** Galilee, preaching the gospel	1:14
1 And they went **into** Capernaum;	1:21
1 on the sabbath day he entered **into** the synagogue,	1:21
1 **throughout** all the region round about Galilee.	1:28
1 they entered **into** the house of Simon and Andrew,	1:29
1 departed **into** a solitary place, and there prayed.	1:35
1 he said unto them, Let us go **into** the next towns,	1:38
1 that I may preach ... **for** therefore came I forth.	1:38
1 And He went **into** their synagogues (NASB)	1:39
1 And he preached ... **throughout** all Galilee,	1:39
1 Moses commanded, **for** a testimony unto them.	1:44
1 Jesus could no more openly enter **into** the city,	1:45
1 again he entered **into** Capernaum after some days;	2:1
1 and it was noised that he was **in** the house.	2:1
1 take up thy bed, and go thy way **into** thine house.	2:11
1 And he went forth again **by** the sea side;	2:13
1 not to call the righteous, but sinners **to** repentance.	2:17

εἰς 1506B

1 And no man putteth new wine **into** old bottles:	Mark 2:22
1 but new wine must be put **into** new bottles.	2:22
1 How he went **into** the house of God	2:26
1 And he entered again **into** the synagogue;	3:1
1 "stand up **in** front of everyone." (NIV)	3:3
1 withdrew himself with his disciples **to** the sea:	3:7
1 And he goeth up **into** a mountain,	3:13
1 and they went **into** an house.	3:19
1 No man can enter **into** a strong man's house,	3:27
1 But he that shall blaspheme **against** the Holy Ghost	3:29
1 **against** the Holy Ghost hath never forgiveness,	3:29
1 so that he entered **into** a ship, and sat in the sea;	4:1
1 some fell **among** thorns, and the thorns grew up,	4:7
1 And other fell **on** good ground,	4:8
1 thirty, sixty, and a hundredfold (NASB) (NT)	4:8
1 some thirty, and some sixty, and some an hundred.	4:8
1 some thirty, and some sixty, and some an hundred.	4:8
1 word which has been sown **in** them. (NASB)	4:15
1 And these are they which are sown **among** thorns;	4:18
1 but that it should come **to** light. (NASB)	4:22
1 Let us pass over **unto** the other side.	4:35
1 and the waves beat **into** the ship,	4:37
1 And they came over **unto** the other side of the sea,	5:1
1 other side ... **into** the country of the Gadarenes.	5:1
1 Send us **into** the swine, that we may enter	5:12
1 into the swine, that we may enter **into** them.	5:12
1 and entered **into** the swine:	5:13
1 herd ran violently down a steep place **into** the sea,	5:13
1 and told it in the city, and in the country.	5:14
1 and told it in the city, and in the country.	5:14
1 And when he was come **into** the ship,	5:18
1 Go home **to** thy friends, and tell them how great	5:19
1 passed over again by ship **unto** the other side,	5:21
1 but rather grew worse, (NT)	5:26
1 go **in** peace, and be whole of thy plague.	5:34
1 cometh **to** the house of the ruler of the synagogue,	5:38
1 and came **into** his own country;	6:1
1 that they should take nothing **for** their journey,	6:8
1 no scrip, no bread, no money **in** their purse:	6:8
1 In what place soever ye enter **into** an house,	6:10
1 shake off the dust under your feet **for** a testimony	6:11
1 Come ye yourselves apart **into** a desert place,	6:31
1 they departed **into** a desert place by ship privately.	6:32
1 that they may go **into** the country round about,	6:36
1 he looked up **to** heaven, and blessed,	6:41
1 he constrained his disciples to get **into** the ship,	6:45
1 and to go **to** the other side before unto Bethsaida,	6:45
1 he departed **into** a mountain to pray.	6:46
1 And he went up **into** the ship;	6:51
1 they came **to** land at Gennesaret, (NASB)	6:53
1 And whithersoever he entered, **into** villages,	6:56
1 into villages, towns, or countryside (NIV) (NT)	6:56
1 into villages, towns, or countryside (NIV) (NT)	6:56
1 that entering **into** him can defile him:	7:15
1 he was entered **into** the house from the people,	7:17
1 thing from without entereth **into** the man,	7:18
1 Because it entereth not **into** his heart,	7:19
1 entereth not into his heart, but **into** the belly,	7:19
1 goeth out **into** the draught, purging all meats?	7:19
1 and went **into** the borders of Tyre and Sidon,	7:24
1 and entered **into** an house,	7:24
1 And when she was come **to** her house,	7:30
1 through Sidon to the Sea of Galilee, (NASB)	7:31
1 and put his fingers **into** his ears,	7:33
1 And looking up **to** heaven, he sighed,	7:34
1 if I send them away fasting **to** their own houses,	8:3
1 And straightway he entered **into** a ship	8:10
1 and came **into** the parts of Dalmanutha.	8:10
1 and entering **into** the ship again departed to	8:13
1 and entering into the ship again departed **to**	8:13
1 When I brake the five loaves **among** five thousand,	8:19
1 And when the seven **among** four thousand,	8:20
1 And he cometh **to** Bethsaida;	8:22
1 and when he had spit **on** his eyes,	8:23
1 And he sent him away **to** his house, saying,	8:26
1 Neither go **into** the town, nor tell it to any	8:26
1 **into** the towns of Caesarea Philippi:	8:27
1 up **into** an high mountain apart by themselves:	Mark 9:2
1 And ofttimes it hath cast him **into** the fire,	9:22
1 it hath cast him into the fire, and **into** the waters,	9:22
1 come out of him, and enter no more **into** him.	9:25
1 And when he was come **into** the house,	9:28
1 The Son of man is delivered **into** the hands of men,	9:31
1 And he came **to** Capernaum:	9:33
1 offend one of these little ones that believe **in** me,	9:42
1 about his neck, and he were cast **into** the sea.	9:42
1 it is better for thee to enter **into** life maimed,	9:43
1 than having two hands to go **into** hell,	9:43
1 hell, **into** the fire that never shall be quenched:	9:43
1 it is better for thee to enter halt **into** life,	9:45
1 than having two feet to be cast **into** hell,	9:45
1 **into** the fire that never shall be quenched:	9:45
1 it is better for thee to enter **into** the kingdom	9:47
1 than having two eyes to be cast **into** hell fire:	9:47
1 and cometh **into** the coasts of Judaea	10:1
1 And they twain shall be one flesh: (NT)	10:8
1 When they were **in** the house again,	10:10
1 as a little child, he shall not enter **therein**.	10:15
1 And when he was gone forth **into** the way,	10:17
1 that have riches enter **into** the kingdom of God!	10:23
1 how hard is it ... to enter **into** the kingdom of God!	10:24
1 than for a rich man to enter **into** the kingdom	10:25
1 And they were in the way going up **to** Jerusalem;	10:32
1 Saying, Behold, we go up **to** Jerusalem;	10:33
1 And they came **to** Jericho.	10:46
1 And when they came nigh **to** Jerusalem,	11:1
1 nigh to Jerusalem, **unto** Bethphage and Bethany,	11:1
1 nigh to Jerusalem, unto Bethphage and Bethany,	11:1
1 Go your way **into** the village over against you:	11:2
1 and as soon as ye be entered **into** it,	11:2
1 And many spread their garments **in** the way:	11:8
1 branches off ... trees, and strowed them **in** the way.	11:8
1 Jesus entered **into** Jerusalem, and into the temple:	11:11
1 Jesus entered into Jerusalem, and **into** the temple:	11:11
1 he went out **unto** Bethany with the twelve.	11:11
1 No man eat fruit of thee hereafter **for** ever.	11:14
1 And they come **to** Jerusalem:	11:15
1 and Jesus went **into** the temple,	11:15
1 Be thou removed, and be thou cast **into** the sea;	11:23
1 And they come again **to** Jerusalem:	11:27
1 is become the head of the corner: (NT)	12:10
1 for You are not partial **to** any, (NASB)	12:14
1 how the people cast money **into** the treasury:	12:41
1 than all they which have cast **into** the treasury:	12:43
1 And as he sat **upon** the mount of Olives	13:3
1 for they shall deliver you up **to** councils;	13:9
1 and **in** the synagogues ye shall be beaten:	13:9
1 **for** they shall deliver you up to councils;	13:9
1 gospel must first be published **among** all nations.	13:10
1 Now the brother shall betray the brother **to** death,	13:12
1 but he that shall endure **unto** the end, ... be saved.	13:13
1 let them that be in Judaea flee **to** the mountains:	13:14
1 is on the housetop not go down **into** the house,	13:15
1 And let him that is **in** the field not turn back again	13:16
1 not turn back again **for** to take up his garment.	13:16
1 Why was this waste of the ointment made?	14:4
1 she hath wrought a good work **on** me.	14:6
1 come aforehand to anoint my body **to** the burying.	14:8
1 gospel ... be preached **throughout** the whole world,	14:9
1 done shall be spoken of **for** a memorial of her.	14:9
1 and saith unto them, Go ye **into** the city,	14:13
1 his disciples went forth, and came **into** the city,	14:16
1 one of the twelve, that dippeth with me **in** the dish.	14:20
1 they went out **into** the mount of Olives.	14:26
1 I will go before you **into** Galilee.	14:28
1 came **to** a place which was named Gethsemane:	14:32
1 Watch ye and pray, lest ye enter **into** temptation.	14:38
1 Son of man is betrayed **into** the hands of sinners.	14:41
1 followed ... even **into** the palace of the high priest:	14:54
1 witness against Jesus to put him **to** death;	14:55
1 And the high priest stood up **in** the midst,	14:60
1 he went out **into** the porch; and the cock crew.	14:68
1 My God, my God, **why** hast thou forsaken me?	15:34
1 And **one** ran and filled a sponge full of vinegar,	15:36

289

εἰς 1506B

1 And the veil of the temple was rent in twain ...... Mark 15:38	1 shall they not both fall into the ditch? .... Luke 6:39
1 women which came up with him unto Jerusalem. 15:41	1 ended all his sayings in the audience of the people, ... 7:1
1 entering into the sepulchre, they saw a young man 16:5	1 he entered into Capernaum. 7:1
1 that he goeth before you into Galilee: 16:7	1 And they that were sent, returning to the house, ... 7:10
1 as they walked, and went into the country. 16:12	1 that he went into a city called Nain; 7:11
1 And he said unto them, Go ye into all the world, ... 16:15	1 What went ye out into the wilderness for to see? 7:24
1 he was received up into heaven, ... 16:19	1 rejected the counsel of God against themselves, ... 7:30
1 his lot was to burn incense when he went into the ... Luke 1:9	1 And he went into the Pharisee's house, ... 7:36
1 my words, which shall be fulfilled in their season. 1:20	1 Seest thou this woman? I entered into thine house, ... 7:44
1 he departed to his own house. 1:23	1 Thy faith hath saved thee; go in peace. 7:50
1 Gabriel was sent from God unto a city of Galilee, ... 1:26	1 other seed fell into the good soil, (NASB) 8:8
1 he shall reign over the house of Jacob for ever; 1:33	1 And that which fell among thorns are they, which, ... 8:14
1 and went into the hill country with haste, ... 1:39	1 that shall not be known and come to light. (NASB) 8:17
1 into the hill country with haste, into a city of Juda; 1:39	1 that he went into a ship with his disciples: 8:22
1 And entered into the house of Zacharias, ... 1:40	1 Let us go over unto the other side of the lake. 8:22
1 the voice of thy salutation sounded in mine ears, ... 1:44	1 and there came down a storm of wind on the lake; 8:23
1 them that fear him from generation to generation. 1:50	1 And they arrived at the country of the Gadarenes, ... 8:26
1 our fathers, to Abraham, and to his seed for ever. 1:55	1 and was driven of the devil into the wilderness. 8:29
1 and returned to her own house. 1:56	1 because many devils were entered into him. 8:30
1 to guide our feet into the way of peace. 1:79	1 would not command them to go out into the deep. 8:31
1 all went to be taxed, every one into his own city. 2:3	1 that he would suffer them to enter into them. 8:32
1 out of the city of Nazareth, into Judaea, ... 2:4	1 devils out of the man, and entered into the swine: 8:33
1 unto the city of David, which is called Bethlehem; 2:4	1 down a steep place into the lake, and were choked. 8:33
1 the angels were gone away from them into heaven, ... 2:15	1 and went and told it in the city and in the country. 8:34
1 they brought him to Jerusalem, to present him 2:22	1 and went and told it in the city and in the country. 8:34
1 And he came by the Spirit into the temple: 2:27	1 he went up into the ship, and returned back again. 8:37
1 Then took he him up in his arms, and blessed God, ... 2:28	1 Return to thine own house, and show how great 8:39
1 A light to lighten the Gentiles, ... 2:32	1 besought him that he would come into his house: 8:41
1 is set for the fall and rising again of many in Israel; 2:34	1 which had spent all her living upon physicians, ... 8:43
1 and for a sign which shall be spoken against; 2:34	1 thy faith hath made thee whole; go in peace. 8:48
1 returned into Galilee, to their own city Nazareth. 2:39	1 And when he came into the house, he suffered no 8:51
1 returned into Galilee, to their own city Nazareth. 2:39	1 he said unto them, Take nothing for your journey, ... 9:3
1 Now his parents went to Jerusalem every year 2:41	1 And whatsoever house ye enter into, there abide, ... 9:4
1 went up to Jerusalem after the custom of the feast. 2:42	1 dust from your feet for a testimony against them. 9:5
1 they turned back again to Jerusalem, seeking him. 2:45	1 that one of the old prophets was risen again. 9:8
1 he went down with them, and came to Nazareth, ... 2:51	1 and went aside privately into a desert place 9:10
1 And he came into all the country about Jordan, ... 3:3	1 that they may go into the towns and country 9:12
1 the baptism of repentance for the remission of sins; 3:3	1 except we should go and buy meat for all this 9:13
1 and the crooked shall be made straight, (NT) 3:5	1 looking up to heaven, he blessed them, and brake, ... 9:16
1 and the rough ways shall be made smooth; (NT) 3:5	1 and went up into a mountain to pray. 9:28
1 good fruit is hewn down, and cast into the fire. 3:9	1 and they feared as they entered into the cloud. 9:34
1 I indeed baptize you with water; 3:16	1 Let these sayings sink down into your ears, ... 9:44
1 and will gather the wheat into his garner; 3:17	1 shall be delivered into the hands of men. 9:44
1 and was led by the Spirit into the wilderness, ... 4:1	1 he stedfastly set his face to go to Jerusalem, ... 9:51
1 the devil, taking him up into an high mountain, ... 4:5	1 and entered into a village of the Samaritans, ... 9:52
1 And he brought him to Jerusalem, ... 4:9	1 his face was as though he would go to Jerusalem. 9:53
1 returned in the power of the Spirit into Galilee: 4:14	1 And they went to another village. 9:56
1 came to Nazareth, where he had been brought up: 4:16	1 bid them farewell, which are at home at my house. 9:61
1 he went into the synagogue on the sabbath day, ... 4:16	1 looking back, is fit for the kingdom (NT) 9:62
1 we heard was done at Capernaum, (NASB) 4:23	1 and looking back, is fit for the kingdom of God. 9:62
1 unto none ... was Elias sent, save unto Sarepta, ... 4:26	1 before his face into every city and place, ... 10:1
1 that they might cast him down headlong. 4:29	1 that he would send forth labourers into his harvest. 10:2
1 And came down to Capernaum, a city of Galilee, ... 4:31	1 And into whatsoever house ye enter, first say, ... 10:5
1 And when the devil had thrown him in the midst, ... 4:35	1 Go not from house to house. 10:7
1 And the fame of him went out into every place 4:37	1 And into whatsoever city ye enter, ... 10:8
1 and entered into Simon's house. 4:38	1 But into whatsoever city ye enter, ... 10:10
1 he departed and went into a desert place: 4:42	1 go your ways out into the streets of the same, ... 10:10
1 to other cities also: for therefore am I sent. 4:43	1 the dust ... which clings to our feet, (NASB) (NT) 10:11
1 kept on preaching in the synagogues (NIV) 4:44	1 certain man went down from Jerusalem to Jericho, ... 10:30
1 And he entered into one of the ships, ... 5:3	1 and brought him to an inn, and took care of him. 10:34
1 Launch out into the deep, and let down your nets 5:4	1 neighbour unto him that fell among the thieves? 10:36
1 and let down your nets for a draught. 5:4	1 that he entered into a certain village: 10:38
1 as Moses commanded, for a testimony unto them. 5:14	1 Martha received him into her house. 10:38
1 the power ... was present for Him (NASB) 5:17	1 And lead us not into temptation; but deliver us 11:4
1 tiling with his couch into the midst before Jesus. 5:19	1 and my children are with me in bed; I cannot rise 11:7
1 and take up thy couch, and go into thine house. 5:24	1 I will return unto my house whence I came out. 11:24
1 and departed to his own house, glorifying God. 5:25	1 for they repented at the preaching of Jonas; 11:32
1 not to call the righteous, but sinners to repentance. 5:32	1 putteth it in a secret place, neither under a bushel, ... 11:33
1 And no man putteth new wine into old bottles; 5:37	1 I will send to them prophets and apostles, (NASB) 11:49
1 But new wine must be put into new bottles; 5:38	1 after he hath killed hath power to cast into hell; 12:5
1 How he went into the house of God, ... 6:4	1 And whosoever shall speak a word against the Son 12:10
1 that he entered into the synagogue and taught: 6:6	1 unto him that blasphemeth against the Holy Ghost 12:10
1 Rise up, and stand forth in the midst. 6:8	1 thou hast much goods laid up for many years; 12:19
1 that he went out into a mountain to pray. 6:12	1 treasure for himself, and is not rich toward God. 12:21
1 And he lifted up his eyes on his disciples, ... 6:20	1 is to day ... and to morrow is cast into the oven; 12:28
1 And unto him that smiteth thee on the one cheek 6:29	1 I am come to send fire on the earth; 12:49
1 and running over, shall men give into your bosom. 6:38	1 and the officer cast thee into prison. 12:58

εἰς 1506B

1 and if it bear fruit, well: (NT)	Luke	13:9
1 and could in no wise lift up herself.		13:11
1 seed, which a man took, and cast into his garden;		13:19
1 and it grew, and waxed a great tree; (NT)		13:19
1 a woman took and hid in three measures of meal,		13:21
1 teaching, and journeying toward Jerusalem.		13:22
1 went into the house of one of the chief Pharisees		14:1
1 of you shall have an ass or an ox fallen into a pit,		14:5
1 When thou art bidden of any man to a wedding,		14:8
1 sit not down in the highest room;		14:8
1 go and sit down in the lowest room;		14:10
1 Go out quickly into the streets and lanes of the city,		14:21
1 Go out into the highways and hedges,		14:23
1 to see if he has enough to complete it? (NASB)		14:28
1 what king, going to make war against another king,		14:31
1 neither fit for the land, nor yet for the dunghill;		14:35
1 neither fit for the land, nor yet for the dunghill;		14:35
1 And when he cometh home, (NT)		15:6
1 and took his journey into a far country,		15:13
1 and he sent him into his fields to feed swine.		15:15
1 And when he came to himself, he said,		15:17
1 I have sinned against heaven, and before thee,		15:18
1 son said … Father, I have sinned against heaven,		15:21
1 and put a ring on his hand, and shoes on his feet;		15:22
1 and put a ring on his hand, and shoes on his feet;		15:22
1 they may receive me into their houses.		16:4
1 in their generation wiser than the children of light.		16:8
1 they may receive you into everlasting habitations.		16:9
1 and every man presseth into it.		16:16
1 was carried by the angels into Abraham's bosom:		16:22
1 that thou wouldest send him to my father's house:		16:27
1 lest they also come into this place of torment.		16:28
1 hanged about his neck, and he cast into the sea,		17:2
1 If thy brother trespass against thee, rebuke him;		17:3
1 And if he trespass against thee seven times in a day,		17:4
1 And it came to pass, as he went to Jerusalem,		17:11
1 And as he entered into a certain village,		17:12
1 shineth unto the other part under heaven;		17:24
1 until the day that Noe entered into the ark,		17:27
1 field should go back for anything. (NIV)		17:31
1 lest by her continual coming she weary me.		18:5
1 Two men went up into the temple to pray;		18:10
1 would not lift up so much as his eyes unto heaven,		18:13
1 but smote upon his breast, saying, God be merciful		18:13
1 I tell you, this man went down to his house		18:14
1 as a little child shall in no wise enter therein.		18:17
1 that have riches enter into the kingdom of God!		18:24
1 than for a rich man to enter into the kingdom		18:25
1 said unto them, Behold, we go up to Jerusalem,		18:31
1 that as he was come nigh unto Jericho,		18:35
1 he ran … climbed a sycamore-fig tree (NIV) (NT)		19:4
1 into a far country to receive for himself a kingdom,		19:12
1 spoken, he went before, ascending up to Jerusalem.		19:28
1 when he was come nigh to Bethphage and Bethany,		19:29
1 Saying, Go ye into the village over against you;		19:30
1 And he went into the temple, and began to cast out		19:45
1 the same is become the head of the corner? (NT)		20:17
1 that so they might deliver him unto the power and		20:20
1 the rich men casting their gifts into the treasury.		21:1
1 their abundance cast in unto the offerings of God:		21:4
1 persecute … delivering you up to the synagogues,		21:12
1 And it shall turn to you for a testimony.		21:13
1 Settle it therefore in your hearts,		21:14
1 them which are in Judaea flee to the mountains;		21:21
1 not them that are in the countries enter thereinto.		21:21
1 and shall be led away captive into all nations:		21:24
1 in the mount that is called the mount of Olives.		21:37
1 Then entered Satan into Judas surnamed Iscariot,		22:3
1 Behold, when ye are entered into the city,		22:10
1 follow him into the house where he entereth in.		22:10
1 the house that he enters (NASB) (NT)		22:10
1 Take this and share it among yourselves; (NASB)		22:17
1 this do in remembrance of me.		22:19
1 go with thee, both into prison, and to death.		22:33
1 go with thee, both into prison, and to death.		22:33
1 and went, as he was wont, to the mount of Olives;		22:39
1 Pray that ye enter not into temptation.		22:40

1 rise and pray, lest ye enter into temptation.	Luke	22:46
1 and brought him into the high priest's house.		22:54
1 things blasphemously spake they against him.		22:65
1 came together, and led him into their council,		22:66
1 Who … for murder, was cast into prison.		23:19
1 that for sedition and murder was cast into prison,		23:25
1 when you come into your kingdom. (NIV)		23:42
1 Father, into thy hands I commend my spirit;		23:46
1 afraid, and bowed down their faces to the earth,		24:5
1 must be delivered into the hands of sinful men,		24:7
1 two of them went that same day to a village		24:13
1 rulers delivered him to be condemned to death,		24:20
1 suffered these things, and to enter into his glory?		24:26
1 drew nigh unto the village, whither they went:		24:28
1 rose up the same hour, and returned to Jerusalem,		24:33
1 and that repentance for forgiveness of sins (NASB)		24:47
1 among all nations, beginning at Jerusalem.		24:47
1 And he led them out as far as to Bethany,		24:50
1 was parted from them, and carried up into heaven.		24:51
1 they worshipped him, and returned to Jerusalem		24:52
1 The same came for a witness,	John	1:7
1 was the true Light, … that cometh into the world.		1:9
1 He came unto his own,		1:11
1 even to them that believe on his name;		1:12
1 begotten Son, which is in the bosom of the Father,		1:18
1 Jesus would go forth into Galilee,		1:43
1 Jesus was called, and his disciples, to the marriage.		2:2
1 and his disciples believed on him.		2:11
1 After this he went down to Capernaum,		2:12
1 and Jesus went up to Jerusalem,		2:13
1 many believed in his name, when they saw		2:23
1 enter the second time into his mother's womb,		3:4
1 he cannot enter into the kingdom of God.		3:5
1 And no man hath ascended up to heaven,		3:13
1 whosoever believeth in him should not perish,		3:15
1 that whosoever believeth in him should not perish,		3:16
1 God sent not his Son into the world to condemn		3:17
1 He that believeth on him is not condemned:		3:18
1 in the name of the only begotten Son of God.		3:18
1 that light is come into the world,		3:19
1 Jesus and his disciples into the land of Judaea;		3:22
1 For John was not yet cast into prison.		3:24
1 He that believeth on the Son hath everlasting life:		3:36
1 He left Judaea, and departed again into Galilee.		4:3
1 Then cometh he to a city of Samaria,		4:5
1 For his disciples were gone away unto the city		4:8
1 I shall give him shall never thirst; (NT)		4:14
1 a well of water springing up into everlasting life.		4:14
1 went her way into the city, and saith to the men,		4:28
1 and gathereth fruit unto life eternal:		4:36
1 and ye are entered into their labours.		4:38
1 believed on him for the saying of the woman,		4:39
1 he departed thence, and went into Galilee.		4:43
1 Then when he was come into Galilee,		4:45
1 for they also went unto the feast.		4:45
1 So Jesus came again into Cana of Galilee,		4:46
1 that Jesus was come out of Judaea into Galilee,		4:47
1 when he was come out of Judaea into Galilee.		4:54
1 and Jesus went up to Jerusalem.		5:1
1 I have no man, … to put me into the pool:		5:7
1 and shall not come into condemnation;		5:24
1 but is passed from death unto life.		5:24
1 that have done good, unto the resurrection of life;		5:29
1 done evil, unto the resurrection of damnation.		5:29
1 that accuseth you, even Moses, in whom ye trust.		5:45
1 And Jesus went up into a mountain,		6:3
1 but what are they among so many?		6:9
1 that prophet that should come into the world.		6:14
1 he departed again into a mountain himself alone.		6:15
1 And entered into a ship,		6:17
1 and went over the sea toward Capernaum.		6:17
1 Then they willingly received him into the ship:		6:21
1 the ship was at the land whither they went.		6:21
1 save that one whereinto his disciples were entered,		6:22
1 that Jesus went not with his disciples into the boat,		6:22
1 they themselves got into the small boats, (NASB)		6:24
1 they also took shipping, and came to Capernaum,		6:24

εἰς 1506B

1 for that meat which endureth **unto** everlasting life,.. John 6:27		
1 that ye believe **on** him whom he hath sent.		6:29
1 and he that believeth **on** me shall never thirst.		6:35
1 which seeth the Son, and believeth **on** him,		6:40
1 He that believeth **on** me hath everlasting life.		6:47
1 if any man eat of this bread, he shall live **for** ever:		6:51
1 he that eateth of this bread shall live **for** ever.		6:58
1 many of his disciples went back, (NT)		6:66
1 Depart hence, and go **into** Judaea,		7:3
1 For neither did his brethren believe **in** him.		7:5
1 Go ye up **unto** this feast:		7:8
1 I go not up yet **unto** this feast:		7:8
1 then went he also up **unto** the feast, not openly,		7:10
1 Jesus went up **into** the temple, and taught.		7:14
1 And many of the people believed **on** him, and said,		7:31
1 will he go **unto** the dispersed among the Gentiles,		7:35
1 He that believeth **on** me, as the scripture hath said,		7:38
1 which they that believe **on** him should receive:		7:39
1 Have any of the rulers ... believed **on** him?		7:48
1 And every man went **unto** his own house.		7:53
1 Jesus went **unto** the mount of Olives.		8:1
1 in the morning he came again **into** the temple,		8:2
1 and with his finger wrote **on** the ground,		8:6
1 again he stooped down, and wrote **on** the ground.		8:8
1 and I speak **to** the world those things		8:26
1 As he spake these words, many believed **on** him.		8:30
1 And the servant abideth not in the house **for** ever:		8:35
1 abideth not ... but the Son abideth ever. (NT)		8:35
1 he shall never see death. (NT)		8:51
1 he shall never taste of death. (NT)		8:52
1 wash **in** the pool of Siloam,		9:7
1 and said unto me, Go **to** the pool of Siloam,		9:11
1 Dost thou believe **on** the Son of God?		9:35
1 Who is he, Lord, that I might believe **on** him?		9:36
1 For judgment I am come into this world,		9:39
1 For judgment I am come into this world,		9:39
1 entereth not by the door **into** the sheepfold,		10:1
1 And I give **unto** them eternal life;		10:28
1 the Father hath sanctified, and sent **into** the world,		10:36
1 **into** the place where John at first baptized;		10:40
1 And many believed **on** him there.		10:42
1 Let us go **into** Judaea again.		11:7
1 he that believeth **in** me, though he were dead,		11:25
1 liveth and believeth **in** me shall never die.		11:26
1 liveth and believeth **in** me shall never die.		11:26
1 the Son of God, which should come **into** the world.		11:27
1 Now Jesus was not yet come **into** the town,		11:30
1 saying, She goeth **unto** the grave to weep there.		11:31
1 she fell down **at** his feet, saying unto him, Lord,		11:32
1 again groaning in himself cometh **to** the grave.		11:38
1 Then many of the Jews ... believed **on** him.		11:45
1 let him thus alone, all men will believe **on** him:		11:48
1 but that also he should gather together **in** one		11:52
1 near to the wilderness, **into** a city called Ephraim,		11:54
1 went thence unto a country near **to** the wilderness,		11:54
1 and many went out of the country up **to** Jerusalem		11:55
1 What think ye, that he will not come **to** the feast?		11:56
1 six days before the passover came **to** Bethany,		12:1
1 **against** the day of my burying hath she kept this.		12:7
1 many of the Jews went away, ... believed **on** Jesus.		12:11
1 next day much people that were come **to** the feast,		12:12
1 they heard that Jesus was coming **to** Jerusalem,		12:12
1 and went forth **to** meet him, and cried, Hosanna:		12:13
1 Except a corn of wheat fall **into** ... ground and die,		12:24
1 that hateth his life ... shall keep it **unto** life eternal.		12:25
1 but for this cause came I **unto** this hour.		12:27
1 heard out of the law that Christ abideth **for** ever:		12:34
1 While ye have light, believe **in** the light,		12:36
1 so many miracles ... yet they believed not **on** him,		12:37
1 among the chief rulers also many believed **on** him;		12:42
1 Jesus cried and said, He that believeth **on** me,		12:44
1 believeth not **on** me, but on him that sent me.		12:44
1 believeth not **on** me, but on him that sent me.		12:44
1 I am come a light **into** the world,		12:46
1 believeth **on** me should not abide in darkness.		12:46
1 he loved them **unto** the end.		13:1
1 the devil having now put **into** the heart of Judas		13:2
1 that the Father had given all things **into** his hands, John 13:3		
1 After that he poureth water **into** a basin,		13:5
1 Peter saith ... Thou shalt never wash my feet. (NT)		13:8
1 Then the disciples looked one **on** another,		13:22
1 And after the sop Satan entered **into** him.		13:27
1 those things that we have need of **against** the feast;		13:29
1 ye believe **in** God, believe also **in** me.		14:1
1 ye believe **in** God, believe also **in** me.		14:1
1 He that believeth **on** me,		14:12
1 Comforter, that he may abide with you **for** ever;		14:16
1 and men gather them, and cast them **into** the fire,		15:6
1 these things they will do **to** you (NASB)		15:21
1 Of sin, because they believe not **on** me;		16:9
1 Spirit of truth, ... he will guide you **into** all truth:		16:13
1 but your sorrow shall be turned **into** joy.		16:20
1 for joy that a man is born **into** the world.		16:21
1 from the Father, and am come **into** the world:		16:28
1 that ye shall be scattered, every man **to** his own,		16:32
1 and lifted up his eyes **to** heaven, and said,		17:1
1 As thou hast sent me **into** the world,		17:18
1 even so have I also sent them **into** the world.		17:18
1 but for them also which shall believe **on** me		17:20
1 that they may be made perfect **in** one;		17:23
1 was a garden, **into** the which he entered,		18:1
1 they went backward, and fell to the ground. (NT)		18:6
1 Put up thy sword **into** the sheath:		18:11
1 and went in with Jesus **into** the palace		18:15
1 Jesus from Caiaphas **unto** the hall of judgment:		18:28
1 they themselves went not **into** the judgment hall,		18:28
1 Then Pilate entered **into** the judgment hall again,		18:33
1 I am a king. **To** this end was I born,		18:37
1 and **for** this cause came I into the world,		18:37
1 and for this cause came I **into** the world,		18:37
1 And went again **into** the judgment hall,		19:9
1 in a place that is called the Pavement,		19:13
1 **into** a place called the place of a skull,		19:17
1 that disciple took her **unto** his own home.		19:27
1 They shall look **on** him whom they pierced.		19:37
1 early, when it was yet dark, **unto** the sepulchre,		20:1
1 and that other disciple, and came **to** the sepulchre.		20:3
1 and came first **to** the sepulchre.		20:4
1 and went **into** the sepulchre,		20:6
1 but wrapped together **in** a place by itself.		20:7
1 other disciple, which came first **to** the sepulchre,		20:8
1 she stooped down, and looked **into** the sepulchre,		20:11
1 she turned herself back, and saw Jesus (NT)		20:14
1 came Jesus and stood **in** the midst,		20:19
1 and put my finger **into** the print of the nails,		20:25
1 and thrust my hand **into** his side,		20:25
1 stood **in** the midst, and said, Peace be unto you.		20:26
1 reach hither thy hand, and thrust it **into** my side:		20:27
1 went forth, and entered **into** a ship immediately;		21:3
1 morning was now come, Jesus stood **on** the shore:		21:4
1 Cast the net **on** the right side of the ship,		21:6
1 and did cast himself **into** the sea.		21:7
1 As soon then as they were come **to** land,		21:9
1 and drew the net **to** land, full (NASB)		21:11
1 Then went this saying abroad **among** the brethren,		21:23
1 And while they looked stedfastly **toward** heaven..... Acts 1:10		
1 why stand ye gazing up **into** heaven?		1:11
1 Jesus, which is taken up from you **into** heaven,		1:11
1 in like manner as ye have seen him go **into** heaven.		1:11
1 Then returned they **unto** Jerusalem		1:12
1 they went up **into** an upper room,		1:13
1 that he might go **to** his own place.		1:25
1 there were Jews living **in** Jerusalem (NASB)		2:5
1 The sun shall be turned **into** darkness,		2:20
1 sun ... **into** darkness, and the moon **into** blood,		2:20
1 a man approved of God **among** you by miracles		2:22
1 For David speaketh **concerning** him,		2:25
1 Because thou wilt not leave my soul **in** hell,		2:27
1 that his soul was not left **in** hell,		2:31
1 For David is not ascended **into** the heavens:		2:34
1 the name of Jesus Christ **for** the remission of sins,		2:38
1 and to all that are afar off, (NT)		2:39
1 Peter and John went up together **into** the temple		3:1
1 to ask alms of them that entered **into** the temple;		3:2

εἰς 1506B

1 about to go **into** the temple asked an alms.	Acts	3:3
1 Peter, fastening his eyes **upon** him with John, said,		3:4
1 And Peter, ... said, Look **on** us.		3:4
1 and entered with them **into** the temple,		3:8
1 be converted, **that** your sins may be blotted out,		3:19
1 and put them **in** hold unto the next day:		4:3
1 and put them in hold **unto** the next day:		4:3
1 that their rulers, and elders, and scribes, (NT)		4:5
1 stone ... which is become the head **of** the corner.		4:11
1 But that it spread no further **among** the people,		4:17
1 By stretching forth thine hand **to** heal;		4:30
1 carried the sick out **into** the streets,		5:15
1 out of the cities round about **unto** Jerusalem,		5:16
1 they entered **into** the temple early in the morning,		5:21
1 and sent **to** the prison to have them brought.		5:21
1 and all, ... were scattered, and brought **to** nought.		5:36
1 speak blasphemous words **against** Moses,		6:11
1 and caught him, and brought him **to** the council,		6:12
1 looking stedfastly **on** him,		6:15
1 and come **into** the land which I shall show thee.		7:3
1 removed him **into** this land, wherein ye now dwell.		7:4
1 removed him into this land, **wherein** ye now dwell.		7:4
1 that he would give it to him **for** a possession,		7:5
1 moved with envy, sold Joseph **into** Egypt:		7:9
1 there was grain **in** Egypt, (NASB)		7:12
1 So Jacob went down **into** Egypt, and died,		7:15
1 And were carried over **into** Sychem,		7:16
1 **to** the end they might not live.		7:19
1 and nourished him **for** her own son.		7:21
1 and would have set them **at** one again,		7:26
1 And now come, I will send thee **into** Egypt.		7:34
1 and in their hearts turned back again **into** Egypt,		7:39
1 have received the law **by** the disposition of angels,		7:53
1 looked up stedfastly **into** heaven,		7:55
1 haling men and women committed them **to** prison.		8:3
1 Then Philip went down **to** the city of Samaria,		8:5
1 only they were baptized **in** the name of the Lord		8:16
1 Thy money perish with thee, (NT)		8:20
1 I perceive that thou art **in** the gall of bitterness,		8:23
1 returned **to** Jerusalem, and preached the gospel		8:25
1 way that goeth down from Jerusalem **unto** Gaza,		8:26
1 and had come to Jerusalem **for** to worship,		8:27
1 they went down both **into** the water, both Philip		8:38
1 But Philip was found **at** Azotus:		8:40
1 preached in all the cities, till he came **to** Caesarea.		8:40
1 and slaughter **against** the disciples of the Lord,		9:1
1 And desired of him letters **to** Damascus		9:2
1 he might bring them bound **unto** Jerusalem.		9:2
1 the Lord said unto him, Arise, and go **into** the city,		9:6
1 they led him ... and brought him **into** Damascus.		9:8
1 and entered **into** the house;		9:17
1 Is this not he who **in** Jerusalem, (NASB)		9:21
1 and came hither **for** that intent,		9:21
1 And when Saul was come **to** Jerusalem,		9:26
1 moved about freely **in** Jerusalem. (NIV)		9:28
1 they brought him down **to** Caesarea,		9:30
1 and sent him forth **to** Tarsus.		9:30
1 they brought him **into** the upper chamber:		9:39
1 are come up **for** a memorial before God.		10:4
1 now send men **to** Joppa, and call for one Simon,		10:5
1 when he had declared ... he sent them **to** Joppa.		10:8
1 and the vessel was received up again **into** heaven.		10:16
1 by an holy angel to send for thee **into** his house,		10:22
1 And the morrow after they entered **into** Caesarea.		10:24
1 Send therefore to Joppa, and call hither Simon,		10:32
1 that through his name whosoever believeth **in** him		10:43
1 And when Peter was come up **to** Jerusalem,		11:2
1 **Upon** the which when I had fastened mine eyes,		11:6
1 unclean hath at any time entered **into** my mouth.		11:8
1 and all were drawn up again **into** heaven.		11:10
1 and we entered **into** the man's house:		11:12
1 Send men **to** Joppa, and call for Simon,		11:13
1 the Gentiles granted repentance **unto** life.		11:18
1 which, when they were come **to** Antioch,		11:20
1 these things came **unto** the ears of the church		11:22
1 departed Barnabas **to** Tarsus, for to seek Saul:		11:25
1 he brought him **unto** Antioch.		11:26
1 came prophets from Jerusalem **unto** Antioch.	Acts	11:27
1 determined to send relief **unto** the brethren		11:29
1 he had apprehended him, he put him **in** prison,		12:4
1 came unto the iron gate that leadeth **unto** the city;		12:10
1 And he departed, and went **into** another place.		12:17
1 And he went down from Judaea **to** Caesarea,		12:19
1 Barnabas and Saul returned **to** (NASB, margin)		12:25
1 Separate me Barnabas and Saul **for** the work		13:2
1 forth by the Holy Ghost, departed **unto** Seleucia;		13:4
1 and from thence they sailed **to** Cyprus.		13:4
1 filled with the Holy Ghost, set his eyes **on** him,		13:9
1 from Paphos, they came **to** Perga in Pamphylia:		13:13
1 John departing from them returned **to** Jerusalem;		13:13
1 they came **to** Antioch in Pisidia,		13:14
1 and went **into** the synagogue on the sabbath day,		13:14
1 he raised up unto them David **to be** their king;		13:22
1 and laid him **in** a sepulchre.		13:29
1 came up with him from Galilee **to** Jerusalem,		13:31
1 now no more to return **to** corruption,		13:34
1 speak further ... **on** the next Sabbath. (NASB)		13:42
1 lo, we turn **to** the Gentiles.		13:46
1 I have set thee **to be** a light of the Gentiles,		13:47
1 that thou shouldest be **for** salvation		13:47
1 as many as were ordained **to** eternal life believed.		13:48
1 and came **unto** Iconium.		13:51
1 that they went both together **into** the synagogue		14:1
1 and fled **unto** Lystra and Derbe, cities of Lycaonia,		14:6
1 and ran in **among** the people, crying out,		14:14
1 he rose up, and came **into** the city:		14:20
1 the next day he departed with Barnabas **to** Derbe.		14:20
1 they returned again **to** Lystra, and to Iconium,		14:21
1 they returned **to** Lystra, and to Iconium, (NASB)		14:21
1 to Lystra, and to Iconium, and **to** Antioch, (NASB)		14:21
1 tribulation enter **into** the kingdom of God.		14:22
1 to the Lord, **on** whom they believed.		14:23
1 throughout Pisidia, they came **to** Pamphylia.		14:24
1 they had spoken the word **in** Perga, (NASB)		14:25
1 they went down **into** Attalia:		14:25
1 And thence sailed **to** Antioch,		14:26
1 the grace of God **for** the work which they fulfilled.		14:26
1 should go up to Jerusalem **unto** the apostles		15:2
1 And when they were come **to** Jerusalem,		15:4
1 **to** Antioch with Paul and Barnabas;		15:22
1 when they were dismissed, they came **to** Antioch:		15:30
1 and went not with them **to** the work.		15:38
1 so Barnabas took Mark, and sailed **unto** Cyprus;		15:39
1 Then came he **to** Derbe and Lystra:		16:1
1 He came to Derbe and then **to** Lystra: (NIV)		16:1
1 were trying to go **into** Bithnia: (NASB)		16:7
1 And they passing by Mysia came down **to** Troas.		16:8
1 saying, Come over **into** Macedonia, and help us.		16:9
1 we endeavoured to go **into** Macedonia,		16:10
1 we came with a straight course **to** Samothracia,		16:11
1 and the next day **to** Neapolis;		16:11
1 And from thence **to** Philippi,		16:12
1 come **into** my house, and abide there.		16:15
1 And it came to pass, as we went **to** prayer,		16:16
1 drew them **into** the marketplace unto the rulers,		16:19
1 they cast them **into** prison,		16:23
1 thrust them **into** the inner prison,		16:24
1 and made their feet fast **in** the stocks.		16:24
1 And when he had brought them **into** his house,		16:34
1 and have cast us **into** prison;		16:37
1 and entered into the house **of** Lydia:		16:40
1 through Amphipolis ... they came **to** Thessalonica,		17:1
1 and sought to bring them **out** to the people.		17:5
1 sent away Paul and Silas by night **unto** Berea:		17:10
1 went **into** the synagogue of the Jews.		17:10
1 thou bringest certain strange things **to** our ears:		17:20
1 which were there spent their time **in** nothing else,		17:21
1 Paul departed from Athens, and came **to** Corinth;		18:1
1 from henceforth I will go **unto** the Gentiles.		18:6
1 entered **into** a certain man's house, named Justus,		18:7
1 and sailed thence **into** Syria,		18:18
1 And he came **to** Ephesus, and left them there:		18:19
1 but he himself entered **into** the synagogue,		18:19
1 keep this feast that cometh **in** Jerusalem:		18:21

293

εἰς 1506B

1 when he had landed **at** Caesarea, and gone up,	Acts	18:22
1 and saluted the church, he went down **to** Antioch.		18:22
1 a certain Jew named Apollos, ... came **to** Ephesus.		18:24
1 And when he was disposed to pass **into** Achaia,		18:27
1 came **to** Ephesus: and finding certain disciples,		19:1
1 **Unto** what then were ye baptized?		19:3
1 And they said, **Unto** John's baptism.		19:3
1 that they should believe **on** him		19:4
1 should come after him, that is, **on** Christ Jesus.		19:4
1 they were baptized **in** the name of the Lord Jesus.		19:5
1 And he went **into** the synagogue,		19:8
1 passed through Macedonia ... to go **to** Jerusalem,		19:21
1 So he sent **into** Macedonia two of them		19:22
1 but he himself stayed **in** Asia for a season.		19:22
1 our **craft** is in danger to be set **at** nought;		19:27
1 Artemis be regarded as worthless (NASB)		19:27
1 they rushed with one accord **into** the theatre.		19:29
1 when Paul would have entered in **unto** the people,		19:30
1 not adventure himself **into** the theatre.		19:31
1 and departed for to go **into** Macedonia.		20:1
1 he came **into** Greece.		20:2
1 as he was about to sail **into** Syria,		20:3
1 and came unto them **to** Troas in five days;		20:6
1 And we went before to ship, and sailed **unto** Assos,		20:13
1 And when he met with us **at** Assos, we took him in,		20:14
1 at Assos, we took him in, and came **to** Mitylene.		20:14
1 and the next day we arrived **at** Samos,		20:15
1 and the next day we came **to** Miletus.		20:15
1 to be **at** Jerusalem the day of Pentecost.		20:16
1 And from Miletus he sent **to** Ephesus,		20:17
1 Ye know, from the first day that I came **into** Asia,		20:18
1 repentance **toward** God, and faith toward our Lord		20:21
1 and faith **toward** our Lord Jesus Christ.		20:21
1 behold, I go bound in the spirit **unto** Jerusalem,		20:22
1 shall grievous wolves enter in **among** you,		20:29
1 And they accompanied him **unto** the ship.		20:38
1 we came with a straight course **unto** Coos,		21:1
1 and the day following **unto** Rhodes,		21:1
1 and from thence **unto** Patara:		21:1
1 And finding a ship sailing over **unto** Phenicia,		21:2
1 we left it on the left hand, and sailed **into** Syria,		21:3
1 and sailed into Syria, and landed **at** Tyre,		21:3
1 that he should not go up **to** Jerusalem.		21:4
1 we took ship; and they returned home again. (NT)		21:6
1 we took ship; and they returned home again. (NT)		21:6
1 we came **to** Ptolemais, and saluted the brethren,		21:7
1 departed, and came **unto** Caesarea:		21:8
1 we entered **into** the house of Philip the evangelist,		21:8
1 shall deliver him **into** the hands of the Gentiles.		21:11
1 besought him not to go up **to** Jerusalem.		21:12
1 to die **at** Jerusalem for the name of the Lord Jesus.		21:13
1 took up our carriages, and went up **to** Jerusalem.		21:15
1 And when we were come **to** Jerusalem,		21:17
1 himself with them entered **into** the temple,		21:26
1 and further brought Greeks also **into** the temple,		21:28
1 supposed that Paul had brought **into** the temple.		21:29
1 he commanded him to be carried **into** the castle,		21:34
1 And as Paul was to be led **into** the castle,		21:37
1 and leddest out **into** the wilderness four thousand		21:38
1 and delivering **into** prisons both men and women.		22:4
1 letters unto the brethren, and went **to** Damascus,		22:5
1 them which were there bound **unto** Jerusalem,		22:5
1 And I fell **unto** the ground,		22:7
1 Arise, and go **into** Damascus;		22:10
1 being led by the hand ... I came **into** Damascus.		22:11
1 And the same hour I looked up **upon** him.		22:13
1 when I was come again **to** Jerusalem,		22:17
1 for I will send thee far hence **unto** the Gentiles.		22:21
1 cast off their clothes, and threw dust **into** the air,		22:23
1 commanded him to be brought **into** the castle,		22:24
1 and brought Paul down, and set him **before** them.		22:30
1 and to bring him **into** the castle.		23:10
1 for as thou hast testified of me **in** Jerusalem,		23:11
1 so must thou bear witness also **at** Rome.		23:11
1 to bring him down **to** you (NASB)		23:15
1 he went and entered **into** the castle, and told Paul.		23:16
1 bring down Paul to morrow **into** the council,		23:20
1 I brought him forth **into** their council:	Acts	23:28
1 told me how that the Jews laid wait **for** the man,		23:30
1 took Paul, and brought him by night **to** Antipatris.		23:31
1 left the horsemen ... and returned **to** the castle:		23:32
1 Who, when they came **to** Caesarea,		23:33
1 I went up **to** Jerusalem to worship. (NASB)		24:11
1 And have hope **toward** God,		24:15
1 I came to bring alms **to** my nation, and offerings.		24:17
1 and heard him concerning the faith **in** Christ.		24:24
1 he ascended from Caesarea **to** Jerusalem.		25:1
1 that he would send for him **to** Jerusalem,		25:3
1 being kept in custody **at** Caesarea, (NASB)		25:4
1 he went down **unto** Caesarea,		25:6
1 Neither **against** the law of the Jews,		25:8
1 neither **against** the temple,		25:8
1 nor yet **against** Caesar,		25:8
1 Wilt thou go up **to** Jerusalem,		25:9
1 Agrippa ... came **unto** Caesarea to salute Festus.		25:13
1 About whom, when I was **at** Jerusalem,		25:15
1 manner of the Romans to deliver any man **to** die,		25:16
1 because I doubted **of** such manner of questions,		25:20
1 I asked him whether he would go **to** Jerusalem,		25:20
1 to be reserved **unto** the hearing of Augustus,		25:21
1 and was entered **into** the place of hearing,		25:23
1 promise made by God **to** our fathers: (NASB)		26:6
1 **Unto** which promise our twelve tribes,		26:7
1 I persecuted them even **unto** strange cities.		26:11
1 Whereupon as I went **to** Damascus with authority		26:12
1 And when we were all fallen **to** the earth,		26:14
1 for I have appeared unto thee **for** this purpose,		26:16
1 from the Gentiles, **unto** whom now I send thee,		26:17
1 and to turn them from darkness **to** light,		26:18
1 them which are sanctified by faith that is **in** me.		26:18
1 and **throughout** all the coasts of Judaea,		26:20
1 Paul, ... much learning doth make thee mad. (NT)		26:24
1 it was determined that we should sail **into** Italy,		27:1
1 meaning to sail by the coasts **of** Asia;		27:2
1 And the next day we touched **at** Sidon.		27:3
1 had sailed ... we came **to** Myra, a city of Lycia.		27:5
1 found a ship of Alexandria sailing **into** Italy;		27:6
1 sailing into Italy; and he put us **therein**.		27:6
1 came **unto** a place which is called The fair havens;		27:8
1 if by any means they might attain **to** Phenice,		27:12
1 fearing lest they should fall **into** the quicksands,		27:17
1 Howbeit we must be cast **upon** a certain island.		27:26
1 fearing lest we should have fallen **upon** rocks,		27:29
1 when they had let down the boat **into** the sea,		27:30
1 and cast out the wheat **into** the sea.		27:38
1 **into** the which they were minded, if ... possible,		27:39
1 they committed themselves **unto** the sea,		27:40
1 hoisted up the mainsail ... and made **toward** shore.		27:40
1 And falling **into** a place where two seas met,		27:41
1 shook off the beast **into** the fire, and felt no harm.		28:5
1 and saw no harm come **to** him,		28:6
1 landing **at** Syracuse, we tarried there three days.		28:12
1 we fetched a compass, and came **to** Rhegium:		28:13
1 and we came the next day **to** Puteoli:		28:13
1 and so we went **toward** Rome.		28:14
1 they came **to** meet us as far as Appii forum,		28:15
1 And when we came **to** Rome,		28:16
1 from Jerusalem **into** the hands of the Romans.		28:17
1 there came many to him **into** his lodging;		28:23
1 called to be an apostle, separated **unto** the gospel	Rom	1:1
1 **for** obedience to the faith among all nations,		1:5
1 spiritual gift, **to** the end ye may be established;		1:11
1 for it is the power of God **unto** salvation		1:16
1 righteousness of God revealed from faith **to** faith:		1:17
1 **so that** they are without excuse:		1:20
1 Wherefore God also gave them up **to** uncleanness		1:24
1 the Creator, who is blessed **for** ever. Amen.		1:25
1 this cause God gave them up **unto** vile affections:		1:26
1 the natural use **into** that which is against nature:		1:26
1 burned in their lust one **toward** another;		1:27
1 God gave them over to a reprobate mind,		1:28
1 the goodness of God leadeth thee **to** repentance?		2:4
1 his uncircumcision be counted **for** circumcision?		2:26
1 more abounded through my lie **unto** his glory;		3:7

εἰς 1506B

1 Christ **unto** all and upon all them that believe:	Rom	3:22
1 **to** declare his righteousness for the remission		3:25
1 **that** he might be just, and the justifier of him		3:26
1 and it was counted unto him **for** righteousness.		4:3
1 his faith is counted **for** righteousness.		4:5
1 faith was reckoned to Abraham **for** righteousness.		4:9
1 **that** he might be the father of all them that believe,		4:11
1 **that** righteousness might be imputed unto them		4:11
1 **in order that** the promise may be certain (NASB)		4:16
1 **that** he might become the father of many nations,		4:18
1 He staggered not **at** the promise of God		4:20
1 therefore it was imputed to him **for** righteousness.		4:22
1 access by faith **into** this grace wherein we stand,		5:2
1 But God commendeth his love **toward** us,		5:8
1 as by one man sin entered **into** the world,		5:12
1 and so death passed **upon** all men,		5:12
1 Jesus Christ, hath abounded **unto** many.		5:15
1 for the judgment was by one **to** condemnation,		5:16
1 the free gift is of many offences **unto** justification.		5:16
1 judgment came **upon** all men to condemnation;		5:18
1 judgment came **upon** all men to condemnation;		5:18
1 gift came **upon** all men unto justification of life.		5:18
1 gift came upon all men **unto** justification of life.		5:18
1 **unto** eternal life by Jesus Christ our Lord.		5:21
1 **into** Jesus Christ were baptized into his death?		6:3
1 into Jesus Christ were baptized **into** his death?		6:3
1 we are buried with him by baptism **into** death:		6:4
1 **that** ye should obey it in the lusts thereof.		6:12
1 **to** that to whom ye yield yourselves servants **to** obey,		6:16
1 whether of sin **unto** death,		6:16
1 or of obedience **unto** righteousness?		6:16
1 teaching **to** which you were committed, (NASB)		6:17
1 uncleanness and to iniquity **unto** iniquity;		6:19
1 servants to righteousness **unto** holiness.		6:19
1 ye have your fruit **unto** holiness,		6:22
1 **that** ye should be married to another,		7:4
1 at work in our bodies, **so that** we bore (NIV)		7:5
1 the commandment, which was ordained **to** life,		7:10
1 the commandment, ... I found to be **unto** death.		7:10
1 Because the carnal mind is enmity **against** God:		8:7
1 not received the spirit of bondage again **to** fear;		8:15
1 the glory which shall be revealed **in** us.		8:18
1 **into** the glorious liberty of the children of God.		8:21
1 work together **for** good to them that love God,		8:28
1 **that** he might be the firstborn among many		8:29
1 who is over all, God blessed **for** ever. Amen.		9:5
1 children of the promise are counted **for** the seed.		9:8
1 Even **for** this same purpose have I raised thee up,		9:17
1 of the same lump to make one vessel **unto** honour,		9:21
1 vessel unto honour, and another **unto** dishonour?		9:21
1 the vessels of wrath fitted **to** destruction:		9:22
1 which he had afore prepared **unto** glory,		9:23
1 hath not attained to the law **of** righteousness.		9:31
1 prayer ... for Israel is, **that** they might be saved.		10:1
1 **for** righteousness to every one that believeth.		10:4
1 Say not ... Who shall ascend **into** heaven?		10:6
1 Or, Who shall descend **into** the deep?		10:7
1 with the heart man believeth **unto** righteousness;		10:10
1 with the mouth confession is made **unto** salvation.		10:10
1 Lord over all is rich **unto** all that call upon him.		10:12
1 How then shall they call **on** him		10:14
1 Yes verily, their sound went **into** all the earth,		10:18
1 and their words **unto** the ends of the world.		10:18
1 Let their table be made a snare, (NT)		11:9
1 table be made ... a trap, (NT)		11:9
1 table be made ... a stumblingblock, (NT)		11:9
1 table be made ... a recompense (NT)		11:9
1 unto the Gentiles, **for** to provoke them to jealousy.		11:11
1 grafted contrary to nature **into** a good olive tree:		11:24
1 For God hath concluded them all in unbelief,		11:32
1 For of him, and through him, and **to** him,		11:36
1 are all things: to whom be glory **for** ever. Amen.		11:36
1 **that** ye may prove what is that good,		12:2
1 **so as** to have sound judgment (NASB)		12:3
1 Be kindly affectioned one **to** another with		12:10
1 Be of the same mind one **toward** another.		12:16
1 For he is the minister of God to thee **for** good.		13:4
1 a revenger **to** execute wrath upon him that doeth	Rom	13:4
1 attending continually **upon** this very thing.		13:6
1 to fulfil the lusts **thereof**.		13:14
1 but not to doubtful disputations.		14:1
1 **For** to this end Christ both died, and rose,		14:9
1 and the building up **of** one another. (NASB)		14:19
1 please his neighbour **for** his good to edification.		15:2
1 were written **for** our learning,		15:4
1 as Christ also received us **to** the glory of God.		15:7
1 **to** confirm the promises made unto the fathers:		15:8
1 peace in believing, **that** ye may abound in hope,		15:13
1 **That** I should be the minister of Jesus Christ		15:16
1 be the minister of Jesus Christ **to** the Gentiles,		15:16
1 **to** make the Gentiles obedient, by word and deed,		15:18
1 Whensoever I take my journey **into** Spain,		15:24
1 I go **unto** Jerusalem to minister unto the saints.		15:25
1 to make a certain contribution **for** the poor saints		15:26
1 I will come by you **into** Spain.		15:28
1 and that my service which I have **for** Jerusalem		15:31
1 who is the firstfruits of Achaia **unto** Christ.		16:5
1 Greet Mary, who bestowed much labour **on** us.		16:6
1 For your obedience is come abroad **unto** all men.		16:19
1 yet I would have you wise **unto** that which is good,		16:19
1 and simple **concerning** evil.		16:19
1 known to all nations **for** the obedience of faith:		16:26
1 known **to** all nations for the obedience of faith:		16:26
1 be glory through Jesus Christ **for** ever. Amen.		16:27
1 by whom ye were called **unto** the fellowship	1 Co	1:9
1 or were ye baptized **in** the name of Paul?		1:13
1 should say that I had baptized **in** mine own name.		1:15
1 God ordained before the world **unto** our glory:		2:7
1 But **with** me it is a very small thing		4:3
1 in a figure transferred **to** myself and to Apollos		4:6
1 unto Satan **for** the destruction of the flesh,		5:5
1 no, not **one** that shall be able to judge		6:5
1 for two, saith he, shall be one flesh. (NT)		6:16
1 fornication sinneth **against** his own body.		6:18
1 the Father, of whom are all things, and we **in** him;		8:6
1 to eat those things which are offered **to** idols;		8:10
1 But when ye sin so **against** the brethren,		8:12
1 wound their weak conscience, ye sin **against** Christ.		8:12
1 I will eat no flesh **while** the world standeth,		8:13
1 **that** I abuse not my power in the gospel.		9:18
1 baptized **unto** Moses in the cloud and in the sea;		10:2
1 **to** the intent we should not lust after evil things,		10:6
1 **upon** whom the ends of the world are come.		10:11
1 or whatsoever ye do, do all **to** the glory of God.		10:31
1 come together not **for** the better, but for the worse.		11:17
1 come together not for the better, but **for** the worse.		11:17
1 What? have ye not houses to eat and to drink **in**?		11:22
1 Take, eat: ... this do **in** remembrance of me.		11:24
1 as oft as ye drink it, **in** remembrance of me.		11:25
1 my brethren, when ye come together to eat, (NT)		11:33
1 that ye come not together **unto** condemnation.		11:34
1 by one Spirit are we all baptized **into** one body,		12:13
1 and have been all made to drink **into** one Spirit.		12:13
1 who shall prepare himself **to** the battle?		14:8
1 for ye shall speak **into** the air.		14:9
1 tongues are **for** a sign, not to them that believe,		14:22
1 or came it **unto** you only?		14:36
1 and his grace which was bestowed **upon** me.		15:10
1 The first man Adam was made a living soul; (NT)		15:45
1 the last Adam was made a quickening spirit. (NT)		15:45
1 that is written, Death is swallowed up **in** victory.		15:54
1 Now concerning the collection **for** the saints,		16:1
1 will I send to bring your liberality **unto** Jerusalem.		16:3
1 that they have addicted themselves **to** the ministry		16:15
1 **that** we may be able to comfort them	2 Co	1:4
1 For as the sufferings of Christ abound in us,		1:5
1 **in** whom we trust that he will yet deliver us;		1:10
1 that for the gift bestowed **upon** us		1:11
1 And to pass by you **into** Macedonia,		1:16
1 of you to be brought on my way **toward** Judaea.		1:16
1 Now he which stablisheth us with you **in** Christ,		1:21
1 that to spare you I came not as yet **unto** Corinth.		1:23
1 the love which I have more abundantly **unto** you.		2:4
1 that ye would confirm your love **toward** him.		2:8

295

εἰς 1506B

1 For to this end also did I write,	2 Co	2:9
1 whether ye be obedient in all things.		2:9
1 when I came to Troas to preach Christ's gospel,		2:12
1 when I came to Troas to preach Christ's gospel,		2:12
1 I went from thence into Macedonia.		2:13
1 To the one we are the savour of death unto death;		2:16
1 and to the other the savour of life unto life.		2:16
1 look intently at the face of Moses (NASB)		3:7
1 look to the end of that which is abolished:		3:13
1 into the same image from glory to glory,		3:18
1 that they might not see the light (NASB)		4:4
1 For we which live are alway delivered unto death		4:11
1 thanksgiving of many redound to the glory of God.		4:15
1 far more exceeding and eternal weight (NT)		4:17
1 that hath wrought us for the selfsame thing is God,		5:5
1 that ye receive not the grace of God in vain.		6:1
1 And will be a Father unto you,		6:18
1 and ye shall be my sons and daughters, (NT)		6:18
1 that ye are in our hearts to die and live with you.		7:3
1 For, when we were come into Macedonia,		7:5
1 but that ye sorrowed to repentance:		7:9
1 For godly sorrow worketh repentance to salvation		7:10
1 his inward affection is more abundant toward you,		7:15
1 abounded unto the riches of their liberality.		8:2
1 the fellowship of the ministering to the saints.		8:4
1 Insomuch that we desired Titus,		8:6
1 so he would also finish in you the same grace also.		8:6
1 your abundance may be a supply for their want,		8:14
1 abundance also may be a supply for your want:		8:14
1 upon the great confidence which I have in you.		8:22
1 he is my partner and fellowhelper concerning you:		8:23
1 Wherefore show ye to them,		8:24
1 and before the churches, the proof of your love,		8:24
1 For as touching the ministering to the saints,		9:1
1 that they would go before unto you,		9:5
1 God is able to make all grace abound toward you;		9:8
1 may abound to every good work:		9:8
1 his righteousness remaineth for ever.		9:9
1 both minister bread for your food,		9:10
1 Being enriched in every thing to all bountifulness,		9:11
1 professed subjection unto the gospel of Christ,		9:13
1 and for your liberal distribution unto them,		9:13
1 liberal distribution unto them, and unto all men;		9:13
1 but being absent am bold toward you:		10:1
1 captivity every thought to the obedience of Christ;		10:5
1 which the Lord hath given us for edification,		10:8
1 for edification, and not for your destruction,		10:8
1 we will not boast of things without our measure,		10:13
1 as though we reached not unto you:		10:14
1 Not boasting of things without our measure,		10:15
1 according to our rule abundantly, (NT)		10:15
1 To preach the gospel in the regions beyond you,		10:16
1 and not to boast in another man's line of things		10:16
1 from the simplicity that is in Christ.		11:3
1 made manifest among you in all things.		11:6
1 stop me of this boasting in the regions of Achaia.		11:10
1 transforming themselves into the apostles of Christ.		11:13
1 Satan himself is transformed into an angel of light.		11:14
1 if a man exalt himself, ... smite you on the face.		11:20
1 Lord Jesus Christ, which is blessed for evermore,		11:31
1 I will come to visions and revelations of the Lord.		12:1
1 How that he was caught up into paradise,		12:4
1 think of me above that which he seeth me to be,		12:6
1 that, if I come again, I will not spare: (NT)		13:2
1 which to you-ward is not weak, but is mighty		13:3
1 live with him by the power of God toward you.		13:4
1 which the Lord hath given me to edification,		13:10
1 given me to edification, and not to destruction.		13:10
1 To whom be glory for ever and ever. Amen.	Gal	1:5
1 so soon removed from him ... unto another gospel:		1:6
1 Neither went I up to Jerusalem		1:17
1 Neither ... to Jerusalem ... but I went into Arabia,		1:17
1 into Arabia, and returned again unto Damascus.		1:17
1 Then after three years I went up to Jerusalem		1:18
1 I came into the regions of Syria and Cilicia;		1:21
1 I went up again to Jerusalem with Barnabas,		2:1
1 by any means I should run, or had run, in vain.		2:2
1 in Peter to the apostleship of the circumcision,	Gal	2:8
1 the same was mighty in me toward the Gentiles:		2:8
1 that we should go unto the heathen,		2:9
1 unto the heathen, and they unto the circumcision.		2:9
1 But when Peter was come to Antioch,		2:11
1 even we have believed in Jesus Christ,		2:16
1 and it was accounted to him for righteousness.		3:6
1 come on the Gentiles through Jesus Christ;		3:14
1 confirmed before of God in Christ, the law,		3:17
1 that it should make the promise of none effect.		3:17
1 shut up unto the faith which should ... be revealed.		3:23
1 law was our schoolmaster to bring us unto Christ,		3:24
1 have been baptized into Christ have put on Christ.		3:27
1 the Spirit of his Son into your hearts, crying, Abba,		4:6
1 lest I have bestowed upon you labour in vain.		4:11
1 the mount Sinai, which gendereth to bondage,		4:24
1 I have confidence in you through the Lord,		5:10
1 only use not liberty for an occasion to the flesh,		5:13
1 and then shall he have rejoicing in himself alone,		6:4
1 have rejoicing in himself alone, and not in another.		6:4
1 For he that soweth to his flesh		6:8
1 but he that soweth to the Spirit		6:8
1 Having predestinated us unto the adoption	Eph	1:5
1 the adoption of children by Jesus Christ to himself,		1:5
1 To the praise of the glory of his grace,		1:6
1 abounded toward us in all wisdom and prudence;		1:8
1 That in the dispensation of the fulness of times		1:10
1 That we should be to the praise of his glory,		1:12
1 That we should be to the praise of his glory,		1:12
1 until the redemption of the purchased possession,		1:14
1 unto the praise of his glory.		1:14
1 faith in the Lord Jesus, and love unto all the saints,		1:15
1 that ye may know what is the hope of his calling,		1:18
1 of his power to us-ward who believe,		1:19
1 for to make in himself of twain one new man,		2:15
1 groweth unto an holy temple in the Lord:		2:21
1 for an habitation of God through the Spirit.		2:22
1 of the grace of God which is given me to you-ward:		3:2
1 by his Spirit in the inner man;		3:16
1 that ye might be filled with all the fulness of God.		3:19
1 throughout all ages, world without end. Amen.		3:21
1 Wherefore he saith, When he ascended up on high,		4:8
1 descended first into the lower parts of the earth?		4:9
1 for the work of the ministry,		4:12
1 for the edifying of the body of Christ:		4:12
1 Till we all come in the unity of the faith,		4:13
1 unto a perfect man,		4:13
1 unto the measure of the stature of the fulness		4:13
1 may grow up into him in all things,		4:15
1 maketh increase of the body unto the edifying		4:16
1 to work all uncleanness with greediness.		4:19
1 whereby ye are sealed unto the day of redemption.		4:30
1 And be ye kind one to another, tenderhearted,		4:32
1 and a sacrifice to God for a sweetsmelling savour.		5:2
1 and they two shall be one flesh. (NT)		5:31
1 but I speak concerning Christ and the church.		5:32
1 but I speak concerning Christ and the church.		5:32
1 and watching thereunto with all perseverance;		6:18
1 Whom I have sent unto you for the same purpose,		6:22
1 For your fellowship in the gospel from the first day	Phlp	1:5
1 That ye may approve things that are excellent;		1:10
1 sincere and without offence till the day of Christ;		1:10
1 unto the glory and praise of God.		1:11
1 rather unto the furtherance of the gospel;		1:12
1 knowing that I am set for the defence of the gospel.		1:17
1 For I know that this shall turn to my salvation		1:19
1 having a desire to depart, (NT)		1:23
1 for your furtherance and joy of faith;		1:25
1 not only to believe on him, but also to suffer		1:29
1 Christ is Lord, to the glory of God the Father.		2:11
1 that I may rejoice in the day of Christ,		2:16
1 that I may rejoice in the day of Christ,		2:16
1 I have not run in vain, neither laboured in vain.		2:16
1 I have not run in vain, neither laboured in vain.		2:16
1 he hath served with me in the gospel.		2:22
1 I might attain unto the resurrection of the dead.		3:11
1 Press on toward the goal for the prize (NASB)		3:14

εἰς 1506B

1 Nevertheless, **whereto** we have already attained,	Phlp	3:16
1 **that** it may be fashioned like unto his glorious		3:21
1 no church communicated **with** me ... but ye only.		4:15
1 ye sent once and again **unto** my necessity.		4:16
1 but I desire fruit that may abound **to** your account.		4:17
1 Now unto God and our Father be glory **for** ever		4:20
1 and of the love which ye have **to** all the saints,	Col	1:4
1 Which is come **unto** you, as it is in all the world;		1:6
1 might walk worthy of the Lord **unto** all pleasing,		1:10
1 and increasing **in** the knowledge of God;		1:10
1 unto all patience and longsuffering with joyfulness;		1:11
1 to be partakers of the inheritance of the saints		1:12
1 translated us **into** the kingdom of his dear Son:		1:13
1 all things were created by him, and **for** him:		1:16
1 by him to reconcile all things **unto** himself;		1:20
1 is given to me **for** you, to fulfil the word of God;		1:25
1 **Whereunto** I also labour,		1:29
1 being knit together in love, and **unto** all riches		2:2
1 to the acknowledgement of the mystery of God,		2:2
1 and the stedfastness of your faith in Christ.		2:5
1 Which all are **to** perish with the using;		2:22
1 Lie not one **to** another,		3:9
1 the new man, which is renewed **in** knowledge		3:10
1 **to** the which also ye are called in one body;		3:15
1 Whom I have sent unto you **for** the same purpose,		4:8
1 are my fellowworkers **unto** the kingdom of God,		4:11
1 For our gospel came not **unto** you in word only,	1 Th	1:5
1 we preached **unto** you the gospel of God.		2:9
1 That ye would walk worthy of God,		2:12
1 of God, who hath called you **unto** his kingdom		2:12
1 to fill up their sins alway: for the wrath is come		2:16
1 to speak **to** the Gentiles that they might be saved,		2:16
1 sent Timotheus, our brother, ... **to** establish you,		3:2
1 yourselves know that we are appointed **thereunto**.		3:3
1 I sent to know your faith, (NT)		3:5
1 tempted you, and our labour be in vain.		3:5
1 praying exceedingly **that** we might see your face,		3:10
1 increase and abound in love one **toward** another,		3:12
1 in love one toward another, and **toward** all men,		3:12
1 and toward all men, even as we do **toward** you:		3:12
1 To the end he may stablish your hearts		3:13
1 God, who hath also given **unto** us his holy Spirit.		4:8
1 for ye yourselves are taught of God **to** love		4:9
1 And indeed ye do it **toward** all the brethren		4:10
1 are alive and remain **unto** the coming of the Lord		4:15
1 in the clouds, **to** meet the Lord in the air:		4:17
1 in the clouds, to meet the Lord **in** the air:		4:17
1 For God hath not appointed us **to** wrath,		5:9
1 but **to** obtain salvation by our Lord Jesus Christ,		5:9
1 both **among** yourselves, and to all men.		5:15
1 both among yourselves, and **to** all men.		5:15
1 the will of God in Christ Jesus **concerning** you.		5:18
1 charity of every one of you all **toward** each other	2 Th	1:3
1 that ye may be counted worthy of the kingdom		1:5
1 **Wherefore** also we pray always for you,		1:11
1 **That** ye be not soon shaken in mind,		2:2
1 so that he as God sitteth **in** the temple of God,		2:4
1 that he might be revealed in his time.		2:6
1 received not the love ... **that** they might be saved.		2:10
1 strong delusion, **that** they should believe a lie:		2:11
1 to salvation through sanctification of the Spirit		2:13
1 **Whereunto** he called you by our gospel,		2:14
1 to the obtaining of the glory of our Lord Jesus		2:14
1 the Lord direct your hearts **into** the love of God,		3:5
1 and **into** the patient waiting for Christ.		3:5
1 make ourselves an ensample **unto** you to follow us.		3:9
1 abide ... at Ephesus, when I went **into** Macedonia,	1 Tm	1:3
1 have turned aside **unto** vain jangling;		1:6
1 counted me faithful, putting me **into** the ministry;		1:12
1 Christ Jesus came **into** the world to save sinners;		1:15
1 should hereafter believe on him **to** life everlasting.		1:16
1 God, be honour and glory **for** ever and ever.		1:17
1 and to come **unto** the knowledge of the truth.		2:4
1 **Whereunto** I am ordained a preacher,		2:7
1 he fall **into** the condemnation of the devil.		3:6
1 lest he fall **into** reproach and the snare of the devil.		3:7
1 which God hath created **to** be received		4:3

1 For therefore we both labour and suffer reproach,	1 Tm	4:10
1 are open beforehand, going before **to** judgment;		5:24
1 For we brought nothing **into** this world,		6:7
1 But they that will be rich fall **into** temptation		6:9
1 a snare, and **into** many foolish and hurtful lusts,		6:9
1 eternal life, **whereunto** thou art also called,		6:12
1 living God, who giveth us richly all things **to** enjoy;		6:17
1 a good foundation **against** the time to come,		6:19
1 **Whereunto** I am appointed a preacher,	2 Tm	1:11
1 which I have committed **unto** him against that day		1:12
1 that they strive not about words to no profit,		2:14
1 and some **to** honour, and some to dishonour.		2:20
1 and some to honour, and some **to** dishonour.		2:20
1 he shall be a vessel **unto** honour, sanctified,		2:21
1 and prepared unto every good work.		2:21
1 repentance **to** the acknowledging of the truth;		2:25
1 who are taken captive by him **at** his will.		2:26
1 For of this sort are they which creep **into** houses,		3:6
1 never able to come to the knowledge of the truth.		3:7
1 which are able to make thee wise **unto** salvation		3:15
1 For Demas ... departed **unto** Thessalonica;		4:10
1 Crescens **to** Galatia, Titus unto Dalmatia.		4:10
1 Crescens to Galatia, Titus **unto** Dalmatia.		4:10
1 Mark, ... for he is profitable to me **for** the ministry.		4:11
1 And Tychicus have I sent to Ephesus.		4:12
1 to whom be glory **for** ever and ever. Amen.		4:18
1 to whom be glory for ever and ever. Amen.		4:18
1 be diligent to come unto me **to** Nicopolis:	Tit	3:12
1 learn to maintain good works **for** necessary uses,		3:14
1 and faith, which thou hast **toward** the Lord Jesus,	Phlm	1:5
1 toward the Lord Jesus, and **toward** all saints;		1:5
1 every good thing which is in you **in** Christ Jesus.		1:6
1 And again, I will be **to** him a Father,	Heb	1:5
1 I will be to him a Father, (NT)		1:5
1 he bringeth in the firstbegotten **into** the world,		1:6
1 Thy throne, O God, is **for** ever and ever:		1:8
1 sent forth **to** minister for them who shall be heirs		1:14
1 was confirmed **unto** us by them that heard him;		2:3
1 in bringing many sons **unto** glory,		2:10
1 to make reconciliation for the sins of the people.		2:17
1 was faithful ... **for** a testimony of those things		3:5
1 They shall not enter **into** my rest.		3:11
1 sware he that they should not enter **into** his rest,		3:18
1 a promise being left us of entering into his rest,		4:1
1 For we which have believed do enter **into** rest,		4:3
1 if they shall enter **into** my rest:		4:3
1 in this place again, If they shall enter **into** my rest.		4:5
1 it remaineth that some must enter **therein**,		4:6
1 For he that is entered **into** his rest,		4:10
1 Let us labour therefore to enter **into** that rest,		4:11
1 and find grace to help **in** time of need.		4:16
1 a priest **for** ever after the order of Melchisedec.		5:6
1 to renew them again **unto** repentance;		6:6
1 is nigh unto cursing; whose end is **to** be burned.		6:8
1 of love, which ye have showed **toward** his name,		6:10
1 and an oath for confirmation is to them an end		6:16
1 and which entereth **into** that within the veil;		6:19
1 high priest **for** ever after the order of Melchisedec.		6:20
1 abideth a priest continually. (NT)		7:3
1 of which tribe Moses spake nothing concerning		7:14
1 a priest **for** ever after the order of Melchisedec.		7:17
1 a priest **for** ever after the order of Melchisedec:		7:21
1 But this man, because he continueth ever, (NT)		7:24
1 to save them to the uttermost that come unto God		7:25
1 he ever liveth to make intercession (NT)		7:25
1 maketh the Son, who is consecrated **for** evermore.		7:28
1 For every high priest is ordained to offer gifts (NT)		8:3
1 I will put my laws **into** their mind,		8:10
1 and I will be **to** them a God,		8:10
1 and they shall be **to** me a people:		8:10
1 the priests went always **into** the first tabernacle,		9:6
1 But into the second went the high priest alone		9:7
1 Which was a figure **for** the time then present,		9:9
1 he entered in once **into** the holy place,		9:12
1 from dead works **to** serve the living God?		9:14
1 **for** the redemption of the transgressions that were		9:15
1 not entered **into** the holy places made with hands,		9:24

297

εἰς 1506B

are the figures of the true; but **into** heaven itself,	Heb 9:24
entereth **into** the holy place every year with blood	9:25
to put away sin by the sacrifice of himself.	9:26
was once offered to bear the sins of many; (NT)	9:28
appear the second time without sin **unto** salvation.	9:28
which they offered year by year continually (NT)	10:1
Wherefore when he cometh **into** the world,	10:5
after he had offered one sacrifice for sins **for** ever,	10:12
he hath perfected **for** ever them that are sanctified.	10:14
to enter into the holiest by the blood of Jesus,	10:19
to provoke unto love and to good works;	10:24
to fall **into** the hands of the living God.	10:31
we are not of them who draw back **unto** perdition;	10:39
but of them that believe **to** the saving of the soul.	10:39
so that things which are seen	11:3
prepared an ark **to** the saving of his house;	11:7
to go out **into** a place which he should after receive	11:8
which he should after receive **for** an inheritance,	11:8
By faith he sojourned in the land of promise,	11:9
Sara herself received strength to conceive seed,	11:11
he had respect **unto** the recompense of the reward.	11:26
Looking **unto** Jesus the author and finisher	12:2
such contradiction of sinners **against** himself,	12:3
It is **for** discipline (NASB)	12:7
that we might be partakers of his holiness.	12:10
the same yesterday, and to day, and **for** ever.	13:8
into the sanctuary by the high priest for sin,	13:11
equip you ... **for** doing his will, (NIV)	13:21
Jesus Christ; to whom be glory **for** ever and ever.	13:21
that we should be a kind of firstfruits	Jas 1:18
let every man be swift to hear, slow to speak, (NT)	1:19
let every man be swift to hear, slow to speak, (NT)	1:19
man be swift to hear, slow to speak, slow **to** wrath;	1:19
But whoso looketh **into** the perfect law of liberty,	1:25
For if there come **unto** your assembly a man	2:2
and draw you **before** the judgment seats?	2:6
and it was imputed unto him **for** righteousness;	2:23
Behold, we put bits **in** the horses' mouths,	3:3
horses' mouths so **that** they may obey (NASB)	3:3
let your laughter be turned to mourning,	4:9
turned to mourning, and your joy **to** heaviness.	4:9
To day or to morrow we will go **into** such a city,	4:13
and the rust **of** them shall be a witness against you,	5:3
are entered **into** the ears of the Lord of sabaoth.	5:4
swear not, ... lest ye fall **into** condemnation,	5:12
unto obedience and sprinkling of the blood	1 Pt 1:2
hath begotten us again **unto** a lively hope	1:3
To an inheritance incorruptible, and undefiled,	1:4
that fadeth not away, reserved in heaven **for** you,	1:4
by the power of God through faith **unto** salvation	1:5
might be found **unto** praise and honour and glory	1:7
in whom, ... now ye see him not, yet believing,	1:8
the grace that should come **unto** you:	1:10
Searching what, or what manner of time (NT)	1:11
it testified beforehand the sufferings **of** Christ,	1:11
which things the angels desire to look **into**.	1:12
Who by him do believe **in** God,	1:21
that your faith and hope might be **in** God.	1:21
unto unfeigned love of the brethren,	1:22
word of God, which liveth and abideth **for** ever.	1:23
But the word of the Lord endureth **for** ever.	1:25
word which by the gospel is preached **unto** you.	1:25
you may grow in respect **to** salvation (NASB)	2:2
as a spiritual house **for** a holy priesthood (NASB)	2:5
the same is made the head of the corner, (NT)	2:7
whereunto also they were appointed.	2:8
a people **for** God's own possession, (NASB)	2:9
out of darkness **into** his marvellous light:	2:9
are sent by him **for** the punishment of evildoers,	2:14
For even **hereunto** were ye called:	2:21
women also, who hoped **in** God, (NASB)	3:5
that your prayers be not hindered.	3:7
blessing; knowing that ye are **thereunto** called,	3:9
and his ears are open **unto** their prayers:	3:12
wherein few, that is, eight souls were saved	3:20
but the answer of a good conscience **toward** God,	3:21
Who is gone **into** heaven, and is on the right hand	3:22
That he no longer should live the rest of his time	1 Pt 4:2
run not with them **to** the same excess of riot,	4:4
for this cause was the gospel preached also to them	4:6
be ye therefore sober, and watch **unto** prayer.	4:7
have fervent charity **among** yourselves:	4:8
Use hospitality one **to** another without grudging.	4:9
even so minister the same one **to** another,	4:10
to whom be praise and dominion **for** ever	4:11
called us **unto** his eternal glory by Christ Jesus,	5:10
To him be glory and dominion **for** ever and ever.	5:11
that this is the true grace of God **wherein** ye stand.	5:12
nor unfruitful **in** the knowledge of our Lord Jesus	2 Pt 1:8
unto you abundantly **into** the everlasting kingdom	1:11
my beloved Son, **in** whom I am well pleased.	1:17
to be reserved **unto** judgment;	2:4
and to reserve the unjust **unto** the day of judgment	2:9
brute beasts, made **to** be taken and destroyed,	2:12
to whom the mist of darkness is reserved **for** ever.	2:17
sow that was washed to her wallowing in the mire.	2:22
reserved unto fire **against** the day of judgment	3:7
but is longsuffering to **us-ward**,	3:9
but that all should come **to** repentance.	3:9
To him be glory both now and **for** ever. Amen.	3:18
but he that doeth the will of God abideth **for** ever.	1 Jn 2:17
For this purpose the Son of God was manifested,	3:8
We know that we have passed from death **unto** life,	3:14
many false prophets are gone out **into** the world.	4:1
God sent his only begotten Son **into** the world,	4:9
and these three agree **in** one.	5:8
He that believeth **on** the Son of God	5:10
has not believed **in** the witness (NASB)	5:10
you that believe on the name of the Son of God;	5:13
ye may believe **on** the name of the Son of God.	5:13
which dwelleth in us, and shall be with us **for** ever.	2 Jn 1:2
For many deceivers are entered **into** the world,	1:7
not this doctrine, receive him not **into** your house,	1:10
faithfully whatsoever thou doest **to** the brethren,	3 Jn 1:5
thou doest to the brethren, and **to** strangers;	1:5
were before of old ordained **to** this condemnation,	Jude 1:4
turning the grace of our God **into** lasciviousness,	1:4
unto the judgment of the great day.	1:6
is reserved the blackness of darkness **for** ever.	1:13
mercy of our Lord Jesus Christ **unto** eternal life.	1:21
dominion and power, both now and **for** ever.	1:25
to him be glory and dominion for ever and ever.	Rev 1:6
and, What thou seest, write **in** a book,	1:11
seven churches which are in Asia; **unto** Ephesus,	1:11
and **unto** Smyrna, and unto Pergamos,	1:11
and unto Smyrna, and **unto** Pergamos,	1:11
and **unto** Thyatira, and unto Sardis,	1:11
and unto Thyatira, and **unto** Sardis,	1:11
and **unto** Philadelphia, and unto Laodicea.	1:11
and unto Philadelphia, and **unto** Laodicea.	1:11
and, behold, I am alive **for** evermore, Amen;	1:18
the devil shall cast some of you **into** prison,	2:10
Behold, I will cast her into a bed,	2:22
commit adultery with her **into** great tribulation,	2:22
sat on the throne, who liveth **for** ever and ever,	4:9
and worship him that liveth **for** ever and ever,	4:10
seven Spirits of God sent forth **into** all the earth.	5:6
and **unto** the Lamb for ever and ever.	5:13
and worshipped him that liveth **for** ever and ever.	5:14
And the stars of heaven fell **unto** the earth,	6:13
hid themselves in the dens and in the rocks	6:15
hid themselves in the dens and in the rocks	6:15
might, be unto our God **for** ever and ever. Amen.	7:12
and cast it **into** the earth: and there were voices,	8:5
and they were cast **upon** the earth:	8:7
mountain burning with fire was cast **into** the sea:	8:8
part of the waters became wormwood; (NT)	8:11
and I saw a star fall from heaven **unto** the earth:	9:1
came out of the smoke locusts **upon** the earth:	9:3
locusts were like unto horses prepared **unto** battle;	9:7
sound of chariots of many horses running **to** battle.	9:9
for an hour, and a day, and a month, and a year,	9:15
and upon the earth lifted up his hand **to** heaven,	10:5
And sware by him that liveth **for** ever and ever,	10:6

1 and have power over waters to turn them **to** blood, Rev	11:6
1 not suffer their dead bodies to be put **in** graves.	11:9
1 And they ascended up **to** heaven in a cloud;	11:12
1 and he shall reign **for** ever and ever.	11:15
1 the stars of heaven, and did cast them **to** the earth:	12:4
1 And the woman fled **into** the wilderness,	12:6
1 Devil, and Satan, ... he was cast out **into** the earth,	12:9
1 the dragon saw that he was cast **unto** the earth,	12:13
1 she might fly **into** the wilderness, **into** her place,	12:14
1 she might fly into the wilderness, **into** her place,	12:14
1 saw one of his heads as it were wounded **to** death;	13:3
1 he opened his mouth **in** blasphemy against God,	13:6
1 if anyone is destined **for** captivity (NASB)	13:10
1 that leadeth into captivity shall go **into** captivity:	13:10
1 fire come down ... **on** the earth in the sight of men,	13:13
1 And the smoke of their torment ascendeth up **for**	14:11
1 And the angel thrust in his sickle **into** the earth,	14:19
1 cast it **into** the great winepress of the wrath of God.	14:19
1 of the wrath of God, who liveth **for** ever and ever.	15:7
1 and no man was able to enter **into** the temple,	15:8
1 pour out the vials of the wrath ... **upon** the earth.	16:1
1 first went, and poured out his vial **upon** the earth;	16:2
1 **upon** the men which had the mark of the beast,	16:2
1 the second angel poured out his vial **upon** the sea;	16:3
1 the third angel poured out his vial **upon** the rivers	16:4
1 his vial **upon** the rivers and fountains of waters;	16:4
1 **to** the battle of that great day of God Almighty.	16:14
1 he gathered them together **into** ... Armageddon.	16:16
1 the seventh angel poured out his vial **into** the air;	16:17
1 And the great city was divided **into** three parts,	16:19
1 carried me away in the spirit **into** the wilderness:	17:3
1 out of the bottomless pit, and go **into** perdition:	17:8
1 and is of the seven, and goeth **into** perdition.	17:11
1 For God hath put in their hearts to fulfil his will,	17:17
1 stone like a great millstone, and cast it **into** the sea,	18:21
1 Alleluia. And her smoke rose up **for** ever and ever.	19:3
1 are called **unto** the marriage supper of the Lamb.	19:9
1 together **unto** the supper of the great God;	19:17
1 These both were cast alive **into** a lake of fire	19:20
1 cast him **into** the bottomless pit, and shut him up,	20:3
1 Gog and Magog, to gather them together **to** battle:	20:8
1 the devil that deceived them was cast **into** the lake	20:10
1 and shall be tormented day and night **for** ever	20:10
1 And death and hell were cast **into** the lake of fire.	20:14
1 was ... in the book of life was cast **into** the lake	20:15
1 And there came unto me **one** of the seven angels	21:9
1 do bring their glory and honour **into** it.	21:24
1 bring the glory and honour of the nations **into** it.	21:26
1 in no wise enter **into** it any thing that defileth,	21:27
1 the leaves ... were **for** the healing of the nations.	22:2
1 and they shall reign **for** ever and ever.	22:5
1 and may enter in through the gates **into** the city.	22:14

Classical Greek and Septuagint Usage

The use of this preposition is extremely widespread in both classical Greek writings and in the Septuagint. In classical occurrences it follows verbs of motion, it has metaphoric usage, it expresses destination, it is used in connection with payments, and has temporal use as well (*Moulton-Milligan*). In other words, *eis* is an extremely flexible preposition and is found, in fact, in places where one might expect to see the word *en* (1706). In an early form of the Greek, the old Attic, it is spelled *es*, where in poetry *eis* was used before vowels and *es* before consonants (Smyth, *Greek Grammar*, p.376). The word occurs thousands of times in the Septuagint.

The New Testament occurrences of *eis* number over 1,700, and it shows the same variety of uses as in the classical writings. Used only with the accusative case, the root meanings of the preposition are "in, within" (Dana and Mantey, *Manual of the Greek New Testament*, p.103). By the Koine period *eis* had overtaken many of the functions of *en*.

New Testament Usage

In addition to the "root meanings" a number of additional English words translate *eis* in the New Testament depending upon its contextual and syntactic usage. In the third volume of Moulton's *Grammar of New Testament Greek* entitled *Syntax*, Nigel Turner (3:266f.) describes five categories of the use of *eis*. First is its normal sense as used with verbs of motion. New Testament examples are abundant. For instance, one might go "into" a city (Matthew 26:18), a house (Matthew 9:7), a synagogue (Acts 17:10), a boat (Matthew 8:23), the world (John 1:9), heaven (Luke 2:15), or the abyss (Luke 8:31) (cf. *Bauer*). Often *eis* combines with action verbs to produce compound forms (e.g., *eiserchomai* [1511], *eisdechomai* [1509], *eisporeuō* [1515], and *eispherō* [1517]). A second category is referred to as a "distributive" use with numbers (see Mark 4:8 where it is a variant to *ev* in many ancient texts). A third class is called a "purposive" (or "temporal" [with reference to a goal in time]) use where *eis* may be translated "up to, until, with a view to." In several occurrences of this usage *eis* is used with *telos* (4904) to mean "fully" or "with a view to the end" (Luke 18:5; John 13:1).

Turner (*Grammar of New Testament Greek*, 3:266) lists a fourth category of the use of *eis* for instances where the preposition substitutes for the Hebrew prefix l^e (e.g., Matthew 14:31; 21:46). A final classification given is a "casual" use of *eis*. In these occurrences *eis* may be translated "because of" (e.g., Matthew 3:11; 10:41; 12:41).

In addition to the standard categories described in various grammars, a variety of miscellaneous uses of *eis* occur as well. For example, it is found in both predicate nominative and predicate accusative constructions (see *Bauer*). Remote meanings for *eis*, therefore, may include "upon, against, among, with respect to, for, as" and "for the purpose of" (Dana

εἰσάγω 1507

and Mantey, pp.103,104). Clearly, to limit the translation of *eis* to a single word such as "into" or "unto" is misleading at best and at worse—incorrect.

STRONG 1519, BAUER 228-30,
MOULTON-MILLIGAN 186-87, KITTEL 2:420-34,
LIDDELL-SCOTT 491-92, COLIN BROWN
3:1171-78,1182-91,1201,1204,12

1507. εἰσάγω eisagō verb
Bring (or) lead in, into.
CROSS-REFERENCE:
ἄγω agō (70)

אָסַף 'āsaph (636), Gather, harvest (Ex 23:10).

בּוֹא bō' (971), Qal: go, come (Ex 18:7); hiphil: bring, let come (Gn 39:14, 2 Chr 28:13, Zec 10:10); hophal: be brought (Gn 43:18, Lv 10:18).

הַב hav (1957), Put, set (2 Sm 11:15).

הָלַךְ hālakh (2050), Go, walk; hiphil: lead (Ez 40:24—Codex Alexandrinus only).

חָזַק chāzaq (2480), Be strong; hiphil: take hold of (Jgs 19:4—Codex Alexandrinus only).

יָצָא yātsā' (3428), Come out, go out; hiphil: bring out, lead out (Ez 42:1).

לָקַח lāqach (4089), Qal: take (Gn 7:2); pual: be brought, taken (Gn 12:15—Codex Alexandrinus only).

נָהַג nāhagh (5268), Lead; piel: lead away, drive away (Dt 4:27).

עֲלַל 'ălal (A6178), Go in; haphel: bring in (Dn 2:24,25—Aramaic); hophal: be brought in (Dn 5:13—Aramaic).

קָדַשׁ qādhash (7227), Be holy; piel: dedicate (Jer 22:7—Codex Alexandrinus only).

קָרָא qārā' (7410), Call (1 Kgs 12:20—Codex Alexandrinus only).

שׁוּב shûv (8178), Return; hiphil: bring back (Ez 47:1).

1. εἰσήγαγεν eisēgagen 3sing indic aor act
2. εἰσήγαγον eisēgagon 3pl indic aor act
3. εἰσαγάγῃ eisagagē 3sing subj aor act
4. εἰσάγαγε eisagage 2sing impr aor act
5. εἰσαγαγεῖν eisagagein inf aor act
6. εἰσάγεσθαι eisagesthai inf pres mid

```
5 and when the parents brought in the child Jesus,.... Luke 2:27
4 and bring in hither the poor, and the maimed,......... 14:21
2 and brought him into the high priest's house........... 22:54
1 spake unto her ... and brought in Peter............ John 18:16
2 our fathers that came after brought in with Jesus .... Acts 7:45
2 they led him ... and brought him into Damascus........ 9:8
1 and further brought Greeks also into the temple...... 21:28
1 supposed that Paul had brought into the temple...... 21:29
6 And as Paul was to be led into the castle,.............. 21:37
6 ordered Paul to be taken into the barracks (NIV)...... 22:24
3 he bringeth in the firstbegotten into the world,....... Heb 1:6
```

This is a compound word (from *agō* [70] and *eis* [1506B]) meaning "to bring" or "lead into" a place. It occurs 10 times in the New Testament, mostly in Luke-Acts. It can function as a priestly term of dedication since it often refers to bringing things or people into the temple, including Jesus (Luke 2:27; 22:54), Peter (John 18:16), Greeks (Acts 21:28,29), and the firstborn (Hebrews 1:6).

STRONG 1521, BAUER 232, MOULTON-MILLIGAN 187-88, LIDDELL-SCOTT 492-93.

1508. εἰσακούω eisakouō verb
Hear, listen to; hear and obey.
COGNATE:
ἀκούω akouō (189)
SYNONYMS:
ἀκολουθέω akoloutheō (188)
ἀκούω akouō (189)
ἐνωτίζομαι enōtizomai (1785)
ἐξακολουθέω exakoloutheō (1795)
ἐπακούω epakouō (1858)
ἐπακροάομαι epakroaomai (1859)
ὑπακούω hupakouō (5057)

אָזַן 'āzan (237), Hiphil: listen, hear (Is 32:9).

חוּשׁ chûsh (2456), Hurry, come quickly (Ps 141:1 [140:1]).

יָשַׁע yāsha' (3588), Hiphil: save (Ps 55:16).

מַעֲנֶה ma'ăneh (4776), Answer (Mi 3:7—Codex Vaticanus only).

עָנָה 'ānâh (6257), Qal: answer, reply (Jb 9:15, Ps 4:1, Mi 3:4); niphal: be answered (Prv 21:13); piel: violate (Jb 37:23—Codex Alexandrinus only).

עָתַר 'āthar (6518), Pray; niphal: be moved by entreaty, respond (Is 19:22).

קָשַׁב qāshav (7477), Hiphil: listen, hear (Ex 4:1, Ps 55:17 [54:17], Is 1:15).

רָצָה rātsâh (7813), Be pleased with (Jb 33:26—only some Sinaiticus texts).

שָׁמַע shāma' (8471), Qal: hear, listen to (Nm 14:22, 1 Kgs 8:29, Mi 7:7); niphal: be heard (Dn 10:12); hiphil: announce (Jer 23:22—Codex Sinaiticus only).

שָׁמַר shāmar (8490), Follow, observe (Ex 16:28, Dt 28:58).

1. εἰσηκούσθη eisēkousthē 3sing indic aor pass
2. εἰσακουσθείς eisakoustheis
   nom sing masc part aor pass
3. εἰσακουσθήσονται eisakousthēsontai
   3pl indic fut pass
4. εἰσακούσονται eisakousontai 3pl indic fut mid

```
3 that they shall be heard for their much speaking..... Matt 6:7
1 Fear not, Zacharias: for thy prayer is heard;........ Luke 1:13
1 And said, Cornelius, thy prayer is heard,.......... Acts 10:31
```

```
4 and yet for all that will they not hear me,......... 1 Co 14:21
2 and was heard in that he feared;................... Heb 5:7
```

Classical Greek and Septuagint Usage
This expression is a compound from the preposition *eis* (1506B) and the verb *akouō* (189), "to hear," and means "to listen to, to give heed to, to hear and obey." It occurs throughout classical sources in reference to hearing requests (by gods from persons or by persons from other persons). In the Septuagint, besides being used of listening to human speech (e.g., Genesis 34:17; 42:21), this verb is widely used to depict God's hearing petitions and requests of individuals (e.g., Genesis 21:17; Exodus 2:24; Psalms 38:15 [LXX 37:15]; 55:2 [51:2]; Sirach 3:5) and of individuals' listening to (or not listening to) God's instructions (e.g., Deuteronomy 1:43,45; Jeremiah 11:10). Most often a form of the Hebrew word *shāmaʿ* stands behind *eisakouō*.

New Testament Usage
Five instances of *eisakouō* are recorded in the New Testament. Its connection with God's "listening" to prayers and petitions continues to be reflected. Thus Gentiles think that "they shall be heard" because of their many words (Matthew 6:7).

Positively, in Luke 1:13 Zechariah's prayer for a child "has been heard" ([NIV] the passive here is another way of saying "God heard"; cf. Acts 10:31 of Cornelius' prayer; Hebrews 5:7 of Jesus' prayers and petitions). Also in typical Old Testament fashion, Paul reminded his readers that Isaiah spoke of the unwillingness of people to "hear" or "listen" to God (1 Corinthians 14:21; cf. Isaiah 28:12 [the Septuagint reads only *akouō*]).

STRONG 1522, BAUER 232, MOULTON-MILLIGAN 188, KITTEL 1:222, LIDDELL-SCOTT 493, COLIN BROWN 2:172-73,175,177.

1509. εἰσδέχομαι eisdechomai verb
Take in, receive, welcome.
COGNATE:
δέχομαι dechomai (1203)
SYNONYMS:
ἀναδέχομαι anadechomai (322)
ἀπέχω apechō (563)
ἀποδέχομαι apodechomai (583)
ἀπολαμβάνω apolambanō (612)
δέχομαι dechomai (1203)
ἐπιδέχομαι epidechomai (1911)
κομίζω komizō (2837)
λαμβάνω lambanō (2956)
μεταλαμβάνω metalambanō (3205)
παραδέχομαι paradechomai (3720)
παραλαμβάνω paralambanō (3741)
προσδέχομαι prosdechomai (4185)
προσλαμβάνω proslambanō (4213)
ὑποδέχομαι hupodechomai (5103)
ὑπολαμβάνω hupolambanō (5112)

קָבַץ qāvats (7192), Qal: gather, assemble (Hb 2:5, Zep 3:8); piel: gather together, assemble (Ez 11:17, Hos 8:10, Zec 10:10).

קְבֻצָה qᵉvutsāh (7194), Gathering (Ez 22:20).

1. εἰσδέξομαι eisdexomai 1sing indic fut mid
```
1 touch not the unclean thing; and I will receive you,..2 Co 6:17
```

This is a compound word from *dechomai* (1203) and *eis* (1506B). It actually occurs only in a quotation of the Septuagint (Isaiah 52:11) at 2 Corinthians 6:17. Christians are compared to a sanctified Israel who is to be "welcomed" from exile among the nations.

STRONG 1523, BAUER 232, MOULTON-MILLIGAN 188, KITTEL 2:57, LIDDELL-SCOTT 494, COLIN BROWN 3:744-45.

1510. εἴσειμι eiseimi verb
Go (in, into).
COGNATE:
εἰμί eimi (1498)
SYNONYMS:
εἰσέρχομαι eiserchomai (1511)
εἰσπορεύω eisporeuō (1515)
ἐμβαίνω embainō (1671)

1. εἰσίασιν eisiasin 3pl indic pres act
2. εἰσιέναι eisienai inf pres act
3. εἰσῄει eisēei 3sing indic imperf act
```
2 about to go into the temple asked an alms.......... Acts 3:3
3 the day following Paul went in with us unto James;.... 21:18
3 himself with them entered into the temple,........... 21:26
1 the priests went always into the first tabernacle,..... Heb 9:6
```

Like *eisagō* (1507), *eiseimi* functions in the New Testament as a priestly term. All four times it is used a person (Peter, John, Paul, or a priest) is "entering" the temple worship precincts (Acts 3:3; 21:18,26; Hebrews 9:6).

STRONG 1524, BAUER 232, MOULTON-MILLIGAN 188, LIDDELL-SCOTT 494.

1511. εἰσέρχομαι eiserchomai verb
Come (in, into), go (in, into), enter.
COGNATE:
ἔρχομαι erchomai (2048)
SYNONYMS:
εἴσειμι eiseimi (1510)

εἰσέρχομαι 1511

εἰσπορεύω eisporeuō (1515)
ἐμβαίνω embainō (1671)

אָהַל 'āhal (163), Camp; piel: be inhabited (Is 13:20—Codex Sinaiticus only).

אָסַף 'āṣaph (636), Gather in (Ex 9:19).

בּוֹא bô' (971), Qal: go in, come (Ex 10:1, 2 Kgs 4:4, Jer 16:5); hiphil: bring, carry (Ex 35:29, 1 Sm 1:24); hophal: be brought (Jer 27:21 [34:21], Ez 40:4).

גָּלָה gālâh (1580), Uncover; niphal: expose oneself, show oneself (1 Sm 14:11).

הָלַךְ hālakh (2050), Qal: go, walk (Ez 37:21); hiphil: bring, take (Jer 32:5 [39:5]).

יָצָא yātsâ' (3428), Go out (1 Chr 14:15—Sixtine Edition only).

יָרַד yāradh (3495), Go down (1 Sm 26:6).

יָשַׁב yāshav (3553), Dwell, stay (Jgs 9:41).

לָקַח lāqach (4089), Take; niphal: be taken (Est 2:16).

נָגַשׁ nāghash (5242), Niphal: come near (Ex 20:21).

עָבַר 'āvar (5882), Pass through, cross over (Dt 34:4, Jos 1:11).

עָלָה 'ālâh (6148), Go up, ascend (Jos 6:5).

עֲלַל 'ălal (A6178), Go in (Dn 2:16,24—Aramaic).

קוּם qûm (7251), Get up, arise (Gn 19:35).

קָרֵב qārēv (7414), Approach (Lv 18:14).

רָאָה rā'âh (7495), See (Jb 33:26).

שָׁכַן shākhan (8331), Inhabit (Is 13:20).

1. εἰσῆλθον eisēlthon 1/3sing/pl indic aor act
2. εἰσῆλθες eisēlthes 2sing indic aor act
3. εἰσῆλθεν eisēlthen 3sing indic aor act
4. εἰσήλθομεν eisēlthomen 1pl indic aor act
5. εἰσήλθετε eisēlthete 2pl indic aor act
6. εἰσέλθῃς eiselthēs 2sing subj aor act
7. εἰσέλθῃ eiselthē 3sing subj aor act
8. εἰσέλθωμεν eiselthōmen 1pl subj aor act
9. εἰσέλθητε eiselthēte 2pl subj aor act
10. εἰσέλθωσιν eiselthōsin 3pl subj aor act
11. εἴσελθε eiselthe 2sing impr aor act
12. εἰσελθόντα eiselthonta nom/acc sing/pl masc/neu part aor act
13. εἰσελθών eiselthōn nom sing masc part aor act
14. εἰσελθόντος eiselthontos gen sing masc part aor act
15. εἰσελθόντι eiselthonti dat sing masc part aor act
16. εἰσελθόντες eiselthontes nom pl masc part aor act
17. εἰσελθόντων eiselthontōn gen pl masc part aor act
18. εἰσελθοῦσα eiselthousa nom sing fem part aor act
19. εἰσελθούσης eiselthousēs gen sing fem part aor act
20. εἰσελθοῦσαι eiselthousai nom pl fem part aor act
21. εἰσελθεῖν eiselthein inf aor act
22. εἰσελθέτω eiselthetō 3sing impr aor act
23. εἰσέλθετε eiselthete 2pl impr aor act
24. εἰσεληλύθατε eiselēluthate 2pl indic perf act
25. εἰσεληλύθασιν eiselēluthasin 3pl indic perf act
26. εἰσέρχεται eiserchetai 3sing indic pres mid
27. εἰσερχόμεθα eiserchometha 1pl indic pres mid
28. εἰσέρχεσθε eiserchesthe 2pl indic pres mid
29. εἰσέρχησθε eiserchēsthe 2pl subj pres mid
30. εἰσερχέσθωσαν eiserchesthōsan 3pl impr pres mid
31. εἰσερχόμενος eiserchomenos nom sing masc part pres mid
32. εἰσερχομένου eiserchomenou gen sing masc part pres mid
33. εἰσερχόμενοι eiserchomenoi nom pl masc part pres mid
34. εἰσερχομένους eiserchomenous acc pl masc part pres mid
35. εἰσερχομένην eiserchomenēn acc sing fem part pres mid
36. εἰσερχόμενον eiserchomenon nom/acc sing neu part pres mid
37. εἰσελεύσομαι eiseleusomai 1sing indic fut mid
38. εἰσελεύσεται eiseleusetai 3sing indic fut mid
39. εἰσελεύσονται eiseleusontai 3pl indic fut mid
40. εἰσελεύσεσθαι eiseleusesthai inf fut mid
41. εἰσήλθατε eisēlthate 2pl indic aor act
42. εἰσελθάτω eiselthatō 3sing impr aor act
43. εἰσέλθατε eiselthate 2pl impr aor act
44. εἰσελήλυθαν eiselēluthan 3pl indic perf act

3 and came into the land of Israel. (NASB)	Matt 2:21
9 in no case enter into the kingdom of heaven.	5:20
11 when thou prayest, enter into thy closet,	6:6
23 Enter ye in at the strait gate: for wide is the gate,	7:13
43 Enter ye in at the strait gate: for wide is the gate,	7:13
33 and many there be which go in thereat:	7:13
38 shall enter into the kingdom of heaven;	7:21
15 And when Jesus was entered into Capernaum,	8:5
14 And when Jesus was entered into Capernaum,	8:5
6 that thou shouldest come under my roof:	8:8
13 there came a certain ruler, and worshipped him,	9:18
13 But when the people were put forth, he went in,	9:25
9 and into any city of the Samaritans enter ye not:	10:5
9 And into whatsoever city or town ye shall enter,	10:11
33 And when ye come into an house, salute it.	10:12
3 How he entered into the house of God,	12:4
21 else how can one enter into a strong man's house,	12:29
12 and they enter in and dwell there:	12:45
36 Not ... which goeth into the mouth defileth a man;	15:11
3 And when he was come into the house,	17:25
12 And when he was come into the house,	17:25
9 ye shall not enter into the kingdom of heaven.	18:3
21 better for thee to enter into life halt or maimed,	18:8
21 it is better for thee to enter into life with one eye,	18:9
21 thou wilt enter into life, keep the commandments.	19:17
38 a rich man shall hardly enter into the kingdom	19:23
21 easier for a camel to go (NASB)	19:24
21 for a rich man to enter the kingdom (NASB)	19:24
21 for a rich man to enter into the kingdom of God.	19:24
14 And when he was come into Jerusalem,	21:10
3 And Jesus went into the temple of God,	21:12
13 And when the king came in to see the guests,	22:11
2 Friend, how camest thou in hither	22:12
28 for ye neither go in yourselves,	23:13
34 neither suffer ye them that are entering to go in.	23:13
21 neither suffer ye them that are entering to go in.	23:13
3 until the day that Noe entered into the ark,	24:38
1 that were ready went in with him to the marriage:	25:10
11 enter thou into the joy of thy lord.	25:21
11 enter thou into the joy of thy lord.	25:23

εἰσέρχομαι 1511

9	Watch and pray, that ye **enter** not into temptation:	Matt 26:41
13	**went in**, and sat with the servants, to see the end.....	26:58
1	**went** into the holy city, and appeared unto many......	27:53
13	on the sabbath day he **entered** into the synagogue,	Mark 1:21
21	Jesus could no more openly **enter** into the city,........	1:45
3	again he **entered** into Capernaum after some days;.....	2:1
13	again he **entered** into Capernaum after some days;.....	2:1
3	How he **went** into the house of God...................	2:26
3	And **he entered** again into the synagogue;.............	3:1
13	No man can **enter** into a strong man's house,...........	3:27
8	into the swine, that we **may enter** into them...........	5:12
1	and **entered** into the swine:...........................	5:13
13	And when he **was come in**, he saith unto them,........	5:39
9	In what place soever ye **enter** into an house,...........	6:10
19	when the daughter of the said Herodias **came in**,......	6:22
18	she **came in** straightway with haste unto the king,......	6:25
3	he **was entered** into the house from the people,........	7:17
13	and **entered** into an house,...........................	7:24
18	certain woman, ... and **came** and fell at his feet:......	7:25
6	Neither **go** into the town, nor tell it to any.............	8:26
6	come out of him, and **enter** no more into him.........	9:25
14	And when he **was come** into the house,................	9:28
21	it is better for thee **to enter** into life maimed,.........	9:43
21	it is better for thee **to enter** halt into life,.............	9:45
21	it is better for thee **to enter** into the kingdom........	9:47
7	as a little child, he **shall** in no wise **enter** therein........	10:15
39	How hardly **shall** they that have riches **enter**.........	10:23
21	how hard is it ... **to enter** into the kingdom of God!..	10:24
21	It is easier for a camel **to go** through.................	10:25
21	than for a rich man **to enter** into the kingdom........	10:25
3	Jesus **entered** into Jerusalem, and into the temple:....	11:11
13	and Jesus **went** into the temple,.......................	11:15
22	neither **enter therein**, to take any thing out...........	13:15
42	neither **enter therein**, to take any thing out...........	13:15
7	And wheresoever he **shall go in**,.......................	14:14
9	Watch ye and pray, lest ye **enter** into temptation......	14:38
3	Joseph ... and **went in** boldly unto Pilate,..............	15:43
20	**entering** into the sepulchre, they saw a young man....	16:5
13	his lot was to burn incense **when he went** into the..	Luke 1:9
13	And the angel **came in** unto her, and said, Hail,......	1:28
3	And **entered** into the house of Zacharias,..............	1:40
3	he **went** into the synagogue on the sabbath day,......	4:16
3	and **entered** into Simon's house.......................	4:38
3	How he **went** into the house of God,...................	6:4
21	that he **entered** into the synagogue and taught:........	6:6
3	he **entered** into Capernaum............................	7:1
6	worthy that thou **shouldest enter** under my roof:......	7:6
13	And he **went** into the Pharisee's house,.................	7:36
1	Seest thou this woman? I **entered** into thine house,....	7:44
1	since ... I **came in** hath not ceased to kiss my feet.....	7:45
8	because many devils **were entered** into him............	8:30
21	that he would suffer them **to enter** into them..........	8:32
3	devils out of the man, and **entered** into the swine:.....	8:33
1	devils out of the man, and **entered** into the swine:.....	8:33
21	besought him that he **would come** into his house:......	8:41
13	And when he **came** into the house, he suffered no....	8:51
21	he suffered no man **to go in**, save Peter, and...........	8:51
9	And whatsoever house ye **enter** into, there abide,......	9:4
21	and they feared as they **entered** into the cloud.........	9:34
3	Then there **arose** a reasoning among them,............	9:46
1	and **entered** into a village of the Samaritans...........	9:52
29	And into whatsoever house ye **enter**, first say,........	10:5
9	And into whatsoever house ye **enter**, first say,........	10:5
29	And into whatsoever city ye **enter**,.....................	10:8
29	But into whatsoever city ye **enter**,.....................	10:10
9	But into whatsoever city ye **enter**,.....................	10:10
3	that he **entered** into a certain village:.................	10:38
12	and **enter in**, and dwell there:..........................	11:26
13	and he **went in**, and sat down to meat................	11:37
5	ye **entered** not in yourselves,...........................	11:52
41	ye **entered** not in yourselves,...........................	11:52
34	and them that **were entering** in ye hindered............	11:52
21	Strive **to enter in** at the strait gate....................	13:24
21	will seek **to enter in**, and shall not be able.............	13:24
21	highways and hedges, and compel them **to come in**,..	14:23
21	And he was angry, and would not **go in**:...............	15:28
15	when he **is come** from the field,.......................	17:7
32	And as he **entered** into a certain village,............	Luke 17:12
3	until the day that Noe **entered** into the ark,...........	17:27
7	as a little child **shall** in no wise **enter** therein.........	18:17
39	How hardly shall they that have riches **enter**.........	18:24
21	is easier for a camel **to go** through a needle's eye,....	18:25
21	than for a rich man **to enter** into the kingdom........	18:25
13	And Jesus **entered** and passed through Jericho........	19:1
3	he **was gone** to be guest with a man that is a sinner...	19:7
13	And he **went** into the temple, and began to cast out..	19:45
30	not them that **were** in the countries **enter** thereinto.....	21:21
3	Then **entered** Satan into Judas surnamed Iscariot,.....	22:3
17	Behold, when ye **are entered** into the city,.............	22:10
21	Pray that ye **enter** not into temptation.................	22:40
9	rise and pray, lest ye **enter** into temptation.............	22:46
20	And they **entered in**, and found not the body.........	24:3
21	suffered these things, and **to enter** into his glory?.....	24:26
3	And he **went in** to tarry with them....................	24:29
21	**enter** the second time into his mother's womb,......	John 3:4
21	he cannot **enter** into the kingdom of God.............	3:5
24	and ye **are entered** into their labours...................	4:38
31	**entereth** not by the door into the sheepfold,...........	10:1
31	But he that **entereth in** by the door...................	10:2
7	by me if any man **enter in**, he shall be saved,.........	10:9
38	and **shall go** in and out, and find pasture.............	10:9
3	And after the sop Satan **entered** into him.............	13:27
3	was a garden, into the which he **entered**,..............	18:1
1	they themselves **went** not into the judgment hall,.....	18:28
3	Then Pilate **entered** into the judgment hall again,.....	18:33
3	And **went** again into the judgment hall,...............	19:9
3	saw the linen clothes lying; yet **went** he not **in**........	20:5
3	and **went** into the sepulchre,..........................	20:6
3	Then **went in** also that other disciple,.................	20:8
1	And when they **were come in**,.......................	Acts 1:13
3	time that the Lord Jesus **went** in and out among us,...	1:21
3	and **entered** with them into the temple,...............	3:8
3	his wife, not knowing what was done, **came in**........	5:7
16	and the young men **came in**, and found her dead,.....	5:10
1	they **entered** into the temple early in the morning,.....	5:21
11	the Lord said unto him, Arise, and go into the city,...	9:6
12	Ananias **coming in**, and putting his hand on him,.....	9:12
3	and **entered** into the house;..........................	9:17
12	an angel of God **coming in** to him,...................	10:3
1	And the morrow after **they entered** into Caesarea.....	10:24
3	the following day he **entered** Caesarea (NASB)........	10:24
21	And as Peter was **coming in**, Cornelius met him,.....	10:25
3	And as he talked with him, he **went in**,...............	10:27
2	saying, "You **went** to uncircumcised men (NASB).....	11:3
2	Saying, Thou **wentest in** to men uncircumcised,......	11:3
3	unclean hath at any time **entered** into my mouth......	11:8
4	and we **entered** into the man's house:.................	11:12
16	which, when they **were come** to Antioch,.............	11:20
16	and **went into** the synagogue on the sabbath day,.....	13:14
21	that they **went** both together into the synagogue......	14:1
3	he rose up, and **came** into the city:...................	14:20
16	tribulation **enter** into the kingdom of God.............	14:22
16	**come** into my house, and abide there.................	16:15
1	and **entered** into the house of Lydia:..................	16:40
3	And Paul, as his manner was, **went in** unto them,....	17:2
3	and **went** to the house of a certain man (NASB).....	18:7
13	but he himself **entered** into the synagogue,...........	18:19
13	And he **went** into the synagogue,.....................	19:8
21	when Paul would **have entered in** unto the people,....	19:30
39	shall grievous wolves **enter** in among you,............	20:29
16	we **entered** into the house of Philip the evangelist,.....	21:8
13	he went and **entered** into the castle, and told Paul....	23:16
16	Who, when they **came** to Caesarea,...................	23:33
17	and **was entered** into the place of hearing,............	25:23
13	to whom Paul **entered in**, and prayed,................	28:8
4	And when we **entered** Rome, (NASB)................	28:16
3	as by one man sin **entered** into the world,.........	Rom 5:12
7	until the fulness of the Gentiles **be come in**...........	11:25
10	**come in** those that are unlearned, or unbelievers,..1	Co 14:23
7	and there **come in** one that believeth not,............	14:24
39	They **shall not enter** into my rest..................	Heb 3:11
40	And to whom sware he that they **should** not **enter**.....	3:18
21	they could not **enter in** because of unbelief............	3:19
21	a promise being left us **of entering** into his rest,........	4:1

εἰσκαλέομαι 1512

27	For we which have believed **do enter** into rest,	Heb 4:3
39	if they **shall enter** into my rest:	4:3
39	in this place again, If they **shall enter** into my rest.	4:5
21	it remaineth that some must **enter** therein,	4:6
1	they to whom it was first preached **entered** not in	4:6
13	For he that **is entered** into his rest,	4:10
21	Let us labour therefore **to enter** into that rest,	4:11
35	and which **entereth** into that within the veil;	6:19
3	Whither the forerunner is for us **entered**,	6:20
3	he **entered** in once into the holy place,	9:12
3	not **entered** into the holy places made with hands,	9:24
26	**entereth** into the holy place every year with blood	9:25
31	Wherefore when he **cometh** into the world,	10:5
7	For if there **come** unto your assembly a man	Jas 2:2
7	and there **come** in also a poor man in vile raiment;	2:2
25	**are entered** into the ears of the Lord of sabaoth.	5:4
44	**are entered** into the ears of the Lord of sabaoth.	5:4
1	For many deceivers are **entered** into the world,	2 Jn 1:7
37	I will **come** in to him, and will sup with him,	Rev 3:20
3	the Spirit of life from God **entered** into them,	11:11
21	and no man was able **to enter** into the temple,	15:8
7	in no wise **enter** into it any thing that defileth,	21:27
10	and may **enter in** through the gates into the city	22:14

This deponent verb, common in Greek literature of all kinds, is a compound of *eis* (1506B), "into," and *erchomai* (2048), "go." It simply denotes "go into, enter." As frequently happens in Koine Greek, the preposition which is in the compound *eis* may appear in conjunction with the compound even though it is redundant (e.g., "enter 'into,'" Matthew 2:21; 7:21; John 3:4; etc.). It also occurs in other constructions such as "enter through" (*eiserchomai dia*), for example, Luke 13:24; John 10:1,2; or less frequently "enter to" (*eiserchomai pros*), Mark 6:25; Luke 1:28.

Eiserchomai can speak of a thought "coming into" mind (Herodotus), wisdom entering someone (Wisdom of Solomon 1:4), the "entering" of the prophetic spirit (Josephus *Antiquities* 4.6.5), demonic spirits that "enter" into men (Mark 9:25; Luke 8:30), and Satan "entering" Judas (Luke 22:3).

Figuratively it can denote the acquiring of something, i.e., "to attain something" (wealth, property, and so on). It is used of the kingdom of God/heaven (Matthew 5:20; 7:21; 19:24; Mark 9:47; 10:15; *et al*); it describes attaining eternal life (Matthew 18:8f.; 19:17; Mark 9:43,45); or it can speak of entering rest (Hebrews 3:11,18; 4:11). (See *Bauer*.)

STRONG 1525, BAUER 232-33, MOULTON-MILLIGAN 188, KITTEL 2:676-78, LIDDELL-SCOTT 494-95, COLIN BROWN 1:320-21.

1512. εἰσκαλέομαι eiskaleomai verb
Invite in.
CROSS-REFERENCE:
  καλέω kaleō (2535)

1. εἰσκαλεσάμενος eiskalesamenos
  nom sing masc part aor mid
1 Then **called** he them **in**, and lodged them. . . . . Acts 10:23

This term of invitation is a compound form of *kaleō* (2535), "call," and *eis* (1506B), "in." It occurs just once in the New Testament when Cornelius the Gentile invited Peter, a Jew, to come to Caesarea (Acts 10:23). *Moulton-Milligan* suggests that the verb seems to denote summoning by word of mouth rather than a formal citation (*parangellō* [3715]).

STRONG 1528, BAUER 233, MOULTON-MILLIGAN 188, KITTEL 3:496 (see "eiskaleō"), LIDDELL-SCOTT 495 (see "eiskaleō"), COLIN BROWN 1:273 (see "eiskaleō").

1513. εἴσοδος eisodos noun
Entering, entrance, access.
CROSS-REFERENCE:
  ὁδός hodos (3461)

בּוֹא bô' (971), Qal: come, enter (Jos 13:5, 2 Kgs 14:25, 2 Chr 26:8); hiphil: lift, wield (Ps 74:5 [73:5]—Codex Vaticanus only).

גָּלָל gālāl (1600), On account of (Gn 30:27—Codex Alexandrinus only).

זִיז zîz (2206), Breast (Is 66:11).

יָצָא yātsâ' (3428), Go out (Ps 121:8 [120:8]).

מָבוֹא māvô' (4136), Entrance, access to the sea (Jgs 1:24, 2 Kgs 11:16, Ez 44:5).

מוֹבָא môvā' (4264), Entrance (Ez 43:11).

סַף ṣaph (5790), Door, threshold (2 Chr 23:4).

פֶּתַח pethach (6860), Entrance (Prv 8:34).

1. εἴσοδος eisodos nom sing fem
2. εἰσόδου eisodou gen sing fem
3. εἴσοδον eisodon acc sing fem

2	When John had first preached before his **coming**	Acts 13:24
3	what manner of **entering in** we had unto you,	1 Th 1:9
3	brethren, know our **entrance** in unto you,	2:1
3	to enter into the holiest by the blood of Jesus,	Heb 10:19
1	For so an **entrance** shall be ministered unto you	2 Pt 1:11

This term can quickly be understood by recognizing its opposite, *exodus*. In Acts 13:24; 1 Thessalonians 1:9; and 2:1 it refers to the "entrance" of the good news into the world through the ministry of John and Paul. In 2 Peter 1:11 the believer enters into the eternal kingdom, and this is accomplished through the blood of Jesus (Hebrews 10:19).

STRONG 1529, BAUER 233, MOULTON-MILLIGAN 188, KITTEL 5:103-9, LIDDELL-SCOTT 496, COLIN BROWN 3:935-37,940-41.

1514. εἰσπηδάω eispēdaō verb

Leap or rush in.

CROSS-REFERENCE:
ἐκπηδάω ekpēdaō (1587B)

בּוֹא bô' (971), Entered, went (Am 5:19).

1. εἰσεπήδησεν eisepēdēsen 3sing indic aor act
2. εἰσεπήδησαν eisepēdēsan 3pl indic aor act

2 and ran in among the people, crying out,	Acts 14:14
1 Then he called for a light, and sprang in,	16:29

This is a term that indicates frantic, impulsive movement. It is translated "leap" or "rush in" in Acts 16:29. In extra-Biblical Greek a bolt of lightning "springs into" view.

STRONG 1530, BAUER 233, MOULTON-MILLIGAN 188, LIDDELL-SCOTT 497.

1515. εἰσπορεύω eisporeuō verb

Go (in), come (in), enter.

COGNATE:
πορεύομαι poreuomai (4057)

SYNONYMS:
εἴσειμι eiseimi (1510)
εἰσέρχομαι eiserchomai (1511)
ἐμβαίνω embainō (1671)

בִּאָה bi'āh (905), Entrance (Ez 8:5—Codex Alexandrinus only).
בּוֹא bô' (971), Come, arrive (Gn 23:10, Ru 4:11, Hg 2:16 [2:17]).
הָלַךְ hālakh (2050), Go, went (Jos 6:13 [6:12]).
יָצָא yātsâ' (3428), Go out, come out (Ex 11:4, Dt 31:2, 1 Sm 18:16).
יָרַד yāradh (3495), Go down (1 Sm 26:6—Codex Alexandrinus only).
מָבוֹא māvô' (4136), Entrance (Ez 26:10).
עָבַר 'āvar (5882), Go over, go across (Dt 4:14, 11:11, 2 Kgs 4:8).
עָלָה 'ālâh (6148), Took, came upon (Jos 10:9).
עֲלַל 'ălal (A6178), Go in (Dn 5:8—Aramaic).

1. εἰσπορεύεται eisporeuetai 3sing indic pres mid
2. εἰσπορεύονται eisporeuontai 3pl indic pres mid
3. εἰσπορευόμενος eisporeuomenos nom sing masc part pres mid
4. εἰσπορευόμενοι eisporeuomenoi nom pl masc part pres mid
5. εἰσπορευομένων eisporeuomenōn gen pl masc part pres mid
6. εἰσπορευομένους eisporeuomenous acc pl masc part pres mid
7. εἰσπορευόμεναι eisporeuomenai nom pl fem part pres mid
8. εἰσπορευόμενον eisporeuomenon nom/acc sing neu part pres mid
9. εἰσεπορεύετο eiseporeueto 3sing indic imperf mid

8 entereth in at the mouth goeth into the belly,	Matt 15:17
2 And they went into Capernaum;	Mark 1:21
7 and the lusts of other things entering in,	4:19
1 and entereth in where the damsel was lying.	5:40
9 And whithersoever he entered, into villages,	6:56
8 that entering into him can defile him:	7:15
8 thing from without entereth into the man,	7:18
1 Because it entereth not into his heart,	7:19
4 and as soon as ye be entered into it,	11:2
4 that they which enter in may see the light.	Luke 8:16
4 that they which come in may see the light.	11:33
2 for those who are wealthy to enter (NASB)	18:24
4 the which at your entering ye shall find a colt tied,	19:30
1 follow him into the house where he entered in.	22:10
5 to ask alms of them that entered into the temple;	Acts 3:2
3 entering into every house, and haling men and	8:3
3 with them coming in and going out at Jerusalem.	9:28
6 and received all that came in unto him,	28:30

This term occurs only in the Synoptic Gospels and Acts. A compound from *eis* (1506B), "in," and *poreuomai* (4057), "go along," it always indicates the place from which one object is entering into another. So Jesus explained to some Pharisees and disciples who lacked understanding that no food outside a man can defile him by going into him (Mark 7:15,18).

STRONG 1531, BAUER 233 (see "eisporeuomai"), MOULTON-MILLIGAN 188 (see "eisporeuomai"), KITTEL 6:578 (see "eisporeuomai"), LIDDELL-SCOTT 497.

1516. εἰστρέχω eistrechō verb

Run in.

CROSS-REFERENCE:
τρέχω trechō (4983)

1. εἰσδραμοῦσα eisdramousa nom sing fem part aor act

1 she opened not the gate for gladness, but ran in,	Acts 12:14

The term is used but once, in Acts 12:14, when in a humorous scene Rhoda leaves Peter at the house gate and "runs in" to alert John Mark's household that Peter is alive. The second part of the compound, *trechō* (4983), is used literally and figuratively ("run the race") throughout the New Testament.

STRONG 1532, BAUER 233, LIDDELL-SCOTT 497.

1517. εἰσφέρω eispherō verb

Bring or lead (in).

CROSS-REFERENCE:
φέρω pherō (5179)

אָסַף 'āsaph (636), Gather (Dt 11:14, 28:38, Jb 39:12).
בּוֹא bô' (971), Qal: go, come (Gn 27:18, Jos 6:19 [6:18], 2 Kgs 23:34); hiphil: bring, put in (Ex 4:6, Hg 1:9); hophal: be brought, be offered (Lv 6:23 [6:30], 2 Kgs 12:14 [12:13], 2 Chr 34:9).

εἰς 1518

לָקַט lāqaṭ (4092), Bring in (Ex 16:5—Codex Alexandrinus only).
קָרָא qārā' (7410), Call, summon (Dn 2:2).
שׁוּב shûv (8178), Hiphil: take out (Ex 4:7).

1. εἰσφέρεις eisphereis 2sing indic pres act
2. εἰσηνέγκαμεν eisēnenkamen 1pl indic aor act
3. εἰσενέγκῃς eisenenkēs 2sing subj aor act
4. εἰσενέγκωσιν eisenenkōsin 3pl subj aor act
5. εἰσενεγκεῖν eisenenkein inf aor act
6. εἰσφέρεται eispheretai 3sing indic pres mid
7. εἰσφέρωσιν eispherōsin 3pl subj pres act

```
3  And lead us not into temptation,................... Matt 6:13
5  and they sought means to bring him in,............ Luke 5:18
4  they might bring him in because of the multitude,....... 5:19
3  And lead us not into temptation; but deliver us....... 11:4
7  when they bring you before (NASB)................ 12:11
1  thou bringest certain strange things to our ears:.... Acts 17:20
2  For we brought nothing into this world,........... 1 Tm 6:7
6  whose blood is brought into the sanctuary......... Heb 13:11
```

Classical Greek and Septuagint Usage

As with most compounds of *eis* (1506B), the preposition functions to give specific direction to the controlling verb (cf. *eiserchomai* [1511], *eiskaleomai* [1512], *eisporeuō* [1515]). In this case *pherō* (5179), "bring" or "carry," is made more precise by the added *eis*; hence, "bring in" is its basic definition.

Eispherō occurs regularly in the Septuagint. Likewise it is found in contemporary Hellenistic literature (e.g., Philo, Josephus); furthermore, it is recorded as early as Homer (Eighth Century B.C.). *Eispherō* (second aorist *eisēnenka*) is the term used in the proverbial comment: "We *brought* nothing *into* the world, thus we are unable to take anything out" (1 Timothy 6:7; *Polycarp to the Philippians* 4:1; Philo *Special Laws* 1.294; cf. Job 1:21 and Ecclesiastes 5:14 for the thought if not the word).

New Testament Usage

Luke used *eispherō* more than any other author (Luke 5:18,19; 11:4; 12:11; Acts 17:20). He paralleled Matthew's only use (Matthew 6:13) in the Lord's Prayer: "Lead us not into temptation." Luke uses it figuratively of receiving a report. New ideas are "brought into" the ears of Paul's Areopagan listeners (Acts 17:20).

Hebrews 13:11 speaks of the high priest's responsibility to carry (used passively here) the blood of sacrificial animals into the Holy of Holies (cf. Leviticus 4:5; 16:27). The writer intimated that Christ, himself the High Priest, brought His own blood into the sanctuary of God as a sin offering.

STRONG 1533, BAUER 233, MOULTON-MILLIGAN 188-89, KITTEL 9:64-65, LIDDELL-SCOTT 497, COLIN BROWN 3:803.

1518. εἷς heis

See word study at number 1506A.

1519. εἰς eis

See word study at number 1506B.

1520. εἶτα eita adv

Then, next, furthermore.

1. εἶτα eita

```
1  afterward, when affliction or persecution ariseth..... Mark 4:17
1  first the blade, then the ear, after that the full corn..... 4:28
1  then the ear, after that the full corn in the ear......... 4:28
1  After that he put his hands again upon his eyes,........ 8:25
1  then cometh the devil, and taketh away the word....Luke 8:12
1  the mother of Jesus saith unto him,................ John 2:13
1  After that he poureth water into a basin,............. 13:5
1  Then saith he to the disciple, Behold thy mother!...... 19:27
1  Then saith he to Thomas, Reach hither thy finger,..... 20:27
1  after that miracles, then gifts of healings,.......... 1 Co 12:28
1  that he was seen of Cephas, then of the twelve;......... 15:5
1  he was seen of James; then of all the apostles......... 15:7
1  Then cometh the end,............................. 15:24
1  For Adam was first formed, then Eve.............. 1 Tm 2:13
1  then let them use the office of a deacon,............. 3:10
1  Furthermore we have had fathers of our flesh...... Heb 12:9
1  Then when lust hath conceived,.................... Jas 1:15
```

This word can function as an adverbial particle of time meaning "afterward." In general and in enumerations it is a transition word meaning "then" or "next." See Mark 4:17; John 13:5; 1 Timothy 2:13, for example. It may be translated "furthermore" in Hebrews 12:9.

STRONG 1534, BAUER 233-34, MOULTON-MILLIGAN 189, LIDDELL-SCOTT 498.

1521. εἴτε eite conj

If.

1. εἴτε eite

```
1  whether prophecy, let us prophesy according to.... Rom 12:6
1  Or ministry, let us wait on our ministering:........... 12:7
1  or he that teacheth, on teaching;..................... 12:7
1  Or he that exhorteth, on exhortation:................. 12:8
1  Whether Paul, or Apollos, or Cephas, or the world, 1 Co 3:22
1  Whether Paul, or Apollos, or Cephas, or the world,..... 3:22
1  Whether Paul, or Apollos, or Cephas, or the world,..... 3:22
1  Whether Paul, or Apollos, or Cephas, or the world,..... 3:22
1  Apollos, or Cephas, or the world, or life, or death,..... 3:22
1  Apollos, or Cephas, or the world, or life, or death,..... 3:22
1  or things present, or things to come; all are yours;...... 3:22
1  or things present, or things to come; all are yours;...... 3:22
1  that are called gods, whether in heaven or in earth,..... 8:5
1  that are called gods, whether in heaven or in earth,..... 8:5
```

1 Whether therefore ye eat, or drink,	1 Co 10:31
1 Whether therefore ye eat, or drink,	10:31
1 or whatsoever ye do, do all to the glory of God.	10:31
1 whether we be Jews or Gentiles,	12:13
1 whether we be Jews or Gentiles,	12:13
1 whether we be bond or free;	12:13
1 whether we be bond or free;	12:13
1 And whether one member suffer,	12:26
1 or one member be honoured,	12:26
1 but whether there be prophecies, they shall fail;	13:8
1 whether there be tongues, they shall cease;	13:8
1 whether there be knowledge, it shall vanish away.	13:8
1 without life giving sound, whether pipe or harp,	14:7
1 without life giving sound, whether pipe or harp,	14:7
1 If any man speak in an unknown tongue,	14:27
1 Therefore whether it were I or they, so we preach,	15:11
1 Therefore whether it were I or they, so we preach,	15:11
1 And whether we be afflicted,	2 Co 1:6
1 or whether we be comforted,	1:6
1 whether present or absent, we may be accepted	5:9
1 present or absent, we may be accepted of him.	5:9
1 to that he hath done, whether it be good or bad.	5:10
1 to that he hath done, whether it be good or bad.	5:10
1 For whether we be beside ourselves, it is to God;	5:13
1 or whether we be sober, it is for your cause.	5:13
1 Whether any do inquire of Titus,	8:23
1 or our brethren be inquired of,	8:23
1 whether in the body, I cannot tell;	12:2
1 or whether out of the body, I cannot tell:	12:2
1 whether in the body, or out of the body,	12:3
1 whether in the body, or out of the body,	12:3
1 receive of the Lord, whether he be bond or free.	Eph 6:8
1 receive of the Lord, whether he be bond or free.	6:8
1 every way, whether in pretence, or in truth,	Phlp 1:18
1 in pretence, or in truth, Christ is preached;	1:18
1 whether it be by life, or by death.	1:20
1 whether it be by life, or by death.	1:20
1 that whether I come and see you, or else be absent,	1:27
1 that whether I come and see you, or else be absent,	1:27
1 visible and invisible, whether they be thrones,	Col 1:16
1 whether they be thrones, or dominions,	1:16
1 thrones, or dominions, or principalities, or powers:	1:16
1 thrones, or dominions, or principalities, or powers:	1:16
1 by him, I say, whether they be things in earth,	1:20
1 things in earth, or things in heaven.	1:20
1 whether we wake or sleep, we should live	1 Th 5:10
1 whether we wake or sleep, we should live	5:10
1 whether by word, or our epistle.	2 Th 2:15
1 whether by word, or our epistle.	2:15
1 whether it be to the king, as supreme;	1 Pt 2:13
1 Or unto governors, as unto them that are sent	2:14

This particle is directly related to *ei* (1479). It usually occurs in duplicate; "if—if," "whether—or." See Romans 12:6-8; 1 Corinthians 3:22.

STRONG 1535, BAUER 234, LIDDELL-SCOTT 498.

1521B. εἶτεν eiten adv
Then, afterwards.

1. εἶτεν eiten

1 first the blade, then the ear, after that the full corn	Mark 4:28
1 then the ear, after that the full corn in the ear.	4:28

A variant to the term *eita* (1520), the Greek word *eiten* means "then," "afterwards," or "next." *Liddell-Scott* reports that this adverb reflects the spelling of a more ancient Greek dialect (Ionic) and is used to denote "the sequence of one act or state upon another." A rare New Testament occurrence of the word is seen at Mark 4:28 in the Parable of the Growing Seed: "For the earth bringeth forth fruit of herself; first the blade, *then* the ear, after that the full corn in the ear" (cf. the variant to the traditional text, i.e., the *Textus Receptus*).

BAUER 234, MOULTON-MILLIGAN 189, LIDDELL-SCOTT 498.

1522. εἴωθα eiōtha verb
Be accustomed, be used to.

1. εἰώθει eiōthei 3sing indic plperf act
2. εἰωθός eiōthos nom/acc sing neu part perf act

1 was wont to release unto the people a prisoner,	Matt 27:15
1 and, as he was wont, he taught them again.	Mark 10:1
2 and, as his custom was, he went into the synagogue	Luke 4:16
2 And Paul, as his manner was, went in unto them,	Acts 17:2

Classical Greek
Eiōtha is actually the perfect tense of the verb *ethō* ("to be accustomed, used to") which appears only in the present participial form in classical Greek.

Septuagint Usage
The term occurs four times in the Septuagint, but only one of these is canonical (Numbers 24:1). The use in that text is the present participial form, and it refers to Balaam's not resorting to sorcery "according to custom" (cf. Susanna 13; cf. 4 Maccabees 1:12).

New Testament Usage
The four instances of *eiōtha* in the New Testament include three Gospel texts (none of which are parallel) and one text in Acts. Every instance is in keeping with the understood usage, "to be accustomed, to be used to." Jesus enters the synagogue "as his custom was" (*kata to eiōthos autō*) (Luke 4:16; cf. Mark 10:1; Acts 17:2). At the time of Jesus' trial the governor was accustomed to releasing a prisoner to the crowd. On that fateful date the crowd demanded Barabbas be released and Jesus crucified (Matthew 27:15).

BAUER 234, MOULTON-MILLIGAN 189, LIDDELL-SCOTT 480 (see "ethō"), COLIN BROWN 2:437.

1523. ἐκ ek prep
From, out of, away from.

1. ἐξ ex gen
2. ἐκ ek gen

2 And Judas begat Phares and Zara of Thamar;	Matt 1:3
2 And Salmon begat Booz of Rachab;	1:5

ἐκ 1523

2 and Booz begat Obed of Ruth;	Matt 1:5
2 of her that had been the wife of Urias;	1:6
1 of whom was born Jesus, who is called Christ.	1:16
2 she was found with child of the Holy Ghost.	1:18
2 that which is conceived in her is of the Holy Ghost.	1:20
2 for out of thee shall come a Governor,	2:6
1 saying, Out of Egypt have I called my son.	2:15
2 God is able of these stones to raise up children	3:9
2 And lo a voice from heaven, saying,	3:17
2 for whatsoever is more than these cometh of evil.	5:37
1 Which of you by taking thought can add one cubit	6:27
2 Let me take the speck out of your eye, (NASB)	7:4
2 first cast out the beam out of thine own eye;	7:5
2 see ... to cast out the mote out of thy brother's eye.	7:5
1 Or what man is there of you, ... his son ask bread,	7:9
2 Wherefore by their fruits ye shall know them.	7:20
2 two possessed with devils, coming out of the tombs,	8:28
2 that house or city, shake off the dust of your feet.	10:14
2 persecute you in this city, flee ye into another:	10:23
1 and one of them shall not fall on the ground	10:29
1 What man shall there be among you,	12:11
2 for the tree is known by his fruit.	12:33
2 for out of the abundance of the heart	12:34
2 A good man out of the good treasure of the heart	12:35
2 out of the evil treasure bringeth forth evil things.	12:35
2 For by thy words thou shalt be justified,	12:37
2 and by thy words thou shalt be condemned.	12:37
2 for she came from the uttermost parts of the earth	12:42
2 The same day went Jesus out of the house,	13:1
2 out of his kingdom all things that offend,	13:41
2 the kingdom of heaven is like unto a net,	13:47
2 and sever the wicked from among the just,	13:49
2 out of his treasure things new and old.	13:52
1 by whatsoever thou mightest be profited by me;	15:5
2 but that which cometh out of the mouth,	15:11
2 But those things which proceed out of the mouth	15:18
2 out of the mouth come forth from the heart;	15:18
2 For out of the heart proceed evil thoughts,	15:19
2 that he would show them a sign from heaven.	16:1
2 and behold a voice out of the cloud, which said,	17:5
2 coming down from the mountain (NASB)	17:9
2 until the Son of man be risen again from the dead.	17:9
1 hundred sheep, and one of them be gone astray,	18:12
1 that if two of you agree on earth (NASB)	18:19
1 That if two of you shall agree on earth as touching	18:19
2 which were so born from their mother's womb:	19:12
2 All these things have I kept from my youth up:	19:20
2 agreed with the labourers for a penny a day,	20:2
2 one on thy right hand, and the other on the left,	20:21
1 one on thy right hand, and the other on the left,	20:21
2 but to sit on my right hand, and on my left,	20:23
1 but to sit on my right hand, and on my left,	20:23
2 Out of the mouth of babes and sucklings	21:16
2 Let no fruit grow on thee henceforward for ever.	21:19
1 whence was it? from heaven, or of men?	21:25
1 whence was it? from heaven, or of men?	21:25
1 If we shall say, From heaven, he will say unto us,	21:25
1 But if we shall say, Of men; we fear the people;	21:26
2 Whether of them twain did the will of his father?	21:31
1 Then one of them, which was a lawyer, asked him	22:35
1 said unto my Lord, Sit thou on my right hand,	22:44
1 the outside of the cup and of the platter,	23:25
1 and some of them ye shall kill and crucify;	23:34
1 some of them shall ye scourge in your synagogues,	23:34
1 not come down to take any thing out of his house;	24:17
2 and the stars shall fall from heaven,	24:29
2 shall gather together his elect from the four winds,	24:31
1 And five of them were wise, and five were foolish.	25:2
2 Give us of your oil; for our lamps are gone out.	25:8
2 And he shall set the sheep on his right hand,	25:33
1 sheep on his right hand, but the goats on the left.	25:33
2 shall the King say unto them on his right hand,	25:34
1 Then shall he say also unto them on the left hand,	25:41
1 I say unto you, that one of you shall betray me.	26:21
1 gave it to them, saying, Drink ye all of it;	26:27
2 I will not drink henceforth of this fruit of the vine,	26:29
2 He went away again the second time, (NT)	26:42
2 and prayed the third time, (NT)	Matt 26:44
2 the Son of man sitting on the right hand of power,	26:64
1 said to Peter, Surely thou also art one of them;	26:73
1 and bought with them the potter's field,	27:7
1 And when they had platted a crown of thorns,	27:29
2 one on the right hand, and another on the left.	27:38
1 one on the right hand, and another on the left.	27:38
1 straightway one of them ran, and took a sponge,	27:48
2 And came out of the graves after his resurrection,	27:53
1 for the angel of the Lord descended from heaven,	28:2
2 coming up out of the water (NASB)	Mark 1:10
2 And there came a voice from heaven, saying,	1:11
1 saying, Hold thy peace, and come out of him.	1:25
1 and cried with a loud voice, he came out of him.	1:26
2 when they were come out of the synagogue,	1:29
2 And when he was come out of the ship,	5:2
2 immediately there met him out of the tombs a man	5:2
2 Come out of the man, thou unclean spirit.	5:8
1 knowing ... that virtue had gone out of him,	5:30
2 That John the Baptist was risen from the dead,	6:14
2 John, whom I beheaded: he is risen from the dead.	6:16
1 give me by and by in a charger the head of John	6:25
2 were sore amazed in themselves beyond measure,	6:51
2 And when they were come out of the ship,	6:54
1 by whatsoever thou mightest be profited by me;	7:11
2 things which proceed out of the man (NASB)	7:15
2 cometh out of the man, that defileth the man.	7:20
2 out of the heart of men, proceed evil thoughts,	7:21
2 he would cast forth the devil out of her daughter.	7:26
2 the devil is gone out of thy daughter.	7:29
2 departing from the coasts of Tyre and Sidon,	7:31
2 and a voice came out of the cloud, saying,	9:7
2 coming down from the mountain (NASB)	9:9
2 till the Son of man were risen from the dead.	9:9
2 what the rising from the dead should mean.	9:10
2 And one of the multitude answered and said,	9:17
1 How long is it ago since this came unto him?	9:21
2 And he said, "From childhood. (NASB)	9:21
1 come out of him, and enter no more into him.	9:25
2 Master, all these have I observed from my youth.	10:20
2 one on thy right hand, and the other on thy left	10:37
1 and the other on thy left hand, in thy glory.	10:37
2 But to sit on my right hand and on my left hand	10:40
1 But to sit on my right hand and on my left hand	10:40
2 and others cut down branches off the trees,	11:8
2 No man eat fruit of thee hereafter for ever.	11:14
2 they saw the fig tree dried up from the roots.	11:20
1 The baptism of John, was it from heaven,	11:30
1 was it from heaven, or of men? answer me.	11:30
1 If we shall say, From heaven;	11:31
1 But if we shall say, Of men;	11:32
2 For when they shall rise from the dead,	12:25
1 shalt love the Lord thy God with all thy heart,	12:30
1 with all thy soul, and with all thy mind,	12:30
1 with all thy soul, and with all thy mind,	12:30
1 with all thy mind, and with all thy strength:	12:30
1 And to love him with all the heart,	12:33
1 all the heart, and with all the understanding,	12:33
1 and with all the soul, and with all the strength,	12:33
1 and with all the soul, and with all the strength,	12:33
2 Sit thou on my right hand,	12:36
2 For all they did cast in of their abundance;	12:44
2 but she of her want did cast in all that she had,	12:44
2 And as he went out of the temple,	13:1
2 one of his disciples saith unto him, Master,	13:1
2 neither enter ... to take any thing out of his house:	13:15
2 And the stars will be falling from heaven, (NASB)	13:25
2 gather together his elect from the four winds,	13:27
1 One of you which eateth with me shall betray me.	14:18
2 one of the twelve, that dippeth with me in the dish.	14:20
1 he gave it to them: and they all drank of it.	14:23
2 I will drink no more of the fruit of the vine,	14:25
2 But he spake the more vehemently, (NT)	14:31
2 the Son of man sitting on the right hand of power,	14:62
1 a maid saw him again, ... This is one of them.	14:69
1 Surely thou art one of them: ... art a Galilaean,	14:70
2 And the second time the cock crew. (NT)	14:72

ἐκ 1523

2	the one on his right hand, and the other on his left.Mark	15:27
1	the one on his right hand, and the other on his left....	15:27
1	when the centurion, which stood over against him,.....	15:39
2	in a sepulchre which was hewn out of a rock,...........	15:46
2	Who shall roll us away the stone from the door.......	16:3
1	he appeared in another form unto two of them,.......	16:12
2	them which had seen him after he was risen...........	16:14
2	and sat on the right hand of God.....................	16:19
1	priest named Zacharias, of the course of Abia:......Luke	1:5
2	and his wife was of the daughters of Aaron,............	1:5
2	standing on the right side of the altar of incense........	1:11
2	with ... Holy Ghost, even from his mother's womb.....	1:15
1	whose name was Joseph, of the house of David;........	1:27
2	be born of thee shall be called the Son of God.........	1:35
2	no one among your relatives who is called (NASB).....	1:61
1	That we should be saved from our enemies,............	1:71
2	and from the hand of all that hate us;.................	1:71
2	we being delivered out of the hand of our enemies.....	1:74
1	the dayspring from on high hath visited us,.............	1:78
2	out of the city of Nazareth, into Judaea,................	2:4
1	out of the city of Nazareth, into Judaea,................	2:4
2	that the thoughts of many hearts may be revealed.....	2:35
2	daughter of Phanuel, of the tribe of Aser:..............	2:36
2	That God is able of these stones to raise up	3:8
1	and a voice came from heaven, which said,............	3:22
2	gracious words which proceeded out of his mouth.......	4:22
1	saying, Hold thy peace, and come out of him..........	4:35
2	And he arose out of the synagogue,.....................	4:38
2	he sat down, and taught the people out of the ship.....	5:3
2	which were come out of every town of Galilee,.........	5:17
2	cast out first the beam out of thine own eye,...........	6:42
2	For every tree is known by his own fruit................	6:44
1	For of thorns men do not gather figs,..................	6:44
2	nor of a bramble bush gather they grapes...............	6:44
2	A good man out of the good treasure of his heart......	6:45
2	and an evil man out of the evil treasure	6:45
2	of the abundance of the heart his mouth speaketh......	6:45
2	support them out of their own means (NASB)..........	8:3
2	there met him out of the city a certain man,...........	8:27
2	man from the city which had devils (NASB)...........	8:27
2	it was said ... that John was risen from the dead;......	9:7
2	And there came a voice out of the cloud, saying,......	9:35
2	that we command fire to come down from heaven,.....	9:54
1	Go not from house to house...........................	10:7
2	the very dust of your city, which cleaveth on us,......	10:11
2	I beheld Satan as lightning fall from heaven...........	10:18
1	shalt love the Lord thy God with all thy heart,.........	10:27
1	and with all thy soul, and with all thy strength,........	10:27
1	and with all thy soul, and with all thy strength,........	10:27
1	and with all thy strength, and with all thy mind;.......	10:27
1	Which of you shall have a friend,.....................	11:5
2	For a friend of mine in his journey is come to me,....	11:6
1	Now suppose one of you fathers is asked (NASB).....	11:11
1	more will your Father in heaven give (NIV)..........	11:13
1	But some of them said, He casteth out devils..........	11:15
2	tempting him, sought of him a sign from heaven.......	11:16
2	certain woman of the company lifted up her voice,.....	11:27
2	for she came from the utmost parts of the earth......	11:31
1	and some of them they shall slay and persecute:.......	11:49
2	and seeking to catch something out of his mouth,......	11:54
1	and not one of them is forgotten before God?........	12:6
2	And one of the company said unto him, Master,......	12:13
2	the abundance of the things which he possesseth.......	12:15
1	And which of you with taking thought can add.......	12:25
1	when he will return from the wedding;................	12:36
1	For which of you, intending to build a tower,.........	14:28
1	he be of you that forsaketh not all that he hath,.......	14:33
1	What man of you, having an hundred sheep,...........	15:4
1	if he lose one of them, doth not leave the ninety......	15:4
2	He longed to fill his stomach with the pods (NIV).....	15:16
2	when I am removed from the stewardship (NASB).....	16:4
2	Make to yourselves friends of the mammon	16:9
2	be persuaded, though one rose from the dead..........	16:31
1	But which of you, having a servant plowing............	17:7
2	when he is come from the field,......................	17:7
1	And one of them, when he saw that he was healed,....	17:15
2	that lighteneth out of the one part under heaven,......	17:24
2	he said, All these have I kept from my youth up...Luke	18:21
2	Out of thine own mouth will I judge thee,.............	19:22
1	baptism of John, was it from heaven, or of men?.....	20:4
1	baptism of John, was it from heaven, or of men?.....	20:4
1	If we shall say, From heaven; he will say,.............	20:5
1	and if we say, Of men; all the people will stone us:...	20:6
2	and the resurrection from the dead,...................	20:35
2	said unto my Lord, Sit thou on my right hand,........	20:42
2	For all these have of their abundance cast in..........	21:4
2	but she of her penury hath cast in all the living.......	21:4
1	some of you shall they cause to be put to death.......	21:16
2	But there shall not an hair of your head perish........	21:18
2	Iscariot, being of the number of the twelve............	22:3
1	For I say unto you, I will not any more eat thereof,...	22:16
1	which of them it was that should do this thing.........	22:23
1	one of them smote the servant.........................	22:50
1	Thou art also of them. And Peter said, ... I am not....	22:58
2	sit on the right hand of the power of God.............	22:69
2	knew that he belonged unto Herod's jurisdiction,......	23:7
1	for he was desirous to see him of a long season,......	23:8
2	one on the right hand, and the other on the left.......	23:33
1	one on the right hand, and the other on the left.......	23:33
2	which came with him from Galilee, followed after,.....	23:55
1	two of them went that same day to a village..........	24:13
1	And the one of them, whose name was Cleopas,......	24:18
1	women also of our company made us astonished,......	24:22
2	and to rise from the dead the third day:...............	24:46
1	until ye be endued with power from on high..........	24:49
1	until ye be endued with power from on high..........	24:49
1	Which were born, not of blood,..................John	1:13
2	not of blood, nor of the will of the flesh,..............	1:13
2	nor of the will of man, but of God....................	1:13
2	nor of the will of man, but of God....................	1:13
2	And of his fulness have all we received,..............	1:16
1	the Jews sent priests ... from Jerusalem to ask him,...	1:19
2	And they which were sent were of the Pharisees.......	1:24
1	I saw the Spirit descending from heaven..............	1:32
2	next day after John stood, and two of his disciples;....	1:35
2	One of the two which heard John speak,..............	1:40
2	of the city of Andrew and Peter. (NASB)	1:44
2	Can there any good thing come out of Nazareth?.....	1:46
2	And when he had made a scourge of small cords,.....	2:15
2	he drove them all out of the temple,..................	2:15
2	When therefore he was risen from the dead,..........	2:22
2	There was a man of the Pharisees,.....................	3:1
1	Except a man be born of water and of the Spirit,......	3:5
2	That which is born of the flesh is flesh;...............	3:6
2	and that which is born of the Spirit is spirit...........	3:6
2	so is every one that is born of the Spirit..............	3:8
2	but he that came down from heaven,..................	3:13
2	between some of John's disciples and the Jews	3:25
2	nothing, except it be given him from heaven..........	3:27
2	he that is of the earth is earthly,......................	3:31
1	he that is of the earth is earthly,......................	3:31
2	and speaketh of the earth:.............................	3:31
2	he that cometh from heaven is above all..............	3:31
2	for God giveth not the Spirit by measure unto him....	3:34
2	Jesus therefore, being wearied with his journey,.......	4:6
2	There cometh a woman of Samaria to draw water:.....	4:7
2	which gave us the well, and drank thereof himself,.....	4:12
2	Whosoever drinketh of this water shall thirst,..........	4:13
2	of the water that I shall give him shall never thirst;.....	4:14
2	for salvation is of the Jews...........................	4:22
2	they went out of the city, and came unto him.........	4:30
2	And many of the Samaritans of that city believed.....	4:39
2	When he heard that Jesus was come out of Judaea.....	4:47
2	when he was come out of Judaea into Galilee.........	4:54
2	but is passed from death unto life.....................	5:24
2	One of his disciples, Andrew,.........................	6:8
2	and likewise of the fishes as much as they would.......	6:11
2	with the fragments of the five barley loaves,...........	6:13
2	Howbeit there came other boats from Tiberias.........	6:23
2	because ye did eat of the loaves, and were filled.......	6:26
2	written, He gave them bread from heaven to eat......	6:31
2	Moses gave you not that bread from heaven;..........	6:32
2	my Father giveth you the true bread from heaven......	6:32
2	the bread ... he which cometh down from heaven,.....	6:33

ἐκ 1523

2	For I came down **from** heaven, not to do mine own John	6:38
1	that of all which he hath given me ... lose nothing,	6:39
2	I am the bread which came down **from** heaven.	6:41
2	he saith, I came down **from** heaven?	6:42
2	This is the bread which cometh down **from** heaven,	6:50
1	that a man may eat **thereof**, and not die.	6:50
2	the living bread which came down **from** heaven:	6:51
2	if any man eat **of** this bread, he shall live for ever:	6:51
2	This is that bread which came down **from** heaven:	6:58
1	This is that bread which came down **from** heaven:	6:58
2	Many therefore **of** his disciples,	6:60
1	But there are some **of** you that believe not.	6:64
1	For Jesus knew **from** the beginning who they were	6:64
2	except it were given unto him **of** my Father.	6:65
2	**From** that time many of his disciples went back,	6:66
2	**From** this time many ... turned back (NIV) (NT)	6:66
1	chosen you twelve, and one **of** you is a devil?	6:70
2	Judas Iscariot ... being one **of** the twelve.	6:71
2	shall know of the doctrine, whether it be **of** God,	7:17
1	and yet none **of** you keepeth the law?	7:19
2	not because it is **of** Moses, but of the fathers;	7:22
2	not because it is of Moses, but **of** the fathers;	7:22
2	Then said some of them **of** Jerusalem,	7:25
2	And many **of** the people believed on him, and said,	7:31
2	**out of** his belly shall flow rivers of living water.	7:38
2	Many **of** the people therefore,	7:40
2	But some said, Shall Christ come **out of** Galilee?	7:41
2	That Christ cometh **of** the seed of David,	7:42
1	And some **of** them would have taken him;	7:44
2	Have any **of** the rulers or of the Pharisees believed	7:48
2	Have any of the rulers or **of** the Pharisees believed	7:48
1	he that came to Jesus by night, being one **of** them,	7:50
2	Art thou also **of** Galilee? Search, and look:	7:52
2	for **out of** Galilee ariseth no prophet.	7:52
2	Ye are **from** beneath; I am from above:	8:23
2	Ye are from beneath; I am **from** above:	8:23
2	ye are **of** this world; I am not of this world.	8:23
2	ye are of this world; I am not **of** this world.	8:23
2	We be not born **of** fornication;	8:41
2	for I proceeded forth and came **from** God;	8:42
2	Ye are **of** your father the devil,	8:44
2	When he speaketh a lie, he speaketh **of** his own:	8:44
1	Which of you convinceth me **of** sin?	8:46
2	He that is **of** God heareth God's words:	8:47
2	ye ... hear them not, because ye are not **of** God.	8:47
2	but Jesus hid himself, and went **out of** the temple,	8:59
2	he saw a man which was blind **from** his birth.	9:1
2	spat on the ground, and made clay of the spittle,	9:6
2	Therefore said some **of** the Pharisees,	9:16
2	Then **again** called they the man that was blind,	9:24
2	**Since** the world began was it not heard	9:32
2	And some **of** the Pharisees which were with him	9:40
2	And other sheep I have, which are not **of** this fold:	10:16
1	And many **of** them said, He hath a devil,	10:20
2	But ye believe not, because ye are not **of** my sheep,	10:26
2	neither shall any man pluck them **out of** my hand.	10:28
2	is able to pluck them **out of** my Father's hand.	10:29
2	good works have I showed you **from** my Father;	10:32
2	but he escaped **out of** their hand,	10:39
2	Bethany, the town **of** Mary and her sister Martha.	11:1
2	And many **of** the Jews came to Martha and Mary,	11:19
1	And some **of** them said, Could not this man,	11:37
2	Then many **of** the Jews which came to Mary,	11:45
1	But some of them went their ways to the Pharisees,	11:46
1	one **of** them, named Caiaphas, ... the high priest	11:49
2	and many went **out of** the country up to Jerusalem	11:55
2	Lazarus was ... whom he raised **from** the dead.	12:1
2	Lazarus was one **of** those reclining (NASB)	12:2
2	house was filled **with** the odour of the ointment.	12:3
2	Then saith one **of** his disciples, Judas Iscariot,	12:4
2	Much people **of** the Jews therefore knew	12:9
2	see Lazarus ... whom he had raised **from** the dead.	12:9
2	with him when he called Lazarus **out of** his grave,	12:17
2	called Lazarus ... and raised him **from** the dead,	12:17
2	And there were certain Greeks **among** them	12:20
2	what shall I say? Father, save me **from** this hour:	12:27
2	Then came there a voice **from** heaven, saying,	12:28
2	And I, if I be lifted up **from** the earth, ... John	12:32
2	heard **out of** the law that Christ abideth for ever:	12:34
2	**among** the chief rulers also many believed on him;	12:42
1	For I have not spoken **of** myself;	12:49
2	that he should depart **out of** this world	13:1
2	riseth **from** supper, and laid aside his garments;	13:4
1	I say unto you, that one **of** you shall betray me.	13:21
2	on Jesus' breast one **of** His disciples (NASB)	13:23
2	If ye were **of** the world,	15:19
2	but because ye are not **of** the world,	15:19
2	but I have chosen you **out of** the world,	15:19
1	these things I said not unto you **at** the beginning,	16:4
1	and none **of** you asketh me, Whither goest thou?	16:5
2	He shall glorify me: for he shall receive **of** mine,	16:14
2	therefore said I, that he shall take **of** mine,	16:15
2	Then said some **of** his disciples among themselves,	16:17
2	I came forth **from** the Father, (NASB)	16:28
2	the men which thou gavest me **out of** the world:	17:6
2	and none of them is lost, but the son **of** perdition;	17:12
2	because they are not **of** the world,	17:14
2	even as I am not **of** the world.	17:14
2	not that thou shouldest take them **out of** the world,	17:15
2	but that thou shouldest keep them **from** the evil.	17:15
2	They are not **of** the world,	17:16
2	are not of the world, even as I am not **of** the world.	17:16
2	and officers **from** the chief priests and Pharisees,	18:3
2	and officers from the chief priests and Pharisees,	18:3
1	**Of** them which thou gavest me have I lost none.	18:9
2	Art not thou also one **of** this man's disciples?	18:17
2	Art not thou also one **of** his disciples? He denied it,	18:25
2	One of the servants of the high priest,	18:26
2	Jesus answered, My kingdom is not **of** this world:	18:36
2	if my kingdom were **of** this world,	18:36
2	Every one that is **of** the truth heareth my voice.	18:37
1	And the soldiers platted a crown **of** thorns,	19:2
2	And **from** thenceforth Pilate sought to release him:	19:12
2	without seam, woven **from** the top throughout.	19:23
2	and seeth the stone taken away **from** the sepulchre.	20:1
2	have taken away the Lord **out of** the sepulchre,	20:2
2	that he must rise again **from** the dead.	20:9
2	But Thomas, one **of** the twelve, called Didymus,	20:24
2	the sons of Zebedee, and two other **of** his disciples.	21:2
2	after that he was risen **from** the dead.	21:14
2	purchased a field **with** the reward of iniquity; Acts	1:18
2	show whether **of** these two thou hast chosen,	1:24
1	apostleship, **from** which Judas by transgression fell,	1:25
2	And suddenly there came a sound **from** heaven	2:2
2	for he is **on** my right hand,	2:25
2	that **of** the fruit of his loins, according to the flesh,	2:30
2	said unto my Lord, Sit thou **on** my right hand,	2:34
2	And a certain man lame **from** his mother's womb	3:2
2	whom God hath raised **from** the dead;	3:15
2	shall ... God raise up unto you **of** your brethren,	3:22
2	shall be destroyed **from among** the people.	3:23
2	through Jesus the resurrection **from** the dead.	4:2
2	as many as were of the kindred **of** the high priest,	4:6
2	ye crucified, whom God raised **from** the dead,	4:10
1	for if this counsel or this work be **of** men,	5:38
2	But if it be **of** God, ye cannot overthrow it;	5:39
2	look you **among** you seven men of honest report,	6:3
2	Then there arose certain **of** the synagogue,	6:9
2	And said unto him, Get thee **out of** thy country,	7:3
2	Get thee out of thy country, and **from** thy kindred,	7:3
2	Then came he **out of** the land of the Chaldaeans,	7:4
2	And delivered him **out of** all his afflictions,	7:10
2	God raise up unto you **of** your brethren,	7:37
2	which brought us out **of** the land of Egypt,	7:40
2	and Jesus standing **on** the right hand of God,	7:55
2	the Son of man standing **on** the right hand of God.	7:56
1	If thou believest **with** all thine heart, thou mayest.	8:37
2	And when they were come up **out of** the water,	8:39
2	a light **from** heaven flashed around him (NASB)	9:3
1	Aeneas, which had kept his bed eight years, (NT)	9:33
2	a centurion **of** the band called the Italian band,	10:1
2	spake unto him again the second time, (NT)	10:15
2	and drink with him after he rose **from** the dead.	10:41
2	And they **of** the circumcision which believed	10:45

310

ἐκ 1523

2	they ... of the circumcision contended with him,	Acts 11:2
2	let down from heaven by four corners;	11:5
2	But the voice answered me again from heaven,	11:9
2	But the voice answered me again from heaven,	11:9
1	some of them were men of Cyprus and Cyrene,	11:20
1	And there stood up one of them named Agabus,	11:28
2	And his chains fell off from his hands.	12:7
2	and hath delivered me out of the hand of Herod,	12:11
2	how the Lord had brought him out of the prison.	12:17
1	And Barnabas and Saul returned from Jerusalem,	12:25
1	and with an high arm brought he them out of it.	13:17
2	Saul the son of Cis, a man of the tribe of Benjamin,	13:21
2	But God raised him from the dead:	13:30
2	as concerning that he raised him up from the dead,	13:34
2	when the Jews were gone out of the synagogue,	13:42
2	being a cripple from his mother's womb,	14:8
1	that Paul and Barnabas, and certain other of them,	15:2
1	to take out of them a people for his name.	15:14
2	For Moses of old time hath in every city	15:21
1	to send chosen men of their own company	15:22
1	which are of the Gentiles in Antioch and Syria and	15:23
1	that certain which went out from us	15:24
1	from which if ye keep yourselves, ye shall do well.	15:29
2	And they went out of the prison,	16:40
2	and risen again from the dead;	17:3
1	And some of them believed,	17:4
1	Therefore many of them believed;	17:12
1	And hath made of one blood all nations of men	17:26
2	in that he hath raised him from the dead.	17:31
2	So Paul departed from among them.	17:33
2	After these things Paul departed from Athens,	18:1
2	Jews to depart from Rome: and came unto them.	18:2
2	they fled out of that house naked and wounded.	19:16
2	ye know that by this craft we have our wealth.	19:25
2	And they drew Alexander out of the multitude,	19:33
2	all with one voice about the space of two hours	19:34
1	Also of your own selves shall men arise,	20:30
2	Philip the evangelist, which was one of the seven;	21:8
2	suddenly there shone from heaven a great light	22:6
2	and shouldest hear the voice of his mouth.	22:14
1	and get thee quickly out of Jerusalem:	22:18
2	and to take him by force from among them,	23:10
1	lie in wait for him of them more than forty men,	23:21
2	he asked of what province he was.	23:34
2	with ... violence took him away out of our hands,	24:7
2	hast been of many years a judge unto this nation,	24:10
2	My manner of life from my youth,	26:4
2	Delivering thee from the people,	26:17
2	from the Gentiles ... to whom I send you (RSV)	26:17
1	should be the first that should rise from the dead,	26:23
1	shall be no loss of any man's life among you,	27:22
2	they cast four anchors out of the stern,	27:29
2	as the shipmen were about to flee out of the ship,	27:30
2	they would have cast anchors out of the foreship,	27:30
2	shall not an hair fall from the head of any of you.	27:34
2	a viper out of the heat, and fastened on his hand.	28:3
2	saw the venomous beast hang on his hand,	28:4
2	he has been saved from the sea, (NASB)	28:4
1	yet was I delivered prisoner from Jerusalem	28:17
2	our Lord, which was made of the seed of David	Rom 1:3
2	by the resurrection from the dead:	1:4
2	righteousness of God revealed from faith to faith:	1:17
2	as it is written, The just shall live by faith.	1:17
1	But unto them that are contentious,	2:8
2	being instructed out of the law;	2:18
2	And shall not uncircumcision which is by nature,	2:27
1	whose praise is not of men, but of God.	2:29
2	whose praise is not of men, but of God.	2:29
1	Therefore by the deeds of the law there shall no	3:20
2	and the justifier of him which believeth in Jesus.	3:26
2	God, which shall justify the circumcision by faith,	3:30
1	For if Abraham were justified by works,	4:2
2	to them who are not of the circumcision only,	4:12
2	For if they which are of the law be heirs,	4:14
2	Therefore it is of faith, that it might be by grace;	4:16
2	not to that only which is of the law,	4:16
2	but to that also which is of the faith of Abraham;	4:16

2	him that raised up Jesus our Lord from the dead;	Rom 4:24
2	Therefore being justified by faith,	5:1
1	for the judgment was by one to condemnation,	5:16
2	the free gift is of many offences unto justification.	5:16
2	that like as Christ was raised up from the dead	6:4
2	Knowing that Christ being raised from the dead	6:9
2	as those that are alive from the dead,	6:13
2	but ye have obeyed from the heart.	6:17
2	even to him who is raised from the dead,	7:4
2	who shall deliver me from the body of this death?	7:24
2	that raised up Jesus from the dead dwell in you,	8:11
2	he that raised up Christ from the dead shall also	8:11
2	yea rather, that is risen again,	8:34
1	and of whom as concerning the flesh Christ came,	9:5
1	For they are not all Israel, which are of Israel:	9:6
1	but when Rebecca also had conceived by one,	9:10
1	according to election might stand, not of works,	9:11
2	not of works, but of him that calleth;	9:11
2	of the same lump to make one vessel unto honour,	9:21
1	not of the Jews only, but also of the Gentiles?	9:24
1	not of the Jews only, but also of the Gentiles?	9:24
2	even the righteousness which is of faith.	9:30
2	Wherefore? Because they sought it not by faith,	9:32
1	but as it were by the works of the law.	9:32
2	describeth the righteousness which is of the law,	10:5
2	But the righteousness which is of faith	10:6
2	that is, to bring up Christ again from the dead.	10:7
2	that God hath raised him from the dead,	10:9
1	So then faith cometh by hearing,	10:17
2	For I also am an Israelite, of the seed of Abraham,	11:1
1	And if by grace, then is it no more of works:	11:6
1	But if it be of works, then is it no more grace:	11:6
1	and might save some of them.	11:14
2	the receiving of them be, but life from the dead?	11:15
2	For if thou wert cut out of the olive tree	11:24
2	There shall come out of Sion the Deliverer,	11:26
1	For of him, and through him, and to him,	11:36
1	as much as lieth in you, live peaceably with all	12:18
1	and thou shalt have praise of the same:	13:3
1	that now it is high time to awake out of sleep:	13:11
2	because he eateth not of faith:	14:23
2	for whatsoever is not of faith is sin.	14:23
2	Salute them which are of Aristobulus' household.	16:10
2	Greet them that be of the household of Narcissus,	16:11
1	But of him are ye in Christ Jesus,	1 Co 1:30
2	spirit of the world, but the spirit which is of God;	2:12
2	might be taken away from among you.	5:2
2	for then must ye needs go out of the world.	5:10
1	away from among yourselves that wicked person.	5:13
2	except it be with consent for a time,	7:5
2	But every man hath his proper gift of God,	7:7
1	but one God, the Father, of whom are all things,	8:6
2	who planteth ... and eateth not of the fruit thereof?	9:7
2	and eateth not of the milk of the flock?	9:7
2	about holy things live of the things of the temple?	9:13
2	which preach the gospel should live of the gospel.	9:14
2	For though I be free from all men,	9:19
2	drank of that spiritual Rock that followed them:	10:4
2	for we are all partakers of that one bread.	10:17
2	For the man is not of the woman;	11:8
1	but the woman of the man.	11:8
2	For as the woman is of the man,	11:12
2	the man also by the woman; but all things of God.	11:12
2	so let him eat of that bread, and drink of that cup.	11:28
2	so let him eat of that bread, and drink of that cup.	11:28
2	Because I am not the hand, I am not of the body;	12:15
2	is it therefore not of the body?	12:15
2	Because I am not the eye, I am not of the body;	12:16
2	is it therefore not of the body?	12:16
2	are the body of Christ, and members in particular.	12:27
2	For we know in part, and we prophesy in part.	13:9
2	For we know in part, and we prophesy in part.	13:9
2	then that which is in part shall be done away.	13:10
2	now I know in part; but then shall I know	13:12
1	of whom the greater part remain unto this present,	15:6
2	if Christ be preached that he rose from the dead,	15:12
2	But now is Christ risen from the dead,	15:20

311

ἐκ 1523

2	The first man is **of** the earth, earthy:	1 Co 15:47
1	the second man is the Lord **from** heaven.	15:47
2	Who delivered us **from** so great a death,	2 Co 1:10
2	bestowed upon us **by** the means of many persons	1:11
1	but the same which is made sorry **by** me?	2:2
2	For **out** of much affliction and anguish of heart	2:4
2	To the one an aroma **from** death to death, (NASB)	2:16
2	to the other an aroma **from** life to life. (NASB)	2:16
1	but as **of** sincerity, but as **of** God,	2:17
2	but as **of** sincerity, but as **of** God,	2:17
1	or letters of commendation **from** you?	3:1
1	Not that we are sufficient **of** ourselves	3:5
2	but our sufficiency is **of** God;	3:5
2	who commanded the light to shine **out of** darkness,	4:6
1	of the power may be **of** God, and not **of** us.	4:7
2	we have a building **of** God,	5:1
1	with our house which is **from** heaven:	5:2
2	and willing rather to be absent **from** the body,	5:8
2	And all things are **of** God,	5:18
2	come out **from** among them, and be ye separate,	6:17
1	that ye might receive damage **by** us in nothing.	7:9
1	and in all diligence, and **in** your love to us,	8:7
2	be a performance also **out** of that which ye have.	8:11
1	But **by** an equality, that now at this time	8:14
1	and your zeal hath provoked very many. (NT)	9:2
2	so let him give; not grudgingly, or **of** necessity:	9:7
2	so let him give; not grudgingly, or **of** necessity:	9:7
2	in perils **by** mine own countrymen,	11:26
1	in perils **by** the heathen, in perils in the city,	11:26
1	which he seeth me to be, or that he heareth **of** me.	12:6
1	For though he was crucified **through** weakness,	13:4
2	yet he liveth **by** the power of God.	13:4
2	but we shall live with him **by** the power of God	13:4
2	God the Father, who raised him **from** the dead;	Gal 1:1
2	he might deliver us **from** this present evil world,	1:4
1	But though we, or an angel **from** heaven,	1:8
2	God, who separated me **from** my mother's womb,	1:15
2	fearing them which were **of** the circumcision.	2:12
1	are Jews by nature, and not sinners **of** the Gentiles,	2:15
1	that a man is not justified **by** the works of the law,	2:16
2	that we might be justified **by** the faith of Christ,	2:16
1	and not **by** the works of the law:	2:16
1	**by** the works of the law shall no flesh be justified.	2:16
1	Received ye the Spirit **by** the works of the law,	3:2
1	Received ye the Spirit ... or **by** the hearing of faith?	3:2
1	doeth he it **by** the works of the law,	3:5
1	**by** the works of the law, or **by** the hearing of faith?	3:5
2	Know ye therefore that they which are **of** faith,	3:7
2	that God would justify the heathen **through** faith,	3:8
2	So then they which be **of** faith are blessed	3:9
1	are **of** the works of the law are under the curse:	3:10
2	it is evident: for, The just shall live **by** faith.	3:11
2	And the law is not **of** faith:	3:12
2	Christ hath redeemed us **from** the curse of the law,	3:13
2	For if the inheritance be **of** the law,	3:18
1	inheritance of the law, it is no more **of** promise:	3:18
2	verily righteousness should have been **by** the law.	3:21
2	the promise **by** faith of Jesus Christ might be given	3:22
2	that we might be justified **by** faith.	3:24
2	God sent forth his Son, made **of** a woman,	4:4
2	the one **by** a bondmaid, the other **by** a freewoman.	4:22
2	the one **by** a bondmaid, the other **by** a freewoman.	4:22
2	was **of** the bondwoman was born after the flesh;	4:23
2	but he **of** the freewoman was by promise.	4:23
2	wait for the hope of righteousness **by** faith.	5:5
2	persuasion cometh not **of** him that calleth you.	5:8
2	shall **of** the flesh reap corruption;	6:8
2	shall **of** the Spirit reap life everlasting.	6:8
2	in Christ, when he raised him **from** the dead,	Eph 1:20
1	saved through faith; and that not **of** yourselves:	2:8
1	Not of works, lest any man should boast.	2:9
1	**Of** whom the whole family in heaven and earth	3:15
2	abundantly above all that we ask or think, (NT)	3:20
1	**From** whom the whole body fitly joined together	4:16
2	communication proceed **out of** your mouth.	4:29
2	Awake thou that sleepest, and arise **from** the dead,	5:14
2	For we are members of his body, **of** his flesh,	5:30
2	members of his body, of his flesh, and **of** his bones.	Eph 5:30
2	doing the will of God **from** the heart;	6:6
1	The one preach Christ of contention, not sincerely,	Php 1:17
1	other **of** love, knowing that I am set for the defence	1:17
2	For I am in a strait **betwixt** two,	1:23
2	Circumcised the eighth day, **of** the stock of Israel,	3:5
1	the tribe of Benjamin, an Hebrew **of** the Hebrews;	3:5
2	mine own righteousness, which is **of** the law,	3:9
2	the righteousness which is **of** God by faith:	3:9
2	attain to the resurrection **from** the dead. (NASB)	3:11
1	**from** whence also we look for the Saviour,	3:20
2	chiefly they that are **of** Caesar's household.	4:22
2	hath delivered us **from** the power of darkness,	Col 1:13
2	who is the beginning, the firstborn **from** the dead;	1:18
2	of God, who hath raised him **from** the dead.	2:12
2	and took it **out** of the way, nailing it to his cross;	2:14
1	**from** which all the body by joints and bands	2:19
2	filthy communication **out of** your mouth.	3:8
2	work at it **with** all your heart, (NIV)	3:23
1	a faithful and beloved brother, who is one **of** you.	4:9
2	called Justus, who are **of** the circumcision.	4:11
1	Epaphras, who is one **of** you, a servant of Christ,	4:12
2	that ye likewise read the epistle **from** Laodicea.	4:16
2	And to wait for his Son **from** heaven,	1 Th 1:10
2	whom he raised **from** the dead, even Jesus,	1:10
2	delivers us **from** the wrath to come (NASB)	1:10
2	For our exhortation was not **of** deceit,	2:3
1	exhortation was not of deceit, nor **of** uncleanness,	2:3
1	Nor **of** men sought we glory, neither of you,	2:6
2	until he be taken **out** of the way.	2 Th 2:7
2	commandment is charity **out of** a pure heart,	1 Tm 1:5
1	whereof cometh envy, strife, railings,	6:4
2	was raised **from** the dead according to my gospel:	2 Tm 2:8
2	Remember that Jesus Christ **of** the seed of David	2:8
2	with them that call on the Lord **out of** a pure heart.	2:22
2	recover themselves **out of** the snare of the devil,	2:26
2	For of this sort are they which creep into houses,	3:6
2	but **out of** them all the Lord delivered me.	3:11
2	and I was delivered **out of** the mouth of the lion.	4:17
2	Grace be with you. Amen.	4:22
2	and deceivers, specially they **of** the circumcision:	Tit 1:10
1	One of themselves, even a prophet of their own,	1:12
1	he that is **of** the contrary part may be ashamed,	2:8
1	Not by works of righteousness which we have done,	3:5
2	Sit **on** my right hand,	Heb 1:13
1	and they who are sanctified are all **of** one:	2:11
1	lest any **of** you be hardened through ... sin.	3:13
1	howbeit not all that came out **of** Egypt by Moses.	3:16
1	any **of** you should seem to come short of it.	4:1
1	For every high priest taken **from among** men	5:1
2	unto him that was able to save him **from** death,	5:7
2	the patriarch Abraham gave the tenth **of** the spoils.	7:4
2	And verily they that are **of** the sons of Levi,	7:5
2	though they come **out** of the loins of Abraham:	7:5
1	But he whose descent is not counted **from** them	7:6
2	there is made of necessity a change also **of** the law.	7:12
1	For it is evident that our Lord sprang **out of** Juda;	7:14
2	by the hand to lead them **out of** the land of Egypt;	8:9
2	appear the second time without sin (NT)	9:28
2	Now the just shall live **by** faith:	10:38
2	were not made **of** things which do appear.	11:3
2	God was able to raise him up, even **from** the dead;	11:19
1	back their dead **by** resurrection; (NASB)	11:35
1	have an altar, **whereof** they have no right to eat	13:10
2	that brought again **from** the dead our Lord Jesus,	13:20
1	And one **of** you say unto them, Depart in peace,	Jas 2:16
2	show me thy faith **without** thy works,	2:18
2	and I will show thee my faith **by** my works.	2:18
1	Was not Abraham our father justified **by** works,	2:21
2	and **by** works was faith made perfect?	2:22
1	Ye see then how that **by** works a man is justified,	2:24
2	by works ... is justified, and not **by** faith only.	2:24
1	also was not Rahab the harlot justified **by** works,	2:25
2	**Out of** the same mouth ... blessing and cursing.	3:10
2	**at** the same place sweet water and bitter?	3:11
2	let him show **out of** a good conversation his works	3:13
2	even **of** your lusts that war in your members?	4:1

ἐκ 1523

2 that he which converteth the sinner **from** the error	Jas	5:20
2 the error of his way shall save a soul **from** death,		5:20
2 by the resurrection of Jesus Christ **from** the dead,	1 Pt	1:3
2 **from** your vain conversation received by tradition		1:18
2 God, that raised him up **from** the dead,		1:21
2 see that ye love one another **with** a pure heart		1:22
2 Being born again, not **of** corruptible seed,		1:23
2 **out** of darkness into his marvellous light;		2:9
2 may **by** your good works, which they shall behold,		2:12
1 let him do it as **of** the ability which God giveth:		4:11
1 And this voice which came **from** heaven we heard,	2 Pt	1:18
1 from day to day with their unlawful deeds;		2:8
2 how to deliver the godly **out** of temptations,		2:9
2 to turn **from** the holy commandment delivered		2:21
1 earth standing **out** of the water and in the water:		3:5
2 is not of the Father, but is of the world.	1 Jn	2:16
2 is not of the Father, but is of the world.		2:16
1 They went out **from** us, but they were not of us;		2:19
1 They went out from us, but they were not **of** us;		2:19
1 but they were not of us; for if they had been **of** us,		2:19
1 but they were not of us; for if they had been of us,		2:19
1 be made manifest that they were not all **of** us.		2:19
2 because ye know it, and that no lie is **of** the truth.		2:21
1 every one that doeth righteousness is born **of** him.		2:29
2 He that committeth sin is **of** the devil;		3:8
2 Whosoever is born **of** God doth not commit sin;		3:9
2 and he cannot sin, because he is born **of** God.		3:9
2 whosoever doeth not righteousness is not **of** God,		3:10
2 Not as Cain, who was **of** that wicked one,		3:12
2 We know that we have passed **from** death unto life,		3:14
2 And hereby we know that we are **of** the truth,		3:19
2 **by** the Spirit which he hath given us.		3:24
2 but try the spirits whether they are **of** God:		4:1
2 Hereby know ye the Spirit **of** God:		4:2
2 that Jesus Christ is come in the flesh is not **of** God:		4:3
2 Ye are **of** God, little children,		4:4
2 They are **of** the world:		4:5
2 therefore speak they **of** the world,		4:5
2 We are **of** God: he that knoweth God heareth us;		4:6
2 he that is not **of** God heareth not us.		4:6
2 **Hereby** know we the spirit **of** truth,		4:6
2 let us love one another: for love is **of** God;		4:7
2 and every one that loveth is born **of** God,		4:7
2 because he hath given us **of** his Spirit.		4:13
2 believeth that Jesus is the Christ is born **of** God:		5:1
1 loveth him also that is begotten **of** him.		5:1
2 whatsoever is born **of** God overcometh the world:		5:4
2 that whosoever is born **of** God sinneth not;		5:18
2 but he that is begotten **of** God keepeth himself,		5:18
2 And we know that we are **of** God,		5:19
2 that I found **of** thy children walking in truth,	2 Jn	1:4
2 and casteth them out **of** the church.	3 Jn	1:10
2 He that doeth good is **of** God:		1:11
2 having saved the people **out** of the land of Egypt,	Jude	1:5
2 others save with fear, pulling them **out** of the fire;		1:23
2 faithful witness, and the first begotten **of** the dead,	Rev	1:5
2 released us **from** our sins (NASB)		1:5
2 **out** of his mouth went a sharp twoedged sword:		1:16
2 and will remove thy candlestick **out** of his place,		2:5
2 that overcometh will I give to eat **of** the tree of life,		2:7
2 blasphemy **by** those who say (NASB)		2:9
1 the devil shall cast some **of** you into prison,		2:10
1 the devil shall cast some **of** you into prison,		2:10
2 shall not be hurt **of** the second death.		2:11
2 And I gave her space to repent **of** her fornication;		2:21
2 great tribulation, except they repent **of** their deeds.		2:22
2 I will not blot out his name **out** of the book of life,		3:5
2 I will make them **of** the synagogue of Satan,		3:9
2 I also will keep thee **from** the hour of temptation,		3:10
2 which cometh down **out** of heaven from my God:		3:12
2 art lukewarm, ... I will spue thee **out** of my mouth.		3:16
2 I counsel thee to buy **of** me gold tried in the fire,		3:18
2 And **out** of the throne proceeded lightnings		4:5
2 And one of the elders saith unto me, Weep not:		5:5
2 behold, the Lion **of** the tribe of Juda,		5:5
2 he came and took the book **out** of the right hand		5:7
2 by thy blood **out** of every kindred, and tongue,		5:9
2 And I saw when the Lamb opened one **of** the seals,	Rev	6:1
2 one **of** the four beasts saying, Come and see.		6:1
2 granted to take peace **from** the earth, (NASB)		6:4
2 avenging our blood **on** those who dwell (NASB)		6:10
2 and island were moved **out** of their places.		6:14
2 of all the tribes of the children of Israel.		7:4
2 **Of** the tribe of Juda were sealed twelve thousand.		7:5
2 **Of** the tribe of Reuben were sealed		7:5
2 **Of** the tribe of Gad were sealed twelve thousand.		7:5
2 **Of** the tribe of Aser were sealed twelve thousand.		7:6
2 **Of** the tribe of Nephthalim were sealed		7:6
2 **Of** the tribe of Manasses were sealed		7:6
2 **Of** the tribe of Simeon were sealed		7:7
2 **Of** the tribe of Levi were sealed twelve thousand.		7:7
2 **Of** the tribe of Issachar were sealed		7:7
2 **Of** the tribe of Zabulon were sealed		7:8
2 **Of** the tribe of Joseph were sealed twelve thousand.		7:8
2 **Of** the tribe of Benjamin were sealed		7:8
2 of all nations, and kindreds, and people,		7:9
2 And one of the elders answered, saying unto me,		7:13
2 These are they which came **out** of great tribulation,		7:14
2 wipe every tear **from** their eyes. (NASB)		7:17
2 ascended up before God **out** of the angel's hand.		8:4
2 took the censer, and filled it **with** fire of the altar,		8:5
2 and there fell a great star **from** heaven,		8:10
2 and many men died **of** the waters,		8:11
2 **by reason of** the other voices of the trumpet		8:13
2 and I saw a star fall **from** heaven unto the earth:		9:1
2 and there arose a smoke **of** the pit,		9:2
2 were darkened **by reason of** the smoke of the pit.		9:2
2 came **out** of the smoke locusts upon the earth:		9:3
2 I heard a voice **from** the four horns of the ... altar,		9:13
2 and **out** of their mouths issued fire and smoke		9:17
2 was the third part of men killed, **by** the fire,		9:18
2 the fire, and **by** the smoke, and by the brimstone,		9:18
2 the fire, and by the smoke, and **by** the brimstone,		9:18
2 the brimstone, which issued **out** of their mouths.		9:18
2 yet repented not **of** the works of their hands,		9:20
2 Neither repented they **of** their murders,		9:21
2 nor **of** their sorceries, nor of their fornication,		9:21
2 nor **of** their fornication, nor of their thefts.		9:21
2 nor of their fornication, nor **of** their thefts.		9:21
2 another mighty angel come down **from** heaven,		10:1
2 and I heard a voice **from** heaven saying unto me,		10:4
2 And the voice which I heard **from** heaven spake		10:8
2 And I took the little book **out** of the angel's hand,		10:10
2 will hurt them, fire proceedeth **out** of their mouth,		11:5
2 the beast that ascendeth **out** of the bottomless pit		11:7
2 And they of the people and kindreds and tongues		11:9
2 the Spirit of life **from** God entered into them,		11:11
2 heard a great voice **from** heaven saying unto them,		11:12
2 **out** of his mouth water as a flood after the woman,		12:15
2 the flood which the dragon cast **out** of his mouth,		12:16
2 and saw a beast rise up **out** of the sea,		13:1
2 I saw one **of** his heads (NASB)		13:3
2 I beheld another beast coming up **out** of the earth;		13:11
2 so that he maketh fire come down **from** heaven		13:13
2 a voice **from** heaven, as the voice of many waters,		14:2
2 because she made all nations drink **of** the wine		14:8
2 The same shall drink **of** the wine of the wrath		14:10
2 And I heard a voice **from** heaven saying unto me,		14:13
2 that they may rest **from** their labours;		14:13
2 And another angel came out **of** the temple,		14:15
2 And another angel came **out** of the temple		14:17
2 And another angel came **out** from the altar,		14:18
2 and blood came **out** of the winepress,		14:20
2 them that had gotten the victory **over** the beast,		15:2
2 the victory over the beast, and **over** his image,		15:2
2 **over** his mark, and over the number of his name,		15:2
2 **over** his mark, and over the number of his name,		15:2
2 And the seven angels came **out** of the temple,		15:6
2 one **of** the four beasts gave unto the seven angels		15:7
2 the temple was filled with smoke **from** the glory		15:8
2 the temple was filled with smoke from the glory		15:8
2 smoke from the glory of God, and **from** his power;		15:8
2 And I heard a great voice **out** of the temple saying		16:1
2 And I heard another **out** of the altar say,		16:7

313

ἐκ 1523

2 and they gnawed their tongues **for** pain,	Rev	16:10
2 **because** of their pains and their sores,		16:11
2 **because** of their pains and their sores,		16:11
2 blasphemed ... and repented not of their deeds.		16:11
2 I saw three unclean spirits like frogs come **out of**		16:13
2 of the dragon, and **out of** the mouth of the beast,		16:13
2 and **out of** the mouth of the false prophet.		16:13
2 a loud voice came **out of** the temple (NASB)		16:17
2 there fell upon men a great hail **out of** heaven,		16:21
2 and men blasphemed God **because** of the plague		16:21
2 And there came one **of** the seven angels		17:1
2 been made drunk **with** the wine of her fornication.		17:2
2 the woman drunken **with** the blood of the saints,		17:6
2 and **with** the blood of the martyrs of Jesus:		17:6
2 and shall ascend **out of** the bottomless pit,		17:8
2 even he is the eighth, and is **of** the seven,		17:11
2 I saw another angel come down **from** heaven,		18:1
2 angel ... the earth was lightened **with** his glory.		18:1
2 For all nations have drunk **of** the wine of the wrath		18:3
2 rich **through** the abundance of her delicacies.		18:3
2 And I heard another voice **from** heaven, saying,		18:4
1 voice from heaven, ... Come **out of** her, my people,		18:4
2 and that ye receive not **of** her plagues.		18:4
2 and all manner vessels of most precious wood,		18:12
2 were made rich ... **by reason of** her costliness!		18:19
1 Rejoice ... for God hath avenged you **on** her.		18:20
2 hath avenged the blood of his servants **at** her hand.		19:2
2 And a voice came **out of** the throne, saying,		19:5
2 And **out of** his mouth goeth a sharp sword,		19:15
2 which sword proceeded **out of** his mouth:		19:21
2 and all the fowls were filled **with** their flesh.		19:21
2 And I saw an angel come down **from** heaven,		20:1
2 Satan shall be loosed **out of** his prison,		20:7
2 and fire came down from God **out of** heaven,		20:9
2 were judged **out of** those things which were written		20:12
2 Jerusalem, coming down from God **out of** heaven,		21:2
2 And I heard a great voice **out of** heaven saying,		21:3
2 wipe away every tear **from** their eyes, (NASB)		21:4
2 I will give unto him that is athirst **of** the fountain		21:6
2 And one **of** the seven angels ... came (NASB)		21:9
2 Jerusalem, descending **out of** heaven **from** God,		21:10
1 twelve pearls: every several gate was **of** one pearl:		21:21
2 proceeding **out of** the throne of God		22:1
2 **out of** the book of life, and **out of** the holy city,		22:19

This extremely versatile preposition can be found in almost all of Greek literature. (*Ex* is used before words starting with vowels.) The discussion below will focus on its function as an independent preposition, though it is a regular component of a compound verb. In its simplest definition it means "from, away from" or "out of." But under different circumstances the preposition has different shades of meaning.

New Testament Usage

First, it particularly denotes the point of departure or separation such as "to rise from (*ek*) the dead" (e.g., John 12:1,9,17; Acts 3:15; 4:10; etc.). "Out of (*ek*, before a vowel *ex*) Egypt have I called my son" (Hosea 11:1; Matthew 2:15) should also be understood in this way. *Ek* also indicates a separation between persons or objects; Jesus prays that His disciples be "(kept) from (*ek*) the evil one" (John 17:15, RSV).

A second basic function of *ek* is to designate direction: Two possessed by demons came "out of" the tombs (Matthew 8:28). "He came up (*anabainō* [303]) out of (*ek*) the water" (Mark 1:10, RSV).

Third, *ek* suggests the source or reason for some event or act, including the "source" of someone. This is evidenced in Nathaniel's question, "Can there any good thing come out of (*ek*) Nazareth?" (John 1:46). In this sense *ek* speaks of something as part of a larger whole such as in the frequent rhetorical question, "Which of you ... ?" (e.g., Luke 11:5,11; 12:25; 14:28; 15:4; 17:7). Similarly, righteousness comes *ek* God and is by faith (Philippians 3:9; i.e., God is the source of righteousness).

Fourth, *ek* can imply cause or reason. Paul asked, "Did you receive the Spirit by works (*ex ergōn*) of the law?" (Galatians 3:2,5, RSV). It may refer to a condition or state of being. Paul admonished Timothy, "The goal of this command is love which comes from (i.e., results from the condition of) a pure heart" (1 Timothy 1:5, NIV). The term may also suggest a basis for some action. "For the tree is known by (*ek*) his fruit" (Matthew 12:33; cf. verse 37).

Fifth, *ek* marks a point in time. According to Matthew 19:12 some men are eunuchs having been "so born from (*ek*) their mother's womb." The rich ruler explained to Jesus that he had kept the commandments *ek neotētos*, "from youth." And Herod had hoped to see Jesus *ex ikanōn chronōn*, "for a long time." Sixth, *ek* expresses means or agency. It may parallel *hupo* (5097) plus the genitive (after passive verbs or after any voice when accompanying the perfect verb). Some examples are Mark 7:11; 12:30,33 (with active verbs); the James series in 2:18 (active verb) 21,22,24,25; 1 Peter 1:23; Revelation 2:11. A similar pattern can be noted with *apo* (570) plus the genitive in Luke 7:35; 16:18; James 1:13; 5:4; Jude 23. *Dia* (1217) plus the genitive exemplifies the same basic idea under yet another imagery. It seems that Hellenistic Greek is simply adding ways of expressing agency through the use of additional prepositions for this purpose, which is in keeping with the growing use of prepositions in places where earlier Greek relied on case alone together with the nature of the circumstance or topic.

Also in keeping with the trend toward the proliferation of prepositions in Hellenistic Greek, on occasion *ek* and *apo* appear to be little more than pleonastic descriptive genitives roughly equivalent to our usage of "of" to link one noun adjectivally to another.

Many other fine distinctions of definition may be drawn (see *Bauer*), but the basic functions of *ek* are outlined above. Context in conjunction with grammar always makes the best guide for determining this preposition's meaning.

STRONG 1537, BAUER 234-36, MOULTON-MILLIGAN 189-90, LIDDELL-SCOTT 498-99, COLIN BROWN 3:1171-74,1176-78,1180-83,1185,1188-90,1198, 1201-3.

1524. ἕκαστος hekastos adj

Each, every.

אָדָם 'ādhām (119), Man, person (Prv 24:12).

אֶחָד 'echādh (259), One (Nm 7:3).

אִישׁ 'îsh (382), Man; one, each one (Lv 19:3, 1 Chr 16:43, Mal 2:10).

אִשָּׁה 'ishshāh (828), Woman; each (of you), one another (Ru 1:8,9, Zec 11:9).

כֹּל kōl (3725), All, every (Pss 6:6, 7:11, 42:3,10 [41:3,10]).

פְּשַׁר pᵉshar (A6843), Interpretation (Dn 2:24,25—Aramaic).

1. ἕκαστον hekaston nom/acc sing masc/neu
2. ἑκάστου hekastou gen sing masc/neu
3. ἕκαστος hekastos nom sing masc
4. ἑκάστῳ hekastō dat sing masc
5. ἑκάστοις hekastois dat pl masc
6. ἑκάστη hekastē nom sing fem
7. ἑκάστην hekastēn acc sing fem
8. ἕκαστοι hekastoi nom pl masc

4 he shall reward **every man** according to his works...Matt	16:27
3 if ye from your hearts forgive not **every one**	18:35
4 to **every man** according to his several ability;	25:15
3 and began **every one** of them to say unto him, ...	26:22
3 and began **every man** to say unto him, ...	26:22
4 and to **every man** his work,.............................Mark	13:34
3 all went to be taxed, **every one** into his own city.....Luke	2:3
4 and he laid his hands on **every one** of them, ...	4:40
1 For **every tree** is known by his own fruit.	6:44
3 doth not **each one** ... on the sabbath loose his ox	13:15
1 So he called **every one** of his lord's debtors	16:5
3 that **every one** of them may take a little. ....John	6:7
3 And **every man** went unto his own house.	7:53
3 that ye shall be scattered, **every man** to his own, ...	16:32
4 and made four parts, to **every soldier** a part;	19:23
1 cloven tongues ... and it sat upon **each** of them. ......Acts	2:3
3 **every man** heard them speak in his own language.	2:6
3 And how hear we **every man** in our own tongue, ...	2:8
3 be baptized **every one** of you in the name of Jesus ...	2:38
1 turning away **every one** of you from his iniquities.	3:26
4 and distribution was made unto **every man**	4:35
3 the disciples, **every man** according to his ability, ...	11:29
2 though he be not far from **every one** of us:	17:27
1 to warn **every one** night and day with tears.	20:31
1 declared **particularly** what things God had wrought	21:19
2 offering should be offered for **every one** of them....Acts	21:26
4 will render to **every man** according to his deeds: .....Rom	2:6
4 but to think soberly, **according** as God hath dealt	12:3
3 Let **every man** be fully persuaded in his own mind.....	14:5
3 then **every one** of us shall give account ... to God......	14:12
3 Let **every one** of us please his neighbour	15:2
3 Now this I say, that **every one** of you saith, ...1 Co	1:12
4 even as the Lord gave to **every man**?	3:5
3 and **every man** shall receive his own reward	3:8
3 **every man** take heed how he buildeth thereupon........	3:10
2 **Every man's** work shall be made manifest:	3:13
3 fire shall try **every man's** work of what sort it is.........	3:13
4 and then shall **every man** have praise of God...........	4:5
3 avoid fornication, let **every man** have his own wife,.....	7:2
6 and let **every woman** have her own husband............	7:2
3 But **every man** hath his proper gift of God,............	7:7
4 But as God hath distributed to **every man**, ...	7:17
1 as the Lord hath called **every one**, so let him walk.....	7:17
3 Let **every man** abide in the same calling	7:20
3 Brethren, let **every man**, wherein he is called, ...	7:24
3 but **every man** another's wealth........................	10:24
3 **every one** taketh before other his own supper:	11:21
4 the Spirit is given to **every man** to profit withal........	12:7
4 dividing to **every man** severally as he will..............	12:11
1 the members **every one** of them in the body,..........	12:18
3 **every one** of you hath a psalm, hath a doctrine,.......	14:26
3 **every man** in his own order: Christ the firstfruits;	15:23
4 and to **every seed** his own body.......................	15:38
3 let **every one** of you lay by him in store, ...	16:2
3 **every one** may receive the things done in his body, ..2 Co	5:10
3 **Every man** according as he purposeth in his heart, ...	9:7
3 But let **every man** prove his own work, ...Gal	6:4
3 For **every man** shall bear his own burden...............	6:5
4 unto **every one** of us is given grace according to .....Eph	4:7
2 the effectual working in the measure of **every part**,......	4:16
3 speak **every man** truth with his neighbour:	4:25
3 Nevertheless let **every one** of you in particular	5:33
3 Knowing ... whatsoever good thing **any man** doeth,......	6:8
3 Look not **every man** on his own things, ...Phlp	2:4
8 Look not **every man** on his own things, ...	2:4
3 but **every man** also on the things of others.............	2:4
8 but **every man** also on the things of others.............	2:4
4 ye may know how ye ought to answer **every man**.....Col	4:6
1 and comforted and charged **every one** of you, ...1 Th	2:11
1 That **every one** of you should know how	4:4
2 charity of **every one** of you all toward each other ....2 Th	1:3
7 exhort one another **daily**, while it is called Today; ...Heb	3:13
1 that **every one** of you do show the same diligence	6:11
3 And they shall not teach **every man** his neighbour,......	8:11
3 **every man** his brother, saying, Know the Lord:.........	8:11
1 By faith Jacob, ... blessed **both** the sons of Joseph;....	11:21
3 But **every man** is tempted, when he is drawn away....Jas	1:14
3 Father, ... judgeth according to **every man's** work, ...1 Pt	1:17
3 As **every man** hath received the gift,....................	4:10
4 unto **every one** of you according to your works......Rev	2:23
3 having **every one** of them harps, and golden vials	5:8
5 white robes were given unto **every one** of them;	6:11
4 white robes were given unto **every one** of them;	6:11
3 were judged **every man** according to their works.......	20:13
3 twelve pearls: every several gate was of one pearl:.....	21:21
1 and yielded her fruit **every month**:	22:2
4 to give **every man** according as his work shall be.......	22:12

This frequent adjective ("each, every" or pronoun "each one, every one") is used literally or substantively to identify entire classes of people and their deeds in the New Testament. Hebrews 3:13 tells us to "exhort one another daily" (literally "*every* day"). Other examples of its literal use can be found in Luke 6:44 and Revelation 22:2. As a substantive *hekastos* occurs over 75 times. In each case it means either "every man" or "every one."

ἑκάστοτε 1525
STRONG 1538, BAUER 236, MOULTON-MILLIGAN 190, LIDDELL-SCOTT 499-500, COLIN BROWN 1:94,576.

1525. ἑκάστοτε hekastote adv
At any time, always.
SYNONYMS:
ἀεί aei (103)
διαπαντός diapantos (1269)
πάντοτε pantote (3704)

1. ἑκάστοτε hekastote

1 to have these things **always** in remembrance......... 2 Pt 1:15

An adverb of time, *hekastote* occurs only once in the New Testament, at 2 Peter 1:15. The reader is "always" to remember the teachings about Jesus Christ. In classical Greek literature (e.g. Herodotus, Fifth Century B.C.) the word denotes "each time" or "on each occasion."

STRONG 1539, BAUER 236, MOULTON-MILLIGAN 191, LIDDELL-SCOTT 500.

1526. ἑκατόν hekaton num
One hundred.

1. ἑκατόν hekaton card

1 and brought forth fruit, some an **hundredfold**,...... Matt 13:8
1 some an **hundredfold**, some sixty, some thirty.......... 13:23
1 How think ye? if a man have an **hundred** sheep,....... 18:12
1 which owed him an **hundred** pence:.................... 18:28
1 some thirty, and some sixty, and some an **hundred**...Mark 4:8
1 some thirtyfold, some sixty, and some an **hundred**....... 4:20
1 sat down in ranks, by **hundreds**, and by fifties.......... 6:40
1 What man of you, having an **hundred** sheep,....... Luke 15:4
1 And he said, An **hundred** measures of oil.............. 16:6
1 And he said, An **hundred** measures of wheat........... 16:7
1 myrrh and aloes, about an **hundred** pound weight...John 19:39
1 full of great fishes, an **hundred** and fifty and three:.... 21:11
1 together were about an **hundred** and twenty,........Acts 1:15
1 one hundred and forty-four thousand (NASB)........Rev 7:4
1 and with him an **hundred** forty and four thousand,..... 14:1
1 but the **hundred** and forty and four thousand,......... 14:3
1 wall thereof, an **hundred** and forty and four cubits,.... 21:17

The number 100 functions as an approximate, round figure in the Gospels: "a hundred sheep" (Matthew 18:12), "by hundreds" (Mark 6:40). Outside the Gospels it is compounded with larger, more exact numbers (cf. Revelation 7:4).

STRONG 1540, BAUER 236, MOULTON-MILLIGAN 191, KITTEL 2:321-28, LIDDELL-SCOTT 500.

1527. ἑκατονταετής
hekatontaetēs adj
A hundred years.

1. ἑκατονταετής hekatontaetēs nom sing fem

1 when he was about an **hundred years old**,........... Rom 4:19

Similar to *hekaton* (1526), the concept of age is added to the meaning when used once in the New Testament at Romans 4:19. Here Paul recognized that Abraham was "about a hundred years old," i.e., an old man.

STRONG 1541, BAUER 236-37, LIDDELL-SCOTT 500.

1528. ἑκατονταπλασίων
hekatontaplasiōn adj
A hundredfold.

1. ἑκατονταπλασίονα hekatontaplasiona
nom/acc sing/pl masc/neu

1 for my name's sake, shall receive an **hundredfold**,.. Matt 19:29
1 he shall receive an **hundredfold** now in this time,.. Mark 10:30
1 sprang up, and bare fruit an **hundredfold**............ Luke 8:8

The term whose components are *hekaton* (1526), "100," and *plasiōn*, "form," means "a hundredfold." In Matthew, Mark, and Luke it occurs as a general, round enumeration of expected increase for serving Christ (Matthew 19:29; Mark 10:30; Luke 18:30).

STRONG 1542, BAUER 237, LIDDELL-SCOTT 500.

1529. ἑκατοντάρχης
hekatontarchēs noun
Centurion.
COGNATE:
ἀρχή archē (741)
SYNONYMS:
ἑκατόνταρχος hekatontarchos (1530)
κεντυρίων kenturiōn (2731)

1. ἑκατοντάρχης hekatontarchēs nom sing masc
2. ἑκατοντάρχῃ hekatontarchē dat sing masc
3. ἑκατονταρχῶν hekatontarchōn gen pl masc
4. ἑκατοντάρχας hekatontarchas acc pl masc

1 there came unto him a **centurion**, beseeching him,...Matt 8:5
1 The **centurion** answered and said, Lord,............ 8:8
2 And Jesus said unto the **centurion**, Go thy way;........ 8:13
1 when the **centurion**, and they that were with him,..... 27:54
1 the **centurion** sent friends to him, saying unto him,.. Luke 7:6
1 Now when the **centurion** saw what was done,.......... 23:47
1 a **centurion** of the band called the Italian band,.....Acts 10:1
1 And they said, Cornelius the **centurion**, a just man,.... 10:22
4 Who immediately took soldiers and **centurions**,........ 21:32
1 When the **centurion** heard that,...................... 22:26
3 Then Paul called one of the **centurions** unto him,........ 23:17
3 And he called unto him two **centurions**, saying,........ 23:23
2 And he commanded a **centurion** to keep Paul,......... 24:23
2 one named Julius, a **centurion** of Augustus' band,...... 27:1
1 there the **centurion** found a ship of Alexandria........ 27:6
1 Nevertheless the **centurion** believed the master........ 27:11
2 Paul said to the **centurion** and to the soldiers,......... 27:31
1 But the **centurion**, willing to save Paul,............... 27:43

Classical Greek and Septuagint Usage

In classical Greek *hekatontarchēs* was used to describe the leader of 100 men. The Septuagint uses it to describe the elders over the people of Israel in the wilderness (Deuteronomy 1:15) as well as military leaders of 100 (1 Samuel 22:7).

New Testament Usage

During the New Testament era *hekatontarchēs* and the alternate form *hekatontarchos* (1530) served as the title for the Roman officer in charge of a century (about 100 men). Mark used the Latin equivalent *kenturiōn* (Mark 15:39-45), the source for the English translation "centurion." The Roman legion was typically composed of 10 cohorts, each containing 500 soldiers. The cohort was divided into six centuries, each led by a centurion. Most men who enlisted in the Roman army looked upon *hekatontarchēs* as the highest rank to which they could rise.

The New Testament generally describes centurions favorably, as in the case of the centurion at Capernaum (Matthew 8:5-13) and the centurion at the cross (Matthew 27:54).

The two centurions mentioned by name in the New Testament are Cornelius (Acts 10:1) and Julius (Acts 27:1), who was evidently detached from his legion to guard the prisoners en route to Rome.

STRONG 1543, BAUER 237, MOULTON-MILLIGAN 191, LIDDELL-SCOTT 500, COLIN BROWN 3:958,964.

1530. ἑκατόνταρχος
hekatontarchos noun
Centurion, captain.

COGNATE:
ἀρχή archē (741)

SYNONYMS:
ἑκατοντάρχης hekatontarchēs (1529)
κεντυρίων kenturiōn (2731)

1. ἑκατόνταρχος hekatontarchos nom sing masc
2. ἑκατοντάρχου hekatontarchou gen sing masc
3. ἑκατοντάρχῳ hekatontarchō dat sing masc
4. ἑκατόνταρχον hekatontarchon acc sing masc
5. ἑκατοντάρχων hekatontarchōn gen pl masc
6. ἑκατοντάρχους hekatontarchous acc pl masc

1 there came unto him a **centurion**, beseeching him,...Matt 8:5
1 The **centurion** answered and said, Lord,................ 8:8
3 And Jesus said unto the **centurion**, Go thy way;........ 8:13
1 when the **centurion**, and they that were with him,...... 27:54
2 And a certain **centurion's** servant, who was dear.... Luke 7:2
1 Now when the **centurion** saw what was done,........... 23:47
6 Who immediately took soldiers and **centurions**,..... Acts 21:32
4 Paul said unto the **centurion** that stood by,............. 22:25
1 When the **centurion** heard that,................... Acts 22:26
1 there the **centurion** found a ship of Alexandria........ 27:6
1 Nevertheless the **centurion** believed the master........ 27:11
1 But the **centurion**, willing to save Paul,............... 27:43
1 the **centurion** delivered the prisoners.................. 28:16

From the components *hekaton* (1526), "100," and *archos* (from *archēs*, "ruler"), *hekatontarchos* means "a leader of 100 men." This form (*-os*) is merely an alternative declension to *hekatontarchēs* (1529), the more widely used form. *Hekatontarchos* occurs 16 times, always in reference to a "centurion" in the Roman army (e.g., Matthew 8:5,8,13; Luke 7:2 [cf. verse 6, the other form]; Acts 22:25; 28:16).

STRONG 1543, BAUER 237, LIDDELL-SCOTT 501, COLIN BROWN 3:958,964.

1530B. ἐκβαίνω ekbainō verb
Go out, come from.

COGNATE:
ὑπερβαίνω huperbainō (5070)

SYNONYMS:
ἐκπορεύω ekporeuō (1594)
ἐξέρχομαι exerchomai (1814)
ἐξιέναι exienai (1821)
χωρέω chōreō (5397)

יָצָא yātsâ' (3428), Go out, come out (Sir 38:18).
עָלָה 'ālâh (6148), Comes up, climbs out (Jos 4:16ff., Is 24:18).

1. ἐξέβησαν exebēsan 3pl indic aor act

1 of that country from whence they **came out**,........ Heb 11:15

Related to the term *apobainō* (571), "get out, turn out, lead," *ekbainō* occurs one time in the New Testament, at Hebrews 11:15 (other manuscripts read *exerchomai* [1814]). This compound verb is comprised of the preposition *ek* (1523), "from, out of, out from," and the word *bainō*, "walk, stand, go on, advance, come," not found in the New Testament (see *Liddell-Scott*). The Hebrews passage refers back to Abraham and Sarah (verses 8-12) who had left Mesopotamia never to return. Verse 15 says, "And truly, if they had been mindful of that country from whence they *came out*, they might have had opportunity to have returned."

BAUER 237, MOULTON-MILLIGAN 191, LIDDELL-SCOTT 501.

1531. ἐκβάλλω ekballō verb
Throw out, drive out, send out.

COGNATE:
βάλλω ballō (900)

ἐκβάλλω 1531

SYNONYMS:
αἴρω airō (142)
βαστάζω bastazō (934)
ἐξαιρέω exaireō (1791)
ἐξαίρω exairō (1792)
ἐξωθέω exōtheō (1840)
λαμβάνω lambanō (2956)

גָּרַס gāraṣ (1685), Hiphil: cause to grind the teeth (Lam 3:16).

גָּרַף gāraph (1687), Swept away (Jgs 5:21—Codex Alexandrinus only).

גָּרַשׁ gārash (1691), Qal: drive out, divorce (Ex 34:11, Lv 21:7, Ez 44:22); piel: drive out (Gn 3:24, Jos 24:18, Prv 22:10); pual: be driven out (Ex 12:39).

דָּרַשׁ dārash (1938), Seek (Ps 109:10 [108:10]).

זָנַח zānach (2269), Hiphil: reject (2 Chr 11:14).

טוּל ṭûl (3014), Hiphil: throw (Jon 1:15); pilpel: throw far away (Is 22:17).

טָרַד ṭāradh (3065), Drip continually (Prv 27:15).

יָצָא yātsâ' (3428), Go out, come out; hiphil: sent out, brought out (2 Chr 23:14, 29:5,16).

יָרַשׁ yārash (3542), Qal: displaces, succeeds (Prv 30:23 [24:58]); hiphil: take possession of, drive out (Ex 34:24, Dt 11:23).

לָקַח lāqach (4089), Use (Jer 23:31).

נָדַח nādhach (5258), Hiphil: march out, came out (2 Chr 13:9).

נָשַׁל nāshal (5577), Piel: drive away (2 Kgs 16:6).

נָתַן nāthan (5598), Give, put (Dt 23:24—only in some Alexandrinus texts).

נָתַשׁ nāthash (5612), Uproot (Jer 12:14,15).

סָעַר sāʿar (5786), Rage; piel: scatter with a storm (Zec 7:14).

עָבַר ʿāvar (5882), Go over, go through; hiphil: put away, remove (2 Chr 15:8).

עָלָה ʿālâh (6148), Go up (Jos 15:8—Codex Vaticanus only).

פָּלַט pālaṭ (6647), Hiphil: rescue (Is 5:29).

קִיא qî' (7287), Hiphil: vomit (Jon 2:10 [2:11]).

שָׁלַח shālach (8365), Qal: let go, send (Jos 24:12—Codex Alexandrinus only); piel: let go (Ex 12:33, Ps 44:2 [43:2]).

שָׁלַךְ shālakh (8390), Hiphil: throw down or away (Lv 1:16, Eccl 3:6, Is 2:20); hophal: be thrown (Jer 22:28).

1. ἐκβάλλω ekballō 1sing indic pres act
2. ἐκβάλλεις ekballeis 2sing indic pres act
3. ἐκβάλλει ekballei 3sing indic pres act
4. ἐκβάλλουσιν ekballousin 3pl indic pres act
5. ἐκβάλλῃ ekballē 3sing subj pres act
6. ἐκβάλλωσιν ekballōsin 3pl subj pres act
7. ἐκβάλλετε ekballete 2pl impr pres act
8. ἐκβάλλων ekballōn nom sing masc part pres act
9. ἐκβάλλοντα ekballonta acc sing masc part pres act
10. ἐκβάλλειν ekballein inf pres act
11. ἐξέβαλεν exebalen 3sing indic aor act
12. ἐξεβάλομεν exebalomen 1pl indic aor act
13. ἐξέβαλον exebalon 3pl indic aor act
14. ἐκβάλω ekbalō 1sing subj aor act
15. ἐκβάλῃ ekbalē 3sing subj aor act
16. ἐκβάλωσιν ekbalōsin 3pl subj aor act
17. ἔκβαλε ekbale 2sing impr aor act
18. ἐκβάλετε ekbalete 2pl impr aor act
19. ἐκβαλών ekbalōn nom sing masc part aor act
20. ἐκβαλόντες ekbalontes nom pl masc part aor act
21. ἐκβαλοῦσα ekbalousa nom sing fem part aor act
22. ἐκβαλεῖν ekbalein inf aor act
23. ἐκβεβλήκει ekbeblēkei 3sing indic plperf act
24. ἐκβαλοῦσιν ekbalousin 3pl indic fut act
25. ἐξέβαλλον exeballon 3pl indic imperf act
26. ἐκβάλλεται ekballetai 3sing indic pres mid
27. ἐκβαλλόμενοι ekballomenoi nom pl masc part pres mid
28. ἐκβαλλομένους ekballomenous acc pl masc part pres mid
29. ἐξεβλήθη exeblēthē 3sing indic aor pass
30. ἐκβληθέντος ekblēthentos gen sing neu part aor pass
31. ἐκβληθήσεται ekblēthēsetai 3sing indic fut pass
32. ἐκβληθήσονται ekblēthēsontai 3pl indic fut pass

14	Let me **pull out** the mote out of thine eye;	Matt 7:4
17	first **cast out** the beam out of thine own eye;	7:5
22	and then shalt thou see clearly to **cast out** the mote	7:5
12	and in thy name have **cast out** devils?	7:22
32	shall **be cast out** into outer darkness:	8:12
11	and he **cast out** the spirits with his word,	8:16
2	If thou **cast** us out, suffer ... into the herd of swine.	8:31
29	But when the people **were put forth**, he went in,	9:25
30	And when the devil **was cast out**, the dumb spake:	9:33
3	**casteth out** devils through the prince of the devils.	9:34
15	that he will **send forth** labourers into his harvest.	9:38
10	power against unclean spirits, **to cast** them **out**,	10:1
7	cleanse the lepers, raise the dead, **cast out** devils:	10:8
15	till he **send forth** judgment unto victory.	12:20
3	This fellow doth not **cast out** devils,	12:24
3	And if Satan **cast out** Satan, he is divided	12:26
1	And if I by Beelzebub **cast out** devils,	12:27
4	by whom do your children **cast** them **out**?	12:27
1	But if I **cast out** devils by the Spirit of God,	12:28
3	treasure of the heart **bringeth forth** good things:	12:35
3	out of the evil treasure **bringeth forth** evil things.	12:35
3	which **bringeth forth** out of his treasure	13:52
26	and **is cast out** into the draught:	15:17
22	Why could not we **cast** him **out**?	17:19
11	and **cast out** all them that sold and bought	21:12
13	they caught him, and **cast** him out of the vineyard,	21:39
18	and **cast** him into outer darkness;	22:13
7	And **cast** ye the unprofitable servant ... darkness:	25:30
18	And **cast** ye the unprofitable servant ... darkness:	25:30
3	the Spirit **driveth** him into the wilderness.	Mark 1:12
11	he healed many ... and **cast out** many devils;	1:34
8	preached in their synagogues ... and **cast out** devils.	1:39
11	straitly charged him, and forthwith **sent** him **away**;	1:43
10	power to heal sicknesses, and **to cast out** devils:	3:15
3	by the prince of the devils **casteth** he out devils.	3:22
10	said ... in parables, How can Satan **cast out** Satan?	3:23
19	But when he **had put** them all **out**,	5:40
25	And they **cast out** many devils,	6:13
5	he would **cast forth** the devil out of her daughter.	7:26

15	he **would cast forth** the devil out of her daughter...	Mark 7:26
16	thy disciples that they **should cast** him **out**;	9:18
22	asked ... privately, Why could not we **cast** him **out**?	9:28
9	Master, we saw one **casting out** devils in thy name,	9:38
17	And if thine eye offend thee, **pluck** it **out**:	9:47
10	and began **to cast out** them that sold and bought	11:15
13	killed him, and **cast** him **out** of the vineyard.	12:8
23	Magdalene, out of whom he **had cast out** seven devils.	16:9
24	In my name shall they **cast out** devils;	16:17
13	And rose up, and **thrust** him out of the city,	Luke 4:29
16	shall reproach you, and **cast out** your name as evil,	6:22
14	let me **pull out** the mote that is in thine eye,	6:42
17	**cast out** first the beam out of thine own eye,	6:42
22	and then shalt thou see clearly **to pull out** the mote	6:42
22	to pull out the mote that is in thy brother's eye.	6:42
19	he put them all out, and took her by the hand,	8:54
6	And I besought thy disciples **to cast** him **out**;	9:40
16	And I besought thy disciples **to cast** him **out**;	9:40
9	Master, we saw one **casting out** devils in thy name;	9:49
5	that he **would send forth** labourers into his harvest.	10:2
15	that he **would send forth** labourers into his harvest.	10:2
15	that he **would send forth** labourers into his harvest.	10:2
19	morrow when he departed, he **took out** two pence,	10:35
8	And he was **casting out** a devil, and it was dumb.	11:14
30	when the devil was gone out, the dumb spake;	11:14
3	He **casteth out** devils through Beelzebub	11:15
10	ye say that I **cast out** devils through Beelzebub.	11:18
1	And if I by Beelzebub **cast out** devils,	11:19
4	by whom do your sons **cast** them **out**?	11:19
1	But if I with the finger of God **cast out** devils,	11:20
28	kingdom of God, and you yourselves **thrust out**.	13:28
1	and tell that fox, Behold, I **cast out** devils,	13:32
10	and began **to cast out** them that sold therein,	19:45
13	and they wounded him also, and **cast** him **out**.	20:12
20	they **cast** him **out** of the vineyard, and killed him.	20:15
11	he **drove** them all **out** of the temple,	John 2:15
14	him that cometh to me I will in no wise **cast out**.	6:37
13	and dost thou teach us? And they **cast** him **out**.	9:34
13	Jesus heard that they **had cast** him **out**;	9:35
15	And when he **putteth forth** his own sheep,	10:4
31	now shall the prince of this world be **cast out**.	12:31
20	And **cast** him **out** of the city, and stoned him:	Acts 7:58
19	But Peter **put** them all **forth**, and kneeled down,	9:40
13	and **expelled** them out of their coasts.	13:50
4	and now do they **thrust us out** privily? nay verily;	16:37
27	and **cast out** the wheat into the sea.	27:38
17	**Cast out** the bondwoman and her son:	Gal 4:30
21	messengers, and **had sent** them **out** another way?	Jas 2:25
3	and **casteth** them **out** of the church.	3 Jn 1:10
17	the court which is without the temple **leave out**,	Rev 11:2

Classical Greek and Septuagint Usage

In classical Greek *ekballō* means "to throw out, expel, or repel." It was used to describe the pushing back of invading enemies, of expulsion from government, and casting out of demons. It can also mean "to send forth or lead forth" without implying violence or evil. The Septuagint generally uses the first meaning of *ekballō*, "to drive out" (Genesis 3:24; Judges 6:9). It could also describe divorce, as in Leviticus 21:7.

The papyri use the word with a wide range of meaning: "to expel a tenant from his land," "to leave an unwanted infant to die," "to banish someone from the tribe or family," "to cast out demons," or "to send out guards."

New Testament Usage

In the New Testament one can find examples of all the earlier meanings. The most common meaning is negative and describes the violent expulsion of something evil or unwanted (John 6:37; 9:34; 3 John 10). It can also have a positive meaning, "to send out" without violence (Matthew 9:38; Luke 10:35; Acts 16:37; James 2:25). Some passages appear to be transitions between the two major meanings (see Mark 1:12 where the Spirit drives Jesus into the wilderness).

STRONG 1544, BAUER 237, MOULTON-MILLIGAN 191, KITTEL 1:527-28, LIDDELL-SCOTT 501, COLIN BROWN 1:453.

1532. ἔκβασις ekbasis noun

A way out, end.

COGNATE:
ὑπερβαίνω huperbainō (5070)

SYNONYMS:
πέρας peras (3872)
συντέλεια sunteleia (4782)
τέλος telos (4904)

1. ἔκβασιν ekbasin acc sing fem

1	will with the temptation also make **a way to escape**,	1 Co 10:13
1	considering the **end** of their conversation.	Heb 13:7

Classical Greek

In classical Greek *ekbasis* refers to "a way out," like the action of disembarking from a ship. It can also denote "an exit or a way of escape," like a mountain pass that would allow a trapped army to escape.

Septuagint Usage

It appears in the Apocrypha with the figurative meaning of death (Wisdom of Solomon 2:17). By this period the word had developed to include the meaning of "end, issue, or result." The papyri give examples of its use as the end of a process, like oil making, or as the product itself, such as the "produce" of the fields.

New Testament Usage

The New Testament uses *ekbasis* only twice. In 1 Corinthians 10:13 it has the former sense of "a way of escape, a path to get away from the struggle with a temptation." Hebrews 13:7 employs *ekbasis* in the later sense of "end" or "issue." The writer exhorted his readers to remember their past leaders and consider the outcome of their lives. The passage could refer to the result of holiness in the lives of leaders still living or to the outcome of the lives of those who had died.

STRONG 1545, BAUER 237-38, MOULTON-MILLIGAN 191, LIDDELL-SCOTT 501.

1533. ἐκβολή ekbolē noun
Jettisoning.
CROSS-REFERENCE:
βάλλω ballō (900)

גָּרַשׁ gārash (1691), Piel: drive out (Ex 11:1).

1. ἐκβολήν ekbolēn acc sing fem
1 they began to **jettison** the cargo; (NASB) .... Acts 27:18

This nautical term is used only at Acts 27:18 when the sailors "jettison" cargo from the sinking ship that carries Paul. The Greek translation of Jonah 1:15 uses the same word in reference to the "jettison" of Jonah to save the battered ship headed for Tarshish.

STRONG 1546, BAUER 238, MOULTON-MILLIGAN 191, LIDDELL-SCOTT 502.

1534. ἐκγαμίζω ekgamizō verb
Marry, give in marriage.
CROSS-REFERENCE:
γαμέω gameō (1053)

1. ἐκγαμίζοντες ekgamizontes
nom pl masc part pres act
2. ἐκγαμίζων ekgamizōn nom sing masc part pres act
3. ἐκγαμίζονται ekgamizontai 3pl indic pres mid
4. ἐξεγαμίζοντο exegamizonto 3pl indic imperf pass

3 they neither marry, nor **are given in marriage**, ... Matt 22:30
1 **marrying** and **giving in marriage**, ... 24:38
4 they married wives, they **were given in marriage**, ... Luke 17:27
2 So then he **that giveth her in marriage** doeth well; ... 1 Co 7:38
2 he **that giveth her not in marriage** doeth better. 7:38

Ekgamizo—a compound from *ek* (1523), "from," and *gamizō* (1053B), "marry"—denotes "marry" or "give in marriage." In a passive voice it refers to one "given in marriage." *Moulton-Milligan* reports that there is little evidence for the word outside of its appearance in the New Testament. The term does not appear in classical literature or in the Septuagint.

New Testament Usage
Its five occurrences in the Greek New Testament (Matthew 22:30; 24:38; Luke 17:27; 20:35; and 1 Corinthians 7:38) are all replaced by *gamizō* in recent editions (Nestle-Aland, 26th; UBS 3rd). The construction of the term seems to be an effort to particularize the sense of "to give away in marriage" (as a father or guardian might "give away" a daughter) or the passive sense, "to be given away." See word study at *gamizō* (1053B).

STRONG 1547, BAUER 238, MOULTON-MILLIGAN 191, LIDDELL-SCOTT 503 (see "ekgameomai").

1535. ἐκγαμίσκω ekgamiskō verb
To give in marriage.
CROSS-REFERENCE:
γαμέω gameō (1053)

1. ἐκγαμίσκονται ekgamiskontai 3pl indic pres mid
1 of this world marry, and **are given in marriage**: ..... Luke 20:34
1 neither marry, nor **are given in marriage**: 20:35

This combination of *ek* (1523) with the frequent *gamiskō* (1054), "to marry," might indicate a passive sense, "be given away in marriage." It is found two times in the New Testament, at Luke 20:34 and 35. Other Greek texts show a variant spelling, *gamiskō*, at these passages. According to *Moulton-Milligan*, *ekgamiskō* appears in no other extant literature, either Biblical or nonbiblical.

STRONG 1548, MOULTON-MILLIGAN 191.

1536. ἔκγονος ekgonos adj
Descendant, grandchild.
CROSS-REFERENCE:
γονεύς goneus (1112)

אַחֲרִית 'achărîth (321), Future (Prv 24:20).
בֵּן bēn (1158), Child, descendant (Is 49:15).
דּוֹר dôr (1810), Generation, those (Prv 30:11ff. [24:34ff.]).
טַף ṭaph (3054), Children, fruit (of the womb) (Dt 30:9, 31:12).
יָלִיד yālîdh (3320), Son, descendant (2 Sm 21:16).
מוֹלֶדֶת môledheth (4274), Children, offspring (Gn 48:6).
פְּרִי pᵉrî (6780), Fruit, young ones (Dt 28:18,51,53).
צֶאֱצָאִים tse'ĕtsā'îm (6889), Offspring, descendants (Is 48:19, 61:9).

1. ἔκγονα ekgona nom/acc pl neu
1 But if any widow have children or **nephews**, ... 1 Tm 5:4

This term denotes one "sprung from" or "born of." It is rendered generally as "descendants," more specifically as "grandchildren, nephews," etc. In the New Testament it occurs only once, in 1 Timothy 5:4.

It is these who, according to Paul, have the responsibility to care for the widows within their family. Here the implication is that these are the children and grandchildren of the widows. Their responsibility is to see that they put their faith into practice by taking care of their own family. They should, according to Bauer's translation of the clause, "make a return to those who brought them up" (see *Bauer*, "amoibē").

STRONG 1549, BAUER 238, MOULTON-MILLIGAN 192, LIDDELL-SCOTT 503.

1537. ἐκδαπανάω ekdapanaō verb
Spend completely, exhaust.

1. ἐκδαπανηθήσομαι ekdapanēthēsomai
1sing indic fut pass
1 And I will very gladly spend and **be spent** for you; 2 Co 12:15

The verb *ekdapanaō* means to be totally spent or exhausted of one's own energy for someone else. It is the intensive form of the verb *dapanaō* (1154) and is used only in 2 Corinthians 12:15 in connection with Paul's willingness to totally sacrifice himself for their souls.

STRONG 1550, BAUER 238, LIDDELL-SCOTT 503.

1538. ἐκδέχομαι ekdechomai verb
Wait for, expect, look forward to.

COGNATES:
ἀπεκδέχομαι apekdechomai (549)
δέχομαι dechomai (1203)
ἐκδοχή ekdochē (1548)

SYNONYMS:
ἀναμένω anamenō (360)
ἀπεκδέχομαι apekdechomai (549)
ἐλπίζω elpizō (1666)
μένω menō (3176)
περιμένω perimenō (3900)
προσδέχομαι prosdechomai (4185)
προσδοκάω prosdokaō (4186)

בָּחַר bāchar (1013), Test, select (2 Sm 19:38—Codex Alexandrinus only, Jb 34:33—Codex Sinaiticus only, Is 66:44—Codex Vaticanus only).

עָרַב 'ārav (6386), Ensure (Gn 43:9, 44:32, Ps 119:122 [118:122]).

קָבַץ qāvats (7192), Piel: gather together, assemble (Hos 9:6, Mi 2:12, Na 3:18).

קָצַר qātsar (7403), Reap, harvest (Hos 8:7).

שִׂים sîm (7947), Ponder, place (Is 57:1).

1. ἐκδέχομαι ekdechomai 1sing indic pres mid
2. ἐκδέχεται ekdechetai 3sing indic pres mid
3. ἐκδέχεσθε ekdechesthe 2pl impr pres mid
4. ἐκδεχόμενος ekdechomenos
nom sing masc part pres mid
5. ἐκδεχομένου ekdechomenou
gen sing masc part pres mid
6. ἐκδεχομένων ekdechomenōn
gen pl masc part pres mid
7. ἐξεδέχετο exedecheto 3sing indic imperf mid

6 **waiting** for the moving of the water............. John 5:3
5 Now while Paul **waited** for them at Athens,........ Acts 17:16
3 ye come together to eat, **tarry** one for another..... 1 Co 11:33
1 for I **look** for him with the brethren.................. 16:11
4 **expecting** till his enemies be made his footstool..... Heb 10:13
7 For he **looked** for a city which hath foundations,....... 11:10
2 the husbandman **waiteth** for the precious fruit........ Jas 5:7
7 when once the longsuffering of God **waited**.......... 1 Pt 3:20

This is a term translated primarily as "expect or wait for something or someone." It may also be rendered "looking for." (See 1 Corinthians 16:11 and Hebrews 11:10.) This verb interjects the element of receiving something with open anticipation. With *heōs* (2175) it means "wait until" (John 5:3; Acts 17:16; James 5:7).

STRONG 1551, BAUER 238, MOULTON-MILLIGAN 192, KITTEL 2:56, LIDDELL-SCOTT 503, COLIN BROWN 2:244-45; 3:745.

1539. ἔκδηλος ekdēlos adj
Quite evident, plain.
CROSS-REFERENCE:
δηλόω dēloō (1207)

1. ἔκδηλος ekdēlos nom sing fem
1 for their folly shall be **manifest** unto all men,....... 2 Tm 3:9

This word may be translated "manifest, quite evident, quite plain" or "conspicuous." Used only in 2 Timothy 3:9, this adjective is an intensive form of *dēlos* (1206), "evident." Other Greek literature translates the term "conspicuous."

STRONG 1552, BAUER 238, MOULTON-MILLIGAN 192, LIDDELL-SCOTT 503-4.

1540. ἐκδημέω ekdēmeō verb
Away from home.
CROSS-REFERENCE:
δῆμος dēmos (1211B)

1. ἐκδημοῦμεν ekdēmoumen 1pl indic pres act
2. ἐκδημοῦντες ekdēmountes
nom pl masc part pres act
3. ἐκδημῆσαι ekdēmēsai inf aor act

1 at home in the body, we **are absent** from the Lord:...2 Co 5:6
3 and willing rather **to be absent** from the body,.......... 5:8
2 present or **absent**, we may be accepted of him.......... 5:9

Classical Greek and Septuagint Usage
Ekdēmeō is related to the root *dēmos* (1213), which originally denoted "a district of land" but later came to include "the people of a city or region." In classical Greek *ekdēmeō* was used by Plato and others to mean "go abroad, go out of the country," or "travel." *Ekdēmeō* does not appear in the Septuagint, but its root, *dēmos*, is used to translate the Hebrew *mishpāchāh*, "race" or "family." The papyri also use the word in the sense of "being away from one's own people or

land." Certain residents of Alexandria had to give notice if they should change residence or "go abroad."

New Testament Usage

All the uses of *ekdēmeō* in the New Testament occur in 2 Corinthians 5:6-9 where the word is paired three times with *endēmeō* (1720), which means "to be at home, in the homeland." Paul declared that he was at home in his physical body but longed for the day when he could say that he was truly at home "with the Lord." At that time, life "in the body" would be *ekdēmeō*, "a journey abroad," away from the homeland where he presently belonged.

STRONG 1553, BAUER 238, MOULTON-MILLIGAN 192, KITTEL 2:63-64, LIDDELL-SCOTT 504, COLIN BROWN 2:788-90.

1541. ἐκδίδωμι ekdidōmi verb
Let out for hire, lease.

CROSS-REFERENCE:
δίδωμι didōmi (1319)

הָיָה hāyâh (2030), Be, have (Lv 21:3).

יָצָא yātsā' (3428), Go out, come out; hiphil: gave, hand over (2 Kgs 12:11 [12:12]).

נָתַן nāthan (5598), Give (Jgs 1:15).

1. ἐξέδοτο exedoto 3sing indic aor mid
2. ἐκδόσεται ekdosetai 3sing indic fut mid
3. ἐξέδετο exedeto 3sing indic aor mid
4. ἐκδώσεται ekdōsetai 3sing indic fut mid

1 and built a tower, and let it **out** to husbandmen, ...	Matt 21:33
3 and built a tower, and let it **out** to husbandmen, ...	21:33
2 will let **out** his vineyard unto other husbandmen, ...	21:41
4 will let **out** his vineyard unto other husbandmen, ...	21:41
1 and built a tower, and let it **out** to husbandmen, ...	Mark 12:1
3 and built a tower, and let it **out** to husbandmen, ...	12:1
1 a vineyard, and let it **forth** to husbandmen, ...	Luke 20:9
3 a vineyard, and let it **forth** to husbandmen, ...	20:9

The denotation of this word, "let out for hire, lease," is consistent throughout classical Greek and the Septuagint. It could include either material things or even people (referring to times when sons were hired out as apprentices; cf. *Bauer*). In the parable of the husbandman and his vineyard the idea expressed is "to lease out for one's own advantage" (Matthew 21:33; Mark 12:1; Luke 20:9).

STRONG 1554, BAUER 238, MOULTON-MILLIGAN 192, LIDDELL-SCOTT 504.

1542. ἐκδιηγέομαι ekdiēgeomai verb
Tell in detail, narrate at length, declare fully.

COGNATE:
ἄγω agō (70)

SYNONYMS:
ἀγγέλλω angellō (31B)
ἀναγγέλλω anangellō (310)
ἀνατίθημι anatithēmi (392)
ἀπαγγέλλω apangellō (514)
διηγέομαι diēgeomai (1328)
ἐξηγέομαι exēgeomai (1817)
εὐαγγελίζω euangelizō (2076)
καταγγέλλω katangellō (2576)
κηρύσσω kērussō (2756)
λέγω legō (2978)

סָפַר sāphar (5807), Piel: declare, acknowledge (Ez 12:16); pual: be related, told (Hb 1:5).

שִׂיחַ sîach (7943), Declare, inform (Jb 12:8).

שָׁעָה shā'âh (8541), Hithpael: look around in anxiety (Sir 44:8).

1. ἐκδιηγῆται ekdiēgētai 3sing subj pres mid
2. ἐκδιηγούμενοι ekdiēgoumenoi nom pl masc part pres mid

1 no wise believe, though a man **declare** it unto you.	Acts 13:41
2 **declaring** the conversion of the Gentiles:	15:3

This is the intensive form of the verb *diēgeomai* (1328), "tell," and is used only twice in the New Testament. In both cases it denotes the declaration of the Word of God (Acts 13:41; 15:3). An example of this word's usage in the Septuagint can be seen in Job 12:8. There Job declared that the earth itself would speak and would teach his accusers.

STRONG 1555, BAUER 238, LIDDELL-SCOTT 504.

1543. ἐκδικέω ekdikeō verb
Avenge, take revenge, punish.

CROSS-REFERENCE:
δικαιόω dikaioō (1338)

דָּרַשׁ dārash (1938), Command, demand (Dt 18:19).

נָקָה nāqâh (5536), Niphal: banished, cut off (Zec 5:3); piel: pardoned (Jl 3:21—Codex Alexandrinus only).

נָקַם nāqam (5541), Qal: avenge, punish (Nm 31:2, Ps 99:8 [98:8], Na 1:2); niphal: be avenged, take revenge (Ex 21:20); piel: avenge (2 Kgs 9:7, Jer 51:36 [28:36]); hophal: punished (Ex 21:21); hithpael: take one's vengeance (Jer 5:9,29, 9:9).

פָּקַד pāqadh (6734), Destroy, punish (1 Sm 15:2, Hos 4:9, Jer 15:3).

פָּרַק pāraq (6811), Hithpael: uprooted, separated (Ez 19:12).

רִיב rîv (7662), Contend, dispute (Is 57:16).

שָׁפַט shāphaṭ (8570), Qal: judge, sentence (Ez 16:38, 23:45, Ob 21); niphal: executing judgment (2 Chr 22:8).

1. ἐκδικεῖς ekdikeis 2sing indic pres act
2. ἐκδικοῦντες ekdikountes nom pl masc part pres act
3. ἐξεδίκησεν exedikēsen 3sing indic aor act
4. ἐκδίκησον ekdikēson 2sing impr aor act
5. ἐκδικῆσαι ekdikēsai inf aor act
6. ἐκδικήσω ekdikēsō 1sing indic fut act

```
4 was a widow ... Avenge me of mine adversary...... Luke 18:3
6 this widow troubleth me, I will avenge her,............ 18:5
2 Dearly beloved, avenge not yourselves,............ Rom 12:19
5 having in a readiness to revenge all disobedience,...2 Co 10:6
1 avenge our blood on them that dwell on the earth?.. Rev 6:10
3 hath avenged the blood of his servants at her hand..... 19:2
```

Classical Greek
This word, which was first attested around 150 B.C., denotes the acts of "to avenge, to outlaw," or "to punish." Etymologically it is related to *ekdikos* (1545), the corresponding adjective, which originally referred to a person who broke the law. Gradually the meaning shifted from "being outlawed" toward the idea of "vengeance" or "punishment" for lawbreakers.

In the papyri *ekdikeō* is used in its legal sense "to decide a case in court" or "to enable a person to obtain his legal rights."

Septuagint Usage
The Septuagint uses *ekdikeō* both to describe God's act in taking vengeance or bringing justice (Deuteronomy 18:19) and to describe judicial proceedings carried out by man under the authority of God (Numbers 31:2).

New Testament Usage
The New Testament uses *ekdikeō* six times, primarily referring to Old Testament concepts. Luke used it to describe legal protection for the persistent widow in the Parable of the Unjust Judge (18:3,5). In 2 Corinthians 10:6 Paul promised that disobedience will be punished. Romans 12:19 forbids private acts of vengeance, while Revelation 6:10 and 19:2 describe God bringing justice on the evil powers of earth.

STRONG 1556, BAUER 238, MOULTON-MILLIGAN 192-93, KITTEL 2:442-44, LIDDELL-SCOTT 504, COLIN BROWN 3:92-93,96-97.

1544. ἐκδίκησις ekdikēsis noun
Vengeance, punishment, vindication.
COGNATE:
δικαιόω dikaioō (1338)
SYNONYMS:
ἐπιτιμία epitimia (1993)
κόλασις kolasis (2824)
τιμωρία timōria (4946)

אַף 'aph (653), Anger (Is 66:15).

מִשְׁפָּט mishpāṯ (5122), Legal decision, sentence (Ez 16:38, 23:45).

נָקָם nāqām (5542), Vengeance, revenge (Dt 32:35, Ez 25:12, Mi 5:15).

נְקָמָה nᵉqāmāh (5543), Vengeance (Nm 31:2, 2 Sm 4:8, Jer 51:11 [28:11]).

פָּקַד pāqadh (6734), Punish (Jer 50:31 [27:31]).

פְּקֻדָּה pᵉquddāh (6735), Punish, destroy (Jer 46:21 [26:10], Ez 9:1, Hos 9:7).

שְׁפוֹט shᵉphôṭ (8565), Punishment, judgment (Ez 23:10).

שָׁפַט shāphaṭ (8570), Judge (Ez 20:4).

שֶׁפֶט shepheṭ (8572), Punishment, judgment (Ex 7:4, Ez 16:41, 30:14).

תֹּאֲנָה tō'ănāh (8712), Seek an occasion for a quarrel (Jgs 14:4).

תּוֹכַחַת tôkhachath (8763), Reproach (Ez 5:15).

1. ἐκδίκησις ekdikēsis nom sing fem
2. ἐκδικήσεως ekdikēseōs gen sing fem
3. ἐκδίκησιν ekdikēsin acc sing fem

```
3 And shall not God avenge his own elect,.......... Luke 18:7
3 I tell you that he will avenge them speedily........... 18:8
2 For these be the days of vengeance,................... 21:22
3 and avenged him that was oppressed,................ Acts 7:24
1 for it is written, Vengeance is mine;............... Rom 12:19
3 yea, what zeal, yea, what revenge!................... 2 Co 7:11
3 taking vengeance on them that know not God,...... 2 Th 1:8
1 Vengeance belongeth unto me, I will recompense,...Heb 10:30
3 are sent by him for the punishment of evildoers,..... 1 Pt 2:14
```

This word is used to refer to the rendering of divine justice. When joined with *antapodidōmi* (464), "to repay," the punishment belongs to God who repays with divine justice. (See Romans 12:19 and Hebrews 10:30.) With *poiein* (see 4020) it denotes "see to it that justice is done" (cf. Luke 18:7f.; Acts 7:24). See also the verb form *ekdikeō* (1543).

STRONG 1557, BAUER 238, MOULTON-MILLIGAN 193, KITTEL 2:445-46, LIDDELL-SCOTT 504, COLIN BROWN 3:92-93,97.

1545. ἔκδικος ekdikos adj
An avenger, the one who punishes or adjures.
CROSS-REFERENCE:
δικαιόω dikaioō (1338)

1. ἔκδικος ekdikos nom sing masc

```
1 a revenger to execute wrath upon him that doeth...Rom 13:4
1 because that the Lord is the avenger of all such,.... 1 Th 4:6
```

Used in 1 Thessalonians 4:6, *ekdikos* shows God's wrath upon the individual who wrongs his brother. The evildoer who rebels against earthly authority is to fear because this authority is the servant of God appointed to preserve good and is the *ekdikos*, "the avenger, the punisher," who brings God's divine punishment upon the culprit, as in Romans 13:4.

STRONG 1558, BAUER 238, MOULTON-MILLIGAN 193, KITTEL 2:444-45, LIDDELL-SCOTT 504, COLIN BROWN 3:92,97.

1546. ἐκδιώκω ekdiōkō verb
Persecute severely, expel by persecuting.
CROSS-REFERENCE:
διώκω diōkō (1371)

בָּרַח bārach (1300), Run away; hiphil: drive out (1 Chr 8:13).

הָדַף hādhaph (1990), Drive away (Dt 6:19).

נָקַם nāqam (5541), Hithpael: revenge, avenge (Ps 44:16 [43:16]).

צָמַת tsāmath (7059), Hiphil: make silent, destroy (Ps 101:5 [100:5]).

רָדַף rādhaph (7579), Pursue, persecute (1 Sm 30:10—Codex Alexandrinus only).

רוּץ rûts (7608), Qal: run (Jer 50:44 [27:44]); hiphil: chase off (Jer 49:19 [29:19]).

רָחַק rāchaq (7651), Be far away; hiphil: remove, move far away (Jl 2:20).

1. ἐκδιωξάντων ekdiōxantōn gen pl masc part aor act
2. ἐκδιώξουσιν ekdiōxousin 3pl indic fut act

2 and some of them they shall slay and persecute:....Luke 11:49
1 and have persecuted us; and they please not God,... 1 Th 2:15

This term is used twice in the New Testament in connection with the persecution of the servants of God. (See Luke 11:49 and 1 Thessalonians 2:15.) *Ekdiōkō* is interchanged with the verb *diōkō* (1371) in some manuscripts.

STRONG 1559, BAUER 239, MOULTON-MILLIGAN 193, LIDDELL-SCOTT 504, COLIN BROWN 2:805-6.

1547. ἔκδοτος ekdotos adj
Given up, delivered up.
CROSS-REFERENCE:
δίδωμι didōmi (1319)

1. ἔκδοτον ekdoton acc sing masc

1 Him, being delivered by the determinate counsel..... Acts 2:23

This word is a verbal adjective denoting "to be given up or delivered up by the will of another." The discourse by Peter on the Day of Pentecost regarding Christ's crucifixion is the only usage of this term in the New Testament (Acts 2:23).

STRONG 1560, BAUER 239, MOULTON-MILLIGAN 193, LIDDELL-SCOTT 505.

1548. ἐκδοχή ekdochē noun
Expectation.
CROSS-REFERENCE:
ἐκδέχομαι ekdechomai (1538)

1. ἐκδοχή ekdochē nom sing fem

1 But a certain fearful looking for of judgment....... Heb 10:27

The idea behind this word is a "reception," a "waiting for" or "looking for" an event to transpire. While related to the verb *ekdechomai* (1538), "expect" or "wait for," this noun interjects the element of fear into the expectation of judgment. It is used once in the New Testament (Hebrews 10:27).

STRONG 1561, BAUER 239, MOULTON-MILLIGAN 193, LIDDELL-SCOTT 505, COLIN BROWN 2:244.

1549. ἐκδύω ekduō verb
Strip, take off, undress (oneself).
CROSS-REFERENCE:
δύνω dunō (1410)

חָלַץ chālats (2603), Qal: offer (Lam 4:3); niphal: rescue, deliver (Prv 11:8).

פָּשַׁט pāshaṭ (6838), Qal: take off, strip off (Lv 16:23, 1 Sm 19:24, Is 32:11); hiphil: take off, strip off (Gn 37:23, 1 Chr 10:9); hithpael: took off (1 Sm 18:4—Codex Alexandrinus only).

פָּתַח pāthach (6858), Open; hithpael: loosen for oneself (Is 52:2).

1. ἐξέδυσαν exedusan 3pl indic aor act
2. ἐκδύσαντες ekdusantes nom pl masc part aor act
3. ἐκδύσασθαι ekdusasthai inf aor mid
4. ἐκδυσάμενοι ekdusamenoi
    nom pl masc part aor mid

2 they stripped him, and put on him a scarlet robe... Matt 27:28
1 they took the robe off from him,...................... 27:31
2 they took the robe off from him,...................... 27:31
1 they took off the purple from him,................ Mark 15:20
2 among thieves, which stripped him of his raiment,..Luke 10:30
4 that being clothed we shall not be found naked......2 Co 5:3
3 not for that we would be unclothed,.................... 5:4

Classical Greek

In classical Greek *ekduō* is used transitively, denoting "to strip or undress someone else." It is also employed in an intransitive sense, usually in the middle voice, to refer to the action of "stripping or undressing oneself." *Ekduō* carries the related meanings of "ridding oneself of, extracting oneself from," or "escaping something" and it is used figuratively to describe "the laying aside of the human body which clothes the spirit."

Septuagint Usage

The Septuagint and papyri use *ekduō* with the same range of definitions. It is used to describe the brothers "stripping off" Joseph's tunic (Genesis 37:23), and to command the complacent Israelite women to "strip themselves" to put on sackcloth (Isaiah 32:11).

New Testament Usage

In the New Testament the same uses of *ekduō* can be found. The word is used in Matthew 27:28,31 and Mark 15:20 to describe the soldiers removing Jesus' outer garment and then removing the purple robe. Luke 10:30 employs the literal sense again in the description of the man who was robbed and stripped, then later helped by the Good Samaritan. *Ekduō* is used figuratively (middle voice) in 2 Corinthians 5:4, meaning "to lay aside the garment of the human body which houses the spirit."

STRONG 1562, BAUER 239, MOULTON-MILLIGAN 193, KITTEL 2:318, LIDDELL-SCOTT 505, COLIN BROWN 1:313-14.

1550. ἐκεῖ ekei adv

There, in that place.

COGNATES:

ἐκεῖθεν ekeithen (1551)
ἐκεῖνος ekeinos (1552)
ἐκεῖσε ekeise (1553)
κἀκεῖ kakei (2517)
κἀκεῖθεν kakeithen (2518)
κἀκεῖνος kakeinos (2519)
ὑπερέκεινα huperekeina (5075)

הָלְאָה hāleʾāh (2042), To there, farther (Gn 19:9, Nm 16:37).

הֲלֹם hălōm (2057), To here, here (Jgs 20:7).

שָׁם shām (8427), There (Gn 2:8, Jer 18:2).

תַּמָּה tammāh (A8869), There (Ezr 6:12—Aramaic).

1. ἐκεῖ ekei

1	and be thou **there** until I bring thee word:	Matt 2:13
1	And was **there** until the death of Herod:	2:15
1	Archelaus did reign ... he was afraid to go **thither**:	2:22
1	Leave **there** thy gift before the altar,	5:24
1	treasure is, **there** will your heart be also.	6:21
1	**there** shall be weeping and gnashing of teeth.	8:12
1	and they enter in and dwell **there**:	12:45
1	**there** shall be wailing and gnashing of teeth.	13:42
1	**there** shall be wailing and gnashing of teeth.	13:50
1	And he did not many mighty works **there**	13:58
1	when the evening was come, he was **there** alone.	14:23
1	and went up into a mountain, and sat down **there**.	15:29
1	Remove hence to **yonder place**;	17:20
1	two or three are ... **there** am I in the midst of them.	18:20
1	multitudes followed him; ... he healed them **there**.	19:2
1	out of the city into Bethany; and he lodged **there**.	Matt 21:17
1	he saw **there** a man ... not on a wedding garment:	22:11
1	**there** shall be weeping and gnashing of teeth.	22:13
1	**there** will the eagles be gathered together.	24:28
1	**there** shall be weeping and gnashing of teeth.	24:51
1	**there** shall be weeping and gnashing of teeth.	25:30
1	Sit ye **here**, while I go and pray **yonder**.	26:36
1	and said unto them that were **there**,	26:71
1	And sitting down they watched him **there**;	27:36
1	Some of them that stood **there**,	27:47
1	And many women were **there** beholding afar off,	27:55
1	**there** was Mary Magdalene, and the other Mary,	27:61
1	**there** shall ye see him: lo, I have told you.	28:7
1	go into Galilee, and **there** shall they see me.	28:10
1	And he was **there** in the wilderness forty days,	Mark 1:13
1	departed into a solitary place, and **there** prayed.	1:35
1	in order that I may preach **there** also; (NASB)	1:38
1	But there were certain of the scribes sitting **there**,	2:6
1	there was a man **there** which had a withered hand.	3:1
1	Now there was **there** nigh unto the mountains	5:11
1	And he could **there** do no mighty work,	6:5
1	**there** abide till ye depart from that place.	6:10
1	and ran afoot **thither** out of all cities,	6:33
1	where they heard he was. (NT)	6:55
1	certain of them that stood **there** said unto them,	11:5
1	or, lo, he is **there**; believe him not:	13:21
1	a large upper room ... **there** make ready for us.	14:15
1	Galilee: **there** shall ye see him, as he said unto you.	16:7
1	while they were **there**, the days were accomplished	Luke 2:6
1	**there** was a man whose right hand was withered.	6:6
1	And there was **there** an herd of many swine	8:32
1	And whatsoever house ye enter into, **there** abide,	9:4
1	if the son of peace be **there**, your peace shall rest	10:6
1	and they enter in, and dwell **there**:	11:26
1	and **there** will I bestow all my fruits and my goods.	12:18
1	where your treasure is, **there** will your heart be	12:34
1	**There** shall be weeping and gnashing of teeth.	13:28
1	and **there** wasted his substance with riotous living.	15:13
1	Neither shall they say, Lo here! or, lo **there**!	17:21
1	or, see **there**: go not after them, nor follow them.	17:23
1	**thither** will the eagles be gathered together.	17:37
1	a certain poor widow casting in **thither** two mites.	21:2
1	a large upper room furnished: **there** make ready.	22:12
1	**there** they crucified him, and the malefactors,	23:33
1	and the mother of Jesus was **there**:	John 2:1
1	And there were set **there** six waterpots of stone,	2:6
1	and they continued **there** not many days.	2:12
1	and **there** he tarried with them, and baptized.	3:22
1	baptizing ... because there was much water **there**:	3:23
1	Now Jacob's well was **there**.	4:6
1	and he abode **there** two days.	4:40
1	And a certain man was **there**,	5:5
1	and **there** he sat with his disciples.	6:3
1	saw that **there** was none other boat **there**,	6:22
1	the people therefore saw that Jesus was not **there**,	6:24
1	and **there** he abode.	10:40
1	And many believed on him **there**.	10:42
1	sought to stone thee; and goest thou **thither** again?	11:8
1	And I am glad for your sakes that I was not **there**,	11:15
1	saying, She goeth unto the grave to weep **there**.	11:31
1	**There** they made him a supper;	12:2
1	people of the Jews ... knew that he was **there**:	12:9
1	and where I am, **there** shall also my servant be:	12:26
1	Jesus ofttimes resorted **thither** with his disciples.	18:2
1	cometh **thither** with lanterns and torches	18:3
1	**There** laid they Jesus therefore	19:42
1	And **there** he found a certain man named AEneas,.	Acts 9:33
1	And **there** they abode long time with the disciples.	14:28
1	and, behold, a certain disciple was **there**,	16:1
1	but Silas and Timotheus abode **there** still.	17:14
1	And he came to Ephesus, and left them **there**:	18:19
1	After I have been **there**, I must also see Rome.	19:21
1	and **there** be judged of these things before me?	25:9
1	And when they had been **there** many days,	25:14
1	**there** shall they be called the children of ... God.	Rom 9:26
1	and to be brought on my way **thitherward** by you,	15:24
1	and where the Spirit of the Lord is, **there** is liberty.	2 Co 3:17

1 for I have determined there to winter	Tit 3:12
1 but there he receiveth them,	Heb 7:8
1 Stand thou there, or sit here under my footstool:	Jas 2:3
1 there is confusion and every evil work.	3:16
1 and continue there a year, and buy and sell,	4:13
1 hast there them that hold the doctrine of Balaam,	Rev 2:14
1 she has a place prepared by God (RSV) (NT)	12:6
1 a place prepared ... that they should feed her there	12:6
1 is nourished for a time, and times, (NT)	12:14
1 not be shut ... for there shall be no night there	21:25
1 And there shall be no night there;	22:5

This word is an adverb of place translated "there," "in that place," or "thither." It is used throughout the New Testament with two different ideas: "to be in a place" (Matthew 2:15) or "to go to a place" (John 11:8).

STRONG 1563, BAUER 239, MOULTON-MILLIGAN 193-94, LIDDELL-SCOTT 505.

1551. ἐκεῖθεν ekeithen adv

From there, thence.

CROSS-REFERENCE:
ἐκεῖ ekei (1550)

שָׁם shām (8427), There (Ex 25:22, 2 Kgs 6:10).

1. ἐκεῖθεν ekeithen

1 going on from thence, he saw other two brethren,	Matt 4:21
1 Thou shalt by no means come out thence,	5:26
1 And as Jesus passed forth from thence,	9:9
1 Jesus departed thence, two blind men followed	9:27
1 he departed thence to teach and to preach	11:1
1 And when he was departed thence,	12:9
1 Jesus ... he withdrew himself from thence:	12:15
1 finished these parables, he departed thence.	13:53
1 departed thence by ship into a desert place apart:	14:13
1 Then Jesus went thence, and departed	15:21
1 And Jesus departed from thence,	15:29
1 he laid his hands on them, and departed thence	19:15
1 And when he had gone a little farther thence,	Mark 1:19
1 And he went out from thence,	6:1
1 there abide till ye depart from that place.	6:10
1 when ye depart thence, shake off the dust	6:11
1 And from thence he arose,	7:24
1 And from thence he arose,	7:24
1 they departed thence, and passed through Galilee;	9:30
1 And he arose from thence, ... into the coasts	10:1
1 house ye enter ... there abide, and thence depart.	Luke 9:4
1 I tell thee, thou shalt not depart thence,	12:59
1 neither ... pass to us, that would come from thence.	16:26
1 Now after two days he departed thence,	John 4:43
1 went thence unto a country near to the wilderness,	11:54
1 and from thence they sailed to Cyprus.	Acts 13:4
1 And from thence to Philippi,	16:12
1 And he departed thence,	18:7
1 sailed unto Assos, there intending to take in Paul:	20:13
1 majority advised to put to sea from there (RSV)	27:12
1 And on either side of the river (NASB)	Rev 22:2

Whereas *ekei* (1550) denotes a stationary position or moving towards a position, *ekeithen* expresses the idea of moving from a position. (See Matthew 4:21 and 12:15.)

STRONG 1564, BAUER 239, MOULTON-MILLIGAN 194, LIDDELL-SCOTT 505.

1552. ἐκεῖνος ekeinos dem-pron

That, those, that one.

CROSS-REFERENCE:
ἐκεῖ ekei (1550)

1. ἐκείνων ekeinōn gen pl masc/fem/neu
2. ἐκείνου ekeinou gen sing masc/neu
3. ἐκεῖνος ekeinos nom sing masc
4. ἐκείνῳ ekeinō dat sing masc
5. ἐκεῖνον ekeinon acc sing masc
6. ἐκεῖνοι ekeinoi nom pl masc
7. ἐκείνοις ekeinois dat pl masc
8. ἐκείνους ekeinous acc pl masc
9. ἐκείνη ekeinē nom sing fem
10. ἐκείνης ekeinēs gen sing fem
11. ἐκείνῃ ekeinē dat sing fem
12. ἐκείνην ekeinēn acc sing fem
13. ἐκεῖναι ekeinai nom pl fem
14. ἐκείναις ekeinais dat pl fem
15. ἐκείνας ekeinas acc pl fem
16. ἐκεῖνο ekeino nom/acc sing neu
17. ἐκεῖνα ekeina nom/acc pl neu

14 In those days came John the Baptist,	Matt 3:1
11 Many will say to me in that day, Lord, Lord,	7:22
11 and the winds blew, and beat upon that house;	7:25
11 and the winds blew, and beat upon that house;	7:27
11 And his servant was healed in the selfsame hour.	8:13
10 And his servant was healed in the selfsame hour.	8:13
10 so that no man might pass by that way.	8:28
10 And the woman was made whole from that hour.	9:22
12 And the fame hereof went abroad into all that land.	9:26
11 spread abroad his fame in all that country.	9:31
10 when ye depart out of that house or city,	10:14
11 It shall be more tolerable ... than for that city.	10:15
11 for it shall be given you in that same hour	10:19
4 At that time Jesus answered and said,	11:25
4 At that time Jesus went on the sabbath day	12:1
2 and the last state of that man is worse than the first.	12:45
11 The same day went Jesus out of the house,	13:1
7 it is given unto you ... but to them it is not given.	13:11
5 selleth all that he hath, and buyeth that field.	13:44
4 At that time Herod the tetrarch heard of the fame	14:1
2 when the men of that place had knowledge of him,	14:35
12 they sent out into all that country round about,	14:35
1 a woman of Canaan came out of the same coasts,	15:22
10 her daughter was made whole from that very hour.	15:28
10 and the child was cured from that very hour.	17:18
5 and take up the fish that first cometh up;	17:27
11 At the same time came the disciples unto Jesus,	18:1
4 but woe to that man by whom the offence cometh!	18:7
3 servant therefore fell down, and worshipped him,	18:26
2 lord of that servant was moved with compassion,	18:27
3 took him by the throat, ... Pay me that thou owest.	18:28
12 after that he had called him, said unto him,	18:32
7 And to those he said, (NASB)	20:4
7 what will he do unto those husbandmen?	21:40
3 But when the king heard thereof, he was wroth:	22:7
8 and destroyed those murderers,	22:7
6 So those servants went out into the highways,	22:10
11 The same day came to him the Sadducees,	22:23
10 neither durst any man from that day forth ask him	22:46
14 woe unto ... them that give suck in those days!	24:19
13 And except those days should be shortened,	24:22
13 for the elect's sake those days shall be shortened.	24:22
1 Immediately after the tribulation of those days	24:29
10 But of that day and hour knoweth no man,	24:36
14 For as in those days ... before the flood (NASB)	24:38

ἐκεῖνος 1552

16	that if the goodman of the house had known..... Matt	24:43
3	Blessed is that servant, whom his lord ... find so.....	24:46
3	But and if that evil servant shall say in his heart,.....	24:48
2	The lord of that servant shall come in a day.....	24:50
13	all those virgins arose, and trimmed their lamps......	25:7
1	After a long time the lord of those servants cometh,..	25:19
4	but woe unto that man by whom the Son............	26:24
3	been good for that man if he had not been born......	26:24
10	until that day when I drink it new with you........	26:29
11	In that same hour said Jesus to the multitudes,.......	26:55
3	Wherefore that field was called, The field of blood,...	27:8
4	Have thou nothing to do with that just man:.........	27:19
3	Saying, Sir, we remember that that deceiver said,.....	27:63
14	And it came to pass in those days,............... Mark	1:9
14	and then shall they fast in those days.................	2:20
11	and then shall they fast in those days.................	2:20
9	divided against itself, that kingdom cannot stand.....	3:24
9	be divided against itself, that house cannot stand......	3:25
7	but unto them that are without,....................	4:11
6	And those are the ones on whom seed (NASB)......	4:20
11	And the same day, when the even was come,.........	4:35
11	in the day of judgment, than for that city...........	6:11
2	come out of the ship, straightway they knew him,.....	6:54
12	And ran through that whole region round about,.....	6:55
17	those are they that defile the man...................	7:15
16	cometh out of the man, that defileth the man........	7:20
14	In those days the multitude being very great,.........	8:1
6	But those husbandmen said among themselves,......	12:7
11	but whatsoever shall be given you in that hour,......	13:11
14	But woe ... to them that give suck in those days!.....	13:17
13	For in those days shall be affliction,.................	13:19
14	But in those days, after that tribulation,.............	13:24
12	after that tribulation, the sun shall be darkened,.....	13:24
10	But of that day and that hour knoweth no man,.....	13:32
4	but woe to that man by whom the Son of man......	14:21
3	good were it for that man ... never been born.......	14:21
10	until that day that I drink it new in the kingdom.....	14:25
9	she went and told them that had been with him,.....	16:10
7	unto the residue: neither believed they them..........	16:13
6	And they went forth, and preached every where,.....	16:20
14	And it came to pass in those days,................ Luke	2:1
14	And in those days he did eat nothing;...............	4:2
14	and then shall they fast in those days................	5:35
11	Rejoice ye in that day, and leap for joy:.............	6:23
11	the stream beat vehemently upon that house,........	6:48
10	it fell; and the ruin of that house was great..........	6:49
11	At that very time He cured many (NASB)...........	7:21
8	that he would suffer them to enter into them.........	8:32
10	will not receive you, when ye go out of that city,.....	9:5
8	and they feared as they entered into the cloud.......	9:34
14	they kept it close, and told no man in those days	9:36
11	it shall be more tolerable in that day for Sodom,.....	10:12
11	be more tolerable ... for Sodom, than for that city.....	10:12
11	there came down a certain priest that way..........	10:31
2	and the last state of that man is worse than the first.	11:26
6	Blessed are those servants,.........................	12:37
6	and find them so, blessed are those servants.........	12:38
3	Blessed is that servant, whom his lord when he......	12:43
3	But and if that servant say in his heart,.............	12:45
2	The lord of that servant will come in a day when.....	12:46
3	And that servant, which knew his lord's will,........	12:47
6	Or those eighteen, upon whom the tower ... fell,.....	13:4
3	So that servant came, and showed his lord these......	14:21
1	none of those men which were bidden shall taste.....	14:24
12	there arose a mighty famine in that land;...........	15:14
10	joined himself to a citizen of that country;..........	15:15
4	Doth he thank that servant because he did..........	17:9
11	In that day, he which shall be upon the housetop,....	17:31
11	And there was a widow in that city;................	18:3
3	down to his house justified rather than the other:.....	18:14
5	down to his house justified rather than the other:.....	18:14
10	tree to see him: for he was to pass that way..........	19:4
8	But those mine enemies, which would not that I.....	19:27
1	And it came to pass, that on one of those days,.......	20:1
5	shall fall upon that stone shall be broken;...........	20:18
2	shall be accounted worthy to obtain that world,......	20:35
14	woe ... to them that give suck, in those days!........	21:23
9	and so that day come upon you unawares......... Luke	21:34
4	but woe unto that man by whom he is betrayed!.....	22:22
3	He was not that Light, but was sent to bear witness John	1:8
3	the only begotten Son, ... he hath declared him........	1:18
3	he that sent me ... the same said unto me,...........	1:33
12	and abode with him that day:.....................	1:39
3	But he spake of the temple of his body..............	2:21
2	I am not the Christ, but that I am sent before him.....	3:28
5	He must increase, but I must decrease..............	3:30
3	when he is come, he will tell us all things...........	4:25
10	And many of the Samaritans of that city believed......	4:39
11	So the father knew that it was at the same hour,.....	4:53
11	and on the same day was the sabbath................	5:9
3	He that made me whole, the same said unto me,......	5:11
3	for what things soever he doeth,....................	5:19
3	He was a burning and a shining light:..............	5:35
3	the Father ... He has borne witness (NASB) (NT).....	5:37
3	for whom he hath sent, him ye believe not...........	5:38
13	and they are they which testify of me................	5:39
3	shall come in his own name, him ye will receive......	5:43
3	ye would have believed me: for he wrote of me.......	5:46
2	But if ye believe not his writings,....................	5:47
16	save that one whereinto his disciples were entered,....	6:22
3	that ye believe on him whom he hath sent...........	6:29
3	sought him at the feast, and said, Where is he?.......	7:11
6	Then came the officers ... and they said unto them,...	7:45
6	Woman, where are those thine accusers?.............	8:10
3	neither came I of myself, but he sent me.............	8:42
3	He was a murderer from the beginning,.............	8:44
3	others said, He is like him: but he said, I am he.......	9:9
3	He answered and said, A man that is called Jesus.....	9:11
3	Then said they unto him, Where is he?..............	9:12
3	He answered and said,.............................	9:25
2	Thou art his disciple; but we are Moses' disciples.....	9:28
3	He answered and said, Who is he, Lord,.............	9:36
3	and it is he that talketh with thee...................	9:37
3	the same is a thief and a robber.....................	10:1
6	parable spake Jesus ... but they understood not.......	10:6
8	If he called them gods,............................	10:35
6	but they thought that he had spoken of ... rest......	11:13
9	As soon as she heard that, she arose quickly,........	11:29
2	Caiaphas, being the high priest that same year,......	11:49
2	but being high priest that year, he prophesied........	11:51
10	Then from that day forth they took counsel.........	11:53
3	the same shall judge him in the last day.............	12:48
3	and Peter saith unto him, (NT)...................	13:6
3	He then lying on Jesus' breast saith unto him,.......	13:25
3	He it is, to whom I shall give a sop,................	13:26
5	And after the sop Satan entered into him............	13:27
3	He then having received the sop went immediately...	13:30
11	At that day ye shall know that I am in my Father,...	14:20
3	hath my commandments, ... he it is that loveth me:...	14:21
3	the Holy Ghost, ... he shall teach you all things,.....	14:26
3	the Spirit of truth, ... he shall testify of me:.........	15:26
3	when he is come, he will reprove the world of sin,...	16:8
3	Howbeit when he, the Spirit of truth, is come,......	16:13
3	He shall glorify me: for he shall receive of mine,.....	16:14
11	And in that day ye shall ask me nothing............	16:23
11	At that day ye shall ask in my name:................	16:26
2	to Caiaphas, ... the high priest that same year........	18:13
3	that disciple was known unto the high priest,........	18:15
3	one of this man's disciples? He saith, I am not.......	18:17
3	Art not thou also one of his disciples? He denied it,..	18:25
6	But they shouted, "Take him away! (NIV)..........	19:15
3	but that he said, I am King of the Jews..............	19:21
10	from that hour ... took her unto his own home.......	19:27
2	for that sabbath day was an high day,...............	19:31
3	and he knows that he is telling the truth, (NASB)...	19:35
6	they say unto her, Woman, why weepest thou?......	20:13
9	She, supposing him to be the gardener..............	20:15
9	She turned herself, and saith unto him, Rabboni;.....	20:16
11	Then the same day at evening,.....................	20:19
11	and that night they caught nothing.................	21:3
3	that disciple whom Jesus loved saith unto Peter,.....	21:7
3	that that disciple should not die:...................	21:23
16	insomuch as that field is called ... field of blood.... Acts	1:19
14	I will pour out in those days of my Spirit;...........	2:18

11	the **same** day there were added ... three thousand	Acts 2:41
2	when he was determined to let **him** go	3:13
2	every soul, which will not hear **that** prophet,	3:23
14	And they made a calf in **those** days,	7:41
11	And at **that** time there was a great persecution	8:1
11	And there was great joy in **that** city	8:8
14	it came to pass in **those** days, that she was sick,	9:37
1	On the morrow, as **they** went on their journey,	10:9
1	but while **they** made ready, he fell into a trance,	10:10
5	Now about **that** time Herod the king stretched	12:1
11	the **same** night Peter was sleeping	12:6
12	when they had preached the gospel to **that** city,	14:21
7	because of the Jews which were in **those** quarters,	16:3
11	And he took them the **same** hour of the night,	16:33
8	sent the serjeants, saying, Let **those** men go	16:35
2	they fled out of **that** house naked and wounded	19:16
5	same time there arose no small stir about that way	19:23
17	And when he had gone over **those** parts,	20:2
6	we took ship; and **they** returned home again	21:6
2	when I could not see for the glory of **that** light,	22:11
5	In the **same** quarters were possessions of the chief	28:7
1	for the end **of those** things is death	Rom 6:21
6	And **they** also, if they abide not still in unbelief,	11:23
4	esteemeth ... to be unclean, to **him** it is unclean	14:14
5	Destroy not **him** with thy meat,	14:15
6	Now **they** do it to obtain a corruptible crown;	1 Co 9:25
7	these things happened **unto them** for ensamples:	10:11
6	eat not for **his** sake that showed it,	10:28
6	Therefore whether it were I or **they**, so we preach,	15:11
9	that the **same** epistle hath made you sorry,	2 Co 7:8
2	that ye through **his** poverty might be rich	8:9
1	your abundance may be a supply for **their** want,	8:14
1	that **their** abundance also may be a supply for your	8:14
3	For not he **that** commendeth himself is approved,	10:18
4	That at **that** time ye were without Christ,	Eph 2:12
11	our testimony among you was believed in **that** day.	2 Th 1:10
12	which I have committed unto him against **that** day.	2 Tm 1:12
11	that he may find mercy of the Lord in **that** day:	1:18
3	yet he abideth faithful: he cannot deny himself	2:13
2	who are taken captive by him at **his** will	2:26
1	**their** folly shall be manifest ... as theirs also was	3:9
11	the righteous judge, shall give me at **that** day:	4:8
2	That being justified by **his** grace,	Tit 3:7
11	Wherefore I was grieved with **that** generation,	Heb 3:10
8	but the word preached did not profit **them**,	4:2
12	Let us labour therefore to enter into **that** rest,	4:11
7	herbs meet **for them** by whom it is dressed,	6:7
9	For if **that** first covenant had been faultless,	8:7
15	will make with the house of Israel after **those** days,	8:10
15	is the covenant that I will make ... after **those** days,	10:16
10	of **that** country from whence they came out,	11:15
6	For if **they** escaped not who refused him that spake	12:25
3	For let not **that** man think that he shall receive	Jas 1:7
16	If the Lord will, we shall live, and do this, or **that**.	4:15
2	but were eyewitnesses of **his** majesty	2 Pt 1:16
3	ought himself also **so** to walk, even as he walked.	1 Jn 2:6
3	hope in him purifieth himself, even as **he** is pure	3:3
3	know **that** he was manifested to take away our sins;	3:5
3	righteousness is righteous, even as **he** is righteous.	3:7
3	because **he** laid down his life for us:	3:16
3	because as **he** is, so are we in this world.	4:17
10	I do not say that **he** shall pray for it.	5:16
14	And in **those** days shall men seek death,	Rev 9:6
11	And the **same** hour was there a great earthquake,	11:13
10	to the battle of **that** great day of God Almighty	16:14

In the classics, the Septuagint, and the New Testament, *ekeinos* points to something conceived of as dissociated from the speaker: "that, those." It contrasts with *houtos* (3642) and *hode* (3455) which mean "this, these."

New Testament Usage

Occurring alone as a pronoun *ekeinos* may refer to a person, thing, or idea—a usage limited mostly to John and 1 John. As an adjective describing another word it refers to "that man, those days." Nearly four-fifths of its occurrences are in the Gospels and Acts. Often writers attach *ekeinos* to *kai* (2504), meaning "and," to form *kakeinos* (2519) when the words would otherwise appear side by side. Related New Testament terms are *ekei* (1550), "there"; *ekeithen* (1551), "from there"; and *ekeise* (1553), "there, to there." *Ekeinos* has three main applications. First, since pointing to something involves separation, *ekeinos* appears in statements of contrast or differentiation and denotes "the person or thing considered more remote": "This man went down to his house justified rather than the other" (Luke 18:14). Second, it often contrasts present time with past or future: "At that time the disciples came to Jesus" (Matthew 18:1, NIV); "Then shall they fast in *those* days" (Luke 5:35).

Differentiation tends further to draw attention to an item. As a result, a third use of *ekeinos* often comes up in situations where emphasis is appropriate. The word may then refer to a well-known person, whether in respect (1 John 3:3,7) or contempt (John 9:28).

STRONG 1565, BAUER 239-40, MOULTON-MILLIGAN 194, LIDDELL-SCOTT 505-6, COLIN BROWN 3:836,846.

1553. ἐκεῖσε ekeise adv

There, at that place, thither.

CROSS-REFERENCE:
ἐκεῖ ekei (1550)

1. ἐκεῖσε ekeise

1	for **there** the ship was to unlade her burden	Acts 21:3
1	to bring them which were **there** bound	22:5

This adverb means "to that place" as opposed to the adverb *ekeithen* (1551), "from that place." It can also be used with the same meaning as *ekei* (1550), "there, in that place." It occurs only twice in the New Testament (Acts 21:3 and 22:5).

STRONG 1566, BAUER 240, MOULTON-MILLIGAN 194, LIDDELL-SCOTT 506.

1554. ἐκζητέω ekzēteō verb

Seek out, seek diligently, require.

COGNATE:
ζητέω zēteō (2195)

SYNONYMS:
ἐπιζητέω epizēteō (1919)

ἐραυνάω eraunaō (2020B)
ζητέω zēteō (2195)

בָּקַר bāqar (1266), Piel: looks after, investigate carefully (Ez 34:12).

בָּקַשׁ bāqash (1272), Piel: seek, demand (Jos 2:22, 2 Sm 4:11, Hos 5:6).

דָּרַשׁ dārash (1938), Qal: inquire, seek (Gn 9:5, 2 Chr 1:5, Ps 53:2 [52:2]); niphal: accounting, reckoning (Gn 42:22); piel: investigate (Ezr 10:16).

זָבַח zāvach (2159), Defeated (2 Chr 28:23).

חָלָה chālâh (2571), Become weak; piel: seek the favor of someone (Dn 9:13).

חָקַר chāqar (2811), Discover, search (Ps 44:20 [43:20], Ez 39:14).

יָרַשׁ yārash (3542), Possess (Am 9:12).

נָבַט nāvaṭ (5202), Hiphil: look (Ps 119:15 [118:15]—only some Sinaiticus texts).

נָצַר nātsar (5526), Keep (Pss 25:10 [24:10], 78:7 [77:7], 119:22 [118:22]).

נָקָה nāqâh (5536), Piel: pardoned (Jl 3:21).

נָקַשׁ nāqash (5550), Niphal: ensnared (Dt 12:30).

פָּקַד pāqadh (6734), Seek out (Is 34:16—Codex Alexandrinus only).

1. ἐκζητῶν ekzētōn nom sing masc part pres act
2. ἐκζητοῦσιν ekzētousin dat pl masc part pres act
3. ἐξεζήτησαν exezētēsan 3pl indic aor act
4. ἐκζητήσωσιν ekzētēsōsin 3pl subj aor act
5. ἐκζητήσας ekzētēsas nom sing masc part aor act
6. ἐκζητηθῇ ekzētēthē 3sing subj aor pass
7. ἐκζητηθήσεται ekzētēthēsetai 3sing indic fut pass

6 may be required of this generation; .... Luke 11:50
7 It shall be required of this generation. 11:51
4 That the residue of men might seek after the Lord, Acts 15:17
1 there is none that seeketh after God. .... Rom 3:11
2 he is a rewarder of them that diligently seek him.... Heb 11:6
5 though he sought it carefully with tears. 12:17
3 Of which salvation the prophets have inquired .... 1 Pt 1:10

Ekzēteō is attested in secular Greek literature no earlier than the First Century B.C., although it appears quite frequently in the Septuagint because of the common Hebrew idiom it often translates. New Testament writers employed it just seven times. As a compound of *ek* (1523), "out of," and *zēteō* (2195), "to seek," *ekzēteō* strengthens the basic idea into "seek out, seek diligently." Unlike the shorter form, *ekzēteō* is not used in the New Testament and seldom in the Septuagint to mean "want" (John 1:38) or "attempt," as in "the Jews sought to kill him" (John 7:1). Other related words are *ekzētēsis* (1554B), *zētēma* (2196), and *zētēsis* (2197).

Two principal applications of *ekzēteō* are made in the Greek New Testament. The first usage means "to seek diligently"; it looks at a concern of the person doing the searching: "For (Esau) found no place of repentance (on the part of his father?), though he *sought* it *carefully* with tears" (Hebrews 12:17; cf. Acts 15:17; Romans 3:11; Hebrews 11:6; 1 Peter 1:10). The second usage means "to require"; it looks at a concern originating beyond the person himself: "(the blood of all the prophets) shall be *required* of this generation" (Luke 11:51; cf. 11:50).

STRONG 1567, BAUER 240, MOULTON-MILLIGAN 194, KITTEL 2:894-95, LIDDELL-SCOTT 506, COLIN BROWN 3:530-32.

1554B. ἐκζήτησις ekzētēsis noun
Useless speculation, subject of inquiry.
CROSS-REFERENCE:
ζητέω zēteō (2195)

1. ἐκζητήσεις ekzētēseis nom/acc pl fem

1 which give rise to mere speculation (NASB) .... 1 Tm 1:4

This compound word, found nowhere outside of Christian writings, occurs one time in the New Testament, at 1 Timothy 1:4. The traditional text (*Textus Receptus*) reads *zētēsis* (2197). (Often a preposition prefixed to a word intensifies the base meaning.) Paul stated that *ekzētēsis* (or *zētēsis*), "useless speculation," would be the result of focusing on "fables and endless genealogies." That would be counterproductive to achieving "the end of the commandment" which is *love* (verse 5).

BAUER 240, LIDDELL-SCOTT 506, COLIN BROWN 3:532.

1555. ἐκθαμβέω ekthambeō verb
Be amazed, be astonished, be alarmed.
COGNATE:
θαυμάζω thaumazō (2273)
SYNONYMS:
ἐκπλήσσω ekplēssō (1592)
ἐξίστημι existēmi (1822)
θαμβέω thambeō (2261)

1. ἐκθαμβεῖσθε ekthambeisthe 2pl impr pres mid
2. ἐκθαμβεῖσθαι ekthambeisthai inf pres mid
3. ἐξεθαμβήθη exethambēthē 3sing indic aor pass
4. ἐξεθαμβήθησαν exethambēthēsan 3pl indic aor pass

3 when they beheld him, were greatly amazed, ... Mark 9:15
4 when they beheld him, were greatly amazed, ... 9:15
2 began to be sore amazed, and to be very heavy; 14:33
4 in a long white garment; and they were affrighted...... 16:5
1 And he saith unto them, Be not affrighted: 16:6

ἔκθαμβος 1556

Classical Greek
This term, meaning "amazed," "distressed," or "alarmed," and its cognates *thambos* (2262), meaning "astonishment" or "fear," and *thambeō* (2261), meaning "trembling" or "astounded," have their roots in the Indo-Germanic term *dhabh*, meaning "to strike." The meaning common to all of these cognates is "astonishment" or "amazement." From this sense developed the transitive meaning "terror" and the passive "to be affrightened." This latter sense became predominant. The compound forms in this cognate family, of which *ekthambeō* is a representative, are intensive; hence, they express strong amazement or fear (Bertram, "thambos," Kittel, 3:4).

New Testament Usage
Ekthambeō, occurring only in Mark, denotes a reaction to an individual or situation. The intensive sense of the term can be seen in 9:15 to describe the crowd's reaction when they saw Jesus; in 14:33 to describe Jesus' reaction to his impending crucifixion; and in 16:5 to describe the reaction of Mary of Magdalene, Mary the mother of James, and Salome when they saw the young man inside the empty tomb.

Strong 1568, Bauer 240, Moulton-Milligan 194, Kittel 3:4-7 (see "ekthambeomai"), Liddell-Scott 506, Colin Brown 2:621,623-24.

1556. ἔκθαμβος ekthambos adj
Be utterly astonished, amazed.
Cross-Reference:
　θαυμάζω thaumazō (2273)

1. ἔκθαμβοι ekthamboi nom pl masc
1 all the people ran together ... greatly wondering......Acts 3:11

This adjective—composed of the preposition *ek* (1523), "out of," which serves to intensify the substantive, and *thambos* (2262), "to be amazed"—is found only once in the New Testament. In Acts 3:11 it is used to show the great amazement of the people at the healing of the lame man.

Strong 1569, Bauer 240, Moulton-Milligan 194, Kittel 3:4-7, Liddell-Scott 506, Colin Brown 2:621,623.

1556B. ἐκθαυμάζω ekthaumazō verb
To be astounded, to be amazed, to wonder.
Cross-Reference:
　θαυμάζω thaumazō (2273)

1. ἐξεθαύμαζον exethaumazon 3pl indic imperf act
1 And they marvelled at him...................... Mark 12:17

A variant to the *Textus Receptus*, *ekthaumazō* occurs one time in the New Testament, at Mark 12:17. A compound form of *ek* (1523), which serves to intensify the verb in composition, and *thaumazō* (2273), "to wonder at" or "to admire," this word is translated "marveled" in the KJV. The context describes the reaction of the Pharisees and Herodians after Jesus avoided yet another trap with His answer, "Render to Caesar the things that are Caesar's, and to God the things that are God's." *Bauer* comments that *ekthaumazō* carries the sense of "grudging admiration."

Bauer 240, Moulton-Milligan 194, Liddell-Scott 506, Colin Brown 2:621,623.

1557. ἔκθετος ekthetos adj
Exposed, abandoned, cast out.
Cross-Reference:
　τίθημι tithēmi (4935)

1. ἔκθετα ektheta nom/acc pl neu
1 so that they cast out their young children,........... Acts 7:19

This adjective—a compound form of the preposition *ek* (1523), "out of," and *tithēmi* (4935), "put, place, lay"—is a New Testament hapax legomenon, i.e., it occurs only once, and describes one who has been "put out." Found only in Acts 7:19, it shows the depravity of the Egyptian king. Not knowing Joseph, the king dealt deceitfully with the Jews and tried to destroy their infants by having them (*ekthetos*) cast out to die.

Strong 1570, Bauer 240, Moulton-Milligan 194, Liddell-Scott 507.

1558. ἐκκαθαίρω ekkathairō verb
Clean out, cleanse thoroughly.
Cognate:
　καθαίρω kathairō (2480)
Synonyms:
　καθαίρω kathairō (2480)
　καθαρίζω katharizō (2483)
　ῥαντίζω rhantizō (4329)

בָּעַר bā'ar (1220), Piel: purge, put away (Jgs 20:13).

בָּרָא bārā' (1282), Create; piel: clear, cut down (Jos 17:18).

דּוּחַ dûach (1792), Hiphil: wash away (Is 4:4).

כָּפַר kāphar (3848), Piel: expiate, atone (Dt 32:43).

1. ἐκκαθάρῃ **ekkatharē** 3sing subj aor act
2. ἐκκαθάρατε **ekkatharate** 2pl impr aor act

2 Purge out therefore the old leaven,	1 Co 5:7
1 If a man therefore **purge** himself from these,	2 Tm 2:21

This verb—a compound form of the preposition *ek* (1523), "out of," and the verb *kathairō* (2480), "make clean"—occurs only twice in the New Testament (1 Corinthians 5:7 and 2 Timothy 2:21). It is rendered "cleanse thoroughly," "clean out," or "purge." In 1 Corinthians 5:7 it is used to show the need to cleanse out the filth through the analogy of the old yeast. Second Timothy 2:21 indicates the righteousness an individual is to strive for by purging himself from ungodliness.

STRONG 1571, BAUER 240, MOULTON-MILLIGAN 194, KITTEL 3:430, LIDDELL-SCOTT 507, COLIN BROWN 3:102.

1559. ἐκκαίω ekkaiō verb

Burn vehemently, be inflamed.

COGNATE:
καίω kaiō (2516)

SYNONYMS:
καίω kaiō (2516)
πυρόω puroō (4306)

אֲזֵה 'ēzēh (A229), Make a fire hotter (Dn 3:22—Aramaic).

בָּעַר bāʻar (1220), Qal: burn, consume (Nm 11:1, Ps 2:12, Jer 4:4); piel: set ablaze, kindle (1 Kgs 21:21 [20:21], Is 50:11, Ez 21:4 [20:48]); hiphil: set on fire, kindle (Ex 22:6, Na 2:13).

דָּלַק dālaq (1875), Qal: set on fire (Ob 18); hiphil: kindle (Ez 24:10—Codex Alexandrinus only).

דָּעַךְ dāʻakh (1906), Pual: be extinguished, quenched (Ps 118:12 [117:12]).

חָדַל chādhal (2403), Cease (Jb 3:17).

חָמַם chāmam (2657), Be or become hot (Ez 24:11—Codex Alexandrinus only).

חָמֵץ chāmēts (2661), Be leavened; hithpael: embittered (Ps 73:21 [72:21]—only some Sinaiticus texts).

חָרָה chārâh (2835), Kindled, burned (2 Sm 24:1).

יָצַת yātsath (3448), Kindle; niphal: provoke (2 Kgs 22:17).

נָכָה nākhâh (5409), Hiphil: harm (Ps 121:6 [120:6]—only some Sinaiticus texts).

נָתַךְ nāthakh (5597), Qal: be poured out (2 Chr 34:25); niphal: be poured out (2 Chr 34:21).

עָוַר ʻāwar (5996), Hiphil: stir up (Ps 78:38 [77:38]).

עָשֵׁן ʻāshen (6478), Burn, smoke (Dt 29:19 [29:20]).

פּוּחַ pûach (6558), Hiphil: speak (Prv 6:19, 14:25, 19:9).

פָּתַח pāthach (6858), Niphal: pour out, break forth (Jer 1:14).

קָדַח qādhach (7203), Kindle (Jer 15:14).

1. ἐξεκαύθησαν **exekauthēsan** 3pl indic aor pass

1 **burned** in their lust one toward another;	Rom 1:27

Classical Greek

From the classical period through the early Christian centuries *ekkaiō* meant "to set on fire," "to (be) burn(ing)," or "to burn out/up." It is a strengthened form of the more frequent verb *kaiō* (2516) of similar import.

Septuagint Usage

Besides literal usage (Exodus 22:6), the Septuagint often uses *ekkaiō* figuratively in statements about wrath being kindled (Deuteronomy 29:20). An unusual usage occurs in Proverbs in reference to telling lies; lying breathes out fiery destruction: "A false witness *utters/flames forth* lies" (6:19; 14:5,25; 19:9). According to one textual reading of Psalm 121:6 (LXX 120:6), a third application refers to sunburn: "The sun will not *burn* you during the day."

New Testament Usage

In the New Testament *ekkaiō* is found only one time and refers to homosexual lust: "In the same way the men also abandoned natural relations with women and were *inflamed* with lust for one another" (Romans 1:27, NIV).

STRONG 1572, BAUER 240, MOULTON-MILLIGAN 194, LIDDELL-SCOTT 508.

1560. ἐκκακέω ekkakeō verb

Lose heart, to faint, be despondent.

CROSS-REFERENCE:
κακός kakos (2527)

1. ἐκκακοῦμεν **ekkakoumen** 1pl indic pres act
2. ἐκκακῶμεν **ekkakōmen** 1pl subj pres act
3. ἐκκακεῖν **ekkakein** inf pres act
4. ἐκκακήσητε **ekkakēsēte** 2pl subj aor act

3 that men ought always to pray, and not to **faint**;	Luke 18:1
1 as we have received mercy, we **faint** not;	2 Co 4:1
1 For which cause we **faint** not;	4:16
2 And let us not be **weary** in well doing.	Gal 6:9
3 I desire that ye **faint** not at my tribulations for you,	Eph 3:13
4 But ye, brethren, be not **weary** in well doing.	2 Th 3:13

Classical Greek

Essentially *ekkakeō*, *enkakeō*, and *egkakeō* (1450B) are the same words with different forms. Hort (the text used by Moulton, *Concordance to the Greek Testament*) reads *enkakeō*, but *Bauer* cites *egkakeō*. *Bauer* records *ekkakeō* as a consistent variant reading of the *Textus Receptus* (at Luke 18:1; 2 Corinthians 4:1,16; Galatians 6:9; Ephesians 3:13; 2 Thessalonians 3:13) for *egkakeō*. (Cf. *Bauer*.) Thus one should consider the terms to have essentially the same meaning of "to lose heart, become tired," or "to despair" (*Bauer*).

Septuagint Usage
Symmachus' version in the Septuagint reads *ekkakeō* in Jeremiah 18:12 and *egkakeō* in Genesis 27:46; Numbers 21:5; Isaiah 7:16 (and Proverbs 3:11 according to Hatch and Redpath's *Concordance to the Septuagint*, not so *Bauer* [Theodotion]).

New Testament Usage
The verb always occurs in a negative construction in the New Testament and becomes, in turn, a positive admonition to "endure" and to be "persistent." The sense of "to be tired" speaks of mental and spiritual "weariness" (Galatians 6:9; 2 Thessalonians 3:13) which might occur in doing good. The command "be not weary in well doing" is actually a positive command to be persistent in good deeds. "Persistence" is surely implied in Jesus' advice to "always . . . pray and *not lose heart*" (RSV, Luke 18:1). Paul and the other gospel ministers did not "give up, lose heart" in spite of circumstances (2 Corinthians 4:1,16; cf. Ephesians 3:13; see also 2 Clement 2:2).

STRONG 1573, BAUER 240, MOULTON-MILLIGAN 194, LIDDELL-SCOTT 508.

1561. ἐκκεντέω ekkenteō verb
Pierce through, transfix.
SYNONYMS:
διϊκνέομαι diikneomai (1332)
νύσσω nussō (3434)

דָּקַר dāqar (1916), Qal: kill (Jgs 9:54, 1 Chr 10:4); pual: defeated, killed (Jer 37:10 [44:10], Lam 4:9).

הָרַג hāragh (2103), Kill (Nm 22:29).

טָעַן ṭāʿan (3053), Pual: be pierced (Is 14:19).

1. ἐξεκέντησαν exekentēsan 3pl indic aor act

1 They shall look on him whom they pierced......... John 19:37
1 shall see him, and they also which pierced him:...... Rev 1:7

Classical Greek and Septuagint Usage
This verb—a compound of the preposition *ek* (1523), "out of," and the verb *kenteō*, "pick, goad, spur"—was used by Aristotle (Fourth Century B.C.) in reference to "pricking out" or "putting out" the eyes. Polybius (Second Century B.C.) used it in reference to "piercing" or "stabbing" (cf. the Septuagint for this sense, at Numbers 22:29, and Joshua 16:10 where it refers to a massacre). It was used with an intransitive sense meaning "to stand out" or "project" in the Second Century A.D.

New Testament Usage
Ekkenteō is used only twice in the New Testament (John 19:37 and Revelation 1:7) where the passage in Zechariah 12:10 seems to be in the mind of the New Testament writer. All three passages seem to refer to Jesus, the One who was *pierced*. In John 19:37 the writer saw the soldier's act of piercing the side of Jesus as a direct fulfillment of the prophecy in Zechariah 12:10. This same prophecy is alluded to in Revelation 1:7 but without the direct application of Zechariah's prophecy as is present in the Gospel account. The mention of *exekentēsan* in Revelation, however, has been interpreted since the earliest periods of the Ancient Church as a means of emphasizing that the One who the world put to death will cause them to wail when He returns as the Almighty in the last days (Schlier, "ekkenteō," *Kittel*, 2:447).

STRONG 1574, BAUER 240, KITTEL 2:446-47, LIDDELL-SCOTT 508.

1562. ἐκκλάω ekklaō verb
Break off, cut off.
CROSS-REFERENCE:
κλάω klaō (2779)

שָׁסַע shāsaʿ (8538), Piel: tear (Lv 1:17).

1. ἐξεκλάσθησαν exeklasthēsan 3pl indic aor pass

1 And if some of the branches be broken off,........ Rom 11:17
1 Thou wilt say then, The branches were broken off,..... 11:19
1 Well; because of unbelief they were broken off,........ 11:20

Classical Usage
Ekklaō is a compound form of two Greek words: the preposition *ek* (1523), meaning "out" or "out of," and the verb *klaō* (2779), meaning "to break" or "to break off." *Ekklaō* is used in the classical work of Plato's *Republic* in the passive to denote "broken off." In the writings of Plutarch it denotes one who has "grown weak" (*Liddell-Scott*).

Septuagint Usage
Leviticus 1:17 is the only Septuagintal use of *ekklaō*. Here it renders the Hebrew term *shiṣaʿ*, "tear open," in a passage which outlines the

manner in which the priest was to offer a dove or pigeon as a burnt offering.

New Testament Usage

Ekklaō appears only three times in the New Testament, in Romans 11:17,19,20. In these texts *ekklaō* is used to picture God's rejection of the unbelieving Jews. The Gentiles, pictured as branches of the wild olive tree, replace the branches that are "broken off"; they are grafted (*enkentrizō* [1454]) into the community of faith (Romans 11:17). This "breaking off" only applied to a segment of the Jews and was a direct result of their unbelief (Romans 11:20). Paul's words serve as a clear warning to the branches who have been grafted in, "lest he also spare not thee." This message is not unique with Paul but has its roots in the prophets of the Old Testament. Hosea's searing indictment (Hosea 4:1-6) reflects God's timeless demand that participation in the covenant is not an issue of national or religious identity; it requires nothing less than an intimate knowledge of the Holy One.

STRONG 1575, BAUER 240, LIDDELL-SCOTT 509.

1563. ἐκκλείω ekkleiō verb

Shut out, exclude, eliminate.

CROSS-REFERENCE:
  κλείω kleiō (2781)

סוּר ṣûr (5681), Turn aside; hiphil: removed, taken away (Jb 34:20—Codex Alexandrinus only).

רָפַשׂ rāphas (7806), Make muddy; hithpael: trample down (Ps 68:30 [67:30]—only some Sinaiticus texts).

1. ἐκκλεῖσαι ekkleisai inf aor act
2. ἐξεκλείσθη exekleisthē 3sing indic aor pass

| 2 | Where is boasting then? It is **excluded**. | Rom 3:27 |
| 1 | they would **exclude** you, that ye might affect them. | Gal 4:17 |

This verb—a compound form of the preposition *ek* (1523), "out of," and the verb *kleiō* (2781), "shut, close, bar"—means "to be shut out." It occurs only twice in the New Testament. In Galatians 4:17 Paul warned that the Judaizers were wanting to exclude the Galatian Christians. In Romans 3:27 Paul said that all boasting was *excluded* from the issue of righteousness because justification comes by faith (cf. verse 28). In both instances *ekkleiō* is used in a polemic where Paul opposed justification by works in favor of justification by faith.

STRONG 1576, BAUER 240, MOULTON-MILLIGAN 194, LIDDELL-SCOTT 509.

1564. ἐκκλησία ekklēsia noun

Assembly, congregation, church.

COGNATE:
  καλέω kaleō (2535)
SYNONYM:
  συναγωγή sunagōgē (4715)

לַהֲקָה lahăqāh (4000), Group (1 Sm 19:20).

מַקְהֵל maqhēl (4882), Assembly, congregation (Pss 26:12 [25:12], 68:26 [67:26]).

קָהָל qāhāl (7235), Assembly, congregation (Dt 18:16, 2 Chr 7:8, Mi 2:5).

קְהִלָּה qᵉhillāh (7236), Assembly (Neh 5:7).

1. ἐκκλησίας ekklēsias gen/acc sing/pl fem
2. ἐκκλησία ekklēsia nom sing fem
3. ἐκκλησίᾳ ekklēsia dat sing fem
4. ἐκκλησίαν ekklēsian acc sing fem
5. ἐκκλησίαι ekklēsiai nom pl fem
6. ἐκκλησιῶν ekklēsiōn gen pl fem
7. ἐκκλησίαις ekklēsiais dat pl fem

4	and upon this rock I will build my **church**;	Matt 16:18
3	neglect to hear them, tell it unto the **church**:	18:17
1	but if he neglect to hear the **church**,	18:17
3	added to the **church** daily such as should be saved.	Acts 2:47
4	And great fear came upon all the **church**,	5:11
3	that was in the **church** in the wilderness	7:38
4	against the **church** which was at Jerusalem;	8:1
4	As for Saul, he made havock of the **church**,	8:3
5	Then had the **churches** rest throughout all Judaea	9:31
2	Then had the **churches** rest throughout all Judaea	9:31
1	these things came unto the ears of the **church**	11:22
3	year they assembled themselves with the **church**,	11:26
1	stretched ... his hands to vex certain of the **church**.	12:1
1	but prayer was made without ceasing of the **church**	12:5
4	Now there were in the **church** that was at Antioch	13:1
4	they had ordained them elders in every **church**,	14:23
4	and had gathered the **church** together,	14:27
1	And being brought on their way by the **church**,	15:3
1	they were received of the **church**,	15:4
3	the apostles and elders, with the whole **church**,	15:22
1	through Syria and Cilicia, confirming the **churches**.	15:41
5	And so were the **churches** established in the faith,	16:5
4	and saluted the **church**, he went down to Antioch	18:22
2	and some another: for the **assembly** was confused;	19:32
3	it shall be determined in a lawful **assembly**.	19:39
4	he dismissed the **assembly**.	19:41
1	and called the elders of the **church**.	20:17
4	to feed the **church** of God,	20:28
1	is a servant of the **church** which is at Cenchrea:	Rom 16:1
5	but also all the **churches** of the Gentiles.	16:4
4	Likewise greet the **church** that is in their house.	16:5
5	The **churches** of Christ salute you.	16:16
1	Gaius mine host, and of the whole **church**,	16:23
1	be glory through Jesus Christ for ever. Amen.	16:27
3	Unto the **church** of God which is at Corinth,	1 Co 1:2
3	as I teach every where in every **church**.	4:17
3	to judge who are least esteemed in the **church**.	6:4
7	And so ordain I in all **churches**.	7:17
3	nor to the Gentiles, nor to the **church** of God:	10:32
5	have no such custom, neither the **churches** of God.	11:16
3	when ye come together in the **church**,	11:18
1	or despise ye the **church** of God,	11:22
3	God hath set some in the **church**, first apostles,	12:28
4	but he that prophesieth edifieth the **church**.	14:4
2	interpret, that the **church** may receive edifying.	14:5
1	that ye may excel to the edifying of the **church**.	14:12
3	Yet in the **church** I had rather speak five words	14:19
2	the whole **church** be come together into one place,	14:23

ἐκκλησία 1564

3	let him keep silence in the **church**;	1 Co 14:28
7	but of peace, as in all **churches** of the saints.	14:33
7	Let your women keep silence in the **churches**:	14:34
3	for it is a shame for women to speak in the **church**.	14:35
4	because I persecuted the **church** of God.	15:9
7	as I have given order to the **churches** of Galatia,	16:1
5	The **churches** of Asia salute you.	16:19
3	with the **church** that is in their house.	16:19
3	unto the **church** of God which is at Corinth,	2 Co 1:1
7	grace ... bestowed on the **churches** of Macedonia;	8:1
6	praise ... is in the gospel throughout all the **churches**;	8:18
6	but who was also chosen of the **churches** to travel	8:19
6	they are the messengers of the **churches**,	8:23
6	and before the **churches**, the proof of your love,	8:24
1	I robbed other **churches**, taking wages of them,	11:8
6	the care of all the **churches**.	11:28
1	is it wherein ye were inferior to other **churches**,	12:13
7	all the brethren ... unto the **churches** of Galatia:	Gal 1:2
4	beyond measure I persecuted the **church** of God,	1:13
7	was unknown by face unto the **churches** of Judaea	1:22
3	to be the head over all things to the **church**,	Eph 1:22
1	known by the **church** the manifold wisdom of God,	3:10
3	Unto him be glory in the **church** by Christ Jesus	3:21
1	even as Christ is the head of the **church**:	5:23
2	Therefore as the **church** is subject unto Christ,	5:24
4	even as Christ also loved the **church**,	5:25
4	he might present it to himself a glorious **church**,	5:27
4	even as the Lord the **church**:	5:29
4	but I speak concerning Christ and the **church**.	5:32
4	Concerning zeal, persecuting the **church**;	Phlp 3:6
2	no **church** communicated with me ... but ye only.	4:15
1	And he is the head of the body, the **church**:	Col 1:18
2	for his body's sake, which is the **church**:	1:24
4	and the **church** which is in his house.	4:15
3	it be read also in the **church** of the Laodiceans;	4:16
3	unto the **church** of the Thessalonians	1 Th 1:1
6	the **churches** of God which in Judaea are in Christ	2:14
3	unto the **church** of the Thessalonians	2 Th 1:1
7	So that we ourselves glory in you in the **churches**	1:4
1	how shall he take care of the **church** of God?	1 Tm 3:5
2	which is the **church** of the living God,	3:15
2	and let not the **church** be charged;	5:16
1	Grace be with you. Amen.	2 Tm 4:22
1	Grace be with you all. Amen.	Tit 3:15
3	beloved Apphia, ... and to the **church** in thy house:	Phlm 1:2
1	in the midst of the **church** will I sing praise	Heb 2:12
3	the general assembly and **church** of the firstborn,	12:23
1	let him call for the elders of the **church**;	Jas 5:14
1	borne witness of thy charity before the **church**:	3 Jn 1:6
3	I wrote unto the **church**: but Diotrephes,	1:9
1	and casteth them out of the **church**.	1:10
7	John to the seven **churches** which are in Asia:	Rev 1:4
7	send it unto the seven **churches** which are in Asia;	1:11
6	seven stars are the angels of the seven **churches**:	1:20
5	the seven candlesticks ... are the seven **churches**.	1:20
1	Unto the angel of the **church** of Ephesus write;	2:1
7	hear what the Spirit saith unto the **churches**;	2:7
1	And unto the angel of the **church** in Smyrna write;	2:8
7	hear what the Spirit saith unto the **churches**;	2:11
1	And to the angel of the **church** in Pergamos write;	2:12
7	hear what the Spirit saith unto the **churches**;	2:17
1	unto the angel of the **church** in Thyatira write;	2:18
5	and all the **churches** shall know that I am he	2:23
7	hear what the Spirit saith unto the **churches**.	2:29
1	And unto the angel of the **church** in Sardis write;	3:1
7	hear what the Spirit saith unto the **churches**.	3:6
1	to the angel of the **church** in Philadelphia write;	3:7
7	hear what the Spirit saith unto the **churches**.	3:13
1	And unto ... the **church** of the Laodiceans write;	3:14
7	hear what the Spirit saith unto the **churches**.	3:22
7	to testify unto you these things in the **churches**.	22:16

Classical Greek

The understanding of *ekklēsia* as a secular term of classical Greek is in part linked to its etymology. It is from *ek* (1523), "from, out from," and *kaleō* (2535), "call"; thus the verb *ekkaleō* meant "to call out, to summon" (by a herald). The noun, therefore, means the resulting "assembly," "congregation," or "those summoned." Normally this summoning was of people, and it was often for political or governmental functions such as a legislative "assembly" or any "assembly of the common people, populus" (*Liddell-Scott*; Schmidt, "ekklēsia," *Kittel*, 3:513; Coenen, "Church," *Colin Brown*, 1:291-307).

One *ekklēsia* in particular functioned for over 100 years and was perhaps one of the most important carriers of Greek democracy. Reaching its zenith in the Fifth Century B.C., it consisted of free, accepted citizens of the town and was regulated by certain laws. Any matter of public interest could be discussed at the assembly, matters such as the changing of laws, the appointment of officials, concerns of war and peace, economic questions, etc. The *ekklēsia* could also function as a court for crimes such as treason. Each citizen had the right to speak or make proposals which would in turn be taken up by the assembly if "there was an expert opinion on the matter." Decisions were made by the process of voting. The vote was decided by either a show of hands, by acclamation, by ballots, or by stones (Coenen, "Church," *Colin Brown*, 1:291).

In addition to its political and public interest function, the *ekklēsia* had religious elements which included an opening prayer and an offering to the local gods. However, one should note that in only three cases was *ekklēsia* used of the cultic guild or meal. The Greeks had a well developed vocabulary to describe their religious gatherings and offerings. Most of these terms are not found in the New Testament. The comparison of two words in particular, however, *ekklēsia* and *sunagōgē* (4715) (derived from the verb *sunagō* [4714], "to bring together"), are of specific interest for Biblical studies. *Ekklēsia* was used in a very restricted sense, while *sunagōgē* was used very broadly. *Sunagōgē* was used especially for the cultic gatherings and various offerings to the pagan deities (ibid., 1:291f.).

Septuagint Usage

Ekklēsia translates only one Hebrew word, i.e., *qāhāl*, and four other terms from the same root. *Qāhāl* principally conveys the idea of a group of people assembling for a variety of purposes: mutual defense (Esther 8:11),

ἐκκλησία 1564

to make war (Joshua 22:12), to worship (2 Chronicles 20:26), to request an idol be built (Exodus 32:1), to transport the ark (1 Kings 8:2), the elders and officers to receive instruction (Deuteronomy 31:28), etc. However, Septuagint translators limited the use of *ekklēsia* almost exclusively to religious contexts.

On one of its most significant occasions in its history, referred to as the "day of the *ekklēsia*" by the Septuagint, Israel received the Law (Deuteronomy 9:10; 18:16; cf. 4:10 Septuagint, no Hebrew equivalent). The qualifier *ekklēsia tou kuriou/theou* also lends credence to the supposition that *ekklēsia* was beginning to take on much more of a religious tone (Deuteronomy 23:1,3; Judges 20:2; 1 Chronicles 28:8; Micah 2:5; cf. 2 Chronicles 20:14).

The assembly (*ekklēsia*, Hebrew *qāhāl*) never stands for a pagan religious gathering. In comparing the two Hebrew terms *qāhāl* (*ekklēsia*) and *ʿēdhāh* (*sunagōgē*), several observations can be made.

First, the broad semantic range of both words makes drawing strict lines of distinction between them difficult and unwarranted at best. Second, *ʿēdhāh* occurs primarily in Exodus, Leviticus, and Numbers, while *qāhāl* appears primarily in Deuteronomy and the books of Chronicles. Third, the primary use of *ʿēdhāh* is to designate the congregation of Israel as an entity, while *qāhāl* often indicates the assembling of people for religious purposes. Of special importance here is the phrase "congregation of the Lord," which according to Lewis is the closest to the "church of the Lord" (rendered by the Septuagint as *ekklēsia kuriou*; "*qāhāl*," *Theological Wordbook of the Old Testament*, 2:790).

In summary, although one must avoid making hard and fast distinctions between these two terms, for both may be used in religious as well as profane contexts, *qāhāl* maintains stronger religious connotations. The Septuagint never translates *ʿēdhāh* by *ekklēsia* but uses *sunagōgē* instead (cf. the juxtaposition of *ʿēdhāh* and *qāhāl* in Leviticus 4:13,14; see Bultmann, *Theology of the New Testament*, p.38).

Thus, from the Septuagint it becomes clear that *ekklēsia* was primarily used as an equivalent for *qāhāl*, a term which to some degree was itself a particular group within the people of God, even when it was translated by *sunagōgē* (e.g., Genesis 35:11; 48:4; Numbers 20:6). *Ekklēsia* was used only infrequently for nonreligious assemblies.

The attitudes of exilic and postexilic Jewish religion and the early Christian community polarized in their identification with these terms and their related concepts. The congregation of Judaism identified itself with the institutional *ʿēdhāh*, while the ancient Christian assembly identified with *qāhāl* and adopted the name *ekklēsia*. To understand how this polarization developed, it is necessary to understand the context out of which it developed.

From the inception of the Covenant at Sinai, it was said of Israel that they were a "kingdom of priests, and a holy nation" (Exodus 19:6). It would be in the midst of the people that God's presence would be manifest, and He ordered that the tabernacle be erected in the midst of the camp where His glory (*kāvôdh*) might be revealed.

Later, this special presence of the Lord was transferred to the temple. In the Psalms the congregation of Israel expressed joy for the grace which they experienced in the presence of the Lord. At their festivals and celebrations in the temple, they declared "Lord, I have loved the habitation of thy house, and the place where thine honor dwelleth" (Psalm 26:8 [LXX 25:8]; cf. 84:2 [83:2]).

As the nation fell into deeper and deeper apostasy, a concept developed of a separation within the congregation, although from the earliest days of the covenant the rebellious were removed from the midst of the congregation (Numbers 16:33). Through the ministry of the later prophets however, the message was clear that a total breach of the covenant had taken place. As a result, the nation was carried into exile.

During the apostasy that characterized the later monarchies of both the Northern and Southern Kingdoms, a major development began to take place in the concept of the congregation as the place where God revealed His glory. As the nation fell into spiritual, moral, and ethical decline, the glory of God which once had been so evident became absent. This situation became even more apparent after the destruction of the temple and during the postexilic period. It was at this time that the concept of the "holy remnant" fully developed. The salvation of Israel as a congregation was dependent on this remnant and their faithfulness to God.

New Testament Usage

After the period of the exile it was the synagogue which dominated the religious life of the Jews. It was in the Greek Diaspora that the synagogue became accepted as the new designation for the ʿēdhāh. The name applied not only to the house of the synagogue but to the congregation of the synagogue as well.

Having this background in mind, it is very interesting that the Gentile Christian congregations did not use the designation of synagogue for their signification. The members of these first Christian congregations came in a large degree from the Jewish synagogues which consisted of both Jews and proselytes. These believers claimed to represent the true Jewish religion (Romans 2:28,29) and the true Israel of God (Romans 9:6). Although these ancient Christian congregations were patterned primarily after the Jewish synagogues, they avoided using the term synagogue. In fact, the term synagogue is used only one time in the New Testament as a designation for a Christian congregation (James 2:2).

The best explanation for this strong aversion by the ancient Christians to adopting the term synagogue seems to be an intense desire to avoid being identified with the Jewish synagogues. In the Roman Empire the synagogues stood as symbols of Jewish law and religion, and the new Christian religion. However, Christian congregations avoided association with this term. Instead, they adopted the term ekklēsia which had fallen out of usage in Jewish circles.

As well as avoiding associations with the Jewish religion, the Christians also chose ekklēsia as a way of distancing themselves from the terms utilized by the pagan Greek cults. Here a multitude of terms would have been at the disposal of the ancient Christians. Secular Gentile authors such as Lucian and Celsus did, however, identify the Christian congregations by the pagan term thiasos. More amazing than this though, the early Church historian Eusebius also used this term for the Church.

The reasons these first Christians chose the neutral term ekklēsia are manifold. One popular suggestion contends that there is a certain phonetical resemblance between the consonants of the Hebrew qāhāl and the Greek ekklēsia. This might correspond with the usual use among Jews of the Diaspora and combine its Hebrew name with a similar Greek or Latin name (e.g., Saul and Paul). The congregation of the New Testament is thus a continuation of the old congregation of Israel, the true Israel, while at the same time distancing itself from the Jewish religion.

Although it is tempting, it is violating sound interpretive principles to draw upon the etymology of the word (in this case ek-kaleō) to make the members of the ekklēsia the "called-out ones." This is true even if the Septuagint translators may have seen this potential. The fact remains that for the New Testament it is the *already developed* sense of the Septuagint (and Hebrew) *plus* the *new* understanding of God's community which shapes the meaning of ekklēsia.

The meaning of ekklēsia (translated "church" in the New Testament except in Acts 19:32,39,41 where it is translated "assembly") becomes problematic for two reasons: (1) The New Testament speaks of the "Church" in a universal sense of the body of believers who are in Christ; and (2) the New Testament also uses ekklēsia to describe the early gatherings of believers in various geographical locations. Thus, the ekklēsia is both an event of the assembling (worldwide) of God's people, and it is also a particular local "church, congregation," or "assembly."

The first striking observation to be made regarding ekklēsia in the New Testament is its absence in the Gospels except for two references in Matthew which are themselves "at odds" (16:18; 18:17). As Coenen notes, this absence "cannot be explained by saying that at the time of their writing the concept was not in current use, since the gospels received their literary form contemporary with or later than the Pauline letters" ("Church," *Colin Brown*, 1:298).

One must conclude that the expression was seen as appropriate after the death and resurrection of the Lord. The future oikodomēsō (see 3481) hints at this in Matthew 16:18 (a reference to the worldwide assembly). But what about Matthew 18:17? It is neither a scene of worldwide unity nor a postresurrectional setting, unless one considers the context in light of 18:1 which does suggest a future setting (cf. 18:14).

It becomes apparent from the Gospels that Jesus considered it part of His mission as Messiah to gather together the eschatological people of God as the prophets had foretold (Matthew 9:36-38; John 10:16; 11:52). As the Messiah, Jesus would restore the true congregation of Israel.

The importance of the concept of this congregation in the ministry of Jesus is also evident in the parables, similes, and analogies He used (e.g., the shepherd and the flock, Luke 12:32; John 10:16). Furthermore, Jesus instituted a new covenant meal (Matthew 26:28). The supper was to be seen as a cultic meal which abolished that of the Old Testament Passover. The Great Commission of Christ and His institution of water baptism served as the consecration rites of the new covenant (Matthew 28:19; Mark 16:16). The institution of these rites was the necessary preparation for the birth of the coming congregation on the Day of Pentecost.

A significant element of the thought of Jesus is the relationship of the congregation to the kingdom of God. These are two distinct threads which are woven together in a most intimate way. The congregation is the manifestation of and a piece of the eschatological reality of the kingdom of God, representative of the royal power of God in the world. The congregation is the people to whom God, by His Messiah, has promised the blessings of the latter time (Matthew 5:3-11); the forgiveness of sins (Matthew 26:28); the gift of the Spirit (Luke 24:49; John 14:26; 15:26; 16:7); the right to address God as "Father" (Matthew 6:9); victory over the power of Satan (Luke 11:20-22); and participation in the gift of eternal life (John 5:24-27).

Acts makes it abundantly clear that Luke, indicative of the New Testament writers, understood *ekklēsia* to be an eschatological term for the New Community of God. The congregation appeared as a part of salvation history on the Day of Pentecost (Acts 2). By faith and baptism into the name of Jesus both Jew and Gentile experienced the eschatological gifts of salvation.

This new expression of the kingdom of God was characterized by several distinct traits: (1) the unifying of the people around the doctrine of the apostles (Acts 2:42); (2) participation in the daily prayers (Acts 2:42); (3) the breaking of bread together (Acts 2:42); (4) a unique love and sense of brotherly fellowship created by the Holy Spirit resulting in a sharing of property (Acts 2:44f.); (5) the powers of the coming world which were mightily active in the healing of the sick (Acts 3:2f.; 4:29f.; 5:15), the raising of the dead (Acts 9:36-40), and victory over demonic powers (Acts 19:11,12).

The early fellowship of believers became the "church" in the local geographical sense (e.g., Acts 5:11; 8:1,3; 11:22; 12:1; 16:5; 20:17). Congregations soon appeared throughout Palestine and Asia Minor, including Samaria, Syria, and Antioch, the center of Paul's mission to the Gentiles (Acts 13:1f.). Throughout Acts and the rest of the New Testament, each local congregation was considered the congregation of God in the proper sense as well. Throughout the New Testament *ekklēsia* expresses both the local and universal dynamics of the Community of Faith under the New Covenant.

Paul's writings deserve much of the credit for forming present-day ecclesiologies (he uses *ekklēsia* over 60 times). They show the nature of the Church as being both local and worldwide. Paul wrote of local assemblies as *ekklēsia* (e.g., 1 Corinthians 1:2; 2 Corinthians 1:1; Galatians 1:2; 1 Thessalonians 1:1), composed of saints and the elect, i.e., the people of God (Romans 1:7; 1 Corinthians 14:33; note Paul avoided *laos* [2967] as a term for God's people).

They were typically gatherings of people inside the homes of believers (Romans 16:5; Colossians 4:15; Philemon 2; cf. 1 Corinthians 16:19; 1 Timothy 3:15). The assemblies are God's, that is, God has created these various meetings, and He is in their midst (1 Corinthians 11:22; 12:28; chapter 14 passim; Ephesians 1:22; 3:21; cf. Matthew 18:20). He is also the chief administrator of the Church through Christ the head (Ephesians 5:23).

Yet Paul also spoke of "the Church" as a worldwide entity made up of smaller churches which share certain principles and teachings (1 Corinthians 15:9; Galatians 1:13; Philippians 3:6; cf. Romans 16:4,16; 1 Corinthians 4:17; 7:17; 11:16).

The idea of an "invisible" church would not have been Paul's view. This concept, albeit "valid" in the sense that the "Lord knows who belongs to Him," was introduced first by Augustine (*City of God*) and perpetuated by John Wycliff (*De ecclesia*), Luther (*Preface to Revelation*), and Calvin (*Institues* 4.1.7) (see editor's remarks in Coenen, "Church," *Colin Brown*, 1:299). The Church consists of believers, but it is not a particular quality of life which draws these individuals together and forms them into a congregation. Rather, it is nothing less than the reality of the resurrected Christ by which they came into existence, by which they live, and around which they gather.

It is this internal, divine mystery of the Church's unity along with the reality of the risen Christ which Paul referred to when he spoke of the congregation as the Body of Christ (1 Corinthians 10:17; 12:13,27; Ephesians 1:23; 2:16; 4:12,16; 5:23,30; Colossians 1:18,24; 2:19; 3:15). The intimacy of this union is further illustrated by Paul's analogy of marriage as a picture of the relationship between the Church and Christ (Ephesians 5:25-32).

The depth of the unity between the Church and Christ becomes the catalyst for a deep, heartfelt fellowship between believers. This solidarity includes Jews and Gentiles (Ephesians 2:11-22) and receives it fullest expression in 1 Corinthians 12:12-27.

In the remainder of the New Testament one is struck with the absence of *ekklēsia* in any of the Petrine material, which is itself replete with a sense of "community" (1 Peter 5:1-5). Peter also proclaimed the unity of believers as God's people but in other imagery (1 Peter 2:9,10).

Hebrews 2:12 mirrors the Old Testament assembly of God and actually cites Psalm 22:22. The scene, too, in Hebrews 12:23 is one of the believers' encounter with the living God in the assembly. Here *ekklēsia* is not so much of a local congregation as it is a sign of the arrival of the new covenant.

The three references in the Third Epistle of John reveal the writer's familiarity with the idea already encountered. The *ekklēsia* was the locus of the new people of God. It especially occurred on the local level (3 John 6,9,10).

The Book of Revelation knows only of "churches." The church is the congregation of the new people of God in particular places. Therefore, *ekklēsia* appears to have been appropriated from the language of the Old Testament (especially the Hebrew *qāhāl*), because it represented the assembly of the people of Israel for religious purposes as God's people. The New Testament writers modified the concept only to assign the term a more technical character. The church is the visible geographically identifiable congregation of the new people of God—wherever they are. God operates in and through the local church with Christ as its head.

We can be assured that the early believers saw themselves as God's new people—the eschatological community of God—the "chosen ones." Their gatherings rapidly became incompatible within the synagogue context. The growth of the *ekklēsia* necessitated leadership and direction, although few are ever outlined (not even in the Pastoral Epistles). The early churches were diverse geographically, ethnically, culturally, and perhaps even in their cultic practices and theories. Nevertheless, a single thread—the lordship of Jesus Christ the Son of God—bound them together into a Body with Christ as its head.

STRONG 1577, BAUER 240-41, MOULTON-MILLIGAN 195, KITTEL 3:501-36, LIDDELL-SCOTT 509, COLIN BROWN 1:291-93,295-304,306-7; 2:731.

1565. ἐκκλίνω ekklinō verb
Turn away from, turn aside.
COGNATE:
κλίνω klinō (2800)
SYNONYMS:
ἀποφεύγω apopheugō (662)
ἐκτρέπω ektrepō (1610)
ἐκφεύγω ekpheugō (1614)
περιΐστημι periistēmi (3889)
στέλλομαι stellomai (4575)
φεύγω pheugō (5180)

בּוֹא bô' (971), Go (Jgs 14:5—Codex Alexandrinus only).

גָּזַר gāzar (1535), Devour (Is 9:20).

דָּלַק dālaq (1875), Chasing (1 Sm 17:53).

חָטָא chāṭā' (2490), Hiphil: lead into sin (Neh 13:26).

חָלַץ chālats (2603), Withdraw (Hos 5:6).

כָּלַם kālam (3757), Niphal: ashamed, shocked (Ez 16:27).

מוֹט môṭ (4267), Waver, totter; hiphil: bring down, cast down (Ps 55:3 [54:3]).

מָנַע māna' (4661), Refrain, hold back (Prv 1:15).

נָאַץ nā'ats (5180), Despise, spurn (Prv 5:12).

נָטָה nāṭāh (5371), Qal: turn, turn aside (Nm 20:17, 2 Sm 2:19, Jer 14:8); hiphil: incline, turn aside (Dt 24:17, 1 Sm 8:3, Ps 141:4 [140:4]).

נָתַשׁ nāthash (5612), Uproot, tear up; niphal: vanish, leave (Jer 18:14).

סָבַב sāvav (5621), Avoid, elude (1 Sm 18:11—Codex Alexandrinus only).

סוּג sûgh (5657), Qal: turned away (Ps 53:3 [52:3]); niphal: turned back (Zep 1:6).

סוּר sûr (5681), Qal: turn, turn away (Gn 19:3, Ps 34:14 [33:14], Mal 2:8); hiphil: turn away, remove (2 Sm 6:10, Prv 28:9).

עָבַט 'āvaṭ (5879), Piel: swerve (Jl 2:7).

עָבַר ʻāvar (5882), Go on (Gn 18:5).
עָרַץ ʻārats (6442), Be alarmed, be terrified (Dt 20:3).
פָּנָה pānâh (6680), Turned (Ex 10:6, 2 Kgs 5:12).
שָׂטָה sāṭâh (7928), Turn, turn aside (Prv 4:15, 7:25).
שָׁגָה shāghâh (8146), Stray, err (Ps 119:21 [118:21]).
שָׁמַט shāmaṭ (8447), Stumble (1 Chr 13:9).

1. ἐξέκλιναν exeklinan 3pl indic aor act
2. ἐκκλινάτω ekklinatō 3sing impr aor act
3. ἐκκλίνατε ekklinate 2pl impr aor act
4. ἐκκλίνετε ekklinete 2pl impr pres act

```
1 They are all gone out of the way,..................Rom 3:12
3 contrary to the doctrine ... and avoid them............16:17
4 contrary to the doctrine ... and avoid them............16:17
2 Let him eschew evil, and do good;..................1 Pt 3:11
```

Classical Greek
Fundamentally, *ekklinō* has to do with "bending out or away." From the classical period onwards that picture was applied to such matters as changing direction, course of action, principles of behavior, and personal relationships.

Septuagint Usage
The Septuagint has many examples where the word refers to "turning aside" from a road while traveling (Genesis 18:5; Judges 4:18). It is often used figuratively of "turning away" from God (1 Samuel 12:20 [LXX 1 Kings 12:20]) or His Word (Joshua 23:6). It applies to "turning away" one's affections to foreign deities (1 Kings 11:2 [LXX 3 Kings 11:2]). In several instances *ekklinō* indicates forsaking one's principles (Exodus 23:2) or perverting justice (1 Samuel 8:3 [LXX 1 Kings 8:3]).

New Testament Usage
The three New Testament usages are figurative. Romans 3:12 quotes Psalm 14:3 to the effect that all men have "turned aside" from seeking God. In Romans 16:17 the readers are encouraged to "avoid" troublemakers; in 1 Peter 3:11 Christians are commanded to "avoid" evil and do good.

STRONG 1578, BAUER 241, MOULTON-MILLIGAN 195, LIDDELL-SCOTT 509.

1566. ἐκκολυμβάω ekkolumbaō verb
Swim away, swim out.

1. ἐκκολυμβήσας ekkolumbēsas
nom sing masc part aor act

```
1 lest any of them should swim out, and escape.......Acts 27:42
```

This is a term denoting "to swim out," "swim away," or "dive out into the sea" (*kolumbaō* [2832] with *ek* [1523]). It is found only in Acts 27:42 in connection with the shipwreck experienced by Paul.

STRONG 1579, BAUER 241, LIDDELL-SCOTT 509.

1567. ἐκκομίζω ekkomizō verb
Carry out.

CROSS-REFERENCE:
κομίζω komizō (2837)

1. ἐξεκομίζετο exekomizeto 3sing indic imperf pass

```
1 behold, there was a dead man carried out,..........Luke 7:12
```

This compound verb—composed of the preposition *ek* (1523), "out of," and the verb *komizō* (2837) "take care of, tend"—is attested from Herodotus (Fifth Century B.C.) onward meaning "to carry out," especially to a place of safety; "to throw out," of provender for horses; "to carry out," of a corpse for burial; "to endure to the end"; and "to receive what is due." In its only New Testament occurrence, Luke 7:12, the verb means "to carry out," referring to a dead man being carried from the city.

STRONG 1580, BAUER 241, MOULTON-MILLIGAN 195, LIDDELL-SCOTT 510.

1568. ἐκκόπτω ekkoptō verb
Cut out, cut down, cut off.

COGNATE:
κόπτω koptō (2847)
SYNONYMS:
ἀποκόπτω apokoptō (604)
κόπτω koptō (2847)

גְּדַד gᵉdhadh (A1444), Cut down (Dn 4:14 [4:11]—Aramaic).

גָּדַע gādhaʻ (1468), Niphal: cut off (Jgs 21:6); piel: cut down (Dt 7:5, 2 Chr 14:3); pual: cut down (Is 9:10—Codex Alexandrinus only).

חֲבַל chăval (A2342), Pael: destroy (Dn 4:23 [4:20]—Aramaic).

כָּרַת kārath (3901), Qal: cut off, cut down (Dt 20:19, 1 Kgs 15:13, Jer 6:6); niphal: cut down (Jb 14:7); hiphil: destroy (Jer 44:7 [51:7]); pual: cut down (Jgs 6:28—Codex Alexandrinus only).

נָכָה nākhâh (5409), Hiphil: attack, defeat (Gn 36:35, Jos 15:16).

נָסַע nāsaʻ (5450), Hiphil: tear down (Jb 19:10).

נָפַל nāphal (5489), Fall; hiphil: knock out, strike (Ex 21:27).

ἐκκρεμάννυμι 1569

נָקַר nāqar (5548), Qal: pick out (Prv 30:17 [24:52]); piel: put out, gouge out (Nm 16:14, Jgs 16:21).

נָתַשׁ nāthash (5612), Uproot (Mi 5:14).

רְעַע rᵉʿaʿ (A7779), Break (Dn 2:40—Aramaic).

1. ἐκκόψω **ekkopsō** 1sing subj aor act
2. ἔκκοψον **ekkopson** 2sing impr aor act
3. ἐκκόψεις **ekkopseis** 2sing indic fut act
4. ἐκκόπτεται **ekkoptetai** 3sing indic pres mid
5. ἐκκόπτεσθαι **ekkoptesthai** inf pres mid
6. ἐξεκόπης **exekopēs** 2sing indic aor pass
7. ἐκκοπήσῃ **ekkopēsē** 2sing indic fut pass

```
4 every tree ... not forth good fruit is hewn down, ..... Matt 3:10
2 And if thy right hand offend thee, cut it off, ........... 5:30
4 that bringeth not forth good fruit is hewn down, ....... 7:19
2 cut them off, and cast them from thee: ................. 18:8
4 which bringeth not forth good fruit is hewn down, ... Luke 3:9
2 cut it down; why cumbereth it the ground? ............ 13:7
3 and if not, then after that thou shalt cut it down. ...... 13:9
7 otherwise thou also shalt be cut off. ................. Rom 11:22
6 For if thou wert cut out of the olive tree ............. 11:24
1 that I may cut off occasion from them .............. 2 Co 11:12
5 that your prayers be not hindered. .................. 1 Pt 3:7
```

Classical Greek
The primary word picture in *ekkoptō* is that of "cutting" (*koptō* [2847]) something "from" (*ek* [1523]) a larger whole. In the classical period it indicated activities like surgical removal, sculpturing out of stone, or cutting trees out of a forest. It could refer less strictly to breaking into a house and then to destroying. In military contexts *ekkoptō* indicates repulsing an enemy. Writers occasionally employed it in regard to minting coins.

Septuagint Usage
In the Septuagint *ekkoptō* denotes "cutting out" or "putting out" a person's eyes (Numbers 16:14; Judges 16:21) or "knocking out" a tooth (Exodus 21:27). Writers regularly used it for cutting down trees (Jeremiah 6:6), especially cutting down the asherahs (Exodus 34:13; Judges 6:25,28). In more metaphoric applications it indicated winning a military encounter (Judges 21:6) or exterminating an enemy camp (Job 42:18, Septuagint only).

New Testament Usage
Of the 10 New Testament references, 5 indicate cutting down trees (Matthew 3:10; 7:19; Luke 3:9; 13:7,9); 2 refer to amputation (Matthew 5:30; 18:8); twice it means pruning tree limbs (Romans 11:22,24). In its only figurative occurrence, Paul used *ekkoptō* to speak about "removing" an excuse for his opponents to take advantage of (2 Corinthians 11:12). First Peter 3:7 should read *egkoptō* (1458).

STRONG 1581, BAUER 241-42, MOULTON-MILLIGAN 195, KITTEL 3:857-60, LIDDELL-SCOTT 510.

1569. ἐκκρεμάννυμι
ekkremannumi verb
Hang on.
CROSS-REFERENCE:
κρεμάννυμι kremannumi (2883)

קָשַׁר qāshar (7489), Bound up (Gn 44:30).

1. ἐξεκρέματο **exekremato** 3sing indic aor mid

1 for all the people were very attentive to hear him... Luke 19:48

This compound verb—composed of the preposition *ek* (1523), "out of," and the verb *kremannumi* (2883), "to hang"—is attested from Hippocrates (Fifth Century B.C.) onward and denotes "to hang from (or) upon" a thing or, in a passive sense, "to hang on by" or "cling." In a figurative sense it means "to be devoted to." In its only New Testament occurrence, Luke 19:48, it is used figuratively regarding the attentiveness of the people listening to Jesus; they literally "hung on" to Jesus' teachings.

STRONG 1582, BAUER 242, KITTEL 3:915-21 (see "ekkremamai"), LIDDELL-SCOTT 510.

1570. ἐκλαλέω **eklaleō** verb
Tell, speak out, disclose.
CROSS-REFERENCE:
λαλέω laleō (2953)

1. ἐκλαλῆσαι **eklalēsai** inf aor act

1 See thou tell no man that thou hast showed these .. Acts 23:22

This compound verb—composed of the preposition *ek* (1523), "out of," and the verb *laleō* (2953), "talk, chat, prattle"—denotes "to blurt out, blab, divulge." It is attested from Demosthenes (Fourth Century B.C.). It occurs only once in the New Testament, Acts 23:22, where the chief captain charged Paul's nephew, "Tell (*eklaleō*) no man that thou hast showed these things to me."

STRONG 1583, BAUER 242, MOULTON-MILLIGAN 195, LIDDELL-SCOTT 511.

1571. ἐκλάμπω **eklampō** verb
To shine (forth), to shine (out).
CROSS-REFERENCE:
λάμπω lampō (2962)

אוֹר ʾôr (213), Become day; hiphil: shine (Ez 43:2).

נָגַהּ nāghahh (5226), Hiphil: lighten, let shine (2 Sm 22:29).

1. ἐκλάμψουσιν **eklampsousin** 3pl indic fut act

1 Then shall the righteous shine forth as the sun ..... Matt 13:43

Eklampō is a compound of the Greek words *ek* (1523), "out of," and *lampō* (2962), "to shine." It appears in classical literature, twice in the Septuagint (2 Kings 22:29 [LXX 4 Kings 22:29]; Ezekiel 43:2), the papyri, and once in the New Testament in Matthew 13:43 where it describes the final condition and eternal radiance of the righteous: They will "shine forth as the sun."

STRONG 1584, BAUER 242, MOULTON-MILLIGAN 195, KITTEL 4:16-28, LIDDELL-SCOTT 511, COLIN BROWN 2:484-86.

1572. ἐκλανθάνομαι
eklanthanomai verb

Forget entirely.

COGNATE:
λανθάνω lanthanō (2963)

SYNONYM:
ἐπιλανθάνομαι epilanthanomai (1935)

1. ἐκλέλησθε eklelēsthe 2pl indic perf mid

1 ye **have forgotten** the exhortation which speaketh... Heb 12:5

This word combines *ek* (1523), "out," and *lanthanō* (2963), "escape (someone's) notice, be hidden," literally meaning "to utterly escape notice." It is a strong verb also meaning "to forget completely or altogether." In the New Testament it is used only in Hebrews 12:5 in the middle voice—"Ye have forgotten." Here the readers of this epistle were reminded of an important principle they had been taught earlier but in the face of trial had forgotten, i.e., "that Scripture links suffering and sonship" (Morris, *Expositor's Bible Commentary*, 12:136).

STRONG 1585, BAUER 242, MOULTON-MILLIGAN 195 (see "eklanthanō"), LIDDELL-SCOTT 511 (see "eklanthanō").

1573. ἐκλέγομαι eklegomai verb

Choose, select, elect.

COGNATES:
ἀπελεγμός apelegmos (554)
ἐκλεκτός eklektos (1575)
ἐκλογή eklogē (1576)
συνεκλεκτός suneklektos (4749)

SYNONYMS:
αἱρετίζω hairetizō (139)
αἱρέω haireō (141)
ἐξαιρέω exaireō (1791)
ἐπιλέγω epilegō (1935B)
κρίνω krinō (2892)
λαμβάνω lambanō (2956)
προχειρίζομαι procheirizomai (4258)
χειροτονέω cheirotoneō (5336)

בָּחַר bāchar (1013), Chose, select (Dt 7:7, 1 Kgs 8:16, Is 40:20).

בָּרָה bārāh (1290), Choose (1 Sm 17:8).

בָּרַר bārar (1331), Qal: chosen (1 Chr 16:41); piel: refine (Dn 11:35).

לָקַח lāqach (4089), Learn, receive (Prv 24:32 [24:47]).

קָבַל qāval (7186), Piel: choose (1 Chr 21:11).

קָבַץ qāvats (7192), Gather (Jl 2:16).

תּוּר tûr (8780), Search (Dt 1:33).

1. ἐξελεξάμην exelexamēn 1sing indic aor mid
2. ἐξελέξω exelexō 2sing indic aor mid
3. ἐξελέξατο exelexato 3sing indic aor mid
4. ἐξελέξασθε exelexasthe 2pl indic aor mid
5. ἐξελέξαντο exelexanto 3pl indic aor mid
6. ἐκλεξάμενος eklexamenos
    nom sing masc part aor mid
7. ἐκλεξαμένους eklexamenous
    acc pl masc part aor mid
8. ἐξελέγοντο exelegonto 3pl indic imperf mid
9. ἐκλεξαμένοις eklexamenois
    dat pl masc part aor mid
10. ἐκλελεγμένος eklelegmenos
    nom sing masc part perf mid

3 whom he **hath chosen**, he hath shortened the days. Mark 13:20
6 his disciples: and of them he **chose** twelve,........ Luke 6:13
10 This is my Son, whom I **have chosen**; (NIV)........... 9:35
3 and Mary **hath chosen** that good part,................ 10:42
8 he marked how they **chose** out the chief rooms;...... 14:7
1 Have not I **chosen** you twelve, ... one ... is a devil? John 6:70
1 I know whom I **have chosen**:........................ 13:18
4 Ye **have** not **chosen** me, but I have chosen you,...... 15:16
1 Ye have not chosen me, but I **have chosen** you,...... 15:16
1 but I **have chosen** you out of the world,............. 15:19
3 unto the apostles whom he **had chosen**:............. Acts 1:2
2 show whether of these two thou **hast chosen**,......... 1:24
5 and they **chose** Stephen, a man full of faith........... 6:5
3 The God of this people of Israel **chose** our fathers,... 13:17
3 that a good while ago God made **choice** among us,... 15:7
7 to send **chosen** men of their own company 15:22
7 to send **chosen** men unto you 15:25
9 to **choose** men and send them to you (RSV)......... 15:25
3 But God **hath chosen** the foolish things............. I Co 1:27
3 and God hath **chosen** the weak things of the world.... 1:27
3 and things which are despised, **hath** God **chosen**,....... 1:28
3 According as he **hath chosen** us in him............. Eph 1:4
3 Hath not God **chosen** the poor of this world........ Jas 2:5

Classical Greek

This verb does occur in an active form in classical Greek, but in the New Testament and almost all of the literature afterwards it occurs only in the middle/passive forms. Etymologically it is derived from the preposition *ek* (1523), "from," plus the verb *legō* (2978), "say." In the middle form the word denotes "to choose or pick" (for oneself). The term can also be used of things chosen for their superiority, beauty, or value (Schrenk, "eklegomai," *Kittel*, 4:144).

Septuagint Usage

The Septuagint's usage of *eklegomai*, too, is almost exclusively the middle or passive voice (but cf. 1 Maccabees 9:25; 11:23). The most common Hebrew original underlying *eklegomai* is *bāchar*. *Eklegomai* plays a major role in the Old Testament concept of "election." God, "because he loved your (Israel's) fathers and chose (*eklegomai*) their descendants (*to sperma auton*) after them..." (Deuteronomy 4:37, RSV; cf. 1 Kings 3:8 [LXX 3 Kings 3:8]; Psalms 33:12 [LXX 32:12]; 47:4 [46:4]; 65:4 [64:4]; Isaiah 14:1; 49:7).

Israel was to know that the "Lord is God in heaven above and on the earth beneath; there is no other" (Deuteronomy 4:37, RSV). God's choice (*hos an eklexetai kurios*) *for* Israel was as important as His choice *of* them (cf. Deuteronomy 12:5,11,14,18,21). But Israel must also choose whom they would serve, either Yahweh (Joshua 24:15,22) or "new gods" (Judges 5:8; 10:14). Often, such as in the selection of a king, the choice of God and man are in conflict (e.g., 1 Samuel [LXX 1 Kings] 8:18; 10:24; 12:13; 16:8-10; 2 Chronicles 6:5ff.; Psalm 78:67ff. [LXX 77:67ff.]). However, the language of *eklegomai* is not restricted to theological choices. It can also refer to secular choices (e.g., 1 Kings 18:25 [LXX 3 Kings 18:25]; 1 Chronicles 19:10; 21:10). (For a fuller discussion on the concept of election in the Old Testament see Quell, "eklegomai," *Kittel*, 4:145-168.)

New Testament Usage

In the Gospels of the New Testament (not in Matthew and only once in Mark [13:20]) *eklegomai* is used of normal decision making (e.g., Luke 10:42; 14:7) as well as for decisions of theological import. Jesus' selection (*eklegomai*) of the Twelve was theologically significant, not only for the Gospel accounts but for the later Church as well (Luke 6:13; John 6:70; cf. Acts 1:2). John's Gospel emphasizes that Jesus—not the disciples—had done the choosing (John 15:16,19; cf. 13:18). Jesus himself was chosen by God. Luke 9:35 refers to Jesus as *ho eklelegmenos* instead of *ho agapētos* as in Matthew 3:17 and Mark 9:7 (cf. 1:11). Both Luke 23:35 and John 1:34 refer to Jesus as *ho eklektos* ("the chosen one"), the latter being a variant reading in some manuscripts.

Similarly, in the Acts of the Apostles the replacement for Judas was "chosen" (*eklegomai*) by God through the process of casting lots (Acts 1:24). Stephen, too, was "chosen" as one of the seven picked to assist in the distribution of the widows' offering (Acts 6:5). Peter declared himself chosen to go to the Gentiles (Acts 15:7), and Paul and Barnabas were "selected" to travel to Antioch with the decisions of the Jerusalem Council (Acts 15:22). Although the reports of the gathering of the new community of God are strangely devoid of election language in Acts, Paul's words resonated with the Old Testament background of God's election of Israel in his speech before the church in Antioch (13:17).

Certainly there are some theological questions raised by the language of election; nevertheless, it is dangerous to pursue such interrogation strictly on the basis of language. After all, Judas was one of the Twelve (chosen, Luke 6:13; John 6:70), and yet he clearly was not among "the elect" in the sense that he was a member of the "chosen people" (cf. Colossians 3:12; 1 Peter 1:1f.). Also, why did Paul endure "for the sake of" (RSV, Greek *dia* [1217]) the elect ones (*tous eklektous*) in order that (*hina* [2419], purposive) they might also obtain (subjunctive, *tuchōsin*) the salvation in Christ Jesus (2 Timothy 2:10)? "Faith" is the ultimate requisite of the elect (Titus 1:1; cf. James 2:5). (See also *eklektos* [1575]; Schrenk, "eklegomai," *Kittel*, 4:172-192; Mendenhall, "Election," *Interpreter's Dictionary of the Bible*, 2:76-82).

STRONG 1586, BAUER 242, MOULTON-MILLIGAN 195 (see "eklegō"), KITTEL 4:144-76, LIDDELL-SCOTT 511 (see "eklegō"), COLIN BROWN 1:536-42.

1574. ἐκλείπω ekleipō verb

Cease, fail, die, come to an end.

CROSS-REFERENCE:
λείπω leipō (2981)

אָזַל 'āzal (234), Go (1 Sm 9:7).

אָמַל 'āmal (543), Pulal: dry up (Na 1:4).

אָסַף 'āsaph (636), Gather; niphal: taken away, dying (Hos 4:3).

אָפֵס 'āphēṣ (674), Be gone, vanish (Gn 47:15,16, Is 29:20).

אֶפֶס 'ephes (675), Leave none (Dt 32:36).

בָּצַר bātsar (1245), Gather; niphal: be impossible (Gn 11:6—Codex Alexandrinus only).

גָּוַע gāwa' (1510), Die (Gn 25:8, Jb 13:19, Zec 13:8).

גָּזַר gāzar (1535), Cut; niphal: cut off (Hb 3:17).

ἐκλείπω 1574

גָּמַר gāmar (1625), Cease, disappear (Ps 12:1 [11:1]).

דָּלַל dālal (1870), Look upward (Is 38:14).

זָנַח zānach (2269), Stink, become foul (Is 19:6).

חָדַל chādhal (2403), Abandon, cease (Gn 18:11, Jgs 5:6, Jer 51:30 [28:30]).

חָדֵל chādhēl (2404), Forsaken, rejected (Is 53:3).

חָלָה chālāh (2571), Qal: become weak or sick (Ez 34:16); niphal: be diseased or weak (Ez 34:21).

חָקַר chāqar (2811), Determine, ascertain (2 Chr 4:18).

חָרֵב chārēv (2818), Dry up (Gn 8:13, Is 19:5).

חָרַר chārar (2893), Niphal: burn, be consumed (Jer 6:29, Ez 15:4).

חָתַת chāthath (2973), Qal: cracked (Jer 14:4); niphal: broken (Is 7:8).

יָאַל yā'al (3082), Niphal: be foolish (Is 19:13).

יָגַע yāghē' (3129), Exhaust, labor (Hb 2:13).

יָעֵף yā'ēph (3396), Exhausted, weary (Jgs 8:15—Sixtine Edition only).

יָצַת yātsath (3448), Niphal: burn up, desolate (Jer 9:10).

כָּזַב kāzav (3694), Piel: fail (Is 58:11).

כָּחַד kāchadh (3701), Niphal: perish, destroy (Zec 11:9).

כָּלָה kālāh (3735), Qal: use up (Gn 21:15, 1 Kgs 17:14, Ps 119:81 [118:81]); piel: consume, end (1 Sm 2:33, Ps 78:33 [77:33]); pual: end, conclude (Ps 72:20 [71:20]).

כָּלָה kālāh (3737), End (Jer 46:28 [26:28]).

כִּלָּיוֹן killāyôn (3750), Failing (Dt 28:65).

כָּרַת kārath (3901), Cut down; niphal: cut off, fail (Jos 3:13, 2 Sm 3:29, Is 55:13).

לָהָה lāhâh (3992), Languish, waste away (Gn 47:13).

לוּז lûz (4005), Hiphil: depart, escape (Prv 4:21).

מוּר mûr (4306), Niphal: change (Jer 48:11 [31:11]).

מוּשׁ mûsh (4318), Depart, disappear (Ex 13:22, Ps 55:11 [54:11], Is 54:10).

מוּת mûth (4322), Die (Jer 42:17,22 [49:17,22]).

נָדַף nādhaph (5264), Qal: blow away (Ps 68:2 [67:2]); niphal: be blown away (Ps 68:2 [67:2]).

נָטָה nāṭâh (5371), Niphal: lengthen, stretch (Jer 6:4).

נָתַשׁ nāthash (5612), Niphal: be uprooted (Jer 31:40 [38:40]).

סוּף ṣûph (5673), Qal: cease, fail (Est 9:28); hiphil: sweep, consume (Zep 1:2,3).

סוּר ṣûr (5681), Depart (Gn 49:10).

עָזַב 'āzav (6013), Leave, vanish (Jer 18:14).

עָטַף 'āṭaph (6063), Grow weak; niphal: faint (Lam 2:11); hithpael: faint, ebb (Ps 107:5 [106:5], Jon 2:7 [2:8]).

עִיף 'îph (6105), Be weary, fainting (Jer 4:31).

עָיֵף 'āyēph (6106), Famished, faint (Gn 25:29,30, Jgs 8:5).

עָלַף 'ālaph (6190), Hithpael: faint (Am 8:13).

פָּנָה pānâh (6680), Pass away (Ps 90:9 [89:9]).

צָדָה tsādhâh (6922), Niphal: destroy, devastate (Zep 3:6).

צָפַן tsāphan (7121), Store up (Jb 21:19).

צַר tsar (7140), Adversity, trouble (Prv 24:10).

שָׁבַת shāvath (8139), Qal: cease (Jos 5:12 [5:11]); hiphil: cause to cease (Jer 36:29 [43:29]).

תָּמַם tāmam (8882), Qal: consume, destroy (Gn 47:15,18, Ps 9:6); niphal: be consumed (Ps 104:35 [103:35]); hiphil: consume, end (2 Sm 20:18, Ez 22:15).

1. ἐκλείπῃ ekleipē 3sing subj pres act
2. ἐκλίπητε eklipēte 2pl subj aor act
3. ἐκλείψουσιν ekleipsousin 3pl indic fut act
4. ἐκλείπητε ekleipēte 2pl subj pres act
5. ἐκλίπῃ eklipē 3sing subj aor act
6. ἐκλιπόντος eklipontos gen sing masc part aor act

```
2 that, when ye fail, they may receive you into ...... Luke 16:9
5 that when it fails, they may receive you (NASB) ....... 16:9
1 But I have prayed for thee, that thy faith fail not: ..... 22:32
5 But I have prayed for thee, that thy faith fail not: ..... 22:32
6 for the sun stopped shining. (NIV) .................... 23:45
3 but thou art the same, and thy years shall not fail. ...Heb 1:12
```

Classical Greek

In the classical through Hellenistic periods several applications were made of the original word picture in *ekleipō*: "to leave out/off." It could mean "to abandon a responsibility or a thing," consequently, "to desert an army or abandon a city." Figuratively, the sun might "eclipse"; someone might "fail," "faint," or even "die."

Septuagint Usage

Found quite frequently in the Septuagint, *ekleipō* extends its imagery over a great variety of situations. Water "evaporates" or is used up (Genesis 8:13; 21:15); a number of things do or do not "cease" (Exodus 13:22; Isaiah 7:8; 54:10); travelers "abandon" highways (Judges 5:6). People "die" (Jeremiah 42:17 [LXX 49:17]; 44:18 [51:18]).

New Testament Usage

By contrast *ekleipō* occurs only three or four times in the New Testament (*Textus Receptus*). In all these cases it could be translated "to cease" or "to fail." "Make friends for yourselves by means of unrighteous mammon (wealth), so that when it *fails* they may receive you into the eternal habitations" (Luke 16:9, RSV). By means of a rather troublesome parable Christ exhorted the disciples to exercise stewardship. He unhesitatingly stated that one's money and worldly wealth are transitory. He did not say *if* the wealth collapses but *when* it does, whether at one's death or at the end of the world, those who have understood the spiritual implications of the use of one's wealth will be welcomed into "eternal habitations" (i.e., heaven) by God and/or possibly those who benefited by the proper use of that wealth, e.g., the poor (Harris, "Tent," *Colin Brown*, 3:812).

In Luke 22:32 Jesus prayed for His disciples that their faith would "fail not." Liefeld properly sees this as a concern of Jesus that Peter's faith would not "give out or disappear completely." He goes on to say that this prayer was answered, even in the face of Peter's denial. For though it was serious and revealed a low level of faith, it does not mean Peter ceased to believe (Expositor's Bible Commentary, 8:1029).

The phrase in Hebrews 1:12, "Thy years shall not *fail*," clearly proclaims the eternality of the Son. He is eternally preexistent (Hebrews 1:10), and as *ekleipō* suggests, there will never come a day when He shall cease to exist. A fourth occurrence is found in several early manuscripts which is reflected in many modern versions. "It was now about the sixth hour, and darkness came over the whole land until the ninth hour, for the sun *stopped* shining" (Luke 23:44,45, NIV).

STRONG 1587, BAUER 242, MOULTON-MILLIGAN 195-96, LIDDELL-SCOTT 511-12, COLIN BROWN 3:248.

1575. ἐκλεκτός eklektos adj
Chosen, select, elect.
CROSS-REFERENCE:
ἐκλέγομαι eklegomai (1573)

בַּד badh (940), Branch (Ez 19:14).

בָּחוּר bāchûr (1005), Choice man (Ps 78:31 [77:31]).

בְּחוּרוֹת bᵉchûrôth (1006), Short (Nm 11:28).

בָּחִיר bāchîr (1008), Chosen (2 Sm 21:6, Ps 106:5 [105:5], Is 65:9).

בָּחַן bāchan (1010), Test (Prv 17:3).

בֹּחַן bōchan (1012), Tested, tried (Is 28:16).

בָּחַר bāchar (1013), Qal: best, chosen (Ex 14:7, Jgs 20:34); niphal: better (Prv 8:19).

בַּר bar (1276), Perfect, undefiled (S/S 6:9).

בַּר bar (1277), Trampled (Am 5:11).

בַּרְבֻּר barbur (1285), Fattened, well fed (1 Kgs 4:23—Codex Alexandrinus only).

בָּרִיא bārî' (1304), Choicest, fat (Gn 41:2,4,5, Hb 1:16, Zec 11:16).

בְּרֻמִּים bᵉrōmîm (1323), Colored, multicolored (Ez 27:24).

בָּרַר bārar (1331), Qal: choice, polished (Neh 5:18, Is 49:2); niphal: pure (2 Sm 22:27, Ps 18:26 [17:26]).

גֵּלָל gᵉlāl (A1602), Large blocks, great blocks (Ezr 5:8—Aramaic).

דְּרוֹר dᵉrôr (1926), Myrrh oil, pure (Ex 30:23).

חֶמְדָּה chemdāh (2631), Desirable, fine (Jer 25:34 [32:34], Hg 2:7 [2:8]).

חֵפֶץ chāphēts (2760), Jewel, stone (Is 54:12).

חֹפֶשׁ chōphesh (2772), Saddlecloth (Ez 27:20).

חָרוּץ chārûts (2845), Diligent (Prv 12:24).

יָקָר yāqār (3479), Precious (Ez 27:22—Codex Alexandrinus only).

מִבְחוֹר mivchôr (4143), Choicest (2 Kgs 19:23).

מִבְחָר mivchār (4144), Choicest, fine (Gn 23:6, Is 22:7, Jer 22:7).

מַנְעַמִּים manʿammîm (4664), Delicacies (Ps 141:4 [140:4]).

פְּרִי pᵉrî (6780), Fruit (Ez 19:12).

צְבִי tsᵉvî (6905), Ornament, glory (Ez 7:20, 25:9).

צַמֶּרֶת tsammereth (7058), Treetop, highest branch (Ez 17:22).

רִי rî (7661), Moisture (Jb 37:11).

1. ἐκλεκτόν eklekton nom/acc sing masc/neu
2. ἐκλεκτός eklektos nom sing masc
3. ἐκλεκτοί eklektoi nom pl masc
4. ἐκλεκτῶν eklektōn gen pl masc
5. ἐκλεκτοῖς eklektois dat pl masc
6. ἐκλεκτούς eklektous acc pl masc
7. ἐκλεκτῆς eklektēs gen sing fem
8. ἐκλεκτῇ eklektē dat sing fem

```
3 for many be called, but few chosen................Matt 20:16
3 For many are called, but few are chosen..............22:14
6 for the elect's sake those days shall be shortened........24:22
6 if it were possible, they shall deceive the very elect.....24:24
6 shall gather together his elect from the four winds,....24:31
6 no flesh should be saved: but for the elect's sake, Mark 13:20
6 to seduce, if it were possible, even the elect..........13:22
6 send his angels, and shall gather together his elect ....13:27
4 And shall not God avenge his own elect,..........Luke 18:7
2 if he be Christ, the chosen of God....................23:35
4 shall lay any thing to the charge of God's elect?.....Rom 8:33
1 Salute Rufus chosen in the Lord, and his mother......16:13
3 as the elect of God, holy and beloved,.............Col 3:12
4 and the Lord Jesus Christ, and the elect angels,.....1 Tm 5:21
6 Therefore I endure all things for the elect's sakes,..2 Tm 2:10
4 an apostle ... according to the faith of God's elect,....Tit 1:1
5 To God's elect, strangers in the world (NIV)........1 Pt 1:1
1 disallowed indeed of men, but chosen of God,..........2:4
1 I lay in Sion a chief corner stone, elect, precious:.......2:6
1 But ye are a chosen generation, a royal priesthood,......2:9
8 The elder unto the elect lady and her children,......2 Jn 1:1
7 The children of thy elect sister greet thee. Amen........1:13
3 are with him are called, and chosen, and faithful....Rev 17:14
```

Classical Greek

This adjective is a derivative of the verb *eklegomai* (1573) meaning "chosen, select, outstanding, of the best quality." Although *eklektos* occurs in literary and nonliterary material, there seems to be no evidence that it was anything other than a secular expression in classical Greek.

In classical Greek it is used in connection with a person or thing which is chosen. The term had its origin in military language and was used in reference to the choosing of men for military service, or the choosing of an individual or group for special duty. The word also has a political sense where it is used in connection with the election of persons to offices or duties. In such elections the background of the candidate and his qualifications were the basis of election. However, it was the election itself that furnished the person with the authority and imposed the specific responsibility upon him (Coenen, "Elect," *Colin Brown,* 1:536).

Changes in the meaning of the word took place which extended it to include individual decisions or choices. The Stoics used *eklektos* in connection with personal decisions or choices between different possibilities. In the papyri *eklektos* is used to convey the selection of specific things because of their quality, for example, the selection of slaves (see *Moulton-Milligan*).

Septuagint Usage

Unlike *eklegomai,* which consistently translates one Hebrew term (*bāchar*) more than any other, *eklektos* translates 19 terms, the two most common being *bāchar* and *bārar*. *Bāchar* is used in the Old Testament in three primary ways: (1) in secular contexts; (2) in contexts where God is the object, e.g., men choose God, His will, and His way; and (3) in contexts where God is the subject.

In secular contexts *eklektos* is often applied to "select" products, such as grain, animals, or other goods (e.g., Nehemiah 5:18; Esdras 5:18 [LXX 2 Esdras 5:18]; Amos 5:11), a use commonly found in papyri (*Moulton-Milligan*). Schrenk notes the use of *eklektos* in connection with persons who are "picked" to fight (Judges 20:16; cf. Josephus *Antiquities* 7.2.2; "eklektos," *Kittel,* 4:182). It is in the secular context that *bāchar* first appears (Genesis 6:2), where it is used for the choosing of a wife. *Bāchar* is also used in connection with the selection of choice grazing land (Genesis 13:11); the choosing of warriors (Exodus 17:9); the selection of a king (1 Samuel 8:18 [LXX 1 Kings 8:18]); the selection of stones for a sling (1 Samuel 17:40 [1 Kings 17:40]); the choosing of an appropriate ox for a sacrifice (1 Kings 18:25 [LXX 3 Kings 18:25]); and the craftsman's selection of choice materials (Isaiah 40:20).

Where God is the object of man's selection, *bāchar* is used very infrequently. The most important occurrences are found in Joshua 24:15,22. Here Joshua laid an ultimatum before the whole congregation of Israel either to choose Jehovah and serve Him, or to choose and serve the gods of the Amorites.

It is interesting to note that *bāchar,* which is the strongest term for God's election of Israel, is also used of the people's choice to serve God. This use of *bāchar* indicates that the Lord's election of Israel does not disregard the decision of the people. Israel could obediently confirm their election or defy the will of God. Israel's choice is a real choice. In Psalms 25:12 and 119:30,173 *bāchar* is used to indicate man's choice of God's will and way.

The dominant use of *bāchar* in the Old Testament, however, is God's election of His people (Deuteronomy 7:6,7; 10:15; 14:2). God is also pictured choosing Jerusalem (1 Kings 8:44,48; 11:13; 2 Kings 21:7; Nehemiah 1:9) and as selecting the great leaders of Israel (Abraham, Nehemiah 9:7; Moses, Psalm 106:23 [LXX 105:23]; Aaron, Psalm 105:26; David, Psalm 78:70).

From a religious point of view the offspring of Abraham His servant, the sons of Jacob, are God's "chosen ones" (*eklektoi autou;* 1 Chronicles 16:13). God has made a covenant with His chosen ones (*tois eklektois mou,* Septuagint; cf. also Psalm 105:6,43 [LXX 104:6,43]; Isaiah 65:9,15). Schrenk notes how *eklektos* develops the motif of the election of Israel as God's chosen people for the translators of the Septuagint even more than the original Hebrew intended. This is verified in the significant employment of *eklektos* where there is no Hebrew counterpart (e.g., Haggai 2:23) and in the term's substituting for such a wide variety of religious concepts ("eklektos," *Kittel,* 4:182f.).

The second most common Hebrew term translated by *eklektos* is *bārar,* "to sort, purge out, sift," and its derivative *bār,* "pure." This rendering adds somewhat of a different nuance to the concept of *eklektos* in the Septuagint. The Hebrew term is probably related to the Akkadian verb *barāru,* meaning "to glitter,"

ἐκλεκτός 1575

and its adjective form *barru* meaning "pure" (of metal). A related Ugaritic root means "to be pure, clean" (Kalland, "bārar," *Theological Wordbook of the Old Testament*, 1:134). Thus, the Septuagint translators made the already present but inferred connection between *eklektos* and purity more direct and obvious.

God shows himself to be pure (*eklektos*) to the pure (*eklektou*) (2 Samuel 22:27 [LXX 2 Kings 22:27]). In the post-script to the genealogy of the descendants of Asher, the Chronicler included a highly favorable commentary concerning the nature of the sons of Asher; they were "choice (*eklektoi*) men" (1 Chronicles 7:40). In 1 Chronicles 9:22 the importance of choosing men of integrity to be gatekeepers of the house of the Lord becomes the context for translating *bārar* with *eklektos*. In another passage only the "choice" lambs were selected to be served at the table of King Artaxerxes (Nehemiah 5:18). Elsewhere, the lover describes his beloved as "the favorite" (*eklektē*) of all those born to her mother (Song of Solomon 6:9 [LXX Canticles 6:8]). Here the concept of election is interwoven with the exegesis of the synagogue where the "bride" equals Israel (Schrenk, "eklektos," *Kittel*, 4:182).

God chose Israel to be a holy nation (Deuteronomy 7:6). Through the pressure of their culture and the ungodly leadership of the false prophets, the people began to believe that they could break the covenant and still retain its blessings (Jeremiah 6:13f.; 7:3f.). Moses warned the people that the privilege of election required responsible living and that sin would be punished (Leviticus 26:14f.; Deuteronomy 28:15f.). In addition, the true prophets warned that the people's sin would bring judgment from God and they would be sent into captivity (Jeremiah 7:28,29). Only a remnant of the people would be left to experience the fulfillment of the promises which God had given His people. The Lord who once chose Israel would again choose Israel (Isaiah 14:1). This new election would take place under a new covenant (Jeremiah 31:31f.) The law of the new covenant would be written on the hearts of men rather than the tablets of stone. This new covenant would be extended to include the Gentiles, offering God's salvation to the ends of the earth (Isaiah 49:6).

These promises to the remnant of Israel have not only national ramifications but personal ones as well. Each person is clearly responsible for his or her own relationship with God (Jeremiah 31:34). This is not the first time the issue of personal accountability appears in the Old Testament, however (cf. Psalm 65:5; Numbers 16:7).

The election doctrine of the Old Testament has its source in the messianic promises, and it is here that the foundation for the election of Israel lies (Genesis 12:3). Furthermore, in the messianic prophecies the election of Israel reaches its climax. A primary element in God's election of this One is the establishment of the way of renewal for those who have forsaken the covenant, once again restoring the people of God (Hosea 1:6-2:1). Not only is the way paved for fallen Israel to return, but all the barriers have been removed allowing the Gentiles to participate in this new election of grace as well (cf. Romans 9:25; 1 Peter 2:9,10).

New Testament Usage

It is out of this deeply religious background of the Old Testament that the New Testament concepts of election develop. The New Testament primarily uses the terms *eklegomai* ("elect"), *eklektos* ("chosen"), and *eklogē* (1576) ("election") to communicate the teaching of election. Just as the Old Testament saw election as the foundation for Israel's relationship with God as the people of God, so also in the New Testament God's election is the catalyst for the establishment of the people of the new covenant—the Church.

In the New Testament the word "election" is used in four primary ways: (1) concerning God's election of Israel as His "chosen people," with privileges and responsibilities different from all other people (Romans 9); (2) concerning the election or choosing of certain individuals for particular services (Galatians 1:15ff.); (3) concerning the choice which God made in Christ to provide mankind with salvation (Ephesians 1:3f.); (4) concerning the Church as an elect body.

In the New Testament the ideas of foreknowledge and predestination are closely connected with the concept of election. Several Greek terms are used to communicate these aspects of God's activity, and each one has the distinct feature of the prefix *pro-*, "before, in advance." These terms include: *prognōsis* (4127), "foreknowledge" (1 Peter 1:2); *proginōskō* (4126), "know beforehand, know in advance" (Romans

8:29); *proetoimazō* (4141), "prepare beforehand" (Romans 9:23); *procheirotoneō* (4259), "choose or appoint beforehand" (Acts 10:41); *proorizō* (4168), "decide upon beforehand, predestine" (Romans 8:29).

Apart from the one or two uses of *eklektos* applied to Jesus, which will be addressed below, *eklektos* in the Synoptic Gospels (10 times) has a decided eschatological flavor. The "chosen" are those who are obedient (Matthew 22:14; cf. the variant 20:16); they endure judgment (Matthew 24:31, parallel Mark 13:27; cf. Luke 18:7) and escape destruction (Mark 13:27). The elect are not to fall prey to a false sense of security, however. Christ makes it clear that in the last days false christs will appear in an attempt to seduce the elect (Mark 13:22).

Jesus is the Chosen One of God (*ho eklektos tou theou*; Luke 23:35; cf. a variant reading at John 1:34). Probably the meanings of "choice" and "excellence" coalesce here (Luke reads *ho eklektos* where Matthew and Mark read *ho agapētos*; cf. Luke 9:35, parallel Matthew 17:5; Mark 9:7). The servanthood of Jesus, i.e., His obedience, is particularly a mark of His being God's Chosen One (cf. Psalm 105:6,42f.; Isaiah 65:9; cf. 1 Peter 1:1ff.). Faithfulness, i.e, obedience, is the sign of the "elect" just as it was for Jesus (Titus 1:1; 1 Peter 1:2, cf. Colossians 3:12ff.; 2 Timothy 2:10-13).

There is a clear allusion in these servant passages to the prophecy in Isaiah 42:1 concerning the Servant of the Lord. This term, "the chosen," is often used of the Messiah in Jewish apocalyptic literature as well (1 Enoch 43:3-5) and was a well-known theme among the people as evidenced by the mocking words of the rulers who scorned Jesus as He was dying (Luke 23:35).

Just as Jesus himself was chosen by the Father and sent into the world, so also Jesus chose 12 disciples (Luke 6:13) out of a larger group and sent them out into the world (Matthew 28:19; John 17:18). The Gospel of John in particular emphasizes that the apostles did not choose Jesus, but He chose them (John 6:70; 13:18). Not only were they chosen from among the large group who followed Jesus, as individuals they were chosen out of the world first of all to salvation, and secondly to be apostles (John 15:16,19). This action on the part of Jesus was similar to those men under the old covenant who were chosen out of the larger group to execute particular duties. Furthermore, the election of the apostles is important not only because of their part in the founding of the Church, but because their election was a firstfruit of the new election which the prophets had spoken of (Isaiah 14:1). Paul called this election "the election of grace" (Romans 11:5).

Paul depicted this election and the election of the Gentiles quite vividly with his analogy of the ingrafting of the wild olive branches (Romans 11:17-24). The Gentiles, who are now grafted into the good olive tree, have their place among the people of God.

There has been a great deal of discussion whether Paul's presentation in Romans 9 is concerned with election unto salvation or whether it is merely a question of the fulfillment of God's salvation and judgment in salvation history (see *Complete Biblical Library, Romans—Corinthians*, pp.673-679). Regardless of how this passage is understood, it serves as a fundamental text for understanding the basic principles of God's election. The apostle demonstrated that the issue at hand here is an election that does not have its origin in the privileges which come by virtue of one's birth or descent (Romans 9:7). Similarly, this election does not take place on the basis of works, but it occurs before the individual has done either good or evil (Romans 9:11). It rests not in the will of the person but is based in the grace and will of God that is revealed to whom God desires (Romans 9:15) and for which God cannot be called to account by man (Romans 9:19,20).

The call to salvation brings the believer into an elect body, the Church. God has predestined that believers are to be conformed to the image of God's Son (Romans 8:29,30). This elect body was in God's plan before the foundation of the world was laid (Ephesians 1:3,4). It is an election resulting in communion with God and participation in a glory that believers cannot claim on the basis of anything that they are or do.

For Paul election is not an end in itself. Those who participate in the elect body have the responsibility to pursue a holy (*hagios* [39]) and blameless (*amōmos* [297]) life (Ephesians 1:4). God's election of the Body demands a moral and religious godliness of the highest degree.

Believers can be confident that nothing can breach the protective wall of God's love and separate them from God. However, this promise is never presented in such a way as to lead believers into a false confidence. Just as it is unthinkable that anything should intrude from the outside and separate the believer from the elect, so it is unthinkable that salvation is the mechanical and unalterable destiny of all who occupy a position among the elect. On the contrary, believers are emphatically admonished to "work out" or complete their salvation (Philippians 2:12). Because it is God who is at work in believers, a heightened sense of fear and awe should be present in believers' lives as they pursue the goal of their salvation (Philippians 3:12-16).

In his sermon on the Day of Pentecost, Peter addressed the Jews concerning Jesus (see Acts 3:20-26). Then, in 1 Peter 2:4-6, he called Christ the "chosen" cornerstone which was rejected by men (cf. the Septuagint translation of Isaiah 28:16), and it is upon this Stone that God's chosen people as living stones are being built into a spiritual house (1 Peter 2:5,9). As those who have chosen to follow Jesus, these believers must recognize that the result (*eis* [1506B]) of their sanctification is to be obedience (1 Peter 1:2). The strong element of the necessity of personal responsibility is clearly evident in 2 Peter 3:17,18. Every one who by faith has become part of this elect body must be careful to "grow in grace, and in the knowledge of our Lord and Saviour Jesus Christ" (verse 18) lest they be led away by the error of the wicked and fall from their stable position.

The use of *eklektos* in 2 John should probably be viewed as a "personified congregation" (Schrenk, "eklektos," *Kittel*, 4:191). The community of the elect is based upon familial imagery: brother/sister (verse 13); father/son (verses 3,9); father/children (verse 4); and mother (i.e., the lady)/children (verse 1). Outside of this community of fellowship there is no "election" (2 John 9,10). It is probably not by accident that the language of election in John's Gospel also falls in a context in which the commandment to love one another is given (John 15:12-17). Therefore, remaining part of the elect body involves active obedience which is expressed most fully in obeying the commandments and loving one another (2 John 5,6).

The New Testament Church demonstrated a firm belief in election, but showed no indication that it was some type of divine fatalism. They recognized that God had chosen them to inherit salvation, yet it is God's will that all should come to a place of repentance and that none perish (2 Peter 3:9). The paradoxical and inexplicable mystery of God's sovereignty to elect the individual is maintained without any limitation being placed on His universal plan of salvation (1 Timothy 2:4; 2 Peter 3:9), nor on the universal efficacy of the atonement (1 Corinthians 5:15; 1 John 2:2). The question is not taken up as a problem that has to be solved or understood by man. God's call to all sinners has a place of great importance (Matthew 11:28; 23:27; Revelation 22:17).

STRONG 1588, BAUER 242, MOULTON-MILLIGAN 196, KITTEL 4:181-92, LIDDELL-SCOTT 512, COLIN BROWN 1:536-41.

1576. ἐκλογή eklogē noun

Selection, choice, chosen.

CROSS-REFERENCE:
ἐκλέγομαι eklegomai (1573)

1. ἐκλογή eklogē nom sing fem
2. ἐκλογῆς eklogēs gen sing fem
3. ἐκλογήν eklogēn acc sing fem

2 for he is a **chosen** vessel unto me, ... Acts 9:15
3 purpose of God according to **election** might stand, ... Rom 9:11
3 is a remnant according to the **election** of grace. 11:5
1 **election** hath obtained it, and the rest were blinded 11:7
3 but as touching the **election**, ... 11:28
3 Knowing, brethren beloved, your **election** of God.... 1 Th 1:4
3 to make your calling and **election** sure: .... 2 Pt 1:10

Classical Greek

Eklogē is the noun form of the verb *eklegomai* (1573). This verb is a compound form of the preposition *ek* (1523), "out of," and *legō* (2978), "collect, pick out, select, choose, say." In classical Greek the term is used for the simple act of choosing. As it developed in use, from military to political vocabulary, it came to be used exclusively for the process of electing, selecting, or a choice.

Septuagint Usage

The noun *eklogē* is almost nonexistent in the Septuagint, occurring only once in Aquila's version at Isaiah 22:7 and once each in both Symmachus' and Theodotion's versions at Isaiah 37:24.

New Testament Usage

Eklogē is found seven times in the New Testament. The emphasis is upon the free choice of God in fulfilling His purposes. In every case it is used with reference to the election of God; however, each reference carries its own nuance. In Acts 9:15, Paul is chosen for apostolic tasks; in Romans 9:11f., Israel is chosen for a historical task; in Romans 11:28, the whole people of Israel are chosen (cf. Romans 9:11); in 1 Thessalonians 1:4, the whole Christian community is chosen; in Romans 11:5,7, a part of Israel is chosen from the whole; and in 2 Peter 1:10, the final election is predicated on being fruitful in the knowledge of Christ (cf. verse 8).

STRONG 1589, BAUER 243, MOULTON-MILLIGAN 196, KITTEL 4:176-81, LIDDELL-SCOTT 512, COLIN BROWN 1:536-37,539-40.

1577. ἐκλύω ekluō verb

Faint or weaken, become despondent.

COGNATE:
λύω luō (3061)

SYNONYMS:
κάμνω kamnō (2548)
κοπιάω kopiaō (2844)

גָּאַל gā'al (1381), Redeem (Jb 19:25).

גָּלָה gālāh (1580), Fly away (Jb 20:28—only some Sinaiticus texts).

זָעֵף zā'ēph (2282), Displeased (1 Kgs 20:43 [21:43]).

יָעֵף yā'ēph (3396), Faint, exhausted (2 Sm 16:2).

יָפַח yāphach (3416), Hithpael: groan, anguish (Jer 4:31).

לָאָה lā'āh (3942), Hiphil: worn out, weary (Jer 12:5).

מָהַהּ māhahh (4244), Hithpalpel: stop oneself (Is 29:9).

עָטַף 'āṭaph (6063), Qal: faint (Lam 2:19); hithpael: swoon, faint (Lam 2:12).

עִיף 'îph (6105), Faint (1 Sm 14:28).

עָיֵף 'āyēph (6106), Exhausted, weary (2 Sm 16:14).

עָלְפֶּה 'ulpeh (6191), Wither, faint (Ez 31:15).

פָּגַר pāghar (6537), Piel: exhausted, faint (1 Sm 30:21).

פָּזַז pāzaz (6581), Be made strong, limber (Gn 49:24).

פָּרַק pāraq (6811), Break off, throw off (Gn 27:40).

פָּתַח pāthach (6858), Open; hithpael: loose oneself, free oneself (Is 52:2—Vaticanus texts only).

קוּץ qûts (7258), Despise (Prv 3:11).

רָכַךְ rākhakh (7690), Be faint-hearted (Dt 20:3).

רָפָה rāphâh (7791), Qal: lose courage (2 Sm 4:1, 2 Chr 15:7, Jer 49:24 [30:13]); piel: weaken, discourage (Ezr 4:4, Jer 38:4 [45:4]); hiphil: abandon (Jos 10:6); hithpael: wait, be slack (Jos 18:3).

רָפֶה rāpheh (7793), Weak, discouraged (2 Sm 17:2).

שָׁמֵם shāmēm (8460), Be deserted, shudder; hithpolel: be faint, exhausted (Dn 8:27).

שָׁפַךְ shāphakh (8581), Pour out; hithpael: be poured out, ebb (Jb 30:16—only some Sinaiticus texts).

1. ἐκλύου ekluou 2sing impr pres mid
2. ἐκλυόμενοι ekluomenoi nom pl masc part pres mid
3. ἐκλυθῶσιν ekluthōsin 3pl subj aor pass
4. ἐκλελυμένοι ekleIumenoi
   nom pl masc part perf mid
5. ἐκλυθήσονται ekluthēsontai 3pl indic fut pass

```
4 because they fainted, and were scattered abroad,.... Matt 9:36
3 not ... away fasting, lest they faint in the way.......... 15:32
5 them away fasting ... they will faint by the way:..... Mark 8:3
2 for in due season we shall reap, if we faint not....... Gal 6:9
2 lest ye be wearied and faint in your minds..........Heb 12:3
4 lest ye be wearied and faint in your minds............. 12:3
1 nor faint when thou art rebuked of him:.............. 12:5
```

Classical Greek

This verb is a compound form of the preposition *ek* (1523), "out of," and the verb *luō* (3061), "to loose" or "destroy." *Ekluō*, occurring from Homer onward, has several applications in Greek literature. In a passive sense it can denote "to be set free." This sense was commonly used in the medical field of setting one free from an illness. It is also used with reference "to relax." Along this same vein in a passive sense the term denotes "to be faint, fail." When used of inanimate objects it could denote "to be unserviceable."

Septuagint Usage

In the Septuagint *ekluō* is used of being freed from yokes (Genesis 27:40; Isaiah 52:2); of weary or feeble hands (Isaiah 13:7; Ezekiel 7:17); of animals (Isaiah 46:1); and of people (Judges 8:15). Figuratively it refers to people who are "slack" in obeying God (Joshua 18:3) or "weary" of the Lord's reproof (Proverbs 3:11).

New Testament Usage

Ekluō is used only six times in the New Testament, always in the passive. Jesus used the word literally concerning the crowd which needed to be fed (Matthew 15:32). They were becoming weary and about to faint (cf. Matthew 9:36; Mark 8:3). In Galatians 6:9 Paul exhorted his readers to "not be *weary* in well doing." And in Hebrews 12:3,5 the writer encouraged his readers not to *faint* when undergoing hardships.

STRONG 1590, BAUER 243, MOULTON-MILLIGAN 196, LIDDELL-SCOTT 513, COLIN BROWN 3:177-78,189.

1578. ἐκμάσσω ekmassō verb

Wipe, wipe off.

1. ἐκμάσσειν ekmassein inf pres act
2. ἐξέμαξεν exemaxen 3sing indic aor act

ἐκμυκτηρίζω 1579

3. ἐκμάξασα ekmaxasa nom sing fem part aor act
4. ἐξέμασσεν exemassen 3sing indic imperf act

4 and **did wipe** them with the hairs of her head,......**Luke 7:38**
2 and **did wipe** them with the hairs of her head,.......... 7:38
2 and **wiped** them with the hairs of her head............ 7:44
3 and **wiped** his feet with her hair,................**John 11:2**
2 and **wiped** his feet with her hair:.................... 12:3
1 and **to wipe** them with the towel.................... 13:5

This compound verb is from the preposition *ek* (1523), "out of," and the verb *massō*, "wipe." It is used five times in the Gospels, always concerning feet. Mary dried Jesus' feet (Luke 7:38,44; John 11:2; 12:3); Jesus dried the disciples' feet (John 13:5).

STRONG 1591, BAUER 243, MOULTON-MILLIGAN 196, LIDDELL-SCOTT 513.

1579. ἐκμυκτηρίζω ekmuktērizō verb
Ridicule, sneer at, deride, scoff at.

לָעַג lāʿagh (4074), Qal: laugh (Ps 2:4); hiphil: mock, scorn (Ps 22:7 [21:7]).

לָעֵג lāʿēgh (4076), Mocked (Ps 35:16 [34:16]).

1. ἐξεμυκτήριζον exemuktērizon 3pl indic imperf act

1 heard all these things: and they **derided** him.......Luke 16:14
1 And the rulers also with them **derided** him, saying,.... 23:35

Luke is the only writer to use this verb in the New Testament (Luke 16:14; 23:35). It is a compound of *ek* (1523) and *muktērizō* (3318). The verb comes from the noun *muktēr*, "nose." It characterizes the enemies of Jesus who sneered at Him. A number of *ek*- compounds were used only by Luke in the New Testament. They may not be emphatic forms but rather "the love of Hellenistic Greek for compounds" (Bertram, "ekmukrērizō," *Kittel*, 4:796). It is used in the Septuagint in Psalms 2:4; 35:16 (LXX 34:16).

STRONG 1592, BAUER 243, KITTEL 4:796-99, LIDDELL-SCOTT 514, COLIN BROWN 3:341.

1580. ἐκνεύω ekneuō verb
Slip away, turn aside, withdraw.
CROSS-REFERENCE:
νεύω neuō (3368)

סוּג sûgh (5657), Deviate; hiphil: store, put away (Mi 6:14).

סוּר sûr (5681), Turn aside, enter (Jgs 4:18—Codex Alexandrinus only).

פָּנָה pānâh (6680), Turn, turn around (2 Kgs 2:24, 23:16).

1. ἐξένευσεν exeneusen 3sing indic aor act

1 for Jesus **had conveyed himself away**,................John 5:13

This verb is used only once in the New Testament concerning Jesus' escape from the crowd (John 5:13). "Had withdrawn" (RSV) is technically an accurate translation. "Had slipped away" (NIV) or "had conveyed himself away" (KJV) express better what happened. Elsewhere the word may mean simply "turn aside" (see 2 Kings 23:16 [LXX 4 Kings 23:16]) or "turned" (2 Kings 2:24 [LXX 4 Kings 2:24]).

STRONG 1593, BAUER 243, MOULTON-MILLIGAN 196, LIDDELL-SCOTT 514.

1581. ἐκνήφω eknēphō verb
Sober up.
CROSS-REFERENCE:
νήφω nēphō (3387)

יָצָא yātsâʾ (3428), Go out (1 Sm 25:37).

יָקַץ yāqats (3477), Awake, arise (Gn 9:24, Hb 2:7).

קִיץ qîts (7301), Hiphil: awake, wake up (Jl 1:5, Hb 2:19).

1. ἐκνήψατε eknēpsate 2pl impr aor act

1 **Awake** to righteousness, and sin not;.............1 Co 15:34

This verb, a compound of *ek* (1523) and *nēphō* (3387), "be sober," literally and figuratively refers to "become sober, to come to one's senses." In its only New Testament use Paul commanded the Corinthians, "Come back to your senses" (1 Corinthians 15:34, NIV). According to *Moulton-Milligan* this term belongs to the higher Koine, pointing to Paul's true Hellenism, and should be given its full force, "Get sober out of your drunken condition."

STRONG 1594, BAUER 243, MOULTON-MILLIGAN 196, KITTEL 4:941, LIDDELL-SCOTT 514, COLIN BROWN 1:514-15.

1582. ἑκούσιος hekousios adj
Willing or deliberate, voluntary, spontaneous.
CROSS-REFERENCE:
εἰμί eimi (1498)

דַּי day (1823), Able, possibility (Neh 5:8).

נָדַב nādhav (5246), Hithpael: those who assist, aid (Ezr 1:6).

נְדָבָה nᵉdhāvāh (5249), Willing, freewill offering (Lv 23:38, Ezr 8:28, Ps 119:108 [118:108]).

עָתַר ʿāthar (6518), Pray, supplicate; niphal: multiply (Prv 27:6).

1. ἑκούσιον hekousion nom/acc sing neu

1 should not be as it were of necessity, but **willingly**...Phlm 1:14

Used once in the New Testament in this adjectival form (*kata hekousion*; Philemon 14), *hekousios* is contrasted with *kata anagkēn* ("by necessity or compulsion"). It is used in the Septuagint for freewill sacrifices (Leviticus 7:6, 23:38.) Though usually employed of the impersonal (an action, for example), a synonym, *hekōn* (1622), is used of people (Romans 8:20). (See the adverbial form *hekousiōs* [1583].)

STRONG 1595, BAUER 243, MOULTON-MILLIGAN 196, KITTEL 2:470, LIDDELL-SCOTT 514-15.

1583. ἑκουσίως hekousiōs adv
Willingly, deliberately, intentionally, voluntarily.
CROSS-REFERENCE:
εἰμί eimi (1498)

1. ἑκουσίως hekousiōs

1 For if we sin **wilfully** after that.................... Heb 10:26
1 not by constraint, but **willingly**;..................... 1 Pt 5:2

This adverbial form is used twice in the New Testament. Peter told the elders to care for the flock willingly, not from compulsion (*anankastōs* [315]; 1 Peter 5:2). Sinning deliberately ("wilfully") after conversion is condemned (Hebrews 10:26).

STRONG 1596, BAUER 243, MOULTON-MILLIGAN 196, LIDDELL-SCOTT 514-15.

1584. ἔκπαλαι ekpalai adv
For a long time, long ago, from of old.
CROSS-REFERENCE:
παλαιός palaios (3683)

1. ἔκπαλαι ekpalai

1 whose judgment now **of a long time** lingereth not,....2 Pt 2:3
1 that by the word of God the heavens were **of old**,...... 3:5

This term is an adverbial compound of *ek* (1523), "from," and *palai* (3682), an adverb denoting past time and meaning "long ago, formerly" (*Bauer*). Used twice in the New Testament, it is a stronger term than *palai*, indicating considerable passage of time. One reference, for example, is to creation (2 Peter 3:5) that occurred "a long time ago."

STRONG 1597, BAUER 243, MOULTON-MILLIGAN 197, LIDDELL-SCOTT 515.

1585. ἐκπειράζω ekpeirazō verb
Put to the test, try, tempt.

CROSS-REFERENCE:
πειράζω peirazō (3847)

נָסָה nāṣâh (5441), Piel: put to the test, try (Dt 6:16, 8:16, Ps 78:18 [77:18]).

1. ἐκπειράζωμεν ekpeirazōmen 1pl subj pres act
2. ἐκπειράζων ekpeirazōn nom sing masc part pres act
3. ἐκπειράσεις ekpeiraseis 2sing indic fut act

3 Thou **shalt not tempt** the Lord thy God............ Matt 4:7
3 It is said, Thou **shalt not tempt** the Lord thy God... Luke 4:12
2 a certain lawyer stood up, and **tempted** him,.......... 10:25
1 Neither let us **tempt** Christ,....................... 1 Co 10:9

Classical Greek
Ekpeirazō is a compound of *ek* (1523) plus *peirazō* (3847), "to tempt" or "to test," and it does not occur in secular Greek, although the middle of the related *ekpeirao* does appear as does another compound, *katapeirao* (Seesman, "ekperiazō," *Kittel*, 6:24). *Moulton-Milligan* in its study of nonliterary sources and papyri does not come across *ekpeirazō* either.

Septuagint Usage
The Septuagint, however, records five instances of *ekpeirazō*, all with the Hebrew counterpart *nāṣâh*, which in the piel means "to put someone to the test" (either people or God). God is not to be tested by His people (Deuteronomy 6:16; cf. Psalm 78:18 [LXX 77:18]). But God "tests" men to know their hearts (Deuteronomy 8:2) and for their benefit (Deuteronomy 8:16).

New Testament Usage
In the New Testament two instances of *ekpeirazō* (Matthew 4:7; Luke 4:12) are direct allusions to the Septuagint text of Deuteronomy 6:16. Jesus replied to Satan, "You shall not test the Lord your God." The term obviously is less pejorative in Luke 10:25; still, Jesus' response to the lawyer's question resembles His reply to Satan at the second temptation (Luke 4:7f.). Satan's temptation, incidentally, was an attack on loyalty to God (idolatry?).

First Corinthians 10:9 is probably a play on the Septuagint record of Israel's putting God to the test in the wilderness. This possibility is strengthened by the immediate context of 10:1-5 which recalls the wilderness experience. "Putting God to the test" again is directly linked to idolatry and, in addition, with pride and immorality (10:8-13).

STRONG 1598, BAUER 243, KITTEL 6:23-36, LIDDELL-SCOTT 515, COLIN BROWN 3:798-99,802.

1586. ἐκπέμπω ekpempō verb
Send away, send forth.

ἐκπερισσοῦ 1586A

CROSS-REFERENCE:
πέμπω pempō (3854)

שָׁלַח shālach (8365), Piel: send, send away (Gn 24:54, 2 Sm 19:31); pual: be sent (Prv 17:11).

1. ἐξέπεμψαν exepempsan 3pl indic aor act
2. ἐκπεμφθέντες ekpemphthentes
nom pl masc part aor pass

2 So they, **being sent forth** by the Holy Ghost,....... Acts 13:4
1 And the brethren immediately **sent away** Paul......... 17:10

This term is a compound of *ek* (1523), "from," and *pempō* (3854), "send." It is one of three compounded terms in the New Testament composed of a preposition and the verb *pempō* (cf. *metapempomai* [3213], "send for, summon" and *propempō* [4170], "accompany, help on one's journey"). All instances of *ekpempō* occur in Luke's writings, and only in Acts when Paul and Barnabas were sent out as missionaries (13:4) and Paul and Silas were sent from Thessalonica for safekeeping (17:10).

STRONG 1599, BAUER 243, MOULTON-MILLIGAN 197, LIDDELL-SCOTT 515.

1586A. ἐκπερισσοῦ ekperissou adv
Exceedingly.

1. ἐκπερισσοῦ ekperissou

1 praying **exceedingly** that we might see your face,.... 1 Th 3:10
1 And to esteem them very **highly** in love................ 5:13

This word appears nowhere in extant literature except at 1 Thessalonians 3:10 and 5:13 in the New Testament. There it combines with the preposition *huper* (5065), "beyond, above," and means "beyond all measure." It is related to the adverb *ekperissōs* (1586B), "exceedingly." For more information, see the word study at *huperekperissou* (5076).

1586B. ἐκπερισσῶς ekperissōs adv
Exceedingly.

CROSS-REFERENCE:
περισσεύω perisseuō (3915)

1. ἐκπερισσῶς ekperissōs

1 But Peter kept saying **insistently**,................. Mark 14:31

The word *ekperissōs*, not found in either the classics or the Septuagint, occurs only once in the New Testament, at Mark 14:31 (in some modern Greek texts). The preposition *ek* (1523) intensifies the force of the adjective *perissos* (3916), which means "abundant," to produce this rare adverbial form. The New International Version, based on Greek manuscripts containing this word, translates *ekperissos* in the following manner: "But Peter insisted *emphatically* (literally, 'said more exceedingly'), 'Even if I have to die with you, I will never disown you.'"

BAUER 243, LIDDELL-SCOTT 515.

1587. ἐκπετάννυμι ekpetannumi verb
Spread out, stretch forth.

SYNONYM:
ἐκτείνω ekteinō (1601)

עוּף 'ûph (5990), Qal: fly, fly away (Jb 20:8, Na 3:16); hithpolel: fly off, fly away (Hos 9:11).

פָּרַץ pārats (6805), Break forth, spread out (Is 54:3).

פָּרַשׂ pārash (6817), Qal: spread out, expose (Ex 9:29, Prv 13:16, Ez 12:13); piel: held out, spread out (Is 65:2).

1. ἐξεπέτασα exepetasa 1sing indic aor act

1 All day long I have **stretched forth** my hands...... Rom 10:21

In classical Greek this word refers to the spreading out of a sail, of hands, and of wings among other meanings (see *Liddell-Scott*). The one New Testament occurrence of *ekpetannumi* is found at Romans 10:21 which is a quote from Isaiah 65:2. As an offering of reconciliation, God "stretched forth" His hands to a disobedient, contradicting people. He offered life and salvation, but Israel refused; they rejected Him first. Notice also Acts 26:1 where Paul "stretched forth the hand" before his testimony in front of Agrippa. Stretching forth of the hands is an expression of earnestness which seeks to engage the attention of an audience. The word also occurs in the early Christian writing, Barnabas (12:4).

STRONG 1600, BAUER 243, MOULTON-MILLIGAN 197, LIDDELL-SCOTT 516.

1587B. ἐκπηδάω ekpēdaō verb
Leap out, rush, spring forth, get up quickly.

COGNATE:
εἰσπηδάω eispēdaō (1514)

SYNONYM:
τρέχω trechō (4983)

זָנַק zānaq (2270), Piel: leap, spring out (Dt 33:22).

יָצָא yātsā' (3428), Go out (Est 4:1).

פָּקַד pāqadh (6734), Niphal: be missed (1 Kgs 20:39 [21:39]).

1. ἐξεπήδησαν exepēdēsan 3pl indic aor act

1 they tore their garments and **rushed out** (RSV)..... Acts 14:14

This compound verb—composed of the preposition *ek* (1523), "out of," and the verb *pēdaō*, "leap, spring"—is a commonly used term for "starting up or getting up quickly." It is used in the Septuagint of Dan, one of the sons of Jacob (Deuteronomy 33:22), in Moses' prophecy concerning the 12 tribes. In the New Testament it is used only once, in Acts 14:14, where Barnabas and Paul ran quickly into the crowd at Lystra to prevent the people from worshiping the servants of God.

BAUER 243, MOULTON-MILLIGAN 197, LIDDELL-SCOTT 516.

1588. ἐκπίπτω ekpiptō verb
Fall off or from, drop away, lose, fail.
COGNATE:
πίπτω piptō (3959)
SYNONYMS:
καταπίπτω katapiptō (2637)
πίπτω piptō (3959)

מָלַל mālal (4589), Wither, cut down (Jb 14:2).
נָבֵל nāval (5209), Fade, fall (Is 28:1,4, 40:8).
נָפַל nāphal (5489), Fall (2 Kgs 6:5, Is 14:12).
נְפַל nᵉphal (A5490), Fall (Dn 7:20—Aramaic).
נָשַׁל nāshal (5577), Slip, fly off (Dt 19:5).
סוּר sûr (5681), Carry away, go away (Jb 15:30).
עָנִי 'ānî (6270), Poor (Jb 24:9).
קָהָה qāhâh (7233), Piel: dull, become blunt (Eccl 10:10).
שָׁלַךְ shālakh (8390), Hiphil: cast off, shed (Jb 15:33).
שַׁלֶּכֶת shallekheth (8392), Fell, cut down (Is 6:13).

1. ἐκπίπτει ekpiptei 3sing indic pres act
2. ἐκπίπτοντες ekpiptontes nom pl masc part pres act
3. ἐξέπεσεν exepesen 3sing indic aor act
4. ἐξεπέσετε exepesete 2pl indic aor act
5. ἐξέπεσον exepeson 3pl indic aor act
6. ἐκπέσητε ekpesēte 2pl subj aor act
7. ἐκπέσωσιν ekpesōsin 3pl subj aor act
8. ἐκπεσεῖν ekpesein inf aor act
9. ἐκπέπτωκας ekpeptōkas 2sing indic perf act
10. ἐκπέπτωκεν ekpeptōken 3sing indic perf act
11. ἐξεπέσατε exepesate 2pl indic aor act
12. ἐξέπεσαν exepesan 3pl indic aor act
13. ἐκπέσωμεν ekpesōmen 1pl subj aor act

2	And the stars of heaven shall fall,	Mark 13:25
5	And his chains fell off from his hands.	Acts 12:7
12	And his chains fell off from his hands.	12:7
7	fearing lest they should fall into the quicksands,	27:17
8	Howbeit we must be cast upon a certain island.	27:26
7	fearing lest we should have fallen upon rocks,	27:29
13	fearing that we might run on the rocks, (RSV)	27:29
8	cut off the ropes of the boat, and let her fall off.	27:32
10	as though the word of God hath taken none effect.	Rom 9:6
1	Charity never faileth:	1 Co 13:8
11	are justified by the law; ye are fallen from grace.	Gal 5:4
3	withereth the grass, and the flower thereof falleth,	Jas 1:11
3	and the flower thereof falleth away:	1 Pt 1:24
6	being led away ... fall from your own stedfastness.	2 Pt 3:17
9	Remember therefore from whence thou art fallen,	Rev 2:5

Classical Greek
Ekpiptō is a compound word formed from the preposition *ek* (1523), "out," and the verb *piptō* (3959), "to fall." Classical Greek witnesses a wide semantic range in the use of *ekpiptō*. It is used of objects which fall out of their place or fall from one place to another; as a nautical expression for a shipwreck or sailors cast overboard; or to express the idea of being driven out or banished. Herodotus used this term somewhat metaphorically to express the idea of being deprived of something (*Liddell-Scott*).

Septuagint Usage
The Septuagint uses *ekpiptō* in translating *nāphal*, which has essentially the same meaning as above. For example, 2 Kings 6:5 (LXX 4 Kings 6:5) refers to the ax *falling* into the water, and Isaiah 14:12 refers to "falling from" heaven.

New Testament Usage
The New Testament demonstrates the same broad semantic range in its use of *ekpiptō* as is seen in classical Greek. First Peter 1:24 designates a "falling" that implies destruction or an end of existence (see Mark 13:25; James 1:11; Revelation 2:5). The New Testament further develops the reader's understanding by recording such events as the chains "falling from" the hands of the apostle Peter (Acts 12:7). Galatians 5:4 mentions a "falling from" or a "losing" of grace, and 2 Peter 3:17 speaks of "losing" one's security. Acts 27:17,26,32 further amplifies the term by using it to refer to a ship drifting off course, not under control, thus, "a loss" of direction.

Ekpiptō is used figuratively of the Word of God in Romans 9:6 to show that it has not failed. Furthermore, we note that love will not "fail" (1 Corinthians 13:8).

STRONG 1601, BAUER 243-44, MOULTON-MILLIGAN 197, KITTEL 6:167-69, LIDDELL-SCOTT 516, COLIN BROWN 1:608.

1589. ἐκπλέω ekpleō verb
Sail away (to or from a place).
CROSS-REFERENCE:
πλέω pleō (3986)

ἐκπληρόω 1590

1. ἐξεπλεύσαμεν exepleusamen 1pl indic aor act
2. ἐκπλεῦσαι ekpleusai inf aor act
3. ἐξέπλει exeplei 3sing indic imperf act

2 so Barnabas took Mark, and **sailed** unto Cyprus; ... Acts 15:39
3 and **sailed** thence into Syria, ... 18:18
1 And we **sailed away** from Philippi 20:6

This compound verb, occurring only three times in the New Testament (Acts 15:39; 18:18; 20:6), combines the preposition *ek* (1523), "out of," and the verb *pleō* (3986), "sail, go by sea." In Acts, Luke recorded the separation of Paul and Barnabas over Mark, the latter two "sailing away" to Cyprus (15:39). Luke also recorded Paul's "sailing" for Syria during his third missionary journey (18:18) and Paul's "sailing" from Philippi to Troas (20:6).

STRONG 1602, BAUER 244, MOULTON-MILLIGAN 197, LIDDELL-SCOTT 517.

1590. ἐκπληρόω ekplēroō verb
Fulfill, completely accomplish.
COGNATE:
   πληρόω plēroō (3997)
SYNONYMS:
   ἀναπληρόω anaplēroō (376)
   ἀνταναπληρόω antanaplēroō (463)
   ἀποτελέω apoteleō (652)
   διανύω dianuō (1268)
   ἐκτελέω ekteleō (1602)
   ἐξαρτίζω exartizō (1806)
   ἐπιτελέω epiteleō (1989)
   ἐργάζομαι ergazomai (2021)
   καταρτίζω katartizō (2645)
   κατεργάζομαι katergazomai (2686)
   πληρόω plēroō (3997)
   ποιέω poieō (4020)
   πράσσω prassō (4097)
   συντελέω sunteleō (4783)
   τελειόω teleioō (4896)
   τελέω teleō (4903)

1. ἐκπεπλήρωκεν ekpeplērōken 3sing indic perf act

1 God hath **fulfilled** the same unto us their children, ..Acts 13:33

From *ek* (1523), "out," and *plēroō* (3997), "fill," this verb is used once in the New Testament (Acts 13:33) and refers to the fulfillment of prophecy. *Plēroō* alone sometimes conveys the same ideas (Acts 13:27). An important related verb is *teleō* (4903), "end" (cf. Acts 13:29).

STRONG 1603, BAUER 244, MOULTON-MILLIGAN 197, KITTEL 6:307-8, LIDDELL-SCOTT 517.

1591. ἐκπλήρωσις ekplērōsis noun
Fullness, filling, fulfillment, completion.

CROSS-REFERENCE:
   πληρόω plēroō (3997)

1. ἐκπλήρωσιν ekplērōsin acc sing fem

1 the **accomplishment** of the days of purification, ... Acts 21:26

This is a rare emphatic noun, the more common word being *plērōma* (3998), "fullness." In the New Testament it is used only in Acts 21:26, indicating that the period of the Nazarite vow had been completed. Luke often used *ek*-compounds.

STRONG 1604, BAUER 244, KITTEL 6:308, LIDDELL-SCOTT 517.

1592. ἐκπλήσσω ekplēssō verb
Be amazed, overwhelmed, strike with astonishment.
COGNATE:
   πλήσσω plēssō (4001)
SYNONYMS:
   ἐκθαμβέω ekthambeō (1555)
   ἐξίστημι existēmi (1822)
   θαμβέω thambeō (2261)

שָׁמֵם shāmēm (8460), Be deserted; hithpolel: destroy oneself (Eccl 7:16 [7:17]).

1. ἐκπλησσόμενος ekplēssomenos
      nom sing masc part pres mid
2. ἐκπλήσσεσθαι ekplēssesthai inf pres mid
3. ἐξεπλάγησαν exeplagēsan 3pl indic aor pass
4. ἐξεπλήσσετο exeplēsseto 3sing indic imperf pass
5. ἐξεπλήσσοντο exeplēssonto 3pl indic imperf pass
6. ἐκκλήσσεσθαι ekklēssesthai inf pres mid
7. ἐκπλήττεσθαι ekplēttesthai inf pres mid
8. ἐκπληττόμενος ekplēttomenos
      nom sing masc part pres mid

5 the people were **astonished** at his doctrine: .... Matt 7:28
7 insomuch that they were **astonished**, ... 13:54
2 insomuch that they were **astonished**, ... 13:54
5 they were exceedingly **amazed**, saying, ... 19:25
5 they were **astonished** at his doctrine, ... 22:33
5 And they were **astonished** at his doctrine: .... Mark 1:22
5 and many hearing him were **astonished**, saying, ... 6:2
5 And were beyond measure **astonished**, saying, ... 7:37
5 And they were **astonished** out of measure, ... 10:26
4 all the people was **astonished** at his doctrine. 11:18
5 all the people was **astonished** at his doctrine. 11:18
3 And when they saw him, they were **amazed**: .... Luke 2:48
5 And they were **astonished** at his doctrine: 4:32
5 they were all **amazed** at the mighty power of God. 9:43
1 being **astonished** at the doctrine of the Lord. .... Acts 13:12
8 being **astonished** at the doctrine of the Lord. 13:12

In the New Testament the most frequent rendering of *ekplēssō* is "amaze, astound," or "overwhelm." It is derived from a compound of *ek* (1523), "out of," and *plēssō* (4001), "strike." This use denotes a profound reaction associated with shock. The term occurs only once in the Septuagint, Ecclesiastes 7:16, where it carries the sense of being "destroyed." The New Testament uses the term in its passive voice; that is, it is used to refer to persons being "astonished" or "amazed" by some person or thing. Of its 13 occurrences in the New Testament, it occurs only once outside of the Gospels, in Acts 13:12.

In the Gospels *ekplēssō* is used exclusively in reference to the activity of Jesus and the effect it had upon those who observed and heard Him (Matthew 7:28; Mark 6:2). A typical usage is found in Mark 1:22, where the people were "amazed" at the teaching of Jesus, and in Mark 7:37 where it is stated they were "beyond measure" or "overwhelmed" with astonishment (cf. Matthew 12:33; 13:54; 19:25; Mark 10:26; 11:18; Luke 2:48; 4:32; and 9:43).

STRONG 1605, BAUER 244, MOULTON-MILLIGAN 197-98, LIDDELL-SCOTT 517, COLIN BROWN 1:529-30.

1593. ἐκπνέω ekpneō verb

Breathe one's last, expire.

CROSS-REFERENCE:
πνέω pneō (4014)

1. ἐξέπνευσεν exepneusen 3sing indic aor act

1 Jesus cried with a loud voice, ... gave up the ghost.	Mark 15:37
1 saw that he so cried out, and gave up the ghost,	15:39
1 and having said thus, he gave up the ghost.	Luke 23:46

This word belongs to a family of words related to *pneuma* (4011), "wind, breath, life." It is a verb combining *ek* (1523), "out," and *pneō* (4014), "blow." It is a euphemism for death (cf. the English word *expire*). It is sometimes used in Greek literature with *bios* (972) and *psuchē* (5425) (both mean "life") as direct objects meaning "to breathe out life," i.e., "to die." In the New Testament it is used without an object and only concerning Jesus' death (Mark 15:37,39; Luke 23:46). The use of *ekpneō* in both of these passages provides a climax for the grueling accounts given by both writers of Christ's crucifixion.

STRONG 1606, BAUER 244, KITTEL 6:452-53, LIDDELL-SCOTT 517, COLIN BROWN 3:689,708.

1594. ἐκπορεύω ekporeuō verb

Go out, come out, proceed from.

COGNATE:
πορεύομαι poreuomai (4057)

SYNONYMS:
ἐκβαίνω ekbainō (1530B)
ἐξέρχομαι exerchomai (1814)
ἐξιέναι exienai (1821)
χωρέω chōreō (5397)

בּוֹא bô' (971), Qal: came, arrive (Jos 15:18, 1 Sm 18:16); hiphil: carry (Jer 17:21).

הָלַךְ hālakh (2050), Go, be exiled (Jer 19:10, 22:10).

חָלַק chālaq (2606), Divide; niphal: scatter, disperse (Jb 38:24).

טָמַן ṭāman (3045), Hide (Jb 3:16).

יָצָא yātsā' (3428), Qal: go out, come out (Gn 24:15, Ps 19:5 [18:5], Jer 6:25); hiphil: (1 Kgs 10:29).

יָצַק yātsaq (3441), Pour out (1 Kgs 22:35).

מוֹצָא môtsā' (4296), Go out, depart, turn away (Dt 8:3, Ps 89:34 [88:34], Ez 12:4).

מוּשׁ mûsh (4318), Leave, depart (Ex 33:11).

נְפַק nᵉphaq (A5494), Go out (Dn 7:10—Aramaic).

סָבַב sāvav (5621), Niphal: turn, go (Jos 15:3).

עָבַר 'āvar (5882), Go out, cross (Jos 15:3,4).

עוּר 'āwar (5996), Niphal: rise up, stir (Jer 25:32 [32:32]).

1. ἐκπορεύεται ekporeuetai 3sing indic pres mid
2. ἐκπορεύονται ekporeuontai 3pl indic pres mid
3. ἐκπορευέσθω ekporeuesthō 3sing impr pres mid
4. ἐκπορευόμενον ekporeuomenon
   nom/acc sing masc/neu part pres mid
5. ἐκπορευομένου ekporeuomenou
   gen sing masc/neu part pres mid
6. ἐκπορευόμενος ekporeuomenos
   nom sing masc part pres mid
7. ἐκπορευόμενοι ekporeuomenoi
   nom pl masc part pres mid
8. ἐκπορευομένων ekporeuomenōn
   gen pl masc part pres mid
9. ἐκπορευομένοις ekporeuomenois
   dat pl masc part pres mid
10. ἐκπορευομένη ekporeuomenē
    nom sing fem part pres mid
11. ἐκπορευμένῃ ekporeumenē
    dat sing fem part pres mid
12. ἐκπορευομένῳ ekporeuomenō
    dat sing neu part pres mid
13. ἐκπορευόμενα ekporeuomena
    nom/acc pl neu part pres mid
14. ἐκπορεύεσθαι ekporeuesthai inf pres mid
15. ἐκπορεύσονται ekporeusontai 3pl indic fut mid
16. ἐξεπορεύετο exeporeueto 3sing indic imperf mid
17. ἐξεπορεύοντο exeporeuonto 3pl indic imperf mid
18. ἐκπορευομένη ekporeuomenē
    dat sing fem part pres mid

16	Then went out to him Jerusalem, and all Judaea,...	Matt 3:5
12	word that **proceedeth** out of the mouth of God.	4:4
4	but **that which cometh** out of the mouth,	15:11
13	But those things **which proceed** out of the mouth	15:18
1	this kind **goeth** not out but by prayer and fasting.	17:21
8	And as they **departed** from Jericho,	20:29
16	there **went** out unto him all the land of Judaea,...	Mark 1:5

7 when ye **depart** thence, shake off the dust	Mark 6:11
13 but the things which **come out** of him,	7:15
1 **goeth out** into the draught, purging all meats?	7:19
4 **cometh** out of the man, that defileth the man.	7:20
2 out of the heart of men, **proceed** evil thoughts,	7:21
1 All these evil things **come** from within,	7:23
5 And when he **was gone forth** into the way,	10:17
5 and as he **went out** of Jericho with his disciples	10:46
16 And when even was come, he **went out** of the city.	11:19
17 When evening came, **they went out** (NASB)	11:19
5 And he **went out** of the temple,	13:1
9 Then said he to the multitude that **came forth**	Luke 3:7
9 gracious words which **proceeded** out of his mouth.	4:22
16 And the fame of him **went out** into every place	4:37
15 And **shall come forth;** they that have done good,	John 5:29
1 Spirit of truth, which **proceedeth** from the Father,	15:26
6 with them coming in and **going out** at Jerusalem.	Acts 9:28
14 and the evil spirits **came out** of them. (RSV)	19:12
14 and that he himself would **depart** shortly thither.	25:4
3 Let no corrupt communication **proceed**	Eph 4:29
10 out of his mouth went a sharp twoedged sword:	Rev 1:16
2 And out of the throne **proceeded** lightnings	4:5
1 and out of their mouths **issued** fire and smoke	9:17
5 the brimstone, which **issued** out of their mouths.	9:18
1 will hurt them, fire **proceedeth out** of their mouth,	11:5
14 which **go forth** unto the kings of the earth	16:14
1 which **go forth** unto the kings of the earth	16:14
1 And out of his mouth **goeth** a sharp sword,	19:15
18 which sword **proceeded** out of his mouth:	19:21
4 **proceeding** out of the throne of God	22:1

This verb is a compound of *ek* (1523), "out," and *poreuomai* (4057), "go." Used over 30 times in the New Testament, it indicates a departure to or from depending on the perspective of the observer. John's use of *ekporeuō* in the fourth Gospel (15:26) describes the Spirit who "proceedeth from the Father." Although it is not John's intent here to discuss the relationship of the members of the Trinity, the use of *ek tou patros* with this verb, which could have otherwise simply implied an "emanation from a divine source or a procession on a mission," makes this appropriate to denote the eternal procession of the Spirit from the Father (Harris, *Colin Brown*, 3:1203). Luke used *ekporeuō* of Festus who was going to "depart" to Caesarea (Acts 25:4).

In the Gospel of Luke (4:37) the verb denotes "spread." Luke used the casting out of the unclean spirit as a point of departure for his account of Jesus' ministry to the outcasts of society. This first miracle resulted in His "fame" (*ēchos* [2256]) or news about Him being "spread" throughout the region.

In Revelation 1:16 *ekporeuō* appears in the account of John's vision of the Son of Man. According to Johnson the metaphor of the sword that "proceeds" from the mouth of the Son of Man is important for three reasons: (1) John refers to it as a characteristic of Christ several times (1:16; 2:12,16; 19:15,21); (2) he used a rare term for *sword* found only in Luke 2:35 in the rest of the New Testament; and (3) there is no scriptural parallel of this with the exception of Isaiah 11:4 (*Expositor's Bible Commentary*, 12:428). That it proceeds from His mouth and is not held in the hand may be a picture of judgment; a judgment that comes from His faithful witness to the saving purposes of God (ibid.).

STRONG 1607, BAUER 244 (see "ekporeuomai"), MOULTON-MILLIGAN 198 (see "ekporeuomai"), KITTEL 6:578-79 (see "ekporeuomai"), LIDDELL-SCOTT 518, COLIN BROWN 3:1202-3 (see "ekporeuomai").

1595. ἐκπορνεύω ekporneuō verb

Indulge in sexual immorality, give oneself to fornication.
CROSS-REFERENCE:
  πορνεύω porneuō (4062)

זָנָה zānâh (2265), Qal: prostitute oneself (Ex 34:15, Jgs 2:17, Jer 3:1); hiphil: practice prostitution (Lv 19:29, 2 Chr 21:13, Hos 5:3).

תַּזְנוּת taznûth (8789), Practice prostitution (Ez 16:20,26).

1. ἐκπορνεύσασαι ekporneusasai
nom pl fem part aor act

1 **giving themselves over to fornication,**	Jude 1:7

This is an intensified form of the verb *porneuō* (4062), "to commit fornication," and points to excessive indulgence in and giving oneself completely to immorality. It is used only once in the New Testament at Jude 7.

STRONG 1608, BAUER 244, KITTEL 6:579-95, LIDDELL-SCOTT 518.

1596. ἐκπτύω ekptuō verb

Despise, disdain, reject, loathe.
CROSS-REFERENCE:
  πτύω ptuō (4287)

1. ἐξεπτύσατε exeptusate 2pl indic aor act

1 ye **despised** not, nor rejected; but received me	Gal 4:14

This term is composed of the verb *ptuō* (4287), "to spit" (note the spitting sound, "puhtoo"), and the preposition *ek* (1523), "out." *Ekptuō* is found only in Galatians 4:14 and has been interpreted as a pagan gesture to ward off or deflect sickness (Schlier, "ekptuō," *Kittel*, 2:448f.). Note that Paul was sick (4:13). But its more probable sense is "to despise or disdain," especially in light of Paul's use of it as the second of a verb pair where the first verb means "to set at naught" or "to consider as nothing" (see *exoutheneō* [1832]).

STRONG 1609, BAUER 244, MOULTON-MILLIGAN 198, KITTEL 2:448-49, LIDDELL-SCOTT 518, COLIN BROWN 2:559.

1597. ἐκριζόω ekrizoō verb
Uproot, pull up by the roots, pluck.
CROSS-REFERENCE:
ῥιζόω rhizoō (4348)

גָּרַשׁ gārash (1691), Banish; piel: drive out (Zep 2:4—Codex Alexandrinus only).
נָתַשׁ nāthash (5612), Uproot, tear up (Jer 1:10).
עָקַר ʿāqar (6369), Niphal: be uprooted (Zep 2:4).
שֹׁרֶשׁ shōresh (8659), Root (Jgs 5:14).

1. ἐκριζώσητε ekrizōsēte 2pl subj aor act
2. ἐκριζώθητι ekrizōthēti 2sing impr aor pass
3. ἐκριζωθέντα ekrizōthenta
    nom/acc pl neu part aor pass
4. ἐκριζωθήσεται ekrizōthēsetai 3sing indic fut pass

1 up the tares, ye root up also the wheat with them...Matt 13:29
4 Father hath not planted, shall be rooted up............ 15:13
2 Be thou plucked up by the root,......................... Luke 17:6
3 without fruit, twice dead, plucked up by the roots;...Jude 1:12

This verb is a compound of two words: *rhizoō* (4348), "to cause to take root," and *ek* (1523), "out of." In the New Testament its uses include: (1) to pull up weeds (and with them the wheat) by the roots (Matthew 13:29); (2) to pull up every plant which the Father has not planted (Matthew 15:13); (3) to describe the unfruitful fruit trees which, having died, have been uprooted (Jude 12); and (4) to describe the power of faith to uproot and remove obstacles (Luke 17:6). As these examples show, the New Testament uses *ekrizoō* not merely in the literal sense of physical removal but in the sense of a spiritual removal, frequently exhibited by judgment and destruction.

STRONG 1610, BAUER 244-45, MOULTON-MILLIGAN 198, KITTEL 6:991, LIDDELL-SCOTT 519, COLIN BROWN 3:865-66,869.

1598. ἔκστασις ekstasis noun
Amazement, trance, ecstasy, displacement of the mind.
CROSS-REFERENCE:
ἐξίστημι existēmi (1822)

דִּבָּה dibbāh (1730), Evil report (Nm 13:32 [13:33]).
זַוְעָה zawʿāh (2196III Dread, horror (2 Chr 29:8).
חָפַז chāphaz (2753), Dismay, alarm (Pss 31:22 [30:22], 116:11 [115:2]).
חֲרָדָה chărādhāh (2832), Trembling, panic (Gn 27:33, 1 Sm 14:15, Ez 26:16).
מְהוּמָה mᵉhûmāh (4245), Turmoil, panic (2 Chr 15:5, Zec 14:13).
פַּחַד pachadh (6586), Fear, terror (1 Sm 11:7, 2 Chr 17:10, 20:29).
רָדָה rādhâh (7575), Rule (Ps 68:27 [67:27]).
שַׂעַר saʿar (7995), Afraid, shuddering (Ez 27:35, 32:10).
שַׁמָּה shammāh (8439), A horrible thing (Jer 5:30).
תִּמָּהוֹן timmāhôn (8871), Madness, confusion (Dt 28:28, Zec 12:4).
תַּרְדֵּמָה tardēmāh (8976), Deep sleep (Gn 2:21, 15:12).

1. ἔκστασις ekstasis nom sing fem
2. ἐκστάσεως ekstaseōs gen sing fem
3. ἐκστάσει ekstasei dat sing fem

3 they were astonished with a great astonishment......Mark 5:42
1 for they trembled and were amazed:................... 16:8
1 And they were all amazed, and they glorified God,..Luke 5:26
2 and they were filled with wonder and amazement....Acts 3:10
1 but while they made ready, he fell into a trance,...... 10:10
3 and in a trance I saw a vision,....................... 11:5
3 while I prayed in the temple, I was in a trance;...... 22:17

Classical Greek and Septuagint Usage
Classical Greek demonstrates a rather diverse usage of this term. Both Hippocrates and Aristotle used the term to indicate "diaplacement or change," as well as the "distraction of the mind due to fear, astonishment, anger, etc." (*Liddell-Scott*). This second use of *ekstasis* emphasizes the change of a state of mind, that is, from normal or peaceful to fear or amazement. The Septuagint translates *ekstasis* as "fear" or "anxiety." However, it also includes the translation of "deep sleep" (Genesis 2:21; 15:12).

New Testament Usage
The New Testament translates *ektasis* as "astonished, amazed" and "trance." This usage can include the element of fear also, as found in Luke 5:26. This may be described as a "fearful astonishment," and the writers of the New Testament seem to have employed the term in just this manner (Mark 5:42; 16:8; Acts 3:10). The translation of "trance," Acts 10:10; 11:5; 22:17, describes a supra-normal event in which the person is taken from the normal state of mind and placed in an awareness of God's making, but without losing consciousness.

STRONG 1611, BAUER 245, MOULTON-MILLIGAN 198, KITTEL 2:449-58, LIDDELL-SCOTT 520, COLIN BROWN 1:527-28.

1599. ἐκστρέφω ekstrephō verb
Turn aside, pervert, change for the worse.
CROSS-REFERENCE:
στρέφω strephō (4613)

הָפַךְ hāphakh (2089), Turn (Am 6:12 [6:13]).

הֶפֶךְ hēphekh (2090), Opposite, contrary (Ez 16:34—Codex Alexandrinus only).

פָּרַק pāraq (6811), Piel: tearing, tear off (Zec 11:16).

צוּד tsûdh (6942), Pilpel: hunt, prey (Ez 13:20).

תַּהְפֻּכָה tahpukhāh (8749), Perverseness (Dt 32:20).

1. ἐξέστραπται exestraptai 3sing indic perf mid

1 Knowing that he that is such is subverted,.......... Tit 3:11

This verb is a compound of *strephō* (4613), "to turn around" or "to change," and *ek* (1523), "out of." It is the opposite of conversion ("to turn to") and denotes "to turn away from." It is used only once in the New Testament at Titus 3:11 where the word denotes: "knowing that such a person *has been turned out* and is sinning" (writer's translation) with the figurative meaning of perversion or crookedness. Such a person is in a state of being completely disoriented from the truth.

STRONG 1612, BAUER 245, LIDDELL-SCOTT 520.

1600. ἐκταράσσω ektarassō verb
Agitate, throw into confusion, disturb completely.
CROSS-REFERENCE:
ταράσσω tarassō (4866)

בָּעַת bāʿath (1227), Piel: made afraid, overwhelm (Ps 18:4 [17:4]).

צָמַת tsāmath (7059), Pilpel: cut off, destroy (Ps 88:16 [87:16]).

1. ἐκταράσσουσιν ektarassousin 3pl indic pres act

1 These men, ... do exceedingly trouble our city,...... Acts 16:20

This verb is a compound of *tarassō* (4866), "to shake or stir up," therefore, "to create disorder or confusion," and *ek* (1523), "out of," which in this case serves to intensify the root. It occurs in the New Testament only at Acts 16:20 in the accusation made against Paul and Silas: "These men ... are throwing our city into an uproar" (NIV).

STRONG 1613, BAUER 245, MOULTON-MILLIGAN 198, LIDDELL-SCOTT 521.

1601. ἐκτείνω ekteinō verb
Stretch out, extend, cast out.

COGNATES:
ἐκτένεια ekteneia (1603)
ἐκτενής ektenēs (1604)
ἐκτενῶς ektenōs (1605)
ἐπεκτείνομαι epekteinomai (1886)
ὑπερεκτείνω huperekteinō (5077)
SYNONYM:
ἐκπετάννυμι ekpetannumi (1587)

הָיָה hāyâh (2030), Be (Ez 13:9).

זָמַם zāmam (2246), Thought, plan (Prv 30:32 [24:67]).

זָרָה zārâh (2306), Scatter; pual: spread (Prv 1:17).

יָשַׁט yāshaṭ (3570), Hiphil: hold out, extend (Est 4:11, 8:4).

יָשָׁר yāshār (3596), Straight, stretched (Ez 1:23).

מָשַׁךְ māshakh (5082), Stretch, join (Hos 7:5).

נָטָה nāṭâh (5371), Qal: stretch out (Ex 7:19, Prv 1:24, Jer 10:12); niphal: be stretched out (Zec 1:16); hiphil: extend, stretch out (Jer 6:12).

נָטַשׁ nāṭash (5389), Leave, throw (Ez 32:4).

נָעַר nāʿar (5469), Shake (Neh 5:13—only some Sinaiticus texts).

נָשָׂא nāsâʾ (5558), Uplift (hand), swear (Ex 6:8, Nm 14:30, Neh 9:15).

פָּרַד pāradh (6754), Spread out, stretched (Ez 1:11).

פָּרַשׂ pāras (6816), Qal: spread out, stretch (Ex 25:20, Hos 5:1); piel: spread out (Is 1:15).

פָּשַׁט pāshaṭ (6838), Rush (Jgs 9:44, 20:37).

קָרַם qāram (7449), Cover with (Ez 37:6).

רוּם rûm (7597), Be high; hiphil: raise, lift up (Gn 14:22).

שָׁלַח shālach (8365), Qal: reach out, send (Ex 4:4, Jgs 5:26, Ez 2:9); piel: stretch out, send (Jb 30:12, Ps 80:11 [79:11], Ez 17:6); pual: be sent (Jgs 5:15—Codex Alexandrinus only).

שְׁלַח sheʿlach (A8366), Lift (a hand) (Ezr 6:12—Aramaic).

שָׁלַךְ shālakh (8390), Hiphil: cast, toss (Ps 60:8 [59:8]).

תּוּר tûr (8780), Go about, turn about; hiphil: searching (2 Sm 22:33—Codex Alexandrinus only).

1. ἐκτείνειν ekteinein inf pres act
2. ἐξέτεινεν exeteinen 3sing indic aor act
3. ἐξετείνατε exeteinate 2pl indic aor act
4. ἔκτεινον ekteinon 2sing impr aor act
5. ἐκτείνας ekteinas nom sing masc part aor act
6. ἐκτενεῖς ekteneis 2sing indic fut act

5 And Jesus put forth his hand, and touched him,..... Matt 8:3
4 Then saith he to the man, Stretch forth thine hand..... 12:13
2 And he stretched it forth; ... it was restored whole,..... 12:13
5 he stretched forth his hand toward his disciples,....... 12:49
5 And immediately Jesus stretched forth his hand,...... 14:31
5 which were with Jesus stretched out his hand,....... 26:51
5 moved with compassion, put forth his hand,........ Mark 1:41
4 he saith unto the man, Stretch forth thine hand........ 3:5
2 Stretch forth thine hand. And he stretched it out:..... 3:5
5 And he put forth his hand, and touched him,...... Luke 5:13
4 he said unto the man, Stretch forth thy hand....... 6:10
3 ye stretched forth no hands against me:............. 22:53
6 thou shalt stretch forth thy hands,................ John 21:18

1 By stretching forth thine hand to heal;	Acts 4:30
5 Then Paul stretched forth the hand,	26:1
1 they would have cast anchors out of the foreship,	27:30

Classical Greek
Classical Greek uses the word in basically the same manner as the New Testament. It is used of the hand or another part of the body extended in order to accomplish some activity. *Ekteinō* is also used to describe the stretching out of the body in sleep. It is not limited only to physical things, for the reference is made to the stretching of the will in determination. The term is employed to describe an action that is peaceful, passive (Matthew 8:3; 12:49), or in anger (Matthew 26:51).

Septuagint Usage
The Septuagint uses *ekteinō* in referring to the Lord stretching out His hand (Jeremiah 1:9) or a man stretching out or laying his hand on another (Genesis 37:22).

New Testament Usage
Ekteinō is translated in the New Testament as "to stretch out" (Matthew 12:13) or "put forth" (Mark 1:41). Its usage is exclusively in reference to stretching forth the hands except for the occasion of Acts 27:30 where one finds a nautical use of the word. There the term is employed to describe the "casting out" of a ship's anchor.

Strong 1614, Bauer 245, Moulton-Milligan 198, Kittel 2:460-63, Liddell-Scott 521.

1602. ἐκτελέω ekteleō verb
Finish, to complete.
Cognate:
τελέω teleō (4903)
Synonyms:
ἀναπληρόω anaplēroō (376)
ἀνταναπληρόω antanaplēroō (463)
ἀποτελέω apoteleō (652)
διανύω dianuō (1268)
ἐκπληρόω ekplēroō (1590)
ἐξαρτίζω exartizō (1806)
ἐπιτελέω epiteleō (1989)
ἐργάζομαι ergazomai (2021)
καταρτίζω katartizō (2645)
κατεργάζομαι katergazomai (2686)
πληρόω plēroō (3997)
ποιέω poieō (4020)
πράσσω prassō (4097)
συντελέω sunteleō (4783)
τελειόω teleioō (4896)
τελέω teleō (4903)

כָּלָה kālāh (3735), Make an end, finish (Dt 32:45).
נָתַשׁ nāthash (5612), Uproot (1 Kgs 14:15—Codex Alexandrinus only).

1. ἐκτελέσαι ektelesai inf aor act

1 laid the foundation, and is not able to finish it,	Luke 14:29
1 man began to build, and was not able to finish.	14:30

This verb is a compound of *teleō* (4903), "to finish" or "to complete," and *ek* (1523), the intensifying "out of" or "from." In the New Testament it appears only in two consecutive verses in Luke 14:29,30 where it is used to express the fact that the builder of the tower was not able to see it through to "completion" because of poor planning.

Strong 1615, Bauer 245, Moulton-Milligan 198, Liddell-Scott 521.

1603. ἐκτένεια ekteneia noun
Perseverance, earnestness, intentness.
Cross-Reference:
ἐκτείνω ekteinō (1601)

1. ἐκτενείᾳ ekteneia dat sing fem

1 instantly serving God day and night, hope to come. Acts 26:7

This noun is a compound form of *teinō*, "to stretch," and the intensifying preposition *ek* (1523), "out of" or "out from." Its verb form in the New Testament is used only to denote "to stretch out the hand," frequently implying earnestness in prayer (Acts 12:5) except in Acts 27:30 where it means "to let out the anchor." The noun is used only in the New Testament at Acts 26:6 where Paul explained to King Agrippa that he was being judged "for the hope of the promise" which God had made to Israel (to send the Messiah). He continued, saying that they still hope to attain that promise by "persistent" worship of God night and day with outstretched hands (a symbol of their earnestness).

Strong 1616, Bauer 245, Moulton-Milligan 198, Kittel 2:464, Liddell-Scott 521.

1604. ἐκτενής ektenēs adj
Eager, earnest, constant, intense, fervent.
Cross-Reference:
ἐκτείνω ekteinō (1601)

1. ἐκτενής ektenēs nom sing fem
2. ἐκτενῆ ektenē acc sing fem

1 but prayer was made without ceasing of the church	Acts 12:5
2 have fervent charity among yourselves:	1 Pt 4:8

Ektenēs, "extended" or "strained," is used in Acts 12:5 as an adverb to describe the manner in which the church prayed for Peter in prison.

ἐκτενῶς 1605

In 1 Peter 4:8 *ektenēs* is used as an adjective describing the depth of the love to be shared among believers. There it may be translated "constant" though still with the thought of its intensity. This admonition directs Christians to not merely show fervent love to one another, but in light of the end (*to telos*) they should make certain their love endures against self-seeking. Only in this can they hope to rid themselves of the sin which divides the community of faith (Fuchs, "ektenēs," *Kittel*, 2;463).

STRONG 1618, BAUER 245, MOULTON-MILLIGAN 198, KITTEL 2:463-64, LIDDELL-SCOTT 521.

1605. ἐκτενῶς ektenōs adv

Eagerly, fervently, constantly, earnestly.
CROSS-REFERENCE:
ἐκτείνω ekteinō (1601)

1. ἐκτενῶς ektenōs
2. ἐκτενέστερον ektenesteron comp

2 And being in an agony he prayed **more earnestly**:.. Luke 22:44
1 but **earnest** prayer for him was made (RSV)........Acts 12:5
1 love one another with a pure heart **fervently**:........1 Pt 1:22

Ektenōs is used in 1 Peter 1:22 in reference to the love among believers. This love should be a deep, earnest love which comes from a pure heart. Some editions also read *ektenōs* instead of *ektenēs* (1604) in Acts 12:5. In the Septuagint the term is used of prayer (Jonah 3:8).

A comparative form, *ektenesteron*, which comes from the adverb, occurs in Luke 22:44 and refers to the way Jesus prayed in the Garden of Gethsemane before His death. By using this word Luke showed the intensity of Jesus' prayer. Jesus prayed "more earnestly" or "more fervently."

STRONG 1619, BAUER 245, MOULTON-MILLIGAN 199, LIDDELL-SCOTT 521, COLIN BROWN 2:868.

1606. ἐκτίθημι ektithēmi verb

Expose, put out, expound.
CROSS-REFERENCE:
τίθημι tithēmi (4935)

גָּלָה gālâh (1580), Open (someone's ear), speak (Jb 36:15)

נָגַע nāgha‘ (5236), Hiphil: reach, came to (Est 4:3, 8:17).

נָטָה nāṭâh (5371), Niphal: stretch out (Zec 1:16—Codex Alexandrinus only).

נָתַן nāthan (5598), Give; niphal: given, published (Est 3:14, 4:8).

1. ἐξέθεντο exethento 3pl indic aor mid
2. ἐκτεθέντα ektethenta acc sing masc part aor pass
3. ἐξετίθετο exetitheto 3sing indic imperf mid
4. ἐκτεθέντος ektethentos gen sing masc part aor pass

2 And when he **was cast out**,.........................Acts 7:21
4 And when he **was exposed**, (RSV)....................7:21
3 and **expounded** it by order unto them, saying,........11:4
1 and **expounded** ... the way of God more perfectly......18:26
3 he **expounded** and testified the kingdom of God,.......28:23

Classical Greek

This is a compound word formed by the proposition *ek* (1523), "out, out from," and *tithēmi* (4935), "to place." In classical Greek *ektithēmi* denotes "to expose" or "abandon," thus "to expose someone or something, abandoning them." This exposure is seen as something that is essentially negative. It is also used of the act of exhibiting or posting something up, and the offering of a prize.

New Testament Usage

The New Testament employs the literal usage in Acts 7:21 in reference to the fact that Moses was "cast out" ("abandoned, exposed"). However, classical Greek, the Apocrypha, Josephus, and the New Testament also use *ektithēmi* metaphorically as "explain" or "expound." Consequently, when used in this manner the exposure is positive in that it is an explanation of something. As in Acts 11:4; 18:26; 28:23, *ektithēmi* is employed in the context of explaining what happened (11:4) and in expounding on the things of God and the Scriptures (18:26; 28:23).

STRONG 1620, BAUER 245, MOULTON-MILLIGAN 199, LIDDELL-SCOTT 522.

1607. ἐκτινάσσω ektinassō verb

Shake off, shake out.
COGNATE:
ἀποτινάσσω apotinassō (654)
SYNONYM:
ἀποτινάσσω apotinassō (654)

בָּקַק bāqaq (1265), Lay waste, emptied (Na 2:2).

חָבַט chāvaṭ (2338), Beat, beat out; niphal: be beaten out (Is 28:27).

נָעַר nā‘ar (5469), Qal: shake (Neh 5:13); niphal: shake free (Jgs 16:20, Jb 38:13, Ps 109:23 [108:23]); piel: shake off, shake out (Ex 14:27, Neh 5:13, Ps 136:15 [135:15]); hithpael: shake off (Is 52:2).

נָפַץ nāphats (5492), Qal: break (Jgs 7:19); piel: bring down, haul down (1 Kgs 5:9).

נָתַר nāthar (5609), Be free; hiphil: make perfect (2 Sm 22:33).

1. **ἐκτινάξατε** ektinaxate 2pl impr aor act
2. **ἐκτιναξάμενος** ektinaxamenos
   nom sing masc part aor mid
3. **ἐκτιναξάμενοι** ektinaxamenoi
   nom pl masc part aor mid

1	that house or city, **shake off** the dust of your feet...	Matt 10:14
1	**shake off** the dust under your feet for a testimony..	Mark 6:11
3	they **shook off** the dust of their feet against them,..	Acts 13:51
2	he **shook** his raiment, and said unto them,............	18:6

Classical Greek
In classical Greek *ektinassō* denotes "to shake out" (as in cleaning garments). It often carries the idea of force or violence, "to expel" or "cast out." It may carry the ideas of creating disturbance, thoroughly searching out, or upsetting. The papyri also confirm the rendering "to shake out."

Septuagint Usage
In the Septuagint *ektinassō* means "to shake off," as dust or leaves, or just "to shake" oneself (as Samson in Judges 16:20). It also often means "to cast out, drive forth, displace, discomfit" (Nehemiah 5:13; Job 38:13; etc.).

New Testament Usage
In the New Testament *ektinassō* means "to shake out or shake off." All four instances in the New Testament reflect not a mere "shaking off" but a symbolic action. Jesus told the disciples to "shake off the dust of your feet" as a testimony against those who rejected their message (Matthew 10:14; Mark 6:11). Paul and Barnabas did that very thing on one occasion (Acts 13:51), and Paul shook out his clothes on another (Acts 18:6). The act apparently denoted a breaking off of further associations.

STRONG 1621, BAUER 245-46, MOULTON-MILLIGAN 199, LIDDELL-SCOTT 522, COLIN BROWN 3:560.

1608. ἕκτος hektos num
Sixth.

1. **ἕκτῳ** hektō ord dat sing masc/neu
2. **ἕκτος** hektos ord nom sing masc
3. **ἕκτη** hektē ord nom sing fem
4. **ἕκτης** hektēs ord gen sing fem
5. **ἕκτην** hektēn ord acc sing fem

5	Again he went out about the **sixth** and ninth hour,	Matt 20:5
4	Now from the **sixth** hour there was darkness..........	27:45
4	And when the **sixth** hour was come,..............	Mark 15:33
1	And in the **sixth** month the angel Gabriel was sent..	Luke 1:26
2	and this is the **sixth** month with her,.................	1:36
3	And it was about the **sixth** hour,.....................	23:44
3	and it was about the **sixth** hour...................	John 4:6
3	about the **sixth** hour: and he saith unto the Jews,.....	19:14
5	upon the housetop to pray about the **sixth** hour:...	Acts 10:9
5	And I beheld when he had opened the **sixth** seal,....	Rev 6:12
2	And the **sixth** angel sounded, and I heard a voice......	9:13

1	Saying to the **sixth** angel which had the trumpet,.....	Rev 9:14
2	And the **sixth** angel poured out his vial...............	16:12
2	The fifth, sardonyx; the **sixth**, sardius;................	21:20

Hektos is used in reference to the sixth month (Luke 1:26,36); the sixth hour or noon (Matthew 20:5; 27:45; Mark 15:33; Luke 23:44; John 4:6; 19:14); the sixth angel (Revelation 9:13,14; 16:12); the sixth seal of a roll (Revelation 6:12); and the sixth precious stone, sardius, in the foundations of the Holy City, the New Jerusalem (Revelation 21:20).

STRONG 1623, BAUER 246, MOULTON-MILLIGAN 199, LIDDELL-SCOTT 523.

1609. ἐκτός ektos adv
Outside, except, without, besides.

1. **ἐκτός** ektos

1	that the **outside** of them may be clean also.........	Matt 23:26
1	saying none **other** things than those which..........	Acts 26:22
1	Every sin that a man doeth is **without** the body;.....	1 Co 6:18
1	he that speaketh with tongues, **except** he interpret,.....	14:5
1	**unless** ye have believed in vain.......................	15:2
1	it is manifest that he is **excepted**,.....................	15:27
1	or whether **out of** the body, I cannot tell:..........	2 Co 12:2
1	whether in the body, or **out of** the body,..............	12:3
1	an accusation, **but** before two or three witnesses.....	1 Tm 5:19

In Matthew 23:26 *ektos* is used with the article, making its translation "the outside" in reference to the outside of a cup. In 1 Corinthians 6:18 and 2 Corinthians 12:2 it refers to what is "outside" the body. In most other passages *ektos* is used as an adverb meaning "except, unless, but" or "other than" (Acts 26:22; 1 Corinthians 14:5; 15:2,27; 1 Timothy 5:19).

STRONG 1622, BAUER 246, MOULTON-MILLIGAN 199, LIDDELL-SCOTT 523.

1610. ἐκτρέπω ektrepō verb
Turn, turn from, avoid, forsake.

SYNONYMS:
ἀνακάμπτω anakamptō (342)
ἀποστρέφω apostrephō (648)
ἀποφεύγω apopheugō (662)
ἐκκλίνω ekklinō (1565)
ἐκφεύγω ekpheugō (1614)
ἐπιστρέφω epistrephō (1978)
περιίστημι periistēmi (3889)
στέλλομαι stellomai (4575)
στρέφω strephō (4613)
ὑποστρέφω hupostrephō (5128)
φεύγω pheugō (5180)

הָפַךְ hāphakh (2089), Turn, makes (Am 5:8).

1. **ἐκτρεπόμενος** ektrepomenos
   nom sing masc part pres mid

ἐκτρέφω 1611

2. ἐξετράπησαν exetrapēsan 3pl indic aor pass
3. ἐκτραπῇ ektrapē 3sing subj aor pass
4. ἐκτραπήσονται ektrapēsontai 3pl indic fut pass

2 have **turned aside** unto vain jangling;	1 Tm 1:6
2 For some are already **turned aside** after Satan.	5:15
1 **avoiding** profane and vain babblings,	6:20
4 from the truth, and shall be **turned** unto fables.	2 Tm 4:4
3 lest that which is lame be **turned out of the way;**	Heb 12:13

Classical Greek and Septuagint Usage
In classical Greek *ektrepō*, "to turn off," denotes a variety of things. When used transitively it can denote "to turn (someone else) aside, off the road" or "to prevent." When used intransitively it refers to the act of "turning (oneself) off the course, turn away from, avoid, get out of another's way, turn and flee, turn (itself) inside out." It is also a medical term which indicates "to be put out of joint." In the Septuagint *ektrepō* is used only in Amos 5:8, "to turn darkness into morning."

New Testament Usage
Ektrepō is used five times in the New Testament. The two primary meanings are "to turn aside," i.e., out of the right way or to something else (1 Timothy 1:6; 5:15; 2 Timothy 4:4), and "to turn away from" in the sense of avoiding (1 Timothy 6:20). The word occurs in one difficult passage, Hebrews 12:13, where it may mean either "be put out of joint, dislocated," "turn aside from the way," or "be avoided."

STRONG 1624, BAUER 246, MOULTON-MILLIGAN 199, LIDDELL-SCOTT 523, COLIN BROWN 3:902-3.

1611. ἐκτρέφω ektrephō verb
Feed, nourish, bring up.
COGNATE:
 τρέφω trephō (4982)
SYNONYMS:
 ἀνατρέφω anatrephō (395)
 παιδεύω paideuō (3674)
 τρέφω trephō (4982)

גָּדַל gādhal (1461), Qal: grow up, brought up (1 Kgs 12:8, 2 Chr 10:10, Jb 31:18); piel: bring up, come (2 Kgs 10:6, Hos 9:12, Jon 4:10).

גָּמַל gāmal (1621), Wean, brought up (1 Kgs 11:20).

חָיָה chāyâh (2513), Qal: survive, live (Zec 10:9); piel: nourish, brought up (2 Sm 12:3); hiphil: preserve, save (Gn 45:7).

כּוּל kûl (3677), Pilpel: provide, nourish (Gn 45:11).

כָּרַע kāraʿ (3895), Bow, crouch down (Jb 39:3).

נָהַל nāhal (5273), Piel: lead, bring through (Gn 47:17, Ps 23:2 [22:2]).

1. ἐκτρέφει ektrephei 3sing indic pres act

2. ἐκτρέφετε ektrephete 2pl impr pres act
3. ἐκτρέφωσιν ektrephōsin 3pl subj pres act

1 but **nourisheth** and **cherisheth** it,	Eph 5:29
2 but **bring** them **up** in the nurture and admonition	6:4

Classical Greek
In classical Greek *ektrephō* refers to "bring up from childhood, rear"; it can be used in this sense of plants, animals, or human children. It often carries the added idea (in the middle voice) "to rear for oneself." *Ektrephō* can denote "to nourish a pregnancy and bring to birth." The papyri provide an instance where it refers to the "nursing of an infant."

Septuagint Usage
In the Septuagint *ektrephō* is used some 19 times with a semantic range which includes from providing simple physical nourishment to the rearing of a child (1 Kings 11:20 [LXX 3 Kings 11:20]; Hosea 9:12, etc.) or an animal (2 Samuel 12:3 [LXX 2 Kings 12:3]; Job 39:3) or even a plant (Jonah's gourd, Jonah 4:10). It sometimes refers to "maintain" or "provide for" (Genesis 45:7,11; Job 31:18). The idea of fond, loving provision or rearing is often involved (2 Samuel 12:3 [LXX 2 Kings 12:3]).

New Testament Usage
In the New Testament *ektrephō* is used only twice. In Ephesians 5:29 one nourishes his own flesh (body), where the primary idea of feeding and otherwise providing for is involved. In Ephesians 6:4 the word is used of bringing up children, and the idea of loving provision is at least implicit.

STRONG 1625, BAUER 246, MOULTON-MILLIGAN 199, LIDDELL-SCOTT 523.

1612. ἔκτρωμα ektrōma noun
Untimely birth, miscarriage, abortive birth.

מוּת mûth (4322), Die (Nm 12:12).

נֵפֶל nēphel (5491), Miscarriage (Jb 3:16, Eccl 6:3).

1. ἐκτρώματι ektrōmati dat sing neu

1 seen of me also, as of **one born out of due time**.	1 Co 15:8

Classical Greek and Septuagint Usage
In classical Greek *ektrōma* can refer to a "miscarriage," "abortion," or "untimely birth" (whether the child lives or not). The key features are the abnormality and the unfinished form of such a birth. Apparently the word could be used even of grown men as a term of contempt. It is not a common word in any Greek literature, having been most often used by Greek

physicians. In its rare occurrence in the papyri it denotes "miscarriage." In the Septuagint *ektrōma* occurs only three times, always of one stillborn (Numbers 12:12; Job 3:16; Ecclesiastes 6:3).

New Testament Usage
The interpretation of the only New Testament usage of the word, 1 Corinthians 15:8, is disputed, mainly because the word in other passages never means "a late birth." Some think, therefore, that Paul was looking at his pre-conversion persecution of the Church as one "stillborn," utterly worthless of his calling as an apostle. Others think he was borrowing a term (note that the definite article is used: *tō ektrōmati*) of reproach that his enemies hurled at him as though he were not a genuine apostle but a "miscarriage." More likely Paul's usage was very general, emphasizing the abnormality of his spiritual birth.

The abnormality of Paul's birth into the family of witnesses as used figuratively in 1 Corinthians 15:8 may thus be comparable to the birth of a late child in a family, indicating he had all the privileges as the rest of the children among those who witnessed the resurrected Lord.

STRONG 1626, BAUER 246, MOULTON-MILLIGAN 200, KITTEL 2:465-67, LIDDELL-SCOTT 524, COLIN BROWN 1:182-83.

1613. ἐκφέρω ekpherō verb
Carry or bring out, produce.
CROSS-REFERENCE:
  φέρω pherō (5179)

חָנַט chānaṭ (2690), Ripen (S/S 2:13).

יָצָא yātsā' (3428), Qal: go out (Am 4:3); hiphil: bring forth, stretch out (Lv 4:12, Ezr 1:7, Jer 50:25 [27:25]).

יָרָה yārâh (3498), Cast (Jos 18:6).

לָקַח lāqach (4089), Took (Jos 7:23).

נְפַק nᵉphaq (A5494), Go out; haphel: take out (Ezr 5:14, 6:5).

נָשָׁא nāshâ' (5565), Exact money, practice usury (Neh 5:11).

שָׁלַח shālach (8365), Piel: let go, set free (1 Kgs 20:42 [21:42]).

שָׁלַךְ shālakh (8390), Hiphil: cast (Jos 18:8).

1. ἐκφέρουσα ekpherousa nom sing fem part pres act
2. ἐκφέρειν ekpherein inf pres act
3. ἐξενέγκατε exenenkate 2pl impr aor act
4. ἐξενέγκαντες exenenkantes nom pl masc part aor act
5. ἐξενεγκεῖν exenenkein inf aor act
6. ἐξοίσουσιν exoisousin 3pl indic fut act
7. ἐξήνεγκεν exēnenken 3sing indic aor act

```
7 and led him out of the town; ..................... Mark 8:23
3 Bring forth the best robe, and put it on him; ...... Luke 15:22
4 and carried him out, and buried him. .............. Acts 5:6
6 the feet ... are at the door, and shall carry thee out..... 5:9
4 carrying her forth, buried her by her husband. ......... 5:10
2 that they brought forth the sick into the streets, ......... 5:15
5 and it is certain we can carry nothing out........... 1 Tm 6:7
1 that which beareth thorns and briers is rejected, ..... Heb 6:8
```

Ekpherō is used to refer to "carry out" or "carry forth." The Septuagint uses *ekpherō* over 70 times to translate 11 Hebrew words. Most often it translates a form of *yātsā'*, generally meaning "come out, come forth, go out, go forth." It occurs seven times in the New Testament. Three of the occurrences, in Acts 5:6-10, refer to "carrying out" the bodies of Ananias and Sapphira who died after lying to the Holy Spirit. It is also used in reference to "bringing forth" garments for the prodigal son (Luke 15:22), "bringing forth" the sick to Peter (Acts 5:15), not being able to "carry out" anything from this world after death (1 Timothy 6:7), and the earth "bringing forth" or "producing" thorns (Hebrews 6:8).

STRONG 1627, BAUER 246, MOULTON-MILLIGAN 200, LIDDELL-SCOTT 524-25.

1614. ἐκφεύγω ekpheugō verb
Flee, run away, escape.
COGNATE:
  φεύγω pheugō (5180)
SYNONYMS:
  ἀποφεύγω apopheugō (662)
  διαφεύγω diapheugō (1303)
  ἐκκλίνω ekklinō (1565)
  ἐκτρέπω ektrepō (1610)
  καταφεύγω katapheugō (2672)
  περιΐστημι periistēmi (3889)
  στέλλομαι stellomai (4575)
  φεύγω pheugō (5180)

חָדַל chādhal (2403), Hold, refrain (Prv 10:19).

יָצָא yātsā' (3428), Come out, flourish (Prv 12:13).

מָלַט mālaṭ (4561), Niphal: get to safety (Sir 16:13).

נוּס nûs (5308), Qal: flee (2 Sm 17:2—Codex Alexandrinus only, Am 5:19—Codex Alexandrinus only); hiphil: hide (Jgs 6:11).

שָׂרִיד sārîdh (8032), Survivor (Sir 40:6).

1. ἐξέφυγον exephugon 1/3sing/pl indic aor act
2. ἐκφύγωσιν ekphugōsin 3pl subj aor act
3. ἐκφυγεῖν ekphugein inf aor act

ἐκφοβέω 1615

4. ἐκπεφευγέναι ekpepheugenai inf perf act
5. ἐκφεύξῃ ekpheuxē 2sing indic fut mid
6. ἐκφευξόμεθα ekpheuxometha 1pl indic fut mid

3 that ye may be accounted worthy to escape .... Luke 21:36
4 supposing that the prisoners had been fled.......... Acts 16:27
3 they fled out of that house naked and wounded........ 19:16
5 that thou shalt escape the judgment of God? .... Rom 2:3
1 was I let down by the wall, and escaped his hands. 2 Co 11:33
2 destruction cometh ... and they shall not escape..... 1 Th 5:3
6 How shall we escape, if we neglect ... salvation;..... Heb 2:3
1 For if those did not escape (NASB)................. 12:25

Classical Greek
This compound verb (*ek* [1523], "from," and *pheugō* [5180], "flee, escape, shun") occurs in Greek literature and papyri from the time of Homer on (ca. Seventh century B.C.). A classical usage of "to be acquitted" (see *Liddell-Scott*) is also attested in papyri (see *Moulton-Milligan*), but this definition does not appear in sacred writings.

Septuagint Usage
Of the approximately 20 instances of *ekpheugō* in the Septuagint, only 6 have Hebrew originals behind them; and of these there are 4 Hebrew equivalents and 1 other form. Thus, the Hebrew behind *ekpheugō* is remote and reflects the breadth of the term. Gideon "escaped" and "hid" from the Midianites (Judges 6:11). The sense of "avoid" occurs in Proverbs 12:13, although the idea of "escape from peril" is always latent (verse 12; cf. Amos 5:19; 2 Maccabees 6:26; 7:35; 3 Maccabees 6:29; Sirach 27:20; 40:6).

New Testament Usage
In the New Testament *ekpheugō* can consistently be interpreted as "to escape" (as from a prison, so Acts 16:27; cf. 2 Corinthians 11:33). The imagery of a snare from which believers can pray to escape is a picture of eschatological distress (Luke 21:36; 1 Thessalonians 5:3). Finally, escape from God's judgment is impossible for the unrepentant or for those who "neglect so great salvation" (Romans 2:3; Hebrews 2:3).

STRONG 1628, BAUER 246-47, MOULTON-MILLIGAN 200, LIDDELL-SCOTT 525, COLIN BROWN 1:558.

1615. ἐκφοβέω ekphobeō verb
Frighten, terrify greatly.
CROSS-REFERENCE:
φοβέω phobeō (5236)

חָרַד chāradh (2829), Be afraid (Lv 26:6, Ez 34:28, Mi 4:4).

חִתִּית chittîth (2959), Terror (Ez 32:27).

חָתַת chāthath (2973), Piel: terrify (Jb 7:14).

1. ἐκφοβεῖν ekphobein inf pres act

1 I may not seem as if I would terrify you by letters. 2 Co 10:9

Ekphobeō is used only once in the New Testament. It is a compound of two words; *ek* (1523), "out," and *phobeō* (5236), "fear." Paul used it in his defense of his ministry in 2 Corinthians 10:9. He did not want to frighten away the Corinthians by the letters he had been writing to them.

STRONG 1629, BAUER 247, MOULTON-MILLIGAN 200, LIDDELL-SCOTT 525.

1616. ἔκφοβος ekphobos adj
Greatly terrified.
CROSS-REFERENCE:
φοβέω phobeō (5236)

1. ἔκφοβος ekphobos nom sing masc
2. ἔκφοβοι ekphoboi nom pl masc

2 he wist not what to say; for they were sore afraid... Mark 9:6
2 he wist not what to say; for they were sore afraid...... 9:6
1 that Moses said, I exceedingly fear and quake:...... Heb 12:21

This word, similar to *ekphobeō* (1615), is a compound word comprised of *ek* (1523), which often serves to intensify words in composition, and *phobos* (5238), "fear." In the case of *ekphobos* it is used as an adjective meaning "outright fear" or "intensive fear." In Mark 9:6 it describes the intense fear felt by the disciples at the Transfiguration. In Hebrews 12:21 it is used in the quotation of Moses' words from Deuteronomy 9:19 when he trembled with fear as he looked at the mountain (Sinai).

STRONG 1630, BAUER 247, LIDDELL-SCOTT 525.

1617. ἐκφύω ekphuō verb
Put forth.
CROSS-REFERENCE:
φύω phuō (5289)

1. ἐκφύῃ ekphuē 3sing subj pres act

1 of the fig tree; ... and putteth forth leaves,......... Matt 24:32
1 her branch is yet tender, and putteth forth leaves,..Mark 13:28

Ekphuō is a compound of two words: *ek* (1523), "out," and *phuō* (5289), "produce." It denotes the action of "cause to grow" and is used only in Matthew 24:32 and Mark 13:28 in the New Testament. Both instances refer to the fig trees that produce leaves. In the same way that this growth signified the advent of summer, so also the advent of the coming of the Son of Man is witnessed by the signs of the end of the age.

STRONG 1631, BAUER 247, MOULTON-MILLIGAN 200, LIDDELL-SCOTT 526.

1618. ἐκχέω ekcheō verb

Pour out, shed, spill.

CROSS-REFERENCE:
 ἐκχύνω ekchunō (1619)

זָקַק zāqaq (2298), Piel: refine (Mal 3:3).

זָרַק zāraq (2323), Sprinkle (2 Kgs 16:15).

יָצַק yātsaq (3441), Qal: pour (Ez 24:3—Codex Alexandrinus only); hophal: anoint, poured out (Ps 45:2 [44:2]).

יָצַת yātsath (3448), Niphal: be kindled (2 Kgs 22:13—Codex Vaticanus only).

מָשַׁךְ māshakh (5082), Spread out, drew along (Jgs 20:37).

נָטַשׁ nāṭash (5389), Leave (Hos 12:14).

נָתַךְ nāthakh (5597), Niphal: be poured out (Jer 7:20—Codex Alexandrinus only).

נָתַן nāthan (5598), Place, put (Ex 30:18, Nm 19:17).

פָּשַׁט pāshaṭ (6838), Rush forward (Jgs 9:44—Codex Alexandrinus only).

רִיק rîq (7671), Hiphil: draw out, brand (Ps 35:3 [34:3], Eccl 11:3, Mal 3:10).

שָׁחַת shāchath (8271), Piel: spill (Gn 38:9).

שָׁפַךְ shāphakh (8581), Qal: pour, spill (Lv 4:7, 1 Sm 25:31, Ez 22:3,4,6); niphal: pour out, shed (Dt 19:10, 1 Kgs 13:5); pual: (Nm 35:33, Ps 73:2 [72:2]); hithpael: ebbs, be poured out (Jb 30:16, Lam 2:12).

שֶׁפֶךְ shephekh (8582), Pour out, thrown (Lv 4:12).

1. ἐξέχεεν execheen 3sing indic aor act
2. ἐξέχεαν exechean 3pl indic aor act
3. ἐξεχεῖτο execheito 3sing indic imperf mid
4. ἐκχέαι ekcheai inf aor act
5. ἐκχεῶ ekcheō 1sing indic fut act
6. ἐκχεῖται ekcheitai 3sing indic pres mid
7. ἐκχέατε ekcheate 2pl impr aor act
8. ἐκχέετε ekcheete 2pl impr pres act

6 else the bottles break, and the wine **runneth out**,	Matt 9:17
6 burst the bottles, and the wine **is spilled**,	Mark 2:22
1 and **poured out** the changers' money,	John 2:15
5 I will **pour out** of my Spirit upon all flesh:	Acts 2:17
5 I will **pour out** in those days of my Spirit;	2:18
1 hath **shed forth** this, which ye now see and hear.	2:33
3 when the blood of thy martyr Stephen **was shed**,	22:20
4 Their feet are swift to **shed blood**:	Rom 3:15
1 Which he **shed** on us abundantly through Jesus	Tit 3:6
7 and **pour out** the vials of the wrath of God	Rev 16:1
8 and **pour out** the vials of the wrath of God	16:1
1 first went, and **poured out** his vial upon the earth;	16:2
1 the second angel **poured out** his vial upon the sea;	16:3
1 the third angel **poured out** his vial upon the rivers	16:4
2 they have **shed** the blood of saints and prophets,	16:6
1 the fourth angel **poured out** his vial upon the sun;	Rev 16:8
1 **poured out** his vial upon the seat of the beast;	16:10
1 And the sixth angel **poured out** his vial	16:12
1 the seventh angel **poured out** his vial into the air;	16:17

Classical Greek and Septuagint Usage

In classical Greek *ekcheō* may denote "to pour out, pour away, pour forth" either literally or metaphorically (as in wasting one's money). It is common in the Septuagint (more than 100 times) where the basic idea "pour out" is developed in a variety of ways. Literally it is used of "pouring" liquids or other matter, as when the priests "poured out" the blood at the base of the altar or "poured out" the drink offering before the Lord. Two of the most frequent metaphoric uses are for the "pouring out" of God's wrath and for the "shedding" of blood as the equivalent of murder. One's soul or heart can also be "poured out." Especially significant is that God's Spirit may be "poured forth" (Joel 2:28,29; Zechariah 12:10), as well as other spiritual blessings (Malachi 3:10).

New Testament Usage

In the New Testament *ekcheō* shows similar variety. It is used literally for the "pouring out" or "spilling" of wine from burst wineskins (Matthew 9:17) and for Jesus' "pouring out" or "scattering" the money in the temple (John 2:15). The metaphoric use for the "pouring forth" of the Spirit is used in Acts 2:17,18,33, as fulfillment of Joel 2:28,29 (cf. Titus 3:6). This use probably takes on the connotation of "lavishing" often associated with the "pouring out" of gifts from above. Another use of *ekcheō* is found in Acts 22:20 where it refers to the "shedding" of blood (cf. Romans 3:15). Lastly, it is used for the "pouring forth" of the vials in Revelation 16, a use that reflects the Old Testament idea of the "pouring out" of God's wrath (verses 1-4,6,8,10,12,17).

STRONG 1632, BAUER 247, MOULTON-MILLIGAN 200, KITTEL 2:467-69, LIDDELL-SCOTT 526, COLIN BROWN 2:523-25,853-55.

1619. ἐκχύνω ekchunō verb

Pour out, shed, spill.

COGNATES:
 αἱματεκχυσία haimatekchusia (130)
 ἐκχέω ekcheō (1618)
 ἐπιχέω epicheō (2006)
 καταχέω katacheō (2677)
 πρόσχυσις proschusis (4236)
 συγχέω suncheō (4648)
 σύγχυσις sunchusis (4650)
 ὑπερεκχύννω huperekchunnō (5078)

ἐκχωρέω 1620

1. **ἐκχυνόμενον** ekchunomenon
   nom/acc sing neu part pres mid
2. **ἐξεχύθη** exechuthē 3sing indic aor pass
3. **ἐξεχύθησαν** exechuthēsan 3pl indic aor pass
4. **ἐκκέχυται** ekkechutai 3sing indic perf mid
5. **ἐκχυθήσεται** ekchuthēsetai 3sing indic fut pass
6. **ἐκχυννόμενον** ekchunnomenon
   nom/acc sing neu part pres mid
7. **ἐκκεχυμένον** ekkechumenon
   nom/acc sing masc/neu part perf mid
8. **ἐξεχύννετο** exechunneto 3sing indic imperf mid

1	all the righteous blood **shed** upon the earth,	Matt 23:35
6	all the righteous blood **shed** upon the earth,	23:35
1	which **is shed** for many for the remission of sins.	26:28
6	which **is shed** for many for the remission of sins.	26:28
1	This is my blood ... which **is shed** for many.	Mark 14:24
6	This is my blood ... which **is shed** for many.	14:24
5	the new wine will burst the bottles, and **be spilled**,	Luke 5:37
1	which **was shed** from the foundation of the world,	11:50
6	which **was shed** from the foundation of the world,	11:50
7	which **was shed** from the foundation of the world,	11:50
1	new testament in my blood, which **is shed** for you.	22:20
6	new testament in my blood, which **is shed** for you.	22:20
2	and all his bowels **gushed out**.	Acts 1:18
4	because that on the Gentiles also **was poured out**	10:45
8	when the blood of Stephen ... **was shed**, (RSV)	22:20
4	the love of God **is shed** abroad in our hearts	Rom 5:5
3	**ran greedily** after the error of Balaam for reward,	Jude 1:11

Ekchunō (or *ekchunnō*), the Hellenistic form of the classical *ekcheō* (1618) (*Bauer*), appears 10 times in the New Testament primarily denoting "to pour out." Three of these passages are located in the account of the Last Supper in which Jesus explained to His disciples how His blood would be "poured out" or "shed" for many (Matthew 26:28; Mark 14:24; Luke 22:20). The same word is used to refer to the blood of martyrs being "poured out" (Matthew 23:35; Luke 11:50). *Ekchunō* is also employed in relation to Judas' death (Acts 1:18), to the "pouring out" of the Holy Spirit on the Gentiles (Acts 10:45), to the vastness of the love of God (Romans 5:5), and to godless men running "greedily ... for reward" (Jude 11).

STRONG 1632, BAUER 247, KITTEL 2:467-69, LIDDELL-SCOTT 527, COLIN BROWN 2:853-54.

1620. ἐκχωρέω ekchōreō verb
Go out, go away, depart from.
CROSS-REFERENCE:
χωρέω chōreō (5397)

בָּרַח bārach (1300), Go away, flee (Am 7:12).
צָפַר tsāphar (7129), Depart (Jude 7:3).
רָמַם rāmōm (7715), Be exalted; niphal: get away (Nm 16:45).

1. **ἐκχωρείτωσαν** ekchōreitōsan 3pl impr pres act

1 let them which are in the midst of it **depart out**; ... Luke 21:21

Ekchōreō is used only once in the New Testament (Luke 21:21). In this passage Jesus advised those in the city (Jerusalem, literally "in her midst") to "depart out" because the destruction of Jerusalem was about to occur.

STRONG 1633, BAUER 247, MOULTON-MILLIGAN 200, LIDDELL-SCOTT 527.

1621. ἐκψύχω ekpsuchō verb
Breathe one's last, die, expire.
CROSS-REFERENCE:
ψυχή psuchē (5425)

כָּהָה kāhâh (3663), Piel: become fainthearted (Ez 21:7).
עִיף ʿîph (6105), Be weary, exhausted (Jgs 4:21—Codex Alexandrinus only).

1. **ἐξέψυξεν** exepsuxen 3sing indic aor act

1 fell down, and **gave up the ghost**: Acts 5:5
1 straightway at his feet, and **yielded up the ghost**: 5:10
1 and he was eaten of worms, and **gave up the ghost**. 12:23

This word appears in classical Greek since Hippocrates (Fifth Century B.C.) primarily as a medical term. *Ekpsuchō* is used three times in the New Testament, and in all three instances it refers to the Lord's striking down a person for his or her sin. It is usually translated "to give up the ghost," meaning "to breathe one's last breath, to expire." All of the occurrences are found in Acts; the first two in reference to Ananias and Sapphira (Acts 5:5,10) and the third in reference to Herod (Acts 12:23).

STRONG 1634, BAUER 247, MOULTON-MILLIGAN 200, LIDDELL-SCOTT 527.

1622. ἑκών hekōn adj
Willingly, of one's own free will, voluntarily.

1. **ἑκών** hekōn nom sing masc
2. **ἑκοῦσα** hekousa nom sing fem

2 creature was made subject to vanity, not **willingly**, ... Rom 8:20
1 For if I do this thing **willingly**, I have a reward: 1 Co 9:17

Hekōn denotes "to do something voluntarily or of one's free will." It is used negatively in Romans 8:20 in speaking of the creation and used positively by Paul in 1 Corinthians 9:17 referring to voluntary preaching of the gospel which he did gladly.

STRONG 1635, BAUER 247, MOULTON-MILLIGAN 200, KITTEL 2:469-70, LIDDELL-SCOTT 527.

1623. ἐλαία elaia noun
Olive tree, olive.

CROSS-REFERENCE:
ἔλαιον elaion (1624)

זַיִת zayith (2215), Olive, olive tree (Dt 8:8, Ps 52:8 [51:8], Zec 4:3).

1. ἐλαίας elaias gen/acc sing/pl fem
2. ἐλαίᾳ elaia dat sing fem
3. ἐλαῖαι elaiai nom pl fem
4. ἐλαιῶν elaiōn gen pl fem

4 come to Bethphage, unto the mount of Olives,		Matt 21:1
4 And as he sat upon the mount of Olives,		24:3
4 they went out into the mount of Olives.		26:30
4 Bethphage and Bethany, at the mount of Olives,		Mark 11:1
4 And as he sat upon the mount of Olives,		13:3
4 they went out into the mount of Olives.		14:26
4 even now at the descent of the mount of Olives,		Luke 19:37
4 and went, as he was wont, to the mount of Olives;		22:39
4 Jesus went unto the mount of Olives.		John 8:1
1 partakest of the root and fatness of the olive tree;		Rom 11:17
2 branches, be grafted into their own olive tree?		11:24
1 Can the fig tree, my brethren, bear olive berries?		Jas 3:12
3 the two olive trees, and the two candlesticks		Rev 11:4

Primarily, *elaia* refers to the "olive tree" (Matthew 21:1), though it may also refer to only the "olive" itself as the fruit of that tree (James 3:12). In some ways the olive tree is a symbol for the nation of Israel (Romans 11:17,24). It is a hardy tree, for from its roots new shoots can spring up. It has also been used metaphorically to identify the two witnesses God will raise up to face the beast in Revelation 11:4.

STRONG 1636, BAUER 247, MOULTON-MILLIGAN 201, LIDDELL-SCOTT 527, COLIN BROWN 2:710-11.

1624. ἔλαιον elaion noun

(Olive) oil.

COGNATES:
ἀγριέλαιος agrielaios (64)
ἐλαία elaia (1623)
καλλιέλαιος kallielaios (2536)

יִצְהָר yitshār (3432), Olive oil (2 Chr 31:5, Hg 1:11).

מְשַׁח mᵉshach (A5067), Oil (Ezr 6:9, 7:22—Aramaic).

סוּךְ sûkh (5665), Anointing oil, lotion (Dn 10:3).

שֶׁמֶן shemen (8467), Olive oil (Lv 2:1, 2 Kgs 4:2, Is 1:6).

1. ἐλαίου elaiou gen sing neu
2. ἐλαίῳ elaiō dat sing neu
3. ἔλαιον elaion nom/acc sing neu

3 took their lamps, and took no oil with them:		Matt 25:3
3 the wise took oil in their vessels with their lamps.		25:4
1 Give us of your oil; for our lamps are gone out.		25:8
2 and anointed with oil many that were sick,		Mark 6:13
2 My head with oil thou didst not anoint:		Luke 7:46
3 and bound up his wounds, pouring in oil and wine,		10:34
1 And he said, An hundred measures of oil.		16:6
3 even thy God, hath anointed thee with the oil		Heb 1:9
2 anointing him with oil in the name of the Lord:		Jas 5:14
3 and see thou hurt not the oil and the wine.		Rev 6:6
3 and frankincense, and wine, and oil, and fine flour,		18:13

Classical Greek

Elaion is the common distinction for the *oil* of the olive, the most common form of oil in the ancient Mediterranean. Oil served as a dietary supplement and a cosmetic, as well as a fuel for lamps. Oil was also used for medicinal purposes and was a major trade item. The kinds and quality of olive oil varied greatly. "Pure" oil was made from olives that were pressed cold. The finest oil came from fresh, green olives that were beaten in a mortar (cf. Exodus 29:40).

Septuagint Usage

The centrality of oil in the life of Israel is evident in the Septuagint. Usually the Hebrew *shemen* ([olive] "oil") is translated by *elaion*. Oil was a medicine (e.g., Isaiah 1:6; Jeremiah 8:22); a dietary staple (e.g., Ezekiel 16:13; cf. the formula "grain, wine, and oil," Deuteronomy 7:13; 11:14; 12:17; Joel 2:19); an export item (Ezekiel 27:17); a fuel (Exodus 27:20; Leviticus 24:2); and a vital part of sacrificial and religious, national ceremony (e.g., Leviticus 2:4; 6:15). This latter aspect is vital for understanding the symbolism of oil throughout the Bible (cf. Schlier, "elaion," *Kittel*, 2:470ff.).

The use of oil in the religious life of the Hebrews is recorded very early in the Old Testament (see Genesis 28:18; 35:14). Later when the tabernacle was erected an anointing oil, which was made of fine ingredients including olive oil (see Exodus 30:22-25), was used to dedicate the ark, the candlestick, the altars, and the various utensils and vessels used by the priests. Oil was also an ingredient in many offerings (Exodus 29:23,40). In addition, Aaron and his sons, as well as the priests who followed them, were anointed with this special oil before entering into the priestly service (Exodus 30:25). Kings too were dedicated for their high office by a similar anointing (1 Samuel 10:1 [LXX 1 Kings 10:1]; 1 Kings 19:16 [3 Kings 19:16]).

In the case of priests, kings, and prophets, anointing with oil (see *chrioō* [5383]) was symbolic of authority. This is especially seen in the prophecies related to the Messiah, whose very title means "the Anointed One." According to the Scriptures (see Isaiah 61:1), He would be "anointed" with the Spirit of God himself. He would also have *all* authority.

New Testament Usage

The practical use of oil continued through the New Testament period. Lamps did not burn without oil (Matthew 25:3,4,8). *Elaion* does not seem to be a symbol for the Holy Spirit here, since the point is not the absence of oil but the failure of the foolish virgins to be prepared. We note in verses 10 and 11 that they apparently returned to the wedding *with* oil, but it was too late.

Mark's single usage (6:13) probably reflects an early church practice of anointing with oil to heal the sick. The same practice is found in James 5:14. These are not the same as a medicinal purpose shown in Luke 10:34 (the story of the Good Samaritan).

Hebrews 1:9, a citation of Psalm 45:7, declares that the Son has been anointed (*chriō*) with the "oil of gladness." France detects an allusion to the messianic task of Jesus similar to Luke 4:18, Acts 4:27, and 10:38 ("Oil," *Colin Brown*, 2:710ff.).

The two instances of *elaion* in Revelation (6:6 and 18:13) are symbolic of oil as a staple of the economy of the land and as a source of revenue (cf. the Old Testament refrain, "grain, wine, oil").

STRONG 1637, BAUER 247-48, MOULTON-MILLIGAN 201, KITTEL 2:470-73, LIDDELL-SCOTT 527, COLIN BROWN 2:710-13.

1625. ἐλαιών elaiōn noun
Olive grove, olive orchard.
1. ἐλαιῶνος elaiōnos gen masc
2. ἐλαιῶν elaiōn nom masc sing

4 at the mount called the mount of Olives,.......... Luke 19:29
4 in the mount that is called the mount of Olives........ 21:37
1 unto Jerusalem from the mount called Olivet,....... Acts 1:12

This word is used to describe the ridge which runs north to south, east of the city of Jerusalem. Popularly called the "Mount of Olives," strictly speaking its title should be "the hill called the olive grove." *Elaiōn* appears only three times: twice in relation to the life of Jesus (Luke 19:29; 21:37) and once in reference to His disciples (Acts 1:12).

STRONG 1638, BAUER 248, MOULTON-MILLIGAN 201, LIDDELL-SCOTT 528, COLIN BROWN 2:710-11.

1626. Ἐλαμίτης Elamitēs name
Elamites.
1. Ἐλαμῖται Elamitai nom pl masc

1 Parthians, and Medes, and Elamites,................ Acts 2:9

Resident of Elam; Jews from Elam were in Jerusalem on the Day of Pentecost (Acts 2:9).

1627. ἐλαττονέω elattoneō verb
Have less or too little.
CROSS-REFERENCE:
ἐλαττόω elattoō (1628)

חָסֵר chāsēr (2741), Qal: not wasted, used up (1 Kgs 17:14,16); hiphil: lack, have too little (Ex 16:18).
חָסֵר chāsēr (2742), Have less, have little (Ex 16:17—Codex Alexandrinus only).
מָעַט māʻaṭ (4745), Be few; hiphil: give less (Ex 30:15).

1. ἠλαττόνησεν elattonēsen 3sing indic aor act

1 and he that had gathered little had no lack.......... 2 Co 8:15

Elattoneō occurs only once in the New Testament, in 2 Corinthians 8:15, where Paul used it in a citation of Exodus 16:18. The Israelites gathered manna according to their personal needs. Everyone had enough. Even the one who gathered a little did not "have too little" an amount.

STRONG 1641, BAUER 248, MOULTON-MILLIGAN 201, LIDDELL-SCOTT 529.

1628. ἐλαττόω elattoō verb
Make inferior, diminish, decrease, make less.
COGNATES:
ἐλαττονέω elattoneō (1627)
ἐλάττων elattōn (1629)
ἐλάχιστος elachistos (1633)
ἐλαχιστότερος elachistoteros (1634)

אָצַל ʼātsal (702), Take away; niphal: diminish (Sir 42:21).
חָסֵר chāsēr (2741), Qal: lack, wanting (Ps 34:10 [33:10], Jer 44:18 [51:18]); piel: made lower (Ps 8:5).
חָסֵר chāsēr (2742), Lacking (2 Sm 3:29).
מָעַט māʻaṭ (4745), Be small, decrease; hiphil: give something smaller (Nm 26:54, 33:54).
קָצַר qātsar (7403), Be short, shortened (Sir 30:24).

1. ἠλάττωσας elattōsas 2sing indic aor act
2. ἐλαττοῦσθαι elattousthai inf pres mid
3. ἠλαττωμένον elattōmenon
    acc sing masc part perf mid

2 He must increase, but I must decrease............. John 3:30
1 Thou madest him a little lower than the angels;...... Heb 2:7
3 who was made a little lower than the angels........... 2:9

Classical Greek
In classical Greek *elattoō* (also spelled *elassoō*), with the basic idea of "lessening," can mean "to make less or smaller, diminish, reduce in amount, lower, degrade, cut down, detract

from, reduce the power of." In the passive voice it can mean "to suffer loss, be depreciated, take less than one's due, get the most of it, be inferior, be at a disadvantage" (see *Bauer*). In the papyri, instances occur when it means "to diminish" (one report in comparison with another) or "to incur loss" (in a leasing arrangement).

Septuagint Usage

In the Septuagint *elattoō* is used some 10 times. It can refer to "be in want of" (1 Samuel 21:15 [LXX 1 Kings 21:15], etc.) or "to be brought low" (1 Samuel 2:5 [LXX 1 Kings 2:5], etc.). It can also denote "to be boiled away" (in cooking, Ezekiel 24:10). It often refers to "making something less than another by comparison" (Numbers 26:54; 33:54).

New Testament Usage

In the New Testament *elattoō* occurs three times. Twice (Hebrews 2:7,9) it refers to man's (and Christ, as man) being "made lower"—"of inferior position"—than angels (fulfilling Psalm 8:5). The other usage, John 3:30, reports John the Baptist's statement that while Christ must increase he must decrease (apparently in prominence) by comparison.

STRONG 1642, BAUER 248, MOULTON-MILLIGAN 201, LIDDELL-SCOTT 529.

1629. ἐλάττων elattōn adj

Inferior, less; smaller, younger; under.

CROSS-REFERENCE:
ἐλαττόω elattoō (1628)

אֲרַע ’ara‘ (A796), Inferior (Dn 2:39—Aramaic).
מַחְסוֹר machsôr (4408), Want, poverty (Prv 22:16).
מָעַט mā‘aṭ (4745), Qal: fewer (Lv 25:16); hiphil: less, little (Ex 16:17, Nm 35:8).
מְעַט mᵉ‘aṭ (4746), Lesser, smaller (Nm 26:54, 33:54).
צָעִיר tsā‘îr (7087), Younger (Gn 25:23).
קָטֹן qāṭōn (7275), Lesser (Gn 1:16).

1. ἐλάσσονι elassoni comp dat sing masc
2. ἐλάσσω elassō comp acc sing masc
3. ἔλαττον elatton comp nom/acc sing neu

```
2 men have well drunk, then that which is worse:..... John 2:10
1 The elder shall serve the younger................... Rom 9:12
3 be taken into the number under threescore years....1 Tm 5:9
3 And without all contradiction the less is blessed..... Heb 7:7
```

Elattōn, the Attic form of the word *elassōn* (see Moulton and Howard, *Grammar of the Greek New Testament*, 2:107), has several different meanings. The first of these is found in John 2:10 in reference to the wine of "lesser" quality. In Romans 9:12 it is used to refer to the "younger" of Rebecca's sons. It means "under" in 1 Timothy 5:9 in speaking of widows under the age of 60. In Hebrews 7:7 it refers to the "lesser" of two people.

STRONG 1640, BAUER 248, KITTEL 4:648-59, LIDDELL-SCOTT 529.

1630. ἐλαύνω elaunō verb

Drive, row.

COGNATE:
συνελαύνω sunelaunō (4750)

הָלַם hālam (2056), Strike (Is 41:7).
יָצַק yātsaq (3441), Cast (Ex 25:12).
נָגַשׂ nāghas (5241), Drive, force, oversee (Zec 10:4—Codex Alexandrinus only).
נָהַג nāhagh (5268), Drive (Sir 38:25).
שַׁיִט shayiṭ (8294), Oar (Is 33:21).

1. ἐλαύνειν elaunein inf pres act
2. ἐληλακότες elēlakotes nom pl masc part perf act
3. ἐλαυνόμεναι elaunomenai
   nom pl fem part pres mid
4. ἐλαυνόμενα elaunomena
   nom/acc pl neu part pres mid
5. ἠλαύνετο ēlauneto 3sing indic imperf pass

```
1 And he saw them toiling in rowing;................ Mark 6:48
5 and was driven of the devil into the wilderness..... Luke 8:29
2 So when they had rowed about five and twenty..... John 6:19
4 also the ships, ... and are driven of fierce winds,..... Jas 3:4
3 clouds that are carried with a tempest;............ 2 Pt 2:17
```

Elaunō conveys the idea of "driving, urging," or "impelling." Outside the New Testament it is used in the sense of driving chariots, driving off stolen horses, and persecution (driving to extremes). Sometimes *elaunō* describes the act of striking with a weapon and forging metal.

The use of *elaunō* in the New Testament parallels some of the word's uses in secular literature. The simple idea of "driving," whether by physical means or spiritual, explains its five occurrences. It is applied to ships driven by oars (Mark 6:48, John 6:19) or wind (James 3:4), to men driven by demons (Luke 8:29), and clouds driven by wind (2 Peter 2:17). The implication in each case is the ability of the subject to control the destiny and direction of the object in the sentence.

STRONG 1643, BAUER 248, MOULTON-MILLIGAN 201-2, LIDDELL-SCOTT 529.

1631. ἐλαφρία elaphria noun

Lightness, inconstancy, fickleness.

ἐλαφρός 1632

1. ἐλαφρίᾳ elaphria dat sing fem
1 I therefore was thus minded, did I use **lightness?** .... 2 Co 1:17

Elaphria is used only once in the New Testament, in 2 Corinthians 1:17. When Paul wrote of his intentions to visit Corinth, he did not do so "lightly" (NIV) or "insincerely."

Strong 1644, Bauer 248, Liddell-Scott 530.

1632. ἐλαφρός elaphros adj
Light, easy to bear.

קָטֹן qāṭōn (7275), Small, simple (Ex 18:26).

קַל qal (7316), Swift (Jb 24:18).

קָלָל qālāl (7328), Burnished (Ez 1:7).

1. ἐλαφρόν elaphron nom/acc sing neu
1 For my yoke is easy, and my burden is **light**. ..... Matt 11:30
1 For our **light** affliction, which is but for a moment, .. 2 Co 4:17

In the New Testament this term occurs only in Matthew 11:30 and 2 Corinthians 4:17. In a negative sense it could mean "light-minded, fickle" and "vacillating." Positive meanings include being "light-footed" or "nimble." In other Greek writings it carries the additional idea of "making light" of a matter, something "light or easy to digest" and shallow.

The occurrence in Matthew describes the burden of Christ which is indeed "light" in comparison with the weight sin lays on a person. In 2 Corinthians Paul declared that persecutions and afflictions are "insignificant" compared to the future glory which awaits God's people, and they can be "easy to bear" with the power Christ provides.

Strong 1645, Bauer 248, Moulton-Milligan 202, Liddell-Scott 530.

1633. ἐλάχιστος elachistos adj
Smallest, least, unimportant.
Cross-Reference:
ἐλαττόω elattoō (1628)

צָעִיר tsā'îr (7087), Little, young (Jos 6:26, 1 Sm 9:21, Is 60:22).

קָטֹן qāṭōn (7275), Least, small (2 Kgs 18:24, Prv 30:24 [24:59]).

1. ἐλαχίστων elachistōn sup gen pl masc/fem/neu
2. ἐλάχιστος elachistos sup nom sing masc
3. ἐλαχίστη elachistē sup nom sing fem
4. ἐλαχίστου elachistou sup gen sing neu
5. ἐλαχίστῳ elachistō sup dat sing neu
6. ἐλάχιστον elachiston sup nom/acc sing neu

3 art not the **least** among the princes of Juda: .... Matt 2:6
1 Whosoever therefore shall break one of these **least** 5:19
2 shall be called the **least** in the kingdom of heaven: 5:19
1 done it unto one of the **least** of these my brethren, ... 25:40
1 as ye did it not to one of the **least** of these, ... 25:45
6 If ye then be not able to do that ... which is **least**, Luke 12:26
5 He that is faithful in that which is **least** is faithful 16:10
5 he that is unjust in the **least** is unjust also in much. ... 16:10
5 because thou hast been faithful in **a very little**, ... 19:17
6 **a very small thing** that I should be judged of you, ... 1 Co 4:3
1 are ye unworthy to judge **the smallest matters?** 6:2
2 For I am the **least** of the apostles, ... 15:9
4 yet are they turned about with **a very small** helm, ... Jas 3:4

Classical Greek and Septuagint Usage
Elachistos is the superlative "least." The other forms are *mikros* (3262), "small," and *elassōn* (see 1629), "smaller" or "less." The concept of "smallness" is found throughout the Old Testament. It is used of size (Deuteronomy 25:13), youth (Genesis 9:24), and significance (Isaiah 22:24). Many times people would refer to themselves as "insignificant" or "small" in God's sight (1 Samuel 9:21 [LXX 1 Kings 9:21]). The rabbis used the term in a negative way, referring to students who had not attained their full stature as scholars and teachers.

New Testament Usage
In the New Testament the situation is much the same as in the Old. *Elachistos* is applied to things "small" in size (James 3:4) and significance (1 Corinthians 6:2). Commands (Matthew 5:19), people (Matthew 25:40), and apostles (1 Corinthians 15:9) are all described this way. Interestingly enough, Christ put a great deal of positive emphasis upon the "small" things, be they teachings (Matthew 5:19) or people, especially children (Matthew 5:19; 18:4). The "small," even the "least" in terms of human significance, are of great importance to God.

Strong 1646, Bauer 248-49, Moulton-Milligan 202, Kittel 4:648-59, Liddell-Scott 530, Colin Brown 2:427-29.

1634. ἐλαχιστότερος
elachistoteros adj
Very least, less than least.
Cross-Reference:
ἐλαττόω elattoō (1628)

1. ἐλαχιστοτέρῳ elachistoterō comp dat sing masc

1 Unto me, who am **less than the least** of all saints, ... Eph 3:8

Elachistoteros (the comparative form of the adjective *elachistos* [1633]) is a word found only in Paul's writings. This word is used in Ephesians 3:8 in Paul's description of himself as "less than the least of all saints."

Strong 1647, Moulton-Milligan 202, Liddell-Scott 530 (see "elachistos"), Colin Brown 2:428-29.

1635. Ἐλεάζαρ Eleazar name
Eleazar.

1. Ἐλεάζαρ Eleazar masc
1 And Eliud begat **Eleazar**;........................ Matt 1:15
1 and **Eleazar** begat Matthan;............................ 1:15

The son of Eliud in the genealogy of Jesus (Matthew 1:15).

1635B. ἐλεάω eleaō verb
Be merciful, show mercy.

חָנַן chānan (2706), Be kind, have pity (Ps 37:26 [36:26], Prv 14:31, 28:8).

נָתַן nāthan (5598), Give (Prv 21:26).

רָחַם rācham (7638), Piel: have mercy, have compassion (Ps 116:5 [115:5]—Codex Sinaiticus only).

1. ἐλεᾶτε eleate 2pl impr pres act
2. ἐλεῶντος eleōntos gen sing masc/neu part pres act

2 but on God who **has mercy**. (NASB)............... Rom 9:16
1 of some have **compassion**, making a difference:...... Jude 1:22
1 and on some have **mercy** with fear, (NASB)............ 1:23

This rare form of the verb *eleeō* (1640) can be found in the Septuagint in Proverbs 21:26 where it alludes to the righteous being "merciful." It occurs 31 times in the New Testament, throughout the Synoptics, and in the writings of Paul, Peter, and Jude. In all of these it is God who is looked to as the source of mercy. We see it especially in the Holy Spirit's reminder through the apostle Paul that God will "have mercy on" whom He wills to "have mercy" (Romans 9:15,16,18). In this particular context it relates to God's sovereign selection of the nation of Israel.

Bauer 249, Moulton-Milligan 202-3 (see "eleeō"), Liddell-Scott 530, Colin Brown 2:594.

1635C. ἐλεγμός elegmos noun
Reproof.
Cross-Reference:
ἐλέγχω elenchō (1638)

גְּעָרָה geʿārāh (1648), Rebuke (Is 50:2).

יָכַח yākhach (3306), Hiphil: reproof (Lv 19:17).

מַר mar (4914), Bitter (Nm 5:18,19,23,24,27).

נָאָצָה neʾātsāh (5181), Blasphemy, disgrace (Is 37:3).

תּוֹכֵחָה tôkhēchāh (8762), Punishment, rebuke (2 Kgs 19:3, Ps 149:7 [148:7]).

תּוֹכַחַת tôkhachath (8763), Reproof, rebuke (Pss 38:14 [37:14], 39:11 [38:10]).

1. ἐλεγμόν elegmon acc sing masc
1 and is useful for teaching, **rebuking**, (NIV)......... 2 Tm 3:16

In the Septuagint this term speaks of God's punishment on Israel because of her rebellion against His will (2 Kings 19:3 [LXX 4 Kings 19:3]; see also Leviticus 19:17; Numbers 5:18,19,23,24,27; Psalm 149:7 [148:7]). In the New Testament it is contained in the classic verse about the inspiration of the Bible (2 Timothy 3:16), and it refers to the "reproof" or "correction" of sin that comes as the Holy Spirit operates through the presentation of Scripture.

Bauer 249, Kittel 2:476, Liddell-Scott 530, Colin Brown 2:140-41.

1636. ἔλεγξις elenxis noun
Rebuke, reproof, refutation.
Cross-Reference:
ἐλέγχω elenchō (1638)

שִׂיחַ sîach (7945), Grooming (Jb 23:2).

1. ἔλεγξιν elenxin acc sing fem
1 But was **rebuked** for his iniquity:.................... 2 Pt 2:16

Elenxis is used in 2 Peter 2:16 in reference to the Old Testament story of Balaam's donkey rebuking him for his wrongdoing. "Rebuke" in this sense carries with it the idea of correction or conviction of sin.

Strong 1649, Bauer 249, Kittel 2:476, Liddell-Scott 530, Colin Brown 2:140,142.

1637. ἔλεγχος elenchos noun
Proof, evident demonstration, conviction.
Cross-Reference:
ἐλέγχω elenchō (1638)

יָכַח yākhach (3306), Niphal: dispute, case (Jb 23:7); hiphil: reprove, correct (Jb 6:26).

תּוֹכֵחָה tôkhēchāh (8762), Rebuke, reckoning (Hos 5:9).

תּוֹכַחַת tôkhachath (8763), Chasten, reprove (Ps 73:14 [72:14], Prv 6:23, Hb 2:1).

1. ἔλεγχος elenchos nom sing masc
2. ἔλεγχον elenchon acc sing masc

2 and is profitable for doctrine, for **reproof**,.......... 2 Tm 3:16
1 the **evidence** of things not seen..................... Heb 11:1

Elenchos is used twice in the New Testament. The KJV translates it "reproof" in 2 Timothy

3:16 and "evidence" in Hebrews 11:1. Related words are widely used, both in the New Testament and other Greek writings.

Septuagint Usage
The Septuagint frequently uses this term in Proverbs for "correction and instruction" (Proverbs 3:11; 9:7; 29:15). A wise man gratefully accepts this guidance from the Lord and learns from it. He realizes that God instructs and disciplines His children as a strict but loving Father.

New Testament Usage
This idea carries over into the New Testament with the concept of "conviction" (John 16:8), especially the conviction based on evidence. Thus the Word of God presents facts to its readers (2 Timothy 3:16) which should cause them to see the need of changing their lives so that they may become more godly.

The Hebrews 11:1 use is related to this idea. God has revealed many things through Christ (Hebrews 1:2), most of which have not been seen yet. Faith is the conviction (or proving) that they will be realized. Abraham is the classic example of this conviction in the unseen but revealed things of God (Romans 4:20,21).

STRONG 1650, BAUER 249, MOULTON-MILLIGAN 202, KITTEL 2:476, LIDDELL-SCOTT 531, COLIN BROWN 1:713; 2:140-42.

1638. ἐλέγχω elenchō verb
Refute, convict, reprove.

COGNATES:
διακατελέγχομαι diakatelenchomai (1240)
ἐλεγμός elegmos (1635C)
ἔλεγξις elenxis (1636)
ἔλεγχος elenchos (1637)

SYNONYMS:
δείκνυμι deiknumi (1161)
ἐξελέγχω exelenchō (1810)
ἐπιδείκνυμι epideiknumi (1910)
ἐπιπλήσσω epiplēssō (1954)
ἐπιτιμάω epitimaō (1992)
νουθετέω noutheteō (3423)
παιδεύω paideuō (3674)
ὑποτίθημι hupotithēmi (5132)

אַשְׁמָה 'ashmāh (846), Guilt (Lv 6:4).

חָקַר chāqar (2811), Examine (Prv 18:17).

יָכַח yākhach (3306), Hiphil: complain, reprove (Gn 21:25, Ps 94:10 [93:10]; Am 5:10); hophal: be chastened (Jb 33:19).

נָגַע nāghaʿ (5236), Piel: smite (2 Chr 26:20).

רָשַׁע rāshaʿ (7855), Be guilty; hiphil: condemn (Jb 15:6).

תּוֹכַחַת tôkhachath (8763), Reproof (Prv 3:11).

1. ἐλέγχω elenchō 1sing indic pres act
2. ἐλέγχει elenchei 3sing indic pres act
3. ἔλεγχε elenche 2sing impr pres act
4. ἐλέγχετε elenchete 2pl impr pres act
5. ἐλέγχειν elenchein inf pres act
6. ἔλεγξον elenxon 2sing impr aor act
7. ἐλέγξει elenxei 3sing indic fut act
8. ἐλέγχεται elenchetai 3sing indic pres mid
9. ἐλεγχόμενος elenchomenos
    nom sing masc part pres mid
10. ἐλεγχόμενοι elenchomenoi
    nom pl masc part pres mid
11. ἐλεγχόμενα elenchomena
    nom/acc pl neu part pres mid
12. ἐλεγχθῇ elenchthē 3sing subj aor pass
13. ἐλέγξαι elenxai inf aor act

```
6  tell him his fault between thee and him alone:.... Matt 18:15
9  the tetrarch, being reproved by him for Herodias ... Luke 3:19
12 lest his deeds should be reproved.................. John 3:20
10 being convicted by their own conscience,...............  8:9
2  Which of you convinceth me of sin?.................... 8:46
7  when he is come, he will reprove the world of sin,.... 16:8
8  he is convinced of all, he is judged of all:........1 Co 14:24
4  have no fellowship ... but rather reprove them.......Eph 5:11
11 But all things that are reproved are made manifest ...  5:13
3  Them that sin rebuke before all,....................1 Tm 5:20
6  reprove, rebuke, exhort with all longsuffering ......2 Tm 4:2
5  both to exhort and to convince the gainsayers........Tit 1:9
3  witness is true. Wherefore rebuke them sharply,.......  1:13
3  speak, and exhort, and rebuke with all authority.......  2:15
9  nor faint when thou art rebuked of him:.......... Heb 12:5
10 and are convinced of the law as transgressors.......Jas 2:9
13 and to convict all the ungodly (NASB)............Jude 1:15
1  As many as I love, I rebuke and chasten:......... Rev 3:19
```

Classical Greek
For the classical Greeks elenchō especially denoted "to disgrace, to put (someone) to shame." Secondly, it referred to "cross-examine, question for the purpose of disproving or reproving, to censure, accuse" (see Liddell-Scott). Later it generally denoted "to examine, to investigate." Elenchō and its companions, elenchos (1637) and elenktikos, are significant words in Greek philosophy, most notably in propositional logic (Büschel, "elenchō," Kittel, 2:475f.).

Septuagint Usage
Elenchō occurs throughout the Septuagint. Ordinarily it is a replacement for the Hebrew yakach (in various tenses), itself a legal term for "to argue" and "to settle a quarrel" (e.g., Genesis 31:37; Job 9:33; 13:3). In a nonlegal sense it could mean "to reproach, reprove" (e.g., Genesis 31:42; Job 13:10; 22:4). At times elenchō could imply "to punish" (e.g., 2 Samuel 7:14 [LXX 2 Kings 7:14]; 2 Chronicles 26:20, Hebrew nāghaʿ; cf. Job 5:17). In the Septuagint God is seen to "reprove, chasten" and "convict" man in order to "instruct" him. Thus the

purpose of correction is positive (Job 5:17: "Happy is the man whom God correcteth"; cf. Proverbs 3:12; 9:8).

New Testament Usage
New Testament usage largely conforms to the pattern in the Septuagint that *elenchō* (which may involve reproof of sin) has as its goal a restoring or an establishing of a relationship, whether that relationship is between persons (Matthew 18:15; 1 Timothy 5:20; 2 Timothy 4:2; Titus 1:13; 2:15; cf. John 8:46) or between a person and God (e.g., John 16:8; Hebrews 12:5).

Nonetheless, such an act of "rebuke" or "reproof" does not necessarily generate success in turning someone away from sin (Luke 3:19). Also the sense of "to expose" should not be overlooked. Sin may be perceptible only to the judgment of God (Ephesians 5:11,13); reproof "exposes" sin (John 3:20) for examination.

The Holy Spirit "convinces" the world of sin; i.e., He proves the charge of sin against the world is valid, but again His motive is redemptive (John 16:8; 1 Corinthians 14:24; Jude 22). Thus the heart of *elenchō*—whether meaning "to expose" or "to reprove"—is the purpose of steering the guilty party toward redemption (see Büschel, "elenchō," *Kittel*, 2:475, who develops this thought more fully).

The word *elenchō* is also used in contexts which imply an unauthorized criticism or accusation. When Jesus said, "Which of you *convinceth* me of sin?" (John 8:46) He was responding to the unjust criticism of His accusers.

STRONG 1651, BAUER 249, MOULTON-MILLIGAN 202, KITTEL 2:473-75, LIDDELL-SCOTT 531, COLIN BROWN 2:140-42,145.

1639. ἐλεεινός eleeinos adj
Miserable, pitiable.
CROSS-REFERENCE:
ἐλεέω eleeō (1640)

1. ἐλεεινός eleeinos nom sing masc
2. ἐλεεινότεροι eleeinoteroi comp nom pl masc

2 we are of all men most miserable.................. 1 Co 15:19
1 and **miserable**, and poor, and blind, and naked:...... Rev 3:17

The adjective *eleeinos* is used twice in the New Testament. In the first occurrence Paul wrote of those who have hope only in this life. They are "most miserable" or "pitiable" of people (1 Corinthians 15:19). In this passage the comparative form (*eleeinoteroi*) functions as a superlative ("most"). Paul emphasized that believers are not only "miserable" but "of all men (the) most miserable" if the Resurrection has not occurred. *Eleeinos* is used again in reference to the church of Laodicea which, in spite of its material richness, was in a "miserable" or "pitiable" condition because of its lukewarmness (Revelation 3:17).

STRONG 1652, BAUER 249, MOULTON-MILLIGAN 202, LIDDELL-SCOTT 531, COLIN BROWN 2:594-97.

1640. ἐλεέω eleeō verb
Have mercy or pity on (someone), show mercy.
COGNATES:
   ἀνελεήμων aneleēmōn (413)
   ἀνέλεος aneleos (413B)
   ἀνίλεως anileōs (446)
   ἐλεεινός eleeinos (1639)
   ἐλεημοσύνη eleēmosunē (1641)
   ἐλεήμων eleēmōn (1642)
   ἔλεος eleos (1643)
SYNONYMS:
   ἀμύνομαι amunomai (290)
   ἀντέχομαι antechomai (469)
   ἀντιλαμβάνομαι antilambanomai (479)
   βοηθέω boētheō (990)
   διακονέω diakoneō (1241)
   οἰκτείρω oikteirō (3489)
   παραγίνομαι paraginomai (3716)
   σπλαγχνίζομαι splanchnizomai (4550)
   συλλαμβάνω sullambanō (4666)
   συμβάλλω sumballō (4671)
   συμπαθέω sumpatheō (4685)
   συμφέρω sumpherō (4702)
   συναντιλαμβάνομαι sunantilambanomai (4729)
   ὠφελέω ōpheleō (5456)

בָּכָה bākhāh (1098), Weep (Jb 27:15).

גָּאַל gāʾal (1381), Redeem (Is 44:23—Codex Alexandrinus only).

חָדַר chādhar (2409), Be partial, show favoritism (Ex 23:3).

חִין chîn (2533), Be graceful (Jb 41:12 [41:3]).

חָמַל chāmal (2654), Spare, have pity (Is 9:19, Ez 5:11, 9:5).

חָנַן chānan (2706), Qal: be gracious to (Dt 28:50, 2 Kgs 13:23, Ps 41:4 [40:4]); polel: be kind, have mercy (Prv 14:21); hophal: favor, show mercy (Prv 21:10).

חָסִיד chāsîdh (2728), One who is faithful (Jer 3:12—Codex Alexandrinus only).

יָטַב yāṭav (3296), Go well, be pleasing; hiphil: show kindness, be good to (Jb 24:21).

נָחַם nācham (5341), Niphal: relent, repent (Ez 24:14); piel: comfort (Zec 1:17, Is 12:1, 49:13).

נָתַן nāthan (5598), Give (Prv 21:26—only some Vaticanus texts).

ἐλεημοσύνη 1641

עָשָׂה 'āsâh (6449), Do, make (Is 44:23).
קָבַץ qāvats (7192), Piel: gather, bring back (Is 54:7).
רָחַם rācham (7638), Piel: show love for, have mercy (Dt 30:3, Ps 116:5 [115:5], Hos 2:4); pual: find compassion, find mercy (Hos 1:6, 14:3 [14:4]).
שׁוּב shûv (8178), Return, bring again (Is 52:8).
שָׁמַע shāma' (8471), Hear (Is 59:2).

1. ἐλεεῖ eleei 3sing indic pres act
2. ἐλεῶ eleō 1sing subj pres act
3. ἐλεῶν eleōn nom sing masc part pres act
4. ἐλεοῦντος eleountos gen sing masc part pres act
5. ἐλεεῖτε eleeite 2pl impr pres act
6. ἠλέησα ēleēsa 1sing indic aor act
7. ἠλέησεν ēleēsen 3sing indic aor act
8. ἐλεήσῃ eleēsē 3sing subj aor act
9. ἐλεήσον eleēson 2sing impr aor act
10. ἐλεῆσαι eleēsai inf aor act
11. ἐλεήσω eleēsō 1sing indic fut act
12. ἠλεήθην ēleēthēn 1sing indic aor pass
13. ἠλεήθημεν ēleēthēmen 1pl indic aor pass
14. ἠλεήθητε ēleēthēte 2pl indic aor pass
15. ἐλεηθῶσιν eleēthōsin 3pl subj aor pass
16. ἐλεηθέντες eleēthentes nom pl masc part aor pass
17. ἠλεημένος ēleēmenos
    nom sing masc part perf mid
18. ἠλεημένοι ēleēmenoi nom pl masc part perf mid
19. ἐλεηθήσονται eleēthēsontai 3pl indic fut pass

19	the merciful: for they shall obtain mercy.	Matt 5:7
9	and saying, Thou son of David, have mercy on us.	9:27
9	Have mercy on me, O Lord, thou son of David;	15:22
9	Lord, have mercy on my son: for he is a lunatic,	17:15
10	Shouldest not thou also have had compassion	18:33
6	Shouldest not thou ... even as I had pity on thee?	18:33
9	Have mercy on us, O Lord, thou son of David.	20:30
9	Have mercy on us, O Lord, thou son of David.	20:31
7	and hath had compassion on thee.	Mark 5:19
9	Jesus, thou son of David, have mercy on me.	10:47
9	Thou son of David, have mercy on me.	10:48
9	Abraham, have mercy on me, and send Lazarus,	Luke 16:24
9	and said, Jesus, Master, have mercy on us.	17:13
9	Jesus, thou son of David, have mercy on me.	18:38
9	the more, Thou son of David, have mercy on me.	18:39
11	I will have mercy on whom I will have mercy,	Rom 9:15
2	I will have mercy on whom I will have mercy,	9:15
4	but of God that sheweth mercy.	9:16
1	hath he mercy on whom he will have mercy,	9:18
14	have now obtained mercy through their unbelief:	11:30
15	through your mercy they also may obtain mercy.	11:31
8	that he might have mercy upon all.	11:32
3	he that sheweth mercy, with cheerfulness.	12:8
17	hath obtained mercy of the Lord to be faithful.	1 Co 7:25
13	as we have received mercy, we faint not;	2 Co 4:1
7	but God had mercy on him; and not on him only,	Phlp 2:27
12	but I obtained mercy, because I did it ignorantly	1 Tm 1:13
12	Howbeit for this cause I obtained mercy,	1:16
18	which had not obtained mercy,	1 Pt 2:10
16	but now have obtained mercy.	2:10
5	of some have compassion, making a difference:	Jude 1:22

Classical Greek and Septuagint Usage
This word appears in classical Greek since the time of Homer (ca. Seventh Century B.C.) as an emotional reaction to seeing someone suffering from an undeserved affliction. It includes aspects of both "awe" and "mercy" in the sense that one can both "feel" and "have pity on someone" (Bultmann, "eleeō," *Kittel*, 2:477ff.). While the noun that describes the emotion (*eleos*) is normally used to translate the Hebrew, *chesed*, in the Septuagint, the verb *eleeō* is used to translate some 16 different Hebrew words in over 70 occurrences. Most commonly it translates *chānan*, which denotes the act of "being gracious to" someone (Genesis 33:11), where God is the giver. The same can also be said of men as being gracious or "taking pity" on someone (2 Kings 13:23 [LXX 4 Kings 13:23]; Psalm 37:21,26 [36:21,26]; Proverbs 14:21).

New Testament Usage
Eleeō occurs frequently in the New Testament where its usual translation is to "have mercy." Like the Septuagint, the New Testament concept of having mercy can be from God to man and from man to man. In the Gospels the usual plea to Jesus was "have mercy on me," often coupled with addressing Him by the Messianic title of "Son of David" (Matthew 9:27; Mark 10:47,48; Luke 18:38,39; also cf. Matthew 15:22; 20:30,31). Matthew 15:22-28 shows that even Gentiles, while not a part of the covenant people (Ephesians 2:12), also have a claim on God's mercy (cf. 1 Peter 2:10). Even when mercy is shown from man to man, frequently the motivation for such acts is the mercy of God (Matthew 18:33; cf. Romans 12:8; 2 Corinthians 4:1; Jude 22). Thus the word focuses upon acts of kindness between individuals who have a mutual relationship. The closer the relationship, the more mercy is expected when needed.

STRONG 1653, BAUER 249, MOULTON-MILLIGAN 202-3, KITTEL 2:477-85, LIDDELL-SCOTT 531, COLIN BROWN 2:594-95.

1641. ἐλεημοσύνη eleēmosunē noun
Kind act, merciful, alms.
CROSS-REFERENCE:
ἐλεέω eleeō (1640)

אֱמֶת 'emeth (583), Truth, faithfulness (Is 38:18).
חֶסֶד chesedh (2721), Truth, faithfulness (Gn 47:29, Prv 3:3, 14:22, 20:28).
צֶדֶק tsedheq (6928), Righteousness (Ps 35:24 [34:24]—only some Sinaiticus texts).
צִדְקָה tsidhqāh (A6929), What is right, righteousness (Dn 4:27 [4:24]—Aramaic).

צְדָקָה tsedhāqāh (6930), Righteousness (Dt 6:25, Pss 24:5 [23:5], 103:6 [102:6]).

1. ἐλεημοσύνη eleēmosunē nom sing fem
2. ἐλεημοσύνην eleēmosunēn acc sing fem
3. ἐλεημοσύναι eleēmosunai nom pl fem
4. ἐλεημοσυνῶν eleēmosunōn gen pl fem
5. ἐλεημοσύνας eleēmosunas acc pl fem

2 Take heed that ye do not your **alms** before men,	Matt	6:1
2 Therefore when thou doest thine **alms**,		6:2
2 But when thou doest **alms**,		6:3
1 That thine **alms** may be in secret:		6:4
2 But rather give **alms** of such things as ye have;	Luke	11:41
2 Sell that ye have, and give **alms**;		12:33
2 to ask **alms** of them that entered into the temple;	Acts	3:2
2 about to go into the temple asked an **alms**.		3:3
2 And they knew that it was he which sat for **alms**		3:10
4 full of good works and **almsdeeds** which she did.		9:36
5 which gave much **alms** to the people,		10:2
3 Thy prayers and thine **alms** are come up		10:4
3 **alms** are had in remembrance in the sight of God.		10:31
5 I came to bring **alms** to my nation, and offerings.		24:17

Classical Greek
The noun *eleēmosunē*, "alms," is related to the verb *eleeō* (1640), "to show mercy, sympathy." Originally *eleēmosunē* had a great deal of semantic overlap with *eleos* (1643), "mercy," but gradually the former came to describe "gifts of mercy." Apparently the term's initial use was in the Septuagint (Daniel 4:27; Tobit passim).

Septuagint Usage
In the Septuagint *eleēmosunē* is equated with *tsedhāqāh*, "righteousness," or in another sense it developed as "mercy." This indicates the religious significance Judaism attached to almsgiving. Such an understanding would contend that neighbors were legally entitled to alms or aid. Righteousness, therefore, was the exercise or fulfillment of that religious obligation in accordance with divine law. Fulfillment of the Law brought (it was thought) reward.

Almsgiving was highly regarded as meritorious in Judaism. The law of Moses imposed taxes for the assistance of the poor. One-tenth of each third year's profit was to be divided between the Levites, the foreigners, the fatherless, and the widows (Deuteronomy 14:28,29; 26:12,13). The poor were entitled to the gleanings of the grain fields and vineyards (Leviticus 19:9,10; 23:22; Deuteronomy 24:20f.; Ruth 2:2f.). The Law instructed its adherents to lend to the poor—without interest (Deuteronomy 15:7-11); every seventh year all debts were to be remitted (Deuteronomy 15:1,2).

New Testament Usage
During the time of Christ each town had trained, professional almsgivers who even used force to exact alms. There were basically two kinds of alms: "Gifts of the chest" was money which accrued on the Sabbath in the offering chest of the synagogue and which was intended for the use of the poor. "Gifts of the cup" were food and money gathered in begging cups. In Judea many beggars made their living by asking alms. They sat in the streets, beside the gates of houses of the rich, or at the entrances to synagogues—in Jerusalem beside the temple gates. We can be fairly assured that Jesus gave alms. Evidently the disciples gave alms from a common fund (John 13:29; cf. 2 Corinthians 8:9).

Jesus underscored the responsibility to give alms. He said: "It is more blessed to give than to receive" (Acts 20:35). He invited His disciples to give alms (Luke 12:33; 16:9f.; cf. 19:8). He conceived almsgiving as a fundamental aspect of true worship, comparable to prayer and fasting (Matthew 6:2f.; cf. Tobit passim). He warned His listeners of the judgment awaiting those who do not show mercy (Matthew 25:41f.; Luke 16:19f.).

Jesus demonstrated the importance of the attitude of the giver. One should not give in order to be noticed by men (Matthew 6:1-4; Luke 14:12-14). Against the prideful "charity" of the Pharisees, Jesus placed the widow's small but heartfelt gift (Mark 12:41-44; cf. 1 Corinthians 13:3). The value of the gift itself has little significance; its value is considered in relation to the means of the giver and the love and self-sacrifice which lie behind the gift. The early Christians took seriously the command to show mercy. Caring for the poor characterized the first congregation in Jerusalem, and it also chose servants from the assembly to administer care to the widows (Acts 4:32; 6:1f.).

STRONG 1654, BAUER 249-50, MOULTON-MILLIGAN 203, KITTEL 2:485-87, LIDDELL-SCOTT 531, COLIN BROWN 2:594-97.

1642. ἐλεήμων eleēmōn adj
Merciful, sympathetic, compassionate.
COGNATE:
  ἐλεέω eleeō (1640)
SYNONYMS:
  ἵλεως hileōs (2412)
  οἰκτίρμων oiktirmōn (3491)

חַנּוּן channûn (2688), Gracious (Ex 34:6, 2 Chr 30:9, Jl 2:13).

חֶסֶד chesedh (2721), Kind, faithful (Prv 11:17, 20:6).

חָסִיד chāsîdh (2728), Faithful (Jer 3:12).

רָחוּם rachûm (7631), Compassionate (Ps 145:8 [144:8]).
שֵׂכֶל sēkhel (7961I), Discretion, good sense (Prv 19:11).

1. ἐλεήμων eleēmōn nom sing masc
2. ἐλεήμονες eleēmones nom pl masc

2	Blessed are the **merciful**: ... shall obtain mercy.	Matt 5:7
1	that he might be a **merciful** and faithful high priest	Heb 2:17

Eleēmōn can be translated "merciful" in the sense of being actively compassionate. It is used of men in Matthew 5:7 and of Christ in Hebrews 2:17. In both instances mercy is an attribute of God lived out on earth.

STRONG 1655, BAUER 250, MOULTON-MILLIGAN 203, KITTEL 2:485, LIDDELL-SCOTT 531, COLIN BROWN 2:594-96.

1643. ἔλεος eleos noun

Mercy, compassion, pity.

COGNATE:
ἐλεέω eleeō (1640)

SYNONYM:
οἰκτιρμός oiktirmos (3490)

חֵן chēn (2682), Favor (Gn 19:19, Nm 11:15, Jgs 6:17).
חֲנִינָה chănînāh (2697), Pity (Jer 16:13).
חֶסֶד cheṣedh (2721), Mercy, kindness (Dt 5:10, 1 Kgs 3:6, Jer 2:2).
יֵשַׁע yēshaʿ (3589), Salvation (Is 45:8).
מֵעִים mēʿîm (4753), Compassion (Is 63:15).
צְדָקָה tsedhāqāh (6930), Right, justice (Is 56:1, Ez 18:19,21).
רָחַם rācham (7638), Piel: mercy, compassion (Jer 31:20 [38:20], Hb 3:2).
רַחַם racham (7641II) Mercy, compassion (Is 47:6, Jer 42:12 [49:2], Dn 9:18).
רָצוֹן rātsôn (7814), Favor (Is 60:10).
תְּחִנָּה techinnāh (8798), Mercy, supplication (Jos 11:20, Jer 36:7 [43:7]).
תַּחֲנוּן tachănûn (8800), Supplication (Dn 9:3).

1. ἔλεον eleon acc sing masc
2. ἔλεος eleos nom/acc sing neu
3. ἐλέους eleous gen sing neu
4. ἐλέει eleei dat sing neu

1	I will have **mercy**, and not sacrifice:	Matt 9:13
2	I will have **mercy**, and not sacrifice,	9:13
1	I will have **mercy**, and not sacrifice,	12:7
2	I will have **mercy**, and not sacrifice,	12:7
1	have omitted ... judgment, **mercy**, and faith:	23:23
2	have omitted ... judgment, **mercy**, and faith:	23:23
2	his **mercy** is on them that fear him from generation	Luke 1:50
3	his servant Israel, in remembrance of his **mercy**;	1:54
2	how the Lord had showed great **mercy** upon her;	1:58
2	To perform the **mercy** promised to our fathers,	1:72
3	Through the tender **mercy** of our God;	1:78
2	And he said, He that showed **mercy** on him.	10:37
3	the riches of his glory on the vessels **of mercy**,	Rom 9:23
4	through your **mercy** they also may obtain mercy.	Rom 11:31
3	that the Gentiles might glorify God for his **mercy**;	15:9
2	peace be on them, and **mercy**, and upon the Israel	Gal 6:16
4	But God, who is rich in **mercy**,	Eph 2:4
2	Grace, **mercy**, and peace, from God our Father	1 Tm 1:2
2	Grace, **mercy**, and peace, from God the Father	2 Tm 1:2
2	Lord give **mercy** unto the house of Onesiphorus;	1:16
2	The Lord grant unto him that he may find **mercy**	1:18
2	Grace, **mercy**, and peace, from God the Father	Tit 1:4
1	but according to his **mercy** he saved us,	3:5
2	but according to his **mercy** he saved us,	3:5
1	unto the throne ... that we may obtain **mercy**,	Heb 4:16
2	unto the throne ... that we may obtain **mercy**,	4:16
2	without **mercy**, that hath showed no **mercy**;	Jas 2:13
2	and **mercy** rejoiceth against judgment.	2:13
3	easy to be entreated, full of **mercy** and good fruits,	3:17
2	Christ, which according to his abundant **mercy**	1 Pt 1:3
2	**mercy**, and peace, from God the Father,	2 Jn 1:3
2	**Mercy** unto you, and peace and love,	Jude 1:2
2	looking for the **mercy** of our Lord Jesus Christ	1:21

Classical Greek

The emotions "mercy," "pity," and "sympathy" are translated *eleos* in classical Greek. *Eleos* more narrowly defined is a response to someone else's condition of distress. There is even an element of fear that the same fate may overcome the observer. Nevertheless, *eleos* is an emotion, not a moral relationship (Bultmann, "eleos," *Kittel*, 2:477f.). Since the gods of the Greek religious system did not convey mercy upon men, there is no Greek term which adequately represents the concept of divine mercy as seen in the Bible.

Septuagint Usage

By far the most common Hebrew term for which *eleos* is equivalent in the Septuagint is *cheṣedh*. It can be translated as "faithfulness, mercy," or "loyalty" (e.g., Genesis 19:19; 24:12,14) but more often (especially by *eleos*) is equated with "kindness, grace, loving-kindness." *Eleos* (Latin *misericordia*) is typical of God's forgiveness (Numbers 14:19; cf. Exodus 34:6,7; Psalms 86:13ff. [LXX 85:13ff.]; 103:17 [102:17]; 136 passim [135]; Sirach 18:11). God's mercy and compassion are hoped for (Psalm 52:8 [LXX 51:8]; Sirach 2:9), and it would not be wrong to say it is an eschatological term (cf. 2 Maccabees 2:7; 7:29; cf. ibid., 2:481) denoting that which conceivably takes place at judgment (e.g., Sirach 5:5-7; 16:11f.; cf. Psalms 103:4 [LXX 102:4]; 119:41ff.,124 [118:41ff.,124]).

Mercy or compassion are also qualities of individuals. Rahab showed the spies *eleos* and asked for *eleos* in return (*cheṣedh*, Joshua 2:12,14), as did the spies from the house of Joseph (Judges 1:24ff.; cf. 1 Samuel 20:8 [LXX 1 Kings 20:8]). God's people are expected to show mercy (Psalm 109:16 [LXX 108:16]; Sirach 28:4).

New Testament Usage

God's desire of "mercy" (*chesedh/eleos*) rather than sacrifice (*zevach/thusia* [2355]) (Hosea 6:6/Matthew 9:13; 12:7) typifies a common theme of Scripture. In imitation of God, humanity is to show compassion toward fellow human beings; Jesus exemplified this as both God and Man (e.g., Matthew 5:7; 18:33; 23:23; Luke 10:36f.; 16:24f.; James 2:13; Jude 22f.).

A more prominent theme of mercy, found most notably in Paul, is that God has granted mercy (*eleos*) to the peoples of the earth. God is rich (*plousios* [4004]) in mercy (Ephesians 2:4), which saves mankind (Titus 3:5; 1 Peter 1:3). Jesus demonstrated this mercy (Mark 5:19; 10:47f.; Luke 17:13); therefore, mercy is both a present reality (Hebrews 4:16) and a future eschatological reality standing in contrast to God's wrath (*orgē* [3572]; cf. Romans 9:23; Jude 21f.).

Throughout Scripture, God is represented as a God of grace as well as of mercy. While "grace" (*charis* [5320B]) speaks of the undeserved goodness God shows men, "mercy" (*eleos*) reflects a goodness which reveals God's pity and compassion toward men. Trench points out that of the two terms "grace" must come first since without it, we do not deserve God's mercy (*Synonyms of the New Testament*, p.156f.). Perhaps it is for this reason that Paul used "grace" and "mercy" in succession where the two stand together (see 1 Timothy 1:2; 2 Timothy 1:2).

STRONG 1656, BAUER 250, MOULTON-MILLIGAN 203, KITTEL 2:477-85, LIDDELL-SCOTT 532, COLIN BROWN 2:593-97.

1644. ἐλευθερία eleutheria noun

Freedom, liberty.

CROSS-REFERENCE:
ἐλευθερόω eleutheroō (1646)

חֹפֶשׁ chōphesh (2772), Liberty (Sir 7:21).

חֻפְשָׁה chuphshāh (2773), Freedom (Lv 19:20).

1. ἐλευθερία eleutheria nom sing fem
2. ἐλευθερίας eleutherias gen sing fem
3. ἐλευθερίᾳ eleutheria dat sing fem
4. ἐλευθερίαν eleutherian acc sing fem

4 into the glorious liberty of the children of God......	Rom	8:21
1 is my liberty judged of another man's conscience?..	1 Co	10:29
1 and where the Spirit of the Lord is, there is liberty.	2 Co	3:17
4 who came in privily to spy out our liberty.............	Gal	2:4
3 Stand fast therefore in the liberty........................		5:1
3 For, brethren, ye have been called unto liberty;.....	Gal	5:13
4 only use not liberty for an occasion to the flesh,.....		5:13
2 But whoso looketh into the perfect law of liberty,....	Jas	1:25
2 as they that shall be judged by the law of liberty....		2:12
4 not using your liberty for a cloak of maliciousness,..	1 Pt	2:16
4 While they promise them liberty,.........................	2 Pt	2:19

When *eleutheria* occurs in the New Testament in most instances it refers to "liberty" or "freedom" from sin (Romans 8:21; 2 Corinthians 3:17; Galatians 5:13; 1 Peter 2:16; 2 Peter 2:19). It can also refer to "freedom" from the Law (Galatians 2:4; 5:1; James 1:25; 2:12).

STRONG 1657, BAUER 250, MOULTON-MILLIGAN 203, KITTEL 2:487-502, LIDDELL-SCOTT 532, COLIN BROWN 1:715-19.

1645. ἐλεύθερος eleutheros adj

Free, independent.

CROSS-REFERENCE:
ἐλευθερόω eleutheroō (1646)

חָפְשִׁי chophshî (2775), Free (Ex 21:5, Dt 15:12, Jer 34:9 [41:9]).

חֹר chōr (2814), Noble (1 Kgs 21:11 [20:11], Eccl 10:17).

שַׂר sar (8015), Official (Jer 29:2 [36:2]).

1. ἐλεύθερος eleutheros nom sing masc
2. ἐλεύθεροι eleutheroi nom pl masc
3. ἐλευθέρων eleutherōn gen pl masc
4. ἐλευθέρους eleutherous acc pl masc
5. ἐλευθέρα eleuthera nom sing fem
6. ἐλευθέρας eleutheras gen sing fem

2 Jesus saith unto him, Then are the children free....	Matt	17:26
2 how sayest thou, Ye shall be made free?...........	John	8:33
2 Son ... make you free, ye shall be free indeed.........		8:36
2 ye were free from righteousness.....................	Rom	6:20
5 she is free from that law;.............................		7:3
1 but if thou mayest be made free, use it rather.......	1 Co	7:21
1 he that is called, being free, is Christ's servant.........		7:22
5 she is at liberty to be married to whom she will;........		7:39
1 Am I not an apostle? am I not free?.....................		9:1
1 Am I not an apostle? am I not free?.....................		9:1
1 For though I be free from all men,.....................		9:19
2 whether we be bond or free;...........................		12:13
1 there is neither bond nor free,..........................	Gal	3:28
6 the one by a bondmaid, the other by a freewoman......		4:22
6 but he of the freewoman was by promise................		4:23
5 But Jerusalem which is above is free,.................		4:26
6 shall not be heir with the son of the freewoman......		4:30
6 not children of the bondwoman, but of the free.......		4:31
1 receive of the Lord, whether he be bond or free......	Eph	6:8
1 Barbarian, Scythian, bond nor free:....................	Col	3:11
2 As free, and not using your liberty for a cloak......	1 Pt	2:16
1 and every free man, hid themselves in the dens......	Rev	6:15
4 small and great, rich and poor, free and bond,.........		13:16
3 and the flesh of all men, both free and bond,.........		19:18

Classical Greek

Basically *eleutheros* means "freedom" or as an adjective, "free, freed" in contrast to enslaved. In classical Greek there were essentially two understandings of "freedom": political and philosophical. The political concept of freedom included freedom from slavery as well as the social freedom enjoyed under a government and its laws. The philosophical ideal of freedom, particularly that expressed in Stoicism, meant freedom of the individual "set apart and under the law of his own nature or of human nature generally" (Schlier, "eleutheros," *Kittel*, 2:483,487-496). These two concepts by their nature collide; one sees freedom in the context of community, the other views freedom as the attainment of autonomy.

Septuagint Usage

In the Septuagint *eleutheros* is not laden with as much political or philosophical baggage. Freedom is normally contrasted with literal slavery (e.g., Exodus 21:2,5,26f.; Deuteronomy 15:12,13; Job 39:5 [Hebrew, *chophshî*]; cf. 1 Maccabees 2:11). Also, the leaders or prominent men of cities are called "free" (RSV, "nobles"; 1 Kings 21:8,11 [LXX 3 Kings 21:8,11; Hebrew, *chôrîm*]; cf. Nehemiah 13:17). However, we see no developed concept of freedom as a religious condition in the Septuagint.

New Testament Usage

The word group *eleutheroō* (1646), *eleutheros*, and *eleutheria* (1644) occurs most consistently in Paul's writings. *Eleutheros*, apart from two uses in John, one in Matthew, one in 1 Peter, and three in John's Revelation, is a Pauline term (16 times).

The majority of the uses of *eleutheros*—both Pauline and non-Pauline alike—reflect a literal understanding of "freedom" as the opposite of slavery. The phrase, the "slave and the free" is a stock polarization which signals the inclusion of all men (e.g., Revelation 6:15; 13:16; 19:18). First Peter 2:16, "As free, and not using your liberty . . . ," moves beyond the literal (note *theou douloi*, verse 16) to some degree; yet the sense is still a more political and social freedom than a freedom from sin. This usage may parallel the Septuagintal understanding of free noble; the context of civil responsibility lends credence to this view (see *Bauer*).

As mentioned, Paul recognized *eleutheros* as descriptive of literal freedom (1 Corinthians 7:21,22; 9:19; 12:13; Galatians 3:28; Ephesians 6:8; Colossians 3:11) or "independence" (choice) (Romans 7:3; 1 Corinthians 7:39). The allegory of Hagar and Sarah (Galatians 4:22-31) is both literal in the story and figurative in the larger sense, as 5:1 makes plain.

Of special significance for Paul was the picture of the *eleutheros* in Christ. Those who were formerly enslaved to sin can be set free by Christ (Romans 6:17-22). Even the literal use in Romans 7:3 leads to an image of freedom in Christ from the law of sin which holds men captive (Romans 7:6). The theme of freedom also recurs in many of Paul's other images (cf. Galatians 4:3,8,9; Epp, *Paul's Diverse Imageries of the Human Situation and His Unifying Theme of Freedom*, pp.100-116; Schlier, "eleutheros," *Kittel*, 2:496-502). However, an important paradox should be noted. Paul considered himself and every man set free from the law by Christ, to now be slaves of Christ (1 Corinthians 7:22)!

John, too, shared the imagery of "slavery"/"freedom" as descriptive of the human condition. The life of the person who is not a child of God, i.e., who has not experienced new birth, is slavery, but the one who has God as his or her Father is "free" (John 8:33ff.). "True freedom" can only be experienced by knowing the "Truth." Truth is the opposite of sin, which John especially portrayed as deception and falsehood (John 8:39-47, especially verse 44). Therefore Paul and John shared the same perspective. Life "in Christ" is a life of freedom. A life outside of Him is enslavement to sin and death.

Strong 1658, Bauer 250, Moulton-Milligan 203, Kittel 2:487-502, Liddell-Scott 532, Colin Brown 1:715-18.

1646. ἐλευθερόω eleutheroō verb

Set free; deliver, liberate.

Cognates:
ἀπελεύθερος apeleutheros (555)
ἐλευθερία eleutheria (1644)
ἐλεύθερος eleutheros (1645)

Synonyms:
ἀπαλλάσσω apallassō (521)
ἀπολύω apoluō (624)
ἐξαιρέω exaireō (1791)
ἐπιλύω epiluō (1941)
λυτρόω lutroō (3056)
λύω luō (3061)

1. ἠλευθέρωσεν ēleutherōsen 3sing indic aor act
2. ἐλευθερώσῃ eleutherōsē 3sing subj aor act
3. ἐλευθερώσει eleutherōsei 3sing indic fut act
4. ἐλευθερωθέντες eleutherōthentes
    nom pl masc part aor pass
5. ἐλευθερωθήσεται eleutherōthēsetai
    3sing indic fut pass

3 and the truth **shall make** you **free**................	John	8:32
2 If the Son therefore **shall make** you **free**,.........		8:36
4 Being then **made free** from sin,................	Rom	6:18
4 But now **being made free** from sin,.............		6:22
1 hath **made** me **free** from the law of sin and death.....		8:2
5 Because the creature itself also **shall be delivered**.....		8:21
1 in the liberty wherewith Christ **hath made** us **free**,....	Gal	5:1

This verb is used in secular Greek of freeing slaves. Paul used the word five times and usually specified that from which one is set free: "from sin" (Romans 6:18,22); "from the law of sin and death" (Romans 8:2); "from the bondage of corruption" (Romans 8:21); and Galatians 5:1, where the context implies the Law. John used the word to translate two sayings of Jesus (8:32,36) where the emphasis is on the source of the power to set free, namely, the truth and the Son.

STRONG 1659, BAUER 250-51, MOULTON-MILLIGAN 203, KITTEL 2:487-502, LIDDELL-SCOTT 532, COLIN BROWN 1:715,717.

1647. ἔλευσις eleusis noun

Coming; advent.
CROSS-REFERENCE:
ἔρχομαι erchomai (2048)

1. ἐλεύσεως eleuseōs gen sing fem

1 showed before of the **coming** of the Just One;........ Acts 7:52

This noun, related to an irregular form of a verb which means "to come, to come back, to return," means simply "the coming." One travels until he comes into the presence of his destination; then others experience his coming, his presence. The word is found only once in the New Testament (Acts 7:52) where Luke used it to translate Stephen's reference to the first "coming of the Just One" (Jesus Christ). The Western text (D) and Irenaeus use it of the second coming of Christ in Luke 21:7; 23:42.

STRONG 1660, BAUER 251, KITTEL 2:675, LIDDELL-SCOTT 532, COLIN BROWN 1:320.

1648. ἐλεφάντινος elephantinos adj

Made of ivory.

שֵׁן shēn (8514), Ivory (1 Kgs 10:18, 2 Chr 9:17, Am 3:15).

שֶׁנְהַבִּים shenhabbîm (8527), Ivory (1 Kgs 10:22—Codex Alexandrinus only).

1. ἐλεφάντινον elephantinon nom/acc sing neu

1 and all manner vessels **of ivory**,................ Rev 18:12

This word appears in classical Greek from the Seventh Century B.C. where it is used to describe "articles made of ivory." The Septuagint uses it 11 times to translate the Hebrew word *shēn* generally meaning "tooth" (of man, Exodus 21:27), but it is also used of "ivory" as a type of animal's tooth (1 Kings 10:18 [LXX 3 Kings 10:18]; see also Ezekiel 27:15; Amos 6:4). This adjective appears only once in the New Testament, at Revelation 18:12, where it refers to "all manner vessels of ivory."

STRONG 1661, BAUER 251, MOULTON-MILLIGAN 203, LIDDELL-SCOTT 532-33.

1649. Ἐλιακείμ Eliakeim name

Eliakim.

1. Ἐλιακείμ Eliakeim masc
2. Ἐλιακίμ Eliakim masc

1 and Abiud begat **Eliakim**; and **Eliakim** begat Azor;..Matt 1:13
1 and Abiud begat **Eliakim**; and **Eliakim** begat Azor;..... 1:13
2 and Abiud begat **Eliakim**; and **Eliakim** begat Azor;..... 1:13
2 and Abiud begat **Eliakim**; and **Eliakim** begat Azor;..... 1:13
2 which was the son **of Eliakim**,................ Luke 3:30

Two individuals in the genealogy of Jesus bear this name: the son of Abiud (Matthew 1:13) and the son of Melea (Luke 3:30).

1650. Ἐλιέζερ Eliezer name

Eliezer.

1. Ἐλιέζερ Eliezer masc

1 which was the son **of Eliezer**,................ Luke 3:29

The son of Jorim in the genealogy of Jesus (Luke 3:29).

1651. Ἐλιούδ Elioud name

Eliud.

1. Ἐλιούδ Elioud masc

1 Sadoc begat Achim; and Achim begat **Eliud**;........ Matt 1:14
1 And **Eliud** begat Eleazar;.................... 1:15

The son of Achim in the genealogy of Jesus (Matthew 1:14,15).

1652. Ἐλισάβετ Elisabet name

Elisabeth.

1. Ἐλισάβετ Elisabet fem

1 daughters of Aaron, and her name was **Elisabeth**.... Luke 1:5
1 no child, because that **Elisabeth** was barren,........... 1:7
1 and thy wife **Elisabeth** shall bear thee a son,........... 1:13

Ἐλισσαῖος 1653

1 And after those days his wife **Elisabeth** conceived,...**Luke** 1:24	
1 And, behold, thy cousin **Elisabeth**, she hath also........ 1:36	
1 into the house of Zacharias, and saluted **Elisabeth**....... 1:40	
1 that, when **Elisabeth** heard the salutation of Mary,...... 1:41	
1 and **Elisabeth** was filled with the Holy Ghost:.......... 1:41	
1 Now **Elisabeth's** full time came that she should be...... 1:57	

The relative of Mary and wife of Zechariah; she was the mother of John the Baptist (Luke 1:5,36,57ff.).

1653. Ἐλισσαῖος Elissaios name
Elisha.

1. Ἐλισσαίου Elissaiou gen masc
2. Ἐλισαίου Elisaiou gen masc

2 many lepers were in Israel in the time of **Eliseus**.... Luke 4:27

Old Testament prophet cited by Jesus for the healing of Naaman the Syrian (Luke 4:27; cf. 2 Kings 5:1-14).

1654. ἑλίσσω helissō verb
Roll up.

SYNONYM:
πτύσσω ptussō (4286)

גָּלַל gālal (1597), Niphal: be rolled up (Is 34:4).

הָלַךְ hālakh (2050), Go; hithpael: go away (1 Kgs 7:8—Codex Vaticanus only).

חָלַף chālaph (2599), Follow, pass by; hiphil: change (Ps 102:26 [101:26]).

1. ἑλίξεις helixeis 2sing indic fut act
2. ἑλισσόμενον helissomenon
nom/acc sing neu part pres mid

1 And as a vesture **shalt thou fold them up,**........... Heb 1:12
2 like a scroll when it is **rolled up** (NASB)........... Rev 6:14

Classical Greek
Helissō (or *heilissō*, Ionic Greek) is a colorful word in classical Greek. It means "to turn around" or "to roll, wind, or wrap" something. Generally, it describes moving in any kind of rapid circular motion. It was used to describe situations from the rowing of an oar to the rolling over of facts in one's mind. It might also refer to the "whirl" of a dance (see *Liddell-Scott*).

Septuagint Usage
Four texts of the Septuagint read *helissō*, and a different Hebrew word is used in each of the three texts which have a Hebrew counterpart. This shows the flexibility of *helissō*. It describes being "caught" (wrapped up) in a net (*diktuon* [1344]) (Job 18:8) or the rolling up of an article of clothing (Psalm 102:26 [LXX 101:26]).

Isaiah 34:4 provides an example which parallels New Testament usage in his image of the heaven "rolled up as a scroll" (*biblion* [968]).

New Testament Usage
The New Testament records *helissō* only twice. The text in Hebrews is an allusion to Psalm 102 (see above). The earth and heavens will be "rolled up" as an old cloak (Hebrews 1:12). The imagery in Revelation 6:14 is of the "rolling up" of a scroll. This, as in Isaiah, is applied to the sky. The overall picture is of the time of eschatological distress (cf. 6:12ff.).

STRONG 1667, BAUER 251, MOULTON-MILLIGAN 203, LIDDELL-SCOTT 534.

1655. ἕλκος helkos noun
Sore, boil, abscess, wound, ulcer.

שְׁחִין sh^echîn (8253), Boil, swelling (Ex 9:9, Lv 13:18ff., Jb 2:7).

1. ἕλκος helkos nom/acc sing neu
2. ἑλκῶν helkōn gen pl neu
3. ἕλκη helkē nom/acc pl neu

3 moreover the dogs came and licked his **sores**.......Luke 16:21
1 fell a noisome and grievous **sore** upon the men..... Rev 16:2
2 because of their pains and their **sores,**................ 16:11

This noun is used three times: once of the sores of Lazarus in Luke 16:21 and twice of the boils and abscesses which will result from the pouring out of the first and fifth bowls of wrath in the vision of John (Revelation 16:2,11). In the Septuagint Deuteronomy 28:35 uses *helkos* of sores which would be God's judgment. Job 2:7 uses it of the boils Satan put on Job. (The Hebrew probably means leprous or cancerous sores, or any disease that causes the skin to break and ooze.)

STRONG 1668, BAUER 251, MOULTON-MILLIGAN 203, LIDDELL-SCOTT 534.

1656. ἑλκόω helkoō verb
Be covered with sores (passive).

1. ἡλκωμένος hēlkōmenos
nom sing masc part perf mid
2. εἱλκωμένος heilkōmenos
nom sing masc part perf mid

1 which was laid at his gate, **full of sores,**...........Luke 16:20
2 which was laid at his gate, **full of sores,**............... 16:20

This verb corresponds to the noun *helkos* (1655). It means "to have sores, boils, or abscesses." Luke used the perfect passive participle of this verb to describe the condition in which Lazarus found himself at the gate of the rich man, namely, "full of sores" (Luke 16:20).

STRONG 1669, BAUER 251, LIDDELL-SCOTT 534.

1657. ἑλκύω helkuō verb
Drag, draw, force, persuade.
SYNONYMS:
    ἀντλέω antleō (498)
    ἀποσπάω apospaō (639)
    ἐξέρχομαι exerchomai (1814)
    κατασύρω katasurō (2663)
    σπάω spaō (4538)
    σύρω surō (4803)

גָּלָה gālāh (1580), Flow away, carry away (Jb 20:28).
גָּרַר gārar (1688), Drag (Hb 1:15).
מָשָׁה māshāh (5056), Hiphil: draw (2 Sm 22:17).
מָשַׁךְ māshakh (5082), Draw, drag (Dt 21:3, Ps 10:9 [9:30], S/S 1:4).
נְגַד nᵉghadh (A5223), Flow, came forth (Dn 7:10—Aramaic).
נוּף nûph (5311), Hiphil: wield (Is 10:15).
שָׂדַד sādhadh (7897), Piel: till, harrow (Jb 39:10).
שָׁאַף shā'aph (8079), Pant (Eccl 1:5, Jer 14:6).
שָׁלַף shālaph (8418), Arm (with sword), draw (Jgs 20:2,15,17,25).

1. ἕλκουσιν helkousin 3pl indic pres act
2. εἵλκυσεν heilkusen 3sing indic aor act
3. εἵλκυσαν heilkusan 3pl indic aor act
4. ἑλκύσῃ helkusē 3sing subj aor act
5. ἑλκύσαι helkusai inf aor act
6. ἑλκύσω helkusō 1sing indic fut act
7. εἷλκον heilkon 3pl indic imperf act

4 except the Father which hath sent me **draw** him:		John 6:44
6 And I, ... will **draw** all men unto me.		12:32
2 Then Simon Peter having a sword **drew** it,		18:10
5 and now they were not able to **draw** it		21:6
2 and **drew** the net to land full of great fishes,		21:11
3 **drew** them into the marketplace unto the rulers,		Acts 16:19
7 they took Paul, and **drew** him out of the temple:		21:30
1 and **draw** you before the judgment seats?		Jas 2:6

Helkuō (also spelled *helkō*) appears eight times in the New Testament. The uniform translation in the KJV is to "draw." Both literal and figurative uses can be identified. It is used of drawing a sword from its scabbard (John 18:10), of bringing a net up onto a shore (John 21:11), of Paul and Silas being dragged into the marketplace in Philippi (Acts 16:19), of bringing Paul out of the temple (Acts 21:30), and of hauling believers before courts (James 2:6).

Vine notes that *helkō* usually signifies an act of relative gentleness, as opposed to *surō* (4803) which means "drag" (*Expository Dictionary*, "Drag"). This distinction may be important when the word is used to describe the divine drawing of men to Christ (John 6:44; 12:32). Both the Song of Solomon (1:4) and Jeremiah (31:3) use this term to describe the inner compulsion or drawing of love. Thus the crucified Saviour draws the attention of all and the faith of some.

STRONG 1670, BAUER 251 (see "helkō"), MOULTON-MILLIGAN 204, KITTEL 2:503-4 (see "helkō"), LIDDELL-SCOTT 534 (see "helkō").

1658. Ἑλλάς Hellas name
Greece.

1. Ἑλλάδα Hellada acc fem

1 he came into **Greece**,	Acts 20:2

Former world power under Alexander the Great, it referred to the Roman province of Achaia located south of Macedonia (Acts 20:2).

1659. Ἕλλην Hellēn name
Greek.

1. Ἕλλην Hellēn nom sing masc
2. Ἕλληνος Hellēnos gen sing masc
3. Ἕλληνι Hellēni dat sing masc
4. Ἕλληνες Hellēnes nom pl masc
5. Ἑλλήνων Hellēnōn gen pl masc
6. Ἕλλησιν Hellēsin dat pl masc
7. Ἕλληνας Hellēnas acc pl masc

5 will he go unto the dispersed among the Gentiles,		John 7:35
7 among the Gentiles, and teach the **Greeks**?		7:35
4 And there were certain **Greeks** among them		12:20
7 spake unto the **Grecians**, preaching the Lord Jesus.		Acts 11:20
5 both of the Jews and also of the **Greeks** believed.		14:1
2 a Jewess, and believed; but his father was a **Greek**:		16:1
1 for they knew all that his father was a **Greek**.		16:3
5 and of the devout **Greeks** a great multitude,		17:4
4 and persuaded the Jews and the **Greeks**.		18:4
4 Then all the **Greeks** took Sosthenes,		18:17
7 the word of the Lord Jesus, both Jews and **Greeks**.		19:10
6 And this was known to all the Jews and **Greeks**		19:17
6 Testifying both to the Jews, and also to the **Greeks**,		20:21
7 and further brought **Greeks** also into the temple,		21:28
6 I am debtor both to the **Greeks**, and ... Barbarians;		Rom 1:14
3 to the Jew first, and also to the **Greek**.		1:16
2 of the Jew first, and also of the **Gentile**;		2:9
3 to the Jew first, and also to the **Gentile**:		2:10
7 both Jews and Gentiles, that they are all under sin;		3:9
2 is no difference between the Jew and the **Greek**:		10:12
4 and the **Greeks** seek after wisdom:		I Co 1:22
6 and unto the **Greeks** foolishness;		1:23
6 them which are called, both Jews and **Greeks**,		1:24

6 neither to the Jews, nor to the Gentiles,	1 Co 10:32
4 whether we be Jews or Gentiles,	12:13
1 neither Titus, who was with me, being a Greek,	Gal 2:3
1 There is neither Jew nor Greek,	3:28
1 Where there is neither Greek nor Jew,	Col 3:11

A native of Greece, used of Timothy's father (Acts 16:1); every New Testament occurrence could be seen as referring to Gentiles, as opposed to Jews (Romans 1:14,16).

1660. Ἑλληνικός Hellēnikos name-adj
Greek.

1. Ἑλληνικοῖς **Hellēnikois** dat pl masc/neu
2. Ἑλληνικῇ **Hellēnikē** dat sing fem

1 in letters of Greek, and Latin, and Hebrew,	Luke 23:38
2 but in the Greek tongue hath his name Apollyon.	Rev 9:11

The Greek language (Luke 23:38; Revelation 9:11).

1660B. Ἑλληνίς Hellēnis name
Greek.

1. Ἑλληνίς **Hellēnis** nom sing fem
2. Ἑλληνίδων **Hellēnidōn** gen pl fem

1 woman was a Greek, a Syrophenician by nation;	Mark 7:26
2 also of honourable women which were Greeks,	Acts 17:12

Gentile, used of the Syrophoenician woman (Mark 7:26), and the leading citizens of Beroea (Acts 17:12).

1661. Ἑλληνιστής Hellēnistēs name
Hellenist, Grecian, Greek-speaking Jew.

1. Ἑλληνιστῶν **Hellēnistōn** gen pl masc
2. Ἑλληνιστάς **Hellēnistas** acc pl masc

1 a murmuring of the Grecians against the Hebrews,	Acts 6:1
2 and disputed against the Grecians:	9:29
2 spake unto the Grecians, preaching the Lord Jesus.	11:20

With the conquests of Alexander the Great in the Fourth Century B.C. and the subsequent rise of the Roman Empire, the Mediterranean world had become relatively unified through easier travel, common language, and shared elements of culture. For purposes of commerce many Jews migrated to commercial centers all around the Mediterranean Sea. As a result differences developed between them and Palestinian Jews. Even though they generally held onto their religious heritage, Jews of the Dispersion adopted the language and—in varying degrees—the customs of Graeco-Roman culture; they became "Hellenized." This background sets the context for the meaning of *Hellēnistēs*. The traditional view has been that Jew versus Greek, or Gentile, distinguished racial and religious matters; but Hebrew versus "Hellenist" distinguished languages and customs between Jews at home and abroad (cf. Lightfoot, *Philippians*, pp.146-148). Hebrews spoke Hebrew (Aramaic) as their mother tongue while "Hellenists" used Greek and/or some other language to which they "were born" (Acts 2:6,8,11).

The Hebrew-Hellenist distinction also tended to correlate with Palestinian Jew and Dispersion Jew. That correlation was not absolute, of course, since in Jerusalem itself there was one synagogue (some think five) apparently for Hellenists (Acts 6:8-15; cf. 6:1-5), the one from which Stephen—and perhaps Saul and Barnabas—originated (Acts 6:36,37; 7:58-81; 11:20,22; 15:36-41). Jews raised outside Palestine might return to their ancestral land, and Jews raised in Palestine might emigrate elsewhere but diligently observe the law of Moses, the traditions of the elders, and Jewish social customs. Paul's family could be an example since he called himself a "Hebrew of Hebrews" (Philippians 3:5) despite being born in Tarsus of Cilicia. *Hellēnistēs* would typically refer to a Jew outside of Palestine, though the word itself stressed which language he spoke.

Hellēnistēs evidently does not appear anywhere earlier than Acts of the Apostles, and there it occurs for certain in only two places. Acts 6:1 records a difficulty in the Jerusalem church because the "Hebrews" had been overlooking widows among the "Hellenists" when dispensing support. The second passage is Acts 9:29 where Paul, having returned to Jerusalem after his conversion, was disputing with the "Hellenists," probably many of the same group whose synagogue earlier was instrumental in getting Stephen executed with Paul's approval.

According to most editions of the Greek text, a third usage appears in Acts 11:20. Describing the persecution of Judaean Christians, Luke says that in general these believers preached the gospel wherever they fled but only to Jews (11:19; cf. 8:4). In Antioch, however, some Cyprians and Cyrenians "began to speak also to the *Hellenists*" (*UBS 3rd*; Wescott-Hort; Majority Text; *Textus Receptus*). When news of this reached Jerusalem, the church sent Barnabas to Antioch, and he in turn traveled on to Tarsus and brought Paul to this new work (11:22-25).

A rather well-attested alternate reading puts "Greeks" (*Hellēnas* [see 1659], *Nestle-Aland 25th*) in place of "Hellenists" (*Hellēnistas*), which makes proper sense under the traditional meaning of the latter term. There would have been nothing unusual about preaching to Greek-speaking Jews. That had already been done in Jerusalem long before (Acts 6), since it was being done elsewhere in this same scattering (11:19). Also, Samaritans had been evangelized without objections (Acts 8:4-25), although they were farther removed from mainstream Judaism than Greek-speaking Jews in Antioch would have been. Yet preaching to these people in Antioch must have been unusual because the term "Hellenists" in Acts 11:20 clearly contrasts with the word "Jews" in 11:19, and because soon afterward Judaizers tried to get them to be circumcised (Acts 15:1-35; cf. Galatians 2:11ff.). It is possible, then, that those actually evangelized in Antioch were in fact Gentiles (possibly "God-fearers," or *sebomenoi*, Gentiles who attended synagogue but were not circumcised so as to be included among proselytes: Luke 7:2-5; Acts 10:2; 13:48-50; 16:14; 17:4,17; 18:7).

The question that remains is how to define *Hellēnistēs* in light of this fact. Various suggestions have been made: (1) that *Hellēnistēs* means "proselyte" since Nicolas, one of the seven, was a proselyte (Acts 6:5); (2) that *Hellēnistēs* and *Hellēn* are synonyms meaning "Gentile" in all three references. If so, one wonders why there were not (recorded) conflicts over their conversion as was the case later in Antioch, why Peter and other Jewish Christians were so skeptical about evangelizing Cornelius' household (Acts 10:1 to 11:18), why the main body of fleeing Christians preached only to Jews, or why the conference on circumcision even occurred. God's granting Gentiles repentance unto life was a new thought as late as Acts 11:18 (cf. 8:14-16; 22:22-24). Furthermore, early Gentile conversions do not fit with the natural expansion of Christianity to increasingly distant groups—Jews, Samaritans, Gentiles (cf. Acts 1:8; Romans 1:16, etc.).

Another view is as follows: (3) that *Hellēnistēs* means simply "Greek-speaking" with no implication about race or religion. If this is so, one wonders what contrast would have been communicated between Acts 11:19 and 11:20. Both groups would have been Greek-speaking. To use in the same sentence a term for Antioch *Gentiles* that could as well be used for *Jews* with whom they are deliberately contrasted would surely be unclear.

On the whole, the easiest proposal seems to be (4) that the principles of textual criticism by themselves are simply inadequate in Acts 11:20. *Hellēnistēs* means "Hellenized Jew," but it is not the right word here even as *Hellēn* is not the right word in Acts 9:29 despite its presence in one major manuscript. The reader needs to interpret the text in light of context and let *Hellnistēs* have its traditional meaning: Greek-speaking Jew.

STRONG 1675, BAUER 252, KITTEL 2:504-16, LIDDELL-SCOTT 536, COLIN BROWN 2:124,126.

1662. Ἑλληνιστί Hellēnisti name-adv
Greek.

1. Ἑλληνιστί Hellēnisti

1 it was written in Hebrew, and Greek, and Latin....	John 19:20
1 Who said, Canst thou speak Greek?...............	Acts 21:37

The Greek language (John 19:20; Acts 21:37).

1663. Ἑλληνίς Hellēnis
See word study at number 1660B.

1664. ἐλλογέω ellogeō verb
To charge, put to one's account.
CROSS-REFERENCE:
λέγω legō (2978)

1. ἐλλόγει ellogei 2sing impr pres act
2. ἐλλογεῖται ellogeitai 3sing indic pres mid
3. ἐλλόγα elloga 2sing impr pres act

2 but sin is not **imputed** when there is no law.........	Rom 5:13
1 or oweth thee ought, **put that on mine account**;.....	Phlm 1:18
3 or oweth thee ought, **put that on mine account**;.........	1:18

In the secular, commercial world of the First Century this verb served as a technical term. It was used by Paul in this sense in Philemon 18 where he told Philemon that if Onesimus had caused him any loss, then he should put it to Paul's account and he (Paul) would repay him. Elsewhere, Paul wrote that sin is not charged against one's account when there is no law (Romans 5:13).

STRONG 1677, BAUER 252, MOULTON-MILLIGAN 204 (see "ellogaō"), KITTEL 2:516-17, LIDDELL-SCOTT 537.

1665. Ἐλμωδάμ Elmōdam name
Elmodam.

1. Ἐλμωδάμ Elmōdam masc
2. Ἐλμαδάμ Elmadam masc

1 which was the son of Elmodam,.....................	Luke 3:28
2 which was the son of Elmodam,.....................	3:28

The son of Er in the genealogy of Jesus (Luke 3:28).

1666. ἐλπίζω elpizō verb
Hope for, expect, trust in.

COGNATES:
  ἀπελπίζω apelpizō (557)
  ἐλπίς elpis (1667)
  προελπίζω proelpizō (4137)

SYNONYMS:
  ἀναμένω anamenō (360)
  ἀπεκδέχομαι apekdechomai (549)
  ἐκδέχομαι ekdechomai (1538)
  προσδέχομαι prosdechomai (4185)
  προσδοκάω prosdokaō (4186)

בָּטַח bāṭach (1019), Trust (2 Kgs 18:5, Ps 4:5, Mi 7:5).

בֶּטַח beṭach (1020), Be safe, be secure (Jb 24:23).

גָּלַל gālal (1597), Trust (Ps 22:8 [21:8]).

דָּרַשׁ dārash (1938), Seek, rally to (Is 11:10).

חָלַל chālal (2591), Be used; hophal: began (Gn 4:26).

חָסָה chāsâh (2725), Seek refuge, trust (Pss 16:1 [15:1], 31:1 [30:1], 91:4 [90:4], 144:2 [143:2]).

חָשַׁק chāshaq (2945), Love (Ps 91:14 [90:14]).

יָחַל yāchal (3282), Piel: wait, hope (Ps 31:24 [30:24], 71:14 [70:14], Is 42:4); hiphil: wait, hope (Pss 38:15 [37:15], 43:5 [42:5]).

נָשָׂא nāsâ' (5558), Lift, carry; piel: long for, desire (Jer 44:14 [51:14]).

קָוָה qāwâh (7245), Wait; piel: wait for, trust (Is 25:9, 26:8).

קָרֵב qārēv (7414), Draw near; piel: soon to come (Ez 36:8).

רְחַץ rᵉchats (A7648), Hithpeel: trust in (Dn 3:28—Aramaic).

שָׂבַר sāvar (7887), Piel: hope, wait (Ps 145:15 [144:15], Is 38:18).

שָׁעַן shā‘an (8550), Niphal: relied on (2 Chr 13:18).

שָׁפַט shāphaṭ (8570), Judge, rule (Is 51:5).

1. ἐλπίζω elpizō 1sing indic pres act
2. ἐλπίζει elpizei 3sing indic pres act
3. ἐλπίζομεν elpizomen 1pl indic pres act
4. ἐλπίζετε elpizete 2pl indic pres act
5. ἐλπίζων elpizōn nom sing masc part pres act
6. ἐλπίζουσαι elpizousai nom pl fem part pres act
7. ἠλπίσαμεν ēlpisamen 1pl indic aor act
8. ἐλπίσατε elpisate 2pl impr aor act
9. ἤλπικεν ēlpiken 3sing indic perf act
10. ἠλπίκαμεν ēlpikamen 1pl indic perf act
11. ἠλπίκατε ēlpikate 2pl indic perf act
12. ἠλπικότες ēlpikotes nom pl masc part perf act
13. ἠλπικέναι ēlpikenai inf perf act
14. ἐλπιοῦσιν elpiousin 3pl indic fut act
15. ἤλπιζεν ēlpizen 3sing indic imperf act
16. ἠλπίζομεν ēlpizomen 1pl indic imperf act
17. ἐλπιζομένων elpizomenōn gen pl neu part pres mid

14	And in his name shall the Gentiles **trust**..........	Matt 12:21
4	if ye lend to them of whom ye **hope** to receive,....	Luke 6:34
15	he **hoped** to have seen some miracle done by him.....	23:8
16	But we **trusted** that it had been he which should.....	24:21
11	that accuseth you, even Moses, in whom ye **trust**...	John 5:45
5	He **hoped** also that money should have been given	Acts 24:26
2	instantly serving God day and night, **hope** to come....	26:7
2	for what a man seeth, why doth he yet **hope** for?...	Rom 8:24
3	But if we **hope** for that we see not,..................	8:25
14	in him shall the Gentiles **trust**......................	15:12
1	for I **trust** to see you in my journey,................	15:24
2	**hopeth** all things, endureth all things..............	1 Co 13:7
12	If in this life only we **have hope** in Christ,...........	15:19
12	If in this life only we **have hope** in Christ,...........	15:19
1	but I **trust** to tarry a while with you,................	16:7
10	in whom we **trust** that he will yet deliver us;.......	2 Co 1:10
1	and I **trust** ye shall acknowledge even to the end;.....	1:13
1	I **trust** also are made manifest in your consciences.....	5:11
7	And this they did, not as we **hoped**,.................	8:5
1	**trust** that ye shall know that we are not reprobates...	13:6
1	But I **trust** in the Lord Jesus to send Timotheus....	Phlp 2:19
1	Him therefore I **hope** to send presently,................	2:23
5	things write I ... **hoping** to come unto thee shortly:	1 Tm 3:14
10	because we **trust** in the living God,..................	4:10
9	is a widow indeed, and desolate, **trusteth** in God,.....	5:5
13	nor **trust** in uncertain riches, but in the living God,....	6:17
1	I **trust** that through your prayers I shall be given..	Phlm 1:22
17	Now faith is the substance of things **hoped** for,....	Heb 11:1
8	be sober, and **hope** to the end for the grace.........	1 Pt 1:13
6	who **trusted** in God, adorned themselves,..............	3:5
1	I **trust** to come unto you, and speak face to face,..	2 Jn 1:12
1	But I **trust** I shall shortly see thee,.................	3 Jn 1:14

This verb means "to put one's expectation and trust for the future in someone or something, to hope for something to come to pass, or to expect to be able to do something." It is a verb which deals with the future in an anticipatory and positive way. *Elpizō* thereby brings the power of the future into the present to give meaning and motivation. Hope involves expectation, trust, and patient waiting.

New Testament Usage
In the New Testament this verb is used to mean "to hope in" or "to trust in" (Matthew 12:21; Romans 15:12; 1 Corinthians 15:19; 2

Corinthians 1:10; 1 Timothy 4:10; 5:5; 6:17), "to hope for" and "to hope that" (Luke 24:21; Acts 24:26; Romans 8:24 [cf. verse 25]; 1 Corinthians 13:7; 2 Corinthians 1:13; 5:11; 8:5; 13:6; Philemon 22; Hebrews 11:1), and "to expect to be able to do something" (Luke 6:34; 23:8; Acts 26:7; Romans 15:24; 1 Corinthians 16:7; Philippians 2:19,23; 1 Timothy 3:14; 2 John 12; 3 John 14). The Septuagint usually uses it of putting one's hope in God or His Word (Psalm 42:5,11 [LXX 41:5,11]; 119:114 [118:114]; 145:15 [144:15]; Isaiah 51:5). (See word study at *elpis* [1667].)

STRONG 1679, BAUER 252, MOULTON-MILLIGAN 204, KITTEL 2:517-33, LIDDELL-SCOTT 537, COLIN BROWN 2:238-46.

1667. ἐλπίς elpis noun
Hope, expectation.
CROSS-REFERENCE:
ἐλπίζω elpizō (1666)

בָּטַח bāṭach (1019), Qal: trust (Is 26:3, 47:10); hiphil: hope, trust (Ps 22:9 [21:9]).

בֶּטַח beṭach (1020), Safety (Jgs 18:7, Ps 4:8, Hos 2:18).

בִּטָּחוֹן biṭṭāchôn (1023), Hope (Eccl 9:4).

חָזוּת chāzûth (2471), Agreement (Is 28:18).

חֶסֶד cheṣedh (2721), Devotion, goodness (2 Chr 35:26).

כֶּסֶל keṣel (3815), Confidence (Ps 78:7 [77:7]).

מַבָּט mabbāṭ (4146), Hope (Zec 9:5—Codex Alexandrinus only).

מִבְטָח mivṭāch (4148), Trust, confidence (Ps 40:4 [39:4], Prv 14:26, Ez 29:16).

מַחְסֶה machṣeh (4406II) Refuge (Pss 14:6 [13:6], 61:3 [60:3], Is 28:15).

נְדִיבָה neḏhîvāh (5260), Honor (Jb 30:15).

נֶפֶשׁ nephesh (5497), Desire (Dt 24:15).

עֶזְרָה 'ezrāh (6046), Help (Is 31:2).

צְבִי tseʿvî (6905), Glorious beauty (Is 28:4,5).

קַו qaw (7242II) Possibly sounds imitating prophetic speech (Is 28:10,13).

רַחַץ rachats (7649), Wash basin (Pss 60:8 [59:8], 108:9 [107:9]).

שֶׂבֶר sēver (7888), Hope (Ps 146:5 [145:5]).

תּוֹחֶלֶת tôcheleth (8760), Hope (Prv 13:12, Lam 3:18).

תִּקְוָה tiqwāh (8951), Expectation, hope (Jb 4:6, 14:7, Prv 11:7, Ez 37:11).

1. ἐλπίς elpis nom sing fem
2. ἐλπίδος elpidos gen sing fem
3. ἐλπίδι elpidi dat sing fem
4. ἐλπίδα elpida acc sing fem
5. ἐλπίδι helpidi dat sing fem

3	moreover also my flesh shall rest in **hope**:	Acts 2:26
1	masters saw that the **hope** of their gains was gone,	16:19
2	of the **hope** and resurrection of the dead	23:6
4	And have **hope** toward God,	24:15
3	**hope** of the promise made of God unto our fathers:	26:6
2	For which **hope**'s sake, king Agrippa,	26:7
1	all **hope** that we should be saved was then taken	27:20
2	for the **hope** of Israel I am bound with this chain.	28:20
4	Who against **hope** believed in hope,	Rom 4:18
3	Who against hope believed in **hope**,	4:18
3	and rejoice in **hope** of the glory of God.	5:2
4	And patience, experience; and experience, **hope**:	5:4
1	And **hope** maketh not ashamed;	5:5
5	him who hath subjected the same in **hope**,	8:20
3	For we are saved by **hope**:	8:24
1	saved by hope: but **hope** that is seen is not hope:	8:24
1	saved by hope: but hope that is seen is not **hope**:	8:24
3	Rejoicing in **hope**; patient in tribulation;	12:12
4	and comfort of the scriptures might have **hope**.	15:4
2	of **hope** fill you with all joy and peace in believing,	15:13
3	peace in believing, that ye may abound in **hope**,	15:13
3	that he that ploweth should plow in **hope**;	1 Co 9:10
2	and that he that thresheth in **hope**	9:10
3	thresheth in hope should be partaker of his **hope**.	9:10
1	And now abideth faith, **hope**, charity, these three;	13:13
1	And our **hope** of you is stedfast,	2 Co 1:7
4	Seeing then that we have such **hope**,	3:12
4	but having **hope**, when your faith is increased,	10:15
4	For we through the Spirit wait for the **hope**	Gal 5:5
1	that ye may know what is the **hope** of his calling,	Eph 1:18
4	having no **hope**, and without God in the world:	2:12
3	even as ye are called in one **hope** of your calling;	4:4
4	According to my earnest expectation and my **hope**,	Phlp 1:20
4	For the **hope** which is laid up for you in heaven,	Col 1:5
2	be not moved away from the **hope** of the gospel,	1:23
1	which is Christ in you, the **hope** of glory:	1:27
2	and patience of **hope** in our Lord Jesus Christ,	1 Th 1:3
1	For what is our **hope**, or joy, or crown of rejoicing?	2:19
4	ye sorrow not, even as others which have no **hope**.	4:13
4	and for an helmet, the **hope** of salvation.	5:8
4	consolation and good **hope** through grace,	2 Th 2:16
2	and Lord Jesus Christ, which is our **hope**;	1 Tm 1:1
3	In **hope** of eternal life, which God, ... promised	Tit 1:2
4	Looking for that blessed **hope**,	2:13
4	be made heirs according to the **hope** of eternal life.	3:7
2	and the rejoicing of the **hope** firm unto the end.	Heb 3:6
2	to the full assurance of **hope** unto the end:	6:11
2	who have fled for refuge to lay hold upon the **hope**	6:18
2	but the bringing in of a better **hope** did;	7:19
2	hold fast the confession of our **hope** (NASB)	10:23
4	hath begotten us again unto a lively **hope**	1 Pt 1:3
4	that your faith and **hope** might be in God.	1:21
2	to every man that asketh you a reason of the **hope**	3:15
4	And every man that hath this **hope** in him	1 Jn 3:3

Classical Greek

The customary Greek terms for hope in the New Testament are the noun *elpis*, "hope," and its verb *elpizō* (1666), "to hope." Both words are used subjectively, such as the expectation of something good (e.g., Romans 4:18; 1 Corinthians 9:10; Philippians 1:20), and objectively, as in reference to hope itself (e.g., Acts 28:20; Romans 8:24; Galatians 5:5; Ephesians 1:18; Colossians 1:5,23,27; 1 Timothy 1:1; Titus 2:13; Hebrews 6:18).

Whereas *elpis/elpizō* in the New Testament always carry a positive sense, in secular Greek they have a more neutral meaning and describe man's projection of the future; *elpis* can even express fear. "What we mean by hope, is called *elpis agathē*, though later *elpis* is often used for hope in our sense" (Bultmann, "elpis," *Kittel*, 2:518; cf. *agathos* [18]).

For the Greek, the nature of hope was shaped by his understanding of man's existence. Existence, to the Greek, was governed by the present which he must accept as it is. But it was also controlled by the inescapable effects of the past and the fortune or misfortune waiting in the future. By his very nature man looks toward the future. Sometimes *elpis* can acquire the sense of a "golden hope for the future" (ibid., 2:519). This recalls the old saying that "hope is the only virtue which man did not lose, the only thing man has left." Such hope can refer to the earthly future as well as existence beyond the present. But the Greeks believed that man's hope is uncertain and consequently dangerous; it invites disappointment. Stoicism had no place for hope in its system of thought. The Roman stoic Seneca defined hope as "an uncertain good."

Although hope was viewed as a natural component of the human condition, it never stood as an expression of any fundamental, religious attitude toward life. When Paul wrote to the Ephesians that they were previously "without hope and without God in the world" (Ephesians 2:12, NIV), he may indeed have been offering us insight into their very attitude toward life.

Septuagint Usage

There is probably no area in which the contrast between the Greek and Hebraic concepts of life appear more clearly than in the differences between their conceptions of hope. The entire attitude toward life and religious experience expressed in the Septuagint is based upon faith and hope in God. Usually this is expressed in the Hebrew by the noun *tiqvah*. Typical of the great disparity between Hebraic and Greek modes of thought concerning this area is the evidence that the principal Hebrew verb for hope is translated into the Greek *elpis* only twice. Twenty-six times *qāwâh* is translated by *hupomenō* (5116), "I endure patiently, I await." On the other hand, *elpizō* most often functions as an equivalent for terms which denote faith and trust: *bāṭach*, "to feel secure, safe" (46 times); *chāshaq*, "to hide, take refuge" (20 times); *yāchal*, "to wait" (16 times). When *elpizō* is associated with the Hebrew words for confidence and trust, the Greek term acquires a content which is rather different from the original sense of the secular understanding. This background made *elpizō/elpis* suitable for the writers of the New Testament as an expression of Christian hope.

Thus, hope in the New Testament as a religious idea is firmly rooted in the Old Testament. God is the ultimate hope of Israel (Psalms 62:6 [LXX 61:6]; 71:5 [70:5]; Jeremiah 14:8; 17:13). The devout Israelite looked to God with assurance (Proverbs 3:26) and with expectation (Psalms 130:7 [LXX 129:7]; 131:3 [130:3]). His mercy and grace are the cornerstones of the hope of the faithful (Psalm 33:18-22 [LXX 32:18-22]). He gives the righteous hope (Psalm 119:47-49). A life in awe of God and in harmony with the will of God gives future hope (Proverbs 23:17,18; cf. 3:21-26; Job 4:6).

Any who desert the Lord, the hope of Israel, will be put to shame at the Judgment (Jeremiah 17:13). The hope of the godless perishes (Job 8:13; cf. Proverbs 10:28), and he who is wise in his own conceit is without hope (Proverbs 26:12). Hope is not based upon the visible (Job 31:24; cf. Psalm 52:9 [LXX 51:9]). The visions and prophecies of the false prophets afforded only false hope (Ezekiel 13:6). The righteous put their trust in God's help and protection in the struggle of life, not only for themselves, but for the sake of the nation (Psalms 39:1-8 [LXX 38:1-8]; 62:1,6; Jeremiah 14:8).

Gradually hope also assumed an eschatological quality (Isaiah 38:18; chapters 40 and on). The expectation of the people, i.e., their hope, was given expression in their waiting for Messiah, whom the Scriptures promised (Zechariah 9:9-12). Messianic redemption became more narrowly defined as Israel's hope. Israel placed its future and hope in the promise of Messiah. The Messiah would bring redemption and salvation (Isaiah 11:1-9; 25:8; 32:16f.). Messiah was also the hope of the Gentiles (Isaiah 42:4). During times of exile, humiliation, or punishment, the godly Israelites had a reason to keep on living because of this hope (Jeremiah 29:11f. [LXX 36:11f.]; 31:17 [38:17]).

In addition to the hope of messianic deliverance Israel looked to God for deliverance beyond their present existence. (Prior to the coming of Jesus, Jewish expectation of a Messiah was viewed as a physical, political enterprise.) Glimpses of eternal hope appear in Psalms 9:19 (LXX 8:19); 16:8-11 (15:8-11); and in Isaiah 25:8. This eternal hope is a resurrection hope (Psalm 16:10 [LXX 15:10]; cf. Acts 2:25-28; 13:35; cf. Daniel 12:2).

New Testament Usage

In the New Testament the verb *elpizō* occurs 31 times and the noun *elpis* 48 times. Although most of the writers of the New Testament used *elpizō/elpis*, they are nevertheless, principally terms which belonged to Paul; he used the noun 36 times and the verb 19 times.

Hope plays an even greater part in the New Testament story than in the drama of the Old Testament. First Peter 1:3 should be recognized as a classic text for understanding hope in the New Testament. The believers knew they were "begotten again unto a lively hope by the resurrection of Jesus Christ from the dead." The hope of the New Testament is characterized as "living" because it is being presently realized. The eschatological hope is in a decisive way beginning to be fulfilled. The Kingdom is at hand! The Messiah is revealed! The resurrection has begun!

Along with these marvelous insights of salvation history, hope is also connected with normal human existence (Luke 6:34; Acts 16:19; 24:26; 27:20). Often hope expresses the longing for fellowship and communion with other Christians (2 John 12; 3 John 14). But above all, hope was linked to the message of the gospel itself.

God and His grace are the real hope of the believer (Acts 24:15; 2 Corinthians 1:10; 1 Timothy 4:10; 5:5; 6:17; 1 Peter 1:21; 3:5). God is even addressed as "the God of hope" (Romans 15:13).

The revelation and saving action of God in Christ resulted in Christ's becoming the hope of believers (1 Corinthians 15:19; 1 Timothy 1:1). Just as devout saints of the Old Testament set their hope on the coming Messiah, so too, believers in the new community set their hope in the One who came in the fullness of time. Christian hope is founded upon the prophetic word (Romans 15:4) and in a historical fact—the death of Christ on the Cross. Therefore, hope is assured (Hebrews 6:18,19), living (1 Peter 1:3), good (2 Thessalonians 2:16), and blessed (Titus 2:13). To be without God and without Christ is tantamount to being without hope (Ephesians 2:12; 1 Thessalonians 4:13).

To an even greater degree than in the Old Testament, the hope of the New Testament is eschatological. Hope is hidden in the heavens (Colossians 1:5); it is a hope of resurrection (cf. 1 Corinthians 15:19); it concerns eternal life which God promised before the world began (Titus 1:2); and it is the hope of the glory of God and Jesus Christ (Romans 5:2; Titus 2:13) in which the body also is to participate in (Romans 8:22f.). When *elpizō/elpis* is used absolutely it usually connotes the eschatological consummation (Romans 8:24; 12:12; 15:13; Ephesians 2:12).

At the center of eschatological hope lies the return of Christ. This event marks the transition between the Christian's present condition and his future glorious condition. The future hope of the Christian is in every way tied to the person of Jesus Christ. He stands as the guarantor of all the promises of God (2 Corinthians 1:20); therefore, hope in Christ is an "anchor for the soul" (Hebrews 6:19, NIV). Because of the critical nature of hope for successful Christian living, believers are admonished to hold it fast (Hebrews 3:6; 6:11; 10:23). While believers are looking for that "blessed hope" (Titus 2:13), they may experience trials and hardships because of their faith, but the living hope will sustain them. It gives joy (Romans 12:12; 15:13), comfort (1 Thessalonians 4:13f.), patience during persecution (1 Thessalonians 1:3), and protection during strife (1 Thessalonians 5:8; cf. Ephesians 6:17). It unifies (Ephesians 4:4), inspires ministry (1 Timothy 4:10), and encourages holiness (1 John 3:3).

Christian hope is never self-centered, either in its motivation or goal; Christ is it impetus. The hope of the Christian is not only a personal hope, but also a universal hope. Christ is hope not only for the Jews (Acts 28:20), but for the nations (Matthew 12:18-21). He is the hope of the world, including all of creation which awaits the "revealing of the sons of God" (Romans 8:18ff.; cf. Matthew 19:28; 2 Peter 3:13).

Faith, hope, and love are esteemed as that which will endure when everything else has perished (1 Corinthians 13:13). These three fundamental elements of the Christian life are often conjoined in the New Testament (Galatians 5:5,6; 1 Thessalonians 1:3; 5:8;

Hebrews 6:10-12; 1 Peter 1:21,22). "Faith is the substance of things hoped for" (Hebrews 11:1), and like Abraham believers must often hope against hope (Romans 4:18). But love "hopeth all things" (1 Corinthians 13:7; cf. Colossians 1:4,5).

STRONG 1680, BAUER 252-53, MOULTON-MILLIGAN 204-5, KITTEL 2:517-33, LIDDELL-SCOTT 537, COLIN BROWN 2:238-46.

1668. Ἐλύμας Elumas name
Elymas.

1. Ἐλύμας Elumas nom masc

1 But **Elymas** the sorcerer for so is his name .... Acts 13:8

Jewish false prophet named Bar-jesus who was struck blind for opposing Paul before Sergius Paulus on the island of Cyprus (Acts 13:8ff.).

1669. ἐλωΐ elōi noun
Eloi.

1. ἐλωΐ elōi

1 saying, **Eloi, Eloi,** lama sabachthani? .... Mark 15:34
1 saying, **Eloi, Eloi,** lama sabachthani? 15:34

This word, which means "My God," occurs in Mark 15:34 and in some manuscripts of Matthew 27:46. Mark's "Eloi, Eloi" represents an Aramaic origin, while Matthew's "Eli, Eli" represents a Hebrew original. Those manuscripts of Matthew which agree with Mark's "Eloi, Eloi" do so probably because of assimilation (Metzger, *Textual Commentary*, p.70). According to Carson (*The Expositor's Bible Commentary*, 8:578), Jesus' cry of agony was probably in Aramaic, the language of everyday life, since *sabachthani* is Aramaic in both Matthew and Mark.

STRONG 1682, BAUER 253, MOULTON-MILLIGAN 205.

1670. ἐμαυτοῦ emautou prs-pron
Myself.

1. ἐμαυτοῦ emautou gen 1sing masc
2. ἐμαυτῷ emautō dat 1sing masc
3. ἐμαυτόν emauton acc 1sing masc

3 a man under authority, having soldiers under **me**: ... Matt 8:9
3 neither thought I **myself** worthy to come .... Luke 7:7
3 under authority, having under **me** soldiers, ... 7:8
1 I can of **mine own** self do nothing: .... John 5:30
1 If I bear witness of **myself,** my witness is not true. 5:31
1 whether it be of God, or whether I speak of **myself.** John 7:17
1 and I am not come of **myself,** 7:28
1 Though I bear record of **myself,** 8:14
1 I am one that bear witness of **myself,** 8:18
1 and that I do nothing of **myself;** 8:28
1 neither came I of **myself,** but he sent me. 8:42
3 If I honour **myself,** my honour is nothing: 8:54
1 but I lay it down of **myself.** 10:18
3 And I, ... will draw all men unto **me.** 12:32
1 For I have not spoken of **myself;** 12:49
3 I will come again, and receive you unto **myself;** 14:3
1 words that I speak unto you I speak not of **myself:** 14:10
1 I will love him, and will manifest **myself** to him. 14:21
3 And for their sakes I sanctify **myself,** 17:19
2 neither count I my life dear **unto myself,** .... Acts 20:24
1 I do the more cheerfully answer for **myself:** 24:10
3 I think **myself** happy, king Agrippa, ... 26:2
2 I verily thought **with myself,** 26:9
2 I have reserved **to myself** seven thousand men, ... Rom 11:4
3 of man's judgment: yea, I judge not **mine own** self. ... 1 Co 4:3
2 For I know nothing **by myself,** 4:4
3 in a figure transferred to **myself** and to Apollos 4:6
3 For I would that all men were even as I **myself.** 7:7
3 yet have I made **myself** servant unto all, ... 9:19
1 not seeking **mine own** profit, ... 10:33
2 But I determined this **with myself,** .... 2 Co 2:1
3 in abasing **myself** that ye might be exalted, ... 11:7
3 I have kept **myself** from being burdensome 11:9
1 of **myself** I will not glory, but in mine infirmities. 12:5
3 I make **myself** a transgressor. .... Gal 2:18
3 Brethren, I count not **myself** to have apprehended: .. Phlp 3:13
3 Whom I would have retained with **me,** .... Phlm 1:13

Classical Greek Usage
Emautou is the reflexive pronoun of the first person singular meaning "myself." Other than *emautou*, meaning "myself" in classical Greek, it is used in an expression in Plato that means "to be master of oneself" (see *Liddell-Scott*).

New Testament Usage
In the New Testament *emautou* is sometimes used with a noun and emphasizes possession as in 1 Corinthians 10:33 (*to emautou sumphoron*, "mine own profit"). At times in the New Testament *emautou* is used with various prepositions to make unique expressions. Used with *apo* (570), "from," *emautou* shows authority. Jesus said (John 5:30), "I can *of mine own self* do nothing." This expression is used frequently in John (7:17,28; 8:28,42; 14:10). With the preposition *ek* (1523), *emautou* also means "authority" (10:18). Here Jesus used *emautou* for emphasis. One also finds *pros emautou*, "to myself." It is to himself and no other that men will be drawn. Jesus spoke about himself, *peri emautou*, in John 8:14.

At times in the New Testament *emautou* is used merely for emphasis. Jesus said (John 14:3), "I will ... receive you unto myself," emphasizing that He and no other will receive His people. Mostly *emautou* is used with a verb and refers back to the subject showing that the subject is acting on its own behalf or is acting on itself in some way (1 Corinthians 9:19).

1671. ἐμβαίνω embainō verb

Go into, step into.

COGNATE:
ὑπερβαίνω huperbainō (5070)

SYNONYMS:
εἴσειμι eiseimi (1510)
εἰσέρχομαι eiserchomai (1511)
εἰσπορεύω eisporeuō (1515)
ἐπιβαίνω epibainō (1895)

בּוֹא bô' (971), Go into, work (Na 3:14).
יָרַד yāradh (3495), Went down (Jon 1:3).
עָלָה 'ālâh (6148), Go up, ascend (Jgs 15:6—Codex Alexandrinus only).

1. ἐνέβη enebē 3sing indic aor act
2. ἐνέβησαν enebēsan 3pl indic aor act
3. ἐμβάς embas nom sing masc part aor act
4. ἐμβάντος embantos gen sing masc part aor act
5. ἐμβάντι embanti dat sing masc part aor act
6. ἐμβάντα embanta acc sing masc part aor act
7. ἐμβάντες embantes nom pl masc part aor act
8. ἐμβάντων embantōn gen pl masc part aor act
9. ἐμβῆναι embēnai inf aor act
10. ἐμβαίνοντος embainontos
    gen sing masc part pres act

```
5  And when he was entered into a ship,......... Matt 8:23
3  And he entered into a ship, and passed over,....... 9:1
6  great multitudes ... so that he went into a ship,...... 13:2
9  Jesus constrained his disciples to get into a ship,... 14:22
8  And when they were come into the ship,......... 14:32
1  He got into the boat, (NASB).................... 15:39
6  so that he entered into a ship, and sat in the sea; ..Mark 4:1
4  And when he was come into the ship,............. 5:18
10 And when he was come into the ship,............. 5:18
9  he constrained his disciples to get into the ship,..... 6:45
3  And straightway he entered into a ship,........... 8:10
3  and entering into the ship again departed to......... 8:13
3  And he entered into one of the ships,........... Luke 5:3
1  that he went into a ship with his disciples:......... 8:22
3  he went up into the ship, and returned back again..... 8:37
3  troubling of the water stepped in was made whole ..John 5:4
7  And entered into a ship,........................ 6:17
2  save that one whereinto his disciples were entered,..... 6:22
2  they also took shipping, and came to Capernaum,..... 6:24
2  went out, and got into the boat; (NASB)............. 21:5
```

This verb is found 18 times in the New Testament, almost exclusively in passages speaking of the act of stepping into a boat (cf. Matthew 8:23; 9:1; Mark 4:1; 5:18; Luke 5:3; 8:22; John 6:17,24; Acts 21:6). The word is also found in John 5:4 about the healing of a sick man at the pool of Bethesda.

STRONG 1684, BAUER 254, MOULTON-MILLIGAN 205, LIDDELL-SCOTT 538.

STRONG 1683, BAUER 253-54, MOULTON-MILLIGAN 205, LIDDELL-SCOTT 538.

1672. ἐμβάλλω emballō verb

Cast into, throw in.

CROSS-REFERENCE:
βάλλω ballō (900)

אָסַף 'āṣaph (636), Gather, put in (Ez 24:4).
בּוֹא bô' (971), Came (Hg 2:16 [2:17]).
טוּל ṭûl (3014), Hiphil: cast, throw (Jon 1:12,15).
נָפַל nāphal (5489), Hiphil: let fall, make fall (1 Sm 18:25—Codex Vaticanus only).
נָתַן nāthan (5598), Put (Ex 25:16 [25:15], Ps 40:3 [39:3], Jer 27:8 [34:8]).
פָּלַח pālach (6642), Piel: cut, shred (2 Kgs 4:39).
פָּקַד pāqadh (6734), Hiphil: commit, plea (Jer 37:21 [44:21]).
רְמָה r°mâh (A7701), Peal: cast, throw (Dn 3:20—Aramaic); hithpeel: cast, be thrown (Dn 3:6,11,15—Aramaic).
שִׂים sîm (7947), Put, throw (Gn 43:22, Nm 23:5, Ez 26:12).
שָׁחַת shāchath (8271), Hiphil: destroy (Jer 11:19).
שָׁלַח shālach (8365), Let go, send; pual: cast, thrust (Jb 18:8).
שָׁלַךְ shālakh (8390), Hiphil: cast, throw down (Ex 15:25, Jos 18:10, Zec 11:13).
שָׁמַר shāmar (8490), Keep (Prv 22:18).
תָּקַע tāqa' (8965), Cast, carry (Ex 10:19—Codex Alexandrinus only).

1. ἐμβαλεῖν embalein inf aor act

```
1 after he hath killed hath power to cast into hell;... Luke 12:5
```

Emballō occurs in the New Testament only in Luke 12:5 where it is used to describe God's power to cast men into hell (Gehenna [see 1060]). Though the term is used figuratively here, Jesus unambiguously taught the reality of hell as an actual place of torment and judgment.

STRONG 1685, BAUER 254, MOULTON-MILLIGAN 205, LIDDELL-SCOTT 538-39.

1673. ἐμβάπτω embaptō verb

Dip in.

COGNATE:
βαπτίζω baptizō (901)

SYNONYMS:
βαπτίζω baptizō (901)
βάπτω baptō (905)

1. ἐμβάψας embapsas nom sing masc part aor act
2. ἐμβαπτόμενος embaptomenos
   nom sing masc part pres mid

```
1 He that dippeth his hand with me in the dish,......Matt 26:23
2 one of the twelve, that dippeth with me in the dish.Mark 14:20
1 to whom I shall give a sop, when I have dipped it. John 13:26
1 when he had dipped the sop, he gave it to Judas....... 13:26
```

This word is found only in Matthew 26:23, its parallel in Mark 14:20, and in the majority of Greek manuscripts of John 13:26. In these passages *embaptō* refers to the ancient custom of dipping a morsel of bread into a bowl containing herbs and other victuals as a part of the annual Passover meal. Jesus used this gesture as a clue to the identity of His betrayer, one who enjoyed the closest table fellowship with Jesus.

STRONG 1686, BAUER 254, LIDDELL-SCOTT 539.

1674. ἐμβατεύω embateuō verb
Set foot upon, enter, pry into.

חָלַק chālaq (2606), Piel: divide, allot (Jos 19:51).
נָחַל nāchal (5336), Divide (Jos 19:49).

1. ἐμβατεύων embateuōn nom sing masc part pres act
1 intruding into those things which he hath not seen, ... Col 2:18

Classical Greek
In classical Greek *embateuō* means "to set foot upon" or "to enter." Euripides used *embateuō* for entering a city. Sophocles used *embateuō* of setting foot upon one's homeland. *Embateuō* also has a legal use in classical Greek meaning "to enter into possession of" (a portion of ground, for example, in Euripides; see *Bauer*).

Embateuō was used frequently in the papyri in its legal sense over a period of six centuries from 3 B.C. onward. It was used, for example, of entering into an inheritance. *Embateuō* appears in the inscriptions discovered at the temple of Apollo at Klaros (see *Bauer*). On the basis of these inscriptions, *embateuō* is said to be a technical expression describing the act of initiation into the mysteries.

Septuagint Usage
Embateuō is used twice in the canonical writings of the Septuagint (Joshua 19:49,51) where it translates the Hebrew *nāchal* which means "to divide up" or "to allot." *Embateuō* is also used in the Apocrypha to describe the task of the historian (2 Maccabees 2:30) where it means "to investigate thoroughly."

New Testament Usage
Embateuō is found once in the New Testament (Colossians 2:18). Its meaning here is a matter of debate. Three models compete for acceptance: (1) *Embateuō* means "to approach in order to investigate." Accordingly, Paul was refuting the quest for knowledge which characterized the "errorists" of Colossae. (2) The dominant interpretation is that *embateuō* is a technical term describing the entry of an initiate into a sanctuary to consult an oracle. Paul, in refuting the "errorists," may have been quoting their terminology. This view has been seriously questioned by recent scholarship. (3) *Embateuō* had been understood in the legal sense of "enter into possession of" with the unexpressed object being heaven. Accordingly, Paul was refuting claims to religious superiority which were validated by claims to higher religious experiences through mystical and ascetic piety. In light of the fact that the context of Colossians 2:18 is a legal one using *cheirographon* (5334), "certificate of debt," and *katabrabeuō* (2574), "defraud, rob of a prize," both legal terms, the third choice may be the correct interpretation.

STRONG 1687, BAUER 254, MOULTON-MILLIGAN 205-6, KITTEL 2:535-36, LIDDELL-SCOTT 539.

1675. ἐμβιβάζω embibazō verb
Put on, cause to enter.
CROSS-REFERENCE:
ἐπιβιβάζω epibibazō (1898)

דָּרַךְ dārakh (1931), Tread; hiphil: lead (Prv 4:11).
רָכַב rākhav (7680), Ride; hiphil: carry, took (2 Kgs 9:28—Codex Alexandrinus only).

1. ἐνεβίβασεν enebibasen 3sing indic aor act
1 sailing into Italy; and he put us therein............ Acts 27:6

In its only occurrence in the New Testament (Acts 27:6) *embibazō* describes the embarkation of Paul and his fellow prisoners from the port of Myra in Lycia. The centurion put the prisoners on board the ship.

STRONG 1688, BAUER 254, MOULTON-MILLIGAN 206, LIDDELL-SCOTT 539.

1676. ἐμβλέπω emblepō verb
Look at, fix one's gaze upon, consider, direct the eyes to.
COGNATE:
βλέπω blepō (984)
SYNONYMS:
ἀτενίζω atenizō (810)
βλέπω blepō (984)
εἶδον eidon (1481)
ἐπιβλέπω epiblepō (1899)
ἐποπτεύω epopteuō (2013)
θεάομαι theaomai (2277)
θεωρέω theōreō (2311)
κατανοέω katanoeō (2627)

ὁράω horaō (3571)
σκοπέω skopeō (4503)

נָבַט nāvaṭ (5202), Piel: look (Is 5:30); hiphil: look (Is 8:22, 22:8,11, 51:1,2,6).

פָּנָה pānâh (6680), Turn toward (Jb 6:28—Codex Alexandrinus only).

צָפָה tsāphâh (7099), Piel: watch (Sir 51:7).

רָאָה rā'âh (7495), Qal: consider, look to (1 Sm 16:7, Is 17:7); niphal: seen (1 Kgs 8:8).

1. ἐμβλέποντες emblepontes
   nom pl masc part pres act
2. ἐνέβλεψεν eneblepsen 3sing indic aor act
3. ἐμβλέψατε emblepsate 2pl impr aor act
4. ἐμβλέψας emblepsas nom sing masc part aor act
5. ἐμβλέψασα emblepsasa nom sing fem part aor act
6. ἐνέβλεπον eneblepon 1sing indic imperf act
7. ἐνέβλεπεν eneblepen 3sing indic imperf act

3 **Behold** the fowls of the air: for they sow not,	Matt 6:26
4 But Jesus **beheld** them, and said unto them,	19:26
2 and he was restored, and **saw** every man clearly.	Mark 8:25
7 and he was restored, and **saw** every man clearly.	8:25
4 Then Jesus **beholding** him loved him,	10:21
4 And Jesus **looking upon** them saith,	10:27
5 she **looked upon** him, and said, And thou also	14:67
4 And he **beheld** them, and said,	Luke 20:17
2 And the Lord turned, and **looked upon** Peter.	22:61
4 And **looking upon** Jesus as he walked, he saith,	John 1:36
4 And when Jesus **beheld** him, he said,	1:42
1 why stand ye **gazing up** into heaven?	Acts 1:11
6 when I **could** not **see** for the glory of that light,	22:11

Classical Greek and Septuagint Usage
In classical Greek *emblepō* is not used extensively but means "to look in the face" or "to look at someone," in the eyes, for example (Plato *Republic* 10.608D). *Emblepō* can mean "to look into" in the sense of "to investigate." The Septuagint uses *emblepō* to translate three Hebrew words: *nāvaṭ*, "to look, to behold, to consider" (Genesis 15:5); *pānâh*, "to turn toward, consider" (Psalm 40:4 [LXX 39:4]); and *rā'âh*, "to look at, consider" (1 Samuel 16:7 [LXX 1 Kings 16:7]).

New Testament Usage
The New Testament uses *emblepō* several times. It usually signifies a look of love, concern, or interest, as in the account of the rich young ruler (Mark 10:21). It can mean "to fix one's gaze upon" or "look at intently" as when the servant girl looked at Peter (Luke 22:56), or when Jesus looked directly at the crowd after telling a parable (Luke 20:17). Jesus turned and looked directly (*emblepō*) at Peter after Peter's third denial (Luke 22:61). *Emblepō* also has a figurative meaning of "to look at" in a spiritual sense, or "to consider" (Matthew 6:26; John 1:36). There is also the possibility that *emblepō* can mean "able to see." Acts 22:11 says Paul was unable to see after he was exposed to the light on the road to Damascus. *Emblepō* is used to describe the sight of the formerly blind man after Jesus healed him (Mark 8:25).

STRONG 1689, BAUER 254, MOULTON-MILLIGAN 206, LIDDELL-SCOTT 539-40, COLIN BROWN 3:519-20.

1677. ἐμβριμάομαι
embrimaomai verb
Scold, to be angry, charge sternly.

1. ἐμβριμώμενος embrimōmenos
   nom sing masc part pres mid
2. ἐνεβριμήσατο enebrimēsato 3sing indic aor mid
3. ἐμβριμησάμενος embrimēsamenos
   nom sing masc part aor mid
4. ἐνεβριμῶντο enebrimōnto 3pl indic imperf mid
5. ἐνεβριμήθη enebrimēthē 3sing indic aor pass

2 and Jesus **straitly charged** them, saying,	Matt 9:30
5 and Jesus **straitly charged** them, saying,	9:30
3 **straitly charged** him, and forthwith sent him away;	Mark 1:43
4 given to the poor. And they **murmured** against her.	14:5
2 he **groaned** in the spirit, and was troubled,	John 11:33
1 Jesus therefore again **groaning** in himself	11:38

Classical Greek
This word literally means "to snort." It was used in classical Greek of the sound that horses make (see *Liddell-Scott*). In a fragment attributed to Euripides it was also used in a sense meaning "to admonish urgently" or "to rebuke."

New Testament Usage
In the New Testament *embrimaomai* is used to mean a "stern warning" as in Matthew 9:30 where Jesus warned the formerly blind men not to spread the news of their healing. It is used with the same meaning in Mark 1:43. On one occasion the word carried the idea of anger, harshness, displeasure, and disgust (Mark 14:5); the woman with the alabaster box of perfume was harshly scolded by some of the disciples. *Embriaomai* was also used of Jesus who was deeply moved in His spirit. One interpretation of John 11:33,38 is that Jesus was filled with divine displeasure at the unbelief of the people. Another is that He was angry at the enemy and deeply moved within His own spirit against death and the misery it brings. The latter view seems to fit the context more closely.

STRONG 1690, BAUER 254, MOULTON-MILLIGAN 206, LIDDELL-SCOTT 540.

1678. ἐμέω emeō verb
Vomit, throw up.

קִיא qî' (7288), Vomit (Is 19:14).

1. ἐμέσαι emesai inf aor act
1 art lukewarm, ... I will **spue** thee out of my mouth... **Rev 3:16**

Related to the Latin *vomere*, *emeō* occurs but once in the New Testament. Thayer states that in Revelation 3:16 *emeō* carries the meaning "to vomit" or "to reject with extreme disgust" (*Greek-English Lexicon*). (Cf. Isaiah 19:14 for the literal meaning.)
STRONG 1692, BAUER 254, MOULTON-MILLIGAN 206, LIDDELL-SCOTT 541.

1679. ἐμμαίνομαι emmainomai verb
Be enraged against (someone).
CROSS-REFERENCE:
μαίνομαι mainomai (3077)

1. ἐμμαινόμενος emmainomenos
nom sing masc part pres mid
1 and **being exceedingly mad** against them, ... Acts 26:11

In the New Testament this verb appears only in Acts 26:11 where it is rendered "being exceedingly mad" in the KJV and "being furiously enraged" in the NASB. Paul used the term to describe the furious rage which at one time had motivated him to pursue Christians in order to have them punished.
STRONG 1693, BAUER 255, MOULTON-MILLIGAN 206, LIDDELL-SCOTT 541.

1680. Ἐμμανουήλ Emmanouēl name
Immanuel.

1. Ἐμμανουήλ Emmanouēl masc
1 and they shall call his name **Emmanuel**, ... Matt 1:23

Prophesied name for the virgin-born Christ meaning "God with us" (Matthew 1:23; cf. Isaiah 7:14).

1681. Ἐμμαοῦς Emmaous name
Emmaus.

1. Ἐμμαοῦς Emmaous fem
1 went that same day to a village called **Emmaus**, ... Luke 24:13

Judean village located about 7 miles northwest of Jerusalem (Luke 24:13).

1682. ἐμμένω emmenō verb
Stay, remain in, continue, abide by.

COGNATE:
μένω menō (3176)
SYNONYMS:
ἀπολείπω apoleipō (614)
αὐλίζομαι aulizomai (829)
διαμένω diamenō (1259)
διατελέω diateleō (1294)
διατρίβω diatribō (1298)
εἰμί eimi (1498)
ἐπιμένω epimenō (1946)
καθίζω kathizō (2495)
καταμένω katamenō (2620)
μένω menō (3176)
παραμένω paramenō (3748)
περιλείπομαι perileipomai (3898)
ὑπομένω hupomenō (5116)

חָכָה chākhâh (2542), Qal: wait; longs (Is 30:18); piel: wait for (Dn 12:12).
כּוּל kûl (3677), Pilpel: clasp, hold in (Sir 6:20).
פָּרַר pārar (6815), Hiphil: break (Jer 31:32 [38:32]).
קָוָה qāwâh (7245), Piel: wait for (Sir 11:21).
קוּם qûm (7251), Qal: stand (Dt 19:5, Is 8:10, Jer 44:28 [51:28]); hiphil: carry out, perform (Nm 23:19, Jer 44:25 [51:25]).

1. ἐμμένει emmenei 3sing indic pres act
2. ἐμμένειν emmenein inf pres act
3. ἐνέμειναν enemeinan 3pl indic aor act
4. ἐνέμεινεν enemeinen 3sing indic aor act

2 and exhorting them **to continue** in the faith, ... Acts 14:22
4 And **he lived** there two whole years (RSV) 28:30
1 Cursed is every one that **continueth** not in all .... Gal 3:10
3 because they **continued** not in my covenant, ... Heb 8:9

Classical Greek
In classical Greek *emmenō* means "to stay in a place," such as in a house. It can also mean "to be true to, to cleave to, to stand by," for example, "articles of government and solemn treaties" (Thucydides; see *Bauer*). When *emmenō* is used of things (e.g., law; cf. Plato *Leges* 844c), it means "to remain fixed or steadfast."

Septuagint Usage
The Septuagint uses *emmenō* to translate a variety of Hebrew words: *chākhâh*, "wait," used mainly of the righteous waiting on the Lord (Isaiah 30:18); *qûm*, "to stand, be valid," used in sayings about abiding by one's word or agreement (Numbers 23:19; Deuteronomy 19:15), "to endure" (Isaiah 7:7); *pārar*, "to break," where *emmenō* is used to indicate that God's people were not continuing in the covenant.

New Testament Usage
Emmenō is used three times in the New Testament. In Acts 14:22 it means "to continue in." Hebrews 8:9 quotes Jeremiah 31:32 and

uses *emmenō* with the negative to indicate a lack of perseverance. Paul, writing in the official, legal style of his day in Galatians 3:10 used *emmenō* in a sense that means "adhere to." Here Paul cited Deuteronomy 27:26 to show the impossibility of keeping the Law as a way of salvation.

STRONG 1696, BAUER 255, MOULTON-MILLIGAN 206, KITTEL 4:576-77, LIDDELL-SCOTT 541-42, COLIN BROWN 3:223,226.

1683. Ἐμμόρ Emmor name

Hamor.

1. Ἐμμόρ **Emmor** masc
2. Ἐμμώρ **Hemmōr** masc

1 bought for a sum of money of the sons of **Emmor** ... Acts 7:16
2 bought for a sum of money of the sons of **Emmor** 7:16

The father of the men who sold Abraham a burial place near Shechem (Acts 7:16).

1684. ἐμός emos adj

Mine, my.

1. ἐμόν **emon** nom/acc sing masc/neu
2. ἐμῷ **emō** dat sing masc/neu
3. ἐμός **emos** nom sing masc
4. ἐμοί **emoi** nom pl masc
5. ἐμούς **emous** acc pl masc
6. ἐμή **emē** nom sing fem
7. ἐμῆς **emēs** gen sing fem
8. ἐμῇ **emē** dat sing fem
9. ἐμήν **emēn** acc sing fem
10. ἐμάς **emas** acc pl fem
11. ἐμοῦ **emou** gen sing neu
12. ἐμά **ema** nom/acc pl neu
13. ἐμῶν **emōn** gen pl neu
14. ἐμοῖς **emois** dat pl neu

1 two or three are gathered together in **my** name, ... Matt 18:20
14 not lawful for me to do what I will with **mine** own? .. 20:15
1 is not **mine** to give, but it shall be given to them 20:23
1 I should have received **mine** own with usury. 25:27
5 shall be ashamed of me and of **my** words .... Mark 8:38
1 But to sit on my right hand ... is not **mine** to give; ... 10:40
5 shall be ashamed of me and of **my** words, ... Luke 9:26
12 thou art ever with me, and all that I have is thine. 15:31
9 this do in remembrance of **me**. 22:19
6 this **my** joy therefore is fulfilled. .... John 3:29
1 **My** meat is to do the will of him that sent me, ... 4:34
6 as I hear, I judge: and **my** judgment is just; 5:30
1 because I seek not **mine** own will, ... 5:30
14 how shall ye believe **my** words? 5:47
1 came down from heaven, not to do **mine** own will, ... 6:38
11 if any man eat of this bread, he shall live for ever: 6:51
3 **My** time is not yet come: 7:6
3 for **my** time is not yet full come. 7:8
6 **My** doctrine is not **mine**, but his that sent me. 7:16
6 **My** doctrine is not **mine**, but his that sent me. 7:16

6 And yet if I judge, **my** judgment is true: .... John 8:16
2 If ye continue in **my** word, ... 8:31
3 kill me, because **my** word hath no place in you. 8:37
9 Why do ye not understand **my** speech? 8:43
1 even because ye cannot hear **my** word. 8:43
1 If a man keep **my** saying, he shall never see death. 8:51
7 Your father Abraham rejoiced to see **my** day: 8:56
12 I am the good shepherd, and know **my** sheep, ... 10:14
13 and know **my** sheep, and am known of **mine**. 10:14
12 and know **my** sheep, and am known of **mine**. 10:14
13 But ye believe not, because ye are not of **my** sheep, .. 10:26
12 **My** sheep hear my voice, and I know them, ... 10:27
3 and where I am, there shall also **my** servant be: 12:26
4 By this shall all men know that ye are **my** disciples, .. 13:35
10 If ye love me, keep **my** commandments. 14:15
3 word which ye hear is not **mine**, but the Father's 14:24
9 Peace I leave with you, **my** peace I give unto you: ... 14:27
4 bear much fruit; so shall ye be **my** disciples. 15:8
8 so have I loved you; continue ye in **my** love. 15:9
6 that **my** joy might remain in you, ... 15:11
6 This is **my** commandment, ... love one another, ... 15:12
11 He shall glorify me: for he shall receive of **mine**, ... 16:14
12 All things that the Father hath are **mine**: 16:15
11 therefore said I, that he shall take of **mine**, ... 16:15
12 And all **mine** are thine, and thine are **mine**; 17:10
12 And all **mine** are thine, and thine are **mine**; 17:10
9 they might have **my** joy fulfilled in themselves. 17:13
9 that they may behold **my** glory, ... 17:24
6 Jesus answered, **My** kingdom is not of this world: 18:36
6 if **my** kingdom were of this world, ... 18:36
4 then would **my** servants fight, ... 18:36
6 but now is **my** kingdom not from hence. 18:36
2 more abounded through **my** lie unto his glory; ..... Rom 3:7
7 **my** heart's desire and prayer to God for Israel is, ... 10:1
1 should say that I had baptized in **mine** own name. 1 Co 1:15
9 she is happier if she so abide, after **my** judgment: 7:40
7 for the seal of **mine** apostleship are ye in the Lord. 9:2
6 **Mine** answer to them that do examine me is this, ... 9:3
9 Take, eat: ... this do in remembrance of **me**. 11:24
2 This cup is the new testament in **my** blood: 11:25
9 as oft as ye drink it, in remembrance of **me**. 11:25
1 For they have refreshed **my** spirit and yours: 16:18
8 The salutation of me Paul with **mine** own hand. 16:21
9 Moreover I call God for a record upon **my** soul, ... 2 Co 1:23
6 that **my** joy is the joy of you all. 2:3
3 he is **my** partner and fellowhelper concerning you: 8:23
9 For ye have heard of **my** conversation in time past .. Gal 1:13
8 I have written unto you with **mine** own hand. 6:11
7 in Jesus Christ for me by **my** coming to you again. Phlp 1:26
9 **mine** own righteousness, which is of the law, ... 3:9
8 The salutation by the hand of me Paul. .... Col 4:18
8 The salutation of Paul with **mine** own hand, ... 2 Th 3:17
7 and the time of **my** departure is at hand. .... 2 Tm 4:6
12 therefore receive him, that is, **mine** own bowels: .. Phlm 1:12
8 I Paul have written it with **mine** own hand, ... 1:19
9 I will ... that ye may be able after **my** decease ..... 2 Pt 1:15
12 than to hear that **my** children walk in truth. .... 3 Jn 1:4
5 and to seduce **my** servants to commit fornication, ... Rev 2:20

Emos is the possessive first person pronoun. It occurs over 75 times in the New Testament. About half of these occurrences are in the Gospel of John, possibly due to the large amount of dialogue in that Gospel (cf. Robertson, *Grammar of the Greek New Testament*, p.288). This term is usually more emphatic than the more commonly used genitive of the personal pronoun. The word is used emphatically in such passages as Matthew 20:15; 25:27; and John 10:14.

STRONG 1699, BAUER 255, MOULTON-MILLIGAN 206-7, LIDDELL-SCOTT 542.

1684B. ἐμπαιγμονή
empaigmonē noun

Mockery, derision.

CROSS-REFERENCE:
παίζω paizō (3678)

1. ἐμπαιγμονῇ empaigmonē dat sing fem

1 mockers will come with their **mocking** (NASB) ...... 2 Pt 3:3

This word comes from the verb *empaizō* which could be translated "I deceive, mock, or trick." *Empaigmonē* is used in the New Testament only in 2 Peter 3:3 where it is found in combination with the noun *empaiktai* (see 1687), "mockers." Hence, it refers to those who in the last days will mock the possibility of the second coming of Christ to the earth.

BAUER 255, MOULTON-MILLIGAN 207 (see "empaigmos"), KITTEL 5:635-36, LIDDELL-SCOTT 542.

1685. ἐμπαιγμός empaigmos noun

Mocking, scoffing, scorn.

CROSS-REFERENCE:
παίζω paizō (3678)

קָלָה qālâh (7319), Niphal: burn (Ps 38:7 [37:7]).

קַלָּסָה qallāsāh (7332), Laughingstock (Ez 22:4).

1. ἐμπαιγμῶν empaigmōn gen pl masc

1 others had trial of cruel **mockings** and scourgings, .. Heb 11:36

Related to *empaizō* (1686), "to mock," *empaigmos* is found only once in the New Testament. Hebrews 11:36 refers to some who experienced "mockings," an experience which very possibly awaited the readers of the epistle. The same word appears in 2 Maccabees 7:7, and the cognate verb *empaizō* is similarly used in 2 Maccabees 7:10. The reference in Hebrews 11:36 may refer to the prophet Jeremiah who complained that he had been made a laughingstock by members of his own family and by the nation (cf. Jeremiah 20:7ff.).

STRONG 1701, BAUER 255, MOULTON-MILLIGAN 207, KITTEL 5:635-36, LIDDELL-SCOTT 542.

1686. ἐμπαίζω empaizō verb

Mock, ridicule, delude.

CROSS-REFERENCE:
παίζω paizō (3678)

בּוּס bûs (983), Loathe (Prv 27:7).

הָלַם hālam (2056), Beat (Prv 23:35).

עָלַל ʻālal (6177), Deal with; hithpael: abuse (Nm 22:29, Jgs 19:25, 1 Chr 10:4).

צָחַק tsāchaq (6978), Laugh, piel: mock, make sport (Gn 39:14,17).

קָלַס qālas (7330), Hithpael: mock (Ez 22:5).

שָׂחַק sāchaq (7925), Qal: laugh (Hb 1:10); piel: frolic, play (Ps 104:26 [103:26]).

תָּעַע tāʻaʻ (8924), Hithpalpel: mocked (2 Chr 36:16).

תַּעְתֻּעִים taʻtuʻîm (8928), Mockery (Jer 10:15).

1. ἐμπαίζοντες empaizontes
nom pl masc part pres act
2. ἐμπαίζειν empaizein inf pres act
3. ἐνέπαιξαν enepaixan 3pl indic aor act
4. ἐμπαίξας empaixas nom sing masc part aor act
5. ἐμπαῖξαι empaixai inf aor act
6. ἐμπαίξουσιν empaixousin 3pl indic fut act
7. ἐνέπαιζον enepaizon 3pl indic imperf act
8. ἐνεπαίχθη enepaichthē 3sing indic aor pass
9. ἐμπαιχθήσεται empaichthēsetai
3sing indic fut pass

8 when he saw that **he was mocked** of the wise men, .. Matt 2:16
5 And shall deliver him to the Gentiles to **mock**, ... 20:19
7 and **mocked** him, saying, Hail, King of the Jews! 27:29
3 and **mocked** him, saying, Hail, King of the Jews! 27:29
3 And after that they **had mocked** him, ... 27:31
1 Likewise also the chief priests **mocking** him, ... 27:41
6 And they **shall mock** him, and shall scourge him, .. Mark 10:34
3 And when they **had mocked** him, ... 15:20
1 Likewise also the chief priests **mocking** 15:31
2 all that behold it begin to **mock** him, ... Luke 14:29
9 and **shall be mocked**, and spitefully entreated, ... 18:32
7 men that held Jesus **mocked** him, and smote him. 22:63
4 **mocked** him, and arrayed him in a gorgeous robe, ... 23:11
7 And the soldiers also **mocked** him, ... 23:36
3 And the soldiers also **mocked** him, ... 23:36

Classical Greek
Secular Greek writers understood *empaizō* to mean "to mock, to ridicule, to scorn." The meaning "to deceive" or "to delude" is attested in papyri and other literature (see *Bauer*; *Moulton-Milligan*). Apparently the word is an intensified form of *paizō* (3678) (cf. *pais* [3679]) which means "to play" (as children), "to sport," or "to jest." This later meaning was also known of *empaizō* (see *Liddell-Scott*).

Septuagint Usage
Empaizō occurs 25 times in the Septuagint, 18 of which have Hebrew originals. Seven Hebrew words (and additional forms) are translated by *empaizō*. Of these, the most significant are as follows: the hithpael of *ʻālal* (6 times), "to make a fool" (of someone) (e.g., Exodus 10:2; Numbers 22:29); and *tsāchaq* (4 times), "to play" (qal) or "to joke" (piel) (e.g., Judges 16:27; cf. verse 25; Psalm 104:26 [LXX 103:26]).

New Testament Usage

Of the 13 occurrences of *empaizō* in the New Testament all occur in the Synoptic Gospels. Each of Mark's three uses are in reference to the "mocking" of Christ by the soldiers and religious leaders either as a prediction (Mark 10:34) or as the actual event (Mark 15:20,31). Matthew's Gospel follows Mark's usage and sequence (Matthew 20:19; 27:31,41) and includes an additional reference (perhaps stylistic) in the same general context of the trial of Jesus (27:29). Matthew's Gospel has a unique usage in the account of the wise men's decision not to return to Herod (RSV, "[Herod] saw that he had been 'tricked' by the wise men" [2:16]).

The meaning of *empaizō* in Luke's Gospel is also the same as Mark's (Luke 18:32; 23:36) and includes an additional usage in the trial narrative (22:63). Luke used *empaizō* in the parable of the man building a tower (14:29); and in an interesting difference from Mark (Mark 15:31) used *ekmuktērizō* (1597), "I ridicule," as a synonym for *empaizō* (Luke 23:35), which he used instead in the following verse (36).

STRONG 1702, BAUER 255, MOULTON-MILLIGAN 207, KITTEL 5:630-35, LIDDELL-SCOTT 543, COLIN BROWN 2:436; 3:340-41.

1687. ἐμπαίκτης empaiktēs noun
Mocker, scoffer, deceiver.
CROSS-REFERENCE:
παίζω paizō (3678)

תַּעֲלוּלִים ta'ălûlîm (8918), Children (Is 3:4).

1. ἐμπαῖκται empaiktai nom pl masc

1 that there shall come in the last days **scoffers**,........ 2 Pt 3:3
1 told you there should be **mockers** in the last time,... Jude 1:18

In its only two occurrences in the New Testament (2 Peter 3:3; Jude 18) the noun *empaiktēs* refers to the scoffers who will appear in the last days, denying Biblical truths and living ungodly lives (cf. Daniel 7:25; Matthew 24:3-5,23-26; 2 Timothy 3:1-7). In 2 Peter 3:3 the specific reference is apparently to the false teachers of chapter 2 who deny Christ will return (cf. Blum, *The Expositor's Bible Commentary*, 12:284).

STRONG 1703, BAUER 255, KITTEL 5:635-36, LIDDELL-SCOTT 543.

1688. ἐμπεριπατέω emperipateō verb
Go about in, walk among.
CROSS-REFERENCE:
περιπατέω peripateō (3906)

הָלַךְ hālakh (2050), Go, walk; hithpael: walk, come from (Lv 26:12, 2 Sm 7:6, Jb 1:7).

1. ἐμπεριπατήσω emperipatēsō 1sing indic fut act

1 I will dwell in them, and **walk in them**;............. 2 Co 6:16

The only occurrence of this word in the New Testament is in 2 Corinthians 6:16 which is a quotation from Leviticus 26:12: "I will dwell in them, and walk in them." The idea of "walking" is usually expressed by *peripateō* (3906). It is doubtful whether the compounded form *emperipateō* has a different meaning; the prefix *em-* (*en-* [see 1706]) is due to the expression "in them" (*en autois*). Since "you" in 2 Corinthians 6:15 is plural, some take *en* (verse 16) to mean "among."

STRONG 1704, BAUER 256, KITTEL 5:940-45, LIDDELL-SCOTT 544, COLIN BROWN 3:943-45.

1688B. ἐμπιπλάω empiplaō
Fill up, satisfy.

This is an alternate spelling of *empiplēmi*. See the word study at number 1689.

1689. ἐμπίμπλημι empimplēmi verb
Fill, satisfy.
COGNATE:
πληρόω plēroō (3997)
SYNONYMS:
ἀνταναπληρόω antanaplēroō (463)
γεμίζω gemizō (1065)
κορέννυμι korennumi (2853)
μεστόω mestoō (3195)
πληρόω plēroō (3997)
συμπληρόω sumplēroō (4696)
χορτάζω chortazō (5361)

דָּשֵׁן dāshēn (1941), Pual: drenched, soaked (Is 34:7).

חָבַשׁ chāvash (2372), Bind, shroud (Jb 40:13 [40:8]).

מָלֵא mālē' (4527), Qal: be full, fill (Ex 15:9, 2 Chr 5:14, Mi 3:8); niphal: be filled (Nm 14:21, Is 2:8, Ez 32:6); piel: fill, satisfy (Dt 6:11, Jb 8:21, Jer 31:25 [38:25]).

מָלֵא mālē' (4529), Full (Dt 34:9, Is 22:2).

מְלֹא me lō' (4530), Miltitude (Is 31:4).

נוּחַ nûach (5299), Hiphil: rest, subside (Ez 24:13).

שָׂבַע sāvē' (7881), Qal: be satisfied (Lv 26:26, Ps 22:26

ἐμπίπτω 1690

[21:26], Jer 50:10 [27:10]); piel: satisfy (Ps 90:14 [89:14], Ez 7:19); hiphil: satisfy (Is 58:11).

שָׂבַע sāvaʿ (7882), Increase (Eccl 5:11).

שִׂבְעָה sovʿāh (7885), Abundance (Is 23:18).

1. ἐμπιπλῶν empiplōn nom sing masc part pres act
2. ἐνέπλησεν eneplēsen 3sing indic aor act
3. ἐνεπλήσθησαν eneplēsthēsan 3pl indic aor pass
4. ἐμπλησθῶ emplēsthō 1sing subj aor pass
5. ἐμπεπλησμένοι empeplēsmenoi nom pl masc part perf mid

```
2 He hath filled the hungry with good things;......... Luke 1:53
5 Woe unto you that are full! for ye shall hunger.......... 6:25
3 When they were filled, he said unto his disciples,.... John 6:12
1 filling our hearts with food and gladness........... Acts 14:17
4 if first I be somewhat filled with your company..... Rom 15:24
```

Classical Greek
In classical Greek *empimplēmi* (an alternate form of *empiplaō* [1688B]) means "to fill quite full." It is based on the root *plē* which means "full." This term is used from Homer on and means "to fill a vessel" so that it can be seen as full (for example, of water). It can also mean "to fill a hungry man full of food" (see *Liddell-Scott*).

Septuagint Usage
In the Septuagint *empimplēmi* usually translates the Hebrew words *māle'* and *sāvaʿ* which mean "to fill full." It is used of prophets and skilled craftsmen who are filled with the Spirit (Exodus 28:3; 31:3). Jeremiah 23:24 speaks of God revealing himself in full measure in the world in contrast to the fact that His glory was formerly only revealed in the tabernacle and first and second temples.

New Testament Usage
In the New Testament *empimplēmi* is used chiefly of physical fullness (Luke 1:53), a "satisfied" condition because one has had plenty to eat (Luke 6:25; John 6:12), as does *empiplaō* which is used only in Acts 14:17. It can also imply a sense of to "enjoy something" by having your "fill" (of someone's "company," Romans 15:24).

STRONG 1705, BAUER 256, MOULTON-MILLIGAN 207, KITTEL 6:128-31, LIDDELL-SCOTT 545, COLIN BROWN 1:733,735.

1690. ἐμπίπτω empiptō verb
Fall into, be entrapped by.
CROSS-REFERENCE:
πίπτω piptō (3959)

גּוּחַ gûach (A1503), Haphel: stir up (Dn 7:2—Aramaic).

כָּרַע kāraʿ (3895), Fall (Is 10:4).

נָפַל nāphal (5489), Fall (Gn 14:10, 1 Chr 21:13, Is 47:11).

פָּגַע pāgaʿ (6534), Meet (Am 5:19).

פָּגַשׁ pāghash (6539), Meet (Prv 17:12).

קָרֵב qārēv (7414), Draw near; hithpael: press upon (Sir 13:10).

1. ἐμπίπτουσιν empiptousin 3pl indic pres act
2. ἐμπέσῃ empesē 3sing subj aor act
3. ἐμπεσόντος empesontos gen sing masc part aor act
4. ἐμπεσεῖν empesein inf aor act
5. ἐμπεσεῖται empeseitai 3sing indic fut mid
6. ἐμπεσοῦνται empesountai 3pl indic fut mid

```
2 and if it fall into a pit on the sabbath day,........ Matt 12:11
6 Will they not both fall into a pit? (NASB).......... Luke 6:39
3 neighbour unto him that fell among the thieves?....... 10:36
5 of you shall have an ass or an ox fallen into a pit,..... 14:5
2 he fall into the condemnation of the devil.......... 1 Tm 3:6
2 lest he fall into reproach and the snare of the devil..... 3:7
1 But they that will be rich fall into temptation........... 6:9
4 to fall into the hands of the living God............. Heb 10:31
```

Classical Greek
This verb is formed by the combination of *en* (1706), "in," and *piptō* (3959), "to fall." Ancient writers understood *empiptō* to mean "to fall into, upon, or in." In a slightly different sense it could mean "to fall upon, to attack" (see *Moulton-Milligan*). Figuratively, in Hellenistic texts especially, *empiptō* could mean "to fall among" (as in "the hands of"), such as "to fall among thieves" (see *Bauer*). In an absolute sense it can mean "to set in, arise," e.g., 1 Clement 43:2: "For when jealousy arose concerning the priesthood . . . ."

Septuagint Usage
The Septuagint generally follows the established classical usage of *empiptō*. Frequently the expression "falling into the hands of (something/someone)" occurs (Judges 15:18; 2 Samuel 24:14 [LXX 2 Kings 24:14]; 1 Chronicles 21:13; Sirach 2:18), as does "falling into a snare" (Tobit 14:10; Proverbs 12:13; Sirach 9:3), or "falling into a pit" (Psalm 7:15; Ecclesiastes 10:8; Sirach 27:26; Isaiah 24:18).

New Testament Usage
The New Testament pattern of usage (seven times) also follows the customary understandings. Both Gospels of Matthew and Luke, in different contexts, employ the phrase "fall into a pit" (Matthew 12:11; Luke 14:5). Luke, in the Parable of the Good Samaritan, speaks of "falling" among thieves (10:36). And in Hebrews 10:31 the phrase "fall into the hands of the living God" is a figurative expression denoting judgment. This stands in contrast to the Septuagint's phrase "hands of the Lord"

which really describes God's mercy (2 Samuel 24:14 [LXX 2 Kings 24:14]; 1 Chronicles 21:13; Sirach 2:18).

Paul used *empiptō* only in 1 Timothy. He consistently understood it in a figurative sense as is reflected in the expressions "fall into judgment" (3:6); "fall into reproach" (3:7); and "fall into temptation" (6:9).

STRONG 1706, BAUER 256, MOULTON-MILLIGAN 207, LIDDELL-SCOTT 545.

1691. ἐμπλέκω emplekō verb

Weave in, entangled, involve.

CROSS-REFERENCE:
πλέκω plekō (3980)

נָפַל nāphal (5489), Fall (Prv 28:18).

1. ἐμπλέκεται **empleketai** 3sing indic pres mid
2. ἐμπλακέντες **emplakentes** nom pl masc part aor pass

1 **entangleth** himself with the affairs of this life;........ 2 Tm 2:4
2 they are again **entangled** therein, and overcome,..... 2 Pt 2:20

Classical Greek

In classical Greek the verb *emplekō* was capable of bearing several different meanings, including "weave in, be entangled in, be involved in, entwine," and "form a connection with." Metaphorically the word was used in the sense of "weave (by subtle art)" (see *Liddell-Scott*). The word is used literally of a sheep or a hare being caught in the thorns (*Bauer*). It is also used of a hostile attack (*Moulton-Milligan*).

Septuagint Usage

In the Septuagint *emplekō* occurs in Proverbs 28:18, "He that walks in crooked ways shall be entangled therein." Here its usage is clearly metaphoric and negative. The one who does not walk blamelessly will suddenly fall because of the way he conducts himself, but deliverance is promised to those who walk blamelessly. The word also occurs in 2 Maccabees 15:17 where Judah's words inspire the young men to engage the heathen, who are trying to endanger the sanctuary and the temple, in battle.

New Testament Usage

Emplekō is found only twice in the New Testament. In 2 Timothy 2:4 Paul wrote that no soldier on active duty "entangleth himself" in the affairs of civilian life. Here the verb was used metaphorically for involvement in worldly things and the resulting ineffectiveness of the Christian so involved. In 2 Peter 2:20 the apostle Peter spoke of being "entangled" in the world's corruption. Both of these occurrences of *emplekō* emphasize the importance of godly separation in the life of a Christian.

STRONG 1707, BAUER 256, MOULTON-MILLIGAN 207, LIDDELL-SCOTT 546.

1692. ἐμπλοκή emplokē noun

Braiding, plaiting (of hair).

CROSS-REFERENCE:
πλέκω plekō (3980)

1. ἐμπλοκῆς **emplokēs** gen sing fem

1 not be that outward adorning of **plaiting** the hair,... 1 Pt 3:3

In classical usage *emplokē* means "a struggle, a scuffle" (see *Moulton-Milligan*), or "a braiding" (*Liddell-Scott*). In the New Testament however, Thayer states that this noun refers to the elaborate gathering of braids into knots (*Greek-English Lexicon*). Its sole occurrence in the New Testament is in 1 Peter 3:3, where Peter wrote of "plaiting the hair" (NIV: "braided hair"). Here, Peter was speaking to wives of ungodly husbands. If these women would be as concerned about an inward adorning (e.g., respectful behavior to their husbands) as some were about braiding their hair and other external adornments, then their husbands might be won to the Lord.

STRONG 1708, BAUER 256, MOULTON-MILLIGAN 207, LIDDELL-SCOTT 546.

1693. ἐμπνέω empneō verb

Breathe in, inhale.

CROSS-REFERENCE:
πνέω pneō (4014)

נֶפֶשׁ nephesh (5497), Soul, person (Jos 10:30,39, 11:11).

נְשָׁמָה nᵉshāmāh (5580), Breath (Dt 20:16, Jos 10:40, 11:14).

1. ἐμπνέων **empneōn** nom sing masc part pres act

1 yet **breathing out** threatenings and slaughter......... Acts 9:1

Classical Greek

A combination of the preposition *en(m)* (1706), "into, in, by," etc., and *pneō* (4014), "to blow," *empneō* means "to blow into or upon." Figuratively in classical usage it means "to be alive (to breathe)," or it can mean "to inspire." The former sense clearly carries over into the Septuagint.

Septuagint Usage

The figurative use, "to live," occurs frequently in the context of the Lord's orders to Israel to "not leave alive anything that breathes" in the cities of inheritance (Deuteronomy 20:16; cf. Joshua 10:28,30,35,37,39,40). The composer of the apocryphal Wisdom of Solomon relates *empneō* to the act of creation in Genesis (2:7, *emphusaō* [1704], Septuagint). He speaks of being "inspired with an active soul" (Wisdom of Solomon 15:11, RSV).

New Testament Usage

The single occurrence of *empneō* in the New Testament is a figurative use which occurs in Acts 9:1. Saul (Paul), prior to his conversion, created an atmosphere of violence around himself and was said to be "breathing out threatenings and slaughter against the disciples." Against this backdrop of hostility toward the purposes of God one reads of Paul's dramatic conversion (cf. Philippians 3:6).

STRONG 1709, BAUER 256, MOULTON-MILLIGAN 207, KITTEL 6:452, LIDDELL-SCOTT 546, COLIN BROWN 3:689.

1694. ἐμπορεύομαι

emporeuomai verb
Trade, traffic in, made a gain of, exploit.

COGNATES:
ἐμπορία emporia (1695)
ἐμπόριον emporion (1696)
ἔμπορος emporos (1697)
πορεύομαι poreuomai (4057)
πορνεύω porneuō (4062)

SYNONYMS:
ἀγοράζω agorazō (58)
πιπράσκω pipraskō (3958)
πωλέω pōleō (4310)

יָבַל yāval (3095), Bring; hophal: bring against (Hos 12:2 [12:1]).

יָצָא yātsā' (3428), Go out (Gn 34:24—Sixtine Edition only).

סָחַר sāchar (5692), Trade, bring (Gn 34:21, 2 Chr 9:14, Ez 27:21).

סַחַר sachar (5693), Be profitable (Prv 3:14).

רָכַל rākhal (7691), Trade, exchange (Ez 27:13).

שָׁבַר shāvar (8132), Buy; hiphil: sell (Am 8:6).

1. ἐμπορευσώμεθα **emporeusōmetha**
    1pl subj aor mid
2. ἐμπορεύσονται **emporeusontai** 3pl indic fut mid
3. ἐμπορευσόμεθα **emporeusometha**
    1pl indic fut mid

1 continue there ... and **buy and sell**, and get gain: ..... Jas 4:13
3 continue there ... and **buy and sell**, and get gain: 4:13
2 with feigned words **make merchandise** of you: .... 2 Pt 2:3

Classical Greek

In early Greek *emporeuomai* was a general term for "travel," but later its meaning was restricted to "travel in business, trade" (Field, "Buy," *Colin Brown*, 1:268). In the Koine period it sometimes had the connotation of "exploit." Thus, Polybius (38.12.10) told of a certain Critolaus who exploited a mob by his eloquent speaking.

Septuagint Usage

In the Septuagint *emporeuomai* appears 11 times translating several Hebrew words for traveling and trading. Apparently, as in the Greek world, those who traveled were associated with those who traded and bartered goods for a living. *Emporeuomai* normally refers to trade in the commercial sense (e.g., Genesis 42:34; Amos 8:6). In one place it is used figuratively of trade in wisdom (Proverbs 3:14).

New Testament Usage

Emporeuomai occurs only twice in the New Testament. In James 4:13 it retains the common secular meaning of "engage in trade" (KJV: "buy and sell"). In 2 Peter 2:3 it is used figuratively to convey the idea of exploitation (KJV: "make merchandise"; NIV: "exploit"; TEV: "make a profit").

STRONG 1710, BAUER 256, MOULTON-MILLIGAN 207, LIDDELL-SCOTT 547-48, COLIN BROWN 1:268.

1695. ἐμπορία emporia noun

Business, merchandise, trade.
CROSS-REFERENCE:
ἐμπορεύομαι emporeuomai (1694)

מַעֲרָב ma'ărāv (4789), Merchandise (Ez 27:13).
סֹחֵר sāchar (5692), Merchant (Ez 27:16).
סַחַר sachar (5693), Profit, merchandise (Is 23:18, 45:14).
סְחֹרָה sᵉchōrāh (5694), Market (Ez 27:15).
רָכַל rākhal (7691), Merchant (Na 3:16).
רְכֻלָּה rᵉkhullāh (7693), Trade, merchandise (Ez 28:5,16,18).

1. ἐμπορίαν **emporian** acc sing fem

1 one to his farm, another to his **merchandise**: .... Matt 22:5

Related to *emporos* (1697), "merchant," *emporia* occurs only in Matthew 22:5 where it is translated "merchandise" (NIV: "business"). The word has a range of meanings, all having to do with a business.

1696. ἐμπόριον emporion noun

Market, merchandise mart, emporium.

CROSS-REFERENCE:
ἐμπορεύομαι emporeuomai (1694)

רָכַל rākhal (7691), Merchant (Ez 27:3).

שָׂפַן sāphan (8008), Hide (Dt 33:19).

1. ἐμπορίου emporiou gen sing neu

1 not my Father's house an house **of merchandise**......**John 2:16**

In classical Greek *emporion* could mean a market center where there was no city (see *Liddell-Scott*). In the New Testament this noun occurs only in John 2:16 in the expression *oikos emporiou*, "a house of merchandise" (NIV: "a market"). In contrast to *agora* (57), "the open marketplace," *emporion* refers to an inside business here. Jesus drove out the money changers who had made the temple, which was meant to be a house of prayer, a market.

STRONG 1712, BAUER 257, MOULTON-MILLIGAN 208, LIDDELL-SCOTT 548.

1697. ἔμπορος emporos noun

Merchant, trader, traveler.

CROSS-REFERENCE:
ἐμπορεύομαι emporeuomai (1694)

מַעֲרָב maʿărāv (4789), Cargo, merchandise (Ez 27:25).

סָחַר sāchar (5692), Merchant (Gn 23:16, 2 Chr 1:16, Is 23:8).

רָכַל rākhal (7691), Merchant, tradesman (Ez 27:15,17).

1. ἐμπόρῳ emporō dat sing masc
2. ἔμποροι emporoi nom pl masc

1	kingdom of heaven is like unto **a merchant** man,...	Matt 13:45
2	and the **merchants** of the earth are waxed rich......	Rev 18:3
2	the **merchants** of the earth shall weep and mourn......	18:11
2	**merchants** of these things, which were made rich......	18:15
2	for thy **merchants** were the great men of the earth;....	18:23

Emporos actually means a wholesale dealer rather than a retailer (*kapēlos*). It is used in Jesus' Parable of the Pearl of Great Price (Matthew 13) and of the merchants who profited from Babylon (Revelation 18). The word can mean a traveler since this is what distinguished the wholesaler from the retailer. In its five occurrences in the New Testament, however, *emporos* means simply "merchant."

STRONG 1711, BAUER 256-57, MOULTON-MILLIGAN 208, LIDDELL-SCOTT 548.

1698. ἐμπρήθω emprēthō verb

Burn, set on fire.

1. ἐνέπρησεν eneprēsen 3sing indic aor act

1 and **burned up** their city......................... Matt 22:7

This word can mean "to inflate, swell up, or burn." In the New Testament it takes on both meanings. Occurring only twice in the New Testament *emprēthō* was used by Jesus in His Parable of the Wedding Feast to describe the destruction of a city by fire (Matthew 22:7). In Acts 28:6 the inhabitants of Malta expected Paul to swell up after being bitten by the serpent he disturbed when picking up wood for a fire. The Maltese people must have known how lethal the type of viper was which fastened onto Paul's hand.

STRONG 1714, BAUER 256 (see "empi[m]prēmi"), MOULTON-MILLIGAN 207, LIDDELL-SCOTT 548.

STRONG 1713, BAUER 257, MOULTON-MILLIGAN 208, LIDDELL-SCOTT 548.

1699. ἔμπροσθεν emprosthen prep

In front of, before, ahead.

1. ἔμπροσθεν emprosthen

1	Let your light so shine **before** men,...............	Matt 5:16
1	Leave there thy gift **before** the altar,..................	5:24
1	Take heed that ye do not your alms **before** men,.......	6:1
1	do not sound a trumpet **before** thee,................	6:2
1	neither cast ye your pearls **before** swine,............	7:6
1	Whosoever therefore shall confess me **before** men,....	10:32
1	him will I confess also **before** my Father.............	10:32
1	But whosoever shall deny me **before** men,...........	10:33
1	him will I also deny **before** my Father................	10:33
1	which shall prepare thy way **before** thee.............	11:10
1	Even so, Father: for so it seemed good **in** thy sight....	11:26
1	And was transfigured **before** them:...................	17:2
1	Even so it is not the will of your Father...............	18:14
1	for ye shut up the kingdom of heaven **against** men:...	23:13
1	And **before** him shall be gathered all nations:.........	25:32
1	But he denied **before** them all, saying,...............	26:70
1	And Jesus stood **before** the governor:................	27:11
1	and they bowed the knee **before** him,................	27:29
1	which shall prepare thy way **before** thee....	Mark 1:2
1	and walked out in **full view** of them all. (NIV).........	2:12
1	mountain ... and he was transfigured **before** them,......	9:2
1	tiling with his couch into the midst **before** Jesus....	Luke 5:19
1	which shall prepare thy way **before** thee...............	7:27
1	even so, Father; for so it seemed good **in** thy sight.....	10:21
1	Whosoever shall confess me **before** men,..............	12:8
1	Son of man also confess **before** the angels of God:.....	12:8
1	a certain man **before** him which had the dropsy.......	14:2
1	he ran **before**, and climbed up into a sycamore tree....	19:4
1	bring hither, and slay them **before** me...............	19:27
1	spoken, he went **before**, ascending up to Jerusalem.....	19:28
1	worthy to escape ... to stand **before** the Son of man....	21:36
1	He that cometh after me is preferred **before** me:....	John 1:15
1	who coming after me is preferred **before** me,..........	1:27
1	After me cometh a man ... preferred **before** me:......	1:30

ἐμπτύω 1700

1 I am not the Christ, but that I am sent **before** him... John 3:28
1 he goeth **before** them, and the sheep follow him: 10:4
1 though he had done so many miracles **before** them, ... 12:37
1 your alms have ascended ... **before** God. (RSV) .... Acts 10:4
1 and beat him **before** the judgment seat. 18:17
1 must all appear **before** the judgment seat of Christ; .. 2 Co 5:10
1 I said unto Peter **before** them all, ... Gal 2:14
1 reaching forth unto those things which are **before**, ... Phlp 3:13
1 in the sight of God and our Father; .... 1 Th 1:3
1 Are not even ye **in the presence** of our Lord Jesus 2:19
1 wherewith we joy for your sakes **before** our God; 3:9
1 your hearts unblameable in holiness **before** God, ... 3:13
1 and shall assure our hearts **before** him. .... 1 Jn 3:19
1 were four beasts full of eyes **before** and behind. ...... Rev 4:6
1 And I fell **at** his feet to worship him. 19:10
1 I fell down to worship **before** the feet of the angel 22:8

Classical Greek
Emprosthen, for the most part a preposition (improper) in the New Testament, functioned as an adverb in the classical period (Blass and DeBrunner, *A Greek Grammar of the New Testament*, p.115). As an adverb it denoted place—"in front of, before," and time—"earlier, previously." Later it moved to a prepositional function (with the genitive). The term occurs in virtually every kind of Greek literature including the papyri and inscriptions.

Septuagint Usage
The Septuagint reads *emprosthen* for 6 Hebrew words and even 10 other forms of those words. In Judges it is used as a temporal adverb: "We are defeating them as *before*" (20:32, NIV). A different reading of the adverb *proteron* by Vaticanus in this text shows the adverbial sense of *emprosthen* (e.g., also Zechariah 1:4; 7:7,12; 8:11).

The prepositional nature of *emprosthen* is also attested in the Septuagint: "Before the porch of the Lord" (2 Chronicles 15:8); "God did send me before you" (Genesis 45:5,7); "before him ... neither after him" (2 Kings 23:25 [LXX 4 Kings 23:25]); "(they) are there before you" (Numbers 14:43).

New Testament Usage
Much of the New Testament's usage is as an improper preposition. The first and third Gospels employ *emprosthen* a total of 28 times (18 in Matthew and 10 in Luke) compared to twice in Mark's. It can mean "in the presence of" or "in the sight of" (Matthew 5:16; 10:32,33; Luke 12:8; 21:36; John 12:37), "ahead" or "before" (Matthew 11:10; Luke 7:27; John 3:28), or "in front of" (Matthew 5:24). John's Gospel exemplifies a temporal understanding of "prior to" (John 1:15,30).

The remainder of the New Testament follows the general pattern of usage seen in the Gospels: "in the presence of" (Galatians 2:14; 1 Thessalonians 1:3; 2:19; 3:9), "in front of" (Revelation 4:6), or "ahead of" (Philippians 3:13).

STRONG 1715, BAUER 257, MOULTON-MILLIGAN 208, LIDDELL-SCOTT 548, COLIN BROWN 3:1205.

1700. ἐμπτύω emptuō verb
Spit upon.
CROSS-REFERENCE:
πτύω ptuō (4287)

יָרַק yāraq (3535), Spit (Nm 12:14, Dt 25:9).

1. **ἐμπτύειν** emptuein inf pres act
2. **ἐνέπτυσαν** eneptusan 3pl indic aor act
3. **ἐμπτύσαντες** emptusantes nom pl masc part aor act
4. **ἐμπτύσουσιν** emptusousin 3pl indic fut act
5. **ἐνέπτυον** eneptuon 3pl indic imperf act
6. **ἐμπτυσθήσεται** emptusthēsetai 3sing indic fut pass

2 Then did they **spit** in his face, and buffeted him; ... Matt 26:67
3 And they **spit upon** him, ... 27:30
4 and **shall spit upon** him, and shall kill him: .... Mark 10:34
1 some began to **spit on** him, and to cover his face, ... 14:65
5 they smote him on the head ... did **spit upon** him, ... 15:19
6 mocked, and spitefully entreated, and **spitted on**: ... Luke 18:32

The simple meaning of this verb is "spit upon" as a sign of contempt. In the New Testament it is used either with the dative case (Mark 10:34; 14:65; 15:19) or with the preposition *eis* (1506B) (Matthew 26:67; 27:30). The verb is found once in the passive voice (Luke 18:32). Each of these passages refer to part of the mocking Jesus endured before crucifixion.

STRONG 1716, BAUER 257, MOULTON-MILLIGAN 208, LIDDELL-SCOTT 548.

1701. ἐμφανής emphanēs adj
Manifest, visible, apparent.
CROSS-REFERENCE:
ἐμφανίζω emphanizō (1702)

כּוּן kûn (3679), Niphal: be established (Is 2:2, Mi 4:1).

1. **ἐμφανής** emphanēs nom sing masc
2. **ἐμφανῆ** emphanē acc sing masc

2 raised up the third day, and **showed** him openly; ... Acts 10:40
1 I was made **manifest** unto them that asked not ..... Rom 10:20

Related to the verb *emphainō*, "show in, exhibit," the adjective *emphanēs* is found only twice in the New Testament. In Acts 10:40 it is used for the open display of Christ after the Resurrection ("caused him to be seen," NIV). In Romans 10:20 it is found in a quotation from Isaiah 65:1 (Septuagint). Here Paul spoke of Isaiah's message concerning God making himself manifest to the Gentiles because Israel had turned away.

STRONG 1717, BAUER 257, MOULTON-MILLIGAN 208, LIDDELL-SCOTT 549, COLIN BROWN 2:488-89.

1702. ἐμφανίζω emphanizō verb
Exhibit, reveal, make known, appear.

COGNATES:
ἐμφανής emphanēs (1701)
φαίνω phainō (5154)

SYNONYMS:
ἀναγγέλλω anangellō (310)
ἀναδείκνυμι anadeiknumi (320)
ἀναφαίνω anaphainō (396)
ἀπαγγέλλω apangellō (514)
ἀποκαλύπτω apokaluptō (596)
γίνομαι ginomai (1090)
γνωρίζω gnōrizō (1101)
δείκνυμι deiknumi (1161)
δηλόω dēloō (1207)
διερμηνεύω diermēneuō (1323)
ἐξηγέομαι exēgeomai (1817)
ἐπιφαίνω epiphainō (1998)
ἑρμηνεύω hermēneuō (2043)
ἐφίστημι ephistēmi (2168)
ἵστημι histēmi (2449)
κατηχέω katēcheō (2697)
κηρύσσω kērussō (2756)
λέγω legō (2978)
μηνύω mēnuō (3245)
ὁράω horaō (3571)
παραγίνομαι paraginomai (3716)
φαίνω phainō (5154)
φανερόω phaneroō (5157)

אָמַר 'āmar (569), Tell, report (Est 2:22).

יָדַע yādhaʻ (3156), Know; hiphil: may know (Ex 33:13).

רָאָה rā'âh (7495), See; hiphil: show (Ex 33:18).

1. ἐμφανίζουσιν emphanizousin 3pl indic pres act
2. ἐμφανίζειν emphanizein inf pres act
3. ἐνεφάνισας enephanisas 2sing indic aor act
4. ἐνεφάνισαν enephanisan 3pl indic aor act
5. ἐμφανίσατε emphanisate 2pl impr aor act
6. ἐμφανίσω emphanisō 1sing indic fut act
7. ἐνεφανίσθησαν enephanisthēsan 3pl indic aor pass
8. ἐμφανισθῆναι emphanisthēnai inf aor pass

```
7 went into the holy city, and appeared unto many... Matt 27:53
6 I will love him, and will manifest myself to him.. John 14:21
2 how is it that thou wilt manifest thyself unto us,....... 14:22
5 ye with the council signify to the chief captain..... Acts 23:15
3 See thou tell no man that thou hast showed these...... 23:22
4 Tertullus, ... informed the governor against Paul... 24:1
4 the chief of the Jews informed him against Paul,....... 25:2
4 and the elders of the Jews informed me,.............. 25:15
8 now to appear in the presence of God for us:........Heb 9:24
1 declare plainly that they seek a country............. 11:14
```

Classical Greek
This term appears in classical Greek from the time of Plato (ca. Fourth Century B.C.). It is another term intensified by the addition of a preposition (in this case en [1706] to the verb [here phanizō]). Emphanizō means "to demonstrate, to show" in a secular sense and "to make manifest" in a religious sense. Passively it means "to become visible." A "quasi-technical sense of this word = 'make an official report' is witnessed in papyri as early as 221 B.C." (Moulton-Milligan).

Septuagint Usage
Emphanizō occurs only four times in the canonical writings of the Septuagint, and it translates four different words. Moses requested that God "manifest himself" (Exodus 33:13, Hebrew yādhaʻ) and "show me (Moses) your glory" (Exodus 33:18; rā'âh; cf. Wisdom of Solomon 1:2). The sense of "to make known" or "to reveal" occurs in Esther 2:22 (cf. Isaiah 3:9, RSV "proclaims" [of sins]; Wisdom of Solomon 18:18; 2 Maccabees 11:29).

New Testament Usage
In the New Testament emphanizō depicts the making of an official report (see above) by Paul to a tribunal (Acts 23:15). This idea "to inform" is echoed throughout Acts (23:22; 24:1; 25:2,15).

The sense of "to demonstrate" occurs in Hebrews 11:14. The notion of "to appear" occurs in Matthew 27:53 of the dead who are raised and who "appear" (cf. Wisdom of Solomon 17:4), and in Hebrews 9:24 of Christ who "appears" in heaven on our behalf.

John may have been echoing the Old Testament idea that God manifests himself to men (Exodus 33:13,18; cf. Philo Allegorical Method 3.101 cited by Bultmann/Luhrmann, "emphanizō," Kittel, 9:7). Jesus "reveals" himself only to those who love Him and who are loved by the Father (John 14:21,22; cf. emphanēs [1701], Acts 10:40f.; Romans 10:20; Isaiah 65:1).

STRONG 1718, BAUER 257, MOULTON-MILLIGAN 208, KITTEL 9:7, LIDDELL-SCOTT 549, COLIN BROWN 2:488-89.

1703. ἔμφοβος emphobos adj
Terrified, frightened.

CROSS-REFERENCE:
φοβέω phobeō (5236)

1. ἔμφοβος emphobos nom sing masc
2. ἔμφοβοι emphoboi nom pl masc
3. ἐμφόβων emphobōn gen pl fem

```
3 And as they were afraid,......................... Luke 24:5
2 But they were terrified and affrighted,................ 24:37
```

1 And when he looked on him, he was **afraid**,	Acts 10:4
2 saw indeed the light, and were **afraid**;	22:9
1 Felix **trembled**, and answered, Go thy way	24:25
2 and the remnant were **affrighted**,	Rev 11:13

In the New Testament *emphobos* regularly denotes great fear. The women going to the tomb of Jesus were terrified by the angels announcing His resurrection (Luke 24:5). The Eleven plus the two Emmaus Road brothers were frightened by Jesus' sudden appearance in their midst (Luke 24:37). Cornelius became startled at the appearance of an angel in response to his prayers (Acts 10:4). Acts 22:9 recounts the fear experienced by those who were with Paul on the road to Damascus when the presence of God suddenly shone brighter than the noonday sun. Acts 24:25 relates the fear of Felix after Paul had preached to him concerning, among other things, the coming judgment. Lastly, Revelation 11:13 tells of the earthquake which killed many people and terrified the rest. This was the first woe.

STRONG 1719, BAUER 257, MOULTON-MILLIGAN 208-9, LIDDELL-SCOTT 550.

1704. ἐμφυσάω emphusaō verb

Breathe on, blow in, infuse.

מָדַד mādhadh (4200), Measure; hithpolel: stretch (1 Kgs 17:21).

נָפַח nāphach (5483), Breathe (Gn 2:7, Ez 37:9).

פּוּחַ pûach (6558), Hiphil: blow, breathe (Ez 21:31).

פּוּץ pûts (6571), Hiphil: attack, dash (Na 2:1).

1. ἐνεφύσησεν enephusēsen 3sing indic aor act

1 And when he had said this, he **breathed on** them, .. John 20:22

Classical Greek

The verb *emphusaō* consists of two elements: *en* (1706), "in," and *phusaō*, "blow." In classical Greek it signified "blowing in" as was done in playing a flute (see *Liddell-Scott*). *Emphusaō* had a similar meaning in the Greek papyri. An example is where the word was used in reference to a medical treatment for sneezing. To stop sneezing a compound extracted from some white hellebore plants was to be blown into the nostrils (cf. *Moulton-Milligan*).

Septuagint Usage

Emphusaō occurs 11 times in the Septuagint and has the significance of breathing upon or into. God breathed into the nostrils of Adam the breath of life, and he became a living being (Genesis 2:7; cf. Wisdom 15:11). In the vision of the dry bones God breathed upon the slain, and they came alive (Ezekiel 37:9). Eliphaz reminded Job that men are weak and transient: "For he (God) blows upon them and they are withered" (Job 4:21). See also Sirach 43:4; Nahum 2:1; Ezekiel 21:31; 22:20.

New Testament Usage

In the New Testament *emphusaō* is found only in John 20:22 where Jesus breathed (*enephusēsen*) on the disciples and said, "Receive ye the Holy Ghost." Most likely the use of *emphusaō* by John refers to the bestowal of life as in the Septuagint in Genesis 2:7; Ezekiel 37:9; and Wisdom of Solomon 15:11. As at the first creation when God breathed life into Adam, so Jesus breathed the Holy Spirit into the disciples, bringing a new creation and spiritual life. By the Spirit the disciples were united to the risen Lord so they shared in His life.

STRONG 1720, BAUER 258, MOULTON-MILLIGAN 209, KITTEL 2:536-37, LIDDELL-SCOTT 551.

1705. ἔμφυτος emphutos adj

Implanted, engrafted.

CROSS-REFERENCE:
φυτεύω phuteuō (5288)

1. ἔμφυτον emphuton acc sing masc

1 and receive with meekness the **engrafted** word, ... Jas 1:21

In nonbiblical Greek this adjective is used mostly in the sense of "implanted by nature, inborn, innate" (cf. *Bauer*). It refers to original capacity in contrast to that which was learned or acquired. Furthermore, *emphutos* is used of that which is bestowed, provided it is thought to be deeply rooted in human nature. That is the meaning of the adjective in James 1:21, the only place it appears in the New Testament. There believers are urged to receive "the engrafted word." "The engrafted word" in James could not be described as an inborn characteristic. The Word of God was to be received as a gift and allowed to become "engrafted," that is, to be bound and attached to their lives in such a way that the two grow together inseparably (cf. John 15).

STRONG 1721, BAUER 258, MOULTON-MILLIGAN 209, LIDDELL-SCOTT 551, COLIN BROWN 3:865,868.

1706. ἐν en prep

In, on, at, within, among, with, by, by means of.

ἐν 1706

1. ἐν en

1 she was found with child of the Holy Ghost. (NT)	Matt 1:18
1 that which is conceived in her is of the Holy Ghost.	1:20
1 Behold, a virgin shall be with child, (NT)	1:23
1 Now when Jesus was born in Bethlehem of Judaea	2:1
1 in Bethlehem ... in the days of Herod the king,	2:1
1 for we have seen his star in the east,	2:2
1 And they said unto him, In Bethlehem of Judaea:	2:5
1 art not the least among the princes of Juda:	2:6
1 and, lo, the star, which they saw in the east,	2:9
1 and slew all the children that were in Bethlehem,	2:16
1 in Bethlehem, and in all the coasts thereof,	2:16
1 In Rama was there a voice heard,	2:18
1 angel ... appeareth in a dream to Joseph in Egypt,	2:19
1 In those days came John the Baptist,	3:1
1 John ... preaching in the wilderness of Judaea,	3:1
1 The voice of one crying in the wilderness,	3:3
1 were baptized ... in Jordan, confessing their sins.	3:6
1 And think not to say within yourselves,	3:9
1 I indeed baptize you with water unto repentance:	3:11
1 baptize you with the Holy Ghost, and with fire:	3:11
1 Whose fan is in his hand,	3:12
1 my beloved Son, in whom I am well pleased.	3:17
1 but by every word that proceedeth ... of God.	4:4
1 in the borders of Zabulon and Nephthalim:	4:13
1 The people which sat in darkness saw great light,	4:16
1 them which sat in the region and shadow of death	4:16
1 brethren, ... in a ship with Zebedee their father,	4:21
1 And Jesus went about all Galilee, teaching	4:23
1 Jesus was going about in all Galilee,	4:23
1 Jesus went about ... teaching in their synagogues,	4:23
1 and all manner of disease among the people.	4:23
1 Rejoice, ... for great is your reward in heaven:	5:12
1 lost his savour, wherewith shall it be salted?	5:13
1 and it giveth light unto all that are in the house.	5:15
1 and glorify your Father which is in heaven.	5:16
1 shall be called the least in the kingdom of heaven:	5:19
1 shall be called great in the kingdom of heaven.	5:19
1 whiles thou art in the way with him;	5:25
1 committed adultery with her already in his heart.	5:28
1 neither by heaven; for it is God's throne:	5:34
1 Nor by the earth; for it is his footstool:	5:35
1 Neither shalt thou swear by thy head,	5:36
1 be ... children of your Father which is in heaven:	5:45
1 even as your Father which is in heaven is perfect.	5:48
1 no reward of your Father which is in heaven.	6:1
1 hypocrites do in the synagogues and in the streets,	6:2
1 hypocrites do in the synagogues and in the streets,	6:2
1 That thine alms may be in secret:	6:4
1 and thy Father which seeth in secret	6:4
1 your Father who sees in secret (NASB)	6:4
1 for they love to pray standing in the synagogues	6:5
1 in the synagogues and in the corners of the streets,	6:5
1 pray to thy Father which is in secret;	6:6
1 and thy Father which seeth in secret	6:6
1 your Father who sees in secret (NASB)	6:6
1 that they shall be heard for their much speaking.	6:7
1 Our Father which art in heaven,	6:9
1 Thy will be done in earth, as it is in heaven.	6:10
1 but unto thy Father which is in secret;	6:18
1 and thy Father, which seeth in secret,	6:18
1 which seeth in secret	6:18
1 But lay up for yourselves treasures in heaven,	6:20
1 If therefore the light that is in thee be darkness,	6:23
1 That even Solomon in all his glory	6:29
1 with what judgment ye judge, ye shall be judged:	7:2
1 and with what measure ye mete, ... be measured	7:2
1 the mote that is in thy brother's eye,	7:3
1 considerest not the beam that is in thine own eye?	7:3
1 and, behold, a beam is in thine own eye?	7:4
1 lest they trample them under their feet,	7:6
1 your Father which is in heaven give good things	7:11
1 which come to you in sheep's clothing,	7:15
1 doeth the will of my Father which is in heaven.	7:21
1 Many will say to me in that day, Lord, Lord,	7:22
1 Lord, my servant lieth at home sick of the palsy,	8:6
1 not found so great faith, no, not in Israel.	Matt 8:10
1 and Isaac, and Jacob, in the kingdom of heaven.	8:11
1 And his servant was healed in the selfsame hour.	8:13
1 And, behold, there arose a great tempest in the sea,	8:24
1 into the sea, and perished in the waters.	8:32
1 certain of the scribes said within themselves,	9:3
1 Wherefore think ye evil in your hearts?	9:4
1 as Jesus sat at meat in the house,	9:10
1 For she said within herself,	9:21
1 spread abroad his fame in all that country.	9:31
1 saying, It was never so seen in Israel.	9:33
1 casteth out devils through the prince of the devils.	9:34
1 teaching in their synagogues, and preaching	9:35
1 every sickness and every disease among the people.	9:35
1 or town ye shall enter, inquire who in it is worthy;	10:11
1 Sodom and Gomorrha in the day of judgment,	10:15
1 I send you forth as sheep in the midst of wolves:	10:16
1 and they will scourge you in their synagogues;	10:17
1 for it shall be given you in that same hour	10:19
1 the Spirit of your Father which speaketh in you.	10:20
1 But when they persecute you in this city,	10:23
1 What I tell you in darkness, that speak ye in light:	10:27
1 What I tell you in darkness, that speak ye in light:	10:27
1 able to destroy both soul and body in hell.	10:28
1 shall confess me before men, (NT)	10:32
1 before my Father which is in heaven.	10:32
1 confess also before my Father which is in heaven.	10:32
1 also deny before my Father which is in heaven.	10:33
1 departed ... to teach and to preach in their cities.	11:1
1 John had heard in the prison the works of Christ,	11:2
1 blessed ... whosoever shall not be offended in me.	11:6
1 A man clothed in soft raiment?	11:8
1 they that wear soft clothing are in kings' houses.	11:8
1 Verily ... Among them that are born of women	11:11
1 least in the kingdom of heaven is greater than he.	11:11
1 It is like unto children sitting in the markets,	11:16
1 It is like unto children sitting in the markets,	11:16
1 It is like unto children sitting in the markets,	11:16
1 wherein most of his mighty works were done,	11:20
1 for if the mighty works, which were done in you,	11:21
1 done in you, had been done in Tyre and Sidon,	11:21
1 they would have repented long ago in sackcloth	11:21
1 more tolerable for Tyre ... at the day of judgment,	11:22
1 if the mighty works, ... had been done in Sodom,	11:23
1 if the mighty works, which have been done in thee,	11:23
1 more tolerable ... Sodom in the day of judgment,	11:24
1 At that time Jesus answered and said,	11:25
1 At that time Jesus went on the sabbath day	12:1
1 which is not lawful to do upon the sabbath day.	12:2
1 Or have ye not read in the law,	12:5
1 the priests in the temple profane the sabbath,	12:5
1 my beloved, in whom my soul is well pleased;	12:18
1 neither shall any man hear his voice in the streets.	12:19
1 And in his name shall the Gentiles trust.	12:21
1 but by Beelzebub the prince of the devils.	12:24
1 And if I by Beelzebub cast out devils,	12:27
1 by whom do your children cast them out?	12:27
1 But if I cast out devils by the Spirit of God,	12:28
1 neither in this world, neither in the world to come.	12:32
1 neither in this world, neither in the world to come.	12:32
1 shall give account thereof in the day of judgment.	12:36
1 three days and three nights in the whale's belly;	12:40
1 three days and ... nights in the heart of the earth.	12:40
1 The men of Nineveh shall rise in judgment	12:41
1 queen of the south shall rise up in the judgment	12:42
1 shall do the will of my Father which is in heaven,	12:50
1 The same day went Jesus out of the house, (NT)	13:1
1 And he spake many things unto them in parables,	13:3
1 when he sowed, some seeds fell by the way side,	13:4
1 Why speakest thou unto them in parables?	13:10
1 Therefore speak I to them in parables:	13:13
1 catcheth away that which was sown in his heart.	13:19
1 Yet hath he not root in himself,	13:21
1 a man which sowed good seed in his field:	13:24
1 while men slept, his enemy came and sowed tares	13:25
1 didst not thou sow good seed in thy field?	13:27
1 and in the time of harvest I will say to the reapers,	13:30

403

ἐν 1706

1 seed, which a man took, and sowed in his field:	Matt 13:31
1 birds of the air come and lodge in the branches	13:32
1 spake Jesus unto the multitude in parables;	13:34
1 saying, I will open my mouth in parables;	13:35
1 so shall it be in the end of this world.	13:40
1 shine ... as the sun in the kingdom of their Father.	13:43
1 the kingdom ... is like unto treasure hid in a field;	13:44
1 So shall it be at the end of the world:	13:49
1 which is instructed unto the kingdom of heaven	13:52
1 he taught them in their synagogue,	13:54
1 And they were offended in him.	13:57
1 not without honour, save in his own country,	13:57
1 save in his own country, and in his own house.	13:57
1 At that time Herod the tetrarch heard of the fame	14:1
1 mighty works do show forth themselves in him.	14:2
1 and put him in prison for Herodias' sake,	14:3
1 the daughter of Herodias danced before them,	14:6
1 And he sent, and beheaded John in the prison.	14:10
1 departed thence by ship into a desert place apart:	14:13
1 were in the ship came and worshipped him,	14:33
1 not ... away fasting, lest they faint in the way.	15:32
1 so much bread in the wilderness,	15:33
1 And they reasoned among themselves, saying,	16:7
1 ye of little faith, why reason ye among yourselves,	16:8
1 but my Father which is in heaven.	16:17
1 thou shalt bind on earth shall be bound in heaven:	16:19
1 thou shalt loose on earth shall be loosed in heaven.	16:19
1 For the Son of man shall come in the glory	16:27
1 till they see the Son of man coming in his kingdom.	16:28
1 my beloved Son, in whom I am well pleased;	17:5
1 but have done unto him whatsoever they listed.	17:12
1 this kind goeth not out but by prayer and fasting.	17:21
1 while they abode in Galilee, Jesus said unto them,	17:22
1 At the same time came the disciples unto Jesus,	18:1
1 Who is the greatest in the kingdom of heaven?	18:1
1 a little child ... and set him in the midst of them,	18:2
1 the same is greatest in the kingdom of heaven.	18:4
1 and that he were drowned in the depth of the sea.	18:6
1 That in heaven their angels do always behold	18:10
1 the face of my Father which is in heaven.	18:10
1 it is not the will of your Father which is in heaven,	18:14
1 ye shall bind on earth shall be bound in heaven:	18:18
1 ye shall loose on earth shall be loosed in heaven.	18:18
1 done for them of my Father which is in heaven.	18:19
1 two or three are ... there am I in the midst of them.	18:20
1 and thou shalt have treasure in heaven:	19:21
1 in the regeneration when the Son of man shall sit	19:28
1 and saw others standing idle in the marketplace,	20:3
1 not lawful for me to do what I will with mine own?	20:15
1 took the twelve disciples apart in the way,	20:17
1 and the other on the left, in thy kingdom.	20:21
1 But it shall not be so among you:	20:26
1 but whosoever will be great among you,	20:26
1 And whosoever will be chief among you,	20:27
1 great multitude spread their garments in the way;	21:8
1 cut ... branches ... and strowed them in the way.	21:8
1 Blessed is he that cometh in the name of the Lord;	21:9
1 in the name of the Lord; Hosanna in the highest.	21:9
1 out all them that sold and bought in the temple,	21:12
1 the blind and the lame came to him in the temple;	21:14
1 and the children crying in the temple,	21:15
1 and found nothing thereon, but leaves only,	21:19
1 all things, whatsoever ye shall ask in prayer,	21:22
1 By what authority doest thou these things?	21:23
1 I in like wise will tell you by what authority I do	21:24
1 began reasoning among themselves, (NASB)	21:25
1 Neither tell I you by what authority I do these	21:27
1 and said, Son, go work to day in my vineyard.	21:28
1 John came unto you in the way of righteousness,	21:32
1 and digged a winepress in it, and built a tower,	21:33
1 they said among themselves, This is the heir;	21:38
1 which shall render him the fruits in their seasons.	21:41
1 Did ye never read in the scriptures,	21:42
1 and it is marvellous in our eyes?	21:42
1 answered and spake unto them again by parables,	22:1
1 how they might entangle him in his talk.	22:15
1 and teachest the way of God in truth,	22:16

1 The same day came to him the Sadducees, (NT)	Matt 22:23
1 in the resurrection whose wife shall she be	22:28
1 For in the resurrection they neither marry,	22:30
1 but are as the angels of God in heaven.	22:30
1 which is the great commandment in the law?	22:36
1 love the Lord thy God with all thy heart,	22:37
1 and with all thy soul, and with all thy mind.	22:37
1 and with all thy soul, and with all thy mind.	22:37
1 On these two commandments hang all the law	22:40
1 How then doth David in spirit call him Lord,	22:43
1 If David then call him Lord, how is he his son?	22:45
1 And love the uppermost rooms at feasts,	23:6
1 and the chief seats in the synagogues,	23:6
1 And greetings in the markets,	23:7
1 for one is your Father, which is in heaven.	23:9
1 Whosoever shall swear by the temple, it is nothing;	23:16
1 whosoever shall swear by the gold of the temple,	23:16
1 Whosoever shall swear by the altar, it is nothing;	23:18
1 but whosoever sweareth by the gift that is upon it,	23:18
1 Whoso therefore shall swear by the altar,	23:20
1 sweareth by it, and by all things thereon.	23:20
1 sweareth by it, and by all things thereon.	23:20
1 And whoso shall swear by the temple,	23:21
1 sweareth by it, and by him that dwelleth therein.	23:21
1 sweareth by it, and by him that dwelleth therein.	23:21
1 And he that shall swear by heaven,	23:22
1 sweareth by the throne of God,	23:22
1 the throne of God, and by him that sitteth thereon.	23:22
1 If we had been in the days of our fathers,	23:30
1 partakers with them in the blood of the prophets.	23:30
1 some of them shall ye scourge in your synagogues,	23:34
1 Blessed is he that cometh in the name of the Lord.	23:39
1 in all the world for a witness unto all nations;	24:14
1 spoken of by Daniel ... stand in the holy place,	24:15
1 which be in Judaea flee into the mountains,	24:16
1 Neither let him which is in the field return back	24:18
1 And woe unto them that are with child, (NT)	24:19
1 woe unto ... them that give suck in those days!	24:19
1 your flight be not ... neither on the sabbath day:	24:20
1 Behold, he is in the desert; go not forth:	24:26
1 behold, he is in the secret chambers; believe it not.	24:26
1 shall appear the sign of the Son of man in heaven:	24:30
1 For as in the days that were before the flood	24:38
1 Then shall two be in the field:	24:40
1 Two women shall be grinding at the mill;	24:41
1 wise servant, ... to give them meat in due season?	24:45
1 But and if that evil servant shall say in his heart,	24:48
1 shall come in a day when he looketh not for him,	24:50
1 and in an hour that he is not aware of,	24:50
1 the wise took oil in their vessels with their lamps.	25:4
1 day nor the hour wherein the Son of man cometh.	25:13
1 went and traded with the same,	25:16
1 had received one went and digged in the earth,	25:18
1 afraid, and went and hid thy talent in the earth:	25:25
1 When the Son of man shall come in his glory,	25:31
1 I was in prison, and ye came unto me.	25:36
1 saw we thee sick, or in prison, and came unto thee?	25:39
1 sick, and in prison, and ye visited me not.	25:43
1 or a stranger, or naked, or sick, or in prison,	25:44
1 But they said, Not on the feast day,	26:5
1 lest there be an uproar among the people.	26:5
1 Now when Jesus was in Bethany,	26:6
1 in Bethany, in the house of Simon the leper,	26:6
1 this gospel shall be preached in the whole world,	26:13
1 He that dippeth his hand with me in the dish,	26:23
1 He that dippeth his hand with me in the dish,	26:23
1 I drink it new with you in my Father's kingdom.	26:29
1 All ye shall be offended because of me this night;	26:31
1 All ye shall be offended because of me this night:	26:31
1 Though all men shall be offended because of thee,	26:33
1 That this night, before the cock crow, (NT)	26:34
1 take the sword shall perish with the sword.	26:52
1 In that same hour said Jesus to the multitudes,	26:55
1 I sat daily with you teaching in the temple,	26:55
1 I sat daily with you teaching in the temple,	26:55
1 Now Peter sat without in the palace:	26:69
1 And he cast down the pieces of silver in the temple,	27:5

ἐν 1706

1 when he was accused of the chief priests	Matt	27:12
1 and a reed in His right hand; (NASB)		27:29
1 destroyest the temple, and buildest it in three days,		27:40
1 Among which was Mary Magdalene, and Mary		27:56
1 and wrapped it in a clean linen cloth, (NASB)		27:59
1 And laid it in his own new tomb,		27:60
1 new tomb, which he had hewn out in the rock:		27:60
1 All power is given unto me in heaven and in earth.		28:18
1 As it is written in the prophets,	Mark	1:2
1 The voice of one crying in the wilderness,		1:3
1 John did baptize in the wilderness,		1:4
1 and were all baptized of him in the river of Jordan,		1:5
1 I indeed have baptized you with water:		1:8
1 but he shall baptize you with the Holy Ghost.		1:8
1 And it came to pass in those days,		1:9
1 my beloved Son, in whom I am well pleased.		1:11
1 And he was there in the wilderness forty days,		1:13
1 repent ye, and believe the gospel. (NT)		1:15
1 casting a net into the sea: for they were fishers.		1:16
1 who also were in the ship mending their nets.		1:19
1 and they left their father Zebedee in the ship		1:20
1 in their synagogue a man with an unclean spirit;		1:23
1 in their synagogue a man with an unclean spirit;		1:23
1 And he preached in their synagogues		1:39
1 but was without in desert places:		1:45
1 it was heard that He was at home. (NASB)		2:1
1 of the scribes ... and reasoning in their hearts,		2:6
1 that they so reasoned within themselves,		2:8
1 Why reason ye these things in your hearts?		2:8
1 as Jesus sat at meat in his house,		2:15
1 as Jesus sat at meat in his house,		2:15
1 fast, while the bridegroom is with them?		2:19
1 and then shall they fast in those days.		2:20
1 went through the corn fields on the sabbath day;		2:23
1 Behold, why do they on the sabbath day?		2:24
1 whether he would heal him on the sabbath day;		3:2
1 by the prince of the devils casteth he out devils.		3:22
1 and said unto them in parables, How can Satan		3:23
1 so that he entered into a ship, and sat in the sea;		4:1
1 And he taught them many things by parables,		4:2
1 and said unto them in his doctrine,		4:2
1 as he sowed, some fell by the way side,		4:4
1 some thirty, and some sixty, and some an hundred.		4:8
1 some thirty, and some sixty, and some an hundred.		4:8
1 some thirty, and some sixty, and some an hundred.		4:8
1 all these things are done in parables:		4:11
1 away the word that was sown in their hearts.		4:15
1 And have no root in themselves,		4:17
1 some thirtyfold, some sixty, and some an hundred.		4:20
1 some thirtyfold, some sixty, and some an hundred.		4:20
1 some thirtyfold, some sixty, and some an hundred.		4:20
1 with what measure ye mete, it shall be measured		4:24
1 then the ear, after that the full corn in the ear.		4:28
1 or with what comparison shall we compare it?		4:30
1 And the same day, when the even was come, (NT)		4:35
1 they took him even as he was in the ship.		4:36
1 And He Himself was in the stern, (NASB)		4:38
1 out of the tombs a man with an unclean spirit,		5:2
1 Who had his dwelling among the tombs;		5:3
1 night and day, he was in the mountains,		5:5
1 he was in the mountains, and in the tombs,		5:5
1 and were choked in the sea.		5:13
1 and began to publish in Decapolis		5:20
1 And when Jesus was passed over again by ship		5:21
1 which had an issue of blood twelve years, (NT)		5:25
1 came in the press behind, ... touched his garment.		5:27
1 knowing in himself that virtue had gone out		5:30
1 turned him about in the press, and said,		5:30
1 he began to teach in the synagogue:		6:2
1 And they were offended at him.		6:3
1 is not without honour, but in his own country,		6:4
1 and among his own kin, and in his own house.		6:4
1 and among his own kin, and in his own house.		6:4
1 in the day of judgment, than for that city.		6:11
1 mighty works do show forth themselves in him.		6:14
1 and bound him in prison for Herodias' sake,		6:17
1 and he went and beheaded him in the prison,		6:27

1 took up his corpse, and laid it in a tomb.	Mark	6:29
1 And they went away in the boat (NASB)		6:32
1 the ship was in the midst of the sea,		6:47
1 And he saw them toiling in rowing;		6:48
1 and they were sore amazed in themselves		6:51
1 they laid the sick in the streets,		6:56
1 In those days the multitude being very great,		8:1
1 them away fasting ... they will faint by the way:		8:3
1 neither had they in the ship		8:14
1 nor tell it to any in the town.		8:26
1 and by the way he asked his disciples,		8:27
1 in this adulterous and sinful generation;		8:38
1 in the glory of his Father with the holy angels.		8:38
1 have seen the kingdom of God come with power.		9:1
1 This kind can come forth by nothing, but by		9:29
1 come forth by nothing, but by prayer and fasting.		9:29
1 and being in the house he asked them,		9:33
1 What was it that ye disputed ... by the way?		9:33
1 held their peace: for by the way they had disputed		9:34
1 he took a child, and set him in the midst of them:		9:36
1 casting out demons in Your name, (NASB)		9:38
1 shall give you a cup of water to drink in my name,		9:41
1 salt ... lost his saltness, wherewith ye season it?		9:50
1 Have salt in yourselves, and have peace		9:50
1 Have salt ... and have peace one with another.		9:50
1 And in the house his disciples asked him again		10:10
1 and thou shalt have treasure in heaven:		10:21
1 he shall receive an hundredfold now in this time,		10:30
1 and in the world to come eternal life.		10:30
1 And they were in the way going up to Jerusalem;		10:32
1 and the other on thy left hand, in thy glory.		10:37
1 But so shall it not be among you:		10:43
1 but whosoever will be great among you,		10:43
1 And whoever wishes to be first among you		10:44
1 received his sight, and followed Jesus in the way.		10:52
1 Blessed is he that cometh in the name of the Lord:		11:9
1 kingdom ... that cometh in the name of the Lord:		11:10
1 in the name of the Lord: Hosanna in the highest.		11:10
1 he came, if haply he might find any thing thereon:		11:13
1 cast out them that sold and bought in the temple,		11:15
1 and shall not doubt in his heart, but shall believe		11:23
1 your Father also which is in heaven may forgive		11:25
1 neither will your Father which is in heaven forgive		11:26
1 to Jerusalem: and as he was walking in the temple,		11:27
1 By what authority doest thou these things?		11:28
1 I will tell you by what authority I do these things.		11:29
1 Neither do I tell you by what authority I do these		11:33
1 And he began to speak unto them by parables.		12:1
1 the Lord's doing, and it is marvellous in our eyes?		12:11
1 In the resurrection therefore, when they shall rise,		12:23
1 but are as the angels which are in heaven.		12:25
1 have ye not read in the book of Moses,		12:26
1 answered and said, while he taught in the temple,		12:35
1 For David himself said by the Holy Ghost,		12:36
1 And he said unto them in his doctrine,		12:38
1 the scribes, which love to go in long clothing,		12:38
1 the scribes, ... love salutations in the marketplaces,		12:38
1 And the chief seats in the synagogues,		12:39
1 and the uppermost rooms at feasts:		12:39
1 but whatsoever shall be given you in that hour,		13:11
1 let them that be in Judaea flee to the mountains:		13:14
1 But woe to them that are with child,		13:17
1 But woe ... to them that give suck in those days!		13:17
1 But in those days, after that tribulation,		13:24
1 and the powers that are in heaven shall be shaken.		13:25
1 coming in the clouds with great power and glory.		13:26
1 no man, no, not the angels which are in heaven,		13:32
1 scribes sought how they might take him by craft,		14:1
1 But they said, Not on the feast day,		14:2
1 being in Bethany in the house of Simon the leper,		14:3
1 being in Bethany in the house of Simon the leper,		14:3
1 She has done a good deed to Me. (NASB) (NT)		14:6
1 until that day that I drink it new in the kingdom		14:25
1 All ye shall be offended because of me this night:		14:27
1 All ye shall be offended because of me this night:		14:27
1 That this day, even in this night, before the cock		14:30
1 I was daily with you in the temple teaching,		14:49

ἐν 1706

1 And as Peter was beneath in the palace,	Mark 14:66
1 who had committed murder in the insurrection.	15:7
1 destroyest the temple, and buildest it in three days,	15:29
1 afar off: among whom was Mary Magdalene,	15:40
1 Who also, when he was in Galilee, followed him,	15:41
1 and took him down, and wrapped him in the linen,	15:46
1 they saw a young man sitting on the right side,	16:5
1 After that he appeared in another form unto two	16:12
1 In my name shall they cast out devils;	16:17
1 They will pick up serpents; (RSV) (NT)	16:18
1 things which are most surely believed among us,	Luke 1:1
1 was in the days of Herod, the king of Judaea,	1:5
1 walking in all the commandments and ordinances	1:6
1 and they both were now well stricken in years.	1:7
1 office before God in the order of his course,	1:8
1 office before God in the order of his course,	1:8
1 And he shall go before him in the spirit and power	1:17
1 to turn the hearts of the fathers to the children,	1:17
1 am an old man, and my wife well stricken in years.	1:18
1 marvelled that he tarried so long in the temple.	1:21
1 marvelled that he tarried so long in the temple.	1:21
1 perceived that he had seen a vision in the temple:	1:22
1 in the days wherein he looked on me,	1:25
1 to take away my reproach among men.	1:25
1 And in the sixth month the angel Gabriel was sent	1:26
1 Lord is with thee: blessed art thou among women.	1:28
1 And, behold, thou shalt conceive in thy womb,	1:31
1 she hath also conceived a son in her old age:	1:36
1 And Mary arose in those days,	1:39
1 the babe leaped in her womb;	1:41
1 Blessed art thou among women,	1:42
1 salutation ... the babe leaped in my womb for joy.	1:44
1 salutation ... the babe leaped in my womb for joy.	1:44
1 He hath showed strength with his arm;	1:51
1 that on the eighth day they came to circumcise	1:59
1 none of thy kindred is called by this name.	1:61
1 abroad throughout all the hill country of Judaea.	1:65
1 they that heard them laid them up in their hearts,	1:66
1 salvation for us in the house of his servant David;	1:69
1 In holiness and righteousness before him,	1:75
1 salvation ... by the remission of their sins,	1:77
1 whereby the dayspring from on high hath visited	1:78
1 To give light to them that sit in darkness	1:79
1 and was in the deserts till the day of his showing	1:80
1 And it came to pass in those days,	2:1
1 while they were there, the days were accomplished	2:6
1 and wrapped him ... and laid him in a manger;	2:7
1 because there was no room for them in the inn.	2:7
1 And there were in the same country shepherds	2:8
1 is born this day in the city of David a Saviour,	2:11
1 wrapped in swaddling clothes, lying in a manger.	2:12
1 Glory to God in the highest, and on earth peace,	2:14
1 and on earth peace, good will toward men.	2:14
1 Mary, and Joseph, and the babe lying in a manger.	2:16
1 Mary kept all ... and pondered them in her heart.	2:19
1 of the angel before he was conceived in the womb.	2:21
1 As it is written in the law of the Lord,	2:23
1 a sacrifice according to ... in the law of the Lord,	2:24
1 And, behold, there was a man in Jerusalem,	2:25
1 And he came by the Spirit into the temple:	2:27
1 and when the parents brought in the child Jesus,	2:27
1 Lord, now lettest thou thy servant depart in peace,	2:29
1 is set for the fall and rising again of many in Israel;	2:34
1 a prophetess, ... she was of a great age, (NT)	2:36
1 all them that looked for redemption in Jerusalem.	2:38
1 they had fulfilled the days, as they returned,	2:43
1 the child Jesus tarried behind in Jerusalem;	2:43
1 supposing him to have been in the company,	2:44
1 sought him among their kinsfolk and acquaintance.	2:44
1 sought him among their kinsfolk and acquaintance.	2:44
1 that after three days they found him in the temple,	2:46
1 in the temple, sitting in the midst of the doctors,	2:46
1 that I must be about my Father's business?	2:49
1 but his mother kept all these sayings in her heart.	2:51
1 And Jesus kept increasing in wisdom (NASB)	2:52
1 Now in the fifteenth year of the reign of Tiberius	3:1
1 unto John the son of Zacharias in the wilderness.	3:2

1 As it is written in the book of the words of Esaias	Luke 3:4
1 The voice of one crying in the wilderness,	3:4
1 and begin not to say within yourselves,	3:8
1 and all men mused in their hearts of John,	3:15
1 baptize you with the Holy Ghost and with fire:	3:16
1 Whose fan is in his hand, and he will thoroughly	3:17
1 this above all, that he shut up John in prison.	3:20
1 Now when all the people were baptized,	3:21
1 my beloved Son; in thee I am well pleased.	3:22
1 and was led by the Spirit into the wilderness,	4:1
1 led about by the Spirit in the wilderness (NASB)	4:1
1 And in those days he did eat nothing:	4:2
1 all the kingdoms of the world in a moment of time.	4:5
1 And Jesus returned in the power of the Spirit	4:14
1 taught in their synagogues, being glorified of all.	4:15
1 he went into the synagogue on the sabbath day.	4:16
1 to set at liberty them that are bruised,	4:18
1 the eyes of all them that were in the synagogue	4:20
1 This day is this scripture fulfilled in your ears.	4:21
1 whatsoever we have heard done in Capernaum,	4:23
1 done in Capernaum, do also here in thy country.	4:23
1 No prophet is accepted in his own country.	4:24
1 many widows were in Israel in the days of Elias,	4:25
1 many widows were in Israel in the days of Elias,	4:25
1 many lepers were in Israel in the time of Eliseus	4:27
1 all they in the synagogue, when they heard these	4:28
1 of Galilee, and taught them on the sabbath days.	4:31
1 at his doctrine: for his word was with power.	4:32
1 And in the synagogue there was a man,	4:33
1 with authority and power he commandeth	4:36
1 And he preached in the synagogues of Galilee.	4:44
1 as the people pressed upon him to hear the word	5:1
1 he sat down, and taught the people out of the ship.	5:3
1 which were in the other ship,	5:7
1 And it came to pass, when he was in a certain city,	5:12
1 And it came to pass, when he was in a certain city,	5:12
1 And he withdrew himself into the wilderness,	5:16
1 And it came to pass on a certain day,	5:17
1 What reason ye in your hearts?	5:22
1 And Levi made him a great feast in his own house:	5:29
1 fast, while the bridegroom is with them?	5:34
1 and then shall they fast in those days,	5:35
1 came to pass on the second sabbath after the first,	6:1
1 that which is not lawful to do on the sabbath days?	6:2
1 And it came to pass also on another sabbath,	6:6
1 whether he would heal on the sabbath day;	6:7
1 And it came to pass in those days,	6:12
1 and continued all night in prayer to God.	6:12
1 Rejoice ye in that day, and leap for joy:	6:23
1 for, behold, your reward is great in heaven:	6:23
1 and your reward shall be great,	6:35
1 And why beholdest thou the mote that is in	6:41
1 perceivest not the beam that is in thine own eye?	6:41
1 let me pull out the mote that is in thine eye,	6:42
1 beholdest not the beam that is in thine own eye?	6:42
1 to pull out the mote that is in thy brother's eye.	6:42
1 I have not found so great faith, no, not in Israel.	7:9
1 And it came to pass the day after, (NT)	7:11
1 saying, That a great prophet is risen up among us;	7:16
1 rumour of him went forth throughout all Judaea,	7:17
1 and throughout all the region round about.	7:17
1 And in that same hour he cured many	7:21
1 blessed ... whosoever shall not be offended in me.	7:23
1 to see? A man clothed in soft raiment?	7:25
1 Behold, they which are gorgeously apparelled, (NT)	7:25
1 they which ... live delicately, are in kings' courts.	7:25
1 Among those that are born of women there is not	7:28
1 but he that is least in the kingdom of God	7:28
1 like unto children sitting in the marketplace,	7:32
1 behold, a woman in the city, which was a sinner,	7:37
1 that Jesus sat at meat in the Pharisee's house,	7:37
1 he spake within himself, saying, This man,	7:39
1 at meat with him began to say within themselves,	7:49
1 And it came to pass afterward,	8:1
1 A sower went out to sow his seed: and as he sowed,	8:5
1 some fell among thorns; and the thorns sprang up	8:7
1 but to others in parables;	8:10

ἐν 1706

1 and **in** time of temptation fall away.	Luke	8:13
1 But that **on** the good ground are they,		8:15
1 which **in** an honest and good heart,		8:15
1 keep it, and bring forth fruit **with** patience.		8:15
1 Now it came to pass **on** a certain day,		8:22
1 neither abode **in** any house, but in the tombs.		8:27
1 neither abode in any house, but **in** the tombs.		8:27
1 an herd of many swine feeding **on** the mountain:		8:32
1 it came to pass, that, **when** Jesus was returned,		8:40
1 But **as** he went the people thronged him.		8:42
1 having an issue of blood twelve years, (NT)		8:43
1 and get victuals: for we are here **in** a desert place.		9:12
1 And it came to pass, **as** he was alone praying,		9:18
1 when he shall come **in** his own glory,		9:26
1 And **as** he prayed, the fashion of his countenance		9:29
1 Who appeared **in** glory, and spake of his decease		9:31
1 decease which he should accomplish **at** Jerusalem.		9:31
1 And it came to pass, **as** they departed from him,		9:33
1 and they feared **as** they entered into the cloud.		9:34
1 **when** the voice was past, Jesus was found alone.		9:36
1 they kept it close, and told no man **in** those days		9:36
1 And it came to pass, that **on** the next day,		9:37
1 Then there arose a reasoning **among** them,		9:46
1 is least **among** you all, the same shall be great.		9:48
1 casting out demons **in** Your name (NASB)		9:49
1 And it came to pass, **when** the time was come		9:51
1 And it came to pass, that, as they went **in** the way,		9:57
1 behold, I send you forth as lambs **among** wolves.		10:3
1 **in** the same house remain, eating and drinking		10:7
1 heal the sick that are **therein**, and say unto them,		10:9
1 it shall be more tolerable **in** that day for Sodom,		10:12
1 for if the mighty works had been done **in** Tyre		10:13
1 in Tyre and Sidon, which have been done **in** you,		10:13
1 while ago repented, sitting **in** sackcloth and ashes.		10:13
1 be more tolerable for Tyre ... **at** the judgment,		10:14
1 the devils are subject unto us **through** thy name.		10:17
1 Notwithstanding **in** this rejoice not,		10:20
1 rejoice, because your names are written **in** heaven.		10:20
1 **In** that hour Jesus rejoiced in spirit, and said,		10:21
1 he rejoiced **in** the Holy Spirit (RSV)		10:21
1 What is written in the law? how readest thou?		10:26
1 and **with** all your soul (NIV)		10:27
1 and **with** all your strength (NIV)		10:27
1 and **with** all your mind (NIV)		10:27
1 there came down a certain priest that way: (NT)		10:31
1 **when** I come again, I will repay thee.		10:35
1 Now it came to pass, **as** they went,		10:38
1 that, **as** he was praying in a certain place,		11:1
1 that, as he was praying **in** a certain place,		11:1
1 Our Father which art **in** heaven,		11:2
1 Thy will be done, as **in** heaven, so in earth.		11:2
1 He casteth out devils **through** Beelzebub.		11:15
1 ye say that I cast out devils **through** Beelzebub.		11:18
1 And if I **by** Beelzebub cast out devils,		11:19
1 by whom do your sons cast them out?		11:19
1 But if I **with** the finger of God cast out devils,		11:20
1 armed keepeth his palace, his goods are **in** peace:		11:21
1 And it came to pass, **as** he spake these things,		11:27
1 queen of the south shall rise up **in** the judgment		11:31
1 The men of Nineve shall rise up **in** the judgment		11:32
1 that the light which is **in** thee be not darkness.		11:35
1 And **as** he spake, a certain Pharisee besought him		11:37
1 for ye love the uppermost seats **in** the synagogues,		11:43
1 uppermost seats ... and greetings **in** the markets.		11:43
1 uppermost seats ... and greetings **in** the markets.		11:43
1 **In** the mean time, when there were gathered		12:1
1 Therefore whatsoever ye have spoken **in** darkness		12:3
1 spoken in darkness shall be heard **in** the light;		12:3
1 and that which ye have spoken **in** the ear in closets		12:3
1 Whosoever shall confess me before men, (NT)		12:8
1 him shall the Son of man also confess (NT)		12:8
1 the Holy Ghost shall teach you **in** the same hour		12:12
1 for a man's life consisteth not **in** the abundance		12:15
1 he thought **within** himself, saying, What shall I do,		12:17
1 So is he that layeth up treasure for himself,		12:21
1 that Solomon **in** all his glory was not arrayed like		12:27
1 God so clothe the grass, which is to day **in** the field,		12:28

1 a treasure **in** the heavens that faileth not,	Luke	12:33
1 And if he shall come **in** the second watch,		12:38
1 or come **in** the third watch, and find them so,		12:38
1 to give them their portion of meat **in** due season?		12:42
1 But and if that servant say **in** his heart,		12:45
1 The lord of that servant will come **in** a day when		12:46
1 and **at** an hour when he is not aware,		12:46
1 Suppose ye that I am come to give peace **on** earth?		12:51
1 there shall be five **in** one house divided,		12:52
1 adversary to the magistrate, as thou art **in** the way,		12:58
1 **at** that season some that told him of the Galilaeans,		13:1
1 eighteen, upon whom the tower **in** Siloam fell,		13:4
1 sinners above all men that dwelt **in** Jerusalem?		13:4
1 certain man had a fig tree planted **in** his vineyard;		13:6
1 he came and sought fruit **thereon**, and found none.		13:6
1 three years I come seeking fruit **on** this fig tree,		13:7
1 And he was teaching **in** one of the synagogues		13:10
1 teaching in one of the synagogues **on** the sabbath.		13:10
1 There are six days **in** which men ought to work:		13:14
1 **in** them therefore come and be healed,		13:14
1 the fowls of the air lodged **in** the branches of it.		13:19
1 and thou hast taught **in** our streets.		13:26
1 and all the prophets, **in** the kingdom of God,		13:28
1 and shall sit down **in** the kingdom of God.		13:29
1 The same day there came certain (NT)		13:31
1 Blessed is he that cometh **in** the name of the Lord.		13:35
1 And it came to pass, **as** he went into the house of		14:1
1 not straightway pull him out **on** the sabbath day?		14:5
1 for thou shalt be recompensed **at** the resurrection		14:14
1 Blessed is he that shall eat bread **in** the kingdom		14:15
1 **with** ten thousand to meet him that cometh against		14:31
1 lost his savour, **wherewith** shall it be seasoned?		14:34
1 not leave the ninety and nine **in** the wilderness,		15:4
1 I say unto you, that likewise joy shall be **in** heaven		15:7
1 Now his elder son was **in** the field:		15:25
1 Then the steward said **within** himself,		16:3
1 He that is faithful **in** that which is least is faithful		16:10
1 in that which is least is faithful also **in** much:		16:10
1 he that is unjust **in** the least is unjust also in much.		16:10
1 he that is unjust in the least is unjust also **in** much.		16:10
1 If therefore ye have not been faithful **in** the		16:11
1 not been faithful **in** that which is another man's,		16:12
1 for that which is highly esteemed **among** men		16:15
1 And **in** hell he lift up his eyes, being in torments,		16:23
1 And in hell he lift up his eyes, being **in** torments,		16:23
1 seeth Abraham afar off, and Lazarus **in** his bosom.		16:23
1 cool my tongue; for I am tormented **in** this flame.		16:24
1 that thou **in** thy lifetime receivedst thy good things,		16:25
1 And **besides** all this, between us (NASB)		16:26
1 be thou planted **in** the sea; and it should obey you.		17:6
1 And it came to pass, **as** he went to Jerusalem,		17:11
1 that, **as** they went, they were cleansed.		17:14
1 so shall also the Son of man be **in** his day.		17:24
1 And as it was **in** the days of Noe, so shall be also		17:26
1 so shall it be also **in** the days of the Son of man.		17:26
1 Likewise also as it was **in** the days of Lot;		17:28
1 **In** that day, he which shall be upon the housetop,		17:31
1 be upon the housetop, and his stuff **in** the house,		17:31
1 is **in** the field, let him likewise not return back.		17:31
1 Two men shall be **in** the field;		17:36
1 There was **in** a city a judge, which feared not God,		18:2
1 And there was a widow **in** that city;		18:3
1 but afterward he said **within** himself,		18:4
1 I tell you that he will avenge them speedily. (NT)		18:8
1 have treasure **in** heaven: and come, follow me.		18:22
1 not receive manifold more **in** this present time,		18:30
1 and **in** the world to come life everlasting.		18:30
1 that **as** he was come nigh unto Jericho,		18:35
1 come down; for to day I must abide **at** thy house.		19:5
1 Do business with this **until** I come back. (NASB)		19:13
1 And it came to pass, that **when** he was returned,		19:15
1 because thou hast been faithful **in** a very little,		19:17
1 thy pound, which I have kept laid up **in** a napkin:		19:20
1 **in** the which at your entering ye shall find a colt:		19:30
1 as he went, they spread their clothes **in** the way.		19:36
1 Blessed be the King that cometh **in** the name of		19:38
1 peace **in** heaven, and glory in the highest.		19:38

407

ἐν 1706

1 peace in heaven, and glory **in** the highest. .... Luke 19:38	1 Did not our heart burn **within** us, ... Luke 24:32
1 hadst known, even thou, at least **in** this thy day, ... 19:42	1 while he talked with us **by** the way, ... 24:32
1 thy children **within** thee; and they shall not leave 19:44	1 And they told what things were done **in** the way, ... 24:35
1 shall not leave **in** thee one stone upon another; 19:44	1 how he was known of them **in** breaking of bread. 24:35
1 and began to cast out them that sold **therein**, ... 19:45	1 Jesus himself stood **in** the midst of them, ... 24:36
1 And he taught daily **in** the temple. 19:47	1 and why do thoughts arise **in** your hearts? 24:38
1 And it came to pass, that **on** one of those days, ... 20:1	1 fulfilled, which were written **in** the law of Moses, ... 24:44
1 as he taught the people **in** the temple, ... 20:1	1 but tarry ye **in** the city of Jerusalem, ... 24:49
1 Tell us, **by** what authority doest thou these things? 20:2	1 **while** he blessed them, he was parted from them, ... 24:51
1 Neither tell I you **by** what authority I do these 20:8	1 And were continually **in** the temple, ... 24:53
1 at the season he sent a servant to the husbandmen, ... 20:10	1 **In** the beginning was the Word, ... John 1:1
1 priests and the scribes the same hour (NT) 20:19	1 The same was **in** the beginning with God. 1:2
1 **in** the resurrection whose wife of them is she? 20:33	1 **In** him was life; and the life was the light of men. 1:4
1 And David himself saith **in** the book of Psalms, ... 20:42	1 **In** him was life; and the life was the light of men. 1:4
1 the scribes, which desire to walk **in** long robes, ... 20:46	1 And the light shineth **in** darkness; 1:5
1 and love greetings **in** the markets, ... 20:46	1 He was **in** the world, ... 1:10
1 and the highest seats **in** the synagogues, ... 20:46	1 the Word was made flesh, and dwelt **among** us, ... 1:14
1 and the chief rooms **at** feasts; 20:46	1 I am the voice of one crying **in** the wilderness, ... 1:23
1 **in** the which there shall not be left one stone upon 21:6	1 John answered them, saying, I baptize **with** water: 1:26
1 So make up your minds (NASB) (NT) 21:14	1 things were done **in** Bethabara beyond Jordan, ... 1:28
1 **In** your patience possess ye your souls. 21:19	1 therefore am I come baptizing **with** water. 1:31
1 them which are **in** Judaea flee to the mountains; 21:21	1 but he that sent me to baptize **with** water, ... 1:33
1 let them which are **in** the midst of it depart out; 21:21	1 same is he which baptizeth **with** the Holy Ghost. 1:33
1 not them that are **in** the countries enter thereinto. 21:21	1 Moses **in** the law, and the prophets, did write, ... 1:45
1 But woe unto them that are **with** child, ... 21:23	1 Behold an Israelite indeed, **in** whom is no guile! 1:47
1 woe ... to them that give suck, **in** those days! 21:23	1 And the third day there was a marriage **in** Cana 2:1
1 distress **in** the land, and wrath **upon** this people. 21:23	1 This beginning of miracles did Jesus **in** Cana 2:11
1 signs **in** the sun, and **in** the moon, and **in** the stars; 21:25	1 And found **in** the temple those that sold oxen 2:14
1 upon the earth distress of nations, **with** perplexity; 21:25	1 and **in** three days I will raise it up. 2:19
1 see the Son of man coming **in** a cloud with power 21:27	1 and wilt thou rear it up **in** three days? 2:20
1 hearts be overcharged **with** surfeiting, ... 21:34	1 Now when he was **in** Jerusalem at the passover, ... 2:23
1 Watch ye therefore, and pray always, (NT) 21:36	1 Now when he was **in** Jerusalem at the passover, ... 2:23
1 And **in** the day time he was teaching **in** the temple; ... 21:37	1 **in** Jerusalem at the passover, **in** the feast day, ... 2:23
1 came early in the morning to him **in** the temple, ... 21:38	1 for he knew what was **in** man. 2:25
1 **when** the passover must be killed. 22:7	1 even the Son of man which is **in** heaven. 3:13
1 until it be fulfilled **in** the kingdom of God. 22:16	1 as Moses lifted up the serpent **in** the wilderness, ... 3:14
1 This cup is the new testament **in** my blood, ... 22:20	1 that everyone who believe **in** him (NIV) 3:15
1 And there was also a strife **among** them, ... 22:24	1 that they are wrought **in** God. 3:21
1 shall not be so: but he that is greatest **among** you, ... 22:26	1 John also was baptizing **in** Aenon near to Salim, ... 3:23
1 but I am **among** you as he that serveth. 22:27	1 and hath given all things **into** his hand. 3:35
1 which have continued with me **in** my temptations. 22:28	1 but the water that I shall give him shall be **in** him 4:14
1 ye may eat and drink at my table **in** my kingdom, ... 22:30	1 Our fathers worshipped **in** this mountain; 4:20
1 that is written must yet be accomplished **in** me, ... 22:37	1 and ye say, that **in** Jerusalem is the place 4:20
1 And being in an agony he prayed more earnestly: 22:44	1 when ye shall neither **in** this mountain, ... 4:21
1 they said ... Lord, shall we smite **with** the sword? 22:49	1 nor yet **at** Jerusalem, worship the Father. 4:21
1 When I was daily with you **in** the temple, ... 22:53	1 shall worship the Father **in** spirit and in truth: 4:23
1 they had kindled a fire **in** the midst of the hall, ... 22:55	1 they that worship him must worship him **in** spirit 4:24
1 set down together, Peter sat down **among** them. 22:55	1 **In** the mean while his disciples prayed him, ... 4:31
1 said Pilate ... I find no fault **in** this man. 23:4	1 And **herein** is that saying true, ... 4:37
1 who himself also was **at** Jerusalem at that time. 23:7	1 that a prophet hath no honour **in** his own country. 4:44
1 who himself also was at Jerusalem **at** that time. 23:7	1 having seen all the things that he did **at** Jerusalem 4:45
1 Then he questioned with him **in** many words; 23:9	1 all the things that he did at Jerusalem **at** the feast: 4:45
1 the same day Pilate and Herod (NT) 23:12	1 whose son was sick **at** Capernaum. 4:46
1 before they were **at** enmity between themselves. 23:12	1 inquired ... the hour **when** he began to amend. 4:52
1 examined him ... have found no fault **in** this man 23:14	1 So the father knew that it was **at** the same hour, ... 4:53
1 Who for a certain sedition made **in** the city, ... 23:19	1 **in** the which Jesus said unto him, Thy son liveth: 4:53
1 one who had been thrown **into** prison (NASB) 23:19	1 there is **at** Jerusalem by the sheep market a pool, ... 5:2
1 I have found no cause of death **in** him: 23:22	1 **In** these lay a great multitude of impotent folk, ... 5:3
1 the days are coming, **in** the which they shall say, ... 23:29	1 angel went down at a certain season **into** the pool, ... 5:4
1 For if they do these things **in** a green tree, ... 23:31	1 which had an infirmity thirty and eight years. (NT) 5:5
1 in a green tree, what shall be done **in** the dry? 23:31	1 but **while** I am coming, another steppeth down 5:7
1 seeing thou art **in** the same condemnation? 23:40	1 and **on** the same day was the sabbath. 5:9
1 remember me when thou comest **into** thy kingdom. 23:42	1 a multitude being **in** that place. 5:13
1 To day shalt thou be with me **in** paradise. 23:43	1 Afterward Jesus findeth him **in** the temple, ... 5:14
1 and laid it **in** a sepulchre that was hewn in stone, ... 23:53	1 because he had done these things on the sabbath 5:16
1 **as** they were much perplexed thereabout, behold, ... 24:4	1 For as the Father hath life **in** himself; 5:26
1 two men stood by them **in** shining garments: 24:4	1 so hath he given to the Son to have life **in** himself; 5:26
1 how he spake unto you when he was yet **in** Galilee, ... 24:6	1 **in** the which all that are in the graves shall hear 5:28
1 two of them went that same day to a village (NT) 24:13	1 in the which all that are **in** the graves shall hear 5:28
1 **while** they communed together and reasoned, ... 24:15	1 ye were willing for a season to rejoice **in** his light. 5:35
1 Art thou only a stranger **in** Jerusalem, ... 24:18	1 And ye have not his word abiding **in** you: 5:38
1 things which are come to pass there **in** these days? 24:18	1 for **in** them ye think ye have eternal life: 5:39
1 things which are come to pass there in these days? 24:18	1 I know ... that ye have not the love of God **in** you. 5:42
1 which was a prophet mighty **in** deed and word 24:19	1 I am come **in** my Father's name, ... 5:43
1 which was a prophet mighty **in** deed and word 24:19	1 if another shall come **in** his own name, ... 5:43
1 **in** all the scriptures the things concerning himself. 24:27	1 Now there was much grass **in** the place. 6:10
1 And it came to pass, **as** he sat at meat with them, ... 24:30	1 Our fathers did eat manna **in** the desert; 6:31

ἐν

1 but should raise it up again at the last day	John 6:39	1 having loved his own which were in the world,	John 13:1
1 will raise him up on the last day. (NASB)	6:40	1 Now there was leaning on Jesus' bosom one	13:23
1 and I will raise him up on the last day. (NASB)	6:44	1 and God is glorified in him.	13:31
1 It is written in the prophets,	6:45	1 If God be glorified in him,	13:32
1 Your fathers did eat manna in the wilderness,	6:49	1 God shall also glorify him in himself,	13:32
1 Except ... drink his blood, ye have no life in you.	6:53	1 By this shall all men know that ye are my disciples,	13:35
1 and I will raise him up at the last day.	6:54	1 if ye have love one to another.	13:35
1 drinketh my blood, dwelleth in me, and I in him.	6:56	1 In my Father's house are many mansions:	14:2
1 drinketh my blood, dwelleth in me, and I in him.	6:56	1 Believest thou not that I am in the Father,	14:10
1 These things said he in the synagogue,	6:59	1 that I am in the Father, and the Father in me?	14:10
1 in the synagogue, as he taught in Capernaum.	6:59	1 Father that dwelleth in me, he doeth the works.	14:10
1 knew in himself that his disciples murmured at it,	6:61	1 Believe me that I am in the Father,	14:11
1 After these things Jesus walked in Galilee:	7:1	1 that I am in the Father, and the Father in me:	14:11
1 for he would not walk in Jewry,	7:1	1 whatsoever ye shall ask in my name, that will I do,	14:13
1 For there is no man that doeth any thing in secret,	7:4	1 that the Father may be glorified in the Son.	14:13
1 and he himself seeketh to be known openly. (NT)	7:4	1 If ye shall ask any thing in my name, I will do it.	14:14
1 he abode still in Galilee.	7:9	1 for he dwelleth with you, and shall be in you.	14:17
1 unto the feast, not openly, but as it were in secret.	7:10	1 At that day ye shall know that I am in my Father,	14:20
1 Then the Jews sought him at the feast,	7:11	1 I am in my Father, and ye in me, and I in you.	14:20
1 And there was much murmuring among the people	7:12	1 I am in my Father, and ye in me, and I in you.	14:20
1 the same is true, and no unrighteousness is in him.	7:18	1 I am in my Father, and ye in me, and I in you.	14:20
1 and ye on the sabbath day circumcise a man.	7:22	1 Ghost, whom the Father will send in my name,	14:26
1 If a man on the sabbath day receive circumcision,	7:23	1 prince of this world ... and hath nothing in me.	14:30
1 made a man every whit whole on the sabbath day?	7:23	1 Every branch in me that beareth not fruit	15:2
1 Then cried Jesus in the temple as he taught,	7:28	1 Abide in me, and I in you.	15:4
1 In the last day, that great day of the feast,	7:37	1 Abide in me, and I in you.	15:4
1 So there was a division among the people	7:43	1 bear fruit of itself, except it abide in the vine;	15:4
1 brought unto him a woman taken in adultery;	8:3	1 no more can ye, except ye abide in me.	15:4
1 and when they had set her in the midst,	8:3	1 He that abideth in me, and I in him,	15:5
1 Now Moses in the law commanded us,	8:5	1 He that abideth in me, and I in him,	15:5
1 and the woman standing in the midst.	8:9	1 If a man abide not in me, he is cast forth	15:6
1 he that followeth me shall not walk in darkness,	8:12	1 If ye abide in me, and my words abide in you,	15:7
1 It is also written in your law,	8:17	1 If ye abide in me, and my words abide in you,	15:7
1 These words spake Jesus in the treasury,	8:20	1 Herein is my Father glorified, that ye bear ... fruit;	15:8
1 as he taught in the temple:	8:20	1 so have I loved you: continue ye in my love.	15:9
1 and ye shall seek me, and shall die in your sins:	8:21	1 keep ... commandments, ye shall abide in my love;	15:10
1 that ye shall die in your sins:	8:24	1 ye shall abide in my love; ... and abide in his love.	15:10
1 believe not that I am he, ye shall die in your sins.	8:24	1 that my joy might remain in you,	15:11
1 If ye continue in my word,	8:31	1 whatsoever ye shall ask of the Father in my name,	15:16
1 And the servant abideth not in the house for ever:	8:35	1 If I had not done among them the works	15:24
1 kill me, because my word hath no place in you.	8:37	1 word might be fulfilled that is written in their law,	15:25
1 and abode not in the truth,	8:44	1 He will guide you into all truth; (NASB)	16:13
1 because there is no truth in him.	8:44	1 And in that day ye shall ask me nothing.	16:23
1 the works of God should be made manifest in him.	9:3	1 Whatsoever ye shall ask the Father in my name,	16:23
1 As long as I am in the world, I am the light	9:5	1 Hitherto have ye asked nothing in my name:	16:24
1 Now it was a Sabbath on the day (NASB)	9:14	1 These things have I spoken unto you in proverbs:	16:25
1 And there was a division among them.	9:16	1 when I shall no more speak unto you in proverbs,	16:25
1 Why herein is a marvellous thing,	9:30	1 At that day ye shall ask in my name:	16:26
1 Thou wast altogether born in sins,	9:34	1 At that day ye shall ask in my name:	16:26
1 was a division ... among the Jews for these sayings.	10:19	1 now are you speaking plainly (NASB) (NT)	16:29
1 And it was at Jerusalem the feast of the dedication,	10:22	1 by this we believe that thou camest	16:30
1 Jesus walked in the temple in Solomon's porch.	10:23	1 that in me ye might have peace.	16:33
1 Jesus walked in the temple in Solomon's porch.	10:23	1 In the world ye shall have tribulation:	16:33
1 the works that I do in my Father's name,	10:25	1 and thine are mine; and I am glorified in them.	17:11
1 Is it not written in your law, I said, Ye are gods?	10:34	1 And now I am no more in the world,	17:11
1 and believe, that the Father is in me, and I in him.	10:38	1 but these are in the world, and I come to thee.	17:11
1 and believe, that the Father is in me, and I in him.	10:38	1 Holy Father, keep through thine own name	17:11
1 he abode two days still in the same place	11:6	1 While I was with them in the world,	17:12
1 Are there not twelve hours in the day?	11:9	1 I kept them in thy name:	17:12
1 But if a man walk in the night, he stumbleth,	11:10	1 and these things I speak in the world,	17:13
1 because there is no light in him.	11:10	1 they might have my joy fulfilled in themselves.	17:13
1 he had lain in the grave four days already.	11:17	1 Sanctify them through thy truth: thy word is truth.	17:17
1 but Mary sat still in the house.	11:20	1 they also might be sanctified through the truth.	17:19
1 I know that he shall rise again in the resurrection	11:24	1 as thou, Father, art in me, and I in thee,	17:21
1 shall rise again in the resurrection at the last day.	11:24	1 as thou, Father, art in me, and I in thee,	17:21
1 but was in that place where Martha met him.	11:30	1 and I in thee, that they also may be one in us:	17:21
1 The Jews then which were with her in the house,	11:31	1 I in them, and thou in me, ... made perfect in one;	17:23
1 Jesus therefore again groaning in himself	11:38	1 I in them, and thou in me, ... made perfect in one;	17:23
1 therefore walked no more openly among the Jews;	11:54	1 love wherewith thou hast loved ... may be in them,	17:26
1 as they stood in the temple,	11:56	1 the love ... may be in them, and I in them.	17:26
1 King of Israel that cometh in the name of the Lord.	12:13	1 I ever taught in the synagogue, and in the temple,	18:20
1 Greeks ... that came up to worship at the feast:	12:20	1 I ever taught in the synagogue, and in the temple,	18:20
1 and he that hateth his life in this world	12:25	1 and in secret have I said nothing.	18:20
1 while longer the light is among you. (NASB)	12:35	1 saith, Did not I see thee in the garden with him?	18:26
1 for he that walketh in darkness knoweth not	12:35	1 unto the Jews, ... I find in him no fault at all.	18:38
1 believeth on me should not abide in darkness.	12:46	1 that I should release unto you one at the passover:	18:39
1 the same shall judge him in the last day.	12:48	1 that ye may know that I find no fault in him.	19:4

ἐν 1706

1 and crucify him: for I find no fault in him.	John 19:6
1 not remain upon the cross on the sabbath day,	19:31
1 Now in the place where he was crucified	19:41
1 and in the garden a new sepulchre,	19:41
1 a new sepulchre, wherein was never man yet laid.	19:41
1 And seeth two angels in white sitting,	20:12
1 Except I shall see in his hands the print of ... nails,	20:25
1 other signs ... which are not written in this book:	20:30
1 that believing ye might have life through his name.	20:31
1 and that night they caught nothing. (NT)	21:3
1 which also leaned on his breast at supper,	21:20
1 after his passion by many infallible proofs,	Acts 1:3
1 but ye shall be baptized with the Holy Ghost	1:5
1 wilt thou at this time restore again the kingdom	1:6
1 which the Father hath put in his own power.	1:7
1 ye shall be witnesses unto me both in Jerusalem,	1:8
1 in Jerusalem, and in all Judaea, and in Samaria,	1:8
1 behold, two men stood by them in white apparel;	1:10
1 And in those days Peter stood up in the midst	1:15
1 Peter stood up in the midst of the disciples,	1:15
1 For he was numbered among us, (RSV)	1:17
1 For it is written in the book of Psalms,	1:20
1 and let no man dwell therein:	1:20
1 time that the Lord Jesus went in and out (NT)	1:21
1 time that the Lord Jesus went in and out (NT)	1:21
1 And when the day of Pentecost was fully come,	2:1
1 And there were dwelling at Jerusalem Jews,	2:5
1 in our own tongue, wherein we were born?	2:8
1 it shall come to pass in the last days, saith God,	2:17
1 I will pour out in those days of my Spirit;	2:18
1 And I will show wonders in heaven above,	2:19
1 which God did by him in the midst of you,	2:22
1 and his sepulchre is with us unto this day.	2:29
1 be baptized every one of you in the name of Jesus	2:38
1 added that day about three thousand (NASB) (NT)	2:41
1 in Jerusalem; and great fear (NASB, margin)	2:43
1 continuing daily with one accord in the temple,	2:46
1 eat ... meat with gladness and singleness of heart,	2:46
1 In the name of Jesus Christ of Nazareth rise up	3:6
1 IN YOUR SEED ALL THE FAMILIES (NASB)	3:25
1 in turning away ... from his iniquities.	3:26
1 through Jesus the resurrection from the dead.	4:2
1 were gathered together in Jerusalem (NASB)	4:5
1 when they had set them in the midst, they asked,	4:7
1 By what power, or by what name, have ye done	4:7
1 what power, or by what name, have ye done this?	4:7
1 by what means he is made whole;	4:9
1 that by the name of Jesus Christ of Nazareth,	4:10
1 by him doth this man stand here before you whole.	4:10
1 Neither is there salvation in any other:	4:12
1 none other name under heaven given among men,	4:12
1 is none other name ... whereby we must be saved.	4:12
1 and earth, and the sea, and all that in them is:	4:24
1 For truly in this city (NASB)	4:27
1 By stretching forth thine hand to heal;	4:30
1 the place was shaken where they were assembled	4:31
1 Neither was there any among them that lacked:	4:34
1 after it was sold, was it not in thine own power?	5:4
1 why hast thou conceived this thing in thine heart?	5:4
1 signs and wonders wrought among the people;	5:12
1 they were all with one accord in Solomon's porch.	5:12
1 and put them in the common prison.	5:18
1 Go, stand and speak in the temple to the people	5:20
1 and found them not in the prison, they returned,	5:22
1 The prison truly found we shut with all safety,	5:23
1 whom ye put in prison are standing in the temple,	5:25
1 whom ye put in prison are standing in the temple,	5:25
1 they set them before the council:	5:27
1 Then stood there up one in the council, a Pharisee,	5:34
1 rose up Judas of Galilee in the days of the taxing,	5:37
1 And daily in the temple, and in every house,	5:42
1 And in those days,	6:1
1 widows were neglected in the daily ministration.	6:1
1 the disciples multiplied in Jerusalem greatly;	6:7
1 did great wonders and miracles among the people.	6:8
1 And all that sat in the council,	6:15
1 in Mesopotamia, before he dwelt in Charran,	7:2
1 in Mesopotamia, before he dwelt in Charran,	Acts 7:2
1 Then came he out ... and dwelt in Charran:	7:4
1 And he gave him none inheritance in it,	7:5
1 That his seed should sojourn in a strange land;	7:6
1 shall they come forth, and serve me in this place.	7:7
1 when Jacob heard that there was corn in Egypt,	7:12
1 And at the second time Joseph was made known	7:13
1 all his kindred, threescore and fifteen souls. (NT)	7:14
1 and laid in the sepulchre that Abraham bought	7:16
1 the sons of Hamor in Shechem (NASB)	7:16
1 the people grew and multiplied in Egypt,	7:17
1 In which time Moses was born,	7:20
1 nourished up in his father's house three months:	7:20
1 Moses was educated in all the learning (NASB)	7:22
1 and was mighty in words and in deeds.	7:22
1 and was mighty in words and in deeds.	7:22
1 Then fled Moses at this saying,	7:29
1 and was a stranger in the land of Madian,	7:29
1 in the wilderness of mount Sina an angel	7:30
1 an angel of the Lord in a flame of fire in a bush.	7:30
1 for the place where thou standest is holy ground.	7:33
1 the affliction of my people which is in Egypt,	7:34
1 and a deliverer by the hand of the angel	7:35
1 the angel which appeared to him in the bush.	7:35
1 showed wonders and signs in the land of Egypt,	7:36
1 in the Red sea, and in the wilderness forty years.	7:36
1 in the Red sea, and in the wilderness forty years.	7:36
1 that was in the church in the wilderness	7:38
1 that was in the church in the wilderness	7:38
1 the angel which spake to him in the mount Sina,	7:38
1 and in their hearts they turned (RSV)	7:39
1 And they made a calf in those days,	7:41
1 and rejoiced in the works of their own hands.	7:41
1 as it is written in the book of the prophets,	7:42
1 by the space of forty years in the wilderness?	7:42
1 Our fathers had the tabernacle (NT)	7:44
1 had the tabernacle of witness in the wilderness,	7:44
1 with Jesus into the possession of the Gentiles,	7:45
1 Howbeit the most High dwelleth not in temples	7:48
1 And at that time there was a great persecution	8:1
1 against the church which was at Jerusalem;	8:1
1 hearing and seeing the miracles which he did. (NT)	8:6
1 And there was great joy in that city.	8:8
1 which beforetime in the same city used sorcery,	8:9
1 Now when the apostles which were at Jerusalem	8:14
1 Thou hast neither part nor lot in this matter:	8:21
1 In his humiliation his judgment was taken away:	8:33
1 And as he journeyed, he came near Damascus:	9:3
1 And there was a certain disciple at Damascus,	9:10
1 Ananias; and to him said the Lord in a vision,	9:10
1 inquire in the house of Judas for one called Saul,	9:11
1 And hath seen in a vision a man named Ananias	9:12
1 evil he hath done to thy saints at Jerusalem:	9:13
1 that appeared unto thee in the way as thou camest,	9:17
1 with the disciples which were at Damascus.	9:19
1 straightway he preached Christ in the synagogues,	9:20
1 them which called on this name in Jerusalem,	9:21
1 and confounded the Jews which dwelt at Damascus,	9:22
1 and let him down by the wall in a basket.	9:25
1 how he had seen the Lord in the way,	9:27
1 and how he had preached boldly at Damascus	9:27
1 preached boldly at Damascus in the name of Jesus.	9:27
1 with them coming in and going out at Jerusalem.	9:28
1 And he spake boldly in the name of the Lord Jesus,	9:29
1 was at Joppa a certain disciple named Tabitha,	9:36
1 it came to pass in those days, that she was sick,	9:37
1 they laid her in an upper chamber.	9:37
1 disciples had heard that Peter was there, (NT)	9:38
1 many days in Joppa with one Simon a tanner.	9:43
1 was a certain man in Caesarea called Cornelius,	10:1
1 He saw in a vision evidently about the ninth hour	10:3
1 Wherein were all manner of fourfooted beasts	10:12
1 Now while Peter doubted in himself	10:17
1 and at the ninth hour I prayed in my house,	10:30
1 behold, a man stood before me in bright clothing,	10:30
1 in the house of one Simon a tanner by the sea side:	10:32
1 But in every nation he that feareth him,	10:35

ἐν 1706

1 things which he did both in the land of the Jews,	...Acts	10:39
1 both in the land of the Jews, and in Jerusalem;		10:39
1 God raised him on the third day (NASB)		10:40
1 them to be baptized in the name of the Lord.		10:48
1 I was in the city of Joppa praying:		11:5
1 and in a trance I saw a vision,		11:5
1 men already come unto the house where I was,		11:11
1 showed us how he had seen an angel in his house,		11:13
1 whereby thou and all thy house shall be saved.		11:14
1 as I began to speak, the Holy Ghost fell on them,		11:15
1 Holy Ghost fell on them, as on us at the beginning.		11:15
1 but ye shall be baptized with the Holy Ghost.		11:16
1 of the church which was in Jerusalem:		11:22
1 year they assembled themselves with the church,		11:26
1 the disciples were called Christians first in Antioch.		11:26
1 And in these days came prophets from Jerusalem		11:27
1 relief unto the brethren which dwelt in Judaea:		11:29
1 Peter therefore was kept in prison:		12:5
1 and a light shined in the prison:		12:7
1 Arise up quickly. And his chains fell off (NT)		12:7
1 And when Peter was come to himself, he said,		12:11
1 there was no small stir among the soldiers,		12:18
1 Now there were in the church that was at Antioch		13:1
1 And when they were at Salamis,		13:5
1 they preached the word of God in the synagogues		13:5
1 any word of exhortation for the people (NT)		13:15
1 exalted the people when they dwelt as strangers		13:17
1 when they dwelt as strangers in the land of Egypt,		13:17
1 suffered he their manners in the wilderness.		13:18
1 destroyed seven nations in the land of Chanaan,		13:19
1 and whosoever among you feareth God,		13:26
1 For they that dwell at Jerusalem, and their rulers,		13:27
1 as it is also written in the second psalm,		13:33
1 Wherefore he saith also in another psalm,		13:35
1 from which ye could not be justified by the law		13:39
1 by him all that believe are justified from all things,		13:39
1 which is spoken of in the prophets,		13:40
1 and perish: for I work a work in your days,		13:41
1 And it came to pass in Iconium,		14:1
1 And there sat a certain man at Lystra,		14:8
1 Said with a loud voice, Stand upright on thy feet.		14:10
1 earth, and the sea, and all things that are therein,		14:15
1 Who in times past suffered all nations to walk		14:16
1 And when they had preached the word in Perga,		14:25
1 that a good while ago God made choice among us,		15:7
1 God had wrought among the Gentiles by them,		15:12
1 being read in the synagogues every sabbath day.		15:21
1 and Silas, chief men among the brethren:		15:22
1 Paul also and Barnabas continued in Antioch,		15:35
1 Let us go again and visit our brethren in every city		15:36
1 by the brethren that were at Lystra and Iconium.		16:2
1 because of the Jews which were in those quarters:		16:3
1 of the apostles and elders which were at Jerusalem.		16:4
1 forbidden ... to preach the word in Asia,		16:6
1 and we were in that city abiding certain days.		16:12
1 I command thee in the name of Jesus Christ		16:18
1 and to all that were in his house.		16:32
1 And he took them the same hour (NT)		16:33
1 now therefore depart, and go in peace.		16:36
1 These were more noble than those in Thessalonica,		17:11
1 the word of God was preached of Paul at Berea,		17:13
1 Now while Paul waited for them at Athens,		17:16
1 his spirit was stirred in him,		17:16
1 disputed he in the synagogue with the Jews,		17:17
1 in the market daily with them that met with him.		17:17
1 Then Paul stood in the midst of Mars' hill,		17:22
1 I found an altar with this inscription,		17:23
1 God that made the world and all things therein,		17:24
1 dwelleth not in temples made with hands;		17:24
1 For in him we live, and move, and have our being;		17:28
1 in the which he will judge the world		17:31
1 he will judge the world in righteousness		17:31
1 by that man whom he hath ordained;		17:31
1 among the which was Dionysius the Areopagite,		17:34
1 And he reasoned in the synagogue every sabbath,		18:4
1 spake the Lord to Paul in the night by a vision,		18:9
1 for I have much people in this city.		18:10
1 teaching the word of God among them.	...Acts	18:11
1 having shorn his head in Cenchrea:		18:18
1 an eloquent man, and mighty in the scriptures,		18:24
1 And he began to speak boldly in the synagogue:		18:26
1 that, while Apollos was at Corinth,		19:1
1 that, while Apollos was at Corinth,		19:1
1 disputing daily in the school of one Tyrannus.		19:9
1 man in whom the evil spirit was leaped on them,		19:16
1 Paul purposed in the spirit,		19:21
1 it shall be determined in a lawful assembly.		19:39
1 These going before tarried for us at Troas.		20:5
1 And upon the first day of the week,		20:7
1 And there were many lights in the upper chamber,		20:8
1 Trouble not yourselves; for his life is in him.		20:10
1 and tarried at Trogyllium;		20:15
1 because he would not spend the time in Asia:		20:16
1 which befell me by the lying in wait of the Jews:		20:19
1 the things that shall befall me there: (NT)		20:22
1 among whom I have gone preaching the kingdom		20:25
1 Wherefore I take you to record this day, (NT)		20:26
1 over the which the Holy Ghost hath made you		20:28
1 inheritance among all them which are sanctified.		20:32
1 So shall the Jews at Jerusalem bind the man		21:11
1 what things God had wrought among the Gentiles		21:19
1 thousands there are among the Jews (NASB)		21:20
1 when they saw him in the temple,		21:27
1 with him in the city Trophimus an Ephesian,		21:29
1 one thing, some another, among the multitude:		21:34
1 I am verily a man which am a Jew, born in Tarsus,		22:3
1 yet brought up in this city at the feet of Gamaliel,		22:3
1 a good report of all the Jews which dwelt there,		22:12
1 while I prayed in the temple, I was in a trance;		22:17
1 while I prayed in the temple, I was in a trance;		22:17
1 and get thee quickly out of Jerusalem: (NT)		22:18
1 he cried out in the council, Men and brethren,		23:6
1 and strove, saying, We find no evil in this man:		23:9
1 to be kept in Herod's judgment hall.		23:35
1 since I went up to Jerusalem for to worship.		24:11
1 neither found me in the temple disputing		24:12
1 neither in the synagogues, nor in the city:		24:12
1 written in the prophets: (NASB)		24:14
1 And herein do I exercise myself,		24:16
1 Whereupon certain Jews from Asia found me		24:18
1 Jews from Asia found me purified in the temple,		24:18
1 if they have found any evil doing in me,		24:20
1 that I cried standing among them,		24:21
1 that Paul should be kept at Caesarea,		25:4
1 he himself would depart shortly thither. (NT)		25:4
1 which among you are able, go down with me,		25:5
1 accuse this man, if there be any wickedness in him.		25:5
1 he had tarried among them more than ten days,		25:6
1 Jews have dealt with me, both at Jerusalem,		25:24
1 which was at the first among mine own nation		26:4
1 at the first among mine own nation at Jerusalem,		26:4
1 instantly serving God day and night, hope to come.		26:7
1 Which thing I also did in Jerusalem:		26:10
1 many of the saints in prison, (NASB)		26:10
1 Whereupon as I went to Damascus with authority		26:12
1 and inheritance among them which are sanctified		26:18
1 But showed first unto them of Damascus,		26:20
1 For these causes the Jews caught me in the temple,		26:21
1 for this thing was not done in a corner.		26:26
1 Almost thou persuadest me to be a Christian. (NT)		26:28
1 were both almost, and altogether (NT)		26:29
1 such as I am, except these bonds. (NT)		26:29
1 And when we had sailed slowly many days,		27:7
1 Paul stood forth in the midst of them, and said,		27:21
1 as we were driven up and down in Adria,		27:27
1 Except these abide in the ship, ye cannot be saved.		27:31
1 we were in all in the ship two hundred ... souls.		27:37
1 In the same quarters were possessions of the chief		28:7
1 others also, which had diseases in the island,		28:9
1 And after three months we departed in a ship		28:11
1 ship of Alexandria, which had wintered in the isle,		28:11
1 because there was no cause of death in me.		28:18
1 and had great reasoning among themselves.		28:29
1 Paul dwelt two whole years in his own ... house,		28:30

411

ἐν 1706

1 promised ... by his prophets in the holy scriptures,	Rom	1:2
1 And declared to be the Son of God with power,		1:4
1 for obedience to the faith among all nations,		1:5
1 Among whom ... ye also the called of Jesus Christ:		1:6
1 To all that be in Rome, beloved of God,		1:7
1 your faith is spoken of throughout the ... world.		1:8
1 I serve with my spirit in the gospel of his Son,		1:9
1 I serve with my spirit in the gospel of his Son,		1:9
1 journey by the will of God to come unto you.		1:10
1 That is, that I may be comforted together with you		1:12
1 with you by the mutual faith both of you and me.		1:12
1 that I might have some fruit among you also,		1:13
1 fruit among you ... even as among other Gentiles,		1:13
1 ready to preach the gospel to you that are at Rome		1:15
1 For therein is the righteousness of God revealed		1:17
1 who hold the truth in unrighteousness;		1:18
1 which may be known of God is manifest in them;		1:19
1 but became vain in their imaginations,		1:21
1 into an image made like to corruptible man,		1:23
1 Wherefore God also gave them up to uncleanness		1:24
1 to dishonour their own bodies between themselves:		1:24
1 Who changed the truth of God into a lie,		1:25
1 burned in their lust one toward another;		1:27
1 men with men working that which is unseemly,		1:27
1 and receiving in themselves that recompense		1:27
1 they did not like to retain God in their knowledge,		1:28
1 for wherein thou judgest another,		2:1
1 unto thyself wrath against the day of wrath		2:5
1 have sinned in the law shall be judged by the law;		2:12
1 show the work of the law written in their hearts,		2:15
1 In the day when God shall judge the secrets of men		2:16
1 restest in the law, and makest thy boast of God,		2:17
1 a light of them which are in darkness,		2:19
1 the form of knowledge and of the truth in the law.		2:20
1 Thou that makest thy boast of the law,		2:23
1 name of God is blasphemed among the Gentiles		2:24
1 For he is not a Jew, which is one outwardly; (NT)		2:28
1 circumcision, which is outward in the flesh: (NT)		2:28
1 circumcision, which is outward in the flesh:		2:28
1 But he is a Jew, which is one inwardly; (NT)		2:29
1 and circumcision is that of the heart, in the spirit,		2:29
1 That thou mightest be justified in thy sayings,		3:4
1 and mightest overcome when thou art judged.		3:4
1 more abounded through my lie unto his glory;		3:7
1 Destruction and misery are in their ways:		3:16
1 it saith to them who are under the law:		3:19
1 through the redemption that is in Christ Jesus:		3:24
1 to be a propitiation through faith in his blood,		3:25
1 through the forbearance of God;		3:25
1 To declare, I say, at this time his righteousness:		3:26
1 when he was in circumcision, or ... uncircumcision?		4:10
1 when ... in circumcision, or in uncircumcision?		4:10
1 Not in circumcision, but in uncircumcision.		4:10
1 Not in circumcision, but in uncircumcision.		4:10
1 which he had yet being uncircumcised: (NT)		4:11
1 which he had being yet uncircumcision. (NT)		4:12
1 access by faith into this grace wherein we stand,		5:2
1 And not only so, but we glory in tribulations also:		5:3
1 the love of God is shed abroad in our hearts		5:5
1 Much more then, being now justified by his blood,		5:9
1 being reconciled, we shall be saved by his life.		5:10
1 we also joy in God through our Lord Jesus Christ,		5:11
1 For until the law sin was in the world:		5:13
1 and the gift by grace, which is by one man,		5:15
1 the gift of righteousness shall reign in life by one,		5:17
1 That as sin hath reigned unto death,		5:21
1 that are dead to sin, live any longer therein?		6:2
1 even so we also should walk in newness of life.		6:4
1 but alive unto God through Jesus Christ our Lord.		6:11
1 Let not sin therefore reign in your mortal body,		6:12
1 that ye should obey it in the lusts thereof.		6:12
1 eternal life through Jesus Christ our Lord.		6:23
1 For when we were in the flesh, the motions of sins,		7:5
1 did work in our members to bring forth fruit		7:5
1 that being dead wherein we were held;		7:6
1 that we should serve in newness of spirit,		7:6
1 wrought in me all manner of concupiscence.		7:8
1 is no more I that do it, but sin that dwelleth in me.	Rom	7:17
1 For I know that in me that is, in my flesh,		7:18
1 For I know that in me that is, in my flesh,		7:18
1 no more I that do it, but sin that dwelleth in me.		7:20
1 But I see another law in my members,		7:23
1 making me a prisoner of the law of sin (NASB)		7:23
1 captivity to the law of sin which is in my members.		7:23
1 condemnation to them which are in Christ Jesus,		8:1
1 For the law of the Spirit of life in Christ Jesus		8:2
1 in that it was weak through the flesh,		8:3
1 sending his own Son in the likeness of sinful flesh,		8:3
1 and for sin, condemned sin in the flesh:		8:3
1 be fulfilled in us, who walk not after the flesh,		8:4
1 then they that are in the flesh cannot please God.		8:8
1 But ye are not in the flesh, but in the Spirit,		8:9
1 But ye are not in the flesh, but in the Spirit,		8:9
1 if so be that the Spirit of God dwell in you.		8:9
1 if Christ be in you, the body is dead because of sin;		8:10
1 that raised up Jesus from the dead dwell in you,		8:11
1 by his Spirit that dwelleth in you.		8:11
1 Spirit of adoption, whereby we cry, Abba, Father.		8:15
1 even we ourselves groan within ourselves,		8:23
1 he might be the firstborn among many brethren.		8:29
1 who is even at the right hand of God,		8:34
1 in all these things we are more than conquerors,		8:37
1 the love of God, which is in Christ Jesus our Lord.		8:39
1 I say the truth in Christ, I lie not,		9:1
1 also bearing me witness in the Holy Ghost,		9:1
1 but, In Isaac shall thy seed be called.		9:7
1 that I might show my power in thee,		9:17
1 name might be declared throughout all the earth.		9:17
1 endured with much longsuffering the vessels		9:22
1 As he saith also in Osee:		9:25
1 that in the place where it was said unto them,		9:26
1 finish the work, and cut it short in righteousness:		9:28
1 I lay in Sion a stumblingstone and rock of offence:		9:33
1 man which doeth those things shall live by them.		10:5
1 Say not in thine heart, Who shall ascend		10:6
1 The word is nigh thee, even in thy mouth,		10:8
1 is nigh thee, even in thy mouth, and in thy heart:		10:8
1 That if thou shalt confess with thy mouth the Lord		10:9
1 shalt believe in thine heart that God hath raised		10:9
1 I was found by those who did not seek (NIV)		10:20
1 Wot ye not what the scripture saith of Elias?		11:2
1 Even so then at this present time also		11:5
1 a wild olive tree, wert grafted in among them,		11:17
1 lest you be wise in your own estimation (NASB)		11:25
1 to every man that is among you,		12:3
1 For as we have many members in one body,		12:4
1 So we, being many, are one body in Christ,		12:5
1 Or ministry, let us wait on our ministering:		12:7
1 or he that teacheth, on teaching;		12:7
1 Or he that exhorteth, on exhortation;		12:8
1 he that giveth, let him do it with simplicity;		12:8
1 he that ruleth, with diligence;		12:8
1 he that showeth mercy, with cheerfulness.		12:8
1 but overcome evil with good.		12:21
1 it is briefly comprehended in this saying,		13:9
1 in this saying, namely, (NT)		13:9
1 as in the day;		13:13
1 Let every man be fully persuaded in his own mind.		14:5
1 I know, and am persuaded by the Lord Jesus,		14:14
1 and peace, and joy in the Holy Ghost.		14:17
1 For he that in these things serveth Christ		14:18
1 nor any thing whereby thy brother stumbleth,		14:21
1 condemneth not himself in that ... he alloweth.		14:22
1 one toward another according to Christ Jesus:		15:5
1 ye may with one mind and one mouth glorify God,		15:6
1 this cause I will confess to thee among the Gentiles,		15:9
1 of hope fill you with all joy and peace in believing,		15:13
1 peace in believing, that ye may abound in hope,		15:13
1 through the power of the Holy Ghost.		15:13
1 being sanctified by the Holy Ghost.		15:16
1 therefore whereof I may glory through Jesus Christ		15:17
1 Through mighty signs and wonders,		15:19
1 by the power of the Spirit of God;		15:19
1 But now having no more place in these parts,		15:23

ἐν 1706

1	for the poor saints which are at Jerusalem.	Rom 15:26
1	duty is also to minister unto them in carnal things.	15:27
1	I shall come in the fulness of the blessing	15:29
1	that ye strive together with me in your prayers	15:30
1	delivered from them that do not believe in Judaea;	15:31
1	I may come unto you with joy by the will of God,	15:32
1	is a servant of the church which is at Cenchrea:	16:1
1	ye receive her in the Lord, as becometh saints,	16:2
1	and that ye assist her in whatsoever business	16:2
1	Greet Priscilla and Aquila my helpers in Christ	16:3
1	who are of note among the apostles,	16:7
1	who also were in Christ before me.	16:7
1	Greet Amplias my beloved in the Lord.	16:8
1	Salute Urbane, our helper in Christ,	16:9
1	Salute Apelles approved in Christ.	16:10
1	the household of Narcissus, which are in the Lord.	16:11
1	Tryphena and Tryphosa, who labour in the Lord.	16:12
1	beloved Persis, which laboured much in the Lord.	16:12
1	Salute Rufus chosen in the Lord, and his mother	16:13
1	Salute one another with an holy kiss.	16:16
1	shall bruise Satan under your feet shortly. (NT)	16:20
1	I Tertius, who wrote this ... salute you in the Lord.	16:22
1	be glory through Jesus Christ for ever. Amen.	16:27
1	Unto the church of God which is at Corinth,	1 Co 1:2
1	to them that are sanctified in Christ Jesus,	1:2
1	with all that in every place call upon the name	1:2
1	grace of God which is given you by Jesus Christ;	1:4
1	That in every thing ye are enriched by him,	1:5
1	That in every thing ye are enriched by him,	1:5
1	by him, in all utterance, and in all knowledge;	1:5
1	as the testimony of Christ was confirmed in you:	1:6
1	So that ye come behind in no gift;	1:7
1	be blameless in the day of our Lord Jesus Christ.	1:8
1	and that there be no divisions among you;	1:10
1	in the same mind and in the same judgment.	1:10
1	in the same mind and in the same judgment.	1:10
1	that there are contentions among you.	1:11
1	to preach the gospel: not with wisdom of words,	1:17
1	For after that in the wisdom of God	1:21
1	But of him are ye in Christ Jesus,	1:30
1	He that glorieth, let him glory in the Lord.	1:31
1	I determined not to know any thing among you,	2:2
1	And I was with you in weakness, and in fear,	2:3
1	And I was with you in weakness, and in fear,	2:3
1	in weakness, and in fear, and in much trembling.	2:3
1	my preaching was not with enticing words	2:4
1	but in demonstration of the Spirit and of power:	2:4
1	your faith should not stand in the wisdom of men,	2:5
1	in the wisdom of men, but in the power of God.	2:5
1	we speak wisdom among them that are perfect:	2:6
1	But we speak the wisdom of God in a mystery,	2:7
1	save the spirit of man which is in him?	2:11
1	not in the words which man's wisdom teacheth,	2:13
1	but which the Holy Ghost teacheth;	2:13
1	but as unto carnal, even as unto babes in Christ.	3:1
1	for whereas there is among you envying, and strife,	3:3
1	because it shall be revealed by fire;	3:13
1	and that the Spirit of God dwelleth in you?	3:16
1	If any man among you seemeth to be wise	3:18
1	man among you seemeth to be wise in this world,	3:18
1	He taketh the wise in their own craftiness.	3:19
1	let no man glory in men. For all things are yours;	3:21
1	Moreover it is required in stewards,	4:2
1	yet am I not hereby justified:	4:4
1	that ye might learn in us not to think of men above	4:6
1	We are fools ... but ye are wise in Christ;	4:10
1	though ye have ten thousand instructors in Christ,	4:15
1	for in Christ Jesus I have begotten you	4:15
1	who is my beloved son, and faithful in the Lord,	4:17
1	into remembrance of my ways which be in Christ,	4:17
1	as I teach every where in every church.	4:17
1	the kingdom of God is not in word, but in power.	4:20
1	the kingdom of God is not in word, but in power.	4:20
1	What will ye? shall I come unto you with a rod,	4:21
1	or in love, and in the spirit of meekness?	4:21
1	commonly that there is fornication among you,	5:1
1	fornication as is not ... named among the Gentiles,	5:1
1	In the name of our Lord Jesus Christ,	1 Co 5:4
1	that the spirit may be saved in the day of the Lord	5:5
1	let us keep the feast, not with old leaven,	5:8
1	neither with the leaven of malice and wickedness;	5:8
1	with the unleavened bread of sincerity and truth.	5:8
1	I wrote unto you in an epistle	5:9
1	and if the world shall be judged by you,	6:2
1	to judge who are least esteemed in the church.	6:4
1	Is it so, that there is not a wise man among you?	6:5
1	Now therefore there is utterly a fault among you,	6:7
1	but ye are justified in the name of the Lord Jesus,	6:11
1	of the Lord Jesus, and by the Spirit of our God.	6:11
1	is the temple of the Holy Ghost which is in you,	6:19
1	therefore glorify God in your body,	6:20
1	glorify God in your body, and in your spirit,	6:20
1	the unbelieving husband is sanctified by the wife,	7:14
1	the unbelieving wife is sanctified by the husband:	7:14
1	or a sister is not under bondage in such cases:	7:15
1	but God hath called us to peace.	7:15
1	And so ordain I in all churches.	7:17
1	Is any called in uncircumcision?	7:18
1	abide in the same calling wherein he was called.	7:20
1	abide in the same calling wherein he was called.	7:20
1	For he that is called in the Lord, being a servant,	7:22
1	Brethren, let every man, wherein he is called,	7:24
1	wherein he is called, therein abide with God.	7:24
1	Nevertheless he that standeth stedfast in his heart,	7:37
1	and hath so decreed in his heart	7:37
1	to be married to whom she will; only in the Lord.	7:39
1	we know that an idol is nothing in the world,	8:4
1	that are called gods, whether in heaven or in earth,	8:5
1	Howbeit there is not in every man that knowledge:	8:7
1	if any ... see thee ... sit at meat in the idol's temple,	8:10
1	through your knowledge he who is weak (NASB)	8:11
1	are not ye my work in the Lord?	9:1
1	for the seal of mine apostleship are ye in the Lord.	9:2
1	For it is written in the law of Moses,	9:9
1	that it should be so done unto me:	9:15
1	that I abuse not my power in the gospel.	9:18
1	Know ye not that they which run in a race run all,	9:24
1	baptized unto Moses in the cloud and in the sea;	10:2
1	baptized unto Moses in the cloud and in the sea;	10:2
1	But with many of them God was not well pleased:	10:5
1	for they were overthrown in the wilderness.	10:5
1	and fell in one day three and twenty thousand.	10:8
1	Whatsoever is sold in the shambles, that eat,	10:25
1	neither the woman without the man, in the Lord.	11:11
1	Judge in yourselves: is it comely that a woman	11:13
1	when ye come together in the church,	11:18
1	I hear that there be divisions among you;	11:18
1	For there must be also heresies among you,	11:19
1	are approved may be made manifest among you.	11:19
1	in eating every one taketh before other his own	11:21
1	What shall I say to you? shall I praise you in this?	11:22
1	Jesus the same night in which he was betrayed:	11:23
1	This cup is the new testament in my blood:	11:25
1	this cause many are weak and sickly among you,	11:30
1	And if any man hunger, let him eat at home;	11:34
1	that no man speaking by the Spirit of God	12:3
1	say that Jesus is the Lord, but by the Holy Ghost.	12:3
1	but it is the same God which worketh all in all.	12:6
1	To another faith by the same Spirit;	12:9
1	to another the gifts of healing by the same Spirit;	12:9
1	by one Spirit are we all baptized into one body,	12:13
1	the members every one of them in the body,	12:18
1	That there should be no schism in the body;	12:25
1	God hath set some in the church, first apostles,	12:28
1	see through a glass, darkly; but then (NT)	13:12
1	except I shall speak to you either by revelation,	14:6
1	by knowledge, or by prophesying, or by doctrine?	14:6
1	by knowledge, or by prophesying, or by doctrine?	14:6
1	by knowledge, or by prophesying, or by doctrine?	14:6
1	it may be, so many kinds of voices in the world,	14:10
1	and he that speaketh shall be a barbarian unto me,	14:11
1	otherwise if you bless in the spirit (NASB)	14:16
1	Yet in the church I had rather speak five words	14:19
1	than ten thousand words in an unknown tongue.	14:19

413

ἐν 1706

1	In the law it is written, With men of other tongues	1 Co 14:21
1	With men of other tongues and other lips	14:21
1	With men of other tongues and other lips	14:21
1	and report that God is in you of a truth	14:25
1	let him keep silence in the church;	14:28
1	but of peace, as in all churches of the saints	14:33
1	Let your women keep silence in the churches:	14:34
1	let them ask their husbands at home:	14:35
1	for it is a shame for women to speak in the church.	14:35
1	which also ye have received, and wherein ye stand;	15:1
1	first of all that which I also received, (NT)	15:3
1	say some among you that there is no resurrection	15:12
1	if Christ be not raised, ... ye are yet in your sins.	15:17
1	also which are fallen asleep in Christ are perished.	15:18
1	If in this life only we have hope in Christ,	15:19
1	If in this life only we have hope in Christ,	15:19
1	If in this life only we have hope in Christ,	15:19
1	For as in Adam all die, even so in Christ shall all	15:22
1	even so in Christ shall all be made alive.	15:22
1	every man in his own order: Christ the firstfruits;	15:23
1	afterward they that are Christ's at his coming.	15:23
1	that God may be all in all.	15:28
1	I protest by your rejoicing which I have in Christ	15:31
1	I have fought with beasts at Ephesus,	15:32
1	for one star differeth from another star in glory.	15:41
1	is sown in corruption; it is raised in incorruption:	15:42
1	is sown in corruption; it is raised in incorruption:	15:42
1	It is sown in dishonour; it is raised in glory:	15:43
1	It is sown in dishonour; it is raised in glory:	15:43
1	it is sown in weakness; it is raised in power:	15:43
1	it is sown in weakness; it is raised in power:	15:43
1	In a moment, in the twinkling of an eye,	15:52
1	In a moment, in the twinkling of an eye,	15:52
1	at the last trump: for the trumpet shall sound,	15:52
1	always abounding in the work of the Lord,	15:58
1	know that your labour is not in vain in the Lord.	15:58
1	For I will not see you now by the way;	16:7
1	But I will tarry at Ephesus until Pentecost.	16:8
1	but conduct him forth in peace,	16:11
1	stand fast in the faith, quit you like men, be strong.	16:13
1	Let all your things be done with charity.	16:14
1	Aquila and Priscilla salute you much in the Lord,	16:19
1	Greet ye one another with an holy kiss.	16:20
1	My love be with you all in Christ Jesus. Amen.	16:24
1	unto the church of God which is at Corinth,	2 Co 1:1
1	with all the saints which are in all Achaia:	1:1
1	be able to comfort them which are in any trouble,	1:4
1	is effectual in the enduring of the same sufferings	1:6
1	of our trouble which came to us in Asia,	1:8
1	But we had the sentence of death in ourselves,	1:9
1	that in simplicity and godly sincerity,	1:12
1	not with fleshly wisdom, but by the grace of God,	1:12
1	not with fleshly wisdom, but by the grace of God,	1:12
1	we have had our conversation in the world,	1:12
1	as ye also are ours in the day of the Lord Jesus.	1:14
1	Jesus Christ, who was preached among you by us,	1:19
1	was not yea and nay, but in him was yea.	1:19
1	For all the promises of God in him are yea,	1:20
1	and in him Amen, unto the glory of God by us.	1:20
1	and given the earnest of the Spirit in our hearts.	1:22
1	that I would not come again to you in heaviness.	2:1
1	for your sakes forgave I it in the person of Christ;	2:10
1	and a door was opened unto me of the Lord,	2:12
1	which always causeth us to triumph in Christ,	2:14
1	the savour of his knowledge by us in every place.	2:14
1	in them that are saved, and in them that perish:	2:15
1	in them that are saved, and in them that perish:	2:15
1	in the sight of God speak we in Christ.	2:17
1	Ye are our epistle written in our hearts,	3:2
1	not in tables of stone, but in fleshly tables	3:3
1	in tables of stone, but in fleshly tables of the heart.	3:3
1	written and engraven in stones, was glorious,	3:7
1	written and engraven in stones, was glorious,	3:7
1	written and engraven in stones, was glorious,	3:7
1	the spirit be rather glorious? (NT)	3:8
1	the ministration of righteousness exceed in glory.	3:9
1	made glorious had no glory in this respect,	3:10
1	much more that which remaineth is glorious. (NT)	2 Co 3:11
1	which veil is done away in Christ.	3:14
1	things of dishonesty, not walking in craftiness,	4:2
1	if our gospel be hid, it is hid to them that are lost:	4:3
1	In whom the god of this world hath blinded	4:4
1	shine out of darkness, hath shined in our hearts,	4:6
1	of the glory of God in the face of Jesus Christ.	4:6
1	But we have this treasure in earthen vessels,	4:7
1	We are troubled on every side, yet not distressed;	4:8
1	Always bearing about in the body the dying	4:10
1	Jesus might be made manifest in our body.	4:10
1	Jesus might be made manifest in our mortal flesh.	4:11
1	So then death worketh in us, but life in you.	4:12
1	So then death worketh in us, but life in you.	4:12
1	have a building of God, ... eternal in the heavens.	5:1
1	in this we groan, earnestly desiring to be clothed	5:2
1	For we that are in this tabernacle do groan,	5:4
1	knowing that, whilst we are at home in the body,	5:6
1	I trust also are made manifest in your consciences.	5:11
1	to answer them which glory in appearance,	5:12
1	in appearance, and not in the heart (NASB)	5:12
1	if any man be in Christ, he is a new creature:	5:17
1	To wit, that God was in Christ,	5:19
1	hath committed unto us the word of reconciliation.	5:19
1	might be made the righteousness of God in him.	5:21
1	and in the day of salvation have I succoured thee:	6:2
1	Giving no offence in any thing,	6:3
1	But in all things approving ourselves	6:4
1	as the ministers of God, in much patience,	6:4
1	in afflictions, in necessities, in distresses,	6:4
1	in afflictions, in necessities, in distresses,	6:4
1	in afflictions, in necessities, in distresses,	6:4
1	In stripes, in imprisonments, in tumults,	6:5
1	In stripes, in imprisonments, in tumults,	6:5
1	In stripes, in imprisonments, in tumults,	6:5
1	in tumults, in labours, in watchings, in fastings;	6:5
1	in tumults, in labours, in watchings, in fastings;	6:5
1	in tumults, in labours, in watchings, in fastings;	6:5
1	By pureness, by knowledge, by longsuffering,	6:6
1	By pureness, by knowledge, by longsuffering,	6:6
1	By pureness, by knowledge, by longsuffering,	6:6
1	by kindness, by the Holy Ghost, by love unfeigned,	6:6
1	by kindness, by the Holy Ghost, by love unfeigned,	6:6
1	by kindness, by the Holy Ghost, by love unfeigned,	6:6
1	By the word of truth, by the power of God,	6:7
1	By the word of truth, by the power of God,	6:7
1	Ye are not straitened in us,	6:12
1	but ye are straitened in your own bowels.	6:12
1	as God hath said, I will dwell in them,	6:16
1	perfecting holiness in the fear of God.	7:1
1	that ye are in our hearts to die and live with you.	7:3
1	but we were troubled on every side;	7:5
1	God, ... comforted us by the coming of Titus;	7:6
1	And not by his coming only,	7:7
1	by the consolation wherewith he was comforted	7:7
1	For though I made you sorry with a letter,	7:8
1	that ye might receive damage by us in nothing.	7:9
1	In all things ye have approved yourselves to be	7:11
1	approved yourselves to be clear in this matter,	7:11
1	but as we spake all things to you in truth,	7:14
1	I have confidence in you in all things.	7:16
1	I have confidence in you in all things.	7:16
1	grace ... bestowed on the churches of Macedonia;	8:1
1	How that in a great trial of affliction	8:2
1	Therefore, as ye abound in every thing, in faith,	8:7
1	and in all diligence, and in your love to us,	8:7
1	see that ye abound in this grace also.	8:7
1	And herein I give my advice:	8:10
1	But by an equality, that now at this time	8:14
1	which put the same earnest care into the heart	8:16
1	praise is in the gospel throughout all the churches;	8:18
1	to travel with us in this gracious work, (NASB)	8:19
1	in this abundance which is administered by us:	8:20
1	we have oftentimes proved diligent in many things,	8:22
1	boasting of you should be in vain in this behalf;	9:3
1	should be ashamed in this same confident boasting.	9:4
1	that ye, always having all sufficiency in all things,	9:8

ἐν 1706

1 Being enriched in every thing to all bountifulness, ... 2 Co 9:11	1 no man is justified by the law in the sight of God, ... Gal 3:11
1 who in presence am base among you, ... 10:1	1 but, The man that doeth them shall live in them. 3:12
1 For though we walk in the flesh, ... 10:3	1 come on the Gentiles through Jesus Christ; 3:14
1 having in a readiness to revenge all disobedience, ... 10:6	1 was ordained by angels in the hand of a mediator. 3:19
1 but they measuring themselves by themselves, ... 10:12	1 are all the children of God by faith in Christ Jesus. 3:26
1 as to you also in preaching the gospel of Christ: 10:14	1 for ye are all one in Christ Jesus. 3:28
1 that is, of other men's labours; 10:15	1 temptation which was in my flesh ye despised not, ... 4:14
1 that we shall be enlarged by you 10:15	1 to be zealously affected always in a good thing, ... 4:18
1 and not to boast in another man's line of things 10:16	1 and not only when I am present with you. 4:18
1 But he that glorieth, let him glory in the Lord. 10:17	1 again until Christ be formed in you, ... 4:19
1 as the serpent beguiled Eve through his subtlety, ... 11:3	1 to change my voice; for I stand in doubt of you. 4:20
1 but we have been thoroughly made manifest (NT) 11:6	1 For this Agar is mount Sinai in Arabia, ... 4:25
1 made manifest among you in all things. 11:6	1 whosoever of you are justified by the law; 5:4
1 and in all things I have kept myself 11:9	1 in Jesus Christ ... circumcision availeth any thing, ... 5:6
1 As the truth of Christ is in me, ... 11:10	1 I have confidence in you through the Lord, ... 5:10
1 stop me of this boasting in the regions of Achaia. 11:10	1 For all the law is fulfilled in one word, ... 5:14
1 wherein they glory, they may be found even as we. 11:12	1 all the law is fulfilled in one word, even in this; 5:14
1 as it were foolishly, in this confidence (NT) 11:17	1 Brethren, if a man be overtaken in a fault, ... 6:1
1 as it were foolishly, in this confidence of boasting. 11:17	1 restore such an one in the spirit of meekness; 6:1
1 Howbeit whereinsoever any is bold, ... 11:21	1 Let him that is taught in the word 6:6
1 I speak foolishly, I am bold also. (NT) 11:21	1 As many as desire to make a fair show in the flesh, ... 6:12
1 in labours more abundant, ... 11:23	1 you circumcised, that they may glory in your flesh. ... 6:13
1 in stripes above measure, ... 11:23	1 glory, save in the cross of our Lord Jesus Christ, ... 6:14
1 in prisons more frequent, in deaths oft. 11:23	1 For in Christ Jesus neither circumcision availeth 6:15
1 in prisons more frequent, in deaths oft. 11:23	1 for I bear in my body the marks of the Lord Jesus. ... 6:17
1 a night and a day I have been in the deep; 11:25	1 an apostle ... to the saints which are at Ephesus, ... Eph 1:1
1 in perils in the city, in perils in the wilderness, ... 11:26	1 to the saints ... and to the faithful in Christ Jesus: 1:1
1 in perils in the city, in perils in the wilderness, ... 11:26	1 who hath blessed us with all spiritual blessings 1:3
1 in perils in the sea, in perils among false brethren; ... 11:26	1 all spiritual blessings in heavenly places in Christ: 1:3
1 in perils in the sea, in perils among false brethren; ... 11:26	1 in the heavenly places in Christ. (NASB) 1:3
1 In weariness and painfulness, in watchings often, ... 11:27	1 According as he hath chosen us in him 1:4
1 In weariness and painfulness, in watchings often, ... 11:27	1 be holy and without blame before him in love: 1:4
1 in hunger and thirst, in fastings often, ... 11:27	1 wherein he hath made us accepted in the beloved. 1:6
1 in hunger and thirst, in fastings often, ... 11:27	1 wherein he hath made us accepted in the beloved. 1:6
1 in fastings often, in cold and nakedness. 11:27	1 In whom we have redemption through his blood, ... 1:7
1 In Damascus the governor under Aretas the king 11:32	1 abounded toward us in all wisdom and prudence; 1:8
1 And through a window in a basket was I let down ... 11:33	1 good pleasure which he hath purposed in himself: 1:9
1 I knew a man in Christ above fourteen years ago, ... 12:2	1 might gather together in one all things in Christ, ... 1:10
1 whether in the body, I cannot tell; 12:2	1 both which are in heaven, and which are on earth; ... 1:10
1 whether in the body, or out of the body, ... 12:3	1 In whom also we have obtained an inheritance, ... 1:11
1 of myself I will not glory, but in mine infirmities. 12:5	1 In whom also we have obtained an inheritance, ... 1:11
1 for my strength is made perfect in weakness. 12:9	1 the praise of his glory, who first trusted in Christ. 1:12
1 therefore will I rather glory in my infirmities, ... 12:9	1 In whom ye also trusted, ... 1:13
1 Therefore I take pleasure in infirmities, ... 12:10	1 in whom also after that ye believed, ye were sealed ... 1:13
1 in reproaches, in necessities, in persecutions, ... 12:10	1 after I heard of your faith in the Lord Jesus, ... 1:15
1 in reproaches, in necessities, in persecutions, ... 12:10	1 and revelation in the knowledge of him: 1:17
1 in reproaches, in necessities, in persecutions, ... 12:10	1 riches of the glory of his inheritance in the saints, ... 1:18
1 in persecutions, in distresses for Christ's sake: 12:10	1 Which he wrought in Christ, when he raised him 1:20
1 signs ... were wrought among you in all patience, ... 12:12	1 and set him at his own right hand in the heavenly 1:20
1 signs ... were wrought among you in all patience, ... 12:12	1 at his own right hand in the heavenly places, ... 1:20
1 in signs, and wonders, and mighty deeds. 12:12	1 every name that is named, not only in this world, ... 1:21
1 we speak before God in Christ: 12:19	1 this world, but also in that which is to come: 1:21
1 Since ye seek a proof of Christ speaking in me, ... 13:3	1 the fulness of him that filleth all in all. 1:23
1 to you-ward is not weak, but is mighty in you. 13:3	1 Wherein in time past ye walked according to 2:2
1 For we also are weak in him, ... 13:4	1 that now worketh in the children of disobedience: 2:2
1 Examine yourselves, whether ye be in the faith; 13:5	1 Among whom also we all had our conversation 2:3
1 how that Jesus Christ is in you, ... 13:5	1 in times past in the lusts of our flesh, ... 2:3
1 Greet one another with an holy kiss. 13:12	1 But God, who is rich in mercy, ... 2:4
1 from him that called you into the grace of Christ ..... Gal 1:6	1 hath quickened us together with Christ, ... 2:5
1 my conversation in time past in the Jews' religion, ... 1:13	1 made us sit together in heavenly places in Christ 2:6
1 And profited in the Jews' religion above many 1:14	1 made us sit together in heavenly places in Christ 2:6
1 above many my equals in mine own nation, ... 1:14	1 That in the ages to come he might show 2:7
1 To reveal his Son in me, ... 1:16	1 the exceeding riches of his grace in his kindness 2:7
1 that I might preach him among the heathen; 1:16	1 of his grace ... toward us through Christ Jesus. 2:7
1 unto the churches of Judaea which were in Christ: ... 1:22	1 created in Christ Jesus unto good works, ... 2:10
1 And they glorified God in me. 1:24	1 hath before ordained that we should walk in them. ... 2:10
1 that gospel which I preach among the Gentiles, ... 2:2	1 that ye being in time past Gentiles in the flesh, ... 2:11
1 spy out our liberty which we have in Christ Jesus, ... 2:4	1 the Circumcision in the flesh made by hands; 2:11
1 But if, while we seek to be justified by Christ, ... 2:17	1 That at that time ye were without Christ, ... 2:12
1 yet not I, but Christ liveth in me: 2:20	1 having no hope, and without God in the world: 2:12
1 and the life which I now live in the flesh 2:20	1 now in Christ Jesus ye who sometimes were far off ... 2:13
1 live by the faith of the Son of God, who loved me, ... 2:20	1 are made nigh by the blood of Christ. 2:13
1 evidently set forth, crucified among you? 3:1	1 Having abolished in his flesh the enmity, ... 2:15
1 and worketh miracles among you, ... 3:5	1 law of commandments contained in ordinances; 2:15
1 In thee shall all nations be blessed. 3:8	1 for to make in himself of twain one new man, ... 2:15
1 every one that continueth not in all things 3:10	1 reconcile both unto God in one body by the cross, ... 2:16
1 things which are written in the book of the law 3:10	1 having slain the enmity thereby: 2:16

415

ἐν 1706

1 we both have access by one Spirit unto the Father....Eph 2:18	1 all the saints in Christ Jesus which are at Philippi,...Phlp 1:1
1 In whom all the building fitly framed together 2:21	1 Always in every prayer of mine for you all 1:4
1 groweth unto an holy temple in the Lord: 2:21	1 that he which hath begun a good work in you 1:6
1 In whom ye also are builded together 2:22	1 to think this ... because I have you in my heart; 1:7
1 for an habitation of God through the Spirit. 2:22	1 in my heart; inasmuch as both in my bonds, ... 1:7
1 by revelation ... as I wrote afore in few words, ... 3:3	1 in the defense and confirmation (NASB) 1:7
1 understand my knowledge in the mystery of Christ 3:4	1 I long after you all in the bowels of Jesus Christ. 1:8
1 Which in other ages was not made known 3:5	1 more and more in knowledge and in all judgment; 1:9
1 unto his holy apostles and prophets by the Spirit; 3:5	1 my bonds in Christ are manifest in all the palace, ... 1:13
1 partakers of his promise in Christ by the gospel: 3:6	1 my bonds in Christ are manifest in all the palace, ... 1:13
1 that I should preach among the Gentiles 3:8	1 And many of the brethren in the Lord, ... 1:14
1 hid in God, who created all things by Jesus Christ: 3:9	1 and I therein do rejoice, yea, and will rejoice. 1:18
1 the principalities and powers in heavenly places 3:10	1 that in nothing I shall be ashamed, ... 1:20
1 which he purposed in Christ Jesus our Lord: 3:11	1 but that with all boldness, as always, ... 1:20
1 In whom we have boldness and access 3:12	1 so now also Christ shall be magnified in my body, ... 1:20
1 and access with confidence by the faith of him. 3:12	1 if I live in the flesh, this is the fruit of my labour: 1:22
1 I desire that ye faint not at my tribulations for you, ... 3:13	1 to abide in the flesh is more needful for you. 1:24
1 the whole family in heaven and earth is named, ... 3:15	1 your rejoicing may be more abundant in Jesus 1:26
1 That Christ may dwell in your hearts by faith; 3:17	1 in Jesus Christ for me by my coming to you again. 1:26
1 that ye, being rooted and grounded in love, ... 3:17	1 hear of your affairs, that ye stand fast in one spirit, ... 1:27
1 according to the power that worketh in us, ... 3:20	1 And in nothing terrified by your adversaries: 1:28
1 Unto him be glory in the church by Christ Jesus 3:21	1 Having the same conflict which ye saw in me, ... 1:30
1 Unto him be glory in the church by Christ Jesus 3:21	1 the same conflict ... and now hear to be in me. 1:30
1 I therefore, the prisoner of the Lord, ... 4:1	1 any consolation in Christ, if any comfort of love, ... 2:1
1 with longsuffering, forbearing one another in love; 4:2	1 Let this mind be in you, which was also in Christ 2:5
1 to keep the unity of the Spirit in the bond of peace. 4:3	1 this mind ... which was also in Christ Jesus: 2:5
1 even as ye are called in one hope of your calling; 4:4	1 Who, being in the form of God, ... 2:6
1 who is above all, and through all, and in you all. 4:6	1 and was made in the likeness of men: 2:7
1 by the sleight of men, and cunning craftiness, ... 4:14	1 That at the name of Jesus every knee should bow, ... 2:10
1 by the sleight of men, and cunning craftiness, ... 4:14	1 ye have always obeyed, not as in my presence only, ... 2:12
1 But speaking the truth in love, ... 4:15	1 but now much more in my absence, ... 2:12
1 the effectual working in the measure of every part, ... 4:16	1 For it is God which worketh in you 2:13
1 unto the edifying of itself in love. 4:16	1 in the midst of a crooked and perverse nation, ... 2:15
1 This I say therefore, and testify in the Lord, ... 4:17	1 among whom ye shine as lights in the world; 2:15
1 as other Gentiles walk, in the vanity of their mind, ... 4:17	1 among whom ye shine as lights in the world; 2:15
1 through the ignorance that is in them, ... 4:18	1 But I trust in the Lord Jesus to send Timotheus 2:19
1 to work all uncleanness with greediness. 4:19	1 I trust in the Lord that I also ... shall come shortly. 2:24
1 have been taught by him, as the truth is in Jesus: 4:21	1 Receive him therefore in the Lord 2:29
1 have been taught by him, as the truth is in Jesus: 4:21	1 Finally, my brethren, rejoice in the Lord. 3:1
1 which after God is created in righteousness 4:24	1 and rejoice in Christ Jesus, ... 3:3
1 whereby ye are sealed unto the day of redemption. 4:30	1 and have no confidence in the flesh. 3:3
1 even as God for Christ's sake hath forgiven you. 4:32	1 Though I might also have confidence in the flesh. 3:4
1 And walk in love, as Christ also hath loved us, ... 5:2	1 If any ... might trust in the flesh, I more: 3:4
1 not be once named among you, as becometh saints; 5:3	1 touching the righteousness which is in the law, ... 3:6
1 hath any inheritance in the kingdom of Christ 5:5	1 And be found in him, not having mine own 3:9
1 but now are ye light in the Lord: 5:8	1 the prize of the high calling of God in Christ Jesus. 3:14
1 For the fruit of the Spirit is in all goodness 5:9	1 glory is in their shame, who mind earthly things. 3:19
1 And be not drunk with wine, wherein is excess; 5:18	1 For our conversation is in heaven; 3:20
1 And be not drunk ... but be filled with the Spirit; 5:18	1 so stand fast in the Lord, my dearly beloved. 4:1
1 singing and making melody in your heart 5:19	1 that they be of the same mind in the Lord. 4:2
1 the Father in the name of our Lord Jesus Christ; 5:20	1 women which laboured with me in the gospel, ... 4:3
1 Submitting yourselves ... in the fear of God. 5:21	1 whose names are in the book of life. 4:3
1 the wives be to their own husbands in every thing. 5:24	1 Rejoice in the Lord alway: 4:4
1 cleanse it with the washing of water by the word, ... 5:26	1 but in every thing by prayer and supplication 4:6
1 Children, obey your parents in the Lord: 6:1	1 keep your hearts and minds through Christ Jesus. 4:7
1 which is the first commandment with promise; 6:2	1 Those things, ... and heard, and seen in me, do: 4:9
1 in the nurture and admonition of the Lord. 6:4	1 But I rejoiced in the Lord greatly, ... 4:10
1 in singleness of your heart, as unto Christ; 6:5	1 in whatsoever state I am, therewith to be content. 4:11
1 knowing that your Master also is in heaven; 6:9	1 every where and in all things I am instructed 4:12
1 Finally, my brethren, be strong in the Lord, ... 6:10	1 every where and in all things I am instructed 4:12
1 strong in the Lord, and in the power of his might. 6:10	1 all things through Christ which strengtheneth me. 4:13
1 against spiritual wickedness in high places. 6:12	1 that in the beginning of the gospel, ... 4:15
1 that ye may be able to withstand in the evil day, ... 6:13	1 For even in Thessalonica ye sent once and again 4:16
1 having your loins girt about with truth, ... 6:14	1 according to his riches in glory by Christ Jesus. 4:19
1 shod with the preparation of the gospel of peace; 6:15	1 according to his riches in glory by Christ Jesus. 4:19
1 in addition to all, taking up (NASB) 6:16	1 Salute every saint in Christ Jesus. 4:21
1 wherewith ye shall be able to quench all ... darts 6:16	1 faithful brethren in Christ which are at Colosse: ......Col 1:2
1 Praying always with all prayer and supplication 6:18	1 To the saints and faithful brethren in Christ 1:2
1 with all prayer and supplication in the Spirit, ... 6:18	1 Since we heard of your faith in Christ Jesus, ... 1:4
1 and watching thereunto with all perseverance 6:18	1 For the hope which is laid up for you in heaven, ... 1:5
1 that I may open my mouth boldly, (NT) 6:19	1 whereof ye heard before in the word 1:5
1 that I may open my mouth boldly, (NT) 6:19	1 Which is come unto you, as it is in all the world; 1:6
1 For which I am an ambassador in bonds: 6:20	1 and bringeth forth fruit, as it doth also in you, ... 1:6
1 that therein I may speak boldly, ... 6:20	1 and knew the grace of God in truth: 1:6
1 beloved brother and faithful minister in the Lord; 6:21	1 Who also declared unto us your love in the Spirit. 1:8
1 that love our Lord Jesus Christ in sincerity. Amen. 6:24	1 his will in all wisdom and spiritual understanding; 1:9
1 all the saints in Christ Jesus which are at Philippi, ...Phlp 1:1	1 being fruitful in every good work, ... 1:10

ἐν 1706

1 and increasing in the knowledge of God;	Col	1:10
1 Strengthened with all might,		1:11
1 partakers of the inheritance of the saints in light:		1:12
1 In whom we have redemption through his blood,		1:14
1 For by him were all things created,		1:16
1 that are in heaven, and that are in earth,		1:16
1 is before all things, and by him all things consist.		1:17
1 that in all things he might have the preeminence.		1:18
1 in him should all fulness dwell;		1:19
1 things in earth, or things in heaven.		1:20
1 and enemies in your mind by wicked works,		1:21
1 In the body of his flesh through death,		1:22
1 gospel, ... which was preached to every creature		1:23
1 Who now rejoice in my sufferings for you,		1:24
1 afflictions of Christ in my flesh for his body's sake,		1:24
1 the glory of this mystery among the Gentiles;		1:27
1 which is Christ in you, the hope of glory:		1:27
1 and teaching every man in all wisdom;		1:28
1 we may present every man perfect in Christ Jesus:		1:28
1 his working, which worketh in me mightily,		1:29
1 his working, which worketh in me mightily.		1:29
1 conflict I have for you, and for them at Laodicea,		2:1
1 for as many as have not seen my face in the flesh;		2:1
1 might be comforted, being knit together in love,		2:2
1 In whom are hid all the treasures of wisdom		2:3
1 any man should beguile you with enticing words.		2:4
1 received Christ Jesus the Lord, so walk ye in him:		2:6
1 Rooted and built up in him,		2:7
1 and stablished in the faith, as ye have been taught,		2:7
1 abounding therein with thanksgiving.		2:7
1 abounding therein with thanksgiving.		2:7
1 For in him dwelleth all the fulness of the Godhead		2:9
1 And ye are complete in him, which is the head		2:10
1 In whom also ye are circumcised		2:11
1 in putting off the body of the sins of the flesh		2:11
1 by the circumcision of Christ:		2:11
1 Buried with him in baptism,		2:12
1 with him in baptism, wherein also ye are risen		2:12
1 in your sins and the uncircumcision of your flesh,		2:13
1 a show of them openly, triumphing over them in it.		2:15
1 a show of them openly, triumphing over them in it.		2:15
1 Let no man therefore judge you in meat,		2:16
1 no man ... judge you in meat, or in drink,		2:16
1 or in respect of an holyday, or of the new moon,		2:16
1 in a voluntary humility and worshipping of angels,		2:18
1 why, as though living in the world,		2:20
1 have indeed a show of wisdom in will worship,		2:23
1 not in any honour to the satisfying of the flesh.		2:23
1 where Christ sitteth on the right hand of God.		3:1
1 and your life is hid with Christ in God.		3:3
1 then shall ye also appear with him in glory.		3:4
1 In the which ye also walked some time,		3:7
1 ye also walked some time, when ye lived in them.		3:7
1 bond nor free: but Christ is all, and in all.		3:11
1 And let the peace of God rule in your hearts,		3:15
1 to the which also ye are called in one body;		3:15
1 Let the word of Christ dwell in you richly		3:16
1 Let the word ... dwell in you richly in all wisdom;		3:16
1 singing with grace in your hearts to the Lord.		3:16
1 singing with grace in your hearts to the Lord.		3:16
1 And whatsoever ye do in word or deed,		3:17
1 And whatsoever ye do in word or deed,		3:17
1 do all in the name of the Lord Jesus,		3:17
1 unto your own husbands, as it is fit in the Lord.		3:18
1 for this is well-pleasing to the Lord. (NASB)		3:20
1 obey ... your masters ... not with eyeservice,		3:22
1 but in singleness of heart, fearing God:		3:22
1 knowing that ye also have a Master in heaven.		4:1
1 and watch in the same with thanksgiving,		4:2
1 and watch in the same with thanksgiving;		4:2
1 Walk in wisdom toward them that are without,		4:5
1 Let your speech be alway with grace,		4:6
1 a faithful minister and fellowservant in the Lord:		4:7
1 always labouring fervently for you in prayers,		4:12
1 stand perfect and complete in all the will of God.		4:12
1 them that are in Laodicea and them in Hierapolis.		4:13
1 them that are in Laodicea and them in Hierapolis.		4:13
1 Salute the brethren which are in Laodicea,	Col	4:15
1 it be read also in the church of the Laodiceans;		4:16
1 the ministry which thou hast received in the Lord,		4:17
1 which is in God the Father and in the Lord Jesus	1 Th	1:1
1 For our gospel came not unto you in word only,		1:5
1 but also in power, and in the Holy Ghost,		1:5
1 but also in power, and in the Holy Ghost,		1:5
1 and in the Holy Ghost, and in much assurance;		1:5
1 as ye know what manner of men we were among		1:5
1 having received the word in much affliction,		1:6
1 to all that believe in Macedonia and Achaia.		1:7
1 believers in Macedonia and in Achaia. (NASB)		1:7
1 out the word ... not only in Macedonia and Achaia,		1:8
1 not only in Macedonia and Achaia, (NASB) (NT)		1:8
1 in every place your faith to God-ward is spread		1:8
1 were shamefully entreated, as ye know, at Philippi,		2:2
1 we were bold in our God to speak unto you		2:2
1 speak ... the gospel of God with much contention.		2:2
1 was not of deceit, nor of uncleanness, nor in guile:		2:3
1 at any time used we flattering words, (NT)		2:5
1 nor a cloak of covetousness; God is witness: (NT)		2:5
1 when we might have been burdensome, (NT)		2:6
1 But we were gentle among you,		2:7
1 which effectually worketh also in you that believe.		2:13
1 the churches of God which in Judaea are in Christ		2:14
1 the churches of God which in Judaea are in Christ		2:14
1 to see your face with great desire.		2:17
1 presence of our Lord Jesus Christ at his coming?		2:19
1 we thought it good to be left at Athens alone;		3:1
1 and our fellowlabourer in the gospel of Christ,		3:2
1 That no man should be moved by these afflictions:		3:3
1 For now we live, if ye stand fast in the Lord.		3:8
1 your hearts unblameable in holiness before God,		3:13
1 at the coming of our Lord Jesus Christ		3:13
1 beseech you, ... and exhort you by the Lord Jesus,		4:1
1 to possess his vessel in sanctification and honour;		4:4
1 Not in the lust of concupiscence,		4:5
1 go beyond and defraud his brother in any matter:		4:6
1 not called us unto uncleanness, but unto holiness.		4:7
1 all the brethren which are in all Macedonia:		4:10
1 For this we say unto you by the word of the Lord,		4:15
1 Lord ... shall descend from heaven with a shout,		4:16
1 with the voice of the archangel,		4:16
1 voice of the archangel, and with the trump of God:		4:16
1 and the dead in Christ shall rise first:		4:16
1 caught up together with them in the clouds,		4:17
1 Wherefore comfort one another with these words.		4:18
1 day of the Lord so cometh as a thief in the night.		5:2
1 as travail upon a woman with child; (NT)		5:3
1 But ye, brethren, are not in darkness,		5:4
1 to know them which labour among you,		5:12
1 and are over you in the Lord, and admonish you;		5:12
1 And to esteem them very highly in love		5:13
1 And be at peace among yourselves.		5:13
1 In every thing give thanks:		5:18
1 for this is the will of God in Christ Jesus		5:18
1 unto the coming of our Lord Jesus Christ.		5:23
1 Greet all the brethren with an holy kiss.		5:26
1 in God our Father and the Lord Jesus Christ:	2 Th	1:1
1 So that we ourselves glory in you in the churches		1:4
1 So that we ourselves glory in you in the churches		1:4
1 in all your persecutions and tribulations		1:4
1 when the Lord Jesus shall be revealed from heaven		1:7
1 In flaming fire taking vengeance on them		1:8
1 When he shall come to be glorified in his saints,		1:10
1 and to be admired in all them that believe		1:10
1 our testimony among you was believed in that day.		1:10
1 and the work of faith with power:		1:11
1 our Lord Jesus Christ may be glorified in you,		1:12
1 Christ may be glorified in you, and ye in him,		1:12
1 that he might be revealed in his time.		2:6
1 with all power and signs and lying wonders,		2:9
1 And with all deceivableness of unrighteousness		2:10
1 unrighteousness in them that perish;		2:10
1 but had pleasure in unrighteousness.		2:12
1 to salvation through sanctification of the Spirit		2:13
1 consolation and good hope through grace,		2:16

417

ἐν 1706

1	and stablish you in every good word and work......	2 Th 2:17
1	And we have confidence in the Lord touching you,.....	3:4
1	command ... in the name of our Lord Jesus Christ,.....	3:6
1	we behaved not ourselves disorderly among you;........	3:7
1	but wrought with labour and travail night and day,.....	3:8
1	there are some which walk among you disorderly,......	3:11
1	we command and exhort in the Lord (NASB)..........	3:12
1	the Lord ... give you peace always by all means.........	3:16
1	which is the token in every epistle: so I write...........	3:17
1	Unto Timothy, my own son in the faith:...........	1 Tm 1:2
1	As I besought thee to abide still at Ephesus,...........	1:3
1	rather than godly edifying which is in faith: so do.......	1:4
1	mercy, because I did it ignorantly in unbelief...........	1:13
1	with faith and love which is in Christ Jesus.............	1:14
1	that in me first Jesus Christ might show forth..........	1:16
1	that thou by them mightest war a good warfare;........	1:18
1	For kings, and for all that are in authority,.............	2:2
1	peaceable life in all godliness and honesty..............	2:2
1	I speak the truth in Christ, and lie not;................	2:7
1	a teacher of the Gentiles in faith and verity.............	2:7
1	I will therefore that men pray every where, (NT).......	2:8
1	that women adorn themselves in modest apparel,......	2:9
1	not with broided hair, or gold, or pearls,................	2:9
1	Let the woman learn in silence with all subjection.....	2:11
1	Let the woman learn in silence with all subjection.....	2:11
1	suffer not a woman to teach, ... but to be in silence.....	2:12
1	woman being deceived was in the transgression........	2:14
1	if they continue in faith and charity and holiness......	2:15
1	having his children in subjection with all gravity;......	3:4
1	the mystery of the faith in a pure conscience...........	3:9
1	grave, not slanderers, sober, faithful in all things.......	3:11
1	great boldness in the faith which is in Christ Jesus....	3:13
1	great boldness in the faith which is in Christ Jesus....	3:13
1	hoping to come to you before long; (NASB) (NT).....	3:14
1	oughtest to behave thyself in the house of God,.......	3:15
1	God was manifest in the flesh,.......................	3:16
1	manifest in the flesh, justified in the Spirit,.............	3:16
1	seen of angels, preached unto the Gentiles,............	3:16
1	believed on in the world, received up into glory........	3:16
1	believed on in the world, received up into glory........	3:16
1	in the latter times some shall depart from the faith,....	4:1
1	Speaking lies in hypocrisy;..........................	4:2
1	in word, in conversation, in charity, in spirit,..........	4:12
1	in word, in conversation, in charity, in spirit,..........	4:12
1	in charity, in spirit, in faith, in purity................	4:12
1	in charity, in spirit, in faith, in purity................	4:12
1	in charity, in spirit, in faith, in purity................	4:12
1	in charity, in spirit, in faith, in purity................	4:12
1	Neglect not the gift that is in thee,....................	4:14
1	give thyself wholly to them;.........................	4:15
1	that thy profiting may appear to all...................	4:15
1	the younger as sisters, with all purity.................	5:2
1	Well reported of for good works;.....................	5:10
1	especially they who labour in the word...............	5:17
1	Charge them that are rich in this world,...............	6:17
1	nor trust in uncertain riches, but in the living God,....	6:17
1	do good, that they be rich in good works,..............	6:18
1	according to the promise of life which is in Christ..	2 Tm 1:1
1	I serve from my forefathers with pure conscience,.....	1:3
1	remembrance of thee in my prayers night and day;.....	1:3
1	remembrance of the unfeigned faith that is in thee,.....	1:5
1	which dwelt first in thy grandmother Lois,.............	1:5
1	and I am persuaded that in thee also...................	1:5
1	which is in thee by the putting on of my hands.........	1:6
1	given us in Christ Jesus before the world began,.......	1:9
1	in faith and love which is in Christ Jesus..............	1:13
1	in faith and love which is in Christ Jesus..............	1:13
1	keep by the Holy Ghost which dwelleth in us..........	1:14
1	they which are in Asia be turned away from me;.......	1:15
1	But, when he was in Rome, he sought me out.........	1:17
1	that he may find mercy of the Lord in that day:........	1:18
1	and in how many things he ministered unto me.......	1:18
1	be strong in the grace that is in Christ Jesus...........	2:1
1	be strong in the grace that is in Christ Jesus...........	2:1
1	and the Lord give thee understanding in all things.....	2:7
1	Wherein I suffer trouble, as an evil doer,..............	2:9
1	also obtain the salvation which is in Christ Jesus......	2:10
1	But in a great house ... not only vessels of gold.....	2 Tm 2:20
1	In meekness instructing those that oppose.............	2:25
1	that in the last days perilous times shall come.........	3:1
1	afflictions, which came unto me at Antioch,...........	3:11
1	which came unto me at Antioch, at Iconium,..........	3:11
1	came unto me at Antioch, at Iconium, at Lystra;.......	3:11
1	live godly in Christ Jesus shall suffer persecution.......	3:12
1	But continue thou in ... which thou hast learned.......	3:14
1	through faith which is in Christ Jesus.................	3:15
1	for correction, for instruction in righteousness:........	3:16
1	rebuke, exhort with all longsuffering and doctrine......	4:2
1	But watch thou in all things,.........................	4:5
1	the righteous judge, shall give me at that day:.........	4:8
1	The cloak that I left at Troas with Carpus,.............	4:13
1	At my first answer no man stood with me,.............	4:16
1	Erastus abode at Corinth,............................	4:20
1	but Trophimus have I left at Miletum sick.............	4:20
1	manifested his word through preaching,.............	Tit 1:3
1	For this cause left I thee in Crete,.....................	1:5
1	faithful children not accused of riot or unruly. (NT)....	1:6
1	may be able by sound doctrine both to exhort and.....	1:9
1	that they may be sound in the faith;...................	1:13
1	that they be in behaviour as becometh holiness,.......	2:3
1	in doctrine showing uncorruptness, gravity,...........	2:7
1	and to please them well in all things;..................	2:9
1	the doctrine of God our Saviour in all things...........	2:10
1	righteously, and godly, in this present world;..........	2:12
1	living in malice and envy, hateful, and hating..........	3:3
1	Not by works of righteousness which we have done,....	3:5
1	Greet them that love us in the faith....................	3:15
1	by the acknowledging of every good thing..........	Phlm 1:6
1	every good thing which is in you in Christ Jesus.......	1:6
1	Wherefore, though I might be much bold in Christ.....	1:8
1	son Onesimus, whom I have begotten in my bonds:.....	1:10
1	ministered unto me in the bonds of the gospel:.........	1:13
1	more unto thee, both in the flesh, and in the Lord?.....	1:16
1	more unto thee, both in the flesh, and in the Lord?.....	1:16
1	Yea, brother, let me have joy of thee in the Lord:.....	1:20
1	Yea, brother, ... refresh my bowels in the Lord.........	1:20
1	Epaphras, my fellowprisoner in Christ Jesus;...........	1:23
1	spake ... unto the fathers by the prophets,............	Heb 1:1
1	Hath in these last days spoken unto us by his Son,.....	1:2
1	sat down on the right hand of the Majesty on high;.....	1:3
1	sat down on the right hand of the Majesty on high;.....	1:3
1	For in that he put all in subjection under him,.........	2:8
1	in the midst of the church will I sing praise...........	2:12
1	For in that he himself hath suffered being tempted,.....	2:18
1	as also Moses was faithful in all his house.............	3:2
1	And Moses verily was faithful in all his house.........	3:5
1	Harden not your hearts, as in the provocation,.........	3:8
1	in the day of temptation in the wilderness:............	3:8
1	FATHERS TRIED ME BY TESTING (NASB).........	3:9
1	So I sware in my wrath, They shall not enter..........	3:11
1	lest there be in any of you an evil heart of unbelief,....	3:12
1	in departing from the living God......................	3:12
1	While it is said, To day if ye will hear his voice,........	3:15
1	harden not your hearts, as in the provocation...........	3:15
1	whose carcases fell in the wilderness?.................	3:17
1	as he said, As I have sworn in my wrath,.............	4:3
1	God did rest the seventh day (NT)....................	4:4
1	in this place again, If they shall enter into my rest.....	4:5
1	Again, he limiteth a certain day, saying in David,......	4:7
1	any man fall after the same example of unbelief........	4:11
1	As he saith also in another place,.....................	5:6
1	Who in the days of his flesh,.........................	5:7
1	Wherein God, willing more abundantly to show.........	6:17
1	in which it was impossible for God to lie,.............	6:18
1	For he was yet in the loins of his father,..............	7:10
1	who is set on the right hand of the throne.............	8:1
1	the throne of the Majesty in the heavens;..............	8:1
1	the pattern showed to thee in the mount...............	8:5
1	in the day when I took them by the hand.............	8:9
1	because they continued not in my covenant,...........	8:9
1	In that he saith, A new covenant, he hath made.......	8:13
1	the first, wherein was the candlestick.................	9:2
1	wherein was the golden pot that had manna,...........	9:4
1	almost all things are by the law purged with blood;.....	9:22

ἐν 1706

1 that the patterns of things in the heavens . . . . Heb 9:23	1 honour and glory at the appearing of Jesus Christ: . . . 1 Pt 1:7
1 every year with blood of others; 9:25	1 the Spirit of Christ which was in them did signify, ... 1:11
1 But in those sacrifices there is a remembrance 10:3	1 have preached the gospel unto you with the Holy 1:12
1 in the volume of the book it is written of me, ... 10:7	1 brought unto you at the revelation of Jesus Christ; 1:13
1 By the which will we are sanctified 10:10	1 according to the former lusts in your ignorance: 1:14
1 sat down on the right hand of God; 10:12	1 so be ye holy in all manner of conversation; 1:15
1 to enter into the holiest by the blood of Jesus, ... 10:19	1 pass the time of your sojourning here in fear: 1:17
1 with a true heart in full assurance of faith, ... 10:22	1 ye have purified your souls in obeying the truth 1:22
1 counted the blood ... wherewith he was sanctified, ... 10:29	1 milk of the word, that ye may grow thereby: 2:2
1 former days, in which, after ye were illuminated, ... 10:32	1 Wherefore also it is contained in the scripture, ... 2:6
1 knowing in yourselves that ye have in heaven 10:34	1 Behold, I lay in Sion a chief corner stone, ... 2:6
1 in heaven a better and an enduring substance. 10:34	1 your conversation honest among the Gentiles: 2:12
1 my soul shall have no pleasure in him. 10:38	1 that, whereas they speak against you as evildoers, ... 2:12
1 For by it the elders obtained a good report. 11:2	1 glorify God in the day of visitation. 2:12
1 dwelling in tabernacles with Isaac and Jacob, ... 11:9	1 Servants, be subject to your masters with all fear; 2:18
1 That in Isaac shall thy seed be called: 11:18	1 neither was guile found in his mouth: 2:22
1 from whence also he received him in a figure. 11:19	1 Who his own self bare our sins in his own body 2:24
1 greater riches than the treasures in Egypt: 11:26	1 behold your chaste conversation coupled with fear. 3:2
1 waxed valiant in fight, ... 11:34	1 in that which is not corruptible, ... 3:4
1 were tempted, were slain with the sword: 11:37	1 But sanctify the Lord God in your hearts: 3:15
1 they wandered about in sheepskins and goatskins, ... 11:37	1 the hope that is in you with meekness and fear: 3:15
1 they wandered about in sheepskins and goatskins; 11:37	1 whereas they speak evil of you, as of evildoers, ... 3:16
1 they wandered in deserts, and in mountains, ... 11:38	1 falsely accuse your good conversation in Christ. 3:16
1 is set down at the right hand of the throne of God. 12:2	1 By which also he went and preached 3:19
1 of the firstborn, which are written in heaven, ... 12:23	1 he went and preached unto the spirits in prison; 3:19
1 as being yourselves also in the body. 13:3	1 in the days of Noah, while the ark was a preparing, ... 3:20
1 Marriage is honourable in all, ... 13:4	1 gone into heaven, and is on the right hand of God; 3:22
1 not profited them that have been occupied therein. 13:9	1 as Christ hath suffered for us in the flesh, ... 4:1
1 in all things willing to live honestly. 13:18	1 the rest of his time in the flesh to the lusts of men, ... 4:2
1 through the blood of the everlasting covenant, ... 13:20	1 when we walked in lasciviousness, lusts, ... 4:3
1 perfect in every good work to do his will, ... 13:21	1 Wherein they think it strange that ye run not 4:4
1 working in you that which is wellpleasing 13:21	1 that God in all things may be glorified 4:11
1 twelve tribes which are scattered abroad, (NT) . . . . . . Jas 1:1	1 concerning the fiery trial which is to try you, ... 4:12
1 be perfect and entire, wanting nothing. (NT) 1:4	1 that, when his glory shall be revealed, ... 4:13
1 But let him ask in faith, nothing wavering. 1:6	1 If ye be reproached for the name of Christ, ... 4:14
1 A double minded man is unstable in all his ways. 1:8	1 but let him glorify God on this behalf. 4:16
1 brother of low degree rejoice in that he is exalted: 1:9	1 the keeping of their souls to him in well doing, ... 4:19
1 But the rich, in that he is made low: 1:10	1 The elders which are among you I exhort, ... 5:1
1 so also shall the rich man fade away in his ways. 1:11	1 Feed the flock of God which is among you, ... 5:2
1 and receive with meekness the engrafted word, ... 1:21	1 that he may exalt you in due time: 5:6
1 like ... man beholding his natural face in a glass: 1:23	1 in your brethren that are in the world. 5:9
1 this man shall be blessed in his deed. 1:25	1 called us unto his eternal glory by Christ Jesus, ... 5:10
1 If any man among you seem to be religious, ... 1:26	1 The church that is at Babylon, ... saluteth you; 5:13
1 visit the fatherless and widows in their affliction, ... 1:27	1 Greet ye one another with a kiss of charity. 5:14
1 the Lord of glory, with respect of persons. 2:1	1 Peace be with you all that are in Christ Jesus. 5:14
1 a man with a gold ring, in goodly apparel, ... 2:2	1 faith with us through the righteousness of God . . . . . . 2 Pt 1:1
1 and there come in also a poor man in vile raiment; 2:2	1 Grace and peace ... through the knowledge of God, ... 1:2
1 Are ye not then partial in yourselves, ... 2:4	1 having escaped the corruption that is in the world 1:4
1 God chosen the poor of this world rich in faith, ... 2:5	1 the corruption that is in the world through lust. 1:4
1 and yet offend in one point, he is guilty of all. 2:10	1 add to your faith virtue; and to virtue knowledge; 1:5
1 And one of you say unto them, Depart in peace, ... 2:16	1 add to your faith virtue; and to virtue knowledge; 1:5
1 offend not in word, the same is a perfect man, ... 3:2	1 And to knowledge temperance; and ... patience; 1:6
1 so is the tongue among our members, ... 3:6	1 to temperance patience; and to patience godliness; 1:6
1 Therewith bless we God, even the Father; 3:9	1 to temperance patience; and to patience godliness; 1:6
1 bless we God, ... and therewith curse we men, ... 3:9	1 And to godliness brotherly kindness; 1:7
1 wise man and endued with knowledge among you? 3:13	1 and to brotherly kindness charity. 1:7
1 show out ... his works with meekness of wisdom. 3:13	1 and be established in the present truth. 1:12
1 if ye have bitter envying and strife in your hearts, ... 3:14	1 I think it meet, as long as I am in this tabernacle, ... 1:13
1 And the fruit of righteousness is sown in peace 3:18	1 to stir you up by putting you in remembrance; 1:13
1 From whence come wars and fightings among you? 4:1	1 when we were with him in the holy mount. 1:18
1 even of your lusts that war in your members? 4:1	1 as unto a light that shineth in a dark place, ... 1:19
1 ask amiss, that ye may consume it upon your lusts. 4:3	1 and the day star arise in your hearts: 1:19
1 The spirit that dwelleth in us lusteth to envy? 4:5	1 there were false prophets also among the people, arise . . 2:1
1 rejoice in your boastings: all such rejoicing is evil. 4:16	1 even as there shall be false teachers among you, ... 2:1
1 Ye have heaped treasure together for the last days. 5:3	1 through covetousness shall they with feigned words 2:3
1 nourished your hearts, as in a day of slaughter. 5:5	1 the filthy conversation of the wicked: (NT) 2:7
1 who spoke in the name of the Lord. (NASB) 5:10	1 For that righteous man dwelling among them, ... 2:8
1 Is any among you afflicted? let him pray. 5:13	1 that walk after the flesh in the lust of uncleanness, ... 2:10
1 Is any sick among you? let him call for the elders 5:14	1 speak evil of the things that they understand not; 2:12
1 anointing him with oil in the name of the Lord: 5:14	1 and shall utterly perish in their own corruption; 2:12
1 Brethren, if any of you do err from the truth, ... 5:19	1 they that count it pleasure to riot in the day time: 2:13
1 through sanctification of the Spirit, ... 1 Pt 1:2	1 sporting themselves with their own deceivings 2:13
1 that fadeth not away, reserved in heaven for you, ... 1:4	1 the dumb ass speaking with man's voice 2:16
1 Who are kept by the power of God through faith 1:5	1 they allure through the lusts of the flesh, ... 2:18
1 ready to be revealed in the last time. 1:5	1 were clean escaped from them who live in error. 2:18
1 Wherein ye greatly rejoice, ... 1:6	1 have escaped ... through the knowledge of the Lord 2:20
1 ye are in heaviness through manifold temptations: 1:6	1 in both which I stir up your pure minds 3:1

ἐν 1706

1 I stir up your pure minds by way of remembrance:..	2 Pt	3:1
1 mockers will come with their mocking (NASB)		3:3
1 day of the Lord will come as a thief in the night;		3:10
1 in the which the heavens shall pass away		3:10
1 and the works that are therein shall be burned up......		3:10
1 to be in all holy conversation and godliness, ...		3:11
1 and a new earth, wherein dwelleth righteousness........		3:13
1 be diligent that ye may be found of him in peace, ...		3:14
1 As also in all his epistles, ...		3:16
1 speaking in them of these things;		3:16
1 in which are some things hard to be understood, ...		3:16
1 grow in grace, and in the knowledge of our Lord		3:18
1 that God is light, and in him is no darkness at all...	1 Jn	1:5
1 and walk in darkness, we lie, and do not the truth:		1:6
1 But if we walk in the light, as he is in the light, ...		1:7
1 But if we walk in the light, as he is in the light, ...		1:7
1 we deceive ourselves, and the truth is not in us.........		1:8
1 we make him a liar, and his word is not in us..........		1:10
1 And hereby we do know that we know him, ...		2:3
1 is a liar, and the truth is not in him.....................		2:4
1 in him verily is the love of God perfected:		2:5
1 hereby know we that we are in him.....................		2:5
1 hereby know we that we are in him.....................		2:5
1 He that saith he abideth in him		2:6
1 which thing is true in him and in you:		2:8
1 which thing is true in him and in you:		2:8
1 that saith he is in the light, and hateth his brother, ...		2:9
1 hateth his brother, is in darkness even until now........		2:9
1 He that loveth his brother abideth in the light, ...		2:10
1 and there is none occasion of stumbling in him.........		2:10
1 But he that hateth his brother is in darkness, ...		2:11
1 is in darkness, and walketh in darkness, ...		2:11
1 ye are strong, and the word of God abideth in you, ...		2:14
1 Love ... neither the things that are in the world.........		2:15
1 love the world, the love of the Father is not in him....		2:15
1 For all that is in the world, the lust of the flesh, ...		2:16
1 Let that therefore abide in you, ...		2:24
1 heard from the beginning shall remain in you, ...		2:24
1 also shall continue in the Son, and in the Father........		2:24
1 also shall continue in the Son, and in the Father........		2:24
1 which ye have received of him abideth in you, ...		2:27
1 even as it hath taught you, ye shall abide in him.......		2:27
1 And now, little children, abide in him;		2:28
1 and not be ashamed before him at his coming..........		2:28
1 to take away our sins; and in him is no sin.............		3:5
1 Whosoever abideth in him sinneth not		3:6
1 for his seed remaineth in him: and he cannot sin, ...		3:9
1 In this the children of God are manifest, ...		3:10
1 He that loveth not his brother abideth in death..........		3:14
1 that no murderer hath eternal life abiding in him........		3:15
1 Hereby perceive we the love of God, ...		3:16
1 how dwelleth the love of God in him?		3:17
1 or with tongue but in deed and truth. (NASB)		3:18
1 And hereby we know that we are of the truth, ...		3:19
1 that keepeth his commandments dwelleth in him, ...		3:24
1 dwelleth in him, and he in him.........................		3:24
1 And hereby we know that he abideth in us, ...		3:24
1 And hereby we know that he abideth in us, ...		3:24
1 Hereby know ye the Spirit of God:		4:2
1 that Jesus Christ is come in the flesh is of God:		4:2
1 confesseth not that Jesus Christ is come in the flesh		4:3
1 and even now already is it in the world.................		4:3
1 because greater is he that is in you, ...		4:4
1 is he that is in you, than he that is in the world.........		4:4
1 In this was manifested the love of God toward us, ...		4:9
1 In this was manifested the love of God toward us, ...		4:9
1 Herein is love, not that we loved God, ...		4:10
1 If we love one another, God dwelleth in us, ...		4:12
1 God dwelleth in us, and his love is perfected in us......		4:12
1 Hereby know we that we dwell in him, ...		4:13
1 Hereby know we that we dwell in him, ...		4:13
1 know we that we dwell in him, and he in us, ...		4:13
1 God dwelleth in him, and he in God...................		4:15
1 God dwelleth in him, and he in God...................		4:15
1 known and believed the love that God hath to us......		4:16
1 and he that dwelleth in love dwelleth in God, ...		4:16
1 and he that dwelleth in love dwelleth in God, ...		4:16
1 dwelleth in love dwelleth in God, and God in him...	1 Jn	4:16
1 Herein is our love made perfect, ...		4:17
1 that we may have boldness in the day of judgment:		4:17
1 because as he is, so are we in this world................		4:17
1 There is no fear in love;		4:18
1 He that feareth is not made perfect in love.		4:18
1 By this we know that we love the children of God, ...		5:2
1 not by water only, but by water and blood..............		5:6
1 not by water only, but by water and blood..............		5:6
1 but with the water and with the blood. (NASB)		5:6
1 For there are three that bear record in heaven, ...		5:7
1 And there are three that bear witness in earth, ...		5:8
1 He that believeth ... hath the witness in himself:		5:10
1 given to us eternal life, and this life is in his Son.......		5:11
1 and the whole world lieth in wickedness.................		5:19
1 and we are in him that is true, ...		5:20
1 even in his Son Jesus Christ. This is the true God, ...		5:20
1 and her children, whom I love in the truth;	2 Jn	1:1
1 For the truth's sake, which dwelleth in us, ...		1:2
1 Christ, the Son of the Father, in truth and love.		1:3
1 that I found of thy children walking in truth, ...		1:4
1 That, as ye have heard ... ye should walk in it.		1:6
1 confess not that Jesus Christ is come in the flesh........		1:7
1 and abideth not in the doctrine of Christ, ...		1:9
1 He that abideth in the doctrine of Christ, ...		1:9
1 the wellbeloved Gaius, whom I love in the truth.	3 Jn	1:1
1 even as thou walkest in the truth.		1:3
1 than to hear that my children walk in truth.		1:4
1 to them that are sanctified by God the Father, ...	Jude	1:1
1 in those things they corrupt themselves.................		1:10
1 These are spots in your feasts of charity, ...		1:12
1 the Lord cometh with ten thousands of his saints, ...		1:14
1 told you there should be mockers in the last time, ...		1:18
1 your most holy faith, praying in the Holy Ghost, ...		1:20
1 Keep yourselves in the love of God, ...		1:21
1 others save with fear, pulling them out of the fire;		1:23
1 before the presence of his glory with exceeding joy, ...		1:24
1 things which must shortly come to pass; (NT)	Rev	1:1
1 and keep those things which are written therein:		1:3
1 John to the seven churches which are in Asia:		1:4
1 and washed us from our sins in his own blood, ...		1:5
1 your brother, and companion in tribulation, ...		1:9
1 and in the kingdom and patience of Jesus Christ, ...		1:9
1 perseverance which are in Jesus (NASB)		1:9
1 was in the isle that is called Patmos, ...		1:9
1 I was in the Spirit on the Lord's day, ...		1:10
1 I was in the Spirit on the Lord's day, ...		1:10
1 send it unto the seven churches which are in Asia;		1:11
1 And in the midst of the seven candlesticks		1:13
1 like unto fine brass, as if they burned in a furnace;		1:15
1 And he had in his right hand seven stars:		1:16
1 countenance was as the sun shineth in his strength......		1:16
1 To the angel of the church in Ephesus (NASB)		2:1
1 he that holdeth the seven stars in his right hand, ...		2:1
1 in the midst of the seven golden candlesticks;		2:1
1 which is in the midst of the paradise of God............		2:7
1 To the angel of the church in Smyrna (NASB)		2:8
1 And to the angel of the church in Pergamos write;		2:12
1 even in those days wherein Antipas was ... martyr, ...		2:13
1 even in those days wherein Antipas was ... martyr, ...		2:13
1 who taught Balac to cast a stumblingblock (NT)		2:14
1 fight against them with the sword of my mouth.........		2:16
1 unto the angel of the church in Thyatira write;		2:18
1 And I will kill her children with death;		2:23
1 But unto you I say, and unto the rest in Thyatira, ...		2:24
1 And he shall rule them with a rod of iron;		2:27
1 And unto the angel of the church in Sardis write;		3:1
1 Thou hast a few names even in Sardis		3:4
1 shall walk with me in white: for they are worthy........		3:4
1 the same shall be clothed in white raiment;		3:5
1 to the angel of the church in Philadelphia write;		3:7
1 will I make a pillar in the temple of my God, ...		3:12
1 To the angel of the church in Laodicea (NASB)		3:14
1 will I grant to sit with me in my throne, ...		3:21
1 and am set down with my Father in his throne.		3:21
1 and, behold, a door was opened in heaven, ...		4:1
1 And immediately I was in the spirit;		4:2

ἐν

1 and, behold, a throne was set in heaven,	Rev 4:2
1 elders sitting, clothed in white raiment;	4:4
1 and in the midst of the throne, and round about	4:6
1 angel proclaiming with a loud voice (NASB)	5:2
1 And no man in heaven, nor in earth,	5:3
1 in the midst of the throne and of the four beasts,	5:6
1 and in the midst of the elders, stood a Lamb	5:6
1 by thy blood out of every kindred, and tongue,	5:9
1 And every creature which is in heaven,	5:13
1 and on the earth, and under the earth,	5:13
1 such as are in the sea, and all that are in them,	5:13
1 that sat on him had a pair of balances in his hand.	6:5
1 I heard a voice in the midst of the four beasts say,	6:6
1 sat on him was Death, and Hell followed with him.	6:8
1 sat on him was Death, and Hell followed with him.	6:8
1 and with death, and with the beasts of the earth.	6:8
1 with white robes, and palms in their hands;	7:9
1 and made them white in the blood of the Lamb.	7:14
1 and serve him day and night in his temple:	7:15
1 silence in heaven about the space of half an hour.	8:1
1 there came hail and fire, mixed with blood (NASB)	8:7
1 creatures which were in the sea, and had life, died;	8:9
1 heard an angel flying through the midst of heaven,	8:13
1 And in those days shall men seek death,	9:6
1 and there were stings in their tails:	9:10
1 whose name in the Hebrew tongue is Abaddon,	9:11
1 And thus I saw the horses in the vision,	9:17
1 their power is in their mouth, and in their tails:	9:19
1 and had heads, and with them they do hurt.	9:19
1 not killed by these plagues yet repented not	9:20
1 And he had in his hand a little book open:	10:2
1 And sware by him that liveth for ever and ever,	10:6
1 created heaven, and the things that therein are,	10:6
1 and the earth, and the things that therein are,	10:6
1 and the sea, and the things which are therein,	10:6
1 But in the days of the voice of the seventh angel,	10:7
1 little book which is open in the hand of the angel	10:8
1 but it shall be in thy mouth sweet as honey.	10:9
1 and it was in my mouth sweet as honey:	10:10
1 and the altar, and them that worship therein.	11:1
1 that it rain not in the days of their prophecy:	11:6
1 to smite the earth with every plague (NASB)	11:6
1 breath of life from God came into them, (NASB)	11:11
1 And they ascended up to heaven in a cloud;	11:12
1 And the same hour was there a great (NT)	11:13
1 in the earthquake were slain ... seven thousand:	11:13
1 and there were great voices in heaven, saying,	11:15
1 And the temple of God was opened in heaven,	11:19
1 was seen in his temple the ark of his testament:	11:19
1 And there appeared a great wonder in heaven;	12:1
1 And she being with child cried (NT)	12:2
1 And there appeared another wonder in heaven;	12:3
1 who was to rule all nations with a rod of iron:	12:5
1 And there was war in heaven:	12:7
1 neither was their place found any more in heaven.	12:8
1 And I heard a loud voice saying in heaven,	12:10
1 rejoice, ye heavens, and ye that dwell in them.	12:12
1 all the world wondered after the beast. (NT)	13:3
1 and his tabernacle, and them that dwell in heaven.	13:6
1 whose names are not written in the book of life	13:8
1 he that killeth with the sword must be killed	13:10
1 with the sword must be killed with the sword.	13:10
1 which dwell therein to worship the first beast,	13:12
1 the voice of harpers harping with their harps:	14:2
1 And in their mouth was found no guile:	14:5
1 And I saw another angel fly in the midst of heaven,	14:6
1 with a loud voice, Fear God, and give glory to him;	14:7
1 followed them, saying with a loud voice,	14:9
1 which is poured out without mixture into the cup	14:10
1 and he shall be tormented with fire and brimstone	14:10
1 Blessed are the dead which die in the Lord	14:13
1 a golden crown, and in his hand a sharp sickle.	14:14
1 with a loud voice to him that sat on the cloud,	14:15
1 angel came out of the temple which is in heaven,	14:17
1 saw another sign in heaven, great and marvellous,	15:1
1 for in them is filled up the wrath of God.	15:1
1 tabernacle of the testimony in heaven was opened:	15:5
1 and every living soul died in the sea.	Rev 16:3
1 power was given unto him to scorch men with fire.	16:8
1 carried me away in the spirit into the wilderness:	17:3
1 a golden cup in her hand full of abominations	17:4
1 and shall eat her flesh, and burn her with fire.	17:16
1 he cried mightily with a strong voice, saying,	18:2
1 in the cup which she hath filled fill to her double.	18:6
1 for she saith in her heart, I sit a queen,	18:7
1 Therefore shall her plagues come in one day,	18:8
1 and she shall be utterly burned with fire:	18:8
1 mighty city! for in one hour is thy judgment come.	18:10
1 decked with gold, and precious stones, and pearls!	18:16
1 city, wherein were made rich all that had ships	18:19
1 were made rich all that had ships in the sea	18:19
1 shall be heard no more at all in thee;	18:22
1 no craftsman, ... shall be found any more in thee;	18:22
1 millstone shall be heard no more at all in thee;	18:22
1 light of a candle shall shine no more at all in thee;	18:23
1 of the bride shall be heard no more at all in thee:	18:23
1 for by thy sorceries were all nations deceived.	18:23
1 And in her was found the blood of prophets,	18:24
1 voice of much people in heaven, saying, Alleluia;	19:1
1 which did corrupt the earth with her fornication,	19:2
1 and in righteousness he doth judge and make war.	19:11
1 the armies which were in heaven followed him	19:14
1 sword, that with it he should smite the nations:	19:15
1 nations: and he shall rule them with a rod of iron:	19:15
1 And I saw an angel standing in the sun;	19:17
1 and he cried out with a loud voice (NASB)	19:17
1 to all the fowls that fly in the midst of heaven,	19:17
1 the false prophet ... with which he deceived them	19:20
1 alive into a lake of fire burning with brimstone.	19:20
1 And the remnant were slain with the sword	19:21
1 holy is he that hath part in the first resurrection:	20:6
1 nations which are in the four quarters of the earth,	20:8
1 of those things which were written in the books,	20:12
1 And the sea gave up the dead which were in it;	20:13
1 hell delivered up the dead which were in them:	20:13
1 And whosoever was not found written in the book	20:15
1 shall have their part in the lake which burneth	21:8
1 away in the spirit to a great and high mountain,	21:10
1 and in them the names of the twelve apostles	21:14
1 And I saw no temple therein:	21:22
1 need of the sun, neither of the moon, to shine in it:	21:23
1 them which are saved shall walk in the light of it:	21:24
1 they which are written in the Lamb's book of life:	21:27
1 In the midst of the street of it,	22:2
1 the throne of God and of the Lamb shall be in it;	22:3
1 the things which must shortly be done. (NT)	22:6
1 unto him the plagues that are written in this book:	22:18
1 and from the things which are written in this book.	22:19

Classical Greek

The most widely used preposition in the New Testament, *en* was also extensively relied upon in Greek literature and nonliterary writings of every kind. As in the New Testament the meaning of *en* is in large part determined by its context; nonetheless, there are four basic functions in classical Greek when *en* occurs with the dative case. Except for some unique New Testament functions, these distinctions hold true for Koine Greek as well. With the dative case (which it always takes unless used adverbially) *en* can function: (1) to denote *location*, "in, among, with, at, etc."; (2) to designate *state or condition*, such as to be "in mourning" or "in fear"; (3) to indicate *manner or means* (instrumental), "by, with"; (4) to indicate *time*, "by" (such as "by night or by day"), "during," "at" (at that time), "in" (the period of). We will see in the New Testament another exclusively Christian use.

En also occurs in compound words frequently for emphasis or clarity (cf. *enischuō* [1749] and *ischuō* [2453]), and in classical Greek it can occur without a case and function as an adverb (*en de* = "and therein"). (See *Liddell-Scott*; Blass and DeBrunner, *A Greek Grammar of the New Testament*, pp.106-109; 117-118; Turner, *Grammer of New Testament Greek*, 3:240,242,252f.,261f.)

Septuagint Usage

Not surprisingly *en* occurs exhaustively in the Septuagint where it often translates the Hebrew preposition *be*. It adheres primarily to classical usage. *En archē epoiesen ho theos ton ouranon kai tēn gēn*, the opening words of the Book of Genesis, "In the beginning . . . ," is an example of a temporal use. The closing sentence of Genesis speaks of the death of Joseph: " . . . *kai ethēkan en tē sorō en Aiguptō*," "and he was placed *in* a coffin *in* Egypt." These verses represent two classic uses of *en* in the locative sense (Genesis 50:26).

New Testament Usage

The New Testament writers were also familiar with *en* (the most widely used preposition, 2700 times). Their understanding was probably affected by Septuagintal usage and was undoubtedly shaped by the "elasticity" of *en*'s function as a preposition. In Hellenistic Greek it became increasingly less precise (ibid., 3:261ff.). This became even more so in Koine Greek. In addition, the New Testament writers were influenced in their understanding by "new" theological issues raised by the gospel. The New Testament usage can be patterned after the four classical functions (above) and by the added "Christianization" of the language precipitated by new life "in" Christ. These following five groups are abbreviated presentations of this extremely diverse preposition.

(1) *Local*. This predominating group reflects the growing imprecision of *en* as a preposition. Frequently *en* plus a noun indicates the location in which something occurs. The early chapters of Matthew report that Jesus was born *en* Bethlehem (2:1,5) and that John the Baptist was preaching *en* the wilderness (3:1). Often this is a geographic reference, but it does not have to be, e.g., "He stood *en mesō autōn*," "in their midst" (Luke 24:36). (See also Matthew 20:3; Mark 6:17,32; Luke 24:35; Acts 5:18; passim.)

(2) *State or condition*. Although some might suggest this is the group under which Christian usage should fall, they would be overlooking the relational dimensions of the Christian use. "State" or "condition" are limited and cannot convey the unique relationship which is not only a "state" but a "life acted out" in relation to another. One of the clearest examples of the implications of "state or condition" occurs in Second Corinthians. Paul wrote, "Rather, as servants of God we commend ourselves in every way: in great endurance; in troubles, hardships and distresses; in beatings, imprisonments and riots; in hard work, sleepless nights and hunger; in purity, understanding, patience and kindness; in the Holy Spirit and in sincere love . . . " (2 Corinthians 6:4-6, NIV). These are all "*en* phrases," outlining Paul's state or condition.

(3) *Manner and means* (instrumental). Here one encounters both normal usage of *en* and some Christian uses which follow the function of the classic instrumental, but have been influenced by Christian theology. These include expressions like "by the name of Jesus Christ (the Lord, etc.)" (Acts 4:10; cf. Luke 9:49, "in thy name"; 10:17, "through thy name") or "baptized with (*en*) the Holy Ghost" (e.g., Acts 1:5).

This category covers the "means" by which something is accomplished. Jesus confronted His onlookers: "But if I with (*en*) the finger of God cast out devils, no doubt the kingdom of God is come upon you" (Luke 11:20). Everyone taking the sword will "perish with (*en*) the sword" (Matthew 26:52). David is said to have called Jesus Lord "by (*en*) the Spirit" (Matthew 22:43, NIV).

Here, too, *en* functions to describe the manner in which something occurs. The Son of Man will come "in (*en*) the glory of his Father" (Mark 8:38). The Kingdom, likewise, comes "with (*en*) power" (Mark 9:1).

(4) *Temporal*. Often a point or a period in time is intended to be conveyed: "And it came to pass also on (*en*) another sabbath" (Luke 6:6, cf. 6:1). It can also denote a larger period of time: "At that time Jesus . . . " (Matthew 11:25; 12:1). One stylistic feature of Luke's Gospel is that he uses the Hebraism *en tō* plus a present infinitive to express time during which something occurs. He used the same

construction plus an aorist to refer to the time after which something occurs (Turner, *Grammar of New Testament Greek*, 4:47).

(5) *Christian usage*. The uniquely Christian understanding of "*en* formulae" is probably recognized most easily in such phrases as "in the Spirit," "in the Lord," "in Christ," etc. Here *en* is employed to denote a close personal relationship. The sense is not a pure instrumental "by" or the locative "in." Turner (*Grammatical Insights*, p.118ff.) calls this use "mystical." How is the believer "in the Spirit" while simultaneously the Spirit of God resides "in" him or her? "Ye are not in the flesh, but in the Spirit, if . . . the Spirit of God dwell in you" (Romans 8:9; cf. Galatians 2:20, the Spirit of Christ lived in Paul). The answer to such questions is not achieved by pressing some grammatical rule of a preposition's function.

Often the locative or "in the sphere of" sense of *en* comes through. The Christian is to live and act "in the sphere" of his or her relationship to God. Believers stand firm "*en kuriō*" ("in the Lord," 1 Corinthians 15:58). Paul informed the Corinthians that he became their father "in Christ Jesus" (1 Corinthians 4:15). Such usages are hard to define exactly. There seems to be a communal bond between those who are "in Christ," and yet there is a personal dimension in the relationship "with" Him.

John, in his First Epistle, seems also to acknowledge a similar relationship using the language of *en*. Those outside of a relationship with God "walk in (*en*) darkness" (1:6), while believers "walk in the light" (1:7; cf. 2:9,11,27,28). Again, to truly come to grips with this phenomenon of language, one must rely upon context for grasping its meaning. Even with that precaution it is uncertain that anyone will ever in this life be able to understand fully what God has done "in Christ."

(6) *Prepositions and Theology*. Often exegetical choices need to be made on the function of a given preposition (e.g., 1 Corinthians 15:28; 2 Corinthians 5:19). Sometimes such decisions may have a profound effect upon the interpretation of a text. From another perspective, though, one should be careful about erecting a "theology of prepositions." The flexibility which characterized prepositions in Koine Greek must always be remembered. Prepositions like *eis* (1506B) and *en* were never full synonyms, but rather, could be used interchangeably. Chances are if a "point of exegesis" rests upon a particular understanding of a preposition rather than the rest of the text, the interpreter should be on his or her guard against eisegesis. At the same time, the interpreter needs to be sensitive to authorial style or to any motif (e.g., "in Christ") that may dominate a writer's style which does have consistent theological undercurrents. (For one of the best discussions on the use of prepositions in the New Testament see Harris, *Colin Brown*, 3:1171-1215.)

STRONG 1722, BAUER 258-61, MOULTON-MILLIGAN 209-10, KITTEL 2:537-43, LIDDELL-SCOTT 551-52, COLIN BROWN 3:1171-78,1182-83,1185-86,1188, 1190-94,1198,1200-1201,1204,1207-10,1212-14.

1707. ἐναγκαλίζομαι
enankalizomai verb
Take in one's arms, embrace.

1. ἐναγκαλισάμενος enankalisamenos
nom sing masc part aor mid

1 and when he had taken him in his arms, ... Mark 9:36
1 And he took them up in his arms, ... 10:16

The verb occurs in the Septuagint in only two places (Proverbs 6:10; 24:33). In both it may be rendered the "folding" of one's arms and refers to a lazy person who, in contrast to one who does vigorous work, folds the hands as though settling down to sleep (Zockler, *The Proverbs of Solomon, Lange's Commentaries*, 5:84). Likewise, the New Testament has only two examples of *enankalizomai*. Both are found in the participle form (*enankalsamenos*) in Mark's Gospel (9:36; 10:16) and refer to Jesus' taking the little children in His arms. The verb corresponds to the statement *en ankalais lambano*, "I take in arms."

STRONG 1723, BAUER 261, MOULTON-MILLIGAN 210, LIDDELL-SCOTT 552.

1708. ἐνάλιος enalios adj
Of the sea, things in the sea.

1. ἐναλίων enaliōn gen pl neu

1 and of serpents, and of things in the sea, is tamed, . . . Jas 3:7

Enalios was common in nonbiblical Greek. According to Thayer the singular form refers to that which was in the sea and the plural to sea creatures (*Greek-English Lexicon*). The sole occurrence of *enalios* in the New Testament is James 3:7, which probably is a reference to Genesis 1:20: "Let the waters bring forth abundantly the moving creature that hath life" (cf. verse 21). Here "living creature(s)" (*psuchōn zōsn*, Septuagint) are sea creatures and are equivalent to James' use of *enalion*, "things in the sea." According to James 3:7 natural creation, including marine life, is in subjection to the human race.

STRONG 1724, BAUER 261, LIDDELL-SCOTT 553-54.

1709. ἔναντι enanti prep
Before, in the presence of.
SYNONYM:
κατέναντι katenanti (2683)

1. ἔναντι enanti

1 while he executed the priest's office **before** God	Luke 1:8
1 your heart is not right **before** God (NASB)	Acts 8:21

This word is an adverb, used as an improper preposition, and is a combination of *en* (1706) and *anti* (470). It is common in the Septuagint and is supposed to be a shortened form of *enantion* (1710); however, it is likely that *enanti* is a dialectal variant which came into Koine Greek from either Crete or Delphi about 300 B.C. (see *Moulton-Milligan*). Thayer notes that when *enanti* appears with the genitive case, its meaning "in the presence of" is in the sense of being part of the space that is opposite (*Greek-English Lexicon*). This preposition is nearly synonymous with *enantion* and *enōpion* (1783) and appears in Luke 1:8 where reference is made to Zechariah's serving "before" God in the temple. It also occurs in Acts 8:21 where it is stated that Simon's heart was not right "in the sight of" God; that is, "in the presence of God," and therefore judgment was imminent.

STRONG 1725, BAUER 261, MOULTON-MILLIGAN 211, LIDDELL-SCOTT 554.

1710. ἐναντίον enantion prep
Before, in the presence or sight of.
SYNONYMS:
ἐνώπιον enōpion (1783)
κατενώπιον katenōpion (2684)

1. ἐναντίον enantion

1 took up the bed, and went forth **before** them all;	Mark 2:12
1 both righteous **in the sight of** God, (NASB)	Luke 1:6
1 could not take hold of his words **before** the people:	20:26
1 a prophet mighty ... **before** God and all the people:	24:19
1 wisdom **in the sight of** Pharaoh king of Egypt;	Acts 7:10
1 and like a lamb dumb **before** his shearer,	8:32
1 I have committed nothing **against** the people,	28:17

This improper preposition is the neuter singular of *enantios*. In classical Greek *enantion* is found rarely with the dative case and means "against." It is more commonly found with the genitive case meaning "before." Examples appear in the Septuagint where *enantion* is followed by either a dative or a genitive case. It occurs in the New Testament with the genitive, always signifying "in someone's presence, before."

STRONG 1726, BAUER 261-62, MOULTON-MILLIGAN 211 (see "enantios"), LIDDELL-SCOTT 554.

1711. ἐναντίος enantios adj
Over against, contrary, hostile toward.

בְּלִיַּעַל bᵉlîyaʿal (1139), Wicked (Na 1:11).

1. ἐναντίος enantios nom sing masc
2. ἐναντίων enantiōn gen pl masc
3. ἐναντίους enantious acc pl masc
4. ἐναντίας enantias gen sing fem
5. ἐναντίον enantion nom/acc sing neu
6. ἐναντία enantia nom/acc pl neu

1 tossed with waves: for the wind was **contrary**.	Matt 14:24
1 for the wind was **contrary** unto them:	Mark 6:48
4 when the centurion, which stood over **against** him,	15:39
6 things **contrary** to the name of Jesus of Nazareth...	Acts 26:9
3 under Cyprus, because the winds were **contrary**.	27:4
2 they please not God, and are **contrary** to all men:	1 Th 2:15
4 he that is of the **contrary** part may be ashamed,	Tit 2:8

The adjective *enantios* has *en* (1706) prefixed to *antios*, "set against." In the New Testament the word is used with reference to a contrary wind (Matthew 14:24; Mark 6:48; Acts 27:4) or with a hostile signification. Paul employed *enantios* in 1 Thessalonians 2:15 to describe the unbelieving Jews who were hostile toward everyone who sought to spread the gospel. Likewise this adjective in the neuter singular is used in Acts 28:17 to signify the ideas of opposition and hostility. It was here Paul declared that he had done nothing contrary to ("hostile toward") the Jewish people or their customs (cf. *Bauer*).

STRONG 1727, BAUER 262, MOULTON-MILLIGAN 211, LIDDELL-SCOTT 554-55.

1712. ἐνάρχω enarchō verb
Begin, make a beginning.

COGNATE:
ἀρχή archē (741)

SYNONYMS:
ἄρχω archō (751)
προενάρχομαι proenarchomai (4138)

חָלַל chālal (2591), Profane; hiphil: begin (Nm 16:47, Dt 2:24,25).

קָצִין qātsîn (7389), Captain, commander (Jos 10:24).

1. ἐναρξάμενος enarxamenos
nom sing masc part aor mid
2. ἐναρξάμενοι enarxamenoi
nom pl masc part aor mid

2 Are ye so foolish? **having begun** in the Spirit,........ Gal 3:3
1 that he which **hath begun** a good work in you....... Phlp 1:6

Enarchō is a verb that consistently appears in the middle voice: *enarchomai*. In classical Greek it was often employed in literature describing religious ceremonies, particularly in reference to initiatory rites and sacrificial offerings. Because of its early use in the language of sacrifice, *enarchomai* has been thought to have sacrificial overtones in the New Testament, where the term appears two times (Galatians 3:3; Philippians 1:6). Paul was the only New Testament writer who used it and always with *epiteleō* (1989), "end, complete." But to see this ordinary word as a sacrificial metaphor in Paul's letters reads too much into it. The Christian life may be described as a sacrifice (Romans 12:1), but in the New Testament *enarchomai* is an ordinary word for "beginning" as is *epiteleō* for "ending" (cf. Vincent, *International Critical Commentary, Philippians and Philemon*, pp.7f.).

STRONG 1728, BAUER 262 (see "enarchomai"), MOULTON-MILLIGAN 211 (see "enarchomai"), LIDDELL-SCOTT 557 (see "enarchomai").

1712B. ἔνατος enatos num
Ninth.

1. ἐνάτης enatēs ord gen sing fem
2. ἐνάτῃ enatē ord dat sing fem
3. ἐνάτην enatēn ord acc sing fem

3 Again he went out about the sixth and **ninth** hour, Matt 20:5
1 was darkness over all the land unto the **ninth** hour..... 27:45
3 about the **ninth** hour Jesus cried with a loud voice,.... 27:46
1 darkness over the whole land until the **ninth** hour. Mark 15:33
2 at the **ninth** hour Jesus cried with a loud voice,........ 15:34
1 a darkness over all the earth until the **ninth** hour...Luke 23:44
3 at the **ninth** hour, the hour of prayer (NASB)....... Acts 3:1
3 About the **ninth** hour of the day (NASB)............. 10:3
3 praying ... during the **ninth** (NASB)................. 10:30

Classical Greek and Septuagint Usage
Enatos is an ordinal number commonly found in Greek literature from the time of Homer on. The Septuagint uses *enatos* to translate the Hebrew *tᵉshîʿî*, "ninth," as well as *tēshaʿ* (or *tishʿāh*), "nine." (Where the latter word is used in the sense of "ninth," compare Jeremiah 39:1 [LXX 46:1], *tᵉshîʿî*; and 39:2 [46:2], *tēshaʿ*, both of which are translated *enatos*.)

New Testament Usage
In the New Testament John referred to the topaz as the ninth foundation of the city wall of New Jerusalem (Revelation 21:20). Most often the term is used to refer to the "ninth hour" of the day, or 3 p.m. (Matthew 20:5; 27:45,46; Mark 15:33,34; Luke 23:44). In the Jewish method of keeping time, a new day (24-hour period) began at 6 p.m. The Jews then divided this day into two 12-hour periods, the "day" and the "night." The first hour of the "day" corresponds to our 7 a.m., the third to our 9 a.m., the sixth to our noon, and so on.

Luke identified the ninth hour as the daily time of prayer for the Jews and other believers (Acts 3:1; 10:3,30). It was at this time, during his daily prayers, that Cornelius had his vision of an angel who instructed him to send for Peter.

In some manuscripts of the New Testament the spelling is *ennatos* (1750), but Westcott and Hort, in their *New Testament in the Original Greek*, opted for the shortened spelling based on its use in other First-Century literature.

BAUER 262, MOULTON-MILLIGAN 211, LIDDELL-SCOTT 557.

1713. ἐνδεής endeēs adj
Poor, needy, destitute.

אֶבְיוֹן ʾevyôn (33), Needy, poor (Dt 15:4, 24:14, Is 41:17).

בַּעַל baʿal (1196), Deserving (Prv 3:27).

חָסֵר chāsēr (2741), Want (Prv 13:25).

חָסֵר chāsēr (2742), Lacking (Prv 7:7, 11:12, 15:21).

מַחְסוֹר machsôr (4408), Poor (Prv 21:17).

רָעֵב rāʿēv (7742), Hungry (Prv 27:7).

1. ἐνδεής endeēs nom sing masc

1 Neither was there any among them that **lacked**:......Acts 4:34

Classical Greek and Septuagint Usage
The New Testament sense of *endeēs* is essentially the same as in classical Greek, the Septuagint, and papyri. In the classical authors the word occurs with such nuances as "in need," "lacking," and "deficient" (cf. *Liddell-Scott*).

ἔνδειγμα 1714

The meaning of *endeēs* is basically no different in the papyri where the term expressed a deficiency in the necessities of life or in money to pay for the funeral of one named Philip (for other examples see *Moulton-Milligan*).

New Testament Usage
In the New Testament *endeēs* is found only in Acts 4:34 where the presence of the Spirit prompted the practical expression of ministry to the material needs of fellow Christians. As a result, there were no needy persons among them. Some believe that this may be taken as a fulfillment of the promise of Deuteronomy 15:4: "There shall be no poor among you (*ouk estai en soi endeēs*, Septuagint)."

STRONG 1729, BAUER 262, MOULTON-MILLIGAN 211, LIDDELL-SCOTT 558.

1714. ἔνδειγμα endeigma noun
Evidence, proof, token.
CROSS-REFERENCE:
   δείκνυμι deiknumi (1161)

1. ἔνδειγμα endeigma nom/acc sing neu

1 a **manifest token** of the righteous judgment of God,..2 Th 1:5

According to Robertson, this passive substantive with the termination of *ma* indicates "a thing proved" (*Word Pictures in the New Testament*, 4:42). The active *endeixis* (1716), "a pointing out, proof," appears three times in the New Testament (Romans 3:24f., 2 Corinthians 8:24, Philippians 1:28). In classical Greek *endeigma* is a rare word. It apparently was employed sparingly only by Plato and Demosthenes (cf. *Bauer*). The only occurrence of *endeigma* in the New Testament is 2 Thessalonians 1:5. This passage speaks of the readers' patience and faith as "*manifest token of the righteous judgment of God*." That is, the constancy of their patience and faith in persecution was "manifested proof" of the righteous judgment of God; it pointed to the glory that will be bestowed in the final judgment and to the justice that will be administered to persecutors.

STRONG 1730, BAUER 262, LIDDELL-SCOTT 558.

1715. ἐνδείκνυμι endeiknumi verb
Show, demonstrate, manifest, point out.
COGNATE:
   δείκνυμι deiknumi (1161)

SYNONYMS:
   δείκνυμι deiknumi (1161)
   ἐπιδείκνυμι epideiknumi (1910)
   ὑποδείκνυμι hupodeiknumi (5101)

גָּמַל gāmal (1621), Render, do (Gn 50:15,17).

לָכַד lākhadh (4058), Qal: take (Jos 7:17); niphal: be taken (Jos 7:15,16,18).

רָאָה rā'âh (7495), See; hiphil: show (Ex 9:16).

1. **ἐνδείκνυνται** endeiknuntai 3pl indic pres mid
2. **ἐνδεικνυμένους** endeiknumenous
        acc pl masc part pres mid
3. **ἐνδείκνυσθαι** endeiknusthai inf pres mid
4. **ἐνεδείξατο** enedeixato 3sing indic aor mid
5. **ἐνεδείξασθε** enedeixasthe 2pl indic aor mid
6. **ἐνδείξωμαι** endeixōmai 1sing subj aor mid
7. **ἐνδείξηται** endeixētai 3sing subj aor mid
8. **ἐνδείξασθαι** endeixasthai inf aor mid
9. **ἐνδείξασθε** endeixasthe 2pl impr aor mid
10. **ἐνδεικνύμενοι** endeiknumenoi
        nom pl masc part pres mid

1 **show** the work of the law written in their hearts,...Rom 2:15
6 that I might **show** my power in thee,................. 9:17
8 What if God, willing to **show** his wrath,............... 9:22
9 Wherefore **show** ye to them,..................... 2 Co 8:24
10 Wherefore **show** ye to them,........................ 8:24
7 That in the ages to come he might **show**........... Eph 2:7
7 Jesus Christ **might show** forth all longsuffering,.... 1 Tm 1:16
4 Alexander the coppersmith **did** me much evil:..... 2 Tm 4:14
2 Not purloining, but **showing** all good fidelity;........Tit 2:10
2 but gentle, **showing** all meekness unto all men......... 3:2
5 of love, which ye **have showed** toward his name,.... Heb 6:10
3 that every one of you **do show** the same diligence...... 6:11

Classical Greek
This multipurpose word is at times a legal term meaning "to inform against (one)"; it could also mean "to mark, point out" (Latin *indicare*). In the middle voice or with a participle following, it carried the sense of "to give proof, exhibit" (*Liddell-Scott*). It was a familiar term to many classical Greek writers (e.g., Homer, Sophocles, Plato, and Euripides). Papyri appear to confirm its use in legal contexts (see *Moulton-Milligan*).

Septuagint Usage
In Genesis, the Septuagint employs *endeiknumi* in a nonlegal sense of "to show." Here the connotation is more of "to do," i.e., if someone "shows" respect it is demonstrated by actions. Joseph's brothers feared Joseph would retaliate against them because of the evil they had shown (*endeiknumi*) him (Genesis 50:15,17; cf. 2 Maccabees 13:9; 2 Timothy 4:14). Exodus suggests that *endeiknumi* means "to show" in the sense of "to prove." God used Pharaoh "to demonstrate or prove" His power so His name would be proclaimed in all the earth (Exodus 9:16; cf. 2 Maccabees 9:8). A rare use of the substantive *endeiktēs* occurs in 2 Maccabees

where the connotation of "informant" comes through (4:1).

New Testament Usage
By the time of the New Testament *endeiknumi* was used exclusively in the middle voice. The parameters of definition resemble the Septuagint's—"to show or demonstrate" (e.g., proof, love) and "to show" in the sense of "to do."

Except for two instances in Hebrews, where it means "to show" (love) or "to demonstrate" (6:10,11), *endeiknumi* occurs exclusively in the Pauline letters (nine times). It can be understood as "to do." Paul wrote that "Alexander the metalworker *did* me a great deal of harm. The Lord will repay him for what he has done" (2 Timothy 4:14, NIV). The idea of "to demonstrate" with the intention of "proving" seems to underlie Romans 9:17 (cf. Exodus 9:16) and especially 2 Corinthians 8:24: "Therefore show (*endeiknumenoi*) ye to them ... the proof (*endeixis*) of your love" (cf. Romans 2:17). The simple notion of "to show" also is attested in Romans 9:22, Ephesians 2:7, Titus 2:10; and 3:2.

STRONG 1731, BAUER 262, MOULTON-MILLIGAN 211, LIDDELL-SCOTT 558.

1716. ἔνδειξις endeixis noun
Demonstration, sign, proof, manifestation.
CROSS-REFERENCE:
δείκνυμι deiknumi (1161)
1. ἔνδειξις endeixis nom sing fem
2. ἔνδειξιν endeixin acc sing fem

2 declare his righteousness for the remission of sins ... Rom 3:25
2 To declare, I say, at this time his righteousness: 3:26
2 and before the churches, the proof of your love, ... 2 Co 8:24
1 which is to them an evident token of perdition, ... Php 1:28

In the New Testament *endeixis* was used only by Paul. It refers to a reality made known by an action. The death of Jesus on the cross was "to declare" (literally "a declaration of") God's righteousness (Romans 3:25). C.K. Barrett translates it "show forth and vindicate" (*Harper's New Testament Commentaries, Romans*, p.79). It can be at the same time negative and positive. The unity of the Philippians was an "evident token of perdition" to opponents but at the same time a "clear omen" (RSV) or "sign" (NIV) of the salvation of the Philippians (Philippians 1:28).

STRONG 1732, BAUER 262, MOULTON-MILLIGAN 211, LIDDELL-SCOTT 558.

1717. ἕνδεκα hendeka num
Eleven.
1. ἕνδεκα hendeka card

1 Then the eleven disciples went away into Galilee, .. Matt 28:16
1 Afterward he appeared unto the eleven .... Mark 16:14
1 and told all these things unto the eleven, ... Luke 24:9
1 and found the eleven gathered together, ... 24:33
1 and he was numbered with the eleven apostles. ...... Acts 1:26
1 But Peter, standing up with the eleven, ... 2:14
1 that he was seen of Cephas, then of the twelve: ... 1 Co 15:5

The name for this Greek numerical is formed from the neuter form of *heis* (1506A), *hen* meaning "one," plus the word for "ten," *deka* (1171). In the New Testament *hendeka* refers only to the disciples who remained after Judas' apostasy (Matthew 28:16; Luke 24:9,33; Acts 1:26; 2:14). In effect, this "11" is the 12 apostles minus 1.

STRONG 1733, BAUER 262, MOULTON-MILLIGAN 211, LIDDELL-SCOTT 558.

1718. ἑνδέκατος hendekatos num
Eleventh.
1. ἑνδέκατος hendekatos ord nom sing masc
2. ἑνδεκάτην hendekatēn ord acc sing fem

2 And about the eleventh hour he went out, ... Matt 20:6
2 that were hired about the eleventh hour, ... 20:9
1 the eleventh, a jacinth; the twelfth, an amethyst. ..... Rev 21:20

This word appears twice in the New Testament. In Revelation 21:20 it is part of the numbering of the 12 gates of the heavenly city, and in Matthew 20:9 it refers to the 11th hour of the day (5 p.m. our time). (See 1717.)

STRONG 1734, BAUER 262, MOULTON-MILLIGAN 211, LIDDELL-SCOTT 558.

1719. ἐνδέχομαι endechomai verb
Be possible, to allow.
CROSS-REFERENCE:
δέχομαι dechomai (1203)
עָרַב 'ārav (6386), Ensure (Ps 119:122 [118:122]—Sixtine Edition only).

1. ἐνδέχεται endechetai 3sing indic pres mid

1 cannot be that a prophet perish out of Jerusalem... Luke 13:33

Classical Greek and Septuagint Usage
This word appears in classical Greek from the time of Herodotus (ca. Fifth Century B.C.) and is used to mean "receive, approve of, admit, allow." Its only occurrence in the canonical portions of the Septuagint concur with this usage. For example, Psalm 119:122 (LXX

ἐνδημέω 1720

118:122) states, "*Receive* thy servant for good ...." However, in the writings of Thucydides (cf. 1.124,140) it is used impersonally to mean "it can be allowed, it is possible." It is this sense of the word that carries over into New Testament usage.

New Testament Usage
Endechomai appears only once in the New Testament. In Luke 13:33 Jesus said, "Nevertheless I must walk today, and tomorrow, and the day following: for it cannot *be* that a prophet perish out of Jerusalem." He was of course referring to His upcoming crucifixion in *Jerusalem*, the very city that had been a focal point of God's relationship with His people. However, Jerusalem had become an evil city. As Schultz points out, "A prophet is nowhere more in danger than in Jerusalem" ("Jerusalem," *Colin Brown*, 2:328).

STRONG 1735, BAUER 262-63, MOULTON-MILLIGAN 212, LIDDELL-SCOTT 559.

1720. ἐνδημέω endēmeō verb
Be at home.
CROSS-REFERENCE:
    δῆμος dēmos (1211B)

1. ἐνδημοῦντες endēmountes
        nom pl masc part pres act
2. ἐνδημῆσαι endēmēsai inf aor act

1 knowing that, whilst we **are at home** in the body,....2 Co 5:6
2 and **to be present** with the Lord......................... 5:8
1 **present** or absent, we may be accepted of him.......... 5:9

The word *endēmeō* (related to *dēmos* [1213]—an organized multitude) is used in classical Greek with the meaning "to be at home" or "to be in one's homeland." In the New Testament this word appears only in 2 Corinthians 5:6,8,9. To "be at home" with the Lord in heaven is to be separated from the fleshly body, that is, physically dead. Ultimately for Paul, pleasing the Lord is of utmost importance whether one dwells in the body or "dwells at home" with the Lord (2 Corinthians 5:9).

STRONG 1736, BAUER 263, MOULTON-MILLIGAN 212, KITTEL 2:63-64, LIDDELL-SCOTT 559, COLIN BROWN 2:788-90.

1721. ἐνδιδύσκω endiduskō verb
Put on clothes, to dress.
SYNONYMS:
    ἀμφιέννυμι amphiennumi (292)
    ἐνδύω enduō (1730)
    ἱματίζω himatizō (2415)

לָבֵשׁ lāvēsh (3980), Qal: wear, be clothed (2 Sm 13:18, Prv 31:21); hiphil: clothe someone (2 Sm 1:24); hithpael: be clothed (Sir 50:11).

1. ἐνεδιδύσκετο enedidusketo 3sing indic imperf mid
2. ἐνδιδύσκουσιν endiduskousin 3pl indic pres act

2 And they **dressed** Him up in purple, (NASB)......Mark 15:17
1 which had devils long time, and ware no clothes,....Luke 8:27
1 which **was clothed** in purple and fine linen,............ 16:19

This word appears three times in the New Testament. It occurs at Luke 8:27 in reference to a man who had not clothed himself since being demon possessed. Jesus used it in the Parable of Lazarus and the Rich Man in telling how the rich man dressed in purple (Luke 16:19). The final occurrence is in reference to the soldiers dressing Jesus in purple (Mark 15:17) as a sign of their mock homage. It was at this time they also placed a crown of thorns on His head.

STRONG 1737, BAUER 263, MOULTON-MILLIGAN 212, LIDDELL-SCOTT 560.

1722. ἔνδικος endikos adj
Just, deserved, in the right.
CROSS-REFERENCE:
    δικαιόω dikaioō (1338)

1. ἔνδικον endikon nom/acc sing fem/neu

1 that good may come? whose damnation is **just**.......Rom 3:8
1 received a **just** recompense of reward;.............. Heb 2:2

Classical Greek
The adjective *endikos* (from *dikē* [1343]) describes things which are "legitimate, deserving," or "right" and people which are "righteous and upright." An adverbial form in classical Greek, *endikōs* meant "justly" or "truly" in a legal sense (*Liddell-Scott*). *Endikos* does not appear in the Septuagint.

New Testament Usage
Two occurrences in the New Testament (Romans 3:8; Hebrews 2:2) are similar references to the "deserved" or "just condemnation" (RSV, Greek *krima* [2890]) or "retribution" (RSV, "penalty," Greek *misthapodosia* [3269]) of those who oppose God's people or His laws. The Book of Hebrews especially illustrates God's beneficent mercy. If God had actually carried out the penalties prescribed by law (*endikos*), there would have been no escape for anyone. The writer of this epistle argued that the punishment will be even greater (still deserved)

for those who reject the superior testimony of Jesus and His apostles concerning the mercy of God (Hebrews 2:2-4).

STRONG 1738, BAUER 263, MOULTON-MILLIGAN 212, LIDDELL-SCOTT 560.

1723. ἐνδόμησις endomēsis adj
Construction, structure, building material.

1. ἐνδόμησις endomēsis nom sing fem
1 And the **building** of the wall of it was of jasper: .... **Rev 21:18**

This word appears only once in the New Testament (Revelation 21:18) according to the *Textus Receptus*. Other modern texts include the word but with an *omega* (ō) rather than an *omicron* (o). It is translated "material" by the NASB, "building" by the KJV, and "structure" by Ford (*The Anchor Bible*, 38:331; also see note 18, 38:334). Neither the NIV nor TEV translate this word.

STRONG 1739, BAUER 263, MOULTON-MILLIGAN 212, LIDDELL-SCOTT 561.

1724. ἐνδοξάζω endoxazō verb
Glorify, honor.
CROSS-REFERENCE:
δοξάζω doxazō (1386)

הָלַל hālal (2054), Praise; hithpael: exult, glory (Is 45:26).
כָּבֵד kāvēdh (3632), Be heavy; niphal: be honored, gain glory (Ex 14:4, 2 Kgs 14:10, Hg 1:8).
עָרַץ ʾārats (6442), Be afraid; niphal: be feared (Ps 89:7 [88:7]).
פָּאַר pāʾar (6526), Hithpael: manifest one's glory (Is 49:3).
פָּלָה pālâh (6640), Be separated; niphal: strip off (Ex 33:16).

1. ἐνδοξασθῇ endoxasthē 3sing subj aor pass
2. ἐνδοξασθῆναι endoxasthēnai inf aor pass

2 When he shall come to be **glorified** in his saints, ... **2 Th 1:10**
1 the name of our Lord Jesus Christ **may be glorified** **1:12**

This word appears only twice in the New Testament (2 Thessalonians 1:10,12). It is built from *doxa* (1385), commonly the "glory" of God. Paul stressed that God's glory means destruction to the wicked, but at the same time "He comes to be glorified in His saints" (verse 10, NASB) and to be the object of "marvel" by the believers. As Paul typically showed, this future expectation has a present implication, i.e., that "the name of our Lord Jesus Christ

may be glorified in you" (verse 12). *Endoxazō* is actually unique to the Septuagint, for when Paul used it in 2 Thessalonians, he was quoting the Septuagint of Psalm 89:7 (LXX 88:7). Because the word has limited use and appears only in the passive voice, it is sometimes shown as the first-person passive *endoxazomai*, although listing it as *endoxazō* (active voice) does not actually change the meaning.

STRONG 1740, BAUER 263 (see "endoxazomai"), MOULTON-MILLIGAN 212, KITTEL 2:254-55 (see "endoxazomai"), LIDDELL-SCOTT 561 (see "endoxazomai"), COLIN BROWN 2:44.

1725. ἔνδοξος endoxos adj
Honored, highly esteemed, splendid, glorious.
CROSS-REFERENCE:
δοξάζω doxazō (1386)

הָדָר hādhar (1991), Nobility (Is 5:14).
יָרֵא yārēʾ (3486), Fear; niphal: terrible, awesome (Dt 10:21, Is 64:3).
כָּבֵד kāvēdh (3632), Be heavy; niphal: honor, noble (Gn 34:19, 2 Sm 23:19, Na 3:10).
כָּבֵד kāvēdh (3633), Great (Is 32:2).
כָּבוֹד kāvôdh (3638), Glory (Is 22:24).
כַּבִּיר kabbîr (3642), Mighty (Jb 34:24).
כּוּן kûn (3679), Stand firm; hiphil: appoint (Jos 4:4).
מַחְמָד machmādh (4398), Glory, beauty (Is 64:11).
עֲלִילָה ʿălîlâh (6173), Deed (Is 12:4).
פֻּארָה puʾrāh (6529), Bough, branch (Is 10:33).
פָּלָא pālāʾ (6623), Niphal: miracle, marvelous thing (Ex 34:10, Jb 5:9, 9:10); hiphil: something wonderful or magnificent (2 Chr 2:9).
פַּרְתְּמִים partemîm (6830), Nobles, princes (Est 1:3, 6:9).
צְבִי tsevî (6905), Glory (Is 13:19, 23:9).
שַׂר sar (8015), Chief, leader (2 Chr 36:14).
תְּהִלָּה tehillâh (8747), Praise (Is 48:9).
תְּרוּעָה terûʿāh (8980), A shout (Nm 23:21).

1. ἐνδόξῳ endoxō dat sing masc
2. ἔνδοξοι endoxoi nom pl masc
3. ἔνδοξον endoxon acc sing fem
4. ἐνδόξοις endoxois dat pl neu

1 Behold, they which are **gorgeously apparelled**, ... **Luke 7:25**
4 all the **glorious** things that were done by him. **13:17**
2 ye are **honourable**, but we are despised. .... **1 Co 4:10**
3 he might present it to himself a **glorious** church, ... **Eph 5:27**

Classical Greek
In classical Greek *endoxos* means "to be honored or esteemed" in the opinions of others. Men held in such high esteem were thought to be "extraordinary" or "magnificent."

Septuagint Usage
The Septuagint uses *endoxos* to refer to honorable men. Most often, however, it relates to the "glorious things" God promised Moses that He would do for His covenant people (cf. Exodus 34:10). In doing so His name would be "glorified" (Isaiah 60:9).

New Testament Usage
Endoxos occurs in the New Testament only four times. Luke used *endoxos* to describe clothes. "Behold, those who are *splendidly* clothed and live in luxury are found in royal palaces" (Luke 7:25, NASB). The word relates to "gorgeously" splendid clothes which were made for the elite. Luke also used the word to refer to the *glorious* acts of Jesus (Luke 13:17).

Paul referred to the Corinthians as "honorable" or "illustrious" when contrasting them with the apostle's condition in 1 Corinthians 4:10. Paul also used the same word to describe the "glorious" estate of the Church in Ephesians 5:27.

STRONG 1741, BAUER 263, MOULTON-MILLIGAN 212, KITTEL 2:254-55, LIDDELL-SCOTT 561, COLIN BROWN 2:44,47.

1726. ἔνδυμα enduma noun
Clothing, garment, raiment.
COGNATE:
  δύνω dunō (1410)
SYNONYMS:
  ἐσθής esthēs (2049B)
  ἱμάτιον himation (2416)
  ἱματισμός himatismos (2417)
  σκέπασμα skepasma (4484)
  χιτών chitōn (5345)

בֶּגֶד beghedh (933), Clothes, garment (Is 63:2).

לְבוּשׁ l*vûsh (3961), Garment, clothes (2 Sm 1:24, Prv 31:22, Lam 4:14).

מִדָּה middāh (4201), Robe, garment (Ps 133:2 [132:2]).

מַלְבּוּשׁ malbûsh (4540), Garment (Zep 1:8).

1. ἔνδυμα enduma nom/acc sing neu
2. ἐνδύματος endumatos gen sing neu
3. ἐνδύμασιν endumasin dat pl neu

```
1  And the same John had his raiment of camel's hair, Matt 3:4
2  life more than meat, and the body than raiment? ....... 6:25
2  And why take ye thought for raiment? ................ 6:28
3  which come to you in sheep's clothing, ............... 7:15
1  a man which had not on a wedding garment; .......... 22:11
1  in hither not having a wedding garment? ............. 22:12
1  was like lightning, and his raiment white as snow: .... 28:3
2  and the body is more than raiment. .............. Luke 12:23
```

The Gospel of Matthew uses this term exclusively with the exception of one occurrence in Luke 12:23. In Matthew (3:4; 6:25; 7:15) *enduma* describes a simple and crude covering (e.g., made of camel's hair), a "raiment" (cf. Luke 12:23). This type of "clothing" is contrasted with a more refined "wedding garment" (Luke 22:11,12) and with the clothing ("raiment") of an angel described as "white as snow" (Matthew 28:3).

STRONG 1742, BAUER 263, MOULTON-MILLIGAN 212, LIDDELL-SCOTT 561.

1727. ἐνδυναμόω endunamoō verb
Strengthen, enable, acquire strength, give power.
COGNATE:
  δύναμαι dunamai (1404)
SYNONYMS:
  βεβαιόω bebaioō (943)
  δυναμόω dunamoō (1406)
  ἐνισχύω enischuō (1749)
  ἐπιστηρίζω epistērizō (1975)
  κραταιόω krataioō (2874)
  κυρόω kuroō (2937)
  σθενόω sthenoō (4454)
  στερεόω stereoō (4583)
  στηρίζω stērizō (4592)

לָבֵשׁ lāvēsh (3980), Come upon (Jgs 6:34, 1 Chr 12:18—Codex Alexandrinus only).

עָזַז 'āzaz (6022), Grew strong, strengthen (Ps 52:7 [51:7]).

1. ἐνδυναμοῦντι endunamounti
      dat sing masc part pres act
2. ἐνεδυνάμωσεν enedunamōsen 3sing indic aor act
3. ἐνδυναμώσαντι endunamōsanti
      dat sing masc part aor act
4. ἐνδυναμοῦ endunamou 2sing impr pres mid
5. ἐνδυναμοῦσθε endunamousthe 2pl impr pres mid
6. ἐνεδυναμώθη enedunamōthē 3sing indic aor pass
7. ἐνεδυναμώθησαν enedunamōthēsan
      3pl indic aor pass
8. ἐνεδυναμοῦτο enedunamouto
      3sing indic imperf pass

```
8  But Saul increased the more in strength, ............. Acts 9:22
6  but was strong in faith, giving glory to God; ........ Rom 4:20
5  Finally, my brethren, be strong in the Lord, ......... Eph 6:10
1  all things through Christ which strengtheneth me .... Phlp 4:13
3  hath enabled me, for that he counted me faithful, ... 1 Tm 1:12
4  be strong in the grace that is in Christ Jesus. ....... 2 Tm 2:1
2  the Lord stood with me, and strengthened me; ........ 4:17
7  out of weakness were made strong, ............... Heb 11:34
```

Classical Greek
In classical Greek *endunamoō* means "to strengthen something or someone." God is often seen as the source of power for those who are physically weak or those who need moral strength.

Septuagint Usage

The Septuagint uses *endunamoō* three times. In Judges 6:34 and 1 Chronicles 12:18 the Greek term replaces the Hebrew word *lāvēsh*, "put on, arm, clothe." Gideon, for example, is said to have been "clothed" with the Spirit of the Lord. The third occurrence of *endunamaō* is at Psalm 52:7 (LXX 51:7) where the KJV uses the phrase "strengthened himself."

New Testament Usage

In the New Testament *endunamoō* means "to strengthen, to enable, to empower." Christ is the source of this strength which is mentioned in Philippians 4:13. The Lord is also the one who inwardly strengthened or enabled Paul to serve (1 Timothy 1:12). *Endunamoō* is used in Ephesians 6:10 to admonish the brethren to be prepared for spiritual warfare by being empowered in the Lord's strength.

Hebrews 11:34 speaks of the Old Testament saints who by faith were "made strong" in the midst of weakness. These were individuals who had conquered kingdoms, put armies to flight, quenched the power of fire—all by receiving this enabling power from God.

STRONG 1743, BAUER 263, MOULTON-MILLIGAN 212, KITTEL 2:284-317, LIDDELL-SCOTT 561-62, COLIN BROWN 2:601.

1728. ἐνδύνω endunō verb

Slip in, creep in, sneak.

1. ἐνδύνοντες endunontes nom pl masc part pres act

1 For of this sort are they which creep into houses, . . . 2 Tm 3:6

In classical Greek the word *endunō* (also spelled *enduō* [1730]) means "to put on (clothes)," "to enter into (a contest)," and more generally, "go into." This word occurs only once in the New Testament (2 Timothy 3:6) where it describes the way evil men (or heretics) *creep into* houses in order to get the confidence of "silly women" (*gunaikaria* [see 1127]) in the church.

STRONG 1744, BAUER 263, MOULTON-MILLIGAN 212, LIDDELL-SCOTT 562.

1729. ἔνδυσις endusis noun

A putting on of clothing, a dressing.
CROSS-REFERENCE:
δύνω dunō (1410)

לְבוּשׁ lᵉvûsh (3961), Garment, outer coat (Jb 41:13 [41:4]).

1. ἐνδύσεως enduseōs gen sing fem

1 and of wearing of gold, or of **putting on** of apparel; 1 Pt 3:3

This word occurs only once in the New Testament (1 Peter 3:3) using the construction *enduseōs imatiōn kosmos* which means literally "putting on of adorning garments." *Endusis* refers to a "dressing" or "adornment" that consists of robes (*Bauer*). This action noun is formed from the common verb *enduō* (1730). In the Septuagint it is used of clothing (Esther 5:1; Job 41:5 [LXX 41:4]).

STRONG 1745, BAUER 263, MOULTON-MILLIGAN 212, LIDDELL-SCOTT 562.

1730. ἐνδύω enduō verb

Dress, clothe oneself, put on.
COGNATE:
δύνω dunō (1410)
SYNONYMS:
ἀμφιέννυμι amphiennumi (292)
ἐνδιδύσκω endidusko (1721)
ἱματίζω himatizō (2415)

חָגַר chāghar (2391), Wearing, gird (2 Sm 6:14).

לְבוּשׁ lᵉvûsh (3961), Clothe, dress (Jer 10:9).

לָבֵשׁ lāvēsh (3980), Qal: put on, clothed (Ex 29:30, 2 Chr 6:41, Ez 9:3); pual: dressed (2 Chr 5:12, 18:9); hiphil: clothe (Gn 41:42, Jb 10:11, Is 61:10).

לְבֵשׁ lᵉvēsh (A3981), Be clothed; haphel: clothe (Dn 5:29—Aramaic).

נָתַן nāthan (5598), Give; put on (Lv 8:7).

עָלָה ʻālāh (6148), Clothe, wear (Ez 44:17).

1. ἐνδύουσιν enduousin 3pl indic pres act
2. ἐνέδυσαν enedusan 3pl indic aor act
3. ἐνδύσατε endusate 2pl impr aor act
4. ἐνεδύσασθε enedusasthe 2pl indic aor mid
5. ἐνδύσηται endusētai 3sing subj aor mid
6. ἐνδυσώμεθα endusōmetha 1pl subj aor mid
7. ἐνδύσησθε endusēsthe 2pl subj aor mid
8. ἐνδύσασθε endusasthe 2pl impr aor mid
9. ἐνδυσάμενος endusamenos
    nom sing masc part aor mid
10. ἐνδυσάμενοι endusamenoi
    nom pl masc part aor mid
11. ἐνδύσασθαι endusasthai inf aor mid
12. ἐνδεδυμένος endedumenos
    nom sing masc part perf mid
13. ἐνδεδυμένον endedumenon
    acc sing masc part perf mid
14. ἐνδεδυμένοι endedumenoi
    nom pl masc part perf mid

15. ἐνεδύσατο enedusato 3sing indic aor mid
16. ἐνδύσαντες endusantes nom pl masc part aor act

7	nor yet for your body, what ye **shall put on**.......	Matt 6:25
13	a man which **had** not **on** a wedding garment:.........	22:11
16	they **stripped** him, and put on him a scarlet robe.....	27:28
2	and **put** his own raiment **on** him,....................	27:31
12	And John was **clothed** with camel's hair,..........	Mark 1:6
7	be shod with sandals; and not **put on** two coats......	6:9
11	be shod with sandals; and not **put on** two coats.......	6:9
1	And they **clothed** him with purple,...................	15:17
2	and **put** his own clothes on him,....................	15:20
15	who had not **put on** any clothing (NASB).........	Luke 8:27
7	neither for the body, what ye **shall put on**...........	12:22
3	Bring forth the best robe, and **put it on** him;........	15:22
7	until ye **be endued with** power from on high.........	24:49
9	upon a set day Herod, **arrayed** in royal apparel,...	Acts 12:21
6	and let us **put on** the armour of light.............	Rom 13:12
8	But **put** ye **on** the Lord Jesus Christ,.................	13:14
11	For this corruptible must **put on** incorruption,.....	1 Co 15:53
11	and this mortal must **put on** immortality...............	15:53
5	this corruptible **shall have put on** incorruption,........	15:54
5	and this mortal **shall have put on** immortality,........	15:54
10	that being **clothed** we shall not be found naked.....	2 Co 5:3
4	have been baptized into Christ **have put on** Christ...	Gal 3:27
11	And that ye **put on** the new man,....................	Eph 4:24
8	And that ye **put on** the new man,....................	4:24
8	**Put on** the whole armour of God,.....................	6:11
10	and **having** on the breastplate of righteousness;......	6:14
10	And **have put on** the new man, which is renewed....	Col 3:10
8	**Put on** therefore, ... bowels of mercies, kindness,......	3:12
10	**putting on** the breastplate of faith and love;........	1 Th 5:8
13	**clothed with** a garment down to the foot,.............	Rev 1:13
14	seven angels ... **clothed** in pure and white linen,......	15:6
14	**clothed in** fine linen, white and clean................	19:14

Classical Greek
According to classical usage *enduō* especially describes the "putting on" of clothes. From that basic meaning it could be used of "taking on" a number of things or of even "entering into" something such as a contest (*Liddell-Scott*).

Septuagint Usage
The Septuagint uses *enduō* to translate *lāvēsh* which refers to the putting on of a garment or to wearing clothes. The use of the word in the Old Testament sometimes refers to the Spirit coming upon an individual: "And the Spirit of God *came upon* Zechariah the son of Jehoiada the priest ... and said unto them, Thus saith God" (2 Chronicles 24:20; cf. 1 Chronicles 12:18).

New Testament Usage
In the New Testament *enduō* was sometimes used in the literal sense of being clothed with a garment. "To dress" or the concept of putting on clothes is reflected in passages like Mark 6:9 and Acts 12:21.

The New Testament also used *enduō* figuratively to depict the putting on of immortality (1 Corinthians 15:53) and being clothed with Christ (Galatians 3:27). Paul admonished the Ephesians to prepare for spiritual warfare by putting on the breastplate of righteousness and girding their loins with truth (6:14). These things are part of the armor of God needed to resist evil.

Strong 1746, Bauer 264, Moulton-Milligan 212-13, Kittel 2:319-20, Liddell-Scott 562, Colin Brown 1:314-15.

1730B. ἐνδώμησις endōmēsis noun
A building, a thing built in.

1. ἐνδώμησις endōmēsis nom sing fem

1 And the **material** of the wall was jasper (NASB).... Rev 21:18

This term is derived from *en* (1706), "in," and *domaō*, "to build." It was used by the ancient Greeks of a building used for religious rites. Josephus used the term once (*Antiquities* 15.9.6) of a wall built into the sea to form a breakwater for a harbor. In most manuscripts of *Antiquities* the word is spelled *endomēsis*.

New Testament Usage
Revelation 21:18 is the only New Testament passage using *endōmēsis*. There the term refers to a wall of the New Jerusalem. W.E. Vine points out that some interpreters take the word to mean a "fabric" or "roofing." Others take it to mean "foundation." But these renderings are improbable (*Expository Dictionary*, "Building").

Bauer 264, Moulton-Milligan 212, Liddell-Scott 562.

1731. ἔνεδρα enedra noun
Plot, ambush.

COGNATE:
  ἐνεδρεύω enedreuō (1732)
SYNONYM:
  ἐπιβουλή epiboulē (1902)
אָרַב 'ārav (717), An ambush (Jos 8:7).
מַאֲרָב ma'rāv (4133), An ambush (Jos 8:9, Ps 10:8 [9:29]).

1. ἔνεδραν enedran acc sing fem

1 the son ... heard of their **ambush** (NASB).......... Acts 23:16
1 **laying wait** in the way to kill him..................... 25:3

This word appears in classical Greek from the Fifth Century B.C. and describes "a sitting in, a lying in wait, an ambush." It was also used metaphorically to mean "treachery." In the Septuagint it translates the Hebrew word *'ārav* which means "lie in wait, lie in ambush" (Joshua 8:7,9; Psalm 10:8 [LXX 9:29]). It occurs only twice in the New Testament. Both references in

Acts describe the treacherous scheming of the Jews against Paul (Acts 23:16; 25:3).

STRONG 1747, BAUER 264, MOULTON-MILLIGAN 213, LIDDELL-SCOTT 562.

1732. ἐνεδρεύω enedreuō verb
Wait to ambush, lie in wait, plot, lurk.
COGNATES:
ἐνέδρα enedra (1731)
ἔνεδρον enedron (1733)

אָרַב 'ārav (717), Qal: lie in wait, ambush (Dt 19:11, Jgs 9:32, Prv 7:12); piel: set in wait (Jgs 9:25); hiphil: set an ambush (1 Sm 15:5).
אֶרֶב 'erev (719), Lie in wait (Jb 38:40).
רָגַל rāghal (7558), Piel: slander (Sir 5:14).
רָמָה rāmāh (7700), Piel: deceive (Prv 26:19).
רָצַד rātsadh (7812), Watch (Sir 14:22).

1. ἐνεδρεύουσιν enedreuousin 3pl indic pres act
2. ἐνεδρεύοντες enedreuontes
   nom pl masc part pres act

2 Laying wait for him, and seeking to catch .... Luke 11:54
1 lie in wait for him of them more than forty men, ... Acts 23:21

Like *enedra* (1731), this word appears in classical Greek from the Fifth Century B.C. and is used in the Septuagint as well (cf. Deuteronomy 19:11; Joshua 8:4; Judges 9:25,32,34; Psalm 10:9 [LXX 9:30]). It means to "lie in wait (for someone)." Acts 23:21 reflects this meaning in reference to the fasting 40 who wanted to kill Paul. This kind of ambush presupposes a plot made beforehand. Such is the case in Luke 11:54 where the Pharisees and the scribes were figuratively "*laying wait* for him (Jesus), and seeking to catch something out of his mouth, that they might accuse him."

STRONG 1748, BAUER 264, MOULTON-MILLIGAN 213, LIDDELL-SCOTT 562.

1733. ἔνεδρον enedron noun
Plot, ambush.
CROSS-REFERENCE:
ἐνεδρεύω enedreuō (1732)

אָרַב 'ārav (717), Qal: lie in ambush, ambush (Jos 8:2,12, Jgs 16:9,12); piel: set men in ambush, lie in wait (Jgs 9:25—Codex Alexandrinus only).
מַאֲרָב ma'rāv (4133), Lie in wait (Jgs 9:35, 2 Chr 13:13).
מָזוֹר māzôr (4335), Make an end (Ob 7).
צְדִיָּה tsedhîyāh (6924), Ambush, lie in wait (Nm 35:20,22).

1. ἔνεδρον enedron nom/acc sing neu

1 Paul's sister's son heard of their lying in wait, ... Acts 23:16

According to *Moulton-Milligan* and *Bauer* this word appears instead of *enedra* (1731) in variant readings of Acts 23:16 and means "treacherous ambush." It is used in the Septuagint more often than the classical term *enedra* and is used in the more general sense of "fraud." In a fourth-century A.D. papyrus it means a "hindrance" or an "obstruction" (*Liddell-Scott*).

STRONG 1749, BAUER 264, MOULTON-MILLIGAN 213, LIDDELL-SCOTT 562.

1734. ἐνειλέω eneileō verb
Wrap up in.

לוּט lût (4011), Wrapped (1 Sm 21:9).

1. ἐνείλησεν eneilēsen 3sing indic aor act

1 and took him down, and wrapped him in the linen, Mark 15:46

This word is used throughout classical Greek to mean "wrap (up), confine (in something)." It is found once in the Septuagint in reference to the sword of Goliath the Philistine which was "wrapped" in a cloth (1 Samuel 21:9 [LXX 1 Kings 21:9]). *Eneileō* occurs only once in the New Testament (Mark 15:46) and refers to the linen cloth used to *wrap* the body of Jesus. Since it was so late in the afternoon, there was an urgency to place Jesus' body in the tomb before sundown when the Sabbath began (Mark 15:42-43). There was no time to perform the usual anointing of the body with spices before wrapping it in linens. When the women came to do this after the Sabbath had ended, they did not know Jesus already had been "anointed" for burial (Mark 14:6-8) and was now resurrected from the dead (Mark 16:6).

STRONG 1750, BAUER 264, MOULTON-MILLIGAN 213, LIDDELL-SCOTT 562.

1735. ἔνειμι eneimi verb
To be within.
CROSS-REFERENCE:
εἰμί eimi (1498)

1. ἐνόντα enonta nom/acc pl neu part pres act

1 But rather give alms of such things as ye have; .... Luke 11:41

Classical Greek
The meaning of *eneimi* is derived almost entirely from secular literature. It is in Homer's classical writings as well as various papyri (e.g., Papyrus of Magdola, Tebtanis Papyri). In these

sources *eneimi* often means "contents" or "what is within." Polybius shortens *eneimi* to *eni* (1746) to mean "possible."

The word is also used in 2 Clement 19:2. Here the writer used *"ta enonta"* to indicate "what was inside." This can relate to what is inside of an object, a house, or a man.

New Testament Usage
Eneimi is used only once in the New Testament, in Luke 11:41. Here Jesus was dealing with the Pharisee's concern about outward cleansing. In verse 41 the Lord was saying, "But rather give alms of *such things as ye have*; and, behold, all things are clean unto you." In the New Testament *eneimi* refers to "internal contents" or "that within." Others take it to mean "as much as is possible." Notice that the previous verse states, "Did not the one who made the outside make the inside also?" (verse 40, NIV). In light of this context, the New International Version translates verse 41 as follows: "But give *what is inside* to the poor . . . ." Williams translates this verse "but dedicate once for all your *inner self*" (*The New Testament: A Translation in the Language of the People*). It is possible that giving "from the heart" is in view here.

STRONG 1751, BAUER 264, MOULTON-MILLIGAN 213, LIDDELL-SCOTT 562-63.

1736. ἕνεκα heneka prep
Because of, on account of, by reason of.

1. εἵνεκεν heineken
2. ἕνεκεν heneken
3. ἕνεκα heneka

2	they which are persecuted **for** righteousness' **sake**:	Matt 5:10
2	shall say ... evil against you falsely, **for** my **sake**.	5:11
2	brought before governors and kings **for** my **sake**,	10:18
2	and he that loseth his life **for** my **sake** shall find it.	10:39
2	will lose his life **for** my **sake** shall find it.	16:25
2	**For** this **cause** shall a man leave father and mother,	19:5
3	**For** this **cause** shall a man leave father and mother,	19:5
2	or wife, or children, or lands, **for** my name's **sake**,	19:29
3	or wife, or children, or lands, **for** my name's **sake**,	19:29
2	but whosoever shall lose his life **for** my **sake**	Mark 8:35
2	**For** this **cause** shall a man leave his father and	10:7
2	or lands, **for** my **sake**, and the gospel's,	10:29
2	**for** My **sake** and for the gospel's **sake**, (NASB)	10:29
2	be brought before rulers and kings **for** my **sake**,	13:9
2	**because** he hath anointed me to preach the gospel	Luke 4:18
1	**because** he hath anointed me to preach the gospel	4:18
3	out your name as evil, **for** the Son of man's **sake**.	6:22
2	but whosoever will lose his life **for** my **sake**,	9:24
2	wife, or children, **for** the kingdom of God's **sake**,	18:29
1	wife, or children, **for** the kingdom of God's **sake**,	18:29
2	before kings and rulers **for** my name's **sake**.	21:12
2	part knew not **wherefore** they were come together.	Acts 19:32
3	part knew not **wherefore** they were come together.	19:32
3	**For** these **causes** the Jews caught me in the temple,	26:21
2	**because** that for the hope of Israel I am bound	Acts 28:20
1	**because** that for the hope of Israel I am bound	28:20
3	**For** thy **sake** we are killed all the day long;	Rom 8:36
2	**For** thy **sake** we are killed all the day long;	8:36
2	**For** meat destroy not the work of God.	14:20
2	**by reason of** the glory that excelleth.	2 Co 3:10
1	**by reason of** the glory that excelleth.	3:10
1	I did it not **for** his **cause** that had done the wrong,	7:12
2	I did it not **for** his **cause** that had done the wrong,	7:12
1	nor **for** his **cause** that suffered wrong,	7:12
2	nor **for** his **cause** that suffered wrong,	7:12
1	but **that** our care for you in the sight of God	7:12
2	but **that** our care for you in the sight of God	7:12

Classical Greek and Septuagint Usage
Heneka was increasingly prominent in extra-Biblical literature from the Third Century B.C. onward (see *Bauer*). It relates to the advantage or benefit of a thing. It occurs extensively in the Septuagint in that same sense (cf. "therefore" in Genesis 2:24; "for this cause" in Exodus 9:16; "because of" in Psalm 5:8).

New Testament Usage
In the New Testament *heneka* means "for the sake of" or "on account of." It was used most often to refer to privation or persecution. Jesus was speaking of destitution when He said, "Whosoever will lose his life for my sake, the same shall save it" (Luke 9:24). Similarly, in Matthew 5:10 *heneka* deals with persecution: "Blessed are they which are persecuted *for* (the sake of) righteousness . . . for theirs is the kingdom of heaven." Here *heneka* relates to suffering for the sake of Christ.

In Luke 4:18 *heneka* is translated by the KJV as "because." "The Spirit of the Lord is upon me, *because* he hath anointed me to preach the gospel to the poor." Although the NIV translates *heneka* "therefore," the Hebrew Scriptures being referred to here (Isaiah 61:1ff.) show the word *ya'an*, "on account of, because." This translation can be noted in 2 Corinthians 3:10 and 7:12.

STRONG 1752, BAUER 264, MOULTON-MILLIGAN 213, LIDDELL-SCOTT 563.

1736B. ἐνενήκοντα enenēkonta num
Ninety.

1. ἐνενήκοντα enenēkonta card

1	does he not leave the **ninety**-nine (NASB)	Matt 18:12
1	over the **ninety**-nine which have not gone (NASB)	18:13
1	does not leave the **ninety**-nine in the open (NASB)	Luke 15:4
1	than over **ninety**-nine righteous persons (NASB)	15:7

Classical Greek and Septuagint Usage
Enenēkonta is the common term for "90," used from the time of Homer on. The suffix, *konta*, indicates "tens," and is used in numbers from

30 to 90. In the Septuagint *enenēkonta* is used to translate the Hebrew *tish'îm* (see Genesis 5:9; Ezekiel 41:12). Frequently it is joined with other numbers in compound expressions (see Ezra 2:16,20 [LXX 1 Esdras 2:16,20]).

New Testament Usage

Enenēkonta is used only four times in the New Testament, in just two passages (Matthew 18:12,13; Luke 15:4,7). Both passages relate the Parable of the Lost Sheep. In each verse the word is used with *ennea* (1751), "9," to form the number "99." In some manuscripts the expression is written as one word, *ennenēkontaennea* (1752), with an extra "n" inserted.

BAUER 265, MOULTON-MILLIGAN 213-14, LIDDELL-SCOTT 563.

1737. ἐνέργεια energeia noun
Working, power, efficiency.

CROSS-REFERENCE:
ἐργάζομαι ergazomai (2021)

1. ἐνεργείας energeias gen sing fem
2. ἐνέργειαν energeian acc sing fem

```
2  according to the working of his mighty power,....... Eph 1:19
2  given ... by the effectual working of his power......... 3:7
2  the effectual working in the measure of every part,..... 4:16
2  according to the working whereby he is able......... Phlp 3:21
2  I also labour, striving according to his working,...... Col 1:29
1  through the faith of the operation of God,............... 2:12
2  him, whose coming is after the working of Satan.... 2 Th 2:9
2  for this cause God shall send them strong delusion,..... 2:11
```

Classical Greek

Energeia ("working") is related to the word *energos* which means "to be at work" or "to set at work." Robinson sometimes translates *energeia* as "might" (Ephesians 3:7) or "effectual working" (Ephesians 4:16) (*Commentary on Ephesians*, pp.79,104).

In several papyri and epigrams *energeia* often related to magical *powers* and to divine or supernatural *action*. Philo spoke of the cosmic and physical powers working in man and in the world around him. This "working" in the universe was seen as mysterious and often disastrous. (See *Liddell-Scott* for a complete listing of these sources.)

Septuagint Usage

The word has no Hebrew counterpart in the Old Testament. *Energeia* is found in Wisdom of Solomon and 2 and 3 Maccabees. Sometimes it relates to cosmic powers that bring terror (Wisdom of Solomon 13:4) but most often to the activity of God who is the Creator and Sustainer of the world (Bertram, "energeō," *Kittel*, 2:653).

New Testament Usage

Energeia is used in the New Testament as relating to the work of divine or demonic powers. Ephesians 1:19,20 says, " ... according to the *working* of his mighty power, which he wrought in Christ, when he raised him from the dead." In 2 Thessalonians 2:9 *energeia* refers to the working of the devil: " ... even him, whose coming is after the *working* of Satan with all power and signs and lying wonders." (See *energeō* [1738].)

STRONG 1753, BAUER 265, MOULTON-MILLIGAN 214, KITTEL 2:652-54, LIDDELL-SCOTT 563-64, COLIN BROWN 3:1147,1151.

1738. ἐνεργέω energeō verb
Work, operate, accomplish.

COGNATE:
ἐργάζομαι ergazomai (2021)

SYNONYMS:
ἐργάζομαι ergazomai (2021)
κατεργάζομαι katergazomai (2686)
ποιέω poieō (4020)

גָּמַל gāmal (1621), Do, bring (Prv 31:12).
פָּעַל pā'al (6713), Do (Is 41:4).
פֹּעַל pō'al (6714), Get (Prv 21:6).

1. ἐνεργεῖ energei 3sing indic pres act
2. ἐνεργοῦσιν energousin 3pl indic pres act
3. ἐνεργοῦντος energountos
   gen sing masc/neu part pres act
4. ἐνεργῶν energōn nom sing masc part pres act
5. ἐνεργεῖν energein inf pres act
6. ἐνήργησεν enērgēsen 3sing indic aor act
7. ἐνεργήσας energēsas nom sing masc part aor act
8. ἐνεργεῖται energeitai 3sing indic pres mid
9. ἐνεργουμένη energoumenē
   nom sing fem part pres mid
10. ἐνεργουμένης energoumenēs
    gen sing fem part pres mid
11. ἐνεργουμένην energoumenēn
    acc sing fem part pres mid
12. ἐνηργεῖτο enērgeito 3sing indic imperf mid
13. ἐνήργηκεν enērgēken 3sing indic perf act

```
2  mighty works do show forth themselves in him.... Matt 14:2
2  mighty works do show forth themselves in him..... Mark 6:14
12 did work in our members to bring forth fruit....... Rom 7:5
4  but it is the same God which worketh all in all.... 1 Co 12:6
1  all these worketh that one and the selfsame Spirit,.... 12:11
10 is effectual in the enduring of the same sufferings.. 2 Co 1:6
8  So then death worketh in us, but life in you......... 4:12
7  For he that wrought effectually in Peter............. Gal 2:8
6  the same was mighty in me toward the Gentiles:....... 2:8
4  and worketh miracles among you,..................... 3:5
9  but faith which worketh by love...................... 5:6
3  worketh all things after the counsel of his own will: Eph 1:11
```

ἐνέργημα 1739

6	Which he **wrought** in Christ, when he raised him...	Eph 1:20
13	Which he **wrought** in Christ, when he raised him......	1:20
3	that now **worketh** in the children of disobedience:.....	2:2
11	according to the power that **worketh** in us,............	3:20
4	For it is God which **worketh** in you...............	Phlp 2:13
5	both to will and **to do** of his good pleasure...........	2:13
11	his working, which **worketh** in me mightily...........	Col 1:29
8	which effectually **worketh** also in you that believe...	1 Th 2:13
8	For the mystery of iniquity doth already **work**:......	2 Th 2:7
9	The **effectual fervent** prayer of a righteous man......	Jas 5:16

Classical Greek

Energeō—from *en* (1706), "in," plus *ergō*, "work"—means "to be in action, to operate." (The English idea of "to energize" in the sense of "to set at work" is close.) In Hellenism, according to Bertram, *energeō* and its cognates were used of "cosmic or physical forces at work in men or the world around" ("*energeō*," *Kittel*, 2:652). *Moulton-Milligan* observes that in papyri *energeō* always has the idea of "*effective* working."

Septuagint Usage

The Septuagint reveals that the Hebrew contained no precise equivalent to the Greek *energeō*, since it translates—out of four canonical appearances—three Hebrew terms and one additional form. It almost has the sense of "to acquire" (Proverbs 21:6) or "to effect, to bring about" (Proverbs 31:12; cf. Numbers 8:24). The divine accomplishments of the Lord are recalled in Isaiah (41:1), a use similar to the Hellenistic understanding (cf. Wisdom of Solomon 15:11; 16:17).

New Testament Usage

Energeō (as well as its cognates) is essentially a Pauline term. Of the word's 21 appearances 18 are attributed to Paul.

Mark 6:14 (cf. Matthew 14:2) employs *energeō* to describe "the powers (*dunameis* [see 1405]) at work" in Jesus. This association of *energeō* with the divine workings of God (Herod may not have attributed the powers of God, but they were seen as supernatural) dominates the New Testament and is extensive in Paul's writings (e.g., 1 Corinthians 12:6,11; Galatians 2:8; 3:5; Ephesians 1:11).

On a cosmic scale, God "operated" through Christ "to effect" salvation (Ephesians 1:20). He also works in and through His people to effect His purpose and will (Galatians 2:8; Ephesians 2:2; cf. 1 Corinthians 16:9; Philippians 2:13; Colossians 1:29; 1 Thessalonians 2:13). Also on this cosmic level evil powers are "at work" to deceive the wicked, "the children of unbelief" (2 Thessalonians 2:9,11; cf. 2 Corinthians 4:12, of death). "The mystery of iniquity" is already at *work* in the world (2 Thessalonians 2:7); therefore, the child of God must seek refuge in the Lord, the only one who has the power to establish (strengthen) (cf. Romans 16:25). Believers have the confidence that God is able to "do exceeding abundantly above all that we ask or think, according to the power that worketh (*energeō*) in us" (Ephesians 3:20).

In a classic passage James wrote that "the prayer of a righteous man has great power in its effects" (5:16, RSV). The emphasis is upon the "effectiveness" of prayer, not that a prayer is "effective." A similar sense of *energeō* can be seen in Hebrews 4:12 where the related noun form *energēs* (1740) occurs: "For the word of God is quick (*zōn*, 'living'), and *powerful*."

Strong 1754, Bauer 265, Moulton-Milligan 214, Kittel 2:652-54, Liddell-Scott 563-64, Colin Brown 3:1147,1151-52.

1739. ἐνέργημα *energēma* noun

Workings or operations.

Cross-Reference:
ἐργάζομαι *ergazomai* (2021)

1. ἐνεργήματα *energēmata* nom/acc pl neu
2. ἐνεργημάτων *energēmatōn* gen pl neu

2	And there are diversities **of operations**,............	1 Co 12:6
1	To another the **working** of miracles;................	12:10

The only two occurrences of *energēma* in the New Testament are in Paul's discussion of spiritual gifts (1 Corinthians 12:6,10). In 1 Corinthians 12:6 Paul made "operations" parallel to "gifts" (verse 4) and "administrations" (verse 5). This reflects a unity in the "spirituals" just as "Spirit" (verse 4), "Lord" (verse 5), and "God" (verse 6) reflect a unity in the Godhead.

Strong 1755, Bauer 265, Moulton-Milligan 214, Kittel 2:652-54, Liddell-Scott 563-64, Colin Brown 3:1147,1151.

1740. ἐνεργής *energēs* adj

Effective, something that is working, active.

Cognate:
ἐργάζομαι *ergazomai* (2021)

Synonyms:
δυνατός *dunatos* (1409)
ἰσχυρός *ischuros* (2451)
κραταιός *krataios* (2873)

1. ἐνεργής *energēs* nom sing masc/fem

1	For a great door and **effectual** is opened unto me,...	1 Co 16:9
1	communication of thy faith may become **effectual**...	Phlm 1:6
1	For the word of God is quick, and **powerful**,........	Heb 4:12

Energēs is related etymologically to *ergon* (2024), "work," and has the concept of useful activity. It is also used in connection with trades or occupations, e.g., metalwork. It was contrasted with useless idleness.

Classical Greek
In classical Greek thought, *energēs* had a social or ethical sense. Thus it denoted work as a burden laid on a man. The word group in Hellenism was used of cosmic or physical forces at work in man or the world around. Man was judged by his works, which were the basis and meaning of life. His works would include his deeds and his manner of conduct as a life-style.

In the papyri *energēs* describes objects which have been made usable. Examples of this would be tilled land or a working mill. So one can see the object as receiving the effects from another source.

Septuagint Usage
While *energēs* is not found in the Septuagint, the works (*erga*) of God are. The activities of God result in His glory and honor. In contrast, the works of man come out of and result in the curse, sin, and vanity.

New Testament Usage
In the New Testament the verb form *energeō* is used almost exclusively for the work of divine or demonic powers. In 1 Corinthians 16:9 Paul implied that it is God who ultimately makes the work effectual; He was opening a "great and *effectual*" door of ministry. In Philemon 6 Paul prayed that Philemon would be active or zealous in sharing the faith in which God had empowered him. Hebrews 4:12 says, "The word of God is quick, and *powerful* (*energēs*)."

STRONG 1756, BAUER 265, MOULTON-MILLIGAN 214, KITTEL 2:652-54, LIDDELL-SCOTT 563-64, COLIN BROWN 3:1147,1151.

1741. ἐνευλογέω eneulogeō verb
Bless, confer benefits.
CROSS-REFERENCE:
εὐλογέω eulogeō (2108)

בָּרָא bārā' (1282), Create; hiphil: fatten (1 Sm 2:29).

בָּרַךְ bārakh (1313), Niphal: be blessed (Gn 18:18); piel: bless (Ps 10:3 [9:24]); hithpael: be blessed (Gn 22:18, Ps 72:17 [71:17]—only some Sinaiticus texts).

1. ἐνευλογηθήσονται eneulogēthēsontai
3pl indic fut pass

1 shall all the kindreds of the earth be blessed........ Acts 3:25
1 In thee shall all nations be blessed................. Gal 3:8

This is a compound form of *eulogeō* (2108), which is the more common term for "bless" (found more than 30 times in the New Testament). *Eneulogeō* combines a noun for "word" (*logos* [3030]) with the adverb "good" or "well" (*eu* [2074]) and the preposition "in" (*en* [1706]). Hence it means "to speak a good word in, to bless." In the New Testament *eneulogeō* is used only two times (Acts 3:25; Galatians 3:8), and it exclusively refers to God blessing someone in contrast to someone blessing God. In both of these passages *eneulogeō* refers to God bestowing providential care and provision toward His people.

STRONG 1757, BAUER 265, KITTEL 2:765, LIDDELL-SCOTT 564 (see "eneulogeomai"), COLIN BROWN 1:206,212.

1742. ἐνέχω enechō verb
Be angry, hold a grudge, be ensnared.
COGNATE:
ἔνοχος enochos (1761)

שָׂטַם sāṭam (7929), Be bitter, sorely (Gn 49:23).

1. ἐνέχειν enechein inf pres act
2. ἐνεῖχεν eneichen 3sing indic imperf act
3. ἐνέχεσθε enechesthe 2pl impr pres mid

2 Therefore Herodias had a quarrel against him,...... Mark 6:19
1 the scribes and the Pharisees began to urge him....Luke 11:53
3 be not entangled again with the yoke of bondage..... Gal 5:1

Classical Greek and Septuagint Usage
In the classical Greek *enechō*, in the active voice, had the connotation of holding fast to an emotion, a state, and so on. In the passive voice it usually denoted having guilt or deserving punishment. In the Septuagint *enechō* follows classical thought. In Exodus 14:4,7 Pharaoh's hardening his heart may be viewed as holding to his emotion. In Jacob's blessing of his sons (Genesis 49:23), he was influenced somewhat by their previous actions.

New Testament Usage
By the New Testament times *enechō* usually carried a negative aura. It conveyed the meaning of "having a grudge against" someone and acting upon that hostility (cf. Mark 6:19, "Herodias had a quarrel against [John]"). The Pharisees "oppose(d) (Jesus) fiercely" (Luke 11:53, NIV).

Another meaning seen in the New Testament is "to be subject to" or "to let oneself become entangled with." This is the spirit of Galatians 5:1 where Paul admonished his readers not to be "entangled again with the yoke of bondage," for Christ has set us free. A more positive angle is contemplated in 2 Thessalonians 1:4 where Paul wrote that he boasted of their perseverance.

In patristic literature *enechō* connoted being at enmity with or attacking someone. In the passive it came across as being bound as in the marriage bond.

STRONG 1758, BAUER 265, MOULTON-MILLIGAN 214, KITTEL 2:828, LIDDELL-SCOTT 565, COLIN BROWN 2:142.

1743. ἐνθάδε enthade adv
Here, in this place.

1. ἐνθάδε enthade

1	he said unto them, Have ye **here** any meat?	Luke 24:41
1	that I thirst not, neither come **hither** to draw	John 4:15
1	Go, call thy husband, and come **hither**.	4:16
1	which was surnamed Peter, were lodged **there**.	Acts 10:18
1	Do thyself no harm: for we are all **here**.	16:28
1	turned ... world upside down are come **hither** also;	17:6
1	Therefore, when they were come **hither**,	25:17
1	dealt with me, both at Jerusalem, and also **here**,	25:24

As an adverb of place *enthade* may refer to the locality where an event occurs or to where a condition exists, as in Luke 24:41 where Jesus asked, "Have ye here (in this place) any meat?" The word may also refer to the locality to which something or someone comes or to which something or someone is brought. See John 4:16: "Call thy husband, and come *hither* (to this place)."

STRONG 1759, BAUER 266, MOULTON-MILLIGAN 214, LIDDELL-SCOTT 566.

1743B. ἔνθεν enthen adv
From here.

הֵנָּה hennāh (2077), Here and there, to and fro (2 Kgs 4:35, Dn 12:5).

1. ἔνθεν enthen

1	Move from **here** to there, (NASB)	Matt 17:20
1	who wish to come over from **here** to you (NASB)	Luke 16:26

Classical Greek
Enthen, like other adverbs ending in *then*, answers the question "whence?" i.e., "From where?" (see Blass and DeBrunner, *A Greek Grammar of the New Testament*, p.56). It may indicate movement from one place to another or action carried on from a specified time onward. The first meaning dates from the time of Homer, perhaps as early as the Eighth Century B.C. The latter meaning can be traced back at least as far as the Third Century B.C. in the writings of Apollonius of Rhodes (cf. *Bauer*). (Later Christian writers [e.g., Clement, ca. A.D. 95] used it with the sense of "from then on" [cf. *Bauer*].)

Septuagint Usage
In the Septuagint *enthen* is most frequently used in the expression *enthen kai enthen*, which translates several Hebrew expressions and which can be translated several ways including, "in all directions," "on both sides," "to and fro," and "on either end" (see Exodus 26:13; 1 Samuel 14:16 [LXX 1 Kings 14:16]; 2 Kings 4:35 [4 Kings 4:35]). In each instance it carries the idea of "place" rather than "time."

New Testament Usage
Enthen is used only twice in the New Testament, Matthew 17:20; Luke 16:26, both times to indicate movement from one place to another. In the latter verse, from the story of the rich man and Lazarus, Jesus indicated that the chasm which separated Lazarus (in Abraham's presence) from the rich man (in Hades) would not allow passage back and forth: " ... nor can anyone cross over *from there* to us" (NIV).

BAUER 266, LIDDELL-SCOTT 566.

1744. ἐνθυμέομαι enthumeomai verb
Think, deliberate on, bring in mind.

COGNATES:
  ἐνθύμησις enthumēsis (1745)
  θυμόω thumoō (2350)

SYNONYMS:
  ἀναλογίζω analogizō (355)
  βλέπω blepō (984)
  βουλεύομαι bouleuomai (1003)
  διαλογίζομαι dialogizomai (1254)
  δοκέω dokeō (1374)
  εἶδον eidon (1481)
  ἐπιβλέπω epiblepō (1899)
  ἔχω echō (2174)
  ἡγέομαι hēgeomai (2216)
  κατανοέω katanoeō (2627)
  κρίνω krinō (2892)
  λογίζομαι logizomai (3023)
  νοέω noeō (3401)
  νομίζω nomizō (3406)
  οἴομαι oiomai (3496)
  συμβάλλω sumballō (4671)
  συμβουλεύω sumbouleuō (4674)
  ὑπολαμβάνω hupolambanō (5112)
  φρονέω phroneō (5262)

דָּמָה dāmâh (1880), Be like; piel: intend (Is 10:7).

זָמַם zāmam (2246), Devise, plan (Lam 2:17—Codex Alexandrinus only).

חָמַד chāmadh (2629), Covet (Jos 7:21).
חָרַם chāram (2868), Hiphil: devoted, keep oneself (Jos 6:18 [6:17]).
חָשַׁק chāshaq (2945), Desire, be attracted (Dt 21:11).
נָחַם nācham (5341), Niphal: grieved, sorry (Gn 6:6).
צָוָה tsāwāh (6943), Piel: decreed, commanded (Lam 2:17—Codex Alexandrinus only).
שִׂים sîm (7947), Purposed, resolved (Dn 1:8).

1. ἐνθυμεῖσθε enthumeisthe 2pl indic pres mid
2. ἐνθυμουμένου enthumoumenou gen sing masc part pres mid
3. ἐνθυμηθέντος enthumēthentos gen sing masc part aor pass

3 But while he thought on these things, behold,....... Matt 1:20
1 Wherefore think ye evil in your hearts?................. 9:4
2 While Peter thought on the vision, the Spirit said...Acts 10:19

The verb *enthumeomai* signifies reflection or musing on a subject or idea. In Matthew 1:20, for instance, the word indicates that Joseph turned over and over in his mind the circumstances and events surrounding the angel's announcement concerning Christ. The word may also refer to one's surmisings or reasonings, as in Matthew 9:4 where Jesus asked some of the teachers of the Law, "Wherefore *think* ye evil in your hearts?"

STRONG 1760, BAUER 266, MOULTON-MILLIGAN 214-15, KITTEL 3:172, LIDDELL-SCOTT 567.

1745. ἐνθύμησις enthumēsis noun
Thought, reasoning, reflection, deliberation.
COGNATE:
ἐνθυμέομαι enthumeomai (1744)
SYNONYMS:
διαλογισμός dialogismos (1255)
διανόημα dianoēma (1264)
διάνοια dianoia (1265)
ἔννοια ennoia (1755)
ἐπίνοια epinoia (1948)
λογισμός logismos (3027)
νόημα noēma (3402)

1. ἐνθυμήσεως enthumēseōs gen sing fem
2. ἐνθυμήσεων enthumēseōn gen pl fem
3. ἐνθυμήσεις enthumēseis acc pl fem

3 And Jesus knowing their thoughts said,............ Matt 9:4
3 Jesus knew their thoughts, and said unto them,........ 12:25
1 or silver, or stone, graven by art and man's device. Acts 17:29
2 a discerner of the thoughts and intents of the heart...Heb 4:12

This word is a noun denoting one's thought processes or reflections. The Greek ending *-sis* often characterizes a class of nouns that express action or process (Greenlee, *Concise Exegetical Grammar*, p.19). *Enthumēsis* may refer to thoughts that grow out of or are typical of one's bent of character. Matthew 9:4 implies that evil men typically have evil thoughts. *Enthumēsis* often refers to more than simple fleeting thoughts; it also refers to reflective plans or designs as in Acts 17:29 where *enthumēsis* signifies an invention originating in the mind of man, i.e., gold, silver, or stone images of God created by the Athenians or perhaps heathen man in general.

STRONG 1761, BAUER 266, MOULTON-MILLIGAN 215, KITTEL 3:172, LIDDELL-SCOTT 567, COLIN BROWN 1:105-6.

1746. ἔνι eni verb
There is, is present.

בֵּן bēn (1158), Son: be a certain age; was (2 Chr 24:15—Codex Alexandrinus only).
הָיָה hāyāh (2030), Be (Prv 14:23).
עָלָה 'ālāh (6148), Go up; be in (1 Kgs 10:17).

1. ἔνι eni 3sing indic pres act

1 there is not among you one wise man (NASB)...... 1 Co 6:5
1 There is neither Jew nor Greek,..................... Gal 3:28
1 there is neither bond nor free,...................... 3:28
1 there is neither male nor female:................... 3:28
1 Where there is neither Greek nor Jew,............Col 3:11
1 Father of lights, with whom is no variableness,...... Jas 1:17

Eni is a form of the Greek verb *enesti* (see *eimi* [1498]), a second-person singular alternate for *ei* ("you are"). It is equivalent to the impersonal form of the verb *be*. *Eni* occurs only with the negative and only six times in the New Testament. It is translated "there is no" or "there is neither" (Jew nor Gentile) when combined with the negating particles *ouk* (see 3620) and *oudeis* (3625) (see *Bauer*).

STRONG 1762, BAUER 266, MOULTON-MILLIGAN 215, LIDDELL-SCOTT 567.

1747. ἐνιαυτός eniautos noun
Year.

אֹרַח 'ōrach (758), Path (Prv 2:19).
שָׁנָה shānāh (8523), Year (Ex 23:14, 1 Kgs 14:21, Jer 11:23).

1. ἐνιαυτοῦ eniautou gen sing masc
2. ἐνιαυτόν eniauton acc sing masc
3. ἐνιαυτούς eniautous acc pl masc

2 To preach the acceptable year of the Lord.......... Luke 4:19
1 Caiaphas, being the high priest that same year,.... John 11:49
1 but being high priest that year, he prophesied....... 11:51
1 to Caiaphas, ... the high priest that same year....... 18:13
2 year they assembled themselves with the church,....Acts 11:26
2 And he continued there a year and six months,....... 18:11

3 observe days, and months, and times, and years......	Gal 4:10
1 went the high priest alone once every year,..........	Heb 9:7
2 every year with blood of others;.....................	9:25
2 which they offered year by year continually..........	10:1
2 a remembrance again made of sins every year.........	10:3
2 and continue there a year, and buy and sell,.........	Jas 4:13
3 by the space of three years and six months............	5:17
2 for an hour, and a day, and a month, and a year,....	Rev 9:15

Classical Greek
Eniautos has referred to a year's length of time from classical times through the patristic age. The exact meaning comes out of the context and genre of the text. The time frame usually has some specificity such as "one year from today." It occurs in relation to the terms of a contract, for example, in rental agreements which have been preserved from the ancients.

Septuagint Usage
The Septuagint uses the term many times. One representative usage is Exodus 12:2 where the Lord tells the Israelites that 10 days before the Passover will begin the first month of their *year*.

New Testament Usage
This same usage is common in the New Testament. For instance, James wrote of Elijah's prayer which held back rain for 3 1/2 *years* (James 5:17). John, in his Gospel, spoke of the high priest for that *year* (John 11:49).

The New Testament also uses *eniautos* in a more general reference to denote a longer, nonspecific time frame. Thinking in terms of messianic eschatology, Luke 4:19 refers to the age of the Messiah, thus the year (*eniautos*) of the Lord's favor is the age of salvation for men.

STRONG 1763, BAUER 266, MOULTON-MILLIGAN 215, LIDDELL-SCOTT 567-68, COLIN BROWN 3:841.

1748. ἐνίστημι enistēmi verb
To place in, be present, at hand, impending.
COGNATE:
  ἵστημι histēmi (2449)
SYNONYMS:
  ἐφίστημι ephistēmi (2168)
  παραγίνομαι paraginomai (3716)
  παρίστημι paristēmi (3798)

עָמַד 'āmadh (6198), Stand, remain (2 Kgs 13:6—Codex Alexandrinus only).

1. ἐνέστηκεν **enestēken** 3sing indic perf act
2. ἐνεστῶτος **enestōtos** gen sing masc part perf act
3. ἐνεστηκότα **enestēkota** acc sing masc part perf act
4. ἐνεστῶσαν **enestōsan** acc sing fem part perf act
5. ἐνεστῶτα **enestōta** nom/acc pl neu part perf act
6. ἐνστήσονται **enstēsontai** 3pl indic fut mid

5 nor things present, nor things to come,.............	Rom 8:38
5 or things present, or things to come; all are yours;..	1 Co 3:22
4 that this is good for the present distress,................	7:26
2 he might deliver us from this present evil world,.....	Gal 1:4
1 as that the day of Christ is at hand.................	2 Th 2:2
6 that in the last days perilous times shall come.......	2 Tm 3:1
3 Which was a figure for the time then present,........	Heb 9:9

Classical Greek and Septuagint Usage
The basic meaning of *enistēmi* is "to be present," suggesting currentness. The thought includes a temporal sense such as "to enter" as in "the entry of summer." A classical usage of *enistēmi*, "to put or set in place," implies causation when used in the present, future, or some aorist tenses. In the passive voice and past tense, *enistēmi* connotes an interjection such as "to be set in, stand in," or "veto." Related to this *enistēmi* can also mean "to interfere or intercede." The canonical portions of the Septuagint use this word in only three places to translate the Hebrew '*āmadh* which generally means "to take one's stand."

New Testament Usage
The allusion to currentness, "to be present" or "have come," prevailed through the passage of time from the Septuagint through the patristic age. Accordingly, this is the common New Testament usage. In Romans 8:38 Paul wrote that nothing "present" or "in the current circumstances" is able to separate us from the love of God. The same sense prevails in 1 Corinthians 3:22; Galatians 1:4; and 2 Thessalonians 2:2.

The term is used with the idea of imminency in 2 Timothy 3:1 and 1 Corinthians 7:26. When used in this way *enistēmi* has the connotation of "threatening circumstances," as is seen in both passages.

STRONG 1764, BAUER 266, MOULTON-MILLIGAN 215, KITTEL 2:543-44, LIDDELL-SCOTT 568-69.

1749. ἐνισχύω enischuō verb
Give strength, strengthen, invigorate.
COGNATE:
  ἰσχύω ischuō (2453)
SYNONYMS:
  βεβαιόω bebaioō (943)
  δυναμόω dunamoō (1406)
  ἐνδυναμόω endunamoō (1727)
  ἐπιστηρίζω epistērizō (1975)
  σθενόω sthenoō (4454)
  στερεόω stereoō (4583)

אָזַר 'āzar (246), Piel: girded, armed (2 Sm 22:40).

אָמֵץ 'āmēts (563), Piel: strengthen, reinforce (2 Chr 24:13, Is 41:10).

גָּבַר gāvar (1428), Triumph, be valiant (Jer 9:3).

חָזַק chāzaq (2480), Qal: be strong, prevail (Jgs 1:28, 2 Kgs 25:3, Dn 11:5); piel: strengthen, give power (Jgs 3:12, Ps 147:13 [147:2], Ez 34:4); hiphil: strengthen, protect (Dn 11:1); hithpael: encourage, be strong (Gn 48:2, Jgs 20:22, 1 Chr 19:13).

כָּבֵד kāvēdh (3633), Severe, grievous (Gn 12:10, 47:4,13).

מָעוֹז māʿôz (4735), Be a refuge, be a hope (Jl 3:16).

מָשַׁךְ māshakh (5082), Bear, handle (Jgs 5:14—Codex Alexandrinus only).

נָהַל nāhal (5273), Guide; hithpael: lead on, move along (Gn 33:14).

נָצַח nātsach (5514), Piel: direct, lead (1 Chr 15:21).

נָצַר nātsar (5526), Keep (Is 42:6).

עוּז ʿûz (5974), Take refuge; hiphil: flee for safety (Jer 6:1).

שָׂדַד sādhadh (7897), Piel: plow, planted (Hos 10:11).

שׂוּר sûr (7917), Struggle, strive (Hos 12:4).

שָׂרָה sārâh (8021), Struggle, strive (Gn 32:28, Hos 12:3).

1. ἐνισχύων **enischuōn** nom sing masc part pres act
2. ἐνίσχυσεν **enischusen** 3sing indic aor act

1 angel unto him from heaven, **strengthening** him.... Luke 22:43
2 when he had received meat, he **was strengthened**..... Acts 9:19

This is a compound term that combines the verb *ischuō* (2453), "to be strong, to have power," with the preposition *en* (1706), "in." Its basic meaning is "to grow strong, to regain one's strength" as when Jacob, who was sick, strengthened himself to meet Joseph and his two sons who came to visit him (Genesis 48:2).

New Testament Usage

The verb *enischuō* may be used both transitively and intransitively. Transitively it means "to give strength, strengthen" as in Luke 22:43 where an angel came to Jesus, strengthening Him. Intransitively the word means "to receive strength, to be strengthened, to grow strong." See Acts 9:19: "And when he had received meat, he was *strengthened*." While the word is used in other literature, these are the only two occurrences in the New Testament.

STRONG 1765, BAUER 266-67, MOULTON-MILLIGAN 215, LIDDELL-SCOTT 569.

1750. ἔννατος ennatos num
Ninth.

1. ἔνατος **enatos** ord nom sing masc
2. ἐννατῆς **ennatēs** ord gen sing fem
3. ἐννάτῃ **ennatē** ord dat sing fem
4. ἐννάτην **ennatēn** ord acc sing fem

4 Again he went out about the sixth and **ninth** hour, Matt 20:5
2 was darkness over all the land unto the **ninth** hour..... 27:45
4 about the **ninth** hour Jesus cried with a loud voice,.... 27:46
2 darkness over the whole land until the **ninth** hour. Mark 15:33
3 at the **ninth** hour Jesus cried with a loud voice,........ 15:34
2 a darkness over all the earth until the **ninth** hour...Luke 23:44
4 at the hour of prayer, being the **ninth** hour.......... Acts 3:1
4 a vision evidently about the **ninth** hour of the day..... 10:3
4 and at the **ninth** hour I prayed in my house,.......... 10:30
1 the **ninth**, a topaz; the tenth, a chrysoprasus;....... Rev 21:20

Ennatos, also spelled *enatos* (1712B), is the ordinal number nine, one of a series. In the New Testament *ennatos* is often used in conjunction with the word *ōra* (5443), "hour," as in Matthew 20:5. Thayer observes that Acts 3:1 identifies the *ninth* as the hour of prayer, about 3 p.m. (*Greek-English Lexicon*).

STRONG 1766, MOULTON-MILLIGAN 216, LIDDELL-SCOTT 569.

1751. ἐννέα ennea num
Nine.

1. ἐννέα **ennea** card

1 does he not leave the **ninety-nine** (NASB)......... Matt 18:12
1 over the **ninety-nine** which have not gone (NASB)..... 18:13
1 does not leave the **ninety-nine** in the open (NASB) Luke 15:4
1 than over **ninety-nine** righteous persons (NASB)....... 15:7
1 there not ten cleansed? but where are the **nine**?....... 17:17

Ennea is indeclinable in Greek; i.e., it has no other grammatical forms. The word is used several times in the parables concerning the "ninety and *nine*" (sheep). In Luke 17:17 *ennea* is used substantively representing the noun *lepers*; i.e., "Where are the *nine* (lepers)?"

STRONG 1767, BAUER 267, LIDDELL-SCOTT 569.

1752. ἐννενηκονταεννέα ennenēkontaennea num
Ninety-nine.

1. ἐννενηκονταεννέα **ennenēkontaennea** card

1 doth he not leave the **ninety and nine**,............. Matt 18:12
1 than of the **ninety and nine** which went not astray...... 18:13
1 not leave the **ninety and nine** in the wilderness,.... Luke 15:4
1 more than over **ninety and nine** just persons,.......... 15:7

In some modern Greek texts, this word is broken down into its two component terms: *enenēkonta* (1736B), "ninety," and *ennea* (1751), "nine." It was made notable by Jesus' use in the parable known as the "Ninety and Nine." (The "and" is absent in the Greek.)

STRONG 1768, LIDDELL-SCOTT 563 (see "enenēkontaenna").

1753. ἐννεός enneos adj
Speechless, dumb, mute, without sound.

אִלֵּם 'illēm (489), Dumb (Is 56:10).

1. ἐννεοί enneoi nom pl masc
2. ἐνεοί eneoi nom pl masc

1 men which journeyed with him stood **speechless**, ... Acts 9:7
2 men which journeyed with him stood **speechless**, ... 9:7

Enneos, also spelled eneos, is used only one time in the New Testament, although it is found in the Septuagint and other literature. Acts 9:7 implies that the men who were "speechless" (eneos) were not simply withholding their speech but were actually unable to speak, i.e., they were dumb because of fright.

STRONG 1769, BAUER 267, MOULTON-MILLIGAN 216, LIDDELL-SCOTT 563 (see "eneos").

1754. ἐννεύω enneuō verb
Nod, make signs, signify.

CROSS-REFERENCE:
νεύω neuō (3368)

קָרַץ qārats (7460), Wink (Prv 6:13, 10:10).

1. ἐνένευον eneneuon 3pl indic imperf act

1 And they made signs to his father, how he would .... Luke 1:62

Enneuō may refer to "making signs by nodding one's head." The one New Testament usage probably means "to signal by using the hands." In Luke 1:62 the people "made signs" (enneuō) to Zechariah urging him to answer a question.

STRONG 1770, BAUER 267, LIDDELL-SCOTT 570.

1755. ἔννοια ennoia noun
Way of thinking, perception, understanding, intention, purpose, conception.

COGNATE:
νοέω noeō (3401)

SYNONYMS:
γνῶσις gnōsis (1102)
διαλογισμός dialogismos (1255)
διανόημα dianoēma (1264)
διάνοια dianoia (1265)
ἐνθύμησις enthumēsis (1745)
ἐπίγνωσις epignōsis (1907)
ἐπίνοια epinoia (1948)
λογισμός logismos (3027)
νόημα noēma (3402)
νοῦς nous (3426)

בִּינָה bînāh (1035), Understanding (Prv 4:1).

דַּעַת da'ath (1907), Prudent, discernment (Prv 18:15).

דֶּרֶךְ derekh (1932), Way, path (Prv 23:19).

מְזִמָּה mᵉzimmāh (4343), Discretion, prudence (Prv 1:4, 5:2, 8:12).

שֵׂכֶל sēkhel (7961I), Understanding (Prv 16:22).

תְּבוּנָה tᵉvûnāh (8722), Understanding (Prv 2:11).

1. ἔννοιαν ennoian acc sing fem
2. ἐννοιῶν ennoiōn gen pl fem

2 a discerner of the thoughts and **intents** of the heart... Heb 4:12
1 arm yourselves likewise with the same **mind**: .... 1 Pt 4:1

In its earliest uses in classical Greek ennoia simply referred to the act of thinking. By extension it later shows meanings such as "reflection, cogitation" (Liddell-Scott). In its New Testament uses ennoia denotes more than a fleeting thought; it carries the idea of thoughts based upon knowledge and perception. For example, 1 Peter 4:1 states, "Forasmuch then as Christ hath suffered for us in the flesh, arm yourselves likewise with the same mind." Here ennoia means "an understanding based upon careful consideration of a pungent truth." Similarly, in Hebrews 4:12 the writer says that the word of God is "a discerner of the thougths and intents of the heart." Here ennoia denotes the "deep-seated thoughts which have developed into character-shaping intentions, motives, or beliefs."

STRONG 1771, BAUER 267, MOULTON-MILLIGAN 216, KITTEL 4:968-71, LIDDELL-SCOTT 570, COLIN BROWN 3:122-23,125,128.

1756. ἔννομος ennomos adj
Lawful, legal, regular, bound by the law.

CROSS-REFERENCE:
νόμος nomos (3414)

1. ἔννομος ennomos nom sing masc
2. ἐννόμῳ ennomō dat sing fem

2 it shall be determined in a **lawful** assembly .... Acts 19:39
1 but **under the law** to Christ, ... 1 Co 9:21

Classical Greek
Ennomos is related etymologically to the word nemō which means "to allot." Ennomos has the overarching connotation of "what is proper." The basic concept has its foundation in the ancient cults, playing a main role in such. Ennomos was related to any kind of existing custom, order, or traditional usage. Thus it had an ethical or philosophical tenor.

As political order was established throughout the Greek city-states, the term took on juridical significance. This legal drift was not distinct from the religioethical sense.

Within the classical Greek *ennomos* could mean that an action or decision was "within the law, legal" or "ordained by law." When speaking of a person the term carried the thought that the individual was "upright, just" or "keeping within the law." Although the term does not appear in the canonical portions of the Septuagint, this interpretation may be seen easily within the Old Testament. *Ennomos* usually refers to the Law under which Israel lived. In Judaism those who kept the Law were upright or *ennomos*, and those who paid no heed to the Law or did not have the Law were *anomos* ("lawless").

As time went on the legal aspect took precedence. Thus by the Third and Fourth centuries A.D. the term referred to "lawfully or legally called functions" whether it was a meeting or a young man coming of adult age.

New Testament Usage
The New Testament offers examples of both the legal and religioethical senses. In Acts 19:39 the term is translated "lawful assembly" to which the riotous crowd were told they should turn for redress of their grievances. In 1 Corinthians 9:21,22 Paul used the typical Jewish differentiation between those under the Law (*ennomos*) and those outside the Law (*anomos*) to defend his rights as an apostle of the gospel.

STRONG 1772, BAUER 267, MOULTON-MILLIGAN 216, KITTEL 4:1087-88, LIDDELL-SCOTT 570, COLIN BROWN 2:446.

1757. ἔννυχος ennuchos adj
At night.

1. ἔννυχον ennuchon nom/acc sing neu
2. ἔννυχα ennucha nom/acc pl neu

1 in the morning, rising up a great while (NT) .... Mark 1:35
2 in the morning, rising up a great while before day, ... 1:35

The adverb *ennuchos*, meaning "at night" or "during the nighttime," is used only once in the New Testament (and quite infrequently in other literature as well). Mark 1:35 tells of Jesus' rising to pray during the night, or early morning (*prōi ennucha lian*), while it was still dark.

STRONG 1773, BAUER 267, MOULTON-MILLIGAN 216, LIDDELL-SCOTT 570-71.

1758. ἐνοικέω enoikeō verb
Live, dwell in, inhabit.

CROSS-REFERENCE:
οἰκέω oikeō (3474)

אָהֵב 'āhēv (154), Love (Is 66:10—Codex Alexandrinus only).
בַּיִת bayith (1041), Be a father to (Is 22:21).
גּוּר gûr (1513), Stay as a foreigner or traveler, live in (Jer 42:17 [49:17], 44:8 [51:2], 49:18 [29:18]).
יָשַׁב yāshav (3553), Dwell, live (Lv 26:32, 2 Kgs 19:26, Is 5:3).
מְלֹא mᵉlō' (4530), Comes forth, is in (Is 34:1).
מִשְׁכָּן mishkān (5088), Dwell, live (Is 32:18).

1. ἐνοικείτω enoikeitō 3sing impr pres act
2. ἐνοικοῦντος enoikountos gen sing neu part pres act
3. ἐνοικοῦν enoikoun nom/acc sing neu part pres act
4. ἐνῴκησεν enōkēsen 3sing indic aor act
5. ἐνοικήσω enoikēsō 1sing indic fut act
6. ἐνοικοῦσα enoikousa nom sing fem part pres act

6 one doing it, but sin which **indwells** (NASB) .... Rom 7:17
3 by his Spirit **that dwelleth** in you. 8:11
2 by his Spirit **that dwelleth** in you. 8:11
5 as God hath said, I will **dwell** in them, ... 2 Co 6:16
1 Let the word of Christ **dwell** in you richly .... Col 3:16
4 which **dwelt** first in thy grandmother Lois, ... 2 Tm 1:5
2 keep by the Holy Ghost which **dwelleth** in us. 1:14

Often used of God dwelling in something or someone, *enoikeō* is a compound form from the word *house*, *oikos* (3486). One important use of this word is to describe the intimate relationship of Jesus Christ or the Holy Spirit and God's people as in Romans 8:11. The meaning of *enoikeō* is closely related to that of *katoikeō* (2700) and seems to be interchangeable when referring to Christ's (God's) relationship to His people. In three places God or His Spirit are said to "dwell" in ("inhabit") His people; once a command is given to "let the word of Christ dwell in you" (Colossians 3:16); and once faith is said to dwell within the believer (2 Timothy 1:5).

STRONG 1774, BAUER 267, MOULTON-MILLIGAN 216, LIDDELL-SCOTT 571, COLIN BROWN 2:247,251.

1758B. ἐνορκίζω enorkizō verb
To cause to swear, to adjure.
CROSS-REFERENCE:
ὁρκίζω horkizō (3589)

שָׁבַע shāvaʻ (8123), Hiphil: make swear, make an oath (Neh 13:25—Codex Alexandrinus only).

1. ἐνορκίζω enorkizō 1sing indic pres act

1 I **adjure** you by the Lord (NASB) .... 1 Th 5:27

Found on grave inscriptions, this word was often used to warn possible intruders away (either grave robbers or the public who might use the tomb for other corpses, cf. *Moulton-Milligan*). The only New Testament usage of this word is found in 1 Thessalonians 5:27. *Enorkizō* is a strong word meaning "to cause to swear" or "to adjure." In this passage Paul "charged" the Thessalonians as emphatically as he possibly could to have the epistle publicly "read to all the holy brethren."

BAUER 267, MOULTON-MILLIGAN 216-17, KITTEL 5:464, LIDDELL-SCOTT 572 (see "enorkizomai").

1759. ἑνότης henotēs noun

Unity, unanimity, oneness.
CROSS-REFERENCE:
εἷς heis (1506A)

1. ἑνότητα **henotēta** acc sing fem

1 to keep the **unity** of the Spirit in the bond of peace. Eph 4:3
1 Till we all come in the **unity** of the faith,............ 4:13

Classical Greek
This noun occurs from the time of Aristotle (ca. Fourth Century B.C.) and is found in the writings of Plutarch (*Bauer* cites *Moralia* 95A; 416E al.) as well as in the Hellenistic-Jewish writing of the Old Testament Pseudepigrapha (e.g., Testament of Zebulon 8:6). "Unity" is the normal meaning of this noun throughout antiquity. *Henotēs* is not found in the Septuagint.

New Testament Usage
The two occurrences of *henotēs* in the New Testament are restricted to the fourth chapter of Ephesians. One other variant reading in Colossians is attested by Western manuscripts (D* itala Vulgate) and by some minor Byzantine witnesses (F G). Its usage there is entirely consonant with the genuine texts; love binds every virtue together in perfect harmony and unity (Colossians 3:14).

Since unity is a major theme of Ephesians (e.g., 2:14-16,18; 4:4-6; 5:31), it is not surprising to find *henotēs* here. Paul urged the Ephesians to be eager "to keep the unity (*henotēs*) of the Spirit" (4:3). Unity is further defined as a state of "peace," *eirēnē* (1503). Love is the key to effecting unity where there is dissension and for prompting growth in the body of Christ (Ephesians 4:12,16). "Unity" therefore is not passive, but active; it seeks to develop more Christlike knowledge and behavior in the community (4:12,13,16).

STRONG 1775, BAUER 267, MOULTON-MILLIGAN 217, LIDDELL-SCOTT 572, COLIN BROWN 2:719,721.

1760. ἐνοχλέω enochleō verb

Annoy, harass, disturb, trouble.
COGNATE:
ὄχλος ochlos (3657)
SYNONYMS:
ἀναστατόω anastatoō (385)
παρενοχλέω parenochleō (3788)

חָלָה chālâh (2571), Be sick, diseased (Gn 48:1, 1 Sm 19:14, Mal 1:13).

1. ἐνοχλῇ **enochlē** 3sing subj pres act
2. ἐνοχλούμενοι **enochloumenoi**
nom pl masc part pres mid

2 who were **troubled** with unclean spirits (NASB)..... Luke 6:18
1 lest any root of bitterness springing up **trouble** you, Heb 12:15

Enochleō means "cause to create ill will" or even genuine discomfort. The word is often used to describe mental or emotional turmoil. In Luke 6:18 *enochleō* is used to denote harassment by evil spirits; those who were "vexed" with unclean spirits came to hear Jesus preach and to be healed. In Hebrews 12:15 *enochleō* refers to troubling that may lead to spiritual ruin. The writer notes that if anyone "misses the grace of God" (NIV) or allows bitterness to grow in his heart, he will be *troubled* and will defile (see *miainō* [3256]) many. These are the only two occurrences in the New Testament.

STRONG 1776, BAUER 267, MOULTON-MILLIGAN 217, LIDDELL-SCOTT 572.

1761. ἔνοχος enochos adj

Guilty, in danger of judgment, liable.
CROSS-REFERENCE:
ἐνέχω enechō (1742)

אָלַף 'ālaph (509), Learn; piel: crafty (Jb 15:5).
דָּם dām (1879), Blood, bloodguilt (Lv 20:9,11,12, Nm 35:27).
מוּת mûth (4322), Die; hophal: be killed, put to death (Gn 26:11).
רָשַׁע rāshaʿ (7855), Be guilty; hiphil: condemn (Is 54:17).
רָשָׁע rāshāʿ (7857), Guilty (Nm 35:31).

1. ἔνοχος **enochos** nom sing masc
2. ἔνοχον **enochon** acc sing masc
3. ἔνοχοι **enochoi** nom pl masc

1 kill shall be **in danger** of the judgment:............. Matt 5:21
1 without a cause shall be **in danger** of the judgment:..... 5:22
1 say ... Raca, shall be **in danger** of the council:......... 5:22

1 say, Thou fool, shall be **in danger** of hell fire.	Matt 5:22
1 They answered and said, He is **guilty** of death.	26:66
1 but is **in danger** of eternal damnation:	Mark 3:29
2 And they all condemned him to be **guilty** of death.	14:64
1 shall be **guilty** of the body and blood of the Lord.	1 Co 11:27
3 were all their lifetime **subject** to bondage.	Heb 2:15
1 and yet offend in one point, he is **guilty** of all.	Jas 2:10

Classical Greek and Septuagint Usage

This word appears from the time of Aristotle (Fourth Century B.C.) and means "held in, bound by, connected with." During that same time period Plato used this word as a legal term meaning "liable to, subject to." The Septuagint makes special use of *enochos* to translate several Hebrew constructions of *dām* (blood). Usually *dām* is translated in the Septuagint by *haima* (blood) which can also mean "bloody deed, murder, blood line, blood relationship." It is this nuance of "blood guilt," i.e., guilt in relationship, that connects *dām* with *enochos*, intensifying both the cause and state of "guilt" (Exodus 22:3; Leviticus 20:9; Numbers 35:27). A person is responsible to something and that responsibility has been transgressed, thus the person is *enochos* of the consequences. (See Kedar-Kopfstein, "dām," *Theological Dictionary of the Old Testament*, 3:236ff.)

New Testament Usage

This same idea of "guilt" carries into the New Testament usage. When used with the dative case as an indirect object, it refers to the legal sense of "guilt." Matthew 5:22 illustrates this: "But I say unto you, That whosoever is angry with his brother without a cause shall be in danger (liable) of the judgment: and whosoever shall say to his brother, Raca, shall be in danger (liable) of the council: but whosoever shall say, Thou fool, shall be in danger (liable) of hell fire." When used in conjunction with a genitive showing possession or relation, it may refer to punishment (Mark 14:64; cf. latter part of Matthew 5:22). It may also indicate the person or thing against whom the sin has been committed. Paul wrote: "Whoever eats the bread or drinks the cup of the Lord in an unworthy manner *will be guilty* (*enochos*) of sinning against the body and blood of the Lord" (1 Corinthians 11:27, NIV). Another use with the genitive alludes to the crime itself. James 2:10 illustrates this where the crime is breaking the whole Law.

James 2:10 and 1 Corinthians 11:27 use the term in a primitive manner. In both the degree of blameworthiness is not in question but the degree of responsibility is. The Levitical laws tended to be grounded in this concept. The guilt offerings outlined in Leviticus 5 and 6 exemplify this usage.

Less often, *enochos* indicates that a person is subject to someone or something. For example, the writer of Hebrews (2:15) said Christ died that He might "free those who all their lives were *held in* (or subject to) slavery by their fear of death" (NIV).

STRONG 1777, BAUER 267-68, MOULTON-MILLIGAN 217, KITTEL 2:828, LIDDELL-SCOTT 572, COLIN BROWN 2:142-43.

1762. ἔνταλμα entalma noun

Commandment, precept.

SYNONYMS:
διάταγμα diatagma (1291)
δόγμα dogma (1372)
ἐντολή entolē (1769)
ἐπιταγή epitagē (1987)

אֲשֻׁר 'ashshur (864), Path (Jb 23:11).

מִצְוָה mitswāh (4851), Commandment, precept (Jb 23:12, Is 29:13).

1. ἐντάλματα entalmata nom/acc pl neu

1 teaching for doctrines the **commandments** of men.	Matt 15:9
1 teaching for doctrines the **commandments** of men.	Mark 7:7
1 after the **commandments** and doctrines of men?	Col 2:22

Septuagint Usage

Entalma does not appear in secular Greek prior to the New Testament. However, it is used in the Septuagint where it translates two Hebrew terms in its four appearances, *'ashur* ("leading, steps," RSV, or "track") and *mitswāh* ("commandment"). The relationship between *entolē* (1769) and *entalma* can be seen in that *mitswāh* usually stands behind *entolē* (also "commandment") in the Septuagint. However, *'ashshur* is never an equivalent to *entolē*. Perhaps *entalma* is less technical in nature; in any event it is overshadowed by *entolē*. At times *entalmata* refers to the Lord's commandment (Job 23:11; cf. the parallelism with verse 12, *entolē*), and they are "of men" (*entalmata anthrōpōn*; Isaiah 29:13, Hebrew *mitswāh*; cf. Isaiah 55:11, Septuagint only).

New Testament Usage

The three New Testament instances of *entalma* are all either allusions to or citations of Isaiah 29:13. Matthew 15:9 and Mark 7:7 are almost identical to the full Septuagintal text of Isaiah; only the word order is significantly different in the New Testament phrase "teaching

ἐνταφιάζω 1763

for doctrines the commandments of men." Colossians is more an allusion to the stock phrase, "commandments and doctrines of men" (2:22).

It's clear that Mark associated *entalma* with *paradosis* (3724)—i.e., tradition (Mark 7:8; cf. 7:3,5). Matthew made the same connection, but he did not add the coup de grace that Mark did (but cf. Matthew 15:2,3,6). Interestingly, the context of Colossians (2:21), "touch not; taste not; handle not," shares a similar concern over hypocritical ritual (cf. Colossians 2:8, *paradosin tōn anthrōpōn*; 2:16,22).

STRONG 1778, BAUER 268, LIDDELL-SCOTT 574.

1763. ἐνταφιάζω entaphiazō verb
Prepare for burial, wrap up, bury.
COGNATE:
    θάπτω thaptō (2267)
SYNONYMS:
    θάπτω thaptō (2267)
    συγκομίζω sunkomizō (4643)

חָנַט chānaṭ (2690), Embalm (Gn 50:2).

1. ἐνταφιάζειν entaphiazein inf pres act
2. ἐνταφιάσαι entaphiasai inf aor act

2 ointment on my body, she did it for my burial..... Matt 26:12
1 as the manner of the Jews is to bury.............John 19:40

This word refers to interring or embalming a body. It is used only twice in the New Testament, in both instances referring to Jesus. The first occurrence is Matthew 26:12 which speaks of Jesus being anointed by a woman in Bethany "to prepare him for burial" (NIV). The second reference is to the preparation of the body of Jesus for burial by Joseph of Arimathea and Nicodemus (John 19:40). As John stated, it was common Jewish practice not to embalm but to preserve the body with spices.

STRONG 1779, BAUER 268, MOULTON-MILLIGAN 217, LIDDELL-SCOTT 575, COLIN BROWN 1:263-65.

1764. ἐνταφιασμός
entaphiasmos noun
Preparation of a body for burial, burial.
COGNATES:
    θαμβέω thambeō (2261)
    θάπτω thaptō (2267)

1. ἐνταφιασμοῦ entaphiasmou gen sing masc
2. ἐνταφιασμόν entaphiasmon acc sing masc

2 come aforehand to anoint my body to the burying. Mark 14:8
1 against the day of my burying hath she kept this... John 12:7

Like *entaphiazō* (1764), *entaphiasmos* is relatively rare and also applies specifically to the acts of preparing a body for burial. In the papyri the cognate *entaphiastēs* denotes an "embalmer" (Hemer, "Bury," *Colin Brown*, 1:264ff.). Both New Testament occurrences (Mark 14:8; John 12:7) refer to the anointing of Jesus at Bethany in the Passion narratives. Evidently, myrrh and aloes were used in the usual preparation practice (cf. John 19:39). However, the enormous value of the spices Mary brought to Jesus represented a costly act of devotion to Christ. In John 12:2-11 Jesus applied her act of devotion to the theme of His own coming crucifixion and burial (parallel in Mark 14:8). To the Jewish mind, the spices used for preservation of the body were a necessary prerequisite of resurrection (ibid., 1:266). Thus Jesus, by responding as He did to Mary's gift, was adding significance to her act of devotion in light of what He was going to do in His death and resurrection.

STRONG 1780, BAUER 268, MOULTON-MILLIGAN 217, LIDDELL-SCOTT 575, COLIN BROWN 1:263-65.

1765. ἐντέλλομαι entellomai verb
Command, enjoin, give orders.
COGNATE:
    ἐντολή entolē (1769)
SYNONYMS:
    διαμαρτύρομαι diamarturomai (1257)
    διαστέλλω diastellō (1285)
    διατάσσω diatassō (1293)
    ἐπιτάσσω epitassō (1988)
    ἐπιτρέπω epitrepō (1994)
    κελεύω keleuō (2724)
    λέγω legō (2978)
    ὁρκίζω horkizō (3589)
    παραγγέλλω parangellō (3715)
    προστάσσω prostassō (4225)
    συντάσσω suntassō (4781)
    τάσσω tassō (4872)

אָמַר 'āmar (569), Direct, command (Jos 11:9, Est 2:15).

אָצַר 'ātsar (709), Store up; hiphil: put in charge (Neh 13:13—only some Sinaiticus texts).

דָּבַר dāvar (1744), Piel: speak, direct (Jos 4:12, 11:23).

דָּבָר dāvār (1745), Word (1 Kgs 13:17).

נָצַר nātsar (5526), Keep, preserve (Prv 5:2).

פָּנָה pānâh (6680), Turn, go (1 Kgs 2:3).

פָּקַד pāqadh (6734), Qal: appoint, charge (2 Chr 36:23, Is 13:11); niphal: be missed (1 Sm 25:7,21); piel: mass together, muster (Is 13:4).

צָוָה tsāwâh (6943), Piel: command (Gn 2:16, Jos 1:7,

Zec 1:6); pual: was commanded (Ex 34:34, Ez 12:7, 37:7).

1. ἐντέλλομαι entellomai 1sing indic pres mid
2. ἐνετειλάμην eneteilamēn 1sing indic aor mid
3. ἐνετείλατο eneteilato 3sing indic aor mid
4. ἐντειλάμενος enteilamenos
   nom sing masc part aor mid
5. ἐντέταλται entetaltai 3sing indic perf mid
6. ἐντελεῖται enteleitai 3sing indic fut mid

6	He shall give his angels **charge** concerning thee:	Matt 4:6
3	For God **commanded**, saying,	15:4
3	Jesus **charged** them, ... Tell the vision to no man,	17:9
3	**command** to give a writing of divorcement,	19:7
2	observe all ... whatsoever I have **commanded** you:	28:20
3	he answered ... What did Moses **command** you?	Mark 10:3
3	said unto them even as Jesus had **commanded**:	11:6
3	and **commanded** the porter to watch.	13:34
6	He **shall give** his angels **charge** over thee,	Luke 4:10
3	Now Moses in the law **commanded** us,	John 8:5
3	as the Father gave me **commandment**, even so I do.	14:31
1	Ye are my friends, if ye do whatsoever I **command**	15:14
1	These things I **command** you, that ye love	15:17
4	had given **commandments** unto the apostles	Acts 1:2
5	For so hath the Lord **commanded** us, saying,	13:47
3	the testament which God hath **enjoined** unto you.	Heb 9:20
3	and gave **commandment** concerning his bones.	11:22

In classical Greek literature this word means "to command, to commission." In Herodotus (Fifth Century B.C.), for example, it refers to the commission of a king or a ruler (Schrenk, "entellomai," *Kittel*, 2:544). At a later time (Fourth Century A.D.) the word meant "to invest with legal powers" and "to authorize to act" (*Liddell-Scott*). Although this word is spelled *entellō* in a few early Greek writings, it is usually seen as a middle deponent verb (always so in the New Testament). The word occurs over 400 times in the Septuagint, most frequently translating the Hebrew word *tsāwāh*, "to command."

In every use of this verb in the New Testament (except Mark 13:34) there is reference to an authority, either a divine (God, angels) or a pivotal figure (Joseph, Moses) in Jewish history, behind the command. The most significant use is in Matthew 28:20 where the resurrected Christ told His disciples to teach "them (nations) to observe all things whatsoever I have *commanded* you." From this comes the phrase "the Great *Commission*."

STRONG 1781, BAUER 268 (see "entellō"), MOULTON-MILLIGAN 217, KITTEL 2:544-45, LIDDELL-SCOTT 575 (see "entellō"), COLIN BROWN 1:331-32,335,337.

1766. ἐντεῦθεν enteuthen adv

From here, cause.

כֹּה kōh (3662), There (Nm 11:31).

1. ἐντεῦθεν enteuthen

1	Remove **hence** to yonder place;	Matt 17:20
1	cast thyself down from **hence**:	Luke 4:9
1	and depart **hence**: for Herod will kill thee.	13:31
1	they which would pass from **hence** to you cannot;	16:26
1	Take these things **hence**;	John 2:16
1	Depart **hence**, and go into Judaea,	7:3
1	even so I do. Arise, let us go **hence**.	14:31
1	but now is my kingdom not **from hence**.	18:36
1	and two others with him, **on either side** one,	19:18
1	and two others with him, **on either side** one,	19:18
1	come they not **hence**, even of your lusts that war	Jas 4:1
1	**on either side** of the river, was there the tree	Rev 22:2
1	**on either side** of the river, was there the tree	22:2

Enteuthen is an adverb of place or source, generally meaning "here, there," or "from here, from there." The meaning of this word is consistent throughout classical Greek (since the Seventh Century B.C.), the Septuagint (see Genesis 37:17; Exodus 11:1; Numbers 11:31; Judges 6:18), and into the New Testament. One example of this adverb functioning as a term denoting place is Luke 4:9 where it is recorded that Satan tempted Jesus saying, "Cast thyself down *from hence*." An instance where it denotes source is James 4:1, "Don't they (fights and quarrels) come from your desires that battle *within* you?" (NIV).

STRONG 1782, BAUER 268, MOULTON-MILLIGAN 217-18, LIDDELL-SCOTT 576.

1767. ἔντευξις enteuxis noun

Prayer, intercession.

SYNONYMS:
   αἴτημα aitēma (154)
   δέησις deēsis (1157)
   εὐχή euchē (2152)
   ἱκετηρία hiketēria (2404)
   προσευχή proseuchē (4194)

1. ἐντεύξεως enteuxeōs gen sing fem
2. ἐντεύξεις enteuxeis acc pl fem

2	prayers, **intercessions**, and giving of thanks,	1 Tm 2:1
1	For it is sanctified by the word of God and **prayer**.	4:5

Classical Greek and Septuagint Usage
Enteuxis was used as a noun in Plato and meant "meeting" or "encounter." In Aristotle's work *Rhetoric* and in 2 Maccabees 4:8 it means "interview." In the papyri and inscriptions, as well as in early Christian writings, the word refers to "official petitions" and to general and specific kinds of prayers. The noun form does not occur in the canonical portions of the Septuagint. Josephus used it for the "claims" of Cleopatra (cf. Bauernfeind, "enteuxis," *Kittel*, 8:244).

New Testament Usage

Enteuxis occurs only twice in the New Testament (1 Timothy 2:1; 4:5). In 1 Timothy 2:1 Paul stacked up three synonyms for prayer without a connector between them and included "thanksgiving" with them. Bauernfeind believes it is best to see no significant distinction between these words for prayer (ibid.). The structure of the passage helps us to understand how this word is to be understood. Verses 1-7 speak of Paul's exhortation for men to pray for rulers. Verse 8 recaps and provides a transition for the next section regarding the conduct of women. In this verse Paul used one of the three words for prayer in verse 1 and simply said that men are to pray in every place.

First Timothy 4:5 says that *enteuxis*, along with the Word of God, sanctifies food. Food is to be received with thanksgiving by those who have faith and who know the truth. Furthermore, "thanksgiving" occurs here with *enteuxis* two times: verses 3 and 4. *Enteuxis* also is found alongside "thanksgiving" in 2:1. In 4:1ff., then, the prayer that sanctifies food is the prayer that is said over the meal when it is eaten. *Enteuxis* refers to this prayer of consecration and thanksgiving. (See *deēsis* [1157], *proseuchē* [4194], *eucharisteō* [2149], and *entunchanō* [1777].)

STRONG 1783, BAUER 268, MOULTON-MILLIGAN 218, KITTEL 8:244-45, LIDDELL-SCOTT 576, COLIN BROWN 2:860-61.

1768. ἔντιμος entimos adj

Held in honor, highly esteemed, valued, precious.

COGNATE:
τιμάω timaō (4939)

SYNONYM:
τίμιος timios (4941)

אַחֵר 'achēr (311), Other (Neh 5:5).

חֹר chōr (2814), Nobles (Neh 2:16, 5:7, 7:5).

יָקַר yāqar (3478), Be precious (1 Sm 26:21, Is 43:4).

יָקָר yāqār (3479), Precious (Is 28:16).

כָּבֵד kāvēdh (3632), Niphal: honorable (Dt 28:58, Is 3:5).

שַׂר sar (8015), Princes (Jb 34:19).

1. ἔντιμος entimos nom sing masc
2. ἔντιμον entimon acc sing masc
3. ἐντίμους entimous acc pl masc
4. ἐντιμότερος entimoteros comp nom sing masc

1 who was **dear** unto him, was sick, and ready to die. Luke 7:2
4 lest **a more honourable** man than thou be bidden 14:8

3 Receive him ... and hold such in reputation: .... Phlp 2:29
2 but chosen of God, and **precious**, ... 1 Pt 2:4
2 I lay in Sion a chief corner stone, elect, **precious**: 2:6

Classical Greek

Entimos, from *timē* (4940), "honor, respect, value," is descriptive of honored or respected men or "valued" objects. Substantivally it denotes "men of high rank or office" (see *Liddell-Scott*). According to papyri one common application of *entimos* is to military veterans who were discharged "with honor" (see *Moulton-Milligan*).

Septuagint Usage

The Septuagint records the comparative use ("more honorable," "more valued," Numbers 22:15, cf. Wisdom of Solomon 18:12) as well as a normal usage in reference to men (Sirach 10:19,20; as a substantive, Nehemiah 2:16; 4:14,19; Job 34:19; Isaiah 3:5). Certain objects are "precious" (Job 28:10; Psalm 72:14 [LXX: 71:14]; Isaiah 28:16, of the "precious" foundation stone of Zion; cf. Tobit 13:16). In the Septuagint, God is rarely called *entimos*, and even then it is done indirectly ("his name," Deuteronomy 28:58; Tobit 3:11).

New Testament Usage

In the New Testament the sense of "valued" refers to the centurion's slave (*doulos* [1395]) whom Jesus healed (Luke 7:2). The comparative usage is also attested in Luke 14:8 where *entimoteros* refers to a wedding guest who is "more honored or esteemed." Paul asked that his fellow-worker Epaphroditus be welcomed with "honor" or "respect" (Philippians 2:29). In 1 Peter two references are drawn from Isaiah 28:16. One is a direct citation of Isaiah (1 Peter 2:6), and the other (2:4) leads to the conclusion that Peter was again applying the text. Christ—the *precious*, chosen, living cornerstone (verse 6)—makes believers living stones which build the "spiritual house" of a holy priesthood (1 Peter 2:4ff.).

STRONG 1784, BAUER 268-69, MOULTON-MILLIGAN 218, LIDDELL-SCOTT 576, COLIN BROWN 2:48-49.

1769. ἐντολή entolē noun

Command, order, decree, injunction.

COGNATE:
ἐντέλλομαι entellomai (1765)

SYNONYMS:
διάταγμα diatagma (1291)
δόγμα dogma (1372)
ἔνταλμα entalma (1762)
ἐπιταγή epitagē (1987)

ἐντολή 1769

בְּרִית bᵉrîth (1311), Covenant (1 Kgs 11:11).
דָּבָר dāvār (1745), Word; command (Dt 28:14, Jer 19:15).
חֹק chōq (2805), Statutes, decrees (Dt 16:12).
חֻקָּה chuqqāh (2807), Statute (1 Kgs 11:38, Ez 18:21).
טְעֵם tᵉ'ēm (A3052), Regard, attention (Dn 3:12—Aramaic).
יָד yādh (3135), Hand; commandment (2 Chr 29:25).
מִצְוָה mitswāh (4851), Commandment (Dt 6:1,2, 2 Chr 7:19, Jer 35:16 [42:16]).
מִשְׁפָּט mishpāṭ (5122), Judgments (Dt 11:1).
פִּקּוּדִים piqqûdhîm (6740), Commandments, precept (Pss 103:18 [102:18], 119:40,63 [118:40,63]).
קוֹל qôl (7249), Voice (Jos 5:6).
תּוֹכַחַת tôkhachath (8763), Reprimand (Prv 15:5).
תּוֹרָה tôrāh (8784), The Law, law (2 Kgs 21:8, 2 Chr 12:1, 30:16).

1. ἐντολή entolē nom sing fem
2. ἐντολῆς entolēs gen sing fem
3. ἐντολήν entolēn acc sing fem
4. ἐντολαί entolai nom pl fem
5. ἐντολῶν entolōn gen pl fem
6. ἐντολαῖς entolais dat pl fem
7. ἐντολάς entolas acc pl fem

5	break one of these least **commandments**,	Matt 5:19
3	Why do ye ... transgress the **commandment** of God	15:3
3	made the **commandment** of God of none effect	15:6
7	thou wilt enter into life, keep the **commandments**.	19:17
1	which is the great **commandment** in the law?	22:36
1	This is the first and great **commandment**.	22:38
6	On these two **commandments** hang all the law	22:40
3	For laying aside the **commandment** of God,	Mark 7:8
3	Full well ye reject the **commandment** of God,	7:9
3	hardness of your heart he wrote you this **precept**.	10:5
7	Thou knowest the **commandments**,	10:19
1	Which is the first **commandment** of all?	12:28
5	The first of all the **commandments** is,	12:29
1	love the Lord ... this is the first **commandment**.	12:30
1	none other **commandment** greater than these.	12:31
6	walking in all the **commandments** and ordinances	Luke 1:6
3	neither transgressed I ... thy **commandment**:	15:29
7	Thou knowest the **commandments**,	18:20
3	and rested ... according to the **commandment**.	23:56
3	This **commandment** have I received of my Father.	John 10:18
3	and the Pharisees had given a **commandment**,	11:57
7	and the Pharisees had given a **commandment**,	11:57
3	he gave me a **commandment**, what I should say,	12:49
1	I know that his **commandment** is life everlasting:	12:50
3	A new **commandment** I give unto you,	13:34
7	If ye love me, keep my **commandments**.	14:15
7	He that hath my **commandments**,	14:21
3	as the Father gave me **commandment**, even so I do.	14:31
7	If ye keep my **commandments**, ye shall abide	15:10
7	even as I have kept my Father's **commandments**,	15:10
1	This is my **commandment**, ... love one another,	15:12
3	and receiving a **commandment** unto Silas	Acts 17:15
2	But sin, taking occasion by the **commandment**,	Rom 7:8
2	but when the **commandment** came, sin revived,	7:9
1	the **commandment**, which was ordained to life,	7:10
2	For sin, taking occasion by the **commandment**,	7:11
1	and the **commandment** holy, and just, and good.	7:12
2	that sin by the **commandment** might become	7:13
1	and if there be any other **commandment**,	13:9
5	but the keeping of the **commandments** of God.	1 Co 7:19
4	are the **commandments** of the Lord.	14:37
1	are the **commandments** of the Lord.	14:37
5	law of **commandments** contained in ordinances;	Eph 2:15
1	which is the first **commandment** with promise;	6:2
7	touching whom ye received **commandments**:	Col 4:10
3	That thou keep this **commandment** without spot,	1 Tm 6:14
6	heed to Jewish fables, and **commandments** of men,	Tit 1:14
3	have a **commandment** to take tithes of the people	Heb 7:5
2	not after the law of a carnal **commandment**,	7:16
2	a disannulling of the **commandment** going before	7:18
2	Moses had spoken every **precept** to all the people	9:19
2	to turn from the holy **commandment** delivered	2 Pt 2:21
2	and of the **commandment** of us the apostles	3:2
7	that we know him, as he keep us **commandments**.	1 Jn 2:3
7	and keepeth not his **commandments**, is a liar,	2:4
3	Brethren, I write no new **commandment** unto you,	2:7
3	**commandment** which ye had from the beginning.	2:7
1	The old **commandment** is the word	2:7
3	Again, a new **commandment** I write unto you,	2:8
7	we receive ... because we keep his **commandments**,	3:22
1	And this is his **commandment**,	3:23
3	love one another, as he gave us **commandment**.	3:23
7	that keepeth his **commandments** dwelleth in him,	3:24
3	And this **commandment** have we from him,	4:21
7	when we love God, and keep his **commandments**.	5:2
7	the love of God, that we keep his **commandments**:	5:3
4	and his **commandments** are not grievous.	5:3
3	have received a **commandment** from the Father.	2 Jn 1:4
3	lady, not as though I wrote a new **commandment**	1:5
7	this is love, that we walk after his **commandments**.	1:6
1	This is the **commandment**,	1:6
7	which keep the **commandments** of God,	Rev 12:17
7	here are they that keep the **commandments** of God,	14:12
7	Blessed are they that do his **commandments**,	22:14

Classical Greek

In classical Greek *entolē*, derived from the verb *entellomai* (1765), means "I order, I command." Esser notes that "the vb. and the noun occur from the 5th cent. in Aeschylus, Pindar and Herodotus to denote chiefly the instructions given by a person of high social standing to a subordinate" ("Command," *Colin Brown*, 1:331). Schrenk contends that *entolē* and *entellomai* primarily refer to the commands of a king, ruler, or a military leader ("entellomai" *Kittel*, 2:544ff.).

Septuagint Usage

Although *entolē* translates 11 Hebrew words in the Septuagint, *mitswāh*, "commandment," predominates by a wide margin. Only rarely is *entolē* equal to *tôrāh* (e.g., Deuteronomy 17:19; 2 Kings 21:8 [LXX 4 Kings 21:8]; 2 Chronicles 12:1; 30:16). Also playing a minor role, most clearly in the Psalms, is *piqqûdhîm*, "orders, directions." Interestingly, *entolē* is used rather infrequently in both the Minor (not at all) and the Major Prophets (only in Isaiah 48:18; Jeremiah 19:15; 35:16,18 [LXX 42:16,18]; Ezekiel 18:21). These rare occurrences are ordinarily references to God's commandments (qualified by the possessive pronoun *mou*, "my").

In the Pentateuch *entolē* is most important in Deuteronomy where it is equated with God's commandments, i.e., His laws, statutes, and ordinances (e.g., Deuteronomy 4:2; 6:1,2; passim), which are to be closely observed (literally "guarded," *phulassō* [5278]; e.g., Deuteronomy 4:40; 5:26 [LXX 5:29]; 6:17; 7:9; 8:1ff.; cf. Joshua 22:3,5; 1 Samuel 13:13 [LXX 1 Kings 13:13]; 1 Kings 2:3 [LXX 3 Kings 2:3]; 2:43 [3:1]; passim).

Entolē is surprisingly used as the object of Abraham's obedience prior to the giving of the Law on Sinai (Genesis 26:5). It also refers to the "Ten Commandments" written on the tablets of stone (Exodus 24:12, *ton nomon kai tas entolas has egrapsa*). Thus it became recognized as a technical term for the general commandments of the Law, and it acquired a religious meaning which was not otherwise present in classical Greek.

The apocryphal portions of the Septuagint evidently subscribe to this understanding (e.g., 1 Esdras 4:52; 8:7; Tobit 3:4,5; 4:5; Wisdom of Solomon 9:9; 16:6; Sirach 6:37), but Hellenistic-Jewish writers such as Josephus and Philo, preferring instead *nomos* (3414) as a description of God's laws, drifted away from the Septuagintal moorings and were more influenced by Hellenism (ibid., 2:546).

New Testament Usage

Of its wide usage in the New Testament we note its place in the Synoptic Gospels. The "commandments" are *tou kuriou* ("the Lord's") or *tou theou* ("God's") (e.g., Matthew 15:3; Mark 7:8,9; Luke 1:6), but not exclusively. Jesus summarized His own mission as being in concert with the objective of the commandments. He was not set on their abolishment, but He desired to see them obeyed; He even demanded more (e.g., Matthew 19:16-30). Jesus expected a change of motive for fulfilling the Law (Matthew 5:17-20). Positively, He placed the commandments of God against the traditions (*paradosis* [3724]) of men (Matthew 15:3; cf. Mark 7:7f.).

Jesus taught that the commands to love God and to love neighbors could not be separated. Therefore, He spoke of "another commandment" which belonged with "the first" (Matthew 22:39f.; Mark 12:31). The new commandment Jesus gave His disciples was that they should not only love their neighbor, but that they should love them as He loved them. Implicit in the command is that the follower of Christ must be willing to lay down his life for his friend. Nevertheless, a tension between the commandments and the life of faith is present. Matthew's refrain in the Sermon on the Mount, "You have heard it said . . . ," certainly contrasts the old laws with the radical and new expectations of Jesus and His kingdom. But Jesus did not disparage obedience to the commandments; instead, He moved His listeners beyond them.

Johannine Literature

The Johannine corpus affords a different perspective. *Entolas* can be the "orders" of men (John 11:57); Jesus himself was under the "charge" of His Father (John 10:18; 15:10). Like the other Evangelists, John showed that Jesus endorsed obedience to the commandments of God (14:15,21,31; 15:10). The "new commandment" He gave (John 13:34; 15:12) is not in opposition to the "old"; rather, love moves obedience beyond the demands of the Law (1 John 2:3,4,7,8; 3:22ff.; 4:21; 2 John 4,5,6). To obey the commands of Christ is the sign of a believer's love for Him. Even in the Revelation John showed that keeping the "commandments of God" (*entolas tou theou*) is tantamount to having faith (14:12; cf. 12:17).

Pauline Epistles

Paul took a positive stance on the commandments of God and showed them as "holy, just, and good" (Romans 7:12). The commandments of the Law reveal man's sinfulness (Romans 7:8; cf. 2 Peter 2:21), but they do not have the power to bring life since they only "hold us captive to sin." They offer no release (Romans 7:1-4), because only Christ's atoning death breaks the power of the Law (Ephesians 2:15) and reconciles us to God. Paul, likewise, summarized obedience to the commandments in the single command to love. New life promotes a new compliance with God's ways which fulfill the Law (Romans 13:9,10; cf. 1 Corinthians 7:19). Paul considered his own revelation from God for the instruction of the community as *entolē kuriou* (1 Corinthians 14:37), or *entolē* can speak of simple "orders" (Colossians 4:10).

The peculiar use in 1 Timothy is probably not a reference to the Old Testament commandment (6:14, singular, *entolē*). The "charge" or "command" is probably the obligation Timothy had to remain steadfast in his own faith and service in Ephesus (cf. 4:16; 6:11ff.; 6:20).

Epistle to the Hebrews

Hebrews emphasizes the superiority of Christ's status as high priest over the legal conditions for that position. His power over death (Hebrews 7:16) has made Him the "guarantee" (Hebrews 7:22) of a better covenant. Again the inability of the Law is contrasted with the ability of Christ, which is attested by His power over death and the eternal life He brings.

In summary, the word *entolē* is used in at least five distinct ways in the New Testament: (1) concerning the commands of God in the Old Testament (Matthew 15:3; 22:36f.; Mark 7:8f.; Ephesians 2:15; Hebrews 9:19); (2) concerning the Ten Commandments in particular (Matthew 5:19; Mark 10:19; Romans 7:8-13; Ephesians 6:2); (3) concerning commandments of God generally (Luke 1:6; 1 Corinthians 7:19; 1 John 2:3f.; Revelation 12:17); (4) concerning the commandments of the Father to the Son (John 12:49f.; 14:31; 15:10); and (5) concerning the commandments of Christ (John 13:34; 14:15,21; 1 Corinthians 14:37).

STRONG 1785, BAUER 269, MOULTON-MILLIGAN 218, KITTEL 2:545-56, LIDDELL-SCOTT 576, COLIN BROWN 1:330-37.

1770. ἐντόπιος entopios adj
Resident, be of a certain place.

1. ἐντόπιοι entopioi nom pl masc

1 both we, and they of that **place,** besought him . . . . . . Acts 21:12

This adjective, formed from the words *en* (1706), indicating location, and *topos* (4964), "place," occurs only once in the New Testament. In Acts 21:12 *entopios* is used as a substantive and means the "local people" or "inhabitants."

STRONG 1786, BAUER 269, MOULTON-MILLIGAN 218, LIDDELL-SCOTT 577.

1771. ἐντός entos adv
Inside, within.

1. ἐντός entos

1 cleanse first that **which is within** the cup . . . . Matt 23:26
1 for, behold, the kingdom of God is **within** you . . . . . Luke 17:21

Classical Greek and Septuagint Usage
Entos is properly an adverb of place and was used that way in classical and Attic Greek, the Septuagint, the inscriptions, and other Greek documents of the First and Second Centuries A.D. It became an improper preposition which took as its object a noun in the genitive case. In the Septuagint (e.g., Isaiah 16:11; Psalm 103:1 [LXX 102:1]) *entos* refers to the *inside* of man (i.e., the heart). It is used only as an improper preposition in the New Testament. However, it still functions adverbially.

New Testament Usage
Entos is used with several meanings in the various groups of New Testament literature. Often it refers to an object which is *inside* of something or *within* a period of time. The first of two occurrences in the New Testament clearly refers to the former meaning, "inside the cup" (Matthew 23:26). Some take the second New Testament occurrence of *entos* to mean something similar to this latter meaning and translate Luke 17:21 as "the kingdom is *in* you." Others, however, translate it as "*among* you" and mean by it that the Kingdom is among the community of believers. Still, some translate it as "*within*," so as to suggest that the Kingdom is present in Jesus and therefore available to His listeners if they will only "grasp" it.

It is best to understand the meaning of *entos* in view of the immediate context of Luke 17:20-37 and of the greater context of Luke—Acts. Jesus said (17:20,21) the kingdom of God would not come the way the Pharisees normally expected (cf. their idea of Kingdom and Messiah), although the Son of Man as the Messiah in His kingdom will come (17:24-37). Rather, in the interim period, the Kingdom will be present in the world through the power of the Holy Spirit (cf. Luke 24:44-49; Acts 1:1-8).

STRONG 1787, BAUER 269, MOULTON-MILLIGAN 218-19, LIDDELL-SCOTT 577.

1772. ἐντρέπω entrepō verb
Put to shame, be ashamed; to reverence, have respect for.

חָפַר chāphar (2763), Be ashamed (Ps 35:26 [34:26], Jer 50:12 [27:12]).

כָּלַם kālam (3757), Niphal: shame, disgrace (2 Chr 30:15, Ezr 9:6, Is 45:16,17).

כָּנָה kānâh (3777), Piel: flatter (Jb 32:21).

כָּנַע kānaʻ (3789), Niphal: be subdued, be humbled (Lv 26:41, Jgs 3:30, 2 Chr 7:14).

עָנָה ʻānâh (6257), Bend down; niphal: humble oneself (Ex 10:3).

פָּחַד pāchadh (6585), Tremble (Is 44:11).

רָאָה rāʼâh (7495), See; niphal: appear, make one's appearance (Is 16:12).

רָכַךְ rākhakh (7690), Be tender, responsive (2 Chr 34:27).

ἐντρέφω 1773

1. **ἐντρέπων** entrepōn nom sing masc part pres act
2. **ἐντρέπομαι** entrepomai 1sing indic pres mid
3. **ἐντρεπόμενος** entrepomenos
   nom sing masc part pres mid
4. **ἐντραπῇ** entrapē 3sing subj aor pass
5. **ἐντραπήσονται** entrapēsontai 3pl indic fut pass
6. **ἐνετρεπόμεθα** enetrepometha
   1pl indic imperf pass

5 saying, They **will reverence** my son.	Matt 21:37
5 he sent him also ... They **will reverence** my son.	Mark 12:6
3 which feared not God, neither **regarded** man:	Luke 18:2
2 Though I fear not God, nor **regard** man;	18:4
5 they **will reverence** him when they see him.	20:13
1 I write not these things to **shame** you,	1 Co 4:14
4 no company with him, that he **may be ashamed**.	2 Th 3:14
4 he that is of the contrary part **may be ashamed**,	Tit 2:8
6 fathers of our flesh ... and we **gave them reverence**:	Heb 12:9

Classical Greek
The verb *entrepō* was used from the time of Homer to well into the post-Biblical era in two seemingly opposite ways. On the one hand, the word means "I have shame," while on the other, it means "I show respect or honor." This difference of meaning is also reflected in the use of the noun form. Some scholars have thought Paul changed the meaning of *entrepō* from "to respect" to that of "to have shame." They have not noted, however, that both meanings occur in the Septuagint and in early and late extra-Biblical writings. In fact, depending upon the context three meanings may be involved: "to have shame," "to have respect," and "to turn toward someone or something."

Septuagint Usage
In the Septuagint, *entrepō* translated eight Hebrew words. Like *entrepō*, the Hebrew words can be placed into two broad categories as noted above. Most references in which "shame" is meant are in the Psalms. In the Psalms themselves without exception, *entrepō* involves "shame." There the enemies of God will experience shame, while His people will not.

New Testament Usage
In the New Testament *entrepō* is used nine times. In its five occurrences in the Synoptics, the idea of "reverence" or "respect" is intended. However, in Paul's epistles *entrepō* means "to have shame"; in both the active and middle/passive voices the verb means "shame." This is similar to the use of *entrepō* in the Psalms of the Septuagint.

STRONG 1788, BAUER 269, MOULTON-MILLIGAN 219, LIDDELL-SCOTT 577.

1773. ἐντρέφω entrephō verb
Bring up, rear, train, nurture.

CROSS-REFERENCE:
τεκνοτροφέω teknotropheō (4892)

1. **ἐντρεφόμενος** entrephomenos
   nom sing masc part pres mid

1 **nourished up** in the words of faith	1 Tm 4:6

The New Testament uses *entrephō* only in 1 Timothy 4:6. Paul said that if Timothy taught others what was right and wrong, he would confirm himself as a good minister who had been "*brought up* in the truths of the faith and of the good teaching" (NIV) that he had followed. A similar meaning is found in classical Greek where the term means "to be raised up in" or "bred in" the gymnastic school (cf. *Liddell-Scott*; see also "gumnasion," ibid.).

STRONG 1789, BAUER 269, MOULTON-MILLIGAN 219 (see "entrephomai"), LIDDELL-SCOTT 577.

1774. ἔντρομος entromos adj
Trembling through fear, terrified.

1. **ἔντρομος** entromos nom sing masc

1 Then Moses **trembled**, and durst not behold.	Acts 7:32
1 and came **trembling**, and fell down before Paul	16:29
1 that Moses said, I exceedingly fear and **quake**:	Heb 12:21

This word appears in classical Greek since the time of Plato (ca. Fourth Century B.C.). It was originally used to describe the kind of force or power that could make the foundation of a building "tremble" (see *Moulton-Milligan*). It is used only twice in the canonical portions of the Septuagint, and two of its three uses in the New Testament are in connection with Moses "trembling" before God (Acts 7:32; Hebrews 12:21). The third occurrence refers to the jailer's reaction when he thought that Paul and Silas had escaped from prison (Acts 16:29).

STRONG 1790, BAUER 269, MOULTON-MILLIGAN 219, LIDDELL-SCOTT 577.

1775. ἐντροπή entropē noun
Shame, humiliation, confusion.

SYNONYMS:
αἰσχύνη aischunē (151)
ἀσχημοσύνη aschēmosunē (802)
ἀτιμία atimia (813)

כְּלִמָּה kᵉlimmāh (3759), Disgrace, dishonor (Pss 35:26 [34:26], 69:7 [68:7], 109:29 [108:29]).

1. **ἐντροπήν** entropēn acc sing fem

1 I speak to your **shame**. Is it so,	1 Co 6:5
1 I speak this to your **shame**.	15:34

In Greek writings from the Fifth Century B.C. to the Second Century A.D. the noun *entropē* had three meanings: "shame," "respect," and "a turning towards." It is also used a few times in the Septuagint but only two times in the New Testament, in 1 Corinthians 6:5 and 15:34. In each Septuagint occurrence, *entropē* translates the Hebrew word *kᵉlimmāh*, which means "shame, disgrace" (cf. Job 20:3; Psalms 35:26 [LXX 34:26]; 44:15 [43:15]; 69:7,19 [68:7,19]).

Paul did not use "shame" improperly in First Corinthians (i.e., to motivate by guilt) when he wrote, "I speak to your shame." Rather, in both places he was giving instruction to people who were acting sinfully. The basis of their shame was to be their own bad behavior. (See *aidōs* [127], *aischunē* [151].)

STRONG 1791, BAUER 269-70, MOULTON-MILLIGAN 219, LIDDELL-SCOTT 577-78.

1776. ἐντρυφάω entruphaō verb
Revel, carouse, live luxuriously.

עָדַן ʽādhan (5939), Hithpael: luxuriate, enjoy the good life (Neh 9:25—Codex Alexandrinus only).

עָנֹג ʽānōgh (6253), Hithpael: take delight in (Is 55:2, 57:4).

קָלַס qālas (7330), Hithpael: laugh, deride (Hb 1:10).

שַׁעֲשׁוּעִים shaʽăshûʽîm (8562), Something delightful (Jer 31:20 [38:20]).

1. ἐντρυφῶντες entruphōntes
   nom pl masc part pres act
1 sporting themselves with their own deceivings .... 2 Pt 2:13

In classical Greek this verb means "take delight in" (see *Moulton-Milligan*). It is used only five times in the canonical portion of the Septuagint and is found once in the New Testament. Its meaning in 2 Peter 2:13 is "revel," "carouse," and is employed in a negative sense regarding life-style. *Entruphaō* carries the connotation of evil vices which draw people with a facade of bringing happiness and fulfillment.

STRONG 1792, BAUER 270, MOULTON-MILLIGAN 219, LIDDELL-SCOTT 578.

1777. ἐντυγχάνω entunchanō verb
Approach, appeal, plead, address, intercede for.

COGNATES:
   τυγχάνω tunchanō (5018)
   ὑπερεντυγχάνω huperentunchanō (5079)
SYNONYMS:
   αἰτέω aiteō (153)
   δέομαι deomai (1183)
   ἐγγίζω engizō (1443)
   ἐξαιτέω exaiteō (1793)
   ἐπερωτάω eperōtaō (1890)
   ἐρωτάω erōtaō (2049)
   εὔχομαι euchomai (2153)
   ἐφικνέομαι ephikneomai (2167)
   ἐφίστημι ephistēmi (2168)
   καταντάω katantaō (2628)
   λέγω legō (2978)
   παραβάλλω paraballō (3708)
   παραιτέομαι paraiteomai (3729)
   παρακαλέω parakaleō (3731)
   παρέρχομαι parerchomai (3790)
   παρίστημι paristēmi (3798)
   προσάγω prosagō (4175)
   προσέρχομαι proserchomai (4193)
   προσεύχομαι proseuchomai (4195)
   προσπορεύομαι prosporeuomai (4223)
   πυνθάνομαι punthanomai (4299)
   συμβάλλω sumballō (4671)

קְרֵב qᵉrēv (A7415), Give account to (Dn 6:12—Aramaic).

1. ἐντυγχάνει entunchanei 3sing indic pres act
2. ἐντυγχάνειν entunchanein inf pres act
3. ἐνέτυχον enetuchon 3pl indic aor act

3 Jews have dealt with me, both at Jerusalem, ... Acts 25:24
1 because he maketh intercession for the saints .... Rom 8:27
1 who also maketh intercession for us. 8:34
1 how he maketh intercession to God against Israel, ... 11:2
2 seeing he ever liveth to make intercession for them ... Heb 7:25

Entunchanō is a compound formed from the highly complex verb *tunchanō* (5018), "to hit" (a target) (later, "to meet, to happen by chance"), and the preposition *en* (1706) (see *Liddell-Scott*; see also Bauernfeind, "tunchanō," *Kittel*, 8:238ff. for some primary references). In classical usage it means "to meet" (someone), especially by chance. The second principal definition is "to talk with," and thirdly, "to intercede for." *Moulton-Milligan* cites a technical use of this verb as "to petition" or "to appeal" as well as its normal classical sense (cf. Josephus *Antiquities* 12.2.2, of an "appeal" to a king).

In the canonical portions of the Septuagint only Daniel 6:13 (LXX 6:12), which has an Aramaic original (*qᵉrēv*, "approach, step up to"), is translated by *entunchanō*. The idea there may be more of a technical use of "to appeal" (as the context suggests and as the RSV rightly translates). Other instances also convey this technical use while others could be translated "to pray" (e.g., Wisdom of Solomon 8:21 [LXX 8:20]; 16:28; cf. 1 Maccabees 8:32).

ἐντυλίσσω 1778

The meaning "to read" is introduced in 2 Maccabees (2:25; 15:39). *Bauer* cites other instances of this usage in Philo and Josephus (*Antiquities* 1.1.3; 12.4.10).

New Testament Usage

Only five occurrences of *entunchanō* are recorded in the New Testament. A negative sense of "to appeal" is to be understood in Acts (25:24). In a positive sense the Spirit "intercedes" (both *huperentunchanō* [5079] and *entunchanō*) on behalf of God's people (Romans 8:27; cf. verse 26). Jesus, too, eternally "intercedes" on our behalf (*huper humōn*; Romans 8:34) as high priest (Hebrews 7:25).

STRONG 1793, BAUER 270, MOULTON-MILLIGAN 219, KITTEL 8:242-44, LIDDELL-SCOTT 578, COLIN BROWN 2:882.

1778. ἐντυλίσσω entulissō verb
Wrap (up), fold up, roll in.
SYNONYM:
πτύσσω ptussō (4286)

1. ἐνετύλιξεν enetulixen 3sing indic aor act
2. ἐντετυλιγμένον entetuligmenon
   nom/acc sing neu part perf mid

1 the body, he **wrapped** it in a clean linen cloth,..... Matt 27:59
1 And he took it down, and **wrapped** it in linen,..... Luke 23:53
2 but **wrapped together** in a place by itself........... John 20:7

The three New Testament passages which use this word all relate to the death and resurrection of Jesus. Matthew 27:59 and Luke 23:53 speak of Joseph "wrapping" the body of Jesus in a linen cloth. John 20:7, on the other hand, speaks of the burial cloth once placed around the head of Jesus still wrapped together like a turban after the Resurrection.

STRONG 1794, BAUER 270, MOULTON-MILLIGAN 219, LIDDELL-SCOTT 578.

1779. ἐντυπόω entupoō verb
Carve, impress, engrave.
CROSS-REFERENCE:
τύπος tupos (5020)

פִּתּוּחַ pittûach (6855), Engraving (Ex 39:30 [36:39]—Codex Alexandrinus only).

1. ἐντετυπωμένη entetupōmenē
   nom sing fem part perf mid

1 written and **engraven** in stones, was glorious,........ 2 Co 3:7

This is a hapax legomenon, a word used only once in the New Testament. *Entupoō* occurs in 2 Corinthians 3:7 with the meaning "engrave, carve." The reference is to the ministry of Moses which Paul said was the "ministry that brought death ... engraved in letters of stone" (NIV).

STRONG 1795, BAUER 270, MOULTON-MILLIGAN 219, LIDDELL-SCOTT 578.

1780. ἐνυβρίζω enubrizō verb
Insult, outrage, treat contemptuously.
CROSS-REFERENCE:
ὑβρίζω hubrizō (5036)

1. ἐνυβρίσας enubrisas nom sing masc part aor act

1 and **hath done despite** unto the Spirit of grace?..... Heb 10:29

This verb is a compound of *en* (1706) plus *hubrizō* (5036) and means "treat in an arrogant or spiteful manner, scoff at, insult." In the Oxyrhynchus Papyri this word is used in a construction that translates, "she continues her outrageous behavior and *insulting conduct* towards me" (see *Moulton-Milligan*). The only New Testament passage in which this word occurs is Hebrews 10:29. Here it is used in connection with the statement about God's punishment upon the one "who has *insulted* the Spirit of grace" (NIV). Those who are apostate not only treat the sacred new covenant sealed by the blood of Christ as an "unholy thing" (i.e., a common or profane object of no account), they also treat the Holy Spirit with contempt.

STRONG 1796, BAUER 270, MOULTON-MILLIGAN 219, KITTEL 8:295-307, LIDDELL-SCOTT 578.

1781. ἐνυπνιάζω enupniazō verb
To dream, envision.

חָזָה châzâh (2463), See (Is 56:10).
חֲלוֹם chălôm (2573), Dream (Jer 27:9 [34:9]).
חָלַם châlam (2593), Qal: dream (Gn 37:5,6, Jgs 7:13, Is 29:8); hiphil: dream (Jer 29:8 [36:8]).

1. ἐνυπνιαζόμενοι enupniazomenoi
   nom pl masc part pres mid
2. ἐνυπνιασθήσονται enupniasthēsontai
   3pl indic fut pass

2 and your old men **shall dream** dreams:............. Acts 2:17
1 Likewise also these filthy **dreamers** defile the flesh,.. Jude 1:8

Enupniazō carries the connotation of supernatural activity while one is sleeping, especially in the sense of dreaming. Used only twice in the New Testament, the word is neutral concerning judgment regarding good or evil in the dreaming. Hence, in Acts 2:17 the word is used to describe dreaming activity of which God is the source. In Jude 8 the emphasis is upon the "dreamers" (participial form) who had crept in "unawares" (verse 4) and who defile their bodies, defy their Creator, and deride the angels (cf. verse 9).

STRONG 1797, BAUER 270 (see "enupniazomai"), MOULTON-MILLIGAN 219-20 (see "enupniazomai"), KITTEL 8:545-56 (see "enupniazomai"), LIDDELL-SCOTT 579.

1782. ἐνύπνιον enupnion noun

A dream.

SYNONYM:
ὄναρ onar (3540)

חֲלוֹם chălôm (2573), Dream (Gn 40:9, 1 Sm 28:6, Zec 10:2).

חָלַם chālam (2593), Dream (Jer 23:25).

חֵלֶם chēlem (A2595), Dream (Dn 2:4,5,6, 4:2—Aramaic).

נֶפֶשׁ nephesh (5497), Soul, person (Is 29:8).

1. ἐνύπνια enupnia nom/acc pl neu
2. ἐνυπνίοις enupniois dat pl neu

1 and your old men shall dream **dreams:** .... Acts 2:17
2 and your old men shall dream **dreams:** 2:17

Classical Greek and Septuagint Usage

In classical Greek this word is used to describe a "thing seen in sleep," "a vision in sleep," i.e., "a dream" (see *Liddell-Scott*). This could refer to either a "mere dream" or a "significant, prophetic" one. It is used over 50 times in the Septuagint, usually to translate *chălôm* which is a common word for "dream."

New Testament Usage

Its only use in the New Testament is in Acts 2:17. Luke was quoting Peter's reference to Joel 2:28ff. which is to be taken as a prophetic passage that saw the beginning of its fulfillment at Pentecost. The events of Pentecost included the following prophecy: "Your old men will dream dreams." This was a result of the outpouring of the Spirit on "all flesh" and signaled that the end times had begun. In this context it is improbable that Luke was using *enupnion* to refer to a "mere dream," but rather was implying that there is a significant, supernatural element in them.

STRONG 1798, BAUER 270, MOULTON-MILLIGAN 220, KITTEL 8:545-56, LIDDELL-SCOTT 579, COLIN BROWN 1:511-12.

1783. ἐνώπιον enōpion prep

Before, in the sight or presence of.

SYNONYMS:
ἐναντίον enantion (1710)
κατενώπιον katenōpion (2684)

1. ἐνώπιον enōpion

1 And they were both righteous **before** God, ... Luke 1:6
1 For he shall be great in the **sight** of the Lord, ... 1:15
1 And he shall go **before** him in the spirit and power 1:17
1 I am Gabriel, that stand in the **presence** of God; 1:19
1 In holiness and righteousness **before** him, ... 1:75
1 for you will go on **before** the Lord (NIV) 1:76
1 If thou ... wilt worship me, all shall be thine. (NT) 4:7
1 means to bring him in, and to lay him **before** him. 5:18
1 And immediately he rose up **before** them, ... 5:25
1 she declared unto him **before** all the people 8:47
1 and not one of them is forgotten **before** God? 12:6
1 But he that denieth me **before** men shall be denied 12:9
1 shall be denied **before** the angels of God. 12:9
1 We have eaten and drunk in thy **presence,** 13:26
1 thou have worship in the **presence** of them that sit 14:10
1 there is joy in the **presence** of the angels of God 15:10
1 I have sinned against heaven, and **before** thee, ... 15:18
1 I have sinned against heaven, and in thy **sight,** 15:21
1 Ye are they which justify yourselves **before** men; 16:15
1 among men is abomination in the **sight** of God. 16:15
1 and, behold, I, having examined him **before** you, ... 23:14
1 And their words seemed to them as idle tales, ... 24:11
1 And he took it, and did eat **before** them. 24:43
1 signs ... did Jesus in the **presence** of his disciples, .. John 20:30
1 I foresaw the Lord always **before** my face, ... Acts 2:25
1 by him doth this man stand here **before** you whole. 4:10
1 Whether it be right in the **sight** of God 4:19
1 And the saying pleased the whole multitude: (NT) 6:5
1 Whom they set **before** the apostles: 6:6
1 Who found favour **before** God, ... 7:46
1 for thy heart is not right in the **sight** of God. 8:21
1 to bear my name **before** the Gentiles, ... 9:15
1 are come up for a memorial **before** God. 10:4
1 behold, a man stood **before** me in bright clothing, ... 10:30
1 alms are had in remembrance in the **sight** of God. 10:31
1 Now therefore are we all here present **before** God, ... 10:33
1 but spake evil of that way **before** the multitude, ... 19:9
1 books together, and burned them **before** all men: 19:19
1 and gave thanks to God in presence of them all: 27:35
1 there shall no flesh be justified in his **sight:** .... Rom 3:20
1 Provide things honest in the **sight** of all men. 12:17
1 Hast thou faith? have it to thyself **before** God. 14:22
1 That no flesh should glory in his **presence.** .... 1 Co 1:29
1 to every man's conscience in the **sight** of God. ...... 2 Co 4:2
1 our care for you in the **sight** of God might appear 7:12
1 not only in the **sight** of the Lord, ... 8:21
1 but also in the **sight** of men. 8:21
1 behold, **before** God, I lie not. .... Gal 1:20
1 For this is good and acceptable in the **sight** of God 1 Tm 2:3
1 for that is good and acceptable **before** God. 5:4
1 Them that sin rebuke **before** all, ... 5:20
1 I charge thee **before** God, and the Lord Jesus 5:21
1 professed a good profession **before** many witnesses. 6:12
1 in the sight of God, ... and **before** Christ Jesus, ... 6:13
1 charging them **before** the Lord that they strive not .. 2 Tm 2:14
1 I charge thee therefore **before** God, ... 4:1
1 any creature that is not manifest in his **sight:** .... Heb 4:13
1 that which is wellpleasing in his **sight,** 13:21
1 Humble yourselves in the **sight** of the Lord, ... Jas 4:10
1 which is in the **sight** of God of great price. .... 1 Pt 3:4
1 and do those things that are pleasing in his **sight.** ... 1 Jn 3:22
1 borne witness of thy charity **before** the church: ...... 3 Jn 1:6
1 from the seven Spirits which are **before** his throne; ... Rev 1:4
1 cast a stumblingblock **before** the children of Israel, ... 2:14
1 for I have not found thy works perfect **before** God. 3:2
1 but I will confess his name **before** my Father, ... 3:5
1 his name before my Father, and **before** his angels. 3:5
1 behold, I have set **before** thee an open door, ... 3:8

1 make them to come and worship **before** thy feet,	Rev 3:9
1 seven lamps of fire burning **before** the throne,	4:5
1 And **before** the throne there was a sea of glass	4:6
1 The four and twenty elders fall down **before** him	4:10
1 cast their crowns **before** the throne, saying,	4:10
1 four and twenty elders fell down **before** the Lamb,	5:8
1 stood **before** the throne, and before the Lamb,	7:9
1 stood before the throne, and **before** the Lamb,	7:9
1 **before** the throne on their faces, and worshipped	7:11
1 Therefore are they **before** the throne of God,	7:15
1 I saw the seven angels which stood **before** God;	8:2
1 upon the golden altar which was **before** the throne.	8:3
1 ascended up **before** God out of the angel's hand.	8:4
1 four horns of the golden altar which is **before** God,	9:13
1 candlesticks standing **before** the God of the earth.	11:4
1 the four and twenty elders, which sat **before** God	11:16
1 and the dragon stood **before** the woman	12:4
1 which accused them **before** our God day and night.	12:10
1 all the power of the first beast **before** him,	13:12
1 fire come down ... on the earth in the **sight** of men,	13:13
1 which he had power to do in the **sight** of the beast;	13:14
1 they sung as it were a new song **before** the throne,	14:3
1 and **before** the four beasts, and the elders:	14:3
1 they are without fault **before** the throne of God.	14:5
1 and brimstone in the **presence** of the holy angels,	14:10
1 and in the **presence** of the Lamb:	14:10
1 for all nations shall come and worship **before** thee;	15:4
1 great Babylon came in remembrance **before** God,	16:19
1 false prophet that wrought miracles **before** him,	19:20
1 I saw the dead, small and great, stand **before** God;	20:12

Classical Greek and Septuagint Usage

Enōpion functions as an improper preposition which takes an object in the genitive case. The prepositional phrase, nonetheless, still functions adverbially. Several other Greek words in many cases convey the same meanings as *enōpion*: e.g., *enantion* (1710), *enanti* (1709), and *emprosthen* (1699). (In fact, two codices, A and B, of the Septuagint at Judges 2:11 and 3:12 interchange *enanti* and *enōpion*.) Other references use these synonyms side by side. *Enōpion* is actually the neuter form of the adjective *enōpios* (which does not occur in the New Testament). It derives from a combination of two words, *en* (1706) and *opion*, and generally means "before," either in terms of space, sight, relationships, time, or rank. However, a number of different words translate *enōpion*.

Enōpion occurs in writings from the time of Homer to those well beyond the New Testament era. This word is used frequently by the Septuagint translators and by the New Testament writers. The majority of the New Testament references are in Luke–Acts and Revelation. Matthew and Mark did not use the term *enōpion*.

New Testament Usage

Enōpion in Luke–Acts describes relationships— people whom God approves and appoints to serve Him. Furthermore, the relationships which this word depicts are dynamic. For instance, Luke 1:15,17 says that the angel's assessment of John the Baptist's ministry was that he would be great *before* (*enōpion*) the Lord and that he would go *before* (*enōpion*) Him "in the spirit and power of Elijah." In like manner, Gabriel who stands "in the presence (*enōpion*) of God" was sent to speak to Zechariah (1:19; see also Luke 1:75; Revelation 8:2). Luke's use of *enōpion* in these instances follows the same pattern as that which occurs in Samuel's priestly ministry before the Lord, as translated in the Septuagint of 1 Samuel 2:11,18,21 (LXX 1 Kings 2:11,18,21).

Enōpion expresses relational qualities in another way. It depicts salvation or judgment in a legal, forensic manner (i.e., in terms of a court or judicial scene). A person is righteous (or not) *before* God. Both Luke (Acts 4:19) and Paul (Romans 3:20, "There shall no flesh be justified in his sight") used the word in this manner. In judgment men will stand *before* God (Revelation 20:12).

Some of the references speak of moral relationships *among* men and *with* God. For example, Romans 12:17 reads, "Recompense to no man evil for evil. Provide things honest in the *sight* (*enōpion*) of all men" (see also Romans 14:22; Galatians 1:20).

Enōpion also expresses a public manifestation of someone or something for special effect, such as a testimony. Acts 4:10, for instance, relates that the sick man stood *among*, or *before*, the elders of the people healed and in good health (see also Acts 6:5,6; 19:9,19; 27:35; 2 Corinthians 8:21; 1 Timothy 5:20).

STRONG 1799, BAUER 270-71, MOULTON-MILLIGAN 220, LIDDELL-SCOTT 579 (see "enōpios"), COLIN BROWN 3:1044.

1784. Ἐνώς Enōs name

Enos.

1. Ἐνώς Enōs masc

1 Which was the son **of Enos,**	Luke 3:38

The son of Seth in the genealogy of Jesus (Luke 3:38).

1785. ἐνωτίζομαι enōtizomai verb

Give ear to, pay attention to, listen to.
SYNONYMS:
ἀκούω akouō (189)

εἰσακούω eisakouō (1508)
ἐπακούω epakouō (1858)
ἐπακροάομαι epakroaomai (1859)
ὑπακούω hupakouō (5057)

אָזַן 'āzan (237), Hiphil: hear (Ex 15:26, Neh 9:30, Is 1:2).

יָחַל yāchal (3282), Hiphil: wait (Jb 32:11).

קָשַׁב qāshav (7477), Hiphil: listen (Jb 33:31, Jer 8:6, 23:18).

שָׁמַע shāmaʿ (8471), Hear; hiphil: tell, proclaim (Is 44:8).

1. ἐνωτίσασθε enōtisasthe 2pl impr aor mid

1 be this known unto you, and hearken to my words:.. Acts 2:14

Although *enōtizomai* only occurs in Acts 2:14 in the New Testament, it is an important word. The word means "to give ear to," "to pay close attention to something."

Septuagint Usage

Enōtizomai has not been documented prior to or during the Koine era outside the Septuagint, Acts, and the Testaments of Reuben and Issachar. One theory states that the word was, nonetheless, used in vernacular Greek, while another says that the word came into usage in the Septuagint through Hebrew influence (i.e., a "Hebraism"). The word is found frequently in the Septuagint most often translating the Hebrew word *'āzan*. Many times it introduces a serious speech (e.g., Numbers 23:18; Jude 5:3; Testament Reuben 1:5; Testament Issachar 1:1) or is found within a serious speech or prophetic utterance (e.g., Genesis 4:23; Nehemiah 9:30). In the Psalms (e.g., 5:1; 39:12 [LXX 38:12]; 49:1 [48:1]; 55:1 [54:1]) the word is used in the introduction to prayers. In Nehemiah 9:30 it is used negatively: Israel did not "give ear" (i.e., obey) to the word of the prophets, and thus God judged the nation. In Ecclesiastes 12:9 the piel stem of the Hebrew verb means "to weigh or consider carefully." In Psalm 10:17 the noun form of the verb (meaning "to give special attention to") used with another verb refers to God answering prayer. Likewise, in 1 Samuel 9:15 (LXX 1 Kings 9:15) the noun form used with another verb means "to reveal."

New Testament Usage

It is thus significant for Luke to use this word in Acts 2:14. *Enōtizomai* occurs here in the introduction of Peter's Pentecost message. This introduction was based upon Old Testament speech, prophetic forms, and Hellenistic oratory. These Septuagint and Hellenistic forms would be of particular importance for the readers and listeners, for they would be Jews and proselytes from the diaspora who would be especially familiar with the Greek Bible. The beginning of Peter's sermon on the Day of Pentecost contains *enōtizomai* which means the people should pay special attention to his words and obey them. That they did this is evident from their response (Acts 2:37). By obeying Peter's message they would be saved and receive the gift of the Spirit. In this sense the inner action of paying close attention is significantly attached to *faithful obedience*.

STRONG 1801, BAUER 271, MOULTON-MILLIGAN 220, KITTEL 5:559, LIDDELL-SCOTT 579, COLIN BROWN 2:175.

1786. Ἐνώχ Henōch name

Enoch.

1. Ἐνώχ Henōch masc
2. Ἐνώχ Enōch masc

2 which was the son of Enoch,........................ Luke 3:37
2 Enoch was translated that he should not see death; Heb 11:5
1 Enoch also, the seventh from Adam, prophesied..... Jude 1:14

The son of Jared in the genealogy of Jesus (Luke 3:37); as a result of his life of faith he was translated to heaven without seeing death (Hebrews 11:5).

1787. ἕξ hex num

Six.

1. ἕξ hex card

1 And after six days Jesus taketh Peter, James, and.. Matt 17:1
1 And after six days Jesus taketh with him Peter,.... Mark 9:2
1 heaven was shut up three years and six months,... Luke 4:25
1 There are six days in which men ought to work:....... 13:14
1 And there were set there six waterpots of stone,.... John 2:6
1 Forty and six years was this temple in building,......... 2:20
1 six days before the passover came to Bethany,......... 12:1
1 Moreover these six brethren accompanied me,......Acts 11:12
1 And he continued there a year and six months,........ 18:11
1 two hundred and seventy-six persons (NASB).......... 27:37
1 by the space of three years and six months............ Jas 5:17
1 And the four beasts had each of them six wings..... Rev 4:8
1 his number is six hundred and sixty-six (NASB)....... 13:18

Various theories of symbolism regarding the number six abound. The most popular is that six is the number of humanity. Although there may be some weight to this belief in particular instances, care should be given so as not to build esoteric theories around numerology. *Hex* appears in such texts as Matthew 17:1; Luke 4:25; John 12:1; and James 5:17 without anything but the very literal meaning of "six."

STRONG 1803, BAUER 271, MOULTON-MILLIGAN 220, LIDDELL-SCOTT 579, COLIN BROWN 2:688,700.

1788. ἐξαγγέλλω exangellō verb
Proclaim, report, publicly declare.
CROSS-REFERENCE:
ἀγγέλλω angellō (31B)

יָדַע yādhaʿ (3156), Niphal: know (Prv 12:16).

סָפַר sāphar (5807), Qal: record, tell of (Ps 56:8 [55:8]); piel: make known, declare (Pss 9:14, 73:28 [72:28], 119:13 [118:13]).

1. ἐξαγγείλητε exangeilēte 2pl subj aor act

1 that ye should show forth the praises of him .... 1 Pt 2:9

Exangellō is one of a large family of words meaning "preach, proclaim, report." (See *angellō* [31B] and its cognates.) Its only New Testament occurrence is in 1 Peter 2:9 where the translation would be "to declare the praises" or "to share the good news" of the Christian faith. The "praises" referred to are the life, miracles, death, and resurrection of Jesus, who is the Christ. The sharing or "declaring" is both in life-style and in word.

STRONG 1804, BAUER 271, MOULTON-MILLIGAN 220, KITTEL 1:69-70, LIDDELL-SCOTT 580, COLIN BROWN 3:44-46.

1789. ἐξαγοράζω exagorazō verb
Redeem, deliver, buy back, rescue.
CROSS-REFERENCE:
ἀγοράζω agorazō (58)

1. ἐξηγόρασεν exēgorasen 3sing indic aor act
2. ἐξαγοράσῃ exagorasē 3sing subj aor act
3. ἐξαγοραζόμενοι exagorazomenoi
nom pl masc part pres mid

1 Christ hath redeemed us from the curse of the law, ... Gal 3:13
2 To redeem them that were under the law, ... 4:5
3 Redeeming the time, because the days are evil. ...... Eph 5:16
3 toward them that are without, redeeming the time. ... Col 4:5

Classical Greek
Exagorazō comes from the preposition *ek* (1523) (*ex* before a vowel), "out, out from," and the verb *agorazō* (58), "to buy" (from the marketplace; cf. the noun *agora* [57], "marketplace"). Thus this verb means "to buy, to ransom, to redeem" (cf. the noun *exagorasia*, "a ransom"). The term became widely used of "buying slaves" or of "redeeming slaves" in the marketplace. For example, in the "north market" of ancient Corinth there was a slave market where it is said that as many as 100 slaves were auctioned off each day. This was a typical trait of cities in the ancient world.

Septuagint Usage
Exagorazō occurs only one time in the Septuagint in Daniel 2:8 (Theodotion). It replaces the Aramaic word *zᵉvan*, "to buy." Here both the Hebrew and the Greek are used metaphorically of "buying" time, i.e., "gaining time" (cf. the NIV).

New Testament Usage
Christ is said to "redeem" or to "buy back" those in bondage by the price of His own blood (1 Peter 1:18). This would be the basis of Paul's injunction: "Therefore glorify God in your body, and in your spirit, which are God's" (1 Corinthians 6:20), i.e., it is the basis of God's claim upon the lives of believers.

The word is used metaphorically in Galatians 3:13 and 4:5 of the believer's redemption by Christ from the Law and its curse. It also occurs in Colossians 4:5—"redeeming the time"; that is, make the best use of the time. (In Revelation 5:9 and 14:3,4 *agorazō* means "to purchase" and is translated "redeemed." "Thou art worthy ... for thou wast slain, and hast *redeemed* [purchased] us to God by thy blood out of every kindred, and tongue, and people, and nation." The expression is used of those who sang "a new song before the throne ... which were *redeemed* [purchased out] from the earth.")

Exagorazō is related in meaning to *lutroō* (3056), "to free on receipt of a ransom" (akin to *lutron* [3055], a "ransom"). It signifies "to release by paying a ransom price." While both words refer to redeem, *exagorazō* focuses on the price paid while *lutroō* denotes the actual deliverance, i.e., the setting at liberty. It is one of the most meaningful words in the Bible in that it expresses the purpose for which God gave His Son (cf. Galatians 3:13; 4:5).

STRONG 1805, BAUER 271, MOULTON-MILLIGAN 220, KITTEL 1:124-28, LIDDELL-SCOTT 580, COLIN BROWN 1:267-68.

1790. ἐξάγω exagō verb
Lead out, bring out.
COGNATE:
ἄγω agō (70)
SYNONYM:
προάγω proagō (4113)

אֲבַד ʾăvadh (A7), Perish; haphel: kill (Dn 2:12—Aramaic).

בּוֹא bôʾ (971), Go, come; hiphil: bring (Ex 6:8—only some Vaticanus texts).

יָצָא yātsâʾ (3428), Qal: went out, set out (Gn 11:31);

hiphil: brought out (Lv 23:43, Ps 18:19 [17:19], Ez 11:7); hophal: brought out (Jer 38:22 [45:22]).

כָּרַת kārath (3901), Niphal: cut off (Jl 1:5—only some Sinaiticus texts).

לָקַח lāqach (4089), Bring, set (Ex 14:11, Jer 35:3 [42:3]).

נָזַל nāzal (5320), Hiphil: flow (Is 48:21).

עָבַר ʿāvar (5882), Go over; hiphil: take away, brought (2 Chr 35:23,24).

עָלָה ʿālâh (6148), Go up; hiphil: bring up (Ex 3:8, Nm 21:5, Neh 9:18).

פָּלַט pālaṭ (6647), Piel: deliver (Jb 23:7).

קְטַל qᵉṭal (A7273), Pael: kill (Dn 2:14—Aramaic).

רוּץ rûts (7608), Run; hiphil: bring quickly (Gn 41:14—Codex Alexandrinus only).

שָׁלַח shālach (8365), Piel: let go, set free (1 Kgs 20:42 [21:42]—Codex Alexandrinus only).

שָׁרַץ shārats (8650), Bring forth, teem (Gn 1:20,21).

תָּאַר tā'ar (8716), Went out, went from (Jos 15:9—Codex Alexandrinus only).

תָּעָה tā'âh (8912), Hiphil: wander (Gn 20:13).

1. ἐξάγει exagei 3sing indic pres act
2. ἐξάγουσιν exagousin 3pl indic pres act
3. ἐξήγαγεν exēgagen 3sing indic aor act
4. ἐξαγαγέτωσαν exagagetōsan 3pl impr aor act
5. ἐξαγαγών exagagōn nom sing masc part aor act
6. ἐξαγαγόντες exagagontes nom pl masc part aor act
7. ἐξαγαγεῖν exagagein inf aor act

```
3 and led him out of the town;................. Mark 8:23
2 and led him out to crucify him................... 15:20
3 And he led them out as far as to Bethany,..... Luke 24:50
1 his own sheep by name, and leadeth them out..... John 10:3
5 opened the prison ... brought them forth, and said,.. Acts 5:19
3 He brought them out,............................. 7:36
3 which brought us out of the land of Egypt,....... 7:40
3 how the Lord had brought him out of the prison.. 12:17
3 and with an high arm brought he them out of it.. 13:17
4 but let them come themselves and fetch us out... 16:37
6 came and besought them, and brought them out,... 16:39
5 and leddest out into the wilderness four thousand .. 21:38
7 by the hand to lead them out of the land of Egypt;.. Heb 8:9
```

Classical Greek and Septuagint Usage

In classical Greek this word is very common in custom-house receipts meaning "export" (see *Moulton-Milligan*). By the Third Century B.C. it was also used of persons, and meant "lead out," "lead away," and included the idea of "release" (e.g. "bring out of" prison, "bring forth into the world" cf. *Liddell-Scott*). It is used over 150 times in the Septuagint, usually to translate *yātsâ'* which generally means to "go out" or "take out."

New Testament Usage

In the New Testament *exagō* is used most often in Acts (eight occurrences). It is interesting to note that seven of the eight appearances in Acts describe either an apostle being led out of prison or Moses leading the Israelites out of Egypt. Similarly, Mark 15:20 describes how Jesus was "led out" to be crucified.

STRONG 1806, BAUER 271, MOULTON-MILLIGAN 220, LIDDELL-SCOTT 580.

1791. ἐξαιρέω exaireō verb

Pluck out, take out, tear out.

COGNATE:
αἱρέω haireō (141)

SYNONYMS:
αἱρετίζω hairetizō (139)
αἱρέω haireō (141)
ἀναδίδωμι anadidōmi (323)
ἀπαλλάσσω apallassō (521)
ἀπολύω apoluō (624)
διασῴζω diasōzō (1289)
ἐκβάλλω ekballō (1531)
ἐκλέγομαι eklegomai (1573)
ἐλευθερόω eleutheroō (1646)
ἐξορύσσω exorussō (1830)
ἐπιλέγω epilegō (1935B)
ἐπιλύω epiluō (1941)
κρίνω krinō (2892)
λαμβάνω lambanō (2956)
λυτρόω lutroō (3056)
λύω luō (3061)
προχειρίζομαι procheirizomai (4258)
ῥύομαι rhuomai (4363)
σῴζω sōzō (4834)
χειροτονέω cheirotoneō (5336)

בָּחַר bāchar (1013), Chosen, prefer (Jb 36:21, Is 48:10).

גָּאַל gā'al (1381), Redeem, deliver (Is 60:16, Jer 31:11 [38:11]).

חָלַץ chālats (2603), Take off; piel: deliver, rescue (Lv 14:40, 2 Sm 22:20, Ps 50:15 [49:15]).

יָצָא yātsā' (3428), Come out, go out, hiphil: pass under (Jer 34:13 [41:13]).

יָשַׁע yāshaʿ (3588), Hiphil: deliver (Jer 42:11 [49:11]).

לָקַח lāqach (4089), Niphal: taking (Jb 5:5—Codex Alexandrinus only).

מָלַט mālaṭ (4561), Niphal: escape (Eccl 7:26 [7:27]); piel: save, deliver (1 Kgs 1:12, Ez 33:5).

נָצַל nātsal (5522), Hiphil: save, rescue (Ex 3:8, 1 Chr 16:35, Hos 5:14).

נְצַל nᵉtsal (A5523), Haphel: deliver, rescue (Dn 3:29—Aramaic).

נָצַר nātsar (5526), Preserve, protect (Pss 64:1 [63:1], 140:4 [139:4]).

עָבַת ʿāvath (5893), Piel: desire (Mi 7:3 [7:4]).

עָזַר ʿāzar (6038), Help (Jos 10:6).

פָּלַט pālaṭ (6647), Piel: deliver (2 Sm 22:1, Pss 37:40 [36:40], 71:2 [70:2]).

פָּצָה pātsâh (6722), Deliver, rescue (Ps 144:7 [143:7]).

רָדָה rādhâh (7575), Scoop out, take out (Jgs 14:9).

שֵׁיזִב shêziv (A8288), Haphel: rescue, save (Dn 3:15,17, 6:14,16—Aramaic).

1. **ἔξελε** exele 2sing impr aor act
2. **ἐξαιρούμενος** exairoumenos nom sing masc part pres mid
3. **ἐξειλόμην** exeilomēn 1sing indic aor mid
4. **ἐξείλετο** exeileto 3sing indic aor mid
5. **ἐξέληται** exelētai 3sing subj aor mid
6. **ἐξελέσθαι** exelesthai inf aor mid
7. **ἐξειλάμην** exeilamēn 1sing indic aor mid
8. **ἐξείλατο** exeilato 3sing indic aor mid

1 And if thy right eye offend thee, **pluck it out**,	Matt 5:29
1 And if thine eye offend thee, **pluck it out**,	18:9
4 And **delivered** him out of all his afflictions,	Acts 7:10
8 And **delivered** him out of all his afflictions,	7:10
6 and am come down **to deliver** them.	7:34
4 and hath **delivered** me out of the hand of Herod,	12:11
8 and hath **delivered** me out of the hand of Herod,	12:11
3 then came I with an army, and **rescued** him,	23:27
7 then came I with an army, and **rescued** him,	23:27
2 **Delivering** thee from the people,	26:17
5 he might **deliver** us from this present evil world,	Gal 1:4

In the New Testament *exaireō* may refer to a violent extraction (Matthew 5:29); to taking one out of indescribable circumstances ("set free, deliver, rescue," see Acts 7:10); or to taking one away by force (Acts 23:27). *Exaireō* can also mean "deliver, select" or "choose out" Acts 26:17. In all of the above occurrences, as well as over 75 occurrences in the Septuagint (translating no fewer than 15 different Hebrew words), this term carries with it the implication of implicit danger. Thus it is a strong verb used to describe an unquestionably necessary form of removal.

STRONG 1807, BAUER 271-72, MOULTON-MILLIGAN 221, LIDDELL-SCOTT 581-82.

1792. ἐξαίρω exairō verb
Remove, drive away, lift up.

COGNATE:
αἴρω airō (142)

SYNONYMS:
αἴρω airō (142)
βαστάζω bastazō (934)
ἐκβάλλω ekballō (1531)
ἐξωθέω exōtheō (1840)
λαμβάνω lambanō (2956)
τίθημι tithēmi (4935)

אָבַד 'āvadh (6), Piel: destroy (Nm 33:52).

אָסַף 'āsaph (636), Gather up, draw up (Gn 49:33).

בָּעַר bā'ar (1220), Burn; piel: purge, get rid of (Dt 21:9, 22:22,24, 2 Chr 19:3).

גָּאוֹן gā'ôn (1377), Pride (Is 16:6).

גְּדַד gᵉdhadh (A1444), Cut down (Dn 4:23 [4:20]—Aramaic).

גָּדַע gādha' (1468), Niphal: broken (Ez 6:6).

גָּרַע gāra' (1686), Diminish, reduce (Ez 16:27).

גָּרַשׁ gārash (1691), Piel: drive out (Jgs 2:3).

הָרַס hāras (2117), Demolish, destroy (Mi 5:10 [5:11]).

טָמֵא ṭāmē' (3041), Become unclean; piel: defile (Is 30:22).

יָבֵשׁ yāvêsh (3111), Hiphil: dry up (Jer 51:36 [28:36]—Codex Sinaiticus only).

יָצָא yātsā' (3428), Qal: gone, departed (Lam 1:6, Ez 10:19—Codex Alexandrinus only); hiphil: bring, take (Ez 20:38—Codex Alexandrinus only).

יָרַשׁ yārash (3542), Take possession of; niphal: be poor (Prv 20:13); hiphil: cast out, drive out (Jgs 1:27ff., 2 Kgs 21:2).

כָּחַד kāchadh (3701), Hiphil: destroy (Zec 11:8).

כָּרַת kārath (3901), Qal: cut off (1 Kgs 20:16 [20:15]—Codex Alexandrinus only); niphal: fail (1 Kgs 8:25, 2 Chr 7:18, Ob 9); hiphil: cut off (1 Sm 20:15, Zep 1:3, Ez 14:8); hophal: be rooted out, cut off (Jl 1:9).

מוֹט môṭ (4267), Waver; niphal: move, uproot (Prv 12:3).

מָנַע māna' (4661), Keep, keep back (Jer 48:10 [31:10]).

מַסַּע massa' (4702), Set out, journey (Nm 10:2).

נָטַר nāṭar (5386), Take vengeance (Na 1:2).

נָסַח nāsach (5442), Tear out; niphal: pluck, uproot (Dt 28:63).

נָסַע nāsa' (5450), Qal: set out, journey (Nm 10:12,13, Ezr 8:31, Jer 4:7); hiphil: went (Ex 15:22).

נָשָׂא nāsâ' (5558), Qal: lift up, pardon (Nm 24:2, Ez 11:22, Mi 7:18); niphal: lifted up (Jer 51:9 [28:9], Ez 1:19ff.).

נָשַׁל nāshal (5577), Drive away (Dt 7:1).

נָתַשׁ nāthash (5612), Uproot (Dt 29:28, 2 Chr 7:20, Jer 18:7).

סָגַר sāghar (5646), Shut; hiphil: deliver (Am 6:8).

סוּר sûr (5681), Qal: remove, take away (1 Kgs 15:14, Am 6:7); hiphil: took away, remove (Jos 7:13, 2 Chr 17:6, Zec 9:7).

סָלָה sālâh (5733), Piel: reject (Lam 1:15).

סָלַף sālaph (5751), Piel: distort (Dt 16:19).

סְעָרָה sᵉ'ārāh (5788), Whirlwind, windstorm (Ez 1:4, 13:11,13).

סָפָה sāphâh (5793), Take, destroy (Ps 40:14 [39:14]).

עָבַר 'āvar (5882), Go over; hiphil: cut off, banish (Zec 13:2).

עוּר 'āwar (5996), Hiphil: awaken (Zec 4:1—Codex Vaticanus only).

רָגַע rāgha' (7567), Hiphil: give rest, bring rest (Jer 50:34 [27:34]).

שָׂכִיר sākhîr (7957), Hiphil: raise, lift up (Gn 41:44, Is 62:10); hophal: cast down, brought low (Dn 8:11).

שָׁחַת shāchath (8271), Hiphil: destroy (Jer 51:20 [28:20]).

שָׁמַד shāmadh (8436), Niphal: be destroyed (Hos 10:8); hiphil: destroy (Nm 33:52, 1 Chr 5:25, Am 9:8).

1. ἐξαρεῖτε exareite 2pl indic fut act
2. ἐξαρθῇ exarthē 3sing subj aor pass
3. ἐξάρατε exarate 2pl impr aor act

2 that he that hath done this deed might be taken	1 Co 5:2
1 Therefore put away ... that wicked person.	5:13
3 Therefore put away ... that wicked person.	5:13

Classical Greek

This term is a compound of the preposition *ek* (1523), "out, from" (*ex* before a vowel), and the verb *airō* (142), "to take." The resulting meaning is "to take away." The range of definition in classical Greek includes "to lift up" and "to lift off the earth" (see *Liddell-Scott*). It can also describe "rising," passively "being raised" (from the ground), or "removing" something (from its place). In the middle form it depicts "carrying something away."

Septuagint Usage

Exairō is an extremely common word in the Septuagint where it replaces as many as 37 different Hebrew terms as well as several variations of these. Furthermore, the term is very versatile in definition. It is used of someone "rising" to his feet (e.g., Genesis 29:1) or of someone lifting his hands (e.g., Leviticus 9:22). It also refers to the "setting out" of the camps of the tribes of Israel (e.g., Numbers 2:9,16,24,31).

On a number of occasions the word refers to the disciplinary action of "forcibly taking" someone (evil) from one place to another (e.g., Deuteronomy 17:5), in other words "driving them out" (cf. verses 7,12; 19:19; 21:9,21). This, too, was used of God's military action against Israel's enemies (e.g., Judges 1:20,21,27, etc.; cf. God's action, Amos 9:8; 1 Maccabees 14:14). *Exairō* thus hints at a religious action. For example, "to drive away, do away" with something evil was commendable (e.g., Sirach 49:2, of Josiah's taking away the "abominations of iniquity" [idols]; cf. 2 Chronicles 15:17, of Asa who did not take away the "high places" out of Israel). Therefore, in one sense it denotes divine judgment (e.g., 2 Chronicles 7:20; Amos 2:9; Obadiah 9).

New Testament Usage

The two times that *exairō* appears in the New Testament it comes from the pen of the apostle Paul (1 Corinthians 5:2,13). In 1 Corinthians the usage is significant because Paul was alluding to Deuteronomy, either 17:7 or 24:7: "Therefore put away (*exairō*) from among yourselves that wicked person" (1 Corinthians 5:13). Paul altered the tense of the verb to read an imperative rather than the future. Clearly Paul understood *exairō* in an almost technical sense here. It describes the divinely prescribed disciplinary action to be taken by the community. Paul appealed to the Old Testament as precedent for such action.

STRONG 1808, BAUER 272, MOULTON-MILLIGAN 221, LIDDELL-SCOTT 582.

1793. ἐξαιτέω exaiteō verb

Ask for, demand, request.

COGNATE:
αἰτέω aiteō (153)

SYNONYMS:
αἰτέω aiteō (153)
δέομαι deomai (1183)
ἐντυγχάνω entunchanō (1777)
ἐπερωτάω eperōtaō (1890)
ἐπιζητέω epizēteō (1919)
ἐρωτάω erōtaō (2049)
λέγω legō (2978)
παραιτέομαι paraiteomai (3729)
παρακαλέω parakaleō (3731)
πυνθάνομαι punthanomai (4299)

1. ἐξῃτήσατο exētēsato 3sing indic aor mid

1 Simon, behold, Satan hath desired to have you, ... Luke 22:31

Exaiteō is a compound verb from *ex* (see 1523) + *aiteō* (153), "ask for, demand." It is used only once in Luke's Gospel (22:31) where Jesus stated, "Satan has *asked* to sift you (*humas*, second person plural pronoun referring to the disciples) as wheat" (NIV). The sense is that Satan "demanded" to have the opportunity to tempt Peter and the rest of those who were present. (Cf. the story of Job in this sense.)

STRONG 1809, BAUER 272, MOULTON-MILLIGAN 221, KITTEL 1:194, LIDDELL-SCOTT 582, COLIN BROWN 2:855-56,858 (see "exaiteomai").

1794. ἐξαίφνης exaiphnēs adv

Suddenly, unexpectedly.

פִּתְאֹם pith'ōm (6849), Suddenly (Prv 24:22, Mal 3:1, Jer 6:26).

פֶּתַע petha' (6875), Suddenly (Hb 2:7).

רֶגַע regha' (7569), Suddenly (Is 47:9).

1. ἐξαίφνης exaiphnēs

ἐξακολουθέω 1795

1 Lest coming **suddenly** he find you sleeping.........Mark 13:36
1 And **suddenly** there was with the angel a multitude..Luke 2:13
1 lo, a spirit taketh him, and he **suddenly** crieth out;......9:39
1 and **suddenly** there shined round about him a light...Acts 9:3
1 **suddenly** there shone from heaven a great light........22:6

This adverb appears in the New Testament five times. It is found, for example, in connection with Paul's vision of Christ on the Damascus Road. Acts 9:3 and 22:6 says, "suddenly" a light appeared to Paul from heaven.

STRONG 1810, BAUER 272, MOULTON-MILLIGAN 221, LIDDELL-SCOTT 582.

1795. ἐξακολουθέω
exakoloutheō verb
Follow after, imitate.

COGNATE:
ἀκολουθέω akoloutheō (188)

SYNONYMS:
ἀκολουθέω akoloutheō (188)
εἰσακούω eisakouō (1508)
ἐπακολουθέω epakoloutheō (1857)
ἐπακούω epakouō (1858)
κατακολουθέω katakoloutheō (2598)
μιμέομαι mimeomai (3265)
παρακολουθέω parakoloutheō (3738)
συνακολουθέω sunakoloutheō (4721)
ὑπακούω hupakouō (5057)

פָּנָה pānâh (6680), Turn, look (Is 56:11).

פָּתָה pāthâh (6853), Be naive; niphal: be deceived (Jb 31:9).

1. ἐξακολουθήσαντες exakolouthēsantes
nom pl masc part aor act
2. ἐξακολουθήσουσιν exakolouthēsousin
3pl indic fut act

1 For we **have not followed** cunningly devised fables,..2 Pt 1:16
2 And many **shall follow** their pernicious ways;..........2:2
1 **following** the way of Balaam the son of Bosor,.........2:15

Second Peter is the only letter in which we find *exakoloutheō*. It occurs in 1:16; 2:2,15, and means "follow, pursue." It is used in a figurative sense nature (e.g., "many will follow their shameful ways," 2:2, NIV); however, the figurative always has practical implications in life-styles.

STRONG 1811, BAUER 272, MOULTON-MILLIGAN 221, KITTEL 1:215, LIDDELL-SCOTT 582, COLIN BROWN 1:480-81.

1796. ἑξακόσιοι hexakosioi num
Six hundred.

1. ἑξακοσίων hexakosiōn card gen sing masc/neu
2. ἑξακόσιοι hexakosioi card nom masc

2 his number is **six hundred** and sixty-six (NASB)....Rev 13:18
1 the space of a thousand and **six hundred** furlongs......14:20

This common number occurs only twice in the New Testament, both times in Revelation (13:18; 14:20). In 13:18 the number *600* is combined with *60* and *6*. Some have surmised that *6* may be symbolic of humanity and *3*, the number of the Trinity; thus the Antichrist will be a man claiming to be God. Others take *666* to be the sum of the numerical value of the letters of his name, taking the first letter of the alphabet to be 1, the second 2, etc. (For a full discussion of this topic, see the *Commentary* and *Overview* in *The Complete Biblical Library, Revelation*.) In 14:20 the 600 Greek furlongs (stades) equal about 177 miles.

STRONG 1812, BAUER 272, LIDDELL-SCOTT 582.

1797. ἐξαλείφω exaleiphō verb
Wipe, blot, or smear out, obliterate.

CROSS-REFERENCE:
ἀλείφω aleiphō (216)

גָּרַע gāraʿ (1686), Diminish; niphal: disappear, done away with (Nm 27:4 [27:3]).

חֲמוֹר chămôr (2645), Donkey (Jgs 15:16).

חֲמוֹר chămôr (2646), Heap (Jgs 15:16).

טוּחַ ṭûach (3012), Qal: plaster, coat (Lv 14:42, 1 Chr 29:4); niphal: be plastered (Lv 14:43,48).

מָחָה māchâh (4364), Qal: destroy (Gn 7:4, Ps 9:5); niphal: be destroyed (Dt 25:6, Ps 69:28 [68:28]); hiphil: blot out (Neh 13:14, Jer 18:23).

מַשְׁחִית mashchîth (5072), Destroy (Ez 25:15).

שָׁחַת shāchath (8271), Piel: destroy, devestate (Gn 9:15, Ez 20:17, Hos 11:9); hiphil: destroy (Ez 9:8).

1. ἐξαλείψας exaleipsas nom sing masc part aor act
2. ἐξαλείψω exaleipsō 1sing indic fut act
3. ἐξαλείψει exaleipsei 3sing indic fut act
4. ἐξαλειφθῆναι exaleiphthēnai inf aor pass

4 be converted, that your sins **may be blotted out**,......Acts 3:19
1 **Blotting out** the handwriting of ordinances..........Col 2:14
2 I will not **blot out** his name out of the book of life,..Rev 3:5
3 God shall **wipe away** all tears from their eyes..........7:17
3 And God shall **wipe away** all tears from their eyes;....21:5

Classical Greek
The term *exaleiphō* is derived from the word *aleiphō* (216), "to anoint, smear" (often with oil), and the preposition *ek* (1523). In this instance the preposition serves to intensify the action of the verb. Other classical meanings include "to rub," "to polish," or "to plaster." Metaphorically it thus meant "to wipe out, obliterate, destroy" (Packer, "Destroy," *Colin Brown*, 1:471).

Septuagint Usage

There are around 35 instances of *exaleiphō* in the Septuagint. Normally the Hebrew word it replaces is *māchâh*, "wipe off, wipe out, destroy" (in a variety of forms). It also substitutes for four other terms, although only *shāchath*, "to exterminate, render useless" (in various forms), occurs a significant number of times.

Exaleiphō functions in a very ordinary sense in 1 Chronicles of covering the roof of the temple with gold (29:4), but for the most part it functions metaphorically. *Exaleiphō* is used of God's decision to "wipe" everything from the face of the earth with the Flood (Genesis 7:4,23). In similar judgment language God declared that He would "blot out" the Amalekite people from the memory of all (Exodus 17:14) and that He will "blot out" of His book those who sin against Him (Exodus 32:32,33).

Positively the Psalmist requested that God "blot out" his transgressions (Psalm 51:1,9 [LXX 50:1,9]). In the Book of Isaiah God himself declares: "I, even I, am (*ego eimi* [see *The Complete Biblical Library, John,* especially pp.99,597-601]) he that blotteth out thy transgressions" (Isaiah 43:25; cf. Jeremiah 18:23).

New Testament Usage

The five New Testament usages of *exaleiphō* all reflect the Septuagint's understanding of the term. One instance occurs in Acts 3:19, which possibly picks up on the imagery used by the Psalmist and Isaiah: God is the One who "blots out" sins. The same might hold true in Colossians 2:14. The context is clearly one of forgiveness of sins (verse 13). Christ "wiped out" (NIV reads "canceled") the written debt against us and nailed it to the Cross.

In language similar to that of Exodus (32:32,33), John the Revelator wrote that God will never "blot out" from the Book of Life the names of those who overcome (Revelation 3:5). Later, in chapters 7 (verse 17) and 21 (verse 4) John wrote that God will "wipe away" all tears from the eyes of the faithful.

STRONG 1813, BAUER 272, MOULTON-MILLIGAN 221, LIDDELL-SCOTT 583, COLIN BROWN 1:471.

1798. ἐξάλλομαι exallomai verb

Leap up, spring.

CROSS-REFERENCE:
ἅλλομαι hallomai (240)

הוּם hûm (2016), Hiphil: be noisy (Mi 2:12).
פָּצַח pātsach (6723), Break forth (Is 55:12).
קָלַל qālal (7327), Bc swifter (Hb 1:8).
רָקַד rāqadh (7833), Piel: leap (Jl 2:5).

1. ἐξαλλόμενος exallomenos
nom sing masc part pres mid
1 And he leaping up stood, and walked, ... Acts 3:8

This word is used only one time in the New Testament, in the familiar story of the healing of the man at the temple gate called Beautiful (Acts 3). Upon his healing the man "jumped up" or "leaped up" and walked (verse 8).

STRONG 1814, BAUER 272, MOULTON-MILLIGAN 221, LIDDELL-SCOTT 583.

1799. ἐξανάστασις exanastasis noun

Resurrection, rising from (death).
CROSS-REFERENCE:
ἀνίστημι anistēmi (448)

1. ἐξανάστασιν exanastasin acc sing fem
1 I might attain unto the resurrection of the dead..... Phlp 3:11

This interesting compound word translated "resurrection" was employed by Paul in Philippians 3:11. This is the only passage in which this form of the word for resurrection is found. The word comes from a combination of the preposition *ek* (1523) meaning "out of" and the common Greek term for resurrection, *anastasis* (384). The emphasis here is on Paul's (and the Christian's) future hope of a *bodily* resurrection from or "out from among" the dead.

STRONG 1815, BAUER 272, MOULTON-MILLIGAN 221, KITTEL 1:371-72, LIDDELL-SCOTT 584, COLIN BROWN 3:259,278.

1800. ἐξανατέλλω exanatellō verb

Spring up, start up.
CROSS-REFERENCE:
ἀνατέλλω anatellō (391)

זָרַח zārach (2311), Shine, dawn (Ps 112:4 [111:4]).
צָמַח tsāmach (7048), Hiphil: grow, bud (Gn 2:9, Pss 132:17 [131:17], 147:8 [146:8]).

1. ἐξανέτειλεν exaneteilen 3sing indic aor act
1 and forthwith they sprung up, ... Matt 13:5
1 and immediately it sprang up, ... Mark 4:5

Limited to the Gospels of Matthew and Mark (Matthew 13:5; Mark 4:5), this term means "spring up, sprout." It is employed in both Gospels in connection with the Parable of the Sower. The seed which fell upon the rocky places "sprang up" quickly.

STRONG 1816, BAUER 272, LIDDELL-SCOTT 584.

1801. ἐξανίστημι exanistēmi verb
Raise up, stand up.

COGNATE:
ἀνίστημι anistēmi (448)

SYNONYMS:
διεγείρω diegeirō (1320)
ἐγείρω egeirō (1446)
ἐξεγείρω exegeirō (1809)

חָיָה chāyâh (2513), Be alive; piel: preserve (Gn 19:32,34).

יָקַץ yāqats (3477), Awaken (1 Kgs 18:27).

נָקַם nāqam (5541), Niphal: take revenge (Ez 25:15).

עָמַד 'āmadh (6198), Got up, stand up (Est 7:7—only some Sinaiticus texts).

פָּרַח pārach (6775), Risen, grown (Ez 7:11).

קוּם qûm (7251), Qal: rise up, get up (Ex 21:19, Jgs 3:20, Ob 1); hiphil: raise up, hold up (Jb 4:4); polel: raise up (Is 61:4).

קִיץ qîts (7301), Hiphil: awake (Is 29:8).

שִׁית shîth (8308), Grant, appoint (Gn 4:25).

שָׁכַם shākham (8326), Hiphil: get up, rise early (Is 37:36).

1. ἐξανέστησαν exanestēsan 3pl indic aor act
2. ἐξαναστήσῃ exanastēsē 3sing subj aor act

2 take his wife, and **raise up** seed unto his brother... Mark 12:19
2 and **raise up** seed unto his brother.............. Luke 20:28
1 But there **rose up** certain ... of the Pharisees....... Acts 15:5

Classical Greek
Exanistēmi comes from the preposition *ek* (1523) and the verb *anistēmi* (448), meaning "to raise up" (from the preposition *ana* [301], "up, again," and the verb *histēmi* [2449], "to stand"). Both *exanistēmi* and *anistēmi* are virtually synonymous with *egeirō* (1446), "to raise up." The term could be used of "waking" someone from sleep. It quite regularly carries a causal sense, "to make rise," when used in the present, imperfect, and future tenses (see *Liddell-Scott*). Other meanings include "to remove," "to drive out," or "to expel." Although belief in the "raising" of the dead was rather limited among the Greeks, *anistēmi* language was used to convey the concept (see Oepke, "anistēmi," *Kittel*, 1:369,371).

Septuagint Usage
The Septuagint ordinarily uses *exanistēmi* to translate the Hebrew word *qûm*, "to rise" (22 out of 32 times). It is used in the phrase "to raise up *seed*" i.e., *offspring* (Genesis 4:25; 19:32,34), an expression recurring in the New Testament.

Exanistēmi speaks of "rising up" in ambush (Joshua 8:7,18,19) or of someone "rising" up from his chair (Judges 3:20; Esther 7:7). Other meanings include "rising" from sleep (Isaiah 37:36) or the "increasing" of emotions (Ezekiel 7:11). Figuratively the weak were "raised up" by Job's words (4:4). Elsewhere, God "revives" the injured among the people of God (Hosea 6:2 [LXX 6:3]).

New Testament Usage
Exanistēmi is found three times in the New Testament. The most specific use of *exanistēmi* is "to raise up seed" (Mark 12:19; Luke 20:28). It has to do with the Hebrew custom concerning levirate marriages (literally, "brother-marriages"), whereby the childless widow of a deceased brother was to be married to the deceased man's brother for the express purpose of "raising up seed" (Deuteronomy 25:5). The idea behind the custom was to resurrect a "family line."

The intransitive form of the word is used in Acts 15:5 concerning the "rising up" of a movement of Jewish believers in the Early Christian Church. This included Pharisees who took the position that Gentiles should submit to circumcision in the tradition of becoming proselytes to the Jewish faith.

STRONG 1817, BAUER 272, MOULTON-MILLIGAN 221-22, KITTEL 1:368-71, LIDDELL-SCOTT 585, COLIN BROWN 3:259 (see "exanhistēmi").

1802. ἐξαπατάω exapataō verb
Deceive thoroughly, delude.

COGNATE:
ἀπατάω apataō (534)

SYNONYMS:
ἀπατάω apataō (534)
παραλογίζομαι paralogizomai (3745)
πλανάω planaō (3966)
φρεναπατάω phrenapataō (5258)

תָּלַל tālal (8853), Hiphil: act deceitfully (Ex 8:29).

1. ἐξαπατῶσιν exapatōsin 3pl indic pres act
2. ἐξαπατάτω exapatatō 3sing impr pres act
3. ἐξηπάτησεν exēpatēsen 3sing indic aor act
4. ἐξαπατήσῃ exapatēsē 3sing subj aor act
5. ἐξαπατηθεῖσα exapatētheisa
    nom sing fem part aor pass

3 **deceived** me, and by it slew me................... Rom 7:11
1 and fair speeches **deceive** the hearts of the simple...... 16:18
2 Let no man **deceive** himself....................... 1 Co 3:18

3 as the serpent **beguiled** Eve through his subtlety,... 2 Co 11:3
4 Let no man **deceive** you by any means:............. 2 Th 2:3
5 it was the woman who was **deceived** (NIV)......... 1 Tm 2:14

Apatē (535) means "deception" or "illusion"; *exapatē* means "deceit." *Apataō* (534) is "deceive"; *exapataō* has essentially the same meaning, although often with a stronger sense. Sin and desire are seen as "enticing" one (e.g., "the simple" [Romans 16:18]; Eve [2 Corinthians 11:3]), and 1 Corinthians 3:18 speaks of a man deceiving himself.

STRONG 1818, BAUER 273, MOULTON-MILLIGAN 222, KITTEL 1:384-85, LIDDELL-SCOTT 586, COLIN BROWN 2:457-59.

1803. ἐξάπινα exapina adv
Suddenly, unexpectedly.

פִּתְאֹם pith'ōm (6849), Suddenly (Jos 11:7, Ps 64:4 [63:4]).

1. ἐξάπινα exapina

1 And **suddenly**, when they had looked round about,..Mark 9:8

This is a very rare form of the adverb *exapinēs*, which is a variation of *exaiphnēs* (1794). *Exapina* occurs in the New Testament only in Mark 9:8. It is also found in *The Shepherd of Hermas*, "Lest the master come *suddenly* and find . . . " (see *Bauer*). The earlier form *exaiphnēs* occurs more frequently and also means "suddenly" (e.g., Mark 13:36; Luke 2:13). The idea of "unexpectedly" is implied.

STRONG 1819, BAUER 273, MOULTON-MILLIGAN 222, LIDDELL-SCOTT 586.

1804. ἐξαπορέω exaporeō verb
Be in great difficulty, utter despair, to be without resource.

פּוּן pûn (6566), Be helpless (Ps 88:15 [87:15]).

1. ἐξαπορούμενοι exaporoumenoi
nom pl masc part pres mid
2. ἐξαπορηθῆναι exaporēthēnai inf aor pass

2 insomuch that we **despaired** even of life:............ 2 Co 1:8
1 we are perplexed, but not **in despair**;.................. 4:8

This word represents the state of being at a loss for resources. Such distress may range from shortage of money to despairing of life itself. Generally, the meaning is "great distress to the point of despair." This sense of "utter despair" is what Paul had in mind when he used the word in 2 Corinthians 4:8: "We are perplexed, but not in despair."

STRONG 1820, BAUER 273, MOULTON-MILLIGAN 222, LIDDELL-SCOTT 586.

1805. ἐξαποστέλλω exapostellō verb
Send forth, send away.
CROSS-REFERENCE:
ἀποστέλλω apostellō (643)

אָבַד 'āvadh (6), Destroy (Jer 49:38 [25:17]).

גָּרַשׁ gārash (1691), Piel: drive out (Jos 24:12).

הָלַךְ hālakh (2050), Qal: go (1 Kgs 22:49 [22:50]—Codex Vaticanus only); hiphil: lead away (Jb 12:19).

יָצָא yātsâ' (3428), Qal: went out, left (Jgs 3:19); hiphil: brought out (Gn 45:1, Ex 6:13, 2 Kgs 11:12).

מַחֲשֶׁבֶת machăsheveth (4422II) Think, seem (Est 8:5).

מִשְׁלֹחַ mishlōach (5095I), Sending, giving (Est 9:19,22).

סוּר sûr (5681), Turn aside; hiphil: get rid of, remove (1 Kgs 15:12).

שׁוּב shûv (8178), Return; hiphil: answer, reply (Est 4:15).

שִׁלּוּחִים shillûchîm (8360), Give (Mi 1:14).

שָׁלַח shālach (8365), Qal: send (Gn 24:40, 1 Sm 16:20, Am 7:10); piel: gave over, let go (Ex 9:1, Ps 81:12 [80:12], Jer 3:1); pual: be sent (Ob 1); hiphil: let loose, stretch out (Ez 14:13, Am 8:11).

1. ἐξαπέστειλεν exapesteilen 3sing indic aor act
2. ἐξαπέστειλαν exapesteilan 3pl indic aor act
3. ἐξαποστελῶ exapostelō 1sing indic fut act
4. ἐξαποστέλλω exapostellō 1sing indic/subj pres act
5. ἐξαπεστάλη exapestalē 3sing indic aor pass

1 and the rich he hath **sent** empty **away**.............. Luke 1:53
2 husbandmen beat him, and **sent** him **away** empty....... 20:10
2 entreated him ... and **sent** him **away** empty.......... 20:11
4 I am **sending forth** the promise (NASB)............... 24:49
1 was corn in Egypt, he **sent out** our fathers first....... Acts 7:12
2 and **sent** him **forth** to Tarsus........................ 9:30
2 and they **sent forth** Barnabas,....................... 11:22
1 Now I know ... that the Lord **hath sent** his angel,...... 12:11
5 word of this salvation is **sent out** (NASB)............. 13:26
2 And then immediately the brethren **sent away** Paul.... 17:14
3 for I will **send** thee far hence unto the Gentiles....... 22:21
1 God **sent forth** his Son, made of a woman,........... Gal 4:4
1 God hath **sent forth** the Spirit of his Son............. 4:6

Classical Greek
Found in classical literature from the time of Polybius, *exapostellō* is nearly identical in its usage as *apostellō* (643), a related term. Like *apostellō*, this verb is a rather general expression denoting various acts of sending away, commissioning, banishing, etc. The *ek* (1523) prefix gives this verb a local force and emphasizes the source or sender.

Septuagint Usage
Similar to its use in classical Greek, *exapostellō* is a rather common expression in the Septuagint, occurring most often as a replacement for the

Hebrew word *shālach*, "to send" (in various tenses). Essentially it is interchangeable with *apostellō*, although it occurs less frequently. Typically it can denote either something or someone that is God-sent (e.g., Genesis 3:23; 24:40; Exodus 3:12, of Israel). It can also depict nondivine sending (e.g., Genesis 25:6; Leviticus 14:7,53; 2 Samuel 3:14 [LXX 2 Kings 3:14]).

On a few occasions the objects sent are "messengers" (e.g., Judges 6:35; 2 Kings 1:16 [LXX 4 Kings 1:16]) or "men" (Judges 20:12). God also sends His prophet (Judges 6:8), His mercy (Psalm 57:3 [LXX 56:3]), His help (Psalm 20:2 [19:2]), and His light (Psalm 43:3 [42:3]). Conversely, God sends judgment (literally "fire," Amos 1:4,7,10,12; 2:2; cf. Jeremiah 28:16 [LXX 35:16]; 49:37 [25:16]) as well.

New Testament Usage

In Galatians 4:4 the local sense of *exapostellō* emphasizes the source of the Incarnation, "when the fulness of time was come, God *sent* forth his Son, made of a woman, made under the law." The primary force of the word is that of "sending from." In this case the Sender is God (*ek*, "out of"), and the historical conditions have only to do with the mode of His coming: (1) "made of a woman" (i.e., the virgin Mary) and (2) "made under the law." These relate to the cultural, spiritual, and physical matrix in which the Lord was born and grew up.

Exapostellō is also used of the Holy Spirit (Galatians 4:6): "God hath sent forth the Spirit of his Son into your hearts, crying, Abba, Father" (cf. Luke 24:49; Acts 2:4). In Acts it is said that the angel was *sent* from the Lord to deliver Peter from prison (Acts 7:12).

Jacob is said to have *sent out* his sons to Egypt for food in time of famine. Paul was *sent* of the Lord to the Gentiles (Acts 22:21). In his sermon in Antioch of Pisidia Paul used the word in reference to the "word of this salvation" which was *sent* to the God-fearers of Antioch (Acts 13:26).

In some cases the word means to "send away" (Luke 1:53). In every instance there is a clear emphasis on the sender and on the purpose for which the one sent is being sent. Few words express the mission of the Church more powerfully.

STRONG 1821, BAUER 273, MOULTON-MILLIGAN 222, KITTEL 1:406, LIDDELL-SCOTT 586, COLIN BROWN 1:126-28.

1806. ἐξαρτίζω exartizō verb

Finish, accomplish, completely furnish, fully equip.

COGNATE:
  ἄρτιος artios (734)

SYNONYMS:
  ἀναπληρόω anaplēroō (376)
  ἀνταναπληρόω antanaplēroō (463)
  ἀποτελέω apoteleō (652)
  διανύω dianuō (1268)
  ἐκπληρόω ekplēroō (1590)
  ἐκτελέω ekteleō (1602)
  ἐπιτελέω epiteleō (1989)
  ἐργάζομαι ergazomai (2021)
  καταρτίζω katartizō (2645)
  κατεργάζομαι katergazomai (2686)
  πληρόω plēroō (3997)
  ποιέω poieō (4020)
  πράσσω prassō (4097)
  συντελέω sunteleō (4783)
  τελειόω teleioō (4896)
  τελέω teleō (4903)

חָבַר chāvar (2357), Pual: be joined (Ex 28:7—Sixtine Edition only).

1. ἐξαρτίσαι exartisai inf aor act
2. ἐξηρτισμένος exērtismenos
    nom sing masc part perf mid

1 And when we **had accomplished** those days, ... Acts 21:5
2 **thoroughly furnished** unto all good works. . . . . 2 Tm 3:17

In Acts 21:5 the word is used of days. The sense is that the time was complete: "When our days there were ended" (RSV). In 2 Timothy 3:17, the idea is of preparation being thorough (complete), or of our being "fully prepared" or "equipped."

STRONG 1822, BAUER 273, MOULTON-MILLIGAN 222, KITTEL 1:475-76, LIDDELL-SCOTT 587-88, COLIN BROWN 3:349-51.

1807. ἐξαστράπτω exastraptō verb

Flash, gleam like lightning, radiate, glisten.

בָּרָק bārāq (1326), Flash (Na 3:3).
לָקַח lāqach (4089), Take; hithpael: flashing (Ez 1:4).
קָלַל qālal (7328), Polish, burnish (Dn 10:6).

1. ἐξαστράπτων exastraptōn
    nom sing masc part pres act

1 and his raiment was white and **glistering**. . . . . Luke 9:29

This is a verb which refers to a dazzling brilliance and could be translated "flashing forth like lightning." In its only New Testament occurrence its form is that of an adjective used to describe Jesus' garment at the Transfiguration (Luke 9:29). *Astrapē* (790) means "lightning" and is used to describe the appearance of the angel who rolled the stone back from Jesus' grave. *Astrapē* is also the word used in the Septuagint to describe the lightnings on Mount Sinai when Moses met with God (Exodus 19:16). *Exastraptō* has essentially the same meaning and is the word used to describe the appearance of Ezekiel's vision of God (Ezekiel 1:4,7), and the flashing weapons of Nahum 3:3.

STRONG 1823, BAUER 273, MOULTON-MILLIGAN 222, LIDDELL-SCOTT 588.

1808. ἐξαυτῆς exautēs adv

At once, immediately, at the instant.

SYNONYMS:
εὐθέως eutheōs (2091)
εὐθύς euthus (2098)
παραχρῆμα parachrēma (3777)
ταχέως tacheōs (4878)

1. ἐξαυτῆς exautēs

1 I want you to give me **right away** the head (NASB) Mark 6:25
1 **Immediately** therefore I sent to thee; .... Acts 10:33
1 And, behold, **immediately** there were three men 11:11
1 Who **immediately** took soldiers and centurions, ... 21:32
1 I sent **straightway** to thee, ... 23:30
1 Him therefore I hope to send **presently**, ... Phlp 2:23

This is an adverb meaning "immediately" or "at once," although it is translated "presently" or "soon" in Philippians 2:23. *Autēs* means "self" or "the same." The sense seems to be "at this same (moment)" or "at once."

STRONG 1824, BAUER 273, MOULTON-MILLIGAN 222, LIDDELL-SCOTT 588.

1809. ἐξεγείρω exegeirō verb

Arouse, raise up, appear.

COGNATE:
ἐγείρω egeirō (1446)

SYNONYMS:
ἀνίστημι anistēmi (448)
διεγείρω diegeirō (1320)
ἐγείρω egeirō (1446)
ἐξανίστημι exanistēmi (1801)

בָּעַר bāʿar (1220), Burn; hiphil: consume, take away (1 Kgs 16:3).

חִיל chîl (2523), Be in labor; polel: bring, bring forth (Prv 25:23).

חַי chay (2508), Life (Is 38:16).

טוּל ṭûl (3014), Hiphil: sent (Jon 1:4).

יָעַד yāʿadh (3366), Designate; hiphil: be turned, be directed (Ez 21:16).

יָקַץ yāqats (3477), Awake, wake up (Gn 41:21, Ps 78:65 [77:65]).

עָבַר ʿāvar (5882), Hiphil: crossed, went over (2 Sm 19:18).

עוּר ʿāwar (5996), Qal: arise, be awake (Jgs 5:12, Ps 7:6, Hb 2:19); niphal: be stirred up, be raised up (Jl 3:12, Jer 50:41 [27:41]); polel: stir up, raise (2 Sm 23:18, Ps 80:2 [79:2], S/S 8:5); hiphil: stirred, moved (2 Chr 36:22, Ps 35:23 [35:23], Jer 51:1 [28:1]); hithpael: awake, rouse oneself (Is 51:17).

קוּם qûm (7251), Qal: rise, get up (Nm 10:35, Est 8:4, Ps 119:62 [118:62]); hiphil: raise up (2 Sm 12:11, Hb 1:6, Zec 11:16).

קִיץ qîts (7301), Hiphil: awake (1 Sm 26:12, Ps 3:5, Jer 31:26 [38:26]).

רָדָה rādhâh (7575), Rule, govern (Nm 24:19).

שָׂגַב sāghav (7891), Be high (Jb 5:11).

שָׁמַד shāmadh (8436), Hiphil: destroyed (Am 2:9—Codex Alexandrinus only).

1. ἐξήγειρα exēgeira 1sing indic aor act
2. ἐξεγερεῖ exegerei 3sing indic fut act
3. ἐξήγειρεν exēgeiren 3sing indic aor act
4. ἐξεγείρει exegeirei 3sing indic pres act

1 Even for this same purpose **have I raised** thee up, ... Rom 9:17
2 and will also **raise up** us by his own power. .... 1 Co 6:14
3 and will also **raise up** us by his own power. 6:14
4 and will also **raise up** us by his own power. 6:14

Classical Greek

This compound verb from *ek* (1523) plus *egeirō* (1446), "I raise," means "to awaken" (from sleep) and then "to raise from the dead" (Aeschylus, Fifth Century B.C., see *Bauer*). A metaphorical usage, "to arouse" is also attested in classical Greek (see *Liddell-Scott*).

Septuagint Usage

Exegeirō is a versatile word used extensively in the Septuagint, translating 17 different Hebrew words. Most commonly a form of *ʿāwar*, "to awake, to stir, to arouse" (also used as an equivalent to *egeirō*), lies behind *exegeirō*. The idea of "to awaken from sleep" occurs regularly (e.g., of Jacob following his dream of the ladder, Hebrew *yāqats*; Genesis 28:16; cf. Psalm 3:5).

In another sense *exegeirō* carries images of warlike force and power. Perhaps "to muster" would not be inaccurate. Moses invoked the Lord to "arise" before the ark (Numbers 10:35; cf. Psalms 7:6; 35:23 [LXX 34:23]; 44:23 [43:23]; 59:4 [58:4]). The sense of "to destroy" occurs in Amos 2:9 (cf. the violent sea in Jonah 1:4,11,13; see also Joel 3:7; Zechariah 2:13). Thus the image consistently evokes an almost military summons for preparedness, a violent, hurried "stirring" into action (Isaiah 41:2; 51:9,17; 52:1; Jeremiah 6:1,22f.; 50:41 [LXX

27:41]; 51:1 [28:1]; cf. 2 Maccabees 13:4). The idea of "to raise from the dead" is not present except in Daniel 12:2.

New Testament Usage
Exegeirō is a Pauline word used twice in the New Testament. Paul (Romans 9:17) substituted *exegeirō*, "to raise up," for *diatēreō* (1295), "to maintain," the Septuagint's reading of this Old Testament text (Exodus 9:16; Hebrew *'āmadh*). Paul's point was that all of us, like Pharaoh, are utterly dependent upon God for mercy. Only His mercy permitted Pharaoh to live (RSV translates the Hebrew "to let live").

Paul declared that God both has raised Jesus (*egeirō*, aorist), and He "will raise" (*exegeirō*, future, see Metzger, *Textual Commentary* for the basis of this textual decision) believers through His power (1 Corinthians 6:14). Such a realization and assurance of the promise of bodily resurrection should be an incentive for pure and holy living (cf. verse 18).

STRONG 1825, BAUER 273, MOULTON-MILLIGAN 222, KITTEL 2:338, LIDDELL-SCOTT 589.

1809B. ἔξειμι exeimi verb
Go out, depart.
COGNATE:
εἰμί eimi (1498)
SYNONYMS:
ἀναλύω analuō (358)
ἀναχωρέω anachōreō (400)
ἀπαλλάσσω apallassō (521)
ἀπέρχομαι aperchomai (562)
ἀποβαίνω apobainō (571)
ἀπολύω apoluō (624)
ἀποχωρέω apochōreō (666)
ἀφίημι aphiēmi (856)
ἀφίστημι aphistēmi (861)
διαχωρίζω diachōrizō (1310)
ἐγκαταλείπω enkataleipō (1452)
ἐκβαίνω ekbainō (1530B)
ἐκπορεύω ekporeuō (1594)
ἐξέρχομαι exerchomai (1814)
μεταίρω metairō (3202)
παράγω paragō (3717)
ὑπάγω hupagō (5055)
χωρέω chōreō (5397)

1. ἐξιόντων exiontōn gen pl masc part pres act
2. ἐξιέναι exienai inf pres act
3. ἐξῄεσαν exēesan 3pl indic imperf act

1 when the Jews were gone out of the synagogue,.... Acts 13:42
3 for to come to him with all speed, they departed....... 17:15
2 ready to depart on the morrow;........................ 20:7
2 cast themselves first into the sea, and get to land:..... 27:43

The word *exeimi* is spelled the same in this form as the word for "it is possible or lawful," but the spellings are often different in actual use. This word is a combination of *ek* (1523), "out of," and *eimi* (1498), "to go." Its meaning is "go out" or "depart," although in context it sometimes is rendered "come out" instead of "go out." In Acts 27:43 it is used with *epi tēn gēn* meaning "get to land."

STRONG 1826, BAUER 273-74, MOULTON-MILLIGAN 222, LIDDELL-SCOTT 589, COLIN BROWN 2:606.

1810. ἐξελέγχω exelenchō verb
Convict.
SYNONYM:
ἐλέγχω elenchō (1638)

יָכַח yākhach (3306), Hiphil: judge, settle disputes (Is 2:4, Mi 4:3).

1. ἐξελέγξαι exelenxai inf aor act

1 and to convince all that are ungodly among them....Jude 1:15

This word is used in both the Septuagint and Apocrypha. For example Isaiah 2:4 and Micah 4:3 state that the Lord will "rebuke." It occurs just once in the New Testament. Jude 15 says the Lord will "convict" of sin. The concept is that of revealing sin and reproving for sin.

STRONG 1827, BAUER 274, MOULTON-MILLIGAN 222, LIDDELL-SCOTT 590.

1811. ἐξέλκω exelkō verb
Drag out, draw out.

יָרַשׁ yārash (3542), Take possession of; hiphil: cast out (Jb 20:15).
מִיץ mîts (4468), Churning (Prv 30:33 [24:68]).
מָשַׁךְ māshakh (5082), Pull, draw (Gn 37:28).
נָתַק nāthaq (5607), Pual: be drawn away (Jgs 20:31—Codex Alexandrinus only).
שָׁאַף shā'aph (8079), Desire, long for (Jb 36:20).

1. ἐξελκόμενος exelkomenos
nom sing masc part pres mid

1 he is drawn away of his own lust, and enticed........ Jas 1:14

This word denotes to "drag away" or "draw out." Joseph's brothers "drew" him up "out" of the pit to sell him to the Ishmaelites (Genesis 37:28). In its only New Testament occurrence *exelkō* is used of the effect a person's desires can have on him, as they threaten to entice or "pull" him "away" and "drag" him into captivity to sin (James 1:14).

STRONG 1828, BAUER 274, MOULTON-MILLIGAN 222-23, LIDDELL-SCOTT 590.

1812. ἐξέραμα exerama noun
Vomit, what has been vomited.

1. ἐξέραμα exerama nom/acc sing neu

1 The dog is turned to his own **vomit** again; .... 2 Pt 2:22

This little used word is related to the verb *exeraō*. *Exeraō* denotes to "purge" or "vomit" and it is also used in reference to the discharge from wounds. The noun *exerama* occurs only once in the Bible, at 2 Peter 2:22. Although this is a reference to Proverbs 26:11, the word used in the Septuagint version of Proverbs is *emeton* (from *emetos*), "to vomit." According to Kelly the point of this proverb is "to show in a shocking way the folly and shame of reverting voluntarily to the moral squalor of paganism" (*Thornapple Commentaries, Epistles of Peter and Jude*, p.350).

STRONG 1829, BAUER 274, MOULTON-MILLIGAN 223, LIDDELL-SCOTT 590.

1813. ἐξεραυνάω exeraunaō verb
Search out in detail, inquire carefully.

CROSS-REFERENCE:
ἐραυνάω eraunaō (2020B)

חָפַשׂ chāphas (2769), Qal: search out, plot (Ps 64:6 [63:6], Prv 2:4); niphal: be searched out (Ob 6); piel: search, track (1 Sm 23:23, Am 9:3, Zep 1:12); pual: be searched (Ps 64:6 [63:6]).

חָקַק chāqaq (2809), Poal: command (Jgs 5:14).

חָקַר chāqar (2811), Spy out (1 Chr 19:3).

חָשַׂף chāsaph (2911), Strip off bark (Jl 1:7).

נָצַר nātsar (5526), Keep, observe (Ps 119 [118]:2,69,115,129).

נָקַשׁ nāqash (5550), Piel: catch, seize (Ps 109:11 [108:11]).

שָׁאַל shā'al (8068), Inquire (Dt 13:14).

1. ἐξηρεύνησαν exēreunēsan 3pl indic aor act

1 **prophets** have **inquired and searched diligently**, ... 1 Pt 1:10

In classical Greek it is often used of "scientific, philosophical and religious investigation (particularly in Philo and Plato)" (Seitz, "Seek," *Colin Brown*, 3:533). The word appears frequently in the Septuagint. The idea of a thorough search is seen in 1 Samuel 23:23 (LXX 1 Kings 23:23), "I will search him out throughout all the thousands of Judah." *Exeraunaō*—from the old root *ereunaō*—occurs only in 1 Peter 1:10 in the New Testament. Here the word denotes a very careful, diligent, and precise search, even to the minute detail.

Exeraunaō is used to describe the zeal with which the prophets sought to understand the salvation promised through Christ. The use of this word fits Peter's vocabulary which points consistently throughout the epistle to the precious value of Christ's sacrifice for us.

STRONG 1830, BAUER 274, MOULTON-MILLIGAN 223, KITTEL 2:655-57 (see "exereunaō"), LIDDELL-SCOTT 590, COLIN BROWN 3:532-33.

1813B. ἐξεραυνέω exerauneō verb
Inquire carefully.

CROSS-REFERENCE:
ἐραυνάω eraunaō (2020B)

1. ἐξηραύνησαν exēraunēsan 3pl indic aor act

This is an alternate spelling of *exeraunaō*. See the word study at number 1813.

1814. ἐξέρχομαι exerchomai verb
Go out, come out, issue, depart, send forth.

COGNATE:
ἔρχομαι erchomai (2048)

SYNONYMS:
ἀναλύω analuō (358)
ἀναχωρέω anachōreō (400)
ἀπαλλάσσω apallassō (521)
ἀπέρχομαι aperchomai (562)
ἀποβαίνω apobainō (571)
ἀπολύω apoluō (624)
ἀποχωρέω apochōreō (666)
ἀφίημι aphiēmi (856)
ἀφίστημι aphistēmi (861)
διαχωρίζω diachōrizō (1310)
ἐγκαταλείπω enkataleipō (1452)
ἐκβαίνω ekbainō (1530B)
ἐκπορεύω ekporeuō (1594)
ἐξιέναι exienai (1821)
μεταίρω metairō (3202)
παράγω paragō (3717)
ὑπάγω hupagō (5055)
χωρέω chōreō (5397)

אָסַף 'āsaph (636), Gather; niphal: be gathered (Jgs 10:17—Codex Alexandrinus only).

בָּהַל bāhal (963), Niphal: be terrified (Jer 51:32 [28:32]).

בּוֹא bô' (971), Go, come (Nm 10:9, 2 Kgs 23:17, Jer 31:9 [38:9]).

הָלַךְ hālakh (2050), Go, walk (Gn 12:1, Jer 22:22).

יָצָא yātsâ' (3428), Qal: go out, come forth (Ex 4:14, Ps 19:4 [18:4], Is 48:3); hiphil: carry out, brought out (Dt 16:1, Ez 12:6,7); hophal: be brought out (Ez 38:8).

כָּרַת kārath (3901), Cut off (Jl 1:9—only some Sinaiticus texts).

ἐξέρχομαι 1814

לָקַח lāqach (4089), Receive (Jb 27:13—Codex Alexandrinus only).

מוֹצָא môtsā' (4296), What proceeds from (Nm 30:12 [30:13]).

מִיצִיאֵו mîtsî'ēw (4469), Came into, went into (2 Chr 32:21).

נָזַל nāzal (5320), Flow (Nm 24:7).

נָסַע nāsa' (5450), Qal: went out, went forth (Nm 11:31); niphal: pulled down, departed (Is 38:12).

נְפַק nᵉphaq (A5494), Come out, come forth (Dn 3:26, 5:5—Aramaic).

עָבַר 'āvar (5882), Go into, go down (Jb 33:28—Codex Alexandrinus only).

עָטַף 'āṭaph (6063), Fail, faint (Is 57:16).

עָלָה 'ālāh (6148), Came up, out (Ex 1:10, Jos 19:10, Is 11:16).

צָבָא tsāvā' (6892), Go with, accompany (1 Sm 28:1).

רוּץ rûts (7608), Run (Jos 8:19, 2 Sm 18:21).

תָּמַם tāmam (8882), Be used up, spent (Gn 47:18).

1. ἐξῆλθον exēlthon 1/3sing/pl indic aor act
2. ἐξῆλθες exēlthes 2sing indic aor act
3. ἐξῆλθεν exēlthen 3sing indic aor act
4. ἐξήλθομεν exēlthomen 1pl indic aor act
5. ἐξήλθετε exēlthete 2pl indic aor act
6. ἐξέλθῃς exelthēs 2sing subj aor act
7. ἐξέλθῃ exelthē 3sing subj aor act
8. ἐξέλθητε exelthēte 2pl subj aor act
9. ἔξελθε exelthe 2sing impr aor act
10. ἐξέλθατε exelthate 2pl impr aor act
11. ἐξελθόντα exelthonta
    nom/acc sing/pl masc/neu part aor act
12. ἐξελθόντος exelthontos
    gen sing masc/neu part aor act
13. ἐξελθών exelthōn nom sing masc part aor act
14. ἐξελθόντι exelthonti dat sing masc part aor act
15. ἐξελθόντες exelthontes nom pl masc part aor act
16. ἐξελθόντων exelthontōn gen pl masc part aor act
17. ἐξελθοῦσα exelthousa nom sing fem part aor act
18. ἐξελθοῦσαν exelthousan acc sing fem part aor act
19. ἐξελθοῦσαι exelthousai nom pl fem part aor act
20. ἐξελθεῖν exelthein inf aor act
21. ἐξελήλυθα exelēlutha 1sing indic perf act
22. ἐξελήλυθεν exelēluthen 3sing indic perf act
23. ἐξεληλύθατε exelēluthate 2pl indic perf act
24. ἐξεληλύθασιν exelēluthasin 3pl indic perf act
25. ἐξελήλυθει exelēluthei 3sing indic plperf act
26. ἐξεληλυθότας exelēluthotas
    acc pl masc part perf act
27. ἐξεληλυθός exelēluthos
    nom/acc sing neu part perf act
28. ἐξέρχεται exerchetai 3sing indic pres mid
29. ἐξέρχονται exerchontai 3pl indic pres mid
30. ἐξερχώμεθα exerchōmetha 1pl subj pres mid
31. ἐξέρχεσθε exerchesthe 2pl impr pres mid
32. ἐξερχόμενος exerchomenos
    nom sing masc part pres mid
33. ἐξερχόμενοι exerchomenoi
    nom pl masc part pres mid
34. ἐξερχομένων exerchomenōn
    gen pl masc part pres mid
35. ἐξέρχεσθαι exerchesthai inf pres mid
36. ἐξελεύσεται exeleusetai 3sing indic fut mid
37. ἐξελεύσονται exeleusontai 3pl indic fut mid
38. ἐξήρχετο exērcheto 3sing indic imperf mid
39. ἐξήρχοντο exērchonto 3pl indic imperf mid
40. ἐξήλθατε exēlthate 2pl indic aor act
41. ἐξῆλθαν exēlthan 3pl indic aor act
42. ἐξελθούσῃ exelthousē dat sing fem part aor act
43. ἐξεληλυθυῖαν exelēluthuian
    acc sing fem part perf act
44. ἐξέλθετε exelthete 2pl impr pres act

36	for out of thee **shall come** a Governor,	Matt 2:6
6	Thou shalt by no means **come out** thence,	5:26
37	shall be cast out into outer darkness:	8:12
33	two possessed with devils, **coming out** of the tombs,	8:28
15	Go. And when they **were come out**,	8:32
3	behold, the whole city **came out** to meet Jesus:	8:34
3	And the fame hereof **went abroad** into all that land.	9:26
15	But they, when they **were departed**,	9:31
34	As they **went out**, ... brought to him a dumb man	9:32
8	who ... worthy; and there abide till ye **go thence**.	10:11
33	when ye **depart** out of that house or city,	10:14
5	What **went ye out** into the wilderness to see?	11:7
40	What **went ye out** into the wilderness to see?	11:7
5	But what **went ye out** for to see?	11:8
40	But what **went ye out** for to see?	11:8
5	But what **went ye out** for to see? A prophet?	11:9
40	But what **went ye out** for to see? A prophet?	11:9
15	Then the Pharisees **went out**, and held a council	12:14
7	When the unclean spirit **is gone out** of a man,	12:43
1	will return into my house from whence I **came out**;	12:44
13	The same day **went** Jesus **out** of the house,	13:1
3	saying, Behold, a sower **went forth** to sow;	13:3
37	the angels **shall come forth**,	13:49
13	And Jesus **went forth**, and saw a great multitude,	14:14
28	out of the mouth **come forth** from the heart,	15:18
29	For out of the heart **proceed** evil thoughts,	15:19
13	Then Jesus **went thence**, and departed	15:21
17	a woman of Canaan **came out** of the same coasts,	15:22
3	rebuked the devil; and he **departed** out of him:	17:18
13	But the same servant **went out**,	18:28
3	**went out** early in the morning to hire labourers	20:1
13	And he **went out** about the third hour,	20:3
13	Again he **went out** about the sixth and ninth hour,	20:5
13	And about the eleventh hour he **went out**,	20:6
3	left them, and **went out** of the city into Bethany;	21:17
15	So those servants **went out** into the highways,	22:10
13	Jesus **went out**, and departed from the temple:	24:1
8	Behold, he is in the desert; **go not forth**:	24:26
28	For as the lightning **cometh out** of the east,	24:27
1	and **went forth** to meet the bridegroom.	25:1
31	the bridegroom cometh; **go ye out** to meet him.	25:6
1	they **went out** into the mount of Olives.	26:30
5	Are ye **come out** as against a thief with swords	26:55
40	Are ye **come out** as against a thief with swords	26:55
11	And when he **was gone out** into the porch,	26:71
13	And he **went out**, and wept bitterly.	26:75
33	as they **came out**, they found a man of Cyrene,	27:32
3	let us see whether Elias will **come** to save him.	27:49
15	And **came out** of the graves after his resurrection,	27:53
19	And they **departed** quickly from the sepulchre;	28:8
9	saying, Hold thy peace, and **come out** of him.	Mark 1:25
3	and cried with a loud voice, he **came out** of him.	1:26

ἐξέρχομαι 1814

3 And immediately his fame **spread abroad** .... Mark 1:28	15 go your ways **out** into the streets of the same, ... Luke 10:10
15 when they **were come out** of the synagogue, ... 1:29	13 morrow when he **departed**, he took out two pence, ... 10:35
13 when they **were come out** of the synagogue, ... 1:29	12 when the devil **was gone out**, the dumb spake; 11:14
3 rising up a great while before day, **he went out**, ... 1:35	7 When the unclean spirit **is gone** out of a man, ... 11:24
21 that I may preach ... for therefore **came I forth**. 1:38	1 I will return unto my house whence I **came out**. 11:24
1 that I may preach ... for therefore **came I forth**. 1:38	12 And when He left there, (NASB) 11:53
13 But he **went out**, and began to publish it much, ... 1:45	6 I tell thee, thou **shalt** not **depart** thence, ... 12:59
3 took up the bed, and **went forth** before them all; 2:12	9 saying unto him, Get thee **out**, and depart hence: 13:31
3 And **he went forth** again by the sea side; 2:13	20 bought ... ground, and I must needs **go** and see it: ... 14:18
15 And the Pharisees **went forth**, ... 3:6	13 bought ... ground, and I must needs **go** and see it: ... 14:18
1 they **went out** to lay hold on him: for they said, ... 3:21	9 **Go out** quickly into the streets and lanes of the city, .. 14:21
3 Hearken; Behold, there **went out** a sower to sow: 4:3	9 **Go out** into the highways and hedges, ... 14:23
14 And when he was **come out** of the ship, ... 5:2	13 therefore **came** his father **out**, and entreated him. 15:28
12 And when he was **come out** of the ship, ... 5:2	3 But the same day that Lot **went out** of Sodom 17:29
9 **Come out** of the man, thou unclean spirit. 5:8	32 and at night he **went out**, and abode in the mount 21:37
11 And the unclean spirits **went out**, ... 5:13	13 he **came out**, and went, ... to the mount of Olives; 22:39
1 And they **went out** to see what it was that was done ... 5:14	23 Be ye **come out**, as against a thief, with swords 22:52
18 knowing in himself that virtue **had gone out** 5:30	40 Be ye **come out**, as against a thief, with swords 22:52
3 And he **went out** from thence, ... 6:1	13 And Peter **went out**, and wept bitterly. 22:62
8 there abide till ye **depart from** that place. 6:10	20 The day following Jesus would **go forth** .... John 1:43
15 **went out**, and preached that men should repent. 6:12	1 they **went out** of the city, and came unto him. 4:30
17 And she **went forth**, and said unto her mother, ... 6:24	3 Now after two days he **departed** thence, ... 4:43
13 And Jesus, when he **came out**, saw much people, ... 6:34	39 **went out** one by one, beginning at the eldest, ... 8:9
16 And when they **were come out** of the ship, ... 6:54	1 for I **proceeded forth** and came from God, ... 8:42
22 the devil **is gone out** of thy daughter. 7:29	3 but Jesus hid himself, and **went out** of the temple, ... 8:59
27 she found the devil **gone out**, ... 7:30	36 and **shall go** in and **out**, and find pasture. 10:9
13 **departing** from the coasts of Tyre and Sidon, ... 7:31	3 but he **escaped out** of their hand, ... 10:39
1 the Pharisees **came forth**, and began to question 8:11	3 that she rose up hastily and **went out**, ... 11:31
3 And Jesus **went out**, and his disciples, ... 8:27	3 And he that was dead **came forth**, ... 11:44
9 **come out** of him, and enter no more into him. 9:25	1 and **went forth** to meet him, and cried, Hosanna: 12:13
3 and rent him sore, and **came out** of him: 9:26	3 and that he **was come** from God, and went to God; 13:3
20 This kind can **come forth** by nothing, but by 9:29	3 having received the sop **went** immediately **out**: 13:30
15 they **departed** thence, and passed through Galilee; 9:30	3 Therefore, when he **was gone out**, Jesus said, ... 13:31
3 he **went out** unto Bethany with the twelve. 11:11	1 and have believed that I **came out** from God. 16:27
16 they **were come** from Bethany, he was hungry: 11:12	1 **I came forth** from the Father, ... 16:28
1 his disciples **went forth**, and came into the city, ... 14:16	2 this we believe that thou **camest forth** from God. 16:30
1 they **went out** into the mount of Olives. 14:26	1 and have known surely that I **came out** from thee, ... 17:8
5 Are ye **come out**, as against a thief, with swords 14:48	3 he **went forth** with his disciples 18:1
40 Are ye **come out**, as against a thief, with swords 14:48	13 **went forth**, and said unto them, Whom seek ye? 18:4
3 he **went out** into the porch; and the cock crew. 14:68	3 **went forth**, and said unto them, Whom seek ye? 18:4
19 **went out** quickly, and fled from the sepulchre; 16:8	3 Then **went out** that other disciple, ... 18:16
15 And they **went forth**, and preached every where, ... 16:20	3 Pilate then **went out** unto them, and said, ... 18:29
13 when he **came out**, he could not speak unto them: Luke 1:22	3 **went out** again unto the Jews, and saith unto them, ... 18:38
3 that there **went out** a decree from Caesar Augustus, ... 2:1	3 Pilate therefore **went forth** again, and saith 19:4
3 and there **went out** a fame of him through all 4:14	3 Then **came** Jesus **forth**, wearing the crown 19:5
9 saying, Hold thy peace, and **come out** of him. 4:35	3 And he bearing his cross **went forth** 19:17
3 he **came out** of him, and hurt him not. 4:35	3 and forthwith **came** there **out** blood and water. 19:34
29 commandeth ... unclean spirits, and they **come out**. 4:36	3 Peter therefore **went forth**, ... to the sepulchre. 20:3
38 And devils also **came out** of many, crying out, ... 4:41	1 They **went forth**, and entered into a ship. 21:3
39 And devils also **came out** of many, crying out, ... 4:41	3 Then went this saying abroad among the brethren, ... 21:23
13 he **departed** and went into a desert place: 4:42	3 time that the Lord Jesus **went** in and **out** among us, Acts 1:21
9 **Depart** from me; for I am a sinful man, O Lord. 5:8	9 said unto him, **Get** thee **out** of thy country, ... 7:3
3 And after these things he **went forth**, ... 5:27	13 Then **came** he **out** of the land of the Chaldaeans, ... 7:4
3 that he **went out** into a mountain to pray, ... 6:12	37 and after that **shall** they **come forth**, and serve me 7:7
20 that he **went out** into a mountain to pray, ... 6:12	38 **came out** of many that were possessed with them: 8:7
38 there **went** virtue out of him, and healed them all. 6:19	39 **came out** of many that were possessed with them: 8:7
3 rumour of him **went forth** throughout all Judaea, ... 7:17	3 And on the morrow Peter **went away** with them, ... 10:23
23 What **went** ye **out** into the wilderness for to see? 7:24	3 **departed** Barnabas to Tarsus, for to seek Saul: 11:25
40 What **went** ye **out** into the wilderness for to see? 7:24	13 And he **went out**, and followed him; 12:9
23 But what **went** ye **out** for to see? 7:25	15 they **went out**, and passed on through one street; 12:10
40 But what **went** ye **out** for to see? 7:25	13 And he **departed**, and went into another place. 12:17
23 But what **went** ye **out** for to see? A prophet? Yea, ... 7:26	3 the next day he **departed** with Barnabas to Derbe. 14:20
40 But what **went** ye **out** for to see? A prophet? Yea, ... 7:26	15 that certain which **went out** from us 15:24
25 called Magdalene, out of whom went seven devils, ... 8:2	3 And Paul chose Silas, and **departed**, ... 15:40
3 A sower **went out** to sow his seed: and as he sowed, ... 8:5	20 Him would Paul have **to go forth** with him; 16:3
14 And when he **went forth** to land, ... 8:27	20 we endeavoured **to go** into Macedonia, ... 16:10
20 he had commanded the unclean spirit to **come out** 8:29	4 And on the sabbath we **went out** of the city 16:13
11 Then **went** the devils out of the man, ... 8:33	20 in the name of Jesus Christ **to come out** of her. 16:18
1 Then they **went out** to see what was done; 8:35	3 And he **came out** the same hour. 16:18
25 out of whom the devils **were departed**, ... 8:35	3 masters saw that the hope of their gains **was gone**, ... 16:19
3 out of whom the devils **were departed**, ... 8:35	15 now therefore depart, and go in peace. (NT) 16:36
25 the man out of whom the devils **were departed** 8:38	20 and desired them **to depart** out of the city, ... 16:39
18 for I perceive that virtue **is gone** out of me. 8:46	15 And they **went out** of the prison, ... 16:40
43 for I perceive that virtue **is gone** out of me. 8:46	1 they comforted them, and **departed**. 16:40
31 house ye enter ... there abide, and thence **depart**. 9:4	41 they comforted them, and **departed**. 16:40
33 will not receive you, when ye **go** out of that city, ... 9:5	3 So Paul **departed** from among them. 17:33
33 And they **departed**, and went through the towns, ... 9:6	3 after he had spent some time there, he **departed**, ... 18:23

471

35	and the evil spirits **went out** of them.	Acts 19:12
3	and **departed** for to go into Macedonia.	20:1
3	talked a long while, ... so he **departed**.	20:11
15	we **departed** and went our way;	21:5
15	we that were of Paul's company **departed**,	21:8
9	and **get** thee quickly out of Jerusalem:	22:18
17	there **came** a viper out of the heat,	28:3
1	they **came** to meet us as far as Appii forum,	28:15
3	Yes verily, their sound **went** into all the earth,	Rom 10:18
20	for then must ye needs **go** out of the world.	1 Co 5:10
3	What? **came** the word of God from you?	14:36
1	I **went** from thence into Macedonia.	2 Co 2:13
44	**come out** from among them, and be ye separate,	6:17
10	**come out** from among them, and be ye separate,	6:17
3	of his own accord he **went** unto you.	8:17
1	when I **departed** from Macedonia,	Php 4:15
22	your faith to God-ward **is spread abroad**;	1 Th 1:8
15	howbeit not all that **came out** of Egypt by Moses.	Heb 3:16
26	though they **come out** of the loins of Abraham:	7:5
20	to **go out** into a place which he should after receive	11:8
3	and he **went out**, not knowing whither he went.	11:8
1	of that country from whence they **came out**,	11:15
30	Let us **go forth** therefore unto him without	13:13
28	Out of ... mouth **proceedeth** blessing and cursing.	Jas 3:10
1	They **went out** from us, but they were not of us;	1 Jn 2:19
41	They **went out** from us, but they were not of us;	2:19
24	many false prophets **are gone out** into the world.	4:1
1	deceivers have **gone out** into the world, (NASB)	2 Jn 1:7
1	Because that for his name's sake they **went forth**,	3 Jn 1:7
41	Because that for his name's sake they **went forth**,	1:7
7	and he **shall go** no more out:	Rev 3:12
3	and he **went forth** conquering, and to conquer.	6:2
3	And there **went out** another horse that was red:	6:4
1	**came** out of the smoke locusts upon the earth:	9:3
3	And another angel **came out** of the temple,	14:15
3	And another angel **came out** of the temple	14:17
3	And another angel **came out** from the altar,	14:18
3	and blood **came** out of the winepress,	14:20
1	And the seven angels **came out** of the temple,	15:6
3	**came** a great voice out of the temple of heaven,	16:17
44	voice from heaven, ... **Come out** of her, my people,	18:4
10	voice from heaven, ... **Come out** of her, my people,	18:4
3	And a voice **came** out of the throne, saying,	19:5
42	the sword which **came** from the mouth (NASB)	19:21
36	And **shall go out** to deceive the nations	20:8

Classical Greek
In early literature *exerchomai* refers to going out of a place, of words which go out of a man, of sicknesses which leave a man, and of time which passes. It is usually used of living beings.

Septuagint Usage
In the Septuagint the word is used of coming forth out of the earth and of the fruit of a man's body or lips. It especially refers to works that proceed from God.

New Testament Usage
In the New Testament *exerchomai* is used most often in narrative accounts to refer to a person going away from some place (see Matthew 8:28). In that same vein it speaks of someone leaving another person's presence (see Luke 5:8). At times it goes further than just a general coming or going to refer to someone going forth to do a set thing, such as preaching (Mark 6:12; 16:20; Luke 6:12) or to do a job (Matthew 13:3).

Exerchomai can also mean something that comes forth from a man: rumors, statements, evil thoughts (see Matthew 15:18,19). Of special significance are the references to demons coming out of a person (see Matthew 12:43; Mark 1:26).

In an even more special sense John 8:42 refers to Jesus as coming from God. This relationship between the Father and the Son is interwoven throughout John's gospel. Jesus' entire life and ministry was dominated by this consciousness of having been commissioned by the Father (Ladd, *New Testament Theology*, p.248). The context here of Christ's divine commission prevents this from being interpreted as some form of neo-platonic emanation. When Jesus said here that He is "from" (*ek* [1523]) the Father, this preposition denotes origin (Morris, *New International Commentary on the New Testament, John*, p.462); this is not a statement of the origin of Christ's nature but the origin of His mission.

The Church is also better understood from *exerchomai*, as it speaks of the proclamation of the Word of God (see 1 Corinthians 14:36) and shows that the Word of God goes out from the Church (see 1 Thessalonians 1:8). The people of God are to come out from among nonbelievers in their life-style (2 Corinthians 6:17).

STRONG 1831, BAUER 274-75, MOULTON-MILLIGAN 223, KITTEL 2:678-80, LIDDELL-SCOTT 591-92, COLIN BROWN 1:320-21.

1815. ἔξεστιν exestin verb
It is lawful, it is permitted, it is possible.
CROSS-REFERENCE:
εἰμί eimi (1498)

יָצָא yātsā' (3428), Come out (Ex 28:35 [28:31]).

1. ἔξεστιν exestin 3sing indic pres act
2. ἐξόν exon nom/acc sing neu part pres act

1	Behold, thy disciples do that which **is not lawful**	Matt 12:2
2	which was not **lawful** for him to eat,	12:4
1	saying, Is it **lawful** to heal on the sabbath days?	12:10
1	it is **lawful** to do well on the sabbath days.	12:12
1	John said ... It is not **lawful** for thee to have her.	14:4
1	It is not meet to take the children's bread,	15:26
1	Is it **lawful** for a man to put away his wife	19:3
1	Is it not **lawful** for me to do what I will	20:15
1	Is it **lawful** to give tribute unto Caesar, or not?	22:17
1	It is not **lawful** for to put them into the treasury,	27:6
1	on the sabbath day that which **is not lawful**?	Mark 2:24
1	which is not **lawful** to eat but for the priests,	2:26
1	Is it **lawful** to do good on the sabbath days,	3:4
1	It is not **lawful** for thee to have thy brother's wife.	6:18
1	Is it **lawful** for a man to put away his wife?	10:2
1	Is it **lawful** to give tribute to Caesar, or not?	12:14

ἔξεστιν 1815

1 Why do ye that which is not **lawful** to do	Luke 6:2
1 which it is not **lawful** to eat but for the priests	6:4
1 Is it **lawful** on the sabbath days to do good,	6:9
1 Is it **lawful** to heal on the sabbath day?	14:3
1 Is it **lawful** for us to give tribute unto Caesar,	20:22
1 it is not **lawful** for thee to carry thy bed.	John 5:10
1 It is not **lawful** for us to put any man to death:	18:31
2 let me freely speak unto you of the patriarch	Acts 2:29
1 If thou believest with all thine heart, thou mayest.	8:37
1 customs, which **are** not **lawful** for us to receive,	16:21
1 unto the chief captain, May I speak unto thee?	21:37
1 **lawful** for you to scourge a man that is a Roman,	22:25
1 All things **are lawful** unto me,	1 Co 6:12
1 all things **are lawful** for me,	6:12
1 All things **are lawful** for me,	10:23
1 all things **are lawful** for me,	10:23
2 which it is not **lawful** for a man to utter.	2 Co 12:4

Classical Greek

Exestin is generally an impersonal verb meaning "it is allowed, it is permitted" (i.e., lacking a subject, but cf. when followed by an infinitive [Turner, *Grammar of New Testament Greek*, 3:291f.]). *Exestin* is the same word as *exesti* and has exactly the same meaning, "it is lawful" or "it is possible." The only difference is in spelling, *exestin* having what is called a variable or movable *nu* (Greek "n") attached to the end of the word.

The variable *nu* was seldom used in classical Greek. In Koine Greek it was commonly attached to *exesti* and some other verb forms, especially third person singular forms of past tense verbs. Byzantine grammarians said the movable *nu* was added to avoid the vowel at the end of the verb from coming together with the vowel at the beginning of the next word (as the "an" is used in English in place of "a"). However, no clear rule was ever observed. Older Greek manuscripts of the New Testament have it, whereas the later ones do not. Therefore, edited Greek texts based on older manuscripts regularly have *exestin*, and those based on more recent aged manuscripts, such as the *Textus Receptus*, have *exesti*. Formally *exesti* is the third person singular form of the verb·*exeimi*; however, that verb does not occur (*Bauer*).

Exestin depicts both the "opportunity" to do something as well as the "ability." In addition, it also suggests that the action taken is not prohibited by some higher authority or court. Thus in the legal realm it particularly suggests something either required or forbidden by the law (see Foerster, "exestin," *Kittel*, 2:560).

In classical Greek it may mean "it is possible," as when some men thought it might be possible to talk to Xenophon at breakfast (Xenophon *Anabasis* 4.3.10). It can also mean "it is permitted" or "lawful," as when only sucklings were permitted to be sacrificed on the golden altar at Babylon (Herodotus 1.183). Other meanings include being "proper" or being "able." *Exestin* is common in Josephus with the meanings "it is possible, it is allowed," and "it is permitted" (*Liddell-Scott*).

Septuagint Usage

There are 10 occurrences of *exesti* in the Septuagint. Only three of these are canonical, and there is no single Hebrew equivalent. The variation in manuscripts reading *exesti* coupled with the lack of a Hebrew counterpart suggests it was not as suited to Old Testament legal situations as it was to Greek. Only Ezra 4:14 (LXX 2 Esdras 4:14) in canonical material comes close to that meaning (it was not "proper" [NIV] to see the king dishonored; cf. Leviticus 13:57; Numbers 21:13, which in no way resemble this understanding).

In the later, noncanonical writings *exesti* can carry the legal overtones found in the New Testament. It concerns a decision of the Jewish leaders and their priests that their appointment of Simon as high priest, with all the authority that position had, could not be challenged (1 Maccabees 14:41-44). The word is also used concerning certain individuals (only the high priest and certain priests) who "were allowed" to enter the Holy of Holies (3 Maccabees 1:11; cf. 5:18). Elsewhere it is used of "opportunity" (4 Maccabees 1:12; cf. 17:7).

New Testament Usage

In the New Testament the word *exesti* means "it is permitted." It is found most frequently in the Synoptic Gospels and in Acts. In almost every case it refers to things permitted or to things not permitted by the Torah (the Law). The Law was called the Torah (Hebrew, meaning "teaching," or Greek, *nomos* [3414]). It had to do with the standards of conduct which the Word of God either required or prohibited among the people of God. *Exesti* implies and acknowledges the authority of the Word of God or an authority prescribed by what is proper and permitted.

Hence the Word of God (Torah) was the "yardstick," or the standard of motivation and conduct that continually guided the conversation and actions of Jesus and the disciples. It had to do with what the Word of God said about eating (Matthew 12:4), about the Sabbath (Matthew 12:2,10), about marriage (Matthew 19:3-5), and about taxes (Matthew 22:17). Sometimes

ἐξετάζω 1816

the use of the word *exesti* was put as a question, "Is it permitted?" (Acts 21:37).

In Acts and in certain of Paul's epistles the word is used in the generic sense meaning "to permit," for example, "Let me freely (permit me to) speak" (Peter in Acts 2:29). Paul wrote about "unspeakable words" (KJV), i.e., "words unlawful to utter" (2 Corinthians 12:4). In the latter case the meaning probably is "words not possible to utter."

STRONG 1832, BAUER 275 (see "exesti"), MOULTON-MILLIGAN 223 (see "exesti"), KITTEL 2:560-61, LIDDELL-SCOTT 592 (see "exesti"), COLIN BROWN 2:606,611 (see "exesti").

1816. ἐξετάζω exetazō verb

Inquire, search out, question, examine.
SYNONYMS:
　ἀνακρίνω anakrinō (348)
　ἐραυνάω eraunaō (2020B)
　ζητέω zēteō (2195)
בָּחַן bāchan (1010), Examine, try (Ps 11:4 [10:5]).
דָּרַשׁ dārash (1938), Investigate, inquire (Dt 19:18).
חָקַר chāqar (2811), Spy out (Sir 3:21).

1. ἐξετάσατε exetasate 2pl impr aor act
2. ἐξετάσαι exetasai inf aor act

1 Go and **search** diligently for the young child; .... Matt 2:8
1 or town ye shall enter, **inquire** who in it is worthy; 10:11
2 none of the disciples durst **ask** him, Who art thou? John 21:12

Classical Greek
In secular Greek *exetazō* often has the meaning of "questioning someone" in a judicial sense, and refers especially to torture being used to get testimony from a person.

Septuagint Usage
The Septuagint's use of *exetazō* gives a sense of its Biblical meaning. It is used, for instance, in Deuteronomy 13:14 of making a careful investigation if wickedness is found in a town; if the investigation verified the wickedness, the town was destroyed. *Exetazō* has a similar idea in Deuteronomy 19:18 in speaking of a judge making a careful inquiry into whether a witness had testified maliciously against another person. In 1 Chronicles 28:9 David used *exetazō* to tell Solomon that the Lord makes a careful investigation or search of human hearts. Solomon was thus encouraged to serve the Lord wholeheartedly.

New Testament Usage
While this verb is common in Greek, it is used only three times in the New Testament. Two different ideas are found in those three uses. In Matthew 2:8 it means to make a careful search for someone, to utilize every avenue possible to locate him. In this case the Magi were to search carefully until they found Jesus and then report to Herod. *Exetazō* also carries the idea of "examining" someone's character. In Matthew 10:11 it has this idea in regard to examining people to find a worthy person whose house one might stay in. Finally, in John 21:12 it takes this meaning in the negative sense of the disciples not asking or searching out Jesus' identity.

STRONG 1833, BAUER 275, MOULTON-MILLIGAN 223, LIDDELL-SCOTT 592.

1817. ἐξηγέομαι exēgeomai verb

Explain, interpret, recount, narrate, declare.
COGNATES:
　ἄγω agō (70)
　διηγέομαι diēgeomai (1328)
　διήγησις diēgēsis (1329)
SYNONYMS:
　ἀναγγέλλω anangellō (310)
　ἀνατίθημι anatithēmi (392)
　ἀπαγγέλλω apangellō (514)
　ἀποδείκνυμι apodeiknumi (579)
　δείκνυμι deiknumi (1161)
　διερμηνεύω diermēneuō (1323)
　διηγέομαι diēgeomai (1328)
　ἐκδιηγέομαι ekdiēgeomai (1542)
　ἐμφανίζω emphanizō (1702)
　ἐρεύγομαι ereugomai (2027)
　ἑρμηνεύω hermēneuō (2043)
　καταγγέλλω katangellō (2576)
　κηρύσσω kērussō (2756)
　λέγω legō (2978)
　ὁρίζω horizō (3587)
　φθέγγομαι phthengomai (5187)
　φράζω phrazō (5255)
יָדָה yādhāh (3142), Hiphil: confess (Prv 28:13).
יָרָה yārāh (3498), Hiphil: teach, determine (Lv 14:57).
סָפַר ṣaphar (5807), Piel: declare, tell (Jgs 7:13, 2 Kgs 8:5, Jb 28:27).

1. ἐξηγουμένων exēgoumenōn
　　　　　　　　gen pl masc part pres mid
2. ἐξηγήσατο exēgēsato 3sing indic aor mid
3. ἐξηγησάμενος exēgēsamenos
　　　　　　　　nom sing masc part aor mid
4. ἐξηγεῖτο exēgeito 3sing indic imperf mid
5. ἐξηγοῦντο exēgounto 3pl indic imperf mid

5 And they **told** what things were done in the way, .. Luke 24:35
2 the only begotten Son, ... he **hath declared** him. ...... John 1:18
3 when he **had declared** all these things unto them, ... Acts 10:8
1 **declaring** what miracles and wonders God had 15:12
2 Simeon **hath declared** how God at the first 15:14
4 **declared** particularly what things God had wrought 21:19

In many classical Greek writings *exēgeomai* means "lead, show the way to," but this meaning does not occur in Scripture (*Bauer*). It appears in ancient Greek writings of priests or oracles communicating divine messages to man. In the New Testament Jesus "declared" the Father (John 1:18). The apostles and others "recounted" or "declared" the content of divinely inspired dreams (Acts 10:8), and the works of God (Acts 15:12).

STRONG 1834, BAUER 275, MOULTON-MILLIGAN 223, KITTEL 2:908, LIDDELL-SCOTT 593, COLIN BROWN 1:573-76.

1818. ἑξήκοντα hexēkonta num
Sixty.

1. ἑξήκοντα hexēkonta card

1 brought forth fruit, ... some **sixty**fold,	Matt 13:8
1 some an hundredfold, some **sixty**, some thirty.	13:23
1 some thirty, and some **sixty**, and some an hundred.	Mark 4:8
1 some thirtyfold, some **sixty**, and some an hundred.	4:20
1 was from Jerusalem about **threescore** furlongs.	Luke 24:13
1 taken into the number under **threescore** years old,.	1 Tm 5:9
1 a thousand two hundred and **threescore** days,	Rev 11:3
1 a thousand two hundred and **threescore** days.	12:6
1 and his number is Six hundred **threescore** and six.	13:18

This number appears frequently in the Septuagint and several times in the New Testament. This form is often used with other numbers involving sixty, as in three hundred sixty-five (Numbers 3:50) or six hundred sixty-six (Revelation 13:18). In the King James Version it is sometimes translated "threescore" (cf. Luke 24:13; 1 Timothy 5:9).

STRONG 1835, BAUER 276, MOULTON-MILLIGAN 223, LIDDELL-SCOTT 593.

1819. ἑξῆς hexēs adv
Next.

1. ἑξῆς hexēs

1 And it came to pass the **day after**,	Luke 7:11
1 And it came to pass, that on the **next** day,	9:37
1 and the **day following** unto Rhodes,	Acts 21:1
1 on the morrow I sat on the judgment seat,	25:17
1 the **next day** they lightened the ship;	27:18

The principal idea of *hexēs* is "in sequence, successively." When used with reference to time or place, the idea is "next." In the New Testament all occurrences of this word refer to time sequence. *Tē hexēs* is then "on the next" (day). In Luke 7:11 the preposition *en* (1706) is used, changing the meaning slightly, yet keeping the idea of succession. In this instance the word *chronos* (5385) is assumed after *hexēs*, giving "next succeeding time" or "soon afterward."

STRONG 1836, BAUER 276, MOULTON-MILLIGAN 224, LIDDELL-SCOTT 594.

1820. ἐξηχέω exēcheō verb
To sound forth, ring out.

הָמוֹן hāmôn (2066), Multitudes (Joel 3:14).
קוֹל qôl (7249), Sound, thunder (Sir 40:13).

1. ἐξήχηται exēchētai 3sing indic perf mid

1 For from you **sounded out** the word of the Lord	1 Th 1:8

Exēcheō means "sound forth" or "resound" as in 1 Thessalonians 1:8 where Paul spoke of the word of the Lord which "sounded out" from the Thessalonian Christians. This vivid word has gained the attention of expositors as far back as Chrysostom. It has often been thought that the imagery was derived from the sounding of a trumpet or the rolling of thunder, and the use of the perfect tense here denotes the continuing activity (Morris, *New International Commentary on the New Testament, 1 and 2 Thessalonians*, p.61). The message being sounded out is "the word which comes from the Lord" (subjective genitive), rather than "the word which tells of the Lord" (ibid.). This event is described by Karl Barth as "*God's act,*" (*The Word of God*, p.125). He goes on to say that nothing else will satisfy waiting people and nothing else will satisfy the will of God than for He himself to be revealed in this event (ibid.).

STRONG 1837, BAUER 276, LIDDELL-SCOTT 594.

1821. ἐξιέναι exienai verb
To depart.

This is an infinitive form of the verb *exeimi*. See the word study at number 1809B.

1821B. ἕξις hexis noun
Practice, habit, use.
CROSS-REFERENCE:
ἔχω echō (2174)

בָּרִיא bārî' (1304), Fat, portion (Dn 1:15).
גָּבֹהַּ gāvōahh (1393), Height (1 Sm 16:7).
גְּוִיָּה gᵉwîyāh (1505), Carcass (Jgs 14:9—Codex Alexandrinus only).
זִיו zîw (A2204), Countenance, face (Dn 7:28—Aramaic).

1. ἕξιν hexin acc sing fem

1 by reason **of use** have their senses exercised	Heb 5:14

This form appears in the New Testament only at Hebrews 5:14. It refers to a thoroughly established habit or skill achieved through repetition. Here the writer held up as a model those who were "ethically mature" by virtue of their experience and skill in discerning good and evil (Bruce, *New International Commentary on the New Testament, Hebrews,* p.109).

STRONG 1838, BAUER 276, LIDDELL-SCOTT 595, COLIN BROWN 2:657; 3:562,926.

1822. ἐξίστημι existēmi verb

Confuse, astound, amaze, to be insane, be amazed or astonished.

COGNATES:
ἔκστασις ekstasis (1598)
ἵστημι histēmi (2449)

SYNONYMS:
διαχωρίζω diachōrizō (1310)
ἐκθαμβέω ekthambeō (1555)
ἐκπλήσσω ekplēssō (1592)
θαμβέω thambeō (2261)
μαίνομαι mainomai (3077)

הָלַל hālal (2054), Poel: make a fool of (Jb 12:17).

הָמַם hāmam (2072), Scatter, cause trouble (Jos 10:10, 2 Sm 22:15, 2 Chr 15:6).

חָדָה chādhâh (2397), Rejoice (Ex 18:9).

חָדַר chādhar (2409), Enter, close in on (Ez 21:14).

חָרַד chāradh (2829), Qal: tremble, be afraid (Ex 19:18, 1 Sm 28:5, Is 32:11); hiphil: strike with terror, make afraid (2 Sm 17:2).

חָרֵד chārēdh (2830), Fear, tremble (1 Sm 4:13).

חָתַת chāthath (2973), Niphal: be terrified (1 Sm 17:11, Ez 2:6).

יָצָא yātsâ' (3428), Return, restore (Gn 42:28).

יָרֵא yārē' (3486), Fear, be afraid (Ez 2:6).

לָבֵשׁ lāvēsh (3980), Put on, clothe oneself (Ez 26:16).

מָהַהּ māhahh (4244), Hithpalpel: stun, stay (Is 29:9).

מָהַר māhar (4257), Hurry; niphal: sweep away, carry headlong (Jb 5:13).

מוּג mûgh (4265), Waver; niphal: be disheartened, fainthearted (Jer 49:23 [30:12]).

מָסַס māsas (4701), Niphal: dissolve, melt (Jos 2:11).

נָדַד nādhadh (5252), Flee (Is 10:31, 16:3, Jer 9:10).

נוּעַ nûaʻ (5309), Shake, move (Is 7:2).

נָטַף nātaph (5382), Drip (Jgs 5:4—Codex Alexandrinus only).

עֻלְפֶּה 'ulpeh (6191), Wilting (Ez 31:15).

עָמַד 'āmadh (6198), Stand (Jgs 9:44—Codex Alexandrinus only).

פּוּג pûgh (6555), Be numb, stunned (Gn 45:26—Codex Alexandrinus only).

פָּחַד pāchadh (6585), Tremble, fear (Hos 3:5, Mi 7:17).

רָדָה rādhâh (7575), Hiphil: subdue, rule (Is 41:2).

רָדַם rādham (7578), Niphal: sleep deeply (Jgs 4:21).

רָחַב rāchav (7620), Swell, be enlarged (Is 60:5).

רָנַן rānan (7728), Shout with joy (Lv 9:24).

שָׂעַר sāʻar (7994), Shudder, be afraid (Ez 27:35, 32:10).

שָׁגָה shāghâh (8146), Stagger (Is 28:7).

שָׁמֵם shāmēm (8460), Qal: be horrified, shudder (1 Kgs 9:8, Is 52:14, Jer 2:12); niphal: be horrified (Jer 4:9).

תָּמַהּ tāmahh (8867), Look in amazement, look aghast (Gn 43:33, Is 13:8).

1. ἐξιστῶν existōn nom sing masc part pres act
2. ἐξέστη exestē 3sing indic aor act
3. ἐξέστημεν exestēmen 1pl indic aor act
4. ἐξέστησαν exestēsan 3pl indic aor act
5. ἐξεστακέναι exestakenai inf perf act
6. ἐξίστασθαι existasthai inf pres mid
7. ἐξίστατο existato 3sing indic imperf mid
8. ἐξίσταντο existanto 3pl indic imperf mid
9. ἐξιστάνων existanōn nom sing masc part pres act

8 And all the people were **amazed**, and said,........	Matt 12:23
6 that they were all **amazed**, and glorified God,......	Mark 2:12
2 out to lay hold on him: ... He is **beside himself**..........	3:21
4 they were **astonished** with a great astonishment.........	5:42
8 and they were sore **amazed** in themselves..............	6:51
8 were **astonished** at his understanding and answers....	Luke 2:47
4 And her parents were **astonished**:......................	8:56
4 women also of our company made us **astonished**,......	24:22
8 And they were all **amazed** and **marvelled**,...........	Acts 2:7
8 And they were all **amazed**, and were in doubt,..........	2:12
1 and **bewitched** the people of Samaria,.................	8:9
9 and **bewitched** the people of Samaria,.................	8:9
5 because that of long time he had **bewitched** them.......	8:11
7 he continued with Philip, and **wondered**,...............	8:13
8 But all that heard him were **amazed**, and said;.........	9:21
4 of ... circumcision which believed were **astonished**,.....	10:45
4 and saw him, they were **astonished**....................	12:16
3 For whether we **be beside ourselves**, it is to God:....	2 Co 5:13

Classical Greek

In secular usage *existēmi,* "to remove something from its place" or "to alter," takes on the idea of driving something or someone from the right path, dislodging someone from his opinion, or changing utterly. Another common usage occurs in the sense of "resigning" one's property, since the ownership of the property would be altered.

Septuagint Usage

In the Septuagint the word *existēmi* occurs 75 times and translates 30 different words. While the word often signifies the idea of fright resulting from natural causes (Genesis 27:33; 43:33), more often it expresses the idea of terror before the Lord or His judgments (Jeremiah 4:9; Ezekiel 26:16) (Oepke, "existēmi," *Kittel,* 2:459f.). In general the Septuagint use of the word *existēmi* describes emotions involving anxiety, astonishment, and terror, and is most frequently found in the context of supernatural experience (ibid.).

New Testament Usage

In the New Testament *existēmi* builds on the classical and septuagintal uses to make three distinct emphases. Each emphasis suggests a mental altering of a person or a mental shifting of one's mind from one thing to another.

(1) In two places *existēmi* refers to someone losing his mind, experiencing mental imbalance. In Mark (3:21) Jesus' family suggested that "He is out of his mind" (NIV), because of the extraordinary nature of His ministry and person. Mark's purpose in using the word was to emphasize those extraordinary qualities in Jesus, a thrust the word carries often in its use in the Gospels. In 2 Corinthians (5:13) Paul said, "If we are out of our mind (*existēmi*), it is for the sake of God" (NIV).

(2) *Existēmi* also refers in a general sense to amazing people. Again two passages use this meaning. After the women had visited the empty tomb of Jesus and made their report to Jesus' other followers, the men on the road to Emmaus reported to Jesus that the women "astonished" them with their story (Luke 24:22). Acts 8:9,11 says Simon the Sorcerer "amazed all the people of Samaria" (NIV). In both cases *existēmi* suggests amazement at the supernatural.

(3) A group of uses of *existēmi* contain the specific sense of astonishment at the revelation of the divine glory. Each of these uses appears in the Gospels and Acts. There is astonishment at the remarkable understanding and teaching of Jesus in the temple when He was 12 (Luke 2:47). Four times the Gospel writers indicate that people were amazed at one of the healing miracles of Jesus (Matthew 9:8; 12:23; Mark 2:12; Luke 8:56). In Acts the use of *existēmi* switches from a direct reference, to amazement at the works of Jesus, to amazement at the supernatural works and conversions of the Church (Acts 2:7; 8:13; 9:21; 10:45; 12:16).

STRONG 1839, BAUER 276, MOULTON-MILLIGAN 224, KITTEL 2:459-60, LIDDELL-SCOTT 595, COLIN BROWN 1:527-28.

1823. ἐξισχύω exischuō verb

Be able, be strong enough, be capable.

COGNATE:
ἰσχύω ischuō (2453)
SYNONYMS:
δύναμαι dunamai (1404)
ἰσχύω ischuō (2453)

1. ἐξισχύσητε **exischusēte** 2pl subj aor act

1 May be able to comprehend with all saints .... Eph 3:18

This word is very similar to *ischuō* (2453) in meaning. It is related to the adjective *ischuros* (2451) meaning "strong" or "powerful." In its only occurrence in the New Testament the meaning is that of "being able" to comprehend (Ephesians 3:18).

STRONG 1840, BAUER 276, MOULTON-MILLIGAN 224, LIDDELL-SCOTT 595.

1824. ἕξις hexis

See word study at number 1821B.

1825. ἔξοδος exodos noun

An exit, departure, death.

CROSS-REFERENCE:
ὁδός hodos (3461)

בּוֹא bô' (971), Qal: goings, comings (Ps 121:8 [120:8]); hiphil: something that is lifted up (Ps 74:5—[73:5] only some Sinaiticus texts).

דֶּרֶךְ derekh (1932), Way, path (Ez 16:25—Codex Alexandrinus only).

חוּץ chûts (2445), Outside, street (2 Sm 1:20, Prv 1:20, Lm 4:1).

יָצָא yātsâ' (3428), Qal: movement (Nm 33:38, 2 Chr 23:8, Is 37:28); hiphil: import (2 Chr 9:28).

מוֹצָא môtsā' (4296), Movements (2 Sm 3:25, Ps 19:6 [18:6], Ez 42:11).

מוֹצָאָה môtsā'āh (4298), Origin (Mi 5:2).

צֹאָה tsō'āh (6884), Dung, excrement (Prv 30:12 [24:35]).

צִנָּה tsinnāh (7065), Cold (Prv 25:13).

תּוֹצָאוֹת tôtsā'ôth (8777), Starting point (Prv 4:23).

1. ἐξόδου **exodou** gen sing fem
2. ἔξοδον **exodon** acc sing fem

2 Who appeared in glory, and spake of his decease .... Luke 9:31
1 of the departing of the children of Israel; .... Heb 11:22
2 I will ... that ye may be able after my decease .... 2 Pt 1:15

Classical Greek

The word *exodos* denotes a "way" (*hodos* [3461]) "out" (*ek* [1523]). In classical Greek it can refer to a military expedition, an "exit" from something, or even an argument (see *Liddell-*

Scott). From papyri it is clear that in commercial language an *exodos* can be a "payment" or an "expense" (see *Moulton-Milligan*).

Septuagint Usage
Exodos is the title given to the Second Book of Moses by the Septuagintal translators (Codex Alexandrinus adds "from Egypt"). Israel's "exodus, departure" from Egypt is tagged thus later (Exodus 19:1; cf. Numbers 33:38; 1 Kings 6:1; Psalms 105:38 [LXX 104:38]; 114:1 [113:1]); but *exodus* does not usually have any technical aspect (Numbers 35:26; Judges 5:4,31; 1 Samuel 29:6 [LXX 1 Kings 29:6], of a military expedition). The ordinary Hebrew equivalents to *exodos* are *yātsâʾ* (in various tenses) and *chûts*.

New Testament Usage
Beyond the Septuagint and into the Hellenistic period *exodos* acquired a more technical dimension. Both Philo (*Life of Moses* 2.248; cf. *Bauer*) and Josephus (*Against Apion* 1.25; *Antiquities* 5.1.20) use the term in this way. So, too, the Book of Hebrews recalls Israel's *exodos* from Egypt (11:22). Luke 9:31 seems to use the word euphemistically for "death" (as in 2 Peter 1:15; cf. Josephus *Antiquities* 4.8.2; cf. *Bauer*). (The KJV translates it "decease" in both places.) It may also refer to the whole event including Christ's death, resurrection, and ascension.

Strong 1841, Bauer 276, Moulton-Milligan 224, Kittel 5:103-9, Liddell-Scott 596, Colin Brown 3:935-37,940.

1826. ἐξολοθρεύω exolothreuō verb
Be utterly destroyed, be rooted out.
Cross-Reference:
ὀλοθρεύω olothreuō (3508)

אָבַד ʾāvadh (6), Become lost, perish; piel: destroy (Ez 6:3).

בָּעַר bāʿar (1220), Burn; piel: get rid of, take away (2 Sm 4:11).

גָּדַע gādhaʿ (1468), Cut off (1 Sm 2:31).

הָדַף hādhaph (1990), Drive away (Jos 23:5).

חָרַם chāram (2868), Hiphil: destroy utterly, completely (Dt 3:6, Jos 10:1, 2 Chr 32:14); hophal: be utterly destroyed (Ex 22:20—Codex Alexandrinus only).

יָרַשׁ yārash (3542), Hiphil: dispossess, drive out (Dt 7:17, Jos 23:13, Ps 44:2 [43:2]).

כָּחַד kāchadh (3701), Hiphil: destroy (Ps 83:4 [82:4]).

כָּלָה kālâh (3735), Piel: destroy (2 Chr 8:8—Sixtine edition only); pual: be desolate (Ez 35:15—Codex Alexandrinus only).

כָּרַת kārath (3901), Qal: cut off, cut down (Jgs 6:26, 2 Kgs 18:4, Ez 31:12); niphal: be cut off, removed (Gn 17:14, Zec 14:2); hiphil: destroy (Lv 26:30, Ps 34:16 [33:16], Is 48:9).

מַשְׁחִית mashchîth (5072), Destroy (2 Chr 20:23, 22:4).

נָחַל nāchal (5336), Inherit (Ps 82:8 [81:8]—only some Sinaiticus texts).

נָכָה nākhâh (5409), Hiphil: strike down (Jos 11:14).

נָשַׂג nāsagh (5560), Hiphil: overtake (1 Chr 21:12).

עָכַר ʿākhar (6138), Kill by stoning (Jos 7:25).

צָמַת tsāmath (7059), Hiphil: silence, cut off (Pss 18:40 [17:40], 143:12 [142:12]).

רָזָה rāzâh (7612), Famish, destroy (Zep 2:11).

שָׁדַד shādhadh (8161), Spoil, destroy (Jer 47:4 [29:4], 51:53 [28:53]).

שָׁחַת shāchath (8271), Niphal: become corrupt, spoiled (Ex 8:24); piel: devastate, destroy (Jos 22:33); hiphil: destroy (Dt 10:10, 2 Chr 21:7, Jer 36:29 [43:29]).

שָׁמַד shāmadh (8436), Niphal: perish, be destroyed (Dt 12:30, Ps 83:10 [82:10], Jer 48:8 [31:8]); hiphil: destroy (Dt 1:27, Jos 23:15, Ps 106:23 [105:23]).

1. ἐξολεθρευθήσεται **exolethreuthēsetai**
   3sing indic fut pass
2. ἐξολοθρευθήσεται **exolothreuthēsetai**
   3sing indic fut pass

2 **shall be destroyed** from among the people........... Acts 3:23
1 **shall be destroyed** from among the people................ 3:23

This term (also spelled *exolethreuō*) occurs only once in the New Testament (Acts 3:23) where Peter quoted from the Old Testament (Leviticus 23:29). It is very common in the Septuagint and in other Jewish and Christian writings, but it is otherwise rare. Several times in the Septuagint it is said that the unrighteous person "will be cut off from his people." It is also the word used to describe how Israel was to utterly destroy the Canaanites (cf. Judges 1:17; 2:3).

Strong 1842, Bauer 276, Moulton-Milligan 224, Kittel 5:170-71, Colin Brown 1:465.

1827. ἐξομολογέω exomologeō verb
Confess fully, acknowledge, praise, promise.
Cognate:
ὁμολογέω homologeō (3533)
Synonyms:
ἐπαγγέλλομαι epangellomai (1846)
ὁμολογέω homologeō (3533)

הֲדָרָה hadhārāh (1997), Praise (2 Chr 20:21).

הָלַל hālal (2054), Piel: praise (1 Chr 23:30, 2 Chr 5:13, 23:12).

יְדָא yᵉdhāʾ (A3137), Haphel: praise (Dn 2:23—Aramaic).

יָדָה yādhâh (3142), Hiphil: praise, give thanks (2 Sm 22:50, Pss 6:5, 52:9 [51:9], 118:1 [117:1]); hithpael: confess (2 Chr 30:22, Dn 9:4,20).

סָפַר sāphar (5807), Count; piel: proclaim (Sir 51:1).

שָׁבַע shāvaʿ (8123), Niphal: swear (Is 45:23 [45:24]).

1. ἐξωμολόγησεν exōmologēsen 3sing indic aor act
2. ἐξομολογοῦμαι exomologoumai 1sing indic pres mid
3. ἐξομολογεῖσθε exomologeisthe 2pl impr pres mid
4. ἐξομολογούμενοι exomologoumenoi nom pl masc part pres mid
5. ἐξομολογήσηται exomologēsētai 3sing subj aor mid
6. ἐξομολογήσομαι exomologēsomai 1sing indic fut mid
7. ἐξομολογήσεται exomologēsetai 3sing indic fut mid

```
4 were baptized ... in Jordan, confessing their sins.....Matt 3:6
2 I thank thee, O Father, Lord of heaven and earth,.....11:25
4 were all baptized of him ... confessing their sins.....Mark 1:5
2 I thank thee, O Father, Lord of heaven and earth, Luke 10:21
1 he promised, and sought opportunity to betray.........22:6
4 And many that believed came, and confessed,......Acts 19:18
7 and every tongue shall confess to God.............Rom 14:11
6 this cause I will confess to thee among the Gentiles,... 15:9
5 every tongue should confess that Jesus ... is Lord,... Phlp 2:11
7 every tongue should confess that Jesus ... is Lord,...... 2:11
3 Confess your faults one to another, and pray.........Jas 5:16
6 but I will confess his name before my Father,........Rev 3:5
```

Classical Greek

Exomolgeō is the intensive form of the more often used verb *homologeō* (3533). Both verbs mean "to confess," but *exomologeō* has the more intensive thrust of confessing freely, openly, and fully. They may be used interchangeably, but *exomologeō* was often used when the author wished to express more strongly an open confession.

Septuagint Usage

In the Septuagint *exomologeō* usually means "to praise." Leah offered praise to God at the birth of Judah (Genesis 29:35); David expressed praise in a song (2 Samuel 22:50 [LXX 2 Kings 22:50]); and the Psalms repeatedly express praise (Psalms 7:17; 9:1). *Exomologeō* is also translated "confess" in the Septuagint, first for acknowledging God (1 Kings 8:33,35 [LXX 3 Kings 8:33,35]), and also for admitting one's sin (Daniel 9:4,5).

New Testament Usage

These same meanings carry over to the New Testament, but "acknowledge" is used more often. In Acts 19:18 the Ephesians openly acknowledged their sin, as did the people who repented at the preaching of John (Matthew 3:6), indicating their conversion. Such confession of sin should be made when seeking prayer for healing (James 5:16). Paul used *exomologeō* in Romans 14:11, but it is unclear whether he meant confession of sin to God or acknowledgment to God of who Jesus is.

This latter sense of acknowledgment does appear in the New Testament. Paul expressed this idea in Romans 15:9 and in his hymn of Philippians 2:11. Jesus turned this around to also suggest that He will acknowledge believers before God (Revelation 3:5).

Praise is indicated in the parallel passages of Matthew 11:25 and Luke 10:21. In all these uses *exomologeō* carries the idea of the openness of the expression. This same idea of openness is used in a negative way when Judas "promised" to help betray Jesus for the chief priests and scribes (Luke 22:6).

STRONG 1843, BAUER 277, MOULTON-MILLIGAN 224, KITTEL 5:199-220, LIDDELL-SCOTT 597 (see "exomologeomai"), COLIN BROWN 1:344-46.

1828. ἐξορκίζω exorkizō verb

Adjure, charge under oath.

COGNATE:
ὁρκίζω horkizō (3589)

SYNONYMS:
διαμαρτύρομαι diamarturomai (1257)
διαστέλλω diastellō (1285)
διατάσσω diatassō (1293)
ἐντέλλομαι entellomai (1765)
ἐπιτάσσω epitassō (1988)
κελεύω keleuō (2724)
λέγω legō (2978)
ὁρκίζω horkizō (3589)
παραγγέλλω parangellō (3715)
προστάσσω prostassō (4225)
συντάσσω suntassō (4781)
τάσσω tassō (4872)

אָלָה ʾālâh (426), Pronounce a curse (Jgs 17:2—Codex Alexandrinus only).

שָׁבַע shāvaʿ (8123), Hiphil: cause to swear (Gn 24:3).

1. ἐξορκίζω exorkizō 1sing indic pres act

```
1 I adjure thee by the living God,..................Matt 26:63
```

Classical Greek

This verb (from *ek* [1523] and *horkizō* [3589]) means "to make (one) take an oath," "to cause (someone) to swear (with an oath)." In nonbiblical Greek it appears often in the sense of "to invoke" a deity or "to adjure" as in the exorcism of evil spirits (cf. Acts 19:13 the variant reading *exorkizomen* for *horkizō*, and the noun *exorkistēs* [1829], an "exorcist").

Septuagint Usage
Exorkizō occurs three times in the Septuagint. In Genesis 24:3f. Abraham made his servant "swear" that he would not allow Isaac to marry a Canaanite or to leave the land. Also King Ahab "adjured" the prophet Micaiah to speak the truth in his prophecy (1 Kings 22:16 [LXX 3 Kings 22:16]). In Judges 17:2 *exorkizō* refers to the "cursing" of something.

New Testament Usage
The only instance of *exorkizō* in the New Testament is in Matthew's account of Jesus before the high priest (26:63). The high priest "adjured" (i.e., he tried to make Him take an oath) Jesus "by the living God" to tell him plainly whether or not He was the Messiah. In light of Jesus' response, *su eipas* ("thou hast said"), the question is, Does this contradict Matthew 5:33,34? That is, did Jesus take an oath? Schneider offers a plausible resolution. Jesus' response, *su eipas*, should not be understood as an *acceptance* of the high priest's compelling; rather, it should be regarded as a *refusal* to comply with him. Jesus' reply is not "you said it (correctly)," but "you tell me." Then Jesus declared the facts of what the priest would witness—a description of the Son of Man, the Messiah, judging the world. Thus Jesus refused to take an oath and allowed the high priest to judge for himself (cf. Mark 14:62; "exorkizō," *Kittel*, 5:464f.).

STRONG 1844, BAUER 277, MOULTON-MILLIGAN 225, KITTEL 5:464-66, LIDDELL-SCOTT 598, COLIN BROWN 3:473,476,737-38.

1829. ἐξορκιστής exorkistēs noun
Exorcist.
CROSS-REFERENCE:
ὁρκίζω horkizō (3589)

1. ἐξορκιστῶν exorkistōn gen pl masc
1 Then certain of the vagabond Jews, exorcists,...... Acts 19:13

A rare term in ancient Greek literature, this word occurs in the New Testament only at Acts 19:13. The impact of Paul's ministry and the signs and wonders that followed his preaching the message of Christ are clearly seen in this passage. The undeniable power that came in the proclamation of Jesus' name began to draw the attention of some wandering Jewish exorcists. According to Bruce, the Jewish exorcists were held in high regard by those in ancient times who practiced magic (*New International Commentary on the New Testament, Acts*, p.390). Interestingly, there was a tendency among some Jews to use the name of Jesus in healing. This practice was denounced in the rabbinical writings (ibid.).

STRONG 1845, BAUER 277, KITTEL 5:464-66, LIDDELL-SCOTT 598, COLIN BROWN 3:473,476,737-38.

1830. ἐξορύσσω exorussō verb
Dig out, dig through.
SYNONYM:
ἐξαιρέω exaireō (1791)

נָקַר nāqar (5548), Qal: put out (1 Sm 11:2); piel: gouge out (Jgs 16:21—Codex Alexandrinus only).

1. ἐξορύξαντες exoruxantes nom pl masc part aor act
1 and when they had broken it up, they let down..... Mark 2:4
1 ye would have plucked out your own eyes,........... Gal 4:15

Exorussō, "dig out" (as to dig out of the ground), is frequently used in reference to the eyes. Putting out the right eye was a war strategy, handicapping the enemy; hence the frequent reference to the eye. When referring to the eye it is more appropriately translated "plucked out" as in Galatians 4:15. In the Septuagint this term is used of Samson (Judges 16:21). In Mark 2:4 the word is also used of "breaking up" an opening in a roof.

STRONG 1846, BAUER 277, MOULTON-MILLIGAN 225, LIDDELL-SCOTT 598.

1830B. ἐξουδενέω exoudeneō verb
Treat with contempt.
COGNATES:
ἐξουδενόω exoudenoō (1831)
ἐξουθενέω exoutheneō (1832)

בּוּז bûz (972), Despise, scorn (2 Kgs 19:21—Codex Vaticanus only, S/S 8:1—Codex Alexandrinus only).
בּוּס bûs (983), Trample, tread on (Ps 44:5 [43:5]).
בָּזָה bāzâh (995), Despise (Ez 22:8—Codex Vaticanus only).
מָאַס mā'as (4128), Refuse, reject (Ez 21:10).

1. ἐξουδενηθῇ exoudenēthē 3sing subj aor pass
1 he must suffer many things, and be set at nought.... Mark 9:12

This word appears as a variant of *exoudenoō* in some modern Greek texts (cf. Nestle-Aland

26th). (See the *Textual Apparatus* in *Complete Biblical Library, Mark*, p.238; cf. word study at number 1831.)

BAUER 277, MOULTON-MILLIGAN 225, LIDDELL-SCOTT 598, COLIN BROWN 1:74.

1831. ἐξουδενόω exoudenoō verb
Despise, treat with contempt.
CROSS-REFERENCE:
ἐξουδενέω exoudeneō (1830B)
בּוּז bûz (972), Despise (Zec 4:10).
בּוּס bûṣ (983), Trample, tread on (Ps 60:12 [59:12]).
בָּזָה bāzâh (995), Qal: despise (2 Sm 6:16, Pss 22:24 [21:24], 102:17 [101:17]); niphal: be despised (Pss 15:4 [14:4], 119:141 [118:141], Mal 2:9).
בָּעַר baʿar (1221), Be foolish, senseless (Ps 73:22 [72:22]).
מָאַס māʾas (4128), Qal: abhor, reject (1 Sm 16:1, Ps 78:59 [77:59]); niphal: melt away, vanish (Ps 58:7 [57:7]).
מָסַס māsas (4701), Niphal: become weak (1 Sm 15:9).
סָלָה sālâh (5733), Push down, reject (Ps 119:118 [118:118]).

1. ἐξουδενωθῇ exoudenōthē 3sing subj aor pass
1 he must suffer many things, and **be set at nought**.... Mark 9:12

Exoudenoō, also written *exoudeneō* (1830B), *exouthenoō*, and *exoutheneō* (1832), means "despise, reject, set at naught, scorn." *Exoudeneō* occurs frequently in the Septuagint but only once in the New Testament. In Mark 9:12 Jesus told Peter, James, and John what was to become of the Son of man: "That he must suffer many things, and *set at nought*." There are several New Testament occurrences of the form *exoutheneō*. Regardless of the spelling, the meaning is "consider or treat someone or something as despicable and contemptible." There does seem to be some variation in the intensity of the feeling the word conveys from one occurrence to another. (See *exoutheneō* [1832].)

STRONG 1847, BAUER 277 (see "exoudeneō"), LIDDELL-SCOTT 598.

1832. ἐξουθενέω exoutheneō verb
Despise utterly, disdain; make of no account.
COGNATE:
ἐξουδενέω exoudeneō (1830B)
SYNONYMS:
καταφρονέω kataphroneō (2675)
περιφρονέω periphroneō (3925)

בּוּז bûz (972), Despise (Prv 1:7).
בָּזָה bāzâh (995), Despise (1 Sm 2:30).
כָּשַׁל kāshal (3911), Stumble, totter; hiphil: turn against, fall upon (Ps 64:8 [63:8]).
מָאַס māʾas (4128), Forsake, reject (1 Sm 8:7).
שַׁאֲנָן shaʾănān (8077), At ease, complacent (Am 6:1).

1. ἐξουθενεῖς exoutheneis 2sing indic pres act
2. ἐξουθενείτω exoutheneitō 3sing impr pres act
3. ἐξουθενεῖτε exoutheneite 2pl impr pres act
4. ἐξουθενοῦντας exouthenountas
  acc pl masc part pres act
5. ἐξουθενήσατε exouthenēsate 2pl indic aor act
6. ἐξουθενήσῃ exouthenēsē 3sing subj aor act
7. ἐξουθενήσας exouthenēsas
  nom sing masc part aor act
8. ἐξουθενηθείς exouthenētheis
  nom sing masc part aor pass
9. ἐξουθενημένος exouthenēmenos
  nom sing masc part perf mid
10. ἐξουθενημένους exouthenēmenous
  acc pl masc part perf mid
11. ἐξουθενημένα exouthenēmena
  nom/acc pl neu part perf mid
12. ἐξουθενωθῇ exouthenōthē 3sing subj aor pass

12 he must suffer many things, and **be set at nought**... Mark 9:12
4 that they were righteous, and **despised** others:.... Luke 18:9
7 And Herod with his men of war set him **at nought**,... 23:11
8 the stone which was **set at nought** of you builders,.. Acts 4:11
2 Let not him that eateth **despise** ... that eateth not; Rom 14:3
1 or why dost thou **set at nought** thy brother?.......... 14:10
11 and things which **are despised**, hath God chosen,... 1 Co 1:28
10 to judge who are least esteemed in the church......... 6:4
6 Let no man therefore **despise** him:.................... 16:11
9 and his speech **contemptible**...................... 2 Co 10:10
5 temptation which was in my flesh ye **despised** not,.. Gal 4:14
3 **Despise** not prophesyings......................... 1 Th 5:20

Classical Greek
Bauer cites evidence of the term *exoutheneō* having various forms in the classical period and suggests its meaning there—"to treat with contempt, to despise"—is consistent into the New Testament period. (Orthographically also *exoudeneō* [1830B], *exoudenoō* [1831], and *exouthenoō*; see Blass and Debrunner, *Greek Grammar of the New Testament*, p.18.)

Septuagint Usage
The Septuagint's evidence confirms this last suggestion; its manuscripts witness the same orthographic tension between *exoutheneō* and *exoudeneō* (e.g., 1 Samuel 10:19 [LXX 1 Kings 10:19]; Judith 13:17; Psalm 51:17 [LXX 50:17]). Normally *bāzâh* ("to despise") and *māas* ("to reject") lie behind *exoutheneō*. It is used of Israel's "forsaking" or "rejecting" of God (1 Samuel [LXX 1 Kings] 8:7; 10:19; cf. 15:23,26), but it can also refer to human rejection of things or persons (Psalm 15:4

[LXX 14:4]). On the other hand, God does not despise the afflicted or the humble (Psalms 22:24 [LXX 21:24]; 51:17 [50:17]), but He does "reject" the ungodly (Psalm 53:5 [LXX 52:5]).

New Testament Usage
Aside from the orthographic difficulties at Mark 9:12 (perhaps an allusion to Psalm 118:22), the New Testament (12 times) reads the form *exoutheneō*. Even at Mark 9:12 the meaning is the same. Herod treated Jesus with contempt (Luke 23:11—"set at nought"; cf. Romans 14:3,10), and Jesus' teachings were rejected by those who considered themselves righteous (Luke 18:9; cf. 1 Thessalonians 5:20). He himself is the rejected cornerstone (Acts 4:11/Psalm 118:22). Paul's speaking ability and personal presence were "of no account" (RSV) in the estimation of the Corinthians (2 Corinthians 10:10; cf. 1 Corinthians 1:28).

Within the Christian community there also existed the possibility of contempt. For example, Romans 14:1-12 warns against the "strong" in faith despising the "weak." Also, it appears that Timothy became an object of disdain because of his youth (1 Corinthians 16:11; cf. 1 Timothy 4:12) and Paul because of his physical weakness (Galatians 4:14) and his speech (1 Corinthians 10:10). Even the gifts of the Holy Spirit given for the edification of the Church may have been treated with contempt. In this connection Paul wrote, "Despise not prophesyings" (1 Thessalonians 5:20).

STRONG 1848, BAUER 277, MOULTON-MILLIGAN 225 (see "exoudeneō"), LIDDELL-SCOTT 598, COLIN BROWN 1:74.

1833. ἐξουσία exousia noun

Authority, right, power.

COGNATE:
ἐξουσιάζω exousiazō (1834)

SYNONYMS:
δύναμις dunamis (1405)
ἰσχύς ischus (2452)
κράτος kratos (2877)
κυριότης kuriotēs (2936)

מֶמְשָׁלָה memshālāh (4617), Dominion, kingdom (2 Kgs 20:13, Ps 114:2 [113:2]).

מָשַׁל māshal (5090), Have authority (Sir 45:17).

שִׁלְטוֹן shilṭôn (8378), Power (Eccl 8:8).

שָׁלְטָן sholṭān (A8380), Dominion (Dn 4:3 [3:33], 7:12,14—Aramaic).

שַׁלִּיט shallîṭ (A8385), Rule (Dn 4:26 [4:23]—Aramaic).

1. ἐξουσίας exousias gen/acc sing/pl fem
2. ἐξουσία exousia nom sing fem
3. ἐξουσίᾳ exousia dat sing fem
4. ἐξουσίαν exousian acc sing fem
5. ἐξουσίαι exousiai nom pl fem
6. ἐξουσιῶν exousiōn gen pl fem
7. ἐξουσίαις exousiais dat pl fem

4	For he taught them as one having **authority**,	Matt 7:29
4	For I am a man under **authority**,	8:9
4	that ye may know that the Son of man hath **power**	9:6
4	God, which had given such **power** unto men.	9:8
4	he gave them **power** against unclean spirits,	10:1
3	By what **authority** doest thou these things?	21:23
4	and who gave thee this **authority**?	21:23
3	I in like wise will tell you by what **authority** I do	21:24
3	Neither tell I you by what **authority** I do these	21:27
2	All **power** is given unto me in heaven and in earth.	28:18
4	for he taught them as one that had **authority**,	Mark 1:22
4	with **authority** commandeth he ... unclean spirits,	1:27
4	Son of man hath **power** on earth to forgive sins,	2:10
4	**power** to heal sicknesses, and to cast out devils:	3:15
4	and gave them **power** over unclean spirits;	6:7
3	By what **authority** doest thou these things?	11:28
4	and who gave thee this **authority** to do these things?	11:28
3	I will tell you by what **authority** I do these things.	11:29
3	Neither do I tell you by what **authority** I do these	11:33
4	left his house, and gave **authority** to his servants,	13:34
4	devil said unto him, All this **power** will I give thee,	Luke 4:6
3	at his doctrine: for his word was with **power**.	4:32
3	with **authority** and power he commandeth	4:36
4	that ye may know that the Son of man hath **power**	5:24
4	For I also am a man set under **authority**,	7:8
4	and gave them power and **authority** over all devils;	9:1
4	Behold, I give unto you **power** to tread on serpents	10:19
4	after he hath killed hath **power** to cast into hell;	12:5
1	the synagogues, and unto magistrates, and **powers**,	12:11
4	been faithful ... have thou **authority** over ten cities.	19:17
3	Tell us, by what **authority** doest thou these things?	20:2
4	or who is he that gave thee this **authority**?	20:2
3	Neither tell I you by what **authority** I do these	20:8
3	deliver him unto ... **authority** of the governor.	20:20
2	but this is your hour, and the **power** of darkness.	22:53
1	knew that he belonged unto Herod's **jurisdiction**,	23:7
4	to them gave he **authority** to become the sons of God,	John 1:12
4	hath given him **authority** to execute judgment also,	5:27
4	I have **power** to lay it down,	10:18
4	and I have **power** to take it again.	10:18
4	As thou hast given him **power** over all flesh,	17:2
4	knowest thou not that I have **power** to crucify thee,	19:10
4	to crucify thee, and have **power** to release thee?	19:10
4	Thou couldest have no **power** at all against me,	19:11
3	which the Father hath put in his own **power**.	Acts 1:7
3	after it was sold, was it not in thine own **power**?	5:4
4	Saying, Give me also this **power**,	8:19
4	And here he hath **authority** from the chief priests	9:14
4	having received **authority** from the chief priests;	26:10
1	Whereupon as I went to Damascus with **authority**	26:12
1	and from the **power** of Satan unto God,	26:18
4	Hath not the potter **power** over the clay,	Rom 9:21
7	Let every soul be subject unto the higher **powers**.	13:1
2	For there is no **power** but of God:	13:1
5	the **powers** that be are ordained of God.	13:1
3	Whosoever therefore resisteth the **power**,	13:2
4	Wilt thou then not be afraid of the **power**?	13:3
4	but hath **power** over his own will,	1 Co 7:37
2	take heed lest by any means this **liberty** of yours	8:9
4	Have we not **power** to eat and to drink?	9:4
4	Have we not **power** to lead about a sister, a wife,	9:5
4	have not we **power** to forbear working?	9:6
1	If others be partakers of this **power** over you,	9:12
3	we have not used this **power**; but suffer all things,	9:12
3	that I abuse not my **power** in the gospel.	9:18

ἐξουσία 1833

4	to have **power** on her head because of the angels...	1 Co 11:10
4	put down all rule and all **authority** and power...	15:24
1	I should boast somewhat more of our **authority**,...	2 Co 10:8
4	according to the **power** which the Lord hath given...	13:10
1	Far above all principality, and power, and **might**,...	Eph 1:21
1	according to the prince of the **power** of the air,...	2:2
7	the principalities and **powers** in heavenly places...	3:10
1	but against principalities, against **powers**,...	6:12
1	hath delivered us from the **power** of darkness,...	Col 1:13
5	thrones, or dominions, or principalities, or **powers**:...	1:16
1	which is the head of all principality and **power**:...	2:10
1	And having spoiled principalities and **powers**,...	2:15
4	Not because we have not **power**,...	2 Th 3:9
7	to be subject to principalities and **powers**,...	Tit 3:1
4	have no **right** to eat which serve the tabernacle...	Heb 13:10
6	angels and **authorities** and powers...	1 Pt 3:22
2	be glory and majesty, **dominion** and power,...	Jude 1:25
4	to him will I give **power** over the nations:...	Rev 2:26
2	**power** was given unto them over the fourth part...	6:8
2	locusts ... and unto them was given **power**,...	9:3
4	as the scorpions of the earth have **power**...	9:3
2	and their **power** was to hurt men five months...	9:10
5	their **power** is in their mouth, and in their tails:...	9:19
2	their **power** is in their mouth, and in their tails:...	9:19
4	These have **power** to shut heaven,...	11:6
4	and have **power** over waters to turn them to blood,...	11:6
2	kingdom of our God, and the **power** of his Christ:...	12:10
4	his power, and his seat, and great **authority**...	13:2
4	they worshipped the dragon which gave **power**...	13:4
2	and **power** was given unto him to continue...	13:5
2	and **power** was given him over all kindreds,...	13:7
4	And he exerciseth all the **power** of the first beast...	13:12
4	out from the altar, which had **power** over fire;...	14:18
4	God, which hath **power** over these plagues:...	16:9
4	but receive **power** as kings one hour with the beast...	17:12
4	shall give their power **and strength** unto the beast...	17:13
4	I saw another angel ... having great **power**;...	18:1
4	on such the second death hath no **power**,...	20:6
2	that they may have **right** to the tree of life,...	22:14

Exousia appears frequently in the texts of all types of ancient Greek literature. It is a derivative of *exestin* (1815) which means "it is possible" or "it is lawful." Denotations of *exousia* include an authority to rule, one bearing such authority, the sphere controlled by this authority, and the power to do something. It is closely related to *dunamis* (1405) but differs by its intent of the delegation of authority rather than the capability of the inherent power of *dunamis* (cf. Betz, "Might," *Colin Brown*, 2:606). Two verbs incorporate its meaning: *exousiazō* (1834), "to have power," and *katexousiazō* (2685), "to exercise authority."

Classical Greek

In classical Greek *exousia* is found as early as the Fifth Century B.C. writings of Thucydides. It was used by Antiphon Orator meaning "an ability to do something," as long as there are no hindrances (Foerster, "exousia," *Kittel*, 2:562). Generally, the term denotes the right to act according to legal or moral standards. Thus it is often used in an official sense to describe the authority of a king or other ruler (Plato *Definitiones* 415b,c; cf. *Bauer*). Derived meanings are "authoritative position" and in the plural, "authorities" (Betz, "Might," *Colin Brown*, 2:607).

Septuagint Usage

The sense of "authority to rule" is also found in the Septuagint where *exousia* occurs about 50 times. It usually replaces the Hebrew word *memshālāh*, meaning "the territory of one's dominion" as in Psalm 114:2 (LXX 113:2) and Jeremiah 51:28 (LXX 28:28). It may also translate various forms of the Aramaic word *sholṭān*, "ruling power" or "dominion," as it does throughout Daniel (7:12,14, etc.). In those references, and others in the Apocrypha, *sholṭān* describes the authority of world rulers who are ultimately dependent on supernatural sources for their power, i.e., God delegates their authority to them (ibid.). The Septuagint's use of *exousia* for God's power is an excellent means of communicating the idea of the absolute sovereignty of God (Foerster, "exousia," *Kittel*, 2:565). In fact, Josephus and Philo also used the term in this manner, in addition to the concepts of "freedom of action, the ruling power of officials," and "authorities." Ultimately, human governments will deteriorate and be overthrown by the Son of Man who is invested with the glory, might, and authority to rule over all people forever (Betz, "Might," *Colin Brown*, 2:608).

New Testament Usage

In the New Testament *exousia* appears 103 times, displaying usages from the entire range of meaning found in classical Greek and the Septuagint. The basic idea of "authority" or "right" is used of God, Jesus Christ, and the believer. In relation to God, that authority is absolute and arbitrary (Acts 1:7). God's power is absolute and unlimited. As the Creator He may exercise His authority over His creation, as a potter over the clay (Romans 9:21; cf. Isaiah 29:16; 45:9; Jeremiah 18:6). God alone will judge all the earth for only He has the power and authority to condemn mankind to eternal destruction (Luke 12:5; cf. ibid.).

With respect to Jesus, *exousia* has been delegated by the Father (John 17:2), though no less complete (Matthew 28:18) or authoritative (John 5:27). He also had authority to heal sickness (Matthew 8:8-10) and to forgive sins (Matthew 9:2f.); the Jews of that day believed such authority was reserved for God alone (Matthew 9:3,8; Mark 2:7). Unlike the scribes and Pharisees, Jesus taught as one who had authority (Matthew 7:28,29; cf. John 7:46,

483

ἐξουσιάζω 1834

"Never man spake like this man"). Jesus spoke as one who had more authority than Moses and the prophets (Matthew 5:21-48). His authority enabled Him to control His own life (John 10:18), to equip and send out His disciples (Matthew 28:18), to give eternal life (John 17:2), and to execute judgment (John 5:27).

Believers, too, receive delegated authority from God for sonship (John 1:12) and service (2 Corinthians 10:8). The meanings of "authority" and "power to do something" are integrally related. Jesus acted with *exousia* in His teaching (Luke 4:36) and miraculous works (Matthew 9:6,8), as did His disciples once He delegated it to them (Mark 3:15). This included power and authority to cast out demons and heal the sick (Luke 9:1). Power and authority were also given to the church leadership to facilitate its functioning (Titus 1:13) and to correct its members in matters of faith (Titus 2:15; cf. 2 Corinthians 10:8; 13:10).

Exousia is also used with several other denotations in the New Testament. It refers to those who hold governing powers, the "authorities" (Luke 12:11). Furthermore, the dominion or sphere of control of such rulers, their "jurisdiction," is indicated (Luke 23:7). Then, in a clearly different kind of authority, *exousia* is used with *archai* to signify supernatural powers (Ephesians 1:21; 2:2; Colossians 1:16). Lastly, according to Louw and Nida *exousia* is used in 1 Corinthians 11:10 as a means of symbolizing authority (the implications of which remain controversial) (*Greek-English Lexicon*, 1:476).

Ultimately, "all rule, authority, power, and dominion" (Ephesians 1:21; cf. Colossians 1:16) are subject to Christ, who is their "head" (Colossians 2:10; cf. 1 Peter 3:22). Because of this believers are assured of the final victory in all struggles against the principalities, powers, and rulers of darkness of this age (Ephesians 6:12).

STRONG 1849, BAUER 277-79, MOULTON-MILLIGAN 225, KITTEL 2:562-74, LIDDELL-SCOTT 599, COLIN BROWN 2:606-11,615-16.

1834. ἐξουσιάζω exousiazō verb

Have power over someone, exercise authority, be subjected.

COGNATES:
εἰμί eimi (1498)
ἐξουσία exousia (1833)
κατεξουσιάζω katexousiazō (2685)

מָשַׁל māshal (5090), Rule, exercise dominion over (Neh 9:37, Eccl 9:17, 10:4).

שָׁלַט shālaṭ (8375), Qal: rule, lord over (Neh 5:15, Eccl 2:19, 8:9); hiphil: empower, enable (Eccl 6:2).

שִׁלְטוֹן shilṭôn (8378), Have (Eccl 8:4).

שַׁלִּיט shallîṭ (8384), Rule (Eccl 7:19 [7:20], 8:8).

שַׁלִּיט shallîṭ (A8385), Authorized, permitted (Ezr 7:24—Aramaic).

1. ἐξουσιάζει exousiazei 3sing indic pres act
2. ἐξουσιάζοντες exousiazontes
    nom pl masc part pres act
3. ἐξουσιασθήσομαι exousiasthēsomai
    1sing indic fut pass

2 and they that exercise authority upon them .... Luke 22:25
3 but I will not be brought under the power of any ..... 1 Co 6:12
1 The wife hath not power of her own body, ... 7:4
1 the husband hath not power of his own body, ... 7:4

Classical Greek

Exousiazō means "having the possibility, the right, and the power over someone," often over someone who himself is in a position of authority. In its general Greek meaning, the one who has this right or power is able to do with something or someone as he sees fit.

Septuagint Usage

In the Septuagint *exousiazō* is used to refer to someone who is over or under the authority of another. In 1 Samuel 3:1 (LXX 1 Kings 3:1) it refers to Samuel ministering under Eli, and in Nehemiah 5:15 the word takes this meaning in a negative sense to refer to authorities "lording it over the people." *Exousiazō* also refers to supremacy in a more general sense, especially in Ecclesiastes: a person has control over another's work (2:19); "a king's word is supreme" (8:4, NIV); and a wise man's words "are more to be heeded than the shouts of a ruler of fools" (9:17, NIV).

New Testament Usage

There are only three New Testament uses of *exousiazō*, each of which refers to the right or power over something or someone. In Luke 22:25 it has a general reference to "those who exercise authority" over someone. In 1 Corinthians 7:4 it takes on the New Testament idea of Christians giving up their rights. This verse indicates that both a husband and his wife give up the right or authority over their own bodies. In 1 Corinthians 6:12 Paul used *exousiazō* passively to indicate he "will not be mastered by anything" (NIV).

STRONG 1850, BAUER 279, MOULTON-MILLIGAN 225,

KITTEL 2:574-75, LIDDELL-SCOTT 599, COLIN BROWN 2:606,611.

1835. ἐξοχή exochē noun
Prominence, stand out, eminence.
CROSS-REFERENCE:
ἔχω echō (2174)

שֵׁן shēn (8514), Crag (Jb 39:28).

1. ἐξοχήν exochēn acc sing fem
1 the chief captains, and **principal** men of the city, ... Acts 25:23

The basic meaning of this word is "projection" or "prominence," e.g., a mountain peak. In its only occurrence in the Septuagint it is translated "upon the crag (projecting point) of the rock" (Job 39:28). *Exochē* is used with the preposition *kata* (2567) in its only New Testament occurrence (Acts 25:23). Here "prominence, jutting out" takes on a symbolic sense of standing out, rather than that of physically doing so. Hence it may be translated "eminent, principal, prominent, or leading" men of the city.

STRONG 1851, BAUER 279, MOULTON-MILLIGAN 225-26, LIDDELL-SCOTT 599.

1836. ἐξυπνίζω exupnizō verb
Awaken, arouse.
CROSS-REFERENCE:
ὕπνος hupnos (5096)

יָקַץ yāqats (3477), Awake, wake up (Jgs 16:14, 1 Kgs 3:15).

עוּר 'āwar (5996), Be awake, stir oneself; niphal: be raised up, arouse (Jb 14:12).

1. ἐξυπνίσω exupnisō 1sing subj aor act
1 but I go, that **I may awake** him out of sleep. .... John 11:11

Ek (1523) has the basic meaning of "out of" and *upnoō* means "to go to sleep." Generally this compound verb refers to normal sleep, but in Job 14:12 and John 11:11 it refers to a waking from the dead. *Exupnizō* is a variation of the more literary form *aphupnizō*, literally "away from sleep."

STRONG 1852, BAUER 279, MOULTON-MILLIGAN 226, KITTEL 8:545-56, LIDDELL-SCOTT 599-600, COLIN BROWN 1:442.

1837. ἔξυπνος exupnos adj
Awakened, aroused.

CROSS-REFERENCE:
ὕπνος hupnos (5096)

1. ἔξυπνος exupnos nom sing masc
1 the keeper of the prison **awaking out of his sleep**, ...Acts 16:27

This adjective has essentially the same meaning as the verb *exupnizō* (1836). In Acts 16:27 the adjective *exupnos* is used with *ginomai* (1090), "to become." This construction expresses a passive sense: that he "became awakened out of his sleep."

STRONG 1853, BAUER 279, MOULTON-MILLIGAN 226, KITTEL 8:545-56, LIDDELL-SCOTT 599-600.

1838. ἔξω exō adv
Out, outside, without.

1. ἔξω exō

1 thenceforth good for nothing, but to be cast **out**, ...	Matt 5:13
1 as you go **out** of that house (NASB)	10:14
1 behold, his mother and his brethren stood **without**, ...	12:46
1 thy mother and thy brethren stand **without**, ...	12:47
1 gathered the good ... but cast the bad **away**.	13:48
1 left them, and went **out** of the city into Bethany;	21:17
1 they caught him, and cast him **out** of the vineyard, ...	21:39
1 Now Peter sat **without** in the palace:	26:69
1 And he went **out**, and wept bitterly.	26:75
1 but was **without** in desert places: .... Mark	1:45
1 and, standing **without**, sent unto him, calling him.	3:31
1 thy mother and thy brethren **without** seek for thee.	3:32
1 but unto them **that are without**, ...	4:11
1 he would not send them away **out** of the country.	5:10
1 and led him **out** of the town;	8:23
1 the door **without** in a place where two ways met;	11:4
1 And when even was come, he went out **of** the city.	11:19
1 killed him, and cast him **out** of the vineyard.	12:8
1 he went **out** into the porch; and the cock crew.	14:68
1 people were praying **without** at the time of incense. Luke	1:10
1 And rose up, and thrust him **out** of the city, ...	4:29
1 Thy mother and thy brethren stand **without**, ...	8:20
1 he put them all **out**, and took her by the hand, ...	8:54
1 begin to stand **without**, and to knock at the door, ...	13:25
1 kingdom of God, and you yourselves thrust **out**.	13:28
1 cannot be that a prophet perish **out** of Jerusalem.	13:33
1 nor yet for the dunghill; but men cast it **out**.	14:35
1 they cast him **out** of the vineyard, and killed him.	20:15
1 And Peter went **out**, and wept bitterly.	22:62
1 And he led them **out** as far as to Bethany, ...	24:50
1 him that cometh to me I will in no wise cast **out**. ... John	6:37
1 and dost thou teach us? And they cast him **out**.	9:34
1 Jesus heard that they had cast him **out**;	9:35
1 he cried with a loud voice, Lazarus, come **forth**.	11:43
1 now shall the prince of this world be cast **out**.	12:31
1 he is cast **forth** as a branch, and is withered;	15:6
1 But Peter stood at the door **without**.	18:16
1 Pilate therefore went **out** to them, (NASB)	18:29
1 Pilate therefore went **forth** again, and saith	19:4
1 saith unto them, Behold, I bring him **forth** to you, ...	19:4
1 Then came Jesus **forth**, wearing the crown	19:5
1 Pilate ... heard that saying, he brought Jesus **forth**, ...	19:13
1 But Mary stood **without** at the sepulchre weeping:	20:11
1 commanded them to go aside **out** of the council, ... Acts	4:15
1 and the keepers standing **without** before the doors:	5:23
1 commanded to put the apostles **forth** a little space;	5:34
1 And cast him **out** of the city, and stoned him:	7:58
1 But Peter put them all **forth**, and kneeled down, ...	9:40
1 and, having stoned Paul, drew him **out** of the city, ...	14:19
1 And on the sabbath we went **out** of the city	16:13
1 And brought them **out**, and said, Sirs, ...	16:30

1 till we were **out** of the city:	Acts 21:5
1 they took Paul, and drew him **out** of the temple:	21:30
1 pursuing them even to **foreign** cities. (NASB)	26:11
1 have I to do to judge them also that are **without**?	1 Co 5:12
1 But them that are **without** God judgeth.	5:13
1 but though our **outward** man perish,	2 Co 4:16
1 Walk in wisdom toward **them that are without,**	Col 4:5
1 may walk honestly toward them that are **without,**	1 Th 4:12
1 those beasts, ... are burned **without** the camp.	Heb 13:11
1 Wherefore Jesus also, ... suffered **without** the gate.	13:12
1 unto him **without** the camp, bearing his reproach.	13:13
1 love casteth **out** fear: because fear hath torment.	1 Jn 4:18
1 and he shall go no more **out:**	Rev 3:12
1 the court which is without the temple leave **out,**	11:2
1 And the winepress was trodden **without** the city,	14:20
1 For **without** are dogs, and sorcerers,	22:15

Classical Greek
Exō may be designated simply as an adverb of place, or in some cases, as a preposition followed by the genitive case. In the nursing contracts of the papyri *exō* occurs as an adverb in connection with the provision to care for a child outside (*exō*) of the home but within (*esō* [2059]) the city. The word is also used in the papyri as a preposition. One example is the phrase *exō herou bomon*, which has reference to "being outside of the protection of the temple and altar" (see *Moulton-Milligan*).

Septuagint Usage
Exō appears in the Septuagint over 75 times, translating 4 different Hebrew words, usually some form of *chûts* ("outside, abroad"). A typical example of how *exō* is used as an adverb of place can be found in Genesis 15:5 where God promised Abram a son: "And he brought him forth *abroad*, and said, Look now toward heaven . . . ." In Exodus 29:14 *exō* is used as a preposition in a passage where God told Moses how to consecrate Aaron and his sons.

New Testament Usage
Similarly *exō* is used in the New Testament both as an adverb and preposition. Many examples can be cited from the New Testament to illustrate its adverbial use. Mark 11:4 makes reference to the colt tied outside (*exō*) at the door. There are a number of passages in which *exō* modifies some form of the verb *histēmi* (2449). For example, Matthew 12:46 indicates Jesus' relatives, seeking to speak with Him, were standing outside (*exō*) a house which He had entered (cf. Mark 3:31; Luke 8:20; 13:25; John 18:16; 20:11).

Among the New Testament examples of *exō* as a preposition is Hebrews 13:11f. In the Jewish sacrificial system blood was offered to God, but the bodies of the victims were burned *outside* of the city. Also, in Matthew 10:14 the disciples were instructed by Jesus that before they departed from (*exō*) a house or city where their word was not received, they were to shake off the dust from their feet (cf. Luke 4:29; Acts 4:15; 14:19).

As in some Greek literature dated prior to the First Century, there are examples in the New Testament where *exō* functions as a substantive or as an adjective. In either case *exō* stands with an article. Its substantive use occurs in Mark 4:11, where it is stated that Jesus spoke in parables to those *outside* (*exō*) of the circle of disciples (cf. 1 Corinthians 5:12; Colossians 4:5; 1 Thessalonians 4:12). The only New Testament examples of the adjectival use of *exō* are Acts 26:11 and 2 Corinthians 4:16. The passage in Acts distinguishes the "outside cities" (*tas exō poleis*), that is, non-Jewish, from the cities that were Jewish, while the Corinthian reference employs *exō* to describe "the external" man (in contrast to the inward man).

STRONG 1854, BAUER 279, MOULTON-MILLIGAN 226, KITTEL 2:575-76, LIDDELL-SCOTT 600.

1839. ἔξωθεν exōthen adv
Outside, from without, outwardly, externally.

1. ἔξωθεν exōthen

1 the **outside** of the cup and of the platter,	Matt 23:25
1 which indeed appear beautiful **outward,**	23:27
1 so ye also **outwardly** appear righteous unto men,	23:28
1 There is nothing from **without** a man,	Mark 7:15
1 thing **from without** entereth into the man,	7:18
1 Now do ye Pharisees make clean the **outside**	Luke 11:39
1 did not he that made that which is **without**	11:40
1 **without** were fightings, within were fears.	2 Co 7:5
1 have a good report of them which are **without;**	1 Tm 3:7
1 Whose adorning let it not be that **outward**	1 Pt 3:3
1 And leave **out** the court which is (NASB)	Rev 11:2
1 which is **outside** the temple (NASB)	11:2
1 was trodden **outside** the city (NASB)	14:20

Classical Greek and Septuagint Usage
This word is comprised of *exō* (1838), "outside," plus the suffix *then*. Greek words with the suffix *then* answer the question, "From where?" However, *then* is stereotyped and meaningless for the most part in *exōthen* (Blass and DeBrunner, *Greek Grammar of the New Testament*, p.56). Although *exōthen* occurs less frequently in the Septuagint than *exō*, it is used most often to translate various forms of the same Hebrew word, *chûts*, meaning "outside, abroad." Like *exō*, *exōthen* is also used as an adverb of place (2 Kings 6:6 [LXX 4 Kings 6:6]) and as a preposition (Exodus 26:35).

(See *Moulton-Milligan* for one example in the papyri.)

New Testament Usage

In the New Testament *exōthen* is employed 13 times and thus is much less frequent than *exō*. But like *exō* it is utilized in the New Testament both as an adverb and a preposition.

There are more New Testament examples of *exōthen* as an adverb. Mark 7:18 says that nothing from outside (*exōthen*) can defile a person. In the question of Luke 11:40 *exōthen* stands in contrast to *esōthen* (2060), "inside," where Jesus pointed out the folly of being so careful to keep material objects clean while the heart is polluted. Similarly, in Matthew 23:27 Jesus spoke about the Pharisees who, like whitewashed tombs, appeared beautiful outwardly (*exōthen*), but inwardly they were full of dead men's bones and uncleanness. Paul's letters have two occurrences of *exōthen* and both are adverbs. In 2 Corinthians Paul wrote about outward conflicts (*exōthen machai*) in Macedonia, and in 1 Timothy 3:7 he referred to the non-Christian world as "those who are outside" (*tōn exōthen*).

As to the prepositional usage of *exōthen*, only a few examples appear in the New Testament. There is ambiguity as to whether *exōthen* in Matthew 23:25 and Luke 11:39 functions as a preposition (Robertson, *Grammar of the Greek New Testament*, p.642). But clear examples are found in Mark and Revelation. (1) Mark 7:15 records Jesus' statement that things outside (*exōthen*) a man cannot defile him; (2) Revelation 11:2 refers to the court that is outside (*exōthen*) of the temple. (3) Revelation 14:20 describes the winepress that was trampled outside (*exōthen*) the city of Jerusalem.

The only example of the adjectival usage of this word in the New Testament is 1 Peter 3:3, where it emphasizes that true beauty for the Christian woman consists not of outward (*exōthen*) adorning but of inward graces of the soul.

Strong 1855, Bauer 279-80, Moulton-Milligan 226, Liddell-Scott 600.

1840. ἐξωθέω exōtheō verb

To push out, drive out, expel, propel.
Synonyms:
ἐκβάλλω ekballō (1531)
ἐξαίρω exairō (1792)

דּוּחַ dûach (1792), Hiphil: spew out, cast out (Jer 51:34 [28:35]).

דָּחָה dāchâh (1815), Push; pual: cast down, throw down (Ps 36:12 [35:12]).

כָּאָה kā'âh (3630), Niphal: turn back, return (Dn 11:30).

לָקַח lāqach (4089), Take away (Mi 2:9).

נָדָא nādhâ' (5245), Hiphil: cause to sin (2 Kgs 17:21).

נָדַד nādhadh (5252), Flee; hophal: cast aside, thrust away (2 Sm 23:6).

נָדַח nādhach (5258), Qal: banished person (2 Sm 14:14); niphal: be cast out (2 Sm 14:14); hiphil: cast out (Ps 5:10, Jer 24:9).

נָדַף nādhaph (5264), Blow away; niphal: be blown away (Is 41:2).

נָסַח nāsach (5442), Tear out (Prv 2:22).

רָחַק rāchaq (7651), Hiphil: remove, send far away (Jl 3:6).

תָּעָה tā'âh (8912), Hiphil: lead astray (Jer 50:6 [27:6]).

1. ἔξωσεν exōsen 3sing indic aor act
2. ἐξῶσαι exōsai inf aor act

1 God drave out before the face of our fathers,........Acts 7:45
2 if it were possible, to thrust in the ship................ 27:39

Classical Greek

This word is a compound form consisting of *ex* (i.e., *ek* [1523]), "out of," and *ōtheō*, "thrust, push, force onward or away." The simple form *ōtheō* is much more common in classical Greek than the compound. (See *Moulton-Milligan* for examples of *exōtheō* in the papyri.)

Septuagint Usage

Exōtheō occurs frequently in the Septuagint. Deuteronomy 13:5 refers to a prophet or dreamer who led people to follow other gods. In so doing, he "thrusted" them out of the way in which the Lord commanded them to walk. Many more examples can be cited from the Septuagint where the meaning of *exōtheō* is "thrust out" (2 Samuel [LXX 2 Kings] 14:13,14; 23:6; 2 Kings 17:21 [LXX 4 Kings 17:21]; Psalms 5:10; 36:12 [LXX 35:12]; Isaiah 41:2; Jeremiah 8:3; 23:2; etc.). In the Septuagint the word usually translates *nādhach*.

New Testament Usage

In the New Testament *exōtheō* occurs only twice, both in the Book of Acts. In 7:45 the word is used to refer to God's driving out the inhabitants of Canaan so that Israel could receive the promised inheritance. But in 27:39 the same word has reference to the ship on which Paul was sailing to Rome. It was caught in a storm, and to bring it to shore the ship was "thrust out upon" or "driven upon" the beach.

ἐξώτερος 1841

STRONG 1856, BAUER 280, MOULTON-MILLIGAN 226, LIDDELL-SCOTT 600.

1841. ἐξώτερος exōteros adj
Outer, outside.

חִיצוֹן chîtsôn (2535), Outer (1 Kgs 6:29,30, Ez 10:5, 42:6ff.).

חָצֵר chātsēr (2793), Courtyard, court (Ez 41:15, 42:6).

קִיצוֹן qîtsôn (7303), Outermost (Ex 26:4).

1. ἐξώτερον exōteron comp nom/acc sing neu

1 shall be cast out into **outer** darkness:	Matt 8:12
1 and cast him into **outer** darkness;	22:13
1 cast ye ... unprofitable servant into **outer** darkness:	25:30

Although some lexicons treat *exōteros* as a unique word, it is actually the comparative form of the term *exō* (1838), "outside." *Bauer* states that the idea of "outside" is seen with respect to something which is "inside" and that *exōteros* is used in a superlative sense in the New Testament to mean "farthest" or "extreme" (cf. a Septuagint occurrence at Exodus 26:4 which describes the "*uttermost* edge" of a curtain). In its New Testament occurrences the unbelieving Jew (Matthew 8:12), the person who made light of the king's gracious invitation (Matthew 22:13), and the unfaithful servant (Matthew 25:30) were thrown *outside* (*exōteros*) into the darkness (NIV). They were excluded from the blessings of God's kingdom.

STRONG 1857, BAUER 280, MOULTON-MILLIGAN 226, LIDDELL-SCOTT 600-601.

1842. ἔοικα eoika verb
Be like, resemble.

1. ἔοικεν eoiken 3sing indic perf act

1 For he that wavereth is like a wave of the sea	Jas 1:6
1 he is like unto a man beholding his natural face in	1:23

Classical Greek
Eoika is fairly common in classical Greek. Actually it is a perfect form of the verb *eikō* (1493), although its use in that capacity is rare. Generally *eoika* functions as a present tense verb, and it means "to be like, to seem, to seem likely, possible, or to be fitting, seemly" (see *Liddell-Scott*). It is not found in the Septuagint.

New Testament Usage
Two instances of *eoika* are present in the New Testament, occurring in James (1:6,23). Both texts reveal that *eoika* means "to be like." Thus in two similes the author of James describes the doubter as "like a wave of the sea" and the one who only listens to the word as "like a man who looks at his face in a mirror and, after looking at himself, goes away and immediately forgets what he looks like" (NIV).

BAUER 280, MOULTON-MILLIGAN 226, LIDDELL-SCOTT 601, COLIN BROWN 2:286.

1843. ἑορτάζω heortazō verb
To keep or celebrate a festival or feast.

CROSS-REFERENCE:
ἑορτή heortē (1844)

חָגַג chāghagh (2379), Celebrate (Ex 5:1, Dt 16:15, Zec 14:16).

1. ἑορτάζωμεν heortazōmen 1pl subj pres act

1 let us keep the feast, not with old leaven,	1 Co 5:8

Classical Greek and Septuagint Usage
Festivals were part of life in the ancient world. In classical Greek the verb *heortazō* expresses either the idea of keeping a festival (holiday) or celebrating by the observance of a festival (see *Liddell-Scott*). This verb occurs frequently in the Septuagint for the word *chāghagh* and is often used in reference to the Feast of the Passover or the Feast of Tabernacles (Exodus 5:1; 12:14; 23:14; Leviticus 23:39; Numbers 29:12; Deuteronomy 16:15; Isaiah 30:29; Zechariah 14:15,18,19).

New Testament Usage
The only occurrence of *heortazō* in the New Testament is in 1 Corinthians 5:8. Its use there is based on the Passover custom of getting rid of all leaven from the household and eating only unleavened bread during the Feast. Paul warned the believers at Corinth against the leaven of malice and wickedness. So as a figurative characterization of the Christian life, Paul exhorted the Corinthian believers to practice celebrating (*heortazōmen*) the true Christian feast of the Passover by replacing malice and wickedness with sincerity and truth.

STRONG 1858, BAUER 280, MOULTON-MILLIGAN 226, LIDDELL-SCOTT 601, COLIN BROWN 1:624,631,634.

1844. ἑορτή heortē noun
Festival, feast.

CROSS-REFERENCE:
ἑορτάζω heortazō (1843)

חַג chagh (2374), Feast, festival (Ex 23:15, 2 Chr 7:8, Am 8:10).

חֹדֶשׁ chōdhesh (2415), Feast, festival (1 Kgs 12:33).

מוֹעֵד mô'ēdh (4287), Appointed time, set feast (Lv 23:4, 1 Chr 23:31, Zep 3:18).

1. ἑορτή heortē nom sing fem
2. ἑορτῆς heortēs gen sing fem
3. ἑορτῇ heortē dat sing fem
4. ἑορτήν heortēn acc sing fem

```
3 But they said, Not on the feast day,.............. Matt 26:5
4 Now at that feast the governor was wont to release.... 27:15
3 But they said, Not on the feast day,............. Mark 14:2
4 at that feast he released unto them one prisoner,...... 15:6
3 Jerusalem every year at the feast of the passover.... Luke 2:41
2 went up to Jerusalem after the custom of the feast..... 2:42
1 Now the feast of unleavened bread drew nigh,......... 22:1
4 he must release one unto them at the feast........... 23:17
3 in Jerusalem at the passover, in the feast day,.....John 2:23
3 all the things that he did at Jerusalem at the feast:...... 4:45
4 for they also went unto the feast................... 4:45
1 After this there was a feast of the Jews;............. 5:1
1 And the passover, a feast of the Jews, was nigh........ 6:4
1 Now the Jews' feast of tabernacles was at hand........ 7:2
4 Go ye up unto this feast:.......................... 7:8
1 I go not up yet unto this feast:..................... 7:8
1 then went he also up unto the feast, not openly,..... 7:10
3 Then the Jews sought him at the feast,.............. 7:11
2 Now about the midst of the feast Jesus went up....... 7:14
2 In the last day, that great day of the feast,.......... 7:37
4 What think ye, that he will not come to the feast?.... 11:56
4 next day much people that were come to the feast,... 12:12
3 Greeks ... that came up to worship at the feast:..... 12:20
2 Now before the feast of the passover,............... 13:1
4 those things that we have need of against the feast;... 13:29
1 keep this feast that cometh in Jerusalem:..........Acts 18:21
2 or in respect of an holyday, or of the new moon,....Col 2:16
```

Classical Greek
In classical Greek *heortē* is used in several different ways. Homer used it for a "feast" or "festival." For later writers, such as Aeschylus and Thucydides, it sometimes had the meaning of "sport" or "play" (see *Liddell-Scott*).

Septuagint Usage
The Septuagint employs *heortē* to translate *chagh*, referring to the holy feasts of Israel (compare Nahum 2:1 [LXX 1:15] to Proverbs 15:15, where *mishteh* is used of a banquet). Thus Exodus 23:14-16 uses *heortē* for three of the great feasts of the Jewish religion: Unleavened Bread (Passover), Harvest (Pentecost), and Ingathering (Tabernacles).

New Testament Usage
The New Testament carries over the Septuagint's use of *heortē* for a Jewish feast. There it is used especially of Passover (John 13:1) and Tabernacles (John 7:2). Paul also used the term in Colossians 2:16 to refer to the annual Jewish feasts in general, as opposed to the monthly (new moon) and weekly (Sabbath) celebrations.

Strong 1859, Bauer 280, Moulton-Milligan 226, Liddell-Scott 601, Colin Brown 1:624,626,628,632.

1845. ἐπαγγελία epangelia noun
Promise.

Cognate:
ἐπαγγέλλομαι epangellomai (1846)

Synonym:
ἐπάγγελμα epangelma (1847)

אֲגֻדָּה 'ăghuddāh (89), Firmament, foundation (Am 9:6).
סִפְרָה siphrāh (5815), Book, record (Ps 56:8 [55:8]).
פָּרָשָׁה pārāshāh (6825), Exact amount, sum (Est 4:7).

1. ἐπαγγελίας epangelias gen/acc sing/pl fem
2. ἐπαγγελία epangelia nom sing fem
3. ἐπαγγελίᾳ epangelia dat sing fem
4. ἐπαγγελίαν epangelian acc sing fem
5. ἐπαγγελίαι epangeliai nom pl fem
6. ἐπαγγελιῶν epangeliōn gen pl fem
7. ἐπαγγελίαις epangeliais dat pl fem

```
4 behold, I send the promise of my Father upon you: Luke 24:49
4 but wait for the promise of the Father,............Acts 1:4
4 and having received of the Father the promise......... 2:33
2 For the promise is unto you, and to your children,..... 2:39
1 But when the time of the promise drew nigh,.......... 7:17
4 hath God according to his promise................... 13:23
4 that the promise which was made unto the fathers,.... 13:32
4 ready, looking for a promise from thee............... 23:21
1 hope of the promise made of God unto our fathers:... 26:6
2 For the promise, that he should be the heir........Rom 4:13
2 and the promise made of none effect:................ 4:14
4 the end the promise might be sure to all the seed;..... 4:16
4 He staggered not at the promise of God............... 4:20
5 and the service of God, and the promises;............. 9:4
1 children of the promise are counted for the seed....... 9:8
1 For this is the word of promise,...................... 9:9
1 to confirm the promises made unto the fathers:....... 15:8
5 For all the promises of God in him are yea,....... 2 Co 1:20
1 Having therefore these promises, dearly beloved,...... 7:1
4 receive the promise of the Spirit through faith....... Gal 3:14
5 to Abraham and his seed were the promises made..... 3:16
4 that it should make the promise of none effect:....... 3:17
1 inheritance be of the law, it is no more of promise:..... 3:18
1 but God gave it to Abraham by promise.............. 3:18
6 Is the law then against the promises of God?......... 3:21
2 the promise by faith of Jesus Christ might be given..... 3:22
4 Abraham's seed, ... heirs according to the promise..... 3:29
1 but he of the freewoman was by promise............. 4:23
1 we, ... as Isaac was, are the children of promise...... 4:28
1 ye were sealed with that holy Spirit of promise,.....Eph 1:13
1 and strangers from the covenants of promise,........ 2:12
1 partakers of his promise in Christ by the gospel:...... 3:6
3 which is the first commandment with promise;....... 6:2
4 having promise of the life that now is,............. 1 Tm 4:8
4 according to the promise of life which is in Christ ..2 Tm 1:1
1 a promise being left us of entering into his rest,..... Heb 4:1
1 through faith and patience inherit the promises......... 6:12
1 had patiently endured, he obtained the promise....... 6:15
1 abundantly to show unto the heirs of promise......... 6:17
1 and blessed him that had the promises............... 7:6
7 which was established upon better promises.......... 8:6
4 might receive the promise of eternal inheritance..... 9:15
4 done the will of God, ye might receive the promise..... 10:36
1 By faith he sojourned in the land of promise,......... 11:9
1 and Jacob, the heirs with him of the same promise:... 11:9
1 not having received the promises,................... 11:13
1 and he that had received the promises offered........ 11:17
```

6 wrought righteousness, obtained **promises**,	Heb	11:33
4 And these all, ... received not the **promise**:		11:39
2 And saying, Where is the **promise** of his coming?	2 Pt	3:4
1 The Lord is not slack concerning his **promise**,		3:9
2 This then is the **message** which we have heard	1 Jn	1:5
2 And this is the **promise** that he hath promised us,		2:25
2 the **message** that ye heard from the beginning,		3:11

Classical Greek

The noun *epangelia*, "promise," like the verbs *epangellomai* (1846) and *euangelizō* (2076) and the noun *euangelion* (2077), is derived from the stem *angel-* (cf. *angelos* [32], "messenger"). Originally *epangellomai* and *epangelia* were synonymous with these other terms ("to report"); however, gradually they narrowed in definition. In classical literature *epangelia* is actually a legal term for a "declaration of a claim" or a "public denouncement" of someone who had violated a public trust (*Liddell-Scott*; cf. Schniewind and Friedrich, "epangellō," *Kittel*, 2:576).

It further progressed to mean an "offer" or a "promise," which approximates the New Testament usage. Later it became a technical term for "voluntary payment." Schniewind and Friedrich note only one example in secular Greek to a promise from God to man, despite an apparently recognized sacral role of the word "promise" in the various religions of Hellenism (ibid., 2:578f.).

Septuagint Usage

Epangelia occurs in the Septuagint six times, three of which are canonical (Esther 4:7; Psalm 56:8 [LXX 55:8]; Amos 9:6; cf. 1 Esdras 1:7; 1 Maccabees 10:15; 4 Maccabees 12:9). The Hebrew is inconsistent behind the word (but cf. the verb), and the usage largely follows the classical definitions throughout.

Despite the absence of the terminology of "promise" in the Septuagint, the concept is present in Old Testament thought (see Hoffmann, "Promise," *Colin Brown*, 3:69f.). What God promises, i.e., what He says He will do (see Schniewind and Friedrich, "epangellō," *Kittel*, 2:579 for a discussion of the traditional link between *dāvar*, *'āmar*, and "promise"), is fulfilled again and again and is inherently necessary to any Old Testament understanding of God.

The first promise of God mentioned in the Old Testament occurs in the story of man's fall in the Garden of Eden. After Adam and Eve disobeyed God, the Lord promised that the Seed of the woman would crush the head of the serpent (cf. Genesis 3:15). A second promise is located in Genesis 9:11 where the Lord vowed never again to destroy mankind by a flood. But perhaps the primary point of origin for understanding "promise" in the Old Testament is God's promise to Abraham (Genesis 12:1-3; Hoffmann, "Promise," *Colin Brown*, 3:69). Paul was the principal spokesman for the New Testament's reaction to this concept. The union of Abraham, "promise," and the Law—so common in Paul's writings—was not unknown prior to or at least contemporary with Paul (Syriac Apocalypse of Baruch [2 Baruch] 57:2; 59:2; cf. 57:1; Testament of Joseph 20:1; also noted by Schniewind and Friedrich, "epangellō," *Kittel*, 2:579; Schniewind also lists rabbinic sources which tie keeping the Law to being a recipient of Abraham's promises).

Later in Israel's history, God promised His captive people He would deliver them out of the hand of their Egyptian masters and would take them to the "promised land" of Canaan (cf. Exodus 3:8-10). In conjunction with the covenant delivered on Sinai during the wilderness wanderings, the Lord promised that if Israel would obey His commandments they would be "a peculiar treasure (i.e., a special possession) unto me above all people" (Exodus 19:5). Innumerable promises of this type were pronounced throughout Israel's history (cf. Deuteronomy 28:1-14).

The bond between promise and covenant emerges in other Biblical texts (Isaiah chapter 42; Jeremiah 31:31-34; cf. Ezekiel 36:26-28) as does the idea that in the future a new relationship would be established with God through His Spirit (Isaiah 44:1-5; Joel 2:28ff.) for all peoples (Isaiah 42:6; 49:6; cf. Genesis 12:3: "And in thee [Abraham] shall all families of the earth be blessed").

All things considered, the very nature of the old covenant God established with Israel had the characteristic of a promise. Furthermore, when Israel's tribulation was at its worse—when the nation was rebellious and in captivity—they received the clearest, most direct promise of their coming Messiah (e.g., the prophecies contained in Isaiah and Daniel).

New Testament Usage

The New Testament's concept of *epangelia* expands upon the premise that the Old Testament promises of God are to some extent fulfilled in Christ. The concept of "promise," therefore, is not monolithic; God's promises involve Jesus himself, His ministry, the salvation He brings, the consummation of God's promises to Abraham, and the promise of the Spirit. In fact, Jesus made promises on behalf of the Father which were fulfilled (see *plēroō* [3997]) following His ascension or which remain to be realized.

Luke alone of the Evangelists used *epangelia*, and he did so in a theologically significant passage (Luke 24:49). Jesus departed from the earth after having assured His disciples He would "send (*apostellō* [643]) the promise of my Father." This was realized in the Upper Room, and in his subsequent sermon on the Day of Pentecost, Peter explained that the arrival of the Spirit was indeed the fulfillment of Jesus' words (Acts 1:4; 2:33). "Promise" is repeatedly explained in terms of the Old Testament promises (Acts 2:33,39; cf. Joel 2:28-30; Acts 7:17 [to Abraham]; 13:23; 26:6 [to the promise of resurrection, cf. 26:8]). Since the Spirit is the verification of the reality of the Resurrection and proof that Christ ascended (Acts 2:33), which was witnessed ("which ye now see and hear"), it is clear that "promise" covers a wide range of God's acts in history and not just one single event.

Paul's writings are replete with promise language. He, more than any other writer, assessed God's promise to Abraham in light of the Law and new life in Christ. Like Luke, Paul associated *epangelia* with the Holy Spirit (Galatians 3:14; Ephesians 1:13), and he equated this with the Abrahamic covenant of Genesis 12 (Galatians 3:14-18; cf. Romans 4:16; Galatians 4:23,28). Paul argued that the Law was not the vehicle of promise, particularly not of righteousness and salvation (Romans 4:13f.). Instead, faith in God became the vehicle. This faith, then, is equivalent to believing that God has the power to do what He has promised to do. For this reason, Abraham stands as an example of someone who had an unshakable certainty that God has the power to do what He has promised (cf. Romans 4:20,21). In addition, chapter 4 of Romans makes it clear that the fulfillment of the promises are guaranteed only because of God's grace and sovereign faithfulness. There is no longer an implied contingency, as there was under the old covenant, that Law must be fulfilled if the promise is to be experienced.

In the third chapter of Galatians Paul developed the contrast between Law and promise more fervently. He emphasized that the two are mutually independent. In fact, he pointed out that the "promise" ceases to be a promise if there is any connection to fulfilling the conditions of the Law (verses 12,18). Furthermore, if one seeks to gain the promised inheritance through obedience to the precepts of the Law, one will lose what has been promised. The promise was given by grace to Abraham hundreds of years prior to the introduction of the Law. The Law given to Israel through Moses was not added in order to replace or to compete with the promise. On the contrary, the Law was added as a preparatory schoolmaster designed to bring Israel to a faith in Christ (cf. verses 19-26). In view of these truths, Galatians 3:14 proclaims that "the blessing of Abraham" comes to Gentile as well as Jew through Jesus Christ so that "we might receive the promise of the Spirit through faith" (cf. Acts 2:16,17,33).

Second only to Paul in "promise theology" is the author of Hebrews (if it is not Paul). Again "promise" is related to Abraham (6:15; 7:6; 11:17), as are covenantal promises (8:6; 9:15). "Promise" is also regarded as the eternal life to be inherited by the faithful (9:15; cf. 10:35,36; 11:17-19; 1 John 2:25). Thus, not only is "promise" a referent to the promises of Abraham but to the promises the believer receives which may or may not be realized in this present existence (Hebrews 11:39; cf. 12:26; James 1:12; 2:15; 2 Peter 3:13). The Book of Hebrews reveals that the "better promises" in Christ form an already/not yet situation for the believer. Some of the promises are to be fulfilled in His second coming. Nevertheless, the promises in Christ are superior to the promises given Abraham because Jesus is the guarantor of a better agreement (Hebrews 7:22; 8:6). Therefore, just like the heroes of the Faith described in chapter 11, believers are to be strengthened by considering the faithfulness of the One who gave the promise (10:23).

In the second epistle of Peter, the writer also focused on God's promises, especially those which are not yet fulfilled. Because the return of Christ is delayed, scoffers ask, "Where is the promise of his coming?" (2 Peter 3:4). Against this the apostle assured that "the Lord is not slack concerning his promise, as some men count slackness" (3:9). In fact, His delay is an aspect of His magnanimous character, His longsuffering patience, and His compassion for the lost: Jesus is "not willing that any should perish, but that all should come to repentance" (3:9). But again, until that Day, believers are to have an unswerving trust in the certitude of God's promises (cf. 1:19). These promises concern life in Christ (2 Timothy 1:1), the crown of life (James 1:12), and eternal life (Titus 1:2; 1 John 2:25). They involve both the "here and now" as well as the future. They will reach their climax in the fulfillment of the promise foretelling a "new heavens and a new earth" (2 Peter 3:13).

Strong 1860, Bauer 280, Moulton-Milligan 226-27, Kittel 2:576-85, Liddell-Scott 602, Colin Brown 3:68-72.

1846. ἐπαγγέλλομαι
epangellomai verb

Promise.

Cognates:
ἀγγέλλω angellō (31B)
ἐπαγγελία epangelia (1845)
ἐπάγγελμα epangelma (1847)
προεπαγγέλλομαι proepangellomai (4139)

Synonyms:
ἐξομολογέω exomologeō (1827)
ὁμολογέω homologeō (3533)

אָמַר 'āmar (569), Promise (Est 4:7).

1. ἐπαγγελλόμενοι epangellomenoi
    nom pl masc part pres mid
2. ἐπαγγελλομέναις epangellomenais
    dat pl fem part pres mid
3. ἐπηγγείλατο epēngeilato 3sing indic aor mid
4. ἐπηγγείλαντο epēngeilanto 3pl indic aor mid
5. ἐπαγγειλάμενος epangeilamenos
    nom sing masc part aor mid
6. ἐπαγγειλάμενον epangeilamenon
    acc sing masc part aor mid
7. ἐπήγγελται epēngeltai 3sing indic perf mid

```
4 they were glad, and promised to give him money...Mark 14:11
3 yet he promised that he would give it to him........Acts 7:5
7 what he had promised, he was able ... to perform....Rom 4:21
7 seed should come to whom the promise was made;...Gal 3:19
2 But which becometh women professing godliness....1 Tm 2:10
1 some professing have erred concerning the faith......... 6:21
3 which God, ... promised before the world began;...Tit 1:2
5 For when God made promise to Abraham,..........Heb 6:13
5 for he is faithful that promised;...................... 10:23
6 she judged him faithful who had promised........... 11:11
7 but now he hath promised, saying,.................... 12:26
3 the Lord hath promised to them that love him......Jas 1:12
3 and heirs of the kingdom which he hath promised.... 2:5
1 While they promise them liberty,...................2 Pt 2:19
3 And this is the promise that he hath promised us,... 1 Jn 2:25
```

Classical Greek

In classical Greek the verb *epangellō* has a variety of meanings. Primarily it means "to declare" or "to make known." Around 400 B.C., Thucydides, a Greek historian, used *epangellō* in a military sense meaning to order mobilization of an army. About the same time Plato employed it in reference to declaring war (see *Liddell-Scott*).

By the Hellenistic age *epangellō* dropped out of Koine Greek and was replaced by *epangellomai*. In the papyri it is often used of a promise to pay money or to make a donation. Inscriptions from the era use the term for the promise of a gift to a new emperor (see *Moulton-Milligan*).

Septuagint Usage

The Septuagint seldom uses *epangellomai*, perhaps because of its negative association with broken promises. For example, Proverbs 13:12 says that one who helps is better than one who merely promises. In Esther 4:7 the term is used, as in the Koine papyri, for a promise of money. Only in the Apocrypha is *epangellomai* used of God's promises to man. (See 3 Maccabees 2:10.)

New Testament Usage

In the New Testament *epangellomai* is used in two primary ways: "to promise" and "to profess." Like the Septuagint and the Koine papyri, Mark 14:11 speaks of promised money—in this case to Judas for his betrayal of Jesus. Unlike the Septuagint, the New Testament usually uses *epangellomai* to refer to God's promises to man. (For examples, see Acts 7:5; Romans 4:21; Hebrews 6:13.) Only once, in 2 Peter 2:19, is the word used of a false or broken promise.

Paul is the only New Testament writer who employed *epangellomai* for the act of professing. He did so twice in his first letter to Timothy. In 2:10 Paul spoke of women who profess godliness. Later, in 6:21, he referred to those who had professed false doctrine and had departed from the faith.

Strong 1861, Bauer 280-81, Moulton-Milligan 227, Kittel 2:576-85 (see "epangellō"), Liddell-Scott 602 (see "epangellō"), Colin Brown 3:68,70 (see "epangellō").

1847. ἐπάγγελμα epangelma noun

A promise, announcement.

Cognate:
ἐπαγγέλλομαι epangellomai (1846)
Synonym:
ἐπαγγελία epangelia (1845)

1. ἐπάγγελμα epangelma nom/acc sing neu
2. ἐπαγγέλματα epangelmata nom/acc pl neu

2 exceeding great and precious **promises:** .... 2 Pt 1:4
1 we, according to his **promise,** look for new heavens 3:13

Classical Greek

The word *epangelma* is related to the verb *epangellō* (*epi* [1894], "upon"; *angellō* [31B], "proclaim, announce"). Its meaning overlaps a great deal with *epangelia* (1845), which is used with reference to the promises of God in the New Testament (except Acts 23:31). In classical Greek *epangelma* means "announcement," "order," or "promise" (Hoffman, "Promise," *Colin Brown*, 3:71). This word is not found in the Septuagint.

New Testament Usage

In the New Testament *epangelma* is used twice and is found only in the Epistle of 2 Peter. This epistle sought to stir up hope in the second coming of Christ when it had become subject to ridicule by scoffers. The concept *epangelma* is restricted to the promise of the return of Christ and entrance into the eternal kingdom. That which points to this final reality is described as "exceeding great and precious promises" (*epangelmata*, 2 Peter 1:4). According to God's promise (*epangelma*) the Lord will return, and Christians are to "look for new heavens and a new earth, wherein dwelleth righteousness" (3:13).

STRONG 1862, BAUER 281, KITTEL 2:585-86, LIDDELL-SCOTT 602, COLIN BROWN 3:68,71.

1848. ἐπάγω epagō verb

Bring on or upon, inflict.

CROSS-REFERENCE:
  ἄγω agō (70)

אָנַף 'āneph (613), Be angry (1 Kgs 8:46).
בּוֹא bô' (971), Qal: come up, come against (Jgs 9:24, Ho 13:15, Am 5:9); hiphil: bring upon, brought forth (Gn 20:9, 2 Chr 7:22, Is 7:17).
גָּמַל gāmal (1621), Has done (Is 63:7).
חָתַם chātam (2505), Refrain, hold back (Is 48:9).
חֲלִיפָה chălîphāh (2588), A fresh wave of troops (Jb 10:17).
מָשַׁךְ māshakh (5082), Draw, lure (Jgs 4:7).
נָהַג nāhagh (5268), Qal: lead, take (1 Sm 30:22—Codex Alexandrinus only); piel: led forth, brought in (Ps 78:26 [77:26]).
נָחָה nāchâh (5328), Hiphil: lead (Prv 6:22).

נָטָה nāṭâh (5371), Qal: extend, stretch out (Jb 38:5); hiphil: stretch out (Is 31:3).
נָכָה nākhâh (5409), Hiphil: strike (Ez 22:13—Codex Vaticanus only).
נָשָׂא nāsā' (5558), Qal: lift, raise (Dt 28:49, Is 10:24); hiphil: bring upon, bear (Lv 22:16).
עָבַר 'āvar (5882), Hiphil: pass over, sent over (Gn 8:1, Ez 5:1).
עָלָה 'ālâh (6148), Qal: go with, come up (Ex 33:5); hiphil: bring over, bring upon (Dt 28:61).
עָנָה 'ānâh (6257), Answer; piel: overwhelm, afflict (Ps 88:7 [87:7]).
פָּעַל pā'al (6713), Do (Jb 22:17).
פָּצַר pātsar (6732), Be stubborn, be arrogant (1 Sm 15:23).
פָּקַד pāqadh (6734), Punish (Ex 32:34, Is 24:21, 27:1).
פְּקֻדָּה pᵉquddāh (6735), Store up, lay up (Is 15:7).
קָדַשׁ qādhash (7227), Piel: send against, prepare against (Jer 22:7).
קָרָא qārā' (7410), Call (Hg 1:11).
שׂוּשׂ sûs (7919), Rejoice (Zep 3:17).
שִׂים sîm (7947), Command (Ex 15:26, Ez 39:21).
שׁוּב shûv (8178), Qal: come back, return (Est 9:25); hiphil: turn upon, turn against (Ex 15:19, Am 1:8, Is 1:25).
שִׁית shîth (8308), Bring upon (Is 15:9).
שָׁלַח shālach (8365), Piel: send (Ez 14:19—Codex Alexandrinus only).
שָׁמֵם shāmēm (8460), Hiphil: brought upon (1 Sm 5:6).
שָׁפַךְ shāphakh (8581), Pour out (Is 42:25).

1. ἐπάγοντες epagontes nom pl masc part pres act
2. ἐπάξας epaxas nom sing masc part aor act
3. ἐπαγαγεῖν epagagein inf aor act

3 and intend **to bring** this man's blood upon us........ Acts 5:28
1 and **bring upon** themselves swift destruction.......... 2 Pt 2:1
2 **bringing in** the flood upon the world 2:5

Classical Greek

The verb is a compound of *epi* (1894), "on, upon," and *agō* (70), "bring, lead." It is common in ancient writings. In addition to its meaning of "bring on (upon)," *epagō* is used in classical Greek to urge on as hunters do dogs, to invite allies, to call in as witnesses, etc. (see *Liddell-Scott*).

Septuagint Usage

Often *epagō* is used figuratively to bring something upon someone, usually something evil. This use is found not only in classical Greek but in the Septuagint and the New Testament. God promised to bring evil on apostate Israel and Judah (Jeremiah 6:19; 11:11). Moses announced that God would bring the plague of death on the firstborn of the Egyptians (Exodus 11:1). *Epagō* also is employed in the Septuagint to express the idea of bringing sin(s) upon someone (Genesis 20:9; Exodus 32:21,34; 34:7). But in a few instances this verb is used positively (cf. Jeremiah 32:42 [LXX 39:42]).

New Testament Usage

Epagō is a rare word in the New Testament and (as seen above) it is used with reference to some form of evil. It occurs in Acts 5:28 where the high priest said to the apostles that they "intend to bring this man's blood upon us," that is, to make them answerable for the violent death of Christ. The term appears twice in 2 Peter 2. Verse 1 refers to false teachers who will advocate damnable heresies, denying even the lordship of Christ and in so doing "*bring upon* themselves swift destruction." As an example of how God punishes the unrighteous, verse 5 refers to God's *bringing* the flood *on* the ungodly in Noah's time.

STRONG 1863, BAUER 281, MOULTON-MILLIGAN 227, LIDDELL-SCOTT 602-3.

1849. ἐπαγωνίζομαι
epagōnizomai verb
Fight, contend for, struggle.
CROSS-REFERENCE:
 ἀγωνίζομαι agōnizomai (74)

1. ἐπαγωνίζεσθαι epagōnizesthai inf pres mid

1 and exhort you that ye **should earnestly contend** ..... Jude 1:3

Classical Greek

This compound verb, consisting of *epi* (1894) and *agōnizomai* (74), is an intensive and means "to carry on a conflict, contest, debate, or legal suit" (Stauffer, "agōn," *Kittel*, 1:135). The word is employed in classical Greek to refer to fighting a war or to a struggle in politics or law (cf. Ringwald, "Fight," *Colin Brown*, 1:645). In the Septuagint the compounds of *agōnizomai* are altogether absent.

New Testament Usage

The only occurrence of the compound *epagōnizomai* in the New Testament is Jude 3, where it signifies contending or striving together for the faith of the gospel. But the simplex *agōnizomai* is employed twice in the Gospels (Luke 13:24; John 18:36).

 The other compounds of *agōnizomai* are found in several of the New Testament books (see Romans 15:30; Hebrews 11:33; 12:4).

Though Paul never used *epagōnizomai* in his epistles, he did use *agōnizomai* to denote contending for a prize (as in the gymnastic games; cf. 1 Corinthians 9:25) and as a metaphor for the struggle with difficulties and dangers arising from those antagonistic to the gospel (Colossians 1:29; 1 Timothy 4:10).

STRONG 1864, BAUER 281, MOULTON-MILLIGAN 227, LIDDELL-SCOTT 603, COLIN BROWN 1:644-46.

1850. ἐπαθροίζω epathroizō verb
To gather together.
CROSS-REFERENCE:
 ἀθροίζω athroizō (119B)

1. ἐπαθροιζομένων epathroizomenōn
     gen pl masc part pres mid

1 And when the people **were gathered thick together,** Luke 11:29

Classical Greek

This word is a compound form consisting of the preposition *epi* (1894), "upon, on," and the verb *athroizō* (119B), "collect, gather." The preposition suggests the concentration of the verb's action upon some object (Rienecker, *Linguistic Key to the Greek New Testament*, 1:174). *Liddell-Scott* indicates that *epathroizō* is found in Plutarch's *Antonius*. This word is not found in the Septuagint; however, the simple form *athroizō* is used several times to translate *qāvats*, "assemble, gather" (Genesis 49:2; 2 Kings 6:24 [LXX 4 Kings 6:24]).

New Testament Usage

The only passage in the New Testament in which the word is used is Luke 11:29. In this verse *epathroizō* is in the middle voice and means "were gathering together unto him." The idea is that many people were gathering together unto Jesus in increasing numbers so that they were crowding Him. The simple form, *athroizō*, occurs in Luke 24:33 and another compound form, *sunathroizō*, in Acts 12:12.

STRONG 1865, BAUER 281, LIDDELL-SCOTT 603 (see "epathroizomai").

1851. Ἐπαινετός Epainetos name
Epenetus.

1. Ἐπαινετόν Epaineton acc masc

1 Salute my wellbeloved **Epaenetus,** .... Rom 16:5

 Recipient of a greeting from Paul; the first convert to Christ in Asia (Romans 16:5).

1852. ἐπαινέω epaineō verb
To praise, to approve.
COGNATE:
αἰνέω aineō (134)
SYNONYMS:
αἰνέω aineō (134)
εὐλογέω eulogeō (2108)

הָלַל hālal (2054), Piel: praise (Gn 12:15, Pss 10:3 [9:24], 56:3 [55:3]); poel: taunt, reproach (Ps 102:8 [101:8]); hithpael: (Pss 63:11 [62:11], 105:3 [104:3]).

שָׁבַח shāvach (8099), Piel: praise, glorify (Ps 147:12 [147:1], Eccl 8:15).

1. ἐπαινῶ epainō 1sing indic pres act
2. ἐπῄνεσεν epēnesen 3sing indic aor act
3. ἐπαινέσω epainesō 1sing subj aor act
4. ἐπαινέσατε epainesate 2pl impr aor act
5. ἐπαινεσάτωσαν epainesatōsan 3pl impr aor act

2 And the lord commended the unjust steward,......Luke 16:8
4 Praise the Lord, ... and laud him, all ye people....Rom 15:11
5 Praise the Lord, ... and laud him, all ye people........ 15:11
1 Now I praise you, brethren,.......................1 Co 11:2
1 in this that I declare unto you I praise you not,....... 11:17
3 What shall I say to you? shall I praise you in this?.... 11:22
1 shall I praise you in this? I praise you not............. 11:22

Classical Greek
The verb is a compound form. As a prefix the preposition *epi* (1894) intensifies the verb *aineō* (134), "to praise or exalt." In classical Greek the verb *epaineō* means "to approve, sanction, to praise, give a public mark of esteem" (Schultz, "Praise," *Colin Brown*, 3:816f.).

Septuagint Usage
In the Septuagint *epaineō* appears in a number of passages (Genesis 12:15; Judges 6:20; Psalms 10:3 [LXX 9:24]; 34:2 [33:2]; 44:8 [43:8]; 56:3 [55:3]; 63:11 [62:11]; etc.). Genesis 12:15 speaks of the rulers under Pharaoh who praised (*epainesan*) Sarah for her exceptional beauty. In Psalm 56:4 (LXX 55:4) the Psalmist says, "I will praise (*epaineō*) his word." Almost as a rule, where *epaineō* is a translation of the Hebrew *hālal*, it refers to man's praise or commendation of another person or of himself. When *epaineō* translates the Hebrew *shābach*, generally the reference is to man's praise of God (Psalms 63:3 [LXX 62:3]; 117:1 [116:1]).

New Testament Usage
Epaineō is used five times in the New Testament (Luke 16:8; Romans 15:11; 1 Corinthians 11:2,17,22). Of these verses the verb appears only once in relation to God (Romans 15:11). In the other four verses it refers to man's praise or commendation of man.

STRONG 1867, BAUER 281, MOULTON-MILLIGAN 227, LIDDELL-SCOTT 603-4, COLIN BROWN 3:816-17.

1853. ἔπαινος epainos noun
Praise, commendation.
COGNATE:
αἰνέω aineō (134)
SYNONYMS:
αἴνεσις ainesis (133)
αἶνος ainos (136)

הָדָר hādhār (1994), Splendor, glory (1 Chr 16:27).

חֶמְדָּה chemdāh (2631), Something desirable (2 Chr 21:20).

תְּהִלָּה tᵉhillāh (8747), Praise, glory (Ps 22:3,25 [21:3,25]).

1. ἔπαινος epainos nom sing masc
2. ἔπαινον epainon acc sing masc

1 whose praise is not of men, but of God.............Rom 2:29
2 and thou shalt have praise of the same:................ 13:3
1 and then shall every man have praise of God........1 Co 4:5
1 praise is in the gospel throughout all the churches;.. 2 Co 8:18
2 To the praise of the glory of his grace,...............Eph 1:6
2 That we should be to the praise of his glory,........... 1:12
2 unto the praise of his glory............................. 1:14
2 unto the glory and praise of God...................Phlp 1:11
1 if there be any virtue, and if there be any praise,...... 4:8
2 might be found unto praise and honour and glory... 1 Pt 1:7
2 and for the praise of them that do well................ 2:14

Classical Greek
Epainos, "praise, approval" (cf. the verb *epaineō* [1852] and the noun *ainos*), was recognized during the classical period and by the later philosophical ethicists as a worthy pursuit (Preisker, "epainos," *Kittel*, 2:586). This idea of "recognition" was widely applied to individual praise, public recognition, or to the approval of objects (e.g., a city). "Praise" was highly prized by ancient societies except the Stoic moralists who sought to escape the accolades of men (ibid., 2:587f.).

Septuagint Usage
Whereas *epainos* is almost exclusively a secular term in classical Greek, in the Septuagint (10 times, usually the Hebrew *tᵉhillāh*) "praise" or "recognition" generally belongs to God (e.g., 1 Chronicles 16:35; Psalms 22:3 [LXX 21:3]; 35:28 [34:28]; Sirach 39:10). Nonetheless, men too are recipients of "praise" (2 Chronicles 21:20; Sirach 44:8,15). God himself may offer His "approval" to men (Wisdom of Solomon 15:19). Inanimate objects are also considered "recognized" (of virtue [rational judgment], 4 Maccabees 1:22).

New Testament Usage
Except for two Petrine usages *epainos* is strictly Pauline (nine times). Paul adopted the classical assumption that men can receive "recognition" or "approval" from others (Romans 2:29; 13:3; 2 Corinthians 8:18; cf. Philippians 4:8; 1 Peter 2:14). From a religious perspective

God's recognition—ultimately eschatological—is greater than the recognition of men (Romans 2:29; 1 Corinthians 4:5; cf. Matthew 6:1,5,16f.). Peter shared this same understanding (1 Peter 1:7).

The enigmatic refrain "to the praise of his glory" (*eis epainon tēs doxēs autou*; cf. Ephesians 1:6,12,14) proclaims Paul's thanksgiving for the magnificence of God's grace and provision in Christ and the Holy Spirit (cf. Philippians 1:11).

STRONG 1868, BAUER 281, MOULTON-MILLIGAN 227, KITTEL 2:586-88, LIDDELL-SCOTT 604, COLIN BROWN 2:874; 3:816-17.

1854. ἐπαίρω epairō verb

Raise, lift up, be lifted up (with pride).

COGNATE:
  αἴρω airō (142)
SYNONYMS:
  αἴρω airō (142)
  ὑψόω hupsoō (5150)

אָנֵף 'ānēph (613), Be angry (1 Kgs 8:46—Codex Alexandrinus only).
גָּבַהּ gāvahh (1391), Be haughty (Jer 13:15).
גִּבּוֹר gibbôr (1399), Be mighty (Jgs 11:1, Ezr 7:28).
דָּמַם dāmam (1887), Be still, keep still (Jer 47:6 [29:6]).
טוּל ṭûl (3014), Hiphil: throw (1 Sm 20:33).
מַסָּע maṣṣā' (4703), Reach, lay at (Jb 41:26 [41:17]—only some Sinaiticus texts).
מֹעַל mōʻal (4764), Lift up (Neh 8:6).
מַשָּׂא maśśā' (5014), Be a burden (2 Chr 35:3—Codex Alexandrinus only).
מַשּׁוּאוֹת mashshû'ôth (5061), Place set (Ps 73:18 [72:18]).
נוּעַ nûaʻ (5309), Shake, move (Is 6:4).
נוּף nûph (5311), Hiphil: raise up, lift up (Jb 31:21).
נָטָה nāṭâh (5371), Hiphil: stretch out (Ex 10:13).
נָטִיל nāṭîl (5373), Bear, trade with (Zep 1:11).
נָסַע nāsaʻ (5450), Tear out, start out; hiphil: cause to blow, loose (Ps 78:26 [77:26]).
נָשָׂא nāśā' (5558), Qal: lift up (Nm 6:26, 2 Sm 20:21, Ez 18:6); niphal: be lifted up (Ps 24:7 [23:7], Prv 30:13 [24:36], Is 6:1); piel: lift up, carry (2 Sm 5:12, Ps 28:9 [27:9]); hithpael: lift oneself up, raise oneself (1 Kgs 1:5, Ez 17:14).
נְשָׂא nᵉśā' (A5559), Carry; hithpaal: rise up (Ezr 4:19—Aramaic).
נָשִׂיא nāśî' (5562), Bring up (1 Kgs 8:1—Codex Alexandrinus only).
נָשָׁא nāshā' (5565), Lend; hiphil: deceive, trick (2 Kgs 18:29, 19:10, Ob 3).
נָתַן nāthan (5598), Give; set (Ps 8:1).
סָלָה ṣālâh (5733), Pual: esteem, consider (Lm 4:2).
עָלָה ʻālâh (6148), Go up; niphal: be exalted (Ps 47:9 [46:9]).
עָרָה ʻārâh (6408), Lay bare; hithpael: spread, flourish (Ps 37:35 [36:35]).
רוּם rûm (7597), Be high, arise; niphal: lift up (Ez 10:15—Codex Alexandrinus only); hiphil: lift up, pick up (Nm 20:11, Ps 74:3 [73:3], 1 Kgs 11:27).
שָׁעַן shāʻan (8550), Niphal: lean (Prv 3:5).

1. ἐπαίροντας epairontas acc pl masc part pres act
2. ἐπῆρεν epēren 3sing indic aor act
3. ἐπῆραν epēran 3pl indic aor act
4. ἐπάρατε eparate 2pl impr aor act
5. ἐπάρας eparas nom sing masc part aor act
6. ἐπάραντες eparantes nom pl masc part aor act
7. ἐπάρασα eparasa nom sing fem part aor act
8. ἐπᾶραι eparai inf aor act
9. ἐπαίρεται epairetai 3sing indic pres mid
10. ἐπαιρόμενον epairomenon nom/acc sing neu part pres mid
11. ἐπήρθη epērthē 3sing indic aor pass
12. ἐπῆρκεν epērken 3sing indic perf act

```
6  And when they had lifted up their eyes,............ Matt 17:8
5  And he lifted up his eyes on his disciples,......... Luke 6:20
7  certain woman of the company lifted up her voice,.... 11:27
5  And in hell he lift up his eyes, being in torments,.... 16:23
8  would not lift up so much as his eyes unto heaven,... 18:13
4  then look up, and lift up your heads;................ 21:28
5  and he lifted up his hands, and blessed them......... 24:50
4  behold, I say unto you, Lift up your eyes,.......... John 4:35
5  When Jesus then lifted up his eyes,.................. 6:5
2  hath lifted up his heel against me................... 13:18
12 hath lifted up his heel against me................... 13:18
2  and lifted up his eyes to heaven, and said,.......... 17:1
5  and lifted up his eyes to heaven, and said,.......... 17:1
11 while they beheld, he was taken up;............. Acts 1:9
2  Peter, ... lifted up his voice, and said unto them,...... 2:14
3  they lifted up their voices,.......................... 14:11
3  and then lifted up their voices, and said,............ 22:22
6  and hoisted up the mainsail to the wind,............. 27:40
10 that exalteth itself against the knowledge of God, 2 Co 10:5
9  if a man exalt himself, ... smite you on the face....... 11:20
1  lifting up holy hands, without wrath and doubting. 1 Tm 2:8
```

Classical Greek

In classical Greek the most common meaning of *epairō* is "to lift up something," such as an object. Secondarily, it is sometimes used figuratively of "exalting oneself."

Septuagint Usage

The Septuagint expresses these same meanings. For example, Exodus 10:13 says, "Moses stretched forth his rod," while Zephaniah 1:11 uses *epairō* in the figurative sense: " . . . and all that were exalted by silver have been utterly destroyed." Additionally, the Septuagint uses *epairō* to indicate the act of rising up in opposition to someone. (See 1 Maccabees 8:5, where two kings rise up in battle against Rome.)

Epairō is also sometimes employed to indicate the lifting up of hands in prayer, as in Psalm 134:2 (LXX 133:2).

New Testament Usage

The New Testament follows the Septuagint closely in its usage of *epairō*. Most often it is used literally of lifting up some part of the body, usually the eyes (cf. Matthew 17:8). Sometimes it refers to raising one's voice to be heard, as when Peter preached to the crowd on the Day of Pentecost (Acts 2:14). As in the Septuagint, *epairō* can also indicate a gesture connected with prayer, raising the hands or eyes. (See Luke 18:13 and 1 Timothy 2:8).

Other passages use *epairō* figuratively of exalting oneself or of opposing someone. Second Corinthians 11:20 speaks of bearing with anyone who "exalts himself." At the same time, Paul wrote of "casting down imaginations, and every high thing that *exalteth itself* (*epairō*) against the knowledge of God . . ." (2 Corinthians 10:5). Thus, the idea of military opposition is extended to the intellectual arena. Jesus also used *epairō* to characterize the opposition to Him, when He quoted Psalm 41:9 at the Last Supper: "He that eateth bread with me hath lifted up his heel against me" (John 13:18).

Finally, in Acts 1:9, *epairō* is used to describe Christ's ascension to heaven: "And when he had spoken these things, while they beheld, he was *taken up*; and a cloud received him out of their sight."

STRONG 1869, BAUER 281-82, MOULTON-MILLIGAN 227, KITTEL 1:186, LIDDELL-SCOTT 604.

1855. ἐπαισχύνομαι

epaischunomai verb

Be ashamed (of), feel shame for.

COGNATE:
αἰσχύνω aischunō (152)

SYNONYMS:
αἰσχύνω aischunō (152)
καταισχύνω kataischunō (2587)

בּוֹשׁ bôsh (991), Be ashamed (Ps 119:6 [118:6]).

חָפֵר châphar (2763), Be ashamed (Is 1:29—Codex Alexandrinus only).

נָשָׂא nāsâ' (5558), Lift, carry; accept, show partiality (Jb 34:19).

1. ἐπαισχύνομαι epaischunomai 1sing indic pres mid
2. ἐπαισχύνεται epaischunetai 3sing indic pres mid
3. ἐπαισχύνεσθε epaischunesthe 2pl indic pres mid
4. ἐπῃσχύνθη epēschunthē 3sing indic aor pass
5. ἐπαισχυνθῇς epaischunthēs 2sing subj aor pass
6. ἐπαισχυνθῇ epaischunthē 3sing subj aor pass
7. ἐπαισχυνθήσεται epaischunthēsetai 3sing indic fut pass
8. ἐπαισχύνθη epaischunthē 3sing indic aor pass

```
6 Whosoever therefore shall be ashamed of me........Mark 8:38
7 of him also shall the Son of man be ashamed,..........  8:38
6 shall be ashamed of me and of my words,..............Luke 9:26
7 of him shall the Son of man be ashamed,...............  9:26
1 For I am not ashamed of the gospel of Christ:.......Rom 1:16
3 in those things whereof ye are now ashamed?..........  6:21
5 Be not thou therefore ashamed of the testimony.....2 Tm 1:8
1 nevertheless I am not ashamed: for I know whom......  1:12
4 refreshed me, and was not ashamed of my chain:......  1:16
8 refreshed me, and was not ashamed of my chain:......  1:16
2 he is not ashamed to call them brethren,...........Heb 2:11
2 wherefore God is not ashamed.....................  11:16
```

Classical Greek

In classical Greek this intensive form of *epi* (1894) + *aischunō* (152) means "to be ashamed of or at" (someone or something). The definition is further developed in Biblical materials.

Septuagint Usage

The Septuagint is essentially responsible for the development of the definition, since it is here the Hebraic concepts of "humiliation, shame, and disgrace" converge. Bultmann asserts that in the Septuagint the compounds (particularly *ep-* and *kat-*) of *aischunomai* are "fully interchangeable" with one another ("epaischunō," *Kittel*, 1:189). Manuscript variations confirm this.

Although *aischunō* is common, *epaischunomai* occurs only three times in the Septuagint. Behind the Greek are *bôsh* (Psalm 119:6 [LXX 118:6]), *châpher* (Isaiah 1:29), and *nāsā'* (Job 34:19). In each of these texts "shame" is an inadequate translation unless the fullness of what this involves is explained. The context in each case is judgment—either present vindication (i.e., not to be put to shame, Psalm 119:6) or eschatological triumph (i.e., the wicked are put to shame [causative force] while Zion is redeemed [Isaiah 1:27-29]; see H.C. Kee, *The Linguistic Background of "Shame,"* pp.133-147).

New Testament Usage

Eleven instances of *epaischunomai* occur in the New Testament. The eschatological vindication of the faithful and the "putting to shame" of the wicked, a common Old Testament theme, is almost certainly at work in some texts. The usage in Mark 8:38 is undoubtedly a play on this (parallel Luke 9:26; cf. Psalm 25:1ff.; Jeremiah 17:18; see ibid., pp.145ff.).

Epaischunomai can also be used of social, intellectual, or religious "humiliation" or "embarrassment." When Paul claimed he was "not ashamed" of the gospel, he was not simply saying "he was proud of it"; rather, the scandal of the Cross inevitably brings hardship to the believer (Romans 1:16; see Cranfield, *International Critical Commentary, Romans,* 1:86).

"To be ashamed" of Christ is further explained as avoiding suffering (2 Timothy 1:8,12). One should endure suffering because of an eschatological perspective which realizes by faith that the righteous will be vindicated. Thus by the example he set in his own life, Paul encouraged Timothy "not to be ashamed" (cf. Psalm 25:1-3; Mark 8:38). This thought resonates with the eschatological perspective endorsed by the Old Testament saints and recognized by God. He is "not ashamed" to be called their God (Hebrews 11:16). Christ identified himself with believers through His suffering. Having effected their salvation through suffering, He is not ashamed to call believers His brothers and sisters (Hebrews 2:11).

STRONG 1870, BAUER 282, KITTEL 1:189-91 (see "epaischunō"), LIDDELL-SCOTT 604, COLIN BROWN 3:562-64.

1856. ἐπαιτέω epaiteō verb
To beg, to ask for.
CROSS-REFERENCE:
αἰτέω aiteō (153)

שָׁאַל shā'al (8068), Ask; piel: beg (Ps 109:10 [108:10]).

1. ἐπαιτεῖν epaitein inf pres act
2. ἐπαιτῶν epaitōn nom sing masc part pres act

1 I cannot dig; **to beg** I am ashamed............ Luke 16:3
2 blind man was sitting by the road **begging**: (NASB).... 18:35

Classical Greek and Septuagint Usage
This word consists of two elements: *epi* (1894) plus *aiteō* (153). Thayer says ancient authors, such as Sophocles and Josephus, used *epaiteō* with the sense of to beg as a mendicant (cf. Bauer; Josephus *Wars of the Jews* [2.14.6]). It has the same meaning in the Septuagint, as in Psalm 109:10 (LXX 108:10): "Let his children be continually vagabonds, wanderers and beg" (cf. Sirach 40:28).

New Testament Usage
The word occurs only twice in the New Testament, both times in Luke's Gospel. In 16:3 the unrighteous steward revealed his attitude toward begging: "to beg I am ashamed" (*epaitein*). In 18:35 reference is made to a certain blind man who was sitting by the roadside begging (*epaitōn*). The word used here means to ask again and again and thus beg for alms.

STRONG 1871, BAUER 282, MOULTON-MILLIGAN 227-28, LIDDELL-SCOTT 604.

1857. ἐπακολουθέω
epakoloutheō verb
Follow, come after, verify.
COGNATE:
ἀκολουθέω akoloutheō (188)
SYNONYMS:
ἀκολουθέω akoloutheō (188)
ἐξακολουθέω exakoloutheō (1795)
κατακολουθέω katakoloutheō (2598)
μιμέομαι mimeomai (3265)
παρακολουθέω parakoloutheō (3738)
συνακολουθέω sunakoloutheō (4721)

אַחַר 'achar (313), When, afterward (Dt 12:30, Jos 14:8).

הָלַךְ hālakh (2050), Come (Is 55:3).

מָלֵא mālē' (4527), Fill; do something completely (Sir 46:6).

תּוּשִׁיָּה tûshîyāh (8786), Counsel, offer (Jb 26:3).

1. ἐπακολουθοῦσιν epakolouthousin
3pl indic pres act
2. ἐπακολουθούντων epakolouthountōn
gen pl neu part pres act
3. ἐπηκολούθησεν epēkolouthēsen 3sing indic aor act
4. ἐπακολουθήσητε epakolouthēsēte 2pl subj aor act

2 confirming the word with signs **following**. Amen....Mark 16:20
3 if she have diligently **followed** every good work...... 1 Tm 5:10
1 men's sins ... and some men they **follow after**........... 5:24
4 an example, that ye should **follow** his steps:......... 1 Pt 2:21

Classical Greek
The verb is comprised of two elements *epi* (1894), "after, close upon," and *akoloutheō* (188), "follow." In classical Greek this verb is used in a number of ways such as to follow after someone, to pursue an enemy, to follow mentally what is said, or to follow in the sense of complying with instructions (see *Liddell-Scott*).

Septuagint Usage
Epakoloutheō is used also in the Septuagint. There are commands not to *follow* after idols and mediums (Leviticus 19:4,31) but to *follow* the ways of the Lord (Isaiah 55:3). Caleb claimed to have *followed faithfully* the Lord, and Moses had sworn earlier to give him land for having *followed* after the Lord (Joshua 14:8,9,15).

New Testament Usage

The term *epakoloutheō* is found in only four passages in the New Testament and in each instance it is figurative. It is used in 1 Timothy 5:10 of one who "*diligently followed* every good work." According to 1 Timothy 5:24, "Some men's sins are open beforehand, going before to judgment; and some men they *follow* after." The New English Bible reads, "There are others whose offenses have not yet *overtaken* them," which brings out the force of *epi* prefixed to *akoloutheō*. First Peter 2:21 exhorts readers to "follow" in the steps of Christ. This matter must be taken seriously, though "follow" here has a figurative meaning since Jesus can no longer be followed literally from place to place.

Moulton-Milligan cites a number of examples from the papyri where *epakoloutheō* means to be "personally present at," "to see to," "conform to," "concur with," but observes that one development in the meaning of the verb was "verify," as did signatures on a series of tax receipts. An interesting parallel to this use is Mark 16:20 where it speaks of signs which *follow hard upon* the preaching of the gospel. The meaning is not that signs merely follow but that as a kind of authenticating signature they "verify" the preached word of God (cf. *Moulton-Milligan*).

STRONG 1872, BAUER 282, MOULTON-MILLIGAN 228, KITTEL 1:215, LIDDELL-SCOTT 605, COLIN BROWN 1:480-81.

1858. ἐπακούω epakouō verb

Hear, listen to.

COGNATE:
  ἀκούω akouō (189)
SYNONYMS:
  ἀκολουθέω akoloutheō (188)
  ἀκούω akouō (189)
  εἰσακούω eisakouō (1508)
  ἐνωτίζομαι enōtizomai (1785)
  ἐξακολουθέω exakoloutheō (1795)
  ἐπακροάομαι epakroaomai (1859)
  πειθαρχέω peitharcheō (3842)
  πειθώ peithō (3843B)
  ὑπακούω hupakouō (5057)

אָזַן 'āzan (237), Hiphil: listen, listen to (Is 8:9).

אָמַר 'āmar (569), Say, speak (2 Chr 32:24).

מַעֲנֶה ma'ăneh (4776), Answer (Mi 3:7—Codex Alexandrinus only).

עָנָה 'ānâh (6257), Qal: answer (Gn 30:33, 1 Sm 8:18, Hos 2:22); niphal: be answered (Prv 21:13—Codex Sinaiticus only).

עָשָׂה 'āsâh (6449), Do, perform (Dt 26:14—Codex Vaticanus only).

עָתַר 'āthar (6518), Pray; niphal: pray, entreat (Gn 25:21, 2 Sm 21:14, Ezr 8:23).

קָשַׁב qāshav (7477), Pay attention, hearken (2 Chr 33:10, Dn 9:19).

רָדַד rādhadh (7574), Subdue (Is 45:1).

שָׁמַע shāma' (8471), Qal: hear, listen to (Gn 16:11, 2 Chr 24:17, Dn 9:17); niphal: be heard (2 Chr 30:27).

1. ἐπήκουσα epēkousa 1sing indic aor act

1 For he saith, I have heard thee in a time accepted,.. 2 Co 6:2

Classical Greek

In classical Greek *epakouō* means "to hear" or "to listen to." The latter meaning also came to be used as a technical term for the way a deity hears prayers. Thus Lucian (ca. A.D. 125) spoke of the place in heaven where Zeus heard prayers at a particular time of day.

Septuagint Usage

The Septuagint utilizes *epakouō* to translate several Hebrew words, the two most common being *shāma'* ("to hear," as in Genesis 17:20, and "to obey," Judges 2:17), and *'ānâh* ("to respond," Isaiah 49:8).

New Testament Usage

Epakouō only appears once in the New Testament. In 2 Corinthians 6:2 (a quote of Isaiah 49:8) it refers to God's hearing the prayers of His people.

STRONG 1873, BAUER 282, MOULTON-MILLIGAN 228, KITTEL 1:222, LIDDELL-SCOTT 605, COLIN BROWN 2:172-73,175,178.

1859. ἐπακροάομαι epakroaomai verb

To listen to, to hear.

COGNATE:
  ἀκούω akouō (189)
SYNONYMS:
  ἀκούω akouō (189)
  εἰσακούω eisakouō (1508)
  ἐνωτίζομαι enōtizomai (1785)
  ἐπακούω epakouō (1858)
  ὑπακούω hupakouō (5057)

1. ἐπηκροῶντο epēkroōnto 3pl indic imperf mid

1 and the prisoners heard them..................... Acts 16:25

Classical Greek and Septuagint Usage

Epakroaomai is a compound verb form consisting of *epi* (1894) plus *akroaomai*. This rare word appears in the classical writings of the comic poets and a few other ancient writers

ἐπάν 1860

(see Knowling, *Expositors Greek Testament*, 2:350). A cognate (*epakroasis*) appears in the Septuagint (1 Samuel 15:22 [LXX 1 Kings 15:22]).

New Testament Usage
In the New Testament the word occurs only in Acts 16:25, where it apparently signifies attentive hearing. God gave to Paul and Silas in prison songs at midnight, and the prisoners *were listening* with rapt attention.

STRONG 1874, BAUER 282, MOULTON-MILLIGAN 228, LIDDELL-SCOTT 605, COLIN BROWN 2:172,175.

1860. ἐπάν epan conj
When, after, as soon as.

1. ἐπάν epan

1 when ye have found him, bring me word again,	Matt 2:8
1 But when a stronger than he shall come upon him,	Luke 11:22
1 but when thine eye is evil,	11:34

Classical Greek and Septuagint Usage
Epan (*epei* [1878] + *an* [300]) is a temporal conjunction and is similar to *hote* (3616) and *hotan* (3615). The word appears in Homer and a number of other ancient authors. It is employed by Josephus and in the Septuagint with the aorist subjunctive (*Antiquities* 8.12.3; Esther 5:13).

New Testament Usage
In the New Testament *epan* occurs only three times and in each case it is used with the subjunctive, expressing an indefinite idea. Matthew 2:8 reads, "When (*epan*) ye have found him . . . ." Luke 11:22 says, "But when (*epan*) a stronger than he shall come upon him, and overcome him . . . ." Luke 11:34 states, "When (*epan*) thine eye is single . . . ."

STRONG 1875, BAUER 282, MOULTON-MILLIGAN 230, LIDDELL-SCOTT 606.

1861. ἐπάναγκες epanankes adv
By compulsion, necessarily.
CROSS-REFERENCE:
  ἀναγκάζω anankazō (313)

1. ἐπάναγκες epanankes

1 no greater burden than these **necessary** things;	Acts 15:28

Classical Greek
This word is comprised of two elements: *epi* (1894) plus *anankē* (316), "necessity," and can best be described as an adverb of necessity. It occurs in a number of the ancient Greek authors but it is not found in the Septuagint.

The Oxyrhynchus Papyri illustrate well the way this adverb is used. For example, the officials of the village of Takona pledged to repay the seed corn borrowed from Flavius Apion in these words: "We will pay back without fail (*epanankes*) the same amount of corn . . . " (see *Moulton-Milligan*).

Josephus described a father who evidently brought false charges against his son for plotting against him, and he reminded the village council that there was a law in his country that "if a man's parents, after accusing him, placed their hands on his head, the bystanders were bound (*epanankes*) to stone him . . ." (*Antiquities* 16.11.2).

New Testament Usage
Epanankes occurs only once in the New Testament. According to Acts 15:28 the decision of the council at Jerusalem was not to lay on the Gentile believers any burden besides those which were absolutely necessary: abstaining from those things offered to idols, from blood, from the meat of strangled animals, and from unchastity (*porneias* [4061]).

STRONG 1876, BAUER 282, MOULTON-MILLIGAN 228-29, LIDDELL-SCOTT 607.

1862. ἐπανάγω epanagō verb
To lead up, bring up, put out, return.
CROSS-REFERENCE:
  ἄγω agō (70)

רִיק rîq (7671), Empty out, pour out (Zec 4:12).

1. ἐπανάγων epanagōn nom sing masc part pres act
2. ἐπανάγαγε epanagage 2sing impr aor act
3. ἐπαναγαγεῖν epanagagein inf aor act
4. ἐπαναγαγών epanagagōn nom sing masc part aor act

1 Now in the morning as he **returned** into the city,	Matt 21:18
4 Now in the morning as he **returned** into the city,	21:18
3 that he would **thrust out** a little from the land.	Luke 5:3
2 **Launch out** into the deep, and let down your nets	5:4

Classical Greek
This word is a double-compound verb consisting of *epi* (1894), *ana* (301), and *agō* (70). It is found in Xenophon and in a number of later Greek writers.

Septuagint Usage
In several incidences *epanagō* was used as a nautical term for men and ships putting out to sea. A typical example is 2 Maccabees 12:4

where a ship puts out into the deep (*eis to bathos*). Another common meaning for *epanagō* is that of leading back or returning. Second Maccabees 9:21 speaks about returning to the city (*eis tēn polin*).

New Testament Usage
In the New Testament *epanagō* appears three times. When Jesus got into a boat and asked Simon to *put out* a little from shore, the term is used in the nautical sense (Luke 5:3,4). Matthew 21:18 says Jesus "returned" (*epanogan*) to the city of Jerusalem because He was hungry.
Strong 1877, Bauer 282, Moulton-Milligan 229, Liddell-Scott 607.

1863. ἐπαναμιμνήσκω
epanamimnēskō verb
To remind again.
Cross-Reference:
μιμνήσκω mimnēskō (3267)

1. ἐπαναμιμνήσκων epanamimnēskōn
nom sing masc part pres act
1 as putting you in mind, because of the grace .... Rom 15:15

Classical Greek
Epanamimnēskō is a compound form of *epi* (1894) and *ana* (301) prefixed to *mimnēskō* (3267). It denotes "to call back to mind again." It is found in classical writers such as Plato, Demosthenes, Aristotle, etc. and is used to express the idea of reminding someone of something or someone.

New Testament Usage
This word does not appear in the Septuagint and it is found only once in the New Testament. In Romans 15:15 Paul stated that he was calling again to his readers' remembrance (*epanamimnēskō*) some points of Christian teaching. He was calling to their minds again and jogging their memories about clearly established principles and commands of the gospel.
Strong 1878, Bauer 282, Liddell-Scott 607.

1864. ἐπαναπαύω epanapauō verb
Rest on, settle on, rely on.
Cognate:
ἀναπαύω anapauō (372)
Synonyms:
ἀναπαύω anapauō (372)
ἡσυχάζω hēsuchazō (2248)
καταλύω kataluō (2617)
καταπαύω katapauō (2634)

κοπάζω kopazō (2841)
σιγάω sigaō (4456)
σιωπάω siōpaō (4478)

נוּחַ nûach (5299), Qal: settle, rest (Nm 11:25,26, 2 Kgs 2:15); hiphil: let, allow (Jgs 16:26—Codex Alexandrinus only).

שָׁעַן shā'an (8550), Niphal: lean, rest on (2 Kgs 5:18, Mi 3:11, Ez 29:7).

1. ἐπαναπαύῃ epanapauē 2sing indic pres mid
2. ἐπαναπαύσεται epanapausetai 3sing indic fut mid
3. ἐπαναπαήσεται epanapaēsetai 3sing indic fut pass

2 your peace shall rest upon it: if not, it shall turn to Luke 10:6
3 your peace shall rest upon it: if not, it shall turn to 10:6
1 restest in the law, and makest thy boast of God, ... Rom 2:17

Septuagint Usage
Epanapauō is a late word found neither in works in classical Greek nor in the Koine papyri. It is, however, used by the Septuagint to translate *nûach*, "to rest on" or "to take one's rest" (cf. Numbers 11:25, "the Spirit rested upon" the 70 elders of Israel), and *shā'an*, "to lean on" or "to find rest or support" (see Micah 3:11).

In two Septuagint passages (Job 3:13,17 and Daniel 12:13) *epanapauō* has the sense of one's rest (*nûach*) in death. However, this usage is not carried over into the New Testament.

New Testament Usage
The New Testament uses *epanapauō* only twice. It is found in Luke 10:6 where it means "to rest upon." It is also found in Romans 2:17. There Paul spoke of the Jews "leaning" or "relying upon the Law," perhaps referring back, in word and in purpose, to Micah's denunciation of Israel's false pride (Micah 3:11).
Strong 1879, Bauer 282-83 (see "epanapouomai"), Moulton-Milligan 229 (see "epanapouomai"), Kittel 1:351, Liddell-Scott 607-8, Colin Brown 3:258.

1865. ἐπανέρχομαι
epanerchomai verb
Return, come back again.
Cognate:
ἔρχομαι erchomai (2048)
Synonyms:
ἀποστρέφω apostrephō (648)
ἐπιστρέφω epistrephō (1978)
στρέφω strephō (4613)
ὑποστρέφω hupostrephō (5128)

בּוֹא bô' (971), Go, come (Gn 33:18—Sixtine edition only).

הָלַךְ hālakh (2050), Go, walk (Prv 3:28).

שׁוּב shûv (8178), Return (Lv 25:13, Jb 7:7).

ἐπανίστημι 1866

1. ἐπανελθεῖν epanelthein inf aor act
2. ἐπανέρχεσθαι epanerchesthai inf pres mid

2 when I come again, I will repay thee.............Luke 10:35
1 And it came to pass, that when he was returned,...... 19:15

Classical Greek and Septuagint Usage
Epanerchomai, "coming back to a specific place" or "at a later time" appears in the Septuagint at Proverbs 3:28 where it expresses the idea of a command that forbids telling one's neighbor to "go and *come again*." In 2 Maccabees 4:36 the term indicates that Antiochus Epiphanes *returned* from the region of Cilicia to Jerusalem.

Josephus employed the word in reference to the dove which Noah sent from the ark. After the bird found no place to land, it then "returned" to the ark (*Antiquities* 1.3.5; cf. *Wars of the Jews* 7.5.2).

New Testament Usage
The New Testament uses the word only in the Gospel of Luke. In 10:35 the Good Samaritan promised to "come again" to the inn and pay the rest of the bill. The same idea of leaving and returning is expressed in 19:11ff. where Jesus told the parable of the nobleman who had gone into a far country to receive a kingdom and then "returned" (verse 15).

STRONG 1880, BAUER 283, MOULTON-MILLIGAN 229, LIDDELL-SCOTT 608.

1866. ἐπανίστημι epanistēmi verb
Rise up against, rebel.
CROSS-REFERENCE:
   ἵστημι histēmi (2449)

דָּרַךְ dārakh (1931), Tread (Jb 22:15—only some Alexandrinus texts).

הָפַךְ hāphakh (2089), Turn; niphal: turn against (Jb 19:19).

עוּר 'āwar (5996), Be awake; hiphil: arouse (Dn 11:2); hithpael: be stirred up (Jb 17:8).

עָמַד 'āmadh (6198), Stand (Jgs 6:31).

צוּר tsûr (6961), Set up against, strengthen against (Is 9:11).

קוּם qûm (7251), Qal: rise against, attack (Dt 22:26, 2 Sm 14:7, Ps 86:14 [85:14]); hithpolel: rise up, rebel (Jb 20:27).

1. ἐπαναστήσονται epanastēsontai 3pl indic fut mid

1 and the children shall rise up against their parents, Matt 10:21
1 and children shall rise up against their parents,.... Mark 13:12

Classical Greek
This word consists of three elements: *epi* (1894), *ana* (301), and *histēmi* (2449) and means "to set up." It often signifies rising up or coming to power against someone.

Septuagint Usage
In the *War of the Jews* Josephus used this word to indicate the rise of tyrants to power (1.9) as well as the rise of people in rebellion against a tyrant ruler (2.3.1). In the Septuagint, Judith 5:11 uses *epanistēmi* in the context of the rising up of Pharaoh to overpower the Israelites and to bring them into slavery (cf. 16:17; Deuteronomy 33:11).

New Testament Usage
The term in the New Testament expresses the same idea found in classical and Septuagint uses. Matthew 10:21 foretells how children will "rise up against" their parents to the degree that the parents are slain (cf. Mark 13:12). Here the term is used of the betrayal of family members in the face of persecution. "The demand for radical commitment which is inherent in the gospel takes precedence over other loyalties and may disrupt the deepest ties between men," (Lane, *New International Commentary on the New Testament*, Mark, p.463).

STRONG 1881, BAUER 283, MOULTON-MILLIGAN 229, LIDDELL-SCOTT 609.

1867. ἐπανόρθωσις epanorthōsis noun
Correction, rectification, straightening up again.
CROSS-REFERENCE:
   ὀρθός orthos (3580)

1. ἐπανόρθωσιν epanorthōsin acc sing fem

1 for correction, for instruction in righteousness:......2 Tm 3:16

Classical Greek and Septuagint Usage
The word consists of *epi* (1894) plus *anothōsis* and signifies "correction, reformation," or "restoring to an upright state." In the works of many of the Greek writers it has to do with the correction or improvement of life and character (Polybius; Epictetus; Enchiridion; cf. *Bauer*).

Philo wrote about the "improvement" (*epanorthōsis*) of human conduct that takes various forms such as dealing with the state, management of a house, legislative control of society, etc. (He also used the term in *On Drunkenness* 22:91; cf. also *Allegorical Interpretation* 2.21.85.) In the Septuagint, in the apocryphal writings of 1 Esdras 8:52 and 1 Maccabees 14:34, *epanorthōsis* is also used with the sense of improvement of life.

New Testament Usage

The only place this word occurs in the New Testament is 2 Timothy 3:16 where it refers to the improvement of character. According to this passage, one purpose of Holy Scripture is "correction" (*epanorthōsis*), that is, restoring persons to an upright state or setting their moral feet on the path of righteousness.

Strong 1882, Bauer 283, Moulton-Milligan 229, Kittel 5:450-51, Liddell-Scott 609, Colin Brown 3:351-52.

1868. ἐπάνω epanō prep

Above, over before, more than, on.

1. ἐπάνω epanō

1 star, ... before them, till it came and stood **over**	Matt	2:9
1 A city that is set **on** an hill cannot be hid.		5:14
1 put **on** them their clothes, ... they set him thereon.		21:7
1 put **on** them their clothes, ... they set him **thereon**.		21:7
1 but whosoever sweareth by the gift that is **upon** it,		23:18
1 sweareth by it, and by all things **thereon**.		23:20
1 the throne of God, and by him that sitteth **thereon**.		23:22
1 And set up **over** his head his accusation written,		27:37
1 came and rolled back the stone ... and sat **upon** it.		28:2
1 might have been sold **for more than** three hundred	Mark	14:5
1 And he stood **over** her, and rebuked the fever;	Luke	4:39
1 Behold, I give unto you power to tread **on** serpents		10:19
1 men that walk **over** them are not aware of them.		11:44
1 been faithful ... have thou authority **over** ten cities.		19:17
1 said likewise to him, Be thou also **over** five cities.		19:19
1 He that cometh from above is **above** all:	John	3:31
1 he that cometh from heaven is **above** all.		3:31
1 was seen **of above** five hundred brethren at once;	1 Co	15:6
1 and his name that sat **on** him was Death,	Rev	6:8
1 and shut him up, and set a seal **upon** him,		20:3

Classical Greek and Septuagint Usage

Epanō is comprised of the preposition *epi* (1894) and the adverb *anō* (504). It is used as an adverb or preposition and has a number of different meanings depending on the context in which it occurs. The Septuagint illustrates this point. In Genesis 18:2 *epanō* refers to three men standing "by" or "in the presence of" Abraham (cf. also 2 Samuel 24:20 [LXX 2 Kings 24:20]). But a completely different meaning is indicated in Exodus 30:14 where the Lord instructed Moses to number all the people 20 years old and above (*epanō*).

New Testament Usage

As in classical Greek *epanō* is used in the New Testament both as an adverb and a preposition. Only three examples of its use as an adverb can be cited. Jesus pronounced a woe on the Pharisees because they were like unmarked graves which men walked "over" (*epanō*) without recognizing them (Luke 11:44). Some of those present at the anointing of Jesus at Bethany declared that the jar of expensive perfume could have been sold for "more than" (*epanō*) a year's wages (Mark 15:4; cf. 1 Corinthians 15:6).

As a preposition *epanō* is used 15 times in the New Testament (Robertson, *Grammar of the Greek New Testament*, p.642). An example is Luke 19:17 where a faithful servant is promised authority "over" (*epanō*) 10 cities. John the Baptist affirmed Christ's superiority to himself, but to this truth the apostle John added that Christ is "above" (*epanō*) all men (John 3:31). As a preposition it can also express authority and power, but in Matthew 5:14 it has the meaning of "upon" rather than "above." Jesus declared that a city "on" (*epanō*) a hill cannot be hid (cf. Matthew 11:7; 23:18,20; 28:2; Revelation 6:8; 20:3).

Strong 1883, Bauer 283, Moulton-Milligan 229, Liddell-Scott 609.

1868B. ἐπάρατος eparatos adj

Accursed.

Cross-Reference:
κατάρα katara (2641)

1. ἐπάρατοι eparatoi nom pl masc

1 which does not know the Law is **accursed**. (NASB)	John	7:49

This word appears only in John 7:49, although a similar form of the word is used in Galatians 3:10,13. In both references the word deals with one who is cursed as a result of an improper relationship to the Law. In the passage in John it is a term of judgment used by the Pharisees. Referring to Deuteronomy 27:26, the Pharisees noted that those who did not confirm the Law by obeying it were cursed. The Pharisees' claim was that those believing in Jesus were not following the Law (cf. John 7:48).

Bauer 283, Moulton-Milligan 229, Kittel 1:451, Liddell-Scott 610, Colin Brown 1:416-17.

1869. ἐπαρκέω eparkeō verb

Aid, avail for, relieve.

Cross-Reference:
ἀρκέω arkeō (708)

1. ἐπαρκείτω eparkeitō 3sing impr pres act
2. ἐπήρκεσεν epērkesen 3sing indic aor act
3. ἐπαρκέσῃ eparkesē 3sing subj aor act
4. ἐπαρκείσθω eparkeisthō 3pl subj aor act

2 if she have relieved the afflicted,	1 Tm 5:10
1 that believeth have widows, let them relieve them,	5:16
4 that believeth have widows, let them relieve them,	5:16
3 that it may relieve them that are widows indeed.	5:16

Classical Greek

This is a compound verb from *epi* (1894) and *arkeō* (708). According to Thayer the verb *arkeō* means "to possess unfailing strength" or "to be strong sufficiently to ward off and withstand any danger" (*Greek-English Lexicon*). *Eparkeō* is common in classical Greek and expresses the similar meaning of being strong enough to deal adequately with danger or injury (Vincent, *Word Studies in the New Testament*, 4:262). There are examples of ancient writers using *eparkeō* with the simple meaning "to aid" (Homer; Josephus *Antiquities* 8.4.3 and various papyri; cf. *Bauer*).

The only two occurrences in the Septuagint are in the First Book of Maccabees. In 1 Maccabees 8:26 *eparkeō* is used to mean "help" in a technical sense of military assistance, while in 11:35 it refers to money "remitted" to the Jews from collected tithes and tolls.

New Testament Usage

The idea of "help" or "aid" is the meaning of *eparkeō* in the New Testament. The only two examples occur in 1 Timothy 5. In verse 10 Paul instructed Timothy in the treatment of widows. For a widow to receive assistance from the church she must have "*relieved* (*eparkeō*) the afflicted." In verse 16 the verb occurs twice. If a Christian woman had an aged widow in her home, she was to "relieve" (*eparkeō*) her needs so the burden would not fall on the church. If the church were not burdened, it would be able to "relieve" (*eparkeō*) the widows who were destitute.

STRONG 1884, BAUER 283, MOULTON-MILLIGAN 229, LIDDELL-SCOTT 610.

1869B. ἐπάρχειος eparcheios adj

Governed province or region belonging to an eparch or prefect.
CROSS-REFERENCE:
ἀρχή archē (741)

1. ἐπαρχείῳ **eparcheiō** dat sing masc/neu

This word does not appear in classical Greek or the Septuagint but has limited use in the papyri (see *Bauer*). Its single occurrence in Acts 25:1 is consistent with that in the papyri in that it identifies a "province" that had been entrusted as a responsibility to an eparch or prefect. Such a territory would be seen as an area which was an eparch's personal duty to oversee and control. This clearly communicates why Paul's first dealings with Festus would be charged with anticipation and tensions since Festus had recently taken personal responsibility of this territorial sphere and would be eager to assert his authority.

BAUER 283, LIDDELL-SCOTT 611.

1870. ἐπαρχία eparchia noun

Province.
CROSS-REFERENCE:
ἀρχή archē (741)

מְדִינָה mᵉdhînāh (4224), Province (Est 4:11—only some Sinaiticus texts).

1. ἐπαρχίας **eparchias** gen sing fem
2. ἐπαρχίᾳ **eparchia** dat sing fem
3. ἐπαρχείας **eparcheias** gen sing fem
4. ἐπαρχείᾳ **eparcheia** dat sing fem

1 he asked of what **province** he was.	Acts 23:34
3 he asked of what **province** he was.	23:34
2 Now when Festus was come into the **province**,	25:1
4 Now when Festus was come into the **province**,	25:1

Eparchia is a word used for administrative purposes. It does not appear in classical Greek but it has limited use in the papyri and Septuagint. When Esther promised to intercede for her people she knew, as did all who lived in the king's "provinces," that to enter the king's court uninvited was to risk death (Esther 4:11). The Babylonian and Persian Empires were divided into provinces (Daniel 2:49; 3:3). The Persian king, Darius the Great, had dominion from India to Ethiopia. He divided his empire into satrapies or large provinces which were subdivided into smaller districts or provinces (*New Westminster Dictionary of the Bible*, "Darius").

The administrative divisions of the Roman Empire encompassed two kinds of provinces: imperial and senatorial. The imperial provinces needed to be kept under control by a military force and were directly under the jurisdiction of the emperor, whereas the senate administered the senatorial provinces.

New Testament Usage

The only places where *eparchia* appears in the New Testament are Acts 23:34 and 25:1. In both passages it is "used like the Latin *provincia*" to denote province or sphere of duty (*Moulton-Milligan*) and means "an area ruled by a governor." The implication of Felix' question in Acts 23:34 is that he considered delivering Paul to the jurisdiction of the governor of his home "province," Cilicia. According to Acts 25:1 Festus, taking up his duties as governor of the "province" of Judea, determined to visit Jerusalem at his earliest convenience.

STRONG 1885, BAUER 283 (see "eparcheia"), MOULTON-MILLIGAN 229-30 (see "eparcheia"), LIDDELL-SCOTT 611.

1871. ἔπαυλις epaulis noun
Dwelling, homestead, residence.

גְּדֵרָה geˉdhērāh (1477), Sheepfold (Nm 32:16,24,36).

חַוָּה chawwāh (2427), Small town, settlement (Nm 32:41).

חָצֵר chātsēr (2793), Settlement, farm (Lv 25:31, Jos 15:45, Is 62:9).

טִירָה tîrāh (3029), Camp (Gn 25:16, Nm 31:10, Ps 69:25 [68:25]).

נָוֶה nāweh (5295), House, resting place (Prv 3:33, Is 65:10).

קִרְיַת חֻצוֹת qiryath chutsôth (7444), Huzoth (Num 22:39).

רְחֹב reˉchôv (7624), Streets (Ps 144:14 [143:14]).

1. ἔπαυλις epaulis nom sing fem
1 Let his **habitation** be desolate,..................... Acts 1:20

Classical Greek
A compound form of *epi* (1894), "upon," and *aulē* (827), "courtyard, sheepfold, house" or "farm," *epaulis* essentially refers to a "place to pass the night" or a "dwelling." In classical Greek *epaulis* has the meaning of a "steading" or a "sheepfold" (Herodotus 1.111; Polybius 5.35.3), a "farm building" or "country house" (Diodorus Siculus 12:43), or "quarters for military personnel" (Polybius 16.15.5; cf. *Liddell-Scott*).

Septuagint Usage
The word is common in the Septuagint, but the context in which *epaulis* occurs determines its precise meaning. In Genesis 25:16 it is used in reference to the "encampments" of the sons of Ishmael, but in Exodus 8:13 it refers to "courtyards" that were invaded by frogs during the first plague on Egypt. In Leviticus 25:31 *epaulis* has the meaning of an "unwalled village."

New Testament Usage
The only use of *epaulis* in the New Testament is found in Acts 1:20 where Peter applied Psalm 69:25 to Judas. In this passage *epaulis* has the meaning of a "dwelling place." Psalm 69:25 had foretold the desolation of Judas' "habitation," that is, the estate that he owned.

STRONG 1886, BAUER 283, MOULTON-MILLIGAN 230, LIDDELL-SCOTT 611.

1872. ἐπαύριον epaurion adv
The next day.

SYNONYM:
αὔριον aurion (833)

מָחָר māchār (4417), Tomorrow (Gn 30:33—Sixtine edition only).

מׇחֳרָת mochŏrāth (4420), The following day, the next day (Ex 9:6, 1 Sm 20:27, Jon 4:7).

1. ἐπαύριον epaurion
1 Now the **next day**, that followed ... preparation,.... Matt 27:62
1 on the **morrow**, when they ... come from Bethany, Mark 11:12
1 The **next day** John seeth Jesus coming unto him,.... John 1:29
1 **next day** after John stood, and two of his disciples;..... 1:35
1 The **day following** Jesus would go forth................ 1:43
1 The **day following**,..................................... 6:22
1 **next day** much people that were come to the feast,.... 12:12
1 On the **morrow**, as they went on their journey,..... Acts 10:9
1 And on the **morrow** Peter went away with them,....... 10:23
1 And the **morrow** after they entered into Caesarea...... 10:24
1 the **next day** he departed with Barnabas to Derbe...... 14:20
1 ready to depart on the **morrow**;....................... 20:7
1 And the **next day** we that were of Paul's company..... 21:8
1 On the **morrow**, because he would have known........ 22:30
1 the **morrow** they left the horsemen to go with him,.... 23:32
1 and the **next day** sitting on the judgment seat.......... 25:6
1 And on the **morrow**, when Agrippa was come,........ 25:23

This adverb appears over 25 times in the Septuagint and 17 times in the New Testament, 10 of which are found in the Book of Acts. It is usually preceded by the definite article and translated "tomorrow" or "on the next day."

STRONG 1887, BAUER 283, MOULTON-MILLIGAN 230, LIDDELL-SCOTT 612.

1873. ἐπαυτοφώρῳ epautophōrō adv
(Caught) in the act (of theft).

1. ἐπαυτοφώρῳ **epautophōrō**
1 this woman was taken in adultery, **in the very act**.... John 8:4

Typically *autophōros* occurs in an adverbial construction with the preposition *epi* (1894) and means "caught in the very act (*auto*) of theft (*phōr*)." This is true for the classical writings (see *Bauer*, "autophōros") as well as the New Testament. It occurs in the Septuagint only in a versional reading at Job 34:11 (Symmachus).

Bauer notes that it was especially used of adulterers caught in the act (ibid.). This fits its sole New Testament appearance in the passage

Ἐπαφρᾶς 1874

about the woman "caught in the very act of" adultery (John 7:53 to 8:11).
STRONG 1888.

1874. Ἐπαφρᾶς Epaphras name
Epaphras.

1. Ἐπαφρᾶς Epaphras nom masc
2. Ἐπαφρᾶ Epaphra gen masc

2	also learned of **Epaphras** our dear fellowservant,.....	Col 1:7
1	**Epaphras**, who is one of you, a servant of Christ,.......	4:12
1	**Epaphras**, my fellowprisoner in Christ Jesus;........	Phlm 1:23

The fellow servant and fellow prisoner of Paul who may have founded the church in Colossae where he ministered (Colossians 1:7; Philemon 23).

1875. ἐπαφρίζω epaphrizō verb
To foam up or out.

1. ἐπαφρίζοντα epaphrizonta
   nom/acc pl neu part pres act

1 waves of the sea, **foaming** out their own shame;..... Jude 1:13

This verb is from *epi* (1894), "upon," and *aphrizō* (868), "foam at the mouth." It was used by one writer in the Second Century B.C. to mean "foam up." *Epaphrizō* can be translated "cause to splash up like foam" or "vomit forth," referring to the way in which the waves of the sea foam up at the land's edge. It is used metaphorically in Jude 13 where the writer spoke of godless men who "foam out" their shame.

STRONG 1890, BAUER 283-84, LIDDELL-SCOTT 612.

1876. Ἐπαφρόδιτος
Epaphroditos name
Epaphroditus.

1. Ἐπαφροδίτου Epaphroditou gen masc
2. Ἐπαφρόδιτον Epaphroditon acc masc

2	to send to you **Epaphroditus**, my brother,..........	Phlp 2:25
1	having received of **Epaphroditus** the things............	4:18
1	grace of our Lord Jesus ... be with you all. Amen.......	4:23

The gift bearing messenger sent to Paul by the Philippians; he is called Paul's brother, fellow worker, and fellow soldier (Philippians 2:25).

1877. ἐπεγείρω epegeirō verb
Arouse against, incite against, stir up.

COGNATE:
ἐγείρω egeirō (1446)
SYNONYMS:
ἀνασείω anaseiō (381)
διεγείρω diegeirō (1320)
παροτρύνω parotrunō (3813)
συγχέω suncheō (4648)

יָרַד yāradh (3495), Go down; hiphil: bring down (Is 43:14).

סָכַךְ sākhakh (5718), Cover, hide; pilpel: stir up, set against (Is 19:2).

עוּר 'āwar (5996), Be awake; hiphil: stir up (1 Chr 5:26, 2 Chr 21:16, Is 13:17); polel: stir up, rouse up (Zec 9:13—Codex Alexandrinus only).

קוּם qûm (7251), Qal: stand up, arise (2 Sm 18:31); hiphil: raise up, rouse (1 Sm 3:12, 22:8, Mi 5:5).

1. ἐπήγειραν epēgeiran 3pl indic aor act

1	and **raised** persecution against Paul and Barnabas,..	Acts 13:50
1	But the unbelieving Jews **stirred up** the Gentiles,......	14:2

This verb, from *epi* (1894), "upon," (here perhaps intensifying the verb) and *egeirō* (1446), "raise" is used twice in the New Testament and is generally translated "rouse up" or "awaken." It is used widely in the Septuagint where it means to "be aroused against someone" or "rise up or revolt against someone." The word is found only at Acts 13:50 and Acts 14:2 in the New Testament. In these passages it describes the actions of the Jews against Paul as "stirring up" the crowds against him.

STRONG 1892, BAUER 284, MOULTON-MILLIGAN 230, LIDDELL-SCOTT 612-13.

1878. ἐπεί epei conj
When, after; because, since, otherwise.
SYNONYMS:
ἐπειδή epeidē (1879)
ἐπειδήπερ epeidēper (1880)
ὅτι hoti (3617)

1. ἐπεί epei

1	I forgave thee all ... **because** thou desiredst me:....	Matt 18:32
1	**because** they held him to be a prophet. (NASB)......	21:46
1	**because** it is the price of blood......................	27:6
1	the even was come, **because** it was the preparation,	Mark 15:42
1	How shall this be, **seeing** I know not a man?.......	Luke 1:34
1	Now **when** he had ended all his sayings................	7:1
1	**because** Judas had the bag,.......................	John 13:29
1	The Jews therefore, **because** it was the preparation,....	19:31
1	The Jews therefore, **because** it was the preparation,....	19:31
1	for **then** how shall God judge the world?...........	Rom 3:6
1	And if by grace, **then** is it no more of works:........	11:6
1	**otherwise** work is no more work.....................	11:6
1	**otherwise** thou also shalt be cut off..................	11:22
1	for **then** must ye needs go out of the world.........	1 Co 5:10
1	**else** were your children unclean;...................	7:14
1	**forasmuch** as ye are zealous of spiritual gifts,.........	14:12
1	**Else** when thou shalt bless with the spirit,............	14:16
1	**Else** what shall they do which are baptized............	15:29

1 Seeing that many glory after the flesh,	2 Co 11:18
1 Since ye seek a proof of Christ speaking in me,	13:3
1 Forasmuch then as the children are partakers	Heb 2:14
1 Seeing therefore it remaineth that some must enter	4:6
1 for that he ... also is compassed with infirmity	5:2
1 hard to be uttered, seeing ye are dull of hearing	5:11
1 because he could swear by no greater,	6:13
1 otherwise it is of no strength at all	9:17
1 For then must he often have suffered	9:26
1 For then would they not have ceased to be offered?	10:2
1 because she judged him faithful	11:11

Classical Greek and Septuagint Usage

In classical Greek *epei* is a conjunction frequently used to show time ("since, when, after," etc.) or cause ("because, since, for, for otherwise," etc.). The Septuagint utilizes *epei* the same way. Hence, Genesis 15:17 uses *epei* to indicate time ("When the sun went down . . ."), while Psalm 38:20 (LXX 37:20) has a causal sense ("They . . . are mine adversaries; follow the thing that good is").

New Testament Usage

In the New Testament *epei* is used some 26 times to show causation. (For example: Matthew 18:32; Luke 1:34; Romans 3:6; 1 Corinthians 14:12.) On the other hand, Luke 7:1 (a disputed reading) is the only passage which employs *epei* in its temporal sense ("Now *when* he had ended all his sayings . . ."). Most recent editions of the Greek text show another conjunction, *epeidē* (1879), instead.

Strong 1893, Bauer 284, Moulton-Milligan 230, Liddell-Scott 613.

1879. ἐπειδή epeidē conj

When, after; because, since then.

Synonyms:
ἐπεί epei (1878)
ἐπειδήπερ epeidēper (1880)
ὅτι hoti (3617)

1. ἐπειδή epeidē

1 because they took him for a prophet	Matt 21:46
1 When He had completed all His discourse (NASB)	Luke 7:1
1 For a friend of mine in his journey is come to me,	11:6
1 but seeing ye put it from you,	Acts 13:46
1 Mercurius, because he was the chief speaker	14:12
1 Forasmuch as we have heard,	15:24
1 For after that in the wisdom of God	1 Co 1:21
1 For the Jews require a sign,	1:22
1 seeing he understandeth not what thou sayest?	14:16
1 For since by man came death,	15:21
1 not for that we would be unclothed,	2 Co 5:4
1 For he longed after you all,	Phlp 2:26

Epeidē has two uses—the temporal and the causal. The temporal use, found in many ancient writings and in 1 Corinthians 1:21, can be translated "when" or "after." The causal usage, more predominant in the New Testament, is translated "since," "since then," or "because." In Matthew 21:46 the Pharisees wanted to seize Jesus "*because* they took him for a prophet."

Strong 1894, Bauer 284, Moulton-Milligan 230, Liddell-Scott 614.

1880. ἐπειδήπερ epeidēper conj

Inasmuch as, since.

Synonyms:
ἐπεί epei (1878)
ἐπειδή epeidē (1879)

1. ἐπειδήπερ epeidēper

1 Forasmuch as many have taken in hand to set forth	Luke 1:1

This is a causal conjunction in ancient writings translated "inasmuch as" or "since," usually referring to a fact already known. Translated at Luke 1:1 as "forasmuch as," Luke used this word to introduce the reason for his account.

Strong 1895, Bauer 284, Moulton-Milligan 230, Liddell-Scott 614.

1881. ἐπεῖδον epeidon verb

Look upon, concern oneself (with).

Cross-Reference:
εἶδον eidon (1481)

יָדַע yādha‘ (3156), Observe, know; piel: cause to know (Jb 38:12—Codex Alexandrinus only).

נָבַט nāvaṭ (5202), Hiphil: look (Ps 92:11 [91:11]).

צָפָה tsāphâh (7099), Qal: keep guard, watch (Gn 31:49); piel: keep watch, watch (Jer 48:19 [31:19]).

רָאָה rā’âh (7495), See, regard (1 Chr 17:17, Ps 22:17 [21:17], Ob 13).

רְאִי rŏ’î (7503), See (Gn 16:13).

שָׁעָה shā‘âh (8541), Look, look with favor at (Gn 4:4).

1. ἐπεῖδεν epeiden 3sing indic aor act
2. ἔπιδε epide 2sing impr aor act

1 in the days wherein he looked on me,	Luke 1:25
2 And now, Lord, behold their threatenings:	Acts 4:29

This term is the past tense form of the verb *ephoraō* from *epi* (1894), "upon," and *horaō* (3571), "look." In classical Greek, the papyri, and the Septuagint, the word means "fix one's glance upon," "look at," or "concern oneself with." In some writings this verb is used of God's concern with human affairs. *Epeidon* is also used to denote "look with favor on" something or someone. The Lord "looked on" Mary with favor and took away her disgrace (Luke 1:25). The early believers asked God to

ἐπείπερ 1882

consider them, to "*behold* their threatenings" (Acts 4:29).

STRONG 1896, BAUER 284, MOULTON-MILLIGAN 230, LIDDELL-SCOTT 614.

1882. ἐπείπερ epeiper conj
Since indeed.

1. ἐπείπερ epeiper

1 Seeing it is one God, which shall justify	Rom 3:30

This is a conjunction with a causal usage. In the papyri and other ancient writings it is rendered "since indeed." It is used in Romans 3:30 where Paul gave the reason God is the God of both Jews and Gentiles.

STRONG 1897, BAUER 284, MOULTON-MILLIGAN 231, LIDDELL-SCOTT 614.

1883. ἐπεισαγωγή epeisagōgē noun
Introduction, bringing in.

CROSS-REFERENCE:
ἀγωγή agōgē (71)

1. ἐπεισαγωγή epeisagōgē nom sing fem

1 but the bringing in of a better hope did;	Heb 7:19

This term is from *epi* (1894), "upon," and the verb *eisagō* (1507), "bring (or) lead in, into." In extra-Biblical literature the verb is used in marriage contracts, forbidding a man to "introduce" another woman into his house (take an additional wife, cf. *Bauer*). It is translated as "bringing in" in Hebrews 7:19 where the writer referred to the "better hope." This hope has been "introduced" (RSV) and replaces the former order based on the Law.

STRONG 1898, BAUER 284, MOULTON-MILLIGAN 231, LIDDELL-SCOTT 614-15.

1883B. ἐπεισέρχομαι
epeiserchomai verb
Rush in suddenly (with force).

CROSS-REFERENCE:
ἔρχομαι erchomai (2048)

1. ἐπεισελεύσεται epeiseleusetai 3sing indic fut mid

1 for it will come upon all those who dwell (NASB)	Luke 21:35

Found only in Luke 21:35, this word refers to a "coming upon" with great force and sudden surprise. Unlike the passive impression of a "snare" as used in Luke 21:35, this snare comes upon those who are unaware as an almost violent, forceful invasion. The clear impression of this word is that the great day of the coming of the Son of Man will be a devastating surprise to those caught unaware.

BAUER 284, MOULTON-MILLIGAN 231, LIDDELL-SCOTT 614-15.

1884. ἔπειτα epeita adv
Then, thereupon, thereafter.

1. ἔπειτα epeita

1 Then the Pharisees and scribes asked him,	Mark 7:5
1 Then said he to another, ... how much owest thou?	Luke 16:7
1 Then after that saith he to his disciples,	John 11:7
1 after that miracles, then gifts of healings,	1 Co 12:28
1 then miracles, then gifts of healings, (NASB)	12:28
1 After that, he was seen of above five hundred	15:6
1 After that, he was seen of James;	15:7
1 afterward they that are Christ's at his coming.	15:23
1 and afterward that which is spiritual.	15:46
1 Then after three years I went up to Jerusalem	Gal 1:18
1 Afterwards I came into the regions of Syria	1:21
1 Then fourteen years after I went up again	2:1
1 Then we which are alive and remain	1 Th 4:17
1 and after that also King of Salem,	Heb 7:2
1 first for his own sins, and then for the people's:	7:27
1 from above is first pure, then peaceable, gentle,	Jas 3:17
1 for a little time, and then vanisheth away.	4:14

Classical Greek and Septuagint Usage

In classical Greek *epeita* (from *epi* [1894] and *eita* [1520]) means "thereupon," "therefore," or "then." It marks the sequence from one thing to another. It also means "immediately" or "afterwards" when emphatically expressing an event immediately following another. Sometimes it means "therefore" or "then" (like *oun* [3631]), indicating causal succession of events. In the papyri *epeita* means "next" or "then." It may mark the chronological sequence of events or it may be used to give the successive order of things. The three uses of *epeita* in the Septuagint (Numbers 19:19; Isaiah 16:2; 4 Maccabees 6:3) do not translate a specific Hebrew word.

New Testament Usage

In the New Testament *epeita* is used primarily to indicate a succession of events (Luke 16:7; James 4:14). Often it is used with *prōton* (4270), "first," to denote a logical order or priority: "And God hath set some in the church, first (*prōton*) apostles, secondarily prophets ... after that (*epeita*) miracles, then *epeita* gifts of healings ... " (1 Corinthians 12:28; see also Hebrews 7:2). Both ideas of priority and sequence can be present (1 Corinthians 15:23,46; 1 Thessalonians 4:17).

STRONG 1899, BAUER 284, MOULTON-MILLIGAN 231, LIDDELL-SCOTT 615.

1885. ἐπέκεινα epekeina prep
Beyond, farther on.

1. ἐπέκεινα epekeina
1 and I will carry you away **beyond** Babylon.......... Acts 7:43

This adverb is used in the Septuagint and other ancient writings with the meanings "farther on" or "beyond." Typically this is an adverb of distance, but it can also be used of time. God told Moses that all of His commandments must be kept from the day they were given to all generations "henceforward" (Numbers 15:23). The only New Testament reference, Acts 7:43, refers to an exile "beyond Babylon."

STRONG 1900, BAUER 284, LIDDELL-SCOTT 616.

1886. ἐπεκτείνομαι
epekteinomai verb
Stretch out, stretch forward, strain.
CROSS-REFERENCE:
ἐκτείνω ekteinō (1601)

1. ἐπεκτεινόμενος epekteinomenos
nom sing masc part pres mid
1 **reaching forth** unto those things which are before,... Phlp 3:13

Used only in the middle form in the New Testament, this word comes from *epi* (1894), "upon," and *ekteinō* (1601), "stretch out farther." It is translated "stretch out" or "strain," usually toward something. Possibly it is a metaphor from a foot race and is used at Philippians 3:13,14 as "*reaching forth* unto those things which are before" in order to attain the "prize."

STRONG 1901, BAUER 284, MOULTON-MILLIGAN 231 (see "epekteinō"), LIDDELL-SCOTT 616 (see "epekteinō"), COLIN BROWN 1:649.

1887. ἐπενδύομαι ependuomai verb
Put on, clothe.
CROSS-REFERENCE:
δύνω dunō (1410)

1. ἐπενδύσασθαι ependusasthai inf aor mid
1 to be **clothed upon** with our house ... from heaven:.. 2 Co 5:2
1 for that we would be unclothed, but **clothed upon**,...... 5:4

This verb is from *epi* (1894), "upon," and *enduō* (1730), "clothe." In ancient writings it is translated as "put on." Literally the word refers to "outer garments" or "armor." Figuratively the word can refer to "characteristics," "virtues," or "intentions." In 2 Corinthians 5:2,4 Paul wrote about the believer being "clothed" with his heavenly dwelling. Only the middle form (deponent) occurs in the New Testament.

STRONG 1902, BAUER 284-85, KITTEL 2:320-21 (see "ependuō"), LIDDELL-SCOTT 617 (see "ependuō"), COLIN BROWN 1:313-14,316.

1888. ἐπενδύτης ependutēs noun
Outer garment, coat.
CROSS-REFERENCE:
δύνω dunō (1410)
מְעִיל meʿîl (4752), Robe (2 Sm 13:18).

1. ἐπενδύτην ependutēn acc sing masc
1 girt his fisher's **coat** unto him, for he was naked,... John 21:7

This is a noun of scant usage by ancient writers. Vine states, "The word is found in John 21:7, where it apparently denotes a kind of linen frock, which fishermen wore when at their work" (*Expository Dictionary*, "Clothing").

STRONG 1903, BAUER 285, LIDDELL-SCOTT 617.

1889. ἐπέρχομαι eperchomai verb
Come upon, approach, overtake.
COGNATE:
ἔρχομαι erchomai (2048)
SYNONYMS:
διέρχομαι dierchomai (1324)
ἔρχομαι erchomai (2048)
ἐφικνέομαι ephikneomai (2167)
ἥκω hēkō (2223)
καταντάω katantaō (2628)
παραγίνομαι paraginomai (3716)
παρέρχομαι parerchomai (3790)
παρίστημι paristēmi (3798)
προσέρχομαι proserchomai (4193)
φθάνω phthanō (5185)

אָתָה ʾāthâh (885), Come (Is 41:23).
בּוֹא bôʾ (971), Go, come (Gn 42:21, 2 Chr 22:1, Mi 3:11).
גּוּז gûz (1500), Pass by (Ps 90:10 [89:10]).
גִּיחַ gîach (1554), Hiphil: came forth, charged out (Jgs 20:33).
הָלַךְ hālakh (2050), Go, walk (Neh 5:9—Codex Sinaiticus only).
חָלַף chālaph (2599), Pass by (Jb 4:15).
טוּל ṭûl (3014), Hophal: cast, throw (Prv 16:33).
יָצָא yātsâʾ (3428), Go out, come out (Jer 30:23 [37:23]—Codex Sinaiticus only).
נָגַר nāghar (5240), Niphal: persecute, hound someone (Jb 20:28).
נָפַל nāphal (5489), Fall (1 Sm 11:7).

נָתַךְ nāthakh (5597), Be poured out (Dn 9:11).

עָבַר ʿāvar (5882), Qal: go over, through (Nm 5:14, Jb 15:19, Na 3:19); hiphil: cause to understand (Nm 8:7).

עָלָה ʿālâh (6148), Go up, ascend (Lv 16:9).

עָרָה ʿārâh (6408), Pour out; niphal: be poured out (Is 32:15).

פָּלַס pālas (6668), Piel: observe, consider (Prv 5:6).

פִּתְאֹם pithʾōm (6849), Sudden fear, surprise (Prv 3:25).

קוּם qûm (7251), Arise (Jb 25:3).

רָאָה rāʾâh (7495), See (Prv 27:12).

רִיב rîv (7662), Oppose, plead against (Jb 23:6).

שׁוּב shûv (8178), Reproof, rebuke (Lv 14:43, Jos 24:20, Prv 26:11).

שִׁית shîth (8308), Show, perform (Ex 10:1).

שָׁכַן shākhan (8331), Settle, dwell (Jb 3:5).

תְּבוּאָה tᵉvûʾāh (8721), Root out, uproot (Jb 31:12).

1. **ἐπῆλθον** epēlthon 3pl indic aor act
2. **ἐπέλθῃ** epelthē 3sing subj aor act
3. **ἐπελθών** epelthōn nom sing masc part aor act
4. **ἐπελθόντος** epelthontos gen sing neu part aor act
5. **ἐπερχομένοις** eperchomenois dat pl masc part pres mid
6. **ἐπερχομέναις** eperchomenais dat pl fem part pres mid
7. **ἐπερχομένων** eperchomenōn gen pl neu part pres mid
8. **ἐπελεύσεται** epeleusetai 3sing indic fut mid
9. **ἐπῆλθαν** epēlthan 3pl indic aor act

```
8  The Holy Ghost shall come upon thee,............. Luke 1:35
3  But when a stronger than he shall come upon him,..... 11:22
7  those things which are coming on the earth:.......... 21:26
8  For as a snare shall it come on all them that dwell.... 21:35
4  after that the Holy Ghost is come upon you:......... Acts 1:8
2  these things which ye have spoken come upon me....... 8:24
2  Beware therefore, lest that come upon you,........... 13:40
1  And there came thither certain Jews from Antioch..... 14:19
9  And there came thither certain Jews from Antioch..... 14:19
5  That in the ages to come he might show..............Eph 2:7
6  for your miseries that shall come upon you.......... Jas 5:1
```

Classical Greek

In classical Greek *eperchomai* (from *epi* [1894] plus *erchomai* [2048]) means "to draw near," such as the coming forward of the speaker and the coming of a time or event. It also means "to come upon or overtake with hostile intent," thus "to attack or accuse" (*Moulton-Milligan*). The latter meaning is the most prevalent in the papyri with the additional meaning "to press upon" (as for taxes in arrears) and "to oppress with demands."

Septuagint Usage

The Septuagint uses *eperchomai* to translate 24 Hebrew words, frequently *bôʾ*, "to come" (to, in, upon), and *ʿāvar*, "to go" (over, through, upon). These usually refer to things, events, or conditions which come upon mankind.

New Testament Usage

In the New Testament, except for its use in Ephesians 2:7 and James 5:1, *eperchomai* occurs only in the writings of Luke. All the above meanings are also used in the New Testament, especially of eschatological times or happenings which are unpleasant. In addition, *eperchomai* is associated with the Holy Spirit who "comes upon" those blessed by God (Luke 1:35; Acts 1:8). This "coming upon" from above by the Holy Spirit brings power (*dunamis* [1405]).

STRONG 1904, BAUER 285, MOULTON-MILLIGAN 231, KITTEL 2:680-81, LIDDELL-SCOTT 618, COLIN BROWN 1:320,322.

1890. ἐπερωτάω eperōtaō verb

Ask for, inquire, interrogate.

COGNATE:
ἐρωτάω erōtaō (2049)

SYNONYMS:
αἰτέω aiteō (153)
δέομαι deomai (1183)
ἐντυγχάνω entunchanō (1777)
ἐξαιτέω exaiteō (1793)
ἐρωτάω erōtaō (2049)
λέγω legō (2978)
παραιτέομαι paraiteomai (3729)
παρακαλέω parakaleō (3731)
πυνθάνομαι punthanomai (4299)

בָּקַשׁ bāqash (1272), Piel: seek, look for (Is 65:1).

דָּרַשׁ dārash (1938), Inquire, seek (Dt 18:11, 1 Kgs 22:5, Is 19:3).

עָנָה ʿānâh (6257), Answer (Zec 4:4,12).

שָׁאַל shāʾal (8068), Qal: ask, request (Gn 43:7, 1 Sm 10:22, Is 30:2); piel: inquire (2 Sm 20:18).

שְׁאֵל shᵉʾēl (A8069), Ask, require (Dn 2:10—Aramaic).

1. **ἐπερωτῶσιν** eperōtōsin dat pl masc/neu indic/part pres act
2. **ἐπερωτᾷς** eperōtas 2sing indic pres act
3. **ἐπερωτάτωσαν** eperōtatōsan 3pl impr pres act
4. **ἐπερωτῶντα** eperōtōnta acc sing masc part pres act
5. **ἐπερωτᾶν** eperōtan inf pres act
6. **ἐπηρώτησεν** epērōtēsen 3sing indic aor act
7. **ἐπηρώτησαν** epērōtēsan 3pl indic aor act
8. **ἐπερώτησον** eperōtēson 2sing impr aor act
9. **ἐπερωτήσας** eperōtēsas nom sing masc part aor act
10. **ἐπερωτῆσαι** eperōtēsai inf aor act
11. **ἐπερωτήσω** eperōtēsō 1sing indic fut act
12. **ἐπηρώτα** epērōta 3sing indic imperf act

13. ἐπηρώτων epērōtōn 3pl indic imperf act
14. ἐπερωτηθείς eperōtētheis
   nom sing masc part aor pass
15. ἐπερωτῶ eperōtō 1sing indic pres act
16. ἐπερωτῶντες eperōtōntes
   nom pl masc part pres act
17. ἐπερωτήσατε eperōtēsate 2pl impr aor act

7	And they asked him, saying, Is it lawful to heal... Matt	12:10
7	tempting desired him ... show them a sign	16:1
13	tempting desired him ... show them a sign	16:1
7	And his disciples asked him, saying,	17:10
7	came to him the Sadducees, ... and asked him,	22:23
6	asked him a question, tempting him, and saying,	22:35
6	the Pharisees were gathered ... Jesus asked them,	22:41
10	neither durst any man from that day forth ask him	22:46
6	and the governor asked him, saying,	27:11
12	And he asked him, What is thy name?............ Mark	5:9
1	Then the Pharisees and scribes asked him,	7:5
13	his disciples asked him concerning the parable.	7:17
12	And he asked them, How many loaves have ye?	8:5
12	he asked him if he saw ought.	8:23
12	and by the way he asked his disciples,	8:27
12	He continued by questioning them, (NASB)	8:29
13	And they asked him, saying, Why say the scribes	9:11
6	he asked the scribes, What question ye with them?	9:16
6	And he asked his father, How long is it ago since	9:21
13	disciples asked him privately, Why could not we	9:28
10	they understood not ... and were afraid to ask him.	9:32
12	and being in the house he asked them,	9:33
7	And the Pharisees came to him, and asked him,	10:2
13	And the Pharisees came to him, and asked him,	10:2
7	And in the house his disciples asked him again	10:10
13	And in the house his disciples asked him again	10:10
12	one running, and kneeled to him, and asked him,	10:17
11	I will also ask of you one question, and answer me,..	11:29
7	unto him the Sadducees, ... and they asked him,	12:18
13	unto him the Sadducees, ... and they asked him,	12:18
6	that he had answered them well, asked him,	12:28
10	And no man after that durst ask him any question.	12:34
13	Peter and James and John and Andrew asked him	13:3
12	Peter and James and John and Andrew asked him	13:3
6	stood up in the midst, and asked Jesus, saying,	14:60
12	Again the high priest asked him, ... said unto him,	14:61
6	Pilate asked him, Art thou the King of the Jews?	15:2
6	asked him again, saying, Answerest thou nothing?	15:4
12	asked him again, saying, Answerest thou nothing?	15:4
6	he asked him whether he had been any while dead.	15:44
4	both hearing them, and asking them questions...... Luke	2:46
13	people asked him, saying, What shall we do then?	3:10
13	And the soldiers likewise demanded of him, saying,	3:14
11	I will ask you one thing; Is it lawful on the sabbath	6:9
15	I will ask you one thing; Is it lawful on the sabbath	6:9
13	disciples asked him, ... What might this parable be?	8:9
6	And Jesus asked him, saying, What is thy name?	8:30
6	his disciples were with him: and he asked them,	9:18
10	and they feared to ask him of that saying.	9:45
14	And when he was demanded of the Pharisees,	17:20
6	a certain ruler asked him, saying, Good Master,	18:18
6	and when he was come near, he asked him,	18:40
7	And they asked him, saying, Master, we know	20:21
7	of the Sadducees, ... and they asked him,	20:27
5	And after that they durst not ask him any question	20:40
7	And they asked him, ... when shall these things be?	21:7
13	they struck him on the face, and asked him,	22:64
6	And Pilate asked him, saying,	23:3
6	he asked whether the man were a Galilaean.	23:6
12	Then he questioned with him in many words;	23:9
17	his parents said, "he is of age; ask him." (NASB) John	9:23
6	Then asked he them again, Whom seek ye?	18:7
2	Why askest thou me? ask them which heard me,	18:21
8	Why askest thou me? ask them which heard me,	18:21
13	they asked of him, saying, Lord,............ Acts	1:6
6	and the high priest asked them,	5:27
9	he asked of what province he was.	23:34
1	made manifest unto them that asked not after me. Rom	10:20
3	let them ask their husbands at home:............. 1 Co	14:35

Classical Greek
In classical Greek usage *eperōtaō* (from *epi* [1894] plus *erōtaō* [2049]) means "to consult or put a question to someone." In later Greek it is a more technical term used for asking a formal question either at a meeting or in the process of making a contract or accepting the terms of a treaty. In Greek religion *eperōtaō* means "to put a question or a request to a god" (cf. *Bauer*).

Septuagint Usage
The Septuagint uses *eperōtaō* to translate *shā'al*, "to ask." It occurs most generally in the historical books (e.g., 2 Samuel 2:1 [LXX 2 Kings 2:1]; 1 Chronicles 10:13; cf. Jeremiah 21:2).

New Testament Usage
In the New Testament *eperōtaō* is used 56 times and is most frequently found in Mark. It carries the basic sense of "to ask," but three nuances of meaning are found: (1) asking or seeking after something, like a sign (Matthew 16:1; Romans 10:20); (2) probing someone for something, such as the judicial examination (with investigation) and counterquestioning that the Pharisees used with Jesus (Matthew 22:35: Mark 12:28); (3) approaching an authority for answers (Luke 2:46; 9:45; 1 Corinthians 14:35). *Eperōtaō* may indicate intensity since it can mean "demanding" rather than just "asking" (*erōtaō*). Thus *erōtaō* is translated "to pray," but *eperōtaō* is not.

STRONG 1905, BAUER 285, MOULTON-MILLIGAN 231, KITTEL 2:687-88, LIDDELL-SCOTT 618, COLIN BROWN 2:879-80.

1891. ἐπερώτημα eperōtēma noun
Inquiry, demand, question, request.
CROSS-REFERENCE:
ἐρωτάω erōtaō (2049)

1. ἐπερώτημα eperōtēma nom/acc sing neu

1 but the answer of a good conscience toward God,... 1 Pt 3:21

Classical Greek
Related to the more complex verb *eperōtaō* (1890), *eperōtēma* is a noun meaning a "question," usually one directed to another person and given in hopes of securing a binding answer (Angel, "Prayer," *Colin Brown*, 2:879). Evidence in the papyri suggests that it acquired some of the technical dimensions of the verb,

ἐπέχω 1892

and can refer to a "pledge" or "agreement" of a contract (*Moulton-Milligan*).

Septuagint Usage
Eperōtēma occurs only in Theodotion's Daniel (4:14) and in the apocryphal Sirach 33:3 (read only by Codex Sinaiticus). Daniel reads it against the Hebrew *sheʾēlāʾ*, "request, petition" (cf. 1 Samuel 1:17 [LXX 1 Kings 1:17]; 1 Kings 2:16 [LXX 3 Kings 2:16]).

New Testament Usage
The single instance of *eperōtēma* in the New Testament falls in a baptismal passage in 1 Peter. Various modern versions reflect the difficulty in interpretation. Does baptism, which in corresponding fashion saved Noah, save believers as: *suneidēseōs agathēs eperōtēma eis theon* (Greek); "the *answer* of a good conscience toward God" (1 Peter 3:21, KJV); "an *appeal* to God for a clear conscience" (RSV); "the *ability* to face God with a clear conscience" (Phillips); "the *promise made* to God from a good conscience" (*GNB*); "the *pledge* of a good conscience toward God" (NIV). The New International Version is in all likelihood correct here in reading *eperōtēma* as a "pledge." The confessional/baptismal context (cf. 1 Peter 3:15,21) together with the lexical data (see *Moulton-Milligan*) warrant such a conclusion. Note too that early baptismal liturgies and confessions may have been of the question/answer variety (Angel, "Prayer," *Colin Brown*, 2:881).

STRONG 1906, BAUER 285, MOULTON-MILLIGAN 231-32, KITTEL 2:688-89, LIDDELL-SCOTT 618, COLIN BROWN 2:879-81.

1892. ἐπέχω epechō verb
Hold fast, hold upon, retain, apply, give attention to, detain.

COGNATE:
 ἔχω echō (2174)
SYNONYMS:
 ἀντέχομαι antechomai (469)
 ἔχω echō (2174)
 κατέχω katechō (2692)
 κρατέω krateō (2875)

בִּין bîn (1032), End (Jb 18:2).
בָּצַע bātsaʿ (1239), Cut off (Jb 27:8).
חָדַל chādhal (2403), End, refrain (1 Kgs 22:15, 2 Chr 18:5).
יָחַל yāchal (3282), Hiphil: wait (Gn 8:10,12).
לָאָה lāʾâh (3942), Become tired; niphal: be tired (Jer 6:11).
מָנַע mānaʿ (4661), Retain, withhold; niphal: be withheld (Jl 1:13—only some Sinaiticus texts).
עָצַר ʿātsar (6352), Slow down, slack (2 Kgs 4:24).
קָוָה qāwâh (7245), Piel: wait (Jb 30:26).

1. ἔπεχε epeche 2sing impr pres act
2. ἐπέχων epechōn nom sing masc part pres act
3. ἐπέχοντες epechontes nom pl masc part pres act
4. ἐπέσχεν epeschen 3sing indic aor act
5. ἐπεῖχεν epeichen 3sing indic imperf act

2 he marked how they chose out the chief rooms; .... Luke 14:7
5 And he gave heed unto them, ... Acts 3:5
4 but he himself stayed in Asia for a season. 19:22
3 Holding forth the word of life; .... Phlp 2:16
1 Take heed unto thyself, and unto the doctrine; ...... 1 Tm 4:16

Classical Greek
The basic idea of *epechō* (from *epi* [1894] plus *echō* [2174]) is "to hold or have." The *epi* prefix adds various nuances depending on the context. In classical Greek the following are common: (1) "to hold towards—aim at, launch out against," (2) "to hold out or forth—present, offer," (3) "to hold back oneself or another—wait, desist, hinder," and (4) "to hold power over—command, prevail."

Septuagint Usage
The Septuagint uses *epechō* to translate nine Hebrew words which primarily concern restraining oneself. The most frequent are *chādhal*, "to leave off or desist" (Judges 20:28), and *qāwâh*, "to expect or wait for" (Job 30:26).

New Testament Usage
Epechō occurs only five times in the New Testament and it is used the same as in the papyri, except in Philippians 2:16 where some claim it means "holding fast" (the Word of life). But it may mean "to hold forth or present," or "to give heed or attend to" (the Word of life). In the papyri *epechō* regularly means "pay attention" or "give heed to" (as used in Luke 14:7; Acts 3:5; 1 Timothy 4:16) and "delay, stay, suspend, wait" or "refrain from" (as used in Acts 19:22).

STRONG 1907, BAUER 285, MOULTON-MILLIGAN 232, LIDDELL-SCOTT 619-20.

1893. ἐπηρεάζω epēreazō verb
Insult, treat abusively, revile, slander.

1. ἐπηρεάζοντες epēreazontes
 nom pl masc part pres act
2. ἐπηρεαζόντων epēreazontōn
 gen pl masc part pres act

2 and pray for them which despitefully use you, ... Matt 5:44

2	and pray for them which **despitefully use** you	Luke 6:28
1	**falsely accuse** your good conversation in Christ	1 Pt 3:16

Moulton-Milligan cites an example from the papyri where the parents of a wasteful youth "are taking precautions lest he should *deal despitefully* with us." At 1 Peter 3:16 the word is rendered "falsely accuse" one's "good conversation (conduct)." In Matthew 5:44 and Luke 6:28 the word is translated "mistreat" or "despitefully use."

STRONG 1908, BAUER 285, MOULTON-MILLIGAN 232, LIDDELL-SCOTT 620.

1894. ἐπί epi prep

On, upon, at, by, before, over, against, across.

1. ἐφ' eph'
2. ἐπ' ep'
3. ἐπί epi

3	**about** the time they were carried away to Babylon:	Matt 1:11
3	he heard that Archelaus did reign **in** Judaea	2:22
3	Pharisees and Sadducees come **to** his baptism,	3:7
3	cometh Jesus from Galilee **to** Jordan unto John,	3:13
3	Spirit of God descending ... and lighting **upon** him:	3:16
2	It is written, Man shall not live **by** bread alone,	4:4
3	but **by** every word that proceedeth ... of God.	4:4
3	and setteth him **on** a pinnacle of the temple,	4:5
3	and **in** their hands they shall bear thee up,	4:6
3	but **on** a candlestick; and it giveth light unto all	5:15
3	Therefore if thou bring thy gift **to** the altar,	5:23
3	but whosoever shall smite thee **on** thy right cheek,	5:39
3	maketh his sun to rise **on** the evil and on the good,	5:45
3	and sendeth rain **on** the just and on the unjust.	5:45
3	Thy will be done **in** earth, as it is in heaven.	6:10
3	Lay not up for yourselves treasures **upon** earth,	6:19
3	can add one cubit **unto** his stature?	6:27
3	a wise man, which built his house **upon** a rock:	7:24
3	and it fell not: for it was founded **upon** a rock.	7:25
3	which built his house **upon** the sand:	7:26
3	the people were astonished **at** his doctrine:	7:28
3	a man sick of the palsy, lying **on** a bed:	9:2
3	Son of man hath power **on** earth to forgive sins,	9:6
3	Matthew, sitting **at** the receipt of custom:	9:9
1	**as long as** the bridegroom is with them?	9:15
3	a piece of new cloth **unto** an old garment,	9:16
2	lay thy hand **upon** her, and she shall live.	9:18
2	house be worthy, let your peace come **upon** it:	10:13
3	And ye shall be brought **before** governors	10:18
3	and the children shall rise up **against** their parents,	10:21
3	hear in the ear, that preach ye **upon** the housetops.	10:27
3	shall not fall **on** the ground without your Father.	10:29
3	Think not that I am come to send peace **on** earth:	10:34
1	Take my yoke **upon** you, and learn of me;	11:29
2	I will put my spirit **upon** him,	12:18
1	Satan cast out Satan, he is divided **against** himself;	12:26
1	then the kingdom of God is come **unto** you,	12:28
3	he stretched forth his hand **toward** his disciples,	12:49
3	and the whole multitude stood **on** the shore.	13:2
3	Some fell **upon** stony places,	13:5
3	And some fell **among** thorns;	13:7
3	But other fell **into** good ground,	13:8
2	And **in** them is fulfilled the prophecy of Esaias,	13:14
3	But he that received the seed **into** stony places,	13:20
3	But he that received seed **into** the good ground	13:23
3	Which, when it was full, they drew **to** shore,	13:48
3	Give me here John Baptist's head **in** a charger.	14:8
3	And his head was brought **in** a charger,	14:11
3	and was moved with compassion **toward** them,	Matt 14:14
3	commanded the multitude to sit down **on** the grass,	14:19
3	Jesus went unto them, walking **on** the sea.	14:25
3	And when the disciples saw him walking **on** the sea,	14:26
3	if it be thou, bid me come unto thee **on** the water.	14:28
3	he walked **on** the water, to go to Jesus.	14:29
3	they came **to** land at Gennesaret (NASB)	14:34
3	I have compassion **on** the multitude,	15:32
3	the multitude to sit down **on** the ground.	15:35
3	and **upon** this rock I will build my church;	16:18
3	thou shalt bind **on** earth shall be bound in heaven:	16:19
3	thou shalt loose **on** earth shall be loosed in heaven.	16:19
3	they fell **on** their face, and were sore afraid.	17:6
3	receive ... little child **in** my name receiveth me.	18:5
3	that a millstone were hanged **about** his neck,	18:6
3	and goeth **into** the mountains, and seeketh	18:12
3	I say unto you, he rejoiceth more of that sheep,	18:13
3	than **of** the ninety and nine which went not astray.	18:13
3	that **in** the mouth of two or three witnesses	18:16
3	Whatsoever ye shall bind **on** earth	18:18
3	and whatsoever ye shall loose **on** earth	18:18
3	That if two of you shall agree **on** earth as touching	18:19
2	have patience **with** me, and I will pay thee all.	18:26
2	Have patience **with** me, and I will pay thee all.	18:29
3	except it be **for** fornication, ... shall marry another,	19:9
3	**in** the throne of his glory,	19:28
3	ye also shall sit **upon** twelve thrones,	19:28
3	meek, and sitting **upon** an ass,	21:5
3	EVEN **ON** A COLT, THE FOAL (NASB)	21:5
2	and laid **on** them their garments (NASB)	21:7
3	when he saw a fig tree **in** the way, he came to it,	21:19
2	when he saw a fig tree **in** the way, he came **to** it,	21:19
3	whosoever shall fall **on** this stone shall be broken:	21:44
1	but **on** whomsoever it shall fall,	21:44
3	his own farm, another **to** his business (NASB)	22:5
3	Go ye therefore **into** the highways,	22:9
3	they were astonished **at** his doctrine.	22:33
3	the Pharisees ... were gathered together. (NT)	22:34
3	The scribes and the Pharisees sit **in** Moses' seat:	23:2
3	and lay them **on** men's shoulders;	23:4
3	And call no man your father **upon** the earth:	23:9
1	That **upon** you may come all the righteous blood	23:35
3	all the righteous blood shed **upon** the earth,	23:35
3	All these things shall come **upon** this generation.	23:36
3	shall not be left here one stone **upon** another,	24:2
3	And as he sat **upon** the mount of Olives,	24:3
3	many shall come **in** my name, saying, I am Christ;	24:5
3	For nation shall rise **against** nation,	24:7
2	For nation shall rise **against** nation,	24:7
3	and kingdom **against** kingdom:	24:7
3	which be in Judaea flee **into** the mountains:	24:16
3	Let him which is **on** the housetop not come down	24:17
3	see the Son of man coming **in** the clouds of heaven	24:30
3	know that it is near, even **at** the doors.	24:33
3	whom his lord hath made ruler **over** his household,	24:45
3	That he shall make him ruler **over** all his goods.	24:47
2	I have gained **beside** them five talents more.	25:20
3	thou hast been faithful **over** a few things,	25:21
3	I will make thee ruler **over** many things:	25:21
2	I have gained two other talents **beside** them.	25:22
3	thou hast been faithful **over** a few things,	25:23
3	I will make thee ruler **over** many things:	25:23
3	then shall he sit **upon** the throne of his glory:	25:31
1	**Inasmuch as** ye have done it unto one of the least	25:40
1	**Inasmuch as** ye did it not to one of the least	25:45
3	and poured it **on** his head, as he sat at meat.	26:7
3	in that she hath poured this ointment **on** my body,	26:12
3	And he went a little farther, and fell **on** his face,	26:39
1	Jesus said ... Friend, **wherefore** art thou come?	26:50
3	Then came they, and laid hands **on** Jesus,	26:50
3	Are ye come out as **against** a thief with swords	26:55
3	of power, and coming **in** the clouds of heaven.	26:64
3	When he was set down **on** the judgment seat,	27:19
1	His blood be **on** us, and **on** our children.	27:25
1	His blood be **on** us, and **on** our children.	27:25
2	and gathered **unto** him the whole band of soldiers.	27:27
3	a crown of thorns, they put it **upon** his head,	27:29

ἐπί 1894

3	and a reed **in** his right hand:	Matt 27:29
3	and **upon** my vesture did they cast lots.	27:35
2	and we shall believe **in** Him (NASB)	27:42
2	down from the cross, and we will believe him.	27:42
3	He trusted **in** God; let him deliver him now,	27:43
3	was darkness **over** all the land unto the ninth hour.	27:45
3	rolled a great stone **to** the door of the sepulchre,	27:60
3	And if this come to the governor's ears, (NT)	28:14
3	All power is given unto me in heaven and **in** earth.	28:18
2	and the Spirit like a dove descending **upon** him:	Mark 1:10
3	And they were astonished **at** his doctrine:	1:22
2	but stayed out **in** unpopulated areas; (NASB)	1:45
1	let down the bed **wherein** the sick of the palsy lay.	2:4
3	Son of man hath power **on** earth to forgive sins,	2:10
3	he saw Levi ... sitting **at** the receipt of custom,	2:14
3	seweth a piece of new cloth **on** an old garment:	2:21
3	in the days of Abiathar the high priest,	2:26
3	being grieved **for** the hardness of their hearts,	3:5
1	And if a kingdom be divided **against** itself,	3:24
1	And if a house be divided **against** itself,	3:25
1	if Satan rise up **against** himself, and be divided,	3:26
3	the whole multitude was by the sea **on** the land.	4:1
3	And some fell **on** stony ground,	4:5
3	they likewise which are sown **on** stony ground;	4:16
3	And these are they which are sown **among** thorns;	4:18
3	And these are they which are sown **on** good ground;	4:20
3	a candle ... and not to be set **on** a candlestick?	4:21
3	as if a man should cast seed **into** the ground;	4:26
3	which, when it is sown **in** the earth,	4:31
3	is less than all the seeds that be **in** the earth:	4:31
3	And he was **in** the hinder part of the ship,	4:38
3	hinder part of the ship, asleep **on** a pillow:	4:38
2	much people gathered **unto** him;	5:21
2	and trembling, knowing what was done **in** her,	5:33
3	give me by and by in a charger the head of John	6:25
3	and commanded his head to be brought:	6:27
3	And brought his head in a charger,	6:28
2	and was moved with compassion **toward** them,	6:34
3	sit down by companies **upon** the green grass.	6:39
3	midst of the sea, and he alone **on** the land.	6:47
3	he cometh unto them, walking **upon** the sea,	6:48
3	But when they saw him walking **upon** the sea,	6:49
3	For they considered not the miracle **of** the loaves:	6:52
3	they came **into** the land of Gennesaret,	6:53
3	began to carry about **in** beds those that were sick,	6:55
3	and her daughter laid **upon** the bed.	7:30
3	I have compassion **on** the multitude,	8:2
2	satisfy these ... with bread here **in** the wilderness?	8:4
3	commanded the people to sit down **on** the ground:	8:6
3	After that he put his hands again **upon** his eyes,	8:25
3	as snow; so as no fuller **on** earth can white them.	9:3
3	and how it is written **of** the Son of man,	9:12
2	they have done unto him ... as it is written **of** him.	9:13
3	and he fell **on** the ground, and wallowed foaming.	9:20
1	if thou canst do any thing, have compassion **on** us,	9:22
3	such children **in** my name, receiveth me:	9:37
3	man which shall do a miracle **in** my name,	9:39
2	marry another, committeth adultery **against** her.	10:11
2	put his hands **upon** them, and blessed them.	10:16
3	he was sad **at** that saying, and went away grieved:	10:22
3	And the disciples were astonished **at** his words.	10:24
3	how hard is it for them that trust in riches	10:24
1	ye shall find a colt tied, **whereon** never man sat;	11:2
3	the door without **in** a place where two ways met;	11:4
2	cast their garments on him; and he sat **upon** them.	11:7
2	when he came to it, he found nothing but leaves;	11:13
3	all the people was astonished **at** his doctrine.	11:18
2	but teachest the way of God **in** truth:	12:14
2	And they marvelled **at** him.	12:17
3	how **in** the bush God spake unto him, saying,	12:26
2	Well, Master, thou hast said the truth: (NT)	12:32
3	there shall not be left one stone **upon** another,	13:2
3	many shall come **in** my name, saying, I am Christ;	13:6
3	For nation shall rise **against** nation,	13:8
2	For nation shall rise **against** nation,	13:8
3	rise against nation, and kingdom **against** kingdom:	13:8
3	and ye shall be brought **before** rulers and kings	13:9
3	and children shall rise up **against** their parents,	Mark 13:12
3	And let him that is **on** the housetop not go down	13:15
3	know that it is nigh, even **at** the doors.	13:29
3	he went forward a little, and fell **on** the ground,	14:35
2	And they laid their hands **on** him, and took him.	14:46
3	Are ye come out, as **against** a thief, with swords	14:48
3	having a linen cloth cast **about** his naked body;	14:51
3	And straightway **in** the morning the chief priests	15:1
3	And they bring him **unto** the place Golgotha,	15:22
2	they parted his garments, casting lots **upon** them,	15:24
1	darkness **over** the whole land until the ninth hour.	15:33
3	and rolled a stone **unto** the door of the sepulchre,	15:46
3	came **unto** the sepulchre at the rising of the sun.	16:2
3	they shall lay hands **on** the sick,	16:18
2	saw him, he was troubled, and fear fell **upon** him.	Luke 1:12
2	and many shall rejoice **at** his birth.	1:14
3	of Israel shall he turn **to** the Lord their God.	1:16
3	to turn the hearts of the fathers to the children,	1:17
3	when she saw him, she was troubled **at** his saying,	1:29
3	he shall reign **over** the house of Jacob for ever;	1:33
3	The Holy Ghost shall come **upon** thee,	1:35
3	And my spirit hath rejoiced **in** God my Saviour.	1:47
3	hath regarded the low estate of his (NT)	1:48
3	called him Zacharias, **after** the name of his father.	1:59
3	And fear came on all that dwelt round about them:	1:65
3	keeping watch **over** their flock by night.	2:8
3	Glory to God in the highest, and **on** earth peace,	2:14
3	glorifying and praising God **for** all the things	2:20
3	and the Holy Ghost was **upon** him.	2:25
3	**at** those things which were spoken of him.	2:33
2	and the grace of God was **upon** him.	2:40
3	were astonished **at** his understanding and answers.	2:47
2	Annas and Caiaphas being the high priests, (NT)	3:2
2	**in** the high priesthood of Annas (NASB)	3:2
3	word of God came **unto** John the son of Zacharias	3:2
3	this **above** all, that he shut up John in prison.	3:20
2	descended in a bodily shape like a dove **upon** him,	3:22
2	That man shall not live **by** bread alone,	4:4
3	not live by bread alone, but **by** every word of God.	4:4
3	and set him **on** a pinnacle of the temple,	4:9
3	And in their hands they shall bear thee up,	4:11
2	The Spirit of the Lord is **upon** me,	4:18
3	and wondered **at** the gracious words	4:22
2	I tell you **of** a truth, many widows were in Israel	4:25
3	heaven was shut up three years (NT)	4:25
3	when great famine was **throughout** all the land;	4:25
3	many lepers were in Israel **in the time** of Eliseus	4:27
1	the brow of the hill **whereon** their city was built,	4:29
3	And they were astonished **at** his doctrine:	4:32
3	were all amazed, and spake (NT)	4:36
3	the other cities ... **for** I was sent for this (NASB)	4:43
3	nevertheless **at** thy word I will let down the net.	5:5
3	**at** the draught of the fishes which they had taken:	5:9
3	And when they had brought their ships **to** land,	5:11
3	who seeing Jesus fell **on** his face,	5:12
3	And, behold, men brought **in** a bed a man	5:18
3	they went **upon** the housetop,	5:19
3	Son of man hath power **upon** earth to forgive sins,	5:24
1	and took up that **whereon** he lay,	5:25
3	named Levi, sitting **at** the receipt of custom:	5:27
3	putteth a piece of a new garment **upon** an old;	5:36
3	he came down with them, and stood **in** the plain,	6:17
3	And unto him that smiteth thee **on** the one cheek	6:29
3	for he is kind **unto** the unthankful and to the evil.	6:35
3	and laid the foundation **on** a rock:	6:48
3	could not shake it: for it was founded **upon** a rock.	6:48
3	is like a man ... built an house **upon** the earth;	6:49
2	when the Lord saw her, he had compassion **on** her,	7:13
3	thou gavest me no water **for** my feet:	7:44
3	some fell **upon** a rock; ... soon as it was sprung up,	8:6
3	And other fell **on** good ground, and sprang up,	8:8
3	They **on** the rock are they, ... receive the word	8:13
3	but setteth it **on** a candlestick,	8:16
3	And when he went forth **to** land,	8:27
3	and gave them power and authority **over** all devils,	9:1
2	dust from your feet for a testimony **against** them.	9:5
3	look **upon** my son: for he is mine only child.	9:38

ἐπί 1894

3	they were all amazed **at** the mighty power of God... Luke	9:43
3	But while they wondered every one **at** all things	9:43
3	Whosoever shall receive this child **in** my name	9:48
3	Master, we saw one casting out devils **in** thy name;	9:49
2	No man, having put his hand **to** the plow,	9:62
2	your peace shall rest **upon** it: if not, it shall turn to	10:6
1	shall rest upon it: if not, it shall turn **to** you again	10:6
1	The kingdom of God is come nigh **unto** you	10:9
1	that the kingdom of God is come nigh **unto** you	10:11
3	and **over** all the power of the enemy:	10:19
3	set him **on** his own beast, ... brought him to an inn,	10:34
3	And **on** the morrow when he departed,	10:35
3	Thy will be done, as in heaven, so **in** earth.	11:2
1	Every kingdom divided **against** itself ... desolation;	11:17
3	and a house divided **against** a house falleth.	11:17
1	If Satan also be divided **against** himself,	11:18
1	no doubt the kingdom of God is come **upon** you.	11:20
1	taketh from him all his armour **wherein** he trusted,	11:22
3	neither under a bushel, but **on** a candlestick,	11:33
3	shall be proclaimed **upon** the housetops.	12:3
3	And when they bring you **unto** the synagogues,	12:11
1	Man, who made me a judge or a divider **over** you?	12:14
3	taking thought can add **to** his stature one cubit?	12:25
3	whom his lord shall make ruler **over** his household,	12:42
3	that he will make him ruler **over** all that he hath.	12:44
3	I have come to cast fire **upon** the earth; (NASB)	12:49
3	three **against** two, and two against three.	12:52
3	three against two, and two **against** three.	12:52
1	The father shall be divided **against** the son,	12:53
3	The father shall be divided **against** the son,	12:53
3	against the son, and the son **against** the father;	12:53
3	the mother **against** the daughter,	12:53
3	and the daughter **against** the mother;	12:53
3	the mother in law **against** her daughter in law,	12:53
3	and the daughter in law **against** her mother in law.	12:53
3	When you see a cloud rising **in** the west (NASB)	12:54
3	thou goest with thine adversary **to** the magistrate,	12:58
1	eighteen, **upon** whom the tower in Siloam fell,	13:4
3	all the people rejoiced **for** all the glorious things	13:17
2	with ten thousand to meet him that cometh **against**	14:31
3	and go **after** that which is lost, until he find it?	15:4
3	found it, he layeth it **on** his shoulders, rejoicing,	15:5
3	joy ... be in heaven **over** one sinner that repenteth,	15:7
3	more than **over** ninety and nine just persons,	15:7
3	there is joy ... **over** one sinner that repenteth.	15:10
3	and ran, and fell **on** his neck, and kissed him.	15:20
3	And **beside** all this, between us and you there is	16:26
3	and seven times in a day turn again **to** thee, saying,	17:4
3	fell down **on** his face at his feet, giving him thanks:	17:16
3	In that day, he which shall be **upon** the housetop,	17:31
3	in that night there shall be two men **in** one bed;	17:34
3	Two women shall be grinding together; (NT)	17:35
3	And he would not **for** a while: but afterward	18:4
2	his own elect, ... though he bear long **with** them?	18:7
3	shall he find faith **on** the earth?	18:8
1	parable unto certain which trusted **in** themselves	18:9
3	and climbed up **into** a sycamore tree to see him:	19:4
3	And when Jesus came **to** the place, he looked up,	19:5
1	saying, We will not have this man to reign **over** us.	19:14
3	then gavest not thou my money **into** the bank,	19:23
2	which would not that I should reign **over** them,	19:27
1	shall find a colt tied, **whereon** yet never man sat:	19:30
3	and they cast their garments **upon** the colt,	19:35
2	come near, he beheld the city, and wept **over** it,	19:41
3	For the days shall come **upon** thee,	19:43
3	shall not leave in thee one stone **upon** another;	19:44
2	shall fall **upon** that stone shall be broken;	20:18
1	but **on** whomsoever it shall fall,	20:18
2	scribes the same hour sought to lay hands **on** him;	20:19
2	but teachest the way of God truly: (NT)	20:21
3	they marvelled **at** his answer, and held their peace.	20:26
3	even Moses showed **at** the bush,	20:37
3	there shall not be left one stone **upon** another,	21:6
3	many shall come in my name, saying, I am Christ;	21:8
1	said he unto them, Nation shall rise **against** nation,	21:10
2	said he unto them, Nation shall rise **against** nation,	21:10
3	rise against nation, and kingdom **against** kingdom:	21:10
1	before all these, they shall lay their hands **on** you, Luke	21:12
3	**before** kings and rulers for my name's sake.	21:12
3	for there shall be great distress **in** the land,	21:23
3	**upon** the earth distress of nations, with perplexity;	21:25
1	and so that day come **upon** you unawares.	21:34
3	For as a snare shall it come **on** all them that dwell	21:35
3	all them that dwell **on** the face of the whole earth.	21:35
3	of him that betrayeth me is with me on the table.	22:21
3	ye may eat and drink **at** my table in my kingdom,	22:30
3	sit **on** thrones judging the twelve tribes of Israel.	22:30
3	And when he was **at** the place, he said unto them,	22:40
3	as ... drops of blood falling down **to** the ground.	22:44
2	and the elders, which were come **to** him,	22:52
3	Be ye come out, as **against** a thief, with swords	22:52
2	ye stretched forth no hands **against** me:	22:53
2	Of a truth this fellow also was with him:	22:59
3	multitude of them arose, and led him **unto** Pilate.	23:1
2	Daughters of Jerusalem, weep not **for** me,	23:28
1	but weep **for** yourselves, and for your children.	23:28
3	but weep for yourselves, and **for** your children.	23:28
3	they begin to say to the mountains, Fall **on** us;	23:30
3	And when they were come **to** the place, ... Calvary,	23:33
2	And a superscription also was written **over** him	23:38
1	a darkness **over** all the earth until the ninth hour.	23:44
3	And all the people that came together to that sight,	23:48
3	in the morning, they came **unto** the sepulchre;	24:1
3	Then arose Peter, and ran **unto** the sepulchre;	24:12
3	women ... which were early **at** the sepulchre;	24:22
3	of them which were with us went **to** the sepulchre,	24:24
3	to believe all that the prophets have spoken: (NT)	24:25
3	remission of sins should be preached **in** his name	24:47
1	behold, I send the promise of my Father **upon** you:	24:49
2	from heaven like a dove, and it abode upon him..... John	1:32
1	**Upon** whom thou shalt see the Spirit descending,	1:33
2	see the Spirit descending, and remaining **on** him,	1:33
3	ascending and descending **upon** the Son of man.	1:51
2	whosoever believeth **in** him should not perish,	3:15
2	but the wrath of God abideth **on** him.	3:36
3	wearied with his journey, sat thus **on** the well:	4:6
3	And **upon** this came his disciples,	4:27
3	there is at Jerusalem **by** the sheep market a pool,	5:2
2	miracles which he did **on** them that were diseased.	6:2
3	his disciples went down **unto** the sea,	6:16
3	they see Jesus walking **on** the sea,	6:19
3	the ship was **at** the land whither they went.	6:21
2	but no man laid hands **on** him,	7:30
2	but no man laid hands **on** him.	7:44
2	caught in adultery, **in** the very act (NASB)	8:4
1	without sin ... let him first cast a stone **at** her.	8:7
3	Then took they up stones to cast **at** him:	8:59
3	anointed the eyes of the blind man with the clay,	9:6
3	clay **upon** mine eyes, and I washed, and do see.	9:15
2	It was a cave, and a stone lay **upon** it.	11:38
2	when he had found a young ass, sat **thereon**,	12:14
3	behold, thy King cometh, sitting **on** an ass's colt.	12:15
2	remembered ... these things were written **of** him,	12:16
2	hath lifted up his heel **against** me.	13:18
3	He then lying **on** Jesus' breast saith unto him,	13:25
3	I have glorified thee **on** the earth:	17:4
2	knowing all things that should come **upon** him,	18:4
2	and sat down **in** the judgment seat	19:13
3	And Pilate wrote a title, and put it **on** the cross.	19:19
3	and **for** my vesture they did cast lots.	19:24
3	that the bodies should not remain **upon** the cross	19:31
3	came **to** Jesus, and saw that he was dead already,	19:33
3	And the napkin, that was **about** his head,	20:7
3	again to the disciples **at** the sea of Tiberias;	21:1
3	morning was now come, Jesus stood **on** the shore:	21:4
3	and drew the net **to** land full of great fishes,	21:11
3	which also leaned **on** his breast at supper,	21:20
1	after that the Holy Ghost is come **upon** you:........ Acts	1:8
3	together were about an hundred and twenty, (NT)	1:15
1	time that the Lord Jesus went in and out **among** us,	1:21
3	and the lot fell **upon** Matthias;	1:26
3	they were all with one accord **in** one place.	2:1
1	cloven tongues ... and it sat **upon** each of them.	2:3
3	I will pour out of my Spirit **upon** all flesh:	2:17

515

ἐπί 1894

3	And **on** my servants and **on** my handmaidens	Acts 2:18
3	And on my servants and **on** my handmaidens	2:18
3	wonders in heaven ... signs **in** the earth beneath;	2:19
2	moreover also my flesh shall rest **in** hope:	2:26
3	he would raise up Christ to sit **on** his throne;	2:30
3	be baptized every one of you **in** the name of Jesus	2:38
3	wonders and signs were done by the apostles.	2:43
3	And all that believed were together, (NT)	2:44
3	those who were being saved (NIV) (NT)	2:47
3	Now Peter and John went up ... into the temple	3:1
3	**at** the hour of prayer, being the ninth hour.	3:1
3	sat for alms **at** the Beautiful gate of the temple:	3:10
3	amazement **at** that which had happened unto him.	3:10
3	all the people ran together unto them **in** the porch	3:11
3	Ye men of Israel, why marvel ye **at** this?	3:12
3	And his name **through** faith	3:16
3	And it came to pass **on** the morrow,	4:5
3	If we this day be examined **of** the good deed	4:9
3	But that it spread no **further** among the people,	4:17
3	that they speak henceforth to no man **in** this name.	4:17
3	not to speak at all nor teach **in** the name of Jesus.	4:18
3	for all men glorified God **for** that which was done.	4:21
1	**on** whom this miracle of healing was showed.	4:22
3	were gathered together against the Lord, (NT)	4:26
2	For **of** a truth against thy holy child Jesus,	4:27
3	For **of** a truth **against** thy holy child Jesus,	4:27
3	And now, Lord, behold their threatenings: (NT)	4:29
3	and great grace was **upon** them all.	4:33
3	fear came **on** all them that heard these things.	5:5
3	the feet ... are **at** the door, and shall carry thee out.	5:9
1	And great fear came **upon** all the church,	5:11
3	and **upon** as many as heard these things.	5:11
3	and laid them **on** beds and couches,	5:15
3	And laid their hands **on** the apostles,	5:18
3	with the guards standing **at** the doors. (NIV)	5:23
3	that ye should not teach **in** this name?	5:28
3	and intend to bring this man's blood **upon** us.	5:28
3	Jesus, whom ye slew and hanged **on** a tree.	5:30
3	what ye intend to do as **touching** these men.	5:35
3	that they should not speak **in** the name of Jesus,	5:40
3	whom we may appoint **over** this business.	6:3
2	made him governor **over** Egypt and all his house.	7:10
1	made him governor over Egypt and all his house.	7:10
1	Now there came a dearth **over** all the land of Egypt	7:11
2	Then another king ... became ruler **of** Egypt. (NIV)	7:18
3	it came **into** his heart to visit his brethren	7:23
1	Who made thee a ruler and a judge **over** us?	7:27
1	THE PLACE ON WHICH YOU ARE (NASB)	7:33
1	saying, Who made thee a ruler and a judge?	7:35
2	and they gnashed **on** him with their teeth.	7:54
2	and ran **upon** him with one accord,	7:57
3	**against** the church which was at Jerusalem;	8:1
2	and made great lamentation **over** him.	8:2
2	For as yet he was fallen **upon** none of them:	8:16
2	Then laid they their hands **on** them,	8:17
2	these things which ye have spoken come **upon** me.	8:24
3	**unto** the way that goeth down from Jerusalem	8:26
3	who had the charge of all her treasure,	8:27
3	and sitting **in** his chariot read Esaias the prophet.	8:28
3	He was led as a sheep **to** the slaughter;	8:32
3	came **unto** a certain water: and the eunuch said,	8:36
3	And he fell **to** the earth,	9:4
3	and go **into** the street which is called Straight,	9:11
2	and putting his hands **on** him said, Brother Saul,	9:17
3	he might bring them bound **unto** the chief priests?	9:21
3	AEneas, which had kept his bed eight years, (NT)	9:33
3	Lydda and Saron saw him, and turned **to** the Lord.	9:35
3	and many believed **in** the Lord.	9:42
3	Peter went up **upon** the housetop to pray	10:9
3	but while they made ready, he fell **into** a trance,	10:10
2	and a certain vessel descending **unto** him,	10:11
3	and let down **to** the earth:	10:11
3	This was done thrice: (NT)	10:16
3	had made inquiry ... and stood **before** the gate,	10:17
3	and fell down at his feet, and worshipped him.	10:25
2	Of a truth I perceive that God is no respecter	10:34
3	whom they slew and hanged **on** a tree:	10:39
3	Holy Ghost fell **on** all them which heard the word.	Acts 10:44
3	because that **on** the Gentiles also was poured out	10:45
3	And this was done three times: (NT)	11:10
3	men already come **unto** the house where I was,	11:11
2	as I began to speak, the Holy Ghost fell **on** them,	11:15
1	Holy Ghost fell on them, as **on** us at the beginning.	11:15
3	unto us, who believed **on** the Lord Jesus Christ;	11:17
3	upon the persecution that arose **about** Stephen	11:19
3	great number believed, and turned **unto** the Lord.	11:21
1	should be great dearth **throughout** all the world:	11:28
3	which came to pass in the days **of** Claudius Caesar.	11:28
3	came **unto** the iron gate that leadeth unto the city;	12:10
3	he came **to** the house of Mary the mother of John,	12:12
3	made Blastus the king's chamberlain (NT)	12:20
3	sat **upon** his throne, and made an oration	12:21
3	now, behold, the hand of the Lord is **upon** thee,	13:11
2	And immediately there fell **on** him a mist	13:11
3	being astonished **at** the doctrine of the Lord.	13:12
3	And he was seen many days of (NT)	13:31
1	Beware therefore, lest that come **upon** you,	13:40
3	and raised persecution **against** Paul and Barnabas,	13:50
2	they shook off the dust of their feet **against** them,	13:51
3	abode they speaking boldly **in** the Lord,	14:3
3	bearing witness **to** the word of his grace (NASB)	14:3
3	Said with a loud voice, Stand upright **on** thy feet.	14:10
3	brought oxen and garlands **unto** the gates,	14:13
3	turn from these vanities **unto** the living God,	14:15
3	to put a yoke **upon** the neck of the disciples,	15:10
3	to take out of them a people **for** his name.	15:14
1	all the Gentiles, **upon** whom my name is called,	15:17
2	all the Gentiles, **upon** whom my name is called,	15:17
3	which from among the Gentiles are turned **to** God:	15:19
3	they rejoiced **for** the consolation.	15:31
3	And this did she many days. (NT)	16:18
3	drew them into the marketplace **unto** the rulers,	16:19
3	And they said, Believe **on** the Lord Jesus Christ,	16:31
3	and three sabbath days reasoned with them (NT)	17:2
3	they drew Jason ... **unto** the rulers of the city,	17:6
3	brethren sent away Paul to go as it were **to** the sea:	17:14
3	they took him, and brought him **unto** Areopagus,	17:19
3	for to dwell **on** all the face of the earth,	17:26
3	Your blood be **upon** your own heads; I am clean:	18:6
3	Paul, and brought him **to** the judgment seat,	18:12
3	they desired him to tarry longer time (NT)	18:20
2	hands upon them, the Holy Ghost came **on** them;	19:6
3	and spake boldly **for** the space of three months;	19:8
3	And this continued **by the space of** two years;	19:10
3	So that from his body were brought **unto** the sick	19:12
3	to call **over** them which had evil spirits the name	19:13
3	man in whom the evil spirit was leaped **on** them,	19:16
3	and fear fell **on** them all,	19:17
3	all with one voice **about** the space of two hours	19:34
3	And there sat **in** a window a certain young man	20:9
3	Paul was long preaching (NT)	20:9
1	and talked a long while, (NT)	20:11
3	And we went before **to** ship, and sailed unto Assos,	20:13
3	We went ... to the ship and sailed **for** Assos (NIV)	20:13
3	And they all wept sore, and fell on Paul's neck,	20:37
3	Sorrowing most of all **for** the words ... he spake,	20:38
3	and we kneeled down **on** the shore, and prayed.	21:5
1	We have four men which have a vow **on** them;	21:23
2	and be at charges **with** them,	21:24
2	stirred up all the people, and laid hands **on** him,	21:27
2	soldiers and centurions, and ran down **unto** them:	21:32
3	And when he came **upon** the stairs, so it was,	21:35
3	Paul stood on the stairs,	21:40
3	in every synagogue them that believed **on** thee:	22:19
3	to say **before** thee what they had against him.	23:30
3	that I be not **further** tedious unto thee,	24:4
3	Commanding his accusers to come **unto** thee:	24:8
3	Who ought to have been here **before** thee,	24:19
3	while I stood **before** the council,	24:20
1	I am on trial **before** you today. (NIV)	24:21
3	and the next day sitting **on** the judgment seat	25:6
2	and there be judged of these things **before** me?	25:9
3	Then said Paul, I stand **at** Caesar's judgment seat,	25:10
3	appealed unto Caesar? **unto** Caesar shalt thou go.	25:12

ἐπί 1894

3 on the morrow I sat **on** the judgment seat,	Acts	25:17
1 Wherefore I have brought him forth **before** you,		25:26
3 and specially **before** thee, O king Agrippa,		25:26
3 **before** touching all the things		26:2
2 And now I stand and am judged **for** the hope		26:6
3 But rise, and stand **upon** thy feet:		26:16
3 and from the power of Satan **unto** God,		26:18
3 that they should repent and turn to God,		26:20
3 when neither sun nor stars in many days appeared,		27:20
3 cast themselves first into the sea, and get **to** land:		27:43
3 And the rest, some **on** boards,		27:44
3 and some **on** broken pieces of the ship.		27:44
3 that they escaped all safe to land.		27:44
3 a bundle of sticks, and laid them **on** the fire,		28:3
3 but **after** they had looked a great while,		28:6
2 and were desired to tarry **with** them seven days:		28:14
3 always in my prayers; making request,	Rom	1:10
3 **against** all ungodliness and unrighteousness of men,		1:18
3 **against** them which commit such things.		2:2
3 **upon** every soul of man that doeth evil,		2:9
3 Christ unto all and **upon** all them that believe:		3:22
3 but believeth **on** him that justifieth the ungodly,		4:5
3 this blessedness then **upon** the circumcision only,		4:9
3 blessedness ... or **upon** the uncircumcision also?		4:9
2 Who against hope believed in hope,		4:18
3 if we believe **on** him that raised up Jesus our Lord		4:24
2 and rejoice **in** hope of the glory of God.		5:2
1 passed upon all men, **for** that all have sinned:		5:12
3 even over them that had not sinned,		5:14
3 **after** the similitude of Adam's transgression,		5:14
1 in those things **whereof** ye are now ashamed?		6:21
1 law hath dominion **over** a man as long as he liveth?		7:1
2 him who hath subjected the same in hope,		8:20
2 him who hath subjected the same in hope,		8:20
3 who is **over** all, God blessed for ever. Amen.		9:5
3 the riches of his glory **on** the vessels of mercy,		9:23
3 a short work will the Lord make **upon** the earth.		9:28
2 whosoever believeth **on** him shall not be ashamed.		9:33
2 Whosoever believeth **on** him shall not be ashamed.		10:11
2 jealousy **by** them that are no people,		10:19
3 and **by** a foolish nation I will anger you.		10:19
2 and **by** a foolish nation I will anger you.		10:19
1 **inasmuch as** I am the apostle of the Gentiles,		11:13
3 **on** them which fell, severity;		11:22
3 which fell, severity; but **toward** thee, goodness,		11:22
3 so doing thou shalt heap coals of fire **on** his head.		12:20
2 of them that reproached thee fell **on** me.		15:3
2 **in** him shall the Gentiles trust.		15:12
2 lest I should build **upon** another man's foundation:		15:20
3 I am glad therefore on your **behalf**:		16:19
1 I am rejoicing **over** you (NASB)		16:19
3 **for** the grace of God which is given you by Jesus	1 Co	1:4
3 neither have entered **into** the heart of man,		2:9
3 Now if any man build **upon** this foundation gold,		3:12
3 to law **before** the unjust, and not before the saints?		6:1
3 to law before the unjust, and not **before** the saints?		6:1
3 goeth to law ... and that **before** the unbelievers.		6:6
3 come together again, that Satan tempt (NT)		7:5
3 he behaveth himself uncomely **toward** his virgin,		7:36
1 is bound by the law **as long as** her husband liveth;		7:39
3 that are called gods, whether in heaven or **in** earth,		8:5
3 **through** thy knowledge ... the weak brother perish,		8:11
3 that he that ploweth should plow in hope;		9:10
2 thresheth in hope should be partaker **of** his hope.		9:10
3 to have power **on** her head because of the angels.		11:10
3 When ye come together therefore **into** one place,		11:20
3 Rejoiceth not in iniquity,		13:6
3 the unlearned say Amen **at** thy giving of thanks,		14:16
3 the whole church be come together **into** one place,		14:23
3 so falling down **on** his face he will worship God,		14:25
3 I am glad **of** the coming of Stephanas		16:17
3 Who comforteth us **in** all our tribulation,	2 Co	1:4
1 that we should not trust **in** ourselves,		1:9
1 but in God which raiseth the dead:		1:9
3 Moreover I call God for a record **upon** my soul,		1:23
3 having confidence **in** you all,		2:3
3 And not as Moses, which put a veil **over** his face,		3:13
3 untaken away **in** the reading of the old testament;	2 Co	3:14
3 when Moses is read, the veil is **upon** their heart.		3:15
1 because we do not want to be (NASB) (NT)		5:4
3 I am exceeding joyful in all our tribulation.		7:4
1 consolation wherewith he was comforted in you,		7:7
3 Therefore we were comforted **in** your comfort:		7:13
3 exceedingly the more joyed we **for** the joy of Titus,		7:13
3 even so our boasting, which I made **before** Titus,		7:14
2 soweth bountifully shall reap also bountifully. (NT)		9:6
2 soweth bountifully shall reap also bountifully.		9:6
3 they glorify God **for** your professed subjection		9:13
1 for the exceeding grace of God **in** you.		9:14
3 Thanks be unto God **for** his unspeakable gift.		9:15
3 wherewith I think to be bold **against** some,		10:2
1 let him consider this again **within** himself (NASB)		10:7
2 that the power of Christ may rest **upon** me.		12:9
3 and have not repented **of** the uncleanness		12:21
3 **In** the mouth of two or three witnesses		13:1
3 Cursed is every one that hangeth **on** a tree:	Gal	3:13
3 He saith not, And to seeds, as **of** many;		3:16
3 but as of one, And to thy seed, which is Christ.		3:16
1 Now I say, **That** the heir, as long as he is a child,		4:1
3 turn ye again **to** the weak and beggarly elements,		4:9
2 For, brethren, ye have been called unto liberty;		5:13
3 peace be **on** them, and mercy, and **upon** the Israel		6:16
3 peace be on them, ... and **upon** the Israel of God.		6:16
3 things **in** the heavens and things (NASB)	Eph	1:10
3 both which are in heaven, and which are **on** earth;		1:10
3 making mention of you **in** my prayers,		1:16
1 of his grace ... **toward** us through Christ Jesus.		2:7
3 created in Christ Jesus **unto** good works,		2:10
3 And are built **upon** the foundation of the apostles		2:20
3 family in heaven and earth is named, (NT)		3:15
3 One God and Father of all, who is **above** all,		4:6
3 let not the sun go down **upon** your wrath:		4:26
3 wrath of God **upon** the children of disobedience.		5:6
3 and thou mayest live long on the earth.		6:3
3 **Above** all, taking the shield of faith,		6:16
3 I thank my God **upon** every remembrance of you,	Phlp	1:3
3 **For** your fellowship in the gospel from the first day		1:5
3 offered **upon** the sacrifice and service of your faith,		2:17
3 lest I should have sorrow **upon** sorrow.		2:27
3 the righteousness which is of God **by** faith:		3:9
1 **for** which also I am apprehended of Christ Jesus.		3:12
3 I press toward the mark **for** the prize		3:14
1 **wherein** ye were also careful,		4:10
3 that are in heaven, and that are **in** earth,	Col	1:16
3 by him, I say, whether they be things **in** earth,		1:20
3 on things above, not on things **on** the earth.		3:2
3 your members which are **upon** the earth;		3:5
3 wrath ... cometh **on** the children of disobedience:		3:6
3 And **above** all these things put on charity,		3:14
3 making mention of you **in** our prayers;	1 Th	1:2
2 for the wrath is come upon them to the uttermost.		2:16
1 we were comforted **over** you in all our affliction		3:7
3 we were comforted over you **in** all our affliction		3:7
3 **for** all the joy wherewith we joy for your sakes		3:9
3 For God hath not called us **unto** uncleanness,		4:7
1 our testimony **among** you was believed in that day.	2 Th	1:10
2 and by our gathering together **unto** him,		2:1
3 and exalteth himself **above** all that is called God,		2:4
1 And we have confidence in the Lord **touching** you,		3:4
3 should hereafter believe **on** him to life everlasting.	1 Tm	1:16
3 the prophecies which went before **on** thee,		1:18
3 because we trust **in** the living God,		4:10
3 is a widow indeed, and desolate, trusteth **in** God,		5:5
3 an accusation, but **before** two or three witnesses.		5:19
3 **before** Pontius Pilate witnessed a good confession;		6:13
3 nor trust **in** uncertain riches, but in the living God,		6:17
3 hope on ... riches, but **on** God, (NASB)		6:17
3 wrangle about words, which is (NASB) (NT)	2 Tm	2:14
3 but **to** the subverting of the hearers.		2:14
3 for they will increase **unto** more ungodliness.		2:16
3 But they shall proceed no **further**:		3:9
3 and seducers shall wax worse and worse, (NT)		3:13
3 from the truth, and shall be turned **unto** fables.		4:4
2 **In** hope of eternal life, which God, ... promised	Tit	1:2

517

ἐπί 1894

1	Which he shed **on** us abundantly through Jesus	Tit 3:6
3	making mention of thee always **in** my prayers,	Phlm 1:4
3	For we have great joy and consolation **in** thy love,	1:7
2	Hath **in** these last days spoken unto us by his Son,	Heb 1:2
3	and didst set him **over** the works of thy hands:	2:7
2	And again, I will put my trust **in** him.	2:13
3	But Christ as a son **over** his own house;	3:6
3	let us go on **unto** perfection;	6:1
3	from dead works, and of faith **toward** God,	6:1
2	which drinketh in the rain that cometh oft **upon** it,	6:7
2	for **under** it the people received the law,	7:11
1	For he **of** whom these things are spoken	7:13
3	of the things which we have spoken this is the sum:	8:1
3	For if he were **on** earth, he should not be a priest,	8:4
3	which was established **upon** better promises.	8:6
3	make a new covenant **with** the house of Israel	8:8
3	the house of Israel and **with** the house of Judah:	8:8
3	and write them **in** their hearts:	8:10
3	Which stood only **in** meats and drinks,	9:10
3	transgressions that were **under** the first testament,	9:15
3	For a testament is of force after men are dead:	9:17
3	now once **in** the end of the world hath he appeared	9:26
3	I will put my laws **into** their hearts,	10:16
3	and **in** their minds will I write them;	10:16
3	And having an high priest **over** the house of God;	10:21
3	died without mercy **under** two or three witnesses:	10:28
3	God testifying **of** his gifts:	11:4
3	that they were strangers and pilgrims **on** the earth.	11:13
3	and worshipped, leaning **upon** the top of his staff.	11:21
3	after they were compassed **about** seven days.	11:30
3	wandering **in** deserts and mountains (NASB)	11:38
3	a few days chastened us ... but he **for** our profit,	12:10
3	escaped not who refused him that spake **on** earth,	12:25
3	have respect **to** him that weareth the gay clothing,	Jas 2:3
1	that worthy name **by** the which ye are called?	2:7
3	when he had offered Isaac his son **upon** the altar?	2:21
3	ye rich men, weep and howl **for** your miseries	5:1
3	lived in pleasure **on** the earth, and been wanton;	5:5
2	and hath long patience **for** it,	5:7
2	call for the elders ... and let them pray **over** him,	5:14
3	and it rained not **on** the earth by the space of three	5:17
3	be sober, and hope to the end **for** the grace	1 Pt 1:13
2	but was manifest **in** these last times for you,	1:20
2	he that believeth **on** him shall not be confounded.	2:6
3	bare our sins in his own body **on** the tree,	2:24
3	but are now returned **unto** the Shepherd	2:25
3	who trusted **in** God, adorned themselves,	3:5
3	For the eyes of the Lord are **over** the righteous,	3:12
3	the face of the Lord is **against** them that do evil.	3:12
1	for the spirit of glory and of God resteth **upon** you:	4:14
2	Casting all your care **upon** him; for he careth	5:7
1	I think it meet, **as long as** I am in this tabernacle,	2 Pt 1:13
3	The dog is turned **to** his own vomit again;	2:22
2	that there shall come **in** the last days scoffers,	3:3
2	And every man that hath this hope **in** him	1 Jn 3:3
3	with malicious words: and not content **therewith**,	3 Jn 1:10
2	**In** the last time there shall be mockers (NASB)	Jude 1:18
2	all kindreds of the earth shall wail **because** of him.	Rev 1:7
2	he laid his right hand **upon** me, saying unto me,	1:17
3	seven stars which thou sawest **in** my right hand,	1:20
3	white stone, and **in** the stone a new name written,	2:17
1	I will put **upon** you none other burden.	2:24
3	to him will I give power **over** the nations:	2:26
3	thou shalt not watch, I will come **on** thee as a thief,	3:3
3	shalt not know what hour I will come **upon** thee.	3:3
3	temptation, which shall come **upon** all the world,	3:10
3	to try them that dwell **upon** the earth.	3:10
2	and I will write **upon** him the name of my God,	3:12
3	Behold, I stand **at** the door, and knock:	3:20
3	and one sat **on** the throne.	4:2
1	**upon** the seats I saw four and twenty elders sitting,	4:4
3	and they had **on** their heads crowns of gold.	4:4
3	honour and thanks to him that sat **on** the throne,	4:9
3	elders fall down before him that sat **on** the throne,	4:10
3	saw in the right hand of him that sat **on** the throne	5:1
3	saw in the right hand of him that sat **on** the throne	5:1
3	And no man in heaven, nor **in** earth,	5:3
3	of the right hand of him that sat **upon** the throne.	Rev 5:7
3	kings and priests: and we shall reign **on** the earth.	5:10
3	and **on** the earth and under the earth (NIV)	5:13
3	such as are in the sea, and all that are in them,	5:13
3	power, be unto him that sitteth **upon** the throne,	5:13
2	a white horse: and he that sat **on** him had a bow;	6:2
2	him that sat **thereon** to take peace from the earth,	6:4
2	and he that sat **on** him had a pair of balances	6:5
3	power was given unto them **over** the fourth part	6:8
3	avenge our blood on them that dwell **on** the earth?	6:10
1	And said to the mountains and rocks, Fall **on** us,	6:16
3	from the face of him that sitteth **on** the throne,	6:16
3	angels standing **on** the four corners of the earth,	7:1
3	that the wind should not blow **on** the earth,	7:1
3	not blow on the earth, nor **on** the sea,	7:1
3	blow on the earth, nor on the sea, nor on any tree.	7:1
3	sealed the servants of our God **in** their foreheads.	7:3
3	which sitteth **upon** the throne, and unto the Lamb.	7:10
3	before the throne **on** their faces, and worshipped	7:11
3	that sitteth **on** the throne shall dwell among them.	7:15
2	that sitteth on the throne shall dwell **among** them.	7:15
2	neither shall the sun light **on** them, nor any heat.	7:16
3	shall lead them **unto** living fountains of waters:	7:17
3	And another angel came and stood **at** the altar,	8:3
3	**upon** the golden altar which was before the throne.	8:3
3	and it fell **upon** the third part of the rivers,	8:10
3	the rivers, and **upon** the fountains of waters;	8:10
3	woe, to the inhabiters **of** the earth	8:13
3	which have not the seal of God **in** their foreheads.	9:4
3	**on** their heads were as it were crowns like gold,	9:7
1	And they had a king **over** them, which is the angel	9:11
2	They had as king **over** them the angel (NIV)	9:11
3	which are bound in the great river Euphrates.	9:14
2	I saw the horses ... and them that sat **on** them,	9:17
3	with a cloud: and a rainbow was **upon** his head,	10:1
3	and he set his right foot **upon** the sea,	10:2
3	right foot upon the sea, and his left foot **on** the earth,	10:2
3	And the angel which I saw stand **upon** the sea	10:5
3	and **upon** the earth lifted up his hand to heaven,	10:5
3	And sware ... that there should be time no **longer**:	10:6
3	which standeth **upon** the sea and upon the earth.	10:8
3	which standeth upon the sea and **upon** the earth.	10:8
3	Thou must prophesy again **before** many peoples,	10:11
3	and have power **over** waters to turn them to blood,	11:6
3	dead bodies shall lie in the street of the great city,	11:8
3	that dwell **upon** the earth shall rejoice over them,	11:10
2	that dwell upon the earth shall rejoice **over** them,	11:10
3	prophets tormented them that dwelt **on** the earth.	11:10
2	the Spirit of life from God entered **into** them,	11:11
3	entered into them, and they stood **upon** their feet;	11:11
3	and great fear fell **upon** them which saw them.	11:11
3	elders, which sat before God **on** their seats,	11:16
3	fell **upon** their faces, and worshipped God,	11:16
3	and **upon** her head a crown of twelve stars:	12:1
3	seven heads ... and seven crowns **upon** his heads.	12:3
3	And the dragon was wroth **with** the woman,	12:17
3	And I stood **upon** the sand of the sea,	13:1
3	seven heads ... and **upon** his horns ten crowns,	13:1
3	and **upon** his heads the name of blasphemy.	13:1
3	and power was given him **over** all kindreds,	13:7
3	all that dwell **upon** the earth shall worship him,	13:8
3	to the earth in the presence of man. (NASB)	13:13
3	And deceiveth them that dwell **on** the earth	13:14
3	saying to them that dwell **on** the earth,	13:14
3	a mark **in** their right hand, or in their foreheads:	13:16
3	a mark in their right hand, or **in** their foreheads:	13:16
3	and, lo, a Lamb stood **on** the mount Sion,	14:1
3	his Father's name written **in** their foreheads.	14:1
3	the eternal gospel to proclaim **to** those (NIV)	14:6
3	gospel to preach unto them that dwell **on** the earth,	14:6
3	who live on the earth—to every nation, (NIV)	14:6
3	receive his mark **in** his forehead, or in his hand,	14:9
3	receive his mark in his forehead, or **in** his hand,	14:9
3	**upon** the cloud one sat like unto the Son of man,	14:14
2	Son of man, having **on** his head a golden crown,	14:14
3	with a loud voice to him that sat **on** the cloud,	14:15
3	And he that sat **on** the cloud thrust in his sickle	14:16

3 thrust in his sickle on the earth;	Rev 14:16
3 out from the altar, which had power over fire;	14:18
3 stand on the sea of glass, having the harps of God.	15:2
3 first went, and poured out his vial upon the earth;	16:2
3 on the people who had the mark (NIV)	16:2
3 the fourth angel poured out his vial upon the sun;	16:8
3 God, which hath power over these plagues:	16:9
3 poured out his vial upon the seat of the beast;	16:10
3 his vial upon the great river Euphrates;	16:12
3 which go forth unto the kings of the earth	16:14
3 seventh angel poured out his bowl upon (NASB)	16:17
3 such as was not since men were upon the earth,	16:18
3 there fell upon men a great hail out of heaven,	16:21
3 of the great whore that sitteth upon many waters:	17:1
3 I saw a woman sit upon a scarlet coloured beast,	17:3
3 And upon her forehead was a name written,	17:5
3 and they that dwell on the earth shall wonder,	17:8
3 whose names were not written in the book of life	17:8
2 are seven mountains, on which the woman sitteth.	17:9
3 the ten horns which thou sawest upon the beast,	17:16
3 which reigneth over the kings of the earth.	17:18
2 the kings ... shall bewail her, and lament for her,	18:9
2 the merchants ... shall weep and mourn over her;	18:11
3 every shipmaster, and all the company in ships,	18:17
3 they cast dust on their heads, and cried,	18:19
2 Rejoice over her, thou heaven, and ye holy	18:20
3 and of all that were slain upon the earth.	18:24
3 and worshipped God that sat on the throne, saying,	19:4
2 he that sat upon him was called Faithful and True,	19:11
3 and on his head were many crowns;	19:12
1 upon white horses, clothed in fine linen,	19:14
3 on his vesture and on his thigh a name written,	19:16
3 on his vesture and on his thigh a name written,	19:16
2 the flesh of horses, and of them that sit on them,	19:18
3 to make war against him that sat on the horse,	19:19
3 with the sword of him that sat upon the horse,	19:21
3 having the key ... and a great chain in his hand.	20:1
2 And I saw thrones, and they sat upon them,	20:4
3 his mark upon their foreheads, or in their hands;	20:4
3 his mark upon their foreheads, or in their hands;	20:4
3 on such the second death hath no power,	20:6
3 And they went up on the breadth of the earth,	20:9
2 I saw a great white throne, and him that sat on it,	20:11
3 And he that sat upon the throne said,	21:5
2 away in the spirit to a great and high mountain,	21:10
3 the spirit to a mountain great and high (NIV)	21:10
3 had twelve gates, and at the gates twelve angels,	21:12
2 and on them were the twelve names (NASB)	21:14
3 measured ... twelve thousand furlongs. (NT)	21:16
3 and his name shall be in their foreheads.	22:4
2 for the Lord God will give them light (NIV) (NT)	22:5
3 that they may have right to the tree of life,	22:14
3 to testify unto you these things in the churches.	22:16
2 If anyone adds anything to them (NIV)	22:18
2 unto him the plagues that are written in this book:	22:18

Understanding the meaning of *epi*, or any preposition, involves grammar. The principle is to begin with the root idea of the case of the preposition's object, add the basic root meaning of the preposition itself, and then combine the idea of the context. The result of the above process will be the meaning of *epi* in a given place. The preposition *epi* appears with (that is, its object may occur in) the genitive, locative/dative, and accusative cases. The basic root meaning of *epi* is "upon" and implies contact with its object rather than resting above or over (*huper* [5065]). *Epi* is the opposite of "under" (*hupo* [5097]).

The particular emphases of the cases (of the object) as they are joined with *epi* are as follows: (1) The genitive emphasizes contact, either actual or intended. Thus *epi* means "upon, on, at, by, before." (2) The locative/dative emphasizes not so much contact, though this is involved, as general position. It concerns the effects of the contact and thus means "up, on, at, over, before, against, in, on account of, on the basis of." (3) The accusative case emphasizes motion or direction, that is, some action which takes place on the object. *Epi* with the accusative case is the most common, being employed more often than all the other case uses combined. *Epi* with the accusative may mean "upon, on, up to, to, over, as far as, across, at." In composition (that is, when prefixed to a verb) *epi* retains its root idea and signifies the influence (of the verb's action) upon or over something. *Epi* may also emphasize or intensify the verb's meaning (as in *epiginōskō* [1906], "to know thoroughly"). In composition it also can have the meaning "toward, against, upward" (see *epechō* [1892] as an example of a compound verb [*epi* plus *echō* (2174)] with various meanings due to *epi*).

STRONG 1909, BAUER 285-89, MOULTON-MILLIGAN 232-35, LIDDELL-SCOTT 621-23, COLIN BROWN 3:1171-77,1181,1193-96,1201,12

1895. ἐπιβαίνω epibainō verb
Mount, board, go up (or) upon, walk upon.
COGNATE:
   ὑπερβαίνω huperbainō (5070)
SYNONYMS:
   ἀναβαίνω anabainō (303)
   ἀνέρχομαι anerchomai (422)
   ἐμβαίνω embainō (1671)
   προσαναβαίνω prosanabainō (4178)

דָּרַךְ dārakh (1931), Tread (Dt 1:36, 1 Sm 5:5, Ps 91:13 [90:13]).

הָיָה hāyâh (2030), Become, made (Jb 17:6—Codex Vaticanus only).

הָלַךְ hālakh (2050), Go, walk (Jer 18:15).

הָפַךְ hāphakh (2089), Turn; niphal: turn against (Jb 30:21).

חָנָה chānâh (2684), Encamp, settle (Na 3:17).

יָצַב yātsav (3429), Hithpael: take one's stand, position (Hb 2:1).

עָלָה 'ālâh (6148), Go up, ascend (Jos 15:6, Prv 21:22, Jer 46:4 [26:4]).

ἐπιβάλλω 1896

עָמַד 'āmadh (6198), Stand, take one's stand (Ez 10:18).
צָעַד tsā'adh (7081), Walk, step (Jer 10:5).
רָכַב rākhav (7680), Ride (Gn 24:61, 2 Kgs 9:25, Zec 9:9).

1. ἐπέβην epebēn 1sing indic aor act
2. ἐπέβημεν epebēmen 1pl indic aor act
3. ἐπιβάς epibas nom sing masc part aor act
4. ἐπιβάντες epibantes nom pl masc part aor act
5. ἐπιβεβηκώς epibebēkōs
   nom sing masc part perf act
6. ἐπιβαίνειν epibainein inf pres act
7. ἐνέβημεν enebēmen 1pl indic aor act

5	meek, and sitting upon an ass, ... Matt 21:5
1	Ye know, from the first day that I came into Asia, Acts 20:18
4	over unto Phenicia, we went aboard, and set forth...... 21:2
6	not to go on to Jerusalem. (NIV) 21:4
2	we took ship; and they returned home again. 21:6
7	we took ship; and they returned home again. 21:6
3	Now when Festus was come into the province, ... 25:1
4	entering into a ship of Adramyttium, we launched, ... 27:2

This verb is a compound of *epi* (1894), "upon," and *bainō*, "go." There are two main uses of the word. The first contains the idea of "boarding" or "mounting." Many ancient writers used this word when describing the boarding of ships. The word is used to indicate the mounting of camels (Genesis 24:61) and donkeys (Zechariah 9:9; Matthew 21:5). The second use could be translated as "set foot in." This use can be found in ancient writings and in the New Testament. In extra-Biblical literature the verb was sometimes used to denote hostile intent (for example, a band of robbers; cf. *Moulton-Milligan*). At Acts 20:18 and Acts 25:1 it is used to describe Paul's entering certain provinces.

STRONG 1910, BAUER 289, MOULTON-MILLIGAN 235, LIDDELL-SCOTT 623-24.

1896. ἐπιβάλλω epiballō verb

Throw over or upon, lay on, put on.
CROSS-REFERENCE:
βάλλω ballō (900)

אָרְבָה 'orbāh (723), Spread out (Is 25:11).
בּוֹא bô' (971), Go, come (Prv 18:17).
הָדָה hādhâh (1979), Stretch out, put (Is 11:8).
מִשְׁלוֹחַ mishlôach (5095II) Subject, came to obey (Is 11:14).
מִשְׁלָח mishlāch (5096), Put your hand to (Dt 12:7, 15:10, 28:8).
נָדַח nādhach (5258), Force, put (Dt 20:19).
נוּף nûph (5311), Hiphil: lift up, use (Dt 27:5, Is 11:15).

נָטָה nāṭâh (5371), Extend, stretch out (Is 5:25, 34:11).
נָטַשׁ nāṭash (5389), Went out, went forth (Nm 11:31).
נָפַל nāphal (5489), Fall; hiphil: cause to fall, to sleep (Gn 2:21, Is 34:17).
נָשָׂא nāsā' (5558), Took notice, cast eyes upon (Gn 39:7).
נָתַן nāthan (5598), Lay (a hand) upon (Ex 7:4, Nm 16:47).
עָבַר 'āvar (5882), Sent out, go out (Dt 24:5).
עָלָה 'ālâh (6148), Qal: come upon, wear (Lv 19:19, Nm 19:2); hiphil: cover (Jos 7:6).
פָּרַשׂ pārash (6817), Spread over, stretch out (Nm 4:6ff., Hos 7:12).
קָדַם qādham (7207), Piel: come before (Is 37:33).
שִׂים sîm (7947), Put, set (Ex 5:8, 1 Kgs 20:6 [21:6], Prv 23:2).
שׁוּב shûv (8178), Turn, return; hiphil: turn (Ps 81:14 [80:14]).
שִׁית shîth (8308), Qal: put, set (Gn 48:14, Ex 21:22); hophal: demand, be imposed (Ex 21:30).
שָׁלַח shālach (8365), Stretch out, send (Gn 22:12, 2 Sm 18:12).
שָׁלַךְ shālakh (8390), Hiphil: throw (Ps 108:9 [107:9]).

1. ἐπιβάλλει epiballei 3sing indic pres act
2. ἐπιβάλλον epiballon
   nom/acc sing neu part pres act
3. ἐπέβαλεν epebalen 3sing indic aor act
4. ἐπέβαλον epebalon 3pl indic aor act
5. ἐπιβάλω epibalō 1sing subj aor act
6. ἐπιβαλών epibalōn nom sing masc part aor act
7. ἐπιβαλεῖν epibalein inf aor act
8. ἐπιβαλοῦσιν epibalousin 3pl indic fut act
9. ἐπέβαλλεν epeballen 3sing indic imperf act
10. ἐπιβάλλουσιν epiballousin 3pl indic pres act
11. ἐπέβαλαν epebalan 3pl indic aor act

1	No man putteth a piece of new cloth unto an old .. Matt 9:16
4	Then came they, and laid hands on Jesus, ... 26:50
9	and the waves beat into the ship, ... Mark 4:37
4	cast their garments on him; and he sat upon him. 11:7
10	cast their garments on him; and he sat upon him. 11:7
4	And they laid their hands on him, and took him. 14:46
11	And they laid their hands on him, and took him. 14:46
6	And when he thought thereon, he wept. 14:72
1	putteth a piece of a new garment upon an old; ..... Luke 5:36
6	No man, having put his hand to the plow, ... 9:62
2	give me the portion of goods that falleth to me. 15:12
7	scribes the same hour sought to lay hands on him; ... 20:19
8	before all these, they shall lay their hands on you, ... 21:12
3	but no man laid hands on him, ... John 7:30
3	but no man laid hands on him. 7:44
4	they laid hands on them, and put them in hold ..... Acts 4:3
4	And laid their hands on the apostles, ... 5:18
3	Herod the king stretched forth his hands 12:1
4	stirred up all the people, and laid hands on him, ... 21:27
11	stirred up all the people, and laid hands on him, ... 21:27
5	not that I may cast a snare upon you, ... 1 Co 7:35

Classical Greek

Epiballō is a compound formed from the preposition *epi* (1894), "upon, on," plus the verb *ballō* (900), "throw, cast." In classical writings there exists a wide range of definitions including "beat" (lay on blows) and "throw upon" (one object upon another). Also attested is the idea of "throwing oneself upon," especially in a hostile manner but also in a positive way (see *Liddell-Scott*).

Septuagint Usage

As many as 21 Hebrew terms are rendered by *epiballō* (used over 70 times) alone or in conjunction with other Greek words. Although no single term overwhelmingly stands behind *epiballō*, forms of *shālach*, "stretch out, lay upon," are used more than any other (cf. also *shîth*, "put, set, lay"). The diversity of meaning seen in classical usage is also apparent in the Septuagint.

For example, it is used in the phrase "put a hand to" (something), (Deuteronomy 12:7,18; 15:10). It can also describe "putting something over something else" (Numbers 4:6-8). In another use it reflects the hostile idea of "doing harm." The angel of the Lord called to Abraham, "Lay not thine hand upon the lad" (Genesis 22:12; cf. 2 Samuel 18:12 [LXX 2 Kings 18:12]). In 2 Maccabees it is used of expenses "incurred" (e.g., 3:3; 9:16) or of an "attack" (12:9; cf. 1 Kings 20:6 [LXX 3 Kings 20:6]).

New Testament Usage

Epiballō occurs 18 times in the New Testament. The majority of occurrences are found in the Gospels with Luke having the most instances. It is used in Jesus' sayings about "putting" unshrunk cloth "upon" an old garment (Matthew 9:16; Luke 5:36) and "putting" a hand "to" the plow (Luke 9:62). Intransitively ("without an object") Mark used it of waves which "broke over" the boat in which Jesus and His disciples traveled (Mark 4:37, NIV). Paul spoke of not wanting to "cast a snare upon" the Corinthians (1 Corinthians 7:35; cf. "restrict," NIV).

Frequently the word is used in a hostile sense of the religious leaders who wanted to "seize" Jesus (literally "lay hands upon"; Matthew 26:50; Mark 14:46; Luke 20:19; cf. 21:12; John 7:30,44). This meaning is also attested in Acts of the religious leaders' "seizing" (cf. NIV) Peter and John and putting them in jail (4:3; cf. 5:18; 12:1; 21:27). Implicit in this is the idea of a violent or forceful seizure.

STRONG 1911, BAUER 289-90, MOULTON-MILLIGAN 235, KITTEL 1:528-29, LIDDELL-SCOTT 624.

1897. ἐπιβαρέω epibareō verb

Burden, be heavy upon.
CROSS-REFERENCE:
βαρέω bareō (911)

1. ἐπιβαρῶ epibarō 1sing subj pres act
2. ἐπιβαρῆσαι epibarēsai inf aor act

1 but in part: that I may not **overcharge** you all. . . . . . . 2 Co 2:5
2 we would not be **chargeable** unto any of you, ... 1 Th 2:9
2 that we might not be **chargeable** to any of you: . . . . . 2 Th 3:8

This is a verb from *epi* (1894), "upon," and *bareō* (911), "to burden." Its range of possible meanings include: "be too severe with, weigh down, bear hard upon, overcharge," or "burden." In the papyri the word is used of years, of taxation, and of voyages (cf. *Moulton-Milligan*). The "burden" could be a metaphor for both *trouble* and a *heavy load*. In 2 Corinthians 2:5 it is a "burden of words" that Paul was referring to; he did not want to say too much. In 1 Thessalonians 2:9 and 3:8 it means a "material burden."

STRONG 1912, BAUER 290, MOULTON-MILLIGAN 235, LIDDELL-SCOTT 624, COLIN BROWN 1:261.

1898. ἐπιβιβάζω epibibazō verb

Put on, cause to mount, set upon.
COGNATES:
ἀναβιβάζω anabibazō (305)
ἐμβιβάζω embibazō (1675)
καταβιβάζω katabibazō (2572)
προβιβάζω probibazō (4123)
συμβιβάζω sumbibazō (4673)
τελέω teleō (4903)

דָּרַךְ dārakh (1931), Qal: walk, trample (Hb 3:15); hiphil: enable to go, make walk (Hb 3:19).

יָרַד yāradh (3495), Go down; hiphil: bring down (2 Chr 23:20).

רָכַב rākhav (7680), Hiphil: ride, cause to ride (1 Kgs 1:33, 2 Kgs 13:16, Ps 66:12 [65:12]).

1. ἐπεβίβασαν epebibasan 3pl indic aor act
2. ἐπιβιβάσας epibibasas nom sing masc part aor act
3. ἐπιβιβάσαντες epibibasantes
                nom pl masc part aor act

2 **set** him **on** his own beast, ... brought him to an inn, Luke 10:34
1 garments upon the colt, and they **set** Jesus **thereon**. 19:35
3 provide them beasts, that they **may set** Paul **on**, ... Acts 23:24

This term is rare and when followed by *epi* (1894) could also mean "load upon." This usage can be found in the Apocrypha. The word is used at Luke 19:35 where Jesus was "set thereon" the colt before entering Jerusalem. The only other New Testament uses of *epibibazō*

ἐπιβλέπω **1899**

are found in Luke 10:34 and Acts 23:24 which also refer to someone being "set on" an animal for transport.

STRONG 1913, BAUER 290, LIDDELL-SCOTT 625.

1899. ἐπιβλέπω epiblepō verb
Look at, look, gaze upon.

COGNATE:
βλέπω blepō (984)

SYNONYMS:
ἀναλογίζω analogizō (355)
ἀτενίζω atenizō (810)
ἀφοράω aphoraō (865)
βλέπω blepō (984)
βουλεύομαι bouleuomai (1003)
διαλογίζομαι dialogizomai (1254)
δοκέω dokeō (1374)
εἶδον eidon (1481)
ἐμβλέπω emblepō (1676)
ἐνθυμέομαι enthumeomai (1744)
ἐποπτεύω epopteuō (2013)
ἔχω echō (2174)
ἡγέομαι hēgeomai (2216)
θεάομαι theaomai (2277)
θεωρέω theōreō (2311)
κατανοέω katanoeō (2627)
κρίνω krinō (2892)
λογίζομαι logizomai (3023)
νοέω noeō (3401)
νομίζω nomizō (3406)
ὁράω horaō (3571)
συμβάλλω sumballō (4671)
συμβουλεύω sumbouleuō (4674)
φρονέω phroneō (5262)

אוֹר ʼôr (213), Be bright; hiphil: cause to shine, look with favor (Dn 9:17).

בָּעַט bāʻaṭ (1192), Kick at, scorn (1 Sm 2:29).

בָּקַשׁ bāqash (1272), Piel: sought to, straining to (Zec 6:7).

נָבַט nāvaṭ (5202), Hiphil: look, look out (Gn 19:26, 1 Kgs 19:6, Lam 2:20).

נָהָה nāhâh (5269), Niphal: sought after, lamented after (1 Sm 7:2).

נָטָה nāṭâh (5371), Hiphil: bend down (Hos 11:4).

נָטַף nāṭaph (5382), Hiphil: prophesy against (Ez 20:46, 21:2).

פָּנָה pānâh (6680), Qal: have respect for, look with favor (Lv 26:9, 2 Sm 9:8, Mal 2:13); piel: prepare the way (Mal 3:1); hiphil: turn back, look back (Na 2:8).

צָפָה tsāphâh (7099), Qal: behold, watch (Ps 66:7 [65:7]); piel: watch, wait for (Mi 7:7).

צְפַצְפָה tsaphtsāphāh (7128), Set, planted (Ez 17:5).

רָאָה rāʼâh (7495), See, behold (1 Sm 9:16, Ps 142:4 [141:4], Jer 4:23).

שָׁגַח shāghach (8148), Hiphil: look, watch (Ps 33:14 [32:14]).

שׁוּב shûv (8178), Turn back, return (Zec 1:16—only some Sinaiticus texts).

שׁוּט shûṭ (8198), Polel: look throughout, range throughout (2 Chr 16:9).

שָׁקַף shāqaph (8625), Hiphil: look down (Gn 19:28).

1. ἐπέβλεψεν epeblepsen 3sing indic aor act
2. ἐπιβλέψητε epiblepsēte 2pl subj aor act
3. ἐπίβλεψον epiblepson 2sing impr aor act
4. ἐπιβλέψαι epiblepsai inf aor act

1 **hath regarded** the low estate of his handmaiden: .... Luke 1:48
3 **look** upon my son: for he is mine only child. 9:38
4 **look** upon my son: for he is mine only child. 9:38
2 **have respect** to him that weareth the gay clothing, ... Jas 2:3

Classical Greek
This compound—from the preposition *epi* (1894), "upon, on," and the verb *blepō* (984), "see"—means "look upon," often with the prefix intensifying the verb, "look intently." This is the basic classical use; in addition it can mean "look upon with envy" (*Liddell-Scott*).

Septuagint Usage
In the Septuagint *epiblepō* is rather common, and it translates 15 Hebrew terms. Most often either a form of *pānâh* ("face, from") or *nāvaṭ* ("look at, glance") is behind *epiblepō*. Typically it describes "looking on" something, such as Lot's wife's or Abraham's "looking back" upon Sodom (Genesis 19:26,28; cf. 2 Samuel [LXX 2 Kings] 1:7; 2:20).

It can also describe God's "looking upon" Israel with favor (Leviticus 26:9; cf. 2 Chronicles 6:19; Tobit 3:3; Judith 6:19). The Psalmist cried for God to "look upon" his petitions (Psalms 13:3 [LXX 12:3]; 25:16 [24:16]). This seems to be a favorite word of the Septuagint translators for God's "watching" His people as well as all the peoples of the earth (e.g., also Psalms 33:13,14 [LXX 32:13,14]; 102:19 [101:19]; 104:32 [103:32]; Sirach 23:19). God's very act of "looking upon" His people dispenses mercy and justice; that is, it indicates God's response to their cries for help (cf. Psalms 86:16 [LXX 85:16]; 102:17 [101:17]; Sirach 36:1). Conversely, individuals must "look to" God for mercy and hope (Micah 7:7; Zechariah 12:10). It is this usage which may have affected the New Testament's use of the term.

New Testament Usage
Epiblepō occurs only three times in the New Testament. Two are credited to Luke and one to James. Its use in Luke is similar to that in the Septuagint (see Luke 1:48). God's looking upon the "low estate of his handmaiden" recalls

its usage so common in the Psalms (e.g., Psalm 102:17; cf. 138:6 [not *epiblepō* here]). Luke's telling of the man who begged Jesus to "look upon" his son (implying that this would help) is similar to Septuagintal usage.

James also understood *epiblepō* as a very positive term, although he denounced showing favoritism ("show special attention," NIV) to the wealthy, especially at the expense of the poor (James 2:3).

STRONG 1914, BAUER 290, LIDDELL-SCOTT 625.

1900. ἐπίβλημα epiblēma noun

A patch.
CROSS-REFERENCE:
 βλέπω blepō (984)

מִטְפַּחַת miṭpachath (4441), Claok, mantle (Is 3:22).

1. ἐπίβλημα epiblēma nom/acc sing neu

1 a **piece** of new cloth unto an old garment,..........Matt 9:16
1 seweth a **piece** of new cloth on an old garment:.....Mark 2:21
1 putteth a **piece** of a new garment upon an old;......Luke 5:36
1 and the **piece** that was taken out of the new............5:36

Many ancient writers used this word to describe a piece of clothing used as a covering. At Isaiah 3:22 the word is translated as "mantles," "capes" or "cloaks." In the New Testament the word is translated simply as a "patch" and is used when Jesus referred to sewing unshrunk cloth on a garment (Matthew 9:16; Mark 2:21; Luke 5:36).

STRONG 1915, BAUER 290, MOULTON-MILLIGAN 236, LIDDELL-SCOTT 625.

1901. ἐπιβοάω epiboaō verb

Cry out to or against.
COGNATE:
 βοάω boaō (987)
SYNONYMS:
 ἀναβοάω anaboaō (308)
 ἀνακράζω anakrazō (347)
 βοάω boaō (987)
 ἐπιφωνέω epiphōneō (2003)
 κράζω krazō (2869)
 κραυγάζω kraugazō (2878)
 φωνέω phōneō (5291)

1. ἐπιβοῶντες epiboōntes nom pl masc part pres act

1 **crying** that he ought not to live any longer.........Acts 25:24

This verb is used once in the Apocrypha (Wisdom of Solomon 14:1) of a sailor's "crying out" (in dependence) to his wooden idol and in other ancient writings of an aroused mob (*Bauer*). It could also be translated "raise an outcry by way of complaint" or "exclaim vehemently." In Acts 25:24 it is rendered "crying" and refers to the Jewish community's shouting concerning whether Paul ought to live or die.

STRONG 1916, BAUER 290, MOULTON-MILLIGAN 236, LIDDELL-SCOTT 625.

1902. ἐπιβουλή epiboulē noun

Plot, scheme.
COGNATE:
 βούλομαι boulomai (1007)
SYNONYM:
 ἐνέδρα enedra (1731)

1. ἐπιβουλή epiboulē nom sing fem
2. ἐπιβουλῆς epiboulēs gen sing fem
3. ἐπιβουλαῖς epiboulais dat pl fem

1 But their **laying await** was known of Saul............Acts 9:24
2 And when the Jews **laid wait** for him, (NT)...........20:3
3 which befell me by the **lying in wait** of the Jews:......20:19
2 told me how that the Jews **laid wait** for the man,......23:30

This noun denotes "a plan" (*boulē* [1005]) "against" (*epi* [1894]). In the Septuagint (including the Apocrypha) the noun refers to a "plot." It is usually a plot against someone. Each of the four New Testament occurrences in Acts refers to the plots of the Jews directed against Paul (Acts 9:24; 20:3,19; 23:30).

STRONG 1917, BAUER 290, MOULTON-MILLIGAN 236, LIDDELL-SCOTT 626, COLIN BROWN 3:468.

1903. ἐπιγαμβρεύω epigambreuō verb

Become kin through marriage.

חָתַן chāthan (2967), Hithpael: joined by marriage, related by marriage (1 Sm 18:22f., 2 Chr 18:1).

יָבַם yāvam (3101), Piel: marry (Gn 38:8—Sixtine edition only).

1. ἐπιγαμβρεύσει epigambreusei 3sing indic fut act

1 his brother **shall marry** his wife, and raise up seed Matt 22:24

This verb is a term meaning "become related by marriage." In the Septuagint it is translated "become son-in-law." It refers to marrying the next of kin, usually the brother-in-law of a levirate marriage. In the New Testament it occurs at Matthew 22:24 where the Sadducees questioned Jesus concerning the Mosaic marriage law of marrying a deceased brother's wife.

ἐπίγειος 1904
STRONG 1918, BAUER 290, MOULTON-MILLIGAN 236, LIDDELL-SCOTT 626.

1904. ἐπίγειος epigeios adj
Earthly, worldly.
CROSS-REFERENCE:
γῆ gē (1087)

1. ἐπιγείων epigeiōn gen pl masc/neu
2. ἐπίγειος epigeios nom sing fem
3. ἐπίγεια epigeia nom/acc pl neu

3	If I have told you **earthly things**,	John 3:12
3	are also celestial bodies, and bodies **terrestrial**:	1 Co 15:40
1	and the glory of the **terrestrial** is another.	15:40
2	**earthly** house of this tabernacle were dissolved,	2 Co 5:1
1	of things in heaven, and **things in earth**,	Phlp 2:10
3	glory is in their shame, who mind **earthly things**.	3:19
2	not from above, but is **earthly**, sensual, devilish.	Jas 3:15

Classical Greek
In classical Greek *epigeios*—from *epi* (1894), "on, upon," and *gē* (1087), "earth" (in contrast to "heaven") or "land"—means "earthly" or "terrestrial." Josephus used it twice of "earthly" creatures (i.e., "beasts"; *Antiquities* 6.9.4; 8.2.5). The Testament of Judah contrasts the "earthly matters" of a king with the "heavenly matters" of a priest (21:3). (See also references to Plato and Plutarch; cf. Sasse, "epigeios," *Kittel*, 1:680f.) The word does not occur in the Septuagint.

New Testament Usage
The seven New Testament instances of *epigeios* reflect a dualism between the "heavenly" and the "earthly." John (3:12) records Jesus' comments to Nicodemus that he would hardly believe "heavenly things" (*ta epourania*) since he did not believe the "earthly things" (*ta epigeia*) which Jesus had just told him. Such a contrast is not necessarily disparaging of earthly matters. The same can be said of its use in 1 Corinthians (e.g., 15:40; at the same time, the contrast is developed to highlight the superiority of the heavenly; cf. 1 Corinthians 15:42-44,47,48). In other texts "earthly" carries a definitely inferior meaning and suggests "worldly" or "sinful" or "fleshly" passions (Philippians 3:19; James 3:15). The temporal contrast between heaven as eternal and earth as temporal (intimated in 1 Corinthians 15:40) is illustrated in 2 Corinthians 5:1 (our "earthly house" [our body]). The usage in Philippians 2:10 reveals an expression used to encompass every aspect of creation, "in heaven, and . . . in earth (*epigeiōn*), and . . . under the earth," which will confess Jesus is Lord.

STRONG 1919, BAUER 290, MOULTON-MILLIGAN 236, KITTEL 1:680-81, LIDDELL-SCOTT 627, COLIN BROWN 1:517-18.

1905. ἐπιγίνομαι epiginomai verb
Come up, arise, spring up, arrive upon.
CROSS-REFERENCE:
γίνομαι ginomai (1090)

1. ἐπιγενομένου epigenomenou
   gen sing masc part aor mid
1 and after one day the south wind blew, ... Acts 28:13

The use of this verb in classical writings, papyri, and the Septuagint refers to the wind "coming up." Ancient writers also used this verb to refer to the "coming on" of the night. In the papyri *epiginomai* is a common reference to time. In a certain papyrus "the verb is used of lambs 'born after' a first registration" (*Moulton-Milligan*). In the New Testament the verb is used in Acts 28:13 to refer to the south wind "coming up."

STRONG 1920, BAUER 290, MOULTON-MILLIGAN 236, LIDDELL-SCOTT 627 (see "epigignomai").

1906. ἐπιγινώσκω epiginōskō verb
Know exactly, completely; know again, recognize, acknowledge; learn, find out, ascertain, perceive, understand.
COGNATE:
γινώσκω ginōskō (1091)
SYNONYMS:
αἰσθάνομαι aisthanomai (143)
ἀντιλαμβάνομαι antilambanomai (479)
βλέπω blepō (984)
γινώσκω ginōskō (1091)
γνωρίζω gnōrizō (1101)
εἶδον eidon (1481)
ἐπίσταμαι epistamai (1971)
θεωρέω theōreō (2311)
καταλαμβάνω katalambanō (2608)
καταμανθάνω katamanthanō (2618)
κατανοέω katanoeō (2627)
νοέω noeō (3401)
οἶδα oida (3471)
ὁράω horaō (3571)
παρακολουθέω parakoloutheō (3738)
σκοπέω skopeō (4503)
συνίημι suniēmi (4770)

בִּין bîn (1032), Hiphil: give thought to, understand (Prv 14:8); hithpolel: consider, understand (Jer 30:24 [37:24]—Codex Sinaiticus only).

יָדַע yādha' (3156), Qal: know, find out (Gn 31:32, Ru 3:18, Hos 5:4); niphal: be known, remembered (Gn 41:31); hiphil: make known (Hb 3:2).

ἐπιγινώσκω 1906

יָדַע yᵉdhaʿ (A3157), Know (Dn 4:32 [4:29], 6:10—Aramaic).

נָכַר nākhar (5421), Niphal: be recognized (Lam 4:8); hiphil: recognize, know (Gn 27:23, Neh 6:12, Is 61:9).

רָאָה rāʾâh (7495), See (Est 3:5).

שָׂכַל sākhal (7959), Hiphil: consider, regard (Jb 34:27).

1. ἐπιγινώσκετε epiginōskete 2pl indic/impr pres act
2. ἐπιγινώσκεις epiginōskeis 2sing indic pres act
3. ἐπιγινώσκει epiginōskei 3sing indic pres act
4. ἐπιγινωσκέτω epiginōsketō 3sing impr pres act
5. ἐπέγνωτε epegnōte 2pl indic aor act
6. ἐπέγνωσαν epegnōsan 3pl indic aor act
7. ἐπιγνῷς epignōs 2sing subj aor act
8. ἐπιγνῷ epignō 3sing subj aor act
9. ἐπιγνούς epignous nom sing masc part aor act
10. ἐπιγνόντες epignontes nom pl masc part aor act
11. ἐπιγνόντων epignontōn gen pl masc part aor act
12. ἐπιγνοῦσιν epignousin dat pl masc part aor act
13. ἐπιγνοῦσα epignousa nom sing fem part aor act
14. ἐπιγνῶναι epignōnai inf aor act
15. ἐπεγνωκόσιν epegnōkosin dat pl masc part perf act
16. ἐπεγνωκέναι epegnōkenai inf perf act
17. ἐπεγίνωσκον epeginōskon 3pl indic imperf act
18. ἐπιγινωσκόμενοι epiginōskomenoi nom pl masc part pres mid
19. ἐπεγνώσθην epegnōsthēn 1sing indic aor pass
20. ἐπιγνώσομαι epignōsomai 1sing indic fut mid
21. ἐπιγνώσεσθε epignōsesthe 2pl indic fut mid
22. ἐπέγνωμεν epegnōmen 1pl indic aor act
23. ἐπεγνωκόσι epegnōkosi dat pl masc part perf act

21	Ye shall know them by their fruits.	Matt 7:16
21	Wherefore by their fruits ye shall know them.	7:20
3	and no man knoweth the Son, but the Father;	11:27
3	neither knoweth any man the Father, save the Son,	11:27
10	when the men of that place had knowledge of him,	14:35
6	Elias is come already, and they knew him not,	17:12
9	immediately when Jesus perceived in his spirit	Mark 2:8
9	knowing in himself that virtue had gone out	5:30
6	people saw them departing, and many knew him,	6:33
10	come out of the ship, straightway they knew him,	6:54
7	thou mightest know the certainty of those things,	Luke 1:4
6	perceived that he had seen a vision in the temple:	1:22
9	But when Jesus perceived their thoughts,	5:22
13	when she knew that Jesus sat at meat	7:37
9	knew that he belonged unto Herod's jurisdiction,	23:7
14	eyes were holden that they should not know him.	24:16
6	And their eyes were opened, and they knew him;	24:31
17	And they knew that it was he which sat for alms	Acts 3:10
17	they marvelled; and they took knowledge of them,	4:13
10	Which when the brethren knew,	9:30
13	And when she knew Peter's voice,	12:14
11	But when they knew that he was a Jew,	19:34
10	But when they knew that he was a Jew,	19:34
8	might know wherefore they cried so against him.	22:24
9	was afraid, after he knew that he was a Roman,	22:29
14	I wanted to know why they were accusing (NIV)	23:28
14	examining of whom thyself mayest take knowledge	24:8
14	You can easily verify (NIV)	24:11
2	have I done no wrong, as thou very well knowest.	25:10
17	And when it was day, they knew not the land:	27:39
6	then they knew that the island was called Melita	Acts 28:1
22	we found out that the island was called (NIV)	28:1
10	Who knowing the judgment of God,	Rom 1:32
20	but then shall I know even as also I am known	1 Co 13:12
19	but then shall I know even as also I am known.	13:12
4	acknowledge that the things that I write unto you	14:37
1	therefore acknowledge ye them that are such.	16:18
1	than what ye read or acknowledge;	2 Co 1:13
21	and I trust ye shall acknowledge even to the end;	1:13
5	As also ye have acknowledged us in part,	1:14
18	As unknown, and yet well known;	6:9
1	Know ye not your own selves,	13:5
5	and knew the grace of God in truth:	Col 1:6
15	of them which believe and know the truth.	1 Tm 4:3
16	not to have known the way of righteousness,	2 Pt 2:21
12	than, after they have known it, to turn from	2:21

Classical Greek

Epiginōskō is a compound from *epi* (1894) *ginōskō* (1091), "I know." For the most part it overlaps significantly with *ginōskō*, but in a finer sense it can mean "to observe" (visually), "to look up," hence "to recognize." Classical usage also attests to meanings of "to discover" and "to resolve, decide" (*Liddell-Scott*). *Moulton-Milligan* defines *epiginōskō* as "knowing arrived at by the attention being directed to (*epi*) a particular person or object."

Septuagint Usage

The overlap between *epiginōskō* and *ginōskō* is supported by the Septuagintal usage of the terms. Both translate the Hebrew *bîn*, *yādhaʿ*, (qal, niphal, hiphil), *nākhar*, *rāʾâh*, and the Aramaic *yᵉdhaʿ*. Also, manuscripts (especially Alexandrinus) vary readings of *epiginōskō/ginōskō* (e.g., Exodus 14:4; Deuteronomy 33:9; 1 Kings 20:41 [LXX 3 Kings 20:41]; Wisdom of Solomon 5:7).

The visual sense of "to recognize" is common (e.g., Genesis 27:23; 37:32,33; Ruth 3:14; 1 Kings 20:41 [LXX 3 Kings 20:41]), as is "to recognize" by other means (1 Samuel 26:17 [LXX 1 Kings 26:17], a voice; Sirach 9:13; 12:12). "To acknowledge" or "to show partiality" is another definition (e.g., Deuteronomy 1:17; Ruth 2:10,19). "To know" in the sense of intimate or religious knowledge is conveyed (e.g., Job 24:13; 34:27; Psalm 79:8 [LXX 78:6]; Hosea 2:20; Sirach 23:27). *Epiginōskō* may refer to God's ability "to know" (Sirach 15:19; 18:12). A striking refrain occurs in Ezekiel: "Ye/they shall know (*epiginosesthe/epiginosontai*) that I am (*egō*) the Lord" (e.g., Ezekiel 5:13; 6:7,10).

New Testament Usage

Epiginōskō occurs over 40 times in the Greek New Testament. In the Gospels it is found only in the Synoptic Evangelists (17 times). (John apparently preferred *ginōskō* [over 50 times].)

Mark is followed by Matthew only once (Mark 6:54, parallel Matthew 14:35) and by Luke only once (Mark 2:8, parallel Luke 5:22). Matthew reads *epiginōskō* once in a parallel passage where, except for Luke's reading of *ginōskō*, the wording is almost identical (Matthew 11:27, parallel Luke 10:22). Thus there is further evidence that the two terms demonstrate great semantic overlap. Luke regularly equated *epiginōskō* with visual recognition (Luke 24:16,31; cf. Matthew 14:35; Mark 6:33) and mental knowledge (Luke 1:4,22; 7:37; 23:7; cf. Matthew 7:16,20).

Luke used *epiginōskō* in Acts (11 times; *ginōskō* 16 times). He repeatedly used it as a term for recognition (Acts 3:10; 4:13; 12:14; 19:34), and he employed it for the gaining of mental knowledge (9:30; 23:28; 28:1).

Paul used *epiginōskō* and *ginōskō* interchangably on a number of occasions (of mental or spiritual "knowing"; Romans 1:32; 1 Corinthians 13:12; 2 Corinthians 1:13,14; 6:9; 13:5; 1 Timothy 4:3; cf. 2 Peter 2:21). The word can imply mental acknowledgment (1 Corinthians 14:37) or, as is seen in the Septuagint, *epiginōskō* can be read as "to show partiality" (1 Corinthians 16:18).

It is doubtful that *epiginōskō* played any role in alleged Gnostic heresies in the Early Church, although the same may not be true for the substantive *epignōsis*, which may be an anti-Gnostic device. This may be especially true in 2 Peter which uses the verb twice in reference to correct knowledge of God and which employs the noun four times (cf. also 2 Peter's use of *ginōskō* [1091] and *gnōsis* [1102] and the word studies on the same).

(See also Schmitz, "Knowledge," *Colin Brown*, 2:392-406; Bultmann, "ginōskō," *Kittel*, 1:713f.)

STRONG 1921, BAUER 291, MOULTON-MILLIGAN 236-37, KITTEL 1:689-714, LIDDELL-SCOTT 627, COLIN BROWN 2:392,397-99.

1907. ἐπίγνωσις epignōsis noun
Knowledge, recognition, consciousness.
COGNATE:
  γινώσκω ginōskō (1091)
SYNONYMS:
  γνῶσις gnōsis (1102)
  ἔννοια ennoia (1755)
דַּעַת da‛ath (1907), Knowledge, insight (Prv 2:5, Hos 4:1,6).

1. ἐπίγνωσις epignōsis nom sing fem
2. ἐπιγνώσεως epignōseōs gen sing fem
3. ἐπιγνώσει epignōsei dat sing fem
4. ἐπίγνωσιν epignōsin acc sing fem

3	they did not like to retain God in their **knowledge**,..	Rom 1:28
1	for by the law is the **knowledge** of sin.................	3:20
4	a zeal of God, but not according to **knowledge**.........	10:2
3	and revelation in the **knowledge** of him:.............	Eph 1:17
2	and of the **knowledge** of the Son of God,...............	4:13
3	more and more in **knowledge** and in all judgment;...	Phlp 1:9
4	ye might be filled with the **knowledge** of his will.....	Col 1:9
4	and increasing in the **knowledge** of God;...............	1:10
3	and increasing in the **knowledge** of God;...............	1:10
4	to the **acknowledgment** of the mystery of God,.........	2:2
4	the new man, which is renewed in **knowledge**...........	3:10
4	and to come unto the **knowledge** of the truth.......	1 Tm 2:4
4	repentance to the **acknowledging** of the truth;......	2 Tm 2:25
4	never able to come to the **knowledge** of the truth.......	3:7
4	of God's elect, and the **acknowledging** of the truth....	Tit 1:1
3	by the **acknowledging** of every good thing..........	Phlm 1:6
4	that we have received the **knowledge** of the truth,..	Heb 10:26
3	Grace and peace ... through the **knowledge** of God,..	2 Pt 1:2
2	through the **knowledge** of him that hath called us.......	1:3
4	nor unfruitful in the **knowledge** of our Lord Jesus.......	1:8
3	**knowledge** of the Lord and Saviour Jesus Christ,........	2:20

Classical Greek
Among classical writers the primary use of *epignōsis* was to denote "recognition, knowledge." *Epignōsis* and *gnōsis* (1102) demonstrate significant semantic overlap. It should be remembered that for the Greek "knowledge" was chiefly an objective, verifiable experience (Bultmann, "ginōskō," *Kittel*, 1:691).

Septuagint Usage
The close relationship between *epignōsis* and *gnōsis* is apparent from the Septuagint, which uses both terms to translate the Hebrew term *da‛ath* as "knowledge, ability, discernment" (cf. 1 Kings 7:14 [LXX 3 Kings 7:14]; Ecclesiastes 1:17). However, *epignōsis* appears only eight times (if all variant readings are accepted). *Epignōsis* refers to the skill of a craftsman (1 Kings 7:14 [LXX 3 Kings 7:14]), but it especially describes the "knowledge" or "recognition" of God (Judith 9:14; Proverbs 2:5; Hosea 4:1; 6:6).

New Testament Usage
In the New Testament *epignōsis* is especially a Pauline term occurring elsewhere only in Hebrews and 2 Peter (four times). Paul employed *epignōsis* in a religious sense most frequently. Negatively, "consciousness" (cf. NIV) of sin comes through the Law (Romans 3:20). One can (or cannot) have "knowledge" of God (Romans 1:28; 10:2), His Son (Ephesians 4:13), and His will (Colossians 1:9).

"Knowledge" of the truth is synonymous with salvation (1 Timothy 2:4; cf. 2 Timothy 2:25; 3:7; Titus 1:1; cf. Hebrews 10:26). Second Peter likewise refers to "knowledge" of God (2 Peter 1:2,3) and Christ (1:8; 2:20). Such knowledge comes via the Holy Spirit (Ephesians 1:17) and contributes to spiritual growth (Colossians 3:10; cf. 2 Peter 1:2-8).

Strong 1922, Bauer 291, Moulton-Milligan 237, Kittel 1:689-714, Liddell-Scott 627, Colin Brown 2:392,397,400-401,403,405.

1908. ἐπιγραφή epigraphē noun
Inscription, title.
Cross-Reference:
γράφω graphō (1119)

1. ἐπιγραφή epigraphē nom sing fem
2. ἐπιγραφήν epigraphēn acc sing fem

1 Whose is this image and **superscription**?		Matt 22:20
1 Whose is this image and **superscription**?		Mark 12:16
1 **superscription** of his accusation was written over,		15:26
2 a penny. Whose image and **superscription** hath it?		Luke 20:24
1 And a **superscription** also was written over him		23:38

This noun, a compound of *epi* (1894), "upon," and *graphē* (1118), "writing," is translated "writing upon" or "inscription." In the papyri the word is used of a mark or title of honor (cf. *Moulton-Milligan*). In the New Testament the word can be used of the legends on coins (Matthew 22:20; Mark 12:16; Luke 20:24) or of the title fastened on a cross showing the cause of the criminal's condemnation (Mark 15:26).

Strong 1923, Bauer 291, Moulton-Milligan 237, Liddell-Scott 628, Colin Brown 3:489.

1909. ἐπιγράφω epigraphō verb
Write on or in, inscribe.
Cross-Reference:
γράφω graphō (1119)

כָּתַב kāthav (3918), Write, record (Nm 17:2, Prv 7:3).

1. ἐπιγράψω epigrapsō 1sing indic fut act
2. ἐπεγέγραπτο epegegrapto 3sing indic plperf pass
3. ἐπιγεγραμμένη epigegrammenē
   nom sing fem part perf mid
4. ἐπιγεγραμμένα epigegrammena
   nom/acc pl neu part perf mid

3 **superscription** of his accusation **was written** over,		Mark 15:26
2 I found an altar with this **inscription**,		Acts 17:23
1 and **write** them in their hearts:		Heb 8:10
1 and in their minds will I **write** them;		10:16
4 had twelve gates, ... and names **written** thereon,		Rev 21:12

Classical Greek
This compound from the preposition *epi* (1894), "upon, on," and *graphō* (1119), "write, mark," means "mark upon, inscribe." Other uses of the term include "sign, register, address." As a legal technical term it can mean "set down" (in an indictment), "register, assess." Also it is used of "ascribing" or "claiming" credit for something (cf. *Liddell-Scott*).

Septuagint Usage
Seven instances of *epigraphō* are recorded in the Septuagint, but only five of these have a Hebrew counterpart (despite the fact that all seven appear in canonical books). The corresponding Hebrew word in each instance is *kāthav*, "write." Twice it refers to the names of the 12 leaders which were written upon their staffs (Numbers 17:2,3 [used with *epi*]). The image of the heart as a tablet upon which ordinances are "written" was familiar to the author of Proverbs (7:3) as well as to Jeremiah, who wrote of a new covenant written upon hearts instead of on tables of stone (31:33). Similarly Isaiah 44:5 tells of an outpouring of the Spirit when men will write upon their hands "the Lord's" as an indication of their allegiance to God.

New Testament Usage
Only five texts read *epigraphō* in the New Testament. Mark used it of the "inscription" (*epigraphē*) which was "written over" Jesus' head at the Crucifixion (15:26; cf. Matthew's reading of *graphō* and John 19:19). In Acts 17:23 the word refers to an inscription on the pagan altar in Athens. In Revelation 21:12 it speaks of the names of the 12 tribes "written thereon" the gates of the heavenly city.

The Book of Hebrews cites Jeremiah 31:33 and specifically applies that passage to the new covenant ushered in by Jesus' death on the cross (cf. 8:10; 10:16). The covenant of the Spirit is written in the believer's heart, not in books of rules or tablets of stone.

Strong 1924, Bauer 291, Moulton-Milligan 237, Liddell-Scott 628, Colin Brown 3:489-90.

1910. ἐπιδείκνυμι epideiknumi verb
Show, point out, demonstrate, exhibit.
Cognate:
δείκνυμι deiknumi (1161)
Synonyms:
ἀποδείκνυμι apodeiknumi (579)
δείκνυμι deiknumi (1161)
δηλόω dēloō (1207)
ἐλέγχω elenchō (1638)
ἐνδείκνυμι endeiknumi (1715)

ἐπιφαίνω epiphainō (1998)
ὑποδείκνυμι hupodeiknumi (5101)
ὑποτίθημι hupotithēmi (5132)
φανερόω phaneroō (5157)

בּוֹא bô' (971), Go, come; hiphil: bring (Is 37:26).

פּוּחַ pûach (6558), Hiphil: speak, give testimony (Prv 12:17).

1. ἐπιδεικνύς epideiknus nom sing masc part pres act
2. ἐπέδειξεν epedeixen 3sing indic aor act
3. ἐπιδείξατε epideixate 2pl impr aor act
4. ἐπιδεῖξαι epideixai inf aor act
5. ἐπιδεικνύμεναι epideiknumenai
   nom pl fem part pres mid

4 that he would **show** them a sign from heaven	Matt 16:1
3 **Show** me the tribute money	22:19
4 **to show** him the buildings of the temple	24:1
3 Go **show** yourselves unto the priests	Luke 17:14
3 **Show** me a penny. Whose image and	20:24
2 he **showed** them his hands and his feet	24:40
5 and **showing** the coats and garments	Acts 9:39
1 **showing** by the scriptures that Jesus was Christ	18:28
4 willing more abundantly **to show** unto the heirs	Heb 6:17

Classical Greek
The preposition *epi* (1894) and the verb *deiknumi* (1161), "show," combine to make *epideiknumi*. The intensive force of the preposition results in the meaning "exhibit" or "display" in a general sense. Other classical uses involve "pointing out"; the emphatic form can also mean "prove" (through demonstration), "demonstrate" (cf. *Liddell-Scott*).

Septuagint Usage
In the Septuagint *epideiknumi* translates two Hebrew words in the only two texts with a Hebrew counterpart (Proverbs 12:17; Isaiah 37:26). The remaining 17 instances occur in apocryphal material or in texts lacking a corresponding Hebrew word (e.g., Esther 2:3). "Explain" seems to be the sense in Tobit 4:20 (Codex B), while "be an example" should perhaps be understood in Judith 8:24. To "show" the blessing of the Lord the congregation bows down in worship (Sirach 50:21 [the RSV curiously translates this "receive"]).

New Testament Usage
The New Testament's use of *epideiknumi* is restricted to nine texts: three belong to Matthew, five to Luke (two in Acts), and one to the author of Hebrews. The Pharisees and Sadducees tested Jesus by asking Him to "show" them a sign from heaven (Matthew 16:1). They wanted Jesus to "prove" (through a miracle) that He was who He claimed to be. Their request categorized them as sign seekers who would never be given a sign except that of Jonah (verse 4). On the other hand, in Luke's Gospel (17:14) Jesus' command to the lepers to "Go 'show' yourselves unto the priests" seems more intended to be "proof" for the priests (cf. Mark 1:44, "for a testimony unto [*eis* (1506B), witness against] them").

"To point out" is the idea in Matthew 24:1 (Luke's account reads simply "behold," a request made by the disciples rather than a setting recalled by the evangelist). "Display" or "show" is the idea in Acts 9:39, but in 18:28 the record says Apollos "proved" (was "showing," KJV) from the Scriptures that Jesus is the Messiah. "To make very clear" is the NIV's understanding of *epideiknumi* in Hebrews 6:17. The context of promise and covenant recalls the legal idea of "prove" or "demonstrate." In any case, God "demonstrated" the certainty of His promises by affirming an oath by himself (6:14ff.).

STRONG 1925, BAUER 291-92, MOULTON-MILLIGAN 237, LIDDELL-SCOTT 629.

1911. ἐπιδέχομαι epidechomai verb
Welcome, receive hospitably, admit, accept.

COGNATE:
δέχομαι dechomai (1203)

SYNONYMS:
ἀναδέχομαι anadechomai (322)
ἀποδέχομαι apodechomai (583)
ἀπολαμβάνω apolambanō (612)
δέχομαι dechomai (1203)
εἰσδέχομαι eisdechomai (1509)
κομίζω komizō (2837)
λαμβάνω lambanō (2956)
μεταλαμβάνω metalambanō (3205)
παραδέχομαι paradechomai (3720)
παραλαμβάνω paralambanō (3741)
προσδέχομαι prosdechomai (4185)
προσλαμβάνω proslambanō (4213)
ὑποδέχομαι hupodechomai (5103)
ὑπολαμβάνω hupolambanō (5112)

1. ἐπιδέχεται epidechetai 3sing indic pres mid

1 but Diotrephes, ... **receiveth** us not	3 Jn 1:9
1 neither doth he himself **receive** the brethren	1:10

This verb comes from *epi* (1894), "up," and *dechomai* (1203), "receive." It has two uses. The first is to "receive someone as a guest." This usage can be found in the papyri, the classical writings, and the Septuagint. The second use means "accept" and "not reject." This usage can be found in the Apocrypha and the classical writings. *Epidechomai* is used in the papyri referring to "accepting" the terms of a lease and of taxes (cf. *Moulton-Milligan*). This second usage of the verb is found in the New

Testament at 3 John 9,10 where it is negatively applied to Diotrephes who refused to accept "the brethren." His lack of hospitality toward those who labor in the church was strongly condemned.

STRONG 1926, BAUER 292, MOULTON-MILLIGAN 237, LIDDELL-SCOTT 630.

1912. ἐπιδημέω epidēmeō verb

Visit, sojourn, reside in (temporarily), make oneself at home in.

CROSS-REFERENCE:
δῆμος dēmos (1211B)

1. ἐπιδημοῦντες epidēmountes
nom pl masc part pres act

1 and strangers of Rome, Jews and proselytes,	Acts 2:10
1 which were there spent their time in nothing else,	17:21

The meaning of this word is well documented in early Greek literature since the Fifth Century B.C. It describes how a stranger or visitor may temporarily "dwell" in a place. It is not used in the Septuagint, but in Acts 2:10 the word is used of Romans who were visiting Jerusalem at the time of Pentecost. Acts 17:21 tells of Paul's interaction with the Athenian philosophers and "strangers *which were there.*"

STRONG 1927, BAUER 292, MOULTON-MILLIGAN 237-38, LIDDELL-SCOTT 630.

1913. ἐπιδιατάσσομαι
epidiatassomai verb

Make additions to, to ordain besides.
CROSS-REFERENCE:
τάσσω tassō (4872)

1. ἐπιδιατάσσεται epidiatassetai 3sing indic pres mid

1 no man disannulleth, or addeth thereto.	Gal 3:15

This compound term (comprised of *epi* [1894], *dia* [1217], and *tassō* [4872], "order, place in a fixed spot") is a technical term found only in Christian writings. In its only New Testament usage (Galatians 3:15) it means "to make an addition to a will." When Paul discussed the relation between the Promise and the Law in Galatians 3:15ff., he introduced an illustration from ordinary human experience and compared the promise of God to Abraham with the covenant of a man, i.e., a "will." The many legal terms used in the passage make it clear that Paul was using the word in the sense of Hellenistic law. This illustration from the legal field throws credible light on God's dealings throughout the history of redemption. As a valid will cannot be contested or altered by additions, so the promise of God which is His original "testament" cannot be invalidated by the Law.

STRONG 1928, BAUER 292, MOULTON-MILLIGAN 238, LIDDELL-SCOTT 630.

1914. ἐπιδίδωμι epididōmi verb

Give, hand over, deliver, give up.
COGNATE:
δίδωμι didōmi (1319)
SYNONYMS:
ἀναδίδωμι anadidōmi (323)
ἀποδίδωμι apodidōmi (586)
διαδίδωμι diadidōmi (1233)
δίδωμι didōmi (1319)
δωρέομαι dōreomai (1426)
ἐπιφέρω epipherō (2002)
ἐπιχορηγέω epichorēgeō (2007)
κοινωνέω koinōneō (2814)
μεταδίδωμι metadidōmi (3200)
παραβάλλω paraballō (3708)
παραδίδωμι paradidōmi (3722)
παρέχω parechō (3792)
προστίθημι prostithēmi (4227)
χαρίζομαι charizomai (5319)

בּוֹא bô' (971), Qal: was brought, was reported (Est 9:11); hiphil: bring (Am 4:1).

מוּת mûth (4322), Die; polel: kill (1 Sm 14:13).

נָתַן nāthan (5598), Give, bear (Gn 49:21).

1. ἐπέδωκαν epedōkan 3pl indic aor act
2. ἐπιδόντες epidontes nom pl masc part aor act
3. ἐπιδώσω epidōsō 1sing indic fut act
4. ἐπιδώσει epidōsei 3sing indic fut act
5. ἐπεδίδου epedidou 3sing indic imperf act
6. ἐπεδόθη epedothē 3sing indic aor pass

4 if his son ask bread, will he give him a stone?	Matt 7:9
4 Or if he ask a fish, will he give him a serpent?	7:10
6 And there was delivered unto him the book	Luke 4:17
4 a son shall ask bread ... will he give him a stone?	11:11
4 will he for a fish give him a serpent?	11:11
4 if he shall ask an egg, will he offer him a scorpion?	11:12
5 and blessed it, and brake, and gave to them	24:30
1 And they gave him a piece of a broiled fish,	24:42
3 He it is, to whom I shall give a sop,	John 13:26
1 they delivered the epistle:	Acts 15:30
2 not bear up into the wind, we let her drive. (NT)	27:15

Classical Greek

The preposition *epi* (1894), "upon, on, over on," and the verb *didōmi* (1319), "give," combine to form the verb *epididōmi*, which in classical writings has the meanings of "give, bestow" (often in a positive sense) as well as "hand over, deliver, offer (in a bribe)." In other circumstances the idea behind *epididōmi* was intransitive (lacking an object). Here it could mean "increase, advance" (see *Liddell-Scott*).

Septuagint Usage
Occurring infrequently in the Septuagint (16 times) *epididōmi* has no exact Hebrew counterpart. Three Hebrew terms stand behind the five texts with Hebrew originals. They describe the kind of "giving" that takes place in birth (Genesis 49:21), the "giving" of one's attention (1 Esdras 9:41), or the "giving" of information (Esther 9:11). The author of Sirach used it in a more theological vein of the giving of one's self (*psuchē* [5425] or *kardia* [2559]) to the pursuit of Wisdom and the things of God (6:32; cf. 38:30,34; 39:5).

New Testament Usage
Epididōmi finds only limited use in the New Testament. All but 5 of its 11 appearances come from Luke, but the 2 in Matthew are paralleled in Luke (cf. Matthew 7:9,10; Luke 11:11,12). Some manuscripts read *epididōmi* twice in Luke 11:11. To "give" something, such as a book (Luke 4:17), a stone (Luke 11:11 with parallels), or bread (Luke 24:30; cf. verse 42), is the common usage. It is used of "giving in to" the force of the wind in Acts 27:15.

STRONG 1929, BAUER 292, MOULTON-MILLIGAN 238, LIDDELL-SCOTT 630-31.

1915. ἐπιδιορθόω epidiorthoō verb
Correct (in addition).
CROSS-REFERENCE:
  ὀρθός orthos (3580)

1. ἐπιδιορθώσῃ epidiorthōsē 2sing subj aor mid
2. ἐπιδιορθώσῃς epidiorthōsēs 2sing subj aor act

1 shouldest set in order the things that are wanting,.....Tit 1:5
2 shouldest set in order the things that are wanting,....... 1:5

This verb, meaning "to set in order" or "correct" is confined to Titus 1:5 in the New Testament. Literally it means "set right" or "correct in addition to what has already been corrected."

STRONG 1930, BAUER 292, MOULTON-MILLIGAN 238, LIDDELL-SCOTT 631.

1916. ἐπιδύω epiduō verb
Set (of the sun).

בּוֹא bô' (971), Go down (Dt 24:15, Jos 8:29, Jer 15:9).

1. ἐπιδυέτω epiduetō 3sing impr pres act

1 let not the sun go down upon your wrath:........... Eph 4:26

This word means "set (upon) of the sun" and is confined to only one usage in the New Testament. It is related to *dunō* (1410), "to sink into," which is also used of the setting of the sun (cf. Mark 1:32; Luke 4:40). According to Vine, the sun, moon, and stars are described as "sinking into the sea" when they set (*Expository Dictionary*, "Set"). Paul used the word in Ephesians 4:26, "*Let not* the sun *go down* upon your wrath," perhaps in reference to the Mosaic law (Deuteronomy 24:13,15) where all "transactions" between two or more parties were to be settled before sundown. Paul was not referring to simple business matters or disputes but to exasperating anger between people that could easily degenerate to bitterness and sin if allowed to simmer overnight.

STRONG 1931, BAUER 292, LIDDELL-SCOTT 632.

1917. ἐπιείκεια epieikeia noun
Gentleness, graciousness, clemency.
COGNATE:
  ἐπιεικής epieikēs (1918)
SYNONYM:
  πραΰτης prautēs (4099)

שְׁלֵוָה sh°lēwāh (A8359), Prosperity (Dn 4:27 [4:24]—Aramaic).

1. ἐπιεικείας epieikeias gen sing fem
2. ἐπιεικείᾳ epieikeia dat sing fem

2 wouldest hear us of thy **clemency** a few words......Acts 24:4
1 by the meekness and **gentleness** of Christ,......... 2 Co 10:1

In 2 Corinthians 10:1 *epieikeia* refers to the "gentleness" of Christ as a model for Paul and the Christian community. As the governor, Felix was urged to manifest a "clemency" corresponding to his high office (Acts 24:4). Likewise, Christians should show *epieikeia* in virtue of their heavenly calling given to them by God. In its broadest sense the word can also mean a "temperate mode of life."

STRONG 1932, BAUER 292, MOULTON-MILLIGAN 238, KITTEL 2:588-90, LIDDELL-SCOTT 632, COLIN BROWN 2:256-59.

1918. ἐπιεικής epieikēs adj
Fitting, yielding, gentle.

COGNATE:
ἐπιείκεια epieikeia (1917)

SYNONYM:
ἤπιος ēpios (2239)

סַלָּח ṣallāch (5740), Mercy (Ps 86:5 [85:5]).

1. ἐπιεικῇ epieikē acc sing masc
2. ἐπιεικέσιν epieikesin dat pl masc
3. ἐπιεικεῖς epieikeis acc pl masc
4. ἐπιεικής epieikēs nom sing fem
5. ἐπιεικές epieikes nom/acc sing neu

5	Let your **moderation** be known unto all men.	Phlp 4:5
1	not greedy of filthy lucre; but **patient**,	1 Tm 3:3
3	to be no brawlers, but **gentle**,	Tit 3:2
4	from above is first pure, then peaceable, **gentle**,	Jas 3:17
2	to your masters ... not only to the good and **gentle**,	1 Pt 2:18

Classical Greek

This adjective from *epi* (1894), "upon, unto," and *eikos*, "probable, reasonable" (cf. the noun *epieikeia*), is somewhat complex in classical Greek. The idea of "fitting" or "suitable" is common. The adverbial form is well known. A sense of "moderation" is affixed to the term, particularly when it occurs in a moral sense (cf. Trench's comments on the noun *epieikeia* in *Synonyms of the New Testament*, pp.153ff.). *Epieikēs* can mean "yielding" or "reasonable" or even "considerate." Preisker asserts that consideration directed to humanity might be termed *epieikēs* after the fashion of *eusebēs* (2133), which was a disposition toward the gods ("epiekēs," *Kittel*, 2:588ff., also *Bauer* as opposite to *asebēs* [759] in Diodorus Siculus 16.32.2; cf. Josephus *Antiquities* 10.5.2).

Septuagint Usage

Epieikēs occurs only twice in the Septuagint (Esther 8:13b; and Psalm 86:5 [LXX 85:5]; cf. the adverb and the noun). Each time it translates the Hebrew *ṣallāch*. God is "good and forgiving," i.e., "equitable, yielding"; He does not exact the deserved punishment from those who call upon Him (Psalm 86:5 [LXX 85:5], RSV).

New Testament Usage

Paul employed *epieikēs* in Philippians (4:5) as a neuter adjective for an abstract noun which is virtually "untranslatable" (see Hawthorne, *Word Biblical Commentary*, 43:182). The modern versions confirm Hawthorne's observations of this paradigmatic text: "forbearance," RSV; "moderation," KJV; "reputation for gentleness," Phillips; "magnanimity," NEB; "gentle attitude," GNB; and "gentleness," NIV. As Hawthorne notes (ibid.), the same can be said for other uses. *Epieikēs* resonates with such noble concepts as "peaceableness" (1 Timothy 3:3; Titus 3:2), "open to reason, full of mercy" (James 3:17), and "good things" (1 Peter 2:18). But a precise correspondence is elusive. "Gentle toleration for others, in spite of having justification for intolerance," might aptly state the essence of *epieikēs*.

Christ is the model for a community bereft of harmony in which Paul, as an apostle, had every right to severely chasten. But Paul followed Christ and exerted restraint instead; nevertheless, his *epieikēs* was not "sentimental," and the Corinthians were not to exploit it (2 Corinthians 10:1, *epieikeia*; cf. Preisker, "epieikeia," *Kittel*, 2:589f.).

STRONG 1933, BAUER 292, MOULTON-MILLIGAN 238, KITTEL 2:588-90, LIDDELL-SCOTT 632, COLIN BROWN 2:256-59.

1919. ἐπιζητέω epizēteō verb

Search for, seek after, desire to know; wish for, demand, desire.

COGNATE:
ζητέω zēteō (2195)

SYNONYMS:
ἐκζητέω ekzēteō (1554)
ἐραυνάω eraunaō (2020B)
ζητέω zēteō (2195)

בָּקַשׁ bāqash (1272), Piel: seek (1 Sm 20:1).

דָּרַשׁ dārash (1938), Inquire (2 Kgs 1:3, 2 Chr 18:6, Is 62:12).

פָּקַד pāqadh (6734), Charge, accuse (2 Sm 3:8).

1. ἐπιζητῶ epizētō 1sing indic pres act
2. ἐπιζητεῖ epizētei 3sing indic pres act
3. ἐπιζητοῦμεν epizētoumen 1pl indic pres act
4. ἐπιζητεῖτε epizēteite 2pl indic pres act
5. ἐπιζητοῦσιν epizētousin 3pl indic pres act
6. ἐπεζήτησεν epezētēsen 3sing indic aor act
7. ἐπιζητήσας epizētēsas nom sing masc part aor act
8. ἐπεζήτουν epezētoun 3pl indic imperf act

2	For after all these things do the Gentiles **seek**:	Matt 6:32
5	For after all these things do the Gentiles **seek**:	6:32
2	evil and adulterous generation **seeketh** after a sign;	12:39
2	wicked and adulterous generation **seeketh** ... sign;	16:4
2	Why **doth** this generation **seek** after a sign?	Mark 8:12
8	the multitudes were **searching** for Him, (NASB)	Luke 4:42
2	This is an evil generation: they **seek** a sign;	11:29
2	these things do the nations of the world **seek** after:	12:30
5	these things do the nations of the world **seek** after:	12:30
7	And when Herod **had sought** for him,	Acts 12:19
6	and **desired** to hear the word of God.	13:7
2	if ye **inquire** any thing concerning other matters,	19:39
2	Israel hath not obtained that which he **seeketh** for;	Rom 11:7
1	Not because I **desire** a gift: but I **desire** fruit	Phlp 4:17
1	but I **desire** fruit that may abound to your account.	4:17
5	declare plainly that they **seek** a country.	Heb 11:14
3	no continuing city, but we **seek** one to come.	13:14

Classical Greek
This compound verb from *epi* (1894) (intensive here) and *zēteō* (2195), "seek," means "seek after, search for" in classical Greek. Other meanings include "seek intellectually" (inquire) or "search further." In a stronger sense it can mean "demand" (see *Liddell-Scott*).

Septuagint Usage
Twenty-one occurrences of *epizēteō* can be found in the Septuagint, the majority of which are canonical. Of the three Hebrew terms behind *epizēteō*, *dārash*, "seek, inquire," dominates. It can be used of "asking" a question (1 Samuel 20:1 [LXX 1 Kings 20:1]), which at times means something stronger than a mere inquiry (cf. 2 Samuel 3:8 [LXX 2 Kings 3:8], "accuse," NIV).

It is also used of "consulting" a pagan oracle (2 Kings 1:2,3,6 [LXX 4 Kings 1:2,3,6] [Baalzebub]) or of "inquiring" of a prophet of the Lord (or the Lord himself) concerning future events or present circumstances (2 Kings [LXX 4 Kings] 3:11; 8:8; 22:18). *Epizēteō* also refers to the renewal of a relationship with God (Hosea 3:5; 5:15).

New Testament Usage
Epizēteō appears 13 times in the New Testament. It depicts the "demand" for a sign by the "evil and adulterous generation" (Matthew 12:39; 16:4). In reference to "desires" it is used of the Gentiles who "seek" (cf. NIV "run after") to satisfy their desires for food and clothing. The believer is to "seek" (*zēteō*) instead the kingdom of God and His righteousness (Matthew 6:32f.; Luke 12:30; cf. Philippians 4:17). The idea of desire is latent in Sergius Paulus' "seeking" to hear the word of God (Acts 13:7).

In Acts 12:19 it describes Herod's making a thorough search (cf. NIV) for Peter. From a different perspective it characterizes the "searching" of the patriarchs for a better land (Hebrews 11:14; 13:14, of searching for the coming city).

Paul declared in Romans 11:7 that what Israel sought so earnestly it did not obtain, but the elect did. Here the "earnest seeking" (*epizēteō*) of Israel was not good. What Israel had previously sought was to become righteous through the works of the Law (cf. Romans 9:31). Only the "elect," that is, those living by faith, obtained righteousness as Abraham so vividly illustrates.

STRONG 1934, BAUER 292, MOULTON-MILLIGAN 238-39, KITTEL 2:895-96, LIDDELL-SCOTT 633, COLIN BROWN 3:530-31.

1920. ἐπιθανάτιος epithanatios adj
Condemned to death.
CROSS-REFERENCE:
θανατόω thanatoō (2266)

1. ἐπιθανατίους epithanatious acc pl masc

1 us the apostles last, as it were **appointed to death:** .... 1 Co 4:9

Epithanatios is derived from the root word *thanatos* (2265) which refers to the act of dying or the state of death. It is also used of mortal danger, the manner of death, and the death penalty. *Epithanatios* occurs only once in the New Testament, in 1 Corinthians 4:9, where Paul claimed that apostles are on public display—like men "appointed to death" in the arena.

STRONG 1935, BAUER 292, LIDDELL-SCOTT 633.

1921. ἐπίθεσις epithesis noun
Laying on (of hands).
CROSS-REFERENCE:
ἐπιτίθημι epitithēmi (1991)

עֲגָבָה 'ăghāvāh (5897), Sensual desire (Ez 23:11).
קֶשֶׁר qesher (7490), Conspiracy (2 Chr 25:27).

1. ἐπιθέσεως epitheseōs gen sing fem

1 through **laying on** of the apostles' hands .... Acts 8:18
1 with the **laying on** of the hands of the presbytery.... 1 Tm 4:14
1 which is in thee by the **putting on** of my hands...... 2 Tm 1:6
1 doctrine of baptisms, and **of laying on** of hands, ... Heb 6:2

Classical Greek
For classical authors *epithesis* (from the preposition *epi* [1894], "upon," and the verb *tithēmi* [4935], "to place, put") denoted the act of "setting (something) on its base" or the "placing (of something) upon" something else (either literally or figuratively). Further meanings include "set upon, attack" (see *Liddell-Scott*).

Septuagint Usage
In the Septuagint *epithesis* is used infrequently, a total of five times, only two of which have Hebrew originals. Of these texts *epithesis* can describe a "conspiracy" (Hebrew *qesher*, 2 Chronicles 25:27) or the "deceived sensual desire" of Aholibah (Hebrew *'ăghāvāh*, Ezekiel 23:11). Later versions, such as Aquila's, use it more often (e.g., Genesis 27:35; Psalm 43:1; Proverbs 11:1). The notion of "deceit"

comes through many of these texts. None of these meanings really contribute to the New Testament's use of *epithesis*. However, the use of the verb *epitithēmi* (1991), which was frequently used in describing the "laying on" of hands in a religious ceremony (e.g., Exodus 19:10,19; Leviticus 1:4; 3:2,8), is similar to the New Testament understanding.

New Testament Usage

The New Testament uses *epithesis* (and for the most part the verb too) exclusively in terms of the "laying on" of hands for either healing or to impart the Spirit. The latter was a practice of early Christianity and perhaps also of the contemporary Hellenistic world (so Maurer, "epithesis," *Kittel*, 8:160f.; and Oepke, "igomai," *Kittel*, 3:196).

The uses of *epithesis* in Acts and the Pastoral Epistles clearly refer to the impartation of the Spirit or a gift of the Spirit for ministry (which includes Timothy's "ordination," 1 Timothy 4:14). However, the idea is also present in the use of the verb, so no tight lines of distinction would be drawn (e.g., Matthew 9:18; 19:13, healings; Acts 6:6, "appointment" of the seven deacons; and Acts 8:17, the reception of the Spirit).

Acts 8:18 expressly states that it was through the "*laying on* of the apostles' hands" that the Spirit was given (*didotai* [see 1319]) to the Samaritans. Likewise, Timothy was given (*edothē*) a gift (*charisma* [5321]) for the purposes of ministry through the laying on of the hands of the leaders (1 Timothy 4:14; cf. 2 Timothy 1:6).

The text of Hebrews 6:2 is not so simple to decipher. Here "laying on the hands" appears in conjunction with instruction about "baptisms" (not the plural), "resurrection," and "judgment." One can only assume that the "laying on of hands" was an early Christian rite probably modified from Jewish practices (as were the "baptisms"). At least it was associated with the giving of the Spirit, healing, or special commissioning.

STRONG 1936, BAUER 293, MOULTON-MILLIGAN 239, KITTEL 8:159-61, LIDDELL-SCOTT 634.

1922. ἐπιθυμέω epithumeō verb

Desire, long for; lust for, after.

COGNATE:
ἐπιθυμία epithumia (1924)

SYNONYMS:
ἐπιποθέω epipotheō (1955)
ζηλόω zēloō (2189)

אָוָה ’āwâh (181), Piel: desire, crave (1 Sm 2:16, 2 Sm 3:21, 1 Kgs 11:37); hithpael: desire, long for (2 Sm 23:15, Ps 106:14 [103:14], Jer 17:16).

אַוָּה ’awwāh (182), Craving, longing (Dt 18:6).

אָמַר ’āmar (569), Say (1 Sm 20:4).

בָּחַר bāchar (1013), Select, choose (Is 1:29).

חָמַד chāmadh (2629), Qal: desire (Ex 34:24, Dt 7:25, Mi 2:2); piel: take great delight in (S/S 2:3).

חָפֵץ chāphēts (2759), Be eager for, take delight in (Is 58:2).

חָשַׁק chāshaq (2945), Desire (2 Chr 8:6).

כָּסַף kāsaph (3826), Niphal: deeply long for (Gn 31:30).

רָוָה rāwâh (7588), Hiphil: fill with, lavish on (Is 43:24).

שָׁאַל shā’al (8068), Wish for, desire (Dt 14:26).

תָּאֵב tā’ēv (8703), Long for (Ps 119:40 [118:40]).

תַּאֲבָה ta’ăvāh (8704), Longing (Ps 119:20 [118:20]).

תַּאֲוָה ta’ăwāh (8707), Longing, desire (Jb 33:20, Is 26:8).

1. ἐπιθυμεῖ epithumei 3sing indic pres act
2. ἐπιθυμοῦμεν epithumoumen 1pl indic pres act
3. ἐπιθυμεῖτε epithumeite 2pl indic pres act
4. ἐπιθυμοῦσιν epithumousin 3pl indic pres act
5. ἐπιθυμῶν epithumōn nom sing masc part pres act
6. ἐπεθύμησα epethumēsa 1sing indic aor act
7. ἐπεθύμησαν epethumēsan 3pl indic aor act
8. ἐπιθυμῆσαι epithumēsai inf aor act
9. ἐπιθυμήσεις epithumēseis 2sing indic fut act
10. ἐπιθυμήσετε epithumēsete 2pl indic fut act
11. ἐπιθυμήσουσιν epithumēsousin 3pl indic fut act
12. ἐπεθύμει epethumei 3sing indic imperf act

8	looketh on a woman **to lust** after her hath	Matt 5:28
7	have **desired** to see those things which ye see,	13:17
12	And he would fain have filled his belly	Luke 15:16
5	And **desiring** to be fed with the crumbs which fell	16:21
10	when ye **shall desire** to see one of the days	17:22
6	With desire **I have desired** to eat this passover	22:15
6	I have coveted no man's silver, or gold, or apparel.	Acts 20:33
9	except the law had said, Thou shalt not covet.	Rom 7:7
9	Thou **shalt** not covet;	13:9
7	should not lust after evil things, as they also **lusted**.	1 Co 10:6
1	For the flesh **lusteth** against the Spirit,	Gal 5:17
1	the office of a bishop, he **desireth** a good work.	1 Tm 3:1
2	And we **desire** that every one of you	Heb 6:11
3	Ye lust, and have not: ye kill, and **desire** to have	Jas 4:2
4	which things the angels **desire** to look into	1 Pt 1:12
11	**shall desire** to die, and death shall flee from them.	Rev 9:6

Classical Greek

In classical literature *epithumeō* means "desire for, long for"; it is neither a negative nor positive impulse. The term can be used of a longing for food, of "political attachments" (see *Liddell-Scott*), or of sensual desires. It can simply denote a "desire" to do something. Büschel notes that the *epithum-* word group in Greek philosophy generally is an ethical rather than religious concept; thus it is only one among the four chief passions, "pleasure, fear, and grief" ("thumos," *Kittel*, 3:168ff.).

Septuagint Usage

The Septuagint translators utilized *epithumeō* for as many as 10 Hebrew terms. In a majority of instances it translates a form of *'āwâh*, "long for" (e.g., for food, Numbers 11:4; of personal choice, 1 Samuel 2:16 [LXX 1 Kings 2:16]; of sexual desire, Deuteronomy 5:18; of desiring a neighbor's wife, Judith 16:22; of the desire for wisdom, Sirach 1:26; of the desire for God's law, Psalm 119:20 [LXX 118:20] [*ta'ăvāh*]). There are hints that "desire" or "craving" often stood over against God. This is most clear in the wilderness account where the Israelites' desire for other food was regarded as a major sin which was recalled by later Judaism (cf. Numbers 11:4ff.; Psalm 106:14 [LXX 105:14]; Wisdom of Solomon 16:3; 1 Corinthians 10:6).

New Testament Usage

In the New Testament *epithumeō* rarely retains its suggestion of sexual desire. Jesus cautioned against looking at a woman in lust (Matthew 5:28). Also negatively Paul recalled the Old Testament commands not to covet (Romans 7:7; 13:9). Negatively *epithumeō* describes the (evil) desire for wealth (Acts 20:33; cf. James 4:2).

The word can refer to the simple "desire" for food and drink common to all humanity (Luke 15:16; 16:21), or it can depict a "longing" for some event or thing. Implicitly this longing is often not satisfied (e.g., Matthew 13:17; Luke 17:22; James 4:2; 1 Peter 1:12; Revelation 9:6). Neutrally *epithumeō* is used of Jesus' desire to eat the Passover with His disciples (Luke 22:15) and the desire of the author of Hebrews that his readers remain diligent to the end (Hebrews 6:11).

STRONG 1937, BAUER 293, MOULTON-MILLIGAN 239, KITTEL 3:168-71, LIDDELL-SCOTT 634-35, COLIN BROWN 1:456-57.

1923. ἐπιθυμητής epithumētēs noun
One who desires.
CROSS-REFERENCE:
  ἐπιθυμία epithumia (1924)

אָוָה 'āwâh (181), Hithpael: craving, lust (Nm 11:34).

1. ἐπιθυμητάς epithumētas acc pl masc

1 to the intent we should not **lust after evil things**,... 1 Co 10:6

This noun describes "one who desires" (cf. the related noun *epithumia* [1924] and the verb *epithumeō* [1922]). Although it does not necessarily have negative overtones (i.e., "one who lusts"), it can and does in the Septuagint (Numbers 11:34; Proverbs 1:22). The single instance of *epithumētēs* in the New Testament (1 Corinthians 10:6) could be neutral apart from the qualifying *kakon* (see 2527), "evil things," and apart from Paul's use of the cognate verb which he clearly used in a negative manner (e.g., Romans 7:7; 13:9).

STRONG 1938, BAUER 293, MOULTON-MILLIGAN 239, KITTEL 3:172, LIDDELL-SCOTT 634-35.

1924. ἐπιθυμία epithumia noun
Desire, longing, craving.
COGNATES:
  ἐπιθυμέω epithumeō (1922)
  ἐπιθυμητής epithumētēs (1923)
  θυμόω thumoō (2350)
SYNONYMS:
  εὐδοκία eudokia (2086)
  ὄρεξις orexis (3578)
  ὁρμή hormē (3593)

אָוָה 'āwâh (181), Hithpael: craving, desire (Prv 13:4).
אַוָּה 'awwâh (182), Craving, longing (Dt 12:15, Jer 2:24).
אַשְׁפָּה 'ashpâh (855), Full quiver (Ps 127:5 [126:5]).
חָמַד chāmadh (2629), Desire (Jb 20:20, Prv 12:12).
חֶמְדָּה chemdâh (2631), Desire of women (Dn 11:37).
חֲמֻדוֹת chămudhôth (2632), Choice food, treasure (Dn 10:3, 11:43).
חֵשֶׁק chēsheq (2946), Desire (2 Chr 8:6).
כָּסַף kāsaph (3826), Niphal: deeply long for (Gn 31:30).
לֵב lēv (3949), Heart (Prv 6:25).
מַאֲוַי ma'ăway (4112), Desires (Ps 140:8 [139:8]).
מַחְמָד machmādh (4398), Something sweet (S/S 5:16).
עֲדִי 'ădhî (5927), Satisfaction from good things (Ps 103:5 [102:5]).
רָצוֹן rātsôn (7814), Desire, something that pleases (Gn 49:6).
תַּאֲוָה ta'ăwâh (8707), Longing, desire (Dt 9:22, Ps 38:9 [37:9], Prv 21:25).

1. ἐπιθυμίας epithumias gen/acc sing/pl fem
2. ἐπιθυμία epithumia nom sing fem
3. ἐπιθυμίᾳ epithumia dat sing fem
4. ἐπιθυμίαν epithumian acc sing fem
5. ἐπιθυμίαι epithumiai nom pl fem
6. ἐπιθυμιῶν epithumiōn gen pl fem
7. ἐπιθυμίαις epithumiais dat pl fem

ἐπιθυμία 1924

Ref	Text	Citation
5	and the **lusts** of other things entering in,	Mark 4:19
3	With **desire** I have desired to eat this passover	Luke 22:15
1	and the **lusts** of your father ye will do.	John 8:44
7	uncleanness through the **lusts** of their own hearts,	Rom 1:24
7	that ye should obey it in the **lusts** thereof.	6:12
4	for I had not known **lust**, except the law had said,	7:7
4	wrought in me all manner of **concupiscence**.	7:8
1	to fulfil the **lusts** thereof.	13:14
4	and ye shall not fulfil the **lust** of the flesh.	Gal 5:16
7	crucified the flesh with the affections and **lusts**.	5:24
7	in times past in the **lusts** of our flesh,	Eph 2:3
1	which is corrupt according to the deceitful **lusts**;	4:22
4	having a **desire** to depart, and to be with Christ;	Phlp 1:23
4	evil **concupiscence**, and covetousness,	Col 3:5
3	to see your face with great **desire**.	1 Th 2:17
1	Not in the **lust** of concupiscence,	4:5
1	a snare, and into many foolish and hurtful **lusts**,	1 Tm 6:9
1	Flee also youthful **lusts**: but follow righteousness,	2 Tm 2:22
7	women laden with sins, led away with divers **lusts**,	3:6
1	after their own **lusts** shall they heap ... teachers,	4:3
1	denying ungodliness and worldly **lusts**,	Tit 2:12
7	deceived, serving divers **lusts** and pleasures,	3:3
1	he is drawn away of his own **lust**, and enticed.	Jas 1:14
2	when **lust** hath conceived, it bringeth forth sin:	1:15
7	according to the former **lusts** in your ignorance:	1 Pt 1:14
6	I beseech you ... abstain from fleshly **lusts**,	2:11
7	the rest of his time in the flesh **to** the **lusts** of men,	4:2
7	when we walked in lasciviousness, **lusts**,	4:3
3	the corruption that is in the world through **lust**.	2 Pt 1:4
3	that walk after the flesh in the **lust** of uncleanness,	2:10
7	they allure through the **lusts** of the flesh,	2:18
1	scoffers, walking after their own **lusts**,	3:3
1	scoffers, walking after their own **lusts**,	3:3
2	For all that is in the world, the **lust** of the flesh,	1 Jn 2:16
2	and the **lust** of the eyes, and the pride of life,	2:16
2	And the world passeth away, and the **lust** thereof:	2:17
1	complainers, walking after their own **lusts**;	Jude 1:16
1	who should walk after their own ungodly **lusts**.	1:18
1	the fruits that thy soul **lusted** after are departed	Rev 18:14

Classical Greek

Epithumia in classical Greek was originally an ethically neutral term. It depicted the desires and wishes within everyone which determine both good or evil actions. Gradually, however, it acquired the more familiar sense of an improper (morally or ethically) desire.

Septuagint Usage

Epithumeō (1922) and the noun *epithumia* occur in the Septuagint about 50 times each. Usually they replace the Hebrew *'āwâh* and *chāmadh* which can denote a good or even commendable desire (Genesis 31:30; cf. Isaiah 58:2). They may be ethically neutral in definition (Deuteronomy 12:20f.), or they may convey evil desire (Numbers 11:4,34; Deuteronomy 9:22).

New Testament Usage

In the New Testament the verb *epithumeō* appears 16 times and the noun *epithumia* 38 times. The verb ordinarily has a positive sense (but cf. Matthew 5:28 and Paul's usage). The noun is understood positively in connection with Jesus' desire to eat the Passover meal with His disciples (Luke 22:15), in reference to Paul's desire to be with the Lord (Philippians 1:23), and concerning his longing to see the believers in Thessalonica again (1 Thessalonians 2:17). Perhaps the term is neutral in Revelation 18:14, but aside from the locations mentioned above, it always signifies an evil or sinful "desire." The places which reflect this negative sense have the greatest theological import.

Humanity's natural desires belong to its original physical and spiritual makeup. However, as a result of the Fall these desires were distorted until they exerted an unnatural control over humanity's shattered image of God (Ephesians 4:17-19).

Thus humanity in its present sinful state is—apart from the saving grace of God—serving "divers lusts and pleasures" (Titus 3:3; cf. Romans 1:24-32; Ephesians 4:22). Given over to its evil desires and passions humanity is destroying not only itself but creation as well (Romans 1:24-32).

Humanity's "sinful *lusts*" are particularly revealed in its sinful nature, manifest expressly in sexual, moral, and ethical rebellion against God (Romans 6:12; 7:23,24; 8:13). This includes not only physical desires; *epithumia* attacks the very fabric of humanity's spiritual existence. Evil desires of whatever kind are seated in the heart, in the center of the personality: "For from within, out of the heart of men, proceed evil thoughts, adulteries, fornications, murders, thefts, covetousness, wickedness, deceit, lasciviousness, an evil eye, blasphemy, pride, foolishness: all these evil things come from within, and defile the man" (Mark 7:21-23).

Epithumia plays an important part in Paul's theology. Except for Philippians 1:23 and 1 Thessalonians 2:17, the term always carries a pejorative sense. When he speaks of "desire" and "longing" in a positive sense he chooses another group of words (*epipotheō* [1955]; cf. also *epipothēsis* [1956], *epipothētos* [1957], *epipothia* [1958]).

To Paul, *epithumia* motivates the actions of the fallen human being. The "old man" is corrupt "according to the deceitful lusts" and contrasts with the "new man" of the believer which God "created in righteousness and true holiness" (Ephesians 4:22-24). But even within the believer the old nature, the sinful nature (often translated "the flesh"), challenges the believer's new man. The believer cannot permit these sinful inclinations to rule his or her life. If they remain unchecked they may jeopardize the faith of the believer: "For if you live according to the flesh you will die, but if by the Spirit you put to death the deeds of the body you will live" (Romans 8:13, RSV). "Walk in the Spirit, and ye shall not fulfil the lust of the flesh. For the flesh lusteth against the Spirit, and the Spirit against the flesh: and these are contrary the one to the other" (Galatians 5:16f.). The battle of the Christian is waged not only with patent sinful acts (Galatians 5:19) but against the desires of the sinful nature. Nevertheless, those belonging to Christ have crucified the sinful nature with its passions and desires (Galatians 5:24).

In the General Epistles *epithumia* resembles Paul's attitude. James considered *epithumia* as something which lures and entices man to sin (James 1:14). Peter wrote of the "former lusts" (1 Peter 1:14); i.e., desires which belonged to the old life. A believer is to avoid these since they wage war against the soul (1 Peter 2:11). The corruption in the world comes through *epithumia* (2 Peter 1:4), and Jude exposed spiritual deceivers as typically those who live according to their own desires (Jude 16-18).

With John the triad of "the lust of the flesh, and the lust of the eyes, and the pride of life" are considered characteristic of the world (see *kosmos* [2862]) and worldly life-style (1 John 2:16). A believer cannot love these things because to do so would be a denial of his love for God. Therefore, the desires of the "flesh" are not only a compelling force within each individual, but they are the larger force of the world itself. Jesus traced this evil tendency to its progenitor—the devil: "Ye are of your father the devil, and the lusts of your father ye will do" (John 8:44). The "flesh," the evil desires and schemes of the fallen world, and the devil have enlisted each other to fight against believers.

The writers of the New Testament speak of evil passions in harsh terms and depict them as having infiltrated virtually every aspect of life (2 Peter 3:3; cf. Romans 1:24; Ephesians 4:22; Colossians 3:5; 1 Timothy 6:9; 2 Timothy 2:22; Titus 2:12; 1 Peter 4:2,3; 2 Peter 2:10; 1 John 2:16; Jude 18).

The believer is to walk no longer "after the flesh" (i.e., controlled by the old nature). Instead, he is to walk "after the Spirit" (Romans 8:4). By the Spirit the "inner man" is renewed (Ephesians 4:23; Romans 12:2). The one living in or by the Spirit does not fulfill the desires of the flesh (Galatians 5:16). A new drive and purpose replaces the desires of the sinful nature; this enables a Christian to "put to death" *epithumia* (Colossians 3:5, RSV) in progressing toward holiness.

The New Testament speaks with great sobriety of the detriment of living according to the desires of the "flesh." But it is important not to misunderstand or misinterpret what is meant. Fulfilling the *epithumia* of the sinful nature, "the flesh" (murder, envy, theft, adultery, etc.), is a distortion, corruption, and perversion of the God-given, God-sanctioned desires of humankind. God condemns the evil *epithumia* not the natural impulses themselves or the fulfilling of these desires under God-condoned conditions. To mistakenly conclude that "the lust of the flesh" corresponds only to sexual desire—so that the claim of putting to death the desires of the flesh results in sexual abstention or a renunciation of marriage—is explicitly rejected (Colossians 2:21-23; 1 Timothy 4:1-6). The Christian's ethic is fundamentally not ascetic. Suppression of the natural desires in a sanctioned context (e.g., marriage) should only take place by mutual consent, only for a short time, and only for the purpose of prayer (1 Corinthians 7:5). Sexual abstention can be practiced by those who have a gift of grace for it (1 Corinthians 7:7). Some special ministries in the kingdom of God can even demand it (Matthew 19:12). The pleasure received from marital relationships is "to be received with thanksgiving by those who believe and know the truth" (1 Timothy 4:3,4, RSV). Prolonged voluntary sexual abstention in the marriage relationship is not only abnormal, but it is potentially destructive (1 Corinthians 7:5).

Strong 1939, Bauer 293, Moulton-Milligan 239, Kittel 3:168-71, Liddell-Scott 634-35, Colin Brown 1:456-58.

1925. ἐπικαθίζω epikathizō verb

Sit, sit down (on).
Cross-Reference:
καθίζω kathizō (2495)

יָשַׁב yāshav (3553), Sit (Lv 15:20).

רָכַב rākhav (7680), Qal: ride, mount and ride (2 Sm 13:29, 22:11); hiphil: cause to ride (1 Kgs 1:38,44, 2 Kgs 10:16).

שָׁכַן shākhan (8331), Settle; hiphil: cause to settle, remain (Ez 32:4).

1. ἐπεκάθισεν epekathisen 3sing indic aor act
2. ἐπεκάθισαν epekathisan 3pl indic aor act

1 put on them their clothes, ... they set him thereon. Matt 21:7
2 put on them their clothes, ... they set him thereon..... 21:7

Epikathizō occurs only once in the New Testament, Matthew 21:7. There it is used of Jesus who "sat upon" the garments that were placed on the donkey and colt. Elsewhere in Biblical writings *epikathizō* appears eight times in the Septuagint (e.g., Genesis 31:34; Leviticus 15:20; 2 Samuel 13:29 [LXX 2 Kings 13:29]).
STRONG 1940, BAUER 293, MOULTON-MILLIGAN 239, LIDDELL-SCOTT 635.

1926. ἐπικαλέω epikaleō verb

Call, name, give a name to, call upon, appeal to.

COGNATE:
καλέω kaleō (2535)

SYNONYMS:
ἀναβοάω anaboaō (308)
ἀνακράζω anakrazō (347)
ἀναφωνέω anaphōneō (398)
βοάω boaō (987)
ἐπιβοάω epiboaō (1901)
ἐπιφωνέω epiphōneō (2003)
καλέω kaleō (2535)
κράζω krazō (2869)
μετακαλέομαι metakaleomai (3203)
μεταπέμπομαι metapempomai (3213)
παρακαλέω parakaleō (3731)
προσκαλέομαι proskaleomai (4200)
συγκαλέω sunkaleō (4630)
φωνέω phōneō (5291)

זָכַר zākhar (2226), Mention, remember; hiphil: acknowledge, trust (Ps 20:7 [19:7]—only some Sinaiticus texts).

מָצָא mātsâ' (4834), Find (Prv 8:12).

נָקַב nāqav (5529), Specify, designate; niphal: be designated (2 Chr 28:15).

עָשָׂה 'āsâh (6449), Do (2 Kgs 23:17).

קָרָא qārā' (7410), Qal: call, proclaim (Gn 4:26, 1 Sm 23:28, Ps 50:15 [49:15]); niphal: be called (Dt 28:10, 2 Chr 6:33, Am 9:12); pual: be called, be named (Ez 10:13).

שִׂים sîm (7947), Put (Dt 12:21, 14:24, 2 Chr 6:20).

שָׁכַן shākhan (8331), Qal: dwell, settle (Ex 29:45,46, Dt 12:5); piel: let dwell, make dwell (Dt 12:11, 14:23, 26:2).

שֻׁם shum (A8430), Name (Dn 2:26—Aramaic).

1. ἐπικαλοῦμαι epikaloumai 1sing indic pres mid
2. ἐπικαλεῖται epikaleitai 3sing indic pres mid
3. ἐπικαλεῖσθε epikaleisthe 2pl indic pres mid
4. ἐπικαλούμενος epikaloumenos nom sing masc part pres mid
5. ἐπικαλουμένου epikaloumenou gen sing masc part pres mid
6. ἐπικαλούμενον epikaloumenon acc sing masc part pres mid
7. ἐπικαλουμένων epikaloumenōn gen pl masc part pres mid
8. ἐπικαλουμένοις epikaloumenois dat pl masc part pres mid
9. ἐπικαλουμένους epikaloumenous acc pl masc part pres mid
10. ἐπικαλεῖσθαι epikaleisthai inf pres mid
11. ἐπεκλήθη epeklēthē 3sing indic aor pass
12. ἐπικαλέσηται epikalesētai 3sing subj aor mid
13. ἐπικληθείς epiklētheis nom sing masc part aor pass
14. ἐπικαλεσάμενος epikalesamenos nom sing masc part aor mid
15. ἐπικαλεσαμένου epikalesamenou gen sing masc part aor mid
16. ἐπικληθέντα epiklēthenta acc sing masc part aor pass
17. ἐπικληθέν epiklēthen nom/acc sing neu part aor pass
18. ἐπικαλέσασθαι epikalesasthai inf aor mid
19. ἐπικέκλησαι epikeklēsai 2sing indic perf mid
20. ἐπικέκληται epikeklētai 3sing indic perf mid
21. ἐπεκέκλητο epekeklēto 3sing indic plperf mid
22. ἐπικαλέσονται epikalesontai 3pl indic fut mid
23. ἐπεκάλεσαν epekalesan 3pl indic aor act
24. ἐπικαλέσωνται epikalesōntai 3pl subj aor mid

13 and Lebbaeus, whose **surname** was Thaddaeus;....Matt 10:3
23 have called the head ... Beelzebul, (NASB) 10:25
6 Then entered Satan into Judas **surnamed** Iscariot, Luke 22:3
11 Joseph ... who was **surnamed** Justus, and Matthias. Acts 1:23
12 shall **call on** the name of the Lord shall be saved...... 2:21
13 who by the apostles was **surnamed** Barnabas,.......... 4:36
6 And they stoned Stephen, **calling upon** God,........ 7:59
9 to bind all that **call on** thy name..................... 9:14
9 them which **called on** this name in Jerusalem,......... 9:21
2 and call for one Simon, whose **surname** is Peter:..... 10:5
4 asked whether Simon, which was **surnamed** Peter,........ 10:18
2 and call hither Simon, whose **surname** is Peter;....... 10:32
6 and call for Simon, whose **surname** is Peter;.......... 11:13
5 of John, whose **surname** was Mark;................... 12:12
16 took with them John, whose **surname** was Mark....... 12:25
6 took with them John, whose **surname** was Mark....... 12:25
20 all the Gentiles, upon whom my name **is called**,...... 15:17
6 namely, Judas **surnamed** Barsabas, and Silas,......... 15:22
14 away thy sins, **calling on** the name of the Lord...... 22:16
1 may deliver me unto them. **I appeal** unto Caesar...... 25:11
19 answered, Hast thou **appealed** unto Caesar?.......... 25:12
15 But when Paul **had appealed** to be reserved.......... 25:21
15 and that he himself **hath appealed** to Augustus,....... 25:25
21 set at liberty, if he **had not appealed** unto Caesar..... 26:32
18 I was constrained **to appeal** unto Caesar;........... 28:19
9 Lord over all is rich unto all **that call upon him**... Rom 10:12
12 whosoever **shall call upon** the name of the Lord...... 10:13
22 How then **shall they call on** him.................... 10:14
24 How then **shall they call on** him.................... 10:14
8 with all that in every place **call upon** the name ....1 Co 1:2
1 Moreover I **call** God for a record upon my soul,... 2 Co 1:23
7 with them that **call on** the Lord out of a pure heart.2 Tm 2:22

ἐπικαλέω 1926

10 God is not ashamed to be called their God:	Heb 11:16
17 that worthy name by the which ye are called?	Jas 2:7
3 And if ye call on the Father,	1 Pt 1:17

Classical Greek

This expression in classical Greek denotes the act of "invoking" or "summoning" a god "to a sacrifice or as witness to an oath" (*Liddell-Scott*). Formally it is a compound from the preposition *epi* (1894), "upon, on," and the verb *kaleō* (2535), "name, call, invite." Other ideas include the act of inviting the god's graciousness to be upon an individual; thus, "to pray" is a legitimate definition. Also, "to call on" for aid, "to appeal to" are recognized meanings. Here the middle form, *epikaleomai* is often used. *Epikaleō* is also used of "calling someone by his name," or passively, "to be called by name" (see *Liddell-Scott*; cf. Schmidt, "kaleō," *Kittel*, 3:487-491,496-500).

Septuagint Usage

Epikaleō occurs in the Septuagint as a translation for nine Hebrew words, however, *qārā'* (in various forms), clearly predominates. The Septuagint reflects a semitechnical understanding of *epikaleō*. First, its object is regularly "the name of the Lord" or "the Lord" (e.g., Genesis 4:26; 12:8; 13:4; 21:3; 2 Samuel 6:2 [LXX 2 Kings 6:2]; and so on). Thus it becomes associated with divine worship (Genesis 12:8; 13:4), and in one sense "to pray" is a justifiable translation of *epikaleō* (Deuteronomy 4:7; Psalm 4:1; cf. Schmidt, ibid., 3:499f.). It is even used in the technical sense in reference to other gods. The prophets of Baal "call(ed) on" the name of Baal, but he did not respond (1 Kings 18:25-28 [LXX 3 Kings 18:25-28]; cf. Judith 3:8). The technical understanding became so great that "those calling upon the Lord" became a description used by the psalmist for the faithful of God (e.g., Psalms 99:6 [LXX 98:6]; 145:18 [144:18]).

Second, *epikaleō* occurs in a nontechnical sense of "naming" something (e.g., Genesis 33:20; 1 Kings 7:21 [LXX 3 Kings 7:21]). But even here there are at times divine associations with the name of God (e.g., Deuteronomy 12:5,11,21,26; 14:23; 2 Chronicles 6:20). In the apocryphal writings the technical understanding was utilized (e.g., Judith 6:21; 2 Maccabees 3:15), but the nontechnical sense was also used (e.g., 1 Maccabees 2:2,4,5).

New Testament Usage

The meaning of *epikaleō* in the New Testament is clearly similar to that of the Septuagint. It is mostly absent in the Gospels (occurring only at Matthew 10:3 and Luke 22:3), but Luke employed it in Acts extensively (22 times). Elsewhere Paul used it six times and the author of Hebrews, James, and Peter each used it once.

Luke used it of "naming" a person or place in 13 of his 22 times (e.g., Acts 1:23; 4:36; 10:5; 11:13; etc.). But he also used it in the technical sense of "invoking, calling upon" the Lord or His name. "Whosoever *shall call* on the name of the Lord shall be saved" (Acts 2:21; cf. Joel 2:32) reveals clearly the technical understanding. It is synonymous with "praying" in Acts 7:59: Stephen "called upon" (i.e., "asked") the Lord to receive his spirit. Luke also identified followers of Jesus as those who "call upon" the name of the Lord (Acts 9:14,21; cf. 15:17).

Paul, like Luke, equated "calling upon the name of the Lord" with salvation; he even cited Joel 2:32, just as Luke did (Acts 2:21; cf. Romans 10:12-19). He also associated those calling upon the name of the Lord Jesus Christ with the Church. Here there is an indirect statement of Jesus' deity. He is clearly the "name of the Lord" to whom believers must turn. The technical understanding cannot be overlooked (1 Corinthians 1:2). Paul took an Old Testament formula and applied it to Jesus (cf. 2 Timothy 2:22). The more classical understanding of "to summon" (a witness) occurs in 2 Corinthians 1:23. Paul "called upon" God to witness his actions on behalf of the Corinthians.

Elsewhere in the New Testament *epikaleō* retains its technical overtones. Passively, God is not ashamed "to be called" the God of those who live by faith (Hebrews 11:16). James used the phrase "that worthy name by the which ye are called" as a reference to God or Jesus (James 2:7). The phrase comes from the Septuagint, and it indicates a relationship, especially a relationship with God (Deuteronomy 28:10; 2 Chronicles 7:14; Isaiah 43:7; Amos 9:12) (Davids, *New International Greek New Testament Commentary, James*, p.113). "Prayer" may be the thought in 1 Peter 1:17, but perhaps again *epikaleō* defines or identifies the one belonging to God. Peter's audience "called upon God" rather than the pagan idols they formerly worshiped (cf. 1 Peter 1:18; 4:3).

STRONG 1941, BAUER 294, MOULTON-MILLIGAN 239,

KITTEL 3:496-500, LIDDELL-SCOTT 635-36, COLIN BROWN 2:874.

1927. ἐπικάλυμμα epikalumma noun
Covering, veil; pretext.
CROSS-REFERENCE:
καλύπτω kaluptō (2543)

מִכְסֶה mikhṣeh (4510), Covering (Ex 26:14).

מָסָךְ māsākh (4689), Covering (2 Sm 17:19).

1. ἐπικάλυμμα epikalumma nom/acc sing neu

1 not using your liberty for **a cloak** of maliciousness,...1 Pt 2:16

Epikalumma is understood both figuratively ("pretext") and literally ("covering" [of any animal's orifice]) in ancient sources (see *Liddell-Scott*). In the Septuagint it is used of the "covering" of skins over the tabernacle (Exodus 26:14; 39:34 [LXX 39:21]). A "covering" over a well concealed Jonathan and Ahimaaz (2 Samuel 17:19 [LXX 2 Kings 17:19]). The New Testament reflects the figurative sense in 1 Peter 2:16 which speaks of those who use freedom as a "pretext" or "cover-up" (NIV) for evil.
STRONG 1942, BAUER 294, LIDDELL-SCOTT 636.

1928. ἐπικαλύπτω epikaluptō verb
Cover.
COGNATE:
καλύπτω kaluptō (2543)
SYNONYMS:
ἀποκρύπτω apokruptō (607)
καλύπτω kaluptō (2543)
κατακαλύπτω katakaluptō (2589)
κρύπτω kruptō (2900)
περικαλύπτω perikaluptō (3891)
συγκαλύπτω sunkaluptō (4631)

חָפָה chāphâh (2750), Cover (2 Sm 15:30, Jer 14:4).

כָּסָה kāṣâh (3803), Qal: cover, forgive (Ps 32:1 [31:1]); piel: cover (Jb 16:18 [16:19], Ps 44:19 [43:19], Jer 3:25); pual: be covered (Gn 7:20).

לוּט lûṭ (4011), Hiphil: wrap up, cover (1 Kgs 19:13).

סָכַר sākhar (5727), Niphal: be stopped up, closed (Gn 8:2—Codex Alexandrinus only).

סָרַח sārach (5831), Hang over (Ex 26:12—Codex Alexandrinus only).

פָּרַשׂ pāras (6816), Spread (Nm 4:11).

1. ἐπεκαλύφθησαν epekaluphthēsan
3pl indic aor pass

1 Blessed ... and whose sins **are covered**.............Rom 4:7

This verb (related to *kaluptō* [2543], "cover, conceal, hide") occurs in classical and Septuagintal Greek. Although it translates as many as six Hebrew terms, most often it renders a form of *kāṣâh*, "cover, conceal" (e.g., Genesis 7:19; Job 16:18 [LXX 16:19]; Psalm 32:1 [LXX 31:1]). The sole New Testament use is read in Romans 4:7, an allusion to Psalm 32:1 (LXX 31:1): "Blessed are they ... whose sins are covered." The parallelism of the verse suggests that "being covered" here equals "being forgiven."
STRONG 1943, BAUER 294, LIDDELL-SCOTT 636.

1929. ἐπικατάρατος epikataratos adj
Cursed.
CROSS-REFERENCE:
κατάρα katara (2641)

אָרַר ’ārar (803), Curse (Gn 3:14, Dt 27:15ff., Jer 11:3).

1. ἐπικατάρατος epikataratos nom sing masc
2. ἐπικατάρατοι epikataratoi nom pl masc

2 this people who knoweth not the law **are cursed**.....John 7:49
1 **Cursed** is every one that continueth not in all........Gal 3:10
1 **Cursed** is every one that hangeth on a tree:............ 3:13

This word, meaning "cursed," is extremely rare outside of Biblical Greek (see *Moulton-Milligan* for a tomb inscription, ca. Second Century A.D., using this word), and it may not have existed prior to the Septuagint.

Septuagint Usage
The Septuagint records *epikataratos* over 40 times. Most frequently it translates *’ārar*, "to inflict with a curse." As a result of Adam's disobedience all of creation is "cursed" (Genesis 3:14,17), as was the ground cursed for Cain since he murdered his brother (Genesis 4:11). Especially relevant is the proclaiming of "curses" upon those who violate the (often unseen) ordinances of God (with particular reference to those just given; Deuteronomy 27:15,16, passim; 27:26; Psalm 119:21 [LXX 118:21]; cf. Jeremiah 11:3; 17:5. (See also in the Septuagint the verbs *epikatareomai* and *kataraomai* [2642].)

New Testament Usage
Two New Testament usages of *epikataratos* occur in Galatians (3:10,13). (The *Textus Receptus* also reads *epikataratos* at John 7:49 where the Pharisees said that the crowd, which did not know the Law, was "cursed.") Paul argued in Galatians that anyone who seeks to justify himself through the works of the Law is under a curse (*epikataratos*) if he does not do everything (*pas* [3817B], added to the Septuagint here of Deuteronomy 27:26) the

Law prescribes. Paul understood this as the *whole* Law rather than only the ordinances of Deuteronomy 27 (Galatians 3:10). Paul contended that even if one were to do the Law perfectly, it would not result in justification (cf. e.g., Philippians 3:6).

Christ, however, fulfilled the Law and bore its penalty by becoming *epikataratos* on man's behalf (*huper hēmōn*) (Paul read *epikataratos* against the Septuagint's *kekatēramenos*; Deuteronomy 21:23) through the death on the Cross, that is, hanging on a tree (Galatians 3:13).

Nevertheless, Christ's fulfillment of the Law is not all that justifies believers. His becoming "accursed" was for their sakes, not His. "For if the inheritance (the promise the Spirit, verse 14) be of the law, it is no more of promise: but God gave it to Abraham by promise" (Galatians 3:18). Christ, too, is the promise that makes faith possible (cf. Galatians 3:14-29). (See also Bruce, *New International Greek Testament Commentary, Galatians*, pp.157-168; the Epistle of Barnabas applies a similar analogy of "cursed" to Jesus as the scapegoat of Leviticus 16.)

STRONG 1944, BAUER 294, MOULTON-MILLIGAN 239-40, KITTEL 1:451, LIDDELL-SCOTT 636, COLIN BROWN 1:416-17.

1930. ἐπίκειμαι epikeimai verb

Lie upon, press around, press upon, be urgent.
CROSS-REFERENCE:
    κεῖμαι keimai (2719)

הָכַר hākhar (2039), Hiphil: attack (Jb 19:3).
חָמַס chāmas (2659), Scheme against (Jb 21:27).
נָתַן nāthan (5598), Attach, fasten to (Ex 39:31 [36:40]).

1. ἐπίκειται epikeitai 3sing indic pres mid
2. ἐπικειμένου epikeimenou
    gen sing masc part pres mid
3. ἐπικείμενον epikeimenon
    nom/acc sing neu part pres mid
4. ἐπικείμενα epikeimena
    nom/acc pl neu part pres mid
5. ἐπικεῖσθαι epikeisthai inf pres mid
6. ἐπέκειτο epekeito 3sing indic imperf mid
7. ἐπέκειντο epekeinto 3pl indic imperf mid

5 people **pressed upon** him to hear the word of God,.. Luke 5:1
7 And they **were instant** with loud voices,............... 23:23
6 It was a cave, and a stone **lay upon** it............. John 11:38
3 they saw a fire of coals there, and fish **laid thereon**,.... 21:9
2 and no small tempest **lay on** us,................... Acts 27:20

1 for necessity **is laid upon** me;...................... 1 Co 9:16
4 **imposed** on them until the time of reformation....... Heb 9:10

Classical Greek
Epikeimai plays a number of roles in classical Greek. Functionally it serves as a passive to *epitithēmi* (1991), "lay (or) put upon." It can refer to doors being "closed" ("put to") or to one object being "set upon" another. But in another sense it could denote the violent action of "pressing upon" someone or something (i.e., "attack" an enemy). It also implied "being urgent" about something (see *Liddell-Scott*).

Septuagint Usage
Epikeimai occurs in only three canonical texts in the Septuagint, and each has a different Hebrew original. There are four apocryphal readings. In Exodus 39:31 (LXX 36:40) it refers to "attaching" the sacred diadem to the turban of the priest. Job's "comforters" "lay upon" (i.e., "attacked") him with their words, according to Job 19:3 (cf. 21:27). First Maccabees 6:57 illustrates the idea of "pressing upon urgently"; here it is the affairs of the kingdom.

New Testament Usage
Seven instances of *epikeimai* are recorded in the New Testament. The literal use is illustrated in such texts as John 11:38 which speaks of the stone that "lay upon" the tomb of Lazarus (cf. John 21:9). Figuratively, it also describes the "pressing" of the crowd upon Jesus. Implicit here is the sense of urgency which becomes more explicit in texts like Luke 23:23 (of the insistent cries that Jesus be crucified) and 1 Corinthians 9:16 (of Paul's feeling compelled to preach the gospel). Acts 27:20 tells of how the storm "lay on" (cf. NIV's "raging") those on the ship.

STRONG 1945, BAUER 294, MOULTON-MILLIGAN 240, KITTEL 3:655, LIDDELL-SCOTT 637.

1930B. ἐπικέλλω epikellō verb

Run aground, bring to shore.

1. ἐπέκειλαν epekeilan 3pl indic aor act

1 **ran the vessel aground**; (NASB)................... Acts 27:41

Epikellō is a purely poetical term found one time in the New Testament, Acts 27:41 (see variant to the *Textus Receptus*). It fits well with the word-picture Paul painted in Acts 27 of his shipwreck experience. The word means "to bring ashore," or more specifically, "to run a ship aground."

BAUER 294, MOULTON-MILLIGAN 240, LIDDELL-SCOTT 637.

1931. Ἐπικούρειος Epikoureios name
Epicurean.

1. Ἐπικουρείων Epikoureiōn gen pl masc

1 Then certain philosophers of the **Epicureans**,....... Acts 17:18

A follower of the Greek philosopher Epicurus who taught that pleasure was the highest goal of life (Acts 17:18).

1932. ἐπικουρία epikouria noun
Help.
SYNONYMS:
ἀντίλημψις antilēmpsis (481)
βοήθεια boētheia (989)

1. ἐπικουρίας epikourias gen sing fem

1 Having therefore obtained **help** of God,............Acts 26:22

This term is rare in Biblical writings occurring only in one text in the apocryphal portions of the Septuagint (Wisdom of Solomon 13:18). Its use there depicts general "help" or "aid" such as was being sought from idols. In the only New Testament occurrence (Acts 26:22) Paul used it in his speech before Agrippa. He spoke of the "help" God granted him by enabling him to avoid capture by those Jews who sought to kill him in the temple at Jerusalem.

STRONG 1947, BAUER 294-95, MOULTON-MILLIGAN 240, LIDDELL-SCOTT 640.

1933. ἐπικρίνω epikrinō verb
Decide, determine; give sentence.
CROSS-REFERENCE:
κρίνω krinō (2892)

1. ἐπέκρινεν epekrinen 3sing indic aor act

1 Pilate **gave sentence** ... should be as they required. Luke 23:24

In classical and Hellenistic sources *epikrinō* has both legal and nonlegal nuances. Thus the Septuagint reads that the death sentence was passed (2 Maccabees 4:47) or that destruction had been "decreed" (3 Maccabees 4:2). In the single New Testament instance (Luke 23:24) Pilate "decided" to grant the demands of the maddened mob.

STRONG 1948, BAUER 295, MOULTON-MILLIGAN 240, LIDDELL-SCOTT 641.

1934. ἐπιλαμβάνομαι
epilambanomai verb
Take hold of, grasp, catch, be concerned with, take an interest in, help.
COGNATE:
λαμβάνω lambanō (2956)
SYNONYMS:
ἀγρεύω agreuō (63)
ἁρπάζω harpazō (720)
ἔχω echō (2174)
θηρεύω thēreuō (2317)
καταλαμβάνω katalambanō (2608)
κρατέω krateō (2875)
λαμβάνω lambanō (2956)
πιάζω piazō (3945)
συλλαμβάνω sullambanō (4666)
συναρπάζω sunarpazō (4734B)

אָחַז 'āchaz (270), Lay hold of, catch (Ex 4:4, Jgs 16:3, Is 5:29).

חָזַק chāzaq (2480), Be strong; hiphil: take hold of, seize (Dt 25:11, 1 Kgs 1:50, Jer 49:24 [30:13]).

עָדָה 'ādhāh (5917), Adorn oneself, take up (Jer 31:4 [38:4]).

קָמַט qāmaṭ (7344), Seize (Jb 16:8).

קָרָא qārā' (7410), Come upon, happen unto (Jer 44:23 [51:33]).

שָׁקַק shāqaq (8630), Rush, run (Jl 2:9).

תָּפַשׂ tāphas (8945), Take hold, seize (1 Kgs 11:30, Is 3:6, Ez 30:21).

1. ἐπιλαμβάνεται epilambanetai 3sing indic pres mid
2. ἐπελάβετο epelabeto 3sing indic aor mid
3. ἐπιλάβωνται epilabōntai 3pl subj aor mid
4. ἐπιλαβοῦ epilabou 2sing impr aor mid
5. ἐπιλαβόμενος epilabomenos
    nom sing masc part aor mid
6. ἐπιλαβομένου epilabomenou
    gen sing masc part aor mid
7. ἐπιλαβόμενοι epilabomenoi
    nom pl masc part aor mid
8. ἐπιλαβέσθαι epilabesthai inf aor mid

2 Jesus stretched forth his hand, and **caught** him,.... Matt 14:31
5 And **he took** the blind man by the hand,.......... Mark 8:23
5 And Jesus, ... **took** a child, and set him by him,..... Luke 9:47
5 And **he took** him, and healed him, and let him go;.... 14:4
3 that they might **take hold** of his words,................. 20:20
8 could not **take hold** of his words before the people:.... 20:26
7 they **laid hold upon** one Simon, a Cyrenian,.......... 23:26
5 But Barnabas **took** him,........................Acts 9:27
7 they **caught** Paul and Silas,........................ 16:19
7 they **took** him, and brought him unto Areopagus,...... 17:19
7 Then all the Greeks **took** Sosthenes,................... 18:17
7 and the people ran together: and they **took** Paul,..... 21:30
2 Then the chief captain came near, and **took** him,..... 21:33
5 Then the chief captain **took** him by the hand,......... 23:19
4 Fight ... good fight of faith, **lay hold** on eternal life, 1 Tm 6:12

ἐπιλανθάνομαι 1935

3 that they **may lay hold** on eternal life................1 Tm 6:19
1 For verily he **took** not on him the nature of angels;..Heb 2:16
1 but he **took on** him the seed of Abraham................2:16
6 in the day when I **took** them by the hand..............8:9

Classical Greek and Septuagint Usage

Epilambanomai is actually the middle form, deponent verb from *epilambanō*, which occurs in classical and Septuagintal literature but not in the New Testament. "Seize, grasp, catch, lay hold of" are the primary meanings of this common verb. It may indicate both a violent seizure or a trustful holding of the hand. It is used in the Septuagint, papyri, as well as by classical authors such as Herodotus. The context determines whether the action is favorable or unfavorable.

In the Septuagint the form *epilambanō* appears over 45 times. Six of these are not canonical. As many as seven Hebrew originals stand behind *epilambanō*, but two, *'āchaz* ("lay hold of, seize") and *chāzaq* (hiphil, "take hold"), are used more frequently.

Physically, this word depicts Jacob's "grasping" Esau's heel at their birth (Genesis 25:26), or of God's instructing Moses to "seize" the staff that had become a serpent (Exodus 4:4; cf. Judges 16:3; 2 Samuel 13:11 [LXX 2 Kings 13:11]). It can be used as an image for an army's "taking" a city (cf. Joel 2:9). Positively, it can speak of God's "taking" Israel by the hand and leading her out of Egypt (Jeremiah 31:32 [LXX 38:32]). Negatively the word describes disaster which "overtakes" the disobedient (Jeremiah 44:23 [LXX 51:23]).

New Testament Usage

Only the form *epilambanomai* appears in the New Testament. The sense of "help" is implied when Jesus "caught" (and thereby rescued) Peter from the perils of the sea (Matthew 14:31). Although lexical evidence is not entirely consistent, it is striking that whenever Jesus "took" (*epilambanomai*) an individual he was healed (e.g., Mark 8:23; Luke 9:47; 14:4). In the Epistle to the Hebrews this sense is also present. God "helps" His people, not the angels (Hebrews 2:16, twice; cf. Hebrews 8:9/ Jeremiah 31:32 [LXX 38:32]).

Negatively the word also describes the forceful "seizing" or "catching" of persons, sometimes against their will (Luke 20:20,26 of the scheming of the spies to "trap" Jesus; 23:26; Acts 16:19), and sometimes in compliance with it (Acts 9:27; 17:19). Physical violence is definitely implied in Acts 18:17 and 21:30 and should probably be understood elsewhere (Acts 21:33).

The force of *epilambanomai* is also present when used in a figurative sense. Paul advised Timothy to "seize, lay hold of" eternal life, which is truly life (1 Timothy 6:12,19). The context of the letter as a whole indicates that Paul wanted Timothy to make a stand for the gospel (cf. 1 Timothy 1:3,18,19; 4:6ff.,11-15).

STRONG 1949, BAUER 295, MOULTON-MILLIGAN 240, KITTEL 4:9 (see "epilambanō"), LIDDELL-SCOTT 642 (see "epilambanō"), COLIN BROWN 3:747.

1935. ἐπιλανθάνομαι

epilanthanomai verb

Forget, overlook, neglect.

COGNATE:
λανθάνω lanthanō (2963)

SYNONYM:
ἐκλανθάνομαι eklanthanomai (1572)

מָחָה māchâh (4364), Wipe out or off; niphal: be forgotten (Sir 3:14).

נוּחַ nûach (5299), Hiphil: leave, forsake (Jer 14:9).

נָשָׁה nāshâh (5567), Qal: forget (Lam 3:17); niphal: be forgotten (Is 44:21).

נְשִׁיָּה nᵉshîyāh (5570), Forgetting (Ps 88:12 [87:12]).

שָׁכַח shākhach (8319), Qal: forget (Dt 6:12, Ps 10:11 [9:32], Is 49:14); niphal: be forgotten (Dt 31:21, Eccl 2:16, Jer 23:40); piel: cause something to be forgotten (Lam 2:6); hiphil: cause to forget (Jer 23:27).

שָׁכֵחַ shākhēach (8321), Forget (Is 65:11).

1. ἐπιλανθάνεσθε epilanthanesthe 2pl impr pres mid
2. ἐπιλανθανόμενος epilanthanomenos
   nom sing masc part pres mid
3. ἐπελάθετο epelatheto 3sing indic aor mid
4. ἐπελάθοντο epelathonto 3pl indic aor mid
5. ἐπιλαθέσθαι epilathesthai inf aor mid
6. ἐπιλελησμένον epilelēsmenon
   nom/acc sing neu part perf mid

4 his disciples ... they **had forgotten** to take bread....Matt 16:5
4 Now the disciples **had forgotten** to take bread,......Mark 8:14
6 and not one of them is **forgotten** before God?.....Luke 12:6
2 **forgetting** those things which are behind,............Phlp 3:13
5 For God is not unrighteous **to forget** your work......Heb 6:10
1 Be not forgetful to entertain strangers:................13:2
1 But to do good and to communicate **forget** not:.......13:16
3 straightway **forgetteth** what manner of man he was....Jas 1:24

Classical Greek

Appearing also in the active form (-ō) in classical writings where it means "cause to forget," *epilanthanomai* (more commonly *epilēthomai* in classical Greek) means "forget, neglect" (see *Liddell-Scott*).

542

Septuagint Usage

The active form dominates the Septuagint. Frequently *epilanthonomai* occurs in negative injunctions to Israel "not to neglect or forget" their convenant obligations (e.g., Deuteronomy 4:23,31; cf. Psalm 119:16,61,83,93 [LXX 118:16,61,83,93]). Synonymous with forgetting God's covenant is forgetting or neglecting God himself, especially in His role as Saviour (Deuteronomy 6:12; 8:11,14; cf. 32:15-18).

God, however, is the one who does not forget the righteous (e.g., Sirach 44:10; Isaiah 49:15ff.), despite the fact that He is forgotten (Psalm 9:12; cf. verses 13,17,18; Jeremiah 18:15), and despite the fact that some may feel they have been forgotten (Psalm 44:24 [LXX 43:24]; cf. verses 17,20; Isaiah 49:14). God will forget past "troubles" (Isaiah 65:16, here probably referring to the punishment meted out for Israel's unfaithfulness).

In the Septuagint *epilanthanomai* plays a special role in describing the relationship between God and His people. To "forget" God is tantamount to being "unfaithful" to the covenant. God, who can only be faithful, will not forget His people despite circumstances.

New Testament Usage

Eight occurrences of *eiplambanomai* are found in the New Testament. Two are parallel texts: a comment about the disciples' "forgetting" to take bread with them (Matthew 16:5; Mark 8:14). The Old Testament understanding of God as incapable of forgetting His people is mirrored plainly in Luke 12:6. If God does not "forget" the sparrows, how much more will He not neglect His people's needs.

Paul wisely counseled his Philippian readers concerning running the Christian race: "Forgetting what is behind and straining toward what is ahead, I press on toward the goal to win the prize for which God has called me heavenward in Christ Jesus" (3:13,14, NIV). Like a good runner, Paul knew he could not run well if he concerned himself with past obstacles, regrets, or mistakes.

"Neglect" is more the idea in Hebrews 13:16. Believers should not neglect having fellowship (*koinōnia* [2815]) with one another. Neither should Christians neglect showing hospitality to "strangers." This is not simply because they might be "entertaining angels." Rather, hospitality to the stranger and foreigner—believers are themselves strangers in this world—is fundamental to proper Christian behavior. What is more: "God is not unjust; he will not forget your work and the love you have shown him as you have helped his people and continue to help them" (Hebrews 6:10, NIV).

STRONG 1950, BAUER 295, MOULTON-MILLIGAN 240-41, LIDDELL-SCOTT 642 (see "epilanthanō").

1935B. ἐπιλέγω epilegō

Call, name; call upon, select, choose.

COGNATE:
λέγω legō (2978)

SYNONYMS:
αἱρετίζω hairetizō (139)
αἱρέω haireō (141)
ἐκλέγομαι eklegomai (1573)
ἐξαιρέω exaireō (1791)
ἐπονομάζω eponomazō (2012)
καλέω kaleō (2535)
λαμβάνω lambanō (2956)
λέγω legō (2978)
ὀνομάζω onomazō (3550)
προσαγορεύω prosagoreuō (4174)
προχειρίζομαι procheirizomai (4258)
φωνέω phōneō (5291)
χειροτονέω cheirotoneō (5336)
χρηματίζω chrēmatizō (5372)

בָּחַר bāchar (1013), Select, choose (Ex 18:25, Jos 8:3, 2 Sm 17:1).

בָּעַר bāʻar (1220), Burn; piel: cut off (1 Kgs 14:10).

קָבַץ qāvats (7192), Gather, bring into (Est 2:3).

1. ἐπιλεγομένη **epilegomenē**
nom sing fem part pres mid
2. ἐπιλεξάμενος **epilexamenos**
nom sing masc part aor mid

1 which is called in the Hebrew tongue Bethesda,..... John 5:2
2 And Paul chose Silas, and departed,............... Acts 15:40

Epilegō, from *epi* (1894), "upon, on," and *legō* (2978), "say, speak," basically means "name, call" or "pick, choose." The Septuagint especially uses it of "choosing" individuals for religious, military, or social tasks (e.g., Exodus 17:9; 18:25; 2 Samuel 10:9 [LXX 2 Kings 10:9]). The middle voice (*epilegomai*) appears in the New Testament. There the idea of something's being "called" (something else) appears (John 5:2, an explanatory remark), as well as the idea of "selecting" someone for a task (Acts 15:40).

STRONG 1951, BAUER 295, MOULTON-MILLIGAN 241, LIDDELL-SCOTT 643.

1936. ἐπιλείπω epileipō verb

Leave behind, fail.

ἐπιλείχω 1936B

CROSS-REFERENCE:
λείπω leipō (2981)

שָׁאַר shā'ar (8080), Remain; hiphil: leave remaining (Ob 5).

1. ἐπιλείψει epileipsei 3sing indic fut act
1 for the time would fail me to tell of Gedeon, ... Heb 11:32

This verb is composed of the preposition *epi* (1894) and the verb *leipō* (2981), "leave." In this instance the preposition has a slight intensifying force. Thus *epileipō* means "leave" or (passively) "be left" (behind). It occurs only in a questionable reading in the Septuagint (Obadiah 1:5) and only once in the New Testament. In the Epistle to the Hebrews the author used *epileipō* of time which threatens to "leave behind," i.e., "the time *would fail*" before he recounted all of the heroes of the faith (11:32).

STRONG 1952, BAUER 295, MOULTON-MILLIGAN 241, LIDDELL-SCOTT 643.

1936B. ἐπιλείχω epileichō verb
Lick, lick over.

1. ἐπέλειχον epeleichon 3pl indic imperf act
1 dogs were coming and licking his sores. (NASB) ... Luke 16:21

This verb appears only once in the New Testament. In Jesus' account of the Rich Man and Lazarus, Luke 16:21 says, "The dogs came and *licked* his sores." This was a particularly poignant way to describe the extent of Lazarus' destitution.

BAUER 295, MOULTON-MILLIGAN 241, LIDDELL-SCOTT 643.

1937. ἐπιλεξάμενος
epilexamenos verb
Having chosen.

This is a participial form of *epilegō*. See the word study at number 1935B.

1938. ἐπιλησμονή epilēsmonē noun
Forgetfulness.

1. ἐπιλησμονῆς epilēsmonēs gen sing fem
1 continueth therein, he being not a forgetful hearer, ... Jas 1:25

This rather rare term occurs once in the Septuagint at Sirach 11:27. How easily one forgets the good times when faced with the bad. The sole use in the New Testament (James 1:25) concerns the one who does not "forget" what he has heard. "Not forgetting" here is tantamount to "doing" what one has heard, a consistent understanding in the New Testament (James 1:25; cf. Luke 6:46-49).

STRONG 1953, BAUER 295, LIDDELL-SCOTT 643.

1939. ἐπίλοιπος epiloipos adj
Left, remaining, other.
CROSS-REFERENCE:
λείπω leipō (2981)

יָתַר yāthar (3613), Niphal: remainder (Lv 27:18).
יֶתֶר yether (3615), Remainder (Is 38:10, Mi 5:3).
שָׁאַר shā'ar (8080), Niphal: remainder (Dt 19:20).
שְׁאֵרִית she'ērîth (8086), Remainder, what is left (Jer 25:20 [32:20], 44:14 [51:14]).

1. ἐπίλοιπον epiloipon acc sing masc
1 the rest of his time in the flesh to the lusts of men, .. 1 Pt 4:2

The preposition *epi* (1894) and the noun *loipos* (3036), "the rest, remainder," unite to create the adjective *epiloipos*, "remaining." It occurs both in classical and Septuagintal writings frequently in reference to "remaining time" (e.g., Leviticus 27:18; Isaiah 38:12), although as a plural substantive it can refer to people (Deuteronomy 19:20; 21:21). The New Testament uses *epiloipos* only once (1 Peter 4:2) in reference to how a believer should "arm" himself with the mind of Christ (4:1) so that he will live the "*rest* of his time" doing the will of God.

STRONG 1954, BAUER 295, MOULTON-MILLIGAN 241, LIDDELL-SCOTT 644.

1940. ἐπίλυσις epilusis noun
Interpretation, explanation.
COGNATE:
ἐπιλύω epiluō (1941)
SYNONYM:
ἑρμηνεία hermēneia (2042)

1. ἐπιλύσεως epiluseōs gen sing fem
1 no prophecy ... is of any private interpretation. ...... 2 Pt 1:20

This term is rare in Biblical writings. It does not appear in the Septuagint except in some versional witnesses. Aquila thus reads it of the "interpretation" of dreams (Genesis 40:8; cf. Symmachus at Hosea 3:4 with "ephod"). In the New Testament only 2 Peter 1:20 reads *epilusis*. There the author reminded his readers either that prophecy of Scripture is not subject to private interpretation or that prophecy is not the result of the prophet's own interpretation (on resolving this question see Bauckham, *Word Biblical Commentary*, 50:229ff.).

STRONG 1955, BAUER 295, MOULTON-MILLIGAN 241, KITTEL 4:328-35,337, LIDDELL-SCOTT 644, COLIN BROWN 1:576-78.

1941. ἐπιλύω epiluō verb
Explain, interpret, decide, settle.

COGNATES:
ἐπίλυσις epilusis (1940)
λύω luō (3061)

SYNONYMS:
ἀπαλλάσσω apallassō (521)
ἀπολύω apoluō (624)
βουλεύομαι bouleuomai (1003)
ἐλευθερόω eleutheroō (1646)
ἐξαιρέω exaireō (1791)
κρίνω krinō (2892)
λυτρόω lutroō (3056)
λύω luō (3061)

1. ἐπέλυεν epeluen 3sing indic imperf act
2. ἐπιλυθήσεται epiluthēsetai 3sing indic fut pass

1 he expounded all things to his disciples............. Mark 4:34
2 it shall be determined in a lawful assembly......... Acts 19:39

Epiluō, "loosen, untie," or in a more general sense "set free, release," can particularly apply to "solving" or "unraveling" problems, or (especially in Biblical usage) divine mysteries (see *Liddell-Scott*). The latter usage appears only in Aquila's version of the Septuagint, for example in reference to the interpretation of Pharaoh's dreams (Genesis 40:8; 41:8,12).

New Testament Usage
Epiluō is used only twice in the New Testament. In Mark 4:34 it means "expound, explain more fully, solve further." It was necessary for the disciples to stay close to Jesus because of His habit of unfolding truth developmentally. To the multitudes He spoke in parables, but He "expounded" His meaning in private as He enabled the disciples to better understand the mysteries of the kingdom of heaven.

Epiluō is used in Acts 19:39 to denote the determination of a legal question in a lawful assembly. The town clerk declared that the matter under question could not be settled by a mob in riot. It must be dealt with by an assembly called formally into session. Roman officials were the only ones empowered to call for such an assemblage.

STRONG 1956, BAUER 295-96, MOULTON-MILLIGAN 241, KITTEL 4:328-35,337, LIDDELL-SCOTT 644, COLIN BROWN 1:576-78.

1942. ἐπιμαρτυρέω epimartureō verb
Testify to, bear witness.

COGNATE:
μαρτυρέω martureō (3113)

SYNONYMS:
διαμαρτύρομαι diamarturomai (1257)
μαρτυρέω martureō (3113)

עוּד 'ûdh (5967), Hiphil: summon, call for (1 Kgs 2:42, Neh 9:29,30, Am 3:13).

1. ἐπιμαρτυρῶν epimarturōn
nom sing masc part pres act

1 and testifying that this is the true grace of God..... 1 Pt 5:12

A member of the large *martureō* (3113) word group, *epimartureō* is composed of the preposition (here intensifying) *epi* (1894) and the verb *martureō*. It replaces the Hebrew *'ûdh* seven times in the Septuagint and means "testify to" (e.g., Nehemiah 9:29f.; Amos 3:13). Its sole use in the New Testament, at 1 Peter 5:12, concerns the author's own estimation of what he has accomplished in his letter: "I have written briefly, exhorting (encouraging you, NIV), and *testifying* that this is the true grace of God."

STRONG 1957, BAUER 296, MOULTON-MILLIGAN 241, KITTEL 4:508-10, LIDDELL-SCOTT 644-45, COLIN BROWN 3:1042.

1943. ἐπιμέλεια epimeleia noun
Care, attention, concern.

CROSS-REFERENCE:
μέλω melō (3169)

שִׁקּוּי shiqqûy (8616), Nourishment, marrow (Prv 3:8).

1. ἐπιμελείας epimeleias gen sing fem

1 go unto his friends to refresh himself. (NT)........ Acts 27:3

This term was very common among classical authors and means "care, attention" (cf. the verb *epimeleomai* [1944]). In the papyri it is also common and concerns caring for either individuals, property, or duties (see *Moulton-Milligan*). The term appears over 10 times in the Septuagint but only once in canonical material with a Hebrew original (Proverbs 3:8; cf. Proverbs 3:22; 13:4; Wisdom of Solomon 13:13; 1 Maccabees 16:14). One reading of *epimeleia* occurs in the New Testament. In Acts

ἐπιμελέομαι 1944

27:3 it describes Paul's friends being allowed to give "care" to his needs (cf. NIV "provide for his needs").

STRONG 1958, BAUER 296, MOULTON-MILLIGAN 241-42, LIDDELL-SCOTT 645-46.

1944. ἐπιμελέομαι epimeleomai verb
Care for, take care of, look after.
COGNATES:
  Μελχί Melchi (3167)
  μέλω melō (3169)

1. ἐπεμελήθη epemelēthē 3sing indic aor pass
2. ἐπιμελήθητι epimelēthēti 2sing impr aor pass
3. ἐπιμελήσεται epimelēsetai 3sing indic fut pass

1 and brought him to an inn, and took care of him... Luke 10:34
2 to the host, and said unto him, Take care of him;...... 10:35
3 how shall he take care of the church of God?....... 1 Tm 3:5

In classical sources *epimeleomai* means "take care of, manage." It functions in a variety of contexts from the exercise of public duty, to taking care of or tending to someone or something (see *Liddell-Scott*). It is relatively rare in the Septuagint occurring in only five texts, only one of which is canonical (Genesis 44:21, of Joseph's wanting to "look after" Benjamin; cf. Proverbs 27:23 [LXX 22:25]; Sirach 30:25). Only Luke's Gospel and 1 Timothy use *epimelomai* in the New Testament. In the Gospel it refers to the Good Samaritan's "caring for" the injured man (10:34) and his instructions to the innkeeper to "take care" of him (10:35). In 1 Timothy 3:5 it is used of the elder who must be able to "rule" (manage) (*proistēmi* [4150]) his own home if he is to be trusted with "caring for" the household of God.

STRONG 1959, BAUER 296, MOULTON-MILLIGAN 242, LIDDELL-SCOTT 645-46.

1945. ἐπιμελῶς epimelōs adv
Carefully, diligently.
COGNATE:
  μέλω melō (3169)
SYNONYMS:
  ἀκριβῶς akribōs (197)
  σπουδαίως spoudaiōs (4560)

אָסְפַּרְנָא 'oṣparnā' (A643), Decree, do accordingly (Ezr 6:8,12,13—Aramaic).

רַק raq (7828), Only (Gn 6:5).

שָׁחַר shāchar (8264), Piel: be prompt, careful (Prv 13:24).

1. ἐπιμελῶς epimelōs

1 and seek diligently till she find it?................ Luke 15:8

In early Greek literature *epimelōs* means to perform a service carefully. This word is confined to only one usage in the New Testament in reference to the Parable of the Lost Coin (Luke 15:8) where a woman hunted "carefully," or searched "diligently," for her lost coin.

STRONG 1960, BAUER 296, MOULTON-MILLIGAN 242.

1946. ἐπιμένω epimenō verb
Stay, remain, continue, persist, persevere.
COGNATE:
  μένω menō (3176)
SYNONYMS:
  ἀπολείπω apoleipō (614)
  αὐλίζομαι aulizomai (829)
  διαμένω diamenō (1259)
  διατελέω diateleō (1294)
  διατρίβω diatribō (1298)
  εἰμί eimi (1498)
  ἐμμένω emmenō (1682)
  καθίζω kathizō (2495)
  καταμένω katamenō (2620)
  μένω menō (3176)
  παραμένω paramenō (3748)
  περιλείπομαι perileipomai (3898)
  ὑπομένω hupomenō (5116)

מָהַהּ māhahh (4244), Hithpalpel: tarry, delay (Ex 12:39).

1. ἐπιμένετε epimenete 2pl indic pres act
2. ἐπίμενε epimene 2sing impr pres act
3. ἐπιμενόντων epimenontōn
                gen pl masc part pres act
4. ἐπιμένειν epimenein inf pres act
5. ἐπέμεινα epemeina 1sing indic aor act
6. ἐπεμείναμεν epemeinamen 1pl indic aor act
7. ἐπιμείνῃς epimeinēs 2sing subj aor act
8. ἐπιμείνωσιν epimeinōsin 3pl subj aor act
9. ἐπιμεῖναι epimeinai inf aor act
10. ἐπιμενῶ epimenō 1sing indic fut act
11. ἐπιμενοῦμεν epimenoumen 1pl indic fut act
12. ἐπέμενεν epemenen 3sing indic imperf act
13. ἐπέμενον epemenon 3pl indic imperf act
14. ἐπιμένῃς epimenēs 2sing subj pres act
15. ἐπιμένωμεν epimenōmen 1pl subj pres act
16. ἐπιμένωσιν epimenōsin 3pl subj pres act

13 So when they continued asking him,............... John 8:7
9 Then prayed they him to tarry certain days........ Acts 10:48
12 But Peter continued knocking:...................... 12:16
4 persuaded them to continue in the grace of God...... 13:43
9 Notwithstanding it pleased Silas to abide there still.... 15:34
6 And finding disciples, we tarried there seven days:... 21:4
3 And as we tarried there many days,................. 21:10
6 landing at Syracuse, we tarried there three days...... 28:12
9 and were desired to tarry with them seven days:..... 28:14
11 Shall we continue in sin, that grace may abound?.. Rom 6:1
15 Shall we continue in sin, that grace may abound?...... 6:1

7	if thou **continue** in his goodness:	Rom 11:22
14	if thou **continue** in his goodness:	11:22
8	And they also, if they **abide** not still in unbelief,	11:23
16	And they also, if they **abide** not still in unbelief,	11:23
9	but I trust to **tarry** a while with you,	1 Co 16:7
10	But I will **tarry** at Ephesus until Pentecost.	16:8
5	to see Peter, and **abode** with him fifteen days.	Gal 1:18
4	to **abide** in the flesh is more needful for you.	Phlp 1:24
1	If ye **continue** in the faith grounded and settled,	Col 1:23
2	and unto the doctrine; **continue** in them:	1 Tm 4:16

Classical Greek and Septuagint Usage

Continuous action is implied in the use of *epimenō* in classical and Koine Greek from the days of Homer as well as in the Septuagint (Exodus 12:39). It is translated variously, "to stay over, remain, persevere, abide in, continue in, tarry."

New Testament Usage

In John 8:7 Jesus responded to the "continued" questioning of the assembled men by stooping down to write in the sand. The scribes did not accept the silence of Jesus as sufficient answer, so they kept repeating their question. The use of *epimenō* with a participle indicates a dramatic moment.

The figurative use of the word is illustrated in Peter's "continued" knocking at the door after his release from prison. The use of the participle adds a natural touch, and the emphasis is on his continued, persistent knocking (Acts 12:16).

The figurative sense of continuing in a state of sin is indicated by *epimenō* in Romans 6:1. Paul rejected the question on the ground that such repetitious sinning is incompatible with the completed work of Christ. Paul said that the liberty of the believer through justification is not license for continuing in sin. He admonished the believer to continue actively in the righteousness of God and not to abide in unbelief (Romans 11:22,23).

The literal use of *epimenō* appears in Acts (21:4,10; 28:12,14) indicating that the journeys of Paul involved a number of times when it was necessary to remain in a place for a given period of time.

STRONG 1961, BAUER 296, MOULTON-MILLIGAN 242, LIDDELL-SCOTT 646, COLIN BROWN 3:223,227-28.

1947. ἐπινεύω epineuō verb

Give consent.

COGNATE:
  νεύω neuō (3368)
SYNONYMS:
  συγκατατίθημαι sunkatatithēmai (4635)
  συνευδοκέω suneudokeō (4759)

נָכַר nākhar (5421), Niphal: pretend, disguise (Prv 26:24).

1. ἐπένευσεν epeneusen 3sing indic aor act

1 to tarry longer time with them, he **consented** not; ...Acts 18:20

In extra-Biblical literature this word refers to "one giving consent by a nod." In the New Testament this term is used only in Acts 18:20 where Paul in Ephesus was asked by Prisiclla and Aquila to stay a little while longer. However, Paul "consented not" to stay in Ephesus.

STRONG 1962, BAUER 296, MOULTON-MILLIGAN 242, LIDDELL-SCOTT 648.

1948. ἐπίνοια epinoia noun

Thought, intent.

COGNATE:
  νοέω noeō (3401)
SYNONYMS:
  γνώμη gnōmē (1100)
  διαλογισμός dialogismos (1255)
  διανόημα dianoēma (1264)
  διάνοια dianoia (1265)
  ἐνθύμησις enthumēsis (1745)
  ἔννοια ennoia (1755)
  λογισμός logismos (3027)
  νόημα noēma (3402)
  νοῦς nous (3426)

1. ἐπίνοια epinoia nom sing fem

1 the **thought** of thine heart may be forgiven thee......Acts 8:22

Classical Greek and Septuagint Usage

Epinoia is related to the Greek word *nous* (3426), "mind," and is used in classical Greek in the general sense of "a thought, notion, idea." It is sometimes used to describe a person's "power of thought," "inventiveness," or the thing he had invented. Writers occasionally used *epinoia* to mean "an afterthought, second thoughts." The term often refers to a "purpose, plan, design." It is used eight times in the Septuagint with similar meanings (e.g., Wisdom of Solomon 6:16; 9:14).

New Testament Usage

Epinoia appears only once in the New Testament, in Acts 8:22, where Peter warned the former magician Simon to pray that God would forgive his sinful thought, *epinoia*, that he could purchase the Holy Spirit. The context shows that the word in this instance was used in the bad sense of an evil plan or plot (Reinecker, *Linquistic Key to Greek New Testament*, 1:279).

STRONG 1963, BAUER 296, MOULTON-MILLIGAN 242, LIDDELL-SCOTT 648.

1949. ἐπιορκέω epiorkeō verb
Swear falsely, break one's oath.
CROSS-REFERENCE:
ὁρκίζω horkizō (3589)

1. ἐπιορκήσεις epiorkēseis 2sing indic fut act

1 Thou shalt not forswear thyself, ... Matt 5:33

In classical Greek the word *epiorkeō* (sometimes spelled *ephiorkeo*) occasionally means simply "to swear" but usually refers to a false oath. *Moulton-Milligan* describes its use in the legal formula: "If my oath is kept (*euorkeō*), may it be well with me; but if false (*epiorkeō*), the reverse."

The New Testament uses it only in Matthew 5:33 where Jesus described one of the traditional interpretations of the Old Testament regulations. The verse contrasts it with the virtue of performing any vow made to God and thus refers in this context to the sin of making a solemn vow to God and not carrying it out. The word can also be used to describe an assertion reinforced by a reference to God, one which is intentionally deceptive.

STRONG 1964, BAUER 296, MOULTON-MILLIGAN 242, KITTEL 5:466-67, LIDDELL-SCOTT 649.

1950. ἐπίορκος epiorkos adj
Perjured, falsely sworn.
CROSS-REFERENCE:
ὁρκίζω horkizō (3589)
שָׁבַע shāva' (8123), Swear (Zec 5:3).

1. ἐπιόρκοις epiorkois dat pl masc

1 for menstealers, for liars, for perjured persons, ... 1 Tm 1:10

Classical Greek and Septuagint Usage
Though the word is an adjective, it is more often used as a substantive meaning "a false oath" or "one who swears a false oath." In the *Iliad* it is used to describe a vow made with good intentions but not kept because of interference from the gods (see *Liddell-Scott*). In general it means failing to tell the truth, even when testimony was backed by an oath, or failing to keep a promise that had been made with an oath. Its only Septuagintal use is found in Zechariah 5:3.

New Testament Usage
The only use of the word in the New Testament is in 1 Timothy 1:10 where Paul included "perjurers" in a list of extreme examples of sinners who fell under the condemnation of the Old Testament law. The context suggests that *epiorkos* was a particularly flagrant violation of the Law's provisions such as the command against taking God's name in vain.

STRONG 1965, BAUER 296, KITTEL 5:466, LIDDELL-SCOTT 649.

1951. ἐπιοῦσα epiousa noun
Next.
CROSS-REFERENCE:
εἰμί eimi (1498)

1. ἐπιούσῃ epiousē dat sing fem

1 And the next day he showed himself unto them ..... Acts 7:26
1 and the next day to Neapolis; 16:11
1 and came the next day over against Chios; 20:15
1 the day following Paul went in with us unto James; 21:18
1 And the night following the Lord stood by him, ... 23:11

This word is actually the feminine participle form of *epeimi*, "to come upon, come near, approach." Both in classical Greek and in the New Testament the participle form is almost always used, generally to modify a word denoting time. In such constructions it means "next, following." Its use in Psalm 27:1 (LXX 26:1) shows it does not always necessarily mean tomorrow but can indicate the coming day in general (Mundle, "Bread" *Colin Brown*, 1:251). The New Testament uses it exclusively in Acts to indicate "on the next day" (*tē epiousa hēmera*, e.g., Acts 7:26; 16:1) and once to mean "the next night" (*tē epiousa nukti*, Acts 23:11).

STRONG 1966, BAUER 284 (see "epeimi"), LIDDELL-SCOTT 614 (see "epeimi").

1952. ἐπιούσιος epiousios adj
Daily, necessary for existence; for the following day, for the future.
CROSS-REFERENCE:
εἰμί eimi (1498)

1. ἐπιούσιον epiousion acc sing masc

1 Give us this day our daily bread. .... Matt 6:11
1 Give us day by day our daily bread. .... Luke 11:3

Epiousios appears only in the Lord's Prayer recorded in Matthew 6:11 and Luke 11:3. It does not seem to have clear roots in classical Greek and it is found only in one papyrus, thus shedding no clear light on this difficult word. Most likely it comes from a linguistic derivation of *ha epiousa* meaning "the day which follows" or "the day which is before us" (see *Bauer*). The difficulty with finding an exact derivation of the word seems to spring from the problem of finding a real Greek equivalent for the Hebrew and Aramaic concept contained in the word.

The Septuagint sheds light on the fact that *epiousios* is not an indicator of time but of measure. In Proverbs 30:8 the word is translated "the amount appropriate to the individual." Thus the New Testament usage of this word seems to indicate the Lord had in mind not chronological time but appropriate sustenance needed by Him and His disciples. Foerster translates the Matthew 6:11 passage as saying "the bread which we need give us today" ("epiousios," *Kittel*, 2:590ff.). Thus the prayer Jesus taught His disciples was for bread that was adequate for that day (day by day) to release them from anxiety over tomorrow.

STRONG 1967, BAUER 296-97, MOULTON-MILLIGAN 242-43, KITTEL 2:590-99, LIDDELL-SCOTT 649, COLIN BROWN 1:251.

1953. ἐπιπίπτω epipiptō verb

Fall upon, approach eagerly, come upon.
CROSS-REFERENCE:
πίπτω piptō (3959)

בָּכָה bākhâh (1098), Weep (Gn 45:14—Codex Alexandrinus only).

חָלַק chālaq (2606), Divide; niphal: divide oneself (Gn 14:15—Sixtine edition only).

מָלַל mālal (4589), Dry up, wither (Jb 18:16).

נָפַל nāphal (5489), Qal: fall (Ex 15:16, 2 Sm 17:9, Dn 10:7); hiphil: let fall (Nm 35:23).

עָלַם ʻālam (6180), Hithpael: withdraw, melt (Jb 6:16).

1. ἐπιπίπτειν epipiptein inf pres act
2. ἐπέπεσεν epepesen 3sing indic aor act
3. ἐπέπεσον epepeson 3pl indic aor act
4. ἐπιπεσών epipesōn nom sing masc part aor act
5. ἐπιπεσόντες epipesontes nom pl masc part aor act
6. ἐπιπεπτωκός epipeptōkos nom/acc sing neu part perf act
7. ἐπέπεσαν epepesan 3pl indic aor act

1 that they **pressed upon** him for to touch him, ... Mark 3:10
2 saw him, he was troubled, and fear **fell upon** him. ...Luke 1:12
2 and ran, and **fell on** his neck, and kissed him. 15:20
4 He then **lying** on Jesus' breast saith unto him, ... John 13:25
6 For as yet he was **fallen upon** none of them: .... Acts 8:16
2 but while they made ready, he **fell** into a trance, ... 10:10
2 Holy Ghost **fell on** all them which heard the word..... 10:44
2 as I began to speak, the Holy Ghost **fell on** them, ... 11:15
3 And immediately there **fell on** him a mist 13:11
2 and fear **fell on** them all, ... 19:17
2 And Paul went down, and **fell on** him, ... 20:10
5 And they all wept sore, and **fell on** Paul's neck, ... 20:37
3 of them that reproached thee **fell on** me. .... Rom 15:3
7 of them that reproached thee **fell on** me. 15:3
2 and terror **struck** those who saw them. (NIV) ...... Rev 11:11

Classical Greek

The word *piptō* (3959), "to fall," and the word *epi* (1894), "upon," join together to form *epipiptō*, "to fall upon" or "pressed upon." Its use in classical Greek can indicate both falling (upon) intentionally or unintentionally. This action, however, does not carry with it implied guilt in the moral sense of the word.

Septuagint Usage

The Septuagint also translates forms of *nāphal* with almost equivalent meaning when it uses the word *piptō*. Old Testament wisdom literature uses the word frequently. At times it is used figuratively (e.g., Job 4:13; 33:15; of fear of "falling"), but it can function literally (e.g. Job 6:16, of "falling [melting?] snow").

New Testament Usage

In the New Testament the word is used most often in a literal, concrete sense. Mark 3:10 and Acts 20:10,37 indicate a literal falling or pressing upon one's neck as an expression of love or desire for affection or attention. *Epipiptō* is also used metaphorically when in Luke 1:12 abstractions like fear and darkness can be said to fall upon someone. Likewise, reproach may fall upon someone, as in Romans 15:3. Even this text bears out the fact that the word is never used in the New Testament with hostile intent. Another aspect of the word's usage is seen in Acts (10:10,44; 11:15; 13:11; 19:7) which indicates a suddenness with which the "falling upon" occurs.

STRONG 1968, BAUER 297, MOULTON-MILLIGAN 243, LIDDELL-SCOTT 651.

1954. ἐπιπλήσσω epiplēssō verb

Strike, rebuke.
COGNATE:
πλήσσω plēssō (4001)
SYNONYMS:
ἐλέγχω elenchō (1638)
ἐπιτιμάω epitimaō (1992)
νουθετέω noutheteō (3423)

1. ἐπιπλήξῃς epiplēxēs 2sing subj aor act

1 **Rebuke** not an elder, but entreat him as a father; ... 1 Tm 5:1

This verb is not common in secular writings, but the cognate noun does appear with the meaning of "a severe rebuke, a punishment." Its noun form occurs once in the Septuagint (2 Maccabees 7:33).

Its only use in the New Testament is Paul's instruction in 1 Timothy 5:1 to treat elders respectfully. The literal meaning of *epiplēssō* was "to strike, beat upon" with physical blows. Paul, however, used the figurative meaning "to rebuke or censure severely." The word presents the picture of one striking another verbally, rather than with blows of the fist.

STRONG 1969, BAUER 297, MOULTON-MILLIGAN 243, LIDDELL-SCOTT 651.

1955. ἐπιποθέω epipotheō verb
Long for, desire.
COGNATES:
    ἐπιπόθησις epipothēsis (1956)
    ἐπιπόθητος epipothētos (1957)
    ἐπιποθία epipothia (1958)
SYNONYMS:
    ἐπιθυμέω epithumeō (1922)
    ζηλόω zēloō (2189)

גָּרַס gāraṣ (1685), Consume, break (Ps 119:20 [118:20]).

הָבַל hāval (1960), Trust (Ps 62:10 [61:10]).

חָמַל chāmal (2654), Feel pity for (Dt 13:8).

יָאַב yā'av (3078), Long for (Ps 119:131 [118:131]).

כָּסַף kāṣaph (3826), Niphal: deeply long for (Ps 84:2 [83:2]).

עָרַג 'āragh (6405), Pant for, long for (Ps 42:1 [41:1]).

רָחַף rāchaph (7646), Piel: hover, flutter over (Dt 32:11).

תָּאֵב tā'ēv (8703), Long for (Ps 119:174 [118:174]).

1. ἐπιποθῶ epipothō 1sing indic pres act
2. ἐπιποθεῖ epipothei 3sing indic pres act
3. ἐπιποθῶν epipothōn nom sing masc part pres act
4. ἐπιποθοῦντες epipothountes
    nom pl masc part pres act
5. ἐπιποθούντων epipothountōn
    gen pl masc part pres act
6. ἐπιποθήσατε epipothēsate 2pl impr aor act

1 For I long to see you, that I may impart unto you	Rom 1:11
4 earnestly desiring to be clothed upon	2 Co 5:2
5 which long after you for the exceeding grace	9:14
1 For God is my record, how greatly I long after you	Php 1:8
3 he longed after you all, and was full of heaviness,	2:26
4 desiring greatly to see us, as we also to see you:	1 Th 3:6
3 Greatly desiring to see thee,	2 Tm 1:4
2 The spirit that dwelleth in us lusteth to envy?	Jas 4:5
6 babes, desire the sincere milk of the word,	1 Pt 2:2

Classical Greek
Believed to have been in circulation since the time of Herodotus (ca. Fifth Century B.C.), this compound verb—*epi* (1894) + *potheō* (since Homer, Seventh Century B.C.)—means "to yearn for or after."

Septuagint Usage
The Hebrew behind the Septuagintal usage evidences that a direct equivalent did not exist for the Hebrew, thus *epipotheō* was extremely flexible. Out of 10 texts with Hebrew counterparts, there are 8 different Hebrew terms. The clearest example of the Greek comes through in Psalm 42: "As a hart longs (*epipotheō*) for flowing streams, so longs (*epipotheō*) my soul for thee, O God" (RSV, verse 1; Hebrew *'āragh*; cf. Deuteronomy 13:8; 32:11, which show the difficulty in translating the Hebrew).

New Testament Usage
The New Testament instances of *epipotheō* are restricted to seven Pauline texts, one in James, and one in 1 Peter. Paul frequently described himself to his readers as "longing to see or be with them" (Romans 1:11; Philippians 1:8; 2:26; 1 Thessalonians 3:6; 2 Timothy 1:4; cf. 2 Corinthians 9:14); or, he shared his longing to be with God (2 Corinthians 5:2; cf. 1 Peter 2:2, "yearning for the pure spiritual milk" [*logikos* (3024)]). In a controversial passage, James 4:5 seems to refer back to the Old Testament theme that God "longs" for His creation, and if the spirit He has created man with turns toward the world His jealousy is aroused. (For a discussion of whether or not God is the subject of this verse see Davids, *New International Greek New Testament Commentary, James*, pp.163-165.)

STRONG 1971, BAUER 297-98, LIDDELL-SCOTT 652, COLIN BROWN 1:456-58.

1956. ἐπιπόθησις epipothēsis noun
Longing, desire.
CROSS-REFERENCE:
    ἐπιποθέω epipotheō (1955)

1. ἐπιπόθησιν epipothēsin acc sing fem

1 when he told us your **earnest desire**,	2 Co 7:7
1 yea, what **vehement desire**, yea, what zeal,	7:11

This noun occurs only twice in the New Testament (2 Corinthians 7:7,11), but it is part of a word group occurring a total of 13 times. Paul used *epipothēsis* and its cognates more often than any other New Testament writer, always in situations of "desire" or "longing" in a positive sense.

The word describes man's inner longing for something, his striving for some goal or object of desire. In both the two New Testament occurrences of *epipothēsis*, it refers to the Corinthian believers' desire to see Paul even after receiving his rebuke of their sinful behavior.

STRONG 1972, BAUER 298, LIDDELL-SCOTT 652, COLIN BROWN 1:458 (see "epithumia").

1957. ἐπιπόθητος epipothētos adj
Longed for, desired.
CROSS-REFERENCE:
ἐπιποθέω epipotheō (1955)

1. ἐπιπόθητοι epipothētoi nom pl masc

1 my brethren, dearly beloved and **longed for**,......... Phlp 4:1

This adjective appears only once in the New Testament, in Philippians 4:1, where Paul described the Philippian believers as his "longed for" ones. *Epipothētos* is not common in classical Greek and does not appear in the Septuagint. The related verb *epithumeō* (1922) is used several times in the Septuagint and translates at least eight different Hebrew words. It is an intensified form of an earlier verb that means "to desire." The passage reflects Paul's very deep personal longing for his cherished fellow believers in Philippi.

STRONG 1973, BAUER 298, LIDDELL-SCOTT 652.

1958. ἐπιποθία epipothia noun
Longing, desire.
CROSS-REFERENCE:
ἐπιποθέω epipotheō (1955)

1. ἐπιποθίαν epipothian acc sing fem

1 **a great desire** these many years to come unto you; Rom 15:23

This word and others in its word group are not used extensively in classical Greek but do occur several times in the New Testament. Paul in particular used the whole word group for "desire or longing," always in a positive sense, in contrast to *epithumia* (1924) which often carried a negative connotation. *Epipothia* itself appears in Romans 15:23, where Paul claimed he had possessed a longing to visit the Roman believers for many years. The word implies a strong emotional desire for something not yet possessed. It also appears in 2 Corinthians 7:11 as a variant reading, where Paul noted that the Corinthians had experienced godly sorrow, and this resulted in a longing for godly things.

STRONG 1974, BAUER 298, LIDDELL-SCOTT 652, COLIN BROWN 1:458.

1959. ἐπιπορεύομαι
epiporeuomai verb
Go to, journey to.
CROSS-REFERENCE:
πορεύομαι poreuomai (4057)

אַחַר 'achar (313), After (Lv 26:33).
עָבַר 'āvar (5882), Go through (Ez 39:14).

1. ἐπιπορευομένων epiporeuomenōn
gen pl masc part pres mid

1 and were come to him out of every city,............. Luke 8:4

Classical Greek
Classical Greek writers used *epiporeuomai* with the meaning "go, travel, march to, march over" often followed by a noun specifying the destination. It sometimes appears in a figurative sense, "to go through, run through" a topic or activity. In general, it includes the implication of arriving at the intended person or place.

New Testament Usage
The only New Testament use is in Luke 8:4, where the writer described the great crowds that had journeyed from a variety of cities to join the gatherings around Jesus. The word occurs in the present participle form, perhaps suggesting that such people were constantly arriving, generally because of the warnings against casual listening that Jesus issued in His Parable of the Sower.

STRONG 1975, BAUER 298, MOULTON-MILLIGAN 243, LIDDELL-SCOTT 652.

1960. ἐπιρράπτω epirrhaptō verb
Sew, sew on.

1. ἐπιρράπτει epirrhaptei 3sing indic pres act
2. ἐπιράπτει epiraptei 3sing indic pres act

1 **seweth** a piece of new cloth on an old garment:.... Mark 2:21
2 **seweth** a piece of new cloth on an old garment:........ 2:21

This word means to sew pieces of cloth together. It was sometimes followed by *epi* (1894) referring to sewing a patch onto a garment. It appears in the New Testament only in Mark 2:21, where Jesus used the illustration of sewing a patch of unshrunken cloth onto an old garment to show the incompatibility of combining the old garment of Judaism with the new realities of the Kingdom.

STRONG 1976, BAUER 298 (see "epiraptō"), LIDDELL-SCOTT 654.

1961. ἐπιρρίπτω epirrhiptō verb
Throw, cast.
COGNATE:
ῥίπτω rhiptō (4352)
SYNONYMS:
βάλλω ballō (900)
ῥίπτω rhiptō (4352)

ἐπίσημος 1962

נָפַל nāphal (5489), Fall; hiphil: cut off, conquer (Jos 23:4).

שָׁלַךְ shālakh (8390), Hiphil: throw down, throw away (Nm 35:22, 1 Kgs 19:19, Na 3:6); hophal: be thrown (Ps 22:10 [21:10]).

1. ἐπιρρίψαντες epirrhipsantes nom pl masc part aor act
2. ἐπιρίψαντες epiripsantes nom pl masc part aor act

1 and they cast their garments upon the colt,........ Luke 19:35
2 and they cast their garments upon the colt,............ 19:35
1 Casting all your care upon him; for he careth....... 1 Pt 5:7
2 Casting all your care upon him; for he careth.......... 5:7

Classical Greek
Epirrhiptō is a compound word made up of *rhiptō* (4352), "to throw off," "to cast off," and *epi* (1894), "upon." Classical Greek usage carries meanings such as throwing things to the ground. It also includes a possibility of casting persons to the ground (of "throwing on or toward") in the process of appealing to deity in prayer.

Septuagint Usage
Hebrew background as seen in the Septuagint carries examples of God's throwing the hailstones at His people's enemies in Joshua 10:11. Most pertinent to a foundation for its New Testament usage is the experience of God's casting the sinners' sin behind Him (Isaiah 38:17), or God's invitation to the believer to cast his burdens on the Lord (Psalm 55:22 [LXX 54:22]).

New Testament Usage
New Testament usages of *epirrhiptō* are both literal (Luke 19:35) and figurative (1 Peter 5:7). Of interest is the fact that the 1 Peter usage is an admonition which applies to the community of believers as a whole. The word *pasan* (see 3817B), which is used in the verse, indicates a real imperative. This use of *epirrhiptō* signals a need for commitment to God's rule as a corporate entity. It is the community of believers which casts all its care on the Lord and in so doing sees its burden lifted and given over to the Lord. Of course, it must be remembered that the community of believers is made up of individuals, so each person may apply the promise to himself.

STRONG 1977, BAUER 298, MOULTON-MILLIGAN 243 (see "epiriptō"), KITTEL 6:991-93 (see "epiriptō"), LIDDELL-SCOTT 654.

1962. ἐπίσημος epismos adj
Outstanding, notorious.

COGNATE:
σημαίνω sēmainō (4446)
SYNONYM:
ἐπιφανής epiphanēs (2000)
קָשַׁר qāshar (7489), Strong ones (Gn 30:42).

1. ἐπίσημον episēmon acc sing masc
2. ἐπίσημοι episēmoi nom pl masc

1 they had then a **notable** prisoner, called Barabbas. Matt 27:16
2 who are **of note** among the apostles,............... Rom 16:7

Classical Greek
Episēmos is used in classical Greek in both a literal sense, "having a mark or insignia," and a figurative sense, "notable, remarkable." The literal meaning is used to describe a person or thing bearing a distinctive mark or image. It is especially used of "coined" or "stamped" money, as opposed to simple lumps of gold or silver. Ancient writers spoke of offerings bearing inscriptions, or epileptic patients "bearing the marks" of their disease. The figurative meaning is used of things, such as a remarkable bed or a notable fortune. It is also used to describe persons, such as a man "notable" for wisdom. At times, the word can carry a bad sense, "conspicuous, notorious," as in the case of one who was notorious for loving the applause of crowds (see *Liddell-Scott*).

Septuagint Usage
The Septuagint uses *episēmos* in a good sense. Genesis 30:42 describes the stronger cattle born to Jacob's flocks, rendering the Hebrew *qāshar* "well-knit, strong, vigorous." Apocryphal portions of the Septuagint use the word to describe an outstanding man, a special festival day, or a prominent, easily visible location (Rengstorf, "sussēmon," *Kittel*, 7:269).

Greek papyri of the First Century employ *episēmos* to describe literal examples of marking such as a shop on which is the "number" 50, a district with the "number" 16, or the common classical idea of "coined" money bearing a stamped image. One will has been found mentioning graveside ceremonies on the "high" days, or special ceremonial days of the cemeteries (see *Moulton-Milligan*).

New Testament Usage
The New Testament uses *episēmos* only twice, in Romans 16:7 and Matthew 27:16. In the Romans passage Paul described Andronicus and Junia as those being "notable" among the apostles. Though there has been debate over whether these people were numbered among the apostles or simply recognized by the apostles, the term *episēmos* retains the same meaning

for either interpretation. It is an obvious use of the positive sense of *epis̄emos* to describe Christians who were conspicuous for their good qualities, recognized as possessors of distinctively admirable traits.

Matthew 27:16 uses the term to describe Barabbas as a "conspicuous" prisoner who was ultimately released in place of Jesus. The parallel in Mark 15:7 shows that Barabbas had been involved in an uprising against the Roman government, committing murder in the process. Thus the word is generally translated "notorious" here. D.A. Carson, however, notes that Barabbas' role as an insurrectionist may have made him a hero in the eyes of the common people; in their eyes, he would be "notable," not "notorious" (*Expositor's Bible Commentary*, 8:568f.).

STRONG 1978, BAUER 298, MOULTON-MILLIGAN 243, KITTEL 7:266-67, LIDDELL-SCOTT 656.

1963. ἐπισιτισμός episitismos noun
Food, provisions.
CROSS-REFERENCE:
    σῖτος sitos (4476)

צֵידָה tsêdhāh (6990), Provisions (Gn 45:21, Jos 9:11, 1 Sm 22:10).

1. ἐπισιτισμόν episitismon acc sing masc

1 and get **victuals**: for we are here in a desert place... **Luke 9:12**

In classical Greek *episitismos* refers to the activity of furnishing oneself with provisions or of foraging. It can also describe the stock of food which was gathered. The Septuagint uses it specifically of the provisions for a journey (Genesis 42:25; 45:21). By New Testament times it could be used as a general term for any kind of nourishment. *Episitismos* occurs in the New Testament only in Luke's account of the feeding of the 5,000 (Luke 9:12), when the disciples recommended sending the crowd away to find something to eat in the surrounding villages and countryside.

STRONG 1979, BAUER 298, MOULTON-MILLIGAN 243, LIDDELL-SCOTT 656.

1964. ἐπισκέπτομαι
episkeptomai verb
Look for, inspect, visit, look after.
CROSS-REFERENCE:
    ἐπίσκοπος episkopos (1969)

בָּחַן bāchan (1010), Test (Mal 3:10).
בָּקַר bāqar (1266), Piel: look on, examine (Lv 13:36, Ps 27:4, Ez 34:11).
בְּקַר bᵉqar (A1268), Pael: search, investigate (Ezr 4:15,19, 6:1, 7:14—Aramaic); hithpaal: be investigated, conduct a search (Ezr 5:17—Aramaic).
בַּקָּרָה baqqārāh (1270), Look after, seek out (Ez 34:12—Codex Alexandrinus only).
בָּקַשׁ bāqash (1272), Piel: seek (Zec 11:16).
דָּרַשׁ dārash (1938), Qal: demand, require (2 Chr 24:6, Ez 20:40); niphal: search, sought for (1 Chr 26:31).
יָלַד yāladh (3314), Bear, bring forth; hithpael: declare pedigree, indicate ancestry (Nm 1:18—Codex Alexandrinus only).
נָחַם nācham (5341), Piel: comfort (Jb 2:11).
פָּקַד pāqadh (6734), Qal: visit, show concern for (Ex 4:31, Ru 1:6, Hos 4:14); niphal: be called, be appointed (Jgs 21:3, 2 Kgs 10:19, Neh 7:1); hithpael: be mustered, be numbered (Jgs 20:15,17); hothpaal: be mustered, be numbered (1 Kgs 20:27 [21:27]).
שׂוּשׂ sûs (7919), Rejoice (Jer 32:41 [39:41]).
תּוּר tûr (8780), Spy out (Nm 14:34).

1. ἐπισκέπτῃ episkeptē 2sing indic pres mid
2. ἐπισκέπτεσθαι episkeptesthai inf pres mid
3. ἐπεσκέψατο epeskepsato 3sing indic aor mid
4. ἐπεσκέψασθε epeskepsasthe 2pl indic aor mid
5. ἐπισκεψώμεθα episkepsōmetha 1pl subj aor mid
6. ἐπισκέψασθε episkepsasthe 2pl impr aor mid
7. ἐπισκέψασθαι episkepsasthai inf aor mid
8. ἐπισκέψεται episkepsetai 3sing indic fut mid

4 I was sick, and ye **visited** me:..................... Matt 25:36
4 sick, and in prison, and ye **visited** me not............. 25:43
3 for he **hath visited** and redeemed his people,........ Luke 1:68
3 the dayspring from on high **hath visited** us,............. 1:78
8 the dayspring from on high **hath visited** us,............. 1:78
3 and, That God **hath visited** his people.................. 7:16
6 **look** ye out among you seven men of honest report, Acts 6:3
7 it came into his heart to **visit** his brethren............... 7:23
3 declared how God at the first did **visit** the Gentiles,.... 15:14
5 Let us go again and **visit** our brethren in every city.... 15:36
1 or the son of man, that thou **visitest** him?........... Heb 2:6
2 To **visit** the fatherless and widows................... Jas 1:27

Classical Greek
Episkeptomai is used in classical Greek in a variety of ways such as "to look upon" or "to have regard for." It is also used to designate the activity of a king (or some other authority figure) visiting and looking over his responsibility for purposes of ruling properly. Some usages also refer to visiting sick persons, either by friends or by a doctor (cf. *Moulton-Milligan*).

Septuagint Usage
The Septuagint usage of this word is quite extensive (over 150 times) and takes on a strong religious meaning, particularly as it is used to

denote God's loving concern and care for the people and promises contained in the covenant. Jeremiah 9:25 and Psalm 89:32 (LXX 88:32) also carry the implication of God's visitation with punishment for the purpose of bringing people to repentance.

New Testament Usage
The concept of God's coming (visitation) or His intervention with care and concern continues from the Septuagint into the New Testament (cf. Luke 7:16 and Hebrews 2:6). In addition the New Testament usage of the word carries with it an increased focus on basic attitude rather than isolated activity. Jesus taught that His followers are not to live solely for themselves but for others (Matthew 25:31-46). The uses of *episkeptomai* in the Book of Acts continue the Gospels' focus on concern and responsibility for others (Acts 15:36, e.g.).

STRONG 1980, BAUER 298, MOULTON-MILLIGAN 243-44, KITTEL 2:599-605, LIDDELL-SCOTT 656, COLIN BROWN 1:188-91.

1964B. ἐπισκευάζομαι
episkeuazomai verb
Make preparations, make ready, pack up.
CROSS-REFERENCE:
κατασκευάζω kataskeuazō (2650)

בָּדַק bādhaq (954), Repair (2 Chr 34:10).

חָדַשׁ chādhash (2412), Piel: repair, restore (2 Chr 24:4,12).

חָזַק chāzaq (2480), Be strong; piel: strengthen, repair (2 Chr 29:3).

כָּבָה kāvâh (3637), Be extinguished, go out (1 Sm 3:3).

עָלָה 'ālâh (6148), Go up; hiphil: bring up, set up (Ex 30:8).

1. ἐπισκευασάμενοι episkeuasamenoi
nom pl masc part aor mid
1 And after these days we got ready (NASB)........ Acts 21:15

Only Luke used this deponent verb in the New Testament (Acts 21:15). It describes the efforts which went into the "preparations" for Paul's last journey to Jerusalem from Caesarea.

The Septuagint and papyri also use the word. The papyri, however, do not attest the meaning which Luke gives to the word (*Moulton-Milligan*). In the Septuagint its main sense is "to repair" (2 Chronicles 24:4,12; 29:3; 34:10; 1 Maccabees 12:37). Other classical literature reflects the same sense as its New Testament occurrence (e.g., Aristophanes; cf. *Liddell-Scott*).

BAUER 298, MOULTON-MILLIGAN 244, LIDDELL-SCOTT 656 (see "episkeuazō").

1965. ἐπισκηνόω episkēnoō verb
Take up residence in.
CROSS-REFERENCE:
σκηνόω skēnoō (4492)

1. ἐπισκηνώσῃ episkēnōsē 3sing subj aor act
1 that the power of Christ may rest upon me......... 2 Co 12:9

This word is not common in classical Greek, and it does not appear in the Septuagint. It occurs only once in the New Testament, in 2 Corinthians 12:9. However, additional information may be learned from a study of its cognates, such as *skēnos* (4491), "tent," or *skēnoō* (4492), "to pitch a tent, to dwell."

Classical Greek
In classical Greek *episkēnoō* means "to enter, take up residence in a tent or dwelling" (Michaelis, "episkēnoō," *Kittel*, 7:386). The word group generally is connected with the idea of a tent or temporary shelter and often implies the transitory nature of a residence.

Septuagint Usage
Skēnē (4488) or *skēnos*, "tent," is used in the Septuagint to describe the usual tent dwellings of the people, the booths used at the Feast of Tabernacles, and the tabernacle itself. Hughes suggests that Jews of the New Testament period would see a reference to the tabernacle in this word, since the root *skēn* is suggestive of the Hebrew *shāchan*, "abide," which serves as the base for *shekinah*, the glory which descended on the mercy seat in the tabernacle (*New International Commentary on New Testament, Second Corinthians*, pp.452f.).

New Testament Usage
The New Testament employs this word group in ways that illuminate Paul's usage of *episkēnoō* in 2 Corinthians 12:9. In John 1:14 *skēnoō* describes Christ's coming to take up His dwelling place among men. This image also appears in Revelation where God is pictured as dwelling among the redeemed in glory (7:15; 12:12; 13:6; 21:3). Paul used *skēnos*, "tent," in 2 Corinthians 5:1,4 to describe the earthly body as a temporary tent, in contrast to the heavenly body which will become the believer's eternal dwelling place.

In 2 Corinthians 12:9 Paul used *episkēnoō* to proclaim his willingness to be weak. His weakness opened the way for the power of Christ to take up quarters within him. This may picture the reality of God's Spirit taking up residence in his frail tent of a body, much as the *shekinah* glory descended on the tent in the wilderness. As Colin Brown says, "Paul was painfully aware of its (the physical body) inadequacy as an organ for either the human spirit or the Holy Spirit when compared to the resurrection body" ("Tent," *Colin Brown*, 3:814).

STRONG 1981, BAUER 298, MOULTON-MILLIGAN 244, KITTEL 7:386-87, LIDDELL-SCOTT 656, COLIN BROWN 3:814 (see "skēnē").

1966. ἐπισκιάζω episkiazō verb
Cast a shadow, overshadow.
CROSS-REFERENCE:
σκιά skia (4494)

סָכַךְ sākhakh (5718), Qal: cover (Ps 140:7 [139:7]); hiphil: cover, protect (Ps 91:4 [90:4]).

שָׁכַן shākhan (8331), Settle (Ex 40:35).

1. ἐπισκιάζουσα episkiazousa
    nom sing fem part pres act
2. ἐπεσκίασεν epeskiasen 3sing indic aor act
3. ἐπισκιάσῃ episkiasē 3sing subj aor act
4. ἐπισκιάσει episkiasei 3sing indic fut act
5. ἐπεσκίαζεν epeskiazen 3sing indic imperf act

2 behold, a bright cloud **overshadowed** them: . . . . Matt 17:5
1 And there was a cloud that **overshadowed** them: . . . . Mark 9:7
4 the power of the Highest **shall overshadow** thee: . . . . . Luke 1:35
2 there came a cloud, and **overshadowed** them: 9:34
5 there came a cloud, and **overshadowed** them: 9:34
3 the shadow of Peter passing by **might overshadow** . . . . Acts 5:15

Classical Greek
Episkiazō is used in classical Greek with the meaning of "to shade" or "to overshadow." It is used in a metaphysical sense as an obscuring that distorts the true perspective of an object to be known. It is considered a negative detraction from the object in question.

Septuagint Usage
The term is used several times in the Septuagint where it is understood as a proof and work of power. Exodus 40:35 contains the account of the cloud which overshadowed Moses' tent. That cloud manifested divine presence by being a shadow over the tent.

New Testament Usage
The New Testament usages are found only in the Gospels and the Book of Acts. *Episkiazō* symbolizes the presence of God overshadowing (being with) and providing healing power in ministry situations. The Gospels use the word to indicate God's presence in the accounts of the transfiguration of Jesus in Matthew 17:15, Mark 9:7, and Luke 9:34 (indicated by a bright cloud). Luke 1:35 includes a metaphor of the power of the Most High resting upon (overshadowing) Mary the mother of Jesus. Acts 5:15 tells of those who were healed by the presence of God as they came into contact with Peter's shadow. Thus all five usages of the word in the New Testament show God's power and glory.

STRONG 1982, BAUER 298, MOULTON-MILLIGAN 244, KITTEL 7:399-400, LIDDELL-SCOTT 657, COLIN BROWN 3:553,555.

1967. ἐπισκοπέω episkopeō verb
Oversee, care for.
CROSS-REFERENCE:
ἐπίσκοπος episkopos (1969)

דָּרַשׁ dārash (1938), Care for (Dt 11:12).

יָדַע yādhaʿ (3156), Know, observe (Est 2:11).

נָצַח nātsach (5514), Piel: supervise (2 Chr 34:12).

פָּקַד pāqadh (6734), Miss, call to account; niphal: be visited by, be touched by (Prv 19:23).

1. ἐπισκοποῦντες episkopountes
    nom pl masc part pres act

1 **Looking diligently** lest any man fail of the grace . . . . Heb 12:15
1 **taking the oversight** thereof, not by constraint, ... 1 Pt 5:2

Classical Greek
In classical Greek *episkopeō* stresses involved action and accountable concern. It is not used to denote a singular action; instead, it is the expression of an attitude or disposition that is typical of gods in their watching over their subjects.

Septuagint Usage
In the Septuagint the word is used only five times for a variety of Hebrew words. It usually carries a connotation of taking oversight and finding out about something (cf. Deuteronomy 11:12; Proverbs 19:23).

New Testament Usage
The New Testament usage carries several noteworthy concepts. The diligent accountability called for in Hebrews 12:15 is an attitude which should be expressed by an entire group of believers, not just an appointed official. The congregation in this verse is seen as having

responsibility together. In 1 Peter 5:2 *episkopeō* shows the nature of care for a congregation. It is not to be oversight by constraint or for money. It is ministry to be done in love and concern as an example to the flock. A definitive summary of the usage of *episkopeō* would be "exercising careful oversight." The word implies fulfillment of the responsibility. The focus is not the position of authority but rather a ministry of loving service.

STRONG 1983, BAUER 298-99, MOULTON-MILLIGAN 244, KITTEL 2:599-605, LIDDELL-SCOTT 657, COLIN BROWN 1:188-90.

1968. ἐπισκοπή episkopē noun

Visitation, inspection, position or office as an overseer or bishop.

CROSS-REFERENCE:
ἐπίσκοπος episkopos (1969)

בִּקֹּרֶת biqqōreth (1271), Punishment, scourging (Lv 19:20).

יִרְאָה yir'āh (3488), Fear, fear of God (Jb 6:14).

סוֹד sôdh (5660), Secret, intimate (Jb 29:4).

פָּקַד pāqadh (6734), Visit, aid (Gn 50:24,25, Nm 7:2, Jb 31:14).

פְּקֻדָּה pᵉquddāh (6735), Service, office (Nm 4:16, Ps 109:8 [108:8], Jer 10:15).

צָפַן tsāphan (7121), Secret or treasured place (Ez 7:22).

רָצָה rātsāh (7813), Something that pleases, delights (Jb 34:9).

1. ἐπισκοπῆς episkopēs gen sing fem
2. ἐπισκοπήν episkopēn acc sing fem

1 thou knewest not the time of thy **visitation**.........	Luke 19:44
2 and his **bishopric** let another take.................	Acts 1:20
1 If a man desire the **office of a bishop**,...........	1 Tm 3:1
1 glorify God in the day of **visitation**..................	1 Pt 2:12

Classical Greek and Septuagint Usage

Episkopē is found rarely in secular Greek but frequently in the Septuagint. It can mean "protection" or "care" (Job 10:12; Proverbs 29:13), or it can refer to the office of an overseer (Psalm 109:8 [LXX 108:8]). The dominant meaning, however, is "visitation," especially the visitation of God.

Visitation can have a positive or negative connotation. It is used in the context of a day of judgment and punishment (e.g., Numbers 16:29; Jeremiah 6:15; 10:15). Positive meanings include "deliverance" as in the Exodus from Egypt (Genesis 50:24f.; Exodus 3:16), "material blessing" (Isaiah 23:17), and in later literature "forgiveness" (Sirach 18:20).

New Testament Usage

The New Testament uses *episkopē* primarily to refer to "the Day of the Lord," an occasion of sanctification for the believers but one of judgment for the world. Jesus used the term in describing His offer of salvation to His own people which they rejected, thereby transforming the "season of visitation" from one of blessing to one of destruction (Luke 19:44). In reference to Isaiah 10:3, 1 Peter 2:12 speaks of the "day of visitation" as an incentive for believers to live holy lives. The other two uses of *episkopē* in the New Testament refer to the position of overseer or bishop (Acts 1:20; 1 Timothy 3:1).

STRONG 1984,

1969. ἐπίσκοπος episkopos noun

Overseer, one who inspects or superintends, bishop.

COGNATES:
ἀλλοτριοεπίσκοπος allotrioepiskopos (242)
ἐπισκέπτομαι episkeptomai (1964)
ἐπισκοπέω episkopeō (1967)
ἐπισκοπή episkopē (1968)

אֵל 'ēl (418), God (Jb 20:29).

נָגַשׂ nāghas (5241), Officer, Governor (Is 60:17).

פָּקַד pāqadh (6734), Qal: commander, officer (Nm 31:14, 2 Kgs 11:15); hophal: be set, overseer (2 Chr 34:12,17).

פְּקֻדָּה pᵉquddāh (6735), Guard, officer (Nm 4:16, 2 Kgs 11:18).

פָּקִיד pāqîdh (6746), Deputy, officer (Jgs 9:28, Neh 11:9).

1. ἐπίσκοπον episkopon acc sing masc
2. ἐπισκόποις episkopois dat pl masc
3. ἐπισκόπους episkopous acc pl masc

3 which the Holy Ghost hath made you **overseers**,....	Acts 20:28
2 to all the saints ... with the **bishops** and deacons:....	Php 1:1
1 A **bishop** then must be blameless,.................	1 Tm 3:2
1 Grace be with you. Amen........................	2 Tm 4:22
1 a **bishop** must be blameless, as the steward of God;...	Tit 1:7
1 Grace be with you all. Amen.....................	3:15
1 unto the Shepherd and **Bishop** of your souls.........	1 Pt 2:25

Classical Greek

In secular Greek several related terms are used for the "oversight" of persons or things. The term *episkopos*, "overseer" (from *epi* [1894], "upon, over," + *skopos* [4504], "one who watches"), was originally a religious expression which referred to gods who "guarded" or "protected" (i.e., "watched over") individuals or cities. Later it could refer to individuals who had a trusted position in a *polis* (4032), "city," or in the state. These *episkopoi* are associated with other persons of authority, but it is difficult to determine precisely their duties and functions—they may have been of a changing character (Coenen, "Bishop," *Colin Brown*, 1:189).

Septuagint Usage
The word group in the Septuagint corresponds to different derivations of the Hebrew root *pāqadh*, "to take care of, to have supervision over." Oddly enough, *episkopos* only rarely replaces the Hebrew *pāqîdh*, "superintendent, commander," or "chief" (e.g., Nehemiah 11:9,14,22). Therefore one should not attempt to make any connection between this Old Testament position and the office of "bishop" which appears in the Early Church (ibid.).

New Testament Usage
The word *episkopos* occurs five times in the New Testament. Once it concerns Jesus Christ, "the overseer of our souls" (1 Peter 2:25). Twice the context is the position ("office" here might be pressing the evidence) of *episkopos* in the local church (1 Timothy 3:2; Titus 1:7). Once *episkopos* conjoins with *diakonos* (1243) in a text which may very well refer to "offices" in the local church (Philippians 1:1; even here the exact nature of this appellative is elusive).

From Acts 20:28 (cf. verse 17) it is evident that *episkopos* was at times used interchangeably with *presbuteros* (4104), "elder." In the ancient Christian congregations there were *epiksopoi* and/or *presbuteroi* in each local congregation (cf. Acts 14:23; 20:17; Philippians 1:1; Titus 1:5; James 5:14). To Jews, the term "elder" was long in use as the leader or "ruler" of the synagogue. To Gentiles, "elder" might mean simply "an old man". Thus the Greek term *episkopos* helped to define the office held by a person. (See article on *presbuteros* [4104].)
STRONG 1985, BAUER 299, MOULTON-MILLIGAN 244-45, KITTEL 2:608-20, LIDDELL-SCOTT 657, COLIN BROWN 1:188-91.

1970. ἐπισπάω epispaō verb
Pull over.
CROSS-REFERENCE:
σπάω spaō (4538)

מָשַׁךְ māshakh (5082), Drag, draw (Is 5:18).
שָׁאַב shā'av (8056), Draw (Na 3:14).
תָּפַשׂ tāphas (8945), Take hold of (Gn 39:12).

1. ἐπισπάσθω epispasthō 3sing impr pres mid
1 let him not **become uncircumcised**..................1 Co 7:18

Classical Greek and Septuagint Usage
In classical Greek *epispaō* means "to draw, drag, pull, allure, induce, win," or "obtain." The Septuagint and later Jewish literature use the word in the classical sense (Genesis 39:12; Isaiah 5:18; Nahum 3:14; 4 Maccabees 5:2; Josephus *Antiquities* 14.15.5).

In Jewish and Christian experience, however, the word takes on a specialized meaning in addition to the classical usage. It becomes a reference to a surgical procedure which reverses circumcision by pulling the foreskin back to its original position. In the Maccabean era some Jewish men who participated in the Greek games underwent this operation since all athletes participated naked. Circumcision was a source of embarrassment to the Jewish participants who were conspicuously different from the other athletes. To the pious Jews this was an act of rank apostasy. Josephus and 1 Maccabees mention this reversal of circumcision but use a different word to express it (*Antiquities* 12.5.1; 1 Maccabees 1:15).

New Testament Usage
In the New Testament *epispaō* appears only once in 1 Corinthians 7:18 where Paul referred to the act of concealing circumcision. In the context Paul opposed both the circumcision of Gentile believers and the surgical reversal of circumcision for Jewish believers.
STRONG 1986, BAUER 299 (see "epispaomai"), MOULTON-MILLIGAN 245, LIDDELL-SCOTT 658.

1970B. ἐπισπείρω epispeirō verb
Sow afterward, sow in addition.
CROSS-REFERENCE:
σπείρω speirō (4540)

1. ἐπέσπειρεν epespeiren 3sing indic aor act
1 his enemy came and **sowed tares** (NASB)..........Matt 13:25

Epispeirō was a term used widely in ancient agricultural circles. It is a compound of *epi* (1894), "upon, over," and *speirō* (4540), "sow seed." The practice of replanting was not uncommon in ancient agriculture where fresh seed might be sown in places where the first sowing did not produce. A field might also be sown a second time in order to produce a second crop, different from the first yet compatible with regard to growing conditions. Such was the case in Matthew 13:25, the only New Testament occurrence of *epispeirō*. In one of His kingdom parables Jesus told about a man who sowed seed in his field. Then, "while men slept, his enemy came and sowed tares among the wheat." The problem was not with a second sowing, but with the second sower, an enemy whose crop would not be compatible with what was sown first.

BAUER 300, MOULTON-MILLIGAN 245, LIDDELL-SCOTT 658.

1971. ἐπίσταμαι epistamai verb
Understand, know, comprehend.
COGNATE:
  ἵστημι histēmi (2449)
SYNONYMS:
  αἰσθάνομαι aisthanomai (143)
  γινώσκω ginōskō (1091)
  γνωρίζω gnōrizō (1101)
  ἐπιγινώσκω epiginōskō (1906)
  καταλαμβάνω katalambanō (2608)
  νοέω noeō (3401)
  οἶδα oida (3471)
  ὁράω horaō (3571)
  παρακολουθέω parakoloutheō (3738)
  συνίημι suniēmi (4770)

בִּין bîn (1032), Understand, perceive (Jb 38:20).
דַּעַת daʻath (1907), Knowledge (Prv 15:2).
יָדַע yādhaʻ (3156), Know, understand (Nm 20:14, Jos 2:9, Is 48:8).
שָׂכַל sākhal (7959), Hiphil: understand, see (Is 41:20).

1. ἐπίσταμαι epistamai 1sing indic pres mid
2. ἐπίσταται epistatai 3sing indic pres mid
3. ἐπίστασθε epistasthe 2pl indic pres mid
4. ἐπίστανται epistantai 3pl indic pres mid
5. ἐπιστάμενος epistamenos
  nom sing masc part pres mid

```
1 I know not, neither understand I what thou sayest. Mark 14:68
3 Ye know how that it is an unlawful thing.......... Acts 10:28
3 ye know how that a good while ago................. 15:7
5 knowing only the baptism of John..................... 18:25
1 Jesus I know, and Paul I know; but who are ye?...... 19:15
3 ye know that by this craft we have our wealth....... 19:25
3 Ye know, from the first day that I came into Asia,.. 20:18
4 they know that I imprisoned and beat................. 22:19
5 Forasmuch as I know that thou hast been............. 24:10
2 For the king knoweth of these things,................ 26:26
5 He is proud, knowing nothing,....................... 1 Tm 6:4
5 and he went out, not knowing whither he went..... Heb 11:8
3 Whereas ye know not what shall be on the morrow... Jas 4:14
4 they know not: but what they know naturally,...... Jude 1:10
```

Throughout classical Greek, Septuagintal, and Christian literature *epistamai* means either "to be acquainted with" or "to understand." The first meaning, "to be acquainted with," is the dominant one: it indicates having knowledge of something. *Epistamai* is used mostly by Luke; 9 of its 14 occurrences in the New Testament are found in Acts. In Acts 18:25 it is used to indicate that Apollo knew only of John's baptism prior to his meeting Priscilla and Aquila.

The second meaning, "to understand," occurs in the New Testament only twice. In 1 Timothy 6:4 the heretic is described as void of understanding (*mēden epistamenos*). In Mark 14:68 when Peter was confronted with the accusation, "You too were with Jesus," he denied it with these words, "I neither know (*oida* [3471]) nor understand (*epistamai*) what you are talking about" (NASB).

STRONG 1987, BAUER 300, MOULTON-MILLIGAN 245, LIDDELL-SCOTT 658-59, COLIN BROWN 3:122.

1971B. ἐπίστασις epistasis noun
Attack, approach, onset, pressure, burden, attention.
CROSS-REFERENCE:
  ἵστημι histēmi (2449)

1. ἐπίστασις epistasis nom sing fem
2. ἐπίστασιν epistasin acc sing fem

```
2 did not find me ... causing a riot (NASB) (NT).... Acts 24:12
1 there is the daily pressure upon me (NASB)....... 2 Co 11:28
```

This noun occurs twice in the New Testament. It means "attack" or "upset" in Acts 24:12 and, most likely, "pressure" in 2 Corinthians 11:28. Alternatives to the latter translation would be "attention, oversight," or "hindrance." Not only did Paul face regular persecution for the gospel, but he also had the daily pressure (or "burden, concern") for the churches. He equated this *epistasis* with *hē merimna*, "the concern," for the churches.

BAUER 300, MOULTON-MILLIGAN 245, LIDDELL-SCOTT 659.

1972. ἐπιστάτης epistatēs noun
Master, overseer, superintendent, administrator.
COGNATE:
  ἵστημι histēmi (2449)
SYNONYMS:
  δεσπότης despotēs (1197)
  κύριος kurios (2935)

נָגִיד nāghîdh (5233), Overseer, supervisor (2 Chr 31:12).
נֹגֵשׂ nāghas (5241), Officer, foreman (Ex 5:14).
נָצַח nātsach (5514), Piel: overseer, foreman (2 Chr 2:2).
פָּקִיד pāqîdh (6746), One in charge, officer (Jer 29:26 [36:26], 52:25).
רָדָה rādhāh (7575), Officer, foreman (1 Kgs 5:16).

שַׂר sar (8015), Taskmaster, slave master (Ex 1:11).

1. ἐπιστάτα epistata voc sing masc

1 Master, we have toiled all the night,	Luke 5:5
1 and awoke him, saying, Master, master, we perish.	8:24
1 and awoke him, saying, Master, master, we perish.	8:24
1 Master, the multitude throng thee and press thee,	8:45
1 Peter said unto Jesus, Master, it is good for us	9:33
1 Master, we saw one casting out devils in thy name;	9:49
1 and said, Jesus, Master, have mercy on us.	17:13

Classical Greek
This word occurs in a wide range of meanings in classical Greek. It can denote "one who stands near," as in the case of one who stands behind the front-rank soldier in battle. Or it can refer to "one who stands or is mounted upon," like a charioteer (*Liddell-Scott*). More often, it refers to one who was set over some area of responsibility, whether as one who watches over herds, an inspector of public works, the leader of a temple, a music teacher, or the head of an athletic training group. The president of the ruling council of Athens was called an *epistatēs*. It was used at times for an overseer or headmaster of a group of children being educated (Oepke, "epistatēs," *Kittel*, 2:622f.).

Septuagint Usage
In the Septuagint *epistatēs* maintains its general meaning of one in authority in a variety of settings. It is used in Exodus 1:11 and 5:14 of the Egyptian overseers who directed the Jewish forced labor crews. In 1 Kings 5:16 (LXX 3 Kings 5:16) and 2 Chronicles 2:2 it is used of the foremen who supervised the quarry workers who prepared materials for Solomon's temple. Elsewhere, the word describes the officer in charge of the garrison when Jerusalem fell to Babylon (2 Kings 25:19 [LXX 4 Kings 25:19]), or the Levite who supervised the storage of offerings brought to the temple (2 Chronicles 31:12).

New Testament Usage
In the New Testament only Luke used *epistatēs*, always as a title addressed directly to Jesus. It is a translation of the Aramaic, *rabbi*. In five of the six occurrences it is spoken by one or more of Jesus' disciples. The other occasion is a usage by the 10 lepers who approached Jesus to ask for healing (Luke 17:13). Examination of the parallels in Matthew and Mark shows that Luke used *epistatēs* for the Hebrew *rabbi*, or "teacher" (Luke 9:33; cf. Mark 9:5), perhaps as a way to make the concept clearer to his Hellenistic audience. He also employed it as an equivalent of *didaskalos* (1314), "teacher" (Luke 8:24; cf. Mark 4:38; 9:38; Luke 9:49).

Other uses are Luke 5:5 and 8:45. The word itself is broader than either of its equivalents, however. It implies authority of any kind which produces an attitude of obedience. It also carries the thought of a person of high status. The usage lends itself well to the situation portrayed in the Gospels, i.e., of a fellowship marked by a close personal relationship, yet filled with deep respect.

STRONG 1988, BAUER 300, MOULTON-MILLIGAN 245, KITTEL 2:622-23, LIDDELL-SCOTT 659, COLIN BROWN 2:595; 3:115.

1973. ἐπιστέλλω epistellō verb
To write or inform by a letter.
COGNATES:
  ἐπιστολή epistolē (1976)
  στέλλομαι stellomai (4575)
SYNONYM:
  γράφω graphō (1119)

שָׁלַח shālach (8365), Send (1 Kgs 5:8—Codex Alexandrinus only, Neh 6:19—Codex Vaticanus only).

1. ἐπέστειλα epesteila 1sing indic aor act
2. ἐπεστείλαμεν epesteilamen 1pl indic aor act
3. ἐπιστεῖλαι episteilai inf aor act

3 But that we write unto them,	Acts 15:20
2 we have written and concluded	21:25
1 for I have written a letter unto you in few words.	Heb 13:22

Classical Greek
In classical Greek this word is used to mean "to send or announce a message, direction, or administrative order." It can refer to a command given by word of mouth, but usually it refers to something that is written. Thus the noun derivation *epistolē* (1976), "epistle," is "that which is transmitted by the messenger," i.e., the "letter" itself (Rengstorf, "epistellō," *Kittel*, 7:593f.).

Septuagint Usage
This verb is used in a similar way in the Septuagint and other Jewish writings. *Epistellein* is the Greek translation of the Hebrew *shālah* which means "to send" a message orally or in written form (2 Kings 5:8 [LXX 4 Kings 5:8]; Nehemiah 6:19). Lacquer has demonstrated from the letters of emperors and magistrates of this period that *epistellō* "always meant write rather than send" (*Moulton-Milligan*).

New Testament Usage
In the New Testament *epistellō* means "to send a communication, to inform, or instruct by letter." The writer of Hebrews said, "For I *have written a letter unto* you in a few words"

(Hebrews 13:22). In another occurrence of this word the resolution of the Jerusalem Council was *to write and inform* the Gentile Christians of its decision together with its instructions (Acts 15:20). Rengstorf has concluded that "the few instances of the verb (in the New Testament) ... bring out clearly the authoritative and almost official nature of the primitive Christian epistle" ("epistellō," *Kittel*, 7:593).

STRONG 1989, BAUER 300, MOULTON-MILLIGAN 245-46, KITTEL 7:593-95, LIDDELL-SCOTT 660, COLIN BROWN 1:246-49.

1974. ἐπιστήμων epistēmōn adj
Expert, skillful, experienced.

בִּין bîn (1032), Niphal: have understanding (Dt 1:13, 4:6, Is 5:21).

חָכַם chākham (2549), Be wise, become wise (Sir 10:25).

יָדַע yādhaʻ (3156), Be known, be respected (Dt 1:15).

שָׂכַל sākhal (7959), Hiphil: understand, see (Dn 1:4).

שָׂכְלְתָנוּ sokhlᵉthānû (A7962), Insight (Dn 5:12—Aramaic).

1. ἐπιστήμων epistēmōn nom sing masc

1 Who is a wise man and **endued with knowledge** .... Jas 3:13

In both classical and Septuagintal usage *epistēmōn* means "knowing, wise, prudent," especially being acquainted with an area of skill. It was used of those versed in the sea, skilled in the building craft, or expert in evil. Doerksen says that it refers to a specialist, one possessing professional knowledge of a field (*James*, p.86). It is coupled with *sophia* (4531), "wisdom," in the Septuagint in Deuteronomy 1:13,15; 4:6. The same pair appears in the only New Testament use of the word in James 3:13, where the writer exhorted those who claim the status of being wise and expert to display their virtues in behavior.

STRONG 1990, BAUER 300, MOULTON-MILLIGAN 246, LIDDELL-SCOTT 660.

1975. ἐπιστηρίζω epistērizō verb
Strengthen, further support, confirm, establish beside.
COGNATE:
στηρίζω stērizō (4592)
SYNONYMS:
βεβαιόω bebaioō (943)
δυναμόω dunamoō (1406)
ἐνδυναμόω endunamoō (1727)
ἐνισχύω enischuō (1749)
σθενόω sthenoō (4454)
στερεόω stereoō (4583)
στηρίζω stērizō (4592)

יָעַץ yāʻats (3398), Guide, counsel (Ps 32:8 [31:8]).

כּוּן kûn (3679), Niphal: stand firm support (Jgs 16:26—Codex Alexandrinus only).

נָחֵת nāchēth (5365), Niphal: pierce, stick in (Ps 38:2 [37:2]).

נָצַב nātsav (5507), Niphal: stand (Gn 28:13).

סָמַךְ sāmakh (5759), Qal: lie hard or heavily on (Ps 88:7 [87:7]); niphal: rely on, held up by (Ps 71:6 [70:6]).

רָפַק rāphaq (7805), Lean (S/S 8:5).

שָׁעַן shāʻan (8550), Niphal: lean (2 Sm 1:6).

1. ἐπιστηρίζων epistērizōn
 nom sing masc part pres act
2. ἐπιστηρίζοντες epistērizontes
 nom pl masc part pres act
3. ἐπεστήριξαν epestērixan 3pl indic aor act

2 **Confirming** the souls of the disciples, ... Acts 14:22
3 exhorted the brethren ... and **confirmed** them. 15:32
1 through Syria and Cilicia, **confirming** the churches. 15:41
1 **strengthening** all the disciples. 18:23

Classical Greek and Septuagint Usage
In classical Greek both *epistērizō* and its root *stērizō* were used with the meaning "to support, to cause to lean on," in examples such as a vine supported by a stake or an old man leaning on a staff (cf. *Liddell-Scott*). The Septuagint uses it in similar ways, such as Samson leaning against the pillars in the Philistine temple (Judges 16:26,29).

New Testament Usage
The New Testament uses of the word appear only in Acts, each time in contexts where Paul or others were attempting to strengthen other believers. The purpose was to make these Christians more firm and stronger in their faith, especially in the face of trials. On Paul's first missionary journey he and Barnabas used the latter portion of their trip to strengthen the new believers in Lystra, Iconium, and Derbe (Acts 14:22). After the Jerusalem Council the official delegation included Judas and Silas who spoke to the church at Antioch to strengthen them (Acts 15:32). Paul began his second missionary journey by going through Syria and Cilicia strengthening the churches (Acts 15:41). And at the start of his third trip Paul made one more tour through the area he had covered earlier for the purpose of strengthening the churches (Acts 18:23).

STRONG 1991, BAUER 300, KITTEL 7:653-57, LIDDELL-SCOTT 660.

1976. ἐπιστολή epistolē noun
Letter, epistle, written message.

COGNATE:
ἐπιστέλλω epistellō (1973)

SYNONYM:
γράμμα gramma (1115)

אִגְּרָא 'igg^erā' (A101II) Letter (Ezr 4:11—Aramaic).
אִגֶּרֶת 'iggereth (104), Letter, official letter (2 Chr 30:1, Neh 2:7ff., Est 9:26).
כְּלִי k^elî (3747), Vessel, boat (Is 18:2).
כְּתָב k^ethāv (3920), Writing, text (Est 3:14).
סֵפֶר sēpher (5809), Writing, letter (Is 39:1).
שִׂטְנָה siṭnāh (7932), Accusation (Ezr 4:6).

1. ἐπιστολή epistolē nom sing fem
2. ἐπιστολῆς epistolēs gen sing fem
3. ἐπιστολῇ epistolē dat sing fem
4. ἐπιστολήν epistolēn acc sing fem
5. ἐπιστολαί epistolai nom pl fem
6. ἐπιστολῶν epistolōn gen pl fem
7. ἐπιστολαῖς epistolais dat pl fem
8. ἐπιστολάς epistolas acc pl fem

8 And desired of him letters to Damascus		Acts 9:2
4 they delivered the epistle:		15:30
8 from whom also I received letters		22:5
4 And he wrote a letter after this manner:		23:25
4 and delivered the epistle to the governor,		23:33
4 I Tertius, who wrote this epistle, salute you		Rom 16:22
3 I wrote unto you in an epistle		1 Co 5:9
6 whomsoever ye shall approve by your letters,		16:3
6 epistles of commendation to you,		2 Co 3:1
1 Ye are our epistle written in our hearts,		3:2
1 to be the epistle of Christ ministered by us,		3:3
3 For though I made you sorry with a letter,		7:8
1 that the same epistle hath made you sorry,		7:8
6 I may not seem as if I would terrify you by letters		10:9
5 For his letters, say they, are weighty and powerful;		10:10
6 as we are in word by letters when we are absent,		10:11
1 And when this epistle is read among you,		Col 4:16
4 that this epistle be read unto all the holy brethren.		1 Th 5:27
2 nor by word, nor by letter as from us,		2 Th 2:2
2 whether by word, or our epistle.		2:15
2 And if any man obey not our word by this epistle,		3:14
1 which is the token in every epistle: so I write.		3:17
1 and shall hide a multitude of sins.		Jas 5:20
1 Peace be with you all that are in Christ ... Amen.		1 Pt 5:14
4 This second epistle, beloved, I now write unto you;		2 Pt 3:1
7 As also in all his epistles,		3:16
1 Little children, keep yourselves from idols. Amen.		1 Jn 5:21
1 The children of thy elect sister greet thee. Amen.		2 Jn 1:13
1 Our friends salute thee. Greet the friends by name.		3 Jn 1:14
1 and power, both now and for ever. Amen.		Jude 1:25

Classical Greek
Originally *epistolē* was a message of any kind, either written or verbal. The construction *ex epistolē* meant "by command." In a more restricted sense it meant "letter" (*Liddell-Scott*).

Septuagint Usage
Five different Hebrew terms are translated by *epistolē* in the Septuagint. The predominant words translated by *epistolē* are *'igg^erā'* and *'iggereth* (letter). Often *epistolē* refers to a written document or letter of correspondence (e.g., 2 Chronicles 30:1; Maccabean writings passim), sometimes more specifically a "letter of recommendation" (e.g., Nehemiah 2:7,8,9; cf. Nehemiah 6:5), or perhaps "written orders or decrees" (Esther 3:13,14; 8:13).

New Testament Usage
Epistolē occurs 24 times in the Greek New Testament and invariably refers to a "letter, epistle" (e.g., Acts 15:30; 23:25; Romans 16:22; 1 Corinthians 5:9; 1 Thessalonians 5:27); nevertheless, the sense of "letter" as an official decree or order (Acts 9:2; cf. Acts 22:5) or a "letter of recommendation" (2 Corinthians 3:1-3) are also present.

Each *epistolē* received the apostolic authority of its author for the early Christian communities. The *epistolais* formed a major portion of early instruction and discipline (2 Thessalonians 3:14; cf. 1 Corinthians 5:9; Colossians 4:16; 2 Peter 3:1,16).

STRONG 1992, BAUER 300-301, MOULTON-MILLIGAN 246, KITTEL 7:593-95, LIDDELL-SCOTT 660, COLIN BROWN 1:246-48.

1977. ἐπιστομίζω epistomizō verb
Silence, cover the mouth.

CROSS-REFERENCE:
στόμα stoma (4601)

1. ἐπιστομίζειν epistomizein inf pres act

1 Whose mouths must be stopped,		Tit 1:11

Classical Greek
Epistomizō is not used in the Septuagint, but it does occur in classical Greek to mean "bridle, curb," as in guiding and restraining a horse. It is also used figuratively of restraining enemies. A second meaning refers to flute players who would mute the voice of their instrument by putting on the mouthpiece. This leads to the broader definition of "silence, cause to be stopped up or silenced" (cf. *Liddell-Scott*).

New Testament Usage
The New Testament uses the word *epistomizō* only in Titus 1:11 where Paul prescribed it as a treatment for the false teachers disrupting the congregations in Crete. The meaning "bridle, hinder, prevent" is possible, but it seems more appropriate to see the meaning "to stop the mouth, silence." Kent says it means to silence the false teachers as effectively as putting a gag in the mouth (*Pastoral Epistles*, p.223).

ἐπιστρέφω 1978

STRONG 1993, BAUER 301, MOULTON-MILLIGAN 246, LIDDELL-SCOTT 660.

1978. ἐπιστρέφω epistrephō verb
Turn, turn back, return.

COGNATES:
ἐπιστροφή epistrophē (1979)
στρέφω strephō (4613)

SYNONYMS:
ἀνακάμπτω anakamptō (342)
ἀποστρέφω apostrephō (648)
ἐκτρέπω ektrepō (1610)
ἐπανέρχομαι epanerchomai (1865)
περιΐστημι periistēmi (3889)
στρέφω strephō (4613)
ὑποστρέφω hupostrephō (5128)

אָסַף 'āṣaph (636), Take in, admit (Jos 20:4—Codex Alexandrinus only).

בּוֹא bô' (971), Return, come back (1 Kgs 22:27).

בָּחַן bāchan (1010), Test, prove (Mal 3:10).

הָלַךְ hālakh (2050), Go, walk (1 Sm 30:22—Codex Alexandrinus only).

הָפַךְ hāphakh (2089), Qal: turn, turn around (1 Kgs 22:34, 2 Kgs 5:26); niphal: be turned, changed (1 Sm 4:19, Dn 10:8); hophal: be turned against (Jb 30:15).

חָשַׁב chāshav (2913), Purpose, determine (Lam 2:8).

כָּנַע kāna' (3789), Niphal: humble oneself (2 Chr 33:19).

נָבַט nāvaṭ (5202), Hiphil: look, gaze (Is 63:15, Lam 1:12).

נָגַשׁ nāghash (5242), Come near, approach (Jer 30:21 [37:21]—Codex Alexandrinus only).

נָפַל nāphal (5489), Fall, get down (2 Kgs 5:21, 1 Chr 12:19).

נָשַׂג nāsagh (5560), Hiphil: put one's hand to (1 Sm 14:26).

סָבַב sāvav (5621), Qal: turn, go about (1 Sm 15:12, Ps 71:21 [70:21], Ez 42:19 [42:18]); niphal: turn, change direction (Ez 1:9, 10:16); hiphil: change, turn around (2 Kgs 23:34, 2 Chr 6:3).

סָבִיב sāvîv (5623), Round about, turn about (Ez 42:16f. [42:17,19]).

סוּג sûgh (5657), Niphal: become disloyal, turned away (Ps 78:57 [77:57]).

סוּר sûr (5681), Go away, leave (Jgs 20:8).

עָזַב 'āzav (6013), Leave (Gn 39:6—Codex Alexandrinus only).

פָּנָה pānâh (6680), Qal: turn, turn away (Dt 1:7, Jgs 18:21, Prv 17:8); hiphil: turn, turn to leave (1 Sm 10:9).

שִׂים sîm (7947), Set (Ez 35:2).

שׁוּב shûv (8178), Qal: turn back, return (Ex 4:20, 1 Kgs 8:48, Hos 3:5); polel: restore (Ps 23:3 [22:3]); hiphil: bring back, turn back (Jgs 11:9, 2 Chr 19:4, Is 49:6); hophal: be brought back (Jer 27:16 [34:16]).

שׁוֹבֵב shôvēv (8182), Backsliding, faithless (Jer 3:22).

שָׁלַח shālach (8365), Qal: send (1 Kgs 8:44); piel: let go (Is 45:13).

שָׁמַע shāma' (8471), Listen, obey (Jer 12:17, 34:10 [41:10]).

שָׁפַךְ shāphakh (8581), Build up, cast up (Dn 11:15).

תְּשׁוּבָה t°shûvāh (9007), Turn of the year, in the spring (2 Sm 11:1, 1 Kgs 20:26 [21:26]).

1. ἐπιστρέφετε epistrephete 2pl indic pres act
2. ἐπιστρέφουσιν epistrephousin
   dat pl masc part pres act
3. ἐπέστρεψα epestrepsa 1sing indic aor act
4. ἐπέστρεψεν epestrepsen 3sing indic aor act
5. ἐπεστρέψατε epestrepsate 2pl indic aor act
6. ἐπέστρεψαν epestrepsan 3pl indic aor act
7. ἐπιστρέψῃ epistrepsē 3sing subj aor act
8. ἐπιστρέψωσιν epistrepsōsin 3pl subj aor act
9. ἐπιστρεψάτω epistrepsatō 3sing impr aor act
10. ἐπιστρέψατε epistrepsate 2pl impr aor act
11. ἐπιστρέψας epistrepsas
    nom sing masc part aor act
12. ἐπιστρέψαντες epistrepsantes
    nom pl masc part aor act
13. ἐπιστρέψαι epistrepsai inf aor act
14. ἐπιστρέφειν epistrephein inf aor act
15. ἐπιστρέψω epistrepsō 1sing indic fut act
16. ἐπιστρέψει epistrepsei 3sing indic fut act
17. ἐπεστράφητε epestraphēte 2pl indic aor pass
18. ἐπιστραφῶσιν epistraphōsin 3pl subj aor pass
19. ἐπιστραφήτω epistraphētō 3sing impr aor pass
20. ἐπιστραφείς epistrapheis
    nom sing masc part aor pass

20	But Jesus **turned** him about, and when he saw her,	Matt 9:22
19	if it be not worthy, let your peace **return** to you......	10:13
15	I will **return** into my house from whence I came......	12:44
15	I will **return** into my house from whence I came......	12:44
8	should understand ... and **should be converted**,......	13:15
9	Neither let him which is in the field **return** back......	24:18
8	lest at any time they **should be converted**,.........	Mark 4:12
20	**turned** him about in the press, and said,...............	5:30
20	he had **turned about** and looked on his disciples,......	8:33
9	And let him that is in the field not **turn** back **again**..	13:16
16	And many of the children of Israel **shall he turn** ...	Luke 1:16
13	**to turn** the hearts of the fathers to the children,......	1:17
6	And the shepherds **returned**, glorifying and......	2:20
6	they **returned** to Galilee, to their own city (NASB)....	2:39
4	her spirit **came again**, and she arose straightway:......	8:55
7	and seven times in a day **turn again** to thee, saying,..	17:4
9	is in the field, let him likewise not **return** back......	17:31
11	when thou **art converted**, strengthen thy brethren......	22:32
18	nor understand with their heart, and **be converted**,	John 12:40
20	Then Peter, **turning about**,..........................	21:20
10	Repent ye therefore, and **be converted**,...............Acts	3:19
6	Lydda and Saron saw him, and **turned** to the Lord.....	9:35
11	and **turning** him to the body said, Tabitha, arise.......	9:40
4	great number believed, and **turned** unto the Lord.....	11:21
14	preach unto you that ye **should turn** from these......	14:15
2	which from among the Gentiles **are turned** to God:...	15:19
12	Let us **go again** and visit our brethren in every city ...	15:36
11	being grieved, **turned** and said to the spirit,..........	16:18
13	and **to turn** them from darkness to light,..............	26:18
14	that they should repent and **turn** to God,.............	26:20
8	and **should be converted**, and I should heal them......	28:27

7	Nevertheless when it **shall turn** to the Lord,	2 Co 3:16
1	**turn** ye again to the weak and beggarly elements,	Gal 4:9
5	and how ye **turned** to God from idols	1 Th 1:9
7	if any of you do err ... and one **convert** him;	Jas 5:19
11	that he which **converteth** the sinner from the error	5:20
17	but are now **returned** unto the Shepherd	1 Pt 2:25
13	**to turn** from the holy commandment delivered	2 Pt 2:21
11	The dog **is turned** to his own vomit again;	2:22
3	And I **turned** to see the voice that spake with me	Rev 1:12
11	And being **turned**, I saw seven golden candlesticks;	1:12

Classical Greek

This highly complex term in classical Greek—from *epi* (1894), "on, upon," and *strephō* (4613), "turn"—was widely used in antiquity. It means "to turn around" and possesses many shades of meaning including "to turn, to repel" an enemy or "to pay attention" (*Liddell-Scott*). People can be "turned," i.e., "changed," or in a religious sense "converted" to something. Nonetheless, this should not be construed as the Biblical concept of *conversion* (see Bertram, "epistrephō," *Kittel*, 7:722ff. who also gathers primary data on lexical usage).

Septuagint Usage

Epistrephō is a major word in the Septuagint. Bertram observes that the compound (*epistrephō* and *epistrophē* [1979]) "occurs 579 times in the LXX, 408 times for *shûv*, 30 for *sāvav*, 24 for *pānāh*, 11 for *hāphakh* and another 27 for 17 Hebrew verbs" (ibid., 7:723).

A normal sense of "to return" (to a location) is frequent in the Pentateuch (e.g., Genesis 8:12; 21:32; 37:30; Exodus 4:18,20). A religious understanding of "to return" to the Lord occurs in Deuteronomy 4:30. This early usage paved the way for a development of the concept, which may have its antecedents in the phrase "to return to Egypt"—a synonym of apostasy (Deuteronomy 31:20; Jeremiah 2:27; 11:10; Bertram, ibid., 7:724; cf. Deuteronomy 30:2,10; Nehemiah 1:9; 9:28). "Return" is the cry of the Lord to His people, especially in the Prophets (Isaiah 6:10; 44:22; 55:7; Jeremiah 4:1; Hosea 3:5; 5:4; 6:1; 7:10; 14:2,3; Joel 2:12; Amos 4:6,8-11; Haggai 2:17; Zechariah 1:3.) *Epistrephō* also describes God's "returning" or "bringing back" Israel to its former prosperous state (Lamentations 2:14; cf. 5:21; Hosea 6:11; Joel 3:1; Amos 9:14; Zephaniah 2:7). The NIV probably has the better translation, "restore the fortunes." The association with *epistrephō* and repentance is evident in the apocryphal writings of the Septuagint (e.g., Sirach 21:6; Tobit 13:6) but not to the degree of the prophetic writings of the canonical portions (cf. 1 Maccabees passim). Bertram observes the limited use in the pseudepigrapha as well (ibid., 7:725; e.g., Testaments of: Issachar 6:3; Daniel 5:9; Naphtali 4:3; Judah 3:10).

New Testament Usage

Epistrephō occurs over 35 times in the New Testament. Fifteen instances are found in the Synoptic Gospels and two in the Gospel of John (12:40; 21:20). Apparently *epistrephō* can be used interchangably with *strephō* in certain contexts (Mark 8:33; cf. Matthew 16:23, parallel). It can denote "to return" in the physical sense (Matthew 12:44; Mark 13:16; Luke 2:20), or it can describe the "return" of life to a dead body (Luke 8:55; cf. Acts 9:40).

Not surprisingly Luke in his Gospel and in Acts follows the Old Testament religious understanding of *epistrephō* found in the prophetic writings of the Septuagint (Luke 1:16,17; Acts 3:19; 9:35; 14:15; 15:19; 26:18,20). Mark (paralleled by Matthew) also was aware of this same concept (Mark 4:12 [Matthew 13:16]; see Isaiah 6:10; cf. Acts 28:27).

The Epistles recognize primarily the religious idea of "returning to God" (2 Corinthians 3:16; 1 Peter 2:25) in contrast to "turning to" "weak and beggarly elemental spirits" (Galatians 4:9, RSV). Just as in the Acts and the Gospels, religious turning may involve turning "away from," *apo* (570), one thing and turning "to," *pros* (4172B), another—in this case God (1 Thessalonians 1:9; cf. Acts 26:18).

In the New Testament *epistrephō* quite often serves as a technical term for *conversion* with all of its implications. True conversion not only involves saying "yes" to God; it also includes saying "no" to sin, for it is sin which separates man from God (cf. Isaiah 59:2). The "negative" side of conversion, i.e., turning from the power of Satan, is just as present as the "positive" side, i.e., turning to God (Acts 26:18). The literal sense also occurs in 2 Peter 2:22 (cf. Proverbs 26:11) where the fate of those who turn from God is described.

STRONG 1994, BAUER 301, MOULTON-MILLIGAN 246, KITTEL 7:722-29, LIDDELL-SCOTT 661, COLIN BROWN 1:353-55.

1979. ἐπιστροφή epistrophē noun

Conversion, a turning (away from idolatry).

ἐπισυνάγω 1980

CROSS-REFERENCE:
ἐπιστρέφω epistrephō (1978)
מִשְׁפָּט mishpāṭ (5122), Similar, like (Ez 42:11).
שׁוּב shûv (8178), Arrival (Ez 47:7).
תְּשׁוּקָה tᵉshûqāh (9010), Desire (S/S 7:10).

1. ἐπιστροφήν epistrophēn acc sing fem
1 declaring the conversion of the Gentiles: .... Acts 15:3

Classical Greek
In classical literature *epistrophē* primarily refers to the act of "turning about, turning away," or "turning around" as in maneuvering a ship or changing a person's position. Sometimes in philosophical writings it has a figurative meaning: "turning one's attention to pious devotion to the divine" (cf. *Moulton-Milligan*). Linked with the verb *poieō* (4020), it also has the figurative meaning "to give attention to."

Septuagint Usage
In the Septuagint *epistrophē* and its verb cognate *epistrephō* are used literally (e.g., Judges 8:9; Ezekiel 47:7). They also are used figuratively to indicate repentance. The word is employed to express the theological implications of the Hebrew term *shûv*. It is from this that the Greek word acquires its higher religious meaning.

New Testament Usage
Although the Septuagint used *epistrophē/epistrephō* extensively for "conversion," the New Testament writers preferred *metanoia* (3211) and *metanoeō* (3210) in referring to repentance. The verbal form *epistrephō* (1978) is used 36 times in the New Testament, half of which express the act of repenting or converting. *Epistrophē*, however, occurs only once in the New Testament, in Acts 15:3, where it is used to express the "conversion of the Gentiles."

STRONG 1995, BAUER 301, MOULTON-MILLIGAN 246, KITTEL 7:722-29, LIDDELL-SCOTT 661-62, COLIN BROWN 1:354-55.

1980. ἐπισυνάγω episunagō verb
Gather together.

COGNATE:
συνάγω sunagō (4714)

SYNONYMS:
ἀθροίζω athroizō (119B)
συλλέγω sullegō (4667)
συνάγω sunagō (4714)
συναθροίζω sunathroizō (4718)
συστρέφω sustrephō (4814)
τρυγάω trugaō (5007)

אָסַף ’āsaph (636), Qal: gather (Hb 2:5, Zec 14:2); niphal: be gathered (Zec 12:3); piel: be a rearguard (Is 52:12).
יָסַד yāsadh (3354), Lay the foundations of; niphal: conspire (Ps 31:13 [30:13]).
יָעַד yā‘adh (3366), Niphal: gather, assemble (2 Chr 5:6).
כָּנַס kānas (3788), Piel: gather, assemble (Ps 147:2 [146:2]).
כְּנַשׁ kᵉnash (A3798), Assemble (Dn 3:2—Aramaic).
לָוָה lāwâh (4004), Niphal: join, cleave to (Dn 11:34).
מָלֵא mālē’ (4529), Loudly, from a multitude (Jer 12:6).
סָאַן sā’an (5615), Every (Is 9:5).
צֹהַר tsōhar (6936), Cover, finish above (Gn 6:16).
קָבַץ qāvats (7192), Qal: gather, assemble (1 Kgs 18:20); niphal: be gathered, be assembled (Ps 102:22 [101:22]); piel: gather together (Ps 106:47 [105:47]).
קָהַל qāhal (7234), Niphal: assemble (2 Chr 20:26).
שׁוּב shûv (8178), Return; hiphil: bring back, draw back (Gn 38:29).

1. ἐπισυνάγει episunagei 3sing indic pres act
2. ἐπισυναγαγεῖν episunagagein inf aor act
3. ἐπισυνάξαι episunaxai inf aor act
4. ἐπισυνάξει episunaxei 3sing indic fut act
5. ἐπισυνάξουσιν episunaxousin 3pl indic fut act
6. ἐπισυναχθεισῶν episunachtheisōn
    gen pl fem part aor pass
7. ἐπισυνηγμένη episunēgmenē
    nom sing fem part perf mid
8. ἐπισυναχθήσονται episunachthēsontai
    3pl indic fut pass

2 often would I have gathered thy children together,.. Matt 23:37
1 as a hen gathereth her chickens under her wings,...... 23:37
1 as a hen gathereth her chickens under her wings,...... 23:37
5 shall gather together his elect from the four winds,..... 24:31
7 And all the city was gathered together at the door...Mark 1:33
4 send his angels, and shall gather together his elect..... 13:27
6 when there were gathered together................. Luke 12:1
3 often would I have gathered thy children together,..... 13:34
8 there also will the vultures be gathered. (NASB)....... 17:37

The word simply means "to collect and bring to a place, to gather together," either people or things. It is used of accumulated interest. The New Testament uses it with essentially the same meaning as *sunagō* (4714), its root word. Jesus lamented over the hardness of Jerusalem in the face of His desire to gather them for protection as a hen would gather her chicks (Matthew 23:37 and its parallel, Luke 13:34). He also used the word in His prophetic discourse to describe the work of God's angels in gathering the elect from the four winds (Matthew 24:34; Mark 13:27). The term is used for the crowds which gathered around Christ (Mark 1:33; Luke 12:1), and Luke 17:37 employs it in the Lord's reply to the question of where the Son of Man's return would be. He stated that as vultures gather where a body is, so the place of the coming of the Son of Man will be equally obvious to all.

STRONG 1996, BAUER 301, MOULTON-MILLIGAN 247, LIDDELL-SCOTT 662, COLIN BROWN 2:33.

1981. ἐπισυναγωγή episunagōgē noun

A gathering together, assembly.

CROSS-REFERENCE:
συνάγω sunagō (4714)

1. ἐπισυναγωγῆς episunagōgēs gen sing fem
2. ἐπισυναγωγήν episunagōgēn acc sing fem

1 and by our **gathering together** unto him,............ 2 Th 2:1
2 Not forsaking the **assembling** of ourselves together, Heb 10:25

Classical Greek

Though other members of this word group are quite common, *episunagōgē* itself is not a frequently used term. It is rare in classical Greek and the papyri where it is used to describe "a gathering or being gathered together." One inscription from the island of Syme, on a first-century B.C. monument honoring a notable citizen, mentions that "the collection" (*episunagōgē*) of the disputed money took a long time. Thus it was used to describe the act of gathering. Other usages from the classical period include the idea of "summing up," for example, a collective view of a topic. The introduction of the third volume of a multi-volume work describes its contents as a "collection" of thoughts left over from the two prior volumes (*Moulton-Milligan*). It could therefore mean the results of a collecting process.

Septuagint Usage

The word appears only once in the Septuagint, in 2 Maccabees 2:7, where it is used to describe the Lord's gathering and restoring the nation of Israel from its dispersion. The connection with eschatological ideas of hope for the future is continued in its New Testament uses.

New Testament Usage

Episunagōgē is used twice in the New Testament, in 2 Thessalonians 2:1 and Hebrews 10:25. It carries the meaning of "the act of gathering together" and also "the congregation thus assembled" (Hiebert, *Thessalonian Epistles*, p.301). The Thessalonians passage connects *episunagōgē* closely with the *parousia* (3814), or presence of the returning Lord, and includes both living and dead believers in a final assembly before God. The *epi* (1894) probably shows that the gathering is focused toward a particular point, namely Christ himself. It is not the people who assemble themselves, but He himself assembles them.

The other passage, Hebrews 10:25, speaks of the normal assembly of Christians for worship. Bruce cites the view that the *epi* can mean "in addition to," thus describing meetings that Jewish Christians might attend to supplement their normal synagogue services (*New International Commentary on New Testament*, Hebrews, p.254). But no evidence exists for this usage elsewhere, and it is more likely that the writer meant the regular worship services of the churches. Here again, there is a link with the prophetic; the context which follows pictures contemporary church meetings as a foretaste of the ultimate assembly that lies in the future.

STRONG 1997, BAUER 301, MOULTON-MILLIGAN 247, KITTEL 7:841-43, LIDDELL-SCOTT 662, COLIN BROWN 2:33.

1982. ἐπισυντρέχω episuntrechō verb

Run together, rush together.

CROSS-REFERENCE:
τρέχω trechō (4983)

1. ἐπισυντρέχει episuntrechei 3sing indic pres act

1 Jesus saw that the people **came running together**,... Mark 9:25

This word is related to *trechō* (4983), meaning "run," and the compound prefixes add the idea of running "together." It does not appear in Greek literature outside the New Testament. The single occurrence in the New Testament, Mark 9:25, is used to describe a crowd rushing together to watch Jesus cast out a demon. It pictures a group of people converging on a single point.

STRONG 1998, BAUER 301, MOULTON-MILLIGAN 247, LIDDELL-SCOTT 662.

1983. ἐπισύστασις episustasis noun

Uprising, disturbance, insurrection.

CROSS-REFERENCE:
ἵστημι histēmi (2449)

נָצָה nātsâh (5510), Community, congregation (Nm 26:9).
עֵדָה ʿēdhāh (5920), Company, followers (Nm 16:40).

1. ἐπισύστασις episustasis nom sing fem
2. ἐπισύστασιν episustasin acc sing fem

2 neither **raising up** the people,............... Acts 24:12	
1 that which **cometh upon** me daily,............ 2 Co 11:28	

Classical Greek and Septuagint Usage
Classical authors used *episustasis* to mean "gathering, riotous meeting, insurrection," or "collection." It appears three times in the Septuagint (Numbers 16:40; 26:9; 1 Esdras 5:78), primarily to describe the unruly mob which followed Korah in his revolt against the authority of Moses. It generally includes the thought of people coming together with a hostile intent.

New Testament Usage
The word occurs twice in the New Testament: in Acts 24:12, where Paul denied any involvement in "disturbances" at the temple in Jerusalem; and in 2 Corinthians 11:28, where the apostle listed *episustasis* as part of the pressures and persecutions that characterized his apostolic ministry. Some writers see the use in 2 Corinthians as a reference to opposition from church leaders; however, most commentators take it in a general sense referring to the pressures involved in daily care of the churches. In both New Testament passages *episustasis* is used in the Majority text; some early manuscripts employ *epistasis* (1971B) instead, meaning "oversight, attention," or "pressure."

STRONG 1999, BAUER 301-2, MOULTON-MILLIGAN 247, LIDDELL-SCOTT 663, COLIN BROWN 1:292.

1984. ἐπισφαλής episphalēs adj
Dangerous, likely to fall.

1. ἐπισφαλοῦς episphalous gen sing masc

1 and when sailing was now **dangerous**,............ Acts 27:9

Classical Greek and Septuagint Usage
In classical Greek literature this word carries the meaning of being "prone to fall, unstable, precarious," or "dangerous." Its cognate, *sphallō*, means "making to fall" or "to overthrow" by "tripping up" (as in wrestling). In the Septuagint it is found in Wisdom of Solomon 9:14.

New Testament Usage
In its New Testament usage the adjective *episphalēs* means "unsafe" or "dangerous." Its sole New Testament occurrence is Acts 27:9, where Luke alluded to the danger of embarking on a voyage in the Mediterranean too late in the season. Bruce says that the period between September 14 and November 11 was considered dangerous, and all navigation on the open sea would cease after that date (*New International Commentary on the New Testament, Acts*, p.481). When the ship's captain ignored Paul's warning, the vessel was caught in a massive storm, proving that what Paul had said was correct.

STRONG 2000, BAUER 302, MOULTON-MILLIGAN 247, LIDDELL-SCOTT 663.

1985. ἐπισχύω epischuō verb
Be strong, urgent.

CROSS-REFERENCE:
ἰσχύω ischuō (2453)

1. ἐπίσχυον epischuon 3pl indic imperf act

1 And they were the **more fierce**, saying,............ Luke 23:5

Classical Greek and Septuagint Usage
The word means "to make strong" or "powerful," as in strengthening a city's defenses. It also has an intransitive use, "to be strong, to grow strong, to prevail." The prefix *epi* (1894) results in the idea "to add up in strength" (Rienecker, *Linguistic Key to the Greek New Testament*, 1:209). In the Septuagint it is found in Sirach 29:1 and 1 Maccabees 6:6.

New Testament Usage
Luke 23:5 is the only occurrence of *epischuō* in the New Testament. Here the intransitive use of the word describes the urgency with which the leading priests and the crowds pressured Pilate for the death of Jesus. When the governor claimed that he found no cause for executing his prisoner, the Jews increased their urgency of speech and insisted that He truly was worthy of death.

STRONG 2001, BAUER 302, MOULTON-MILLIGAN 247, LIDDELL-SCOTT 663.

1986. ἐπισωρεύω episōreuō verb
Heap up, accumulate.

SYNONYM:
σωρεύω sōreuō (4839)

1. ἐπισωρεύσουσιν episōreusousin 3pl indic fut act

1 shall they **heap** to themselves teachers,............ 2 Tm 4:3

Classical Greek
The compound verb *episōreuō* means "to heap on to." It comes from the noun *sōros*, "a heap, pile," often used of piles of grain. Outside of the New Testament it is found no earlier than the Second Century A.D. when the verb was used for the excessive accumulation of business,

for overloading a person with difficulties, and for adding further examples to those already given. In each case it carries the connotation of significantly increasing the number or amount.

New Testament Usage
Although the word does not appear in the Septuagint, it is used once in the New Testament, in 2 Timothy 4:3. Here Paul used the verb figuratively to describe the period of apostasy when people will "heap to themselves" teachers who will cater to their own wishes. The quantity of teachers seems to be a substitute for the lack of spiritual quality.

STRONG 2002, BAUER 302, MOULTON-MILLIGAN 247, KITTEL 7:1096, LIDDELL-SCOTT 663.

1987. ἐπιταγή epitagē noun
Command, decree, injunction.

COGNATE:
τάσσω tassō (4872)

SYNONYMS:
διάταγμα diatagma (1291)
δόγμα dogma (1372)
ἔνταλμα entalma (1762)
ἐντολή entolē (1769)

פִּתְגָם pithgām (A6852), Word, reply (Dn 3:16—Aramaic).

1. ἐπιταγῆς epitagēs gen sing fem
2. ἐπιταγήν epitagēn acc sing fem

2 according to the **commandment** of the everlasting...	Rom 16:26
2 this by permission, and not of **commandment**........	1 Co 7:6
2 Now concerning virgins I have no **commandment**......	7:25
2 I speak not by **commandment**,......................	2 Co 8:8
2 by the **commandment** of God our Saviour,..........	1 Tm 1:1
2 the **commandment** of God our Saviour;.............	Tit 1:3
1 speak, and exhort, and rebuke with all **authority**.......	2:15

Classical Greek
Epitagē, found no earlier than the Second Century B.C., denotes an "ordinance, disposition, order," and "statute." It is often used as a technical term with *kata* (2567) in a recognized formula similar to our official notices "by order of" (cf. *Liddell-Scott*). On occasion the phrase is used to describe votive offerings given "at the command of" the deity involved.

Septuagint Usage
This word occurs in the Septuagint six times. In Wisdom of Solomon 18:5 and 19:6 it refers to God's "commands," while the other occurrences are general references to any ruler's "orders" or "decrees." The only canonical occurrence is in Daniel 3:16 where Shadrach, Meshach, and Abednego responded to Nebuchadnezzar's demand that they worship him or be cast into a furnace.

New Testament Usage
The New Testament uses are all in Paul's writings, and he used it simply with the definition "command." It continues the meaning of a command from a superior, a legitimate authority, which must be obeyed. The word is also used of commands from royalty or from deity. Except in 1 Corinthians 7:25 and Titus 2:15 it appears only in the phrase *kat' epitagēn*. In Romans 16:26 Paul wrote that the gospel was being made known by the *command* of God. First Corinthians has two interesting references: 7:6 explains that Paul's advice to marry was a recommendation, not a *command*; and 7:25 explains that he had no direct *command* from the Lord concerning virgins. Second Corinthians 8:8 deals with the offering being gathered for the poor in Jerusalem. Paul made it clear that he was not *commanding* them to give—merely recommending it. According to 1 Timothy 1:1 and Titus 1:3 Paul wrote that he had been placed in the position of spreading the gospel by *command* of God. In the final reference in Titus 2:15 Paul instructed the young preacher to speak to his people with the authority of a *command*.

STRONG 2003, BAUER 302, MOULTON-MILLIGAN 247, KITTEL 8:36-37, LIDDELL-SCOTT 663.

1988. ἐπιτάσσω epitassō verb
Command, order.

COGNATE:
τάσσω tassō (4872)

SYNONYMS:
διαμαρτύρομαι diamarturomai (1257)
διαστέλλω diastellō (1285)
διατάσσω diatassō (1293)
ἐντέλλομαι entellomai (1765)
ἐξορκίζω exorkizō (1828)
ἐπιτρέπω epitrepō (1994)
κελεύω keleuō (2724)
λέγω legō (2978)
ὁρκίζω horkizō (3589)
παραγγέλλω parangellō (3715)
προστάσσω prostassō (4225)
συντάσσω suntassō (4781)
τάσσω tassō (4872)

אָמַר 'āmar (569), Say, command (Dn 1:18, 2:2).

אֲמַר 'ămar (A570), Say, command (Dn 2:46, 3:19,20—Aramaic).

יָסַד yāsadh (3354), Piel: appoint, command (Est 1:8).

נָתַן nāthan (5598), Give, grant (Est 8:11).

צָוָה tsāwāh (6943), Piel: order, direct (Gn 49:33); pual: be ordered, receive a command (Ez 24:18).

ἐπιτελέω 1989

קוּם qûm (7251), Arise, stand; hiphil: establish, bring to (Ps 107:29 [106:29]).

1. **ἐπιτάσσω** epitassō 1sing indic pres act
2. **ἐπιτάσσει** epitassei 3sing indic pres act
3. **ἐπιτάσσειν** epitassein inf pres act
4. **ἐπέταξας** epetaxas 2sing indic aor act
5. **ἐπέταξεν** epetaxen 3sing indic aor act
6. **ἐπιτάξῃ** epitaxē 3sing subj aor act

2 with authority **commandeth** he ... unclean spirits,	Mark 1:27
5 and **commanded** his head to be brought:	6:27
5 And he **commanded** them to make all sit down	6:39
1 Thou dumb and deaf spirit, I **charge** thee,	9:25
2 and power he **commandeth** the unclean spirits,	Luke 4:36
2 for he **commandeth** even the winds and water,	8:25
6 would not **command** them to go out into the deep.	8:31
4 said, Lord, it is done as thou **hast commanded**,	14:22
5 high priest Ananias **commanded** them ... to smite	Acts 23:2
3 **to enjoin** thee that which is convenient,	Phlm 1:8

Classical Greek and Septuagint Usage

In classical, Septuagintal, and Koine Greek *epitassō* means "to command," and it is used to describe a superior giving specific instructions to a subordinate. Two additional usages occur in classical Greek: (1) "to place next, to place behind," or "to place in reserve," and (2) "to place in command over" a group, such as military guards (cf. *Moulton-Milligan*). In the Septuagint *epitassō* is used to translate seven Hebrew words, most frequently *'āmar* ("command," cf. Daniel 2:2) and *tsāwâh* ("command," cf. Genesis 49:33).

New Testament Usage

In the New Testament *epitassō* is used for commands given by Jesus to demons (Mark 1:27; Luke 4:36; 8:31), to people (Mark 6:39), and to a stormy wind (Luke 8:25). It also is used to describe commands by Herod (Mark 6:27), the high priest (Acts 23:2), and the master in one of Christ's parables (Luke 14:22). In Philemon 8 Paul chose not to issue a command in the case of Onesimus.

STRONG 2004, BAUER 302, MOULTON-MILLIGAN 247, LIDDELL-SCOTT 664, COLIN BROWN 1:341.

1989. ἐπιτελέω epiteleō verb

Bring to an end, finish, complete, accomplish, fulfill.

COGNATE:
 τελέω teleō (4903)
SYNONYMS:
 ἀναπληρόω anaplēroō (376)
 ἀνταναπληρόω antanaplēroō (463)
 ἀποτελέω apoteleō (652)
 διανύω dianuō (1268)
 ἐκπληρόω ekplēroō (1590)
 ἐκτελέω ekteleō (1602)
 ἐξαρτίζω exartizō (1806)
 ἐργάζομαι ergazomai (2021)
 καταρτίζω katartizō (2645)
 κατεργάζομαι katergazomai (2686)
 πληρόω plēroō (3997)
 ποιέω poieō (4020)
 πράσσω prassō (4097)
 συντελέω sunteleō (4783)
 τελειόω teleioō (4896)
 τελέω teleō (4903)

בָּצַע bātsa' (1239), Piel: finish, complete (Zec 4:9).

דָּחַף dāchaph (1821), Spurred on, hastened (Est 8:14).

זְמָן z^emān (2249), At the appointed time (Est 9:27).

כָּלָה kālāh (3735), Qal: consume, destroy (Dn 11:16); piel: complete, end (1 Sm 3:12).

עָשָׂה 'āsâh (6449), Do, perform (Nm 23:23).

קָטַר qātar (7281), Let go up in smoke; hophal: be wholly burnt, burned completely (Lv 6:22—Codex Vaticanus only).

1. **ἐπιτελῶ** epitelō 1sing indic pres act
2. **ἐπιτελοῦντες** epitelountes nom pl masc part pres act
3. **ἐπιτελεῖν** epitelein inf pres act
4. **ἐπιτελέσῃ** epitelesē 3sing subj aor act
5. **ἐπιτελέσατε** epitelesate 2pl impr aor act
6. **ἐπιτελέσας** epitelesas nom sing masc part aor act
7. **ἐπιτελέσαι** epitelesai inf aor act
8. **ἐπιτελέσει** epitelesei 3sing indic fut act
9. **ἐπιτελεῖσθε** epiteleisthe 2pl indic pres mid
10. **ἐπιτελεῖσθαι** epiteleisthai inf pres mid

1 and I **do cures** to day and to morrow,	Luke 13:32
6 When therefore I **have performed** this,	Rom 15:28
2 **perfecting** holiness in the fear of God.	2 Co 7:1
4 so he would also **finish** in you the same grace also.	8:6
5 Now therefore **perform** the doing of it;	8:11
7 be a **performance** also out of that which ye have.	8:11
9 are ye now **made perfect** by the flesh?	Gal 3:3
8 **will perform** it until the day of Jesus Christ:	Phlp 1:6
3 when he was about **to make** the tabernacle:	Heb 8:5
2 first tabernacle, **accomplishing** the service of God.	9:6
10 knowing that the same afflictions **are accomplished**	1 Pt 5:9
9 knowing that the same afflictions **are accomplished**	5:9

Classical Greek

This intensive compound of *epi* (1894) + *teleō* (4903) simply means "to complete, finish," or "accomplish." It is to be noted that oracles and prophecies were often regarded as "fulfilled" (*epiteleō*) or not fulfilled (*Liddell-Scott*). Otherwise it had no special function. It could also be said that one "fulfilled" an obligation or duty. These were often religious duties (cf. Delling, "epiteleō," *Kittel*, 8:61; e.g., Josephus *Antiquities* 1.2.1; 4.5.5; 9.11.7, of sacrifices offered; cf. *Moulton-Milligan*).

Septuagint Usage

In the Septuagint *epiteleō* translates seven Hebrew words; only nine texts have Hebrew counterparts. Rituals are "performed" (Leviticus

6:22) and tasks are "completed" (1 Esdras 4:55; 5:73; 6:4,14,28). At the religious level prophecies are "fulfilled" (1 Samuel 3:12 [LXX 1 Kings 3:12]; cf. 1 Esdras 8:16).

New Testament Usage
Of its 11 occurrences in the New Testament 8 are Pauline. Paul spoke of the completion of a task (Romans 15:28) and of the fulfillment of an obligation toward God (2 Corinthians 7:1). The spiritual completion of believers is contrasted with their beginning (*enarchō* [1712], in both texts; it was used as a sacrificial technical term since Euripides, cf. *Bauer*, Galatians 3:3; Philippians 1:6).

The cultic significance of the term is found in Hebrews 9:6 as well as an ordinary sense (8:5). Its use in 1 Peter 5:9 carries the sense of obligation found in cultic use but with a secular application: "The same experience of suffering *is required* of your brotherhood throughout the world" (RSV).

STRONG 2005, BAUER 302, MOULTON-MILLIGAN 247-48, KITTEL 8:61-62, LIDDELL-SCOTT 665.

1990. ἐπιτήδειος epitēdeios adj
Necessary, suitable, needful.

1. ἐπιτήδεια epitēdeia nom/acc pl neu

1 not those things which are needful to the body; .... Jas 2:16

Classical Greek and Septuagint Usage
In classical Greek *epitēdeios* sometimes means "suitable, made or adapted for a particular use," or "convenient." It can also mean a chariot fit to ride in or a person who was easy to live with. It could carry the related meaning of "deserving," as in the case of the one who deserved to be ostracized or struck (cf. *Liddell-Scott*). A second meaning, "necessary, useful," also appears. It describes things which are usable for a certain purpose, or persons who are favorable to the speaker. It also is used to describe the necessities of life, such as food and other provisions. In the Septuagint the word appears in numerous places, such as 1 Chronicles 28:2; Wisdom of Solomon 4:5; and 1 Maccabees 4:46 with similar usage.

Papyri inscriptions illustrate the idiom *ta epitēdeia*, "the necessities of life." One text mentions the task of furnishing "provisions for an impending official visit." Another describes a husband who undertakes to provide *ta epitēdeia* for his divorced wife in a manner appropriate for her rank (cf. *Moulton-Milligan*).

New Testament Usage
The New Testament uses the phrase in James 2:16 with its normal meaning, "the necessities of life," describing the care required for one who is hungry and cold. Some manuscripts also use the word in Acts 24:25 with its other meaning of "convenient" when the Roman governor Felix postponed further discussion of the gospel until a more "suitable" time.

STRONG 2006, BAUER 302, MOULTON-MILLIGAN 248, LIDDELL-SCOTT 665-66.

1991. ἐπιτίθημι epitithēmi verb
Lay or put upon, impose.

COGNATES:
ἐπίθεσις epithesis (1921)
τίθημι tithēmi (4935)

בּוֹא bô' (971), Come (2 Chr 28:17).

גּוּר gûr (1513), Lie in wait (Ps 59:3 [58:3]).

הָתַת hāthath (2133), Polel: assault, mischief against (Ps 62:3 [61:3]).

זִיד zîdh (2202), Qal: treat arrogantly (Ex 18:11); hiphil: scheme against, come upon (Ex 21:14).

זָמַם zāmam (2246), Imagine, plan (Gn 11:6).

יָדָה yādhâh (3142), Piel: throw at, cast (Lam 3:53).

יָצַק yātsaq (3441), Pour out (Is 44:3).

יָקֹשׁ yāqosh (3483), Lay a snare, set a trap (Jer 50:24 [27:24]).

נוּחַ nûach (5299), Settle, rest; hiphil: lay upon, set (1 Sm 6:18, 1 Kgs 13:29, Ez 40:42).

נוּף nûph (5311), Hiphil: wave (Lv 14:24, Nm 5:25, 2 Kgs 5:11).

נִיב nîv (5391), Fruit (Mal 1:12).

נָפַל nāphal (5489), Fall: hithpael: fall on, attack (Gn 43:18).

נָשָׂא nāsâ' (5558), Lift up (Gn 42:26).

נָתַן nāthan (5598), Qal: put, set (Lv 14:28,29, Nm 11:25, 2 Kgs 18:14); niphal: be given (Est 9:14—only some Sinaiticus texts).

סָבַב sāvav (5621), Turn; hiphil: change (2 Kgs 24:17).

סָמַךְ sāmakh (5759), Support, lay on (Ex 29:10, Lv 8:14, 2 Chr 29:23).

עָגַב 'āghav (5896), Have desire for (Ez 23:5,7,9).

עָלָה 'ālâh (6148), Go up; hiphil: bring up, raise (Ex 40:4, Nm 8:2, Ez 27:30).

עָמַס 'āmas (6227), Load (Gn 44:13).

עָרַךְ 'ārakh (6424), Lay (Gn 22:9).

עָשָׂה 'āsâh (6449), Do, make (Ex 25:17, 36:36 [37:4]).

פָּקַד pāqadh (6734), Make a search, call to account; hiphil: commit, assign (1 Kgs 14:27).

ἐπιτίθημι 1991

פָּשַׁט pāshaṭ (6838), Raid, invade (1 Sm 23:27, 27:8, 2 Chr 25:13).

קָטַר qāṭar (7281), Hiphil: offer incense, burn incense (Ex 29:13, Lv 1:13,15, Nm 16:40).

קָשַׁר qāshar (7489), Qal: conspire, plot against (2 Chr 24:21, 33:24); hithpael: conspired against (2 Chr 24:25,26).

קֶשֶׁר qesher (7490), Be treasonous (2 Chr 23:13).

רוּם rûm (7597), Hiphil: lift up, exalt (Ez 21:26).

רָכַב rākhav (7680), Ride; hiphil: carry or move in a cart (1 Chr 13:7).

שִׂים sîm (7947), Put, set (Gn 37:34, 1 Kgs 18:25, Zec 6:11).

שָׁוָה shāwâh (8187), Be like; piel: lay upon, bestow on (Ps 21:5 [20:5]).

שָׁחַת shāchath (8271), Hiphil: destroy, steal (Jer 49:9 [29:9]).

שִׁית shîth (8308), Put, lay (Ru 3:15).

1. ἐπιτίθησιν epitithēsin 3sing indic pres act
2. ἐπετίθουν epetithoun 3pl indic imperf act
3. ἐπιτιθέασιν epititheasin 3pl indic pres act
4. ἐπιτιθῇ epitithē 3sing subj pres act
5. ἐπιτίθει epitithei 2sing impr pres act
6. ἐπέθηκεν epethēken 3sing indic aor act
7. ἐπέθηκαν epethēkan 3pl indic aor act
8. ἐπιθῶ epithō 1sing subj aor act
9. ἐπιθῇς epithēs 2sing subj aor act
10. ἐπιθῇ epithē 3sing subj aor act
11. ἐπίθες epithes 2sing impr aor act
12. ἐπιθείς epitheis nom sing masc part aor act
13. ἐπιθέντος epithentos gen sing masc part aor act
14. ἐπιθέντα epithenta acc sing masc part aor act
15. ἐπιθέντες epithentes nom pl masc part aor act
16. ἐπιθεῖναι epitheinai inf aor act
17. ἐπιθήσει epithēsei 3sing indic fut act
18. ἐπιθήσουσιν epithēsousin 3pl indic fut act
19. ἐπιτίθεσθαι epitithesthai inf pres mid
20. ἐπέθεντο epethento 3pl indic aor mid
21. ἐπιτεθῇ epitethē 3sing subj aor pass
22. ἐπιθήσεται epithēsetai 3sing indic fut mid
23. ἐπιτιθείς epititheis nom sing masc part pres act
24. ἐπιθῆσαι epithēsai 3sing opt aor act
25. ἐπετίθεσαν epetithesan 3pl indic imperf act

11	lay thy hand upon her, and she shall live..........	Matt 9:18
10	that he **should put** his hands on them, and pray:......	19:13
12	he **laid** his hands on them, and departed thence.......	19:15
7	put on them their clothes, ... they set him thereon....	21:7
3	and lay them on men's shoulders;...................	23:4
7	a crown of thorns, **they put** it upon his head,.........	27:29
7	And **set up** over his head his accusation written,.....	27:37
6	And Simon he **surnamed** Peter;................Mark 3:16
6	**surnamed** them Boanerges, ... The sons of thunder:....	3:17
21	a candle ... and not **to be set** on a candlestick?........	4:21
9	I pray thee, come and lay thy hands on her,..........	5:23
12	save that he **laid** his hands upon a few sick folk,......	6:5
10	and they beseech him **to put** his hand upon him........	7:32
12	and **put** his hands upon him,.....................	Mark 8:23
6	After that he **put** his hands again upon his eyes,.......	8:25
18	they **shall lay** hands on the sick,.....................	16:18
12	and he **laid** his hands on every one of them,.......Luke 4:40
23	and he **laid** his hands on every one of them,..........	4:40
1	but setteth it on a candlestick,.......................	8:16
15	stripped him ... and wounded him, (NT).............	10:30
6	And he **laid** his hands on her:.....................	13:13
1	found it, **he layeth** it on his shoulders, rejoicing.......	15:5
7	Simon, a Cyrenian, ... on him they **laid** the cross,....	23:26
6	**anointed** the eyes of the blind man with the clay,..	John 9:6
6	He said unto them, He **put** clay upon mine eyes,......	9:15
7	platted a crown of thorns, and **put** it on his head,....	19:2
7	they **laid** their hands on them......................	Acts 6:6
2	Then **laid** they their hands on them,..................	8:17
25	Then **laid** they their hands on them,..................	8:17
8	that on whomsoever I lay hands,......................	8:19
14	Ananias coming in, and **putting** his hand **on him**,......	9:12
12	and **putting** his hands on him said, Brother Saul,......	9:17
15	fasted and prayed, and **laid** their hands on them,.....	13:3
16	**to put** a yoke upon the neck of the disciples,.........	15:10
19	**to lay** upon you no greater burden than these........	15:28
15	And when they **had laid** many stripes upon them,.....	16:23
22	and no man **shall set** on thee to hurt thee:............	18:10
13	And when Paul **had laid** his hands upon them,........	19:6
13	a bundle of sticks, and **laid** them on the fire,.........	28:3
12	and **laid** his hands on him, and healed him...........	28:8
20	they **laded** us with such things as were necessary......	28:10
5	**Lay** hands suddenly on no man,....................	1 Tm 5:22
6	he **laid** his right hand upon me, saying unto me,....	Rev 1:17
4	If any man **shall add** unto these things,..............	22:18
10	If any man **shall add** unto these things,..............	22:18
17	God **shall add** unto him the plagues.................	22:18

Classical Greek and Septuagint Usage

In classical Greek *epitithēmi* refers to the act of "laying, placing, or putting one thing upon another." Of particular importance in Jewish and Christian literature is the use of *epitithēmi* in the expression "to lay hands upon." In making a sacrifice the priest placed his hands on the head of the animal (Leviticus 16:21). Hands were laid on persons when blessing (e.g., Genesis 48:18) or ordaining to an office (e.g., Numbers 27:18; Deuteronomy 34:9).

New Testament Usage

The New Testament uses the conventional meaning found in secular Greek (e.g., Matthew 27:29,37; Luke 23:53). It also applies the Old Testament's specialized use of *epitithēmi* (or *epithesis* [1921]) with *cheira* (see 5331), "hands," to indicate a special dispensation of divine grace, in particular, to confer power upon ordination or conversion (e.g., Acts 6:6; 8:17ff.; 13:3; 1 Timothy 4:14; 2 Timothy 1:6). The phrase is also used to indicate the means by which the Holy Spirit was imparted to believers in Samaria (Acts 8). In Matthew 19:13,15 Jesus is portrayed as laying His hands on children to bless them. The act is also presented as a means by which Jesus and His followers performed healings (e.g., Matthew 9:18; Mark 5:23; 6:5; 7:32; 8:23; Luke 13:13; Acts 28:8).

STRONG 2007, BAUER 302-3, MOULTON-MILLIGAN

248, Kittel 8:159-61, Liddell-Scott 666, Colin Brown 2:151.

1992. ἐπιτιμάω epitimaō verb

Rebuke, censure, warn, admonish.

COGNATES:
ἐπιτιμία epitimia (1993)
τιμάω timaō (4939)

SYNONYMS:
ἐλέγχω elenchō (1638)
ἐπιπλήσσω epiplēssō (1954)
νουθετέω noutheteō (3423)

גָּעַר gāʻar (1647), Reproach, rebuke (Gn 37:10, Ru 2:16, Ps 9:5).

1. ἐπιτιμῶν epitimōn nom sing masc part pres act
2. ἐπιτιμᾶν epitiman inf pres act
3. ἐπετίμησεν epetimēsen 3sing indic aor act
4. ἐπετίμησαν epetimēsan 3pl indic aor act
5. ἐπιτιμῆσαι epitimēsai 3sing opt aor act
6. ἐπιτίμησον epitimēson 2sing impr aor act
7. ἐπιτιμήσας epitimēsas nom sing masc part aor act
8. ἐπετίμα epetima 3sing indic imperf act
9. ἐπετίμων epetimōn 3pl indic imperf act

3 Then he arose, and **rebuked** the winds and the sea;..Matt	8:26
3 And **charged** them ... should not make him known:....	12:16
3 **charged** he his disciples that they should tell no.......	16:20
2 Then Peter took him, and began to **rebuke** him,.......	16:22
1 Then Peter took him, and began to **rebuke** him,.......	16:22
3 And Jesus **rebuked** the devil;........................	17:18
4 little children, ... and the disciples **rebuked** them......	19:13
3 And the multitude **rebuked** them,.....................	20:31
3 And Jesus **rebuked** him, saying, Hold thy peace,....Mark	1:25
8 **charged** ... that they should not make him known.......	3:12
3 And he arose, and **rebuked** the wind,..................	4:39
3 **charged** them that they should tell no man of him.......	8:30
2 And Peter took him, and began to **rebuke** him,.........	8:32
3 **rebuked** Peter, saying, Get thee behind me, Satan:.....	8:33
3 he **rebuked** the foul spirit, saying unto him,...........	9:25
9 and his disciples **rebuked** those that brought them.....	10:13
4 and his disciples **rebuked** those that brought them.....	10:13
9 many **charged** him that he should hold his peace:......	10:48
3 And Jesus **rebuked** him, saying, Hold thy peace,....Luke	4:35
3 And he stood over her, and **rebuked** the fever;........	4:39
1 he **rebuking** them suffered them not to speak:..........	4:41
3 and **rebuked** the wind and the raging of the water:.....	8:24
7 And he straitly **charged** them, and commanded........	9:21
3 **rebuked** the unclean spirit, and healed the child,.......	9:42
3 But he turned, and **rebuked** them, and said,...........	9:55
6 If thy brother trespass against thee, **rebuke** him;.......	17:3
4 but when his disciples saw it, they **rebuked** them......	18:15
9 but when his disciples saw it, they **rebuked** them......	18:15
9 they which went before **rebuked** him,.................	18:39
6 said unto him, Master, **rebuke** thy disciples...........	19:39
8 But the other answering **rebuked** him, saying,.........	23:40
1 But the other answering **rebuked** him, saying,.........	23:40
6 **rebuke**, exhort with all longsuffering and doctrine... 2 Tm	4:2
5 but said, The Lord **rebuke** thee..................... Jude	1:9

Classical Greek

In classical Greek the verb *epitimaō* can mean both "to honor" and "to censure or penalize." The positive and negative meanings are similar to those carried by the English word *citation*.

Septuagint Usage

In the Septuagint the word usually has the negative meaning indicating rebuke (e.g., Genesis 37:10; Ruth 2:16; Psalms 106:9 [LXX 105:9]; 119:21 [118:21]; Zechariah 3:2). In later Jewish literature it can also mean "to punish" (e.g., 3 Maccabees 2:24; Josephus *Antiquities* 18.4.6). God's rebuke effects judgment and wonder-working (Job 26:11; Psalms 106:9 [LXX 105:9]; 107:29 [106:29]; Isaiah 55:10f.).

New Testament Usage

The New Testament follows the lead of the Septuagint in that it uses the word to express rebuke or warning. *Epitimaō* is used for rebuking people (e.g., Mark 8:32,33; 10:13,48; Luke 9:55; 19:39; 23:40) and for rebuking demons in order to silence them and to effect their exorcism (e.g., Mark 1:25; 9:25). Jesus cured a fever by rebuking it (Luke 4:39) and stilled a storm by rebuking it (Mark 4:39). The noun cognate *epitimia* (1993) occurs in 2 Corinthians 2:6 where Paul called for "censure" or "punishment" to be applied to wayward members of the congregation.

Strong 2008, Bauer 303, Moulton-Milligan 248, Kittel 2:623-26, Liddell-Scott 666-67, Colin Brown 1:572-73.

1993. ἐπιτιμία epitimia noun

Punishment, penalty.

COGNATE:
ἐπιτιμάω epitimaō (1992)

SYNONYMS:
ἐκδίκησις ekdikēsis (1544)
κόλασις kolasis (2824)
τιμωρία timōria (4946)

1. ἐπιτιμία epitimia nom sing fem

1 Sufficient to such a man is this **punishment**,......... 2 Co	2:6

Classical Greek and Septuagint Usage

Classical writers used *epitimia* primarily in two ways: to refer to "citizenship," with all its civil rights and privileges, and to refer to "punishment" or "penalty." The Septuagint adopted the second sense of the term, namely, "punishment," in Wisdom of Solomon 3:10. The term carries the implication of causing an offender to suffer the deserved conseqcuences of his sin, whether simply a rebuke or a more substantial penalty.

New Testament Usage

The only New Testament occurrence of this word, 2 Corinthians 2:6, may refer to the

ἐπιτρέπω 1994

disciplinary actions meted out by the Corinthian church in the case of the member who had been involved in incest (cf. 1 Corinthians 5:1f.). In this case the penalty was expulsion from the fellowship of the church.

STRONG 2009, BAUER 303, MOULTON-MILLIGAN 248-49, KITTEL 2:627, LIDDELL-SCOTT 667, COLIN BROWN 1:572.

1994. ἐπιτρέπω epitrepō verb
Allow, permit, give permission.

COGNATES:
    ἀνατρέπω anatrepō (394)
    ἀποτρέπω apotrepō (659)
    ἐπιτροπή epitropē (1995)
    ἐπίτροπος epitropos (1996)
    μετατρέπω metatrepō (3216B)
    περιτρέπω peritrepō (3922)
    προτρέπομαι protrepomai (4247)
    τρόπος tropos (4999)

SYNONYMS:
    διαμαρτύρομαι diamarturomai (1257)
    διαστέλλω diastellō (1285)
    διατάσσω diatassō (1293)
    ἐάω eaō (1432)
    ἐντέλλομαι entellomai (1765)
    ἐπιτάσσω epitassō (1988)
    κελεύω keleuō (2724)
    ὁρκίζω horkizō (3589)
    παραγγέλλω parangellō (3715)
    προστάσσω prostassō (4225)
    συντάσσω suntassō (4781)
    τάσσω tassō (4872)

אָמַר 'āmar (569), Say, command (Est 9:14).
עָזַב 'āzav (6013), Leave (Gn 39:6—Sixtine Edition only).
עָרַךְ 'ārakh (6424), Prepare, put in order (Jb 32:14).

1. ἐπιτρέπω epitrepō 1sing indic pres act
2. ἐπιτρέπῃ epitrepē 3sing subj pres act
3. ἐπέτρεψεν epetrepsen 3sing indic aor act
4. ἐπιτρέψῃ epitrepsē 3sing subj aor act
5. ἐπίτρεψον epitrepson 2sing impr aor act
6. ἐπιτρέψαντος epitrepsantos
              gen sing masc part aor act
7. ἐπιτρέπεται epitrepetai 3sing indic pres mid
8. ἐπετράπη epetrapē 3sing indic aor pass
9. ἐπιτέτραπται epitetraptai 3sing indic perf mid

```
5 Lord, suffer me first to go and bury my father....... Matt 8:21
5 suffer us to go away into the herd of swine............. 8:31
3 suffered you to put away your wives:................. 19:8
3 And forthwith Jesus gave them leave............... Mark 5:13
3 Moses suffered to write a bill of divorcement,......... 10:4
4 that he would suffer them to enter into them........ Luke 8:32
3 to enter into them. And he suffered them................ 8:32
5 Lord, suffer me first to go and bury my father.......... 9:59
5 but let me first go bid them farewell,................... 9:61
3 away the body of Jesus: and Pilate gave him leave. John 19:38
5 I beseech thee, suffer me to speak unto the people. Acts 21:39
6 And when he had given him licence,................... 21:40
7 Thou art permitted to speak for thyself................. 26:1
3 and gave him liberty to go unto his friends............. 27:3
8 but Paul was suffered to dwell by himself.......... Acts 28:16
9 for it is not permitted unto them to speak;......... 1 Co 14:34
7 for it is not permitted unto them to speak;............. 14:34
2 trust to tarry a while with you, if the Lord permit...... 16:7
4 trust to tarry a while with you, if the Lord permit...... 16:7
1 But I suffer not a woman to teach,................. 1 Tm 2:12
2 And this will we do, if God permit.................. Heb 6:3
```

Epitrepō is a compound verb combining the preposition *epi* (1894), meaning "on, to, toward," and *trepō*, meaning "lead" or "guide." Its primary meaning suggests "to lead or direct someone into something," hence "allow" or "permit."

Classical Greek and Septuagint Usage
In classical Greek *epitrepō* means "to allow or grant permission." In the Septuagint (Genesis 39:6) Joseph is said to have certain responsibilities "entrusted" or "committed" to his care (see also Job 32:14). The Septuagint adds the meaning of "commission with duty or responsibility." It is related to the primary meaning in that one is "permitted" to assume certain responsibilities.

New Testament Usage
In the New Testament *epitrepō* most frequently means "allow" or "permit" as in Matthew 8:21 where it could be translated "Lord, first let me go and bury my father" (NIV). In Mark 5:13, John 19:38, and Acts 21:39 it carries the sense of release from restraint in order to have freedom of choice. For example, in Mark 5:13 Legion gained freedom from being sent away, and instead was permitted to enter a herd of swine (see verses 8-13).

Epitrepō differs from *aphiēmi* (856) which is occasionally translated "allow" or "permit" in that *aphiēmi* lacks the sense of release from restraint. For example, in Matthew 7:4, "*Allow* me to remove the speck . . . ," *aphiēmi* suggests a request that would meet no resistance. *Epitrepō*, on the other hand, carries the sense of release from a restraining activity to freedom or permission to engage in a preferred activity. Paul's request in Acts 21:39 to preach the gospel in the face of a restraining order best illustrates this nuance.

STRONG 2010, BAUER 303, MOULTON-MILLIGAN 249, LIDDELL-SCOTT 667-68.

1995. ἐπιτροπή epitropē noun
Authority, permission, guardianship, commission.

CROSS-REFERENCE:
    ἐπιτρέπω epitrepō (1994)

1. ἐπιτροπῆς epitropēs gen sing fem
1 authority and **commission** from the chief priests, ... Acts 26:12

Classical Greek and Septuagint Usage

A compound noun, *epitropē* is formed by the preposition *epi* (1894), "upon, over," and *tropē* (4998), "a turning" (which comes from the verb *trepō*, "to turn"). The verb *epitrepō* (1994) means "to turn to, transfer onto," hence "to entrust, commit" or "to allow, permit, give leave." Thus the noun carries the idea of "commission, permission, power, authority, guardianship." In the classics *epitropē* is often used of legal guardian and trusteeships and sometimes of the office of the Roman procurator. It occurs only once in the Septuagint (2 Maccabees 13:14).

New Testament Usage

In its only appearance in the New Testament (Acts 26:12), Paul's use of the term (in conjunction with "authority," *exousia* [1833]) in his defense before Agrippa suggests the fullness of the legal permission and authority entrusted to him by the high priest and Sanhedrin for the purpose of destroying the Church.

Strong 2011, Bauer 303, Moulton-Milligan 249, Liddell-Scott 668-69.

1996. ἐπίτροπος epitropos noun

Manager, foreman, steward, guardian.

Cognate:
ἐπιτρέπω epitrepō (1994)

Synonym:
οἰκονόμος oikonomos (3485)

1. ἐπιτρόπου epitropou gen sing masc
2. ἐπιτρόπῳ epitropō dat sing masc
3. ἐπιτρόπους epitropous acc pl masc

2 the lord of the vineyard saith unto his **steward,** .... Matt 20:8
1 And Joanna the wife of Chuza Herod's **steward,** .... Luke 8:3
3 But is under **tutors** and governors until the time .... Gal 4:2

Classical Greek

In classical Greek *epitropos* is used in three primary ways: in a vocational sense it denotes "manager" or "foreman"; in politics it refers to a "governor" or "procurator"; and in a family context it denotes a "guardian." In the papyri it is used most frequently in this third sense as a guardian of children, and secondly in the political sense of a governor. The term does not occur in the Septuagint.

New Testament Usage

Of the three occurrences in the New Testament (Matthew 20:8; Luke 8:3; Galatians 4:2) the Gospel references use *epitropos* in the sense of a household servant. While this servant had authority over land or people, he served as an underling manager over property that belonged to his employer. *Doulos* (1395), "servant," on the other hand, signifies a slave with no authority.

A more frequently used and closely related term is *oikonomos* (3485) which is found alongside *epitropos* in Galatians 4:2: "He is subject to guardians (*epitropos*) and trustees (*oikonomos*)" (NIV). In three occurrences in the Epistles *oikonomos* is used in the unique sense of being stewards of God (Titus 1:7), of His mysteries (1 Corinthians 4:1), or of His grace (1 Peter 4:10). *Oikonomos*, then, assumes theological overtones which are not found in *epitropos*. *Epitropos* is used in a common sense and occurs less frequently in the New Testament than the more theologically significant *oikonomos*.

Strong 2012, Bauer 303, Moulton-Milligan 249, Liddell-Scott 668-69, Colin Brown 1:349.

1997. ἐπιτυγχάνω epitunchanō verb

To obtain, succeed, attain to.

Cross-Reference:
τυγχάνω tunchanō (5018)

חָרַךְ chārakh (2865), Roast? scare away? (Prv 12:27).
צָלֵחַ tsālēach (7014), Hiphil: be successful, succeed (Gn 39:2).

1. ἐπέτυχεν epetuchen 3sing indic aor act
2. ἐπέτυχον epetuchon 3pl indic aor act
3. ἐπιτυχεῖν epituchein inf aor act

1 Israel hath not **obtained** that which he seeketh for; Rom 11:7
1 election **hath obtained** it, and the rest were blinded.... 11:7
1 had patiently endured, he **obtained** the promise....... Heb 6:15
2 wrought righteousness, **obtained** promises,............. 11:33
3 ye kill, and desire to have, and cannot **obtain:**........ Jas 4:2

Classical Greek

Epitunchanō is a compound verb formed of the preposition *epi* (1894), "upon, over," and *tunchanō* (5018) (in the transitive, "to hit the mark, reach, obtain, experience," and in the intransitive, "to happen to be, to befall, hit upon, succeed"). The root noun is *tuchē* meaning "fortune, fate, providence." Properly the verb means "to hit the mark, be successful," hence "to light or hit upon, obtain, attain."

Septuagint Usage

The term occurs twice in the Septuagint and generally means being successful in one's endeavors. It is used in connection with the *success* of Joseph (Genesis 39:2) and with the deceitful man's failure *to capture* his bounty (Proverbs 27:12).

New Testament Usage
The term is used five times in the New Testament. It can be translated "to obtain" (Romans 11:7 twice; Hebrews 6:15), "to receive" (Hebrews 11:33), or "to attain" (James 4:2; see *Moulton-Milligan*). In all these instances the word suggests the idea of "to secure for one's own possession."

STRONG 2013, BAUER 303-4, MOULTON-MILLIGAN 249, LIDDELL-SCOTT 669.

1998. ἐπιφαίνω epiphainō verb
To appear, dawn upon, bring to light, become visible, known.

COGNATES:
  ἐπιφάνεια epiphaneia (1999)
  ἐπιφανής epiphanēs (2000)
  φαίνω phainō (5154)

SYNONYMS:
  ἀναφαίνω anaphainō (396)
  ἀποδείκνυμι apodeiknumi (579)
  ἀποκαλύπτω apokaluptō (596)
  γίνομαι ginomai (1090)
  δείκνυμι deiknumi (1161)
  δηλόω dēloō (1207)
  ἐμφανίζω emphanizō (1702)
  ἐφίστημι ephistēmi (2168)
  ἵστημι histēmi (2449)
  ὀπτάνω optanō (3563)
  ὁράω horaō (3571)
  παραγίνομαι paraginomai (3716)
  φαίνω phainō (5154)
  φανερόω phaneroō (5157)

אוֹר 'ôr (213), Become day, be bright; hiphil: shine, cause to shine (Nm 6:25, Pss 31:16 [30:16], 118:27 [117:27]).

גָּלָה gālâh (1580), Uncover; niphal: appear, reveal oneself (Gn 35:7—Codex Alexandrinus only); hiphil: take into exile, deport (Ez 39:28).

זָרַח zārach (2311), Go forth, shine (Dt 33:2).

יָרֵא yārē' (3486), Fear; niphal: be feared, be fearful (Zep 2:11).

מָצָא mātsâ' (4834), Reach, find; niphal: be found (Jer 29:14 [36:14]).

פָּנָה pānâh (6680), Turn, turn around (Ez 17:6).

1. ἐπιφαινόντων **epiphainontōn** gen pl neu part pres act
2. ἐπιφᾶναι **epiphanai** inf aor act
3. ἐπεφάνη **epephanē** 3sing indic aor pass

2 To give light to them that sit in darkness .... Luke 1:79
1 when neither sun nor stars in many days **appeared**, Acts 27:20
3 For the grace of God ... hath **appeared** to all men, ... Tit 2:11
3 love of God our Saviour toward man **appeared**, ... 3:4

Classical Greek
This is a compound word made up of the preposition *epi* (1894), "being on, upon, supported by, super," and the verb *phainō* (5154), "to cause to shine, to shed light, to be bright, to become evident, to appear to the mind." The verb, intensified by the preposition *epi*, means "to bring to light, to shine upon, to be made manifest, to appear." The root form is *phōs* (5292B), "light." The noun form is *epiphaneia* (1999), "appearance, manifestation, advent, dawn," which is used of the second coming of Christ (1 Timothy 6:14) and of the first coming (2 Timothy 1:10). This verb occurs in classical literature from the time of Theognis (Sixth Century B.C.).

Septuagint Usage
Epiphainō is used 15 times in the Septuagint, e.g., Deuteronomy 33:2; Jeremiah 36:14; there are 9 additional occurrences in the Apocrypha. *Epiphainō* translates six different Hebrew words in the following places: Numbers 6:25; Deuteronomy 33:2; Jeremiah 36:14; Ezekiel 17:6; Daniel 9:17; Zephaniah 2:11.

New Testament Usage
This word appears only four times in the New Testament. In the active voice it is used literally of the appearance of the stars (Acts 27:20) and metaphorically of the imminent messianic fulfillment in which light is given to those in darkness (Luke 1:79). In the passive voice it is used of the manifestation of God's saving grace (Titus 2:11) and of His kindness and love for man in Christ (Titus 3:4). God's grace and love have been brought to light, revealed in Christ.

STRONG 2014, BAUER 304, MOULTON-MILLIGAN 249-50, KITTEL 9:7-10, LIDDELL-SCOTT 669, COLIN BROWN 3:317-19.

1999. ἐπιφάνεια epiphaneia noun
Appearing, appearance, epiphany, manifestation.

CROSS-REFERENCE:
  ἐπιφαίνω epiphainō (1998)

יָרֵא yārē' (3486), Fear; niphal: be awesome (2 Sm 7:23).

1. ἐπιφανείας **epiphaneias** gen sing fem
2. ἐπιφανείᾳ **epiphaneia** dat sing fem
3. ἐπιφάνειαν **epiphaneian** acc sing fem

2 shall destroy with the **brightness** of his coming: .... 2 Th 2:8
1 until the **appearing** of our Lord Jesus Christ: .... 1 Tm 6:14
1 by the **appearing** of our Saviour Jesus Christ, ... 2 Tm 1:10
3 shall judge ... at his **appearing** and his kingdom; 4:1

3 but unto all them also that love his **appearing**......2 Tm 4:8
3 and the glorious **appearing** of the great God.........Tit 2:13

Classical Greek

In classical Greek the noun *epiphaneia*, "appearance, revelation, manifestation," and its companion verb *epiphainō* (1998), "to be revealed, to appear" (an intensive form of *phainō* [5154]), originally stood for the simple, outward, "visible" appearance of someone or something. However, like the related *epiphanēs* (2000), *epiphaneia* came to mean more; i.e., "the brilliant, spectacular" appearance of something or someone. The "revelation" of a hidden deity is how the expression came to be understood in later Hellenism. A king who claimed deity might refer to himself as the "manifestation" of a deity, such as the Syrian king Antiochus IV Epiphanes. The same could be said for those emperors who added "Augustus" to their names. In addition, an *epiphaneia* might refer to a feast celebrating the birth of a "god," the accession of a king to a throne, or a ruler's return from exile.

Septuagint Usage

In the Septuagint the *phōs* word group (to which *epiphaneia* belongs) generally translates the Hebrew *'ôr* which in the hiphil means "to cause to shine." The expression occurs in the blessing of Aaron: "The Lord make (cause) his face to shine upon you!" (Numbers 6:25; cf. Psalms 31:16 [LXX 30:16]; 67:1 [66:1]; 80:3,7,19 [79:3,7,19]; 119:135 [118:135]). Theodotion's version has the term in Daniel 9:17. Additionally the Septuagint employs *epiphainō* for several other Hebrew words including *gālâh* (of God's revelation of himself to Jacob at Bethel [Genesis 35:7] or to returned Israel [Ezekiel 39:29]); *mātsâ'* (when the Lord permits himself to be found [Jeremiah 29:14]); and *zārach* (in reference to the Lord who "appeared" [Deuteronomy 33:2]).

It is also significant that *epiphanēs* translates the Hebrew *yārē'*, "awful, fear-inspiring." Thus Semitic shades of meaning are added to the *epiphaneia* idea which were not originally part of the Greek definition. When the context is God's revelation of himself, one can quite naturally assume the experience will generate "reverance, fear, or awe." *Epiphanēs* is also associated with the great and terrible Day of the Lord (Joel 2:11; 3:14; Malachi 4:5; cf. Judges 13:6; Habakkuk 1:7; Malachi 1:14). Such a meaning is found in the New Testament (Acts 2:20).

New Testament Usage

In the New Testament *epiphaneia* functions exclusively in reference to the "manifestation" or "revelation" of Jesus Christ—His first advent or His final return. It is the *epiphaneia* which the believer longs for (2 Timothy 4:8; Titus 2:13; cf. 1 Timothy 6:14) and which lies at the heart of Christian proclamation (2 Timothy 4:1).

Especially significant is 2 Thessalonians 2:8 where Paul used the puzzling expression *tē epiphaneia tēs parousias*, "the brightness of his coming" or "the appearance of his return." The parousia signals the arrival of the Lord and His presence. Thus all of time draws to a close at the "dawning" of His presence/coming.

STRONG 2015, BAUER 304, MOULTON-MILLIGAN 250, KITTEL 9:7-10, LIDDELL-SCOTT 669-70, COLIN BROWN 3:317-19.

2000. ἐπιφανής epiphanēs adj
Manifest, conspicuous, illustrious, splendid.

COGNATE:
  ἐπιφαίνω epiphainō (1998)
SYNONYM:
  ἐπίσημος episēmos (1962)
יָרֵא yārē' (3486), Fear; niphal: be feared, be dreadful (1 Chr 17:21, Jl 2:11, Mal 1:14).
מָרָא mārā' (4916), Be rebellious (Zep 3:1).

1. ἐπιφανῆ epiphanē acc sing fem

1 great and **notable** day of the Lord come:............Acts 2:20

Classical Greek and Septuagint Usage

Epiphanēs is a compound adjective composed of *epi* (1894), "upon, over," and *phanēs*, "bright, conspicuous," from *phainō* (5154), "to bring to light, appear"—hence the idea of "brilliant, illustrious, splendid." In ancient times the term was frequently used as a royal title, thus Antiochus IV (ca. 215–163 B.C.) surnamed himself *Epiphanes*, "the brilliant, splendid one." The term is used 15 times in the Septuagint.

New Testament Usage

In the New Testament *epiphanēs* occurs only once (Acts 2:20). It is used with reference to the coming of the Day of the Lord, part of a quote from the Septuagint translation of Joel 2:31 (LXX 3:4). The Hebrew original carries the idea of "to be feared, awe-inspiring," whereas the Greek carries more the idea of "brilliant, notable."

STRONG 2016, BAUER 304, MOULTON-MILLIGAN 250, LIDDELL-SCOTT 669-70.

2001. ἐπιφαύσκω epiphauskō verb
Arise, appear, shine upon, give light to.
SYNONYMS:
λάμπω lampō (2962)
φαίνω phainō (5154)
φωτίζω phōtizō (5297)

אָהַל 'āhal (163), Hiphil: shine (Jb 25:5).

הָלַל hālal (2054), Praise; hiphil: shine, radiate (Jb 31:26).

1. ἐπιφαύσει epiphausei 3sing indic fut act

1 and Christ shall give thee light..................... Eph 5:14

Classical Greek
This verb is the compound of *epi* (1894), "upon, over," and the verb *phauskō*, "to shine, show, disclose" (*phauskō* appears in the classics only in compounds with *dia* [1217], *epi* [1894], and *hupo* [5097], and the reduplicated *piphauskō*). Often *epiphauskō* is used in an astronomical sense of the shining of the heavenly luminaries.

Septuagint Usage
Epiphauskō occurs three times in the Septuagint, only in Job. It is used of the moon (25:5) and sun shining (31:26). (See also 41:10 [LXX 41:9].)

New Testament Usage
Its only occurrence in the New Testament is Ephesians 5:14 which is probably a remnant of an Early Church hymn quoted by Paul. Here "Christ shall give thee light" is literally, "Christ shall shine upon you" or "shine out for you."

STRONG 2017, BAUER 304, MOULTON-MILLIGAN 250, LIDDELL-SCOTT 670.

2002. ἐπιφέρω epipherō verb
Bring over or upon, pronounce, inflict.
COGNATE:
φέρω pherō (5179)
SYNONYMS:
δίδωμι didōmi (1319)
δωρέομαι dōreomai (1426)
ἐπιδίδωμι epididōmi (1914)
ἐπιχορηγέω epichorēgeō (2007)
κομίζω komizō (2837)
παρέχω parechō (3792)
προσάγω prosagō (4175)
προστίθημι prostithēmi (4227)
προσφέρω prospherō (4232)
φέρω pherō (5179)

הָלַךְ hālakh (2050), Float, lift up (Gn 7:18).

נוּף nûph (5311), Hiphil: raise, shake (Zec 2:9).

רָזַם rāzam (7618), Wink, flash (Jb 15:12).

רָחַף rāchaph (7646), Piel: hover, move over (Gn 1:2).

שׁוּב shûv (8178), Return; hiphil: bring (Prv 26:15).

שָׁלַח shālach (8365), Let go, raise a hand (Gn 37:22, 1 Sm 22:17, 26:9).

1. ἐπιφέρων epipherōn nom sing masc part pres act
2. ἐπιφέρειν epipherein inf pres act
3. ἐπενεγκεῖν epenenkein inf aor act
4. ἐπέφερον epepheron 3pl indic imperf act
5. ἐπιφέρεσθαι epipheresthai inf pres mid

5 So that from his body were brought unto the sick...Acts 19:12
4 they brought none accusation ... as I supposed:........ 25:18
1 Is God unrighteous who taketh vengeance?..........Rom 3:5
2 supposing to add affliction to my bonds:............ Phlp 1:16
3 durst not bring against him a railing accusation,..... Jude 1:9

Classical Greek and Septuagint Usage
In classical Greek *epipherō* means "to bring upon or grant something to someone." It has a secondary meaning of "pronouncing (a judgment) or inflicting (punishment)." In the papyri it carries the force of producing or presenting something to someone. In the Septuagint it is frequently used in the context of laying hands on someone in the sense of attacking or capturing (1 Samuel [LXX 1 Kings] 24:7; 26:11; Esther 8:7), though in a few instances it has the simple meaning of moving or carrying (Genesis 1:2; 7:8).

New Testament Usage
Of the five occurrences of *epipherō* in the New Testament, three of them carry the sense of placing something on someone, whether it be an accusation (Acts 25:18), wrath (Romans 3:5), or a judgment (Jude 9). In Acts 19:12 it is used in the sense of carrying away an item.

The uniqueness of this verb is seen in its contrast to the cognate verb *pherō* (5179) which lacks the prepositional prefix *epi* (1894). *Pherō* has the meaning "to bring or carry" as in Mark 1:32, "They brought unto him all that were diseased." *Epipherō* does contain the sense of "bear or carry"; however, it includes the idea of a destination or termination. While *pherō* places emphasis on the activity of carrying, *epipherō* is concerned with the destination of that which is being carried. For this reason, *epipherō* is used in Jude 9 where it speaks of Michael bringing a reviling accusation against the devil.

STRONG 2018, BAUER 304, MOULTON-MILLIGAN 250, LIDDELL-SCOTT 670.

2003. ἐπιφωνέω epiphōneō verb
Call out loudly, shout.
COGNATE:
φωνέω phōneō (5291)

SYNONYMS:
ἀναβοάω anaboaō (308)
ἀνακράζω anakrazō (347)
βοάω boaō (987)
ἐπιβοάω epiboaō (1901)
κράζω krazō (2869)
κραυγάζω kraugazō (2878)
φωνέω phōneō (5291)

1. ἐπεφώνει **epephōnei** 3sing indic imperf act
2. ἐπεφώνουν **epephōnoun** 3pl indic imperf act

2 But they **cried**, saying, Crucify him, crucify him.... Luke 23:21
1 And the people **gave a shout**,......................Acts 12:22
2 some **were shouting** one thing (NASB)................ 21:34
2 might know wherefore they **cried** so against him....... 22:24

Classical Greek and Septuagint Usage
Occurring from Sophocles (Fifth Century B.C.) on, *epiphōneō* is a compound verb made up of *epi* (1894), "upon, over, super," with the verb *phōneō* (5291), "to produce a sound, call out, speak loudly." This verb is not used in the canonical portions of the Septuagint, though it does occur three times in the Apocrypha (1 Esdras 9:47; 2 Maccabees 1:23; 3 Maccabees 7:13).

New Testament Usage
In the New Testament this term is used only by Luke. It appears four times and always in connection with a crowd or mob shouting out in protest (Luke 23:21; Acts 22:24), acclamation (Acts 12:22), or accusation (Acts 21:34).

STRONG 2019, BAUER 304, MOULTON-MILLIGAN 250, LIDDELL-SCOTT 672.

2004. ἐπιφώσκω epiphōskō verb
To dawn, break forth, draw near, shine forth.
CROSS-REFERENCE:
φωτίζω phōtizō (5297)

הָלַל hālal (2054), Praise; hiphil: shine, let shine (Jb 41:18 [41:9]—Codex Alexandrinus only).

1. ἐπιφωσκούσῃ **epiphōskousē**
    dat sing fem part pres act
2. ἐπέφωσκεν **epephōsken** 3sing indic imperf act

1 In the end of the sabbath, **as it began to dawn**..... Matt 28:1
2 day was the preparation, and the **sabbath drew on.** Luke 23:54

Classical Greek and Septuagint Usage
Epiphōskō is a compound word formed from the verb *phōskō*, "to dawn," and the prefix *epi* (1894), "upon, over." It occurs only once in the Septuagint (Job 41:10) and then only in some manuscripts (other manuscripts use *epiphauskō* [2001]).

New Testament Usage
In the New Testament the term is found twice. Once it refers to the coming, or dawning, of the first day of the week (Matthew 28:1). The second occurrence refers to the beginning or arrival of the Sabbath (Luke 23:54).

STRONG 2020, BAUER 304, MOULTON-MILLIGAN 250, LIDDELL-SCOTT 672.

2005. ἐπιχειρέω epicheireō verb
To put the hand on, to undertake, attempt, try.
COGNATE:
χείρ cheir (5331)
SYNONYM:
πειράω peiraō (3849)

גָּמַל gāmal (1621), Reward, repay (2 Chr 20:11).
חָשַׁב chāshav (2913), Plot, wicked device (Est 9:25).

1. ἐπεχείρησαν **epecheirēsan** 3pl indic aor act
2. ἐπεχείρουν **epecheiroun** 3pl indic imperf act

1 Forasmuch as many **have taken in hand** to set forth..Luke 1:1
2 but they **went about** to slay him..................... Acts 9:29
1 **took upon them** to call over them..................... 19:13

Classical Greek
The compound verb *epicheireō*, from the preposition *epi* (1894), "over, upon," and the noun *cheir* (5331), "hand, paw," means "to put the hand on," hence "to put the hand to, to work at, undertake," or "attempt."

Septuagint Usage
This verb occurs 12 times in the Septuagint including 8 times in the Apocrypha. It generally means "to attack," "to attempt," or "to make an attempt on." It was used with reference to attacking the Jewish people (2 Chronicles 20:11) and the temple (Ezra 7:23 [LXX 2 Esdras 7:23]), and the attempt to cause harm to the Jews in exile (Esther 9:25).

New Testament Usage
Epicheireō occurs three times in the New Testament exclusively in Lucan writings. In each case the verb is followed by an infinitive and is usually translated "to attempt" or "to undertake." The general sense is "to endeavor to perform a task" such as that of compiling an account (Luke 1:1; see Marshall, *New International Greek Testament Commentary, Luke*, p.41), attempting to take someone's life (Acts 9:29), or the casting out of evil spirits (Acts 19:13).

STRONG 2021, BAUER 304-5, MOULTON-MILLIGAN 250-51, LIDDELL-SCOTT 672-73.

2006. ἐπιχέω epicheō verb
To pour upon, pour over, pour in.

ἐπιχορηγέω 2007

CROSS-REFERENCE:
ἐκχύνω ekchunō (1619)

זָקַק zāqaq (2298), Distill (Jb 36:27).

יָצַק yātsaq (3441), Qal: dish up, pour out (Gn 28:18, Lv 8:12, 2 Kgs 3:11); hiphil: fill up (2 Kgs 4:5); hophal: be emptied, be poured out (Lv 21:10).

נָתַן nāthan (5598), Qal: give, put (Lv 2:15); hophal: be put on (Lv 11:38).

רִיק rîq (7671), Hiphil: pour out, empty (Zec 4:12).

שִׂים sîm (7947), Put, set (Lv 5:11).

1. ἐπιχέων epicheōn nom sing masc part pres act
1 and bound up his wounds, **pouring in oil and wine,** Luke 10:34

Classical Greek and Septuagint Usage
Used from Homer on, *epicheō* is a compound word formed by the preposition *epi* (1894), "upon, over," and the verb *cheō*, "to pour out, gush forth." This word is used 22 times in the Septuagint, often in connection with sacrifices (Leviticus 2:1), worship (Genesis 35:14), and anointing of priests (Exodus 29:7) and kings (1 Samuel 10:1 [LXX 1 Kings 10:1]; 2 Samuel 9:3 [LXX 2 Kings 9:3]). Only in Job 36:27 does it refer to the downpour of rain.

New Testament Usage
The only occurrence of *epicheō* in the New Testament is in the Parable of the Good Samaritan. The good neighbor "poured" oil and wine on the wounds of the robbed and injured man (Luke 10:34).

STRONG 2022, BAUER 305, MOULTON-MILLIGAN 251, LIDDELL-SCOTT 673.

2007. ἐπιχορηγέω epichorēgeō verb
Furnish, provide, give, grant, fully supply.

COGNATE:
χορηγέω chorēgeō (5359)

SYNONYMS:
ἀποδίδωμι apodidōmi (586)
δίδωμι didōmi (1319)
δωρέομαι dōreomai (1426)
ἐπιδίδωμι epididōmi (1914)
ἐπιφέρω epipherō (2002)
παρέχω parechō (3792)
προστίθημι prostithēmi (4227)
χορηγέω chorēgeō (5359)

1. ἐπιχορηγῶν epichorēgōn nom sing masc part pres act
2. ἐπιχορηγήσατε epichorēgēsate 2pl impr aor act
3. ἐπιχορηγούμενον epichorēgoumenon nom/acc sing neu part pres mid
4. ἐπιχορηγηθήσεται epichorēgēthēsetai 3sing indic fut pass

1 Now he that **ministereth** seed to the sower.......... 2 Co 9:10
1 He therefore that **ministereth** to you the Spirit,....... Gal 3:5
3 having nourishment **ministered,** and knit together,..... Col 2:19
2 **add** to your faith virtue; and to virtue knowledge;... 2 Pt 1:5
4 For so an entrance shall be **ministered** unto you........ 1:11

Classical Greek
Epichorēgeō in classical Greek means "to give, provide for," or "support" someone or something at one's own expense. The papyri, while favoring the simple form *chorēgeō* (5359), employ the compound verb *epichorēgeō* to emphasize the generous nature of the one who is providing (*Moulton-Milligan*).

Septuagint Usage
Epichorēgeō occurs only twice in the apocryphal writings in the Septuagint. If a wife "provides" (cf. RSV's "supports") for her husband it brings wrath and disgrace (Sirach 25:22). Second Maccabees 4:9 speaks of "being granted" permission.

New Testament Usage
In the New Testament this word maintains the primary meaning of "providing for" or "supplying" as in 2 Corinthians 9:10 (NIV): "He who *supplies* seed to the sower...." In four of its five occurrences the verb is used in the context of supplying or increasing in spiritual dimensions, as in 2 Peter 1:5-11 where one is exhorted to supplement his faith with virtue, and virtue with knowledge, etc.

Second Corinthians 9:10 provides insight into *epichorēgeō* where it is used parallel with the simple form *chorēgeō*. "He who supplies (*epichorēgeō*) seed to the sower and bread for food will also supply (*chorēgeō*) and increase your store of seed..." (NIV). In this verse *chorēgeō* and *plēthunō* (3989) combine to make the equivalent of *epichorēgeō*. This possibly suggests that the prepositional prefix *epi* (1894) adds an element of intensity to the simple verb *chorēgeō*, i.e., "to provide or supply with generosity and without restraint."

STRONG 2023, BAUER 305, MOULTON-MILLIGAN 251, LIDDELL-SCOTT 673.

2008. ἐπιχορηγία epichorēgia noun
Supply, provision, support, aid.

CROSS-REFERENCE:
χορηγέω chorēgeō (5359)

1. ἐπιχορηγίας epichorēgias gen sing fem
1 compacted by that which every joint **supplieth,**....... Eph 4:16
1 and the **supply** of the Spirit of Jesus Christ,......... Phlp 1:19

Epichorēgia is a compound noun formed by the preposition *epi* (1894), "over, above," and

chorēgia, "support to defray the cost of a public chorus." Two other cognates add color to the meaning: *choreia* refers to "a choral dance with music," and *chorēgos* speaks of "one who pays for the staging of a play accompanied with a chorus." The root meaning of *epichorēgia* is "sufficient support of provision for a choral dance troupe," hence the metaphoric meaning of "abundant support, ample supply" (cf. *Moulton-Milligan*). The term occurs twice in the New Testament, once of the "ample supply" of the Spirit (Philippians 1:19), and once of the "support provided" by and to the parts of the Body (Ephesians 4:16).
STRONG 2024, BAUER 305, MOULTON-MILLIGAN 251, LIDDELL-SCOTT 673.

2009. ἐπιχρίω epichriō verb

Spread or smear on, anoint.
COGNATE:
χρίω chriō (5383)
SYNONYMS:
ἀλείφω aleiphō (216)
ἐγχρίω enchriō (1465)
μυρίζω murizō (3324)
χρίω chriō (5383)

1. ἐπέχρισεν epechrisen 3sing indic aor act

1 **anointed** the eyes of the blind man with the clay,... John 9:6
1 Jesus made clay, and **anointed** mine eyes,.............. 9:11

Classical Greek
In classical Greek *epichriō* means "to spread or smear something on someone." It is most often used in a medical context where the eyes are anointed with salve. In the papyri the verb is used in essentially the same way, i.e., to anoint (the eyes) with medication.

Septuagint Usage
Epichriō does not occur in the Septuagint. However, the simple form *chriō* (5383) does occur and carries the meaning of "commissioning with an office" (e.g., 1 Samuel 9:16 [LXX 1 Kings 9:16]) or "imparting a spiritual element" to someone or something (e.g., Exodus 28:37; 2 Samuel 1:21 [LXX 2 Kings 1:21]).

New Testament Usage
Epichriō occurs twice in the New Testament, in John 9:6 and 11. In both references it means to anoint the eyes with a substance (clay), ostensibly to cure them. The context, however, clearly suggests that a miracle took place, and that the anointing with clay was incidental to the actual healing. Perhaps Jesus formed clay with the dust of the earth and His own spittle in order to convey truth beyond that which the actual healing of the blind man expressed.
STRONG 2025, BAUER 305, MOULTON-MILLIGAN 251, LIDDELL-SCOTT 673.

2010. ἐποικοδομέω
epoikodomeō verb

Build (on, upon or up).
CROSS-REFERENCE:
οἰκοδομέω oikodomeō (3481)

1. ἐποικοδομεῖ epoikodomei 3sing indic pres act
2. ἐποικοδομοῦντες epoikodomountes
  nom pl masc part pres act
3. ἐπῳκοδόμησεν epōkodomēsen 3sing indic aor act
4. ἐποικοδομῆσαι epoikodomēsai inf aor act
5. ἐποικοδομούμενοι epoikodomoumenoi
  nom pl masc part pres mid
6. ἐποικοδομηθέντες epoikodomēthentes
  nom pl masc part aor pass
7. ἐποικοδόμησεν epoikodomēsen 3sing indic aor act

4 word of his grace, which is able to **build** you **up**,... Acts 20:32
1 laid the foundation, and another **buildeth** thereon.... 1 Co 3:10
1 every man take heed how he **buildeth** thereupon........ 3:10
1 Now if any man **build** upon this foundation gold,...... 3:12
3 If any man's work abide which he **hath built**............ 3:14
7 If any man's work abide which he **hath built**........... 3:14
6 And **are built** upon the foundation of the apostles ....Eph 2:20
5 Rooted and **built up** in him,....................... Col 2:7
2 **building up** yourselves on your most holy faith,......Jude 1:20

Classical Greek
In classical Greek *epoikodomeō* means "to build upon" something or add to something already existing. It is used both in the context of adding on to buildings and in a figurative sense of encouraging or establishing someone in something. In the papyri it is used figuratively: "build on it (a sound foundation) your firmness and unshaken resolve" (*Moulton-Milligan*). The word does not occur in the Septuagint.

New Testament Usage
Of the eight occurrences of *epoilokomeō* in the New Testament four are found in 1 Corinthians 3:10-14. Here Paul referred to a builder who builds upon (*epoikodomeō*) the foundation laid by another. The quality of the workmanship and materials used will determine the quality of the finished product. The intent of Paul is found in his construction metaphor. His emphasis was not on constructing a building on a foundation but on establishing and confirming a new believer in his faith. The other four occurrences reflect this same figurative use of *epoikodomeō* (Acts 20:32; Ephesians 2:20; Colossians 2:7; Jude 20).

The related verb *oikodomeō* (3481), outside of Paul's writings, is most often used in reference to the actual construction of a building (cf. Matthew 7:24; Mark 12:1, etc.). By New Testament times the compound form *epoikodomeō* acquired the figurative usage almost exclusively and thus became a technical term for building up in spiritual character or qualities.

STRONG 2026, BAUER 305, MOULTON-MILLIGAN 251, KITTEL 5:147-48, LIDDELL-SCOTT 675, COLIN BROWN 2:251,253.

2011. ἐποκέλλω epokellō verb
To run ashore, run aground, land.

1. ἐπώκειλαν epōkeilan 3pl indic aor act
1 ran the ship aground; and the forepart stuck fast, ... Acts 27:41

The compound verb *epokellō* is formed by *epi* (1894), "over, above," and *okellō* (also *kellō*), "to run ashore, aground, put to shore, land." It is a navigational term meaning "to run ashore, be wrecked, run aground, put into harbor." In the classics *epokallō* appears from Herodotus (Fifth Century B.C.) on. The verb is found once in the New Testament (Acts 27:41) where it is used of Paul's shipwreck on Melita (Malta).

STRONG 2027, BAUER 305, LIDDELL-SCOTT 675.

2012. ἐπονομάζω eponomazō verb
To name, call, give a nickname or a second name.

COGNATES:
ὄνομα onoma (3549)
πανουργία panourgia (3696)

SYNONYMS:
ἐπιλέγω epilegō (1935B)
καλέω kaleō (2535)
λέγω legō (2978)
ὀνομάζω onomazō (3550)
προσαγορεύω prosagoreuō (4174)
φωνέω phōneō (5291)
χρηματίζω chrēmatizō (5372)

זָכַר zākhar (2226), Remember; hiphil: cause to be honored, record (Ex 20:24).

נָקַב nāqav (5529), Curse, blaspheme (Lv 24:11).

קָרָא qārā' (7410), Call, give a name to (Gn 4:26, Ex 2:10, Jos 22:34).

שִׂים sîm (7947), Put, establish (Dt 12:5, 2 Chr 12:13).

1. ἐπονομάζῃ eponomazē 2sing indic pres mid
1 thou art called a Jew, and restest in the law, ... Rom 2:17

Eponomazō is a compound verb formed by adding the preposition *epi* (1894), "upon, over," to the verb *onomazō* (3550), "to give a name, call." It means "to apply a name to, surname, call by name." This verb, which occurs in the classics from Herodotus (Fifth Century B.C.) on, can be found numerous times in the Septuagint but only once in the New Testament. Paul used it in the present passive (or middle) form, "You are being called a Jew" or "You call yourself a Jew" (Romans 2:17).

STRONG 2028, BAUER 305, MOULTON-MILLIGAN 251, KITTEL 5:282, LIDDELL-SCOTT 676, COLIN BROWN 2:648,652,655.

2013. ἐποπτεύω epopteuō verb
To observe, catch sight of, regard.

COGNATES:
ἐπόπτης epoptēs (2014)
ὀπτάνω optanō (3563)

SYNONYMS:
ἀτενίζω atenizō (810)
βλέπω blepō (984)
εἶδον eidon (1481)
ἐμβλέπω emblepō (1676)
ἐπιβλέπω epiblepō (1899)
θεάομαι theaomai (2277)
θεωρέω theōreō (2311)
καταμανθάνω katamanthanō (2618)
κατανοέω katanoeō (2627)
ὁράω horaō (3571)
σκοπέω skopeō (4503)

1. ἐποπτεύσαντες epopteusantes
nom pl masc part aor act
2. ἐποπτεύοντες epopteuontes
nom pl masc part pres act

1 may by your good works, which they **shall behold**, ... 1 Pt 2:12
2 may by your good works, which they **shall behold**, ... 2:12
1 **behold** your chaste conversation coupled with fear. 3:2

Epopteuō is a compound verb formed by adding the preposition *epi* (1894), "over, upon," to the verb *opsomai* (or *horaō* [3571]), "to see, catch sight of." It is the verb form of *epoptēs* (2014), "observer, overseer." The verb carries the idea of "to witness with the eye, observe, look on, be an eyewitness." In the classics it is used of gods and emperors observing the deeds of men, or of someone meditating on or studying something. Used from Homer on, it is not found in the Septuagint, except in Symmachus' text (Psalms 10:14; 33:13). It is used twice in the New Testament, both times in 1 Peter. Peter implored believers to do good works which unbelievers "shall behold" (1 Peter 2:12). Peter also encouraged believing wives with unbelieving husbands to be submissive so that when their husbands "beheld" their purity they might be won over to faith in Christ (3:1,2).

STRONG 2029, BAUER 305, MOULTON-MILLIGAN 251, KITTEL 5:373-75, LIDDELL-SCOTT 676, COLIN BROWN 3:512,515.

2014. ἐπόπτης epoptēs noun
Eyewitness, spectator.
CROSS-REFERENCE:
ἐποπτεύω epopteuō (2013)

1. ἐπόπται epoptai nom pl masc
1 but were **eyewitnesses** of his majesty............... 2 Pt 1:16

Classical Greek
Two basic meanings of *epoptēs* were known in antiquity: (1) an "overseer" (from *epi* [1894], "upon, on," plus *opt-*, "one who looks") and (2) as a technical term (along with the verb *epopteuō* [2013]) in the Greek mystery religions for one who had "come to have a share in vision (of the mysteries)," an "eyewitness" (Michaelis, "autoptēs," *Kittel*, 5:373; cf. *Moulton-Milligan*).

Septuagint Usage
Despite the absence of the verbal form, the noun *epoptēs* does occur in the Septuagint, once in the apocryphal addition to Esther (5:1, RSV) and three times in the apocryphal 2 and 3 Maccabees. In every case God is *epoptēs*, the omniscient One who "looks on" and sees both the peril of His people and the evil of those who oppress them (Michaelis, "autoptēs," *Kittel*, 5:373). He will bring aid to His people (2 Maccabees 3:39) and judgment to their enemies (2 Maccabees 7:35; cf. 3 Maccabees 2:21).

New Testament Usage
Epoptēs is a hapax legomenon (used only once) in the Greek New Testament and found only in 2 Peter 1:16 (the verb *epopteuō* is restricted to Peter's first epistle, 2:12; 3:2). The writer contrasted "cleverly devised myths"—which were not appealed to as evidence for the power and coming of Jesus Christ—with the reliable "eyewitness" who saw firsthand the majesty (*megaleiotēs* [3139]) of Christ. This "majesty" is further explained as the Transfiguration recorded in the Gospels (Matthew 17:1-9; Mark 9:2-10; Luke 9:28-36).

STRONG 2030, BAUER 305, MOULTON-MILLIGAN 251-52, KITTEL 5:373-75, LIDDELL-SCOTT 676, COLIN BROWN 1:189.

2015. ἔπος epos noun
Word, utterance, saying.

1. ἔπος epos nom/acc sing neu
1 as I may so say, Levi also, who receiveth tithes,...... Heb 7:9

Classical Greek and Septuagint Usage
This noun, used from Homer on, generally denotes "that which is uttered in words," hence "speech, tale, verse." The verb *epō*, "to say, name," first used by Nicander (Second Century B.C.), was perhaps coined from this noun. *Epos* occurs only once in the Septuagint, and that in the Apocrypha (Sirach 44:5, translated "verse"), though in some manuscripts it appears in Zechariah 7:3 instead of *etos* (2073), "year," an easily explainable copyist's error.

New Testament Usage
In the New Testament *epos* appears only once (Hebrews 7:9), where it is used in a paraphrastic construction with *legō* (2978), "to say, speak." In this passage it means "to venture to speak, one might perhaps venture to say," or literally, "to say the (right) word." *Epos* is distinct from *logos* (3030), the more common term for "word."

STRONG 2031, BAUER 305, MOULTON-MILLIGAN 252, LIDDELL-SCOTT 676, COLIN BROWN 3:1081.

2016. ἐπουράνιος epouranios adj
Heavenly, celestial.
COGNATE:
οὐρανός ouranos (3636)
SYNONYM:
οὐράνιος ouranios (3634)
שַׁדַּי shadday (8163), Name of deity identified with Yahweh, Almighty God, My destroyer, God of the Mountain (Ps 68:14 [67:14]).

1. ἐπουρανίου epouraniou gen sing masc/fem
2. ἐπουρανίων epouraniōn gen pl masc/neu
3. ἐπουράνιος epouranios nom sing masc
4. ἐπουράνιοι epouranioi nom pl masc
5. ἐπουρανίῳ epouraniō dat sing fem
6. ἐπουράνιον epouranion acc sing fem
7. ἐπουράνια epourania nom/acc pl neu
8. ἐπουρανίοις epouraniois dat pl neu

3 So likewise shall my **heavenly** Father do also....... Matt 18:35
7 shall ye believe, if I tell you of **heavenly things**?..... John 3:12
7 are also **celestial** bodies, and bodies terrestrial:..... 1 Co 15:40
2 but the glory of the **celestial** is one,................... 15:40
3 the **heavenly**, such are they also that are heavenly..... 15:48
4 the **heavenly**, such are they also that are **heavenly**...... 15:48
1 we shall also bear the image of the **heavenly**.......... 15:49
8 all spiritual blessings in **heavenly** places in Christ:.... Eph 1:3
8 at his own right hand in the **heavenly** places,........... 1:20
8 made us sit together in **heavenly** places in Christ....... 2:6

8 the principalities and powers in **heavenly** places	Eph 3:10
8 against spiritual wickedness in **high** places.	6:12
2 **of things in heaven,** and things in earth,	Phlp 2:10
6 and will preserve me unto his **heavenly** kingdom:	2 Tm 4:18
1 holy brethren, partakers of the **heavenly** calling,	Heb 3:1
1 and have tasted of the **heavenly** gift,	6:4
2 unto the example and shadow of **heavenly** things,	8:5
7 but the **heavenly** things themselves with better	9:23
1 they desire a better country, that is, an **heavenly**:	11:16
5 the city of the living God, the **heavenly** Jerusalem,	12:22

Classical Greek

The adjective *epouranios* means "heavenly" (from *epi* [1894], "at," and *ouranios* [3634], "heavenly"), or in a substantive usage either "the gods above" (*hoi epouranioi*) or the "things (i.e., phenomena) of heaven" (neuter, *ta epourania*). The emphasis of the term is on the location—not in the sense of "sky" but as the dwelling place of the divine.

Septuagint Usage

Epouranios is relatively rare in the Septuagint, being found only at Psalm 68:14 (LXX 67:14) in the canonical Scriptures in reference to "the Almighty" (RSV; Hebrew *shadday*). Theodotion (Codex Alexandrinus) reads *epouranios* at Daniel 4:26 (4:23 Masoretic Text) instead of *ouranios*. Second Maccabees writes of God "dwelling in heaven" (RSV; *ho tēn katoikian epouranion*, 3:39; cf. 3 Maccabees 6:28; 7:6).

New Testament Usage

Epouranios is descriptive of God only in a variant reading in Matthew 18:35. Modern critical versions read *ho ouranios*. The Gospel of John records the only other Gospel text with *epouranios* (3:12). There Jesus contrasted "heavenly things" (*ta epourania*) with "earthly things" (*ta epigeia*). A similar contrast occurs in Paul's writings (1 Corinthians 15:40; cf. 15:48,49; Philippians 2:10).

Ephesians has the repeated formula *en tois epouraniois*, "in the heavenly (places)" (1:3,20; 2:6; 3:10; 6:12). This should not be considered as solely the residence of God, for in "the heavenlies" ("high places" KJV) there is warfare against "spiritual wickedness," evil of a supernatural order (Ephesians 6:12). *En tois epouraniois* is the cosmic level at which the effects of salvation are realized (Ephesians 2:6; cf. 2 Timothy 4:18) and at which the battle is both fought and won (Ephesians 6:12).

Hebrews considers "heavenly" as descriptive of the present effects of the sacrifice of Christ (3:1), especially as over against the former "shadow." Thus the "heavenly," which is far superior to the former, is realized in the present by faith. Moreover, it will be realized in actuality in the future (Hebrews 8:5; 9:23; 11:26; 12:22).

STRONG 2032, BAUER 305-6, MOULTON-MILLIGAN 252, KITTEL 5:538-42, LIDDELL-SCOTT 677, COLIN BROWN 2:188,191-92,194,196.

2017. ἑπτά hepta num

Seven.

1. ἑπτά hepta card

1 and taketh with himself **seven** other spirits	Matt 12:45
1 And they said, **Seven,** and a few little fishes.	15:34
1 And he took the **seven** loaves and the fishes,	15:36
1 of the broken meat that was left **seven** baskets full.	15:37
1 Neither the **seven** loaves of the four thousand,	16:10
1 Until seven times: but, Until seventy times **seven.**	18:22
1 Now there were with us **seven** brethren:	22:25
1 the second also, and the third, unto the **seventh.**	22:26
1 whose wife shall she be of the **seven**?	22:28
1 How many loaves have ye? And they said, **Seven...**	Mark 8:5
1 and he took the **seven** loaves, and gave thanks,	8:6
1 of the broken meat that was left **seven** baskets.	8:8
1 And when the **seven** among four thousand,	8:20
1 And they said, **Seven.**	8:20
1 were **seven** brethren: and the first took a wife,	12:20
1 And the **seven** had her, and left no seed:	12:22
1 whose wife ... for the **seven** had her to wife.	12:23
1 Magdalene, out of whom he had cast **seven** devils.	16:9
1 and had lived with an husband **seven** years	Luke 2:36
1 called Magdalene, out of whom went **seven** devils,	8:2
1 and taketh to him **seven** other spirits more wicked	11:26
1 There were therefore **seven** brethren:	20:29
1 third took her; and in like manner the **seven** also:	20:31
1 whose wife ... is she? for **seven** had her to wife.	20:33
1 look ye out among you **seven** men of honest report,	Acts 6:3
1 destroyed **seven** nations in the land of Chanaan,	13:19
1 And there were **seven** sons of one Sceva, a Jew,	19:14
1 to Troas in five days; where we abode **seven** days.	20:6
1 And finding disciples, we tarried there **seven** days:	21:4
1 Philip the evangelist, which was one of the **seven**;	21:8
1 And when the **seven** days were almost ended,	21:27
1 and were desired to tarry with them **seven** days:	28:14
1 after they were compassed about **seven** days.	Heb 11:30
1 John to the **seven** churches which are in Asia:	Rev 1:4
1 from the **seven** Spirits which are before his throne;	1:4
1 sent it unto the **seven** churches which are in Asia;	1:11
1 And being turned, I saw **seven** golden candlesticks;	1:12
1 And in the midst of the **seven** candlesticks	1:13
1 And he had in his right hand **seven** stars:	1:16
1 The mystery of the **seven** stars which thou sawest	1:20
1 seven stars ... and the **seven** golden candlesticks.	1:20
1 seven stars are the angels of the **seven** churches:	1:20
1 seven stars are the angels of the **seven** churches:	1:20
1 and the **seven** candlesticks which thou sawest	1:20
1 the seven candlesticks ... are the **seven** churches.	1:20
1 These things saith he that holdeth the **seven** stars	2:1
1 in the midst of the **seven** golden candlesticks;	2:1
1 These things saith he that hath the **seven** Spirits	3:1
1 These things saith he that hath the **seven** Spirits	3:1
1 seven lamps of fire burning before the throne,	4:5
1 which are the **seven** Spirits of God.	4:5
1 a book written within ... sealed with **seven** seals.	5:1
1 open the book, and to loose the **seven** seals thereof.	5:5
1 a Lamb ... having **seven** horns and **seven** eyes,	5:6
1 a Lamb ... having **seven** horns and **seven** eyes,	5:6
1 seven Spirits of God sent forth into all the earth.	5:6
1 the Lamb opened the first of the **seven** seals (NIV)	6:1
1 I saw the **seven** angels which stood before God;	8:2
1 and to them were given **seven** trumpets.	8:2
1 the **seven** angels which had the seven trumpets	8:6

1 the seven angels which had the **seven** trumpets	Rev 8:6
1 **seven** thunders uttered their voices	10:3
1 when the **seven** thunders had uttered their voices,	10:4
1 Seal up those ... which the **seven** thunders uttered,	10:4
1 in the earthquake were slain ... **seven** thousand:	11:13
1 red dragon, having **seven** heads and ten horns,	12:3
1 **seven** heads ... and **seven** crowns upon his heads	12:3
1 out of the sea, having **seven** heads and ten horns,	13:1
1 **seven** angels having the **seven** last plagues;	15:1
1 **seven** angels having the **seven** last plagues;	15:1
1 And the **seven** angels came out of the temple,	15:6
1 came out of the temple, having the **seven** plagues,	15:6
1 one of the four beasts gave unto the **seven** angels	15:7
1 **seven** golden vials full of the wrath of God,	15:7
1 **seven** plagues of the **seven** angels were fulfilled.	15:8
1 **seven** plagues of the **seven** angels were fulfilled.	15:8
1 voice out of the temple saying to the **seven** angels,	16:1
1 pour out the **seven** bowls of God's wrath (NIV)	16:1
1 And there came one of the **seven** angels	17:1
1 one of the **seven** angels which had the **seven** vials,	17:1
1 beast, ... having **seven** heads and ten horns.	17:3
1 beast ... which hath the **seven** heads and ten horns.	17:7
1 The **seven** heads are **seven** mountains,	17:9
1 The **seven** heads are **seven** mountains,	17:9
1 And there are **seven** kings: five are fallen,	17:10
1 even he is the eighth, and is of the **seven**,	17:11
1 And there came unto me one of the **seven** angels	21:9
1 had the **seven** vials full of the **seven** last plagues,	21:9
1 had the **seven** vials full of the **seven** last plagues,	21:9

Classical Greek and Septuagint Usage
Hepta is an indeclinable adjective, from Homer on, designating the cardinal numeral "seven." The ordinal numeral "seventh" is the cognate *hebdomos* (1436), "week." In addition to the usual common literal meaning this numeral is used often in the classics in a mystical or metaphoric way, i.e., seven islands, seven sages, seven wonders. In the Septuagint *hepta* is the translation of the Hebrew numeral *shevaʻ* (or *shivʻāh*). It is interesting that in the New Testament, when speaking of the seventh day, the Biblical writers transliterated the Hebrew rendering it *sabbaton* (4378) or *sabbata* (English, "sabbath"). *Hepta* occurs often in the New Testament, usually in the normal literal sense but occasionally in a metaphoric sense (Revelation 1:4, "seven Spirits").

New Testament Usage
In the New Testament as indeed throughout all Scripture, perhaps stemming from the 7 days of creation, the numeral "seven" often suggests completeness, totality, perfection, fullness. This appears in some of the narrative portions; e.g., seven demons were cast out of Mary Magdalene (Mark 16:9), seven officials were selected to aid in the benevolence program (Acts 6:3), seven brothers were said to have entered consecutively into a levirate marriage relationship with their deceased brother's widow (Matthew 22:25). The idea of completeness is also seen in Christ's prescription for forgiveness, "seventy times seven" (Matthew 18:22).

It is more fully noticed in Revelation where there are many groupings of seven. In this book there are seven each of the following: churches (1:4), Spirits (1:4, a metaphoric usage signifying the completeness or perfections of the Holy Spirit), candlesticks or lamp stands (1:12), stars (1:16), lamps of fire (4:5), seals (5:1), horns (5:6), eyes (5:6), angels (8:2), trumpets (8:2), thunders (10:3), heads (on the red dragon, 12:3; on the beast out of the sea, 13:1; and on the scarlet colored beast, 17:3), crowns on the red dragon (12:3), plagues (15:1), vials (15:7), mountains (17:9), and kings (17:10). Some believe the period of the tribulation of 7 years (Daniel 9:27) is divided into two 3 1/2-year periods during which time there follow in succession the breaking of the seven seals, blowing of the seven trumpets, sounding of the seven thunders, and pouring out of the seven vials (cf. Revelation 12:6; 13:5).

Used as a substantive with the definite article, *hepta* designates a fixed group. The seven church officials (Acts 6:3) became known as "the seven" (Acts 21:8), much like the designation "the twelve" (Acts 6:2).

STRONG 2033, BAUER 306, MOULTON-MILLIGAN 252, KITTEL 2:627-35, LIDDELL-SCOTT 677, COLIN BROWN 2:690-92.

2017B. ἑπτάκις heptakis adv
Seven times.

שֶׁבַע *shevaʻ* (8124), Seven, seven times (Lv 26:18,24, Prv 24:16).

1. ἑπτάκις heptakis

1 and I forgive him? till **seven times**?	Matt 18:21
1 Until **seven times**: but, Until seventy times seven.	18:22
1 And if he trespass against thee **seven times** in a day,	Luke 17:4
1 and **seven times** in a day turn again to thee, saying,	17:4

Septuagint Usage
Heptakis is the adverbial form of the numeral *hepta* (2017), "seven." In the Septuagint it is used both in the metaphoric sense (Genesis 4:24; Proverbs 24:16, "much, mighty, sufficient, intense") and in the literal sense (2 Kings [LXX 4 Kings] 4:35; 5:10). In the literal sense it is usually used in relationship to ceremonial ritual such as bowing down in worship seven times (Genesis 33:3) and sprinkling seven times (blood, Leviticus 4:6; oil, Leviticus 8:11; blood and water, Leviticus 14:7).

New Testament Usage
In the New Testament *heptakis* appears four times: Matthew 18:21,22 and twice in Luke

17:4. In both passages it is used of the fullness of forgiveness, "seven times."

STRONG 2034, BAUER 306, MOULTON-MILLIGAN 252, KITTEL 2:627-35, LIDDELL-SCOTT 678.

2018. ἑπτακισχίλιοι
heptakischilioi num
Seven thousand.
CROSS-REFERENCE:
χιλιάς chilias (5342)

1. ἑπτακισχιλίους heptakischilious card acc masc
1 I have reserved to myself **seven thousand** men,..... Rom 11:4

A compound adjective formed by the adverb *heptakis* (2017B), "seven times," and the numeral *chilioi* (5343), "thousand," this term means "seven thousand." Used often in the Septuagint *heptakischilioi* occurs only once in the New Testament (Romans 11:4) in reference to God's answer to Elijah, "I have reserved to myself *seven thousand* men, who have not bowed the knee to the image of Baal" (cf. 1 Kings 19:18 [LXX 3 Kings 19:18]).

STRONG 2035, BAUER 306, KITTEL 2:627-35, LIDDELL-SCOTT 678.

2019. ἑπτάκις heptakis
See word study at number 2017B.

2020. Ἔραστος Erastos name
Erastus.

1. Ἔραστος Erastos nom masc
2. Ἔραστον Eraston acc masc
2 that ministered unto him, Timotheus and **Erastus**;.. Acts 19:22
1 **Erastus** the chamberlain of the city saluteth you,... Rom 16:23
1 **Erastus** abode at Corinth:........................ 2 Tm 4:20

The name *Erastos* refers to two people in the New Testament: (1) a companion of Paul who was sent to Macedonia and who remained in Corinth (Acts 19:22; 2 Timothy 4:20); (2) a Corinthian Christian in charge of the city's public works (Romans 16:23).

2020B. ἐραυνάω eraunaō verb
To search, examine, investigate.
COGNATES:
ἀνεξεραύνητος anexeraunētos (416B)
ἀνεξερεύνητος anexereunētos (417)
ἐξεραυνάω exeraunaō (1813)
ἐξεραυνέω exerauneō (1813B)
SYNONYMS:
ἀνακρίνω anakrinō (348)
ἐκζητέω ekzēteō (1554)
ἐξετάζω exetazō (1816)
ἐπιζητέω epizēteō (1919)
ζητέω zēteō (2195)

1. ἐραυνᾶτε eraunate 2pl indic/impr pres act
2. ἐραυνᾷ erauna 3sing indic pres act
3. ἐραυνῶν eraunōn nom sing masc part pres act
4. ἐραυνῶντες eraunōntes nom pl masc part pres act
5. ἐραύνησον eraunēson 2sing impr aor act
1 You **search** the Scriptures, (NASB)................John 5:39
5 from Galilee, are you? **Search**, and see (NASB)....... 7:52

A later form (from about 1 A.D. on) of the classical *ereunaō* (2028), *eraunaō* is a verb meaning "to search, trace out, explain, investigate." The noun form *ereuna* means "a search, an examination." Appearing from Homer on, this verb occurs many times in the Septuagint. In the New Testament it appears six times (John 5:39; 7:52; Romans 8:27; 1 Corinthians 2:10; 1 Peter 1:11; Revelation 2:23), always with the meaning of in-depth searching. In John it "refers to the penetrating examination of scripture to obtain its meaning" (Seitz, "Seek," *Colin Brown*, 3:533). In 1 Peter 1:11 *eraunaō* means "to look into" or "peer into." Interestingly enough, all three Persons of the Trinity "search" the inner parts of man (the intents), the Father (Romans 8:27), the Son (Revelation 2:23), and the Spirit (1 Corinthians 2:10).

BAUER 306, MOULTON-MILLIGAN 252, KITTEL 2:655-57, LIDDELL-SCOTT 686, COLIN BROWN 3:532-33.

2021. ἐργάζομαι ergazomai verb
Work, be active, do accomplish, carry out, perform.
COGNATES:
ἀγαθοεργέω agathoergeō (14)
ἀμπελουργός ampelourgos (287)
γεωργέω geōrgeō (1084)
γεώργιον geōrgion (1085)
γεωργός geōrgos (1086)
δημιουργός dēmiourgos (1211)
ἐνέργεια energeia (1737)
ἐνεργέω energeō (1738)
ἐνέργημα energēma (1739)
ἐνεργής energēs (1740)
ἐργασία ergasia (2022)
ἐργάτης ergatēs (2023)
ἔργον ergon (2024)
εὐεργεσία euergesia (2087)
εὐεργετέω euergeteō (2088)

ἐργάζομαι 2021

εὐεργέτης euergetēs (2089)
ἱερουργέω hierourgeō (2394)
κακοῦργος kakourgos (2528)
κατεργάζομαι katergazomai (2686)
λειτουργέω leitourgeō (2982)
οἰκουργός oikourgos (3487B)
πανουργία panourgia (3696)
περιεργάζομαι periergazomai (3883)
περίεργος periergos (3884)
προσεργάζομαι prosergazomai (4192)
ῥᾳδιουργία rhadiourgia (4325)
συνεργέω sunergeō (4753)
συνεργός sunergos (4754)
συνυπουργέω sunupourgeō (4795)

Synonyms:
ἀναπληρόω anaplēroō (376)
ἀνταναπληρόω antanaplēroō (463)
ἀποτελέω apoteleō (652)
διανύω dianuō (1268)
ἐκπληρόω ekplēroō (1590)
ἐκτελέω ekteleō (1602)
ἐνεργέω energeō (1738)
ἐξαρτίζω exartizō (1806)
ἐπιτελέω epiteleō (1989)
καταρτίζω katartizō (2645)
κατεργάζομαι katergazomai (2686)
κατεστρώννυμι katestrōnnumi (2689)
πληρόω plēroō (3997)
ποιέω poieō (4020)
πράσσω prassō (4097)
συντελέω sunteleō (4783)
τελειόω teleioō (4896)
τελέω teleō (4903)

אָרַג 'āragh (730), Weave (Is 19:9).

בָּגַד bāghadh (931), Treat faithlessly, deal faithlessly (Ps 59:5 [58:5]).

גָּמַל gāmal (1621), Do, render (Prv 3:30).

חָטַב chāṭav (2497), Gather, cut (2 Chr 2:10).

לָקַשׁ lāqash (4095), Piel: rake up (Jb 24:6).

מְלָאכָה mᵉlā'khāh (4536), Work, service (1 Chr 25:1).

מַעֲשֶׂה ma'ăseh (4801), Doing, something done, work (Nm 31:51).

סַחַר sachar (5693), Business profit (Prv 31:18).

עָבַד 'āvadh (5856), Qal: work, perform, serve (Ex 20:9, Prv 12:11, Jer 27:6 [34:6]); niphal: be tilled, be cultivated (Dt 21:4, Eccl 5:9 [5:8], Ez 36:34); pual: be worked (Dt 21:3).

עֲבֹדָה 'ăvōdhāh (5865), Work, labor (1 Chr 27:26).

עָשָׂה 'āsâh (6449), Do, make, perform (Ex 31:4,5, 35:10).

עָשׂוֹת 'āshôth (6472), Wrought (Ez 27:19).

פָּעַל pā'al (6713), Make, commit, do, perform (Ps 5:5, Is 44:12, Mi 2:1).

פֹּעַל pō'al (6714), Work, working (Is 45:9).

שָׂדַד sādhadh (7897), Piel: draw a boundary furrow, harrow (Is 28:24).

שָׁתָה shāthāh (8686), Weave (Is 19:10).

1. ἐργάζεσθε ergazesthe 2pl indic/impr pres mid
2. ἐργάζομαι ergazomai 1sing indic pres mid
3. ἐργάζῃ ergazē 2sing indic pres mid
4. ἐργάζεται ergazetai 3sing indic pres mid
5. ἐργάζονται ergazontai 3pl indic pres mid
6. ἐργαζώμεθα ergazōmetha 1pl subj pres mid
7. ἐργάζου ergazou 2sing impr pres mid
8. ἐργαζόμενος ergazomenos
   nom sing masc part pres mid
9. ἐργαζομένῳ ergazomenō
   dat sing masc part pres mid
10. ἐργαζόμενοι ergazomenoi
    nom pl masc part pres mid
11. ἐργαζομένους ergazomenous
    acc pl masc part pres mid
12. ἐργάζεσθαι ergazesthai inf pres mid
13. εἰργάσατο eirgasato 3sing indic aor mid
14. εἰργασάμεθα eirgasametha 1pl indic aor mid
15. εἰργάσαντο eirgasanto 3pl indic aor mid
16. ἐργάσῃ ergasē 2sing subj aor mid
17. εἰργασμένα eirgasmena
    nom/acc pl neu part perf mid
18. εἰργάζετο eirgazeto 3sing indic imperf mid
19. ἠργάσατο ērgasato 3sing indic aor mid
20. ἠργάσαντο ērgasanto 3pl indic aor mid
21. ἠργάζετο ērgazeto 3sing indic imperf mid
22. ἠργάζοντο ērgazonto 3pl indic imperf mid
23. εἰργάσασθε eirgasasthe 2pl indic aor mid

10	depart from me, ye that **work** iniquity.	Matt 7:23
7	and said, Son, go **work** to day in my vineyard.	21:28
13	went and **traded** with the same,	25:16
19	went and **traded** with the same,	25:16
13	for she hath **wrought** a good work upon me.	26:10
19	for she hath **wrought** a good work upon me.	26:10
13	she hath **wrought** a good work on me.	Mark 14:6
19	she hath **wrought** a good work on me.	14:6
12	There are six days in which men ought **to work**:	Luke 13:14
17	that they are **wrought** in God.	John 3:21
4	My Father **worketh** hitherto, and I **work**.	5:17
2	My Father **worketh** hitherto, and I **work**.	5:17
1	**Labour** not for the meat which perisheth,	6:27
6	What ... do, that we **might work** the works of God?	6:28
3	may see, and believe thee? what dost thou **work**?	6:30
12	I must **work** the works of him that sent me,	9:4
12	the night cometh, when no man can **work**.	9:4
8	and **worketh** righteousness, is accepted with him.	Acts 10:35
2	and perish: for I **work** a work in your days,	13:41
18	he abode with them, and **wrought**:	18:3
21	he abode with them, and **wrought**:	18:3
9	to every man that **worketh** good, to the Jew first,	Rom 2:10
9	Now to him that **worketh** is the reward ... of debt.	4:4
9	But to him that **worketh** not,	4:5
4	Love **worketh** no ill to his neighbour:	13:10
10	And labour, **working** with our own hands:	1 Co 4:12
12	have not we power to forbear **working**?	9:6
10	Do ye not know that they which minister	9:13
4	for he **worketh** the work of the Lord, as I also do.	16:10
4	Godly sorrow **brings** repentance that leads (NASB)	2 Co 7:10
6	let us **do** good unto all men, especially unto	Gal 6:10
8	**working** with his hands the thing which is good,	Eph 4:28
1	do it heartily, as to the Lord, and not unto men;	Col 3:23
10	labour and travail: for **labouring** night and day,	1 Th 2:9
12	and **to work** with your own hands,	4:11
10	but **wrought** with labour and travail night and day,	2 Th 3:8
12	that if any would not **work**, neither should he eat.	3:10
11	**working** not at all, but are busybodies.	3:11
10	with quietness they **work**, and eat their own bread.	3:12
15	**wrought** righteousness, obtained promises,	Heb 11:33
20	**wrought** righteousness, obtained promises,	11:33

4	anger ... does not **achieve** ... righteousness (NASB)	Jas 1:20
1	But if ye have respect to persons, ye **commit** sin,	2:9
14	we lose not those things which we **have wrought**,	2 Jn 1:8
23	we lose not those things which we **have wrought**,	1:8
16	faithfully whatsoever thou **doest** to the brethren,	3 Jn 1:5
5	sailors, and as many as trade **by sea**, stood afar off,	Rev 18:17

Classical Greek

Ergazomai, a deponent verb from the noun *ergon* (2024), functions in classical Greek much like the modern understanding of "to work." It can speak of "to work" or "to labor" in a business or trade; it can simply mean "to do" or "to make, accomplish" (to work at something); or it can also refer to "working" some material (e.g., clay, land, or wood) (see *Liddell-Scott*).

Since work contributed to culture and society it was generally regarded in a positive fashion, and it was held to be part of mankind's lot and purpose in life. Manual labor per se was not disparaged, although some forms of trade were frowned upon because they made little contribution to society (Kitto, *The Greeks*, pp.239-243). Some philosophies esteemed work as an ideal. It was recognized as altogether superior to "idleness," which did not profit the individual or society (cf. Bertram, "ergon," *Kittel*, 2:635f.; Hahn, "Work," *Colin Brown*, 3:1147f. who note the relationship between work and virtue [*aretē* (697)] in Plato and Aristotle).

Septuagint Usage

The classical understanding of this word is repeated in the Septuagint. Although 14 different Hebrew terms are translated by *ergazomai*, 2 (in various forms) are especially equated with it: *'āvadh*, "to work, to serve," and *pā'al*, "to work, to accomplish." In the Pentateuch *'āshāh*, "to do" or "to make," is also rendered by *ergazomai*.

Land and other materials are "worked" (e.g., Genesis 2:5; 3:23; 4:2; 4:12; Exodus 31:4,5). "To work" is mankind's lot in life (Exodus 20:9; Deuteronomy 5:13). The priests are to work in the Lord's service (Numbers 3:7; 8:11,15,19). Those who oppose God and His people are regularly termed "evildoers" or "workers of iniquity" (e.g., Psalms 5:5; 6:8; 14:4 [LXX 13:4]; 28:3 [27:3]; 36:12 [35:12]; passim; Proverbs 10:29), while the godly "work righteousness" (Psalm 15:2 [LXX 14:2]). Yet God the King effects (i.e., works) salvation (Psalm 74:12 [LXX 73:12]).

New Testament Usage

In the New Testament *ergazomai* can describe the general act of working; i.e., physical labor (e.g., Romans 4:4; 1 Corinthians 4:12; Ephesians 4:28; 2 Thessalonians 3:10,11,12). But in a theological sense it can express the practice of obedience to God—working righteousness or doing good deeds (the noun *ergon* is especially significant here; e.g., Acts 10:35; Romans 4:5; Hebrews 11:33; cf. John 3:21; Galatians 6:10; James 1:20).

The believer's responsibility to "work righteousness" is not that deeds (especially "works" of the Law) have the power to justify; rather, righteousness is effected by faith alone (Romans 4:5; cf. Romans 3:20,27,28; Titus 3:5). Faith promotes righteousness (Hebrews 11:33), so certain "works" have a positive nature (e.g., 1 Corinthians 15:58; 16:10; cf. 1 Timothy 2:10; 3:1; 5:10; 6:18; cf. Titus 1:16; 2:14). For Paul, work was necessary for the maintenance of life and was a vital component of his strategy for spreading the gospel. First Thessalonians 2:9 is a clear statement of his approach to ministry: "For ye remember, brethren, our labor and travail: for laboring night and day, because we would not be chargeable unto any of you, we preached unto you the gospel of God." His trade as a tent maker allowed Paul to present the gospel free of charge, even though he taught that one who sowed "spiritual things" was entitled to reap "carnal things" (financial) from them (1 Corinthians 9:11). In addition, he commanded that Christians should work with their hands so that they would be able to give to those who were in need (Ephesians 4:28; 1 Thessalonians 4:11,12). Paul went so far as to say that "if any would not work, neither should he eat" (2 Thessalonians 3:10). This injunction was a stiff warning to the idle, disorderly "busybodies" within the churches (verse 11).

Jesus' own actions (*poieō* [4020] can be a synonym for *ergazomai*) incited the Jewish leaders to plot His death (John 5:15,16). Jesus stated, in the same context that what He *did* (including working signs) were the same *actions* (works) as His Father's, "My Father is working still (*eōs arti ergazetai*), and I am working (*kagō ergazomai*)" (John 5:17, RSV; cf. 9:4; Acts 13:41).

Moreover, Jesus urged His disciples to "work" for food which would last for eternal life (John 6:27) rather than for momentary satisfaction. He explained that such "work" actually involves faith in himself (6:29). When the disciples requested that Jesus "work" a sign for them to see, Jesus explained that He himself, like the manna in the wilderness which was a sign for the fathers, was the bread from heaven which had come down bringing eternal life. Thus God works to reveal himself to the world through Jesus who works the works of the Father (John 9:4).

Aside from the "spiritual" work mentioned above, Jesus also discussed manual labor as a necessary and integral part of life. Work is often mentioned in the parables of the Lord as a natural activity. For example, the brother of the prodigal worked with his father (Luke 15:13-19); the faithful servant who did the work expected of him was rewarded by his master (Matthew 24:45); two of the three servants who were given "talents" from their master were commended for their faithful work (Matthew 25:14-23). (For further information on the subject of "work," see the word study at *ergon* [2024].)

STRONG 2038, BAUER 306-7, MOULTON-MILLIGAN 252, KITTEL 2:635-52, LIDDELL-SCOTT 681, COLIN BROWN 3:1147,1149-50,1156-58.

2022. ἐργασία ergasia noun

Trade, profit, gain, practice (of something), diligence.

COGNATE:
ἐργάζομαι ergazomai (2021)

SYNONYMS:
κέρδος kerdos (2742)
τέχνη technē (4926)

מְלָאכָה mᵉlā'khāh (4536), Work, labor, service (Lv 13:51, 1 Chr 26:29, Ez 15:3).

מַעֲשֶׂה maʻăseh (4801), Doing, something done, work (Ex 26:1, Nm 31:20).

עֶבֶד ʻevedh (5860), Deed (Eccl 9:1).

עֲבֹדָה ʻăvōdhāh (5865), Work, labor (Gn 29:27, 1 Chr 26:30, Ps 104:23 [103:23]).

פֹּעַל pōʻal (6714), Work, working, deed (Ru 2:12, Is 1:31, 41:24).

פְּעֻלָּה pᵉʻullāh (6715), Work (2 Chr 15:7).

1. ἐργασίας ergasias gen sing fem
2. ἐργασίαν ergasian acc sing fem

2 give **diligence** that thou mayest be delivered from .. Luke 12:58
2 brought her masters much **gain** by soothsaying: ..... Acts 16:16
1 masters saw that the hope of their **gains** was gone, ... 16:19
2 brought no small **gain** unto the craftsmen; 19:24
1 ye know that by this **craft** we have our wealth. 19:25
2 to **work** all uncleanness with greediness. .... Eph 4:19

Classical Greek

In classical Greek *ergasia* usually means a "productive labor." It may also denote the "profit" or "earnings" from the labor, a "trade" or "business," or even a "guild of workers." In the papyri *ergasia* is used for "bodily labor," a "business" or "trade" (such as a goldsmith's business), or a "guild" (see *Bauer*).

Septuagint Usage

The Septuagint uses *ergasia* primarily in the sense of the "labor, work, or service rendered" (Genesis 29:27; Ruth 2:12), or as "the product of one's labor" (Exodus 26:1; Numbers 31:20; Ezekiel 15:5). It is often used in connection with the duties of the priests in the temple (2 Chronicles 24:12). In both classical Greek and the Septuagint *ergasia* is contrasted with idleness or laziness.

New Testament Usage

Ergasia is used four different ways in the New Testament. It may refer to a type of employment, that is, a "trade" or "craft" (Acts 19:25). Second, it may refer to the "earnings" from one's labor, the "profit" or "gain" (Acts 16:16,19; 19:24). Third, it may refer to the actual "practice of something," such as in Ephesians 4:19, "to *work* all uncleanness." Finally, *ergasia* may refer to the "effort" involved in an activity, the "diligence" or "pains" to be applied to a certain task. In Luke 12:58 "give diligence" means "to do your utmost."

STRONG 2039, BAUER 307, MOULTON-MILLIGAN 252-53, LIDDELL-SCOTT 681-82, COLIN BROWN 3:1147,1149-50.

2023. ἐργάτης ergatēs noun

Workman or laborer, doer.

CROSS-REFERENCE:
ἐργάζομαι ergazomai (2021)

1. ἐργάτης ergatēs nom sing masc
2. ἐργάτην ergatēn acc sing masc
3. ἐργάται ergatai nom pl masc
4. ἐργατῶν ergatōn gen pl masc
5. ἐργάτας ergatas acc pl masc

3 harvest ... is plenteous, but the **labourers** are few; ... Matt 9:37
5 that he will send forth **labourers** into his harvest. 9:38
1 for the **workman** is worthy of his meat. 10:10
5 went out early in the morning to hire **labourers** 20:1
4 agreed with the **labourers** for a penny a day, ... 20:2
5 Call the **labourers**, and give them their hire, ... 20:8
3 harvest truly is great, but the **labourers** are few; ... Luke 10:2
5 that he would send forth **labourers** into his harvest. 10:2
1 for the **labourer** is worthy of his hire. 10:7
3 depart from me, all ye **workers** of iniquity. 13:27
5 together with the **workmen** of like occupation, ... Acts 19:25
3 For such are false apostles, deceitful **workers**, ... 2 Co 11:13
6 beware of evil **workers**, beware of the concision. .... Phlp 3:2
1 And, The **labourer** is worthy of his reward. .... 1 Tm 5:18

ἔργον 2024

```
2  a workman that needeth not to be ashamed, ........ 2 Tm 2:15
4  Behold, the hire of the labourers who have reaped ... Jas 5:4
```

Although primarily used in a literal sense to refer to agricultural workers, such as a field hand (Matthew 20:1; cf. 10:10; Luke 10:7; 1 Timothy 5:18), *ergatēs* can be used figuratively to refer to any kind of worker, even apostles and teachers (2 Corinthians 11:13; Philippians 3:2; cf. 2 Timothy 2:15). It is also used to describe "a doer" or "one who does something," such as "workers of iniquity" (Luke 13:27).

STRONG 2040, BAUER 307, MOULTON-MILLIGAN 253, LIDDELL-SCOTT 682, COLIN BROWN 3:1147,1149-50.

2024. ἔργον ergon noun

Work, deed, action, occupation, task, thing, matter.

COGNATE:
ἐργάζομαι ergazomai (2021)

SYNONYMS:
κόπος kopos (2845)
μόχθος mochthos (3313)
ποίησις poiēsis (4022)
πόνος ponos (4051)
πρᾶξις praxis (4093)

אֹרַח 'ōrach (758), Path, way (Jb 13:27).
גְּמוּל gᵉmûl (1618), Doings (Is 3:11).
דָּבָר dāvār (1745), Things (1 Kgs 18:36).
דֶּרֶךְ derekh (1932), Way, path (Jb 34:21, 36:23).
חֹק chōq (2805), Portion (Prv 31:15).
יְגִיעַ yᵉghîaʿ (3127), Labor, work (Jb 10:3, 39:11).
כְּלִי kᵉlî (3747), Household furnishings (Nm 4:16).
לֶקַח leqach (4090), Teaching (Jb 11:4).
מָלֵא mālē' (4527), Piel: set jewels (Ex 31:5).
מְלָאכָה mᵉlā'khāh (4536), Work, labor, service (Dt 16:8, Neh 5:16, Jer 18:3).
מַס maṣ (4671), Compulsory labor, overseer of forced labor (Ex 1:11).
מַעֲבָד maʿăbādh (4719), Deed (Jb 34:25).
מַעֲלָל maʿălāl (4770), Deed (Ps 77:11 [76:11], Is 3:10).
מַעֲשֶׂה maʿăseh (4801), Doing, something done, work (Ex 32:16, 2 Kgs 19:18, Jer 51:18 [28:18]).
מִפְעָל miphʿāl (4821), Work, deed (Pss 46:8 [45:8], 66:5 [65:5], Prv 8:22).
מַשָּׂא massā' (5014), Burden, load (Nm 4:27—only some Vaticanus texts).
מַת math (5139), Men, people (Jb 11:11).
סִבְלוֹת ṣivlôth (5633), Forced labor (Ex 1:11).
עָבַד ʿāvadh (5856), Work, do service (Nm 7:5).
עֲבֹדָה ʿăvōdhāh (5865), Work, labor, service (Ex 2:23, Nm 3:31, 1 Chr 25:1).
עֲבֻדָּה ʿăvuddāh (5866), Slaves, servants (Jb 1:3).
עֲבִידָה ʿăvîdhāh (A5881), Work (Ezr 4:24, 5:8, 6:7—Aramaic).
עֲלִילָה ʿălîlāh (6173), Deed, action (Ps 105:1 [104:1]).
עֲלִילִיָּה ʿălîlîyāh (6174), Deed (Jer 32:19 [39:19]).
עֵצָה ʿētsāh (6332), Advice (Jb 21:16).
עָשָׂה ʿāsāh (6449), Do, make (Jb 4:17, Prv 20:12, Jl 2:11).
פָּעַל pāʿal (6713), Make (Jb 36:3, Prv 16:4 [16:2]).
פֹּעַל pōʿal (6714), Deed, work (Dt 32:4, 2 Sm 23:20, Hb 3:2).
פְּעֻלָּה pᵉullāh (6715), Reward, wages, work, deed (Ps 109:20 [108:20], Prv 10:16, Is 40:10).
פְּקֻדָּה pᵉquddāh (6735), Office (2 Chr 23:18).
רָעָה rāʿāh (7749), Wickedness (Jer 44:9 [51:9]—Codex Alexandrinus only).
תּוֹעֵבָה tôʿēvāh (8774), Something abominable or detestable (Prv 13:19).

1. ἔργον ergon nom/acc sing neu
2. ἔργου ergou gen sing neu
3. ἔργῳ ergō dat sing neu
4. ἔργα erga nom/acc pl neu
5. ἔργων ergōn gen pl neu
6. ἔργοις ergois dat pl neu

```
4  that they may see your good works, ................ Matt 5:16
4  John had heard in the prison the works of Christ, ..... 11:2
5  Yet wisdom is vindicated by her deeds (NASB) ........ 11:19
4  but do not ye after their works: ..................... 23:3
4  But all their works they do for to be seen of men: ..... 23:5
1  for she hath wrought a good work upon me. ......... 26:10
1  and to every man his work, ........................ Mark 13:34
1  she hath wrought a good work on me. ................ 14:6
6  Truly ye bear witness that ye allow the deeds of ... Luke 11:48
3  which was a prophet mighty in deed and word ......... 24:19
4  because their deeds were evil. ..................... John 3:19
4  lest his deeds should be reproved. ................... 3:20
4  that his deeds may be made manifest, ................ 3:21
1  to do the will of him ... and to finish his work. ........ 4:34
4  and he will show him greater works than these, ....... 5:20
4  for the works which the Father hath given me ......... 5:36
4  the same works that I do, bear witness of me, ......... 5:36
4  What ... do, that we might work the works of God? .... 6:28
1  This is the work of God, that ye believe .............. 6:29
4  disciples also may see the works that thou doest. ..... 7:3
4  I testify of it, that the works thereof are evil. .......... 7:7
1  I have done one work, and ye all marvel. ............. 7:21
4  ye would do the works of Abraham. .................. 8:39
4  Ye do the deeds of your father. ...................... 8:41
4  the works of God should be made manifest in him. ..... 9:3
4  I must work the works of him that sent me, ........... 9:4
4  the works that I do in my Father's name, ............. 10:25
4  good works have I showed you from my Father; ....... 10:32
1  for which of those works do ye stone me? ........... 10:32
2  For a good work we stone thee not; ................. 10:33
4  If I do not the works of my Father, believe me not. .... 10:37
6  believe the works: that ye may know, and believe, ..... 10:38
4  Father that dwelleth in me, he doeth the works. ...... 14:10
4  or else believe me for the very works' sake. .......... 14:11
4  the works that I do shall he do also; ................. 14:12
4  the works which none other man did, ................ 15:24
1  I have finished the work which thou gavest me ....... 17:4
1  for if this counsel or this work be of men, ........... Acts 5:38
6  and was mighty in words and in deeds. .............. 7:22
6  and rejoiced in the works of their own hands. ........ 7:41
5  full of good works and almsdeeds which she did. ..... 9:36
```

ἔργον 2024

1	Separate me Barnabas and Saul for the **work**	Acts 13:2
1	and perish: for I work **a work** in your days,	13:41
1	and perish: for I **work** a work in your days,	13:41
1	the grace of God for the **work** which they fulfilled	14:26
4	all his **works** from the beginning of the world	15:18
1	and went not with them to the **work**	15:38
4	turn to God, and do **works** meet for repentance	26:20
4	will render to every man according to his **deeds**:	Rom 2:6
2	To them who by patient continuance in well **doing**	2:7
1	show the **work** of the law written in their hearts,	2:15
5	Therefore by the **deeds** of the law there shall no	3:20
5	By what law? of **works**? Nay: ... by the law of faith.	3:27
5	is justified by faith without the **deeds** of the law.	3:28
5	For if Abraham were justified by **works**,	4:2
5	whom God imputeth righteousness without **works**,	4:6
5	according to election might stand, not of **works**,	9:11
5	but as it were by the **works** of the law.	9:32
5	And if by grace, then is it no more of **works**:	11:6
5	But if it be of **works**, then is it no more grace:	11:6
1	otherwise **work** is no more work.	11:6
1	otherwise work is no more **work**.	11:6
5	For rulers are not a terror to good **works**,	13:3
3	For rulers are not a terror to good **works**,	13:3
4	let us therefore cast off the **works** of darkness,	13:12
1	For meat destroy not the **work** of God.	14:20
3	to make the Gentiles obedient, by word and **deed**,	15:18
1	Every man's **work** shall be made manifest:	1 Co 3:13
1	fire shall try every man's **work** of what sort it is.	3:13
1	If any man's **work** abide which he hath built	3:14
1	If any man's **work** shall be burned,	3:15
1	that he that hath done this **deed** might be taken	5:2
1	are not ye my **work** in the Lord?	9:1
3	always abounding in the **work** of the Lord,	15:58
1	for he worketh the **work** of the Lord, as I also do.	16:10
1	may abound to every good **work**:	2 Co 9:8
3	such will we be also in **deed** when we are present.	10:11
4	whose end shall be according to their **works**.	11:15
5	that a man is not justified by the **works** of the law,	Gal 2:16
5	and not by the **works** of the law:	2:16
5	by the **works** of the law shall no flesh be justified.	2:16
5	Received ye the Spirit by the **works** of the law,	3:2
5	doeth he it by the **works** of the law,	3:5
5	are of the **works** of the law are under the curse:	3:10
4	Now the **works** of the flesh are manifest,	5:19
1	But let every man prove his own **work**,	6:4
5	Not of **works**, lest any man should boast.	Eph 2:9
6	created in Christ Jesus unto good **works**,	2:10
1	for the **work** of the ministry,	4:12
6	And have no fellowship with the unfruitful **works**	5:11
1	that he which hath begun a good **work** in you	Phlp 1:6
2	if I live in the flesh, this is the fruit **of my labour**:	1:22
1	for the **work** of Christ he was nigh unto death,	2:30
3	being fruitful in every good **work**,	Col 1:10
6	and enemies in your mind by wicked **works**,	1:21
3	And whatsoever ye do in word or **deed**,	3:17
2	Remembering without ceasing your **work** of faith,	1 Th 1:3
1	very highly in love for their **work's** sake.	5:13
1	and the **work** of faith with power:	2 Th 1:11
3	and stablish you in every good word and **work**.	2:17
5	professing godliness with good **works**.	1 Tm 2:10
2	the office of a bishop, he desireth a good **work**.	3:1
6	Well reported of for good **works**;	5:10
3	if she have diligently followed every good **work**.	5:10
4	the good **works** of some are manifest beforehand;	5:25
6	do good, that they be rich in good **works**,	6:18
4	with an holy calling, not according to our **works**,	2 Tm 1:9
1	and prepared unto every good **work**.	2:21
1	thoroughly furnished unto all good **works**.	3:17
1	endure afflictions, do the **work** of an evangelist,	4:5
4	The Lord reward him according to his **works**:	4:14
2	the Lord shall deliver me from every evil **work**,	4:18
6	that they know God; but in **works** they deny him,	Tit 1:16
1	and unto every good **work** reprobate.	1:16
1	showing thyself a pattern of good **works**:	2:7
5	a peculiar people, zealous of good **works**.	2:14
1	obey magistrates, to be ready to every good **work**,	3:1
5	Not by **works** of righteousness which we have done,	3:5
5	might be careful to maintain good **works**.	Tit 3:8
5	learn to maintain good **works** for necessary uses,	3:14
4	and the heavens are the **works** of thine hands:	Heb 1:10
4	and didst set him over the **works** of thy hands:	2:7
4	proved me, and saw my **works** forty years.	3:9
5	although the **works** were finished	4:3
5	God did rest the seventh day from all his **works**.	4:4
5	he also hath ceased from his own **works**,	4:10
5	the foundation of repentance from dead **works**,	6:1
2	For God is not unrighteous to forget your **work**	6:10
5	purge your conscience from dead **works**	9:14
5	to provoke unto love and to good **works**:	10:24
3	perfect in every good **work** to do his will,	13:21
1	But let patience have her perfect **work**,	Jas 1:4
2	not a forgetful hearer, but a doer **of the work**,	1:25
4	a man say he hath faith, and have not **works**?	2:14
4	faith, if it hath not **works**, is dead, being alone.	2:17
4	a man may say, Thou hast faith, and I have **works**:	2:18
5	show me thy faith without thy **works**,	2:18
5	and I will show thee my faith by my **works**.	2:18
5	know, ... that faith without **works** is dead?	2:20
5	Was not Abraham our father justified by **works**,	2:21
6	Seest thou how faith wrought with his **works**,	2:22
5	and by **works** was faith made perfect?	2:22
5	Ye see then how that by **works** a man is justified,	2:24
5	also was not Rahab the harlot justified by **works**,	2:25
5	so faith without **works** is dead also.	2:26
4	let him show out of a good conversation his **works**	3:13
4	Father, ... judgeth according to every man's **work**,	1 Pt 1:17
5	may by your good **works**, which they shall behold,	2:12
6	from day to day with their unlawful **deeds**;	2 Pt 2:8
4	and the **works** that are therein shall be burned up.	3:10
4	that he might destroy the **works** of the devil.	1 Jn 3:8
4	Because his own **works** were evil,	3:12
3	neither in tongue; but in **deed** and in truth.	3:18
6	is partaker of his evil **deeds**.	2 Jn 1:11
4	I will remember his **deeds** which he doeth,	3 Jn 1:10
5	and to convince all ... of all their ungodly **deeds**	Jude 1:15
4	know thy **works**, and thy labour, and thy patience,	Rev 2:2
4	and repent, and do the first **works**;	2:5
4	that thou hatest the **deeds** of the Nicolaitanes,	2:6
4	I know thy **works**, and tribulation, and poverty,	2:9
4	I know thy **works** and where thou dwellest,	2:13
4	I know thy **works**, and charity, and service,	2:19
4	and faith, and thy patience, and thy **works**;	2:19
5	great tribulation, except they repent of their **deeds**.	2:22
5	unto every one of you according to your **works**.	2:23
4	overcometh, and keepeth my **works** unto the end,	2:26
4	I know thy **works**, ... hast a name that thou livest,	3:1
4	for I have not found thy **works** perfect before God.	3:2
4	I know thy **works**: ... set before thee an open door,	3:8
4	know thy **works**, that thou art neither cold nor hot:	3:15
5	yet repented not of the **works** of their hands,	9:20
4	they may rest from ... their **works** do follow them.	14:13
4	saying, Great and marvellous are thy **works**,	15:3
5	blasphemed ... and repented not of their **deeds**.	16:11
4	double unto her double according to her **works**:	18:6
4	the dead were judged ... according to their **works**.	20:12
4	were judged every man according to their **works**.	20:13
4	to give every man according as his **work** shall be.	22:12

Classical Greek

"Work" is the basic equivalency of this noun (cf. the verb *ergazomai* [2021]) from which many different shades of meaning evolve, as do many compounds. Work includes commercial and agricultural occupations, trade, and fishing. It is also descriptive of the labor of the fine arts such as painting, sculpture, and literary artistry (see Bertram, "ergon," *Kittel*, 2:635). Often, work was given an ethical or moral value. Hence, a work could be described as "good" (*agathos* [18]) or as "evil" (*ponēros* [4050]).

Work was, for the most part, regarded positively in ancient Greek thought, especially if it contributed to society. Work was particularly contrasted with "idleness"; thus it invariably denoted activity. Consequently, "deed" (*ergon*) may be contrasted with "word" (*logos* [3030]) (e.g., of the same juxtaposition: Sirach 3:8; Luke 24:19; Colossians 3:17; Josephus *Against Apion* 2.2.2).

Work also denoted "what is wrought, the result of work or the product of the process of work" (Bertram, "ergon," *Kittel*, 2:636), i.e., a "work of art," a "literary work." Eventually it weakened in definition and meant merely "thing" or "matter."

Septuagint Usage

The versatility of *ergon* is reiterated by the Septuagint where it translates 27 different Hebrew words. Among the most common are *ʿāsâh/maʿăseh*, *mᵉlāʾkhāh*, and various forms of *ʿāvadh*. It is often the object of *poieō* (4020), "to do, make" (a synonym of *ergazomai*; e.g., Genesis 2:2; Exodus 12:16; 31:15; 36:1; Deuteronomy 5:13).

Ergon (cf. *ergazomai*) also describes the labor of the Levites and priests (e.g., Numbers 3:7,8,26). Nonetheless, to work on the Sabbath would violate the religion of Israel (Leviticus 23:3,7,8,21,35).

Theologically "works of justice make life" (*erga dikaion zōēn poiei*; Proverbs 10:16; cf. Isaiah 32:17; Zephaniah 2:3). Yet man was never made blameless before God because of "works" (Job 4:17). Worshiping the "works of men's hands" is extremely abominable before God (e.g., Isaiah 2:8; 17:8; Jeremiah 1:16; Micah 5:13), but God's marvelous works are "the works of his hands" (Psalms 8:4,7; 90:16 [LXX 89:16]; 138:8 [137:8]; Isaiah 29:23). A "work" of God may be a miracle (Deuteronomy 11:3; cf. Sirach 48:14; see Hahn, "Work," *Colin Brown*, 3:1148).

Concerning the works of God, His creative acts are perhaps the most evident. The heavens, the earth, and all things on the earth are representative of the manifold works of God (cf. Genesis 1, 2; Nehemiah 9:6; Psalms 24:1,2 [LXX 23:1,2]; 104:5 [103:5]; Isaiah 37:16). In addition, God "worked" through His chosen people Israel effectuating the plan of redemption. Although He created all people, Israel held a unique place among the nations, for it was through Israel that the kingdom of God was to be established upon the earth.

The Septuagintal understanding of *ergon* is most notably colored by the association of *ergon* with the fall of humanity. Influenced by Hellenistic values, "work" (rather than "anguish") became a curse of the Fall (Genesis 3:16, Septuagint addition). Consequently, Hellenistic Judaism developed the concept that work (all work) was punishment for sin and thus, by association, evil. Human actions became generally regarded as "wicked and corrupt" (e.g., Job 11:14; 21:16). Nevertheless, certain kinds of work were considered holy, such as temple service or, naturally, keeping the Law. This led to the idea—based upon the premise that God rewards according to man's deeds (a concept in itself essentially correct)—that righteousness could be procured through "works" (cf. Proverbs 24:12; Jeremiah 25:14; Lamentations 3:64; Matthew 16:27). It is to this distortion that the New Testament understanding of *ergon* addresses itself.

New Testament Usage

The works of God are also revealed in the salvation and redemption which came through Jesus Christ. His supernatural entrance into history and humanity is the work of God (Luke 1:68-79). The miracles of Christ, which prove His deity and His messianic mission, are the work of God (John 5:19,20,36; 10:25,37; cf Matthew 11:2-5). The Atonement itself is the work of God: "God was in Christ, reconciling the world unto himself" (2 Corinthians 5:19). This work of salvation continues in and through the Church (Ephesians 4:11-16). The preaching of the gospel to the peoples of the world, therefore, is also the work of God (Ephesians 3:1-7). This all leads to the final goal of the redemption work of God: the establishment of His kingdom on earth (Matthew 19:28; Acts 3:21).

Aside from the traditional use of *ergon* to describe labor, a task, or a deed (e.g., Matthew 11:19; 23:3; John 3:20; Acts 5:38), work in the New Testament may also refer to any deed which testifies of God (e.g., John 5:36; 6:28,29; 7:3,21; 9:3,4). But more significant is the use of *erga* (plural) as a technical term for "deeds" of keeping the Law (e.g., Romans 2:15; 3:20,28; Galatians 2:16; 3:2,5,10; cf. John 8:39) or for the "good deeds" which are to punctuate

Christian life-style (e.g., Matthew 5:16; 1 Corinthians 15:58; 2 Corinthians 9:8; Ephesians 2:10; Colossians 1:10; 1 Timothy 2:10; 3:1; 5:10; passim; Hebrews 10:24). Hearing, i.e., faith, by itself is inadequate as a *response* to God's grace; one must also be a "doer of the work" (James 1:25; cf. James 2:14,18,20).

In contrast, evil works or deeds of lawlessness are the trademarks of those who reject God and will be judged by Him (John 3:19; cf. Romans 2:6; 1 Corinthians 3:13; Colossians 1:21; 2 Timothy 4:18; Hebrews 9:14; 1 Peter 1:17; 1 John 3:12). These oppose God and His servants (Luke 11:48; John 8:41). Such "evildoers" are not just corrupted by sin, they violently oppose God and worship the "works of their hands" just as the rebellious Israelites resisted God in the old economy (Acts 7:41; see above on the Septuagint).

In certain contexts *ergon* more specifically denotes "gospel labor." Timothy was to do the "work of an evangelist" and resist the false teachers threatening his church (2 Timothy 4:5). The role of the overseer (*episkopos*) is a "noble task" (1 Timothy 3:1, RSV). Moreover, Paul reminded the Corinthians of his work *en kuriō*, "in the Lord" (1 Corinthians 16:10; cf. Philippians 2:30).

STRONG 2041, BAUER 307-8, MOULTON-MILLIGAN 253, KITTEL 2:635-52, LIDDELL-SCOTT 682-83, COLIN BROWN 3:1147-52.

2025. ἐρεθίζω erethizō verb
Excite, arouse, provoke, irritate, embitter.
SYNONYMS:
παραπικραίνω parapikrainō (3754)
προκαλέω prokaleō (4151)

גָּרָה gārâh (1667), Hithpael: venture into struggle, mobilize for battle (Dn 11:10,25).
מָרָה mārâh (4947), Be refractory, be obstinate (Dt 21:20).
סֵתֶר sēther (5848), Secrecy, backbiting (Prv 25:23).
רָדַף rādhaph (7579), Piel: pursue (Prv 19:7).

1. ἐρεθίζετε erethizete 2pl impr pres act
2. ἠρέθισεν ērethisen 3sing indic aor act

2 and your zeal **hath provoked** very many............ 2 Co 9:2
1 Fathers, **provoke** not your children to anger,......... Col 3:21

The word *erethizō* means "to excite or provoke," especially with the intent of causing the subject to change. In 2 Corinthians 9:2 provoking is equated with encouragement or stimulation. The negative sense of "irritate, embitter" is found in Colossians 3:21, in reference to "*provoke* not your children," as well as in the Septuagint (1 Maccabees 15:40).

STRONG 2042, BAUER 308, MOULTON-MILLIGAN 253, LIDDELL-SCOTT 684.

2026. ἐρείδω ereidō verb
Jam fast, become fixed.

אָמֵץ 'āmēts (563), Piel: strengthen (Prv 31:17).
שׁוּב shûv (8178), Return, come again (Jb 17:10).
שָׁמַר shāmar (8490), Protect, stand guard (Prv 3:26).
תָּמַךְ tāmakh (8881), Take hold of, grasp (Prv 5:5, 11:16).
תָּפַשׂ tāphas (8945), Piel: catch (Prv 30:28 [24:63]).

1. ἐρείσασα ereisasa nom sing fem part aor act

1 ran the ship aground; and the forepart **stuck fast,**...Acts 27:41

The verb *ereidō* means "to strike firmly against something" causing it to jam fast. The only New Testament usage describes what happened to the bow of a ship driven ashore (Acts 27:41).

STRONG 2043, BAUER 308, MOULTON-MILLIGAN 253, LIDDELL-SCOTT 684-85.

2027. ἐρεύγομαι ereugomai verb
Speak aloud or utter, proclaim.
SYNONYMS:
ἀγγέλλω angellō (31B)
ἀναγγέλλω anangellō (310)
ἀνατίθημι anatithēmi (392)
ἀπαγγέλλω apangellō (514)
ἀποδείκνυμι apodeiknumi (579)
ἀποκρίνω apokrinō (605B)
διαλέγομαι dialegomai (1250)
διηγέομαι diēgeomai (1328)
ἐκδιηγέομαι ekdiēgeomai (1542)
ἐξηγέομαι exēgeomai (1817)
ἑρμηνεύω hermēneuō (2043)
καταγγέλλω katangellō (2576)
κηρύσσω kērussō (2756)
κραυγάζω kraugazō (2878)
λαλέω laleō (2953)
λέγω legō (2978)
ὁμιλέω homileō (3519)
φθέγγομαι phthengomai (5187)

נָבַע nāva' (5218), Hiphil: pour out (Ps 19:2 [18:2]).
שָׁאַג shā'agh (8057), Roar (Hos 11:10, Am 3:4,8).
שֶׁרֶץ sherets (8651), Swarming things, tiny water life (Lv 11:10).

1. ἐρεύξομαι ereuxomai 1sing indic fut mid

1 **I will utter** things which have been kept secret..... Matt 13:35

During the Koine period the word *ereugomai* simply meant "to tell, speak," or "proclaim."

The earlier usage of the word was, however, much more forceful—"to belch, to vomit," or "to spew out of the mouth" (of an oxen or other animal). *Ereugomai* is found once in the New Testament, at Matthew 13:35, where Jesus said He was fulfilling Psalm 78:2. No trace of the early usage can be detected here.

STRONG 2044, BAUER 308, MOULTON-MILLIGAN 253, LIDDELL-SCOTT 686.

2028. ἐρευνάω ereunaō verb
Search or examine.

בָּקַשׁ bāqash (1272), Piel: seek, look for (Jgs 6:29).

חָפַשׂ chāphas (2769), Qal: search out, check (Prv 20:27); piel: look, track (Gn 31:35, 1 Kgs 20:6 [21:6], 2 Kgs 10:23).

חָקַר chāqar (2811), Spy out (2 Sm 10:3).

חָשַׂף chāsaph (2911), Strip the bark from (Jl 1:7).

מָשַׁשׁ māshash (5135), Piel: feel through, rummage through (Gn 31:37).

סָלַל sālal (5744), Pile up (Jer 50:26 [27:26]).

שָׁאַל shā'al (8068), Ask, investigate (Dt 13:14).

1. ἐρευνᾷ ereuna 3sing indic pres act
2. ἐρευνᾶτε ereunate 2pl impr pres act
3. ἐρευνῶν ereunōn nom sing masc part pres act
4. ἐρευνῶντες ereunōntes nom pl masc part pres act
5. ἐρεύνησον ereunēson 2sing impr aor act

2	Search the scriptures;	John 5:39
5	Art thou also of Galilee? Search, and look:	7:52
3	And he that searcheth the hearts knoweth	Rom 8:27
1	for the Spirit searcheth all things,	1 Co 2:10
4	Searching what, or what manner of time	1 Pt 1:11
3	that I am he which searcheth the reins and hearts:	Rev 2:23

The term *ereunaō*, occurring several times in the *Textus Receptus* (cf. John 5:39; Romans 8:27; Revelation 2:23), is the classical form of the word *eraunaō* (2020B). Its basic meaning is "to search diligently." The thought in John 5:39 is to not only read the Scriptures but thoroughly and thoughtfully investigate them. A prior meaning of the word dealt with the act of animals sniffing out or tracking down their prey (see *Liddell-Scott*).

STRONG 2045, BAUER 308, KITTEL 2:655-57, LIDDELL-SCOTT 686, COLIN BROWN 2:856.

2029. ἐρέω ereō verb
Say or speak.

1. εἴρηκα eirēka 1sing indic perf act
2. εἴρηκας eirēkas 2sing indic perf act
3. εἴρηκεν eirēken 3sing indic perf act
4. εἰρήκατε eirēkate 2pl indic perf act
5. εἰρήκασιν eirēkasin 3pl indic perf act
6. εἴρηκαν eirēkan 3pl indic perf act
7. εἰρήκει eirēkei 3sing indic plperf act
8. εἰρηκότος eirēkotos gen sing masc part perf act
9. ἐρῶ erō 1sing indic fut act
10. ἐρεῖς ereis 2sing indic fut act
11. ἐρεῖ erei 3sing indic fut act
12. ἐροῦμεν eroumen 1pl indic fut act
13. ἐρεῖτε ereite 2pl indic fut act
14. ἐροῦσιν erousin 3pl indic fut act
15. εἴρηται cirētai 3sing indic perf mid
16. εἰρημένον eirēmenon nom/acc sing neu part perf mid
17. εἰρηκέναι eirēkenai inf perf act

10	Or how wilt thou say to thy brother,	Matt 7:4
14	Many will say to me in that day, Lord, Lord,	7:22
9	and in the time of harvest I will say to the reapers,	13:30
13	ye shall say unto this mountain,	17:20
13	ye shall say, The Lord hath need of them;	21:3
9	I in like wise will tell you by what authority I do	21:24
11	If we shall say, From heaven; he will say unto us,	21:25
11	shall the King say unto them on his right hand,	25:34
11	And the King shall answer and say unto them,	25:40
11	Then shall he say also unto them on the left hand,	25:41
8	remembered the word ... which said unto him,	26:75
9	I will tell you by what authority I do these things.	Mark 11:29
11	he will say, Why then did ye not believe him?	11:31
16	to offer a sacrifice according to that which is said	Luke 2:24
15	And Jesus answering said unto him, It is said,	4:12
13	Ye will surely say unto me this proverb, Physician,	4:23
11	And whosoever shall speak a word against the Son	12:10
9	And I will say to my soul, Soul, thou hast much	12:19
11	and he shall answer and say unto you,	13:25
11	But he shall say, I tell you, I know you not	13:27
11	he that bade thee and him come and say to thee,	14:9
11	he may say to you, 'Friend, move up (NASB)	14:10
9	and will say unto him, Father, I have sinned,	15:18
11	having a servant ... will say unto him by and by,	17:7
11	And will not rather say unto him,	17:8
14	Neither shall they say, Lo here! or, lo there!	17:21
14	And they shall say to you, See here; or, see there;	17:23
13	Why do ye loose him? thus shall ye say unto him,	19:31
11	he will say, Why then believed ye him not?	20:5
13	And ye shall say unto the goodman of the house,	22:11
3	they went, and found as he had said unto them:	22:13
7	they went, and found as he had said unto them:	22:13
14	the days are coming, in the which they shall say,	23:29
2	is not thy husband: in that saidst thou truly.	John 4:18
1	And he said, Therefore said I unto you,	6:65
7	Howbeit Jesus spake of his death:	11:13
3	even as the Father said unto me, so I speak.	12:50
1	And now I have told you before it come to pass,	14:29
1	but I have called you friends;	15:15
16	this is that which was spoken by the prophet Joel;	Acts 2:16
4	these things which ye have spoken come upon me.	8:24
3	he said on this wise,	13:34
16	which is spoken of in the prophets;	13:40
5	as certain also of your own poets have said,	17:28
7	Sorrowing ... for the words which he spake,	20:38
10	Thou shalt not speak evil of the ruler of thy people.	23:5
12	what shall we say? Is God unrighteous	Rom 3:5
12	What shall we say then that Abraham our father,	4:1
16	according to that which was spoken,	4:18
12	What shall we say then? Shall we continue in sin,	6:1
12	What shall we say then? is the law sin?	7:7
12	What shall we then say to these things?	8:31
12	What shall we say then? Is there unrighteousness	9:14
10	wilt say then unto me, Why doth he yet find fault?	9:19

11 Shall the thing formed say to him that formed it,...	Rom 9:20
12 What shall we say then? That the Gentiles,...........	9:30
10 Thou wilt say then, The branches were broken off,...	11:19
11 the unlearned say Amen at thy giving of thanks,..	1 Co 14:16
14 or unbelievers, will they not say that ye are mad?....	14:23
11 some man will say, How are the dead raised up?.....	15:35
9 for I will say the truth: but now I forbear,.........	2 Co 12:6
3 he said unto me, My grace is sufficient for thee:......	12:9
9 and again I say, Rejoice.........................	Phlp 4:4
3 But to which of the angels said he at any time,.....	Heb 1:13
3 as he said, As I have sworn in my wrath,............	4:3
3 For he spake in a certain place of the seventh day.....	4:4
15 as it is said, To day if ye will hear his voice,........	4:7
3 Then said he, Lo, I come to do thy will, O God......	10:9
17 for after saying, (NASB)............................	10:15
3 for he hath said, I will never leave thee,.............	13:5
11 a man may say, Thou hast faith, and I have works:..	Jas 2:18
1 And I said unto him, Sir, thou knowest.............	Rev 7:14
9 I will tell thee the mystery of the woman,...........	17:7
6 again they said, Alleluia. And her smoke rose up.....	19:3

This word occurs over 50 times in the New Testament. Various forms of this verb—"will say, shall say, have said"—indicate not just speaking of words; rather, they indicate that the forcefulness of the speaker is emerging in a command, affirmation, or objection (Mark 17:20; Luke 2:24; Acts 2:16; Hebrews 4:7). The speaker is not only verbalizing a thought but emphasizing it as well (Luke 13:27; John 11:13; Hebrews 13:5). It is used as the future tense for *legō* (2978) and *eipon* (1500) (Luke 12:10; Romans 9:14). (It is also sometimes listed as the future tense of the almost obsolete *eirō*.)

STRONG 2046, LIDDELL-SCOTT 686, COLIN BROWN 3:532.

2030. ἐρημία erēmia noun
Uninhabited place, desert, wilderness.
COGNATE:
  ἔρημος erēmos (2031)
SYNONYM:
  ἔρημος erēmos (2031)

חָרֵב chārēv (2817), Lie in ruins (Is 60:12).

חָרְבָּה chorbāh (2823), Waste (Ez 35:4).

שְׁמָמָה sh^emāmāh (8463), Desolation (Ez 35:9).

1. ἐρημίας erēmias gen sing fem
2. ἐρημίᾳ erēmia dat sing fem
3. ἐρημίαις erēmiais dat pl fem

2 so much bread in the **wilderness**,.................	Matt 15:33
1 satisfy these ... with bread here in the **wilderness**?..	Mark 8:4
2 in perils in the city, in perils in the **wilderness**,.....	2 Co 11:26
3 they wandered in **deserts**, and in mountains,......	Heb 11:38

The word *erēmia* describes an uninhabited place or region, not necessarily incapable of supporting life, but one that is sparsely, if at all, populated. It may also denote an area that was inhabited at one time, but has been laid to waste or abandoned. It is used only a few times in the Septuagint, usually to translate the Hebrew term *chārēv*, meaning "dry, waste, desolate" (Isaiah 60:12; Ezekiel 35:4). Matthew 15:33 translates *erēmia* "wilderness."

STRONG 2047, BAUER 308-9, MOULTON-MILLIGAN 253, KITTEL 2:657-59, LIDDELL-SCOTT 686, COLIN BROWN 3:1004,1007.

2031. ἔρημος erēmos noun
Desert, wilderness, grassland, desolate.
COGNATES:
  ἐρημία erēmia (2030)
  ἔρημος erēmos (2032)
  ἐρημόω erēmoō (2033)
  ἐρήμωσις erēmōsis (2034)
SYNONYM:
  ἐρημία erēmia (2030)

בָּמָה bāmāh (1154), Heights (Ez 36:2).

חָרְבָּה chorbāh (2823), Waste, ruins (Lv 26:31, Ezr 9:9, Is 5:17).

יְשִׁימוֹן y^eshîmôn (3574), Desert, wilderness (Nm 23:28).

מִדְבָּר midhbār (4198), Pasturage, wilderness, desert (Ex 3:1, 1 Kgs 2:34, Jer 22:6).

מוֹרָשׁ môrāsh (4313), Possession, inheritance (Is 14:23).

נֶגֶב neghev (5221), Negeb, desert land (Gn 12:9, Nm 13:17 [13:18], Is 21:1).

עֲרָבָה 'ărāvāh (6400), Desert, steppe (Jb 39:6, Is 35:1, Zec 14:10).

שַׁמָּה shammāh (8439), What is horrible, devastation (Is 24:12, Jer 2:15).

שְׁמָמָה shim^emāh (8464), Desolation (Ez 35:7).

תֹּהוּ tōhû (8744), Emptiness (Is 34:11).

1. ἐρήμου erēmou gen sing fem
2. ἐρήμῳ erēmō dat sing fem
3. ἔρημον erēmon acc sing fem
4. ἐρήμοις erēmois dat pl fem
5. ἐρήμους erēmous acc pl fem

2 John ... preaching in the **wilderness** of Judaea,......	Matt 3:1
2 The voice of one crying in the **wilderness**,.............	3:3
3 was Jesus led up of the Spirit into the **wilderness**.......	4:1
3 What went ye out into the **wilderness** to see?..........	11:7
2 Behold, he is in the **desert**; go not forth:.............	24:26
2 The voice of one crying in the **wilderness**,............	Mark 1:3
2 John did baptize in the **wilderness**,.....................	1:4
3 the Spirit driveth him into the **wilderness**...............	1:12
2 And he was there in the **wilderness** forty days,........	1:13
3 and was led by the Spirit into the **wilderness**,........	Luke 4:1
5 and was driven of the devil into the **wilderness**.......	8:29
2 I am the voice of one crying in the **wilderness**,......	John 1:23
2 as Moses lifted up the serpent in the **wilderness**,.....	3:14
2 Our fathers did eat manna in the **desert**;..............	6:31
2 Your fathers did eat manna in the **wilderness**,.........	6:49
1 went thence unto a country near to the **wilderness**,....	11:54
2 in the **wilderness** of mount Sina an angel............	Acts 7:30
2 in the Red sea, and in the **wilderness** forty years.......	7:36
2 that was in the church in the **wilderness**................	7:38
2 by the space of forty years in the **wilderness**?..........	7:42

2 had the tabernacle of witness in the **wilderness**,	Acts 7:44
2 suffered he their manners in the **wilderness**.	13:18
3 and leddest out into the **wilderness** four thousand	21:38
2 for they were overthrown in the **wilderness**.	1 Co 10:5
2 in the day of temptation in the **wilderness**:	Heb 3:8
2 whose carcases fell in the **wilderness**?	3:17
3 And the woman fled into the **wilderness**,	Rev 12:6
3 she might fly into the **wilderness**, into her place,	12:14
3 carried me away in the spirit into the **wilderness**:	17:3

Classical Greek and Septuagint Usage

Appearing from Homer (Eighth or Seventh Century B.C.) on, the substantive *eremos* occurs numerous times in the Septuagint. The adjective means "solitary, lonely, deserted." Hence as a substantive, *eremos* refers to "a place which is deserted, a solitary place, wilderness." It is used of wilderness or grassland as opposed to cultivated and inhabited land.

New Testament Usage

Eremos occurs many times in the New Testament, especially in the Gospels and Acts. It often refers to the barren wilderness of Judea (Matthew 3:1) and also to the wilderness of Sinai (John 3:14; Acts 7:30). John used the term in Revelation to speak of the place to which Israel will flee for providential protection during the Great Tribulation (12:6,14) and as the setting of his vision of the woman on the scarlet beast (17:3).

STRONG 2048, BAUER 309, KITTEL 2:657-59, LIDDELL-SCOTT 687.

2032. ἔρημος erēmos adj

Desolate, abandoned, desert, solitary (place).

CROSS-REFERENCE:
ἔρημος erēmos (2031)

חָרֵב chārēv (2818), Waste, desolate (Neh 2:17, Jer 33:10 [40:10], Ez 36:35).

חֹרֶב chōrev (2821), Devastation (Is 61:4).

חָרָבָה chārāvāh (2824), Dry land (2 Kgs 2:8, Ez 30:12).

כָּחַד kāchadh (3701), Niphal: be destroyed, be effaced (Jb 15:28).

מְשַׁמָּה mᵉshammāh (5103), Desert, desolation (Is 15:6).

צִיָּה tsîyāh (6993), Dry country, waterless region (Ps 63:1 [62:1]).

שָׁמֵם shāmēm (8460), Be desolated, be deserted (Ez 35:12).

שָׁמֵם shāmēm (8462), Desolate, deserted (Dn 9:17).

שְׁמָמָה shᵉmāmāh (8463), Desolate (Ex 23:29, Is 17:9, Ez 35:15).

1. ἔρημος erēmos nom sing masc/fem
2. ἐρήμῳ erēmō dat sing masc/fem
3. ἔρημον erēmon acc sing masc/fem
4. ἐρήμοις erēmois dat pl masc/fem
5. ἐρήμου erēmou gen sing fem

3 departed thence by ship into **a desert** place apart:	Matt 14:13
1 This is a **desert** place, and the time is now past;	14:15
1 Behold, your house is left unto you **desolate**.	23:38
3 departed into a **solitary** place, and there prayed.	Mark 1:35
4 but was without in **desert** places:	1:45
3 Come ye yourselves apart into a **desert** place,	6:31
3 they departed into a **desert** place by ship privately.	6:32
1 This is a **desert** place,	6:35
4 and was in the **deserts** till the day of his showing	Luke 1:80
2 unto John the son of Zacharias in the **wilderness**.	3:2
2 The voice of one crying in the **wilderness**,	3:4
3 by the Spirit in the **wilderness** (NASB)	4:1
3 he departed and went into **a desert** place:	4:42
4 And he withdrew himself into the **wilderness**,	5:16
3 What went ye out into the **wilderness** for to see?	7:24
3 and went aside privately into a **desert** place	9:10
2 and get victuals: for we are here in a **desert** place.	9:12
1 Behold, your house is left unto you **desolate**:	13:35
2 not leave the ninety and nine in the **wilderness**,	15:4
1 Let his habitation be **desolate**,	Acts 1:20
1 down from Jerusalem unto Gaza, which is **desert**.	8:26
5 for the **desolate** hath many more children than she	Gal 4:27

Classical Greek and Septuagint Usage

The word *eremos* is properly an adjective, but it may also be used as a noun. In classical Greek it is primarily used as an adjective meaning "desolate, lonely," or "solitary." *Eremos* may describe places which have been abandoned or which have very few if any inhabitants. It may describe persons or animals. When *eremos* is used of human beings, it frequently refers to poor, friendless persons. It may also modify words pertaining to court decisions where one party does not appear and the other party wins by default.

In the papyri *eremos* describes a village which has been deserted as well as a beach which is desertlike. It is also used in the legal sense of "default" when one party fails to appear (see *Moulton-Milligan*). The Septuagint almost always uses *eremos* as a noun meaning "desert" or "wilderness." But it may be used as an adjective meaning "desolate" (Nehemiah 2:17).

New Testament Usage

In the New Testament *eremos*, when used as an adjective, normally describes places which are "abandoned, desolate," or "unpopulated." In Matthew 14:13 Jesus probably went into a lonely or solitary place rather than a desert place. In Matthew 23:38 *eremos* describes the word house: "Your house is left . . . desolate." This could refer back to God's warnings in the Old Testament of leaving the temple in "ruin" (Jeremiah 22:5 [LXX 22:6]), meaning worthless and uninhabited, as a punishment for disobedience (cf. 1 Kings 9:7,8 [LXX 3 Kings 9:7,8]). In Galatians 4:27 it describes a woman.

A desolate woman in this passage means one who is childless, not one who has been deserted by her husband.

STRONG 2048, BAUER 309, MOULTON-MILLIGAN 253-54, LIDDELL-SCOTT 687, COLIN BROWN 3:1004,1007.

2033. ἐρημόω erēmoō verb
Lay waste, depopulate, make desolate.
CROSS-REFERENCE:
ἔρημος erēmos (2031)

בָּלַק bālaq (1149), Devastate (Is 24:1).

חָרֵב chārēv (2817), Qal: dry up, lie in ruins (Is 34:10); niphal: be laid in ruins (Ez 26:19); pual: be dried (Jgs 16:7—Codex Alexandrinus only); hiphil: dry up, make desolate, lay in ruins (2 Kgs 19:17, Is 37:18, Jer 51:36 [28:36]); hophal: be devastated, be made desolate (Ez 26:2).

חָרֵב chārēv (2818), Desolate (Neh 2:3).

חֲרַב chărav (A2819), Hophal: be devastated, be destroyed (Ezr 4:15—Aramaic).

חָרְבָּה chorbāh (2823), Waste (Ez 33:24, 38:12).

חָרַם chāram (2868), Hiphil: split, dry up (Is 11:15).

מְשַׁמָּה meshammāh (5103), Desert, desolation (Ez 33:29, 35:3).

שָׁאָה shā'āh (8059), Lie desolate (Is 6:11).

שָׁבַר shāvar (8132), Break, break down; niphal: be broken down (Is 24:10).

שָׁלַךְ shālakh (8390), Throw down; hophal: be thrown down (Dn 8:11).

שָׁמַד shāmadh (8436), Hiphil: exterminate (Lv 26:30).

שָׁמֵם shāmēm (8460), Qal: be deserted, be desolated (Ez 33:28); niphal: be made desolate (Lv 26:22, Ps 69:25 [68:25], Is 33:8); hiphil: make deserted, be made desolate (Ps 79:7 [78:7]); hophal: desolation (Lv 26:43).

שְׁמָמָה shemāmāh (8463), Desolation (Is 1:7, Ez 35:7).

1. ἐρημοῦται erēmoutai 3sing indic pres mid
2. ἠρημώθη erēmōthē 3sing indic aor pass
3. ἠρημωμένην erēmōmenēn
   acc sing fem part perf mid

1 kingdom divided ... is brought to desolation;	Matt 12:25
1 divided against itself is brought to desolation;	Luke 11:17
3 the whore, and shall make her desolate and naked,	Rev 17:16
2 For in one hour so great riches is come to nought......	18:17
2 for in one hour is she made desolate...................	18:19

The word *erēmoō* refers to the act which causes a place to become desolate or wasteful. It also expresses the idea of abandonment, desertion, or loneliness. In Matthew 12:25 Jesus spoke of a kingdom ravaged by civil war—the results are depopulation and loss of wealth (cf. Revelation 18:17; see also *Bauer*).

STRONG 2049, BAUER 309, MOULTON-MILLIGAN 254, KITTEL 2:657-59, LIDDELL-SCOTT 687, COLIN BROWN 3:1004-8.

2034. ἐρήμωσις erēmōsis noun
Desolation, devastation, destruction.
CROSS-REFERENCE:
ἔρημος erēmos (2031)

חָרְבָּה chorbāh (2823), Place of ruin, waste (Jer 7:34, 25:18 [32:18], 44:6 [51:6]).

שַׁמָּה shammāh (8439), What is horrible, horror (2 Chr 30:7, Ps 73:19 [72:19]).

שָׁמֵם shāmēm (8460), Qal: be deserted, be desolated (Dn 8:13, 9:18, 12:11); polel: desolate, destroy (Dn 11:31); hophal: desolation (Lv 26:34,35).

1. ἐρήμωσις erēmōsis nom sing fem
2. ἐρημώσεως erēmōseōs gen sing fem

2 therefore shall see the abomination of desolation,..	Matt 24:15
2 when ye shall see the abomination of desolation,...	Mark 13:14
1 then know that the desolation thereof is nigh.......	Luke 21:20

The term *erēmōsis* generally describes the state of being alone or abandoned. It is used several times in the Septuagint to translate forms of the Hebrew terms *chorbāh* or *shāmēm*, both meaning "desolate, deserted." One very notable exception is the Septuagint version of Daniel 12:11 where the phrase *to Bdelugma tēs erēmōseōs*, "the abomination of desolation," appears. In Daniel 12:11 the Hebrew appears to signify "the abomination which causes (spiritual) desolation" (Beasley-Murray, "Abomination of Desolation," *Colin Brown*, 1:74ff.).

Two of the three New Testament occurrences of *erēmōsis* are the use of that same phrase "the abomination of desolation" (Matthew 24:15; Mark 13:14). Although there is much controversy over the specificity of who or what that phrase refers to, it is safe to say Jesus used the term in foretelling the desecration and ultimate destruction of the temple and the city of Jerusalem. Jesus viewed this destruction in the light of the coming Day of the Lord, as did the Old Testament prophets before Him.

STRONG 2050, BAUER 309, KITTEL 2:660, LIDDELL-SCOTT 687, COLIN BROWN 3:1004-8.

2035. ἐρίζω erizō verb
Quarrel or cry against, strive.

ἐριθεία 2036

גָּרָה gārâh (1667), Hithpael: venture into struggle (2 Kgs 14:10).

מָרָה mārâh (4947), Be refractory, be obstinate (1 Sm 12:14,15).

1. ἐρίσει erisei 3sing indic fut act

1 He shall not strive, nor cry;..................... Matt 12:19

From the word *eris* (2038), *erizō* means "strife, contention," and refers to quarreling, wrangling, or debating. It occurs only once in the New Testament, in Matthew 12:19, as the fulfillment of Isaiah's prophecy that God's Servant, the Messiah, would not *strive*.

STRONG 2051, BAUER 309, MOULTON-MILLIGAN 254, LIDDELL-SCOTT 687-88.

2036. ἐριθεία eritheia noun

Strife, selfish ambition.

COGNATE:
 ἔρις eris (2038)
SYNONYMS:
 ἔρις eris (2038)
 μάχη machē (3135)
 στάσις stasis (4565)
 φιλονεικία philoneikia (5216)

1. ἐριθεία eritheia nom sing fem
2. ἐριθείας eritheias gen sing fem
3. ἐριθείαν eritheian acc sing fem
4. ἐριθείαι eritheiai nom pl fem

2 But unto them that are **contentious**,................ Rom 2:8
4 lest there be debates, envyings, wraths, **strifes**,..... 2 Co 12:20
4 emulations, wrath, **strife**, seditions, heresies,.......... Gal 5:20
2 The one preach Christ of **contention**, not sincerely,.. Phlp 1:16
3 Let nothing be done through **strife** or vainglory;........ 2:3
3 if ye have bitter envying and **strife** in your hearts,.... Jas 3:14
1 For where envying and **strife** is,...................... 3:16

Classical Greek

Bauer notes that *eritheia* (also spelled *erithia*) is found antecedent to New Testament times only in Aristotle "where it denotes a self-seeking pursuit of political office by unfair means." *Moulton-Milligan*, basing its conclusions on the evidence of later papyri, contends that "selfish" rather than "factious"—a translation often encountered (e.g., Romans 2:8: "contentious" [KJV]; "factious" [RSV]; cf. NEB, GNB, NIV)—is preferred. Nonetheless, *Bauer* does not rule out "strife or contentiousness" since the context may include *eris* (2038), "discord," at one time considered the source of derivation for *eritheia*. One need not demand consistency.

New Testament Usage

Of its seven appearances in the Greek New Testament five are Pauline and two occur in James. The context of Romans favors reading *eritheia* as "self-seeking" in contrast to those seeking glory, honor, and immortality (2:7f.). The proximity of Philippians 1:15 ("some indeed preach Christ even of envy and strife") also favors the idea of "selfish ambition" (1:17, NIV), meaning that some were even preaching with wrong motives out of a sense of competition with Paul. In both the sin lists of Galatians (5:20) and 2 Corinthians (12:20), given the larger context of each letter, "strife" might be preferred, but again it is strife motivated by personal selfishness.

James' two texts (3:14,16) are more ambiguous. But here too the selfish ambition coalesces with strife to produce "party spirit" which stands over against peace. As James sees it, the struggle is basically internal.

STRONG 2052, BAUER 309, MOULTON-MILLIGAN 254, KITTEL 2:660-61, LIDDELL-SCOTT 688.

2037. ἔριον erion noun

Wool.

עֲמַר ʻămar (A6241), Wool (Dn 7:9—Aramaic).

צֶמֶר tsemer (7055), Wool (Ps 147:16 [147:5], Is 1:18, Ez 34:3).

1. ἔριον erion nom/acc sing neu
2. ἐρίου eriou gen sing neu

2 with water, and scarlet **wool**, and hyssop,........... Heb 9:19
1 His head and his hairs were white like **wool**,........ Rev 1:14

Throughout classical, Septuagintal, and New Testament periods the word *erion* denoted "wool." Wool is thought of as one of the riches of the Orient. Of its two occurrences in the New Testament, Hebrews 9:19 is an example of a literal reference to "wool," while Revelation 1:14 uses it metaphorically to describe Jesus' head and hair as "white like wool" (cf. Daniel 7:9; Isaiah 1:18). This description suggests wisdom and dignity (see Leviticus 19:32; Proverbs 16:31) as well as the purity of the "son of man."

STRONG 2053, BAUER 309, MOULTON-MILLIGAN 254, LIDDELL-SCOTT 688-89.

2038. ἔρις eris noun

Strife, discord, contention, quarrels.

COGNATE:
 ἐριθεία eritheia (2036)
SYNONYMS:
 ἐριθεία eritheia (2036)
 μάχη machē (3135)

στάσις stasis (4565)
φιλονεικία philoneikia (5216)

מָרָה mārâh (4947), Be refractory, be obstinate (Ps 139:20 [138:20]).

רִיב rîv (7663), Dispute, strife (Sir 40:5).

1. ἔρις eris nom sing fem
2. ἔριδος eridos gen sing fem
3. ἔριδι eridi dat sing fem
4. ἔριν erin acc sing fem
5. ἔρεις ereis nom/acc pl fem
6. ἔριδες erides nom pl fem

2 full of envy, murder, **debate**, deceit, malignity;	Rom 1:29
3 not in **strife** and envying.	13:13
6 that there are **contentions** among you.	1 Co 1:11
1 for whereas there is among you envying, and **strife**,	3:3
5 lest there be **debates**, envyings, wraths, strifes,	2 Co 12:20
1 lest there be **debates**, envyings, wraths, strifes,	12:20
5 Idolatry, witchcraft, hatred, **variance**, emulations,	Gal 5:20
1 Idolatry, witchcraft, hatred, **variance**, emulations,	5:20
4 Some ... preach Christ even of envy and **strife**;	Phlp 1:15
1 whereof cometh envy, **strife**, railings,	1 Tm 6:4
5 whereof cometh envy, **strife**, railings,	6:4
5 and contentions, and **strivings** about the law;	Tit 3:9
4 and contentions, and **strivings** about the law;	3:9

Classical Greek

In classical writings *eris* refers to "strife, contention," or "quarrels" which may be expressed in battle (cf. Josephus *Antiquities* 14.16.1) or in rivalry. Positively *eris* could be "zeal" for something good or noble. As a proper name Eris was a goddess, the sister of Ares, the god of war (see *Liddell-Scott*).

Septuagint Usage

The single canonical occurrence of *eris* in the Septuagint is in Psalm 139:20 (LXX 138:20). The Hebrew behind it is uncertain, but it may be *mārâh*, "to be obstinate." The RSV translates the verse (according to the Hebrew) "men who maliciously defy thee (God)." Three instances of *eris* in the apocryphal Sirach are all in accord with the classical usage of "strife, discord" (e.g., 28:11; 40:5,9).

New Testament Usage

Eris is exclusively a Pauline expression in the New Testament (nine times) and always denotes something negative. Often it conjoins other crimes that are typical of rebellion against God (Romans 1:29; cf. Galatians 5:20) or against society in general (Romans 13:13). It especially falls in "lists" of sins which depict the activity of false members of the community of faith (2 Corinthians 12:20; 1 Timothy 6:4; cf. Titus 3:9; Philippians 1:15). Here too the classical sense is maintained; *eris* means "strife, discord," or "contention."

STRONG 2054, BAUER 309, MOULTON-MILLIGAN 254, LIDDELL-SCOTT 689.

2039. ἐρίφιον eriphion noun

Kid or goat.

1. ἐρίφια eriphia nom/acc pl neu

1 sheep on his right hand, but the **goats** on the left...	Matt 25:33

This word is derived from *eriphos* (2040) which also means "kid" or "he-goat." Use of this derivative in Matthew 25:33 suggests contempt for those described as the goats. They represent the "wicked" in this scene of final judgment, while the sheep represent the "righteous." This separation of sheep and goats reflected the normal practice in Palestine. While it was not unusual for both sheep and goats to graze together, they were usually herded into separate folds at the end of the day (see Day, "Goats," *International Standard Bible Encyclopedia*, 2:492).

STRONG 2055, BAUER 309, MOULTON-MILLIGAN 254, LIDDELL-SCOTT 689, COLIN BROWN 1:114.

2040. ἔριφος eriphos noun

Kid or goat.

גְּדִי gᵉdhî (1454), Kid, young animal (Gn 38:17, Jgs 6:19, S/S 1:8).

כַּר kar (3861), Young ram (Am 6:4).

עֵז ʿēz (6008), Goat (Gn 27:9).

עַתּוּד ʿattûdh (6500), Ram, he-goat (Jer 51:40 [28:40]).

שָׂעִיר sāʿîr (7988), He-goat (Gn 37:31, Ez 43:25, 45:23).

1. ἔριφον eriphon acc sing masc
2. ἐρίφων eriphōn gen pl masc

2 as a shepherd divideth his sheep from the **goats**:	Matt 25:32
1 and yet thou never gavest me **a kid**,	Luke 15:29

The goat was a comparatively worthless animal in New Testament times. Its main value was its use in sacrifices and for feasts. Its use in Luke 15:29, where the prodigal's elder brother bemoaned the fact that he never received even a kid, which was a cheaper food than beef, reveals the relative value of the goat. (See also *tragos* [4970].) In the Old Testament goats may have been an important part of an utilitarian economy, but in the New Testament even the wearing of goatskins was considered a sign of extreme poverty (cf. Hebrews 11:37).

STRONG 2056, BAUER 309, LIDDELL-SCOTT 689, COLIN BROWN 1:114.

2041. Ἑρμᾶς Hermas name

Hermas.

ἑρμηνεία 2042

1. Ἑρμᾶν Herman acc masc

1 Salute Asyncritus, Phlegon, **Hermas**, Patrobas,..... Rom 16:14
1 **Hermas** and the brethren with them (NASB).......... 16:14

Recipient of a greeting from Paul (Romans 16:14).

2042. ἑρμηνεία hermēneia noun
Interpretation, translation.
Cognate:
  ἑρμηνεύω hermēneuō (2043)
Synonym:
  ἐπίλυσις epilusis (1940)

1. ἑρμηνεία hermēneia nom sing fem
2. ἑρμηνείαν hermēneian acc sing fem

1 to another the **interpretation** of tongues:.......... 1 Co 12:10
2 hath a revelation, hath an **interpretation**.............. 14:26

This term denotes the interpretation of words in a different language. Another derivation, Hermes (see 2044), is the Greek name for the pagan god Mercury who was heralded as the messenger of the gods. It is used in 1 Corinthians 14:26 to teach the importance of disciplined interpretation of speaking in tongues. It also occurs in 1 Corinthians 12:10 as one of the manifestations of the Holy Spirit. The meaning of this word carries with it more than the cognitive task of literal translation; implicit in the "interpretation" is the idea of "explanation." This idea can further be seen in the development of *hermēneia* in the modern Greek Velvendos dialect where *hormēnia* means "counsel, advice" (see *Moulton-Milligan*).

Strong 2058, Bauer 310, Moulton-Milligan 254, Kittel 2:661-66, Liddell-Scott 690, Colin Brown 1:579-82,584.

2043. ἑρμηνεύω hermēneuō verb
Explain, translate, interpret.
Cognates:
  διερμηνευτής diermēneutēs (1322)
  διερμηνεύω diermēneuō (1323)
  δυσερμήνευτος dusermēneutos (1414)
  ἑρμηνεία hermēneia (2042)
  μεθερμηνεύω methermēneuō (3148)
Synonyms:
  δείκνυμι deiknumi (1161)
  διερμηνεύω diermēneuō (1323)
  διηγέομαι diēgeomai (1328)
  ἐμφανίζω emphanizō (1702)
  ἐξηγέομαι exēgeomai (1817)
  μεθερμηνεύω methermēneuō (3148)
  ὁρίζω horizō (3587)
  φράζω phrazō (5255)

תִּרְגֵּם tirgēm (8975), Translate (Ezr 4:7).

1. ἑρμηνεύεται hermēneuetai 3sing indic pres mid
2. ἑρμηνευόμενος hermēneuomenos
nom sing masc part pres mid
3. ἑρμηνευόμενον hermēneuomenon
nom/acc sing neu part pres mid

3 Rabbi, which is to say, **being interpreted**, Master,.... John 1:38
1 Cephas, which is **by interpretation**, A stone............. 1:42
1 which is **by interpretation**, Sent....................... 9:7
2 first being **by interpretation** King of righteousness,....Heb 7:2

Classical Greek and Septuagint Usage
The word *hermēneuō* comes from Hermes (see 2044), the name of the Greek god of communication. In classical Greek *hermēneuō* usually means to "translate" a foreign language into a language one can understand. It may also mean to "explain" or "interpret" a written or spoken communication, or even to "express" one's ideas in words. In the Septuagint the word means to "translate" a foreign language.

New Testament Usage
Hermēneuō occurs four times in the New Testament. Each time it is used in reference to translating a Hebrew or Aramaic word into Greek. This was usually done for the sake of the Gentile readers who did not know Hebrew or Armaic (Rabbi, John 1:38; Cephas, John 1:42; Siloam, John 9:7). In Hebrews 7:2 the author translates (or perhaps interprets) the name Melchizedek in order to draw a comparison with Christ. In Hebrew the name Melchizedek means "king of righteousness." Some manuscripts have *hermēneuō* in Luke 24:27 where it would mean "to explain" or "to expound." The English word *hermeneutics*, "the study of the methods and principles of (Bible) interpretation," is rooted in this Greek term.

Strong 2059, Bauer 310, Moulton-Milligan 254, Kittel 2:661-66, Liddell-Scott 690, Colin Brown 1:579-81,584.

2044. Ἑρμῆς Hermēs name
Hermes.

1. Ἑρμῆν Hermēn acc masc

1 called Barnabas, Jupiter; and Paul, **Mercurius**,...... Acts 14:12
1 Greet Asyncritus, Phlegon, **Hermes**, (NASB)........ Rom 16:14
1 **Hermes**, and the brethren which are with them......... 16:14

Hermēs was the name of a Greek god mentioned in Acts 14:12. He is not mentioned in the Septuagint, the Apocrypha, or pseudepigrapha. He corresponded to the Roman deity Mercury (*Mercurius*) and was identified with the planet Mercury. The term *Hermēs* provides the base for *hermēneuō* (2043), the

Greek word for "proclaim, interpret, translate" (cf. *hermeneutics*, the science of interpretation). The name originated from *herma*, a guidepost for travelers.

Hermes, half brother of Apollo and son of Zeus and Maia, was known primarily as the messenger of the gods; therefore as god of communication and eloquence he became the patron of orators. Known for trickery and cunning, he was god of gain and good luck and so became patron of both thieves and traders. A fertility god, his image appeared with phallic symbols on statues and doorposts of houses. As Psychopompos he guided the souls of the dead to Hades and was identified with the Egyptian god Thoth as revealer of immortality. His symbols were winged shoes (messenger), a purse (gain), and a golden rod which represented a shepherd's staff, a herald's staff, or magic powers.

When a plot was laid against the lives of Paul and Barnabas, on their first missionary tour, they fled from Iconium in Phrygia to Lystra in Lycaonia and began preaching there. After Paul healed a lifelong cripple, the inhabitants decided he and Barnabas were gods in the form of men. They called Barnabas Zeus and Paul Hermes "because he was the chief speaker" (Acts 14:8-12), obviously focusing on the primary role of Hermes. A local Lycaonian legend known from Ovid (*Metamorphoses* 8) has Zeus and his attendant appearing to a husband and wife in neighboring Phrygia. This couple, named Philemon and Baucis, were rewarded for entertaining them unawares.

F.F. Bruce cites a third-century inscription that contains Lycaonian names in connection with a statue of Hermes that was dedicated to Zeus, and a stone altar discovered near Lystra dedicated to the "Hearer of Prayer" and Hermes (*New International Commentary on the New Testament, Acts*, pp.274f.). Commentators have suggested that Paul's experience in Lystra provided the background for his statements in Galatians: "Though ... an angel (messenger) from heaven, preach any other gospel unto you than that which we have preached unto you, let him be accursed" (1:8); "Ye ... received me as an angel (messenger) of God" (4:14). The ancient deities of Lycaonia had by this time been assimilated into their Greek counterparts.

Hermēs was also the name of a man, otherwise unknown, that Paul mentioned once (Romans 16:14). He and four others had "brethren ... with them," implying that the group constituted a household church with Hermes as perhaps one of its five leaders. Slaves often had this name, so Hermes was possibly a slave like Onesimus (Colossians 4:9; Philemon 10), especially since a high percentage of Rome's inhabitants were slaves. Another of the five, called *Hermas*, the Doric form of the name, was considered by Origen to be the author of *The Shepherd of Hermes*. The same root appears also in the name *Hermogenēs* (2045), "born of Hermes," a man who "turned away from" Paul (2 Timothy 1:15).

STRONG 2060, BAUER 310, MOULTON-MILLIGAN 254-55, LIDDELL-SCOTT 690-91.

2045. Ἑρμογένης Hermogenēs name
Hermogenes.

1. Ἑρμογένης Hermogenēs nom masc

1 of whom are Phygellus and **Hermogenes**............ 2 Tm 1:15

One of the Christians in Asia who deserted Paul in his time of trouble (2 Timothy 1:15).

2046. ἑρπετόν herpeton noun
Snake, reptile.

SYNONYMS:
δράκων drakōn (1398)
ὄφις ophis (3653)

חַיָּה chayyāh (2516), Animals (Gn 1:28).
כַּר kar (3861), Ram (Is 16:1).
רִמָּה rimmāh (7704), Maggot (Sir 10:11).
רָמַשׂ rāmas (7718), Swarm, teem (Lv 20:25, Dt 4:18).
רֶמֶשׂ remes (7719), Small animals, reptiles (Gn 1:24ff., Ps 104:25 [103:25]).
שֶׁרֶץ sherets (8651), Swarming things (Gn 1:20, Lv 11:20,21, Dt 14:19).

1. ἑρπετά herpeta nom/acc pl neu
2. ἑρπετῶν herpetōn gen pl neu

1 and wild beasts, and **creeping things**,............... Acts 10:12
1 and wild beasts, and **creeping things**,.................. 11:6
2 and fourfooted beasts, and **creeping things**........... Rom 1:23
2 and **of serpents**, and of things in the sea, is tamed,... Jas 3:7

The word *herpeton* refers to a creeping creature. It is related to the word *herpō*, "to creep." Romans 1:23 includes creatures in a list of false gods. This is a reference to the serpent worship which was part of many pagan cults prior to and during New Testament times. (Also see Acts 10:12; 11:6; and James 3:7.)

Ἐρυθρά Θάλασσα 2047

Strong 2062, Bauer 310, Moulton-Milligan 255, Liddell-Scott 691.

2047. Ἐρυθρά Θάλασσα
Eruthra Thalassa name
Red sea.
1. Ἐρυθρᾷ Θαλάσσῃ Eruthra Thalassē dat fem
2. Ἐρυθράν Θάλασσαν Eruthran Thalassan acc fem

1 in the Red sea, and in the wilderness forty years..... Acts 7:36
2 By faith they passed through the Red sea.......... Heb 11:29

The site of miracles and faith where Israel escaped from Egypt (Acts 7:36; Hebrews 11:29).

2047B. ἐρυθρός eruthros
Red.

Eruthros is used to speak of the red color of wine, blood, or copper. It is also used in the name *Red* Sea (Acts 7:36; Hebrews 11:29). The origin of the root, *rudh*, "red," is uncertain. (See number 2047.)

Strong 2063, Bauer 310, Moulton-Milligan 255, Liddell-Scott 693.

2048. ἔρχομαι erchomai verb
Come, go (rare), appear.

Cognates:
ἀνέρχομαι anerchomai (422)
ἀντιπαρέρχομαι antiparerchomai (489)
ἀπέρχομαι aperchomai (562)
διεξέρχομαι diexerchomai (1320C)
διέρχομαι dierchomai (1324)
εἰσέρχομαι eiserchomai (1511)
ἔλευσις eleusis (1647)
ἐξέρχομαι exerchomai (1814)
ἐπανέρχομαι epanerchomai (1865)
ἐπεισέρχομαι epeiserchomai (1883B)
ἐπέρχομαι eperchomai (1889)
κατέρχομαι katerchomai (2687)
παρεισέρχομαι pareiserchomai (3784)
παρέρχομαι parerchomai (3790)
περιέρχομαι perierchomai (3885)
προέρχομαι proerchomai (4140)
προσέρχομαι proserchomai (4193)
συνεισέρχομαι suneiserchomai (4747)
συνέρχομαι sunerchomai (4755)

Synonyms:
διαπορεύω diaporeuō (1273)
διέρχομαι dierchomai (1324)
διοδεύω diodeuō (1347)
ἐπέρχομαι eperchomai (1889)
ἐφικνέομαι ephikneomai (2167)

ἥκω hēkō (2223)
καταντάω katantaō (2628)
παραγίνομαι paraginomai (3716)
παραπορεύομαι paraporeuomai (3760)
παρέρχομαι parerchomai (3790)
παρίστημι paristēmi (3798)
πορεύομαι poreuomai (4057)
προσέρχομαι proserchomai (4193)
φθάνω phthanō (5185)

אָחַז 'āchaz (270), Lay hold of, seize (Jb 18:9).

אֹרַח 'ōrach (758), Path, traveller (Jb 31:32).

אָתָה 'āthâh (885), Qal: come (Jb 3:25); hiphil: bring (Jer 12:9).

אֲתָה 'āthâh (A886), Come (Ezr 4:12, 5:3, Dn 3:2—Aramaic).

בּוֹא bô' (971), Qal: come, go (Gn 35:6, 1 Sm 7:1, Is 41:25); hiphil: bring (2 Chr 8:18, Ezr 8:18).

דֶּרֶךְ derekh (1932), Way, path (Prv 14:12).

הָיָה hāyâh (2030), Be, is (1 Kgs 8:18).

הָלַךְ hālakh (2050), Go, walk (Nm 22:16, 1 Chr 19:5, Ps 80:2 [79:2]).

הִנֵּה hinnêh (2079), Behold (1 Kgs 18:7).

חָבֵר chāvēr (2358), Comrade, companion (Jgs 20:11—Codex Alexandrinus only).

חָלַל chālal (2591), Profane; hiphil: begin (Jer 25:29 [32:29]—Codex Alexandrinus only).

יָאַשׁ yā'ash (3085), Niphal: despair of, desist from (1 Sm 27:1).

יָסַף yāsaph (3362), Hiphil: go on, do again (Prv 23:35).

יָפַע yāpha' (3423), Hiphil: let shine (Jb 3:4).

יָצָא yātsâ' (3428), Come out, go out (2 Kgs 2:3, 18:18, 2 Chr 21:19).

יָרַד yāradh (3495), Go down (1 Sm 29:4).

יָשַׁב yāshav (3553), Sit down (1 Sm 20:24).

לָקַח lāqach (4089), Receive (Jb 27:13).

מָבוֹא māvô' (4136), Entrance (1 Chr 4:39).

מוּל mûl (4272II) In front of, opposite (1 Sm 14:5—Codex Vaticanus only).

מַסַּע massa' (4702), Departure, day's marches (Gn 13:3).

נָדָה nādhâh (5255), Piel: believe something to be far away (Am 6:3).

נָפַל nāphal (5489), Fall on, attack (Jb 1:15, Is 9:8).

נָצַב nātsav (5507), Niphal: step up to, stand up to (Ex 5:20).

נָשָׁא nāshâ' (5565), Lend; hiphil: trick deceive (Ps 55:15 [54:15]).

עָבַר 'āvar (5882), Go by (Lv 27:32).

עָדָה 'ādhâh (5917), Walk (Jb 28:8—Codex Alexandrinus only).

עָלָה 'ālâh (6148), Go up, come up, sprout (Am 7:1).

עָרָה 'ārâh (6408), Niphal: be poured out (Is 32:15).

פָּגַע pāga' (6534), Reach (Jos 16:7).

ἔρχομαι 2048

קָבַץ qāvats (7192), Niphal: gather, assemble (1 Chr 11:1).
קָרֵב qārēv (7414), Draw near, approach (Jgs 19:13—Codex Alexandrinus only).
שׁוּב shûv (8178), Return (2 Chr 10:5).

1. ἦλθον ēlthon 1/3sing/pl indic aor act
2. ἦλθες ēlthes 2sing indic aor act
3. ἦλθεν ēlthen 3sing indic aor act
4. ἤλθομεν ēlthomen 1pl indic aor act
5. ἤλθετε ēlthete 2pl indic aor act
6. ἔλθω elthō 1sing subj aor act
7. ἔλθῃς elthēs 2sing subj aor act
8. ἔλθῃ elthē 3sing subj aor act
9. ἔλθωσιν elthōsin 3pl subj aor act
10. ἐλθέ elthe 2sing impr aor act
11. ἐλθέτω elthetō 3sing impr aor act
12. ἐλθόντα elthonta
    nom/acc sing/pl masc/neu part aor act
13. ἐλθών elthōn nom sing masc part aor act
14. ἐλθόντος elthontos gen sing masc part aor act
15. ἐλθόντι elthonti dat sing masc part aor act
16. ἐλθόντες elthontes nom pl masc part aor act
17. ἐλθόντων elthontōn gen pl masc part aor act
18. ἐλθόντας elthontas acc pl masc part aor act
19. ἐλθοῦσα elthousa nom sing fem part aor act
20. ἐλθούσης elthousēs gen sing fem part aor act
21. ἐλθοῦσαι elthousai nom pl fem part aor act
22. ἐλθόν elthon nom/acc sing neu part aor act
23. ἐλθεῖν elthein inf aor act
24. ἐλήλυθα elēlutha 1sing indic perf act
25. ἐλήλυθας elēluthas 2sing indic perf act
26. ἐλήλυθεν elēluthen 3sing indic perf act
27. ἐληλύθει elēluthei 3sing indic plperf act
28. ἐληλύθεισαν elēlutheisan 3pl indic plperf act
29. ἐληλυθότα elēluthota acc sing masc part perf act
30. ἐληλυθότες elēluthotes nom pl masc part perf act
31. ἐληλυθυῖαν elēluthuian acc sing fem part perf act
32. ἔρχομαι erchomai 1sing indic pres mid
33. ἔρχῃ erchē 2sing indic pres mid
34. ἔρχεται erchetai 3sing indic pres mid
35. ἐρχόμεθα erchometha 1pl indic pres mid
36. ἔρχονται erchontai 3pl indic pres mid
37. ἔρχωμαι erchōmai 1sing subj pres mid
38. ἔρχηται erchētai 3sing subj pres mid
39. ἔρχου erchou 2sing impr pres mid
40. ἐρχέσθω erchesthō 3sing impr pres mid
41. ἔρχεσθε erchesthe 2pl impr pres mid
42. ἐρχόμενον erchomenon
    nom/acc sing masc/neu part pres mid
43. ἐρχομένῳ erchomenō
    dat sing masc/neu part pres mid
44. ἐρχόμενος erchomenos
    nom sing masc part pres mid
45. ἐρχομένου erchomenou
    gen sing masc part pres mid
46. ἐρχόμενοι erchomenoi nom pl masc part pres mid
47. ἐρχομένων erchomenōn gen pl masc part pres mid
48. ἐρχομένους erchomenous
    acc pl masc part pres mid
49. ἐρχομένη erchomenē nom sing fem part pres mid
50. ἐρχομένης erchomenēs gen sing fem part pres mid
51. ἐρχομένην erchomenēn acc sing fem part pres mid
52. ἐρχόμενα erchomena
    nom/acc pl neu part pres mid
53. ἔρχεσθαι erchesthai inf pres mid
54. ἐλεύσομαι eleusomai 1sing indic fut mid
55. ἐλεύσεται eleusetai 3sing indic fut mid
56. ἐλευσόμεθα eleusometha 1pl indic fut mid
57. ἐλεύσονται eleusontai 3pl indic fut mid
58. ἠρχόμην ērchou 2sing indic imperf mid
59. ἤρχετο ērcheto 3sing indic imperf mid
60. ἤρχοντο ērchonto 3pl indic imperf mid
61. ἦλθε ēlthe 3sing indic aor act
62. ἤλθαμεν ēlthamen 1pl indic aor act
63. ἤλθατε ēlthate 2pl indic aor act
64. ἦλθαν ēlthan 3pl indic aor act
65. ἔλθητε elthēte 2pl subj aor act
66. ἐλθάτω elthatō 3sing impr aor act

4	seen his star ... and **are come** to worship him.	Matt 2:2
13	that I may **come** and worship him also.	2:8
13	star, ... before them, till it **came** and stood over	2:9
16	And when they **were come** into the house,	2:11
3	and **came** into the land of Israel.	2:21
13	And he **came** and dwelt in a city called Nazareth:	2:23
48	Pharisees and Sadducees **come** to his baptism,	3:7
44	but he that **cometh** after me is mightier than I,	3:11
33	need ... baptized of thee, and **comest** thou to me?	3:14
42	Spirit of God descending ... and **lighting** upon him:	3:16
13	he **came** and dwelt in Capernaum,	4:13
1	Think not that **I am come** to destroy the law,	5:17
1	I am not **come** to destroy, but to fulfil.	5:17
13	and then **come** and offer thy gift.	5:24
11	Thy kingdom **come**. Thy will be done in earth,	6:10
66	Thy kingdom **come**. Thy will be done in earth,	6:10
36	which **come** to you in sheep's clothing,	7:15
1	and the floods **came**, and the winds blew,	7:25
64	and the floods **came**, and the winds blew,	7:25
1	and the floods **came**, and the winds blew,	7:27
13	there came a leper and worshipped him, saying,	8:2
13	Jesus saith unto him, I will **come** and heal him.	8:7
39	and to another, **Come**, and he **cometh**;	8:9
34	and to another, **Come**, and **he cometh**;	8:9
13	And when Jesus **was come** into Peter's house,	8:14
15	And when he **was come** to the other side	8:28
14	And when he **was come** to the other side	8:28
2	**art thou come** hither to torment us before the time?	8:29
3	passed over, and **came** into his own city.	9:1
16	many publicans and sinners **came** and sat down	9:10
1	for **I am** not **come** to call the righteous,	9:13
57	bridegroom is with them? but the days **will come**,	9:15
13	there **came** a certain ruler, and worshipped him,	9:18
13	but **come** and lay thy hand upon her,	9:18
13	And when Jesus **came** into the ruler's house,	9:23
15	And when he **was come** into the house,	9:28
11	house be worthy, let your peace **come** upon it:	10:13
66	house be worthy, let your peace **come** upon it:	10:13
8	not ... cities of Israel, till the Son of man be **come**.	10:23
1	Think not that **I am come** to send peace on earth:	10:34
1	**I came** not to send peace, but a sword.	10:34
1	For **I am come** to set a man ... against his father,	10:35
44	And said unto him, Art thou he **that should come**,	11:3
53	this is Elias, which was for **to come**.	11:14

ἔρχομαι 2048

3	For John **came** neither eating nor drinking,	Matt 11:18
3	The Son of man **came** eating and drinking,	11:19
3	**he went** into their synagogue:	12:9
3	for **she came** from the uttermost parts of the earth	12:42
22	and when he **is come**, he findeth it empty, swept,	12:44
3	and the fowls **came** and devoured them up:	13:4
1	and the fowls **came** and devoured them up:	13:4
12	and the fowls **came** and devoured them up:	13:4
34	understandeth it not, then **cometh** the wicked one,	13:19
3	his enemy **came** and sowed tares among the wheat,	13:25
23	birds of the air **come** and lodge in the branches	13:32
3	sent the multitude away, and **went** into the house:	13:36
13	And when he **was come** into his own country,	13:54
16	buried it, and **went** and told Jesus.	14:12
3	He **came** to them, walking upon the sea (NASB)	14:25
23	if it be thou, bid me **come** unto thee on the water.	14:28
10	And he said, **Come**.	14:29
23	he walked on the water, **to go** to Jesus.	14:29
3	he walked on the water, **to go** to Jesus.	14:29
16	were in the ship **came** and worshipped him,	14:33
1	**they came** into the land of Gennesaret.	14:34
19	Then **came** she and worshipped him, saying,	15:25
3	and **came** nigh unto the sea of Galilee;	15:29
3	and **came** into the coasts of Magdala.	15:39
16	And when his disciples were **come** to the other side,	16:5
13	Jesus **came** into the coasts of Caesarea Philippi,	16:13
23	any man will **come** after me, let him deny himself,	16:24
53	For the Son of man **shall come** in the glory	16:27
42	till they see the Son of man **coming** in his kingdom.	16:28
23	Why then say the scribes that Elias must first **come**?	17:10
34	Elias truly shall first **come**, and restore all things.	17:11
3	But I say unto you, That Elias is **come** already,	17:12
17	And when they were **come** to the multitude,	17:14
17	And when they were **come** to Capernaum,	17:24
12	And when he **came** into the house, (NASB)	17:25
23	for it must needs be that offences **come**;	18:7
34	but woe to that man by whom the offence **cometh**!	18:7
3	the Son of man is **come** to save that which was lost.	18:11
16	**came** and told unto their lord all that was done.	18:31
3	and **came** into the coasts of Judaea beyond Jordan;	19:1
23	and forbid them not, **to come** unto me:	19:14
16	when they **came** ... received every man a penny.	20:9
16	But when the first **came**, they supposed ... more;	20:10
3	the Son of man **came** not to be ministered unto,	20:28
1	and **were come** to Bethphage,	21:1
34	Behold, thy King **cometh** unto thee,	21:5
44	Blessed is he **that cometh** in the name of the Lord;	21:9
3	when he saw a fig tree in the way, **he came** to it,	21:19
15	And when he **was come** into the temple,	21:23
14	And when he **was come** into the temple,	21:23
3	John **came** unto you in the way of righteousness,	21:32
8	When the lord therefore of the vineyard **cometh**,	21:40
23	bidden to the wedding: and they would not **come**.	22:3
8	That upon you may **come** all the righteous blood	23:35
44	Blessed is he that **cometh** in the name of the Lord.	23:39
57	many **shall come** in my name, saying, I am Christ;	24:5
42	see the Son of man **coming** in the clouds of heaven.	24:30
3	And knew not until the flood **came**,	24:39
34	for ye know not what hour your Lord **doth come**.	24:42
34	in what watch the thief would **come**,	24:43
34	an hour as ye think not the Son of man **cometh**.	24:44
13	whom his lord when he **cometh** shall find so doing.	24:46
23	shall say in his heart, My lord delayeth his **coming**;	24:48
34	the bridegroom **cometh**; go ye out to meet him.	25:6
3	And while they went to buy, the bridegroom **came**;	25:10
36	Afterward **came** also the other virgins,	25:11
34	day nor the hour wherein the Son of man **cometh**.	25:13
34	After a long time the lord of those servants **cometh**,	25:19
13	money to the exchangers, and then at my **coming**	25:27
8	When the Son of man shall **come** in his glory,	25:31
5	I was in prison, and ye **came** unto me.	25:36
63	I was in prison, and ye **came** unto me.	25:36
4	saw we thee sick, or in prison, and **came** unto thee?	25:39
34	Then **cometh** Jesus with them	26:36
34	**cometh** unto the disciples, and findeth them asleep,	26:40
13	And he **came** and found them asleep again:	26:43
34	**cometh** he to his disciples, and saith unto them,	26:45
3	lo, Judas, one of the twelve, **came**,	Matt 26:47
42	of power, and **coming** in the clouds of heaven.	26:64
16	when they **were come** unto a place called Golgotha,	27:33
34	let us see whether Elias **will come** to save him.	27:49
3	**came** a rich man of Arimathaea, named Joseph,	27:57
16	lest his disciples **come** by night, and steal him	27:64
3	**came** Mary Magdalene and the other Mary to see	28:1
16	behold, some of the watch **came** into the city,	28:11
16	His disciples **came** by night, and stole him	28:13
34	There **cometh** one mightier than I after me,	Mark 1:7
3	that Jesus **came** from Nazareth of Galilee,	1:9
3	Jesus **came** into Galilee, preaching the gospel	1:14
2	art thou **come** to destroy us?	1:24
1	they **entered** into the house of Simon and Andrew,	1:29
3	they **entered** into the house of Simon and Andrew,	1:29
3	And He **went** into their synagogues (NASB)	1:39
34	And there **came** a leper to him, beseeching him,	1:40
60	and they **came** to him from every quarter.	1:45
36	they **come** unto him, bringing one sick of the palsy,	2:3
59	and all the multitude **resorted** unto him,	2:13
1	I **came** not to call the righteous, but sinners	2:17
36	and **they come** and say unto him,	2:18
57	But the days **will come**, when the bridegroom	2:20
1	a great multitude, ... **came** unto him.	3:8
36	and they **went** into an house.	3:19
34	and they **went** into an house.	3:19
36	There **came** then his brethren and his mother,	3:31
34	There **came** then his brethren and his mother,	3:31
3	and the fowls of the air **came** and devoured it up.	4:4
34	when they have heard, Satan **cometh** immediately,	4:15
34	Is a candle **brought** to be put under a bushel,	4:21
8	kept secret, but that it **should come** abroad.	4:22
1	And they **came** over unto the other side of the sea,	5:1
1	the people **came** to see what it was (NASB)	5:14
36	And **they come** to Jesus,	5:15
34	there **cometh** one of the rulers of the synagogue,	5:22
13	I pray thee, **come** and lay thy hands on her,	5:23
19	but rather grew worse,	5:26
19	**came** in the press behind, ... touched his garment.	5:27
3	**came** and fell down before him,	5:33
36	**came** from the ruler of the synagogue's house	5:35
36	**cometh** to the house of the ruler of the synagogue,	5:38
3	and **came** into his own country,	6:1
34	and **came** into his own country;	6:1
1	they **came** and took up his corpse,	6:29
64	they **came** and took up his corpse,	6:29
46	for there were many **coming** and going,	6:31
34	he **cometh** unto them, walking upon the sea,	6:48
1	they **came** into the land of Gennesaret,	6:53
16	certain of the scribes, which **came** from Jerusalem.	7:1
19	certain woman ... and **came** and fell at his feet:	7:25
3	he **came** unto the sea of Galilee,	7:31
3	and **came** into the parts of Dalmanutha.	8:10
34	And he **cometh** to Bethsaida;	8:22
36	And he **cometh** to Bethsaida;	8:22
23	he said unto them, Whosoever will **come** after me,	8:34
8	when he **cometh** in the glory of his Father	8:38
31	till they have seen the kingdom of God **come**	9:1
3	and a voice **came** out of the cloud, saying,	9:7
23	Why say the scribes that Elias must first **come**?	9:11
13	Elias verily **cometh** first, and restoreth all things;	9:12
26	But I say unto you, That Elias is indeed **come**,	9:13
13	And when he **came** to his disciples,	9:14
16	And when he **came** to his disciples,	9:14
3	And he **came** to Capernaum:	9:33
1	And he **came** to Capernaum:	9:33
34	and **cometh** into the coasts of Judaea	10:1
53	Suffer the little children **to come** unto me,	10:14
43	and in the world **to come** eternal life.	10:30
3	the Son of man **came** not to be ministered unto,	10:45
36	And they **came** to Jericho:	10:46
34	And they **came** to Jericho:	10:46
3	casting away his garment, rose, and **came** to Jesus.	10:50
44	Blessed is he **that cometh** in the name of the Lord:	11:9
49	kingdom ... **that cometh** in the name of the Lord:	11:10
3	he **came**, if haply he might find any thing thereon:	11:13
13	when he **came** to it, he found nothing but leaves;	11:13

ἔρχομαι 2048

36	And **they come** to Jerusalem:	Mark 11:15
36	And they **come** again to Jerusalem:	11:27
36	there **come** to him the chief priests,	11:27
55	he **will come** and destroy the husbandmen,	12:9
16	And when they **were come**, they say unto him,	12:14
36	Then **come** unto him the Sadducees.	12:18
19	And there **came** a certain poor widow,	12:42
57	many **shall come** in my name, saying, I am Christ;	13:6
42	And then shall they see the Son of man **coming**,	13:26
34	ye know not when the master of the house **cometh**,	13:35
13	Lest **coming** suddenly he find you sleeping.	13:36
3	there **came** a woman having an alabaster box	14:3
1	his disciples went forth, and **came** into the city,	14:16
34	And in the evening he **cometh** with the twelve.	14:17
36	**came** to a place which was named Gethsemane:	14:32
34	And he **cometh**, and findeth them sleeping,	14:37
65	that you **may not come** into temptation (NASB)	14:38
13	And again He **came** and found them (NASB)	14:40
34	he **cometh** the third time, and saith unto them,	14:41
3	the hour **is come**; behold, the Son of man is betrayed	14:41
13	soon as he **was come**, he goeth straightway to him,	14:45
42	of power, and **coming** in the clouds of heaven.	14:62
34	there **cometh** one of the maids of the high priest:	14:66
42	Simon a Cyrenian, ... **coming** out of the country,	15:21
34	see whether Elias will **come** to take him down.	15:36
3	which also waited for the kingdom of God, **came**,	15:43
13	which also waited for the kingdom of God, **came**,	15:43
21	sweet spices, that they **might come** and anoint him.	16:1
36	**came** unto the sepulchre at the rising of the sun.	16:2
21	**entering** into the sepulchre, they saw a young man	16:5
8	that the mother of my Lord **should come** to me?	Luke 1:43
1	the eighth day **they came** to circumcise the child;	1:59
1	And **they came** with haste, and found Mary,	2:16
64	And **they came** with haste, and found Mary,	2:16
3	And **he came** by the Spirit into the temple:	2:27
1	went a day's journey; and they sought him among	2:44
3	he went down with them, and **came** to Nazareth,	2:51
3	And he **came** into all the country about Jordan,	3:3
1	Then **came** also publicans to be baptized,	3:12
34	but one mightier than I **cometh**,	3:16
3	**came** to Nazareth, where he had been brought up:	4:16
2	Jesus of Nazareth? **art** thou **come** to destroy us?	4:34
1	and the people sought him, and **came** unto him,	4:42
18	that they should **come** and help them.	5:7
1	And **they came**, and filled both the ships,	5:7
64	And **they came**, and filled both the ships,	5:7
30	which were **come** out of every town of Galilee,	5:17
24	I **came** not to call the righteous, but sinners	5:32
57	But the days **will come**, when the bridegroom shall	5:35
1	which **came** to hear him, and to be healed	6:17
44	Whosoever **cometh** to me, and heareth my sayings,	6:47
13	beseeching him that he **would come** and heal	7:3
23	neither thought I myself worthy **to come**	7:7
39	and to another, **Come**, and he **cometh**;	7:8
34	and to another, **Come**, and he **cometh**;	7:8
44	saying, Art thou he **that should come**?	7:19
44	Art thou he **that should come**?	7:20
26	For John the Baptist **came** neither eating bread nor	7:33
26	The Son of man **is come** eating and drinking;	7:34
34	then **cometh** the devil, and taketh away the word	8:12
8	that shall not be known and **come** abroad.	8:17
1	and **came** to Jesus, and found the man,	8:35
64	and **came** to Jesus, and found the man,	8:35
3	And, behold, there **came** a man named Jairus,	8:41
3	she **came** trembling, and falling down before him,	8:47
34	yet spake, there **cometh** one from the ruler	8:49
13	And when He **had come** to the house, (NASB)	8:51
23	If any man will **come** after me, let ... deny himself,	9:23
53	If any man will **come** after me, let ... deny himself,	9:23
8	when he **shall come** in his own glory,	9:26
3	the Son of man is not **come** to destroy men's lives,	9:56
53	city and place, whither he himself would **come**.	10:1
13	**came** and looked on him, and passed by on	10:32
3	But a certain Samaritan, ... **came** where he was:	10:33
11	Hallowed be thy name. Thy kingdom **come**.	11:2
66	Hallowed be thy name. Thy kingdom **come**.	11:2
22	he **cometh**, he findeth it swept and garnished.	11:25
3	for she **came** from the utmost parts of the earth	Luke 11:31
14	that when he **cometh** and knocketh,	12:36
13	whom the lord when he **cometh** shall find watching:	12:37
8	And if he **shall come** in the second watch,	12:38
8	or **come** in the third watch, and find them so,	12:38
34	had known what hour the thief **would come**,	12:39
34	Son of man **cometh** at an hour when ye think not.	12:40
13	whom his lord when he **cometh** shall find so doing.	12:43
53	say in his heart, My lord delayeth his **coming**;	12:45
1	I am **come** to send fire on the earth;	12:49
34	straightway ye say, There **cometh** a shower;	12:54
3	he **came** and sought fruit thereon, and found none.	13:6
32	three years I **come** seeking fruit on this fig tree,	13:7
46	in them therefore **come** and be healed,	13:14
44	Blessed is he that **cometh** in the name of the Lord.	13:35
23	went into the house of one of the chief Pharisees	14:1
13	he that bade thee and him **come** and say to thee,	14:9
8	that when he that bade thee **cometh**,	14:10
41	were bidden, **Come**; for all things are now ready.	14:17
23	I have married a wife, ... therefore I cannot **come**.	14:20
34	If any man **come** to me, and hate not his father,	14:26
34	doth not bear his cross, and **come** after me,	14:27
43	with ten thousand to meet him that **cometh** against	14:31
13	And when he **cometh** home, he calleth together	15:6
13	And when he **came** to himself, he said,	15:17
3	And he arose, and **came** to his father.	15:20
44	and as he **came** and drew nigh to the house,	15:25
3	But as soon as this thy son **was come**,	15:30
46	moreover the dogs **came** and licked his sores.	16:21
9	lest they also **come** into this place of torment.	16:28
23	It is impossible but that offences **will come**:	17:1
34	but woe unto him, through whom they **come**!	17:1
34	when the kingdom of God **should come**,	17:20
34	The kingdom of God **cometh** not with observation:	17:20
57	And he said unto the disciples, The days **will come**,	17:22
3	and the flood **came**, and destroyed them all.	17:27
59	was a widow in that city; and she **came** unto him,	18:3
49	lest by her continual **coming** she weary me.	18:5
13	Nevertheless when the Son of man **cometh**,	18:8
53	Suffer little children **to come** unto me,	18:16
43	and in the world **to come** life everlasting.	18:30
3	And when Jesus **came** to the place, he looked up,	19:5
3	For the Son of man **is come** to seek and to save	19:10
32	delivered them ten pounds, ... Occupy till I **come**.	19:13
3	the second **came**, saying, Lord, thy pound hath	19:18
3	And another **came**, saying, Lord, behold, here is	19:20
13	that at my **coming** I might have required mine own	19:23
44	Blessed be the King that **cometh** in the name of	19:38
55	He **shall come** and destroy these husbandmen,	20:16
57	these things which ye behold, the days **will come**,	21:6
57	many **shall come** in my name, saying, I am Christ;	21:8
42	And then shall they see the Son of man **coming**	21:27
3	Then **came** the day of unleavened bread,	22:7
8	of the vine, until the kingdom of God **shall come**.	22:18
13	rose up from prayer, and **was come** to his disciples,	22:45
45	Simon, a Cyrenian, **coming** out of the country,	23:26
42	Simon, a Cyrenian, **coming** out of the country,	23:26
36	the days **are coming**, in the which they shall say,	23:29
1	And when they **came** to the place (NASB)	23:33
7	remember me when thou **comest** into thy kingdom.	23:42
1	in the morning, they **came** unto the sepulchre,	24:1
1	they **came**, saying, that they had also seen a vision.	24:23
3	The same **came** for a witness,	John 1:7
42	was the true Light, ... that **cometh** into the world.	1:9
3	He **came** unto his own,	1:11
44	He that **cometh** after me is preferred before me:	1:15
44	who **coming** after me is preferred before me,	1:27
42	The next day John seeth Jesus **coming** unto him,	1:29
34	After me **cometh** a man ... preferred before me:	1:30
1	therefore am I **come** baptizing with water.	1:31
41	He saith unto them, **Come** and see.	1:39
1	They **came** and saw where he dwelt,	1:39
64	They **came** and saw where he dwelt,	1:39
39	Philip saith unto him, **Come** and see.	1:46
42	Jesus saw Nathanael **coming** to him,	1:47
3	The same **came** to Jesus by night,	3:2
25	we know that thou art a teacher **come** from God:	3:2

ἔρχομαι 2048

34	but canst not tell whence it **cometh**,..............	John 3:8
26	that light **is come** into the world,...............	3:19
34	hateth the light, neither **cometh** to the light,......	3:20
34	But he that doeth truth **cometh** to the light,......	3:21
3	After these things **came** Jesus and his disciples......	3:22
1	And they **came** unto John, and said unto him,......	3:26
64	And they **came** unto John, and said unto him,......	3:26
36	the same baptizeth, and all men **come** to him.......	3:26
44	He that **cometh** from above is above all:...........	3:31
44	he that **cometh** from heaven is above all............	3:31
34	Then **cometh** he to a city of Samaria,...............	4:5
34	There **cometh** a woman of Samaria to draw water:.....	4:7
37	that I thirst not, neither **come** hither to draw........	4:15
10	Go, call thy husband, and **come** hither...............	4:16
34	Woman, believe me, the hour **cometh**,...............	4:21
34	But the hour **cometh**, and now is,.................	4:23
34	I know that Messias **cometh**, which is called Christ:...	4:25
8	when he **is come**, he will tell us all things............	4:25
1	And upon this **came** his disciples,...................	4:27
64	And upon this **came** his disciples,...................	4:27
60	they went out of the city, and **came** unto him........	4:30
34	yet four months, and then **cometh** harvest?.........	4:35
1	So when the Samaritans were **come** unto him,.......	4:40
3	Then when he **was come** into Galilee,.................	4:45
1	for they also **went** unto the feast...................	4:45
3	So Jesus **came** again into Cana of Galilee,..........	4:46
13	when he **was come** out of Judaea into Galilee.........	4:54
32	but while I am **coming**, another steppeth down......	5:7
34	and shall not **come** into condemnation;.............	5:24
34	The hour **is coming**, and now is,...................	5:25
34	Marvel not at this: for the hour **is coming**,..........	5:28
23	ye will not **come** to me, that ye might have life.....	5:40
24	I **am come** in my Father's name,...................	5:43
8	if another **shall come** in his own name,.............	5:43
34	and saw a great company **come** unto him,..........	6:5
44	This is of a truth that prophet that **should come**.....	6:14
53	that they would **come** and take him by force,.......	6:15
60	and **went** over the sea toward Capernaum...........	6:17
27	and Jesus **was** not **come** to them..................	6:17
3	Howbeit there **came** other boats from Tiberias.......	6:23
1	Howbeit there **came** other boats from Tiberias.......	6:23
1	they also took shipping, and **came** to Capernaum,...	6:24
44	he that **cometh** to me shall never hunger;..........	6:35
42	him that **cometh** to me I will in no wise cast out.....	6:37
23	No man can **come** to me, except.................	6:44
34	and hath learned of the Father, **cometh** unto me.....	6:45
23	no man can **come** unto me, except it were given.....	6:65
38	but when Christ **cometh**, no man knoweth............	7:27
24	and I **am** not **come** of myself,.....................	7:28
27	because his hour **was** not yet **come**................	7:30
8	When Christ **cometh**, will he do more miracles........	7:31
23	and where I am, thither ye cannot **come**.............	7:34
23	and where I am, thither ye cannot **come**?............	7:36
40	If any man thirst, let him **come** unto me,............	7:37
34	But some said, Shall Christ **come** out of Galilee?.....	7:41
34	That Christ **cometh** of the seed of David,............	7:42
1	Then **came** the officers to the chief priests............	7:45
13	he that **came** to Jesus by night, being one of them,...	7:50
59	and all the people **came** unto him;...................	8:2
1	for I know whence I **came**, and whither I go;.......	8:14
32	ye cannot tell whence I **come**, and whither I go.....	8:14
27	for his hour **was** not yet **come**....................	8:20
23	whither I go, ye cannot **come**.......................	8:21
23	because he saith, Whither I go, ye cannot **come**.....	8:22
24	neither **came** I of myself, but he sent me............	8:42
34	the night **cometh**, when no man can work...........	9:4
3	and washed, and **came** seeing........................	9:7
1	For judgment I **am come** into this world,............	9:39
1	that ever **came** before me are thieves and robbers:...	10:8
34	The thief **cometh** not, but for to steal, and to kill,....	10:10
1	I **am come** that they might have life,................	10:10
42	seeth the wolf **coming**, and leaveth the sheep,........	10:12
1	And many **resorted** unto him, and said,.............	10:41
13	Then when Jesus **came**,.............................	11:17
3	Then when Jesus **came**,.............................	11:17
28	And many of the Jews **came** to Martha and Mary,...	11:19
34	as soon as she heard that Jesus **was coming**,.........	11:20

44	the Son of God, which **should come** into the world.	John 11:27
34	she arose quickly, and **came** unto him................	11:29
59	she arose quickly, and **came** unto him................	11:29
27	Now Jesus **was** not yet **come** into the town,........	11:30
3	Then when Mary **was come** where Jesus was,......	11:32
39	They said unto him, Lord, **come** and see............	11:34
34	again groaning in himself **cometh** to the grave........	11:38
16	Then many of the Jews which **came** to Mary,.......	11:45
57	Romans **shall come** and take ... place and nation.....	11:48
8	What think ye, that he **will** not **come** to the feast?...	11:56
3	six days before the passover **came** to Bethany,......	12:1
1	and they **came** not for Jesus' sake only,............	12:9
13	next day much people that **were come** to the feast,...	12:12
34	they heard that Jesus **was coming** to Jerusalem,......	12:12
44	King of Israel that **cometh** in the name of the Lord...	12:13
34	behold, thy King **cometh**, sitting on an ass's colt.....	12:15
34	Philip **cometh** and telleth Andrew:..................	12:22
34	Andrew and Philip **came**, (NASB)..................	12:22
26	hour **is come**, that the Son ... should be glorified.....	12:23
1	but for this cause **came** I unto this hour.............	12:27
3	Then **came** there a voice from heaven, saying,......	12:28
24	I **am come** a light into the world,...................	12:46
1	I judge him not: for I **came** not to judge the world,..	12:47
26	when Jesus knew that his hour **was come**............	13:1
3	when Jesus knew that his hour **was come**............	13:1
34	Then **cometh** he to Simon Peter:....................	13:6
23	Whither I go, ye cannot **come**;......................	13:33
32	I **will come** again, and receive you unto myself;......	14:3
34	no man **cometh** unto the Father, but by me.........	14:6
32	I will not leave you comfortless: I **will come** to you...	14:18
56	Father will love him, and we **will come** unto him,.....	14:23
32	I go away, and **come again** unto you................	14:28
34	for the prince of this world **cometh**,.................	14:30
1	If I **had** not **come** and spoken unto them,..........	15:22
8	But when the Comforter **is come**,...................	15:26
34	yea, the time **cometh**, that whosoever killeth you.....	16:2
8	that when the time **shall come**,......................	16:4
55	for if I go not away, the Comforter **will** not **come**...	16:7
8	for if I go not away, the Comforter **will** not **come**...	16:7
13	when he **is come**, he will reprove the world of sin,....	16:8
8	Howbeit when he, the Spirit of truth, **is come**,.......	16:13
52	and he will show you things to **come**................	16:13
3	hath sorrow, because her hour **is come**:..............	16:21
34	the time **cometh**, ... no more speak ... in proverbs,....	16:25
24	from the Father, and am **come** into the world:.......	16:28
34	Behold, the hour **cometh**, yea, is now come,........	16:32
34	Behold, the hour **cometh**, yea, is now come,........	16:32
26	Father, the hour **is come**; glorify thy Son,...........	17:1
32	but these are in the world, and I **come** to thee........	17:11
32	And now **come** I to thee; and these things I speak...	17:13
34	**cometh** thither with lanterns and torches............	18:3
52	knowing all things that should **come** upon him,......	18:4
24	and for this cause **came** I into the world,............	18:37
60	began **to come up** to Him, ... "Hail, King (NASB)....	19:3
1	**came** the soldiers, and brake the legs of the first,.....	19:32
16	**came** to Jesus, and saw that he was dead already,....	19:33
3	He **came** therefore, and took the body of Jesus......	19:38
1	He **came** therefore, and took the body of Jesus......	19:38
3	And there **came** also Nicodemus,...................	19:39
13	which at the first **came** to Jesus by night,...........	19:39
34	The first day ... **cometh** Mary Magdalene early,......	20:1
34	Then she runneth, and **cometh** to Simon Peter,......	20:2
60	and that other disciple, and **came** to the sepulchre...	20:3
3	and **came** first to the sepulchre.....................	20:4
34	Then **cometh** Simon Peter following him,...........	20:6
13	other disciple, which **came** first to the sepulchre,.....	20:8
34	Mary Magdalene **came** and told the disciples........	20:18
3	**came** Jesus and stood in the midst,..................	20:19
3	Thomas, ... was not with them when Jesus **came**.....	20:24
34	then **came** Jesus, the doors being shut,..............	20:26
35	They say unto him, We also go with thee..............	21:3
1	And the other disciples **came** in a little ship;.........	21:8
34	Jesus then **cometh**, and taketh bread,................	21:13
32	If I will that he tarry till I **come**,...................	21:22
32	but, If I will that he tarry till I **come**,...............	21:23
55	**shall** so **come** in like manner as ye have seen him..	Acts 1:11
23	great and notable day of the Lord **come**:.............	2:20

604

ἔρχομαι 2048

9	when the times of refreshing **shall come**	Acts 3:19
1	And being let go, they **went** to their own company,	4:23
45	the shadow of Peter **passing by** might overshadow	5:15
3	Now there **came** a dearth over all the land of Egypt	7:11
27	and **had come** to Jerusalem for to worship,	8:27
1	**they came** unto a certain water:	8:36
23	preached in all the cities, till he **came** to Caesarea.	8:40
58	that appeared unto thee in the way as thou **camest,**	9:17
27	and **came** hither for that intent,	9:21
1	Therefore **came** I unto you without gainsaying,	10:29
3	by four corners; and it **came** even to me:	11:5
1	Moreover these six brethren **accompanied** me,	11:12
16	who **came** to Antioch and began speaking (NASB)	11:20
1	**came** unto the iron gate that leadeth unto the city;	12:10
64	**came** unto the iron gate that leadeth unto the city;	12:10
3	he **came** to the house of Mary the mother of John,	12:12
1	from Paphos, they **came** to Perga in Pamphylia:	13:13
16	and **went** into the synagogue and sat down (NASB)	13:14
34	But, behold, there **cometh** one after me,	13:25
43	the next sabbath day **came** almost the whole city	13:44
1	and **came** unto Iconium.	13:51
1	throughout Pisidia, they **came** to Pamphylia.	14:24
1	when they were dismissed, they **came** to Antioch:	15:30
16	After they **were come** to Mysia,	16:7
16	but let them **come** themselves and fetch us out.	16:37
16	And they **came** and besought them,	16:39
1	through Amphipolis ... they **came** to Thessalonica,	17:1
1	they **came** thither also, and stirred up the people.	17:13
9	and Timotheus for **to come** to him with all speed,	17:15
3	Paul departed from Athens, and **came** to Corinth;	18:1
29	lately **come** from Italy, with his wife Priscilla,	18:2
3	**entered** into a certain man's house, named Justus,	18:7
51	keep this feast that **cometh** in Jerusalem:	18:21
23	**came** to Ephesus: and finding certain disciples,	19:1
42	believe on him which **should come** after him,	19:4
3	hands upon them, the Holy Ghost **came** on them;	19:6
60	And many that believed **came,** and confessed,	19:18
23	our craft is in danger to **be set** at nought;	19:27
3	he **came** into Greece,	20:2
4	and **came** unto them to Troas in five days;	20:6
4	at Assos, we took him in, and **came** to Mitylene.	20:14
4	and the next day we **came** to Miletus.	20:15
4	we **came** with a straight course unto Coos,	21:1
1	departed, and **came** unto Caesarea:	21:8
4	departed, and **came** unto Caesarea:	21:8
13	And when he **was come** unto us,	21:11
25	for they will hear that thou **art come.**	21:22
1	being led by the hand ... I **came** into Damascus.	22:11
13	**Came** unto me, and stood, and said unto me,	22:13
23	the chief priests and all their council to **appear,**	22:30
53	Commanding his accusers to **come** unto thee:	24:8
14	And on the morrow, when Agrippa **was come,**	25:23
4	**came** unto a place which is called The fair havens;	27:8
4	and we **came** the next day to Puteoli:	28:13
4	and so we **went** toward Rome.	28:14
62	and so we **went** toward Rome.	28:14
64	**came** ... as far as the Market of Appius (NASB)	28:15
4	And when we **came** to Rome,	28:16
1	they **came** to him at his lodging (NASB)	28:23
23	journey by the will of God **to come** unto you.	Rom 1:10
23	that oftentimes I purposed **to come** unto you,	1:13
8	Let us do evil, that good **may come?**	3:8
20	but when the commandment **came,** sin revived,	7:9
54	At this time **will I come,** ... Sarah shall have a son.	9:9
23	I have been much hindered from **coming** to you.	15:22
23	a great desire these many years **to come** unto you;	15:23
54	take my journey into Spain, **I will come** to you:	15:24
44	And I am sure that, when I **come** unto you,	15:29
54	**I shall come** in the fulness of the blessing	15:29
6	**I may come** unto you with joy by the will of God,	15:32
13	**I may come** unto you with joy by the will of God,	15:32
13	And I, brethren, when I **came** to you,	1 Co 2:1
1	**came** not with excellency of speech or of wisdom,	2:1
8	Therefore judge nothing ... until the Lord **come,**	4:5
45	are puffed up, as though I would not **come** to you.	4:18
54	But **I will come** to you shortly, if the Lord will,	4:19
6	What will ye? **shall I come** unto you with a rod,	4:21
8	ye do show the Lord's death till he **come.**	1 Co 11:26
6	And the rest will I set in order when I **come.**	11:34
8	But when that which is perfect is **come,**	13:10
6	if I **come** unto you speaking with tongues,	14:6
36	and with what body **do they come?**	15:35
6	that there be no gatherings when I **come.**	16:2
54	Now I **will come** unto you,	16:5
8	if Timotheus **come,** see that he may be with you	16:10
8	that he **may come** unto me:	16:11
8	desired him to **come** unto you with the brethren:	16:12
8	but his will was not at all **to come** at this time;	16:12
55	he **will come** when he shall have convenient time.	16:12
23	I was minded **to come** unto you before,	2 Co 1:15
23	and **to come** again out of Macedonia unto you,	1:16
1	that to spare you I **came** not as yet unto Corinth.	1:23
23	that I would not **come** again to you in heaviness.	2:1
13	And I wrote this same unto you, lest, when I **came,**	2:3
13	when I **came** to Troas to preach Christ's gospel,	2:12
17	For, when we **were come** into Macedonia,	7:5
9	Lest haply if they of Macedonia come with me,	9:4
44	For if he that **cometh** preacheth another Jesus,	11:4
16	brethren which **came** from Macedonia supplied:	11:9
54	**I will come** to visions and revelations of the Lord.	12:1
23	Behold, the third time I am ready **to come** to you;	12:14
13	For I fear, lest, when I **come,**	12:20
12	And lest, when I **come** again,	12:21
14	And lest, when I **come** again,	12:21
32	This is the third time I **am coming** to you.	13:1
6	to all other, that, if I **come** again, I will not spare:	13:2
1	I **came** into the regions of Syria and Cilicia;	Gal 1:21
3	But when Peter was **come** to Antioch,	2:11
23	For before that certain **came** from James,	2:12
1	but when they **were come,** he withdrew	2:12
3	but when they **were come,** he withdrew	2:12
8	seed **should come** to whom the promise was made;	3:19
23	But before faith **came,** we were kept under the law,	3:23
20	But after that faith is **come,**	3:25
3	But when the fulness of the time was **come,**	4:4
13	And **came** and preached peace to you	Eph 2:17
34	because of these things **cometh** the wrath of God	5:6
26	**have fallen** out rather unto the furtherance	Php 1:12
13	that whether I **come** and see you, or else be absent,	1:27
54	But I trust ... that I also myself **shall come** shortly,	2:24
34	For which things' sake the wrath of God **cometh**	Col 3:6
8	if he **come** unto you, receive him;	4:10
50	Jesus, which delivered us from the wrath **to come**	1 Th 1:10
23	Wherefore we would **have come** unto you,	2:18
14	But now when Timotheus **came** from you unto us,	3:6
34	that the day of the Lord so **cometh** as a thief	5:2
8	When he **shall come** to be glorified in his saints,	2 Th 1:10
8	that day **shall** not **come,** except there come a falling	2:3
3	Christ Jesus **came** into the world to save sinners;	1 Tm 1:15
23	and **to come** unto the knowledge of the truth.	2:4
23	things write I ... hoping **to come** unto thee shortly:	3:14
32	Till I **come,** give attendance to reading,	4:13
23	never able **to come** to the knowledge of the truth.	2 Tm 3:7
23	Do thy diligence **to come** shortly unto me:	4:9
44	The cloak ... when thou **comest,** bring with thee,	4:13
23	Do thy diligence **to come** before winter:	4:21
23	be diligent **to come** unto me to Nicopolis:	Tit 3:12
42	which drinketh in the rain that **cometh** oft upon it,	Heb 6:7
36	Behold, the days **come,** saith the Lord,	8:8
44	he that **shall come** will come, and will not tarry.	10:37
34	and he went out, not knowing whither he **went.**	11:8
38	with whom, if he **come** shortly, I will see you.	13:23
57	that there **shall come** in the last days scoffers,	2 Pt 3:3
34	and as ye have heard that antichrist **shall come,**	1 Jn 2:18
29	that Jesus Christ **is come** in the flesh is of God:	4:2
29	confesseth not that Jesus Christ is **come** in the flesh	4:3
34	whereof ye have heard that it **should come;**	4:3
13	This is he that **came** by water and blood,	5:6
42	confess not that Jesus Christ is **come** in the flesh.	2 Jn 1:7
34	**come** any unto you, and bring not this doctrine,	1:10
23	I trust **to come** unto you, and speak face to face,	1:12
47	when the brethren **came** and testified of the truth.	3 Jn 1:3
6	Wherefore, if I **come,** I will remember his deeds	1:10
3	the Lord **cometh** with ten thousands of his saints,	Jude 1:14

44	peace, from him which is, ... and which **is to come**;..	Rev 1:4
34	**cometh** with clouds; and every eye shall see him,......	1:7
44	which is, and which was, and which **is to come**,........	1:8
32	or else I **will come** unto thee quickly,.................	2:5
32	Repent; or else I **will come** unto thee quickly,.........	2:16
53	temptation, which shall **come** upon all the world,......	3:10
32	I **come** quickly: hold that fast which thou hast,........	3:11
44	God Almighty, which was, and is, and **is to come**......	4:8
3	he **came** and took the book out of the right hand......	5:7
39	one of the four beasts saying, **Come** and see............	6:1
39	I heard the second beast say, **Come** and see...........	6:3
39	I heard the third beast say, **Come** and see.............	6:5
39	the voice of the fourth beast say, **Come** and see........	6:7
3	For the great day of his wrath **is come**;...............	6:17
1	arrayed in white robes? and whence **came** they?.......	7:13
46	These are they which **came** out of great tribulation,....	7:14
3	And another angel **came** and stood at the altar,.......	8:3
36	and, behold, there **come** two woes more hereafter......	9:12
34	and, behold, there **come** two woes more hereafter......	9:12
34	and, behold, the third woe **cometh** quickly............	11:14
44	Almighty, which art, and wast, and **art to come**;......	11:17
3	the nations were angry, and thy wrath **is come**,.......	11:18
3	glory to him; **for** the hour of his judgment is **come**:...	14:7
3	and reap: for the time **is come** for thee to reap;.......	14:15
32	I **come** as a thief. Blessed is he that watcheth,........	16:15
3	And there **came** one of the seven angels.............	17:1
3	and one is, and the other is not yet **come**;............	17:10
8	when he **cometh**, he must continue a short space......	17:10
3	mighty city! for in one hour is thy judgment **come**....	18:10
3	for the marriage of the Lamb **is come**,................	19:7
3	And there **came** unto me one of the seven angels.....	21:9
32	Behold, I **come** quickly: blessed is he that	22:7
32	behold, I **come** quickly; and my reward is with me,...	22:12
10	And the Spirit and the bride say, **Come**..............	22:17
39	And the Spirit and the bride say, **Come**..............	22:17
10	And let him that heareth say, **Come**..................	22:17
39	And let him that heareth say, **Come**..................	22:17
11	And let him that is athirst **come**......................	22:17
40	And let him that is athirst **come**......................	22:17
32	He which testifieth ... Surely I **come** quickly..........	22:20
39	I **come** quickly. Amen. Even so, **come**, Lord Jesus....	22:20

Erchomai is a general word expressing motion. The motion may either be toward the speaker (in which case it means "come") or away from the speaker (in which case it means "go"). English has two separate words to express these ideas, but Greek can use the same word. *Erchomai* may be used with reference to persons, animals, or things which are coming or going.

Classical Greek and Septuagint Usage
In classical Greek the word is used of persons, birds, ships, spears, wind, storms, stars, time, events, feelings, sounds, danger, commands, etc. A similar variety of subjects used with *erchomai* may be found throughout the history of the word. In the Septuagint *erchomai* is often used in reference to the coming of the Messiah (Psalm 118:26 [LXX 117:26]; Daniel 7:13). One of the uses of this word in the papyri was to express the coming of the end.

New Testament Usage
In the New Testament *erchomai* usually means "come." The idea of going away is normally expressed by other words. Only rarely does it mean "go" (or "went"), as in John 21:3. *Erchomai* is often used in the sense of making an appearance. This is especially to be observed in references to the appearance of the Messiah among men (John 7:31; 1 John 5:6). The expression "the Coming One" is commonly used as a messianic title (Matthew 11:3; Hebrews 10:37). *Erchomai* often refers to prophetic events, conveying either the thought of imminency or certainty (1 Thessalonians 1:10). It may even refer to the "coming to" one's senses (Luke 15:17) or to the illness of a woman "becoming" worse (Mark 5:26).

STRONG 2064, BAUER 310-11, MOULTON-MILLIGAN 255, KITTEL 2:666-75, LIDDELL-SCOTT 694-95, COLIN BROWN 1:319-22.

2049. ἐρωτάω erōtaō verb

Ask, request (something).

COGNATES:
  διερωτάω dierōtaō (1325)
  ἐπερωτάω eperōtaō (1890)
  ἐπερώτημα eperōtēma (1891)

SYNONYMS:
  αἰτέω aiteō (153)
  δέομαι deomai (1183)
  ἐντυγχάνω entunchanō (1777)
  ἐξαιτέω exaiteō (1793)
  ἐπερωτάω eperōtaō (1890)
  λέγω legō (2978)
  παραιτέομαι paraiteomai (3729)
  παρακαλέω parakaleō (3731)
  πυνθάνομαι punthanomai (4299)

אָמַר ʼāmar (569), Say (Ex 3:13).

חָקַר chāqar (2811), Investigate (Dt 13:14).

שָׁאַל shāʼal (8068), Qal: ask, inquire of (Gn 37:15, 1 Sm 19:22, Jer 48:19 [31:19]); piel: inquire (2 Sm 20:18).

שְׁאֵל sheʼēl (A8069), Ask (Ezr 5:10—Aramaic).

1. ἐρωτᾷ erōta 3sing indic/subj pres act
2. ἐρωτῶ erōtō 1sing indic pres act
3. ἐρωτῶμεν erōtōmen 1pl indic pres act
4. ἐρωτῶν erōtōn nom sing masc part pres act
5. ἐρωτῶντες erōtōntes nom pl masc part pres act
6. ἐρωτώντων erōtōntōn gen pl masc part pres act
7. ἐρωτᾶν erōtan inf pres act
8. ἐρωτήσω erōtēsō 1sing indic/subj fut/aor act
9. ἠρώτησεν ērōtēsen 3sing indic aor act
10. ἠρώτησαν ērōtēsan 3pl indic aor act
11. ἐρωτήσῃ erōtēsē 3sing subj aor act
12. ἐρωτήσωσιν erōtēsōsin 3pl subj aor act
13. ἐρωτήσατε erōtēsate 2pl impr aor act
14. ἐρωτῆσαι erōtēsai inf aor act

15. ἐρωτήσετε erōtēsete 2pl indic fut act
16. ἠρώτα ērōta 3sing indic imperf act
17. ἠρώτων ērōtōn 3pl indic imperf act
18. ἐρωτᾷς erōtas 2sing indic pres act
19. ἐρώτησον erōtēson 2sing impr aor act
20. ἠρώτουν ērōtoun 3pl indic imperf act

17	And his disciples came and **besought** him,	Matt 15:23
20	And his disciples came and **besought** him,	15:23
16	he **asked** his disciples, saying, Whom do men say	16:13
18	"Why are you **asking** Me (NASB)	19:17
8	I also **will ask** you one thing, which if ye tell me,	21:24
10	they ... with the twelve **asked** of him the parable.	Mark 4:10
17	they ... with the twelve **asked** of him the parable.	4:10
20	they ... with the twelve **asked** of him the parable.	4:10
16	and she **besought** him that he would cast forth	7:26
16	He **was asking** them, "How many loaves (NASB)	8:5
10	great fever; and they **besought** him for her.	Luke 4:38
9	and **prayed** him that he would thrust out a little	5:3
4	**beseeching** him that he would come and heal	7:3
17	they came to Jesus, they **besought** him instantly,	7:4
16	Pharisees **desired** him that he would eat with him.	7:36
10	round about **besought** him to depart from them;	8:37
9	round about **besought** him to depart from them;	8:37
14	and they feared **to ask** him of that saying.	9:45
16	a certain Pharisee **besought** him to dine with him:	11:37
1	a certain Pharisee **besought** him to dine with him:	11:37
2	needs go and see it: I **pray** thee have me excused.	14:18
2	I go to prove them: I **pray** thee have me excused.	14:19
1	an ambassage, and **desireth** conditions of peace.	14:32
2	Then he said, I **pray** thee therefore, father,	16:27
1	And if any man **ask** you, Why do ye loose him?	19:31
8	I will also **ask** you one thing; and answer me:	20:3
8	And if I also **ask** you, ye will not answer me,	22:68
9	And Pilate **asked** Him, saying, (NASB)	23:3
12	the Jews sent priests ... from Jerusalem **to ask** him,	John 1:19
10	And **they asked** him, What then? Art thou Elias?	1:21
10	And they **asked** him, and said unto him,	1:25
17	In the mean while his disciples **prayed** him,	4:31
17	they **besought** him that he would tarry with them:	4:40
16	and **besought** him that he would come down,	4:47
10	Then **asked** they him, What man is that which said	5:12
5	So when they continued **asking** him,	8:7
10	And his disciples **asked** him, saying, Master,	9:2
17	Then again the Pharisees also **asked** him	9:15
10	And they **asked** them, saying, Is this your son,	9:19
13	he is of age; **ask** him: he shall speak for himself.	9:21
13	Therefore said his parents, He is of age; **ask** him.	9:23
17	and **desired** him, saying, Sir, we would see Jesus.	12:21
8	And I **will pray** the Father, and he shall give you	14:16
1	and none of you **asketh** me, Whither goest thou?	16:5
7	Now Jesus knew that they were desirous **to ask** him,	16:19
15	And in that day ye **shall ask** me nothing.	16:23
8	that I **will pray** the Father for you:	16:26
1	and needest not that any man **should ask** thee:	16:30
2	I **pray** for them: I **pray** not for the world,	17:9
2	I **pray** for them: I **pray** not for the world,	17:9
2	I **pray** not that thou shouldest take them out	17:15
2	Neither **pray** I for these alone,	17:20
9	The high priest then **asked** Jesus of his disciples,	18:19
18	Why do you **question** Me? (NASB)	18:21
19	Why askest thou me? **Question** those (NASB)	18:21
10	**besought** Pilate that their legs might be broken,	19:31
9	**besought** Pilate that he might take away the body	19:38
17	they **asked** him, Lord, are you (NIV)	Acts 1:6
16	about to go into the temple **asked** an alms.	3:3
10	Then **prayed** they him to tarry certain days.	10:48
17	and **desired** them to depart out of the city.	16:39
6	they **desired** him to tarry longer time with them,	18:20
9	and **prayed** me to bring this young man unto thee,	23:18
14	The Jews have agreed **to desire** thee that	23:20
2	And I **entreat** thee also, true yokefellow,	Phlp 4:3
3	Furthermore then we **beseech** you, brethren,	1 Th 4:1
3	And **we beseech** you, brethren,	5:12
3	Now we **beseech** you, brethren,	2 Th 2:1
11	is a sin unto death: I do not say that he **shall pray**	1 Jn 5:16
2	And now I **beseech** thee, lady,	2 Jn 1:5

Classical Greek and Septuagint Usage

In classical Greek *erōtaō* usually means "to ask a question" in order to gain information. It may also mean "to challenge a person" or "to request something from someone." In the Septuagint the primary meaning of *erōtaō* is "to ask for information." A fairly common use of *erōtaō* in the Septuagint is in connection with prayers to God. Prayers using *erōtaō* are generally requests for guidance. The Christian use of *erōtaō* in prayers to God is documented by an inscription in a Roman catacomb (see *Moulton-Milligan*).

New Testament Usage

In the New Testament *erōtaō* primarily means "to ask for information" (John 5:12) or "to request someone to do something" (John 4:40; 19:31). On the other hand, its related term *aiteō* (153) usually means "to ask for something which one wants for himself, to request, or demand." As such, *erōtaō* is generally more conversational in form and at times may express a more intimate relation between the parties than *aiteō* would. It should be noted that Jesus always used *erōtaō* in His prayers to the Father (John 14:16), whereas the disciples used *aiteō* in their prayers to God.

The word *erōtaō* does not appear to denote the asking between equals as some have suggested, nor does *aiteō* refer to an inferior requesting something of a superior. There are many exceptions to both ideas in the Septuagint and the New Testament. The context, not the word, will reveal the status of the persons involved. The focus of the words themselves seems to be more on the way something is asked rather than on who is doing the asking.

STRONG 2065, BAUER 311-12, MOULTON-MILLIGAN 255, KITTEL 2:685-87, LIDDELL-SCOTT 695-96, COLIN BROWN 2:855-57,879-80,885.

2049B. ἐσθής esthēs noun

Clothing.

COGNATE:
ἔσθησις esthēsis (2050)

SYNONYMS:
ἔνδυμα enduma (1726)
ἱμάτιον himation (2416)
ἱματισμός himatismos (2417)
σκέπασμα skepasma (4484)
χιτών chitōn (5345)

ἔσθησις 2050

1. ἐσθῆτι **esthēti** dat sing fem
2. ἐσθῆτα **esthēta** acc sing fem

2 mocked him, and arrayed him in a gorgeous **robe**,..	Luke 23:11
1 stood near them in dazzling **apparel** (NASB)	24:4
1 behold, two men stood by them in white **apparel**;....	Acts 1:10
1 behold, a man stood before me in bright **clothing**,.....	10:30
2 upon a set day Herod, arrayed in royal **apparel**,.......	12:21
1 a man with a gold ring, in goodly **apparel**,............	Jas 2:2
1 and there come in also a poor man in vile **raiment**;.....	2:2
2 have respect to him that weareth the gay **clothing**,......	2:3

From classical Greek down into New Testament times *esthēs* appears to have the same meaning. It is always a general word meaning "clothing." The word may be used to refer to a variety of different kinds of clothing in the same way the English word *clothing* may refer to anything from a wedding dress to an athlete's attire. The particular kind of clothing is indicated by the context, not by the word itself.

Classical Greek and Septuagint Usage
In classical Greek *esthēs* is used to refer to the dress of a prophetess, to the clothing of a mourner, to clean clothing, or to simple attire (see *Liddell-Scott*). In the papyri it refers to a soldier's uniform, to woolen clothing, to a long robe, or to expensive clothing (see *Moulton-Milligan*). The Septuagint uses it of a holy mantle and a soldier's uniform.

New Testament Usage
Esthēs occurs six times in the New Testament. Again it is a general word for clothing. The context will help determine what kind of clothing is being referred to. *Esthēs* may refer to a beautiful robe (Luke 23:11), to the radiant apparel of angels (Acts 1:10; 10:30), to the clothing of kings (Acts 12:21), to the expensive clothes of the rich (James 2:2), or to the dirty clothes of the poor (James 2:2).

STRONG 2066, BAUER 312, MOULTON-MILLIGAN 255-56, LIDDELL-SCOTT 696, COLIN BROWN 1:312.

2050. ἔσθησις esthēsis noun
Clothing, garments.
CROSS-REFERENCE:
ἐσθής esthēs (2049B)

1. ἐσθήσεσιν **esthēsesin** dat pl fem
2. ἐσθήσεσι **esthēsesi** dat pl fem

1 two men stood by them in shining **garments**:.......	Luke 24:4
2 two men in white **clothing** stood (NASB)...........	Acts 1:10

As in Luke 24:4, some forms of the word *esthesis* suggest ornate, goodly, unusual garments or clothing. It was used of the "royal apparel" worn by King Herod (Acts 12:21). It is related to *esthēs* (2049B).

STRONG 2067, MOULTON-MILLIGAN 256, LIDDELL-SCOTT 696.

2051. ἐσθής esthēs
See word study at number 2049B.

2052. ἐσθίω esthiō verb
Eat, get sustenance.
COGNATES:
κατεσθίω katesthiō (2688)
συνεσθίω sunesthiō (4756)
SYNONYMS:
γεύω geuō (1083)
καταπίνω katapinō (2636)
κατεσθίω katesthiō (2688)
τρώγω trōgō (5017)

אָכַל 'ākhal (404), Qal: eat, consume (Lv 22:6ff., 2 Kgs 4:41ff., Is 36:16); niphal: be eaten, be consumed (Ex 13:7, Ez 45:21); hiphil: feed (Ru 2:14, 2 Chr 18:26, Ez 3:3).

אֲכַל 'ăkhal (A405), Eat, devour (Dn 4:33 [4:30], 7:7—Aramaic).

אָכְלָה 'okhlāh (408), Food (Ex 16:15).

בָּרָה bārāh (1290), Eat, receive a diet (2 Sm 13:6,10).

יָנַק yānaq (3352), Suck (Is 60:16).

מַאֲכָל ma'ăkhāl (4120), Food (Gn 40:17).

נָפַל nāphal (5489), Fall, be allotted (Ez 47:22).

נָשָׂא nāsâ' (5558), Take away (Jb 32:22).

שָׁמֵן shāmēn (8466), Fat (Dt 32:15).

1. ἐσθίετε **esthiete** 2pl indic/impr pres act
2. ἐσθίει **esthiei** 3sing indic pres act
3. ἐσθίουσιν **esthiousin** 3pl indic pres act
4. ἐσθίῃ **esthiē** 3sing subj pres act
5. ἐσθίητε **esthiēte** 2pl subj pres act
6. ἐσθίωσιν **esthiōsin** 3pl subj pres act
7. ἐσθιέτω **esthietō** 3sing impr pres act
8. ἐσθίων **esthiōn** nom sing masc part pres act
9. ἐσθίοντι **esthionti** dat sing masc part pres act
10. ἐσθίοντα **esthionta** acc sing masc part pres act
11. ἐσθίοντες **esthiontes** nom pl masc part pres act
12. ἐσθιόντων **esthiontōn** gen pl masc part pres act
13. ἐσθίοντας **esthiontas** acc pl masc part pres act
14. ἐσθίειν **esthiein** inf pres act
15. φάγω **phagō** 1sing subj aor act
16. φάγῃς **phagēs** 2sing subj aor act
17. φάγῃ **phagē** 3sing subj aor act
18. φάγωμεν **phagōmen** 1pl subj aor act
19. φάγητε **phagēte** 2pl subj aor act
20. φάγωσιν **phagōsin** 3pl subj aor act
21. φάγοι **phagoi** 3sing opt aor act
22. φάγε **phage** 2sing impr aor act

ἐσθίω 2052

23. φάγετε **phagete** 2pl impr aor act
24. φαγόντες **phagontes** nom pl masc part aor act
25. φαγεῖν **phagein** inf aor act
26. ἤσθιον **ēsthion** 3pl indic imperf act
27. ἔφαγον **ephagon** 1/3sing/pl indic aor act
28. ἔφαγεν **ephagen** 3sing indic aor act
29. ἐφάγομεν **ephagomen** 1pl indic aor act
30. ἐφάγετε **ephagete** 2pl indic aor act
31. φάγεσαι **phagesai** 2sing indic fut mid
32. φάγεται **phagetai** 3sing indic fut mid
33. φάγονται **phagontai** 3pl indic fut mid
34. ἤσθιεν **ēsthien** 3sing indic imperf act

19	what ye **shall eat**, or what ye shall drink;	Matt 6:25
18	What **shall** we **eat**? or, What shall we drink?	6:31
2	Why **eateth** your Master with publicans and	9:11
8	For John came neither **eating** nor drinking,	11:18
8	The Son of man came **eating** and drinking,	11:19
14	and began to pluck the ears of corn, and **to eat**.	12:1
28	into the house of God, and did **eat** the showbread,	12:4
27	into the house of God, and did **eat** the showbread,	12:4
25	which was not lawful for him **to eat**,	12:4
25	They need not depart; give ye them **to eat**.	14:16
27	And they did all **eat**, and were filled:	14:20
11	they that **had eaten** were about five thousand men,	14:21
6	for they wash not their hands when **they eat** bread.	15:2
25	but **to eat** with unwashen hands defileth not a man.	15:20
2	yet the dogs **eat** of the crumbs which fall	15:27
20	with me now three days, and have nothing **to eat**:	15:32
27	And they **did all eat**, and were filled.	15:37
11	they that **did eat** were four thousand men,	15:38
14	and **to eat** and drink with the drunken;	24:49
4	and **to eat** and drink with the drunken;	24:49
25	For I was an hungered, and ye gave me **meat**:	25:35
25	For I was an hungered, and ye gave me no **meat**,	25:42
25	Where ... we prepare for thee **to eat** the passover?	26:17
12	And as they **did eat**, he said, Verily I say unto you,	26:21
12	And as they were **eating**, Jesus took bread,	26:26
23	and said, Take, **eat**; this is my body.	26:26
8	and he **did eat** locusts and wild honey;	Mark 1:6
10	And when the scribes and Pharisees saw him **eat**	2:16
2	And when the scribes and Pharisees saw him **eat**	2:16
34	And when the scribes and Pharisees saw him **eat**	2:16
2	he **eateth** and drinketh with publicans and sinners?	2:16
28	and did **eat** the showbread, which is not lawful	2:26
25	which is not lawful **to eat** but for the priests,	2:26
25	so that they could not so much as **eat** bread.	3:20
25	that something should be given her **to eat**.	5:43
25	and they had no leisure so much as **to eat**.	6:31
20	buy themselves bread: ... they have nothing **to eat**.	6:36
25	answered and said unto them, Give ye them **to eat**.	6:37
25	go and buy ... bread, and give them **to eat**?	6:37
27	And they **did all eat**, and were filled.	6:42
24	And they that **did eat** of the loaves were about	6:44
13	And when they saw some of his disciples **eat** bread	7:2
3	And when they saw some of his disciples **eat** bread	7:2
3	except they wash their hands oft, **eat** not,	7:3
3	except they wash, they **eat** not.	7:4
5	but **eat** bread with unwashen hands?	7:5
2	dogs under the table **eat** of the children's crumbs.	7:28
3	dogs under the table **eat** of the children's crumbs.	7:28
20	and having nothing **to eat**,	8:1
20	been with me three days, and have nothing **to eat**:	8:2
27	So they **did eat**, and were filled:	8:8
24	And they that **had eaten** were about four thousand:	8:9
21	No man **eat** fruit of thee hereafter for ever.	11:14
16	go and prepare that thou **mayest eat** the passover?	14:12
15	where I **shall eat** the passover with my disciples?	14:14
12	And as they sat and **did eat**, Jesus said, Verily I say	14:18
8	One of you **which eateth** with me shall betray me.	14:18
12	And as they **did eat**, Jesus took bread, and blessed,	14:22
23	gave to them, and said, Take, **eat**: this is my body.	14:22
28	And in those days he **did eat** nothing:	Luke 4:2
1	**do ye eat** and drink with publicans and sinners?	5:30
3	disciples of the Pharisees; but thine **eat** and drink?	5:33
26	his disciples plucked the ears of corn, and **did eat**,	6:1
28	house of God, and did take and **eat** the showbread,	6:4
25	which it is not lawful **to eat** but for the priests	6:4
8	For John the Baptist came neither **eating** bread nor	7:33
8	The Son of man is come **eating** and drinking,	7:34
17	Pharisees desired him that he **would eat** with him.	7:36
25	she arose ... and he commanded to give her **meat**.	8:55
25	But he said unto them, Give ye them **to eat**.	9:13
27	And they **did eat**, and were all filled:	9:17
11	**eating** and drinking such things as they give;	10:7
1	**eat** such things as are set before you:	10:8
22	take thine ease, **eat**, drink, and be merry.	12:19
19	no thought for your life, what **ye shall eat**;	12:22
19	And seek not ye what ye **shall eat**,	12:29
14	and **to eat** and drink, and to be drunken;	12:45
29	We **have eaten** and drunk in thy presence,	13:26
25	**to eat** bread on the sabbath day, that they watched.	14:1
32	Blessed is he that **shall eat** bread in the kingdom,	14:15
26	filled ... belly with the husks that the swine **did eat**:	15:16
24	the fatted calf, ... and let us **eat**, and be merry:	15:23
15	and serve me, till I **have eaten** and drunken;	17:8
31	and afterward thou **shalt eat** and drink?	17:8
26	They **did eat**, they drank, they married wives,	17:27
26	it was in the days of Lot; they **did eat**, they drank,	17:28
18	Go and prepare us the passover, that we **may eat**.	22:8
15	where I **shall eat** the passover with my disciples?	22:11
25	With desire I have desired **to eat** this passover	22:15
15	For I say unto you, I will not any more **eat** thereof,	22:16
5	ye **may eat** and drink at my table in my kingdom,	22:30
28	And he took it, and **did eat** before them.	24:43
22	his disciples prayed him, saying, Master, **eat**.	John 4:31
25	I have meat **to eat** that ye know not of.	4:32
25	Hath any man brought him ought **to eat**?	4:33
20	Whence shall we buy bread, that these **may eat**?	6:5
27	nigh unto the place where they **did eat** bread,	6:23
30	because ye **did eat** of the loaves, and were filled.	6:26
27	Our fathers **did eat** manna in the desert;	6:31
25	written, He gave them bread from heaven **to eat**.	6:31
27	Your fathers did **eat** manna in the wilderness,	6:49
17	that a man **may eat** thereof, and not die.	6:50
17	if any man **eat** of this bread, he shall live for ever:	6:51
25	How can this man give us his flesh **to eat**?	6:52
19	Except ye **eat** the flesh of the Son of man,	6:53
27	not as your fathers did **eat** manna, and are dead:	6:58
20	but that they **might eat** the passover.	18:28
28	and neither did **eat** nor drink.	Acts 9:9
22	came a voice to him, Rise, Peter; kill, and **eat**.	10:13
27	for I **have** never **eaten** any thing that is common	10:14
22	a voice saying unto me, Arise, Peter; slay and **eat**.	11:7
25	neither **eat** nor drink till they had killed Paul.	23:12
25	will neither **eat** nor drink till they have killed him:	23:21
14	and when he had broken it, he began **to eat**.	27:35
25	For one believeth that he **may eat** all things:	Rom 14:2
2	**eat** all things: another, who is weak, **eateth** herbs.	14:2
8	Let not him that **eateth** despise ... that eateth not;	14:3
10	Let not him that eateth despise ... that **eateth** not;	14:3
8	let not him which **eateth** not judge him that eateth:	14:3
10	let not him which eateth not judge him that **eateth**:	14:3
8	He that **eateth**, eateth to the Lord,	14:6
2	He that eateth, **eateth** to the Lord,	14:6
8	and he that **eateth** not, to the Lord he eateth not,	14:6
2	and he that eateth not, to the Lord he **eateth** not,	14:6
9	but it is evil for that man who **eateth** with offence.	14:20
25	It is good neither **to eat** flesh, nor to drink wine,	14:21
17	And he that doubteth is damned if he **eat**,	14:23
3	**eat** it as a thing offered unto an idol;	I Co 8:7
18	for neither, if we **eat**, are we the better;	8:8
18	neither, if we **eat** not, are we the worse.	8:8
14	**to eat** those things which are offered to idols;	8:10
15	I will **eat** no flesh while the world standeth,	8:13
25	Have we not power **to eat** and to drink?	9:4
2	who planteth ... and **eateth** not of the fruit thereof?	9:7
2	and **eateth** not of the milk of the flock?	9:7
3	about holy things **live** of the things of the temple?	9:13

609

ἔσθω 2052B

27	And did all **eat** the same spiritual meat;	1 Co 10:3
25	sat down **to eat** and drink, and rose up to play;	10:7
11	are not they which **eat** of the sacrifices partakers	10:18
1	Whatsoever is sold in the shambles, that **eat**,	10:25
1	whatsoever is set before you, **eat**,	10:27
1	**eat** not for his sake that showed it,	10:28
1	Whether therefore ye **eat**, or drink,	10:31
25	this is not **to eat** the Lord's supper.	11:20
25	in **eating** every one taketh before other his own	11:21
14	What? have ye not houses **to eat** and to drink in?	11:22
23	**eat**: this is my body, which is broken for you:	11:24
5	For as often as ye **eat** this bread,	11:26
4	Wherefore whosoever **shall eat** this bread,	11:27
7	so **let him eat** of that bread, and drink of that cup.	11:28
8	For he that **eateth** and drinketh unworthily,	11:29
2	**eateth** and drinketh damnation to himself,	11:29
25	my brethren, when ye come together **to eat**,	11:33
7	And if any man hunger, let him **eat** at home;	11:34
18	let us **eat** and drink; for to morrow we die.	15:32
29	Neither **did we eat** any man's bread for nought;	2 Th 3:8
7	that if any would not work, neither **should** he **eat**.	3:10
6	with quietness they work, and **eat** their own bread.	3:12
14	which shall **devour** the adversaries.	Heb 10:27
25	have no right **to eat** which serve the tabernacle.	13:10
32	and **shall eat** your flesh as it were fire.	Jas 5:3
25	that overcometh will I give **to eat** of the tree of life,	Rev 2:7
25	**to eat** things sacrificed unto idols,	2:14
25	will I give **to eat** of the hidden manna,	2:17
25	and **to eat** things sacrificed unto idols.	2:20
27	and as soon as I **had eaten** it, my belly was bitter.	10:10
33	and **shall eat** her flesh, and burn her with fire.	17:16
19	That ye **may eat** the flesh of kings,	19:18

Classical Greek and Septuagint Usage

In classical Greek *esthiō*, as well as *phagō* (which provides certain missing tenses), denoted the process of eating in order to sustain life. When combined with the verb *pinō* (3956), "drink," a stock expression is generated ("eating and drinking") which carries with it the notion of fellowship or participation. This association with fellowship is also found in the Old Testament. David complained (Psalm 41:9 [LXX 40:9]) that his "familiar friend . . . which did eat" (*ho esthiōn artous mou*) of David's food had rebelled against him. Eating could also have a religious significance for the Greek. Certain types of worship, particularly in the "mystery religions," were involved with eating and drinking. The "peace (fellowship) offering" (Leviticus 3) is an expression of eating as a worship function in the Old Testament, as were the laws concerning "permitted" foods (Leviticus 11). Eating and drinking were always construed by the Jews as emblematic of the blessings of God to be enjoyed with thanksgiving (Ecclesiastes 2:24,25 and throughout the book). But, from the foundation of the world, sin has involved man's abuse of something originally good. So drunkenness and gluttony were regarded as sinful debauchery.

New Testament Usage

In the New Testament Jesus defended himself against such a charge (Matthew 11:18,19) by replying that John the Baptist failed to eat or drink, and they charged him with having a demon. But when Jesus ate and drank, they accused Him of being a glutton and a drunkard (cf. Luke 7:33,34).

The notion of fellowship is clearly conveyed when Jesus spoke of the reprobate servant who began "to eat and drink with the drunken" (Matthew 24:49; cf. Luke 12:45). It also lies at the root of the accusation that Jesus ate with tax collectors and sinners (Matthew 9:11; cf. Luke 15:1,2, *sunesthiō* [4756], "eats with"). Participation is implied in Revelation 2:7, where "to eat of the tree of life" (cf. Genesis 2:9; Revelation 22:2,14) clearly indicates sharing in that life. In John 6:48-58 Jesus declared that it is necessary to eat His flesh and drink His blood (6:53) to have life. Jesus said he who does this "dwelleth in me, and I in him" (6:56).

Paul's attitude toward meats offered to idols (1 Corinthians 8) is better understood if one views eating as a worship function. Those who are "strong" see it only as a natural function. But Paul wrote that the "strong" must consider the "weaker brother" who, before his conversion, viewed eating these sacrifices as a form of idol worship, and it still offended him. Eating as a legitimate form of worship to God is seen in the eating of the Passover (Matthew 26:17-30; Mark 14:12-26; Luke 22:7-28), which became the Lord's Supper for the Church (1 Corinthians 11:23-34).

STRONG 2068, BAUER 312-13, MOULTON-MILLIGAN 256, KITTEL 2:689-95, LIDDELL-SCOTT 696, COLIN BROWN 2:271,277.

2052B. ἔσθω esthō verb

Eat.

1. ἔσθητε **esthēte** 2pl subj pres act
2. ἔσθων **esthōn** nom sing masc part pres act
3. ἔσθοντες **esthontes** nom pl masc part pres act

2	and he **did eat** locusts and wild honey;	Mark 1:6
3	**eating** and drinking such things as they give:	Luke 10:7
1	ye **may eat** and drink at my table in my kingdom,	22:30

This word is an alternate spelling of *esthiō* (2052). The form *esthō* is attested as early as Homer (ca. Eighth Century B.C.) as well as in the third-century B.C. ostraca and the Septuagint (cf. *Bauer*). See the word study at number 2052.

BAUER 313, LIDDELL-SCOTT 697.

2053. Ἐσλί Esli name
Esli.

1. Ἐσλί Esli masc
2. Ἐσλί Hesli masc

2 which was the son of Esli,........................ Luke 3:25

The son of Naggai in the genealogy of Jesus (Luke 3:25).

2054. ἔσοπτρον esoptron noun
Mirror.

1. ἐσόπτρου esoptrou gen sing neu
2. ἐσόπτρῳ esoptrō dat sing neu

1 For now we see through a glass, darkly;........... 1 Co 13:12
2 like ... a man beholding his natural face in a glass:... Jas 1:23

Mirrors in ancient times were made of highly polished metal; the image reflected was hazy and imperfect. Used figuratively in the New Testament, a mirror indicates the imperfect image believers have, the fleeting glance of heavenly things, or the fact that heavenly things are seen indirectly (1 Corinthians 13:12).

Strong 2072, Bauer 313, Moulton-Milligan 256, Kittel 1:178-80; 2:696, Liddell-Scott 697, Colin Brown 2:756.

2055. ἑσπέρα hespera noun
Evening.

Synonym:
ὄψιος opsios (3662)

עֶרֶב 'ārav (6386), Become evening (Jgs 19:9).
עֲרָב 'ărāv (6390), Desert, wasteland, (Arabia?) (Is 21:13).
עֶרֶב 'erev (6394), Evening (Gn 1:5,8,13, 2 Sm 11:2, Ps 104:23 [103:23]).
עֲרָבָה 'ărāvāh (6400), Desert, waterless region (1 Sm 23:24).
עַתָּה 'attāh (6498), Now (Ru 2:7).

1. ἑσπέρα hespera nom sing fem
2. ἑσπέρας hesperas gen sing fem
3. ἑσπέραν hesperan acc sing fem

3 for it is toward evening, and the day is far spent... Luke 24:29
1 in hold unto the next day: for it was now eventide... Acts 4:3
2 testified ... from morning till evening.................. 28:23

Throughout classical Greek and the Septuagint this word was used in a literal sense to delineate time, "evening, (at) eve, (at) nightfall." Metaphorically it described one whose life was wearing to its *eve*; however, the New Testament usage depicts its literal meaning exclusively. Luke is the only writer to use *hespera*, and in each case he referred to it to describe a time of day (Luke 24:29; Acts 4:3; 28:23).

Strong 2073, Bauer 313, Moulton-Milligan 256, Liddell-Scott 697.

2056. Ἐσρώμ Esrōm name
Hezron.

1. Ἐσρώμ Esrōm masc
2. Ἐσρώμ Hesrōm masc

2 and Phares begat Esrom; and Esrom begat Aram;... Matt 1:3
2 and Phares begat Esrom; and Esrom begat Aram;...... 1:3
2 which was the son of Esrom,........................ Luke 3:33

The son of Pharez in the genealogy of Jesus (Matthew 1:3; Luke 3:33).

2056B. ἑσσόομαι hessoomai verb
Be weaker, inferior; be defeated, overcome.

1. ἡσσώθητε hēssōthēte 2pl indic aor pass

1 what respect were you treated as inferior (NASB)..2 Co 12:13

Classical Greek

Hessoomai is an Ionic dialect variant of *hēssoomai*, "be less than, weaker than, inferior to," or "be beaten, be overcome." It is related to the comparative form *hēssōn* (2247B), "lesser, inferior, weaker." In the New Testament it is equivalent to the variant *hēttaomai*.

New Testament Usage

Hessoomai is used by two New Testament writers, Paul and Peter. Paul used it in the sense of "inferior" in his attempts to reason with the Corinthians, "In what respect were you treated as *inferior to* the rest of the churches . . . ?" (2 Corinthians 12:13, NASB). Peter used it in two consecutive verses in the other sense, "be overcome": "For by what a man *is overcome*, by this he is enslaved. For if after they have escaped . . . they *are* again . . . *overcome* . . ." (2 Peter 2:19,20, NASB).

Bauer 313, Liddell-Scott 698.

2057. ἔσχατος eschatos adj
Last, least, final, farthest, extreme, latter.

Cross-Reference:
ἐσχάτως eschatōs (2058)

אָחוֹר 'āchôr (268), Behind, the future (Ps 139:5 [138:5], Is 41:23).
אַחַר 'achar (313), Afterward, after (Nm 31:2, Jos 10:14).

ἔσχατος 2057

אַחֲרוֹן 'achărôn (315), Later, future, last (Dt 24:3, 2 Chr 16:11, Dn 11:29).

אַחֲרֵי 'ochŏrî (A319), End (Dn 2:28—Aramaic).

אַחֲרִית 'achărîth (321), End, outcome, future (Nm 24:14, Prv 5:11, Jer 17:11).

אָסַף 'āsaph (636), Gather; piel: form a rear guard (Nm 10:25).

אֶפֶס 'ephes (675), Extremity, end (Is 45:22).

אָרַח 'ārach (755), Wander, wanderer (Jer 9:2).

אֹרַח 'ōrach (758), Path (Jb 8:13).

גָּדוֹל gādhôl (1448), Great (Jos 1:4).

יַרְכָּה yarkāh (3526), Rear, most distant part (Jer 6:22, Ez 38:6).

מֶרְחָק merchāq (4963), Remote, distant (Is 8:9).

סוּף sûph (5675), Reed, aquatic plant (Jon 2:6).

סוֹף sôph (5677), End (1 Kgs 9:26).

קָצֶה qātseh (7381), End, extremity (Dt 28:49, Ps 135:7 [134:7], Jer 51:16 [28:16]).

שְׁבִיעִי sh^evî'î (8113), Seventh (Lv 23:16).

תַּכְלִית takhlîth (8832), Extremity (Jb 11:7).

1. ἐσχάτων eschatōn gen pl masc/fem
2. ἐσχάτου eschatou gen sing masc/neu
3. ἔσχατον eschaton nom/acc sing masc/neu
4. ἔσχατος eschatos nom sing masc
5. ἐσχάτῳ eschatō dat sing masc
6. ἔσχατοι eschatoi nom pl masc
7. ἐσχάτους eschatous acc pl masc
8. ἐσχάτη eschatē nom sing fem
9. ἐσχάτῃ eschatē dat sing fem
10. ἐσχάταις eschatais dat pl fem
11. ἐσχάτας eschatas acc pl fem
12. ἔσχατα eschata nom/acc pl neu

3	till thou hast paid the **uttermost** farthing...........	Matt 5:26
12	and the **last** state of that man is worse than the first.	12:45
6	But many that are first shall be **last**;................	19:30
6	first shall be **last**; and the **last** shall be first........	19:30
1	beginning from the **last** unto the first................	20:8
6	Saying, These **last** have wrought but one hour,......	20:12
5	I will give unto this **last**, even as unto thee..........	20:14
6	So the **last** shall be first, and the first **last**:.........	20:16
6	So the **last** shall be first, and the first **last**:.........	20:16
4	They say unto him, The first.....................	21:31
8	so the **last** error shall be worse than the first........	27:64
4	desire to be first, the same shall be **last** of all,.....	Mark 9:35
6	many that are first shall be **last**; and the **last** first.....	10:31
6	many that are first shall be **last**; and the **last** first.....	10:31
3	one son, ... he sent him also **last** unto them, saying,..	12:6
8	**last** of all the woman died also.....................	12:22
3	**last** of all the woman died also.....................	12:22
12	and the **last** state of that man is worse than the first.	Luke 11:26
3	till thou hast paid the very **last** mite.................	12:59
6	And, behold, there are **last** which shall be first,......	13:30
6	and there are first which shall be **last**...............	13:30
3	and thou begin with shame to take the **lowest** room...	14:9
3	go and sit down in the **lowest** room;.................	14:10
9	but should raise it up again at the **last** day.........	John 6:39
9	and I will raise him up at the **last** day...............	6:40
9	and I will raise him up at the **last** day...............	6:44
9	and I will raise him up at the **last** day...............	6:54
9	In the **last** day, that great day of the feast,............	7:37
1	beginning at the eldest, even unto the **last**:........	John 8:9
9	shall rise again in the resurrection at the **last** day.....	11:24
9	the same shall judge him in the **last** day............	12:48
2	Samaria, and unto the **uttermost** part of the earth.....	Acts 1:8
10	it shall come to pass in the **last** days, saith God,........	2:17
2	be for salvation unto the **ends** of the earth..........	13:47
7	I think that God hath set forth us the apostles **last**,	1 Co 4:9
3	And **last** of all he was seen of me also...............	15:8
4	The **last** enemy that shall be destroyed is death......	15:26
4	the **last** Adam was made a quickening spirit.........	15:45
9	at the **last** trump: for the trumpet shall sound,.......	15:52
10	that in the **last** days perilous times shall come......	2 Tm 3:1
1	Hath in these **last** days spoken unto us by his Son,	Heb 1:2
2	Hath in these **last** days spoken unto us by his Son,....	1:2
10	Ye have heaped treasure together for the **last** days...	Jas 5:3
5	ready to be revealed in the **last** time................	1 Pt 1:5
1	but was manifest in these **last** times for you,.........	1:20
2	but was manifest in these **last** times for you,.........	1:20
12	**latter end** is worse with them than the beginning....	2 Pt 2:20
2	that there shall come in the **last** days scoffers,........	3:3
1	that there shall come in the **last** days scoffers,........	3:3
8	Little children, it is the **last** time:................	1 Jn 2:18
8	whereby we know that it is the **last** time.............	2:18
2	told you there should be mockers in the **last** time,....	Jude 18
4	I am Alpha and Omega, the first and the **last**:......	Rev 1:11
4	Fear not; I am the first and the **last**:.................	1:17
4	These things saith the first and the **last**,..............	2:8
12	and the **last** to be more than the first................	2:19
11	seven angels having the seven **last** plagues;...........	15:1
1	had the seven vials full of the seven **last** plagues,.....	21:9
4	the beginning and the end, the first and the **last**......	22:13

Classical Greek

The adjective (perhaps from *ek* [1523], "out from, away from") functions to denote the limits of space. In the "last" as opposed to the first in a line, or in terms of rank or order, the *eschatos* was the "worst." Perhaps *eschatos* originally depicted the "farthest" in any direction; this is closest to the prepositional meaning. It refers to the "last" as in the final events in a series (cf. the English word *eschat-ology*, the study of "last things"). The Greeks, however, had "no developed eschatological understanding of time; i.e., one directed towards a future goal or end of the historical process" (Link, "Goal," *Colin Brown*, 2:55).

Septuagint Usage

In the Septuagint *eschatos* conforms to normal classical usage. *Eschatos* contrasts *prōtos* 4270B, "first," in a common formula expressing totality ("from beginning to end," cf. 2 Chronicles 16:11; 20:34; 25:26; 26:22; 28:26). The "last" is also a sequential term (Deuteronomy 24:3; Nehemiah 8:18), and it functions as a spatial word (Deuteronomy 28:49; cf. Joshua 1:4). The prophets used the phrase "the ends of the earth" repeatedly (e.g., Isaiah 45:22; 48:20; 49:6; etc.). Temporally it denotes the final days of one's life (Deuteronomy 31:29). Most of these texts have *'achar* in one form or another as the Hebrew equivalency.

It was not until the advent of the prophetic writings that *eschatos* acquired significant theological implications, usually in the phrase "last days" (*en tais eschatais hēmerais* or *ep' eschatou ton hēmeron*). It is primarily from this basis that the New Testament developed its understanding of *eschatos* as a theological expression.

Most critically for the prophets, "end time" is a time of God's saving activity (Isaiah 2:2; Hosea 3:5; Micah 4:1) as well as His judgment (Jeremiah 23:20; 30:24 [LXX 37:24]; Ezekiel 38:16). Daniel's apocalyptic flavor is enhanced with "last days" predictions (Daniel [Septuagint] 2:28,45; 10:14).

A similar understanding of "last days" is reflected in the Dead Sea Scrolls of the Qumran community (Commentary on Habakkuk [1QpHab] 2:5; Damascus Document [CD] 4:4). That group also saw this time as the time of the reappearance of the "Teacher of Righteousness" (CD 6:11) (see Link, "Goal," *Colin Brown*, 2:56 for a fuller discussion of Qumran and rabbinic Judaism).

New Testament Usage

Apart from a normal usage following the classical patterns of space, time, sequence, or rank (e.g., Matthew 5:26; 12:45; 19:30; Mark 12:6; Acts 1:8; 1 Corinthians 4:9; Revelation 1:17; 2:8), *eschatos* is theologically significant and relevant to New Testament theology as a whole.

In the Synoptic Gospels there is no "last days" language, although the concept of the *eschaton*, especially captured in the reversal of roles—"the first will be (future) last (*eschatos*) . . . "—is implicit (e.g., Mark 9:35; 10:31 with parallels cf. ibid., 2:57).

John's Gospel knows the "last day" (singular) to be the day of resurrection (6:39,40,44,54; 11:24); Peter understood it as the time of salvation (1 Peter 1:5). But it will be the day of judgment for those rejecting Jesus and His Word (John 12:48).

In Acts Luke stated that the "last days" are the age of the Spirit instituted at Pentecost. Luke wrote "last days" (*en tais eschatais hēmerais*) for "afterwards" (*meta tauta* [in the Septuagint]) in his citation of Joel 2:28 at Acts 2:17 (cf. Hebrews 1:2; 1 Peter 1:20 of the manifestation of Christ). Lastly, other New Testament passages emphasize that these times, i.e., the "last days," are perilous because of the assault of sin's forces (2 Timothy 3:1; cf. 2 Peter 3:3; 1 John 2:18; Jude 18).

STRONG 2078, BAUER 313-14, MOULTON-MILLIGAN 256, KITTEL 2:697-98, LIDDELL-SCOTT 699-700, COLIN BROWN 2:55-59.

2058. ἐσχάτως eschatōs adv

Finally, to the uttermost, at the end of (life).
CROSS-REFERENCE:
  ἔσχατος eschatos (2057)

1. ἐσχάτως eschatōs

1 My little daughter lieth at the point of death:........Mark 5:23

This obscure word related to *eschatos* (2057) occurs only once in the New Testament, at Mark 5:23. It is, however, used in classical Greek writings as early as the Fifth Century B.C. where it means "to the uttermost, in the end," and "exceedingly." Accompanied by *echei* in Mark's Gospel, *eschatōs* carries the meaning of "the last extremity." The KJV translates it "at the point of death."

STRONG 2079, BAUER 314, MOULTON-MILLIGAN 256, LIDDELL-SCOTT 699-700, COLIN BROWN 2:55.

2059. ἔσω esō adv

In, into, inside, within, inner.

1. ἔσω esō

1 went **in**, and sat with the servants, to see the end...Matt 26:58
1 followed ... even **into** the palace of the high priest: Mark 14:54
1 And the soldiers led him away **into** the hall,.......... 15:16
1 after eight days again his disciples were **within**,.... John 20:26
1 when we had opened, we found no man **within**...... Acts 5:23
1 I delight in the law of God after the **inward** man:... Rom 7:22
1 do not ye judge them that are **within**?............... 1 Co 5:12
1 yet our **inner** man is being renewed (NASB)........2 Co 4:16
1 by his Spirit in the **inner** man;..................... Eph 3:16

Esō is an adverb of place implying movement in or describing the state of being within. In Romans 7:22 it is used to refer to the inward or spiritual side of man's nature. This does not refer to the introspective, inward-looking man, but to his essential being, often expressed in terms of the heart (*kardia* [2559]) versus his outward appearance (Ephesians 3:16; cf. 2 Corinthians 4:16). First Corinthians 5:12 uses the word to describe those believers who are within the Christian community, as opposed to the pagans who are without or outside.

STRONG 2080, BAUER 314, MOULTON-MILLIGAN 256, KITTEL 2:698-99, LIDDELL-SCOTT 700, COLIN BROWN 2:566.

2060. ἔσωθεν esōthen adv

Inward, within, from inside.

ἐσώτερος 2061

פְּנִימָה pᵉnîmāh (6687), Inside (Ps 45:13 [44:13]).
פְּנִימִי pᵉnîmî (6688), Inner (Ez 41:17, 42:15).

1. ἔσωθεν esōthen

1	but **inwardly** they are ravening wolves.	Matt 7:15
1	but **within** they are full of extortion and excess.	23:25
1	but are **within** full of dead men's bones,	23:27
1	but **within** ye are full of hypocrisy and iniquity.	23:28
1	For **from within**, out of the heart of men,	Mark 7:21
1	All these evil things come **from within**,	7:23
1	**from within** shall answer and say, Trouble me not:	Luke 11:7
1	**inward part** is full of ravening and wickedness.	11:39
1	did not he ... make that which is **within** also?	11:40
1	yet the **inward** man is renewed day by day.	2 Co 4:16
1	without were fightings, **within** were fears.	7:5
1	and they were full of eyes **within**:	Rev 4:8
1	a book written **within** and on the backside,	5:1
1	the court which is without the temple (NT)	11:2

The word *esōthen* is an adverb of place meaning "from inside" or "within." It is used in the New Testament mainly to express the inner or spiritual nature of man in contrast to the outward show or appearance; e.g., Matthew 7:15, "but inwardly they are ravening wolves."

STRONG 2081, BAUER 314, MOULTON-MILLIGAN 256, LIDDELL-SCOTT 700.

2061. ἐσώτερος esōteros adj

That which is within or innermost.

חִיצוֹן chîtsōn (2535), Outer (Ez 40:17,34).
עֶלְיוֹן ʽelyôn (6169), Upper (2 Chr 23:20).
פְּנִימָה pᵉnîmāh (6687), Inside (1 Kgs 6:30, Ez 41:3).
פְּנִימִי pᵉnîmî (6688), Inner (1 Chr 28:11, 2 Chr 4:22, Ez 46:1).

1. ἐσωτέραν esōteran comp acc sing fem
2. ἐσώτερον esōteron comp nom/acc sing neu

1	thrust them into the **inner** prison,	Acts 16:24
2	and which entereth into that **within** the veil;	Heb 6:19

Technically speaking, this term is the comparative form of *esō* (2059). It refers to the innermost part. In Acts 16:24 the inner prison was the worst part of a prison where no light and little air could enter. In Hebrews 6:19 *esōteros* speaks of that which is within the veil, or curtain, which is the unseen or heavenly world, the heavenly Holy of Holies.

STRONG 2082, BAUER 314, MOULTON-MILLIGAN 256, LIDDELL-SCOTT 700, COLIN BROWN 3:794.

2062. ἑταῖρος hetairos noun

Companion, friend.
SYNONYMS:
κοινωνός koinōnos (2817)
μέτοχος metochos (3223)

חָבֵר chāvēr (2358), Comrade, companion (S/S 1:7, 8:13).
מֵרֵעַ mērēaʽ (4991), Intimate friend, close friend (Jgs 14:11—Codex Alexandrinus only).
רֵעַ rēaʽ (7739), Comrade, companion, friend (2 Sm 13:3, Jb 30:29).
רֵעֶה rēʽeh (7751), Friend, fellow (2 Sm 16:17, 1 Kgs 4:5).

1. ἑταῖρε hetaire voc sing masc
2. ἑταίροις hetairois dat pl masc

2	like unto children ... and calling unto their **fellows**,	Matt 11:16
1	But he answered one of them, and said, **Friend**,	20:13
1	And he saith unto him, **Friend**,	22:12
1	Jesus said ... **Friend**, wherefore art thou come?	26:50

Classical Greek and Septuagint Usage
From earliest times in classical literature this word has indicated one who is associated with someone else in terms of companionship and/or comradeship. The Hebrew word (*rēʽeh*) that it most often translates in the Septuagint also means "companion," although it sometimes renders *chāvēr*, "friend." Josephus used the term to address fellow soldiers. Among the rabbis the Hebrew equivalent came to mean a colleague or associate (see *Bauer*).

New Testament Usage
In the New Testament the word is used only three times: in Matthew 20:13; 22:12; and 26:50 (Matthew 11:16 reads *heterois* [see 2066], "others," in the earlier manuscripts). Each time the word is used it is in the form of an address. *Hetairos* occurs in the Parable of the Laborers in the Vineyard as a means of address for the vineyard owner when he answered his grumbling worker: "*Friend*, I do thee no wrong" (Matthew 20:13). It appears on the lips of the king in the Parable of the Marriage Feast (Matthew 22:12) when he addressed the man without a wedding garment: "*Friend*, how camest thou in hither not having a wedding garment?" It was also used by Jesus to address Judas when he betrayed the Lord (Matthew 26:50). Each use of the word indicates the existence of a bond between speaker and hearer which the hearer has somehow disregarded or even spurned. In many cases generosity is shown on the part of the speaker, in spite of the self-assertion of the hearer.

Finally, the word is to be distinguished from its related term *philos* (5220B), "beloved." Jesus called His disciples *philoi*, never *hetairoi* (John 15:14,15).

In a variant of Luke 23:32 in p75 *hetairoi* can refer to "political partisans" in reference to the two criminals crucified with Jesus (see *Bauer*).

Strong 2083, Bauer 314, Moulton-Milligan 256-57, Kittel 2:699-701, Liddell-Scott 700, Colin Brown 1:259-60.

2063. ἑτερόγλωσσος
heteroglōssos adj
Speaking a foreign language.
CROSS-REFERENCES:
γλῶσσα glōssa (1094)
ἕτερος heteros (2066)

1. ἑτερογλώσσοις **heteroglōssois** dat pl masc

1 With men of **other tongues** and other lips.......... 1 Co 14:21

This word finds its roots in two other words, *heteros* (2066), "another, different," and *glōssa* (1094), "tongue." Its use in 1 Corinthians 14:21 refers to the occasion in the Old Testament where God spoke to the Israelites through the foreign language of their Assyrian foes (Isaiah 28:11ff.). Paul used this word to teach a lesson concerning speaking in tongues.

Strong 2084, Bauer 314, Moulton-Milligan 257, Kittel 1:726-27, Liddell-Scott 701, Colin Brown 2:739-41; 3:1078-79.

2064. ἑτεροδιδασκαλέω
heterodidaskaleō verb
Teach a different (i.e., heretical) doctrine.
CROSS-REFERENCES:
διδάσκω didaskō (1315)
ἕτερος heteros (2066)

1. ἑτεροδιδασκαλεῖ **heterodidaskalei**
3sing indic pres act
2. ἑτεροδιδασκαλεῖν **heterodidaskalein** inf pres act

2 charge some that they **teach no other doctrine**,...... 1 Tm 1:3
1 If any man **teach otherwise**, and consent not............ 6:3

This compound verb from *heteros* (2066), "other, another kind," and *didaskaleō*, "I teach," literally means "to teach other (in effect, heretical) teaching." It does not appear in pre-Christian literature and it is found in the New Testament only in 1 Timothy 1:3 and 6:3.

New Testament Usage
Within the context of the Pastoral Epistles it is obvious that the presence of false teachers, "those who teach other teachings," in the community at Ephesus had prompted Paul to write to Timothy. The precise nature of this "false doctrine" (TEV) is not known. Its character, however, is known (e.g., 1 Timothy 1:6,7; 2 Timothy 4:3ff.). Paul urged Timothy to remain in Ephesus for the express purpose (*hina* [2419]) of commanding some in the community to stop teaching false doctrine (1:3). Such false teaching resisted sound doctrine (the true teachings) and ran counter to the gospel's prescriptions for holy living (6:3).

False teaching always threatened the Church (e.g., 2 Corinthians 11:4,12-15; Galatians 2:4) and continued to do so into the early centuries. Ignatius, the Bishop of Antioch (died ca. A.D. 108), warned Polycarp to stand firm against false teaching (Ignatius To Polycarp 3:1) "as an anvil that is smitten" (see *Liddell-Scott*). It is interesting that he qualified such resistance in terms of suffering and endurance (cf. 2 Timothy 2:3ff.). (See also the word study at *hairesis* [138].)

Strong 2085, Bauer 314, Kittel 2:163, Liddell-Scott 701, Colin Brown 3:766,768.

2065. ἑτεροζυγέω
heterozugeō verb
Intermixing.
CROSS-REFERENCES:
ἕτερος heteros (2066)
ζυγός zugos (2201)

1. ἑτεροζυγοῦντες **heterozugountes**
nom pl masc part pres act

1 ye not **unequally yoked together** with unbelievers:....2 Co 6:14

Heterozugeō, a verb used just once in the New Testament (2 Corinthians 6:14), means "intermixing." The single reference in the Septuagint (Leviticus 19:19) and its use in the New Testament (*ktēnē heterozuga*) are in the context of intermixing animal species (cattle). The idea of "not belonging together" can be found as early as the Zenon Papyri in Hellenistic times. "Unequally yoked together with" or "mismated with" in 2 Corinthians 6:14 is in the context of believer/unbeliever incompatability. Paul combined it with two other words, "partnership," *metochē* (3222), and "fellowship," *koinōnia* (2815).

Strong 2086, Bauer 314, Moulton-Milligan 257, Kittel 2:901, Liddell-Scott 701, Colin Brown 2:739,741; 3:1160,1164.

2066. ἕτερος **heteros** adj
Other, another.
COGNATES:
ἑτερόγλωσσος heteroglōssos (2063)

ἕτερος 2066

ἑτεροδιδασκαλέω heterodidaskaleō (2064)
ἑτεροζυγέω heterozugeō (2065)
ἑτέρως heterōs (2067)

SYNONYM:
ἄλλος allos (241)

אָח 'āch (250), Other (Ex 16:15, Nm 14:4).

אֶחָד 'echādh (259), One, another (Jer 24:2, Dn 8:13, Zec 11:7).

אָחוֹת 'āchôth (269), Each other (Ex 26:3, Ez 3:13).

אַחֵר 'achēr (311), Other, another (Ex 20:3, 2 Kgs 17:7, Is 48:11).

אַחֲרוֹן 'achărôn (315), Later, future (Pss 48:13 [47:13], 102:18 [101:18]).

אָחֳרָן 'ochŏrān (A322), Another (Dn 3:29—Aramaic).

אִישׁ 'îsh (382), Each, each one (Ex 16:15, Is 13:8).

אִשָּׁה 'ishshāh (828), Each (Ex 26:3, Ez 3:13).

זֶה zeh (2172), This, that (Jb 1:16, Is 44:5).

זָר zār (2299), Strange, other (Ex 30:9).

חָדָשׁ chādhāsh (2413), New (Ex 1:8).

כֹּל kōl (A3726), Any, any other (Dn 3:28—Aramaic).

נֵכָר nēkhār (5424), Something foreign (Jos 24:20).

עוֹד 'ôdh (5968), Once more, again, beside (Gn 37:9, Is 47:8).

רֵעַ rēaʿ (7739), Each other (Is 34:14).

רְעוּת rᵉʿûth (7757), Each other (Is 34:16).

שֵׁנִי shēnî (8529), Second (Dn 8:3).

1. ἕτερον heteron nom/acc sing masc/neu
2. ἑτέρῳ heterō dat sing masc/neu
3. ἑτέρων heterōn gen pl masc/neu
4. ἑτέροις heterois dat pl masc/neu
5. ἕτερος heteros nom sing masc
6. ἑτέρου heterou gen sing masc
7. ἕτεροι heteroi nom pl masc
8. ἑτέρους heterous acc pl masc
9. ἑτέρα hetera nom sing/pl fem
10. ἑτέρας heteras gen sing fem
11. ἑτέρᾳ hetera dat sing fem
12. ἑτέραν heteran acc sing fem
13. ἕτεραι heterai nom pl fem
14. ἑτέραις heterais dat pl fem

1	for either he will hate the one, and love the **other**;	Matt 6:24
6	else he will hold to the one, and despise the **other**.....	6:24
5	And **another** of his disciples said unto him,............	8:21
12	persecuted in one place, flee to **another** (NASB).....	10:23
1	he that should come, or do we look for **another**?.....	11:3
4	who call out to the **other** children, (NASB)........	11:16
9	and taketh with himself seven **other** spirits.........	12:45
8	lame, blind, dumb, maimed, and many **others**,........	15:30
7	some, Elias; and **others**, Jeremias,.................	16:14
2	father went to the **other** son and said (NIV)........	21:30
11	After that he appeared in **another** form unto two	Mark 16:12
9	many **other** things in his exhortation preached he...	Luke 3:18
14	I must preach the kingdom of God to **other** cities.....	4:43
2	which were in the **other** ship,.......................	5:7
2	And it came to pass also on **another** sabbath,........	6:6
1	thou he that should come? or look we for **another**?...	7:19
5	one owed five hundred pence, and the **other** fifty.....	7:41
13	and Susanna, and many **others**,....................	Luke 8:3
1	some fell upon a rock; ... soon as it was sprung up,....	8:6
1	some fell among thorns; and the thorns sprang up.....	8:7
1	And **other** fell on good ground, and sprang up,........	8:8
1	the fashion of his countenance was **altered**,...........	9:29
12	And they went to **another** village..................	9:56
1	And he said unto **another**, Follow me. But he said,....	9:59
5	And **another** also said, Lord, I will follow thee;.......	9:61
8	After these things the Lord appointed **other**	10:1
7	And **others**, tempting him, sought of him a sign	11:16
9	and taketh to him seven **other** spirits more wicked....	11:26
5	And **another** said, I have bought five yoke of oxen,....	14:19
5	And **another** said, I have married a wife,.............	14:20
2	what king, going to make war against **another** king,...	14:31
2	Then said he to **another**, ... how much owest thou?...	16:7
1	for either he will hate the one, and love the **other**;...	16:13
6	else he will hold to the one, and despise the **other**....	16:13
12	putteth away his wife, and marrieth **another**,........	16:18
5	the one shall be taken, and the **other** shall be left.....	17:34
9	the one shall be taken, and the **other** left.............	17:35
5	the one shall be taken, and the **other** left.............	17:36
5	the one a Pharisee, and the **other** a publican.........	18:10
5	And **another** came, saying, Lord, behold, here is.....	19:20
1	And again he sent **another** servant:.................	20:11
5	And after a little while **another** saw him, and said,...	22:58
9	And many **other** things blasphemously spake they....	22:65
7	And there were also two **other**, malefactors,.........	23:32
5	But the **other** answering rebuked him, saying,.......	23:40
9	And again **another** scripture saith,.................	John 19:37
5	and his bishoprick let **another** take................	Acts 1:20
14	and began to speak with **other** tongues,.............	2:4
7	**Others** mocking said, ... men are full of new wine......	2:13
4	with many **other** words did he testify and exhort,.....	2:40
1	none **other** name under heaven given among men,....	4:12
5	Till **another** king arose, which knew not Joseph......	7:18
6	of himself, or of some **other** man?...................	8:34
1	And he departed, and went into **another** place.......	12:17
2	Wherefore he saith also in **another** psalm,...........	13:35
3	teaching and preaching ... with many **others** also.....	15:35
1	saying that there is **another** king, one Jesus..........	17:7
1	which were there spent their time in nothing **else**,...	17:21
7	a woman named Damaris, and **others** with them.....	17:34
3	if ye inquire any thing concerning **other matters**,.....	19:39
11	and the **next day** we arrived at Samos,................	20:15
1	one part were Sadducees, and the **other** Pharisees,...	23:6
8	they delivered Paul and certain **other** prisoners......	27:1
11	And the **next day** we touched at Sidon...............	27:3
1	for wherein thou judgest **another**,..................	Rom 2:1
1	Thou therefore which teachest **another**,.............	2:21
2	she be married to **another** man,.....................	7:3
2	though she be married to **another** man...............	7:3
2	that ye should be married to **another**,...............	7:4
1	But I see **another** law in my members,...............	7:23
9	Nor height, nor depth, nor any **other** creature,.......	8:39
1	for he that loveth **another** hath fulfilled the law.....	13:8
9	and if there be any **other** commandment,.............	13:9
5	and **another**, I am of Apollos; are ye not carnal?...	1 Co 3:4
6	of you be puffed up for one against **another**............	4:6
1	Dare any of you, having a matter against **another**,.....	6:1
5	and that there is none **other** God but one.............	8:4
6	but every man **another's** wealth......................	10:24
6	Conscience, I say, not thine own, but of the **other:**...	10:29
2	To **another** faith by the same Spirit;.................	12:9
2	to **another** divers kinds of tongues;..................	12:10
5	but the **other** is not edified.........................	14:17
3	With men of **other** tongues and **other** lips..........	14:21
3	With men of **other** tongues and **other** lips..........	14:21
9	but the glory of the celestial is **one**,.................	15:40
9	and the glory of the terrestrial is **another**............	15:40
3	but by occasion of the forwardness **of others**,.......	2 Co 8:8
1	or if ye receive **another** spirit,.......................	11:4
1	or **another** gospel, which ye have not accepted,......	11:4
1	so soon removed from him ... unto **another** gospel:..	Gal 1:6
1	But **other** of the apostles saw I none, save James.....	1:19
1	have rejoicing in himself alone, and not in **another**.....	6:4
14	Which in **other** ages was not made known..........	Eph 3:5
3	but every man also on the things **of others**.........	Php 2:4

1	any **other** thing that is contrary to sound doctrine;	1 Tm 1:10
8	men, who shall be able to teach **others** also.	2 Tm 2:2
2	As he saith also in **another** place,	Heb 5:6
1	what **further** need was there that **another** priest	7:11
10	For he ... pertaineth to **another** tribe,	7:13
5	of Melchisedec there ariseth **another** priest,	7:15
7	**others** had trial of cruel mockings and scourgings,	11:36
11	messengers, and had sent them out **another** way?	Jas 2:25
1	who art thou that judgest **another**?	4:12
10	over to fornication, and going after **strange** flesh,	Jude 1:7

This word must be studied in conjunction with its synonym, *allos* (241). Although sometimes a distinction is hard to see, where they are used together, *allos* means: (1) "one" of a series; and (2) "another" of a similar nature. On the other hand, *heteros* is used to indicate: (1) "one" of two, and thus (2) "another" of a dissimilar nature. Thus Luke 23:32 says "two other (*heteroi*) men, both criminals," were also led out to be crucified with Jesus. In Matthew 11:3 Jesus was asked if He is the One that should come, or do we look for another (different) One. In Mark 16:12 Jesus is said to have appeared in another (different) form (i.e., in one He had not assumed before) in His resurrection appearance. *Heteros* can also mean neighbor or one other than oneself (e.g., 1 Corinthians 6:1; 10:24,29; 14:17; Galatians 6:4).

The "otherness" expressed by *heteros* explains a great deal in the New Testament. To "speak in other tongues" (*lalein heterais glōssais*) thus means to speak in a language different from one's own (Acts 2:4). And "others" (*heteroi*; i.e., those who were unbelievers) said that those who received the Spirit at Pentecost were drunk with new wine, denying the work of the Spirit. In the same manner Paul inquired of the Galatians as to why they departed from the grace of God to another, that is, different (*heteros*) gospel (Galatians 1:6), which is not another (*allos*, "similar") (Galatians 1:7).

STRONG 2087, BAUER 315, MOULTON-MILLIGAN 257, KITTEL 2:702-4, LIDDELL-SCOTT 702, COLIN BROWN 2:739-40,742.

2067. ἑτέρως heterōs adv
Otherwise, differently.
CROSS-REFERENCE:
ἕτερος heteros (2066)

1. ἑτέρως heterōs

1	and if in **any thing** ye be otherwise minded,	Php 3:15

An adverbial form of the adjective *heteros* (2066), "another," *heterōs* is found in classical Greek writings from the time of Homer (ca. Eighth Century B.C.). It occurs only once in the New Testament in Philippians 3:15. In the passage preceding verse 15 Paul discussed "perfection" (see *telos* [4904]) and pressing toward the mark (verse 14). Verse 15 states, "Let us therefore, as many as be perfect (*telos*), be thus minded: and if in anything ye be *otherwise* minded, God shall reveal even this unto you." Commenting on this passage and on the word *heterōs*, Selter remarks, "The last point is evidently directed at the claim to special revelations. Paul is confident that by being realistic and patient, they will grow in insight" ("Other," *Colin Brown*, 2:741).

STRONG 2088, BAUER 315, MOULTON-MILLIGAN 257, LIDDELL-SCOTT 702, COLIN BROWN 2:739,741.

2068. ἔτι eti adv
Yet, still, in addition, also.

אֶחָד 'echādh (259), One, another (1 Chr 17:21).

אַךְ 'akh (395), Only (Gn 18:32, Ex 10:17).

אַף 'aph (652), Even, also, indeed (Neh 9:18, Ps 16:7,9 [15:7,9]).

גַּם gām (1612), Even, also (Ps 8:7, Is 43:13).

הִנֵּה hinnēh (2079), Behold (Is 29:8).

נָא nā' (5167), Please (Nm 23:13).

עַד ʿadh (5912), As long as, until (2 Kgs 9:22, Neh 7:3).

עוֹד ʿôdh (5968), Still, again, beside (Ex 4:18, Eccl 3:16, Jer 49:7 [29:7]).

רַק raq (7828), Only (Ex 8:29).

שָׁם shām (8427), There, then (Is 28:10,13).

1. ἔτι eti

1	it is thenceforth good for nothing, (NT)	Matt 5:13
1	While he **yet** talked to the people,	12:46
1	While he **yet** spake, ... cloud overshadowed them:	17:5
1	then take with thee one or two **more**,	18:16
1	these ... I kept from my youth up: what lack I **yet**?	19:20
1	And while he **yet** spake, lo, Judas, ... came,	26:47
1	what **further** need have we of witnesses?	26:65
1	that that deceiver said, while he was **yet** alive,	27:63
1	While he **yet** spake, there came from the ruler	Mark 5:35
1	why troublest thou the Master any **further**?	5:35
1	have ye your heart **yet** hardened?	8:17
1	Having **yet** therefore one son, his wellbeloved,	12:6
1	immediately, while he **yet** spake, cometh Judas,	14:43
1	and saith, What need we any **further** witnesses?	14:63
1	with ... Holy Ghost, even from his mother's womb.	Luke 1:15
1	While he **yet** spake, there cometh one from the	8:49
1	as he was **yet** a coming, the devil threw him down,	9:42
1	as thou hast commanded, and **yet** there is room.	14:22
1	and his own life **also**, he cannot be my disciple.	14:26
1	Or else, while the other is **yet** a great way off,	14:32
1	But when he was **yet** a great way off,	15:20
1	for thou mayest be **no longer** steward.	16:2
1	**Yet** lackest thou one thing: sell all that thou hast,	18:22
1	Neither can they die **any more**:	20:36
1	that this that is written must **yet** be accomplished	22:37
1	And while he **yet** spake, behold a multitude,	22:47

ἑτοιμάζω 2069

1 immediately, while he yet spake, the cock crew.	Luke 22:60
1 And they said, What need we **any further** witness?	22:71
1 how he spake unto you when he was yet in Galilee,	24:6
1 while they yet believed not for joy, and wondered,	24:41
1 I spake unto you, while I was yet with you,	24:44
1 Say not ye, There are yet four months,	John 4:35
1 Yet a little while am I with you,	7:33
1 was **still** in the place where Martha (NASB)	11:30
1 therefore walked no **more** openly among the Jews;	11:54
1 Yet a little while is the light with you.	12:35
1 Little children, yet a little while I am with you.	13:33
1 Yet a little while, and the world seeth me no more;	14:19
1 Yet a little while, and the world seeth me no more;	14:19
1 Hereafter I will not talk much with you: (NT)	14:30
1 because I go to my Father, and ye see me no **more**;	16:10
1 I have yet many things to say unto you,	16:12
1 she remembereth no **more** the anguish,	16:21
1 when I shall no **more** speak unto you in proverbs,	16:25
1 And now I am no **more** in the world,	17:11
1 early, when it was yet dark, unto the sepulchre,	20:1
1 and **now** they were not able to draw it	21:6
1 **moreover** also my flesh shall rest in hope:	Acts 2:26
1 yet breathing out threatenings and slaughter	9:1
1 While Peter yet spake these words,	10:44
1 And Paul after this tarried there yet a good while,	18:18
1 and **further** brought Greeks also into the temple,	21:28
1 why yet am I also judged as a sinner?	Rom 3:7
1 For when we were yet without strength,	5:6
1 while we were **still** helpless ... Christ died (NASB)	5:6
1 love toward us, in that, while we were yet sinners,	5:8
1 that are dead to sin, live **any longer** therein?	6:2
1 wilt say then unto me, Why doth he yet find fault?	9:19
1 not able to bear it, neither yet now are ye able.	1 Co 3:2
1 For ye are yet carnal: ... is among you envying,	3:3
1 and yet show I unto you a more excellent way.	12:31
1 if Christ be not raised, ... ye are yet in your sins.	15:17
1 in whom we trust that he will yet deliver us;	2 Co 1:10
1 do I seek to please men? for if I yet pleased men,	Gal 1:10
1 And I, brethren, if I yet preach circumcision,	5:11
1 why do I yet suffer persecution?	5:11
1 this I pray, that your love may abound yet more	Phlp 1:9
1 when I was yet with you, I told you these things?	2 Th 2:5
1 For he was yet in the loins of his father,	Heb 7:10
1 what **further** need was there that another priest	7:11
1 And it is yet far more evident:	7:15
1 and their iniquities will I remember no **more**.	8:12
1 while as the first tabernacle was yet standing:	9:8
1 should have had no **more** conscience of sins.	10:2
1 their sins and iniquities will I remember no **more**.	10:17
1 yet a little while, and he that shall come will come,	10:37
1 and by it he being dead yet speaketh.	11:4
1 And what shall I **more** say?	11:32
1 **yea**, moreover of bonds and imprisonment:	11:36
1 Yet once more I shake not the earth only,	12:26
1 And this word, Yet once more,	12:27
1 and he shall go no **more** out:	Rev 3:12
1 that they should rest yet for a little season,	6:11
1 shall hunger no **more**, neither thirst any more;	7:16
1 shall hunger no **more**, neither thirst any **more**;	7:16
1 and, behold, there come two woes **more** hereafter.	9:12
1 neither was their place found **any more** in heaven.	12:8
1 thrown down, and shall be found no more at all.	18:21
1 shall be heard no **more** at all in thee;	18:22
1 no craftsman, ... shall be found any **more** in thee;	18:22
1 the sound of a millstone shall be heard no **more**	18:22
1 light of a candle shall shine no **more** at all in thee;	18:23
1 of the bride shall be heard no **more** at all in thee;	18:23
1 that he should deceive the nations **no more**,	20:3
1 were passed away; and there was no **more** sea.	21:1
1 And there shall be no more death, neither sorrow,	21:4
1 neither shall there be any **more** pain:	21:4
1 And there shall be no **more** curse:	22:3
1 And there shall be no night there (NT)	22:5
1 He that is unjust, let him be unjust still:	22:11
1 and he which is filthy, let him be filthy **still**:	22:11
1 and he that is righteous, let him be righteous **still**:	22:11
1 and he that is holy, let him be holy **still**.	22:11

This is an adverb that means "yet" or "still." It is used commonly in the Septuagint, usually to translate the Hebrew term ʿodh, generally meaning "again, still." It can be used to indicate constancy, permanence (2 Samuel 3:35 [LXX 2 Kings 3:35]), or action that goes on continually (Genesis 46:26). In the New Testament it is used in statements referring to past (Hebrews 7:10), present (Luke 14:32), or future time (Luke 1:15). Besides references referring to time it can also mean "in addition" as in Hebrews 11:36, or "also" as in Luke 14:26.

STRONG 2089, BAUER 315-16, MOULTON-MILLIGAN 258, LIDDELL-SCOTT 703.

2069. ἑτοιμάζω hetoimazō verb

Put or keep in readiness, prepare.

COGNATES:
ἑτοιμασία hetoimasia (2070)
ἕτοιμος hetoimos (2071)
ἑτοίμως hetoimōs (2072)
προετοιμάζω proetoimazō (4141)

SYNONYMS:
καταρτίζω katartizō (2645)
κατασκευάζω kataskeuazō (2650)
κατεργάζομαι katergazomai (2686)
ποιέω poieō (4020)

בָּרָא bārā' (1282), Create; piel: clear ground (Ez 21:19—Codex Alexandrinus only).

חוּשׁ chûsh (2456), Hurry (Ps 119:60 [118:60]).

יָטַב yāṭav (3296), Hiphil: do well, do better than (Mi 7:3, Na 3:8).

יָכַח yākhach (3306), Hiphil: determine, assign (Gn 24:14,44).

כּוּן kûn (3679), Niphal: stand firm, be stable, be ready (1 Sm 20:31, Jb 12:5, Prv 16:12); polel: set up, prepare, establish (Ex 15:17, 2 Sm 7:24, Ps 99:4 [98:4]); hiphil: establish, prepare, determine (Nm 23:1, 1 Chr 17:11, Is 14:21); hophal: be established, set up firmly, be made ready (Prv 21:31, Is 30:33, Na 2:5).

מָשַׁח māshach (5066), Spread oil over (Is 21:5).

סוּר sûr (5681), Turn aside; hiphil: remove (2 Chr 35:12).

עוּר ʿâwar (5996), Stir oneself up (Jb 41:10 [41:1]).

עָרַךְ ʿārakh (6424), Prepare (Nm 23:4, Ps 78:19 [77:19]).

עָשָׂה ʿâsâh (6449), Make, prepare (Est 5:14, 6:14).

עָתֹד ʿâthōdh (6497), Hithpael: destined (Jb 15:28).

פּוּק pûq (6572), Hiphil: gain (Prv 8:35).

פָּלַג pālagh (6629), Piel: cut open, split (Jb 38:25).

פָּנָה pānâh (6680), Turn to the side; piel: clear (Gn 24:31).

פָּקַד pāqadh (6734), Miss, call to account; niphal: be called up, be summoned (Ez 38:8).

ἑτοιμασία 2070

רָבַץ rāvats (7547), Lie down, settle; hiphil: cover, set (Is 54:11).

תּוּר tûr (8780), Reconnoiter, spy out (Ez 20:6).

תָּכַן tākhan (8834), Examine; niphal: be examined (1 Sm 2:3); pual: counted out (2 Kgs 12:11—Sixtine Edition only).

1. ἑτοίμαζε hetoimaze 2sing impr pres act
2. ἡτοίμασα hētoimasa 1sing indic aor act
3. ἡτοίμασας hētoimasas 2sing indic aor act
4. ἡτοίμασεν hētoimasen 3sing indic aor act
5. ἡτοίμασαν hētoimasan 3pl indic aor act
6. ἑτοιμάσω hetoimasō 1sing subj aor act
7. ἑτοιμάσωμεν hetoimasōmen 1pl subj aor act
8. ἑτοίμασον hetoimason 2sing impr aor act
9. ἑτοιμάσατε hetoimasate 2pl impr aor act
10. ἑτοιμάσας hetoimasas nom sing masc part aor act
11. ἑτοιμάσαι hetoimasai inf aor act
12. ἑτοιμασθῇ hetoimasthē 3sing subj aor pass
13. ἡτοίμασται hētoimastai 3sing indic perf mid
14. ἡτοιμασμένον hētoimasmenon
    nom/acc sing masc/neu part perf mid
15. ἡτοιμασμένοι hētoimasmenoi
    nom pl masc part perf mid
16. ἡτοιμασμένοις hētoimasmenois
    dat pl masc part perf mid
17. ἡτοιμασμένην hētoimasmenēn
    acc sing fem part perf mid
18. ἑτοιμάσαντες hetoimasantes
    nom pl masc part aor act
19. ἡτοίμακα hētoimaka 1sing indic perf act
20. ἑτοιμάσομεν hetoimasomen 1pl indic fut act

9	Prepare ye the way of the Lord,	Matt 3:3
13	for whom it is prepared of my Father.	20:23
2	Behold, I have prepared my dinner:	22:4
19	Behold, I have prepared my dinner:	22:4
17	inherit the kingdom prepared for you.	25:34
14	fire, prepared for the devil and his angels:	25:41
7	Where ... we prepare for thee to eat the passover?	26:17
5	and they made ready the passover.	26:19
9	Prepare ye the way of the Lord,	Mark 1:3
13	it shall be given to them for whom it is prepared.	10:40
7	Where wilt thou that we go and prepare	14:12
9	a large upper room ... there make ready for us.	14:15
5	and they made ready the passover.	14:16
18	the chief priests ... held a consultation (NASB)	15:1
11	to make ready a people prepared for the Lord.	Luke 1:17
11	go before the face of the Lord to prepare his ways;	1:76
3	thou hast prepared before the face of all people;	2:31
9	Prepare ye the way of the Lord,	3:4
11	a village of the Samaritans, to make ready for him.	9:52
3	shall those things be, which thou hast provided?	12:20
10	knew his lord's will, and prepared not himself,	12:47
8	Make ready wherewith I may sup, and gird thyself,	17:8
9	Go and prepare us the passover, that we may eat.	22:8
7	Where wilt thou that we prepare?	22:9
9	a large upper room furnished: there make ready.	22:12
5	and they made ready the passover.	22:13
5	they returned, and prepared spices and ointments;	23:56
5	bringing the spices which they had prepared,	24:1
11	I go to prepare a place for you.	John 14:2
6	And if I go and prepare a place for you,	14:3
9	Make ready two hundred soldiers	Acts 23:23
4	which God hath prepared for them that love him.	1 Co 2:9
14	and prepared unto every good work.	2 Tm 2:21

1	But withal prepare me also a lodging:	Phlm 1:22
4	for he hath prepared for them a city.	Heb 11:16
5	the seven angels ... prepared themselves to sound.	Rev 8:6
16	locusts were like unto horses prepared unto battle;	9:7
15	the four angels were loosed, which were prepared	9:15
14	where she hath a place prepared of God,	12:6
12	the way of the kings of the east might be prepared.	16:12
4	and his wife hath made herself ready.	19:7
17	prepared as a bride adorned for her husband.	21:2

Classical Greek and Septuagint Usage

From Homer on, this verb meant "to get ready, prepare" in classical Greek. In the Septuagint it translates the Hebrew verbs meaning "create" and "make." A case in point is the final clause in Proverbs 3:19, "By understanding hath he established (*hētoimasen*) the heavens." Another is 2 Samuel 7:24 (LXX 2 Kings 7:24): "For thou hast confirmed (*hētoimasas*) to thyself thy people Israel."

New Testament Usage

The same range of meaning evident in classical and Septuagintal Greek may be seen in the New Testament. In John 14:3 Jesus spoke of "preparing" a place for the disciples in His "Father's house" (see verse 2), i.e., in heaven. Tenney states, "The imagery of a dwelling place ('rooms' ['mansions,' KJV]) is taken from the oriental house in which the sons and daughters have apartments under the same roof as their parents" (*Expositor's Bible Commentary, John*, p.143). In Acts 23:23 the Roman tribune ordered two centurions, "Make ready (*hetoimasate*) two hundred soldiers to go to Caesarea." Paul said (1 Corinthians 2:9) that human eye or ear has not witnessed, nor has man even considered, the things God has prepared (*hētoimasen*) for those who love Him. Paul appealed to Philemon (verse 22) to prepare (*hetoimaze*) him a place to stay. Hebrews 11:16 says that God has prepared (*hētoimasen*) a city for the faithful. The word can be used in reference to preparation of both people and things.

Strong 2090, Bauer 316, Moulton-Milligan 258, Kittel 2:704-6, Liddell-Scott 703, Colin Brown 3:116-17.

2070. ἑτοιμασία hetoimasia noun

Readiness, preparation, equipment.

Cognate:
  ἑτοιμάζω hetoimazō (2069)
Synonym:
  παρασκευή paraskeuē (3765)

כּוּן kûn (3679), Stand firm; hiphil: prepare (Ps 65:9 [64:9], Na 2:3).

ἔτοιμος 2071

מָכוֹן mākhôn (4487), Foundation, support (Ezr 2:68, Ps 89:14 [88:14]).

מְכוֹנָה mᵉkhônāh (4488), Place, foundation (Ezr 3:3, Zec 5:11).

תְּכוּנָה tᵉkhûnāh (8828), Arrangement, furnishing (Ez 43:11—Codex Alexandrinus only).

1. ἑτοιμασία hetoimasia dat sing fem

1 shod with the **preparation** of the gospel of peace; .... **Eph 6:15**

Used once in the New Testament, in Ephesians 6:15, this term means "readiness" or "preparation." It is related to the word *hetoimazō* (2069), "to put or keep in readiness." Psalms 10:17 (LXX 9:38); 65:9 (64:9); 89:14 (88:14) are Septuagintal usages which may have bearing on the meaning in Ephesians. As such, the gospel of Christ to which the "soldier" has been reconciled becomes his foundation or foothold for the battle at hand (Wood, *Expositor's Bible Commentary*, 11:88). Wood also suggests another understanding of this difficult phrase. In secular literature this same term is used for the tackling of a ship. Therefore, readiness to preach the gospel message is seen as part of the soldiers "equipment" (cf. Paul's reference in Ephesians 2:17 to Isaiah 52:7 and the feet of the herald; ibid.).

STRONG 2091, BAUER 316, MOULTON-MILLIGAN 258, KITTEL 2:704-6, LIDDELL-SCOTT 703, COLIN BROWN 3:116-18.

2071. ἕτοιμος hetoimos adj
Ready, prepared.
CROSS-REFERENCE:
ἑτοιμάζω hetoimazō (2069)

כּוּן kûn (3679), Niphal: be ready, be established (Ex 19:11, Ps 38:17 [37:17], Mi 4:1); hiphil: prepare (Jos 4:3).

כָּסַף kāṣaph (3826), Long, be eager (Ps 17:12).

מָכוֹן mākhôn (4487), Dwelling, abode (Ex 15:17, 1 Kgs 8:39, Ps 33:14 [32:14]).

מָרַט māraṭ (4965), Qal: burnish (Ez 21:11); pual: be burnished (Ez 21:10).

עָרַךְ ʻārakh (6424), Put in order, all in order (2 Sm 23:5).

עִתִּי ʻittî (6501), Available (Lv 16:21).

עָתִיד ʻāthîdh (6503), Coming event, ready (Dt 32:35, Est 3:14).

צָנַע tsānaʻ (7076), Hiphil: live cautiously or carefully (Mi 6:8).

1. ἕτοιμοι hetoimoi nom pl masc/fem
2. ἕτοιμος hetoimos nom sing masc
3. ἑτοίμους hetoimous acc pl masc
4. ἑτοίμην hetoimēn acc sing fem
5. ἑτοίμῳ hetoimō dat sing neu
6. ἕτοιμον hetoimon nom/acc sing neu
7. ἕτοιμα hetoima nom/acc pl neu

7 and all things are **ready**: come unto the marriage... Matt 22:4
2 saith he to his servants, The wedding is **ready**,........ 22:8
1 Therefore be ye also **ready**;........................ 24:44
1 that were **ready** went in with him to the marriage:.... 25:10
6 a large upper room furnished and **prepared**:....... Mark 14:15
1 Be ye therefore **ready** also: ... Son of man cometh Luke 12:40
7 were bidden, Come; for all things are now **ready**....... 14:17
2 Lord, I am **ready** to go with thee, both into prison,.... 22:33
2 but your time is alway **ready**....................... John 7:6
1 we, or ever he come near, are **ready** to kill him..... Acts 23:15
1 and now are they **ready**, looking for a promise........ 23:21
4 that the same might be **ready**,...................... 2 Co 9:5
5 having in a **readiness** to revenge all disobedience,...... 10:6
7 man's line of things made **ready** to our hand........... 10:16
3 obey magistrates, to be **ready** to every good work,.... Tit 3:1
4 **ready** to be revealed in the last time.................. 1 Pt 1:5
1 be **ready** always to give an answer to every man........ 3:15

This term is found 17 times in the New Testament. The Gospels contain nine of these references; with Matthew perhaps having the strongest meaning, because each of the four references speaks of "end time" significance. Readiness both of things (Mark 14:15) and people (Luke 12:40) are included. The papyri also refer to the making ready of things (statements regarding corn and money) and people (getting the harvesters ready; see *Moulton-Milligan*).

STRONG 2092, BAUER 316, MOULTON-MILLIGAN 258, KITTEL 2:704-6, LIDDELL-SCOTT 703-4, COLIN BROWN 3:116.

2072. ἑτοίμως hetoimōs adv
Readily, be willing.
CROSS-REFERENCE:
ἑτοιμάζω hetoimazō (2069)

אָסְפַּרְנָא ʼoṣparnāʼ (A643), Exactly, eagerly (Ezr 7:17,21,26—Aramaic).

עֲתִיד ʻăthîdh (A6504), Ready to (Dn 3:15—Aramaic).

1. ἑτοίμως hetoimōs

1 for I am **ready** not to be bound only,.............. Acts 21:13
1 Behold, the third time I am **ready** to come to you; 2 Co 12:14
1 him that is **ready** to judge the quick and the dead.... 1 Pt 4:5

This adverb, which means "readily," is used three times in the New Testament (Acts 21:13; 2 Corinthians 12:14; 1 Peter 4:5). In the first two references the idea is that of "being willing" (used with the infinitive). *Hetoimōs* is related to *hetoimazō* (2069), "to prepare."

STRONG 2093, BAUER 316, MOULTON-MILLIGAN 258, LIDDELL-SCOTT 703-4.

2073. ἔτος etos noun
Year.

יוֹם yôm (3219), Day (Jb 38:21).
יוֹם yôm (A3220), Day (Dn 4:34 [4:31]—Aramaic).
עִדָּן ʿiddān (A5944), Year (Dn 4:16,32 [4:13,29]—Aramaic).
שָׁנָה shānāh (8523), Year (Gn 5:3ff., 2 Kgs 8:1, Ez 1:1).
שְׁנָה sh°nāh (A8525), Year (Ezr 5:11,13, Dn 7:1—Aramaic).

1. ἔτει etei dat sing neu
2. ἔτος etos nom/acc sing neu
3. ἔτη etē nom/acc pl neu
4. ἐτῶν etōn gen pl neu
5. ἔτεσιν etesin dat pl neu

3	was diseased with an issue of blood twelve years,	Matt 9:20
3	which had an issue of blood twelve years,	Mark 5:25
4	for she was of the age of twelve years.	5:42
3	and had lived with an husband seven years	Luke 2:36
4	she was a widow of about fourscore and four years,	2:37
2	Now his parents went to Jerusalem every year	2:41
4	And when he was twelve years old,	2:42
1	Now in the fifteenth year of the reign of Tiberius	3:1
4	Jesus himself began to be about thirty years of age,	3:23
3	heaven was shut up three years and six months,	4:25
4	had one only daughter, about twelve years of age,	8:42
4	a woman having an issue of blood twelve years,	8:43
3	thou hast much goods laid up for many years;	12:19
3	three years I come seeking fruit on this fig tree,	13:7
2	let it alone this year also, till I shall dig about it,	13:8
3	which had a spirit of infirmity eighteen years,	13:11
3	lo, these eighteen years, be loosed from this bond	13:16
3	Lo, these many years do I serve thee,	15:29
5	Forty and six years was this temple in building,	John 2:20
3	which had an infirmity thirty and eight years.	5:5
3	Thou art not yet fifty years old,	8:57
4	For the man was above forty years old,	Acts 4:22
3	and entreat them evil four hundred years.	7:6
4	And when forty years were expired,	7:30
3	in the Red sea, and in the wilderness forty years.	7:36
3	by the space of forty years in the wilderness?	7:42
4	AEneas, which had kept his bed eight years,	9:33
5	about the space of four hundred and fifty years,	13:20
3	by the space of forty years.	13:21
3	And this continued by the space of two years;	19:10
4	hast been of many years a judge unto this nation,	24:10
4	Now after many years I came to bring alms	24:17
4	a great desire these many years to come unto you;	Rom 15:23
4	I knew a man in Christ above fourteen years ago,	2 Co 12:2
3	Then after three years I went up to Jerusalem	Gal 1:18
4	Then fourteen years after I went up again	2:1
3	which was four hundred and thirty years after,	3:17
4	taken into the number under threescore years old,	1 Tm 5:9
3	but thou art the same, and thy years shall not fail.	Heb 1:12
3	proved me, and saw my works forty years.	3:9
3	But with whom was he grieved forty years?	3:17
3	that one day is with the Lord as a thousand years,	2 Pt 3:8
3	and a thousand years as one day.	
3	and Satan, and bound him a thousand years,	Rev 20:2
3	till the thousand years should be fulfilled:	20:3
3	lived and reigned with Christ a thousand years.	20:4
3	not again until the thousand years were finished.	20:5
3	and shall reign with him a thousand years.	20:6
3	And when the thousand years are expired,	20:7

This term is found 49 times in the New Testament and over 450 times in the Septuagint, where in almost every case it translates *shānāh* meaning "year" or "yearly" (e.g., 2 Kings 25:27 [LXX 4 Kings 25:27]). It can refer to age (John 8:57) and a span of time (Revelation 20:4). *Kata etos*, which means "yearly" (Luke 2:41), and *apo etōn* (Luke 8:43; Romans 15:23), "for many years," are two common grammatical constructions using *etos* found in the New Testament.

STRONG 2094, BAUER 316-17, MOULTON-MILLIGAN 258, LIDDELL-SCOTT 704.

2074. εὖ eu adv
Well, do good, show kindness, do well, act properly.

SYNONYM:
καλῶς kalōs (2544)

1. εὖ eu

1	Well done, thou good and faithful servant:	Matt 25:21
1	Well done, good and faithful servant;	25:23
1	and whensoever ye will ye may do them good:	Mark 14:7
1	And he said unto him, Well, thou good servant:	Luke 19:17
1	from which if ye keep yourselves, ye shall do well.	Acts 15:29
1	That it may be well with thee,	Eph 6:3

Classical Greek
Properly an adverb, *eu* is a diverse term in classical Greek. Besides being a common prefix meaning "good, well," *eu* is also used alone. In these cases it can mean "well" in the sense of thorough, accurate, or good as a moral quality. It can also function as a substantive, meaning "what is right, ideal, proper." As an exclamation it meant "well done!" (*Liddell-Scott*).

Septuagint Usage
In the Septuagint *eu* is used almost exclusively in conjunction with verbs. Thus, one can "do good," "be good, kind," or "understand well." For example, Pharaoh treated Abraham "well" because he desired what he thought was Abraham's sister—Sarah (Genesis 12:16; cf. Exodus 1:20). God promised the people of Israel that if they obeyed His covenant stipulations things would "go well" for them (e.g., Deuteronomy 12:25,28; 22:7).

New Testament Usage
As in all Greek literature, *eu* is a common prefix to verbs, but only six instances of *eu* by itself are attested in the New Testament. It functions as an interjection in three texts ("Well done"; Matthew 25:21,23; Luke 19:17). "Doing good" to the poor is commended whenever possible (Mark 14:7). In a slightly different understanding, the leaders of the apostolic council advised the Gentiles that they would "do well" if they followed the advice of the council (Acts 15:29).

Εὔα 2075

The Old Testament promise that obedience results in things "going well" is still applicable in the New (Ephesians 6:3).

STRONG 2095, BAUER 317, MOULTON-MILLIGAN 259, LIDDELL-SCOTT 704.

2075. Εὔα Eua name
Eve.

1. Εὔα **Eua** nom fem
2. Εὔαν **Euan** acc fem
3. Εὔα **Heua** nom fem
4. Εὔαν **Heuan** acc fem

4 as the serpent beguiled Eve through his subtlety,... 2 Co 11:3
1 For Adam was first formed, then Eve.............. 1 Tm 2:13

The wife of Adam who became the first sinner when she was deceived by the serpent (2 Corinthians 11:3; 1 Timothy 2:13).

2076. εὐαγγελίζω euangelizō verb
Bring or announce good news, proclaim, preach (the gospel).

COGNATES:
ἀγγέλλω angellō (31B)
εὐαγγέλιον euangelion (2077)
εὐαγγελιστής euangelistēs (2078)
προευαγγελίζομαι proeuangelizomai (4142)

בָּשַׂר bāsar (1339), Piel: bring news, make known (1 Sm 31:9, 2 Sm 1:20, Is 40:9); hithpael: receive news (2 Sm 18:31).

1. εὐηγγέλισεν **euēngelisen** 3sing indic aor act
2. εὐαγγελίσαι **euangelisai** inf aor act
3. εὐαγγελίζομαι **euangelizomai** 1sing indic pres mid
4. εὐαγγελίζεται **euangelizetai** 3sing indic pres mid
5. εὐαγγελιζόμεθα **euangelizometha** 1pl indic pres mid
6. εὐαγγελίζονται **euangelizontai** 3pl indic pres mid
7. εὐαγγελίζωμαι **euangelizōmai** 1sing subj pres mid
8. εὐαγγελίζηται **euangelizētai** 3sing subj pres mid
9. εὐαγγελιζόμενος **euangelizomenos** nom sing masc part pres mid
10. εὐαγγελιζομένου **euangelizomenou** gen sing masc part pres mid
11. εὐαγγελιζομένῳ **euangelizomenō** dat sing masc part pres mid
12. εὐαγγελιζόμενοι **euangelizomenoi** nom pl masc part pres mid
13. εὐαγγελιζομένων **euangelizomenōn** gen pl masc part pres mid
14. εὐαγγελίζεσθαι **euangelizesthai** inf pres mid
15. εὐηγγελισάμην **euēngelisamēn** 1sing indic aor mid
16. εὐηγγελίσθη **euēngelisthē** 3sing indic aor pass
17. εὐηγγελίσατο **euēngelisato** 3sing indic aor mid
18. εὐηγγελισάμεθα **euēngelisametha** 1pl indic aor mid
19. εὐηγγελίσαντο **euēngelisanto** 3pl indic aor mid
20. εὐαγγελισαμένου **euangelisamenou** gen sing masc part aor mid
21. εὐαγγελισθέντες **euangelisthentes** nom pl masc part aor pass
22. εὐαγγελισάμενοι **euangelisamenoi** nom pl masc part aor mid
23. εὐαγγελισαμένων **euangelisamenōn** gen pl masc part aor mid
24. εὐαγγελισθέν **euangelisthen** nom/acc sing neu part aor pass
25. εὐαγγελίσασθαι **euangelisasthai** inf aor mid
26. εὐηγγελισμένοι **euēngelismenoi** nom pl masc part perf mid
27. εὐηγγελίζετο **euēngelizeto** 3sing indic imperf mid
28. εὐαγγελίσωμαι **euangelisōmai** 1sing subj aor mid
29. εὐαγγελίσηται **euangelisētai** 3sing subj aor mid
30. εὐηγγελίζοντο **euēngelizonto** 3pl indic imperf mid

6 and the poor have the gospel preached to them.....Matt 11:5
25 sent to speak ... and to show thee these glad tidings. Luke 1:19
3 behold, I bring you good tidings of great joy,......... 2:10
27 many other things in his exhortation preached he...... 3:18
14 because he hath anointed me to preach the gospel..... 4:18
25 because he hath anointed me to preach the gospel..... 4:18
25 I must preach the kingdom of God to other cities..... 4:43
6 to the poor the gospel is preached..................... 7:22
9 showing the glad tidings of the kingdom of God:...... 8:1
12 preaching the gospel, and healing every where....... 9:6
4 since that time the kingdom of God is preached,..... 16:16
10 taught the people ... and preached the gospel,........ 20:1
12 they ceased not to teach and preach Jesus Christ....Acts 5:42
12 went every where preaching the word................. 8:4
11 preaching the things concerning the kingdom........ 8:12
19 returned to Jerusalem, and preached the gospel....... 8:25
30 were preaching the gospel to many (NASB)........... 8:25
17 the same scripture, and preached unto him Jesus..... 8:35
27 and passing through he preached in all the cities,..... 8:40
9 preaching peace by Jesus Christ: he is Lord of all:.... 10:36
12 spake unto the Grecians, preaching the Lord Jesus.... 11:20
5 And we declare unto you glad tidings,................ 13:32
12 And there they preached the gospel.................. 14:7
12 preach unto you that ye should turn from these...... 14:15
22 when they had preached the gospel to that city,...... 14:21
12 after they had preached the gospel (NASB)........... 14:21
12 teaching and preaching the word of the Lord,....... 15:35
25 had called us for to preach the gospel unto them...... 16:10
27 he preached unto them Jesus, and the resurrection.... 17:18
25 ready to preach the gospel to you that are at Rome Rom 1:15
13 the feet of them that preach the gospel of peace,..... 10:15
13 and bring glad tidings of good things!................ 10:15
14 Yea, so have I strived to preach the gospel,.......... 15:20
14 sent me not to baptize, but to preach the gospel:... 1 Co 1:17
7 For though I preach the gospel,....................... 9:16
7 yea, woe is unto me, if I preach not the gospel!....... 9:16
28 yea, woe is unto me, if I preach not the gospel!....... 9:16
9 Verily that, when I preach the gospel,................ 9:18
15 unto you the gospel which I preached unto you,..... 15:1
15 if ye keep in memory what I preached unto you,..... 15:2
25 To preach the gospel in the regions beyond you,...2 Co 10:16
15 have preached to you the gospel of God freely?...... 11:7
8 or an angel from heaven, preach any other gospel...Gal 1:8
29 or an angel from heaven, preach any other gospel.... 1:8
18 any other gospel ... we have preached unto you,..... 1:8
4 If any man preach any other gospel unto you........ 1:9
24 gospel which was preached of me is not after man...... 1:11

7	that I might **preach** him among the heathen;	Gal 1:16
4	now **preacheth** the faith which once he destroyed.	1:23
15	I **preached** the gospel unto you at the first.	4:13
17	and **preached** peace to you which were afar off,	Eph 2:17
25	that I should **preach** among the Gentiles	3:8
20	**brought us good tidings** of your faith and charity,	1 Th 3:6
26	For unto us was the **gospel preached**,	Heb 4:2
21	they to whom it **was first preached** entered not in	4:6
23	have **preached the gospel** unto you with the Holy	1 Pt 1:12
24	this is the word which by the **gospel is preached**	1:25
16	was the **gospel preached** also to ... dead,	4:6
1	as he hath **declared** to his servants the prophets.	Rev 10:7
2	having the everlasting gospel **to preach** unto them	14:6

Classical Greek

This verb is related to the noun *angelos* (32), "messenger." Originally the term stood for proclaiming a military victory, "to bring good news" of various content from the battlefield. Such messages were not always reliable since deceptive messages were often brought. Due to political motives or in order to boost morale of the troops, false reports of victory were not uncommon. This naturally led to a certain degree of skepticism among those who received the message.

Gradually the meaning of *euangelizō* expanded. It was used of public political decrees or of private messages of a joyous nature. In Hellenism the term acquired a religious-sacral significance in connection with an oracle. In this circumstance *euangelizō* might imply "to promise" something.

Septuagint Usage

In the Septuagint the verb translated the Hebrew *bāsar*, "to proclaim, to tell." Friedrich maintains that *bāsar* inherently referred to a joyous message, whereas *euangelizomai* (its usual form) acquired a positive meaning by being the translator's choice for a counterpart of the Hebrew. This, he says, is characteristic of all the Semitic languages with this stem, in contrast to Latin and modern languages which do not have any special word stem for "joyous message." If *bāsar* functioned in connection with the proclaiming of a bad message, it was because of the expanded sense found in the original battlefield context ("euangelizomai," *Kittel*, 2:707ff.).

An example of this can be seen in 1 Samuel 31:9 (LXX 1 Kings 31:9). There it is recorded that the Philistines proclaimed in the temple of their idols the "joyous" message of their defeat of Saul and his army. In this context *bāsar* receives an added religious sense because the proclamation of victory is a cultic action. The original definition, however, is a "good message" (1 Kings 1:42 [LXX 3 Kings 1:42]). In those circumstances in which an additional modifier is used, it is only to reinforce the positive meaning of the stem (ibid.).

Bāsar makes noteworthy appearances in a religious sense in the Psalms and in Isaiah. The Lord is the giver of victory and salvation: He gives songs of victory and joyous announcements (cf. Psalms 40:10 [LXX 39:9]; 68:11,12 [67:11,12]; cf. 1 Samuel 18:6 [LXX 1 Kings 18:6]; Psalm 96:2f.).

The term occurs with similar effect in Isaiah 41:27 and 52:7. Here the messenger comes bearing glad tidings. This connection to *euangelizomai* in the New Testament is made explicitly in Romans 10:15. Both *euangelizomai* and *euangelion* in the New Testament receive their prehistory from the Old Testament rather than from secular Greek. And although *euangelion* does not occur in a religious sense in the Septuagint, the New Testament understands *euangelizomai* as an event locked in salvation history, such as occurs in the eschatological "preaching" of Isaiah. Thus the writers of the New Testament were only indirectly influenced by the religious/philosophical thought of Hellenism (but cf. Jewish writers like Philo and Josephus who were thoroughly immersed in the Hellenistic mode of thought).

New Testament Usage

Different forms of *euangelizomai* appear over 50 times in the New Testament. The term is used in its active form only twice (Revelation 10:7; 14:6). Passively it can describe the message that is preached (Luke 16:16; Galatians 1:11; 1 Peter 1:25). The verb describes preaching Christ (Acts 5:42), the Word (Acts 8:4), the kingdom of God (Acts 8:12), "the faith" (Galatians 1:23), peace (Ephesians 2:17), and "the unsearchable riches of Christ" (Ephesians 3:8). The compound *proeuangelizomai* (4142) refers to the essential equality of the faith of Abraham in God's promise and the New Testament faith. God's promise to Abraham that "in thee shall all families of the earth be blessed" (Genesis 12:3) was "good news" in which Abraham placed his trust (Galatians 3:8f.).

Euangelizomai principally denotes "preaching the gospel." When *euangelizomai* is conjoined with *euangelion* the added emphasis should not be ignored. (Cf. *euangelion* [2077].)

STRONG 2097, BAUER 317, MOULTON-MILLIGAN 259, KITTEL 2:707-21 (see "euangelizomai"),

εὐαγγέλιον 2077

LIDDELL-SCOTT 704-5 (see "euangelizomai"), COLIN BROWN 2:107,110.

2077. εὐαγγέλιον euangelion noun

Good news, gospel.

CROSS-REFERENCE:
εὐαγγελίζω euangelizō (2076)

בְּשׂוֹרָה bᵉsōrāh (1342), Messenger's reward, good news (2 Sm 4:10, 18:22,25).

1. εὐαγγέλιον euangelion nom/acc sing neu
2. εὐαγγελίου euangeliou gen sing neu
3. εὐαγγελίῳ euangeliō dat sing neu

1	and preaching the **gospel** of the kingdom,	Matt 4:23
1	and preaching the **gospel** of the kingdom,	9:35
1	And this **gospel** of the kingdom shall be preached	24:14
1	Wheresoever this **gospel** shall be preached	26:13
1	alway, even unto the end of the world. Amen.	28:20
2	The beginning of the **gospel** of Jesus Christ,	Mark 1:1
1	preaching the **gospel** of the kingdom of God,	1:14
3	repent ye, and believe the **gospel**.	1:15
2	my sake and the **gospel's**, the same shall save it.	8:35
2	or lands, for my sake, and the **gospel's**,	10:29
1	**gospel** must first be published among all nations.	13:10
1	Wheresoever this **gospel** shall be preached	14:9
1	and preach the **gospel** to every creature.	16:15
1	confirming the word with signs following. Amen.	16:20
1	in the temple, praising and blessing God. Amen.	Luke 24:53
2	by my mouth should hear the word of the **gospel**,	Acts 15:7
1	to testify the **gospel** of the grace of God.	20:24
1	called to be an apostle, separated unto the **gospel**	Rom 1:1
3	I serve with my spirit in the **gospel** of his Son,	1:9
1	For I am not ashamed of the **gospel** of Christ:	1:16
1	judge ... by Jesus Christ according to my **gospel**.	2:16
3	But they have not all obeyed the **gospel**.	10:16
1	As concerning the **gospel**,	11:28
1	to the Gentiles, ministering the **gospel** of God,	15:16
1	I have fully preached the **gospel** of Christ.	15:19
2	fulness of the blessing of the **gospel** of Christ.	15:29
1	is of power to stablish you according to my **gospel**,	16:25
2	I have begotten you through the **gospel**.	1 Co 4:15
3	lest we should hinder the **gospel** of Christ.	9:12
1	which preach the **gospel** should live of the **gospel**.	9:14
2	which preach the **gospel** should live of the **gospel**.	9:14
1	I may make the **gospel** of Christ without charge,	9:18
3	that I abuse not my power in the **gospel**.	9:18
1	And this I do for the **gospel's** sake,	9:23
1	Moreover, brethren, I declare unto you the **gospel**	15:1
1	when I came to Troas to preach Christ's **gospel**,	2 Co 2:12
1	if our **gospel** be hid, it is hid to them that are lost:	4:3
2	lest the light of the glorious **gospel** of Christ,	4:4
3	praise is in the **gospel** throughout all the churches;	8:18
1	professed subjection unto the **gospel** of Christ,	9:13
3	as to you also in **preaching** the **gospel** of Christ:	10:14
1	or another **gospel**, which ye have not accepted,	11:4
1	have preached to you the **gospel** of God freely?	11:7
1	so soon removed from him ... unto another **gospel**:	Gal 1:6
1	and would pervert the **gospel** of Christ.	1:7
1	**gospel** which was preached of me is not after man.	1:11
1	that **gospel** which I preach among the Gentiles,	2:2
2	the truth of the **gospel** might continue with you.	2:5
1	the **gospel** of the uncircumcision was committed	2:7
2	not uprightly according to the truth of the **gospel**,	2:14
1	the word of truth, the **gospel** of your salvation:	Eph 1:13
2	partakers of his promise in Christ by the **gospel**:	3:6
2	shod with the preparation of the **gospel** of peace;	6:15
2	to make known the mystery of the **gospel**,	6:19
1	For your fellowship in the **gospel** from the first day	Phlp 1:5
2	and in the defence and confirmation of the **gospel**,	1:7
2	rather unto the furtherance of the **gospel**;	1:12
2	knowing that I am set for the defence of the **gospel**.	Phlp 1:17
2	be as it becometh the **gospel** of Christ:	1:27
2	striving together for the faith of the **gospel**;	1:27
1	he hath served with me in the **gospel**.	2:22
3	women which laboured with me in the **gospel**,	4:3
2	that in the beginning of the **gospel**,	4:15
2	heard before in the word of the truth of the **gospel**;	Col 1:5
2	be not moved away from the hope of the **gospel**,	1:23
1	For our **gospel** came not unto you in word only,	1 Th 1:5
1	speak ... the **gospel** of God with much contention.	2:2
1	allowed of God to be put in trust with the **gospel**,	2:4
1	not the **gospel** of God only, but also our own souls,	2:8
1	we preached unto you the **gospel** of God.	2:9
3	and our fellowlabourer in the **gospel** of Christ,	3:2
3	that obey not the **gospel** of our Lord Jesus Christ:	2 Th 1:8
2	Whereunto he called you by our **gospel**,	2:14
1	the glorious **gospel** of the blessed God,	1 Tm 1:11
3	but be thou partaker of the afflictions of the **gospel**	2 Tm 1:8
2	life and immortality to light through the **gospel**:	1:10
1	was raised from the dead according to my **gospel**:	2:8
2	ministered unto me in the bonds of the **gospel**:	Phlm 1:13
3	of them that obey not the **gospel** of God?	1 Pt 4:17
1	having the everlasting **gospel** to preach unto them	Rev 14:6

Classical Greek

The original classical definition of the noun *euangelion* was a "reward for bringing a good message." But the term also stood for the message itself. It became a general term for the triumphant message from the battlefield, and it was used for joyous political proclamations or for personal messages of good news (cf. *euangelizō* [2076]).

Its service in the Greco-Roman world is of special interest in association with the emperor cult. In one instance it was used of the Emperor Augustus in an allusion to his so-called divinity: "But the birthday of the god was for the world the beginning of tidings of joy on his account" (*Moulton-Milligan*). To the first Christians the emperor was a false lord (*kurios* [2935]) who claimed divine rule, something which belongs to the Lord Jesus Christ alone. In the same way, the *eungelion* of the emperor cult was a false gospel which opposed the gospel of Christ. Linguistically, however, these two terms formed a background for the preaching of Jesus Christ as *Lord*. Therefore, when Paul spoke of "another gospel," a very literal sense can be understood, because he lived in an age of "gospel preaching." When Christians used the term *euangelion*, they were speaking the familiar language of the day.

Septuagint Usage

Euangelion does not occur in the singular in the Septuagint; but in the plural form it describes, as in classical Greek, a reward for bringing a good message (2 Samuel [LXX 2 Kings] 4:10; 18:22). The Hebrew behind it is *bᵉsōrāh*. In 2 Samuel 18:20,22 (LXX 2 Kings 18:20,22) this word could be translated "good tidings." It is rendered *euangelia* by the Septuagint translators. This derivative of *euangelion* does not occur in the New Testament (cf. 2 Samuel 18:25,27 [LXX 2 Kings 18:25,27]). Interestingly, the noun *never* functions in a religious capacity in the Old Testament (Friedrich, "euangelion," *Kittel*, 2:721).

New Testament Usage

Euangelion has a broad semantic range in the New Testament. Nevertheless, this variety should be examined and understood in light of the basic concept that the gospel is a message of victory. According to its Greek heritage, as well as its acquired Hebrew background via the Septuagint, *euangelion* describes a good report from the battlefield, a message of victory. Moreover, this is its essential meaning in the New Testament. The gospel is the message of Christ's victory over the enemy; the strong one has been conquered by the One who is stronger (Matthew 12:29). Therefore this gospel is to be preached to the poor and to the captives who will be set at liberty by its power (cf. Luke 4:18).

Although *euangelion* is a principal word for the New Testament proclamation, it is remarkably unevenly distributed among the different writers. Matthew and Mark jointly have the term 12 times; in the Gospel of Luke and in John's Gospel it is not found at all. (However, the verbal form *euangelizō*, "to preach the gospel," occurs quite regularly in the writings of Luke.) Twice *euangelion* is recorded in Acts; once in the First Epistle of Peter; and once in the Book of Revelation.

The other 60 instances are attributed to Paul. In about half of these Paul used *euangelion* in an absolute sense, i.e., without any qualifying definition. For the apostle, as well as for his readers, there was only one gospel.

Since the term does not appear in either the earliest or the latest New Testament writings (except for Revelation 14:6), there is no way of being certain precisely when *euangelion* was first used as a technical term for Christian proclamation. Nonetheless, in all probability this transpired very early. By the time Paul wrote his first epistle, it was evidently already regarded as such. The same can be said for Acts. In the Synoptic Gospels *euangelion*/*euangelizō* denote the message and preaching of Jesus. Especially remarkable is Jesus' use of these terms as descriptive of His own ministry.

The frequent occurrence in Paul's writings should be regarded as evidence that early on the term held special significance given by the Spirit to Paul. Undoubtedly his theological understanding of "good news" helped to shape the understanding of the expression in early Christian vocabulary.

Paul twice summarized the essential message of Christian proclamation, i.e., the gospel (Romans 1:1ff. and 1 Corinthians 15:1ff.). The Christian message of salvation is both a proclamation of and an interpretation of the facts of salvation history. Thus one word, *euangelion*, summarizes the Christ event— His incarnation, His earthly life, His death on the cross, His resurrection, His ascension. The gospel is neither legal commandments nor philosophy; it is not even religion in the human sense of the word. Rather, it is the message of God's action in Christ, executed within the framework of human history—what God has done to make our salvation possible.

The proclamation of this message is the creative word of God in action. It changes darkness into light and death into life. It is the power of God for salvation (Romans 1:16). This same word becomes active in those who believe (1 Thessalonians 2:13). The gospel receives many qualifying descriptions. It is referred to as the gospel of God and Jesus Christ (e.g., Mark 1:14; Romans 1:1; 15:19; 1 Corinthians 9:12; 1 Thessalonians 1:8), the gospel of God's grace (Acts 20:24), the gospel of the kingdom of God (Matthew 4:23, 9:35; Luke 8:1; Acts 8:12), the gospel of the Son of God (Romans 1:1-3), the gospel of God's Son (Mark 1:1; Romans 1:9), the gospel of Jesus Christ (Mark 1:1), the gospel of Christ (Romans 15:19; 1 Corinthians 9:12; 2 Corinthians 2:12; 9:13; 10:14; Galatians 1:7; Philippians 1:27; 1 Thessalonians 3:2), the gospel of our Lord Jesus (1 Thessalonians 1:8), the gospel of Jesus (Acts 8:35), the gospel of the glory of Christ (2 Corinthians 4:4), the gospel of the unsearchable riches of Christ (Ephesians 3:8), and the gospel of "your" salvation (Ephesians 1:13). As an eternal gospel (Revelation 14:6) of peace (Ephesians 6:15) it is "ours" (2 Corinthians 4:3; 1 Thessalonians 1:5).

In addition to the above qualifying descriptions, other phrases are used in the New Testament to describe the gospel. For example, the content of its message is signified as "the preaching of the cross" (1 Corinthians 1:18) and also the "witness of the resurrection of the Lord Jesus" (Acts 4:33). Elsewhere the gospel message is referred to as the word of God's grace (Acts 14:3), the word of salvation (Acts 13:26), the word of reconciliation (2 Corinthians 5:19), the word of truth (Ephesians 1:13), the word of faith (Romans 10:8), and the word of life (Philippians 2:16). Nevertheless, the main emphasis of the message is contained in the phrase "preach Christ" (cf. Acts 8:5; Colossians 1:28).

The content of the gospel message is further explained in Romans 1:17 which states that "therein is the righteousness of God revealed from faith to faith." Here Paul explained that faith and not obedience to the Law brings righteousness. This righteousness is "from faith to faith"; that is, faith in Christ alone produces righteousness, but it is the preaching (hearing) of the gospel that creates faith (cf. Romans 10:17). Where the gospel is permitted to produce faith and where it is received in faith, "it is the power of God unto salvation" (Romans 1:16). Only then does the gospel bring peace (Ephesians 2:17; 5:16), hope (Colossians 1:23), and eternal life (Titus 1:1-3).

Believers are not to be ashamed of it (Romans 1:16; 2 Timothy 1:8) and are to govern their life-style by it (Philippians 1:27). Though believers may be called upon to suffer on account of the gospel (Philippians 1:16), yet they must continue to proclaim it to the ends of the earth (2 Timothy 4:2). It alone heralds the sound words of truth, salvation, reconciliation, and grace (e.g., Acts 13:26; 14:3; 2 Corinthians 5:19; Ephesians 1:13). Only the gospel is the word of life (Philippians 2:16).

See the verb *euangelizō* (2076) for further information.

STRONG 2098, BAUER 317-18, MOULTON-MILLIGAN 259, COLIN BROWN 2:721-36, LIDDELL-SCOTT 704-5, COLIN BROWN 2:107-14.

2078. εὐαγγελιστής euangelistēs noun
Preacher of the gospel, evangelist.
CROSS-REFERENCE:
εὐαγγελίζω euangelizō (2076)

1. εὐαγγελιστοῦ euangelistou gen sing masc
2. εὐαγγελιστάς euangelistas acc pl masc

1 we entered into the house of Philip the evangelist, ..Acts 21:8
2 some, evangelists; and some, pastors and teachers; ... Eph 4:11
1 endure afflictions, do the work of an evangelist, ... 2 Tm 4:5

Related to *euangelizō* (2076), "announce good news," this term denotes a "preacher of the gospel" or "evangelist." In a secular sense this word identifies one who proclaimed "oracular announcements" (*Moulton-Milligan*). It occurs three times in the New Testament: referring to Philip as "the evangelist" (Acts 21:8), to Christ's gift of "evangelists" to the Church (Ephesians 4:11), and to Timothy who was to do the work of an "announcer of the gospel" (2 Timothy 4:5). Opinion differs on whether it is the title of an office or a function. It seems that originally it described a function rather than an office, for all the apostles were evangelists. However, not all evangelists were apostles, and in the three New Testament occurrences the evangelists were subordinate to the apostles (Friedrich, "euangelistēs," *Kittel*, 2:736f.).

STRONG 2099, BAUER 318, MOULTON-MILLIGAN 259, KITTEL 2:736-37, LIDDELL-SCOTT 705, COLIN BROWN 2:107,114.

2079. εὐαρεστέω euaresteō verb
Please, be pleasing.
CROSS-REFERENCE:
ἀρέσκω areskō (694)

הָלַךְ hālakh (2050), Hithpael: walk, walk around, move back and forth (Gn 6:9, 48:15, Pss 26:3 [25:3], 35:14 [34:14]).

שָׁרַת shārath (8664), Piel: serve, wait on (Gn 39:4—Codex Alexandrinus only).

1. εὐαρεστῆσαι euarestēsai inf aor act
2. εὐηρεστηκέναι euērestēkenai indic perf act
3. εὐαρεστεῖται euaresteitai 3sing indic pres mid
4. εὐαρεστηκέναι euarestēkenai inf perf act

2 he had this testimony, that he pleased God......... Heb 11:5
4 he had this testimony, that he pleased God......... 11:5
1 But without faith it is impossible to please him:....... 11:6
3 for with such sacrifices God is well pleased............ 13:16

Classical Greek and Septuagint Usage
This word is a compound of the adverb *eu* (2074), "well," and the verb *areskō* (694), derived from the root *ar*, "to fit." In classical Greek *areskō* means "to make peace with" or "reconcile" someone. In the Septuagint *euaresteō* translates *yithhallēkh* (from *hālakh*) in the phrase *yithhallēkh ethhā'ĕlōhîm*, "walk with God," in Genesis 5:22,24.

New Testament Usage
Euaresteō is found three times in the New Testament, all three in the Book of Hebrews.

The word carries the same meaning as the Septuagintal usage when it refers to Enoch's life that pleased God (Hebrews 11:5). The writer to the Hebrews said it is impossible for a person to please God unless he has faith (Hebrews 11:6). In Hebrews 13:16 *euaresteō* shows God's pleasure in the believer's good works.

STRONG 2100, BAUER 318, MOULTON-MILLIGAN 259, KITTEL 1:456-57, LIDDELL-SCOTT 706, COLIN BROWN 2:814-17.

2080. εὐάρεστος euarestos adj
Pleasing, acceptable.
COGNATE:
  ἀρέσκω areskō (694)
SYNONYMS:
  ἀπόδεκτος apodektos (582)
  δεκτός dektos (1178)
  εὐπρόσδεκτος euprosdektos (2124)

1. εὐάρεστος euarestos nom sing masc
2. εὐάρεστοι euarestoi nom pl masc
3. εὐαρέστους euarestous acc pl masc
4. εὐάρεστον euareston nom/acc sing fem/neu

4	holy, **acceptable** unto God,	Rom 12:1
4	that good, and **acceptable**, and perfect, will of God.	12:2
1	is **acceptable** to God, and approved of men.	14:18
2	present or absent, we may be **accepted** of him.	2 Co 5:9
4	Proving what is **acceptable** unto the Lord.	Eph 5:10
4	a sacrifice acceptable, **wellpleasing** to God.	Phlp 4:18
4	obey ... for this is **well pleasing** unto the Lord.	Col 3:20
3	and **to please** them well in all things;	Tit 2:9
4	working in you that which is **wellpleasing**	Heb 13:21

The use of this adjective in the New Testament is most interesting as eight of the nine New Testament references are by Paul, yet they are found in five different books. Eight of the nine references speak of that which is acceptable to God, whether it is the believer's body (Romans 12:1), labor (2 Corinthians 5:9), sacrifice (Philippians 4:18), obedience (Colossians 3:20), etc. Hebrews 13:21 adds that the believer's good works are "well-pleasing" *through* Jesus Christ.

STRONG 2101, BAUER 318, MOULTON-MILLIGAN 259, KITTEL 1:456-57, LIDDELL-SCOTT 706, COLIN BROWN 2:814-17.

2081. εὐαρέστως euarestōs adv
Acceptably.
CROSS-REFERENCE:
  ἀρέσκω areskō (694)

1. εὐαρέστως euarestōs
1 we may serve God **acceptably** with reverence .... Heb 12:28

This adverb is found only in Hebrews 12:28 and refers to serving God "acceptably, in an acceptable manner" (see *euarestos* [2080]). It does not appear in the Septuagint and it is only rarely used in non-Christian writings.

STRONG 2102, BAUER 318-19, MOULTON-MILLIGAN 259, LIDDELL-SCOTT 706.

2082. Εὔβουλος Euboulos name
Eubulus.

1. Εὔβουλος Euboulos nom masc
1 **Eubulus** greeteth thee, and Pudens, and Linus, ... 2 Tm 4:21

A Christian in Rome who greeted Timothy (2 Timothy 4:21).

2082B. εὖγε euge adv
Good! Well! Well done!

אָח 'āch (251), Alas (Ez 6:11).
הֶאָח he'āch (1955), Aha (Pss 35:21 [34:21], 70:3 [69:3], Ez 26:2).

1. εὖγε euge
1 he said to him, '**Well done**, good slave (NASB) .... Luke 19:17

This term is a compound of the adverb *eu* (2074), "well, good," and the intensifying enclitic particle *ge* (1058). It functions as an exclamatory phrase "well done!" This term is often used to signify approval or confirmation of what is previously said (*Liddell-Scott*). When used with a verb it means "well" or "rightly," i.e., something that is said "well" or "rightly" spoken. *Euge* is found in the New Testament (as a variant to *eu* found in the *Textus Receptus*) in the Parable of the Ten Pounds (Luke 19:11-27). In this parable the nobleman said to one of his faithful servants, "Well!" or "Well done!" (Cf. Matthew 25:21,23.)

BAUER 319, LIDDELL-SCOTT 707-8.

2083. εὐγενής eugenēs adj
Wellborn, highborn, noble-minded, high-minded.
CROSS-REFERENCE:
  γίνομαι ginomai (1090)

גָּדוֹל gādhôl (1448), Great (Jb 1:3).

1. εὐγενής eugenēs nom sing masc
2. εὐγενεῖς eugeneis nom pl masc
3. εὐγενέστεροι eugenesteroi comp nom pl masc

εὐδία 2084

1	**nobleman** went into a far country to receive	Luke 19:12
3	These were more **noble** than those in Thessalonica,	Acts 17:11
2	not many mighty, not many **noble**, are called:	1 Co 1:26

This adjective is used frequently in classical Greek where discussions exist concerning adoption and social status (e.g., "the son of well-born and free parents," see *Moulton-Milligan*). Septuagintal usage is limited to Job 1:3, and there are only three New Testament references: Luke 19:12; Acts 17:11; and 1 Corinthians 1:26. Paul used it to say that not many "noble" are called (1 Corinthians 1:26), while Luke records the open words of Jesus' Parable of the Ten Minas: "A certain *nobleman* went into a far country ... " (Luke 19:12).

STRONG 2104, BAUER 319, MOULTON-MILLIGAN 259-60, LIDDELL-SCOTT 708 (see "eugeneia"), COLIN BROWN 1:187-88.

2084. εὐδία eudia noun
Fair weather.

1. εὐδία eudia nom sing fem

1	It will be **fair weather:** for the sky is red	Matt 16:2

Used just once in the New Testament (Matthew 16:2), this term means "fair weather." It is not used in the Septuagint except in the Apocrypha, Ecclesiasticus 3:15. It may be used metaphorically, as on the Rosetta Stone and in the papyri, in which case it can mean "peace" or "rest of mind" (see *Moulton-Milligan*).

STRONG 2105, BAUER 319, MOULTON-MILLIGAN 260, LIDDELL-SCOTT 709, COLIN BROWN 3:1000,1002.

2085. εὐδοκέω eudokeō verb
Be well pleased, delight in, approve, consent.

COGNATES:
δοκέω dokeō (1374)
εὐδοκία eudokia (2086)
συνευδοκέω suneudokeō (4759)

SYNONYMS:
ἐπινεύω epineuō (1947)
συγκατατίθημαι sunkatatithēmai (4635)
συμφωνέω sumphōneō (4707)
συνευδοκέω suneudokeō (4759)

אָבָה 'āvâh (13), Accede, consent (Jgs 11:17).

חָמַד chāmadh (2629), Desire (Ps 68:16 [67:16]).

חָפֵץ chāphēts (2759), Take pleasure in (2 Sm 22:20, Ps 51:19 [50:19]).

יָשַׁר yāshar (3595), Be straight, be upright (Hb 2:4).

נָתַן nāthan (5598), Give (Jgs 15:18).

פַּחְדָּה pachdāh (6588), Fear, dread (Jer 2:19).

צָלֵחַ tsālēach (7014), Qal: be effective, be of use (Is 54:17—Codex Alexandrinus only); hiphil: be successful, succeed (1 Chr 29:23).

קָדַד qādhadh (7199), Bow down, kneel down (Gn 24:26,48).

רָצָה rātsâh (7813), Qal: be pleased with, enjoy, be favorable to (Lv 26:34, 2 Chr 10:7, Hg 1:8); hiphil: cause to be paid off, make good (Lv 26:34).

1. εὐδοκῶ eudokō 1sing indic pres act
2. εὐδοκεῖ eudokei 3sing indic pres act
3. εὐδοκοῦμεν eudokoumen 1pl indic pres act
4. ηὐδόκησα eudokēsa 1sing indic aor act
5. εὐδόκησα eudokēsa 1sing indic aor act
6. εὐδόκησας eudokēsas 2sing indic aor act
7. εὐδόκησεν eudokēsen 3sing indic aor act
8. εὐδοκήσαμεν eudokēsamen 1pl indic aor act
9. εὐδόκησαν eudokēsan 3pl indic aor act
10. εὐδοκήσαντες eudokēsantes nom pl masc part aor act
11. ηὐδοκήσαμεν eudokēsamen 1pl indic aor act
12. ηὐδοκοῦμεν eudokoumen 1pl indic imperf act
13. ηὐδόκησαν eudokēsan 3pl indic aor act
14. ηὐδόκησεν eudokēsen 3sing indic aor act

5	my beloved Son, in whom I **am well pleased**	Matt 3:17
4	my beloved Son, in whom I **am well pleased**	3:17
7	my beloved, in whom my soul **is well pleased:**	12:18
14	my beloved, in whom my soul **is well pleased:**	12:18
5	my beloved Son, in whom I **am well pleased;**	17:5
4	my beloved Son, in whom I **am well pleased;**	17:5
5	my beloved Son, in whom I **am well pleased**	Mark 1:11
4	my beloved Son; in thee I **am well pleased**	Luke 3:22
5	my beloved Son; in thee I **am well pleased**	3:22
7	for it is your Father's **good pleasure** to give you	12:32
9	For it hath **pleased** them of Macedonia and Achaia	Rom 15:26
13	For it hath **pleased** them of Macedonia and Achaia	15:26
9	It hath **pleased** them verily;	15:27
13	It hath **pleased** them verily;	15:27
7	it **pleased** God by the foolishness of preaching	1 Co 1:21
7	But with many of them God was not **well pleased:**	10:5
3	and **willing** rather to be absent from the body,	2 Co 5:8
1	Therefore I take **pleasure** in infirmities,	12:10
7	But when it **pleased** God,	Gal 1:15
7	it **pleased** the Father that in him should all fulness	Col 1:19
3	we were **willing** to have imparted unto you,	1 Th 2:8
12	we were **willing** to have imparted unto you,	2:8
8	we thought it good to be left at Athens alone;	3:1
11	we thought it good to be left at Athens alone;	3:1
10	but had **pleasure** in unrighteousness	2 Th 2:12
6	and sacrifices for sin thou hast had no **pleasure**	Heb 10:6
6	neither **hadst pleasure therein;**	10:8
2	my soul shall **have no pleasure** in him	10:38
5	my beloved Son, in whom I **am well pleased**	2 Pt 1:17

In nearly all of its occurrences in the New Testament this term means "be well pleased." However, in 2 Thessalonians 2:8, 3:1, and 2 Corinthians 5:8 it may mean "willing, thought it good," and "willing" respectively. The New Testament refers to several who are being "pleased": God (seven times relating to Christ), Paul, the Macedonians and Achaians, and sinners (2 Thessalonians 2:12). Four times there is reference to God *not* being pleased (1 Corinthians 10:5; Hebrews 10:6,8,38). Other Greek writings give evidence of a variety of renderings, one of which is "consent," as in legal matters (see *Liddell-Scott*).

STRONG 2106, BAUER 319, MOULTON-MILLIGAN 260, KITTEL 2:738-42, LIDDELL-SCOTT 710, COLIN BROWN 2:383,780-81,817-18,820.

2086. εὐδοκία eudokia noun

Goodwill, favor, good pleasure, wish, desire.
COGNATE:
  εὐδοκέω eudokeō (2085)
SYNONYMS:
  ἐπιθυμία epithumia (1924)
  ὄρεξις orexis (3578)
  ὁρμή hormē (3593)

רָצוֹן rātsôn (7814), Favor, what is acceptable, desire (Pss 5:12, 69:13 [68:13], 145:16 [144:16]).

תִּרְצָה tirtsāh (8995), Tirzah (S/S 6:4 [6:3]).

1. εὐδοκία eudokia nom sing fem
2. εὐδοκίας eudokias gen sing fem
3. εὐδοκίαν eudokian acc sing fem

```
1 Even so, Father: for so it seemed good in thy sight. Matt 11:26
1 and on earth peace, good will toward men,......... Luke 2:14
2 and on earth peace, good will toward men............ 2:14
1 even so, Father; for so it seemed good in thy sight..... 10:21
1 my heart's desire and prayer to God for Israel is,.. Rom 10:1
3 according to the good pleasure of his will,............ Eph 1:5
3 mystery of his will, according to his good pleasure..... 1:9
3 preach Christ ... and some also of good will:........ Phlp 1:15
2 both to will and to do of his good pleasure............ 2:13
3 and fulfil all the good pleasure of his goodness,..... 2 Th 1:11
```

The term *eudokia* is almost completely restricted to Jewish literature and occurs for the first time in the Greek Bible. "It is not even found in the Hellenistic koine" (including Josephus and Philo) (Schrenk, "eudokia," *Kittel*, 2:742f.).

Septuagint Usage

Eudokia occurs in the canonical writings of the Septuagint once in 1 Chronicles, which has an uncertain Hebrew original, and once in the Song of Solomon (6:4 [LXX 6:3]). The remaining eight instances appear in the Psalms. *Rātsôn* ("favor") is the Hebrew term it translates. The Chronicler recalled that David appointed Asaph to sing thanksgiving to the Lord. In the song the writer invoked the "favor" of God upon the hearts of those seeking the Lord (1 Chronicles 16:10). The Psalms also speak of God's favor upon His people (Psalms 5:12; 19:14 [LXX 18:14]; 51:18 [50:18]; 89:17 [88:17]; 106:4 [105:4]; cf. 69:13 [68:13]).

The apocryphal writing of Sirach uses *eudokia* 16 times. "Those who fear the Lord will seek his approval (*eudokia*)" (RSV, Sirach 2:15f.; cf. 32:14 [LXX 35:14]; 35:3,16 [32:3,16]), but those "favoring" their desires (*epithumia* [1924]) will become the "laughingstock of their enemies" (RSV, Sirach 18:31; cf. 34:18 [LXX 31:18]). The word can also describe simple human satisfaction reflected in choice: "As clay in the hand of the potter—for all his ways are as he pleases (*eudokia*)—" (Sirach 33:13 [LXX 36:13]; see also Schrenk for rabbinic examples of *eudokia*, ibid., 2:745).

New Testament Usage

Eudokia occurs three times in the Gospels. Matthew 11:26 and Luke 10:21 share the same tradition that it is God's favor/pleasure to disclose the "hidden things." Here there is the union of the ideas of choice or will and favor (cf. the RSV's good translation "gracious will").

God's favor is likewise understood in Luke 2:14. God's peace is among men of His favor, "to men on whom his favor rests" (NIV), rather than being "good will (*eudokia*) toward men" (KJV). Again the merging of favor and will should not be overlooked. (The problem around which this interpretation revolves is textual, i.e., whether to read *eudokia* [nominative] or *eudokias* [genitive]. For a discussion of the basis for the textual preference of the genitive see Metzger, *Textual Commentary*, p.133.)

Paul's writings contain the remaining six instances of *eudokia*. He also associated *eudokia* with the "gracious will" of God manifest in His salvation (Ephesians 1:5,9). But *eudokia* can also refer to human "favor" or "desire" or "choice" (Romans 10:1; Philippians 1:15, here of "good," albeit mistaken, "intention"; cf. Philippians 2:13; 2 Thessalonians 1:11).

STRONG 2107, BAUER 319, MOULTON-MILLIGAN 260, KITTEL 2:742-51, LIDDELL-SCOTT 710, COLIN BROWN 2:817-20.

2087. εὐεργεσία euergesia noun

Good deed, service, benefit.
CROSS-REFERENCE:
  ἐργάζομαι ergazomai (2021)

עֲלִילָה 'ălîlāh (6173), Deed, action (Ps 78:11 [77:11]).

1. εὐεργεσίας euergesias gen sing fem
2. εὐεργεσίᾳ euergesia dat sing fem

```
2 the good deed done to the impotent man,.......... Acts 4:9
1 are faithful and beloved, partakers of the benefit.... 1 Tm 6:2
```

This term is found in classical Greek documents mentioning "benefits" that increased the welfare of an empire. In the Septuagint it is used in Psalm 78:11 (LXX 77:11) to refer to God's "wonders." Used just twice in the New Testament, *euergesia* means "good deed" as in Acts 4:9 or "benefit" as in 1 Timothy 6:2.

STRONG 2108, BAUER 319-20, MOULTON-MILLIGAN 260, KITTEL 2:654-55, LIDDELL-SCOTT 712, COLIN BROWN 3:1152.

2088. εὐεργετέω euergeteō verb
Do good, benefit.
COGNATE:
ἐργάζομαι ergazomai (2021)
SYNONYMS:
ἀγαθοεργέω agathoergeō (14)
ἀγαθοποιέω agathopoieō (15)
גָּמַל gāmal (1621), Render, do (Ps 13:6 [12:6]).
גָּמַר gāmar (1625), Requite, avenge (Ps 57:2 [56:2]).

1. εὐεργετῶν euergetōn nom sing masc part pres act

1 Jesus of Nazareth ... who went about **doing good**, ... Acts 10:38

"Doing good," a reference to Jesus' works on earth, is found in Acts 10:38. This is the only instance of this word in the New Testament. (Cf. Luke 22:25, *euergetēs* [2089].) In the Old Testament, several references to God's actions toward individuals are seen in Psalms 13:6 (LXX 12:6); 57:2 (56:2); 116:7 (115:7). In other Greek writings petitions commonly end with a request to be relieved (i.e., to be a recipient of another's "doing good" to them).

STRONG 2109, BAUER 320, MOULTON-MILLIGAN 260-61, LIDDELL-SCOTT 712, COLIN BROWN 3:1147,1152.

2089. εὐεργέτης euergetēs noun
Benefactor.
CROSS-REFERENCE:
ἐργάζομαι ergazomai (2021)

1. εὐεργέται euergetai nom pl masc

1 that exercise authority ... are called **benefactors**. ... Luke 22:25

This is a princely title or the title of an important person meaning "benefactor." In classical Greek the word is a regular title. It is used in a petition to the prefect; to refer to emperors and a king; and with reference to Gaius, the physician to Emperor Claudius (see *Moulton-Milligan*). It is found only in Luke 22:25 in the New Testament where Jesus mentioned the title with contempt and forbade His disciples to allow themselves to be called *euergetēs*. Only Christ can rightly be called *euergetēs* because of who He is and what He does (cf. Acts 10:38). Betram states, "The proper position of men as mediators of the divine benefits is that of servants" (Luke 22:26) ("euergetēs," *Kittel*, 2:654f.).

STRONG 2110, BAUER 320, MOULTON-MILLIGAN 261, KITTEL 2:654-55, LIDDELL-SCOTT 712, COLIN BROWN 3:1147,1152.

2090. εὔθετος euthetos adj
Fit, suitable, usable.
CROSS-REFERENCE:
τίθημι tithēmi (4935)
מָצָא mātsā' (4834), Find (Ps 32:6 [31:6]).

1. εὔθετος euthetos nom sing masc
2. εὔθετον eutheton nom/acc sing fem/neu

1 and looking back, is **fit** for the kingdom of God..... Luke 9:62
2 neither **fit** for the land, nor yet for the dunghill;....... 14:35
2 herbs **meet** for them by whom it is dressed,......... Heb 6:7

Originally this term meant "well placed," but later it came to mean "fit, usable, suitable, convenient" (see *Bauer*). The only Septuagint reference is Psalm 32:6 (LXX 31:6) where the Psalmist refers to penitent prayer in a "fit" time. Other Greek references include the idea of one being "suitable for a place or office." New Testament usage is limited to Luke 9:62, referring to someone; and Luke 14:35 and Hebrews 6:7, referring to something.

STRONG 2111, BAUER 320, MOULTON-MILLIGAN 261, LIDDELL-SCOTT 714.

2091. εὐθέως eutheōs adv
At once, immediately.
SYNONYMS:
ἐξαυτῆς exautēs (1808)
εὐθύς euthus (2098)
παραχρῆμα parachrēma (3777)
ταχέως tacheōs (4878)
פִּתְאֹם pith'ōm (6849), Suddenly, surprisingly (Jb 5:3).

1. εὐθέως eutheōs

1 **straightway** left their nets, and followed him.........Matt 4:20
1 they **immediately** left the ship and their father,.......... 4:22
1 And **immediately** his leprosy was cleansed............... 8:3
1 and **forthwith** they sprung up,....................... 13:5
1 And **straightway** Jesus constrained his disciples........ 14:22
1 But **straightway** Jesus spake unto them, saying,....... 14:27
1 And **immediately** Jesus stretched forth his hand,....... 14:31
1 and **immediately** their eyes received sight,............... 20:34
1 and **straightway** ye shall find an ass tied,............... 21:2
1 and **straightway** he will send them.................... 21:3

1 **Immediately** after the tribulation of those days	Matt 24:29
1 and **straightway** took his journey	25:15
1 received the five talents went **at once** (NIV)	25:16
1 And **forthwith** he came to Jesus, ... and kissed him	26:49
1 And **immediately** the cock crew	26:74
1 **straightway** one of them ran, and took a sponge,	27:48
1 And **straightway** coming up out of the water,	Mark 1:10
1 And **immediately** the Spirit driveth him	1:12
1 And **straightway** they forsook their nets,	1:18
1 And **straightway** he called them:	1:20
1 and **straightway** on the sabbath day he entered	1:21
1 And **forthwith**, when they were come out	1:29
1 lay sick of a fever, and **anon** they tell him of her	1:30
1 and **immediately** the fever left her,	1:31
1 **immediately** the leprosy departed from him,	1:42
1 straitly charged him, and **forthwith** sent him away;	1:43
1 And **straightway** many were gathered together,	2:2
1 **immediately** when Jesus perceived in his spirit	2:8
1 And **immediately** he arose, took up the bed,	2:12
1 and **straightway** took counsel with the Herodians	3:6
1 and **immediately** it sprang up,	4:5
1 when they have heard, Satan cometh **immediately**,	4:15
1 **immediately** receive it with gladness;	4:16
1 **immediately** they are offended	4:17
1 **immediately** he putteth in the sickle,	4:29
1 **immediately** there met him out of the tombs a man	5:2
1 And **forthwith** Jesus gave them leave	5:13
1 And **straightway** the fountain of her blood	5:29
1 And Jesus, **immediately** knowing in himself	5:30
1 **As soon as** Jesus heard the word that was spoken,	5:36
1 And **straightway** the damsel arose, and walked;	5:42
1 she came in **straightway** with haste unto the king,	6:25
1 And **immediately** the king sent an executioner,	6:27
1 And **straightway** he constrained his disciples	6:45
1 And **immediately** he talked with them,	6:50
1 come out of the ship, **straightway** they knew him,	6:54
1 And **straightway** his ears were opened,	7:35
1 And **straightway** he entered into a ship	8:10
1 And **immediately** all the people,	9:15
1 when he saw him, **straightway** the spirit tare him;	9:20
1 And **straightway** the father of the child cried out,	9:24
1 And **immediately** he received his sight,	10:52
1 and **as soon as** ye be entered into it,	11:2
1 and **straightway** he will send him hither.	11:3
1 **immediately**, while he yet spake, cometh Judas,	14:43
1 soon as he was come, he goeth **straightway** to him,	14:45
1 And **straightway** in the morning the chief priests	15:1
1 And **immediately** the leprosy departed from him	Luke 5:13
1 having drunk old wine **straightway** desireth new:	5:39
1 and **immediately** it fell; and the ruin of that house	6:49
1 they may open unto him **immediately**.	12:36
1 **straightway** ye say, There cometh a shower;	12:54
1 not **straightway** pull him out on the sabbath day?	14:5
1 having a servant ... will say unto him **by and by**,	17:7
1 first come to pass; but the end is not **by and by**.	21:9
1 And **immediately** the man was made whole,	John 5:9
1 and **immediately** the ship was at the land	6:21
1 having received the sop went **immediately** out:	13:30
1 and **immediately** the cock crew	18:27
1 And **immediately** there fell from his eyes	Acts 9:18
1 **straightway** he preached Christ in the synagogues,	9:20
1 and made thy bed. And he arose **immediately**.	9:34
1 and **forthwith** the angel departed from him.	12:10
1 **immediately** we endeavoured to go	16:10
1 And the brethren **immediately** sent away Paul	17:10
1 And then **immediately** the brethren sent away Paul	17:14
1 and **forthwith** the doors were shut.	21:30
1 Then **straightway** they departed from him	22:29
1 **immediately** I conferred not with flesh and blood:	Gal 1:16
1 **straightway** forgetteth what manner of man he was.	Jas 1:24
1 But I trust I shall **shortly** see thee,	3 Jn 1:14
1 And **immediately** I was in the spirit;	Rev 4:2

This term of action, which means "immediately" or "straightway," is significantly present in Mark's Gospel where it is used 40 of the 80 times in the New Testament. Several of these Markan references relate to immediate physical healing (Mark 1:31,42; 7:35; 10:52). Septuagint usage is confined to Joshua 6:11 (LXX 6:10). There is a portrayal of action, immediacy, and/or excitement with the use of this adverb. The more common New Testament form, however, is *euthus* (see the discussion at number 2098 in this volume).

STRONG 2112, BAUER 320, MOULTON-MILLIGAN 261, LIDDELL-SCOTT 714, COLIN BROWN 3:833-34,837.

2092. εὐθυδρομέω euthudromeō verb

Run a straight course.

1. εὐθυδρομήσαμεν euthudromēsamen
    1pl indic aor act
2. εὐθυδρομήσαντες euthudromēsantes
    nom pl masc part aor act

1 we came with a **straight course** to Samothracia,	Acts 16:11
2 we came with a **straight course** unto Coos,	21:1

This verb is not found in the Septuagint, but it is used twice in the New Testament in reference to the sailing of a ship (Acts 16:11; 21:1). It must be distinguished from *euthunō* (2096) and *euthunein* which mean "make straight" or "straighten" and which are used in the Septuagint and classical Greek.

STRONG 2113, BAUER 320, LIDDELL-SCOTT 715.

2093. εὐθυμέω euthumeō verb

Be cheerful, cheer up, keep up one's courage.

COGNATE:
   θυμόω thumoō (2350)

SYNONYMS:
   εὐψυχέω eupsucheō (2155)
   θαρρέω tharrheō (2269)
   θαρσέω tharseō (2270)
   τολμάω tolmaō (4958)

1. εὐθυμεῖ euthumei 3sing indic pres act
2. εὐθυμεῖτε euthumeite 2pl impr pres act
3. εὐθυμεῖν euthumein inf pres act

3 And now I exhort you **to be of good cheer**:	Acts 27:22
2 sirs, **be of good cheer**: for I believe God,	27:25
1 Is any **merry**? let him sing psalms.	Jas 5:13

This verb, which means "be cheerful," is found only in Acts 27:22,25 and James 5:13 in the New Testament. Its meaning may shade to "taking hope" or "taking heart" (Acts 27:22,25) or being outwardly "merry" (James 5:13) in singing. Psalm 32:11 (LXX 31:11) and Proverbs 15:15 (both in Symmachus' text) are the only two occurrences in the Septuagint.

εὔθυμος 2094

STRONG 2114, BAUER 320, MOULTON-MILLIGAN 261, LIDDELL-SCOTT 715.

2094. εὔθυμος euthumos adj
Cheerful, having good courage.
CROSS-REFERENCE:
θυμόω thumoō (2350)

1. εὔθυμοι euthumoi nom pl masc
1 Then were they all of good cheer,............. Acts 27:36

Rarely used in the New Testament, this adjective means "cheerful." Its only occurrence in the Septuagint is in 2 Maccabees 11:26. In the New Testament it is found only in Acts 27:36 where it means "encouraged" or "good cheer." (See also euthumeō [2093] which is used twice in Acts 27.)

STRONG 2115, BAUER 320, MOULTON-MILLIGAN 261, LIDDELL-SCOTT 715.

2094B. εὐθυμότερον
euthumoteron adv
More cheerfully.

This is the comparative form of euthumōs. See word study at number 2095.

2095. εὐθύμως euthumōs adv
Cheerfully.
CROSS-REFERENCE:
θυμόω thumoō (2350)

1. εὐθυμότερον euthumoteron comp
2. εὐθύμως euthumōs

1 I do the **more cheerfully** answer for myself:........ Acts 24:10
2 so I **gladly** make my defense (NIV).................... 24:10

This word is not found in the Septuagint, and it is rare in other Greek writings. Its only occurrence in the New Testament is in Acts 24:10 where Paul made his defense "cheerfully" before the governor. Here it is used in a comparative manner. The adjective form (euthumos [2094]) is found in Acts 27:36.

BAUER 320, MOULTON-MILLIGAN 261, LIDDELL-SCOTT 715.

2096. εὐθύνω euthunō verb
Make straight, straighten, steer (straight).

יָשַׁר yāshar (3595), Please (1 Sm 18:26).
נָטָה nāṭāh (5371), Extend, stretch out; hiphil: turn aside, incline (Nm 22:23, Jos 24:23).

1. εὐθύνοντος euthunontos
gen sing masc part pres act
2. εὐθύνατε euthunate 2pl impr aor act

2 **Make straight** the way of the Lord,................John 1:23
1 turned about ... whithersoever the governor listeth.... Jas 3:4

Rare in the New Testament (found only in John 1:23 and James 3:4), this verb conveys two basic ideas. During the Intertestamental Period its usage was largely in a moral or behavioral sense: "Make your ways straight" or "May God direct/straighten your path" (e.g., Sirach 2:6). The other prominent use had to do with the imagery of navigation, piloting a ship on a sure course. James employed it in this sense (James 3:4), while John the Baptist used the verb in a more figurative way that contained a moral meaning, "*Make straight* the way of the Lord" (John 1:23).

STRONG 2116, BAUER 320-21, MOULTON-MILLIGAN 261-62, LIDDELL-SCOTT 715-16.

2097. εὐθύς euthus adj
Straight, right, upright.
SYNONYM:
ὀρθός orthos (3580)

בַּר bar (1276), Pure (Ps 73:1 [72:1]).
יָשַׁר yāshar (3595), Qal: please (Jgs 14:3); piel: level (Is 45:13).
יָשָׁר yāshār (3596), Straight, level, right, upright (Ps 49:14 [48:14], Hos 14:9 [14:10]).
יֹשֶׁר yōsher (3598), Straightness, uprightness (Ps 25:21 [24:21], Prv 2:13).
כּוּן kûn (3679), Niphal: stand firm, be stable (Ps 78:37 [77:37]).
מִישׁוֹר mîshôr (4473), Level ground, plain, righteousness (1 Kgs 20:23,25 [21:23,25], Ps 27:11 [26:11], Is 40:4).
מֵישָׁרִים mêshārîm (4478), Level way, uprightness (Ps 58:1 [57:1], Is 26:7).
נֶגֶד neghedh (5224), Before (Gn 33:12).
נֹכַח nōkhach (5415), What lies opposite, directly in front of (Ez 46:9).
נָכֹחַ nākhōach (5416), What is straight, what is right (Is 59:14).
שְׁפִי sh⁽e⁾phî (8576), Caravan track, worn path (Nm 23:3 [23:4], Jer 3:2).

תָכַן tākhan (8834), Examine; niphal: be in order, be fair (Ez 33:17,20).

1. **εὐθεῖα** eutheia nom sing fem
2. **εὐθείαν** eutheian acc sing fem
3. **εὐθείας** eutheias acc pl fem

3 Prepare ye the way ... make his paths **straight**.	Matt 3:3
3 Prepare ye the way ... make his paths **straight**.	Mark 1:3
3 Prepare ye the way ... make his paths **straight**.	Luke 3:4
2 and the crooked shall be made **straight**,	3:5
3 and the crooked shall be made **straight**,	3:5
1 for thy heart is not **right** in the sight of God.	Acts 8:21
2 and go into the street which is called **Straight**,	9:11
3 wilt thou not cease to pervert the **right** ways	13:10
2 have forsaken the **right** way, and are gone astray,	2 Pt 2:15

Classical Greek

In classical Greek the adjective *euthus* has both a literal and a figurative meaning. Literally it is used in the spatial sense of "straight, level, direct." It is often used this way to describe roads. Figuratively it is used in the moral sense of "straightforward, upright, true, sincere, honest."

Septuagint Usage

In the Septuagint, as in classical Greek, the adjective *euthus* is used both in a literal and figurative sense. A usage that stands out in the Psalms is the expression "upright heart" (e.g., Psalms 7:10; 32:11 [LXX 31:11]; 37:14 [36:14]; 73:1 [72:1]; 125:4 [124:4]).

New Testament Usage

In the New Testament *euthus* is used adjectivally in eight instances. In the majority of cases it refers to paths, roads, ways. In Acts 9:11 it is used in a literal sense to designate a specific thoroughfare, "the street which is called Straight."

In six instances *euthus* is used with reference to paths, ways, roads in a figurative sense. In Acts 13:10 and 2 Peter 2:15 the right "way" is essentially the way that leads to God. In a sense, the "right way" is a designation for true religion. Matthew 3:3, Mark 1:3, and Luke 3:4 quote Isaiah 40:3 with reference to John the Baptist's role of making the paths of the Lord "straight," that is, preparing the people for the message and ministry of Jesus. In addition, Luke 3:5 explicitly contrasts the straight with the crooked (*skolios* [4501]) way.

It is only in Acts 8:21 that the adjective *euthus* is used in a context other than that of path, road, or way. Here it designates a heart that is not "right" or "upright" from God's perspective.

STRONG 2117, BAUER 321, MOULTON-MILLIGAN 262, LIDDELL-SCOTT 716, COLIN BROWN 3:833-34,837.

2098. εὐθύς euthus adv

Immediately, at once, forthwith, straightway.

SYNONYMS:
ἐξαυτῆς exautēs (1808)
εὐθέως eutheōs (2091)
παραχρῆμα parachrēma (3777)
ταχέως tacheōs (4878)

הִנֵּה hinnēh (2079), Behold! (Gn 24:45, 38:29).

פִּתְאֹם pith'ōm (6849), Suddenly, surprisingly (Jb 5:3—Codex Alexandrinus only).

1. **εὐθύς** euthus

1 Jesus, ... went up **straightway** out of the water:	Matt 3:16
1 heareth the word, and **anon** with joy receiveth it;	13:20
1 persecution ariseth ... **by and by** he is offended.	13:21
1 **immediately** Jesus spoke to them, saying, (NASB)	14:27
1 and **straightway** ye shall find an ass tied,	21:2
1 and **immediately** he will send them (NASB)	21:3
1 And **immediately** the cock crew.	26:74
1 **immediately** coming up out of the water, (NASB)	Mark 1:10
1 And **immediately** the Spirit driveth him	1:12
1 And they **immediately** left the nets (NASB)	1:18
1 And **immediately** He called them; (NASB)	1:20
1 and **immediately** on the Sabbath (NASB)	1:21
1 **just then** there was in their synagogue (NASB)	1:23
1 And **immediately** his fame spread abroad	1:28
1 And **immediately** after they had come out (NASB)	1:29
1 **immediately** they spoke to Him (NASB)	1:30
1 And **immediately** the leprosy left him (NASB)	1:42
1 and **immediately** sent him away, (NASB)	1:43
1 And **immediately** Jesus, aware in His spirit (NASB)	2:8
1 he rose and **immediately** took up (NASB)	2:12
1 and **immediately** began taking counsel (NASB)	3:6
1 and **immediately** it sprang up (NASB)	4:5
1 **immediately** Satan comes (NASB)	4:15
1 **immediately** receive it with joy; (NASB)	4:16
1 **immediately** they fall away. (NASB)	4:17
1 he **immediately** puts in the sickle, (NASB)	4:29
1 **immediately** a man from the tombs (NASB)	5:2
1 And **immediately** the flow of her blood (NASB)	5:29
1 **immediately** Jesus, perceiving in Himself (NASB)	5:30
1 **immediately** the girl got up (NASB)	5:42
1 **immediately** they were ... astounded. (NASB)	5:42
1 **immediately** she came in haste (NASB)	6:25
1 **immediately** the king sent an executioner (NASB)	6:27
1 And **immediately** He made His disciples (NASB)	6:45
1 But **immediately** He spoke with them (NASB)	6:50
1 **immediately** the people recognized Him, (NASB)	6:54
1 hearing ... a woman ... **immediately** came (NASB)	7:25
1 and the impediment of his tongue (NASB) (NT)	7:35
1 And **immediately** He entered the boat (NASB)	8:10
1 **immediately**, when the entire crowd saw (NASB)	9:15
1 **immediately** the spirit threw him (NASB)	9:20
1 **Immediately** the boy's father cried out (NASB)	9:24
1 And **immediately** he received his sight, (NASB)	10:52
1 and **immediately** as you enter it. (NASB)	11:2
1 and **immediately** he will send it back here (NASB)	11:3
1 **immediately** while He was still speaking (NASB)	14:43
1 he **immediately** went up to Him (NASB)	14:45
1 **immediately** a cock crowed a second (NASB)	14:72
1 **immediately** held a consultation (NASB)	15:1
1 and **immediately** it collapsed, (NASB	Luke 6:49
1 he went out **immediately** (NASB)	John 13:30
1 and shall **straightway** glorify him.	13:32
1 and **forthwith** came there out blood and water.	19:34
1 went forth, and entered into a ship **immediately**;	21:3
1 **immediately** the object was taken up (NASB)	Acts 10:16

Classical Greek and Septuagint Usage

In classical Greek the adverb *euthus* has the temporal meaning of "immediately, at once,

εὐθύτης 2099

forthwith, straightway." This is also the meaning in the six Septuagint uses (e.g., Genesis 24:45; 38:29; Job 3:11).

New Testament Usage

It has been argued that in the New Testament *euthus* at times acts as an inferential conjunction meaning "so then, so now then," and "by and by." This usage has especially been suggested for Mark 1:21,23,29. At the most this is a very minor use of *euthus*, and there is by no means a scholarly consensus that it is used in this way at all. The most common meaning of the adverb *euthus* in the New Testament is "immediately, at once, forthwith, straightway." (See Matthew 13:20f.; Mark 1:10,12; Luke 6:49.)

No discussion of the adverb *euthus* is complete without reference to the adverb *eutheōs* (2091). While a few scholars have attempted to distinguish between the meanings of these two terms, it is generally agreed that they are equivalent in meaning. In fact, these two adverbs are often interchanged in the Biblical manuscripts. (Compare Matthew 4:20,22; 14:31; Luke 12:36.)

Differences in usage between *euthus* and *eutheōs* relate not to meaning but to writing style. While in Hellenistic Greek *eutheōs* is generally more common than *euthus*, the reverse is true in the writings of Philo and Josephus. *Euthus* is found in Luke 6:49, Acts 10:16, and a few other places. In the Gospel of John both *euthus* and *eutheōs* are given prominence. In the *Textus Receptus eutheōs* is by far the adverb most used in Mark. The critical Greek editions of the New Testament, however, have substituted *euthus* for *eutheōs* in the vast majority of passages in Mark.

STRONG 2117, BAUER 321, MOULTON-MILLIGAN 262, LIDDELL-SCOTT 716, COLIN BROWN 3:833-34,837.

2099. εὐθύτης euthutēs noun

Righteousness, uprightness.

יָשָׁר yāshār (3596), Upright, what is right (Pss 37:37 [36:37], 111:8 [110:8]).

יֹשֶׁר yōsher (3598), Straightness, uprightness, rightly (1 Kgs 9:4, Ps 119:7 [118:7], Eccl 12:10).

יִשְׁרָה yishrāh (3599), Sincerity (1 Kgs 3:6).

מִישׁוֹר mîshôr (4473), Level, fairness (Pss 26:12 [25:12], 45:6 [44:6]).

מֵישָׁרִים mêshārîm (4478), Level way, uprightness, truth, justly (Pss 9:8, 99:4 [98:4], S/S 1:4).

תָּמִים tāmîm (8879), Sincerely, honestly (Jos 24:14).

1. εὐθύτητος euthutētos gen sing fem

1 of righteousness is the sceptre of thy kingdom........Heb 1:8

Occurring only once in the New Testament, this adjective's meaning comes, in a large degree, from its parent verb *euthunō* (2096), "make straight." Its appearance in early Christian literature is in all instances figurative (*Bauer*). God's scepter is *euthutēs*, "righteous," in the sense that it is a visible sign of a righteous kingship, a righteous kingdom (Hebrews 1:8).

STRONG 2118, BAUER 321, LIDDELL-SCOTT 716.

2100. εὐκαιρέω eukaireō verb

Have (a favorable) time, leisure, opportunity.

CROSS-REFERENCE:
καιρός kairos (2511)

1. εὐκαιρήσῃ eukairēsē 3sing subj aor act
2. ηὐκαίρουν ēukairoun 3pl indic imperf act
3. εὐκαίρουν eukairoun 3pl indic imperf act

2 and they had no leisure so much as to eat.......... Mark 6:31
3 and they had no leisure so much as to eat............... 6:31
3 which were there spent their time in nothing else,.. Acts 17:21
2 which were there spent their time in nothing else,..... 17:21
1 he will come when he shall have convenient time.... 1 Co 16:12

Classical Greek

The verb *eukaireō* appears rather late in Greek literature. It first came into prominence during the time of the historian Polybius who died ca. 128 B.C. As such it can be classified as having originated in Koine Greek.

In secular Greek the primary meaning of *eukaireō* is "to have a favorable opportunity, time, or leisure." Secondary meanings are "to devote one's leisure" (to a thing), "to enjoy good times," "to prosper." The term *eukaireō* is not found in the Septuagint although several related terms are (e.g., Psalm 104:27 [LXX 103:27], *eukairos* [2102]; 2 Maccabees 14:29).

New Testament Usage

In the New Testament *eukaireō* occurs three times and basically reflects the usage of secular Greek. In Mark 6:31 it has the sense of "having time" or "leisure." Similarly, in 1 Corinthians 16:12 the meaning is probably that of "having a favorable opportunity." It should be noted that the emphasis in the use of *eukaireō* is on the opportunity of doing something rather than on the extent of time itself.

In Acts 17:21 the meaning of *eukaireō* as "having time" or "leisure" cannot be ruled out completely. It appears, however, that the secondary Koine meaning, "to devote or spend one's time," is more appropriate.

STRONG 2119, BAUER 321, MOULTON-MILLIGAN 262, LIDDELL-SCOTT 717, COLIN BROWN 3:833,837.

2101. εὐκαιρία eukairia noun
Favorable opportunity, the right moment.
CROSS-REFERENCE:
καιρός kairos (2511)

עֵת 'ēth (6496), Time, a point of time, the right time (Pss 9:9, 10:1 [9:22], 145:15 [144:15]).

1. εὐκαιρίαν eukairian acc sing fem

1 that time he sought **opportunity** to betray him......Matt 26:16
1 and sought **opportunity** to betray him unto them...Luke 22:6

Eukairia first appears in the writings of Plato (Fourth Century B.C.). It appears five times in the Septuagint, three of which are canonical (e.g., Psalms 9:9; 10:1 [LXX 9:22]; 145:15 [144:15]). It is found in the Gospels twice, both times referring to the moment of Judas' betrayal of Jesus (cf. Matthew 26:16; Luke 22:6). As a derivative of *kairos* (2511) it seems to convey a particular time of some importance, a moment that alone is suitable for a specific action.

STRONG 2120, BAUER 321, MOULTON-MILLIGAN 262, KITTEL 3:462, LIDDELL-SCOTT 717, COLIN BROWN 3:833,837.

2102. εὔκαιρος eukairos adj
Well-timed, suitable, opportune time.
CROSS-REFERENCE:
καιρός kairos (2511)

עֵת 'ēth (6496), Time, the right time (Ps 104:27 [103:27]).

1. εὐκαίρου eukairou gen sing fem
2. εὔκαιρον eukairon acc sing fem

1 And when a **convenient day** was come,.............Mark 6:21
2 and find grace to help in **time of need**..............Heb 4:16

This adjective, known from the classical period, appears only infrequently in Biblical writings. In the New Testament *eukairos* appears only twice. It describes Herodias' taking advantage of the "opportunity" to have John the Baptist killed (Mark 6:21). In Hebrews 4:16 the author explains that the throne of grace is available to believers *eukairos*. Most interpret this as "in our time of need" (cf. NIV, KJV, NASB, RSV). Some perceive that the perspective of opportunity is God's rather than man's: "at the (i.e., God's) appropriate time" (Delling, "eukairos," *Kittel*, 3:462). Probably the former is to be preferred because of the emphasis on the confidence the believer has in approaching God.

STRONG 2121, BAUER 321, MOULTON-MILLIGAN 262, KITTEL 3:462, LIDDELL-SCOTT 717, COLIN BROWN 3:833,837.

2103. εὐκαίρως eukairōs adv
Conveniently, appropriately, in season.
CROSS-REFERENCE:
καιρός kairos (2511)

1. εὐκαίρως eukairōs

1 he sought how he might **conveniently** betray him...Mark 14:11
1 Preach the word; be instant **in season**,.............2 Tm 4:2

Eukairōs, an adverb, is relatively rare. It can be found once in the Septuagint, in the apocryphal Sirach. A certain sense of promptness is conveyed here, so the "right time" to repay a vow is "as soon as possible" (Sirach 18:22). In its two New Testament uses it refers to a "convenient" time for doing something. Mark 6:31 seems to mean they could not find a convenient time or opportunity to eat. It describes Judas' seeking to betray Jesus "conveniently" (Mark 14:11). More complex is its use in 2 Timothy 4:2. There it is uncertain whether Paul's command to Timothy (to stand ready to "reprove, rebuke, exhort" [all part of "preach the word," the first imperative], *eukairōs akairōs*, "in season, out of season") is from Timothy's perspective or that of his hearers.

STRONG 2122, BAUER 321, MOULTON-MILLIGAN 262, LIDDELL-SCOTT 717, COLIN BROWN 3:833,837-38.

2104. εὔκοπος eukopos adj
Easy.
CROSS-REFERENCE:
κοπιάω kopiaō (2844)

1. εὐκοπώτερον eukopōteron comp nom/acc sing neu

1 For whether is **easier**, to say,.....................Matt 9:5
1 **easier** for a camel to go through the eye of a needle,...19:24
1 Whether is it **easier** to say to the sick of the palsy,..Mark 2:9
1 It is **easier** for a camel to go through.................10:25
1 Whether is **easier**, to say, Thy sins be forgiven......Luke 5:23
1 And it is **easier** for heaven and earth to pass,.........16:17
1 is **easier** for a camel to go through a needle's eye,.....18:25

Found only as a comparative adjective (*eukopōteros*) in the New Testament, it gives the impression of work done "without effort" or "with ease." It is commonly employed when setting up a contrast between one thing and another.

Three situations are mentioned in the Gospels which encompass all the seven occurrences of the term in the New Testament. First, there is the account of the healing of the paralytic where Jesus asked, "For whether is *easier*, to say, Thy sins be forgiven thee; or to say, Arise, and walk?" (Matthew 9:5; cf. Mark 2:9 and Luke 5:23). In the account of the rich young ruler Jesus stated, "It is easier for a camel to go through the eye of a needle, than for a rich man to enter into the kingdom of God" (Matthew 19:24; cf. Mark 10:25 and Luke 18:25). Interestingly, in these two instances Jesus made the point that with God it is not a matter of one condition being easier than the other, for God can just as well forgive sins as He can heal. And He can just as easily make a camel pass through a needle's eye as He can allow heavenly entrance for a rich man, for with God all things are possible. The last instance of *eukopos* is found in Luke without any implication as to God's ability (Luke 16:17). It is simply a contrast between heaven and earth passing away and the Law remaining intact.

STRONG 2123, BAUER 321, MOULTON-MILLIGAN 262, LIDDELL-SCOTT 718.

2105. εὐλάβεια eulabeia noun
Awe, reverence, fear of God.
CROSS-REFERENCE:
εὐλαβέομαι eulabeomai (2106)

דְּאָגָה deʾāghāh (1722), Anxiety (Jos 22:24).

1. εὐλαβείας eulabeias gen sing fem
1 and was heard in that he feared;............Heb 5:7
1 acceptably with reverence and godly fear:..........12:28

Classical Greek
In early classical Greek the noun *eulabeia* denotes "caution, discretion, circumspection." Three other uses are also seen. In a negative way caution developed into fear in the sense of "anxiety, dread." In a positive way caution became fear in the religious sense of "reverence, piety, veneration, awe." In addition, *eulabeia* took on the meaning of "timidity," implying that caution can easily be viewed as over caution. It is interesting to note that the Stoics saw *eulabeia* as a positive characteristic of the age.

Septuagint Usage
In the Septuagint the noun *eulabeia* occurs only three times, although the verb is fairly common (e.g., Exodus 3:6; Jeremiah 5:22). In Proverbs 28:14 it refers to "religious fear" or "awe," while in Joshua 22:24 and Wisdom 17:8 it denotes fear in the sense of "concern" or "anxiety."

New Testament Usage
In the New Testament the use of *eulabeia* is restricted to two occurrences in Hebrews. Some commentators have argued that both Hebrews 5:7 and 12:28 refer to fear in the sense of "anxiety" or even "dread." Most interpreters, however, conclude that at least one or even both of these passages refer to fear in terms of "religious reverence" or "awe," in other words, to a "godly fear."

Thus, in New Testament usage *eulabeia* as fear of God is not a dishonorable fear. It is not a fear that paralyzes man in the presence of grave danger, but rather a prudent fear or attitude of circumspection and caution as man stands in reverent awe before his God.

STRONG 2124, BAUER 321, MOULTON-MILLIGAN 262, KITTEL 2:751-54, LIDDELL-SCOTT 720, COLIN BROWN 2:90-91.

2106. εὐλαβέομαι eulabeomai verb
Be afraid, be concerned, reverence, respect.
COGNATES:
εὐλάβεια eulabeia (2105)
εὐλαβής eulabēs (2107)
λαμβάνω lambanō (2956)
SYNONYMS:
σέβομαι sebomai (4431)
φοβέω phobeō (5236)

גּוּר gûr (1513), Be afraid (1 Sm 18:15).

דָּאַג dāʾagh (1720), Fear, be in dread (Is 57:11).

דְּחַל deḥal (A1819), Pael: fear, be afraid (Dn 4:5—Aramaic).

הַס haṣ (2085), Hush! Quiet! (Hb 2:20, Zep 1:7, Zec 2:13).

חִיל chîl (2523), Tremble (Jer 5:22).

חָסָה chāsâh (2725), Seek refuge (Prv 30:5 [24:28], Na 1:7).

חָסִיד chāsîdh (2728), One who is faithful or devout (Prv 2:8).

חָשַׁב chāshav (2913), Value, esteem (Mal 3:16).

יָגֹר yāghōr (3133), Be afraid (Jer 22:25).

יָרֵא yārēʾ (3486), Fear, be afraid (Ex 3:6, 1 Sm 18:29).

עָלַז ʿālaz (6159), Exult (Jer 15:17).

עָרַץ ʿārats (6442), Be startled, alarmed, terrified (Jb 13:25).

פָּחַד pāchadh (6585), Tremble (Jb 3:25—Codex Alexandrinus only).

שָׁמַר shāmar (8490), Watch, guard; niphal: be careful (Dt 2:4).

1. εὐλαβηθείς eulabētheis nom sing masc part aor pass

1 fearing lest Paul should have been pulled in pieces Acts 23:10
1 By faith Noah, ... moved with fear, ... Heb 11:7

Classical Greek
In classical Greek the oldest meaning of the verb *eulabeomai* is "to take care, be cautious, be circumspect, be on guard." Two other meanings appear in later Greek. *Eulabeomai* came to include the meaning of "to fear" both in the negative sense of "to be afraid" and in the positive sense of "to revere, pay honor to, stand in awe of."

Septuagint Usage
In the Septuagint the original meaning of *eulabeomai* as "to take care" is by no means absent. The meaning "to fear," however, predominates. Especially significant are the references to the fear of God. While there are about 40 occurrences of this verb in the Septuagint, this frequency is relatively low in comparison to another word for fear, the verb *phobeō* (5236) (e.g., Zechariah 1:7; Jeremiah 4:1).

New Testament Usage
In the New Testament the verb *eulabeomai* occurs only twice. Both the positive and negative aspects of fear are reflected. In Acts 23:10 *eulabeomai* is used to refer to fearing in the sense of apprehension or concern. While some interpreters also suggest this meaning for Hebrews 11:7, it is much more likely that here this verb is used in the religious sense. Noah did not act so much out of fear and anxiety but out of reverence resulting from his devotion to God.

Although the verb *eulabeomai* and the noun *eulabeia* (2105) have a religious sense in classical Greek, it is clear that these terms do not form the primary terminology which refers to the fear of God in the New Testament.

STRONG 2125, BAUER 321-22, MOULTON-MILLIGAN 262, LIDDELL-SCOTT 720, COLIN BROWN 2:90-91.

2107. εὐλαβής eulabēs adj
Devout, reverent.
COGNATE:
  εὐλαβέομαι eulabeomai (2106)
SYNONYMS:
  εὐσεβής eusebēs (2133)
  θεοσεβής theosebēs (2294)

חָסִיד chāsîdh (2728), One who is faithful or devout (Mi 7:2).

1. εὐλαβής eulabēs nom sing masc
2. εὐλαβεῖς eulabeis nom pl masc

1 and the same man was just and **devout**, ... Luke 2:25
2 **devout** men, out of every nation under heaven. ...... Acts 2:5
2 And **devout** men carried Stephen to his burial, ... 8:2
1 Ananias, a man who was **devout** (NASB) 22:12

Septuagint Usage
The basic meaning of this adjective is "devout, pious, reverent" (cf. the verb *eulabeomai* [2106] and the noun *eulabeia* [2105]). In Biblical writings as well as the Apocrypha *eulabēs* is almost always used of "reverence" directed toward God (cf. Deuteronomy 2:4). This reverence concerns separation from ritual defilement in the Old Testament (Leviticus 15:31), and it is often associated with "awe" or "fear" of God (cf. the use of the verb, Exodus 3:6). Those who are "devout" are the faithful of God (Sirach 11:17; Micah 7:2; cf. Proverbs 2:8, the use of the verb).

New Testament Usage
In the New Testament *eulabēs* is reserved for describing "religious reverence, godliness," or "piety." It is also limited to Luke and Acts in reference to "devout" Jews (e.g., Simeon, Luke 2:25; Jews attending the Feast of Pentecost, Acts 2:5; those who buried Stephen, Acts 8:2; and Ananias, Acts 22:12). It is obvious that Luke used *eulabēs* in an extremely positive sense. Devout Jews were those who responded to the gospel and became believers. Luke did not denigrate Jewish piety (i.e., keeping the Law), because those who *truly* kept the Law and its spirit responded to the message that Jesus is Messiah.

STRONG 2126, BAUER 322, MOULTON-MILLIGAN 262-63, KITTEL 2:751-54, LIDDELL-SCOTT 720, COLIN BROWN 2:90-91.

2108. εὐλογέω eulogeō verb
Speak well of, praise, extol, bless.
COGNATES:
  ἐνευλογέω eneulogeō (1741)
  εὐλογητός eulogētos (2109)
  εὐλογία eulogia (2110)
  κατευλογέω kateulogeō (2690B)
SYNONYMS:
  αἰνέω aineō (134)
  ἐπαινέω epaineō (1852)
  χαριτόω charitoō (5323)

בָּרַךְ bārakh (1313), Qal: be blessed, be praised (Gn 14:19, Ru 2:19, Jer 17:7); niphal: wish for oneself a blessing

εὐλογέω 2108

(Gn 12:3—Codex Alexandrinus only); piel: bless, praise (Dt 2:7, 1 Chr 13:14, Ps 103:1,2 [102:1,2]); pual: be blessed, be praised (2 Sm 7:29, Ps 113:2 [112:2], Prv 20:21); hithpael: bless oneself (Is 65:16).

בְּרַךְ b⁵khrakh (A1315), Pael: bless (Dn 2:19,20—Aramaic).

בְּרָכָה b⁵rākhāh (1318), Blessing, capitulation (Is 19:24, 36:16).

הֲדַר hădhar (A1992), Pael: glorify (Dn 5:23—Aramaic).

הָלַל hālal (2054), Piel: praise (Is 38:18, 64:11).

יָדָה yādhâh (3142), Hiphil: praise (Is 12:1, 38:19).

יָרֵא yārē' (3486), Fear, be afraid (Is 25:3).

יָתַר yāthar (3613), Hiphil: pour out an abundance on (Dt 30:9).

כָּבֵד kāvēdh (3632), Weigh heavily; piel: honor (Is 25:3).

נָגַן nāghan (5235), Piel: play a stringed instrument (Is 38:20).

רָנַן rānan (7728), Shout with joy; hiphil: make a shout for joy (Jb 29:13).

רָצָה rātsâh (7813), Be pleased with, be favorable to (2 Sm 24:23).

שְׁבַח sh⁵vach (A8100), Praise (Dn 5:4—Aramaic).

1. εὐλογοῦμεν **eulogoumen** 1pl indic pres act
2. εὐλογεῖτε **eulogeite** 2pl impr pres act
3. εὐλογῶν **eulogōn** nom sing masc part pres act
4. εὐλογοῦντα **eulogounta**
     acc sing masc part pres act
5. εὐλογοῦντες **eulogountes**
     nom pl masc part pres act
6. εὐλογεῖν **eulogein** inf pres act
7. εὐλόγησεν **eulogēsen** 3sing indic aor act
8. εὐλογήσῃς **eulogēsēs** 2sing subj aor act
9. εὐλογήσας **eulogēsas** nom sing masc part aor act
10. εὐλόγηκεν **eulogēken** 3sing indic perf act
11. εὐλογήσω **eulogēsō** 1sing indic fut act
12. ηὐλόγει **ēulogei** 3sing indic imperf act
13. εὐλογεῖται **eulogeitai** 3sing indic pres mid
14. εὐλογοῦνται **eulogountai** 3pl indic pres mid
15. εὐλογημένος **eulogēmenos**
     nom sing masc part perf mid
16. εὐλογημένοι **eulogēmenoi**
     nom pl masc part perf mid
17. εὐλογημένη **eulogēmenē**
     nom sing fem part perf mid
18. εὐλογῇς **eulogēs** 2sing subj pres act
19. εὐλόγει **eulogei** 2sing impr pres act
20. εὐλογηθήσονται **eulogēthēsontai**
     3pl indic fut pass
21. ηὐλόγησεν **ēulogēsen** 3sing indic aor act

```
2  But I say unto you, ... bless them that curse you,.. Matt 5:44
7  and looking up to heaven, he blessed, and brake,..... 14:19
21 and looking up to heaven, he blessed, and brake,..... 14:19
15 Blessed is he that cometh in the name of the Lord;... 21:9
15 Blessed is he that cometh in the name of the Lord.... 23:39
16 Come, ye blessed of my Father,..................... 25:34
9  Jesus took bread, and blessed it, and brake it,.... Matt 26:26
7  he looked up to heaven, and blessed,............. Mark 6:41
9  And they had a few small fishes: and he blessed,...... 8:7
12 put his hands upon them, and blessed them........... 10:16
19 put his hands upon them, and blessed them.......... 10:16
15 Blessed is he that cometh in the name of the Lord:... 11:9
17 Blessed be the kingdom of our father David,......... 11:10
9  And as they did eat, Jesus took bread, and blessed,... 14:22
17 Lord is with thee: blessed art thou among women. Luke 1:28
17 Blessed art thou among women,...................... 1:42
15 and blessed is the fruit of thy womb................. 1:42
3  his tongue loosed, and he spake, and praised God..... 1:64
7  Then took he him up in his arms, and blessed God,... 2:28
7  And Simeon blessed them,........................... 2:34
2  Bless them that curse you, and pray for them........ 6:28
7  looking up to heaven, he blessed, and brake,...... 9:16
15 Blessed is he that cometh in the name of the Lord... 13:35
15 Blessed be the King that cometh in the name of..... 19:38
7  and blessed it, and brake, and gave to them......... 24:30
7  and he lifted up his hands, and blessed them........ 24:50
6  while he blessed them, he was parted from them,.... 24:51
5  in the temple, praising and blessing God. Amen...... 24:53
15 Hosanna: Blessed is the King of Israel........... John 12:13
4  raised up his Son Jesus, sent him to bless you,..... Acts 3:26
2  Bless them which persecute you: bless,........... Rom 12:14
2  bless, and curse not............................... 12:14
1  being reviled, we bless;........................ 1 Co 4:12
1  The cup of blessing which we bless,............... 10:16
8  Else when thou shalt bless with the spirit,...... 14:16
18 Else when thou shalt bless with the spirit,....... 14:16
14 So then they which be of faith are blessed........ Gal 3:9
9  who hath blessed us with all spiritual blessings..... Eph 1:3
3  Saying, Surely blessing I will bless thee,........ Heb 6:14
11 Saying, Surely blessing I will bless thee,.......... 6:14
9  who met Abraham ... and blessed him;................ 7:1
10 and blessed him that had the promises............... 7:6
7  and blessed him that had the promises............... 7:6
13 And without all contradiction the less is blessed... 7:7
7  By faith Isaac blessed Jacob and Esau.............. 11:20
7  By faith Jacob, ... blessed both the sons of Joseph;... 11:21
1  Therewith bless we God, even the Father;......... Jas 3:9
5  Not rendering evil ... but contrariwise blessing;..... 1 Pt 3:9
```

Classical Greek

The prefix *eu* (2074), "good," and the verb *legō* (2978), "I say or speak," form this compound verb which means "to speak good of, to praise, to honor" (cf. the noun *eulogia* [2110], "praise"). Although *eulogeō* rarely means "I bless" in secular Greek, there are inscriptions which support the role of *eulogeō* in other religious contexts (*Moulton-Milligan*; cf. Beyer, "eulogeō," *Kittel*, 2:754f.).

Septuagint Usage

Eulogeō occurs throughout the Septuagint (over 400 times), usually in a religious context. There it translates 11 Hebrew terms. Normally *bārakh*, in various tenses, stands behind *eulogeō*. This important Old Testament term means "to bless" (for success, power, fertility, or prosperity) or "to praise" (God) in a thankful spirit. The latter often occurs in common phrases or formulas (e.g., Deuteronomy 28:12; Psalm 103:22 [LXX 102:22]; Sirach 39:15; cf. Daniel [Septuagint] 3:51-90 [35 times]). God is often asked to bless His people, or He is seen as the One who does (Deuteronomy 26:15; 27:12; 2 Chronicles

31:10; Sirach 45:15; Isaiah 19:25). God is frequently blessed/praised because of His *cheṣedh* ("faithful love, kindness") and *'ĕmeth* ("faithfulness"). Those who are recipients of God's favor often manifest these same qualities (Deuteronomy 15:14; 1 Samuel 23:21 [LXX 1 Kings 23:21]; 1 Kings 10:9 [LXX 3 Kings 10:9]). *Eulogeō* is used in standard greetings (2 Kings 4:29 [LXX 4 Kings 4:29]; 1 Chronicles 16:43). The praise of the Lord by His people was central to the religion of Israel (Genesis 24:48; Deuteronomy 8:10; Psalm 26:12 [LXX 25:12]; Tobit 13:6,15; Isaiah 12:1). (For more on the Old Testament usage of *eulogeō* see ibid., 2:755-759.)

New Testament Usage
The New Testament has been thoroughly influenced by the Septuagint/Old Testament concept of "to bless" or "to praise" as a religious function in its presentation of *eulogeō* (see *eulogia, eulogētos* [2109]). *Eulogeō* is used frequently in the Synoptic Gospels (25 times; cf. John, only 1), and of those it is more often found in Luke (13 times). The citation of or allusion to Psalm 118:26 (LXX 117:26) in messianic reference to Jesus occurs in all four Gospels, often more than once (e.g., Matthew 21:9; 23:39; Mark 11:9f.; Luke 13:35; 19:38; John 12:13): "Blessed is he that cometh in the name of the Lord."

Eulogeō can describe the offering of thanks to God for food (in this case the elements of the Last Supper), a common Jewish practice (Matthew 26:26; Luke 24:30; 1 Corinthians 10:16). In describing persons, Mary is highly "favored" or "praised" (Luke 1:28,42), because the "fruit of (her) womb" is "blessed" (Luke 1:42; see article on *eulogētos*). "To praise" is often a good translation (Luke 2:28; 24:53), while a formal type of blessing is pictured in Luke 24:50 when Jesus blessed the disciples as He left them (cf. Matthew 25:34).

God pronounces blessing (*makarios* [3079]) on those who suffer for His sake (e.g., Luke 6:22). But the faithful believers are to bless (*eulogeō*) those at whose hands they are suffering (Luke 6:28; Romans 12:14; 1 Peter 3:9).

Inherent in the Biblical idea of blessing is that the greater blesses the lesser (see Oswalt, "bārak," *Theological Wordbook of the Old Testament*, 1:132) (e.g., Genesis 24:60; 1 Kings 8:14 [LXX 3 Kings 8:14]). This is the premise for the author of Hebrews who argued that Melchizedek—who is a type of Christ—is superior to Abraham (Hebrews 7:1,7); hence, Christ's high priesthood is superior to the levitical priesthood. God's promise to Abraham is fulfilled by faith to the faithful (Genesis 12:3; cf. Galatians 3:9; Ephesians 1:3; Hebrews 6:14). (See also Link, "Blessing," *Colin Brown*, 1:206-215.)

STRONG 2127, BAUER 322, MOULTON-MILLIGAN 263, KITTEL 2:754-63, LIDDELL-SCOTT 720-21, COLIN BROWN 1:206-7,212-13.

2109. εὐλογητός eulogētos adj
Blessed, praised.
COGNATE:
  εὐλογέω eulogeō (2108)
SYNONYM:
  μακάριος makarios (3079)

בָּרַךְ bārakh (1313), Be blessed, be praised (Gn 9:26, 1 Sm 15:13, Ps 72:18 [71:18]).

בְּרַךְ bᵉrakh (A1315), Be blessed (Dn 3:28—Aramaic).

בְּרָכָה bᵉrākhāh (1318), Blessing (Gn 12:2—Codex Alexandrinus only).

1. εὐλογητός eulogētos nom sing masc
2. εὐλογητοῦ eulogētou gen sing masc

2 Art thou the Christ, the Son of the **Blessed**?	Mark 14:61
1 **Blessed** be the Lord God of Israel;	Luke 1:68
1 the Creator, who is **blessed** for ever. Amen.	Rom 1:25
1 who is over all, God **blessed** for ever. Amen.	9:5
1 **Blessed** be God, even the Father of our Lord Jesus	2 Co 1:3
1 Lord Jesus Christ, which is **blessed** for evermore,	11:31
1 **Blessed** be the God and Father of our Lord Jesus	Eph 1:3
1 **Blessed** be the God and Father of our Lord Jesus	1 Pt 1:3

Septuagint Usage
An adjective based upon the union of the prefix *eu* (2074), "good," and the verb *legō* (2978) (cf. the verb *eulogeō* [2108]), according to Thayer *eulogētos* is especially a Biblical and ecclesiastical term (*Greek English Lexicon*). It appears in the Septuagint numerous times, always translating some form of *bārakh* ("blessed"). The term is almost invariably applied to God (e.g., Genesis 9:26; 14:20; Exodus 18:10; Ruth 2:20; 4:14; 2 Samuel 18:28 [LXX 2 Kings 18:28]; Tobit 3:11; Psalms throughout; cf. Tobit 11:14, of angels, Codex Siniaticus).

New Testament Usage
The New Testament likewise restricts the application of *eulogētos* to God. Thus Christ is "the Son of the Blessed (One)" (Mark 14:61). God is frequently called "blessed" in open thanksgivings (2 Corinthians 1:3; Ephesians

εὐλογία 2110

1:3; 1 Peter 1:3). The title also appears in other doxologies directed to God such as Zechariah's song (Luke 1:68; cf. Romans 1:25; 9:5).

STRONG 2128, BAUER 322, KITTEL 2:764, LIDDELL-SCOTT 720-21, COLIN BROWN 1:206-7,210,212-13.

2110. εὐλογία eulogia noun
Praise, flattery, blessing, consecration, bounty.
CROSS-REFERENCE:
  εὐλογέω eulogeō (2108)

בְּכֹרָה bekhōrāh (1112), Rank as firstborn (1 Chr 5:1,2).

בָּרַךְ bārakh (1313), Qal: be blessed (Nm 23:11, Jos 24:10); piel: bless (Jos 24:10); pual: be blessed (Dt 33:13).

בְּרָכָה berākhāh (1318), Blessing (Gn 27:38, Jos 15:19, Ps 109:17 [108:27]).

פְּרִי perî (6780), Result (Is 27:9).

תַּאֲוָה ta'ăwāh (8707), Desire (boundary ? cf. tāwâh [8757] (Gn 49:26).

1. εὐλογία eulogia nom sing fem
2. εὐλογίας eulogias gen sing fem
3. εὐλογίᾳ eulogia dat sing fem
4. εὐλογίαν eulogian acc sing fem
5. εὐλογίαις eulogiais dat pl fem

2 fulness of the **blessing** of the gospel of Christ......	Rom 15:29
2 and **fair speeches** deceive the hearts of the simple......	16:18
2 The cup of **blessing** which we bless,................	1 Co 10:16
4 and make up before hand your **bounty**,.............	2 Co 9:5
4 as a matter of **bounty**, and not as of covetousness.......	9:5
5 soweth **bountifully** shall reap also bountifully............	9:6
5 soweth bountifully shall reap also **bountifully**............	9:6
1 **blessing** of Abraham might come on the Gentiles.....	Gal 3:14
4 receive the promise of the Spirit through faith..........	3:14
3 who hath blessed us with all spiritual **blessings**.......	Eph 1:3
2 receiveth **blessing** from God:.......................	Heb 6:7
4 when he would have inherited the **blessing**,............	12:17
1 Out of ... mouth proceedeth **blessing** and cursing.....	Jas 3:10
4 thereunto called, that ye should inherit a **blessing**....	1 Pt 3:9
4 and strength, and honour, and glory, and **blessing**.....	Rev 5:12
1 heard I saying, **Blessing**, and honour, and glory,......	5:13
1 Saying, Amen: **Blessing**, and glory, and wisdom,........	7:12

Many words in the New Testament demonstrate a further development of the meanings in secular Greek, but the word group of which *eulogia* belongs has as its source of meaning the religious ideas associated with the Septuagint. It means "fine words" or "a good thing" (*eu* [2074], "good," *logia* [3022], "word/thing"). The idea of blessing, like cursing, presupposes a certain worldview. For there to be blessing, there must be "beings and forces from which good and life and power derive, as well as those from which evil comes" (Beyer, "eulogia," *Kittel*, 2:755). From the 16 occurrences in the New Testament, there are 5 general meanings of the word *eulogia*: (1) "praise" (Revelation 5:12,13; 7:12); (2) "flattery" (Romans 16:18); (3) "blessing" as an act derived from people (James 3:10) and as a "benefit" from God (Ephesians 1:3; Hebrews 6:7; 12:17; 1 Peter 3:9)—possibly both nuances being contained in Galatians 3:14; (4) "consecration" (1 Corinthians 10:16); and (5) "bounty" (2 Corinthians 9:5f.; Hebrews 6:7).

STRONG 2129, BAUER 322-23, MOULTON-MILLIGAN 263, KITTEL 2:754-63, LIDDELL-SCOTT 720-21, COLIN BROWN 1:206,212-14.

2111. εὐμετάδοτος eumetadotos adj
Generous, ready to give.
CROSS-REFERENCE:
  δίδωμι didōmi (1319)

1. εὐμεταδότους eumetadotous acc pl masc

1 **ready to distribute**, willing to communicate;.........	1 Tm 6:18

This adjective occurs only once in the New Testament, in 1 Timothy 6:18. It conveys the sense of being ready to give in an empathetic manner (literally *meta* [3196] plus *didōmi* [1319], "give with," is intensified by the prefix *eu* [2074]). The emphasis, however, does not stop with merely the attitude of giving but includes carrying out the action. *Eumetadotos* implies the specific giving or sharing of one's worldly goods, whatever they may be. In this sense, then, acts or deeds of mercy are in mind.

STRONG 2130, BAUER 323, MOULTON-MILLIGAN 263, LIDDELL-SCOTT 722.

2112. Εὐνείκη Euneikē name
Eunice.

1. Εὐνείκῃ Euneikē dat fem
2. Εὐνίκῃ Eunikē dat fem

1 in thy grandmother Lois, and thy mother **Eunice**;...	2 Tm 1:5
2 in thy grandmother Lois, and thy mother **Eunice**;.......	1:5

The faithful mother of Timothy (2 Timothy 1:5). Also spelled *Eunikē*.

2113. εὐνοέω eunoeō verb
Be well disposed, be friendly.
CROSS-REFERENCE:
  νοέω noeō (3401)

דְּבֵק deveq (A1741), Stick or hold together (Dn 2:43—Aramaic).

1. εὐνοῶν eunoōn nom sing masc part pres act
1 Agree with thine adversary quickly, ... Matt 5:25

Though found frequently in classical Greek, this verb is found only once in the New Testament, at Matthew 5:25. As a reference to general dealings between persons, it is almost always translated "be well disposed, friendly, agree, attached, wish well, meet halfway." The parable in Matthew is a portrait of the looming threat of judgment day; therefore it is urgent for those with hostilities toward another to reestablish that relationship in peace (literally become "well minded" [*eu* (2074), "well"; *nous* (3426), "mind"]). It is a charge to go beyond well-intentioned inclinations to a dramatic change of relations.

STRONG 2132, BAUER 323, MOULTON-MILLIGAN 263, KITTEL 4:971-73, LIDDELL-SCOTT 723.

2114. εὔνοια eunoia noun

Goodwill.
CROSS-REFERENCE:
νοέω noeō (3401)

1. εὐνοίας eunoias gen sing fem
2. εὔνοιαν eunoian acc sing fem
2 husband render unto the wife due benevolence: ...... 1 Co 7:3
1 With good will doing service, as to the Lord, ... Eph 6:7

Classical Greek and Septuagint Usage

The noun *eunoia* is derived from the adverb *eu* (2074) meaning "well" and the noun *nous* (3426) meaning "mind." Reflecting these components, in classical Greek the primary meaning of *eunoia* is "goodwill, favor, benevolence, kindness." Often this noun is used with reference to the attitude of rulers or any type of superiors to those under them. A secondary meaning of *eunoia* is "gift," that is, a gift that is essentially a sign of goodwill. For example, it designated the gifts from the subject states to the Athenian commanders (see *Liddell-Scott*). In the Septuagint the noun *eunoia* has the basic meaning of "goodwill."

New Testament Usage

In the New Testament *eunoia* occurs only once. In Ephesians 6:7 it refers to the proper attitude of a slave towards his master. A slave is to serve his master with goodwill. This may well include such characteristics as zeal, enthusiasm, loyalty, devotion, affection.

Later in Koine Greek, especially in Jewish and Christian circles, *eunoia* also came to refer to affection between relatives and devotion or loyalty of a subject to a ruler, including a slave to his master.

STRONG 2133, BAUER 323, MOULTON-MILLIGAN 263, KITTEL 4:971-73, LIDDELL-SCOTT 723.

2115. εὐνουχίζω eunouchizō verb

Emasculate, make a eunuch.
CROSS-REFERENCE:
εὐνοῦχος eunouchos (2116)

1. εὐνούχισαν eunouchisan 3pl indic aor act
2. εὐνουχίσθησαν eunouchisthēsan 3pl indic aor pass
2 which were made eunuchs of men: .... Matt 19:12
1 which have made themselves eunuchs 19:12

This verb does not appear in classical Greek until the Fourth Century B.C., and it is not used in the Septuagint. However, the Septuagint does use the noun *eunouchos* (2116) from which comes our English word *eunuch*. The idea of castration was basically alien to Western society until the great influx of Oriental culture which was a result of the extensive conquests of Alexander the Great (Schneider, "eunouchizō," *Kittel,* 2:765). The Old Testament strictly forbids castration of both man and beast; it goes against the divine will in creation (Deuteronomy 17:16ff.; 23:2-9). The rabbis thus taught that marriage was obligatory to all males in light of Genesis 1:28 (ibid., 2:767).

New Testament Usage

In the only New Testament use of the verb, Jesus transcended the rabbinic view. In Matthew 19:12 He set in contrast three examples of becoming a eunuch: (1) those who are so from birth, (2) those who are so as a result of other men, and (3) those who are so because of choice. The first two ways were the limits to the rabbinic understanding; the third way of becoming a eunuch had not before been elaborated by anyone, thus reinforcing the fact that the point of Jesus' words rests there. This last way should be understood figuratively, not literally, for Jesus would have abhorred castration like all true Jews. He had in mind those who voluntarily forego sexual companionship in order to render total service for the Kingdom's sake. (See also the word study for *eunouchos* [2116], "eunuch.")

However, it is only fair to say that the Early Church was divided as to whether Jesus' words were to be taken figuratively or literally (ibid., 2:765).

εὐνοῦχος 2116

STRONG 2134, BAUER 323, KITTEL 2:765-68, LIDDELL-SCOTT 724, COLIN BROWN 1:559-60.

2116. εὐνοῦχος eunouchos noun
Eunuch.

CROSS-REFERENCE:
εὐνουχίζω eunouchizō (2115)

סָרִיס sārîs (5835), Eunuch, eunuch who is a court official (Gn 40:2, 1 Kgs 22:9, Jer 52:25).

1. εὐνοῦχος eunouchos nom sing masc
2. εὐνοῦχοι eunouchoi nom pl masc

2	For there are some **eunuchs**,	Matt 19:12
2	and there are some **eunuchs**,	19:12
2	and there be **eunuchs**, ... made themselves eunuchs....	19:12
1	a man of Ethiopia, an **eunuch** of great authority	Acts 8:27
1	And the **eunuch** answered Philip, and said,	8:34
1	came unto a certain water: and the **eunuch** said,	8:36
1	both Philip and the **eunuch**; and he baptized him.	8:38
1	away Philip, that the **eunuch** saw him no more:	8:39

Classical Greek
The term *eunouchos*, "a eunuch," refers to "one in charge of the women," a "chamberlain." Because of that position the man was castrated so as to not pose a threat to the owner. It was also used of castrated animals, and in a figurative sense it could refer to a date without the pit. The heritage of the term is most apparent in its usage as an adjective for "watching the bed, sleepless" (*Liddell-Scott*).

Septuagint Usage
The Hebrew word *sārîs*, "eunuch," lies behind *eunouchos* in the Septuagint. This term was also the title of a "court official" who, according to an ancient practice, was castrated (e.g., Esther 1:10; 2:3f.; 4:4f.). However, there is not conclusive evidence that all court officials (*sāris*) were indeed eunuchs (e.g., 1 Kings 22:9 [LXX 3 Kings 22:9]; 2 Chronicles 18:8; Esther 1:1, cf. verse 10). On occasion the torment endured by a eunuch was employed as an image of anguish (Sirach 20:4; 30:20).

The ancient world had differing views of eunuchs. On the one hand, in the religious cults of Asia Minor, becoming a eunuch transformed one into a state of existence more like the deity; as such this view was embraced by the cult's adherents (Schneider, "eunouchos," *Kittel*, 2:765-768). On the other hand, the rabbinic view considered the eunuch as being in violation of God's command to be fruitful and multiply (Genesis 1:28). Further, eunuchs were excluded from the Israelite community of worship (Deuteronomy 23:1). However, Isaiah 56:3-5 promises a future worship community with eunuchs. (Acts 8:26ff. may be seen as a fulfillment of this promise.)

New Testament Usage
The term occurs in only two New Testament contexts: Matthew 19:12 and Acts 8:26ff. The word apparently had two dominant meanings referred to in Matthew 19:12. To these Jesus added a third type, those who have made themselves eunuchs for the sake of the Kingdom. Undoubtedly the rabbinic view provided the backdrop for Matthew 19:12. The response of Jesus was given to a question about celibacy versus marriage (verse 10). With this context in view it is certain that Jesus was not recommending self-emasculation as a path to higher spirituality. Rather, Jesus was making an exception to the rabbinic view of marriage as obligatory. This exception is based on dedication to the kingdom of heaven over and above one's commitment to the natural order. Some believers in the early centuries did take it literally, however.

Acts 8:27 speaks of the Ethiopian eunuch who was a court official for Candace. Whether or not this person was emasculated is questionable, although normally *eunouchos* refers to one in that condition.

STRONG 2135, BAUER 323, MOULTON-MILLIGAN 263, KITTEL 2:765-68, LIDDELL-SCOTT 724, COLIN BROWN 1:559-61.

2116B. Εὐοδια Euodia name
Euodias.

This is an alternate spelling of *Euōdia*. See the word study at number 2157.

2117. εὐοδόομαι euodoomai verb
Get along well, prosper, succeed, gain.

נָחָה nāchāh (5328), Qal: lead (Gn 24:27); hiphil: lead (Gn 24:48—Codex Alexandrinus only).

פָּרַץ pārats (6805), Determine; niphal: what is determined (1 Chr 13:2).

צָלֵחַ tsālēach (7014), Qal: be successful (Jer 12:1); hiphil: be successful, make succeed (Gn 39:3, 2 Chr 20:20, Dn 8:24f.).

צְלַח ts^elach (A7015), Haphel: prove a success, prosper (Ezr 5:8—Aramaic).

קָרָה qārâh (7424), Happen, come; hiphil: let something happen, ordain (Gn 24:12).

רָצָה rātsâh (7813), Be pleased with, be favorable to (Jer 14:10).

שָׂכַל sākhal (7959), Hiphil: have success (Prv 17:8).

1. εὐοδοῦται euodoutai 3sing indic pres mid
2. εὐοδῶται euodōtai 3sing subj pres mid
3. εὐοδοῦσθαι euodousthai inf pres mid
4. εὐοδωθήσομαι euodōthēsomai 1sing indic fut pass

4 I might have a prosperous journey ... to come .... Rom 1:10
2 as God hath prospered him, ... 1 Co 16:2
3 I wish above all things that thou mayest prosper ..... 3 Jn 1:2
1 and be in health, even as thy soul prospereth. 1:2

The verb literally means "be led along a good road" or "have a good journey" (*eu* [2074], "good"; *hodos* [3461], "way"). Each of its uses in the New Testament (Romans 1:10; 1 Corinthians 16:2; 3 John 2) is clearly metaphoric. *Euodoō* describes prospering and succeeding in the normal courses of life, both materially and spiritually. It is important to note that the passive voice of this verb indicates or implies that God is the true source of our prosperity and success.

STRONG 2137, BAUER 323 (see "euodoō"), MOULTON-MILLIGAN 263 (see "euodoō"), KITTEL 5:109-14 (see "euodoō"), LIDDELL-SCOTT 724 (see "euodoō").

2117B. εὐπάρεδρος euparedros adj
Attendance on; devotion to.

1. εὐπάρεδρον euparedron acc sing

1 to secure undistracted devotion (NASB) .... 1 Co 7:35

This word results from the combining of the adverbial prefix *eu* (2074), "well, properly, rightly," and the compound adjective *paredros*, "seated beside," or just "beside, next to, near." The resulting form, *euparedros*, means "proper attendance on" or "devotion to" someone.

New Testament Usage
Euparedros has not been found in sources earlier than the New Testament and appears there only once. In 1 Corinthians 7:35 Paul linked it with *euschēmōn* (2139) in describing the desirable attitude toward God, "That you may live in a right way (*euschēmon*) in undivided *devotion* (*euparedros*) to the Lord" (NIV; compare the NASB, "This I say ... to promote what is seemly [*euschēmon*] and to secure undisturbed *devotion* [*euparedros*] to the Lord").

BAUER 324, LIDDELL-SCOTT 725.

2118. εὐπειθής eupeithēs adj
Obedient, compliant.
CROSS-REFERENCE:
πείθω peithō (3844)

1. εὐπειθής eupeithēs nom sing fem

1 easy to be entreated, full of mercy and good fruits, ...Jas 3:17

In Biblical Greek the adjective is found only at James 3:17. It has been variously translated as "persuadable, willing to yield, easy to entreat, compliant," etc. The force of this adjective includes the sense of "agreeability." It is more than mere acquiescence. Vine says it comes from *eu* (2074), "well," and *peithomai* (see 3844), "to obey," and indicates a "readiness to obey" (*Expository Dictionary*, "Intreat"). James used it to describe the availability and attributes of the "wisdom that is from above" (3:17).

STRONG 2138, BAUER 324, MOULTON-MILLIGAN 263-64, LIDDELL-SCOTT 726.

2119. εὐπερίστατος euperistatos adj
Easily ensnaring, entangling, besetting.
CROSS-REFERENCE:
ἵστημι histēmi (2449)

1. εὐπερίστατον euperistaton acc sing fem

1 and the sin which doth so easily beset us, ... Heb 12:1

The difficulty of translating this adjective, besides its single occurrence in the Bible (Hebrews 12:1), is its scarcity in extra-Biblical texts. The New Testament context is one of a race with a great audience observing the runner. The difficulty in translation lies in explaining the way sin in general (not specific sins) hinders the progress of the spiritual athlete. Since the notions of a hindrance and an obstacle are implied within the verse, we should probably agree with those who view sin as that which "trips up, entangles," or "impedes" otherwise normal movement. The Christian is to lay aside sin because it hampers spiritual progress (literally "it stands in the way") and is therefore dangerous.

STRONG 2139, BAUER 324, MOULTON-MILLIGAN 264, LIDDELL-SCOTT 726.

2120. εὐποιΐα eupoiia noun
Doing good.
CROSS-REFERENCE:
ποιέω poieō (4020)

1. εὐποιΐας eupoiias gen sing fem

1 **But to do good and to communicate forget not:** ..... Heb 13:16

Although this compound noun is found only once in the entire New Testament (Hebrews 13:16), its simple cognate *poieō* (4020), "do," is used quite frequently. *Eupoiia* refers to the concrete practice of giving away material resources, i.e., the sharing of what one has with others. Doing "good deeds" (with regard to personal belongings) admittedly often entails great sacrifices, but these acts are pleasing to God.

STRONG 2140, BAUER 324, MOULTON-MILLIGAN 264, LIDDELL-SCOTT 727.

2121. εὐπορέω euporeō verb
Have plenty, be well-off.
CROSS-REFERENCE:
πορεύομαι poreuomai (4057)

מָצָא mātsā' (4834), Find (Lv 25:28).

נָשַׂג nāsagh (5560), Hiphil: be able to afford (Lv 25:49).

1. ηὐπορεῖτο ēuporeito 3sing indic imperf mid
2. εὐπορεῖτο euporeito 3sing indic imperf mid

1 the disciples, every man according to his **ability**, ... Acts 11:29
2 the disciples, every man according to his **ability**, ... 11:29

Classical Greek and Septuagint Usage
This verb occurs only once in the New Testament, in Acts 11:29. There its form is the middle voice. The precise nuance of the middle is difficult to ascertain since there are no active-voice usages with which to compare it. It is to be noted that classical Greek uses the verb in the middle voice also.

The Septuagint uses the verb form three times (possibly four; cf. Leviticus 25:28). Twice it occurs in the passive voice: "If he be prospered by means of (his) hand ... " (Leviticus 25:26; verse 49 uses a plural noun with a future passive participle). This is an attempt to render into Greek the causative force of the Hebrew which implies that the hand causes prosperity. The language pictures a theology of industrious labor. A definite work ethic is contained in the phraseology of the Old Testament. The apocryphal Wisdom of Solomon 10:10 uses the active voice. Wisdom "prospered" (RSV) the righteous man.

New Testament Usage
In the context of Acts 11:29 *euporeō* seems to have a *stative* force, that is, "Every man according to his ability (to the extent that he *was prosperous*), determined ...." The related noun form occurs at Acts 19:25 where Demetrius told his fellow craftsmen that their "wealth" or "prosperity" (*euporia*) stemmed from making idols and that Christianity threatened their financial well-being. Note that the prosperity of the Antioch disciples did not lead to self-indulgence. It led, rather, to generosity toward those in need. Active involvement in the needs of others was the concrete result of the Antiochene prosperity. Discipleship leads to fellowship.

STRONG 2141, BAUER 324, MOULTON-MILLIGAN 264, LIDDELL-SCOTT 727-28.

2122. εὐπορία euporia noun
Prosperity, wealth, riches.
CROSS-REFERENCE:
πορεύομαι poreuomai (4057)

חַיִל chayil (2524), Army (2 Kgs 25:10—Codex Alexandrinus only).

1. εὐπορία euporia nom sing fem

1 ye know that by this craft we have our **wealth**. ..... Acts 19:25

This Greek term denotes a high standard of living achieved through one's work, whether that work is easy or hard. Demetrius greedily feared that the "wealth" or "prosperity" which he and his guild enjoyed was being undermined by Paul's witness (Acts 19:25). This is the only time the word is used in the New Testament.

STRONG 2142, BAUER 324, MOULTON-MILLIGAN 264, LIDDELL-SCOTT 727-28.

2123. εὐπρέπεια euprepeia noun
Beauty, beautiful appearance, comeliness, gracefulness.
CROSS-REFERENCE:
πρέπω prepō (4100)

גֵּאוּת gē'ûth (1378), Majesty (Ps 93:1 [92:1]).

הָדָר hādhār (1994), Splendor, grandeur (Prv 31:25, Lam 1:6, Ez 16:14).

מִכְלָל mikhlāl (4497), Perfection (Ps 50:2 [49:2]).

מָעוֹן mā'ôn (4737), Dwelling, habitation (Ps 26:8 [25:8]).

נָוֶה nāweh (5295), Abode, residence, habitation (2 Sm 15:25).

נָעִים nā'îm (5456), Prosperity, good fortune (Jb 36:11).

1. εὐπρέπεια euprepeia nom sing fem

1 and the **grace** of the fashion of it perisheth: .... Jas 1:11

Found only in James 1:11, the noun is part of a Hebrew idiom for "beauty," in this case the beauty of a flower. Literally it reads, "the beauty (*euprepeia*) of its countenance." The translation "grace" (KJV) should be understood in this sense. The word *euprepeia* is related to the verb *prepō* (4100) which means "be fitting, be seemly."

STRONG 2143, BAUER 324, MOULTON-MILLIGAN 264, LIDDELL-SCOTT 728.

2124. εὐπρόσδεκτος

euprosdektos adj

Acceptable, pleasant, well-received, approved.

COGNATE:
    δέχομαι dechomai (1203)

SYNONYMS:
    ἀπόδεκτος apodektos (582)
    δεκτός dektos (1178)
    εὐάρεστος euarestos (2080)

1. **εὐπρόσδεκτος euprosdektos** nom sing masc/fem
2. **εὐπροσδέκτους euprosdektous** acc pl fem

1 the offering up of the Gentiles might be **acceptable**, Rom 15:16
1 I have for Jerusalem may be **accepted** of the saints;.... 15:31
1 behold, now is the **accepted** time;................... 2 Co 6:2
1 it is **accepted** according to that a man hath,............. 8:12
2 **acceptable** to God by Jesus Christ................... 1 Pt 2:5

Classical Greek

This adjective is derived from *prosdechomai* (4185), "to receive favorably." The *eu* (2074) prefix emphasizes the positive aspect of the reception; thus it means "pleasant, acceptable," and it is much like the term *dektos* (1178), "acceptable." *Euprosdektos*, unlike its parent word *dektos*, does not occur in the Septuagint; nevertheless it would probably not be incorrect to assume that *euprosdektos* contains some of the same cultic significance that *dektos* has in the Septuagint ("to offer an acceptable sacrifice," e.g., Jeremiah 6:20; cf. Exodus 28:38; Leviticus 1:4).

New Testament Usage

The usage of *euprosdektos* (five times) in the New Testament is entirely in accord with understanding it as the closely related term *dektos*, which retains its cultic significance (cf. Philippians 4:18). Paul, directed by the Spirit, clearly associated *euprosdektos* with cultic imagery in Romans 15:16 (of the Gentiles as an "acceptable" offering to God) as does Peter in 1 Peter 2:5 (of believers' acceptable sacrifices to God). The cultic sense may be intended in 2 Corinthians 8:12 as well. The context totally allows for the image of "acceptable sacrificial giving" (cf. verses 1-7).

However, Paul also regarded *euprosdektos* as a secular term. He hoped that his actions would be "acceptable" to those in Jerusalem (Romans 15:31). And from a different perspective, playing upon Isaiah 49:8 (*dektos*, Septuagint), Paul declared that now is indeed the "accepted time" of God's salvation (2 Corinthians 6:2; cf. verse 1).

STRONG 2144, BAUER 324, MOULTON-MILLIGAN 264, KITTEL 2:58-59, LIDDELL-SCOTT 728, COLIN BROWN 3:744,746.

2125. εὐπρόσεδρος euprosedros adj

Constant, devoted, faithfully attending.

1. **εὐπρόσεδρον euprosedron** nom/acc sing neu

1 ye **may attend upon the Lord without distraction**..... 1 Co 7:35

The manuscripts underlying the King James Version supply this term as a variant to the more attested *euparedros* (2117B), the only difference being the matter of a preposition in the middle of the word. The meanings are the same: "giving single and undivided devotion" to the Lord. Taken literally the word conveys the imagery of someone "sitting fixed and near" another. The only place it appears in the New Testament is 1 Corinthians 7:35 where Paul indicated that the goal of his teaching on moral matters was that the Corinthians could "*attend upon* (literally 'be devoted to') the Lord without distraction."

STRONG 2145, BAUER 324, LIDDELL-SCOTT 728.

2126. εὐπροσωπέω euprosōpeō verb

Make a good showing, make a fair appearance.

CROSS-REFERENCE:
    πρόσωπον prosōpon (4241)

1. **εὐπροσωπῆσαι euprosōpēsai** inf aor act

1 As many as desire **to make a fair show** in the flesh,...Gal 6:12

This verb is rare with only one occurrence in the New Testament (Galatians 6:12). Until recently it was thought to have been introduced by Paul. But papyri dating to 114 B.C. have turned up other instances of its use (cf. *Moulton-Milligan*). Paul's opponents in Galatia were concerned about an "external showing," about "having a good appearance, exhibiting a good face" (*eu* [2074], "good"; *prosōpon* [4241], "face") amidst the crowd. Paul's own concern was the opposite; it was the Spirit's inward work in his converts that was important to him (cf. 4:19; 5:16ff.). His caricature of the Judaizers showed the contrast between outward appearance and inward reality.

STRONG 2146, BAUER 324, MOULTON-MILLIGAN 264, KITTEL 6:779, LIDDELL-SCOTT 728.

2127. εὐρακύλων eurakulōn noun

Northeast wind, Euroaquilo, northeaster.

1. **εὐρακύλων eurakulōn** nom sing masc

1 a violent wind, called Euraquilo; (NASB) .... Acts 27:14

Eurakulōn is apparently a Greek-Latin hybrid word used by sailors. It appears to be a compound of the Greek word *euros*, "east wind" (later, "southeast wind"), with the Latin *aquilo*, "north wind." Thus its apparent meaning is "northeast wind."

It appears in the oldest New Testament manuscripts and the Latin versions in Acts 27:14 in place of *eurokludōn* (2129).

BAUER 324, MOULTON-MILLIGAN 264, LIDDELL-SCOTT 729.

2128. εὑρίσκω heuriskō verb

Find, discover, obtain, ascertain, contrive.

COGNATES:

ἀνευρίσκω aneuriskō (427)
ἐφευρετής epheuretēs (2164)

SYNONYMS:

ἐπιγινώσκω epiginōskō (1906)
θεωρέω theōreō (2311)
καταλαμβάνω katalambanō (2608)

אָמַר 'āmar (569), Say; niphal: be said (Dn 8:26).

בּוֹא bô' (971), Qal: go, come (2 Chr 30:25, Jb 28:20); hophal: be brought (2 Kgs 12:9).

בָּקַע bāqa' (1260), Hatch; niphal: be hatched (Is 59:5).

בָּקַשׁ bāqash (1272), Piel: seek (Dn 9:3).

דָּרַךְ dārakh (1931), Walk; hiphil: let walk (Is 48:17).

יָתַר yāthar (3613), Niphal: be left over, remain over (1 Kgs 15:18).

מָלַט mālaṭ (4561), Piel: leave undisturbed (2 Kgs 23:18—Codex Alexandrinus only).

מָצָא mātsā' (4834), Qal: meet by chance, find, obtain (Gn 18:28, 1 Kgs 1:3, Eccl 8:17); niphal: be found (Ex 35:24, 2 Kgs 16:8, Mi 1:13); hiphil: make something happen to someone (Jb 34:11).

נָשָׂא nāsâ' (5558), Carry off, win, obtain (Est 2:9,15,17).

נָשַׂג nāsagh (5560), Hiphil: overtake, be able to afford, appear (Lv 5:11, Nm 6:21, Jer 42:16 [49:16]).

עֲבַד 'ăvadh (A5857), Do, commit (Dn 6:22—Aramaic).

פּוּק pûq (6572), Hiphil: gain (Prv 12:2).

רָאָה rā'âh (7495), Qal: see (Jgs 18:9—Codex Alexandrinus only); niphal: appear (Jgs 6:12—Codex Alexandrinus only).

שְׁכַח sh^ekhach (A8320), Haphel: find (Ezr 4:15,19, 7:16, Dn 2:25—Aramaic); hithpeel: be found, find oneself (Ezr 6:2, Dn 6:22—Aramaic).

שָׁמַר shāmar (8490), Observe, keep (Prv 2:20).

1. **εὑρίσκον heuriskon** nom/acc sing/pl neu indic/part pres/imperf act
2. **εὑρίσκω heuriskō** 1sing indic pres act
3. **εὑρίσκει heuriskei** 3sing indic pres act
4. **εὑρίσκομεν heuriskomen** 1pl indic pres act
5. **εὑρίσκοντες heuriskontes** nom pl masc part pres act
6. **εὗρον heuron** 1/3sing/pl indic aor act
7. **εὗρες heures** 2sing indic aor act
8. **εὗρεν heuren** 3sing indic aor act
9. **εὕρομεν heuromen** 1pl indic aor act
10. **εὕρω heurō** 1sing subj aor act
11. **εὑρήσῃς heurēsēs** 2sing subj aor act
12. **εὕρῃ heurē** 3sing subj aor act
13. **εὕρωμεν heurōmen** 1pl subj aor act
14. **εὕρητε heurēte** 2pl subj aor act
15. **εὕρωσιν heurōsin** 3pl subj aor act
16. **εὕροιεν heuroien** 3pl opt aor act
17. **εὑρών heurōn** nom sing masc part aor act
18. **εὑρόντες heurontes** nom pl masc part aor act
19. **εὑροῦσα heurousa** nom sing fem part aor act
20. **εὑροῦσαι heurousai** nom pl fem part aor act
21. **εὑρεῖν heurein** inf aor act
22. **εὕρηκα heurēka** 1sing indic perf act
23. **εὑρήκαμεν heurēkamen** 1pl indic perf act
24. **εὑρηκέναι heurēkenai** inf perf act
25. **εὑρήσεις heurēseis** 2sing indic fut act
26. **εὑρήσει heurēsei** 3sing indic fut act
27. **εὑρήσομεν heurēsomen** 1pl indic fut act
28. **εὑρήσετε heurēsete** 2pl indic fut act
29. **εὑρήσουσιν heurēsousin** 3pl indic fut act
30. **εὑρισκόμεθα heuriskometha** 1pl indic pres mid
31. **εὑρέθην heurethēn** 1sing indic aor pass
32. **εὑρέθη heurethē** 3sing indic aor pass
33. **εὑρέθημεν heurethēmen** 1pl indic aor pass
34. **εὑρέθησαν heurethēsan** 3pl indic aor pass
35. **εὑρεθῶ heurethō** 1sing subj aor pass
36. **εὑρεθῇ heurethē** 3sing subj aor pass
37. **εὑρεθῆτε heurethēte** 2pl subj aor pass
38. **εὑρεθῶσιν heurethōsin** 3pl subj aor pass
39. **εὑρεθείς heuretheis** nom sing masc part aor pass
40. **εὑράμενος heuramenos** nom sing masc part aor mid
41. **εὑρεθῆναι heurethēnai** inf aor pass
42. **εὑρεθησόμεθα heurethēsometha** 1pl indic fut pass

εὑρίσκω 2128

43. εὑρίσκετο **heurisketo** 3sing indic imperf pass
44. εὕραμεν **heuramen** 1pl indic aor act
45. εὗραν **heuran** 3pl indic aor act
46. εὕρῃς **heurēs** 2sing subj aor act
47. ηὕρισκον **hēuriskon** 1/3sing/pl indic imperf act
48. εὑρεθήσεται **heurethēsetai** 3sing indic fut pass
49. ηὑρίσκετο **hēurisketo** 3sing indic imperf mid

32	she **was found** with child of the Holy Ghost........ Matt	1:18
14	when ye **have found** him, bring me word again,.......	2:8
6	they **saw** the young child with Mary his mother,.......	2:11
28	seek, and ye **shall find**;..............................	7:7
3	and he that seeketh **findeth**;.........................	7:8
5	narrow is the way, ... and few there be that **find** it.....	7:14
6	not **found** so great faith, no, not in Israel.............	8:10
17	He that **findeth** his life shall lose it:.................	10:39
26	and he that loseth his life for my sake **shall find** it....	10:39
28	and ye **shall find** rest unto your souls................	11:29
3	through dry places, seeking rest, and **findeth** none.....	12:43
3	and when he is come, he **findeth** it empty, swept,.....	12:44
17	treasure ... the which when a man **hath found**,........	13:44
17	Who, when he **had found** one pearl of great price,....	13:46
26	will lose his life for my sake **shall find** it.............	16:25
25	thou **shalt find** a piece of money:....................	17:27
21	And if so be that he **find** it, verily I say unto you,....	18:13
8	went out, and **found** one of his fellowservants,........	18:28
8	he went out, and **found** others standing idle,.........	20:6
28	and straightway ye **shall find** an ass tied,.............	21:2
8	and **found** nothing thereon, but leaves only,..........	21:19
14	and as many as ye **shall find**, bid to the marriage.....	22:9
6	and gathered together all as many as **they found**,.....	22:10
26	whom his lord when he cometh **shall find** so doing....	24:46
3	cometh unto the disciples, and **findeth** them asleep,...	26:40
3	And he came and **found** them asleep again:..........	26:43
8	And he came and **found** them asleep again:..........	26:43
6	But **found** none: ... though many false witnesses......	26:60
6	many false witnesses came, yet **found they** none......	26:60
6	they **found** a man of Cyrene, Simon by name:........	27:32
18	when they **had found** him, they said unto him,..... Mark	1:37
6	when they **had found** him, they said unto him,.......	1:37
8	**she found** the devil gone out,........................	7:30
28	ye **shall find** a colt tied, whereon never man sat;.....	11:2
6	and **found** the colt tied by the door...................	11:4
26	he came, if haply he **might find** any thing thereon:...	11:13
8	when he came to it, **he found** nothing but leaves;.....	11:13
12	Lest coming suddenly he **find** you sleeping...........	13:36
6	into the city, and **found** as he had said unto them:....	14:16
3	And he cometh, and **findeth** them sleeping,..........	14:37
8	when he returned, he **found** them asleep again,.......	14:40
1	sought for witness against Jesus ... and **found** none....	14:55
47	sought for witness against Jesus ... and **found** none....	14:55
7	Fear not, ... for thou **hast found** favour with God...Luke	1:30
28	**shall find** the babe wrapped in swaddling clothes,......	2:12
18	when they **found** him not, they turned back again.....	2:45
6	that after three days they **found** him in the temple,....	2:46
8	he **found** the place where it was written,.............	4:17
18	And when they **could** not **find** by what way........	5:19
15	that they **might find** an accusation against him........	6:7
6	I **have** not **found** so great faith, no, not in Israel......	7:9
6	**found** the servant whole that had been sick...........	7:10
6	and came to Jesus, and **found** the man,.............	8:35
45	and came to Jesus, and **found** the man,.............	8:35
15	and get victuals: for we are here in a desert place......	9:12
32	when the voice was past, Jesus **was found** alone.......	9:36
28	seek, and ye **shall find**;.............................	11:9
3	and he that seeketh **findeth**;........................	11:10
1	seeking rest; and **finding** none, he saith,.............	11:24
3	he cometh, he **findeth** it swept and garnished........	11:25
26	whom the lord when he cometh **shall find** watching:..	12:37
12	or come in the third watch, and **find** them so,........	12:38
26	whom his lord when he cometh **shall find** so doing....	12:43
8	he came and sought fruit thereon, and **found** none....	13:6
2	I come seeking fruit on this fig tree, and **find** none:..	13:7
12	and go after that which is lost, until **he find** it?.......	15:4
17	he **hath found** it, he layeth it on his shoulders,....Luke	15:5
6	for I **have found** my sheep which was lost............	15:6
12	and seek diligently till **she find** it?...................	15:8
19	And when she **hath found** it, she calleth her friends...	15:9
6	for I **have found** the piece which I had lost...........	15:9
32	dead, and is alive again; he was lost, and **is found**....	15:24
32	and is alive again; and was lost, and **is found**.........	15:32
34	**are** not **found** that returned to give glory to God,.....	17:18
26	**shall** he **find** faith on the earth?.....................	18:8
28	the which at your entering ye **shall find** a colt tied,...	19:30
6	and **found** even as he had said unto them............	19:32
1	And **could** not **find** what they might do:............	19:48
6	they went, and **found** as he had said unto them:......	22:13
8	he **found** them sleeping for sorrow,...................	22:45
9	We **found** this fellow perverting the nation,..........	23:2
44	We **found** this fellow perverting the nation,..........	23:2
2	said Pilate ... I **find** no fault in this man..............	23:4
6	examined him ... **have found** no fault in this man.....	23:14
6	I **have found** no cause of death in him:...............	23:22
6	**found** the stone rolled away from the sepulchre.......	24:2
6	**found** not the body of the Lord Jesus.................	24:3
20	And when they **found** not his body, they came,......	24:23
6	and **found** it even so as the women had said:.........	24:24
6	and **found** the eleven gathered together,..............	24:33
3	He first **findeth** his own brother Simon,.......... John	1:41
23	and saith unto him, We **have found** the Messias,.....	1:41
3	and **findeth** Philip, and saith unto him, Follow me.....	1:43
3	Philip **findeth** Nathanael, and saith unto him,.........	1:45
23	We **have found** him, of whom Moses ... did write,.....	1:45
8	And **found** in the temple those that sold oxen.........	2:14
3	Afterward Jesus **findeth** him in the temple,............	5:14
18	And when they **had found** him on the other side.......	6:25
28	Ye shall seek me, and **shall** not **find** me:..............	7:34
27	Whither will he go, that we **shall** not **find** him?........	7:35
28	Ye shall seek me, and **shall** not **find** me:..............	7:36
17	and when he **had found** him, he said unto him,........	9:35
26	and shall go in and out, and **find** pasture.............	10:9
8	he **found** that he had lain in the grave four days......	11:17
17	when he **had found** a young ass, sat thereon;.........	12:14
2	unto the Jews, ... I **find** in him no fault at all..........	18:38
2	that ye may know that I **find** no fault in him..........	19:4
2	and crucify him: for I **find** no fault in him............	19:6
28	Cast the net on the right side ... and ye **shall find**.....	21:6
5	**finding** nothing how they might punish them,........Acts	4:21
6	and the young men came in, and **found** her dead,.....	5:10
45	and the young men came in, and **found** her dead,.....	5:10
6	and **found** them not in the prison, they returned,.....	5:22
9	The prison truly **found** we shut with all safety,........	5:23
9	when we had opened, we **found** no man within.......	5:23
37	lest haply ye **be found** even to fight against God,.....	5:39
1	and our fathers **found** no sustenance..................	7:11
47	and our fathers **found** no sustenance..................	7:11
8	Who **found** favour before God,......................	7:46
21	desired to **find** a tabernacle for the God of Jacob,.....	7:46
32	But Philip **was found** at Azotus:.....................	8:40
12	that if he **found** any of this way,.....................	9:2
8	And there he **found** a certain man named AEneas,.....	9:33
3	and **found** many that were come together............	10:27
17	And when he **had found** him,........................	11:26
17	Herod had sought for him, and **found** him not,.......	12:19
6	they **found** a certain sorcerer, a false prophet,........	13:6
6	I **have found** David the son of Jesse,.................	13:22
18	And though they **found** no cause of death in him,....	13:28
18	And when they **found** them not,.....................	17:6
6	I **found** an altar with this inscription,.................	17:23
16	if haply they might feel after him, and **find** him,......	17:27
17	And **found** a certain Jew named Aquila,..............	18:2
17	came to Ephesus: and **finding** certain disciples,.......	19:1
21	came to Ephesus: and **finding** certain disciples,.......	19:1
6	and **found** it fifty thousand pieces of silver............	19:19
18	And **finding** a ship sailing over unto Phenicia,........	21:2
4	and strove, saying, We **find** no evil in this man:......	23:9
6	Whom I **perceived** to be accused of questions........	23:29
18	For we **have found** this man a pestilent fellow,.......	24:5
6	neither **found** me in the temple disputing.............	24:12
6	Jews from Asia **found** me purified in the temple,.....	24:18
6	if they **have found** any evil doing in me,..............	24:20

647

εὑρίσκω 2128

17 there the centurion **found** a ship of Alexandria	Acts 27:6
6 And sounded, and **found** it twenty fathoms:	27:28
6 they sounded again, and **found** it fifteen fathoms.	27:28
18 Where we **found** brethren,	28:14
24 as pertaining to the flesh, hath **found**?	Rom 4:1
32 the commandment, ... I **found** to be unto death.	7:10
2 but how to perform that which is good I **find** not.	7:18
2 I **find** then a law, that, when I would do good,	7:21
31 I **was found** of them that sought me not;	10:20
36 that a man **be found** faithful.	1 Co 4:2
30 Yea, and we **are found** false witnesses of God;	15:15
21 because I **found** not Titus my brother:	2 Co 2:13
42 that being clothed we **shall** not **be found** naked.	5:3
15 of Macedonia come ... and **find** you unprepared,	9:4
38 wherein they glory, they **may be found** even as we.	11:12
10 I **shall** not **find** you such as I would,	12:20
35 and that I **shall be found** unto you such as	12:20
33 we ourselves also **are found** sinners,	Gal 2:17
39 And **being found** in fashion as a man,	Phlp 2:8
35 And **be found** in him, not having mine own	3:9
8 he sought me out very diligently, and **found** me.	2 Tm 1:17
21 The Lord grant unto him that he **may find** mercy	1:18
13 and **find** grace to help in time of need.	Heb 4:16
40 **having obtained** eternal redemption for us.	9:12
43 **was** not **found**, because God had translated him:	11:5
49 **was** not **found**, because God had translated him:	11:5
8 for he **found** no place of repentance,	12:17
36 might **be found** unto praise and honour and glory	1 Pt 1:7
32 neither was guile **found** in his mouth:	2:22
48 and everything in it **will be laid bare**. (NIV)	2 Pt 3:10
41 be diligent that ye **may be found** of him in peace,	3:14
22 that I **found** of thy children walking in truth,	2 Jn 1:4
7 and hast **found** them liars:	Rev 2:2
22 for I **have** not **found** thy works perfect before God.	3:2
32 I wept much, because no man **was found** worthy	5:4
29 shall men seek death, and **shall** not **find** it;	9:6
32 neither **was** their place **found** any more in heaven.	12:8
32 And in their mouth **was found** no guile:	14:5
34 and the mountains **were** not **found**.	16:20
11 and thou **shalt find** them no more at all.	18:14
29 and thou **shalt find** them no more at all.	18:14
36 thrown down, and **shall be found** no more at all.	18:21
36 no craftsman, ... **shall be found** any more in thee;	18:22
32 And in her **was found** the blood of prophets,	18:24
32 fled away; and there **was found** no place for them.	20:11
32 And whosoever **was** not **found** written in the book	20:15

Classical Greek

Heuriskō demonstrates a wide semantic range in classical and Hellenistic Greek. Essentially it means "find, discover." This "finding" ranges in scope from finding objects to discovering information or insight. "Find" a way, i.e., "devise, invent," is also an attested use. Moreover, "to find" money was another way of saying one "earned" it, or a valuable article might "find" a good price (*Liddell-Scott*).

Septuagint Usage

Being quite common in the Septuagint, *heuriskō* translates as many as 15 different Hebrew words. Ordinarily, however, a form of *mātsā'*, "find," corresponds to *heuriskō*. Its usage essentially repeats the classical pattern. For example, Cain lamented that anyone "finding" him would want to kill him (Genesis 4:14,15; cf. 38:20,22). The word is used of Enoch who "was not (found)" after God took him (Genesis 5:24) and of Noah who "found" favor in God's sight (Genesis 6:8; Sirach 44:17; cf. Genesis 33:8; 34:11; Exodus 34:9; 1 Samuel 20:29 [LXX 1 Kings 20:29]; also used of finding human favor).

New Testament Usage

The verb occurs over 175 times in the New Testament. Each text in order cannot be discussed, but basic categories can be given which will point out the various nuances of nearly all occurrences of the text.

The most basic sense of the verb is seen where it simply takes a direct object, i.e., "to find" *something* or *someone*. The passive voice, "to be found," has the same meaning, but what is grammatically the object in the active voice becomes the subject in the passive voice. The passive voice is used, then, to emphasize that which was found rather than those who find something (e.g., Romans 10:20). A special use of the passive voice is found when it is used in a negative aspect, "not to be found," meaning "to cease to exist" (Revelation 12:8; 16:20; 18:14,21ff.).

At times the object of the verb gives a special sense to the verb, as in "to find favor" (Luke 1:30; Acts 7:46) with the meaning "to be pleasing"; "to find a temple" (Acts 7:46), which is similar to the English usage "to found" or "originate" something. Paul also used the verb to express a "discovery" or realization of the truth after reflection upon experience (Romans 4:1; 7:10,21). Further, the verb is related to the legal sphere in the sense of "finding fault" or grounds for accusation (Luke 23:2,14,22; John 18:38; 19:4,6; Acts 23:9; 24:5,20; Revelation 14:5).

Further nuances of the verb are brought out by its association with complementary verbs, as in seeking and finding, losing and finding, and coming and finding.

Seeking and finding are associated over 20 times in the New Testament. The connotation of the ideas is that finding comes as the reward for the effort of seeking: "Seek, and ye shall *find*" (Matthew 7:7). To find that which is sought brings resolution to the need which motivated the search.

An important subset of seeking and finding is the association of the terms *losing* and *finding*. When the two are used together it speaks of restoration. That which is lost is restored, and the original state of wholeness is reinstated. "For this my son was dead, and is alive again;

he was lost, and is *found*" (Luke 15:24). The appropriate response is rejoicing (Luke 15:5,9,32).

The most frequent use of the verb *heuriskō* is when it is paired with a verb about "coming." This word association reflects the language of the journey. It speaks of the conditions a traveler finds upon arrival at a destination. Many examples could be given, but the ultimate example is how the language of the journey rivets our attention on what the Lord will "find" when He comes (Mark 13:34-37).

STRONG 2147, BAUER 324-25, MOULTON-MILLIGAN 264-65, KITTEL 2:769-70, LIDDELL-SCOTT 729-30, COLIN BROWN 3:527-30.

2129. εὐροκλύδων eurokludōn noun
(South)east wind.
CROSS-REFERENCE:
κατακλυσμός kataklusmos (2597)

1. εὐροκλύδων eurokludōn nom sing masc

1 against it a tempestuous wind, called **Euroclydon**. . . . Acts 27:14

Eurokludōn has commonly been interpreted as a compound of *euros*, "(south)east wind," and *kludōn* (2803), "waves." Thus the name was understood as signifying "a southeast wind stirring up great waves." Alternate suggestions connect it with *eurus*, "broad, wide," thus a wind causing "wide waves." Another explains it as a simple scribal miswriting of *eurakulōn* (2127), "northeast wind."

Eurokludōn seems to appear only in the later New Testament manuscripts in Acts 27:14. The oldest manuscripts have *eurakulōn*. (See also *tuphōnikos* [5030].)

STRONG 2148, BAUER 325-26, LIDDELL-SCOTT 730.

2130. εὐρύχωρος euruchōros adj
Broad, spacious, roomy.
CROSS-REFERENCE:
χωρέω chōreō (5397)

גֹּרֶן gōren (1681), Threshing floor (2 Chr 18:9).

מֶרְחָב merchāv (4962), Wideness, open space, broad place (Ps 31:8 [30:8], Hos 4:16).

רָחַב rāchav (7620), Make wide; niphal: be broad (Is 30:23).

1. εὐρύχωρος euruchōros nom sing fem

1 for wide is the gate, and **broad** is the way, ... Matt 7:13

In the Septuagint this adjective is used of an open pasture (Isaiah 30:23) and a large field (Hosea 4:16). From *eurus*, "broad," and *chōra* (5396), "place," both instances connote the freedom and prosperity which the land expanses provide. The only New Testament occurrence carries the same meaning of "broad, spacious," and "roomy" (Matthew 7:13). Ironically, the "broad" way now affords not blessing but cursing. The doctrine of the two ways is seen here: narrow leads to life; broad is a detour to death.

STRONG 2149, BAUER 326, MOULTON-MILLIGAN 265, LIDDELL-SCOTT 731.

2131. εὐσέβεια eusebeia noun
Piety, godliness.
COGNATE:
σέβομαι sebomai (4431)
SYNONYMS:
θεοσέβεια theosebeia (2293)
ὁσιότης hosiotēs (3604)

חֶסֶד cheṣedh (2721), Loyalty, faithfulness (Sir 49:3).

יִרְאָה yir'āh (3488), Fear of God (Prv 1:7, Is 33:6).

1. εὐσέβεια eusebeia nom sing fem
2. εὐσεβείας eusebeias gen sing fem
3. εὐσεβείᾳ eusebeia dat sing fem
4. εὐσέβειαν eusebeian acc sing fem
5. εὐσεβείαις eusebeiais dat pl fem

3 as though by our own power or **holiness** . . . . Acts 3:12
3 peaceable life in all **godliness** and honesty . . . . 1 Tm 2:2
2 great is the mystery of **godliness**: 3:16
4 and exercise thyself rather unto **godliness**. 4:7
1 but **godliness** is profitable unto all things, ... 4:8
4 and to the doctrine which is according to **godliness**; 6:3
4 supposing that gain is **godliness**: 6:5
1 But **godliness** with contentment is great gain. 6:6
4 follow after righteousness, **godliness**, faith, love, ... 6:11
2 Having a form **of godliness**, but denying the power . . 2 Tm 3:5
4 the truth which is after **godliness**; . . . . Tit 1:1
4 all things that pertain unto life and **godliness**, ... 2 Pt 1:3
4 to temperance patience; and to patience **godliness**; 1:6
3 And to **godliness** brotherly kindness; 1:7
5 to be in all holy conversation and **godliness**, ... 3:11

Classical Greek

This noun—from the stem *seb-* and the adverb *eu* (2074), "well"—is an important member of the very common *seb-* word group. The usage of *eusebeia* in ancient times suggests that the term had come to be associated primarily with the idea of religious "piety, godliness," or "reverence toward the gods." In a nonreligious sense it spoke of "respect," such as a parent is to receive from a child. But increasingly *eusebeia* lost its domestic flavor and became almost exclusively a religious term denoting "right conduct before the gods." This, of course, included the concept of proper social conduct (Foerster, "eusebeia," *Kittel*, 7:175ff.).

Evidence from papyri and inscriptions indicate that *eusebeia* was a chief term for denoting religious piety in the Hellenistic world (*Moulton-Milligan*). It was regarded as one of the many virtues (*aretai* [see 697]) and not the source of all other virtues. The opposite of *eusebeia* is *asebeia* (757), "godlessness, impiety" (Foerster, "eusebeia," *Kittel*, 7:178; he also discusses Philo's and Josephus' use of this word group on 7:179-181).

Septuagint Usage

The extremely Hellenistic character of *eusebeia* is confirmed by the Septuagint, because it appears primarily in the Hellenistic writings of 1 Esdras, Wisdom of Solomon, Sirach, 2 Maccabees, 3 Maccabees, and 4 Maccabees. The remaining members of the word group follow this same tendency. Often *eusebeia* is understood in these Hellenistic-Jewish writings as synonymous with keeping God's law (e.g., 4 Maccabees 5:19ff.).

Of the four canonical texts which are translated by *eusebeia* two are in Proverbs (1:7, Hebrew *yir'āh*; 13:11 [no Hebrew original]), and two are in Isaiah (11:2 [*yir'ath YHWH*, a messianic text]; 33:6 [*yir'āh*]). The concept in each text is "reverence" or "fear/awe" towards God. The writer of Proverbs summarized the general concept of *eusebeia*: "The *fear* (*reverence*) of the Lord is the beginning of knowledge" (1:7). Thus even here *eusebeia* is not an isolated quality; rather it is the essence of trusting God.

New Testament Usage

Eusebeia (cf. also the rest of the word group) occurs in what are generally regarded as the hellenized writings of the New Testament: Acts (only at 3:12; cf. 10:2,7), the Pastoral Epistles, and 2 Peter.

Of crucial importance for understanding the entire thrust of the Pastoral Epistles is recognizing that *eusebeia*, "godliness," is *the* Christian attitude and conduct, the heart of the Faith. Thus Paul modified the Hellenistic concept of *eusebeia* as one virtue among many. *Eusebeia* became both life-style and religion for the believing community (1 Timothy 2:2). Paul declared, "Great indeed, we confess, is the mystery of our *religion* (*eusebeia*)" (1 Timothy 3:16, RSV). Although this translation may stretch the point ("our" is not present in the original), it does pick up the nuance that *eusebeia* is the essence of the believer's faith. Particularly in light of the problem of false teachers in Ephesus, *eusebeia* stands as the true doctrine of the Faith as over against the "godlessness" (*asebeia*, 1 Timothy 1:9; cf. 2 Timothy 2:16) and "godless legends" (*GNB*, virtually "old wives' tales") of the false teachers (1 Timothy 4:7-10; 6:3,5,6; cf. Titus 1:1; 2 Timothy 3:5; see Fee, *Good News Commentary, 1 and 2 Timothy, Titus*, for a complete discussion of this problem).

Second Peter also conjoins general Christian life-style and conduct with *eusebeia* (1:3; 3:11), but it can, moreover, be one of many godly attributes endorsed for the Christian's character and building of faith (2 Peter 1:6,7). The use of the related adjective *eusebēs* (2133) substantivally suggests that Peter regarded "those living godly lives" (2:9) as synonymous with those who are "righteous" (*dikaios* [1335B], cf. verses 7,8 as in contrast with verse 9, *adikos* [93]).

Thus generally for Christian writers *eusebeia* is "godly conduct," the essence of the Faith. Specific behavior is not outlined; rather a general attitude of piety towards God, respect for humanity, as well as regard for the truth of the gospel are signs of true *eusebeia*.

Strong 2150, Bauer 326, Moulton-Milligan 265, Kittel 7:175-85, Liddell-Scott 731, Colin Brown 2:91-95.

2132. εὐσεβέω eusebeō verb

Worship, revere, respect, show piety toward.
Cross-Reference:
σέβομαι sebomai (4431)

1. εὐσεβεῖτε eusebeite 2pl indic pres act
2. εὐσεβεῖν eusebein inf pres act

1 Whom therefore ye ignorantly **worship**,............ Acts 17:23
2 let them learn first **to show piety at home**,.......... 1 Tm 5:4

Classical Greek

Among classical and later Hellenistic writers *eusebeō* (from *eu* [2074], "well," + *sebomai* [4431], "show awe, reverence") especially meant to "show reverence" in a religious sense. However, in a broad sense one could show "respect" for all the various orders of life including domestic, national, and also international. This word expressed one of the core aspects of Greek religion, and to "show piety" was to align oneself with the orders (especially social) that were controlled by the gods (Foerster, "eusebeō," *Kittel*, 7:176ff.).

Septuagint Usage
The verb does not occur in the Septuagint until very late and only in apocryphal material (once in Susanna and four or five times in 4 Maccabees). Since these writings are very much the product of Hellenistic Judaism it is not surprising that the usage reflects the Greek understanding of *eusebeō*. Jews applied it to their own "reverence" of the Creator (4 Maccabees 11:5,23). The influence of Hellenism is illustrated clearly in 4 Maccabees 18:2 which speaks of "devout reason (as) . . . master of emotions" (RSV). In Susanna 64 it is applied to Daniel's being "respected" among the people (probably because of his great standing before God).

New Testament Usage
The verb form occurs only twice in the New Testament, each time in association with non-Jewish (i.e., Hellenistic) circumstances. Once it appears with a god as its object and once with humans. This dual reference is quite consistent with its nonbiblical usage, so a general sense of "revere" might be suggested as its meaning.

Acts 17:23 says the Athenians "worshiped" an unknown god. The divine recipient of this reverence was proclaimed by Paul to be the Creator-God who established the very order to which the people of Athens gave so much reverent concern in the Areopagus (see verses 26-28). Paul declared that the one God raised from the dead, not dead idols raised by men, is this God's standard of judgment (verse 31).

First Timothy 5:4 is grammatically difficult to understand because the subject of "learn" is unexpressed. Was it the widows who were to learn to "show piety" at home to children or grandchildren? Or was it the children and/or grandchildren who were to "show piety" to the widows by supporting them so the church was not overly burdened? The latter obviously fits the context and makes the most sense practically. Moreover, it fits best with the idea of alignment with the established order. Responsibility to the familial order will fulfill the younger generation's duty to those who reared them, and it will establish a witness to the church's concern for that established order.

STRONG 2151, BAUER 326, MOULTON-MILLIGAN 265, KITTEL 7:175-85, LIDDELL-SCOTT 731-32, COLIN BROWN 2:91-93.

2133. εὐσεβής eusebēs adj
Devout, godly, reverent, religious.
COGNATE:
 σέβομαι sebomai (4431)
SYNONYMS:
 εὐλαβής eulabēs (2107)
 θεοσεβής theosebēs (2294)

חָסִיד chāsîdh (2728), One who is faithful or devout (Mi 7:2).
טוֹב ṭôv (3005), Good (Sir 39:27).
נָדִיב nādhîv (5259), Noble, generous (Is 32:8).
פָּחַד pāchadh (6585), Tremble (Sir 37:12).
צַדִּיק tsaddîq (6926), Righteous, godly, just (Is 24:16, 26:7).

1. **εὐσεβής eusebēs** nom sing masc
2. **εὐσεβῆ eusebē** acc sing masc
3. **εὐσεβεῖς eusebeis** acc pl masc

1 A **devout** man, and one that feared God . . . . Acts 10:2
2 and a **devout** soldier of them that waited on him 10:7
1 one Ananias, a **devout** man according to the law, ... 22:12
3 how to deliver the **godly** out of temptations, ... 2 Pt 2:9

Of the four instances in which this adjective appears in the New Testament, three are found in Acts. Luke did not use the word to speak of Christians, per se, but of God fearers (such as Cornelius in Acts 10:2,7) and Jews (such as Ananias in Acts 22:12). The root *sebomai* (4431) means "fall back before, shrink from." This would be done out of holy fear or respect of some dignitary, perhaps a parent, or maybe in ritual to a deity. Luke did not use this term for believers, for theirs is not a reverence "according to the law" (Acts 22:12), the meaning for which he reserved the word. The other occurrence of *eusebēs* is found in 2 Peter 2:9 where it clearly includes believers as those who are "godly" and thus spared.

STRONG 2152, BAUER 326, MOULTON-MILLIGAN 265, KITTEL 7:175-85, LIDDELL-SCOTT 731-32, COLIN BROWN 2:91-94.

2134. εὐσεβῶς eusebōs adv
In a godly manner, piously, religiously.
CROSS-REFERENCE:
 σέβομαι sebomai (4431)

1. **εὐσεβῶς eusebōs**

1 all that will live **godly** ... shall suffer persecution. . . . 2 Tm 3:12
1 we should live soberly, righteously, and **godly**, ... Tit 2:12

Found only in the Pastoral Epistles (2 Timothy 3:12; Titus 2:12), this adverb is derived from the word *sebomai* (4431) which means "fall back before," or "shrink from" out of fear and respect. This stance would be evoked by confronting a parent, a deity, or any other superior. It is significant that the term is qualified in 2 Timothy 3:12 ("All that will live godly *in Christ Jesus* . . ."), for a person could be "godly" with respect to any god or object of devotion. The focus in the Pastorals is on that way and character of life customary to the gospel. By itself *eusebōs* cannot adequately describe this particular life-style, which is why it is surrounded by words and phrases that illustrate its meaning (cf. 2 Timothy 4:10f.; Titus 2:12ff.).

STRONG 2153, BAUER 326, MOULTON-MILLIGAN 266, LIDDELL-SCOTT 731-32.

2135. εὔσημος eusēmos adj
Easily recognizable, clear, distinct, intelligible.
CROSS-REFERENCE:
σημαίνω sēmainō (4446)

כֶּסֶא keṣeʼ (3801), Full moon (Ps 81:3 [80:3]).

1. εὔσημον eusēmon acc sing masc

1 utter by the tongue words **easy to be understood**,... 1 Co 14:9

In general Koine usage, the Greek adjective means "that which is distinguishable" about something. Literally it refers to "something which gives good signs" (*eu* [2074], "good"; *sēmeion* [4447], "sign"). The only New Testament occurrence is in 1 Corinthians 14:9 where Paul called for clear and intelligible speech ("easy to be understood") among those gathered for public worship. The context shows his concern that speaking in tongues should be interpreted in order to edify others.

STRONG 2154, BAUER 326, MOULTON-MILLIGAN 266, KITTEL 2:770, LIDDELL-SCOTT 732.

2136. εὔσπλαγχνος eusplanchnos adj
Compassionate, tenderhearted.
CROSS-REFERENCE:
σπλαγχνίζομαι splanchnizomai (4550)

1. εὔσπλαγχνοι eusplanchnoi nom pl masc

1 And be ye kind one to another, **tenderhearted**,......Eph 4:32
1 love as brethren, **be pitiful**, be courteous:............ 1 Pt 3:8

This term—from *eu* (2074), "good," and *splanchnon* (4551), "inward parts"—was originally a medical term denoting the "intestines, bowels," or "*tender* parts." Gradually the physical meaning shifted to the metaphoric sense of "affection" and "*tender* mercies." In nonbiblical Greek this term was applied to human virtues in general. In the New Testament (Ephesians 4:32; 1 Peter 3:8) this word is used to describe the specifically Christian characteristic of compassion or tenderheartedness.

STRONG 2155, BAUER 326, KITTEL 7:548-59, LIDDELL-SCOTT 732, COLIN BROWN 2:599-600.

2137. εὐσχημόνως euschēmonōs adv
Becomingly, properly, decently.
CROSS-REFERENCE:
σχῆμα schēma (4828)

1. εὐσχημόνως euschēmonōs

1 Let us walk **honestly**,........................... Rom 13:13
1 Let all things be done **decently** and in order........1 Co 14:40
1 may walk **honestly** toward them that are without,....1 Th 4:12

This is the adverbial form of *euskēmōn* (2139). It signifies the characteristics of being "acceptable, honest," or "becoming." These are used of both internal and external aspects of the thing being described. The adverb, however, is limited to the inward aspects and is translated (in Romans 13:13; 1 Corinthians 14:40; 1 Thessalonians 4:12) "honestly, decently, becomingly." This trait is one that is observable to all people, believers and unbelievers alike.

STRONG 2156, BAUER 327, MOULTON-MILLIGAN 266, LIDDELL-SCOTT 734.

2138. εὐσχημοσύνη euschēmosunē noun
Propriety, modesty.
CROSS-REFERENCE:
σχῆμα schēma (4828)

1. εὐσχημοσύνην euschēmosunēn acc sing fem

1 uncomely parts have more abundant **comeliness**.....1 Co 12:23

The focus of this term is the external appearance, conveying the sense of "propriety, decorum, external beauty." Thus it has the sense of "presentability" (of clothing) and "modesty" (in concealment). The unpresentable parts of the human body are given "greater presentability," i.e., are "treated with special modesty" (1 Corinthians 12:23, NIV). In the Septuagint it appears at Proverbs 1:25.

Strong 2157, Bauer 327, Moulton-Milligan 266, Liddell-Scott 734, Colin Brown 1:206.

2139. εὐσχήμων euschēmōn adj
Presentable, honorable, reputable, well formed.
CROSS-REFERENCE:
σχῆμα schēma (4828)

1. εὐσχήμων euschēmōn nom sing masc
2. εὐσχημόνων euschēmonōn gen pl fem
3. εὐσχήμονας euschēmonas acc pl fem
4. εὔσχημον euschēmon nom/acc sing neu
5. εὐσχήμονα euschēmona nom/acc pl neu

1 Joseph of Arimathaea, an **honourable** counsellor,.. Mark 15:43
3 stirred up the devout and **honourable** women,...... Acts 13:50
2 also of **honourable** women which were Greeks,........ 17:12
4 but for **that which is comely**,....................... 1 Co 7:35
5 For our **comely parts** have no need:.................. 12:24

Classical Greek
A compound of *eu* (2074), "good," and *schēma* (4828), *euschēmōn* generally means "elegant in figure, bearing." If used of objects it means "decent, becoming, honorable, noble" (*Liddell-Scott*).

Septuagint Usage
Euschēmōn occurs only in Proverbs 11:25 in the Septuagint. The use lacks a Hebrew original, but in contrast to *thumōdēs*, "fierce," (like an animal) its meaning of "respectable," or perhaps "civilized," seems fitting.

New Testament Usage
The word occurs five times in the New Testament. It is found in two types of grammatical constructions: as a noun and as an adjective. Its meaning varies according to its use.

Paul used it twice as a noun. First Corinthians 7:35 gives the reason Paul had spoken as he did in the preceding verses. The time is short (verse 29), the form of this world is passing away (verse 31). This reality bears on the Christian's use of the world and its institutions. There is propriety (*euschēmōn*) to the manner in which Christians relate to the world. The proper use of this perishing world is outlined in what precedes verse 35.

The other noun usage is in 1 Corinthians 12:24 where Paul spoke of our "comely" (*euschēmōn*) body parts. The contrasting word "uncomely" (*aschēmon* [see 803]) parts is found in the preceding verse. The perspective of human perception about the body plays no role in the body of Christ. The categories of *euschēmon* (verse 24) and *aschēmon* (verse 23) do not apply to the body of Christ, because all members were baptized by one Spirit into the Body (1 Corinthians 12:13), and God has placed each member right where He chooses (1 Corinthians 12:18).

The word is used three times as an adjective, at Mark 15:42 and Acts 13:50 and 17:12. Joseph of Arimathea is an "honorable" counselor (*euschēmōn bouleutēas*), in the former passage, and the prominent social status of recently converted women is mentioned in the two Acts references (*gunaikas tas euschēmonas*). Even those in the "social elite" are addressed by the gospel.

Strong 2158, Bauer 327, Moulton-Milligan 266, Kittel 2:770-72, Liddell-Scott 734.

2140. εὐτόνως eutonōs adv
Powerfully, vehemently, forcefully.

1. εὐτόνως eutonōs

1 and scribes stood and **vehemently** accused him......Luke 23:10
1 he **mightily** convinced the Jews, and that publicly,.. Acts 18:28

A compound term—from *eu* (2074), "good," and *teinō*, "to stretch"—this word means "powerfully," "vigorously," or even "vehemently." The Jews "vehemently" denounced Christ (Luke 23:10) just as, years later, Apollos powerfully argued for Him and "mightily convinced" the Jews of his day (Acts 18:28). In the Septuagint it appears at Joshua 6:8 (LXX 6:7).

Strong 2159, Bauer 327, Moulton-Milligan 266, Liddell-Scott 735.

2141. εὐτραπελία eutrapelia noun
Indecent or vulgar jesting, improper jokes.

1. εὐτραπελία eutrapelia nom sing fem

1 Neither filthiness, nor foolish talking, nor **jesting**,.... Eph 5:4

Coming from *eu* (2074), "good", and *trephō* (4982), "turning," this term means "quick-witted, mentally sharp," or "witty." In classical Greek it was used in a good sense. Aristotle placed this type of humor between "buffoonery and boorishness," terming it "childish humor" (cf. *Liddell-Scott*). Paul used it in a much more negative way, referring to indecent, off-color humor (Ephesians 5:4).

Strong 2160, Bauer 327, Moulton-Milligan 266, Liddell-Scott 735.

2142. Εὔτυχος Eutuchos name
Eutychus.

1. Εὔτυχος Eutuchos nom masc
1 in a window a certain young man named **Eutychus,** Acts 20:9

A young man who fell to his death but was then returned to life when Paul prayed (Acts 20:9).

2143. εὐφημία euphēmia noun
Good report, good reputation, commendation.
CROSS-REFERENCE:
  φημί phēmi (5183)

1. εὐφημίας euphēmias gen sing fem
1 by evil report and **good report:** .... 2 Co 6:8

This compound literally means "the speaking of good terms or words." The New Testament usage is that of "good report, good reputation," or "praise" (2 Corinthians 6:8).
STRONG 2162, BAUER 327, MOULTON-MILLIGAN 266-67, LIDDELL-SCOTT 736-37.

2144. εὔφημος euphēmos adj
Of good report, well spoken of, reputable.
CROSS-REFERENCE:
  φημί phēmi (5183)

1. εὔφημα euphēma nom/acc pl neu
1 whatsoever things are **of good report;** .... Phlp 4:8

This adjective appears in classical Greek since the Fifth Century B.C. reflecting a variety of meanings, one of which also appears in the New Testament. Its only New Testament occurrence, in Philippians 4:8, refers to things that can be described as "admirable" (NIV), "of good report" (KJV), or "gracious" (RSV). The common ground for these meanings attempts to positively describe an attractive moral character.
STRONG 2163, BAUER 327, MOULTON-MILLIGAN 267, LIDDELL-SCOTT 736-37.

2145. εὐφορέω euphoreō verb
Be fruitful, fertile, producing plenty.
CROSS-REFERENCE:
  φέρω pherō (5179)

1. εὐφόρησεν euphorēsen 3sing indic aor act
1 **ground of a ... rich man brought forth plentifully:** ...Luke 12:16

The components of this compound verb mean to "bear well"; *eu* (2074), "good," plus *pherō* (5179), "bring, bear." New Testament usage is consistent with that in classical Greek when applied to farmland. Its only New Testament occurrence is in Luke 12:16 where Jesus began to tell the Parable of the Rich Fool saying, "The ground of a certain rich man *brought forth plentifully*." Unfortunately the rich man did not respond properly to his prosperity.
STRONG 2164, BAUER 327, MOULTON-MILLIGAN 267, LIDDELL-SCOTT 737.

2146. εὐφραίνω euphrainō verb
To make glad; be happy, glad, rejoice, be merry.
COGNATES:
  εὐφροσύνη euphrosunē (2148)
  φρονέω phroneō (5262)
SYNONYMS:
  ἀγαλλιάω agalliaō (21)
  χαίρω chairō (5299)

אָגַר 'āghar (100), Gather in, harvest (Dt 28:39).

בּוֹא bô' (971), Go, come (1 Sm 16:5).

גִּיל gîl (1559), Shriek, ecstatically, shout with joy (Is 41:16).

גִּיל gîl (1561), Rejoicing (Hos 9:1).

הָמָה hāmâh (2064), Be unsteady, be restless (Ps 77:3 [76:3]).

חָדָה chādhâh (2397), Piel: make happy (Ps 21:6 [20:6]).

חָלַל chālal (2591), Qal: play the flute (Ps 87:7 [86:7]); piel: make use of (Dt 20:6).

יָחַד yāchadh (3265), Piel: determine exclusively (Ps 86:11 [85:11]).

כּוּן kûn (3679), Niphal: be ready (Prv 22:18).

לִיץ lîts (4054), Mock, ridicule; hithpolal: give oneself airs, act as a scoffer (Is 28:22).

מוּג mûgh (4265), Polel: soften, make dissolve (Ps 65:10 [64:10]).

מָשׂוֹשׂ māsôs (5026), Joy (Is 62:5).

נָשָׂא nāsâ' (5558), Lift up (Is 42:11).

רָנַן rānan (7728), Qal: shout with joy (Is 24:14, 42:11); piel: shout with joy, proclaim in shouts of joy (1 Chr 16:33, Is 26:19); pual: be joyful in shouts (Is 16:10); hiphil: ring out a shout of joy (Dt 32:43).

רָעַף rā'aph (7780), Hiphil: let drip (Is 45:8).

שָׂגַב sāghav (7891), Pual: be protected (Prv 29:25).

שׂוּשׂ sûs (7919), Rejoice (Dt 28:63, Is 35:1, 65:19).

שִׂים sîm (7947), Set (Ez 23:41).

שָׂחַק sāchaq (7925), Qal: laugh (Prv 31:25); piel: be happy (Prv 8:30).

שָׂמַח sāmach (7975), Qal: rejoice, be joyful (Lv 23:40,

εὐφραίνω 2146

1 Sm 2:1, Ps 68:3 [67:3]); piel: make glad, allow to rejoice (Dt 24:5, 2 Chr 20:27, Hos 7:3); hiphil: make rejoice (Ps 89:42 [88:42]).

שָׂמֵחַ sāmēach (7976), Filled with joy, glad (Dt 16:15, 1 Kgs 1:40, Prv 15:13).

שִׂמְחָה simchāh (7977), Joy, festival (Jgs 16:23, Prv 12:20).

שָׂשׂוֹן sāsôn (8050), Joy, exultation (Jer 7:34).

שִׁיר shîr (8302), Song (Is 30:29).

שָׁעַע shāʿaʿ (8551), Pilpel: treat fondly (Ps 94:19 [93:19]).

שַׁעֲשׁוּעִים shaʿāshûʿîm (8562), Delight, rapture (Prv 8:31).

1. εὐφραίνων euphrainōn
   nom sing masc part pres act
2. εὐφραίνου euphrainou 2sing impr pres mid
3. εὐφραίνεσθε euphrainesthe 2pl impr pres mid
4. εὐφραινόμενος euphrainomenos
   nom sing masc part pres mid
5. εὐφραίνεσθαι euphrainesthai inf pres mid
6. εὐφράνθη euphranthē 3sing indic aor pass
7. εὐφρανθῶ euphranthō 1sing subj aor pass
8. εὐφρανθῶμεν euphranthōmen 1pl subj aor pass
9. εὐφράνθητι euphranthēti 2sing impr aor pass
10. εὐφράνθητε euphranthēte 2pl impr aor pass
11. εὐφρανθῆναι euphranthēnai inf aor pass
12. εὐφρανθήσονται euphranthēsontai
    3pl indic fut pass
13. εὐφραίνοντο euphrainonto 3pl indic imperf pass
14. εὐφραίνονται euphrainontai 3pl indic pres mid
15. ηὐφράνθη ēuphranthē 3sing indic aor pass

2 take thine ease, eat, drink, and be merry.	Luke 12:19
8 the fatted calf, ... and let us eat, and be merry:	15:23
5 lost, and is found. And they began to be merry.	15:24
7 that I might make merry with my friends:	15:29
11 It was meet that we should make merry,	15:32
4 rich man, ... and fared sumptuously every day:	16:19
6 Therefore did my heart rejoice,	Acts 2:26
15 Therefore did my heart rejoice,	2:26
13 and rejoiced in the works of their own hands.	7:41
10 And again he saith, Rejoice, ye Gentiles,	Rom 15:10
1 who is he then that maketh me glad,	2 Co 2:2
9 Rejoice, thou barren that bearest not;	Gal 4:27
12 make merry, and shall send gifts one to another;	Rev 11:10
14 make merry, and shall send gifts one to another;	11:10
3 rejoice, ye heavens, and ye that dwell in them.	12:12
2 Rejoice over her, thou heaven, and ye holy	18:20

Classical Greek

In classical Greek *euphrainō*, in the active voice, means "to cheer" or "to gladden." In the passive voice it means "to be glad" or "to rejoice." A variety of events or situations could cause such a mood. *Euphrainō* is especially associated with banquets and their consequent merriment.

Septuagint Usage

The Septuagint uses *euphrainō*, a synonym of *agalliaō* (21) and *chairō* (5299), to describe rejoicing on the part of various individuals. Many times it is used to translate *sāmēach*. Generally speaking, *euphrainō* is used in four ways in the Septuagint. (1) The enemies of God's people "rejoice" when Israel or the righteous are defeated or caused to suffer (Psalm 35:15 [LXX 34:15]; Judges 16:23). (2) Joy is expressed in God's ability and willingness to help or save an individual (Psalms 5:11; 9:2; 16:9 [LXX 15:9]; 32:11 [31:11]; 40:16 [39:16]). Israel "rejoices" over victory in battle (2 Chronicles 20:27). (3) *Euphrainō* is used especially in relation to the religious activities of Israel. This includes both sacrifices and feasts (Deuteronomy 12:7; 14:26; 16:11; 26:11; 27:7) as well as Solomon's coronation (1 Kings 1:45,46 [LXX 3 Kings 1:45,46]). (4) Growing out of the "rejoicing" in religious activities is the use of *euphrainō* in eschatological contexts. Psalms 96:11 (LXX 95:11) and 97:1 (96:1) describe such "rejoicing" in the eschatological Jerusalem where there will no longer be the voice of weeping (Isaiah 65:19).

New Testament Usage

In the New Testament *euphrainō* appears in the writings of Luke, Paul, and in Revelation. *Euphrainō* is associated with rejoicing at a banquet. It appears four times in reference to the rejoicing at the return of the prodigal son (Luke 15:11-32). On the other hand, Luke used *euphrainō* to depict individuals who selfishly eat and drink (Luke 12:19; 16:19). The term was employed by Stephen (Acts 7:41) when he was discussing the revelry of the Children of Israel as they worshiped the golden calf. It seems they celebrated their victory by sending gifts to one another.

Euphrainō is also used for "rejoicing" over the salvation given by the Lord. This includes the vindication of the Messiah (Acts 2:26) and the expression of joy over the mystery of the Gentiles being incorporated into the people of God (Romans 15:10; Galatians 4:27). Paul used *euphrainō* to emphasize the special joy which comes through the fellowship of the Christian community (2 Corinthians 2:2).

As in the Septuagint, *euphrainō* occurs in eschatological contexts. When the two witnesses sent by God are killed (Revelation 11:10), the inhabitants of the world will "rejoice." The inhabitants of heaven are depicted as rejoicing when Satan is hurled to earth (Revelation 12:12). In addition, the heavens are summoned to "rejoice" when the fall of Babylon takes place (Revelation 18:20).

STRONG 2165, BAUER 327, MOULTON-MILLIGAN 267,

KITTEL 2:772-75, LIDDELL-SCOTT 737, COLIN BROWN 2:354-57,361.

2147. Εὐφράτης Euphratēs name
Euphrates.

1. Εὐφράτῃ Euphratē dat masc
2. Εὐφράτην Euphratēn acc masc

1 which are bound in the great river **Euphrates**......... **Rev 9:14**
2 his vial upon the great river **Euphrates**;............... **16:12**

An important river in western Asia described as "great" in both the Old and New Testaments (Revelation 9:14; 16:12).

2148. εὐφροσύνη euphrosunē noun
Joyfulness, cheerfulness, gladness.
COGNATE:
εὐφραίνω euphrainō (2146)
SYNONYMS:
ἀγαλλίασις agalliasis (20)
χαρά chara (5315)

אַהֲבָה 'ahăvāh (157), Love (Zep 3:17—only some Sinaiticus texts).

גְּדוּלָּה gᵉdhûllāh (1449II) Greatness, majesty (Est 1:4).

גִּיל gîl (1561), Rejoicing (Jer 48:33 [31:33]).

חֶדְוָה chedhwāh (A2401), Joy (Ezr 6:16—Aramaic).

מָשׂוֹשׂ māsôs (5026), Joy (Is 24:8, 60:15, Hos 2:11).

מִשְׁתֶּה mishteh (5136), Feast, banquet (Est 9:19).

נֵבֶל nēvel (5213), Harp (Is 14:11).

נָוֶה nāweh (5295), Abode, residence, habitation (Is 35:7).

נָתַן nāthan (5598), Lift up; hithpael: exalt oneself (Prv 30:32 [24:67]).

סִכְלוּת sikhlûth (5724), Foolishness (Eccl 2:3—Sixtine Edition only).

צְדָקָה tsᵉdhāqāh (6930), Righteousness (Is 61:10).

רִנָּה rinnāh (7726), Shout of joy (Ps 105:43 [104:43], Is 14:7, 49:13).

רָנַן rānan (7728), Piel: shout with joy (Is 52:9).

רְנָנָה rᵉnānāh (7729), Shout of joy (Jb 3:7, 20:5).

שׂוּשׂ sûs (7919), Rejoice (Is 65:18).

שְׂחֹק sᵉchōq (7926), Laughter (Prv 14:13).

שָׂמַח sāmach (7975), Qal: rejoice, be joyful (Ez 35:14); piel: make glad, allow to rejoice (Jgs 9:13—Codex Alexandrinus only).

שִׂמְחָה simchāh (7977), Joy, festival (Nm 10:10, Neh 8:17, Jl 1:16).

שָׂשׂוֹן sāsôn (8050), Joy, exultation (Is 12:3, 22:13, Jer 15:16).

שֶׁמֶן shemen (8467), Oil, olive oil (Is 25:6).

1. εὐφροσύνης euphrosunēs gen sing fem

1 shalt make me full **of joy** with thy countenance...... **Acts 2:28**
1 filling our hearts with food and **gladness**............... **14:17**

One of several overlapping terms translated "joy," "cheerfulness," or "gladness," this word focuses on the inward or spiritual basis for such joy. In the New Testament such bases are the order of creation (Acts 14:17) and God's presence (Acts 2:28). In the Septuagint it is used most often to translate *simchāh*, which means "fulness of joy" (e.g., Psalm 16:11 [LXX 15:11], the Old Testament verse quoted in Acts 2:28).

STRONG 2167, BAUER 328, MOULTON-MILLIGAN 267, KITTEL 2:772-75, LIDDELL-SCOTT 737, COLIN BROWN 2:354-55.

2149. εὐχαριστέω eucharisteō verb
To be thankful, give thanks, return thanks, pray.
COGNATES:
εὐχαριστία eucharistia (2150)
εὐχάριστος eucharistos (2151)
χαίρω chairō (5299)
SYNONYM:
ἀνθομολογέομαι anthomologeomai (435)

1. εὐχαριστῶ eucharistō 1sing indic pres act
2. εὐχαριστεῖς eucharisteis 2sing indic pres act
3. εὐχαριστεῖ eucharistei 3sing indic pres act
4. εὐχαριστοῦμεν eucharistoumen 1pl indic pres act
5. εὐχαριστεῖτε eucharisteite 2pl impr pres act
6. εὐχαριστῶν eucharistōn
   nom sing masc part pres act
7. εὐχαριστοῦντες eucharistountes
   nom pl masc part pres act
8. εὐχαριστεῖν eucharistein inf pres act
9. εὐχαρίστησεν eucharistēsen 3sing indic aor act
10. εὐχαρίστησαν eucharistēsan 3pl indic aor act
11. εὐχαριστήσας eucharistēsas
    nom sing masc part aor act
12. εὐχαριστήσαντος eucharistēsantos
    gen sing masc part aor act
13. εὐχαριστηθῇ eucharistēthē 3sing subj aor pass
14. ηὐχαρίστησαν ēucharistēsan 3pl indic aor act

11 the seven loaves and the fishes, and **gave thanks**, ..**Matt 15:36**
11 Jesus took bread, and blessed it, and brake it, ... **26:26**
11 And he took the cup, and **gave thanks**, ... **26:27**
11 And he took the seven loaves, and **gave thanks**, ... **Mark 8:6**
11 he took the cup, and when he **had given thanks**, ... **14:23**
6 fell down on his face at his feet, giving him **thanks:Luke 17:16**
1 God, I **thank** thee, that I am not as other men are,... **18:11**
11 And he took the cup, and **gave thanks**, and said, ... **22:17**
11 And he took bread, and **gave thanks**, and brake it, ... **22:19**
11 and when he **had given thanks**, ... **John 6:11**
9 and when he **had given thanks**, ... **6:11**
12 after that the Lord **had given thanks**: **6:23**
1 Father, I **thank** thee that thou hast heard me......... **11:41**

9	and gave thanks to God in presence of them all:..	Acts 27:35
11	he thanked God, and took courage..................	28:15
1	I thank my God through Jesus Christ for you all,..	Rom 1:8
10	glorified him not as God, neither were thankful;.......	1:21
14	glorified him not as God, neither were thankful;.......	1:21
1	I thank God through Jesus Christ our Lord.............	7:25
3	for he giveth God thanks;...........................	14:6
3	to the Lord he eateth not, and giveth God thanks.....	14:6
1	unto whom not only I give thanks,..................	16:4
1	I thank my God always on your behalf,...........	1 Co 1:4
1	I thank God that I baptized none of you,...........	1:14
1	evil spoken of for that for which I give thanks?.......	10:30
11	And when he had given thanks, he brake it,.........	11:24
2	For thou verily givest thanks well,....................	14:17
1	I thank my God, I speak with tongues more than.....	14:18
13	thanks may be given by many on our behalf.......	2 Co 1:11
6	Cease not to give thanks for you,..................	Eph 1:16
7	Giving thanks always for all things unto God..........	5:20
1	I thank my God upon every remembrance of you,..	Phlp 1:3
4	We give thanks to God and the Father of our Lord	Col 1:3
7	Giving thanks unto the Father,.......................	1:12
7	giving thanks to God and the Father by him...........	3:17
4	We give thanks to God always for you all,...........	1 Th 1:2
4	For this cause also thank we God without ceasing,.....	2:13
5	In every thing give thanks:..........................	5:18
8	We are bound to thank God always for you,.......	2 Th 1:3
8	we are bound to give thanks alway to God for you,.....	2:13
1	I thank my God, making mention of thee always...	Phlm 1:4
4	We give thee thanks, O Lord God Almighty,......	Rev 11:17

Classical Greek and Septuagint Usage

The compound verb *eucharisteō* is formed by adding the suffix *eu* (2074), "good, well, kind," to the verb *charisteō*, "to give freely, bestow a favor, gratify." Primarily it means "to give thanks." The cognate *charis* (5320B), "grace, attractiveness, favor," has been incorporated by New Testament writers into Christian thinking and has taken on the special meaning of "grace," God's gracious favor toward His own. The verb, occurring as early as the Third Century B.C., has the basic meaning of "to show someone a favor" and hence "oblige" (*Moulton-Milligan*). And because a favor deserves an obligation of thanks, the verb developed the meaning "to be thankful," hence "to give thanks, return thanks." This idea of giving thanks also had a general meaning of "to pray" in Philo and elsewhere. The verb occurs in the Septuagint, six times in the Apocrypha.

New Testament Usage

In the New Testament *eucharisteō* can be found 39 times. All but once (Romans 16:4) it is used of giving thanks to God. Though this term originally meant "to bestow favor on" and eventually included the meaning of "to pray" (Fourth Century A.D., cf. *Bauer*), in the New Testament it always means "to be thankful, return thanks" and almost always to God. The verb is used of Christ at the feeding of the 5,000 (John 6:11, though interestingly enough, the Synoptic Gospels use the verb "to bless" [*eulogeō* (2108)]; Matthew 14:19; Mark 6:41; Luke 9:16), the feeding of the 4,000 (Matthew 15:36; Mark 8:6; Luke 17:16), the raising of Lazarus (John 11:41), and the initiation of the Lord's Supper (Matthew 26:27; Mark 14:23; Luke 22:17,19; 1 Corinthians 11:24). This last usage gave rise to entitling the Communion service and/or its elements "the Eucharist."

In all his epistles except 2 Corinthians, Galatians, and the Pastoral Epistles, Paul used this verb in the introductory portion to share with his readers his appreciation to God for them. When Paul used the term in his writing it was often connected with terms or phrases like "always" (1 Corinthians 1:4), "cease not" (Ephesians 1:16), "all things" (Ephesians 5:20), and "upon every remembrance" (Philippians 1:3). Thanksgiving is expressed as an obligation in 2 Thessalonians 1:3 and 2:13, "We are bound . . . ." As Paul remembered his friends, he would often burst into thanksgiving for them, which in turn would lead to prayer on their behalf (Ephesians 1:16,17; Philemon 4-6). Thanksgiving and prayer are closely interrelated; doing the one leads to doing the other.

A way to glorify God is to be thankful. Ungratefulness to God for His bounty is basis for condemnation (Romans 1:21). Thanksgiving to God will never cease; even in heaven the 24 elders worship God by giving Him thanks for who He is (Revelation 1:17).

STRONG 2168, BAUER 328, MOULTON-MILLIGAN 267, KITTEL 9:407-15, LIDDELL-SCOTT 738, COLIN BROWN 2:855,874; 3:817-20.

2150. εὐχαριστία eucharistia noun

Thankfulness, gratitude, thanksgiving, prayer of thanksgiving.

CROSS-REFERENCE:
    εὐχαριστέω eucharisteō (2149)

1. εὐχαριστίας eucharistias gen/acc sing/pl fem
2. εὐχαριστία eucharistia nom sing fem
3. εὐχαριστίᾳ eucharistia dat sing fem
4. εὐχαριστίαν eucharistian acc sing fem
5. εὐχαριστιῶν eucharistiōn gen pl fem

1	most noble Felix, with all thankfulness.............	Acts 24:3
3	the unlearned say Amen at thy giving of thanks,...	1 Co 14:16
4	might through the thanksgiving of many redound....	2 Co 4:15
4	which causeth through us thanksgiving to God..........	9:11
5	is abundant also by many thanksgivings unto God;......	9:12
2	but rather giving of thanks...........................	Eph 5:4
1	by prayer and supplication with thanksgiving........	Phlp 4:6
3	abounding therein with thanksgiving.................	Col 2:7
3	and watch in the same with thanksgiving;.............	4:2
4	what thanks can we render to God again for you,...	1 Th 3:9
1	and giving of thanks, be made for all men;.........	1 Tm 2:1

εὐχάριστος 2151

1 with **thanksgiving** of them which believe	1 Tm 4:3
1 if it be received with **thanksgiving**:	4:4
4 honour and **thanks** to him that sat on the throne,	Rev 4:9
2 and **thanksgiving**, and honour, and power,	7:12

Classical Greek

This common word in antiquity means "gratitude, thanksgiving"; generally such thanksgiving is directed toward the gods. *Eucharistia* is indirectly derived from *eu* (2074), "well," and *charizomai* (5319), "to show favor, kindness." It may denote either an attitude of "thankfulness" or an act of "thanksgiving."

Septuagint Usage

Oddly enough the Hebrew language knows no direct equivalent to *eucharistia* despite the concept of "offering thanks" to God in the thank offering or in thanksgiving songs (Conzlemann, "eucharisteō," *Kittel*, 9:409). In the apocryphal literature *eucharistia* occurs four times: Esther 8:13; Wisdom of Solomon 16:28; Sirach 37:11; 2 Maccabees 2:27. It is not always directed toward God (e.g., Sirach 37:11; 2 Maccabees 2:27). (*Eucharistia* is also read by Aquila in several texts, e.g., Leviticus 7:12; Psalm 42:5.)

New Testament Usage

Eucharistia is the Greek word from which we derive the English term "*Eucharist*" the "Lord's Supper." However, such a technical usage of the noun (cf. possibly the verb in Matthew 26:27; Mark 14:23; Luke 22:17,19; John 6:11; 1 Corinthians 11:24) is foreign to the New Testament. In fact, Paul spoke of his "gratitude" to Felix that the nation was enjoying peace and reform (Acts 24:3). *Eucharistia* is probably not an allusion to the Lord's Supper even in 1 Timothy 4:3,4. Instead, it is probably simply a reference to the practice of offering thanks to God for food.

Ordinarily *eucharistia* (and its verbal companion, e.g., 2 Thessalonians 2:13; Philemon 4; Revelation 11:17) is related to general prayer or supplication to God (e.g., 2 Corinthians 4:15; 9:11,12; Ephesians 5:4; Philippians 4:6; 1 Timothy 2:1; etc.). But the usage in 1 Corinthians 14:16 is an interesting reference to the offering of thanksgiving (*eucharistia*) in the context of speaking in tongues (cf. 14:13ff.).

Early in the history of the Church *eucharistia* did become a technical term for the Eucharist, not only in the early "apostolic" writings outside of the canon (e.g., *Didache* 9:1,5; Ignatius *To The Ephesians* 13:1; *To The Philadelphians* 4), but some New Testament manuscripts witness the technical usage. At 1 Corinthians 10:16 some read *to potērion tēs eucharistias*, "the cup of thanksgiving," for *to potērion tēs eulogias*, "the cup of blessing."

STRONG 2169, BAUER 328-29, MOULTON-MILLIGAN 267, KITTEL 9:407-15, LIDDELL-SCOTT 738, COLIN BROWN 2:874; 3:817-19.

2151. εὐχάριστος eucharistos adj

Grateful, thankful.

CROSS-REFERENCE:
  εὐχαριστέω eucharisteō (2149)

חֵן chēn (2682), Pleasant, gracious (Prv 11:16).

1. εὐχάριστοι eucharistoi nom pl masc

| 1 ye are called in one body; and be ye **thankful** | Col 3:15 |

This term is often used of cities that are grateful to a benefactor for favors bestowed upon them (cf. *Bauer*). The application of this word to the believer's attitude toward God admirably fits this sense (Colossians 3:15). In the Septuagint, at Proverbs 11:16, it translates *chēn* which means "gracious, winning, agreeable."

STRONG 2170, BAUER 329, MOULTON-MILLIGAN 267-68, KITTEL 9:407-15, LIDDELL-SCOTT 738, COLIN BROWN 2:874; 3:817.

2152. εὐχή euchē noun

Oath, vow, prayer.

COGNATE:
  προσεύχομαι proseuchomai (4195)

SYNONYMS:
  δέησις deēsis (1157)
  ἔντευξις enteuxis (1767)
  ἱκετηρία hiketēria (2404)
  προσευχή proseuchē (4194)

בָּעוּ bāʿû (A1188), Petition, prayer (Dn 6:7—Aramaic).

נָדַר nādhar (5265), Make a vow (Nm 30:11, Mal 1:14).

נֶדֶר nēdher (5266II) Vow (Nm 30:12ff., Ps 50:14 [49:14], Jon 1:16).

נָזַר nāzar (5324), Dedicate oneself to a deity; hiphil: abstain, take a Nazarite vow (Nm 6:6).

נֵזֶר nēzer (5325), Consecration, head of hair (Nm 6:7ff.,12f.,18,21).

תְּפִלָּה tᵉphillāh (8940), Prayer (Jb 16:18).

1. εὐχή euchē nom sing fem
2. εὐχήν euchēn acc sing fem

| 2 shorn his head in Cenchrea: for he had a **vow** | Acts 18:18 |

2 We have four men which have **a vow** on them; ..... Acts 21:23
1 And the **prayer** of faith shall save the sick, ... Jas 5:15

Classical Greek
Among classical writers *euchē* denoted a "prayer" or "vow" offered to the gods. The *euchē* represented one's "wish" or "desire." In a negative sense a *euchē* could be a "curse" (i.e., a prayer for harm) upon another (*Liddell-Scott*).

Septuagint Usage
The Septuagint frequently uses *euchē* in place of *nēdher* and *nēzer*. Most often *euchē* means a "vow" (Numbers 30:3). It can also signify a specific kind of offering (Deuteronomy 12:6,11). In the Old Testament a vow was taken upon oneself voluntarily (Deuteronomy 23:21-23) and implied that something would be delivered to God at a specific point in time. A variety of items could serve as a "vow," including a life of service rendered by the one who made the vow (Leviticus 27:2ff.). In Numbers 21:1-3 an entire city was placed under a ban as the result of a "vow" the Israelites took in order to help secure a military victory.

One special use of *euchē* deserves closer examination. Numbers 6:1-21 is devoted to a discussion of the Nazarite vow. This *euchē* was voluntary and open to both men and women. It covered a limited period of time. It involved such a consecrated dedication to God that the vow called for rigorous steps to ensure purity. Not only did the Nazarite abstain from wine and strong drink, he also abstained from all fruit of the vine (i.e., grapes, raisins). In addition, the Nazarite was to grow his hair long and wear it unbound as a symbol of strength in honor of the Lord. Also he was to have no association with the dead. Special purification rites were prescribed in the extraordinary event of contact with the dead (Numbers 6:9-12). On the final day of the vow, certain sacrifices were offered including the hair cut from the consecrated head. The significance of the vow was a demonstration of one's dedication to God.

New Testament Usage
Euchē occurs but three times in the New Testament. Twice it is best understood as "vow." Paul cut his hair at Cenchreae due to a vow he had taken (Acts 18:18). Some believe this was a modified Nazarite vow. Acts 21:23 speaks of four men who had made a Nazarite vow. To demonstrate that he did not want to abolish Judaism, Paul was asked to pay for the sacrifices these four men were to present on the last day of the vow. This was in accordance with the Law (Numbers 6:21) and contemporary practice, as when Herod Agrippa I paid for the expense of many Nazarites (Josephus *Antiquities* 19.6.1).

Only in James 5:15 is *euchē* used for "prayer." The context is that of the prayer of faith offered on behalf of the sick. Such a prayer is prayed with the expectation that God will act. The prayer will result, if in accordance with the divine will, in the healing (not saving) of the sick person. Sin is sometimes seen as the cause of illness (Mark 2:5; John 5:14; 1 Corinthians 11:30). If sin causes the illness in that particular case, the prayer will be instrumental in both spiritual and physical healing.

STRONG 2171, BAUER 329, MOULTON-MILLIGAN 268, KITTEL 2:775-806, LIDDELL-SCOTT 739, COLIN BROWN 2:861,867.

2153. εὔχομαι euchomai verb
Pray (for), wish (for).
COGNATE:
προσεύχομαι proseuchomai (4195)
SYNONYMS:
βούλομαι boulomai (1007)
δέομαι deomai (1183)
ἐντυγχάνω entunchanō (1777)
θέλω thelō (2286)
προσεύχομαι proseuchomai (4195)

אָסַר 'āsar (646), Bind oneself to a vow of abstention (Nm 30:10).

בְּעָה beʿâh (A1187I) Request (Dn 6:7,12,13—Aramaic).

נָדָה nādhâh (5255), Piel: suppose to be far away (Am 6:3—Codex Alexandrinus only).

נָדַר nādhar (5265), Make a vow (Gn 31:13, Dt 12:11, Is 19:21).

נֶדֶר nedher (5266I), Vow (Prv 20:25).

נָזִיר nāzîr (5319), Nazarite (Nm 6:13,18ff.).

נָזַר nāzar (5324), Dedicate oneself to a deity; hiphil: abstain, take a Nazarite vow (Nm 6:5).

נָשָׂא nāsaʾ (5558), Lift up; piel: long to (Jer 22:27).

עָתַר ʿāthar (6518), Qal: pray, plead (Ex 8:30, 10:18); hiphil: pray, plead (Ex 8:8f.,28f., Jb 22:27).

פָּלָא pālāʾ (6623), Be too hard, difficult; hiphil: do in a strange or surprising way (Lv 27:2).

פָּלַל pālal (6663), Hithpael: pray (Nm 11:2, 2 Kgs 20:2, Jb 42:8).

תְּפִלָּה tephillāh (8940), Prayer (Jer 7:16).

1. **εὔχομαι** euchomai 1sing indic pres mid
2. **εὐχόμεθα** euchometha 1pl indic pres mid

3. εὔχεσθε euchesthe 2pl impr pres mid
4. εὐξαίμην euxaimēn 1sing opt aor mid
5. ηὐχόμην ēuchomēn 1sing indic imperf mid
6. ηὔχοντο ēuchonto 3pl indic imperf mid

4	And Paul said, I would to God, that not only thou,	Acts 26:29
6	anchors out of the stern, and wished for the day	27:29
5	For I could wish that myself were accursed	Rom 9:3
1	Now I pray to God that ye do no evil;	2 Co 13:7
2	Now I pray to God that ye do no evil;	13:7
2	and this also we wish, even your perfection	13:9
3	Confess your faults ... and pray one for another,	Jas 5:16
1	I wish above all things that thou mayest prosper	3 Jn 1:2

Classical Greek

In classical Greek *euchomai* demonstrates a wide range of meanings. In its simplest state it means "offer prayer, pray that." Associated with this is the meaning "vow." A third sense is "boast, profess loudly." Usually it connotes a boasting that one was justified in doing (*Liddell-Scott*).

Septuagint Usage

The Septuagint frequently uses *euchomai* in place of *nādhar*. Most often *euchomai* means "make a vow." These vows include the Nazarite vow (Numbers 6), various voluntary offerings (Deuteronomy 12:11), and even questionable vows such as Jephthah sacrificing his own daughter due to a vow (Judges 11:30,39). *Euchomai* can also mean "pray." Here the emphasis is upon intercessory prayer. This includes Moses praying for Pharaoh (Exodus 8:8,9,28-30), Aaron (Deuteronomy 9:20), Israel (Deuteronomy 9:26), and Job praying for his friends (Job 42:10). On one occasion Jeremiah is instructed not to offer intercessory prayer for his people (Jeremiah 7:16). Prayer can also be offered on one's own behalf as with Hezekiah (2 Kings 20:2 [LXX 4 Kings 20:2]). Only once does *euchomai* mean "wish" in the Septuagint (Jeremiah 22:27).

New Testament Usage

The New Testament uses *euchomai* in two ways. Twice Paul used *euchomai* to mean "pray." On both occasions (2 Corinthians 13:7,9) the word appears in contexts of intercessory prayer. In his final warnings to the Corinthian church Paul informed them he prayed that they do nothing wrong (verse 7) and for their restoration (verse 9). James also used *euchomai* for intercessory prayer (5:16). He instructed the believers to pray for one another. The primary concern here is healing. Having previously hinted at the occasional relationship between sin and illnesses, James encouraged the believers to inform one another of their faults and needs so the community would be better prepared to pray for one another. The emphasis is not upon open confession but intercessory prayer.

There are New Testament passages where *euchomai* is used to express a strong wish or desire. Paul could "wish" that he were *anathema* (329) for his people's sake (Romans 9:3). Sometimes it is difficult to distinguish whether *euchomai* means "wish" or "prayer" as when Paul said he would continue to pray (or desire) that Agrippa be converted (Acts 26:29). *Euchomai* expresses the hope (or prayer) that dawn would soon come after Paul's shipwreck (Acts 27:29). The phrase "I *wish* above all things that thou mayest prosper and be in health, even as thy soul prospereth," found in 3 John 2, is a common formula in letters of the First Century. While it may be taken as a prayer, it is more likely a standard literary greeting which expressed the wishes of the writer.

STRONG 2172, BAUER 329, MOULTON-MILLIGAN 268, KITTEL 2:775-806, LIDDELL-SCOTT 739, COLIN BROWN 2:861-62,867,873.

2154. εὔχρηστος euchrēstos adj

Useful, serviceable, profitable.

COGNATE:
χρηστεύομαι chrēsteuomai (5376)

SYNONYM:
ὠφέλιμος ōphelimos (5457)

חֵפֶץ chēphets (2761), Joy, pleasure (Prv 31:13).

1. εὔχρηστον euchrēston nom/acc sing masc/neu
2. εὔχρηστος euchrēstos nom sing masc

1	sanctified, and meet for the master's use,	2 Tm 2:21
2	Mark, ... for he is profitable to me for the ministry	4:11
1	but now profitable to thee and to me:	Phlm 1:11

This compound adjective means "useful" or "profitable" as opposed to *achrēstos* (883) which signifies "not useful." The term is applied to both persons and things. In the Septuagint, at Proverbs 31:13, it translates *chēphets* in referring to the "profitable" work of one's hands. Paul discussed what one must do in order to be "*meet* for the master's use" (2 Timothy 2:21); and in 2 Timothy 4:11 Paul said Mark was "profitable" for the ministry. *Euchrēstos* also occurs in Philemon 11 as a wordplay on the name Onesimus which means "useful" or "profitable."

STRONG 2173, BAUER 329, MOULTON-MILLIGAN 268, LIDDELL-SCOTT 739.

2155. εὐψυχέω eupsucheō verb

To be glad, in good spirits, cheerful, encouraged.

COGNATE:
ψυχή psuchē (5425)

SYNONYMS:
εὐθυμέω euthumeō (2093)
θαῤῥέω tharrheō (2269)
θαρσέω tharseō (2270)
τολμάω tolmaō (4958)

1. εὐψυχῶ **eupsuchō** 1sing subj pres act

1 that I also **may be of good comfort**,................ Phlp 2:19

This verb means either "to have courage" or "to be glad." Paul's one use of it (Philemon 2:19) falls into the latter category, "be of good comfort." The former may be seen in the occurrence of this word in epitaphs, though here it may also have the sense of "farewell" (cf. *Bauer*).

STRONG 2174, BAUER 329, MOULTON-MILLIGAN 268, LIDDELL-SCOTT 739-40, COLIN BROWN 3:687.

2156. εὐωδία euōdia noun

Aroma, fragrance, sweet smelling.

CROSS-REFERENCE:
ὄζω ozō (3467)

נִיחֹחַ nîchōach (5394I), Soothing (Lv 2:2, Nm 15:3, Ez 16:19).

1. εὐωδία **euōdia** nom sing fem
2. εὐωδίας **euōdias** gen sing fem

1 For we are unto God **a sweet savour** of Christ,...... 2 Co 2:15
2 and a sacrifice to God for **a sweetsmelling savour**..... Eph 5:2
2 an odour **of a sweet smell**, a sacrifice acceptable,.... Phlp 4:18

Classical Greek

The term *euōdia*, "savor, fragrance, aroma," is made up of *eu* (2074), "well, good," and *ozō* (3467), "to smell, to give off an aroma." In antiquity the odor of something was regarded as indicative of its character. Thus the odor/aroma carried the essence and quality of its originator.

Septuagint Usage

In the Old Testament aroma plays an important role in the worship of Israel (e.g., Leviticus 1:9,17; Numbers 15:3; cf. Ezekiel 6:13 of idols). Fragrant incense was burned in the sanctuary and the various offerings were burned in belief that their aroma would be pleasing to the Lord, i.e., He would be satisfied with the sacrifice.

New Testament Usage

This forms the background for the three texts in which Paul used the term. First and foremost, the fragrant offering of Christ has been made to God through the Cross; furthermore, it has been offered on our behalf, and God has accepted it (Ephesians 5:2). Moreover, the apostle considered the heralds of the gospel as the fragrance of the gospel—of Christ to God (2 Corinthians 2:15). To some it is an aroma of death to death (judgment); to others it is of life to life (salvation, 2 Corinthians 2:14-17).

Just as the self-sacrifice of Christ for others was a savory offering to God, the gift which the congregation in Philippi had collected for Paul was a "sweet smell, a sacrifice acceptable, well-pleasing to God" (Philippians 4:18).

STRONG 2175, BAUER 329, MOULTON-MILLIGAN 268-69, KITTEL 2:808-10, LIDDELL-SCOTT 740, COLIN BROWN 3:599-601.

2157. Εὐωδία Euōdia name

Euodias.

1. Εὐωδίαν **Euōdian** acc fem
2. Εὐοδίαν **Euodian** acc fem

1 I beseech **Euodias**, and beseech Syntyche,........... Phlp 4:2
2 I beseech **Euodias**, and beseech Syntyche,............ 4:2

A woman who worked with Paul in Philippi. Paul requested that she and Syntyche "be of the same mind in the Lord" (Philippians 4:2).

2158. εὐώνυμος euōnumos adj

Left.

SYNONYM:
ἀριστερός aristeros (704)

צָפוֹן tsāphôn (7103), North (Jos 13:3).
שְׂמֹאל sᵉmō'l (7972II) Left, left side, northward (Nm 20:17, 2 Chr 3:17, Ez 16:46).
שְׂמֹאל sim'ēl (7973), Hiphil: go to the left (Ez 21:16).
שְׂמָאלִי sōmā'lî (7974), On the left (2 Kgs 11:11).

1. εὐώνυμον **euōnumon** acc sing masc/fem
2. εὐωνύμων **euōnumōn** gen pl neu

2 one on thy right hand, and the other on **the left**,...Matt 20:21
2 but to sit on my right hand, and on **my left**,........ 20:23
2 sheep on his right hand, but the goats on **the left**.... 25:33
2 Then shall he say also unto them on **the left hand**,.... 25:41
2 one on the right hand, and another on **the left**........ 27:38
2 and the other on thy **left hand**, in thy glory........ Mark 10:37
2 But to sit on my right hand, and on my **left hand**...... 10:40
2 the one on his right hand, and the other on **his left**.... 15:27
1 we left it **on the left hand**, and sailed into Syria,.... Acts 21:3
1 right foot upon the sea, ... his **left** foot on the earth, Rev 10:2

This is one of the two New Testament words translated "left" (see *aristeros* [704]). Literally this term means "good name" or "good omen." It is applied to bad omens which came "from the left." Thus a "good name" is given to a bad message. *Euōnumos* is used as an adjective, "left-hand," or in prepositional phrases indicating position ("on the left"). Although New Testament usage of *euōnumos* is primarily neutral (e.g., Acts 21:3; Revelation 10:2), there is one usage which retains its original pejorative sense where at the Last Judgment the sheep will be placed on Jesus' right, but the goats will be placed on His "left" (Matthew 25:33,41). In the Septuagint the word usually translates *semōl* meaning "left" (cf. Exodus 14:22,29; Ezekiel 16:46).

STRONG 2176, BAUER 329-30, MOULTON-MILLIGAN 269, LIDDELL-SCOTT 740, COLIN BROWN 2:148.

2159. ἐφάλλομαι ephallomai verb
To leap upon, spring upon.
CROSS-REFERENCE:
ἅλλομαι hallomai (240)
צָלֵחַ tsālēach (7014), Be strong, be powerful (1 Sm 10:6, 16:13).

1. ἐφαλλόμενος ephallomenos
nom sing masc part pres mid
2. ἐφαλόμενος ephalomenos
nom sing masc part aor mid

1 man in whom the evil spirit was **leaped on them**,... Acts 19:16
2 man in whom the evil spirit was **leaped on them**,...... 19:16

The consistent meaning of this word throughout Greek literature is "to leap upon." This verb is usually followed by a direct object, most frequently a person as in Acts 19:16. In the Septuagint it translates *tsālēach* at 1 Samuel (LXX 1 Kings) 10:6; 11:6; and 16:13, all of which refer to the Holy Spirit "coming upon" someone.

STRONG 2177, BAUER 330, MOULTON-MILLIGAN 269, LIDDELL-SCOTT 740.

2160. ἐφάπαξ ephapax adv
At once, once for all.
COGNATE:
πᾶς pas (3817B)
SYNONYM:
ἅπαξ hapax (526)

1. ἐφάπαξ ephapax

1 For in that he died, he died unto sin **once**:......... Rom 6:10
1 was seen of above five hundred brethren **at once**;.. 1 Co 15:6
1 for this he did **once**, when he offered up himself..... Heb 7:27
1 he entered in **once** into the holy place,............. Heb 9:12
1 the offering of the body of Jesus Christ **once for all**.... 10:10

This compound adverb, from *epi* (1894), "upon," plus *hapax* (526), "once," is an emphatic term best translated "at once, once for all." In four of its New Testament occurrences it emphasizes the singularity and uniqueness of Christ's sacrifice and its results (Romans 6:10; Hebrews 7:27; 9:12; 10:10). It can also mean "at one time" as in 1 Corinthians 15:6 where Christ appeared to more than 500 simultaneously.

STRONG 2178, BAUER 330, MOULTON-MILLIGAN 269, KITTEL 1:383-84, LIDDELL-SCOTT 740, COLIN BROWN 2:716-18,725.

2161. Ἐφεσῖνος Ephesinos name-adj
Of Ephesus.

1. Ἐφεσίνης Ephesinēs gen sing fem

1 Unto the angel of the church of **Ephesus** write;...... Rev 2:1

A reference to the church (or more specifically "the angel of the church") which received a message from the resurrected Saviour (Revelation 2:1).

2162. Ἐφέσιος Ephesios name-adj
Ephesian.

1. Ἐφεσίων Ephesiōn gen pl masc
2. Ἐφεσίους Ephesious acc pl masc
3. Ἐφέσιοι Ephesioi nom pl masc
4. Ἐφέσιον Ephesion acc masc

1 cried out, saying, Great is Diana of the **Ephesians**...Acts 19:28
1 cried out, Great is Diana of the **Ephesians**............ 19:34
3 he said, Ye men **of Ephesus**, what man is there 19:35
1 knoweth not how that the city of the **Ephesians**....... 19:35
4 with him in the city Trophimus an **Ephesian**,.......... 21:29
2 that love our Lord Jesus Christ in sincerity. Amen....Eph 6:24
1 Grace be with you. Amen...................... 2 Tm 4:22

A resident of the city of Ephesus; of Trophimus (Acts 21:29).

2163. Ἔφεσος Ephesos name
Ephesus.

1. Ἐφέσου Ephesou gen fem
2. Ἐφέσῳ Ephesō dat fem
3. Ἔφεσον Epheson acc fem

3 And he came to **Ephesus**, and left them there:..... Acts 18:19
1 And he sailed from **Ephesus**........................ 18:21
3 a certain Jew named Apollos, ... came to **Ephesus**..... 18:24
3 came to **Ephesus**: and finding certain disciples,......... 19:1
3 all the Jews and Greeks also dwelling at **Ephesus**;..... 19:17

1	that not alone at **Ephesus**,	Acts 19:26
3	For Paul had determined to sail by **Ephesus**,	20:16
3	And from Miletus he sent to **Ephesus**,	20:17
2	I have fought with beasts at **Ephesus**,	1 Co 15:32
2	But I will tarry at **Ephesus** until Pentecost.	16:8
2	an apostle ... to the saints which are at **Ephesus**,	Eph 1:1
2	As I besought thee to abide still at **Ephesus**,	1 Tm 1:3
2	many things he ministered unto me at **Ephesus**,	2 Tm 1:18
3	And Tychicus have I sent to **Ephesus**.	4:12
3	seven churches which are in Asia; unto **Ephesus**,	Rev 1:11
2	To the angel of the church in **Ephesus** (RSV)	2:1

Seaport city of Asia Minor visited by Paul on his second missionary journey. It was known for its temple of Artemis (Acts 19:1ff.) (see 730).
STRONG 2181.

2164. ἐφευρετής epheuretēs noun
Inventor, contriver, discoverer.
CROSS-REFERENCE:
εὑρίσκω heuriskō (2128)

1. ἐφευρετάς epheuretas acc pl masc

1	despiteful, proud, boasters, **inventors** of evil things,..	Rom 1:30

Used only once in the New Testament, this compound noun means "inventor" or "contriver." It comes from the verb *epheuriskō*, itself a compound from *heuriskō* (2128), "to find." It is consistently used throughout Greek literature in the negative sense. In Romans 1:30 Paul discussed the fate of the reprobate, who included "*inventors* of evil things."
STRONG 2182, BAUER 330, MOULTON-MILLIGAN 269, LIDDELL-SCOTT 743.

2165. ἐφημερία ephēmeria noun
Class, division.
CROSS-REFERENCE:
ἡμέρα hēmera (2232)

מַחֲלֹקֶת machălōqeth (4393), Division (1 Chr 28:1, 2 Chr 31:15, 35:4).

מְלָאכָה mᵉlā'khāh (4536), Service (2 Chr 13:10).

מִשְׁמָר mishmār (5110), Division (Neh 12:24).

מִשְׁמֶרֶת mishmereth (5111), Duty (2 Chr 31:17, Neh 13:30).

1. ἐφημερίας ephēmerias gen sing fem

1	priest named Zacharias, of the **course** of Abia:	Luke 1:5
1	office before God in the order of his **course**,	1:8

Classical Greek and Septuagint Usage
Ephēmeria is a compound word literally meaning "daily" (*epi* [1894], "by" or "on," + *hēmera* [2232], "day"). This word does not appear before the First Century B.C. in classical Greek but it is used in the Septuagint in two ways. It can mean either the "service rendered by the priests" (1 Chronicles 25:8; 2 Chronicles 13:10; Nehemiah 13:30) or *ephēmeria* can stand for a "division" or "class" of priests (1 Chronicles 23:6; 28:13).

First Chronicles 24:1-19 indicates there were 24 divisions of priests. Each division was composed of four to nine families, all of which traced their lineage to Aaron. Several of these classes never returned from exile. Consequently, to preserve the divisions the remaining families were divided into 24 groups. For this reason Josephus could refer to the four families of priests (*Against Apion* 2.8).

Due to the large number of priests in each *ephēmeria*, it was necessary to determine which priest in a division would serve (offer incense) in the temple on a given day. The opportunity to offer incense came but once in a lifetime (*Mishnah* Tamid 5:2). This selection was accomplished through the casting of lots.

New Testament Usage
The New Testament uses *ephēmeria* on two occasions, Luke 1:5,8. Both verses refer to Zechariah, a member of the division of Abijah which was the eighth class (1 Chronicles 24:10). Zechariah had been chosen to offer incense in the temple. This honor had come late in life for him. Yet Zechariah's service would be long remembered due to the promise which was given to him in the temple. Zechariah would father a child named John. This son would play a vital role in salvation history, preparing the way for the Messiah himself.
STRONG 2183, BAUER 330, MOULTON-MILLIGAN 269, LIDDELL-SCOTT 743-44.

2166. ἐφήμερος ephēmeros adj
Daily, for the day.
CROSS-REFERENCE:
ἡμέρα hēmera (2232)

1. ἐφημέρου ephēmerou gen sing fem

1	or sister be naked, and destitute of **daily** food,	Jas 2:15

This compound adjective comes from *epi* (1894), "upon," and *hēmera* (2232), "day." The significance is "for the day" or "daily." The term comes into English in the word *ephemeral*. Used once in the New Testament (James 2:15), it signifies food lasting "for a day," or "daily" food.
STRONG 2184, BAUER 330, MOULTON-MILLIGAN 269, LIDDELL-SCOTT 743-44.

2167. ἐφικνέομαι ephikneomai verb
To come to, to reach.

SYNONYMS:
διέρχομαι dierchomai (1324)
ἐπέρχομαι eperchomai (1889)
ἔρχομαι erchomai (2048)
ἥκω hēkō (2223)
καταντάω katantaō (2628)
παραγίνομαι paraginomai (3716)
παρέρχομαι parerchomai (3790)
παρίστημι paristēmi (3798)
προσέρχομαι proserchomai (4193)
φθάνω phthanō (5185)

1. **ἐφικνούμενοι** ephiknoumenoi
nom pl masc part pres mid
2. **ἐφικέσθαι** ephikesthai inf aor mid

2 a measure to **reach** even unto you............ 2 Co 10:13
1 as though we **reached** not unto you:............. 10:14

This verb is consistently translated "to come to" or "to reach." It occurs in the New Testament with the preposition *eis* (1506B), indicating who or what was reached (2 Corinthians 10:14), and with *achri* (884), meaning "as far as" someone (2 Corinthians 10:13).

STRONG 2185, BAUER 330, LIDDELL-SCOTT 744-45.

2168. ἐφίστημι ephistēmi verb
Stand by or near, approach, appear, be present.

COGNATE:
ἵστημι histēmi (2449)

SYNONYMS:
ἀναφαίνω anaphainō (396)
γίνομαι ginomai (1090)
ἐγγίζω engizō (1443)
ἐμφανίζω emphanizō (1702)
ἐντυγχάνω entunchanō (1777)
ἐπέρχομαι eperchomai (1889)
ἐπιφαίνω epiphainō (1998)
ἵστημι histēmi (2449)
ὁράω horaō (3571)
παραβάλλω paraballō (3708)
παραγίνομαι paraginomai (3716)
παρίστημι paristēmi (3798)
προσάγω prosagō (4175)
προσεγγίζω prosengizō (4189)
προσέρχομαι proserchomai (4193)
προσπορεύομαι prosporeuomai (4223)
φαίνω phainō (5154)

חָזַק chāzaq (2480), Become strong; hiphil: make strong (Jer 51:12 [28:12]).

יָצַב yātsav (3429), Hithpael: take one's stand (Jer 46:14 [26:14]).

כָּסָה kāsāh (3803), Piel: cover (Ez 31:15—Codex Alexandrinus only).

לָחַם lācham (4032), Niphal: attack (Jer 21:2).

מָנַע mānaʿ (4661), Hold back (Ez 31:15—Codex Alexandrinus only).

נָצַב nātsav (5507), Niphal: be standing (Nm 23:6, Am 9:1); be in charge (Ru 2:5,6); hiphil: set up (Jos 6:26, 1 Kgs 16:34).

נָצָה nātsāh (5510), Hiphil: strive against (Nm 26:9—Codex Alexandrinus only).

נָתַן nāthan (5598), Set (Lv 17:10, 20:3); make someone to be something (Is 3:4).

סָמַךְ sāmakh (5759), Uphold (Is 63:5).

עוּף ʿûph (5990), Hiphil: fly (Prv 23:5).

עָמַד ʿāmadh (6198), Qal: stand (Nm 14:14, 1 Sm 17:51, Zec 1:10,11); hiphil: set (Neh 6:1).

פָּקַד pāqadh (6734), Qal: appoint (Jer 50:44 [27:44], 51:27 [28:27]); hiphil: appoint (Nm 1:50).

קוּם qûm (7251), Stand, arise; hiphil: raise (Jos 7:26, 8:29).

רָפַף rāphaph (7804), Poal: tremble (Jb 26:11—Codex Alexandrinus only).

שִׂים sîm (7947), Appoint (Ex 1:11); set (Lv 20:5); turn into (Is 21:4).

שָׂכַל sākhal (7959), Hiphil: understand (Neh 8:13).

שׁוּב shûv (8178), Return; hiphil: restore (2 Sm 8:3, Is 1:26).

שִׁית shîth (8308), Set (Ex 7:23); apply (Prv 22:17).

שָׁנָה shānāh (8521), Piel: change (Jb 14:20).

שָׁפַת shāphath (8609), Put on (2 Kgs 4:38).

1. **ἐπέστη** epestē 3sing indic aor act
2. **ἐπέστησαν** epestēsan 3pl indic aor act
3. **ἐπιστῇ** epistē 3sing subj aor act
4. **ἐπίστηθι** epistēthi 2sing impr aor act
5. **ἐπιστάς** epistas nom sing masc part aor act
6. **ἐπιστάντες** epistantes nom pl masc part aor act
7. **ἐπιστᾶσα** epistasa nom sing fem part aor act
8. **ἐφέστηκεν** ephestēken 3sing indic perf act
9. **ἐφεστώς** ephestōs nom sing masc part perf act
10. **ἐφεστῶτα** ephestōta acc sing masc part perf act
11. **ἐφίσταται** ephistatai 3sing indic pres mid

1 And, lo, the angel of the Lord **came upon** them,... Luke 2:9
7 And she **coming** in that instant gave thanks............ 2:38
5 And he **stood** over her, and rebuked the fever;........ 4:39
7 and **came** to him, and said, Lord,..................... 10:40
2 the chief priests and the scribes **came upon** him...... 20:1
3 and so that day **come** upon you unawares........... 21:34
2 two men **stood** by them in shining garments:......... 24:4
2 and the Sadducees, **came upon** them,............... Acts 4:1
6 the scribes, and **came upon** him, and caught him,...... 6:12
2 had made inquiry ... and **stood** before the gate,....... 10:17
2 men already come unto the house where I was,....... 11:11
1 behold, the angel of the Lord **came upon** him,........ 12:7
6 and **assaulted** the house of Jason,..................... 17:5
5 Came unto me, and **stood**, and said unto me,........ 22:13
9 I also was **standing by**, and consenting,............... 22:20
5 And the night following the Lord **stood by** him,..... 23:11
5 then **came** I with an army, and rescued him,........ 23:27
10 because of the **present** rain, and ... the cold......... 28:2
11 then sudden destruction **cometh** upon them,........ 1 Th 5:3

| 4 | Preach the word; be instant in season, | 2 Tm 4:2 |
| 8 | and the time of my departure is at hand. | 4:6 |

Classical Greek

Ephistēmi is a compound word (*epi* [1894], "on" or "upon," + *histēmi* [2449], "to stand"). In classical Greek *ephistēmi* can mean "to stand by or near." In the Third Century B.C. it was used in ancient papyri to indicate "delaying" or "holding up" (cf. *Moulton-Milligan*). Many times it is used of someone or something coming suddenly upon an individual or a thing. It can also mean "to be in authority over" or "to be in charge of" something.

Septuagint Usage

In the Septuagint *ephistēmi* is used in several ways. Many times it means "to stand by or beside" (Genesis 24:43; Numbers 23:6,17; 1 Samuel 22:17 [LXX 1 Kings 22:17]; 2 Samuel 1:10 [LXX 2 Kings 1:10]; Amos 9:1), "to stand before" (Judges 3:19), or "to stand among" (Zechariah 1:10,11). On a number of occasions *ephistēmi* means "to appoint" (Leviticus 26:16; Numbers 1:50; Isaiah 1:26), "to set someone in authority over others" (Exodus 1:11; Isaiah 3:4), or "to stand over another in authority" (1 Samuel 17:51 [LXX 1 Kings 17:51]). *Ephistēmi* can also mean "to give attention to" or "to pay attention" (Exodus 7:23; Nehemiah 8:13; Isaiah 41:22), and it is sometimes used to express opposition (Leviticus 17:10; 19:16; 20:3,5,6; 26:17). The setting in place of gates (Joshua 6:26; 1 Kings 16:34 [LXX 3 Kings 16:34]; Nehemiah 6:1), stones (Joshua 7:26; 8:29), monuments (1 Chronicles 18:3), and even a snare (Jeremiah 5:27) are described by the use of *ephistēmi*.

New Testament Usage

In the New Testament *ephistēmi* occurs primarily in the writings of Luke. It can denote the arrival of supernatural messengers (Luke 2:9; 24:4; Acts 12:7) or a less spectacular arrival (Luke 10:40; Acts 11:11). It is used to describe a sudden arrival, many times involving hostility (Luke 4:39; 20:1; Acts 4:1; 6:12; 17:5; 23:27), or an imminent departure (2 Timothy 4:6). *Ephistēmi* can also mean "to stand before or by someone or something" (Acts 10:17; 22:13,20; 23:11). The coming of sudden destruction or judgment is prophesied by the use of *ephistēmi* (Luke 21:34; 1 Thessalonians 5:3). And 2 Timothy 4:2 admonishes the believer to *always be prepared* to preach the Word.

STRONG 2186, BAUER 330-31, MOULTON-MILLIGAN 269, LIDDELL-SCOTT 745.

2169. Ἐφραΐμ Ephraim name

Ephraim.

1. Ἐφραΐμ Ephraim masc

1 near to the wilderness, into a city called **Ephraim**,..John 11:54

The name of a village near the desert where Jesus withdrew with His disciples (John 11:54).

2170. ἐφφαθά ephphatha verb

Be opened.

1. ἐφφαθά ephphatha

1 and saith unto him, **Ephphatha**, that is, Be opened. Mark 7:34

This is the Greek spelling of an Aramaic imperative verb *ethpethoch* which means "be opened!" Mark (7:34) translates it by the Greek word *dianoichtheti* (see 1266) which also means "be opened!" In this passage the inoperative eyes and ears of the deaf and dumb man were considered closed; hence this term describes their healing.

STRONG 2188, BAUER 331, COLIN BROWN 2:560-729.

2170B. ἐχθές echthes adv

Yesterday.

אֶמֶשׁ 'emesh (582), Yesterday evening (Gn 19:34); yesterday (2 Kgs 9:26).

אֶתְמוֹל 'ethmôl (896II), Previously, formerly (1 Sm 19:7, 2 Sm 5:2); yesterday (Ps 90:4 [89:4]).

תְּמוֹל t\`môl (8873), Before, formerly (Ex 5:7, Jos 3:4, 1 Chr 11:2).

1. ἐχθες echthes

1	"Yesterday at the seventh hour (NASB)	John 4:52
1	as you killed the Egyptian yesterday? (NIV)	Acts 7:28
1	the same yesterday and today, (NASB)	Heb 13:8

Echthes is an adverb denoting the time of action for the verb it modifies, e.g., "the day before the present" (John 4:52; Acts 7:28). It is used of the past in its entirety in Hebrews 13:8, "Jesus Christ the same yesterday (from eternity), and today, and for ever." (See word study *chthes* [5340].)

BAUER 331, MOULTON-MILLIGAN 269, LIDDELL-SCOTT 748.

2171. ἔχθρα echthra noun

Enmity, hostility.

CROSS-REFERENCE:
  ἐχθρός echthros (2172)

ἐχθρός 2172

אָיַב ’āyav (342), Be an enemy (Is 63:10, Mi 2:8).
אֵיבָה ’êvāh (343), Enmity (Gn 3:15, Nm 35:22).
אַף ’aph (653), Anger (Ez 35:11).
אָרַב ’ōrev (720), Ambush (Jer 9:8).
שִׂנְאָה sin’āh (7985), Hatred (Nm 35:20, Prv 10:18, 26:26).

1. ἔχθρα echthra nom sing fem
2. ἔχθρᾳ echthra dat sing fem
3. ἔχθραν echthran acc sing fem
4. ἔχθραι echthrai nom pl fem

```
2  before they were at enmity between themselves.....Luke 23:12
1  Because the carnal mind is enmity against God:.....Rom 8:7
4  Idolatry, witchcraft, hatred, variance, emulations,.....Gal 5:20
3  Having abolished in his flesh the enmity,..............Eph 2:15
3  having slain the enmity thereby:......................    2:16
1  the friendship of the world is enmity with God?......Jas 4:4
```

Classical Greek

This noun (cf. the adjective *echthros* [2172]) refers to "enmity, hatred" or "hostility" in ancient Greek. Papyri suggest the lesser sense of "quarrel" might be intended when *echthra* is qualified by *idios* (2375), "private" or "personal" (cf. *Moulton-Milligan*). Nonetheless, national/ethnic hatred is clearly understood in some instances (e.g., the Hellenistic Greek of Josephus' *Antiquities* 4.2.4).

Septuagint Usage

Echthra (Hebrew *’êvāh*) characterizes the relationship God enacted between the woman and the serpent (Genesis 3:15). The strong impulse behind enmity is related in Numbers where the distinction is made between murder prompted by *echthra* and murder without it (35:20,22). (Compare the implied intensity of *echthra* in Proverbs 6:35 which sees reconciliation or compensation for a state of enmity impossible.)

New Testament Usage

Apart from theologically insignificant texts like Luke 23:12 and the nondescript use in Galatians 5:20 (one item in a "sin list"), the New Testament speaks most plainly, through Paul and James, that sinful humanity is at "enmity" with God. Either the sinful nature (Romans 8:7) or the past or present affiliations (James 4:4; cf. Ephesians 2:14ff.) prevent fellowship with God; i.e., they cause enmity. But Christ, through His sacrificial death, has "broken down the middle wall of partition (or hatred, *echthra*)" between humanity (Jews and Gentiles) and between God and mankind (Ephesians 2:14). He has reconciled believers to God and has brought the hostility (*echthra*) to an end (Ephesians 2:16).

STRONG 2189, BAUER 331, MOULTON-MILLIGAN 269, KITTEL 2:815, LIDDELL-SCOTT 748, COLIN BROWN 1:553-55.

2172. ἐχθρός echthros adj

Hated, hostile; an enemy, the enemy (Satan).

COGNATE:
ἔχθρα echthra (2171)

SYNONYM:
ἀντίδικος antidikos (473)

אָיַב ’āyav (342), Be an enemy to (Ex 23:22).
אֵיבָה ’êvāh (343), Enmity (Ez 35:5).
אָכַל ’ākhal (404), Devour (Jer 30:16 [37:16]—Codex Sinaiticus only).
אָרַב ’ārav (717), Lie in wait (1 Sm 22:8,13).
גּוֹי gôy (1504), Nation (Zec 9:10).
זָר zār (2299), Stranger (Prv 6:1).
מַת math (5139), Men (Ps 17:14 [16:14]).
עָר ‘ār (A6384), Enemy (Dn 4:19 [4:16]—Aramaic).
צָמַת tsāmath (7059), Hiphil: destroy (Ps 69:4 [68:4]).
צַר tsar (7141), Adversary, enemy (Dt 33:7, 2 Sm 24:13, Ez 39:23).
צָרַר tsārar (7173), Be hostile toward (Is 11:13); enemy (Est 9:10, Ps 6:7).
קוּם qûm (7251), Hithpael: rise up (Ps 139:21 [138:21]).
רַע rā‘ (7737II) Evil (Prv 20:22).
שָׂנֵא sānē’ (7983), Qal: hate (Jb 8:22); enemy (Ex 23:5, Prv 25:21); piel: hater (Ps 81:15 [80:15]).
שׁוֹרֵר shôrēr (8234), Enemy (Ps 92:11 [91:11]).

1. ἐχθρός echthros nom sing masc
2. ἐχθροῦ echthrou gen sing masc
3. ἐχθρόν echthron acc sing masc
4. ἐχθρέ echthre voc sing masc
5. ἐχθροί echthroi nom pl masc
6. ἐχθρῶν echthrōn gen pl masc
7. ἐχθρούς echthrous acc pl masc

```
3  love thy neighbour, and hate thine enemy..........Matt 5:43
7  But I say unto you, Love your enemies,...............   5:44
5  a man's foes shall be they of his own household.......10:36
1  his enemy came and sowed tares among the wheat,....13:25
1  He said unto them, An enemy hath done this..........13:28
1  The enemy that sowed them is the devil;.............13:39
7  till I make thine enemies thy footstool?............22:44
7  till I make thine enemies thy footstool......Mark 12:36
6  That we should be saved from our enemies,........Luke 1:71
6  we being delivered out of the hand of our enemies.... 1:74
7  Love your enemies, do good to them which hate......  6:27
7  But love ye your enemies, and do good, and lend,....  6:35
2  and over all the power of the enemy:.................10:19
7  But those mine enemies, which would not that I......19:27
5  that thine enemies shall cast a trench about thee,.....19:43
7  Till I make thine enemies thy footstool..............20:43
7  Until I make thy foes thy footstool...............Acts 2:35
4  thou enemy of all righteousness,......................13:10
5  when we were enemies, we were reconciled to God..Rom 5:10
5  they are enemies for your sakes,.....................11:28
1  Therefore if thine enemy hunger, feed him;...........12:20
7  reign, till he hath put all enemies under his feet....1 Co 15:25
```

1 The last enemy that shall be destroyed is death.....	1 Co 15:26
1 become your enemy, because I tell you the truth?....	Gal 4:16
7 that they are the enemies of the cross of Christ:.....	Phlp 3:18
7 and enemies in your mind by wicked works,.........	Col 1:21
7 Yet count him not as an enemy,.....................	2 Th 3:15
3 until I make thine enemies thy footstool?...........	Heb 1:13
5 expecting till his enemies be made his footstool.......	10:13
1 a friend of the world is the enemy of God...........	Jas 4:4
7 of their mouth, and devoureth their enemies:.......	Rev 11:5
5 they ascended ... and their enemies beheld them......	11:12

Classical Greek
The adjective *ekthros* means "hostile, hated." Perhaps it was related to *ektos* (1609), "outside." (See article on *echthra* [2171], "enmity.")

Septuagint Usage
The Septuagint records *echthros* more than 450 times. Among other terms it is regularly an equivalent to the Hebrew *'āyav*. In the Old Testament "enemies" usually refer to enemies of Israel; consequently these "enemies" were God's enemies because they opposed the chosen people (Exodus 23:22; Joshua 7:8; 2 Samuel 12:14 [LXX 2 Kings 12:14]). But *echthros* may equally refer to personal enemies. The ungodly are enemies of the pious (Psalms 5:8f.; 55:3 [LXX 54:3]).

New Testament Usage
Echthros functions in different capacities in the New Testament, but primarily it refers to those who oppose God. The unsaved are "alienated and enemies" because of their hostile minds and their evil deeds (Colossians 1:21).

The enemy of God inherently is an enemy of Christ (Romans 15:3; cf. Psalm 69:9). In one of His parables Jesus indirectly warned of the judgment that will come upon His enemies—those who do not want God as their ruler (Luke 19:27). All the Synoptic Evangelists record Jesus' citation of Psalm 110:1: "The LORD said unto my Lord, Sit thou at my right hand, until I make thine *enemies* thy footstool" (Matthew 22:41f.; Mark 12:35f.; Luke 20:42f.).

The one believing in Christ will encounter his own personal enemies, above all, the devil (Matthew 13:39; cf. Ephesians 6:11; 1 Peter 5:8). Likewise, the world will hate the believer (cf. John 7:7; James 4:4). Even a believer's own family may become his enemy (Matthew 10:36). The last enemy to be defeated is death (1 Corinthians 15:26).

The believer is responsible to pray for personal enemies (Matthew 5:44). He should try to win them by overcoming evil with good (Romans 12:20).

STRONG 2190, BAUER 331, MOULTON-MILLIGAN 270, KITTEL 2:811-14, LIDDELL-SCOTT 748, COLIN BROWN 1:553-54.

2173. ἔχιδνα echidna noun
Poisonous snake, viper, adder.

1. ἔχιδνα echidna nom sing fem
2. ἐχιδνῶν echidnōn gen pl fem

2 he said unto them, O generation of vipers,..........	Matt 3:7
2 O generation of vipers,..............................	12:34
2 Ye serpents, ye generation of vipers,.................	23:33
2 O generation of vipers, who hath warned you.......	Luke 3:7
1 a viper out of the heat, and fastened on his hand...	Acts 28:3

Translated "viper" in the KJV, this term is always used in the negative sense, whether of reptile (Acts 28:3) or, metaphorically, of people (e.g., Matthew 3:7; 12:34; 23:33; Luke 3:7). *Echidna* focuses on the evil, dangerous character of the creature in contrast to the more common word for snake, *ophis* (3653).

STRONG 2191, BAUER 331, MOULTON-MILLIGAN 270, KITTEL 2:815-16, LIDDELL-SCOTT 748.

2174. ἔχω echō verb
Have, hold, keep, preserve, possess, cling to.

COGNATES:
    ἀνέχομαι anechomai (428)
    ἀντέχομαι antechomai (469)
    ἀπέχω apechō (563)
    ἕξις hexis (1821B)
    ἐξοχή exochē (1835)
    ἐπέχω epechō (1892)
    κακουχέω kakoucheō (2529)
    κατέχω katechō (2692)
    μετέχω metechō (3218)
    παρέχω parechō (3792)
    περιέχω periechō (3886)
    περιοχή periochē (3905)
    προέχω proechō (4143)
    προσέχω prosechō (4196)
    συγκακουχέομαι sunkakoucheomai (4629)
    συνευωχέομαι suneuōcheomai (4760)
    συνέχω sunechō (4762)
    συνοχή sunochē (4779)
    ὑπερέχω huperechō (5080)
    ὑπεροχή huperochē (5085)
    ὑπέχω hupechō (5092)

SYNONYMS:
    ἀναλογίζω analogizō (355)
    ἀντέχομαι antechomai (469)
    ἁρπάζω harpazō (720)
    βλέπω blepō (984)
    βουλεύομαι bouleuomai (1003)
    διαλογίζομαι dialogizomai (1254)
    δοκέω dokeō (1374)
    δράσσομαι drassomai (1399)
    εἶδον eidon (1481)
    ἐνθυμέομαι enthumeomai (1744)

ἔχω 2174

ἐπέχω epechō (1892)
ἐπιβλέπω epiblepō (1899)
ἐπιλαμβάνομαι epilambanomai (1934)
ἡγέομαι hēgeomai (2216)
καταλαμβάνω katalambanō (2608)
κατανοέω katanoeō (2627)
κατέχω katechō (2692)
κρατέω krateō (2875)
κρίνω krinō (2892)
λαμβάνω lambanō (2956)
λογίζομαι logizomai (3023)
νοέω noeō (3401)
νομίζω nomizō (3406)
οἴομαι oiomai (3496)
πιάζω piazō (3945)
συλλαμβάνω sullambanō (4666)
συμβάλλω sumballō (4671)
συμβουλεύω sumbouleuō (4674)
συναρπάζω sunarpazō (4734B)
φρονέω phroneō (5262)

אָהֵב 'āhēv (154), Love (Prv 1:22).
אָחַז 'āchaz (270), Seize, take hold of (Jb 18:20, 21:6, 30:16).
אַחַר 'achar (313), After (Gn 41:23, 2 Sm 21:1).
אִיתַי 'îthay (A390), Are (Dn 3:15—Aramaic).
אֵצֶל 'ētsel (703), Beside, by (Lv 6:10, 1 Kgs 1:9, Ez 1:19).
אֵת 'ēth (882), Near (Jgs 4:11).
בַּעַל bā'al (1195), Have (Dn 8:6,20).
דָּבַק dāvaq (1740), Holdfast (Dt 30:20).
הָיָה hāyâh (2030), Be (Ex 28:32 [28:28]); become (Jb 30:9).
הִנֵּה hinnēh (2079), Behold! Lo! (Gn 8:11, 18:10, Is 62:11).
חָבַר chāvar (2357), Join (Ex 26:3).
חָזַק chāzaq (2480), Be strong; hiphil: holdfast (Jb 2:3).
חָלַק chālaq (2606), Piel: distribute (Jb 21:17).
יָאַל yā'al (3082), Hiphil: take on (Gn 18:31).
יֵשׁ yēsh (3552), Is (Gn 23:8, Nm 22:29).
כּוּן kûn (3679), Niphal: be prepared (Neh 8:10).
כָּתַב kāthav (3918), Write (Jb 31:35).
לְבוּשׁ levûsh (3961), Clothes (Est 4:2).
לָקַח lāqach (4089), Bring (Gn 38:23); take (Hos 13:11, Am 6:13 [6:14]).
מוּל mûl (4272II) Opposite (Dt 11:30).
מָחֳרָת mochŏrāth (4420), The next day (1 Chr 10:8).
מָלַט mālaṭ (4561), Let escape, save; hithpael: escape (Jb 19:20).
מָצָא mātsā' (4834), Qal: find (Ex 33:12, Prv 28:23); niphal: be in a certain place (Gn 19:15).
נֶגֶד neghedh (5224), Opposite (Ez 42:1).
נָשָׂא nāsā' (5558), Set (Dt 24:15); carry (Jos 6:8 [6:7]).
נָתַן nāthan (5598), Give (Est 3:11).
עַל 'al (6142), Next to (Nm 2:5,12); on (Nm 7:9).

עִם 'im (6196), From (Jgs 9:37); near (2 Sm 13:23).
עָצַר 'ātsar (6352), Recover (2 Chr 13:20).
צָפַן tsāphan (7121), Conceal (Jb 10:13).
רַב rav (7521), Enough (Nm 16:3).
רָבַץ rāvats (7547), Lie (Gn 49:25).
שִׂים sîm (7947), Set (Jer 9:8).
שָׁכַב shākhav (8311), Qal: ravish (Dt 28:30); niphal: be ravished (Is 13:16).
שָׁלוֹם shālôm (8361), Welfare (Gn 43:27).

1. ἔχω echō 1sing indic/subj pres act
2. ἔχετε echete 2pl indic/impr pres act
3. ἔχεις echeis 2sing indic pres act
4. ἔχει echei 3sing indic pres act
5. ἔχομεν echomen 1pl indic pres act
6. ἔχουσιν echousin 3pl indic pres act
7. ἔχῃ echē 3sing subj pres act
8. ἔχωμεν echōmen 1pl subj pres act
9. ἔχητε echēte 2pl subj pres act
10. ἔχωσιν echōsin 3pl subj pres act
11. ἔχοι echoi 3sing opt pres act
12. ἔχοιεν echoien 3pl opt pres act
13. ἔχε eche 2sing impr pres act
14. ἐχέτω echetō 3sing impr pres act
15. ἔχοντα echonta nom/acc sing/pl masc/neu part pres act
16. ἔχοντος echontos gen sing masc/neu part pres act
17. ἔχων echōn nom sing masc part pres act
18. ἔχοντι echonti dat sing masc part pres act
19. ἔχοντες echontes nom pl masc part pres act
20. ἐχόντων echontōn gen pl masc part pres act
21. ἔχοντας echontas acc pl masc part pres act
22. ἔχουσα echousa nom sing fem part pres act
23. ἐχούσης echousēs gen sing fem part pres act
24. ἐχούσῃ echousē dat sing fem part pres act
25. ἔχουσαν echousan acc sing fem part pres act
26. ἔχουσαι echousai nom pl fem part pres act
27. ἐχούσαις echousais dat pl fem part pres act
28. ἔχον echon nom/acc sing neu part pres act
29. ἔχειν echein inf pres act
30. ἔσχον eschon 1/3sing/pl indic aor act
31. ἔσχες esches 2sing indic aor act
32. ἔσχεν eschen 3sing indic aor act
33. σχῶ schō 1sing subj aor act
34. ἔσχηκα eschēka 1sing indic perf act
35. ἔσχηκεν eschēken 3sing indic perf act
36. ἐσχήκαμεν eschēkamen 1pl indic perf act
37. ἐσχηκότα eschēkota acc sing masc part perf act
38. ἕξεις hexeis 2sing indic fut act
39. ἕξει hexei 3sing indic fut act
40. ἕξετε hexete 2pl indic fut act
41. ἕξουσιν hexousin 3pl indic fut act
42. εἶχον eichon 1/3sing/pl indic imperf act
43. εἶχες eiches 2sing indic imperf act

ἔχω 2174

44. εἶχεν eichen 3sing indic imperf act
45. εἶχε eiche 3sing indic imperf act
46. εἴχομεν eichomen 1pl indic imperf act
47. εἴχετε eichete 2pl indic imperf act
48. ἐχομένῃ echomenē dat sing fem part pres mid
49. ἐχομένας echomenas acc pl fem part pres mid
50. ἐχόμενα echomena nom/acc pl neu part pres mid
51. ἔχουσι echousi 3pl indic pres act
52. ἔσχομεν eschomen 1pl indic aor act
53. σχῶμεν schōmen 1pl subj aor act
54. σχῆτε schēte 2pl subj aor act
55. εἴχοσαν eichosan 3pl indic imperf act
56. εἶχαν eichan 1/3sing/pl indic imperf act

22	she was found with child of the Holy Ghost. (NT) Matt	1:18
39	Behold, a virgin shall be with child,	1:23
44	And the same John had his raiment of camel's hair,	3:4
5	think not ... We have Abraham to our father:	3:9
1	I have need to be baptized of thee,	3:14
21	and they brought unto him all sick people (NT)	4:24
4	there rememberest that thy brother hath ought	5:23
2	love them which love you, what reward have ye?	5:46
1	otherwise ye have no reward of your Father	6:1
2	your Father knoweth what things ye have need of,	6:8
17	For he taught them as one having authority,	7:29
17	a man under authority, having soldiers under me:	8:9
21	cast out the spirits ... and healed all that were sick:	8:16
6	The foxes have holes, and the birds ... have nests:	8:20
4	but the Son of man hath not where to lay his head.	8:20
4	that ye may know that the Son of man hath power	9:6
6	They that be whole need not a physician, (NT)	9:12
19	whole need not a physician, but they that are sick.	9:12
15	scattered abroad, as sheep having no shepherd.	9:36
17	He that hath ears to hear, let him hear.	11:15
4	John came ... and they say, He hath a devil.	11:18
17	there was a man which had his hand withered.	12:10
39	that shall have one sheep,	12:11
44	stony places, where they had not much earth:	13:5
29	because they had no deepness of earth:	13:5
29	and because they had no root, they withered away.	13:6
17	Who hath ears to hear, let him hear.	13:9
4	For whosoever hath, to him shall be given,	13:12
4	but whosoever hath not, from him shall be taken	13:12
4	from him shall be taken away even that he hath.	13:12
4	Yet hath he not root in himself,	13:21
4	from whence then hath it tares?	13:27
17	Who hath ears to hear, let him hear.	13:43
4	for joy thereof goeth and selleth all that he hath,	13:44
44	went and sold all that he had, and bought it.	13:46
29	John said ... It is not lawful for thee to have her.	14:4
42	because they counted him as a prophet.	14:5
6	They need not depart; give ye them to eat. (NT)	14:16
5	We have here but five loaves, and two fishes.	14:17
21	and brought unto him all that were diseased;	14:35
19	having with them those that were lame,	15:30
6	with me now three days, and have nothing to eat.	15:32
2	Jesus saith unto them, How many loaves have ye?	15:34
2	because you have no bread? (NASB)	16:8
4	for he is a lunatic, and sore vexed:	17:15
9	If ye have faith as a grain of mustard seed,	17:20
15	rather than having two hands or two feet to be cast	18:8
15	than having two eyes to be cast into hell fire.	18:9
16	But forasmuch as he had not to pay,	18:25
44	and his wife, and children, and all that he had,	18:25
4	and his wife, and children, and all that he had,	18:25
1	good thing shall I do, that I may have eternal life?	19:16
33	good thing shall I do, that I may have eternal life?	19:16
38	and thou shalt have treasure in heaven:	19:21
17	went away sorrowful: for he had great possessions.	19:22
4	ye shall say, The Lord hath need of them;	21:3
9	If ye have faith, and doubt not,	21:21
6	we fear the people; for all hold John as a prophet.	21:26
44	But what think ye? A certain man had two sons; Matt	21:28
53	let us kill him, and seize his inheritance. (NASB)	21:38
42	because they took him for a prophet.	21:46
17	in hither not having a wedding garment?	22:12
17	Moses said, If a man die, having no children,	22:24
17	married a wife, deceased, and, having no issue,	22:25
30	whose wife shall she be ... for they all had her.	22:28
27	And woe unto them that are with child,	24:19
3	afraid, ... lo, there thou hast that is thine.	25:25
18	and give it unto him which hath ten talents.	25:28
18	For unto every one that hath shall be given,	25:29
16	but from him that hath not shall be taken away	25:29
4	shall be taken away even that which he hath.	25:29
22	came unto him a woman having an alabaster box	26:7
2	For ye have the poor always with you;	26:11
2	poor always with you; but me ye have not always.	26:11
5	what further need have we of witnesses?	26:65
42	they had then a notable prisoner, called Barabbas.	27:16
2	Pilate said unto them, Ye have a watch:	27:65
17	for he taught them as one that had authority, Mark	1:22
21	they brought unto him all that were diseased,	1:32
21	he healed many that were sick of divers diseases,	1:34
49	he said unto them, Let us go into the next towns,	1:38
4	that ye may know that the Son of man hath power	2:10
6	They that are whole have no need of the physician,	2:17
19	no need of the physician, but they that are sick:	2:17
6	as long as they have the bridegroom with them,	2:19
32	when he had need, and was an hungred,	2:25
17	there was a man there which had a withered hand.	3:1
18	saith unto the man which had the withered hand,	3:3
18	saith unto the man which had the withered hand,	3:3
18	saith unto the man which had the withered hand,	3:3
42	for to touch him, as many as had plagues.	3:10
29	And to have power to heal sicknesses,	3:15
4	scribes ... from Jerusalem said, He hath Beelzebub,	3:22
4	Satan ... he cannot stand, but hath an end.	3:26
4	against the Holy Ghost hath never forgiveness,	3:29
4	Because they said, He hath an unclean spirit.	3:30
44	fell on stony ground, where it had not much earth;	4:5
29	because it had no depth of earth:	4:5
29	and because it had no root, it withered away.	4:6
17	He that hath ears to hear, let him hear.	4:9
4	He that hath ears to hear, let him hear.	4:9
6	And have no root in themselves,	4:17
4	If any man have ears to hear, let him hear.	4:23
7	For he that hath, to him shall be given:	4:25
4	For he that hath, to him shall be given:	4:25
4	and he that hath not, from him shall be taken even	4:25
4	from him shall be taken even that which he hath.	4:25
2	are ye so fearful? how is it that ye have no faith?	4:40
44	Who had his dwelling among the tombs;	5:3
37	was possessed with the devil, and had the legion,	5:15
4	My little daughter lieth at the point of death: (NT)	5:23
29	It is not lawful for thee to have thy brother's wife	6:18
15	because they were as sheep not having a shepherd:	6:34
6	buy themselves bread: ... they have nothing to eat.	6:36
2	He saith unto them, How many loaves have ye?	6:38
21	began to carry about in beds those that were sick,	6:55
4	If any man have ears to hear, let him hear.	7:16
44	whose young daughter had an unclean spirit,	7:25
20	and having nothing to eat,	8:1
6	been with me three days, and have nothing to eat:	8:2
2	How many loaves have ye? And they said, Seven.	8:5
42	And they had a few small fishes: and he blessed,	8:7
56	And they had a few small fishes: and he blessed,	8:7
42	neither had they in the ship	8:14
5	saying, It is because we have no bread.	8:16
6	saying, It is because we have no bread.	8:16
2	Why reason ye, because ye have no bread?	8:17
2	have ye your heart yet hardened?	8:17
19	Having eyes, see ye not?	8:18
19	having ears, hear ye not? and do ye not remember?	8:18
15	unto thee my son, which hath a dumb spirit;	9:17
15	than having two hands to go into hell,	9:43
15	than having two feet to be cast into hell,	9:45
15	than having two eyes to be cast into hell fire:	9:47
2	Salt is good: but if the salt have lost his saltness,	9:50

ἔχω 2174

3	sell whatsoever thou **hast**, and give to the poor, ..	Mark 10:21
38	and thou **shalt have** treasure in heaven:	10:21
17	went away grieved: for he **had** great possessions.	10:22
19	How hardly shall they that **have** riches enter	10:23
4	say ye that the Lord **hath** need of him;	11:3
25	And seeing a fig tree afar off **having** leaves, ...	11:13
2	answering saith unto them, **Have** faith in God.	11:22
2	forgive, if **ye have** ought against any:	11:25
42	for all men **counted** John, that he was a prophet	11:32
17	**Having** yet therefore one son, his wellbeloved, ...	12:6
44	**Having** yet therefore one son, his wellbeloved, ...	12:6
30	whose wife ... for the seven **had** her to wife.	12:23
44	but she of her want did cast in all that **she had**, ...	12:44
27	But woe to them that **are** with child, ...	13:17
22	there came a woman **having** an alabaster box	14:3
2	For **ye have** the poor with you always, ...	14:7
2	ye may do them good: but me **ye have** not always.	14:7
44	She hath done what she **could**:	14:8
32	She hath done what she could:	14:8
5	What need we any further witnesses? (NT)	14:63
44	for they trembled and were amazed: (NT)	16:8
41	lay hands on the sick, and **they shall** recover.	16:18
5	We **have** Abraham to our father: for I say	Luke 3:8
17	He that **hath** two coats, let him impart to him that	3:11
18	two coats, let him impart to him that **hath** none;	3:11
17	and he that **hath** meat, let him do likewise.	3:11
17	which **had** a spirit of an unclean devil, ...	4:33
42	all they that **had** any sick with divers diseases	4:40
4	that ye may know that the Son of man **hath** power ...	5:24
6	They that are whole need not a physician; (NT)	5:31
19	need not a physician; but they that **are** sick.	5:31
18	and said to the man which **had** the withered hand, ...	6:8
17	who was dear unto him, **was** sick, and ready to die.	7:2
17	under authority, **having** under me soldiers, ...	7:8
4	For John ... came ... and ye say, He **hath** a devil.	7:33
1	I **have** somewhat to say unto thee. And he saith, ...	7:40
20	when they **had** nothing to pay, he ... forgave them	7:42
29	it withered away, because it lacked moisture. (NT)	8:6
17	he cried, He that **hath** ears to hear, let him hear.	8:8
6	and these **have** no root, which for a while believe, ...	8:13
7	for whosoever **hath**, to him shall be given;	8:18
7	and whosoever **hath** not, from him shall be taken	8:18
29	shall be taken even that which he seemeth **to have**.	8:18
44	which **had** devils long time, and ware no clothes, ...	8:27
17	which **had** devils long time, and ware no clothes, ...	8:27
29	neither money; neither **have** two coats apiece.	9:3
21	and healed them that **had** need of healing.	9:11
6	Foxes **have** holes, and birds of the air have nests;	9:58
4	but the Son of man **hath** not where to lay his head. ...	9:58
39	Which of you **shall have** a friend, ...	11:5
1	and I **have** nothing to set before him?	11:6
28	be full of light, **having** no part dark, ...	11:36
20	and after that have no more that they **can** do.	12:4
15	after he hath killed **hath** power to cast into hell;	12:5
1	because I **have** no room where to bestow my fruits? ..	12:17
3	thou **hast** much goods laid up for many years;	12:19
1	But I **have** a baptism to be baptized with;	12:50
44	certain man **had** a fig tree planted in his vineyard;	13:6
22	which **had** a spirit of infirmity eighteen years, ...	13:11
48	to day, and to morrow, and the day **following**:	13:33
6	shalt be blessed; for **they** cannot recompense thee:	14:14
1	bought ... ground, and I **must** needs go and see it:	14:18
13	needs go and see it: I pray thee **have** me excused.	14:18
13	I go to prove them: I pray thee **have** me excused.	14:19
4	the cost, whether he **have** sufficient to finish it?	14:28
17	He that **hath** ears to hear, let him hear.	14:35
17	What man of you, **having** an hundred sheep, ...	15:4
6	just persons, which need no repentance. (NT)	15:7
22	Either what woman **having** ten pieces of silver, ...	15:8
44	And he said, A certain man **had** two sons;	15:11
44	was a certain rich man, which **had** a steward;	16:1
1	**have** five brethren; that he may testify unto them, ...	16:28
6	**have** Moses and the prophets; let them hear them.	16:29
47	If ye **had** faith as a grain of mustard seed, ...	17:6
2	If ye **had** faith as a grain of mustard seed, ...	17:6
17	**having** a servant plowing or feeding cattle, ...	17:7
4	Doth he thank that servant because he did (NT)	17:9
3	sell all that thou **hast**, and distribute unto the poor,	Luke 18:22
38	and thou **shalt have** treasure in heaven: and come, ...	18:22
19	How hardly **shall** they that **have** riches enter	18:24
17	been faithful ... **have** thou authority over ten cities. ...	19:17
42	thy pound, which I **have kept** laid up in a napkin:	19:20
18	and give it to him that **hath** ten pounds.	19:24
4	And they said unto him, Lord, he **hath** ten pounds. ...	19:25
18	That unto every one which **hath** shall be given;	19:26
16	and from him that **hath** not, even that he hath	19:26
4	even that he **hath** shall be taken away from him.	19:26
4	Because the Lord **hath** need of him.	19:31
4	And they said, The Lord **hath** need of him.	19:34
4	a penny. Whose image and superscription **hath** it?	20:24
17	If any man's brother die, **having** a wife, ...	20:28
30	whose wife ... is she? for seven **had** her to wife.	20:33
44	her penury hath cast in all the living that she **had**.	21:4
27	But woe unto them that **are** with child, ...	21:23
17	But now, he that **hath** a purse, let him take it, ...	22:36
17	he that **hath** no sword, let him sell his garment, ...	22:36
4	for the things concerning me **have** an end.	22:37
5	What need we any further witness? (NT)	22:71
44	he **must** release one unto them at the feast.	23:17
4	and see; for a spirit **hath** not flesh and bones, ...	24:39
15	spirit hath not flesh and bones, as ye see me **have**. ...	24:39
2	he said unto them, Have ye here any meat?	24:41
42	And when they wanted wine, ...	John 2:3
6	They **have** no wine.	2:3
44	And needed not that any should testify (NT)	2:25
7	should not perish, but **have** eternal life.	3:15
7	should not perish, but **have** everlasting life.	3:16
17	He that **hath** the bride is the bridegroom:	3:29
4	He that believeth on the Son **hath** everlasting life:	3:36
3	thou **hast** nothing to draw with, ...	4:11
3	from whence then **hast** thou that living water?	4:11
1	woman answered and said, I **have** no husband.	4:17
1	Thou hast well said, I **have** no husband:	4:17
31	For thou **hast had** five husbands;	4:18
3	and he whom thou now **hast** is not thy husband:	4:18
1	I **have** meat to eat that ye know not of.	4:32
4	that a prophet **hath** no honour in his own country.	4:44
32	inquired ... when he began to amend. (NT)	4:52
22	Bethesda, **having** five porches.	5:2
17	which **had** an infirmity thirty and eight years.	5:5
4	knew that he **had been** ... a long time in that case, ...	5:6
1	I **have** no man, ... to put me into the pool:	5:7
4	**hath** everlasting life, ...	5:24
4	For as the Father **hath** life in himself;	5:26
29	so hath he given to the Son **to have** life in himself;	5:26
1	But I **have** greater witness than that of John:	5:36
2	And ye **have** not his word abiding in you:	5:38
29	for in them ye think ye **have** eternal life:	5:39
9	ye will not come to me, that ye **might have** life.	5:40
2	I know ... that ye **have** not the love of God in you. ...	5:42
4	There is a lad here, which **hath** five barley loaves, ...	6:9
7	believeth on him, **may have** everlasting life:	6:40
4	He that believeth on me **hath** everlasting life.	6:47
2	Except ... drink his blood, ye **have** no life in you.	6:53
4	and drinketh my blood, **hath** eternal life;	6:54
3	thou **hast** the words of eternal life.	6:68
3	The people answered and said, Thou **hast** a devil:	7:20
10	tempting him, that they **might have** to accuse him. ...	8:6
39	but **shall have** the light of life.	8:12
1	I **have** many things to say and to judge of you:	8:26
5	**we have** one Father, even God.	8:41
3	that thou art a Samaritan, and **hast** a devil?	8:48
4	Jesus answered, I **have** not a devil;	8:49
3	Now we know that thou **hast** a devil, ...	8:52
3	Thou **art** not yet fifty years old, ...	8:57
4	he is of age; ask him: he shall speak for himself.	9:21
4	Therefore said his parents, He is of age; ask him.	9:23
47	If ye were blind, ye **should have** no sin:	9:41
10	I am come that they **might have** life, ...	10:10
10	and that they might **have** it more abundantly.	10:10
1	And other sheep I **have**, which are not of this fold: ...	10:16
1	I **have** power to lay it down, ...	10:18
1	and I **have** power to take it again.	10:18
4	And many of them said, He **hath** a devil, ...	10:20

670

ἔχω 2174

15	he **had lain** in the grave four days already....... John	11:17
44	but because he was a thief, and **had** the bag,........	12:6
17	but because he was a thief, and **had** the bag,........	12:6
2	For the poor always ye **have** with you;..............	12:8
2	poor always ye have ... but me ye **have** not always....	12:8
2	Walk while ye **have** the light,.......................	12:35
2	While ye **have** light, believe in the light,..........	12:36
4	**hath** one that judgeth him:.........................	12:48
3	If I wash thee not, thou **hast** no part with me.......	13:8
4	He that is washed needeth not (NT).................	13:10
44	because Judas **had** the bag,.........................	13:29
5	Buy those things that **we have** need of...............	13:29
9	if ye **have** love one to another......................	13:35
17	He that **hath** my commandments,.....................	14:21
4	prince of this world ... and **hath** nothing in me......	14:30
4	Greater love **hath** no man than this,.................	15:13
42	If I had not come ... they **had** not **had** sin:.........	15:22
55	If I had not come ... they **had** not **had** sin:.........	15:22
6	but now they **have** no cloak for their sin.............	15:22
42	I had not done ... works ... they **had** not **had** sin:.....	15:24
55	I had not done ... works ... they **had** not **had** sin:.....	15:24
1	I **have** yet many things to say unto you,..............	16:12
4	All things that the Father **hath** are mine:............	16:15
4	A woman when she is in travail **hath** sorrow,.........	16:21
2	And ye now therefore **have** sorrow:...................	16:22
40	And ye now therefore **have** sorrow:...................	16:22
3	and needest not that any man should ask (NT)......	16:30
9	that in me ye **might have** peace.......................	16:33
2	In the world ye **shall have** tribulation:..............	16:33
40	In the world ye **shall have** tribulation:..............	16:33
42	glory which I **had** with thee before the world was.....	17:5
10	they **might have** my joy fulfilled in themselves........	17:13
17	Then Simon Peter **having** a sword drew it,...........	18:10
5	We **have** a law, and by our law he ought to die,......	19:7
1	knowest thou not that I **have** power to crucify thee,..	19:10
1	to crucify thee, and **have** power to release thee?.....	19:10
43	Thou couldest **have** no power at all against me,......	19:11
4	he that delivered me ... **hath** the greater sin.........	19:11
5	priests answered, We **have** no king but Caesar.......	19:15
9	that believing ye **might have** life through his name....	20:31
2	Jesus saith unto them, Children, **have** ye any meat?...	21:5
28	which is from Jerusalem a sabbath day's journey.... Acts	1:12
42	were together, and **had** all things common;...........	2:44
44	parted them to all men, as every man **had** need.......	2:45
19	and **having** favour with all the people.................	2:47
1	but such as I **have** give I thee:.......................	3:6
42	they **could** say nothing against it......................	4:14
44	unto every man according as he **had** need.............	4:35
4	Then said the high priest, Are these things so?......	7:1
20	came out of many that **were possessed** with them:.....	8:7
4	And here he **hath** authority from the chief priests......	9:14
42	Then **had** the churches rest throughout all Judaea.....	9:31
44	Then **had** the churches rest throughout all Judaea.....	9:31
21	Thou wentest in to men uncircumcised, (NT)........	11:3
29	But she constantly affirmed that it **was** even so......	12:15
42	and they **had** also John to their minister..............	13:5
4	and perceiving that he **had** faith to be healed,........	14:9
4	For Moses of old time **hath** in every city.............	15:21
6	visit our brethren ... and see how they **do**............	15:36
25	certain damsel **possessed with** a spirit of divination....	16:16
11	whether those things were so........................	17:11
44	shorn his head in Cenchrea: for he **had** a vow.........	18:18
21	to call over them which **had** evil spirits the name.....	19:13
6	**have** a matter against any man, the law is open,......	19:38
51	**have** a matter against any man, the law is open,......	19:38
48	and the **next day** we came to Miletus..................	20:15
1	neither **count** I my life dear unto myself,.............	20:24
1	for **I am** ready not to be bound only,.................	21:13
19	We have four men which **have** a vow on them;........	21:23
48	and the **next day** purifying himself with them........	21:26
4	for he **hath** a certain thing to tell him................	23:17
15	who **hath** something to say unto thee.................	23:18
3	What is that thou **hast** to tell me?....................	23:19
25	And he wrote a letter **having** this form: (NASB).....	23:25
15	**to have** nothing laid to his charge worthy of death....	23:29
29	saying that these things **were** so.....................	24:9
17	And **have** hope toward God,.........................	24:15
29	**to have** always a conscience void of offence....... Acts	24:16
17	**to have** always a conscience void of offence..........	24:16
12	and object, if they **had** ought against me.............	24:19
29	to keep Paul, and **to let him have** liberty,.............	24:23
28	Felix trembled, ... Go thy way for this time; (NT)....	24:25
11	he which is accused **have** the accusers face to face,...	25:16
42	**had** certain questions ... of their own superstition,....	25:19
1	I **have** no certain thing to write unto my lord.........	25:26
33	I **might have** somewhat to write......................	25:26
1	I **might have** somewhat to write......................	25:26
15	discovered a certain creek with a shore, (NT)........	27:39
19	others also, which **had** diseases in the island,.........	28:9
17	not that I **had** ought to accuse my nation of..........	28:19
19	and **had** great reasoning among themselves..........	28:29
33	that I **might have** some fruit among you also,...... Rom	1:13
29	they did not like **to retain** God in their knowledge,....	1:28
15	For when the Gentiles, which **have** not the law,......	2:14
19	**having** not the law, are a law unto themselves:........	2:14
15	which **hast** the form of knowledge and of the truth....	2:20
4	he **hath** whereof to glory; but not before God.........	4:2
5	we **have** peace with God through our Lord Jesus	5:1
8	we **have** peace with God through our Lord Jesus	5:1
36	By whom also we **have** access by faith................	5:2
47	What fruit had ye then in those things................	6:21
2	ye **have** your fruit unto holiness......................	6:22
4	Now if any man **have** not the Spirit of Christ,........	8:9
19	which **have** the firstfruits of the Spirit,................	8:23
22	but when Rebecca also **had** conceived by one,........	9:10
4	**Hath** not the potter power over the clay,.............	9:21
6	I bear them record that they **have** a zeal of God,.....	10:2
5	For as we **have** many members in one body,........	12:4
4	and all members **have** not the same office:...........	12:4
19	**Having** then gifts differing according to the grace.....	12:6
38	and thou **shalt have** praise of the same:..............	13:3
3	**Hast** thou faith? have it to thyself before God........	14:22
13	Hast thou faith? **have** it to thyself before God........	14:22
8	and comfort of the scriptures **might have** hope........	15:4
1	I **have** therefore whereof I may glory through Jesus ...	15:17
17	But now **having** no more place in these parts,........	15:23
17	and **having** a great desire these many years..........	15:23
5	But we **have** the mind of Christ..................... I Co	2:16
3	and what **hast** thou that thou didst not receive?......	4:7
9	though ye **have** ten thousand instructors in Christ,.....	4:15
29	that one **should have** his father's wife.................	5:1
17	Dare any of you, **having** a matter against another,.....	6:1
9	ye **have** judgments of things pertaining to this life,....	6:4
2	because ye go to law one with another. (NT).........	6:7
2	which ye **have** of God, and ye are not your own?......	6:19
14	avoid fornication, let every man **have** his own wife,...	7:2
14	and let every woman **have** her own husband..........	7:2
4	But every man **hath** his proper gift of God,...........	7:7
4	If any brother **hath** a wife that believeth not,.........	7:12
4	woman which **hath** an husband that believeth not,....	7:13
1	Now concerning virgins I **have** no commandment.....	7:25
41	Nevertheless such **shall have** trouble in the flesh:.....	7:28
19	they that **have** wives be as though they had none;.....	7:29
19	they that have wives be as though they had none;.....	7:29
17	standeth stedfast in his heart, **having** no necessity,.....	7:37
4	but **hath** power over his own will,.....................	7:37
29	and I think also that I **have** the Spirit of God.........	7:40
5	we know that we all **have** knowledge.................	8:1
15	For if any man see thee which **hast** knowledge........	8:10
5	**Have** we not power to eat and to drink?..............	9:4
5	**Have** we not power to lead about a sister, a wife,......	9:5
5	**have** we not power to forbear working?..............	9:6
1	For if I do this thing willingly, I **have** a reward:......	9:17
17	**having** his head covered, dishonoureth his head.......	11:4
29	**to have** power on her head because of the angels.....	11:10
5	we **have** no such custom, neither the churches........	11:16
2	What? **have** ye not houses to eat and to drink in?....	11:22
21	and shame them that **have** not?......................	11:22
4	For as the body is one, and **hath** many members,.....	12:12
1	cannot say unto the hand, I **have** no need of thee:....	12:21
1	again the head to the feet, I **have** no need of you.....	12:21
4	uncomely parts **have** more abundant comeliness.......	12:23
4	For our comely parts **have** no need:..................	12:24
6	**Have** all the gifts of healing?.........................	12:30

671

ἔχω

1	have not charity, I am become as sounding brass,	1 Co 13:1
1	And though I **have** the gift of prophecy,	13:2
1	and though I **have** all faith,	13:2
1	and **have** not charity, I am nothing.	13:2
1	and **have** not charity, it profiteth me nothing.	13:3
4	every one of you **hath** a psalm, hath a doctrine,	14:26
4	every one of you hath a psalm, **hath** a doctrine,	14:26
4	hath a doctrine, **hath** a tongue, hath a revelation,	14:26
4	hath a doctrine, hath a tongue, **hath** a revelation,	14:26
4	hath a revelation, **hath** an interpretation.	14:26
1	I protest by your rejoicing which I **have** in Christ	15:31
6	for some **have** not the knowledge of God:	15:34
36	But we **had** the sentence of death in ourselves,	2 Co 1:9
9	that ye **might have** a second benefit;	1:15
1	I **should have** sorrow from them of whom	2:3
33	I **should have** sorrow from them of whom	2:3
1	but that ye might know the love which I **have**	2:4
34	I **had** no rest in my spirit,	2:13
5	such trust **have** we through Christ to God-ward:	3:4
19	Seeing then that we **have** such hope,	3:12
19	Therefore seeing we **have** this ministry,	4:1
5	But we **have** this treasure in earthen vessels,	4:7
19	We **having** the same spirit of faith,	4:13
5	we **have** a building of God,	5:1
9	that ye **may have** somewhat to answer	5:12
19	as **having** nothing, and yet possessing all things.	6:10
19	**Having** therefore these promises, dearly beloved,	7:1
35	were come into Macedonia, our flesh **had** no rest,	7:5
29	be a performance also out of that which ye **have**.	8:11
7	it is accepted according to that a man **hath**,	8:12
4	and not according to that he **hath** not.	8:12
19	that ye, always **having** all sufficiency in all things,	9:8
19	**having** in a readiness to revenge all disobedience,	10:6
19	but **having** hope, when your faith is increased,	10:15
1	Behold, the third time **I am** ready to come to you;	12:14
5	spy out our liberty which we **have** in Christ Jesus,	Gal 2:4
32	For it is written, that Abraham **had** two sons,	4:22
23	more children than she which **hath** an husband.	4:27
39	and then **shall** he **have** rejoicing in himself alone,	6:4
5	As we **have** therefore opportunity, let us do good	6:10
8	As we **have** therefore opportunity, let us do good	6:10
5	In whom we **have** redemption through his blood,	Eph 1:7
52	In whom we **have** redemption through his blood,	1:7
19	**having** no hope, and without God in the world:	2:12
5	we both **have** access by one Spirit unto the Father.	2:18
5	In whom we **have** boldness and access	3:12
7	that he **may have** to give to him that needeth.	4:28
18	that he **may have** to give to him that needeth.	4:28
4	**hath** any inheritance in the kingdom of Christ	5:5
25	not **having** spot, or wrinkle, or any such thing;	5:27
29	to think this ... because I **have** you in my heart;	Php 1:7
17	**having** a desire to depart, and to be with Christ;	1:23
19	**Having** the same conflict which ye saw in me,	1:30
19	that ye be likeminded, **having** the same love,	2:2
1	For I **have** no man likeminded,	2:20
33	lest I **should have** sorrow upon sorrow.	2:27
2	Receive him ... and **hold** such in reputation:	2:29
17	Though I might also **have** confidence in the flesh.	3:4
17	found in him, not **having** mine own righteousness,	3:9
2	them which walk so as ye **have** us for an ensample.	3:17
2	the love which you **have** for all the saints, (NASB)	Col 1:4
5	In whom **we have** redemption through his blood,	1:14
1	that ye knew what great conflict I **have** for you,	2:1
15	**have** indeed a show of wisdom in will worship,	2:23
7	if any man **have** a quarrel against any:	3:13
2	knowing that ye also **have** a Master in heaven.	4:1
4	bear him record, that he **hath** a great zeal for you,	4:13
29	so that we need not to speak any thing. (NT)	1 Th 1:8
5	what manner of entering in we **had** unto you,	1:9
52	what manner of entering in we **had** unto you,	1:9
2	and that ye **have** good remembrance of us always,	3:6
2	ye need not that I write unto you: (NT)	4:9
5	ye need not that I write unto you:	4:9
9	and that ye **may have** lack of nothing.	4:12
19	ye sorrow not, even as others which **have** no hope.	4:13
2	ye **have** no need that I write unto you,	5:1
24	as travail upon a woman with child; (NT)	5:3
5	Not because we **have** not power,	2 Th 3:9
1	And I thank Christ Jesus our Lord,	1 Tm 1:12
17	**Holding** faith, and a good conscience;	1:19
15	**having** his children in subjection with all gravity;	3:4
29	Moreover he must **have** a good report	3:7
21	**Holding** the mystery of the faith	3:9
22	**having** promise of the life that now is,	4:8
4	But if any widow **have** children or nephews,	5:4
26	**Having** damnation, because they have cast off	5:12
4	If any man or woman that believeth **have** widows,	5:16
10	rebuke before all, that others also may fear. (NT)	5:20
15	and they that **are** otherwise cannot be hid.	5:25
19	And they that **have** believing masters,	6:2
19	And **having** food and raiment let us be ... content.	6:8
17	Who only **hath** immortality,	6:16
1	I thank God, whom I serve (NT)	2 Tm 1:3
1	that without ceasing I **have** remembrance of thee	1:3
13	Hold fast the form of sound words, (NT)	1:13
39	And their word will eat as doth a canker: (NT)	2:17
5	**having** this seal, The Lord knoweth	2:19
19	**Having** a form of godliness, but denying the power	3:5
17	the husband of one wife, **having** faithful children	Tit 1:6
17	**having** no evil thing to say of you.	2:8
3	and faith, which thou **hast** toward the Lord Jesus,	Phlm 1:5
5	For we **have** great joy and consolation in thy love,	1:7
30	For we **have** great joy and consolation in thy love,	1:7
17	Wherefore, though I might **be** much bold in Christ	1:8
3	If thou **count** me therefore a partner,	1:17
15	him that **had** the power of death, that is, the devil;	Heb 2:14
4	**hath** more honour than the house.	3:3
19	Seeing then that we **have** a great high priest,	4:14
5	**have** not an high priest which cannot be touched	4:15
2	ye **have** need that one teach you again	5:12
19	and are become such as **have** need of milk,	5:12
20	by reason of use **have** their senses exercised	5:14
50	and things that **accompany** salvation,	6:9
44	because he could swear by no greater, (NT)	6:13
8	we might **have** a strong consolation,	6:18
5	Which hope we **have** as an anchor of the soul,	6:19
17	**having** neither beginning of days, nor end of life;	7:3
6	**have** a commandment to take tithes of the people	7:5
15	and blessed him that **had** the promises.	7:6
4	continueth ever, **hath** an unchangeable priesthood.	7:24
4	Who needeth not daily, (NT)	7:27
21	law maketh men high priests which **have** infirmity;	7:28
5	this is the sum: We **have** such an high priest,	8:1
29	that this man **have** somewhat also to offer.	8:3
44	Then verily the first covenant **had** also ordinances	9:1
45	Then verily the first covenant **had** also ordinances	9:1
22	Which **had** the golden censer,	9:4
22	wherein was the golden pot that **had** manna,	9:4
23	while as the first tabernacle **was** yet standing:	9:8
17	the law **having** a shadow of good things to come,	10:1
29	**should have had** no more conscience of sins.	10:2
19	**Having** therefore, brethren, boldness to enter	10:19
29	knowing in yourselves that ye **have** in heaven	10:34
4	which **hath** great recompense of reward.	10:35
2	For ye **have** need of patience,	10:36
25	For he looked for a city which **hath** foundations,	11:10
42	they **might have had** opportunity to have returned.	11:15
29	than to enjoy the pleasures of sin (NT)	11:25
19	Wherefore seeing we also **are** compassed about	12:1
46	**have had** fathers of our flesh which corrected us,	12:9
8	we receiving a kingdom ... let us **have** grace,	12:28
5	we receiving a kingdom ... let us **have** grace,	12:28
5	**have** an altar, whereof they have no right to eat	13:10
6	**have** no right to eat which serve the tabernacle.	13:10
5	For here **have** we no continuing city,	13:14
5	for we trust we **have** a good conscience,	13:18
14	But let patience **have** her perfect work,	Jas 1:4
2	**have** not the faith of our Lord Jesus Christ,	2:1
29	a man say he **hath** faith, and have not works?	2:14
7	a man say he hath faith, and **have** not works?	2:14
7	faith, if it **hath** not works, is dead, being alone.	2:17
3	a man may say, Thou **hast** faith, and I have works:	2:18
1	a man may say, Thou hast faith, and I **have** works:	2:18
2	if ye **have** bitter envying and strife in your hearts,	3:14

ἔχω

2	Ye lust, and **have** not: ye kill, and desire	Jas	4:2
2	yet ye **have** not, because ye ask not.		4:2
19	**Having** your conversation honest	1 Pt	2:12
19	not **using** your liberty for a cloak of maliciousness,		2:16
19	**Having** a good conscience;		3:16
18	him that **is** ready to judge the quick and the dead.		4:5
19	**have** fervent charity among yourselves:		4:8
29	**to have** these things always in remembrance.	2 Pt	1:15
5	We **have** also a more sure word of prophecy;		1:19
19	**Having** eyes full of adultery,		2:14
19	heart they **have** exercised with covetous practices;		2:14
32	But **was** rebuked for his iniquity:		2:16
9	that ye also **may have** fellowship with us:	1 Jn	1:3
5	If we say that **we have** fellowship with him,		1:6
5	we **have** fellowship one with another,		1:7
5	If we say that **we have** no sin,		1:8
5	we **have** an advocate with the Father, Jesus Christ		2:1
47	commandment which ye **had** from the beginning.		2:7
2	But ye **have** an unction from the Holy One,		2:20
4	denieth the Son, the same **hath** not the Father:		2:23
4	the one who confesses the Son **has** the Father (NASB)		2:23
2	and ye need not that any man teach you: (NT)		2:27
8	when he shall appear, we **may have** confidence,		2:28
53	when he shall appear, we **may have** confidence,		2:28
17	And every man that **hath** this hope in him		3:3
4	and ye know that no murderer **hath** eternal life		3:15
7	But whoso **hath** this world's good,		3:17
15	and seeth his brother **have** need,		3:17
5	then **have** we confidence toward God.		3:21
4	known and believed the love that God **hath** to us.		4:16
8	that we **may have** boldness in the day of judgment:		4:17
4	love casteth out fear: because fear **hath** torment.		4:18
5	And this commandment **have** we from him,		4:21
4	He that believeth ... **hath** the witness in himself:		5:10
17	He that **hath** the Son **hath** life;		5:12
4	He that **hath** the Son **hath** life;		5:12
17	and he that **hath** not the Son of God **hath** not life.		5:12
4	and he that **hath** not the Son of God **hath** not life.		5:12
2	that ye may know that ye **have** eternal life,		5:13
5	And this is the confidence that we **have** in him,		5:14
5	that we **have** the petitions that we desired of him.		5:15
46	but that which we **had** from the beginning,	2 Jn	1:5
4	and abideth not in the doctrine ... **hath** not God.		1:9
4	he **hath** both the Father and the Son.		1:9
17	**Having** many things to write unto you,		1:12
1	I **have** no greater joy than to hear that my children	3 Jn	1:4
42	I **had** many things to write, but I will not with ink		1:13
30	it **was** needful for me to write unto you,	Jude	1:3
19	separate themselves, sensual, **having** not the Spirit,		1:19
17	And he **had** in his right hand seven stars:	Rev	1:16
1	and **have** the keys of hell and of death.		1:18
3	And **hast** borne, and **hast** patience,		2:3
1	Nevertheless I **have** somewhat against thee,		2:4
3	But this thou **hast**, that thou hatest the deeds		2:6
17	He that **hath** an ear, let him hear		2:7
40	and ye **shall have** tribulation ten days:		2:10
17	He that **hath** an ear, let him hear.		2:11
17	These things saith he which **hath** the sharp sword		2:12
1	But I **have** a few things against thee,		2:14
3	**hast** there them that hold the doctrine of Balaam,		2:14
3	So **hast** thou also ... doctrine of the Nicolaitanes,		2:15
17	He that **hath** an ear, let him hear		2:17
17	who **hath** his eyes like unto a flame of fire,		2:18
1	Notwithstanding I **have** a few things against thee,		2:20
6	rest in Thyatira, as many as **have** not this doctrine,		2:24
2	that which ye **have** already hold fast till I come.		2:25
17	He that **hath** an ear, let him hear		2:29
17	These things saith he that **hath** the seven Spirits		3:1
3	thou **hast** a name that thou livest, and art dead.		3:1
3	Thou **hast** a few names even in Sardis		3:4
17	He that **hath** an ear, let him hear		3:6
17	he that is true, he that **hath** the key of David,		3:7
3	no man can shut it: for thou **hast** a little strength,		3:8
3	I come quickly: hold that fast which thou **hast**,		3:11
17	He that **hath** an ear, let him hear		3:13
1	increased with goods, and **have** need of nothing;		3:17
17	He that **hath** an ear, let him hear		3:22
30	and they **had** on their heads crowns of gold.	Rev	4:4
28	and the third beast **had** a face as a man,		4:7
17	and the third beast **had** a face as a man,		4:7
42	And the four beasts **had** each of them six wings		4:8
17	And the four beasts **had** each of them six wings		4:8
6	and they rest not day and night, saying, Holy, (NT)		4:8
28	a Lamb ... **having** seven horns and seven eyes,		5:6
17	a Lamb ... **having** seven horns and seven eyes,		5:6
19	**having** every one of them harps, and golden vials		5:8
17	a white horse: and he that sat on him **had** a bow;		6:2
17	and he that sat on him **had** a pair of balances		6:5
42	and for the testimony which they **held**:		6:9
15	**having** the seal of the living God:		7:2
17	another angel came ... **having** a golden censer;		8:3
19	the seven angels which **had** the seven trumpets		8:6
15	creatures which were in the sea, and **had** life, died;		8:9
6	as the scorpions of the earth **have** power.		9:3
6	which **have** not the seal of God in their foreheads.		9:4
42	And they **had** hair as the hair of women,		9:8
42	**had** breastplates, as it were breastplates of iron;		9:9
6	And they **had** tails like unto scorpions,		9:10
6	And they **had** a king over them, which is the angel		9:11
4	but in the Greek tongue **hath** his name Apollyon.		9:11
45	Saying to the sixth angel which **had** the trumpet,		9:14
17	Saying to the sixth angel which **had** the trumpet,		9:14
21	**having** breastplates of fire, and of jacinth,		9:17
26	their tails were like unto serpents, and **had** heads,		9:19
44	And **he had** in his hand a little book open:		10:2
17	And **he had** in his hand a little book open:		10:2
6	These **have** power to shut heaven,		11:6
6	and **have** power over waters to turn them to blood,		11:6
22	And she **being** with child cried, travailing in birth,		12:2
17	red dragon, **having** seven heads and ten horns,		12:3
4	where she **hath** a place prepared of God,		12:6
17	devil is come down unto you, **having** great wrath,		12:12
4	because he knoweth that he **hath** but a short time.		12:12
20	and **have** the testimony of Jesus Christ.		12:17
28	out of the sea, **having** seven heads and ten horns,		13:1
4	If any man **have** an ear, let him hear.		13:9
44	out of the earth; and he **had** two horns like a lamb,		13:11
4	to the beast, which **had** the wound by a sword,		13:14
17	might buy or sell, save he that **had** the mark,		13:17
17	**hath** understanding count the number of the beast:		13:18
26	**having** his Father's name written		14:1
15	**having** the everlasting gospel to preach unto them		14:6
6	and they **have** no rest day nor night,		14:11
17	Son of man, **having** on his head a golden crown,		14:14
17	another angel ... he also **having** a sharp sickle.		14:17
17	out from the altar, which **had** power over fire;		14:18
18	with a loud cry to him that **had** the sharp sickle,		14:18
21	seven angels **having** the seven last plagues;		15:1
21	stand on the sea of glass, **having** the harps of God.		15:2
19	came out of the temple, **having** the seven plagues,		15:6
21	upon the men which **had** the mark of the beast,		16:2
16	God, which **hath** power over these plagues:		16:9
20	one of the seven angels which **had** the seven vials,		17:1
28	beast, ... **having** seven heads and ten horns.		17:3
15	beast, ... **having** seven heads and ten horns.		17:3
22	stones and pearls, **having** a golden cup in her hand		17:4
16	beast ... which **hath** the seven heads and ten horns.		17:7
17	And here is the mind which **hath** wisdom.		17:9
6	These **have** one mind, and shall give their power		17:13
22	which reigneth over the kings of the earth. (NT)		17:18
15	I saw another angel ... **having** great power;		18:1
19	were made rich all that **had** ships in the sea		18:19
20	of thy brethren that **have** the testimony of Jesus:		19:10
17	and he **had** a name written, that no man knew,		19:12
4	he **hath** on his vesture and on his thigh a name		19:16
15	an angel ... **having** the key of the bottomless pit		20:1
17	holy is he that **hath** part in the first resurrection:		20:6
4	on such the second death **hath** no power,		20:6
20	**had** the seven vials full of the seven last plagues,		21:9
25	**Having** the glory of God: and her light was like		21:11
25	**had** a wall great and high, and had twelve gates,		21:12
22	**had** a wall great and high, and had twelve gates,		21:12
25	had a wall great and high, and **had** twelve gates,		21:12
22	had a wall great and high, and **had** twelve gates,		21:12

28 And the wall of the city **had** twelve foundations,	Rev 21:14
17 And the wall of the city **had** twelve foundations,	21:14
44 **had** a golden reed to measure the city,	21:15
4 And the city **had** no need of the sun,	21:23
6 no night there; and they need no candle, (NT)	22:5

Classical Greek

Echō, "I have," or *echein*, "to have," means "to have, hold, or possess." In classical Greek, however, there are so many shades of meaning that the context must be the determining factor.

Septuagint Usage

Echō's usage in the Septuagint is relatively rare. Accordingly, there is no fixed rule employed by the translators where *echō* is used (there are almost 60 Hebrew words or phrases translated by *echō*). However, *echō* still covers (through various Hebrew words it replaces) the full range of meaning in the Septuagint as it does in classical and Hellenistic usage (Hanse, "echō," *Kittel*, 2:817).

New Testament Usage

The New Testament also covers this full range of meaning in its use of *echō*. A sample of *echō*'s many usages is as follows: (1) to have in the hand (Revelation 1:16; 6:5; 10:2); (2) to possess (Matthew 19:21; 26:7; Acts 2:44); (3) to have or possess a wife, husband, relative, or friend (Luke 11:5; 1 Corinthians 7:12,13); (4) to have spiritual gifts or God's Spirit (1 Corinthians 7:7; 12:30 to 13:3); (5) must or have to (Luke 12:50; Acts 23:19); (6) to have a demon (Mark 5:15; 7:25; Luke 7:33; Acts 19:13) (from *Bauer*). Generally speaking, *echō*'s meanings fall within two general categories: spatial and possessional meanings (ibid., 2:816).

In denoting spatial categories, *echō* has a wide range of meanings, yet its principal meaning is "to have" or "to hold." A person, for example, may have a disease or may hold a glass of water (in this sense "having" a glass of water.) The theological significance of this use lies in the material sense of having. The emphasis here is upon something "present." Thus a person may "have" the Holy Spirit in the same sense in which the body has a disease; that is, a disease is present in the body (see Eichler, "Fellowship," *Colin Brown*, 1:636).

The possessional category is also full of significant meaning. A person, for example, may "have" children, a wife, etc.; or God may "have" a chosen people. A dominant sense of spiritual "having" is to be noted in the New Testament. This usage is particularly apparent in the writings of John and Paul. For example, "He that *hath* the Son *hath* life" (1 John 5:12) or "if any man *have* not the Spirit of Christ, he is none of his" (Romans 8:9). The emphasis here falls upon the possession of "life" or the possession of "the Spirit." The reverse is also true; that is, the Spirit may "have" or "possess" a person. This usage is found in the classical Greek writers in reference to demon possession or having a demon. (See Homer, Plato, Plotinus; cf. *Bauer*.) The New Testament also uses the word to denote "having" fellowship with God and one another (1 John 1:3).

Perhaps the most significant New Testament application of *echō* is when it demonstrates the Christian's relationship to God. The Christian is said "to have" (*echō*) God's Spirit (1 Corinthians 7:40). Here it is to be understood that it is not the mind (*nous* [3426], as the Greeks taught) but spirit (*pneuma* [4011]), which God breaths or instills into man at the new birth, which brings real life. In the New Testament, men have *nous*, but only Christians have *pneuma* or, more strictly, "have" a share in the one Spirit of God and of Christ (Hanse, "echō," *Kittel*, 2:816). So man does not possess spirit or life. Even the Christian does not possess it in the individual sense. But he "has" spirit in the *metochos* (3223) (sharing or participating) sense as seen in Hebrews 3:14; 6:4; and 1 John 1:6,7.

So then, Christians "have" God's Spirit which brings God's life, grace, peace, spiritual gifts, and salvation. These things are not possessed individually (for they are God's) but shared (*metochos*) with Christ in God (Colossians 3:2-4, 1 John 5:12). For Christ is the believer's life, and only in Him does the believer live.

STRONG 2192, BAUER 331-34, MOULTON-MILLIGAN 270, KITTEL 2:816-27, LIDDELL-SCOTT 749-51, COLIN BROWN 1:635-638.

2175. ἕως *heōs* conj

Till, until, while, as long as.

1. ἕως *heōs*

1 So all the generations from Abraham to David	Matt 1:17
1 from David **until** the carrying away into Babylon	1:17
1 **unto** Christ are fourteen generations.	1:17
1 And knew her not **till** she had brought forth	1:25
1 star, ... before them, **till** it came and stood over	2:9
1 and be thou there **until** I bring thee word:	2:13
1 And was there **until** the death of Herod:	2:15
1 verily I say unto you, **Till** heaven and earth pass,	5:18
1 in no wise pass from the law, **till** all be fulfilled.	5:18
1 **whiles** thou art in the way with him;	5:25

ἕως 2175

1	till thou hast paid the uttermost farthing	Matt 5:26
1	who ... worthy; and there abide till ye go thence	10:11
1	not ... cities of Israel, till the Son of man be come	10:23
1	And from the days of John the Baptist **until** now	11:12
1	all the prophets and the law prophesied **until** John	11:13
1	Capernaum, which art exalted **unto** heaven,	11:23
1	Capernaum, ... shalt be brought down **to** hell:	11:23
1	till he send forth judgment unto victory	12:20
1	both to grow together **until** the harvest; (NASB)	13:30
1	and hid in ... meal, till the whole was leavened	13:33
1	**while** he sent the multitudes away	14:22
1	till they see the Son of man coming in his kingdom	16:28
1	**until** the Son of man be risen again from the dead	17:9
1	how long shall I be with you? (NT)	17:17
1	how long shall I suffer you? (NT)	17:17
1	and I forgive him? till seven times?	18:21
1	Until seven times: but, Until seventy times seven	18:22
1	Until seven times: but, Until seventy times seven	18:22
1	cast him into prison, till he should pay the debt	18:30
1	till he should pay all that was due unto him	18:34
1	beginning from the last **unto** the first	20:8
1	the second also, and the third, **unto** the seventh	22:26
1	till I make thine enemies thy footstool	22:44
1	**unto** the blood of Zacharias son of Barachias,	23:35
1	Ye shall not see me henceforth, till ye shall say,	23:39
1	not since the beginning of the world **to** this time,	24:21
1	and shineth even **unto** the west;	24:27
1	his elect ... from one end of heaven **to** the other	24:31
1	shall not pass, till all these things be fulfilled	24:34
1	And knew not **until** the flood came,	24:39
1	**until** that day when I drink it new with you	26:29
1	Sit ye here, **while** I go and pray yonder	26:36
1	My soul is exceeding sorrowful, **even unto** death:	26:38
1	followed him afar off **unto** the high priest's palace,	26:58
1	field was called, The field of blood, **unto** this day	27:8
1	was darkness over all the land **unto** the ninth hour	27:45
1	was rent in twain from the top **to** the bottom;	27:51
1	that the sepulchre be made sure **until** the third day,	27:64
1	with you alway, even **unto** the end of the world	28:20
1	there abide till ye depart from that place	Mark 6:10
1	I will give it thee, **unto** the half of my kingdom	6:23
1	**while** he sent away the people	6:45
1	till they have seen the kingdom of God come	9:1
1	how long shall I be with you? (NT)	9:19
1	be with you? how long shall I suffer you? (NT)	9:19
1	till I make thine enemies thy footstool	12:36
1	of the creation which God created **unto** this time,	13:19
1	from ... the earth **to** the uttermost part of heaven	13:27
1	**until** that day that I drink it new in the kingdom	14:25
1	Gethsemane: ... Sit ye here, **while** I shall pray	14:32
1	My soul is exceeding sorrowful **unto** death:	14:34
1	followed ... even into the palace of the high priest	14:54
1	darkness over the whole land **until** the ninth hour	15:33
1	was rent in twain from the top **to** the bottom	15:38
1	and was in the deserts till the day of his showing	Luke 1:80
1	Let us now go even **unto** Bethlehem,	2:15
1	was a widow **until** she was eighty-four. (NIV)	2:37
1	and led him **unto** the brow of the hill	4:29
1	and the people sought him, and came **unto** him,	4:42
1	not taste of death, till they see the kingdom of God	9:27
1	perverse generation, **how long** shall I be with you,	9:41
1	thou, Capernaum, which art exalted **to** heaven,	10:15
1	art exalted to heaven, shalt be thrust down **to** hell	10:15
1	From the blood of Abel **unto** ... blood of Zacharias,	11:51
1	and how am I straitened till it be accomplished!	12:50
1	till thou hast paid the very last mite	12:59
1	let it alone this year also, till I shall dig about it,	13:8
1	woman took and hid ... till the whole was leavened	13:21
1	**until** the time come when ye shall say,	13:35
1	and go after that which is lost, **until** he find it?	15:4
1	and seek diligently till she find it?	15:8
1	The law and the prophets were **until** John:	16:16
1	and serve me, till I have eaten and drunken;	17:8
1	delivered them ten pounds, ... Occupy till I come	19:13
1	Till I make thine enemies thy footstool	20:43
1	This generation shall not pass ... till all be fulfilled	21:32
1	**until** it be fulfilled in the kingdom of God	22:16
1	of the vine, **until** the kingdom of God shall come	Luke 22:18
1	crow ... **until** you have denied three (NASB)	22:34
1	And Jesus answered and said, Suffer ye thus **far**	22:51
1	beginning from Galilee **to** this place	23:5
1	a darkness over all the earth **until** the ninth hour	23:44
1	**until** ye be endued with power from on high	24:49
1	And he led them out **as far as** to Bethany,	24:50
1	And they filled them **up to** the brim	John 2:7
1	but thou hast kept the good wine **until** now	2:10
1	My Father worketh **hitherto**, and I work	5:17
1	beginning at the eldest, even **unto** the last:	8:9
1	the works of him that sent me, **while** it is day:	9:4
1	did not believe ... **until** they called the parents	9:18
1	How long dost thou make us to doubt?	10:24
1	Walk **while** ye have the light,	12:35
1	**While** ye have light, believe in the light,	12:36
1	cock shall not crow, till thou hast denied me thrice	13:38
1	**Hitherto** have ye asked nothing in my name:	16:24
1	If I will that he tarry till I come,	21:22
1	but, If I will that he tarry till I come,	21:23
1	Samaria, and **unto** the uttermost part of the earth	Acts 1:8
1	**unto** that same day that he was taken up from us,	1:22
1	Until I make thy foes thy footstool	2:35
1	**unto** the days of David;	7:45
1	they all gave heed, from the least **to** the greatest,	8:10
1	preached in all the cities, till he came to Caesarea	8:40
1	that he would not delay to come to them	9:38
1	travelled **as far as** Phenice, and Cyprus,	11:19
1	Barnabas, that he should go **as far as** Antioch	11:22
1	**until** Samuel the prophet	13:20
1	be for salvation **unto** the ends of the earth	13:47
1	sent Paul out to go **as far as** the sea (NASB)	17:14
1	that conducted Paul brought him **unto** Athens:	17:15
1	till we were out of the city:	21:5
1	**until** that an offering should be offered	21:26
1	neither eat nor drink till they had killed Paul	23:12
1	that we will eat nothing **until** we have slain Paul	23:14
1	will neither eat nor drink till they have killed him:	23:21
1	ready two hundred soldiers to go to Caesarea,	23:23
1	him to be kept till I might send him to Caesar	25:21
1	I persecuted them even unto strange cities. (NT)	26:11
1	testified ... from morning till evening	28:23
1	there is none that doeth good, no, not one. (NT)	Rom 3:12
1	and ears that they should not hear; **unto** this day	11:8
1	Who shall also confirm you **unto** the end,	1 Co 1:8
1	Therefore judge nothing ... **until** the Lord come,	4:5
1	and are the offscouring of all things **unto** this day	4:13
1	for some with conscience of the idol **unto** this hour	8:7
1	of whom the greater part remain **unto** this present,	15:6
1	But I will tarry at Ephesus **until** Pentecost	16:8
1	and I trust ye shall acknowledge even **to** the end;	2 Co 1:13
1	But even **unto** this day, when Moses is read,	3:15
1	such an one caught up **to** the third heaven	12:2
1	**until** he be taken out of the way	2 Th 2:7
1	Till I come, give attendance to reading,	1 Tm 4:13
1	**until** I make thine enemies thy footstool?	Heb 1:13
1	all shall know me, from the least **to** the greatest	8:11
1	expecting till his enemies be made his footstool	10:13
1	Be patient ... **unto** the coming of the Lord	Jas 5:7
1	**until** he receive the early and latter rain	5:7
1	that shineth in a dark place, **until** the day dawn,	2 Pt 1:19
1	hateth his brother, is in darkness even **until** now	1 Jn 2:9
1	saying, How long, O Lord, holy and true,	Rev 6:10
1	**until** their fellowservants also and their brethren,	6:11
1	But the rest of the dead lived not again **until**	20:5

Heōs serves as a common conjunction and a preposition in classical, Septuagintal, and Biblical Greek. In the New Testament *heōs* has a variety of functions. *Heōs* appears much more frequently in the Gospels and Acts than in the rest of the New Testament.

The majority of occurrences denote the end of a period of time or the beginning of a period of time. When used in this way *heōs* means "until" or "unto." In particular, *heōs* designates the time at which the kingdom of God will be consummated (Matthew 10:23; 16:28; 26:29; Mark 9:1; Luke 9:27). Occasionally *heōs* means "while" (Matthew 14:22; 26:36; Mark 6:45; 14:32; John 9:4). It sometimes is used to ask "how long" (Matthew 17:17; Mark 9:19; Revelation 6:10), and on at least one occasion (Luke 24:50) *heōs* is translated "as far as" (cf. Acts 11:19,22).

STRONG 2193, BAUER 334-35, MOULTON-MILLIGAN 270-71, LIDDELL-SCOTT 751-52.

Manuscripts

Egyptian Papyri

Note: (a) designates the section of the New Testament on which the manuscript is based; (b) designates the century in which it is believed the manuscript was written (using the Roman numerals); (c) provides information on the present location of the manuscript.

p1 (a) Gospels; (b) III; (c) Philadelphia, University of Pennsylvania Museum, no. E2746.

p2 (a) Gospels; (b) VI; (c) Florence, Museo Archeologico, Inv. no. 7134.

p3 (a) Gospels; (b) VI, VII; (c) Vienna, Österreichische Nationalbibliothek, Sammlung Papyrus Erzherzog Rainer, no. G2323.

p4 (a) Gospels; (b) III; (c) Paris, Bibliothèque Nationale, no. Gr. 1120, suppl. 2º.

p5 (a) Gospels; (b) III; (c) London, British Museum, P. 782 and P. 2484.

p6 (a) Gospels; (b) IV; (c) Strasbourg, Bibliothèque de la Université, 351^r, 335^v, 379, 381, 383, 384 copt.

p7 (a) Gospels; (b) V; (c) now lost, was in Kiev, library of the Ukrainian Academy of Sciences.

p8 (a) Acts; (b) IV; (c) now lost; was in Berlin, Staatliche Museen, P. 8683.

p9 (a) General Epistles; (b) III; (c) Cambridge, Massachusetts, Harvard University, Semitic Museum, no. 3736.

p10 (a) Paul's Epistles; (b) IV; (c) Cambridge, Massachusetts, Harvard University, Semitic Museum, no. 2218.

p11 (a) Paul's Epistles; (b) VII; (c) Leningrad, State Public Library.

p12 (a) General Epistles; (b) late III; (c) New York, Pierpont Morgan Library, no. G. 3.

p13 (a) General Epistles; (b) III, IV; (c) London, British Museum, P. 1532 (verso), and Florence, Biblioteca Medicea Laurenziana.

p14 (a) Paul's Epistles; (b) V (?); (c) Mount Sinai, St. Catharine's Monastery, no. 14.

p15 (a) Paul's Epistles; (b) III; (c) Cairo, Museum of Antiquities, no. 47423.

p16 (a) Paul's Epistles; (b) III, IV; (c) Cairo, Museum of Antiquities, no. 47424.

p17 (a) General Epistles; (b) IV; (c) Cambridge, England, University Library, gr. theol. f. 13 (P), Add. 5893.

p18 (a) Revelation; (b) III, IV; (c) London, British Museum, P. 2053 (verso).

p19 (a) Gospels; (b) IV, V; (c) Oxford, Bodleian Library, MS. Gr. bibl. d. 6 (P.).

p20 (a) General Epistles; (b) III; (c) Princeton, New Jersey, University Library, Classical Seminary AM 4117 (15).

p21 (a) Gospels; (b) IV, V; (c) Allentown, Pennsylvania, Library of Muhlenberg College, Theol. Pap. 3.

p22 (a) Gospels; (b) III; (c) Glasgow, University Library, MS. 2-x. 1.

p23 (a) General Epistles; (b) early III; (c) Urbana, Illinois, University of Illinois, Classical Archaeological and Art Museum, G. P. 1229.

p24 (a) Revelation; (b) IV; (c) Newton Center, Massachusetts, Library of Andover Newton Theological School.

p25 (a) Gospels; (b) late IV; (c) now lost, was in Berlin, Staatliche Museen, P. 16388.

p26 (a) Paul's Epistles; (b) c. 600; (c) Dallas, Texas, Southern Methodist University, Lane Museum.

p27 (a) Paul's Epistles; (b) III; (c) Cambridge, England, University Library, Add. MS. 7211.

Manuscripts Continued

p28 (a) Gospels; (b) III; (c) Berkeley, California, Library of Pacific School of Religion, Pap. 2.

p29 (a) Acts; (b) III; (c) Oxford, Bodleian Library, MS. Gr. bibl. g. 4 (P.).

p30 (a) Paul's Epistles; (b) III; (c) Ghent, University Library, U. Lib. P. 61.

p31 (a) Paul's Epistles; (b) VII; (c) Manchester, England, John Rylands Library, P. Ryl. 4.

p32 (a) Paul's Epistles; (b) c. 200; (c) Manchester England, John Rylands Library, P. Ryl. 5.

p33 (a) Acts; (b) VI; (c) Vienna, Österreichische Nationalbibliothek, no. 190.

p34 (a) Paul's Epistles; (b) VII; (c) Vienna, Österreichische Nationalbibliothek, no. 191.

p35 (a) Gospels; (b) IV (?); (c) Florence, Biblioteca Medicea Laurenziana.

p36 (a) Gospels; (b) VI; (c) Florence, Biblioteca Medicea Laurenziana.

p37 (a) Gospels; (b) III, IV; (c) Ann Arbor, Michigan, University of Michigan Library, Invent. no. 1570.

p38 (a) Acts; (b) c. 300; (c) Ann Arbor, Michigan, University of Michigan Library, Invent. no. 1571.

p39 (a) Gospels; (b) III; (c) Chester, Pennsylvania, Crozer Theological Seminary Library, no. 8864.

p40 (a) Paul's Epistles; (b) III; (c) Heidelberg, Universitätsbibliothek, Inv. Pap. graec. 45.

p41 (a) Acts; (b) VIII; (c) Vienna, Österreichische Nationalbibliothek, Pap. K.7541-8.

p42 (a) Gospels; (b)VII, VIII; (c) Vienna, Österreichische Nationalbibliothek, KG 8706.

p43 (a) Revelation; (b) VI, VII; (c) London, British Museum, Pap. 2241.

p44 (a) Gospels; (b) VI, VII; (c) New York, Metropolitan Museum of Art, Inv. 14-1-527.

p45 (a) Gospels, Acts; (b) III; (c) Dublin, Chester Beatty Museum; and Vienna, Osterreichische Nationalbibliothek, P. Gr. Vind. 31974.

p46 (a) Paul's Epistles; (b) c. 200; (c) Dublin, Chester Beatty Museum, and Ann Arbor, Michigan, University of Michigan Library, Invent. no. 6238.

p47 (a) Revelation; (b) late III; (c) Dublin, Chester Beatty Museum.

p48 (a) Acts; (b) late III; (c) Florence, Museo Medicea Laurenziana.

p49 (a) Paul's Epistles; (b) late III; (c) New Haven, Connecticut, Yale University Library, P. 415.

p50 (a) Acts; (b) IV, V; (c) New Haven, Connecticut, Yale University Library, P. 1543.

p51 (a) Paul's Epistles; (b) c. 400; (c) London British Museum.

p52 (a) Gospels; (b) early II; (c) Manchester, John Rylands Library, P. Ryl. Gr. 457.

p53 (a) Gospels, Acts; (b) III; (c) Ann Arbor, Michigan, University of Michigan Library, Invent. no. 6652.

p54 (a) General Epistles; (b) V, VI; (c) Princeton, New Jersey, Princeton University Library, Garrett Depos. 7742.

p55 (a) Gospels; (b) VI, VII; (c) Vienna, Österreichische Nationalbibliothek, P. Gr. Vind. 26214.

p56 (a) Acts; (b) V, VI; (c) Vienna, Österreichische Nationalbibliothek, P. Gr. Vind. 19918.

p57 (a) Acts; (b) IV, V; (c) Vienna, Österreichische Nationalbibliothek, P. Gr. Vind. 26020.

p58 (a) Acts; (b) VI; (c) Vienna, Österreichische Nationalbibliothek, P. Gr. Vind. 17973, 36133[54], and 35831.

p59 (a) Gospels; (b) VII; (c) New York, New York University, Washington Square College of Arts and Sciences, Department of Classics, P. Colt. 3.

p60 (a) Gospels; (b) VII; (c) New York, New York University, Washington Square College of Arts and Sciences, Department of Classics, P. Colt. 4.

p61 (a) Paul's Epistles; (b) c. 700; (c) New York, New York University, Washington Square College of Arts and Sciences, Department of Classics, P. Colt. 5.

p62 (a) Gospels; (b) IV; (c) Oslo, University Library.

p63 (a) Gospels; (b) c. 500; (c) Berlin, Staatliche Museen.

p64 (a) Gospels; (b) c. 200; (c) Oxford, Magdalen College Library.

p65 (a) Paul's Epistles; (b) III; (c) Florence, Biblioteca Medicea Laurenziana.

p66 (a) Gospels; (b) c. 200; (c) Cologny/Genève, Bibliothèque Bodmer.

p67 (a) Gospels; (b) c. 200; (c) Barcelona, Fundación San Lucas Evangelista, P. Barc. 1.

p68 (a) Paul's Epistles; (b) VII (?); (c) Leningrad, State Public Library, Gr. 258.

p69 (a) Gospels; (b) III; (c) place (?)

p70 (a) Gospels; (b) III; (c) place (?)

p71 (a) Gospels; (b) IV; (c) place (?)

p72 (a) General Epistles; (b) III, IV; (c) Cologny/Genève, Bibliothèque Bodmer.

p73 (a) Gospels; (b)—; (c) Cologny/Genève, Bibliothèque Bodmer.

p74 (a) Acts, General Epistles; (b) VII; (c) Cologny/Genève, Bibliothèque Bodmer.

p75 (a) Gospels; (b) early III; (c) Cologny/Genève, Bibliothèque Bodmer.

p76 (a) Gospels; (b) VI; (c) Vienna, Österreichische Nationalbibliothek, P. Gr. Vind. 36102.

Major Codices

01, aleph:	Sinaiticus
02, A:	Alexandrinus
03, B:	Vaticanus
04, C:	Ephraemi Rescriptus
05, D:	Bezae Cantabrigiensis
06, E:	Claromontanus

Manuscripts Continued

Majuscules

No.	Contents	Century
01, *aleph*	Total New Testament	4th
02, A	Total New Testament	5th
03, B	New Testament, Revelation	4th
04, C	Total New Testament	5th
05, D	Gospels, Acts	6th
06, D	Paul's Epistles	6th
07, E	Gospels	8th
08, E	Acts	6th
09, F	Gospels	9th
010, F	Paul's Epistles	9th
011, G	Gospels	9th
012, G	Paul's Epistles	9th
013, H	Gospels	9th
015, H	Paul's Epistles	6th
016, I	Paul's Epistles	5th
017, K	Gospels	9th
018, K	Acts, Paul's Epistles	9th
019, L	Gospels	8th
020, L	Acts, Paul's Epistles	9th
021, M	Gospels	9th
022, N	Gospels	6th
023, O	Gospels	6th
024, P	Gospels	6th
025, P	Acts, Paul's Epistles, Revelation	9th
026, Q	Gospels	5th
028, S	Gospels	10th
029, T	Gospels	9th
030, U	Gospels	9th
031, V	Gospels	9th
032, W	Gospels	5th
033, X	Gospels	10th
034, Y	Gospels	9th
036,	Gospels	10th
037,	Gospels	9th
038,	Gospels	9th
039,	Gospels	9th
040,	Gospels	6th-8th
041,	Gospels	9th
042,	Gospels	6th
043,	Gospels	6th
044,	Gospels, Acts, Paul's Epistles	8th-9th

In addition to these manuscripts identified by a letter (letter uncials), there are 200 other numbered majuscule manuscripts. Even though most of these manuscripts are very valuable, there is not enough room to list them all. Our apparatus gives the official numbers, 046, 047 etc.

Minuscules

There are about 2800 of these. A total classification of these is only possible in specialized literature dealing with textual criticism.

Early Versions

Abbrev.	Name	Century
it	Itala, early Latin	II-IV
vul	Vulgate, Latin	IV-V
old syr	Old Syrian	II-III
syr pesh	Peshitta	V
got	Gothic	IV
arm	Armenian	IV-V
geo	Georgian	V
cop	Coptic	VI
nub	Nubian	VI
eth	Ethiopian	VI

Early Church Fathers

Athanasius, deacon of Alexandria; key figure at the Council of Nicea (325) where he attacked Arianism; he defended the Nicean claim that Christ was of the same substance as God; intimate friend of Origen; died 373.

Athenagoras, Christian philosopher of Athens ca. 178; he was one of the most articulate writers of the early Christian apologists.

Augustine, 354–430, convert of Ambrose and bishop of Hippo; his writings have dominated the development of theology in the Western Church since the Middle Ages; wrote *Confessions* and *The City of God*; he advanced the principle "Believe in order to understand."

Basil the Great, 329–379, bishop of Caesarea; one of the Cappadocian fathers and highly influential in the Eastern Church; he was one of the first great defenders of the divinity of the Holy Spirit; his formula "one substance, three persons" is still the accepted expression of the Trinity.

Bede, the Venerable; one of the great church historians of the Middle Ages; wrote *Ecclesiastical History of the English People*; he popularized the calendar which uses the birth of Christ as the baseline.

Chrysostom, 350–407, bishop of Constantinople, known also as "Golden Mouth"; he remains one of the greatest expositors and preachers in the history of the Church.

Clemens Alexandrinus, Clement of Alexandria; one of the founders of Christian literature; he created new terminology in the language of the Greeks to express the ideas of the Faith.

Clemens Romanus, Clement of Rome; traditionally a fellow laborer with Peter and Paul; bishop of Rome in 91; his letter 1 Clement provides insight into the life of the Church shortly after the apostles.

Cyprian, bishop of Carthage in 248, martyred in 258; wrote "The Unity of the Church"; taught the gift of salvation limited to the Roman Catholic Church; he was an outstanding churchman and administrator.

Cyrillus Alexandrinus, Clement of Alexandria, died ca. 444; appointed patriarch of Alexandria in 412; main focus was to oppose Nestorianism; convened the Council of Alexandria, 430, and the Council of Ephesus, 431; his primary contribution was to preserve the unity of Christ, though later he was accused of reviving Apollinarianism.

Cyrillus Hierosolymitanaus, Cyril of Jerusalem, 315–386; bishop of Jerusalem; known widely for his *Catechetical Lectures* which provide detail about the rites and ceremonies of the Church at this time.

Ephraim of Syrus, Ephraim the Syrian, deacon of Edessa; born in early days of Constantine's rule (ca. 306), died 373; known as the "Great Light of the Syrian Church," he was very influential in shaping the ritual of the Syrian church; renowned mystic and teacher, writer of hymns and commentaries.

Eusebius of Caesarea, ca. 260–340; a prolific writer and author of first full scale history of the Church; he was highly instrumental in shaping Byzantium's political ideals.

Gregory Thaumaturgus, disciple of Origen, bishop of Neocaesarea in 240; said to have had the gift to work miracles which he used regularly; wrote *A Declaration of Faith* (on the Trinity), and *Panegyric* which gives insight into the origins of Roman law.

Hippolytus, a bishop and contemporary with Origen; one of the most learned and eminent scholars of the Third Century; he opposed the popes of his day and wrote *Apostolic Tradition* which details the ordaining and ordering of ministers.

Ignatius, bishop of Antioch, martyred ca. 110; a forceful opponent of Docetism; claimed to have the gift of prophesy; he saw the Eucharist as a means of maintaining unity in the Church and stressing the humanity of Jesus.

Irenaeus, 140–202, disciple of Polycarp; bishop of Lyons in 177; countered the Gnostics in his works *Against Heresies* and *Proof of the Apostolic Tradition*; stressed the full humanity and deity of Jesus; he developed idea that the Church preserved the canon of truth for interpreting Scripture.

Early Church Fathers Continued

Jerome, ca. 342–420, also called Hieronymus; one of the most eminent scholars of the Latin fathers; he is the author of the translation of the Scriptures called the Vulgate.

Justin Martyr, martyred 165; Christian philosopher and most noted apologist of the Second Century; he helped to synthesize philosophy and theology; wrote *First Apology* and *Dialogue with Trypho*.

Origen, 185–254; considered by some the greatest scholar and voluminous writer of the Early Church in the East; was responsible for the *Hexapala*; he expressed his faith in the structures of Platonism, and was one of the great champions of allegorical hermeneutics.

Tertullian, died ca. 220; was the first Christian writer to use Latin; rejected any synthesis of theology and philosophy and coined the phrase, "What has Athens to do with Jerusalem"; his writings include *Against Marcion*, defending the use of the Old Testament by Christians, *Against Praxeas*, outlining the doctrine of the Trinity, and *On the Soul*, the first Christian writing on psychology.

Books of the Old and New Testament

Old Testament Books

Genesis
Exodus
Leviticus
Numbers
Deuteronomy
Joshua
Judges
Ruth
1 Samuel
2 Samuel
1 Kings
2 Kings
1 Chronicles
2 Chronicles
Ezra
Nehemiah
Esther
Job
Psalms
Proverbs
Ecclesiastes
Song of Solomon
Isaiah
Jeremiah
Lamentations
Ezekiel
Daniel
Hosea
Joel
Amos
Obadiah
Jonah
Micah
Nahum
Habakkuk
Zephaniah
Haggai
Zechariah
Malachi

New Testament Books

Matthew
Mark
Luke
John
Acts
Romans
1 Corinthians
2 Corinthians
Galatians
Ephesians
Philippians
Colossians
1 Thessalonians
2 Thessalonians
1 Timothy
2 Timothy
Titus
Philemon
Hebrews
James
1 Peter
2 Peter
1 John
2 John
3 John
Jude
Revelation

Books of the Apocrypha and Pseudepigrapha

Old Testament Apocryphal Books

Additions to the Book of Esther
Baruch
Bel and the Dragon
Ecclesiasticus (Sirach)
1 Esdras
2 Esdras
Judith
Letter of Jeremiah
1 Maccabees
2 Maccabees
Prayer of Azariah
Prayer of Manasseh
Song of the Three Young Men
Susanna
Tobit
Wisdom of Solomon

New Testament Apocryphal Books

Gospels
Arabic Gospel of the Infancy
Armenian Gospel of the Infancy
Assumption of the Virgin
Book of the Resurrection of Christ by Bartholomew the Apostle
Gospel According to the Egyptians
Gospel According to the Hebrews
Gospel of Bartholomew
Gospel of Basilides
Gospel of the Birth of Mary
Gospel of the Ebionites
Gospel of Marcion
Gospel of Matthias
Gospel of the Nazarenes
Gospel of Peter
Gospel of Philip
Gospel of Pseudo-Matthew
Gospel of Thomas
History of Joseph the Carpenter
Protevangelium of James

Acts
Acts of Andrew
Acts of Andrew
Acts of Andrew and Matthias
Acts of Andrew and Paul
Acts of Barnabas
Acts of James the Great
Acts of John
Acts of John by Prochorus
Acts of Paul
Acts of Peter
Acts of Peter and Andrew
Acts of Peter and Paul
Acts of Philip
Acts of Pilate
Acts of Thaddaeus
Acts of Thomas
Apostolic History of Abdias
Ascents of James
Fragmentary Story of Andrew
Martyrdom of Matthew
Passion of Paul
Passion of Peter
Passion of Peter and Paul
Preaching of Peter
Slavonic Acts of Peter

Epistles
Apocryphal Epistle of Titus
Epistle of the Apostles
Epistle to the Laodiceans
Epistle of Lentalus
Epsitles of Christ and Abgarus
Epistles of Paul and Seneca
Third Epistle to the Corinthians

Apocalypses
Apocalypse of James
Apocalypse of Paul
Apocalypse of Peter
Revelation of Stephen
Apocalypse of Thomas
Apocalypse of the Virgin

Books of the Pseudepigrapha

Apocalypse of Baruch
Apocryphon of Genesis
Aristeas
Assumption of Moses
3 Baruch
Book of Mysteries
Damascus Document
Description of the New Jerusalem
Enoch
2 Enoch
Hodayoth
Jubilees
Life of Adam and Eve
Liturgy of Three Tongues of Fire
Lives of the Prophets
3 Maccabees
4 Maccabees
Martyrdom of Isaiah
Paralipomena of Jeremiah
Psalms of Joshua
Psalms of Solomon
Pseudo-Jeremianic work
Sibylline Oracles
Testament of Job
Testament of Levi
Testaments of the Twelve Patriarchs
War Scroll

Orders and Tractates of the Mishnah and the Talmud

Division 1: Zeraim *Seeds*
Berakoth *Blessings*
Peah *Gleanings*
Demai *Produce not Certainly Tithed*
Kilaim *Two Kinds*
Shebiith *The Seventh Year*
Terumoth *Heave Offerings*
Maaseroth *Tithes*
Maaser Sheni *Second Tithe*
Hallah *Dough Offering*
Orlah *The Fruit of Young Trees*
Bikkurim *First Fruits*

Division 2: Moed *Feast*
Shabbath *Sabbath*
Erubin *Mixtures*
Pesahim *Passover*
Shekalim *The Shekel Dues*
Yoma *The Day of Atonement*
Sukkah *The Feast of Tabernacles*
Yom Tob *Festival Days*
Rosh ha-Shanah *New Year*
Taanith *The Days of Fasting*
Megillah *Scroll of Esther*
Moed Katan *Minor Feast*
Hagigah *The Festival Offering*

Division 3: Nashim *Women*
Yebamoth *Sisters-in-law*
Ketuboth *Marriage Deeds*
Nedarim *Vows*
Nazir *Nazirite Vow*
Sotah *The Suspected Adulteress*
Gittin *Bills of Divorce*
Kiddushin *Betrothals*

Division 4: Nezekin *Damages*
Baba Kamma *First Gate*
Baba Metzia *Middle Gate*
Baba Bathra *Last Gate*
Sanhedrin *The Sanhedrin*
Makkoth *Stripes*
Shebuoth *Oaths*
Eduyoth *Testimonies*
Abodah Zarah *Unlawful Worship*
Aboth *Fathers*
Horayoth *Instructions*

Division 5: Kodashim *Sacred Things*
Zebahim *Animal Offerings*
Menahoth *Meal Offerings*
Hullin *Slaughtering of Animals*
Bekhoroth *Firstlings*
Arakhin *Valuations*
Temurah *Substituted Offering*
Kerithoth *Excisions*
Meilah *Trespass*
Tamid *The Daily Whole Offering*
Middoth *Measurements*
Kinnim *Nests*

Division 6: Tohoroth *Cleannesses*
Kelim *Vessels*
Oholoth *Tents*
Negaim *Plagues*
Parah *The Red Heifer*
Tohoroth *Cleannesses*
Mikwaoth *Pools of Water*
Niddah *The Menstruant*
Makshirin *Predisposers*
Zabim *Persons that Suffer a Flux*
Tebul Yom *One Immersed on the Day*
Yadaim *Hands*
Uktzin *Stalks*

Bibliography

Resource Tools

BAUER (BAGD)
Bauer, Walter, William F. Arndt, and F. Wilbur Gingrich. *A Greek-English Lexicon of the New Testament and other Early Christian Literature.* Rev. ed. by F. Wilbur Gingrich and Frederick W. Danker. Chicago: The University of Chicago Press. 1979.

COLIN BROWN (NIDNTT)
Brown, Colin, ed. *The New International Dictionary of New Testament Theology.* 4 vols. Grand Rapids: Zondervan Publishing House. 1975.

KITTEL (TDNT)
Kittel, G., and G. Friedrich. *Theological Dictionary of the New Testament.* Trans. by G. W. Bromiley. 10 vols. Grand Rapids: William B. Eerdmans Publishing Co. 1972.

LIDDELL–SCOTT (LSJ)
Liddell, H. G., and R. Scott. *A Greek-English Lexicon.* 9th. ed. Ed. by H. Stuart Jones and R. McKenzie. Oxford: Clarendon. 1940.

MOULTON–MILLIGAN (M-M)
Moulton, J.H., and G. Milligan. *The Vocabulary of the Greek Testament Illustrated from the Papyri and Other Non-Literary Sources.* London: Hodder and Stoughton. 1914–1930. Reprint. Grand Rapids: Wm. B. Eerdmans Publishing Company. 1985.

STRONG
Strong, James. *The Exhaustive Concordance of the Bible.* 1890. Reprint. Nashville: Abingdon Press. 1977.

(Parenthetical abbreviations found in Study Bible.)

Modern Greek Texts

Aland, K. et al. in cooperation with the Institute for New Testament Textual Research. *The Greek New Testament.* 2nd ed. London: United Bible Societies. 1968. (Also known as UBS.)

Aland, K. et al. in cooperation with the Institute for New Testament Textual Research. *The Greek New Testament.* 3rd ed. New York: United Bible Societies. 1975. (Also known as UBS.)

Nestle, E., and K. Aland. *Novum Testamentum Graece.* 25th ed. Stuttgart: Wurtembergische Bibelanstalt. 1963. (Also known as Nestle-Aland or NA 25.)

Nestle, E., and K. Aland. et al. *Novum Testamentum Graece.* 26th ed. Stuttgart: Deutsche Bibelstiftung. 1979. (Also known as Nestle-Aland or NA 26.)

General Bibliography

Abbott, T. K. *Ephesians and Colossians. The International Critical Commentary.* Ed. by S. R. Driver, A. Plummer, and C. A. Briggs. Edinburgh: T. and T. Clark. 1968.

Abbott-Smith, G. *A Manual Greek Lexicon of the New Testament.* New York: Charles Scribner's Sons. 1937.

Achtemeier, Paul J. *Harper's Bible Dictionary.* New York: Harper and Row. 1985.

Albright, W. F., and C. S. Mann. *Matthew.* Vol. 26 of *The Anchor Bible.* Ed. by William Foxwell Albright and David Noel Freedman. Garden City, NY: Doubleday and Company, Inc. 1971.

Alford, Henry. *Alford's Greek Testament.* 3 vols. Grand Rapids: Baker Book House. 1980.

Allen, W. C. *A Critical and Exegetical Commentary on the Gospel According to St. Matthew. The International Critical Commentary.* Ed. by S. R. Driver, A. Plummer, and C. A. Briggs. Edinburgh: T. and T. Clark. 1912.

Archer, Gleason L. *Encyclopedia of Bible Difficulties.* Grand Rapids: Zondervan Publishing House. 1982.

Bauckham, Richard J. *Jude, 2 Peter.* Vol. 50 of *Word Biblical Commentary.* Ed. by David A. Hubbard, et al. Waco, TX: Word Books. 1983.

Barclay, William. *The Gospel of John. The Daily Study Bible.* Rev. ed. Philadelphia: The Westminster Press. 1975.

Barclay, William. *The Gospel of Mark. The Daily Study Bible.* Rev. ed. Philadelphia: The Westminster Press. 1975.

Barclay, William. *New Testament Words.* Philadelphia: The Westminster Press. 1974.

Barrett, C. K. *A Commentary on the Epistle to the Romans. Harper's New Testament Commentaries.* Ed. by Henry Chadwick. New York: Harper and Row. 1957.

Barrett, C. K. *A Commentary on the First Epistle to the Corinthians. Harper's New Testament Commentaries.* Ed. by Henry Chadwick. New York: Harper and Row. 1968.

Barrett, C. K. *The New Testament Background: Selected Documents.* New York: Harper and Row. 1961.

Barth, Karl. *The Epistle to the Romans.* Trans. by Edwyn C. Hoskyns. London: Oxford University Press. 1933.

Barth, Karl. *The Word of God and the Word of Man.* Trans. by Douglas Horton. New York: Harper and Brothers, Publishers. 1957.

Bauer, Walter. *Griechisch-deutsches Worterbuch zu den Schriften des Neuen Testaments und der fruhchristlichen Literatur.* Ed. by Kurt and Barbara Aland. New York: Walter de Gruyter. 1988.

Bauer, Walter, William F. Arndt, and F. Wilbur Gingrich. *A Greek-English Lexicon of the New Testament and other Early Christian Literature.* Rev. ed. by F. Wilbur Gingrich and Frederick W. Danker. Chicago: The University of Chicago Press. 1979.

Baylis, Charles P. "The Woman Caught in Adultery: A Test of Jesus as the Greater Prophet." *Biblio Theca Sacra* 146 (April–June 1989): 171-184.

Beasley-Murray, G. R. *Baptism in the New Testament.* Grand Rapids: William B. Eerdmans Publishing Co. 1973.

Bickerman, E. J. "The Name of Christians." *Harvard Theological Review* 42, no. 1 (January 1949): 109-124.

Bibliography Continued

Bigg, Charles. *A Critical and Exegetical Commentary on the Epistles of St. Peter and St. Jude.* The International Critical Commentary. Ed. by S. R. Driver, A. Plummer, and C. A. Briggs. Edinburgh: T. and T. Clark. 1978.

Black, David Alan. "Ephesian Address." *Grace Theological Journal* 2 (1981): 59-73.

Blass, F. *Philology of the Gospels.* Amsterdam: B. R. Gruner. 1969.

Blass, F., and A. DeBrunner. *A Greek Grammar of the New Testament and Other Early Christian Literature.* Trans. by Robert W. Funk. Chicago: The University of Chicago Press. 1974.

Blum, Edwin A. *2 Peter.* In *Hebrews—Revelation.* Vol. 12 of *The Expositor's Bible Commentary.* Ed. by Frank E. Gaebelein. Grand Rapids: Zondervan Publishing House. 1981.

Bornkamm, Gunther. *Jesus of Nazareth.* Trans. by Irene and Fraser McLuskey. New York: Harper. 1960.

Botterweck, G. Johannes, and Helmer Ringgren, eds. *Theological Dictionary of the Old Testament.* 5 vols. Trans. by Geoffrey Bromiley, et al. Grand Rapids: William B. Eerdmans Publishing Co. 1974.

Brown, Colin, ed. *The New International Dictionary of New Testament Theology.* 4 vols. Grand Rapids: Zondervan Publishing House. 1975.

Brown, Raymond E. *The Gospel According to St. John.* Vols. 29 and 29a of *The Anchor Bible.* Ed. by William Foxwell Albright and David Noel Freedman. Garden City, NY: Doubleday and Company, Inc. 1978.

Brown, Francis, Samuel Driver, and Charles A. Briggs. *The New Brown-Driver-Briggs-Gesenius Hebrew and English Lexicon of the Old Testament.* Peabody, MA: Hendrickson Publishers. 1979.

Bruce, A. B. *The Synoptic Gospels.* In *The Synoptic Gospels and John.* Vol. 1 of *The Expositor's Greek Testament.* Ed. by W. Robertson Nicoll. Grand Rapids: William B. Eerdmans Publishing Co. 1951.

Bruce, F. F. *The Acts of the Apostles.* Vol. 5 of *Tyndale New Testament Commentaries.* Ed. by R. V. G. Tasker. Grand Rapids: William B. Eerdmans Publishing Co. 1952.

Bruce, F. F. *The Acts of the Apostles: The Greek Text.* London: The Tyndale Press. 1956.

Bruce, F. F. *The Book of Acts.* The New International Commentary on the New Testament. Ed. by F. F. Bruce. Grand Rapids: William B. Eerdmans Publishing Co. 1979.

Bruce, F. F. *The Epistle of Paul to the Romans.* Vol. 6 of *Tyndale New Testament Commentaries.* Ed. by R. V. G. Tasker. Grand Rapids: William B. Eerdmans Publishing Co. 1963.

Bruce, F. F. *The Epistle to the Hebrews.* The New International Commentary on the New Testament. Ed. by F. F. Bruce. Grand Rapids: William B. Eerdmans Publishing Co. 1964.

Bruce, F. F. *The Epistles to the Colossians, to Philemon, and to the Ephesians.* The New International Commentary on the New Testament. Ed. by F. F. Bruce. Grand Rapids: William B. Eerdmans Publishing Co. 1984.

Bruce, F. F. *1 and 2 Thessalonians.* Word Biblical Commentary. Ed. by David A. Hubbard, et al. Waco, TX: Word Books. 1982.

Bruce, F. F. *Galatians.* New International Greek Testament Commentary. Ed. by I. Howard Marshall and W. Ward Gasque. Grand Rapids: William B. Eerdmans Publishing Co. 1982.

Bruce, F. F. *The Gospel of John: Introduction, Exposition, and Notes.* Grand Rapids: William B. Eerdmans Publishing Co. 1983.

Bruce, F. F. *The Hard Sayings of Jesus.* The Jesus Library. Ed. by Michael Green. Downers Grove, IL: InterVarsity Press. 1983.

Bruce, F. F. *New Testament Development of Old Testament Themes.* Grand Rapids: William B. Eerdmans Publishing Co. 1969.

Bruce, F. F. *Paul, Apostle of the Heart Set Free.* Grand Rapids: William B. Eerdmans Publishing Co. 1977.

Bruce, F. F., and E. K. Simpson. *Ephesians and Colossians. The New International Commentary on the New Testament.* Ed. by F. F. Bruce. Grand Rapids: William B. Eerdmans Publishing Co. 1975.

Bultmann, Rudolf. *The Gospel of John.* Trans. by G. R. Beasley-Murray. Philadelphia: The Westminster Press. 1975.

Bultmann, Rudolf. *Primitive Christianity in its Contemporary Setting.* Trans. by R. H. Fuller. New York: The World Publishing Company. 1972.

Burdick, Donald W. *Oida and Ginōskō in the Pauline Epistles.* In *New Dimensions in New Testament Study.* Ed. by Richard N. Longenecker and Merrill C. Tenney. Grand Rapids: Zondervan Publishing House. 1974.

Burrows, Millar. *The Dead Sea Scrolls.* New York: Viking Press. 1955.

Carson, D. A. *Matthew.* In *Matthew, Mark, and Luke.* Vol. 8 of *The Expositor's Bible Commentary.* Ed. by Frank E. Gaebelein. Grand Rapids: Zondervan Publishing House. 1984.

Casson, Lionel. *Ships and Seamanship in the Ancient World.* Princeton: Princeton University Press. 1971.

Chamberlain, William D. *An Exegetical Grammar of the Greek New Testament.* New York: The Macmillan Company. 1952.

Charles, R. H. *The Revelation of St. John.* 2 vols. *The International Critical Commentary.* Ed. by S. R. Driver, A. Plummer, and C. A. Briggs. Edinburgh: T. and T. Clark. 1971.

Clark, Stephen B. *Man and Woman in Christ: An Examination of the Roles of Men and Women in the Light of Scripture and the Social Sciences.* Ann Arbor, MI: Servant Books. 1980.

Conzelmann, Hans. *1 Corinthians.* Ed. by George W. McRae, and trans. by James W. Leitch. *Hermeneia.* Ed. by Helmut Koester, et al. Philadelphia: Fortress Press. 1975.

Cook, Barbara. *Ordinary Women, Extraordinary Strength.* Lynnwood: Aglow Publications. 1988.

Craigie, Peter C. *Deuteronomy. The New International Commentary on the Old Testament.* Ed. by R. K. Harrison. Grand Rapids: William B. Eerdmans Publishing Co. 1976.

Cranfield, C. E. B. *The Epistle to the Romans.* 2 vols. *The International Critical Commentary.* Rev. ed. Ed. by J. A. Emerton and C. E. B. Cranfield. Edinburgh: T. and T. Clark. 1979.

Cross, F. L. *The Oxford Dictionary of the Christian Church.* Oxford: Oxford University Press. 1974.

Dana, H. E., and Julius R. Mantey. *A Manual of the Greek New Testament.* New York: The Macmillan Co. 1955.

Daube, David. "Jesus and the Samaritan Woman: The Meaning of *Sugchraomai*." *Journal of Biblical Literature* 69 (1950): 137-147.

Davids, Peter H. *The Epistle of James: A Commentary on the Greek Text. New International Greek Testament Commentary.* Ed. by I. Howard Marshall and W. Ward Gasque. Grand Rapids: William B. Eerdmans Publishing Co. 1982.

Deissmann, G. Adolf. *Bible Studies.* Winona Lake, IN: Alpha Publications. 1979.

Dibelius, Martin. *James.* Trans. by Michael A. Williams. *Hermeneia.* Ed. by Helmut Koester, et al. Philadelphia: Fortress Press. 1976.

Dodd, C. H. *The Apostolic Preaching of the Cross.* Grand Rapids: Baker Book House. 1980.

Dodd, C. H. *The Interpretation of the Fourth Gospel.* Cambridge: Cambridge University Press. 1972.

Bibliography Continued

Doerksen, Vernon. *James*. Chicago: Moody Press. 1983.

Dods, Marcus. *The Epistle to the Hebrews*. In *Thessalonians–James*. Vol. 4 of *The Expositor's Greek Testament*. Ed. by W. Robertson Nicoll. Grand Rapids: William B. Eerdmans Publishing Co. 1974.

Douglas, J. D., ed. *The Illustrated Bible Dictionary*. 3 vols. Wheaton: Tyndale House Publishers. 1980.

Douglas, J. D. *New Bible Dictionary*. 2d ed. Wheaton: Tyndale House Publishers. 1982.

Dunn, James D. G. *Jesus and the Spirit*. Philadelphia: The Westminster Press. 1975.

Dunn, James D. G. *Romans 9–16*. Vol. 38b of Word Biblical Commentary. Ed. by David A. Hubbard, et al. Waco, TX: Word Books. 1988.

Eadie, John. *Ephesians*. Vol. 2 of *The John Eadie Greek Text Commentaries*. Grand Rapids: Baker Book House. 1979.

Earle, Ralph. *Word Meanings in the New Testament*. 6 vols. Grand Rapids: Baker Book House. 1984.

Edersheim, Alfred. *The Life and Times of Jesus the Messiah*. 2 vols. Grand Rapids: William B. Eerdmans Publishing Co. 1972.

Eichrodt, Walter. *Theology of the Old Testament*. 2 vols. Trans. by J. A. Baker. Philadelphia: The Westminster Press. 1967.

Ellis, E. Earle. *Paul's Use of the Old Testament*. Grand Rapids: William B. Eerdmans Publishing Co. 1957.

Ellis, E. Earle. *Prophecy and Hermeneutic in Early Christianity*. Grand Rapids: William B. Eerdmans Publishing Co. 1978.

English, E. Schugler. *Rethinking the Rapture*. Traveller's Rest, SC: Southern Bible Book House. 1954.

Fee, Gordon D. *1 and 2 Timothy, Titus. A Good News Commentary*. Ed. by W. Ward Gasque. San Francisco: Harper and Row. 1984.

Fee, Gordon D. *The First Epistle to the Corinthians. The New International Commentary on the New Testament*. Ed. by F. F. Bruce. Grand Rapids: William B. Eerdmans Publishing Co. 1987.

Fitzmyer, Joseph A. *The Gospel According to Luke*. Vol. 28 of *The Anchor Bible*. Ed. by William Foxwell Albright and David Noel Freedman. Garden City, NY: Doubleday and Company, Inc. 1982.

Forbes, R. J., ed. *Studies in Ancient Technology*. 9 vols. Leiden: E. J. Brill. 1965.

Ford, J. Massyngberde. *Revelation*. Vol. 38 of *The Anchor Bible*. Ed. by William Foxwell Albright and David Noel Freedman. Garden City, NY: Doubleday and Company, Inc. 1975.

Foulkes, Francis. *The Epistle of Paul to the Ephesians*. Vol. 10 of *Tyndale New Testament Commentaries*. Ed. by R. V. G. Tasker. Grand Rapids: William B. Eerdmans Publishing Co. 1983.

Furnish, Victor Paul. *2 Corinthians*. Vol. 32a of *The Anchor Bible*. Ed. by William Foxwell Albright and David Noel Freedman. Garden City, NY: Doubleday and Company, Inc. 1984.

Gartner, Betril Edgar. *The Temple and the Community in Qumran and the New Testament*. Cambridge: Cambridge University Press. 1965.

Gehman, Henry Snyder, ed. *The New Westminster Dictionary of the Bible*. Philadelphia: The Westminster Press. 1970.

Gemsler, B. *The Rîv or Controversy Pattern in Hebrew Mentality*. In *Wisdom in Israel and in the Ancient Near East*. Ed. by M. Noth and D. W. Thomas. *Supplements to Vetus Testamentum*, vol. 3. Leiden: E. J. Brill. 1969.

Gesenius, Wilhelm. *Gesenius' Hebrew Grammar.* 2d English ed., ed. and rev. by E. Kautzsch and A. E. Cowley. Oxford: Clarendon Press. 1910.

Glover, T. R. *The Conflict of Religions in the Early Roman Empire.* Washington: Canon Press. 1974.

Grant, Robert McQueen. *Gnosticism and Early Christianity.* 2d ed. New York: Columbia University Press. 1966.

Green, Michael. *The Second Epistle of Peter and the Epistle of Jude.* Vol. 18 of *Tyndale New Testament Commentaries.* Ed. by R. V. G. Tasker. Grand Rapids: William B. Eerdmans Publishing Co. 1975.

Green, Samuel G. *Handbook to the Grammar of the Greek Testament.* London: The Religious Tract Society. N.d.

Greenlee, J. Harold. *A Concise Exegetical Grammar of New Testament Greek.* Grand Rapids: William B. Eerdmans Publishing Co. 1963.

Greenlee, J. Harold. *A New Testament Greek Morpheme Lexicon.* Grand Rapids: Zondervan Publishing House. 1983.

Grimm, C. L. Wilibald. *A Greek-English Lexicon of the New Testament.* 4th ed., trans. and rev. by Joseph Henry Thayer. Edinburgh: T. and T. Clark. 1956.

Gundry, Robert. *Matthew: A Commentary on His Literary and Theological Art.* Grand Rapids: William B. Eerdmans Publishing Co. 1982.

Guthrie, Donald. *The Letter to the Hebrews.* Vol. 20 of *Tyndale New Testament Commentaries.* Ed. by R. V. G. Tasker. Grand Rapids: William B. Eerdmans Publishing Co. 1983.

Guthrie, Donald. *The Pastoral Epistles.* Vol. 14 of *Tyndale New Testament Commentaries.* Ed. by R. V. G. Tasker. Grand Rapids: William B. Eerdmans Publishing Co. 1957.

Guthrie, Donald, and J. A. Motyer. *The New Bible Commentary: Revised.* Grand Rapids: William B. Eerdmans Publishing Co. 1981.

Guthrie, W. K. C. *The Greeks and Their Gods.* Boston: Beacon Press. 1949.

Hagner, Donald A. *Hebrews. A Good News Commentary.* Ed. by W. Ward Gasque. San Francisco: Harper and Row. 1983.

Harner, Philip B. *The "I Am" of the Fourth Gospel.* Facet Books: Biblical Series, no. 26. Philadelphia: Fortress Press. 1970.

Hastings, James, et al., eds. *Dictionary of the Bible.* New York: Charles Scribner's Sons. 1951.

Hatch, Edwin, and Henry A. Redpath, eds. *A Concordance to the Septuagint.* 2 vols. Reprint. Grand Rapids: Baker Book House. 1983.

Hawthorne, Gerald F. *Philippians.* Vol. 43 of *Word Biblical Commentary.* Ed. by David A. Hubbard, et al. Waco, TX: Word Books. 1983.

Hemer, Colin J. *The Letters to the Seven Churches of Asia in Their Local Setting.* Journal for the Study of the New Testament Supplement Series, vol. 11. Ed. by David Hill. Sheffield, England: JSOT Press. 1986.

Hendriksen, William. *Exposition of the Pastoral Epistles. New Testament Commentary.* Grand Rapids: Baker Book House. 1957.

Hengel, Martin. *Judaism and Hellenism.* Trans. by John Bowden. Philadelphia: Fortress Press. 1981.

Hiebert, D. Edmond. *1 Timothy.* Chicago: Moody Press. 1957.

Hiebert, D. Edmond. *The Thessalonian Epistles.* Chicago: Moody Press. 1971.

Bibliography Continued

Hiebert, D. Edmond. *Titus.* In *Ephesians–Philemon.* Vol. 11 of *The Expositor's Bible Commentary.* Ed. by Frank E. Gaebelein. Grand Rapids: Zondervan Publishing House. 1978.

Hobart, William Kirk. *The Medical Language of St. Luke.* Dublin: Hodges, Figgis, and Co. 1882.

Hodge, Charles. *A Commentary on 1 and 2 Corinthians.* Edinburgh: The Banner of Truth Trust. 1974.

Hopkins, David C. "Life on the Land: The Subsistence Struggles of Early Israel." *Biblical Archeologist* 50 (September 1987): 179-190.

Hort, Fenton John Anthony. *Judaistic Christianity.* Ed. by J. O. F. Murray. Grand Rapids: Baker Book House. 1980.

Horton, Stanley M. *What the Bible Says about the Holy Spirit.* Springfield, MO: Gospel Publishing House. 1976.

Howard, J. Keir. "Neither Male nor Female: An Examination of the Status of Women in the New Testament." *Evangelical Quarterly* 55, no. 1 (1983): 31-42.

Hughes, Philip E. *The Second Epistle to the Corinthians.* The New International Commentary on the New Testament. Ed. by F. F. Bruce. Grand Rapids: William B. Eerdmans Publishing Co. 1962.

Jackson, F. J. Foakes, and Kirsopp Lake. *The Beginnings of Christianity.* 5 vols. London: Macmillan and Company, Limited. 1920.

Jagersma, Henk. *A History of Israel from Alexander the Great to Bar Kochba.* Trans. by John Bowden. Philadelphia: Fortress Press. 1986.

Jart, Una. "The Precious Stones in the Revelation of St. John 21:18-21." *Studia Theologica* 24 (1970): 150-181.

Jeremias, Joachim. *The Eucharistic Words of Jesus.* London: SCM Press. 1966.

Jeremias, Joachim. *Jerusalem in the Time of Jesus.* Philadelphia: Fortress Press. 1987.

Jeremias, Joachim. *The Parables of Jesus.* New York: Charles Scribner's Sons. 1963.

Kaseman, Ernst. *Perspectives on Paul.* Trans. by Margaret Kohl. Philadelphia: Fortress Press. 1974.

Kee, H. C. *The Linguistic Background of Shame in the New Testament.* In *On Language, Culture, and Religion: In Honor of Eugene A. Nida.* Ed. by Matthew Black and William A. Smalley. The Hague: Mouton. 1974.

Kelly, J. N. D. *A Commentary on the Epistles of Peter and Jude.* Thornapple Commentaries. Reprint. Grand Rapids: Baker Book House. 1981.

Kent, Homer. *The Pastoral Epistles.* Chicago: Moody Press. 1958.

Kittel, G., and G. Friedrich. *Theological Dictionary of the New Testament.* Trans. by G. W. Bromiley. 10 vols. Grand Rapids: William B. Eerdmans Publishing Co. 1972.

Kitto, H. D. F. *The Greeks.* Middlesex: Penguin Books. 1951.

Klein, Ralph W. *1 Samuel.* Vol. 10 of *Word Biblical Commentary.* Ed. by John D. Watts, et al. Waco, TX: Word Books. 1983.

Knight, George W. "*Authenteō* in Reference to Women in 1 Timothy 2:12." *New Testament Studies* 30 (1984): 143-157.

Knowling, R. J. *The Acts of the Apostles*. In *Acts–1 Corinthians*. Vol. 2 of *The Expositor's Greek Testament*. Ed. by W. Robertson Nicoll. Grand Rapids: William B. Eerdmans Publishing Co. 1974.

Koester, Helmut. *History, Culture and Religion of the Hellenistic Age*. Philadelphia: Fortress Press. 1982.

Kroeger, Catarine C. "Ancient Heresies and a Strange Greek Verb." *The Reformed Journal* 29, no. 3 (1979): 12-15.

Kummel, Werner Georg. *Introduction to the New Testament*. Rev. ed. Ed. by Howard Clark Kee. Nashville: Abingdon Press. 1975.

Ladd, George Eldon. *The Presence of the Future*. Grand Rapids: William B. Eerdmans Publishing Co. 1974.

Lane, William L. *The Gospel of Mark*. *The New International Commentary on the New Testament*. Ed. by F. F. Bruce. Grand Rapids: William B. Eerdmans Publishing Co. 1978.

Lenski, R. C. H. *The Interpretation of the Acts of the Apostles*. Minneapolis: Augsburg Publishing House. 1964. Lenski, R. C. H. *The Interpretation of the Epistles of St. Peter, St. John, and St. Jude*. Minneapolis: Augsburg Publishing House. 1966.

Lenski, R. C. H. *The Interpretation of the Epistles to the Hebrews and James*. Minneapolis: Augsburg Publishing House. 1966.

Lenski, R. C. H. *The Interpretation of St. Paul's Epistles to the Colossians, to the Thessalonians, to Timothy, to Titus, and to Philemon*. Minneapolis: Augsburg Publishing House. 1966.

Lenski, R. C. H. *The Interpretation of St. Paul's First and Second Epistles to the Corinthians*. Minneapolis: Augsburg Publishing House. 1964.

Lichtheim, Miriam. *The Old and Middle Kingdoms*. Vol. 1 of *Ancient Egyptian Literature*. Los Angeles: University of California Press. 1975.

Liddell, H. G., and R. Scott. *A Greek-English Lexicon*. 9th ed., ed. by H. Stuart Jones and R. McKenzie. Oxford: Clarendon Press. 1940.

Liefeld, Walter L. *Luke*. In *Matthew, Mark, and Luke*. Vol. 8 of *The Expositor's Bible Commentary*. Ed. by Frank E. Gaebelein. Grand Rapids: Zondervan Publishing House. 1984.

Lightfoot, J. B. *The Epistle of St. Paul to the Galatians*. Grand Rapids: Zondervan Publishing House. 1974.

Lightfoot, J. B. *Matthew–Mark*. Vol. 2 of *A Commentary on the New Testament from the Talmud and Hebraica*. Grand Rapids: Baker Book House. 1979.

Lightfoot, J. B. *Saint Paul's Epistle to the Philippians*. Grand Rapids: Zondervan Publishing House. 1953.

Lightfoot, J. B. *Saint Paul's Epistles to the Colossians and to Philemon*. New York: The Macmillan Company. 1897.

Lightfoot, R. H. *St. John's Gospel: A Commentary*. Ed. by C. F. Evans. Oxford: Oxford University Press. 1956.

Limet, Henri. "The Cuisine of Ancient Sumer." *Biblical Archeologist* 50 (September 1987): 132-147.

Lockyer, Hebert, ed. *Nelson's Illustrated Bible Dictionary*. Nashville: Thomas Nelson. 1986.

Lohse, Eduard. *Colossians and Philemon*. Ed. by Helmut Koester, and trans. by William R. Poehlmann and Robert J. Karris. *Hermeneia*. Ed. by Helmut Koester, et al. Philadelphia: Fortress Press. 1982.

Bibliography Continued

Longenecker, Richard N. *The Acts of the Apostles.* In *John–Acts.* Vol. 9 of *The Expositor's Bible Commentary.* Ed. by Frank E. Gaebelein. Grand Rapids: Zondervan Publishing House. 1981.

Louw, Johannes P. and Eugene A. Nida, eds. *Greek-English Lexicon of the New Testament Based on Semantic Domains.* 2 vols. New York: United Bible Societies. 1988.

Machen, J. Gresham. *New Testament Greek for Beginners.* New York: The Macmillan Company. 1957.

Mackie, George M. *Bible Manners and Customs.* New York: Flemming H. Revell Co. N.d.

Marshall, I. Howard. *The Acts of the Apostles.* Vol. 5 of *Tyndale New Testament Commentaries.* Ed. by R. V. G. Tasker. Grand Rapids: William B. Eerdmans Publishing Co. 1980.

Marshall, I. Howard. *The Gospel of Luke. New International Greek Testament Commentary.* Ed. by I. Howard Marshall and W. Ward Gasque. Grand Rapids: William B. Eerdmans Publishing Co. 1978.

Marshall, I. Howard. *The Meaning of Reconciliation.* In *Unity and Diversity in New Testament Theology: Essays in Honor of George E. Ladd.* Ed. by Robert A. Guelich. Grand Rapids: William B. Eerdmans Publishing Co. 1978.

Mayor, Joseph B. *The Epistle of St. James.* Minneapolis: Klock and Klock Christian Publishers. 1977.

McDonald, H. Dermot. *Commentary on Colossians and Philemon.* Waco, TX: Word Books. 1982.

Metzger, Bruce M. *Lexical Aids for Students of New Testament Greek.* Princeton: Bruce M. Metzger. 1978.

Metzger, Bruce M. *A Textual Commentary on the Greek New Testament.* London: United Bible Societies. 1971.

Miranda, Jose. *Christianity is Communism.* In *Third World Liberation Theologies.* Ed. by Deane William Ferm. Maryknoll, NY: Orbis Books. 1986.

Moffatt, James. *The Revelation of St. John the Divine.* In *1 Peter–Revelation.* Vol. 5 of *The Expositor's Greek Testament.* Ed. by W. Robertson Nicoll. Grand Rapids: William B. Eerdmans Publishing Co. 1951.

Moo, Douglas J. "1 Timothy 2:11-15: Meaning and Significance." *Trinity Journal* 1, no. 1 (1980): 62-83.

Morris, Leon. *The First and Second Epistles to the Thessalonians. The New International Commentary on the New Testament.* Ed. by F. F. Bruce. Grand Rapids: William B. Eerdmans Publishing Co. 1959.

Morris, Leon. *The Gospel According to John. The New International Commentary on the New Testament.* Ed. by F. F. Bruce. Grand Rapids: William B. Eerdmans Publishing Co. 1973.

Morris, Leon. *Hebrews.* In *Hebrews–Revelation.* Vol. 12 of *The Expositor's Bible Commentary.* Ed. by Frank E. Gaebelein. Grand Rapids: Zondervan Publishing House. 1981.

Morris, Leon. *The Revelation of St. John.* Vol. 20 of *Tyndale New Testament Commentaries.* Ed. by R. V. G. Tasker. Grand Rapids: William B. Eerdmans Publishing Co. 1969.

Morrish, George. *A Concordance of the Septuagint.* Grand Rapids: Zondervan Publishing House. 1976.

Moule, C. F. D. *An Idiom Book of New Testament Greek.* Cambridge: Cambridge University Press. 1986.

Moulton, J. H., and W. F. Howard. *Accidence and Word Formation.* Vol. 2 of *Grammar of New Testament Greek.* Edinburgh: T. and T. Clark. 1979.

Moulton, J. H., and G. Milligan. *The Vocabulary of the Greek Testament Illustrated from the Papyri and Other Non-Literary Sources.* London: Hodder and Stoughton. 1914-1930. Reprint. Grand Rapids: William B. Eerdmans Publishing Co. 1985.

Moulton, W. F., et al. *A Concordance to the Greek New Testament*. Edinburgh: T. and T. Clark. 1897.

Mounce, Robert H. *Revelation. The New International Commentary on the New Testament*. Ed. by F. F. Bruce. Grand Rapids: William B. Eerdmans Publishing Co. 1977.

Muhly, James D. *The Bronze Age Setting*. In *The Coming of the Age of Iron*. Ed. by Theodore A. Wertime and James D. Muhly. New Haven: Yale University Press. 1980.

Muller, J. J. *The Epistles of Paul to the Philippians and to Philemon. The New International Commentary on the New Testament*. Ed. by F. F. Bruce. Grand Rapids: William B. Eerdmans Publishing Co. 1955.

Murphy-O'Connor, Jerome. "1 Corinthians 11:2-16 Once Again." *Catholic Biblical Quarterly* 50, no. 2 (April 1988): 265-274.

Murray, John. *The Epistle to the Romans. The New International Commentary on the New Testament*. Ed. by F. F. Bruce. Grand Rapids: William B. Eerdmans Publishing Co. 1965.

Negev, Abraham. "Understanding the Nabateans." *Biblical Archeology Review* 14 (November–December 1988): 26-45.

Orr, William F., and James Arthur Walther. *1 Corinthians*. Vol. 26 of *The Anchor Bible*. Ed. by William Foxwell Albright and David Noel Freedman. Garden City, NY: Doubleday and Company, Inc. 1976.

O'Brien, Peter T. *Colossians and Philemon*. Vol. 44 of *Word Biblical Commentary*. Ed. by David A. Hubbard, et al. Waco, TX: Word Books. 1982.

Osiek, Carolyn. *Galatians*. Vol. 22 of *New Testament Message: A Biblical Theological Commentary*. Wilmington: Michael Glazier, Inc. 1980.

Pfeifer, Charles F., and Howard F. Vos. *The Wycliffe Historical Geography of Bible Lands*. Chicago: Moody Press. 1967.

Plummer, Alfred. *A Critical and Exegetical Commentary on the Gospel According to St. Luke. The International Critical Commentary*. Ed. by S. R. Driver, A. Plummer, and C. A. Briggs. Edinburgh: T. and T. Clark. 1969.

Radford, Lewis B. *The Epistle to Colossians and the Epistle to Philemon. Westminster Commentaries*. Ed. by Walter Lock and D. C. Simpson. London: Melhuen and Co. Ltd. 1931.

Rapinsky, Michael. "The Camel in Ancient Arabia." *Antiquity* 49 (1979): 295-298.

Reicke, Bo Ivar. *The New Testament Era: The World of the Bible from 500 B.C. to A.D. 100*. Philadelphia: Fortress Press. 1968.

Reiling, J., and J. L. Swellengvebel. *A Translator's Handbook on the Gospel of Luke*. London: United Bible Society. 1971.

Ridderbos, Herman J. *Paul: An Outline of His Theology*. Trans. by Rohn Richard deWitt. Grand Rapids: William B. Eerdmans Publishing Co. 1975.

Ridderbos, Herman J. *Studies in Scripture and its Authority*. Grand Rapids: William B. Eerdmans Publishing Co. 1978.

Rienecker, Fritz. *Linguistic Key to the Greek New Testament*. 2 vols. Grand Rapids: Zondervan Publishing House. 1980.

Robertson, Archibald Thomas. *A Grammar of the Greek New Testament in the Light of Historical Research*. Nashville: Broadman Press. 1934.

Robertson, Archibald Thomas. *Word Pictures in the New Testament*. 6 vols. Nashville: Broadman Press. 1931.

Bibliography Continued

Robinson, J. Armitage. *Commentary on Ephesians.* Grand Rapids: Kregel Publications. 1979.

Rose, H. J. *A Handbook of Greek Mythology.* New York: E. P. Dutton and Co., Inc. 1959.

Russell, David S. *The Method and Message of Jewish Apocalyptic.* Philadelphia: The Westminster Press. 1964.

Sanday, William, and Arthur Headlam. *A Critical and Exegetical Commentary on the Epistle to the Romans. The International Critical Commentary.* Ed. by S. R. Driver, A. Plummer, and C. A. Briggs. Edinburgh: T. and T. Clark. 1897.

Scarborough, John. *Facets of Hellenic Life.* Boston: Houghton Mifflin Company. 1976.

Schmithals, Walter. *Paul and the Gnostics.* Trans. by John E. Steely. Nashville: Abingdon Press. 1972.

Selwyn, Edward Gordon. *The First Epistle of St. Peter.* Grand Rapids: Baker Book House. 1981.

Sevier, Paul. *Images of the Church in the New Testament.* Philadelphia: The Westminster Press. 1960.

Sherwin-White, Adrian Nicholas. *Roman Society and Roman Law in the New Testament.* Grand Rapids: Baker Book House. 1978.

Sidebottom, E. M. *James, Jude, 2 Peter. The New Century Bible Commentary.* Grand Rapids: William B. Eerdmans Publishing Co. 1982.

Smalley, Stephen. *1, 2, 3 John.* Vol. 51 of *Word Biblical Commentary.* Ed. by David A. Hubbard, et al. Waco, TX: Word Books. 1984.

Smith, J. B. *Greek-English Concordance to the New Testament.* Scottsdale, PA: Herald Press. 1974.

Smyth, Herbert Weir. *Greek Grammar.* Cambridge: Harvard University Press. 1984.

Snodgrass, Anthony M. *Iron and Early Metallurgy in the Mediterranean.* In *The Coming of the Age of Iron.* Ed. by Theodore A. Wertime and James D. Muhly. New Haven: Yale University Press. 1980.

Spence, H. D. M., and J. Marshall Lang. *St. Luke.* In *Mark and Luke.* Vol. 16 of *The Pulpit Commentary.* Grand Rapids: William B. Eerdmans Publishing Co. 1950.

Stagg, Frank. *New Testament Theology.* Nashville: Broadman Press. 1962.

Stagg, Frank. *Polarities of Man's Existence in Biblical Perspective.* Philadelphia: The Westminster Press. 1973.

Stein, Robert H. *The Method and Message of Jesus' Teachings.* Philadelphia: The Westminster Press. 1978.

Summers, Ray. *Worthy is the Lamb.* Nashville: Broadman Press. 1951.

Temkin, Owsei. *The Falling Sickness.* 2d ed. Baltimore: The Johns Hopkins Press. 1971.

Tenney, Merrill C. *The Zondervan Pictorial Encyclopedia of the Bible.* 5 vols. Grand Rapids: Zondervan Publishing House. 1975.

Thayer, Joseph Henry. *Thayer's Greek-English Lexicon of the New Testament.* Grand Rapids: Associated Publishers Authors, Inc. N.d.

Theissen, Henry C. *Introduction to the New Testament.* Grand Rapids: William B. Eerdmans Publishing Co. 1950.

Thrall, Margaret E. *Greek Participles in the New Testament*. Grand Rapids: William B. Eerdmans Publishing Co. 1962.

Tigoy, Jeffrey H. "On the Term Phylacteries." *Harvard Theological Review* 72 (January–April 1979): 45-54.

Trench, Richard C. *Synonyms of the New Testament*. 8th ed. Greenwood: The Attic Press, Inc. 1961.

Turner, Nigel. *Christian Words*. Nashville: Thomas Nelson Publishers. 1982.

Turner, Nigel. *Grammatical Insights into the New Testament*. Edinburgh: T. and T. Clark. 1965.

Turner, Nigel. *Style*. Vol. 4 of *A Grammar of New Testament Greek*. Edinburgh: T. and T. Clark. 1976.

Turner, Nigel. *Syntax*. Vol. 3 of *A Grammar of New Testament Greek*. Edinburgh: T. and T. Clark. 1980.

Tyler, Alice F. *Freedom's Ferment*. New York: Harper and Row. 1962.

Vaughan, Curtis. *Colossians*. In *Ephesians–Philemon*. Vol. 11 of *The Expositor's Bible Commentary*. Ed. by Frank E. Gaebelein. Grand Rapids: Zondervan Publishing House. 1978.

Vaughan, Curtis, and Virtus E. Gideon. *A Greek Grammar of the New Testament*. Nashville: Broadman Press. 1979.

Vincent, Marvin R. *The Epistles to the Philippians and to Philemon*. The International Critical Commentary. Ed. by S. R. Driver, A. Plummer, and C. A. Briggs. Edinburgh: T. and T. Clark. 1972.

Vincent, Marvin R. *Word Studies in the New Testament*. 4 vols. Grand Rapids: William B. Eerdmans Publishing Co. 1946.

Vine, W. E. *An Expository Dictionary of New Testament Words*. Nashville: Royal Publishers, Inc. 1952.

Walbank, F. W. *A Historical Commentary on Polybius*. 3 vols. Oxford: Clarendon Press. 1967.

Waldbaum, Jane C. *The First Archaeological Appearance of Iron and the Transition to the Iron Age*. In *The Coming of the Iron Age*. Ed. by Theodore A. Wertime and James D. Muhly. New Haven: Yale University Press. 1980.

Walters, Peter. *The Text of the Septuagint*. Ed. by D. W. Gooding. Cambridge: Cambridge University Press. 1973.

Walvoord, John F. *The Revelation of Jesus Christ*. Chicago: Moody Press. 1966.

Ward, Ronald A. *Commentary on 1 and 2 Timothy and Titus*. Waco, TX: Word Books. 1980.

Wescott, B. F. *The Epistle to the Hebrews*. Grand Rapids: William B. Eerdmans Publishing Co. 1955.

Wessel, Walter W. *Mark*. In *Matthew, Mark and Luke*. Vol. 8 of *The Expositor's Bible Commentary*. Ed. by Frank E. Gaebelein. Grand Rapids: Zondervan Publishing House. 1984.

Wight, Fred H. *Manners and Customs of Bible Lands*. Chicago: Moody Press. 1953.

Wigram, George W. *The Englishman's Greek Concordance*. Grand Rapids: Baker Book House. 1979.

Wilkinson, John. *Jerusalem as Jesus Knew It: Archaelogy as Evidence*. London: Thames and Hudson. 1978.

Wilson, John A. *The Intellectual Adventure of Ancient Man*. Ed. by H. and H. A. Frankfort. Chicago: The University of Chicago Press. 1946.

Wolff, Hans Walter. *Hosea*. Ed. by Paul D. Hanson, and trans. by Gary Stansell. *Hermeneia*. Ed. by Frank M. Cross, et al. Philadelphia: Fortress Press. 1974.

Bibliography Continued

Wood, A. Skevington. *Ephesians.* In *Ephesians–Philemon.* Vol. 11 of *The Expositor's Bible Commentary.* Ed. by Frank E. Gaebelein. Grand Rapids: Zondervan Publishing House. 1978.

Wurthwein, Ernst. *The Text of the Old Testament.* Trans. by Erroll F. Rhodes. Grand Rapids: William B. Eerdmans Publishing Co. 1979.

Yeager, Randolph O. *The Renaissance New Testament.* 8 vols. Gretna, LA: Pelican Publishing Company. 1980.

Young, Edward J. *The Book of Isaiah.* 3 vols. *The New International Commentary on the Old Testament.* Grand Rapids: William B. Eerdmans Publishing Co. 1972.

Zarins, Zuris. "The Camel in Ancient Arabia: A Further Note." *Antiquity* 52 (1978): 44-46.

Zockler, Otto. *The Proverbs of Solomon.* Ed. and trans. by Charles A. Aiken. In *Proverbs, Ecclesiastes, and the Song of Solomon.* Vol. 10 of *Commentary on the Holy Scriptures by John Lange.* Ed. and trans. by Philip Schaff. Grand Rapids: Zondervan Publishing House. 1969.

General Reference Sources by Title

This list is provided to make it easier for the reader to find the source material in those instances where only the title of the general reference is cited in text without the editor(s) or compiler(s).

The Analytical Greek Lexicon Revised. Harold K. Moulton. Grand Rapids: Zondervan Publishing House. 1977.

The Assyrian Dictionary. Ed. by A. Leo Oppenheim. 21 vols. Chicago: The Oriental Institute of the University of Chicago. 1968.

Biblico-Theological Lexicon of New Testament Greek. August Hermann Cremer. 4th ed. Edinburgh: T. and T. Clark. 1962.

A Concise Hebrew and Aramaic Lexicon of the Old Testament. William L. Holladay. Grand Rapids: William B. Eerdmans Publishing Co. 1980.

A Critical Lexicon and Concordance to the English and Greek New Testament. Ethelbert W. Bullinger. 8th ed. London: The Lamp Press, Ltd. 1957.

A Dictionary of Life in Bible Times. Willy Corswant. Trans. by Arthur Heathcote. London: Hodder and Stoughton. 1960.

Expository Dictionary of Bible Words. Lawrence O. Richards. Grand Rapids: Zondervan Publishing House. 1985.

An Expository Dictionary of New Testament Words. W. E. Vine. Nashville: Royal Publishers, Inc. 1952.

A Greek-English Lexicon of the New Testament and Other Early Christian Literature. W. A. Bauer, William F. Arndt, and F. Wilbur Gingrich. 2nd ed. Revised and augmented by F. Wilbur Gingrich and Frederick W. Danker. Chicago: The University of Chicago Press. 1979.

A Greek-English Lexicon. H. G. Liddell and R. Scott. 9th ed. Ed. by H. Stuart Jones and R. McKenzie. Oxford: Oxford University Press. 1940.

Greek-English Lexicon of the New Testament. Joseph Henry Thayer. 4th ed. Grand Rapids: Baker Book House. 1979.

Greek-English Lexicon of the New Testament Based on Semantic Domains. Ed. by Johannes P. Louw and Eugene A. Nida. 2 vols. New York: United Bible Societies. 1988.

A Homeric Dictionary. Georg Autenreith. Trans. by Robert P. Keep. Norman, OK: University of Oklahoma Press. 1972. *The International Standard Bible Encyclopedia.* Ed. by Geoffrey W. Bromiley. 4 vols. Grand Rapids: William B. Eerdmans Publishing Co. 1979.

The Interpreter's Dictionary of the Bible. Ed. by George Arthur Buttrick. 5 vols. Nashville: Abingdon Press. 1962.

The New Bible Dictionary. Ed. by J. D. Douglas. 2d ed. Wheaton: Tyndale House Publishers. 1982.

The New International Dictionary of New Testament Theology. Ed. by Colin Brown. 4 vols. Grand Rapids: Zondervan Publishing House. 1975.

Bibliography Continued

The New Standard Jewish Encyclopedia. Ed. by Cecil Roth and Geoffrey Wigoder. 5th ed. Garden City, NY: Doubleday and Company, Inc. 1977.

The New Westminster Dictionary of the Bible. Ed. by Henry Snyder Gehman. Philadelphia: The Westminster Press. 1970.

A Patristic Greek Lexicon. G. W. H. Lampe. Oxford: The Clarendon Press. 1961.
A Reader's Greek-English Lexicon of the New Testament. Sakae Kubo. Berrien Springs: Andrews University Press. 1975.

Theological Dictionary of the New Testament. Ed. by G. Kittel and G. Friedrich. 10 vols. Trans. by G. W. Bromiley. Grand Rapids: William B. Eerdmans Publishing Co. 1964-1977.

Theological Wordbook of the Old Testament. Ed. by R. Laird Harris, Gleason J. Archer, Jr., and Bruce K. Waltke. 2 vols. Chicago: Moody Press. 1980.

The Vocabulary of the Greek Testament Illustrated from the Papyri and Other Non-Literary Sources. J. H. Moulton and G. Milligan. London: Hodder and Stoughton. 1914-1930. Reprint. Grand Rapids: William B. Eerdmans Publishing Co. 1985.

The Zondervan Pictorial Bible Dictionary. Ed. by Merrill C. Tenney. Grand Rapids: Zondervan Publishing House. 1972.

Literature of Antiquity

The "Literature of Antiquity" (8th century B.C. to 16th century A.D.) refers to the noncanonical quotations and references found in one or all of the volumes of the *Greek-English Dictionary*. Also included are the sources where these materials may be found in print, many of which contain English translations.

Aeschylus.*
  Agamemnon.
  Prometheus Bound.

Anaxandrides.

The Apostolic Fathers.*
  1 Clement.
  The Didache.
  The Epistle of Barnabas.
  The Epistle to Diognetus.
  The Epistle to the Philippians of St. Polycarp.
  The Epistles of St. Ignatius.
  The Martyrdom of Polycarp.
  The Shepherd of Hermas.

Aristophanes.*
  Thesmophriazusae.

Aristotle.*
  Analytica Priora (Prior Analytics).
  The Athenian Constitution.
  De Caelo (On the Heavens).
  Ethica Nicomachea (Nichomachean Ethics).
  Historia Animalium (The History of Animals).
  De Longitudine et Brevitate Vitae (On Length and Shortness of Life).
  Meteorologica.
  Mirabilia (*De Mirabilibus Auscultationibus*, On Marvelous Things Heard).
  (*Politics*).
  Problemata (Problems).
  Rhetorica (Rhetoric).

The Babylonian Talmud. Ed. by I. Epstein. London: The Soncino Press. 1948.

Cicero.*
  In Verrem.
  Letters to Atticus.

Demosthenes.*
  De Corona and De Falsa Legatione.
  Orations.

Diodorus Siculus.*
  Library of History.

Bibliography Continued

Diogenes Laertius.*
  Lives of Eminent Philosophers.

Dionysius of Halicarnassus.*
  Roman Antiquities.

Epictetus.*
  Discourses.

Epicurus. *To Menoeceus.* In *Letters, Principal Doctrines and Vatican Sayings.* Trans. by Russel M. Geer. Indianapolis: The Bobbs-Merrill Company, Inc. 1964.

Euripides.*
  Supplices.

Flavius Josephus. *The Complete Works of Flavius Josephus.* Trans. by William Whiston. Grand Rapids: Kregel Publications. 1960.
  Against Apion.
  Antiquities of the Jews.
  Wars of the Jews.

Herodotus.*

Hesiod.*
  Fragmenta.
  Theogony.
  Works and Days.

Hippocrates.*
  De Fracturis (On Fractures).
  Prognostikon (The Book of Prognostics).

Homer.*
  Iliad.
  Odyssey.

Justin. *Apology.* In *St. Justin Martyr.* Vol. 6, *The Fathers of the Church.* Washington, D.C.: The Catholic University of America Press. 1977.

Lucian.*
  Tyrannicida (The Tyrannicide).
  Philopseudes (The Lover of Lies).

Lycurgus. In *Minor Attic Orators.**

Marcus Aurelius. *Lucretius, Epictetus, Marcus Aurelius.* Trans. by George Long. *Great Books of the Western World.* Chicago: William Benton, Publisher. 1971.

Methodius. *The Symposium: A Treatise on Chastity.* Trans. by Herbert Musurillo. Vol. 27 of *Ancient Christian Writers.* New York: Newman Press. 1958.

The Mishna: Translated from the Hebrew with Introduction and Brief Explanatory Notes. Trans. by Herbert Danby. Oxford: Oxford University Press. 1933.

Mishnayoth. 7 vols. Ed. by Philip Blackman. New York: Judaica Press, Inc. 1964.

The Old Testament Pseudepigrapha. 2 vols. Ed. by James H. Charlesworth. Garden City, NY: Doubleday and Company, Inc. 1983.

Pausanias.*
  Description of Greece.

Philo.*
  De Mutatione Nominum (On the Change of Names).
  De Opificio Mundi (On the Creation).
  Quid Rerum Divinarum Heres (Who Is the Heir of Divine Things?).
  De Specialibus Legibus (On the Special Books).
  De Somniis (On Dreams).
  De Vita Mosis (The Life of Moses).

Philostratus.*
  Vitae Sophistarum (The Lives of the Sophists).

Pindar.*
  The Odes of Pindar.

Plato.*
  Euthyphro, Apology, Crito, Phaedo, Phaedrus.
  Legum Allegoriae.
  Lysis, Symposium, Gorgias.
  Philebus.
  Republic.
  Timaeus, Critias, Clitophon, Menexenus, Epistulae.

Pliny.*
  Natural History.

Plotinus.*

Plutarch.*
  Demetrius.
  Moralia.

Polybius.*
  The Histories.

Propertius.*

Seneca.*
  Moral Essays.

The Talmud of the Land of Israel. Ed. by Jacob Neusner, et al. Chicago: University of Chicago Press. 1988.

Bibliography Continued

Tertullian. *Against Marcion.* In *Latin Christianity: Its Founder Tertullian.* Vol. 3 of *The Ante-Nicene Fathers.* Ed. by Alexander Roberts and James Donaldson. Edinburgh. 1867. Reprint. Grand Rapids: William B. Eerdmans Publishing Co. 1973.

Theophrastus.*
  Characteres.

Thucydides.*

Vettius Valens. *Astrologus.* In *The Greek Anthology and other Ancient Greek Epigrams.* Ed. and trans. by Peter Jay. New York: Oxford University Press. 1973.

Xenophon.*
  Anabasis.
  Constitution of the Lacedaimonians. In *Scripta Minora.*
  Cyropaedia (*Institutio Cyri.*)
  Memorabilia.

*The Loeb Classical Library. Cambridge: Harvard University Press.

Sin cesar (EKTENES: P.359. 1604)